Encyclopedia *of* Careers *and*

Vocational Guidance

Seventeenth Edition

Volume 6

Career Articles, Psy–Z

Ferguson's

An Infobase Learning Company

Encyclopedia of Careers and Vocational Guidance, Seventeenth Edition

Copyright © 2018 by Infobase Learning

Ferguson's
An Infobase Learning Company
132 West 31st Street
New York, NY 10001

Library of Congress Cataloging-in-Publication Data

Names: Ferguson Publishing.
Title: Encyclopedia of careers and vocational guidance.
Description: Seventeenth edition. | New York, NY : Fergusons, [2017] |
    Includes bibliographical references and index. |
Identifiers: LCCN 2017011340 (print) | LCCN 2017021276 (ebook) | ISBN
    9781438177144 (ebook) | ISBN 9780816085149 (6 volume set)
Subjects: LCSH: Vocational guidance—Handbooks, manuals, etc.—Juvenile
    literature. | Occupations—Handbooks, manuals, etc.—Juvenile literature.
Classification: LCC HF5381 (ebook) | LCC HF5381 .E52 2017 (print) | DDC
    331.702—dc23
LC record available at https://lccn.loc.gov/2017011340

Ferguson's books are available at special discounts when purchased in bulk quantities for businesses, associations, institutions, or sales promotions. Please call our Special Sales Department in New York at (212) 967-8800 or (800) 322-8755.

You can find Ferguson's on the World Wide Web at http://www.infobasepublishing.com.

Text design by David Strelecky
Composition by Newgen
Cover printed by Sheridan Books, Inc., Ann Arbor, MI
Book printed and bound by Sheridan Books, Inc., Ann Arbor, MI
Date printed: October 2017

Printed in the United States of America

Contents

Volume 6: Career Articles Psy–Z

Psychiatric Technicians

■ OVERVIEW

Psychiatric technicians work with people with mental illness, emotional disturbances, or developmental disabilities. Their duties vary considerably depending on place of work, but may include helping patients with hygiene and housekeeping and recording patients' pulse, temperature, and respiration rates. Psychiatric technicians participate in treatment programs by having one-on-one sessions with patients, under a nurse's or counselor's direction.

Another prime aspect of the psychiatric technician's work is reporting observations of patients' behavior to medical and psychiatric staff. Psychiatric technicians may also fill out admitting forms for new patients, contact patients' families to arrange conferences, issue medications from the dispensary, and maintain records. There are approximately 58,450 psychiatric technicians employed in the United States.

■ HISTORY

Although some people with mental illness were treated as early as the 15th century in institutions like the Hospital of Saint Mary of Bethlehem in London (whose name was often shortened to Bedlam, hence the modern word "bedlam"), the practice of institutionalizing people with mental disorders did not become common until the 17th century.

During the 17th, 18th, and even into the 19th centuries, treatment of patients with mental illness was quite crude and often simply barbarous. This state of affairs started to change as medical practitioners began to see mental illness as a medical problem. During the late 18th and early 19th centuries, hospitals began concentrating on keeping patients clean and comfortable, building their self-respect, and treating them with friendliness and encouragement. This method of treating mental illness resulted in the establishment of specially designed institutions for the care of mental patients.

Beginning in the 1940s, mental health institutions sought more effective therapeutic services for their patients, including more social activities and innovative treatment programs. Treatment shifted from a sole reliance on state mental hospitals to provision of more services in general hospitals and community mental health centers.

The object was to shorten periods of institutionalization and to decrease the stigma and dislocation associated with treatment in mental hospitals. However, these changes also sharply increased personnel needs. One strategy for dealing with this has been to train more professionals: psychiatrists, psychologists, social workers, nurses, and others. Another strategy has focused on training more nonprofessionals: aides, attendants, orderlies, and others.

The drive to develop new therapies and the trend toward deinstitutionalizing patients have led to the creation of a new category of mental health worker with a training level between that of the professional and the nonprofessional. Workers at this level are usually referred to as paraprofessionals or technicians, and in the mental health field they are known as psychiatric technicians or mental health technicians.

■ THE JOB

Psychiatric technicians not only take over for or assist professionals in traditional treatment activities, but they also provide new services in innovative ways. They may work with alcohol and drug abusers, psychotic or emotionally disturbed children and adults, developmentally disabled people, or the aged. They must be skilled and specially trained.

Psychiatric technicians are supervised by health professionals, such as registered nurses, counselors, therapists, or, more and more frequently, senior psychiatric technicians. Psychiatric technicians work as part of a team of mental health care workers and provide physical and mental rehabilitation for patients through recreational, occupational, and psychological readjustment programs.

In general, psychiatric technicians help plan and implement individual treatment programs. Specific duties vary according to work setting, but they may include the following: interviewing

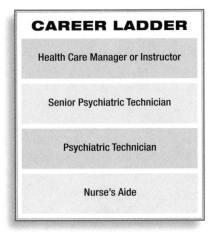

CAREER LADDER

Health Care Manager or Instructor

Senior Psychiatric Technician

Psychiatric Technician

Nurse's Aide

and information gathering; working in a hospital unit admitting, screening, evaluating, or discharging patients; record keeping; making referrals to community agencies; working for patients' needs and rights; visiting patients at home after their release from a hospital; and participating in individual and group counseling and therapy.

Psychiatric technicians endeavor to work with patients in a broad, comprehensive manner and to see each patient as a person whose peculiar or abnormal behavior stems from an illness or disability. They strive to help each patient achieve a maximum level of functioning. This means helping patients strengthen social and mental skills, accept greater responsibility, and develop confidence to enter into social, educational, or vocational activities.

In addition, psychiatric technicians working in hospitals handle a certain number of nursing responsibilities. They may take temperature, pulse and respiration rates; measure blood pressure; and help administer medications and physical treatments. In many cases, technicians working in hospitals will find themselves concerned with all aspects of their patients' lives—from eating, sleeping, and personal hygiene to developing social skills and improving self-image.

Technicians working in clinics, community mental health centers, halfway houses, day hospitals, or other non-institutional settings also perform some specialized tasks. They interview newly registered patients and their relatives and visit patients and their families at home. They also administer psychological tests, participate in group activities, and write reports about their observations for supervising psychiatrists or other mental health professionals. They try to ease the transition of patients leaving hospitals and returning to their communities. They may refer patients to and arrange for consultations with mental health specialists. They may also help patients resolve problems with employment, housing, and personal finance.

Most psychiatric technicians are trained as generalists in providing mental health services. But some opportunities exist for technicians to specialize in a particular aspect of mental health care. For example, some psychiatric technicians specialize in the problems of mentally disturbed children. Others work as counselors in drug and alcohol abuse programs or as members of psychiatric emergency or crisis-intervention teams.

Another area of emphasis is working in community mental health. Technicians employed in this area are sometimes known as *human services technicians*. They use rehabilitation techniques for non-hospitalized patients who have problems adjusting to their social environment. These technicians may be primarily concerned with drug and alcohol abuse, parental effectiveness, the elderly, or problems in interpersonal relationships. Human services technicians work in social welfare departments, child care centers, preschools, vocational rehabilitation workshops, and schools for the learning disabled, emotionally disturbed, and mentally handicapped. This concentration is particularly popular in college curricula, according to the American Association of Psychiatric Technicians, although it has yet to find wide acceptance in the job market.

With slightly different training, psychiatric technicians may specialize in the treatment of developmentally disabled people. These technicians, sometimes referred to as *DD techs,* work with patients with such activities as supervising recreational activities or teaching patients basic skills. They generally work in halfway houses, state hospitals, training centers, or state and local service agencies. These jobs are among the easiest psychiatric technician jobs to get, and many techs start out in this area. On average, however, the pay of the DD tech is considerably less than that of other psychiatric technicians.

■ EARNINGS

Salaries for psychiatric technicians vary according to geographical area and work setting: technicians in California generally receive substantially higher wages than those in other areas of the country, and technicians in community settings generally receive higher salaries than those in institutional settings. Psychiatric technicians earned median salaries of $31,140 in May 2015, according to the U.S. Department of Labor. The lowest 10 percent earned less than $20,780, and the highest 10 percent earned $60,690 or more. Technicians who worked in psychiatric and substance abuse hospitals earned mean annual salaries of $37,450.

Most psychiatric technicians receive fringe benefits, including health insurance, sick leave, and paid vacations. Technicians working for state institutions or agencies will probably also be eligible for financial assistance for further education.

■ WORK ENVIRONMENT

Psychiatric technicians work in a variety of settings, and their working conditions vary accordingly. Typically they work 40 hours a week, five days a week, although one may be a weekend day. Some psychiatric technicians work evening or night shifts, and all technicians may sometimes be asked to work holidays.

For the most part, the physical surroundings are pleasant. Most institutions, clinics, mental health centers, and agency offices are kept clean and comfortably furnished. Technicians who work with the mentally ill must nonetheless adjust to an environment that is normally chaotic and sometimes upsetting. Some patients are acutely depressed and withdrawn or excessively agitated and excited. Some patients may become unexpectedly violent and verbally abusive. However, institutions treating these kinds of patients maintain enough staff to keep the patients safe and to protect workers from physical harm. Psychiatric technicians who make home visits may also sometimes encounter unpleasant conditions.

Finally, psychiatric technicians work not only with individuals, but often with the community as well. In that role, technicians can be called upon to advocate for their patients by motivating community agencies to provide services or by obtaining exceptions to rules when needed for individuals or groups of patients. Successful psychiatric technicians become competent in working and dealing with various decision-making processes of community and neighborhood groups.

■ EXPLORING

Prospective psychiatric technicians can gather personal experience in this field in a number of ways. You can apply for a job as a nurse's aide at a local general hospital. In this way you gain direct experience providing patient care. If such a job requires too much of a time commitment, you might consider volunteering at a hospital part-time or during the summer. Volunteering is an excellent way to become acquainted with the field, and many techs' full-time jobs evolve from volunteer positions. Most volunteers must be 21 years of age to work in the mental health unit. Younger students who are interested in volunteering can often find places in the medical records department or other areas to get their feet in the door.

People interested in this career might also consider volunteering at their local mental health association or a local social welfare agency. In some cases, the mental health association can arrange opportunities for volunteer work inside a mental hospital or mental health clinic. Finally, either on your own or with your teachers, you can arrange a visit to a mental health clinic. You may be able to talk with staff members and observe firsthand how psychiatric technicians do their jobs.

A psychiatric technician counsels a patient with depression. (Monkey Business Images. Shutterstock.)

■ EDUCATION AND TRAINING REQUIREMENTS
High School

A high school diploma is the minimum education requirement to find work as a psychiatric technician, although in many cases psychiatric technicians are expected to have a certificate or associate's degree. In general, high school students should take courses in English, biology, psychology, and sociology.

Postsecondary Training

The two-year postsecondary training programs usually lead to an associate of arts or associate of science degree. It is important to note that many hospitals prefer to hire applicants with bachelor's degrees.

In general, study programs include human development, personality structure, the nature of mental illness, and, to a limited extent, anatomy, physiology, basic

TALKING ABOUT MENTAL HEALTH

Depression: A serious, but usually treatable, medical illness that negatively affects the way people think, feel, and act. Depression affects nearly one in 10 adults each year.

Neurosis: A mental and emotional disorder that affects only part of the personality. A neurosis does not disturb the use of language, and it is accompanied by various physical, physiological, and mental disturbances, the most usual being anxieties or phobias.

Obsessive-compulsive disorder: A neurosis that results in the patient's compulsion to carry out certain acts, no matter how odd or illogical or repetitive they are. This sort of neurosis is evident once the obsession or compulsive act interferes with normal life. For example, a person obsessed with cleanliness might take a dozen or more showers a day.

Paranoid schizophrenia: The most common and destructive of the psychotic disorders, characterized by departure from reality, inability to think clearly, difficulty feeling and expressing emotions, and a retreat into a fantasy life.

Phobias: Irrational or overblown fears that prevent a person from living a normal life.

Post-traumatic stress disorder: A psychiatric disorder that can occur in people who have witnessed or experienced life-threatening events such as terrorist attacks, war, violence, natural disasters, or serious accidents.

Psychiatric technician: An allied mental health professional who provides direct patient care to people with mental illness, emotional disturbances, or developmental disabilities.

Psychiatrist: A physician who attends to patients' mental, emotional, and behavioral symptoms.

Psychologist: A mental health professional who teaches, counsels, conducts research, or administers programs to understand people and help people understand themselves. Psychologists hold doctorates in psychology. Most cannot prescribe medication.

Psychosis: Disintegration of personality and loss of contact with the outside world; more severe than neurosis.

nursing, and medical science. Other subjects usually include some introduction to basic social sciences so that technicians can better understand relevant family and community structures; an overview of the structure and functions of institutions that treat patients; and most important, practical instruction.

■ CERTIFICATION, LICENSING, AND SPECIAL REQUIREMENTS
Certification or Licensing

Psychiatric technicians must be licensed in California and several other states. Ask your guidance or placement counselors for more information about licensing requirements in your state. Voluntary certification is available through the American Association of Psychiatric Technicians. To receive basic certification, you will need to take a multiple-choice exam covering topics on mental disorders and developmental disabilities. Those who pass the test receive the designation nationally certified psychiatric technician and can place the initials NCPT after their names. To attain higher levels of certification, applicants must pass an essay test. Depending on the employer, a certified technician may qualify for higher pay than a noncertified worker.

Most mental health technology programs emphasize interviewing skills. Such training guides technicians to correctly describe a patient's tone of voice and body language so that they are well equipped to observe and record behavior that will be interpreted by the treatment team and sometimes even a court of law. Some programs also teach administration of selected psychological tests. You may also gain knowledge and training in crisis intervention techniques, child guidance, group counseling, family therapy, behavior modification, and consultation skills.

■ EXPERIENCE, SKILLS, AND PERSONALITY TRAITS

Any experience one can obtain in the field of mental health care—such as an internship, volunteering, or a part-time job—will be useful for aspiring psychiatric technicians.

Because psychiatric technicians interact with people, you must be sensitive to others' needs and feelings. Some aspects of sensitivity can be learned, but this requires willingness to listen, being extremely observant, and risking involvement in situations that at first may seem ambiguous and confusing. In addition, you need to be willing to look at your own attitudes and behaviors and to be flexible and open about changing them. The more you know about yourself, the more effective you will be in helping others.

Patience, understanding, and resilience are required in working with people whose actions may be disagreeable and unpleasant because of their illnesses. Patients can be particularly adept at finding a person's weaknesses and exploiting them. This is not a job for the tenderhearted. A sense of responsibility and the ability to remain calm in emergencies are also essential characteristics.

EMPLOYMENT PROSPECTS

Employers

Psychiatric technicians work in a variety of settings: the military, hospitals, mental hospitals, community mental health centers, psychiatric clinics, schools and day centers for the developmentally disabled, and social service agencies. They also work at residential and nonresidential centers, such as geriatric nursing homes, child or adolescent development centers, and halfway houses.

Other potential places of employment for psychiatric technicians include correctional programs and juvenile courts, schools for the blind and deaf, community action programs, family service centers, and public housing programs. Approximately 58,450 psychiatric technicians are employed in the United States.

Starting Out

Graduates from mental health and human services technology programs can usually choose from a variety of job possibilities. College career services offices can be extremely helpful in locating employment. Students can follow want ads or apply directly to the clinics, agencies, or hospitals of their choice. Job information can also be obtained from each state's department of mental health.

ADVANCEMENT PROSPECTS

Working as a psychiatric technician is still a relatively new occupation, and sequences of promotions have not yet been clearly defined. Seeking national certification through the AAPT is one way to help to set up a career path in this field. Advancement normally takes the form of being given greater responsibilities with less supervision. It usually results from gaining experience, developing competence and leadership abilities, and continuing formal and practical education. In cases where promotions are governed by civil service regulations, advancement is based on experience and test scores on promotion examinations.

In large part, advancement is linked to gaining further education. Thus, after working a few years, technicians may decide to obtain a bachelor's degree in psychology. Advanced education, coupled with previous training and work experience, greatly enhances advancement potential. For instance, with a bachelor's degree, experienced technicians may be able to find rewarding positions as instructors in programs to train future mental health workers.

OUTLOOK

Employment for psychiatric technicians is expected to grow as fast as the average for all careers through 2024, according to the U.S. Department of Labor. Demand for technicians is expected to continue in large part because of a well-established trend of returning patients to their communities after shorter and shorter periods of hospitalization. This trend has encouraged development of comprehensive community mental health centers and has led to a strong demand for psychiatric technicians to staff these facilities. The passage of the Affordable Care Act has increased the number of people with access to mental health care, which will increase demand for psychiatric technicians. Opportunities will also be good in facilities that treat older people with cognitive mental diseases, such as Alzheimer's disease; in prisons; and in outpatient care centers for people with developmental disabilities, mental illness, and substance abuse problems.

Concerns over rising health care costs should increase employment levels for technicians, because they and other paraprofessionals can take over some functions of higher paid professionals. This kind of substitution has been demonstrated to be an effective way of reducing costs without reducing quality of care.

UNIONS AND ASSOCIATIONS

Psychiatric technicians who work for government agencies can join the American Federation of Government Employees, a union that represents government workers. Those who work in California can join the California Association of Psychiatric Technicians, a professional association and union that represents 14,000 state-licensed technicians who work in state programs that serve people with mental illnesses and developmental disabilities. The American Association of Psychiatric Technicians provides certification.

TIPS FOR ENTRY

1. Visit http://psychtechs.org/jobs.shtml for job listings.
2. Work as a volunteer or administrative worker at a mental health facility to obtain introductory experience and make networking contacts.
3. Talk to psychiatric technicians about their careers. Ask them for advice on breaking into the field.

FOR MORE INFORMATION

For information on certification and careers, contact
American Association of Psychiatric Technicians (AAPT)
1220 S Street, Suite 100
Sacramento, CA 95811-7138
Tel: (800) 391-7589
Fax: (916) 329-9145
E-mail: aapt@psychtechs.net
http://www.psychtechs.org

Psychiatric technicians who work for government agencies can join the American Federation of Government Employees, a union that represents government workers.

American Federation of Government Employees, AFL-CIO (AFGE)

80 F Street, NW

Washington, D.C. 20001

Tel: (202) 737-8700

E-mail: comments@afge.org

https://www.afge.org

For more information on careers, education, and union membership, contact

California Association of Psychiatric Technicians (CAPT)

1220 S Street, Suite 100

Sacramento, CA 95811-7138

Tel: (800) 677-2278; (916) 329-9140

Fax: (916) 329-9145

http://psychtechs.net

HIGHEST PAYING JOBS

Psychiatrists

■ OVERVIEW

Psychiatrists are physicians who attend to patients' mental, emotional, and behavioral symptoms. They try to help people function better in their daily lives. Psychiatrists generally specialize by treatment methods, based on their chosen fields. They may explore a patient's beliefs and history. They may prescribe medicine, including tranquilizers, antipsychotics, and antidepressants. If they specialize in treating children, they may use play therapy. There are 24,060 psychiatrists employed in the United States.

■ HISTORY

The greatest advances in psychiatric treatment came in the latter part of the 19th century. Emil Kraepelin, a German psychiatrist, made an important contribution when he developed a classification system for mental illnesses that is still used for diagnosis. Sigmund Freud, the famous Viennese psychiatrist, developed techniques for analyzing human behavior that have strongly influenced the practice of modern psychiatry. Freud first lectured in the United States in 1909. Swiss psychiatrist Carl Jung, a former associate of Freud's, revolutionized the field with his theory of a collective unconscious.

Another great change in treatment began in the 1950s with the development of medication that could be used in treating psychiatric problems, such as depression and anxiety.

■ THE JOB

Psychiatrists are medical doctors (M.D.'s) who treat people suffering from mental and emotional illnesses that make it hard for them to cope with everyday living or to behave in socially acceptable ways. Psychiatrists treat problems ranging from being irritable and feeling frustrated to losing touch with reality. Some people, in addition to having a mental illness, may also engage in destructive behavior such as abusing alcohol or drugs or committing crimes. Others may have physical symptoms that spring from mental or emotional disorders. People with mental illness were once so misunderstood and stigmatized by society that they were kept, chained and shackled, in asylums. Today society recognizes that emotional or mental illnesses need to be diagnosed and treated just like any other medical problem.

Some psychiatrists run general practices, treating patients with a variety of mental disorders. Others may specialize in working with certain types of therapy or kinds of patients, such as the chronically ill. When meeting a client for the first time, psychiatrists conduct an evaluation of the client, which involves talking with the person about his or her current circumstances and getting a medical history. In some cases, the psychiatrist will give the client a physical examination or order laboratory tests if he or she feels the client's problem may have a physical cause. Next, the psychiatrist decides on a treatment plan for the client. This may involve medications, psychotherapy, or a combination of these approaches.

As medical doctors, psychiatrists can prescribe medications that affect a client's mood or behavior, such as tranquilizers or antidepressants. Scientific advancements in both the understanding of how the human brain functions and the creation of more effective drugs with fewer side effects have helped make medications an important element in the treatment of mental illness. Some psychiatrists will only supervise the medication aspect of a client's treatment and refer the client to another health professional, such as a psychologist, for the psychotherapy aspect of treatment. These psychiatrists often work in private practices and focus on the chemical aspects of a person's illness to find medication to help that client. Other psychiatrists, often those working in hospitals or in small cities and towns, may be the providers of both medication management and psychotherapy.

Psychotherapy, sometimes called talk therapy, is perhaps the best-known type of treatment for mental illness. By having the client talk about problems he or she faces, the therapist helps the client uncover and understand the feelings and ideas that form the root of his or her problems and, thus, overcome emotional pain. Talk therapy can be used with individuals, groups, couples, or families.

Another therapeutic method that some psychiatrists use is behavior therapy or behavior modification therapy. This therapy focuses on changing a client's behavior and may involve teaching the client to use meditation and relaxation techniques as well as other treatment methods, such as biofeedback, a process in which electronic monitors are used to measure the effects that thoughts and feelings have on bodily functions like muscle tension, heart rate, or brain waves. This method allows the client to learn how to consciously control his or her body through stress reduction.

Free association is a technique in which the client is encouraged to relax and talk freely. The therapist's aim is to help the client uncover troubling subconscious beliefs or conflicts and their causes. Dreams may also be examined for hints about the subconscious mind. Subconscious conflicts are believed to cause neurosis, an emotional disorder in which the patient commonly exhibits anxious behavior.

In addition to those working in general psychiatry, there are psychiatrists who specialize in working with certain groups or in certain areas. These specialists include the following:

Child psychiatrists work with youth and usually their parents as well.

At the opposite end of the age scale are *geriatric psychiatrists,* who specialize in working with older individuals.

Industrial psychiatrists are employed by companies to deal with problems that affect employee performance, such as alcoholism or absenteeism.

Forensic psychiatrists work in the field of law. They evaluate defendants and testify on their mental states. They may help determine whether or not defendants understand the charges against them and if they can contribute to their own defense.

Other health professionals who may work with mentally ill people include *psychologists,* who may see clients but are unable to prescribe medications because they are not physicians, and *neurologists,* physicians specializing in problems of the nervous system. In some cases, a person's disturbed behavior results from disorders of the nervous system, and neurologists diagnose and treat these conditions.

■ EARNINGS

Psychiatrists' earnings are determined by the kind of practice they have and its location, their experience, and the number of patients they treat. Like other physicians, their average income is among the highest of any occupation.

Physicians who were still in their residencies earned an average of between $51,586 to $67,236 in the 2014–2015 academic year, according to a survey by the Association of American Medical Colleges.

The median salary for a general psychiatrist in May 2015 was $187,200, according to the U.S. Department of Labor (DOL). Ten percent of psychiatrists earned less than $59,430. The DOL reports the following mean annual salaries for psychiatrists by employer: offices of physicians, $188,110; psychiatric and substance abuse hospitals, $191,150; outpatient care centers, $205,410; general medical and surgical hospitals, $186,260; and state government, $210,810.

Psychiatrists who are employed by health care institutions receive fringe benefits such as health insurance and paid vacation and sick days. Those who are self-employed must provide their own benefits.

■ WORK ENVIRONMENT

Psychiatrists in private practice set their own schedules and usually work regular hours. They may work some evenings or weekends to see patients who cannot take time off during business hours. Most psychiatrists, however, put in long workdays, averaging 55 hours a week, according to American Medical Association statistics. Like other physicians, psychiatrists are always on call.

QUICK FACTS

ALTERNATE TITLE(S)
Child Psychiatrists, Forensic Psychiatrists, Geriatric Psychiatrists, Industrial Psychiatrists

DUTIES
Treat people who suffer from mental and emotional illnesses

SALARY RANGE
$51,586 to $187,200 to $210,810+

WORK ENVIRONMENT
Primarily Indoors

BEST GEOGRAPHIC LOCATION(S)
Nationwide; most opportunities available in major metropolitan areas

MINIMUM EDUCATION LEVEL
Medical Degree

SCHOOL SUBJECTS
Biology, Psychology, Sociology

EXPERIENCE
Four- to five-year residency required

PERSONALITY TRAITS
Outgoing, Problem-Solving, Scientific

SKILLS
Interpersonal, Research, Scientific

CERTIFICATION OR LICENSING
Required

SPECIAL REQUIREMENTS
None

EMPLOYMENT PROSPECTS
Good

ADVANCEMENT PROSPECTS
Fair

OUTLOOK
Much Faster than the Average

NOC
3111

O*NET-SOC
29-1066.00

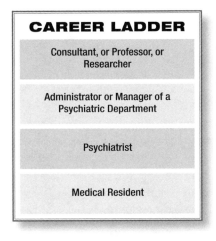

CAREER LADDER

Consultant, or Professor, or Researcher

Administrator or Manager of a Psychiatric Department

Psychiatrist

Medical Resident

Psychiatrists in private practice typically work in comfortable office settings. Some private psychiatrists also work as hospital staff members, consultants, lecturers, or teachers.

Salaried psychiatrists work in private hospitals, state hospitals, and community mental health centers. They also work for government agencies, such as the U.S. Department of Health and Human Services, the Department of Defense, and the Department of Veterans Affairs. Psychiatrists who work in public facilities often bear heavy workloads. Changes in treatment have reduced the number of patients in hospitals and have increased the number of patients in community health centers.

■ EXPLORING

You can easily explore this job by reading as much as you can about the field and the work. To learn about different types of psychotherapies, you may want to read *Essential Psychotherapies: Theory and Practice*, edited by Alan Gurman and Stanley Messer (The Guilford Press, 2013). You can also talk with your school counselor or psychology teacher about helping you arrange an information interview with a local psychiatrist. If this is not possible, try to get an information interview with any physician, such as your family doctor, to ask about the medical school experience.

A psychiatrist takes notes while listening to a patient. (Alexander Raths. Shutterstock.)

An excellent way to explore this type of work is to do volunteer work in health care settings, such as hospitals, clinics, or nursing homes. While you may not be taking care of people with psychiatric problems, you will be interacting with patients and health care professionals. This experience will benefit you when it's time to apply to medical schools and will give you a feel for working with those who are ill.

As a college student, you may be able to find a summer job as a hospital orderly, nurse's aide, psychiatric aide, or ward clerk.

■ EDUCATION AND TRAINING REQUIREMENTS
High School

If working as a psychiatrist sounds interesting to you, you should start preparing for college and medical school while you are still in high school. Do this by taking a college preparatory curriculum and concentrating on math and science classes. Biology, chemistry, and physics as well as algebra, geometry, and calculus will all be helpful. You can also start learning about human behavior by taking psychology, sociology, and history classes. In addition, take English classes to develop your communication skills—much of a psychiatrist's work involves speaking, listening, and record keeping.

Postsecondary Training

When you are deciding what college to attend, keep in mind that you'll want one with a strong science department, excellent laboratory facilities, and a strong humanities department. You may want to check *Medical School Admissions Requirements*, a publication from the Association of American Medical Colleges (AAMC, https://students-residents.aamc.org/applying-medical-school/applying-medical-school-process/deciding-where-apply/medical-school-admission-requirements), to see what specific college classes you should take in preparation for medical school. Some colleges or universities offer a premed major; other possible majors include chemistry and biology. No matter what your major, though, you can count on taking biology, chemistry, organic chemistry, physics, and psychology classes. Medical schools look for well-rounded individuals, however, so be sure to take other classes in the humanities and social sciences. The AAMC reports that most people apply to medical school after their junior year of college. Most medical schools require the Medical College Admission Test as part of their application, so you should take this test your junior or even sophomore year.

In medical school, students must complete a four-year program of medical studies and supervised clinical work leading to their M.D. degrees. Students will once again concentrate on studying the sciences during their first two years; in addition, they will learn about taking a person's medical history and how to do an examination. The next two years are devoted to clinical work, which is when students first begin to see patients under supervision.

After receiving an M.D., physicians who plan to specialize in psychiatry must complete a residency. In the first year, they work in several specialties, such as internal medicine and pediatrics. Then they work for three years in a psychiatric hospital or a general hospital's psychiatric ward. Here they learn how to diagnose and treat various mental and emotional disorders or illnesses. Some psychiatrists continue their education beyond this four-year residency. To become a child psychiatrist, for example, a doctor must train for at least three years in general residency and two years in child psychiatry residency. Part of psychiatrists' training involves undergoing therapy themselves.

Other Education or Training

Continuing education opportunities are provided by many national and state organizations, including the American Association for Geriatric Psychiatry, American Medical Association, and American Psychiatric Association. Contact these organizations for more information.

■ CERTIFICATION, LICENSING, AND SPECIAL REQUIREMENTS
Certification or Licensing

All physicians must be licensed in order to practice medicine. After completing the M.D., graduates must pass a licensing test given by the board of medical examiners for the state in which they want to work. The American Board of Psychiatry and Neurology (ABPN) is the certifying board for all psychiatrists regardless of their specialty. To become an ABPN-certified psychiatrist you will need to pass a written and an oral test. Certification subspecialties include addiction psychiatry, brain injury medicine, child and adolescent psychiatry, clinical neurophysiology, forensic psychiatry, geriatric psychiatry, hospice and palliative medicine, pain medicine, psychosomatic medicine, and sleep medicine.

■ EXPERIENCE, SKILLS, AND PERSONALITY TRAITS

There is no way to obtain direct experience in high school, but it's a good idea to take as many health, psychology, and science classes as possible and participate in science and health clubs. During your medical training, you will gain experience by completing a residency in internal medicine (or pediatrics) and psychiatry.

KEY TERMS IN PSYCHIATRY

WORDS TO KNOW

Bipolar disorder: A very treatable brain disorder that causes shifts in a person's energy level, mood, and ability to function.

Cognitive: Pertaining to thoughts or thinking.

Compulsion: Repetitive ritualistic behavior that aims to reduce stress or prevent an occurrence.

Electroconvulsive therapy: A medical treatment that involves applying electrical currents to the brain; it is used most often to treat severe depression.

Obsession: Persistent, recurring thought or image experienced as intrusive and distressing to the self.

Psychoanalysis: A method of treating mental disorders by bringing unconscious fears and conflicts into the conscious mind.

Psychosomatic: A physical illness caused or aggravated by a mental condition.

Psychotherapy: The treatment of mental disorders by psychological, rather than physical, means.

Schizophrenia: A chronic disorder of the brain that affects more than 1 percent of the population. Symptoms can include hallucinations, delusions, trouble with concentration and thinking, and a lack of motivation.

Seasonal affective disorder: A mental disorder that causes the gradual or sudden onset of depression during the fall and winter months.

Source: American Psychiatric Association

To complete the required studies and training, students need outstanding mental ability and perseverance. Psychiatrists must be emotionally stable so they can deal with their patients objectively. Psychiatrists must be perceptive, able to listen well, and able to work well with others. They must also be dedicated to a lifetime of learning, as new therapeutic techniques and medications are constantly being developed.

■ EMPLOYMENT PROSPECTS
Employers

There are 24,060 psychiatrists working in the United States. Approximately half of practicing psychiatrists work in private practice; many others combine private practice with work in a health care institution. These institutions include private hospitals, state mental hospitals, medical schools, community health centers, and government health agencies. Psychiatrists may also work at correctional facilities, for health maintenance organizations, or in nursing homes. They are employed throughout the country.

PSYCHIATRY AND PSYCHOTHERAPY

LEARN MORE ABOUT IT

Corey, Gerald. *Theory and Practice of Counseling and Psychotherapy,* 10th ed. Salt Lake City, Utah: Brooks Cole, 2016.

Hales, Robert E., Stuart C. Yudofsky, and Laura Weiss Roberts. (eds.) *The American Psychiatric Publishing Textbook of Psychiatry,* 6th ed. Arlington, Va.: American Psychiatric Publishing, 2014.

Harvey, Pat, and Britt H. Rathbone. *Dialectical Behavior Therapy for At-Risk Adolescents: A Practitioner's Guide to Treating Challenging Behavior Problems.* Oakland, Calif.: New Harbinger Publications, 2014.

Linde, Paul R. *Danger to Self: On the Front Line with an ER Psychiatrist.* Berkeley, Calif.: University of California Press, 2011.

Norris, Donna M., Geetha Jayaram, and Annelle B. Primm. (eds.) *Women in Psychiatry: Personal Perspectives.* Arlington, Va.: American Psychiatric Publishing, 2012.

Starting Out

Psychiatrists in residency can find job leads in professional journals and through professional organizations such as the American Psychiatric Association. Many are offered permanent positions with the same institution where they complete their residency.

ADVANCEMENT PROSPECTS

Most psychiatrists advance in their careers by enlarging their knowledge and skills, clientele, and earnings. Those who work in hospitals, clinics, and mental health centers may become administrators. Those who teach or concentrate on research may become department heads.

OUTLOOK

The U.S. Department of Labor predicts that employment for physicians will grow much faster than the average for all careers through 2024. Opportunities for psychiatrists in private practice and salaried positions are good. Employment for physicians who work in outpatient mental health and substance abuse centers and in residential mental health and substance abuse facilities is expected to grow much faster than the average for all occupations. Demand is great for child psychiatrists, and other specialties are also in short supply, especially in rural areas and public facilities.

A number of factors contribute to this shortage. Growing population and increasing life span add up to more people who need psychiatric care; rising incomes and the passage of the Affordable Health Care Act have enabled more people to afford treatment; and higher educational levels make more people aware of the importance of mental health care.

Psychiatrists are also needed as researchers to explore the causes of mental illness and develop new ways to treat it.

UNIONS AND ASSOCIATIONS

Most psychiatrists are not members of unions, but some may be represented by the Doctors Council SEIU or another union. Professional associations that provide useful resources (publications, continuing education, networking opportunities, etc.) include the American Medical Association and the American Psychiatric Association. Many receive board certification from the American Board of Psychiatry and Neurology. The Association of American Medical Colleges represents all accredited U.S. and Canadian medical schools, major teaching hospitals and health systems, and academic and scientific societies. The Canadian Psychiatric Association represents the professional interests of psychiatrists who work in Canada. Other helpful agencies/organizations include the National Institute of Mental Health and Mental Health America.

TIPS FOR ENTRY

1. To learn more about the field, read:
   - *JAMA Psychiatry* (http://archpsyc.jamanetwork.com/journal.aspx)
   - *Psychiatric News* (http://psychnews.psychiatryonline.org)
   - *American Journal of Geriatric Psychiatry* (http://www.ajgponline.org)
2. For job listings, visit:
   - http://www.aagponline.org
   - http://www.mentalhealthamerica.net/career-center
   - http://www.jamacareercenter.com
3. Join the American Medical Association (AMA), American Association for Geriatric Psychiatry (AAGP), and other professional associations to access training and networking resources, industry publications, and employment opportunities.
4. The AMA and AAGP offers mentoring programs for students, residents, and fellows. These are excellent ways to make networking contacts and grow in your career.

FOR MORE INFORMATION

For information on board certification, contact

American Board of Psychiatry and Neurology Inc. (ABPN)
2150 East Lake Cook Road, Suite 900
Buffalo Grove, IL 60089-1875

Tel: (847) 229-6500

Fax: (847) 229-6600

http://www.abpn.com

For more information on becoming a doctor as well as current health care news, visit the AMA Web site.

American Medical Association (AMA)

330 North Wabash Avenue, Suite 39300

Chicago, IL 60611-5885

Tel: (800) 621-8335

http://www.ama-assn.org

For comprehensive information on careers in psychiatry, contact

American Psychiatric Association (APA)

1000 Wilson Boulevard, Suite 1825

Arlington, VA 22209-3901

Tel: (800) 368-5777; (703) 907-7322

E-mail: apa@psych.org

http://www.psych.org

To learn more about careers in medicine and how to apply to medical schools, visit the following Web site:

Association of American Medical
Colleges (AAMC)

655 K Street, NW, Suite 100

Washington, D.C. 20001-2399

Tel: (202) 828-0400

http://www.aamc.org

For information on education, advocacy, and certification for Canadian psychiatrists, contact

Canadian Psychiatric Association (CPA)

141 Laurier Avenue West, Suite 701

Ottawa, ON K1P 5J3

Canada

Tel: (800) 267-1555; (613) 234-2815

Fax: (613) 234-9857

E-mail: cpa@cpa-apc.org

http://www.cpa-apc.org

Most psychiatrists are not members of unions, but some may be represented by the Doctors Council SEIU.

Doctors Council SEIU

50 Broadway, 11th Floor, Suite 1101

New York, NY 10004

Tel: (855) 362-7348

E-mail: info@doctorscouncil.org

http://www.doctorscouncil.org

For information on mental health, contact

Mental Health America (MHA)

500 Montgomery Street, Suite 820

Alexandria, VA 22314

Tel: (800) 969-6642; (703) 684-7722

Fax: (703) 684-5968

http://www.mentalhealthamerica.net

For information on mental health issues, contact

National Institute of Mental Health (NIMH)

Science Writing, Press, and Dissemination Branch

6001 Executive Boulevard, Room 6200, MSC 9663

Bethesda, MD 20892-9663

Tel: (866) 615-6464

Fax: (301) 443-4279

E-mail: nimhinfo@nih.gov

http://www.nimh.nih.gov

Psychologists

■ OVERVIEW

Psychologists teach, counsel, conduct research, or administer programs to understand people and help people understand themselves. Psychologists examine individual and group behavior through testing, experimenting, and studying personal histories.

Psychologists normally hold doctorates in psychology. Unlike psychiatrists, they are not medical doctors and most cannot prescribe medication in most states (clinical psychologists in Illinois, Louisiana, and New Mexico may prescribe medication to patients). Approximately 173,900 psychologists are employed in the United States.

■ HISTORY

The first syllable in psychology derives from *psyche*, a Greek word meaning soul. The second half of psychology contains the root of the word *logic*. Thus, psychology translates as "the science of the soul."

Early philosophers emphasized differences between body and soul. Plato, for example, believed they were two entirely different parts. Modern scholars tend to emphasize the unity between mind and body rather than their dissimilarity.

The founder of experimental psychology, Wilhelm Wundt, held both an M.D. and a Ph.D. A physician, he taught at the University of Leipzig, where his title was professor of philosophy. Like Wundt, German scholars of the 19th century were committed to the scientific method. Discovery by experiment was considered the only respectable way for learned thinkers to work. Thus it was not thought strange that in 1879, Wundt set up an experimental laboratory to conduct research on human behavior. Many people who later became famous psychologists in the United States received their training under Wundt.

QUICK FACTS

ALTERNATE TITLE(S)
Child Psychologists, Clinical Psychologists, Consumer Psychologists, Counseling Psychologists, Developmental Psychologists, Educational Psychologists, Engineering Psychologists, Experimental Psychologists, Forensic Psychologists, Industrial-Organizational Psychologists, Psychometrists, School Psychologists, Social Psychologists

DUTIES
Treat people who suffer from mental and emotional illnesses; conduct research on the human mind, behaviors, and mental and emotional illnesses

SALARY RANGE
$40,920 to $70,580 to $158,900+

WORK ENVIRONMENT
Primarily Indoors

BEST GEOGRAPHIC LOCATION(S)
Nationwide; most opportunities available in major metropolitan areas

MINIMUM EDUCATION LEVEL
Master's Degree

SCHOOL SUBJECTS
Biology, Psychology, Sociology

EXPERIENCE
Internship, residency

PERSONALITY TRAITS
Outgoing, Problem-Solving, Scientific

SKILLS
Interpersonal, Research, Scientific

CERTIFICATION OR LICENSING
Required

SPECIAL REQUIREMENTS
None

EMPLOYMENT PROSPECTS
Good

ADVANCEMENT PROSPECTS
Good

OUTLOOK
Much Faster than the Average

NOC
4151

O*NET-SOC
19-3031.00, 19-3031.01, 19-3031.02, 19-3031.03, 19-3032.00

At the turn of the 20th century, Russian physiologist Ivan Pavlov discovered a key aspect of behaviorist theory while studying the process of digestion. While experimenting on dogs, he found that they began to salivate in anticipation of their food. He discovered that if he rang a bell before presenting their meat, the dogs associated the sound of a bell with mealtime. He then would ring the bell but withhold the food. The dogs' saliva flowed anyway, whether or not they saw or smelled food. Pavlov called this substitute stimulus a "conditioned response." Many psychologists began to incorporate the theory of conditioned response into their theories of learning.

One of the most famous pioneers in psychology was Sigmund Freud, whose work led to many of the modern theories of behavior. Freud lived and practiced in Vienna, Austria, until Hitler's forces caused him to flee to England. His work on the meaning of dreams, the unconscious, and the nature of various emotional disturbances has had a profound effect upon the profession and practice of psychology for more than 70 years, although many psychologists now disagree with some of his theories.

Many Americans have contributed greatly to the science that seeks to understand human behavior: William James, Robert Woodworth, E. L. Thorndike, Clark Hull, B. F. Skinner, and others.

■ THE JOB

Psychology is both a science and a profession. As a science, it is a systematic approach to the understanding of people and their behavior; as a profession, it is the application of that understanding to help solve human problems. Psychology is a rapidly growing field, and psychologists work on a great variety of problems.

The field of psychology is so vast that no one person can become an expert in all of its specialties. The psychologist usually concentrates on one specialty. Many specialists use overlapping methodologies, theories, and treatments.

Many psychologists teach some area of basic psychology in colleges and universities. They are also likely to conduct research and supervise graduate student work in an area of special interest.

Clinical psychologists concern themselves with people's mental, emotional, and behavioral disorders. They assess and treat problems ranging from normal psychological crises, such as adolescent rebellion or middle-age loss of self-esteem, to extreme conditions, such as severe depression and schizophrenia.

Some clinical psychologists work almost exclusively with children. They may be staff members at a child guidance clinic or a treatment center for children at a large general hospital. *Child psychologists* and other clinical psychologists may engage in private practice, seeing clients at offices. Clinical psychologists comprise the largest group of specialists.

Developmental psychologists study how people develop from birth through old age. They describe, measure, and explain age-related changes in behavior, stages of emotional development, universal traits and individual differences, and abnormal changes in development. Many developmental psychologists teach and do research in colleges and universities. Some specialize in programs for children in day care centers, preschools, hospitals, or clinics. Others specialize in programs for the elderly.

Social psychologists study how people interact with one other, and how individuals are affected by their environment. Social psychology has developed from four sources: sociology, cultural anthropology, psychiatry, and psychology. Social psychologists are interested in individual and group behavior. They study the ways groups influence individuals and vice versa. They study different kinds of groups: ethnic, religious, political, educational, family, and many others. The social psychologist has devised ways to research group nature, attitudes, leadership patterns, and structure.

Counseling psychologists work with people who have problems they find difficult to face alone. These clients are not usually mentally or emotionally ill, but they are emotionally upset, anxious, or struggling with some conflict within themselves or their environment. By helping people solve their problems, make decisions, and cope with everyday stresses, the counseling psychologist actually is working in preventive mental health.

School psychologists frequently do diagnosis and remediation. They may engage primarily in preventive and developmental psychology. Many school psychologists are assigned the duty of testing pupils surmised to be exceptional. Other school psychologists work almost entirely with children who have proven to be a problem to themselves or to others and who have been referred for help by teachers or other members of the school system. Many school psychologists are concerned with pupils who reveal various kinds of learning disabilities. School psychologists may also be called upon to work with relationship problems between parents and children.

Industrial-organizational psychologists are concerned with the relation between people and work. They deal with organizational structure, worker productivity, job satisfaction, consumer behavior, personnel training and development, and the interaction between humans and machines. Industrial-organizational psychologists may work with a sales department to help salespeople become more effective. Some study assembly line procedures and suggest changes to reduce monotony and increase worker responsibility. Others plan various kinds of tests to help screen applicants for employment. Industrial-organizational psychologists conduct research to determine qualities that seem to produce the most efficient employees or help management develop programs to identify staff with management potential. They may be asked to investigate and report on certain differences of opinion between a supervisor and one of the workers. Some may design training courses to indoctrinate new employees or counsel older employees on career development or retirement preparation.

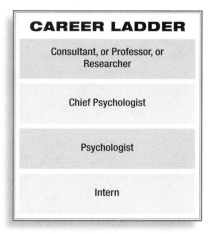

CAREER LADDER

Consultant, or Professor, or Researcher

Chief Psychologist

Psychologist

Intern

Forensic psychologists are psychologists with additional training in legal issues who regularly provide the judicial system with their professional expertise in a variety of matters.

Other industrial psychologists, referred to as *engineering psychologists,* help engineers and technicians design systems that require workers or consumers and machines to interact. They also develop training aids for those systems.

Consumer psychologists are interested in consumer reactions to products or services. These psychologists may be asked to determine the kinds of products the public will buy. They may study, for instance, whether people prefer big cars or little cars. They might be asked to make decisions about the most appealing ways to present a product through advertising. Many of today's most established advertising, promotion, and packaging practices have been influenced by the opinions and advice of consumer psychologists. Consumer psychologists also

A psychologist listens intently to a patient during a session. (Olimpik. Shutterstock.)

ALFRED ADLER

MOVERS AND SHAKERS

Austrian psychologist Alfred Adler (1870-1937) was founder of the school of individual psychology. He believed that humans strive throughout their lives to achieve contentment and fulfillment, in an attempt to compensate for strong feelings of inferiority developed in childhood. Most persons are able to compensate satisfactorily; those who are unsuccessful develop neuroses. Adler explained his theories in *The Theory and Practice of Individual Psychology* (1918), *Understanding Human Nature* (1927), and *Pattern of Life* (1930).

Adler was born in Vienna. He received a degree in medicine from the University of Vienna in 1895. In 1902, Adler became associated with Sigmund Freud, founder of psychoanalysis. Rejecting Freud's emphasis upon sex as a significant motive behind human behavior, Adler broke with Freud in 1911 and spent much of his time after 1925 lecturing in the United States.

try to improve product acceptability and safety in addition to helping the consumer make better decisions.

Psychometrists work with intelligence, personality, and aptitude tests used in clinics, counseling centers, schools, and businesses. They administer tests, score them, and interpret results as related to standard norms. Psychometrists also study methods and techniques used to acquire and evaluate psychological data. They may devise new, more reliable tests. These specialists are usually well trained in mathematics, statistics, and computer programming and technology.

The *educational psychologist* is concerned primarily with how people teach, learn, and evaluate learning. Many educational psychologists are employed on college or university faculties, and they also conduct research into learning theory. Educational psychologists are also interested in the evaluation of learning.

Experimental psychologists conduct scientific experiments on particular aspects of behavior, either animal or human. Much experimental study is done in learning, in physiological psychology (the relationship of behavior to physiological processes), and in comparative psychology (sometimes called animal psychology). Many experimental psychological studies are carried out with animals, partly because their environments can be carefully controlled.

Many psychologists of all kinds find that writing skills are helpful. They may write up the results of research efforts for a scholarly journal. Psychologists prepare papers for presentation at professional association meetings and sometimes write books or articles. As consultants or industrial psychologists, they may write instruction manuals. Educational psychologists may prepare test manuals.

Some psychologists become administrators who direct college or university psychology departments or personnel services programs in a school system or industry. Some become agency or department directors of research in scientific laboratories. They may be promoted to department head in a state or federal government agency. *Chief psychologists* in hospitals or psychiatric centers plan psychological treatment programs, direct professional and nonprofessional personnel, and oversee psychological services provided by the institution.

■ EARNINGS

Because the psychology field offers so many different types of employment possibilities, salaries for psychologists vary greatly. In addition, the typical conditions affecting salaries, such as the person's level of education, professional experience, and location, also apply. The U.S. Department of Labor reports that clinical, counseling, and school psychologists earned median salaries of $70,580 in May 2015. Salaries ranged from less than $40,920 to $116,960 or more. The department also reports the following mean annual earnings for clinical, counseling, and school psychologists by employer: offices of other health practitioners, $83,230; elementary/secondary schools, $74,130; outpatient care centers, $70,770; and individual and family services, $68,440. Industrial-organizational psychologists earned salaries that ranged from less than $52,270 to $158,900 or more, with an average salary of $77,350.

Benefits for full-time workers include vacation and sick time, health, and sometimes dental, insurance, and pension or 401(k) plans. Self-employed psychologists must provide their own benefits.

■ WORK ENVIRONMENT

Psychologists work under many different conditions. Those who work as college or university teachers usually have offices in a building on campus and access to a laboratory in which they carry out experiments.

Offices of school psychologists may be located in the school system headquarters. They may see students and their parents at those offices, or they might work in space set aside for them in several schools within the school district that they may visit regularly.

Psychologists in military service serve in this country or overseas. They may be stationed in Washington, D.C., and assigned to an office job, or they may be stationed with other military personnel at a post or, more likely, in a military hospital.

Psychologists employed in government work in such diverse places as public health or vocational rehabilitation agencies, the Department of Veterans Affairs, the Peace Corps, the U.S. Office of Education, or a state department of education. Their working conditions depend largely on the kind of jobs they have. They may be required to travel a lot or to produce publications. They may work directly with people or be assigned entirely to research.

Some psychologists are self-employed. Most work as clinical psychologists and have offices where they see clients individually. Others work as consultants to business firms. Self-employed psychologists rent or own their office spaces and arrange their own work schedules.

▣ EXPLORING

If you are interested in psychology, explore the field by taking psychology classes in high school and reading all you can about the subject, including biographies of and works by noted psychologists. In addition, make an appointment to talk about the profession with a psychologist who may work at a nearby school, college, hospital, or clinic. Use the Internet to learn more about mental health issues by visiting Web sites, such as that of Mental Health America at http://www.mentalhealthamerica.net or the American Psychological Association at http://www.apa.org.

If being involved with patient care interests you, gain experience in the health care field by volunteering at a local hospital or clinic. In addition, volunteer opportunities may exist at local nursing homes, where you will also have the chance to work with clients needing some type of assistance. If doing research work sounds appealing to you, consider joining your school's science club, which may offer the opportunity to work on projects, document the process, and work as part of a team.

▣ EDUCATION AND TRAINING REQUIREMENTS
High School

Because you will need to continue your education beyond high school in order to become a psychologist, you should enroll in college preparatory courses. Your class schedule should concentrate on English courses, computer science, mathematics, and sciences. Algebra, geometry, and calculus are important to take, as are biology, chemistry, and physics. You should take social science courses, such as psychology and sociology. You should also take a modern foreign language, such as French or German, because reading comprehension of these languages is one of the usual requirements for obtaining the doctorate degree.

Postsecondary Training

A doctorate in psychology (Ph.D. or Psy.D.) is recommended. While most new doctorates in the psychology field received a Ph.D., the number of Psy.D. recipients has increased over the past decade. Some positions are available to people with a master's degree, but they are jobs of lesser responsibility and lower salaries than those open to people with a doctorate.

Psychology is an obvious choice for your college major, but not all graduate programs require entering students to have a psychology bachelor's degree. Nevertheless, your college studies should include a number of psychology courses, such as experimental psychology, developmental psychology, and abnormal psychology. You should also take classes in statistics as well as such classes as English, foreign language, and history to complete a strong liberal arts education.

Course work at the master's degree level usually involves statistics, ethics, and industrial and organizational content. If you want to work as a school psychologist, you will need to complete a supervised, year long internship at a school after receiving your degree.

Some doctoral programs accept students with master's degrees; in other cases, students enter a doctoral program with only a bachelor's degree. Because entrance requirements vary, you will need to research the programs you are interested in to find out their specific requirements. The doctorate degree typically takes between four and seven years to complete for those who begin their studies with only the bachelor's degree. Course work will include studies in various areas of psychology and research (including work in quantitative research methods). Those who focus on research often complete a yearlong postdoctoral fellowship. Those who want to work as clinical, counseling, or school psychologists must complete a one-year supervised internship. Frequently those who are interested in clinical, counseling, or school psychology will get the Psy.D., because this degree emphasizes clinical rather than research work. Most states, however, require school psychologists to have the specialist degree Ed.S. in school psychology, which requires completion of two years of full-time graduate study and one year in a full-time internship. Those interested in clinical, counseling, or school psychology should attend a program accredited by the American Psychological Association (APA).

Unlike psychiatrists, psychologists do not need to attend medical school.

Other Education or Training

In order to maintain their licensing, psychologists must complete continuing education (CE) seminars, webinars, and other learning opportunities that are provided by professional associations at the national, state, and local levels. The American Psychological Association, for example, offers online courses, classes, and workshops on topics ranging from ethics and legal issues to practice specialties and mental, emotional, and behavioral disorders. The National Association of School Psychologists, Society for Industrial & Organizational Psychology, and the American College of Forensic Psychology also provide CE opportunities. Contact these organizations for more information.

■ CERTIFICATION, LICENSING, AND SPECIAL REQUIREMENTS
Certification or Licensing

The American Board of Professional Psychology offers voluntary specialty certification in a number of areas, including clinical psychology, clinical neuropsychology, and counseling, forensic, industrial-organizational, and school psychology. Requirements for certification include having a doctorate in psychology, professional experience, appropriate postdoctoral training, and the passing of an examination. Those who fulfill these requirements receive the designation of diplomate.

The National Association of School Psychologists (NASP) awards the nationally certified school psychologist designation to applicants who complete educational requirements, an internship, and pass an examination. More than 30 states recognize the designation.

Psychologists in independent practice or those providing any type of patient care, such as clinical, counseling, and school psychologists, must be licensed or certified by the state in which they practice. Psychologists must complete one or more of the following to become licensed: a pre-doctoral or post-doctoral supervised experience, an internship, a residency program, or one to two years of professional experience. They must also pass an examination. Check with your state's licensing board for specific information.

■ EXPERIENCE, SKILLS, AND PERSONALITY TRAITS

Because psychology is such a broad field, various personal attributes apply to different psychology positions. Those involved in research, for example, should be analytical, detail oriented, and have strong math and writing skills. Those working with patients should be "people persons," able to relate to others, and have excellent listening skills. They must have a desire to help people understand themselves and others. No matter what their area of focus, however, all psychologists should be committed to lifelong learning since our understanding of humans is constantly evolving. A basic curiosity is required as well as a fascination with the way the human mind works.

■ EMPLOYMENT PROSPECTS
Employers

Approximately 173,900 psychologists are employed in the United States. About one-fourth of psychologists are self-employed. Clinical psychologists may teach at colleges or universities. Or, clinical psychologists may work with patients in a private practice or a hospital, where they provide therapy after evaluation through special tests.

Many developmental psychologists teach and research in colleges and universities. Some specialize in programs for children in day care centers, preschools, hospitals, or clinics.

Social psychologists often teach and conduct research in colleges or universities. They also work for agencies of the federal or state government or in private research firms. Some work as consultants. An increasing number of social psychologists work as researchers and personnel managers in such nontraditional settings as advertising agencies, corporations, and architectural and engineering firms.

Counseling psychologists work in college or university counseling centers; they also teach in psychology departments. They may be in private practice. Or they may work at a community health center, a marriage counseling agency, or a federal agency such as the Department of Veterans Affairs.

Forensic psychologists work for government agencies (including those in law enforcement), hospitals, prisons, drug rehabilitation centers, law firms, community health centers that offer specialized services, and in private practice. Others teach at colleges and universities.

Consumer psychologists study consumer reactions to products or services. They are hired by advertising, promotion, and packaging companies.

Psychometrists may be employed in colleges and universities, testing companies, private research firms, or government agencies.

Educational psychologists may work for test publishing firms devising and standardizing tests of ability, aptitude, personal preferences, attitudes, or characteristics.

Starting Out

Those entering the field with only a bachelor's degree will face strong competition for few jobs. The university career services office or a psychology professor may be able to help such a student find a position assisting a psychologist at a health center or other location. Those with a baccalaureate degree can also pursue careers in business administration, sales, and secondary education. Positions beyond the assistant level, however, will be very difficult to attain. Those graduating from master's or doctorate degree programs will find more employment opportunities. Again, university career services offices may be able to provide these graduates with assistance. In addition, contacts made during an internship may offer job leads. Joining professional organizations and networking with members is also a way to find out about job openings. In addition, these organizations, such as the American Psychological Association, often list job vacancies in their publications for members.

■ ADVANCEMENT PROSPECTS

For those who have bachelor's or master's degrees, the first step to professional advancement is to complete a doctorate degree. After that, advancement will depend on the area of psychology in which the person is working. For example, a psychologist teaching at a college or university may advance through the academic ranks from instructor to professor. Some college teachers who enjoy administrative work become department heads.

Psychologists who work for state or federal government agencies may, after considerable experience, be promoted to head a section or department. School psychologists might become directors of pupil personnel services. Industrial psychologists can rise to managerial or administrative positions.

After several years of experience, many psychologists enter private practice or set up their own research or consulting firms.

■ OUTLOOK

The U.S. Department of Labor projects that employment for psychologists will grow much faster than the average for all occupations through 2024. More employment opportunities will be in schools, hospitals, social service agencies, mental health centers, substance abuse treatment clinics, consulting firms, and private companies. Increased emphasis on health maintenance and illness prevention as well as growing interest in psychological services for special groups, such as children or the elderly, will create demand for psychologists. Many of these areas depend on government funding, however, and could be adversely affected in an economic downswing when spending is likely to be curtailed. Many openings should be available in business and industry, and the outlook is very good for psychologists who are in full-time independent practice.

Prospects look best for those with doctorates in applied areas, such as clinical, counseling, health, industrial/organizational, and school psychology, and for those with extensive technical training in quantitative research methods and computer applications. Postdoctorates are becoming increasingly crucial in the fields of research psychology that deal with behavior based on biology.

Forensic psychologists will be increasingly needed in coming years to serve as expert witnesses and to offer legal consulting services to law firms.

Competition for jobs will be tougher for those with master's or bachelor's degrees. Most job candidates with bachelor's degrees, in fact, will not be able to find employment in the psychology field beyond assistant-level jobs at such places as rehabilitation centers. Some may work as high school psychology teachers if they meet state teaching certification requirements.

■ UNIONS AND ASSOCIATIONS

Some psychologists belong to unions that specifically serve those in the government or education sectors. Professional associations that provide useful resources (publications, continuing education, networking opportunities, etc.) include the American Psychological Association, National Association of School Psychologists, American College of Forensic Psychology, and the Society for Industrial & Organizational Psychology. The American Board of Professional Psychology and the American Board of Forensic Psychology provide certification to psychologists. The Association of State and Provincial Psychology Boards is an organization of psychology licensing boards in the United States and Canada. The Canadian Psychological Association represents the professional interests of psychologists in Canada.

■ TIPS FOR ENTRY

1. To learn more about the field, read:
   - *The American Psychologist* (http://www.apa.org/pubs/journals)
   - *American Journal of Forensic Psychology* (http://www.forensicpsychology.org)
   - *School Psychology Review* (http://www.nasponline.org/resources-and-publications)
   - *The Industrial-Organizational Psychologist* (http://my.siop.org/tipdefault)
2. Join professional associations to access training and networking resources, industry publications, and employment opportunities. The American Psychological Association (APA) offers membership categories for high school and college students and professionals.
3. Talk to psychologists about their careers. The APA offers a database of psychologists at http://locator.apa.org.
4. For job listings, visit:
   - http://www.apa.org/careers
   - http://nasponline-jobs.careerwebsite.com/home/home.cfm?site_id=15381&cust_code=nasp
   - http://www.siop.org/JobNet

◾ FOR MORE INFORMATION

For information on board certification, contact

American Board of Forensic Psychology (ABFP)
http://www.abfp.com

For information on specialty certification, contact

**American Board of Professional
        Psychology (ABPP)**
600 Market Street, Suite 201
Chapel Hill, NC 27516-4056
Tel: (919) 537-8031
Fax: (919) 537-8034
E-mail: office@abpp.org
http://www.abpp.org

For information about the American Journal of Forensic Psychology, contact

American College of Forensic Psychology
PO Box 5899
Balboa Island, CA 92662
Tel: (760) 929-9777
Fax: (844) 812-9426
E-mail: psychlaw@sover.net
http://www.forensicpsychology.org

For more on careers in psychology and mental health issues, contact

American Psychological Association (APA)
750 First Street, NE
Washington, D.C. 20002-4242
Tel: (800) 374-2721
Fax: (202) 336-5500
http://www.apa.org

For licensing information, visit

**Association of State and Provincial Psychology
        Boards (ASPPB)**
PO Box 3079
Peachtree City, GA 30269-7079
Tel: (678) 216-1175
Fax: (678) 216-1176
E-mail: asppb@asppb.org
http://www.asppb.net/

For a list of Canadian psychology departments providing graduate programs, contact

Canadian Psychological Association (CPA)
141 Laurier Avenue West, Suite 702
Ottawa, ON K1P 5J3
Canada
Tel: (888) 472-0657; (613) 237-2144
Fax: (613) 237-1674
E-mail: cpa@cpa.ca
http://www.cpa.ca

For a whimsical introduction to psychology, visit

ePsych
http://epsych.msstate.edu

For more information on certification and becoming a school psychologist, including graduate school information, contact

**National Association of School
        Psychologists (NASP)**
4340 East-West Highway, Suite 402
Bethesda, MD 20814-4468
Tel: (301) 657-0270
Fax: (866) 331-NASP
E-mail: (301) 657-0275
http://www.nasponline.org

For more information about education and careers, contact

**Society for Industrial & Organizational
        Psychology (SIOP)**
440 East Poe Road, Suite 101
Bowling Green, OH 43402-1355
Tel: (419) 353-0032
Fax: (419) 352-2645
E-mail: SIOP@siop.org
http://www.siop.org

Public Interest Lawyers

◾ OVERVIEW

Lawyers, or *attorneys,* help clients know their rights under the law and then help them achieve these rights before a judge, jury, government agency, or other legal forum, such as an arbitration panel. Lawyers represent individuals and for-profit and nonprofit organizations. Lawyers often choose a field of law in which to specialize. Lawyers specializing in public interest law provide a wide range of services to those who otherwise could not afford legal representation. They also work for organizations advocating for a particular cause. Their work is often done *pro bono*—for the public good—voluntarily and without payment. The American Bar Association, the largest association for legal professionals, has a Standing Committee on Pro Bono and Public Service. Approximately 609,930 lawyers work in the United States today in various legal specialties.

◾ HISTORY

The tradition of governing people by laws has been established over centuries. Societies have built up systems of law that have been studied and drawn upon by later governments. The earliest known law is the Code of Hammurabi, developed about 1800 B.C. by the ruler of the Sumerians. Another early set of laws was the Law of Moses, known as the Ten Commandments. Every set of laws, no matter when they were introduced, has been accompanied by the need for someone to explain those laws and help others live under them.

The great orators of ancient Greece and Rome set up schools for young boys to learn by apprenticeship the many skills involved in pleading a law case. To be an eloquent speaker was the greatest advantage. The legal profession has matured since those earlier times; a great deal of training and an extensive knowledge of legal matters are required of the modern lawyer and judge.

Much modern European law was organized and refined by legal experts assembled by Napoleon; their body of law was known as the Napoleonic Code. English colonists coming to America brought English common law, from which American laws have grown. In areas of the United States that were heavily settled by Spanish colonists, there are traces of Spanish law. As the population in the country grew, along with business, those who knew the law were in high demand. The two main kinds of law are *civil* and *criminal,* but many other specialty areas are also prevalent today. When our country was young, most lawyers were general law practitioners— they knew and worked with all the laws for their clients' sakes. Today, there are many more lawyers who specialize in areas such as tax law, corporate law, intellectual property law, and public interest law.

Public interest law in the United States developed in the late 1800s, according to the National Legal Aid & Defender Association. The German Society of New York founded what is considered to be the first civil legal assistance program for poor people in 1876. The organization was formed to protect the rights of recent German immigrants. Later, it expanded its services to advocate for other groups and was renamed the Legal Aid Society of New York in 1890. It is still serving the disadvantaged today.

In the early 1920s, the American Bar Association created the Special Committee on Legal Aid Work and encouraged other legal associations to do the same. By the 1950s, legal aid programs were available in nearly every major U.S. city.

In 1964, the U.S. government began providing federal funding for civil legal assistance to poor people, which created strong growth for public interest law organizations.

In 1986, students from 14 law schools created the National Association for Public Interest Law (now known as Equal Justice Works) to advance the profession of public interest law.

Today, public interest law is a popular and rewarding career option for lawyers who are interested in helping the disadvantaged attain better lives.

■ THE JOB

Public interest lawyers (PILs) may have different specialties, but all direct their services to a particular group of clients— those who may not have the means to pay for legal counsel. PILs often provide their services pro bono, for little or no fee. While the majority of their clients are individuals who are poor or on fixed incomes, PILS may also do work for public interest groups with a range of advocacy issues, such as the environment, adoption, or immigration.

Many PILs work for government-funded legal aid clinics and offices. For example, lawyers working for the Migrant Farm Worker Division of Texas RioGrande Legal Aid (TRLA) provide legal assistance to seasonal or migrant agricultural workers, some with alien status. These workers are mostly of Latino heritage. The TRLA provides civil legal service at no cost; its funding comes from a combination of support from the federal government and private foundations. Lawyers employed by the TRLA represent the rights of their clients regarding housing, employment, public benefits, and civil rights issues. They may also propose changes in welfare training and educational materials and services to these migrant workers. Lawyers working in this capacity are paid an annual salary, though much less compared to

---

QUICK FACTS

ALTERNATE TITLE(S)
Public Defenders, Public Interest Attorneys

DUTIES
Provide legal services to those who otherwise could not afford legal representation; work for organizations advocating for a particular cause such as environmental justice or human rights

SALARY RANGE
$44,600 to $51,000 to $84,500+

WORK ENVIRONMENT
Primarily Indoors

BEST GEOGRAPHIC LOCATION(S)
Nationwide

MINIMUM EDUCATION LEVEL
Law Degree

SCHOOL SUBJECTS
English, Government, Speech

EXPERIENCE
Internship or clerkship

PERSONALITY TRAITS
Organized, Problem-Solving, Realistic

SKILLS
Business Management, Leadership, Organizational

CERTIFICATION OR LICENSING
Required

SPECIAL REQUIREMENTS
None

EMPLOYMENT PROSPECTS
Fair

ADVANCEMENT PROSPECTS
Good

OUTLOOK
About as Fast as the Average

NOC
4112

O*NET-SOC
23-1011.00

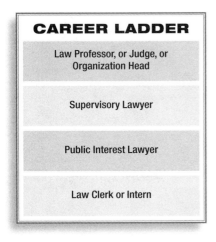

CAREER LADDER

Law Professor, or Judge, or
Organization Head

Supervisory Lawyer

Public Interest Lawyer

Law Clerk or Intern

attorneys employed at a private firm.

Public defenders can also be considered public interest lawyers. Low income, or indigent, people charged with a crime are often assigned a public defender to assist with their legal defense. Public defender agencies, at the state and federal level, are supported by public funding. Full-time public defenders specialize in criminal law—offenses committed against society or the state, such as theft, murder, or arson. They interview clients and witnesses to ascertain facts in a case, correlate their findings with known cases, and prepare a case to defend a client against the charges made. They conduct a defense at the trial, examine witnesses, and summarize the case with a closing argument to a jury.

Other PILs choose to provide legal counsel or work as advocates for nonprofit organizations. For example, a public interest lawyer may serve as the director of legal services and advocacy for an HIV/AIDS organization. Duties for someone in this position might include influencing the policies and positions of the executive and legislative branches of the federal government regarding HIV/AIDS, monitoring HIV/AIDS issues and helping lead community alliances against the disease, and educating the public about political candidates' positions regarding HIV/AIDS. Other lawyers working for this advocacy group might provide legal representation, offer technical advice, and participate in interviews and forums about HIV/AIDS.

Lawyers employed at private legal firms may also practice public interest law. Many support the work of various organizations and charities by providing their legal expertise pro bono. In fact, the American Bar Association urges its members to render at least 50 hours of *pro bono publico* legal services a year.

■ EARNINGS

Public interest lawyers earn salaries that vary depending on the type, size, and location of their employer. PILs who are employed by government agencies typically earn more than those employed by nonprofit organizations or foundations.

The National Association for Law Placement reports the following starting salaries for public interest lawyers by specialty in 2014: civil legal services, $44,600; public defenders, $50,400; and public interest organizations, $46,000. Salaries for lawyers with five years' experience ranged from less than $51,000 to $63,600 or more. Public interest lawyers with 11–15 years' experience had earnings that ranged from less than $65,000 to more than $84,500. PILs who are employed by government agencies typically earn more than those who work for nonprofit organizations and foundations.

Benefits for lawyers who work full time include vacation and sick time, health, and sometimes dental, insurance, and pension or 401(k) plans. Self-employed lawyers must provide their own benefits.

■ WORK ENVIRONMENT

Offices and courtrooms are usually pleasant, although busy, places to work. Public interest lawyers also spend significant amounts of time in law libraries or record rooms, in the homes and offices of clients, and sometimes in the jail cells of clients or prospective witnesses. Many lawyers never work in a courtroom. Unless they are directly involved in litigation, they may never perform at a trial.

Some courts, such as small claims, family, or surrogate, may have evening hours to provide flexibility to the community. Criminal arraignments may be held at any time of the day or night. Court hours for most lawyers are usually regular business hours, with a one-hour lunch break. Often lawyers have to work long hours, spending evenings and weekends preparing cases and materials and working with clients. In addition to the work, the lawyer must always keep up with the latest developments in the profession. Also, it takes a long time to become a qualified lawyer, and it may be difficult to earn an adequate living until the lawyer gets enough experience to develop an established private practice.

Public interest lawyers who are employed at law firms must often work grueling hours to advance in the firm. Spending long weekend hours doing research and interviewing people should be expected.

■ EXPLORING

If you think a career in public interest law might be right up your alley, there are several ways you can find out more about the field before making that final decision. First, sit in on a trial or two at your local or state courthouse. Write down questions you have and terms or actions you do not understand. Then, talk to your school counselor and ask for help in setting up a telephone or in-person interview with a lawyer. Ask questions and get the scoop on what the career is really all about. Also, talk to your counselor or political science teacher about starting or joining a job-shadowing program. Job-shadowing programs allow you to follow a person in a certain career around for a day or two to get an idea of what goes on in a typical day. You may even be invited to help out with a few minor duties.

You can also search the Internet for general information about public interest lawyers and current court cases. After you have done some research and talked to a lawyer and you still think you are destined for law school, try to get a part-time job in a law office—preferably one that specializes in public interest law. Ask your counselor for help.

If you are already in law school, you might consider becoming a student member of the American Bar Association. Student members receive *Student Lawyer,* a magazine that contains useful information for aspiring lawyers. Sample articles from the magazine can be read at http://abaforlawstudents.com/stay-informed/student-lawyer-magazine/.

■ EDUCATION AND TRAINING REQUIREMENTS
High School
A high school diploma, a college degree, and three years of law school are minimum requirements for a law degree. A high school diploma is a first step on the ladder of education that a lawyer must climb. If you are considering a career in law, courses such as government, history, social studies, and economics provide a solid background for entering college-level courses. Speech courses are also helpful to build strong communication skills necessary for the profession. Foreign language classes, particularly Spanish, are also useful. In addition, you can take advantage of any computer-related classes or experience you can get, because public interest lawyers often use technology to research and interpret the law, from surfing the Internet to searching legal databases.

Postsecondary Training
To enter any law school approved by the American Bar Association, you must satisfactorily complete at least three, and usually four, years of college work. Most law schools do not specify any particular courses for prelaw education. Usually a liberal arts track is most advisable, with courses in English, history, economics, social sciences, logic, and public speaking. A college student planning on specialization in a particular area of law, however, might also take courses significantly related to that area, such as economics or political science. Some students interested in careers in public law earn bachelor's degrees in nonprofit management or social work.

Those interested should contact several law schools to learn more about any requirements and to see if they will accept credits from the college the student is planning to attend.

Currently, 205 law schools in the United States are approved by the American Bar Association; others, many of them night schools, are approved by state authorities only. Most of the approved law schools, however, do have night sessions to accommodate part-time students. Part-time courses of study usually take four years.

Law school training consists of required courses such as legal writing and research, contracts, criminal law, constitutional law, torts, and property. The second and third years may be devoted to specialized courses of interest to the student, such as public interest law. The study of cases and decisions is of basic importance to the law student, who will be required to read and study thousands of these cases. A degree of juris doctor (J.D.) or bachelor of laws (LL.B.) is usually granted upon graduation. Some law students considering specialization, research, or teaching may go on for advanced study.

Most law schools require that applicants take the Law School Admission Test (LSAT), where prospective law students are tested on their critical thinking, writing, and reasoning abilities.

Certification
Some lawyers choose to earn a master of laws (LL.M) degree, an advanced law certification that helps them advance professionally. LL.M programs, which typically last one year, are offered in many areas—such as child and family law, dispute resolution, energy/environment/natural resources, general law, human rights, litigation/trial advocacy, and public interest law. A first law degree is required for admission to LL.M programs. Visit http://www.lsac.org/llm for more information or http://www.americanbar.org/groups/legal_education/accreditation.html for a list of LL.M specialties and the law schools that offer them.

Other Education or Training
The American Bar Association, American Immigration Lawyers Association, Equal Justice Works, National Association for Law Placement, National Association of Counsel for Children, National Employment Lawyers Association, National Legal Aid and Defender Association, and national, state, and local bar and professional associations offer a variety of continuing education (CE) classes, conference sessions, workshops, and webinars. Contact these organizations for more information. Additionally, most law firms provide in-house CE opportunities to their employees.

■ CERTIFICATION, LICENSING, AND SPECIAL REQUIREMENTS
Certification or Licensing
The National Board of Legal Specialty Certification offers voluntary board certification in civil pretrial practice, civil law, criminal law, family law, and Social Security

LAW IN THE PUBLIC INTEREST   LEARN MORE ABOUT IT

Edwards, Lee. *Bringing Justice to the People: The Story of the Freedom-Based Public Interest Law Movement.* Westminster, Md.: Heritage Books, 2004.

Fontaine, Valerie. *The Right Moves: Job Search and Career Development Strategies for Lawyers,* 2nd ed. Washington, D.C.: National Association for Law Placement, 2013.

Morrison, Alan B., and Diane Chin. *Beyond the Big Firm: Profiles of Lawyers Who Want Something More.* New York: Aspen Publishers, 2007.

Schmedemann, Deborah A. *Thorns and Roses: Lawyers Tell Their Pro Bono Stories.* Durham, N.C.: Carolina Academic Press, 2010.

disability advocacy. The National Association of Counsel for Children provides the child welfare law certification to attorneys who serve in the role of child's attorney (including guardian ad litem, law guardian, attorney ad litem), parent's attorney, and agency/department/government attorney. The specialization area as approved by the American Bar Association is defined as "the practice of law representing children, parents or the government in all child protection proceedings including emergency, temporary custody, adjudication, disposition, foster care, permanency planning, termination, guardianship, and adoption. Child welfare law does not include representation in private child custody and adoption disputes where the state is not a party." Specialized voluntary certification for elder law attorneys is provided by the National Elder Law Foundation. Contact these organizations for more information on certification requirements.

Every state requires that lawyers be admitted to the bar of that state before they can practice. They require that applicants graduate from an approved law school and that they pass a written examination in the state in which they intend to practice. In a few states, graduates of law schools within the state are excused from these written examinations. After lawyers have been admitted to the bar in one state, they can practice in another state without taking a written examination if the states have reciprocity agreements; however, they will be required to meet certain state standards of good character and legal experience and pay any applicable fees.

■ EXPERIENCE, SKILLS, AND PERSONALITY TRAITS

Experience as a public interest law intern or clerk is highly recommended.

Successful public interest lawyers need to be effective communicators, work well with people, and be able to find creative solutions to problems. PILs must also be compassionate, with a strong desire to help others, especially the disadvantaged. Oftentimes PILs are not rewarded financially, but rather with the knowledge of helping those unable to help themselves.

■ EMPLOYMENT PROSPECTS
Employers

Approximately 609,930 lawyers are employed in the United States. The list of PIL employers is endless—ranging from government agencies, to nonprofit organizations, to advocacy groups. Organizations such as Equal Justice Works (http://www.equaljusticeworks.org) offer programs for lawyers to match their pro bono legal services to individuals or areas that need them most. Many private law firms also encourage their lawyers to provide pro bono work or volunteer in other capacities.

Starting Out

Beginning lawyers often work as law clerks or as assistants to senior lawyers doing research work and other routine tasks. After a few years of experience, they may be assigned their own cases; some may choose to go into private practice specializing in public interest law.

Many new lawyers are recruited by law firms or other employers directly from law school. Recruiters come to the school and interview possible hires. Other new graduates can get job leads from local and state bar associations.

■ ADVANCEMENT PROSPECTS

Lawyers, if they choose to pursue the specialty of public interest law, can advance by being assigned more responsibilities within their organization or firm. They can lead entire projects, take on higher profile cases, or represent an advocacy group. Public defenders can be promoted from the state to the federal level. Some public interest lawyers become law professors or judges.

■ OUTLOOK

According to the *Occupational Outlook Handbook,* employment for lawyers is expected to grow about as fast as the average for all occupations through 2024, but record numbers of law school graduates have created strong competition for jobs, even though the number of graduates has begun to level off. Continued population growth and increased numbers of legal cases involving environmental, human rights, international law, elder abuse, and sexual harassment issues, among others, will create a steady demand for public interest lawyers. Law services will be more accessible to the middle-income public with the popularity of prepaid legal services and clinics.

Despite the relatively low salaries earned by public interest lawyers, there is strong competition for these jobs. Most lawyers enter the specialty after several years practicing law and completing internships or fellowships in public interest law.

■ UNIONS AND ASSOCIATIONS

Public interest lawyers who are employed by the government can become members of the American Federation of Government Employees. Many lawyers join the American Academy of Adoption Attorneys, American Bar Association, American Immigration Lawyers Association, National Association of Counsel for Children (NACC), National Association of Women Lawyers, National Employment Lawyers Association, or the National Legal Aid & Defender Association. The National Board of Legal Specialty Certification, National Elder Law Foundation, and the NACC provide certification to public interest lawyers. Other important organizations for lawyers include the Association of American Law Schools, Equal Justice Works, Law School Admission Council, and the National Association for Law Placement.

■ TIPS FOR ENTRY

1. Visit http://www.psjd.org/Public_Interest_Career_Fair_and_Events_Calendar to access a list of public interest career fairs throughout the United States.
2. Use the NALP Directory of Legal Employers (http://www.nalpdirectory.com) to search for employers by location, employer type, practice areas, and other criteria.
3. Visit the following Web sites for job listings:
   - http://www.nlada.org/job-board
   - http://careers.aila.org/jobseekers
   - http://www.naccchildlaw.org/networking
   - http://www.abalcc.org
   - http://www.nela.org
   - http://www.psjd.org
4. Conduct information interviews with public interest lawyers and ask them for advice on preparing for and entering the field.

■ FOR MORE INFORMATION

For information on membership and continuing education, contact

American Academy of Adoption
Attorneys (AAAA)
PO Box 33053
Washington, D.C. 20033-0053

Tel: (202) 832-2222
E-mail: info@adoptionattorneys.org
http://www.adoptionattorneys.org

For more information about public interest law, contact

American Bar Association Standing Committee
on Pro Bono and Public Service and the Center
for Pro Bono
321 North Clark Street
Chicago, IL 60654-7598
Fax: (312) 988-5483
E-mail: abaprobono@americanbar.org
http://www.americanbar.org/groups/probono_public
_service/contact_us.html

Some attorneys who work in the government sector are members of AFGE. Contact the organization for more details.

American Federation of Government Employees,
AFL-CIO (AFGE)
80 F Street, NW
Washington, D.C. 20001
Tel: (202) 737-8700
E-mail: comments@afge.org
https://www.afge.org

For information on immigration law, contact

American Immigration Lawyers
Association (AILA)
1331 G Street, NW, Suite 300
Washington, D.C. 20005-3142
Tel: (202) 507-7600
Fax: (202) 783-7853
E-mail: membership@aila.org
http://aila.org

For information on law schools, contact

Association of American Law Schools (AALS)
1614 20th Street, NW
Washington, D.C. 20009-1001
Tel: (202) 296-8851
Fax: (202) 296-8869
E-mail: aals@aals.org
http://www.aals.org

For more information about public interest law, contact

Equal Justice Works
1730 M Street, NW, Suite 800
Washington, D.C. 20036-4511
Tel: (202) 466-3686
E-mail: info@equaljusticeworks.org
http://www.equaljusticeworks.org

For information about admission to law school, contact
> **Law School Admission Council (LSAC)**
> 662 Penn Street
> Newtown, PA 18940
> Tel: (215) 968-1001
> http://www.lsac.org

NALP is "an association of over 2,500 legal career professionals who advise law students, lawyers, law offices, and law schools in North America and beyond."
> **The National Association for Law**
> **Placement (NALP)**
> 1220 19th Street, NW, Suite 401
> Washington, D.C. 20036-2405
> Tel: (202) 835-1001
> Fax: (202) 835-1112
> E-mail: info@nalp.org
> http://www.nalp.org

For information, contact
> **National Association of Counsel for**
> **Children (NACC)**
> 13123 E. 16th Avenue, B390
> Aurora, CO 80045
> Tel: (888) 828-NACC; (303) 864-5320
> E-mail: Advocate@NACCchildlaw.org
> http://www.naccchildlaw.org

For information about elder law, contact
> **National Elder Law Foundation (NELF)**
> 6336 N. Oracle Rd., Ste. 326, #136
> Tucson, AZ 85704
> Tel: (520) 881-1076
> Fax: (520) 203-0277
> http://www.nelf.org

For more information about public interest law, contact
> **National Legal Aid & Defender Association**
> **(NLADA)**
> 1901 Pennsylvania Avenue, NW, Suite 500
> Washington, D.C. 20006
> Tel: (202) 452-0620
> Fax: (202) 872-1031
> http://www.nlada.org

PSJD is an "online clearinghouse for law students and lawyers to connect with public interest job listings and career-building resources."
> **PSJD**
> 1220 19th Street, NW, Suite 401
> Washington, D.C. 20036-2405
> Tel: (202) 296-0076
> Fax: (202) 835-1112
> E-mail: PSJD@nalp.org
> http://www.psjd.org

Public Opinion Researchers

■ OVERVIEW

Public opinion researchers, also known as *survey researchers,* help measure public sentiment about various products, services, or social issues by gathering information from a sample of the population through questionnaires and interviews. They collect, analyze, and interpret data and opinions to explore issues and forecast trends. Their poll results help business people, politicians, and other decision makers determine what's on the public's mind. Approximately 13,650 survey researchers are employed in the United States, many of whom combine full-time work in government, academia, or business with part-time consulting work in another setting.

■ HISTORY

Public opinion research began in a rudimentary way in the 1830s and 1840s when local newspapers asked their readers to fill out unofficial ballots indicating for whom they had voted in a particular election. Since that time, research on political issues has been conducted with increasing frequency—especially during presidential election years. However, public opinion research is most widely used by businesses to determine what products or services consumers like or dislike.

As questionnaires and interviewing techniques have become more refined, the field of public opinion research has become more accurate at reflecting the individual attitudes and opinions of the sample groups. Companies like Gallup and Harris Interactive conduct surveys for a wide range of political and economic purposes. Although some people continue to question the accuracy and importance of polls, they have become an integral part of our social fabric.

■ THE JOB

Public opinion researchers conduct interviews and gather data that accurately reflect public opinions. They do this so that decision makers in business and politics have a better idea of what people want on a wide range of issues. Public opinion is sometimes gauged by interviewing a small percentage of the population containing a variety of people who closely parallel the larger population in terms of age, race, income, and other factors. At other times, researchers interview people who represent a certain demographic group. Public opinion researchers may help a company implement a new marketing strategy or help a political candidate decide which campaign issues the public considers important.

Researchers use a variety of methods to collect and analyze public opinion. The particular method depends on the target audience and the type of information desired. For example, if the owner of a shopping mall is interested in gauging the opinions of shoppers, the research company will most likely station interviewers in selected areas around the mall so they can question the shoppers. On the other hand, an advertising firm may be interested in the opinions of a particular demographic group, such as working mothers or teenagers. In this case, the research firm would plan a procedure (such as a telephone survey) providing access to that group. Other field collection methods include interviews in the home and at work as well as questionnaires that are filled out by respondents and then returned through the mail.

Planning is an important ingredient in developing an effective survey method. After they receive an assignment, researchers decide what portion of the population they will survey and develop questions that will result in an accurate gauging of opinion. Researchers investigate whether previous surveys have been done on a particular topic, and if so, what the results were.

It is important that exactly the same procedures be used throughout the entire data collection process so that the survey is not influenced by the individual styles of the interviewers. For this reason, the process is closely monitored by supervisory personnel. Research assistants help train survey interviewers, prepare survey questionnaires and related materials, and tabulate and code survey results.

Other specialists within the field include *market research analysts,* who collect, analyze, and interpret survey results to determine what they mean. They prepare reports and make recommendations on subjects ranging from preferences of prospective customers to future sales trends. They use mathematical and statistical models to analyze research. Research analysts are careful to screen out unimportant or invalid information that could skew their survey results. Some research analysts specialize in one industry or area. For example, *agricultural marketing research analysts* prepare sales forecasts for food businesses, which use the information in their advertising and sales programs. *Survey workers* conduct public opinion interviews to determine people's buying habits or opinions on public issues. Survey workers contact people in their homes, at work, at random in public places, or via the telephone, questioning the person in a specified manner, usually following a questionnaire format.

Public opinion researchers are sometimes mistaken for telemarketers. In general, public opinion researchers are conducting serious research and collecting opinions, whereas telemarketers ultimately are in the business of sales.

■ EARNINGS

Starting salaries vary according to the skill and experience of the applicant, the nature of the position, and the size of the company. Survey researchers earned a median salary of $53,920 in May 2015, according to the U.S. Department of Labor. Earnings ranged from less than $22,300 to $99,500 or more. Those in academic positions may earn somewhat less than their counterparts in the business community, but federal government salaries are competitive with those in the private sector.

Most full-time public opinion researchers receive the usual medical, pension, vacation, and other benefits that other professional workers do. Managers may also receive bonuses based on their company's performance.

■ WORK ENVIRONMENT

Public opinion researchers usually work a standard 40-hour week, although they may have to work overtime occasionally if a project has a tight deadline. Those in supervisory positions may work especially long hours overseeing the collection and interpretation of information.

When conducting telephone interviews or organizing or analyzing data, researchers work in comfortable offices, with computers and data processing equipment close at hand. When collecting information via personal interviews or questionnaires, it is not unusual to spend time in shopping malls, on the street, or in private homes. Some evening and weekend

QUICK FACTS

ALTERNATE TITLE(S)
Agricultural Marketing Research Analysts, Market Research Analysts, Survey Researchers, Survey Workers

DUTIES
Measure public sentiment about various products, services, or social issues by gathering information through questionnaires and interviews

SALARY RANGE
$22,300 to $53,920 to $99,500+

WORK ENVIRONMENT
Indoors/Outdoors

BEST GEOGRAPHIC LOCATION(S)
Nationwide; most opportunities available in metropolitan areas

MINIMUM EDUCATION LEVEL
Bachelor's Degree

SCHOOL SUBJECTS
English, Social Studies, Speech

EXPERIENCE
Internship; volunteer or part-time experience

PERSONALITY TRAITS
Curious, Organized, Outgoing

SKILLS
Interpersonal, Organizational, Research

CERTIFICATION OR LICENSING
Recommended

SPECIAL REQUIREMENTS
None

EMPLOYMENT PROSPECTS
Good

ADVANCEMENT PROSPECTS
Good

OUTLOOK
Faster than the Average

NOC
1454

O*NET-SOC
13-1161.00, 19-3022.00

CAREER LADDER

Marketing Research Director or Business Owner

Supervisor

Public Opinion Researcher

Interviewer or Data Analyst

Survey Worker

work may be involved because people are most readily available to be interviewed at those times. Some research positions may include assignments that involve travel, but these are generally short assignments.

■ EXPLORING

High school students can often work as survey workers for a telemarketing firm or other consumer research company. Work opportunities may also be available through which you can learn about the coding and tabulation of survey data. Actual participation in a consumer survey may also offer insight into the type of work involved in the field. You should also try to talk with professionals already working in the field to learn more about the profession.

■ EDUCATION AND TRAINING REQUIREMENTS
High School

Because the ability to communicate in both spoken and written form is crucial for this job, you should take courses in English, speech, and social studies while in high school. In addition, take mathematics (especially statistics) and any courses in journalism or psychology that are available. Knowledge of a foreign language is also helpful.

Postsecondary Training

A college degree in marketing or survey research, statistics, economics, or business administration provides a good background for public opinion researchers. A degree in sociology or psychology will be helpful for those interested in studying consumer demand research or opinion research, while work in statistics or engineering might be more useful for those interested in certain types of industrial or analytical research.

Because of the increasingly sophisticated techniques used in public opinion research, most employers expect researchers to be familiar with computer applications, and many require a master's degree in business administration, sociology, educational psychology, or political science. While a doctorate is not necessary for most researchers, it is highly desirable for those who plan to become involved with complex research studies or work in an academic environment.

Other Education or Training

Keeping up with industry developments is key to success as a public opinion researcher. Professional associations often provide continuing education (CE) opportunities. For example, the American Association for Public Opinion Research offers webinars such as "Methods for Cross-Cultural Survey Design," "Questionnaire Design," and "Twitter and Public Opinion Research: Who, What, When, Where, Why and How!" CASRO offers webinars on project management, survey methods and trends, and professional skills. The Advertising Research Foundation, American Marketing Association, and the Marketing Research Association also provide CE opportunities. Contact these organizations for more information.

■ CERTIFICATION, LICENSING, AND SPECIAL REQUIREMENTS
Certification or Licensing

The Marketing Research Association offers the professional researcher certification to those who meet professional experience and educational requirements and pass an exam. While voluntary, becoming certified is an excellent way to demonstrate to potential employers that you're highly skilled and have met the highest standards that have been established by your industry.

■ EXPERIENCE, SKILLS, AND PERSONALITY TRAITS

Those wishing to enter the field of public opinion research should obtain as much experience as possible in high school and college by participating in internships, volunteering, or working at a part-time job at a public opinion or market research firm.

Public opinion researchers who conduct interviews must be outgoing and enjoy interacting with a wide variety of people. Because much of the work involves getting people to reveal their personal opinions and beliefs, you must be a good listener and as nonjudgmental as possible. You must be patient and be able to handle rejection, as some people may be uncooperative during the interviewing process.

If you choose to work in data analysis, you should be able to pay close attention to detail and spend long hours analyzing complex data. You may experience some pressure when required to collect data or solve a problem within a specified period of time. If you intend to plan questionnaires, you will need good analytical skills and a strong command of the English language.

■ EMPLOYMENT PROSPECTS
Employers

Approximately 13,650 survey researchers are employed in the United States, including those who work in public opinion polling. Most public opinion researchers are employed by private companies, such as public and private research firms and advertising agencies. They also work for government agencies and for various colleges and universities, often in research and teaching capacities. As is usually the case, those with the most experience and education should find the greatest number of job opportunities. Gaining experience in a specific area (such as food products) can give prospective researchers an edge.

Starting Out

Many people enter the field in a support position such as a survey worker, and with experience become interviewers or work as data analysts. Those with applicable education, training, and experience may begin as interviewers or data analysts. College career counselors can often help qualified students find an appropriate position in public opinion research. Contacts can also be made through summer employment or by locating public and private research companies in the phone book.

■ ADVANCEMENT PROSPECTS

Advancement opportunities are numerous in the public opinion research field. Often a research assistant will be promoted to a position as an interviewer or data analyst and, after sufficient experience in these or other aspects of research project development, become involved in a supervisory or planning capacity.

With a master's degree or doctorate, a person can become a manager of a large private research organization or marketing research director for an industrial or business firm. Those with extended work experience in public opinion research and with sufficient credentials may choose to start their own companies. Opportunities also exist in university teaching or research and development.

■ OUTLOOK

Employment of survey research workers is expected to grow faster than the average for all careers through 2024, according to the U.S. Department of Labor. The increasingly competitive economy means that businesses will need to be more efficient and effective in their use of advertising funds, and will need survey researchers to help in this arena. Also, public policy groups and all levels of government are hiring more survey researchers to help identify a variety of issues. Job opportunities should be ample for those trained in public opinion research, particularly those with graduate degrees in market or survey research, statistics, or the social sciences. Those who specialize in marketing, mathematics, and statistics will have the best opportunities. Marketing research

WHAT IS POLITICAL TELEMARKETING?

DID YOU KNOW?

Political telemarketing—sometimes called "push polling"—is a telemarketing technique conducted under the guise of a legitimate poll. What is the difference?

■ The purpose of a legitimate poll or survey is to obtain opinions; the goal of political telemarketing is to "push" voters away from a particular candidate and toward another.

■ Legitimate polling firms disclose their true names or the research company conducting the interview; political telemarketers often do not disclose their names or those whom they represent.

■ Legitimate polls are usually at least five minutes in duration and consist of many questions; political telemarketing calls are typically 30 to 60 seconds and only involve one or two questions.

■ The major difference is that legitimate polls and surveys provide information to respondents in an effort to determine the public's opinion on an issue or candidate. Political telemarketing is a campaign technique designed solely to influence potential voters.

Source: Marketing Research Association

firms, financial services organizations, health care institutions, advertising firms, and insurance firms are potential employers.

Despite the prediction of good employment growth, aspiring public opinion researchers should realize that the field is very small and competition is very strong for jobs. Those with a bachelor's degree may have a hard time landing a job. Additionally, the DOL reports that employment growth may slow as a result of changing research methods. For example, "collecting information from social media sites and data mining—finding trends in large sets of existing data—are expected to reduce the need for some traditional survey methods, such as telephone interviews."

■ UNIONS AND ASSOCIATIONS

Public opinion researchers do not belong to unions, but they can join professional associations such as the American Association for Public Opinion Research, American Marketing Association, and the Marketing Research Association. The Advertising Research Foundation and CASRO are membership organizations for advertising agencies and marketing research firms.

■ TIPS FOR ENTRY

1. Read *Public Opinion Quarterly* (http://poq.oxford journals.org) and the *CASRO Journal* (https://www.casro.org/?page=journal) to learn more about the field.

2. Join the American Association for Public Opinion Research (AAPOR) and other professional associations to access networking opportunities; receive discounts on conferences, continuing education classes, and publications; and receive special member-only career resources.

3. Attend the AAPOR Annual Conference to network and participate in continuing education opportunities.

4. Visit http://jobs.aapor.org for job listings.

5. Try to get a summer job doing statistical research with your local government or a marketing research firm.

■ FOR MORE INFORMATION

For more information on market research, contact

Advertising Research Foundation (ARF)
432 Park Avenue South, 6th Floor
New York, NY 10016-8013
Tel: (212) 751-5656
Fax: (212) 689-1859
E-mail: new-member-info@thearf.org
http://www.thearf.org

For information on membership and graduate programs, contact

American Association for Public Opinion Research (AAPOR)
One Parkview Plaza, Suite 800
Oakbrook Terrace, IL 60181
Tel: (847) 686-2230
Fax: (847) 686-2251
http://www.aapor.org

For information on careers, contact

American Marketing Association (AMA)
130 E. Randolph St., 22nd Floor
Chicago, IL 60601
Tel: (800) 262-1150; (312) 542-9000
Fax: (312)542-9001
https://www.ama.org

For career information and other resources, contact

Marketing Research Association (MRA)
1156 15th Street, NW, Suite 302
Washington, D.C. 20005-1745
Tel: (202) 800-2545
http://www.marketingresearch.org

Public Relations Managers

■ OVERVIEW

Public relations managers are responsible for influencing the public's image and recognition of their client, be it a large corporation, a service, or an individual. This is done through a carefully set plan of public appearances, public relations campaigns, press releases, surveys, and other scheduled events. Public relations managers, especially at large corporations, oversee the work of many staff members such as public relations specialists, researchers, designers, and administrators. There are approximately 60,380 public relations and fund-raising managers employed in the United States.

■ HISTORY

The origins of public relations date back to the time of ancient Greece, when philosophers such as Socrates and Plato used their oratory skills to persuade the public to agree with their views.

One of the first public relations specialists was Ivy Ledbetter Lee, a newspaper reporter. He was hired by the Standard Oil Company, as well as the family of John D. Rockefeller Jr., to manage the company crisis brought on by unrest by coal miners. Another early industry pioneer was Edward Bernays, often referred to as the "father of public relations." He listed actors, presidents, the government, nonprofit organizations, and large corporations as clients. One of his most memorable and successful public relations campaigns was for Proctor & Gamble's Ivory Soap. Public surveys indicated the nation's preference for unscented soap. He capitalized on the fact that Ivory Soap so happened to be the only unscented soap on the market. Bernays organized sporting events such as soap yacht races in New York's Central Park, and nationwide contests such as the annual Ivory soap sculpting contest, promoting the product to the public. All events were widely covered in the media.

Chester Burger, another pioneer, was one of the first public relations professionals to use the medium of television to tell a story. His clientele included Sears Roebuck, the American Cancer Society, and Texas Instruments, Inc.

In 1947, the Public Relations Society of America was founded as a way to establish industry standards and provide support and education for public relations professionals. In the 1950s, it established the "Code for the Professional Standards for the Practice of Public Relations," which is still widely used by the industry.

■ THE JOB

Public relations managers may supervise a team of public relations specialists or an entire department. Specialists, designers, artists, copywriters, media relations specialists, and administrative assistants are just a few of the workers who report to the public relations manager. Public relations managers work in all types of industries. For example, medical products and services companies rely on public relations managers to lead teams that raise public awareness and interest in a drug that is currently being reviewed by the Food and Drug Administration. Public relations managers are indispensable to politicians during election times in bringing the candidate's views and message to the voters, while at the same time negatively defining their opponents. Those in the entertainment or sports industries also rely on public relations managers to develop public relations campaigns to raise their Q-rating—a person's measure of visibility and likeability—in hopes of also increasing their market potential.

When creating a publicity program, public relations managers first identify the target audience—the group of people specifically affected by the product, service, idea, or individual being promoted. Once the target audience is ascertained, the manager then assigns tasks—such as writing press releases and arranging personal appearances and interviews—to his or her staff. After the project is assigned, managers monitor their staff and the progress of the campaign to ensure that everything is going as planned. They rely heavily on research to do their jobs. They may tweak or revise a plan according to the results of public surveys, opinion polls, or demographic analyses. They may also alter a plan after consultation with company executives or input from their staff.

Supervision is an important part of the job. Public relations managers review new programs and publicity campaigns, and are responsible for their implementation and success. An unfavorable review or client dissatisfaction will ultimately be the manager's responsibility to rectify. Conducting staff performance reviews, maintaining databases, and determining departments budgets are also part of the manager's job description.

Public relations managers may work with the advertising, marketing, or financial departments of their company to create newsletters, brochures, annual reports, or the content of the company's Web site. Company executives may confer with managers before giving interviews or addressing major stockholders. Public relations managers often act as the corporate spokesperson when giving interviews or responding to requests from the media for information about the company or its products or services.

■ EARNINGS

Public relations managers had median annual earnings of $104,140 in May 2015, according to the U.S. Department of Labor. Salaries ranged from less than $56,890 to $187,200 or more annually. However, many factors may affect salary, such as the size and industry of a business, its location, and the overall size of the public relations department. The department reports the following mean salaries for public relations managers by type of employer: advertising, public relations, and related services, $153,710; professional, labor, political, and similar organizations, $115,330; colleges, universities, and professional schools, $112,330; and grant-making and giving services, $109,760. Many firms offer benefits and compensation packages, including retirement plans, health and life insurance, or stock options that will further increase a manager's annual compensation.

■ WORK ENVIRONMENT

Public relations managers, especially those employed by large corporations, may have their own spacious office, or simply a desk in a cubicle, if at a smaller firm. Some high-level managers may enjoy benefits such as a company car, expense accounts, or access to free merchandise or services from different vendors.

The daily pace of a public relations office is usually busy and exciting, especially when workers are in the middle of an important publicity campaign, or when they are tackling multiple projects.

QUICK FACTS

ALTERNATE TITLE(S)
None

DUTIES
Develop and implement strategies that promote a positive image for their clients (large corporation, nonprofit, individual, etc.); manage public relations staff

SALARY RANGE
$56,890 to $104,140 to $187,200+

WORK ENVIRONMENT
Primarily Indoors

BEST GEOGRAPHIC LOCATION(S)
Opportunities available throughout the country, but are best in large, urban areas

MINIMUM EDUCATION LEVEL
Bachelor's Degree

SCHOOL SUBJECTS
Business, English, Speech

EXPERIENCE
Several years required

PERSONALITY TRAITS
Organized, Outgoing, Problem-Solving

SKILLS
Business Management, Leadership, Public Speaking

CERTIFICATION OR LICENSING
Recommended

SPECIAL REQUIREMENTS
None

EMPLOYMENT PROSPECTS
Fair

ADVANCEMENT PROSPECTS
Good

OUTLOOK
About as Fast as the Average

NOC
0124

O*NET-SOC
11-2031.00

CAREER LADDER

Consultant or PR Firm Owner

Director of Public Relations

Public Relations Manager

Public Relations Specialist

Public Relations Assistant

Expect long hours—55- to 60-hour workweeks may be the norm at some firms. Approximately 40 percent of PR managers work more than 40 hours per week. Functions are often scheduled on evenings or weekends, which may affect a manager's personal or family time.

■ EXPLORING

You can explore this field by doing promotional work for a school club or participating in other activities that catch your interest. For example, you can write a press release about an upcoming fund-raising activity sponsored by the student council and send it out to the local media. Have the school photography club take pictures of the event as well. Finally, send a report about the fund-raising project's success, along with photos or video footage, to the local newspaper, town news bulletin, district Web site, or local cable channel.

You can also explore this career by developing your managerial skills in general. Whether you're involved in drama, sports, school publications, or a part-time job, there are managerial duties associated with any organized activity. These can involve planning, scheduling, managing other workers or volunteers, fund-raising, or budgeting.

■ EDUCATION AND TRAINING REQUIREMENTS
High School

You can prepare for a career as a public relations manager by taking college preparatory classes. Concentrate on courses that will improve your communication skills, such as speech, English, and creative writing. Also, you should aim to study business-related subjects such as marketing, economics, public relations, management, and computer science.

Postsecondary Training

Most public relations mangers have a bachelor's or master's degree in public relations, communications, English, or journalism. Others have entered the industry with a business, fine arts, or liberal arts degree, though with some concentration in public relations, advertising, or communications. Useful college classes include psychology, sociology, business, economics, social media marketing, and any art medium. Graduate and professional degrees are common at the managerial level. Visit http://prsa.vendorguides.com for a list of colleges and universities that offer degrees in public relations.

Other Education or Training

The Public Relations Society of America offers a wealth of continuing education (CE) classes, webinars, seminars and workshops on leadership, management, staff development, crisis communications strategy, digital media, social media, and other topics. The International Association of Business Communicators, Canadian Public Relations Society, National Management Association, National School Public Relations Association, and the Public Affairs Council also offer CE resources. Contact these organizations for more information.

■ CERTIFICATION, LICENSING, AND SPECIAL REQUIREMENTS
Certification of Licensing

Many candidates on the executive track find it very helpful to pursue certification in this field. The Public Relations Society of America, International Association of Business Communicators, and the Canadian Public Relations Society accredit public relations workers who meet specific educational and work experience requirements and pass a comprehensive examination. Contact these organizations for more information.

■ EXPERIENCE, SKILLS, AND PERSONALITY TRAITS

Several years of experience in lower-level public relations positions is needed to enter the ranks of management.

Having excellent communication skills, the ability to work on multiple projects, and superior management skills are imperative to becoming a successful public relations manager. Managing an entire department, dealing with other business executives, or interacting with a difficult client are often daily tests for workers in this career. You must be able to work well under stressful situations and tight deadlines, be able to delegate responsibilities, and effectively communicate your ideas to various staff members.

Other traits considered important for public relations managers are intelligence, decisiveness, intuition, creativity, honesty, loyalty, a sense of responsibility, and planning abilities.

■ EMPLOYMENT PROSPECTS
Employers

Approximately 60,380 public relations and fund-raising managers are employed in the United States. While employment opportunities exist in every industry, jobs may be more plentiful with businesses that provide some type of service. Examples include health care—hospitals, clinics, medical equipment manufacturers; educational services—publishers or universities and colleges; professional, scientific, or technical services—financial institutions and planners, smartphone manufacturers, software developers, or laboratories. Public relations managers may need to relocate because many management track jobs at desirable companies are located in larger, more urban areas.

Starting Out

You will first need experience in lower-level public relations jobs before advancing to a managerial position. As an assistant, your duties may include updating databases, assembling media kits, or helping with the many details of a fund-raising event. With more experience, you may be given more responsibilities or assigned more prestigious accounts and projects.

To break into a public relations firm, visit your college career services office for job leads. In addition, many firms advertise job listings in newspapers and on Internet job boards.

■ ADVANCEMENT PROSPECTS

Promotion to director of public relations or other executive positions within a company are common advancement routes for managers. To stay competitive, you may want to continue your education, either with a master's degree in public relations or business administration.

Another advancement possibility includes moving to a company with a larger public relations budget and staff, and possibly higher compensation. Some experienced managers may opt to start their own public relations firm, or work as a public relations consultant on a freelance basis.

Advancement may be accelerated by participating in advanced training programs sponsored by industry and trade associations or by enrolling in continued education programs at colleges and universities. Firms sometimes offer tuition reimbursement for these programs. Managers committed to improving their knowledge of the field and of related disciplines—especially computer information systems—will have the best opportunities for advancement.

■ OUTLOOK

Employment for public relations managers is expected to grow about as fast as the average for all occupations through 2024, according to the U.S. Department of Labor. The high level of competition between certain businesses, especially those specializing in products and

A public relations manager coaches a model on how to convey a designer's look and message when walking down the runway during New York Fashion Week. (Anton Oparin. Shutterstock.)

services, will create a demand for seasoned public relations specialists and managers to promote their companies as better than the rest.

Also, the Internet has had a global impact on business performance. Employers will look for candidates with superior computer skills and ease with Internet-based (especially social media-oriented) communication and promotions. Businesses that have international dealings may look for managers fluent in the language and customs of other countries.

■ UNIONS AND ASSOCIATIONS

Public relations managers do not typically belong to unions. The Public Relations Society of America (PRSA) is the major membership organization for PR professionals. Membership benefits include access to free webinars, discounts on PRSA conferences and events, access to

TOP EMPLOYERS OF PUBLIC RELATIONS MANAGERS, MAY 2015

FAST FACTS

Employer	#Employed	Mean Salary
Colleges, universities, and professional schools	8,480	$112,300
Management of companies and enterprises	6,250	$136,860
Advertising, public relations, and related services	5,580	$153,710
Professional, labor, political, and similar organizations	4,630	$115,330
Grantmaking and giving services	3,520	$109,760

Source: U.S. Department of Labor

discussion boards and member directories, and networking opportunities. The International Association of Business Communicators is another leading organization for PR professionals. It offers accreditation, networking opportunities, and useful publications. The Canadian Public Relations Society represents the professional interests of PR workers in Canada. Other helpful organizations include the PR Council, National Management Association, and the Public Affairs Council.

■ TIPS FOR ENTRY

1. Read *Public RelationsTactics, Public Relations Journal,* and *The Public RelationsStrategist* (all available at http://www.prsa.org/Intelligence) and visit the Resources section of the IABC's Web site (http://www.iabc.com/cw) to learn more about the field.
2. For job listings, visit:
   • http://www.prsa.org/jobcenter
   • http://jobs.iabc.com
3. Visit http://www.prsa.org/Network/FindAFirm/Search for a database of PR firms.
4. Attend the PRSA International Conference to network and participate in continuing education opportunities.
5. Talk to public relations managers about their careers. Ask them for advice on breaking into the field.

■ FOR MORE INFORMATION

This professional association for public relations professionals offers an accreditation program and opportunities for professional development.

Canadian Public Relations Society (CPRS)
4195 Dundas Street West, Suite 346
Toronto, ON M8X 1Y4
Canada
Tel: (416) 239-7034
Fax: (416) 239-1076
E-mail: admin@cprs.ca
http://www.cprs.ca

For information about certification, contact
International Association of Business Communicators (IABC)
155 Montgomery Street, Suite 1210
San Francisco, CA 94104
Tel: (415) 544-4700; (415) 544-4700
Fax: (415) 544-4747
E-mail: member_relations@iabc.com
http://www.iabc.com

To learn more about a career in management, contact
National Management Association (NMA)
2210 Arbor Boulevard
Dayton, OH 45439-1506
Tel: (937) 294-0421
Fax: (937) 294-2374
E-mail: nma@nma1.org
http://nma1.org

For career information and PR news, contact
PR Council
32 East 31st Street
New York, NY 10016
Tel: (646) 588-0139
E-mail: contact@prcouncil.net
http://prcouncil.net

For useful publications and information on continuing education, contact
Public Affairs Council
2121 K Street, NW, Suite 900
Washington, D.C. 20037-1891
Tel: (202) 787-5950
Fax: (202) 787-5942
E-mail: pac@pac.org
http://pac.org

For statistics, salary surveys, and information on careers, accreditation, and student membership, contact

Public Relations Society of America (PRSA)
120 Wall St., 21st Floor
New York, NY 10005
Tel: (212) 460-1400
http://www.prsa.org

Public Relations Specialists

■ OVERVIEW

Public relations (PR) specialists develop and maintain programs that present a favorable public image for an individual or organization. They provide information to the target audience (generally, the public at large) about the client, its goals and accomplishments, and any further plans or projects that may be of public interest.

PR specialists may be employed by corporations, government agencies, nonprofit organizations, or almost any type of organization. Many PR specialists hold positions in public relations consulting firms or work for advertising agencies. There are approximately 240,700 public relations specialists in the United States.

■ HISTORY

The first public relations counsel was a reporter named Ivy Ledbetter Lee, who in 1906 was named press representative for a group of coal mine operators. Labor disputes were becoming a large concern of the operators, and they had run into problems because of their continual refusal to talk to the press and the hired miners. Lee convinced the mine operators to start responding to press questions and supply the press with information on mine activities.

During and after World War II, the rapid advancement of communications techniques prompted firms to realize they needed professional help to ensure their messages were given proper public attention. Manufacturing firms that had turned their production facilities over to the war effort returned to the manufacture of peacetime products and enlisted the aid of public relations professionals to forcefully and convincingly bring products and the company name before the buying public.

Large business firms, labor unions, and service organizations, such as the American Red Cross, Boy Scouts of America, and the YMCA, began to recognize the value of establishing positive, healthy relationships with the public that they served and depended on for support.

The need for effective public relations was often emphasized when circumstances beyond a company's or institution's control created unfavorable reactions from the public.

Public relations specialists must be experts at representing their clients before the media. The rapid growth of the public relations field since 1945 is testimony to the increased awareness in all industries of the need for professional attention to the proper use of media and the proper public relations approach to the many publics of a firm or an organization—customers, employees, stockholders, contributors, and competitors.

■ THE JOB

Public relations specialists perform a variety of tasks. They may be employed primarily as writers, creating reports, news releases, and booklet texts. Others write speeches or create copy for radio, TV, or film sequences. These workers often spend much of their time contacting the press, radio, and TV as well as magazines on behalf of the employer. They also use social media, such as Facebook and Twitter, to convey their client's message to target audiences and the general public. Some PR specialists work more as editors than writers, fact-checking and rewriting employee publications, newsletters, shareholder reports, and other management communications.

Specialists may choose to concentrate in graphic design, using their background knowledge of art and layout for developing brochures, booklets, and photographic communications. Other PR workers handle special events, such as press parties, convention

QUICK FACTS	
ALTERNATE TITLE(S)	Fund-raisers, Lobbyists
DUTIES	Develop and implement strategies that present a favorable public image for an individual or organization
SALARY RANGE	$31,690 to $56,770 to $110,080+
WORK ENVIRONMENT	Primarily Indoors
BEST GEOGRAPHIC LOCATION(S)	New York, Los Angeles, Chicago, and other major cities, but opportunities exist in all regions
MINIMUM EDUCATION LEVEL	Bachelor's Degree
SCHOOL SUBJECTS	English, Journalism, Speech
EXPERIENCE	Internship; volunteer or part-time experience
PERSONALITY TRAITS	Organized, Outgoing, Problem-Solving
SKILLS	Business Management, Interpersonal, Public Speaking
CERTIFICATION OR LICENSING	Recommended
SPECIAL REQUIREMENTS	None
EMPLOYMENT PROSPECTS	Fair
ADVANCEMENT PROSPECTS	Good
OUTLOOK	About as Fast as the Average
NOC	1123
O*NET-SOC	11-2031.00, 27-3031.00

CAREER LADDER

Consultant or PR Firm Owner

Director of Public Relations

Public Relations Manager

Public Relations Specialist

Public Relations Research Assistant or Trainee

exhibits, open houses, or anniversary celebrations.

PR specialists must be alert to any and all company or institutional events that are newsworthy. They prepare news releases and direct them toward the proper media. Specialists working for manufacturers and retailers are concerned with efforts that will promote sales and create goodwill for the firm's products. They work closely with the marketing and sales departments in announcing new products, preparing displays, and attending occasional dealers' conventions.

A large firm may have a director of public relations who is a vice president of the company and in charge of a staff that includes writers, artists, researchers, and other specialists. Publicity for an individual or a small organization may involve many of the same areas of expertise but may be carried out by a few people or possibly even one person.

Many PR workers act as consultants (rather than staff) of a corporation, association, college, hospital, or other institution. These workers have the advantage of being able to operate independently, state opinions objectively, and work with more than one type of business or association.

PR specialists are called upon to work with the public opinion aspects of almost every corporate or institutional problem. These can range from the opening of a new manufacturing plant to a college's dormitory dedication to a merger or sale of a company.

Public relations professionals may specialize. *Lobbyists* try to persuade legislators and other office holders to pass laws favoring the interests of the firms or people they represent. *Fund-raising directors* develop and direct programs designed to raise funds for social welfare agencies and other nonprofit organizations.

Early in their careers, public relations specialists become accustomed to having others receive credit for their behind-the-scenes work. The speeches they draft will be delivered by company officers, the magazine articles they prepare may be credited to the president of the company, and they may be consulted to prepare the message to stockholders from the chairman of the board that appears in the annual report.

■ EARNINGS

Public relations specialists had median annual earnings of $56,770 in May 2015, according to the U.S. Department of Labor. Salaries ranged from less than $31,690 to more than $110,080. The department reports the following mean salaries for public relations specialists by type of employer: professional, scientific, and technical services, $59,430; religious, grantmaking, civic, professional, and similar organizations, 56,160; state and local government, excluding education and hospitals, $55,500; state, local, and private educational services, $52,260; and health care and social assistance, $50,300.

Many PR workers receive a range of fringe benefits from corporations and agencies employing them, including bonus/incentive compensation, stock options, profit sharing/pension plans/401(k) programs, medical benefits, life insurance, financial planning, maternity/paternity leave, paid vacations, and family college tuition. Bonuses can range from 5 to 100 percent of base compensation and often are based on individual and/or company performance.

■ WORK ENVIRONMENT

Public relations specialists generally work in offices with adequate administrative support, regular salary increases, and expense accounts. They are expected to make a good appearance in tasteful, conservative clothing. They must have social poise, and their conduct in their personal life is important to their firms or their clients. Public relations specialists may have to entertain business associates.

The PR specialist seldom works conventional office hours for many weeks at a time; although the workweek may consist of 35 to 40 hours, these hours may be supplemented by evenings and even weekends when meetings must be attended and other special events covered. Time behind the desk may represent only a small part of the total working schedule. Travel is often an important and necessary part of the job.

The life of the PR worker is so greatly determined by the job that many consider this a disadvantage. Because the work is concerned with public opinion, it is often difficult to measure the results of performance and to sell the worth of a public relations program to an employer or client. Competition in the consulting field is keen, and if a firm loses an account, some of its personnel may be affected. The demands it makes for anonymity will be considered by some as one of the profession's less inviting aspects. Public relations involves much more hard work and a great deal less glamour than is popularly supposed.

■ EXPLORING

Almost any experience in working with other people will help you to develop strong interpersonal skills, which are crucial in public relations. The possibilities are almost endless. Summer work on a newspaper or trade paper or with a radio or television station may give insight into communications media. Working as a volunteer on a political campaign can help you to understand the ways in which people can be persuaded. Being selected as a page for the U.S. Congress or a state legislature will help you grasp the fundamentals of government processes. A job in retail will help you to understand some of the principles of product presentation. A teaching job will develop your organization and presentation skills. These are just some of the jobs that will let you explore areas of public relations.

■ EDUCATION AND TRAINING REQUIREMENTS
High School

While in high school, take courses in English, journalism, public speaking, humanities, and languages because public relations is based on effective communication with others. Courses such as these will develop your skills in written and oral communication as well as provide a better understanding of different fields and industries to be publicized.

Postsecondary Training

Most people employed in public relations service have a college degree. Major fields of study most beneficial to developing the proper skills are public relations, English, communications, business, and journalism. Some employers feel that majoring in the area in which the public relations person will eventually work is the best training. Knowledge of business administration is most helpful as is innate talent for selling. A graduate degree may be required for managerial positions. People with a bachelor's degree in public relations can find staff positions with either an organization or a public relations firm. Visit http://prsa.vendorguides.com for a list of colleges and universities that offer degrees in public relations.

Many colleges and graduate schools offer degree programs or special courses in public relations. In addition, many other colleges offer at least courses in the field. Public relations programs are sometimes administered by the journalism or communication departments of schools. In addition to courses in theory and techniques of public relations, interested individuals may study organization, management and administration, and practical applications and often specialize in areas such as business, government, and nonprofit organizations. Other preparation includes courses in creative writing, psychology, communications, advertising, and journalism.

Public relations workers confer over the guest list backstage at a fashion show. (Anton Oparin. Shutterstock.)

Other Education or Training

The Public Relations Society of America offers a wealth of continuing education classes, webinars, seminars, and workshops on topics such as crisis communications strategy, public relations writing, branding strategies, digital media, social media, and community relations and employee communications. The International Association of Business Communicators, Canadian Public Relations Society, National School Public Relations Association, and the Public Affairs Council also provide CE resources. Contact these organizations for more information.

■ CERTIFICATION, LICENSING, AND SPECIAL REQUIREMENTS
Certification or Licensing

The Public Relations Society of America, International Association of Business Communicators, and the Canadian Public Relations Society accredit public

MUSEUM OF PUBLIC RELATIONS

DID YOU KNOW?

In late 1997, Spector & Associates debuted the Museum of Public Relations on the Internet. The museum is meant to provide a history and examples of successful public relations programs for industry, education, and government, using photographs and stories. Read about such public relations trendsetters as Edward L. Bernays, Moss Kendrix, Carl R. Byoir, Arthur W. Page, and Chester Burger. For more information, visit http://prmuseum.com.

relations workers who meet educational and work experience requirements and pass a comprehensive examination. Such accreditation is a sign of competence in this field, although it is not a requirement for employment.

■ EXPERIENCE, SKILLS, AND PERSONALITY TRAITS

Any experience one can obtain in the field of public relations—such as an internship, volunteering, or a part-time job—will be useful for aspiring PR professionals.

Today's public relations specialist must be a businessperson first, both to understand how to perform successfully in business and to comprehend the needs and goals of the organization or client. Additionally, successful PR specialists are strong writers and speakers, and have good interpersonal, leadership, problem-solving, and organizational skills.

■ EMPLOYMENT PROSPECTS

Employers

Public relations specialists hold about 240,700 jobs. Workers may be paid employees of the organization they represent or they may be part of a public relations firm that works for organizations on a contract basis. Others are involved in fund-raising or political campaigning. Public relations may be done for a corporation, retail business, service company, utility, association, nonprofit organization, or educational institution.

Most PR firms are located in large cities that are centers of communications. New York, Chicago, San Francisco, Los Angeles, and Washington, D.C., are good places to start a search for a public relations job. Nevertheless, there are many good opportunities in cities across the United States.

Starting Out

There is no clear-cut formula for getting a job in public relations. Individuals often enter the field after gaining preliminary experience in another occupation closely allied to the field, usually some segment of communications, and frequently, in journalism. Coming into public relations from newspaper work is still a recommended route. Another good method is to gain initial employment as a public relations trainee or intern, or as a clerk, secretary, or research assistant in a public relations department or a counseling firm.

■ ADVANCEMENT PROSPECTS

In some large companies, an entry-level public relations specialist may start as a trainee in a formal training program for new employees. In others, new employees may expect to be assigned to work that has a minimum of responsibility. They may assemble clippings or do rewrites on material that has already been accepted. They may make posters or assist in conducting polls or surveys, or compile reports from data submitted by others.

As workers acquire experience, they are typically given more responsibility. They write news releases, direct polls or surveys, or advance to writing speeches for company officials. Progress may seem to be slow, because some skills take a long time to master.

Some advance in responsibility and salary in the same firm in which they started. Others find that the path to advancement is to accept a more rewarding position in another firm.

The goal of many public relations specialists is to open an independent office or to join an established consulting firm. To start an independent office requires a large outlay of capital and an established reputation in the field. However, those who are successful in operating their own consulting firms probably attain the greatest financial success in the public relations field.

■ OUTLOOK

Employment of public relations professionals is expected to grow about as fast as the average for all careers through 2024, according to the U.S. Department of Labor. Competition will be keen for beginning jobs in public relations because so many job seekers are enticed by the perceived glamour and appeal of the field; those with both education and experience will have an advantage. Opportunities will be stronger in some industries than others.

Most large companies have some sort of public relations resource, either through their own staff or through the use of a firm of consultants. Most are expected to expand their public relations activities, creating many new jobs. Smaller companies are increasingly hiring public relations specialists, adding to the demand for these workers. The growing use of social media by businesses and other organizations will create increasing opportunities for public relations specialists, who will be needed to help their employers use this valuable tool to reach consumers and the general public. Additionally, when corporate scandals surface, public relations specialists will be hired to help improve the images of companies and regain the trust of the public.

UNIONS AND ASSOCIATIONS

Public relations specialists do not typically belong to unions. The Public Relations Society of America (PRSA) is the major membership organization for PR specialists. Membership benefits include access to free webinars, discounts on PRSA conferences and events, access to discussion boards and member directories, and networking opportunities. The International Association of Business Communicators is another leading organization for PR professionals. It offers accreditation, networking opportunities, and useful publications. The Canadian Public Relations Society represents the professional interests of PR workers in Canada. Other helpful organizations include the PR Council, Public Affairs Council, and the National School Public Relations Association.

TIPS FOR ENTRY

1. Read *Public Relations Tactics* and *The Public Relations Strategist* (both available at http://www .prsa.org/Intelligence) to learn more about the field.
2. Visit http://www.prsa.org/Jobcenter/career _resources/career_level/entry_level for detailed information about launching a career in public relations including PR job descriptions, an *Ask the Experts* electronic forum, and advice on preparing resumes and acing job interviews.
3. Volunteer for a local nonprofit organization or acquire a part-time job with the local government to see how they handle their promotions and interactions with the media.

FOR MORE INFORMATION

This professional association for public relations professionals offers an accreditation program and opportunities for professional development.

Canadian Public Relations Society (CPRS)
4195 Dundas Street West, Suite 346
Toronto, ON M8X 1Y4
Canada
Tel: (416) 239-7034
Fax: (416) 239-1076
E-mail: admin@cprs.ca
http://www.cprs.ca

For information on accreditation, contact
International Association of Business Communicators (IABC)
155 Montgomery Street, Suite 1210
San Francisco, CA 94104

> ### GET ADVICE FROM A MENTOR
> **DID YOU KNOW?**
>
> The Public Relations Society of America (PRSA) has a College of Fellows mentoring program that allows participants to receive career advice from accredited professionals with 20 years or more of experience. The College of Fellows is a group of senior PR experts elected to the College because they have "left a significant footprint on the public relations profession." They offer their business knowledge to individuals who are considering changing jobs, trying to advance into a management position, or facing other professional challenges. PRSA members register for the service online and are then matched with a College of Fellows member who has volunteered to consult on the topic they need help with. For information, see the Communities section of the PRSA Web site at http://www.prsa.org.

Tel: (800) 776-4222; (415) 544-4700
Fax: (415) 544-4747
E-mail: member_relations@iabc.com
http://www.iabc.com

For information on school public relations, contact
National School Public Relations Association (NSPRA)
15948 Derwood Road
Rockville, MD 20855-2123
Tel: (301) 519-0496
Fax: (301) 519-0494
E-mail: info@nspra.org
http://www.nspra.org

For career information and PR news, contact
PR Council
32 East 31st Street
New York, NY 10016
Tel: (646) 588-0139
http://prcouncil.net

For useful publications and information on continuing education, contact
Public Affairs Council
2121 K Street, NW, Suite 900
Washington, D.C. 20037-1891
Tel: (202) 787-5950
Fax: (202) 787-5942
E-mail: pac@pac.org
http://pac.org

For statistics, salary surveys, and information on careers, accreditation, and student membership, contact

Public Relations Society of America (PRSA)
120 Wall St., 21st Floor
New York, NY 10005
Tel: (212) 460-1400
E-mail: memberservice@prsa.org
http://www.prsa.org

Public Transportation Operators

■ OVERVIEW

Public transportation operators include drivers of school buses, intercity buses, local commuter buses, and local transit railway systems, such as subways and streetcars. Many drivers run a predetermined route within a city or metropolitan area, transporting passengers from one designated place to another. Intercity drivers travel between cities and states, transporting passengers and luggage on more lengthy trips. Some public transportation operators are required to handle additional special duties, such as transporting passengers with disabilities. There are approximately 665,000 bus drivers and 12,600 subway and streetcar operators employed in the United States.

■ HISTORY

In both the United States and Europe, public transportation systems were first developed in the 19th century. As early as 1819, there was a successful horse-drawn bus service in Paris. The idea was subsequently adopted in other major cities, such as New York and London.

The first subway system, initially four miles long, was opened in London in the 1860s. The railcars were powered by steam until 1890, when the system was converted to electricity. New York, Chicago, Paris, Budapest, and many other cities followed with their own subway systems. Streetcar, or trolley, lines and elevated tracks were also built around this time. The first electric-powered elevated train system opened in Chicago in 1895.

The 20th century began with a new vehicle for public transportation: the gasoline-powered bus. Various cities throughout the United States established bus services in the first decade of the century. Trucks fitted with seats and automobiles lengthened for increased seating capacity were among the first buses. As roads improved and better equipment became available, bus systems expanded.

Toward the middle of the 20th century, some transit systems came under the ownership of automotive- or oil-related businesses that had little interest in maintaining trolley lines. Around the same time, bus systems began to receive government assistance because of greater routing flexibility and other advantages. By the 1950s, buses had largely replaced the country's trolley lines, as increased ownership of private automobiles also reduced the demand for trolleys. Subways and elevated tracks, however, stayed in service, as did a few of the trolley systems, notably in San Francisco. In the latter half of the 20th century, some American cities, such as Washington, D.C., and San Francisco, built new subway systems, while others expanded their existing underground lines.

■ THE JOB

The work of an *intercity bus driver* commonly begins at the terminal, where he or she prepares a trip report form and inspects the bus. Safety equipment, such as a fire extinguisher and a first-aid kit, as well as the vehicle's brakes, lights, steering, oil, gas, water, and tires are checked. The driver then supervises the loading of baggage, picks up the passengers, collects fares or tickets, and answers questions about schedules and routes.

At the final destination, the intercity driver oversees the unloading of passengers and baggage and then prepares a report on the trip's mileage, fares, and time, as required by the U.S. Department of Transportation. Another report must be completed if an accident or unusual delay occurs.

Intercity bus drivers may make only a single one-way trip to a distant city or a round trip each day, stopping at towns and cities along the route. Drivers who operate chartered buses typically pick up groups, drive them to their destination, and remain with them until it is time for the return trip.

Within a town, city, or extended urban area, *local commuter bus drivers* run routes with scheduled stops every few blocks. As passengers board the bus, the driver notes passes and discount cards; collects payment; and issues transfers. At the end of the day, drivers of local transit buses turn in trip sheets, which might include records of fares received, the trips made, and any delays or accidents during their shift.

To aid the driver and discourage robbery, local bus drivers in most major cities do not give change. Passengers instead deposit their exact fare or token in a tamper-resistant box; electronic equipment in the box then counts the bills and coins and displays the transaction total. Many public transportation systems now use fare card swipe systems in which a customer pays his or her fare by passing a pre-loaded debit card over an electronic scanner.

School bus drivers run a predetermined route in the mornings and in the afternoons, transporting students to and from school. Occasionally, they drive students and faculty to other events, such as sports competitions or field trips. Though they do not have to collect fares from their passengers, school bus drivers are responsible for maintaining order on the bus. They must be aware of school policies and standards and enforce these rules during the ride.

All bus drivers must operate their vehicles carefully during trips. They are required to follow established schedules, but they must do so within the legal speed limits. Bus drivers are also responsible for regulating the interior lights and the heating and air-conditioning systems.

Drivers of subway, streetcar, and other local railway systems have many of the same duties as bus drivers. *Subway/elevated train drivers* control trains that transport passengers throughout cities and suburbs. They usually sit in special compartments at the front of the first car, from which they start, slow, and stop the train. Drivers obey traffic signals along routes that run underground, at surface levels, or elevated above ground.

Operators announce stops over the loudspeaker, open and close doors, and make sure passengers get on and off safely. In order to remain on schedule, they control the speed and the amount of time spent at each station. When the train malfunctions or emergencies occur, drivers contact dispatchers for help and may have to instruct passengers on how to evacuate the train cars.

In general, all public transportation operators must make announcements and answer questions from passengers concerning schedules, routes, transfer points, and addresses. They are also required to enforce safety regulations established by the transit company or the government.

■ EARNINGS

Earnings for public local transportation operators vary by location and experience. According to the U.S. Department of Labor, the May 2015 median salary for local and intercity bus drivers was $38,290. The lowest 10 percent earned less than $22,310 and the highest 10 percent earned more than $62,240. School bus drivers on average made less, with a median salary of $29,490. The lowest 10 percent earned less than $18,210 and the highest 10 percent earned $45,670 or more. Subway and streetcar operators earned salaries that ranged from less than $42,120 to $78,440 or more, with a median of $62,360.

Almost all public transportation operators belong to a union, such as the Amalgamated Transit Union or the Transport Workers Union of America. Wages and benefits packages are usually determined through bargaining agreements between these unions and the management of the transit system. Benefits often include paid health and life insurance, sick leave, free transportation on their line or system, and as much as four weeks of vacation per year.

■ WORK ENVIRONMENT

Public transportation operators work anywhere from 20 to 40 hours per week. About half of all drivers work full time. The U.S. Department of Transportation restricts all drivers from working more than 10 hours per day or more than 60 hours per week. New drivers often work part time, though they may be guaranteed a minimum number of hours.

Schedules for intercity bus drivers may require working nights, weekends, and holidays. Drivers may also have to spend nights away from home, staying in hotels at company expense. Senior drivers who have regular routes typically have regular working hours and set schedules, while others must be prepared to work on short notice.

Local transit drivers and subway operators usually have a five-day workweek, with Saturdays and Sundays considered regular workdays. Some of these employees work evenings and night shifts. In order to accommodate commuters, many work split shifts, such as four hours in the morning and four hours in the afternoon and evening, with time off in between.

QUICK FACTS

ALTERNATE TITLE(S)
Intercity Bus Drivers, Local Commuter Bus Drivers, School Bus Drivers, Subway/Elevated Train Drivers

DUTIES
Transport passengers via buses, subway/elevated trains, and streetcars

SALARY RANGE
$18,210 to $38,290 to $78,440+

WORK ENVIRONMENT
Primarily Indoors

BEST GEOGRAPHIC LOCATION(S)
Opportunities best in large, urban areas

MINIMUM EDUCATION LEVEL
High School Diploma

SCHOOL SUBJECTS
English, Mathematics, Speech

EXPERIENCE
On-the-job training

PERSONALITY TRAITS
Conventional, Hands On, Realistic

SKILLS
Interpersonal, Mechanical/Manual Dexterity, Public Speaking

CERTIFICATION OR LICENSING
Required

SPECIAL REQUIREMENTS
Must meet age and license requirements; must pass physical examinations

EMPLOYMENT PROSPECTS
Good

ADVANCEMENT PROSPECTS
Poor

OUTLOOK
About as Fast as the Average

NOC
7512

O*NET-SOC
53-3021.00, 53-3022.00, 53-4041.00

CAREER LADDER

Dispatcher or Station Manager

Supervisor

Experienced Driver

Part-Time, Substitute Driver

The lack of direct supervision is one of the advantages of being a public transportation operator. Intercity bus drivers may also enjoy traveling as a benefit. Disadvantages include weekend, holiday, or night shifts, and, in some cases, being called to work on short notice. Operators with little seniority may be laid off when business declines.

Although driving a bus or rail car is usually not physically exhausting, operators are exposed to tension from maneuvering their vehicle on heavily congested streets or through crowded stations. They may also feel stressed from dealing with passengers—including those who are unruly or difficult.

■ EXPLORING

Any job that requires driving can provide you with important experience for a job as a public transportation operator. Possibilities include a part-time or summer job as a delivery driver.

You may also benefit from talking personally with a bus driver or subway operator. Those already employed with bus or rail companies can give you a good, detailed description of the pros and cons of the position.

■ EDUCATION AND TRAINING REQUIREMENTS
High School

While still in high school, take English and speech classes to improve your communication skills. Math skills may also be needed to calculate fares and make change. Finally, sign up for a driver's education class to learn the rules of the road.

Postsecondary Training

Qualifications and standards for bus drivers are established by state and federal regulations. Federal regulations require drivers who operate vehicles designed to transport 16 or more passengers to obtain a commercial license (CDL). In order to receive a CDL, applicants must pass a written exam and a driving test in the type of vehicle they will be operating.

While many states' minimum age requirement for drivers is 18, federal regulations require that interstate bus drivers be at least 21 years old and in good general health. They must pass a physical exam every two years, checking for good hearing, vision, and reflexes. They must also be able to speak, read, and write English well enough to fill out reports, read signs, and talk to passengers. In addition to these minimum requirements, many employers prefer drivers over 24 years old with at least a high school diploma and previous truck or bus driving experience.

Bus companies and local transit systems train their drivers with two to eight weeks of classroom and on-the-road instruction. In the classroom, trainees learn federal and company work policies, state and local driving regulations, and other general safe driving practices. They also learn how to handle the public, read schedules, determine fares, and keep records.

For subway operator jobs, local transit companies prefer applicants 21 years of age or older with at least a high school diploma. As with bus drivers, good vision, hearing, and reflexes are necessary, as well as a clean driving record.

New operators are generally trained both in the classroom and on the job in programs that range from one to six months. Operators must then pass qualifying exams covering operations, troubleshooting, and emergency procedures.

■ CERTIFICATION, LICENSING, AND SPECIAL REQUIREMENTS
Certification or Licensing

There are no certification requirements for public transportation operators. A commercial driver's license is required to work as a bus driver.

Other Requirements

Candidates must meet age, license, and physical requirements for each job. For instance, interstate bus drivers must be at least 21 years old and local transit companies prefer applicants 21 years of age or older. Drivers who operate vehicles designed to transport 16 or more passengers must have a commercial driver's license and must also meet hearing and vision requirements.

■ EXPERIENCE, SKILLS, AND PERSONALITY TRAITS

You will not be able to obtain hands-on experience as a public transportation driver until you receive on-the-job training, but you can hone your driving skills by getting your driver's license and learning the rules of the road.

Bus and rail car drivers must have good reflexes and quick reaction time, and must drive safely under all circumstances. Because operators are required to deal regularly with passengers, it is also important that they be courteous and levelheaded. An even temperament comes in handy when driving in heavy or fast-moving traffic or during bad weather conditions. Drivers should be able to stay alert and attentive to the task at hand. They must be dependable and responsible, because the lives of their passengers are in their hands.

■ EMPLOYMENT PROSPECTS
Employers
There are approximately 665,000 bus drivers currently employed in the United States. About 75 percent are employed by a school system or a company that provides contract school bus service. The second largest group of bus drivers work for private and local transit systems, and the remainder work as intercity and charter drivers. There are approximately 12,600 subway and streetcar operators, located almost exclusively in major urban areas.

Starting Out
If you are interested in the field, you should directly contact public transportation companies as well as government and private employment agencies. Labor unions, such as the Amalgamated Transit Union, might know about available jobs. Positions for drivers can also be found in the classified section of the newspaper.

After completing the training program, new drivers often initially are given only special or temporary assignments—for example, substituting for a sick employee, driving an extra bus or rail car during commuter rush hours, or driving a charter bus to a sporting event. These new drivers may work for several years in these part-time, substitute positions before gaining enough seniority for a regular route.

■ ADVANCEMENT PROSPECTS
Advancement is usually measured by greater pay and better assignments or routes. For example, senior drivers or rail car operators may have routes with lighter traffic, weekends off, or higher pay rates. Although opportunities for promotion are limited, one option for advancement is to move into supervisory or training positions. Experienced drivers can become *dispatchers* (workers who assign drivers their bus or train route, determine whether buses or trains are running on time, and send out help when there is a breakdown or accident). Other managerial positions also exist. Experienced subway or streetcar operators, for example, may become station managers.

■ OUTLOOK
Employment for public transportation operators is expected to grow as fast as the average for all occupations through 2024, according to the *Occupational Outlook Handbook*. As the population increases, local and intercity travel will also increase. Future government efforts to reduce traffic and pollution through greater funding

A bus driver sits in the driver's seat of an all-electric bus in New York City. (Marc A. Hermann. MTA New York City Transit.)

of public transportation could also greatly improve job opportunities. In addition, thousands of job openings are expected to occur each year because of the need to replace workers who retire or leave the occupation.

Because many of these positions offer relatively high wages and attractive benefits, however, job seekers may face heavy competition. Those who have good driving records and are willing to work in rapidly growing metropolitan areas will have the best opportunities.

■ UNIONS AND ASSOCIATIONS
Almost all public transportation operators belong to a union, such as the Transport Workers Union of America or the Amalgamated Transit Union. The American Public Transit Association is a group of public organizations, companies, and government agencies that are engaged in the areas of bus, paratransit, commuter rail, light rail, subways, waterborne passenger services, and high-speed

PUBLIC TRANSPORTATION BY THE NUMBERS

FAST FACTS

- In 2014, Americans took 10.8 billion trips on public transportation. This was the highest annual ridership number in 58 years.
- People board public transportation 35 million times each weekday.
- Public transportation ridership increased by 39 percent from 1995 through 2014.
- More than 7,200 organizations provide public transportation in the United States.
- More than 400,000 people are employed in the public transportation industry.

Source: American Public Transit Association

rail. The National School Transportation Association is a professional organization for transportation-related private contractors, manufacturers, and suppliers.

■ TIPS FOR ENTRY

1. Read *In Transit* (http://www.atu.org/media/intransit) and *Passenger Transport* (http://www.apta.com/passengertransport) to learn more about the field.
2. Conduct information interviews with public transportation operators and ask them for advice on preparing for and entering the field.
3. Join the Transport Workers Union of America or the Amalgamated Transit Union to increase your chances of landing a job and receiving fair pay for your work.

■ FOR MORE INFORMATION

For information on union membership, contact
Amalgamated Transit Union, AFL-CIO/CLC (ATU)
10000 New Hampshire Avenue
Silver Spring, MD 20903
Tel: (888) 240-1196; (301) 431-7100
Fax: (301) 431-7117
http://www.atu.org

For career information, contact
American Public Transit Association (APTA)
1300 I Street, NW, Suite 1200 East
Washington, D.C. 20005
Tel: (202) 496-4800
Fax: (202) 496-4324
http://www.apta.com

For industry information, contact
National School Transportation Association (NSTA)
122 South Royal Street
Alexandria, VA 22314-3328
Tel: (703) 684-3200
E-mail: info@yellowbuses.org
http://www.yellowbuses.org

For information on union membership and careers in public transportation, contact
Transport Workers Union of America (TWU)
501 3rd Street, NW, 9th Floor
Washington, D.C. 20001-2790
Tel: (202) 719-3900
Fax: (202) 347-0454
E-mail: okorin@twu.org
http://www.twu.org

Publicists

■ OVERVIEW

There are two types of *publicists*: those who work for companies, movie studios, recording companies, sports teams, and other organizations and those who work for individuals such as CEOs, actors, musicians, and professional athletes. *Publicists* who are employed by companies and organizations handle the daily press operations for the organization. They handle media relations, arrange interviews, ensure that the correct information is distributed to the press, and write press releases. Those who work for individuals try to enhance their client's image by casting them in a positive light via newspaper, magazine, television, and Internet stories and other methods. Publicists are sometimes called *press agents, public relations (PR) directors, marketing directors,* or *directors of communication.*

■ HISTORY

Publicists have long been experts at influencing the public's perception of a business, organization, or individual. Using press releases, photographs, and other forms of media, publicists gain public recognition for their client. Publicists also take advantage of the popularity of the Internet by creating video news releases, e-mail press releases, e-mail invitations, polls, and surveys. The popularity of publications and Web sites, reality television shows, talk shows, entertainment programs, and countless cable channels covering the entertainment, sports, business, and other industries have provided publicists a huge outlet for media coverage.

■ THE JOB

Publicists are responsible for obtaining positive attention and name recognition for their clients. They achieve this by developing a publicity plan that may incorporate a variety of methods—press kits, news releases, photographs, personal appearances, and promotions. Using their many contacts and media savvy, publicists can turn a new restaurant or club into the latest hotspot, or reverse the fading career of a former A-list actor. Publicists may also be called to perform damage control—sometimes spinning a negative incident into a positive one, or at the very least, making a story less harmful to the client's reputation. A publicist's talents can be applied to many industries. The following paragraphs detail the many career options available to publicists.

Entertainment

In the entertainment industry, where being at the right parties and nightclubs can further an actor's public image and career, having a good publicist is an asset. Publicists promote actors and actresses by getting them invited to parties and premiers and involved in charity events and social causes that will make the individual more visible and attractive to the press and the public. They may schedule radio and television interviews, press junkets, personal appearances, television and radio interviews, and photo sessions to help promote an upcoming project. They often work closely with managers, agents, image consultants, and stylists to help the actor or actress portray a certain image that is favorable to the public. At times, a publicist may be called on to "spin" or interpret a negative incident into one less career damaging.

Sports

Publicists who work in the sports industry are responsible for the promotion of a team or athlete. They write press releases, hold press conferences, and arrange media interviews and tours. They often work with the public relations, advertising, and marketing departments of professional sports teams to create press releases, game programs, brochures, recruiting kits, media kits, and fan newsletters.

Publicists may also work to generate fan interest in a sports team or athlete by scheduling special events before, during, and after competitions; creating ticket or product promotions; and organizing music or fireworks displays.

Publishing

Publicists help promote an author's latest work by sending it to reporters, writers, and book reviewers employed at newspapers, trade papers, magazines, and Web sites.

They may schedule and advertise a multi-city book tour, including signings and reading at bookstores, schools, and libraries. Publicists may book an author, especially if he or she is well known, for interviews and personal appearances on television and radio shows, as well as on the Internet. They may also promote the author's work for special awards and industry recognition.

Hospitality

The hospitality industry relies on publicists to promote its properties. Publicists employed in this industry often send press releases and media kits to travel magazines, travel agents, convention planners, and frequent guests of the hotel to create interest in the properties. Publicists may fine-tune or tailor media kits and other promotional material to attract a particular audience. For example, material sent to travel magazine editors would spotlight the hotel's unique spa services or nearby attractions; convention planners and travel agents would be sent highlights of the hotel's meeting facilities and guest rooms. Hospitality publicists also promote entertainment options found at hotels. A publicist employed by a Las Vegas hotel, for example, would tout its high-roller casinos, lounge acts and shows, or world-class dining. They might also showcase special events held at the hotel such as a New Year's Eve extravaganza or a poker tournament.

Restaurants

Besides delicious food and impeccable service, restaurants rely on good publicity to attract

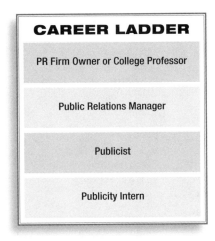

CAREER LADDER

| PR Firm Owner or College Professor |
| Public Relations Manager |
| Publicist |
| Publicity Intern |

clientele. Publicists working in the restaurant industry need to promote their clients in a way that makes them stand out from the crowd. They work with restaurant owners to identify an appropriate image for the restaurant and the type of customers it wishes to attract—whether tourists, business people, young and hip urban professionals, families with children, or another demographic group. Publicists plan special events such as wine tastings, holiday theme parties, and fashion shows as a way to attract new diners to their establishment. These events may be listed in a calendar or flyer mailed or e-mailed to local media or frequent patrons, or they may be posted on popular social media sites. Publicists may invite the media to special events in hopes of garnering publicity in the form of a positive restaurant review or a mention in an upcoming column. Publicists may invite local television or radio personalities to do a live broadcast from the restaurant or bar to get additional publicity.

■ EARNINGS

Publicists earn anywhere from $20,000 to more than $250,000 per year. Those just starting out might earn less, while those with proven track records command higher salaries. According to the Department of Labor, publicists had median annual salaries of $56,770 in May of 2015. Salaries ranged from $31,690 to $110,080. Publicists who work for high-profile individuals can earn higher salaries.

Most full-time positions provide life and medical insurance, pension, vacation, and holiday benefits.

■ WORK ENVIRONMENT

During busy times, publicists may work 12- to 20-hour days, seven days a week. Some publicists travel with their clients, while others do not. Either way, this job is very time-consuming. Successful publicists have flexible schedules and are accessible to their clients at any time during the day or night.

■ EXPLORING

Ask your teacher or counselor to set up an information interview with a publicist. Volunteer to handle various public relations-type duties for your high school sports teams or clubs. Run for student council or another leadership position at school to gain experience with public speaking and management.

■ EDUCATION AND TRAINING REQUIREMENTS
High School

As a publicist, you are the voice of the person or organization that you represent, so it is very important to be an effective communicator. Take classes in English, writing, and journalism to hone your writing skills, and take speech classes to help you learn how to compose your ideas and thoughts and convey them to an audience. You should also take other college preparatory classes, such as math, business, science, and foreign language. A general knowledge of history, sociology, psychology, and current events will also be useful.

Postsecondary Training

Most publicists are college graduates with degrees in public relations, marketing, communications, or journalism. A college degree is essential, according to the Public Relations Society of America. Visit http://prsa

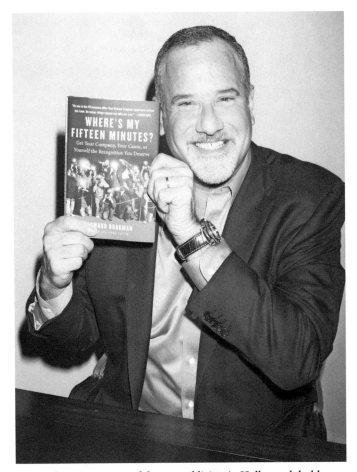

Howard Bragman, one of the top publicists in Hollywood, holds a copy of his book Where's My Fifteen Minutes? *(carrie-nelson. Shutterstock.)*

.vendorguides.com for a list of colleges and universities that offer degrees in public relations.

Other Education or Training

The Public Relations Society of America offers continuing education classes, webinars, seminars, and workshops on crisis communications strategy, public relations writing, branding strategies, digital media, social media, and other topics. The International Association of Business Communicators and the Entertainment Publicists Professional Society also provide CE resources. Contact these organizations for more information.

■ CERTIFICATION, LICENSING, AND SPECIAL REQUIREMENTS
Certification or Licensing

The Public Relations Society of America and the International Association of Business Communicators accredit public relations workers who meet specific education requirements, have related work experience, and pass a comprehensive examination. This certification will help show prospective employers that you possess a high level of knowledge and experience.

■ EXPERIENCE, SKILLS, AND PERSONALITY TRAITS

Any experience one can obtain in the field of public relations—via internships, volunteer opportunities, or a part-time job—will be useful for aspiring publicists.

In order to be a successful publicist, you should be outgoing and able to get along with many different types of people. You should also be creative, organized, and able to work well under stress, since you will likely interact with big-name clients. Strong oral and written communication skills are a must in this profession.

■ EMPLOYMENT PROSPECTS
Employers

Publicists work for public relations firms that handle publicity for companies, sports teams, and other organizations. Others work directly for companies. Some are self-employed, working directly with clients.

Starting Out

The best way to become a publicist is by gaining experience while you are in college. Many internships are available at this level, and landing one is the best way to get your foot in the door. As an intern, you may be asked to contribute to publications and write and prepare press releases. This will give you a great opportunity not only to learn how to generate all of this material, but also to begin collecting samples of your writing and to develop

---

PUBLICITY AND PR PRACTICES — LEARN MORE ABOUT IT

Breakenridge, Deirdre K. *Social Media and Public Relations: Eight New Practices for the PR Professional.* Upper Saddle River, N.J.: FT Press, 2012.

Kleiman, Jessica and Meryl Weinsaft Cooper. *Be Your Own Publicist: How to Use PR Techniques to Get Noticed, Hired and Rewarded at Work.* Franklin Lakes, N.J.: Career Press, 2011.

Scott, David Meerman. *The New Rules of Marketing and PR: How to Use Social Media, Online Video, Mobile Applications, Blogs, News Releases, and Viral Marketing to Reach Buyers Directly,* 5th ed. Hoboken, N.J.: John Wiley & Sons, 2015.

Wilcox, Dennis L. and Glen T. Cameron. *Public Relations: Strategies and Tactics,* 11th ed. Upper Saddle River, N.J.: Pearson Education, 2014.

---

your clip file. Every interviewer you meet will ask you for your clip file, since it provides proof of your journalistic and public relations writing skills. Established public relations companies may also offer in-house training programs.

■ ADVANCEMENT PROSPECTS

Publicists advance by gaining employment with more prestigious organizations, companies, or individuals, by becoming public relations managers, or by opening their own public relations firms. Others leave the field to teach public relations at colleges and universities.

■ OUTLOOK

The U.S. Department of Labor predicts that employment of public relations specialists in general is expected to increase about as fast as the average for all occupations through 2024, but the number of applicants with degrees in the communications fields (journalism, public relations, and advertising) is expected to exceed the number of job openings. Publicists with expertise in social media will be in demand. Job opportunities will also arise from the need to replace publicists retiring from the field or leaving their positions for other opportunities.

■ UNIONS AND ASSOCIATIONS

Publicists do not typically belong to unions. The Public Relations Society of America (PRSA) is the major membership organization for publicists. Membership benefits include the opportunity to view free webinars, discounts on PRSA conferences and events, access to discussion boards and member directories, and networking opportunities. Other membership organizations for publicists include the International Association of Business Communicators and the Entertainment Publicists Professional Society.

■ TIPS FOR ENTRY

1. Read *Public Relations Tactics* and *The Public Relations Strategist* (both available at http://www.prsa.org/Intelligence) to learn more about the field.
2. Visit http://www.prsa.org/Jobcenter/career_resources/career_level/entry_level for detailed information about launching a career in public relations including PR job descriptions, an Ask the Experts electronic forum, and advice on preparing resumes and acing job interviews.
3. For job listings, visit:
   - http://www.prsa.org/jobcenter
   - http://jobs.iabc.com
4. Visit http://www.prsa.org/Network/FindAFirm/Search for a database of PR firms.

■ FOR MORE INFORMATION

For information on working as an entertainment publicist, contact

Entertainment Publicists Professional Society (EPPS)
PO Box 5841
Beverly Hills, CA 90209-5841
E-mail: info@eppsonline.org
http://www.eppsonline.org

For information on accreditation, contact

International Association of Business Communicators (IABC)
155 Montgomery Street, Suite 1210
San Francisco, CA 94104
Tel: (800) 776-4222; (415) 544-4700
Fax: (415) 544-4747
E-mail: member_relations@iabc.com
http://www.iabc.com

For information on careers and accreditation in public relations, contact

Public Relations Society of America (PRSA)
120 Wall St., 21st Floor
New York, NY 10005
Tel: (212) 460-1400
E-mail: memberservice@prsa.org
http://www.prsa.org

Publicity Photographers

■ OVERVIEW

Photographers take pictures of people, places, objects, and events, using a variety of cameras and photographic equipment. They work in the publishing, advertising, public relations, science, and business industries, as well as provide personal photographic services. They may also work as fine artists, videographers, and cinematographers. There are approximately 50,070 photographers employed in the United States.

■ HISTORY

The word *photograph* means "to write with light." Although the art of photography goes back only about 150 years, the two Greek words that were chosen and combined to refer to this skill quite accurately describe what it does.

The discoveries that led eventually to photography began early in the 18th century when a German scientist, Dr. Johann H. Schultze, experimented with the action of light on certain chemicals. He found that when these chemicals were covered by dark paper they did not change color, but when they were exposed to sunlight, they darkened. A French painter named Louis Daguerre became the first photographer in 1839, using silver-iodide-coated plates and a small box. To develop images on the plates, Daguerre exposed them to mercury vapor. The daguerreotype, as these early photographs came to be known, took minutes to expose and the developing process was directly to the plate. There were no prints made.

Although the daguerreotype was the sensation of its day, it was not until George Eastman invented a simple camera and flexible roll film that photography began to come into widespread use in the late 1800s. After exposing this film to light and developing it with chemicals, the film revealed a color-reversed image, which is called a negative. To make the negative positive (a.k.a. print a picture), light must be shone though the negative on to light-sensitive paper. This process can be repeated to make multiple copies of an image from one negative.

One of the most important developments in recent years is digital photography. In digital photography, instead of using film, pictures are recorded on microchips, which can then be downloaded onto a computer's hard drive. They can be manipulated in size, color, and shape, virtually eliminating the need for a darkroom.

New methods (such as digital photography) and new creative mediums (such as the Internet) have created many new opportunities for photographers, including those employed by public relations firms, corporations, nonprofit organizations, and government agencies.

■ THE JOB

Many photographers rely on public relations work or corporate photography for a large bulk of their assignments. They are often hired by the public relations department of a corporation to take formal portraits of executives or shoot photos to accompany a press release or for use on a Web site or in brochures. Photographers are often hired to document special events such as the opening of a new facility, a community event, or a corporate-sponsored charitable event. Some photographers may be asked to film an event for use in a video or Internet release.

Photography is both an artistic and technical occupation. There are many variables in the process that a knowledgeable photographer can manipulate to produce a clear image or a more abstract work of fine art. First, photographers know how to use cameras and can adjust focus, shutter speeds, aperture, lenses, and filters. They know about the types and speeds of films. Photographers also know about light and shadow, deciding when to use available natural light and when to set up artificial lighting to achieve desired effects.

Most photographers today use digital cameras, rather than traditional silver-halide film cameras (for which film is developed in a laboratory). With this technology, film is replaced by microchips that record pictures in digital format. Pictures can then be downloaded onto a computer's hard drive. Using special software, photographers edit the images on the screen and place them directly onto the layout of a Web site or brochure. Most photographers continually experiment with photographic processes to improve their technical proficiency or to create special effects.

Many times, photographers work with public relations professionals such as designers and writers to create publicity campaigns. Some photographers write for trade and technical journals, teach photography in schools and colleges, act as representatives of photographic equipment manufacturers, sell photographic equipment and supplies, produce documentary films, or do freelance work.

■ EARNINGS

The U.S. Department of Labor reports that salaried photographers had median annual earnings of $31,710 in May 2015. Salaries ranged from less than $18,850 to more than $72,200. Photographers earned the following mean annual salaries by employer: motion picture and video firms, $70,350; radio and television broadcasting companies, $45,680; newspaper, periodical, book, and directory publishers, $45,310; and other professional, scientific, and technical services firms, $35,860.

Self-employed photographers often earn more than salaried photographers, but their earnings depend on general business conditions. In addition, self-employed photographers do not receive the benefits that a company provides its employees.

Photographers in salaried jobs usually receive benefits such as paid holidays, vacations, and sick leave and medical insurance.

■ WORK ENVIRONMENT

Work conditions vary based on the job and employer. Many publicity photographers work a 35- to 40-hour workweek, but may have to work at night and on weekends when outreach programs, award dinners, and other events are held. Freelancers often work longer, more irregular hours.

In general, photographers work under pressure to meet deadlines and satisfy customers. Freelance photographers have the added pressure of uncertain incomes and have to continually seek out new clients.

For freelance photographers, the cost of equipment can be quite expensive, with no assurance that the money spent will be repaid through income from future assignments. For all photographers, flexibility is a major asset.

QUICK FACTS

ALTERNATE TITLE(S)
None

DUTIES
Take photographs of people, places, and objects using a variety of cameras and photographic equipment

SALARY RANGE
$18,850 to $31,710 to $72,200+

WORK ENVIRONMENT
Indoors/Outdoors

BEST GEOGRAPHIC LOCATION(S)
Opportunities are available throughout the country, but are best in large, urban areas

MINIMUM EDUCATION LEVEL
High School Diploma, Some Postsecondary Training

SCHOOL SUBJECTS
Art, Business, Journalism

EXPERIENCE
Experience as an assistant essential

PERSONALITY TRAITS
Artistic, Creative, Outgoing

SKILLS
Digital Media, Drawing/Design, Interpersonal

CERTIFICATION OR LICENSING
Recommended

SPECIAL REQUIREMENTS
None

EMPLOYMENT PROSPECTS
Good

ADVANCEMENT PROSPECTS
Good

OUTLOOK
Little Change or More Slowly than the Average

NOC
5221

O*NET-SOC
27-4021.00

CAREER LADDER

Business Owner

Manager

Staff Photographer

Photographic Apprentice, Trainee, or Assistant

◼ EXPLORING

Photography is a field that anyone with a camera can explore. To learn more about this career, you can join high school camera clubs, yearbook or newspaper staffs, photography contests, and community hobby groups. You can also seek a part-time or summer job in a photo studio or camera shop, or work as a developer in a laboratory or processing center.

If you are interested in becoming a publicity photographer, volunteer to take photographs for community and nonprofit organizations in your area. This will give you a good introduction to the field, and even allow you the chance to have your work published in press releases and at an organization's Web site. Start a blog that features your photographs. Talk to photographers about their careers. Visit http://findaphotographer.org and http://aspp.com/find-a-pro/search-pros for lists of media photographers. Finally, consider becoming a high school- or college-level member of American Photographic Artists.

◼ EDUCATION AND TRAINING REQUIREMENTS
High School

While in high school, take as many art classes and photography classes that are available. Chemistry is useful for understanding developing and printing processes. You can learn about photo editing software and digital photography in computer and art classes, and business classes will help if you are considering a freelance career.

Postsecondary Training

A college education is not required to become a photographer, although college training probably offers the most promising assurance of success if you decide to pursue a career in fields such as industrial, news, or scientific photography. There are degree programs at the associate's, bachelor's, and master's levels. Many, however, become photographers with no formal education beyond high school.

Professional Photographers of America offers a merit degree program in which photographers can earn the following designations: master of photography, photographic craftsman, and master artist.

To become a photographer, you should have a broad technical understanding of photography plus as much practical experience with cameras as possible. Take many

different kinds of photographs with a variety of cameras and subjects. Learn how to develop photographs and use photo-editing software.

Other Education or Training

Continuing education events, seminars, classes, and other activities are offered by many professional associations, including American Photographic Artists, American Society of Media Photographers, American Society of Picture Professionals, and the Professional Photographers of America. Contact these organizations for more information.

◼ CERTIFICATION, LICENSING, AND SPECIAL REQUIREMENTS
Certification or Licensing

The Professional Photographic Certification Commission, which is affiliated with Professional Photographers of America, offers certification to general photographers. Visit http://www.ppa.com/cpp for more information.

◼ EXPERIENCE, SKILLS, AND PERSONALITY TRAITS

The best way to obtain experience in the field is to work as an assistant to a publicity photographer. Contact photographers in your area to inquire about opportunities.

You should possess manual dexterity, good eyesight and color vision, and artistic ability to succeed in this line of work. You need an eye for form and line, an appreciation of light and shadow, and the ability to use imaginative and creative approaches to photographs or film, especially in commercial work. In addition, you should be patient and accurate and enjoy working with detail.

Self-employed (or freelance) photographers need good business skills. They must be able to manage their own studios, including hiring and managing assistants and other employees, keeping records, and maintaining photographic and business files. Marketing and sales skills are also important to a successful freelance photography business.

◼ EMPLOYMENT PROSPECTS
Employers

About 50,070 photographers work in the United States, nearly 60 percent of whom are self-employed. Most jobs for photographers are provided by photographic or commercial art studios; other employers include public relations and advertising firms, newspapers and magazines, radio and TV broadcasting, film companies, government agencies, and manufacturing firms. Colleges, universities, and other educational institutions employ photographers to prepare promotional and educational materials.

Starting Out

Some photographers enter the field as apprentices, trainees, or assistants. Trainees may work in a darkroom, camera shop, or developing laboratory. They may move lights and arrange backgrounds for a publicity photographer. Assistants spend many months learning this kind of work before they move into a job behind a camera.

Many large cities offer schools of photography, which may be a good way to start in the field. Beginning photographers may work for a public relations firm, newspapers, or magazine in their area. Other photographers choose to go into business for themselves as soon as they have finished their formal education. Setting up a studio may not require a large capital outlay, but beginners may find that success does not come easily.

■ ADVANCEMENT PROSPECTS

Because photography is such a diversified field, there is no usual way in which to get ahead. Those who begin by working for someone else may advance to owning their own businesses. Commercial photographers may gain prestige as more of their pictures are placed in well-known trade journals or popular magazines. A few photographers may become celebrities in their own right by making contributions to the art world or the sciences.

■ OUTLOOK

Employment of photographers will increase by 3 percent through 2024, according to the *Occupational Outlook Handbook,* or more slowly than the average for all occupations. Photography is a highly competitive field. While the Internet has enabled professional photographers to market their services to a wider audience, digital photography has intensified the competition. More people have access to digital photography equipment and are able to take and store pictures, reducing the barrier of entry into this profession. Now more than ever, there are far more photographers than positions available (especially in large, metropolitan areas). Only those who are extremely talented and highly skilled can support themselves as self-employed photographers. Many photographers take pictures as a sideline while working another job.

Despite slower-than-average growth, there will continue to be demand for new images in business, education, communication, marketing, and research.

■ UNIONS AND ASSOCIATIONS

Publicity photographers are not represented by unions, but they can obtain useful resources and

A publicity photographer sits atop a ladder to capture photos of runners during a marathon. (txking. Shutterstock.)

professional support from the following organizations: American Photographic Artists, American Society of Media Photographers, American Society of Picture Professionals, and Professional Photographers of America (PPA). College students who are pursuing a major in photography or digital media can become members of the PPA. American Photographic Artists offers membership options for high school and college students. The Professional Photographic Certification Commission provides certification.

■ TIPS FOR ENTRY

1. Start developing a portfolio of your work so that you are ready to begin looking for jobs once you graduate. Include only your best work.
2. Create your own Web site that showcases your photography and advertises your services.
3. Read industry publications such as *ASMP Professional Business Practices in Photography* (http://asmp.org) and *The Picture Professional* (http://aspp.com/the-picture-professional) to learn more about trends in the industry and potential employers.
4. Join professional associations to access training and networking opportunities, industry publications, and employment opportunities.

Top Independent U.S. Public Relations Firms by Revenue, 2015

Firm	Revenue (millions)	Location	Web Site
1. Edelman	$854.58	New York	http://www.edelman.com
2. APCO Worldwide	$119.86	Washington, D.C.	http://www.apcoworldwide.com
3. WE	$98.78	Bellevue, Wash.	https://www.we-worldwide.com
4. W2O Group	$95.01	San Francisco	http://www.w2ogroup.com
5. Ruder Finn	$74.0	New York	http://www.ruderfinn.com
6. Finn Partners	$71.48	New York	http://www.finnpartners.com
7. LEWIS	$68.59	San Francisco	http://www.teamlewis.com
8. ICR	$56.21	New York	http://www.icrinc.com/
9. Zeno Group	$47.34	Norwalk, Ct.	http://zenogroup.com
10. PadillaCRT	$34.81	Minneapolis	http://www.padillacrt.com

Source: J.R. O'Dwyer Company, Inc.

5. Participate in internships or part-time jobs that are arranged by your college's career services office.

■ FOR MORE INFORMATION

For information on careers and information on membership for high school and college students, contact

American Photographic Artists (APA)
2055 Bryant Street
San Francisco, CA 94110-2125
E-mail: members@apanational.org
http://apanational.org

The ASMP promotes the rights of photographers, educates its members in business practices, and promotes high standards of ethics.

American Society of Media Photographers (ASMP)
P.O. Box 1810
Traverse City, MI 49685-1810
Tel: (877) 771-2767
Fax: (231) 946-6180
E-mail: asmp@vpconnections.com
http://asmp.org

For information on membership and publications, contact
American Society of Picture Professionals (ASPP)
E-mail: membership@aspp.com
http://www.aspp.com

This organization provides training, publishes its own magazine, and offers various services for its members.

Professional Photographers of America (PPA)
229 Peachtree Street, NE, Suite 2200
Atlanta, GA 30303-1608

Tel: (800) 786-6277; (404) 522-8600
Fax: (404) 614-6400
http://www.ppa.com

Purchasing Agents

■ OVERVIEW

Purchasing agents work for businesses and other large organizations, such as hospitals, universities, and government agencies. They buy raw materials, machinery, supplies, and services required for the organization. They must consider cost, quality, quantity, and time of delivery. Purchasing agents and buyers hold approximately 443,200 jobs in the United States.

■ HISTORY

Careers in the field of purchasing are relatively new and came into real importance only in the last half of the 20th century. The first purchasing jobs emerged during the Industrial Revolution, when manufacturing plants and businesses became bigger. This led to the division of management jobs into various specialties, one of which was buying.

By the late 1800s, buying was considered a separate job in large businesses. Purchasing jobs were especially important in the railroad, automobile, and steel industries. The trend toward creating specialized buying jobs was reflected in the founding of professional organizations, such as the National Association of Purchasing Agents (now the Institute for Supply Management) and the American Purchasing Society. It was not until after World War II, however, with the expansion of the U.S. government and the increased complexity of business practices, that the job of purchasing agent became firmly established.

■ THE JOB

Purchasing agents generally work for organizations that buy at least $100,000 worth of goods a year. Their primary goal is to purchase the best quality materials for the best price. To do this, the agent must consider the exact specifications for the required items, cost, quantity discounts, freight handling or other transportation costs, and delivery time. In the past, much of this information was obtained by comparing listings in catalogs and trade journals, interviewing suppliers' representatives, keeping up with current market trends, examining sample goods, and observing demonstrations of equipment. Increasingly, information can be found through computer databases, and most purchasing transactions are now handled through the Internet. Sometimes agents visit plants of company suppliers. The agent is responsible for following up on orders and ensuring that goods meet the order specifications.

Purchasing agents also frequently work with other employees as part of a "team buying" process. For example, before placing an order, they will meet with design engineers to discuss the product's design, or with production supervisors to learn more about the quality of purchased goods, or with receiving department managers to hash out shipping issues. Gathering this information from various perspectives improves the quality of the purchase.

Most purchasing agents work in firms that have fewer than five employees in their purchasing department. In some small organizations, there is only one person responsible for making purchases. Very large firms, however, may employ as many as 100 purchasing agents, each responsible for specific types of goods. In such organizations there is usually a purchasing director or purchasing manager.

Some purchasing agents seek the advice of *purchase-price analysts,* who compile and analyze statistical data about the manufacture and cost of products. Based on this information, they can make recommendations to purchasing personnel regarding the feasibility of producing or buying certain products and suggest ways to reduce costs.

Purchasing agents often specialize in a particular product or field. For example, *procurement engineers* specialize in aircraft equipment. They establish specifications and requirements for construction, performance, and testing of equipment.

Field contractors negotiate with farmers to grow or purchase fruits, vegetables, or other crops. These agents may advise growers on methods, acreage, and supplies, and arrange for financing, transportation, or labor recruitment.

Head tobacco buyers are engaged in the purchase of tobacco on the auction warehouse floor. They advise other buyers about grades and quantities of tobacco and suggest prices.

Grain buyers manage grain elevators. They are responsible for evaluating and buying grain for resale and milling. They are concerned with the quality, market value, shipping, and storing of grain.

Grain broker-and-market operators buy and sell grain for investors through the commodities exchange. Like other brokers, they work on a commission basis.

■ EARNINGS

How much a purchasing agent earns depends on various factors, including the employer's sales volume. Mass merchandisers, such as discount or chain department stores, pay among the highest salaries. According to May 2015 U.S. Department of Labor data, earnings for purchasing agents, except wholesale, retail, and farm products ranged from less than $37,850 to for the lowest 10 percent to more than $99,960 for the top 10 percent. Median salaries were $62,220. Purchasing agents and buyers of farm products had median annual earnings of $56,270 in May 2015, with salaries that ranged from $31,220 to $101,180 or more.

QUICK FACTS

ALTERNATE TITLE(S)
Procurement Engineers, Purchasing Managers, Purchase-Price Analysts

DUTIES
Buy raw materials, supplies, machinery, and services for their organizations

SALARY RANGE
$31,220 to $62,220 to $101,180+

WORK ENVIRONMENT
Primarily Indoors

BEST GEOGRAPHIC LOCATION(S)
Opportunities are available throughout the country

MINIMUM EDUCATION LEVEL
High School Diploma

SCHOOL SUBJECTS
Business, Economics, Mathematics

EXPERIENCE
Internship

PERSONALITY TRAITS
Hands On, Organized, Social

SKILLS
Interpersonal, Organizational, Sales

CERTIFICATION OR LICENSING
Recommended

SPECIAL REQUIREMENTS
None

EMPLOYMENT PROSPECTS
Good

ADVANCEMENT PROSPECTS
Good

OUTLOOK
Little Change or More Slowly than the Average

NOC
1225

O*NET-SOC
11-3061.00, 13-1021.00, 13-1023.00

CAREER LADDER

Vice-President of Purchasing

Purchasing Director or Purchasing Manager

Experienced Purchasing Agent

Entry-Level Purchasing Agent

In addition to their salaries, buyers often receive cash bonuses based on performance and may be offered incentive plans, such as profit sharing and stock options. Most buyers receive the usual company benefits, such as vacation, sick leave, life and health insurance, and pension plans. They generally also receive an employee's discount of 10 to 20 percent on merchandise purchased for personal use.

■ WORK ENVIRONMENT

Working conditions for a purchasing agent are similar to those of other office employees. They usually work in offices that are pleasant, well lighted, and clean. Work is year-round and generally steady because it is not particularly influenced by seasonal factors. Most have 40-hour workweeks, although overtime is not uncommon. In addition to regular hours, agents may have to attend meetings, read and prepare reports, visit suppliers' plants, or travel. While most work is done indoors, some agents occasionally need to inspect goods outdoors or in warehouses.

It is important for purchasing agents to have good working relations with others. They must interact closely with suppliers as well as with personnel in other departments of the company. Because of the importance of their decisions, purchasing agents sometimes work under great pressure.

■ EXPLORING

If you are interested in becoming a purchasing agent, you can learn more about the field through a summer job in the purchasing department of a business. Even working as a stock clerk can offer some insight into the job of purchasing agent or buyer. You may also learn about the job by talking with an experienced purchasing agent or reading publications on the field such as *Professional Purchasing* (http://www.american-purchasing.com). Keeping abreast of economic trends, fashion styles, or other indicators may help you to predict the market for particular products. Making educated and informed predictions is a basic part of any buying job.

■ EDUCATION AND TRAINING REQUIREMENTS
High School

Most purchasing and buying positions require at least a bachelor's degree. Therefore, while in high school, take a college preparatory curriculum. Helpful classes include English, business, mathematics, social science, and economics.

Postsecondary Training

Although it is possible to obtain an entry-level purchasing job with only a high school diploma, many employers prefer or require college graduates for the job. College work should include courses in general economics, purchasing, accounting, statistics, and business management. A familiarity with computers also is desirable. Some colleges and universities offer majors in purchasing, but other business-related majors are appropriate as well.

Purchasing agents with a master's degree in business administration, engineering, technology, economics, or finance tend to have the best jobs and highest salaries. Companies that manufacture machinery or chemicals may require a degree in engineering or a related field. A civil service examination is required for employment in government purchasing positions.

In addition to formal education, newly hired purchasing agents also receive on-the-job training that can last a year or more.

Other Education or Training

Continuing education (CE) opportunities are provided by many professional associations. For example, the American Purchasing Society offers courses and seminars such as "Fundamentals of Business Buying and Purchasing Management," "The Science and The Art of Negotiation," "Body Language," and "How to Plan Your Career and Prepare Your Resume." The Institute for Supply Management and NIGP: The Institute for Public Procurement also provide CE classes, webinars, and workshops. Contact these organizations for more information.

■ CERTIFICATION, LICENSING, AND SPECIAL REQUIREMENTS
Certification or Licensing

There are no specific licenses or certification requirements imposed by law for purchasing agents. There are, however, several professional organizations to which many purchasing agents belong, including the Institute for Supply Management, NIGP: The Institute for Public Procurement, and the American Purchasing Society. These organizations offer certification to applicants who meet educational and other requirements and who pass the necessary examinations.

The Institute for Supply Management offers the certified professional in supply management and certified professional in supplier diversity designations. NIGP: The Institute for Public Procurement and the Universal Public Procurement Certification Council offer the certified public purchasing officer and the certified professional public buyer designations. The American Purchasing Society offers the certified purchasing professional (CPP), the certified professional purchasing manager (CPPM), the certified green purchasing professional (CGPP), the certified professional in distribution and warehousing (CPDW), and the certified professional purchasing consultant (CPPC) designations. Although certification is not essential, it is a recognized mark of professional competence that enhances a purchasing agent's opportunities for promotion to top management positions.

▪ EXPERIENCE, SKILLS, AND PERSONALITY TRAITS

Aspiring purchasing agents should take as many math and business classes as possible and participate in internships to gain experience in the field.

Purchasing agents should have calm temperaments and have confidence in their decision-making abilities. Because they work with other people, they need to be diplomatic, tactful, and cooperative. A thorough knowledge of business practices and an understanding of the needs and activities of the employer are essential, as is knowledge of the relevant markets. It also is helpful to be familiar with social and economic changes in order to predict the amounts or types of products to buy.

▪ EMPLOYMENT PROSPECTS
Employers

There are approximately 443,200 purchasing agents and buyers currently working in the United States. They work for a wide variety of businesses, both wholesale and retail, as well as for government agencies. Employers range from small stores, where buying may be only one function of a manager's job, to multinational corporations, where a buyer may specialize in one type of item and buy in enormous quantity. Nearly every business that sells products requires someone to purchase the goods to be sold. These businesses are located nearly everywhere there is a community of people, from small towns to large cities. Of course, the larger the town or city, the more businesses and thus more buying positions. Larger cities provide the best opportunities for higher salaries and advancement.

Starting Out

Students without a college degree may be able to enter the field as clerical workers and then receive on-the-job

THE BASICS OF PURCHASING

LEARN MORE ABOUT IT

Burt, David, Sheila Petcavage, and Richard Pinkerton. *Proactive Purchasing in the Supply Chain: The Key to World-Class Procurement.* New York: McGraw-Hill Professional, 2011.

Monczka, Robert M., et al. *Purchasing and Supply Chain Management,* 6th ed. Independence, Ky.: Cengage Learning, 2015.

O'Brien, Jonathan. *Category Management in Purchasing: A Strategic Approach to Maximize Business Profitability,* 3rd ed. Philadelphia: Kogan Page Publishers, 2015.

O'Brien, Jonathan. *Negotiation for Purchasing Professionals.* Philadelphia: Kogan Page Publishers, 2013.

training in purchasing. A college degree, though, is usually required for higher positions. College and university career services offices offer assistance to graduating students in locating jobs.

Entry into the purchasing department of a private business can be made by direct application to the company. Some purchasing agents start in another department, such as accounting, shipping, or receiving, and transfer to purchasing when an opportunity arises. Many large companies send newly hired agents through orientation programs, where they learn about goods and services, suppliers, and purchasing methods.

Another means of entering the field is through the military. Service in the Quartermaster Corps of the Army or the procurement divisions of the Navy or Air Force can provide excellent preparation either for a civilian job or a career position in the service.

▪ ADVANCEMENT PROSPECTS

In general, purchasing agents begin by becoming familiar with departmental procedures, such as keeping inventory records, filling out forms to initiate new purchases, checking purchase orders, and dealing with vendors. With more experience, they gain responsibility for selecting vendors and purchasing products. Agents may become junior buyers of standard catalog items, assistant buyers, or managers, perhaps with overall responsibility for purchasing, warehousing, traffic, and related functions. The top positions are head of purchasing, purchasing director, materials manager, and vice-president of purchasing. These positions include responsibilities concerning production, planning, and marketing.

Many agents advance by changing employers. Frequently an assistant purchasing agent for one firm will be hired as a purchasing agent or head of the purchasing department by another company.

OUTLOOK

Employment of purchasing agents and buyers overall is likely to grow more slowly than the average for all occupations through 2024, according to the U.S. Department of Labor (DOL). Computerized purchasing methods and the increased reliance on a select number of suppliers boost the productivity of purchasing personnel and have somewhat reduced the number of new job openings. But as more and more schools, state and local governments, health care organizations, and other service-related organizations turn to professional purchasing agents to help reduce costs, they will become good sources of employment.

The DOL predicts that job opportunities for purchasing agents and buyers will grow by only 2 percent through 2024, due to outsourcing of certain procurement functions, growing public sector adoption of cooperative purchasing agreements, and and declines in manufacturing. Employment of purchasing managers is expected to grow only 1 percent during the same time period.

Most job openings will arise from the need to replace workers who retire or otherwise leave their jobs. Demand will be strongest for those with a master's degree in business administration or supply chain management or an undergraduate degree in purchasing. Among firms that manufacture complex machinery, chemicals, and other technical products, the demand will be for graduates with a master's degree in engineering, another field of science, or business administration. Graduates of two-year programs in purchasing or materials management should continue to find good opportunities, especially in smaller companies.

UNIONS AND ASSOCIATIONS

Purchasing agents do not typically belong to unions, but they often join professional associations such as the American Purchasing Society, Institute for Supply Management, and NIGP: The Institute for Public Procurement. These organizations provide career support, network opportunities, continuing education classes and seminars, publications, and other resources. According to its Web site, the National Retail Federation is the "world's largest retail trade association, representing retailers from the United States and more than 45 countries." Its Web site offers information on education and careers in retail.

TIPS FOR ENTRY

1. Read *Professional Purchasing* (http://www.american-purchasing.com) and *Inside Supply Management* (https://www.instituteforsupplymanagement.org/pubs/ISMMag/?&navItemNumber=30166) to learn more about the field.
2. Check job listings on these Web sites:
   - http://jobs.nrf.com
   - http://www.nigp.org
   - http://www.american-purchasing.com
   - https://www.instituteforsupplymanagement.org
3. Joining a professional association is a great way to learn more about purchasing and advance your career. Associations provide many benefits to their members. For example, members of the American Purchasing Society receive free advice on preparing resumes and locating jobs, discounts on continuing education classes, useful industry and salary publications, and many other resources. Other membership organizations include the Institute for Supply Management and NIGP: The Institute for Public Procurement.

FOR MORE INFORMATION

For career and certification information, contact
American Purchasing Society (APS)
PO Box 256
Aurora, IL 60507-0256
Tel: (630) 859-0250
Fax: (630) 859-0270
E-mail: propurch@propurch.com
http://www.american-purchasing.com

For career and certification information and lists of colleges with purchasing programs, contact
Institute for Supply Management (ISM)
2055 East Centennial Circle
Tempe, AZ 85284-1898
Tel: (800) 888-6276; (480) 752-6276
Fax: (480) 752-7890
https://www.instituteforsupplymanagement.org

For information on education and careers in the retail industry, contact
National Retail Federation (NRF)
1101 New York Ave., NW
Washington, D.C. 20005
Tel: (800) 673-4692; (202) 783-7971
Fax: (202) 737-2849
http://www.nrf.com

For information on certification and purchasing careers in government, contact

NIGP: The Institute for Public Procurement (NIGP)
2411 Dulles Corner Park, Suite 350
Herndon, VA 20171
Tel: (800) 367-6447; (703) 736-8900
Fax: (703) 736-9639
E-mail: customercare@nigp.org
http://www.nigp.org

Purohitas

■ OVERVIEW

Purohitas are female priests who lead worship services, officiate at festivals, and perform ceremonies and rituals in Hindu temples and in the homes of devotees. They are also known as *temple priests* and *family priests.* There were an estimated 1,600 purohitas in India in 2014, according to the Bhandarkar Oriental Research Institute in Pune, India. They also work throughout Asia (especially in India) as well as in Western countries such as the United States, Canada, and the United Kingdom.

■ HISTORY

Hinduism is considered to be the world's oldest living religion—with roots dating to 2000 B.C. The religion originated around the Indus Valley near the Indus River in what is now modern day India and Pakistan. "Most traditions within Hinduism share certain distinctive, core beliefs despite the absence of an identifiable beginning in history, single founder, central religious establishment, or sole authoritative scripture," according to the Hindu American Foundation. "Two of these core beliefs are that of the oneness of existence (No one is superior, none inferior. All are brothers marching forward to prosperity.) and pluralism (May all beings be happy. May all beings be healthy. May all beings experience prosperity. May none in the world suffer.)."

Until the last 45 years or so, priests in India traditionally were men who came from the Brahmin caste (which includes those in sacred and teaching professions). But this was not always the case. In the Vedic era (c. 1500–c. 500 B.C.E.) in India—during which the *Vedas,* the oldest scriptures of Hinduism, were composed—women enjoyed equal freedom to pursue knowledge and study the holy scriptures. According to the Vedas, "Men and women, being equal halves of one substance—are equal in every respect." Women also appeared frequently in the *Rigveda* (a collection of Vedic Sanskrit hymns) in priest-like positions, composing/singing hymns and making sacrifices. Yet, despite the equality espoused in ancient Hindu texts and the fact that there is no scriptural constraint against women becoming priests, women have been strongly discouraged from becoming priests—especially in India. Other geographic areas have a tradition of female Hindu priesthood. For hundreds of years, females have been allowed to serve as priests in Bali, Indonesia.

In India, the restriction against women priests began loosening in the mid-1970s when a philanthropist named Shankar Hari Thatte first trained women priests in Pune, India. "He wanted to impart knowledge of the Vedic texts and learning, and chose children to begin with," according to an article from the Inter Press Service International Association about the increase in the number of female priests. "But seeing their indiscipline and disinterest, he decided to teach their mothers instead." Thatte established the Udyan Prasad Karyalaya in Pune to train the first class of women priests. The classes were free, and lasted four months. Pune continued to be a hotbed of training for women priests. In the early 1980s, Shankarrao Thatte, the owner of a marriage hall in Pune, launched the Shankar Seva Samiti, a school to train female priests. The Jnana Prabodhini School was also founded during this time in Pune to train female priests. In addition, temples and learning centers in Hyderabad (the capital of the state of Telangana) and Mumbai (the

QUICK FACTS

ALTERNATE TITLE(S)
Family Priests, Temple Priests

DUTIES
Lead worship and perform ceremonies and rituals in Hindu temples and devotees' homes

SALARY RANGE
$0 to $28,750 to $65,150+

WORK ENVIRONMENT
Primarily Indoors

BEST GEOGRAPHIC LOCATION(S)
Opportunities are available throughout the country, but are best in large U.S. cities

MINIMUM EDUCATION LEVEL
Some Postsecondary Training

SCHOOL SUBJECTS
Foreign Language, Religion, Speech

EXPERIENCE
Three to five years of experience as an assistant purohita

PERSONALITY TRAITS
Hands On, Helpful, Outgoing

SKILLS
Foreign Language, Interpersonal, Public Speaking

CERTIFICATION OR LICENSING
Recommended

SPECIAL REQUIREMENTS
Brahmin caste may be required at some temples

EMPLOYMENT PROSPECTS
Fair

ADVANCEMENT PROSPECTS
Fair

OUTLOOK
About as Fast as the Average

NOC
4154

O*NET-SOC
21-2011.00

CAREER LADDER

Temple Administrator

Purohita

Assistant Purohita

Temple Volunteer

capital of the state of Maharashtra) have a tradition of being supportive of female priests.

Today, Hinduism is the third-largest religion in the world with approximately one billion devotees (including 2.5 million in the United States).

▇ THE JOB

According to the Hindu American Foundation, Hinduism is "not divided by denomination, but by other categories, including deity traditions, sampradaya, parampara, and darsana. Most Hindus belong to one of four major deity traditions— Shaiva, Shakta, Vaishnava, and Smarta." For more information on Hindu deity traditions, major schools of thought, and holy scriptures visit http://www.haf site.org.

Job responsibilities for purohitas vary by deity traditions, size of the congregation, and other criteria, but typical duties include:

- conducting daily prayers (pujas), rituals, festivals, and special deity ceremonies in the temple and Hindu family residences; in some traditions, purohitas are only allowed to perform these duties in people's homes (those who do so are known as *family priests*), while others perform these duties in both homes and temples
- performing samskaras (rites of passage in a human being's life described in ancient Sanskrit texts) such as Jathakarma (birth of a child), Namakaranam (new child naming ceremony), Vivaham (wedding), Upaakarma (thread-changing ceremony for student-scholars), Nishchayathartham (wedding engagement), Varalakshmi Vratham (prosperity and happiness for one's family), Antima Sanskar (funeral), and various homam/havan (purification) rituals (In some traditions, purohitas are not involved in funeral ceremonies.)
- leading Stotra recitation (a melodically sung hymn)
- playing musical instruments such as the harmonium and tabla
- developing and executing spiritual and religious programs for seniors, children, and other diverse audiences
- ensuring that the temple is maintained with sacredness and cleanliness

- preparing special food offerings (prasadam) for Hindu worship services
- helping to raise money for the temple through various fundraising activities

▇ EARNINGS

The U.S. Department of Labor does not collect salary information for purohitas, but it does report that religious workers-not otherwise classified earned salaries that ranged from $18,280 to $65,150 in May 2015, with median earnings of $28,750.

In India, annual salaries for archakas (male priests) are quite low—the equivalent of $540 to $900 (in U.S. currency), according to New Delhi Television. Earnings for purohitas are in this range, but slightly lower. Some purohitas do not receive a salary, but are paid a fee for each ritual or ceremony they perform. Others do not accept pay because they consider their work a "divine calling."

A full-time Hindu priest in the United States receives paid vacation, sick, and personal days; medical, dental, and life insurance; and a 401(k) retirement plan. Some temples provide year-end bonuses and a vehicle allowance.

▇ WORK ENVIRONMENT

"In a Hindu temple there is often a multiplicity of simultaneous proceedings and ceremonies," according to *Hinduism Today*. "In one corner, an extended family, or clan, with its hundreds of tightly knit members, may be joyously celebrating a wedding. At another shrine a lady might be crying in front of the Deity, saddened by some misfortune and in need of solace. Elsewhere in the crowded precincts, a baby is being blessed, and several groups of temple musicians are filling the chamber with the shrill sounds of the nagasvaram [a double-reed melody instrument] and drum. After the puja reaches its zenith, brahmin priests move in and out of the sanctum, passing camphor and sacred ash and holy water to hundreds of worshipers crowding eagerly to get a glimpse of the Deity. All of this is happening at once, unplanned and yet totally organized."

Priests are very busy and often travel during religious festivals. For example, a purohita might travel to dozens of homes in a five- or 10-mile radius to perform pujas during the 10-day Ganesha Chaturthi, an elaborate festival that celebrates the birth of Lord Ganesha—the supreme God of wisdom and prosperity.

A purohita who works in the West may wear Western-style clothing rather than the traditional white austere priestly garments.

▇ EXPLORING

You can obtain a good introduction to Hindu religious vocations by working as a temple volunteer. In this

SHRUTI AND SMRITI—HEARD AND REMEMBERED

Hindu sacred texts are classified generally into two categories: Shruti ("heard" in Sanskrit) and Smriti ("memory" in Sanskrit). According to the Hindu American Foundation, Shruti "consists of what Hindus believe to be eternal truths akin to natural law. These texts are revered as 'revealed' or divine in origin and are believed to contain the foundational truths of Hinduism. Smriti is distinguished from Shruti in terms of its origin. Teachings in Smriti texts are meant to remind adherents about the eternal truths of Shruti, and read and interpreted in light of changing circumstances over kala (time), desha (land), and guna (personality)." Here's a brief overview of the best-known texts:

SHRUTI

Vedas: The word "veda" means knowledge. They contain hymns, incantations, and rituals. The four *Vedas* are the *Rig Veda* (the oldest), *Sama, Yajur,* and *Atharva.*

Upanishads: The more than 100 *Upanishads* explore methods of understanding God, oneself, and the world around us.

SMRITI

Upavedas: There are four main texts in the Upavedas:

- *Ayurveda:* cover the science of health and life
- *Dhanurveda:* science of warfare
- *Gandharvaveda:* an examination of art forms and aesthetics
- *Arthashastra:* guidance on public administration, governance, politics, and economy

Puranas: The 18 major *Puranas* and many minor ones teach the meaning of the *Upanishads* and *Vedas* through stories and parables.

Ramayana: An epic, popular tale of a prince named Rama (whom Hindus believe is an incarnation of the God Vishnu) who undergoes years of exile and challenges while fighting demons and searching for his beloved wife Sita. After Rama overcomes these challenges and rescues his wife, he returns to rule his kingdom, inaugurating a golden age for humanity.

Mahabharata: This historical epic, which has more than 100,000 verses, focuses on the struggle for sovereignty between two groups of cousins and themes such as truth, justice, self-sacrifice, devotion to God, and the ultimate futility of war.

Bhagavad Gita: This is the primary scripture of Hinduism, but it's actually a small portion of the *Mahabharata*. It is composed in the form of a dialogue between one of the story's protagonists and Krishna (a major Hindu deity) about what to do in situations where there is no clear right and wrong and how to achieve liberation from the cycle of death and rebirth.

Agama Shastras: These texts provide guidance on the practical aspects of devotion and worship.

Source: Hindu American Foundation

position, you might greet visitors, clean the temple, and assist office staff in their duties. Talk to a purohita about her career and the rewards and challenges of being a female priest in a male-dominated occupation. Visit http://www.hindutemples.us for a list of Hindu temples in the United States. Biographies of resident priests are sometimes provided at these sites, which can help you to identify potential purohitas to contact regarding an interview. Visit a temple and observe a purohita performing puja. *Hinduism Today* offers a helpful primer on visiting a temple and the various aspects of the service at https://www.hinduismtoday.com/modules/smartsection/item.php?itemid=5315. The Hindu American Foundation provides a wealth of information about the career of priest and other temple jobs at its Web site, http://www.hafsite.org. Finally, check out the following resources to learn more about Hinduism:

- *Hinduism For Dummies* (For Dummies, 2011)
- *The Illustrated Encyclopedia of Hinduism* (Lorenz Books, 2012)

- *The Little Book of Hindu Deities: From the Goddess of Wealth to the Sacred Cow* (Plume, 2006)
- Hindupedia: http://www.hindupedia.com

■ EDUCATION AND TRAINING REQUIREMENTS
High School

Aspiring purohitas who plan to work in a temple in the United States must be proficient in English, Sanskrit (the primary sacred language of Hinduism), Hindi, and Telegu. They may also need to be proficient, or at least have working knowledge, of regional Indian languages such as Bengali, Tamil, Malayalam, and Kannada, or the languages spoken in the countries where they work. Few, if any, American high schools teach Indian languages, but Indian community centers and local colleges offer language classes. Additionally, if you live in New Jersey, Connecticut, and Maryland, you can take Hindi classes offered by the nonprofit organization HindiUSA (http://www.hindiusa.info).

In addition to religion and philosophy courses, other useful classes include business, accounting, music, science, mathematics, speech, and computer science.

Postsecondary Education

The length of training for female priests is usually shorter than it is for male priests. Purohita training programs in India typically last anywhere from six months to a year, although some purohitas train with a guru (expert teacher) for longer periods. In addition to traditional religious schools, some charitable organizations also train women to become priests.

Many U.S.-based Hindu temples require job applicants to have an undergraduate degree. Some purohitas have degrees in Hindu studies, Southeast Asian Studies, or an applicable foreign language such as Sanskrit, Hindi, or Bengali.

Some purohitas also have secular careers (e.g., social workers, teachers, doctors, engineers, lawyers, etc.). In these instances, they would earn degrees in their respective fields. For example, a social worker would have a degree in social work and a teacher would have a degree in education.

Other Education or Training

Throughout their lives, purohitas must continue to develop spiritually and expand their language proficiency, knowledge of business practices, and ability to use computer software for temple business. To do so, they attend spiritual retreats, work with a master teacher, and take courses offered by colleges, universities, and business and technology associations.

Certification

The Graduate Theological Union, through its Mira and Ajay Shingal Center for Dharma Studies, offers a six-course certificate program that culminates in the awarding of a certificate in Hindu studies. Earning this certificate doesn't make you a purohita, but it will provide you with a deeper understanding of Hinduism. Visit http://www.gtu.edu/academics/areas/hindu-studies for more information. Some purohitas improve their language skills by earning undergraduate and graduate certificates in an Indian language or English. Contact schools in your area to learn about available programs.

■ CERTIFICATION, LICENSING, AND SPECIAL REQUIREMENTS
Certification or Licensing

Hinduism is a highly decentralized religion, and there is no standard certification or licensing for purohitas. Organizations such as Arya Pratinidhi Sabha America, which represents Arya Samajs and Vedic Temples in North America, offer certification to members of their sects.

Other Requirements

In the past, Hindu priests typically hailed from the Brahmin caste, but today, they can come from any caste provided that they have requisite training and that the governing Agama Shastras (temple rules) allow it.

■ EXPERIENCE, SKILLS, AND PERSONALITY TRAITS

To work in an American Hindu temple, you'll need to have three to five years of experience as a purohita or assistant purohita. Temples in India or other Asian countries with a significant Hindu population may require less experience.

Strong communication and interpersonal skills, and knowledge of English and Indian languages (especially Sanskrit), are extremely important in this career. You should also be caring, compassionate, have wisdom and patience, and be a good listener because you will be asked to counsel congregants during challenging times in their lives (e.g., illness, deaths in the family, job loss, etc.). Many U.S.-based temples require priests to be proficient in basic business principles and the use of Microsoft Word and Excel. Other important traits include strong leadership, organizational, and time-management skills.

In addition to personal and professional skills, purohitas must have deep knowledge and understanding of Hindu religious and classical texts such as the *Bhagavad Gita, Vedas, Upanishads, Agama Shastras, Puranas,* and the *Ramayana.*

■ EMPLOYMENT PROSPECTS
Employers
Purohitas are employed by Hindu temples, which are located throughout the world (but most commonly in India, Nepal, Mauritius, Fiji, and Bhutan). They are also hired by individuals to perform religious rituals and ceremonies in their homes. More than 200 Hindu temples are located in the United States; many are found in California, Texas, and New York.

Starting Out
Many women begin training to become purohitas in middle age after raising their families, but an increasing number are choosing to pursue this vocation in their 20s. Some purohitas have fathers or husbands who were priests (archakas).

In the United States, those seeking priest positions should contact Hindu temples directly to inquire about job openings. A list of Hindu temples in the United States can be found at http://shaivam.org/siddhanta/toi_usa .htm.

■ ADVANCEMENT PROSPECTS
An experienced purohita might become the administrator of her temple, while keeping her priestly responsibilities. Although those in religious vocations are not typically motivated by the accrual of wealth, some purohitas choose to work at larger temples to earn higher pay or receive a better benefits package. Some purohitas have secular jobs as teachers, nurses, social workers, dentists, doctors, and lawyers, among many other careers.

■ OUTLOOK
The percentage of Americans who practice Hinduism nearly doubled from 2007 to 2014, according to *America's Changing Religious Landscape,* a report from the Pew Research Center, which suggests that there is good demand for purohitas. But if you consider the actual numbers of devotees to Hinduism in the United States (2.5 million), the relatively small number of Hindu temples in the United States (200 or so), the small number of women priests, and concerns by some groups about the appropriateness of women serving as priests, the employment outlook is a bit more sobering. Opportunities in certain cities or regions of India and other predominantly Hindu countries that have a tradition of encouraging women to become Buddhist priests—such as cities in the Indian states of Telangana and Maharashtra—will be better, but the number of purohitas is still small.

Because pay is traditionally low for Hindu priests, a growing number of male priests are leaving the field to pursue jobs that allow them to better support their families. In addition, fewer men are training for the priesthood because of salary issues and increasing opportunities in other careers. If these trends continue, employment opportunities for purohitas will improve.

■ UNIONS AND ASSOCIATIONS
Purohitas are not members of unions. The Hindu American Foundation offers an overview of Hinduism, information on religious vocations, and many other resources at its Web site, http://www.hafsite.org.

■ TIPS FOR ENTRY
1. Read *Hinduism Today* (http://www.hinduismtoday .com) to learn more about the religion.
2. Visit http://www.australiancouncilofhinduclergy .com/uploads/5/5/4/9/5549439/female_hindu _priests.pdf to read "Female Hindu priests in India are making strides in a male-dominated profession."
3. Talk to purohitas about their careers. Ask them for advice on entering the profession.

■ FOR MORE INFORMATION
For information on Hinduism and religious vocations, contact

Hindu American Foundation
910 Seventeenth Street, NW, Suite 316A
Washington, D.C. 20006-2601
Tel: (202) 223-8222
Fax: (202) 223-8004
http://www.hafsite.org

Quality Control Engineers and Technicians

■ OVERVIEW
Quality control engineers plan and direct procedures and activities that will ensure the quality of materials and goods. They select the best techniques for a specific process or method, determine the level of quality needed, and take the necessary action to maintain or improve quality performance. *Quality control technicians* assist quality control engineers in devising quality control procedures and methods, implement quality control techniques, test and inspect products during different phases of production, and compile and evaluate statistical data to monitor quality levels.

■ HISTORY

Quality control technology is an outgrowth of the Industrial Revolution, which began in England in the 18th century. Each person involved in the manufacturing process was responsible for a particular part of the process. The worker's responsibility was further specialized by the introduction of manufacturing with interchangeable parts in the late 18th and early 19th centuries. In a manufacturing process using this technique, a worker concentrated on making just one component, while other workers concentrated on creating other components. Such specialization led to increased production efficiency, especially as manufacturing processes became mechanized during the early part of the 20th century. It also meant, however, that no one worker was responsible for the overall quality of the product. This led to the need for another kind of specialized production worker whose primary responsibility was not one aspect of the product but rather its overall quality.

This responsibility initially belonged to the mechanical engineers and technicians who developed the manufacturing systems, equipment, and procedures. After World War II, however, a new field emerged that was dedicated solely to quality control. Along with specially trained persons to test and inspect products coming off assembly lines, new instruments, equipment, and techniques were developed to measure and monitor specified standards.

At first, quality control engineers and technicians were primarily responsible for random checks of products to ensure they met all specifications. This usually entailed testing and inspecting either finished products or products at various stages of production.

During the 1980s, a renewed emphasis on quality spread across the United States. Faced with increased global competition, especially from Japanese manufacturers, many U.S. companies sought to improve quality and productivity. Quality improvement concepts such as Total Quality Management (TQM), Six Sigma, continuous improvement, quality circles, and zero defects gained popularity and changed the way in which companies viewed quality and quality control practices. A new philosophy emerged, emphasizing quality as the concern of all individuals involved in producing goods and directing that quality be monitored at all stages of manufacturing, not just at the end of production or at random stages of manufacturing.

Today, most companies focus on improving quality during all stages of production, with an emphasis on preventing defects rather than merely identifying defective parts. There is an increased use of sophisticated automated equipment that can test and inspect products as they are manufactured. Automated equipment includes cameras, X-rays, lasers, scanners, metal detectors, video inspection systems, electronic sensors, and machine vision systems that can detect the slightest flaw or variance from accepted tolerances. Many companies use statistical process control to record levels of quality and determine the best manufacturing and quality procedures. Quality control engineers and technicians work with employees from all departments of a company to train them in the best quality methods and to seek improvements to manufacturing processes to further improve quality levels.

Many companies today are seeking to conform to international standards for quality, such as ISO (International Organization for Standardization) 9000, in order to compete with foreign companies and to sell products to companies around the world. These standards are based on concepts of quality of industrial goods and services and involve documenting quality methods and procedures.

■ THE JOB

Quality control engineers develop, implement, and direct processes and practices that result in a desired level of quality for manufactured parts. They identify standards to measure the quality of a part or product, analyze factors that affect quality, and determine the best practices to ensure quality.

Quality control engineers set up procedures to monitor and control quality, devise methods to improve quality, and analyze quality control methods for effectiveness, productivity, and cost factors. They are involved in all aspects of quality during a product's life cycle. Not only do they focus on ensuring quality during production operations, they are also involved in product design and evaluation. Quality control engineers may be specialists who work with engineers and industrial designers during the design phase of a product, or they may work with sales and marketing professionals to evaluate reports from consumers on how well a product is performing. Quality control engineers are responsible for ensuring that all incoming materials used in a finished product meet required standards and that all instruments and automated equipment used to test and monitor parts during production perform properly. They supervise and direct workers involved in assuring quality, including quality control technicians, inspectors, and related production personnel.

Quality control technicians work with quality control engineers in designing, implementing, and maintaining quality systems. They test and inspect materials and products during all phases of production in order to ensure that they meet specified levels of quality. They may test random samples of products or monitor production workers and automated equipment that inspect products during manufacturing. Using engineering blueprints, drawings, and specifications, they measure and inspect parts for dimensions, performance, and mechanical, electrical, and chemical properties. They establish tolerances, or acceptable deviations from engineering specifications, and they direct manufacturing personnel in identifying rejects and items that need to be reworked. They monitor production processes to ensure that machinery and equipment are working properly and are set to established specifications.

Quality control technicians also record and evaluate test data. Using statistical quality control procedures, technicians prepare charts and write summaries about how well a product conforms to existing standards. Most importantly, they offer suggestions to quality control engineers on how to modify existing quality standards and manufacturing procedures. This helps to achieve the optimum product quality from existing or proposed new equipment.

Quality control technicians may specialize in any of the following areas: product design, incoming materials, process control, product evaluation, inventory control, product reliability, and research and development. Nearly all industries employ quality control technicians.

■ EARNINGS

Earnings vary according to the type of work, the industry, and the geographical location. According to a spring 2016 survey by the National Association of Colleges and Employers, the average beginning salary for new graduates with bachelor's degrees in engineering was $63,764. According to the U.S. Department of Labor, the median yearly income for industrial production managers (a category that includes quality control engineers) was $93,940 in May 2015. The lowest paid 10 percent earned less than $56,640 and the highest paid 10 percent made more than $162,240.

CAREER LADDER

Quality Control Director, or Operations Manager, or Professor

Quality Control Engineer

Quality Control Technician

The average annual salary for industrial engineering technicians was $53,780 in May 2015. Salaries ranged from $33,910 to $83,000 or more. Most beginning quality control technicians who are graduates of two-year technical programs earn lower salaries, while more experienced and senior technicians with special skills or experience may earn much more.

Most companies offer benefits that include paid vacations, paid holidays, and health insurance. Actual benefits depend on the company but may also include pension plans, profit sharing, 401(k) plans, and tuition assistance programs.

■ WORK ENVIRONMENT

Quality control engineers and technicians work in a variety of settings, and their conditions of work vary accordingly. Most work in manufacturing plants, though the type of industry determines the actual environment. For example, quality control engineers in the metals industry usually work in foundries or iron and steel plants. Conditions there are hot, dirty, and noisy. Other factories, such as those in the electronics or pharmaceutical industries, are generally quiet and clean. Most engineers and technicians have offices separate from the production floor, but they still need to spend a fair amount of time there. Engineers and technicians involved with testing and product analysis work in comfortable surroundings, such as a laboratory or workshop. Even in these settings, however, they may be exposed to unpleasant fumes and toxic chemicals. In general, quality control engineers and technicians work inside and are expected to do some light lifting and carrying (usually not more than 20 pounds). Because many manufacturing plants operate 24 hours a day, some quality control technicians may need to work second or third shifts.

As with most engineering and technical positions, the work can be both challenging and routine. Engineers and

A quality control worker performs an inspection on a product. (**Andrew Bassett. Shutterstock.**)

technicians can expect to find some tasks repetitious and tedious. In most cases, though, the work provides variety and satisfaction from using highly developed skills and technical expertise.

■ EXPLORING

Quality control engineers and technicians work with scientific instruments; therefore, you should take academic or industrial arts courses that introduce you to different kinds of scientific or technical equipment. You should also take electrical and machine shop courses, mechanical drawing courses, and chemistry courses with lab sections. Joining a radio, computer, or science club is also a good way to gain experience and to engage in team-building and problem-solving activities. Active participation in clubs is a good way to learn skills that will benefit you when working with other professionals in manufacturing and industrial settings.

Join the Technology Student Association (TSA), which provides students a chance to explore career opportunities in science, technology, engineering, and mathematics, enter academic competitions, and participate in summer exploration programs. TSA administers a competition that allows high school students to use their technology skills. The Tests of Engineering Aptitude, Mathematics and Science (http://teams.tsaweb.org) is an engineering problem competition.

You should check out the American Society for Engineering Education's precollege Web site, http://egfi-k12.org, for general information about careers in engineering, as well as answers to frequently asked questions about engineering.

Keep in mind that quality control activities and quality control professionals are often directly involved with manufacturing processes. If it is at all possible, try to get a part-time or summer job in a manufacturing setting, even if you are not specifically in the quality control area. Although your work may mean doing menial tasks, it will give you firsthand experience in the environment and demonstrate the depth of your interest to future employers.

■ EDUCATION AND TRAINING REQUIREMENTS
High School

To prepare for these careers, take high school classes in mathematics (including algebra, geometry, and statistics), physical sciences, physics, and chemistry. You should also take shop, mechanical drawing, and computer courses. In addition, take English courses that develop your reading skills, your ability to write well-organized reports with a logical development of ideas, and your ability to speak comfortably and effectively in front of a group.

Postsecondary Training

Quality control engineers generally have a bachelor's degree in engineering. Many quality control engineers receive degrees in industrial or manufacturing engineering. Some receive degrees in metallurgical, mechanical, electrical, chemical engineering, or in business administration, depending on where they plan to work. A master's or doctoral degree is required for most jobs in research and higher education, and for supervisory and administrative positions.

ABET sets minimum education standards for educational programs in engineering. Graduation from an ABET-accredited school is a requirement for becoming licensed in many states, so it is important to select an accredited school. Visit the ABET Web site, http://www.abet.org, for a list of accredited schools.

College engineering programs vary based on the type of engineering program. Most programs take four to five years to complete and include courses in mathematics, physics, and chemistry. Other useful courses include statistics, logistics, business management, and technical writing.

Educational requirements for quality control technicians vary by industry. Most employers of quality control technicians prefer to hire applicants who have received some specialized training. A small number of positions for technicians require a bachelor of arts or science degree. In most cases, though, completion of a two-year technical program is sufficient. Students enrolled in such a program at a community college or technical school take courses in the physical sciences, mathematics, materials control, materials testing, and engineering-related subjects.

Other Education or Training

Several associations offer continuing education opportunities. The American Society for Quality provides a variety of seminars, workshops, and courses on the basics of quality control and management, how to develop and prosper in a consulting business, and leadership and problem-solving skills. ASTM International offers seminars and other training programs for those involved in testing materials and quality assurance. Contact these organizations for more information.

■ CERTIFICATION, LICENSING, AND SPECIAL REQUIREMENTS

Certification or Licensing

Although there are no licensing or certification requirements designed specifically for quality control engineers or technicians, some need to meet special requirements that apply only within the industry employing them. Many quality control engineers and technicians pursue voluntary certification from professional organizations to indicate that they have achieved a certain level of expertise. The American Society for Quality (ASQ), for example, offers certification at a number of levels including quality engineer certification and quality technician certification. Requirements include having a certain amount of work experience, having proof of professionalism (such as being a licensed professional engineer), and passing a written examination. Many employers value this certification and take it into consideration when making new hires or giving promotions.

Engineers whose work may affect the life, health, or safety of the public must be registered according to regulations in all 50 states and the District of Columbia. Licensing requirements vary from state

ENGINEERING AND IMPROVING QUALITY   LEARN MORE ABOUT IT

Benbow, Donald W., et al. *The Certified Quality Technician Handbook,* 2nd ed. Milwaukee, Wisc.: ASQ Quality Press, 2012.

Benbow, Donald W., and Hugh W. Broome. *The Certified Reliability Engineer Handbook,* 2nd ed. Milwaukee, Wisc.: ASQ Quality Press, 2013.

Besterfield, Dale H. *Quality Improvement,* 9th ed. Upper Saddle River, N.J.: Prentice Hall, 2012.

Brussee, Warren. *Statistics for Six Sigma Made Easy,* 2nd ed. New York: McGraw-Hill, 2012.

Griffith, Gary K. *The Quality Technician's Handbook*, 6 ed. New York: Pearson, 2013.

to state. In general, however, they involve graduating from an accredited school, having four years of work experience, and passing the eight-hour Fundamentals of Engineering exam and the eight-hour Principles and Practice of Engineering exam. Depending on your state, you can take the Fundamentals exam shortly before your graduation from college or after you have received your bachelor's degree. At that point you will be an engineer-in-training. Once you have fulfilled all the licensure requirements, you receive the designation professional engineer. Visit the National Council of Examiners for Engineering and Surveying Web site, http://www.ncees.org, for more information on licensure.

■ EXPERIENCE, SKILLS, AND PERSONALITY TRAITS

Take as many math and science classes as possible and participate in internships and other experiential opportunities to gain experience in the field.

Quality control engineers need scientific and mathematical aptitudes, strong interpersonal skills, and leadership abilities. Good judgment is also needed, as quality control engineers must weigh all the factors influencing quality and determine procedures that incorporate price, performance, and cost factors. Other important traits include organizational skills and a willingness to continue to learn throughout one's career.

Quality control technicians should do well in mathematics, science, and other technical subjects and be comfortable using the language and symbols of mathematics and science. They should have good eyesight and good manual skills, including the ability to use hand tools. They must also be able to follow technical instructions and make sound judgments about technical matters. They should have orderly minds and be able to maintain records, conduct inventories, and estimate quantities.

■ EMPLOYMENT PROSPECTS
Employers
There are approximately 169,390 industrial production managers (a group that includes quality control engineers) and 62,290 industrial engineering technicians working in the United States. The majority of quality control engineers and technicians are employed in the manufacturing sector of the economy. Because engineers and technicians work in all areas of industry, their employers vary widely in size, product, location, and prestige.

Starting Out
Students enrolled in two-year technical schools may learn of openings for quality control technicians through their schools' career services office. Recruiters often visit these schools and interview graduating students for technical positions. Quality control engineers may also learn of job openings through their schools' job placement services, recruiters, and job fairs. In many cases, employers prefer to hire engineers who have some work experience in their particular industry. For this reason, applicants who have had summer or part-time employment or participated in a work-study or internship program have greater job opportunities.

Students may also learn about openings through employment Web sites or by using the services of state and private employment services. They may also apply directly to companies that employ quality control engineers and technicians. Students can identify and research such companies by using job resource guides and other reference materials available on the Internet and at most public libraries.

■ ADVANCEMENT PROSPECTS
Quality control technicians usually begin their work under the direct and constant supervision of an experienced technician or engineer. As they gain experience or additional education, they are given assignments with greater responsibilities. They can also become quality control engineers with additional education. Promotion usually depends on additional training as well as job performance. Technicians who obtain additional training have greater chances for advancement opportunities.

Quality control engineers may have limited opportunities to advance within their companies. However, because quality control engineers work in all areas of industry, they have the opportunity to change jobs or companies to pursue more challenging or higher paying positions. Quality control engineers who work in companies with large staffs of quality personnel can become quality control directors or advance to operations management positions. Some quality control engineers become college professors or researchers.

■ OUTLOOK
The employment outlook for quality control engineers and technicians depends, to some degree, on general economic conditions. Through 2024, the U.S. Department of Labor projects a 4 percent decline in employment for the field of industrial production management, which includes quality control engineers and technicians. Factors contributing to this decline are better technology, which has increased productivity, and a greater reliance on manufacturing workers to constantly monitor the quality of their own work. However, the roles of the quality control engineer and technicians are vital to production and cannot be eliminated. Thus, there will still be new jobs to replace people retiring from or otherwise leaving this field.

Many companies are making vigorous efforts to make their manufacturing processes more efficient, lower costs, and improve productivity and quality. Opportunities for quality control engineers and technicians should be good in the food and beverage industries and at pharmaceutical firms, electronics companies, and chemical companies. Quality control engineers and technicians may also find employment in industries using robotics equipment or in the aerospace, biomedical, bioengineering, environmental controls, and transportation industries. Declines in employment in some industries may occur because of the increased use of automated equipment that tests and inspects parts during production operations.

■ UNIONS AND ASSOCIATIONS
Some engineers may be represented by the International Federation of Professional and Technical Engineers (http://www.ifpte.org) and other unions. Major organizations for quality control engineers and technicians include the American Society for Quality and ASTM International.

■ TIPS FOR ENTRY
1. Read publications such as *Quality Progress* (http://asq.org/qualityprogress/index.html) and *Standardization News* (http://www.astm.org/

MAGS_NEWSLETTERS) to learn more about the field.

2. Participate in the National Society of Professional Engineers' mentoring program (https://www.nspe.org/resources/career-center/mentoring-resources).

3. Join professional associations such as the American Society for Quality and the ASTM International to access training and networking resources, industry publications, and employment opportunities.

4. Visit http://asq.org/career/index.html for job listings.

5. Become certified by the American Society for Quality in order to show employers that you have met the highest standards established by your industry.

■ FOR MORE INFORMATION

For information on certification and student chapters, contact

American Society for Quality (ASQ)
PO Box 3005
Milwaukee, WI 53201-3005
Tel: (800) 248-1946; (414) 272-8575
Fax: (414) 272-1734
E-mail: help@asq.org
http://www.asq.org

ASTM International offers seminars and other training programs for those involved in testing materials and quality assurance. Visit its Web site to read articles from its magazine,

ASTM International (ASTM)
100 Barr Harbor Drive
PO Box C700
West Conshohocken, PA 19428-2959
Tel: (877) 909-2786; (610) 832-9585
http://www.astm.org

Some engineers may be represented by the International Federation of Professional & Technical Engineers. Contact the union for more information.

International Federation of Professional & Technical Engineers (IFPTE)
501 3rd Street, NW, Suite 701
Washington, D.C. 20001
Tel: (202) 239-4880
Fax: (202) 239-4881
E-mail: generalinfo@ifpte.org
http://www.ifpte.org

Rabbis

■ OVERVIEW

Rabbis are the spiritual leaders of Jewish religious congregations. They interpret Jewish law and tradition and conduct religious services on the Sabbath (a daylong period of rest and worship from Friday evening to Saturday evening) and holy days. Rabbis perform wedding ceremonies and funeral services, counsel members of the congregation, visit the sick, and often take part in community and interfaith affairs. Most rabbis serve one of the four main types of Jewish congregations: Orthodox, Conservative, Reform, and Reconstructionist. The remaining congregations are other unaffiliated streams of Judaism.

■ HISTORY

The term rabbi comes from a Hebrew word meaning master, and it has been used to describe Jewish leaders and scholars for the last 2,000 years. During the Talmudic period (from the first to the fifth century A.D.), the term was used to refer to preachers and scholars.

Over the centuries, rabbis became the leading religious authorities in Jewish communities. It has only been in the last 150 years that rabbis have become salaried officials in religious congregations.

■ THE JOB

Regardless of their congregational affiliation, all rabbis have similar responsibilities. Their primary duty is conducting religious services on the Sabbath and on holy days. They also officiate at weddings, funerals, and other rites of passage in the Jewish tradition. Rabbis further serve their congregations by counseling members and visiting the sick, as well as supervising and even teaching some religious education courses.

Within Judaism, the rabbi has an elevated status in spiritual matters, but most Jewish synagogues and temples have a relatively democratic form of decision making in which all members participate. Rabbis of large congregations spend much of their time working with their staffs and various committees. They often receive assistance from an associate or assistant rabbi.

Naturally, the Jewish traditions differ among themselves in their view of God and of history. These differences also extend to such variations in worship as the wearing of head coverings, the extent to which Hebrew is used during prayer, the use of music, the level of congregational participation, and the status of women. Whatever their particular point of view might be, all rabbis help their congregations learn and understand Jewish traditions and the role of faith in everyday life.

QUICK FACTS

ALTERNATE TITLE(S)
None

DUTIES
Serve as the spiritual leaders of Jewish religious congregations

SALARY RANGE
$30,000 to $44,250 to $409,756

WORK ENVIRONMENT
Primarily Indoors

BEST GEOGRAPHIC LOCATION(S)
Nationwide

MINIMUM EDUCATION LEVEL
Master's Degree

SCHOOL SUBJECTS
Business, Psychology, Religion

EXPERIENCE
Internship

PERSONALITY TRAITS
Helpful, Problem-Solving, Social

SKILLS
Interpersonal, Public Speaking, Teaching

CERTIFICATION OR LICENSING
Required

SPECIAL REQUIREMENTS
Orthodox seminaries accept only men, but all other denominations accept men and women into the rabbinate

EMPLOYMENT PROSPECTS
Good

ADVANCEMENT PROSPECTS
Fair

OUTLOOK
About as Fast as the Average

NOC
4154

O*NET-SOC
21-2011.00

Many rabbis take on additional responsibilities in the community at large. They may become involved with such social concerns as poverty and drug abuse, or they may take part in interfaith activities with ministers of other religions.

A small but significant number of rabbis do not serve as congregational leaders. They instead serve as educators at colleges, universities, and Jewish schools and seminaries, as writers and scholars, or as chaplains at hospitals or in the armed forces.

■ EARNINGS

Salaries for rabbis vary according to the size, branch, location, and financial status of their congregations. Information is limited, but the earnings of rabbis tend to range from $50,000 to $100,000. Smaller congregations offer salaries on the lower end of the scale, usually between $30,000 and $50,000 a year. The U.S. Bureau of Labor Statistics reports that the average salary for all clergy was $44,250 in May 2015.

Senior or solo Reform rabbis earned salaries that ranged from $83,200 to $409,756 in 2015, according to a study conducted by the Union for Reform Judaism and the Central Conference of American Rabbis. Associate Reform rabbis earned salaries that ranged from $87,969 to $225,000, and assistant Reform rabbis had earnings that ranged from $85,000 to $122,500.

Benefits include health insurance, paid vacations, pensions, and car and housing allowance. Rabbis usually receive gifts or fees for officiating at weddings and other ceremonies. Some congregations may allow their rabbi to teach at local universities or other settings to earn additional income.

■ WORK ENVIRONMENT

Rabbis work long hours. Like all clergy, rabbis are on call at any hour of the day or night. This can make a rabbi's private life difficult at times, particularly if he or she is married and has a family. As far as accommodations and professional offices are concerned, rabbis are usually well provided for by their congregations.

There is no such thing as a standard workweek. Rabbis have to divide their time between religious services, administrative duties, and pastoral care of their congregations as they see fit. They must also take time for personal prayer and the continuing study of Jewish faith and traditions. Rabbis are generally independent in their positions, responsible only to the board of directors of their congregation rather than to any formal hierarchy.

■ EXPLORING

Those interested in becoming a rabbi should talk with his or her own rabbi and others involved in the work of the synagogue or temple to get a clearer idea of the rewards and responsibilities of this profession. Choosing a career as a rabbi requires a good deal of levelheaded self-assessment of your suitability for the rabbinate. Prospective rabbis should also spend time in prayer to determine whether they are called to this ministry.

Aspiring rabbis may volunteer at a temple or synagogue in order to get better acquainted with the work of rabbis. Most Jewish seminaries are also eager to speak and work with young people to help them learn about the rabbinate before making a firm decision about it.

■ EDUCATION AND TRAINING REQUIREMENTS
High School

Many aspiring rabbis informally begin their training early in life in Jewish grade schools and high schools. Aspiring rabbis should take all religious and Hebrew language courses available to them. It is also important to study English and communications to become an effective leader. Business and mathematics courses are a good foundation for administrative work as the leader of a congregation.

Postsecondary Training

Completion of a course of study in a seminary is a prerequisite for ordination as a rabbi. Entrance requirements, curriculum, and length of the seminary program vary depending on the particular branch of Judaism. Prospective rabbis normally need to complete a bachelor's degree before entering the seminary. Degrees in Jewish studies, philosophy, and even English and history can fulfill seminary entrance requirements. It is advisable to study Hebrew at the undergraduate level if at all possible. Seminarians without a solid background in Jewish studies and the Hebrew language may have to take remedial courses.

While seminary studies differ between the four movements of Judaism, there are many similarities between them. Most seminary programs lead to the master of arts in Hebrew letters degree and ordination as a rabbi. With more advanced study, some students earn the doctor of Hebrew letters degree. Most master's programs last about five years, and many of them include a period of study in Jerusalem. It is becoming more common for seminarians to complete internships—usually as assistants to experienced rabbis in the area—as part of their educational requirements.

The general curriculum of ordination for all branches of Judaism includes courses in the Torah, the Talmud (post-biblical writings), rabbinic literature, Hebrew philosophy, Jewish history, and theology. Students should expect to study Hebrew for both verbal and written skills. Courses are also offered in education, public speaking, and pastoral psychology. Practical courses in conducting religious services are usually required. Training for leadership in community service and religious education may be available to those who wish to serve outside the traditional synagogue situation.

Other Education or Training

Rabbis never stop learning during their careers, and some rabbinical organizatuions offer continuing education classes, webinars, and workshops to help them stay up to date. For example, the Central Conference of American Rabbis offers seminars such as "Developing Jewish Young Adults: From High School to College and Beyond," "The First 100 Days For Every Rabbi in Job Transition," and "Building Skills for Community-Based and Small Congregational Rabbinic Work." It also offers educational opportunities at its annual conference. Contact the conference for more information.

■ CERTIFICATION, LICENSING, AND SPECIAL REQUIREMENTS
Certification or Licensing

There are no certification requirements for rabbis. All states require rabbis to be licensed (ordained) to perform marriage ceremonies.

Other Requirements

Conservative, Reform, and Reconstructionist seminaries accept women and allow them to be ordained as rabbis. The Orthodox congregation does not officially recognize women as rabbis and only men are allowed to attend Orthodox seminaries.

■ EXPERIENCE, SKILLS, AND PERSONALITY TRAITS

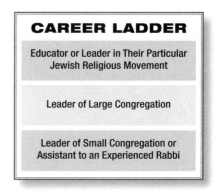

CAREER LADDER

Educator or Leader in Their Particular Jewish Religious Movement

Leader of Large Congregation

Leader of Small Congregation or Assistant to an Experienced Rabbi

Rabbis obtain experience by taking classes and participating in an internship in the seminary. Most importantly, rabbis must feel a calling to religious life. They must believe that they have received a call from God to serve others.

In addition to the ordination requirements, a primary consideration in choosing a career in the clergy is a strong religious faith coupled with the desire to help others. Rabbis should be able to communicate effectively and supervise others. They must have self-confidence, initiative, and the ability to deal with pressure. They need to be impartial and attentive when listening to the troubles and worries of congregants. They must be tactful and compassionate in order to deal with people of many backgrounds. They must set a high moral and ethical standard for the members of their congregation. Orthodox seminaries accept only men, but all other denominations accept men and women into the rabbinate.

■ EMPLOYMENT PROSPECTS
Employers

Most rabbis are employed by their congregations. Others work for schools, colleges, seminaries, and publications.

A rabbi reads a prayer in a synagogue. (Pavel L Photo and Video. Shutterstock.)

CANTORS

If you are considering a ministry in the Jewish faith and have a good singing voice, you might think about becoming a cantor. *Cantors* are singers who lead the liturgies in synagogues. They are professionals who have almost as much training as rabbis. They generally need to earn a master of arts in sacred music degree before undergoing investiture as a cantor. While working on the MA, cantors study the Hebrew language, Jewish history, and the chants used for daily services as well as high holy days. Many also take part in internships at local synagogues to gain practical experience. For someone with a love of music and the Jewish faith, this can be a very rewarding career. The American Conference of Cantors (http://www.accantors.org) can provide more information.

Some serve as chaplains in hospitals or in the various branches of the armed forces.

Starting Out

Only ordained rabbis can work in this profession. Many newly ordained rabbis find jobs through the seminary from which they graduated or through professional rabbinical organizations within their particular Jewish movement. With the growing popularity of internships for seminaries, it is possible that these will lead to permanent positions after ordination. Rabbis generally begin their careers as leaders of small congregations, assistants to experienced rabbis, directors of Hillel foundations on college campuses, or chaplains in the armed forces.

■ ADVANCEMENT PROSPECTS

With experience, rabbis may acquire their own or larger congregations or choose to remain in their original position. The pulpits of large, well-established synagogues and temples are usually filled by rabbis of considerable experience. They may also choose to open new synagogues in growing communities that require more religious facilities. Others may discover that their talents and abilities are most useful in teaching, fund-raising, or leadership positions within their particular movement.

■ OUTLOOK

The U.S. Department of Labor predicts average employment growth for all clergy through 2024. Job opportunities for rabbis are good for all four major branches of Judaism. Orthodox rabbis should have good job prospects as older rabbis retire and smaller communities become large enough to hire their own rabbi. Conservative and Reform rabbis should also have excellent employment opportunities, especially because of retirement and new Jewish communities. Reconstructionist rabbis should find very good opportunities because this branch of Judaism is growing rapidly.

Opportunities exist in Jewish communities throughout the country. Small communities in the South, Midwest, and Northwest offer the best opportunities for those rabbis who do not mind receiving less compensation and working away from big metropolitan areas.

■ UNIONS AND ASSOCIATIONS

Rabbis do not belong to unions, but many join rabbinical organizations such as the Central Conference of American Rabbis and the Rabbinical Assembly.

■ TIPS FOR ENTRY

1. Visit http://huc.edu/academics/become-rabbi to read Become a Rabbi.
2. Talk to rabbis about their careers. Ask them for advice on entering the profession.

■ FOR MORE INFORMATION

The following organization serves ordained rabbis but can be of some help to those considering the ministry.

Central Conference of American Rabbis (CCAR)
355 Lexington Avenue
New York, NY 10017-6603
Tel: (212) 972-3636
E-mail: info@ccarnet.org
http://ccarnet.org

The following educational institution has four campuses: Cincinnati, New York, Los Angeles, and Jerusalem. Visit its Web site to learn about the different schools and the training required to become a rabbi.

Hebrew Union College-Jewish Institute of Religion (HUC-JIR)
http://www.huc.edu

For information on the Reconstructionist branch of Judaism, contact

Jewish Reconstructionist Communities
1299 Church Road
Wyncote, PA 19095
Tel: (215) 576-0800
http://www.jewishrecon.org

For information on training programs, contact

Jewish Theological Seminary (JTS)
3080 Broadway
New York, NY 10027-4650

Tel: (212) 678-8000

http://www.jtsa.edu

For information on the Conservative branch of Judaism, contact

Rabbinical Assembly (RA)

3080 Broadway

New York, NY 10027-4650

Tel: (212) 280-6000

E-mail: info@rabbinicalassembly.org

http://rabbinicalassembly.org

For information on the Orthodox branch of Judaism, contact

Rabbinical Council of America (RCA)

305 Seventh Avenue, 12th Floor

New York, NY 10001-6008

Tel: (212) 807-9000

http://www.rabbis.org

For information on training, contact

Reconstructionist Rabbinical College (RRC)

1299 Church Road

Wyncote, PA 19095-1824

Tel: (215) 576-0800

E-mail: info@rrc.edu

http://www.rrc.edu

Radiation Protection Technicians

◼ OVERVIEW

Radiation protection technicians, also known as *health physics technicians* and *nuclear technicians,* monitor radiation levels, protect workers, and decontaminate radioactive areas. They work under the supervision of nuclear scientists, engineers, or power plant managers and are trained in the applications of nuclear and radiation physics to detect, measure, and identify different kinds of nuclear radiation. They possess knowledge of federal regulations and permissible levels of radiation.

◼ HISTORY

All forms of energy have the potential to endanger life and property. This potential existed with the most primitive uses of fire, and it exists in the applications of nuclear power. Special care must be taken to prevent uncontrolled radiation in and around nuclear power plants. Skilled nuclear power plant technicians are among the workers who monitor and control radiation levels.

Around 1900, scientists discovered that certain elements give off invisible rays of energy. These elements are said to be radioactive, which means that they emit radiation. Antoine-Henri Becquerel, Marie Curie, and Pierre Curie discovered and described chemical radiation before the turn of the century. In 1910, Marie Curie isolated pure radium, the most radioactive natural element, and in 1911 she was awarded the Nobel Prize for chemistry for her work related to radiation.

Scientists eventually came to understand that radiation has existed in nature since the beginning of time, not only in specific elements on Earth, such as uranium, but also in the form of cosmic rays from outer space. All parts of the Earth are constantly bombarded by a certain background level of radiation, which is considered normal or tolerable.

During the 20th century, research into the nature of radiation led to many controlled applications of radioactivity, ranging from X-rays to nuclear weapons. One of the most significant of these applications is the use of nuclear fuel to produce energy. Nuclear power reactors produce heat that is used to generate electricity.

Scientists are still trying to understand the biological effects of radiation exposure, but we know that short-term effects include nausea, hemorrhaging, and fatigue; long-range and more dangerous effects include cancer, lowered fertility, and possible birth defects. These factors have made it absolutely clear that if radiation energy is to be used for any purpose, the entire process must be

QUICK FACTS

ALTERNATE TITLE(S)
Health Physics Technicians, Nuclear Technicians

DUTIES
Monitor radiation levels, protect workers, and decontaminate radioactive areas

SALARY RANGE
$47,730 to $80,260 to $103,750+

WORK ENVIRONMENT
Indoors/Outdoors

BEST GEOGRAPHIC LOCATION(S)
Large, metropolitan areas

MINIMUM EDUCATION LEVEL
Associate's Degree

SCHOOL SUBJECTS
English, Mathematics, Physics

EXPERIENCE
Internships

PERSONALITY TRAITS
Hands On, Scientific, Technical

SKILLS
Math, Mechanical/Manual Dexterity, Scientific

CERTIFICATION OR LICENSING
None

SPECIAL REQUIREMENTS
May need federal security clearance for some jobs

EMPLOYMENT PROSPECTS
Good

ADVANCEMENT PROSPECTS
Good

OUTLOOK
Decline

NOC
2263

O*NET-SOC
19-4051.00, 19-4051.02

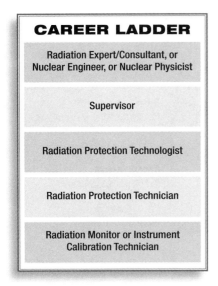

CAREER LADDER

Radiation Expert/Consultant, or
Nuclear Engineer, or Nuclear Physicist

Supervisor

Radiation Protection Technologist

Radiation Protection Technician

Radiation Monitor or Instrument
Calibration Technician

controlled. Thus, appropriate methods of radiation protection and monitoring have been developed. The radiation protection technician's job is to ensure that these methods are employed accurately, safely, and consistently.

◾ THE JOB

Radiation protection technicians protect workers, the general public, and the environment from overexposure to radiation. Many of their activities are highly technical. They measure radiation and radioactivity levels in work areas and in the environment by collecting samples of air, water, soil, plants, and other materials. They record test results and inform the appropriate personnel when tests reveal deviations from acceptable levels. They help power plant workers set up equipment that automatically monitors processes within the plant and records deviations from established radiation limits, and they calibrate and maintain such equipment using hand tools.

Radiation protection technicians work efficiently with people of different technical backgrounds. They instruct operations personnel in making the necessary adjustments to correct problems such as excessive radiation levels, discharges of radionuclide materials above acceptable levels, or improper chemical levels. They also prepare reports for supervisory and regulatory agencies.

Radiation protection technicians are concerned with ionizing radiation, particularly three types known by the Greek letters alpha, beta, and gamma. Ionization occurs when atoms split and produce charged particles. If these particles strike the cells in the body, they cause damage by upsetting well-ordered chemical processes.

In addition to understanding the nature and effects of radiation, technicians working in nuclear power plants must understand the principles of nuclear power plant systems. They have a thorough knowledge of the instrumentation that is used to monitor radiation in every part of the plant and its immediate surroundings. They also play an important role in educating other workers about radiation monitoring and control.

Radiation protection technicians deal with three fundamental concepts of radiation: time, distance from the radiation source, and shielding. When considering time, technicians know that certain radioactive materials break down into stable elements in a matter of days or even minutes. Other materials, however, continue to emit radioactive particles for thousands of years. Radiation becomes less intense in proportion to its distance from the source, so distance is an important concept in controlling radiation exposure. Shielding is used to protect people from radiation exposure. Appropriate materials with a specific thickness must be used to block emissions of radioactive particles.

Because radiation generally cannot be seen, heard, or felt, radiation protection technicians use special instruments to detect and measure it and to determine the extent of radiation exposure. Technicians use devices that measure the ionizing effect of radiation on matter to determine the presence of radiation and, depending on the instrument used, the degree of radiation danger in a given situation.

Two such devices are Geiger counters, which measure levels of radioactivity, and dosimeters, which measure received radiation doses. Dosimeters are often in the form of photographic badges worn by personnel and visitors. These badges are able to detect radioactivity because it shows up on photographic film. Radiation protection technicians calculate the amount of time that personnel may work safely in contaminated areas, considering maximum radiation exposure limits and the radiation level in the particular area. They also use specialized equipment to detect and analyze radiation levels and chemical imbalances.

Finally, although the radiation that is released into the environment surrounding a nuclear facility is generally far less than that released through background radiation sources, radiation protection technicians must be prepared to monitor people and environments during abnormal situations and emergencies.

Under normal working conditions, technicians monitor the work force, the plant, and the nearby environment for radioactive contamination; test plant workers for radiation exposure, both internally and externally; train personnel in the proper use of monitoring and safety equipment; help nuclear materials handling technicians prepare and monitor radioactive waste shipments; perform basic radiation orientation training; take radiation contamination and control surveys, air sample surveys, and radiation level surveys; maintain and calibrate radiation detection instruments using standard samples to determine accuracy; ensure that radiation protection regulations, standards, and procedures are followed and records are kept of all regular measurements and radioactivity tests; and carry out decontamination procedures that ensure the safety of plant workers and the continued operation of the plant.

EARNINGS

The earnings of radiation protection technicians who are beginning their careers depend on the radiation safety program in which they work (nuclear power, federal or state agencies, research laboratories, medical facilities, etc.). They may begin as salaried staff or be paid hourly wages. Technicians who receive hourly wages usually work in shifts and receive premium pay for overtime.

The U.S. Department of Labor reports that median hourly earnings of nuclear technicians were $38.59 in May 2015, or $80,260 a year. Wages ranged from less than $22.95 per hour to more than $49.88 per hour, or $47,730 to $103,750 per year.

Earnings are affected by whether technicians remain in their entry-level jobs or become supervisors and whether they become registered radiation protection technologists.

Technicians usually receive benefits, such as paid holidays and vacations, insurance plans, and retirement plans. Because of the rapid changes that occur in the radiation safety industry, many employers pay for job-related study and participation in workshops, seminars, and conferences.

WORK ENVIRONMENT

Depending on the employer, work environments vary from offices and control rooms to relatively cramped and cold and hot areas of power plants. They may also be required to take radiation readings outside plants in a variety of weather conditions.

Of all power plant employees, radiation protection technicians are perhaps best able to evaluate and protect against the radiation hazards that are an occupational risk of this field. The safety of all plant workers depends on the quality and accuracy of their work.

Radiation protection technicians wear film badges or carry pocket monitors to measure their exposure to radiation. Like all other nuclear power plant employees, technicians wear safety clothing, and radiation-resistant clothing may be required in some areas. This type of clothing contains materials that reduce the level of radiation before it reaches the human body. Other protective gear includes hearing and eye protection and respirators.

In some of the work done by radiation protection technicians, radiation shielding materials, such as lead and concrete, are used to enclose radioactive materials while the technician manipulates these materials from outside the contaminated area. These procedures are called hot-cell operations. In some areas, automatic

A radiation protection technician uses a detector to measure levels of radiation. (Staff Sgt. Mark Miranda. U.S. Army.)

alarm systems are used to warn of radiation hazards so that proper protection can be maintained.

EXPLORING

Ask your school counselor to help you learn more about this career. You can also obtain information from the occupational information centers at community and technical colleges.

Your science teacher may be able to arrange field trips and invite speakers to describe various careers. Nuclear reactor facilities are unlikely to provide tours, but they may be able to furnish literature on radiation physics and radiation control. Radiation protection technicians employed at nuclear-related facilities may be invited to speak about their chosen field.

Radiation is used for medical diagnosis and treatment in hospitals all over the country. Radiology departments of local hospitals often provide speakers for science or career classes.

In addition, a utilities company with a nuclear-fired plant may be able to offer you a tour of the visitor's center at the plant, where much interesting and valuable information about nuclear power plant operation is available. Small reactors used for experiments, usually affiliated with universities and research centers, may also give tours.

EDUCATION AND TRAINING REQUIREMENTS
High School

You should have a solid background in mathematics and science. Take four years of English, at least two years of mathematics including algebra, and at least one year of physical science, preferably physics with laboratory instruction. Computer programming and applications, vocational machine shop operations, and blueprint

HOW RADIATION IS USED

FAST FACTS

- About 70 percent of Americans have received X-rays or radiation therapy.
- In the United States, 10 million nuclear medicine procedures are performed at hospitals and radiology centers annually.
- Nuclear energy provides nearly 20 percent of electricity in the United States.
- In a 2015 Bisconti Research Inc. survey, 69 percent of adults supported nuclear energy, and 62 percent believed that the industry should build more nuclear power plants in the future.
- The U.S. Department of Transportation and the U.S. Nuclear Regulatory Commission oversee the transportation of radioactive material in the United States. Almost all of the radioactive material that is transported is used for research, educational, medical, or industrial purposes.

Source: U.S. Nuclear Regulatory Commission; Nuclear Energy Institute

reading will also provide you with a good foundation for further studies.

Postsecondary Training

After high school, you will need to study at a two-year technical school or community college. Several public or private technical colleges offer programs designed to prepare nuclear power plant radiation protection technicians. Other programs, called nuclear technology or nuclear materials handling technology, also provide a good foundation. You should be prepared to spend from one to two years in postsecondary technical training taking courses in chemistry, physics, laboratory procedures, and technical writing. Because the job entails accurately recording important data and writing clear, concise technical reports, technicians need excellent writing skills.

A typical first year of study for radiation protection technicians includes introduction to nuclear technology, radiation physics, mathematics, electricity and electronics, technical communications, radiation detection and measurement, inorganic chemistry, radiation protection, blueprint reading, quality assurance and quality control, nuclear systems, computer applications, and radiation biology.

Course work in the second year includes technical writing, advanced radiation protection, applied nuclear chemistry, radiological emergencies, advanced chemistry, radiation shielding, radiation monitoring techniques,

advanced radionuclide analysis, occupational safety and health, nuclear systems and safety, radioactive materials disposal and management, and industrial economics.

Visit http://www.nei.org/Careers-Education/Education-Resources/Nuclear-Energy-Training-Education-Programs for information on nuclear energy training and education programs.

Students who graduate from nuclear technician programs are usually hired by nuclear power plants and other companies and institutions involved in nuclear-related activities. These employers provide a general orientation to their operations and further training specific to their procedures.

■ CERTIFICATION, LICENSING, AND SPECIAL REQUIREMENTS
Certification or Licensing

At present, there are no special requirements for licensing or certification of nuclear power plant radiation protection technicians. Some graduates of radiation control technology programs, however, may want to become nuclear materials handling technicians. For this job, licensing may be required, but the employer will usually arrange for the special study needed to pass the licensing test.

Radiation protection professionals may become registered by satisfying work experience/training requirements and completing an examination that consists of 150 multiple-choice questions from the following general categories: applied radiation protection, detection and measurements, and fundamentals. This examination is administered by the National Registry of Radiation Protection Technologists. Professionals who successfully complete this examination are known as registered radiation protection technologists. Registration is not the same as licensing and does not guarantee professional ability, but it can help a technician demonstrate their professional competence to prospective employers.

■ EXPERIENCE, SKILLS, AND PERSONALITY TRAITS

Take as many math and science classes as possible and participate in internships to gain experience in the field.

The work of a radiation protection technician is very demanding. Technicians must have confidence in their ability to measure and manage potentially dangerous radioactivity on a daily basis. Radiation protection technicians play an important teaching role in the nuclear energy-fueled power plant. They must know the control measures required for every employee and be capable of explaining the reasons for such measures. Because abnormal conditions sometimes develop in the nuclear power industry, technicians must be able to withstand the stress, work long hours without making mistakes, and participate as a cooperating member of a team of experts.

Successful technicians are usually individuals who are able to confidently accept responsibility, communicate effectively in person and on paper, and enjoy doing precise work. Their participation is vital to the successful application of nuclear technology.

Federal security clearances are required for workers in jobs that involve national security. Nuclear Regulatory Commission (NRC) clearance is required for both government and private industry employees in securing related positions. Certain projects may necessitate military clearance with or without NRC clearance. Employers usually help arrange such clearances.

■ EMPLOYMENT PROSPECTS
Employers
Radiation protection technicians are employed by government agencies, such as the Department of Energy and the Department of Defense, as well as electric power utilities that operate nuclear plants. Other than utilities, technicians are employed by nuclear materials handling and processing facilities, regulatory agencies, nondestructive testing firms, radiopharmaceutical industries, nuclear waste handling facilities, nuclear service firms, and national research laboratories.

Starting Out
The best way to enter this career is to graduate from a radiation control technology program and make use of the school's career services office to find your first job. Another excellent way to enter the career is to join the U.S. Navy and enter its technical training program for various nuclear specialties.

Graduates of radiation control technology programs are usually interviewed and recruited while in school by representatives of companies with nuclear facilities. At that time, they may be hired with arrangements made to begin work soon after graduation. Graduates from strong programs may receive several attractive job offers.

Entry-level jobs for graduate radiation protection technicians include the position of *radiation monitor*. This position involves working in personnel monitoring, decontamination, and area monitoring and reporting. Another entry-level job is *instrument calibration technician*. These technicians test instrument reliability, maintain standard sources, and adjust and calibrate instruments. *Accelerator safety technicians* evaluate nuclear accelerator operating procedures and shielding to ensure personnel safety. *Radiobiology technicians* test

the external and internal effects of radiation in plants and animals, collect data on facilities where potential human exposure to radiation exists, and recommend improvements in techniques or facilities.

Hot-cell operators conduct experimental design and performance tests involving materials of very high radioactivity. *Environmental survey technicians* gather and prepare radioactive samples from air, water, and food specimens. They may handle nonradioactive test specimens for test comparisons with National Environmental Policy Act standards. *Reactor safety technicians* study personnel safety through the analysis of reactor procedures and shielding and through analysis of radioactivity tests.

■ ADVANCEMENT PROSPECTS
A variety of positions are available for experienced and well-trained radiation protection technicians. *Research technicians* develop new ideas and techniques in the radiation and nuclear field. *Instrument design technicians* design and prepare specifications and tests for use in advanced radiation instrumentation. *Customer service specialists* work in sales, installation, modification, and maintenance of customers' radiation control equipment. *Radiochemistry technicians* prepare and analyze new and old compounds, utilizing the latest equipment and techniques. *Health physics technicians* train new radiation monitors, analyze existing procedures, and conduct tests of experimental design and radiation safety. *Soil evaluation technicians* assess soil density, radioactivity, and moisture content to determine sources of unusually high levels of radioactivity. *Radioactive waste analysts* develop waste disposal techniques, inventory stored waste, and prepare waste for disposal.

By completing additional training, technicians can become nuclear power reactor operators, nuclear engineers, and nuclear physicists.

Some of the most attractive opportunities for experienced radiation protection technicians include working as radiation experts for a company or laboratory, or acting as consultants. Consultants may work for nuclear engineering or nuclear industry consulting firms or manage their own consulting businesses.

■ OUTLOOK
In 2016 the Nuclear Energy Institute (NEI) reported that two new nuclear reactors were being built in South Carolina, along with two in Georgia and one in Tennessee. According to the NEI, "the U.S. Department of Energy projects that demand for electricity in the United States will rise 22 percent by 2040. That means our nation will need hundreds of new power plants to provide electricity for our homes and continued economic growth.

Maintaining nuclear energy's current 20 percent share of electricity production will require building one reactor every year starting in 2016, or 20 to 25 new reactors by 2040, according to DOE forecasts."

Nevertheless, the Department of Labor (DOL) projects a 5 percent employment decline for technicians through 2024, due to productivity increases at traditional power generation facilities and competition from solar and wind energy. However, the DOL indicates that good opportunities will exist in the areas of nuclear medical technology, waste management safety, environmental remediation, and defense (nuclear security).

■ UNIONS AND ASSOCIATIONS

Radiation protection technicians who work for government agencies can join the American Federation of Government Employees and other unions. The American Nuclear Society and the Health Physics Society are membership organizations for nuclear professionals. The Nuclear Energy Institute is a membership organization for companies that operate nuclear power plants, fuel suppliers and service companies, companies involved in nuclear medicine and nuclear industrial applications, radionuclide and radio-pharmaceutical companies, universities and research laboratories, and other nuclear-related firms and organizations.

■ TIPS FOR ENTRY

1. Read *Nuclear News* (http://www.ans.org/pubs/magazines/nn) and *Health Physics Journal* (http://hps.org/hpspublications/journal.html) to learn more about the field.
2. Visit http://hps.org/students/careers.html to read a brochure on careers in health physics.
3. Visit http://www.nei.org/Careers-Education/Careers-in-the-Nuclear-Industry to read Careers in the Nuclear Industry.
4. Join the American Nuclear Society and the Health Physics Society to access networking and mentoring opportunities, members-only job listings, continuing education classes, and other resources.

■ FOR MORE INFORMATION

Radiation protection technicians who work for government agencies can join the American Federation of Government Employees.

American Federation of Government Employees, AFL-CIO (AFGE)
80 F Street, NW
Washington, D.C. 20001
Tel: (202) 737-8700
E-mail: comments@afge.org
https://www.afge.org

For information on careers, publications, scholarships, and seminars, contact

American Nuclear Society (ANS)
555 North Kensington Avenue
LaGrange Park, IL 60526-5535
Tel: (800) 323-3044; (708) 352-6611
Fax: (708) 352-0499
http://www.ans.org

This professional organization promotes the practice of radiation safety. For information on the latest issues, radiation facts, and membership, contact

Health Physics Society (HPS)
1313 Dolley Madison Boulevard, Suite 402
McLean, VA 22101-3953
Tel: (703) 790-1745
E-mail: hps@BurkInc.com
http://hps.org

For information on registration, contact

National Registry of Radiation Protection Technologists (NRRPT)
PO Box 3084
Westerly, RI 02891-0936
Tel: (401) 637-4811
Fax: (401) 637-4822
E-mail: nrrpt@nrrpt.org
http://www.nrrpt.org

This organization is dedicated to the peaceful use of nuclear technologies. Visit its Web site for information on careers and nuclear energy.

Nuclear Energy Institute (NEI)
1201 F Street, NW, Suite 1100
Washington, D.C. 20006-3708
Tel: (202) 739-8000
Fax: (202) 785.4019
E-mail: membership@nei.org
http://www.nei.org

Radio and Television Announcers

■ OVERVIEW

Radio and television announcers present news and commercial messages from a script. They identify the station, announce station breaks, and introduce and close shows. Interviewing guests, making public service announcements, and conducting panel discussions may also be part of the announcer's work. In small stations, the local announcer may keep the program log, run the transmitter, and cue the changeover to network broadcasting as well as write scripts or rewrite news releases. Approximately 30,390 people are employed as announcers in the United States.

■ HISTORY

Guglielmo Marconi, a young Italian engineer, first transmitted a radio signal in his home in 1895. Radio developed rapidly as people began to comprehend the tremendous possibilities. The stations KDKA in Pittsburgh and WWWJ in Detroit began broadcasting in 1920. Within 10 years, there were radio stations in all the major cities in the United States, and broadcasting had become a big business. The National Broadcasting Company became the first network in 1926 when it linked together 25 stations across the country. The Columbia Broadcasting System was organized in the following year. In 1934, the Mutual Broadcasting Company was founded. The years between 1930 and 1950 may be considered the zenith years of the radio industry. With the coming of television, radio broadcasting took second place in importance as entertainment for the home—but radio's commercial and communications value should not be underestimated.

Discoveries that led to the development of television can be traced as far back as 1878, when William Crookes invented a tube that produced the cathode ray. Other inventors who contributed to the development of television were Vladimir Zworykin, a Russian-born scientist who came to this country at the age of 20 and is credited with inventing the iconoscope before he was 30; Charles Jenkins, who invented a scanning disk, using vacuum tubes and photoelectric cells; and Philo Farnsworth, who invented an image dissector. WNBT and WCBW, the first commercially licensed television stations, went on the air in 1941 in New York. Both suspended operations during World War II but resumed them in 1946 when television sets began to be manufactured on a commercial scale.

As radio broadcasting was growing across the country in its early days, the need for announcers grew. They identified the station and brought continuity to broadcasts by linking one program with the next as well as participating in many programs. In the early days (and even today in smaller stations) announcers performed a variety of jobs around the station. When television began, many radio announcers and newscasters started to work in the new medium, and the jobs and job skills have evolved over the years. Television news broadcasting requires specialized on-camera personnel—anchors, television news reporters, broadcast news analysts, consumer reporters, and sports reporters (sportscasters).

In addition to being broadcast via transmitters, radio and television stations now also broadcast via satellite technology and on the Internet.

QUICK FACTS

ALTERNATE TITLE(S)
Commentators, Disc Jockeys, News Anchors, Newscasters, Sportscasters

DUTIES
Present news and commercial messages from a script on radio and television programs; also may interview guests, make public service announcements, conduct panel discussions, and perform other duties

SALARY RANGE
$18,000 to $30,960 to $86,780+

WORK ENVIRONMENT
Primarily Indoors

BEST GEOGRAPHIC LOCATION(S)
Opportunities exist throughout the country, but are best in large, urban areas

MINIMUM EDUCATION LEVEL
High School Diploma, Some Postsecondary Training

SCHOOL SUBJECTS
English, Journalism, Speech

EXPERIENCE
Internship; Volunteer, or part-time experience at a college or for-profit station

PERSONALITY TRAITS
Conventional, Social, Talkative

SKILLS
Interpersonal, Performance, Music, and Acting, Public Speaking

CERTIFICATION OR LICENSING
None

SPECIAL REQUIREMENTS
None

EMPLOYMENT PROSPECTS
Fair

ADVANCEMENT PROSPECTS
Fair

OUTLOOK
Decline

NOC
5231

O*NET-SOC
27-3011.00

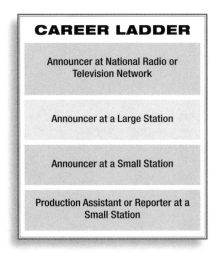

CAREER LADDER

Announcer at National Radio or
Television Network

Announcer at a Large Station

Announcer at a Small Station

Production Assistant or Reporter at a
Small Station

■ THE JOB

Some announcers merely announce; others do a multitude of other jobs, depending on the size of the station. But the nature of their announcing work remains the same.

An announcer is engaged in an exacting career. The necessity for finishing a sentence or a program segment at a precisely planned moment makes this a demanding and often tense career. It is absolutely essential that announcers project a sense of calm to their audiences, regardless of the activity and tension behind the scenes.

The announcer who plays recorded music interspersed with a variety of advertising material and informal commentary is called a *disc jockey*. This title arose when most music was recorded on conventional flat records, or discs. Today much of the recorded music used in commercial radio stations is on compact disc or digital audio files. Disc jockeys serve as a bridge between the music itself and the listener. They may perform such public services as announcing the time, the weather forecast, or important news. It can be a lonely job, since many disc jockeys are the only person in the studio. But because their job is to maintain the good spirits of their audience and to attract new listeners, disc jockeys must possess the ability to be relaxed and cheerful.

Unlike the more conventional radio or television announcer, the disc jockey is not bound by a written script. Except for the commercial announcements, which must be read as written, the disc jockey's statements are usually spontaneous. Disc jockeys usually are not required to play a musical selection to the end; they may fade out a record when it interferes with a predetermined schedule for commercials, news, time checks, or weather reports.

Announcers who cover sports events for the benefit of the listening or viewing audience are known as *sportscasters*. This is a highly specialized form of announcing, as sportscasters must have extensive knowledge of the sports that they cover, plus the ability to describe events quickly, accurately, and compellingly.

Often the sportscaster will spend several days with team members, observing practice sessions, interviewing players and coaches, and researching the history of an event or of the teams to be covered. The more information that a sportscaster can acquire about individual team members, the tradition of the contest, the team's ratings and history, and the community in which the event takes place, the more interesting the coverage is to the audience.

The announcer who specializes in reporting the news to the listening or viewing public is called a *newscaster*. This job may require simply reporting facts, or it may include editorial commentary. Newscasters may be given the authority by their employers to express their opinions on news items or the philosophies of others. They must make judgments about which news is important and which is not. In some instances, they write their own scripts based on facts that are furnished by international news bureaus or local reporters. In other instances, they read text exactly as it is prepared by newswriters. They may make as few as one or two reports each day if they work on a major news program, or they may broadcast news for five minutes every hour or half-hour. Their delivery is usually dignified, measured, and impersonal.

The *news anchor* generally summarizes and comments on one aspect of the news at the end of the scheduled broadcast. This kind of announcing differs noticeably from that practiced by the sportscaster, whose manner may be breezy and interspersed with slang, or from the disc jockey, who may project a humorous, casual, or intimate image.

The newscaster may specialize in certain aspects of the news, such as economics, politics, or military activity. Newscasters also introduce films and interviews prepared by news reporters that provide in-depth coverage and information on the event being reported. *News analysts,* often called *commentators,* interpret specific events and discuss how these may affect individuals or the nation. They may have a specified daily slot for which material must be written, recorded, or presented live. They gather information that is analyzed and interpreted through research and interviews and cover public functions such as political conventions, press conferences, and social events.

Smaller television stations may have an announcer who performs all the functions of reporting, presenting, and commenting on the news as well as introducing network and news service reports.

Many television and radio announcers have become well-known public personalities in broadcasting. They may serve as masters of ceremonies at banquets and other public events.

■ EARNINGS

Salaries for announcers vary widely, but generally they are low. The exceptions are those announcers who work for major networks and stations that serve large metropolitan areas.

The U.S. Department of Labor reports that median hourly earnings for radio and television announcers were $14.88 in May 2015, which is about $30,960 a year. The lowest paid 10 percent made less than $8.65 an hour ($18,000 a year) and the highest paid 10 percent made more than $41,72 an hour ($86,780 a year).

Nationally known announcers and newscasters who appear regularly on network television programs receive salaries that may be quite impressive. For those who become top television personalities in large metropolitan areas, salaries also are quite rewarding.

Most radio or television stations broadcast 24 hours a day. Although much of the material may be prerecorded, announcing staff must often be available and as a result may work considerable overtime or split shifts, especially in smaller stations. Evening, night, weekend, and holiday duty may provide additional compensation.

■ WORK ENVIRONMENT

Work in radio and television stations is usually very pleasant. Almost all stations are housed in modern facilities. The maintenance of electronic equipment requires temperature and dust control, and people who work around such equipment benefit from the precautions taken to preserve it.

Announcers' jobs may provide opportunities to meet well-known people. Being at the center of an important communications medium can make the broadcaster more keenly aware of current issues and divergent points of view than the average person.

Announcers and newscasters usually work a 40-hour week, but they may work irregular hours. They may report for work at a very early hour in the morning or work late into the night. Some radio stations operate on a 24-hour basis. All-night announcers may be alone in the station during their working hours. Technology has allowed some overnight shows to be recorded during the day, thus eliminating the need for live overnight announcers.

■ EXPLORING

If you are interested in a career as an announcer, try to get a summer job at a radio or television station. Although you will probably not have the opportunity to broadcast, you may be able to judge whether or not this type of work appeals to you as a career.

Any chance to speak or perform before an audience should be welcomed. Join the speech or debate team to build strong speaking skills. Appearing as a speaker or performer can show whether or not you have the stage

A sports announcer reviews footage before a baseball game. (Michiel de Wit. Shutterstock.)

presence necessary for a career in front of a microphone or camera.

Many colleges and universities have their own radio and television stations and offer courses in radio and television. You can gain valuable experience working at college-owned stations. Some radio stations, cable systems, and TV stations offer financial assistance, internships, and co-op work programs, as well as scholarships and fellowships.

■ EDUCATION AND TRAINING REQUIREMENTS
High School

Although there are no formal educational requirements for entering the field of radio and television announcing, most large stations prefer college-educated applicants. The general reason for this preference is that announcers with broad educational and cultural backgrounds are better prepared to successfully meet a variety of unexpected or emergency situations. The greater the knowledge of geography, history, literature, the arts, political science, music, science, and of the sound and structure of the English language, the greater the announcer's value.

TALKING ON THE AIR

WORDS TO KNOW

Air check: An audio sample of a disc jockey or announcer's best on-air work that is submitted to program directors during the job search; also known as an **audition tape.**

FCC: The Federal Communications Commission is an independent federal agency that regulates television, cable, and radio.

Format: The type of content that is broadcast on a radio station, such as music, news, or talk shows.

Internet radio: Radio programming that is delivered over the Internet.

Newscast: The program that airs the news on television or radio.

Ratings: Determined by Nielsen (television) or Arbitron (radio), ratings help rank the stations and attract advertising dollars.

Satellite: An electronic device that orbits the Earth and transmits television, radio, and other communications signals.

Satellite radio: Radio programming that is broadcast via satellite; satellite radio, unlike traditional radio broadcasts, can reach listeners over thousands of miles.

Script: The written copy read by the reporters.

Teleprompter: For television broadcasts, this machine projects the script for on-air reporters to read.

In high school, therefore, you should focus on a college preparatory curriculum. In that curriculum, you should learn how to write and use the English language in literature and communication classes, including speech. Subjects such as history, government, economics, and a foreign language are also important.

It's a good idea to take as many computer science and multimedia classes as possible since announcers at some stations may be asked to update Web sites, develop an active presence on social media, and use databases to manage information.

Postsecondary Training

A strong liberal arts background with an emphasis in journalism, English, political science, or economics is advised, as well as a telecommunications or communications major. Participation in internships and work on your college's radio or television station is also highly recommended.

Once hired, announcers also participate in on-the-job training in which they learn how to operate the station's equipment.

■ CERTIFICATION, LICENSING, AND SPECIAL REQUIREMENTS
Certification or Licensing

No certification or licensing is required to become a radio or television announcer.

■ EXPERIENCE, SKILLS, AND PERSONALITY TRAITS

Those wishing to enter the field of announcing should obtain as much experience as possible in high school and college by participating in internships, working at their school's radio or television station, or by volunteering or working part time at a local station.

You must have a pleasing voice and personality in order to find success as an announcer. You must be levelheaded and able to react calmly in the face of a major crisis. People's lives may depend on an announcer's ability to remain calm during a disaster. There are also many unexpected circumstances that demand the skill of quick thinking. For example, if guests who are to appear on a program do not arrive or become too nervous to go on the air, you must compensate immediately and fill the airtime. You must smooth over an awkward phrase, breakdown in equipment, or other technical difficulty.

Good diction and English usage, thorough knowledge of correct pronunciation, and freedom from regional dialects are very important. A factual error, grammatical error, or mispronounced word can bring e-mails and phone calls of criticism to station managers.

If you aspire to a career as a television announcer, you must present a good appearance and have no nervous mannerisms. Neatness, cleanliness, and careful attention to the details of proper dress are important. The successful television announcer must have the combination of sincerity and showmanship that attracts and captures an audience.

Broadcast announcing is a highly competitive field. Station officials will pay particular attention to recorded auditions of your delivery or, in the case of television, to video-recorded demos of sample presentations.

■ EMPLOYMENT PROSPECTS
Employers

Approximately 30,390 announcers are employed in the United States. Some work on a freelance basis on individual assignments for networks, stations, advertising agencies, and other producers of commercials. Many announcers work part time.

Some companies own several television or radio stations; some belong to networks such as ABC, CBS, NBC, or Fox, while others are independent. While radio and television stations are located throughout the United

States, major markets where better-paying jobs are found generally near large metropolitan areas.

Starting Out

One way to enter this field is to apply for an entry-level job rather than an announcer position. It is also advisable to start at a small station. Most announcers start in jobs such as production secretary, production assistant, researcher, or reporter in small stations. As opportunities arise, it is common for announcers to move from one job to another. You may be able to find work as a disc jockey, sportscaster, or news reporter. Network jobs are few, and the competition for them is great. You must have several years of experience as well as a college education to be considered for these positions.

You must audition before you will be employed as an announcer. You should carefully select audition material to show a prospective employer the full range of your abilities. In addition to presenting prepared materials, you may be asked to read material that you have not seen previously, such as a commercial, news release, dramatic selection, or poem.

■ ADVANCEMENT PROSPECTS

Most successful announcers advance from small stations to large ones. Experienced announcers usually have held several jobs. The most successful announcers may be those who work for the networks. Usually, because of network locations, announcers must live in or near the country's largest cities.

Some careers lead from announcing to other aspects of radio or television work. More people are employed in sales, promotion, and planning than in performing; often they are paid more than announcers. Because the networks employ relatively few announcers in proportion to the rest of the broadcasting professionals, a candidate must have several years of experience and specific background in several news areas before being considered for an audition. These top announcers are usually college graduates.

■ OUTLOOK

Employment of radio and television announcers is projected to decline 14 percent through 2024, according to the U.S. Department (DOL). Openings will result mainly from those who leave the industry or the labor force. Industry consolidation, advances in technology that allow fewer announcers to do more work, and the increasing use of voice-tracking, which allows announcers to pre-record content and distribute it for use at multiple stations, are limiting employment opportunities for announcers. Competition for entry-level employment

---

TOP TELEVISION MARKETS

FAST FACTS

Nielsen ranks the television markets, and TV announcers interested in moving up always know the number of the station where they would like to work. The top 15 markets are as follows:

1. New York
2. Los Angeles
3. Chicago
4. Philadelphia
5. Dallas/Ft. Worth
6. San Francisco/Oakland/San Jose
7. Washington, D.C. (Hagerstown, Md.)
8. Houston
9. Boston (Manchester)
10. Atlanta
11. Tampa-St. Petersburg (Sarasota)
12. Phoenix (Prescott)
13. Detroit
14. Seattle-Tacoma
15. Minneapolis-St. Paul

Source: Nielsen, 2016–2017 television season, http://www.nielsen.com

---

in announcing during the coming years is expected to be keen, as the broadcasting industry always attracts more applicants than are needed to fill available openings. There is a better chance of working in radio than in television because there are more radio stations. Local television stations usually carry a high percentage of network programs and need only a very small staff to carry out local operations.

The DOL reports that "Internet radio may positively influence occupation growth. Start-up costs for Internet radio stations are relatively lower than for land-based radio. These stations can cheaply target a specific demographic or listening audience and create new opportunities for announcers."

The trend among major networks, and to some extent among many smaller radio and TV stations, is toward specialization in such fields as sportscasting or weather forecasting. Newscasters who specialize in such areas as business, consumer, and health news should have an advantage over other job applicants.

■ UNIONS AND ASSOCIATIONS

Union membership may be required for employment with large stations in major cities, and it is a necessity with the networks. The largest talent union is SAG-AFTRA, and some announcers may also be members of the National Association of Broadcast Employees and Technicians. Most small stations, however, hire nonunion workers. Other useful organizations for announcers include the Broadcast Education Association, National Association of Broadcasters, National Association of Farm Broadcasting, National Cable & Telecomunications Association, and the Radio Television Digital News Association.

■ TIPS FOR ENTRY

1. Work on your high school or college radio or television station to obtain experience.
2. Try to land an internship at a radio or television station.
3. Visit the following Web sites to learn more about job opportunities for announcers:
   - http://AirTalents.com
   - http://BestRadioJobs.com
   - http://tvandradiojobs.com
4. Be willing to relocate. It may improve your job prospects.

■ FOR MORE INFORMATION

For a list of schools offering degrees in broadcasting as well as scholarship information, contact
Broadcast Education Association (BEA)
1771 N Street, NW
Washington, D.C. 20036-2891
Tel: (202) 602-0584
Fax: (202) 609-9940
E-mail: HELP@BEAweb.org
http://www.beaweb.org

For information on union membership, contact
National Association of Broadcast Employees and Technicians–Communications Workers of America (NABET-CWA)
501 Third Street, NW
Washington, D.C. 20001-2797
Tel: (202) 434-1254
Fax: (202) 434-1426
E-mail: nabet@nabetcwa.org
http://www.nabetcwa.org

For broadcast education, support, and scholarship information, contact
National Association of Broadcasters (NAB)
1771 N Street, NW
Washington, D.C. 20036-2800

Tel: (202) 429-5300
E-mail: nab@nab.org
http://www.nab.org

For information on farm broadcasting, contact
National Association of Farm Broadcasting (NAFB)
1100 Platte Falls Road, PO Box 500
Platte City, MO 64079-0500
Tel: (816) 431-4032
Fax: (816) 431-4087
E-mail: info@nafb.com
http://nafb.com

For information on the cable television industry, contact
National Cable & Telecommunications Association (NCTA)
25 Massachusetts Avenue, NW, Suite 100
Washington, D.C. 20001-1434
Tel: (202) 222-2300
Fax: (202) 222-2514
E-mail: info@ncta.com
http://www.ncta.com

For scholarship and internship information, contact
Radio Television Digital News Association (RTDNA)
529 14th Street, NW, Suite 1240
Washington, D.C. 20045-2520
Fax: (202) 223-4007
http://www.rtdna.org

For information on union membership, contact
Screen Actors Guild - American Federation of Television and Radio Artists (SAG-AFTRA)
5757 Wilshire Boulevard, 7th Floor
Los Angeles, CA 90036-3600
Tel: (855) 724-2387
E-mail: sagaftrainfo@sagaftra.org
http://www.sagaftra.org

Radio and Television Program Directors

■ OVERVIEW

Radio and television program directors plan and schedule program material for stations and networks. They determine what entertainment programs, news broadcasts, and other program material their organizations offer to the public. At a large network, the program director may supervise a large programming staff. At a small station, one person may manage the station and also handle all programming duties.

HISTORY

Radio broadcasting in the United States began after World War I. The first commercial radio station, KDKA in Pittsburgh, came on the air in 1920 with a broadcast of presidential election returns. About a dozen radio stations were broadcasting by 1921. In 1926, the first national network linked stations across the country. According to the Federal Communications Commission (FCC), there were 15,489 radio stations in the United States as of June 30, 2016.

The first public demonstration of television in the United States came in 1939 at the opening of the New York World's Fair. Further development was limited during World War II, but by 1953 there were about 120 stations. There were 1,385 commercial television stations in the United States as of June 30, 2016. according to the FCC.

In 2009, the FCC required all television broadcast stations to switch their broadcasts from analog to digital (known as high-definition television), which carries more information. Many stations are now using digital recording devices and computers for editing and storage, and many major network shows now use digital cameras and equipment. Radio is also transitioning to digital broadcasting, such as through satellite radio services that listeners subscribe to.

Today, many people are also watching television and cable programming and listening to radio stations on the Internet via computers, tablet computers, and smartphones.

THE JOB

Program directors plan and schedule program material for radio and television stations and networks. They work in both commercial and public broadcasting and may be employed by individual radio or television stations, regional or national networks, or cable television systems.

Program directors oversee material including entertainment programs, public service programs, newscasts, sportscasts, and commercial announcements. Program directors decide what material is broadcast and when it is scheduled; they work with other staff members to develop programs and buy programs from independent producers. They are guided by such factors as the budget available for program material, the

audience their station or network seeks to attract, their organization's policies on content and other matters, and the kinds of products advertised in the various commercial announcements.

In addition, program directors may set up schedules for the program staff, audition and hire announcers and other on-air personnel, and assist the sales department in negotiating contracts with sponsors of commercial announcements. The duties of individual program directors are determined by such factors as whether they work in radio or television, for a small or large organization, for one station or a network, or in a commercial or public operation.

At small radio stations the owner or manager may be responsible for programming, but at larger radio stations and at television stations the staff usually includes a program director. At medium to large radio and television stations the program director usually has a staff that includes such personnel as music librarians, music directors, editors for recorded segments, and writers. Some stations and networks employ public service directors. It is the responsibility of these individuals to plan and schedule radio or television public service programs and announcements in such fields as education, religion, and civic and government affairs. Networks often employ *broadcast operations directors*, who coordinate the activities of the personnel who prepare network program schedules, review program schedules, issue daily corrections, and advise affiliated stations on their schedules.

QUICK FACTS

ALTERNATE TITLE(S)
News Directors, Operations Directors, Production Managers, Sports Directors

DUTIES
Plan and schedule programming for stations and networks

SALARY RANGE
$54,108 to $67,132 to $80,175+

WORK ENVIRONMENT
Primarily Indoors

BEST GEOGRAPHIC LOCATION(S)
Opportunities exist throughout the country, but are best in large, urban areas

MINIMUM EDUCATION LEVEL
Bachelor's Degree

SCHOOL SUBJECTS
Business, Social Studies, Speech

EXPERIENCE
Several years experience required

PERSONALITY TRAITS
Hands On, Organized, Problem-Solving

SKILLS
Business Management, Leadership, Organizational

CERTIFICATION OR LICENSING
None

SPECIAL REQUIREMENTS
None

EMPLOYMENT PROSPECTS
Fair

ADVANCEMENT PROSPECTS
Fair

OUTLOOK
Faster than the Average

NOC
5131

O*NET-SOC
27-2012.02, 27-2012.03

CAREER LADDER

Station Manager

Radio and Television Program Director

Assistant Radio and Television Program Director

News or Production Director

Reporter or Production Assistant

Program directors must carefully coordinate the various elements for a station while keeping in tune with the listeners, viewers, advertisers, and sponsors.

Other managers in radio and television broadcasting include *production managers*, *operations directors*, *news directors*, and *sports directors*. The work of program directors usually does not include the duties of *radio directors* or *television directors*, who direct rehearsals and integrate all the elements of a performance.

EARNINGS

Salaries for radio and television program directors vary widely based on such factors as size and location of the station, whether the station is commercial or public, and experience of the director. Radio and television program directors earned median annual salaries of $67,132 in September 2016, according to Salary.com. Salaries ranged from less than $54,108 to $80,175 or more. Television program directors generally earn more than their counterparts in radio.

Both radio and television program directors usually receive health and life coverage benefits and sometimes yearly bonuses as well.

WORK ENVIRONMENT

Program directors at small stations often work 44–48 hours a week and frequently work evenings, late at night, and on weekends. At larger stations, which have more personnel, program directors usually work 40-hour weeks.

Program directors frequently work under pressure because of the need to maintain precise timing and meet the needs of sponsors, performers, and other staff members.

Although the work is sometimes stressful and demanding, program directors usually work in pleasant environments with creative staffs. They also interact with the community to arrange programming and deal with a variety of people.

EXPLORING

If your high school or college has a radio or television station, volunteer to work on the staff. You can also look for part-time or summer jobs at local radio or television stations. You may not be able to plan the programming at a local station, but you will see how a station works and be able to make contacts with those in the field. If you can't find a job at a local station, at least arrange for a visit and ask to talk to the personnel. You may be able to "shadow" a program director for a day—that is, follow that director for the workday and see what his or her job entails.

EDUCATION AND TRAINING REQUIREMENTS
High School

If you are interested in this career, you should take courses that develop your communication skills in high school. Such classes include English, debate, and speech. You should also take business courses to develop your management skills; current events and history courses to develop your understanding of the news and the trends that affect the public's interests; and such courses as dance, drama, music, and visual art to expand your understanding of the creative arts. Finally, don't neglect your computer skills. You will probably be using computers throughout your career to file reports, maintain schedules, plan future programming projects, and promote your station on the Internet.

Postsecondary Training

Those with the most thorough educational backgrounds will find it easiest to advance in this field. A college degree, therefore, is recommended for this field. Possible majors for those interested in this work include radio and television production and broadcasting, communications, liberal arts, or business administration. Useful classes include English, economics, business administration, history, computer, and media classes. You may also wish to acquire some technical training that will help you understand the engineering aspects of broadcasting.

CERTIFICATION, LICENSING, AND SPECIAL REQUIREMENTS
Certification or Licensing

There are no certification or licensing requirements for radio and television program directors.

EXPERIENCE, SKILLS, AND PERSONALITY TRAITS

Extensive technical and on-air experience in either radio or television is required to become a program director.

Program directors must be creative, alert, and adaptable people who stay up to date on the public's interests and attitudes and are able to recognize the potential in new ideas. They must be able to work under pressure and be willing to work long hours, and they must be able to work with all kinds of people. Program directors must also be good managers who can make decisions, oversee costs and deadlines, and attend to details.

■ EMPLOYMENT PROSPECTS
Employers
Program directors work for broadcast television, radio, or cable television stations throughout the United States. Large conglomerates own some stations, while others are owned individually. While radio and television stations are located all over the country, the largest stations with the highest paid positions are located in large metropolitan areas.

Starting Out
Program director jobs are not entry-level positions. A degree and extensive experience in the field is required. Most program directors have technical and on-air experience in either radio or television. While you are in college you should investigate the availability of internships, since internships are almost essential for prospective job candidates. Your college career services office should also have information on job openings. Private and state employment agencies may also prove useful resources. You can also send resumes to radio and television stations or apply in person.

Beginners should be willing to relocate, as they are unlikely to find employment in large cities. They usually start at small stations with fewer employees, allowing them a chance to learn a variety of skills.

■ ADVANCEMENT PROSPECTS
Most beginners start in entry-level jobs and work several years before they have enough experience to become program directors. Experienced program directors usually advance by moving from small stations to larger stations and networks or by becoming station managers.

■ OUTLOOK
All radio and television stations, cable television systems, and regional and national networks employ program directors or have other employees whose duties include programming. According to the U.S. Department of Labor, employment of program directors is expected to increase faster than the average for all industries through 2024. However, the broadcasting industry has been impacted by consolidation, introduction of new technologies, greater use of prepared programming, and competition from other media.

Competition for radio and television program director jobs is strong. There are more opportunities for beginners in radio than there are in television. Most radio and television stations in large cities hire only experienced workers.

Radio program director discusses a broadcast schedule with a disc jockey. (DmitriMaruta. Shutterstock.)

New radio and television stations and new cable television systems are expected to create some additional openings for program directors, but some radio stations are eliminating program director positions by installing automatic programming equipment or combining those responsibilities with other positions. On the other hand, many radio stations are building their own HD (digital broadcast) radio stations, which could create more jobs in the years to come.

■ UNIONS AND ASSOCIATIONS
Radio and television program directors do not belong to unions. Useful organizations for program directors include the Broadcast Education Association, National Association of Broadcasters, National Association of Farm Broadcasting, National Cable & Telecommunications Association, and the Radio Television Digital News Association.

■ TIPS FOR ENTRY
1. Work on your high school or college radio or television station to obtain experience.
2. Try to land an internship at a radio or television station.
3. Visit the following Web sites to learn more about job opportunities:
   - http://AirTalents.com
   - http://BestRadioJobs.com
   - http://tvandradiojobs.com
   - http://www.rtdna.org/channel/find_a_job
4. Be willing to relocate. Small-market stations are more likely to hire inexperienced program directors than those located in large cities such as New York and Chicago.

PROGRAMMING LINGO

WORDS TO KNOW

Adjacency: A commercial announcement positioned immediately before or after a specific program.

Coverage: The percentage of households in a signal area.

Dayparts: Segments of the television or radio broadcast day.

Fixed position: An advertisement that must run at a specific time.

Frequency: The number of times an advertisement or promotion will run.

HD radio: Radio that is digitally broadcast; HD Radio is a trademark of the digital technology company iBiquity.

HDTV: High definition television.

O & O station: A station owned and operated by a network.

PSA: A public service announcement provided free by a radio or television station for an organization.

Preemption: The interruption of regularly scheduled programming.

Rating: Estimated size of audience.

Simulcast: Simultaneous broadcast of the same program on two different stations.

Spot: Purchased broadcast time.

Storyboard: Layout for advertisement or sequence.

Sweep: Television and radio survey periods when audience listening habits are measured.

Syndicated program: A program offered by an independent organization for sale to stations.

■ FOR MORE INFORMATION

For a list of schools offering degrees in broadcasting, contact

Broadcast Education Association (BEA)
1771 N Street, NW
Washington, D.C. 20036-2891
Tel: (202) 602-0584
Fax: (202) 609-9940
E-mail: HELP@BEAweb.org
http://www.beaweb.org

For broadcast education, support, and scholarship information, contact

National Association of Broadcasters (NAB)
1771 N Street, NW
Washington, D.C. 20036-2800
Tel: (202) 429-5300
E-mail: nab@nab.org
http://www.nab.org

For information on farm broadcasting, contact

National Association of Farm Broadcasting (NAFB)
1100 Platte Falls Road, PO Box 500
Platte City, MO 64079-0500
Tel: (816) 431-4032
Fax: (816) 431-4087
E-mail: info@nafb.com
http://nafb.com

For information on the cable television industry, contact

National Cable & Telecommunications Association
25 Massachusetts Avenue, NW, Suite 100
Washington, D.C. 20001-1434
Tel: (202) 222-2300
Fax: (202) 222-2514
E-mail: info@ncta.com
http://www.ncta.com

For scholarship and internship information, contact

Radio Television Digital News Association (RTNDA)
529 14th Street, NW, Suite 1240
Washington, D.C. 20045-2520
Fax: (202) 223-4007
http://www.rtdna.org

Radio Producers

■ OVERVIEW

Radio producers plan, rehearse, and produce live or recorded programs. They work with the music, on-air personalities, sound effects, and technology to put together an entire radio show. They schedule interviews and arrange for promotional events.

According to the Federal Communications Commission, there were 15,489 radio stations in the United States as of June 30, 2016. Larger stations employ radio producers, while smaller stations may combine those duties with those of the program director or disc jockey. While most radio producers work at radio stations, some work to produce a particular show and then sell that show to various stations. Approximately 25,470 radio and television producers and directors are employed in the United States.

■ HISTORY

As long as radio has existed, people have been behind the scenes to make sure that what the audience hears is what the station wants them to hear. A wide variety of administrative, programming, and technical people work behind the scenes of radio shows to create a professional broadcast.

Scheduled broadcasting began with a program broadcast by radio station KDKA in Pittsburgh. By 1923, 2.5 million radios had been sold. In the 1930s, radio personalities were household names, and even then, numerous people worked behind the scenes, arranging interviews and coordinating production. Today, radio reaches more than 90 percent of people age 12 and over on a weekly basis, according to a 2014 report by Arbitron.

Before television, radio producers would direct the on-air soap operas as well as the news, weather, and music. With the added technology of today's radio broadcast, radio producers are even more important in mixing the special effects, locations, personalities, and formats in ways that create a good radio show.

The Internet has made the radio producer's job easier in some ways and more challenging in others. Web sites specifically for producers provide a community where ideas can be exchanged for shows, news, jokes, and more. However, with the new frontier of broadcasting on the Internet, radio producers have one more duty to add to their long list of responsibilities.

■ THE JOB

The identity and style of a radio program is a result of the collaborations of on-air and off-air professionals. Radio disc jockeys talk the talk during a broadcast, and producers walk the walk behind the scenes. But in many situations, particularly with smaller radio stations, the disc jockey and the show's producer are one in the same person.

Also, many show producers have disc jockey experience. This experience, combined with technical expertise, helps producers effectively plan their shows.

Radio producers rely on the public's very particular tastes—differences in taste allow for many different kinds of radio to exist, to serve many different segments of a community. In developing radio programs, producers take into consideration the marketplace—they listen to other area radio stations and determine what's needed and appreciated in the community, and what there may already be too much of. They conduct surveys and interviews to find out what the public wants to hear. They decide which age groups they want to pursue and develop a format based on what appeals to these listeners. These decisions result in a station's identity, which is very important. Listeners associate a station with the kind of music it plays, how much music it plays, the type of news and conversation presented, and the station's on-air personalities.

Based on this feedback, and on additional market research, radio disc jockeys/producers devise music playlists and music libraries. They each develop an individual on-air identity, or personality, and they invite guests who will interest their listeners. Keeping a show running on time is also the responsibility of a producer. This involves carefully weaving many different elements into a show, including music, news reports, traffic reports, and interviews. Radio producers may also be responsible for technical controls such as operating the sound volume levels, recording software, and the switchboard.

Radio producers write copy for and coordinate on-air commercials, which are usually recorded in advance. They also devise contests, from large public events to small, on-air trivia competitions.

Though a majority of radio stations have music formats, radio producers also work for 24-hour news stations, public broadcasting, and talk radio. Producing news programs and radio documentaries involves a great deal of research, booking guests, writing scripts, and interviewing.

■ EARNINGS

According to the U.S. Department of Labor, median annual earnings for radio and television producers and directors were $72,020 in May 2015. The lowest paid 10 percent of all producers and directors in all entertainment fields make less than $31,780 a year, and the highest paid 25 percent make more than $104,780. Like many radio jobs, there is a wide salary range resulting from differences in market size and station size of each radio station.

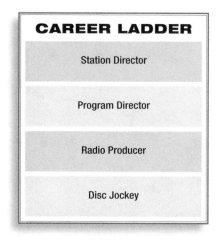

CAREER LADDER

Station Director

Program Director

Radio Producer

Disc Jockey

Most large stations offer typical benefits to full-time employees, including health and life insurance.

◼ WORK ENVIRONMENT

Radio producers generally work indoors in a busy environment, although some location and outdoor work might be required. The atmosphere at a radio station is generally very pleasant; however, smaller stations may not be modern, with much of the investment going into high-tech equipment for the broadcasts.

Full-time radio producers usually work more than 40 hours per week planning, scheduling, and producing radio shows. Also, according to the schedule of their shows, early morning, late night, or weekend work might be required. Radio is a 24-hours-a-day, seven-days-a-week production, requiring constant staffing.

Producers work with disc jockeys and program directors in planning radio shows, and they also work with advertising personnel to produce radio commercials. In addition to this collaboration, they may work alone doing research for the show. Working with the public is another aspect of the radio producer's job. Promotions and events may require contact with businesspeople and listeners.

◼ EXPLORING

Getting your feet wet early is a good idea for all radio careers. Small radio stations are often willing to let young, inexperienced people work either behind-the-scenes or on-air. Getting a job or an internship at one of the small stations in your area may be as simple as asking for one.

Many high schools and universities have on-site radio stations where students can get hands-on experience at all different levels. As you explore the career further, you might want to interview a radio producer to make sure that the job requirements and description are still of interest to you.

Since most people don't start out as a producer, experience in any area of radio is helpful, so talk to local disc jockeys or program directors as well.

◼ EDUCATION AND TRAINING REQUIREMENTS
High School

Writing skills are valuable in any profession, but especially in radio. Take composition and literature courses,

and other courses that require essays and term papers. Journalism courses will not only help you develop your writing skills, but they will also teach you about the nature and history of media. You'll learn about deadlines and how to put a complete project (such as a newspaper or yearbook) together. Speech courses are also necessary for on-air experience.

Business courses and clubs frequently require students to put together projects; starting any business is similar to producing your own radio show. Use such a project as an opportunity to become familiar with the market research, interviewing, and writing that are all part of a radio producer's job. For both the future radio producer and the future disc jockey, a theater department offers great learning opportunities. Drama or theater classes, which are frequently involved in productions, may provide opportunities for learning about funding, advertising, casting, and other fundamentals similar to a radio production.

If your school has a radio station, get involved with it in any way you can. Also check with your local radio stations; some may offer part-time jobs to high school students interested in becoming producers and disc jockeys.

Postsecondary Training

Most journalism and communications schools at universities offer programs in broadcasting. Radio producers and announcers often start their training in journalism schools, and they receive hands-on instruction at campus radio stations. These broadcasting programs are generally news-centered, providing great opportunities for students interested in producing news programs, daily newscasts, and documentaries. News directors and program managers of radio stations generally want to hire people who have a good, well-rounded education with a grounding of history, geography, political science, and literature.

◼ CERTIFICATION, LICENSING, AND SPECIAL REQUIREMENTS
Certification or Licensing

There are no certification or licensing requirements for radio producers.

◼ EXPERIENCE, SKILLS, AND PERSONALITY TRAITS

Aspiring radio producers can gain excellent experience by working on their high school, college, or community radio station as disc jockeys, assistant producers, producers, or in other positions.

In order to be a successful radio producer, you should be well versed in the English language (or the language in which you broadcast) and be a creative thinker who can combine several elements into one project. The ability to understand technical equipment and coordinate it with on-air events is also necessary.

A healthy curiosity about people and the world will help radio producers find new topics for news shows, new guests for call-ins, and new ideas for music formats. There are no physical requirements to be a radio producer, although those starting as disc jockeys need a strong, clear voice to be heard over the airwaves.

■ EMPLOYMENT PROSPECTS

Employers

The U.S. Department of Labor reports that 25,470 radio and television producers and directors are employed in the United States.

Many stations combine the position of radio producer with that of the disc jockey or program director, so depending on the size of the station and market, producers may or may not be able to find a suitable employer.

Due to the Telecommunications Act of 1996, companies can own an unlimited number of radio stations nationwide with an eight-station limit within one market area, depending on the size of the market. When this legislation took effect, mergers and acquisitions changed the face of the radio industry, with automation and networking reducing the number of employees needed by stations. Consolidation of both radio and television broadcasting stations continues to this day.

Starting Out

Radio producers usually start work at radio stations in any capacity possible. After working for a while in a part-time position gaining experience and making connections, a young, dedicated producer will find opportunities to work in production or on-air.

Both experience and a college education are generally needed to become a radio producer. It is best if both your experience and your education are well rounded, with exposure to on-air and off-air positions as well as a good working knowledge of the world in which we live.

Although some future producers begin their first radio jobs in paid positions, many serve unpaid internships or volunteer to help run their college or high school station. Even if this entry-level work is unpaid, the experience gained is one of the key necessities to furthering a career in any type of radio work.

With experience as a disc jockey or behind-the-scenes person, an aspiring radio producer might try to land a position at another station, most likely within a station and format they are used to.

A radio producer uses monitors and a soundboard when recording a show. (dotshock. Shutterstock.)

■ ADVANCEMENT PROSPECTS

Radio producers are a key link in putting together a radio show. Once they have experience coordinating all the elements that go into a radio production, it is possible to move into a program director position or, possibly in the future, to general manager.

Another way to advance is to move from being the producer of a small show to a larger one, or move from a small station to a larger one. Some producers move into the freelance arena, producing their own shows that they sell to several radio stations.

■ OUTLOOK

The U.S. Department of Labor predicts faster-than-average employment growth for all producers (radio and television) through 2024. However, job growth in the radio industry, specifically, has been curtailed by several factors in recent years. In the past, radio station ownership was highly regulated by the government, limiting the number of stations a person or company could own. Recent deregulation has made multiple-station ownership and consolidation of offices possible. Radio stations now are bought and sold at a more rapid pace. This may result in a radio station changing formats as well as entire staffs. Though some radio producers are able to stay at a station over a period of several years, people going into radio should be prepared to change employers at some point in their careers.

Another trend that is affecting jobs in radio producing is the increasing use of programming created by services outside the broadcasting industry. Satellite radio, in which subscribers pay a monthly fee for access to radio stations, has become a threat to smaller, more marginal

RADIO HISTORY

DID YOU KNOW?

- While Franklin D. Roosevelt is well known for his fireside chats via the radio, it was Woodrow Wilson who was the first president to broadcast over the radio. In 1918, he used a radio broadcast to talk to troops stationed on vessels in the Atlantic Ocean.

- When Orson Welles broadcast his realistic version of H. G. Wells's *War of the Worlds* there was a panic in America when people thought Martian spacecrafts had actually landed. This incident prompted the Federal Communications Commission to order that there be no more fictional news bulletins.

- In 1994, the first radio broadcast was streamed over the Internet, and the first 24-hour Web-only radio station was started. By 2012, 40 percent of Americans listened to online radio for nearly 10 hours a week.

- XM Radio launched the first satellite radio service in March of 2001, opening a new market for broadcasting where listeners subscribe to the service and use proprietary devices to listen to channels. Competitor Sirius radio launched in 2002. In 2008 the companies merged to become Sirius XM Radio.

Source: The Media History Project

stations. Also, increased use of mobile devices such as smartphones and MP3 players has negatively affected the industry. One bright spot, however, is that there may be an increase in technical and production jobs due to the growth of HD (digital broadcast) radio stations.

Competition is usually keen for all radio jobs. Graduates of college broadcasting programs are finding a scarcity of work in media. Paid internships will also be difficult to find—many students of radio will have to work for free for a while to gain experience. Radio producers may find more opportunities as freelancers, developing their own programs independently and selling them to stations.

■ UNIONS AND ASSOCIATIONS

Radio producers do not belong to unions. Useful organizations for producers include the Alliance for Women in Media, Broadcast Education Association, National Association of Broadcasters, and the Radio Television Digital News Association. The Federal Communications Commission is a U.S. government agency that "regulates interstate and international communications by radio, television, wire, satellite and cable in all 50 states, the District of Columbia, and U.S. territories."

■ TIPS FOR ENTRY

1. Work on your high school or college radio station to obtain experience.
2. Visit the following Web sites to learn more about job opportunities for announcers:
   - http://www.rtdna.org/channel/find_a_job
   - http://BestRadioJobs.com
   - http://tvandradiojobs.com
3. Try to land an internship at a radio station.
4. Apply for producer positions at small radio stations to get your foot in the door.

■ FOR MORE INFORMATION

For information on careers for women in radio and television, as well as scholarships and internships, contact
Alliance for Women in Media and
  Foundation (AWM)
2365 Harrodsburg Road, A325
Lexington, KY 40504
Tel: (202) 750-3664
http://allwomeninmedia.org

For a list of schools offering degrees in broadcasting as well as scholarship information, contact
Broadcast Education Association (BEA)
1771 N Street, NW
Washington, D.C. 20036-2891
Tel: (202) 602-0584
Fax: (202) 609-9940
E-mail: HELP@BEAweb.org
http://www.beaweb.org

The FCC offers information on media guidelines, including all radio laws. For more information, contact
Federal Communications Commission (FCC)
445 12th Street, SW
Washington, D.C. 20554-0004
Tel: (888) 225-5322
Fax: (866) 418-0232
http://www.fcc.gov

For information on union membership, contact
National Association of Broadcast Employees
  and Technicians–Communications Workers of
  America (NABET-CWA)
501 3rd Street, NW
Washington, D.C. 20001-2760
Tel: (202) 434-1254
Fax: (202) 434-1426
E-mail: nabet@nabetcwa.org
http://nabetcwa.org

For broadcast education, support, and scholarship information, contact

National Association of Broadcasters (NAB)
1771 N Street, NW
Washington, D.C. 20036-2800
Tel: (202) 429-5300
E-mail: nab@nab.org
http://www.nab.org

For scholarship and internship information, contact

Radio Television Digital News Association (RTNDA)
529 14th Street, NW, Suite 1240
Washington, D.C. 20045-2520
Fax: (202) 223-4007
http://www.rtdna.org

Radiologic Technologists

■ OVERVIEW

Radiologic technologists operate equipment that creates images of a patient's body tissues, organs, and bones for the purpose of medical diagnoses and therapies. These images allow physicians to know the exact nature of a patient's injury or disease, such as the location of a broken bone or the confirmation of an ulcer.

Before an X-ray examination, radiologic technologists may administer drugs or chemical mixtures to the patient to better highlight internal organs. They place the patient in the correct position between the X-ray source and film and protect body areas that are not to be exposed to radiation. After determining the proper duration and intensity of the exposure, they operate the controls to beam X-rays through the patient and expose the photographic film or record the image on video or as a digital file.

They may also operate computer-aided imaging equipment that does not involve X-rays and may help to treat diseased or affected areas of the body by exposing the patient to specified concentrations of radiation for prescribed times. Radiologic technologists hold about 195,590 jobs in the United States.

■ HISTORY

Radiography uses a form of electromagnetic radiation to create an image on photographic film, or on video or a digital file. Unlike photography, where the film is exposed to ordinary light rays (the most familiar kind of electromagnetic radiation), in radiography the film is exposed to X-rays, which have shorter wavelengths and different energy levels.

X-rays were discovered by Wilhelm Conrad Roentgen in 1895. X-rays, or Roentgen rays, are generated in a glass vacuum tube (an X-ray tube) that contains two differently charged electrodes, one of which gives off electrons. When the electrons travel from one electrode to the other, some of the energy they emit is X-radiation. X-rays are able to pass through skin and muscle and other soft body tissue, while bones and denser objects show up as white images on the photographic emulsion when film is exposed to X-rays. A picture of the inside of the body can thus be developed.

All forms of radiation are potentially harmful. Exposure to ultraviolet radiation may tan the skin, but it can also result in burning and other damage to tissue, including the development of cancer cells. Low-level infrared radiation can warm tissues, but at higher levels it cooks them like microwaves do; the process can destroy cells. Protective measures to avoid all unnecessary exposure to radiation must be taken whenever X-rays are used, because they can have both short- and long-term harmful effects.

There are other forms of diagnostic imaging that do not expose patients to any potentially harmful radiation. Sound waves are used in ultrasound technology, or sonography, to obtain a picture of internal organs. High-frequency sound waves beamed into the patient's body bounce back and create echoes that can be recorded on a paper strip, photograph, video, or digital file. Ultrasound is very frequently employed to

---

QUICK FACTS

ALTERNATE TITLE(S)
None

DUTIES
Operate equipment that creates images of a patient's body tissues, organs, and bones for the purpose of medical diagnoses and therapies

SALARY RANGE
$38,110 to $56,670 to $81,660+

WORK ENVIRONMENT
Primarily Indoors

BEST GEOGRAPHIC LOCATION(S)
Nationwide; most opportunities available in major metropolitan areas

MINIMUM EDUCATION LEVEL
High School Diploma, Some Postsecondary Training

SCHOOL SUBJECTS
Biology, Chemistry, Physics

EXPERIENCE
Internship

PERSONALITY TRAITS
Hands On, Outgoing, Technical

SKILLS
Interpersonal, Math, Scientific

CERTIFICATION OR LICENSING
Required

SPECIAL REQUIREMENTS
None

EMPLOYMENT PROSPECTS
Good

ADVANCEMENT PROSPECTS
Good

OUTLOOK
Faster than the Average

NOC
3215

O*NET-SOC
29-2034.00

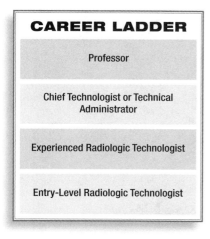

CAREER LADDER

Professor

Chief Technologist or Technical Administrator

Experienced Radiologic Technologist

Entry-Level Radiologic Technologist

determine the size and development of a human fetus. Magnetic resonance imaging (MRI) uses magnetic fields, radio waves, and computers to create images of the patient's body.

The use of imaging techniques that do not involve radiation grew rapidly during the 1980s and 1990s because of the safety of these techniques and because of great improvements in computer technology. Computers can now handle a vast quantity of data much more rapidly, making it possible to enhance images to great clarity and sharpness.

■ THE JOB

All radiological work is done at the request of and under the supervision of a physician. Just as a prescription is required for certain drugs to be dispensed or administered, so must a physician's request be issued before a patient can receive any kind of imaging procedure.

There are four primary disciplines in which radiologic technologists may work: radiography (taking X-ray pictures or radiographs), nuclear medicine, radiation therapy, and sonography. In each of these medical imaging methods, the technologist works under the direction of a physician who specializes in interpreting the pictures produced by X-rays, other imaging techniques, or radiation therapy. Technologists can work in more than one of these areas. Some technologists specialize in working with a particular part of the body or a specific condition.

X-ray pictures, or radiographs, are the most familiar use of radiologic technology. They are used to diagnose and determine treatment for a wide variety of afflictions, including ulcers, tumors, and bone fractures. Chest X-ray pictures can determine whether a person has a lung disease. Radiologic technologists who operate X-ray equipment first help the patient prepare for the radiologic examination. After explaining the procedure, they may administer a substance that makes the part of the body being imaged more clearly visible on the film, video, or digital file. (Note: digital imaging technology is increasingly being used by imaging facilities today and may eventually replace film.) They make sure that the patient is not wearing jewelry or other metal that would obstruct the X-rays. They position the person sitting, standing, or lying down so that the correct view of the body can be radiographed, and then they cover adjacent

areas with lead shielding to prevent unnecessary exposure to radiation.

The technologist positions the X-ray equipment at the proper angle and distance from the part to be radiographed and determines exposure time based on the location of the particular organ or bone and thickness of the body in that area. The controls of the X-ray machine are set to produce pictures of the correct density, contrast, and detail. Placing the photographic film or digital recording device closest to the body part being x-rayed, the technologist takes the requested images, repositioning the patient as needed. Typically, there are standards regarding the number of views to be taken of a given body part. The film is then developed (or the video or digital file is prepared) for the radiologist or other physician to interpret.

In a fluoroscopic examination (a more complex imaging procedure that examines the gastrointestinal area), a beam of X-rays passes through the body and onto a fluorescent screen, enabling the physician to see the internal organs in motion. For these, the technologist first prepares a solution of barium sulfate to be administered to the patient, either rectally or orally, depending on the exam. The barium sulfate increases the contrast between the digestive tract and surrounding organs, making the image clearer. The technologist follows the physician's guidance in positioning the patient, monitors the machine's controls, and takes any follow-up radiographs as needed.

Radiologic technologists may learn other imaging procedures such as computed tomography (CT) scanning, which uses X-rays to get detailed cross-sectional images of the body's internal structures, and MRI, which uses radio waves, powerful magnets, and computers to obtain images of body parts. These diagnostic procedures have become more common and usually require radiologic technologists to undergo additional on-the-job training.

Other specialties within the radiography discipline include mammography and cardiovascular interventional technology. In addition, some technologists may focus on radiography of joints and bones, or they may be involved in such areas as angiocardiography (visualization of the heart and large blood vessels) or neuroradiology (the use of radiation to diagnose diseases of the nervous system).

Radiologic technologists perform a wide range of duties, from greeting patients and putting them at ease by explaining the procedures to developing the finished film or preparing the video or digital image. Their administrative tasks include maintaining patients' records, recording equipment usage and maintenance, organizing work schedules, and managing a radiologist's private practice or hospital's radiology department. Some radiologic technologists teach in programs to educate other technologists.

■ EARNINGS

Salaries for radiologic technologists compare favorably with those of similar health care professionals. According to the U.S. Department of Labor, median annual earnings of radiologic technologists and technicians were $56,670 in May 2015. The lowest paid 10 percent, which typically includes those just starting out in the field, earned less than $38,110. The highest paid 10 percent, which typically includes those with considerable experience, earned more than $81,660. Median annual earnings of radiologic technologists and technicians who worked in medical and diagnostic laboratories were $57,830 in May 2015. Those who worked in hospitals earned a mean salary of $59,820, and those who worked in offices of medical doctors earned $54,290.

Most technologists take part in their employers' vacation and sick leave provisions. In addition, most employers offer benefits such as health insurance and pensions.

■ WORK ENVIRONMENT

Full-time technologists generally work eight hours a day, 40 hours a week. In addition, they may be on call for some night emergency duty or weekend hours, which pays in equal time off or additional compensation.

In diagnostic radiologic work, technologists perform most of their tasks while on their feet. They move around a lot and often are called upon to lift patients who need help in moving.

Great care is exercised to protect technologists from radiation exposure. Each technologist wears a badge that measures radiation exposure, and records are kept of total exposure accumulated over time. Other routine precautions include the use of safety devices (such as lead aprons, lead gloves, and other shielding) and the use of disposable gowns, gloves, and masks. Careful attention to safety procedures has greatly reduced or eliminated radiation hazards for the technologist.

Radiologic technology is dedicated to conserving life and health. Technologists derive satisfaction from their work, which helps promote health and alleviate human suffering. Those who specialize in radiation therapy need to be able to handle the close relationships they inevitably develop while working with very sick or dying people over a period of time.

■ EXPLORING

There is no way to gain direct experience in this profession without the appropriate qualifications. However, it is possible to learn about the duties of radiologic technologists by

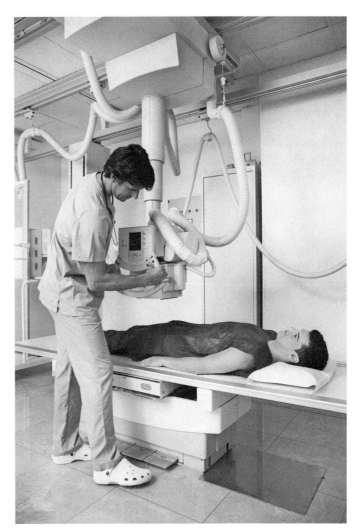

A radiologic technologist adjusts the position of an X-ray machine. (Tyler Olson. Shutterstock.)

talking with them and observing the facilities and equipment they use. It is also possible to have interviews with teachers of radiologic technology. Ask your school counselor or a science teacher to help you contact local hospitals or schools with radiography programs to locate technologists who are willing to talk to an interested student.

As with any career in health care, volunteering at a local hospital, clinic, or nursing home provides an excellent opportunity for you to explore your interest in the field. Most hospitals are eager for volunteers, and working in such a setting will give you a chance to see health care professionals in action, as well as to have some patient contact.

■ EDUCATION AND TRAINING REQUIREMENTS
High School

If this career interests you, take plenty of math and science classes in high school. Biology, anatomy, chemistry,

MEDICAL IMAGING TECHNIQUES

DID YOU KNOW?

In addition to X-rays, radiological technologists can specialize in other types of diagnostic medical imaging techniques. Some of these include:

Computed Tomography (CT Scan): Uses X-rays in conjunction with computer imaging to diagnose soft tissues in the body in detailed, three-dimensional form.

Magnetic Resonance Imaging (MRI): Uses strong magnetic fields, radio waves, and complex computer programs to make precise measurements of internal organs.

Ultrasound: High frequency sound waves are used to visualize soft tissue structures. Ultrasound is vital to obstetrical imaging as it allows safe observation of an in utero fetus. It is also used in the treatment of kidney stones and other procedures.

and physics classes will be particularly useful to you. Take computer classes to become comfortable working with this technology. English classes will help you improve your communication skills. You will need these skills both when interacting with the patients and when working as part of a health care team. Finally, consider taking photography classes. Photography classes will give you experience with choosing film, framing an image, and developing photographs.

Postsecondary Training

After high school, you will need to complete an education program in radiography. Programs range in length from one to four years. Depending on length, the programs award a certificate, associate's degree, or bachelor's degree. Two-year associate's degree programs are the most popular option.

Educational programs are available in hospitals, medical centers, colleges and universities, and vocational and technical institutes. It is also possible to get radiologic technology training in the armed forces.

The Joint Review on Education in Radiologic Technology accredits certificate, associate degree, and bachelor's degree programs. To enter an accredited program, you must be a high school graduate; some programs require one or two years of higher education. You will complete both classroom training and clinical training (which will provide you with hands-on experience working with patients and imaging technology). Courses in radiologic technology education programs include anatomy, physiology, patient care, physics, radiation

protection, medical ethics, principles of imaging, medical terminology, radiobiology, and pathology. For some supervisory or administrative jobs in this field, a bachelor's or master's degree may be required.

Other Education or Training

The American Society of Radiologic Technologists offers continuing education (CE) courses on radiologic practice issues, patient care, and leadership. The Society of Diagnostic Medical Sonography also provides CE classes and webinars. Contact these organizations for more information.

■ CERTIFICATION, LICENSING, AND SPECIAL REQUIREMENTS
Certification or Licensing

Radiologic technologists can become certified through the American Registry of Radiologic Technologists (ARRT) after graduating from an accredited program in radiography, radiation therapy, or nuclear medicine. After becoming certified, many technologists choose to register with the ARRT. Registration is an annual procedure required to maintain the certification. Registered technologists meet the following three criteria: They agree to comply with the ARRT rules and regulations, comply with the ARRT standards of ethics, meet continuing education requirements every two years and complete continuing qualifications requirements every 10 years. Only technologists who are currently registered can designate themselves as ARRT registered technologists and use the initials RT after their names. Although registration and certification are voluntary, many jobs are open only to technologists who have acquired these credentials.

In addition to receiving primary certification in various imaging disciplines, radiologic technologists can receive advanced qualifications in mammography, computed tomography, magnetic resonance imaging, quality management, bone densitometry, cardiac-interventional radiography, vascular-interventional radiography, sonography, vascular sonography, or breast sonography. As the work of radiologic technologists grows increasingly complex and employment opportunities become more competitive, the desirability of registration and certification will also grow.

Most states require practicing radiologic technologists to be licensed. You will need to check with the state in which you hope to work about its specific licensure requirements.

■ EXPERIENCE, SKILLS, AND PERSONALITY TRAITS

Participation in radiologic technology internships while in college will provide useful experience.

Radiologic technologists should be responsible individuals with a mature and caring nature. They should be personable and enjoy interacting with all types of people, including those who are very ill. A compassionate attitude is essential to deal with patients who may be frightened or in pain.

■ EMPLOYMENT PROSPECTS

Employers

There are approximately 195,590 radiologic technologists working in the United States. According to the U.S. Department of Labor, about 58 percent of these technologists work in hospitals. Radiologic technologists also find employment in doctors' offices and clinics, at X-ray labs, and in nursing homes and outpatient care facilities.

Starting Out

With more states regulating the practice of radiologic technology, certification by the appropriate accreditation body for a given specialty is quickly becoming a necessity for employment. If you get your training from a school that lacks accreditation or if you learn on the job, you may have difficulty in qualifying for many positions, especially those with a wide range of assignments. If you are enrolled in a hospital educational program, you may be able to get a job with the hospital upon completion of the program. If you are in a degree program, get help in finding a job through your school's career services office.

■ ADVANCEMENT PROSPECTS

Many radiologic technologists are employed in hospitals where there are opportunities for advancement to administrative and supervisory positions such as chief technologist or technical administrator. Other technologists develop special clinical skills in advanced imaging procedures, such as CT scanning or MRI. Some radiologic technologists qualify as instructors. Radiologic technologists who hold bachelor's degrees have more opportunities for advancement. The technologist who wishes to become a teacher or administrator will find that a master's degree and considerable experience are necessary.

■ OUTLOOK

Overall, employment for radiologic technologists is expected to grow faster than the average through 2024, according to the U.S. Department of Labor. Major reasons for this growth are the passage of the Affordable Health Care Act, which has allowed more people to become eligible for health insurance; the development of new technologies, which are making many imaging modalities less expensive and more apt to be performed by radiologic

technicians; and the increasing elderly population in the United States, which will create a need for radiologic technologists' services. The demand for qualified technologists in some areas of the country far exceeds the supply. This shortage is particularly acute in rural areas and small towns. Those who are willing to relocate to these areas may improve their chances of landing a job. Radiologic technologists who are trained to do more than one type of imaging procedure will also find that they have increased job opportunities. Those specializing in CT and MRI should have better odds of securing work as these are being increasingly used as diagnostic tools.

In the years to come, increasing numbers of radiologic technologists will be employed in settings outside of hospitals, such as physicians' offices, clinics, health maintenance organizations, laboratories, government agencies, and diagnostic imaging centers. This pattern will be part of the overall trend toward lowering health care costs by delivering more care outside of hospitals. Nevertheless, hospitals will remain the major employers of radiologic technologists for the near future. Because of the increasing importance of radiologic technology in the diagnosis and treatment of disease, it is unlikely that hospitals will do fewer radiologic procedures than in the past. Instead, they try to do more on an outpatient basis and on weekends and evenings. This should increase the demand for part-time technologists and thus open more opportunities for flexible work schedules.

■ UNIONS AND ASSOCIATIONS

Radiologic technologists who work for government agencies can join unions that represent government workers. Unions specifically for health care professionals include the National Union of Healthcare Workers and Service Employee International Union. Major membership organizations for radiologic technologists include the American Society of Radiologic Technologists and the Society of Diagnostic Medical Sonography. The American Registry of Radiologic Technologists offers certification to radiologic technologists. The Canadian Association of Medical Radiation Technologists represents the professional interests of technologists in Canada.

■ TIPS FOR ENTRY

1. Read books and journals such as *Radiologic Technology* and *Radiation Therapist* (both are available at http://www.asrt.org/main/news-research/asrt-journals-magazines) to learn more about the field.
2. Join the American Society of Radiologic Technologists (ASRT) to access member-only

career resources, scholarships, publications, discounts on conferences, and other resources.

3. Visit http://www.healthecareers.com/asrt and http://www.sdms.org/resources/careers/job-board for job listings.

4. The ASRT offers detailed information on career paths at https://www.asrt.org/main/careers/careers-in-radiologic-technology.

■ FOR MORE INFORMATION

For information on certification and educational programs, contact

American Registry of Radiologic Technologists (ARRT)
1255 Northland Drive
St. Paul, MN 55120-1139
Tel: (651) 687-0048
http://www.arrt.org

For information on education and careers, contact

American Society of Radiologic Technologists (ASRT)
15000 Central Avenue, SE
Albuquerque, NM 87123-3909
Tel: (800) 444-2778; (505) 298-4500
Fax: (505(298-5063
E-mail: memberservices@asrt.org
http://www.asrt.org

For career and education information, contact

Canadian Association of Medical Radiation Technologists (CAMRT)
1300-180 rue Elgin Street
Ottawa, ON K2P 2K3
Canada
Tel: (800) 463-9729; (613) 234-0012
Fax: (613) 234-1097
E-mail: info@camrt.ca
http://www.camrt.ca

NUHW's mission is "to hold health care corporations accountable to the public, to establish better working conditions and higher standards of care, and to give our members a stronger voice in the workplace." Contact the union for more details.

National Union of Healthcare Workers (NUHW)
1100 Vermont Avenue NW, Suite 1200
Washington, D.C. 20005
Tel: (866) 968-NUHW
http://nuhw.org

Some health care workers belong to SEIU. Contact the union for more information.

Service Employees International Union (SEIU)
1800 Massachusetts Ave., NW
Washington, D.C. 20036
Tel: (800) 424-8592; (202) 730-7000
http://www.seiu.org

For information about education and careers, contact

Society of Diagnostic Medical Sonography (SDMS)
2745 Dallas Parkway, Suite 350
Plano, TX 75093-8730
Tel: (800) 229-9506
Fax: (214) 473-8563
http://www.sdms.org

Railroad Conductors

■ OVERVIEW

Railroad conductors supervise trains and train crews on passenger trains, on freight trains, or in the rail yards. They are responsible for keeping track of the train's operating instructions and of its makeup and cargo. There are approximately 42,330 railroad conductors and yardmasters employed in the United States.

■ HISTORY

The term conductor is likely to conjure up an image of the man who calls "All aboard!" before a train leaves the station. In the early days of the railroad, this association was accurate. Today, however, railroad conductors are more than a passenger liaison. With today's smaller crews, conductors and engineers often make up the entire crew aboard a train.

On many early passenger trains, the railroad conductor's most important task was to see to the comfort and safety of the passengers. For the first conductors, this was no simple task. The earliest trains had seats bolted to platforms that looked much like today's flat cars. There were no roofs over those cars, and passengers were consequently exposed to the elements, such as rain and wind, and to flying sparks from the tinderboxes of locomotives. More often than not, the conductor had to extinguish fires started by flying sparks on the train and in passengers' clothing.

By the 1870s, as trains crossed the unsettled western areas of the United States, the conductor's job became even more difficult and dangerous. Outlaws frequently attacked trains or tore up tracks and damaged bridges.

Once rail came to be a popular method of both passenger and freight transportation in the latter half of the 1800s and early 1900s, railroad companies had the means to improve the quality of their locomotives and trains.

As locomotives and trains became more complex machines, conductors became well versed in all areas of train operation. They were required to know a lot about all aspects of a train, from the engines, cars, and cargo to the track and signal systems. Today's conductors are responsible for the proper functioning of the entire train.

■ THE JOB

Railroad conductors fall into two basic categories: road conductors and yard conductors (or yardmasters). Within the category of road conductors are included conductors of both freight and passenger trains, although their duties vary somewhat. The conductor is in charge of the train in its entirety, including all equipment and the crew.

Before a freight or passenger train departs from the terminal, the road conductor receives orders from the dispatcher regarding the train's route, timetable, and cargo. He or she then confers with the engineer and other members of the train crew, if necessary. During the run, conductors may receive additional communication by radio, such as information on track conditions or the instruction to pull off at the next available stop. They then relay this information to the engineer via a two-way radio. Conductors also receive information about any operating problems while underway and may make arrangements for repairs or removal of defective cars. They use a radio or cell phone to keep dispatchers informed about the status of the trip.

Conductors on freight trains are responsible for getting bills of loading, lists of cars in their train, and written orders from the station agent and dispatcher. They keep records of each car's content and eventual destination and see to it that cars are dropped off and picked up along the route as specified. Both before and during the run, they inspect the cars to make sure everything is as it should be.

On passenger trains, conductors see to it that passenger cars are clean and that passengers are seated and comfortable. They collect tickets and cash and attend to the passengers' needs. At stops, they supervise the disembarking of the passengers and tell the engineer when it is safe to pull out of the station. If an accident occurs, conductors take charge and direct passengers and other crew members.

Yard conductors are usually stationed at a switching point or terminal where they signal the engineer and

QUICK FACTS

ALTERNATE TITLE(S)
Road Conductors, Yard Conductors, Yardmasters

DUTIES
Supervise trains and train crews on passenger trains, on freight trains, or in rail yards

SALARY RANGE
$38,450 to $55,930 to $77,940+

WORK ENVIRONMENT
Indoors/Outdoors

BEST GEOGRAPHIC LOCATION(S)
Opportunities exist throughout the country

MINIMUM EDUCATION LEVEL
High School Diploma

SCHOOL SUBJECTS
English, Geography, Technical/Shop

EXPERIENCE
Several years experience required

PERSONALITY TRAITS
Hands On, Outgoing, Realistic

SKILLS
Interpersonal, Mechanical/Manual Dexterity, Organizational

CERTIFICATION OR LICENSING
Required

SPECIAL REQUIREMENTS
Some conductor must be at least 21 years old; must be able to lift at least 80 pounds; drug tests

EMPLOYMENT PROSPECTS
Fair

ADVANCEMENT PROSPECTS
Fair

OUTLOOK
Decline

NOC
7362

O*NET-SOC
53-4031.00

direct the work of switching crews that assemble and disassemble the trains. Based on knowledge of train schedules, the yard conductor or yard foreman is responsible for seeing that cars destined to arrive at various points along one of many routes are put together and ready to leave on time. He or she sends cars to special tracks for unloading and sends other cars to tracks to await being made into trains. Conductors tell switching crews which cars to couple or uncouple and which switches to throw to

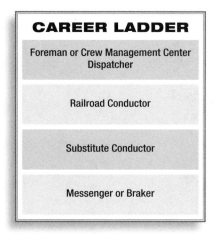

CAREER LADDER

Foreman or Crew Management Center Dispatcher

Railroad Conductor

Substitute Conductor

Messenger or Braker

divert the locomotive or cars to the proper tracks. Today, many yards are mechanized. In this case, yard conductors supervise the movement of cars through electronic monitoring devices.

All conductors perform strenuous work outside in all weather conditions and travel extensively. Usually, conductors are required to work on-call, on an as-needed basis. Railroads expect conductors, as well as most of their other employees, to be available to work 24 hours a day, seven days a week in all weather conditions. A certain time period is allotted, usually 12 hours, from the time of call to report to work.

EARNINGS

As is the case with most rail occupations, the daily wage or hourly rate varies with the size of the railroad. Other factors that affect wages are the type of service, number of cars on the train, and the location of the train's run. For example, conductors receive extra pay on trains passing through mountainous regions. Usually, basic wages, as well as fringe benefits, for conductors are guaranteed by union contract.

According to the U.S. Department of Labor, median hourly earnings of railroad conductors and yardmasters were $26.89 in May 2015, making a median annual salary $55,930. Wages ranged from less than $18.49 (a full-time salary of $38,450) to more than $37.47 an hour (a full-time salary of $77,940).

Conductors, like other railroad workers, receive a generous benefits package including health and life insurance, paid holidays and vacations, sick leave, and a pension plan. In addition to retirement plans sponsored by unions and railroads, conductors are eligible for Social Security and other government benefits.

WORK ENVIRONMENT

Road conductors spend much of their time traveling and must be away from home on a constant basis. While assigned to the extra board, they usually have irregular hours. Once they receive a regular assignment, however, they may maintain a regular schedule and remain on a run for years. Although the basic workweek is eight hours for five days a week, days and nights are not considered different, and Sunday is treated as a workday. Along with other members of the train's crew, conductors

work extra hours, including nights, weekends, and holidays, when travel is especially heavy. Mandatory rest periods are required for safety purposes. If a conductor is required to "lay over" while awaiting a train to return to the home terminal, he or she must pay for meals and other living expenses.

In addition to being a leader among other members of the train crew, the conductor also has the most direct and frequent contact with the public. The position can carry heavy responsibilities; it can also be very rewarding.

EXPLORING

A visit to a rail yard might give you some insight into the work of a yard conductor and into the operations of railroads in general. It might be possible to arrange to talk with a conductor who works on a freight train or a passenger train for further insight. It might even be possible to obtain summer or part-time work for a railroad company.

Many conductors have an engineering or mechanical background, so you may find it helpful to explore such areas in high school through vocational clubs or classes. The Technical Student Association (TSA) is a nationwide organization that provides training and competitions for students in science, engineering, technology, and mathematics. Visit the TSA Web site (http://www.tsaweb.org) for more information about joining or starting a chapter.

EDUCATION AND TRAINING REQUIREMENTS
High School

If you are interested in becoming a conductor, you will benefit from taking as many shop classes as possible. Any course that teaches electrical principles is particularly helpful. Because on-board computers are increasingly used in this profession, computer training would be a plus. Finally, academic subjects such as English and speech are also important because conductors are required to write some reports and speak to fellow workers and passengers.

Postsecondary Training

Many conductors acquire much of the knowledge to assume their positions through years of practical experience in other positions on the railroad. Railroads prefer that applicants for these jobs have high school diplomas, but further education, outside of the railroad's training school, is not typically required. To be eligible for a conductor's position, you must pass examinations testing your knowledge of signals, timetables, air brakes, operating rules, and related subjects. Once hired, conductors complete one to three months of training on railroad operating procedures, how to interact with passengers, ticketing procedures, and other topics.

Certification

A few colleges and organizations offer certificates in railroad operations. For example, the National Academy of Railroad Sciences and Johnson County Community College offer certificates in locomotive-electrical, locomotive-mechanical, railroad operations, and other railroad-related areas.

■ CERTIFICATION, LICENSING, AND SPECIAL REQUIREMENTS
Certification or Licensing

New conductors are required to pass a certification exam that has been designed and administered by their employer (and approved by the Federal Railroad Administration). Yard conductors may be required to hold a commercial driver's license in order to operate trucks and other heavy vehicles.

Other Requirements

You must pass an entrance-to-service medical examination and must pass further physicals at regular intervals. You are also required to take tests that screen for drug use. Some conductor jobs require applicants to be at least 21 years old. You must be able to lift 80 pounds, as is required when replacing knuckles that connect rail cars.

■ EXPERIENCE, SKILLS, AND PERSONALITY TRAITS

Many conductors enter the field after obtaining several years of experience in entry-level positions (such as messenger or braker) in the railroad industry.

Since conductors are responsible for overseeing the activities of the other crew members and for dealing with the public, you must be capable of assuming responsibility, directing the work activities of others, and acting as the railroad's representative to passengers. A conductor must have a good working knowledge of the operation of the train and of its mechanical details. In addition, you must be self-sufficient and capable of occupying free hours because much of the time is spent away from home. Finally, it is important that you have good judgment skills, be dependable, and be able to make quick, responsible decisions.

■ EMPLOYMENT PROSPECTS
Employers

Railroad conductors may be employed by passenger lines or freight lines. They may work for one of the major railroads, such as BNSF Railway Company, Norfolk

An Amtrak railroad conductor waves from the dinette car. (Spirit of America. Shutterstock.)

Southern, or CSX, or they may work for one of the more than 500 smaller short-line railroads across the country. Many of the passenger lines today are commuter lines located near large metropolitan areas. Railroad conductors who work for freight lines may work in a rural or an urban area and will travel more extensively than the shorter, daily commuter routes passenger railroad conductors make. There are 42,330 railroad conductors and yardmasters working in the United States, according to the Bureau of Labor Statistics.

Starting Out

The method of becoming a conductor varies and is usually determined by a particular railroad company. Most often, you must start at an entry-level job—such as *messenger* or *janitor*—and work your way up to *foreman* or *conductor* positions. After acquiring experience, you may be considered for the position of *conductor*. Some companies promote experienced personnel to conductor positions. At other companies, there is a specific sequence of jobs and training required before you become a conductor.

For example, one of the major railroads, Norfolk Southern, requires class and field training for freight service trainees to become conductor trainees. Field experience includes training with yard, local, and through freight crews. Completion of written exams is also required. Conductor trainees for Norfolk Southern undergo locomotive engineer training, including 12 to 14 months of field training. The railroad lists the following duties for its conductor trainees: operate track switches, couple cars, and work on freight trains in yard operations and on the road. To learn more about Norfolk Southern, visit http://www.nscorp.com/content/nscorp/en.html.

RAILWAY MUSEUMS

DID YOU KNOW?

The history of railroads continues to interest people of all ages even today—years after the railroad's heyday as the nation's chief means of transportation. Railway museums can be found all over the country and are a great way to get a feel for how much railroads affected the average American's life in the early 20th century. Large railway museums boast large collections of restored locomotives—passenger, freight and streetcars. The Illinois Railway Museum (http://www.irm.org), located in Union, Ill., bills itself as the largest railroad museum in the United States. Visitors can see locomotives and cars, as well as artifacts, such as buildings, signals, telegraph apparatus, signage, tickets, caps, and badges. Some unique cars and locomotives in the museum's collection include the Electroliner, the Nebraska Zephyr, the only remaining Chicago streamlined PCC streetcars, the first GP7 diesel engine, the only interurban sleeping car, and an 1859 horsecar. On the West Coast, the Golden Gate Railroad Museum (http://www.ggrm.org) offers an extensive collection of cars and locomotives. Its collection includes the Southern Pacific 2472, a steam locomotive built in 1921; the Atchison-Topeka-Santa Fe 2356 diesel locomotive built in 1948 by the American Locomotive Company; and passenger cars built in the 1920s by Pullman.

Thus, you must first seek employment at a lower-level job with a railroad company. Direct contact with unions and railroad companies is recommended if you want more information about an entry-level job. Such jobs serve as training for future conductors, as you will be required to know all aspects of train operation.

ADVANCEMENT PROSPECTS

When conductors first begin their careers, they are seldom assigned regular full-time positions. Instead, they are put on a list called an "extra board" (meaning their names are on a board of people who are available 24/7) and are called in only when the railroad needs a substitute for a regular employee. On most railroads, conductors who are assigned to the extra board may work as brakers if there are not enough conductor runs available that month. The first form of promotion, then, is receiving a regular assignment as a conductor. Conductors who show promise and ability may eventually be promoted to managerial positions or *crew management center dispatcher,* who schedule locomotive engineers and conductors by using a computerized calling system.

OUTLOOK

The U.S. Department of Labor predicts that employment for railroad conductors will decline through 2024. Rail passenger services to many points have been discontinued. Although the volume of railroad freight business is expected to increase in the coming years, the use of mechanization, automation, and larger, faster trains is expected to reduce the need for new conductors. Computers are now used to keep track of empty freight cars, match empty cars with the closest load, and dispatch trains. Also, new work rules that allow two- and three-person crews instead of the traditional five-person crews are becoming more widely used, and these factors combine to lessen the need for conductors and other crew workers. Some employment growth may occur, however, due to the 2008 Rail Safety Improvement Act, which increases the number of hours crews must rest between shifts. More workers will be needed to fill in these gaps.

Also, many older rail workers—locomotive engineers and conductors in particular—are expected to retire from the field in the coming years. Job openings will arise from the need to replace them with qualified workers.

UNIONS AND ASSOCIATIONS

Almost three-quarters of railroad employees are members of a union, such as the International Association of Sheet Metal, Air, Rail and Transportation Workers (SMART) and the Brotherhood of Locomotive Engineers and Trainmen. The Association of American Railroads and the American Short Line & Regional Railroad Association are membership organizations for railroads. The Federal Railroad Administration is an agency of the U.S. Department of Transportation that regulates more than 760 railroads (including 27 passenger, eight switching and terminal, approximately 134 tourist/excursion/historical, and 640 freight railroads). The National Academy of Railroad Sciences offers training for railroad professionals.

TIPS FOR ENTRY

1. Contact railroads directly to learn about job openings. The American Short Line & Regional Railroad Association provides a list of its members at http://www.aslrra.org/web/Members/Directory/web/Dir/RR_Member_Search_NM.aspx?&hkey=9450250f-beac-4459-ae9c-9ed5a13a9101.
2. Visit http://freightrailworks.org/topic/jobs to learn more about railroad careers.
3. Read *Locomotive Engineers & Trainmen News* (http://www.ble-t.org/pr/journal) to learn more about the field.

4. Visit the following Web sites for job listings: http://www.railjobs.com and http://www.rrb.gov/PandS/Jobs/rrjobs.asp.

■ FOR MORE INFORMATION

For information on small railroads, contact

American Short Line & Regional Railroad Association (ASLRRA)
50 F Street, NW, Suite 7020
Washington, D.C. 20001-1507
Tel: (202) 628-4500
Fax: (202) 628-6430
http://www.aslrra.org

For general information on the railroad industry, contact

Association of American Railroads (AAR)
425 Third Street, SW
Washington, D.C. 20024-3206
Tel: (202) 639-2100
http://www.aar.org

For information on union membership, contact

Brotherhood of Locomotive Engineers and Trainmen (BLET)
7061 East Pleasant Valley Road
Independence, OH 44131
Tel: (216) 241-2630
E-mail: PresStaff@ble-t.org
http://www.ble-t.org

For information on railroading and federal regulations, contact

Federal Railroad Administration (FRA)
1200 New Jersey Avenue, SE
Washington, D.C. 20590-0001
Tel: (202) 493-6014
http://www.fra.dot.gov

For conductor training program information and other resources, contact

National Academy of Railroad Sciences (NARS)
12345 College Boulevard
Overland Park, KS 66210-1283
Tel: (800) 228-3378
Fax: (913) 319-2603
http://www.narstraining.com

SMART is "the largest railroad operating union in North America, with more than 500 Transportation locals." For information, contact

International Association of Sheet Metal, Air, Rail and Transportation Workers (SMART)
1750 New York Avenue, NW, 6th Floor
Washington, D.C. 20006
Tel: (800) 457-7694; (202) 662-0800
E-mail: info@smart-union.org
https://smart-union.org

Range Managers

■ OVERVIEW

Range managers work to maintain and improve grazing lands on public and private property. They research, develop, and carry out methods to improve and increase the production of forage plants, livestock, and wildlife without damaging the environment; develop and carry out plans for water facilities, erosion control, and soil treatments; restore rangelands that have been damaged by fire, pests, and undesirable plants; and manage the upkeep of range improvements, such as fences, corrals, and reservoirs. Approximately 36,000 conservation scientists, including range managers, are employed in the United States.

■ HISTORY

Early in history, primitive peoples grazed their livestock wherever forage was plentiful. As the supply of grass and shrubs became depleted, they simply moved on, leaving the stripped land to suffer the effects of soil erosion. When civilization grew and the nomadic tribes began to establish settlements, people began to recognize the need for conservation and developed simple methods of land terracing, irrigation, and the rotation of grazing lands.

Much of the same thing happened in the United States. The rapid expansion across the continent in the 19th century was accompanied by the destruction of plant and animal life and the abuse of the soil. Because the country's natural resources appeared inexhaustible, the cries of alarm that came from a few concerned conservationists went unheeded. It was not until after 1890 that conservation became a national policy. Today many state and federal agencies are actively involved in protecting the nation's soil, water, forests, and wildlife.

Rangelands cover more than a billion acres of the United States, mostly in the western states and Alaska. Many natural resources are found there: grass and shrubs for animal grazing, wildlife habitats, water from vast watersheds, recreation facilities, and valuable mineral and energy resources. In addition, rangelands are used by scientists who conduct studies of the environment.

◼ THE JOB

Range managers are sometimes known as *range scientists, range ecologists,* and *range conservationists.* Their goal is to maximize range resources without damaging the environment. They accomplish this in a number of ways.

To help ranchers attain optimum production of livestock, range managers study the rangelands to determine the number and kind of livestock that can be most profitably grazed, the grazing system to use, and the best seasons for grazing. The system they recommend must be designed to conserve the soil and vegetation for other uses, such as wildlife habitats, outdoor recreation, and timber.

Grazing lands must continually be restored and improved. Range managers study plants to determine which varieties are best suited to a particular range and to develop improved methods for reseeding. They devise biological, chemical, or mechanical ways of controlling undesirable and poisonous plants, and they design methods of protecting the range from grazing damage.

Range managers also develop and help carry out plans for water facilities, structures for erosion control, and soil treatments. They are responsible for the construction and maintenance of such improvements as fencing, corrals, and reservoirs for stock watering. Following drastic events such as wildfires, floods, droughts, and mineral, oil, and gas extractions, range managers assess and implement rehabilitation and land reclamation techniques.

Although range managers spend a great deal of time outdoors, they also work in offices, consulting with other conservation specialists, preparing written reports, and doing administrative work.

Rangelands have more than one use, so range managers often work in such closely related fields as wildlife and watershed management, forest management, and recreation. Soil conservationists and naturalists are concerned with maintaining ecological balance both on the range and in the forest preserves.

◼ EARNINGS

According to the U.S. Department of Labor, in May 2015, conservation scientists earned from less than $37,380 to more than $91,830 per year, with $61,110 as the median salary. Those working as foresters earned a median salary of $58,230 per year and from less than $38,660 up to $84,980.

Range managers are also eligible for paid vacations and sick days, health and life insurance, and other benefits.

◼ WORK ENVIRONMENT

Range managers, particularly those just beginning their careers, spend a great deal of time on the range. That means they must work outdoors in all kinds of weather. They usually travel by car or small plane, but in rough country they use four-wheel-drive vehicles or get around on horseback or on foot. When riding the range, managers may spend a considerable amount of time away from home, and the work is often quite strenuous.

As range managers advance to administrative jobs, they spend more time working in offices, writing reports, and planning and supervising the work of others. Range managers may work alone or under direct supervision; often they work as part of a team. In any case, they must deal constantly with people—not only their superiors and coworkers but with the general public, ranchers, government officials, and other conservation specialists.

◼ EXPLORING

As a high school student, you can test your appetite for outdoor work by applying for summer jobs on ranches or farms. Other ways of exploring this occupation include a field trip to a ranch or interviews with or lectures by range managers, ranchers, or conservationists. Any volunteer work with conservation organizations—large or small—will give you an idea of what range managers do and will help you when you apply to colleges and for employment.

As a college student, you can get more direct experience by applying for summer jobs in range management with such federal agencies as the Forest Service, the

Natural Resources Conservation Service, and the Bureau of Land Management. This experience may better qualify you for jobs when you graduate.

■ EDUCATION AND TRAINING REQUIREMENTS
High School

If you are interested in pursuing a career in range management, you should begin planning your education early. Since you will need a college degree for this work, take college preparatory classes in high school. Your class schedule should include the sciences, such as earth science, biology, and chemistry. Take mathematics and economics classes. Any computer courses that teach you to use databases and word processing programs will also be beneficial. You will frequently use computers during your career to keep records, file reports, and do planning. English courses will also help you develop your research, writing, and reading skills. You will need all of these skills in college and beyond.

Postsecondary Training

The minimum educational requirement for range managers is usually a bachelor's degree in range management or range science. To be hired by the federal government, you will need at least 42 credit hours in plant, animal, or soil sciences and natural resources management courses, including at least 18 hours in range management. If you would like a teaching or research position, you will need a graduate degree in range management. Advanced degrees may also prove helpful for advancement in other jobs.

To receive a bachelor's degree in range management, students must have acquired a basic knowledge of biology, chemistry, physics, mathematics, and communication skills. Specialized courses in range management combine plant, animal, and soil sciences with the principles of ecology and resource management. Students are also encouraged to take electives, such as economics, statistics, forestry, hydrology, agronomy, wildlife, animal husbandry, computer science, and recreation.

While a number of schools offer some courses related to range management, only 10 colleges and universities in the United States have degree programs in range management or range science that are accredited by the Society of Range Management. More than 40 other schools offer course work or degrees in range management or range science.

Other Education or Training

The Society for Range Management offers symposia and workshops on range management-related issues. Past offerings included "Strategic Grazing Management for Complex Adaptive Systems" and "Climate Change in Western Rangelands." Contact the society for more information.

■ CERTIFICATION, LICENSING, AND SPECIAL REQUIREMENTS
Certification or Licensing

The Society for Range Management offers the certified range management consultant and certified professional in rangeland management designations. Although voluntary, these certifications demonstrate a professional's commitment to the field and the high quality of his or her work. Requirements for certification include having a bachelor's degree and at least five years of experience in the field as well as passing a written exam.

■ EXPERIENCE, SKILLS, AND PERSONALITY TRAITS

Previous experience in range management positions (part-time jobs, internships, volunteerships) while in college is highly recommended.

Range managers need to be familiar with geographic information systems and remote sensing data (aerial photographs and other imagery taken from airplanes and satellites) for mapping forest and range areas and evaluating trends in forest and land use. A working knowledge of hand-held computers, global positioning systems (GPS),

CAREER LADDER

| Consultant, or Researcher, or Professor |
| Manager or Supervisor |
| Experienced Range Manager |
| Entry-Level Range Manager |

A range manager records data on grouse populations in Idaho. (Stephen Ausmus. USDA.)

WHAT IS A RANGE?

The Society for Range Management defines rangeland and range resources as follows: "Rangelands are the world's largest land type. Comprising over 40 percent of the Earth's land, rangelands consist of prairies, grasslands, deserts, alpine, savanna, marshes and some types of forests. The primary components of rangelands are native grasses, shrubs and other native plants. These lands are extremely productive and rich in biodiversity…"

The term range can also include forestlands that have grazing resources, or seeded lands that are managed like rangeland. Range resources are not limited to the grazable forage, but may include wildlife, water, and many other benefits.

Source: http://www.rangelands.org

and Internet-based applications is useful in this work. Along with their technical skills, range managers must be able to speak and write effectively and to work well with others. Range managers need to be self-motivated and flexible. They are generally persons who do not want the restrictions of an office setting and a rigid schedule. They should have a love for the outdoors as well as good health and physical stamina for the strenuous activity that this occupation requires.

■ EMPLOYMENT PROSPECTS
Employers
The U.S. Department of Labor reports that there are 36,500 conservation scientists, including range managers, employed in the United States. The majority of range managers are employed by the federal government in the Forest Service, the Bureau of Land Management (BLM), or the Natural Resources Conservation Service (NRCS). State governments employ range managers in game and fish departments, state land agencies, and extension services.

In private industry, the number of range managers is increasing. They work for coal and oil companies to help reclaim mined areas, for banks and real estate firms to help increase the revenue from landholdings, and for private consulting firms and large ranches. Some range managers with advanced degrees teach and do research at colleges and universities. Others work overseas with U.S. and United Nations agencies and with foreign governments.

Starting Out
The usual way to enter this occupation is to apply directly to the appropriate government agencies. People interested in working for the federal government may contact the Department of Agriculture's Forest Service or the NRCS, or the Department of the Interior's Bureau of Indian Affairs or the BLM. Others may apply to local state employment offices for jobs in state land agencies, game and fish departments, or agricultural extension services. Your school's career services office should have listings of available jobs.

■ ADVANCEMENT PROSPECTS
Range managers may advance to administrative positions in which they plan and supervise the work of others and write reports. Others may go into teaching or research. An advanced degree is often necessary for the higher-level jobs in this field. Another way for range managers to advance is to enter business for themselves as range management consultants or ranchers.

■ OUTLOOK
This is a small occupation, and most of the openings will arise when older, experienced range managers retire or leave the occupation. In fact, the Society for Range Management reports that it is "concerned about the future management of rangelands because approximately 25 to 33 percent of rangeland managers are likely to retire within the next 10 years." On the other hand, the U.S. Department of Labor predicts that employment for conservation scientists and foresters, a category that includes range managers, will grow by 7 percent through 2024, or as fast as the average for all careers.

The need for range managers should be stimulated by a growing demand for wildlife habitats, recreation, and water as well as by an increasing concern for the environment. A greater number of large ranches will employ range managers to improve range management practices and increase output and profitability. Range specialists will also be employed in larger numbers by private industry to reclaim lands damaged by oil and coal exploration. A small number of new jobs will result from the need for range and soil conservationists to provide technical assistance to owners of grazing land through the Natural Resources Conservation Service.

An additional demand for range managers could be created by the conversion of rangelands to other purposes, such as wildlife habitats and recreation. Federal employment for these activities, however, depends on the passage of legislation concerning the management of range resources, an area that is always controversial. Smaller budgets may also limit employment growth in this area.

■ UNIONS AND ASSOCIATIONS
Range managers do not belong to unions. The Society for Range Management is the leading organization for range

managers. It offers certification, scholarships, publications, career information, and student programs. It also accredits postsecondary range management programs.

▣ TIPS FOR ENTRY

1. Read *Rangeland Ecology & Management* and *Rangelands* (both available at http://www.srmjournals.org) to learn more about the field.
2. Visit https://www.usajobs.gov for job opportunities with the federal government.
3. Participate in range management internships or part-time jobs that are arranged by your college's career services office.

▣ FOR MORE INFORMATION

This organization provides career, education, scholarship, and certification information. Student membership is also available through its International Student Conclave.

Society for Range Management
6901 South Pierce Street, Suite 225
Littleton, CO 80128-7206
Tel: (303) 986-3309
Fax: (303) 986-3892
E-mail: info@rangelands.org
http://www.rangelands.org

For information about career opportunities in the federal government, contact

U.S. Department of Agriculture Natural Resources Conservation Service
1400 Independence Avenue, SW
Washington, D.C. 20250-0002
Tel: (202) 720-7246
http://www.nrcs.usda.gov

For information on careers, contact

U.S. Department of Agriculture U.S. Forest Service
1400 Independence Avenue, SW
Washington, D.C. 20250-1111
Tel: (800) 832-1355
http://www.fs.fed.us

For information on careers, contact

U.S. Department of the Interior Bureau of Indian Affairs
Office of Public Affairs, MS-3658-MIB
1849 C Street, NW
Washington, D.C. 20240-0001
Tel: (202) 208-3710
Fax: (202) 501-1516
http://www.bia.gov

To learn more about career opportunities with the BLM, contact

U.S. Department of the Interior Bureau of Land Management (BLM)
1849 C Street, NW
Washington, D.C. 20240-0001
Tel: (202) 208-3801
Fax: (202) 208-5242
E-mail: blm_wo_newmedia@blm.gov
http://www.blm.gov

To learn more about career opportunities with the NPS, contact

U.S. Department of the Interior National Park Service (NPS)
1849 C Street, NW
Washington, D.C. 20240-0001
Tel: (202) 208-3818
http://www.nps.gov

Real Estate Agents and Brokers

▣ OVERVIEW

Real estate brokers are licensed to manage their own real estate businesses and sell, rent, or manage the property of others. *Real estate agents* are salespeople who are either self-employed or hired by brokers. Sometimes, the term agent is applied to both real estate brokers and agents. There are approximately 421,000 real estate agents and real estate brokers employed in the United States. They may also be called *real estate buyer's agents and brokers.*

▣ HISTORY

Three factors contributed to the rise of the modern real estate business: first, the general increase in the total population and in the number of pieces of real estate for sale, second, the growing percentage of people owning property, and third, the complexity of laws regarding the transfer of real estate. These factors led to the need for experienced agents, on whom both sellers and buyers increasingly rely.

Professionalization of the real estate field developed rapidly in the 20th century. In 1908, the National Association of Realtors was founded. This huge trade group has encouraged the highest ethical standards for the field and has lobbied hard in Congress for many of the tax advantages that homeowners and property owners now enjoy. Today, the organization has 1 million

QUICK FACTS

ALTERNATE TITLE(S)
Real Estate Buyer's Agents and
    Brokers

DUTIES
Represent buyers during real
    estate transactions (real estate
    agent); sell, rent, or manage
    the property of others (real
    estate broker)

SALARY RANGE
$21,780 to $43,370 to
    $110,560+ (real estate agents)
$23,400 to $56,860 to
    $166,940+ (real estate
    brokers)

WORK ENVIRONMENT
Primarily Indoors

BEST GEOGRAPHIC LOCATION(S)
Opportunities exist in all regions

MINIMUM EDUCATION LEVEL
High School Diploma

SCHOOL SUBJECTS
Business, English, Mathematics

EXPERIENCE
One to three years experience
    as a licensed sales agent to
    be eligible for licensing as
    a broker

PERSONALITY TRAITS
Enterprising, Organized,
    Outgoing

SKILLS
Business Management,
    Interpersonal, Sales

CERTIFICATION OR LICENSING
Required

SPECIAL REQUIREMENTS
Must be at least 18 years old

EMPLOYMENT PROSPECTS
Good

ADVANCEMENT PROSPECTS
Good

OUTLOOK
Little Change or More Slowly
    than the Average

NOC
6232

O*NET-SOC
41-9021.00, 41-9022.00

members and also serves as a self-regulatory organization for the real estate brokerage industry.

■ THE JOB

The primary responsibility of real estate brokers and agents is to help clients buy, sell, rent, or lease a piece of real estate. Real estate is defined as a piece of land or property and all improvements attached to it. The property may be residential, commercial, or agricultural. When people wish to put property up for sale or rent, they contract with real estate brokers to arrange the sale and to represent them in the transaction. This contract with a broker is called a listing.

One of the main duties of brokers is to actively solicit listings for the agency. They develop leads for potential listings by distributing promotional items, by advertising in local publications, and by showing other available properties in open houses. They also spend a great deal of time on the phone exploring leads gathered from various sources, including personal contacts.

Once a listing is obtained, real estate agents analyze the property to present it in the best possible light to prospective buyers. They have to recognize and promote the property's strong selling points. A residential real estate agent might emphasize such attributes as a home's layout or proximity to schools, for example. Agents develop descriptions to be used with photographs of the property in ads and promotions on Web sites and in print literature. Many real estate Web sites now feature what's know as 360 (as

in 360 degrees) virtual real estate tours, videos that walk viewers through properties. To make a piece of real estate more attractive to prospective buyers, agents may also advise homeowners on ways to improve the look of their property to be sold.

Agents must also determine the fair market value for each property up for sale. They compare their client's real estate with similar properties in the area that have recently been sold to decide upon a fair asking price. The broker and any agents of the brokerage work to obtain the highest bid for a property because their earnings are dependent on the sale price. Owners usually sign a contract agreeing that if their property is sold, they will pay the agent a percentage of the selling price.

When the property is ready to be shown for sale, agents contact buyers and arrange a convenient time for them to see the property. If the property is vacant, the broker usually retains the key. To adjust to the schedules of potential buyers, agents frequently show properties in the late afternoon or evening and on weekends. Because a representative of the broker's firm is usually on the premises in each house, weekend showings are a good way to put part-time or beginning agents to work.

An agent may have to meet several times with a prospective buyer to discuss and view available properties. When the buyer decides on a property, the agent must bring the buyer and seller together at terms agreeable to both. In many cases, different brokers will represent the seller and buyer. Agents may have to present several counteroffers to reach a compromise suitable to both parties.

Once the contract is signed by both the buyer and the seller, the agent must see to it that all terms of the contract are carried out before the closing date. For example, if the seller has agreed to repairs or a home inspection, the agent must make sure these are carried out or the sale cannot be completed.

Brokers often provide buyers with information on loans to finance their purchase. They also arrange for title searches and title insurance. A broker's knowledge, resourcefulness, and creativity in arranging financing that is favorable to the buyer can mean the difference between success and failure in closing a sale. In some cases, agents assume the responsibilities of closing the sale, but the closing process is increasingly handled by lawyers or loan officers.

Commercial or agricultural real estate agents operate in much the same fashion. Their clients usually have specific and prioritized needs. For example, a trucking firm might require their property to be located near major highways. These real estate specialists often conduct extensive searches to meet clients' specifications. They usually make fewer but larger sales, resulting in higher commissions.

In addition to selling real estate, some brokers rent and manage properties for a fee. Some brokers combine other types of work, such as selling insurance or practicing law, with their real estate businesses.

■ EARNINGS

Compensation in the real estate field is based largely upon commission. Agents usually split commissions with the brokers who employ them, in return for providing the office space, advertising support, sales supervision, and the use of the broker's good name. When two or more agents are involved in a transaction (for example, one agent listing the property for sale and another selling it), the commission is usually divided between the two on the basis of an established formula. Agents can earn more if they both list and sell the property.

According to the U.S. Department of Labor, median annual earnings of salaried real estate agents, including commission, were $43,370 in May 2015. Salaries ranged from less than $21,780 to more than $110,560. Median annual earnings of salaried real estate brokers, including commission, were $56,860 in May 2015, with salaries ranging from less than $23,400 to $166,940 or higher.

Agents and brokers may supplement their incomes by appraising property, placing mortgages with private lenders, or selling insurance. Since earnings are irregular and economic conditions unpredictable, agents and brokers should maintain sufficient cash reserves for slack periods.

Real estate agents and brokers who work for a company usually receive benefits such as vacation days, sick leave, health and life insurance, and a savings and pension program. Those who are self-employed must provide their own benefits.

■ WORK ENVIRONMENT

One glance at the property advertisements in any newspaper will offer a picture of the high degree of competition found within the field of real estate. In addition to full-time workers, the existence of many part-time agents increases competition.

Beginning agents must accept the frustration inherent in the early months in the business. Earnings are often irregular before a new agent has built a client base and developed the skills needed to land sales.

After agents become established, many work over 40 hours a week, including evenings and weekends, to best cater to their clients' needs. Despite this, agents work on their own schedules and are free to take a day off when they choose. Some do much of their work out of their own homes. However, successful agents will spend little time in an office; they are busy showing properties to potential buyers or meeting with sellers to set up a listing.

Real estate positions are found in every part of the country but are concentrated in large urban areas and in smaller, rapidly growing communities. Regardless of the size of the community in which they work, good agents should know its economic life, the personal preferences of its citizens, and the demand for real estate.

CAREER LADDER

Real Estate Business Owner or Sales Manager

Real Estate Broker

Real Estate Agent

Real Estate Agent Trainee

■ EXPLORING

Contact local real estate brokers and agents for useful information on the field and to talk one-on-one with

A real estate agent greets a couple during a home viewing.
(Goodluz. Shutterstock.)

TOP-PAYING STATES FOR REAL ESTATE AGENTS, MAY 2015	FAST FACTS	

State	Mean $$$	# of Workers
New York	$100,090	6,500
Hawaii	$83,620	220
Massachusetts	$78,760	2,340
Illinois	$76,800	5,070
Colorado	$76,590	3,660

Source: Bureau of Labor Statistics

an employee about their job. You can also obtain information on licensing requirements from local real estate boards or from the real estate departments of each state. Securing part-time and summer employment in a real estate office will provide you with practical experience.

■ EDUCATION AND TRAINING REQUIREMENTS
High School

There are no standard educational requirements for the real estate field. However, high school courses in English, business, computer science, math, and a foreign language such as Spanish would help to prepare you for communicating with clients and handling sales.

Postsecondary Training

An increasing percentage of real estate agents and brokers have some college education. As property transactions have become more complex, many employers favor applicants with more education. Some colleges and universities offer associate's and bachelor's degrees in real estate, but mostly they offer certificates. Courses in psychology, economics, sociology, statistics, accounting, marketing, finance, business administration, and law are helpful. Learning a foreign language can also be useful in working with clients from other countries. Real estate associations at the national and state level also provide training. Some agents and brokers are required to participate in training programs provided by their employers.

The National Association of Realtors (NAR) offers a master of real estate degree via its REALTOR University. The following specializations are available: Residential Real Estate Sales, Marketing, and Management; Real Estate Association Management; Real Estate Asset and Property Management; Commercial Real Estate Investment and Analysis; and Real Estate Appraisal and Valuation Services. Contact the NAR for more information.

Certification

Many colleges and universities offer certificates in real estate. Contact schools in your area to learn more about available programs.

Other Education or Training

The National Association of Realtors and the Society of Industrial and Office Realtors offer a wealth of continuing education opportunities for real estate agents and brokers. Contact these organizations for more information.

■ CERTIFICATION, LICENSING, AND SPECIAL REQUIREMENTS
Certification or Licensing

The National Association of Realtors, Real Estate Buyer's Agent Council, Realtors Land Institute, Institute of Real Estate Management, Council of Residential Specialists, and the Society of Industrial and Office Realtors offer voluntary certification to real estate professionals. Contact these organizations for more information.

Every state (and the District of Columbia) requires that real estate agents and brokers be licensed. For the general license, most states require agents to have between 30 and 90 hours of classroom training, and pass a written examination on real estate fundamentals and relevant state laws. Prospective brokers must pass a more extensive examination and complete between 60 and 90 hours of classroom training. Additionally, many states require brokers to have one to three years' experience selling property or a formal degree in real estate.

State licenses are usually renewed annually without examination, but many states require agents to fulfill continuing education requirements in real estate. Agents who move to another state must qualify under the licensing laws of that state. To supplement minimum state requirements, many agents take courses in real estate principles, laws, financing, appraisal, and property development and management.

Other Requirements

In most states, real estat agents and brokers must be at least 18 years old.

■ EXPERIENCE, SKILLS, AND PERSONALITY TRAITS

No experience is needed to become a real estate agent, but sales experience is a definite plus. Brokers typically need one to three years of experience as a licensed sales agent to be eligible for licensing.

Successful brokers and agents must be willing to study the changing trends of the industry to keep their skills updated. Residential real estate agents must keep up with the latest trends in mortgage financing, construction, and community development. They must have a thorough knowledge of the housing market in their assigned communities so they can identify which neighborhoods will best fit their clients' needs and budgets, and they must be familiar with local zoning and tax laws. Agents and brokers must also be good negotiators to act as go-betweens between buyers and sellers.

In most cases, educational experience is less important than the right personality. Brokers want agents who possess a pleasant personality, exude honesty, and maintain a neat appearance. Agents must work with many different types of people and inspire their trust and confidence. They need to express themselves well and show enthusiasm to motivate customers. They should also be well organized and detail oriented, and have a good memory for names, faces, and business details.

■ EMPLOYMENT PROSPECTS
Employers
There are approximately 421,000 real estate agents and brokers currently employed in the United States; agents hold about 81 percent of the jobs. Many work part time, supplementing their income with additional jobs in law, finance, or other fields.

Agents work in small offices, larger organizations, or for themselves. (Nearly 51 percent of real estate agents and brokers are self-employed.) Opportunities exist at all levels, from large real estate firms specializing in commercial real estate to smaller, local offices that sell residential properties. Much of agents' work is independent; over time, they can develop their own client bases and set their own schedules. Many real estate agents and brokers work part time, supplementing their income with additional jobs in law, finance, or other fields.

Starting Out
The typical entry position in this field is as an agent working for a broker with an established office. Another opportunity may be through inside sales, such as with a construction firm building new housing developments. Prospective agents usually apply directly to local real estate firms or are referred through public and private employment services. Brokers looking to hire agents may run newspaper advertisements. Starting out, prospective agents often contact firms in their own communities, where their knowledge of area neighborhoods can work to their advantage.

The beginning agent must choose between the advantages of joining a small or a large organization. In a small office, the newcomer will train informally under an experienced agent. Their duties will be broad and varied but

TOP-PAYING STATES FOR REAL ESTATE BROKERS, MAY 2015

FAST FACTS

State	Mean $$$	#of Workers
District of Columbia	$148,730	150
New Hampshire	$132,600	190
Nevada	$121,440	330
Ohio	$119,680	790
Hawaii	$118,630	340

Source: Bureau of Labor Statistics

possibly menial. However, this is a good chance to learn all the basics of the business, including gaining familiarity with the databases used to locate properties or sources of financing. In larger firms, the new agent often proceeds through a more standardized training process and specializes in one aspect of the real estate field, such as commercial real estate, mortgage financing, or property management.

■ ADVANCEMENT PROSPECTS
While many successful agents develop professionally by expanding the quality and quantity of their services, others seek advancement by entering management or by specializing in residential or commercial real estate. An agent may enter management by becoming the head of a division of a large real estate firm. Other agents purchase an established real estate business, join one as a partner, or set up their own offices. Self-employed agents must meet state requirements and obtain a broker's license.

Agents who wish to specialize have a number of available options. They may develop a property management business. In return for a percentage of the gross receipts, *property managers* operate apartment houses or multiple-tenant business properties for their owners. Property managers are in charge of renting (including advertising, tenant relations, and collecting rents), building maintenance (heating, lighting, cleaning, and decorating), and accounting (financial recording and filing tax returns).

Agents can also become *appraisers*, estimating the current market value of land and buildings, or *real estate counselors*, advising clients on the suitability of available property. Experienced brokers can also join the real estate departments of major corporations or large government agencies.

■ OUTLOOK
The country's expanding population also creates additional demand for real estate services. A trend

toward mobility, usually among Americans in their prime working years, indicates a continued need for real estate professionals. In addition, a higher percentage of affluence among this working group indicates that more Americans will be able to own their own homes.

An increase in agents' use of technology, such as computers, smartphones, and databases, has greatly improved productivity. Real estate Web sites now allow agents and customers to view multiple property listings without leaving the office. However, the use of this technology may eliminate marginal jobs, such as part-time workers, who may not be able to invest in this technology and compete with full-time agents. Job growth is potentially limited by the fact that many potential customers are conducting their own searches for property using the Internet.

The field of real estate is easily affected by changes in the economy. Periods of prosperity bring a lot of business. Conversely, a downturn leads to a lower number of real estate transactions, resulting in fewer sales and commissions for agents and brokers. Beginning real estate agents and brokers face keen competition from those who are well established, and more experienced in the field. Ambitious people with strong selling and communication skills will fare the best in the job market.

■ UNIONS AND ASSOCIATIONS

Real estate agents and brokers are not represented by unions. The major professional association for agents and brokers in the United States is the National Association of Realtors. It offers publications, continuing education classes, networking events, industry research, and other resources to its members. Other helpful organizations include the Association of Real Estate License Law Officials, National Association of Exclusive Buyer Agents, and the Society of Industrial and Office Realtors. Agents and brokers in Canada are represented by the Canadian Real Estate Association.

■ TIPS FOR ENTRY

1. Visit SelectLeaders.com and http://www.reales tatejobsite.com/ for job listings.
2. Join professional associations such as the National Association of Realtors to access industry publications, training and networking opportunities, and job listings.
3. Ask agents in your area to suggest possible employers and job opportunities.
4. Obtain sales experience in order to make yourself more attractive to potential employers.

5. Look around your neighborhood to see which realtors have the most homes for sale. These agencies might offer the best hiring prospects.

■ FOR MORE INFORMATION

For information on licensing, contact
Association of Real Estate License Law Officials
150 North Wacker Drive, Suite 920
Chicago, IL 60606-1682
Tel: (312) 300-4800
Fax: (312) 300-4807
E-mail: support@arello.org
http://www.arello.org

For information on careers in Canada, contact
Canadian Real Estate Association
200 Catherine Street, 6th Floor
Ottawa, ON K2P 2K9
Canada
Tel: (800) 842-2732; (613) 237-7111
Fax: (613) 234-2567
E-mail: info@crea.ca
http://crea.ca

For career information, contact
National Association of Exclusive Buyer Agents
1481 N. Eliseo Felix Way, #100
Avondale, Arizona 85323
Tel: (800) 986-2322; (623) 399-4699
E-mail: naeba@naeba.info
http://www.naeba.org

For information on state and local associations, professional designations, real estate courses, and publications, contact
National Association of Realtors
430 North Michigan Avenue
Chicago, IL 60611-4087
Tel: (800) 874-6500
http://www.realtor.org

For information on commercial real estate, contact
Society of Industrial and Office Realtors
1201 New York Avenue, NW, Suite 350
Washington, D.C. 20005-6126
Tel: (202) 449-8200
Fax: (202) 216-9325
E-mail: admin@sior.com
http://www.sior.com

Real Estate Clerks

OVERVIEW

Real estate clerks perform a variety of clerical tasks that help real estate-related businesses, such as realtors and construction firms, run smoothly. Approximately 34,800 clerks are employed in the offices of real estate agents and brokers in the United States.

HISTORY

There has always been a need for clerks in the real estate industry, but technological advances (including the Internet and the use of databases such as the Multiple Listing Service) have increased the need for qualified clerks. Today, clerks play a key role in the real estate industry—helping construction managers, realtors, real estate developers, and other industry professionals do their jobs quickly and efficiently.

THE JOB

Real estate clerks perform a wide variety of tasks that help real estate agents, real estate developers, construction managers, construction inspectors, building managers, and other real estate professionals do their jobs. These tasks include maintaining files; sorting mail; drafting correspondence; keeping records; typing copies of lists of rental or sales properties for submission to real estate databases or for listing in newspaper want ads; answering telephone calls about available properties or a need for services; making photocopies; preparing mailings (including announcements for open houses or rent notices to tenants); operating office equipment such as photocopiers, fax machines, and switchboards; computing, classifying, recording, and verifying financial data; and producing and processing bills and collecting payments from customers.

In small companies, real estate clerks perform most or all of the aforementioned duties. In larger companies, clerks may have more specialized duties. The following paragraphs detail the specialties available for people who work as clerks in the real estate industry:

File clerks review and classify letters, documents, articles, and other information and then file this material so it can be quickly retrieved at a later time. This information may be in electronic or paper format.

Billing clerks keep records and up-to-date accounts of all business transactions. They type and send bills for services or products and update files to reflect payments. They also review incoming invoices to ensure that the requested products have been delivered and that the billing statements are accurate and paid on time.

Bookkeeping clerks keep systematic records and current accounts of financial transactions for real estate management companies, and developers. The bookkeeping records of a firm or business are a vital part of its operational procedures because these records reflect the assets and the liabilities, as well as the profits and losses, of the operation.

EARNINGS

Salaries for real estate clerks vary depending on the size and geographic location of the company and the skills of the worker. Some new clerks may only earn a low wage ($9.28 an hour, or $19,300 annually) until they gain experience. The U.S. Department of Labor reports that clerks who are employed in the offices of real estate agents and brokers earned mean annual salaries of $31,820 in May 2016.

Benefits for real estate clerks depend on the employer; however, they usually include such items as health insurance, retirement or 401(k) plans, and paid vacation days.

WORK ENVIRONMENT

Most real estate clerks work an average of 37 to 40 hours per week. Clerks in the real estate industry may work evenings and weekends, as much of the business conducted in this field occurs during nontraditional business hours. Although clerks perform a variety of tasks, the job itself can be fairly routine and repetitive. Clerks often interact with accountants, real estate agents, and other office personnel and may work under close supervision.

EXPLORING

A good way to learn more about the work of clerks is to perform clerical or bookkeeping tasks for a school club or organization. Your school may also have a school-to-work program that can provide you with part-time

---

QUICK FACTS

ALTERNATE TITLE(S)
Billing Clerks, Bookkeeping Clerks, File Clerks

DUTIES
Perform a variety of clerical tasks such as filing, data entry, and billing

SALARY RANGE
$19,300 to $31,820 to $50,410+

WORK ENVIRONMENT
Primarily Indoors

BEST GEOGRAPHIC LOCATION(S)
Opportunities exist in all regions

MINIMUM EDUCATION LEVEL
High School Diploma

SCHOOL SUBJECTS
Business, English, Mathematics

EXPERIENCE
None required

PERSONALITY TRAITS
Conventional, Helpful, Organized

SKILLS
Interpersonal, Math, Organizational

CERTIFICATION OR LICENSING
Recommended

SPECIAL REQUIREMENTS
None

EMPLOYMENT PROSPECTS
Good

ADVANCEMENT PROSPECTS
Good

OUTLOOK
Little Change or More Slowly than the Average

NOC
1411

O*NET-SOC
43-9061.00

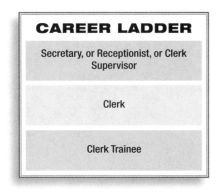

CAREER LADDER

Secretary, or Receptionist, or Clerk Supervisor

Clerk

Clerk Trainee

on-the-job training with local businesses, such as real estate agencies, newspapers and magazines that focus on the real estate industry, law firms that specialize in real estate, and financial institutions. You might also ask your school counselor to help arrange an information interview with a clerk—especially one who is employed in the real estate industry.

■ EDUCATION AND TRAINING REQUIREMENTS
High School
Take courses in English, mathematics, computer science (especially database management), and as many business-related subjects, such as keyboarding and bookkeeping, as possible to prepare for this career.

Postsecondary Education
A high school diploma is usually sufficient to enter this field, but clerks who have received postsecondary training covering office machine operation, the use of computers, and bookkeeping will have the best employment prospects. These courses are offered by business schools and community colleges.

Other Education or Training
The Association of Executive and Administrative Professionals and the International Association of Administrative Professionals offer classes and seminars for clerks and other administrative professionals. Topics

Real estate offices often hire clerks to assist with paperwork and administrative tasks. (Leondardo da. Shutterstock.)

include Microsoft Excel, Microsoft Word, personal productivity, office politics, business etiquette, and basic administrative assistant fundamentals. Contact these organizations for more information.

■ CERTIFICATION, LICENSING, AND SPECIAL REQUIREMENTS
Certification or Licensing
Although there is no specific certification available for real estate clerks, the International Association of Administrative Professionals offers certification for general administrative professionals (including office clerks). Contact the association for more information.

■ EXPERIENCE, SKILLS, AND PERSONALITY TRAITS
No experience is needed to become a real estate clerk, but any experience you can obtain in an office setting will be useful.

Successful real estate clerks have strong computer skills, are excellent communicators, and are able to concentrate on repetitive tasks for long periods of time. They also have the ability to work well with others and are dependable, trustworthy, and have a neat personal appearance.

■ EMPLOYMENT PROSPECTS
Employers
Approximately 34,800 clerks are employed in the offices of real estate agents and brokers. Other major employers include real estate developers, finance and insurance companies, advertising agencies, local government, health care and social assistance organizations, administrative and support services companies, and professional, scientific, and technical services industries.

Starting Out
To secure an entry-level position, contact real estate-related companies directly. Newspaper ads and temporary-work agencies are also good sources for finding jobs in this field.

■ ADVANCEMENT PROSPECTS
Real estate clerks typically advance by learning new skills and being tasked with more complicated assignments. Clerks who demonstrate leadership ability may be asked to supervise other clerks, while others may be promoted to different clerical positions, such as secretary or receptionist. Some clerks may earn a college degree or other specialized training in order to advance to professional

positions such as accountant, real estate agent, or construction manager.

OUTLOOK

The U.S. Department of Labor reports that employment for office clerks who work in the real estate industry is expected to grow more slowly than the average for all occupations through 2024 due to difficult economic times that have slowed home and business sales throughout the United States. Clerks who pursue jobs in industries (such as health care or professional, scientific, and technical services) that have a more promising employment outlook will have the best opportunities.

Despite this prediction, there will still be many jobs available for real estate clerks due to the size of this field and a high turnover rate. Opportunities will be best for clerks who have strong computer skills and knowledge of business software that is commonly used in the real estate industry.

UNIONS AND ASSOCIATIONS

Real estate clerks are not represented by unions, but they can obtain useful resources and professional support from the Association of Executive and Administrative Professionals, International Association of Administrative Professionals, and National Association of Realtors.

TIPS FOR ENTRY

1. Visit the following Web sites for job listings: http://SelectLeaders.com and http://www.flipdog.com/jobs/usa/real-estate. Professional associations also often offer job listings at their Web sites.
2. Obtain certification from the International Association of Administrative Professionals to improve your chances of landing a job.
3. Participate in internships or part-time jobs that are arranged by your college's career services office.
4. Apply for any type of entry-level job in the real estate industry.

FOR MORE INFORMATION

For information on seminars, conferences, and news on the industry, contact

Association of Executive and Administrative Professionals
900 South Washington Street, Suite G-13
Falls Church, VA 22046-4009
Tel: (703) 237-8616
Fax: (703) 533-1153
E-mail: headquarters@theaeap.com
http://www.theaeap.com

REAL ESTATE OFFICE ADMINISTRATION   LEARN MORE ABOUT IT

Clark, James L., and Lyn R. Clark. *HOW 13: A Handbook for Office Professionals,* 13th ed. Independence, Ky.: Cengage Learning, 2013.
Cooperman, Susan H. *Professional Office Procedures,* 5th ed. Upper Saddle River, N.J.: Prentice Hall, 2011.
Oliverio, Mary Ellen, William R. Pasewark, and Bonnie R. White. *The Office: Procedures and Technology,* 6th ed. Independence, Ky.: Cengage Learning, 2012.
Reilly, John W., and Marie S. Spodek. *The Language of Real Estate,* 7th ed. Fort Lauderdale, Fla.: Dearborn Real Estate Education/Kaplan, Inc., 2013.

For information on certification, contact

International Association of Administrative Professionals
10502 North Ambassador Drive, Suite 100
Kansas City, MO 64153-1278
Tel: (816) 891-6600
Fax: (816) 891-9118
http://www.iaap-hq.org

For information on the real estate industry, contact

National Association of Realtors
430 North Michigan Avenue
Chicago, IL 60611-4087
Tel: (800) 874-6500
http://www.realtor.org

For free office career and salary information and job listings, visit

OfficeTeam
Tel: (877) 358-9770
https://www.roberthalf.com/officeteam

Real Estate Developers

OVERVIEW

Real estate developers envision, organize, and execute construction or renovation projects for commercial or private use. This process involves negotiations with property owners, real estate agents, investors, lending institutions such as banks and insurance companies, architects, lawyers, general contractors, government officials, and other

QUICK FACTS

ALTERNATE TITLE(S)
Real Estate Entrepreneurs

DUTIES
Develop land for residential or
commercial use; negotiate
with property owners, real
estate agents, investors, and
lending institutions; oversee
finance and project planning;
hire and manage contractors
and other workers

SALARY RANGE
$60,000 to $90,000 to
$1,000,000+

WORK ENVIRONMENT
Indoors/Outdoors

BEST GEOGRAPHIC LOCATION(S)
The best opportunities are
available in urban areas,
although jobs can be found
throughout the country

MINIMUM EDUCATION LEVEL
High School Diploma

SCHOOL SUBJECTS
Business, Economics,
Mathematics

EXPERIENCE
Experience as an assistant highly
recommended

PERSONALITY TRAITS
Enterprising, Organized,
Outgoing

SKILLS
Building/Trades, Business
Management, Financial

CERTIFICATION OR LICENSING
None

SPECIAL REQUIREMENTS
None

EMPLOYMENT PROSPECTS
Fair

ADVANCEMENT PROSPECTS
Fair

OUTLOOK
About as Fast as the Average

NOC
0121

O*NET-SOC
N/A

interested parties. Developers may work independently as consultants or in partnership with other professionals involved in real estate development.

HISTORY

The United States is a relatively young country without a long history of densely populated cities. In Europe, however, there is evidence of urban areas from as far back as 3,000 years ago. In areas of early Roman settlement, archaeologists have discovered the remnants of street grids, sewage lines, and uniform construction indicating some level of formal planning. Since the Middle Ages, cities like Paris have had municipal regulations governing the placement and use of buildings.

Such planning and regulations emerge when many people try to live harmoniously in a limited space. In these situations, land is expensive. Construction of homes, roads for travel, or public buildings for commerce and government requires a substantial investment of money. The developer is the entrepreneur who sees an opportunity to make money by providing services, in the form of buildings or infrastructure, to the community. The developer's role is to envision development, organize investors to fund land purchase and construction, and oversee the project.

Individuals have played this role in much the same way as long as people have lived in settled communities. What has changed, and what continues to change, are the zoning laws and building codes regulating development and the tax laws affecting the organization of the development entity.

THE JOB

The developer's actual day-to-day activities vary depending on the type and size of the project. A developer may be involved in purchasing 500 suburban acres and developing 1,000 condominiums, a couple of parks, a golf course, and a small shopping center with a grocery store, full-service dry cleaner, video rental store, and health club. Or a developer may renovate and remodel an existing structure, such as a warehouse, for use as a restaurant and office space.

Whether a group of investors approaches the developer or the developer searches out investors, the first step is to structure the development entity, a group made up of the project owner (the person or group who will receive the profits or suffer the losses from the proposed development), the investors who put up the initial equity funds, and the developer. In many cases, the developer is the owner. These individuals may establish a development entity with only one owner, a partnership with a lead owner, a limited partnership, or a corporation that sells stock to stockholders.

The legal definitions of each type of entity vary according to locale, and the benefits and risks of each are quite different. The developer, who facilitates the process of structuring the contract, is concerned with three main issues—managing risk, gathering equity to facilitate borrowing money, and creating a functioning structure with a limited number of people involved in decision-making.

The developer's job at the beginning of a project has been compared to pitching a tent in high wind—the toughest thing is getting the first corner nailed down. In negotiating with potential investors, the developer brings all interested parties to the table to secure an initial commitment of equity funds. Without equity, the developer is unable to approach banks or insurance companies for loans to complete the project.

The developer might come to the table with $100,000 of personal money to invest—or none. With an excellent track record and a solid proposal, the developer's involvement in the project may be enough to secure the confidence of potential investors. But the developer must show a willingness to protect these investors by creating a development entity that exposes them to only reasonable risk.

Most investors want to risk only the equity money they contribute. In other words, if the project fails, they do not want to be held liable for all the money lost. The contract therefore must protect their other assets, such as their homes, savings accounts, and other investments, in case of a default on the loans. The contract must be written in such a way that the investors are willing to accept the risk involved.

After securing the equity necessary to convince financial institutions to participate in the project, the developer approaches these institutions (primarily banks and insurance companies) to secure financing.

Most development projects require both short-term and long-term financing. Banks often provide the money to buy land and complete construction. However, to receive this short-term financing, sometimes called a construction loan, the developer must already have equity funds from the investors. The equity money might equal from 10 to 40 percent of the total amount of the loan.

Insurance companies are the most common providers of long-term financing, which is used to pay off the construction loan. Long-term financing commitments are based on the economic projections of the completed development and usually must be obtained before securing short-term financing. Occasionally one institution will provide both the short-term and long-term financing, but this is less likely to happen with larger projects.

Another participant in real estate financing is the government. Sometimes a municipal government will issue a bond to raise money from taxes. These funds may provide long-term financing to a private developer for the construction of a stadium, for example, or for some infrastructure improvement, such as widening the streets. Municipal governments frequently participate in projects to develop run-down areas of the city. In exchange for shouldering some of the financial risk, the city stands to benefit from the increased productivity of the renovated neighborhood.

Before receiving a building permit, the real estate developer may have to complete impact studies to assess how the proposed project will affect the community and the environment. He or she may also have to meet with the zoning board if there are regulations that the new building will be unable to meet.

At this stage, the project needs an architect. The architect's first job usually is to hire a structural engineer and a mechanical engineer. Together they create the building plans, which the developer submits to the building department.

This process of creating the plans involves consideration of economics, aesthetic architectural concerns, building codes, and other legal constraints imposed by the community. This is one of the most exciting and important times in the development process. Through the competition of the interests of all the involved parties, the best use for the site evolves, and the project is born.

While waiting for the building permit to be issued, the developer also puts the building plans out for bids

from general contractors. The general contractor selected for the job hires subcontractors, such as carpenters, plumbers, roofers, and drywallers.

In applying for the building permit and preparing to break ground on the construction site, developers spend a lot of time dealing with government regulations. They must make sure that they understand and meet building codes designed to ensure the safety of future occupants. Windows in a residential building, for example, must have a certain number of square feet for light and a certain number for ventilation.

Developers must be aware not only of building codes but also of laws affecting construction. New buildings, for example, must meet handicap access codes to comply with the Americans with Disabilities Act.

On large projects, such as the development of a skyscraper, the developer will contract out much of the work, such as public relations and advertising, the completion of impact studies, and the general contractor's job. On smaller projects, however, the developer may perform some or all of these functions.

As general contractor, the developer is involved on a daily basis with work at the construction site. If someone else is hired as general contractor, the developer may only be involved at weekly construction meetings, where the architect, engineers, and various subcontractors discuss progress and changes necessary in the plans.

In either case, the developer, who is ultimately responsible for the success or failure of the project, must be knowledgeable about all aspects of the development process and capable of hiring a group of people who can work successfully as a team. Though the developer may or may not be an investor who stands to lose money, the developer's career is on the line with every project.

If a developer secures city approval and necessary funds to construct a new office building in a highly visible spot, the whole city may be watching. The local government officials may have used their influence to change zoning laws in favor of the project. Therefore, their reputations may also be riding on the building's success. If, for example, the construction costs exceed the initial estimates, and the developer is unable to raise the additional money to cover the costs, construction on the building may be halted at any stage, and the empty shell may stand for years as an eyesore in the community.

CAREER LADDER

Developer of Large Properties

Developer

Developer Trainee or Assistant

An architect discusses building plans with a real estate developer. (bikeriderlondon. Shutterstock.)

Failure to complete such projects successfully inhibits the developer's ability to secure investors and government cooperation in the future. Depending on the terms of the developer's contract, it may also mean that the developer is never compensated for the time and work spent on the project.

Once the project is complete, the developer's role depends on the specifications set forth by the development entity. With a high-rise residential building, for example, the developer may be involved in selling or renting the apartments. As an owner in the project, the developer may be involved in the management of rental property for many years.

■ EARNINGS

There is no set pay scale for real estate developers. How much they make depends on their skill and experience, the size of the projects on which they work, the structure established for their payment in the development entity contract, and the successful completion of the project. Some real estate developers become millionaires. An exceptional few become billionaires, such as President Donald Trump,

chairman and CEO of the Trump Organization and founder of Trump Entertainment Resorts, who developed properties across the United States and overseas before being elected president of the United States.

Sometimes, developers are contracted by a group of individual investors or a company to manage a project. In this case they may work out a consulting agreement with a certain secured fee up front, preset fees paid throughout the duration of the project, and some percentage of the profits once the project is complete. Or the agreement may contain some combination of these payment options.

A less experienced developer will often shoulder more risk on a project to gain expertise and complete work that will improve the developer's reputation. In these instances, developers may be undercompensated or not paid at all for their time and effort if the project fails.

In March 2015, PayScale.com reported that real estate development managers had a median salary of approximatly $90,000. Salaries ranged from $60,000 to $146,000. Developers of large properties can earn millions of dollars annually.

■ WORK ENVIRONMENT

Real estate developers are often highly visible individuals in the community. It is important that they have excellent communication skills, be able to work with all kinds of people, and enjoy the speculative nature of their business.

Developers spend a great deal of time negotiating with executives in banks and insurance companies, government officials, and private or corporate business investors. A certain professionalism and comfort in executive situations is necessary for success.

However, some developers report to the job site every day, don a hard hat, and oversee the work of roofers, plumbers, and electricians. The developer must be flexible enough to adjust to the job's varying demands.

In addition to staying in touch with investors and overseeing the project, developers sometimes may need to respond to the public and the media. Controversial, high-profile projects often put the developer under a spotlight, requiring excellent public relations skills.

Real estate developers, because of the complexity of their jobs and the often large sums of money at stake, work under a great deal of pressure and stress. While the level of risk and the potential profit depend on the developer's role in the development entity, those who like a steady schedule with a dependable paycheck may not be well suited to this career.

Hours can be long and frequently vary with the type of project and stage of development. Developers may have to attend city council meetings or neighborhood meetings in the evening if they are seeking changes in zoning laws before applying for a building permit. In addition to having the potential to earn a large sum of money, developers enjoy the satisfaction of seeing a project evolve from its inception through various stages of planning and finally into a finished, usable structure.

Though their work depends on the cooperation of other individuals and organizations, developers also enjoy a certain level of independence and flexibility in their lifestyles. As entrepreneurs, they shoulder a lot of personal risk for their businesses, but this brings with it great opportunities to do creative work and positively influence their communities while potentially earning a handsome profit.

■ EXPLORING

Read the real estate section of the local newspaper and follow the building and development activities in the community to gain exposure to this industry. A local librarian should also be able to refer you to books and magazines about real estate development. Sometimes a teacher or school counselor will be able to arrange for a developer or other real estate professional to visit and talk about his or her work.

You can also prepare for your career by working in the offices of the following professionals: real estate developers, lawyers practicing within the real estate industry, architects, and general contractors. Spending time in any of these offices will introduce you to the general milieu of the real estate developer's world. The early exposure can also help you decide in which of these areas you most want to develop expertise.

You can gain good experience in certain aspects of real estate development by doing public relations, publicity, or advertising work and participating in fund-raising campaigns for school and community organizations. Volunteering with a housing advocacy organization, such as Habitat for Humanity, may provide opportunities to learn about home construction, bank financing, and legal contracts. To gain confidence and develop a business sense, take on leadership roles at school and in extracurricular activities, such as the student council or the business club.

■ EDUCATION AND TRAINING REQUIREMENTS
High School

There are no specific educational requirements or certifications for becoming a real estate developer, but many developers have college degrees, and some have advanced degrees. While you are in high school, you can prepare for a career in real estate development by pursuing a

DEVELOPING REAL ESTATE   LEARN MORE ABOUT IT

Brueggeman, William, and Jeffrey Fisher. *Real Estate Finance and Investments,* 14th ed. New York: McGraw-Hill/Irwin, 2010.

Long, Charles. *Finance for Real Estate Development.* Washington, D.C.: Urban Land Institute, 2011.

Peiser, Richard, and David Hamilton. *Professional Real Estate Development: The ULI Guide to the Business.* Washington, D.C.: Urban Land Institute, 2012.

Rybczynski, Witold. *Last Harvest: From Cornfield to New Town: Real Estate Development from George Washington to the Builders of the Twenty-First Century, and Why We Live in Houses Anyway.* New York: Scribner, 2008.

broad-based liberal arts curriculum that will prepare you for a college education. In addition, courses in business, economics, finance, mathematics, speech communications, drafting, and shop will be helpful.

Postsecondary Training

Schools generally do not offer a specific curriculum that leads to a career as a real estate developer. Because the position requires a broad base of knowledge as well as some experience in the business community, most people become real estate developers after leaving an earlier career.

There are a few schools that offer undergraduate degrees in real estate, usually as a concentration within a general business degree program. Ohio State University, for example, offers a bachelor's degree specialization in real estate. There are even fewer graduate degree programs in real estate development, such as the University of Southern California's master's degree in real estate development. The Massachusetts Institute of Technology offers a one-year master's degree program in real estate development. Some schools offer master of business administration programs with a concentration in real estate.

Graduate degrees in law, business, and architecture are among the most beneficial to the real estate developer. If you are interested in pursuing an advanced degree in one of these areas, you should complete the necessary preparatory work as an undergraduate.

The National Association of Realtors (NAR) offers a master of real estate degree via its REALTOR University. The following specializations are available: Commercial Real Estate Investment and Analysis; Residential Real Estate Sales, Marketing, and Management; Real Estate Association Management; Real Estate Asset and Property

Management; and Real Estate Appraisal and Valuation Services. Contact the NAR for more information.

To pursue a law degree, you need a strong background in the liberal arts, including English, philosophy, history, and government. Good preparation for a master's degree in business includes course work in finance, marketing, accounting, business communications, and higher-level mathematics. An advanced degree in architecture requires an emphasis on drafting, mathematics, engineering, and physics.

Other Education or Training

The National Association of Realtors offers continuing education opportunities for real estate professionals. Contact the association for more information.

■ CERTIFICATION, LICENSING, AND SPECIAL REQUIREMENTS
Certification or Licensing

There are no certification or licensing requirements for real estate developers.

■ EXPERIENCE, SKILLS, AND PERSONALITY TRAITS

Experience working in real estate development as an assistant is highly recommended for aspiring real estate developers.

Real estate development is regarded as one of the most challenging careers in the real estate industry. You must have the ability to speculate about the economy and envision profitable ventures in addition to having a broad knowledge of the legal, financial, political, and construction issues related to development. Consequently, a background in law, architecture, or general contracting can be highly beneficial.

It is useful to have a working knowledge of both zoning laws and building codes. While it is the architect's primary responsibility to ensure that the plans ultimately submitted to the building department will be approved, the knowledgeable developer may decide it is appropriate to seek a variance in zoning or code. This is most common with non-safety issues, such as the number of parking spaces required. A municipality might grant a variance if you present a convincing case that the project will create a significant number of jobs for the community.

You must also understand the marketplace. For this reason, experience in appraising, leasing, or selling real estate can prove very helpful. Real estate brokers who lease office space often have excellent contacts and knowledge for entering the development business. They know where the potential tenants are, and they understand the issues involved in developing large buildings

for commercial use. You must also grasp the basics of finance to structure the development entity effectively.

■ EMPLOYMENT PROSPECTS
Employers

Real estate developers often work independently or open offices in communities that have property with the potential for development. The activity of the real estate marketplace will dictate the number of opportunities in a given community.

Starting Out

There is no specific way to become a real estate developer. Successful real estate developers are always central to the project, facilitating communication among the various participants. This often requires finely tuned diplomatic skills. Their proven track record, professional manner, and influence in the real estate world are their biggest assets. They have the ability to sell ideas and secure large sums of money from investors and lending institutions.

Most developers do not begin their careers in this field. They frequently have backgrounds as lawyers, architects, real estate brokers, or general contractors, positions that allow them to gain the expertise and contacts necessary for success in real estate development.

Many real estate developers secure work because they have an established reputation. Their contacts and knowledge in a particular community or type of real estate allow them to work more effectively than others. But developers are also successful because of their abilities in analyzing the marketplace, structuring solid investment proposals, facilitating the creation of the development entity, and overseeing projects.

■ ADVANCEMENT PROSPECTS

The real estate developer is really at the top of the profession. Advancement involves larger, more prestigious projects and earning more money. Such achievements may take several years. It is important to keep in mind that even the most successful developers suffer setbacks when projects fail. For those not-so-successful developers, such setbacks can end a career.

■ OUTLOOK

The outlook for real estate developers is subject to the fluctuations of the general economy. In the early-to-mid 2000s, economic conditions were excellent for real estate developers. Record-low interest rates roused many formerly depressed areas of the country to renewed economic vigor. But housing prices declined in 2006 and 2007, which, along with other factors, caused the housing market to crash in late 2008. Many attribute the recent financial crisis in the United States to the real estate bubble, which occurred when housing and real estate values increased at a rate that outpaced income levels. Real estate prices were then drastically reduced. But economic conditions are never fixed or stable. In addition, the real estate market can be quite strong in some parts of the country and weak in others. The U.S. Department of Labor does not provide information about real estate developers specifically, but does predict average employment growth for property, real estate, and community association managers. Because of the growing population, more people are living in developments managed by third-party property management companies. Opportunities are expected to be the best in the development of apartment buildings, condominiums, homeowner associations, and senior housing.

■ UNIONS AND ASSOCIATIONS

Real estate developers are not represented by unions, but they can obtain useful resources and professional support from the National Association of Realtors.

■ TIPS FOR ENTRY

1. For real estate industry job listings, visit: http://www.selectleaders.com and http://www.flipdog.com/jobs/usa/real-estate.
2. Participate in internships with a real estate developer that are arranged by your college's career services office.
3. Apply for entry-level jobs with real estate developers. Take advantage of these opportunities to make networking contacts and learn as much as you can about the industry.

■ FOR MORE INFORMATION

For information about educational programs, publications, and industry-related events, visit

MIT Center for Real Estate
77 Massachusetts Avenue, Building 9-343
Cambridge, MA 02139-4307
Tel: (617) 253-4373
Fax: (617) 258-6991
E-mail: mit-cre@mit.edu
http://mitcre.mit.edu

For information on the real estate industry, contact

National Association of Realtors
430 North Michigan Avenue
Chicago, IL 60611-4087
Tel: (800) 874-6500
http://www.realtor.org

Visit these Web sites for industry information.

RealEstateDeveloper.com
http://www.realestatedeveloper.com

The Real Estate Library
E-mail: mschaffer@relibrary.com
http://www.relibrary.com

Real Estate Educators

■ OVERVIEW

Real estate educators, or r*eal estate teachers,* provide postsecondary instruction to students wishing to enter the real estate industry. They also offer continuing education opportunities or training to those already committed to a real estate career. They teach in colleges and universities, as well as in smaller classroom settings such as park districts, for-profit proprietary schools, conferences, and real estate corporations. Many belong to the Real Estate Educators Association, which serves the interests of real estate teachers nationwide.

■ HISTORY

In American colonial times, organized adult education was started to help people make up for schooling missed as children or to help people prepare for jobs. Apprenticeships were an early form of vocational education in the American colonies as individuals were taught a craft by working with a skilled person in a particular field.

Peak periods in adult education typically occurred during times of large-scale immigration. Evening schools filled with foreign-born persons eager to learn the language and culture of their new home and to prepare for the tests necessary for citizenship.

In 1911, Wisconsin established the first State Board of Vocational and Adult Education in the country, and in 1917 the federal government supported the continuing education movement by funding vocational training in public schools for individuals over the age of 14. Immediately after World War II, the federal government took another large stride in financial support of adult and vocational education by creating the G.I. Bill of Rights, which provided money for veterans to pursue further job training.

Today, colleges and universities, vocational high schools, private trade schools, private businesses, and other organizations offer adults the opportunity to prepare for a specific occupation or pursue personal enrichment. Real estate, with its many opportunities, is a popular choice. Today, real estate education is available throughout the United States, in different disciplines and venues. Many schools' real estate curriculum is accredited by either the National Association of Realtors or meets licensure requirements as dictated by the state in which the schools are located.

■ THE JOB

Real estate education classes take place in a variety of settings, such as high schools, colleges and universities, community centers, and businesses. The responsibilities of a real estate teacher are similar to those of a schoolteacher and include planning and conducting lectures, grading homework, evaluating students, writing and preparing reports, and counseling students.

When employed at colleges or universities, real estate educators are referred to as *instructors* or *professors*. They hold an advanced degree in real estate or related field, such as business or law. In addition, many have years of practical real estate experience. This expertise and insight adds greatly to the instruction they provide their students. Students who complete these types of programs graduate with an undergraduate or graduate degree in real estate, or a business degree with a concentration in real estate.

A larger number of real estate educators teach at community colleges, vocational schools, for-profit real estate schools, or park districts. Many, but not all, educators at this level hold a college degree in real estate or business. Others obtain their positions solely on the merit of their career experience. They may teach classes for college credit towards a certificate

or associate's degree. Others may teach a one-session adult enrichment class or noncredit courses lasting for an entire semester. They may teach classes pertaining to property appraisal standards and ethics, real estate law, mortgage brokering, commercial property management, or countless other topics. Educators at this level may also prepare students for exams needed to obtain a real estate broker's license or property appraiser's license. They may teach certification classes such as those needed to become a home inspector.

Many real estate teachers are also employed by real estate corporations to provide their staff additional education or training. The Real Estate Educators Association (REAA) estimates that between 5,000 to 6,000 educators are employed throughout the United States to provide agents and brokers information on the latest trends and developments in contract law, mortgage financing and disclosure, and other topics. Other real estate teachers are tapped to provide sales agents additional training to boost job performance.

Well-known and respected professionals in the real estate industry are often contracted by associations or corporations to teach seminars at conferences and training sessions. Their advice, approach, and experience are often inspirational to those still climbing the real estate corporate ladder.

Whether teaching in higher education or a continuing education classroom, real estate teachers, in addition to giving lectures, assign textbook readings and homework assignments. They prepare and administer exams and grade essays and presentations. Real estate teachers also meet with students individually to discuss class progress and grades. Some courses are conducted as part of a long-distance education program (traditionally known as correspondence courses). Many of these classes are now taught online. For these classes, teachers prepare course materials, assignments, and work schedules to be sent to students, and then grade the work when the students turn it in.

■ EARNINGS

Earnings vary widely according to the subject, the number of courses taught, the teacher's experience, and the geographic region where the institution is located. According to the U.S. Department of Labor, self-enrichment education teachers earned an average salary of $36,680 in May 2015. The lowest paid 10 percent of these workers made less than $19,050, while the highest paid 10 percent earned $73,610 or more.

Because many real estate teachers are employed part time, they are often paid by the hour or by the course, with no health insurance or other benefits. Hourly rates range from $9 to $35.

Benefits for full-time workers include paid vacation, health, disability, life insurance, and retirement or pension plans. Some employers also offer profit-sharing plans. Self-employed teachers must provide their own benefits.

WORK ENVIRONMENT

Working conditions vary according to the type of class being taught, the location, and the number of students participating. Courses are usually taught in a classroom setting but may also be in a work setting, conference room, or online. Those teaching at conferences or training real estate professionals at their offices often travel to the conference or work site. Class sizes vary, ranging from one-on-one instruction to large lectures attended by many individuals.

High school and college real estate teachers only work nine or 10 months a year, with summers off. Part-time teachers work 20 hours or less, depending on how many classes they teach. Some real estate teachers, especially those employed in nonacademic settings, primarily work in the evenings or on weekends, though many corporate trainers will work during regular office hours.

EXPLORING

Some high schools offer real estate classes as part of their business curriculum. If this is the case at your school, enroll in such classes and take the initiative to discuss your career choice with the teacher. This is a great way to learn about the highs and lows of the industry, plus you'll get a professional's opinion on your future goals.

Registering for a continuing education or vocational education course at your local park district or community college is another way of discovering the skills and disciplines needed to succeed in this field.

Are you wondering if you have what it takes to be a teacher? Try volunteering in your school's peer tutoring program. Not only will you be introduced to the requirements of teaching, but also you'll more than likely earn community service points needed to graduate high school. You could also volunteer to assist in special educational activities at a nursing home, church, synagogue, mosque, or community center.

EDUCATION AND TRAINING REQUIREMENTS
High School

While in high school, you should take college preparatory classes such as business, English, math, history, and government. Speech and communications courses will help you prepare for speaking in front of groups of people. Writing skills are very important because you'll be preparing reports, lesson plans, and grading essays. Take classes such as English and social studies, which often require written reports to help you perfect your research and writing skills. Teachers use computers to do research, write reports, calculate and report grades, as well as to conduct online lessons. Increase your computer comfort level by taking all the computer classes your school has to offer.

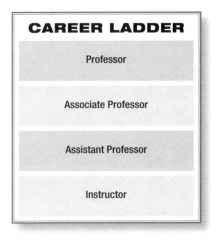

CAREER LADDER

Professor

Associate Professor

Assistant Professor

Instructor

Postsecondary Education

Before becoming a real estate teacher, you'll need to gain some professional experience in this area. A bachelor's degree is often required in real estate, business, or a related field, though some colleges and universities will

Real estate educators teach classes on property appraisal and marketing, mortgage brokering, and more. (auremar. Shutterstock.)

SURVEY SAYS

DID YOU KNOW?

More than 8 in 10 Americans believe that purchasing a home is a good financial decision, and 68 percent believe that now is a good time to buy a home. Also more than half of renters put owning their own home at the top of their priority list. This is up significantly from just three years ago. The feeling among Americans polled is that the housing market will continue to improve, with 89 percent expecting real estate sales to increase or at least remain the same.

Source: Housing Pulse Survey 2015; National Association Of Realtors

only consider those with a master's degree or higher. Many faculty members teaching at top-tier conferences hold advanced degrees in real estate or business or law degrees with concentrations in real estate.

However, many teachers offering instruction at park district or adult enrichment classes are hired based more on their specific skills. For example, a person with expertise in real estate sales will be a prime candidate to conduct property sales training courses.

Other Education or Training

The Real Estate Educators Association provides webinars on interacting successfully with students from different backgrounds and other topics. It also provides educational sessions at its annual conference. Past offerings included "How to Accelerate Learning in the Online World," "21st Century Technology Update for Real Estate Educators," and "Curriculum and Course Design 101." The National Association of Realtors also offers continuing education opportunities for real estate professionals. Contact these organizations for more information.

■ CERTIFICATION, LICENSING, AND SPECIAL REQUIREMENTS

Certification or Licensing

The Real Estate Educators Association (REEA) offers the distinguished real estate instructor (DREI) certification to those who complete training and successfully pass an examination. This designation is awarded to individuals who have proven knowledge of their industry and excellent teaching experience in a classroom setting. The DREI certification must be renewed every three years. Contact the REEA for more information on this particular certification as well as other links to industry certification opportunities as accredited by the National Association of Realtors.

■ EXPERIENCE, SKILLS, AND PERSONALITY TRAITS

Experience as a teacher or in a particular real estate specialty (such as sales or financing) is required to become a successful real estate educator.

As a teacher, you should be able to interact with students at different skill levels, including some who might not have learned proper study habits or who have a different first language. This requires patience, as well as the ability to track the progress of each individual student. Good communication skills are essential, as you'll need to explain things clearly and to answer questions completely. Other important traits include good organizational and leadership skills.

■ EMPLOYMENT PROSPECTS

Employers

Adult education teachers, including those teaching real estate classes, can find work in a variety of different schools and education programs. Community and junior colleges offer classes in real estate ranging from property management and appraisal to broker administration. Park districts often have adult enrichment classes available in a variety of real estate-related interests.

Teachers are also hired for long-distance education programs and to lead continuing education courses for corporations and professional associations.

Starting Out

Most people entering this field have some professional experience in real estate, a desire to share that knowledge with other adults, and a teaching certificate or academic degree. Real estate teachers with previous practical experience in the market are highly regarded.

When pursuing work as a real estate teacher, you should contact colleges, private trade schools, vocational high schools, or other appropriate institutions that have real estate programs in place to receive additional information about employment opportunities.

Many colleges, technical schools, and state departments of education offer job lines or bulletin boards of job listings. Check with your area park district for possible employment opportunities. You can also often find job openings in the classifieds of local newspapers or journals. Try the Vandema Web site (http://www.vandema.com/Journals.htm) for a list of magazines pertaining to the commercial real estate industry.

■ ADVANCEMENT PROSPECTS

Advancement for a skilled educator teaching classes at a community college or park district may mean a larger class load, higher pay, or additional teaching assignments dealing with different real estate specialties. They may also work toward a goal of someday teaching full time at a larger college or university. Teaching at this level may require a master's degree or doctorate.

Many educators, especially those with a good reputation, are tapped to speak at real estate seminars or provide continuing education classes at industry conferences.

OUTLOOK

Employment opportunities for real estate educators should be favorable in coming years. The housing market has stabilized and recovered since the last recession creating a stronger real estate market. The Bureau of Labor Statistics projects faster than average growth for postsecondary instructors, including real estate educators, through 2024. Educators will be needed to teach those interested in entering the field or to give additional training to those seeking career advancement.

Teaching opportunities can be found at any college or university offering undergraduate and graduate degrees in real estate. However, the majority of employment opportunities can be found at the local level—at high schools, junior colleges, proprietary schools, or park districts. Also, many real estate corporations, financial institutions, or law firms that deal with real estate issues want their employees trained in the latest skills and technology. They often hire real estate educators to conduct at work training seminars or conferences to present the latest developments in say, real estate tax law, or licensure reviews.

UNIONS AND ASSOCIATIONS

Unions that represent the interests of real estate educators include the American Federation of Teachers and National Education Association. Some educators become members of the Real Estate Educators Association, which offers certification and professional support. Other useful organizations include the American Association for Adult and Continuing Education, American Association of University Professors, Association for Career and Technical Education, and National Association of Realtors.

TIPS FOR ENTRY

1. Try to land a position as an instructor at a college or university.
2. Join the Real Estate Educators Association (REEA) to access training, networking, and employment opportunities.
3. Become certified by the REEA as a means to demonstrate your skill as an educator.
4. Gain as much experience in the real estate industry as possible to increase your qualifications.

FOR MORE INFORMATION

For information about conferences and publications, contact

American Association for Adult and Continuing Education
1827 Powers Ferry Road, Building 14, Suite 100
Atlanta, GA 30339
Tel: (678) 271-4319
Fax: (404) 393.9506
E-mail: office@aaace.org
http://www.aaace.org

For information about careers and education, contact
American Association of University Professors
1133 19th Street, NW, Suite 200
Washington, D.C. 20036-3655
Tel: (202) 737-5900
Fax: (202) 737-5526
E-mail: aaup@aaup.org
http://www.aaup.org

For information on union membership, contact
American Federation of Teachers
555 New Jersey Avenue, NW
Washington, D.C. 20001-2029
Tel: (202) 879-4400
http://www.aft.org

For information about publications, current legislation, and programs, contact
Association for Career and Technical Education
1410 King Street
Alexandria, VA 22314-2749
Tel: (800) 826-9972
Fax: (703) 683-7424
E-mail: acte@acteonline.org
http://www.acteonline.org

For industry news and employment opportunities, contact
National Association of Realtors
430 North Michigan Avenue
Chicago, IL 60611-4087
Tel: (800) 874-6500
http://www.realtor.org

For information on union membership, contact
National Education Association
1201 16th Street, NW
Washington, D.C. 20036-3290
Tel: (202) 833-4000
Fax: (202) 822-7974
http://www.nea.org

For information about certification, contact
Real Estate Educators Association
7739 East Broadway, #337
Tuscon, AZ 85710-3941
Tel: (520) 609-2380
E-mail: MemberCare@REEA.org
https://www.reea.org

Real Estate Lawyers

OVERVIEW

Lawyers who specialize in legal issues regarding real estate are called *real estate lawyers* or *real estate attorneys*. They provide advice on title and deed transfers, mortgage contracts, financing options, and other real estate topics. Real estate lawyers handle private, industrial, and commercial holdings. The American College of Real Estate Lawyers is a national organization that promotes high professional standards in the practice of real estate law.

HISTORY

The tradition of governing people by laws has been established over centuries. Societies have built up systems of law that have been studied and drawn upon by later governments. The earliest known law is the Code of Hammurabi, developed about 1800 B.C. by the ruler of the Sumerians. Another early set of laws was the law of Moses, known as the Ten Commandments. Every set of laws, no matter when they were introduced, has been accompanied by the need for someone to explain those laws and help others live under them.

The great orators of ancient Greece and Rome set up schools for young boys to learn by apprenticeship the many skills involved in pleading a law case. To be an eloquent speaker was the greatest advantage. The legal profession has matured since those earlier times; a great deal of training and an extensive knowledge of legal matters are required of the modern lawyer and judge.

Much modern European law was organized and refined by legal experts assembled by Napoleon (1769–1821); their body of law was known as the Napoleonic Code. English colonists coming to America brought English common law, from which American laws have grown. In areas of the United States that were heavily settled by Spanish colonists, there are traces of Spanish law. As the population in the country grew, along with business, those who knew the law were in high demand.

Today, many lawyers choose to specialize in a particular area of the law. Real estate law, for example, deals with legal issues regarding the sale or rental of property, as well as construction-related issues.

THE JOB

Real estate lawyers handle all legal issues involving real property transactions such as the transfer of titles and deeds, obtaining mortgages, zoning, and tenant concerns. Their knowledge of real estate law is essential whether working on the sale of a bungalow or a multimillion-dollar skyscraper development. Individuals may retain the services of a lawyer to help them negotiate complicated details of a purchase, sale, or lease of property. Corporations also use the legal expertise of real estate lawyers when acquiring land for development, rehabbing existing property, or battling to change zoning boundaries or laws.

The purchase of a house or building can be intimidating; no wonder many people often retain lawyers to successfully guide them through this process. Lawyers first discuss the details of the purchase with their client. What type of property is the individual interested in purchasing—a single-family house, a multi-unit dwelling, a commercial property, or a mixed-use property? In the example of a home sale, the real estate lawyer may ask the following questions: What are the client's present living arrangements—do they own property, or are they currently leasing or renting? Is the offer contingent on the sale of their current residence? Does the property have a lien against it? Lawyers may also be asked to give advice or referrals regarding financing options, real estate agencies, mortgage brokers, or home inspectors. Lawyers will also follow the same steps when representing the seller. In addition, they may draft a property disclosure report. Lawyers will review any pending contracts or riders, explain confusing terminology, initiate any changes, or draft/execute a punch list.

Lawyers also represent their clients at closing. They make sure contracts and other documents are in order, tax and escrow calculations are accurate, and answer any questions from their clients. For cases under litigation, lawyers will represent their client in court.

Owners of a multi-unit apartment building often enlist the expertise of a real estate lawyer to help with problem tenants. Condominium homeowner's associations often hire a real estate expert to draft or review their by-laws—a list of regulations to be followed by members. Lawyers may also prepare a declaration—a list of regulations, which helps form a sense of unity with homeowners within a subdivision or living community.

Real estate lawyers may also work on larger, multi-property cases. They are often retained by big corporations to negotiate the sale or purchase of a high-rise building, office building, warehouse, or open parcel of land. In such cases, titles must be inspected and zoning laws reviewed. Sometimes the lawyer finds it necessary to initiate the process of rezoning the desired location from residential to commercial, or vice versa. Lawyers may also help in bidding for the property's final price.

Local governments also retain the services of real estate lawyers to help with various projects. For example, if town officials want to build an entertainment and sports complex on an undeveloped piece of land, lawyers may need to investigate public records and deeds to establish title to the property. They then negotiate a fair price with the owner. They also handle zoning issues, land inspections, and surveyors' reports before construction can begin.

■ EARNINGS

Incomes generally increase as the lawyer gains experience and becomes better known in the field. The beginning lawyer in solo practice may barely make ends meet for the first few years. The National Association for Law Placement, reports that first-year associate lawyers earned salaries that ranged from $68,000 to $160,000 in 2015, depending on the size of their firm. Lawyers with one to three years of experience earned salaries that ranged from $68,000 to $175,000; with four to nine years of experience, $85,000 to $235,000; and with 10 to 12 years of experience, $101,250 to $275,000.

According to the U.S. Department of Labor, the May 2015 median salary for lawyers was $115,820, although some senior partners earned well over $1 million a year. Ten percent earned less than $55,870. General attorneys in the federal government received $138,860. State and local government attorneys generally made less, earning $82,550 and $90,710, respectively.

Lawyers usually receive paid vacations and holidays, sick leave, hospitalization and insurance benefits, and pension programs. Some employers also offer profit-sharing plans. Lawyers who have their own firms must provide their own benefits.

■ WORK ENVIRONMENT

Law offices are usually pleasant, although busy, places to work. Lawyers also spend significant amounts of time in law libraries or record rooms, and in the homes and offices of clients. They may also do onsite visits or investigations of property for a particular case. They may represent clients at closings or court appearances.

Often real estate lawyers have to work long hours, spending evenings and weekends preparing cases and materials and working with clients. In addition to the work, the lawyer must always keep up with the latest developments in the industry. Also, it takes a long time to become a qualified lawyer, and it may be difficult to earn an adequate living until the lawyer gets enough experience to develop an established private practice.

Real estate lawyers who are employed at law firms must often work grueling hours to advance in the firm. Spending long weekend hours doing research and interviewing people should be expected. Some travel may be necessary, especially when dealing with property located out of state, or if the law firm has satellite offices.

■ EXPLORING

If you think a career as a lawyer might be right for you, there are several ways you can find out more about it before making a final decision. First, sit in on a trial or two at your local or state courthouse. Try to focus mainly on the lawyer and take note of what they do. Write down questions you have and terms or actions you don't understand. Then, talk to your school counselor and ask for help in setting up a telephone or in-person interview with a lawyer. Ask questions and get the scoop on what those careers are really all about. Also, talk to your counselor or political science teacher about starting or joining a job-shadowing program. Can they connect you with a law firm in your area that specializes in real estate law? Job shadowing programs allow you to follow a person in a certain career around for a day or two to get an idea of what goes on in a typical day. You may even be invited to help out with a few minor duties.

CAREER LADDER

Senior Partner or General Counsel

Junior Partner

Real Estate Lawyer

Law Clerk

Paralegal

You can also search the Internet for general information about lawyers and current court cases. After you've done some research and talked to a lawyer, and you still think you are destined for law school, try to get a part-time job in a law office. Ask your counselor for help.

If you are already in law school, you might consider becoming a student member of the American Bar Association. Student members receive *Student Lawyer*, a magazine that contains useful information for aspiring lawyers. Sample articles from the magazine can be read at http://www.americanbar.org/groups/law_students.html. Additionally, the ABA publishes specialty publications for real estate lawyers such as *The Construction Lawyer*. Visit http://www.americanbar.org/publications_cle/publications.html for more information. Additionally, the American College of Construction Lawyers publishes the *Journal of the American College of Construction Lawyers* (http://www.accl.org).

■ EDUCATION AND TRAINING REQUIREMENTS
High School
A high school diploma, a college degree, and three years of law school are minimum requirements for a law degree. A high school diploma is a first step on the ladder of education that a lawyer must climb. If you are considering a career in law, courses such as business, government, history, social studies, and economics provide a solid background for entering college-level courses. Speech courses are also helpful to build strong communication skills necessary for the profession. Take as many writing classes as possible during high school to strengthen your writing skills. Lawyers spend a tremendous amount of time writing briefs, contracts, and depositions for their cases. Also take advantage of any computer-related classes or experience you can get, because lawyers often use technology to research and interpret the law, from surfing the Internet to searching legal databases.

Postsecondary Education
To enter a law school approved by the American Bar Association (ABA), you must satisfactorily complete at least three, and usually four, years of college work. Most law schools do not specify any particular courses for pre-law education. Usually a liberal arts track is most advisable, with courses in English, history, economics, social sciences, logic, and public speaking. A college student planning to specialize in real estate law might also take courses significantly related to this area, such as business or economics. Those interested should contact several law schools to learn more about any special requirements and to see if they will accept credits from the college the student is planning to attend. It would also be wise to investigate the school's real estate law program.

Most law schools require that applicants take the Law School Admission Test (LSAT), where prospective law students are tested on their critical thinking, writing, and reasoning abilities.

Currently, 203 law schools in the United States are approved by the ABA; others, many of them night schools, are approved by state authorities only. Most of the approved law schools, however, do have night sessions to accommodate part-time students. Part-time courses of study usually take four years. The ABA currently does not accredit online law education programs.

Law school training in real estate consists of required courses such as legal writing and research, commercial real estate finance, public housing redevelopment, real estate investment and transactions, and real estate structuring. A degree of juris doctor (J.D.) or bachelor of laws (LL.B.) is usually granted upon graduation.

Certification
Some lawyers choose to earn a master of laws (LL.M) degree, an advanced law certification that helps them advance professionally. LL.M programs, which typically last one year, are offered in many areas—such as general law, litigation/trial advocacy, and real estate/land development. A first law degree is required for admission to LL.M programs. Visit http://www.lsac.org/llm for more information. Visit http://www.americanbar.org/groups/legal_education/resources/accreditation.html for a list of LL.M specialties and the law schools that offer them.

Other Education or Training
The American Bar Association, National Association for Law Placement, and state and local bar associations offer a variety of continuing education opportunities. Contact these organizations for more information. Additionally, most law firms provide in-house continuing education opportunities to their employees. Some even offer mentorship programs that pair new lawyers with experienced lawyers to help them prepare for the field.

◼ CERTIFICATION, LICENSING, AND SPECIAL REQUIREMENTS
Certification or Licensing
The National Board of Legal Specialty Certification offers voluntary board certification in civil pretrial practice, civil law, and other areas. Contact the board for more information.

Every state requires that lawyers be admitted to the bar of that state before they can practice. They require that applicants graduate from an approved law school and that they pass a written examination in the state in which they intend to practice. In a few states, graduates of law schools within the state are excused from these written examinations. After lawyers have been admitted to the bar in one state, they can practice in another state without taking a written examination if the states have reciprocity agreements; however, they will be required to meet certain state standards of good character and legal experience and pay any applicable fees.

Many lawyers who specialize in real estate law also carry a brokers' license. A real estate broker acts as an agent for others in buying or selling property. Licensure is obtained after sufficient course work and the successful completion of an examination. Check with your state for specific licensure requirements as they may differ from state to state.

◼ EXPERIENCE, SKILLS, AND PERSONALITY TRAITS
Experience as a real estate law intern is highly recommended.

Lawyers must be effective communicators, work well with people, and be able to find creative solutions to problems, such as complex court cases or real estate issues. They should also have strong ethics. Cases are often complex, and a lawyer might be tempted to cut corners or not act in an ethical way in order to earn more money or speed up legal proceedings. Other important traits include strong research skills, the ability to direct the work of others, and excellent time-management skills.

◼ EMPLOYMENT PROSPECTS
Employers
Private law firms specializing in real estate law are just one avenue of employment for lawyers, either as an associate, or sole practitioner. Real estate lawyers may also hold positions as house counsel for businesses, such as a real estate brokerage firm or developer. Some may choose to represent banks and mortgage companies. Others may be employed by local government to work on zoning laws or other real estate-related legal issues.

Real estate lawyers provide advice and manage legal issues pertaining to property transactions. (LDprod. Shutterstock.)

Starting Out
The first steps to entering the law profession are graduation from an approved law school and passing a state bar examination. Usually beginning lawyers do not go into solo practice right away. It is often difficult to become established, and additional experience is helpful to the beginning lawyer. Also, most lawyers do not specialize in a particular branch of law without first gaining experience. Beginning lawyers usually work as assistants to experienced real estate lawyers. At first they do mainly research and routine work. After a few years of successful experience, they may be promoted to junior partner, or be ready to go out on their own and specialize in real estate law. Other choices open to the beginning lawyer include joining an established law firm or entering into partnership with another lawyer. Positions are also available with banks, business corporations such as large title and mortgage companies, insurance companies, and with government agencies at different levels.

Many new lawyers are recruited by law firms or other employers directly from law school. Recruiters come to the school and interview possible hires. Other new graduates can get job leads from local and state bar associations.

You may also want to check out the American Bar Association Web site, which often posts employment opportunities and job fairs in its Career Center section. State bar associations will also provide job leads located in their state. Use the Internet to find out if your state has an association catering to the interests of real estate lawyers.

◼ ADVANCEMENT PROSPECTS
Lawyers with outstanding ability can expect to go a long way in their profession. Novice lawyers generally start as

FROM CONTRACT TO ZONING LAW

Contract: A legal agreement between two parties.

Deed: A legal document that conveys title to a property.

Deposition: Sworn testimony that is given outside of a courtroom.

Escrow: An item of value, money, or documents deposited with a third party to be delivered upon the fulfillment of a condition.

Legal brief: A written legal document that is presented in court to support a client's case.

Lien: A legal claim against a property to seek repayment for an unpaid debt.

Litigation: To contest in court.

Mortgage: A loan given to an individual to purchase a home or other property.

Property disclosure report: A document that is required by law to list any relevant information such as past flooding, presence of mold, or other concerns.

Punch list: A list of issues that need to be addressed before the sale is complete.

Tax: A financial charge that people are required to pay to local, state, and federal governments.

Tenant: An individual who pays rent to live in an apartment or other type of housing.

Title: A legal document that provides proof of ownership of a home, land, vehicle, or other type of property.

Zoning law: A government regulation that stipulates the type and size of a building or structure that can be built on a particular area of land; for example, a zoning law may prohibit the construction of a building taller than five stories on a particular city block.

law clerks, but as they prove themselves and develop their abilities, many opportunities for advancement will arise. They may be promoted to junior partner in a law firm or establish their own practice. Lawyers may enter politics and become mayors, congressmen, or other government leaders. Others may become judges specializing in real estate law. Top positions are available in business, too, for the qualified lawyer. Lawyers working for the federal government advance according to the civil service system. Experienced lawyers may also choose to teach real estate law at colleges and universities. Some may become real estate developers.

■ OUTLOOK

According to the *Occupational Outlook Handbook*, employment for lawyers in general is expected grow about as fast as the average for all careers through 2024.

A large number of law school graduates have created strong competition for jobs, but employment of real estate lawyers in particular may grow by as much as 20 percent, much faster than the average, in the same period, according to the Bureau of Labor Statistics.

Continued population growth and typical business activities will create demand for lawyers who specialize in real estate law. Opportunities may be plentiful in areas of the United States experiencing high population growth, such as the Southwestern states, and in areas where the real estate industry has recovered. An increase in population can translate to private and commercial construction needs.

Law services will be more accessible to the middle-income public with the popularity of prepaid legal services and clinics. However, stiff competition has and will continue to urge some lawyers to look outside the legal profession for employment. Administrative and managerial positions in real estate companies, banks, insurance firms, and government agencies are typical areas where legal training is useful.

The top 10 percent of the graduating seniors of the country's best law schools will have more opportunities with well-known law firms and jobs on legal staffs of corporations, in government agencies, and in law schools in the next few decades. Lawyers in solo practice will find it hard to earn a living until their practice is fully established. The best opportunities exist in small towns or suburbs of large cities, where there is less competition and new lawyers can meet potential clients more easily.

Graduates with lower class rankings and from lesser-known schools may have difficulty in obtaining the most desirable positions.

■ UNIONS AND ASSOCIATIONS

Real estate lawyers who are employed by the government can become members of the American Federation of Government Employees. Many real estate lawyers join the American College of Real Estate Lawyers, American Bar Association, American College of Construction Lawyers, DRI, and the International Association of Attorneys and Executives in Corporate Real Estate. Other important organizations for lawyers include the Association of American Law Schools, Law School Admission Council, and National Association for Law Placement.

■ TIPS FOR ENTRY

1. Working as a law intern or law clerk can help you make valuable industry contacts and lead to a permanent job.
2. Visit the Web sites of law firms that specialize in real estate law to access job listings. Additionally,

use the NALP Directory of Legal Employers (http://www.nalpdirectory.com) to search for employers by location, employer type, practice areas, and other criteria.

3. Network at state and national bar association career events, conferences, and seminars.

4. Join professional associations such as the American College of Real Estate Lawyers and American Bar Association to access training and networking opportunities, industry publications, and employment opportunities.

5. Visit http://www.americanbar.org/resources_for_lawyers/careercenter.html for job listings.

■ FOR MORE INFORMATION

For information about law student services, academic programs, and publications offered by the ABA, contact

American Bar Association (ABA)
Section of Real Property, Trust & Estate Law
321 North Clark Street
Chicago, IL 60654-7598
Tel: (800) 285-2221; (312) 988-5000
http://www.americanbar.org/groups/real_property
_trust_estate.html

For information about membership requirements, contact

American College of Real Estate Lawyers
11300 Rockville Pike, Suite 903
Rockville, MD 20852-3034
Tel: (301) 816-9811
Fax: (301) 816-9786
http://www.acrel.org

For information on law programs, contact

Association of American Law Schools
1614 20th Street, NW
Washington, D.C. 20009-1001
Tel: (202) 296-8851
Fax: (202) 296-8869
E-mail: aals@aals.org
http://www.aals.org

For information on the Law School Admission Test and choosing and paying for law school, contact

Law School Admission Council
662 Penn Street
Newtown, PA 18940-2176
Tel: (215) 968-1001
http://www.lsac.org

For information on choosing a law school, law careers, salaries, and alternative law careers, contact

National Association for Law Placement
1220 19th Street, NW, Suite 401
Washington, D.C. 20036-2405
Tel: (202) 835-1001
Fax: (202) 835-1112
E-mail: info@nalp.org
http://www.nalp.org

Real Estate Writers

■ OVERVIEW

Writers who cover the real estate industry are referred to as *real estate writers*. They report on trends in housing developments, commercial business transactions, architecture, real estate financial concerns, and other topics for inclusion in print, broadcast, or online media. The National Association of Real Estate Editors is a nationwide group that is dedicated to advancing the careers of editors, writers, columnists, and freelancers specializing in real estate-related news.

■ HISTORY

The modern publishing age began in the 18th century. Printing became mechanized, and the novel, magazine, and newspaper developed. The first newspaper in the American colonies appeared in the early 18th century, but it was Benjamin Franklin who, as editor and writer, made the *Pennsylvania Gazette* one of the most influential in setting a high standard for his fellow American journalists. Franklin also published the first magazine in the colonies, *The American Magazine*, in 1741.

Advances in the printing trades, photoengraving, retailing, and the availability of capital produced a boom in newspapers and magazines in the 19th century. Further mechanization in the printing field, such as the use of the Linotype machine, high-speed rotary presses, and special color reproduction processes, set the stage for still further growth in the book, newspaper, and magazine industry.

In addition to the print media, the broadcasting industry has contributed to the development of the professional writer. Radio, television, and the Internet are sources of information, education, and entertainment that provide employment for thousands of journalistic writers.

Many newspapers now have special sections or columns devoted to a particular topic of interest to readers—such as real estate. Entire magazines cover different aspects of the real estate industry, from construction to real estate sales and management. Tremendous growth in the real estate industry has resulted in increased coverage and the need for talented writers to report and comment on the news. Today, real estate-related topics are covered in newspapers, popular magazines, industry journals and Web sites, and broadcast media.

■ THE JOB

Real estate writers report on developments in the real estate industry; their reports appear in a variety of media—print, broadcast, or online. They may also prepare marketing material for industry associations.

Staff writers employed by real estate-related magazines and journals write news stories or feature articles. Topics vary, but all deal with real estate issues. For example, staff writers may be assigned finance-based articles debating the merits of interest-only loans vs. traditional fixed-rate loans; articles detailing the green building movement's effect on modern architecture; or business-related articles such as the estimated economic effects of the development of a large tract of commercial property in a rundown business district. Many staff writers work on different articles as assigned by editors; some are permanently assigned a particular area of interest, or beat.

A reporter who is assigned real estate-related stories on a regular basis is called a *real estate columnist*. Columnists are regarded as experts in their field. Aside from regular written articles, columnists may answer real estate questions from readers. Their work may appear in a newspaper's daily edition or Sunday special section, or in a monthly magazine. Oftentimes, their photo accompanies their byline.

Critics are reporters with extensive knowledge of a particular field—such as real estate. For example, *architecture critics* may comment on the aesthetic effects of a new skyscraper on a city's skyline or decry the destruction of 200-year-old row houses in a rapidly gentrifying area. Critics usually have additional training or education related to their industry.

Real estate writers work for a variety of media. They may write material for textbooks used in real estate classes. Others may work for the public relations department of an organization or association producing newsletters or press releases. They may also place reports on behalf of a news station or a real estate Web site.

When working with a new assignment, writers begin gathering as much information as possible about the subject through library research, interviews, the Internet, observation, and other methods. They keep extensive notes from which they will draw material for their project. Once the material has been organized and arranged in logical sequence, writers prepare a written outline. The process of developing a piece of writing is exciting, although it can also involve detailed and solitary work. After researching an idea, a writer might discover that a different perspective or related topic would be more effective, entertaining, or marketable.

When working on assignment, writers usually submit their outlines to an editor or other company representative for approval. Then they write a first draft, trying to put the material into words that will have the desired effect on their audience. They often rewrite or polish sections of the material as they proceed, always searching for just the right way of imparting information or expressing an idea or opinion. A manuscript may be reviewed, corrected, and revised numerous times before a final copy is submitted. Even after that, an editor may request additional changes.

Real estate writers can be employed either as in-house staff or as freelancers. Pay varies according to experience and the position, but freelancers must provide their own office space and equipment such as computers and fax machines. Freelancers also are responsible for keeping tax records, sending out invoices, negotiating contracts, and providing their own health insurance. Freelancers obtain assignments by sending out query letters and writing samples to publications and organizations. While there is much freedom in their daily work hours, freelancers sometimes find it hard to find steady employment.

■ EARNINGS

In May 2015, median earnings for all salaried writers were $60,250 a year, according to the U.S. Department of Labor. The lowest 10 percent earned less than $29,230, while the highest 10 percent earned $114,530 or more. Writers employed in the real estate field earned average wages of $53,600 to $58,770.

In addition to their salaries, many real estate writers earn some income from freelance work. Part-time freelancers may earn from $5,000 to $15,000 a year. Freelance earnings vary widely. Full-time established freelance writers may earn $75,000 or more a year.

Typical benefits may be available for full-time salaried employees including sick leave, vacation pay, and health, life, and disability insurance. Retirement plans may also be available, and some companies may match employees' contributions. Some companies may also offer stock-option plans.

Freelance writers do not receive benefits and are responsible for their own medical, disability, and life insurance. They do not receive vacation pay, and when they aren't working, they aren't generating income. Retirement plans must also be self-funded and self-directed.

■ WORK ENVIRONMENT

Working conditions vary for journalistic writers. Although their workweek usually runs 35 to 40 hours, many writers work overtime. A publication that is issued frequently has more deadlines closer together, creating greater pressures to meet them. The work is especially hectic on newspapers and at broadcasting companies, which operate seven days a week. Writers often work nights and weekends to meet deadlines or to cover a late-developing story.

Most writers work independently, but they often must cooperate with editors, artists, photographers, graphic designers, and rewriters who may have widely differing ideas of how the materials should be prepared and presented.

Physical surroundings range from comfortable private offices to noisy, crowded newsrooms filled with other workers typing and talking on the telephone. Some writers must confine their research to the library or telephone interviews, but others may travel to other cities or countries or to local sites, such as new housing developments, press conferences, groundbreaking ceremonies, or other offices.

The work is arduous, but most writers are seldom bored. Real estate writers must keep up to date on the latest trends and developments in the industry, be it new building technology to keep heating costs low, or revisions in real estate tax laws. The most difficult element is the continual pressure of deadlines. People who are the most content as writers enjoy and work well with deadline pressure.

■ EXPLORING

As a high school or college student, you can test your interest and aptitude in the field of writing by serving as a reporter or writer on school newspapers, yearbooks, and literary magazines. Various writing courses and workshops will offer you the opportunity to sharpen your writing skills.

CAREER LADDER

Real Estate Editor

Real Estate Writer

Editorial Assistant or Junior Staff Writer

Small community newspapers and local radio stations often welcome contributions from outside sources, although they may not have the resources to pay for them. Jobs in bookstores, magazine shops, and even newsstands will offer you a chance to become familiar with various publications.

You can also obtain information on writing as a career by visiting local newspapers, publishers, or radio and television stations and interviewing some of the writers who work there. Contact a local real estate company and find out if it has any part-time employment opportunities; this is a great way to familiarize yourself with the industry.

The National Association of Real Estate Editors does not offer student membership status, but it does allow public access to its archive of industry news developments and newsletters at its Web site. Check out these sections to get a feel for the real estate world.

Reading is a great way to explore the real estate industry. Don't limit yourself to newspapers. Browse through industry journals such as *Realtor Magazine* (http://www.realtor.org/publications/realtor-magazine), a leading publication sponsored by the National Association of Realtors that covers real estate business and news.

■ EDUCATION AND TRAINING REQUIREMENTS
High School

While in high school, build a broad educational foundation by taking courses in English, literature, foreign languages, history, general science, business, and social studies. Such classes usually require written reports, which will ultimately help you to develop your writing style. It's important to also take computer classes to become familiar with computers and to improve the speed and accuracy of your keyboarding skills. Many writers are also now required to take their own photographs and videos, so it is a good idea to take photography and videography classes if they are offered.

Blair Kamin

Blair Kamin has served as the architecture critic for the *Chicago Tribune* since 1992. In 1999, he won the Pulitzer Prize for Criticism. He also serves as a contributing editor to *Architectural Record* magazine and is the author of *Why Architecture Matters: Lessons From Chicago* (University of Chicago Press, 2001) and *Terror and Wonder: Architecture in a Tumultuous Age* (University of Chicago Press, 2010).

Kamin received the Pulitzer Prize for Criticism for his work that spotlighted the "problems and promise" of Chicago's lakefront. He encouraged Chicago leaders and residents to reimagine the lakefront to improve access—especially to underserved minority communities along the lake on the South Side of Chicago. His articles also encouraged the city to reassess its land-use plans for a former steel plant on the city's far south lakefront.

Kamin has received more than 30 awards during his career, including the George Polk Award for Criticism (1996), the American Institute of Architects' Institute Honor for Collaborative Achievement (1999), and the American Institute of Architects' Presidential Citation (2004).

Source: Chicago Tribune

Real estate writers don't just report on property sales—they often write about the style and design of a building or community. It is a good idea to enroll in such classes as art, architecture, and design to build your knowledge of these fields.

Postsecondary Education

Most, if not all, employers seek candidates with a college education. The type of degree in demand varies from employer to employer. Many successful writers have a liberal arts background, with majors ranging from English to philosophy to social science. Still others have real estate or business degrees. Many employers desire candidates with a degree in communications or journalism. Journalism, especially, is highly regarded because of the strong emphasis on writing and industry-relevant classes such as newspaper and magazine writing, publication management, book publishing, and Internet writing.

There are some traditional colleges and universities, such as the University of Cincinnati (http://www.business.uc.edu/realestate/academics), that offer a business degree with a concentration in real estate. While this degree focuses on the business side of the industry, there are several classes that would definitely give

valuable knowledge and training to any real estate editor-in-training.

In addition to formal course work, most employers look for practical writing experience. If you have worked on high school or college newspapers, yearbooks, or literary magazines, or if you have worked for small community newspapers or radio stations, even in an unpaid position, you will be a more attractive candidate. Many magazines, newspapers, and radio and television stations have summer internship programs that provide valuable training if you want to learn about the publishing and broadcasting businesses. Interns do many simple tasks, such as running errands and answering phones, but some may be asked to perform research, conduct interviews, or even write some minor pieces. Turn to the Internet for a list of publications covering the real estate industry. Many magazines post their writer's guidelines, or any job openings. Visit http://www.vandema.com for links to real estate journals and publications.

Other Education or Training

A variety of webinars, conference seminars, and other continuing education opportunities are offered by professional associations such as the Construction Writers Association, National Association of Realtors, MPA-The Association of Magazine Media, and the Society of Professional Journalists. Topics include editing, writing, interviewing, social media, technology, and real estate trends.

■ CERTIFICATION, LICENSING, AND SPECIAL REQUIREMENTS
Certification or Licensing

There are no certification or licensing requirements for real estate writers.

■ EXPERIENCE, SKILLS, AND PERSONALITY TRAITS

Any experience working or volunteering as a writer or working in real estate will be useful for aspiring real estate writers.

To be a real estate writer, you should be creative and able to express ideas clearly, have a broad general knowledge, be skilled in research techniques, and be computer literate. Other assets include curiosity, persistence, initiative, resourcefulness, and an accurate memory. For some jobs—with a newspaper or a television news organization, for example, where the activity is hectic and deadlines are short—the ability to concentrate and produce under pressure is essential. Above all, you should have a strong interest in real estate-related issues and topics.

■ EMPLOYMENT PROSPECTS
Employers
Real estate writers can find employment with all types of media—print, broadcast, and online. The most obvious sources of employment are with newspapers and industry journals, but don't count out industry associations, educational publications, law firms specializing in real estate law, and the government.

The major newspaper, magazine, and book publishers and broadcasting companies account for the concentration of journalistic writers in large cities such as New York, Chicago, Los Angeles, Boston, Philadelphia, San Francisco, and Washington, D.C. Opportunities with small publishers and broadcasting companies can be found throughout the country. Freelance writers can work from a home base and report on topics per assignment.

Starting Out
A fair amount of experience is required to gain a high-level position in the field. Most real estate writers start out in entry-level positions such as junior staff writer, or editorial assistant. Don't be discouraged if your first writing job is not related to real estate. It is more important to get solid writing experience under your belt, and then move the direction of your writing to real estate-related topics.

Entry-level jobs may be listed with college career services offices, or obtained by applying directly to the employment departments of individual publishers or broadcasting companies. Graduates who previously served internships with these companies often have the advantage of knowing someone who can give them a personal recommendation. Want ads in newspapers and trade journals are another source for jobs. Because of the competition for positions, however, few vacancies are listed with public or private employment agencies. Don't forget to check association Web sites, which often post job openings, dates of upcoming job fairs, and other networking opportunities. The NAREE, for example, holds an annual conference giving editors, reporters, columnists, freelancers, and authors who cover the real estate industry a chance to discuss trends and network with their peers.

Get your clippings in order, especially those that are real estate related. Employers usually are interested in samples of published writing. These are often assembled in an organized portfolio or scrapbook. Bylined or signed articles are more credible (and, as a result, more useful) than stories whose source is not identified.

Beginning positions as junior staff writers usually involve library research, preparation of rough drafts for part or all of a report, cataloging, and other related writing tasks. At times, they may be given an assignment to complete independently. Such tasks are generally carried on under the supervision of a senior writer.

■ ADVANCEMENT PROSPECTS
Most real estate writers find their first jobs as editorial, production, or research assistants. Advancement may be more rapid in small media companies, where beginners learn by doing a little bit of everything and may be given writing tasks immediately. At large publishers or broadcast companies, duties are usually more compartmentalized. Assistants in entry-level positions are assigned such tasks as research and fact checking, but it generally takes much longer to advance to full-scale writing duties.

Promotion into higher-level positions may come with the assignment of more important articles and stories to write, or it may be the result of moving to another company. A staff writer at a real estate magazine that covers the Midwest may switch to a similar position at a more prestigious publication that covers the entire United States. Or a news writer may switch to a different media as a form of advancement. Newspaper writers may move to cover the industry for an online site, or broadcast real estate reports for a local television station or cable channel.

As staff writers become more experienced in a particular aspect of the real estate industry they may be permanently assigned that beat. Writers may also be given a regular by-line column. The *New York Times*, for example, has several columnists that cover the real estate industry in general, as well as special interest areas such as architecture and new housing developments. Special features usually appear in weekly sections of the paper that deal with home or housing concerns.

Freelance or self-employed writers earn advancement in the form of bigger projects and larger fees as they gain exposure and establish their reputations.

■ OUTLOOK
Employment for writers is expected to be only fair through 2024, with employment growth of about 2 percent. The picture is somewhat bleaker for real estate writers, with an expected decline of almost 1.5 percent over the same period. Employment opportunities will be available at newspapers, industry journals, book publishers, associations, broadcast and online media, and at real estate associations. There will always be some demand for real estate writers, but the current weak state

of the real estate market is prompting reduced demand for writers.

People entering this field should realize that the competition for jobs is extremely keen. Beginners, especially, may have difficulty finding employment. Of the thousands who graduate each year with degrees intending to establish a career as a real estate writer, many turn to other occupations when they find that applicants far outnumber the job openings available. College students would do well to keep this in mind and prepare for an unrelated alternate career in the event they are unable to obtain a position as writer.

■ UNIONS AND ASSOCIATIONS

Real estate writers may obtain union representation from the National Writers Union. They also may join professional associations such as the Construction Writers Association, National Association of Real Estate Editors, and Society of Professional Journalists. Other useful organizations for real estate writers include the Accrediting Council on Education in Journalism and Mass Communications (which accredits postsecondary programs), Association for Education in Journalism and Mass Communication (a nonprofit, educational association of journalism and mass communication educators, students, and media professionals), and National Association of Realtors (the leading organization for real estate agents, brokers, and other professionals).

■ TIPS FOR ENTRY

1. Write as often as you can and create a portfolio of your work to show potential employers.
2. If you are an expert regarding real estate, start a blog or Twitter account to raise your profile and attract the interest of potential employers.
3. Read real estate-related journals to learn what types of topics they cover, as well as obtain contact information for editorial staff members who are responsible for hiring. Suggestions include *Realtor Magazine* (http://www.realtor.org/publications/realtor-magazine) and *The Real Estate Professional* (http://www.therealestatepro.com).
4. Apply for entry-level jobs in the real estate industry in order to gain experience in the field.
5. Join professional associations to access training and networking opportunities, industry publications, and employment opportunities.

■ FOR MORE INFORMATION

For a list of accredited programs in journalism and mass communications, visit the council's Web site.

Accrediting Council on Education in Journalism and Mass Communications
Stauffer-Flint Hall, 1435 Jayhawk Boulevard
Lawrence, KS 66045-0001
Tel: (785) 864-3973
Fax: (785) 864-5225
http://www.acejmc.org/

This organization provides general educational information on all areas of journalism, including newspapers, magazines, television, and radio.

Association for Education in Journalism and Mass Communication
234 Outlet Pointe Boulevard
Columbia, SC 29210-5667
Tel: (803) 798-0271
Fax: (803) 772-3509
http://www.aejmc.org

For information on writing careers in the construction industry, contact

Construction Writers Association
E-mail: info@constructionwriters.org
http://www.constructionwriters.org

For information regarding membership, conferences, and employment opportunities, contact

National Association of Real Estate Editors
1003 NW 6th Terrace
Boca Raton, FL 33486-3455
Tel: (561) 391-3599
Fax: (561) 391-0099
http://www.naree.org

For industry news and employment opportunities, contact

National Association of Realtors
430 North Michigan Avenue
Chicago, IL 60611-4087
Tel: (800) 874-6500
http://www.realtor.org

For information about working as a writer and union membership, contact

National Writers Union
256 West 38th Street, Suite 703
New York, NY 10018-9807
Tel: (212) 254-0279
Fax: (212) 254-0673
E-mail: nwu@nwu.org
http://www.nwu.org

This organization for journalists has campus and online chapters.

Society of Professional Journalists
Eugene S. Pulliam National Journalism Center
3909 North Meridian Street
Indianapolis, IN 46208-4011
Tel: (317) 927-8000
Fax: (317) 920-4789
http://www.spj.org

Real-Time Captioners

■ OVERVIEW

Real-time captioners, also known as *broadcast captioners,* operate a computer-aided transcription (CAT) stenotype system to create closed captions for use in live television broadcasts, in classroom instruction, or in other scenarios requiring live translating or interpreting on the computer. Computer-aided real-time translation, or CART, refers to the use of machine steno shorthand skills to produce real-time text on a computer. Generally, captioning systems use a modified stenotype machine connected to a computer. The real-time captioner inputs the captions phonetically (transcription or speech sounds) on the steno machine, and the sounds are then translated into English words by the computer using a special dictionary created by the captioner. During a live broadcast, the captions are entered as the program progresses, much as a court reporter transcribes a trial as it progresses. The input data is sent along telephone lines to the broadcast point, where the caption codes become part of the television signal.

■ HISTORY

Real-time captioning technology arose from a need to make live broadcasts accessible to people who are deaf or hard of hearing. To meet this need, the National Captioning Institute (NCI), founded in 1979, became the chief architect of the computer-based technology needed to bring captions to real-time audiences nationwide. At first, the NCI provided captions only for prerecorded programs. Captions were prepared in advance by people who were not court reporters. It soon became apparent, however, that captions were needed for live television, so the NCI went to work developing a system that could prepare captions for live broadcast.

The NCI first introduced real-time captioning to eager audiences in April 1982 when it captioned the Academy Awards. Today, real-time captioners create captions for a wide range of live broadcasts on network, cable, syndication, and pay-per-view services. All programs on prime-time schedules of the four major commercial networks are now captioned, many by real-time captioners.

Real-time captions are generated within seconds after a word is spoken. They are made possible by highly skilled court reporters, who receive months of specialized retraining to become first-class real-time captioners.

■ THE JOB

The refined skills of real-time captioners are called upon every day to bring the latest news, sports, and entertainment to a diverse group consisting not only of the deaf and hard-of-hearing, but also young children learning to read and those learning English as a second language. While captioning a live program, meeting, or other event may seem rather straightforward on the surface, there is a great deal of work, anxiety, and preparation that goes into ensuring that the words appearing on screen come out as smoothly and effortlessly as possible. Real-time captioning requires much dexterity and discipline to be able to reach the higher speeds required—250 words a minute—and good brain-to-hand coordination to get it all down quickly and accurately.

There is also much preparation work that must be done by real-time captioners before they can caption a live television broadcast. It takes about one and a half to two hours to prepare for an average news broadcast, using preparation materials obtained from the broadcaster

QUICK FACTS

ALTERNATE TITLE(S)
Broadcast Captioners

DUTIES
Operate computer-aided transcription (CAT) stenotype systems to create closed captions for use in live television broadcasts and other settings

SALARY RANGE
$27,180 to $49,500 to $90,510+

WORK ENVIRONMENT
Primarily Indoors

BEST GEOGRAPHIC LOCATION(S)
Opportunities exist throughout the country

MINIMUM EDUCATION LEVEL
Bachelor's Degree

SCHOOL SUBJECTS
Computer Science, English, Journalism

EXPERIENCE
Previous court or field reporting experience is highly recommended

PERSONALITY TRAITS
Conventional, Hands On, Technical

SKILLS
Digital Media, Mechanical/Manual Dexterity

CERTIFICATION OR LICENSING
Required

SPECIAL REQUIREMENTS
None

EMPLOYMENT PROSPECTS
Fair

ADVANCEMENT PROSPECTS
Fair

OUTLOOK
Little Change or More Slowly than the Average

NOC
N/A

O*NET-SOC
N/A

CAREER LADDER

Supervisor

Experienced Real-Time Captioner

Entry-Level Real-Time Captioner

Court Reporter

and the captioner's own research. (Special broadcasts such as holiday parades, the Super Bowl, or the Olympics can take days or even weeks of preparation.) Captioners call this pre-show preparation dictionary-building.

Captioners working for established captioning houses will usually have access to all types of reference materials—everything from *Star Stats: Who's Whose in Hollywood* to the *Congressional Staff Directory*. Captioners working on their own will want to think about what kinds of materials to include in their own libraries.

Real-time captioners prepare for a job by going through resource materials to find words that might come up during a broadcast, and then develop steno codes that they will use to "write" these words when the words come up during the broadcast. It is important that captioners test all the briefs developed for complicated names to make sure they are translating properly. Because captioners will hear names and words during the broadcast that they have not prepared dictionary entries for, they must learn to "write around" the actual words and listen for titles. In this way captioners can write "The former Secretary of State" instead of "Condoleezza Rice," for example.

While striving to keep them to a minimum, captioners will occasionally make mistakes that go out over the air. For example, in real-time captioning, the phrase "Olympic tryouts," which would require the captioner to type five key strokes on a stenotype machine, might come out (and actually did) as "old limp pig tryouts" if strokes are entered that the computer cannot match correctly.

CART reporters also work in classroom settings, where they might be seen with a notebook computer and steno keyboard, sitting next to a deaf person. CART reporters write down everything that happens, making sure the notebook computer screen is turned so the deaf person can see it. To help the client better understand what is going on, they may paraphrase or interpret the proceedings, rather than create a verbatim record, as in a courtroom. Real-time reporters can also cover meetings, with captions shown on large projection screens. Additionally, computer technology allows highly skilled court reporters to provide real-time captioning in the courtroom, which has great value for large numbers of deaf or hard-of-hearing judges, attorneys, and litigants, or those who have difficulty understanding English. Also, judges and attorneys can scroll back to earlier statements during the trial and mark text for later reference.

One major difference between real-time captioning for television broadcast and other live-display settings and verbatim reporting, as is frequently done in courtrooms and lawyers' offices, is that captioning's main purpose is to let the viewer who is deaf or hard-of-hearing understand the story being told on the screen. It is not enough to listen only for the phonetic strokes; the real-time captioner must also listen for context.

Before beginning even limited on-air captioning, captioner trainees must spend at least three to six months in training, eight hours a day, five days a week, and up to one year of real-time captioning before doing certain specialized programming. As a vital part of the production team, captioners must also become intimately familiar with the programs they are captioning to know what to expect and to anticipate the unexpected.

A typical day for a captioner trainee would include preparing for a practice broadcast by creating a job dictionary, then writing that practice broadcast for supervisors, who would make suggestions as to editing, brief form, style, and format. Later, the trainee would review the broadcast and make the necessary dictionary entries. Trainees would sit in on a variety of broadcasts with more experienced captioners.

Real-time captioning for television is generally performed in a production control room, equipped with several television sets and networked computer systems, giving the environment a high-tech look and feel. Sometimes, one captioner will write a show alone; sometimes two captioners will share a show, depending on whether there are commercials or not. No captioner can maintain a high accuracy level without taking regular breaks. On a show with no commercials, two captioners will typically switch back and forth about every 10 minutes.

As a show gets closer to airtime, the environment in the control room becomes tense, as the real-time captioner scrambles to get last-minute information in the computer. Then a deep breath, and the countdown begins… "Good evening, I'm Diane Sawyer."

The captioner strokes the steno keys while listening to the live broadcast, transcribing the broadcast accurately while inserting correct punctuation and other symbols. (Double arrows at the beginning of a sentence indicate that a new speaker is speaking.) Those strokes are converted to electronic impulses, which travel through a cable to the computer. The steno strokes are matched with the correct entries on the captioner's personal dictionary. That data is then sent by modem to the broadcast site, where it gets added to the broadcaster's video signal. Within two to three seconds, people across the country can see those captions—if they have televisions with a built-in decoder chip or a set with a decoder connected to it.

Some kinds of captioning can be done from home, mainly broadcasts for local television stations. The equipment needed (which may be provided by the employer) includes a computer, modem, steno machine, and the appropriate software. Captioners may even choose to work for companies that specialize in producing captions remotely, with just an audio feed, thereby allowing more home-based operations. Getting started in the business, however, usually requires an on-site presence, until confidence and trust is established. Obviously, live events that are not broadcast require a real-time captioner on site.

■ EARNINGS

Earning power for real-time captioners is dependent upon many variables and is often region-specific and a product of "what the market will bear." In large captioning organizations, real-time captioners can make anywhere from $30,000 for a recent graduate in training to $75,000 or even higher for those experienced and tireless workers who always volunteer for extra hours, overflow work, etc., and who are capable of captioning all kinds of programming. Trainee salaries increase once the captioner goes on the air.

Salaries for real-time captioners are often in line with salaries for court reporters. According to the Bureau of Labor Statistics, average salaries for court reporters were between $27,180 to $90,510 in May 2015; median salaries were $49,500.

A fringe benefit of working for a captioning agency for most reporters (particularly students just out of school) is that such agencies generally provide all the equipment. Large captioning organizations also offer benefits, such as vacation and health insurance, likely to be provided at a courthouse for court reporters but not at a freelance firm of deposition reporters, for instance.

■ WORK ENVIRONMENT

Real-time captioning for television broadcast is not a nine-to-five job. While many reporting jobs require erratic hours, broadcast captioning is done seven days a week, around the clock. Real-time captioners producing captions for television broadcast will likely work nights, weekends, or holidays, as directed. Shows can air at 5:30 in the morning, at midnight on a Saturday night, or during Thanksgiving dinner.

AT THE MOVIES

DID YOU KNOW?

Although deaf and hard-of-hearing viewers have been able to enjoy real-time captioning on television for some time, they did not have access to similar technology at movie theaters (unless a film is subtitled). This began to change in 1997 with the introduction of the Rear Window Captioning System, which was developed by Boston public broadcasting station WGBH and Rufus Butler Seder. With Rear Window, captions are displayed from a light-emitting diode (LED) display screen at the back of the theater. Deaf and hard-of-hearing viewers receive these captions on a portable screen that makes it look as if the captions are projected on the actual movie screen. The portable screen can be used at any seat in the theater. Many theaters across the country and in Canada have installed Rear Window to meet industry and consumer demand.

Source: MoPix, Media Access Group at WGBH, http://ncam.wgbh.org/mopix

Given the irregularity of TV schedules, several shifts are needed to cover programming hours scheduled throughout the day. It is imperative that captioners be flexible and dependable and that they not get fatigued, so they can maintain high accuracy levels. How many hours a day a captioner is on the air depends on the level of experience. If new to the air, captioners may do only one or two shows a day, as it takes longer to prepare for a broadcast and review the result in the beginning. An experienced captioner may be on the air three to five hours a day, writing captions for short programs, news broadcasts, or sporting events. In the broadcast setting, real-time captioners do not have to produce transcripts, which eliminates the long hours that go along with that aspect of reporting.

Real-time captioning work can be physically demanding. Along with suffering the mental stress of performing in a live environment, real-time captioners may also be subject to repetitive stress injury, a prevalent industrial hazard for those who perform repeated motions in their daily work. Carpal tunnel syndrome, a type of repetitive stress injury, sometimes afflicts real-time captioners after several years. It can cause prickling sensation or numbness in the hand and sometimes a partial loss of function.

■ EXPLORING

Although some core classes on captioning technology are being introduced into court reporting and other stenographic curricula around the country, it is still a "hit or miss" situation, with many schools simply intimidated by the new technology. Good programs exist, however, that are providing beneficial exposure and actually working with local TV stations and area colleges to provide both news captioning and real-timing or steno interpreting in the classroom for deaf students and those with disabilities.

A smart way to prepare for real-time captioning, according to a real-time captioner who hires new graduates for a captioning company, is to practice by transcribing or writing newspaper articles or those from news magazines. Along with helping to build vocabulary skills, this exercise enables you to focus on conflict resolution by seeing the word in print, helps to familiarize you with difficult foreign names and words, and increases awareness of current events, both national and international.

While honing your skills, you may also get good exposure by working with local organizations, such as the Association of Late Deafened Adults, Hearing Loss Association of America, the National Association of the Deaf, the Alexander Graham Bell Association for the Deaf and Hard of Hearing, and other nonprofit groups that might eventually need captioning services. Although the pay will not be as high as it would at a captioning house, the job satisfaction level will be high. It is important to keep in mind that while the major captioning companies do sometimes hire people with little or no training for internships or on-the-job training, there is no substitute for experience.

■ EDUCATION AND TRAINING REQUIREMENTS
High School
You should take typing and computer courses to increase your keyboard speed and accuracy and to develop an understanding of word processing programs. Because you'll be working with a variety of news, sports, and entertainment programs, you should keep up on current events by taking journalism, social studies, and government courses. English composition and speech classes can help you develop your vocabulary and grammar skills.

Postsecondary Training
You should first complete training to become a *court and conference reporter* (*stenographer*), which takes anywhere from two to four years. An associate's or bachelor's degree in court and conference reporting, or satisfactory completion of other two-year equivalent programs, is usually required. Because of the additional training needed to learn computer and English grammar skills, some two-year programs have become three-year programs. In fact, many real-time reporters and their employers believe that additional formal education in the arts and sciences is needed to perform the work properly and to adapt to the swift technological changes taking place. They are urging the National Court Reporters Association (NCRA), to which most captioners and other reporters belong, to require a bachelor's degree for entry into the court reporting profession, which would extend to captioning as well. About 100 postsecondary vocational and technical schools and colleges offer court reporter training programs, and NCRA has certified approximately 50 programs, many of which offer courses in real-time reporting and computer-aided transcription. A few four-year college programs already exist, to allow students a well-rounded background. A degree in English (or the primary language in which captioning will be done) or linguistics would be helpful. Others argue, however, that while a formal education is beneficial, many court reporters who never earned a four-year degree are working successfully with high skill levels.

Even after graduating from court reporting school, you will have to undergo more specialized training, during which you'll hone your reporting skills to achieve the proficiency needed to create broadcast-quality captions.

Other Education or Training
Real-time captioners must participate in continuing education classes and webinars to stay up to date with industry developments and become eligible to renew their certification. The National Court Reporters Association and the National Verbatim Reporters Association, along with state-level court reporting associations, provide continuing education opportunities. Contact these organizations for more information.

■ CERTIFICATION, LICENSING, AND SPECIAL REQUIREMENTS
Certification or Licensing
Typically, the reporter considering real-time captioning work has passed the registered professional reporter, certified realtime reporter, or certified broadcast captioner exams given by the National Court Reporters Association, or a comparable state certification exam. Potential employers may even require applicants to be certified. Additionally, the National Verbatim Reporters Association offers the following certifications: certified verbatim reporter, certificate of merit, real-time verbatim reporter, registered broadcast captioner, and registered CART provider.

Some states require court reporters (or voice writers) to pass a test and earn state licensure.

■ EXPERIENCE, SKILLS, AND PERSONALITY TRAITS

You should have extreme proficiency in machine shorthand skills and an ability to perform under pressure. Familiarity with CAT systems is usually preferred, as is previous court or field reporting experience. It generally takes several years of court reporting experience to be able to transcribe complex testimony with the high levels of speed and accuracy that real-time captioning demands.

Real-time captioners must also possess an incredible amount of concentration. Besides typing accurately at speeds of 200 to 250 words a minute to keep up with the fastest natural speakers, they must also anticipate commercial breaks so as not to cut off captions in mid-sentence, insert appropriate punctuation marks and symbols, and watch their own translation closely to correct any problems on the spot.

■ EMPLOYMENT PROSPECTS
Employers

Captioners are employed primarily by captioning companies such as the National Captioning Institute (NCI) and VITAC. These companies contract with broadcasters and production companies to caption live and recorded events. Captioners work either as full-time employees for captioning companies or as freelancers (that is, independent contractors).

Starting Out

You should seek employment at one of the few large captioning companies in the country or contact station managers at your local television stations to inquire about real-time captioning positions. As with many other businesses, the best approach may be simply to start calling the leading companies in the field and the local companies and see who is hiring. Gallaudet University, a postsecondary institution that provides education for deaf and hard of hearing students, provides useful information about captioning on its Web site, http://www.gallaudet.edu.

Before securing a real-time captioning position, you may have to "audition" as part of a pre-interview screening process that involves preparing raw steno notes from a sample recorded program. The notes are then analyzed, with employment consideration based on the results of the evaluation and job experience. A good way to prepare for employment evaluation is to practice on the kind of material you wish to caption and to offer to demonstrate your skills.

■ ADVANCEMENT PROSPECTS

Advancement for a real-time captioner is dependent upon performance, with salary increases and promotions to more responsible positions awarded with greater proficiency and tenure. Skilled real-time captioners may advance to supervisory positions.

■ OUTLOOK

The development of automated voice and speech systems—the computer programs that automatically convert speech to written text—may have some effect on the court reporting field, but there are no current systems that can accurately handle multiple speakers, and it's unlikely that such technology will exist in the near future. Therefore, captioners and court reporters will be in demand for years to come. The U.S. Department of Labor (DOL) predicts that employment for all court reporting occupations will grow slower than average, around 2 percent, for all careers through 2024. It reports that "all new television programming will continue to need closed captioning. Broadcasters are adding closed captioning to their online programming in order to comply with new federal regulations." Court reporters who are certified and who specialize in CART, broadcast captioning, or webcasting services will have the best job opportunities. Those with skills in foreign-language captioning will also have good employment prospects.

Digital and high-definition TV (DTV and HDTV) also continue to make captioning more desirable and useful to more people, thereby increasing demand for captioners. DTV and HDTV enhancements allow viewers with poor vision to adjust text-size, styles, and fonts. They also allow for more non-English letters, as well as more information transmitted per minute.

Captioners should focus first on the area where they want to live and work. To caption area news or city council meetings in a local area or do conventions in a large hotel, captioners must first obtain some costly supplies. These include a laptop or notebook computer, a compatible steno writer, cables, modem, and captioning software. Captioners may also need a character generator to project onto a large convention screen.

Captioners should learn the basic real-time skills that will enable them to do any live translating or interpreting on the computer. With such skills, they will be eligible for a variety of positions, including working in a computer-integrated courtroom; taking real-time depositions for attorneys; providing accompanying litigation support, such as key word indexing; real-timing or captioning in the classroom; or doing broadcast captioning. The future looks great for those who qualify themselves to perform real-time translation.

Other opportunities for the real-time captioner include working with hospitals that specialize in cochlear implants. For late-deafened adults who learned English before sign language, if they learned to sign at all, captions provide a far greater comprehension level. Additionally, some local news stations across the country are working to expand and improve the quality of their local captioning capabilities, providing yet another source of potential employment for the real-time captioner.

UNIONS AND ASSOCIATIONS

Real-time captioners do not belong to unions, but many join the National Court Reporters Association and the National Verbatim Reporters Association. According to its Web site, the National Captioning Institute "supplies world-class captioning services for broadcast and cable television, webcasting, home video and DVD, and government and corporate video programming."

TIPS FOR ENTRY

1. Talk to real-time captioners about their careers. Visit the National Verbatim Reporters Association's Web site, http://www.nvra.org, for a list of captioners in your area.
2. Visit http://www.careersincourtreporting.com for information on careers in court reporting and broadcast captioning.
3. Visit http://www.ncra.org/Education/joblist.cfm?navItemNumber=530 for job listings.

FOR MORE INFORMATION

The NCI Web site features historical information, a list of captioning terms, and employment information.

National Captioning Institute (NCI)
3725 Concorde Parkway, Suite 100
Chantilly, VA 20151-1157
Tel: (703) 917-7600
Fax: (703) 917-7628
E-mail: mail@ncicap.org
http://www.ncicap.org

Visit the NCRA Web site for extensive career and certification information, as well as information about technology, education programs, and access to its publications.

**National Court Reporters
    Association (NCRA)**
12030 Sunrise Valley Drive, Suite 400
Reston, VA 20191
Tel: (800) 272-6272; (703) 556-6272
Fax: (703) 391-0629
E-mail: msic@ncra.org
http://www.ncraonline.org

For information about certification and other resources, contact
National Verbatim Reporters Association
629 North Main Street
Hattiesburg, MS 39401-3429
Tel: (601) 582-4345
E-mail: nvra@nvra.org
http://www.nvra.org

Receptionists

OVERVIEW

Receptionists—so named because they receive visitors in places of business—have the important job of giving a business's clients and visitors a positive first impression. Also called *information clerks*, these front-line workers are the first communication sources who greet clients and visitors to an office, answer their questions, and direct them to the people they wish to see. Receptionists also answer telephones, take and distribute messages for other employees, and make sure no one enters the office unescorted or unauthorized. Many receptionists perform additional clerical duties. *Switchboard operators* perform similar tasks but primarily handle equipment that receives an organization's telephone calls. There are 1,028,600 receptionists and information clerks employed throughout the United States.

HISTORY

In the 18th and 19th centuries, as businesses began to compete with each other for customers, merchants and other business people began to recognize the importance of giving customers the immediate impression that the business was friendly, efficient, and trustworthy. These businesses began to employ hosts and hostesses, workers who would greet customers, make them comfortable, and often serve them refreshments while they waited or did business with the owner. As businesses grew larger and more diverse, these hosts and hostesses (only recently renamed receptionists) took on the additional duties of answering phones, keeping track of workers, and directing visitors to the employee they needed to see. Receptionists also began to work as information dispensers, answering growing numbers of inquiries from the public. In the medical field, as services expanded, more receptionists were needed to direct patients to physicians and clinical services and to keep track of appointments and payment information.

Receptionists have become indispensable to business and service establishments. It is hard to imagine most medium-sized or large businesses functioning without them. Today, receptionists field inquiries through complex voicemail systems, as well as personal computers and other electronic devices. They also use the Internet for various search tasks. There are now also *virtual receptionists*, who perform most of the basic receptionist duties off site.

■ THE JOB

The receptionist is a specialist in human contact: The most important part of a receptionist's job is dealing with people in a courteous and effective manner. Receptionists greet customers, clients, patients, and salespeople, take their names, and determine the nature of their business and the person they wish to see. The receptionist then pages the requested person, directs the visitor to that person's office or location, or makes an appointment for a later visit. Receptionists usually keep records of all visits by writing down the visitor's name, purpose of visit, person visited, and date and time. They may also be responsible for having clients and visitors fill out applications or paperwork pertaining to their visit.

Most receptionists answer the telephone at their place of employment; many operate switchboards or paging systems. These workers usually take and distribute messages for other employees and may receive and distribute mail. Receptionists may perform a variety of other clerical duties, including keying in and filing correspondence and other paperwork, proofreading, preparing travel vouchers, and preparing outgoing mail. In some businesses, receptionists are responsible for monitoring the attendance of other employees. In businesses where employees are frequently out of the office on assignments, receptionists may keep track of their whereabouts to ensure that they receive important phone calls and messages. Many receptionists use computers and word processors in performing their clerical duties.

Receptionists are partially responsible for maintaining office security, especially in large firms. They may require all visitors to sign in and out and carry visitors' passes during their stay. Since visitors may not enter most offices unescorted, receptionists usually accept and sign for packages and other deliveries.

Receptionists are frequently responsible for answering inquiries from the public about a business's nature and operations. To answer these questions efficiently and in a manner that conveys a favorable impression, a receptionist must be as knowledgeable as possible about the business's products, services, policies, and practices and familiar with the names and responsibilities of all other employees. They must be careful, however, not to divulge classified information such as business procedures or employee activities that a competing company might be able to use. This part of a receptionist's job is so important that some businesses call their receptionists information clerks.

A large number of receptionists work in physicians' and dentists' offices, hospitals, clinics, and other health care establishments. Workers in medical offices receive patients, take their names, have them fill out forms, and escort them to examination rooms. They make future appointments for patients and may prepare statements and collect bill payments. In hospitals, receptionists obtain patient information, assign patients to rooms, and keep records on the dates they are admitted and discharged.

In other types of industries, the duties of these workers vary. Receptionists in hair salons arrange appointments for clients and may escort them to stylists' stations. Workers in bus or train companies answer inquiries about departures, arrivals, and routes. *In-file operators* collect and distribute credit information to clients for credit purposes. *Registrars, park aides,* and *tourist-information assistants* may be employed as receptionists at public or private facilities. Their duties may include keeping a record of the visitors entering and leaving the facility, as well as providing information on services that the facility provides. *Information clerks, automobile club information clerks,* and *referral-and-information aides* provide answers to questions by telephone or in person from current or potential clients and keep a record of all inquiries.

QUICK FACTS

ALTERNATE TITLE(S)
Information Clerks

DUTIES
Greet clients and visitors to an office, answer their questions, and direct them to the people they wish to see; answer telephone calls and take and distribute messages for other employees

SALARY RANGE
$19,070 to $27,300 to $39,350+

WORK ENVIRONMENT
Primarily Indoors

BEST GEOGRAPHIC LOCATION(S)
Opportunities exist throughout the country

MINIMUM EDUCATION LEVEL
High School Diploma

SCHOOL SUBJECTS
Business, Computer Science, Speech

EXPERIENCE
On-the-job training

PERSONALITY TRAITS
Conventional, Outgoing, Talkative

SKILLS
Interpersonal, Organizational, Public Speaking

CERTIFICATION OR LICENSING
Recommended

SPECIAL REQUIREMENTS
None

EMPLOYMENT PROSPECTS
Good

ADVANCEMENT PROSPECTS
Fair

OUTLOOK
About as Fast as the Average

NOC
1414

O*NET-SOC
43-4171.00

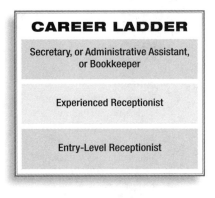

CAREER LADDER

Secretary, or Administrative Assistant, or Bookkeeper

Experienced Receptionist

Entry-Level Receptionist

Switchboard operators may perform specialized work, such as operating switchboards at police district offices to take calls for assistance from citizens. Or, they may handle airport communication systems, including public address paging systems and courtesy telephones, or serve as *answering-service operators,* who record and deliver messages for clients who cannot be reached by telephone.

■ EARNINGS

Earnings for receptionists vary widely with the education and experience of the worker and type, size, and geographic location of the business. The median annual salary for receptionists was $27,300 in May 2015, according to the U.S. Department of Labor (DOL), with salaries ranging from $19,070 to $39,350 or higher. The DOL reports that receptionists earned the following mean salaries by employer: offices of dentists, $32,730; offices of physicians, $29,450; offices of other health practitioners, $27,300; and personal care services, $23,230.

Receptionists are usually eligible for paid holidays and vacations, sick leave, medical and life insurance coverage, and a retirement plan of some kind.

■ WORK ENVIRONMENT

Because receptionists usually work near or at the main entrance to the business, their work area is one of the first places a caller sees. Therefore, these areas are usually pleasant and clean and are carefully furnished and decorated to create a favorable, businesslike impression. Work areas are almost always air-conditioned, well lit, and relatively quiet, although a receptionist's phone rings frequently. Receptionists work behind a desk or counter and spend most of their workday sitting, although some standing and walking is required when filing or escorting visitors to their destinations. The job may be stressful at times, especially when a worker must be polite to rude callers.

Most receptionists work 35–40 hours a week. Some may work weekend and evening hours, especially those in medical offices. Switchboard operators may have to work any shift of the day if their employers require 24-hour phone service, such as hotels and hospitals. These workers usually work holidays and weekend hours.

■ EXPLORING

A good way to obtain experience in working as a receptionist is through a high school work-study program. Students participating in such programs spend part of their school day in classes and the rest working for local businesses. This arrangement will help you gain valuable practical experience before you look for your first job. High school guidance counselors can provide information about work-study opportunities.

■ EDUCATION AND TRAINING REQUIREMENTS
High School

You can prepare for a receptionist or switchboard operator position by taking courses in business procedures, office machine operation, business math, English, and public speaking. You should also take computer science courses (such as word processing and spreadsheet application), as computers are used in nearly all offices.

Postsecondary Training

Most employees require receptionists to have a high school diploma. Some businesses prefer to hire workers who have completed post-high school courses at a junior college or business school. If you are interested in post-high school education, you may find courses in basic bookkeeping and principles of accounting helpful. This type of training may lead to a higher paying receptionist job and a better chance for advancement. Many employers require typing, switchboard, computer, and other clerical skills, but they may provide some on-the-job training, as the work is typically entry level.

Certification

Many community colleges and business and secretarial schools offer certificates in business or office operations.

A receptionist greets an office visitor. (Andresr. Shutterstock.)

Contact schools in your area to learn about available programs.

■ CERTIFICATION, LICENSING, AND SPECIAL REQUIREMENTS
Certification or Licensing
There are no certification or licensing requirements for receptionists. Those who wish to hone their skills and enhance their chances to secure work can receive certification from the National Association of Professional Receptionists (NAPR). Qualifications for the certified professional receptionist designation include one-year membership to NAPR, at least five years of relevant work experience, and a diploma or certificate from an accredited business or secretarial school, or continuing education certificates. The International Association of Administrative Professionals also provides certification to administrative professionals. Contact these organizations for more information.

■ EXPERIENCE, SKILLS, AND PERSONALITY TRAITS
No experience is needed to work as a receptionist, but those with prior work experience will increase their chances of landing a job, getting promoted, and possibly earning higher pay.

To be a good receptionist, you must be well groomed, have a pleasant voice, and be able to express yourself clearly. Because you may sometimes deal with demanding people, a smooth, patient disposition and good judgment are important. All receptionists need to be courteous and tactful. A good memory for faces and names also proves very valuable. Most important are good listening and communications skills and an understanding of human nature.

■ EMPLOYMENT PROSPECTS
Employers
According to the U.S. Department of Labor, approximately 1,028,600 people are employed as receptionists and information clerks. Many work in service-providing industries, with offices of physicians, dentists, and other health care practitioners employing about 31 percent of all receptionists and information clerks. Factories, wholesale and retail stores, and service providers also employ a large percentage of these workers. About one in three receptionists work part time.

Starting Out
While you are in high school, you may be able to learn of openings with local businesses through your school counselors or newspaper want ads and employment Web

---

TOP-PAYING INDUSTRIES AND MEAN ANNUAL SALARIES FOR RECEPTIONISTS, MAY 2015
FAST FACTS

- U.S. Postal Service: $57,770
- Rail transportation: $50,600
- Natural Gas Distribution: $40,380
- Shoe Stores: $38,060
- Insurance and Employee Benefit Funds: $37,420

Source: U.S. Department of Labor

---

sites. Local state employment offices frequently have information about receptionist work. You should also contact area businesses for whom you would like to work; many available positions are not advertised in the paper because they are filled so quickly. Temporary-work agencies are a valuable resource for finding jobs, too, some of which may lead to permanent employment. Friends and relatives may also know of job openings.

■ ADVANCEMENT PROSPECTS
Advancement opportunities are limited for receptionists, especially in small offices. The more clerical skills and education workers have, the greater their chances for promotion to such better-paying jobs as secretary, administrative assistant, or bookkeeper. College or business school training can help receptionists advance to higher-level positions. Many companies provide training for their receptionists and other employees, helping workers gain skills for job advancement.

■ OUTLOOK
Overall employment for receptionists is expected to grow faster than the average for all careers through 2024, according to the *Occupational Outlook Handbook*. Many openings will occur due to the occupation's high turnover rate. Opportunities will be best for those with a variety of clerical and computer skills and work experience. Growth in jobs for receptionists is expected to be greater than for other clerical positions because automation will have little effect on the receptionist's largely interpersonal duties and because of an anticipated growth in the number of businesses providing services. In addition, more and more businesses are learning how valuable a receptionist can be in furthering their public relations efforts and helping them convey a positive image.

The employment outlook for receptionists varies by employment sector. For example, job opportunities for receptionists in the health care industry will grow by nearly 25 percent (or much faster than the average for all careers) through 2024 because of the growing aging population (which will require more medical care) and the passage of the Affordable Care Act (which will allow more people to be covered by health insurance—and create demand for more staff at health care facilities). On the other hand, employment is expected to decline for receptionists who work in the manufacturing, retail, information, and broadcasting industries.

UNIONS AND ASSOCIATIONS

Receptionists are not represented by unions, but many join the American Society of Administrative Professionals, Association of Executive and Administrative Professionals, International Association of Administrative Professionals, and the National Association of Professional Receptionists. These organizations provide publications, job listings, networking opportunities, and certification.

TIPS FOR ENTRY

1. Join professional associations to access networking resources, industry publications, and employment opportunities.
2. Read *OfficePro* (https://www.iaap-hq.org/page/OfficeProMagazine) to learn more about successful office practices.
3. Talk with receptionists about their careers. Ask them for advice on breaking into the field.
4. For job listings, visit:
   - http://careers.iaap-hq.org
   - http://jobs.theaeap.com

FOR MORE INFORMATION

For information on education and careers, contact
American Society of Administrative Professionals
121 Free Street
Portland, ME 04101-3919
Tel: (888) 960-ASAP; (207) 842-5500
E-mail: custserv@divcom.com
http://www.asaporg.com

For information on membership, contact
Association of Executive and Administrative Professionals
900 South Washington Street, Suite G-13
Falls Church, VA 22046-4009
Tel: (703) 237-8616
Fax: (703) 533-1153
E-mail: headquarters@theaeap.com
http://theaeap.com/

For information on careers, contact
International Association of Administrative Professionals
10502 North Ambassador Drive, Suite 100
Kansas City, MO 64153-1278
Tel: (816) 891-6600
Fax: (816) 891-9118
http://www.iaap-hq.org

For certification information, job listings, and other resources, visit
National Association of Professional Receptionists
PO Box 104
College Park, MD 20741-0104
Tel: (877) 709-5051; (301) 220-1613
E-mail: rredrick@receptionservices.com
http://www.receptionists.us

Recreation Workers

OVERVIEW

Recreation workers help groups and individuals enjoy and use their leisure time constructively. They organize and administer physical, social, and cultural programs. They also operate recreational facilities and study recreation needs. There are approximately 379,300 recreation workers employed in the United States.

HISTORY

Americans enjoy more leisure time today than at any other period in history. The introduction of new technology, along with changing labor laws, has shrunk the workday and workweek. Workers receive increased vacation time, often setting their own flexible hours and, in many cases, retiring at an earlier age. The use of labor-saving devices and convenience foods in the home adds more free hours to a family's time, while increased income provides extra money for recreational activities.

During the last generation, leisure has become a time for planned activity. New services and revolutionized old ones have been developed to help Americans find beneficial ways in which to use their spare time.

Organized recreation has been of great value to those in nursing homes and other extended-care facilities. The occupations in recreation work grew out of the awareness that people were happier when they participated in activities. Today's recreation professionals are specialists in motivating people. They are trained, responsible leaders who understand and are sensitive to human needs and who are dedicated to helping people help themselves through recreation.

■ THE JOB

Recreation workers plan, organize, and direct recreation activities for people of all ages, social and economic levels, and degrees of physical and emotional health. The exact nature of their work varies and depends on their individual level of responsibility.

Recreation workers employed by local governments and voluntary agencies include *recreation supervisors,* who coordinate recreation center directors, who in turn supervise *recreation leaders* and *aides.* With the help of volunteer workers, they plan and carry out programs at community centers, neighborhood playgrounds, recreational and rehabilitation centers, prisons, hospitals, and homes for children and the elderly, often working in cooperation with social workers and sponsors of the various centers.

Recreation supervisors plan programs to meet the needs of the people they serve. Well-rounded programs may include arts and crafts, dramatics, music, dancing, swimming, games, camping, nature study, and other pastimes. Special events may include festivals, contests, pet and hobby shows, and various outings. Recreation supervisors also create programs for people with special needs, such as the elderly or people in hospitals. Supervisors have overall responsibility for coordinating the work of the recreation workers who carry out the programs and supervise several recreation centers or an entire region.

Recreation center directors run the programs at their respective recreation buildings, indoor centers, playgrounds, or day camps. In addition to directing the staff of the facility, they oversee the safety of the buildings and equipment, handle financial matters, and prepare reports. *Directors of recreation and parks* develop and manage recreation programs in parks, playgrounds, and other settings.

Recreation or activity leaders, with the help of recreation aides, work directly with assigned groups and are responsible for the daily operations of a recreation program. They organize and lead activities such as drama, dancing, sports and games, camping trips, and other recreations. They give instruction in crafts, games, and sports, and they work with other staff on special projects and events. Leaders help train and direct volunteers and perform other tasks as required by the director. *Activity specialists* provide instruction and coaching primarily in one activity, such as art, music, drama, swimming, or tennis.

In industry, recreation leaders plan social and athletic programs for employees and their families. Bowling leagues, softball teams, picnics, and dances are examples of company-sponsored activities. In addition, an increasing number of companies provide exercise and fitness programs for their employees.

Camp counselors lead and instruct children and adults in nature-oriented forms of recreation at camps or resorts. Activities usually include swimming, hiking, horseback riding, and other outdoor sports and games, as well as instruction in nature and folklore. Camp counselors teach skills such as wood crafting, leather working, and basket weaving. Some camps offer specialized instruction in subjects such as music, drama, gymnastics, and computers. In carrying out the programs, camp counselors are concerned with the safety, health, and comfort of the campers. Counselors are supervised by a camp director.

Another type of recreation worker is the *social director,* who plans and organizes recreational activities for guests in hotels and resorts or for passengers aboard a ship. Social directors usually greet new arrivals and introduce them to other guests, explain the recreational facilities, and encourage guests to participate in planned activities. These activities may include card parties, games, contests, dances, musicals, or field trips and may require setting up equipment, arranging for transportation, or planning decorations, refreshments, or entertainment. In general, social directors try to create a friendly atmosphere, paying particular attention to lonely guests and trying to ensure that everyone has a good time.

QUICK FACTS

ALTERNATE TITLE(S)
Activity Specialists, Camp Counselors, Directors of Recreation and Parks, Recreation Aides, Recreation Center Directors, Recreation Leaders, Recreation Supervisors, Social Directors

DUTIES
Plan and organize recreational activities for people of all ages

SALARY RANGE
$17,660 to $23,320 to $40,880+

WORK ENVIRONMENT
Primarily Outdoors

BEST GEOGRAPHIC LOCATION(S)
Nationwide

MINIMUM EDUCATION LEVEL
Bachelor's Degree

SCHOOL SUBJECTS
Music, Physical Education, Theater/Dance

EXPERIENCE
On-the-job trainings; several years experience for management

PERSONALITY TRAITS
Athletic, Hands On, Social

SKILLS
Interpersonal, Public Speaking, Teaching

CERTIFICATION OR LICENSING
Required

SPECIAL REQUIREMENTS
None

EMPLOYMENT PROSPECTS
Good

ADVANCEMENT PROSPECTS
Good

OUTLOOK
Faster than the Average

NOC
4167

O*NET-SOC
39-9032.00

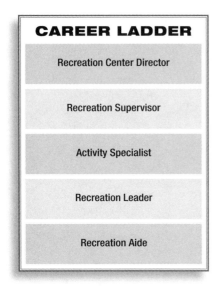

CAREER LADDER

Recreation Center Director

Recreation Supervisor

Activity Specialist

Recreation Leader

Recreation Aide

■ EARNINGS

The U.S. Department of Labor reports that in May 2015, full-time recreation workers earned a median salary of $23,320. Wages ranged from less than $17,660 to more than $40,880 a year. Some top-level managers can make considerably more. The average salary for federally employed recreation workers was $51,780; state-employed recreation workers earned $38,030 per year.

Benefits for salaried recreation workers depend on the employer; however, they usually include such items as health insurance, retirement or 401(k) plans, and paid vacation days. Self-employed recreation workers must provide their own benefits.

■ WORK ENVIRONMENT

Physical conditions vary greatly from outdoor parks to nursing homes for the elderly. A recreation worker can choose the conditions under which he or she would like to work. Recreation workers with an interest in the outdoors may become camp counselors. Those who have an interest in travel may seek a job as a social director on a cruise ship. There are opportunities for people who want to help the elderly or mentally handicapped, as well as for people with an interest in drama or music. Recreation directors typically spend most of their time indoors, in an office.

A recreation worker conducts a swim class for children at a community pool. (wavebreakmedia. Shutterstock.)

Generally, recreation workers must work while others engage in leisure activities. Most recreation workers work 44-hour weeks. But they should expect, especially those just entering the field, some night and weekend work. A compensating factor is the pleasure of helping people enjoy themselves.

Many of the positions are part time or seasonal, and many full-time recreation workers spend more time performing management duties than in leading hands-on activities.

■ EXPLORING

The best way to learn more about this field is through firsthand experience. You can see if this type of work is for you through a part-time, summer, or volunteer job in a recreation department, neighborhood center, camp, or other recreation-oriented organization. It is essential to be comfortable with people, so take on any jobs or activities that will expose you to a variety of people. Also consider participating in clubs and other activities that will boost your proficiency in areas like crafts, sports, and music.

■ EDUCATION AND TRAINING REQUIREMENTS
High School

High school students interested in recreation work should get a broad liberal arts and cultural education and acquire at least a working knowledge of arts and crafts, music, dance, drama, athletics, and nature study.

Postsecondary Training

Acceptable college majors include parks and recreation management, leisure studies, fitness management, and related disciplines. A degree in any liberal arts field may be sufficient if the person's education includes courses relevant to recreation work.

In industrial recreation, employers usually prefer applicants with a bachelor's degree in recreation and a strong background in business administration. Some jobs require specialized training in a particular field, such as art, music, drama, or athletics. Others need special certifications, such as a lifesaving certificate to teach swimming.

Approximately 80 recreation administration, leisure studies, and related baccalaureate programs are accredited by the Council on Accreditation of Parks, Recreation, Tourism and Related Professions. Students may also pursue a master's degree or doctorate (Ph.D.) in the field.

Certification

The American Camp Association (ACA) awards certificates to individuals who complete online training. The following certificates are available: entry-level program staff certificate, experienced program staff certificate, middle manager certificate, and camp director certificate. Contact the ACA for more information.

■ CERTIFICATION, LICENSING, AND SPECIAL REQUIREMENTS
Certification or Licensing

Many recreation professionals become certified to demonstrate their professional competence. The National Recreation and Park Association (NRPA) provides certification to recreation workers. More than 40 states have adopted NRPA standards for park/recreation professionals. The NRPA offers four certifications: certified park and recreation professional, certified park and recreation executive, aquatic facility operator, and certified playground safety inspector. To obtain certification, applicants must meet educational and experience requirements and pass an examination. Contact the NRPA for more information.

The federal government employs many recreation leaders in national parks, the armed forces, the Department of Veterans Affairs, and correctional institutions. It may be necessary to pass a civil service examination to qualify for these positions.

Specialized certification may be required depending on the job. For instance, a recreation worker for water-related activities must earn a lifesaving certificate.

■ EXPERIENCE, SKILLS, AND PERSONALITY TRAITS

No experience is required for entry-level positions; several years of experience are required for management positions such as recreation director.

Recreation workers must enjoy working with people of different ages and circumstances. They may also have a passion for sports or crafts that they want to share with others. Personal qualifications for recreation work include an outgoing personality, an even temperament, and the ability to lead and influence others. Strong communication skills for speaking to and directing large groups are a must, as are problem-solving skills; recreation workers must be able to adjust activities to suit the needs and abilities of a variety of participants. Recreation workers also should have good health and stamina and should be able to stay calm and think clearly and quickly in emergencies.

■ EMPLOYMENT PROSPECTS
Employers

There are about 379,300 recreation workers, not counting summer workers or volunteers, employed in the United

---

AMERICAN LEISURE TIME

FAST FACTS

According to the U.S. Bureau of Labor Statistics, in 2015

- On an average day, individuals age 15 and over spent half of their leisure time—2.8 hours per day—watching TV.
- Americans spent 1.71 additional hours in leisure and sport activities on weekends than during weekdays.
- Employed adults living in households without children engaged in leisure activities on average for 5.2 hours per day, over an hour more than employed adults living with a child under 6 years old.
- Men were slightly more likely than women to participate in sports, exercise, or recreation on any given day. Also, men typically spent more time in these activities than did women: 1.8 hours versus 1.3hours.
- Participants reported doing the following sports, exercise, and recreation activities most frequently: walking (28.7 percent), using cardiovascular equipment (16.4 percent), and weightlifting/strength training (9.8 percent).

Source: Bureau of Labor Statistics

States. About 30 percent work for local government agencies, and about 15 percent are employed by nursing and residential care facilities, such as halfway houses, institutions for delinquent youths, and group homes or commercial recreation establishments and private industry. Another 10 percent work for civic and social membership organizations such as the Boy Scouts, Girl Scouts, YMCA, or YWCA.

Starting Out

College career services offices are useful in helping graduates find employment. Most college graduates begin as either recreation leaders or specialists and, after several years of experience, they may become recreation directors. A few enter trainee programs leading directly to recreation administration within a year or so. Those with graduate training may start as recreation directors.

■ ADVANCEMENT PROSPECTS

Recreation leaders without graduate training will find advancement limited, but it is possible to obtain better paying positions through a combination of education and experience. With experience it is possible to become a recreation director. With further experience, directors may become supervisors and eventually head of all recreation departments or divisions in a city. Some recreation professionals become consultants.

■ OUTLOOK

The U.S. Department of Labor predicts that employment opportunities for recreation workers will increase by 10 percent through 2024, or faster than the average for all occupations. The expected expansion in the recreation field will result from increased leisure time and income for the population as a whole, along with a continuing interest in fitness and health and a growing elderly population in nursing homes, senior centers, and retirement communities. There is also a demand for recreation workers to conduct activity programs for special needs groups.

Two areas promising the most favorable opportunities for recreation workers are the commercial recreation and social service industries. Commercial recreation establishments include amusement parks, sports and entertainment centers, wilderness and survival enterprises, tourist attractions, vacation excursions, hotels and other resorts, camps, health spas, athletic clubs, and apartment complexes. New employment opportunities will arise in social service agencies such as senior centers, halfway houses, children's homes, and day-care programs for the mentally or developmentally disabled.

Recreation programs that depend on government funding are most affected in times of economic downturns when budgets are reduced. This means that competition will increase significantly for jobs in the private sector. Due to such predicted budget reductions, employment for recreation workers in local government is predicted to grow more slowly than the average for all other occupations.

In any case, competition is expected to be keen because the field is open to college graduates regardless of major; as a result, there are more applicants than there are job openings. Opportunities for staff positions will be best for individuals who have formal training in recreation and for those with previous experience. Those with graduate degrees will have the best opportunities for administrative or supervisory positions.

■ UNIONS AND ASSOCIATIONS

Membership with professional organizations, such as the National Recreation and Park Association, can provide networking, advocacy, and career advancement benefits.

■ TIPS FOR ENTRY

1. Gain experience by taking on volunteer, part-time, or summer jobs as a camp counselor or recreation aide.
2. Work or volunteer with as many different people as possible to become more outgoing and to build communication skills.
3. Become proficient in as many areas as possible, such as music, crafts, sports, and other activities.

Developing a speciality or a focus may increase your chances in landing a job.

■ FOR MORE INFORMATION

For information regarding industry trends, accredited institutions, and conventions, contact

American Alliance for Health, Physical Education, Recreation and Dance
1900 Association Drive
Reston, VA 20191-1598
Tel: (800) 213-7193; (703) 476-3400
Fax: (703) 476-9527
http://www.shapeamerica.org/

For information on certification qualifications, contact

American Camp Association
5000 State Road 67 North
Martinsville, IN 46151-7902
Tel: (800) 428-2267; (765) 342-8456
Fax: (765) 342-2065
E-mail: contactus@ACAcamps.org
http://www.acacamps.org

For information about owning and running a camp, contact

Camp Owners and Directors Association
Tel: (520) 577-7925
E-mail: Codacamp@gmail.com
http://coda.camp/

For information on the recreation industry, career opportunities, and certification qualifications, contact

National Recreation and Park Association
22377 Belmont Ridge Road
Ashburn, VA 20148-4501
Tel: (800) 626-6772
E-mail: customerservice@nrpa.org
http://www.nrpa.org

Recreational Therapists

■ OVERVIEW

Recreational therapists, also known as *therapeutic recreation specialists,* plan, organize, direct, and monitor medically approved recreation programs for patients in hospitals, clinics, and various community settings. These therapists use recreational activities to assist patients with mental, physical, or emotional disabilities to achieve the maximum possible functional independence. Recreational therapists hold about 18,600 jobs in the United States.

HISTORY

The field of therapy has expanded in the past few decades to include recreational therapy as a form of medical treatment. Its use grew out of the realization that soldiers suffering from battle fatigue, shock, and emotional trauma respond positively to organized recreation and activity programs.

As a result, therapy for people in nursing homes, hospitals, mental institutions, and adult care facilities is no longer limited to physical therapy. Experiments have shown that recovery is aided by recreational activities such as sports, music, art, gardening, dance, drama, field trips, and other pastimes. Elderly people are healthier and more alert when their days are filled with activities, field trips, and social get-togethers. People with disabilities can gain greater self-confidence and awareness of their own abilities when they get involved with sports, crafts, and other activities. People recovering from drug or alcohol addiction can reaffirm their self-worth through directed hobbies, clubs, and sports. The recreational therapist is a health professional who organizes these types of activities and helps patients take an active role in their own recovery.

THE JOB

Recreational therapists work with people who are mentally, physically, or emotionally disabled. They are professionals who employ leisure activities as a form of treatment, much as other health practitioners use surgery, drugs, nutrition, exercise, or psychotherapy. Recreational therapists strive to minimize patients' symptoms, restore function, and improve their physical, mental, and emotional well-being. Enhancing the patient's ability to take part in everyday life is the primary goal of recreational therapy; interesting and rewarding activities are the means for working toward that goal.

Recreational therapists work in a number of different settings, including mental hospitals, psychiatric day hospitals, community mental health centers, nursing homes, adult day care programs, residential facilities for the mentally disabled, school systems, and prisons. They can work as individual staff members, as independent consultants, or as part of a larger therapeutic team. They may get personally involved with patients or direct the work of assistants and support staff.

QUICK FACTS

ALTERNATE TITLE(S)
Art Therapists, Dance/Movement Therapists, Horticultural Therapists, Industrial Therapists, Music Therapists, Orientation Therapists, Therapeutic Recreation Specialists

DUTIES
Plan, organize, direct, and monitor medically approved recreation programs for patients in hospitals, clinics, and various community settings

SALARY RANGE
$28,020 to $45,890 to $71,790+

WORK ENVIRONMENT
Primarily Indoors

BEST GEOGRAPHIC LOCATION(S)
Nationwide; most opportunities available in major metropolitan areas

MINIMUM EDUCATION LEVEL
Bachelor's Degree

SCHOOL SUBJECTS
Biology, Chemistry, Psychology

EXPERIENCE
Volunteer or part-time experience

PERSONALITY TRAITS
Athletic, Helpful, Social

SKILLS
Interpersonal, Organizational, Teaching

CERTIFICATION OR LICENSING
Required

SPECIAL REQUIREMENTS
None

EMPLOYMENT PROSPECTS
Good

ADVANCEMENT PROSPECTS
Fair

OUTLOOK
About as Fast as the Average

NOC
3144

O*NET-SOC
29-1125.00

The recreational therapist first confers with the doctors, psychiatrists, social workers, physical therapists, occupational therapists, and other professionals on staff to coordinate their efforts in treatment. The recreational therapist needs to understand the nature of the patient's ailment, current physical and mental capacities,

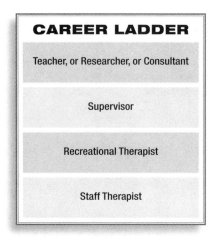

CAREER LADDER

Teacher, or Researcher, or Consultant

Supervisor

Recreational Therapist

Staff Therapist

emotional state, and prospects for recovery. The patient's family and friends are also consulted to find out the patient's interests and hobbies. With this information, the recreational therapist then plans an agenda of activities for that person.

To enrich the lives of people in hospitals and other institutions, recreational therapists use imagination and skill in organizing beneficial activities. Sports, games, arts and crafts, movie screenings, field trips, hobby clubs, and dramatics are only a few examples of activities that can enrich the lives of patients. Some therapists specialize in certain areas. *Dance/movement therapists* plan and conduct dance and body movement exercises to improve patients' physical and mental well-being. *Art therapists* work with patients in various art methods, such as drawing, painting, and ceramics, as part of their therapeutic and recovery programs. Therapists may also help patients by having them spend time with pets and other animals, such as horses. *Music therapists* design programs for patients that can involve solo or group singing, playing in bands, rhythmic and other creative activities, listening to music, or attending concerts. Even flowers and gardening can prove beneficial to patients, as is proved by the work of *horticultural therapists*. When a treatment team feels that regular employment would help certain patients, an *industrial therapist* arranges a productive job for the patient in an actual work environment, one that will have the greatest therapeutic value based on the patient's needs and abilities. *Orientation therapists* for the blind work with people who have recently lost their sight, helping them to readjust to daily living and independence through training and exercise. All of these professional therapists plan their programs to meet the needs and capabilities of patients. They also carefully monitor and record each patient's progress and report it to the other members of the medical team.

As part of their jobs, recreational therapists need to understand their patients and set goals for their progress accordingly. A patient having trouble socializing, for example, may have an interest in playing chess but be overwhelmed by the prospect of actually playing, since that involves interaction with another person. A therapist would proceed slowly, first letting the patient observe a number of games and then assigning a therapeutic

assistant to serve as a chess partner for weeks or even months, as long as it takes for the patient to gain enough confidence to seek out other patients for chess partners. The therapist makes a note of the patient's response, modifies the therapy program accordingly, and shares the results with other professionals on the team. If a patient responds more enthusiastically to the program, works more cooperatively with others, or becomes more disruptive, the therapist must note these reactions and periodically reevaluate the patient's activity program.

Responsibilities and elements of the job can vary, depending on the setting in which the recreational therapist works. In nursing homes, the therapist often groups residents according to common or shared interests and ability levels and then plans field trips, parties, entertainment, and other group activities. The therapist documents residents' responses to the activities and continually searches for ways of heightening residents' enjoyment of recreational and leisure activities, not just in the facility but in the surrounding community as well. Because nursing home residents are likely to remain in the facility for months or even years, the activities program makes a big difference in the quality of their lives. Without the stimulation of interesting events to look forward to and participate in, the daily routine of a nursing home can become monotonous and depressing, and some residents are apt to deteriorate both mentally and physically. In some nursing homes, recreational therapists direct the activities program. In others, activities coordinators plan and carry out the program under the part-time supervision of a consultant who is either a recreational or occupational therapist.

The therapist in a community center might work in a day-care program for the elderly or in a program for mentally disabled adults operated by a county recreation department. No matter what the disability, recreational therapists in community settings face the added logistical challenge of arranging transportation and escort services, if necessary, for prospective participants. Coordinating transportation is less of a problem in hospitals and nursing homes, where the patients all live under one roof. Developing therapeutic recreation programs in community settings requires a large measure of organizational ability, flexibility, and ingenuity.

■ EARNINGS

Salaries of recreational therapists vary according to educational background, experience, certification, and region of the country. Recreational therapists had median earnings of $45,890 in May 2015, according to the U.S. Department of Labor. The lowest paid 10 percent earned less than $28,020 a year, while the highest paid 10 percent earned more than $71,790 annually. Employment setting is also an important factor in determining salary. Recreational therapists employed by nursing facilities earned average incomes of $43,000 in 2015. Those employed by federal agencies earned $66,050, while those who worked at state agencies earned $49,590. Consultants and educators may earn higher salaries.

Therapists employed at hospitals, clinics, and other facilities generally enjoy a full benefits package, including health insurance and vacation, holiday, and sick pay. Consultants and self-employed therapists must provide their own benefits.

■ WORK ENVIRONMENT

Working conditions vary, but recreational therapists generally work in a ward, a specially equipped activity room, or at a nursing home. In a community setting, recreational therapists may interview subjects and plan activities in an office, but they might work in a gymnasium, swimming pool, playground, or outdoors on a nature walk when leading activities. Therapists may also work on horse ranches, farms, and other outdoor facilities catering to people with disabilities.

The job may be physically tiring because therapists are often on their feet all day and may have to lift and carry equipment. Recreational therapists generally work a standard 40-hour week, although weekend and evening hours may be required. Supervisors may have to work overtime, depending on their workload.

■ EXPLORING

If you are interested in a career in recreational therapy, you can find part-time or summer work as a sports coach or referee, park supervisor, or camp counselor. Volunteer work in a nursing home, hospital, or care facility for disabled adults is also a good way to learn about the daily realities of institutional living. These types of facilities are always looking for volunteers to work with and visit patients. Working with people with physical, mental, or emotional disabilities can be stressful, and volunteer work is a good way for you to test whether you can handle this kind of stress.

■ EDUCATION AND TRAINING REQUIREMENTS
High School

You can prepare for a career as a recreational therapist by taking your high school's college preparatory program. This should include science classes, such as biology and chemistry, as well as mathematics and history classes. You can begin to gain an understanding of human behavior by taking psychology and sociology classes. For exposure to a variety of recreation specialties, take physical

A recreational therapist leads an exercise class for seniors. (De Visu. Shutterstock.)

education, art, music, and drama classes. Verbal and written communication skills are essential for this work, so take English and speech classes. This job will require you to write reports and work with databases, so computer science skills are also essential.

Postsecondary Training

More than 100 recreational therapy programs, which offer degrees ranging from the associate to the doctoral level, are currently available in the United States. While associate degrees in recreational therapy exist, such a degree will allow you only to work at the paraprofessional level. To be eligible for an entry-level professional position as a recreational therapist, you will need a bachelor's degree. Acceptable majors are recreational therapy, therapeutic recreation, and recreation with a concentration in therapeutic recreation. A typical four-year bachelor's degree program includes courses in both natural science (such as biology, behavioral science, and human anatomy) and social science (such as psychology and sociology). Courses more specific to the profession include programming for special populations; rehabilitative techniques including self-help skills, mobility, signing for the deaf, and orientation for the blind; medical equipment; current treatment approaches; legal issues; and professional ethics. In addition, you will need to complete a supervised internship or field placement lasting a minimum of 480 hours.

Those with degrees in related fields can enter the profession by earning master's degrees in therapeutic recreation. Advanced degrees are recommended for those seeking advancement to supervisory, administrative,

THERAPEUTIC RECREATION
LEARN MORE ABOUT IT

Austin, David R. *Therapeutic Recreation: Processes and Techniques,* 6th ed. Champaign, Ill.: Sports Publishing LLC, 2009.

Best-Martini, Elizabeth, Mary Anne Weeks, and Priscilla Wirth. *Long Term Care for Activity Professionals and Recreational Therapists,* 5th ed. Enumclaw, Wash.: Idyll Arbor, 2008.

Dattilo, John. *Facilitation Techniques in Therapeutic Recreation.* State College, Pa.: Venture, 2000.

Robertson, Terry, and Terry Long. *Foundations of Therapeutic Recreation.* Champaign, Ill.: Human Kinetics, 2007.

Stumbo, Norma, and Carol Ann Peterson. *Therapeutic Recreation Program Design: Principles and Procedures,* 5th ed. San Francisco: Benjamin Cummings, 2008.

Wilhite, Barbara, and Jean Keller. *Therapeutic Recreation: Cases and Exercises,* 2nd ed. State College, Pa.: Venture, 2001.

and teaching positions. These requirements will become stricter as more professionals enter the field.

Other Education or Training

Continuing education is increasingly becoming a requirement for professionals in this field. Many therapists attend conferences and seminars and take additional university courses. A number of professional organizations (for example, the National Therapeutic Recreation Society, the American Therapeutic Recreation Association, and the American Alliance for Health, Physical Education, Recreation, and Dance) offer continuing education opportunities.

■ CERTIFICATION, LICENSING, AND SPECIAL REQUIREMENTS
Certification or Licensing

A number of states regulate the profession of therapeutic recreation. Licensing is required in some states; professional certification (or eligibility for certification) is required in others; titling is regulated in some states and at some facilities. In other states, many hospitals and other employers require recreational therapists to be certified. Certification is recommended for recreational therapists as a way to show professional accomplishment. It is available through the National Council for Therapeutic Recreation Certification. To receive certification you must meet eligibility requirements, including

education and experience, as well as pass an exam. You are then given the title of certified therapeutic recreation specialist. Because of the variety of certification and licensing requirements, you must check with both your state and your employer for specific information on your situation.

■ EXPERIENCE, SKILLS, AND PERSONALITY TRAITS

Experience as a volunteer or part-time aide, along with education and work experience, are needed to obtain certification.

Most people become interested in recreation therapy because they have compassion for those who need help. To be a successful recreational therapist, you must be kind and gentle when providing therapy to clients, as much as you should enjoy and be enthusiastic about the activities in which you involve your clients. You will also need patience and a positive attitude. Since this is people-oriented work, therapists must be able to relate to many different people in a variety of settings. They must be able to deal assertively and politely with other health care workers, such as doctors and nurses, as well as with the clients themselves and their families. In addition, successful therapists must be creative and have strong communication and listening skills in order to develop and explain activities to patients.

■ EMPLOYMENT PROSPECTS
Employers

Recreational therapists hold almost 18,600 jobs, according to the U.S. Department of Labor. About 35 percent of these jobs are at hospitals and 20 percent at nursing care facilities. Other employers include hospitals, residential facilities, adult day care centers, and substance abuse centers, and state and local government agencies. Some therapists are self-employed. Employment opportunities also exist in long-term rehabilitation, home health care, correctional facilities, psychiatric facilities, and transitional programs.

Starting Out

There are many methods for finding out about available jobs in recreational therapy. A good place to start is the job notices and want ads printed in the local newspapers, bulletins from state park and recreation societies, and publications of the professional associations previously mentioned. A useful Internet resource for job listings include The Therapeutic Recreation Directory (http://www.recreationtherapy.com). State employment agencies and human service departments will know of job openings in state hospitals. College career services offices might also be able to put new recreational therapy graduates in touch with prospective employers. Internship programs are sometimes available, offering good opportunities to find potential full-time jobs.

Recent graduates should also make appointments to meet potential employers personally. Most colleges and universities offer career counseling services. Most employers will make themselves available to discuss their programs and the possibility of hiring extra staff. They may also guide new graduates to other institutions currently hiring therapists. Joining professional associations, both state and national, and attending conferences are good ways to meet potential employers and colleagues.

■ ADVANCEMENT PROSPECTS

Newly graduated recreational therapists generally begin as *staff therapists*. Advancement is chiefly to supervisory or administrative positions, usually after some years of experience and continuing education. Some therapists teach, conduct research, or do consulting work on a contract basis; a graduate degree is essential for moving into these areas.

Many therapists continue their education but prefer to continue working with patients. For variety, they may choose to work with new groups of people or get a job in a new setting, such as moving from a retirement home to a facility for the disabled. Some may also move to a related field, such as special education, or sales positions involving products and services related to recreational therapy.

■ OUTLOOK

The U.S. Department of Labor predicts that employment for recreational therapists will grow faster than the average for all careers through 2024. Increased life expectancies for the elderly and for people with developmental disabilities such as Down Syndrome will create opportunities for recreational therapists. Most openings for therapists will be in health care and assisted living facilities because of the increasing numbers and greater longevity of the elderly. There is also greater public pressure to regulate and improve the quality of life in retirement centers, which may mean more jobs and increased scrutiny of recreational therapists. Strong employment growth is also expected in offices of health practitioners, outpatient care centers, and the offices of physical, occupational and speech therapists, and audiologists. The incidence of alcohol and drug dependency problems is also growing,

creating a demand for qualified therapists to work in short-term alcohol and drug abuse clinics.

Expansion of the school-age population and the extension of federally funded services for disabled students will also increase demand for recreational therapists in schools.

Growth in hospital jobs is not expected to be as strong. Many of the new jobs created will be in hospital-based adult day care programs or in units offering short-term mental health services. Because of economic and social factors, no growth is expected in public mental hospitals. Many of the programs and services formerly offered there are being shifted to community residential facilities for the disabled. Community programs for special populations are expected to expand significantly. Therapists with a bachelor's degree in therapeutic recreation and certification will have better chances of securing work.

■ UNIONS AND ASSOCIATIONS

Recreational therapists should be members of the American Therapeutic Recreation Association, which offers continuing education classes, publications, and networking opportunities.

■ TIPS FOR ENTRY

1. Take a college preparatory program in high school, because you will need a variety of skills including computer, psychology, science, language and communication, business, athletics, and the arts to be a successful recreational therapist.
2. Earn a bachelor's degree in recreational therapy and become licensed in your state.
3. Take on part-time or summer work as a counselor or coach, and work part time in a nursing home or hospital.
4. Consider pursuing an advanced degree to open the door to more advanced positions and higher salaries.
5. Attend conferences and seminars to continue your education once in the field.

■ FOR MORE INFORMATION

For career information and resources, contact
American Alliance for Health, Physical Education, Recreation and Dance
1900 Association Drive
Reston, VA 20191-1598
Tel: (800) 213-7193; (703) 476-3400
Fax: (703) 476-9527
http://www.aahperd.org

For career information, networking opportunities, and job listings, contact

American Therapeutic Recreation Association
629 North Main Street
Hattiesburg, MS 39401-3429
Tel: (601) 450-2872
Fax: (601) 582-3354
E-mail: academy@atra-online.com
http://www.atra-online.com/

For information about a career as a child life specialist, contact

Association of Child Life Professionals (ACLP)
1820 N Fort Myer Dr Suite 520
Arlington, VA 22209
Tel: (800) 252-4515; (571) 483-4500
Fax: (571) 483-4482
E-mail: certification@childlife.org
http://www.childlife.org

To learn more contact

Canadian Therapeutic Recreation Association
P.O. Box 448
Russell, ON K4R 1E3
Canada
E-mail: ctra@canadian-tr.org
http://www.canadian-tr.org

For information on certification, contact

National Council for Therapeutic Recreation Certification
7 Elmwood Drive
New City, NY 10956-5136
Tel: (845) 639-1439
Fax: (845) 639-1471
E-mail: nctrc@nctrc.org
http://www.nctrc.org

For industry-related programs and resources, visit

National Therapeutic Recreation Society (NTRS)
22377 Belmont Ridge Road
Ashburn, VA 20148-4501
Tel: (800) 626-6772
E-mail: membership@nrpa.org
http://www.nrpa.org

Recycling Coordinators

■ OVERVIEW

Recycling coordinators manage recycling programs for city, county, or state governments or large organizations, such as colleges or military bases. They work with waste haulers and material recovery facilities to arrange for collecting, sorting, and processing recyclables such as aluminum, glass, and paper from households and businesses. Recycling coordinators are often responsible for educating the public about the value of recycling as well as instructing residents on how to properly separate recyclables in their homes. Recycling coordinators keep records of recycling rates in their municipality and help set goals for diversion of recyclables from the waste stream.

■ HISTORY

Coordinating recycling has a brief history as the job is known today. Only in the 1980s and early 1990s did many states begin setting recycling goals, creating the need for recycling coordinators at the local level. Prior to that time, private citizen groups or industry led most recycling efforts, so there was little need for municipal recycling coordinators. While much of today's recycling is driven by a desire to improve the environment, earlier recycling was often driven by economic forces. During the Great Depression, individual citizens or groups, such as the Boy Scouts, held newspaper drives and turned the newspaper over to a recycler. The recycler paid a minimal amount for the collection of the newspapers and then generally sold the newspaper to industry, which recycled or otherwise reused the newspaper. During World War II, shortages in raw materials to support the war prompted citizens to hold drives for aluminum, rubber, paper, and scrap metal; this time the spirit of recycling was patriotic as well as economic.

Other than times of shortage, governments had little concern for how people disposed of waste, simply because there was relatively little waste. Municipalities had been dumping, burning, burying, or otherwise disposing of residents' waste for years with little consequence. In 1898, New York City opened the first garbage-sorting plant in the United States, recycling some of its trash. The first aluminum recycling plants were built in the early 1900s in Chicago and Cleveland. By the 1920s, about 70 percent of U.S. cities had limited recycling programs, according to the League of Women Voters.

By 1960, the United States recycled about 7 percent of its municipal waste. In the mid-1960s, the federal government began to take greater interest in municipal waste-handling methods. Part of the Solid Waste Disposal Act of 1965 granted money for states to develop waste-handling programs. The Resource Conservation and Recovery Act of 1970 and 1976 amendments defined types of municipal solid waste (MSW) and spelled out minimum standards for waste handling.

State and federal governments, such as branches of the Environmental Protection Agency (EPA), were the earliest to hire people who specialized in recycling. These recycling experts usually acted in an advisory capacity to local governments that were trying to develop their own programs.

In the 1990s, more states began to set recycling goals, driving the increase in need for recycling coordinators. By 1998, all but six states had set formal recycling goals. These goals are generally stated in terms of the percentage of waste to be diverted from ending up in a landfill. Most states set goals between 20 and 50 percent. To encourage counties to make the effort at a local level, many state governments offered grants to counties to fund new recycling programs, and many counties found they needed a full-time person to coordinate the new effort. Initially, only the most populous counties qualified for the grants to afford a recycling program because they could divert the highest volume from landfills. The EPA reports that in 2012, Americans generated about 251 million tons of waste, of which nearly 35 percent was recycled and composted. In other words, on average, each person in the United States recycled and composted approximately 1.51 pounds of the nearly 4.38 pounds of waste he or she generated every day.

■ THE JOB

As recycling becomes more widespread, fewer recycling coordinators are faced with the task of organizing a municipal program from scratch. Instead, recycling coordinators work to improve current recycling rates in several ways. While recycling coordinators spend some time on administrative tasks, such as meeting with waste haulers and government officials and writing reports, they often need a considerable amount of time for public-education efforts. Only a small portion of the average recycling coordinator's job is spent sitting behind a desk.

Educating the public on proper separation of recyclables as well as explaining the need for recycling are a large part of a recycling coordinator's job. Good verbal communication skills are essential for a recycling coordinator to succeed in this role. Getting people who

QUICK FACTS

ALTERNATE TITLE(S)
None

DUTIES
Manage recycling programs for city, county, state governments, or other large organizations; educate the public about the importance of recycling

SALARY RANGE
$28,630 to $49,670 to $100,000+

WORK ENVIRONMENT
Primarily Indoors

BEST GEOGRAPHIC LOCATION(S)
Opportunities are available throughout the country, but are best in large, urban areas

MINIMUM EDUCATION LEVEL
Bachelor's Degree

SCHOOL SUBJECTS
Business, Earth Science, Government

EXPERIENCE
Internship; Volunteer or part-time experience

PERSONALITY TRAITS
Organized, Problem-Solving, Realistic

SKILLS
Business Management, Leadership, Organizational

CERTIFICATION OR LICENSING
None

SPECIAL REQUIREMENTS
None

EMPLOYMENT PROSPECTS
Good

ADVANCEMENT PROSPECTS
Fair

OUTLOOK
About as Fast as the Average

NOC
4161

O*NET-SOC
53-1021.01

haven't recycled before to start doing so can take some convincing. Recycling coordinators spread their message by speaking to community groups, businesses, and schools. They use persuasive speaking skills to urge people to do the extra work of peeling labels from and washing bottles and jars instead of just throwing them out, and separating newspapers, magazines, cardboard, and other types of paper. Even as recycling increases in this

CAREER LADDER

Recycling or Solid Waste Management Consultant

Recycling Coordinator—Large City

Recycling Coordinator—Small Municipality

country, many people are accustomed to disposing of trash as quickly as possible without giving it a second thought. It is the task of a recycling coordinator to get people to change such habits, and how well a recycling coordinator is able to do this can make the difference in the success of the entire program.

In some communities, recycling coordinators have economics on their side when it comes to getting people to change their habits. In so-called pay-as-you-throw programs, residents pay for garbage disposal based on how much waste their household produces. So recycling, although it may mean extra work, makes sense because it saves the homeowner money. For example, residents may be charged extra for any waste they set out at the curb beyond one garbage can per week. In communities with these programs, recycling rates tend to be higher, and recycling coordinators have an easier task of convincing people to recycle. Another part of a recycling coordinator's role as educator is answering questions about how recyclables are to be separated. Especially with new programs, residents often have questions about separating recyclables, such as what type of paper can be set out with newspaper, whether labels should be peeled from jars, and even keeping track of which week of the month or day of the week they should set their recyclables out with the trash. Fielding these types of calls always demands some portion of a recycling coordinator's time.

Most recycling coordinators spend a minimal amount of time on record keeping, perhaps 5 percent, one coordinator estimates. The coordinator is responsible for making monthly, or sometimes quarterly, reports to state and federal government agencies. Recycling coordinators also fill out grant applications for state and federal funding to improve their programs.

Some recycling coordinators work on military bases or college campuses. The goal of a recycling coordinator in one of these settings is the same as a municipal recycling coordinator—getting people to recycle. Their responsibilities may differ, however. The recycling coordinator on a college campus, for example, has a new set of residents every year to educate about the college's recycling program.

Recycling coordinators who come up with creative uses for waste may find opportunities in other fields as well. For example, recycling of computers and computer parts is a growing area. Some with knowledge in this area have founded their own companies or work for computer manufacturers.

■ EARNINGS

Salaries vary widely for recycling coordinators depending upon their level of experience and the region in which the job is located. For example, positions in areas with a higher cost of living, such as California, Arizona, New York, and Washington, D.C., for example, tend to pay higher salaries to recycling coordinators.

According to the U.S. Department of Labor, median annual earnings of first line supervisors/managers of helpers, laborers, and material movers (a category that includes recycling coordinators) were $49,670 in May 2015, with salaries ranging from $28,630 to $76,040. Recruiter.com estimated that recycling coordinators earn betwen $32,000 and $48,000 annually. Very experienced recycling coordinators who manage the recycling programs of large cities can earn more than $100,000 annually.

Benefits vary, but most local governments offer full-time employees a benefit package that generally includes paid health insurance; a retirement plan; and holiday, vacation, and sick pay.

■ WORK ENVIRONMENT

Recycling coordinators are essentially administrators. As such, they primarily work indoors, either in their offices or in meetings or giving speeches. Recycling coordinators need to watch costs, understand markets, and work within budgets. They should be able to be firm with contractors when necessary. They need to demonstrate good judgment and leadership, and they may need to justify their decisions and actions to city council members or others. Stresses are part of the job, including dealing with government bureaucracy, dips in community participation, services that fall short of expectations, fluctuating markets for recyclables, and other less-than-ideal situations.

Generally, recycling coordinators work 40 hours per week if they are full-time employees. Some positions may be part time, but for both work arrangements, working hours are generally during the day with weekends off. Occasionally, recycling coordinators may need to attend meetings in the evening, such as a county or city board meeting, or speak before a community group that meets at night. Facility or landfill tours that a recycling coordinator may arrange or participate in to generate publicity for the program may be offered on weekends. Recycling coordinators may leave the office setting to visit the material recovery facility, which can be noisy and dirty if compacting equipment and conveyers are running.

■ EXPLORING

You can start to explore a career as a recycling coordinator by familiarizing yourself with the issues involved in the field. Why is sorting garbage so costly? Why are some materials recycled and not others? Where are the markets? What are some creative uses for recyclable materials? Find out what's going on both nationally and in your area. Some states have more extensive recycling programs than others; for example, some have bottle deposit laws or other innovative programs to boost recycling efforts. Get to know who's doing what and what remains to be done. Read books on the topic and industry-related magazines; two informative publications are *Recycling Today* (http://www.recyclingtoday.com) and *Resource Recycling* (http://www.resource-recycling.com).

Arrange a tour of a local material recovery facility and talk with the staff there. You might even volunteer to work for a recycling organization. Large and small communities often have groups that support recycling with fund drives and information campaigns. Also, most municipal public meetings and workshops are good places to learn about how you can help with recycling in your community.

■ EDUCATION AND TRAINING REQUIREMENTS
High School

Recycling coordinators need a variety of skills, so taking a variety of classes in high school is a good start. Classes in business, economics, and civics are a good idea to help build an understanding of the public sector in which most recycling coordinators work. Knowledge of how local governments and markets for recycled materials function is something you will need to know later, and civics and economics courses provide this framework. English and speech classes are vital to developing good oral and written communication skills that you use to spread the word about the importance of recycling. Mathematics and science will prove useful in setting recycling goals and understanding how recycling helps the environment.

Postsecondary Training

Until recently, people with widely varying backgrounds and experience were becoming recycling coordinators. Enthusiasm, an understanding of recycling issues, and business acumen were more important than any specific degree or professional background. This is still true to some extent, as colleges generally don't offer degrees in recycling coordination. Instead, a bachelor's degree in environmental studies, environmental resources management, environmental education, or a related area and strong communication skills are desirable. Some

A recycling coordinator talks about good recycling practices at a local environmental awareness fair. (Joseph Sohm. Shutterstock.com)

schools offer minors in integrated waste management. Classes may include public policy, source reduction, transformation technology (composting/waste energy) and landfills.

Other Education or Training

The National Recycling Coalition offers continuing education (CE) opportunities via webinars and at its annual conference. Past webinars included "Understanding Domestic and Global Recycling Commodity Markets," "Sustainability Efforts in the Healthcare Industry: Focus on Plastics Recycling," and "Biodegradable Plastic Resins: Debunking the Myths." The National Waste & Recycling Association also provides CE classes and workshops. Contact these organizations for more information.

■ CERTIFICATION, LICENSING, AND SPECIAL REQUIREMENTS
Certification or Licensing

There are no certification or licensing requirements for recycling coordinators.

■ EXPERIENCE, SKILLS, AND PERSONALITY TRAITS

Experience as an intern, volunteer, or part-time employee at a recycling program is recommended for obtaining an entry-level position, but more experience will be needed to advance to higher level work.

Useful personal skills include good communication and people skills for interacting with staff, contractors, government officials, and the public. Leadership, persuasiveness, and creativity (the ability to think of new ways to use collected materials, for example) also are important.

DON'T TRASH THAT TV!

Although technology has made many aspects of life more enjoyable and convenient, items such as personal computers, cell phones, and televisions become outdated almost as soon as you walk out of the store. It almost seems as if you can open the paper the next day and find a newer model with more features and an "improved" design. Since many consumers want the newest and most advanced technology available, and since old electronics tend to do little more than collect dust, there is an ever increasing amount of old electronic equipment showing up in today's garbage. A recent study estimates that at least 500 million personal computers have become obsolete, and subsequently junked, in the United States since 1997. One problem with simply throwing these items out with your regular garbage is the possible contaminants they contain. For example, televisions and computer monitors contain cathode ray tubes (CRTs), which contain significant amounts of lead. Other electronic products contain nickel, cadmium, and other heavy metals that can be dangerous to humans and the environment.

Thus, the National Recycling Coalition recommends that you check with your state or local recycling board to see how to properly dispose of electronic equipment. Your town or county may even have regular pickup dates for such materials. You can also contact the manufacturer of your computer, television, or other electronic device to see if they offer recycling services or can put you in touch with a local organization that does.

As an alternative, and especially if the equipment still works, consider donating it to a charitable organization, small business, or local school that might have a need for it. For information on how and where to recycle your electronic equipment, visit http://www.epa.gov/osw/conserve/materials/ecycling/donate.htm. Taking the time to consider what to do with your obsolete electronics can make an important difference in the environment and in everyone's quality of life.

Source: National Recycling Coalition

■ EMPLOYMENT PROSPECTS

Employers

Recycling coordinators are almost exclusively employed by some level of government; they oversee recycling programs at the city, county, or state level. A limited number of recycling coordinators may find work with waste haulers that offer recycling coordination as part of their contracts to municipalities. Recycling coordinators work in communities of all sizes—from rural

countywide programs to urban ones. When states first mandated recycling, larger counties that generated more waste generally were the first to hire recycling coordinators. However, as more states set and achieve higher recycling goals, smaller cities and even rural areas need someone to coordinate their growing programs. At the state level, state environmental protection agencies or community development agencies may employ coordinators to administer state grants to and advise local recycling programs all over the state. Large organizations, such as colleges or military bases, are other employers of recycling coordinators.

Starting Out

A first job as a recycling coordinator is most likely to be with a smaller municipal program. Most colleges have a network of career referral services for their graduates, and city or county governments with openings for recycling coordinators often use these services to advertise positions to qualified graduates. Positions at the state level may also be available. Someone with previous experience with waste management projects, issues, and operations, in addition to the right educational background, is likely to get the more sought-after positions in larger cities and state governments. You can get hands-on experience through internships, volunteering, cooperative education, summer employment, or research projects.

You can gain experience during summers off from college, or if necessary, after college by volunteering or serving an internship with a recycling program in your area. If internships aren't available, paid work at a waste facility is a way to earn money over the summer and learn the very basics of recycling. Volunteering for a waste management consulting firm or nonprofit environmental organization is another way to get practical experience with recyclables. Most colleges have their own recycling programs, and you may find part-time work during the school year in your own college's recycling program. Contact the physical plant operations department or student employment services at your school.

■ ADVANCEMENT PROSPECTS

In most cases, the position of recycling coordinator is the top spot in the recycling program. Advancement isn't really an option, unless the coordinator moves to another, perhaps larger, municipal program, to a private employer, or in some cases, to a different field. There is a fair amount of turnover in the field because recycling coordinator positions, in many cases, are training ground for college graduates who eventually move on to other fields where they use skills they developed as recycling coordinators. Because recycling coordinators develop so many useful skills, they often find work in related fields, such as small business administration and nonprofit organizations or as government administrators.

Since many states have waste-handling projects, someone with good experience at the local level might move into a state-level job, such as recycling expert, a position in some states' waste-handling departments. Opportunities with private businesses that have in-house recycling needs or with solid waste management consultants or businesses might also constitute advancement. Finally, recycling coordinators also have the opportunity to expand their own programs. Through their efforts, a modest program with a limited staff and budget could blossom into a full-scale, profitable venture for the community. The coordinator could conceivably extend the scope of the program; improve links with state or local government officials, the public, and private business and industry; receive more funding; add staff; and otherwise increase the extent and prominence of the program.

OUTLOOK

The percentage of municipal solid waste that is recycled has grown from 10.1 percent in 1985 to 34.5 percent in 2012, according to the Environmental Protection Agency. This suggests that there will be growing demand for recycling coordinators. As states strive to meet their increasingly ambitious waste-reduction and recycling goals, people who can make it happen on the local level are going to be crucial. Although the recycling industry is subject to business fluctuations, demand and new technologies have created a viable market for recycled materials.

The recycling industry is also subject to political and social trends. Jobs will decline under administrations that do not allocate as much money for environmental concerns. On the other hand, more jobs may become available as engineers and technicians are attracted by the higher salaries offered in more popular technology- and finance-oriented fields. Environmental careers such as this one are also starting to be recognized as their own field, and not just subspecialties of other fields, such as civil engineering.

Nationwide, the waste management and recycling industries will need more people to run recovery facilities, design new recycling technologies, come up with new ways to use recyclables, and do related work. Private businesses are also expected to hire recycling coordinators to manage in-house programs.

UNIONS AND ASSOCIATIONS

Recycling coordinators do not belong to unions. The National Recycling Coalition is a nonprofit organization of recycling coordinators and related professionals. The National Waste & Recycling Association represents companies that collect and manage garbage and recycling and medical waste. The American Forest and Paper Association is a national trade association of companies that make up more than 75 percent of U.S. pulp, paper, paper-based packaging and wood building materials. It offers information on sustainability and paper recycling at its Web site.

TIPS FOR ENTRY

1. Read *Recycling Today* (http://www.recyclingtoday.com) and *Resource Recycling* (http://www.resource-recycling.com) to learn more about the field.
2. Attend the Resource Recycling Conference (http://rrconference.com/) to network and participate in continuing education opportunities.
3. Visit http://jobs.environmentalistseveryday.org/jobseekers for job listings.

FOR MORE INFORMATION

For up-to-date information on recycling, contact
American Forest and Paper
   Association
1101 K Street, NW, Suite 700
Washington, D.C. 20005-4210
Tel: (800) 878-8878
E-mail: info@afandpa.org
http://www.afandpa.org

This organization provides technical information, education, training, outreach, and advocacy services.
National Recycling Coalition
1220 L St NW, Suite 100-155
Washington, D.C. 20005-4018
Tel: (202) 618-2107
E-mail: info@NRCrecycles.org
http://nrcrecycles.org

For information on solid waste management, contact
National Waste & Recycling
   Association
4301 Connecticut Avenue, NW, Suite 300
Washington, D.C. 20008-2304
Tel: (800) 424-2869; (202) 244-4700
Fax: (202) 966-4824
E-mail: info@wasterecycling.org
https://wasterecycling.org/

Reflexologists

■ OVERVIEW

Reflexologists base their work on the theory that reflexes, specific points on the hands and feet, correspond to specific points on other parts of the body. They apply pressure to the feet or hands of their clients in order to affect the areas of the body that correspond to the areas that they are manipulating. Reflexologists believe that their work promotes overall good health, helps clients relax, and speeds the healing process.

■ HISTORY

Reflexology—or something similar to it—was practiced thousands of years ago. More than 4,000 years ago, the Chinese learned that foot massage was a useful adjunct to the practice of acupuncture. Many modern practitioners of reflexology believe that reflexology utilizes the principles on which acupuncture and traditional Chinese medicine are based. A 4,000-year-old fresco that appears in the tomb of Ankhmahor, physician to a pharaoh, in the Egyptian city of Saqqara depicts the practice of foot massage. In North America, the Cherokee people have emphasized the importance of the feet in health, partly because it is through the feet that human beings connect with the earth. Zone theory, which provides a theoretical basis for reflexology, existed in Europe as early as the 1500s.

Although reflexology is an ancient practice, its modern form originated in the early 20th century. William Fitzgerald, a Ct.-based physician who was an ear, nose, and throat specialist, revived the practice of reflexology in the West in 1913, when he found that applying pressure to a patient's hands or feet just before surgery decreased the level of pain experienced by the patient. In 1917, Fitzgerald wrote *Zone Therapy, or Relieving Pain at Home*, which described his work. Fitzgerald believed that "bioelectrical energy" flows from points in the feet or hands to specific points elsewhere in the body, and he thought that applying tourniquets and various instruments to the feet or hands enhanced the flow of energy. He set out to map the flow of that energy, and in the process he set up correspondences between areas on the feet or hands and areas throughout the body.

The next important figure in modern reflexology was Eunice Ingham, a physiotherapist who had worked with Joseph Shelby Riley, a follower of William Fitzgerald. Riley had decided against using instruments to manipulate the feet and hands, opting to use his hands instead. Ingham practiced and taught extensively, mapped the correspondences between the reflexes and the parts of the body, and wrote books chronicling her work with her patients, which helped to promote the field of reflexology. She went on to found the organization now known as the International Institute of Reflexology (IIR), which continues to promote the Original Ingham Method of Reflexology. Ultimately, Ingham became known as the mother of modern reflexology. Her students have played major roles in spreading reflexology throughout the world.

■ THE JOB

Reflexologists believe that the standing human body is divided vertically into 10 zones, five zones on each side of the imaginary vertical line that divides the body in two. On both sides, the zone closest to the middle is zone one, while the zone farthest from the middle is zone five. These zones also appear on the hands and feet. Reflexologists believe that by massaging a spot in a zone on the foot, they can stimulate a particular area in the corresponding zone of the body. By massaging the reflex in the middle of the big toe, for example, a reflexologist attempts to affect the pituitary gland, which is the corresponding body part.

Reflexologists also believe that their ministrations help their clients in two other ways. First, they believe that their treatments reduce the amount of lactic acid in the feet. Lactic acid is a natural waste product of the metabolic process, and its presence in large quantities is unhealthful. Second, they believe that their treatments break up calcium crystals that have built up in the nerve endings of the feet. It is their theory that the presence of these crystals inhibits the flow of energy, which is increased when the crystals are removed. Reflexologists also emphasize that their techniques improve circulation and promote relaxation.

It is worth noting that modern science has not validated the theoretical basis of reflexology, which is even less well accepted in the scientific world than are some other alternative therapies. Yet it is also worth noting that some therapies whose underlying theories have not been validated by science have been shown to be effective. Relatively few scientific studies of reflexology have been completed, but much research is underway at present, and it is likely that reflexology will be better understood in the near future.

An initial visit to a reflexologist generally begins with the practitioner asking the client questions about his or her overall health, medical problems, and the reason for the visit. The reflexologist makes the client comfortable and begins the examination and treatment.

Although most reflexologists, such as the followers of Eunice Ingham, use their hands to work on their clients' feet or hands, some prefer to use instruments. In either case, the reflexologist works on the feet and looks for sore spots, which are thought to indicate illness or other problems in the corresponding part of the body. On occasion, the problem will not be manifested in the corresponding organ or part of the body but will instead be manifested elsewhere within the zone. Usually, the reflexologist will spend more time on the sore spots than on other parts of the foot. On the basis of information provided by the client and information obtained by the reflexologist during the examination, the reflexologist will recommend a course of treatment that is appropriate for the client's physical condition. In some cases, such as those of extreme illness, the reflexologist may ask the client to check with his or her physician to determine whether the treatment may be in conflict with the physician's course of treatment. Most reflexologists will not treat a client who has a fever. In addition, because reflexology treatments tend to enhance circulation, it is sometimes necessary for a client who is taking medication to decrease the dosage, on the advice of a doctor, to compensate for the increased circulation and the resulting increased effectiveness of the medication.

One of the most important aspects of the reflexologist's skill is knowing exactly how much pressure to apply to a person's feet. The pressure required for a large, healthy adult, for example, would be too much for a young child or a baby. Different foot shapes and weights may also require different levels of pressure. The practitioner must also know how long to work on the foot, since the benefits of the treatment may be offset if the treatment lasts too long. In her book *Reflexology Today*, Doreen E. Bayly, one of Ingham's students, recalled that Ingham once told her: "If you work on the reflex too long, you are undoing the good you have done." Ingham recommended 30-minute sessions, but most modern reflexologists conduct 45-minute or 60-minute sessions unless the client's condition dictates otherwise.

Most reflexologists work primarily on feet, but some work on the hands or even the ears. If a foot has been injured or amputated, it is acceptable to work on the hands. For the most part, reflexologists work on the feet because the feet are so sensitive. In addition, feet that are encased in shoes during most of the day typically require more attention than hands do. Furthermore, the feet, because of their size, are easier to manipulate. It is somewhat more difficult to find the reflexes on the hands.

EARNINGS

There are no reliable figures to indicate what reflexologists earn per year. NaturalHealers.com reports that earnings for reflexologists parallel those for massage therapists. The Bureau of Labor Statistics cited average yearly earnings of $43,170 for those in the profession. The lowest paid earned no more than $18,860, while the highest paid earned $74,860 or more.

Some practitioners may charge as little as $15 per hour, while a small number of well-respected reflexologists in large cities may earn $100 or even substantially more per hour. Thus earnings are determined by a combination of skill, experience, client base, and the number of hours per week a reflexologist chooses to work. Many do not work 40 hours per week doing reflexology exclusively.

As of October 2016, Payscale.com reported salaries of around $38,000 for entry-level reflexologists up to $57,000 for those with many years of experience. Typically, it takes quite some time for new practitioners to build up a practice, so many of them rely on other sources of income in the beginning. Many reflexologists offer other holistic treatments and therapies, which means that they do not rely on reflexology to provide all their income.

WORK ENVIRONMENT

Reflexologists almost always work in their homes or in their own offices. Although some reflexologists may have office help, most work alone. For this reason, practitioners must be independent enough to work effectively on schedules of their own devising. Because they must make their clients comfortable in order to provide effective treatment, they generally try to make their workplaces as pleasant and relaxing

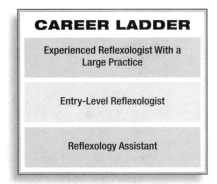

CAREER LADDER

Experienced Reflexologist With a
Large Practice

Entry-Level Reflexologist

Reflexology Assistant

as possible. Many practitioners play soothing music while they work. Some, especially those who practice aromatherapy as well as reflexology, use scents to create a relaxed atmosphere.

EXPLORING

The best way to learn about the field of reflexology is to speak with reflexologists. Call practitioners and ask to interview them. Find reflexologists in your area if you can, but do not hesitate to contact people in other areas. There is no substitute for learning from those who actually do the work. Although most reflexologists run one-person practices, it may be possible to find clerical work of some kind with a successful practitioner in your area, especially if you live in a large city.

Read as much as you can on the subject. Many books are currently available, and many more will be available in the near future, since the field is growing rapidly. Look for information on reflexology in magazines and Web sites that deal with alternative medicine and bodywork. Learn as much as you can about alternative therapies. You may find that you wish to practice a number of techniques in addition to reflexology.

EDUCATION AND TRAINING REQUIREMENTS
High School

Because the practice of reflexology involves utilizing the correspondences between reflexes and the various parts of the body, a student who has some knowledge of medicine and anatomy will have an advantage. Study biology, chemistry, and health—anything that relates to the medical sciences. Since reflexologists must make their clients comfortable and gain their trust, some study of psychology may be useful. You might also investigate areas of bodywork and alternative medicine that are not taught in school. If you have some knowledge or practical skill in some area of massage (shiatsu or Swedish massage, for example), you will have a head start, especially since some states require reflexologists to be licensed massage therapists.

Postsecondary Training

The single most important part of a reflexologist's training is the completion of a rigorous course of study and practice, such as that provided by the International Institute of Reflexology. Many courses are available, and they range from one-day sessions designed to train people to work

on themselves or their partners to comprehensive courses that require a commitment of nine months or longer on the part of the student. Naturally, if you wish to practice professionally you should select a comprehensive course. Correspondence courses are available, but any reputable correspondence course will require you to complete a required number of hours of supervised, hands-on work. Some aspects of the technique must be demonstrated, not simply read, especially concerning the amount of pressure that the reflexologist should apply to different kinds of feet. Many reflexologists offer services other than reflexology, and you may wish to also train in other kinds of massage, aromatherapy, or another kind of bodywork. Such training may increase the likelihood that you will make a decent living, especially at the beginning of your career.

Other Education or Training

The International Institute of Reflexology and the Reflexology Association of America provide continuing education classes, webinars, and workshops that help reflexologists keep their skills up to date and maintain their certification. Contact these organizations for more information.

CERTIFICATION, LICENSING, AND SPECIAL REQUIREMENTS
Certification or Licensing

In some states, such as North Dakota, New Hampshire, Washington, and Tennessee, a reflexologist who has completed a course given by a reputable school of reflexology can be licensed specifically as a reflexologist. In most states, however, reflexologists are subject to the laws that govern massage therapists. That often means that you must complete a state-certified course in massage before being licensed to practice reflexology. In many cases, reflexologists are subject to laws that are designed to regulate massage parlors. In some places, these laws require you to be subjected to disease testing and walk-in inspections by police. It is common for those who are medical doctors or licensed cosmetologists to be exempt from massage-licensing regulations. Because there is such wide variation in the law, anyone who wishes to practice reflexology should carefully study state and local regulations before setting up shop.

It is recommended that you enroll in a course that requires a substantial number of hours of training and certifies you upon graduation. If you are at least 18 years old, have a high school diploma or its equivalent, have completed a course that requires at least 110 hours of training, and have at least 90 documented postgraduate reflexology sessions, you can apply for certification from the American Reflexology Certification Board (ARCB), an organization that seeks to promote reflexology by recognizing competent practitioners. In addition to meeting age, training, and experience requirements, applicants must take and pass a three-part examination (written, practical, and documentation). Certification is purely voluntary, but a high score from the ARCB is a good sign that a practitioner is competent.

■ EXPERIENCE, SKILLS, AND PERSONALITY TRAITS

Aspiring reflexologists should obtain hands-on clinical experience with clients while in school. Additionally, any volunteer or part-time experience in the office of a reflexologist will provide a useful introduction to the field.

Reflexologists work closely with their clients, so it is essential that you be friendly, open, and sensitive to the feelings of others. You must be able to gain your clients' trust, make them comfortable and relaxed, and communicate well enough with them to gather the information that they need in order to treat them effectively. It is highly unlikely that an uncommunicative person who is uncomfortable with people will be able to build a reflexology practice. In addition, you must be comfortable making decisions and working alone. Most reflexologists have their own practices, and anyone who sets up shop will need to deal with the basic tasks and problems that all business owners face: advertising, accounting, taxes, legal requirements, and so forth.

■ EMPLOYMENT PROSPECTS
Employers

For the most part, reflexologists work for themselves, although they may work at businesses that include reflexology as one of a number of services that they provide. It is probably wise to assume that you are going to run your own business, even if you do end up working for another organization. In most cases, organizations that use reflexologists bring them in as independent contractors rather than employees.

Starting Out

You should begin by taking the best, most comprehensive course of study you can find from a school that will certify you as a practitioner. After that, if you have not found an organization that you can work for, begin to practice on your own. You may rent an office or set up shop at home in order to save money. You may begin by working part time, so that you can earn money by other means while you are getting your business underway. Be sure to investigate the state and local laws that may affect you.

To run your own business, you need to be well versed in basic business skills. You may want to take courses in

A reflexologist applies pressure to a client's foot. (Ambrophoto. Shutterstock.)

business or seek advice from the local office of the Small Business Administration (http://www.sba.gov). Seek advice from people you know who run their own businesses. Your financial survival will depend on your business skills, so be sure that you know what you are doing.

■ ADVANCEMENT PROSPECTS

Because most reflexologists work for themselves, advancement in the field is directly related to the quality of treatment they provide and their business skills. Reflexologists advance by proving to the members of their community that they are skilled, honest, professional, and effective.

■ OUTLOOK

Although no official government analysis of the future of reflexology has yet been conducted, it seems safe to say that the field is expanding much more rapidly than

PRACTICING REFLEXOLOGY

LEARN MORE ABOUT IT

Davies, Clair, Amber Davies, and David G.
Simons. *The Trigger Point Therapy Workbook: Your Self-Treatment Guide for Pain Relief*, 3rd ed. Oakland, Calif.: New Harbinger Publications, 2013.

Faure-Alderson, Martine. *Total Reflexology: The Reflex Points for Physical, Emotional, and Psychological Healing.* Rochester, Vt.: Healing Arts Press/Inner Traditions, 2008.

Keet, Louise. *The Reflexology Bible: The Definitive Guide to Pressure Point Healing.* New York: Sterling Publishing Company, 2009.

Kunz, Barbara. *Complete Reflexology for Life.* New York: DK Adult, 2009.

the average for all fields. Although science still views it with skepticism, reflexology has become relatively popular in a short period of time. It has certainly benefited from the popular acceptance of alternative and complementary medicine and therapies in recent years, particularly because it is a holistic practice that aims to treat the whole person rather than the symptoms of disease or discomfort. Because reflexology treatments entail little risk to the client in most cases, they provide a safe and convenient way to improve health. The U.S. Department of Labor projects that employment of massage therapists will grow much faster than the average for all careers through 2024 at 22 percent, and it is possible that employment in reflexology will grow similarly.

■ UNIONS AND ASSOCIATIONS

Reflexologists do not belong to unions, but they often join membership organizations such as the International Institute of Reflexology and the Reflexology Association of America. The American Reflexology Certification Board provides voluntary certification to reflexologists. The American Commission for Accreditation of Reflexology Education and Training accredits reflexology training programs.

■ TIPS FOR ENTRY

1. Talk to reflexologists about their careers. Ask them for advice on breaking into the field. Visit http://reflexology-usa.net/referrals.htm and http://reflexology-usa.org/practitioners/.
2. Join the Reflexology Association of America and the International Institute of Reflexology (IIR)

to take advantage of networking opportunities, continuing education classes and workshops, and other resources that will help you build a successful practice.
3. Read the IIR's blog (http://www.reflexologyusa.net) to learn more about the field.

■ FOR MORE INFORMATION

The ARCB was created in order to promote reflexology by recognizing competent practitioners. It provides voluntary testing for working reflexologists and maintains lists of certified practitioners and educational programs.

American Reflexology Certification Board (ARCB)
2586 Knightsbridge Road, SE
Grand Rapids, MI 49546-6755
Tel: (303) 933-6921
Fax: (303) 904-0460
E-mail: info@arcb.net
http://www.arcb.net

The IIR promotes the Original Ingham Method of Reflexology, providing seminars worldwide as well as a thorough certification program. The Institute also sells books and charts.

International Institute of Reflexology (IIR)
5650 First Avenue North, PO Box 12642
St. Petersburg, FL 33733-2642
Tel: (727) 343-4811
Fax: (727) 381-2807
E-mail: info@reflexology-usa.net
http://www.reflexology-usa.net

Laura Norman provides training classes and certification in reflexology, as well as books, videos, and reflexology products.

Laura Norman Wellness
http://www.lauranormanreflexology.com

Visit this organization's Web site for membership information, school listings, articles and interviews, and other resources.

Reflexology Association of America
PO Box 44324
Madison, WI 53744
Tel: 980-234-0159
E-mail: InfoRAA@reflexology-usa.org
http://www.reflexology-usa.org

Refuse Collectors

■ OVERVIEW

Refuse collectors gather garbage and other discarded materials set out by customers along designated routes in urban and rural communities and transport the materials to sanitary landfills or incinerator plants for disposal. Refuse collectors may specialize in collecting certain types of material, such as recyclable glass, newsprint, or aluminum. There are approximately 114,000 refuse and recyclable materials collectors working in the United States.

■ HISTORY

Refuse, or the solid waste generated by a community, has presented problems for just about every society throughout history; previously, the accepted method for disposal of refuse was burning at home or haphazard dumping into open pits or waterways. In the past couple of centuries, heavier population concentrations and industrial growth have vastly increased the quantity of refuse produced, making unregulated dumping impractical as well as unhealthy. As waste disposal has become more regulated, the job of the waste hauler has changed as well.

The first sanitary landfill was opened in 1912. In a sanitary landfill, refuse gathered from a community is deposited in a large pit in shallow layers, compacted, and covered daily with earth. Sealed in, the refuse undergoes slow, natural decomposition. When the pit is full, the top is sealed over and the land is available for reuse, often as a public park or other recreational area. Landfills are increasingly regulated in regard to their location, operation, and closure. The number of landfills, which peaked nationwide in the mid-1980s, is now dropping as communities fight against having landfills in their midst. The result is fewer, larger landfills that are located in communities that favor the jobs that the landfill offers. As a result, refuse collectors who transport waste to landfills may spend greater parts of their workday driving longer distances to the landfill.

Increases in recycling have also changed the job of the refuse collector. In more and more communities around the United States, people separate out materials such as glass bottles, metal cans, newspapers, certain plastics, and other designated refuse for recycling, thus limiting the flow of refuse into landfills and incinerators. The sale of recyclable materials can help to reduce the cost of the refuse disposal operation. Refuse collectors are the ones who pick up recyclables in most communities, sometimes on the same day, and even in the same truck, as the garbage is collected. Some trucks are equipped with separate bins for refuse and recyclables. Other refuse collectors may pick up only recyclables, usually in larger communities. The trend toward recycling requires refuse collectors who deal with these items to be familiar with how they are to be properly separated.

Another form of reclaiming materials is the composting of plant wastes, such as grass clippings, brush, and leaves, in community compost heaps. Composting is a way to decompose this material into mulch, which is rich in minerals and can be reclaimed for fertilizer. This mulch, or compost, may be used by the municipality or made available to its citizens. Refuse collectors sometimes pick up yard wastes and are therefore required to know when the resident has used the proper container for grass clippings.

■ THE JOB

In general, refuse collection teams of two or three workers drive along established routes and empty household trash containers into garbage trucks. The refuse, which is often mechanically compacted in the truck, is taken to a landfill or other appropriate disposal facility.

Refuse workers may collect all kinds of solid wastes, including food scraps, paper products, and plastics. Depending on local requirements, the refuse may be loose in containers, in packaging such as plastic bags, in preapproved containers that indicate recyclable materials, or, for newspapers and magazines, tied in bundles. When the

CAREER LADDER

Garbage-Collection Supervisor or
Recycling Coordinator

Refuse Collector-Driver

Refuse Collector-Garbage Loader/
Unloader

truck is full, the workers drive with the load to the disposal site and empty the truck. Workers may also pick up cast-off furniture, old appliances, or other large, bulky items, although usually such items are collected only on certain days.

An average day for refuse collectors often begins before dawn with an inspection of the truck that includes checking lights, tires, testing air and oil pressure gauges, and making sure a spill kit is on board. Refuse collectors who work on commercial routes or pickup dumpsters stay in contact with dispatchers via radio or cellular phone to learn where they are needed to pick up. Refuse collectors gas up their trucks as needed and recheck the truck's vital equipment at the end of the day.

As they move along their routes, refuse collectors are constantly getting on and off the truck to lift trash containers onto the truck. The containers are often heavy. Sometimes the different work duties are divided among the workers, with the driver doing only the driving all day long. In other cases, the workers alternate between driving and loading and unloading throughout the day.

Some employers send refuse collectors on routes alone, and they are responsible for driving the truck and loading the refuse. Usually, however, refuse collectors working alone have special routes, such as driving a truck that can lift and empty dumpsters. The refuse collector operates the levers and buttons that lift and dump the dumpster's contents into the truck. This kind of system is particularly useful for apartment buildings, construction sites, and other locations that need containers so large they are too heavy to empty by hand. The use of mechanical hoists on trucks makes refuse pickup much faster and more efficient.

Some trucks are built with multiple bins, so that recyclable items that customers have set out separately, such as aluminum or newspaper, can be kept separate in the truck and later taken to buyers. In some communities, the pickup days and the company responsible for disposal are different for recyclable materials than for other mixed general refuse.

Garbage-collection supervisors direct and coordinate the tasks of the various workers involved in the collecting and transporting of refuse. They make work assignments and monitor and evaluate job performance.

■ EARNINGS

Earnings of refuse collectors vary widely depending on their employer, union status, and other factors. Beginning refuse collectors who work for small, private firms and are not union members are sometimes paid at hourly wages not far above the federal minimum wage. Median annual earnings of refuse and recyclable materials collectors in May 2015 were $36,370 a year for full-time work, according to the U.S. Bureau of Labor Statistics. Salaries range from less than $19,860 to more than $58,790. In general, workers employed by large cities under union contracts make more money, and those working for small companies without union contracts make less.

Refuse collectors get overtime pay for working extra hours, during the evenings, or on weekends. They may receive paid time during each shift to shower and change clothes. Union workers receive benefits such as health insurance and paid sick leave and vacation days. Most full-time workers with private companies also receive benefits, although they may not receive as desirable a benefits package.

A refuse collector operates a garbage truck. (Dmitry Kalinovsky. Shutterstock.)

■ WORK ENVIRONMENT

Refuse workers must work outdoors in all kinds of weather, including cold, snow, rain, and heat, and they must handle dirty, smelly objects. The work is active and often strenuous, requiring the lifting of heavy refuse containers, hopping on and off the truck constantly, and operating hoists and other equipment. Workers often encounter garbage that is not packed correctly. Because there is a danger of infection from raw garbage, they must wear protective gloves and are sometimes provided with uniforms. Workers must always be aware of the dangers of working around traffic and mechanical compactors. Most workers wear heavy steel-toe boots to help avoid foot injuries from accidentally dropping containers or large objects. New employees receive instruction on safety precautions they will need to take as well as instructions about their responsibilities.

Most refuse collectors work during weekday daylight hours, with regular shifts totaling 35 to 40 hours per week. Many workers put in slightly longer hours. Many workers begin their shifts in the predawn hours, while other workers routinely work in the evenings. In emergencies (for removal of storm-downed tree branches, for instance), weekend hours may be necessary. Workers who drive the trucks must have a commercial driver's license, and federal law prohibits CDL drivers from working more than 60 hours per week.

■ EXPLORING

If you are thinking about getting into this kind of work, you may find it helpful to talk with experienced workers in similar jobs. In some areas, there may be opportunities for summer or part-time work, although workers in these positions generally have to meet the same requirements as full-time employees. Contact local recycling centers to check on availability of volunteer or part-time work. A job as a furniture mover or truck driver is another way to learn about some of the responsibilities of refuse collectors. Any experience you can gain in a related job that requires physical strength and reliability is useful to test your work endurance. Experience as a material handler, equipment cleaner, helper, or laborer would be useful.

■ EDUCATION AND TRAINING REQUIREMENTS
High School

Employers prefer applicants who are high school graduates. Workers who hope to advance to a supervisory position ought to have at least a high school diploma. High school classes that may be helpful include any shop classes that provide hands-on learning opportunities and physical education classes that teach you how to develop strength and endurance. A good understanding of basic

---

WHERE DOES THE GARBAGE GO?

DID YOU KNOW?

Talk to anyone in the solid waste management industry today, and it's unlikely you'll hear them use the word *dump*. Yesterday's dumps are today's landfills—highly regulated and carefully engineered. Open land dumps have been banned in the United States. When refuse collectors pick up garbage at the curbside, the garbage is usually crushed once it's deposited into the truck. When the collector takes the waste to the landfill, the garbage is compacted even further to reduce volume and conserve landfill space. Landfills are expensive to build and maintain, so every effort is made to make the best use of them. Once the garbage is dumped at the landfill, it is covered with a layer of earth. The earth reduces odors and keeps away disease-carrying pests, such as rats and flies. Building today's landfills requires extensive planning, engineering, monitoring, and supervision. Many landfills are made with liners of compacted clay (as thick as 10 feet) or impermeable materials such as plastic to prevent contamination of soil and water outside the landfill. Another method of preventing contamination is a drainage system in which rainwater and runoff are pumped to the surface, where they are treated and discharged. When landfills reach their capacity, they are sealed and covered with a layer of clay and dirt, where grass is planted, and the large hill that is left can be used for recreational purposes. To see an example of 10 landfills that were turned into nature preserves, visit WebEcoist's Web site, http://www.webecoist.com/2009/05/10/garbage-to-green-10-landfills-turned-into-nature-preserves.

---

math and English is also necessary to read instructions and operate equipment for the job.

Postsecondary Training

Generally, employers will hire people without work experience or specific training. Most employers, however, do require workers to be at least 18 years old and physically able to perform the work. Some employers provide on-the-job training to new hires that can last up to three months.

■ CERTIFICATION, LICENSING, AND SPECIAL REQUIREMENTS
Certification or Licensing

Workers who drive collection trucks need a commercial driver's license (CDL). In some areas, where the workers alternate jobs, a CDL is required even of those who are generally loaders. A clean driving record is often a

FOOD WASTE

DID YOU KNOW?

When you are just unable to finish that second helping that you were sure you needed, do you wrap it up and save the leftovers, or do you simply throw out the uneaten portion? If you're like many Americans, you probably do the latter. Food waste, which consists of uneaten portions of meals and food left over from cooking preparations, is the second largest component of generated waste by weight, and the largest component of discarded waste by weight. According to the Natural Resources Defense Council, the average American throws away more than 20 pounds of food every month, or 240 pounds per year. Food waste is 70 percent water and 30 percent solids, and can decompose into methane in landfills. The U.S. Department of Agriculture (USDA) estimates that Americans throw out higher percentages of fresh fruits and vegetables and dairy and grain products than meat, nuts, and processed foods. More than 60 million homes and 500,000 businesses have in-sink food disposers that compost food waste and divert it from landfills. Composting on a large-scale can be expensive, but projects in Seattle, San Francisco, and Toronto are breaking new ground. Also, the USDA is looking into ways to improve composting methods for this type of garbage.

Source: Waste360

necessity. Refuse collectors may have to pass a civil service test in order to work for a city or town.

Other Requirements

Refuse collectors must generally be at least 18 years old and capable of lifting heavy items.

■ EXPERIENCE, SKILLS, AND PERSONALITY TRAITS

No experience is needed to work as a refuse collector, but those with prior work experience will increase their chances of landing a job, getting promoted, and possibly earning higher pay.

Refuse workers need to be physically fit and able to lift heavy objects. Sometimes a health examination is required for employment. Employers look for workers who are reliable and hardworking.

Experience in driving a truck and in loading and unloading heavy material is helpful. Many refuse workers, especially those in metropolitan areas, are members of a union such as the International Brotherhood of Teamsters. Those who work for private firms might not be unionized.

■ EMPLOYMENT PROSPECTS
Employers

Approximately 114,000 refuse and recyclable materials collectors are employed in the United States. In the past, refuse collectors were employed almost exclusively by municipalities. Today, refuse collectors may work for private waste haulers that contract with local governments or even specialized firms, such as recycling haulers. Some local governments still operate their own waste-hauling programs, and in these communities, refuse collectors are city employees. But many have found it more cost-effective to contract with private waste haulers who employ their own refuse collectors. Similar jobs may be found at landfills, where workers are needed to assist drivers in dumping collected refuse, or at material recovery facilities (MRFs), where recyclables are taken. MRFs need workers to separate materials, load and unload trucks, and operate equipment such as balers that condense the recyclables into large, dense bales.

Starting Out

To apply for refuse collector jobs, contact your local city government's personnel department or department of sanitation. Employees in these offices may be able to supply information on job openings and local requirements. If you are interested in working for a private disposal firm, contact the firm directly. You can find listings for specific job opportunities through the state employment service, employment Web sites, or newspaper classified ads. Contacting a waste disposal union's local branch and becoming a member may help you land a job when one becomes available in your area.

■ ADVANCEMENT PROSPECTS

Opportunities for advancement are usually limited for refuse collectors. Those who work for municipal governments may be able to transfer to better-paying jobs in another department of city government, such as public works. Sometimes advancement means becoming the driver of a refuse truck, rather than a worker who loads and unloads the truck. In larger organizations, refuse collectors who prove to be reliable employees may be promoted to supervisory positions, where they coordinate and direct the activities of other workers. Others may develop a knowledge of recyclables, for example, and help coordinate a waste hauler's recycling business.

■ OUTLOOK

The U.S. Department of Labor predicts that employment for refuse and recyclable material collectors will grow as fast as average for all careers through 2024 as a result of the growing U.S. population (which is generating more garbage and recyclable materials). As communities encourage more recycling and more resource recovery technologies, more varied pickup services may tend to require more workers, expanding the employment opportunities in both the public and private sector. Additionally, job turnover is high in this field. Every year, many positions will become available as workers transfer to other jobs or leave the workforce.

Opportunities will be best in heavily populated regions in and near big cities, where the most waste is generated. In cities, increasing use of mechanized equipment for lifting and emptying large refuse containers may decrease the need for these workers.

A trend that favors use of large, nationally based waste management corporations is eliminating smaller competitors in some areas. This suggests that job security may depend on the size of the employer. As recycling becomes more lucrative, large companies may concentrate on this aspect of waste disposal.

UNIONS AND ASSOCIATIONS

Refuse collectors may be members of the International Brotherhood of Teamsters and other unions. The National Waste & Recycling Association represents the private-sector waste and recycling industry in the United States.

TIPS FOR ENTRY

1. Talk with refuse collectors about their careers. Ask them for advice on preparing for and entering the field.
2. Be willing to relocate. It may open more job opportunities.
3. Join the International Brotherhood of Teamsters to increase your chances of landing a job and receiving fair pay for your work.

FOR MORE INFORMATION

The following is a national union whose members include refuse collectors:

International Brotherhood of Teamsters
25 Louisiana Avenue, NW
Washington, D.C. 20001-2130
http://www.teamster.org

To learn more about the garbage and solid waste industry, contact

National Waste & Recycling Association
4301 Connecticut Avenue, NW, Suite 300
Washington, D.C. 20008-2304
Tel: (800) 424-2869; (202) 244-4700
Fax: (202) 966-4824
E-mail: info@wasterecycling.org
https://wasterecycling.org/

Regional and Local Officials

OVERVIEW

Regional and local officials hold positions in the legislative, executive, and judicial branches of government at the local level. They include mayors, commissioners, and city and county council members. These officials direct regional legal services, public health departments, and police protection. They serve on housing, budget, and employment committees and develop special programs to improve communities.

HISTORY

The first U.S. colonies adopted the English shire form of government. This form was 1,000 years old and served as the administrative arm of both the national and local governments; a county in medieval England was overseen by a sheriff (a title which comes from the original term shire reeve) appointed by the crown and was represented by two members in Parliament.

When America's founding fathers wrote the Constitution, they didn't make any specific provisions for the governing of cities and counties. This allowed state governments to define themselves; when drawing up their own constitutions, the states essentially considered county governments to be extensions of the state government.

City governments, necessary for dealing with increased industry and trade, evolved during the 19th century. Population growth and suburban development helped to strengthen local governments after World War I. County governments grew even stronger after World War II, due to counties' rising revenues and increased independence from the states. The National Association of Counties states that today's counties are "the most flexible, locally responsive and creative governments in the United States," and that they "vividly express" the slogan "Think globally, act locally."

THE JOB

There are a variety of different forms of local government across the country, but they all share similar concerns. County and city governments make sure that the local streets are free of crime as well as free of potholes. They create and improve regional parks and organize music festivals and outdoor theater events to be staged in these parks. They identify community problems and help to solve them in original ways. For example, King County in Washington State, in an effort to solve the problem of unemployment among those recently released from jail, developed a baking training program for county inmates. The inmates' new talents with danishes and bread loaves opened up opportunities for good-paying jobs in grocery store bakeries all across the county.

The Innovative Farmers of Michigan Program, which was organized in Huron, Tuscola, and Sanilac Counties, was developed to introduce new methods of farming to keep agriculture part of the county's economy. The program studies new cover-crops, tillage systems, and herbicides, with two primary goals: reduce the amount of sediment entering the Saginaw Bay and alter farming practices to reduce nutrient and pesticide runoff while retaining profitability for the farmers. In Onondaga County, N.Y., the public library started a program of basic reading instruction for deaf adults. In Broward County, Fla., a program provides a homelike setting for supervised visitation and parenting training for parents who are separated from their children due to abuse or domestic violence.

The needs for consumer protection, water quality, and affordable housing increase every year. Regional or local officials are elected to deal with issues such as public health, legal services, housing, and budget and fiscal management. They attend meetings and serve on committees. They know about the industry and agriculture of the area as well as the specific problems facing constituents, and they offer educated solutions, vote on laws, and generally represent the people in their districts.

There are two forms of county government: the commissioner/administrator form, in which the county board of commissioners appoints an *administrator* who serves the board, and the council/executive form, in which a *county executive* is the chief administrative officer of the district and has the power to veto ordinances enacted by the county board. A county government may include a *chief executive*, who directs regional services; council members, who are the county legislators; a county clerk, who keeps records of property titles, licenses, etc.; and a *county treasurer*, who is in charge of the receipt and disbursement of money.

County government funds come from taxes, state aid, fees, and grants. A city government funds its projects and programs with money from sales tax and other local taxes, block grants, and state aid. Directing these funds and services are elected executives. *Mayors* are elected by the general populace to serve as the heads of city governments. Their specific functions vary depending on the structure of their government. In mayor-council governments, both the mayor and the city council are popularly elected. The council is responsible for formulating city ordinances, but the mayor exercises control over the actions of the council. In such governments, the mayor usually plays a dual role, serving not only as chief executive officer but also as an agent of the city government responsible for such functions as maintaining public order, security, and health. In a commission government, the people elect a number of *commissioners*, each of whom serves as head of a city department. The presiding commissioner is usually the mayor. The final type of municipal government is the council/manager form. Here, the council members are elected by the people, and one of their functions is to hire a *city manager* to administer the city departments. A mayor is elected by the council to chair the council and officiate at important municipal functions.

■ EARNINGS

In general, salaries for government officials tend to be lower than what the official could make working in the private sector. In many local offices, officials volunteer their time, work only part time, or are given a nominal salary. One example of salary waiving is former New York Mayor Bloomberg, who amassed great wealth through his media business prior to election to office; he declined to receive a city salary, and instead accepted $1 per year for his services.

In general, salaries for government officials tend to be lower than what the official could make working in the private sector. In many local offices, officials volunteer their time or work only part time. Local government managers earned mean annual salaries of $96,570 in May 2013, according to the U.S. Department of Labor (DOL). Chief executives in local government had mean annual earnings of $110,230. In general, salaries for city managers range from $50,000 to $175,000 or more annually. Local government chief appointed officials earned salaries that ranged from $25,264 to $368,282 in 2015, according to the International City/County Management Association.

The DOL reports that government legislators earned median annual salaries of $20,500 in May 2015. Salaries generally ranged from less than $16,950 to $91,960 or more, although some officials earn nothing at all.

A job with a local or regional government may or may not provide benefits. Some positions may include accounts for official travel and other expenses.

■ WORK ENVIRONMENT

Most government officials work in a typical office setting. Some may work a regular 40-hour week, while others work long hours and weekends. Though some positions may only be considered part time, they may take up nearly as many hours as full-time work. Officials have the opportunity to meet with the people of the region, but they also devote a lot of time to clerical duties. If serving a large community, they may have assistants to help with phones, filing, and preparing documents.

Because officials must be appointed or elected in order to keep their jobs, determining long-range career plans can be difficult. There may be extended periods of unemployment, where living off of savings or other jobs may be necessary. Because of the low pay of some positions, officials may have to work another job even while they serve in office. This can result in little personal time and the need to juggle many different responsibilities at once.

■ EXPLORING

Depending on the size of your city or county, you can probably become involved with your local government at a young age. Your council members and other government officials should be more accessible to you than state and federal officials, so take advantage of that. Visit the county court house and volunteer in whatever capacity you can with county-organized programs, such as tutoring in a literacy program or leading children's reading groups at the public library.

You can also become involved with local elections. Many candidates for local and state offices welcome young people to assist with campaigns. As a volunteer, you may make calls, post signs, and get to see a candidate at work. You will also have the opportunity to meet others who have an interest in government, and the experience will help you to gain a more prominent role in later campaigns.

Another way to learn about government is to become involved in an issue that interests you. Maybe there's an old building in your neighborhood you'd like to save from destruction, or maybe you have some ideas for youth programs or programs for senior citizens. Research what's being done about your concerns and come up with solutions to offer to local officials.

CAREER LADDER

U.S. Senator/Representative or Other National Elected or Appointed Official

Regional or State Official

Local Official

■ EDUCATION AND TRAINING REQUIREMENTS
High School

Courses in government, civics, and history will give you an understanding of the structure of government. English courses are important because you will need good writing skills to communicate with constituents and other government officials. Math and accounting will help you develop analytical skills for examining statistics and demographics. Journalism classes will develop research and interview skills for identifying problems and developing programs.

Postsecondary Training

To serve on a local government, your experience and understanding of the city or county are generally more important than your educational background. Some

Former New York City mayor Michael Bloomberg and former police commissioner Ray Kelly march in the 2013 Columbus Day Parade. (lev radin. Shutterstock.)

MODEL COUNTY PROGRAMS

The National Association of Counties (NACO) sponsors achievement awards that recognize innovative government programs and projects in such areas as arts and historic preservation, children and youth, and employment and training. Here are a few of the NACO's "Model County Programs."

- Students in the local schools of Jane City, Va., were invited to draw an ideal playground. Volunteers and donations were then sought by the Parks and Recreation Department, and "Kidsburg" was built from these student designs.
- Johnson County, Kans., introduced a program to increase the number of older volunteers in public schools for tutoring and for speaking to students in the Living History Program, which features stories of the past.
- After Hurricane Andrew, many lost pets could not be returned to their owners because of loss of identification and lack of communication among humane organizations. In response, Orange County, Fla., has developed disaster planning kits and new animal shelters in the event of future natural disasters.
- After Hurricane Katrina, St. Tammany Parish in La. arranged the Mobile Community Information Center, a converted recreational vehicle that brought information and government services to residents for emergency and non-emergency needs.
- The Baltimore County Commission on Disabilities collaborated with U.S. Homeland Security & Emergency to create a training DVD to help personnel at agencies and organizations throughout the country work more effectively and compassionately with people with disabilities.

mayors and council members are elected to their positions because they've lived in the region for a long time and have had experience with local industry and other concerns. For example, someone with years of farming experience may be the best candidate to serve a small agricultural community. Voters in local elections may be more impressed by a candidate's previous occupations and roles in the community than they are by a candidate's postsecondary degrees.

That said, most regional and local officials still hold an undergraduate degree, and many hold a graduate degree. Popular areas of study include public administration, law, economics, political science, history, and English.

Regardless of your major as an undergraduate, you are likely to be required to take classes in English literature, statistics, foreign language, western civilization, and economics.

Certification

The National League of Cities offers the Certificate of Achievement in Leadership Program to help participants develop key skills necessary for excellence in leadership. Members earn educational credits toward the certificate by attending leadership seminars at the organization's annual conferences and other events.

Other Education or Training

The International City/County Management Association provides Web conferences and workshops and other continuing education opportunities. Topics include ethics, management skills, staff development, leadership, and financial management. The National League of Cities offers workshops, conference seminars, webinars, and a Leadership Fellowship Program. The National Association of Counties provides conference seminars and workshops, Web-based education, and a County Leadership Institute. Topics include social media, disaster planning, and leadership. Contact these organizations for more information.

■ CERTIFICATION, LICENSING, AND SPECIAL REQUIREMENTS
Certification or Licensing

The International City/County Management Association offers a voluntary credentialing program for government managers who meet education and experience requirements. Contact the association for more information.

■ EXPERIENCE, SKILLS, AND PERSONALITY TRAITS

Many regional and local officials have prior experience as community activists or working on political campaigns, in law enforcement, or in business.

To be successful in this field, you must deeply understand the city and region you serve. You need to be knowledgeable about the local industry, private businesses, and social problems. You should also have lived for some time in the region in which you hope to hold office.

You also need good people skills to be capable of listening to the concerns of constituents and other officials and exchanging ideas with them. Other useful qualities are problem-solving and negotiation skills and creativity to develop innovative programs.

■ EMPLOYMENT PROSPECTS

Employers

Every city in the United States requires the services of local officials. In some cases, the services of a small town or suburb may be overseen by the government of a larger city or by the county government. According to the National Association of Counties, 48 states have operational county governments—a total of over 3,069 counties. (Conn. and R.I. are the only two states without counties.) Counties range in size from the 82 residents in Loving County, Tex., to the more than 9.8 million residents of Los Angeles County in Calif. There are also about 40 governments that are consolidations of city and county governments; New York, Denver, and San Francisco are among them.

Starting Out

There is no direct career path for gaining public office. The way you pursue a local office will be greatly affected by the size and population of the region in which you live. When running for mayor or council of a small town, you may have no competition at all. On the other hand, to become mayor of a large city, you need extensive experience in the city's politics. If you are interested in pursuing a local position, research the backgrounds of your city mayor, county commissioner, and council members to get an idea of how they approached their political careers.

Some officials stumble into government offices after some success with political activism on the grassroots level. Others have had success in other areas, such as agriculture, business, and law enforcement, and use their experience to help improve the community. Many local politicians started their careers by assisting in someone else's campaign or advocating for an issue.

■ ADVANCEMENT PROSPECTS

Some successful local and regional officials maintain their positions for many years. Others hold local office for only one or two terms, then return full time to their businesses and other careers. You might also choose to use a local position as a stepping stone to a position of greater power within the region or to a state office. Many mayors of the largest cities run for governor or state legislature and may eventually move into federal office.

■ OUTLOOK

Though the form and structure of state and federal government are not likely to change, the form of your local and county government can be altered by popular vote. Every election, voters somewhere in the country are deciding whether to keep their current forms of government or to introduce new forms. But these changes don't greatly affect the number of officials needed to run your local government. Employment for local and regional officials is unlikely to change much in the near future.

The chances of holding office will be greater in a smaller community, where fewer people may seek a position. Cities and other high-population areas may present more opportunities for appointed and elected posts, but with stiffer competition for them. The races for part-time and nonpaying offices will also be less competitive and can be a good way to get a foot in the door.

The issues facing a community will have the most effect on the jobs of local officials. In a city with older neighborhoods, officials deal with historic preservation, improvements in utilities, and water quality. In a growing city with many suburbs, officials have to make decisions regarding development, roads, and expanded routes for public transportation.

The federal government has made efforts to shift costs to the states. If this continues, states may offer less aid to counties. A county government's funds are also affected by changes in property taxes.

■ UNIONS AND ASSOCIATIONS

Regional and local officials are not represented by unions. The major professional organization for regional and local officials, especially city managers, is the International City/County Management Association. The NASPAA accredits degree programs in public affairs and administration. The National League of Cities is a membership organization for cities, villages, and towns, and the National Association of Counties represents our nation's counties.

■ TIPS FOR ENTRY

1. Join professional associations such as the International City/County Management Association (ICMA) to access training and networking resources, industry publications, and employment opportunities. Attend the ICMA Annual Conference (http://icma.org/en/icma/events/conference) and other industry events to network and to interview for jobs.
2. Read publications such as *Public Management* (http://webapps.icma.org/pm/9401) to learn more about the field.
3. For job listings, visit:
   - http://icma.org/en/icma/career_network/home
   - http://www.naco.org/PROGRAMS/JOBS ONLINE
   - http://www.publicservicecareers.org

4. Participate in internships or part-time jobs that are arranged by your college's career services office. Additionally, ICMA offers information on internships at its Web site, http://icma.org/en/icma/career_network/job_seekers/interns.

■ FOR MORE INFORMATION

For information about the forms of city and county governments around the country and to learn about programs sponsored by local and regional governments, contact

International City/County Management Association (ICMA)
777 North Capitol Street, NE, Suite 500
Washington, D.C. 20002-4201
Tel: (800) 745-8780; (202) 962-3680
Fax: (202) 962-3500
E-mail: membership@icma.org
http://www.icma.org

For information on education and careers, contact
National Association of Counties (NAC)
660 North Capitol Street, NW, Suite 400
Washington, D.C. 20001-1450
Tel: (888) 407-6226; (202) 393-6226
Fax: (202) 393-2630
http://www.naco.org

For information on cities, contact
National League of Cities (NLC)
660 North Capitol Street, NW, Suite 450
Washington, D.C. 20004-1701
Tel: (877) 827-2385
http://www.nlc.org

For more information on finding a school, the MPA degree, and public affairs work, contact
Network of Schools of Public Policy, Affairs, and Administration (NASPAA)
1029 Vermont Avenue, NW, Suite 1100
Washington, D.C. 20005-3517
Tel: (202) 628-8965
Fax: (202) 626-4978
E-mail: naspaa@naspaa.org
http://www.naspaa.org

For information on education and careers, visit
PublicServiceCareers.org
http://www.publicservicecareers.org

MOST NEW JOBS

Registered Nurses

■ OVERVIEW

Registered nurses (RNs) help individuals, families, and groups to improve and maintain health and to prevent disease. They care for the sick and injured in hospitals and other health care facilities, physicians' offices, private homes, public health agencies, schools, camps, and industry. Some registered nurses are employed in private practice. RNs hold more than 2.7 million jobs in the United States.

■ HISTORY

Modern ideas about hospitals and nursing as a profession did not develop until the 19th century. The life and work of Florence Nightingale were a strong influence on the profession's development. Nightingale, who came from a wealthy, upper-class British family, dedicated her life to improving conditions in hospitals, beginning in an army hospital during the Crimean War. In the United States, many of Nightingale's ideas were put into practice for the care of the wounded during the Civil War. The care, however, was provided by concerned individuals who nursed, rather than by professionally trained nurses. They had not received the kind of training that is required for nurses today.

The first school of nursing in the United States was founded in Boston in 1873. In 1938, New York State passed the first state law requiring that practical nurses be licensed. Even though the first school for the training of practical nurses was started more than 75 years ago, and the establishment of other schools followed, the training programs then lacked uniformity.

After the 1938 law was passed, a movement emerged to have organized training programs that would assure new standards in the field. The role and training of nurses have undergone radical changes since the first schools opened.

Education standards for nurses have been improving constantly since that time. Today's nurse is a highly educated, licensed health care professional. Extended programs of training are offered throughout the country, and all states have enacted laws to assure training standards are maintained and to assure qualification for licensure. Nurses are a vital part of the health care system.

■ THE JOB

Registered nurses work under the direct supervision of nursing departments and in collaboration with physicians. Approximately 59 percent of all nurses work in hospitals, where they may be assigned to general, operating room, or maternity room duty. They may also care for sick children or be assigned to other hospital units, such as emergency rooms, intensive care units, or outpatient clinics. There are many different kinds of RNs.

General duty nurses work together with other members of the health care team to assess the patient's condition and to develop and implement a plan of health care. These nurses may perform such tasks as taking patients' vital signs, administering medication and injections, recording the symptoms and progress of patients, changing dressings, assisting patients with personal care, conferring with members of the medical staff, helping prepare a patient for surgery, and completing any number of duties that require skill and understanding of patients' needs.

Surgical nurses oversee the preparation of the operating room and the sterilization of instruments. They assist surgeons during operations and coordinate the flow of patient cases in operating rooms.

Maternity nurses, or *neonatal nurses*, help in the delivery room, take care of newborns in the nursery, and teach mothers how to feed and care for their babies.

The activities of staff nurses are directed and coordinated by *head nurses* and *charge nurses*. Heading up the entire nursing program in the hospital is the *nursing service director*, who administers the nursing program to maintain standards of patient care. The nursing service director advises the medical staff, department heads, and the hospital administrator in matters relating to nursing services and helps prepare the department budget.

Private duty nurses may work in hospitals or in a patient's home. They are employed by the patient they are caring for or by the patient's family. Their service is designed for the individual care of one person and is carried out in cooperation with the patient's physician.

Office nurses usually work in the office of a dentist, physician, or health maintenance organization (HMO). An office nurse may be one of several nurses on the staff or the only staff nurse. If a nurse is the only staff member, this person may have to combine some clerical duties with those of nursing, such as serving as receptionist, making appointments for the doctor, helping maintain patient records, sending out monthly statements, and attending to routine correspondence. If the physician's staff is a large one that includes secretaries and clerks, the office nurse will concentrate on screening patients, assisting with examinations, supervising the examining rooms, sterilizing equipment, providing patient education, and performing other nursing duties.

Occupational health nurses, or *industrial nurses*, are an important part of many large firms. They maintain a clinic at a plant or factory and are usually occupied in rendering preventive, remedial, and educational nursing services. They work under the direction of an industrial physician, nursing director, or nursing supervisor. They may advise on accident prevention, visit employees on the job to check the conditions under which they work, and advise management about the safety of such conditions. At the plant, they render treatment in emergencies.

School nurses may work in one school or in several, visiting each for a part of the day or week. They may supervise the student clinic, treat minor cuts or injuries, or give advice on good health practices. They may examine students to detect conditions of the eyes or teeth that require attention. They also assist the school physician.

Community health nurses, also called *public health nurses*, require specialized training for their duties. Their job usually requires them to spend part of the time traveling from one assignment to another. Their duties may differ greatly from one case to another. For instance, in one day they may have to instruct a class of expectant mothers, visit new parents to help them plan proper care for the baby, visit an aged patient requiring special care, and conduct a class in nutrition. They usually possess many varied nursing skills and are often called upon to resolve unexpected or unusual situations.

Administrators in the community health field include *nursing directors*, *educational directors*, and *nursing supervisors*. Some nurses go into

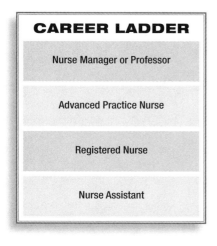

CAREER LADDER

Nurse Manager or Professor

Advanced Practice Nurse

Registered Nurse

Nurse Assistant

nursing education and work with nursing students to instruct them on theories and skills they will need to enter the profession. Nursing instructors may give classroom instruction and demonstrations or supervise nursing students on hospital units. Some instructors eventually become nursing school directors, university faculty, or deans of a university degree program. Nurses also have the opportunity to direct staff development and continuing education programs for nursing personnel in hospitals.

Advanced practice nurses are nurses with training beyond that required to have the RN designation. There are four primary categories of nurses included in this category: *nurse-midwives*, *clinical nurse specialists*, *nurse anesthetists*, and *nurse practitioners*.

Some nurses are consultants to hospitals, nursing schools, industrial organizations, and public health agencies. They advise clients on such administrative matters as staff organization, nursing techniques, curricula, and education programs. Other administrative specialists include *educational directors* for the state board of nursing, who are concerned with maintaining well-defined educational standards, and *executive directors* of professional nurses' associations, who administer programs developed by the board of directors and the members of the association.

Some nurses choose to enter the armed forces. All types of nurses, except private duty nurses, are represented in the military services. They provide skilled nursing care to active-duty and retired members of the armed forces and their families. In addition to basic nursing skills, *military nurses* are trained to provide care in various environments, including field hospitals, on-air evacuation flights, and onboard ships. Military nurses actively influence the development of health care through nursing research. Advances influenced by military nurses include the development of the artificial kidney (dialysis unit) and the concept of the intensive care unit.

■ EARNINGS

According to the U.S. Department of Labor (DOL), registered nurses had median annual earnings of $67,490 in May 2015. Salaries ranged from less than $46,360 to more than $101,630. Earnings of RNs vary according to employer. According to the DOL, those who worked at hospitals earned $69,510; registered nurses employed in physicians' offices earned $60,820; those working in home health care services earned $63,840; and RNs who worked at nursing care facilities earned $60,370.

Salary is determined by several factors: setting, education, and work experience. Most full-time nurses are given flexible work schedules as well as health and life insurance; some are offered education reimbursement and year-end bonuses. A staff nurse's salary is often limited only by the amount of work he or she is willing to take on. Many nurses take advantage of overtime work and shift differentials. Some nurses hold more than one job.

■ WORK ENVIRONMENT

Most nurses work in facilities that are clean and well lighted and where the temperature is controlled, although some work in rundown inner-city hospitals in less-than-ideal conditions. Many nurses work eight-hour shifts. Those in hospitals generally work any of three shifts: 7:00 A.M. to 3:00 P.M.; 3:00 P.M. to 11:00 P.M.; or 11:00 P.M. to 7:00 A.M. Some nurses may work 10- to 12-hour shifts. Approximately 20 percent of registered nurses work part time.

Nurses spend much of the day on their feet, either walking or standing. Handling patients who are ill or infirm can also be very exhausting. Nurses who come in contact with patients with infectious diseases must be especially careful about cleanliness and sterility. Although many nursing duties are routine, many responsibilities are unpredictable. Sick persons are often very demanding, or they may be depressed or irritable. Despite this, nurses must maintain their composure and should be cheerful to help the patient achieve emotional balance.

Community health nurses may be required to visit homes that are in poor condition or very dirty. They may also come in contact with social problems, such as family violence. The nurse is an important health care provider and in many communities he or she is the sole provider.

Both the office nurse and the industrial nurse work regular business hours and are seldom required to work overtime. In some jobs, such as where nurses are on duty in private homes, they may frequently travel from home to home and work with various cases.

■ EXPLORING

You can explore your interest in nursing in a number of ways. Read books on careers in nursing and talk with high school guidance counselors, school nurses, and local public health nurses. Visit hospitals to observe the work and talk with hospital personnel to learn more about the daily activities of nursing staff.

Some hospitals now have extensive volunteer service programs in which high school students may work after school, on weekends, or during vacations in order both to render a valuable service and to explore their interests in nursing. There are other volunteer work experiences available with the Red Cross or community health services. Camp counseling jobs sometimes offer related experiences. Some schools offer participation in Future Nurses programs.

The Internet is full of resources about nursing. Check out Discover Nursing (http://www.discovernursing.com) and the American Nurses Association's Web site (http://www.nursingworld.org).

■ EDUCATION AND TRAINING REQUIREMENTS
High School

If you are interested in becoming a registered nurse, you should take mathematics and science courses, including biology, chemistry, and physics. Health courses will also be helpful. English and speech courses should not be neglected because you must be able to communicate well with patients. Take computer science classes because nurses frequently use computers to "chart" patients and complete continuing education classes and seminars.

Postsecondary Training

There are three basic kinds of training programs that you may choose from to become a registered nurse: associate's degree, diploma, and bachelor's degree. Deciding on which of the three training programs to pursue depends on your career goals. A bachelor's degree in nursing is required for most supervisory or administrative positions, for jobs in public health agencies, and for admission to graduate nursing programs. A master's degree is usually necessary to prepare for a nursing specialty or to teach. For some specialties, such as nursing research, a Ph.D. is essential.

There are many bachelor's degree programs in nursing in the United States, which can take up to five years to complete, in some cases. The graduate of this program receives a bachelor of science in nursing (B.S.N.) degree. The associate degree in nursing (A.D.N.) is awarded after completion of a two-year study program that is usually offered in a junior or community college. Nursing students receive hospital training at cooperating hospitals in the general vicinity of the community college. The

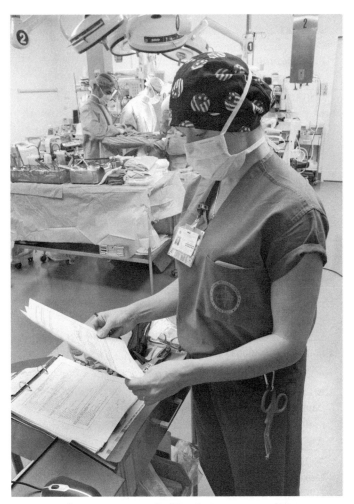

A registered nurse reviews a checklist during surgery. (Mass Communication Specialist 3rd Class Jake Berenguer. U.S. Navy.)

diploma program, which usually lasts three years, is conducted by hospitals and independent schools, although the number of these programs is declining. At the conclusion of each of these programs, you become a graduate nurse, but not, however, a registered nurse. To obtain the RN designation you must pass a licensing examination required in all states.

Nurses can pursue postgraduate training that allows them to specialize in certain areas, such as emergency room, operating room, premature nursery, or psychiatric nursing. This training is sometimes offered through hospital on-the-job training programs.

Other Education or Training

Registered nurses must continue to learn throughout their careers in order to keep their skills up to date and comply with licensing and certification and recertification requirements. Many nursing association provide continuing education (CE) opportunities in the form

Unusual Nursing Specialties   DID YOU KNOW?

Forensic nursing applies nursing science to public or legal proceedings. Forensic nurses help in the scientific investigation and treatment of trauma and/or death of victims and perpetrators of abuse, violence, criminal activity and traumatic accidents. They provide direct services to individual clients; provide consultation services to nursing and medical- and law-related agencies; and provide expert court testimony in cases dealing with trauma and death investigation processes.

Nursing informatics combines nursing science with computer science, information processing theory, and technology. Nurses in this specialty design, implement, and manage information technology and systems that enhance nursing education, clinical practice, and research through networking, education, and professional activities.

Transcultural nursing focuses on the cultural beliefs, values, and practices of people to help them maintain and regain their health, or face death in meaningful ways. Nurses in this specialty try to understand cultures and their specific care needs and how to provide care that fits their ways rather than automatically imposing traditional Western medical practices on them. They provide culturally congruent care for well, sick, disabled, or dying patients of Mexican, Vietnamese, Japanese, African, Anglo, and other cultures and subcultures.

of Web-based educational courses, conferences, seminars, webinars, and workshops. Contact nursing associations in your practice area for information on CE opportunities.

■ CERTIFICATION, LICENSING, AND SPECIAL REQUIREMENTS
Certification or Licensing
Many professional nursing associations provide voluntary certification to registered nurses. For example, the Board of Certification for Emergency Nursing awards the certified transport registered nurse designation to those who pass an examination and meet other requirements. The American Nurses Credentialing Center, a subsidiary of the American Nurses Association, provides a variety of certification credentials.

All states, the District of Columbia, and U.S. territories require a license to practice nursing. To obtain a license, graduates of approved nursing schools must pass a national examination. Nurses may be licensed by more than one state. In some states, continuing education is a condition for license renewal. Different titles require different education and training levels.

■ EXPERIENCE, SKILLS, AND PERSONALITY TRAITS
Nursing students should gain experience by completing several nursing internships, or clinical rotations (ideally in their practice specialty, such as emergency nursing), as part of their postsecondary training.

You should enjoy working with people, and be especially sensitive and effective in working with those who may experience fear or anger because of an illness. Patience, compassion, and calmness are qualities needed by anyone working in this career. In addition, you must be able to give directions as well as follow instructions and work as part of a health care team. Anyone interested in becoming a registered nurse should also have a strong desire to continue learning, because new tests, procedures, and technologies are constantly being developed within medicine.

■ EMPLOYMENT PROSPECTS
Employers
More than 2.7 million registered nurses are employed in the United States. About 61 percent of registered nurses work in hospitals, 7 percent work in offices of physicians, 7 percent in nursing care facilities, 6 percent in home health care services, and 6 percent for the government. The rest work in managed-care facilities, clinics, industry, private homes, schools, camps, and government agencies. Some nurses work part time.

Starting Out
The only way to become a registered nurse is through completion of one of the three kinds of educational programs, plus passing the licensing examination. Registered nurses may apply for employment directly to hospitals, nursing homes, home care agencies, temporary nursing agencies, companies, and government agencies that hire nurses. Jobs can also be obtained through college career services offices, by signing up with employment agencies specializing in placement of nursing personnel, or through the state employment office. Other sources of jobs include nurses' associations, professional journals, and newspaper want ads.

■ ADVANCEMENT PROSPECTS
Increasingly, administrative and supervisory positions in the nursing field go to nurses who have earned at least the bachelor of science degree in nursing. Nurses with many years of experience who are graduates of a diploma program may achieve supervisory positions, but

requirements for such promotions have become more difficult in recent years and in many cases require at least the B.S.N. degree.

Nurses with bachelor's degrees are usually those who are hired as public health nurses. Nurses with master's degrees are often employed as clinical nurse specialists, faculty, instructors, supervisors, or administrators.

RNs can pursue graduate degrees to become advanced practice nurses, who have greater responsibilities and command higher salaries.

■ OUTLOOK

The nursing field is the largest of all health care occupations, and employment prospects for nurses are good. The U.S. Department of Labor (DOL) projects that registered nurses will have the second-largest number of new jobs for all professions through 2024: nearly 439,000 new nursing jobs will be added to the field. Registered nurses with at least a bachelor's degree in nursing will have the best job prospects.

There has been a serious shortage of nurses in recent years. Many nurses are expected to leave the profession in the coming years because of unsatisfactory working conditions, including low pay, severe understaffing, high stress, physical demands, mandatory overtime, and irregular hours. The shortage will also be exacerbated by the increasing numbers of baby-boomer aged nurses who are expected to retire, creating more open positions than there are graduates of nursing programs.

The faster-than-average job growth in this field is also a result of improving medical technology that will allow for treatments of many more diseases and health conditions. Nurses will be in strong demand to work with the rapidly growing population of senior citizens in the United States. Another factor that is prompting growth is the passage of the Affordable Care Act, which has greatly increased the number of Americans who are eligible for health insurance. As more people sign up for insurance, demand is growing for more health care professionals, including nurses, to provide care to them.

Employment in home care and nursing homes is expected to grow rapidly. Though more people are living well into their 80s and 90s, many need the kind of long-term care available at a nursing home. Also, because of financial reasons, patients are being released from hospitals sooner and admitted into nursing homes. Many nursing homes have facilities and staff capable of caring for long-term rehabilitation patients, as well as those afflicted with Alzheimer's. Many nurses will also be needed to help staff the growing number of outpatient facilities, such as HMOs, group medical practices, and ambulatory surgery centers.

NURSING FUNDAMENTALS   LEARN MORE ABOUT IT

Ackley, Betty J., and Gail B. Ladwig. *Nursing Diagnosis Handbook: An Evidence-Based Guide to Planning Care,* 10th ed. Philadelphia: Mosby, 2013.

Dewit, Susan C. *Saunders Student Nurse Planner: A Guide to Success in Nursing School,* 10th ed. Philadelphia: W. B. Saunders Co., 2014.

Evangelist, Thomas, et al. *McGraw-Hill's Nursing School Entrance Exams,* 2nd ed. New York: McGraw-Hill, 20012.

Lagerquist, Sally Lambert. *Davis's NCLEX-RN Success,* 3rd ed. Philadelphia: F.A. Davis Company, 2012.

Lewis, Sharon L., et al. *Medical-Surgical Nursing: Assessment and Management of Clinical Problems,* 9th ed. Philadelphia: Mosby, 2013.

Potter, Patricia A., Anne G. Perry et al. *Fundamentals of Nursing,* 8th ed. Philadelphia: Mosby, 2012.

Skidmore-Roth, Linda. *Mosby's 2015 Nursing Drug Reference,* 28th ed. Philadelphia: Mosby, 2014.

Van Leeuwen, Anne M., et al. *Davis's Comprehensive Handbook of Laboratory and Diagnostic Tests with Nursing Implications,* 5th ed. Philadelphia: F.A. Davis Company, 2013.

Advanced practice nursing specialties will be in great demand. The DOL predicts that employment for nurse anesthetists, nurse midwives, and nurse practitioners will grow by 31 percent through 2024, or much faster than the average for all careers.

■ UNIONS AND ASSOCIATIONS

Some registered nurses are represented by National Nurses United; the American Federation of State, County, and Municipal Employees; and other national and local unions. The American Nurses Association is a membership organization for registered nurses. It offers publications, continuing education classes and webinars, networking opportunities, and other valuable resources. The American Association of Colleges of Nursing represents more than 725 member schools of nursing; these schools offer a mix of baccalaureate, graduate, and post-graduate programs. The American Nurses Credentialing Center, along with many other nursing organizations, provides certification to registered nurses. The National League for Nursing is a membership organization for nurse faculty and leaders in nursing education. The National Organization for Associate Degree Nursing bills itself as the "voice for associate degree nursing."

▓ TIPS FOR ENTRY

1. Visit the following Web sites for job listings:
   - http://www.healthecareers.com
   - http://nursepath.com
   - http://www.nurse.com/students/careersinnursing.html
2. Read *The American Nurse* and *American Nurse Today* (both are available at http://nursingworld.org/MainMenuCategories/ANAMarketplace/ANAPeriodicals) to learn more about the field.
3. Join nursing associations to access training and networking resources, industry publications, and employment opportunities. Volunteer for association committees, special interest groups, and workgroups to raise your profile and make networking contacts.
4. Conduct information interviews with registered nurses and ask for advice on landing a job.

▓ FOR MORE INFORMATION

Visit the AACN Web site to access a list of member schools and career information.

American Association of Colleges of Nursing (AACN)
One Dupont Circle, NW, Suite 530
Washington, D.C. 20036-1135
Tel: (202) 463-6930
Fax: (202) 785-8320
http://www.aacn.nche.edu

For information about opportunities as an RN, contact
American Nurses Association (ANA)
8515 Georgia Avenue, Suite 400
Silver Spring, MD 20910-3492
Tel: (800) 274-4262
Fax: (301) 628-5001
E-mail: memberinfo@ana.org
http://www.nursingworld.org

For information on certification, contact
American Nurses Credentialing Center (ANCC)
8515 Georgia Ave, Suite 400
Silver Spring, MD 20910-3492
Tel: (800) 284-2378
http://www.nursecredentialing.org

Discover Nursing, sponsored by Johnson & Johnson Services Inc., provides information on nursing careers, nursing schools, and scholarships.
Discover Nursing
Tel: (888) 981-9111
http://www.discovernursing.com

For information about membership for nursing educators, contact
National League for Nursing (NLN)
2600 Virginia Avenue, NW
Washington, D.C. 20037-1905
Tel: (800) 669-1656
E-mail: generalinfo@nln.org
http://www.nln.org

For information on membership, contact
Organization for Associate Degree Nursing (OADN)
7794 Grow Drive
Pensacola, FL 32514-7072
Tel: (877) 966-6236
Fax: (850) 484-8762
E-mail: oadn@oadn.org
https://www.oadn.org/

Rehabilitation Counselors

▓ OVERVIEW

Rehabilitation counselors provide counseling and guidance services to people with disabilities to help them resolve life problems and to train for and locate work that is suitable to their physical and mental abilities, interests, and aptitudes. There are approximately 120,100 rehabilitation counselors working in the United States.

▓ HISTORY

Today it is generally accepted that people with disabilities can and should have the opportunity to become as fully independent as possible in all aspects of life, from school to work and social activities. In response to the needs of disabled war veterans, Congress passed the first Vocational Rehabilitation Act in 1920. The act set in place the Vocational Rehabilitation Program, a federal-state program that provides for the delivery of rehabilitation services, including counseling, to eligible people with disabilities.

The profession of rehabilitation counseling has its roots in the Rehabilitation Act, which allowed for funds to train personnel. What was at first a job title developed into a fully recognized profession as it became evident that the delivery of effective rehabilitation services required highly trained specialists. Early efforts for providing rehabilitation counseling and other services were often directed especially toward the nation's veterans. In

1930, the Veterans Administration was created to supply support services to veterans and their families, and in 1989, the U.S. Department of Veterans Affairs was created as the 14th cabinet department in the U.S. government.

The passage of the Americans with Disabilities Act in 1990 recognized the rights and needs of people with disabilities and developed federal regulations and guidelines aimed at eliminating discrimination and other barriers preventing people with disabilities from participating fully in school, workplace, and public life. Many state and federal programs have since been created to aid people with disabilities. In 2009, the Twenty-first Century Communications and Video Accessibility Act (H.R. 3101) was introduced to Congress for debate, "to ensure that individuals with disabilities have access to emerging Internet Protocol-based communication and video programming technologies in the 21st Century."

■ THE JOB

Rehabilitation counselors work with people with disabilities to identify barriers to medical, psychological, personal, social, and vocational functioning and to develop a plan of action to remove or reduce those barriers.

Clients are referred to rehabilitation programs from many sources. Sometimes they seek help on their own initiative; sometimes their families bring them in. They may be referred by a physician, hospital, or social worker, or they may be sent by employment agencies, schools, or accident commissions. A former employer may seek help for the individual.

The counselor's first step is to determine the nature and extent of the disability and evaluate how that disability interferes with work and other life functions. This determination is made from medical and psychological reports as well as from family history, educational background, work experience, and other evaluative information.

The next step is to determine a vocational direction and plan of services to overcome the handicaps to employment or independent living.

The rehabilitation counselor coordinates a comprehensive evaluation of a client's physical functioning abilities and vocational interests, aptitudes, and skills. This information is used to develop vocational or independent-living goals for the client and the services necessary to reach those goals. Services that the rehabilitation counselor may coordinate or provide include physical and mental restoration, academic or vocational training, vocational counseling, job analysis, job modification or reasonable accommodation, and job placement. Limited financial assistance in the form of maintenance or transportation assistance may also be provided.

The counselor's relationship with the client may be as brief as a week or as long as several years, depending on the nature of the problem and the needs of the client.

■ EARNINGS

The U.S. Department of Labor reports that median annual earnings of rehabilitation counselors were $34,390 in May 2015. Salaries ranged from less than $20,950 to more than $60,750.

Rehabilitation counselors employed by the federal government generally start at the GS-9 or GS-11 level. In 2015, the basic GS-9 salary was $45,530. Those with master's degrees generally began at the GS-11 level, with a salary of $50,790 in 2015. Salaries for federal government workers vary according to the region of the country in which they work. Those working in areas with a higher cost of living receive additional locality pay.

Counselors employed by government and private agencies and institutions generally receive health insurance, pension plans, and other benefits, including vacation, sick, and holiday pay. Self-employed counselors must provide their own benefits.

■ WORK ENVIRONMENT

Rehabilitation counselors work approximately 40 hours each week and do not usually have to work during evenings or weekends. They work both in the office and in the field. Depending on the type of training required, lab space and workout or therapy rooms may be available. Rehabilitation counselors must usually keep detailed accounts of their progress with clients and write reports. They may spend many hours traveling about the community to visit employed clients, prospective employers, trainees, or training programs.

CAREER LADDER

Professor

Manager or Supervisor

Experienced Rehabilitation Counselor

Entry-Level Rehabilitation Counselor

Rehabilitation Counseling Intern

■ EXPLORING

To explore a career in which you work with people with disabilities, look for opportunities to volunteer or work in this field. One possibility is to be a counselor at a children's camp for disabled youngsters. You can also volunteer with a local vocational rehabilitation agency or a facility such as Easter Seals or Goodwill. Other possibilities include reading for the blind or leading a hobby or craft class at an adult day care center. And don't forget volunteer opportunities at a local hospital or nursing home. Even if your only responsibility is to escort people to the X-ray department or talk to patients to cheer them up, you will gain valuable experience interacting with people who are facing challenging situations.

■ EDUCATION AND TRAINING REQUIREMENTS
High School

To prepare for a career in rehabilitation counseling, take your high school's college prep curriculum. These classes should include several years of mathematics and science, such as biology and chemistry. To begin to gain an understanding of people and societies, take history, psychology, and sociology classes. English classes are important because you will need excellent communication skills for this work. Some of your professional responsibilities will include documenting your work and doing research to provide your clients with helpful information; to do these things you will undoubtedly be working with computers. Therefore, you should take computer science classes so that you are skilled in using them. In addition, you may want to consider taking speech and a foreign language, both of which will enhance your communication skills.

Postsecondary Training

Although some positions are available for people with a bachelor's degree in rehabilitation counseling, these positions are usually as aides and offer limited advancement opportunities. Most employers require the rehabilitation counselors working for them to hold master's degrees. Before receiving your master's, you will need to complete a bachelor's degree with a major in behavioral sciences, social sciences, or a related field. Another option is to complete an undergraduate degree in rehabilitation

counseling. The Council for Accreditation of Counseling and Related Educational Programs has accredited institutions in the United States, Canada, and Mexico that offer programs in counselor education. If you decide on an undergraduate degree in rehabilitation, it is recommended you attend an accredited program. Keep in mind, however, that even if you get an undergraduate degree in rehabilitation, you will still need to attend a graduate program to qualify for most counselor positions. No matter which undergraduate program you decide on, you should concentrate on courses in sociology, psychology, physiology, history, and statistics as well as courses in English and communications. Several universities now offer courses in various aspects of physical therapy and special education training. Courses in sign language, speech therapy, and a foreign language are also beneficial.

Master's programs in rehabilitation counseling include courses in medical aspects of disability, psychosocial aspects of disability, testing techniques, statistics, personality theory, personality development, abnormal psychology, techniques of counseling, occupational information, and vocational training and job placement. A supervised internship is also an important aspect of a program. Students who wish to have a thorough education in rehabilitation counseling can secure a graduate degree through programs accredited by the Council on Rehabilitation Education.

Other Education or Training

Continuing education opportunities are provided by the Commission on Rehabilitation Counselor Certification, American Rehabilitation Counseling Association, and the National Rehabilitation Counseling Association. Contact these organizations for more information.

■ CERTIFICATION, LICENSING, AND SPECIAL REQUIREMENTS
Certification or Licensing

The counseling profession is regulated in nearly every state and the District of Columbia. This regulation may be in the form of credentialing, registry, certification, or licensure. Regulations, however, vary by state and sometimes by employer. For example, an employer may require certification even if the state does not. You will need to check with your state's licensing board as well as your employer for specific information about your circumstances.

Across the country, many employers now require their rehabilitation counselors to be certified by the Commission on Rehabilitation Counselor Certification (CRCC). The purpose of certification is to provide assurance that professionals engaged in rehabilitation counseling meet set standards and maintain those standards through continuing education. To become certified, counselors must pass an extensive multiple-choice examination to demonstrate their knowledge of rehabilitation counseling. The CRCC requires the master's degree as the minimum educational level for certification. Applicants who meet these certification requirements receive the designation of certified rehabilitation counselor (CRC).

Most state government rehabilitation agencies require future counselors to meet state civil service and merit system regulations. The applicant must take a competitive written examination and may also be interviewed and evaluated by a special board.

■ EXPERIENCE, SKILLS, AND PERSONALITY TRAITS

Those wishing to enter the field should obtain as much experience as possible in college by participating in internships, volunteering, or working at a part-time job at an organization that provides rehabilitation counseling services.

The most important personal attribute required for rehabilitation counseling is the ability to get along well with other people. Rehabilitation counselors work with many different kinds of clients and must be able to see situations and problems from their client's point of view. They must be both patient and persistent. Rehabilitation may be a slow process with many delays and setbacks. The counselor must maintain a calm, positive manner even when no progress is made.

■ EMPLOYMENT PROSPECTS

Employers

Approximately 120,100 rehabilitation counselors are employed in the United States. Rehabilitation counselors work in a variety of settings. The majority of rehabilitation counselors work for state agencies; some also work for local and federal agencies. Employment opportunities are available in rehabilitation centers, mental health agencies, prisons, developmental disability agencies, sheltered workshops, training institutions, and schools (colleges and elementary and secondary schools).

Starting Out

School career services offices are the best places for the new graduate to begin the career search. In addition, the National Rehabilitation Counseling Association and the American Rehabilitation Counseling Association (a division of the American Counseling Association) are sources for employment information. The new counselor

People with disabilities use the aid of a rehabilitation counselor to help them adapt to their workplace. (goodluz. Shutterstock.)

may also apply directly to agencies for available positions. Vocational rehabilitation agencies employ nearly 36,000 rehabilitation counselors. The Department of Veterans Affairs employs rehabilitation counselors to assist with the rehabilitation of disabled veterans. Many rehabilitation counselors are employed by private for-profit or nonprofit rehabilitation programs and facilities. Others are employed in industry, schools, hospitals, and other settings, while others are self-employed.

■ ADVANCEMENT PROSPECTS

The rehabilitation counselor usually receives regular salary increases after gaining experience in the job. He or she may move from relatively easy cases to increasingly challenging ones. Counselors may advance into such positions as administrator or supervisor after several years of counseling experience. It is also possible to find related counseling and teaching positions, which may represent advancement in other fields.

■ OUTLOOK

The passage of the Americans with Disabilities Act of 1990 increased the demand for rehabilitation counselors. As more local, state, and federal programs are initiated that are designed to assist people with disabilities and as private institutions and companies seek to comply with this new legislation, job prospects are promising. Budget pressures may serve to limit the number of new rehabilitation counselors to be hired by government agencies; however, the overall outlook remains excellent.

Employment for rehabilitation counselors is expected to grow by 9 percent, faster than average for all careers, through 2024, according to the U.S. Department of Labor. Some of this growth can be attributed to the advances in

REHABILITATION BASICS

LEARN MORE ABOUT IT

Chan, Fong, et al. *Certified Rehabilitation Counselor Examination Preparation: A Concise Guide to the Rehabilitation Counselor Test.* New York: Springer Publishing Company, 2011.

Hays, Danica G. *Assessment in Counseling: A Guide to the Use of Psychological Assessment Procedures,* 5th ed. Alexandria, Va.: American Counseling Association, 2012.

Parker, Randall M., and Jeanne Boland Patterson. *Rehabilitation Counseling: Basics and Beyond,* 5th ed. Austin, Tex.: Pro-Ed, 2011.

Van Voorhis, Patricia, and Emily J. Salisbury. *Correctional Counseling and Rehabilitation,* 8th ed. Philadelphia: Elsevier, 2013.

medical technology that are saving more lives, as well as the elderly population living longer and needing rehabilitation counseling. In addition, more employers are offering employee assistance programs that provide mental health and alcohol and drug abuse services. Counselors will also be needed to work with veterans who have been injured during their military service and with those who have learning disabilities and autism spectrum disorders.

■ UNIONS AND ASSOCIATIONS

Rehabilitation counselors who work for government agencies can join the American Federation of Government Employees and the American Federation of State, County and Municipal Employees, unions that represent government workers. Membership organizations for counselors include the American Rehabilitation Counseling Association, National Rehabilitation Association, and the National Rehabilitation Counseling Association. The Council on Rehabilitation Education and the Council for Accreditation of Counseling and Related Educational Programs accredit counseling education programs. The Commission on Rehabilitation Counselor Certification provides certification. The National Clearinghouse of Rehabilitation Training Materials, which is sponsored by the Rehabilitation Services Administration, provides a wealth of information about rehabilitation counseling.

■ TIPS FOR ENTRY

1. Visit http://www.rehabjobs.org to read *Careers in Vocational Rehabilitation.*
2. To learn more the field, read:
   - *Rehabilitation Counseling Bulletin* (http://www.arcaweb.org)
   - *Journal of Applied Rehabilitation Counseling* (http://nrca-net.org/index_files/jarc.htm)
   - *Journal of Rehabilitation* (http://www.nationalrehab.org)
3. Use social media to stay up to date on industry developments and learn about job openings. Many professional associations are embracing social media to stay in touch with members and others who are interested in rehabilitation counseling. For example, the National Rehabilitation Association has a presence on Facebook, LinkedIn, and Twitter.

■ FOR MORE INFORMATION

For general information on careers in rehabilitation counseling, visit

American Rehabilitation Counseling Association
http://www.arcaweb.org

For information on certification, contact

Commission on Rehabilitation Counselor Certification
1699 East Woodfield Road, Suite 300
Schaumburg, IL 60173-4957
Tel: (847) 944-1325
Fax: (847) 944-1346
E-mail: info@crccertification.com
http://www.crccertification.com

For listings of CORE-approved programs as well as other information, contact

Council on Rehabilitation Education (CORE)
1699 East Woodfield Road, Suite 300
Schaumburg, IL 60173-4957
Tel: (847) 944-1345
Fax: (847) 944-1346
http://www.core-rehab.org

For information on a variety of resources, visit

National Clearinghouse of Rehabilitation Training Materials
New Editions Consulting Inc.
103 W. Broad St., Suite 400
Falls Church, VA 22046
E-mail: NCRTM@neweditions.net
https://ncrtm.ed.gov/

For information on membership, contact

National Rehabilitation Association (NRA)
PO Box 150235
Alexandria, VA 22315-0235

Tel: (888) 258-4295; (703) 836-0850

Fax: (703) 836-0848

E-mail: info@nationalrehab.org

http://www.nationalrehab.org

For news on legislation, employment, and other information, contact

National Rehabilitation Counseling Association

PO Box 4480

Manassas, VA 20108-4480

Fax: (703) 361-2489

E-mail: nrcaoffice@aol.com

http://nrca-net.org

Renewable Energy Careers

■ OVERVIEW

Renewable energy is defined as a clean and unlimited source of power or fuel. This energy is harnessed from different sources such as wind, sunlight (solar), water (hydro), organic matter (biomass), and the earth's internal heat (geothermal). Unlike nonrenewable energy sources like oil, natural gas, or coal, or nuclear energy, renewable energy is not based on extracting a limited resource.

The renewable energy industry is actually a vast group of sub-industries that offer employment opportunities for people with many different educational backgrounds. *Engineers, scientists, architects, farmers, technicians, operators, mechanics, lawyers, businesspeople, sales workers, human resource and public affairs specialists*, as well as a host of administrative support workers make their living by researching, developing, installing, and promoting renewable energy. The National Renewable Energy Laboratory estimates that renewable energy industries will provide at least 300,000 new jobs for American workers in the next two decades.

■ HISTORY

Renewable energy resources have been used for centuries. Windmills have long been used to grind grain or pump water. The sun has always been used as a source of heat. In 1839, Edmund Becquerel, an early pioneer in solar energy, discovered the photoelectric effect—the production of electricity from sunlight. The power of water that is stored and released from dams has been used for generating electricity. This type of electricity is known as hydropower electricity. Hot springs and underground reservoirs, products of geothermal energy, have long been used as sources of heat. People have burned trees or other organic matter, known as biomass, for warmth or cooking purposes.

The early technology of harnessing and producing renewable energy as a source of power or fuel was under-developed and expensive. Because of this, the majority of our power needs have been met using nonrenewable resources such as natural gas or fossil fuels. Our use of fossil fuels has caused our nation to rely heavily on foreign sources to meet demand. Our declining national supply of nonrenewable natural resources, coupled by public awareness of the soaring costs and environmental damage caused by the mining, processing, and use of conventional energy sources, have shed new light on renewable energy sources as a viable solution to our energy needs.

Today, "green" sources of power have earned respect as an important alternative to nonrenewable resources. New research and technology in the past 30 years have enabled self-renewing resources to be harnessed more efficiently and at a lower cost than in the past. Deregulation and a restructuring of the conventional power industries by the Energy Policy Act of 1992 have presented the public with more choices. And the American Recovery and Reinvestment Act of 2009 included more than $80 billion in clean energy investments. Tax incentives at the state and federal level make buying green power more affordable to consumers and for the utility companies. Renewable

QUICK FACTS

ALTERNATE TITLE(S)
Varies by profession

DUTIES
Research, develop, install, and promote renewable energy resources

SALARY RANGE
$22,390 to $55,160 to $146,820+

WORK ENVIRONMENT
Indoors/Outdoors

BEST GEOGRAPHIC LOCATION(S)
Opportunities are available throughout the country

MINIMUM EDUCATION LEVEL
High School Diploma, Bachelor's Degree

SCHOOL SUBJECTS
Chemistry, Earth Science, Mathematics

EXPERIENCE
Internship

PERSONALITY TRAITS
Problem-Solving, Social, Technical

SKILLS
Interpersonal, Math, Scientific

CERTIFICATION OR LICENSING
Required

SPECIAL REQUIREMENTS
Varies based on position and employer

EMPLOYMENT PROSPECTS
Good

ADVANCEMENT PROSPECTS
Good

OUTLOOK
Faster than the Average

NOC
0112, 2112, 2113, 2123, 2131, 2134, 2148, 2151, 2212, 7441

O*NET-SOC
11-2011.01, 11-9199.10, 13-1199.05, 17-2051.00, 17-2071.00, 17-2141.00, 17-2141.01, 17-2199.03, 17-2199.10, 17-2199.11, 41-4011.07, 47-1011.03

CAREER LADDER

Manager or Consultant

Experienced Renewable
Energy Worker

Entry-Level Renewable
Energy Worker

energy sources are used to produce more than 13 percent of all electricity in the United States, according to the U.S. Department of Energy.

■ THE JOB

The renewable energy industry can be broken down into the following sub-industries: wind, solar, hydropower, geothermal, bioenergy, and fuel cell technology. A wide variety of career options are available to workers with a high school diploma to advanced degrees. Additionally, many career skills are transferable from one sub-industry to another.

Wind

According to the American Wind Energy Association, every state in the United States has either an operational wind energy project or a wind-related manufacturing facility. Approximately 88,000 people are employed in the wind energy industry. In 2015, wind energy made up 35 percent of all renewable energy in the United States, according to the Energy Information Administration (EIA).

The wind turbine is the modern, high-tech equivalent of yesterday's windmill. A single wind turbine can harness the wind's energy to generate enough electricity to power a house or small farm. Wind plants, also called wind farms, are a collection of high-powered turbines that can generate electricity for tens of thousands of homes. In order to achieve this capacity, a variety of technical workers are employed in the wind power industry. Electrical, mechanical, and aeronautical engineers design and test the turbines as well as the wind farms. *Meteorologists* help to identify prime locations for new project sites, and may serve as consultants throughout the duration of a project. Skilled construction workers build the farms; *windsmiths*, sometimes called *mechanical or electrical technicians*, operate and maintain the turbines and other equipment on the farm.

Solar

In 2015, solar energy made up 5 percent of all renewable energy in the United States, according to the EIA. Its potential as a major energy source is largely untapped.

There are different ways to turn the sun's energy into a useful power source. The most common technology today uses photovoltaic (PV) cells. When a PV cell is directly struck by sunlight, the materials inside it absorb this light. Simply put, the activity of absorption frees electrons, which then travel through a circuit. Electrons traveling through a circuit produce electricity. Many PV cells can be linked together to produce unlimited amounts of electricity.

The Concentrating Solar Power (CSP) technologies use mirrors to focus sunlight onto a receiver. The receiver collects sunlight as heat, which can be used directly, or generated into electricity. The three CSP methods used are parabolic troughs, power towers, and parabolic dishes. Parabolic troughs can produce solar electricity inexpensively compared to the other methods, and can generate enough power for large-scale projects. Power towers can also generate power for large-scale projects, while parabolic dishes are used for smaller scale projects. Using solar collectors and storage tanks, the sun's energy can be used to heat water for swimming pools or buildings. Many schools, hospitals, prisons, and government facilities use solar technology for their water use. A building's design or construction materials can also utilize the sun's energy for its heating and light through passive solar design, water heating, or with electrical PV cells.

Skilled workers are needed for all aspects of solar technology. *Electrical, mechanical, and chemical engineers* work in research and development departments. *Architects*, many of whom specialize in passive solar design and construction, design solar-powered structures. *Technicians, electricians, installers,* and *construction workers* build and maintain solar projects.

Hydropower

Hydropower is the largest and least expensive type of renewable energy in the United States. In 2015, hydropower energy made up 46 percent of all renewable energy in the United States, according to the EIA.

Hydropower uses the energy of flowing water to produce electricity. Water is retained in a dam or reservoir. When the water is released, it passes through and spins a turbine. The movement of the turbine in turn spins generators, which produces electricity. In "run of the river" projects, dams are not needed. Canals or pipes divert river water to spin turbines.

Electrical and mechanical engineers and technicians design, construct, and maintain hydropower projects. *Biologists* and other *environmental scientists* assess the effects of hydropower projects on wildlife and the environment. *Fish farmers* develop fish screens and ladders and other migration-assisting devices. *Recreation managers* and *trail planners* manage and preserve the land surrounding the reservoir or dam.

Geothermal

The Geothermal Energy Association states that the United States produces more geothermal energy than any other country, yet geothermal energy generates less than 1 percent of total U.S. electricity. In 2015, geothermal energy made up 3 percent of all renewable energy in the United States, according to the EIA. Geothermal heat comes from the heat within the Earth. Water heated from geothermal energy is tapped from its underground reservoirs and used to heat buildings, grow crops, or melt snow. This direct use of geothermal energy can also be used to generate electricity.

Most water and steam reservoirs are located in the western United States. However, dry rock drilling, a process that drills deeper into the Earth's magma, is an innovation that will eventually allow geothermal projects to be undertaken almost anywhere.

Employment opportunities in the geothermal industry are excellent for *geologists*, *geochemists*, and *geophysicists*, who are needed to research and locate new reservoirs. *Hydraulic engineers*, *reservoir engineers*, and *drillers* work together to reach and maintain the reservoir's heat supply.

The building of new geothermal projects requires the work of electricians, welders, mechanics, and construction workers. *Drilling workers*, *machinists*, and *mechanics* also are needed to keep the drilling equipment in good order. *Environmental scientists*, *chemists*, and other scientists are needed to research and develop new technology to reach other geothermal sources of energy.

Bioenergy

Bioenergy electricity generation accounts for 11 percent of all renewable energy generated in the United States, according to the U.S. Department of Energy.

Bioenergy is the energy stored in biomass—organic matter such as trees, straw, or corn. Bioenergy is the second largest source of renewable energy. It can be used directly, as is the case when we burn wood for cooking or heating purposes. Indirect uses include the production of electricity using wood waste or other biomass waste as a source of power. Another important biomass byproduct is ethanol, which is converted from corn. However, in the past several years, researchers have found that growing biofuels such as corn in an un-sustainable manner can actually be harmful to the environment. Carol Werner, executive director of the Environmental and Energy Study Institute, says that the most environmentally friendly biofuels should be made from agricultural waste products (non-edible food products) and from biomass grown on non-agricultural lands.

Chemists, *biochemists*, *biologists*, and *agricultural scientists* work together to find faster and less costly ways to produce bioenergy. *Engineers*, *construction workers*, *electricians*, and *technicians* build and maintain bioenergy

Workers install solar energy panels on a roof. (Dennis Schroeder. U.S. Department of Energy.)

conversion plants. *Farmers* and *foresters* raise and harvest crops or other sources of biomass. *Truck drivers* transport crops to the conversion plants.

Fuel Cell Technology

Until recently, all motor vehicles were powered by gasoline and internal combustion engines. While effective and reliable, these systems cause considerable pollution—especially as the number of vehicle owners in the world continues to grow rapidly.

Manufacturers have developed cleaner power options for vehicles such as the electric car, or the gas/electric hybrid. The fuel cell is another option currently in development. A fuel cell is a highly efficient device that generates electricity. According to the Fuel Cell and Hydrogen Energy Association, "fuel cells can run on a variety of fuels, including natural gas and hydrogen. Hydrogen is a clean, carbon-free fuel readily available from a variety of sources. When powered by hydrogen, fuel cells emit only water vapor as a byproduct. Fuel cells can run at any time of day and produce nearly zero noise. They are reliable, safe, and never need recharging."

Fuel cell technology workers design, study, modify, and build fuel cell components or provide support to workers who do these tasks. Careers in the field range from technical positions such as engineer and technician to support jobs in sales, human resources, and clerical support.

Non-Technical Careers: All Sectors

Within all sectors of the renewable energy industry, non-technical workers are also needed to perform clerical duties, manage workers, sell, market, and advertise products, maintain records, and educate the public. *Sales and marketing professionals*, *advertising workers*, *secretaries*, *receptionists*, *customer service representatives*, *media*

WHY SHOULD YOU CARE ABOUT RENEWABLE ENERGY?

- **Save the environment:** Renewable energy is clean energy. It can be converted with little or no negative impacts on the environment.
- **Future generations:** Renewable energy sources can never be depleted. This means the technology we set up today to gather power and fuel will benefit generations to come.
- **The economy:** The renewable energy industry is labor intensive. Many different types of jobs are needed in research, construction, production, and maintenance—many of which are located at or near the project site. Investment dollars are kept close to home, fueling local economies in particular, and that of the United States as a whole.
- **Energy independence:** Using renewable energy sources helps curb U.S. dependence on fuel from foreign nations.

relations specialists, personnel and human resources specialists, accountants, information technology workers, and *educators* are just some of the types of nontechnical workers who work in this industry.

EARNINGS

Very little salary information is available for specific jobs in each sub-industry. However, according to the U.S. Department of Labor (DOL), the median salary for electrical engineers was $93,010 in May 2015. Overall, engineers earn salaries that range from less than $59,420 to $146,820 or more annually. Mechanics who worked as electrical and electronics repairers of commercial and industrial equipment had a median salary of $55,160 in May 2015. Geoscientists earned an average salary of $89,700, hydrologists earned $79,550, and geological technicians averaged $55,610 per year. Farmers and agricultural managers' salaries vary due to weather conditions and other factors that affect crop production. Agricultural managers had a median salary of $64,170 per year.

Annual salaries for nontechnical workers vary according to the position, type and size of the employer, and job responsibilities. The DOL reported that human resources managers had a median salary of $104,440 in May 2015. Architects averaged $76,100 and lawyers earned about $115,820 per year. Sales managers earned about $113,860 per year. Administrative services managers earned about $86,110 per year. Secretaries earned salaries that ranged from $22,390 to $60,640 or more. Administrative workers employed by nonprofit organizations tend to earn slightly less than their corporate counterparts.

Most employees receive a standard benefits package including medical insurance, paid vacation and sick days, and a retirement savings program.

WORK ENVIRONMENT

Work environment will vary depending on the industry and the type of position a worker holds. For example, meteorologists in the wind industry may need to travel to distant sites in order to better gauge wind capabilities for a proposed wind turbine project. Solar industry technicians often travel from site to site in order to install or maintain equipment needed for solar projects such as homes, buildings, or thermal generators. Hydropower industry employees perform much of their work outdoors. Biologists and fisheries managers work at or near ponds and rivers. Recreation managers often find themselves developing outdoor walking paths and trails near hydroelectric projects to ensure that vegetation and wildlife are protected. In the geothermal industry, drilling crews work outdoors when they operate heavy drilling tools to locate new reservoirs. Farmers employed by bio energy companies work outdoors tending their biomass crops. All workers who work outdoors must deal with occasionally extreme weather conditions such as high wind, rain, sleet, snow, and temperature extremes.

Administrative support staff, industry educators, research and development workers, sales and marketing staff, and other non-technical workers often work indoors in comfortable offices. Many scientists work in laboratories, which are clean, comfortable, and well lit. Most employees work a standard 40-hour week. Important projects or deadlines may require overtime and weekend work.

EXPLORING

Volunteering is one way to explore the renewable energy industry. You can find energy fairs or conventions in your area by contacting energy associations. Your duties may consist of handing out brochures or other simple tasks, but you will have the opportunity to learn about the industry and make contacts.

Many professional associations have student chapters or junior clubs. The National Society of Professional Engineers, for example, has local student chapters specifically designed to help college students learn more about careers in engineering. In addition to providing information about different engineering disciplines, student chapters promote contests, and offer information on scholarships and internships.

Industry associations also hold many competitions designed to promote their particular renewable energy sector. Visit the National Renewable Energy Laboratory's Web site (http://www.nrel.gov/learning/student_resources.html) for a list of student programs and competitions held throughout the United States. One such contest is the Junior Solar Sprint Car Competitions (http://www.nrel.gov/education/jss_hfc.html) held in Colorado for middle school students. The contest calls for the construction and racing of solar-powered cars. There is also a contest that involves battery-powered vehicles. Contestants learn about renewable energy technologies and concepts in a fun, challenging, and exciting setting.

■ EDUCATION AND TRAINING REQUIREMENTS
High School
For many jobs in the renewable energy industry, it pays to have a strong background in science and mathematics. For example, earth science, agriculture, and biology classes will be useful if you plan to work in the hydropower industry researching the effects of a new hydropower project on the surrounding vegetation and animal life. Mathematics, earth science, and chemistry classes will be helpful if you plan to work in the geothermal energy industry identifying and harvesting possible sources of geothermal energy from within the earth. Physics classes will be helpful if you plan to work in the wind industry designing windmills and turbine engines to capture and convert wind energy into electricity, or "green" buildings and homes of the future.

You need not be technically gifted in science and math in order to succeed in the renewable energy industry. Computer classes are useful for workers who run design programs, organize research, and maintain basic office records. Finance, accounting, communications, and English classes will be helpful to anyone who is interested in working in the business end of the industry. Taking a foreign language is highly useful since a majority of renewable energy companies are located abroad.

Postsecondary Training
Most technical jobs in this industry require at least an associate's or bachelor's degree. Courses of study range from environmental science and mathematics to architecture and meteorology. Many people who are employed in the research and development or technical departments of their respective renewable sub-industry have bachelor's or master's degrees in electrical, chemical, or mechanical engineering. Some scientists have graduate degrees in engineering or the sciences (such as biology, physics, or chemistry).

ALL ABOUT ALTERNATIVE ENERGY   FAST FACTS

- The Romans were among the first to use geothermal energy to heat their homes.
- The first fuel cell was built in 1839. Sir William Robert Grove, a Welsh lawyer and physicist, created what he called the "Grove gas voltaic battery," which was actually a primitive fuel cell. It did not create enough electricity to be useful.
- Albert Einstein was truly a pioneer in renewable energy: In 1921, he won the Nobel Prize in Physics for his groundbreaking experiments in solar power and photovoltaics.
- A solar-powered aircraft set a world record in 1990 when it flew across the United States (in 21 stages) using no fuel at all.
- All it takes is a wind speed of about 14 mph to convert wind energy to electricity, and just one wind turbine can produce enough electricity to power up to 300 homes.

Source: "The Natural Solution: Ten Facts About Renewable Energy," by Ana Caistor-Arendar

---

A growing number of colleges offer classes, certificates, and degrees in renewable energy, including Georgia Tech, Purdue University, the University of California (at both Davis and Irvine), and the University of Wisconsin. San Juan College, located in Farmington, New Mexico, offers an associate's degree or one-year certificate with emphasis in photovoltaic and solar thermal systems.

Visit the following Web sites for lists of programs: http://energy.gov/eere/education/education-homepage and http://www.irecusa.org/training-directory.

Four-year degrees in liberal arts, business, or other professional degrees are not required, but are recommended for many non-technical jobs. For example, a *community affairs representative* or *public relations specialist* should have a communications or journalism background.

Certification
Certificate programs in renewable energy are provided by colleges and universities, professional associations (such as the Midwest Renewable Energy Association), and private organizations (such as National Solar Trainers). Contact these providers for more information.

Other Education or Training
The Renewable Fuels Association offers continuing education opportunities (CE) at its National Ethanol Conference. The Geothermal Resources Council offers workshops and seminars at its annual meeting and

trade show. Topics include drilling, economics, environmental aspects of geothermal activity, financing, geochemistry, geology, geophysics, heat pumps, legal aspects, management, non-electric uses, and reservoir engineering. Many other professional associations (such as the American Solar Energy Society, American Wind Energy Association, and the National Hydropower Association) provide CE classes, webinars, and conferences in their particular specialty.

■ CERTIFICATION, LICENSING, AND SPECIAL REQUIREMENTS
Certification or Licensing

The Association of Energy Engineers (AEE) offers certification in more than 25 specialties. To be considered for certification, a candidate must meet eligibility standards such as a minimum of three years of relevant work experience and membership in a professional organization. Most programs consist of classroom work and an examination.

Certification and licensing requirements for other jobs in the renewable industry will vary according to the position. Solar panel installers must be certified in order to work on most projects, especially government contracts. Different associations offer certification needs and continuing education training. For example, the Midwest Renewable Energy Association offers certification for those working with photovoltaics. Other organizations that offer certification include the North American Board of Certified Energy Practitioners and the National Institute for Certification in Engineering Technologies.

Contractors in the solar industry must apply for certification to ensure their structures are sound and to industry standards. Check the industry trade associations for specifics on project certification.

Most states require engineers to be licensed. There are two levels of licensing for engineers. Professional engineers (PEs) have graduated from an accredited engineering curriculum, have four years of engineering experience, and have passed a written exam. Engineering graduates need not wait until they have four years of experience, however, to start the licensure process. Those who pass the Fundamentals of Engineering examination after graduating are called engineers in training (EIT) or engineer interns (EI). The EIT certification is usually valid for 10 years. After acquiring suitable work experience, EITs can take the second examination, the Principles and Practice of Engineering exam, to gain full PE licensure. For more information on licensing and examination requirements, visit the National Council of Examiners for Engineering and Surveying's Web site, http://www.ncees.org.

Electricians may require licensure depending on the requirements of their job, as well as the industry sector for which they are employed. All states and the District of Columbia require that architects be licensed before contracting to provide architectural services in that particular state. Though many work in the field without licensure, only licensed architects are required to take legal responsibility for all work.

Truck drivers must meet federal requirements and any requirements established by the state where they are based. All drivers must obtain a state commercial driver's license. Truck drivers involved in interstate commerce must meet requirements of the U.S. Department of Transportation.

■ EXPERIENCE, SKILLS, AND PERSONALITY TRAITS

Any experience—such as an internship or volunteer opportunity—that you can obtain working at a renewable energy-related employer will be useful preparation for the field. One of the best ways to gain experience in the field is to participate in an internship while in college. This will help you to to explore career paths, learn about your industry, and make valuable networking contacts. These contacts will come in handy when you are looking for a job.

It's not absolutely necessary to be a technical genius to do well in this industry. Some of the technical side can be learned while on the job. However, it is important to have an interest in environmental issues.

Teamwork is important within all sectors of renewable energy. The ability to work with large groups of people, with varying backgrounds and technical knowledge, is a must. Other important traits include strong organizational and communication skills, as well as an interest in continuing to learn throughout one's career.

■ EMPLOYMENT PROSPECTS
Employers

The renewable energy industry is a large and diverse field. Employment opportunities in each sector exist at manufacturing or research and development companies, both large and small; utilities; government organizations; and nonprofit groups and agencies. Research or education opportunities can be found at universities or trade associations. Because the benefits of renewable energy are a global concern, many employment opportunities can be found outside of the United States.

It is important to note that while employment in the renewable energy industry can be found nationwide, some sectors of the industry tend to be clustered in specific regions of the United States. A good example of this is the wind power industry. Although wind is everywhere, different sections of the United States are windier than other areas. For this reason, wind-related projects tend to be most concentrated in the western states of California and Texas, other western states such as Colorado and Oklahoma, the Pacific Northwest (especially Oregon), and the Midwest (especially Illinois, Iowa, and Minnesota), and the Mid-Atlantic. Approximately 80,700 people are employed in the wind energy industry, according to the American Wind Energy Association.

There are a wide variety of employment opportunities in solar energy. Contractors, dealers, distributors, builders, utilities, government agencies, manufacturers, installers, and research and development companies can be found throughout the United States.

As of November 2013, nearly 142,700 people spent at least 50 percent of their work time on solar-related projects, according to The Solar Foundation. The foundation reports that the top five states for solar jobs are (in descending order): California, Arizona, New Jersey, Massachusetts, and New York. Manufacturers of solar power components and equipment are located throughout the United States. Large plants are located in California, Colorado, Georgia, Massachusetts, Michigan, New Mexico, Ohio, Oregon, Tennessee, Texas, and Wisconsin.

Currently, most geothermal employment opportunities in the United States exist where most geothermal reservoirs are located—in the western states. As of 2013, the Geothermal Energy Association (GEA) reports that geothermal electric power is generated, or in the process of being developed, in the following states: Alaska, Arizona, California, Hawaii, Idaho, Nevada, New Mexico, North Dakota, Oregon, Texas, Utah, Washington, and Wyoming. Other states, such as Colorado, Louisiana, and Mississippi, are expected to begin generating electric power via geothermal technology in the next several years. However, since magma is located everywhere under the Earth's surface, better technology and more powerful tools enable geothermal-related projects to be found throughout the United States. Workers are also employed by construction subcontractors and suppliers of power and cooling systems components, many of which are located in Georgia, Kansas, Louisiana, Maryland, Nebraska, Nevada, Ohio, Oklahoma, Pennsylvania, and Texas. The GEA estimates that 13,100 people are directly employed in the geothermal industry.

Hydropower plants are found throughout the United States. Hydropower projects can be separated into two categories: large hydropower projects run by the federal electric utilities and operated by the Bureau of Reclamation and the Army Corps of Engineers, and nonfederal hydropower dams—about 2,600—licensed by the Federal Energy Regulatory Commission. According to the National Hydropower Association, the top 10 hydropower generating states are Washington, Oregon, California, New York, Montana, Idaho, Tennessee, Alabama, Arizona, and South Dakota.

Biomass is bulky and thus costly to transport. Because of this, bioenergy projects are located where biomass crops are grown. This is a great benefit for many rural areas of the United States since jobs and their economic benefits are kept close to home. Opportunities for bioenergy and biofuels workers are available throughout the United States, although certain areas of the country may offer better opportunities than others. For example, the majority of ethanol production takes place in the Midwest. The top states for ethanol production are Iowa, Nebraska, Illinois, Indiana, Minnesota, and South Dakota.

There are approximately 3,600 people directly employed in the U.S. fuel cell industry, according to Fuel Cells 2000. More than 7,000 people are employed in the supply chain segment of the industry. Employers of fuel cell technology workers include automotive manufacturers with hydrogen vehicle programs, companies that manufacture fuel cells and related technology, merchant hydrogen producers, colleges and universities that conduct fuel cell and hydrogen research, and government agencies that conduct research in the field (most significantly, the U.S. Department of Energy and its National Laboratories, and the U.S. Department of Defense Fuel Cell Test and Evaluation Center, which is operated by Concurrent Technologies Corporation). According to the *State of the States: Fuel Cells in America 2013*, the top states for fuel cell research, development, and manufacturing are California, Connecticut, New York, Ohio, and South Carolina. States identified as "rising stars" in the fuel cell industry include Delaware, New Jersey, and Texas.

Starting Out

Industry associations are a rich source of information, especially when you are looking for your first job. Association Web sites feature the latest industry news, project developments, market forecasts, and government policies. Professional associations, such as the AEE, also offer career advice and job postings on their Web sites.

Many companies recruit on campus or at job fairs. Check with your school's career center for upcoming fairs in your area. Other good job hunting resources are trade journals, some of which may have job advertisements in their classifieds sections. Check out notable renewable energy publications and blogs, such as *Solar Industry* (http://www.solarindustrymag.com), *Solar Today* (http://ases.org), and Into the Wind: The AWEA Blog (http://www.aweablog.org).

Internships are also a great way to get relevant work experience, not to mention valuable contacts. Many of the larger energy companies and nonprofit groups offer internships (either with pay or for course credit) to junior or senior level college students. For example, the National Renewable Energy Laboratory offers both undergraduate and graduate students the opportunity to participate in its many research and development programs.

■ ADVANCEMENT PROSPECTS

Typical advancement paths depend on the type of position. For example, solar panel installers may advance to positions of higher responsibility such as managing other workers. With experience, they may opt to start their own business specializing in panel installation and maintenance. Engineers may start with a position at a small company with local interests and advance to a position of higher responsibility within that same company, for example, director of research and development. Or they may move on to a larger, more diverse company such as a public utility, whose interests may cover a broader area.

A nontechnical employee with a background in communications, for example, may advance from the human resource department of a windmill turbine manufacturing company to handle media and communication requests for a state's energy program. With the proper expertise and credentials, he or she may advance to direct a nonprofit organization representing a sector of the renewable energy industry.

■ OUTLOOK

Prospects are bright for green-industry jobs. The International Renewable Energy Agency reported that more than 760,000 people worked in this field in the United States, with a total workforce of more than 8.1 million around the world as of 2015. Their report, *Renewable Energy and Jobs Annual Report 2016*, measured 6 percent employment growth in the U.S. and 5 percent globally from 2014. Solar and wind energy employment rose 11 percent and 5 percent respectively, while employment in bioenergy and hydropower remained flat or declined.

The fast growth of solar and wind industries can be attributed to lower production costs. Better technology and equipment have lowered the cost of wind- and solar-generated electricity. This almost matches the cost of electricity generated by conventional methods such as coal or nuclear.

The United States is expected to continue increasing its renewable energy usage, but its pace may be dampened by cheap fossil fuels made available through new mining and drilling technology. The United States has greatly increased its wind capacity in the 21st century. The U.S. Department of Energy reports that in the United States, installed wind electricity capacity grew from 6 billion kilowatthours (kWh) in 2000 to about 191 billion in 2015. This is good news for windsmiths, engineers, meteorologists, electricians, and other technical workers.

Solar energy use is already well established in high-value markets such as remote power, satellites, and communications. Industry experts are working to improve current technology and lower costs to bring solar generated electricity, hot water systems, and solar optimized buildings to the public. The manufacturing of PV cell systems also presents many employment opportunities. The Solar Energy Industries Association reported that installed solar capacity in the United States in 2015 reached 25 gigawatts, up from only 2 gigawatts in 2010. Much of this growth has been driven by improved and more affordable solar technology. If the trend continues, it should fuel steady growth.

Hydropower is a leading renewable energy resource because of its abundance and ability to produce electricity inexpensively without harmful emissions. However, some dams and other water reservoirs have been found to harm fish and wildlife located in or near the project site. The industry has responded to such claims by hiring specialists to protect vegetation and wildlife affected by hydropower projects. Two factors may limit growth in the hydropower industry. First, most potential sites for hydropower projects have already been utilized. Second, the licensing process for hydropower projects is slow and inefficient. License requests must be reviewed and approved by federal and state agencies, which often have a conflict in goals and regulations, making it difficult to obtain a license.

Improved technological advances, such as more powerful drilling tools, have helped the geothermal energy industry grow in the past few years. Employment opportunities are greatest in the West (especially in California, Idaho, Nevada, Oregon, and Utah) for the direct use, or drilling, of geothermal energy, and in the Midwest for geothermal heat pumps. However, with advances in technology, employment opportunities will be plentiful throughout the United States. Long delays in obtaining geothermal land leases from the government could hinder the growth of this industry.

Bioenergy is also experiencing steady growth. Interest in bioenergy will not only stem from its electricity potential, but also the biofuels converted from biomass such as ethanol biobutanal, and biodiesel. The U.S. Department of Agriculture estimates that 17,000 jobs are created for every million gallons of ethanol, an important biomass byproduct, produced. Employment opportunities will exist for chemists, engineers, and other agricultural scientists.

The U.S. Department of Energy reports that interest in advanced water power—such as ocean, river, and tidal currents—has been growing in recent years, "with many protype projects in testing stages and permits being filed with the Federal Energy Regulatory Commission.

Public interest in renewable energy has grown in the last decade. Research has brought better technology, lowered generating costs, and even developed other uses for renewable energy. However, there are still many barriers that hinder this industry's growth potential: lack of infrastructure to transport renewable energy reliably, competition for local distribution, and lack of government funding for additional research and projects. Additionally, the U.S. Department of Energy reports that "growing domestic production of natural gas and crude oil continues to reshape the U.S. energy economy, with crude oil production approaching the historical high achieved in 1970 of 9.6 million barrels per day." This increased domestic production of nonrenewable energy resources may limit employment growth in the renewable energy industry.

■ UNIONS AND ASSOCIATIONS

Some renewable energy workers may be represented by the International Federation of Professional and Technical Engineers, American Federation of Government Employees, International Brotherhood of Teamsters, International Brotherhood of Electrical Workers, and other unions.

Major professional organizations for renewable energy engineers are as follows by sector: wind (American Wind Energy Association); solar (American Solar Energy Society, Solar Electric Power Association, Solar Energy Industries Association, and The Solar Foundation); hydropower (Hydro Research Foundation, National Hydropower Association, International Hydropower Association, and Ocean Renewable Energy Coalition); geothermal (Geothermal Education Office, Geothermal Energy Association, and the Geothermal Resources Council); biofuels (Renewable Fuels Association); and fuel cell technology (Fuel Cell & Hydrogen Energy Association and CSA International). The Association of Energy Engineers represents the professional interests of engineers who are employed in the renewable energy industry. The National Council of

Examiners for Engineering and Surveying (http://www.ncees.org) provides licensure to engineers. Other professional organizations include the Interstate Renewable Energy Council and the Midwest Renewable Energy Association.

The U.S. Department of Energy's Office of Energy Efficiency and Renewable Energy is a government agency that provides resources for those interested in renewable energy.

There are many other professional associations for engineers such as the Society of Civil Engineers, Institute of Electrical and Electronics Engineers, and the Institute of Industrial Engineers. Check the *Encyclopedia of Associations*, which is published by Gale Cengage Learning, for associations in your field of interest. It is available in many community and school libraries.

■ TIPS FOR ENTRY

1. To learn more about the field, read publications such as:
   - *Windpower Monthly* (http://www.windpowermonthly.com/windpower-weekly)
   - *Solar Industry* (http://www.solarindustrymag.com)
   - *Solar Today* (http://ases.org)
   - *International Journal on Hydropower and Dams* (http://www.hydropower-dams.com)
   - *Geothermal Education Weekly* (http://www.geo-energy.org/updates.aspx)
   - *Geothermal Resources Council Bulletin* (http://www.geothermal.org)
   - *Biofuels Digest* (http://biofuelsdigest.com)
   - *Fuel Cell & Hydrogen Energy Connection* (http://www.fchea.org)
2. Visit the following Web sites for job listings:
   - http://www.nspe.org/resources/career-center
   - http://www.awea.org
   - http://www.ases.org
   - http://www.seia.org/solar-jobs
   - http://solarliving.jobamatic.com/a/jbb/find-jobs
   - http://www.homepower.com/jobs
   - http://www.hydrofoundation.org/job-postings.html
   - http://www.geothermal.org/employment.html
   - http://www.fuelcellmarkets.com
   - http://www.jobsinfuelcells.com.
3. Participate in internships or part-time jobs that are arranged by your college's career services office. Visit http://energy.gov/eere/education/clean-energy-jobs-and-career-planning for information on internships, fellowships, and scholarships.

■ FOR MORE INFORMATION

For industry news and updates, publications, conferences, career opportunities, and membership information, contact

American Solar Energy Society
2525 Arapahoe Avenue, E4-253
Boulder, CO 80302-6720
E-mail: info@ases.org
http://www.ases.org

For industry news and updates, publications, conferences, career opportunities, and membership information, contact

American Wind Energy Association
1501 M Street, NW, Suite 1000
Washington, D.C. 20005-1769
Tel: (202) 383-2500
Fax: (202) 383-2505
http://www.awea.org

For information on careers, employment opportunities, membership, and industry surveys, contact

Association of Energy Engineers
3168 Mercer University Drive
Atlanta, GA 30341
Tel: (770) 447-5083
http://www.aeecenter.org

Visit the association's Web site for a wealth of information on the fuel cell industry.

Fuel Cell & Hydrogen Energy Association
1211 Connecticut Avenue, NW, Suite 600
Washington, D.C. 20036-2705
Tel: (202) 261-1331
http://www.fchea.org

For general information on the geothermal industry and educational teaching guides, contact

Geothermal Education Office
664 Hilary Drive
Tiburon, CA 94920-1446
Fax: (415) 435-7737
E-mail: 24hrcleanpower@gmail.com
http://geothermal.marin.org

For industry news and updates, publications, conferences, career opportunities, and membership information, contact

Geothermal Energy Association
209 Pennsylvania Avenue, SE
Washington, D.C. 20003-1107

Tel: (202) 454-5261
Fax: (202) 454-5265
http://www.geo-energy.org

For information on geothermal energy and membership, contact

Geothermal Resources Council
PO Box 1350
Davis, CA 95617-1350
Tel: (530) 758-2360
Fax: (530) 758-2839
http://www.geothermal.org

For industry information, contact

Hydro Research Foundation
3124 Elk View Drive
Evergreen, CO 80439-7961
Tel: (720) 722-0HRF
E-mail: info@hydrofoundation.org
http://hydrofoundation.org

For information about renewable energy, contact

Interstate Renewable Energy Council
PO Box 1156
Latham, NY 12110-1156
Tel: (518) 458-6059
E-mail: info@irecusa.org
http://www.irecusa.org

For information on solar tours, energy fairs, industry workshops, or certification, contact

Midwest Renewable Energy Association
7558 Deer Road
Custer, WI 54423-9734
Tel: (715) 592-6595
E-mail: info@midwestrenew.org
http://www.the-mrea.org

For industry news and updates, publications, conferences, career opportunities, and membership information, contact

National Hydropower Association
25 Massachusetts Avenue, NW, Suite 450
Washington, D.C. 20001-7405
Tel: (202) 682-1700
Fax: (202) 682-9478
E-mail: help@hydro.org
http://www.hydro.org

For more background information on renewable energy, careers, and internships, contact

National Renewable Energy Laboratory
15013 Denver West Parkway
Golden, CO 80401-3111

Tel: (303) 275-3000

http://www.nrel.gov

For information on careers, certification and licensing, membership benefits, or local chapters, contact

National Society of Professional Engineers

1420 King Street

Alexandria, VA 22314-2794

Tel: (703) 684-2800

Fax: (703) 684-2821

http://www.nspe.org

For industry news and updates, general information on bioenergy, contact

Renewable Fuels Association

425 Third Street, SW, Suite 1150

Washington, D.C. 20024-3231

Tel: (202) 289-3835

http://www.ethanolrfa.org

For trade news and updates, publications, conferences, career opportunities, and membership information, contact

Solar Energy Industries Association

600 14th Street, NW, Suite 400

Washington, D.C. 20005

Tel: (202) 682-0556

E-mail: info@seia.org

http://www.seia.org

For general information about the renewable energy industry plus email and phone contacts for different initiatives dedicated to furthering it, go to

U.S. Department of Energy Office of Energy Efficiency and Renewable Energy

1000 Independence Avenue, SW

Washington, D.C. 20585

http://energy.gov/eere/office-energy-efficiency-renewable-energy

Renewable Energy Engineers

■ OVERVIEW

Renewable energy is defined as a clean and unlimited source of power or fuel. This energy is harnessed from different sources such as wind, sunlight (solar), water (hydro), organic matter (biomass), and the earth's internal heat (geothermal). Unlike non-renewable energy sources like oil, natural gas, or coal, or nuclear energy, renewable energy is not based on extracting a limited resource. Renewable energy sources provided about 13 percent of the electricity generated in the United States in 2015.

Renewable energy engineers are problem-solvers who use the principles of mathematics and science to perform a variety of tasks in the renewable energy industry such as research and designing wind turbines, geothermal plants, and solar photovoltaic cells. Other engineers work in testing, production, maintenance, or management. Engineers work in a variety of fields. In fact, more than 25 engineering specialties are recognized by professional engineering societies. There are more than 1.5 million engineers employed in the United States.

■ HISTORY

People have been using different forms of renewable energy resources for centuries. Windmills have long been used to grind grain or pump water. The sun has always been used as a source of heat. In 1839, Edmond Becquerel, an early pioneer in solar energy, discovered the photoelectric effect, or the production of electricity from sunlight. The power of water that is stored and released from dams has been used for generating electricity. This type of electricity is known as hydropower electricity. Hot springs and underground reservoirs, products of geothermal energy, have long been used as sources of heat. People have also

---

QUICK FACTS

ALTERNATE TITLE(S)
Biomass Engineers, Fuel Cell Engineers, Geothermal Energy Engineers, Hydropower Engineers, Reservoir Engineers, Solar Engineers, Wind Engineers

DUTIES
Use the principles of mathematics and science to perform a variety of tasks in the renewable energy industry

SALARY RANGE
$53,120 to $93,010 to $157,610+

WORK ENVIRONMENT
Indoors/Outdoors

BEST GEOGRAPHIC LOCATION(S)
Varies by subspecialty

MINIMUM EDUCATION LEVEL
Bachelor's Degree, Master's Degree

SCHOOL SUBJECTS
Chemistry, Earth Science, Mathematics, Physics

EXPERIENCE
Internships

PERSONALITY TRAITS
Curious, Problem-Solving, Technical

SKILLS
Computer, Math, Scientific

CERTIFICATION OR LICENSING
Required

SPECIAL REQUIREMENTS
None

EMPLOYMENT PROSPECTS
Good

ADVANCEMENT PROSPECTS
Good

OUTLOOK
Little Change or More Slowly than the Average

NOC
2148

O*NET-SOC
17-2051.00, 17-2071.00, 17-2141.00, 17-2141.01, 17-2199.03, 17-2199.10, 17-2199.11

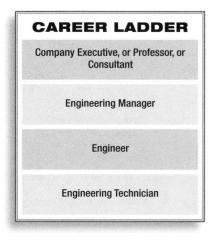

CAREER LADDER

Company Executive, or Professor, or Consultant

Engineering Manager

Engineer

Engineering Technician

burned trees or other organic matter, known as biomass, for warmth or cooking purposes.

The early technology used in harnessing and producing renewable energy as a source of power or fuel, however, was underdeveloped and expensive. Because of this, the majority of our power needs have been met using nonrenewable resources such as natural gas or fossil fuels. Our use of fossil fuels has caused our nation to rely heavily on foreign sources to meet demand. Our declining national supply of some major nonrenewable natural resources, coupled by public awareness of the soaring costs and environmental damage caused by the mining, extraction, processing, and use of conventional energy sources, have shed new light on renewable energy sources as a viable solution to our energy needs.

Today, "green" sources of power have earned respect as an important alternative to nonrenewable resources. New research and technology in the past 25 years have enabled self-renewing resources to be harnessed more efficiently and at a lower cost than in the past. The Energy Policy Act of 1992 (which deregulated and restructured the conventional power industries) and the Energy Policy Act of 2005 (which promoted the development of renewable energy resources by offering tax incentives and loan guarantees to the private sector) have presented the public with more choices. Tax incentives at the state and federal level make buying green power more affordable to consumers and for utility companies. The Energy Independence and Security Act of 2007 has also prompted growth in the renewable energy industry.

■ THE JOB

Renewable energy sources provided about 13 percent of the electricity generated in the United States in 2015. The renewable energy industry can be broken down into the following sub-industries: wind, solar, hydropower, geothermal, bioenergy, and fuel cell technology. A wide variety of career options are available to engineers. Additionally, many career skills are transferable from one sub-industry to another. The following sections provide an overview of each renewable energy sector and detail career opportunities for engineers in each industry.

Wind

According to the American Wind Energy Association, every state in the U.S. has either an operational wind energy project or a wind-related manufacturing facility. In 2015, wind energy made up 35 percent of all renewable energy in the United States, according to the Energy Information Administration (EIA).

The wind turbine is the modern, high-tech equivalent of yesterday's windmill. A single wind turbine can harness the wind's energy to generate enough electricity to power a house or small farm. Wind plants, also called wind farms, are a collection of high-powered turbines that can generate electricity for tens of thousands of homes. In addition to development on land, wind projects are also being developed offshore.

The wind industry is very competitive. There are hundreds of companies that manufacture turbines and related components. Companies are constantly seeking ways to make wind turbines more reliable, efficient, and powerful while keeping costs manageable. In order to achieve these improvements, many types of engineers are employed in research and development. *Aerospace*, *civil* (with specializations in construction, geotechnical, structural, and transportation engineering), *computer*, *electrical*, *environmental*, *health and safety*, *industrial*, *materials*, and *mechanical engineers* design and test the turbines.

Solar

In 2015, solar energy made up 5 percent of all renewable energy in the United States, according to the Energy Information Administration. Its potential as a major energy source is largely untapped.

There are different ways to turn the sun's energy into a useful power source. The most common technology today uses photovoltaic (PV) cells. When a PV cell is directly hit by sunlight, the materials inside it absorb this light. Simply put, the activity of absorption frees electrons, which then travel through a circuit. Electrons traveling through a circuit produce electricity. Many PV cells can be linked together to produce unlimited amounts of electricity.

The concentrating solar power (CSP) technologies use mirrors or lenses to focus sunlight onto a receiver. The receiver collects sunlight as heat, which can be used directly or generated into electricity. The four CSP methods used are parabolic trough systems, power towers, parabolic dishes, and compact linear Fresnel systems that concentrate thermal energy to power a conventional steam turbine. Parabolic troughs can produce solar electricity inexpensively compared to the other methods, and they can generate enough power for large-scale projects.

Power towers can also generate power for large-scale projects, while parabolic dishes are used for smaller-scale projects. Flat mirrors are used in compact linear Fresnel systems, which allows for more reflectors to be added to a solar array. This technology allows solar infrastructure to use less land surface than other technologies.

Using solar collectors and storage tanks, the sun's energy can be used to heat water for swimming pools or buildings. Many schools, hospitals, prisons, and government facilities use solar technology for their water use. This technology can also be used for cooling. Desiccant systems remove moisture from the air, thereby making it more comfortable. Absorption chiller systems are the most common solar cooling systems. These systems produce air-conditioning without using electricity.

A building's design or construction materials can also utilize the sun's energy for the building's heating and light through passive solar design or water heating, or with electrical PV cells.

Solar engineers work in any number of areas of engineering products that help harness energy from the sun. They research, design, and develop new products, or they may work in testing, production, or maintenance. They collect and manage data to help design solar systems. Types of products solar engineers work on include solar panels, solar-powered technology, communications and navigation systems, heating and cooling systems, and even cars. Solar engineers are frequently electrical, mechanical, civil, *chemical,* industrial, or materials engineers who are working on solar projects and designing photovoltaic systems. Solar engineers with a degree in civil engineering, for example, may work in solar power plant construction. They use their knowledge of materials science and engineering theory to design and oversee the construction of solar power plants and related infrastructure (such as roads, support structures, and foundations). Others with backgrounds in electrical engineering work in solar power plant operations, controlling and monitoring transmission and electrical generation devices.

Hydropower

In 2015, hydropower energy made up 46 percent of all renewable energy in the United States, according to the Energy Information Administration.

Hydropower uses the energy of flowing water to produce electricity. Water is retained in a dam or reservoir. When the water is released, it passes through and spins a turbine. The movement of the turbine in turn spins generators, and that spinning produces electricity. In "run of the river" projects, dams are not needed. Canals or pipes divert river water to spin turbines.

In addition to hydropower generated via dams or reservoirs, scientists are currently studying several other types of hydroenergy generation techniques. According to the U.S. Department of Energy (DOE), *wave energy technologies* "extract energy directly from surface waves or from pressure fluctuations below the surface." These waves can be turned into electricity by onshore or offshore systems. Wave energy can only be harnessed in certain areas of the world. In the United States, the northeastern and northwestern coasts offer the best prospects for viable wave-based generation.

Tidal energy involves the harnessing of tides into electricity. According to the DOE, tides can be harnessed only if the difference between high and low tides is more than 16 feet. There are only about 40 places on Earth where this is the case, including sites in the Pacific Northwest and Atlantic Northeast. Tidal energy is harvested by using barrages or dams, tidal fences, and tidal turbines.

Ocean thermal energy conversion (OTEC) involves converting the heat energy stored in oceans into electricity. According to the DOE, OTEC "works best when the temperature between the warmer, top layer of the ocean and the colder, deep ocean water is about 36 degrees Fahrenheit. These conditions exist in tropical coastal areas, roughly between the Tropic of Capricorn and the Tropic of Cancer." OTEC has been around for about 80 years, but it is not yet cost competitive with traditional power technologies.

Hydropower engineers design, construct, and maintain hydropower projects. They typically have backgrounds in civil (especially construction, geotechnical, hydraulic, and structural) engineering, electrical engineering, and mechanical engineering.

Geothermal

In 2015, geothermal energy made up 3 percent of all renewable energy in the United States, according to the Energy Information Administration.

Geothermal heat comes from the heat within the earth. Water heated from geothermal energy is tapped from its underground reservoirs and used to heat buildings, grow crops, or melt snow. This direct use of geothermal energy can also be used to generate electricity. Most water and steam reservoirs are located in the western United States. However, dry rock drilling, a process that drills deeper into the Earth's magma, is an innovation that will eventually allow geothermal projects to be undertaken almost anywhere.

Hydraulic engineers, reservoir engineers, and *drillers* work together to reach and maintain the reservoir's heat supply. Geothermal engineers with backgrounds in chemical, civil, electrical, manufacturing, mechanical,

Engineers prepare a wind turbine for atmospheric testing. (Stephen Ausmus. USDA.)

performance/systems, project, and quality engineering play an important role in plant design and construction, developing the complex mechanical and electrical systems, as well as the power unit systems, that are part of plant infrastructure.

Bioenergy

In 2015, bioenergy made up 11 percent of all renewable energy in the United States, according to the Energy Information Administration. Bioenergy can be used to generate electricity and produce heat. It can also be used to produce *biofuels*, which are used in place of fossil fuels to power vehicles and for small heating applications. Bioenergy can be derived from wood, construction and consumer waste, landfill gas, and liquid biofuels such as ethanol for use in generating electricity, producing heat, and fueling vehicles.

Engineers help design and build bioenergy and biofuels plants. Civil, electrical, industrial, and mechanical engineers develop designs for plants and process equipment using computer-aided design and computer-aided industrial design software. They work closely with architects, developers, business owners, construction crews, and others to make sure the work is done according to specifications.

Fuel Cell Technology

Until recently, all motor vehicles were powered by gasoline and internal combustion engines. While effective and reliable, these systems cause considerable pollution—especially with the increasing number of vehicle owners in the world. Manufacturers have developed cleaner power options for vehicles such as the electric car, or the gas/electric hybrid. The fuel cell is another option currently in development. A fuel cell is a highly efficient device that generates electricity. According to the Fuel Cell and Hydrogen Energy Association, "fuel cells can run on a variety of fuels, including natural gas and hydrogen. Hydrogen is a clean, carbon-free fuel readily available from a variety of sources. When powered by hydrogen, fuel cells emit only water vapor as a byproduct. Fuel cells can run at any time of day and produce nearly zero noise. They are reliable, safe, and never need recharging." In addition to use in powering motor vehicles, fuel cells are used in a wide range of applications, from stationary electricity generation to portable electronics. They are only in the developmental phase in the automobile industry, but are in regular use in markets in which they can provide performance and environmental benefits. These markets include backup power systems, specialty vehicles (such as airport ground vehicles and fork lifts), portable power units, and combined heat and power production.

Fuel cell engineers use their engineering expertise to design fuel cell systems, subsystems, stacks, assemblies, and components. They typically have backgrounds in chemical, electrical, industrial, materials, and mechanical engineering.

■ EARNINGS

The DOL does not provide comprehensive salary information for renewable energy engineers. It does provide salary data for engineers in all industries. It reports that engineers, by specialty, earned the following salary ranges in May 2015: chemical, $59,470 to $157,610+; industrial, $53,300 to $126,920+; materials, $53,120 to $144,720+; and mechanical, $53,640 to $128,430+. Electrical engineers earn a median salary of $93,010, with the lowest 10 percent earning $59,240 or less and the highest 10 percent earning $146,820 or more.

Employers offer a variety of benefit packages, which can include any of the following: paid holidays, vacations, and sick days; personal days; medical, dental, and life insurance; profit-sharing plans; 401(k) plans; retirement and pension plans; and educational assistance programs.

■ WORK ENVIRONMENT

Work environments for engineers vary by subsector and specialty. Engineers may work in laboratories and offices, as well as outdoors, depending on the project. For example, wind engineers travel frequently to inspect turbine installations or wind turbine manufacturing processes. Solar engineers work in office buildings, laboratories, or industrial plants. They may spend time outdoors at solar power plants, and they may also spend time traveling to different plants and worksites in the United States as well as overseas. College engineering professors work in comfortable classrooms, laboratories, and offices, although some may supervise learning opportunities in the field.

■ EXPLORING

Participation in science and engineering fairs can be an invaluable experience for a high school student interested in engineering. Through these fairs, students learn to do their own research and applications in an engineering field. By developing a project for a fair, students begin to learn how to think like an engineer by creatively using their academic knowledge to solve real-life problems.

Join the Technology Student Association, which provides students a chance to explore career opportunities in science, technology, engineering, and mathematics, enter academic competitions, and participate in summer exploration programs. Visit http://www.tsaweb.org for more information.

The U.S. Department of Labor offers many helpful publications on green careers—including those in wind energy and solar power—at its Web site, http://www.bls.gov/green/greencareers.htm. You should also check out the American Society for Engineering Education's pre-college Web site, http://egfi-k12.org, for general information about careers in engineering, as well as answers to frequently asked questions about engineering. In addition, the society offers *Engineering, Go For It!,* a comprehensive brochure about careers for a small fee. Here are two additional Web sites that provide good information on careers: Energy4Me (http://www.energy4me.org) and Get Into Energy (http://www.getintoenergy.com).

Talk to renewable energy engineers about their careers. Ask your science teacher or school counselor for help setting up interviews.

■ EDUCATION AND TRAINING REQUIREMENTS
High School

Engineers in the renewable energy industry need a strong background in science and mathematics. For example, mathematics, earth science, and chemistry classes will be helpful if you plan to work in the geothermal energy industry identifying and harvesting possible sources of

---

RENEWABLE RESOURCES IN THE U.S.

DID YOU KNOW?

Renewable energy resources accounted for 13.44 percent of total U.S. energy production in 2015, according to the U.S. Department of Energy. They provided more than 12 percent of total U.S. utility-scale electricity generation.

---

geothermal energy from within the earth. Physics classes will be helpful if you plan to work in the wind industry designing windmills and turbine engines to capture and convert wind energy into electricity.

Other important classes include computer science, computer-aided design, shop, English, and speech. Those interested in management careers should take business and accounting classes. Taking a foreign language is highly useful since a majority of renewable energy companies are located abroad.

Postsecondary Education

Engineers need at least a bachelor's degree to enter the field. Students typically complete at least one internship as part of their college training. Those who conduct research, manage workers, or teach college classes typically need a graduate-level degree, often a Ph.D. The Interstate Renewable Energy Council offers a database of postsecondary renewable energy training programs at http://www.irecusa.org/training-directory. The U.S. Department of Energy provides a list of programs at http://energy.gov/eere/education/education-homepage. The following paragraphs provide more information on educational paths in each renewable energy subdiscipline.

Most wind engineers have a bachelor of science in an engineering specialty, such as electrical, civil, environmental, industrial, materials, or mechanical engineering. Many companies prefer to hire engineers with master of science degrees, so those who pursue advanced degrees may have better odds of securing work. Engineers also receive extensive on-the-job training. More information about wind energy technology and educational programs can be found at https://energy.gov/eere/wind/wind-energy-technologies-office.

Most solar engineers have a bachelor of science degree in an engineering specialty, such as electrical, civil, mechanical, or chemical engineering.

Hydropower engineers usually have a minimum of a bachelor's degree in renewable energy engineering or in their particular discipline such as civil, electrical, or mechanical engineering.

Geothermal engineers usually have bachelor's degrees in their particular specialty (such as mechanical or civil engineering).

Bioenergy/biofuels engineers may have a bachelor's or advanced degree in electrical, electronics, industrial, mechanical, or even civil engineering.

Fuel cell engineers typically have bachelor's degrees in chemical, electrical, industrial, materials, or mechanical engineering, along with extensive course work in fuel cell technology. The Office of Energy Efficiency and Renewable Energy provides a good resource for exploring careers and education in this field: https://energy.gov/eere/education/explore-careers-fuel-cell-technologies

Certification

Certificate programs in renewable energy are provided by colleges and universities, professional associations (such as the Midwest Renewable Energy Association), and private organizations (such as National Solar Trainers). Contact these providers for more information.

Other Education or Training

Continuing education (CE) opportunities are provided by many professional associations. For example, the American Wind Energy Association offers educational sessions at its annual conference that cover technical, scientific, and business issues. The Geothermal Resources Council offers workshops and seminars at its annual meeting and trade show. Topics include drilling, economics, the environmental aspects of geothermal activity, financing, geochemistry, geology, geophysics, heat pumps, legal aspects, management, non-electric uses, and reservoir engineering. The Renewable Fuels Association provides CE opportunities at its National Ethanol Conference.

The American Society for Engineering Education offers continuing education opportunities for engineers via its annual conference and other events. The National Society of Professional Engineers provides webinars for student members of the society. Past webinars included "Career Success in Engineering: A Guide for Students and New Professionals," "Ethics and Professionalism for Students and Young Engineers," "How to Get Your First Job," and "Engineering Your Career with a High Quality Social Network Web Seminar." The Society of Women Engineers offers conference sessions, webinars, and other education resources on topics such as leadership, career development, and special issues for women in engineering.

Other organizations that offer continuing education classes, webinars, conference workshops, and other opportunities include the American Institute of Chemical Engineers, American Solar Energy Society, Association of Energy Engineers, Canadian Hydropower Association, Fuel Cell & Hydrogen Energy Association, Geothermal Energy Association, International Hydropower Association, Interstate Renewable Energy Council, Midwest Renewable Energy Association, National Hydropower Association, National Society of Professional Engineers, SAE International, Society of Women Engineers, Solar Electric Power Association, Solar Energy Industries Association, and The Solar Foundation.

■ CERTIFICATION, LICENSING, AND SPECIAL REQUIREMENTS
Certification or Licensing

The Association of Energy Engineers provides certification in a variety of specialties. SME offers certification to manufacturing engineers. To be considered for certification, a candidate must meet eligibility standards such as a minimum of three years of relevant work experience and membership in a professional organization. Most programs consist of classroom work and an examination.

Most states require engineers to be licensed. There are two levels of licensing for engineers. Professional engineers (PEs) have graduated from an accredited engineering curriculum, have four years of engineering experience, and have passed a written exam. Engineering graduates need not wait until they have four years experience, however, to start the licensure process. Those who pass the Fundamentals of Engineering examination after graduating are called engineers in training (EIT) or engineer interns (EI). The EIT certification usually is valid for 10 years. After acquiring suitable work experience, EITs can take the second examination, the Principles and Practice of Engineering exam, to gain full PE licensure. For more information on licensing and examination requirements, visit the National Council of Examiners for Engineering and Surveying's Web site, http://www.ncees.org.

■ EXPERIENCE, SKILLS, AND PERSONALITY TRAITS

Take as many math and science classes as possible and participate in internships and other experiential opportunities to gain experience in the field.

Students who are interested in becoming renewable energy engineers should enjoy solving problems, developing logical plans, and designing things. They should have a strong interest and ability in science and mathematics, as well as knowledge of renewable energy technologies. Engineers often work on projects in teams, so prospective engineers should be able to work well both alone and with others. Other important traits include strong communication skills and an interest in continuing to learn throughout their careers.

▪ EMPLOYMENT PROSPECTS
Employers

More than 1.6 million engineers are employed in the United States. The renewable energy industry is a large and diverse field. Employment opportunities in each sector exist at manufacturing or research and development companies, both large and small; utilities; government organizations; and nonprofit groups and agencies. Research or education opportunities can be found at universities or trade associations. Because the benefits of renewable energy are a global concern, many employment opportunities can be found outside of the United States.

It is important to note that while employment in the renewable energy industry can be found nationwide, some sectors of the industry tend to be clustered in specific regions of the United States. A good example of this is the wind power industry. Although wind is everywhere, different regions of the United States are windier than others. For this reason, wind-related projects tend to be most concentrated in the Midwest, Southwest, and Northeast regions of the United States. As of 2016, the top five U.S. states by total wind capacity (in descending order) are Texas, Iowa, California, Oklahoma, Illinois, and Kansas. There are more than 550 wind-related manufacturing facilities in the United States. Much wind turbine manufacturing is located in the Midwest and Southeast. Approximately 88,000 people are employed in the wind energy industry, according to the American Wind Energy Association.

There are a wide variety of employment opportunities available in the solar energy industry. Contractors, dealers, distributors, builders, utilities, government agencies, manufacturers, installers, and research and development companies can be found throughout the United States. The Southwest has the greatest potential for solar energy, although solar energy development has increased in other areas of the United States. As of 2015, nearly 208,859 worked in solar-related industries, according to The Solar Foundation. The foundation reports that the top five states for solar jobs are (in descending order): Nevada, Massachusetts, Vermont, Hawaii, and California.

The International Renewable Energy Agency (IREA) estimated 35,000 workers employed directly in the geothermal industry as of 2014-2015. Employment in this field still lags behind other renewable energy industries in part due to the expense of implementing it and the availability of cheaper alternatives, such as natural gas. The majority of geothermal employment opportunities in the United States exist where most geothermal reservoirs are located in the western states, especially in rural areas. As of 2016, the Geothermal Energy Association reported geothermal electric power being generated in Alaska, California, Hawaii, Idaho, Nevada, New Mexico, Oregon, and Utah, with planned capacity additions in those states as well as Colorado and North Dakota. Other states, such as Arizona, Louisiana, Mississippi, Montana, Texas, Washington, and Wyoming, are exploring generating electric power via geothermal technology. However, since magma is located everywhere under the Earth's surface, better technology and more powerful tools may enable geothermal-related projects to be found throughout the United States. Geothermal energy workers are employed by government agencies such as the Bureau of Land Management and Forest Service that review and approve licensing requests from geothermal energy contractors. They also conduct geothermal energy research for the U.S. Department of Energy, the U.S. Department of the Interior (National Park Service, U.S. Geological Survey), and other agencies. Developers of geothermal energy resources are major employers of workers in the field. Workers are also employed by construction subcontractors and suppliers of power and cooling systems components, many of which are located in Georgia, Kansas, Louisiana, Maryland, Nebraska, Nevada, Ohio, Oklahoma, Pennsylvania, and Texas.

Approximately 300,000 people are currently employed in the U.S. hydropower industry, according to the National Hydropower Association (NHA). Hydropower plants are found throughout the United States. Hydropower projects can be separated into two categories: large hydropower projects run by the federal electric utilities and operated by the Bureau of Reclamation (http://www.usbr.gov) and the Army Corps of Engineers (http://www.usace.army.mil), and nonfederal hydropower dams licensed by the Federal Energy Regulatory Commission. According to the NHA, the top 10 hydropower generating states are Washington, Oregon, New York, California, Alabama, Tennessee, Montana, Idaho, North Carolina, and Arizona.

Biomass is bulky and thus costly to transport. Because of this, bioenergy projects are located where biomass crops are grown. This is a great benefit for many rural areas of the United States since jobs and their economic benefits are kept close to home. Opportunities for bioenergy and biofuels workers are available throughout the United States, although certain areas of the country may offer better opportunities than others. For example, the majority of ethanol production takes place in the Midwest. The top states for ethanol production are Iowa, Nebraska, Illinois, Indiana, Minnesota, and South Dakota.

Employers of fuel cell technology workers include automotive manufacturers with hydrogen vehicle programs, companies that manufacture fuel cells and related technology, merchant hydrogen producers, colleges and universities that conduct fuel cell and hydrogen research, and government agencies that conduct research in the field (most significantly, the U.S. Department of Energy and its National Laboratories, and the U.S. Department of Defense Fuel Cell Test and Evaluation Center, which is operated by Concurrent Technologies Corporation). The applications for fuel cells are varied and so are the types of jobs. According to the *State of the States: Fuel Cells in America 2016,* the top three states for fuel cell research, development, and manufacturing are California, Connecticut, and New York. Other states with favorable views of fuel cells include Colorado, Hawaii, Massachusetts, New Jersey, and Ohio.

Starting Out

Industry and professional associations are a rich source of information, especially when you are looking for your first job. Association Web sites feature the latest industry news, project developments, market forecasts, and government policies, and also offer career advice and job postings on their Web sites.

Many companies recruit on campus or at job fairs. Check with your school's career center for upcoming fairs in your area. Other good job hunting resources are trade journals, some of which may have job advertisements in their classifieds sections.

Internships are also a great way to get relevant work experience, not to mention valuable contacts. Many of the larger energy companies and nonprofit groups, as well as government employers, offer internships (either with pay or for course credit) to junior- or senior-level college students. For example, the National Renewable Energy Laboratory offers both undergraduate and graduate students the opportunity to participate in its many research and development programs.

■ ADVANCEMENT PROSPECTS

Engineers may start with a position at a small company with local interests and advance to a position of higher responsibility within that same company, for example, engineering manager or director of research and development. Or they may move on to a larger, more diverse company such as a public utility, whose interests may cover a broader area. Some teach engineering at colleges and universities or work as consultants.

■ OUTLOOK

Overall, prospects are bright for green-industry jobs. According to the International Renewable Energy Agency, green energy businesses employed more than 760,000 workers in the United States and 8.1 million worldwide as of 2015. This represented 6 percent employment growth from the past year in the U.S. and 5 percent globally. The same report, *Renewable Energy and Jobs Annual Report 2016,* identified strong growth in solar and wind energy employment, which increased 11 percent and 5 percent respectively from 2014. Slow growth and declines occurred in bioenergy and hydropower due to low production and a drop in construction of new installations. Much of the industry's employment and highest growth occurred in Brazil, China, Germany, India, Japan, and the United States.

For engineers, however, the prospects are tepid. Overall growth for engineering professions related to renewable energy are forecast to grow between 0 and 5 percent through 2024, according to the Bureau of Labor Statistics. Electrical engineers are predicted to see no growth in employment while mechanical engineers may enjoy growth of five percent. The BLS projects 2 percent growth for chemical engineers and 1 percent for industrial engineers and materials engineers.

Many factors will determine future growth for renewable energy professions. The availability of cheap coal, natural gas, and oil can slow investment in renewable energy systems. New or improved technologies may spur growth of on type of renewable energy and shift resources there. Also, geopolitical trends and developments can affect government and corporate energy policies and access to resources, which may influence the industry. Federal and state regulations regarding the environment and use of fossil fuels will also influence future growth. As energy demands grow and technology improves, however, the demand for alternative sources of power seems set to increase steadily in coming years.

■ UNIONS AND ASSOCIATIONS

Some engineers may be represented by the International Federation of Professional and Technical Engineers (http://www.ifpte.org) and other unions.

The Association of Energy Engineers represents the professional interests of engineers who are employed in the renewable energy industry. Major professional organizations for renewable energy engineers are as follows by sector: wind (American Wind Energy Association); solar (American Solar Energy Society, Solar Electric Power Association, Solar Energy Industries Association, and The Solar Foundation); hydropower (Hydro Research Foundation, National Hydropower Association, International Hydropower Association, and Ocean Renewable Energy Coalition);

geothermal (Geothermal Education Office, Geothermal Energy Association, and the Geothermal Resources Council); biofuels (Renewable Fuels Association); and fuel cell technology (Fuel Cell & Hydrogen Energy Association and CSA International). Other professional organizations include the Interstate Renewable Energy Council and the Midwest Renewable Energy Association.

The National Council of Examiners for Engineering and Surveying (http://www.ncees.org) provides licensure to engineers. SME offers certification to manufacturing engineers. The Association of Energy Engineers offers certification in a variety of specialties.

The U.S. Department of Energy's Office of Energy Efficiency and Renewable Energy is a government agency that provides resources for those interested in renewable energy.

■ TIPS FOR ENTRY

1. To learn more about the field, read industry publications, such as:
   - *Windpower Monthly* (http://www.windpower monthly.com/windpower-weekly)
   - *Solar Industry* (http://www.solarindustrymag .com)
   - *Solar Today* (http://ases.org)
   - *International Journal on Hydropower and Dams* (http://www.hydropower-dams.com)
   - *Geothermal Education Weekly* (http://www.geo -energy.org/updates.aspx)
   - *Geothermal Resources Council Bulletin* (http:// www.geothermal.org)
   - *Biofuels Digest* (http://biofuelsdigest.com)
   - *Fuel Cell & Hydrogen Energy Connection* (http:// www.fchea.org)
2. Visit the following Web sites for job listings:
   - http://www.nspe.org/resources/career-center
   - http://www.awea.org
   - http://www.ases.org
   - http://www.seia.org/solar-jobs
   - http://solarliving.jobamatic.com/a/jbb/ find-jobs
   - http://www.homepower.com/jobs
   - http://www.hydrofoundation.org/job-postings .html
   - http://www.geothermal.org/employment.html
   - http://www.fuelcellmarkets.com
   - http://www.jobsinfuelcells.com
3. Participate in internships or part-time jobs that are arranged by your college's career services office. Visit http://energy.gov/eere/education/clean-energy-jobs-and-career-planning for information on internships, fellowships, and scholarships.

4. Join professional associations to access training and networking resources, industry publications, and employment opportunities.
5. Visit http://energy.gov/eere/education/explore-clean-energy-careers for comprehensive information on careers in renewable energy.

■ FOR MORE INFORMATION

For industry news and updates, publications, conferences, career opportunities, and membership information, contact

American Solar Energy Society
2525 Arapahoe Avenue, E4-253
Boulder, CO 80302-6720
E-mail: info@ases.org
http://www.ases.org

For industry news and updates, publications, conferences, career opportunities, and membership information, contact

American Wind Energy Association
1501 M Street, NW, Suite 1000
Washington, D.C. 20005-1769
Tel: (202) 383-2500
Fax: (202) 383-2505
http://www.awea.org

For information on careers, employment opportunities, membership, and industry surveys, contact

Association of Energy Engineers
3168 Mercer University Drive
Atlanta, GA 30341
Tel: (770) 447-5083
http://www.aeecenter.org

Visit the association's Web site for a wealth of information on the fuel cell industry.

Fuel Cell & Hydrogen Energy Association
1211 Connecticut Avenue, NW, Suite 600
Washington, D.C. 20036-2705
Tel: (202) 261-1331
http://www.fchea.org

For general information on the geothermal industry and educational teaching guides, contact

Geothermal Education Office
664 Hilary Drive
Tiburon, CA 94920-1446
Fax: (415) 435-7737
E-mail: 24hrcleanpower@gmail.com
http://geothermal.marin.org

For industry news and updates, publications, conferences, career opportunities, and membership information, contact

Geothermal Energy Association
209 Pennsylvania Avenue, SE
Washington, D.C. 20003-1107
Tel: (202) 454-5261
Fax: (202) 454-5265
http://www.geo-energy.org

For information on geothermal energy and membership, contact

Geothermal Resources Council
PO Box 1350
Davis, CA 95617-1350
Tel: (530) 758-2360
Fax: (530) 758-2839
http://www.geothermal.org

For industry information, contact

Hydro Research Foundation
3124 Elk View Drive
Evergreen, CO 80439-7961
Tel: (720) 722-0HRF
E-mail: info@hydrofoundation.org
http://hydrofoundation.org

For information about renewable energy, contact

Interstate Renewable Energy Council
PO Box 1156
Latham, NY 12110-1156
Tel: (518) 621-7379
E-mail: info@irecusa.org
http://www.irecusa.org

For information on energy fairs and industry workshops, contact

Midwest Renewable Energy Association
7558 Deer Road
Custer, WI 54423-9734
Tel: (715) 592-6595
E-mail: info@midwestrenew.org
https://www.midwestrenew.org

For industry news and updates, publications, conferences, and information on careers, contact

National Hydropower Association
25 Massachusetts Avenue, NW, Suite 450
Washington, D.C. 20001-7405
Tel: (202) 682-1700
Fax: (202) 682-9478
E-mail: help@hydro.org
http://www.hydro.org

For more background information on renewable energy, careers, and internships, contact

National Renewable Energy Laboratory
15013 Denver West Parkway
Golden, CO 80401-3111
Tel: (303) 275-3000
http://www.nrel.gov

For information on careers, licensing, membership benefits, and local chapters, contact

National Society of Professional Engineers
1420 King Street
Alexandria, VA 22314-2794
Tel: (703) 684-2800
Fax: (703) 684-2821
http://www.nspe.org

For general information about the renewable energy industry, contact

Office of Energy Efficiency and Renewable Energy
1000 Independence Avenue, SW
Washington, D.C. 20585
Tel: (877) 337-3463
http://www.eere.energy.gov

For industry news, updates, and general information on bioenergy, contact

Renewable Fuels Association
425 Third Street, SW, Suite 1150
Washington, D.C. 20024-3231
Tel: (202) 289-3835
http://www.ethanolrfa.org

For trade news and updates, publications, conferences, career opportunities, and membership information, contact

Solar Energy Industries Association
600 14th Street, NW, Suite 400
Washington, D.C. 20005
Tel: (202) 682-0556
E-mail: info@seia.org
http://www.seia.org

Reporters

■ OVERVIEW

Reporters are the foot soldiers for newspapers, magazines, Internet news organizations, and television and radio broadcast companies. They gather and analyze information about current events and write stories for publication or for broadcasting. Reporters and *correspondents* hold about 54,400 jobs in the United States.

HISTORY

Newspapers are the primary disseminators of news in the United States. People read newspapers to learn about the current events that are shaping their society and societies around the world. Newspapers give public expression to opinion and criticism of government and societal issues, and, of course, provide the public with entertaining, informative reading.

Newspapers are able to fulfill these functions because of the freedom given to the press. However, this was not always the case. The first American newspaper, published in 1690, was suppressed four days after it was published. And it was not until 1704 that the first continuous newspaper appeared in the American colonies.

One early newspaperman who later became a famous writer was Benjamin Franklin. Franklin worked for his brother at a Boston newspaper before publishing his own paper two years later in 1723 in Philadelphia.

A number of developments in the printing industry made it possible for newspapers to be printed more cheaply. In the late 19th century, new types of presses were developed to increase production, and more importantly, the Linotype machine was invented. The Linotype mechanically set letters so that handset type was no longer necessary. This dramatically decreased the amount of prepress time needed to get a page into print. Newspapers could respond to breaking stories more quickly, and late editions with breaking stories became part of the news world.

These technological advances, along with an increasing population, factored into the rapid growth of the newspaper industry in the United States. In 1776, there were only 37 newspapers in the United States. Today hundreds of daily and weekly newspapers are published across the country.

As newspapers grew in size and widened the scope of their coverage, it became necessary to increase the number of employees and to assign them specialized jobs. Reporters have always been the heart of newspaper staffs. However, in today's complex world, with the public hungry for news as it occurs, reporters and correspondents are involved in all media—not only newspapers, but magazines, radio, television, and the Internet as well. Today, many newspapers are available in both online and print versions.

THE JOB

Reporters collect information on newsworthy events and prepare stories for newspaper or magazine publication, for radio or television broadcast, or for publication on the Internet. The stories may simply provide information about local, state, or national events, or they may present opposing points of view on issues of current interest. In this latter capacity, the press plays an important role in monitoring the actions of public officials and others in positions of power.

Stories may originate as an assignment from an editor or as the result of a lead, or news tip. Good reporters are always on the lookout for good story ideas. To cover a story, they gather and verify facts by interviewing people involved in or related to the event, examining documents and public records, observing events as they happen, and researching relevant background information. Reporters generally take notes or use a recording device as they collect information and write their stories once they return to their offices. They may take photos and edit accompanying video material. They are also increasingly being asked to write and maintain content for newspapers' Web sites. In order to meet a deadline, they may have to e-mail or telephone the stories to rewriters, who write or transcribe the stories for them. After the facts have been gathered and verified, the reporters transcribe their notes, organize their material, and determine what emphasis, or angle, to give the news. The story is then written to meet prescribed standards of editorial style and format.

The basic functions of reporters are to observe events objectively and impartially, record them accurately, and

QUICK FACTS

ALTERNATE TITLE(S)
Correspondents, Critics, Editorial Writers, Feature Writers, General Assignment Reporters, News Reporters, Syndicated News Columnists, Topical Reporters

DUTIES
Observe and research events; collect facts about these events through research and conducting interviews; write stories that clearly communicate information to readers, viewers, and listeners

SALARY RANGE
$21,390 to $36,360 to $81,580+

WORK ENVIRONMENT
Indoors/Outdoors

BEST GEOGRAPHIC LOCATION(S)
Any geographic location

MINIMUM EDUCATION LEVEL
Bachelor's Degree

SCHOOL SUBJECTS
English, History, Journalism

EXPERIENCE
Writing, reporting, and editing experience

PERSONALITY TRAITS
Curious, Organized, Outgoing

SKILLS
Public Speaking, Research, Writing

CERTIFICATION OR LICENSING
None

SPECIAL REQUIREMENTS
None

EMPLOYMENT PROSPECTS
Fair

ADVANCEMENT PROSPECTS
Fair

OUTLOOK
Decline

NOC
5123

O*NET-SOC
27-3022.00

CAREER LADDER

Editor

Editorial Writer

Columnist

Correspondent

Reporter

explain what the news means in a larger, societal context. Within this framework, there are several types of reporters.

The most basic is the *news reporter*. This job sometimes involves covering a beat, which means that the reporter may be assigned to consistently cover news from an area such as the local courthouse, police station, or school system. It may involve receiving general assignments, such as a story about an unusual occurrence or an obituary of a community leader. *General assignment reporters* are usually assigned to cover general events such as accidents, political rallies, celebrities' visits, or business closings. Large daily papers may assign teams of reporters to investigate social, economic, or political events and conditions.

Many newspaper, wire service, and magazine reporters specialize in one type of story, either because they have a particular interest in the subject or because they have acquired the expertise to analyze and interpret news in that particular area. *Topical reporters* cover stories for a specific department, such as medicine, politics, foreign affairs, sports, consumer affairs, finance, science, business, education, labor, or religion. They sometimes write features explaining the history that has led up to certain events in the field they cover. *Feature writers* generally write longer, broader stories than news reporters, usually on more upbeat subjects, such as fashion, art, theater, travel, and social events. They may write about trends, for example, or profile local celebrities. *Editorial writers* and *syndicated news columnists* present viewpoints that, although based on a thorough knowledge, are opinions on topics of popular interest. Columnists write under a byline and usually specialize in a particular subject, such as politics or government activities. *Critics* review restaurants, books, works of art, movies, plays, musical performances, and other cultural events.

Specializing allows reporters to focus their efforts, talent, and knowledge on one area of expertise. It also gives them more opportunities to develop deeper relationships with contacts and sources, which is necessary to gain access to the news.

Correspondents report events in locations distant from their home offices. They may report news by mail,

telephone, fax, or computer from rural areas, large cities throughout the United States, or foreign countries. Many large newspapers, magazines, and broadcast companies have one correspondent who is responsible for covering all the news for the foreign city or country where they are based. These reporters are known as *foreign correspondents*.

Reporters on small or weekly newspapers not only cover all aspects of the news in their communities, but may also take photographs, write editorials and headlines, lay out pages, edit wire-service copy, and help with general office work. *Television reporters* may have to be photogenic as well as talented and resourceful: They may at times present live reports, filmed by a mobile camera unit at the scene where the news originates, or they may tape interviews and narration for later broadcast.

■ EARNINGS

There are great variations in the earnings of reporters. Salaries are related to experience, the type of employer for which the reporter works, geographic location, and whether the reporter is covered by a contract negotiated by the Newspaper Guild.

According to the Bureau of Labor Statistics, the median annual wage for reporters and correspondents was $36,360 in May 2015. The lowest paid 10 percent of these workers earned $21,390 or less per year, while the highest paid 10 percent made $81,580 or more annually. The mean annual salary for reporters in radio and television was $53,530.

Benefits for salaried reporters depend on the employer; however, they usually include such items as health insurance, retirement or 401(k) plans, and paid vacation days. Self-employed reporters must provide their own benefits.

■ WORK ENVIRONMENT

Reporters work under a great deal of pressure in settings that differ from the typical business office. Their jobs generally require a five-day, 35- to 40-hour week, but overtime and irregular schedules are very common. Reporters employed by morning papers start work in the late afternoon and finish around midnight, while those on afternoon or evening papers start early in the morning and work until early or mid-afternoon. Foreign correspondents often work late at night to send the news to their papers in time to meet printing deadlines.

The day of the smoky, ink-stained newsroom has passed, but newspaper offices remain hectic places. Reporters have to work amid the clatter of computer keyboards and other machines, loud voices engaged in telephone conversations, and the bustle created by people hurrying about. An atmosphere of excitement prevails, especially as press deadlines approach.

Travel is often required in this occupation, and some assignments may be dangerous, such as covering wars, political uprisings, fires, floods, and other events of a volatile nature.

■ EXPLORING

You can explore a career as a reporter by talking to reporters and editors at local newspapers and radio and TV stations. You can also interview the admissions counselor at the school of journalism closest to your home.

In addition to taking courses in English, journalism, social studies, speech, computer science, and typing, high school students can acquire practical experience by working on school newspapers or on a church, synagogue, or mosque newsletter. Part-time and summer jobs on newspapers provide invaluable experience to the aspiring reporter.

College students can develop their reporting skills in the laboratory courses or workshops that are part of the journalism curriculum. College students might also accept jobs as campus correspondents for selected newspapers. People who work as part-time reporters covering news in a particular area of a community are known as *stringers* and are paid only for those stories that are printed.

Journalism scholarships, fellowships, and assistantships are offered by universities, newspapers, foundations, and professional organizations to college students. Many newspapers and magazines offer summer internships to journalism students to provide them with practical experience in a variety of basic reporting and editing duties. Students who successfully complete internships are usually placed in jobs more quickly upon graduation than those without such experience.

■ EDUCATION AND TRAINING REQUIREMENTS
High School

High school courses that will provide you with a firm foundation for a reporting career include English, journalism, history, social studies, communications, typing, and computer science. Speech courses will help you hone your interviewing skills, which are necessary for success as a reporter. In addition, it will be helpful to take college prep courses, such as foreign language, math, and science.

Postsecondary Training

You will need at least a bachelor's degree to become a reporter, and a graduate degree will give you a great advantage over those entering the field with lesser degrees. Many editors prefer applicants with degrees in journalism because their studies include liberal arts

A reporter interviews Secretary of Agriculture Tom Vilsack. (Thomas Witham. USDA.)

courses as well as professional training in journalism. Some editors consider it sufficient for a reporter to have a good general education from a liberal arts college.

More than 1,500 institutions offer programs in journalism or communications, or related programs. Many colleges offer programs in journalism leading to a bachelor's degree. In these schools, a majority of a student's time is devoted to a liberal arts education and the rest to the professional study of journalism, with required courses such as introductory mass media, basic reporting and copyediting, history of journalism, and press law and ethics. Students are encouraged to select other journalism courses according to their specific interests.

Journalism courses and programs are also offered by many community and junior colleges. Graduates of these programs are prepared to go to work directly as general assignment reporters, but they may encounter difficulty when competing with graduates of four-year programs. Credit earned in community and junior colleges may be transferable to four-year programs in journalism at other colleges and universities. Journalism training may also be obtained in the armed forces.

Some schools offer a master's or graduate degree in journalism. Graduate degrees may prepare students specifically for careers in news or as journalism teachers, researchers, and theorists, or for jobs in advertising or public relations.

A reporter's liberal arts training should include courses in English (with an emphasis on writing), sociology, political science, economics, history, psychology, business, speech, and computer science. Knowledge of foreign languages is also useful. To be a reporter in a specialized field, such as science or finance, requires concentrated course work in that area.

EMPLOYMENT HIGHLIGHTS FOR REPORTERS, MAY 2015

FAST FACTS

EMPLOYMENT HIGHLIGHTS

- Newspapers employed nearly 23,000 analysts and reporters.
- Television broadcasters employed more than 11,000.
- Radio employed only a little more than 3,000.
- Other information services, which includes broadcasting and publishing exclusive to the Internet, employed about 3,600 workers.

EARNINGS HIGHLIGHTS

- Independent reporters and correspondents earned the highest average salary, $65,940 annually.
- Those working in other information services earned $65,460
- Radio and television reporters averaged $51,430 per year.
- Reflecting the sharp decline in print news media, reporters working for print publications earned only $40,860 per year on average.

Source: U.S. Department of Labor, May 2015

Other Education or Training

A variety of webinars, conference seminars, digital journalism training sessions, and other continuing education opportunities are offered by professional associations such as the American Copy Editors Society, American Society of News Editors, MPA-The Association of Magazine Media, Online News Association, and the Society of Professional Journalists. Topics include writing, editing, interviewing, social media, and technology. Contact these organizations for more information.

■ CERTIFICATION, LICENSING, AND SPECIAL REQUIREMENTS
Certification or Licensing

There are no certification or licensing requirements for reporters.

■ EXPERIENCE, SKILLS, AND PERSONALITY TRAITS

Any experience working or volunteering as a writer, reporter, or editor in print, online, and broadcast journalism will be useful for aspiring reporters.

To be a successful reporter, you must be dedicated to obtaining hard facts, finding reliable sources, and conducting effective interviews. You need to be detail oriented and should enjoy working under tight deadlines. Reporters must also be good communicators, who can relate facts in a clear, easy-to-follow style. You should enjoy interacting with people of various races, cultures, religions, economic levels, and social statuses.

In order to succeed as a reporter, it is crucial that you have good typing skills, since you will type your stories using word processing programs. Although not essential, knowledge of shorthand or speedwriting makes note taking easier, and familiarity with news photography is an asset. Proficiency in multimedia and strong computer skills and database knowledge are essential. Reporters should also be inquisitive, aggressive, and persistent.

■ EMPLOYMENT PROSPECTS
Employers

Of the approximately 54,400 reporters and correspondents employed in the United States, more than 46 percent work for newspapers, periodical, book, and directory publishers. About 28 percent work in radio and television broadcasting.

Starting Out

Jobs in this field may be obtained through college career services offices or by applying directly to the personnel departments of individual employers. If you have some practical experience, you will have an advantage; you should be prepared to present a portfolio of material you wrote as a volunteer or part-time reporter, or other writing samples.

Most journalism school graduates start out as general assignment reporters or copy editors for small publications. A few outstanding journalism graduates may be hired by large city newspapers or national magazines. They are trained on the job. But they are the exception, as large employers usually require several years' experience. As a rule, novice reporters cover routine assignments, such as reporting on civic and club meetings, writing obituaries, or summarizing speeches. As you become more skilled in reporting, you will be assigned to more important events or to a regular beat, or you may specialize in a particular field.

■ ADVANCEMENT PROSPECTS

Reporters may advance by moving to larger newspapers or press services, but competition for such positions is unusually keen. Many highly qualified reporters apply for these jobs every year.

A select number of reporters eventually become columnists, correspondents, editorial writers, editors, or top executives. These important and influential positions represent the top of the field, and competition is strong for them.

Many reporters transfer the contacts and knowledge developed in newspaper reporting to related fields, such as public relations, advertising, or preparing copy for radio and television news programs.

■ OUTLOOK

The U.S. Department of Labor reports that employment for newspaper and magazine reporters and correspondents is expected to decline rapidly through 2024 because of mergers, consolidations, and closures in the newspaper and magazine industries, as well as declining advertising revenue.

Because of an increase in the number of small community and suburban daily and weekly newspapers, opportunities will be best for journalism graduates who are willing to relocate and accept relatively low starting salaries. With experience, reporters on these small papers can move up to editing positions or may choose to transfer to reporting jobs on larger newspapers or magazines.

Openings will be limited on big city dailies. While individual papers may enlarge their reporting staffs, little or no change is expected in the total number of these newspapers. Applicants will face strong competition for jobs on large metropolitan newspapers. Experience is a definite requirement, which rules out most new graduates unless they possess credentials in an area for which the publication has a pressing need. Occasionally, a beginner can use contacts and experience gained through internship programs and summer jobs to obtain a reporting job immediately after graduation.

Opportunities will be somewhat better for television and radio reporters with employment anticipated to grow about as fast as average, but broadcasting stations in major news markets generally prefer experienced reporters. For beginning correspondents, small stations with local news broadcasts will continue to replace staff who move on to larger stations or leave the business. Network hiring has been cut drastically in the past few years and will probably continue to decline.

Much stronger employment growth is expected for reporters in online-only newspapers and magazines, given the increasing importance of online news sources.

Overall, the prospects are best for graduates who have majored in news-editorial journalism and completed an internship while in school. The top graduates in an accredited program will have a great advantage, as will talented technical and scientific writers. Small

newspapers prefer to hire beginning reporters who are acquainted with the community and are willing to help with photography and other aspects of production. Without at least a bachelor's degree in journalism, applicants will find it increasingly difficult to obtain even an entry-level position. Beginning reporters may find more opportunities through freelancing.

Those with doctorates and practical reporting experience may find teaching positions at four-year colleges and universities, while highly qualified reporters with master's degrees may obtain employment in journalism departments of community and junior colleges.

■ UNIONS AND ASSOCIATIONS

Reporters may obtain union representation from the National Writers Union. They also may join professional associations such as the Society of Professional Journalists. Other useful organizations for reporters include the Association for Education in Journalism and Mass Communication, MPA-The Association of Magazine Media, and the Newspaper Association of America.

■ TIPS FOR ENTRY

1. In high school, work as a reporter or editor on your school newspaper.
2. Keep up with the news online and in print every day to stay on top of current events and learn how news is reported.
3. Apply to a college that offers a journalism major.
4. Work with your college career office to locate job openings for reporters.

■ FOR MORE INFORMATION

This organization provides general educational information on all areas of journalism, including newspapers, magazines, television, and radio.

Association for Education in Journalism and Mass Communication
234 Outlet Pointe Boulevard
Columbia, SC 29210-5667
Tel: (803) 798-0271
Fax: (803) 772-3509
http://www.aejmc.org

To find out about paid summer internships in reporting and editing, contact
Dow Jones Newspaper Fund
PO Box 300
Princeton, NJ 08543-0300
Tel: (609) 452-2820

Fax: (609) 520-5804

E-mail: djnf@dowjones.com

https://www.newsfund.org

For industry information, events, training, and networking, contact

MPA—The Association of Magazine Media

757 Third Avenue, 11th Floor

New York, NY 10017

Tel: (212) 872-3700

E-mail: mpa@magazine.org

http://www.magazine.org/

To learn more about this labor union for writers, contact

National Writers Union (NWU)

256 West 38th Street, Suite 703

New York, NY 10018

Tel: (212) 254-0279

Fax: (212) 254-0673

E-mail: membership@nwu.org

https://nwu.org/

For information on industry facts and figures, contact

Newspaper Association of America

4401 Wilson Boulevard, Suite 900

Arlington, VA 22203-1867

Tel: (571) 366-1000

E-mail: info@newsmediaalliance.org

http://www.naa.org

For information on union membership, contact

The Newspaper Guild, Communications Workers of America

501 Third Street, NW, 6th Floor

Washington, D.C. 20001-2797

Tel: (202) 434-7177

Fax: (202) 434-1472

E-mail: guild@cwa-union.org

http://www.newsguild.org

For industry information, resources, training, and networking, contact

Society of Professional Journalists (SPJ)

Eugene S. Pulliam National Journalism Center

3909 N. Meridian St.

Indianapolis, IN 46208

Tel: (317) 927-8000

Fax: (317) 920-4789

http://www.spj.org/

Reservation and Ticket Agents

■ OVERVIEW

Reservation and ticket agents are employed by airlines, bus companies, railroads, and cruise lines to help customers in several ways. Reservation agents make and confirm travel arrangements for passengers by using computers and manuals to determine timetables, taxes, and other information.

Ticket agents sell tickets in terminals or in separate offices. Like reservation agents, they also use computers and manuals containing scheduling, boarding, and rate information to plan routes and calculate ticket costs. They determine whether seating is available, answer customer inquiries, check baggage, and direct passengers to proper places for boarding. They may also announce arrivals and departures and assist passengers in boarding. There are approximately 138,810 reservation and ticket agents employed in the United States.

■ HISTORY

Since the earliest days of commercial passenger transportation (by boat or stagecoach), someone has been responsible for making sure that space is available and that everyone on board pays the proper fare. As transportation grew into a major industry over the years, the job of making reservations and selling tickets became a specialized occupation.

The airline industry experienced its first boom in the early 1930s. By the end of that decade, millions of people were flying each year. Since the introduction of passenger-carrying jet planes in 1958, the number of people traveling by air has multiplied many times over. Airlines now employ the majority of reservation and ticket agents.

A number of innovations have helped make the work of reservation and ticket agents easier and more efficient. The introduction of automated telephone services allows customers to check on flight availability or arrival and departure times without having to wait to speak to an agent. Computers have both simplified the agents' work and put more resources within their reach. Since the 1950s, many airlines have operated computerized scheduling and reservation systems, either individually or in partnership with other airlines. Until recently, these systems were not available to the general consumer. In the last decade, however, the growth of the Internet has permitted travelers to access scheduling and rate information, make reservations, and purchase tickets without contacting an agent. Airlines now offer electronic tickets, which they expect will eventually replace the traditional paper ticket. Despite these innovations, there will always be a need for reservation and ticketing agents, primarily for safety and security purposes. These employees still fill a vital role in the transportation industry.

■ THE JOB

Airline reservation agents are sales agents who work in large central offices run by airline companies. Their primary job is to book and confirm reservations for passengers on scheduled flights. At the request of the customer or a ticket agent, they plan the itinerary and other travel arrangements. While some veteran agents may still use timetables, airline manuals, reference guides, and tariff books, this work is generally performed using specialized computer programs.

Computers are used to make, confirm, change, and cancel reservations. After asking for the passenger's destination, desired travel time, and airport of departure, reservation agents type the information into a computer and quickly obtain information on all flight schedules and seating availability. If the plane is full, the agent may suggest an alternative flight or check to see if space is available on another airline that flies to the same destination. Agents may even book seats on competing airlines, especially if their own airline can provide service on the return trip.

Reservation agents also answer telephone inquiries about such things as schedules, fares, arrival and departure times, and cities serviced by their airline. They may maintain an inventory of passenger space available so they can notify other personnel and ticket stations of changes and try to book all flights to capacity. Some reservation agents work in more specialized areas, handling calls from travel agents or booking flights for members of frequent flyer programs. Agents working with international airlines must also be informed of visa regulations and other travel developments. This information is usually supplied by the senior reservation agent, who supervises and coordinates the activities of the other agents.

In the railroad industry, *train reservation clerks* perform similar tasks. They book seats or compartments for passengers, keep station agents and clerks advised on available space, and communicate with reservation clerks in other towns.

General transportation ticket agents for any mode of travel (air, bus, rail, or ship) sell tickets to customers at terminals or at separate ticket offices. Like reservation agents, they book space for customers. In addition, they use computers to prepare and print tickets, calculate fares, and collect payment. At the terminals they check and tag luggage, direct passengers to the proper areas for boarding, keep records of passengers on each departure, and help with customer problems, such as lost baggage or missed connections. *Airline ticket agents* may have additional duties, such as paging arriving and departing passengers and finding accommodations or new travel arrangements for passengers in the event of flight cancellations.

In airports, *gate agents* assign seats, issue boarding passes, make public address announcements of departures and arrivals, and help elderly or disabled passengers board the planes. In addition, they may also provide information to disembarking passengers about ground transportation, connecting flights, and local hotels.

Regardless of where they work, reservation and transportation ticket agents must be knowledgeable about their companies' policies and procedures, as well as the standard procedures of their industry. They must be aware of the availability of special promotions and services and be able to answer any questions customers may have.

■ EARNINGS

According to the U.S. Department of Labor, reservation and transportation ticket agents earned median salaries of $35,170 in 2015. The lowest paid 10 percent of these workers made about $20,870 per year, while the highest paid 10 percent earned more than $56,750 annually.

Most agents can earn overtime pay; many employers also pay extra for night work. Benefits vary according to the place of

---

QUICK FACTS

ALTERNATE TITLE(S)
Airline Reservation Agents, Airline Ticket Agents, Gate Agents, General Transportation Ticket Agents, Train Reservation Clerks

DUTIES
Make and confirm travel plans using computer systems; check baggage; respond to customer and traveler inquiries

SALARY RANGE
$20,870 to $35,170 to $56,750+

WORK ENVIRONMENT
Primarily Indoors

BEST GEOGRAPHIC LOCATION(S)
Any geographic area

MINIMUM EDUCATION LEVEL
High School Diploma, Some Postsecondary Training

SCHOOL SUBJECTS
Business, Computer Science, English

EXPERIENCE
Customer service internship or part-time job

PERSONALITY TRAITS
Helpful, Organized, Outgoing

SKILLS
Interpersonal, Organizational

CERTIFICATION OR LICENSING
None

SPECIAL REQUIREMENTS
None

EMPLOYMENT PROSPECTS
Fair

ADVANCEMENT PROSPECTS
Fair

OUTLOOK
Decline

NOC
6523, 6524

O*NET-SOC
43-4181.00

CAREER LADDER

Supervisor

Gate Agent

Ticketing/Reservation Agent

work, experience, and union membership; however, most receive vacation and sick pay, health insurance, and retirement plans. Agents, especially those employed by the airlines, often receive free or reduced-fare transportation for themselves and their families.

■ WORK ENVIRONMENT

Reservation and ticket agents generally work 40 hours per week. Those working in reservations typically work in cubicles with their own computer terminals and telephone headsets. They are often on the telephone and behind their computers all day long. Conversations with customers and computer activity may be monitored and recorded by their supervisors for evaluation and quality reasons. Agents might also be required to achieve sales or reservations quotas. During holidays or when special promotions and discounts are being offered, agents are especially busy. At these times or during periods of severe weather, passengers may become frustrated. Handling customer frustrations can be stressful, but agents must maintain composure and a pleasant manner when speaking with customers.

Ticket agents working in airports and train stations face a busy and noisy environment. They may stand most of the day and lift heavy objects such as luggage and packages. During holidays and busy times, their work can become

Ticketing agents who work in airports assist customers with their reservations, seating assignments, and baggage. (Takashi Usui. Shutterstock)

extremely hectic as they process long lines of waiting customers. Storms and other factors may delay or even cancel flights, trains, and bus services. Like reservation agents, ticket agents may be confronted with upset passengers, but must be able to maintain composure at all times.

■ EXPLORING

You may wish to apply for part-time or summer work with transportation companies in their central offices or at terminals. A school counselor can help you arrange an information interview with an experienced reservation and transportation ticket agent. Talking to an agent directly about his or her duties can help you to become more familiar with transportation operations.

■ EDUCATION AND TRAINING REQUIREMENTS
High School

Reservation and ticket agents are generally required to have at least a high school diploma. Applicants should be able to type and have good communication and problem-solving skills. Because computers are being used more and more in this field, you should have a basic knowledge of computers and computer software. Previous experience working with the public is also helpful for the job. Knowledge of geography and foreign languages are other valuable skills, especially for international service agents.

Postsecondary Training

Some college is preferred, although it is not considered essential for the job. Some colleges now offer courses specifically designed for ticket reservations.

Reservation agents are given about a month of classroom instruction. Here they will be taught how to read schedules, calculate fares, and plan itineraries. They learn how to use computer programs to get information and reserve space efficiently. They also study company policies and government regulations that apply to the industry.

Transportation ticket agents receive less training, consisting of about one week of classroom instruction. They learn how to read tickets and schedules, assign seats, and tag baggage. This is followed by one week of on-the-job training, working alongside an experienced agent. After mastering the simpler tasks, the new ticket agents are trained to reserve space, create tickets, and handle the boarding gate.

■ CERTIFICATION, LICENSING, AND SPECIAL REQUIREMENTS
Certification or Licensing

There are no certification or licensing requirements for reservation and ticket agents.

■ EXPERIENCE, SKILLS, AND PERSONALITY TRAITS

Aspiring reservation and ticket agents should try to obtain experience in customer service via internships, part-time jobs, or volunteer opportunities.

Reservation agents should have a thorough knowledge of the transportation industry. They should know how to work with sophisticated computer systems; deal effectively with the general public; listen carefully to questions from customers and answer them clearly; and they should be detail-oriented and work well under pressure.

Because you will be in constant contact with the public, professional appearance, a clear and pleasant speaking voice, and a friendly personality are important qualities. You need to be tactful in keeping telephone time to a minimum without alienating your customers. In addition, you should enjoy working with people, have a good memory, and be able to maintain your composure when working with harried or unhappy travelers. Agents form a large part of the public image of their company.

■ EMPLOYMENT PROSPECTS

Employers

Reservation and ticket agents hold approximately 138,810 jobs in the United States. Commercial airlines are the main employers. However, other transportation companies, such as rail, ship, and bus lines, also require their services.

Starting Out

To find part-time or summer work, apply directly to the personnel or employment offices of transportation companies. Ask your school counselor or college placement director for information about job openings, requirements, and possible training programs. Additionally, contact transportation unions for lists of job openings.

■ ADVANCEMENT PROSPECTS

With experience and a good work record, some reservation and ticket agents can be promoted to supervisory positions. They can also become city and district sales managers for ticket offices. Beyond this, opportunities for advancement are limited. However, achieving seniority within a company can give an agent the first choice of shifts and available overtime.

■ OUTLOOK

Employment for reservation and ticket agents is expected to decline by approximately 1.4 percent through 2024, according to the U.S. Department of Labor. Technology is changing the way consumers purchase tickets. Ticketless

PLANNING A VACATION?   DID YOU KNOW?

In recent years, much of the work of a reservation and ticket agent has been placed directly into the hands of anyone with access to the Internet. Travel Web sites such as Expedia (http://www.expedia.com), Kayak (http://www.kayak.com), Travelocity (http://www.travelocity.com), and Orbitz (http://www.orbitz.com) enable users to plan every detail of a trip, from arranging a shuttle to the airport, to booking a flight, hotel, or rental car, or to buying a complete cruise package. Most sites also contain detailed information on local attractions, dining, and nightlife. The next time you and your family or friends are taking a trip, offer to act as the reservation and ticket agent by doing online research on the flights, cars, or hotel rooms that best meet everyone's needs. Start by comparing prices on the sites mentioned above, or search on the sites of individual airlines and hotels. Also visit sites such as Hotwire (http://www.hotwire.com) and Priceline (http://www.priceline.com) that sometimes provide access to fares that are far below the going rates (but that are subject to restrictions). The Internet holds a wealth of travel information, and performing searches like this, even just for fun, will provide valuable exposure to this career.

travel and electronic ticketing—automated reservations ticketing—is reducing the need for agents. In addition, many airports now have computerized kiosks that allow passengers to reserve and purchase tickets themselves. Passengers can also access information about fares and flight times on the Internet, where they can also make reservations and purchase tickets. However, for security reasons, all of these services cannot be fully automated, so the need for reservation and transportation ticket agents will never be completely eliminated.

Most openings will occur as experienced agents transfer to other occupations or retire. Competition for jobs is fierce due to declining demand, low turnover, and because of the glamour and attractive travel benefits associated with the industry.

Overall, the transportation industry will remain heavily dependent on the state of the economy. During periods of recession or public fear about the safety of air travel, passenger travel generally declines and transportation companies are less likely to hire new workers, or may even resort to layoffs.

■ UNIONS AND ASSOCIATIONS

Useful professional organizations and government agencies for those working in this field include the Association of American Railroads, Cruise Lines International Association, Federal Aviation Administration, the Travel and Tourism Research Association, and the United Nations World Tourism Organization. These groups provide industry information or advocacy, networking, and training opportunities. Other organizations for travel professionals may also be helpful.

■ TIPS FOR ENTRY

1. Talk to your school counselor about summer jobs with transportation companies, like railroads.
2. Plan or organize a vacation for family members or friends to become familiar with transportation schedules and pricing.
3. Volunteer or find a part-time job with an emphasis on customer service or public relations.
4. Contact airlines, bus companies, and rail companies directly to learn more about job opportunities.

■ FOR MORE INFORMATION

For information about travel by rail, contact
Association of American Railroads (AAR)
425 Third Street, SW
Washington, D.C. 20024
Tel: (202) 639-2100
https://www.aar.org/Pages/HomePages.aspx

For information about cruises, contact
Cruise Lines International Association (CLIA)
1201 F Street, NW, Suite 250
Washington D.C. 20004
Tel: (202) 759-9370
E-mail: info@cruising.org
http://www.cruising.org

For information on the airline industry, contact the FAA.
Federal Aviation Administration (FAA)
800 Independence Avenue, SW, Room 810
Washington, D.C. 20591-0004
Tel: (866) 835-5322
http://www.faa.gov

Learn more about the tourism industry, including job postings, by visiting
Travel and Tourism Research Association
5300 Lakewood Road
Whitehall, MI 49461
Tel: (248) 708-8872
Fax: (248) 814-7150
E-mail: info@ttra.com
http://www.ttra.com

For statistics on international travel and tourism, visit the following Web site.
United Nations World Tourism Organization
Capitán Haya 42
28020 Madrid
Spain
Tel: +34 91 567 81 00
Fax: +34 91 571 37 33
E-mail: omt@unwto.org
http://www.unwto.org

Resort Workers

■ OVERVIEW

Resort workers assist the public at spas, luxury hotels, casinos, theme parks, and lodges. Employment opportunities range from entry-level *housekeepers* and *retail clerks* to highly specialized *game attendants* and *ski instructors*. Each worker is necessary to ensure the smooth daily operation of the business and comfort of resort patrons. Club Med, the largest resort chain in the world, employs about 23,000 workers, called Gentils Organizers, every season.

■ HISTORY

The travel and tourism industry has enjoyed steady growth over the years. Factors such as the rising number of two-income families, easier, affordable means of travel, and the public's love for fun and relaxation have triggered the increase of travel destinations in the United States and abroad. There are different kinds of resorts, each catered to meet specific tastes, expectations, and budgets. Here are some of the more popular types of resorts:

Beach Resorts

Great locations and warm, temperate climates make beach resorts popular vacation destinations. The same factors create tough competition when it comes to employment at such resorts. Does the idea of working in the Florida Keys or Hawaiian Islands sound attractive to you? Beach resorts offer outdoor activities such as snorkeling, surfing, sailing, and swimming. Here's the downside: The high cost of living in such regions can eat into your paycheck.

Alpine Resorts

Alpine resorts are popular winter vacation destinations—offering downhill skiing, sledding, and snowboarding. Many alpine resorts market warm weather activities such as hiking and biking in the off season. However, some resort areas, especially those located in Colorado, have a high cost of living.

Adventure Resorts

Dude ranches and rafting companies are some examples of adventure travel options. They are generally smaller operations and employ fewer workers, and many applicants are attracted to the exciting atmosphere. Most adventure resorts are found in out-of-the-way locations. As a result, if you crave big-city night life during your off hours, this may not be the option for you.

Eco Resorts

Eco resorts, or ecological resorts, strive to make the best use of natural resources readily available to them. Everything from the construction of the resort to the food, towels, bath accessories, and activities reflects a mission to be in harmony with the natural environment and have little to no impact on the surroundings. These resorts usually offer eco tours and opportunities for resort visitors to volunteer on ecological projects.

Hotels, Spas, and Casinos.

They are the biggest employers in the industry, offering many entry-level positions, as well as openings for specially trained *dealers*, *concierges*, *golf instructors*, and *masseurs*. Busy seasons vary, though you can expect to have a job year-round. These resorts tend to cater to an upscale clientele, so service standards are quite high and the work atmosphere is more structured. Luxury hotels and spas are located throughout the United States; the larger casino/resorts are located in the gambling meccas of Las Vegas and Atlantic City.

Theme Parks

Theme and amusement parks, located throughout the country, employ thousands of workers every year. Many job opportunities, such as *ride attendants*, *food service workers*, and *retail sales workers*, are entry-level positions; most are seasonal. Some of the larger theme resorts offer internships, or work/study programs.

■ THE JOB

Resort employment opportunities are endless. Many different positions, all as important as the next, are required for the successful operation of a resort business. Here are some types of jobs typically found in the industry:

Business Department

Accountants, *human resource specialists*, *managers*, *departmental supervisors*, and *general managers*, are just some positions found in the business department of a resort. While industry jobs are seasonal, business department employees work year round. The off season can be quite busy—budgets for the next year are set, marketing and advertising strategies are made, new hires and interns are interviewed. The number of workers employed in the business department is dependent on the size of the resort. A large casino/resort may employ hundreds of business professionals, while a dude ranch may have a single individual responsible for bookkeeping, advertising, and managerial duties. Traditionally, such positions are not considered entry-level but rather require a college degree or prior work experience. Many interns are assigned to a resort's business department.

Food Service

This is one of the largest departments in the industry. Every resort offers food and beverage service, whether simple buffets or elaborate gourmet dinners. *Waiters* and *waitresses* are needed to serve food to resort patrons in dining rooms and restaurants. *Bussers*, or *buspersons*, help set and clear tables and assist the *wait staff* in serving food, especially when dealing with large parties. They may also be asked to fill water glasses and bread baskets. *Dishwashers* clean plates, glasses, utensils, and other cooking or serving implements. *Hosts and hostesses* show diners to their tables, and may take dinner reservations over the phone. They are careful to rotate table occupation so all waiters and waitresses get an equal share of customers. *Prep cooks*, *sous chefs*, and *executive chefs* prepare all meals served at a resort. Some resorts are known for

QUICK FACTS

ALTERNATE TITLE(S)
Game Attendants, Ride Attendants, Ski Instructors

DUTIES
Assist the public at spas, luxury hotels, theme parks, casinos, and lodges

SALARY RANGE
$16,770 to $20,000 to $35,640+ (including tips)

WORK ENVIRONMENT
Indoors/Outdoors

BEST GEOGRAPHIC LOCATION(S)
The Southwest, New England, Florida, Hawaii, Colorado, California, and other popular tourist regions

MINIMUM EDUCATION LEVEL
High School Diploma

SCHOOL SUBJECTS
Business, Mathematics, Speech

EXPERIENCE
Varies by occupation

PERSONALITY TRAITS
Conventional, Helpful, Social

SKILLS
Business Management, Interpersonal

CERTIFICATION OR LICENSING
Required

SPECIAL REQUIREMENTS
Varies by occupation

EMPLOYMENT PROSPECTS
Good

ADVANCEMENT PROSPECTS
Good

OUTLOOK
About as Fast as the Average

NOC
0632, 5254, 6531

O*NET-SOC
11-9081.00, 33-9092.00, 43-4081.00

CAREER LADDER

> Resort Manager

> Department Manager

> Experienced Resort Worker

> Entry-Level Resort Worker

their food service, so the best-trained chefs are often recruited. *Bartenders* mix and serve alcoholic drinks.

Front Desk

Desk clerks and *reservation clerks* assign guests to their hotel room or guest quarters. They are also in charge of giving guests their mail or packages, taking reservations over the phone, collecting payment, and answering any questions regarding the resort. Phone operators work the resort switchboard, field calls, and sometimes take reservations.

Guest Services

Concierges assist resort guests with travel arrangements, reservations, or provide information. The *bell staff*, supervised by the *bell captain*, bring guests' luggage to their room, run short errands, or make deliveries. They may also be asked to drive resort vehicles. *Doormen* open doors for guests and help with the luggage. They may also be asked to hail taxis or provide information or directions.

Housekeeping and Maintenance

A resort's reputation rests largely on its appearance. *Housekeepers*, or *room attendants*, tidy guest rooms and common areas such as the lobby, dining rooms, and the pool and spa. Most housekeeping positions are entry level and need little or no experience. Maintenance workers make repairs throughout the resort, ranging from mending broken chairs to fixing electrical circuits.

Security

Guards are often employed to provide safety and security for all guests. While most guards are uniformed, some wear plainclothes and act as undercover security. Casino resorts employ a large number of security personnel to deter would-be thieves and dishonest gamblers. Security personnel, especially if they are armed, must receive some sort of formal training.

Retail

Retail clerks and *retail managers* work at the shopping galleries and gift shops found at many resorts, selling everything from exclusive clothing labels and cosmetics to souvenirs, candy, and snacks. Most retail positions are entry level.

Child Care and Health Care

Many resorts cater to growing families, and therefore hire *daycare workers* to provide care for patrons' children. Many resorts, especially those that are island-based, also hire a *medical or first aid staff* to tend to guests needing medical attention while on the premises.

Specialty Workers

Specialty workers fill the industry niches or provide services advertised by the particular resort. Most occupations in this category are highly specialized or require particular training, or in some cases, certification and licensure. *Lifeguards* are employed by resorts to supervise beaches and swimming pools. *Ski instructors* provide group or individual lessons for alpine resort patrons. Many beach resorts employ *recreation workers* to manage water activities such as water skiing, snorkeling, scuba diving, sailing, and deep-sea fishing. Dude ranches need *wranglers*, *trail guides*, and *horse groomers*. Theme resorts employ many entertainers for parades, musicals, and shows. Guides work for adventure resorts leading tours of wilderness areas. Casinos hire many people to work as *table dealers*, *pit bosses*, and *change clerks*. Golf resorts need *golf professionals* to give instruction and *caddies* to help guests with their golf bags.

■ EARNINGS

Most entry-level jobs in this industry pay an hourly wage anywhere from minimum wage on up. Waiters and waitresses, bussers, dishwashers, cleaning workers, the bell staff, and doormen earn low hourly salaries that are off-set by tips. Specialty workers who need certification or special training, such as instructors, bartenders, entertainers, lifeguards, wranglers, or blackjack dealers, may be paid a higher hourly wage. Some resorts supply free room and board for their employees, and offer only a small monthly stipend.

The following is a sampling (from the U.S. Department of Labor) of typical salary ranges for resort workers in May 2015: waiters, $16,810 to $35,640 (including tips); maids and housekeeping cleaners, $17,020 to $33,380; lifeguards, ski patrol, and other recreational protective service workers, $16,770 to $30,790; and hotel, motel, and resort desk clerks, $17,070 to $30,800. You should keep in mind, however, that most resort worker jobs are seasonal, so year-round, full-time employment is unlikely at most resorts, especially for entry-level jobs.

Since most jobs are seasonal, very few employee benefits are given apart from free use of resort facilities on off days, and some subsidized or free room and board. Some larger companies provide transportation to and from the resort. Full-time, year-round employees receive a standard benefits package including health insurance and paid sick and vacation time.

■ WORK ENVIRONMENT

All employees, regardless of their position, are expected to work hard. Hours will vary depending on the job and season. Most resort workers work eight hours a day, five or six days a week. Some employers, such as hotels, casinos, and spas, require their employees to wear company uniforms. Many places allow their employees to use the resort facilities on off days. Ski resorts give their employees free lift passes for the season. Employees of beach resorts enjoy swimming and sailing during their free time.

Many resorts offer housing options for their employees, with assignments grouping two or more employees to an apartment or room. Oftentimes, especially if the resort is in a remote location, seasonal workers have no choice but to hang out with each other during their free time.

■ EXPLORING

You can get work-related experience right now—without even leaving your hometown. Get a job at a nearby golf course, hotel, or restaurant. These types of jobs offer a great introduction to the industry, help you hone your people skills, and give your resume substance.

If you're thinking of becoming a swimming instructor, join your school's swim club, or start one yourself. This suggestion goes for whatever activity interests you—skiing, horseback riding, surfing, sailing, etc. Excelling in and enjoying a particular activity is a good stepping-stone for a career in the resort industry.

Check the Internet for resort-related Web sites and employment opportunities, or subscribe to a travel magazine to learn more about travel destinations.

■ EDUCATION AND TRAINING REQUIREMENTS
High School

There really is no specific high school class to take in order to be a successful resort worker (especially since there are dozens of career paths in the resort industry). Rather, a pleasant and outgoing personality and good people skills are what will help you land a job. On the other hand, business, computer science, English, speech, and even foreign language classes will provide basic skills that will come in handy in any career.

Postsecondary Training

If you are interested in something other than an entry-level job, or wish to make this industry a lifelong career,

A waiter pours wine for patrons at a resort restaurant. (Phil Date. Shutterstock.)

then a college education will be very helpful. Many companies look for college graduates with degrees in hospitality, communications, or business management.

■ CERTIFICATION, LICENSING, AND SPECIAL REQUIREMENTS
Certification or Licensing

Most entry-level resort jobs do not require certification or a license. This, however, is not the case with specialty workers. Ski instructors, scuba instructors, child-care workers, and lifeguards, just to name a few, must be certified.

■ EXPERIENCE, SKILLS, AND PERSONALITY TRAITS

No experience is needed to work in entry-level positions, but those with prior work experience will increase their chances of landing a job, getting promoted, and possibly earning higher pay. High-level positions such as nurse or executive require previous work experience.

Resorts are service-oriented so employees are required to be courteous, helpful, and friendly at all times. They are expected to dress and behave properly at all times, even when they are not on call. Some resorts such as Disney World, for example, consider their employees as "the cast," and expect them to be on their best behavior when on stage (working hours).

Employees are expected to mix well with the resort patrons as well as with their coworkers. Only team players are needed in this industry.

Some resorts insist that applicants be trained in CPR and first aid. Check with the human resources department of your potential employer to learn about their requirements.

■ EMPLOYMENT PROSPECTS

Employers

Resorts are located all over the country, from multimillion-dollar hotels to smaller, family-owned adventure companies. Jobs are plentiful. The hard part, especially if relocation is not a problem, is deciding which type of resort to work for. There are several important factors to consider before starting your job search: location, size of company, cost of living, and work availability. Here are profiles of three popular resort regions:

Aspen, Colorado

There are many jobs available in Aspen, such as waiting on tables, housekeeping, or bellhopping. Most pay minimum wage or higher, but tips can greatly increase your weekly salary. Besides world-class venues for skiing, biking, and hiking, spectacular views, and clean mountain air, Aspen attracts a diverse group of people from different backgrounds and interests. Be forewarned: Aspen, as with many other Colorado resort towns, is very expensive. You may have to share the rent with a roommate(s),

or consider finding more affordable housing outside of town. Most resort jobs are seasonal, from mid-October to mid-April. Unless you are fortunate enough to land a job year-round, save up for the off season. The big employer in Aspen is The Aspen Skiing Company, which has seasonal and some year-round work at its four ski areas and three hotel resorts.

Las Vegas, Nevada

Not only is this town a gambler's haven, it is also a place to go for entertainment, culture, sightseeing, and outdoor activities. The growth of mega-resorts catering to a diverse crowd of tourists, from wealthy gamblers to families, has turned Vegas into a hot travel destination. The good news: Most resort jobs in Vegas are year-round. This town is host to the largest business conventions and trade shows, so in addition to entry-level jobs, conference planners, chefs, hotel managers, and entertainers are needed to take care of the millions of conventioneers that come to Vegas each year. Housing in Las Vegas is very affordable. Many apartments advertise one month free as an incentive to potential renters. The bad news: It gets really hot in the summer. With temperatures rising over 100 degrees Fahrenheit, be sure to find out whether your resort job is primarily indoors during the months of June, July, and August. Check out the MGM Resorts International, which owns the Mirage Hotel as well as the Bellagio and other well-known properties.

Martha's Vineyard, Massachusetts

Jobs are available for waitresses/waiters, bartenders, beach lifeguards, or as guides for fishing tours. Most jobs are seasonal, lasting from mid-April to the end of October. Because of the location, a ferry ride away from the mainland, and the relatively small size of the island, housing for workers is costly. Prospective resort workers may want to consider working at some of the larger hotels; the hourly pay may be low, minimum wage or little better, but at least they offer free or subsidized housing. Applicants with hotel or restaurant experience are desired.

Starting Out

This is a popular industry, so it's important to apply early in order to get a choice position. A good rule of thumb is to submit your application at least two seasons in advance. That means no later than early spring for warm weather resorts, and the end of summer for Alpine resorts. Since many resorts recruit heavily at college campuses, and some high schools, your career guidance center would be a good place to start your job search. See if they post job opportunities, or have information on resort companies.

The Internet offers a wealth of information on resort employment. Visit the Web site http://www.resortjobs .com for industry information, tips on how to land the right jobs, and a listing of available positions. You may also want to check the chamber of commerce in a particular town of interest, or check the Internet or your local bookstore for a copy of the local paper.

Your place of residence is an important factor when applying for a resort job, especially with some of the larger Alpine resorts, and almost all resorts in Hawaii. Blame it on the high cost of living at such places. Since employer-provided housing in Hawaii, for example, is scarce, and rental properties and apartments are so expensive, most resorts will not consider applicants without a local address. You should always research the cost of living in an area when considering resort worker jobs.

Recruiters also look for a commitment to stay the length of the season. When new hires leave mid-season, resort managers find themselves scrambling to find a replacement, or the entire department ends up pulling the slack.

■ ADVANCEMENT PROSPECTS

Many employees return to resort jobs year after year. If they spend their first summer in an entry-level position, chances are they can advance to a job with more responsibility the next season. Bussers can advance to a waitstaff position, switchboard operators to a job as a front desk clerk, and housekeepers can become floor managers.

■ OUTLOOK

Until the public has enough of rest and relaxation, or tires of adventure travel and exotic locales, employment prospects in the resort industry will continue to be good. Mega-resorts in Las Vegas, the popularity of all-inclusive vacation packages, and alternative vacation destinations such as eco resorts will supply endless employment opportunities for resort workers. Work in these jobs is subject to economic ups and downs, however, which means a weak economy can diminish employment growth.

Many positions require little experience, but the best positions (more responsibility, higher pay) require more training and education. Management and hospitality graduates, entertainers, activity instructors, and chefs fare better in this respect. Also, applicants with industry exposure, or the ability to speak a foreign language, will be in high demand.

■ UNIONS AND ASSOCIATIONS

Some resort workers belong to unions. For example, hotel desk workers can join UNITE HERE. There are also a number of professional organizations, such as the

CLUB MED
DID YOU KNOW?

At Club Med, one of the world's largest resort chains, you are not called an employee but a *Gentils Organisateurs* (French for Congenial Hosts, and G.O. for short), and you don't work at a resort but rather a village. Club Med, in business since the 1940s, innovated the idea of all-inclusive vacations. That means for one price, you get room and board, entertainment, activities, and all the sun and surf you want. Well, at least for a week or so.

Club Meds are located all over the world and actively recruit young and energetic men and women to staff their villages. The typical G.O. is about 28 years old and works for the company for about two years. Different employment opportunities are available, such as hospitality administration, culinary arts, resort maintenance, child care and health care, sports instruction (both land and water), and entertainment. On off days, G.O.s are encouraged to mingle—share meals, play sports, and plan activities—with the village guests. New hires are assigned to a North American village for at least six months. After that G.O.s can apply to transfer to different villages as demand allows. Besides room and board, a G.O. receives round-trip transportation to their assigned village, health and accident insurance, and a monthly stipend that varies depending upon skill level. Most G.O.s do not work at Club Med to make money but rather for the experience of working with a diverse group of people and a chance to travel to many exotic ports of call. For more information, visit the employment section of Club Med's Web site, http://www.clubmed.us.

American Hotel and Lodging Association, that resort workers can join.

■ TIPS FOR ENTRY

1. Visit http://www.resortjobs.com for job listings.
2. Talk to resort workers about their careers. Ask them for advice on breaking into the field.
3. Land a part-time job at a resort to hone your customer service skills and make industry contacts.

■ FOR MORE INFORMATION

For information on education and careers, contact
American Hotel and Lodging Association
1250 I Street, NW, Suite 1100
Washington, D.C. 20005
Tel: (202) 289-3100
Fax: (202) 289-3199
E-mail: informationcenter@ahla.com
http://www.ahla.com

Respiratory Therapists and Technicians

■ OVERVIEW

Respiratory therapists, also known as *respiratory care practitioners*, evaluate, treat, and care for patients with deficiencies or abnormalities of the cardiopulmonary (heart/lung) system by either providing temporary relief from chronic ailments or administering emergency care where life is threatened. They are involved with the supervision of other respiratory care workers in their area of treatment. *Respiratory technicians* have many of the same responsibilities as therapists; however, technicians do not supervise other respiratory care workers.

Working under a physician's direction, these workers set up and operate respirators, mechanical ventilators, and other devices. They monitor the functioning of the equipment and the patients' response to the therapy and maintain the patient's charts. They also assist patients with breathing exercises, and inspect, test, and order repairs for respiratory therapy equipment. They may demonstrate procedures to trainees and other health care personnel. Approximately 130,700 respiratory therapy workers are employed in the United States.

■ HISTORY

In normal respiration, the chest muscles and the diaphragm (a muscular disc that separates the chest and abdominal cavities) draw in air by expanding the chest volume. When this automatic response is impaired because of illness or injury, artificial means must be applied to keep the patient breathing and to prevent brain damage or death. Respiratory problems can result from many conditions. For example, with bronchial asthma, the bronchial tubes are narrowed by spasmodic contractions, and they produce an excessive amount of mucus. Emphysema is a disease in which the lungs lose their elasticity. Diseases of the central nervous system and drug poisoning may result in paralysis, which could lead to suffocation. Emergency conditions such as heart failure, stroke, drowning, or shock also interfere with the normal breathing process.

Respirators, or ventilators, are mechanical devices that enable patients with cardiorespiratory problems to breathe. The iron lung was designed in 1937 by Philip Drinker and Louise A. Shaw, of the Harvard School of Public Health in Boston, primarily to treat people with polio. It was a cylindrical machine that enclosed the patient's entire body, except the head. This type of respirator is still in use today. The newer ventilators, however, are small dome-shaped breastplates that wrap around the patient's chest and allow more freedom of motion. Other sophisticated, complex equipment to aid patients with breathing difficulties includes mechanical ventilators, apparatuses that administer therapeutic gas, environmental control systems, and aerosol generators.

Respiratory therapists and technicians and their assistants are the workers who operate this equipment and administer care and life support to patients suffering from respiratory problems.

■ THE JOB

Respiratory therapists and technicians treat patients with various cardiorespiratory problems. They may provide care that affords temporary relief from chronic illnesses such as asthma or emphysema, or they may administer life-support treatment to victims of heart failure, stroke, drowning, or shock. These specialists often mean the difference between life and death in cases involving acute respiratory conditions, as may result from head injuries or drug poisoning. Adults who stop breathing for longer than three to five minutes rarely survive without serious brain damage, and an absence of respiratory activity for more than nine minutes almost always results in death. Respiratory therapists carry out their duties under a physician's direction and supervision. Technicians typically work under the supervision of a respiratory therapist and physician, following specific instructions. Therapists and technicians set up and operate special devices to treat patients who need temporary or emergency relief from breathing difficulties. The equipment may include respirators, positive-pressure breathing machines, or environmental control systems. Aerosol inhalants are administered to confine medication to the lungs. Respiratory therapists often treat patients who have undergone surgery because anesthesia depresses normal respiration, thus the patients need some support to restore their full breathing capability and to prevent respiratory illnesses.

In evaluating patients, therapists test the capacity of the lungs and analyze the oxygen and carbon dioxide concentration and potential of hydrogen (pH), a measure of the acidity or alkalinity level of the blood. To measure lung capacity, therapists have patients breathe into an instrument that measures the volume and flow of air during inhalation and exhalation. By comparing the reading with the norm for the patient's age, height, weight, and gender, respiratory therapists can determine whether lung deficiencies exist. To analyze oxygen, carbon dioxide, and pH levels, therapists draw an arterial blood sample, place it in a blood gas analyzer, and relay the results to a physician.

Respiratory therapists watch equipment gauges and maintain prescribed volumes of oxygen or other inhalants. Besides monitoring the equipment to be sure it is operating properly, they observe the patient's physiological response to the therapy and consult with physicians in case of any adverse reactions. They also record pertinent identification and therapy information on each patient's chart and keep records of the cost of materials and the charges to the patients.

Therapists instruct patients and their families on how to use respiratory equipment at home, and they may demonstrate respiratory therapy procedures to trainees and other health care personnel. Their responsibilities include inspecting and testing equipment. If it is faulty, they either make minor repairs themselves or order major repairs.

Respiratory therapy workers include therapists, technicians, and assistants. Differences between respiratory therapists' duties and those of other respiratory care workers' include supervising technicians and assistants, teaching new staff, and bearing primary responsibility for the care given in their areas. At times the respiratory therapist may need to work independently and make clinical judgments on the type of care to be given to a patient. Although technicians can perform many of the same activities as a therapist (for example, monitoring equipment, checking patient responses, and giving medicine), they do not make independent decisions about what type of care to give. *Respiratory assistants* clean, sterilize, store, and generally take care of the equipment but have very little contact with patients.

■ EARNINGS

Respiratory therapists earned a median salary of $57,790 in May 2015, according to the U.S. Department of Labor. The lowest 10 percent earned less than $41,970, and the highest 10 percent earned more than $80,440. Median annual earnings of respiratory therapy technicians were $48,490. Salaries ranged from less than $30,750 to more than $72,300.

Hospital workers receive benefits that include health insurance, paid vacations and sick leave, and pension plans. Some institutions provide additional benefits, such as uniforms and parking, and offer free courses or tuition reimbursement for job-related courses.

■ WORK ENVIRONMENT

Respiratory therapists and technicians generally work in extremely clean, quiet surroundings. They usually work 40 hours a week, which may include nights and weekends because hospitals are in operation 24 hours a day, seven days a week. The work requires long hours of standing and may be very stressful during emergencies.

A possible hazard is that the inhalants these employees work with are highly flammable. The danger of fire is minimized, however, if the workers test equipment regularly and are strict about taking safety precautions. As do workers in many other health occupations, respiratory therapists run a risk of catching infectious diseases. Careful adherence to proper procedures minimizes the risk.

QUICK FACTS

ALTERNATE TITLE(S)
Respiratory Assistants,
    Respiratory Care Practitioners

DUTIES
Evaluate, treat, and care
    for patients with various
    cardiorespiratory problems

SALARY RANGE
$30,750 to $48,490 to
    $72,300+ (technicians)
$41,970 to $57,790 to
    $80,440+ (therapists)

WORK ENVIRONMENT
Primarily Indoors

BEST GEOGRAPHIC LOCATION(S)
Opportunities available
    throughout the country

MINIMUM EDUCATION LEVEL
Associate's Degree

SCHOOL SUBJECTS
Biology, Chemistry, Health

EXPERIENCE
Internship

PERSONALITY TRAITS
Outgoing, Social, Technical

SKILLS
Interpersonal, Mechanical/
    Manual Dexterity, Scientific

CERTIFICATION OR LICENSING
Required

SPECIAL REQUIREMENTS
None

EMPLOYMENT PROSPECTS
Good

ADVANCEMENT PROSPECTS
Good

OUTLOOK
Faster than the Average

NOC
3214

O*NET-SOC
29-1126.00, 29-2054.00

CAREER LADDER

Department Manager or Professor

Chief Respiratory Therapist

Respiratory Therapist

Respiratory Technician

Respiratory Assistant

■ EXPLORING

Hospitals are excellent places to obtain part-time and summer employment. They have a continuing need for helpers in many departments. Even though the work may not be directly related to respiratory therapy, you will gain knowledge of the operation of a hospital and may be in a position to get acquainted with respiratory therapists and observe them as they carry out their duties. If part-time or temporary work is not available, you may wish to volunteer your services.

Ask your school counselor or health teacher to help set up interviews with or lectures by respiratory therapy practitioners from a local hospital.

■ EDUCATION AND TRAINING REQUIREMENTS
High School

To prepare for a career in this field while you are still in high school, take health and science classes, including biology, chemistry, and physics. Mathematics and statistics classes will also be useful to you since much of this work involves using numbers and making calculations. Take computer science courses to become familiar with using technical and complex equipment and to become familiar with programs you can use to document your work. Since some of your responsibilities may include working directly with patients to teach them therapies, take English classes to improve your communication skills. Studying a foreign language may also be useful.

Postsecondary Training

Formal training is necessary for entry to this field. Training is offered at the postsecondary level by hospitals, medical schools, colleges and universities, trade schools, vocational-technical institutes, and the armed forces. To be eligible for a respiratory therapy program, you must have graduated from high school. Visit http://www.coarc.com/36.html for a list of accredited educational programs in respiratory therapy. Formal training in this field is available in hospitals and other non-collegiate settings as well. Local hospitals can provide information on training opportunities.

Accredited respiratory therapy programs combine class work with clinical work. Programs vary in length,

depending on the degree awarded. A certificate program generally takes one year to complete, an associate's degree usually takes two years, and a bachelor's degree program typically takes four years. In addition, it is important to note that some advanced-level programs will prepare you for becoming a registered respiratory therapist (RRT), while entry-level programs will prepare you for becoming a certified respiratory therapist (CRT). RRT-prepared graduates will be eligible for jobs as respiratory therapists once they have been certified. CRT-prepared graduates, on the other hand, are only eligible for jobs as respiratory technicians after certification. The areas of study for both therapists and technicians cover human anatomy and physiology, chemistry, physics, microbiology, and mathematics. Technical studies include courses such as patient evaluation, respiratory care pharmacology, pulmonary diseases, and care procedures.

There are no standard hiring requirements for assistants. Department heads in charge of hiring set the standards and may require only a high school diploma.

Other Education or Training

The American Association for Respiratory Care offers continuing education webinars, classes, and workshops. Past offerings included "Respiratory Therapists of the Future," "Pulmonary Rehabilitation," "Asthma Self-Management," "Dealing with Difficult People," and "Ethical Decisions Encountered in Respiratory Therapy." Contact the association for more information.

■ CERTIFICATION, LICENSING, AND SPECIAL REQUIREMENTS
Certification or Licensing

The National Board for Respiratory Care (NBRC) offers the voluntary certified respiratory therapist (CRT) and registered respiratory therapist (RRT) designations to graduates of Committee on Accreditation for Respiratory Care-accredited and Commission on Accreditation of Allied Health Education Programs-accredited programs. You must have at least an associate's degree to be eligible to take the CRT exam. Anyone desiring certification must take the CRT exam first. After successfully completing this exam, those who are eligible can take the RRT exam. CRTs who meet further education and experience requirements can qualify for the RRT credential. Certification is highly recommended because most employers require this credential. Those who are designated CRT or are eligible to take the exam are qualified for technician jobs that are entry-level or generalist positions. Employers usually require those with supervisory positions or those in intensive care specialties to have the RRT (or RRT eligibility).

The NBRC also offers specialty certification exams in adult critical care, neonatal/pediatric respiratory care, pulmonary function technology, and sleep disorders.

A license is required by all states, except Alaska, to practice as a respiratory therapist. Also, most employers require therapists to maintain a cardiopulmonary resuscitation certification. Requirements vary, so you will need to check with your state's regulatory board for specific information. The NBRC Web site provides helpful contact information for state licensure agencies at http://apps.nbrc.org/statelic/.

■ EXPERIENCE, SKILLS, AND PERSONALITY TRAITS

Working as a respiratory therapy assistant and participation in internships while in college will provide useful experience for aspiring respiratory technicians and therapists.

Respiratory therapists and technicians must enjoy working with people. You must be sensitive to your patients' physical and psychological needs because you will be dealing with people who may be in pain or who may be frightened. The work of respiratory workers is of great significance. Respiratory therapists and technicians are often responsible for the lives and well being of people already in critical condition. You must pay strict attention to detail, be able to follow instructions and work as part of a team, and remain cool in emergencies. Mechanical ability and manual dexterity are necessary to operate much of the respiratory equipment.

■ EMPLOYMENT PROSPECTS
Employers

Approximately 130,700 respiratory therapy workers are employed in the United States. About 81 percent of respiratory therapy jobs are in hospital departments of respiratory care, anesthesiology, or pulmonary medicine. The rest are employed by oxygen equipment rental companies, ambulance services, nursing homes, home health agencies, and physicians' offices. Many respiratory therapists hold a second job.

Starting Out

Graduates of Committee on Accreditation for Respiratory Care- and Commission on Accreditation of Allied Health Education Programs-accredited respiratory therapy training programs may use their school's career services offices to help them find jobs. Otherwise, they may apply directly to the individual local health care facilities.

High school graduates may apply directly to local hospitals for jobs as respiratory therapy assistants. If your goal is to become a therapist or technician, however, you

A respiratory therapist holds a nebulizer over a patient's face during treatment. (Ermolaev Alexander. Shutterstock.)

will need to enroll in a formal respiratory therapy educational program.

■ ADVANCEMENT PROSPECTS

Many respiratory therapists start out as assistants or technicians. With appropriate training courses and experience, they advance to the therapist level. Respiratory therapists with sufficient experience may be promoted to assistant chief or chief therapist. With graduate education, they may be qualified to teach respiratory therapy at the college level or move into administrative positions such as director.

■ OUTLOOK

Employment for respiratory therapists is expected to grow faster than the average for all careers through 2024, about 12 percent, according to the Department of Labor, as a result of the growing middle-aged and elderly population with respiratory conditions such as chronic bronchitis, asthma, emphysema, pneumonia, and other disorders. The increasing demand for respiratory therapists is the result of other factors also. The field of neonatal care is growing, and there are continuing advances in treatments for victims of heart attacks and accidents and for premature babies.

Employment opportunities for respiratory therapists should be very favorable in the rapidly growing field of home health care (where employment is expected to grow by 53 percent through 2024), although this area accounts for only a small number of respiratory

RESPIRATORY THERAPY NEWS AND EDUCATION PROGRAMS

ONLINE RESOURCES

Find educational programs, school listings, publications, research, and other resources at these Web sites.

Accredited Respiratory Therapy Programs
http://www.aarc.org/education/accredited_programs

ExploreHealthCareers.org: Respiratory Therapist
http://explorehealthcareers.org/en/Career/23/Respiratory_Therapist

Mayo Clinic: Respiratory Career Overview
http://www.mayo.edu/mshs/careers/respiratory-care

Respiratory Care
http://rc.rcjournal.com

RT Magazine
http://www.rtmagazine.com

therapy jobs. In addition to jobs in home health agencies and hospital-based home health programs, there should be numerous openings for respiratory therapists in equipment rental companies and in firms that provide respiratory care on a contract basis. In addition, employment is expected to grow due to respiratory therapists' increasing role in case management, disease prevention, emergency care, and the early detection of pulmonary disorders.

In contrast, employment of respiratory therapy technicians is forecast to decline by 19 percent during the same period, with a loss of approximately 2,000 jobs, according to the Bureau of Labor Statistics.

■ UNIONS AND ASSOCIATIONS

Respiratory therapists and technicians who work for government agencies can join the American Federation of Government Employees and the American Federation of State, County and Municipal Employees. Other unions for health care professionals include the National Union of Healthcare Workers and Service Employee International Union. The American Association for Respiratory Care is the major professional organization for respiratory care professionals. It offers network opportunities, continuing education classes and webinars, publications, and other resources. The Committee on Accreditation for Respiratory Care and the Commission on Accreditation of Allied Health Education Programs accredit respiratory and other health care programs. The National Board for Respiratory Care provides information on licensing and certification.

■ TIPS FOR ENTRY

1. Read *AARC Times* (http://www.aarc.org/members_area/aarc_times) and *ADVANCE for Respiratory Care and Sleep Medicine* (http://respiratory-care-sleep-medicine.advanceweb.com) to learn more about the field.
2. The American Association for Respiratory Care offers a wealth of articles on career development at its Web site, http://www.aarc.org/career.
3. Visit http://www.aarc.org/career/job_bank for job listings.

■ FOR MORE INFORMATION

For information on scholarships, continuing education, job listings, and careers in respiratory therapy, contact
American Association for Respiratory Care
9425 North MacArthur Boulevard, Suite 100
Irving, TX 75063-4706
Tel: (972) 243-2272
Fax: (972) 484-2720
E-mail: info@aarc.org
http://www.aarc.org

For more information on accredited programs, contact
Commission on Accreditation of Allied Health Education Programs
25400 U.S. Highway 19 North, Suite 158
Clearwater, FL 33763
Tel: (727) 210-2350
Fax: (727) 210-2354
E-mail: mail@caahep.org
http://www.caahep.org

For a list of CoARC-accredited training programs, contact
Committee on Accreditation for Respiratory Care (CoARC)
1248 Harwood Road
Bedford, TX 76021-4244
Tel: (817) 283-2835
Fax: (817) 354-8519
http://www.coarc.com

For information on licensing and certification, contact
National Board for Respiratory Care
18000 West 105th Street
Olathe, KS 66061-7543
Tel: (888) 341-4811; (913) 895-4900
Fax: (913) 712-9283
E-mail: nbrc-info@nbrc.org
http://www.nbrc.org

Restaurant and Food Service Managers

■ OVERVIEW

Restaurant and food service managers are responsible for the overall operation of businesses that serve food. Food service work includes the purchasing of a variety of food, selection of the menu, preparation of the food, and, most importantly, maintenance of health and sanitation levels. It is the responsibility of managers to oversee staffing for each task in addition to performing the business and accounting functions of restaurant operations. There are approximately 305,000 food service managers employed in the United States.

■ HISTORY

The word restaurant comes from the French word *restaurer*, meaning "to restore." It is believed that the term was first used in its present sense in the 18th century by a soup vendor in Paris, who offered his customers a choice of soups, or restoratives (restaurants). The first restaurants in the United States were patterned after European restaurants and coffeehouses. During the 20th century, many innovations in the restaurant industry led to the development of new kinds of eating establishments, including the cafeteria, Automat, counter-service restaurant, drive-in, and fast food chain. Today's restaurants offer a wide array of foods from all cultures, and many now also cater to specific diets such as vegetarian, vegan, and raw food. Restaurant and food managers have a variety of options in choosing their career path.

■ THE JOB

Restaurant and food service managers work in restaurants ranging from elegant hotel dining rooms to fast food restaurants. They may also work in food service facilities ranging from school cafeterias to hospital food services. Whatever the setting, these managers coordinate and direct the work of the employees who prepare and serve food and perform other related functions. *Restaurant managers* set work schedules for wait staff and host staff. *Food service managers* are responsible for buying the food and equipment necessary for the operation of the restaurant or facility, and they may help with menu planning. They inspect the premises periodically to ensure compliance with health and sanitation regulations. Restaurant and food service managers perform many clerical and financial duties, such as keeping records, directing payroll operations, handling large sums of money, and taking inventories. Their work usually involves much

contact with customers and vendors, such as taking suggestions, handling complaints, and creating a friendly atmosphere. Restaurant managers generally supervise any advertising or sales promotions for their operations.

In some very large restaurants and institutional food service facilities, one or more *assistant managers* and an *executive chef* or *food manager* assist the manager. These specially trained assistants oversee service in the dining room and other areas of the operation and supervise the kitchen staff and preparation of all foods served.

Restaurant and food service managers are responsible for the success of their establishments. They continually analyze every aspect of its operation and make whatever changes are needed to guarantee its profitability.

These duties are common, in varying degrees, to both owner-managers of relatively small restaurants and to nonowner-managers who may be salaried employees in large restaurants or institutional food service facilities. The owner-manager of a restaurant is more likely to be involved in service functions, sometimes operating the cash register, waiting on tables, and performing a wide variety of tasks.

■ EARNINGS

The earnings of salaried restaurant and food service managers vary a great deal, depending on the type and size of the establishment. According to the U.S. Department of Labor, median annual earnings of food service managers were $48,690 in May 2015. The lowest paid

QUICK FACTS

ALTERNATE TITLE(S)
Food Service Managers, Restaurant Managers

DUTIES
Manage restaurants and food service facilities; hire and train workers; prepare budgets; plan menus; order supplies; ensure that proper health and sanitation levels are maintained; prepare advertising and marketing campaigns

SALARY RANGE
$28,780 to $48,690 to $83,010+

WORK ENVIRONMENT
Primarily Indoors

BEST GEOGRAPHIC LOCATION(S)
Opportunities exist throughout the country

MINIMUM EDUCATION LEVEL
High School Diploma, Some Postsecondary Training

SCHOOL SUBJECTS
Business, Health, Mathematics

EXPERIENCE
Food service experience required

PERSONALITY TRAITS
Conventional, Helpful, Outgoing

SKILLS
Business Management, Interpersonal, Leadership

CERTIFICATION OR LICENSING
Recommended

SPECIAL REQUIREMENTS
None

EMPLOYMENT PROSPECTS
Good

ADVANCEMENT PROSPECTS
Good

OUTLOOK
About as Fast as the Average

NOC
0631

O*NET-SOC
11-9051.00, 35-1012.00

CAREER LADDER

Restaurant Owner-Manager

Restaurant and Food Service Manager

Executive Chef or Food Manager

Assistant Manager

Pantry Supervisor or Food Manager

10 percent earned less than $28,780, and the highest paid 10 percent earned more than $83,010. Those in charge of full-service restaurants earned about $51,000, while those who worked in traveler accommodation establishments earned $62,570 per year in 2015. In addition to a base salary, most managers receive bonuses based on profits, which can range from $2,000 to $7,500 a year.

Many restaurants furnish meals to employees during their work hours. Annual bonuses, group plan pensions, hospitalization, medical, and other benefits may be offered to restaurant managers.

■ WORK ENVIRONMENT

Work environments are usually pleasant, and the atmospheres can range from calm to chaotic, depending upon the nature of the restaurant and its patrons. There is usually a great deal of activity involved in preparing and serving food to large numbers of people, and managers usually work 40 to 48 hours per week. In some cafeterias, especially those located within an industry or business establishment, hours are regular, and little evening work is required. Many restaurants serve late dinners, however, necessitating the manager to remain on duty during a late-evening work period.

■ EXPLORING

Practical restaurant and food service experience is usually easy to get. In colleges with curriculum offerings in these areas, summer jobs in all phases of the work are available and, in some cases, required. Some restaurant and food service chains provide on-the-job training in management. Another way to learn more about the field is to talk to a manager about his or her career.

■ EDUCATION AND TRAINING REQUIREMENTS
High School

Take a business-oriented curriculum, with classes in accounting, finance, and mathematics. Computers are key tool used by managers, so take as many computer science classes as possible, especially those in database management. Take English and speech classes to brush up on your communication skills. Since many restaurant

workers speak Spanish as their first language, it is a good idea to take Spanish so that you will be better able to communicate with your staff.

The National Restaurant Association Educational Foundation offers ProStart, a two-year career-building program for high school students who are interested in careers in culinary arts and food service management. Students gain experience in the field via classes and mentored work experience in food service operations. They also have the opportunity to participate in the National ProStart Invitational, a culinary and management competition in which students demonstrate their skills and compete for scholarships. Visit http://www.nraef.org/Students/ProStart for more information.

Postsecondary Training

Educational requirements for restaurant and food service managers vary greatly. In many cases, no specific requirements exist and managerial positions are filled by promoting experienced food and beverage preparation and service workers. However, as more colleges offer programs in restaurant and institutional food service management—programs that combine academic work with on-the-job experience—more restaurant and food service chains are seeking individuals with this training.

Many colleges and universities offer four-year programs leading to a bachelor's degree in restaurant and hotel management or institutional food service management. Some individuals qualify for management training by earning an associate's degree or other formal award below the bachelor's degree level from one of the nearly 1,000 community and junior colleges, technical institutes, or other institutions that offer programs in these fields. Students hired as management trainees by restaurant chains and food service management companies undergo vigorous training programs.

Those interested in working at higher-end restaurants, chains, or opening their own restaurant should earn at least a bachelor's degree in restaurant management or a related field.

Other Education or Training

The National Restaurant Association provides member-only webinars and other continuing education opportunities. Topics include marketing, social media, regulatory and labor challenges, and food safety. It also offers the ManageFirst program for college students to help them develop the professional skills that are necessary to become successful restaurant and food service managers. The National Restaurant Association Educational Foundation offers a variety of continuing education opportunities for food service workers and managers.

For example, its ServSafe Food Handler Program provides training in five areas: basic food safety, personal hygiene, cross-contamination and allergens, time and temperature, and cleaning and sanitation. The American Hotel & Lodging Educational Institute and Restaurants Canada also provide continuing education workshops and seminars. Contact these organizations for more information.

■ CERTIFICATION, LICENSING, AND SPECIAL REQUIREMENTS
Certification and Licensing

The National Restaurant Association Educational Foundation offers a voluntary food service management professional certification to restaurant and food service managers. Additionally, the International Food Service Executives Association provides the certified food manager and certified food executive voluntary certification designations. Contact these organizations for more information.

■ EXPERIENCE, SKILLS, AND PERSONALITY TRAITS

Any volunteer or paid experience working in the food service industry and managing others will be useful for aspiring restaurant and food service managers. Experience in all areas of restaurant and food service work is an important requirement for successful managers. Managers must be familiar with the various operations of the establishment: food preparation, service operations, sanitary regulations, and financial functions.

One of the most important requirements for restaurant and food service managers is to have good business knowledge. They must possess a high degree of technical knowledge in handling business details, such as buying large items of machinery and equipment and large quantities of food. Desirable personality characteristics include poise, self-confidence, and an ability to get along with people. Managers may be on their feet for long periods, and the hours of work may be both long and irregular. Other important traits include good organizational, time management, and leadership skills; a detail-oriented personality; good problem-solving skills; reliability; and a neat and clean appearance.

■ EMPLOYMENT PROSPECTS
Employers

Approximately 305,000 food service managers are employed in the United States. Restaurants and food service make up one of the largest and most active sectors of the nation's economy. Employers include restaurants of various sizes, hotel dining rooms, ships, trains,

A restaurant manager discusses reservations with the chef. (wave breakmedia. Shutterstock.)

institutional food service facilities, and many other establishments where food is served. No matter the size or style of the establishment, managers are needed to oversee the operation and to ensure that records are kept, goals are met, and things run smoothly. About 38 percent of restaurant and food service managers are self employed. They own independent restaurants or other small food service establishments.

Starting Out

Many restaurants and food service facilities provide self-sponsored, on-the-job training for prospective managers. There are still cases in which people work hard and move up the ladder within the organization's workforce, finally arriving at the managerial position. More and more, people with advanced education and specialized training move directly into manager-trainee positions and then on to managerial positions.

■ ADVANCEMENT PROSPECTS

In large restaurants and food service organizations, promotion opportunities frequently arise for employees with knowledge of the overall operation. Experience in all aspects of the work is an important consideration for the food service employee who desires advancement. The employee with knowledge of kitchen operations may advance from pantry supervisor to food manager, assistant manager, and finally restaurant or food service manager. Similar advancement is possible for dining room workers with knowledge of kitchen operations.

Advancement to top executive positions is possible for managers employed by large restaurant and institutional food service chains. A good educational background and

TOP-PAYING STATES FOR FOOD MANAGERS, MAY 2015

FAST FACTS

- New Jersey: $34.35 per hour ($71,440 annually)
- Delaware: $34.20 per hour ($71,330 annually)
- Rhode Island: $33.17 per hour ($69,000 annually)
- New York: $32.54 per hour ($67,690 annually)
- Florida: $32.44 per hour ($67,470 annually)

Source: U.S. Department of Labor

some specialized training are increasingly valuable assets to employees who hope to advance.

■ OUTLOOK

According to the U.S. Department of Labor, jobs will grow as fast as the averge through 2024. Many job openings will arise from the need to replace managers retiring from the workforce. Also, population growth will result in an increased demand for full-service restaurants and, in turn, a need for managers to oversee them. As the elderly population increases, managers will be needed to staff dining rooms located in hospitals and nursing homes. Opportunities will also be good for managers in special food services such as schools, health care facilities, hotels, and other businesses that contract out their food service needs (especially nursing and residential care facilities). The demand for quick food is expected to grow, creating more jobs for food service managers in convenience and grocery stores, and in retail and recreation industries. More jobs are expected to open up in full-service restaurants and limited-service eating places. Those with bachelor's or associate's degrees in restaurant, hospitality, or institutional food service management will have the strongest employment opportunities.

Economic downswings have a great effect on eating and drinking establishments. During a recession, people have less money to spend on luxuries such as dining out, thus hurting the restaurant business. However, greater numbers of working parents and their families are finding it convenient to eat out or purchase carryout food from restaurants.

■ UNIONS AND ASSOCIATIONS

Restaurant and food service managers are not represented by unions, but they can obtain useful resources and professional support from the National Restaurant Association and Educational Foundation, International Food Service Executives Association, and International Council on Hotel, Restaurant, and Institutional

Education. Restaurant and food service managers in Canada often join Restaurants Canada.

■ TIPS FOR ENTRY

1. Visit the following Web sites for job listings:
   - http://www.restaurant.org/Restaurant-Careers
   - http://www.careerbuilder.com
   - http://www.hcareers.com
2. Read publications about food service, hospitality, and tourism to learn more about trends in the industry and potential employers at https://www.chrie.org/i4a/pages/index.cfm?pageid=3275.
3. Become certified by the National Restaurant Association Educational Foundation and the International Food Service Executives Association in order to show employers that you have met the highest standards established by your industry.
4. Use social media such as Facebook, LinkedIn, and Twitter to stay up to date on industry developments and learn about job openings.

■ FOR MORE INFORMATION

For information on educational programs, contact

International Council on Hotel, Restaurant and Institutional Education
2810 North Parham, Suite 230
Richmond, VA 23294-4422
Tel: (804) 346-4800
Fax: (804) 346-5009
E-mail: membership@chrie.org
http://www.chrie.org

For information on certification, contact

International Food Service Executives Association
4955 Miller Street, Suite 107
Wheat Ridge, CO 80033-2294
Tel: (800) 893-5499
E-mail: ifseahqoffice@gmail.com
http://www.ifsea.com

For information on careers, contact

National Restaurant Association
2055 L Street, NW, Suite 700
Washington, D.C. 20036-4985
Tel: (800) 424-5156; (202) 331-5900
Fax: (202) 331-2429
E-mail: membership@restaurant.org
http://www.restaurant.org

For information on careers, training programs, and scholarships, contact

National Restaurant Association Educational Foundation
2055 L Street, NW
Washington, D.C. 20036-4983
Tel: (800) 424-5156
http://www.nraef.org

For information on careers in Canada, contact

Restaurants Canada
1155 Queen Street West
Toronto, ON M6J 1J4
Canada
Tel: (800) 387-5649; (416) 923-8416
Fax: (416) 923-1450
E-mail: info@restaurantscanada.org
http://www.crfa.ca

Retail Business Owners

■ OVERVIEW

Retail business owners are entrepreneurs who start or buy their own businesses or franchise operations. They are responsible for all aspects of a business operation, from planning and ordering merchandise to overseeing day-to-day operations. Retail business owners sell such items as clothing, household appliances, groceries, jewelry, and furniture.

■ HISTORY

Retailing is a vital commercial activity, providing customers with an opportunity to purchase goods and services from various types of merchants. The first retail outlets in America were trading posts and general stores. At trading posts, goods obtained from Native Americans were exchanged for items imported from Europe or manufactured in other parts of the country. As villages and towns grew, trading posts developed into general stores and began to sell food, farm necessities, and clothing. Typically run by a single person, these stores sometimes served as the post office and became the social and economic center of their communities.

Since World War II, giant supermarkets, discount houses, chain stores, and shopping malls have grown in popularity. Even so, individually owned businesses still thrive, often giving customers more personal and better-informed service. Moreover, despite the large growth in retail outlets and the increased competition that has accompanied it, retailing still provides the same basic, important function it did in the early years of the United States.

■ THE JOB

Although retail business owners sell a wide variety of products, from apples to automobiles, the basic job responsibilities remain the same. Simply stated, the retail business owner must do everything necessary to ensure the successful operation of a business.

There are five major categories of job responsibilities within a retail establishment: merchandising and buying, store operations, sales promotion and advertising, bookkeeping and accounting, and personnel supervision. Merchandising and buying determine the type and amount of actual goods to be sold. Store operations involve maintaining the building and providing for the movement of goods and personnel within the building. Sales promotion and advertising are the marketing methods used to inform customers and potential customers about the goods and services that are available. In bookkeeping and accounting, records are kept of payroll, taxes, and money spent and received. Managing personnel involves staffing the store with people who are trained and qualified to handle all the work that needs to be done.

The owner must be aware of all aspects of the business operation so that he or she can make informed decisions. Specific duties of an individual owner depend on the size of the store and the number of employees.

QUICK FACTS

ALTERNATE TITLE(S)
None

DUTIES
Start or buy their own businesses or franchises; responsible for merchandising and buying, store operations, sales promotion and advertising, bookkeeping and accounting, and personnel supervision

SALARY RANGE
$15,000 to $58,617 to $146,861+

WORK ENVIRONMENT
Primarily Indoors

BEST GEOGRAPHIC LOCATION(S)
Opportunities are available throughout the country

MINIMUM EDUCATION LEVEL
High School Diploma

SCHOOL SUBJECTS
Business, English, Mathematics

EXPERIENCE
Retail experience required

PERSONALITY TRAITS
Organized, Problem-Solving, Realistic

SKILLS
Business Management, Financial, Leadership

CERTIFICATION OR LICENSING
Required

SPECIAL REQUIREMENTS
None

EMPLOYMENT PROSPECTS
Fair

ADVANCEMENT PROSPECTS
Fair

OUTLOOK
About as Fast as the Average

NOC
0621

O*NET-SOC
N/A

CAREER LADDER

Owner of a Large Business or Multiple Franchises, or Consultant

Retail Business Owner

Retail Manager

Retail Sales Clerk

In a store with more than 10 employees, many of the operational, promotional, and personnel activities may be supervised by a manager. The owner may plan the overall purpose and function of the store and hire a manager to oversee the day-to-day operations. In a smaller store, the owner may also do much of the operational activities, including sweeping the floor, greeting customers, and balancing the accounting books.

In both large and small operations, an owner must keep up to date on product information, as well as on economic and technological conditions that may have an impact on business. This entails reading catalogs about product availability, checking current inventories and prices, and researching and implementing any technological advances that may make the operation more efficient. For example, an owner may decide to purchase data processing equipment to help with accounting functions, as well as to generate a mailing list to inform customers of special sales.

Because of the risks involved in opening a business and the many economic and managerial demands put on individual owners, a desire to open a retail business should be combined with proper management skills, sufficient economic backing, and a good sense of what the public wants. The large majority of retail businesses fail because of a lack of managerial experience on the part of owners.

Franchise ownership, whereby an individual owner obtains a license to sell an existing company's goods or services, grew phenomenally during the 1980s but has tapered off in recent years due to the economic slowdown in 2007. Franchise agreements enable the person who wants to open a business to receive expert advice from the sponsoring company about location, hiring and training of employees, arrangement of merchandise, display of goods, and record keeping. Some entrepreneurs, however, do not want to be limited to the product lines and other restrictions that accompany running a franchise store, or to split their profits with the franchise company. Franchise operations may still fail, but their likelihood of success is greater than that of a totally independent retail store.

■ EARNINGS

Earnings vary widely and are greatly influenced by the ability of the individual owner, the type of product or service being sold, and existing economic conditions. Some retail business owners may earn less than $15,000 a year, while the most successful owners earn hundreds of thousands of dollars or more. PayScale.com reported that owners/operators of small businesses earned median salaries of $58,617 in October 2016. Salaries ranged from $25,521 to $146,861.

■ WORK ENVIRONMENT

Retail business owners generally work in pleasant surroundings. Even so, ownership is a demanding occupation, with owners often working six or seven days a week. Working more than 60 hours a week is not unusual, especially during the Christmas season and other busy times. An owner of a large establishment may be able to leave a manager in charge of many parts of the business, but the owner still must be available to solve any pressing concerns. Owners of small businesses often stay in the store throughout the day, spending much of the time on their feet.

A retail business owner may occasionally travel out of town to attend conferences or to solicit new customers and product information. An owner of a small business, especially, should develop a close relationship with steady customers.

■ EXPLORING

Working full or part time as a sales clerk or in some other capacity within a retail business is a good way to learn about the responsibilities of operating a business. Talking with owners of small shops is also helpful, as is reading periodicals that publish articles on self-employment, such as *Entrepreneur* magazine (http://www.entrepreneur.com/magazine).

Most communities have a chamber of commerce whose members usually will be glad to share their insights into the career of a retail business owner. The Small Business Administration, an agency of the U.S. government, is another possible source of information.

■ EDUCATION AND TRAINING REQUIREMENTS
High School

A high school diploma is important in order to understand the basics of business ownership, though there are no specific educational or experiential requirements for this position. Course work in business administration is helpful, as is previous experience in the retail trade. Hard work, constant analysis, innovation, and evaluation, and sufficient capital are important elements of a successful business venture.

If you are interested in owning a business, you should take courses in mathematics, business management, and in business-related subjects, such as accounting, typing, and computer science. In addition, pursue English and other courses that enhance your communications skills. Specific skill areas also should be developed. For example, if you want to open an electronics repair shop, you should learn as much about electronics as possible.

Owners of small retail businesses often manage the store and work behind the counter. In such a case, the owner of a meat market is the butcher as well.

Postsecondary Training

As the business environment gets more and more competitive, many people are opting for an academic degree in order to get more training. A bachelor's program emphasizing business communications, marketing, business law, business management, and accounting should be pursued. Some people choose to get a master's in business administration or another related graduate degree. There are also special business schools that offer a one- or two-year program in business management. Some correspondence schools also offer courses on how to plan and run a business.

Other Education or Training

The National Retail Federation offers classes and other continuing education opportunities. Topics include customer service, management issues, sales training, buying, store operations, merchandising, and marketing. The Retail Design Institute provides workshops and seminars that educate participants about industry trends and developments in retail store design. The International Franchise Association offers continuing education classes, webinars, and workshops such as "Marketplace Fundamentals," "Cash Flow: How to Prevent Your Cash Flow From Going South," and "Knowledge-Driven Financial Performance." The U.S. Small Business Administration provides online classes in starting, funding, and managing a business at its online Small Business Learning Center (http://www.sba.gov/tools/sba-learning-center/search/training). It also offers in-person seminars and workshops at locations throughout the United States. Contact these organizations for more information.

■ CERTIFICATION, LICENSING, AND SPECIAL REQUIREMENTS
Certification or Licensing

The National Retail Federation Foundation offers the following voluntary designations to retail workers who successfully pass an assessment and meet other requirements: national professional certification in retail

Owner of a florist shop tracks orders on a computer while on the phone. (Kinga. Shutterstock.)

management, national professional certification in sales, national professional certification in customer service, and professional retail business credential. Contact the foundation for more information.

Some franchisers have their own certification process and require their franchisees to go through training. You may also want to receive the certified franchise executive designation offered by the Institute of Certified Franchise Executives, an organization affiliated with the International Franchise Association. This certification involves completing a certain number of courses in topics such as economics and franchise law, participating in events such as seminars or conventions, and work experience.

A business license may be a requirement in some states. Individual states or communities may have zoning codes or other regulations specifying what type of business can be located in a particular area. Check with your state's chamber of commerce or department of revenue for more information on obtaining a license.

■ EXPERIENCE, SKILLS, AND PERSONALITY TRAITS

Previous experience as a sales clerk or manager or in another retail position is generally required for aspiring retail business owners.

Whatever the experience and training, a retail business owner needs a lot of energy, patience, and fortitude to overcome the slow times and other difficulties involved in running a business. Other important personal characteristics include maturity, creativity, and good business judgment. Retail business owners should also be able to motivate employees and delegate authority.

TOP U.S. RETAILERS, 2015

The following were the top retailers in the United States in 2015. Read more about these companies to learn about retail trends.

1. Wal-Mart Stores
2. The Kroger Co.
3. Costco
4. The Home Depot
5. Walgreen
6. Target
7. CVS Caremark
8. Lowe's Companies
9. Amazon.com
10. Safeway

Source: National Retail Federation, *Top 100 Retailers*

■ EMPLOYMENT PROSPECTS

Employers

Retail is the largest private sector employer in the United States, employing more than 14 million Americans, according to the National Retail Federation. More than 95 percent of all U.S. retailers are single-store businesses, and more than 50 percent of all retail companies have fewer than five employees.

Starting Out

Few people start their career as an owner. Many start as a manager or in some other position within a retail business. While developing managerial skills or while pursuing a college degree or other relevant training, you should decide what type of business you would like to own. Many people decide to buy an existing business because it already has a proven track record and because banks and other lending institutions often are more likely to loan money to an existing facility. A retail business owner should anticipate having at least 50 percent of the money needed to start or buy a business. Some people find it helpful to have one or more partners in a business venture.

Owning a franchise is another way of starting a business without a large capital investment, as franchise agreements often involve some assistance in planning and start-up costs. Franchise operations, however, are not necessarily less expensive to run than a totally independent business.

■ ADVANCEMENT PROSPECTS

Because an owner is by definition the boss, there are limited opportunities for advancement. Advancement often takes the form of expansion of an existing business, leading to increased earnings and prestige. Expanding a business can also entail added risk, as it involves increasing operational costs. A successful franchise owner may be offered an additional franchise location or an executive position at the corporate headquarters.

A small number of successful independent business owners choose to franchise their business operations in different areas. Some owners become part-time consultants, while others teach a course at a college or university or in an adult education program. This teaching is often done not only for the financial rewards but as a way of helping others investigate the option of retail ownership.

■ OUTLOOK

The retail field is extremely competitive, and many businesses fail each year. The most common reason for failure is poor management. Thus people with some managerial experience or training will likely have the best chance at running a successful business.

The retail industry is directly affected by the economy and is negatively affected by financial downturns. In addition to overcoming economic slowdowns, retail businesses must also face increased competition from other retailers and direct-marketers, and the growth of Internet businesses in the next decade.

Another factor to consider is changing social and technological trends. Even in a down economy, a business catering to a hot new device or market may thrive, while once-successful business based on past trends or technology may fade fast.

■ UNIONS AND ASSOCIATIONS

Retail business owners do not belong to unions. Useful organizations for retail business owners include the National Retail Federation and the Retail Industry Leaders Association. The American Association of Franchisees & Dealers and the International Franchise Association offer memberships and professional resources to aspiring and current franchise owners. The American Franchisee Association is a national trade association of franchisees and dealers. The Small Business Administration is a federal agency that provides seminars, loans, and other helpful resources to aspiring and current business owners.

■ TIPS FOR ENTRY

1. Participate in retail-oriented internships or part-time jobs that are arranged by your high school or college's career services office.
2. The U.S. Small Business Administration offers comprehensive information about starting and funding a business at http://www.sba.gov/category/

navigation-structure/starting-managing-business/
starting-business.

3. Read *STORES* (http://www.stores.org) and *Entrepreneur* (http://www.entrepreneur.com/magazine) to learn more about the retail industry and starting a business.

4. Visit http://www.franchise.org/franchises.aspx for a database of franchising opportunities.

FOR MORE INFORMATION

For information about buying a franchise and a list of AAFD-accredited franchisers, contact

**American Association of Franchisees &
    Dealers (AAFD)**
PO Box 10158
Palm Desert, CA 92255-1058
Tel: (800) 733-9858; (619) 209-3775
Fax: (866) 855-1988
http://www.aafd.org

For articles about franchising, membership, and seminars, visit

American Franchisee Association
410 S Michigan Ave., Suite 528
Chicago, IL 60605
Tel: (312) 431-0545
Fax: (312) 431-1469
E-mail: spkezios@franchisee.org
http://www.franchisee.org

For general information about franchising, specific franchise opportunities, and publications, contact the IFA.

International Franchise Association (IFA)
1900 K Street, NW, Suite 700
Washington, D.C. 20006
Tel: (202) 628-8000
Fax: (202) 628-0812
http://www.franchise.org

For information on education, careers, and certification in the retail industry, contact

National Retail Federation
1101 New York Ave., NW
Washington, D.C. 20005
Tel: (800) 673-4692; (202) 783-7971
Fax: (202) 737-2849
http://www.nrf.com

For information on jobs in retail, contact

Retail Industry Leaders Association
1700 North Moore Street, Suite 2250
Arlington, VA 22209-1933

Tel: (703) 841-2300
Fax: (703) 841-1184
http://www.rila.org

To learn more about starting, funding, and operating a business, visit

U.S. Small Business Administration
409 Third Street, SW
Washington, D.C. 20416-0002
Tel: (800) 827-5722
E-mail: answerdesk@sba.gov
http://www.sba.gov

Retail Managers

OVERVIEW

Retail managers are responsible for the profitable operation of retail trade establishments. They oversee the selling of food, clothing, furniture, sporting goods, novelties, and many other items. Their duties include hiring, training, and supervising other employees, maintaining the physical facilities, managing inventory, monitoring expenditures and receipts, and maintaining good public relations. Retail managers hold more than 1.2 million jobs in the United States.

HISTORY

In the United States, small, family-owned stores have been around for centuries. The first large chain store began to operate in the late 19th century. One of the aims of early chain stores was to provide staples for the pioneers of the newly settled West. Because chain store corporations were able to buy goods in large quantities and store them in warehouses, they were able to undersell private merchants.

The number of retail stores, especially supermarkets, began to grow rapidly during the 1930s. Stores often were owned and operated by chain corporations, which were able to benefit from bulk buying and more sophisticated storage practices. Cheaper transportation also contributed to the growth of retail stores because goods could be shipped and sold more economically.

Unlike the early family-owned stores, giant retail outlets employed large numbers of people, requiring various levels of management to oversee the business. Retail managers were hired to oversee particular areas within department stores, for example, but higher-level managers also were needed to make more general decisions about a company's goals and policies. Today, retailing is the largest private sector employer in the United States.

QUICK FACTS

ALTERNATE TITLE(S)
None

DUTIES
Operate retail trade
  establishments by performing
  a wide range of duties,
  from hiring, training, and
  supervising staff, to managing
  inventory and maintaining the
  physical facilities

SALARY RANGE
$23,770 to $38,310 to
  $100,000+

WORK ENVIRONMENT
Primarily Indoors

BEST GEOGRAPHIC LOCATION(S)
Opportunities are available
  throughout the country

MINIMUM EDUCATION LEVEL
High School Diploma

SCHOOL SUBJECTS
Business, Economics,
  Mathematics

EXPERIENCE
Retail experience required

PERSONALITY TRAITS
Enterprising, Organized,
  Problem-Solving

SKILLS
Business Management,
  Interpersonal, Leadership

CERTIFICATION OR LICENSING
Recommended

SPECIAL REQUIREMENTS
None

EMPLOYMENT PROSPECTS
Good

ADVANCEMENT PROSPECTS
Good

OUTLOOK
Little Change or More Slowly
  than the Average

NOC
0621, 6211

O*NET-SOC
41-1011.00

■ THE JOB

Retail managers are responsible for every phase of a store's operation. They are often one of the first employees to arrive in the morning and the last to leave at night. Their duties include hiring, training, and supervising other employees, maintaining the physical facilities, managing inventory, monitoring expenditures and receipts, and maintaining good public relations.

Perhaps the most important responsibility of retail managers is hiring and training qualified employees. Managers then assign duties to employees, monitor their progress, promote employees, and increase salaries when appropriate. When an employee's performance is not satisfactory, a manager must find a way to improve the performance or, if necessary, fire him or her.

Managers should be good at working with all different kinds of people. Differences of opinion and personality clashes among employees are inevitable, however, and the manager must be able to restore good feelings among the staff. Managers often have to deal with upset customers, and must attempt to restore goodwill toward the store when customers are dissatisfied.

Retail managers keep accurate and up-to-date records of store inventory. When new merchandise arrives, the manager ensures items are recorded, priced, and displayed or shelved. They must know when stock is getting low and order new items in a timely manner.

Some managers are responsible for merchandise promotions and advertising. The manager may confer with an advertising agency representative to determine appropriate advertising methods for the store. The manager may also decide what products to put on sale for advertising purposes.

The duties of store managers vary according to the type of merchandise sold, the size of the store, and the number of employees. In small, owner-operated stores, managers are often involved in accounting, data processing, marketing, research, sales, and shipping. In large retail corporations, however, managers may be involved in only one or two of these activities.

■ EARNINGS

Salaries depend on the size of the store, the responsibilities of the job, and the number of customers served. According to the U.S. Department of Labor, median annual earnings of supervisors of retail sales workers, including commission, were $38,310 in May 2015. Salaries ranged from less than $23,770 to more than $64,640 per year. Mean annual earnings of grocery store managers were $41,460, and managers of clothing stores earned $40,600. Those who managed automobile dealerships ranked among the highest paid at $80,300. Managers who oversee an entire region for a retail chain can earn more than $100,000.

In addition to a salary and fringe benefits (health insurance, paid vacation, etc.), some stores offer their managers special bonuses, or commissions, which are typically connected to the store's performance. Many stores also offer employee discounts on store merchandise.

■ WORK ENVIRONMENT

Most retail stores are pleasant places to work, and managers are often given comfortable offices. Many, however, work long hours. Managers often work six days a week and as many as 60 hours a week, especially during busy times of the year such as during the holidays. Because holiday seasons are peak shopping periods, it is extremely rare that managers can take holidays off or schedule vacations around a holiday, even if the store is not open on that day.

Although managers usually can get away from the store during slow times, they must often be present if the store is open at night. It is important that the manager be available to handle the store's daily receipts, which are usually put in a safe or taken to a bank's night depository at the close of the business day.

■ EXPLORING

If you are interested in becoming a retail manager, you may be able to find part-time, weekend, or summer jobs in a clothing store, supermarket, or other retail trade establishment. You can gain valuable work experience through such jobs and will have the opportunity to observe the retail industry to determine whether you are interested in pursuing a career in it. You can ask about job openings in the stores you regularly visit, or search for listings on stores' Web sites and on employment sites such as AllRetailJobs.com (http://www.allretailjobs .com). It also is useful to read periodicals that publish articles on the retail field, such as *Stores* (http://www .stores.org), published by the National Retail Federation.

■ EDUCATION AND TRAINING REQUIREMENTS
High School

You will need at least a high school education in order to become a retail manager. Helpful courses include business, mathematics, marketing, and economics. English and speech classes are also important. These courses will teach you to communicate effectively with all types of people, including employees and customers.

Postsecondary Training

Most retail stores prefer applicants with a college degree, and many hire only college graduates. Liberal arts, social sciences, and business are the most common degrees held by retail managers.

To prepare for a career as a retail store manager, take courses in accounting, business, marketing, English, advertising, and computer science. If you are unable to attend college as a full-time student, consider getting a job in a store to gain experience and attend college part time. All managers, regardless of their education, must have good marketing, analytical, communication, and people skills.

Many large retail stores and national chains have established formal training programs, including classroom instruction, for their new employees. The training period may last a week or as long as one year. Training for a department store manager, for example, may include working as a salesperson in several departments in order to learn about the store's operations. Training classes usually include interviewing, customer service skills, inventory management, employee relations, and scheduling. Retail franchise training programs are comprehensive: Trainees usually learn everything about the company's operations, from budgeting, marketing, management, finance, and purchasing, to product preparation, human resource management, and compensation.

Other Education or Training

The National Retail Federation offers classes and other continuing education opportunities. Topics include customer service, management issues, sales training, buying, store operations, merchandising, and marketing. The Retail Design Institute offers workshops and seminars that educate participants about industry trends and developments in retail store design. Contact these organizations for more information.

■ CERTIFICATION, LICENSING, AND SPECIAL REQUIREMENTS
Certification or Licensing

The National Retail Federation Foundation offers the following voluntary

CAREER LADDER

Retail Business Owner

Purchasing Manager, or Buyer, or Purchasing Agent

Retail Manager

Assistant Retail Manager

Retail Sales Worker or Clerk

A grocery store manager organizes a store display. (Tyler Olson. Shutterstock.)

GUIDES TO RETAIL MANAGEMENT

LEARN MORE ABOUT IT

Averwater, Chip. *Retail Truths: The Unconventional Wisdom of Retailing.* Milwaukee, Wisc.: Hal Leonard Corporation, 2013.

Berman, Barry, and Joel R. Evans. *Retail Management: A Strategic Approach,* 12th ed. Upper Saddle River, N.J.: Prentice Hall, 2012.

Levy, Michael, Barton A. Weitz, and Dhruv Grewal. *Retailing Management,* 9th ed. New York: McGraw-Hill, 2013.

Stephens, Doug. *The Retail Revival: Reimagining Business for the New Age of Consumerism.* Hoboken, N.J.: John Wiley & Sons, 2013.

designations to retail workers who successfully pass an assessment and meet other requirements: national professional certification in retail management, national professional certification in sales, national professional certification in customer service, and professional retail business credential. Contact the foundation for more information.

■ EXPERIENCE, SKILLS, AND PERSONALITY TRAITS

Previous experience in the retail industry as an assistant manager or clerk is highly recommended.

To be a successful retail manager, you should have good communication skills, enjoy working with and supervising people, and be willing to put in very long hours. Diplomacy is often necessary when creating schedules for workers and in disciplinary matters. There is a great deal of responsibility in retail management and such positions can be stressful. A calm disposition and ability to handle stress will serve you well.

■ EMPLOYMENT PROSPECTS
Employers

There are more than 1.2 million retail managers in the United States, and about 34 percent are self-employed (many are store owners). Nearly every type of retail business requires management, though small businesses may be run by their owners. Wherever retail sales are made there is an opportunity for a management position, though most people have to begin in a much lower job. The food industry employs more workers than nearly any other, and retail food businesses always need managers, though smaller businesses may not pay very well. In general, the larger the business and the bigger the city, the more a retail manager can earn. Most other retail managers work in grocery and department stores, motor vehicle dealerships, and clothing and accessory stores.

Starting Out

Many new college graduates are able to find managerial positions through their schools' career services offices. Some of the large retail chains recruit on college campuses.

Not all store managers, however, are college graduates. Many store managers are promoted to their positions from jobs of less responsibility within their organization. Some may be in the retail industry for more than a dozen years before being promoted. Those with more education often receive promotions faster.

Regardless of educational background, people who are interested in the retail industry should consider working in a retail store at least part time or during the summer. Although there may not be an opening when the application is made, there often is a high turnover of employees in retail management, and vacancies occur frequently.

■ ADVANCEMENT PROSPECTS

Advancement opportunities in retailing vary according to the size of the store, where the store is located, and the type of merchandise sold. Advancement also depends on the individual's work experience and educational background.

A store manager who works for a large retail chain, for example, may be given responsibility for a number of stores in a given area or region or transferred to a larger store in another city. Willingness to relocate to a new city may increase an employee's promotional opportunities.

Some managers may become purchasing managers, buyers, or purchasing agents. Others may decide to open their own stores after they have acquired enough experience in the retail industry. After working as a retail manager for a large chain of clothing stores, for example, a person may decide to open a small boutique.

Sometimes becoming a retail manager involves a series of promotions. A person who works in a supermarket, for example, may advance from clerk, checker, or bagger to a regular assignment in one of several departments in the store. After a period of time, he or she may become an assistant manager and eventually, a manager.

■ OUTLOOK

Employment of retail managers is expected to grow as fast as the average for all occupations through 2024.

Although retailers have reduced their management staff to cut costs and make operations more efficient, there are still good opportunities in retailing. Opportunities will be best in wholesale clubs, superstores, and discount department stores. Competition for all jobs will continue to be keen, however, and computerized systems for inventory control may reduce the need for some managers. Applicants with the best educational backgrounds and work experience will have the best chances of finding jobs. There will always be a need for retail managers, however, as long as retail stores exist. Retail manager positions are rarely affected by corporate restructuring at retail headquarters; this has a greater impact on home office staff.

UNIONS AND ASSOCIATIONS

Retail managers do not belong to unions. Useful organizations for retail workers include the National Retail Federation and the Retail Industry Leaders Association.

TIPS FOR ENTRY

1. Visit the National Retail Federation's Retail Careers Center (http://www.nrffoundation.com/content/retail-careers-center) for job listings, information on retail education programs, an overview of retail career paths, and career advice.
2. Check with local retailers for job opportunities.
3. Obtain sales experience in order to make yourself more attractive to potential employers.
4. Participate in retail-oriented internships or part-time jobs that are arranged by your high school or college's career services office.

FOR MORE INFORMATION

For information on education and careers in the retail industry, contact

National Retail Federation
325 7th Street, NW, Suite 1100
Washington, D.C. 20004-2825
Tel: (800) 673-4692; (202) 783-7971
Fax: (202) 737-2849
http://www.nrf.com

For information on jobs in retail, contact

Retail Industry Leaders Association
1700 North Moore Street, Suite 2250
Arlington, VA 22209-1933
Tel: (703) 841-2300
Fax: (703) 841-1184
http://www.rila.org

MOST NEW JOBS

Retail Sales Workers

OVERVIEW

Retail sales workers assist customers with purchases by identifying their needs, showing or demonstrating merchandise, receiving payment, recording sales, and wrapping their purchases or arranging for their delivery. They are sometimes called *sales clerks*, *retail clerks*, or *salespeople*. There are more than 4.8 million retail salespersons employed in the United States.

HISTORY

The Industrial Revolution and its techniques of mass production encouraged the development of specialized retail establishments. The first retail outlets in the United States were trading posts and general stores. At trading posts, goods obtained from Native Americans were exchanged for items imported from Europe or manufactured in the eastern United States. Trading posts had to be located on the fringes of settlements and relocated to follow the westward movement of the frontier. As villages and towns grew, what had been trading posts frequently developed into general stores. General stores sold food staples, farm necessities, and clothing. They often served as the local post office and became the social and economic centers of their communities. They were sometimes known as dry goods stores.

A number of changes occurred in the retail field during the second half of the 19th century. The growth of specialized retail stores (such as hardware, feed, grocery, and drugstores) reflected the growing sophistication of available products and customer tastes. The first grocery chain store, which started in New York City in 1859, led to a new concept in retailing. Later, merchants such as Marshall Field developed huge department stores, so named because of their large number of separate departments. Their variety of merchandise, ability to advertise their products, and low selling prices contributed to the rapid growth and success of these stores. Retail sales workers staffed the departments, and they became the stores' primary representatives to the public.

The 20th century witnessed the birth of supermarkets and suburban shopping centers, the emergence of discount houses, and the expansion of credit buying. Today, retailing is the largest private sector employer in

QUICK FACTS

ALTERNATE TITLE(S)
Retail Clerks, Sales Clerks, Salespersons

DUTIES
Perform a wide range of duties at retail stores, from waiting on customers and accepting payment, to stocking goods and preparing window displays

SALARY RANGE
$17,326 to $21,770 to $40,206+

WORK ENVIRONMENT
Primarily Indoors

BEST GEOGRAPHIC LOCATION(S)
Opportunities are available throughout the country, but the vast majority of positions are located in large cities and suburban areas

MINIMUM EDUCATION LEVEL
High School Diploma

SCHOOL SUBJECTS
English, Mathematics, Speech

EXPERIENCE
On-the-job training

PERSONALITY TRAITS
Conventional, Helpful, Outgoing

SKILLS
Interpersonal, Public Speaking, Sales

CERTIFICATION OR LICENSING
Recommended

SPECIAL REQUIREMENTS
Some states set a minimum age of 14 and require at least a high school diploma

EMPLOYMENT PROSPECTS
Excellent

ADVANCEMENT PROSPECTS
Good

OUTLOOK
About as Fast as the Average

NOC
6421

O*NET-SOC
41-2031.00

the United States. Clothing and department stores are the largest employers of sales workers, followed by building material and supplies dealers, and other general merchandise stores. All of these retailers, as well as many others, hire sales workers.

■ THE JOB

Salespeople work in more than 100 different types of retail establishments in a variety of roles. Some, for example, work in small specialty shops where, in addition to waiting on customers, they might check inventory, order stock from sales representatives (or by telephone or e-mail), place newspaper display advertisements, prepare window displays, and rearrange merchandise for sale.

Other salespeople may work in specific departments, such as the furniture department, of a large department store. The employees in a department work in shifts to provide service to customers six or seven days a week. To improve their sales effectiveness and knowledge of merchandise, they attend regular staff meetings. Advertising, window decorating, sales promotion, buying, and market research specialists support the work of retail salespeople.

Whatever they are selling, the primary responsibility of retail sales workers is to interest customers in the merchandise. This might be done by describing the product's features, demonstrating its use, or showing various models and colors. Some retail sales workers must have specialized knowledge, particularly those who sell such expensive, complicated products as stereos, appliances, and personal computers.

In addition to selling, most retail sales workers make out sales checks; receive cash, checks, and charge payments; bag or package purchases; and give change and receipts. Depending on the hours they work, retail sales workers might have to open or close the cash register. This might include counting the money in the cash register; separating charge slips, coupons, and exchange vouchers; and making deposits at the cash office. The sales records they keep are normally used in inventory control. Sales workers are usually held responsible for the contents of their registers, and repeated shortages are cause for dismissal in many organizations.

Sales workers must be aware of any promotions the store is sponsoring and know the store's policies and procedures, especially on returns and exchanges. Also, they often must recognize possible security risks and know how to handle such situations.

Consumers often form their impressions of a store by its sales force. To stay ahead in the fiercely competitive retail industry, employers are increasingly stressing the importance of providing courteous and efficient service. When a customer wants an item that is not on the sales floor, for example, the sales worker might be expected to check the stockroom and, if necessary, place a special order or call another store to locate the item.

■ EARNINGS

Most beginning sales workers start at the federal minimum wage, which is $7.25 an hour. Wages vary greatly, depending primarily on the type of store and the degree of skill required. Businesses might offer higher wages to attract and retain workers.

Department stores or retail chains might pay more than smaller stores. Higher wages are paid for positions requiring a greater degree of skill. Many sales workers also receive a commission (often 4 to 8 percent) on their sales or are paid solely on commission. According to the Department of Labor, median hourly earnings of retail salespersons, including commission, were $10.47 in May 2015. A yearly salary for full-time work therefore averages $21,770. Wages ranged from less than $8.35 ($17,326 a year) to more than $19.33 an hour ($40,206 a year). Sales workers in building material and supplies dealers earned mean hourly wages of $12.06 ($24,120 a year); motor vehicle and parts dealers earned mean hourly wages of $14.79 ($30,763 a year); sporting goods, hobby, book and music stores earned mean hourly wages of $9.80 ($20,384 a year); and clothing and accessories stores earned mean hourly wages of $9.57 ($19,905 a year)

Salespeople in many retail stores are allowed a discount on their own purchases, ranging from 10 to 25 percent. This privilege is sometimes extended to the worker's family. Meals in the employee cafeterias maintained by large stores might be served at a price that is below cost. Many stores provide sick leave, medical and life insurance, and retirement benefits for full-time workers. Most stores give paid vacations.

■ WORK ENVIRONMENT

Retail sales workers generally work in clean, comfortable, well-lighted areas. Those with seniority have reasonably good job security. When business is slow, stores might curtail hiring and not fill vacancies that occur. Most stores, however, are able to weather mild recessions in business without having to release experienced sales workers. During periods of economic recession, competition among salespeople for job openings can become intense.

With more than 3.6 million retail establishments across the country, sales positions are found in every region. An experienced salesperson can find employment in almost any state. The vast majority of positions, however, are located in large cities or suburban areas.

The five-day, 40-hour workweek is the exception rather than the rule in retailing. Most salespeople can expect to work some evening and weekend hours, and longer than normal hours might be scheduled during Christmas and other peak periods. In addition, most retailers restrict the use of vacation time between Thanksgiving and early January. Most sales workers receive overtime pay during Christmas and other rush seasons. Part-time salespeople generally work at peak hours of business, supplementing the full-time staff. Because competition in the retailing business is keen, many retailers work under pressure. The sales worker might not be directly involved but will feel the pressures of the industry in subtle ways. The sales worker must be able to adjust to alternating periods of high activity and dull monotony. No two days—or even customers—are alike. Because some customers are hostile and rude, salespeople must learn to exercise tact and patience at all times.

■ EXPLORING

Because of its seasonal nature, retailing offers numerous opportunities for temporary or part-time sales experience. Most stores add extra personnel during the holiday season. Vacation areas may hire sales employees, usually high school or college students, on a seasonal basis. Fewer sales positions are available in metropolitan areas during the summer, as this is frequently the slowest time of the year.

Another way to learn more about retailing is through "distributive education" programs, created by high schools and junior colleges to combine courses in retailing with part-time work in the field. The distributive education student may receive academic credit for this work experience in addition to regular wages. Store owners cooperating in these programs often hire students as full-time personnel upon completion of the program.

CAREER LADDER

Retail Business Owner

Supervisor or Department Manager

Senior Sales Worker

Retail Sales Clerk

Stock Clerk

■ EDUCATION AND TRAINING REQUIREMENTS
High School

Employers generally prefer to hire high school graduates for most sales positions. Such subjects as English, speech, and mathematics provide a good background for these jobs. Many high schools and two-year colleges have special programs that include courses in merchandising, principles of retailing, and retail selling.

Postsecondary Training

In retail sales, as in other fields, the level of opportunity tends to coincide with the level of a person's education. In many stores, college graduates enter immediately into on-the-job training programs to prepare them for management assignments. Successful and experienced workers who do not have a degree might also qualify for these programs. Useful college courses include economics, business administration, and marketing. Many colleges offer majors in retailing. Executives in many companies express a strong preference for liberal arts graduates, especially those with some business courses or a master's degree in business administration.

Other Education or Training

The National Retail Federation offers classes and other continuing education opportunities. Topics include customer service, management issues, sales training, purchasing, store operations, merchandising, and marketing. The Retail Design Institute offers workshops and seminars that educate participants about industry trends and developments in retail store design. Contact these organizations for more information.

■ CERTIFICATION, LICENSING, AND SPECIAL REQUIREMENTS
Certification or Licensing

The National Retail Federation Foundation offers the following voluntary designations to retail workers who

A salesperson assists a customer with a product in a gourmet foods store. (Tyler Olson. Shutterstock.)

successfully pass an assessment and meet other requirements: national professional certification in retail management, national professional certification in sales, national professional certification in customer service, and professional retail business credential. Contact the foundation for more information.

Other Requirements

Most states have established minimum standards that govern retail employment. Some states set a minimum age of 14, require at least a high school diploma, or prohibit more than eight hours of work a day or 48 hours in any six days. These requirements are often relaxed during the holiday season.

■ EXPERIENCE, SKILLS, AND PERSONALITY TRAITS

Any sales experience you can obtain will be a plus. Get a job at clothing or department stores to gain experience in the retail industry. Contact stores in your area to learn more about opportunities.

The retail sales worker must be in good health. Many selling positions require standing most of the day. The sales worker must have stamina to face the grueling pace of busy times, such as weekends and the Christmas season, while at the same time remaining pleasant and effective. Personal appearance is important. Salespeople should be neat and well groomed and have an outgoing personality.

A pleasant speaking voice, natural friendliness, tact, and patience are all helpful personal characteristics. The sales worker must be able to converse easily with strangers of all ages. In addition to interpersonal skills, sales workers must be equally good with figures. They should be able to add and subtract accurately and quickly and operate cash registers and other types of business machines.

■ EMPLOYMENT PROSPECTS
Employers

More than 4.8 million retail salespersons are employed in the United States. There are many different types of retail establishments, ranging from small specialty shops that appeal to collectors to large retailers that sell everything from eyeglasses to DVD players. The largest employers of retail salespersons are department stores, clothing and accessories stores, building material and garden equipment stores, home furnishings stores, automobile dealers, and sporting goods, hobby, and musical instrument stores. Retail sales workers can have just one or two coworkers or well over 100, depending on the size of the establishment.

Starting Out

If they have openings, retail stores usually hire beginning salespeople who come in and fill out an application. Major department stores maintain extensive personnel departments, while in smaller stores the manager might do the hiring. Occasionally, sales applicants are given an aptitude test.

Young people might be hired immediately for sales positions. Often, however, they begin by working in the stockroom as clerks, helping to set up merchandise displays, or assisting in the receiving or shipping departments. After a while they might be moved up to a sales assignment.

Training varies with the type and size of the store. In large stores, the beginner might benefit from formal training courses that cover sales techniques, store policies, the mechanics of recording sales, and an overview of the entire store. Programs of this type are usually followed by on-the-job sales supervision. The beginner in a small store might receive personal instruction from the manager or a senior sales worker, followed by supervised sales experience.

College graduates and people with successful sales experience often enter executive training programs (sometimes referred to as flying squads because they move rapidly through different parts of the store). As they rotate through various departments, the trainees are exposed to merchandising methods, stock and inventory control, advertising, buying, credit, and personnel. By spending time in each of these areas, trainees receive a broad retailing background designed to help them as they advance into the ranks of management.

■ ADVANCEMENT PROSPECTS

Large stores have the most opportunities for promotion. Retailing, however, is a mobile field, and successful and experienced people can readily change employment. This is one of the few fields where, if the salesperson has the necessary initiative and ability, advancement to executive positions is possible regardless of education.

When first on the job, sales workers develop their career potential by specializing in a particular line of merchandise. They become authorities on a certain product line, such as sporting equipment, women's suits, or building materials. Many good sales workers prefer the role of the *senior sales worker* and remain at this level. Others might be asked to become supervisor of a section. Eventually they might develop into a *department manager, floor manager, division or branch manager,* or *general manager.*

People with sales experience often enter related areas, such as buying. Other retail store workers advance into support areas, such as personnel, accounting, public relations, and credit.

Young people with ability find that retailing offers the opportunity for unusually rapid advancement. Many retail executives are under 35 years of age. It is not uncommon for a person under 35 to be in charge of a retail store or department with an annual sales volume of over $1,000,000. Conversely, a retail executive who makes bad merchandising judgments might quickly be out of a job.

■ OUTLOOK

More than 4.8 million people are employed as sales workers in retail stores of all types and sizes. The employment of sales personnel should grow about as fast as the average for all occupations through 2024, according to the U.S. Department of Labor. Turnover among sales workers is much higher than the average for other occupations. Many of the expected employment opportunities will stem from the need to replace workers. Other

SELLING IN RETAIL

LEARN MORE ABOUT IT

Bell, Judith, and Kate Ternus. *Silent Selling: Best Practices and Effective Strategies in Visual Merchandising,* 4th ed. New York: Fairchild Books, 2011.

Friedman, Harry J. *No Thanks, I'm Just Looking: Sales Techniques for Turning Shoppers into Buyers.* Hoboken, N.J: John Wiley & Sons, 2012.

Gallagher, Richard S. *The Customer Service Survival Kit: What to Say to Defuse Even the Worst Customer Situations.* New York: AMACOM, 2013.

Hudson, Matthew, and Rick Segel. *The Retail Sales Bible: The Great Book of G.R.E.A.T. Selling.* Kissimmee, Fla.: Specific House Publishing, 2011.

positions will result from existing stores' staffing for longer business hours or reducing the length of the average employee workweek.

As drug, variety, grocery, and other stores have rapidly converted to self-service operations, they will need fewer sales workers. At the same time, many products, such as electrical appliances, home audio systems, computers, and sporting goods, do not lend themselves to self-service operations. These products require extremely skilled sales workers to assist customers and explain the benefits of various makes and models. On balance, as easy-to-sell goods will be increasingly marketed in self-service stores, the demand in the future will be strongest for sales workers who are knowledgeable about particular types of products.

During economic recessions, sales volume and the resulting demand for sales workers generally decline. Purchases of costly items, such as cars, appliances, and furniture, tend to be postponed during difficult economic times. In areas of high unemployment, sales of all types of goods might decline. Since turnover of sales workers is usually very high, however, employers often can cut payrolls simply by not replacing all those who leave. Stores that offer a variety of products at low prices, such as general merchandise stores and discount warehouses, are expected to have strong employment growth. Employment at department stores is expected to grow more slowly than the average for all careers through 2024.

There should continue to be good opportunities for temporary and part-time workers, especially during the holidays. Stores are particularly interested in people who, by returning year after year, develop good sales backgrounds.

■ UNIONS AND ASSOCIATIONS

Retail sales workers may be represented by the United Food and Commercial Workers International Union. The National Retail Federation is the world's largest retail trade association. It represents discount and department stores, Main Street merchants, grocers, home goods and specialty stores, wholesalers, and other retailers from the United States and more than 45 countries.

■ TIPS FOR ENTRY

1. Visit the National Retail Federation's Retail Careers Center (http://www.nrffoundation.com/content/retail-careers-center) for job listings, information on retail education programs, an overview of retail career paths, and career advice.
2. Participate in retail-oriented internships or part-time jobs that are arranged by your high school or college's career services office.
3. Become certified by the National Retail Federation in order to show employers that you have met the highest standards set by your industry.
4. Obtain sales experience in order to make yourself more attractive to potential employers.

■ FOR MORE INFORMATION

For information on education and careers in the retail industry, contact

National Retail Federation
1101 New York Ave., NW
Washington, D.C. 20005
Tel: (800) 673-4692; (202) 783-7971
Fax: (202) 737-2849
http://www.nrf.com

For information on union membership, visit

**United Food and Commercial Workers
    International Union**
http://www.ufcw.org

Retirement Planners

■ OVERVIEW

Financial planners help people invest for the future. *Retirement planners* are financial planners who specialize in the financial needs and concerns of people planning for retirement. Some retirement planners work for corporations of all sizes; many others are self-employed. Retirement planners have diverse backgrounds in fields such as banking, accounting, law, and

life insurance. There are approximately 249,400 personal financial advisers working in the United States.

■ HISTORY

In the 20th century, several factors, including population growth, technological advances, and work efficiency, greatly affected employment for older employees. As the pool of young workers grew, employers began to set work age restrictions that were altered by several laws through the years. (One note: In 1986 a federal law was passed that prohibited mandatory retirement for most workers.) The Social Security Act of 1935 gave workers and their families retirement benefits, among other social welfare programs. Depending on the age of retirement, insured workers receive monthly benefits—full benefits are allowed after age 65; early retirement after age 62 allows for 80 percent of benefits. Workers who choose to work beyond age 65 receive increased benefits.

Most people have found Social Security insufficient, especially to maintain their previous standard of living during their retirement years. To supplement retirement income, people have increasingly relied on pension plans, company profit sharing, individual retirement accounts (IRAs), and other forms of investments. Today, most workers are aware of the importance of saving and planning for retirement. They often turn to knowledgeable professionals for financial advice and strategies. The field of retirement planning grew as a specialty from traditional financial planning services. Such planners and counselors are in demand to create and administer financial retirement plans. They also address other important retirement issues such as relocation, medical insurance needs, income tax, wills, and estate planning.

■ THE JOB

Financial planners, especially those specializing in retirement issues, tailor saving strategies to ensure that a client can live a comfortable lifestyle during his or her retirement years.

The first task of retirement planners is to meet with clients (or set up a phone consultation) to gather information. They must ascertain a client's net worth by collecting tax forms, insurance papers, and data regarding income, assets and debts, and trusts, among other information. Then the planner determines what the client's needs and goals will be for his or her retirement years. There is a big difference between simple living and first-class travel to exotic locales. Relocation and medical insurance are also major concerns to address. Once the data is compiled, the retirement planner researches and presents the best means to achieve the client's retirement objectives.

A good retirement planner will assess a client's financial history—pointing out relevant areas such as tax returns, insurance policies, company savings plans, and investments. Planners also identify what areas, if any, a client needs to strengthen, such as improving investment returns or consolidating debts. They will discuss investment preferences and risk levels comfortable to the client. Traditional sources of retirement funds include Social Security, personal savings (IRAs, stocks and bonds, real estate, and other investments), employer-sponsored plans, post-retirement employment, and inheritance.

Retirement planners also help prepare clients for the possibility of incapacity, disability, and the need for chronic-illness care during retirement. Disability income insurance, long-term care insurance, or a medical savings account may be suggested as precautions for such situations. Many companies, in an attempt to restructure or downsize, offer their employees the option for early retirement, complete with incentives. Retirement planners are consulted as to the benefits or downfalls of early retirement.

Many retirement planners stay in frequent touch with their clients, with some checking in quarterly. The economy and stock market are often volatile and clients' needs and situations change, so it is imperative to make constant assessments. A yearly reevaluation is necessary, at minimum. Such considerations are key to maintaining good rapport with clients and helping them to stay on track for a financially stable retirement.

■ EARNINGS

The U.S. Department of Labor reports that median annual earnings for personal financial advisers, which includes retirement planners, were $89,360 in May 2015, with the lowest 10 percent earning less than $39,300, and the highest 25 percent earning more than $187,200. Many retirement planners, especially those who are self-employed, charge their clients an hourly rate for their services or a flat fee for a comprehensive plan. These rates and fees vary according to the complexity of the work the planner must do. Retirement planners sometimes receive commissions on the products they sell, in addition to their standard fees.

Retirement planners who are salaried employees of companies or financial planning firms receive fringe benefits such as health insurance and paid vacation and sick days. Self-employed planners must provide their own benefits.

■ WORK ENVIRONMENT

Most retirement planners work 40 hours or more a week, depending on the number of clients and businesses they represent. The majority of their workday is spent in the office doing research or meeting with clients. However, financial planners may also travel to their client's business, home, or other designated places.

■ EXPLORING

Check out the financial planning information available on the Internet to familiarize yourself with the industry. Visit Web sites such as About. com: Retirement Planning (http://retireplan.about.com). The U.S. Department of Labor also offers the free booklet "What You Should Know about Your Retirement Plan," which can be found at http://www.dol.gov/ebsa/publications/wyskapr.html. Another way to explore the field is through part-time work or an internship with a financial planner or brokerage house. This will allow you to get work experience, and provide an insider's peek at the industry.

Conduct information interviews with financial planners and ask them for advice on preparing for and entering the field. The Financial Planning Association (http://www.fpanet.org/PlannerSearch/PlannerSearch.aspx) and the National Association of Personal Financial Advisors (http://findanadvisor.napfa.org/Home.aspx) offer member lists at their Web sites.

■ EDUCATION AND TRAINING REQUIREMENTS
High School

Take as many business and mathematics courses in high school as possible. Speech classes will help you hone your oral communication skills, while English classes will give you the basics necessary to write reports for your clients.

QUICK FACTS

ALTERNATE TITLE(S)
Financial Planners, Personal Financial Advisers

DUTIES
Help people make financial plans for retirement

SALARY RANGE
$39,300 to $89,360 to $187,200+

WORK ENVIRONMENT
Primarily Indoors

BEST GEOGRAPHIC LOCATION(S)
Opportunities are available throughout the country, but many planners are based in New York, California, and Florida

MINIMUM EDUCATION LEVEL
Bachelor's Degree

SCHOOL SUBJECTS
Business, Economics, Mathematics

EXPERIENCE
Internship, co-op, or part-time job

PERSONALITY TRAITS
Helpful, Organized, Technical

SKILLS
Business Management, Financial, Interpersonal

CERTIFICATION OR LICENSING
Recommended

SPECIAL REQUIREMENTS
None

EMPLOYMENT PROSPECTS
Fair

ADVANCEMENT PROSPECTS
Fair

OUTLOOK
Much Faster than the Average

NOC
1114

O*NET-SOC
13-2052.00

CAREER LADDER

Teacher or Owner of Financial Planning Firm

Experienced Retirement Planner With a Large Client Base

Entry-Level Retirement Planner

Postsecondary Training

A bachelor's degree is generally the basic requirement for a career in retirement planning. Most retirement planners and other financial advisers hold degrees in accounting, business, finance, mathematics, law, or economics, as these directly relate to the type of work that planners do. Courses in taxes, estate planning, and risk management are especially helpful. You should also be sure to take classes in communication and public speaking, as interacting with clients is the cornerstone of this business. Good computer skills are also a must.

Other Education or Training

Keeping up with industry developments is key to success as a retirement planner. Professional associations often provide continuing education opportunities. For example, the Financial Planning Association offers continuing education (CE) classes, workshops, webinars, and seminars on communication and organizational skills, sales and marketing, and business and practice management. The National Association of Personal Financial Advisors also offers CE opportunities. Contact these organizations for more information.

■ CERTIFICATION, LICENSING, AND SPECIAL REQUIREMENTS
Certification or Licensing

Because of their diverse backgrounds, financial planners have many different educational degrees and licenses.

A retirement planner explains investment options to an older couple. (bikeriderlondon. Shutterstock.)

Planners who seek specialized training can earn credentials such as chartered financial consultant (from The American College of Financial Services) or certified financial planner (Certified Financial Planner Board of Standards). Professionals who wish to specialize in retirement issues may opt to become a chartered retirement plans specialist (CRPS) or a chartered retirement planning counselor (CRPC)—both of which are available from the College for Financial Planning. CRPSs advise businesses on employee retirement plans, while CRPCs work with individuals who are retired or nearing retirement age.

Certification requirements vary depending on the specialty, though all programs demand continuing education credits for yearly recertification.

■ EXPERIENCE, SKILLS, AND PERSONALITY TRAITS

Students should obtain as much experience in the field as possible by participating in summer internships, co-ops, and part-time jobs at financial planning firms or with self-employed planners.

This job will require you to be in constant contact with your customers. You will need excellent communication skills, as you must be comfortable dealing with all kinds of people. The most successful planner is highly ethical and able to express and deliver a sense of expertise and professionalism to his or her clients. Other important traits include good research, time-management, and organizational skills.

■ EMPLOYMENT PROSPECTS
Employers

Retirement planners are employed by businesses such as consulting firms, brokerage houses, accounting firms, and banks. Some retirement planners are self-employed. Jobs are located throughout the country, but many personal financial planners are based in New York, California, and Florida. Numerous planners have careers in related fields such as accounting, insurance, real estate, and do consulting on a part-time basis.

Starting Out

Retirement planning is a specialty that takes special training and education. Many people transfer to financial planning after working in related fields. Most college graduates interested in this career would probably start at a brokerage house like Charles Schwab or Merrill Lynch, earning a base salary plus commission.

If your school has a job placement program or career center, take advantage of the information and services it offers. Also, consider job fairs, newspaper want ads—look under finance or employment recruiters. If you can get in touch with a financial planner, pick their brains on the best ways to enter the business.

ADVANCEMENT PROSPECTS

Advancement in this occupation can take several forms. For some, this may mean working toward having a larger, more diverse client base. Others may consider starting their own financial consulting business.

Self-employed retirement planners need to be responsible for numerous details of running a business—accounting, insurance, overhead costs—as well as finding customer leads and referrals. Being your own boss may sound appealing, but it carries much responsibility, not to mention risk. You may first want to speak with others in the industry to weigh the pros and cons of self-employment. Those who run their own businesses advance by developing a solid reputation in the field, growing their client base, and adding more staff and office locations. Others may teach and write about the field.

OUTLOOK

The Bureau of Labor Statistics forecasts remarkable employment growth of 30 percent for personal financial advisors, which includes retirement planners. Demand for financial planners is growing in part because people are living longer due to advances in the medical and health care fields. The U.S. Census Bureau estimated that in 2010 there were 35 million people in the United States who were age 65 or older. By 2030, nearly one in five U.S. residents is expected to be 65 or older; and by 2050, it's projected that there will be 82 million people over 65 years old. In addition, the number of people age 85 or older may more than quadruple by 2050 (increasing from approximately four million in 2000 to 19 million in 2050). Thus, the retirement planning field should grow at a much-faster-than-average rate, as more and more people will be demanding these services.

Job opportunities for financial planners are also growing because the government's Social Security system is often not enough to meet the financial needs of seniors as they continue to live longer and more productively, and because decreased funding for corporate and government pension plans has prompted more people to seek out the services of retirement planners. People are increasingly dependent on savings plans and investments to help maintain a comfortable standard of living through their retirement years. Many people lost money, including their retirement savings, in the recent economic crisis. Some retirees were forced to return to some form of work to increase their earnings. As a result, the focus on sound retirement planning has intensified.

PLANNING FOR RETIREMENT

LEARN MORE ABOUT IT

Brandeburg, Matthew. *Your Guide to the CFP Certification Exam: A Supplement to Financial Planning Coursework and Self-Study Materials,* 4th ed. Dublin, Ohio: Coventry House Publishing, 2013.

Lorette, Kristie, and Peg Stomierowski. *How to Open and Operate a Financially Successful Personal Financial Planning Business.* Ocala, Fla.: Atlantic Publishing Company, 2011.

Matthews, Joseph. *Social Security, Medicare and Government Pensions: Get the Most Out of Your Retirement and Medical Benefits,* 19th ed. Berkeley, Calif.: Nolo, 2014.

Tyson, Eric. *Personal Finance For Dummies,* 7th ed. Hoboken, N.J.: For Dummies, 2012.

Financial planners, especially those who specialize in retirement plans, will be in high demand for their advice and recommendations on the best way to build and manage retirement funds. Job opportunities for certified retirement planners, whether affiliated with a company or self-employed, will be plentiful.

UNIONS AND ASSOCIATIONS

Retirement planners are not members of unions. Popular membership organizations for planners include the Financial Planning Association (FPA) and the National Association of Personal Financial Advisors. The College for Financial Planning, FPA, and the Certified Financial Planner Board of Standards provide certification.

TIPS FOR ENTRY

1. Read the *Journal of Financial Planning* (http://www.fpanet.org/journal) to learn more about the field.
2. Visit http://www.onefpa.org/business-success/Pages/Job-Board.aspx and http://www.napfa.org/career/opportunities for job listings.
3. Take advantage of the Financial Planning Association's MentorMatch program, which matches new planners with experienced professionals. Visit http://connect.onefpa.org/FPANET/Mentoring/AboutMentorMatch for more information.
4. Attend the Financial Planning Association's annual conference and expo (http://fpa-be.org) and other association conferences to network and participate in continuing education opportunities.

■ FOR MORE INFORMATION

For information on certification, contact

Certified Financial Planner Board of Standards

1425 K Street, NW, Suite 500

Washington, D.C. 20005-3673

Tel: (800) 487-1497; (202) 379-2200

Fax: (202) 379-2299

E-mail: mail@CFPBoard.org

http://www.cfp.net

For information on educational opportunities, contact

College for Financial Planning

9000 East Nichols Avenue, Suite 200

Centennial, CO 80112-3406

Tel: (800) 237-9990

Fax: (303) 220-1810

E-mail: enroll@cffp.edu

http://www.cffp.edu

For information on the certified financial planner designation, contact

Financial Planning Association

7535 East Hampden Avenue, Suite 600

Denver, CO 80231-4844

Tel: (800) 322-4237; (303) 759-4900

http://www.fpanet.org

For information on careers in financial planning, contact

**National Association of Personal Financial
   Advisors**

8700 W. Bryn Mawr Avenue, Suite 700N

Chicago, IL 60631

Tel: (888) 333-6659

Fax: (847) 483-5415

E-mail: info@napfa.org

http://napfa.org

Risk Managers

■ OVERVIEW

Risk managers help businesses control risks and losses while maintaining the highest production levels possible. They work in industrial, service, nonprofit, and public-sector organizations. By protecting a company against loss, the risk manager helps it to improve operating efficiency and meet strategic goals. Approximately 555,900 financial managers, including risk managers, are employed in the United States. Risk managers are also known as *risk officers.*

■ HISTORY

Entrepreneurs have always taken steps to prevent losses or damage to their businesses. During the Industrial Revolution, business owners recognized that as production levels increased, risks increased at the same rate. The risks were often managed at the expense of worker health and safety.

Only since the mid-1950s, however, has risk management developed into a specialized field. With the rapid growth of technology came greater and more varied risks. Risk management changed from simply buying insurance against risks to planning a wide variety of programs to prevent, minimize, and finance losses. Today's risk managers analyze data through various software and Internet programs, and help individuals, companies, and government agencies reduce the risk of loss due to accidents, incidents, and catastrophes.

■ THE JOB

Risk management protects people, property, and inventory. For example, factories that use hazardous chemicals require employees to wear protective clothing; department stores use closed-circuit surveillance to minimize shoplifting and vandalism; and manufacturers have a plan of action to follow should their products injure consumers. The five general categories of risks are:

- damage to property,
- loss of income from property damage,
- injury to others,
- fraud or criminal acts, and
- death or injury of employees.

Risk managers first identify and analyze potential losses. They examine the various risk management techniques and select the best ones, including how to pay for losses that may occur. After the chosen techniques are implemented, they closely monitor the results.

Risk management has two basic elements: risk control and risk finance. Risk control involves loss prevention techniques to reduce the frequency and lower the severity of losses. Risk managers make sure operations are safe. They see that employees are properly trained and that workers have and use safety equipment. This often involves conducting safety and loss prevention programs for employees. They make recommendations on the safe design of the workplace and make plans in case of machinery breakdowns. They examine company contracts with suppliers to ensure a steady supply of raw materials.

Risk finance programs set aside funds to pay for losses not anticipated by risk control. Some losses can be covered by the company itself; others are covered by outside sources, such as insurance firms. Risk finance programs try to reduce costs of damage or loss, and include insurance programs to pay for losses.

Risk and insurance managers help companies choose programs to minimize risks and losses due to financial transactions and business operations. For example, companies may incur costs because of a lawsuit against another company, or have to make disability payments to an employee who was injured on the job. Insurance managers help companies obtain insurance against such risks. Risk managers use techniques such as hedging to limit a company's exposure to currency or commodity price changes. Risk managers who specialize in international finance create financial and accounting systems for the banking transactions of multinational organizations. Risk managers are also responsible for calculating and limiting potential operations risk, such as a disgruntled employee damaging the company's finances or a hurricane damaging a factory.

Large organizations often have a risk management department with several employees who each specialize in one area, such as employee-related injuries, losses to plant property, automobile losses, and insurance coverage. Small organizations have risk managers who may serve as safety and training officers in addition to handling workers' compensation and employee benefits.

■ EARNINGS

Risk managers' salaries vary depending on level of responsibility and authority, type of industry, organization size, and geographic region. The U.S. Department of Labor, which classifies risk managers with financial managers, reported a median yearly income for financial managers of $117,900 in May 2015. The lowest paid 10 percent earned less than $63,020, and the highest paid 25 percent earned more than $187,200. PayScale.com reported that senior risk managers earned annual salaries that ranged from $71,524 to $152,338 in March 2014.

Risk managers usually receive benefits, bonuses, paid vacation, health and life insurance, pensions, and stock options.

■ WORK ENVIRONMENT

Risk managers work in a variety of settings, from schools, stores, and government agencies to manufacturers and airlines. Most work in offices, not on the production line, but they may be required to spend some time in production departments. They may have to travel to study risks in other companies or to attend seminars.

QUICK FACTS

ALTERNATE TITLE(S)
Risk Officers

DUTIES
Identify business risks and provide suggestions on how to avoid losses

SALARY RANGE
$63,020 to $117,900 to $187,200+

WORK ENVIRONMENT
Primarily Indoors

BEST GEOGRAPHIC LOCATION(S)
Large metropolitan areas

MINIMUM EDUCATION LEVEL
Bachelor's Degree

SCHOOL SUBJECTS
Business, Economics, Mathematics

EXPERIENCE
Five years experience

PERSONALITY TRAITS
Organized, Problem-Solving, Realistic

SKILLS
Business Management, Financial, Interpersonal

CERTIFICATION OR LICENSING
Recommended

SPECIAL REQUIREMENTS
None

EMPLOYMENT PROSPECTS
Good

ADVANCEMENT PROSPECTS
Good

OUTLOOK
About as Fast as the Average

NOC
0111

O*NET-SOC
13-2099.02

Risk managers usually work long hours, usually more than a 40-hour week. They may have to spend much of their time at a computer, analyzing statistics and preparing reports.

■ EXPLORING

You may wish to ask your family's insurance agent to help you contact a colleague who has commercial accounts and might introduce you to a risk manager for one of their larger clients.

CAREER LADDER

General Manager or Independent Consultant

Risk Manager

Risk Management Trainee

RIMS—The Risk Management society is one of the largest organizations for risk managers. It offers books, monographs, *Risk Management* magazine, education programs, and an annual conference. The Spencer Educational Foundation, affiliated with RIMS, provides annual scholarships to academically outstanding full-time students of risk management and insurance.

■ EDUCATION AND TRAINING REQUIREMENTS
High School

If you are interested in becoming a risk manager, you should plan on getting a bachelor's degree and may at some point consider getting an advanced degree, such as master's of business administration (MBA) or a master's in risk management degree. In high school, therefore, you should take classes that will prepare you for college as well as help you explore this type of work. Take plenty of mathematics classes. Also, take accounting, business, and economics if your school offers these classes. To round out your education, take a variety of science, history, government, and computer classes. And of course, take English classes, which will help you hone your research and writing skills and make you ready for college-level work.

Postsecondary Training

Risk managers generally need a college degree with a broad business background. Depending on the college or university you attend, you may be able to major in risk management or insurance. Many schools offer courses or degrees in insurance and risk management. If your school does not offer these degrees, consider a major in other management or finance areas, such as accounting, economics, engineering, finance, law, management, or political science. No matter what your particular major, your class schedule will most likely include economics, accounting, and mathematics, such as calculus. It is also important to take computer classes that teach you how to deal with using a variety of software programs. Insurance and even banking classes will give you an understanding of these industries and the financial tools they use. Increasingly, some employers are seeking risk managers with a postgraduate degree in finance or real estate or an MBA.

Other Education or Training

Continuing education classes, workshops, online tutorials, and webinars are offered by the American Institute for Chartered Property and Casualty Underwriters, National Alliance for Insurance Education and Research, Public Risk Management Association, and RIMS—The Risk Management Society. Topics include risk assessment, risk control, insuring commercial property, and insuring personal residential property. Contact these organizations for more information.

■ CERTIFICATION, LICENSING, AND SPECIAL REQUIREMENTS
Certification or Licensing

Many organizations require their risk managers to earn the designation associate in risk management (ARM). The ARM program is run jointly by the American Institute for Chartered Property Casualty Underwriters and the Insurance Institute of America. You must take courses and pass exams in the following areas: risk assessment, risk control, and risk financing. The institute also offers the associate in risk management for public entities certification for risk managers who are interested in working in the public sector and the associate in risk management-enterprise risk management.

The National Alliance for Insurance Education and Research offers the certified risk managers international designation. To earn this designation, you must pass exams in five courses covering all major areas of risk management.

Global Risk Management Institute offers an advanced designation in risk management, the RIMS Fellow. Applicants must satisfy educational and experience requirements.

■ EXPERIENCE, SKILLS, AND PERSONALITY TRAITS

Aspiring risk managers should have five years of experience in risk management, insurance, or related areas.

Communications skills are important for risk managers. They must regularly interact with other departments, such as accounting, engineering, finance, human resources, environmental, legal, research and development, safety, and security. They must also be able to communicate with outside sources, such as attorneys, brokers, union officials, consultants, and insurance agents.

Risk managers must have analytical and problem-solving skills in order to foresee potential problem situations and recommend appropriate solutions. They must be able to examine and prepare reports on risk costs, loss statistics, cost-versus-benefit data, insurance costs, and depreciation of assets.

Knowledge of insurance fundamentals and risk financing is necessary. Risk managers must know loss-control issues such as employee health, worker and product safety, property safeguards, fire prevention, and environmental protection.

Management skills help risk managers set goals, plan strategies, delegate tasks, and measure and forecast results. Computer skills and familiarity with business law are also very helpful.

■ EMPLOYMENT PROSPECTS

Employers

Approximately 555,900 financial managers, including risk managers, are employed in the United States. Airlines, banks, insurance companies, manufacturers, government agencies, municipalities, hospitals, retailers, school districts, construction firms, nonprofit organizations, colleges and universities, and other organizations all employ risk managers.

Starting Out

College career services offices can put students in touch with recruiters from industries that employ risk managers. Recent graduates can also search the Internet for risk manager job listings, as well as visit the Web sites of employers of risk managers, such as corporations, service providers, government agencies, and other public and private organizations. Some risk managers join insurance companies, insurance brokerage firms, or consulting firms that provide risk management services to clients.

Some individuals gain experience and education while working in accounting or personnel departments and later move into risk management positions.

■ ADVANCEMENT PROSPECTS

There is good potential for advancement in the risk management field. Many risk managers work in a related field, such as in a human resources department handling employee benefits.

Risk managers may eventually become a *personnel supervisor* or *finance department head*, become a *human resources director*, or join the insurance industry. Some become *independent consultants*. Membership in professional associations that offer networking opportunities can lead to better positions in the field.

Risk managers usually hold mid-level management positions and often report to a financial officer. Some, however, become *vice presidents* or *presidents* of their organizations.

■ OUTLOOK

Since advanced technology continues to increase productivity as well as the potential for disaster, the need for risk

---

RISK CONTROL AND POLICIES

WORDS TO KNOW

Builder's risk insurance: Property insurance that covers structures that are under construction.

Cost of risk: The sum total of items such as insurance premiums, claims and legal expenses, the cost of risk management operation, and other costs related to an organization's attempt to control the impact of adverse events.

Frequency: The likelihood that a loss will occur.

Loss control: The process of reducing the chance that a loss will occur, and if it occurs, reducing the severity of the loss.

Mitigation: Attempts to reduce the significance of negative events.

Risk audit: An independent assessment of a company's risk management practices. Risk audits are done to verify that the company has appropriate risk management controls, and adheres to these controls and is compliant with approved policies and procedures in mitigating risk.

Risk policies and procedures: Most corporate risk management programs have these fundamental control documents.

Risk register: This is a basic document used in risk management control systems that identifies, ranks, and assigns significant risk factors.

Risk/reward ratio: The ratio between profitability and loss, which is often used for trade selection or comparison.

Severity: The amount of damage caused by a loss.

Sources: Risk Limited Corporation; Public Risk Management Association

---

management will continue to grow. Organizations now recognize risk management as an integral and effective tool for cost-containment. The profession will continue to gain recognition in the next decade, so salaries and career opportunities are expected to continue to escalate. The U.S. Department of Labor predicts that employment for financial managers (including risk managers) will grow about as fast as the average for all careers through 2024. Competition for risk management positions is expected to be keen. Those with advanced degrees and certification will have better chances of securing work.

■ UNIONS AND ASSOCIATIONS

Risk managers are not represented by unions, but they can obtain useful resources and professional support from the American Institute for Chartered Property Casualty Underwriters, American Risk and Insurance Association, National Alliance for Insurance Education and Research, Public Risk Management Association, and RIMS—The Risk Management Society.

■ TIPS FOR ENTRY

1. For job listings visit: http://www.rims.org/resources/CareerCenter.
2. Join professional associations to access industry publications, training and networking opportunities, and employment opportunities.
3. Participate in internships or part-time jobs that are arranged by your college's career services office.

■ FOR MORE INFORMATION

For information about the associate in risk management designation, contact

American Institute for Chartered Property Casualty Underwriters
720 Providence Road, Suite 100
Malvern, PA 19355-3433
Tel: (800) 644-2101; (610) 644-2100
Fax: (610) 640-9576
http://www.aicpcu.org

For information on education, research, student memberships, and publications, contact

American Risk and Insurance Association
716 Providence Road
Malvern, PA 19355-3402
Tel: (610) 640-1997
Fax: (610) 725-1007
E-mail: aria@TheInstitutes.org
http://aria.org

For information about the certified risk manager designation, contact

National Alliance for Insurance Education and Research
PO Box 27027
Austin, TX 78755-2027
Tel: (800) 633-2165
Fax: (512) 349-6194
E-mail: alliance@scic.com
http://scic.com

Visit the association's Web site for a risk management glossary and other resources.

Public Risk Management Association
700 South Washington Street, Suite 218
Alexandria, VA 22314-4291
Tel: (703) 528-7701
Fax: (703) 739-0200
E-mail: info@primacentral.org
http://www.primacentral.org

For information on continuing education and the Spencer Educational Foundation, contact

RIMS—The Risk Management Society
5 Bryant Park, 13th Floor
New York, NY 10018
Tel: (212) 286-9292
http://www.rims.org

Robotics Engineers and Technicians

■ OVERVIEW

Robotics engineers design, develop, build, and program robots and robotic devices, including peripheral equipment and computer software used to control robots. *Robotics technicians* assist robotics engineers in a wide variety of tasks relating to the design, development, production, testing, operation, repair, and maintenance of robots and robotic devices.

■ HISTORY

Robots are devices that perform tasks ordinarily performed by humans; they seem to operate with an almost-human intelligence. The idea of robots can be traced back to the ancient Greek and Egyptian civilizations. An inventor from the first century A.D., Hero of Alexandria, invented a machine that would automatically open the doors of a temple when the priest lit a fire in the altar. During the later periods of the Middle Ages, the Renaissance, and the 17th and 18th centuries, interest in robot-like mechanisms lead to the development of automatons, devices that imitate human and animal appearance and activity but perform no useful task.

The Industrial Revolution inspired the invention of many different kinds of automatic machinery. One of the most important robotics inventions occurred in 1804: Joseph-Marie Jacquard's method for controlling machinery by means of a programmed set of instructions recorded on a punched paper tape that was fed into a machine to direct its movements.

The word robot and the concepts associated with it were first introduced in the early 1920s. They made their appearance in a play titled *R.U.R.*, which stands for Rossum's Universal Robots, written by Czechoslovakian dramatist Karel Capek. The play involves human-like robotic machines created to perform manual tasks for their human masters.

During the 1950s and 1960s, advances in the fields of automation and computer science led to the development of experimental robots that could imitate a wide range of human activity, including self-regulated and self-propelled movement (either on wheels or on legs), the ability to sense and manipulate objects, and the ability to select a course of action on the basis of conditions around them.

In 1954, George Devol designed the first programmable robot in the United States. He named it the Universal Automation, which was later shortened to Unimation, which also became the name of the first robot company. Hydraulic robots, controlled by numerical control programming, were developed in the 1960s and were used initially by the automobile industry in assembly line operations. By 1973, robots were being built with electric power and electronic controls, which allowed greater flexibility and increased uses.

Robotic technology has evolved significantly in the past few decades. Early robotic equipment, often referred to as first-generation robots, were simple mechanical arms or devices that could perform precise, repetitive motions at high speeds. They contained no artificial intelligence capabilities. Second-generation robots, which came into use in the 1980s, are controlled by minicomputers and programmed by computer language. They contain sensors, such as vision systems and pressure, proximity, and tactile sensors, which provide information about the outside environment. Third-generation robots, also controlled by minicomputers and equipped with sensory devices, were developed starting in the 1990s. Referred to as "smart" robots, they can work on their own without supervision by an external computer or human being. They are capable of speech recognition and other features. Fourth-generation robots are currently in development and will include features such as artificial intelligence and self-assembly.

The evolution of robots is closely tied to the study of human anatomy and movement of the human body. The early robots were modeled after arms, then wrists. Second-generation robots include features that model human hands. Advanced robots, or androids, resemble human beings superficially, and are able to move around on wheels or a track drive, or walk on human-like legs.

There are currently more than 1.4 million operational industrial robots in the world, and these robots are becoming more sophisticated with each passing year. The

QUICK FACTS

ALTERNATE TITLE(S)
Electromechanical Technicians, Installation Robotics Technicians, Manufacturing Technicians, Robotics Engineers, Robot Mechanics, Robotics Repairmen, Robot Service Technicians, Robotics Technicians

DUTIES
Design, develop, build, and program robots and robotic devices

SALARY RANGE
$53,300 to $95,230 to $151,990+ (engineers)
$59,240 to $93,010 to $146,820+ (technicians)

WORK ENVIRONMENT
Primarily Indoors

BEST GEOGRAPHIC LOCATION(S)
Many robotics manufacturers are located in California, Michigan, Illinois, Indiana, Pennsylvania, Ohio, Connecticut, Texas, British Columbia, and Ontario

MINIMUM EDUCATION LEVEL
High School Diploma, Bachelor's Degree

SCHOOL SUBJECTS
Computer Science, Mathematics, Physics

EXPERIENCE
Internships; any experience with science and mathematics

PERSONALITY TRAITS
Hands On, Scientific, Technical

SKILLS
Math, Mechanical/Manual Dexterity, Scientific

CERTIFICATION OR LICENSING
Recommended

SPECIAL REQUIREMENTS
None

EMPLOYMENT PROSPECTS
Fair

ADVANCEMENT PROSPECTS
Good

OUTLOOK
About as Fast as the Average

NOC
2132, 2232

O*NET-SOC
17-2199.08, 17-3024.01

Washington Post reports that "General Electric has developed spider-like robots to climb and maintain tall wind turbines. Kiva Systems, a company recently purchased by Amazon.com, has orange ottoman-shaped robots that sweep across warehouse floors, pull products off

shelves, and deliver them for packaging." "Baxter," a robot developed by a former MIT scientist, is even more impressive. According to the *CAM Report,* "it has red plastic arms and a cartoon face, and can do the job of two or more workers at plastics and metal manufacturing companies, where it works. If a human comes too close as it works, its eyes widen dramatically and it moves out of the way. Baxter's cost: $22,000—quite affordable for manufacturers."

■ THE JOB

The majority of robotics engineers and technicians work within the field of computer-integrated manufacturing or programmable automation. Using computer science technology, engineers design and develop robots and other automated equipment, including computer software used to program robots.

The title robotics engineer may be used to refer to any engineer who works primarily with robots. In many cases, these engineers may have been trained as *mechanical, electronic, computer,* or *manufacturing engineers.* A small, but growing, number of engineers trained specially in robotics are graduating from colleges and universities with robotics engineering or closely related degrees.

Robotics engineers have a thorough understanding of robotic systems and equipment and know the different technologies available to create robots for specific applications. They have a strong foundation in computer systems and how computers are linked to robots. They also have an understanding of manufacturing production requirements and how robots can best be used in automated systems to achieve cost efficiency, productivity, and quality. Robotics engineers may analyze and evaluate a manufacturer's operating system to determine whether robots can be used efficiently instead of other automated equipment or humans.

Many other types of engineers are also involved in the design, development, fabrication, programming, and operation of robots. Following are brief descriptions of these types of engineers and how they relate to robotics.

Electrical and electronics engineers research, design, and develop the electrical systems used in robots and the power supply, if it is electrical. These engineers may specialize in areas such as integrated circuit theory, lasers, electronic sensors, optical components, and energy power systems.

Mechanical engineers are involved in the design, fabrication, and operation of the mechanical systems of a robot. These engineers need a strong working knowledge of mechanical components such as gripper mechanisms, bearings, gears, chains, belts, and actuators. Some robots are controlled by pneumatic or mechanical power supplies, and these engineers need to be specialists in designing these systems. Mechanical engineers also select the material used to make robots. They test robots once they are constructed.

Computer engineers design the computer systems that are used to program robots. Sometimes these systems are built into a robot and other times they are a part of separate equipment that is used to control robots. Some computer engineers also write computer programs.

Industrial engineers are specialists in manufacturing operations. They determine the physical layout of a factory to best utilize production equipment. They may determine the placement of robotic equipment. They are also responsible for safety rules and practices and for ensuring that robotic equipment is used properly.

CAD/CAM engineers (computer-aided design/computer-aided manufacturing) are experts in automated production processes. They design and supervise manufacturing systems that utilize robots and other automated equipment.

Manufacturing engineers manage the entire production process. They may evaluate production operations to determine whether robots can be used in an assembly line and make recommendations on purchasing robotic equipment. Some manufacturing engineers design robots. Other engineers specialize in a specific area of robotics, such as artificial intelligence, vision systems, and sensor systems. These specialists are developing robots with "brains" that are similar to those of humans.

Robotics technicians assist in all phases of robotics engineering. They install, repair, and maintain finished robots. Others help design and develop new kinds of robotics equipment. Technicians who install, repair, and maintain robots and robotic equipment need knowledge of electronics, electrical circuitry, mechanics, pneumatics, hydraulics, and computer programming. They use hand and power tools, testing instruments, manuals, schematic diagrams, and blueprints.

Before installing new equipment, technicians review the work order and instructional information; verify that the intended site in the factory is correctly supplied with the necessary electrical wires, switches, circuit breakers, and other parts; position and secure the robot in place, sometimes using a crane or other large tools and equipment; and attach various cables and hoses, such as those that connect a hydraulic power unit with the robot. After making sure that the equipment is operational, technicians program the robot for specified tasks, using their knowledge of its programming language. They may write the detailed instructions that program robots or reprogram a robot when changes are needed.

Once robots are in place and functioning, they may develop problems. Technicians then test components and locate faulty parts. When the problem is found, they may replace or recalibrate parts. Sometimes they suggest changes in circuitry or programming, or may install different end-of-arm tools on robots to allow machines to perform new functions. They may train robotics operators in how to operate robots and related equipment and help establish in-house basic maintenance and repair programs at new installations.

Companies that only have a few robots don't always hire their own robotics technicians. Instead they use *robot field technicians* who work for a robotic manufacturer. These technicians travel to manufacturing sites and other locations where robots are used to repair and service robots and robotic equipment.

Technicians involved with the design and development of new robotic devices are sometimes referred to as *robotics design technicians*. As part of a design team, they work closely with robotics engineers. The robotics design job starts as the engineers analyze the tasks and settings to be assigned and decide what kind of robotics system will best serve the necessary functions. Technicians involved with robot assembly, sometimes referred to as *robot assemblers*, commonly specialize in one aspect of robot assembly. Materials handling technicians receive requests for components or materials, then locate and deliver them to the technicians doing the actual assembly or those performing tests on these materials or components. Mechanical assembly technicians put together components and subsystems and install them in the robot. *Electrical assembly technicians* do the same work as mechanical assembly technicians but specialize in electrical components such as circuit boards and automatic switching devices. Finally, some technicians test the finished assemblies to make sure the robot conforms to the original specifications.

Other kinds of robotics technicians include *robot operators*, who operate robots in specialized settings, and *robotics trainers*, who train other employees in the installation, use, and maintenance of robots.

Robotics technicians may also be referred to as *electromechanical technicians, manufacturing technicians, robot mechanics, robotics repairmen, robot service technicians,* and *installation robotics technicians*.

NASA engineers check a robot prototype called the "Mighty Eagle." (Marshall Space Flight Center. Fred Deaton. NASA.)

■ EARNINGS

Earnings and benefits in manufacturing companies vary widely based on the size of the company, geographic location, nature of the production process, and complexity of the robots. The U.S. Department of Labor (DOL) does not report on salaries specific to robotics engineers and technicians, but salary information can be garnered from other engineering disciplines. In general, electrical engineers earned a median starting salary of $95,230 in May 2015. The DOL reports the following salary ranges for engineers by specialty: computer hardware, $65,570 to $167,100; electrical, $59,240 to $146,820; electronics (except computer), $63,430 to $151,990; industrial, $53,300 to $126,920; and mechanical, $53,640 to $128,430.

The DOL reports that electrical and electronic engineering technicians had a median annual salary of $93,010 in May 2015, with earnings ranging from $59,240 to $146,820 or more.

Employers offer a variety of benefits that can include the following: paid holidays, vacations, personal days, and sick leave; medical, dental, disability, and life insurance; 401(k) plans, pension and retirement plans; profit sharing; and educational assistance programs.

■ WORK ENVIRONMENT

Robotics engineers and technicians may work either for a company that manufactures robots or a company that uses robots. Most companies that manufacture robots are

ROBOTICS FUNDAMENTALS

LEARN MORE ABOUT IT

Baichtal, John. *Basic Robot Building With LEGO Mindstorms NXT 2.0.* Indianapolis, Ind.: Que Publishing, 2013.

Baichtal, John. *I, Robot Builder: The Beginner's Guide to Building Robots.* Indianapolis, Ind.: Que Publishing, 2014.

Cook, David. *Robot Building for Beginners,* 2nd ed. New York: Apress Media LLC, 2010.

McComb, Gordon. *Robot Builder's Bonanza,* 4th ed. New York: McGraw-Hill/TAB Electronics, 2011.

Scherz, Paul, and Simon Monk. *Practical Electronics for Inventors,* 3rd ed. New York: McGraw-Hill/TAB Electronics, 2013.

relatively clean, quiet, and comfortable environments. Engineers and technicians may work in an office or on the production floor.

Engineers and technicians who work in a company that uses robots may work in noisy, hot, and dirty surroundings. Conditions vary based on the type of industry within which one works. Automobile manufacturers use a significant number of robots, as do manufacturers of electronics components and consumer goods and the metalworking industry. Workers in a foundry work around heavy equipment and in hot and dirty environments. Workers in the electronics industry generally work in very clean and quiet environments. Some robotics personnel are required to work in clean room environments, which keep electronic components free of dirt and other contaminants. Workers in these environments wear facemasks, hair coverings, and special protective clothing.

Some engineers and technicians may confront potentially hazardous conditions in the workplace. Robots, after all, are often designed and used precisely because the task they perform involves some risk to humans: handling laser beams, arc-welding equipment, radioactive substances, or hazardous chemicals. When they design, test, build, install, and repair robots, it is inevitable that some engineers and technicians will be exposed to these same risks. Plant safety procedures protect the attentive and cautious worker, but carelessness in such settings can be especially dangerous.

In general, most technicians and engineers work 40-hour workweeks, although overtime may be required for special projects or to repair equipment that is shutting down a production line. Some technicians, particularly those involved in maintenance and repairs, may work shifts that include evening, late night, or weekend work.

Field service technicians travel to manufacturing sites to repair robots. Their work may involve extensive travel and overnight stays. They may work at several sites in one day or stay at one location for an extended period for more difficult repairs.

■ EXPLORING

Because robotics is a relatively new field, it is important to learn as much as possible about current trends and recent technologies. Reading books and articles in trade magazines provides an excellent way to learn about what is happening in robotics technologies and expected future trends. Magazines with informative articles include *Servo Magazine* (http://www.servomagazine.com) and *Robot Magazine* (http://www.botmag.com).

You can become a robot hobbyist and build your own robots or buy toy robots and experiment with them. Complete robot kits are available through a number of companies and range from simple, inexpensive robots to highly complex robots with advanced features and accessories. A number of books that give instructions and helpful hints on building robots can be found online and at most public libraries and bookstores. In addition, relatively inexpensive and simple toy robots are available from electronics shops, department stores, and mail order companies.

You can also participate in competitions such as the National Robotics Challenge (http://www.nationalroboticschallenge.org) or International Aerial Robotics Competition, which is sponsored by the Association for Unmanned Vehicle Systems International (http://www.aerialroboticscompetition.org).

The Robotics Institute Summer Scholars Program at Carnegie Mellon University offers summer research programs for junior and senior undergraduate students. To learn more, visit its Web site, http://www.cs.cmu.edu/~summerscholar/Robotics_Institute_Summer_Scholars/Robotics_Summer_Scholars_Program.html.

Another great way to learn about robotics is to attend trade shows. Many robotics and automated machinery manufacturers exhibit their products at shows and conventions. Numerous such trade shows are held every year in different parts of the country. Information about these trade shows is available through association trade publications.

Other activities that foster knowledge and skills relevant to a career in robotics include membership in high school science clubs, participation in science fairs, joining national science and technology associations (such as the Technology Student Association, http://www.tsaweb.org), and pursuing hobbies that involve electronics, mechanical equipment, and model building.

■ EDUCATION AND TRAINING REQUIREMENTS
High School

In high school, you should take as many science, math, and computer classes as possible. Recommended courses are biology, chemistry, physics, algebra, trigonometry, geometry, calculus, graphics, computer science, English, speech, composition, social studies, and drafting. In addition, take shop and vocational classes that teach blueprint and electrical schematic reading, the use of hand tools, drafting, and the basics of electricity and electronics.

Postsecondary Training

Because changes occur so rapidly within this field, it is often recommended that engineers and technicians get a broad-based education that encompasses robotics but does not focus solely on robotics. Programs that provide the widest career base are those in automated manufacturing, which includes robotics, electronics, and computer science.

In order to become an engineer it is necessary to earn a bachelor's degree in engineering. Many colleges and universities throughout the country offer courses in robotics or related technology. Many different types of programs are available. Some colleges and universities offer robotics engineering degrees and others offer engineering degrees with concentrations or options in robotics and manufacturing engineering. For some higher-level jobs, such as robotics designer, a master of science or doctoral degree is required. Carnegie Mellon University has an extensive robotics program and offers baccalaureate, master's, and doctoral degrees in robotics. ABET (http://www.abet.org) accredits college and university programs for engineering.

Although the minimum educational requirement for a robotics technician is a high school diploma, many employers prefer to hire technicians who have received formal training beyond high school. Two-year programs are available in community colleges and technical institutes that grant an associate's degree in robotics. The armed forces also offer technical programs that result in associate's degrees in electronics, biomedical equipment, and computer science. The military uses robotics and other advanced equipment and offers excellent training opportunities to members of the armed forces. This training is highly regarded by many employers and can be an advantage in obtaining a civilian job in robotics.

Other Education or Training

Several associations offer continuing education opportunities. The Robotic Industries Association provides webinars, conference sessions, and other educational opportunities. Recent topics included robotics safety standards and career opportunities in the field. The National Society of Professional Engineers provides webinars for student members of the society. Past webinars included "Career Success in Engineering: A Guide for Students and New Professionals," "Ethics and Professionalism for Students and Young Engineers," "How to Get Your First Job," and "Engineering Your Career with a High Quality Social Network Web Seminar." The Society of Women Engineers offers conference sessions, webinars, and other education resources on topics such as leadership, career development, and special issues for women in engineering. The Society of Manufacturing Engineers and the American Society for Engineering Education also provide continuing education opportunities. Contact these organizations for more information.

■ CERTIFICATION, LICENSING, AND SPECIAL REQUIREMENTS
Certification or Licensing

Some robotics engineers become certified. Certification is a status granted by a technical or professional organization for the purpose of recognizing and documenting an individual's abilities in a specific engineering field. For example, SME offers the certified manufacturing engineer certification to engineers who work in manufacturing and who meet education and experience requirements.

Engineers whose work may affect the life, health, or safety of the public must be registered according to regulations in all 50 states and the District of Columbia. Licensing requirements vary from state to state. In general, however, they involve graduating from an accredited school, having four years of work experience, and passing the eight-hour Fundamentals of Engineering exam and the eight-hour Principles and Practice of Engineering exam. Depending on your state, you can take the Fundamentals exam shortly before your graduation from college or after you have received your bachelor's degree. At that point you will be an engineer-in-training. Once you have fulfilled all the licensure requirements, you receive the designation professional engineer. Visit the National Council of Examiners for Engineering and Surveying's Web site, http://www.ncees.org, for more information on licensure.

■ EXPERIENCE, SKILLS, AND PERSONALITY TRAITS

Take as many math and science classes as possible and participate in internships and other opportunities to gain experience in the field.

Because the field of robotics is rapidly changing, one of the most important requirements for a person

ROBOTS THAT SAVE LIVES

When you think of a robot, you may think of a toy dog or other electronic "pet." But robotics engineers and technicians work on far more serious issues, such as clearing the more than 100 million landmines buried all over the world, particularly in war-ravaged areas.

There are so many still buried, in fact, that experts estimate it could take several centuries to dig up all the mines manually. However, Japanese robotics engineers are working on a variety of machines to make the work both more efficient and safe. One such robot is called the COMET3, which is a bug-shaped device that runs on gasoline. It has two antennas, one containing a metal detector, the other, a marking device. On its six legs, COMET3 moves along an affected area, using its antennas to sense landmines. The device then uses paint to mark locations where metal is detected. COMET3 is also equipped with radar detectors to locate plastic landmines. The radar emits radio waves and senses waves that bounce back.

Roughly 150,000 World War Two-era mines still litter the Baltic Sea, posing a danger to a proposed gas pipeline. BACTEC (Battle Area Clearance, Training, Equipment, and Consultancy), a group that specializes in landmine clearance, will use a specially designed robot to search the ocean floor for bombs blocking the pipeline's path. When the robot detects a mine, a surface ship releases a high-pitched wail to scare away nearby marine mammals, sets off a small explosive to scare away any fish, and then plants and detonates a small charge on the mine.

With the help of these robots, engineers hope to create a database of the exact locations of buried landmines to make detection more accurate.

Source: Asahi.com, *Popular Science*

interested in a career in robotics is the willingness to pursue additional training on an ongoing basis during his or her career. After completing their formal education, engineers and technicians may need to take additional classes in a college or university or take advantage of training offered through their employers and professional associations.

Robotics engineers and technicians need manual dexterity, good hand-eye coordination, and mechanical and electrical aptitude. Other important traits include a detailed-oriented personality, strong communication skills, and an ability to work both independently and as a member of a team, when necessary.

■ EMPLOYMENT PROSPECTS
Employers

The Department of Labor reports that there are more than 1.6 million engineers, including robotics engineers, employed in the United States. Engineering technicians hold approximately 437,440 jobs. Robotics engineers and technicians are employed in virtually every manufacturing industry. With the trend toward automation continuing—often via the use of robots—people trained in robotics can expect to find employment with almost all types of manufacturing companies in the future. Robotics professionals also work in professional, scientific, and technical service industries and for government agencies such as the Department of Defense and NASA.

A large number of robotics manufacturers are found in California, Michigan, Illinois, Indiana, Pennsylvania, Ohio, Connecticut, Texas, British Columbia, and Ontario, although companies exist in many other U.S. states and Canadian provinces.

Starting Out

In the past, most people entered robotics technician positions from positions as automotive workers, machinists, millwrights, computer repair technicians, and computer operators. Companies retrained them to troubleshoot and repair robots rather than hire new workers. Although this still occurs today, there are many more opportunities for formal education and training specifically in robotics engineering, and robotics manufacturers are more likely to hire graduates of robotics programs, both at the technician and engineer levels.

Graduates of two- and four-year programs may learn about available openings through their schools' career services offices. It may also be possible to learn about job openings through want ads in newspapers and trade magazines, through job fairs, and on employment Web sites.

In many cases, it will be necessary to research companies that manufacture or use robots and apply directly to them. Professional engineering and robotics associations may offer publications with classified ads, or other job search information.

Job opportunities may be good at small start-up companies or a start-up robotics unit of a large company. Many times these employers are willing to hire inexperienced workers as apprentices or assistants. Then, when their sales and production grow, these workers have the best chances for advancement.

■ ADVANCEMENT PROSPECTS

Engineers may start as part of an engineering team and do relatively simple tasks under the supervision of a project manager or more experienced engineer. With experience and demonstrated competency, they can move into higher engineering positions. Engineers who demonstrate good interpersonal skills, leadership abilities, and technical expertise may become team leaders, project managers, or chief engineers. Engineers can also move into supervisory or management positions. Some engineers pursue a master's in business. These engineers are able to move into top management positions. Some engineers also develop specialties, such as artificial intelligence, and move into highly specialized engineering positions.

After several years on the job, robotics technicians who have demonstrated their ability to handle more responsibility may be assigned some supervisory work or, more likely, will train new technicians. Experienced technicians and engineers may teach courses at their workplace or find teaching opportunities at a local school or community college.

Other routes for advancement include becoming a sales representative for a robotics manufacturing or design firm or working as an independent contractor for companies that use or manufacture robots.

With additional training and education, such as a bachelor's degree, technicians can become eligible for positions as robotics engineers.

■ OUTLOOK

Employment opportunities for robotics engineers are closely tied to economic conditions in the United States and in the global marketplace. The U.S. Department of Labor predicts that the fields of mechanical and computer hardware engineering will grow more slowly than or about as fast as average through 2024, mainly due to increased foreign competition. Competition for engineering and jobs will be stiff, and opportunities will be best for those that have advanced degrees.

The use of industrial robots is expected to grow as robots become more programmable and flexible and as manufacturing processes become more automated. Growth is also expected in nontraditional applications, such as education, health care, security, and nonindustrial purposes. Future employment in robotics will depend on future demand for new applications, as well as available capital to spend on research and development.

The International Federation of Robotics (IFG) reported that sales of industrial robots reached a record number exceeding 250,000 units in 2015. The electronics and metal industry in particular increased purchases and use of robots. Five countries—China, Germany, Japan, Korea, and the United States—comprised 75 percent of total robot sales. With some forecasts estimating further,

rapid growth in use of robots in years to come, it's clear the industry is expanding.

Job opportunities for engineering technicians vary by specialty. For example, employment for mechanical engineering technicians is expected to grow by 2 percent through 2024 or more slowly than the average for all careers. Job opportunities for industrial engineering technicians will decline during this same time span. Employment is expected to decline about 2 percent for electrical and electronics engineering technicians.

■ UNIONS AND ASSOCIATIONS

Some engineers may be represented by the International Federation of Professional and Technical Engineers (http://www.ifpte.org), the Society of Professional Engineering Employees in Aerospace (http://www.speea.org), and other unions. In addition, many organizations provide useful resources, including the American Society for Engineering Education, Association for Unmanned Vehicle Systems International, General Aviation Manufacturers Association, National Society of Professional Engineers, Robotic Industries Association, Robotics and Automation Society, SME, and the Society of Women Engineers.

■ TIPS FOR ENTRY

1. To learn more about trends in the industry and potential employers, read publications such as:
   - *Servo Magazine* (http://www.servomagazine.com)
   - *Robot Magazine* (http://www.botmag.com)
   - *Unmanned Systems* (http://www.auvsi.org/Publications/UnmannedSystemsMagazine)
   - *Robotics Online Electronic Newsletter* (http://www.robotics.org)
   - *IEEE Robotics & Automation Magazine* (http://www.ieee.org)
2. Participate in the National Society of Professional Engineers' mentoring program (http://www.nspe.org/resources/career-center/mentoring-programs).
3. Visit the following Web sites for job listings:
   - http://careers.robotics.org
   - http://nasajobs.nasa.gov
   - http://www.nspe.org/resources/career-center/job-board/job-board
   - http://careers.swe.org
4. Attend industry conferences to network and to interview for jobs.
5. Join professional associations to access training and networking resources, industry publications, and employment opportunities.

■ FOR MORE INFORMATION

For information on educational programs and to purchase a copy of Engineering: Go For It, contact

American Society for Engineering Education
1818 N Street, NW, Suite 600
Washington, D.C. 20036-2479
Tel: (202) 331-3500
Fax: (202) 265-8504
E-mail: outreach@asee.org
http://www.asee.org

For information on competitions and student membership, contact

Association for Unmanned Vehicle Systems International
2700 South Quincy Street, Suite 400
Arlington, VA 22206-2226
Tel: (703) 845 9671
Fax: (703) 845 9679
E-mail: info@auvsi.org
http://www.auvsi.org

For information on careers and educational programs, contact

IEEE Robotics and Automation Society
445 Hoes Lane
Piscataway, NJ 08854
Tel: 732 562 3906
E-mail: ras@ieee.org
http://www.ieee-ras.org

For information on careers, licensing, membership benefits, and local chapters, contact

National Society of Professional Engineers
1420 King Street
Alexandria, VA 22314-2794
Tel: (703) 684-2800
Fax: (703) 684-2821
http://www.nspe.org

Visit the following NASA Web site for information on robotics education and summer camps and programs.

The Robotics Alliance Project
E-mail: Drew.Price@NASA.gov
http://robotics.nasa.gov

For career information, company profiles, training seminars, and educational resources, contact

Robotic Industries Association
900 Victors Way, Suite 140
Ann Arbor, MI 48108-5210
Tel: (734) 994-6088
Fax: (734) 994-3338
http://www.robotics.org

For information on educational programs, competitions, and student membership in SME, contact

SME
One SME Drive
Dearborn, MI 48128-2408
Tel: (800) 733-4763; (313) 425-3000
Fax: (313) 425-3400
E-mail: service@sme.org
http://www.sme.org

For information on careers and scholarships, contact
Society of Women Engineers
130 East Randolph Street, Suite 3500
Chicago, IL 60601-1269
Tel: (877) 793-4636
E-mail: hq@swe.org
http://societyofwomenengineers.swe.org and http://aspire.swe.org

Roman Catholic Priests

■ OVERVIEW

Roman Catholic priests serve as either diocesan priests (sometimes called *secular priests),* leading individual parishes within a certain diocese, or as *religious priests,* living and working with other members of their religious order. The primary function of all priests is administering the church's seven sacraments: baptism, confirmation, confession, holy communion, marriage, holy orders, and anointing of the sick. Diocesan priests also visit the sick, oversee religious education programs, and generally provide pastoral care to their parishioners. Religious priests often serve as educators and missionaries, or they may be cloistered in a monastery. There were approximately 37,578 Roman Catholic priests in the United States in 2015, most of whom were diocesan priests.

■ HISTORY

Priests and other clergy are part of the hierarchical structure of the Roman Catholic Church. In the Roman Catholic Church, only men can enter priesthood. This hierarchy began historically with Jesus Christ, who is believed by Catholics and other Christians to have been both God and man. Peter, the leader of the twelve apostles, is considered the priestly human successor to Jesus Christ. The spiritual successor of Peter is the pope, who is the leader of the worldwide Roman Catholic Church. The pope appoints bishops who oversee a diocese, a territorial district of the church. The bishops appoint the priests, who are spiritual leaders of individual parishes. Religious priests work under the direction of the superiors of their community and their order.

■ THE JOB

All priests have the same powers bestowed on them through ordination by a bishop, but their way of life, the type of work they do, and the authority to whom they report depends on whether they are members of a religious order or working in a diocese. Diocesan priests generally work in parishes to which they are assigned by their bishop. Religious priests, such as Dominicans, Jesuits, or Franciscans, work as members of a religious community and teach, doing missionary work, or engage in other specialized activities as assigned by their superiors. Both categories of priests teach and hold administrative positions in Catholic seminaries and educational institutions.

Diocesan priests are the spiritual leaders of their congregations. They are responsible for leading liturgical celebrations, especially the Mass. They also provide pastoral care for their parishioners in times of sickness, death, or personal crisis. Diocesan priests oversee the religious education of everyone in their congregation and take care of administrative duties. Some work in parochial schools attached to parish churches or in diocesan high schools. Religious priests perform similar duties but usually in monastic or missionary settings, or in such institutions as boarding schools, medical facilities, and residential homes.

All priests take time each day to nurture their own spiritual lives through Mass, private prayer, and recitation of the Liturgy of the Hours (the offices of Morning Prayer, Evening Prayer, etc.). They also devote time to studying the Bible, church history, and the doctrines and practices of the faith. All of this gives them the spiritual strength necessary to carry out their ministries.

Catholic clergy do not choose their own work assignments; this is done in collaboration with their religious superiors. Work assignments, however, are always made with the interests and abilities of the individual priest in mind. Every effort is made to place a priest in the type of ministry he prepares for. Priests may serve in a wide range of ministries, from counseling full-time and working in social services to being chaplains in the armed forces, prisons, or hospitals.

In response to the shortage of Catholic priests in the United States, there has been strong increase in the number of permanent deacons. Their numbers grew from 898 in 1975 to 17,325 in 2013. Deacons are ordained ministers who perform liturgical functions such as baptisms, marriages, funerals, and to provide various services to the community. Deacons do not take the same vows as priests and thus may hold other jobs, marry, and have families. Deacons are not permitted to perform the sacraments of reconciliation or anointing of the sick. Although they perform many important duties and are of great help in a parish, deacons cannot take the place of ordained priests.

■ EARNINGS

Religious priests take a vow of poverty and are supported by their orders. Any salary that they may receive for writing or other activities is usually turned over to their religious orders. Diocesan priests receive small salaries calculated to cover their basic needs. These salaries vary according to the size of the parish, as well as its location and financial status. SalaryList .com reports that Catholic priests in the Archdiocese of Indianapolis, earned $52,000 in 2014; those in the Diocese of Los Angeles earned $35,672. The U.S. Department of Labor reports that salaries for all clergy ranged from less than $22,380 to $77,220 or more in May 2015.

Additional benefits usually include a monthly travel allowance, room and board in the parish rectory, car allowance, health insurance, retirement benefits, and educational allowance. Priests who teach or do specialized work usually receive a small stipend that is less than that paid to lay persons in similar positions. Occasionally,

QUICK FACTS

ALTERNATE TITLE(S)
Diocesan Priests, Religious Priests, Secular Priests

DUTIES
Provide pastoral care to their parishioners and communities

SALARY RANGE
$0 to $35,672 to $77,220+

WORK ENVIRONMENT
Primarily Indoors

BEST GEOGRAPHIC LOCATION(S)
Nationwide

MINIMUM EDUCATION LEVEL
Bachelor's Degree

SCHOOL SUBJECTS
English, Religion, Speech

EXPERIENCE
Seminar or assistant priest experience

PERSONALITY TRAITS
Helpful, Outgoing, Problem-Solving

SKILLS
Interpersonal, Public Speaking, Teaching

CERTIFICATION OR LICENSING
None

SPECIAL REQUIREMENTS
Only men may become Roman Catholic priests

EMPLOYMENT PROSPECTS
Good

ADVANCEMENT PROSPECTS
Fair

OUTLOOK
About as Fast as the Average

NOC
4154

O*NET-SOC
21-2011.00

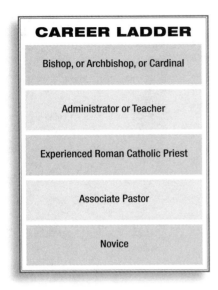

CAREER LADDER

Bishop, or Archbishop, or Cardinal

Administrator or Teacher

Experienced Roman Catholic Priest

Associate Pastor

Novice

priests who do special work are compensated at the same level as a lay person. Priests who serve in the armed forces receive the same amount of pay as other officers of equal rank.

■ WORK ENVIRONMENT

There is no such thing as a standard workweek for diocesan priests. Like all clergy, priests who function as pastors are on call at any hour of the day or night. They may be called to visit the sick or administer last rites at any time of the day or night. They may be asked to counsel families or individuals in times of crisis. Priests also must prepare sermons and keep up with religious and secular events. They may also have a great deal of administrative duties working with staff and various committees. As a result, priests encounter a significant amount of daily stress. A deep prayer life, plus the support of other priests, is necessary to reduce this stress. Parish priests usually live in quiet, simply furnished rectories with other priests. They may have a housekeeper to cook and perform cleaning duties.

Religious priests who live in monasteries devote themselves to liturgical celebration, mental prayer, and manual labor on the monastery grounds. While they do not experience the stresses of parish life, religious priests

Two Roman Catholic priests celebrate mass. (Mass Communication Specialist 2nd Class Joan E. Kretschmer. U.S. Navy.)

do face the challenges of the contemplative life and of living in a small, close community. Religious priests who pursue missionary work must adapt to difficult working conditions, usually in poorer countries and often in uncomfortable climates.

■ EXPLORING

If you are interested in the priesthood, talk with your parish priest and others involved in the pastoral work of the church to get a clearer idea of the rewards and responsibilities. Your priest or diocesan vocations office can put you in touch with a religious order if that is where you would like to serve. Aspiring priests may wish to volunteer at a church or other religious institution to become better acquainted with the type of responsibilities a priest has. Those interested in becoming a religious priest may choose to spend time in a monastery; many monasteries are open to the public for weekend or even weeklong retreats.

In both exploring the priesthood and preparing for it, you should be conscientious about living the Catholic faith as fully as you can—that is the essence of the vocation. Attend Mass and other services frequently; read about church history and doctrine; take part in parish activities. Finally, those with experience in religious ministries will tell you that the very best way to prepare for a vocation and to discern it is to pray.

■ EDUCATION AND TRAINING REQUIREMENTS
High School

Some high schools offer preparation for the priesthood that is similar to that of a college preparatory high school. High school seminary studies focus on English, speech, literature, and social studies. Latin may or may not be required; the study of other foreign languages, such as Spanish, is encouraged. Other recommended high school courses include typing, debating, and music.

Postsecondary Training

Eight years of post-high school study are usually required to become an ordained priest. Candidates for the priesthood often choose to enter at the college level or begin their studies in theological seminaries after college graduation. The liberal arts program offered by seminary colleges stresses philosophy, religion, the behavioral sciences, history, the natural sciences, and mathematics. Some priestly formation programs may insist on seminarians majoring in philosophy.

The additional four years of preparation for ordination are given over entirely to the study of theology, including studies in moral (ethics) and pastoral and dogmatic (doctrine) theology. Other areas of study include church history, scripture, homiletics (the art of preaching), liturgy (worship), and canon (church) law. In the third year of advanced training, candidates undertake fieldwork in parishes and the wider community. Because the work expected of secular and religious priests differs, they are trained in different major seminaries offering slightly varied programs.

Postgraduate work in theology and other fields is available and encouraged for priests, who may earn the master of divinity or master of arts degrees from American Roman Catholic universities, ecclesiastical universities in Rome, or other places around the world. Continuing education for ordained priests in the last several years has stressed sociology, psychology, and the natural sciences.

All Catholic seminaries offer scholarships and grants to qualified students; no one is denied the chance to study for the priesthood because he cannot afford it.

Other Education or Training

The National Federation of Priests' Councils, an organization for bishops, presbyterates, and priests, offers continuing education programs on leadership, conflict resolution, emotional intelligence, and other topics.

■ CERTIFICATION, LICENSING, AND SPECIAL REQUIREMENTS
Certification or Licensing

There are no certification or licensing requirements for Roman Catholic priests.

Other Requirements

Only men may enter the Roman Catholic priesthood.

■ EXPERIENCE, SKILLS, AND PERSONALITY TRAITS

Roman Catholic priests obtain experience in the seminary and by working as an assistant pastor after they are ordained.

Those interested in the priesthood should possess a strong religious faith, coupled with the belief that they have received a special call from God to serve and help others. All other interests and potential vocations should be considered secondary to this call. In addition to a strong desire for helping others, priests need to be able to communicate effectively and supervise others. They must have common sense, initiative, and self-confidence in order to be able to effectively oversee a parish or mission. They must also have compassion, humility, and integrity so as to be able to set an example for others. They must be open-minded and good listeners in order to successfully interact with and help those who seek their counsel.

CELIBACY AND CHASTITY

DID YOU KNOW?

Although priests take a vow of celibacy and sisters and brothers take vows of chastity, their vows amount to essentially the same thing—they will never form romantic or sexual relationships with other people. Some people shy away from religious vocations because of this requirement—but it is actually a blessing to those pursuing full-time ministries within the church. These vows allow priests and religious sisters and brothers to devote all of their time and attention to living out their vocations; if they had spouses and children, they would naturally want and need to give much of their time and attention to them. Vows of celibacy or chastity help men and women to concentrate on spiritual things.

Perhaps more importantly, when priests, sisters, and brothers are living out the call to give themselves to God through the church, they don't want to give themselves to other people through dating or marriage. This doesn't mean that they are cold or distant with others, and it doesn't mean that they don't experience human desires—it means that they seek the spiritual dimensions of love and sacrifice the physical dimensions to God.

A vow of celibacy is required, along with vows of poverty and obedience. Some orders take a special fourth vow, often related to their community, such as a vow of stability to stay in one place or a vow of silence.

■ EMPLOYMENT PROSPECTS
Employers

There were approximately 37,578 Roman Catholic priests in the United States in 2015, most of whom were diocesan priests. While some priests serve in dioceses and others serve in religious orders, all priests ultimately serve the church. Most priests can count on a pretty conventional life in the settings they have chosen: the hustle and bustle of an urban mission, the steady work of a suburban parish or school, or the serenity of a monastery. Still, it is important to be ready and willing to serve wherever the church needs you. For example, a priest who has done an exemplary job in a small suburban parish may be called to work in a bustling urban archdiocese.

Starting Out

Newly ordained diocesan priests generally begin their ministry as associate pastors, while new priests of religious orders are assigned duties for which they are specially trained, such as missionary work. Both diocesan and religious priests work under the supervision of more

THE SEVEN SACRAMENTS

Baptism: The sacrament through which a person is absolved of original sin and becomes a member of the Roman Catholic Church.

Reconciliation: The sacrament in which a person is absolved of his or her sins after confessing them to a priest.

Holy Communion: The sacrament in which a baptized Catholic receives bread and wine that, during the celebration of Mass, have been consecrated by the priest to become the body and blood of Christ.

Confirmation: The sacrament in which a Catholic renews his or her baptismal vows and commits to upholding the principles and doctrines of the Catholic Church.

Marriage: In the presence of a priest or deacon, a man and a woman take vows to commit to each other and God for the rest of their lives.

Holy Orders: The sacrament in which a man is ordained a priest.

Anointing of the sick: The sacrament administered during a time of extreme illness or when death is imminent; a priest anoints the sick person with oil and prays for their soul.

experienced colleagues until they are deemed ready for more responsibility.

ADVANCEMENT PROSPECTS

Because serving God and other people through the church is a priest's main concern, advancing to positions of power or prestige is not an important goal. Most priests do, however, advance to positions of some responsibility or move into altogether different positions. Some may become teachers in seminaries and other educational institutions, or chaplains in the armed forces. The pulpits of large, well-established churches are usually filled by priests of considerable experience. A small number of priests become *bishops, archbishops,* and *cardinals.*

OUTLOOK

The Bureau of Labor Statistics forecasts average employment growth for clergy in general through 2024. There is a shortage of priests in the Roman Catholic Church, however, with the number of priests having declined by about 31 percent since 1985 because of retirement and those leaving the profession for other reasons. Opportunities for positions in the priesthood are increasing and will probably continue to do so for

the foreseeable future. In 2016, there were 25,760 diocesan priests and 11,432 religious priests serving the Roman Catholic Church in the United States. Both numbers showed a slight decline from 2015. Priests are needed in all areas of the country, but the greatest need is in metropolitan areas that have large Catholic populations and in communities near Catholic educational institutions.

UNIONS AND ASSOCIATIONS

Roman Catholic priests who also work in nonreligious careers (such as teaching) may become members of a union or professional association. The National Federation of Priests' Councils is an organization for bishops, presbyterates, and priests. The National Religious Vocation Conference, a membership organization for vocation ministers for religious congregations, promotes vocation awareness, invitation, and discernment to life as a priest or religious sister or brother.

TIPS FOR ENTRY

1. Read *VISION: The Annual Catholic Religious Vocation Discernment Guide* (http://www.digitalvocationguide.org) to learn more about becoming a Roman Catholic priest.
2. Visit http://www.vocationnetwork.org/match and http://www.vocationnetwork.org for assistance in choosing a vocation.
3. Participate in a vocation discernment retreat. Additionally, talk with your parish priest about pursuing a priestly vocation.

FOR MORE INFORMATION

For information on conventions, publications, seminars, and recent news, contact

National Federation of Priests' Councils
333 North Michigan Avenue, Suite 1114
Chicago, IL 60601-4002
Tel: (888) 271-6372; (312) 442-9700
E-mail: nfpc@nfpc.org
http://www.nfpc.org

The NRVC can provide information about all kinds of Catholic vocations.

National Religious Vocation Conference (NVRC)
5401 South Cornell Avenue, Suite 207
Chicago, IL 60615-5664
Tel: (773) 363-5454
Fax: (773) 363-5530
http://www.nrvc.net

Roofers

■ OVERVIEW

Roofers install and repair roofs of buildings using a variety of materials and methods, including built-up roofing, single-ply roofing systems, asphalt shingles, tile, and slate. They may also waterproof and damp-proof walls, swimming pools, and other building surfaces. Approximately 116,410 roofers are employed in the United States.

■ HISTORY

Roofs cover buildings and protect their interiors against snow, rain, wind, temperature extremes, and strong sunlight. The earliest roofs were probably thatched with plant materials such as leaves, branches, or straw. With clay or a similar substance pressed into any open spaces, such a roof can provide good protection from the weather. Roofs constructed on frameworks of thick branches or timbers allowed different roof designs to develop, including the flat and pitched, or sloping, forms that are in use today. When brick and stone began to be used in buildings, people could construct domes and vaults, which are roof forms based on arches.

Throughout most of history, flat roofs have been associated with dry climates, where drainage of water off the roof is seldom a concern. In the 19th century, new roofing and building materials made flat roofs an economical alternative to pitched roofs in somewhat wetter conditions, such as those in much of the United States. Today, flat or very slightly sloped roofs are common on commercial buildings and are also used on some residential buildings. Pitched roofs in various forms have been used for many centuries, largely in climates where drainage is a concern. Most houses have pitched roofs.

All roofs must keep out water. There are two basic types of roof covering that do this: separate shingles, or flat pieces of a waterproof material that are placed so that water cannot get through at the joints; and a continuous layer or sheet membrane of a material that is impermeable to water. Different kinds of roofing materials are appropriate for different kinds of roofs, and each material has its own method of application.

The occupation of roofer has developed along with the various kinds of modern roofing materials. Roofers today must know about how the elements in each roofing system are used, and how water, temperature, and humidity affect the roof. While asphalt shingle roofs on homes may require only relatively simple materials and application procedures, large commercial building roofs can involve complex preparation and layering of materials to produce the necessary protective covering. A recent development in the field is the focus on creating roofing systems that reduce energy costs, are less of a burden on the environment, and have longer life spans than traditional roofs.

■ THE JOB

Although roofers usually are trained to apply most kinds of roofing, they often specialize in either sheet membrane roofing or prepared roofing materials such as asphalt shingles, slate, or tile.

One kind of sheet membrane roofing is called built-up roofing. Built-up roofing, used on flat roofs, consists of roofing felt (fabric saturated in bitumen, a tar-like material) laid into hot bitumen. To prepare for putting on a built-up roof, roofers may apply a layer of insulation to the bare roof deck. Then they spread molten bitumen over the roof surface, lay down overlapping layers of roofing felt, and spread more hot bitumen over the felt, sealing the seams and making the roof watertight. They repeat this process several times to build up as many layers as desired. They then give the top a smooth finish or embed gravel in the top for a rough surface.

Single-ply roofing, a relatively new roofing method, uses a waterproof sheet membrane and employs any of several different types of chemical products. Some roofing consists of polymer-modified bituminous compounds that are rolled out in sheets on the building's insulation. The compound may be remelted on the roof by torch or hot anvil to fuse it to or embed it in hot bitumen in a manner similar to built-up roofing. Other single-ply roofing is made of rubber

QUICK FACTS

ALTERNATE TITLE(S)
None

DUTIES
Install and repair roofs of
  buildings using a variety of
  materials and methods

SALARY RANGE
$24,560 to $36,720 to
  $62,180+

WORK ENVIRONMENT
Primarily Outdoors

BEST GEOGRAPHIC LOCATION(S)
Opportunities exist throughout
  the country

MINIMUM EDUCATION LEVEL
High School Diploma,
  Apprenticeship

SCHOOL SUBJECTS
Mathematics, Physical
  Education, Technical/Shop

EXPERIENCE
Apprenticeship

PERSONALITY TRAITS
Athletic, Hands On, Technical

SKILLS
Building/Trades, Interpersonal,
  Mechanical/Manual Dexterity

CERTIFICATION OR LICENSING
Required

SPECIAL REQUIREMENTS
Most employers hire
  applicants who are at least
  18 years of age

EMPLOYMENT PROSPECTS
Good

ADVANCEMENT PROSPECTS
Good

OUTLOOK
Faster than the Average

NOC
7291

O*NET-SOC
47-2181.00

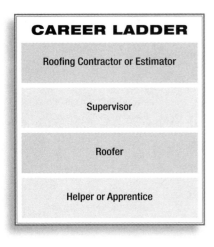

CAREER LADDER

Roofing Contractor or Estimator

Supervisor

Roofer

Helper or Apprentice

or plastic materials that can be sealed with contact adhesive cements, solvent welding, hot air welding, or other methods. Still another type of single-ply roofing consists of spray-in-place polyurethane foam with a polymeric coating. Roofers who apply these roofing systems must be trained in the application methods for each system. Many manufacturers of these systems require that roofers take special courses and receive certification before they are authorized to use the products.

To apply asphalt shingles, a very common roofing material on houses, roofers begin by cutting strips of roofing felt and tacking them down over the entire roof. They nail on horizontal rows of shingles, beginning at the low edge of the roof and working up. Sometimes they must cut shingles to fit around corners, vent pipes, and chimneys. Where two sections of roof meet, they nail or cement flashing, which consists of strips of metal or shingle that make the joints watertight.

Tile and slate shingles, which are more expensive types of residential roofing, are installed slightly differently. First, roofing felt is applied over the wood base. Next, the roofers punch holes in the slate or tile pieces so that nails can be inserted, or they embed the tiles in mortar. Each row of shingles overlaps the preceding row.

Metal roofing is applied by specially trained roofers or by sheet metal workers. One type of metal roof uses metal sections shaped like flat pans, soldered together for weatherproofing and attached by metal clips to the wood below. Another kind of metal roofing, called "standing seam roofing," has raised seams where the sections of sheet metal interlock.

Some roofers waterproof and damp-proof walls, swimming pools, tanks, and structures other than roofs. To prepare surfaces for waterproofing, workers smooth rough surfaces and roughen glazed surfaces. Then they brush or spray waterproofing material on the surface. Damp-proofing is done by spraying a coating of tar or asphalt onto interior or exterior surfaces to prevent the penetration of moisture.

The growing interest in "green" construction and more efficient use of natural resources has led some companies to incorporate landscape roofing systems to their buildings. With this type of roofing, roofers put a waterproof layer down first and test to ensure it is leak free. They next place a roof barrier over it, and then layers of soil in which trees and grass are planted. The plants and greenery on the roof absorb the sun and keep buildings cool in the summer; they also handle storm water runoff.

Roofers use various hand tools in their work, including hammers, roofing knives, mops, pincers, caulking guns, rollers, welders, chalk lines, and cutters.

■ EARNINGS

The earnings of roofers vary widely depending on how many hours they work, geographical location, skills and experience, and other factors. Sometimes bad weather prevents them from working, and some weeks they work fewer than 20 hours. They make up for lost time in other weeks, and if they work longer hours than the standard workweek (usually 40 hours), they receive extra pay for the overtime. While roofers in northern states may not work in the winter, most roofers work year-round.

In May 2015, median hourly earnings of roofers were $17.65, according to the U.S. Department of Labor, or a $36,720 yearly salary for full-time work. Wages ranged from less than $24,560 anually to more than $62,180 annually. Mean annual earnings for foundation, structure, and building exterior contractors were $46,360 annually. Those who worked in residential building construction averaged $49,210 annually.

Hourly rates for apprentices usually start at about 50 to 60 percent of the skilled worker's rate and increase periodically until the pay reaches 90 percent of the full rate during the final six months. Workers who belong to a union usually receive higher hourly wages and fringe benefits.

■ WORK ENVIRONMENT

Roofers work outdoors most of the time they are on the job. They work in the heat and cold, but not in wet weather. Roofs can get extremely hot during the summer. The work is physically strenuous, involving lifting heavy weights, prolonged standing, climbing, bending, and squatting. Roofers must work while standing on surfaces that may be steep and quite high; they must use caution to avoid injuries from falls while working on ladders, scaffolding, or roofs.

■ EXPLORING

High school or vocational school students may be able to get firsthand experience of this occupation through a part-time or summer job as a roofer's helper. It may be possible to visit a construction site to observe roofers at work, but a close look is unlikely, as roofers do most of their work at heights.

■ EDUCATION AND TRAINING REQUIREMENTS
High School

Most employers prefer to hire applicants at least 18 years of age who are in good physical condition and have a good sense of balance. Although a high school education or its equivalent is not required, it is generally preferred. Students can also take courses that familiarize them with some of the skills that are a regular part of roofing work. Beneficial courses include shop, basic mathematics, and mechanical drawing.

Postsecondary Training

Roofers learn the skills they need through on-the-job training or by completing a three-year apprenticeship. Most roofers learn informally on the job while they work under the supervision of experienced roofers. Beginners start as helpers, doing simple tasks like carrying equipment and putting up scaffolding. They gradually gain the skills and knowledge they need for more difficult tasks. Roofers who do not complete apprenticeships may need four or more years of on-the-job training to become familiar with all the materials and techniques they need to know.

Apprenticeship programs generally provide more thorough, balanced training. Apprenticeships are three years in length and combine a planned program of work experience with formal classroom instruction in related subjects. The work portion of the apprenticeship includes a minimum of 1,400 hours each year under the guidance of experienced roofers. Classroom instruction, amounting to at least 144 hours per year, covers such topics as safety practices, how to use and care for tools, and arithmetic.

Other Education or Training

The National Roofing Contractors Association offers educational resources, including seminars and customized training programs, on safety, customer service, project planning, business operations, and other topics. Contact the association for more information.

■ CERTIFICATION, LICENSING, AND SPECIAL REQUIREMENTS
Certification or Licensing

In addition to apprenticeship experience or on-the-job training, all roofers should receive safety training that is in compliance with standards set by the Occupational Safety and Health Administration (OSHA). Workers can get safety training through their employer or through OSHA's Outreach Training Program. The National Roofing Contractors Association University offers the certified roofing torch applicator designation to those

A roofer uses a blowtorch to install roofing material. (Dmitry Kalinovsky. Shutterstock.)

who complete a program that teaches the safe use of roofing torches used to apply polymer-modified bitumen roofing products.

Other Requirements

Some employers have age requirements—often a minimum of 18 years—for job candidates.

■ EXPERIENCE, SKILLS, AND PERSONALITY TRAITS

Previous experience as a helper or apprentice is required to enter the field.

A roofer with a fear of heights will not get far in his or her career. Roofers need a good sense of balance and good hand-eye coordination. Since this work can be dangerous, roofers need to pay attention to detail and be able to follow directions precisely. They should enjoy working outdoors and working with their hands. The work is strenuous, so physical strength and stamina are essential. Roofers may work with architects and other construction workers as well as interact with customers, so they must be able to work as part of a team. To advance in this field, to the position of *estimator* for example,

SIDING, ROOFING, AND TRIM

LEARN MORE ABOUT IT

Chew Yit Lin, Michael. *Construction Technology for Tall Buildings,* 4th ed. Hackensack, N.J.: World Scientific Publishing Company, 2012.

Editors of Creative Publishing International. *Black & Decker Complete Guide to Roofing and Siding,* 3rd ed. Minneapolis, Minn.: Creative Publishing International, 2013.

Editors of Fine Homebuilding. *Siding, Roofing, and Trim,* Rev. ed. Newtown, Conn.: The Taunton Press, 2014.

Luckett, Kelly. *Green Roof Construction and Maintenance.* New York: McGraw-Hill Professional, 2009.

a roofer should also have strong communications and mathematical skills.

■ EMPLOYMENT PROSPECTS

Employers

There are approximately 116,410 people employed as roofers in the United States. Most (about 70 percent) work for established roofing contractors. Approximately 28 percent of roofers are self-employed, and many specialize in residential work.

Starting Out

People who are planning to start out as helpers and learn on the job can directly contact roofing contractors to inquire about possible openings. Job leads may also be located through the local office of the state employment service, online employment sites, or newspaper classified ads. Graduates of vocational schools may get useful information from their schools' placement offices.

People who want to become apprentices can learn about apprenticeships in their area by contacting local roofing contractors, the state employment service, or the local office of the United Union of Roofers, Waterproofers and Allied Workers.

■ ADVANCEMENT PROSPECTS

Experienced roofers who work for roofing contractors may be promoted to supervisory positions in which they are responsible for coordinating the activities of other roofers. Roofers may also become estimators, calculating the costs of roofing jobs before the work is done. Roofers, who have the right combination of personal characteristics, including good judgment, the ability to deal with people, and planning skills, may be able to go into business for themselves as independent roofing contractors.

■ OUTLOOK

Employment for roofers is expected to grow faster than the average for all occupations through 2024, according to the U.S. Department of Labor. Roofers will continue to be in demand for the construction of new buildings, and roofs tend to need more maintenance and repair work than other parts of buildings. About 75 percent of roofing work is on existing structures. Roofers will always be needed for roof repairs and replacement, even during economic downturns when construction activity generally decreases. Also, damp-proofing and waterproofing are expected to provide an increasing proportion of the work done by roofers. On the other hand, more construction workers are completing roofing projects as part of their work, which could impede job growth.

Turnover in this job is high because roofing work is strenuous, hot, and dirty. Many workers consider roofing a temporary job and move into other construction trades. Since roofing is done during the warmer part of the year, job opportunities will probably be best during spring and summer.

■ UNIONS AND ASSOCIATIONS

Some roofers are members of the United Union of Roofers, Waterproofers and Allied Workers. The National Roofing Contractors Association is a membership organization for roofing contractors that offers publications, continuing education opportunities, and other resources.

■ TIPS FOR ENTRY

1. Visit http://www.unionroofers.com/Training-and-Education/Apprenticeship.aspx for information on apprenticeships.
2. Read *Professional Roofing* (http://www.professionalroofing.net) to learn more about the field.
3. Talk to roofers about their careers. Ask them for tips on breaking into the field.

■ FOR MORE INFORMATION

For information on membership benefits and about becoming a professional roofer, contact

National Roofing Contractors Association
10255 West Higgins Road, Suite 600
Rosemont, IL 60018-5607
Tel: (847) 299-9070
Fax: (847) 299-1183
http://www.nrca.net

For information on certification, CERTA, and other educational programs offered by the National Roofing Contractors Association, visit

NRCA Institute
http://www.nrca.net/rp/education/nrca

For information on union membership and careers, contact

United Union of Roofers, Waterproofers and Allied Workers

1660 L Street, NW, Suite 800

Washington, D.C. 20036-5646

Tel: (202) 463-7663

Fax: (202) 463-6906

E-mail: roofers@unionroofers.com

http://www.unionroofers.com

Roustabouts

◼ OVERVIEW

Roustabouts do the routine physical labor and maintenance around oil wells, pipelines, and natural gas facilities. Sample tasks include clearing trees and brush, mixing concrete, manually loading and unloading pipe and other materials onto or from trucks or boats, and assembling pumps, boilers, valves, and steam engines and performing minor repairs on such equipment. Roustabouts find work in approximately 30 states nationwide, especially Texas, Oklahoma, Louisiana, North Dakota, and New Mexico. There are approximately 51,290 roustabouts working in the United States.

◼ HISTORY

In the 19th century, people began to search for oil and extract it from deposits inside the earth. The first exploratory oil well was drilled in 1859 in Titusville, Pennsylvania. After much hard work with crude equipment, the drilling crew struck oil, and within a short time the first oil boom was on.

From the earliest days of drilling for oil, roustabouts have performed the necessary manual labor tasks of clearing the land and preparing the site for drilling. Nowadays, with increasing automation and mechanization in the oil industry, roustabouts routinely operate motorized lifts, power tools, electronic testers, and tablet computers. Although roustabouts still perform such chores as digging trenches or cutting down trees and brush, the advent of labor-saving equipment has enabled roustabouts to assume more maintenance and troubleshooting responsibilities.

◼ THE JOB

Roustabouts perform a wide range of tasks, from picking up trash at well sites to running heavy equipment. Part of their work involves clearing sites that have been selected for drilling and building a solid base for drilling equipment. Roustabouts cut down trees to make way

QUICK FACTS

ALTERNATE TITLE(S)
None

DUTIES
Perform physical labor and maintenance around oil wells, pipelines, and natural gas facilities

SALARY RANGE
$25,160 to $38,700 to $57,240+

WORK ENVIRONMENT
Primarily Outdoors

BEST GEOGRAPHIC LOCATION(S)
Roustabouts find work in about 30 states nationwide, especially Texas, Oklahoma, Louisiana, North Dakota, and New Mexico

MINIMUM EDUCATION LEVEL
High School Diploma

SCHOOL SUBJECTS
Mathematics, Physical Education, Technical/Shop

EXPERIENCE
Little or no formal training or experience is required

PERSONALITY TRAITS
Athletic, Hands On, Technical

SKILLS
Building/Trades, Math, Mechanical/Manual Dexterity

CERTIFICATION OR LICENSING
Required

SPECIAL REQUIREMENTS
Must have a valid driver's license; some positions require a commercial driver's license or crane and forklift operator licenses; must pass drug screenings

EMPLOYMENT PROSPECTS
Good

ADVANCEMENT PROSPECTS
Fair

OUTLOOK
About as Fast as the Average

NOC
8615

O*NET-SOC
47-5071.00

for roads or to reduce fire hazards. They dig trenches for foundations, fill excavated areas, mix up batches of wet concrete, and pour concrete into building forms. Other jobs include loading and unloading pipe and other materials onto or from trucks and boats.

Roustabouts also dig drainage ditches around wells, storage tanks, and other installations. They walk flow lines

CAREER LADDER

Skilled Craftsworker or Machinery Operator

Lead Roustabout

Experienced Roustabout

Entry-Level Roustabout

to locate leaks and clean up spilled oil by bailing it into barrels or other containers. They also paint equipment such as storage tanks and pumping units and clean and repair oil field machinery and equipment.

The tools roustabouts use range from simple hand tools like hammers and shovels to heavy equipment such as backhoes or trackhoes. Roustabouts use heavy wrenches and other hand tools to help break out and replace pipe, valves, and other components for repairs or modifications and truck winches for moving or lifting heavy items. Roustabouts also operate motorized lifts, power tools, and electronic sensors and testers. They may also operate tractors with shredders, forklifts, or ditching machines.

◼ EARNINGS

The earnings of roustabouts vary depending on the branch of the industry they work in, the region of the country, the hours they work, and other factors. Offshore workers generally earn more than on-shore, and roustabouts who work for oil companies generally earn more than those who work for drilling contractors.

Some beginning salaries are on a par with minimum wage, according to the Association of Energy Service Companies. The U.S. Department of Labor reports that the mean annual salary of roustabouts was $38,700 in May 2015. Salaries ranged from less than $25,160 to $57,240 or more annually. Generally, roustabouts receive time and a half for overtime; conversely, employers do not pay them if they finish early during a slow time. Those who work away from home receive additional "sub pay" plus reimbursement for their hotel and other expenses. Most oil rig companies will also cover air fare, medical insurance, and meals.

◼ WORK ENVIRONMENT

Roustabouts work in and around oil fields, on drilling platforms in oceans, on pipelines that transport oil or gas long distances, and at facilities that capture and distribute natural gas. In onshore oil fields or on ocean platforms, roustabouts work outside in all types of weather. On offshore rigs and platforms, they can experience strong ocean currents, violent storms, and bitterly cold winds.

Workers in oil fields on shore may have to contend with extremely hot or cold weather, dust, or insects.

Roustabouts on offshore drilling rigs generally work 12-hour days, seven days a week. After seven days on, they usually get seven days off, although some crews may have to work two to four weeks at a stretch, followed by an equal amount of time off. Workers generally stay on the ocean platform during their whole work shift and return to shore via helicopter or crew boat. It is not unusual for offshore roustabouts to live hundreds of miles from the ocean platform where they work.

In onshore oil fields, roustabouts are more likely to work five-day, 40-hour weeks, although this is not always the case, especially during a "boom." Some roustabouts average between 120 and 130 hours in a two-week pay period. Roustabouts may travel anywhere from a half-mile away to 100 or more miles away to a work site. They take short lunch and other breaks depending on how busy the crew is. The end of the day might come early in the afternoon or in the middle of the night. Many drilling operations work around the clock until either discovering oil or abandoning the location as a dry hole. This requires shifts of workers every day of the week.

Being a roustabout can be stressful due to the long hours and time away from home, family, and friends. Some roustabouts work away from home one to three weeks at a time with only a few days off.

Roustabouts' work is strenuous and potentially dangerous, especially on open-sea drilling platforms. They lift heavy materials and equipment and frequently must bend, stoop, and climb. They have to use caution to avoid falling off derricks and other high places, as well as injuries from being hit by falling objects. They are subject to cuts, scrapes, and sore or strained muscles. Because fire is a hazard around oil operations, roustabouts and other workers must be trained in fire fighting and be ready to respond to emergencies.

Roustabouts who work on drilling crews can expect to move from place to place, since drilling at a site may be completed in a few weeks or months. If they are working at a site that is producing oil, they usually remain there for longer periods of time.

◼ EXPLORING

Talking with someone who has worked as a roustabout or in another oil field operations job would be a very helpful and inexpensive way of exploring this field. Visit the Web sites of oil and gas industry professional associations, as well as leading companies, to learn more about the field.

Those who live near an oil field may be able to arrange a tour by contacting the public relations department of oil companies or drilling contractors. Another option is to drive by oil fields that lie along public roads and public lands and take an unofficial tour by car.

Some summer and other temporary jobs as roustabouts are available, and they provide a good way to find out about this field. Temporary workers can learn firsthand the basics of oil field operations, equipment maintenance, safety, and other aspects of the work. Those individuals who are thinking about this kind of work should also consider entering a two-year training program in petroleum technology to learn about the field.

■ EDUCATION AND TRAINING REQUIREMENTS
High School

Little or no formal training or experience is required to get a job as a roustabout. However, there are more applicants than there are jobs, which allows employers to be selective, choosing people who have previous experience as a roustabout or formal training in a related area. While in high school, classes in mathematics, shop, and technical training will be helpful in preparing to work as a roustabout.

Postsecondary Training

More and more applicants have earned an associate's degree in petroleum technology, which demonstrates their familiarity with oil field operations and equipment. In general, any technical training, specialized courses, or pertinent experience can be a definite advantage in securing a job and later in getting promotions to more responsible positions.

To learn the skills they need, some newly hired roustabouts take courses at junior colleges or self-study courses such as those offered by the University of Texas at Austin (http://www.utexas.edu/ce). Some employers, particularly the major oil companies, help pay for job-related courses that employees take during their own time. Because the turnover rate among roustabouts is fairly high, however, employers are usually reluctant to invest a great deal in specialized training for beginning workers.

Other Education or Training

Roustabouts can learn about continuing education (CE) conferences, tradeshows, professional meetings, and social events by checking out The Rigzone Events Calendar (http://www.rigzone.com/events). Additionally, the American Petroleum Institute, Association of Energy

Two roustabouts work on a pipe on an oil rig. (Rumo. Shutterstock.)

Service Companies, and the Society of Petroleum Engineers provide CE opportunities that will be of interest to roustabouts. Contact these organizations for more information.

■ CERTIFICATION, LICENSING, AND SPECIAL REQUIREMENTS
Certification or Licensing

No professional certifications or special licenses are required for roustabouts.

Other Requirements

Roustabouts need a current valid vehicle operator's license and a good driving record. Depending on the equipment they operate, roustabouts may also need a commercial driver's license as well as crane and forklift operator licenses. Some jobs may require candidates to undergo drug screenings and physical examinations.

DRILLING FOR OIL AND GAS

LEARN MORE ABOUT IT

Hilyard, Joseph. *The Oil & Gas Industry: A Nontechnical Guide.* Tulsa, Okla.: PennWell Corp., 2012.

Hyne, Norman J. *Nontechnical Guide to Petroleum Geology, Exploration, Drilling & Production,* 3rd ed. Tulsa, Okla.: PennWell Corp., 2012.

Kolb, Robert W. *The Natural Gas Revolution: At the Pivot of the World's Energy Future.* Upper Saddle River, N.J.: FT Press, 2013.

Leffler, William L., Richard Pattarozzi, and Gordon Sterling. *Deepwater Petroleum Exploration & Production: A Nontechnical Guide,* 2nd ed. Tulsa, Okla.: PennWell Corp., 2011.

■ EXPERIENCE, SKILLS, AND PERSONALITY TRAITS

Little or no formal training or experience is required to work as a roustabout, but those with prior work experience will increase their chances of landing a job, getting promoted, and possibly earning higher pay.

Roustabouts must be physically fit, with good coordination, agility, and eyesight. They must enjoy working out of doors, be willing to work in extreme weather, and often are required to work more than 40 hours a week. In addition, employers may require that job applicants pass a physical examination and a screening test for drug use before hiring them. Applicants might also have to take aptitude tests to determine their mechanical ability.

Those who become roustabouts should be ready to pitch in with extra work when the situation requires it. They should work well both on their own and as part of a crew. Those on offshore platforms must be able to get along with the same people for extended periods of time.

Roustabouts need to be comfortable with an unpredictable field; at times they do not have steady work, and at other times they work several weeks straight with only a few days off. Many roustabouts have a taste for challenge, travel, and adventure rather than a settled home life. Others look at the job as a short-term way to gain experience, earn money for college or some other specific expense, or to prepare for a better paying job in the energy industry.

■ EMPLOYMENT PROSPECTS
Employers

Approximately 51,290 roustabouts are employed in the United States. Most roustabouts are employed by oil companies, working with production crews around existing oil wells or natural gas facilities. Others work for drilling contractors, which are companies that specialize in drilling new wells. Roustabouts usually work under the supervision of a maintenance superintendent and frequently assist skilled workers such as welders, electricians, and mechanics.

Starting Out

Potential roustabouts can contact drilling contractors or oil or natural gas companies directly about possible job openings. For the names and addresses of oil companies, visit the oil and industry Web site Rigzone (http://www.rigzone.com) or search directories such as Oildex's Oil & Gas Industry Directory (https://www.oildex.com/resources/directory/). Information may also be available through the local office of state employment services. Graduates of technical training programs may find assistance in locating employment through the placement office at their schools.

Roustabouts are usually hired in the field by the maintenance superintendent or by a local company representative. Many roustabouts learn their skills on the job by working under the supervision of experienced workers. Roustabouts with no previous experience are considered "hands" who learn by helping the lead roustabout and crew. They begin with simple jobs, like unloading trucks, and gradually take on more complicated work. As they progress, they learn about oil and natural gas field operations and equipment, safety practices, and maintenance procedures for the machinery.

■ ADVANCEMENT PROSPECTS

A job as a roustabout is usually an entry-level position. To advance, roustabouts will need to prove that they can do the work; advancement to a variety of other jobs comes with experience.

Roustabouts who are part of maintenance and operation crews may advance to such positions as *switcher, gauger, pumper,* or *lease operator.* Those with proven leadership abilities may eventually become *lead roustabout, chief operators* or *maintenance superintendents.* Roustabouts who are on drilling crews may advance to become *roughnecks, floor hands,* or *rotary helpers,* and, later, *derrick operators, drillers,* and *tool pushers,* who are in charge of one or more drilling rigs; they also might become *engineering technicians.* All of these positions represent a special set of responsibilities in a complex operation.

Some companies run their own training programs offering employees the opportunity to take specialized courses in welding, electricity, and other craft areas; roustabouts who participate in such courses may be prepared to advance into such jobs as *welders, electricians, pipefitters,* and other *craftworkers.*

OUTLOOK

Employment for roustabouts is expected to grow 8 percent, about as fast as the average for all careers through 2024, according to the U.S. Department of Labor. Continuing demand for oil and natural gas resources, which will continue to be primary energy sources for decades, will spur employment growth. Turnover is high among roustabouts, especially in offshore drilling. The work is difficult and dirty enough that many people stay in the job only a short time. The need to replace workers who leave will account for many job openings. Workers who have experience or formal training in the field will have the best chance of being hired.

Fluctuating prices of oil and natural gas greatly affect employment in this industry. When oil and gas prices rise sharply, companies invest more money in new technology and employees in order to increase their profits. When oil and gas prices fall, companies may be less inclined to expand domestic and international exploration and production of oil and gas, thus decreasing the number of jobs available.

This industry is greatly affected by environmental concerns, especially when drilling and exploring are limited in sensitive or federally protected areas. In addition, many companies have moved drilling and exploration to locations outside of the United States, which decreases the number of workers needed in this country. However, companies are likely to continue to restructure and look for cost-effective technology that permits new drilling abroad and offshore in the Gulf of Mexico, which would provide jobs for U.S. workers.

UNIONS AND ASSOCIATIONS

Most roustabouts are not union members. Those who are, however, may be represented by United Steelworkers. The American Petroleum Institute and the Association of Energy Service Companies represent companies in the petroleum industry. The Society of Petroleum Engineers is a membership organization that offers publications, continuing education classes and webinars, and other resources.

TIPS FOR ENTRY

1. Read *Well Servicing* (http://www.wellservicing-magazine.com) to learn more about the field.

2. Visit http://www.rigzone.com/jobs/search_jobs.asp for job listings.
3. Talk to roustabouts about their careers. Ask them for advice on breaking into the field.

FOR MORE INFORMATION

For facts and statistics about the petroleum industry, contact
American Petroleum Institute
1220 L Street, NW
Washington, D.C. 20005-4070
Tel: (202) 682-8000
http://www.api.org

For information on well-servicing careers, visit
Association of Energy Service Companies
121 E. Magnolia Street, Suite 103
Friendswood, TX 77546
Tel: (713) 781-0758
Fax: (713) 781-7542
http://www.aesc.net

For information on courses and publications offered through the university's Petroleum Extension Service, visit
Petroleum Extension Service of The University of Texas at Austin
J.J. Pickle Research Campus
10100 Burnet Road, Bldg. 2
Austin, TX 78758-4445
Tel: (800) 687-4132; (512) 471-5940
E-mail: info@petex.utexas.edu
http://www.utexas.edu/ce/petex

For a list of petroleum technology schools, contact
Society of Petroleum Engineers
PO Box 833836
Richardson, TX 75083-3836
Tel: (800) 456-6863; (972) 952-9393
Fax: (972) 952-9435
E-mail: spedal@spe.org
http://www.spe.org

For information on union membership, contact
United Steelworkers
Five Gateway Center
Pittsburgh, PA 15222
Tel: (412) 562-2400
http://www.usw.org

Rubber Goods Production Workers

■ OVERVIEW

Rubber goods production workers make items out of natural and synthetic rubber materials. They soften, shape, cure, cut, mold, and otherwise treat rubber to make thousands of different products, from household goods to parts for spacecrafts.

■ HISTORY

Natural rubber is a pliable, stretchy material made from the milky juice of various tropical plants. Rubber was given its name in 1770 when a chemist observed it could be used to rub away, or erase, pencil marks. The earliest commercial use for rubber was in the 1840s when Charles Goodyear, an American, invented the vulcanization process. Vulcanization improves the properties of rubber, making it more elastic, stronger, and more durable. Beginning as early as 1845, long before bicycles and motor vehicles became common, vulcanized rubber was occasionally used in wheels. Rubber tire-making became an industry in 1888, when John Dunlop, a British surgeon, developed pneumatic tires for bicycles. Not long after that, rubber found an important new market in automobile tires. By the early 20th century, a useful kind of synthetic rubber was being produced to supplement natural rubber supplies for a growing list of purposes, although vehicles depended on tires made of natural rubber until World War II.

Before World War I, most rubber used in the United States was imported from South America. From then until World War II, most rubber came from Southeast Asia. When the supply was cut off by war, the industry entered a crash program and quickly developed new and better kinds of synthetic rubber. Since that time, both natural and synthetic rubber have continued to be important commodities. Today, both are found in countless products, from shoes to conveyor belts, baby bottles to mammoth storage containers, rubber balls to gaskets on spacecraft. Approximately 70 percent of the rubber used in the United States is made into tires for automobiles, trucks, and other vehicles.

■ THE JOB

Rubber goods are formed from natural or synthetic materials. Different products go through different processes, but generally all rubber is heated, shaped, and finished. Most of this work is done by machine.

The first step in rubber goods production is breaking up and mixing the crude rubber. *Rubber cutters* operate machines to cut bales of crude rubber into pieces. *Rubber-mill tenders* tend milling machines that mix, blend, knead, or refine scrap, crude, or synthetic rubber. The machines have corrugated rolls that break the rubber apart and soften it. Rubber is then mixed with chemicals to give it various desirable properties. *Formula weighers* operate tram cars on monorails beneath storage bins to collect and weigh ingredients. Rubber is mixed with ingredients such as zinc oxide, sulfur, stearic acid, or fillers in mixing machines such as banbury mixers. Chemists and others decide which chemicals to use, and they test samples of the mix before further processing. *Foam rubber mixers*, *frothing-machine operators*, and *cement mixers* tend special machines that mix air and chemicals into rubber to produce foam rubber and rubber cement.

Mixed and heated rubber is then shaped in one of several ways. It may be squeezed into sheets, molded in shapes, or extruded into tubing or other forms. *Calender operators* run machines that form rubber sheets of specified thickness. *Sponge-press operators* run machines that form and cure sponge rubber into sheeting for gaskets, insulation, and carpet padding. *Dusting-and-brushing-machine operators* may dust the sheets with talc to keep them from sticking together before further processing. Other workers shape rubber into products using various processes, including building up thin layers (plies) of rubber sheeting. Among these workers and products are *self-sealing-fuel-tank builders*, who make airplane fuel tanks; *belt builders*, *sectional-belt-mold assemblers*, *v-belt builders*, and *belt-builder helpers*, who make rubber belts; and *expansion-joint builders*, who make expansion joints for ends of rubber hoses.

Some rubber is formed by molding. *Pourers* fill curing molds with latex using a hose or a machine lever on a conveyor-belt machine. Some rubber products are formed by injection. Injection-molding-machine tenders inject hot rubber into molds to form molded products. Products such as balloons and rubber gloves are formed by *dippers*, who dip forms into liquid compounded latex rubber to coat them. Most other molded rubber products, including tires, are pressed and heated in molds. Foam-rubber molders make foam cushions and mattresses this way. *Press tenders* make hard objects such as golf and bowling balls. *Arch-cushion press operators* heat-press sponge rubber into arch cushions for rubber shoes and boots. Other molding is done by spraying. *Foam dispensers* spray liquid foam rubber into shaped plastic sheets to make padded dashboards and door panels for vehicles. *Skin formers* shape the plastic sheeting for these products. *Mold strippers* remove molded items from molds and prepare molds for further use . *Mold cleaners* clean, store, and distribute these molds.

The final method of forming rubber is extrusion. In this method, rubber is forced through dies to form continuous shaped rubber products such as tubes and strips. *Extruder operators* and *extruder helpers* set up and run extrusion machines. They select the proper die and install it on the machine, feed rubber stock into the machine, and set the speed at which the rubber is to be forced through the die. *Extruder tenders* regulate and run machines that extrude rubber into strands for elastic yarn. In shoe and boot making, *wink-cutter operators* extrude and cut rubber strips for rubber soles.

Rugs and other fabric goods are often given a rubber backing using calenders, which are machines that press materials between rollers to give a particular finish. Among the workers who operate these machines are four-roll *calender operators*, who use calenders to coat fabric with rubber to a specified thickness. *Calender-let-off operators* use machines to cure and dry fabrics after they are coated. *Calender-wind-up tenders* accumulate the coated fabric into rolls of specified size. *Fabric normalizers* shrink rubberized fabric to increase its strength.

Rubber is cured after it assumes its final shape. In curing, rubber is subjected to heat and pressure to increase its hardness, durability, stability, and elasticity. One such curing process is vulcanization. Foam-rubber sheeting is cured by *foam-rubber curers*, who roll a latex mixture into curing ovens. *Belt-press operators* and *v-belt curers* cure rubber transmission and conveyor belting. *Weather-strip machine operators* mold and vulcanize sponge-rubber beading to make weather-stripping for automobiles.

Rubber sheets, strips, and tubing must be cut into lengths and shapes to form products of specified types and sizes. *Rubber-goods cutter-finishers* use machines to cut, drill, and grind rubber goods, and they verify the sizes of goods using rulers, calipers, gauges, and templates. *Extruder cutters* cut extruded rubber into lengths. *Automatic-die-cutting-machine operators* stamp out rubber shapes using machines with sharp dies. *Roll cutters* use a lathe to cut rolls of rubber or rubberized fabric. *Rubber-cutting-machine tenders* use a guillotine-type

QUICK FACTS

ALTERNATE TITLE(S)
Arch-Cushion Press Operators, Automatic-Die-Cutting-Machine Operators, Band Machine Operators, Belt Builders, Belt-Builder Helpers, Belt-Press Operators, Calender Operators, Calender-Let-Off Operators, Calender-Wind-Up Tenders, Dusting-and-Brushing-Machine Operators, Expansion-Joint Builders, Extruder Cutters, Fabric Normalizers, Foam-Padded-Products Finishers, Foam Rubber Mixers, Machine Skivers, Mat Punchers, Molded-Rubber-Goods Cutters, Roll Cutters, Rubber Curers, Rubber Cutters, Rubber-Cutting-Machine Tenders, Rubber-Goods Cutter-Finishers, Rubber Goods Inspectors, Rubber-Mill Tenders, Sectional-Belt-Mold Assemblers, Self-Sealing-Fuel-Tank Builders, Splitting-Machine Operators, Sponge-Press Operators, Strap-Cutting-Machine Operators, V-Belt Builders, V-Belt Curers, Weather-Strip Machine Operators, Wink-Cutter Operators

DUTIES
Soften, shape, cure, cut, mold, and otherwise treat rubber to make a variety of products

SALARY RANGE
$21,440 to $43,130 to $58,660+

WORK ENVIRONMENT
Primarily Indoors

BEST GEOGRAPHIC LOCATION(S)
Opportunities are available throughout the country, but many rubber goods plants are located in Indiana and Ohio

MINIMUM EDUCATION LEVEL
High School Diploma

SCHOOL SUBJECTS
Chemistry, Mathematics, Technical/Shop

EXPERIENCE
No experience required

PERSONALITY TRAITS
Conventional, Hands On, Technical

SKILLS
Building/Trades, Mechanical/Manual Dexterity

CERTIFICATION OR LICENSING
None

SPECIAL REQUIREMENTS
None

EMPLOYMENT PROSPECTS
Poor

ADVANCEMENT PROSPECTS
Fair

OUTLOOK
Decline

NOC
9214, 9423, 9615

O*NET-SOC
17-3029.09, 51-9021.00, 51-9197.00

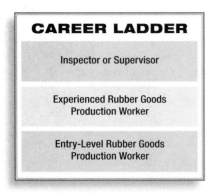

CAREER LADDER

Inspector or Supervisor

Experienced Rubber Goods Production Worker

Entry-Level Rubber Goods Production Worker

machine to cut rubber slabs. *Molded-rubber-goods cutters* use cutting dies to trim molded articles.

Other workers cut rubber for specific products or purposes. These workers include *strap-cutting-machine operators*, who cut leg straps for hip boots; *band machine operators*, who cut rubber bands from special tubing; and *hose cutters,* who cut rubber hose into specified lengths. *Mat punchers* punch automobile floor mats from sheeting. *Splitting-machine operators* cut scrap tires or rubber sheets into pieces for reclamation.

Rubber items made of a single piece of rubber often need to go through a finishing process. *Buffers* may buff items to smooth and polish them; *dippers* may coat them with vinyl. Workers called *openers* pull weather-stripping through a machine to force apart sides stuck together during curing. *Machine skivers* bevel edges of shoe parts to prepare them for cementing or stitching. *Padded-products finishers* repair defects in padded automobile parts by injecting wrinkles and gaps with liquid rubber foam. Other workers do many other specialized finishing tasks, such as splicing tubing, rolling rings on the mouths of balloons, pressing seams on shoes together to make them watertight, and crimping the edges of articles to reinforce them.

The final processing of rubber items may involve assembling several pieces, decorating surfaces, and quality inspections. Workers who assemble items position and cement or stitch pieces together to make such goods as footwear, shock absorbers for airplane gas tanks, pneumatic airplane deicers, inflatable animals and figures for parades, and many other types of rubber goods. Among the specialized workers who decorate rubber goods are those who print designs or lettering on balloons, brand names on rubber hoses, and designs on rubber sheeting that will be made into footwear. Once goods are finished, *rubber goods inspectors* make sure company standards are met and repair defects they find.

EARNINGS

The earnings of workers in rubber goods production vary widely according to the workers' skills, seniority, the hours they work, and other factors. Many workers are members of unions, and their pay is determined by agreements between the union and company management. In general, earnings compare favorably to those of workers in other production jobs in industry. According to the U.S. Bureau of Labor Statistics, mean annual earnings for all rubber production workers were $43,130 in May 2015. Tire builders had median annual earnings of $39,120. Salaries ranged from less than $24,950 to $58,660 or more. Crushing, grinding, and polishing machine setters, operators, and tenders earned median annual salaries of $33,810. Ten percent earned less than $21,440, while 10 percent earned $51,950 or more. Salaries will vary depending on experience, hours worked, and whether or not the job involves supervisory duties. Workers on night shifts are usually paid more than those who work day shifts.

In addition to their regular earnings, rubber goods workers generally receive benefits such as paid vacation days and holidays, sick leave, and employer contributions to pension plans, and life and health insurance.

WORK ENVIRONMENT

Most employees in rubber goods production plants work about 41 hours per week, according to the U.S. Department of Labor. Conditions on the job are generally quite safe. Plants are equipped with special ventilation systems to remove heat, fumes, and dust, and safety features on machinery protect workers from most injuries. Most plants are well lighted and have comfortable heating and cooling systems.

Like most production work, rubber goods jobs often involve repetitive tasks. Working with hot presses, sharp tools, and heavy machinery requires steady nerves and mechanical aptitude.

EXPLORING

During college or technical school training, you may be able to obtain a summer job in a rubber goods plant. The experience can help you decide whether you like the work, and it may also be an advantage if you want full-time employment in the field when you graduate. Another useful experience would be to visit a local rubber goods plant. Some companies allow group tours of their facilities to educate the public about their operations.

EDUCATION AND TRAINING REQUIREMENTS
High School

Because most rubber goods production workers learn their skills on the job, a high school diploma is often the only necessary qualification. Recommended classes include mathematics, speech, English, chemistry, and computer science.

Postsecondary Training

No postsecondary training is required for production jobs, but you will need a college degree if you plan to work as chemist, engineer, researcher, or manager in the rubber goods industry.

■ CERTIFICATION, LICENSING, AND SPECIAL REQUIREMENTS
Certification or Licensing

There are no certification or licensing requirements for rubber goods production workers.

■ EXPERIENCE, SKILLS, AND PERSONALITY TRAITS

Most beginning workers enter the industry with few, if any, specialized skills, and learn what they need to know on the job. Those with prior work experience will increase their chances of landing a job, getting promoted, and possibly earning higher pay.

Production workers need to be in good health and they must have some aptitude for working with machinery and other tools. Other important traits include strong time-management and communication skills and the ability to follow instructions and perform sometimes repetitive tasks. Inspectors must have good eyesight and be able to make quick decisions.

■ EMPLOYMENT PROSPECTS
Employers

Many of the rubber goods plants in the United States are located in Ohio and Indiana, although new plants are springing up in the South. There are rubber plants around the world, especially in Europe, North America, and Japan.

Starting Out

The best way to look for work in this industry is to apply directly to rubber goods plants that may be hiring new employees. Jobs may also be located through the local offices of the state employment service, employment Web sites, newspaper classified ads, or offices of the unions that organize workers in local plants.

■ ADVANCEMENT PROSPECTS

After they have gained experience and shown that they are reliable employees, rubber production workers may

A worker looks up at a stack of large tires in a factory. (Vladimir Melnik. Shutterstock.)

be promoted to positions in which they are responsible for supervising other workers or for performing tasks that require higher skill levels. Some workers eventually become rubber goods inspectors. Taking courses in technical schools or colleges can speed advancement for many workers.

■ OUTLOOK

Overall employment in the rubber industry is predicted to decline through 2024. The Bureau of Labor statistics opportunities for crushing, grinding, and polishing machine setters, operators, and tenders as well as for cutting and slicing machine setters, operators, and tenders will shrink by 8 percent in that period. Employment is expected to decline by 14 percent for tire builders; by 17 percent for hand cutters and trimmers; and by 10 percent for furnace, kiln, oven, drier, and kettle operators and tenders during this same time span. Increasing automation in manufacturing processes and technological advances that make some rubber goods better and longer-lasting have sharply reduced the number of rubber goods production jobs that are available. Those with advanced training, especially knowledge of computer systems that are used to operate high-tech manufacturing equipment, will have the best job prospects.

On the positive side, LMC International Ltd. reports that world rubber consumption is expected to grow to 3.5 percent annually through 2018, with a majority of

ALL ABOUT RUBBER

DID YOU KNOW?

- In the 1490s, Christopher Columbus discovered rubber in Haiti. While there, he observed the natives playing with a ball made from the sap of a tree called *cau-uchu*.
- Rubber grows on plantations in Indonesia, Malaysia, Thailand, and the west coast of Africa. Today, more than 90 percent of the natural rubber supply comes from Southeast Asia,
- Natural rubber is made from saps of certain types of trees and plants, whereas synthetic rubber usually has oil as its base and is composed of chemical compounds.
- Approximately 70 percent of all rubber used is synthetic.

Sources: Alliance Rubber Company; eHow.com; Rubber Manufacturers Association

rubber demand from the motor vehicle sector. Because 70 percent of the rubber industry is devoted to tires for vehicles, rubber goods production will always be related to the state of the automobile industry. When fewer cars are being manufactured and sold, there is less need for workers who make tires. The U.S car industry is recoving from the recent economic downturn, and demand for rubber will likely increase during the next decade.

As new uses for synthetic rubber are developed, probably a smaller portion of the rubber industry will depend on making rubber tires. Instead, new products such as rubber-like paints, waterproofings, and noise-control pads for use in building construction may make up a larger part of the industry's production.

Normal employee turnover in this industry will mean that every year, some openings will become available as experienced workers move into new jobs or leave the workforce altogether.

■ UNIONS AND ASSOCIATIONS

Many rubber goods production workers are members of unions such as United Steelworkers and the International Brotherhood of Teamsters. The Rubber Manufacturers Association is an association for manufacturers of tires, tubes, roofing, sporting goods, mechanical, and industrial products. The International Institute of Synthetic Rubber Producers is a member organization for global synthetic rubber producers.

■ TIPS FOR ENTRY

1. Read *Rubber World* (http://www.rubberworld .com/RWmagazine.asp) to learn more about the field.
2. Conduct information interviews with rubber goods production workers and ask them for advice on preparing for and entering the field.
3. Join United Steelworkers and the International Brotherhood of Teamsters to increase your chances of landing a job and receiving fair pay for your work.

■ FOR MORE INFORMATION

For information on union membership, contact

International Brotherhood of Teamsters
25 Louisiana Avenue, NW
Washington, D.C. 20001-2130
http://www.teamster.org

For information on the rubber industry in North America and worldwide, contact

International Institute of Synthetic Rubber Producers
3535 Briarpark Drive, Suite 250
Houston, TX 77042-5241
Tel: (713) 783-7511
Fax: (713) 783-7253
E-mail: info@iisrp.com
http://www.iisrp.com

The following is an association for manufacturers of tires, tubes, roofing, sporting goods, mechanical, and industrial products.

Rubber Manufacturers Association
1400 K Street, NW, Suite 900
Washington, D.C. 20005-2403
Tel: (202) 682-4800
E-mail: info@rma.org
http://www.rma.org

This union represents workers in various industries, including the rubber industry.

United Steelworkers
60 Boulevard of the Allies
Pittsburgh, PA 15222
Tel: (412) 562-2400
http://www.usw.org

Sales Engineers

■ OVERVIEW

Sales engineers sell technological and scientific products and services to businesses. They have a strong understanding of the parts and functions of the products. They also understand the complex scientific processes that make theses products work and are able to explain the processes to prospective buyers. There were approximately 72,200 sales engineers employed in the United States in May 2015, according to the Department of Labor.

■ HISTORY

Sales engineers perform functions similar to those of salespeople, with the difference being that they sell complex scientific and technical products and services. As the title indicates, the job combines sales and engineers; thus most sales engineers have backgrounds in engineering, science, and/or technology. The sales profession is an old one, but the selling of technical and scientific products grew in the 19th century, when the Industrial Revolution introduced numerous machines and inventions that increased workers' productivity and improved life for many. Salespeople who understood these products and their complex machinery were needed to explain how they worked and their benefits to manufacturers and business owners. For example, salesman who sold equipment to farmers had miniature versions of the machinery, usually in a portable case. They traveled to different farms and demonstrated to farmers how the equipment worked.

The sales profession in general grew and expanded further during the late 1800s and early 1900s as new and faster methods of transportation were introduced. Railroads, automobiles, and later airplanes made it possible for salespeople to travel to more areas and sell their products and services to more people. Factories also grew during this time, manufacturing more parts and tools for equipment and machinery. Manufacturers sold merchandise directly to retail outlets and also to wholesalers, with sales representatives selling the manufactured products to specific territories.

Computers were introduced to the general public in the late 1970s and since the 1980s have become intrinsic to most business and manufacturing operations. Sales engineers may specialize in computer systems as well as telecommunications. Strong knowledge of these fields is required to discuss the benefits with customers and to help improve existing computer systems designs and telecommunications setups in companies.

■ THE JOB

Sales engineers have backgrounds in scientific and technological areas, which enables them to discuss and sell complex products and services to businesses. Their general tasks are much like those of salespeople: they identify prospective customers; conduct research and prepare materials to present to prospects; negotiate prices and close sales. Sales engineers work for companies that design and produce technical products, and they also work at independently owned sales firms. They may work alone or in sales teams. They meet with customers to discuss their equipment needs and assess which products and services are most suited to their business goals and budgets. They also recommend improvements that can be made to machinery and materials that can improve efficiency, explaining to customers the specific production increases and cost savings. Some sales engineers work in research and development also, helping with the identification and development of new products.

■ EARNINGS

Sales engineers earned a median annual salary of $97,650 in May 2015, as reported by the Department of Labor. The lowest 10 percent earned $55,280 and the highest 10 percent earned $165,250 or more. Those who worked in computer systems design and related services earned a higher annual salary ($116,920) compared to

CAREER LADDER

Sales Engineer Manager

Sales Engineer

Engineer

those who worked for machinery, equipment, and supplies merchant wholesalers ($101,740). Sales engineers who specialized in data processing, hosting, and related services earned the highest average annual salary, which was $140,880 in May 2015.

■ WORK ENVIRONMENT

Sales engineers work primarily indoors in offices but they may travel extensively to meet with customers, particularly if they are assigned multiple cities or large territories to cover. The work can be stressful since payment and bonuses are usually linked to the number of sales made during specified time frames. Most sales engineers work full-time hours and about a third work more than 40 hours per week. Their hours can be irregular at times, especially when working with customers who are overseas in different time zones.

■ EXPLORING

A good way to learn more about the everyday life of sales engineers is through an internship. Most sales engineer jobs require previous sales experience, so an internship or part-time job with a company that produces and sells scientific or technical equipment is a great starting point. Familiarity with general sales techniques is important; find classes and read publications offered by professional associations such as the Manufacturers' Representatives Educational Research Foundation and the Manufacturers' Agents National Association.

■ EDUCATION AND TRAINING REQUIREMENTS
High School

Sales engineers have backgrounds in science, math, computers, and other technical areas. A solid foundation for this type of work includes classes in mathematics, computer science, and chemistry. Classes in business and English are also useful for the general sales work that is entailed and to improve communication skills with customers.

Postsecondary Education

A bachelor's degree in engineering or a similar field is usually required to be a sales engineer. Depending on their specialty, sales engineers may have a degree in

business or a science field, such as chemistry. Essential classes are math, physical science, and computer science. Common majors include electrical, mechanical, or civil engineering. Some sales engineers have academic backgrounds in chemical, biomedical, or computer hardware engineering.

■ CERTIFICATION, LICENSING, AND SPECIAL REQUIREMENTS

Certification is voluntary and can enhance skills and improve the chances of employment for sales engineers. Professional associations offer certification to those who meet the work experience requirements and pass the certification exam. For instance, the Manufacturers' Representatives Educational Research Foundation offers certification programs for Certified Sales Professional (CSP) and Certified Professional Manufacturers Representative (CPMR).

■ EXPERIENCE, SKILLS, AND PERSONALITY TRAITS

Sales engineers must have academic backgrounds in the areas in which they specialize. They must also have sales experience and training before they can work independently as sales engineers. In training, they learn sales techniques and may partner with senior-level sales engineers who explain the business practices of their employer, the types of customers they have, and the company's culture. Sales engineers must have strong scientific and technological knowledge to understand the products and services that they sell. They must also have solid interpersonal skills and be able to clearly communicate the benefits of the products to customers. They should be confident, outgoing, and able to make persuasive presentations. Strong problem-solving skills are also needed, particularly when listening to customers' concerns and offering suggestions for customizing products that address these concerns. The desire to continually learn is essential in this field, since technology is constantly changing and sales engineers must keep up to date with the latest innovations in their industry. Retraining is common in the sales engineer profession.

■ EMPLOYMENT PROSPECTS
Employers

Sales engineers work for industrial, scientific, and technological companies, selling advanced, complex products and services to customers. The Department of Labor reported that in May 2015, there were 72,200 sales engineers employed in the United States. Many work for companies that offer computer systems design and related services, and for wholesale electronics markets and agents and brokers. Other employers include machinery, equipment, and supplies merchant wholesalers; and professional and commercial equipment and supplies merchant wholesalers.

Starting Out

Sales engineers start out in entry-level positions, usually training with more senior-level sales engineers. Some have prior sales experience in other technical areas. This is a competitive field with average employment growth expected for the next few years. Those with a bachelor's degree in engineering or other field related to the products and services they sell, along with strong sales skills, will have the best job prospects.

■ ADVANCEMENT PROSPECTS

Sales engineers who succeed in selling products and services may receive higher commissions and bonuses, as well as be assigned larger territories to cover. They may advance to become managers, training and supervising the work of junior and entry-level sales staff. They may also advance their skills by receiving certification in sales specialties and speaking at trade conferences.

■ OUTLOOK

The employment growth for sales engineers is expected to be about 7 percent, which is as fast as the average for all occupations, through 2024, according to the Department of Labor. The continual introduction of new technological products and improvements to previously existing products will require the skill and expertise of sales engineers to sell these products to customers. Strong job growth is predicted in the computer hardware and software areas, and job growth for sales engineers in computer systems design and related services will be much faster than average, at 21 percent through 2024. There will also be good job opportunities at independent sales agencies as manufacturers are increasingly outsourcing their sales staff as a way to curb costs. Sales engineers with solid knowledge of the technical products and services they are selling and strong interpersonal and persuasive abilities will do well in this field.

■ UNIONS AND ASSOCIATIONS

The Manufacturers' Representatives Educational Research Foundation provides certification and training programs, resource materials and publications, and other resources for sales engineer professionals and related workers. The Manufacturers' Agents National

---

SALES ENGINEER: IT'S MORE THAN SALES

DID YOU KNOW?

Sales engineers rely on their background in engineering or other technical or science field in their work. Math and science fans who enjoy continually learning about the latest technologies and who are skilled in the art of persuading others do well in the sales engineering profession. The College Board recommends a good background for this field includes course work in calculus, physics, and chemistry, as well as computer science and computer-aided design. Courses in speech and drama are also beneficial, as is participation in a debate team. The job involves travel and speaking with other people, so those who enjoy working in various locations with different people will excel in this type of work. In addition to sales, sales engineers discuss how products work and the ways they can improve and enhance existing work processes and methods.

The College Board provides insight into the sales engineers' expertise that a manufacturer may need. For example, a toy factory owner has to make many decisions, such as which electronic parts will give their toys extra energy, and what types of materials to use for packaging the toys. Should the packaging be polyethylene or polystyrene? Another decision they may need help making is how much computer memory their managers will need. They hire sales engineers who can advise them on these decisions and sell them the products that best fit their needs.

Source: The College Board, bigfuture.com

Association offers webinars and seminars, publications, and other membership benefits for manufacturers and agents. The National Association of Sales Professionals provides education, career support, and membership benefits for sales professionals.

■ TIPS FOR ENTRY

1. Gain sales experience through an internship or part-time job in a company that produces and sells scientific or technological products and services.
2. Learn more about what sales engineers do through the National Association of Sales Engineers' Web site; this is a student-driven group associated with California Polytechnic State University (also known as Cal Poly): https://nationalsocietyofsalesengineers.org.
3. Explore the educational and certification programs offered by the Manufacturers' Representatives Educational Research Foundation.

FOR MORE INFORMATION

The Manufacturers' Agents National Association provides education, publications, events, and other resources for manufacturers and their representatives.

> **Manufacturers' Agents National
> Association (MANA)**
> 6321 West Dempster Street, Suite 110
> Morton Grove, IL 60053-2848
> Tel: (877) 626-2776; (949) 859-4040
> Fax: (949) 855-2973
> E-mail: mana@manaonline.org
> https://www.manaonline.org

The Manufacturers' Representatives Educational Research Foundation offers certification and training programs, among other resources, for manufacturers' representatives and related workers.

> **Manufacturers' Representatives Educational
> Research Foundation (MRERF)**
> 5460 Ward Road, Suite 125
> Arvada, CO 80002-1818
> Tel: (303) 463-1801
> https://mrerf.org

The National Association of Sales Professionals provides training programs, publications, and a career center for sales professionals.

> **National Association of Sales
> Professionals (NASP)**
> 555 Friendly Street
> Bloomfield, MI 48302
> https://www.nasp.com

Sales Managers

OVERVIEW

Sales managers direct a company's sales program by managing staff, working with dealers and distributors, setting prices for products and services, analyzing sales data, establishing sales goals, and implementing plans that improve sales performance. They may oversee an entire company, a geographical territory of a company's operations, or a specific department within a company. There are 376,300 sales managers employed in the United States.

HISTORY

U.S. retailing grew tremendously in the 1850s and 1860s, with the establishment of such chain organizations as the Great Atlantic & Pacific Tea Company, and firms like Macy's and Marshall Field's, which grew into sizable department stores. Mail-order firms such as Sears & Roebuck and Montgomery Ward gained popularity due to the introduction of low postal rates. Self-service stores came about after World War I, enabling people to make their own shopping choices based on merchandise and displays as opposed to salespeople. The movement to the suburbs in the 1950s and 1960s gave rise to one-stop shopping centers, which were smaller versions of today's malls. Large department stores and merchandisers also established branches in the suburbs to meet growing demand. Shoppers today can choose from a variety of merchandise in specialty stores, department stores, strip malls, mega malls, or discount warehouses, and in person, through catalogs, or on the Internet.

For as long as products and services have been sold, there has been a need for sales managers to manage staff, create sales strategies, oversee the distribution or delivery of goods and services, and establish training programs for sales workers. Sales managers are key players in businesses of all types and sizes.

THE JOB

Most companies that have a national or regional presence employ sales managers to manage the activity of their stores, the merchandise or services sold, and the performance of their sales staff. They may be in charge of multiple stores as determined by their territory. Some sales managers oversee territories that encompass a section of a large city, while others cover entire regions of the United States or abroad.

Sales managers oversee activities of each store's sales staff within their assigned territory. They implement training programs for employees to improve the work flow, interaction with customers, and familiarity with the company's products or services. Sales managers set sales goals for each salesperson, store managers, and the store itself. They monitor a store or stores' monthly or quarterly sales figures to ensure they meet set sales quotas. If not, they make recommendations to increase sales figures. These might include creating new sales presentations or special advertising programs or implementing employee retraining. Sales managers also work with each store manager to devise seasonal advertising campaigns and establish marketing budgets.

If their parent company offers franchising opportunities, sales managers are often responsible for interviewing and assessing potential owners. They explain company policies, procedures, and the principles behind its products or services. Sales managers may analyze potential market locations to determine if a new store would be viable. Once a new franchise is operational, sales managers visit often to inspect the store to ensure it is meeting company safety codes, procedures, and marketing plans.

Sales managers also oversee the quality and quantity of products sold or services rendered. For example, the regional sales manager of a national jewelry chain may inspect the loose diamonds or other gemstones that are purchased from wholesalers to determine if they meet the standards of the parent company. They may increase merchandise orders for each store to keep inventory levels sufficient during holidays or other times of the year when sales increase.

Sales managers may also be involved in product research and development. For example, district or regional managers of stores specializing in home goods may be instrumental in finding new furniture lines, kitchenware, or other accessories to carry in their stores. They often maintain contact with dealers and distributors to ensure imported goods arrive safely and in a timely manner, as well as meet governmental import regulations and procedures.

In addition to being familiar with their store's products, sales managers must also be knowledgeable about their company's work processes. For example, a district sales manager for the McDonald's Corporation must know the proper way to cook, prep, and package each food item on the company's menu.

Other duties of sales managers include monitoring the purchasing preferences of customers, writing reports, and representing the company at trade shows, conventions, and association meetings.

■ EARNINGS

The median annual earnings for sales managers were $113,860 in May 2015, according to the U.S. Department of Labor. The lowest paid 10 percent earned $54,490 or less, while the highest paid 10 percent earned $187,200 or more.

Salary levels vary substantially, depending upon the level of responsibility, length of service, and type, size, and location of the company. Top-level managers in large companies can earn much more than their counterparts in small companies. Also, salaries in large metropolitan areas, such as New York City, are higher than those offered in smaller cities. Most sales managers receive a combination of salary and commissions or salary plus bonuses.

Benefit and compensation packages for managers are usually excellent, and may even include such things as bonuses, stock awards, and company-paid insurance premiums.

■ WORK ENVIRONMENT

Sales managers work in comfortable offices near the departments they direct. Higher-level managers may have spacious, lavish offices and enjoy such privileges as executive dining rooms, company cars, country club memberships, and liberal expense accounts.

Managers often work long hours under intense pressure to meet sales goals. Workweeks consisting of 55 to 60 hours at the office are not uncommon (and often include work at night and on weekends)—in fact, some higher-level managers spend up to 80 hours working each week. These long hours limit time available for family and leisure activities.

Sales departments—especially those at large companies—are usually highly charged with energy and are both physically and psychologically exciting places to work. Managers work with others as a team in a creative environment where a lot of ideas are exchanged among colleagues.

■ EXPLORING

You can explore this career by developing your managerial skills in general. Whether you're involved in drama, sports, school publications, or a part-time job, there are managerial duties associated with any organized activity. These can involve planning, scheduling, managing other workers or volunteers, fund-raising, or budgeting. Additionally, talk with sales managers about their careers to get an idea of the rewards and challenges of this profession.

QUICK FACTS

ALTERNATE TITLE(S)
District Sales Managers, Regional Sales Managers

DUTIES
Direct a company's sales program by managing staff, establishing sales goals, and performing other duties

SALARY RANGE
$54,490 to $113,860 to $187,200+

WORK ENVIRONMENT
Primarily Indoors

BEST GEOGRAPHIC LOCATION(S)
Opportunities are available throughout the country

MINIMUM EDUCATION LEVEL
Bachelor's Degree

SCHOOL SUBJECTS
Business, Mathematics, Speech

EXPERIENCE
One to five years experience required

PERSONALITY TRAITS
Enterprising, Organized, Outgoing

SKILLS
Business Management, Leadership, Sales

CERTIFICATION OR LICENSING
Recommended

SPECIAL REQUIREMENTS
None

EMPLOYMENT PROSPECTS
Good

ADVANCEMENT PROSPECTS
Fair

OUTLOOK
About as Fast as the Average

NOC
0015, 0124, 0601

O*NET-SOC
11-2022.00

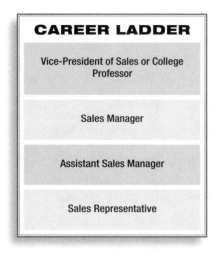

CAREER LADDER

Vice-President of Sales or College Professor

Sales Manager

Assistant Sales Manager

Sales Representative

■ EDUCATION AND TRAINING REQUIREMENTS
High School

If you are interested in a career as a sales manager, you should start preparing in high school by taking college preparatory classes. Because strong communication skills are important, take as many English classes as possible. Speech classes are another way to improve your communication skills. Courses in mathematics, accounting, statistics, business, marketing, advertising, economics, and computer science are also excellent choices to help you prepare for this career.

Postsecondary Training

Many sales managers have a bachelor's degree in business administration, with an emphasis on marketing or sales. Useful general college classes include those in psychology, sociology, business, and economics. Managers often have graduate and professional degrees.

Most managers have worked in lower-level sales jobs, which helps them effectively coordinate the efforts of the whole sales department. Candidates for managerial positions who have extensive experience will have a competitive edge.

A sales manager discusses store finances with a company executive. (imtmphoto. Shutterstock.)

Other Education or Training

The Sales Management Association offers webinars, classes, and workshops to help sales managers keep their skills up to date. Past offerings included "Social Strategies for Sales Leaders," "Assessing Sales Talent for Front-Line and Management Roles," and "New Product Selling: What Works." The American Management Association provides seminars and webcasts on analytical, management and supervisory, project management, leadership, communication, and finance skills. The American Marketing Association and the National Management Association also provide professional development opportunities. Contact these organizations for more information.

■ CERTIFICATION, LICENSING, AND SPECIAL REQUIREMENTS
Certification or Licensing

The Sales Management Association (SMA) offers the certified sales leadership professional and the certified sales operations professional designations to applicants who complete association-endorsed training courses, exams, and in-role requirements. Contact the SMA for more information.

■ EXPERIENCE, SKILLS, AND PERSONALITY TRAITS

Work as a sales manager is not typically an entry-level position. Sales managers need one to five years' experience as sales representatives and purchasing agents before entering the field.

There are a number of personal characteristics that you will need to succeed in this career—including good communication and interpersonal skills, strong organizational skills, and the ability to delegate work to members of your staff. The ability to think on your feet and work well under pressure is also critical. Other traits considered important for sales managers are intelligence, decisiveness, intuition, creativity, strategic vision, honesty, loyalty, and a sense of responsibility.

■ EMPLOYMENT PROSPECTS
Employers

There are approximately 376,300 sales managers in the United States. About 63 percent work in finance, insurance, manufacturing, retail trade, and the wholesale trade industries.

Starting Out

You will first need experience in lower-level sales jobs before advancing to a managerial position. To break into a sales position, contact your college career services office for job leads. In addition, many firms advertise job listings in newspapers and on Internet job boards.

Your first few jobs in sales should give you experience in working with clients, studying the market, and following up on client service. This work will give you a good sense of the rhythm of the job and the type of work required.

■ ADVANCEMENT PROSPECTS

Most management and top executive positions are filled by experienced lower-level workers who have displayed valuable skills, such as leadership, self-confidence, creativity, motivation, decisiveness, and flexibility. In smaller firms, advancement to a management position may come slowly, while promotions may occur more quickly in larger firms.

Advancement may be accelerated by participating in advanced training programs sponsored by industry and trade associations or by enrolling in continued education programs at local universities. These programs are sometimes paid for by the firm. Managers committed to improving their knowledge of the field and of related disciplines—especially computer information systems— will have the best opportunities for advancement.

High-performing sales managers may be promoted to executive-level positions such as vice-president of sales or chief executive officer. Some sales managers become college professors. Others advance by taking sales management positions at larger companies.

■ OUTLOOK

Employment of sales managers is expected to grow about as fast as the average for all occupations through 2024, according to the U.S. Department of Labor. The outlook for sales managers is closely tied to the overall economy. When the economy is good, business expands both in terms of the company's output and the number of people it employs, which creates a need for more managers. Even in economic downturns, though, firms are less likely to lay off sales manager, as opposed to other types of managers, because they help generate profits.

Employment is expected to grow faster than average for sales managers in the following industries: construction; health care; and professional, scientific and technical services. Job opportunities are expected to decline in many manufacturing industries. Additionally, the DOL reports that "growth is expected to be stronger for sales managers involved in business-to-business sales than in business-to-consumer sales, because the rise of online

LARGEST EMPLOYERS OF SALES MANAGERS AND MEAN SALARIES, MAY 2015	FAST FACTS	
Industry	**# Employed**	**Salary**
Management of companies and enterprises	30,980	$143,830
Automobile dealers	26,170	$125,290
Wholesale electronic markets and agents and brokers	16,960	$146,940
Computer systems design and related services	13,610	$154,830
Professional and commercial equipment and supplies	8,750	$148,510

Source: U.S. Department of Labor

shopping will reduce the need for sales calls to individual consumers."

Many job openings will be the result of managers being promoted to better positions, retiring, or leaving their positions to start their own businesses. Even so, the compensation and prestige of these positions make them highly sought-after, and competition to fill openings will be intense. College graduates with experience, a high level of creativity, and strong communication skills should have the best job opportunities.

■ UNIONS AND ASSOCIATIONS

Sales managers are not represented by unions. The Sales Management Association, a membership organization for managers and other sales workers, offers continuing education classes, certification, publications, and other resources. Other important organizations include the American Management Association, American Marketing Association, National Management Association, and the Retail Industry Leaders Association.

■ TIPS FOR ENTRY

1. Read the *Journal of Personal Selling and Sales Management* (http://www.jpssm.org) to learn more about the field.
2. Visit https://careers-amanet.icims.com and http://salesmanagement.org/job-board for job listings.
3. Talk to sales managers about their jobs. Ask them for advice on breaking into the field.

▓ FOR MORE INFORMATION

For news about management trends and resources on career information and finding a job, contact

American Management Association
1601 Broadway
New York, NY 10019-7420
Tel: (877) 566-9441
Fax: (518) 891-0368
E-mail: customerservice@amanet.org
http://www.amanet.org

For information on the practice, study, and teaching of marketing, contact

American Marketing Association
130 E. Randolph St., 22nd Floor
Chicago, IL 60601
Tel: (800) AMA-1150; (312) 542-9000
Fax: (312) 542-9001
https://www.ama.org

For information on a career in management, contact

National Management Association
2210 Arbor Boulevard
Dayton, OH 45439-1580
Tel: (937) 294-0421
Fax: (937) 294-2374
E-mail: nma@nma1.org
http://nma1.org

For information on jobs in retail, contact

Retail Industry Leaders Association
1700 North Moore Street, Suite 2250
Arlington, VA 22209-1933
Tel: (703) 841-2300
Fax: (703) 841-1184
http://www.rila.org

For information on careers and certification, contact

Sales Management Association (SMA)
1440 Dutch Valley Place, NE, Suite 990
Atlanta, GA 30324-5377
Tel: (404) 963-7992
http://salesmanagement.org

Sales Representatives

▓ OVERVIEW

Sales representatives, also called *sales reps*, sell the products and services of manufacturers and wholesalers. They look for potential customers or clients such as retail stores, other manufacturers or wholesalers, government agencies, hospitals, and other institutions; explain or demonstrate their products to these clients; and attempt to make a sale. The job may include follow-up calls and visits to ensure the customer is satisfied.

Sales representatives work under a variety of titles. Those employed by manufacturers are typically called *manufacturers' sales workers* or *manufacturers' representatives*. Those who work for wholesalers are sometimes called *wholesale trade sales workers* or *wholesale sales representatives*. A manufacturers' agent is a self-employed salesperson who agrees to represent the products of various companies. A *door-to-door sales worker* usually represents just one company and sells products directly to consumers, typically in their homes. Sales representatives may be further categorized as *inside sales representatives,* who mostly work in offices and generate sales by making "cold calls" to potential customers, and *outside sales representatives,* who travel frequently to current clients and prospective buyers to make sales. More than 1.8 million people work as manufacturers' and wholesale sales representatives in the United States.

▓ HISTORY

Sales representatives for manufacturers and wholesalers have long played an important role in the U.S. economy. By representing products and seeking out potential customers, they have helped in the efficient distribution of large amounts of merchandise.

The earliest wholesalers were probably the ship "chandlers," or suppliers, of colonial New England, who assembled in large quantities the food and equipment required by merchant ships and military vessels. Ship owners found that a centralized supply source enabled them to equip their vessels quickly.

Various developments in the 19th century made wholesalers more prominent. Factories were becoming larger, thus allowing for huge amounts of merchandise to be manufactured or assembled in a single location. New forms of transportation, especially the railroad, made it more practical for manufacturers to sell their products over great distances. Although some manufacturers would sell their goods directly to retail outlets and elsewhere, many found it easier and more profitable to let wholesalers do this job. Retail stores, moreover, liked working with wholesalers, who were able to sell them a wide range of merchandise from different manufacturers and from different areas of the country and the world.

The sales representatives hired by manufacturers and wholesalers were typically given a specific territory in which to sell their goods. Armed with illustrated product catalogs, special promotional deals, and financial support for advertising, they traveled to prospective customers and tried to explain the important qualities of their products. Competition between sales representatives sometimes was fierce, leading some to be less than scrupulous. Product claims were exaggerated, and retail stores were sometimes supplied with shoddy merchandise. Eventually more fact-based sales pitches were emphasized by manufacturers and wholesalers, who in the long run benefited from having responsible, honest, well-informed representatives. Products also began to be backed by written guarantees of quality.

Meanwhile, some manufacturers employed door-to-door sales workers to sell their products directly to consumers. Direct selling in the United States goes back to the famous "Yankee Peddler" who, during colonial times, traveled by wagon, on horseback, and sometimes on foot, bringing to isolated settlers many products not easily available otherwise. A forerunner of the modern door-to-door sales worker, peddlers also tried to anticipate the settlers' needs and wants. They frequently represented new or unknown products with the hope of creating a demand for them.

Changes in the 20th century, once again including improvements in transportation, brought still more possibilities for sales representatives. Automobiles allowed representatives to travel to many more communities and to carry more product samples and descriptive catalogs. Trucks provided a new means of transporting merchandise. The growth of commercial aviation further expanded the opportunities for salespeople. Sales representatives would eventually be able to travel to customers in New York, Atlanta, Los Angeles, and Minneapolis, for example, all during a single week.

In 2013, the U.S. Department of Labor listed wholesale electronic markets and agents and brokers as the largest employer of sales representatives. Other important fields included printing, publishing, fabricated metal products, chemicals and dyes, electrical and other machinery, and transportation equipment. Among the many establishments helped by sales representatives were retail outlets, which needed a constant supply of clothing, housewares, and other consumer goods, and hospitals, which purchased specialized surgical instruments, drugs, rubber gloves, and thousands of other products from representatives.

■ THE JOB

Manufacturers' representatives and wholesale sales representatives sell goods to retail stores, other manufacturers and wholesalers, government agencies, and various institutions. They usually do so within a specific

QUICK FACTS

ALTERNATE TITLE(S)
Door-to-Door Sales Workers, Inside Sales Representatives, Manufacturers' Representatives, Manufacturers' Sales Workers, Outside Sales Representatives, Wholesale Sales Representatives, Wholesale Trade Sales Workers

DUTIES
Sell the products and services of manufacturers and wholesalers

SALARY RANGE
$38,570 to $59,080 to $153,490+

WORK ENVIRONMENT
Indoors/Outdoors

BEST GEOGRAPHIC LOCATION(S)
Opportunities are available throughout the country

MINIMUM EDUCATION LEVEL
High School Diploma

SCHOOL SUBJECTS
Business, Mathematics, Speech

EXPERIENCE
Previous sales experience useful

PERSONALITY TRAITS
Conventional, Enterprising, Outgoing

SKILLS
Interpersonal, Public Speaking, Sales

CERTIFICATION OR LICENSING
Recommended

SPECIAL REQUIREMENTS
None

EMPLOYMENT PROSPECTS
Good

ADVANCEMENT PROSPECTS
Good

OUTLOOK
About as Fast as the Average

NOC
6221, 6411

O*NET-SOC
41-4011.00, 41-4012.00, 41-9031.00, 41-9091.00

geographical area. Some representatives concentrate on just a few products. An electrical appliance salesperson, for example, may sell 10 to 30 items ranging from food freezers and air conditioners to waffle irons and portable heaters. Representatives of medical supply wholesalers, however, may sell as many as 50,000 items.

The duties of sales representatives usually include locating and contacting potential new clients, keeping

CAREER LADDER

Sales Manager

Manufacturers' Agent, or Sales Engineer, or Industrial Sales Worker

Sales Representative

Office, Stock, or Shipping Clerk

a regular correspondence with existing customers, determining their clients' needs, and informing them of pertinent products and prices. They also travel to meet with clients, show them samples or catalogs, take orders, arrange for delivery, and possibly provide installation. A sales representative must also handle customer complaints, keep up to date on new products, and prepare reports. Many salespeople attend trade conferences, where they learn about products and make sales contacts.

Finding new customers is one of sales representatives' most important tasks. Sales representatives often follow leads suggested by other clients, from advertisements in trade journals, and from participants in trade shows and conferences. They may make "cold calls"(meaning calls without a referral, or "warm lead") to potential clients. Sales representatives frequently meet with and entertain prospective clients during evenings and weekends.

Representatives who sell highly technical machinery or complex office equipment often are referred to as *sales engineers* or *industrial sales workers*. Because their products tend to be more specialized and their client's needs more complex, the sales process for these workers tends to be longer and more involved. Before recommending a product, they may, for example, carefully analyze a customer's production processes, distribution methods, or office procedures. They usually prepare extensive sales presentations that include information on how their products will improve the quality and efficiency of the customers' operations.

Some sales engineers, often with the help of their company's research and development department, adapt products to a customer's specialized needs. They may provide the customer with instructions on how to use the new equipment or work with installation experts who provide this service. Some companies maintain a sales assistance staff to train customers and provide specific information. This permits sales representatives to devote a greater percentage of their time to direct sales contact.

Other sales workers, called *detail people*, do not engage in direct selling activities but strive instead to create a better general market for their companies' products. A detail person for a drug company, for example, may call on physicians and hospitals to inform them of new products and distribute samples.

The particular products sold by the sales representative directly affect the nature of the work. Salespeople who represent sporting goods manufacturers may spend most of their time driving from town to town calling on retail stores that carry sporting equipment. They may visit with coaches and athletic directors of high schools and colleges. A representative in this line may be a former athlete or coach who knows intimately the concerns of his or her customers.

Food manufacturers and wholesalers employ large numbers of sales representatives. Because these salespeople usually know the grocery stores and major chains that carry their products, their main focus is to ensure the maximum sales volume. Representatives negotiate with retail merchants to obtain the most advantageous store and shelf position for displaying their products. They encourage the store or chain to advertise their products, sometimes by offering to pay part of the advertising costs or by reducing the selling price to the merchant so that a special sale price can be offered to customers. Representatives check to make sure that shelf items are neatly arranged and that the store has sufficient stock of their products.

Sales transactions can involve huge amounts of merchandise, sometimes worth millions of dollars. For example, in a single transaction, a washing-machine manufacturer, construction company, or automobile manufacturer may purchase all the steel products it needs for an extended period of time. Salespeople in this field may do much of their business by telephone because the product they sell is standardized and, to the usual customer, requires no particular description or demonstration.

Direct, or door-to-door, selling has been an effective way of marketing various products, such as appliances and housewares, cookware, china, tableware and linens, foods, drugs, cosmetics and toiletries, costume jewelry, clothing, and greeting cards. Like other sales representatives, door-to-door sales workers find prospective buyers, explain and demonstrate their products, and take orders. Door-to-door selling has waned in popularity, and Internet-based selling has taken over much of the door-to-door market.

Several different arrangements are common between companies and their door-to-door sales workers. Under the direct company plan, for example, a sales representative is authorized to take orders for a product, and the company pays the representative a commission for each completed order. Such workers may be employees of the company and may receive a salary in addition to a commission, or they may be independent contractors. They usually are very well trained. Sales workers who sell magazine subscriptions may be hired, trained, and supervised by a *subscription crew leader*, who assigns representatives to specific areas, reviews the orders they take, and compiles sales records.

Under the exhibit plan, a salesperson sets up an exhibit booth at a place where large numbers of people are expected to pass, such as a state fair, trade show, or product exposition. Customers approach the booth and schedule appointments with the salespersons for later demonstrations at home.

The dealer plan allows a salesperson to function as the proprietor of a small business. The salesperson, or dealer, purchases the product wholesale from the company and then resells it to consumers at the retail price, mainly through door-to-door sales.

Under various group plans, a customer is contacted by a salesperson and given the opportunity to sponsor a sales event. In the party plan, for example, the sales representative arranges to demonstrate products at the home of a customer, who then invites a group of friends for the party. The customer who hosts the party receives free or discounted merchandise in return for the use of the home and for assembling other potential customers for the salesperson.

Finally, the COD plan allows representatives to sell products on a cash-on-delivery (COD) basis. In this method, the salesperson makes a sale, perhaps collecting an advance deposit, and sends the order to the company. The company, in turn, ships the merchandise directly to the customer, who in this case makes payment to the delivery person, or to the salesperson. The product is then delivered to the customer and the balance collected.

Whatever the sales plan, door-to-door sales workers have some advantages over their counterparts in retail stores. Direct sellers, for example, do not have to wait for the customer to come to them; they go out and find the buyers for their products. The direct seller often carries only one product or a limited line of products and thus is much more familiar with the features and benefits of the merchandise. In general, direct sellers get the chance to demonstrate their products where they will most likely be used—in the home.

There are drawbacks to this type of selling. Many customers grow impatient or hostile when salespeople come to their house unannounced and uninvited. It may take several visits to persuade someone to buy the product. In a brief visit, the direct seller must win the confidence of the customer, develop the customer's interest in a product or service, and close the sale.

A sales representative helps a client select fabrics. (bikerider-london. Shutterstock.)

■ EARNINGS

Many beginning sales representatives are paid a salary while receiving their training. After assuming direct responsibility for a sales territory, they may receive only a commission (a fixed percentage of each dollar sold). Also common is a modified commission plan (a lower rate of commission on sales plus a low base salary). Some companies provide bonuses to successful representatives.

Because manufacturers' and wholesale sales representatives typically work on commission, salaries vary widely. Some made as little as $38,570 a year in May 2015, according to the U.S. Department of Labor (DOL). The most successful representatives earned more than $153,490. Median annual salaries (including commissions) for sales representatives were $76,190 for those working with technical and scientific products, and $59,080 for those working in other aspects of wholesale and manufacturing.

Earnings can be affected by changes in the economy or industry cycles, and great fluctuations in salary from year to year or month to month are common. Employees who travel usually are reimbursed for transportation, hotels, meals, and client entertainment expenses. Door-to-door sales workers usually earn a straight commission on their sales, ranging from 10 to 40 percent of an item's suggested retail price.

Sales engineers earned salaries that ranged from $55,280 to $165,250 or more in May 2015, according to the DOL.

Sales representatives typically receive vacation days, medical and life insurance, and retirement benefits. However, manufacturers' agents and some door-to-door sales workers do not receive benefits.

GOOD SALES HABITS AND GROWING SALES

LEARN MORE ABOUT IT

Baumgartner, Thomas, et al. *Sales Growth: Five Proven Strategies from the World's Sales Leaders.* Hoboken, N.J.: John Wiley & Sons, 2012.

Lytle, Chris. *The Accidental Salesperson: How to Take Control of Your Sales Career and Earn the Respect and Income You Deserve,* 2nd ed. New York: AMACOM Books, 2012.

Moore, Geoffrey A. *Crossing the Chasm: Marketing and Selling Technology Products to Mainstream Customers,* 3rd ed. New York: HarperCollins, 2014.

Schiffman, Stephan. *The 25 Sales Habits of Highly Successful Salespeople,* 3rd ed. Avon, Mass.: Adams Media, 2008.

■ WORK ENVIRONMENT

Salespeople generally work long and irregular hours. Those with large territories may spend all day calling and meeting customers in one city and much of the night traveling to the place where they will make the next day's calls and visits. Sales workers with a small territory may do little overnight travel but, like most sales workers, may spend many evenings preparing reports, writing up orders, and entertaining customers. Several times a year, sales workers may travel to company meetings and participate in trade conventions and conferences. Irregular working hours, travel, and the competitive demands of the job can be disruptive to ordinary family life.

Sales work is physically demanding. Representatives often spend most of the day on their feet. Many carry heavy sample cases or catalogs. Occasionally, sales workers assist a customer in arranging a display of the company's products or moving stock items. Many door-to-door sellers work in their own community or nearby areas, although some cover more extensive and distant territories. They are often outdoors in all kinds of weather. Direct sellers must treat customers, even those who are rude or impatient, with tact and courtesy.

■ EXPLORING

If you are interested in becoming a sales representative, try to get part-time or summer work in a retail store. Working as a telemarketer is also useful. Some high schools and junior colleges offer programs that combine classroom study with work experience in sales.

Various opportunities exist to gain experience in direct selling. You can take part in sales drives for school or community groups, for instance.

Occasionally manufacturers hire college students for summer assignments. These temporary positions provide an opportunity for the employer and employee to appraise each other. A high percentage of students hired for these specialized summer programs become career employees after graduation. Some wholesale warehouses also offer temporary or summer positions.

■ EDUCATION AND TRAINING REQUIREMENTS
High School

A high school diploma is required for most sales positions, although an increasing number of salespeople are graduates of two- or four-year colleges. In high school, take classes such as business, mathematics, psychology, speech, and economics that will teach you to deal with customers and financial transactions.

Postsecondary Training

Some areas of sales work require specialized college work. Those in engineering sales, for example, usually have a college degree in a relevant engineering field. Other fields that demand specific college degrees include chemical sales (chemistry or chemical engineering), office systems (accounting or business administration), and pharmaceuticals and drugs (biology, chemistry, biotechnology, or pharmacy). Those in less technical sales positions usually benefit from course work in English, speech, psychology, marketing, public relations, economics, advertising, finance, accounting, and business law.

Other Education or Training

The Sales Management Association offers webinars, classes and workshops to help sales reps keep their skills up to date. Past offerings included "Social Strategies for Sales Leaders" and "New Product Selling: What Works." The Direct Marketing Association and the Manufacturers' Agents National Association also offer continuing education opportunities. Contact these organizations for more information.

■ CERTIFICATION, LICENSING, AND SPECIAL REQUIREMENTS
Certification or Licensing

Sales representatives can elevate their marketability by securing designation as a certified sales professional or a certified professional manufacturers' representative, both of which are offered by the Manufacturers' Representatives Education Research Foundation to applicants who complete formal training and pass an exam. Additionally, the Sales Management Association offers the certified sales leadership professional and the certified sales operations professional designations to applicants who complete association-endorsed training courses, exams, and in-role requirements. Contact these organizations for more information.

▣ EXPERIENCE, SKILLS, AND PERSONALITY TRAITS

No previous experience is needed, but any sales experience one can obtain in the field—such as an internship, volunteering, or a part-time job—will be useful.

To be a successful sales representative, you should enjoy working with people. You should also be self-confident and enthusiastic, and self-disciplined. You must be able to handle rejection since only a small number of your sales contacts will result in a sale.

▣ EMPLOYMENT PROSPECTS

Employers

In the United States, nearly 1.8 million people work as manufacturer's and wholesale sales representatives. Around 347,800 work with technical and scientific products. Food, drugs, electrical goods, hardware, and clothing are among the most common products sold by sales representatives.

Starting Out

Firms looking for sales representatives sometimes list openings with high school and college career services offices, as well as with public and private employment agencies. In many areas, professional sales associations refer people to suitable openings. Contacting companies directly also is recommended. A list of manufacturers and wholesalers can be found in telephone books and industry directories, which are available at public libraries and online.

Although some high school graduates are hired for manufacturer's or wholesale sales jobs, many join a company in a nonselling position, such as office, stock, or shipping clerk. This experience allows an employee to learn about the company and its products. From there, he or she eventually may be promoted to a sales position.

Most new representatives complete a training period before receiving a sales assignment. In some cases new salespeople rotate through several departments of an organization to gain a broad exposure to the company's products. Large companies often use formal training programs lasting two years or more, while small organizations frequently rely on supervised sales experience.

Direct selling is usually an easy field to enter. Direct sale companies advertise for available positions in newspapers, in sales workers' specialty magazines, and on television and radio. Many people enter direct selling through contacts they have had with other door-to-door sales workers. Most firms have district or area representatives who interview applicants and arrange the necessary training. Part-time positions in direct selling are common.

▣ ADVANCEMENT PROSPECTS

New representatives usually spend their early years improving their sales ability, developing their product knowledge, and finding new clients. As sales workers gain experience they may be shifted to increasingly large territories or more difficult types of customers. In some organizations, experienced sales workers narrow their focus. For example, an office equipment sales representative may work solely on government contracts.

Advancement to management positions, such as *regional* or *district manager*, also is possible. Some representatives, however, choose to remain in basic sales. Because of commissions, they often earn more money than their managers do, and many enjoy being in the field and working directly with their customers.

A small number of representatives decide to become *manufacturers' agents*, or self-employed salespeople who handle products for various organizations. Agents perform many of the same functions as sales representatives but usually on a more modest scale.

Door-to-door sales workers also have advancement possibilities. Some are promoted to supervisory roles and recruit, train, and manage new members of the sales force. Others become *area*, *branch*, or *district managers*. Many managers of direct selling firms began as door-to-door sales workers.

▣ OUTLOOK

Employment for manufacturers' and wholesale sales representatives is expected to grow at an average rate through 2024, according to the U.S. Department of Labor (DOL). Because of continued economic growth and an increasing number of new products on the market, more sales representatives will be needed to explain, demonstrate, and sell these products to customers. The DOL reports that employment will grow faster or much faster than the average for sales reps in the following industries: construction, health care and social assistance, mining, quarrying, and oil and gas extraction; satellite telecommunications; software publishers; sporting goods stores.

Employment growth is expected to be strongest for sales representatives who are employed by independent sales agencies. These professionals represent product manufacturers and operate on a fee or commission basis. Although this decreases overhead costs for manufacturers, the instability of self-employment is a deterrent in the field of independent sales. Thus, competition for in-house sales positions with wholesalers will be stiff, and jobs will go to applicants with the most experience and technical knowledge.

■ UNIONS AND ASSOCIATIONS

Sales representatives are not represented by unions, but they can obtain useful resources and professional support from the following organizations: Direct Marketing Association, Manufacturers' Agents National Association, and the Sales Management Association (SMA). The Manufacturers' Representatives Educational Research Foundation and SMA provide certification.

■ TIPS FOR ENTRY

1. Join professional associations to access training and networking resources, industry publications, and employment opportunities.
2. Visit http://careercenter.thedma.org/ for job listings.
3. Read *Agency Sales* (http://www.manaonline.org/?cat=10) to learn more about the field.
4. Conduct information interviews with sales representatives and managers, and ask them for advice on preparing for and entering the field.
5. Attend industry conferences to network and participate in continuing education classes.

■ FOR MORE INFORMATION

For information on careers and membership, contact
Direct Marketing Association (DMA)
1333 Broadway, Suite #301
New York, NY 10018
Tel: (212) 790-1500
E-mail: memberservices@the-dma.org
http://www.the-dma.org

For information on membership and publications, contact
**Manufacturers' Agents National
    Association (MANA)**
6321 West Dempster Street, Suite 110
Morton Grove, IL 60053-2848
Tel: (877) 626-2776; (949) 859-4040
Fax: (949) 855-2973
E-mail: MANA@MANAonline.org
http://www.manaonline.org

For information on certification, contact
**Manufacturers' Representatives Educational
    Research Foundation (MRERF)**
5460 Ward Rd., Suite 125
Arvada, CO 80002
Tel: (303) 463-1801

Fax: (303) 379-6024
E-mail: Certify@MRERF.org
https://mrerf.org/

For information on careers and certification, contact
Sales Management Association (SMA)
1440 Dutch Valley Place, NE, Suite 990
Atlanta, GA 30324-5377
Tel: (404) 963-7992
http://salesmanagement.org

School Administrators

■ OVERVIEW

School administrators are leaders who plan and set goals related to the educational, administrative, and counseling programs of schools. They coordinate and evaluate the activities of teachers and other school personnel to ensure that they adhere to deadlines and budget requirements and meet established objectives. There are approximately 235,110 school administrators employed in the United States.

■ HISTORY

The history of school administrators is almost as old as the history of education itself. The first American colonists of the 17th century set up schools in their homes. In the 18th century, groups of prosperous parents established separate schools and employed schoolmasters. In these small early schools, the teachers were also the administrators, charged with the operation of the school as well as with the instruction of the pupils.

In the early 1800s, the importance of education gained recognition among people from all classes of society and the government became involved in providing schooling without cost to all children. Schools grew larger, a more complex system of education evolved, and there developed a demand for educators specializing in the area of administration.

In the United States, each state has its own school system, headed by a state superintendent or commissioner of education who works in conjunction with the state board of education. The states are divided into local school districts, which may vary in size from a large urban area to a sparsely populated area containing a single classroom. The board of education in each district elects a professionally trained superintendent or supervising principal to administer the local schools.

In most school districts the superintendent has one or more assistants, and in a very large district a superintendent may also be assisted by business managers, directors of curriculum, or research and testing personnel. Individual schools within a district are usually headed by a school principal, with one or more assistant principals. The administrative staff of a very large secondary school may also include deans, registrars, department heads, counselors, and others.

The problems of school administrators today are much more complex than in the past and require political as well as administrative skills. School leaders are confronted by such volatile issues as desegregation, school closings and reduced enrollments, contract negotiations with teachers, student and staff safety, violence, and greatly increased costs coupled with public resistance to higher taxes.

■ THE JOB

The occupation of school administrator includes *school district superintendents, assistant superintendents, school principals,* and *assistant principals.* Private schools also have administrators, often known as *school directors* or *headmasters.* Administrators in either public or private schools are responsible for the smooth, efficient operation of an individual school or an entire school system, depending on the size and type of the school or the size of the district. They make plans, set goals, and supervise and coordinate the activities of teachers and other school personnel in carrying out those plans within the established time framework and budget allowance. The general job descriptions that follow refer to administrators in the public school system.

School principals far outnumber the other school administrators and are the most familiar to the students, who often think of them as disciplinarians. Principals spend a great deal of time resolving conflicts that students and teachers may have with one another, with parents, or with school board policies, but their authority extends to many other matters. They are responsible for the performance of an individual school, directing and coordinating educational, administrative, and counseling activities according to standards set by the superintendent and the board of education. They hire and assign teachers and other staff, help them improve their skills, and evaluate their performance. They plan and evaluate the instructional programs jointly with teachers. Periodically, they visit classrooms to observe the effectiveness of the teachers and teaching methods, review educational objectives, and examine learning materials, always seeking ways to improve the quality of instruction.

Principals are responsible for pupils' registration, schedules, and attendance. In cases of severe educational or behavioral problems, they may confer with teachers, students, parents, and counselors and recommend corrective measures. They cooperate with community organizations, colleges, and other schools to coordinate educational services. They oversee the day-to-day operations of the school building and requisition and allocate equipment, supplies, and instructional materials.

A school principal's duties necessitate a great deal of paperwork: filling out forms, preparing administrative reports, and keeping records. They also spend much of each day meeting with people: teachers and other school personnel, colleagues, students, parents, and other members of the community.

In larger schools, usually secondary schools, principals may have one or more assistants. Assistant principals, who may be known as *deans of students,* provide counseling for individuals or student groups related to personal problems, educational or vocational objectives, and social and recreational activities. They often handle discipline, interviewing students, and taking whatever action is necessary in matters such as truancy and delinquency. Assistant principals generally plan and supervise social and recreational programs and coordinate other school activities.

Superintendents manage the affairs of an entire school district, which may range in size from a small town with a handful of schools to a city with a

QUICK FACTS

ALTERNATE TITLE(S)
Assistant Principals, Assistant Superintendents, Headmasters, School Directors, School District Superintendents, School Principals

DUTIES
Oversee educational, administrative, and counseling programs at schools

SALARY RANGE
$59,070 to $90,410 to $131,310+

WORK ENVIRONMENT
Primarily Indoors

BEST GEOGRAPHIC LOCATION(S)
Opportunities are available throughout the country

MINIMUM EDUCATION LEVEL
Master's Degree

SCHOOL SUBJECTS
Business, Government, Psychology

EXPERIENCE
Five years teaching experience

PERSONALITY TRAITS
Helpful, Organized, Problem-Solving

SKILLS
Business Management, Leadership, Teaching

CERTIFICATION OR LICENSING
Required

SPECIAL REQUIREMENTS
None

EMPLOYMENT PROSPECTS
Good

ADVANCEMENT PROSPECTS
Good

OUTLOOK
Little Change or More Slowly than the Average

NOC
0421, 0422

O*NET-SOC
11-9031.00, 11-9032.00, 11-9033.00

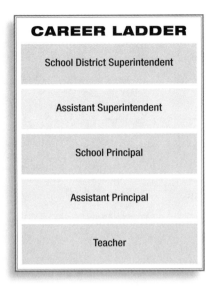

CAREER LADDER

School District Superintendent

Assistant Superintendent

School Principal

Assistant Principal

Teacher

population of millions. Superintendents must be elected by the board of education to oversee and coordinate the activities of all the schools in the district in accordance with board of education standards. They select and employ staff and negotiate contracts. They develop and administer budgets, the acquisition and maintenance of school buildings, and the purchase and distribution of school supplies and equipment. They coordinate related activities with other school districts and agencies. They speak before community and civic groups and try to enlist their support. In addition, they collect statistics, prepare reports, enforce compulsory attendance, and oversee the operation of the school transportation system and provision of health services.

School district superintendents usually have one or more assistants or deputies, whose duties vary depending on the size and nature of the school system. Assistant superintendents may have charge of a particular geographic area or may specialize in activities pertaining, for example, to budget, personnel, or curriculum development.

Boards of education vary in their level of authority and their method of appointment or election to the post of board member. Normally, board members are elected from leaders in the community in business and education. It is not uncommon for the board either to be

President Obama leads a school principal and her students through a tour of the Oval Office. (Pete Souza. White House.)

selected by the mayor or other city administrator, or to be elected directly.

■ EARNINGS

The income of school administrators depends on the position, the level of responsibility, and the size and geographic location of the school or school district.

According to the U.S. Department of Labor, the median annual salary of elementary and secondary school education administrators was $90,410 in May 2015. Salaries ranged from less than $59,070 to more than $131,310.

School administrators also receive a variety of other benefits including health insurance, retirement plans, and vacation and sick leave.

■ WORK ENVIRONMENT

School administrators work a standard 40-hour week, although they often attend meetings or handle urgent matters in the evenings or on weekends. The job requires year-round attention, even during school vacations.

Administrators work in pleasant office environments, usually at a desk. At times, however, they attend meetings elsewhere with PTA members, the school board, and civic groups. Principals and their assistants periodically sit in on classes, attend school assemblies and sporting events, and conduct inspections of the school's physical facilities.

■ EXPLORING

If you attend a private or public school, you're already very familiar with the nature of education and already know many great resources of information, such as your own teachers and school administrators. Talk to your teachers about their work, and offer to assist them with some projects before or after school. School counselors can offer vocational guidance, provide occupational materials, and help students plan appropriate programs of study. You can also learn more about the field by reading books and publications about the field, such as *School Administrator* (http://www.aasa.org/SchoolAdministrator.aspx), published monthly by the American Association of School Administrators.

You can gain experience in the education field by getting a summer job as a camp counselor or day care center aide, working with a scouting group, volunteering to coach a youth athletic team, or tutoring younger students.

■ EDUCATION AND TRAINING REQUIREMENTS
High School

School administration calls for a high level of education and experience. For this reason, you should begin preparing for the job by taking a wide range of college preparatory courses, including English, government, mathematics, psychology, science, music, art, and history. Computer science and business classes will also be beneficial. A broad secondary school education will help you as you pursue your college degrees and gain admittance into strong colleges of education.

Postsecondary Training

Principals and assistant principals are generally required to have a master's degree in educational administration or leadership in addition to five years' experience as a classroom teacher.

School superintendents are usually required to have had graduate training in educational administration, preferably at the doctoral level. Some larger districts require a law degree or a business degree in addition to a graduate degree in education. Candidates for the position of school superintendent generally must have accumulated previous experience as an administrator.

Many universities offer graduate programs in educational administration accredited by the Council for the Accreditation of Educator Preparation. Programs are designed specifically for elementary school principals, secondary school principals, or school district superintendents, and include such courses as school management, school law, curriculum development and evaluation, and personnel administration. A semester of internship and field experience are extremely valuable.

Other Education or Training

The National Association of Elementary School Principals provides educational sessions at its conferences, as well as webinars. Past offerings included "Grit, Mindset, and Determination: The Key to Leading by Influence" and "Moving Ordinary Schools to Extraordinary: Five Essential Skills for Every Effective Principal." The National Association of Secondary School Principals and the American Association of School Administrators also provide continuing education opportunities. Contact these organizations for more information.

■ CERTIFICATION, LICENSING, AND SPECIAL REQUIREMENTS
Certification or Licensing

Most states require administrators to be licensed, however there are no licensing requirements for postsecondary school administrators. Requirements to become licensed may include U.S. citizenship or state residency, graduate training in educational administration, experience, and good health and character. In some states,

candidates must pass a qualifying examination. You can obtain information on specific requirements from the department of education in your state. Principals in private schools do not need a state-issued license.

The American Association of School Administrators offers the National Superintendent Certification Program to help superintendents with less than five years of experience develop their professional skills. Contact the association for more information.

The Educational Testing Service (ETS) offers the School Leaders Licensure Assessment test, which measures whether or not entry-level principals and other school leaders are fit for professional practice. ETS also offers the School Superintendent Assessment test, which measures an administrator's understanding of Interstate School Leaders Licensure Consortium standards.

■ EXPERIENCE, SKILLS, AND PERSONALITY TRAITS

School administrators are generally required to have a master's degree in educational administration in addition to five years' experience as a classroom teacher.

You should have leadership skills necessary for keeping the school operating smoothly. You also need good communication skills and the ability to get along with many different types and ages of people. Strong self-motivation and self-confidence are important for putting your plans into action, and for withstanding criticism.

■ EMPLOYMENT PROSPECTS
Employers

There are approximately 235,110 education administrators employed throughout the United States. Most work in either public or private schools at the elementary or

TOP-PAYING STATES FOR ELEMENTARY AND SECONDARY EDUCATION ADMINISTRATORS, MAY 2015

FAST FACTS

- New Jersey: $124,560
- Connecticut: $124,330
- New York: $114,090
- California: $109,210
- Alaska: $109,090

Source: Bureau of Labor Statistics

secondary level. Some are employed as preschool or child care administrators.

Starting Out

Most school administrators enter the field as teachers. College and university career services offices may help place you in your first teaching job, or you may apply directly to a local school system. Teachers, of course, must meet the requirements for state licensure. Many school districts and state departments of education maintain job listings that notify potential teachers and administrators of openings. Qualified candidates may also come from other administrative jobs, such as curriculum specialist, financial adviser, or director of audiovisual aids, libraries, arts, or special education. The important thing is having experience in organizing and supervising school programs and activities.

ADVANCEMENT PROSPECTS

A teacher may be promoted directly to principal, but more often teachers begin as assistant principals and in time are promoted. Experienced administrators may advance to assistant superintendent and then superintendent. In fact, many school superintendents are former principals who worked their way up the administrative ladder. Each increase in responsibility usually carries a corresponding salary increase.

OUTLOOK

Overall, school administrators can expect as fast as-average employment growth through 2024, according to the *Occupational Outlook Handbook*. Job availability for school administrators varies by region. States with the highest level of employment tend to be those with large populations, such as California, Illinois, New York, Ohio, and Texas. Areas in the south and west where populations are growing may see higher demand.

The number of school administrators employed is determined to a large extent by state and local expenditures for education. Budget cuts affect not only the number of available positions in administration, but also how an administrator can perform his or her job. Administrators in the coming years will have to remain creative in finding funds for their schools. School administrators are also faced with developing additional programs for children as more parents work outside the home. Schools may be expected to help care for children before and after regular school hours.

Administrators may also be overseeing smaller learning environments in the coming years. Research has proven that smaller classrooms and more individual attention not only improve education but also help educators identify students with personal and emotional problems. In order to keep students safe from violence, drug abuse, and street gangs, administrators may be called upon to develop more individualized education.

UNIONS AND ASSOCIATIONS

School administrators do not belong to unions. Many administrators join the American Association of School Administrators, National Association of Elementary School Principals, and the National Association of Secondary School Principals, which provide networking opportunities, leadership training and other continuing education resources, and publications. The Educational Testing Service offers tests which measure administrators' qualifications for licensing.

TIPS FOR ENTRY

1. To learn more about the field, read:
   - *School Administrator* (http://www.aasa.org/SchoolAdministrator.aspx)
   - *Principal Leadership* (https://www.nassp.org/news-and-resources/publications/principal-leadership)
   - *Principal* (https://www.naesp.org/principal-archives)
2. Visit http://aasa-jobs.careerwebsite.com/home/index.cfm?site_id=574 and http://careers.nassp.org/ for job listings.
3. Use social media to stay up to date on industry developments, network, and learn about job openings. Many education associations have a presence on social media. The National Association of Secondary School Principals, for example, has Facebook and LinkedIn pages that you should check out.

■ **FOR MORE INFORMATION**

For information on membership, certification, and careers, contact

**American Association of School
    Administrators (AASA)**
1615 Duke Street
Alexandria, VA 22314-3406
Tel: (703) 528-0700
E-mail: info@aasa.org
http://www.aasa.org

For information on the School Leaders Licensure Assessment and the School Superintendent Assessment tests, contact

Educational Testing Service (ETS)
660 Rosedale Road
Princeton, NJ 08541-2218
Tel: (609) 921-9000
Fax: (609) 734-5410
http://www.ets.org

For information on membership and continuing education, contact

**National Association of Elementary School
    Principals (NAESP)**
1615 Duke Street
Alexandria, VA 22314-3406
Tel: (800) 386-2377; (703) 684-3345
Fax: (800) 396-2377
E-mail: naesp@naesp.org
http://www.naesp.org

For information on membership and continuing education, contact

**National Association of Secondary School
    Principals (NASSP)**
1904 Association Drive
Reston, VA 20191-1537
Tel: (800) 253-7746; (703) 860-0200
E-mail: membership@principals.org
http://www.nassp.org

School Nurses

■ **OVERVIEW**

School nurses focus on students' overall health. They may work in one school or in several, visiting each for a part of the day or week. They may also assist the school physician, if the school employs one. They work with parents, teachers, and other school and professional personnel to meet student's health needs. School nurses promote health and safety, work to prevent illnesses, treat accidents and minor injuries, maintain students' health records, and refer students who may need additional medical attention. School nurses may also oversee health education programs and school health plans. They also administer medication to children and see that special needs students' health requirements are met. School nurses are employed at the elementary, middle, and high school levels. There are nearly 80,000 registered nurses working as school nurses, according to the Health Resources and Services Administration.

■ **HISTORY**

Until the 1800s, nursing was considered a lowly task, relegated to women who were usually in the lower echelons of society. The Civil War highlighted the need for qualified nurses. To raise nursing to an organized, professional status, three nursing schools based on Florence Nightingale's principles of nursing were established in 1873: the Bellevue School of Nursing in New York, the Connecticut Training School at New Haven, and the Boston Training School in Mass.

In an effort to reduce health-related absenteeism in schools, the New York City school system hired Lina Rogers Struthers on October 1, 1902, to serve as a nurse for a one-month trial. She continued her appointment

CAREER LADDER

Registered School Nurse or State
School Nurse Consultant

School Nurse

Nursing Student

after the month ended because of promising results, and two months later she was named superintendent of school nurses, and had a staff of 12 nurses. By February 1903, another 15 nurses were added to the staff. During the first year of this new school-nurse system, health-related absenteeism dropped by nearly 90 percent. The positive results triggered other large cities to hire school nurses, with Philadelphia starting in 1903, Los Angeles in 1904, Boston in 1905, Philadelphia in 1908, and Chicago in 1910.

The school nurse continues to play a vital role in the education and health care systems. In recognition of this role, National School Nurse Day is celebrated each year in May.

■ THE JOB

There's a lot more to school nursing than just applying bandages and taking temperatures. Of course, school nurses care for sick and injured children, but they are also responsible for paperwork, planning, and record keeping. School nurses must assess every child entering kindergarten and make sure the child has had all the required immunizations. In addition, they maintain health records for all students that include a record of state-mandated immunizations. Each year, they take the height and weight of students, perform basic vision screenings, and work with audiologists to conduct hearing tests.

In addition to all their record-keeping tasks, school nurses are frequently a resource for parents or staff members. They communicate with parents when children are ill to determine the best treatment option. They answer questions from parents regarding their children's health and school policies regarding sick days and the administration of medications. School nurses must also develop care plans for any students with special needs.

School nurses are also health educators. Teachers may ask the school nurse to speak to their individual classes when they are covering subjects that deal with health or safety. School nurses may also be required to make presentations on disease prevention, health education, and environmental health and safety to the student body, staff, and parent organizations.

School nurses may be employed on a full- or part-time basis depending on the school's needs, their funding, their size, and their state's or district's requirements.

Some school nurses may also work at private or parochial schools.

■ EARNINGS

School nurses' salaries are determined by several factors—the financial status of the school district, the nurse's experience, and the scope of duties.

According to the U.S. Department of Labor, registered nurses had median annual earnings of $67,490 in May 2015. Salaries ranged from less than $46,360 to more than $101,630. Licensed practical and licensed vocational nurses made a median salary of $43,170 in May 2015. The lowest paid 10 percent made less than $32,040, and the highest paid 10 percent made more than $59,510. School nurses' salaries may differ from these figures, however. Salary.com reported a median annual salary of $46,761 for school nurses at the end of 2016. Salaries ranged from less than $28,803 to $70,120 or more.

Employers offer a variety of benefit packages, which can include any of the following: paid holidays, vacations, and sick days; personal days; medical, dental, and life insurance; profit-sharing plans; 401(k) plans; and retirement and pension plans.

■ WORK ENVIRONMENT

Schools are found in all communities, cities, and rural areas, and learning institutions can vary greatly. School nurses may work in an environment that is a state-of-the-art educational institution in an affluent community, or they may work in a rundown building in the inner city. By the same token, some school nurses may have up-to-date equipment and adequate resources, while others may find that they have restricted funds that inhibit their ability to do their jobs.

School nurses usually work days and may have some time off during the summer months when school is not in session.

The increase in school violence impacts the school nurses' working environment since it is evident that acts of violence can occur in any institution and in any community. School nurses must be prepared to deal with the physical results of violence in their schools.

School nurses may come in contact with infectious diseases and are often exposed to illnesses and injuries. All nursing careers have some health and disease risks; however, adherence to health and safety guidelines greatly minimizes the chance of contracting infectious diseases such as hepatitis and AIDS.

■ EXPLORING

This is one area of nursing for which you don't have far to travel to talk to someone in the career; of course, you should visit your own school nurse. Ask about his or her daily responsibilities and workload and how he or she prepared for this line of work. Ask for suggestions on nursing programs and other tips on starting your career.

See if your school or local institution offers first-aid programs to learn some basic emergency medical procedures such as CPR. Another way to gain experience is through volunteer work at a hospital, nursing home, or other medical facility.

■ EDUCATION AND TRAINING REQUIREMENTS
High School

To prepare for future work as a school nurse, take as many science classes as possible, such as biology and chemistry. Math, health, psychology, computer science, and English classes are also important. Foreign language courses can also be useful in communicating with students and parents from other countries.

Postsecondary Training

State requirements for school nurses vary. Some states have a certification requirement. Others require that their school nurses have bachelor's degrees while some do not require a bachelor's degree but do have specific educational requirements. Some states require their school nurses to be registered nurses. There are three basic kinds of training programs that you may choose from in order to become a registered nurse: associate's degree, diploma, and bachelor's degree. Your career goals will help you determine which training program to opt for. A bachelor's degree in nursing is the most popular method, however, as such a degree is required for most supervisory or administrative positions, for jobs in public health agencies, and for admission to graduate nursing programs. Diplomas are offered by three-year programs at schools of nursing and hospitals, and an associate's degree is obtained from a two-year college.

There is no special program for school nursing; however, most nursing programs have courses geared to the specialty such as health education, child or adolescent psychology, crisis intervention, community health, and growth and development.

Many school nurses are graduates of practical nursing programs, which involve about one year of classroom instruction and supervised clinical practice, which usually takes place in a hospital.

Other Education or Training

The National Association of School Nurses offers online continuing education (CE) classes on topics such as immunizations, infectious diseases, mental health issues, and dealing with the media. It also offers in-person CE

A school nurse checks a student's temperature. (Brian Eichhorn. Shutterstock.)

classes on specialized topics such as diabetes management and childhood obesity. Contact the association for more information.

■ CERTIFICATION, LICENSING, AND SPECIAL REQUIREMENTS
Certification or Licensing

Many states have certification requirements for school nurses, and some have certification programs but they are not required in all circumstances. National certification is available through the National Board for Certification of School Nurses.

Both licensed practical nurses and registered nurses must pass an examination after they have completed a state-approved nursing program. This is required by all states and the District of Columbia.

In addition, some state education agencies set requirements such as nursing experience and competency in specified areas of health and education. Local or regional boards of education may also have certain qualifications that they require of their school nurses.

■ EXPERIENCE, SKILLS, AND PERSONALITY TRAITS

Nursing students gain experience by completing several nursing internships, or clinical rotations, as part of their postsecondary training. Many school nurses have also obtained experience in a non-school nursing setting before specializing in school nursing.

School nurses must have patience and like working with children and teens. They must also be able to work well with teachers, parents, administrators, and other health personnel. School nurses should be able to work independently since they often work alone.

THE ROLE OF THE SCHOOL NURSE

The career of school nurse began in the United States in 1902. According to the National Association of School Nurses, school nurses perform the following important health roles in schools:

- The school nurse provides direct health care to students and staff.
- The school nurse provides leadership for the provision of health services.
- The school nurse provides screening and referral for health conditions.
- The school nurse promotes a healthy school environment.
- The school nurse promotes health.
- The school nurse serves in a leadership role for health policies and programs.
- The school nurse serves as a liaison between school personnel, family, community, and health care providers.

Source: http://www.nasn.org

■ EMPLOYMENT PROSPECTS

Employers

There are more than 80,000 registered nurses working as school nurses, according to the Health Resources and Services Administration. School nurses are employed by private and public schools at the elementary, middle, and high school levels. They also work in parochial schools, vocational schools, and preschools. The National Association of School Nurses reports that school nurses also work for departments of health, public health departments and agencies, hospitals, and hospital districts.

Starting Out

Many new nurses gain practical experience in a nonschool setting before they apply for employment as a school nurse. Nurses can apply directly to hospitals, nursing homes, and companies and government agencies that hire nurses. Jobs can also be obtained through school career services offices, by signing up with employment agencies specializing in placement of nursing personnel, or through the state employment office. Other sources of jobs include nurses' associations, professional journals, newspaper want ads, and Internet job sites. Additionally, the National Association of School Nurses offers job listings at its Web site, http://www.nasn.org.

■ ADVANCEMENT PROSPECTS

Administrative and supervisory positions in the nursing field go to nurses who have earned at least a bachelor of science degree in nursing. Nurses with many years of experience who are graduates of the diploma program may achieve supervisory positions, but requirements for such promotions have become more difficult in recent years and in many cases require at least the bachelor of science in nursing degree.

Some school nurses may advance to the position of *registered school nurse*. These professionals manage and oversee health aides employed in the schools. Others become *state school nurse consultants*, who help school districts and school nurses provide top-quality nursing services to students.

■ OUTLOOK

Nursing specialties will be in great demand in the future. In fact, according to the Bureau of Labor Statistics, nursing will grow 16 percent through 2024, and employment of registered nurses is expected to grow faster than the average for all occupations in the years to come. The outlook for school nurses, however, is mixed. The U.S. Department of Labor reports that employment for nurses in education in general will grow around 6 percent, mostly in private schools. Employment of nurses in state schools may decrease by as much as 16 percent during the same period. As educational systems try to find ways to cut costs, professionals such as school nurses may be eliminated, or jobs may be reduced from full time to part time. Since cuts may vary by region and state, school nurses should be flexible and willing to relocate or to seek other nursing opportunities, if necessary.

■ UNIONS AND ASSOCIATIONS

School nurses can join unions such as the American Federation of State, County, and Municipal Employees (http://www.afscme.org) and the American Federation of Teachers (http://www.aft.org). The main professional organization for school nurses is the National Association of School Nurses, but nurses also can become members of the American Nurses Association (http://www.nursingworld.org), American Society of Registered Nurses (http://www.asrn.org), National League for Nursing (http://www.nln.org), National Association of State School Nurse Consultants (http://www.schoolnurseconsultants.org), and organizations at the state and local levels. The American Association of Colleges of Nursing provides information on educational training programs. The National Board for Certification of School Nurses provides certification to school nurses.

■ TIPS FOR ENTRY

1. For job listings, visit:
   - http://www.nasn.org/RoleCareer/Employment Center
   - http://nursepath.com
   - http://www.nurse.com/students/careersinnursing.html
2. Join the National Association of School Nurses to access training and networking resources, industry publications, and employment opportunities.
3. Become certified in order to show employers that you have met the highest standards set by your professions.
4. Volunteer or acquire a part-time job at a hospital or health care facility.
5. Use social media tools such as LinkedIn and Twitter to stay up to date on industry developments and learn about job openings.

■ FOR MORE INFORMATION

For information on educational programs, contact

American Association of Colleges of Nursing (AACN)
One Dupont Circle, NW, Suite 530
Washington, D.C. 20036-1135
Tel: (202) 463-6930
Fax: (202) 785-8320
E-mail: info@aacn.nche.edu
http://www.aacn.nche.edu

For information on careers, contact

National Association of School Nurses (NASN)
1100 Wayne Avenue, #925
Silver Spring, MD 20910-5642
Tel: (240) 821-1130
Fax: (301) 585-1791
E-mail: nasn@nasn.org
http://www.nasn.org

For more information on the career of state school nurse consultant, contact

National Association of State School Nurse Consultants (NASSNC)
http://www.schoolnurseconsultants.org

For information on certification, contact

National Board for Certification of School Nurses (NBCSN)
2170 S. Parker Rd., Ste. 120
Denver, CO 80231
Tel: (844) 808-6276
E-mail: certification@nbscn.com
http://www.nbcsn.org

Science and Medical Writers

■ OVERVIEW

Science and medical writers translate technical medical and scientific information so it can be disseminated to the general public and professionals in the field. Science and medical writers research, interpret, write, and edit scientific and medical information. Their work often appears in books, technical studies and reports, magazine and trade journal articles, newspapers, company newsletters, and on Web sites, and may be used for radio and television broadcasts. Science and medical writers may also be known as *science and medical authors* or *medical and science communicators.*

■ HISTORY

The skill of writing has existed for thousands of years. Papyrus fragments with writing by ancient Egyptians date from about 3000 b.c., and archaeological findings show that the Chinese had developed books by about 1300 b.c. A number of technical obstacles had to be overcome before printing and the writing profession progressed.

The modern age of publishing began in the 18th century. Printing became mechanized, and the novel, magazine, and newspaper were developed. Developments in the printing trades, photoengraving, retailing, and the availability of capital produced a boom in newspapers and magazines in the 19th century. Further mechanization in the printing field, such as the use of the Linotype machine, high-speed rotary presses, and color-reproduction processes, set the stage for still further growth in the book, newspaper, and magazine industry.

The broadcasting industry has also contributed to the development of the professional writer. Film, radio, and television are sources of entertainment, information, and education that provide employment for thousands of writers. Today, the computer industry and Web sites have also created the need for more writers.

As our world becomes more complex and people seek even more information, professional writers have become increasingly important. And, as medicine and science take giant steps forward and discoveries are being made every day that impact our lives, skilled science and medical writers are needed to document these changes and disseminate the information to the general public and to more specialized audiences.

QUICK FACTS

ALTERNATE TITLE(S)
Medical and Science
    Communicators, Science and
    Medical Authors

DUTIES
Write articles about science-
    and medical-related topics;
    conduct research; interview
    medical and science
    professionals

SALARY RANGE
$29,230 to $60,250 to
    $114,350+

WORK ENVIRONMENT
Primarily Indoors

BEST GEOGRAPHIC LOCATION(S)
Opportunities are available
    throughout the country

MINIMUM EDUCATION LEVEL
Bachelor's Degree

SCHOOL SUBJECTS
Biology, English, Journalism

EXPERIENCE
Prior writing experience required

PERSONALITY TRAITS
Curious, Organized, Scientific

SKILLS
Research, Scientific, Writing

CERTIFICATION OR LICENSING
Recommended

SPECIAL REQUIREMENTS
None

EMPLOYMENT PROSPECTS
Good

ADVANCEMENT PROSPECTS
Good

OUTLOOK
Little Change or More Slowly
    than the Average

NOC
5121

O*NET-SOC
27-3042.00, 27-3043.00

THE JOB

Science and medical writers usually write about subjects related to these fields. Because the medical and scientific subject areas may sometimes overlap, writers often find that they do science writing as well as medical writing. For instance, a medical writer might write about a scientific study that has an impact on the medical field.

Medical and science writing may be targeted for the printed page, the broadcast media, or the Web. It can be specific to one product and one type of writing, such as writing medical information and consumer publications for a specific drug line produced by a pharmaceutical company. Research facilities hire writers to edit reports or write about their scientific or medical studies. Writers who are *public information officers* write press releases that inform the public about the latest scientific or medical research findings. Educational publishers use writers to write or edit educational materials for the medical profession. Science and medical writers also write online articles or interactive courses that are distributed over the Internet.

Science and medical writers usually write for the general public. They translate high-tech information into articles and reports that the general public and the media can understand. For example, writers may write an article about a genetically modified virus-based vaccine that is being developed to treat melanoma or a recombinant fusion protein that has been invented to treat age-related macular degeneration. The writer provides a general overview of the developments and the new medical resources, and breaks down complicated medical terminology and concepts into information that can be understood by the average reader who does not have a scientific or medical background. Good writers who cover the subjects thoroughly have inquisitive minds and enjoy looking for additional information that might add to their articles. They research the topic to gain a thorough understanding of their subject matter. This may require hours of research on the Internet, or in corporate, university, or public libraries. Writers always need good background information regarding a subject before they can write about it.

In order to get the information required, writers may interview professionals such as doctors, pharmacists, scientists, engineers, managers, and others who are familiar with the subject. Writers must know how to present the information clearly so it can be easily understood. This requires knowing the audience and how to reach them. For example, an article may need graphs, photos, or historical facts. Writers sometimes enlist the help of technical or medical illustrators or engineers in order to add a visual dimension to their work.

For example, if reporting on a new heart surgery procedure that will soon be available to the public, writers may need to illustrate how that surgery is performed and what areas of the heart are affected. They may give a basic overview of how the healthy heart works, show a diseased heart in comparison, and report on how this surgery can help the patient. The public will also want to know how many people are affected by this disease, what the symptoms are, how many procedures have been done successfully, where they were performed, what the recovery time is, and if there are any complications. In addition, interviews with doctors and patients can add a personal touch to the story.

Broadcast media need short, precise articles that can be transmitted in a specific time allotment. Writers usually need to work quickly because news-related stores have tight deadlines. Because science and medicine can be so complex, science and medical writers also need to help the audience understand and evaluate the information. Writing for the Web encompasses most journalistic guidelines including time constraints and sometimes space constraints.

Some science and medical writers specialize in their subject matter. For instance, a medical writer may write only about heart disease and earn a reputation as the best writer in that subject area. Science writers may limit their writing or research to environmental science subjects, or may be even more specific and focus only on air pollution issues.

Some writers may choose to be freelance writers either on a full- or part-time basis, or to supplement other jobs.

Freelance science and medical writers are self-employed writers who work with small and large companies, health care organizations, research institutions, or publishing firms on a contract or hourly basis. They may specialize in writing about a specific scientific or medical subject for one or two clients, or they may write about a broad range of subjects for a number of different clients. Many freelance writers write articles, papers, or reports, and then attempt to get them published in newspapers, trade, or consumer publications.

■ EARNINGS

Although there are no specific salary surveys for science and medical writers, salary information for all writers is available. The U.S. Department of Labor reports that the median annual salary for writers in May 2015 was $60,250. Salaries ranged from less than $29,230 to more than $114,350. Median annual earnings for technical writers were $70,240. The lowest 10 percent earned less than $41,610, while the highest 10 percent earned more than $112,220.

Freelance writers' earnings can vary depending on their expertise, reputation, and the articles they are contracted to write.

Most full-time writing positions offer the usual benefits such as insurance, sick leave, and paid vacation. Some jobs also provide tuition reimbursement and retirement benefits. Freelance writers must pay for their own insurance. However, professional associations may offer group insurance rates for their members.

■ WORK ENVIRONMENT

The work environment for science and medical writers depends on the type of writing and the employer. Generally, writers work in an office or research environment. Writers for the news media sometimes work in noisy surroundings. Some writers travel to research information and conduct interviews while other employers may confine research to local libraries or the Internet. In addition, some employers require writers to conduct research interviews over the phone, rather than in person. Some writers work from home-based offices.

Although the workweek usually runs 35 to 40 hours in a normal office setting, many writers may have to work overtime to cover a story, interview people, meet deadlines, or to disseminate information in a timely manner. The newspaper and broadcasting industries deliver the news 24 hours a day, seven days a week. Writers often work nights and weekends to meet press deadlines or to cover a late-developing story.

Each day may bring new and interesting situations. Some stories may even take writers to exotic locations with a chance to interview famous people and write about timely topics. Other assignments may be boring or they may take place in less than desirable settings, where interview subjects may be rude and unwilling to talk. One of the most difficult elements for writers may be meeting deadlines or gathering information. People who are the most content as writers work well with deadline pressure.

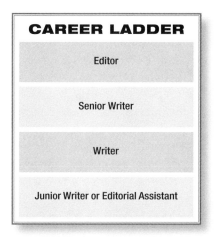

CAREER LADDER

Editor

Senior Writer

Writer

Junior Writer or Editorial Assistant

■ EXPLORING

As a high school or college student, you can test your interest and aptitude in the field of writing by serving as a reporter or writer on school newspapers, yearbooks, and literary magazines. Attending writing workshops and taking writing classes will give you the opportunity to practice and sharpen your skills.

Community newspapers and local radio stations often welcome contributions from outside sources, although they may not have the resources to pay for them. Jobs in bookstores, magazine shops, libraries, and even newsstands offer a chance to become familiar with various publications. If you are interested in science writing, try to get a part-time job in a research laboratory, interview science writers, and read good science writing in major newspapers such as the *New York Times* or the *Wall Street Journal.* Similarly, if your interest is medical writing, work or volunteer in a health care facility, visit with people who do medical writing, and read medical articles in major newspapers. You may also find it helpful to read publications such as the *American Medical Writers Association Journal* (http://www.amwa.org) and *ScienceWriters* (http://www.nasw.org/publications). Information on writing as a career may also be obtained by visiting local newspapers, publishing houses, or radio and television stations and interviewing some of the writers who work there. Career conferences and other guidance programs frequently include speakers from local or national organizations who can provide information on communication careers.

Some professional organizations such as the Society for Technical Communication welcome students as members and have special student membership rates and career information. In addition, participation in

WRITING ABOUT SCIENCE

Blum, Deborah, Mary Knudson, and
Robin Marantz Henig (eds.). *Field Guide for Science Writers: The Official Guide of the National Association of Science Writers,* 2nd ed. New York: Oxford University Press, USA, 2005.

Hayden, Thomas, and Michelle Nijhuis (eds.). *The Science Writers' Handbook: Everything You Need to Know to Pitch, Publish, and Prosper in the Digital Age.* Boston: Da Capo Press, 2013.

James-Enger, Kelly. *Writer for Hire: 101 Secrets to Freelance Success.* New York: Writer's Digest Books, 2012.

Raimes, Ann. *Keys to Successful Writing: A Handbook for College and Career.* Independence, Ky.: Cengage Learning, 2012.

LEARN MORE ABOUT IT

professional organizations gives you the opportunity to meet and visit with people in this career field.

■ EDUCATION AND TRAINING REQUIREMENTS
High School

If you are considering a career as a writer, you should take English, journalism, and communication courses in high school. Computer classes will also be helpful. If you know in high school that you want to do scientific or medical writing, it would be to your advantage to take biology, physiology, chemistry, physics, math, health, psychology, and other science-related courses. If your school offers journalism courses and you have the chance to work on the school newspaper or yearbook, you should take advantage of these opportunities. Part-time employment at health care facilities, newspapers, publishing companies, or scientific research facilities can also provide experience and insight regarding this career. Volunteer opportunities are also available in hospitals and nursing homes.

Postsecondary Training

Although not all writers are college-educated, today's jobs almost always require a bachelor's degree. Many writers earn an undergraduate degree in English, journalism, or liberal arts and then obtain a master's degree in a communications field such as medical or science writing. A good liberal arts education is important since you are often required to write about many subject areas. Science and medical-related courses are highly recommended. You should investigate internship programs that give you experience in the communications department of a corporation, medical institution, or research facility. Some newspapers, magazines, or public relations firms also have internships that give you the opportunity to write.

Some people find that after working as a writer, their interests are strong in the medical or science fields and they evolve into that writing specialty. They may return to school and enter a master's degree program or take some additional courses related specifically to science and medical writing. Similarly, science majors or people in the medical fields may find that they like the writing aspect of their jobs and return to school to pursue a career as a medical or science writer.

Certification

The American Medical Writers Association (AMWA) offers certificates in the following areas: Essential Skills, Business, Composition & Publication, Concepts in Science & Medicine, and Regulatory & Research. Certificates are earned by completing workshops in these areas at the association's annual conference, at chapter conferences, or in AMWA's onsite training programs.

Other Education or Training

The American Medical Writers Association provides self-study workshops on ethics, medical terminology, basic grammar and usage, punctuation, statistics, and other topics. The National Association of Science Writers provides professional development workshops and other continuing education opportunities. The Society of Professional Journalists offers training on-demand videos, workshops, conference seminars, and other learning opportunities. Topics include editing, writing, new media ethics, interviewing, social media, and technology.

■ CERTIFICATION, LICENSING, AND SPECIAL REQUIREMENTS
Certification or Licensing

Certification, while not mandatory, is available from various organizations and institutions. The American Medical Writers Association provides voluntary certification to medical writers.

■ EXPERIENCE, SKILLS, AND PERSONALITY TRAITS

Any experience volunteering as a writer will be useful for those wishing to enter the field. Contact organizations that require the skills of writers.

If you are considering a career as a medical or science writer, you should enjoy writing, be able to write well, and be able to express your ideas and those of others clearly. You should have an excellent knowledge of the English language and have superb grammar and spelling skills. You should be skilled in research techniques and be computer literate and familiar with software programs related to writing and publishing. You should be curious, enjoy learning about new things, and have an interest in science or medicine. You need to be detail-oriented since many of your writing assignments will require that you obtain and relay accurate and detailed information. Interpersonal skills are also important because many jobs require that you interact with and interview scientists, engineers, researchers, and medical personnel. You must be able to meet deadlines and work under pressure.

▧ EMPLOYMENT PROSPECTS
Employers

Pharmaceutical and drug companies, medical research institutions, government organizations, insurance companies, health care facilities, nonprofit organizations, medical publishers, medical associations, and other medical-related industries employ medical writers.

Science writers may also be employed by medical-related industries. In addition, they are employed by scientific research companies, government research facilities, federal, state, and local agencies, manufacturing companies, research and development departments of corporations, and the chemical industries. Large universities and hospitals often employ science writers. Large technology-based corporations and industrial research groups also hire science writers.

Many science and medical writers are employed, often on a freelance basis, by newspapers, magazines, and the broadcast industries as well. Internet publishing is a growing field that hires science and medical writers. Corporations that deal with the medical or science industries also hire specialty writers as their public information officers or to head up communications departments within their facilities.

Starting Out

A fair amount of experience is required to gain a high-level position in this field. Most writers start out in entry-level positions. These jobs may be listed with college placement offices, or you may apply directly to the employment departments of corporations, institutions, universities, research facilities, nonprofit organizations, and government facilities that hire science and medical writers. Many firms now hire writers directly upon application or recommendation of college professors and placement offices. Want ads in newspapers, trade journals, and Internet job boards are another source for jobs.

Participation in an internship in college can provide you with valuable experience and give you the advantage of knowing people who can give you personal recommendations. Internships are also excellent ways to build your portfolio. Employers in the communications field are usually interested in seeing samples of your published writing assembled in an organized portfolio or scrapbook. Working on your college's magazine or newspaper staff can help you build a portfolio. Sometimes small, regional magazines will also buy articles or assign short pieces for you to write. You should attempt to build your portfolio with good writing samples. Be sure to include the type of writing you are interested in doing, if possible.

You may need to begin your career as a junior writer or editor and work your way up. This usually involves library research, preparation of rough drafts for part or all of a report, cataloging, and other related writing tasks. These are generally carried on under the supervision of a senior writer.

Many science and medical writers enter the field after working in public relations departments, the medical profession, or science-related industries. They may use their skills to transfer to specialized writing positions or they may take additional courses or graduate work that focuses on writing or documentation skills.

▧ ADVANCEMENT PROSPECTS

Writers with only an undergraduate degree may choose to get a graduate degree in science or medical writing, corporate communications, document design, or a related program. An advanced degree may open doors to more progressive career options.

Many experienced science and medical writers are often promoted to head writing, documentation, or public relations departments within corporations or institutions. Others take on editorial duties. Some may become recognized experts in their field and their writings may be in demand by trade journals, newspapers, magazines, and the broadcast industry.

As freelance writers prove themselves and work successfully with clients, they may be able to demand increased contract fees or hourly rates.

▧ OUTLOOK

According to the U.S. Department of Labor, there is a lot of competition for writing and editing jobs, and employment for writers should grow more slowly than the average for all careers through 2024. Job opportunities for science and medical writers should be better in certain industries. For example, employment for writers who work for professional, scientific, and technical services firms will grow faster than the average, and job opportunities for writers in the health care industry will grow much faster than the average for all careers. Continued developments in these fields will drive the need for skilled writers to put complex information in terms that a wide and varied audience can understand. Opportunities will also be best with online publications and services, as these continue to grow. Writers who are well versed with new media will also have an advantage in the job market.

■ UNIONS AND ASSOCIATIONS

Writers may obtain union representation from the National Writers Union. They also may join professional associations such as the American Medical Writers Association, Association of Opinion Journalists, National Association of Science Writers, Society for Technical Communication, and the Society of Professional Journalists.

■ TIPS FOR ENTRY

1. Write as often as you can and create a portfolio of your work to show potential employers.
2. Read science and medical journals such as *Science Writers* (http://www.nasw.org/publications) and the *AMWA Journal* (http://www.amwa.org) to learn more about the field.
3. Join professional associations such as the American Medical Writers Association and the National Association of Science Writers to access training and networking resources, job listings, industry publications, and employment opportunities.
4. If you are an expert regarding science or medicine, start a blog or Twitter account to raise your profile and attract the interest of potential employers.

■ FOR MORE INFORMATION

For information on a career in medical writing, contact
American Medical Writers Association (AMWA)
30 West Gude Drive, Suite 525
Rockville, MD 20850-4347
Tel: (240) 238-0940
Fax: (301) 294-9006
E-mail: amwa@amwa.org
http://www.amwa.org

For information on a career in science writing, contact
National Association of Science Writers (NASW)
PO Box 7905
Berkeley, CA 94707-0905
Tel: (510) 647-9500
E-mail: director@nasw.org
http://www.nasw.org

For information about working as a writer and union membership, contact
National Writers Union (NWU)
256 West 38th Street, Suite 703
New York, NY 10018-9807
Tel: (212) 254-0279
Fax: (212) 254-0673
https://nwu.org

For information on scholarships and student memberships aimed at those preparing for a career in technical communication, contact
Society for Technical Communication (STC)
9401 Lee Highway, Suite 300
Fairfax, VA 22031-1803
Tel: (703) 522-4114
Fax: (703) 522-2075
E-mail: stc@stc.org
http://www.stc.org

This organization for journalists has campus and online chapters.
Society of Professional Journalists (SPJ)
3909 North Meridian Street
Indianapolis, IN 46208-4011
Tel: (317) 927-8000
Fax: (317) 920-4789
http://www.spj.org

Screenwriters

■ OVERVIEW

Screenwriters write scripts for entertainment, education, training and sales, films and television programs. Screenwriters may choose themes themselves, or they may write on a theme assigned by a producer or director, sometimes adapting plays, novels, or other works into screenplays. Screenwriting is an art, a craft, and a business. It is a career that requires imagination and creativity, the ability to tell a story using both dialogue and pictures, and the ability to negotiate with producers and studio executives.

■ HISTORY

In 1894, Thomas Edison invented the kinetograph to take a series of pictures of actions staged specifically for the camera. In October of the same year, the first film opened at Hoyt's Theatre in New York. It was a series of acts performed by such characters as a strongman, a contortionist, and trained animals. Even in these earliest motion pictures, the plot or sequence of actions the film would portray was written down before filming began.

Newspaperman Roy McCardell was the first person to be hired for the specific job of writing for motion pictures. He wrote captions for photographs in a weekly entertainment publication. When he was employed by the movie company Biograph to write 10 scenarios, or stories, at $10 apiece, it caused a flood of newspapermen to try their hand at screenwriting.

The early films ran only about a minute and typically captured scenes of movement and exotic places. These films eventually grew into narrative films running between nine and 15 minutes. The demand for original plots led to the development of story departments at each of the motion picture companies in the period from 1910 to 1915. The story departments were responsible for writing the stories and also for reading and evaluating material that came from outside sources. Stories usually came from writers, but some were purchased from actors on the lot. The actor Genevieve (Gene) Gauntier was paid $20 per reel of film for her first scenarios.

There was a continuing need for scripts because usually a studio bought a story one month, filmed the next, and released the film the month after. Some of the most popular stories in these early films were Wild West tales and comedies.

Longer story films began to use titles, and as motion pictures became longer and more sophisticated, so did the titles. In 1909–1910, there was an average of 80 feet of title per 1,000 feet of film. By 1926, the average increased to 250 feet of title per 1,000 feet. The titles included dialogue, description, and historical background.

In 1920, the first Screen Writers Guild was established to ensure fair treatment of writers, and in 1927, the Academy of Motion Picture Arts and Sciences was formed, including a branch for writers. The first sound film, *The Jazz Singer*, was also produced in 1927. Screenwriting changed dramatically to adapt to the new technology.

From the 1950s to the 1980s, the studios gradually declined, and more independent film companies and individuals were able to break into the motion picture industry. The television industry began to thrive in the 1950s, further increasing the number of opportunities for screenwriters. During the 1960s, people began to graduate from the first education programs developed specifically for screenwriting.

Today, most Americans spend countless hours viewing programs on television and movie screens (as well as on computers and mobile electronic devices). Many writers are attempting to write screenplays—especially as more cable companies and video streaming services such as Amazon Prime and Netflix create original programming. This has created an intensely fierce marketplace with many more screenplays being rejected than accepted each year.

■ THE JOB

Screenwriters write dramas, comedies, soap operas, adventures, westerns, documentaries, newscasts, and training films. They may write original stories, or get inspiration from newspapers, magazines, books, or other sources. They may also write scripts for continuing television series. *Continuity writers* in broadcasting create station announcements, previews of coming shows, and advertising copy for local sponsors. Broadcasting scriptwriters usually work in a team, writing for a certain audience, to fill a certain time slot. *Motion picture writers* submit an original screenplay or adaptation of a book to a motion picture producer or studio. *Playwrights* submit their plays to drama companies for performance or try to get their work published in book form.

Screenwriters may work on a staff of writers and producers for a large company. Or they may work independently for smaller companies that hire only freelance production teams. Advertising agencies also hire writers, sometimes as staff, sometimes as freelancers.

Scripts are written in a two-column format, one column for dialogue and sound, the other for video instructions. One page of script equals

QUICK FACTS

ALTERNATE TITLE(S)
Continuity Writers, Motion Picture Writers, Playwrights

DUTIES
Write scripts for television shows, movies, documentaries, and other productions

SALARY RANGE
$15,000 to $127,000 to $1 million+

WORK ENVIRONMENT
Primarily Indoors

BEST GEOGRAPHIC LOCATION(S)
Most opportunities exist in New York and Los Angeles

MINIMUM EDUCATION LEVEL
High School Diploma

SCHOOL SUBJECTS
English, Journalism, Theater/Dance

EXPERIENCE
Previous writing experience recommended

PERSONALITY TRAITS
Creative, Enterprising, Organized

SKILLS
Computer, Performance, Music, and Acting, Writing

CERTIFICATION OR LICENSING
None

SPECIAL REQUIREMENTS
Membership in the Writers Guild of America (WGA) may be required

EMPLOYMENT PROSPECTS
Fair

ADVANCEMENT PROSPECTS
Fair

OUTLOOK
Little Change or More Slowly than the Average

NOC
5121

O*NET-SOC
27-3043.00, 27-3043.05

CAREER LADDER

Director, or Producer, or Award-Winning Screenwriter

Screenwriter

Writer's Assistant or Production Assistant

about one minute of running time, though it varies. Each page has about 150 words and takes about 20 seconds to read. Screenwriters send a query letter outlining their idea before they submit a script to a production company. Then they send a standard release form and wait at least a month for a response. Studios buy many more scripts than are actually produced, and studios often will buy a script only with provisions that the original writer or another writer will rewrite it to their specifications.

EARNINGS

Wages for screenwriters are nearly impossible to track. Some screenwriters make hundreds of thousands of dollars from their scripts, while others write and film their own scripts without any payment at all, relying on backers and loans. Screenwriter Joe Eszterhas made entertainment news in the early 1990s when he received $3 million for each of his treatments for *Basic Instinct*, *Jade*, and *Showgirls*. In the early 2000s, many scripts by first-time screenwriters were sold for between $500,000 and $1 million. Typically, a writer will earn a percentage (approximately 1 percent) of the film's budget. Obviously, a lower budget film pays considerably less than a big production, starting at $15,000 or less.

According to the Writers Guild of America (WGA) 2014 Theatrical and Television Basic Agreement (which runs through mid-2014), earnings for writers of an original screenplay ranged from $45,556 to $127,295.

Screenwriters who are WGA members are also eligible to receive health benefits.

WORK ENVIRONMENT

Screenwriters who choose to freelance have the freedom to write when and where they choose. They must be persistent and patient; only one in 20 to 30 purchased or optioned screenplays is produced.

Screenwriters who work on the staff of a large company, for a television series, or under contract to a motion picture company may share writing duties with others.

Screenwriters who do not live in Hollywood or New York City will likely have to travel to attend script conferences. They may even have to relocate for several weeks while a project is in production. Busy periods before and during film production are followed by long periods of inactivity and solitude. This forces many screenwriters, especially those just getting started in the field, to work other jobs and pursue other careers while they develop their talent and craft.

EXPLORING

One of the best ways to learn about screenwriting is to read and study scripts. It is advisable to watch a motion picture while simultaneously following the script. The scripts for such classic films as *Casablanca, Network,* and *Chinatown* are often taught in college screenwriting courses. You should read film-industry publications, such as *Variety* (http://www.variety.com), *The Hollywood Reporter* (http://www.hollywoodreporter .com), and *The Hollywood Scriptwriter* (http://www .hollywoodscriptwriter.com). There are a number of books about screenwriting, but they are often written by those outside of the industry. These books are best used primarily for learning about the format required for writing a screenplay. There are also computer software programs that assist with screenplay formatting.

The Sundance Institute, a nonprofit organization founded by the actor Robert Redford, offers a variety of programs and activities for aspiring screenwriters, including a five-day writing workshop, a screenplay reading series, and, most notably, an annual film festival.

Most states offer grants for emerging and established screenwriters and other artists. Contact your state's art council for guidelines and application materials. In addition, several arts groups and associations hold annual contests for screenwriters. To find out more about screenwriting contests, consult a reference work such as *The Writer's Market* (http://www.writersmarket .com).

Students may try to get their work performed locally. A teacher may be able to help you submit your work to a local radio or television station or to a publisher of plays.

EDUCATION AND TRAINING REQUIREMENTS
High School

You can develop your writing skills in English, theater, speech, and journalism classes. Belonging to a debate team can also help you learn how to express your ideas within a specific time allotment and framework. History, government, and foreign language can contribute to a well-rounded education, necessary for creating intelligent scripts. A business course can be useful in understanding the basic business principles of the film industry.

Postsecondary Training

There are no set educational requirements for screenwriters. A college degree is desirable, especially a liberal arts education, which exposes you to a wide range of subjects. An undergraduate or graduate film program will likely include courses in screenwriting, film theory, and other subjects that will teach you about the film industry and its history. A creative writing program will involve you with workshops and seminars that will help you develop fiction-writing skills.

Many colleges and universities have film departments, but some of the most respected film schools are the University of California-Los Angeles (http://www.tft.ucla.edu/programs/film-tv-digital-media-department), the University of Southern California (http://cinema.usc.edu), and Columbia University (http://arts.columbia.edu/film). Contact these schools or visit their Web sites for information about course work and faculty.

Other Education or Training

The Writers Guild of America offers members the opportunity to participate in seminars and workshops that cover a variety of topics, such as screenwriting techniques, tax planning, and technology. Contact the guild for more information.

■ CERTIFICATION, LICENSING, AND SPECIAL REQUIREMENTS

Certification or Licensing

There are no certification or licensing requirements for screenwriters.

Other Requirements

Some employers may require candidates to have membership in the Writers Guild of America (WGA) before accepting any written material.

■ EXPERIENCE, SKILLS, AND PERSONALITY TRAITS

Aspiring screenwriters can gain experience by writing screenplays and constantly revising their work. They should sign up for classes and workshops, as well as review the work of award-winning screenwriters.

As a screenwriter, you must be able to create believable characters and develop a story. You must have technical skills, such as dialogue writing, creating plots, and doing research. In addition to creativity and originality, you also need an understanding of the marketplace for your work. You should be aware of what kinds of scripts are in demand by producers. Word processing skills are also helpful.

Screenwriter Billy Ray, writer of Captain Phillips *and* The Hunger Games, *attends the New York Film Festival with his wife.* (Debby Wong. Shutterstock.)

■ EMPLOYMENT PROSPECTS

Employers

Most screenwriters work on a freelance basis, contracting with production companies for individual projects. Those who work for television may contract with a TV production company for a certain number of episodes or seasons.

Starting Out

The first step to getting a screenplay produced is to write a letter to the script editor of a production company describing yourself, your training, and your work. Ask if the editors would be interested in reading one of your scripts. You should also pursue a manager or agent by sending a brief letter describing your project. A list of agents is available from the Writers Guild of America

(WGA). If you receive an invitation to submit more, you will then prepare a synopsis or treatment of the screenplay, which is usually from one to 10 pages. It should be in the form of a narrative short story, with little or no dialogue.

Whether you are a beginning or experienced screenwriter, it is best to have an agent, since studios, producers, and stars often return unsolicited manuscripts unopened to protect themselves from plagiarism charges. Agents provide access to studios and producers, interpret contracts, and negotiate deals.

It is wise to register your script (online registration is $10 for members, $20 for nonmembers) with the Writers Guild of America. Although registration offers no legal protection, it is proof that on a specific date you came up with a particular idea, treatment, or script. You should also keep a detailed journal that lists the contacts you've made, including the people who have read your script.

■ ADVANCEMENT PROSPECTS

Competition is stiff among screenwriters, and a beginner will find it difficult to break into the field. More opportunities become available as a screenwriter gains experience and a reputation, but that is a process that can take many years. Rejection is a common occurrence in the field of screenwriting. Most successful screenwriters have had to send their screenplays to numerous production companies before they find one who likes their work.

Once they have sold some scripts, screenwriters may be able to join the Writers Guild of America (WGA). Membership with the WGA guarantees the screenwriter a minimum wage for a production and other benefits such as arbitration. Some screenwriters, however, writing for minor productions, can have regular work and successful careers without WGA membership.

Those screenwriters who manage to break into the business can benefit greatly from recognition in the industry. In addition to creating their own scripts, some writers are also hired to "doctor" the scripts of others, using their expertise to revise scripts for production. If a film proves very successful, a screenwriter will be able to command higher payment, and will be able to work on high-profile productions. Some of the most talented screenwriters receive awards from the industry, most notably the Academy Award for best original or adapted screenplay.

■ OUTLOOK

Employments for writers in the motion picture industry is expected to change little through 2024, according to the U.S. Department of Labor. Overall employment for writers is forecast to increase only 2 percent with employment in media and communications in general growing 4 percent. Job opportunities for television screenwriters will decline by up to 2.5 percent.

There is intense competition in the television and motion picture industries. As the movie industry grows, cable television expands, and digital technology allows for more programming, new opportunities will emerge. Television networks continue to need new material and new episodes for long-running series. Studios are always looking for new angles on action, adventure, horror, and comedy, and especially romantic comedy stories. The demand for new screenplays should increase slightly in the next decade, but the number of screenwriters is growing at a faster rate. Writers will continue to find opportunities in advertising agencies and educational and training video production houses.

UNIONS AND ASSOCIATIONS

The Writers Guild of America (WGA) represents the professional interests of screenwriters. It has chapters in New York and Los Angeles. Membership in the Writers Guild of America (WGA) may be required for those who work for studios and production companies that are signatories of WGA contracts.

TIPS FOR ENTRY

1. Attend film school and major in screenwriting. Apply for internships at film production companies.
2. Enter your screenplay in screenwriting contests, and look for specialized contests such as the WGA's Feature Writer Access Project: http://www.wga.org/the-guild/advocacy/diversity.
3. Attend film festivals to network with film industry professionals. Visit http://www.filmfestivals.com for more information.
4. Consider hiring an agent to help you promote your work. A list of agents is available from the Writers Guild of America.
5. Look for jobs and/or market your services at Mandy.com.

FOR MORE INFORMATION

Visit the following Web site to read useful articles on screenwriting.

Screenwriter's Utopia

http://www.screenwritersutopia.com

For guidelines on submitting a script for consideration for the Sundance Institute's screenwriting program, contact

Sundance Institute

5900 Wilshire Boulevard, Suite 800

Los Angeles, CA 90036-5041

Tel: (310) 360-1981

Fax: (310) 360-1969

E-mail: institute@sundance.org

http://www.sundance.org

To learn more about the film industry, to read interviews and articles by noted screenwriters, and to find links to many other screenwriting-related sites on the Internet, visit

Writers Guild of America-East Chapter (WGA)

250 Hudson Street, Suite 700

New York, NY 10013-1437

Tel: (212) 767-7800

Fax: (212) 582-1909

http://www.wgaeast.org

To learn more about the film industry, to read interviews and articles by noted screenwriters, and to find links to many other screenwriting-related sites on the Internet, visit

Writers Guild of America-West Chapter (WGA)

7000 West Third Street

Los Angeles, CA 90048-4321

Tel: (800) 548-4532; (323) 951-4000

Fax: (323) 782-4800

http://www.wga.org

Search Engine Optimization Specialists

OVERVIEW

Companies rely on *search engine optimization (SEO) specialists* to help ensure that their Web sites rank high in search results. Search engine optimization specialists identify and implement search engine keywords, tags, social media profiles, or site maps, as well as use HTML coding to improve the company's ranking. They work with Internet consultants, content writers, developers, and designers to improve the ranking of their company's site or sites. SEO specialists are also known as *search engine marketers* and *search marketing analysts.*

HISTORY

The Internet as we know it today began in the early 1990s. In order to find desired content, Internet users relied on search engines such as Yahoo! and Google to lead them to the most popular and relevant Web sites. Each search engine has a unique formula, also known as an algorithm, used to rank Web sites based on content, tags, and hits for search engines users. The higher the rank, the better chance Internet users would visit the site. As more companies began to create Web sites and sell their products and services online, they began to seek out ways to have their sites rank higher on search engine results.

Known as search engine optimization, the process of increasing a page's chances for a better ranking became widely known in the mid-1990s. Search engines were forced to quickly adapt their algorithms in order to avoid manipulation of rankings. Some of the most popular search engines do not disclose the algorithms they use to rank sites, which can include up to 200 different signals. Search engines are constantly updating their algorithms and introducing new features to their users. For example, Google Instant, an offshoot of Google's search engine, predicts and produces results while users are typing in search terms. Google Instant came as a response to the explosion in the number of social media sites and blogs and Google estimates that it saves users two to five seconds on each search.

SEMPO, the leading association in the field, was founded in 2003.

■ THE JOB

When consumers want to find a particular brand, service, or company on the Internet, they often use search engines. The first Web sites that appear as a result of a search are the highest ranked. In order to get their sites ranked high in search results, many companies and other organizations employ search engine optimization (SEO) specialists to make sure their sites attain this visibility.

SEO specialists' main duty is creating a search engine optimization strategy for their clients. They study their client's Web site to identify strengths and weaknesses. SEO specialists make sure section or page titles appearing throughout the Web site are clear cut. Do the titles reflect the content they head? If not, SEO specialists suggest alternate titles, or work with webmasters and writers to create better headlines, which help sites move up in search results. SEO specialists also make sure the Web site uses descriptors, or relevant keywords. For example, if the client's Web site sells sporting goods, then keywords would include not only "sporting goods," but particular types such as "hiking shoes," "camping equipment," or "sporting equipment."

Web sites with extraneous coding, Flash files, and large images hinder search engines from finding them, so SEO specialists often limit their use. However, when image files and Flash files are used, SEO specialists make sure they are well documented for relevant codes, which will help them be more accessible for search engines.

SEO specialists use Hypertext Markup Language (HTML) coding to add text, tables, and images to Web sites. Proper HTML coding is important to ensure content is picked up during search engine activity. SEO specialists also rely on analytical tools such as Google Analytics or Omniture, the latter of which is owned by Adobe Systems.

SEO specialists understand that appealing content is important to get users interested and engaged in a site, and that this content should be updated often to encourage users to keep coming back. They work with the Web site's writers to create appealing content, at times editing their work to make sure the copy is rich with relevant keywords. Some SEO specialists write original content for their clients.

SEO specialists also build a client's system internally, matching protocols to make sure all content is optimized across all types of platforms including Web sites, blogs, social media, video, and portals for retail sales.

Once a search marketing strategy is designed and implemented, SEO specialists continually monitor the site. They monitor and review search engine ranking reports, including paid search campaigns or those from Google or Yahoo, for example, to make sure their client stays highly visible.

SEO specialists also identify and create a keyword portfolio—relevant words to use within the site. This keyword portfolio is especially helpful when writing and tagging new content.

Many SEO specialists are employed by companies and organizations, though a good number work as independent consultants. SEO specialists working as consultants have additional duties pertaining to establishing and running their business. They market and advertise their services to potential clients, make presentations, and have office-related duties including paperwork, billing, and supervision of staff members.

■ EARNINGS

The SEMPO 2015 State of Search Marketing Report found that salaries for digital marketing professionals in general, including search engine optimization specialists, rose about 16 percent from 2013 earnings levels with substantial growth in the number of workers earning $100,000 or more. Payscale. com estimated the national average salary for SEO specialists at $42,499 in 2016. Search engine optimization managers averaged $63,792 in annual earnings, and digital marketing managers brought in an average of $62,539. Indeed.com reported an annual earnings range of $57,000 to $83,000 for SEO professionals, with an average of $71,000. Salaries may continue to rise as companies prioritize optimal search results and as workers gain experience.

Benefits for full-time workers include paid vacation, health, disability, life insurance, and retirement or pension plans. Some employers also offer profit-sharing plans. Self-employed SEO specialists must provide their own benefits.

■ WORK ENVIRONMENT

SEO specialists employed by companies and organizations work a normal 40-hour week, though they may have to work overtime on weekdays or weekends to complete projects. Hours vary for SEO specialists who work as consultants. They are determined by the number of clients they serve or the scope of the project at hand.

SEO specialists spend a great deal of time working at their computer, either running search engine queries, revising or rewriting coding, or analyzing the latest report. While SEO specialists can spend hours, or even days, working independently, they also spend time brainstorming with members from other departments and presenting strategies to prospective clients.

■ EXPLORING

Visiting the Web sites of professional associations in the field is an excellent way to introduce yourself to search engine marketing. SEMPO's Web site, http://www.sempo.org, is a good starting point. It provides many resources, including an overview of the field, a glossary of terms, and information on earnings and employment. Start your own Web site or blog and learn how to move it higher in Web search results. Talk to SEO specialists about their careers and ask questions about their work experience. How did you train for the field? What do you like most and least about your job? What advice would you give to someone who wants to break into the field?

■ EDUCATION AND TRAINING REQUIREMENTS
High School

Useful high school classes include English, speech, computer science, advertising, marketing, psychology, statistics, and foreign languages.

Postsecondary Education

There is no standard educational path for SEO specialists. Some companies only require a high school diploma and on-the-job experience. Others require a bachelor's degree. Typical degrees include marketing, marketing research, Internet marketing, advertising, computer science, information management, new media, journalism, or the liberal arts. Some colleges offer classes in search engine marketing. Contact colleges in your area to see what educational opportunities are available. Aspiring SEO specialists should also complete at least one internship as part of their college education.

CAREER LADDER

Search Engine Optimization Manager/ Executive or Search Marketing Consulting Firm Owner

Search Engine Optimization Specialist

Search Marketing Intern or Entry-Level Worker

Other Education or Training

Professional associations offer training opportunities for SEO specialists. For example, SEMPO offers a variety of webinars such as "The Complicated World of Local Search," "Mobile Trends For Marketers," and "Search Synergy: Maximizing Your Online Shelf Space." Other organizations that offer continuing education classes, webinars, workshops, and videos include the American Marketing Association, eMarketing Association, Interactive Advertising Bureau, International Webmasters Association, and the Word of Mouth Marketing Association.

■ CERTIFICATION, LICENSING, AND SPECIAL REQUIREMENTS
Certification or Licensing

Voluntary certification in Internet marketing is available from the eMarketing Association and the Internet Marketing Association. Contact these organizations for more information.

■ EXPERIENCE, SKILLS, AND PERSONALITY TRAITS

Aspiring SEO specialists should participate in at least one internship during college with a company that uses search engine marketing. Additionally, many companies require applicants to have at least two years' experience in creating, managing, and optimizing search engine marketing campaigns

Successful SEO specialists have a comprehensive understanding of interactive marketing and online media, strong oral and written communication skills, and analytical personalities. They are able to work well independently, as well as in teams, when necessary. Other important traits include organizational skills, the ability

SEO Terms

Blog: An often informal online journal that is updated regularly and appears in reverse chronological order; blogs also often contain photographs, videos, and links to other sites.

Flash: A multimedia platform (incorporating text, audio, video, animation, and interactivity) that has become a popular method of adding animation and interactive features to Web pages; it is also widely used for broadcast animation work.

Hidden text: Text that a search engine sees, but is hidden to the user.

Keyword stuffing: Adding a very large number of keywords into the tags or HTML coding of a Web page.

Search engine: A specialized Web site containing computer-maintained lists of other Web sites; lists are usually organized by subject, name, content, and other categories; users request searches by typing in keywords, or topical words and phrases, and the search engine displays a list of links to related Web sites.

Social media: User-created content (audio, text, video, multimedia) that is published and shared on social media sites such as Facebook, LinkedIn, and Twitter; it can also be defined as the online technology that allows users to share content.

Tags: Keywords added to a Web site to help the site rank higher on search engines; tags are also used to help site visitors find related information at the Web site.

Targeting: Using particular ads and keywords to attract a certain type of customer.

Traffic: The number of visits a Web page receives.

to multitask and meet deadlines, and a willingness to continue to learn throughout one's career.

■ EMPLOYMENT PROSPECTS

Employers

SEO specialists are employed by advertising and marketing firms that offer search marketing services to companies and other organizations that want to reach more customers on the Internet. They are also directly employed by companies that have in-house search optimization workers or departments.

The position of search engine optimization specialist is not typically an entry-level job. Applicants need at least two years of experience before becoming eligible for jobs in the field. Those breaking into the search marketing field often work first as interns or assistants to SEO specialists.

Starting Out

The Web sites of professional associations are a great place to start when searching for jobs. SEMPO, for example, offers job listings at its Web site, http://www.sempo.org/?page=jobs. New graduates can also utilize the services of their college's career services office or apply directly to consulting firms or companies that have a need for SEO specialists.

■ ADVANCEMENT PROSPECTS

SEO specialists with considerable experience and skill in the field can advance to work in managerial positions or leave their companies to open their own search marketing consulting firms.

■ OUTLOOK

Search marketing is a very lucrative industry. eMarketer reported that search marketing generated more than $29 billion in 2016 and predicted that figure to rise steadily through 2019. The field is expected to continue to grow as companies seek to gain an extra edge by improving the search rankings of their Web sites. Changes to search engine algorithms will also motivate companies to invest in SEO in order to adapt and maintain good search results. The growth of mobile Internet technologies is also creating demand for search marketing professionals. Opportunities should be strongest for those with college degrees and extensive experience in the field.

■ UNIONS AND ASSOCIATIONS

SEO specialists are not represented by unions. SEMPO is the major organization for SEO specialists. Other useful organizations include the American Marketing Association, eMarketing Association, Interactive Advertising Bureau, Internet Marketing Association, and the Word of Mouth Marketing Association.

■ TIPS FOR ENTRY

1. Read publications such as *Search Marketing Standard Magazine* (http://www.searchmarketing standard.com) and *Website Magazine* (http://www .websitemagazine.com) to learn more about trends in the industry.

2. State in your social media profiles (LinkedIn, Facebook, etc.) that you are seeking a job in search engine marketing. Use keywords such as "search engine marketing" and "search engine optimization" in your resume. Resume scanners often look

for these and other buzz words to select potential job candidates.

3. Use social media such as Facebook, LinkedIn, and Twitter to stay up to date on industry developments and learn about job openings. Participate in online forums to raise your professional profile.

4. Visit the following Web sites for job listings:
   - http://www.sempo.org/?page=jobs
   - http://www.careerbuilder.com
   - http://www.dice.com
   - http://www.highendcareers.com
   - http://careers.womma.org
   - http://www.jobsinsocialmedia.com
   - http://www.simplyhired.com

5. Participate in internships or part-time jobs that are arranged by your college's career services office.

■ FOR MORE INFORMATION

For information on the practice, study, and teaching of marketing, contact

American Marketing Association
130 E. Randolph St., 22nd Floor
Chicago, IL 60601
Tel: (800) AMA-1150; (312) 542-9000
Fax: (312) 542-9001
https://www.ama.org

The following organization offers certification to Internet marketing professionals,

eMarketing Association
4259 Old Post Road
Charlestown, RI 02813-2571
Tel: (800) 496-2950
Fax: (408) 884-2461
E-mail: eMA@eMarketingAssociation.com
http://www.emarketingassociation.com

For information on continuing education, contact

Interactive Advertising Bureau
116 East 27th Street, 7th Floor
New York, NY 10016-8942
Tel: (212) 380-4700
http://www.iab.net

For information on certification, contact

Internet Marketing Association
E-mail: info@imanetwork.org
http://www.imanetwork.org

For information on search engine marketing and a glossary of terms, visit

SEMPO
401 Edgewater Place, Suite 600
Wakefield, MA 01880-6200
Tel: (781) 876-8866
E-mail: info@sempo.org
http://www.sempo.org

For information of word of mouth marketing, contact

Word of Mouth Marketing Association
65 East Wacker Place, Suite #500
Chicago, IL 60601-7255
Tel: (312) 853-4400
Fax: (312) 233-0063
http://womma.org

Secondary School Teachers

■ OVERVIEW

Secondary school teachers teach students in grades seven through twelve. Specializing in one subject area, such as English or math, these teachers work with five or more groups of students during the day. They lecture, direct discussions, and test students' knowledge with exams, essays, and homework assignments. There are nearly 1 million secondary school teachers employed in the United States.

■ HISTORY

Early secondary education was typically based upon training students to enter the clergy. Benjamin Franklin pioneered the idea of a broader secondary education with the creation of the academy, which offered a flexible curriculum and a wide variety of academic subjects.

It was not until the 19th century, however, that children of different social classes commonly attended school into the secondary grades. The first English Classical School, which was to become the model for public high schools throughout the country, was established in 1821, in Boston. An adjunct to the high school, the junior high school was conceived by Dr. Charles W. Eliot, president of Harvard. In a speech before the National Education Association in 1888, he recommended that secondary studies be started two years earlier than was then the custom. The first such school opened in 1908 in Columbus, Ohio. Another opened a year later in Berkeley, California.

QUICK FACTS

ALTERNATE TITLE(S)
High School Teachers, Middle School Teachers

DUTIES
Teach students in grades seven through twelve

SALARY RANGE
$37,800 to $57,200 to $91,190+

WORK ENVIRONMENT
Primarily Indoors

BEST GEOGRAPHIC LOCATION(S)
Opportunities are available throughout the country

MINIMUM EDUCATION LEVEL
Bachelor's Degree

SCHOOL SUBJECTS
English, History, Mathematics

EXPERIENCE
Student-teaching experience required

PERSONALITY TRAITS
Helpful, Organized, Outgoing

SKILLS
Interpersonal, Public Speaking, Teaching

CERTIFICATION OR LICENSING
Required

SPECIAL REQUIREMENTS
None

EMPLOYMENT PROSPECTS
Good

ADVANCEMENT PROSPECTS
Fair

OUTLOOK
About as Fast as the Average

NOC
4031

O*NET-SOC
25-2022.00, 25-2023.00, 25-2031.00, 25-2032.00

By the early 20th century, secondary school attendance was made mandatory in the United States.

■ THE JOB

Many successful people credit secondary school teachers with helping guide them into college, careers, and other endeavors. A teacher's primary responsibility is to educate students in a specific subject. But secondary teachers also inform students about colleges, occupations, and such varied subjects as the arts, health, and relationships.

Secondary school teachers may teach in a traditional area, such as science, English, history, and math, or they may teach more specialized classes, such as information technology, business, and theater. Many secondary schools are expanding their course offerings to better serve the individual interests of their students. School-to-work programs, which are vocational education programs designed for high school students and recent graduates, involve lab work and demonstrations to prepare students for highly technical jobs. Though secondary teachers are likely be assigned to one specific grade level, they may be required to teach students in surrounding grades as well. For example, a secondary school mathematics teacher may teach algebra to a class of ninth-graders one period and trigonometry to high school seniors the next.

In the classroom, secondary school teachers use a variety of teaching methods. They spend a great deal of time lecturing, but they also facilitate student discussion and develop projects and activities to interest the students in the subject. They show films and videos, use computers and the Internet, and bring in guest speakers. They assign essays, presentations, and other projects. Each individual subject calls upon particular approaches and may involve laboratory experiments, role-playing exercises, shop work, and field trips.

Outside of the classroom, secondary school teachers prepare lectures, lesson plans, and exams. They evaluate student work and calculate grades. In the process of planning their class, secondary school teachers read textbooks, novels, and workbooks to determine reading assignments; photocopy notes, articles, and other handouts; and develop grading policies. They also continue to study alternative and traditional teaching methods to hone their skills. They prepare students for special events and conferences and submit student work to competitions. Many secondary school teachers also serve as sponsors to student organizations in their field. For example, a French teacher may sponsor the French club and a journalism teacher may advise the yearbook staff. Some secondary school teachers also have the opportunity for extracurricular work as athletic coaches or drama coaches. Teachers also monitor students during lunch or break times and sit in on study halls. They may also accompany student groups on field trips and to competitions and events. Some teachers also have the opportunity to escort students on educational vacations to Washington, D.C., other major U.S. cities, and to foreign countries. Secondary school teachers attend faculty meetings, meetings with parents, and state and national teacher conferences.

Some teachers explore their subject area outside of the requirements of the job. English and writing teachers may publish in magazines and journals, business and technology teachers may have small businesses of their own, music teachers may perform and record their music, art teachers may show work in galleries, and sign-language teachers may do freelance interpreting.

■ EARNINGS

Most teachers are contracted to work nine months out of the year, though some contracts are made for 10 or a full 12 months. (When regular school is not in session, teachers are expected to conduct summer teaching, planning, or other school-related work.) In most cases, teachers have the option of prorating their salary for up to 52 weeks.

According to the Bureau of Labor Statistics, the median annual salary for secondary school teachers was $57,200 in May 2013. The lowest 10 percent earned $37,800; the highest 10 percent earned $91,190 or more.

Teachers can also supplement their earnings through teaching summer classes, coaching sports, sponsoring a club, or other extracurricular work.

On behalf of the teachers, unions bargain with schools over contract conditions such as wages, hours, and benefits. A majority of teachers join the American Federation of Teachers or the National Education Association. Depending on the state, teachers usually receive a retirement plan, sick leave, and health and life insurance. Some systems grant teachers sabbatical leave.

WORK ENVIRONMENT

Although the job of the secondary school teacher is not overly strenuous, it can be tiring and trying. Secondary school teachers must stand for many hours each day, do a lot of talking, show energy and enthusiasm, and handle discipline problems. But they also have the reward of guiding their students as they make decisions about their lives and futures.

Secondary school teachers work under generally pleasant conditions, though some older schools may have poor heating and electrical systems. Although violence in schools has decreased in recent years, media coverage of the violence has increased, and so have student fears. In most schools, students are prepared to learn and to perform the work that's required of them. But in some schools, students may be dealing with gangs, drugs, poverty, and other problems, so the environment can be tense and emotional.

School hours are generally 8:00 A.M. to 3:00 P.M., but teachers work more than 40 hours a week teaching, preparing for classes, grading papers, and directing extracurricular activities. As a coach, or as a music or drama director, teachers may have to work some evenings and weekends. Many teachers enroll in masters or doctoral programs and take evening and summer courses to continue their education.

EXPLORING

By going to high school, you have already gained a good sense of the daily work of a secondary school teacher. But the requirements of a teacher extend far beyond the classroom, so ask to spend some time with one of your teachers after school, and ask to look at lecture notes and record-keeping procedures. Interview your teachers about the amount of work that goes into preparing a class and directing an extracurricular activity. To get some firsthand teaching experience, volunteer for a peer tutoring program. Many other teaching opportunities may exist in your community. Look into coaching an athletic team at the YMCA, counseling at a summer camp,

teaching an art course at a community center, or assisting with a community theater production.

EDUCATION AND TRAINING REQUIREMENTS
High School

Follow your guidance counselor's college preparatory program and take advanced classes in such subjects as English, history, science, math, and government. You should also explore an extracurricular activity, such as theater, sports, and debate, so that you can offer these additional skills to future employers. If you already know which subject you'd like to teach, take all available courses in that area. Also be sure to take speech and composition courses to develop your communication skills.

Postsecondary Training

All 50 states and the District of Columbia require teachers to have a bachelor's degree and to have completed an accredited teacher-training program, which includes many hours of supervised teaching. Many colleges and universities in the U.S. offer accredited teacher education programs, most of which are designed to meet the certification requirements for the state in which they are located. Some states may require you to pass a test before being admitted to an education program. You may choose to major in your subject area while taking required education courses, or you may major in secondary education with a

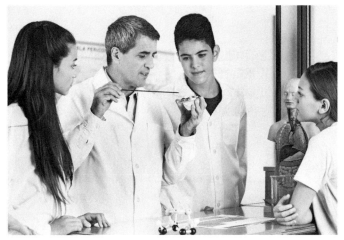

A high school science teacher explains an experiment to his students. (Tyler Olson. Shutterstock.)

TEACHING SECONDARY SCHOOL — LEARN MORE ABOUT IT

Capel, Susan, et al. *Learning to Teach in the Secondary School: A Companion to School Experience,* 6th ed. New York: Routledge, 2013.

Emmer, Edmund T., and Carolyn M. Evertson. *Classroom Management for Middle and High School Teachers,* 9th ed. Upper Saddle River, N.J.: Pearson, 2012.

Kellough, Richard D., and Jionna Carjuzaa. *Teaching in the Middle and Secondary Schools,* 10th ed. Upper Saddle River, N.J.: Pearson, 2012.

Singer, Alan J. *Teaching to Learn, Learning to Teach: A Handbook for Secondary School Teachers,* 2nd ed. New York: Routledge, 2013.

Thompson, Julia G. *Discipline Survival Kit for the Secondary Teacher,* 2nd ed. Hoboken, N.J.: Jossey-Bass, 2010.

concentration in your subject area. Advisers (both in education and in your chosen specialty) will help you select courses.

In addition to a degree, a training period of student teaching in an actual classroom environment is required. Students are placed in schools to work with full-time teachers. During this period, undergraduate students observe the ways in which lessons are presented and the classroom is managed, learn how to keep records of such details as attendance and grades, and get actual experience in handling the class, both under supervision and alone.

Besides licensure and courses in education, prospective high school teachers usually need 24 to 36 hours of college work in the subject they wish to teach. Some states require a master's degree; teachers with master's degrees can earn higher salaries. Private schools generally do not require an education degree.

■ CERTIFICATION, LICENSING, AND SPECIAL REQUIREMENTS
Certification or Licensing
The National Board for Professional Teaching Standards offers voluntary national certification. Contact the board for information on eligibility criteria.

Public school teachers must be licensed under regulations established by the department of education of the state in which they teach. Not all states require licensure for teachers in private or parochial schools. When you've received your teaching degree, you may request that a transcript of your college record be sent to the licensure section of the state department of education. If you have

met licensure requirements, you will receive a certificate and thus be eligible to teach in that state's public schools. In some states, you may have to take additional tests. If you move to another state, you will have to resubmit college transcripts, as well as comply with any other regulations in the new state to be able to teach there.

■ EXPERIENCE, SKILLS, AND PERSONALITY TRAITS
One of the best ways to gain experience in the field is to work as a student teacher, which is often a requirement of your education degree program.

Working as a secondary school teacher, you'll need respect for young people and a genuine interest in their success in life. You'll also need patience; adolescence can be a troubling time for children, and these troubles often affect behavior and classroom performance. Because you'll be working with students who are at very impressionable ages, you should serve as a good role model. You should also be well organized, as you'll have to keep track of the work and progress of many students.

■ EMPLOYMENT PROSPECTS
Employers
Secondary school teachers are needed at public and private schools, including parochial schools, juvenile detention centers, vocational schools, and schools of the arts. They work in middle schools, junior high schools, and high schools. Though some rural areas maintain schools, most secondary schools are in towns and cities of all sizes. Teachers are also finding opportunities in charter schools, which are smaller, deregulated schools that receive public funding.

Starting Out
After completing the teacher certification process, including your months of student teaching, you'll work with your school's career services office to find a full-time position. The departments of education of some states maintain listings of job openings. Many schools advertise teaching positions in the classifieds of the state's major newspapers as well as on their Web sites. You may also directly contact the principals and superintendents of the schools in which you'd like to work. While waiting for full-time work, you can work as a substitute teacher. In urban areas with many schools, you may be able to substitute on a full-time basis.

■ ADVANCEMENT PROSPECTS
Most teachers advance simply by becoming more of an expert in the job that they have chosen. There is usually an increase in salary as teachers acquire experience.

Additional training or study can also bring an increase in salary.

A few teachers with management ability and interest in administrative work may advance to the position of *principal*. Others may advance into supervisory positions, and some may become helping teachers who are charged with the responsibility of helping other teachers find appropriate instructional materials and develop certain phases of their courses of study. Others may go into teacher education at a college or university. For most of these positions, additional education is required. Some teachers also make lateral moves into other education-related positions such as *school counselor* or *resource room teacher*.

■ OUTLOOK

The U.S. Department of Labor predicts that job opportunities for secondary school teachers will grow as fast as average for all careers through 2024 as a result of a decline in student enrollments due to lower birth rates. Enrollments will vary be region, with the largest enrollments occurring in the southern and western United States. Little or no enrollment growth is expected in the Midwest, and enrollment is expected to decline in the Northeast.

Despite the prediction for slow employment growth, there will continue to be opportunities for high school teachers. Many teachers will reach retirement age over the next decade and will need to be replaced. The National Education Association believes this will be a challenge because of the low salaries that are paid to secondary school teachers. Higher salaries will be necessary to attract new teachers and retain experienced ones, along with other changes such as smaller classroom sizes and safer schools. Other challenges for the profession involve attracting more men into teaching. The percentage of male teachers at this level continues to decline.

Teachers who are bilingual and who specialize in subjects such as math, science (especially chemistry and physics), English as a second language, and special education will be in high demand, especially in urban and rural school districts. In order to attract qualified teachers to these areas, some states and cities have started programs to pay for qualified candidates' graduate school or teacher certification education while the candidate works in a school that is in need of teachers. The New York City Teaching Fellows program is one such program. Visit http://www.nycteachingfellows.org for more information.

In order to improve education for all children, changes are being considered by some districts. Some private companies are managing public schools. Though some believe that a private company can afford to provide better facilities, faculty, and equipment, this hasn't been proven. Teacher organizations are concerned about taking school management away from communities and turning it over to remote corporate headquarters. Charter schools and voucher programs are two other controversial alternatives to traditional public education. Charter schools, which are small schools that are publicly funded but not guided by the rules and regulations of traditional public schools, are viewed by some as places of innovation and improved educational methods; others see charter schools as ill-equipped and unfairly funded with money that could better benefit local school districts. Vouchers, which exist only in a few cities, allow students to attend private schools courtesy of tuition vouchers; these vouchers are paid for with public tax dollars. In theory, the vouchers allow for more choices in education for poor and minority students, but private schools still have the option of being highly selective in their admissions. Teacher organizations see some danger in giving public funds to unregulated private schools.

■ UNIONS AND ASSOCIATIONS

Secondary school teachers may join unions such as the American Federation of Teachers and the National Education Association. The National Board for Professional Teaching Standards offers certification. The Council for the Accreditation of Educator Preparation accredits teacher education programs.

■ TIPS FOR ENTRY

1. Visit https://www.teach.org for job listings and advice on preparing a resume and portfolio and acing interviews.
2. Read industry publications, such as *American Teacher* and *American Educator* (both are available at http://www.aft.org/our-news/periodicals), to learn more about trends in your profession.
3. Become certified by the National Board for Professional Teaching Standards in order to show employers that you have met the highest standards established by your profession.
4. Participate in student-teaching opportunities.

■ FOR MORE INFORMATION

For information on union membership, contact
American Federation of Teachers (AFT)
555 New Jersey Avenue, NW
Washington, D.C. 20001-2029
Tel: (202) 879-4400
http://www.aft.org

For information on accredited teacher education programs, contact

Council for the Accreditation of Educator Preparation (CAEP)
1140 19th St., NW, Suite 400
Washington, D.C. 20036
Tel: (202) 223-0077
http://caepnet.org

For information on union membership, contact

National Education Association (NEA)
1201 16th Street, NW
Washington, D.C. 20036-3290
Tel: (202) 833-4000
Fax: (202) 822-7974
http://www.nea.org

For information on careers, certification and licensing, and financial aid, visit

Teach.org
https://www.teach.org

Secret Service Special Agents

■ OVERVIEW

Secret Service special agents are employed by the U.S. Secret Service, part of the Department of Homeland Security. Secret Service agents work to protect the president and other political leaders of the United States, as well as heads of foreign states or governments when they are visiting the United States. Special agents also investigate financial crimes. The U.S. Secret Service employs about 6,300 people, about 3,200 of whom are special agents.

■ HISTORY

The Secret Service was established in 1865 to suppress the counterfeiting of U.S. currency. After the assassination of President William McKinley in 1901, the Secret Service was directed by Congress to protect the president of the United States. Today it is the Secret Service's responsibility to protect the following people: the president and vice president (also president-elect and vice president-elect) and their immediate families; former presidents and their spouses for 10 years after the president leaves office (spouses lose protection if they remarry; all former presidents up to and including President Clinton

receive lifetime protection, as this law changed in 1997); children of former presidents until they are 16 years old; visiting heads of foreign states or governments and their spouses traveling with them, along with other distinguished foreign visitors to the United States and their spouses traveling with them; official representatives of the United States who are performing special missions abroad; major presidential and vice-presidential candidates and, within 120 days of the general presidential election, their spouses.

■ THE JOB

Secret Service special agents are charged with two missions: protecting U.S. leaders or visiting foreign dignitaries (likewise, U.S. leaders on missions to other countries) and investigating the counterfeiting of U.S. currency. Special agents are empowered to carry and use firearms, execute warrants, and make arrests.

When assigned to a permanent protection duty—for the president, for example—special agents are usually assigned to the Washington, D.C., area. They are responsible for planning and executing protective operations for those whom they protect at all times. Agents can also be assigned to a temporary protective duty to provide protection for candidates or visiting foreign dignitaries. In either case, an advance team of special agents surveys each site that will be visited by those whom they protect. Based on their survey, the team determines how much manpower and what types of equipment are needed to provide protection. They identify hospitals and evacuation routes and work closely with local police, fire, and rescue units to develop the protection plan and determine emergency routes and procedures, should the need arise. A command post is then set up with secure communications to act as the communication center for protective activities. The post monitors emergencies and keeps participants in contact with each other.

Before the officials arrive, the *lead advance agent* coordinates all law enforcement representatives participating in the visit. The assistance of military, federal, state, county, and local law enforcement organizations is a vital part of the entire security operation. Personnel are told where they will be posted and are alerted to specific problems associated with the visit. Intelligence information is discussed and emergency measures are outlined. Just prior to the arrival of those whom they protect, checkpoints are established and access to the secure area is limited. After the visit, special agents analyze every step of the protective operation, record unusual incidents, and suggest improvements for future operations.

Protective research is an important part of all security operations. *Protective research engineers* and *protective research technicians* develop, test, and maintain technical devices and equipment needed to provide a safe environment for their charge.

When assigned to an investigative duty, special agents investigate threats against those the Secret Service protects. They also work to detect and arrest people committing any offense relating to coins, currency, stamps, government bonds, checks, credit card fraud, computer fraud, false identification crimes, and other obligations or securities of the United States. Special agents also investigate violations of the Federal Deposit Insurance Act, the Federal Land Bank Act, and the Government Losses in Shipment Act. Special agents assigned to an investigative duty usually work in one of the Secret Service's more than 150 domestic and foreign field offices. Agents assigned to investigative duties in a field office are often called out to serve on a temporary protective operation.

Special agents assigned to investigate financial crimes may also be assigned to one of the Secret Service's three divisions in Washington, D.C., or they may receive help from the divisions while conducting an investigation from a field office. The Counterfeit Division constantly reviews the latest reprographic and lithographic technologies to keep a step ahead of counterfeiters. The Financial Crimes Division aids special agents in their investigation of electronic crimes involving credit cards, computers, cellular and regular telephones, narcotics, illegal firearms trafficking, homicide, and other crimes. The Forensic Services Division coordinates forensic science activities within the Secret Service. The division analyzes evidence such as documents, fingerprints, photographs, and video and audio recordings.

The Secret Service employs a number of specialist positions such as electronics engineers, communications technicians, research psychologists, computer experts, armorers, intelligence analysts, polygraph examiners, forensic experts, security specialists, and more.

Special agents assigned to smaller field offices typically handle a wide variety of criminal investigations. But special agents usually work for a specialized squad in a field office, handling specific investigations like counterfeit currency, forgery, and financial crimes. Special agents may receive case referrals from the Secret Service headquarters, from other law enforcement agencies, or through their own investigations. Investigating counterfeit money requires extensive undercover operations and surveillance. Special agents usually work with the U.S. Attorney's Office and local law enforcement for counterfeiting cases. Through their work, special agents detect and seize millions of dollars of counterfeit money each year—some of which is produced overseas. Special agents working in a fraud squad often receive complaints or

referrals from banking or financial institutions that have been defrauded. Fraud cases involve painstaking and long-term investigations to reveal the criminals, who are usually organized groups or individuals hiding behind

QUICK FACTS

ALTERNATE TITLE(S)
Lead Advance Agents, Protective Research Engineers, Protective Research Technicians

DUTIES
Protect the president and other political leaders of the United States, as well as heads of foreign states or governments when they are visiting the United States; investigate financial crimes

SALARY RANGE
$35,359 to $74,585 to $150,000+

WORK ENVIRONMENT
Indoors/Outdoors

BEST GEOGRAPHIC LOCATION(S)
Opportunities are available in field offices throughout the U.S., but many agents are based in Washington, D.C.

MINIMUM EDUCATION LEVEL
Bachelor's Degree

SCHOOL SUBJECTS
Computer Science, English, Foreign Language

EXPERIENCE
Three years experience in law enforcement or a related field or an equivalent combination of education and experience required

PERSONALITY TRAITS
Helpful, Problem-Solving, Realistic

SKILLS
Interpersonal, Leadership, Organizational

CERTIFICATION OR LICENSING
None

SPECIAL REQUIREMENTS
Applicants must be U.S. citizens and be at least 21 and less than 37 years of age at the time of appointment; must meet physical requirements; undergo background, drug, and polygraph screenings

EMPLOYMENT PROSPECTS
Poor

ADVANCEMENT PROSPECTS
Fair

OUTLOOK
Little Change or More Slowly than the Average

NOC
N/A

O*NET-SOC
33-3021.03

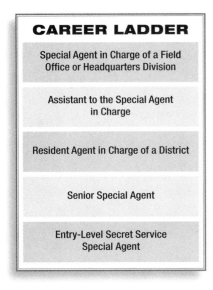

CAREER LADDER

Special Agent in Charge of a Field Office or Headquarters Division

Assistant to the Special Agent in Charge

Resident Agent in Charge of a District

Senior Special Agent

Entry-Level Secret Service Special Agent

false identifications. Special agents working for forgery squads often have cases referred to them from banks or local police departments that have discovered incidents of forgery.

■ EARNINGS

Special agents generally receive Law Enforcement Availability Pay (LEAP) on top of their base pay. Agents usually start at the GS-7 or GS-9 grade levels, which in 2017 were $35,359 and $43,251, respectively, excluding LEAP. (Salaries may be slightly higher in some areas with high costs of living.) Agents automatically advance until they reach the GS-13 level, which in 2017 was $74,584, excluding LEAP. The payscale also includes 10 "Steps" within each grade that can increase these base earnings by anywhere from a few hundred to tens of thousands of dollars. Top officials in the Secret Service are appointed to Senior Executive Service (SES) positions; they do not receive the availability pay. Top SES salaries are well over $150,000 a year.

Benefits for special agents include low-cost health and life insurance, annual and sick leave, paid holidays, and a comprehensive retirement program. In addition, free financial protection is provided to agents and their families in the event of job-related injury or death.

■ WORK ENVIRONMENT

A Secret Service special agent is assigned to a field office or the Washington, D.C., headquarters. Agents on investigative assignments may spend much time doing research with the office as base, or they may be out in the field, doing undercover or surveillance work. Protective and investigative assignments can keep a special agent away from home for long periods of time, depending on the situation. Preparations for the president's visits to cities in the United States generally take no more than a week. However, a large event attracting foreign dignitaries, such as International Monetary Fund/World Bank meetings in various cities, can take months to plan. Special agents at field offices assigned to investigate crimes are called out regularly to serve temporary protective missions. During presidential campaign years, agents typically serve three-week protective assignments, work three weeks back at their field offices, and then start the process over again.

Special agents always work at least 40 hours a week and often work a minimum of 50 hours each week.

Since special agents must travel for their jobs, interested applicants should be flexible and willing to be away from home for periods up to 30 days and sometimes longer. According to the Secret Service, they also must be willing to "work long hours in undesirable conditions on short notice, relocate to duty stations throughout the U.S. and abroad as organizational needs dictate, and work undercover assignments as requested."

One of the drawbacks of being a special agent is the potential danger involved. A special agent was shot in the stomach in 1981 during an assassination attempt on President Ronald Reagan. Other agents have been killed on the job in helicopter accidents, surveillance assignments, and protective operations, to name a few. For most agents, however, the benefits outweigh the drawbacks.

■ EXPLORING

Visit the U.S. Secret Service Web site, http://www.secret service.gov, to learn more about career opportunities. Additionally, the Secret Service offers several programs for students ages 16 through college age to help them gain experience in the field, including the Secret Service Student Temporary Education Employment Program, Student Career Experience Program, and the Student Volunteer Service Program. Visit https://www.secret service.gov/about/faqs/ for more information on these programs. Finally, talk to a Secret Service special agent about his or her career. Ask your social studies or school counselor to help arrange an information interview.

■ EDUCATION AND TRAINING REQUIREMENTS
High School

You can help prepare for a career as a special agent by doing well in high school. You may receive special consideration by the Secret Service if you have computer training, which is needed to investigate computer fraud, or if you can speak a foreign language, which is useful during investigations and while protecting visiting heads of state or U.S. officials who are working abroad. Specialized skills in electronics, forensics, and other investigative areas are highly regarded. Other important classes include physical education, English, speech, and psychology. Aside from school, doing something unique and positive for your city or neighborhood, or becoming involved in community organizations can improve your chances of being selected by the Secret Service.

Postsecondary Training

The Secret Service recruits special agents at the GS-7 and GS-9 grade levels. You can qualify at the GS-7 level in one of three ways: obtain a four-year degree from an accredited college or university; work for at least three years in a criminal investigative or law enforcement field and gain knowledge and experience in applying laws relating to criminal violations; or obtain an equivalent combination of education and experience. You can qualify at the GS-9 level by achieving superior academic scores (defined as a grade point average of at least 2.95 on a 4.0 scale), going to graduate school and studying a directly related field, or gaining an additional year of criminal investigative experience.

All newly hired special agents go through 10 weeks of training in the Criminal Investigator Training Program at the Federal Law Enforcement Training Center in Glynco, Georgia, and then 17 weeks of specialized training at the Secret Service's Special Agent Training Course outside of Washington, D.C. During training, new agents take comprehensive courses in protective techniques, criminal and constitutional law, criminal investigative procedures, use of scientific investigative devices, first aid, the use of firearms, and defensive measures. Special agents also learn about collecting evidence, surveillance techniques, undercover operation, and courtroom demeanor. Specialized training includes skills such as marksmanship, control tactics, water survival skills, and physical fitness. Secret service agents also participate in "real world" emergency situations involving Secret Service protectees. The classroom study is supplemented by on-the-job training, and special agents go through advanced in-service training throughout their careers.

New special agents usually begin work at the field offices where they first applied. Their initial work is investigative in nature and is closely supervised. After six to eight years, agents are usually transferred to a protection assignment.

■ CERTIFICATION, LICENSING, AND SPECIAL REQUIREMENTS
Certification or Licensing
There are no certification or licensing requirements to become a special agents, though agents that carry a firearm must be licensed to do so.

Other Requirements
Special agents must be U.S. citizens; be at least 21 and less than 37 years of age at the time of appointment; have uncorrected vision no worse than 20/60 in each eye, correctable to 20/20 in each eye; be in excellent health and physical condition; pass the Treasury Enforcement Agent Examination; and undergo a complete background investigation, including in-depth interviews, drug screening, medical examination, and polygraph examination.

A Secret Service agent waits for the president outside a limousine. (Pete Souza. White House.)

■ EXPERIENCE, SKILLS, AND PERSONALITY TRAITS
A degree, at least three years of experience in law enforcement or a related area, or an equivalent combination of education and experience are required to become a Secret Service special agent.

The Secret Service is looking for smart, upstanding citizens who will give a favorable representation of the U.S. government. The agency looks for people with strong ethics, morals, and virtues, and then they teach them how to be special agents.

Special agents also need dedication, which can be demonstrated through a candidate's grade point average in high school and college. Applicants must have a drug-free background. Even experimental drug use can be a reason to dismiss an applicant from the hiring process. Special agents also need to be confident and honest—with no criminal background.

■ EMPLOYMENT PROSPECTS
Employers
The Secret Service warns that because they have many well-qualified applicants and few anticipated vacancies, the chance that you will be hired is limited. On top of that, the hiring process can take up to a year or more because of the thoroughness of the selection process.

Starting Out
If you are ready to apply for a special agent job, you can visit the application page on the Secret Service's Web

COUNTERFEIT CURRENCY AND PROTECTIVE BUBBLES

WORDS TO KNOW

Checkpoint: A place set up by law enforcement officials to examine an individual's credentials (driver license, passport, state identification, etc.).

Choke point: A potential ambush site, such as a bridge, where a protectee or motorcade may be more vulnerable to attack.

Counterfeit currency: Money that has not been officially printed by a government.

Forgery: The illegal act of creating something that is not real such as bank or real estate documents or currency.

Protective bubble: A 360-degree virtual boundary of safety that the Secret Service maintains around each of the people it protects. Special agents work to ensure that nothing dangerous penetrates the bubble.

Protectee: A person—usually a political leader of the United States or a foreign dignitary—that the Secret Service is responsible for protecting. Protectees may also include the spouse or family of the primary protectee.

Warrant: A legal order issued to a law enforcement officer by a judge; for example, a warrant may be issued to allow the search of a suspect's home for illegal drugs or stolen goods.

site, at https://www.secretservice.gov/join/apply/. Be sure to check with the Secret Service field office nearest you before submitting your forms, though; the application process can be complicated, and you'll want to make sure you have completed the required paperwork. You can also find the field office in your area on the Secret Service's Web site.

■ ADVANCEMENT PROSPECTS

Generally, special agents begin their careers by spending five to 10 years performing primarily investigative duties at a field office. Then they are usually assigned to a protective assignment for three to five years. After 12 or 13 years, special agents become eligible to move into supervisory positions. A typical promotion path moves special agents to the position of senior agent, then resident agent in charge of a district, assistant to the special agent in charge, and finally special agent in charge of a field office or headquarters division. Promotion is awarded based upon performance, and since the Secret Service employs many highly skilled professionals, competition for promotion is strong.

Special agents can retire after 20 years and after they reach the age of 50. Special agents must retire before the age of 57. Some retired agents are hired by corporations to organize the logistics of getting either people or products from one place to another. Others work as bodyguards, private investigators, security consultants, and local law enforcement officials.

■ OUTLOOK

Compared to other federal law enforcement agencies, the Secret Service is small. The agency focuses on its protective missions and is not interested in expanding its responsibilities. As a result, the Secret Service will likely not grow much, unless the president and Congress decide to expand the agency's duties.

In spite of increased high-alert conditions as a result of terrorist threats, the Secret Service still employs a small number of people, and their new hires each year are limited. Officials anticipate that the job availability could increase slightly over the next few years.

■ UNIONS AND ASSOCIATIONS

Secret Service special agents are not represented by unions, but some join the Association of Former Intelligence Officers (a nonprofit organization for current and former intelligence officers).

■ TIPS FOR ENTRY

1. Visit the Career Fairs page of the U.S. Secret Service's Web site, https://www.secretservice.gov/join/calendar/, to learn more about recruiting opportunities in your area. You can also call (888) 813-8777 for a list of current vacancies.

2. Visit https://www.secretservice.gov/join/careers/ to learn about different career paths in the Secret Service.

3. Conduct information interviews with special agents and ask them for advice on preparing for and entering the field.

■ FOR MORE INFORMATION

This is a nonprofit organization for current and former intelligence officers. Visit its Web site for information on the intelligence community and careers in the field.

Association of Former Intelligence Officers (AFIO)
7700 Leesburg Pike, Suite 324
Falls Church, VA 22043-2618
Tel: (703) 790-0320
Fax: (703) 991-1278
E-mail: afio@afio.com
http://www.afio.com

Your local Secret Service field office or headquarters office can provide more information on becoming a special agent. To learn about careers, download employment applications, and read answers to frequently asked questions, visit the Secret Service's Web site.

U.S. Secret Service
245 Murray Lane, SW, Building 410
Washington, D.C. 20223-0007
Tel: (202) 406-5708; (202) 406-5458
http://www.secretservice.gov

Secretaries

■ OVERVIEW

Secretaries, also called *administrative assistants*, perform a wide range of jobs that vary greatly from business to business. However, most secretaries draft memos, letters, and reports; manage records and information; answer telephones; handle correspondence; schedule appointments; make travel arrangements; and sort mail. The amount of time secretaries spend on these duties depends on the size and type of the office as well as on their own job training. There are nearly 4 million secretaries employed in the United States.

■ HISTORY

Today, as in the past, secretaries play an important role in keeping lines of communication open. Before there were telephones, messages were transmitted by hand, often from the secretary of one party to the secretary of the receiving party. Their trustworthiness was valued because the lives of many people often hung in the balance of certain communications.

Secretaries in the ancient world developed methods of taking abbreviated notes so that they could capture as much as possible of their employers' words. In 16th-century England, the modern precursors of the shorthand methods we know today were developed. In the 19th century, Isaac Pitman and John Robert Gregg developed the shorthand systems that are still used in offices and courtrooms in the United States.

The equipment secretaries use in their work has changed drastically in recent years. Almost every office is automated in some way. Familiarity with machines such as switchboards, photocopiers, fax machines, personal computers, videoconferencing equipment, and cell phones has become an integral part of the secretary's day-to-day work.

QUICK FACTS

ALTERNATE TITLE(S)
Administrative Assistants, Administrative Secretaries, Education Secretaries, Legal Secretaries, Medical Secretaries, Membership Secretaries, Personal Secretaries, Social Secretaries, Technical Secretaries, Virtual Assistants

DUTIES
Perform a variety of administrative and clerical duties in offices; assist employers; coordinate meetings and other functions; represent their employer in a professional manner

SALARY RANGE
$22,390 to $36,500 to $79,500+

WORK ENVIRONMENT
Primarily Indoors

BEST GEOGRAPHIC LOCATION(S)
Opportunities are available throughout the country

MINIMUM EDUCATION LEVEL
High School Diploma

SCHOOL SUBJECTS
Business, Computer Science, English

EXPERIENCE
On-the-job training

PERSONALITY TRAITS
Conventional, Organized, Outgoing

SKILLS
Computer, Interpersonal, Organizational

CERTIFICATION OR LICENSING
Recommended

SPECIAL REQUIREMENTS
None

EMPLOYMENT PROSPECTS
Good

ADVANCEMENT PROSPECTS
Good

OUTLOOK
About as Fast as the Average

NOC
1241

O*NET-SOC
43-6011.00, 43-6012.00, 43-6013.00, 43-6014.00

■ THE JOB

Secretaries perform a variety of administrative and clerical duties. The goal of all their activities is to assist their employers in the execution of their work and to help their companies conduct business in an efficient and professional manner.

CAREER LADDER

Office Manager

Secretarial Supervisor

Executive Secretary

Experienced Secretary

Entry-Level Secretary

Secretaries' work includes processing and transmitting information to the office staff and to other organizations. They operate office machines and arrange for their repair or servicing. These machines include computers, typewriters, videoconferencing technology, photocopiers, scanners, switchboards, and fax machines. Secretaries also order office supplies and perform regular duties such as answering phones, sorting mail and e-mails, managing files, and writing letters, memos, and other correspondence.

Some offices have word processing centers that handle all of the firm's typing. In such a situation, *administrative secretaries* take care of all secretarial duties except for typing and dictation. This arrangement leaves them free to respond to correspondence, prepare reports, do research and present the results to their employers, and otherwise assist the professional staff. Often these secretaries work in groups of three or four so that they can help each other if one secretary has a workload that is heavier than normal.

In many offices, secretaries make appointments for company executives and keep track of the office schedule. They make travel arrangements for the professional staff or for clients, and occasionally are asked to travel with staff members on business trips. Other secretaries might manage the office while their supervisors are away on vacation or business trips.

Secretaries take minutes at meetings, write up reports, and compose and type letters. They will often find their responsibilities growing as they learn the business. Some are responsible for finding speakers for conferences, planning receptions, and arranging public relations programs. Some write copy for brochures or articles before making the arrangements to have them printed or posted to the Internet, or they might use desktop publishing software to create the documents themselves. They greet clients and guide them to the proper offices, and they often supervise and train other staff members and newer secretaries, especially in the use of computer software programs.

Some secretaries perform very specialized work. *Legal secretaries* prepare legal papers including wills, mortgages, contracts, deeds, motions, complaints, and summonses. They work under the direct supervision of an attorney or paralegal. They assist with legal research by reviewing legal journals and organizing briefs for their employers. They must learn an entire specialized vocabulary that is used in legal papers and documents.

Medical secretaries take medical histories of patients; make appointments; prepare and send bills to patients; track and collect bills; process insurance billing; maintain medical files; and pursue correspondence with patients, hospitals, and associations. They assist physicians or medical scientists with articles, reports, speeches, and conference proceedings. Some medical secretaries are responsible for ordering medical supplies. They, too, need to learn an entire specialized vocabulary of medical terms and be familiar with laboratory or hospital procedures.

Technical secretaries, who work for engineers and scientists, use design and database software to prepare reports and papers that often include graphics and mathematical equations. The secretaries maintain a technical library and help with scientific papers by gathering and editing materials.

Social secretaries, often called *personal secretaries*, arrange all of their employer's social activities. They handle private as well as business social affairs and may plan parties, send out invitations, or write speeches for their employers. Social secretaries are often hired by celebrities or high-level executives who have busy social calendars to maintain.

Many associations, clubs, and nonprofit organizations have *membership secretaries* who compile and send out newsletters or promotional materials while maintaining membership lists, dues records, and directories. Depending on the type of club, the secretary may be the one who gives out information to prospective members and who keeps current members and related organizations informed of upcoming events.

Education secretaries work in elementary or secondary schools or on college campuses. They take care of all clerical duties at the school. Their responsibilities may include preparing bulletins and reports for teachers, parents, or students; keeping track of budgets for school supplies or student activities; and maintaining the school's calendar of events. Depending on the position, they work for school administrators, principals, or groups of teachers or professors. Other education secretaries work in administration offices, state education departments, or service departments.

Virtual assistants are a new type of secretarial and office support specialist. Working from a home or remote office, these professionals use the Internet, e-mail, and fax machines to communicate and work with multiple clients in different industries.

EARNINGS

Salaries for secretaries vary widely by region; type of business; and the skill, experience, and level of responsibility of the secretary. Secretaries (except legal, medical, and executive) earned an average of $36,500 annually in May 2015, according to the U.S. Department of Labor (DOL). Salaries ranged from $22,390 to $60,640. Medical secretaries earned salaries averaging $33,040. Ten percent earned less than $22,610, and 10 percent earned $48,670 or more per year. Legal secretaries made an average of $43,200. Salaries for legal secretaries ranged from $26,760 to more than $72,890 annually.

An attorney's rank in the firm will also affect the earnings of a legal secretary; secretaries who work for a partner will earn higher salaries than those who work for an associate. The median salary for executive secretaries and executive administrative assistants was $53,370 in May 2015, according to the DOL, with salaries ranging from less than $33,830 to more than $79,500.

Secretaries, especially those working in the legal profession, earn considerably more if certified. Most secretaries receive paid holidays and two weeks vacation after a year of work, as well as sick leave. Many offices provide benefits including health and life insurance, pension plans, overtime pay, and tuition reimbursement.

WORK ENVIRONMENT

Most secretaries work in pleasant offices with modern equipment. Office conditions vary widely, however. While some secretaries have their own offices and work for one or two executives, others share crowded workspace with other workers.

Most office workers work 35–40 hours a week. Very few secretaries work on the weekends on a regular basis, although some may be asked to work overtime if a particular project demands it.

The work is not physically strenuous or hazardous, although deadline pressure is a factor and sitting for long periods of time can be uncomfortable. Many hours spent in front of a computer can lead to eyestrain or repetitive-motion problems for secretaries. Most secretaries are not required to travel. Part-time and flexible schedules are easily adaptable to secretarial work.

EXPLORING

High school counselors can give interest and aptitude tests to help you assess your suitability for a career as a secretary. Local business schools often welcome visitors, and sometimes offer courses that can be taken in

A secretary takes notes during a meeting with her manager. (Goodluz. Shutterstock.)

conjunction with a high school business course. Work-study programs will also provide you with an opportunity to work in a business setting to get a sense of the work performed by secretaries.

Part-time or summer jobs as *receptionists*, *file clerks*, and *office clerks* are often available in various offices. These jobs are the best indicators of future satisfaction in the secretarial field. You may find a part-time job if you are computer-literate. Cooperative education programs arranged through schools and "temping" through an agency also are valuable ways to acquire experience. In general, any job that teaches basic office skills is helpful.

EDUCATION AND TRAINING REQUIREMENTS
High School

You will need at least a high school diploma to enter this field. To prepare for a career as a secretary, take high school courses in business, English, and speech. Keyboarding and computer science courses will also be helpful.

Postsecondary Training

To succeed as a secretary, you will need good office skills that include rapid and accurate keyboarding skills and good spelling and grammar. You should enjoy handling details. Some positions require typing a minimum number of words per minute, as well as shorthand ability. Knowledge of word processing, spreadsheet, and database management is important, and most employers require it. Knowledge of Internet programs is also useful. Some of these skills can be learned in business education courses taught at vocational and business schools. Special training programs are available for students who want to become medical or legal secretaries or administrative technology assistants.

Other Education or Training

Participating in continuing education (CE) classes is a great way to keep your skills up to date and become a more attractive job candidate. These opportunities are provided by local, state, and national professional associations. For example, the Association of Executive and Administrative Professionals offers classes and webinars, which in the past have included "Administrative Assistant Fundamentals," "Medical Terminology: A Word Association Approach," and "Computer Skills for the Workplace." The International Association of Administrative Professionals offers the Options Technology training program, which provides training in key office tools and prorgrams. The International Virtual Assistants Association, NALS...the association for legal professionals, and Legal Secretaries International Inc. also provide CE workshops, seminars, and webinars. Contact these organizations for more information.

■ CERTIFICATION, LICENSING, AND SPECIAL REQUIREMENTS
Certification or Licensing

Several professional associations provide certification to secretaries. The International Association of Administrative Professionals offers the certified administrative professional (CAP) designation to applicants who meet experience/education requirements and pass a rigorous exam covering a number of general secretarial topics. It also offers a technology applications specialty designation to those who have already earned the CAP designation.

Two general legal secretary certifications are offered by NALS...the association for legal professionals. After some preliminary office training, you can take an examination to receive the accredited legal professional designation. This certification is for legal secretaries with education, but little to no experience. Legal secretaries with three years of experience can become certified as a professional legal secretary/certified legal professional (PLS/CLP). The PLS/CLP certification designates a legal secretary with exceptional skills and experience. Other specific legal secretary certifications are given by Legal Secretaries International Inc. You can become board certified in business law, civil litigation, criminal law, intellectual property, probate, or real estate. An executive legal secretary designation is also available. Applicants must have a minimum of five years of law experience and pass an examination.

The International Virtual Assistants Association also provides certification.

■ EXPERIENCE, SKILLS, AND PERSONALITY TRAITS

No experience is needed, but those with experience are more likely to land jobs, earn higher pay, and get promoted.

Personal qualities are important in this field of work. As a secretary, you will often be the first employee that clients meet, and therefore you must be friendly, poised, and professionally dressed. Because you must work closely with others, you should be personable and tactful. Discretion, good judgment, organizational ability, and initiative are also important. These traits will not only get you hired but will also help you advance in your career.

Some employers encourage their secretaries to take advanced courses and to be trained to use any new piece of equipment in the office. Requirements vary widely from company to company.

■ EMPLOYMENT PROSPECTS
Employers

Nearly 4 million secretaries are employed throughout the United States, making this profession one of the largest in the country. Of this total, 776,600 work as executive secretaries and administrative assistants, 215,500 specialize as legal secretaries, and 527,600 work as medical secretaries. Secretaries are employed in almost every type of industry—from health care, banking, financial services, and real estate to construction, manufacturing, transportation, communications, and retail and wholesale trade. A large number of secretaries are employed by federal, state, and local government agencies.

Starting Out

Most people looking for work as secretaries find jobs through Internet job boards, newspaper want ads, or by applying directly to local businesses. Both private employment offices and state employment services place secretaries, and business schools help their graduates find suitable jobs. Temporary-help agencies are often an excellent way to find jobs, some of which may turn into permanent ones.

■ ADVANCEMENT PROSPECTS

Secretaries often begin by assisting executive secretaries and work their way up by learning the way their business operates. Initial promotions from a secretarial position are usually to jobs such as *secretarial supervisor*, *office manager*, or *administrative assistant*. Depending on other personal qualifications, college courses in business, accounting, or marketing can help the ambitious secretary enter middle and upper management. Training in computer skills can also lead to advancement. Secretaries who become proficient in word processing, for instance, can get jobs as *instructors* or as *sales representatives* for software manufacturers.

Secretaries may choose to advance by taking positions as medical or legal secretaries—occupations that typically pay higher salaries. Many legal secretaries, with additional training and schooling, become *paralegals*. Secretaries in the medical field can advance into the fields of radiological and surgical records or medical transcription.

■ OUTLOOK

The U.S. Department of Labor predicts that overall employment for secretaries will grow slower than the average for all occupations through 2024, but job prospects vary by specialty. Industries such as health care and social assistance, local college and education services, satellite communication, and utility system construction will create the most new job opportunities. As is common with large occupations, the need to replace retiring workers will generate many openings.

Employment for medical secretaries is expected to grow much faster than the average for all careers through 2024. The growing elderly population (an age demographic that typically requires more medical care than the rest of the population) will create many new job opportunities. In fact, 108,200 new jobs for medical secretaries are expected to be available by 2024.

Job opportunities for executive secretaries will decline by 6 percent through 2024 as a result of the growing use of administrative assistants (who receive lower salaries than executive secretaries) and technological advances that allow secretaries to do more work. Computers, fax machines, e-mail, copy machines, and scanners are some technological advancements that have greatly improved the work productivity of secretaries.

Employment for legal secretaries will decline by 4 percent through 2024 as a result of consolidation in the legal industry and the trend toward having paralegals and legal assistants take on more tasks that were formerly handled by secretaries.

Though more professionals are using personal computers for their correspondence, some administrative duties will still need to be handled by secretaries. The personal aspects of the job and responsibilities such as making travel arrangements, scheduling conferences, and transmitting staff instructions have not changed.

Many employers currently complain of a shortage of capable secretaries. Those with skills (especially computer skills) and experience will have the best chances for employment. Specialized secretaries should attain certification in their field to stay competitive.

■ UNIONS AND ASSOCIATIONS

Some secretaries may be represented by the Office & Professional Employees International Union and other unions. The Association of Executive and Administrative Professionals and the International Association of Administrative Professionals are the major professional associations for secretaries. They offer membership, career information, certification, continuing education classes, and networking opportunities. NALS...the association for legal professionals and Legal Secretaries International Inc. are the leading professional associations for legal secretaries. The International Virtual Assistants Association is a membership organization for virtual assistants.

■ TIPS FOR ENTRY

1. Read *OfficePro* (http://www.iaap-hq.org/page/ OfficeProMagazine) and *The Executary* (http:// www.theaeap.com/newsletters) to learn more about careers in general secretarial work. The *NALS docket* (http://www.nals.org/?page_id=85) is a useful publication for legal secretaries.

2. Talk to secretaries about their jobs. Ask them for advice on preparing for and entering the field.

3. Visit the following Web sites for job listings:
   - http://jobs.theaeap.com/home/index.cfm?site_id=427
   - http://careers.iaap-hq.org/home/index.cfm?site_id=11607
   - http://careers.nals.org

4. http://lsintl.legalstaff.com/Common/HomePage.aspx

■ FOR MORE INFORMATION

For information on careers, contact

Association of Executive and Administrative Professionals (AEAP)
900 South Washington Street, Suite G-13
Falls Church, VA 22046-4009
Tel: (703) 237-8616
Fax: (703) 533-1153
E-mail: headquarters@theaeap.com
http://theaeap.com

For information on the certified professional secretary designation, contact

International Association of Administrative Professionals (IAAP)
10502 North Ambassador Drive, Suite 100
Kansas City, MO 64153-1278
Tel: (816) 891-6600
Fax: (816) 891-9118
http://www.iaap-hq.org

For more information on the emerging career of virtual assistant, visit

International Virtual Assistants Association (IVAA)
3773 Howard Hughes Pkwy, Suite 500S
Las Vegas, NV 89169-6014
Tel: (877) 440-2750
Fax: (888) 259-2487
http://www.ivaa.org

For information about certification, contact

Legal Secretaries International Inc.
2951 Marina Bay Drive, Suite 130-641
League City, TX 77573-4078
E-mail: info@legalsecretaries.org
http://www.legalsecretaries.org

For information on certification, job openings, a variety of careers in law, and more, contact

NALS...the association for legal professionals (NALS)
8159 East 41st Street
Tulsa, OK 74145-3313
Tel: (918) 582-5188
Fax: (918) 582-5907
http://www.nals.org

For information regarding union representation, contact

Office & Professional Employees International Union (OPEIU)
80 Eighth Avenue, 20th Floor
New York, NY 10011-7144
Tel: (800) 346-7348
http://www.opeiu.org

For job listings and career and salary information, visit

OfficeTeam
Tel: (855) 549-0489
http://www.roberthalf.com/officeteam

Security Consultants and Guards

■ OVERVIEW

Security consultants and *security guards* (who are also called *security officers*) are responsible for protecting public and private property against theft, fire, vandalism, illegal entry, and acts of violence. They may work for commercial or government organizations or private individuals. More than 1 million security workers are employed in the United States.

■ HISTORY

People have been concerned with protecting valuable possessions since they began accumulating goods. At first, most security plans were rather simple. In earliest times, members of extended families or several families would band together to watch food, clothing, livestock, and other valuables. As personal wealth grew, the wealthier members of a society would often assign some of their servants to protect their property and families from theft and violence. Soldiers often filled this function as well. During the Middle Ages, many towns and villages hired guards to patrol the streets at night as protection against fire, theft, and hostile intrusion. Night watchmen continued to play an important role in the security of many towns and cities until well into the 19th century.

The first public police forces were organized in the middle of the 19th century. These were largely limited to cities, however, and the need for protection and safety of goods and property led many to supplement police forces with private security forces. In the United States, ranchers and others hired armed guards to protect their property. Soon, people began to specialize in offering comprehensive security and detective services. Allan Pinkerton was one of the first such security agents. In 1861, Pinkerton was hired to guard President-elect Abraham Lincoln on his way to his inauguration.

As police forces at local, state, and federal levels were established across the country, night watchmen and other security personnel continued to play an important role in protecting the goods and property of private businesses. The growth of industry created a need for people to patrol factories and warehouses. Many companies hired private security forces to guard factories during strikes. Banks, department stores, and museums employed security guards to watch against theft and vandalism. Other security personnel began to specialize in designing security systems—with considerations including the types of safes and alarms to be used and the stationing of security guards—to protect both public and private facilities. Government and public facilities, such as military facilities, nuclear power facilities, dams, and oil pipelines, also needed security systems and guards to protect them.

Security systems have grown increasingly sophisticated with the introduction of technologies such as cameras, closed-circuit television, video, computers, and motion-sensor devices. The security guard continues to play an important role in the protection of people and property. The increasing use of computers has aided the guard or security technician by protecting electronic data and transmissions. The increasing number of terrorist threats has also led to more frequent use of security services.

■ THE JOB

A security consultant is engaged in protective service work. Anywhere that valuable property or information is present or people are at risk, a security consultant may be called in to devise and implement security plans that offer protection. Security consultants work for a variety of clients, including large stores, art museums, factories, laboratories, data processing centers, and political candidates. They seek to prevent theft, vandalism, fraud, kidnapping, and other crimes. Specific job responsibilities depend on the type and size of the client's company and the scope of the security system required.

Security consultants always work closely with company officials or other appropriate individuals in the development of a comprehensive security program that

---

QUICK FACTS

ALTERNATE TITLE(S)
Bank Guards, Security Officers

DUTIES
Protect public and private property against theft, fire, vandalism, illegal entry, and acts of violence

SALARY RANGE
$24,000 to $97,165 to $200,000+ (consultants)
$18,350 to $24,630 to $45,010+ (guards)

WORK ENVIRONMENT
Indoors/Outdoors

BEST GEOGRAPHIC LOCATION(S)
Opportunities are available throughout the country

MINIMUM EDUCATION LEVEL
High School Diploma, Bachelor's Degree

SCHOOL SUBJECTS
Government, Psychology, Speech

EXPERIENCE
Police or public safety experience recommended; several years experience required for consultants

PERSONALITY TRAITS
Conventional, Hands On, Helpful

SKILLS
Interpersonal, Leadership, Math

CERTIFICATION OR LICENSING
Required

SPECIAL REQUIREMENTS
Applicants must be at least 18 years of age to be eligible for licensing; must pass background screening and meet physical requirements

EMPLOYMENT PROSPECTS
Excellent

ADVANCEMENT PROSPECTS
Good

OUTLOOK
About as Fast as the Average

NOC
6316, 6541

O*NET-SOC
11-9199.07, 13-1199.02, 33-9032.00

---

will fit the needs of individual clients. After discussing goals and objectives with the relevant company executives, consultants study and analyze the physical conditions and internal operations of a client's operation. They learn much by simply observing day-to-day operations.

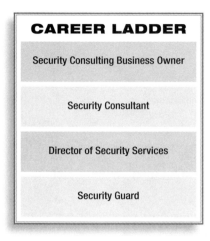

CAREER LADDER

Security Consulting Business Owner

Security Consultant

Director of Security Services

Security Guard

The size of the security budget also influences the type of equipment ordered and methods used. For example, a large factory that produces military hardware may fence off its property and place surveillance devices around the perimeter of the fence. They may also install perimeter alarms and use passkeys to limit access to restricted areas. A smaller company may use only entry-control mechanisms in specified areas. The consultant may recommend sophisticated technology, such as closed-circuit surveillance or ultrasonic motion detectors, alone or in addition to security personnel. Usually, a combination of electronic and human resources is used.

Security consultants not only devise plans to protect equipment but also recommend procedures on safeguarding and possibly destroying classified material. Increasingly, consultants are being called on to develop strategies to safeguard data processing equipment. They may have to develop measures to safeguard transmission lines against unwanted or unauthorized interceptions.

Once a security plan has been developed, the consultant oversees the installation of the equipment, ensures that it is working properly, and checks frequently with the client to ensure that the client is satisfied. In the case of a crime against the facility, a consultant investigates the nature of the crime (often in conjunction with police or other investigators) and then modifies the security system to safeguard against similar crimes in the future.

Many consultants work for security firms that have several types of clients, such as manufacturing and telecommunications plants and facilities. Consultants may handle a variety of clients or work exclusively in a particular area. For example, one security consultant may be assigned to handle the protection of nuclear power plants and another to handle data processing companies.

Security consultants may be called on to safeguard famous individuals or persons in certain positions from kidnapping or other type of harm. They provide security services to officers of large companies, media personalities, and others who want their safety and privacy protected. These consultants, like bodyguards, plan and review client travel itineraries and usually accompany the client on trips, checking accommodations and appointment locations along the way. They often check the backgrounds of people who will interact with the client, especially those who see the client infrequently.

Security consultants are sometimes called in for special events, such as sporting events and political rallies, when there is no specific fear of danger but rather a need for overall coordination of a large security operation. The consultants oversee security preparation—such as the stationing of appropriate personnel at all points of entry and exit—and then direct specific responses to any security problems.

Security officers develop and implement security plans for companies that manufacture or process material for the federal government. They ensure that their clients' security policies comply with federal regulations in such categories as the storing and handling of classified documents and restricting access to authorized personnel only.

Security guards have various titles, depending on the type of work they do and the setting in which they work. They may be referred to as *patrollers* (who are assigned to cover a certain area), *bouncers* (who eject unruly people from places of entertainment), *golf-course rangers* (who patrol golf courses), or *gate tenders* (who work at security checkpoints).

Many security guards are employed during normal working hours in public and commercial buildings and other areas with a good deal of pedestrian traffic and public contact. Others patrol buildings and grounds outside normal working hours, such as at night and on weekends. Guards usually wear uniforms and may carry a nightstick. Guards who work in situations where they may be called upon to apprehend criminal intruders are usually armed. They may also carry a flashlight, a whistle, a two-way radio, and a watch clock, which is used to record the time at which they reach various checkpoints.

Guards in public buildings may be assigned to a certain post or they may patrol an area. In museums, art galleries, and other public buildings, guards answer visitors' questions and give them directions; they also enforce rules against smoking, touching art objects, and so forth. In commercial buildings, guards may sign people in and out after hours and inspect packages being carried out of the building. *Bank guards* observe customers carefully for any sign of suspicious behavior that may signal a possible robbery attempt. In department stores, security guards often work with undercover detectives to watch for theft by customers or store employees. Guards at large public gatherings, such as sporting events and conventions, keep traffic moving, direct people to their seats, and eject unruly spectators. Guards employed at airports limit access to boarding areas to passengers only. They make sure people entering passenger areas have valid tickets and observe passengers and their baggage as they pass through X-ray machines and metal detection equipment.

After-hours guards are usually employed at industrial plants, defense installations, construction sites, and transport facilities such as docks and railroad yards. They make regular rounds on foot or, if the premises are very large, in motorized vehicles. They check to be sure that no unauthorized persons are on the premises, that doors and windows are secure, and that no property is missing. They may be equipped with walkie-talkies to report in at intervals to a central guard station. Sometimes guards perform custodial duties, such as turning on lights and setting thermostats.

In a large organization, a *security officer* is often in charge of the guard force; in a small organization, a single worker may be responsible for all security measures. As more businesses purchase advanced electronic security systems to protect their properties, more guards are being assigned to stations where they monitor perimeter security, environmental functions, communications, and other systems. In many cases, these guards maintain radio contact with other guards patrolling on foot or in motor vehicles. Some guards use computers to store information on matters relevant to security such as visitors or suspicious occurrences during their time on duty.

Security guards work for government agencies or for private companies hired by government agencies. Their task is usually to guard secret or restricted installations domestically or in foreign countries. They spend much of their time patrolling areas, which they may do on foot, on horseback, or in automobiles or aircraft. They may monitor activities in an area through the use of surveillance cameras and video screens. Their assignments usually include detecting and preventing unauthorized activities, searching for explosive devices, standing watch during secret and hazardous experiments, and performing other routine police duties within government installations.

Security guards are usually armed and may be required to use their weapons or other kinds of physical force to prevent some kinds of activities. They are usually not, however, required to remove explosive devices from an installation. When they find such devices, they notify a bomb disposal unit, which is responsible for removing and then defusing or detonating the device.

◼ EARNINGS

Earnings for security consultants vary greatly depending on the consultant's training and experience. Indeed.com reported that security consultants had an average salary of $97,165 in January 2017. Experienced consultants may earn up yo $220,000 per year or more. Many consultants

EFFECTIVE SECURITY

LEARN MORE ABOUT IT

Fennelly, Lawrence J. *Handbook of Loss Prevention and Crime Prevention,* 5th ed. Philadelphia: Butterworth-Heinemann, 2012.

Fischer, Robert J., et al. *Introduction to Security,* 9th ed. Philadelphia: Butterworth-Heinemann, 2012.

Purpura, Philip P. *Security and Loss Prevention: An Introduction,* 6th ed. Philadelphia: Butterworth-Heinemann, 2013.

Sennewald, Charles A. *Effective Security Management*, 5th ed. Philadelphia: Butterworth-Heinemann, 2011.

work on a per-project or contract basis and may be paid with rates of up to $150 per hour or $25,000 per month.

Average starting salaries for security guards and technicians vary according to their level of training and experience, and the location where they work. Median annual earnings for security guards were $24,630 in May 2015, according to the U.S. Department of Labor. Experienced security guards earned more than $45,010 per year, while the least experienced security guards earned less than $18,350 annually. Entry-level guards working for contract agencies may receive little more than the minimum wage. In-house guards generally earn higher wages and have greater job security and better advancement potential.

Depending on their employers, most security consultants and guards receive benefits such as vacation and sick time as well as holidays and medical and dental insurance. Self-employed workers must provide their own benefits.

◼ WORK ENVIRONMENT

Consultants usually divide their time between their offices and a client's business. Much time is spent analyzing various security apparatuses and developing security proposals. The consultant talks with a variety of employees at a client's company, including the top officials, and discusses alternatives with other people at the consulting firm. A consultant makes a security proposal presentation to the client and then works with the client on any modifications. Consultants must be sensitive to budget issues and develop security systems that their clients can afford.

Consultants may specialize in one type of security work (nuclear power plants, for example) or work for a variety of large and small clients, such as museums, data processing companies, and banks. Although there may be a lot of travel and some work may require outdoor activity, there will most likely be no strenuous work.

A consultant may oversee the implementation of a large security system but is not involved in the actual installation process. A consultant may have to confront suspicious people but is not expected to do the work of a police officer.

Security guards and technicians may work indoors or outdoors. In high-crime areas and industries vulnerable to theft and vandalism, there may be considerable physical danger. Guards who work in museums, department stores, and other buildings and facilities remain on their feet for long periods of time, either standing still or walking while on patrol. Guards assigned to reception areas or security control rooms may remain at their desks for the entire shift. Much of their work is routine and may be tedious at times, yet guards must remain constantly alert during their shift. Guards who work with the public, especially at sporting events and concerts, may have to confront unruly and sometimes hostile people. Bouncers often confront intoxicated people and are frequently called upon to intervene in physical altercations.

Many companies employ guards around the clock in three shifts, including weekends and holidays, and assign workers to these shifts on a rotating basis. The same is true for security technicians guarding government facilities and installations. Those with less seniority will likely have the most erratic schedules. Many guards work alone for an entire shift, usually lasting eight hours. Lunches and other meals are often taken on the job, so that constant vigilance is maintained.

■ EXPLORING

Part-time or summer employment as a clerk with a security firm is an excellent way to gain insight into the skills and temperament needed to become a security consultant. Discussions with professional security consultants are another way of exploring career opportunities in this field. You may find it helpful to join a safety patrol at school.

If you are interested in a particular area of security consulting, such as data security, for example, you can join a club or association to learn more about the field. This is a good way to make professional contacts.

Opportunities for part-time or summer work as security guards are not generally available to high school students. You may, however, work as a lifeguard, on a safety patrol, and as a school hallway monitor, which can provide helpful experience.

■ EDUCATION AND TRAINING REQUIREMENTS
High School

Security guards must be high school graduates. In addition, they should expect to receive several weeks

of specialized training in security procedures and technology. Security consultants must have a college degree. Recommended high school classes include physical education, mathematics, government, psychology, and computer science. You should also take English courses to develop your reading and writing skills. You should be able to read manuals, memos, textbooks, and other instructional materials and write reports with correct spelling, grammar, and punctuation. You should also be able to speak to small groups with poise and confidence.

Postsecondary Training

Most companies prefer to hire security consultants who have at least a college degree. An undergraduate or associate's degree in criminal justice, business administration, or related field is best. Course work should be broad and include business management, communications, computer courses, sociology, and statistics. As the security consulting field becomes more competitive, many consultants choose to get a master's in business administration (MBA), computer security, or other graduate degree.

Because many consulting firms have their own techniques and procedures, most require entry-level personnel to complete an on-the-job training program, during the course of which they learn company policies.

Other Education or Training

ASIS International offers continuing education classes, workshops, and webinars on enhanced violence assessment and management, asset protection, security procedures for high-rise buildings, safe school procedures, and other topics. Contact the organization for more information.

■ CERTIFICATION, LICENSING, AND SPECIAL REQUIREMENTS
Certification or Licensing

Many security consultants earn the certified protection professional designation, which is awarded by ASIS International. To be eligible for certification, a consultant must pass a written test and have nine years' work or a combination of a bachelor's degree and work experience in the security profession. ASIS International also offers the professional certified investigator and physical security professional certification designations.

Other Requirements

Virtually every state has licensing or registration requirements for security guards who work for contract security agencies. Registration generally requires that a person newly hired as a guard be reported to the licensing authorities, usually the state police department or special state licensing commission. To be granted a license, individuals generally must be 18 years of age, have no convictions for perjury or acts of violence, pass a background investigation, and complete classroom training on a variety of subjects, including property rights, emergency procedures, and capture of suspected criminals.

Guards employed by the federal government must be U.S. armed forces veterans, have some previous experience as guards, and pass a written examination. Many positions require experience with firearms. In many situations, guards must be bonded.

Security technicians need good eyesight and should be in good physical shape; able to lift at least 50 pounds; climb ladders, stairs, poles, and ropes; and maintain their balance on narrow, slippery, or moving surfaces. They should be able to stoop, crawl, crouch, and kneel with ease.

■ EXPERIENCE, SKILLS, AND PERSONALITY TRAITS

Although there are no specific educational or professional requirements, many security guards have had previous experience with police work or other forms of crime prevention. It is helpful if a person develops an expertise in a specific area. For example, if you want to work devising plans securing data processing equipment, it is helpful to have previous experience working with computers. Consultants need several years' experience in police or investigative work.

For security guards, general good health (especially vision and hearing), alertness, emotional stability, and the ability to follow directions are important characteristics. Military service and experience in local or state police departments are assets. Prospective guards should have clean records. Some employers require applicants to take a polygraph examination or a written test that indicates honesty, attitudes, and other personal qualities. Most employers require applicants and experienced workers to submit to drug screening tests as a condition of employment.

For some hazardous or physically demanding jobs, guards must be under a certain age and meet height and weight standards. For top-level security positions in facilities such as nuclear power plants or vulnerable information centers, guards may be required to complete a special training course. They may also need to fulfill certain relevant academic requirements.

■ EMPLOYMENT PROSPECTS

Employers

More than 1 million security workers are employed in the United States. Security services is one of the largest employment fields in the United States. About 58 percent of all security guards are employed in the investigation and security industry, or contract security firms, in the United States. The remainder are in-house guards employed by various business and government establishments. Many law enforcement officers also work as security guards during their off hours, to supplement their income. They may work at construction sites and apartment complexes, where their presence can ward off crime.

Starting Out

People interested in careers in security services generally apply directly to security companies. Some jobs may be available through state or private employment services. People interested in security guard positions should apply directly to government agencies.

Beginning security personnel receive varied amounts of training. Training requirements are generally increasing as modern, highly sophisticated security systems become more common. Many employers give newly hired security guards instruction before they start the job and also provide several weeks of on-the-job training. Guards receive training in protection, public relations, report writing, crisis deterrence, first aid, and the use of firearms.

Those employed at establishments that place a heavy emphasis on security usually receive extensive formal training. For example, guards at nuclear power plants may undergo several months of training before being placed on duty under close supervision. Guards may be taught to use firearms, administer first aid, operate alarm systems and electronic security equipment, handle emergencies, and spot and deal with security problems.

Many of the less strenuous guard positions are filled by older people who are retired police officers or armed forces veterans. Because of the odd hours required for many positions, this occupation appeals to many people seeking part-time work or second jobs.

Most entry-level positions for security consultants are filled by those with a bachelor's or associate's degree in criminal justice, business administration, or a related field. Those with a high school diploma and some experience in the field may find work with a security consulting firm, although they usually begin as security guards and become consultants only after further training.

■ ADVANCEMENT PROSPECTS

In most cases, security guards receive periodic salary increases, and guards employed by larger security companies or as part of a military-style guard force may increase their responsibilities or move up in rank.

A guard with outstanding ability, especially with some college education, may move up to the position of *chief guard,* gaining responsibility for the supervision and training of an entire guard force in an industrial plant or a department store, or become director of security services for a business or commercial building. A few guards with management skills open their own contract security guard agencies; other guards become licensed private detectives. Experienced guards may become bodyguards for political figures, executives, and celebrities, or choose to enter a police department or other law enforcement agency. Additional training may lead to a career as a corrections officer.

Increased training and experience with a variety of security and surveillance systems may lead security guards into higher-paying security consultant careers. Security consultants with experience may advance to management positions or they may start their own private consulting firms. Instruction and training of security personnel is another advancement opportunity for security guards, consultants, and technicians.

■ OUTLOOK

Employment for guards and other security personnel is expected to increase about as fast as the average for all careers through 2024, as public concern about crime, vandalism, and terrorism continues to grow. Many job openings will be created as a result of the high turnover of workers in this field. Employment prospects will be better in certain industries than others. For example, job opportunites for security guards in the construction industry will grow much faster than the average for all careers, while employment will decline for those who work in the manufacturing industry. Employment for security consultants can be expected to remain steady or rise if threats from crime, terrorism, and vandalsim remain constant.

A factor adding to this demand is the trend for private security firms to perform duties previously handled by police officers, such as courtroom security, and security at public events and in residential neighborhoods. Private security companies employ security technicians to guard many government sites, such as nuclear testing facilities. Private companies also operate many training facilities for government security technicians and guards, as well as providing police services for some communities. More hospitals and nursing homes are also seeking the help of private security firms to protect their facilities.

■ UNIONS AND ASSOCIATIONS

The International Union, Security, Police and Fire Professionals of America represents more than 27,000 security police professionals in the U.S. and Canada. ASIS International is a membership organization for security professionals. It offers networking opportunities, certification, networking groups for young professionals and women, publications, and other resources.

■ TIPS FOR ENTRY

1. For job listings, visit:
   - https://securityjobs.asisonline.org
   - http://www.careerbuilder.com
   - http://www.indeed.com
2. Read *Security Management* and *Protection of Assets* (both available at https://www.asisonline.org/ Publications) to learn more about the field.
3. Become certified by ASIS International in order to show employers that you've met the highest standards established by your industry.

■ FOR MORE INFORMATION

For information on educational programs and certification, contact

ASIS International (ASIS)
1625 Prince Street
Alexandria, VA 22314-2818
Tel: (703) 519-6200
Fax: (703) 519-6299
E-mail: asis@asisonline.org
http://www.asisonline.org

For information on union membership, contact

International Union, Security, Police and Fire Professionals of America (SPFPA)
25510 Kelly Road
Roseville, MI 40866-4932
Tel: (800) 228-7492; (586) 772-7250
Fax: (586) 772-9644
http://www.spfpa.org

Security Systems Installers and Workers

■ OVERVIEW

Security Systems Installers and Workers install and program electronic security equipment in residential and commercial buildings to deter burglars and prevent crimes. They may also install fire alarm systems. They are responsible for maintaining security systems and repairing equipment as needed. They make sure the wiring that they do and the equipment they use meets industry codes. Approximately 64,730 security and fire alarm systems installers were employed in the United States in May 2015, as reported by the Department of Labor.

■ HISTORY

In the 18th century, American colonists were responsible for protecting their communities from crime and enforcing the laws that existed in those early days. The growth of America's population in the 19th century gave rise to densely populated cities and with that came more crime. Municipal police departments were created to patrol areas and protect citizens but they were outnumbered and could only do so much. More services to prevent crimes needed to be added to keep people safe.

The first private security agency in the United States was formed in the 1850s by Allan Pinkerton, a former Chicago detective, who partnered with an attorney from Chicago. Known as the Pinkertons, they prevented train robberies. Around this time Edwin Holmes created the first burglar alarm and by 1866, these alarms were protecting hundreds of customers in New York. Holmes and his son innovated the alarm's technology by connecting it to a clock and later, when telephones were invented, connecting it to the telephone network to transmit alarm signals.

American District Telegraph (now known as ADT) was founded in 1874, in direct competition with the telephone company. When alarms sounded, they sent messenger boys to the alarm sites. These messengers would then use call boxes to contact police or firefighters. Over the years the company expanded to offer security patrols among its services. ADT dominated the market for central-station alarm services by the 1960s; in 1964, the U.S. Justice Department determined that the company was operating a monopoly in restraint of trade, and forced ADT to adopt a uniform national price list and service offerings. In 1997, Tyco International purchased ADT and in 2012, ADT was again introduced as an independent, publicly traded company.

Brink's was founded in 1859 by Perry Brink in Chicago, starting as a parcel delivery company and expanding to include money transport for banks by the 1890s. In the 1920s Brink's experimented with using converted school buses as armored vehicles for transport services. After World War II, the company ramped up its security by using heavily armored cars and operators with heavy weaponry. In the 1980s, Brink's started offering home security alarms, a business that was eventually taken over by ADT. The Wells Fargo Armored Security Corporation,

QUICK FACTS
ALTERNATE TITLE(S)
Security and Fire Alarm Systems Installers
DUTIES
Install, maintain, and repair security and alarm systems and equipment; follow blueprints; demonstrate security systems to customers
SALARY RANGE
$27,310 to $43,420 to $64,350+
WORK ENVIRONMENT
Indoors/Outdoors
BEST GEOGRAPHIC LOCATION(S)
Opportunities exist in all regions; the states with the highest level of employment in California, Texas, Florida, New York, and Virginia
MINIMUM EDUCATION LEVEL
Associate's Degree
SCHOOL SUBJECTS
Computer Science, Mathematics, Technical/Shop
EXPERIENCE
Two to three years of apprenticeship and on-the-job training
PERSONALITY TRAITS
Conventional, Hands On, Problem-Solving
SKILLS
Computer, Math, Mechanical/Manual Dexterity
CERTIFICATION OR LICENSING
Required
SPECIAL REQUIREMENTS
Must be at least 18 years old, complete qualifying education, pass an exam, have no criminal record, and submit proof of a fingerprint completion
EMPLOYMENT PROSPECTS
Good
ADVANCEMENT PROSPECTS
Good
OUTLOOK
Faster than the Average
NOC
6316, 6541
O*NET-SOC
49-2098.00

which was later absorbed into Loomis Armored, was also a spin-off from a delivery service.

Another security system company is G4S Secure Solutions, established in 1954 by George Wackenhut and three other former FBI agents. The company initially specialized in security services for government

CAREER LADDER

Security Systems Supervisor

Security Systems Installer

Security Systems Technician

Apprentice

installations such as the Kennedy Space Center, later expanding into for-profit prison operations.

Since the 1990s, the security system services industry has grown. As of 2016 the security alarm services industry generates $23 billion in revenue and is projected to have steady growth in the coming years, as reported by the market research group IBISWorld. Today there are 56,549 security alarm service businesses in the United States.

■ THE JOB

Security systems installers and workers install, maintain, and repair security and alarm systems, devices, and equipment. They use blueprints for reference to electrical layouts and building plans. They use various tools and methods to install components such as control panels, window and door contacts, sensors, or video cameras and electrical and telephone wiring. When the work is done, they explain to customers how to use the system, demonstrating the steps to take and what to do when a false alarm happens. Installers and workers also make sure circuits and sensors are working. They feed cables through spaces in walls, ceilings, or roofs so that they reach fixture outlets.

■ EARNINGS

The median annual salary for security and fire alarm systems installers was $43,420 in May 2015, according to the Department of Labor. The lowest 10 percent earned $27,310 and the highest 10 percent earned $64,350 or more. The top paying industries for security systems installers and workers were scientific research and development services (paid an annual mean wage of $56,460 in May 2015), state government ($55,450), general medical and surgical hospitals ($53,660), local government ($53,280), and computer systems design and related services ($53,120).

■ WORK ENVIRONMENT

Security systems installers and workers work in security systems offices and travel to residential and commercial buildings to install, maintain, or repair security systems and equipment. They carry tools and equipment that can be heavy. The work may also require climbing on ladders and/or working in cramped, tight spaces to thread

wires through ceilings and roofs. They may work daytime hours, evenings, and/or weekends.

■ EXPLORING

Learn more about the security systems industry by visiting the Web sites of companies such as ADT. Look for the careers section and read about the types of jobs offered and the backgrounds of the people working in the field. Find out from family members and friends if they know someone who works in security systems and see if you can speak with them to learn more about the pros and cons of the job. Explore trade associations such as the Electronic Security Association, among others, to find out about industry news, publications, and upcoming events where there are opportunities for networking with security systems professionals.

■ EDUCATION AND TRAINING REQUIREMENTS
High School

Security systems installers and workers need good math skills, knowledge of electricity and electronics, and the ability to interact well with customers. Classes that help provide a solid foundation for this type of work are math, English, computers, electronics (if offered), and shop.

Postsecondary Education

A bachelor's degree is not required for this field. Most security systems installers and workers attend vocational schools and/or have an associate's degree. Technical knowledge of electronics and electricity is essential, so take classes in these subjects. Many schools offer programs in telecommunications and electrical utilities, which includes classes on electricity, electronics, fiber optics, and microwave transmissions. Classes in computers, English, business, and math are also beneficial.

Other Education or Training

Many security systems companies offer apprenticeship programs and on-the-job training with experienced security systems installers and workers. The training may last from one to two years.

■ CERTIFICATION, LICENSING, AND SPECIAL REQUIREMENTS
Certification or Licensing

Security Systems Installers and Repairers who wish to advance their skills can receive certification through vocational schools and industry associations. Licensing requirements vary by state and by occupation. For example, in New York State, entities that engage in the business of installing, servicing, or maintaining security or fire alarm systems must be licensed by the Department of State.

Other Requirements

Some states, such as New York, may require applicants to be at least 18 years old, have completed 81 hours of qualifying education, pass an alarm installer exam, have no criminal convictions, and submit proof of a finger-print completion.

■ EXPERIENCE, SKILLS, AND PERSONALITY TRAITS

Security systems installers and workers usually have several years of on-the-job training with experienced professionals. They may also have completed an education program to qualify for licensing in the state in which they work. The job requires technical skills, critical thinking, problem solving, quick thinking, and active listening. Security systems install-ers and workers must also have near vision to see objects up close; they also need good hand-eye coordination to handle tools and equipment. Installers and Workers must have solid communication skills to fulfill customers' needs. They must have strong knowledge of computers and electronics, and be knowledgeable about equipment policies and procedures and security systems regulations and codes.

■ EMPLOYMENT PROSPECTS

Employers

There are 64,730 security and fire alarm systems installers and workers employed in the United States. The indus-tries that employ the most workers in this occupation are investigation and security services, building equipment contractors, miscellaneous durable goods merchant wholesalers; household appliances and electronic and electrical goods merchant wholesalers; and machinery, equipment, and supplies merchant wholesalers.

Starting Out

Employers favor job applicants who have vocational training and an undergraduate degree. Security systems installers and workers can receive training while working in the job. They can also take relevant classes through trade associations.

■ ADVANCEMENT PROSPECTS

Security systems installers and workers may work as apprentices for several years and then advance to become technicians. Those who have more years of experience may assume more responsibilities and authority by advancing to supervisor and management-level roles. As managers, they will be responsible for hiring and supervising staff.

WIRELESS SECURITY   ON THE CUTTING EDGE

In the early days of the security systems industry, people had fewer options for protecting themselves and their property. For example, they may have subscribed to a service in which guards would patrol homes and buildings at night, shaking the doors to make sure they were locked. Another system for protection, used mainly by the wealthy, was to place electromagnetic sensors on doors and windows, which would sound a loud alarm if an intruder tried to get in. The security system industry has evolved since then to now offer wireless options to protect people and their possessions.

Wireless security systems include motion detectors and glass-break sensors, which wirelessly communicate with a control panel and sound an alarm when there is a break-in. Wireless monitoring is also known as cellular monitoring; the control panel communicates information to a central monitoring station by using cell towers. This is an effective way to protect homes and buildings because there are no phone lines and therefore burglars can't cut the lines of communication that people need to summon help. People can access these security systems through their computers and mobile devices, giving them the ability to monitor their homes and property wherever they are. They can arm and disarm the systems remotely. Home automation systems also enable them to control the lights, thermostat, and locks.

■ OUTLOOK

The outlook for security systems installers and workers is bright. The Department of Labor predicts 13 percent employment growth, which is faster than the average, through 2024. The security alarm services industry has been growing the past few years, with 4.3 percent annual growth from 2011 to 2016, and increased interest in security systems is expected to continue, according to IBISWorld. As the economy strengthens, more companies are invest-ing in security systems. Stricter fire and safety regulations mandated by the government will also increase demand for security and fire alarm systems. Security systems pre-vent theft and lower insurance costs, making them attrac-tive financial incentives for businesses. Also, technological advances in the industry now enable people to use security systems to monitor their homes from their computers and mobile devices; this is expected to increase the demand for security systems in the coming years.

■ UNIONS AND ASSOCIATIONS

The Electronic Security Association represents, pro-motes, and enhances the growth of the electronic life safety, security, and integrated systems industry. This organization provides educational programs, job training, advocacy, information about industry trends and issues, and opportunities for networking. The Electrical Training Alliance provides apprenticeship and training programs for electrical workers. The Telecommunications Industry Association is a member-driven organization that provides business opportunities, market intelligence, networking events, and various other resources.

■ TIPS FOR ENTRY

1. Visit the Web sites of security and fire alarm systems companies such as ADT to learn more about the types of work they do and the career opportunities.
2. Take telecommunications classes, including classes on electronics and electricity, while in school.
3. Ask friends and family members if they know someone who works in security systems installation; talk to them to learn more about the job.
4. Visit the Web sites of trade associations such as the Electronic Security Association for industry news and to find training programs.

■ FOR MORE INFORMATION

The Electrical Training Alliance offers training programs, a learning center and bookstore, and other resources for electrical workers.

Electrical Training Alliance (ETA)
5001 Howerton Way, Suite N
Bowie, MD 20715-4459
Tel: (888) 652-4007
http://www.electricaltrainingalliance.org

The Electronic Security Association provides government advocacy and professional development tools, products, and services for electronic security professionals.

Electronic Security Association (ESA)
6333 North State Highway 161, Suite 350
Irving, TX 75038-2228
Tel: (888) 447-1689; (972) 807-6800
Fax: (972) 807-6883
http://www.esaweb.org

The Security Industry Association offers educational programs, training, certification, events, and other resources for security industry professionals.

Security Industry Association (SIA)
8405 Colesville Road, Suite 500
Silver Spring, MD 20910-6343
Tel: (301) 804-4700

Fax: (301) 804-4701
http://www.siaonline.org

The Telecommunications Industry Association provides industry standards, news and events, and other resources for the telecommunications industry.

Telecommunications Industry Association (TIA)
1320 North Courthouse Road, Suite 200
Arlington, VA 22201-2598
Tel: (703) 907-7700
Fax: (703) 907-7727
http://www.tiaonline.org

Semiconductor Technicians

■ OVERVIEW

Semiconductor technicians are highly skilled workers who test new kinds of semiconductor devices (which are commonly known as integrated circuits or microchips) being designed for use in many kinds of modern electronic equipment. They may also test samples of devices already in production to assess production techniques. They help develop and evaluate the test equipment used to gather information about the semiconductor devices. Working under the direction provided by engineers in research laboratory settings, they assist in the design and planning for later production or help to improve production yields. Semiconductor technicians are also known as *semiconductor processors*. Approximately 370,00 people are employed in the semiconductor manufacturing industry.

■ HISTORY

Semiconductors and devices utilizing them are found in nearly every electronic product made today, from complicated weapons systems and space technology to personal computers, DVD players, smartphones, and programmable coffeemakers. The manufacturing of semiconductors and microelectronics devices requires the efforts of a variety of people, from the engineers who design them, to the technicians who process, construct, and test them.

Although the word semiconductor is often used to refer to microchips or integrated circuits, a semiconductor is actually the basic material of these devices. Semiconductor materials are so-called because they can be switched to act with properties between that of an insulator, which does not conduct electrical current, and that of a true conductor of electrical current, such as metal.

Silicon is the most common material used as a semiconductor. Other semiconductor materials may be gallium arsenide, cadmium sulfide, and selenium sulfide. Doping, or treating, these materials with substances such as aluminum, arsenic, boron, and phosphorous gives them conducting properties. By applying these substances according to a specifically designed layout, engineers and technicians construct the tiny electronic devices—transistors, capacitors, and resistors—of an integrated circuit. A microchip no larger than a fingernail may contain many thousands of these devices.

■ THE JOB

There are many steps that occur in processing semiconductors into integrated circuits. The technicians involved in these processes are called *semiconductor development technicians* and *semiconductor process technicians*. They may be involved in several or many of the steps of semiconductor manufacturing, depending on where they work. Often, semiconductor technicians function as a link between the engineering staff and the production staff in the large-scale manufacturing of semiconductor products.

The making of semiconductors begins with silicon. The silicon must be extremely pure in order to be of use. The silicon used for semiconductors is heated in a furnace and formed into cylinder rods between one and six inches in diameter and three or more feet in length. These rods are smoothed and polished until they are perfectly round. They are then sliced into wafers that are between one-quarter and one-half millimeter in thickness. Then the wafers are processed, by etching, polishing, heat-treating, and lapping, to produce the desired dimensions and surface finish. After the wafers are tested, measured, and inspected for any defects, they are coated with a photosensitive substance called a photoresist.

The engineering staff and the technicians assigned to assist them prepare designs for the layout of the microchip. This work is generally done using a computer-aided design (CAD) system. The large, completed design is then miniaturized as a photomask when it is applied to the wafer. The photomask is placed over the wafer and the photoresist is developed, much like film in a traditional camera, with ultraviolet light, so that the layout of the microchip is reproduced many times on the same wafer. This work takes place in a specially equipped clean room, or laboratory, that is kept completely free of dust and other impurities. During the miniaturization process, the tiniest speck of dust will ruin the reproduction of the layout onto the wafer.

Next, the wafer is doped with the substances that will give it the necessary conducting properties. Technicians follow the layout, like a road map, when adding these substances. The proper combinations of materials create the various components of the integrated circuit. When this process is complete, the wafer is tested by computerized equipment that can test the many thousands of components in a matter of seconds. Many of the integrated circuits on the wafer will not function properly, and these are marked and discarded. After testing, the wafer is cut up into its individual chips.

The chips are then packaged by placing them in a casing usually made of plastic or ceramic, which also contains metal leads for connecting the microchip into the electronic circuitry of the device for which it will be used. It is this package that is usually referred to as a chip or semiconductor.

Semiconductor process technicians are generally responsible for the fabrication and processing of the semiconductor wafer. *Semiconductor development technicians* usually assist with the basic design and development of rough sketches of a prototype chip; they may be involved in transferring the layout to the wafer and in assembling and testing the semiconductor. Both types of technicians gather and evaluate data on the semiconductor, wafer, or chip. They must ensure that each step of the process precisely meets test specifications, and also identify flaws and problems in the material

QUICK FACTS

ALTERNATE TITLE(S)
Semiconductor Development Technicians, Semiconductor Processors, Semiconductor Process Technicians

DUTIES
Fabricate and process semiconductor wafers; test semiconductor devices and identify flaws and problems in the material and design

SALARY RANGE
$25,310 to $35,390 to $54,820+

WORK ENVIRONMENT
Primarily Indoors

BEST GEOGRAPHIC LOCATION(S)
Opportunities are available throughout the country, but are strongest in California, Texas, Oregon, and Washington

MINIMUM EDUCATION LEVEL
Associate's Degree

SCHOOL SUBJECTS
Computer Science, Mathematics, Technical/Shop

EXPERIENCE
On-the-job training

PERSONALITY TRAITS
Hands On, Problem-Solving, Technical

SKILLS
Computer, Research, Scientific

CERTIFICATION OR LICENSING
Recommended

SPECIAL REQUIREMENTS
None

EMPLOYMENT PROSPECTS
Poor

ADVANCEMENT PROSPECTS
Good

OUTLOOK
Decline

NOC
N/A

O*NET-SOC
51-9141.00

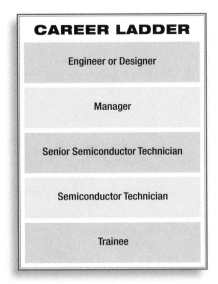

CAREER LADDER

Engineer or Designer

Manager

Senior Semiconductor Technician

Semiconductor Technician

Trainee

and design. Technicians may also assist in designing and building new test equipment, and in communicating test data and production instructions for large-scale manufacture. Technicians may also be responsible for maintaining the equipment and for training operators on its use.

EARNINGS

Semiconductor processors (a category that includes semiconductor technicians) earned a median hourly wage of $17.01, or $35,390 a year, in May 2015, according to the U.S. Department of Labor. Ten percent of all workers earned less than $12.17 an hour ($25,310 a year), while the top 10 percent earned $26.36 or more an hour ($54,820 a year or more). Technicians earning higher salaries have more education or have worked in the industry for many years.

Benefits for semiconductor technicians depend on the employer; however, they usually include such items as health insurance, retirement or 401(k) plans, and paid vacation days.

WORK ENVIRONMENT

The work of semiconductor technicians is not physically strenuous and is usually done in an extremely clean environment. Technicians may work with hazardous chemicals, however, and proper safety precautions must be strictly followed. Because of the large demand for semiconductors and related devices, many facilities operate with two 12-hour shifts, meaning that a technician may be assigned to the night or weekend shift, or on a rotating schedule.

Because of the need for an extremely clean environment, technicians are required to wear clean-room suits (known as bunny suits) to keep dust, lint, and dirt out of the clean room where the production takes place. Their entry and exit into the clean room is controlled to minimize contamination; changing into a clean suit is required for each and every entry to the room.

An important component in most manufacturing processes is the speed with which products are produced. Workers may find themselves under a great deal of pressure to maintain a certain level of production volume. The ability to work well in a sometimes-stressful

environment is an important quality for any prospective semiconductor technician.

EXPLORING

You can develop your interests in computers and microelectronics while in school. Most high schools will be unable to keep up with the rapid advances in electronics technology, and you will need to read and explore on your own. Joining extracurricular clubs in computers or electronics will give you an opportunity for hands-on learning experiences. Joining national science and technology associations such as the Technology Student Association (http://www.tsaweb.org) will also provide useful experience.

You should also begin to seek out the higher education appropriate for your future career interests. Your high school counselor should be able to help you find a training program that will match your career goals.

EDUCATION AND TRAINING REQUIREMENTS
High School

Math and science courses, as well as classes in computer science, are requirements for students wishing to enter the semiconductor and microelectronics field. Physics and chemistry will help you understand many of the processes involved in developing and fabricating semiconductors and semiconductor components. Strong communications skills are also very important.

Postsecondary Training

Technician jobs in microelectronics and semiconductor technology require at least an associate's degree in electronics, microelectronics, or electrical engineering or technology. Students may attend a two-year program at a community college or vocational school. Students interested in a career at the engineering level should consider studying for a bachelor's degree. The trend toward greater specialization within the industry has made a bachelor's degree in engineering or the physical sciences more desirable than an associate's degree.

An electronics engineering program will include courses in electronics theory, as well as math, science, and English courses. Students can expect to study such subjects as the principle and models of semiconductor devices; physics for solid-state electronics; solid-state theory; introduction to VLSI (very-large-scale integration) circuit systems; and basic courses in computer organization, electromagnetic fundamentals, digital and analog laboratories, and the design of circuits and active networks. Companies will also provide additional training on the specific equipment and software they use. Many companies also offer training programs and educational opportunities to employees to increase their skills and their responsibilities.

Courses are available at many community and junior colleges, which may be more flexible in their curriculum and better able to keep up with technological advances than vocational training schools. The latter, however, will often have programs geared specifically to the needs of the employers in their area and may have job placement programs and relationships with the different companies as well. If you are interested in these schools, you should do some research to determine whether the training offered is thorough and that the school has a good placement record. Training institutes should also be accredited by the Accrediting Commission of Career Schools and Colleges (http://www.accsc.org).

Military service may also provide a strong background in electronics. In addition, the tuition credits available to military personnel will be helpful when continuing your education.

Once hired, technicians complete on-the-job training that can last from one month to about a year.

Other Education or Training

Semiconductor technicians must pursue additional training during their careers in order to keep up to date with new technologies and techniques. Many employers offer continuing education (CE) in the form of in-house workshops or outside seminars. Professional associations also provide webinars, workshops, seminars, and classes. For example, the Institute of Electrical and Electronics Engineers provides career enhancement, technical knowledge, and professional development webinars; an eLearning Library; conference seminars and workshops; and other CE opportunities. Contact the institute for more information.

■ CERTIFICATION, LICENSING, AND SPECIAL REQUIREMENTS
Certification or Licensing

Certification is not mandatory, but voluntary certification may prove useful in locating work and in increasing your pay and responsibilities. The International Society of Certified Electronics Technicians (ISCET) offers certification at various levels and fields of electronics. The ISCET also offers a variety of study and training material to help prepare for certification tests.

■ EXPERIENCE, SKILLS, AND PERSONALITY TRAITS

Experience working with electronics via school clubs, competitions, and other activities is highly recommended for aspiring semiconductor technicians.

CLEAN ROOMS, SEMICONDUCTORS, AND WAFERS
WORDS TO KNOW

Adhesion: The ability of materials to stick together.

Circuit: The complete path of an electric current.

Clean room: The area where the semiconductors or microchips are manufactured.

Clean-room suit: The outfit worn by someone in a "clean room." The suit is kept in a changing area where workers must change each day before working in the clean room. Sometimes called a **bunny suit.**

Doping: A manufacturing process in which small amounts of impurities are added to pure semiconductors with the goal of causing large changes in the conductivity of the material.

Evaporation: A method that is commonly used to deposit thin film materials.

Semiconductors: Sometimes called **microchips** or **integrated circuits,** these tiny devices are made from silicon and produced in high-tech manufacturing environments.

Silicon: A nonmetallic chemical element that is used to manufacture microchips.

Silicon Valley: The Silicon Valley is an area in Northern California, named for the many semiconductor and other technical manufacturing companies located there.

Transistors: Printed on the wafers to allow the chips to interact with other parts of the machine that the microchip will become a part of, such as a toaster or a rocket.

Wafer: After the silicon is melted, a single crystal cylinder is produced. This is then sliced into very thin wafers.

A thorough understanding of semiconductors, electronics, and the production process is necessary for semiconductor technicians. Investigative, research, communication, and critical-thinking skills, a detail-oriented personality, dexterity, and knowledge of computers and computer programs are also important.

■ EMPLOYMENT PROSPECTS
Employers

Approximately 370,000 people are employed in the semiconductor industry. Nearly all semiconductor technicians work in the computer and electronic product manufacturing industry. Finding a job in the semiconductor industry may mean living in the right part of the country. Certain states, such as California, Texas, Oregon, and Washington, have many more opportunities than others. Some of the big names in semiconductors include Intel, Motorola, and Texas Instruments. These companies are very large and employ many technicians, but there are smaller and mid-size companies in the industry as well.

Starting Out

Semiconductor technician positions can be located through the job placement office of a community college or vocational training school. Since an associate's degree is recommended, many of these degree programs provide students with job interviews and introductions to companies in the community that are looking for qualified workers.

Internet job boards, and job listings in newspapers or at local employment agencies are also good places for locating job opportunities. Aspiring semiconductor technicians can also find less-skilled positions in the semiconductor industry and work hard for promotion to a technician position. Having more education and training will give you an advantage in the job market for semiconductors and related devices.

■ ADVANCEMENT PROSPECTS

As with any manufacturing industry, the advancement possibilities available to semiconductor technicians will depend on their levels of skill, education, and experience. Technicians may advance to *senior technicians* or may find themselves in supervisory or management positions. Technicians with two-year associate's degrees may elect to continue their education. Often, their course work will be transferable to a four-year engineering program, and many times their employer may help pay for their continuing education. Semiconductor technicians may ultimately choose to enter the engineering and design phases of the field. Also, a background in semiconductor processing and development may lead to a career in sales or purchasing of semiconductor components, materials, and equipment.

■ OUTLOOK

The U.S. Department of Labor predicts there will be a decline (by about 8 percent) in employment in the semiconductor industry through 2024. This decline is due to two main factors: higher productivity and increased imports. Many semiconductor manufacturers have installed new machinery that can produce twice as many wafers as the old machines. This increased automation has streamlined the staff of many manufacturing plants. In addition, manufacturers have begun to build plants in overseas locations where semiconductors can be made more cheaply than in the United States. Imports of more affordable semiconductors from non-U.S. manufacturers are expected to rise in the

coming years, which will lessen the need for semiconductor manufacturing technicians in the United States. As the technology advances, the employment opportunities for semiconductor technicians will continue to decrease.

Some jobs will arise from the need to build the components for new products, as well as to replace the many technicians who will be reaching retirement age. Jobs will go to the technicians with the most education, training, and technical experience.

■ UNIONS AND ASSOCIATIONS

Semiconductor technicians do not belong to unions, but many join professional associations such as the Institute of Electrical and Electronics Engineers. The International Society of Certified Electronics Technicians offers certification. The Semiconductor Industry Association and SEMI are trade organizations that represent the interests of the semiconductor industry.

■ TIPS FOR ENTRY

1. Read publications such as *IEEE Spectrum* (http://spectrum.ieee.org/magazine) and *The High-Tech News* (http://www.eta-i.org/the_high_tech_news.html) to learn more about the field. Additionally, the Institute of Electrical and Electronics Engineers (IEEE) publishes more than 75 journals and periodicals about electrical and electronics engineering and related topics. Visit http://www.ieee.org/publications_standards/publications/journmag/journals_magazines.html for more information.
2. Visit the following Web sites for job listings: http://careers.ieee.org and http://www.iscet.org.
3. Join professional associations such as the IEEE to access training and networking resources, industry publications, and employment opportunities.

■ FOR MORE INFORMATION

For information on careers in electrical and electronics engineering, contact

Institute of Electrical and Electronics Engineers
2001 L Street, NW, Suite 700
Washington, D.C. 20036-4910
Tel: (202) 785-0017
Fax: (202) 785-0835
E-mail: ieeeusa@ieee.org
http://www.ieee.org

For certification information, contact

International Society of Certified Electronics Technicians
3000-A Landers Street
Fort Worth, TX 76107-5642

Tel: (800) 946-0201

Fax: (817) 921-3741

E-mail: info@iscet.org

http://www.iscet.org

For industry information, contact

SEMI

3081 Zanker Road

San Jose, CA 95134-2127

Tel: (408) 943-6900

Fax: (408) 428-9600

E-mail: semihq@semi.org

http://www.semi.org

For information on semiconductors, a glossary of terms, and industry information, contact

Semiconductor Industry Association

1101 K Street, NW, Suite 450

Washington, D.C. 20005-7037

Tel: (866) 756-0715; (202) 446-1700

Fax: (202) 216-9745

http://www.semiconductors.org/

Senior Care Pharmacists

■ OVERVIEW

Pharmacists are health care professionals responsible for the dispensation of prescription and nonprescription medications. They may advise physicians, nurses, or other health care professionals on the use of medications, and they also give patients instructions for taking and storing medicines. *Senior care pharmacists,* who are also known as *geriatric care pharmacists,* have expert knowledge regarding the medical conditions of the elderly and the treatments for these conditions. Many factors must be considered when treating the elderly, making this a complicated process. One factor to keep in mind is that older bodies react differently to medications than younger bodies. In addition, many older people have more than one health problem and take more than one medication. According to the American Society of Consultant Pharmacists, more than 90 percent of American seniors have at least one chronic condition, and more than 75 percent have two. As people get older that number only increases. Because of factors such as these, senior care pharmacists work closely with other members of health-care professionals in caring for a patient. Senior care pharmacists' responsibilities include keeping records on their patients' drug regimens, advising health professionals on what medicines to use and giving training on how to use them, and monitoring patients' progress and adjusting medicines as needed.

■ HISTORY

The title of pharmacist can be traced to ancient Greece. During the time of Aristotle, those who compounded drugs were called *pharmakons.* The word has changed little from its original form and still means approximately the same thing: one who compounds drugs, medicines, or poisons.

Pharmacy as a profession grew slowly in the United States. It is said that one of our earliest pharmacists was Governor John Winthrop of the Massachusetts Bay Colony. He learned to compound drugs because there were no other sources in the colony for obtaining medicines. The first school established to teach pharmacy in this country was the Philadelphia College of Pharmacy, founded in 1822. It is still in operation today as a college of the University of the Sciences in Philadelphia.

In 1906, the Federal Pure Food and Drug Act was passed. The Food and Drug Administration (FDA) was created in 1931. This agency must approve any pharmaceutical before it can be offered for sale in the United States. The field of pharmacy continued to grow, but it was only later in the 20th century that geriatric pharmacy came into existence

CAREER LADDER

Consulting Business Owner or Professor

Experienced Senior Care Pharmacist

Entry-Level Senior Care Pharmacist

as a profession. By the 1950s, some pharmacists had begun to focus on providing pharmacy services to nursing homes. Government health official George Archambault, now known as the founding father of this profession, coined the term "consultant pharmacist" to refer to the pharmacists working (that is, consulting) with nursing homes.

Today, senior care pharmacists, as the consultant pharmacists became known, still provide pharmacy services to nursing facilities. In addition, senior care pharmacists may provide services for elderly people in other environments, such as assisted living facilities, hospices, and home-based care programs. Because our country has a large and growing senior population, the skills and expertise of senior care pharmacists should be increasingly in demand.

■ THE JOB

Senior care pharmacists have expert knowledge of drug products and their effects on elderly patients, the medical conditions affecting the elderly, and the treatments for these conditions. They work in a variety of settings, and their responsibilities vary based on the places of work. In general, however, senior care pharmacists' duties involve consulting with nursing facilities or other long-term care facilities (such as assisted living facilities, hospices, and home-based care programs) about the condition and care of their patients. These pharmacists do on-site visits to meet with their patients, discuss any problems they may be having as well as to discuss a treatment plan, and meet with the other health care professionals who are part of a team caring for the patient.

An important aspect of the senior care pharmacist's work is to conduct regular drug regimen reviews as required by law. For these reviews, senior care pharmacists gather and review information on a patient's medical history, diagnosis, test results, and treatments. In general, they go over any information related to the person's health, including his or her diet. The pharmacist also meets with the patient's doctors, nurses, and any other health professional involved in the patient's care to review treatment plans and goals. Senior care pharmacists then go over the medications prescribed for the patient, checking to make sure the patients are receiving the right medicines, in the right doses, and at the right

times. If the senior care pharmacist discovers a problem with a medication being given, he or she figures out how to correct the situation.

Some of the unique knowledge senior care pharmacists must have includes knowing how a medicine will affect an older person's body, knowing how different medicines will react together in clients who take more than one prescription, knowing if a medication will make an elderly person's existing conditions worse, and, just as important, knowing the life circumstances of the patient. That is, the pharmacist should know the answer to questions such as: Is someone available to give the medication to the patient on a regular basis? Or, if the patient is in an assisted living facility, will he or she remember to take the medicine? Is the patient skipping doses to make a prescription last longer? Can the patient read the instruction label? Does the patient still need the medicine, or has he or she recovered from the illness the medicine was treating? Senior care pharmacists need to be aware of all such factors in order to find appropriate solutions to any problems that may arise.

In addition to having a close relationship with other health care professionals, senior care pharmacists must have close relationships with their clients, treating each as an individual. Because an older person's body processes medication differently than a younger person's, senior care pharmacists must be able to customize medications for their patients so that they achieve the desired results. A pharmacist may suggest, for example, taking two doses of a medicine at different times during the day instead of one large dose that is more difficult for an older person's body to absorb. Many older people regularly take more than one type of drug for a variety of problems. Senior care pharmacists must know when a 70-year-old man, for example, comes in with a prescription for a new arthritis medicine if this medicine will interfere with the effectiveness of the blood pressure medicine he is already taking. If the potential for harmful drug interaction exists, the pharmacist will consult with the doctor and suggest a more appropriate treatment. Another aspect senior care physicians must stay attuned to is how medications interact with vitamins and herbs, an issue that has arisen recently due to more people turning to alternative health treatments.

Senior care pharmacists must also understand a patient's overall health condition. Many older people, for example, have a poor sense of balance, limited vision, or are forgetful. Senior care pharmacists must know if a patient experiences any such problems so that they do not give a medicine that will make the situation worse. For example, if an 82-year-old woman (who has osteoporosis and is unsteady walking) has a prescription for a medicine that has the side effect of causing dizziness, the pharmacist should realize this might aggravate her balance problem and lead to a fall that could cause broken bones. In such a case, the senior care pharmacist will advise her doctor about the problem and recommend a different medication.

Senior care pharmacists also keep detailed records of drugs dispensed to each client. This is extremely important because older people often see more than one doctor for a number of different conditions. The senior care pharmacist may be the only person keeping track of various medicines prescribed by several doctors for one patient. In these cases, the senior care pharmacist is the health care professional who is in the best position to spot a potential adverse drug interaction and recommend a prescription change.

Another responsibility of senior care pharmacists is to answer questions about medications and provide training to other health care workers on how to administer these medications. A senior care pharmacist may spend part of a day or an entire day, for example, giving nurses at a nursing home instruction on how to determine the proper dose of an antibiotic that will be given through an IV. Naturally, senior care pharmacists also spend time in the pharmacy, where their activities include reviewing and documenting incoming prescriptions, supervising pharmacy technicians, checking filled prescriptions for their correctness, and answering questions about medications.

Like all pharmacists, senior care pharmacists must be diligent in maintaining clean and ordered work areas. They must be exceedingly accurate and precise in their calculations, and possess a high degree of concentration in order to reduce the risk of error as they assemble prescriptions. They also must be proficient with a variety of technical devices and computer systems.

■ EARNINGS

Salaries for senior care pharmacists are generally on par with what other pharmacists earn. Some pharmacies view senior care pharmacists as acting as sales representative in addition to their regular duties. In these cases, senior care pharmacists are usually at the higher end of the pay scale. Other factors that influence salaries include location and type of employer and the pharmacist's experience.

According to the U.S. Department of Labor, pharmacists had median yearly incomes of $121,500 in May 2015. The department also reported that the lowest paid 10 percent earned less than $86,790, while the highest paid 10 percent made more than $154,040 annually.

A senior care pharmacist helps a customer with a product. (Belushi. Shutterstock.)

Pharmacists, in addition to salary, often enjoy fringe benefits such as paid vacation time, medical and dental insurance, retirement plans, and sometimes bonuses, depending on the size and type of employer.

■ WORK ENVIRONMENT

Pharmacies must be clean, orderly, well lighted, and well ventilated. They are frequently busy places and this is especially true for those serving a large number of geriatric patients, since older people often take more than one medication at a time. In addition to working in a pharmacy, senior care pharmacists also visit their patients and consult with other members of the patient's health care team. This means there is often travel involved in the senior care pharmacist's work. Additionally, because these pharmacists are in contact with such a variety of people, from elderly people in pain to concerned family members to other health care professionals, they may often need to be diplomatic when advising on why and how medications should be taken.

The two most unfavorable conditions of the pharmacist's practice are the long hours and the necessity to stay on one's feet. Most state laws covering the practice of pharmacy require that there be a pharmacist on duty at all times when a pharmacy is open. This may mean long shifts as, for example, hospital pharmacies are continuously open. Despite these factors, most senior care pharmacists appreciate being involved in health care where they can use their medical and scientific knowledge to help older patients feel better.

Those who run their own businesses have management and financial responsibilities. They must hire employees, keep records on patients, and keep track of

GERIATRIC PHARMACOLOGY   **LEARN MORE ABOUT IT**

Atkinson, Steven. *Geriatric Pharmacology: The Principles of Practice & Clinical Recommendations.* Eau Claire, Wisc.: PHC Publshing Group/PESI Publishing & Media, 2012.

Figg, William, and Cindy H. Chau. *Get Into Pharmacy School: Rx for Success!,* 3rd ed. New York: Kaplan Publishing, 2011.

Galt, Kimberly A., and Michael Galt. *Patient-Centered Care for Pharmacists,* 2nd ed. Bethesda, Md.: American Society of Health-System Pharmacists, 2012.

Hutchinson, Lisa C., and Rebecca B. Sleeper. *Fundamentals of Geriatric Pharmacotherapy: An Evidence-Based Approach.* Bethesda, Md.: American Society of Health-System Pharmacists, 2010.

Katz, Michael, et al. *Pharmacotherapy Principles and Practice Study Guide,* 3rd ed. New York: McGraw-Hill Medical, 2013.

costs. They must make rent or mortgage payments and pay insurance premiums and taxes.

■ EXPLORING

One way to learn more about this profession is to read publications and visit Web sites dedicated to geriatric pharmacy. Another option is to get experience in a pharmacy environment by finding part-time or summer work at a drugstore. Even if you aren't working in the pharmacy, you can get valuable experience dealing with customers and observing the kind of work pharmacists do. If you are a hard worker and demonstrate responsibility, you may be given the chance to assist in the pharmacy, such as entering data in customer computer records, taking inventory on pharmaceuticals, preparing labels, or making deliveries to customers. Part-time or summer work in a nutrition and vitamin store can also give you the opportunity to learn a great deal about dietary supplements and herbal alternatives to pharmaceuticals.

It is also important that you explore how much you enjoy working with the elderly. Part-time or summer work in a nursing home is one way of doing this. In addition, many volunteer opportunities exist for helping older people. These opportunities can be found with organizations and agencies such as the American Red Cross, states' departments of aging, and local Catholic Charities agencies, to name a few. You will benefit from getting involved with helping older people, because you will begin to learn about their particular concerns and needs.

■ EDUCATION AND TRAINING REQUIREMENTS
High School

You can start preparing for this career while you are in high school. Begin by taking a college preparatory curriculum. Be sure to take four years of math courses, including algebra, geometry, and trigonometry, and four years of science, including biology, chemistry, and physics. Take computer science classes so that you are comfortable working with computers, and English classes to develop your research and writing skills. You may also want to take business classes to learn management skills and business basics. Other courses you should take include history, government, a foreign language, and a social science, such as psychology.

Postsecondary Training

The Accreditation Council for Pharmacy Education is the accrediting organization for professional programs in pharmacy that offer the doctor of pharmacy (Pharm.D.), which, since 2005, has completely replaced the bachelor's of science degrees in pharmacy (B.Pharm.). The B.Pharm. degree, and all bachelor's programs in this field, have been terminated. If you want to become a pharmacist, you should plan on getting the doctorate degree, which generally takes six years to complete.

Your first year or two of study does not take place in a school of pharmacy but rather in a general college setting where you will complete pre-pharmacy classes. Studies typically include chemistry, organic chemistry, biology, physics, calculus, statistics, anatomy, English, and social science classes, such as psychology or sociology. After completing this undergraduate work, you will need to gain admission to a school of pharmacy. If you are attending a large university that has a school of pharmacy, you may want to apply there. You may also apply for admission to schools of pharmacy that are not part of your undergraduate school. In addition to completing pre-pharmacy course work, some pharmacy schools require applicants to take the Pharmacy College Admission Test (P-CAT) to be considered for admission.

Once you are in pharmacy school, you will take courses such as the principles of pharmacology, biochemistry, pharmacy law and ethics, and pharmaceutical care. Because geriatric pharmacy is a growing field, more and more schools are offering courses with a focus on the elderly and their pharmaceutical care needs. In addition, your education should include an internship, sometimes known as a clerkship, in which you work under the supervision of a professional pharmacist. When deciding on a school to attend, it is advisable that you consult the *Accreditation Council for Pharmacy Education's Annual Directory of Accredited Professional Programs of Colleges and Schools of Pharmacy.* The directory is available on the council's Web site, https://www.acpe-accredit.org/students/programs.asp.

Other Education or Training

Senior care pharmacists need to complete continuing education (CE) on a regular basis to maintain their certification or licensing, as required by their state. Continuing education may be done through correspondence (written responses to educational material, usually done online) or by attending conferences, workshops, and seminars that are offered by professional associations such as the American Society of Consultant Pharmacists and the American Society of Health-System Pharmacists. Some states may also require CE in particular disease topics and treatments.

■ CERTIFICATION, LICENSING, AND SPECIAL REQUIREMENTS
Certification or Licensing

The Commission for Certification in Geriatric Pharmacy offers voluntary certification to pharmacists who serve geriatric populations. To become certified, pharmacists must currently be a licensed pharmacist, have a minimum of two years of experience as a licensed pharmacist, and pass a written exam that focuses on geriatric pharmacy practice. Those who pass receive the designation of certified geriatric pharmacist. While this is a voluntary certification, professionals in the field highly recommend obtaining it as a demonstration of your specialized skills and knowledge. The Board of Pharmacy Specialties also provides certification.

All 50 states, the District of Columbia, and U.S. territories require practicing pharmacists to be licensed. To become licensed, candidates must have graduated from an accredited pharmacy program, completed an internship under a licensed pharmacist, and passed their state's board examination.

■ EXPERIENCE, SKILLS, AND PERSONALITY TRAITS

Any experience (an internship, part-time job, etc.) in a pharmacy at a senior care facility will provide a useful introduction to the field.

Naturally, senior care pharmacists need to be detail-oriented as well as organized. They also need strong communication and people skills since they interact with doctors, nurses, other health professionals, elderly people who are ill, and sometimes an elderly person's family as well. They must be able to work professionally and often patiently when explaining what a medicine will do, how to take it, when to take it, and so on. Senior care pharmacists should also enjoy being around older people and want to help them. These pharmacists must be committed to a lifetime of learning because the field of medicine continues to grow, making new treatments and new methods of treatment available.

■ EMPLOYMENT PROSPECTS
Employers

Senior care pharmacists traditionally work for nursing home facilities. According to the American Society of Consultant Pharmacists, a number of employers exist within this setting. For example, a senior care pharmacist may work for a small long-term care provider, which provides pharmacy services to several nursing facilities in a small area. A senior care pharmacist can also work for a large long-term care provider, which is a pharmacy providing services to a large number of nursing facilities in a region. A pharmacist in geriatric care can also be hospital-based, working in a hospital's pharmacy and providing services to nursing facilities that are owned or run by the hospital.

There are also a growing number of senior care pharmacists employed in nontraditional settings. These pharmacists may provide services to employers such as assisted living facilities, hospice agencies, and home health programs. In addition, senior care pharmacists may be academically based, teaching at schools of pharmacy; may work in industry for drug companies as administrators or researchers; or may be self-employed, running their own consulting businesses and working with care providers such as nursing facilities, geriatric care managers, and hospice agencies.

Starting Out

Those in geriatric pharmacy often cite the desire to provide in-depth help to their older clients as one reason for starting out in this field. Recent graduates from pharmacy school should be able to get help locating jobs through their schools' career services offices. Professional organizations are also sources of information; the American Society of Consultant Pharmacists provides a listing of companies that hire recent graduates as well as employment listings on its Web site.

Graduates can also apply to and complete residency programs in geriatric pharmacy. Such a residency will give you further training for working in this field and enhance your credentials. The American Society of Health-System Pharmacists accredits residencies, including residencies in pharmacy practice and residencies in geriatric pharmacy. During a residency, which usually lasts one year, pharmacists work full-time and earn a stipend. Residents who complete their programs have excellent employment prospects. Sometimes they are offered jobs at the places of their residencies. Visit http://accred.ashp .org/aps/pages/directory/residencyProgramSearch.aspx for a list of residencies.

Another option is to begin working in a pharmacy that provides services to a general population, gain work experience, and move into geriatric pharmacy practice when the opportunity presents itself.

ADVANCEMENT PROSPECTS

Senior care pharmacists can advance by moving to larger pharmacies for more responsibilities, such as managing a larger staff of pharmacy technicians and working with more nursing facilities than they had in their past jobs. Other senior care pharmacists may consider it an advancement to move into a different area of consulting, for example, changing from nursing facility consulting to long-term care facility consulting. Those in academia advance by becoming full professors, and those in industry may advance by obtaining positions with increased management responsibilities. Some senior care pharmacists with experience may decide to form their own consulting businesses, either alone or in partnership with other pharmacists.

OUTLOOK

The U.S. Department of Labor (DOL) predicts that job opportunities for pharmacists who are employed at nursing and residential care facilities (including those that serve the elderly) will grow slower than average through 2024. The number of available positions is expected to exceed the number of people entering the field, mainly due to pharmacists who are retiring or otherwise leaving the field.

Senior citizens are expected to take an increasing number of prescription medications as a result of continuing medical advances and new drug research. Because of the growing complexity of prescription drugs, pharmacists will be needed to advise them on proper drug selections, medication usages, and dosages. Employment will also be strong for pharmacists in medical care establishments such as doctors' offices, outpatient care centers, hospitals, and home health care services.

Employment will be good for pharmacists at drugstores, which continue to process the majority of prescriptions and will increasingly offer patient care services such as vaccines. Other avenues for geriatric pharmacists include working for pharmaceutical manufacturing companies, especially those that manufacture drugs designed to treat ailments that affect senior citizens. In such contexts, pharmacists can work in research and development, or even in the marketing and advertising of new drug products.

UNIONS AND ASSOCIATIONS

Senior care pharmacists do not belong to unions. The American Society of Consultant Pharmacists and the American Society of Health-System Pharmacists are the leading professional associations for senior care pharmacists. They provide continuing education classes and webinars, networking events, career advice, publications, and much more. The Accreditation Council for Pharmacy Education accredits professional degree programs in pharmacy and providers of continuing pharmacy education. The Commission for Certification in Geriatric Pharmacy and the Board of Pharmacy Specialties provide certification to senior care pharmacists.

TIPS FOR ENTRY

1. Read *The Consultant Pharmacist* (http://www.ascp .com/page/journal) to learn more about the field.
2. Visit the American Society of Health-System Pharmacists' CareerPharm Web site, http://www .ashp.org/menu/careerpharm, which offers job listings, career advice, and other employment-related resources.
3. Read profiles of senior care pharmacists on the Web site of the American Society of Consultant Pharmacists: https://www.ascp.com/page/ meetascp.
4. Participate in a residency program in geriatric pharmacy to increase your skills and make networking contacts. Pharmacists sometimes are offered jobs at the places of their residencies.

FOR MORE INFORMATION

For more information on accredited programs, visit
Accreditation Council for Pharmacy Education
135 South LaSalle Street, Suite 4100
Chicago, IL 60603-4810
Tel: (312) 664-3575
Fax: (312) 664-4652
E-mail: info@acpe-accredit.org
https://www.acpe-accredit.org

For more information about the career of senior care pharmacist, contact
American Society of Consultant Pharmacists
1321 Duke Street
Alexandria, VA 22314-3507
Tel: (800) 355-2727; (703) 739-1300
Fax: (800) 220-1321
E-mail: info@ascp.com
http://ascp.com

The ASHSP has information on careers, geriatric program residencies, and news of interest for those in long-term care.

American Society of Health-System Pharmacists (ASHSP)

7272 Wisconsin Avenue

Bethesda, MD 20814-4836

Tel: (866) 279-0681

E-mail: students@ashp.org

http://www.ashp.org

For information about certification, contact

Board of Pharmacy Specialties

2215 Constitution Avenue, NW

Washington, D.C. 20037-2985

Tel: (202) 429-7591

Fax: (202) 429-6304

E-mail: info@bpsweb.org

http://bpsweb.org

For information about certification, contact

Commission for Certification in Geriatric Pharmacy

1321 Duke Street

Alexandria, VA 22314-3563

Tel: (703) 535-3036

Fax: (202) 429-6304

E-mail: info@ccgp.org

http://www.ccgp.org

Sheet Metal Workers

■ OVERVIEW

Sheet metal workers fabricate, assemble, install, repair, and maintain ducts used for ventilating, air-conditioning, and heating systems. They also work with other articles of sheet metal, including roofing, siding, gutters, downspouts, partitions, chutes, and stainless steel kitchen and beverage equipment for restaurants. Not included in this group are employees in factories where sheet metal items are mass-produced on assembly lines. There are approximately 141,000 sheet metal workers in the United States.

■ HISTORY

Sheet metal did not become important in many products until the development of mills and processes that form various kinds of metal into thin, strong, flat sheets and strips. The processes for making sheet metal have undergone a long series of improvements in the 20th century. As the methods were refined and made more economical, new uses for sheet metal were developed, and making sheet metal products became a well-established skilled craft field. Today, sheet metal workers are concerned with cutting, shaping, soldering, riveting, and other processes to fabricate, install, and maintain a wide range of articles. Heating, ventilating, and air-conditioning systems for all kinds of buildings—residential, commercial, and industrial—provide the most important source of employment for sheet metal workers.

■ THE JOB

Most sheet metal workers handle a variety of tasks in fabricating, installing, and maintaining sheet metal products. Some workers concentrate on just one of these areas. Skilled workers must know about the whole range of activities involved in working with sheet metal.

Many sheet metal workers are employed by building contracting firms that construct or renovate residential, commercial, and industrial buildings. Fabricating and installing air-conditioning, heating, and refrigeration equipment is often a big part of their job. Some workers specialize in adjusting and servicing equipment that has already been installed so that it can operate at peak efficiency. Roofing contractors, federal government agencies, and businesses that do their own alteration and construction work also employ sheet metal workers. Other sheet metal workers are employed in the shipbuilding, railroad, and aircraft industries or in shops that manufacture specialty products such as

QUICK FACTS	
ALTERNATE TITLE(S)	None
DUTIES	Fabricate, assemble, install, repair, and maintain ducts used for ventilating, air-conditioning, and heating systems
SALARY RANGE	$25,760 to $45,750 to $83,230+
WORK ENVIRONMENT	Primarily Indoors
BEST GEOGRAPHIC LOCATION(S)	Opportunities are available throughout the country
MINIMUM EDUCATION LEVEL	Apprenticeship
SCHOOL SUBJECTS	Mathematics, Physics, Technical/Shop
EXPERIENCE	Apprenticeship
PERSONALITY TRAITS	Conventional, Hands On, Technical
SKILLS	Building/Trades, Math, Mechanical/Manual Dexterity
CERTIFICATION OR LICENSING	Recommended
SPECIAL REQUIREMENTS	None
EMPLOYMENT PROSPECTS	Good
ADVANCEMENT PROSPECTS	Good
OUTLOOK	Faster than the Average
NOC	7233
O*NET-SOC	47-2211.00

CAREER LADDER

Independent Sheet Metal Contractor

Job Superintendent

Supervisor

Sheet Metal Worker

Apprentice or Helper

custom kitchen equipment or electrical generating and distributing machinery.

Fabricating is often done in a shop away from the site where the product is to be installed. When fabricating products, workers usually begin by studying blueprints or drawings. After determining the amounts and kinds of materials required for the job, they make measurements and lay out the pattern on the appropriate pieces of metal. They may use measuring tapes and rulers and figure dimensions with the aid of calculators. Then, following the pattern they have marked on the metal, they cut out the sections with hand or power shears or other machine tools. They may shape the pieces with a hand or machine brake, which is a type of equipment used for bending and forming sheet metal, and punch or drill holes in the parts. As a last step before assembly, workers inspect the parts to verify that all of them are accurately shaped. Then they fasten the parts together by welding, soldering, bolting, riveting, cementing, or using special devices such as metal clips. After assembly, it may be necessary to smooth rough areas on the fabricated item with a file or grinding wheel.

Computers play an increasingly important role in several of these tasks. Computerized layout programs help workers plan the layout efficiently, so that all the necessary sections can be cut from the metal stock while leaving the smallest possible amount of waste sheet metal. Computerized laser-cutting machines also help guide saws, shears, and lasers that cut metal, as well as other machines that form the pieces into the desired shapes.

If the item has been fabricated in a shop, it is taken to the installation site. There, the sheet metal workers join together different sections of the final product. For example, they may connect sections of duct end to end. Some items, such as sections of duct, can be bought factory-made in standard sizes, and workers modify them at the installation site to meet the requirements of the situation. Once finished, ductwork may be suspended with metal hangers from ceilings or attached to walls. Sometimes sheet metal workers weld, bolt, screw, or nail items into place. To complete the installation, they may need to make additional sheet metal parts or alter the items they have fabricated.

Some tasks in working with sheet metal, such as making metal roofing, are routinely done at the job site. Workers measure and cut sections of roof paneling, which interlock with grooving at the edges. They nail or weld the paneling to the roof deck to hold it in place and put metal molding over joints and around the edges, windows, and doors to finish off the roof.

■ EARNINGS

Sheet metal workers earned a median hourly wage of $21.99 in May 2015, according to the U.S. Department of Labor. This amounts to a yearly salary of $45,750. Overall, hourly earnings ranged from less than $25,760 a year to more than $83,230 a year. Earnings vary in different parts of the country and tend to be highest in industrialized urban areas. Earnings also vary by industry. For example, in May 2015, construction trade workers earned about $41,020 per year; whereas sheet metal workers employed in ventilation, heating, air-conditioning, and commercial refrigeration equipment manufacturing earned about $50,480 a year. Apprentices begin at about 40 to 50 percent of the rate paid to experienced workers and receive periodic pay increases throughout their training. Some workers who are union members are eligible for supplemental pay from their union during periods of unemployment or when they are working less than full time.

Sheet metal workers who are members of the Sheet Metal Workers' International Association, the industry's main labor union, are entitled to benefits including paid vacation days and holidays, health insurance, pensions to help with retirement savings, supplemental unemployment compensation plans, and so forth.

■ WORK ENVIRONMENT

Most sheet metal workers have a regular 40-hour workweek and receive extra pay for overtime. Most of their work is performed indoors, so they are less likely to lose wages due to bad weather than many other craftworkers involved in construction projects. Some work is done outdoors, occasionally in uncomfortably hot or cold conditions.

Workers sometimes have to work high above the ground (like when they install gutters and roofs) and sometimes in awkward, cramped positions (when they install ventilation systems in buildings). Workers may have to be on their feet for long periods, and they may have to lift heavy objects. Possible hazards of the trade include cuts and burns from machinery and equipment, as well as falls from ladders and scaffolding. Workers must use effective safety practices to avoid injuries and sometimes wear protective gear such as safety glasses.

Sheet metal fabrication shops are usually well ventilated and properly heated and lighted, but at times they are quite noisy.

■ EXPLORING

High school students can gauge their aptitude for and interest in some of the common activities of sheet metal workers by taking such courses as metal shop, blueprint reading, and mechanical drawing. A summer or part-time job as a helper with a contracting firm that does sheet metal work could provide an excellent opportunity to observe workers on the job. If such a job cannot be arranged, it may be possible to visit a construction site and perhaps to talk with a sheet metal worker who can give an insider's view of this job.

■ EDUCATION AND TRAINING REQUIREMENTS

High School

Requirements vary slightly, but applicants for sheet metal training programs must be high school graduates. High school courses that provide a good background include shop classes, mechanical drawing, trigonometry, and geometry.

Postsecondary Training

The best way to learn the skills necessary for working in this field is to complete an apprenticeship. Apprenticeships generally consist of a planned series of on-the-job work experiences plus classroom instruction in related subjects. The on-the-job training portion of apprenticeships, which lasts four to five years, includes about 8,000 hours of work. The classroom instruction totals approximately 600 hours, spread over the years of the apprenticeship. The training covers all aspects of sheet metal fabrication and installation.

Apprentices get practical experience in layout work, cutting, shaping, and installing sheet metal. They also learn to work with materials that may be used instead of metal, such as fiberglass and plastics. Under the supervision of skilled workers, they begin with simple tasks and gradually work up to the most complex. In the classroom, they learn blueprint reading, drafting, mathematics, computer operations, job safety, welding, and the principles of heating, air-conditioning, and ventilating systems.

Apprenticeships may be run by joint committees representing locals of the Sheet Metal Workers' International Association, an important union in the field, and local chapters of the Sheet Metal and Air Conditioning Contractors' National Association. Other apprenticeships are run by local chapters of a contractor group, the Associated Builders and Contractors.

A roofer welds sheet metal to construct a gutter. (racorn. Shutterstock.)

A few sheet metal workers learn informally on the job while they are employed as helpers to experienced workers. They gradually develop skills when opportunities arise for learning. Like apprentices, helpers start out with simple jobs and in time take on more complicated work. However, the training that helpers get may not be as balanced as that for apprentices, and it may take longer for them to learn all that they need to know. Helpers often take vocational school courses to supplement their work experience.

Other Education or Training

Even after they have become experienced and well qualified in their field, sheet metal workers may need to take further training to keep their skills up to date. Such training is often sponsored by unions or paid for by their employers. Additionally, the American Welding Society; Fabricators and Manufacturers Association,

MANUFACTURING SHEET METAL

LEARN MORE ABOUT IT

Barr, Ed. *Professional Sheet Metal Fabrication.* Minneapolis, Minn.: Motorbooks, 2013.

Boljanovic, Vukota. *Sheet Metal Forming Processes and Die Design,* 2nd ed. South Norwalk, Conn.: Industrial Press, 2014.

Joseph, Matt. *Automotive Sheet Metal Forming & Fabrication.* North Branch, Minn.: S-A Design/CarTech, 2011.

Longyard, William H. *Sheet Metal Fab for Car Builders: Make Panels for Cobra, Lotus, Hot Rods & More.* Stillwater, Minn.: Wolfgang Publications, 2014.

Paul, Eddie. *Sheet Metal Fabrication: Techniques and Tips for Beginners and Pros.* Minneapolis, Minn.: Motorbooks, 2008.

International; and the International Training Institute for the Sheet Metal and Air-Conditioning Industry provide continuing education opportunities to sheet metal workers.

■ CERTIFICATION, LICENSING, AND SPECIAL REQUIREMENTS
Certification or Licensing

Voluntary certification can help sheet metal workers keep up with developments in fabrication technology, such as computerized layout and laser-cutting machines, as well as building information modeling (B.I.M.) software. These certifications are provided by equipment manufacturers and other organizations. Also, certification in welding from the American Welding Society can give a sheet metal worker an advantage in the job market.

■ EXPERIENCE, SKILLS, AND PERSONALITY TRAITS

Previous experience as a helper or apprentice is required to become a sheet metal worker.

Sheet metal workers need to be in good physical condition, with good manual dexterity, eye-hand coordination, and the ability to visualize and understand shapes and forms.

■ EMPLOYMENT PROSPECTS
Employers

Approximately 141,000 sheet metal workers are employed in the United States. Most workers in this field are employed by sheet metal contractors; some workers with a great deal of experience go into business for themselves. The U.S. Department of Labor reports that

about 60 percent of all sheet metal workers work in the construction industry, and of these nearly half work for plumbing, heating, and air-conditioning contractors. The rest work for building and roofing finishing contractors.

Starting Out

People who would like to enter an apprentice program in this field can seek information about apprenticeships from local employers of sheet metal workers, such as sheet metal contractors or heating, air-conditioning, and refrigeration contractors; from the local office of the Sheet Metal Workers International Association; or from the local Sheet Metal Apprentice Training office, the joint union-management apprenticeship committee. Information on apprenticeship programs can also be obtained from the local office of the state employment service or the state apprenticeship agency.

People who would rather enter this field as on-the-job trainees can contact contractors directly about possibilities for jobs as helpers. Leads for specific jobs may be located through the state employment service or newspaper classified ads. Graduates of vocational or technical training programs may get assistance from the placement office at their schools.

■ ADVANCEMENT PROSPECTS

Skilled and experienced sheet metal workers who work for contractors may be promoted to positions as *supervisors* and eventually *job superintendents*. Those who develop their skills through further training may move into related fields, such as welding. Some sheet metal workers become specialists in particular activities, such as design and layout work or estimating costs of installations. Some workers eventually go into business for themselves as *independent sheet metal contractors*.

■ OUTLOOK

The U.S. Department of Labor predicts that employment for sheet metal workers will grow as fast as average for all careers through 2024. Employment growth will be related to several factors. Many new residential, commercial, and industrial buildings will be constructed, requiring the skills of sheet metal workers, and many older buildings will need to have new energy-efficient heating, cooling, and ventilating systems installed to replace outdated systems. Existing equipment will need routine maintenance and repair. Decorative sheet metal products are becoming more popular for some uses, a trend that is expected to provide an increasing amount of employment for sheet metal workers. Employment for sheet metal workers in manufacturing will also grow faster than average through 2024 as some work that was previously outsourced to other countries returns to the United States.

Job prospects will vary somewhat with economic conditions. In general, the economy is closely tied to the level of new building construction activity. During economic downturns, workers may face periods of unemployment, while at other times there may be more jobs than skilled workers available to take them. But overall, sheet metal workers are less affected by economic ups and downs than some other craftworkers in the construction field. This is because activities related to maintenance, repair, and replacement of old equipment compose a significant part of their job, and even during an economic slump, building owners are often inclined to go ahead with such work. Sheet metal workers who have apprenticeship training or certification in welding will have better chances to secure work.

UNIONS AND ASSOCIATIONS

Many sheet metal workers are represented by the Sheet Metal Workers' International Association, an important union in the field, and local chapters of the Sheet Metal and Air Conditioning Contractors' National Association. Membership organizations for sheet metal workers include the American Welding Society and the Fabricators and Manufacturers Association, International. The International Training Institute for the Sheet Metal and Air-Conditioning Industry offers a variety of occupational training and continuing education classes.

TIPS FOR ENTRY

1. Visit http://jobs.fmanet.org/ for job listings.
2. Read *Practical Welding Today* (http://fmanet.org) and Eye on Sheet Metal (http://www.sheetmetal-iti.org/eye_on_sheetmetal.asp) to learn more about the field.
3. Talk to sheet metal workers about their careers. Ask them for advice on breaking into the field.

FOR MORE INFORMATION

For information on certification, contact
American Welding Society
8669 NW 36th Street, #130
Miami, FL 33166-6672
Tel: (800) 443-9353; (305) 443-9353
http://www.aws.org

For information about certification, educational programs, and other resources, visit
Fabricators and Manufacturers Association, International
2135 Point Blvd
Elgin, IL 60123

Tel: (888) 394-4362; (815) 399-8700
E-mail: info@fmanet.org
http://www.fmanet.org

For industry and career information, contact
International Training Institute for the Sheet Metal and Air-Conditioning Industry
8403 Arlington Boulevard, Suite 100
Fairfax, VA 22031-4662
Tel: (703) 739-7200
Fax: (703) 683-7461
http://www.sheetmetal-iti.org

For industry information, contact
Sheet Metal and Air Conditioning Contractors' National Association
4201 Lafayette Center Drive
Chantilly, VA 20151-1209
Tel: (703) 803-2980
Fax: (703) 803-3732
E-mail: memberservices@smacna.org
http://www.smacna.org

The Sheet Metal arm of SMART, formerly the Sheet Metal Workers International Association, represents 136,000 members in the sheet metal and related trades. For more information contact
SMART, the International Association of Sheet Metal, Air, Rail and Transportation Workers (SMART)
1750 New York Avenue, NW, 6th Floor
Washington, D.C. 20006-5301
Tel: 800-457-7694; 202-662-0800
E-mail: info@smart-union.org
http://www.smwia.org

Ship's Captains

OVERVIEW

Ship's captains, also known as *masters*, command vessels and oversee crews. They are licensed mariners who make sure procedures are followed to ensure the safety of the crews, cargo, and passengers. They supervise and delegate work to crews, including other officers, and keep records and logs of the ship's activities and movements. According to the Department of Labor, there were 15,770 ship's captains and boat operators employed in the United States in May 2015.

QUICK FACTS

ALTERNATE TITLE(S)
Masters

DUTIES
Operate and maintain ships; ensure safety of crew, passengers, and cargo; supervise crew; keep records of ship's activities and movements; prepare budgets for maintenance and repairs; oversee passenger and cargo loading and unloading.

SALARY RANGE
$38,310 to $76,780 to $134,950+

WORK ENVIRONMENT
Indoors/Outdoors

BEST GEOGRAPHIC LOCATION(S)
Highest levels of employment for ship's captains occur in Louisiana, Texas, Washington, Florida, and Virginia, but opportunities exist in all regions near waterways

MINIMUM EDUCATION LEVEL
Associate's Degree

SCHOOL SUBJECTS
Business, Geography, Mathematics

EXPERIENCE
Several years of deckhand and officer experience

PERSONALITY TRAITS
Hands On, Problem-Solving, Technical

SKILLS
Business Management, Interpersonal, Leadership

CERTIFICATION OR LICENSING
Required

SPECIAL REQUIREMENTS
Must pass a drug screening test and physical with good vision, and hearing; shipboard safety class required; may undergo a background check

EMPLOYMENT PROSPECTS
Fair

ADVANCEMENT PROSPECTS
Fair

OUTLOOK
Faster than the Average

NOC
2273

O*NET-SOC
53-5021.00, 53-5021.01, 53-5021.03

■ HISTORY

The use of boats for transportation of goods and people dates to Egypt in 4000 B.C. Clay tablets from that era depict images of wooden boats with sails being rowed by oarsmen. The Egyptians transported obelisks by boats, initially on the Nile River and later branching out to the Mediterranean and Red seas. The Phoenicians and Greeks further developed ships for trade journeys and for naval warfare.

As water transportation evolved, ships became more specialized based on their purpose. For example, fighting ships were designed to be long and narrow because they needed to be fast while also having enough space to transport large numbers of fighters. Trading ships had more cargo than crew, and thus were round in design and had high decks so they could handle larger seas. By the middle ages, sailing ships had replaced rowing ships, giving rise to more oceanic navigation by various countries across continents and growth in the shipbuilding industry. Starting in the 15th century, overseas trade and exploration grew and more efforts were made to keep as few crew members as possible on the merchant ships to maximize the profits.

The introduction of the steam-powered boat in the 19th century enabled inland and coastal navigation in the United States. The 20th century saw the growth of large passenger liners as tourist travel increased. These boats had the capacity for large numbers of passengers and crews. For instance, the RMS Queen Mary, which was retired in the 1960s, could accommodate 1,957 passengers and had 1,174 officers and crew members.

Today the global deep-sea, coastal, and inland water transportation industry is a $448 billion business. As reported by the market research group IBISWorld, it consists of 32,662 businesses in cargo transportation and passenger transportation.

■ THE JOB

Ship's captains operate and maintain nonmilitary vessels. Their main job is to ensure the safety of their crew, the passengers, and the goods and products that they are transporting on the ships. Typical tasks include supervising the work of crew members and officers, preparing budgets for the ship's maintenance and repairs, keeping records of the ship's activities and travels, overseeing the loading and unloading of passengers and cargo, and interacting with passengers. They may work on cruise ships, ferries, fishing boats, tugboats, freighters, or barges.

Captains work closely with ship's officers, pilots, sailors, deckhands, ship's engineers, and engine room crew. Those who command large deep-sea container ships oversee the transport of manufactured goods and refrigerated cargoes around the world. Captains also work on bulk carriers that transport heavy commodities, such as coal or iron ore, across oceans and the Great Lakes. Captains work on large and small tankers that move oil and other liquid products to different parts of the United States and to other countries. Captains of supply ships transport equipment and supplies to offshore oil and gas platforms. Cruise ship captains oversee large crews and many passengers and may travel for days or weeks. Ferry captains operate boats that carry passengers short distances.

The crew for most deep-sea merchant ships, large coastal ships, or Great Lakes merchant ships typically consists of a ship's captain, a chief engineer, three mates, three assistant engineers, and a number of sailors and marine oilers. Vessels that operate in harbors or rivers are usually smaller and require fewer crew members than merchant and coastal ships. The U.S. Coast Guard regulations determines the number of mariners required for ship's crews.

■ EARNINGS

The average annual salary for captains, mates, and pilots of water vessels was $76,780 in May 2015, according to the Department of Labor. The lowest 10 percent earned $38,310 or less and the highest 10 percent earned $134,950 or more. Salaries vary depending on the water transportation industry. Those who work in deep-sea, coastal, and Great Lakes water transportation earn higher annual salaries (average of $82,390) than those who work in scenic and sightseeing transportation (average of $50,630). The average annual salary for captains, mates, and pilots who are employed in inland transportation is $81,210.

Payscale reported the median salary for ship captains in January 2016 was $99,122. Salaries ranged from $42,936 to $194,016. Ship captains with up to five years of experience earned approximately $50,000 per year.

■ WORK ENVIRONMENT

Ship captains work aboard boats in all types of weather conditions. They may work daytime hours only if they work on a tugboat, ferry, or sightseeing vessel, and return home at the end of each workday. Those who work on cruise ships, freighters, and fishing vessels work and live on the boats for extended periods of time, which could be days, weeks, or months. When they take breaks from work, first mates and officers take over until they return. The long trips at sea and the extended time away from family and home can be stressful. On cruise ships and other large boats accommodations for the captain may be pleasant, including air-conditioning and comfortable living quarters. Many boats now have entertainment systems with satellite TV and Internet and staff chefs and/or cooks.

■ EXPLORING

The first thing to learn is if you have the legs as well as stomach for this type of work, especially if you aim to be at sea for lengthy periods of time. If you live near a port, get a part-time job on a sightseeing or fishing boat. This will give you the opportunity to experience what it's like to work while on a moving vessel. You will also have the opportunity to see what a ship captain does. See if you can set up a time to speak with the captain to ask questions about the job and find out what steps they took to get into the profession. You can also learn more about maritime professions through online exploration. One place to start is by visiting the Web site of the U.S. Department of Transportation's Maritime Administration (MARAD), which features information about the merchant marine and waterborne transportation, as well as a list of maritime colleges and academies.

CAREER LADDER

Ship Captain

First Mate

Deckhand

■ EDUCATION AND TRAINING REQUIREMENTS
High School

Ship's captains must have good communication and organizational skills, in addition to solid maritime knowledge. While in high school, take classes in English, business, math, science, computers, and, if offered, marine science.

Postsecondary Education

Most ship's captains have an associate's or bachelor's degree. Many receive their degrees from maritime colleges or academies. Undergraduate programs include marine transportation, maritime operations and technology, marine engineering, and logistics and intermodal transportation. Other areas that are typically covered are meteorology, electronic navigation, ship construction, and maritime law. Courses in communications, English, business management, computers, and math are also helpful for this type of work.

■ CERTIFICATION, LICENSING, AND SPECIAL REQUIREMENTS
Certification or Licensing

Most ship officers and engineers have the Merchant Marine Credential, which is an endorsement certification issued by the U.S. Coast Guard upon passing a written exam. Captains and mariners who operate ships with U.S. flags must have a Transportation Worker Identification Credential from the Transportation

SHIP HANDLING AND MANAGEMENT

LEARN MORE ABOUT IT

Abrashoff, D. Michael. *It's Your Ship: Management Techniques from the Best Damn Ship in the Navy, 10th Anniversary Ed.* New York: Grand Central Publishing, 2012.

Baudu, Herve. *Ship Handling*. Vlissingen, Netherlands: Dokmar, 2014.

Dickie, John W. *Reeds 21st Century Ship Management*. Brookline, Mass.: Thomas Reed, 2014.

Lavery, Brian. *Ship: The Epic Story of Maritime Adventure*. London: DK, 2010.

Marquet, L. David. *Turn the Ship Around!: A True Story of Turning Followers*. London: Portfolio, 2013.

Paine, Lincoln. *The Sea and Civilization: A Maritime History of the World*. London: Routledge, 2015.

Parrott, Daniel. *Bridge Resource Management for Small Ships: The Watchkeeper's Manual for Limited-Tonnage Vessels*. New York: International Marine and Ragged Mountain Press, 2011.

Security Administration. They must pass a drug screening and take a class on shipboard safety. Ship captains and mariners who operate vessels on open oceans must have the Standards of Training, Certification, and Watchkeeping endorsement from the U.S. Coast Guard. All of these credentials must be renewed every five years.

Ship's captains who also pilot the boats must have a license issued by the state in which they work and licensing requirements vary by state. The U.S. Coast Guard issues licenses for those who work on the Great Lakes.

Other Requirements

Ship's captains can expect to be required to pass a drug screening test as well as a physical to ensure they are healthy and have good vision and hearing. They must also pass training shipboard safety. Some employers may require background checks.

■ EXPERIENCE, SKILLS, AND PERSONALITY TRAITS

Ship's captains have years of experience on the job. Some get their start in entry-level positions as deckhands and work their way up through the ranks by advancing to jobs with increasingly more responsibility. Ship's captains must have strong leadership, management, and communication skills to effectively manage staff and interact with passengers and customers. Knowledge of navigation, logistics, and maritime safety and laws is required.

They must also be problem-solvers and quick thinkers, particularly when faced with emergency situations while operating the ships. The job requires multitasking abilities coupled with interpersonal skills.

■ EMPLOYMENT PROSPECTS
Employers

Ship's captains work for companies that have cruise lines, ferries, sightseeing boats, fishing boats, tugboats, and freighters. There are 15,770 ship and boat captains and operators employed in the United States, according to the Department of Labor. Nearly a quarter of all water transportation workers are employed in inland transportation; 19 percent work in deep sea, coastal, and Great Lakes water transportation; and the remainder are employed in scenic and sightseeing water transportation, in government agencies, or in support activities for water transportation.

Starting Out

Many ship's captains receive training through maritime academies and by starting out as deckhands on ships. They must meet specific requirements, including a certain amount of sea time, to receive a license to work in the United States. Each state issues ship captain licenses and the requirements vary by state. Many states will also allow ship captains to work in the state if they have captain's or ship master's licensing from the U.S. Coast Guard. This is a small, highly competitive field. Those with maritime education, appropriate certification and licensing, and experience in the field improve their job prospects.

■ ADVANCEMENT PROSPECTS

Deckhands with years of experience advance to higher levels, from third mate to chief's mate. They become a ship's captain after meeting work requirements and passing the licensing exam. Once in the job, ship's captains may advance by changing to different types of ships. If they work for a small, scenic water transportation company, they may explore working for larger ships. Those who work in inland transportation may decide to work for ships that travel overseas. They may advance by securing different licenses to operate large vessels with large passenger and cargo capacities. They may also start their own companies, such as a fishing boat or sightseeing boat company.

■ OUTLOOK

The outlook for water transportation workers overall is good. The Department of Labor forecasts 9 percent employment growth through 2024. Ship's captains, mates, and pilots of water vessels are expected to have faster than average employment growth (10 percent) in the coming years. There will be opportunities in freight companies, particularly because of increase in demand for bulk commodities such as petroleum, iron, and grain. Most of the jobs in these areas will be located on the Great Lakes and inland rivers. There may also be more job openings on tanker ships and barges, as domestic oil production has been increasing. Refineries, which are usually near waterways, will need raw crude to be delivered. There should also be employment opportunities on supply ships that operate to support offshore oil platforms. Growth in domestic waterways freight may be limited, however, due to competition from pipelines, railways, and trucks for transporting oil.

Employment in deep-sea shipping is expected to remain steady, particularly due to the significance of keeping a fleet of ships for the defense of the nation. River cruise ships are also gaining popularity and will offer some job opportunities for captains. Captains of cruise lines may have more difficulty in the job market, however, because many cruise lines travel internationally and often hire non-U.S. workers.

■ UNIONS AND ASSOCIATIONS

The American Waterways Operators is a national advocacy group for the U.S. tugboat, towboat, and barge industry. Its members operate on U.S. rivers, coasts, Great Lakes, and harbors. The Lake Carriers' Association represents U.S.-flag vessel operators of the Great Lakes. Its members operate vessels, tugboats, and barges that carry more than 100 million tons of cargo in a year. The commodities carried are primarily iron ore, limestone, and coal. The Passenger Vessel Association offers industry information, networking opportunities, and other resources for U.S. passenger vessel operators and owners.

■ TIPS FOR ENTRY

1. If you live near a port, get a part-time job on a sightseeing boat, fishing boat, or any other type of boat where a crew is employed. This will help you learn if the boat life is for you.
2. Visit the Web sites of maritime colleges and academies to learn more about educational requirements for various careers in water transportation.
3. Visit the Web sites of trade associations such as the Passenger Vessel Association, among others, to learn more the news and events in the industry.

■ FOR MORE INFORMATION

The American Waterways Operators is a national advocate for the U.S. tugboat, towboat, and barge industry.

**American Waterways
   Operators (AWO)**
801 North Quincy Street, Suite 200
Arlington, VA 22203-1999
Tel: (703) 841-9300
Fax: (703) 841-0389
http://www.americanwaterways.com

The Lake Carriers' Association represents and promotes the common interests of U.S.-flag vessel operators on the Great Lakes.

Lake Carriers' Association (LCA)
20325 Center Ridge Road, Suite 720
Rocky River, OH 44116-3572
Tel: (440) 333-4444
Fax: (440) 333-9993
E-mail: info@lcaships.com
http://www.lcaships.com

The Maritime Administration is a U.S. Department of Transportation agency that deals with waterborne transportation.

**Maritime Administration
   (MARAD)**
1200 New Jersey Avenue, SE
Washington, D.C. 20590-3660
Tel: (202) 366-4000
https://www.marad.dot.gov

The Passenger Vessel Association is dedicated to promoting the interests and economic well-being of U.S. passenger vessel owners and operators.

**Passenger Vessel Association
   (PVA)**
103 Oronoco Street, Suite 200
Alexandria, VA 22314-2055
Tel: (800) 807-8360
Fax: (703) 518-5151
E-mail: pvainfo@passengervessel.com
http://www.passengervessel.com

The U.S. Coast Guard National Maritime Center issues credentials for fully qualified mariners.

**U.S. Coast Guard National Maritime Center
   (USCG NMC)**
100 Forbes Drive
Martinsburg, WV 25404-0001
Tel: (888) 427-5662
Fax: (304) 433-5622
https://www.uscg.mil/nmc

Sign Language and Oral Interpreters

■ OVERVIEW

Sign language interpreters help people who use sign language communicate with people who can hear and speak. They translate a message from spoken words to signs, and from signs to spoken words. They are fluent in American Sign Language, and/or sign systems based on English (such as Seeing Essential English, Signing Exact English, and Linguistics of Visual English). *Oral interpreters* help to deliver a spoken message from someone who hears to someone who is deaf. They also have the ability to understand the speech and mouth movements of someone who is deaf or hard of hearing, and to deliver the message to someone who is hearing.

According to the Registry of Interpreters for the Deaf, "American Sign Language is the language used by a majority of people in the Deaf community in the United States, most of Canada, certain Caribbean countries and areas of Mexico. Other areas of the world use their own sign languages, such as England (British Sign Language) and Australia (Australian Sign Language)."

■ HISTORY

Until the 1960s, sign language was considered by many educators to be inferior to spoken and written language. Oralism, the tradition of teaching deaf children to speak and lip-read, was practiced exclusively in deaf schools, and sign language was forbidden.

A child born deaf can learn sign language as naturally as a hearing child learns English, but English does not come naturally to deaf children. Hearing children pick up many of their English words and language skills from listening to all the noise that surrounds them—a radio or TV on in the room; a phone conversation down the hall; older siblings playing in the front yard. Deaf children can only carefully and painstakingly study the English language. They are limited to watching the movement of a person's mouth and to touching a person's neck and throat to learn sounds. Lip-reading is difficult at best, as many words require the same shaping of the lips. Even the best lip-readers can become lost quickly during a normal conversation.

Various forms of sign language were widely used in the 19th century. Laurent Clerc, a deaf Frenchman, and Thomas Gallaudet, a hearing minister, introduced French Sign Language to America in 1816. This system, integrated with the signs Americans were already using, served as the foundation for American Sign Language

(ASL, although the language did not come to be called ASL until the 1960s). It also led to the establishment of the first school for the deaf in Hartford, Connecticut. Many schools for the deaf followed and, by 1867, all of them used sign language in their lessons, resulting in the spread of ASL. But even educators who supported the use of sign language criticized ASL, favoring instead sign systems that followed English sentence structure and word order. (American Sign Language is considered a "natural sign language," a language completely separate from English.)

By the mid-1800s, some educators came to believe that by letting deaf children sign, they were preventing the children from developing speech and English language skills. This led to a conference on deaf education in Milan, Italy, in 1880. There, a resolution was passed to ban all sign language from deaf education. This ban was widely accepted in America, and all schools for the deaf had eliminated ASL from their lessons by 1907. In some classrooms, teachers even tied down the student's hands to prevent them from signing. However, American Sign Language survived. The language was passed secretly from deaf parents to deaf children, from deaf teachers to deaf students. The resilience of the language, through nearly 100 years of oralism, was finally acknowledged with a series of linguistic studies in the 1960s. In the 1970s, ASL was reintroduced to deaf education and is now considered important in the teaching of English to deaf students.

American Sign Language has enabled members of the deaf community to accurately express their cultural values, beliefs, and ideas, and interpreters help to communicate these ideas to the English-speaking majority. The Registry of Interpreters for the Deaf (RID), established in 1964, introduced certification standards in 1972. The Rehabilitation Act of 1973 led the way for better opportunities for deaf people; by mandating interpreters, the legislation gave deaf people access to employment, education, health, and social services. The Americans with Disabilities Act and the Individuals with Disabilities Education Act were both passed in 1990 and guarantee, in some instances, interpreters for deaf students and even deaf workers.

The field is expanding as a result of the introduction of Video Relay Service and Video Remote Interpreting technologies, which allow the deaf community access to real-time video communication with the hearing community.

■ THE JOB

In a classroom in New York City, a deaf teacher instructs hearing students in American Sign Language (ASL). No speaking or writing is allowed. The teacher uses pictures, gestures, and pantomime to teach the meaning of a sign. He stands in front of the class, and without words, emphasizes not only the importance of finger and hand movement, but of a raised eyebrow, a nod, or a smile. The room is filled with people who spend their days speaking to coworkers and friends, talking on the phone, yelling for cabs, and ordering in restaurants. Tonight the classroom is silent but for the occasional clap of a hand, or the buzzing of the fluorescent lights, or laughter.

This class, taught at The Sign Language Center in Manhattan, is composed of people who want access to deaf communities. A social worker wants to be able to communicate with deaf clients; a history teacher wants to interact directly with her deaf students; a man plays Saturday morning basketball games with a deaf neighbor. There's even an anthropologist who wants to communicate with the apes in a study lab. With about a half million Americans using ASL as their main language, ASL has come to be used in many different settings. Deaf actors perform plays using sign language. Deaf poets have developed a body of sign-language literature. Scientists, inventors, school administrators, and many others are making important contributions to society using ASL. Just as speakers of foreign languages sometimes need interpreters to help them express their ideas to English speakers, so do the users of ASL.

Interpreters are also increasingly in demand for doctors, social service workers, and others who work with elderly populations. People over the age of 65, a rapidly growing segment of society, are threatened with a number of disorders that can lead to hearing loss. Though many hearing-impaired elderly people may rely on a hearing aid, others may need to develop some sign language skills.

The Americans with Disabilities Act guarantees the services of interpreters in some situations. Large private companies are required to accommodate employees who have physical limitations. In addition to working with deaf employees, interpreters work in schools helping deaf students learn from English-speaking teachers. They work in legal settings, such as law offices and courtrooms. In hospitals, doctors and nurses need the aid of interpreters in communicating with deaf patients. Social service and religious agencies need interpreters to offer counseling and other services to deaf clients. Deaf audience members rely on interpreters for theatrical or televised performances. When an interpreter is needed, the client can check with the school or theater or social service agency to make sure interpreting is provided. If not, there are interpreter provider organizations that can direct the client to an interpreter. The Registry of Interpreters for the Deaf (RID) publishes state-by-state listings of these organizations, as well as a directory of individual interpreters.

Deaf interpreters translate spoken material into a language that can be understood by the deaf. This may be done in either of two ways. Sign language interpreters translate a speaker's words into ASL using their hands and fingers, and then repeat aloud the deaf person's signed response to the speaker. Oral interpreters carefully mouth words without voicing them aloud for deaf people who can speech-read. *Tactile interpreters* work with deaf individuals who also have a visual impairment and communicate only through touch. *Trilingual interpreters* facilitate communication among an ASL user, an English speaker, and a speaker of another language.

Interpreters must be very visible; proper lighting and backgrounds should contribute to their visibility, not distract from it. Furthermore, they should obtain any written supplements to assist in accurate interpretation. The interpreter's role is only to interpret; they are not part of the conversation, and any personal asides or additions only cause confusion.

This professional distance is part of an established code of ethics for interpreters. Confidentiality is also part of the code, as is impartiality (strong biases toward a subject matter can affect the ability to interpret accurately). An interpreter also has the responsibility of educating the public about deaf issues. Before going to work as an interpreter, candidates should be aware of the complete code of ethics as established by RID.

QUICK FACTS

ALTERNATE TITLE(S)
Deaf Interpreters, Tactile Interpreters, Trilingual Interpreters

DUTIES
Help people who use sign language communicate with people who can hear and speak; translate a message from spoken words to signs, and from signs to spoken words

SALARY RANGE
$23,160 to $44,190 to $78,520+

WORK ENVIRONMENT
Primarily Indoors

BEST GEOGRAPHIC LOCATION(S)
Opportunities are available throughout the country

MINIMUM EDUCATION LEVEL
Bachelor's Degree

SCHOOL SUBJECTS
Foreign Language, Social Studies, Speech

EXPERIENCE
Internships; volunteer experience

PERSONALITY TRAITS
Helpful, Social, Talkative

SKILLS
Foreign Language, Interpersonal, Public Speaking

CERTIFICATION OR LICENSING
Recommended

SPECIAL REQUIREMENTS
None

EMPLOYMENT PROSPECTS
Excellent

ADVANCEMENT PROSPECTS
Fair

OUTLOOK
Much Faster than the Average

NOC
5125

O*NET-SOC
27-3091.00

CAREER LADDER

Interpreting Business Owner

Certified Interpreter

Tutor

EARNINGS

Freelance interpreters can charge by the hour or the day, providing services to a variety of organizations and institutions. Their fees will be determined primarily by their skills and experience. Other factors include the type of certification held, educational background, and previous employer. A beginning interpreter will charge about $12 to $25 per hour, and an experienced interpreter can charge from $50 to $60 per hour.

According to the U.S. Department of Labor, interpreters and translators of all types had median hourly earnings of $21.24 (or $44,190 annually) in May 2015. The lowest paid 10 percent made less than $23,160 annually, and the highest paid 10 percent made more than $78,520 annually.

Interpreters living in large cities like Washington, D.C., New York, Los Angeles, or Chicago will have many opportunities to interpret and will be able to charge more. Living in a city with a deaf college or residential school, or a college where there is a lot of deaf research and cultural study will also increase business opportunities. Some rural areas may offer good, varied work for an interpreter.

WORK ENVIRONMENT

Working as an interpreter can be stressful. When interpreting from ASL to English, or from English to ASL, translators must make many quick decisions. The two languages are very different structurally, and an inexperienced interpreter can get lost in their complexities. In some situations, such as in a court case or in a public presentation or performance, many people are relying on the interpreter's ability to translate messages clearly, quickly, and accurately. But in other situations, such as one-on-one interviews or counseling sessions, things can be more relaxed. Interpreters should only accept the assignments they feel they can perform well and with confidence. This will help lower the stress level.

Generally, interpreters work inside, in a variety of settings, including offices, meeting halls, and classrooms. They may be interpreting for just one person, a small group, or a very large group. Though working directly with many different people, the interpreter's role is limited to that of a translator.

EXPLORING

Many books about sign language and interpreting have been published and can give students a good idea of the demands of the job. To find publications on sign language and interpreting, visit the local library, or contact the Registry of Interpreters for the Deaf for its list of publications. *Train Go Sorry: Inside a Deaf World* (Vintage Books, 1995), by Leah Hager Cohen, is a vivid and authentic account of life as a hearing person within the deaf community. Cohen also describes her experiences as an interpreter and the particular problems with which she was confronted.

Some exposure to American Sign Language will help you decide if interpreting is for you. Try to learn some sign language, or visit a place in your community (such as a religious service, town meeting, or community-sponsored event) where signing is used. If courses in ASL are not available, you should study Spanish, German, French, or any foreign language course, as learning another language will help to improve your translating and comprehension skills.

An excellent way to gain insight into the career of an interpreter is to talk to an interpreter, a teacher of deaf students, or any other professional who works with deaf people. In some cases, you may be allowed to watch an interpreter at work in the courtroom, classroom, or at a presentation.

EDUCATION AND TRAINING REQUIREMENTS
High School

In high school, interested students should take English and composition courses, as well as foreign language courses. ASL is taught in some high schools and some community learning centers.

Postsecondary Training

Many colleges offer sign language courses, courses in deaf culture, and some offer certificate, baccalaureate, and master's programs in deaf studies. Earning a college degree is highly recommended because it will help you to land better jobs and receive higher pay. A postsecondary education will also provide you with the background and skills necessary for passing the certification exams.

Visit the Registry of Interpreters for the Deaf's Web site, https://www.rid.org, for a database of postsecondary programs that offer interpreter education.

Other Education or Training

The Registry of Interpreters for the Deaf offers workshops, classes, and other continuing education opportunities. Recent offerings included "I'm Graduating...Now What?," "Best Practices in Interpreting," and "Deaf-Blind Interpreting." The Alexander Graham Bell Association for the Deaf and Hard of Hearing offers seminars such as "Identifying and Managing Pediatric Hearing Loss" and "Auditory-Verbal Practice: State of the Art." Contact these organizations for more information.

■ CERTIFICATION, LICENSING, AND SPECIAL REQUIREMENTS
Certification or Licensing
The National Interpreter Certification Program is cosponsored by the National Association of the Deaf (NAD) and the Registry of Interpreters for the Deaf (RID). Certification is awarded to applicants who pass a multiple-choice knowledge examination, an interview, and a performance examination. RID/NAD certification is the only national certification for sign language interpreters. The RID/NAD also offer the following specialty certifications: conditional legal interpreting permit-relay, specialist certificate: legal, and specialist certificate: performing arts.

Most qualified sign language interpreters without certification are in the process of getting certified. Tests are expensive and are only offered at various times of the year, at random sites. As a result, interpreters don't take the tests until they are certain they can pass them. Certificants must keep their certification valid by earning continuing education credits via a RID-approved sponsor. Contact RID for further information regarding continuing education requirements.

■ EXPERIENCE, SKILLS, AND PERSONALITY TRAITS
Previous education and experience (via internships, part-time jobs, etc.) are required to work as a sign language or oral interpreter.

Interpreters should be interested in the ways people communicate. They should also be prepared to learn all about complex languages, and to take on the responsibility of conveying accurate messages from one person to another. Sign language and oral interpreting is difficult and demanding work. It requires a thorough understanding of both English and ASL. Interpreters must also be honest and trustworthy—people will be relying upon them to get their messages and meanings across.

Some experience with the deaf community is very important. Though interpreters may spend many hours studying ASL, they will need to see the language in use among deaf people to gain a more complete understanding of ASL. This will require a commitment to a continuing education in deaf culture. Interpreters should be aware of the issues that affect deaf people, such as the debate of ASL versus oralism, or special residential schooling versus mainstreaming into an English-based classroom. They also need to learn about

Sign language interpreters assist a tornado disaster victim in Alabama. (David Fine. FEMA.)

the technological tools used by deaf people: devices that assist in amplification, phone calls, and watching television and movies.

It is also important that interpreters remain on an equal level with the clientele they serve. The interpreter should remain cooperative and respect the client's self-esteem and independence.

■ EMPLOYMENT PROSPECTS
Employers
There is a demand for deaf interpreters in many fields. Possible employers include public health agencies, employment agencies, hearing and speech clinics, hospitals, rehabilitation centers, public schools, trade and technical schools, colleges and universities, business and industry, government agencies, theaters, television stations, churches and religious agencies, law enforcement agencies, and the courts.

Sign language and oral interpreters typically work in one of three categories: as salaried interpreters for an agency that provides interpreting services to individual clients, companies, and organizations; as freelance interpreters who must find their own clients; or as contract interpreters, who work under contract for an agency for a set period of time.

Starting Out
Once sign language skills have been sufficiently developed, interpreting students may then tutor deaf students or volunteer in a social service agency that works with deaf clients. In either case, they should become familiar with the deaf community centers and any other deaf organizations in the area. The more experience with deaf people they acquire, the smoother the certification process will be. Also, to help prepare for certification, students should study the Registry of Interpreters for

KEY SKILLS FOR ORAL INTERPRETERS

DID YOU KNOW?

Oral interpreters must

- be speech-readable
- be naturally expressive when speaking
- have excellent short-term memory
- be able to concentrate for long periods of time in the middle of all kinds of distractions
- have a great knowledge of the English language
- have a degree of flexibility and open-mindedness
- be comfortable in front of large groups of people
- have knowledge of speech production and speechreading
- have physical stamina and endurance
- be able to easily understand the speech of a wide variety of deaf speakers
- be able to speak inaudibly when interpreting to the deaf

Source: Registry of Interpreters for the Deaf

the Deaf (RID) Code of Ethics and books and videos recommended by RID. Once certified, interpreters can be listed in various directories, including directories published by RID.

■ ADVANCEMENT PROSPECTS

Because most interpreters work on a freelance basis, the best way to advance is to take on more clients and to remain active in the community. The key to becoming a successful interpreter is a continued study of language and deaf culture. By being part of a deaf community, interpreters can always improve their grasp of ASL. Just as the English language grows and changes, so does ASL. New developments require new signs, and some old signs become outdated. Also, by staying involved with the deaf community, interpreters can make their services readily available.

To retain certification, interpreters are required to earn continuing education units. Continuing education will allow them to maintain their skills and learn about new developments in interpreting. With a background of continuing education, interpreters can attract more clients and organizations, as well as charge higher fees.

■ OUTLOOK

The U.S. Department of Labor reports that employment for interpreters and translators, including sign language and oral interpreters, is expected to grow by 29 percent, much faster than the average for all careers through 2024. According to the *Occupational Outlook Handbook*, "demand for American Sign Language interpreters is expected to grow rapidly, driven by the increasing use of video relay services, which allow people to conduct online video calls and use a sign language interpreter." Additionally, legislation enacted over the last 20 years has increased demand for interpreters. More deaf students are getting a postsecondary education because of access to classroom interpreters. The elderly population is growing as well, a population threatened with a number of disorders that can lead to hearing impairment. Society recognizes the need to involve more deaf people in the larger community and to pay more attention to deaf culture.

The U.S. Census Bureau reports that "across all age groups, in the United States, approximately 1,000,000 people over five years of age are 'functionally deaf'; more than half are over 65 years of age." Eighteen percent of American adults 45–64 years old, 30 percent of adults 65–74 years old, and 47 percent of adults 75 years old or older have a hearing loss, according to the National Institute on Deafness and Other Communication Disorders.

The role of the sign language interpreter will change as the deaf community changes. An interpreter's job can be greatly affected by the politics of the deaf community. There is much controversy concerning how deaf children should be educated and how involved deaf children need be with the hearing population. Some members of the deaf community want to be classified as a minority group instead of as a disability group; however, this would prevent deaf people from receiving most of the benefits they now receive, including interpreters in the schools. It could also result in difficulty "mainstreaming" deaf students into public schools. Without the interpreters guaranteed by the Americans with Disabilities Act, the parents of deaf students would have to hire their own interpreters, or send their children to residential schools.

For the last few years, however, legislation has fully supported mainstreaming. Government has even been moving toward "full inclusion," or mainstreaming, of all deaf students. This causes concern among many members of the deaf community—full inclusion could mean deaf students would not be allowed the opportunity of a special education environment.

Many more deaf people are enrolling in postsecondary programs, and occupational opportunities have improved for highly educated deaf people. But the overall employment rates for deaf people have not improved much. Interpreters may become more involved in correcting this imbalance; employee assistance programs will need interpreters to help train and integrate deaf people in new jobs. Businesses may also provide special programs for their deaf employees to help them earn promotions. Social services need also to focus on helping young ethnic-minority deaf persons. A number of problems affect this group. Programs need to be established to help them become prepared for postsecondary education.

Because of such legislation as the Americans with Disabilities Act, opportunities will be good for sign language interpreters. In addition, the increased demand for interpreters in the schools and in the workplace has resulted in a shortage of qualified professionals.

UNIONS AND ASSOCIATIONS

Sign language and oral interpreters can join the American Federation of Government Employees, a union that represents government workers. The Registry of Interpreters for the Deaf is a membership organization that "plays a leading role in advocating for excellence in the delivery of interpretation and transliteration services between people who use sign language and people who use spoken language." It offers a wealth of career resources for aspiring and current interpreters. The Alexander Graham Bell Association for the Deaf and Hard of Hearing is an advocacy organization for those with hearing loss. It provides continuing education opportunities and resources for people who are deaf or who have hearing loss. The American Speech-Language-Hearing Association, a membership organization for audiologists; speech-language pathologists; speech, language, and hearing scientists; audiology and speech-language pathology support personnel; and students, provides good background information on hearing disorders.

TIPS FOR ENTRY

1. Search job listings at http://rid.org/listings/browse-categories/4/job-listings/ and http://www.listeningandspokenlanguage.org/Jobs.
2. Join the Registry of Interpreters for the Deaf (RID) to receive a variety of member benefits, including a subscription to VIEWS, the organization's quarterly newsletter, and the Journal of Interpretation; reduced certification, continuing education, and conference fees; access to networking opportunities; and a personal listing on the organization's searchable database for interpreters.
3. Volunteer for RID committees, special interest groups, and workgroups to raise your profile and make networking contacts.

FOR MORE INFORMATION

This organization has programs, publications, and financial aid programs for the hearing-impaired.

Alexander Graham Bell Association for the Deaf and Hard of Hearing
3417 Volta Place, NW
Washington, D.C. 20007-2737
Tel: (202) 337-5220
Fax: (202) 337-8314
E-mail: info@agbell.org
http://listeningandspokenlanguage.org

For information on careers, educational programs, and employment, contact
American Speech-Language-Hearing Association
2200 Research Boulevard
Rockville, MD 20850-3289
Tel: (800) 638-8255
Fax: (301) 296-8580
http://www.asha.org

Visit the following Web site for information on education and careers for ASL interpreters:
Discover Interpreting
E-mail: info@discoverinterpreting.com
http://www.discoverinterpreting.com

For information about certification, contact
Registry of Interpreters for the Deaf (RID)
333 Commerce Street
Alexandria, VA 22314-2801
Tel: (703) 838-0030
Fax: (703) 838-0454
E-mail: ridinfo@rid.org
http://www.rid.org

Signal Mechanics

OVERVIEW

Signal mechanics, or signal and track switch repairers, are railroad employees who install, repair, and maintain the signals, signal equipment, and gate crossings that are part of the traffic control and communications systems along railroad tracks. They keep both electrical and mechanical components of signaling devices in good operating order by routinely inspecting and testing lights, circuits and wiring, crossing gates, and detection devices. There are approximately 8,680 signal and track switch repairers employed in the United States.

HISTORY

Railroad signals were developed to let train crews know about conditions on the track ahead of them. Signaling

QUICK FACTS

ALTERNATE TITLE(S)
Signal and Track Switch
  Repairers, Signal Maintainers

DUTIES
Install, repair, and maintain
  railroad signal equipment

SALARY RANGE
$43,070 to $63,840 to
  $80,590+

WORK ENVIRONMENT
Primarily Outdoors

BEST GEOGRAPHIC LOCATION(S)
Opportunities are available
  throughout the country

MINIMUM EDUCATION LEVEL
High School Diploma, Some
  Postsecondary Training

SCHOOL SUBJECTS
Computer Science, Mathematics,
  Technical/Shop

EXPERIENCE
Apprenticeship

PERSONALITY TRAITS
Conventional, Hands On,
  Technical

SKILLS
Math, Mechanical/Manual
  Dexterity

CERTIFICATION OR LICENSING
None

SPECIAL REQUIREMENTS
None

EMPLOYMENT PROSPECTS
Good

ADVANCEMENT PROSPECTS
Fair

OUTLOOK
Decline

NOC
7242

O*NET-SOC
49-9097.00

systems became necessary in the 19th century when early steam-driven trains began to move so quickly that they ran the risk of colliding with one another. Smooth rails and wheels allowed trains to carry heavy loads easily and efficiently, but as speeds and load weights increased, trains needed longer stopping distances. Train crews had to be sure that they were not headed toward another train coming in the opposite direction on the same track, and they had to maintain a safe distance between trains moving in the same direction.

The first attempt to avoid accidents was the adoption of a timetable system. This system was based on running trains on timed schedules, so that there was always a space between them. However, if a train broke down, the next train's crew had to be informed somehow so that it could react appropriately. In 1837, on a rail line in England, a telegraph system was introduced in which signals were sent on telegraph wires between stations up and down the tracks. The track was divided into blocks, or sections, with a signalman responsible for each block. As trains passed through the blocks, one signalman telegraphed messages to the next block, allowing the next signalman to decide whether it was safe for the train to proceed through that block.

In 1841, a system was devised for communicating with train operators using a mechanical version of semaphore arm signals. At night, when the signal flags could not be seen, a light source was used, with different colored lenses that were rotated in front of it. In time, various codes and rules were developed so that train crews could be kept informed about track conditions ahead as they moved from block to block.

As rail traffic increased, many refinements in signaling systems reduced the chances of human error and helped make train traffic run more smoothly. In 1872, an automatic block system was introduced in which the track itself was part of an electrical circuit, and various signals were activated when the train passed over the track. A modern version of this invention is the moving block system, in which a kind of zone is electronically maintained around a train, and the speed of nearby trains is regulated automatically. Today, traffic control in rail systems is largely centralized and computerized. Many trains and cars can be monitored at one time, and signals and switches can be operated remotely to manage the system with maximum safety and efficiency.

In order for these sophisticated controls to be effective, railroad signals and signaling equipment must function properly. Signal mechanics ensure that this vital equipment is working as intended.

■ THE JOB

Signal mechanics install, maintain, and repair signal equipment. Today's signal equipment includes computerized and electronic equipment detection devices and electronic grade crossing protection. To install signals, workers travel with road crews to designated areas. They place electrical wires, create circuits, and construct railway-highway crossing signals, such as flashers and gates. When signal mechanics install new signals or signal equipment, they or other crew members may have to dig holes and pour concrete foundations for the new equipment, or they may install precast concrete foundations. Because railroad signal systems are sometimes installed in the same areas as underground fiber-optic cables, signal mechanics must be familiar with marking systems and take great care in digging.

Signal mechanics who perform routine maintenance are generally responsible for a specified length of track. They are often part of a team of several signal mechanics, called a signal construction gang. They drive a truck along the track route, stopping to inspect and test crossings, signal lights, interlock equipment, and detection devices. When servicing battery-operated equipment, they check batteries, refilling them with water or replacing them with fresh ones if necessary. They use standard electrical testing devices to check signal circuits and wiring connections, and they replace any defective wiring, burned-out light bulbs, or broken colored lenses on light signals. They clean the lenses with a cloth and cleaning solution and lubricate moving parts on swinging signal arms and crossing gates. They tighten loose bolts, and open and close crossing gates to verify that the circuits and connections in the gates are working.

Signal mechanics are often required to travel long distances as repairs are needed. Many are assigned to a large region by their employer, such as the entire Midwest, or may even be on call to work anywhere in the nation. Generally, employees are responsible for providing their own transportation from their home to the work location. The railroad company pays the cost of hotel rooms and provides a meal allowance. When signal mechanics are required to travel, their workweek may begin on Sunday, when they travel to the work site so they can start early Monday. The workweek may then include four 10-hour days, or may be longer, depending on the urgency of the job.

Sometimes signal mechanics are dispatched to perform repairs at specific locations along the track in response to reports from other rail workers about damaged or malfunctioning equipment. In these cases, the worker analyzes the problem, repairs it, and checks to make sure that the equipment is functioning properly.

Signal mechanics also compile written reports that detail their inspection and repair activities, noting the mileage of the track that they have traveled and the locations where they have done work. Some mechanics may use hand-held computers to prepare reports and record data.

■ EARNINGS

According to the U.S. Department of Labor, signal and track switch repairers, a career that includes signal mechanics, had median hourly earnings of $30.69 (amounting to an annual salary of $63,840) in May 2015. Wages ranged from less than $20.71 per hour ($43,070 a year) to more than $38.74 per hour ($80,590 a year). Workers receive extra pay for overtime work.

In addition to regular earnings, signal mechanics receive fringe benefits such as employer contributions to health insurance and retirement plans, paid vacation days, and travel passes.

■ WORK ENVIRONMENT

Signal department workers do their work outdoors in a variety of weather conditions, sometimes at night. Some workers are regularly scheduled to be on call for emergency repairs.

There is variety in the kinds of signals a mechanic works on, and variety in the location of the work, so the job is rarely boring. In addition, workers in this field can take pride in the importance of their responsibilities, since railroad travel is heavily dependent upon the proper functioning of signals.

■ EXPLORING

A field trip to a rail yard can give you a firsthand idea of the work involved in this occupation. For a personalized view of the work, consider arranging an information interview with a railroad employee who is involved in maintaining communications or control equipment. You or your school counselor may be able to find such a professional through local railroad company offices or local branches of the Brotherhood of Railroad Signalmen. Go to the interview prepared to ask questions about the job. You will find that most people are pleased to talk about their work with those who show a sincere interest.

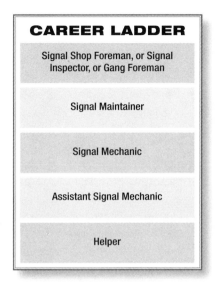

CAREER LADDER

Signal Shop Foreman, or Signal Inspector, or Gang Foreman

Signal Maintainer

Signal Mechanic

Assistant Signal Mechanic

Helper

■ EDUCATION AND TRAINING REQUIREMENTS
High School

Proven mechanical aptitude is very desirable, and a firm knowledge of electricity is a must. Because of the change in signaling technology in the railroad industry, railroads are requiring new job applicants to pass written tests that include AC/DC electronics. Therefore, you should take high school courses in electrical shop and electronics to give you a good background for this work. Take computer classes to familiarize yourself with this technology. Mathematics classes will also give you the skills you need to complete calculations and detailed work. Take English classes to hone your research, writing, and speaking skills. You will need these skills for completing reports.

Postsecondary Training

Signal mechanics must have at least a high school diploma, although some railroads have gone so far as to require applicants to have college degrees in electronics or electrical engineering. Some signal mechanics train for the field by completing an apprenticeship of up to four years. Other railroads will consider applicants who have military experience in electronics, or who possess a two-year degree in electronics from a technical school.

Workers are usually trained both on the job and in the classroom. Some of the biggest railroads have their own schools; the smaller ones often contract to send their employees to those schools. For example, Norfolk Southern sends its signal trainees to its training center in McDonough, Georgia, during which they are paid a training wage and lodging and meals are paid for during the one-week training course.

Subjects studied in the classroom include electrical and electronics theory; mathematics; signal apparatus,

HEAVY EQUIPMENT REPAIRERS

DID YOU KNOW?

In addition to the mechanics who repair and maintain signal equipment, other mechanics are needed to repair all of the heavy equipment necessary to keep a railroad running. These repairers are responsible for repairs to various types of heavy equipment, including tampers, ballast regulators, spike pullers, tie removers and inserters, graders, cranes, bulldozers, and tractors. Repairers are usually assigned to a truck equipped with a company radio, crane, and welder. They are required to have a commercial driver's license to drive these large trucks. Students interested in becoming heavy-equipment mechanics should take any available shop classes in high school, as well as English, speech, and math classes. Good oral communication skills are essential to explain to other workers how to use equipment, and mathematical knowledge is needed to understand blueprints.

protection devices, and circuits; federal railroad administration policies; and procedures related to signaling.

■ CERTIFICATION, LICENSING, AND SPECIAL REQUIREMENTS
Certification or Licensing
There are no certification or licensing requirements for signal mechanics.

■ EXPERIENCE, SKILLS, AND PERSONALITY TRAITS
Aspiring signal mechanics should obtain experience by participating in apprenticeships or by working as helpers to experienced signal mechanics.

Signal mechanics need to be able to climb, stoop, kneel, crouch, and reach, and they should also be agile, with a good sense of balance. They work outdoors in any kind of weather and may have to be active throughout the day, perhaps climbing poles or hand digging with shovels and picks. Good vision, normal hearing, and depth perception are important. Anyone who works with electrical wiring should have good color vision to distinguish color-coded wires. Alertness and quick reflexes are needed for working in potentially dangerous circumstances on ladders, near high-voltage lines, and on moving equipment. Some companies require drug testing of their employees.

■ EMPLOYMENT PROSPECTS
Employers
Approximately 8,680 signal and track switch repairers are employed in the United States. Signal mechanics may be employed by passenger lines or freight lines. They may work for one of the major railroads, such as BNSF Railway Company, Norfolk Southern, or CSX Corporation, or they may work for one of the 500 smaller short-line railroads across the country. Many of the passenger lines today are commuter lines located near large metropolitan areas. Signal mechanics who work for freight lines may work in rural or urban areas and travel more extensively than the shorter, daily commuter routes passenger railroad conductors make.

Starting Out
Prospective signal mechanics can contact the personnel offices of railroad companies for information about job opportunities. Another possibility is to check with the local, state, or national office of the Brotherhood of Railroad Signalmen. Because signal mechanic positions are often union positions, they follow structured hiring procedures, such as specific times of the year when applications are accepted. For instance, Norfolk Southern holds recruiting sessions on college campuses and in other settings. Applications are not sent out for union positions; rather, recruiting sessions are advertised in local newspapers, state job services, and schools. At these sessions, supervisors detail the open positions, answer questions, and oversee the application process. Some applicants may be selected for evaluations, which will be used to help determine who is hired.

On the job, beginners often start out in helper positions, doing simple tasks requiring little special skill. Helpers work under the supervision of experienced signal mechanics. Later, they may become assistants and signal maintainers, based on their seniority and how much they have learned.

■ ADVANCEMENT PROSPECTS
Workers generally advance from *helper* positions to become *assistant signal mechanics*, and from there to positions as *signal maintainers*. Other advanced positions include *signal shop foremen* and *signal inspectors*. These promotions, which are related to workers' seniority, sometimes take a number of years to achieve. Experienced signal mechanics can advance to such supervisory positions as *gang foremen*, directing and coordinating the activities of other signal mechanics. At one railroad, Norfolk Southern, signal mechanics are designated as *assistant signal persons* after qualifying as trainees. After completing two phases of training and based on seniority, assistant signal persons can bid for promotion to a signal maintainer position with territorial maintenance responsibilities.

■ OUTLOOK

The U.S. Department of Labor (DOL) predicts that employment for most railroad transportation occupations, including signal mechanics, will decline through 2024. Despite this prediction, the DOL says that job opportunities will be favorable because a large number of workers in the railroad industry are reaching retirement age. Because of the increasingly complex circuitry involved in the signaling systems, signal maintainers with the strongest technical training will be in the greatest demand in the coming years.

■ UNIONS AND ASSOCIATIONS

Most signal mechanics who work for the larger railroads are required to belong to a union—usually the Brotherhood of Railroad Signalmen. Those who work for the smaller railroads are typically nonunionized. The Association of American Railroads and the American Short Line & Regional Railroad Association are membership organizations for railroads.

■ TIPS FOR ENTRY

1. Search job listings at http://www.brs.org and http://www.rrb.gov/PandS/Jobs/rrjobs.asp.
2. Join the Brotherhood of Railroad Signalmen to increase your chances of landing a job and receiving fair pay for your work.
3. Acquire a part-time job or join a community group with an emphasis on electronics and mechanics.

■ FOR MORE INFORMATION

For information on short line and regional railroads (that account for 9 percent of the rail industry's freight revenue and 12 percent of railroad employment), contact

American Short Line & Regional Railroad Association (ASLRRA)
50 F Street, NW, Suite 7020
Washington, D.C. 20001-1507
Tel: (202) 628-4500
Fax: (202) 628-6430
http://www.aslrra.org

For general information on the railroad industry, contact
Association of American Railroads (AAR)
425 Third Street, SW
Washington, D.C. 20024-3206
Tel: (202) 639-2100
http://www.aar.org

For information on union membership and the career of railroad signal mechanic, contact

Brotherhood of Railroad Signalmen (BRS)
917 Shenandoah Shores Road
Front Royal, VA 22630-6418
Tel: (540) 622-6522
Fax: (540) 622-6532
http://www.brs.org

For information on the railroad industry, visit
Railway Age
55 Broad St., 26th Floor
New York, NY 10004
Tel: (212) 620-7200
Fax: (212) 633-1863
http://www.railwayage.com

For information on magazines for train enthusiasts, visit
Trains.com
http://www.trains.com

Silverware Artisans and Workers

■ OVERVIEW

Silverware artisans include *designers* and *artists*, as well as *silversmiths* or *precious-metal workers*, who are skilled workers and repairers of silver and a variety of other metals, including gold and platinum. Silverware workers manufacture metal utensils used at the table for holding, serving, and handling food and drink, such as platters, pitchers, forks, and spoons.

The creation and manufacturing of silverware falls under a number of other areas as well, such as industrial design, metalworking, commercial art and design, and machine operation. Approximately 28,050 people are employed in the U.S. silverware manufacturing industry.

■ HISTORY

People have used an interesting variety of eating utensils throughout the ages. Dishes, flatware, and cutlery of all kinds have been made from wood, bone, stone, volcanic glass, shell, and a number of metals, including silver, tin, gold, pewter, and stainless steel.

Shells were probably the first rudimentary spoons. Primitive forks were just sticks with sharpened ends. And the first knives, sharpened with bone, wood, or stone, were used not only for cutting food but for warfare as well. By the Middle Ages, eating utensils became ornately decorated and more developed, according to each of their required uses.

QUICK FACTS

ALTERNATE TITLE(S)
Annealers, Finishing Machine Operators, Flatware Designers, Flatware Makers, Flatware Press Operators, Hammersmiths, Hollow Handle Bench Workers, Polishing Machine Operators, Precious-Metal Workers, Profile-Saw Operators, Profile Trimmers, Silversmiths, Solderers

DUTIES
Design, repair, and manufacture silverware

SALARY RANGE
$15,080 to $41,920 to $62,170+

WORK ENVIRONMENT
Primarily Indoors

BEST GEOGRAPHIC LOCATION(S)
A concentration of silverware manufacturing plants is located on the East Coast, especially in New England

MINIMUM EDUCATION LEVEL
High School Diploma, Apprenticeship

SCHOOL SUBJECTS
Art, Mathematics, Technical/Shop

EXPERIENCE
Apprenticeship

PERSONALITY TRAITS
Artistic, Hands On, Technical

SKILLS
Drawing/Design, Mechanical/Manual Dexterity

CERTIFICATION OR LICENSING
None

SPECIAL REQUIREMENTS
None

EMPLOYMENT PROSPECTS
Poor

ADVANCEMENT PROSPECTS
Fair

OUTLOOK
Decline

NOC
5244, 9227, 9537

O*NET-SOC
51-9071.07

With the invention of electroplating in the mid-18th century, the silver-plating industry experienced enormous growth in the United States. The process, which involves coating inexpensive metals with silver, became a common method for producing attractive tableware.

Silversmiths of the day were regarded as sculptors of sorts. Able to shape materials into pieces both attractive and functional, these artisans created not only utensils but also bowls, creamers, teapots, pitchers, cups, and trays.

Paul Revere was perhaps the best-known silversmith in the United States. A number of other craftspeople also played key roles in the emerging silver industry in colonial America. James Geddy Jr., for example, sold a variety of items that both he and other artisans made from 1766 to 1777. These pieces included silver flatware and hollowware, such as teaspoons, tureen ladles, cans, and tongs. Geddy's brother-in-law William Waddill, another well-known colonial silversmith, provided engraving services.

Today, about 60 different kinds of craftspeople work in the industry, transforming silver, stainless steel, nickel, zinc, copper, and other metals into contemporary silverware. Regardless of the metals used, many of the steps in the silverware manufacturing process are essentially the same.

■ THE JOB

Silverware manufacturing requires contributions from many different types of artisans and production workers. The process begins with *flatware designers*, who, after considering current market trends and the products offered by competitors, make sketches or computerized three-dimensional models of styles and patterns for new lines of tableware.

Once management approves proposed designs, they are given to *model makers*, who create handmade, full-size models of all pieces in the line, sculpting or carving them in plastic, clay, or plaster. Based on these models, the designs are often altered. Then model makers prepare models of the final version of the tableware designs, which serve as patterns for the molds and dies that will be used in producing the actual silverware.

Die makers construct dies, which are tools that can stamp, shape, or cut metal. These dies are used to create forks, spoons, knives, and other utensils out of flat sheets of stainless steel, sterling silver, nickel silver, brass, or other metal. *Flatware press operators* feed the sheets into presses that cut the metal into flat blanks roughly the same size and shape as the finished utensils. The blanks are then put into a drop press, which shapes each blank into the desired piece. Next, *flatware makers*, or *annealers*, heat (or anneal) the metal, softening it to help reduce the possibility of warping. Annealed flatware is then immersed in a chemical solution to cool and clean it.

Once all pieces have been thoroughly cleaned, *trimmers* use bench grinding machines or hand files to remove any undesirable irregularities on the surface and to round off edges in accordance with the design. Finally, the flatware is buffed and polished to a smooth finish by *finishing machine operators* or *polishing machine operators.*

While the process just described is used for most flatware, some pieces require the skills of additional specialists as well. The handles of many kinds of knives, for example, are stamped out as two separate halves that are joined together by *solderers* or *hollow handle bench workers.* The handles can be left hollow or filled so that the knife has more weight. *Knife assemblers* then cement the knife blades into the handles. They check the finished pieces for alignment and clean any excess cement from the blade using a metal pick and brush. Inspected knives are placed in a rack to dry, while those that are rejected are set aside on a separate tray.

The manufacturing process for hollowware items such as teapots, trays, and sugar bowls also calls for specialized workers because these pieces can be quite ornate. Most hollowware is made of a base metal, such as brass. The brass comes in rolled sheets, which workers cut into usable sections. *Press operators* mold the brass sheeting into the desired shapes using large presses. Then *profile-saw operators* and *profile trimmers* trim away excess metal from the edges. Other parts of hollowware vessels, such as handles, legs, and border trim, are made separately and attached by silverware assemblers using screws, bolts, pins, or adhesives. These parts may be cast in molds using molten Britannia metal, an alloy similar to pewter. Objects like goblets and candlesticks are stretched and shaped by spinners who use hand tools and bench-lathes.

Silversmiths and *hammersmiths* also create hollowware. Silversmiths are skilled craftworkers who perform many kinds of tasks related to the fabrication of fine hollowware, such as annealing metal, shaping it with various tools, adding embossed designs, and soldering parts. In addition, they repair damaged pieces using hammers, tongs, pliers, dollies, anvils, tracing punches, and other tools. Hammersmiths also repair hollowware using many of the same tools. Both silversmiths and hammersmiths work with not only silver but also a variety of other metals, including pewter, chromium, nickel, and brass.

A final step often used in manufacturing flatware and hollowware is electroplating, a process that uses electric current to coat a metal with one or more thin layers of another metal. Using the electroplating process, workers coat articles made of an inexpensive metal with a precious metal, such as gold, silver, or platinum.

Platers, or *electroplaters,* first clean unplated articles in vats of cleaning solutions. They may initially coat the items with nickel or copper, either of which allows the plating metal to attach to the base metal. Then electroplaters suspend an unplated item and a piece of the plating metal in a tank containing a chemical solution. When they run electricity through the apparatus, plating metal is deposited on the piece, creating an item that looks as attractive as one made entirely of the precious metal. At the end of the process, platers check the finished objects for thickness using such instruments as calipers and micrometers. Platers are also responsible for marking, measuring, and covering any areas that have failed to be plated.

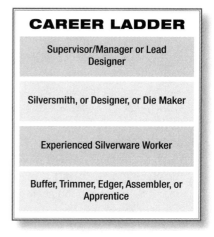

CAREER LADDER

Supervisor/Manager or Lead Designer

Silversmith, or Designer, or Die Maker

Experienced Silverware Worker

Buffer, Trimmer, Edger, Assembler, or Apprentice

■ EARNINGS

Production workers in the silverware industry are often paid an hourly rate. Alternatively, they can earn piecework or incentive rates, which are based on the amount of work they complete. Earnings vary with the particular job and skill level of the worker.

Some unskilled workers start as low as minimum wage ($15,080 annually based on a 40-hour week). However, in time they may be able to increase their pay by earning piecework rates. Earnings are generally higher for workers with special training and skills. The U.S. Department of Labor reports the following mean annual earnings for workers in the jewelry and silver manufacturing industry in May 2015: assemblers and fabricators, $30,900; commercial and industrial designers, $56,950; computer-controlled machine tool operators, metal and plastic, $38,330; machine tool cutting setters, operators, and tenders, metal and plastic, $30,350; machinists, $44,040; team assemblers, $27,290; and tool and die makers, $50,670. Silversmiths and other precious-metal workers earned on average between $19,950 and $62,170 a year, with a median salary of $41,920.

In addition to their regular pay, production workers and designers usually receive such benefits as health insurance, pensions, paid vacation days and sick leave, employee assistance programs, and profit sharing plans. Workers may also be able to buy company products at a discount.

■ WORK ENVIRONMENT

Silverware factories usually have open and pleasant work areas. Many of the machines that silverware production

PAUL REVERE

Known in the history books for his midnight ride, Paul Revere (1735–1818) actually began his professional career as a silversmith. Working as an apprentice to his father, Revere developed a variety of patterns for casting handles and other parts.

When his father died in 1754, Revere was too young to run the shop on his own. However, within a year of returning from the French and Indian War, he began operating what became a very busy and thriving business. In addition to training young people interested in the silversmith trade, Revere employed a number of journeymen who had completed their training but lacked the money to establish their own shops.

Revere was very involved in the fabrication of silver in the early years of his career. After the Revolution, however, he started to establish other businesses. And by the late 1700s, his son Paul took over the daily operation of the silversmith shop.

Source: http://www.paulreverehouse.org

workers use are small but noisy. The work is not physically strenuous, but some jobs, such as operating punch presses, are monotonous. Some employees may be required to lift and carry heavy objects, but mechanical devices perform much of this work.

To avoid injury, workers usually wear protective gear, such as safety glasses, ear protectors, and heavy gloves. Although electroplaters, in particular, are often exposed to strong and hazardous chemicals, factories have ventilation systems installed to remove fumes generated in the electroplating process, and workers receive safety training, as well as special clothing, to reduce any possible risks or danger.

Silverware designers work in well-lit, quiet, modern offices or studios, at drafting tables or computer terminals. They often work alone but spend time consulting with other employees as well. Sometimes they visit production areas to get a feel for the manufacturing process or to check on the progress of their designs.

Designers may travel to attend meetings, seminars, or conventions or to conduct research on design trends in the market.

Workweeks for all silverware industry employees average 40 hours, though flatware designers may have to work additional hours to meet specific deadlines. Similarly, production workers are often required to put in overtime when there are big orders to complete. At other times, companies have very few orders and must lay off manufacturing workers for short periods of time.

■ EXPLORING

A part-time or summer job in a silverware factory can provide you with an excellent opportunity to learn about the silverware industry. However, with relatively few plants in the United States, such jobs are difficult to obtain. For this reason, you may want to consider a position at a metal manufacturing or machining company. Such a position can offer you the experience you'll need when you're ready to look for a job in silverware manufacturing.

If you're interested in silverware design or silversmithing, sampling similar activities will allow you to get a taste of some of the skills you'll need. While in school, take classes in ornamental metalwork, jewelry making, woodworking, ceramics, sketching, and drafting. If these courses are not offered, check to see if your local community college or art center offers more specialized art classes.

You can also read professional magazines about art, design, manufacturing, and industry-specific topics to become familiar with the field and keep abreast of new products, trends, and developments. *Handmade Business* (http://handmade-business.com/), for example, is specifically aimed at craftsworkers, while *Silver Magazine* (http://www.silvermag.com) focuses on the field of silver and the products made from this material. *MetalForming Magazine* (http://www.metalformingmagazine.com) and other trade publications may also be of interest. In addition, you might want to contact Brynmorgen Press (http://www.brynmorgen.com) for books on metalsmithing.

■ EDUCATION AND TRAINING REQUIREMENTS
High School

Although there are no formal educational requirements for silverware manufacturing workers, most employers prefer to hire high school graduates. Courses in mathematics, especially plane geometry, will prove to be valuable once you begin working in the field. Classes in such subjects as drafting, sketching, computer science, and shop are important for aspiring toolmakers, die cutters, machinists, and bench workers.

If you're planning on a career as a silverware designer, art courses at the high school level are a must. In particular, classes in design, computer graphics, drawing, and drafting are essential. In addition, you should take a sampling of liberal arts and business courses, including English, marketing, psychology, and management.

Postsecondary Training

You can obtain postsecondary training through technical or vocational schools, community colleges, art schools, or correspondence courses. Course work usually includes applied mathematics, manufacturing arts, casting, enameling, metalworking, silversmithing, plating, and tool-making. Specialized courses are often offered as well, including tool designing and programming, blueprint reading, and mechanical drawing.

If you aim to become skilled in a specialized craft, you should consider an apprenticeship, which generally lasts four to five years. Apprentices learn on the job as they work in a silverware plant under the supervision of experienced craftworkers. They also receive related classroom instruction. Apprenticeships are the usual method by which workers are trained in silversmithing, soft soldering, spinning, engraving, model making, drafting, machining, tool and die making, and a variety of other areas.

If you are interested in silverware art and design, you will need a college degree in a field such as industrial or applied design, along with training in fine art and the properties of metals. More than 100 schools offer a bachelor's degree in metalsmithing and industrial design. Some colleges also offer master's degrees in these disciplines. Many schools require a prospective designer to complete a year of basic design and art courses before they are allowed formal entry into a design program. Students enrolled in a design program spend many hours designing three-dimensional objects. They gain experience using metalworking and woodworking machines to construct their designs. Among the courses they should take are drafting, drawing, and computer-aided design.

■ CERTIFICATION, LICENSING, AND SPECIAL REQUIREMENTS
Certification or Licensing

There are no specific certification or licensing requirements for silverware artisans and workers.

■ EXPERIENCE, SKILLS, AND PERSONALITY TRAITS

No experience is needed to work in unskilled positions, but those with prior work experience will increase their chances of landing a job, getting promoted, and possibly earning higher pay. Skilled positions such as tool and die makers and designers require the completion of an apprenticeship or previous experience.

To be a silverware manufacturing worker, you need to be precise in your work and have good concentration. You should also have good vision and manual dexterity. Depending on your position, you may have to handle repetitive tasks as part of the job. Die makers, in particular, should be extremely patient, since their work requires highly precise computation. They also need to have mechanical aptitude and physical strength.

If you plan to work in design, you must be artistic and creative and have an eye for color and beauty. To be successful, you should have a thorough knowledge of the flatware industry, specifically the manufacturing techniques that are used in production. In addition, you will need to keep abreast of current trends and develop work accordingly.

Freelance designers must be willing to work long hours. They also need to be organized, detail-minded, self-disciplined, and prepared for possible downtime.

■ EMPLOYMENT PROSPECTS
Employers

About 28,050 people are employed in the U.S. silverware manufacturing industry. Of the plants that manufacture flatware and hollowware in the United States, most are located in New England, particularly in Massachusetts and Connecticut. The major companies in the industry include Gorham (Lenox Corporation), Oneida, Towle (Lifetime Sterling), Wallace, Lunt, and Reed and Barton, with four of the biggest firms accounting for over half of the U.S. market.

Many smaller companies are located in Rhode Island, Maryland, and other parts of the country. Among them are Regent Sheffield, Lifetime Brands, and Tableware International. Foreign manufacturers in Japan, Brazil, and various European countries specialize in the production and design of silverware as well.

In addition to production workers, manufacturing companies employ both staff and freelance flatware designers. These creative professionals also work at independent companies that provide flatware designs to manufacturers, or for upscale retailers such as New York's Tiffany & Co.

Starting Out

You can apply directly, either in person or in writing, to manufacturing firms that may be hiring new workers. Leads to specific jobs can sometimes be found through state employment service offices or help wanted ads in trade publications and local newspapers. If you graduate from a technical training program, you may be able to learn about openings through your school's placement office.

Many newly hired manufacturing workers begin as buffers, trimmers, edgers, or assemblers. Others learn skilled crafts through apprenticeship programs. If you're interested in entering the field as a tool and die maker, keep in mind that these specialists frequently move up from other related jobs, such as machine operators or machinists. (Tool and die makers are frequently considered advanced machinists.)

If you are considering the design side of the silverware industry, check out *Innovation*, the newsletter of the Industrial Designers Society of America (http://www.idsa.org/innovation) for ads placed by companies seeking design professionals. In addition, available positions are frequently posted at the Web sites of industry-related associations, as well as on job bulletin boards at colleges and universities and through school placement offices.

You will find better job opportunities if you obtain some experience in the industry before applying for positions. A part-time or summer job at a flatware company or another related firm can provide such experience. In addition, you should assemble a portfolio of artwork and designs to show potential employers during interviews.

ADVANCEMENT PROSPECTS

Silverware workers who can produce high-quality pieces quickly and consistently have the best chances for advancement. Unskilled workers can apply to become apprentices, learning such specialized skills as soft soldering, engraving, spinning, and toolmaking. Skilled workers may be promoted to supervisory positions.

Production workers with many years of on-the-job experience sometimes move up to positions as silversmiths or designers. Experienced die makers, in particular, may move into supervisory and managerial jobs. Others become *tool designers* or *tool programmers* in related industries.

In the design area, highly skilled professionals may advance to become *lead designers* or *directors* of design departments. At companies where the design department is very small, advancement opportunities are often limited. Instead of promotions, designers at these firms are frequently given more job responsibilities and higher salaries. Well-known, highly experienced designers with strong financial backing can start their own consulting firms or concentrate solely on freelance work.

Production workers and design professionals alike can also advance to other fields that require their skills, such as glass manufacturing, ceramics, and ornamental metalwork.

OUTLOOK

Employment levels in the U.S. silverware industry have been declining for years, and the trend is expected to continue for the foreseeable future, with employment opportunities expected to decline through 2024. Among the reasons for this decline are competition from silverware manufacturers in other countries (especially those in Europe and Asia), high prices for silver and steel, and a decreased demand for expensive gifts, such as flatware settings and tea services.

Like many other fields, the silverware industry is affected by the health of the overall economy. Consumers simply don't buy expensive silverware more than once or twice in a lifetime. Many who are buying silver are increasingly price-conscious and may therefore choose simplicity over formality. On the factory side, many managers are cutting equipment budgets. In sum, reduced levels of customer spending and pessimism about the future of the economy are resulting in fewer opportunities for silverware industry workers.

On the technology front, the implementation of labor-saving machinery is resulting in increased productivity. However, according to the *Occupational Outlook Handbook*, lower skilled workers who manually operate machines are likely to find their positions eliminated because their jobs can be easily automated.

Despite the dreary prospects, some job openings will continue to be available in the field, but most will come about as workers move to other jobs or leave the workforce altogether. In addition, competition for these jobs will be fierce. Designers, silversmiths, tool and die makers, and others who have flexible skills and talents have the best chances for continued employment in their specific specialty. Workers who are willing to participate in continuing education programs and/or relocate will also have a competitive edge within the silverware manufacturing and design industry.

UNIONS AND ASSOCIATIONS

Silverware artisans and workers may be represented by the International Brotherhood of Teamsters and other unions. Other organizations for silverware industry workers include the Industrial Designers Society of America, Manufacturing Jewelers and Suppliers of America, National Tooling and Machining Association, The Silver Institute, and the Society of American Silversmiths.

TIPS FOR ENTRY

1. For job listings, visit:
   - http://www.idsa.org/jobboard
   - http://www.silversmithing.com/jobs.htm
   - http://www.ntma.org/resources
2. Land a part-time job at a silverware manufacturing plant to hone your skills and make industry contacts.
3. Talk with silverware artisans and workers about their careers. Ask them for advice on preparing for and entering the field.

■ FOR MORE INFORMATION

For information on education and careers, contact
Industrial Designers Society of America (IDSA)
555 Grove Street, Suite 200
Herndon, VA 20170-4728
Tel: (703) 707-6000
http://www.idsa.org

This association is a national trade organization supporting the jewelry/metals industry. For information, contact
Manufacturing Jewelers and Suppliers of America (MJSA)
57 John L. Dietsch Square
Attleboro Falls, MA 02763-1027
Tel: (800) 444-6572
Fax: (508) 316-1429
E-mail: info@mjsa.org
http://www.mjsa.org

For information on custom precision manufacturing, contact
National Tooling and Machining Association (NTMA)
1357 Rockside Road
Cleveland, OH 44134-2776
Tel: (800) 248-6862
Fax: (216) 264-2840
E-mail: info@ntma.org
http://www.ntma.org

The Silver Institute serves as the industry's voice in increasing public understanding of the many uses of silver. For information, contact
The Silver Institute
1400 I Street, NW, Suite #550
Washington, D.C. 20005
Tel: (202) 835-0185
http://www.silverinstitute.org

This is the nation's only professional organization solely devoted to the preservation and promotion of contemporary silversmithing, specifically in the areas of hollowware, flatware, and sculpture. For more information, contact
Society of American Silversmiths (SAS)
PO Box 786
West Warwick, RI 02893-0610
Tel: (401) 461-6840
Fax: (401) 828-0162
E-mail: sas@silversmithing.com
http://www.silversmithing.com

Singers

■ OVERVIEW

Professional *singers* perform opera, gospel, blues, rock, jazz, folk, classical, country, and other musical genres before an audience or in recordings. Singers are musicians who use their voices as their instruments. They may perform as part of a band, choir, or other musical ensembles, or solo, whether with or without musical accompaniment. Singers and musicians hold approximately 40,110 jobs in the United States.

■ HISTORY

"Song is man's sweetest joy," said the Greek poet Museaeus in the eighth century B.C. Singers use their voices as instruments of sound and are capable of relating music that touches the soul. The verb *to sing* is related to the Greek term *omphe*, which means voice. In general, singing is related to music and thus to the Muses, the goddesses in Greek mythology who are said to watch over the arts and are sources of inspiration.

Singing, or vocal performance, is considered the mother of all music, and is thought of as an international language. Before musical instruments were created there existed the voice, which has had the longest and most significant influence on the development of all musical forms and materials that have followed.

A precise, formal history of the singing profession is not feasible in an article of this length, for singing evolved in different parts of the world and in diverse ways at various times. A 40,000-year-old cave painting in France suggests the earliest evidence of music; the painting shows a man playing a musical bow and dancing behind several reindeer. Most civilizations have had legends suggesting that gods created song, and many myths suggest that nymphs have passed the art of singing to us. The Chinese philosopher Confucius considered music, with its ability to portray emotions as diverse as joy and sorrow, anger and love, to be a significant aspect of a moral society.

There are certain differences between Eastern and Western music. In general, music of Middle Eastern civilizations has tended to be more complex in its melodies (although music from the Far East is often relatively simple). Western music has been greatly influenced by the organized systems of musical scales of ancient Greece and has evolved through various eras, which were rich and enduring but can be defined in general terms. The first Western musical era is considered to have been the medieval period (c. 850–1450), when the earliest surviving songs were written by 12th century French troubadours and German minnesingers;

QUICK FACTS

ALTERNATE TITLE(S)
Classical Singers, Folk Singers, Gospel Singers, Jazz Singers, Pop/Rock Singers, Professional Singers, Virtuosos

DUTIES
Sing and perform songs for audiences and audio and video recordings

SALARY RANGE
$19,136 to $50,336 to $143,478+

WORK ENVIRONMENT
Primarily Indoors

BEST GEOGRAPHIC LOCATION(S)
New York, Los Angeles, Nashville, Chicago, and Las Vegas

MINIMUM EDUCATION LEVEL
High School Diploma

SCHOOL SUBJECTS
Music, Speech, Theater/Dance

EXPERIENCE
Experience with a variety of singing styles recommended

PERSONALITY TRAITS
Creative, Outgoing, Social

SKILLS
Interpersonal, Performance, Music, and Acting, Public Speaking

CERTIFICATION OR LICENSING
None

SPECIAL REQUIREMENTS
None

EMPLOYMENT PROSPECTS
Fair

ADVANCEMENT PROSPECTS
Fair

OUTLOOK
Little Change or More Slowly than the Average

NOC
5133

O*NET-SOC
27-2042.00, 27-2042.01

these poet-musicians sang of love, nature, and religion. The next periods include the Renaissance (c. 1450–1600), during which the musical attitude was one of calm and self-restraint; the Baroque (c. 1600–1750), a time of extravagance, excitement, and splendor; the Classical (c. 1750–1820), a return to simplicity; and the Romantic (c. 1820–1900), which was a time of strong emotional expression and fascination with nature.

In primitive societies of the past and present, music has played more of a ritualistic, sacred role. In any case, singing has been considered an art form for thousands of years, powerfully influencing the evolution of societies. It is a large part of our leisure environment, our ceremonies, and our religions; the power of song has even been said to heal illness and sorrow. In antiquity, musicians tended to have more than one role, serving as composer, singer, and instrumentalist at the same time. They also tended to be found in the highest levels of society and to take part in events such as royal ceremonies, funerals, and processions.

The function of singing as entertainment was established relatively recently. Opera had its beginnings in the late 16th century in Italy and matured during the following centuries in other European countries. The rise of the professional singer (also referred to as the vocal virtuoso because of the expert talent involved) occurred in the 17th and 18th centuries. At this time, musical composers began to sing to wider audiences, who called for further expression and passion in singing.

Throughout the periods of Western music, the various aspects of song have changed along with general musical developments. Such aspects include melody, harmony, rhythm, tempo, dynamics, texture, and other characteristics. The structures of song are seemingly unlimited and have evolved from plainsong and madrigal, chanson and chorale, opera and cantata, folk and motet, anthem and drama, to today's expanse of pop, rock, country, rap, and so on. The development of radio, television, motion pictures, the Internet, and various types of recordings (LP records, cassettes, compact discs, and digital audio) has had a great effect on the singing profession, creating smaller audiences for live performances yet larger and larger audiences for recorded music.

■ THE JOB

Essentially, singers are employed to perform music with their voices by using their knowledge of vocal sound and delivery, harmony, melody, and rhythm. They put their individual vocal styles into the songs they sing, and they interpret music accordingly. The inherent sounds of the voices in a performance play a significant part in how a song will affect an audience; this essential aspect of a singer's voice is known as its tone.

Classical singers are usually categorized according to the range and quality of their voices, beginning with the highest singing voice, the soprano, and ending with the lowest, the bass; voices in between include mezzo soprano, contralto, tenor, and baritone. Singers perform either alone (in which case they are referred to as soloists) or as members of an ensemble, or group. They sing by either following a score, which is the printed musical text, or by memorizing the material. Also, they may sing either with or without instrumental accompaniment; singing without accompaniment is called a cappella. In opera—which are plays set to music—singers perform the various roles, much as actors do, interpreting the drama with their voices to the accompaniment of a symphony orchestra.

Classical singers may perform a variety of musical styles, or specialize in a specific period; they may give recitals, or perform as members of an ensemble. Classical singers generally undergo years of voice training and instruction in musical theory. They develop their vocal technique and learn how to project without harming their voices. Classical singers rarely use a microphone when they sing; nonetheless, their voices must be heard above the orchestra. Because classical singers often perform music from many different languages, they learn how to pronounce these languages, and often how to speak them as well. Those who are involved in opera work for opera companies in major cities throughout the country and often travel extensively. Some classical singers also perform in other musical areas.

Professional singers tend to perform in a chosen style of music, such as jazz, rock, or blues, among many others. Many singers pursue careers that will lead them to perform for coveted recording contracts, on concert tours, and for television and motion pictures. Others perform in rock, pop, country, gospel, or folk groups, singing in concert halls, nightclubs, and churches and at social gatherings and for small studio recordings. Whereas *virtuosos*, classical artists who are expertly skilled in their singing style, tend to perform traditional pieces that have been handed down through hundreds of years, singers in other areas often perform popular, current pieces, and often songs that they themselves have composed.

Another style of music in which formal training is often helpful is jazz. *Jazz singers* learn phrasing, breathing, and vocal techniques; often, the goal of a jazz singer is to become as much a part of the instrumentation as the piano, saxophone, trumpet, or trombone. Many jazz singers perform *scat* singing, in which the voice is used in an improvisational way much like any other instrument.

Folk singers perform songs that may be many years old, or they may write their own songs. Folk singers generally perform songs that express a certain cultural tradition; while some folk singers specialize in their own or another culture, others may sing songs from a great variety of cultural and musical traditions. In the United States, folk singing is particularly linked to the acoustic guitar, and many singers accompany themselves while singing.

A cappella singing, which is singing without musical accompaniment, takes many forms. A cappella music may be a part of classical music; it may also be a part of folk music, as in the singing of barbershop quartets. Another form, called doo-wop, is closely linked to rock and rhythm and blues music.

Gospel music, which evolved in the United States, is a form of sacred music; *gospel singers* generally sing as part of a choir, accompanied by an organ, or other musical instruments, but may also perform a cappella. Many popular singers began their careers as singers in church and gospel choirs before entering jazz, pop, blues, or rock.

Pop/rock singers generally require no formal training whatsoever. Rock music is a very broad term encompassing many different styles of music, such as heavy metal, punk, rap, rhythm and blues, rockabilly, techno, and many others. Many popular rock singers cannot even sing. But rock singers learn to express themselves and their music, developing their own phrasing and vocal techniques. Rock singers usually sing as part of a band, or with a backing band to accompany them. Rock

singers usually sing with microphones so that they can be heard above the amplified instruments around them.

CAREER LADDER

Music/Voice Teacher or Nationally Known Singer

Singer

Amateur Singer

All singers practice and rehearse their songs and music. Some singers read from music scores while performing; others perform from memory. Yet all must gain an intimate knowledge of their music, so that they can best convey its meanings and feelings to their audience. Singers must also exercise their voices even when not performing. Some singers perform as featured soloists and artists. Others perform as part of a choir or as backup singers adding harmony to the lead singer's voice.

▪ EARNINGS

As with many occupations in the performing arts, earnings for singers are highly dependent on one's professional reputation and thus have a wide range. To some degree, pay is also related to educational background (as it relates to how well one has been trained) and geographic location of performances. In certain situations, such as singing for audio recordings, pay is dependent on the number of minutes of finished music (for instance, an hour's pay will be given for each three and a half minutes of recorded song).

Singing is often considered a glamorous occupation. However, because it attracts so many professionals, competition for positions is very high. Only a small proportion of those who aspire to be singers achieve glamorous jobs and extremely lucrative contracts. Famous opera singers, for example earn $8,000 and more for each performance. Singers in an opera chorus earn between $600 and $800 per week. The average opera soloist earns $1,100 or more a performance, according to MENC: The National Association for Music Education. Classical soloists can receive between $2,000 and $3,000 per performance, while choristers may receive around $70 per performance. For rock singers, earnings can be far higher. Within the overall group of professional singers, studio and opera singers tend to earn salaries that are well respected in the industry; their opportunities for steady, long-term contracts tend to be better than for singers in other areas.

The average hourly wage for singers and musicians with salaried positions was $24.20 in May 2015, according to the U.S. Department of Labor. This wage would amount to $50,336 for a full-time job for a year; however

Country music singers Lindsay Lawler and Chris Roberts perform "God Bless America" during a ceremony at Arlington National Cemetery. (Mass Communication Specialist 2nd Class Kiona Miller. U.S. Navy.)

there is a wide variation in the number of hours worked per year by most singers and musicians, and the U.S. Department of Labor reports that it is rare to have a job that exceeds three to six months. The lowest paid 10 percent earned less than $9.20 an hour (or $19,136 annually), while the highest paid 10 percent earned more than $68.98 an hour (or $143,478 annually).

Top studio and opera singers earn an average of $70,000 per year, though some earn much more. Rock singers may begin by playing for drinks and meals only; if successful, they may earn tens of thousands of dollars for a single performance. Singers on cruise ships generally earn between $750 and $2,000 per week, although these figures can vary considerably. Also, many singers supplement their performance earnings by working at other positions, such as teaching at schools or giving private lessons or even working at jobs unrelated to singing. The U.S. Department of Labor reports that salaries in May 2015 for full-time, postsecondary art, drama, and music teachers ranged from $33,450 to $129,150, with a median annual salary of $65,340.

Singers generally receive no fringe benefits, and must provide their own health insurance and retirement planning.

■ WORK ENVIRONMENT

The environments in which singers work tend to vary greatly, depending on such factors as type of music involved and location of performance area. Professional singers often work in the evenings and during weekends, and many are frequently required to travel. Many singers who are involved in popular productions such as in opera, rock, and country music work in large cities such as New York, Las Vegas, Chicago, Los Angeles, and Nashville. Stamina and endurance are needed to keep up with the hours of rehearsals and performances, which can be long; work schedules are very often erratic, varying from job to job.

■ EXPLORING

Anyone who is interested in pursuing a career as a singer should obviously have a love for music. Listen to recordings and live performances as often as possible, and develop an understanding of the types of music that you enjoy. Singing, alone or with family and friends, is one of the most natural ways to explore music and develop a sense of your own vocal style. Join music clubs at school, as well as the school band if it does vocal performances. In addition, take part in school drama productions that involve musical numbers.

Older students interested in classical music careers could contact trade associations such as the American Guild of Musical Artists, as well as read trade journals. For information and news about popular singers, read *Billboard* magazine (http://www.billboard.com), which can be purchased at many local bookshops and newsstands. Those who already know what type of music they wish to sing should audition for roles in community musical productions or contact trade groups that offer competitions. For example, Opera America (http://www.operaamerica.org) can provide information on competitions, apprentice programs, and performances for young singers interested in opera.

There are many summer programs offered throughout the United States for high school students interested in singing and other performing arts. For example, Stanford University offers its Stanford Jazz Workshop (https://stanfordjazz.org) each summer for students who are 12 to 17 years old. It offers activities in instrumental and vocal music, as well as recreational swimming, tennis, and volleyball. For college students who are 18 years and older, the jazz workshop also has a number of positions available.

Another educational institute that presents a summer program is Boston University's Tanglewood Institute (http://www.bu.edu/cfa/tanglewood), which is geared especially toward very talented and ambitious students between the ages of 15 and 18. It offers sessions in chorus, musical productions, chamber music, classical music, ensemble, instrumental, and vocal practice. Arts and culture field trips are also planned. College students who are at least 20 years old can apply for jobs at the summer Tanglewood programs.

Students interested in other areas of singing can begin while still in high school, or even sooner. Many gospel singers, for example, start singing with their local church group at an early age. Many high school students form their own bands, playing rock, country, or jazz, and can gain experience performing before an audience; some of these young musicians even get paid to perform at school parties and other social functions.

■ EDUCATION AND TRAINING REQUIREMENTS
High School

Many singers require no formal training in order to sing. However, those interested in becoming classical or jazz singers should begin learning and honing their talent when they are quite young. Vocal talent can be recognized in grade school students and even in younger children. In general, however, these early years are a time of vast development and growth in singing ability. Evident changes occur in boys' and girls' voices when they are around 12 to 14 years old, during which time their vocal cords go through a process of lengthening and thickening. Boys' voices tend to change much more so than girls' voices, although both genders should be provided with challenges that will help them achieve their talent goals. Young students should learn about breath control and why it is necessary; they should learn to follow a conductor, including the relationship between hand or baton motions and the dynamics of the music; and they should learn about musical concepts such as tone, melody, harmony, and rhythm.

During the last two years of high school, aspiring singers should have a good idea of what classification they are in, according to the range and quality of their voices: soprano, alto, contralto, tenor, baritone, or bass. These categories indicate the resonance of the voice, soprano being the highest and lightest, bass being the lowest and heaviest. Students should take part in voice classes, choirs, and ensembles. In addition, students should continue their studies in English, writing, social studies, foreign language, and other electives in music, theory, and performance.

There tend to be no formal educational requirements for those who wish to be singers. However, formal education is valuable, especially in younger years. Some students know early in their lives that they want to be singers and are ambitious enough to continue to practice and learn. These students are often advised to attend high schools that are specifically geared toward combined academic and intensive arts education in music, dance, and theater. Such schools can provide valuable preparation and guidance for those who plan to pursue professional careers in the arts. Admission is usually based on results from students' auditions as well as academic testing.

MARIAN ANDERSON — MOVERS AND SHAKERS

The resonant low tones and natural beauty of Marian Anderson's (1897–1993) contralto voice brought her wide acclaim as a singer of spirituals, lieder, and arias. After many years of success on the concert stage, she became the first black singer to join the Metropolitan Opera Company. She made her debut as Ulrica in *A Masked Ball* in 1925.

In 1939, Anderson received national attention when the Daughters of the American Revolution refused to let her sing in Constitution Hall in Washington, D.C., because of her race. Eleanor Roosevelt and others organized a concert at the Lincoln Memorial, and on Easter Sunday morning Anderson sang before an audience of 75,000. In the same year, the singer received the Spingarn Medal for outstanding achievement by a black American.

Anderson toured India and the Far East for the State Department in 1957, and in 1958 became a delegate to the United Nations. She retired from the concert stage in 1965 after a series of farewell concerts. Her autobiography is *My Lord, What a Morning* (1956).

Postsecondary Training

Many find it worthwhile and fascinating to continue their study of music and voice in a liberal arts program at a college or university. Similarly, others attend schools of higher education that are focused specifically on music, such as The Juilliard School (http://www.juilliard.edu) in New York. Such an intense program would include a multidisciplinary curriculum of composition and performance, as well as study and appreciation of the history, development, variety, and potential advances of music. In this type of program, a student would earn a bachelor's degree. To earn a bachelor's degree in music, one would study musicology, which concerns the history, literature, and cultural background of music; the music industry, which will prepare one for not only singing but also marketing music and other business aspects; and professional performance. Specific music classes in a typical four-year liberal arts program would include such courses as introduction to music, music styles and structures, harmony, theory of music, elementary and advanced auditory training, music history, and individual instruction.

In addition to learning at schools, many singers are taught by private singing teachers and voice coaches, who help to develop and refine students' voices. Many aspiring singers take courses at continuing adult education centers, where they can take advantage of courses in beginning and advanced singing, basic vocal techniques, voice coaching, and vocal performance workshops. When one is involved in voice training, he or she must learn about good articulation and breath control, which are very important qualities for all singers. Performers must take care of their voices and keep their lungs in good condition. Voice training, whether as part of a college curriculum or in private study, is useful to many singers, not only for classical and opera singers, but also for jazz singers and for those interested in careers in musical theater. Many highly successful professional singers continue to take voice lessons throughout their careers.

Other Education or Training

The American Composers Forum offers workshops and other learning opportunities. Past workshop topics included copyright law and writing music for film. The American Society of Composers, Authors, and Publishers provides workshops that cover topics such as songwriting, film scoring, and musical theatre scoring. The Society of Composers & Lyricists offers seminars and other continuing education opportunities on music technology, industry trends, and other topics. The Songwriters Guild of America provides songwriting workshops in a variety of cities. Contact these organizations for more information.

■ CERTIFICATION, LICENSING, AND SPECIAL REQUIREMENTS
Certification or Licensing

There are no certification or licensing requirements for singers.

■ EXPERIENCE, SKILLS, AND PERSONALITY TRAITS

To be a successful singer, you should gain as much experience as possible performing in a variety of styles—such as opera, jazz, or popular music.

In other areas of music, learning to sing and becoming a singer is often a matter of desire, practice, and having an inborn love and talent for singing. Learning to play a musical instrument is often extremely helpful in learning to sing and to read and write music. Sometimes it is not even necessary to have a "good" singing voice. Many singers in rock and rap music have less-than-perfect voices. But these singers learn to use their voices in ways that nonetheless provide good expression to their songs, music, and ideas.

■ EMPLOYMENT PROSPECTS
Employers

Approximately 40,110 singers and musicians are employed in the United States. There are many different environments in which singers can be employed, including local lounges, bars, cafes, radio and television, theater productions, cruise ships, resorts, hotels, casinos, large concert tours, and opera companies.

Many singers hire agents, who usually receive a percentage of the singer's earnings for finding them appropriate performance contracts. Others are employed primarily as studio singers, which means that they do not perform for live audiences but rather record their singing in studios for albums, radio, television, and motion pictures.

An important tactic for finding employment as a singer is to invest in a professional-quality recording of your singing that you can send to prospective employers.

Starting Out

There is no single correct way of entering the singing profession. It is recommended that aspiring singers explore the avenues that interest them, continuing to apply and audition for whatever medium or venue suits them. Singing is an extremely creative profession, and singers must learn to be creative and resourceful in the business skills involved in finding opportunities to perform.

High school students should seek out any opportunities to perform, including choirs, school musical productions, and church and other religious functions. Voice teachers can arrange recitals and introduce students to their network of musician contacts.

■ ADVANCEMENT PROSPECTS

In the singing profession and the music industry in general, the nature of the business is such that singers can consider themselves to have "made it" when they get steady, full-time work. A measure of advancement is how well known and respected singers become in their field, which in turn influences their earnings. In most areas, particularly classical music, only the most talented and persistent singers make it to the top of their profession. In other areas, success may be largely a matter of luck and perseverance. A singer on Broadway, for example, may begin as a member of the chorus and eventually become a featured singer. Other singers tend to enjoy working in local performance centers, nightclubs, and other musical environments.

Also, many experienced singers who have had formal training will become voice teachers. Reputable schools such as Juilliard consider it a plus when a student can say that he or she has studied with a master.

■ OUTLOOK

Any employment forecast for singers will most probably emphasize one factor that plays an important role in the availability of jobs: competition. Because so many people pursue musical careers and because there tend to be no formal requirements for employment in this industry (the main qualification is talent), competition is most often very strong. Talented singers who are skilled at promoting themselves on social media and the Internet should have better chances of finding steady work.

According to the U.S. Department of Labor (DOL), employment for singers and musicians is expected to grow slower than average 2024, or more slowly than the average for all careers. Demand for more music performances will create job opportunities for musicians. Singers will be also be needed to sing backup and perform in films, commercials, and television. Growth can be limited by the availability of funding for the arts.

The entertainment industry is expected to grow during the next decade, which will create jobs for singers and other performers. Because of the nature of this work, positions tend to be temporary and part time; in fact, of all members of the American Federation of Musicians, fewer than 2 percent work full time in their singing careers. Thus, it is often advised that those who are intent on pursuing a singing career keep in mind the varied fields other than performance in which their interest in music can be beneficial, such as composition, education, broadcasting, therapy, and community arts management.

Those intent on pursuing singing careers in rock, jazz, and other popular forms should understand the keen competition they will face. There are thousands of singers all hoping to make it; only a very few actually succeed. However, there are many opportunities to perform in local cities and communities, and those with a genuine love of singing and performing should also possess a strong sense of commitment and dedication to their art.

■ UNIONS AND ASSOCIATIONS

Many singers are members of trade unions, which represent them in matters such as wage scales and fair working conditions. Vocal performers who sing for studio recordings are represented by SAG-AFTRA; solo opera singers, solo concert singers, and choral singers are members of the American Guild of Musical Artists. Other useful organizations for singers include Opera America and the National Association of Schools of Music.

■ TIPS FOR ENTRY

1. Keep developing your vocal talents by taking music classes and practicing your singing.
2. Create a demo recording of your best work and submit it to music companies and agents, or start a Web site that spotlights your talents, or post videos of your performances on YouTube.
3. Audition for spots in local musical groups, church choirs, and other organizations.
4. Participate in casting calls and auditions for theater productions.

■ FOR MORE INFORMATION

For professional and artistic development resources, contact
American Composers Forum (ACF)
75 West 5th Street, Suite 522
Saint Paul, MN 55102-1439
Tel: (651) 228-1407
Fax: (651) 291-7978
E-mail: PMarschke@composersforum.org
http://www.composersforum.org

For information on membership in a local union nearest you, developments in the music field, a searchable database of U.S. and foreign music schools, and articles on careers in music, visit the following Web site.
American Federation of Musicians of the United States and Canada (AFM)
1501 Broadway, Suite 600
New York, NY 10036-5601
Tel: (800) 762-3444; (212) 869-1330
http://www.afm.org

The AGMA is a union for professional musicians. The Web site has information on upcoming auditions, news announcements for the field, and membership information.
American Guild of Musical Artists (AGMA)
1430 Broadway, 14th Floor
New York, NY 10018-3308
Tel: (212) 265-3687
Fax: (212) 262-9088
E-mail: AGMA@MusicalArtists.org
http://www.musicalartists.org

For information on its music programs, contact
Boston University, Tanglewood Institute
855 Commonwealth Ave.
Boston, MA 02215
Tel: (617) 353-3350
E-mail: askcfa@bu.edu
http://www.bu.edu/cfa/tanglewood

For a list of colleges and universities that offer music-related programs, contact

National Association of Schools of Music (NASM)
11250 Roger Bacon Drive, Suite 21
Reston, VA 20190-5248
Tel: (703) 437-0700
Fax: (703) 437-6312
E-mail: info@arts-accredit.org
http://nasm.arts-accredit.org

For career and educational information for opera singers, contact

Opera America
330 Seventh Avenue
New York, NY 10001-5010
Tel: (212) 796-8620
Fax: (212) 796-8621
E-mail: info@operaamerica.org
http://www.operaamerica.org

For information on union membership, contact

SAG-AFTRA
5757 Wilshire Boulevard, 7th Floor
Los Angeles, CA 90036-3600
Tel: (855) 724-2387
E-mail: sagaftrainfo@sagaftra.org
http://www.sagaftra.org

For information on jazz performances and events, contact

Stanford University, Jazz Workshop
P.O. Box 20454
Stanford, CA 94309
Tel: (650) 736-0324
Fax: (650) 856-4155
E-mail: info@stanfordjazz.org
http://www.stanfordjazz.org

Ski Resort Workers

▮ OVERVIEW

Ski resorts offer many different types of employment opportunities. Qualified *ski resort workers* are needed to supervise the activities on ski slopes, run operations at the lodge, provide instruction to skiers, and ensure the safety of resort patrons. There are numerous ski resorts located throughout the United States and the world. Jobs are plentiful, though the majority of them are seasonal, lasting from November to April. The National Ski Areas Association represents 313 alpine resorts, which account

for more than 90 percent of skier/snowboarder visits in the United States.

▮ HISTORY

Skiing developed primarily as a means to travel from one place to another. Northern Europeans were the first people to wear skis, which they fashioned from tree branches. Armies have used skis to travel snowy mountain regions since the Middle Ages.

Though people started skiing for pleasure in the 18th century, it was not until the invention of the motorized ski lift in the 1930s that skiing grew in popularity. After World War II, hundreds of resorts opened to accommodate this growing form of recreation. Resorts, offering skiing opportunities combined with comfortable accommodations and entertainment, provided people with a new vacation alternative. In the United States, large ski communities, such as Vail and Aspen in Colorado, developed as a result of the sport. Today, many of these towns' primary sources of revenue stem from skiing and related activities.

There are three types of skiing—Alpine, or downhill; Nordic, or cross-country; and Freestyle, which incorporates acrobatic movements, stunts, and dance elements. Most resorts cater to the Alpine type of skiing. Other popular snow activities are snowboarding and sledding.

▮ THE JOB

Ski resort workers run the gamut from entry level to highly skilled. Each is important for maintaining the order and operations of the resort community. One of the largest departments is ski lift operation. *Ski lift operators* make sure skiers have safe transport. There are several steps taken daily before a ski lift is opened to the public. First, ice, snow, or tree branches are cleared from the machinery and the loading and unloading platforms. Next, all machinery and parts are cleaned and checked for safety. Finally, an experienced member of the lift staff conducts a trial run.

There are three main sections of the lift: bottom, middle terminal, and the top. Workers at all stations help passengers on or off the lift safely. They collect and punch lift tickets, adjust seats or the speed of the lift, and spot check for loose or dangling items that may catch on the lift's machinery. They answer any inquiries passengers may have about the run, or address general questions. They give directions and make sure skiers stay on the slopes and trails designated for their level of expertise—beginner, intermediate, and expert. Workers must sometimes reprimand unruly passengers.

Skiers who monitor the runs and surrounding areas are called the *ski patrol*. Considered the police of the mountains, they are specially trained ski experts responsible for preventing accidents and maintaining the safety standards of the resort. They mark off trails and courses that are not safe for the public. Patrol members also help injured skiers off the slopes and to proper first aid stations, or in extreme cases, to an ambulance. Ski patrol members should be versed in emergency medical techniques, such as CPR and first aid.

A *certified ski instructor* can teach everything from basic maneuvers to more advanced techniques. Whether in group classes or private lessons, ski instructors teach students how to avoid injury by skiing safely and responsibly.

Before skiers head for the moguls, they need proper equipment. Working in the supply houses is an example of an entry-level position. *Ski technicians* assist skiers in getting the proper-sized boots, skis, and poles. They may answer questions regarding equipment and how to use it.

Most ski resorts have chalets or lodges that offer skiers a place to rest and grab refreshments between runs. More often than not, these lodges serve as gathering places in the evenings for drinks and socialization. Some jobs at lodges include *wait staff*, *housekeeping staff*, *gift shop* or *ski shop employees*, *resort managers*, and *human resources staff*.

■ EARNINGS

Salaries for ski resort workers vary depending on the resort, the region where it is located, and the type of position the worker holds. Large, well-established resorts, especially those located in the mountain states and Northeast, tend to pay higher hourly rates. One should bear in mind that most ski resorts operate only seasonally, so many jobs are not available the entire year. Earnings for jobs common among many hospitality or recreational industries tend to be roughly equivalent at ski resorts.

According to Simplyhired.com, in 2017 the median salary for ski resort workers was $55,583. Average earnings for some key positions were reported as ski instructors, $21,681 (Salary.com); ski lift operators, $23,513 (Salaryexpert.com); and ski patrol members, $19,500 (Bureau of Labor Statistics).

Most ski resort employees are given complimentary full- or partial-season ski passes. Some companies also provide their employees with housing at or near the resort. Full-time employees receive the standard benefits package including paid vacation and health insurance.

■ WORK ENVIRONMENT

Ski slopes open at 8:00 A.M. and close at dusk; many resorts light some courses, to allow for night skiing. Ski lift operators, ski patrol, ski instructors, and other employees assigned to outdoor work prepare for the often blustery weather by wearing layers of clothes, waterproof coats, ski pants, boots, hats, and gloves. Some resorts supply their employees with uniform coats and accessories.

There are also indoor positions available for ski resort workers. Employees who enjoy a warm and comfortable workplace and still have great customer contact include lodge workers, gift shop employees, and ski technicians. Most ski resort employees work about 40 hours a week; ski instructors' schedules will vary depending on their class load. Since ski resorts are open seven days a week, employees with low seniority are expected to work weekends and holidays—the busiest times for most resorts.

■ EXPLORING

If you live in one of the 40 states that have ski resorts, you can get an excellent introduction to work in the ski industry by getting a part-time job at a ski resort. If you don't live near a ski resort, a job at a golf course, hotel, or restaurant will also provide good experience.

If you plan on becoming a ski instructor or ski patrol officer, you should hone your skiing skills to improve your chances of landing a job.

Talk to ski resort workers about their careers. Ask them what they like and dislike about their jobs, what a typical workday is like, and other questions that will help you get a good understanding of ski industry careers.

QUICK FACTS

ALTERNATE TITLE(S)
Certified Ski Instructors, Ski Lift Operators, Ski Patrollers, Ski Shop Employees, Ski Technicians

DUTIES
Perform a variety of duties at ski resorts, from providing instruction to skiers, to working on safety patrols and operating ski lift equipment, to providing housekeeping and food and gift shop services

SALARY RANGE
$19,500 to $23,513 to $55,583+

WORK ENVIRONMENT
Indoors/Outdoors

BEST GEOGRAPHIC LOCATION(S)
Colorado, New York, Michigan, Wisconsin, Pennsylvania, California, Minnesota, Vermont, Maine, and New Hampshire

MINIMUM EDUCATION LEVEL
High School Diploma

SCHOOL SUBJECTS
Business, Mathematics, Speech

EXPERIENCE
Varies by position

PERSONALITY TRAITS
Athletic, Conventional, Helpful

SKILLS
Business Management, Foreign Language, Interpersonal

CERTIFICATION OR LICENSING
Required

SPECIAL REQUIREMENTS
None

EMPLOYMENT PROSPECTS
Fair

ADVANCEMENT PROSPECTS
Good

OUTLOOK
About as Fast as the Average

NOC
0632, 5252, 5254, 6421, 6531, 6722

O*NET-SOC
39-3091.00, 33-9092.00

CAREER LADDER

Ski Resort Manager

Department Manager

Experienced Ski Resort Worker

Entry-Level Ski Resort Worker

■ EDUCATION AND TRAINING REQUIREMENTS
High School

Education requirements vary depending on the facility and type of work involved, though most resorts expect at least a high school diploma for their entry-level positions. High school courses that will be helpful include general business, mathematics, speech, and physical education. Learning a foreign language should also be helpful, since many foreign visitors vacation at American ski resorts.

Postsecondary Training

Many resorts prefer to hire college students as seasonal help. Management positions usually require a college degree. Some institutions offer degrees in ski industry management. For example, Sierra Nevada College offers a bachelor's degree in ski business and resort management. Lyndon State College awards a bachelor's degree in mountain recreation management. And Northern Michigan University/Gogebic Community College offer a joint associate degree in ski area management.

A ski instructor coaches a student during a lesson. (Dmitry Fisher. Shutterstock.)

■ CERTIFICATION, LICENSING, AND SPECIAL REQUIREMENTS
Certification or Licensing

Entry-level jobs such as clerks, wait staff, and ski lift operators do not require certification. However, you must be certified to qualify as a professional ski or snowboard instructor. Certification is provided by the Professional Ski Instructors of America–American Association of Snowboard Instructors. Certification consists of skill tests, further education, and on-the-job experience. Satisfactory completion of a certification exam is also required. Ski instructors must be re-certified every one to two years, depending on the region in which they teach.

■ EXPERIENCE, SKILLS, AND PERSONALITY TRAITS

No experience is needed to work in entry-level positions, but those with prior work experience will increase their chances of landing a job, getting promoted, and possibly earning higher pay. High-level positions, such as nurse or executive, require previous work experience.

All employees, especially those who deal with customers, are a reflection of the resort for which they work. Different jobs call for different qualities in a worker. Responsibility is key when working the ski lift, as is tact when confronting troublesome skiers. Ski instructors need to be physically fit, as well as patient and understanding with their students. Ski patrol members must be able to react quickly in emergencies and have the foresight to spot potential trouble situations.

Workers who speak a second language will have an advantage. Many ski enthusiasts from South America travel to the United States for world-class skiing, so workers who are fluent in Spanish or Portuguese will have good job prospects. Most positions can be altered to accommodate employees who are physically challenged. It is best to check with each resort to learn their policies and employee requirements.

■ EMPLOYMENT PROSPECTS
Employers

Approximately 40 states have ski resorts, with the highest number of ski resorts located in Colorado, New York, Michigan, Wisconsin, Pennsylvania, California, Minnesota, Vermont, Maine, and New Hampshire. Colorado is the most popular skiing state, where many communities such as Vail, Aspen, and Telluride have grown around the industry.

Workers who are interested in year-round employment should look for resorts that cater to year-round business. The Aspen Skiing Company, for example, has four mountain ski areas in operation during the winter.

Many employees work the slopes from November to April and the golf courses the rest of the year.

Starting Out

Many resorts actively recruit at college campuses and job fairs. Phone and Skype interviews and online applications are becoming more prevalent in this field. There are also Web sites that operate online employment services. Visit them to find job descriptions, salary expectations, and job benefits.

It would be wise to first compile a list of resorts or locations that interest you. Trade magazines, such as *Powder, the Skier's Magazine* (http://www.powdermag.com) or *SKI* (http://www.skinet.com/ski), as well as your local library, are helpful resources. Apply for work at least two seasons ahead—that means start looking for winter work in the summer to be considered for choice positions.

■ ADVANCEMENT PROSPECTS

Advancement is determined by a worker's experience, skill, level of education, and starting position. Ski lift operators can be promoted to department supervisors of that division, general supervisors, and finally, management. Ski instructors may begin their careers by giving beginner's lessons or children's lessons and then advance to intermediate- or expert-level classes. Experienced instructors with good reputations may develop a following of students. They may also be promoted to department supervisor or management. Lodge employees may be promoted to positions with increased responsibilities such as shift supervisor or manager.

■ OUTLOOK

Emphasis on physical health, interest in sport-related vacations, and growing household incomes point to a bright future for ski resorts and their employees. And weather may not always hamper this industry. Many resorts, using snowmaking devices to create a snow-covered run, can extend the season well into April.

Note, however, that the majority of jobs in this industry are seasonal. Many students use this opportunity to supplement their income during school vacations, as well as fuel their interest in the sport. Some resorts offer year-round employment by shifting their employees to other off-season jobs. Golf course attendants, tour guides, and spa workers are some examples of summer jobs. Workers who are interested in working on the management side of the business should consider pursuing degrees in business management, rehabilitation services, or physical education.

> ## ALTITUDE SICKNESS
> **DID YOU KNOW?**
>
> While generally not a medical emergency, feeling sick or disoriented is common for many people who are first visiting a ski resort in an altitude that is higher than what they are used to. Symptoms of altitude sickness include headache, nausea, fatigue, diarrhea or constipation, difficulty sleeping, agitation, shortness of breath, rapid heartbeat, nasal congestion, and coughing. According to ski professionals in Breckenridge, Colorado, you can minimize these symptoms by taking it easy on the first day or two after you arrive at a ski resort; limiting alcohol consumption, caffeine, and salty foods; eating lightly; drinking plenty of water; and getting adequate sleep.

The travel and tourism industry is affected by the state of our nation's economy. More people will vacation at ski resorts and other travel destinations when they feel that travel is safe and the economy is strong. In bad economic times and periods of uncertainty, people will take fewer vacations. Some regions may suffer warm winters or minimal snowfall. During these times, fewer employment opportunities may be available to workers in the ski resort industry.

■ UNIONS AND ASSOCIATIONS

Some ski resort workers belong to unions; for example, hotel desk workers can join UNITE HERE. There are also a number of professional organizations, such as the American Hotel and Lodging Association, that ski resort workers can join. The National Ski Areas Association represents 313 alpine resorts, which account for more than 90 percent of skier/snowboarder visits in the United States. The Professional Ski Instructors of America–American Association of Snowboard Instructors offer membership, certification, publications, and other resources.

■ TIPS FOR ENTRY

1. To learn more about a career as a ski or snowboard instructor, read:
   - *32 Degrees* (http://www.thesnowpros.org/Publications,VideosResources/32Degrees.aspx)
   - *Powder, the Skier's Magazine* (http://www.powdermag.com)
   - *National Ski Areas Association Journal* (http://www.nsaa.org)
   - *SKI* (http://www.skinet.com/ski)
2. Visit http://www.resortjobs.com for job listings.

3. Use social media to stay up to date on industry developments, network, and learn about job openings. Many associations have social media sites. For example, the Professional Ski Instructors of America has an active presence on Facebook, Twitter, Google+, YouTube, Instagram, LinkedIn, and Pinterest.

■ FOR MORE INFORMATION

For information on employment opportunities and to fill out an online employment application, visit

Aspen Skiing Company
Tel: (800) 525-6200
E-mail: contactus@aspensnowmass.com
http://www.aspensnowmass.com

For industry information, contact

National Ski Areas Association
133 South Van Gordon Street, Suite 300
Lakewood, CO 80228-1706
Tel: (303) 987-1111
Fax: (303) 986-2345
E-mail: nsaa@nsaa.org
http://www.nsaa.org

For information on membership and certification, contact

Professional Ski Instructors of America—
　American Association of Snowboard
　Instructors
133 South Van Gordon Street, Suite 200
Lakewood, CO 80228-1706
Tel: (844) 340-7669
E-mail: memberservices@thesnowpros.org
http://www.thesnowpros.org

For information on employment, travel packages, and resort news, visit

SkiResorts
http://www.skiresorts.com

Social Media Workers

■ OVERVIEW

Social media can be defined as user-created content (audio, text, video, multimedia) that is published and shared on social media sites such as Facebook, LinkedIn, and Twitter; it can also be defined as the online technology that allows users to share content. *Social media workers* have become increasingly important to the success of companies and other organizations. By using social media tools and sites such as Facebook and Twitter, businesses and other organizations can generate more Web traffic, raise their business or organizational profiles, and increase sales. There are many specialties in the field. Careers covered in this article include community managers, social media directors, vice-presidents of social strategy, online reputation managers, chief conversation officers, blogger outreach managers, search engine optimization specialists, bloggers, and podcasters.

■ HISTORY

The Internet as we know it today began in the early 1990s. During the last two decades it has grown to become an integral part of many people's everyday lives. The Internet started out as a place to exchange information, but has now become one of the top ways for companies to reach potential customers. Traditional forms of advertising, such as print ads, billboards, direct mail, flyers, and product testing events, are still used by businesses; however, social media tools and programs are increasingly relied on to "get the word out" about a particular brand or service. Facebook and Twitter are just two of the tools used as a cost-effective way to connect with those already familiar with a product, but also to convince others to buy a company's products or services. The increasing affordability and wide accessibility of computers and smartphones have increased the amount of time an average user spends on the Internet and using social media. In fact, the Pew Research Center's Internet & American Life Project reports that 79 percent of Internet adult users used Facebook in 2016, up from about 65 percent in 2012. Instagram and Pinterest were the next most popular social media platforms, with 32 and 31 percent of adults using them, respectively.

The rapid growth of social media sites and tools on the Internet has created demand for workers who are experts in social media. These workers perform a wide range of duties, from seeking to raise their company's position on search engine results to contacting bloggers to convince them to review their company's products, monitoring chat rooms, and steering negative conversation back to the positive.

■ THE JOB

Careers in social media have grown rapidly in the past several years. Corporations and businesses realize that using social media is a cost-effective, user-friendly, and time-efficient way to promote their brands, products, and services. Government organizations and nonprofits also utilize social media to collect and disseminate information, connect with people, and spread the word about their programs and services. The following paragraphs provide information about some of the most popular social media careers.

Company blogs and forums are useful tools that educate people and create "buzz" about an organization's products and services. *Community managers* oversee the content used in company blogs and activity on forums. They begin new threads of conversation by introducing topics for discussion, perhaps posing questions or asking for reader input. If a discussion gets heated, community managers redirect the focus of the thread. They are on constant watch for defamatory remarks or other negative feedback, which could be damaging to the company's sales or public perception. Community managers also use Facebook fan pages, tweets, and other social media tools to attract new site visitors and keep them coming back to the site.

Social media directors oversee the development and execution of a company's social media strategy. They are responsible for driving word-of-mouth marketing through digital means. Using digital tools such as blogs, podcasts, video sharing and streaming, social networking sites, and various widgets, they are able to create user excitement and brand recognition. Social media directors research social media habits of a target demographic (for example, teens ages 16 to 19), find appropriate social media tools and programs, and plan and implement strategy. Social media directors also take a company's existing marketing materials (surveys, photographs, videos, etc.) and circulate them through various social media channels. At large companies, social media directors often manage staff who handle these duties. At smaller companies, the social media director may be responsible for all these tasks.

Vice presidents of social strategy oversee a company's overall social media policy. In addition to responsibility for social media, they also play a major role in developing their company's overall marketing strategy.

Dissatisfied customers often enter a forum or chat room and vent their feelings to the online world. They might be unhappy with the service they received at a restaurant, the quality of a product they purchased, or the manner in which they were treated by a customer service representative. Justified or not, it is the *online reputation manager*'s responsibility to diffuse the situation. These largely behind-the-scenes workers identify such situations by monitoring social media sites, often perusing tweets, Facebook fan pages, or company Web site forums. Once identified, online reputation managers will redirect comments, or in serious cases, bury the negative

responses to push them far down on search engine results (if a search engine is used). Techniques used to achieve this result include creating new social profile pages, redirecting users to positive links, or re-tagging a post. Online reputation managers also monitor the online reputation of their employer's competitors. By learning what customers are saying about a competitor's products or services, they can help their own company improve its existing products or services or develop new ones.

Chief conversation officers have many of the same duties as the aforementioned careers, but they are responsible for looking at the "big picture" and telling a company's story via social media. This is done by providing commentary and creating, curating, and manipulating content from company blogs and Web sites. Depending on the company's size, this function is filled by a single employee or an entire staff. Chief conversation officers monitor content as well as the context of online conversations. They set the stage for users to comment, and more importantly, set the tone for this stage. They use digital media tools such as an RSS feed or aggregating software to create a community of information and users. For example, when employed by a manufacturer such as Kraft Foods Groups, Inc., chief conversation officers facilitate conversation with users regarding the taste, texture, or shelf life of different products. They manage fan pages, blogs, and news sites to make sure their company's products are discussed positively. Any negative feedback is

QUICK FACTS

ALTERNATE TITLE(S)
Bloggers, Blogger Outreach Managers, Chief Conversation Officers, Community Managers, Online Reputation Managers, Podcasters, Search Engine Marketers, Search Engine Optimization Specialists, Social Media Directors, Vice Presidents of Social Strategy

DUTIES
Use social media tools and other technology to help companies generate more Web traffic, raise their business or organizational profile, and increase sales

SALARY RANGE
$47,750 to $62,250 to $94,250

WORK ENVIRONMENT
Primarily Indoors

BEST GEOGRAPHIC LOCATION(S)
Opportunities exist throughout the country

MINIMUM EDUCATION LEVEL
Bachelor's Degree

SCHOOL SUBJECTS
Business, Computer Science, English

EXPERIENCE
Internship

PERSONALITY TRAITS
Creative, Outgoing, Social

SKILLS
Digital Media, Interpersonal, Writing

CERTIFICATION OR LICENSING
Recommended

SPECIAL REQUIREMENTS
None

EMPLOYMENT PROSPECTS
Good

ADVANCEMENT PROSPECTS
Good

OUTLOOK
Faster than the Average

NOC
1123

O*NET-SOC
15-1199.03, 15-1134.00, 15-1141.00

CAREER LADDER

Social Media Manager/Executive or
Social Media Consulting Firm Owner

Experienced Social Media Worker

Entry-Level Social Media Worker

immediately segregated or deleted.

A blogger's kind words can do wonders for a company's brand, while a single negative remark can do intense damage to a company's reputation. For this reason, many companies rely on the expertise of *blogger outreach managers.* Blogger outreach managers identify popular bloggers who might be encouraged to promote their company's products or services. For example, a blogger outreach manager for a baby product manufacturer would first identify popular bloggers, such as mommy bloggers, and contact them via e-mail, the telephone, or social media sites such as Facebook. When communicating with bloggers, blogging outreach managers must be careful not to sound desperate or pushy. They must convey a friendly, relaxed tone that puts the blogger at ease and makes him or her open to reviewing and promoting the company's product or service. If the conversation goes well, the outreach manager might send the blogger product samples, provide a password so that the blogger can access a service or product online, or send informational and marketing materials such as press releases, photographs, videos, surveys, company statistics, or positive industry reviews. The blogger outreach manager then follows up with the blogger to see if he or she needs more information or plans to talk about the product or service in the blog.

Twitter founder, Biz Stone, speaks about social media. (drserg. Shutterstock.)

When consumers want to find a particular brand, service, or company, they often use search engines. Companies rely on *search engine optimization specialists,* also known as *search engine marketers* and *search marketing analysts,* to help ensure that their Web sites rank high in search results. Search engine optimization specialists identify and implement search engine keywords, tags, social media profiles, or site maps to improve the company's ranking. They work with consultants, content writers, developers, and designers to improve the ranking of their company's site or sites. Search engine optimization specialists are well versed in HTML coding as well as analytical tools such as Google Analytics or Omniture, the latter of which is owned by Adobe Systems.

Bloggers are employed by companies to promote their products and services via the written word (a blog).

Podcasting is the exchange of information using audio or video files (sometimes called vodcasting) that can be played on a computer or portable media device, such as an MP3 player. Podcasts are released to the World Wide Web in regular episodes. People who create and distribute podcasts are called *podcasters.* (Those who create videocasts may be called podcasters or *vodcasters.)* The information available on podcasts covers a wide range of topics, from government and politics to kids and families.

■ EARNINGS

The Creative Group, a division of staffing leader Robert Half International, conducted a survey of creative professionals in 2014. It reports the following salary ranges for social media workers: bloggers, $47,750 to $70,500; search engine optimization specialists, $62,250 to $87,750; social media managers, $67,750 to $94,250; and social media specialists, $54,000 to $77,750.

Benefits for full-time workers include paid vacation, health, disability, life insurance, and retirement or pension plans. Some employers also offer profit-sharing plans. Self-employed social media workers must provide their own benefits.

■ WORK ENVIRONMENT

Most social media professionals work a regular 40-hour week, though total hours may vary depending on the size of the company, the size of their social media staff, and the number and type of projects. Since the Internet is a 24/7 venue, social media workers should expect to work evenings and weekends.

Social media professionals work in comfortable, well-lit offices. A powerful server and the fastest Internet connection are work environment must-haves for this job.

The job can often get frustrating, especially when dealing with hackers (unauthorized intruders to a computer or Internet system), angry customers, and Web trolls (individuals who post offensive or controversial comments in an online forum, chat room, blog, or other setting in order to provoke outrage or otherwise disrupt legitimate conversation). Successful social media professionals are able to multitask; for example, many are able to write Web site entries while interacting with Web forum users. Since new digital tools are produced at a quick rate, social media professionals must spend time familiarizing themselves with the latest widgets, tools, and programs in order to stay technically savvy.

■ EXPLORING

The best way to learn more about social media is to actually use it. Visit popular social media sites such as Facebook and Twitter to learn about the field. You can get an idea of the types of challenges faced by social media professionals by visiting the Web forums at a company's site or their Twitter or Facebook pages. See how social media workers respond to customer complaints and negative comments, and try to think of what you might do to address such issues. Start your own Web site or blog and learn how to move it higher in Web search results. Talk to social media workers about their careers and ask questions. How did you train for the field? What do you like most and least about your job? What advice would you give to someone who wants to break into the field? and What are some emerging jobs in social media?

■ EDUCATION AND TRAINING REQUIREMENTS
High School

Take English and speech classes in high school to help develop your communication skills. Take as many computer science- and Internet-related courses as possible to learn about the technology behind social media applications. Other important classes include advertising, marketing, and psychology.

Postsecondary Education

There is no standard educational path for social media workers. Some have bachelor's degrees in computer science or information management, while others have degrees in advertising, marketing, marketing research, new media, journalism, or the liberal arts. Additionally, an increasing number of colleges and universities throughout the United States are recognizing the popularity of social media careers by adding classes and even majors in digital media and related fields. Check out major and course listings at colleges that you might want to attend to see what educational opportunities are available. Aspiring social media workers should also complete at least one internship as part of their college education.

POSTER'S REMORSE AND OTHER SOCIAL MEDIA IDEAS

WORDS TO KNOW

Forum: A discussion area on a Web site where users who have a shared interest in a topic can comment on existing conversations (or posts) and post their own comments; also called a message board.

Friend: A contact on a social media site such as Facebook; also known as a fan.

Online community: A group of individuals who have shared interests who use social media sites and tools.

Poster's remorse: A feeling of embarrassment and shame one feels after posting inappropriate text, photos, video, or other material at social media sites.

Social media: User-created content (audio, text, video, multimedia) that is published and shared on social media sites such as Facebook, LinkedIn, and Twitter; it can also be defined as the online technology that allows users to share content.

Social networking: The act of interacting with others in an online community.

Social networking sites: Web sites such as Facebook, MySpace, and LinkedIn where users can create biographical and/or professional profiles; post text, video, photographs, and audio; add friends; and communicate with other social media users.

Status: A maximum 140-character description that a user posts that details his or her current activities.

Tweet: A real-time posting of text (limited to 140 characters or less).

Web 2.0: The second generation of Web sites that allow people with little or no technical skill to create, edit, and publish their own creative content; popular Web 2.0 Web sites include Flickr, Digg, and Wikipedia.

Widget: A stand-alone application on a Web site that has a specific purpose (such as presenting news) and that is constantly being updated; also called an applet, badge, or gadget.

Other Education or Training

Professional associations offer training opportunities for social media workers. For example, SEMPO offers a variety of webinars such as "Mobile Trends For Marketers" and "Search Synergy: Maximizing Your Online Shelf Space." The International Webmasters Association offers more than 60 e-classes. Topics include Web content writing, search engine optimization, software, programming languages, and web animation. The Online News Association (ONA) offers free digital journalism training sessions (called ONACamps) at locations throughout the United States. These camps are geared toward "independent, community, non-profit, displaced and employed journalists, bloggers and entrepreneurs." Other organizations that offer continuing education classes, webinars, workshops, and videos include the American Marketing Association, eMarketing Association, Interactive Advertising Bureau, and the Word of Mouth Marketing Association.

■ CERTIFICATION, LICENSING, AND SPECIAL REQUIREMENTS
Certification or Licensing

Voluntary certification in Internet marketing is available from the eMarketing Association and the Internet Marketing Association. Contact these organizations for more information.

■ EXPERIENCE, SKILLS, AND PERSONALITY TRAITS

Aspiring social media workers should participate in at least one internship during college with a company that uses social media. This will allow them to make valuable industry contacts, explore career options, and possibly make such a good impression that they will be offered a job after graduation. Additionally, any experience with social media, especially as it relates to advertising and marketing, will be useful.

To be successful in these careers, you should be an expert in using social media, have strong communication skills, be a good writer, be creative, have an analytical personality, be able to act professionally when interacting with site users, and be willing to continue to learn throughout your career.

■ EMPLOYMENT PROSPECTS
Employers

Social media workers are employed by advertising and marketing firms that offer social media consulting services to companies, nonprofit organizations, and government agencies. They are also directly employed by businesses, nonprofits, and government agencies.

Starting Out

Aspiring social media workers can learn about job openings by visiting job search Web sites that specialize in social media careers, utilizing the services of their college's career services offices, or applying directly to consulting firms or companies that have a need for social media professionals.

■ ADVANCEMENT PROSPECTS

Some of the jobs covered in this article, such as community manager and blogger outreach managers, are entry-level. Others, such as social media director and vice president of social strategy, require holders to have first gained years of experience in marketing and business.

Advancement prospects are good for social media workers who demonstrate initiative, drive, and detailed knowledge of social media applications and technology. With experience, they can move into managerial or executive positions or start their own consulting firms.

■ OUTLOOK

Employment for social media professionals is expected to be good during the next decade. Companies and other organizations have realized the key role the Internet and social media play in selling products and services, ensuring positive publicity and public opinion, and collecting and disseminating information. Opportunities should be strongest for those with college degrees and extensive experience working with social media, especially as it relates to advertising and marketing. Social media is a dynamic field. New apps, platforms, and functions can be expected to sustain demand for talented and innovative workers.

■ UNIONS AND ASSOCIATIONS

Social media workers are not represented by unions, but they can obtain useful resources and professional support from advertising, marketing, and computer professional associations such as the Advertising Educational Foundation, American Advertising Federation, American Marketing Association, American Society for Information Science and Technology, eMarketing Association, Interactive Advertising Bureau, International Internet Marketing Association, Internet Marketing Association, SEMPO, and the Word of Mouth Marketing Association.

■ TIPS FOR ENTRY

1. State in your social media profiles (LinkedIn, Facebook, etc.) that you are seeking a job in social media. Use keywords such as "social media," "community," and "engagement" in your resume. Resume scanners often look for these and other buzz words to select potential job candidates.

2. Use social media such as LinkedIn and Twitter to stay up to date on industry developments and learn about job openings. Participate in online forums to raise your professional profile.

3. Visit the following Web sites for job listings:
   - http://www.sempo.org/?page=jobs
   - http://www.dice.com
   - http://www.highendcareers.com
   - http://careers.womma.org
   - http://www.jobsinsocialmedia.com

4. Participate in internships or part-time jobs that are arranged by your college's career services office.

5. Conduct information interviews with social media workers and ask them for advice on breaking into the field.

■ FOR MORE INFORMATION

For profiles of advertising workers and career information, contact

Advertising Educational Foundation (AEF)
220 East 42nd Street, Suite 3300
New York, NY 10017-5806
Tel: (212) 986-8060
Fax: (212) 986-8061
http://www.aef.com

The AAF combines the mutual interests of corporate advertisers, agencies, media companies, suppliers, and academia. Visit its Web site to learn more about internships, scholarships, college student chapters, and awards.

American Advertising Federation (AAF)
1101 Vermont Avenue NW 5th Floor
Washington, D.C. 20005-3521
Tel: (202) 898-0089
E-mail: aaf@aaf.org
http://www.aaf.org

For information on the practice, study, and teaching of marketing, contact

American Marketing Association (AMA)
130 E. Randolph St., 22nd Floor
Chicago, IL 60601
Tel: (800) AMA-1150; (312) 542-9000
Fax: (312) 542-9001
https://www.ama.org

Check out this professional organization's Web site for industry information.

American Society for Information Science and Technology
8555 16th Street, Suite 850
Silver Spring, MD 20910-2835
Tel: (301) 495-0900
Fax: (301) 495-0810
E-mail: asis@asis.org
http://www.asis.org

For information on certification, contact

eMarketing Association
40 Blue Ridge Dr.
Charlestown, RI 02813
Tel: (800) 496-2950; (401) 622-2369
Fax: (408) 884-2461
E-mail: eMA@eMarketingAssociation.com
http://www.emarketingassociation.com

For information on continuing education, contact

Interactive Advertising Bureau
116 East 27th Street, 7th Floor
New York, NY 10016-8942
Tel: (212) 380-4700
http://www.iab.net

For information on continuing education, contact

International Webmasters Association
119 East Union Street, Suite #A
Pasadena, CA 91103-3951
Tel: (626) 449-3709
Fax: (866) 607-1773
E-mail: Support@iwanet.org
http://www.iwanet.org

For information on certification, contact

Internet Marketing Association
E-mail: info@imanetwork.org
http://www.imanetwork.org

The Online News Association is a membership organization for journalists "whose principal livelihood involves gathering or producing news for digital presentation." Visit its Web site for information on membership.

Online News Association

c/o National Public Radio,

1111 North Capitol Street, NE, 6th Floor

Washington, D.C. 20002-7502

Tel: (646) 290-7900

E-mail: support@journalists.org

http://journalists.org

For more information on blogging, visit

ProBlogger

PO Box 1181

Blackburn North, Victoria 3130

Australia

http://www.problogger.net

For information on search engine marketing and a glossary of terms, visit

SEMPO

401 Edgewater Place, Suite 600

Wakefield, MA 01880-6200

Tel: (781) 876-8866

E-mail: info@sempo.org

http://www.sempo.org

For industry information, contact

Social Networking and Media Association

1600 Wilson Blvd, Suite 400

Arlington, VA 22209

Tel: (866) 670-1402; (202) 360-4402

Fax: (866) 533-0428

https://www.higherlogic.com/home

For information of word of mouth marketing, contact

Word of Mouth Marketing Association

200 East Randolph Street, Suite 5100

Chicago, IL 60601

Tel: (312) 577-7610; (312) 233-0063

http://womma.org

Social Workers

■ OVERVIEW

Social workers help people and assist communities in solving problems. These problems include poverty, racism, discrimination, physical and mental illness, addiction, and abuse. They counsel individuals and families, they lead group sessions, they research social problems, and they develop policy and programs. Social workers are dedicated to empowering people and helping them to preserve their dignity and worth. Approximately 649,300 social workers are employed in the United States. Social workers may also be known as *case workers.*

■ HISTORY

Even before the United States became a country, poverty and unemployment were among society's problems. Almshouses and shelters that provided the homeless with jobs and rooms were established as early as 1657. The social work profession as we know it today, however, has its origins in the "friendly visitor" of the early 1800s; these charity workers went from home to home offering guidance in how to move beyond the troubles of poverty.

At a time when not much financial assistance was available from local governments, the poor relied on friendly visitors for instruction on household budgeting and educating their children. Despite their good intentions, however, the friendly visitors could not provide the poor with all the necessary support. The middle-class women who served as friendly visitors were generally far removed from the experiences of the lower classes. Most of the friendly visitors served the community for only a very short time and therefore did not have the opportunity to gain much experience with the poor. The great difference between the life experiences of the friendly visitors and the experiences of their clients sometimes resulted in serious problems: The self-esteem and ambitions of the poor were sometimes damaged by the moral judgments of the friendly visitors. In some cases, friendly visitors served only to promote their middle-class values and practices. By the late 1800s, many charitable organizations developed in U.S. and Canadian cities. With the development of these organizations came a deeper insight into improving the conditions of the poor. Serving as a friendly visitor came to be considered an apprenticeship; it became necessary for friendly visitors to build better relationships with their clients. Friendly visitors were encouraged to take the time to learn about their clients and to develop an understanding of each client's individual needs. Nevertheless, some sense of moral superiority remained, as these charitable organizations refused assistance to alcoholics, beggars, and prostitutes.

The birth of the settlement house brought charity workers even closer to their clients. Settlement houses served as communities for the poor and were staffed by young, well-educated idealists eager to solve society's problems. The staff people lived among their clients and learned from them. In 1889, Jane Addams established the best known of the settlement houses, a community in Chicago called Hull House. Addams wrote extensively about the problems of the poor, and her efforts to provide solutions to their problems led to the foundation of social work education. She emphasized the importance of an education specific to the concerns of the social worker. By the 1920s, social work master's degree programs were established in many universities.

Theories and methodologies of social work have changed over the years, but the basis of the profession has remained the same: helping people and addressing social problems. As society changes, so do its problems, calling for redefinition of the social work profession. The first three fields of formal social work were defined by setting: medical social work, psychiatric social work, and child welfare. Later, practice was classified by different methodologies: casework, group work, and community organization. Most recently, the social work profession has been divided into two areas—direct practice and indirect practice.

■ THE JOB

After months of physical abuse from her husband, a young woman has taken her children and moved out of her house. With no job and no home, and fearing for her safety, she looks for a temporary shelter for herself and her children. Once there, she can rely on the help of social workers who will provide her and her family with a room, food, and security. The social workers will offer counseling and emotional support to help her address the problems in her life. They will involve her in group sessions with other victims of abuse. They will direct her to job training programs and other employment services. They will set up interviews with managers of low-income housing. As the woman makes efforts to improve her life, the shelter will provide day care for the children. All these resources exist because the social work profession has long been committed to empowering people and improving society.

The social worker's role extends even beyond the shelter. If the woman has trouble getting help from other agencies, the social worker will serve as an advocate, stepping in to ensure that she gets the aid to which she is entitled. The woman may also qualify for long-term assistance from the shelter, such as a second-step program in which a social worker offers counseling and other support over several months. The woman's individual experience will also help in the social worker's research of the problem of domestic violence; with that research, the social worker can help the community come to a better understanding of the problem and can direct society toward solutions. Some of these solutions may include the development of special police procedures for domestic disputes, or court-ordered therapy groups for abusive spouses.

Direct social work practice is also known as clinical practice. As the name suggests, direct practice involves working directly with the client by offering counseling, advocacy, information and referral, and education. Indirect practice concerns the structures through which the direct practice is offered. Indirect practice (a practice consisting mostly of social workers with Ph.D. degrees) involves program development and evaluation, administration, and policy analysis. The vast majority of the more than 130,000 members of the National Association of Social Workers work in direct service roles.

Because of the number of problems facing individuals, families, and communities, social workers find jobs in a wide variety of settings and with a variety of client groups. Many involve working with people of various age groups; others, such as geriatric social work, focus on assisting people from one age group, such as the elderly.

Mental Health and Substance Abuse Care

Mental health care has become the lead area of social work employment. These jobs are competitive and typically go to more experienced social workers. Settings include community mental health centers, where social workers serve mentally ill people and participate in outreach services; state and county mental hospitals, for long-term, inpatient care; facilities of the Department of Veterans Affairs,

CAREER LADDER

Social Work Manager or Director of Social Work Programs

Social Worker

Social Work Assistant/Aide/Technician

involving a variety of mental health care programs for veterans; and private psychiatric hospitals, for patients who can pay directly. Social workers also work with patients who have physical illnesses. They help individuals and their families adjust to the illness and the changes that illness may bring to their lives. They confer with physicians and with other members of the medical team to make plans about the best way to help the patient. They explain the treatment and its anticipated outcome to both the patient and the family. They help the patient adjust to the possible prospect of long hospitalization and isolation from the family.

Child Care/Family Services

Efforts are being made to offer a more universal system of care that would incorporate child care, family services, and community service. Child care services include day care homes, child care centers, and Head Start centers. Social workers in this setting attempt to address all the problems children face from infancy to late adolescence. They work with families to detect problems early and intervene when necessary. They research the problems confronting children and families, and they establish new services or adapt existing services to address these problems. They provide parenting education to teenage parents, which can involve living with a teenage mother in a foster care situation, teaching parenting skills, and caring for the baby while the mother attends school. Social workers alert employers to employees' needs for daytime child care.

Social workers in this area of service are constantly required to address new issues. In recent years, for example, social workers have developed services for families composed of different cultural backgrounds, services for children with congenital disabilities resulting from the mother's drug use, and disabilities related to HIV or AIDS.

Geriatric Social Work

Within this field, social workers provide individual and family counseling services in order to assess the older person's needs and strengths. Social workers help older people locate transportation and housing services. They also offer adult day care services or adult foster care services that match older people with families. Adult protective services protect older people from abuse and neglect,

and respite services allow family members time off from the care of an older person. A little-recognized problem is the rising incidence of AIDS among the elderly; 10 percent of all AIDS patients are aged 50 or over.

School Social Work

In schools, social workers serve students and their families, teachers, administrators, and other school staff members. Education, counseling, and advocacy are important aspects of school social work. With education, social workers attempt to prevent alcohol and drug abuse, teen pregnancy, and the spread of AIDS and other sexually transmitted diseases. They provide multicultural and family life education. They counsel students who are discriminated against because of their sexual orientation or racial, ethnic, or religious background. They also serve as advocates for these students, bringing issues of discrimination before administrators, school boards, and student councils.

A smaller number of social workers are employed in the areas of *social work education* (a field composed of the professors and instructors who teach and train students of social work); *group practice* (in which social workers facilitate treatment and support groups); and *corrections* (providing services to inmates in penal institutions). Social workers also offer counseling, occupational assistance, and advocacy to those with addictions and disabilities, to the homeless, and to women, children, and the elderly who have been in abusive situations.

Client groups expand and change as societal problems change. Social work professionals must remain aware of the problems affecting individuals and communities in order to offer assistance to as many people as possible.

Computers have become important tools for social workers. Client records are maintained on computer databases, allowing for easier collection and analysis of data. Interactive software programs are used to train social workers, as well as to analyze case histories (such as for an individual's risk of HIV infection).

■ EARNINGS

The more education a social worker has completed, the more money he or she stands to make in the profession. The area of practice also determines earnings; the areas of mental health, group services, and community organization and planning provide higher salaries, while elderly and disabled care generally provide lower pay. Salaries also vary among regions. Social workers on the east and west coasts earn higher salaries than those in the Midwest. Earnings in Canada vary from province to province as well. During their first five years of practice, social workers' salaries generally increase faster than in later years.

Social workers in general earned median wages of $45,900 as of May 2015. The lowest paid 10 percent garnered no more than $28,530 annually, and the highest paid took home $76,820 or more. Child, family, and school social workers earned a median salary of $42,350 in May 2015, according to the U.S. Department of Labor. Health care social workers had a median salary of $52,380. Mental health and substance abuse social workers earned a median salary of $42,170.

■ WORK ENVIRONMENT

Social workers do not always work at a desk. When they do, they may be interviewing clients, writing reports, or conferring with other staff members. Depending on the size of the agency, office duties such as writing letters, filing, and answering phones may be performed by an aide or volunteer. Social workers employed at shelters or halfway houses may spend most of their time with clients, tutoring, counseling, or leading groups.

Some social workers have to drive to remote areas to make a home visit. They may go into inner-city neighborhoods, schools, courts, or jails. In larger cities, domestic violence and homeless shelters are sometimes located in rundown or dangerous areas. Most social workers are involved directly with the people they serve and must carefully examine the client's living conditions and family relations. Although some of these living conditions can be pleasant and demonstrate a good home situation, others can be squalid and depressing.

Advocacy involves work in a variety of different environments. Although much of this work may require making phone calls and sending e-mails, faxes, and letters, it also requires meetings with clients' employers, directors of agencies, local legislators, and others. It may sometimes require testifying in court as well.

■ EXPLORING

As a high school student, you may find openings for summer or part-time work as a receptionist or file clerk with a local social service agency. If there are no opportunities for paid employment, you could work as a volunteer. You can also gain good experience by working as a counselor in a camp for children with physical, mental, or developmental disabilities. Your local YMCA, park district, or other recreational facility may need volunteers for group recreation programs, including programs designed for the prevention of delinquency. By reporting for your high school newspaper, you'll have the opportunity to interview people, conduct surveys, and research social

A social worker checks on an elderly client in the hospital. (ChameleonsEye. Shutterstock.)

change, all of which are important aspects of the social work profession.

You could also volunteer a few afternoons a week to read to people in retirement homes or to the blind. Work as a tutor in special education programs is sometimes available to high school students.

■ EDUCATION AND TRAINING REQUIREMENTS
High School

To prepare for a social work career, you should take courses in high school that will improve your communications skills, such as English, speech, composition, and and a foreign language (such as Spanish). On a debate team, you could further develop your skills in communication as well as research and analysis. History, social studies, and sociology courses are important in understanding the concerns and issues of society. Although limited work is available for those with only an associate's degree (as a social work aide or social services technician), the most opportunities exist for people with more advanced degrees in social work.

Postsecondary Training

There are approximately 510 accredited B.S.W. (bachelor's in social work) programs and 155 accredited M.S.W. (master's in social work) programs accredited by the Council on Social Work Education (CSWE). The Group for the Advancement of Doctoral Education lists more than 80 doctoral programs for Ph.D.'s in social work or D.S.W.'s (doctor of social work). The CSWE requires that five areas be covered in accredited bachelor's degree social work programs: human

JANE ADDAMS, FOUNDER OF HULL HOUSE

MOVERS AND SHAKERS

Social worker, reformer, and peace advocate Jane Addams (1860–1935) made Hull House in Chicago world-famous as a settlement house (social-welfare center). She shared the 1931 Nobel Peace Prize with Nicholas Murray Butler, president of Columbia University. She was elected to the Hall of Fame for Great Americans in 1965.

In 1889, Addams and Ellen Gates Starr, a college classmate, leased a decrepit mansion known as Hull House, located in one of Chicago's worst slums. Here Addams, Starr, and other volunteers held classes for immigrants, provided day care for babies, and operated a community center, dispensary, coffee shop, art gallery, theater, gymnasium, and cooperative boardinghouse for working women. Addams solicited financial support, had new buildings erected around Hull House, and recruited volunteer workers, mostly middle- and upper-class women. Hull House became a training center for social workers and a model for similar settlement houses in other parts of the United States.

Addams campaigned for political and social reforms, including woman suffrage, protection of working women, strict child labor laws, recognition of labor unions, improvements in public welfare, more playgrounds, and separate courts for juvenile offenders.

behavior and the social environment; social welfare policy and services; social work practice; research; and field practicum. Most programs require two years of liberal arts study followed by two years of study in the social work major. Also, students must complete a field practicum of at least 400 hours. Graduates of these programs can find work in public assistance or they can work with the elderly or with people with mental or developmental disabilities.

The CSWE offers a directory of accredited social work programs at http://www.cswe.org/Accreditation/Accredited-Programs.aspx.

Although no clear lines of classification are drawn in the social work profession, most supervisory and administrative positions require at least an M.S.W. degree. Master's programs are organized according to fields of practice (such as mental health care), problem areas (substance abuse), population groups (the elderly), and practice roles (practice with individuals, families, or communities). They are usually two-year programs that require at least 900 hours of field practice. Most positions in mental health care facilities require an M.S.W.

Doctoral degrees are also available and prepare students for research and teaching. Most social workers with doctorates go to work in community organizations.

Other Education or Training

The National Association of Social Workers offers online courses, webinars, and other continuing education opportunities. Topics include everyday practice issues, social media, career planning, and ethics. The Association for Childhood Education International, Council on Social Work Education, and the Canadian Association of Social Workers also provide professional development courses. Contact these organizations for more information.

■ CERTIFICATION, LICENSING, AND SPECIAL REQUIREMENTS
Certification or Licensing

Licensing, certification, or registration of social workers is required by all states. To receive the necessary licensing, a social worker will typically have to gain a certain amount of experience and also pass an exam.

The National Association of Social Workers offers two professional social work credentials and 18 specialty certifications (13 for M.S.W.s and five for B.S.W.s). These credentials are particularly valuable for social workers in private practice, as some health insurance providers require them for reimbursement purposes. Contact the association for more information.

■ EXPERIENCE, SKILLS, AND PERSONALITY TRAITS

One way to gain experience in preparation for a career in social work is to help people in need in your community. Volunteer with community and religious organizations and in any other setting where you can help people. College social work students gain valuable practical experience by completing a field practicum of at least 400 hours.

Social work requires great dedication. As a social worker, you have the responsibility of helping whole families, groups, and communities, as well as focusing on the needs of individuals. Your efforts will not always be supported by the society at large; sometimes you must work against a community's prejudice, disinterest, and denial. You must also remain sensitive to the problems of your clients, offering support, and not moral judgment or personal bias. The only way to effectively address new social problems and new client groups is to remain open to the thoughts and needs of all human beings. Assessing situations and solving problems requires clarity of vision and a genuine concern for the well-being of others.

With this clarity of vision, your work will be all the more rewarding. Social workers have the satisfaction of making a connection with other people and helping them through difficult times. Along with the rewards, however, the work can cause a great deal of stress. Hearing repeatedly about the deeply troubled lives of prison inmates, the mentally ill, abused women and children, and others can be depressing and defeating. Trying to convince society of the need for changes in laws and services can be a long, hard struggle. You must have perseverance to fight for your clients against all odds.

■ EMPLOYMENT PROSPECTS
Employers

Approximately 649,300 social workers are employed in the United States. They can be employed in direct or clinical practice, providing individual and family counseling services, or they may work as administrators for the organizations that provide direct practice. Social workers are employed by community health and mental health centers; hospitals and mental hospitals; child care, family services, and community service organizations, including day care and Head Start programs; elderly care programs, including adult protective services and adult day care and foster care; prisons; shelters and halfway houses; schools; courts; and nursing homes.

Starting Out

Most students of social work pursue a master's degree and in the process learn about the variety of jobs available. They also make valuable connections through faculty and other students. Through the university's career services center or an internship program, a student will learn about job openings and potential employers.

A social work education in an accredited program will provide you with the most opportunities, and the best salaries and chances for promotion, but practical social work experience can also earn you full-time employment. A part-time job or volunteer work will introduce you to social work professionals who can provide you with career guidance and letters of reference. Agencies with limited funding may not be able to afford to hire social workers with M.S.W.s and therefore will look for applicants with a great deal of experience and lower salary expectations.

■ ADVANCEMENT PROSPECTS

More attractive and better-paying jobs tend to go to those with more years of practical experience. Dedication to your job, an extensive resume, and good references will lead to advancement in the profession. Also, many social work programs offer continuing education workshops, courses, and seminars. These refresher courses help practicing social workers to refine their skills and to learn about new areas of practice and new methods and problems. The courses are intended to supplement your social work education, not substitute for a bachelor's or master's degree. These continuing education courses can lead to job promotions and salary increases. Social workers with advanced degrees and experience can advance to become social work managers or directors of social work programs. Some become university professors.

■ OUTLOOK

The field of social work is expected to grow 12 percent, faster than the average for all occupations, through 2024, according to the U.S. Department of Labor. The greatest factor for this growth is the increased number of older people who are in need of social services. Social workers that specialize in gerontology will find many job opportunities in nursing homes, hospitals, and home health care agencies. The needs of the future elderly population are likely to be different from those of the present elderly. Currently, the elderly appreciate community living, while subsequent generations may demand more individual care.

Employment for child, family, and school social workers is expected to grow faster than the average for all careers through 2024. Schools will need more social workers to deal with issues such as teenage pregnancies, children from single-parent households, and any adjustment problems recent immigrants may have. The trend to integrate students with disabilities into the general school population will require the expertise of social workers to make the transition smoother. However, job availability in schools will depend on funding given by state and local sources. Demand will increase for child and family social workers as these professionals are needed to investigate alleged cases of child abuse and place children with adoptive families and in foster care.

Job opportunities for health care social workers will grow much faster than the average for all careers through 2024. To help control costs, hospitals are encouraging early discharge for some of their patients. Social workers will be needed by hospitals to help secure health services for patients in their homes. There are also a growing number of people with physical disabilities or impairments staying in their own homes, requiring home health care workers.

Employment of mental health and substance abuse social workers is projected to grow much faster than the average for all careers through 2024. Demand is growing for these specialized social workers because more people are seeking treatment for mental illness and substance use disorders, and the court system is increasingly sending drug offenders to treatment programs rather than to jail.

Increased availability of health insurance funding and the growing number of people able to pay for professional help will create opportunities for those in private practice. Many businesses hire social workers to help in employee assistance programs, often on a contractual basis.

Poverty is still a main issue that social workers address. Families are finding it increasingly challenging to make ends meet on wages that are just barely above the minimum. The problem of fathers who do not make their court-ordered child support payments forces single mothers to work more than one job or rely on welfare. An increased awareness of domestic violence has also pointed up the fact that many homeless and unemployed people are women who have left abusive situations. Besides all this, working with the poor is often considered unattractive, leaving many social work positions in this area unfilled.

Competition for jobs in urban areas will remain strong. However, there is still a shortage of social workers in rural areas; these areas usually cannot offer the high salaries or modern facilities that attract large numbers of applicants.

The social work profession is constantly changing. The survival of social service agencies, both private and public, depends on shifting political, economic, and workplace issues.

Social work professionals are worried about the threat of declassification. Because of budget constraints and a need for more workers, some agencies have lowered their job requirements. When unable to afford qualified professionals, they hire those with less education and experience. This downgrading raises questions about quality of care and professional standards. Just as in some situations low salaries push out the qualified social worker, so do high salaries. In the area of corrections, attractive salaries (up to $40,000 for someone with a two-year associate's degree) have resulted in more competition from other service workers.

Liability is another growing concern. If a social worker, for example, tries to prove that a child has been beaten or attempts to remove a child from his or her home, the worker can potentially be sued for libel. At the other extreme, a social worker can face criminal charges for failure to remove a child from an abusive home. More social workers are taking out malpractice insurance.

■ UNIONS AND ASSOCIATIONS

The U.S. Department of Labor reports that approximately 24 percent of social workers are members of a union or covered by a union contract. Many social workers are members of the National Association of Social Workers. The Association of Social Work Boards provides information on licensing. The Council on Social Work Education offers information on educational programs. Social workers who are employed in Canada can obtain information on education and careers from the Canadian Association for Social Work Education and the Canadian Association of Social Workers.

■ TIPS FOR ENTRY

1. Participate in internships or part-time jobs that are arranged by your college's career services office. Try to acquire work that requires you to frequently interact with people.
2. Visit http://careers.socialworkers.org for job listings.
3. Join the National Association of Social Workers (NASW) to access training and networking resources, industry publications, and employment opportunities.
4. Become certified by the NASW in order to show employers that you have met the highest standards set by your industry.

■ FOR MORE INFORMATION

For information on licensing, contact
Association of Social Work Boards
400 South Ridge Parkway, Suite B
Culpeper, VA 22701-3791
Tel: (800) 225-6880
E-mail: info@aswb.org
http://www.aswb.org

For career information and job listings available in Canada, contact
Canadian Association of Social Workers
383 Parkdale Avenue, Suite 402
Ottawa, ON K1Y 4R4
Canada
Tel: (855) 729-2279; (613) 729-6668
Fax: (613) 729-9608
E-mail: casw@casw-acts.ca
http://www.casw-acts.ca

For information on social work careers and educational programs, contact
Council on Social Work Education
1701 Duke Street, Suite 200
Alexandria, VA 22314-3457
Tel: (703) 683-8080

Fax: (703) 683-8099

E-mail: info@cswe.org

http://www.cswe.org

For information on careers and certification, contact

National Association of Social Workers

750 First Street, NE, Suite 700

Washington, D.C. 20002-4241

Tel: (800) 742-4089; (202) 408-8600

E-mail: membership@naswdc.org

http://www.naswdc.org

Sociologists

■ OVERVIEW

Sociologists study the behavior and interaction of people in groups. They research the characteristics of families, communities, the workplace, religious and business organizations, and many other segments of society. By studying a group, sociologists can gain insight about individuals; they can develop ideas about the roles of gender, race, age, and other social traits in human interaction. This research helps the government, schools, and other organizations address social problems and understand social patterns. In addition to research, a sociologist may teach, publish, consult, or counsel.

■ HISTORY

Sociology has its origins in the 19th century. As a science, it was based on experiment and measurement rather than philosophical speculation. Until an experimental basis for the testing of theory and speculation was devised, the study of society remained in the area of philosophy and not in that of science. Auguste Comte, a French mathematician, is generally credited with being the originator of modern sociology. He coined the term, which is derived from the Latin *socius*, meaning *companion*. His idea was that sociology should become the science that would draw knowledge from all sciences to produce fundamental understandings of human society. It was his feeling that once all sciences were blended together, human society could be viewed as a totality. Comte's theories are not now widely held among scientists; in fact, the development of sociology through the past century has been basically in the opposite direction. It was Emile Durkheim, a French sociologist, who initiated the use of scientific study and research methods to develop and support sociological theories in the early part of the 20th century.

The field has become more specialized as it has grown. The study of the nature of human groups has proved to be all encompassing. Only by specializing in one aspect of this science can scholars hope to form fundamental principles. For example, such areas as criminology and penology, while still technically within the field of sociology, have become very specialized. Working in these areas requires training that is different in emphasis and content from that which is required in other areas of sociology.

■ THE JOB

Curiosity is the main tool of a successful sociologist. Sociologists are intrigued by questions. For example, why do the members of different high school sports teams interact with each other in certain ways? Or why do some people work better in teams than others? What are the opportunities for promotion for workers with disabilities? Sociologists can even be inspired to question social policies based on their everyday experiences. For example, a sociologist reading a newspaper article about someone on a state's death row may wonder what the effect that the state's death penalty has on its crime level. Or an article on a new casino may cause the sociologist to wonder what effects legalized gambling have on the residents of that area. Such curiosity is one of the driving forces behind a sociologist's work.

With thoughtful questions and desire for knowledge, sociologists investigate the origin, development, and functioning of groups of people. This can involve extensively interviewing people or distributing form questionnaires. It

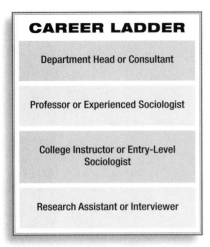

CAREER LADDER

Department Head or Consultant

Professor or Experienced Sociologist

College Instructor or Entry-Level Sociologist

Research Assistant or Interviewer

can involve conducting surveys or researching historical records, both public and personal. A sociologist may need to set up an experiment, studying a cross section of people from a given society. The sociologist may choose to watch the interaction from a distance, or to participate as well as observe.

The information sociologists compile from this variety of research methods is then used by administrators, lawmakers, educators, and other officials engaged in solving social problems. By understanding the common needs, thoughts, patterns, and ideas of a group of people, an organization can better provide for the individuals within those groups. With a sociologist's help, a business may be able to create a better training program for its employees; counselors in a domestic violence shelter may better assist clients with new home and job placement; teachers may better educate students with special needs.

Sociologists work closely with many other professionals. One of the closest working relationships is between sociologists and *statisticians* to analyze the significance of data. Sociologists also work with *psychologists*. Psychologists attempt to understand individual human behavior, while sociologists try to discover basic truths about groups. Sociologists also work with *cultural anthropologists*. Anthropologists study whole societies and try to discover what cultural factors have produced certain kinds of patterns in given communities. Sociologists work with *economists*. The ways in which people buy and sell are basic to understanding how groups behave. They also work with *political scientists* to study systems of government.

Ethnology and ethnography, social sciences that treat the subdivision of humans and their description and classification, are other fields with which sociologists work closely. Problems in racial understanding and cooperation, in failures in communication, and in differences in belief and behavior are all concerns of the sociologist who tries to discover underlying reasons for group conduct.

Sociologists and *psychiatrists* have cooperated to discover community patterns of mental illness and mental health. They have attempted to compare such things as socioeconomic status, educational level, residence, and occupation to the incidence and kind of mental illness to determine in what ways society may be contributing to or preventing emotional disturbances.

Some sociologists choose to work in a specialized field. *Criminologists* specialize in investigations of causes of crime and methods of prevention, and *penologists* investigate punishment for crime, management of penal institutions, and rehabilitation of criminal offenders. *Social pathologists* specialize in the investigation of group behavior that is considered detrimental to the proper functioning of society. *Demographers* are population specialists who collect and analyze vital statistics related to population changes, such as birth, marriages, and death. *Rural sociologists* investigate cultures and institutions of rural communities, while *urban sociologists* investigate origin, growth, structure, composition, and population of cities. *Social welfare research workers* conduct research that is used as a tool for planning and carrying out social welfare programs.

■ EARNINGS

Median annual earnings for sociologists were $73,760 in May 2015, according to the U.S. Bureau of Labor Statistics. The lowest paid 10 percent earned less than $36,200, while the highest paid 10 percent earned more than $145,250. Sociologists working for the scientific research and developments earned mean annual salaries of $97,920. Those employed by state governments earned $63,300. College sociology professors earned median annual salaries of $56,310 in May 2015.

Benefits for full-time workers include health insurance and retirement funds. In some cases, college sociology professors receive stipends for travel related to research, housing allowances, and tuition waivers for dependents.

■ WORK ENVIRONMENT

An academic environment can be ideal for a sociologist intent on writing and conducting research. If required to teach only a few courses a semester, a sociologist can then devote a good deal of time to his or her own work. And having contact with students can create a balance with the research.

The work of a sociologist takes place mostly in the classroom or at a computer writing reports and analyzing data. Some research requires visiting the interview subjects or setting up an experiment within the community of study.

■ EXPLORING

There are books about sociology, and possibly some journals of sociology, in your school and public libraries. By reading recent books and articles you can develop an understanding of the focus and requirements of sociological study. If no specific sociology courses are offered in your high school, courses in psychology, history, or English literature can prepare you for the study of groups and human interaction; within these courses you may be able to write reports or conduct experiments with a sociological slant. A school newspaper, magazine, or journalism course can help you to develop important interview, research, and writing skills, while also heightening your awareness of your community and the communities of others.

■ EDUCATION AND TRAINING REQUIREMENTS
High School

Since a master's degree is recommended, if not required, in this field, you should take college prep courses while in high school. Take English classes to develop composition skills; you will be expected to present your research findings in reports, articles, and books. In addition to sociology classes, you should take other classes in the social sciences, such as psychology, history, and anthropology. Math and business will prepare you for the analysis of statistics and surveys. Government and history classes will help you to understand some of the basic principles of society, and journalism courses will bring you up to date on current issues.

Postsecondary Training

Most sociologists get their undergraduate degree in sociology, but a major in other areas of the liberal arts is also possible. Courses that you will likely take include statistics, mathematics, psychology, logic, and possibly a foreign language. In addition, keep up your computer skills because the computer is an indispensable research and communication tool.

Keep in mind that only limited entry-level positions will be available to you with only a bachelor's degree. New graduates may be able to start as a *research assistant* or *interviewer*. These workers are needed in research organizations, social service agencies, and corporate marketing departments.

Students who go on to get their master's and doctorate degrees will have a wider variety of employment opportunities. With a master's degree, opportunities are available in the federal government, industrial firms, or research organizations. Individuals with specific training in research methods will have an advantage. Those with a master's degree can also teach at the community or junior college level.

More than half of all sociologists hold doctorates. A large majority of the sociologists at the doctoral level

teach in four-year colleges and universities throughout the country. Job candidates fare best if their graduate work includes specialized research and fieldwork.

Other Education or Training

A variety of webinars, conference seminars, and other continuing education (CE) opportunities are offered by professional associations such as the American Sociological Association and the Association for Applied and Clinical Sociology. Contact these organizations for more information.

■ CERTIFICATION, LICENSING, AND SPECIAL REQUIREMENTS
Certification or Licensing

The Association for Applied and Clinical Sociology offers the voluntary certified sociological practitioner designation to those who submit a portfolio of their academic and practice background, current practice, and ethical positions, as well as complete a certification demonstration (which covers their portfolio in more detail) at a professional meeting. Contact the association for more information.

■ EXPERIENCE, SKILLS, AND PERSONALITY TRAITS

Many sociologists pursue careers as college professors. Previous teaching experience (student teaching, etc.) is necessary to become a college teacher; it will take several years at the minimum to gain tenure and advance to the rank of professor.

ESSENTIAL READING FOR SOCIOLOGISTS

DID YOU KNOW?

The International Sociological Association conducted an opinion survey of its members to find the most important books about sociology published in the 20th century. Here are the top five.

1. *Economy and Society,* by Max Weber
2. *The Sociological Imagination,* by Charles Wright Mills
3. *Social Theory and Social Structure,* by Robert K. Merton
4. *The Protestant Ethic and the Spirit of Capitalism,* by Max Weber
5. *The Social Construction of Reality,* by P. L. Berger and T. Luckmann

Source: http://www.isa-sociology.org/en/about-isa/history-of-isa/books-of-the-xx-century/

In addition to the natural curiosity mentioned above, a good sociologist must also possess an open mind. You must be able to assess situations without bias or prejudice that could affect the results of your studies. Social awareness is also important. As a sociologist, you must pay close attention to the world around you, to the way the world progresses and changes. Because new social issues arise every day, you will be frequently reading newspapers, magazines, and reports to maintain an informed perspective on these issues. Many sociologists also use social media and the Internet in general to gather information and conduct research.

Good communication skills are valuable to the sociologist. In many cases, gathering information will involve interviewing people and interacting within their societies. The better your communication skills, the more information you can get from the people you interview.

▪ EMPLOYMENT PROSPECTS
Employers
The majority of sociologists teach in colleges and universities. Some sociologists work for agencies of the federal government. In such agencies, their work lies largely in research, though they may also serve their agencies in an advisory capacity. Some sociologists are employed by private research organizations and nonprofits, and some work in management consulting firms. Sociologists also work with various medical groups and with physicians. Some sociologists are self-employed, providing counseling, research, or consulting services.

Starting Out
Many sociologists find their first jobs through the career services offices of their colleges and universities. Some are placed through the professional contacts of faculty members. A student in a doctorate program will make many connections and learn about fellowships, visiting professorships, grants, and other opportunities.

Those who wish to enter a research organization, industrial firm, or government agency should apply directly to the prospective employer. If you have been in a doctorate program, you should have research experience and publications to list on your resume, as well as assistantships and scholarships.

▪ ADVANCEMENT PROSPECTS
Sociologists who become college or university teachers may advance through the academic ranks from instructor to full professor. Those who like administrative work may become a head of a department. Publications of books and articles in journals of sociology will assist in a professor's advancement.

Those who enter research organizations, government agencies, or private business advance to positions of responsibility as they acquire experience. Salary increases usually follow promotions.

▪ OUTLOOK
Employment for sociologists is expected to decline for all careers through 2024, according to the U.S. Department of Labor (DOL). Opportunities are best for those with broad training and education in analytical, methodological, conceptual, and qualitative and quantitative analysis and research. Competition will be strong in all areas, however, as many sociology graduates continue to enter the job market. The DOL reports that "candidates with an advanced degree, strong statistical and research skills, and a background in applied sociology will have the best job prospects."

As the average age of Americans rises, more opportunities of study will develop for those working with the elderly. Sociologists who specialize in gerontology will have opportunities to study the aging population in a variety of environments. Sociologists will find more opportunities in marketing, as companies conduct research on specific populations, such as the children of baby boomers. The Internet is also opening up new areas of sociological research; sociologists, demographers, market researchers, and other professionals are studying online communities and their impact.

▪ UNIONS AND ASSOCIATIONS
The majority of sociologists are employed as college educators. Unions that represent the interests of college professors include the American Federation of Teachers and the National Education Association. The American Association of University Professors' purpose is to "advance academic freedom and shared governance, to define fundamental professional values and standards for higher education, and to ensure higher education's contribution to the common good." The American Sociological Association is the leading professional organization for sociologists. It provides career resources, job listings, publications, continuing education classes and webinars, and other useful resources. The Association for Applied and Clinical Sociology, another popular organization for sociologists, provides certification and continuing education opportunities.

▪ TIPS FOR ENTRY
1. Sociology students who plan to become college teachers should subscribe to the *Chronicle of Higher Education* (http://chronicle.com) to learn about trends in higher education and to access job listings.

2. To learn more about the field, read:
   - *American Sociological Review* (http://www.asanet.org/journals/journals.cfm)
   - *Teaching Sociology* (http://www.asanet.org/teaching/resources.cfm)
   - *Journal of Applied Social Science* (http://journals.sagepub.com/home/jax)
3. Conduct information interviews with sociologists and ask them for advice on preparing for and entering the field.
4. Join the American Sociological Association (ASA) and other professional associations to take advantage of training and networking resources, industry publications, and employment opportunities. Members of the ASA receive access to job listings, discounts on publications and conferences, networking opportunities, and other resources.

■ FOR MORE INFORMATION

For information about careers, education, and union membership, contact

American Association of University Professors

1133 19th Street, NW, Suite 200

Washington, D.C. 20036-3655

Tel: (202) 737-5900

Fax: (202) 737-5526

E-mail: aaup@aaup.org

http://www.aaup.org

For information on union membership, contact

American Federation of Teachers (AFT)

555 New Jersey Avenue, NW

Washington, D.C. 20001-2029

Tel: (202) 879-4400

http://www.aft.org

ASA offers career publications as well as job information.

American Sociological Association (ASA)

1430 K Street, NW, Suite 600

Washington, D.C. 20005-2529

Tel: (202) 383-9005

E-mail: info@asanet.org

http://www.asanet.org

To learn about sociologists working outside academia, contact

Association for Applied and Clinical Sociology

Eastern Michigan University

926 East Forest Avenue

Ypsilanti, MI 48198-3823

Tel: (734) 845-1206

E-mail: sac_aacs@emich.edu

http://www.aacsnet.net/

For information on union membership, contact

National Education Association (NEA)

1201 16th Street, NW

Washington, D.C. 20036-3290

Tel: (202) 833-4000

Fax: (202) 822-7974

http://www.nea.org

> **MOST NEW JOBS**

Software Application Developers

■ OVERVIEW

Software application developers devise applications, often referred to as apps, such as word processing programs, data storage programs, and spreadsheet programs that make it possible for computers to complete given tasks and to solve problems. They also design and build Web browsing applications and software applications for mobile devices such as smartphones. Once a need in the market has been identified, software developers first conceive of the program on a global level by outlining what the program will do. Then they write the specifications from which programmers code computer commands to perform the given functions. Software application developers are also known as *mobile application developers, software application builders,* and *software application designers.* Approximately 718,400 software application developers are employed in the United States.

■ HISTORY

Software application developers create programs to do almost anything—from online banking to finding driving directions to word processing to tracking baseball standings. With the extensive proliferation of computers and smartphones in our society, there is an excellent market for user-friendly, imaginative, and high-performance software applications.

Application software is the type of software that is most familiar to computer users. This category includes word-processing, spreadsheets, and e-mail packages commonly used in business; games, accounting, and reference software used by the average consumer;

Web browsing applications; social media applications; and subject- or skill-based software used in schools.

Software applications for smartphones and other handheld, Internet-enabled devices have become very popular in recent years. In 2002, the Treo line of handheld computing/telecommunications devices was released by Handspring. Users could download or sync third-party applications for use with the device. But according to *Five Technology Trends to Watch 2011,* a report by the Consumer Electronics Association (CEA), it took another six years for mobile apps as we know them today to emerge.

Apple launched the original iPhone on January 9, 2007. Contrary to popular lore, Apple did not initially focus on app development for this mobile device. Instead it stressed the telecommunication aspects of the iPhone. Demand grew for mobile apps for the iPhone, and in October of that year, Apple announced that it would release a software development kit for mobile application developers who were interested in creating apps for iPhones.

The Apple App store opened on July 10, 2008, and applications began selling briskly. Today, they are ubiquitous on handheld, Internet-enabled telecommunications/computing devices produced by Apple, Google, and other manufacturers.

The CEA reports that "there are more than 250,000 apps in Apple's iTunes Store; 100,000 apps in the Android Marketplace; and thousands of apps across a multiplicity of other platforms." In 2016, 77 percent of adults in the United States had mobile phones that are app friendly, according to the Pew Research Center. As a result of these developments, the career of mobile application developer has emerged to meet market demands.

■ THE JOB

Applications, or programs, are sets of codes that instruct computers on how to perform. *Software application developers* create these by developing and/or writing this code. Developers must consider every aspect of how an application will function, what users will do with it, and what might go wrong. They must also think about the interface—or the look of the app and how users interact with it.

Application developers may create programs for wide use, such as word processing, photo editing, or mapping software, or they may create specialized programs for professionals, such as accountants or doctors. Some companies specialized in custom software, which is often created for businesses or governments and must meet their needs. In some cases, these applications must also comply with specific laws or regulations.

Regardless of whom the end user is, software application developers must begin by defining the goal and purpose of the program. Next, they develop the program architecture and design strategy. Once this is approved and finalized, a team begins writing the program. Once this is done, the program goes through phases of testing, during which errors and bugs are corrected before it is released to the public or delivered to a client.

The growing popularity of smartphones and other mobile computing/telecommunications devices has created a new career specialty: *mobile application developer.* Mobile application developers create applications for smartphones—such as the Apple iPhone, Google Android, or RIM Blackberry—as well as for other handheld, Internet-enabled telecommunications/computing devices. Developing an application for a mobile device is much different than creating one for use on a computer. Mobile app developers need to design software that is user-friendly for the smaller screens of smartphones and other devices. They need to understand how users interact with their devices and design apps that are both functional (for example, stressing touch-screen tools rather than drop-down menus that are incorporated into traditional software applications), but also visually appealing. Mobile app developers need the standard knowledge of HTML, artificial intelligence tools, and object-oriented programming languages such as Java, Python, and C++ that all developers have, but also must be proficient in newer object-oriented programming languages and have knowledge of specific mobile development environments like Google's Android and Apple's iOS.

EARNINGS

Salaries for software application designers ranged from less than $57,340 to $153,710 or more in May 2015, according to the U.S. Department of Labor. They earned median annual salaries of $98,260. At the managerial level, salaries are even higher and can reach $175,000 or more. Mobile application developers earn higher salaries, ranging from $115,250 to $175,750 in 2016, according to Robert Half Technology's *2016 Salary Guide for Technology Professionals.*

Salaries for software application developers vary with the size of the company and by location. Salaries may be higher in areas where there is a large concentration of computer companies, such as the Silicon Valley and San Francisco in northern California and Texas, Virginia, Massachusetts, Washington, and New York.

Most developers work for large companies, which offer a full benefits package that includes health insurance, vacation and sick time, and a profit sharing or retirement plan. Freelance developers must provide their own benefits.

WORK ENVIRONMENT

Software application developers work in comfortable environments. Many computer companies are known for their casual work atmosphere; employees generally do not have to wear suits, except during client meetings. Overall, many software developers work standard weeks. However, they may be required to work overtime near a deadline, and over 25 percent work more than 40 hours per week. It is common in software development to share office or cubicle space with two or three coworkers, which is typical of the team approach to working. Internet technology is also allowing software application developers to work from home or other remote locations. As a software application developer or programmer, much of the day is spent in front of the computer, although a software developer will have occasional team meetings or meetings with clients.

Software application development can be stressful work for several reasons. First, the market for software is very competitive, and companies are pushing to develop more innovative software, including cutting-edge mobile apps, and to get them on the market before competitors do. For this same reason, software application development is also very exciting and creative work. Second, software developers are given a project and a deadline. It is up to the developer and team members to budget their time to finish in the allocated time. Finally, working with programming languages and so many details can be very frustrating, especially when the tiniest glitch means the program will not run. For this reason, software application developers must be patient and diligent.

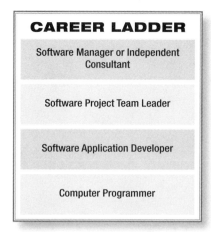

CAREER LADDER

Software Manager or Independent Consultant

Software Project Team Leader

Software Application Developer

Computer Programmer

EXPLORING

Spending a day with a software application developer or programmer will allow you to experience firsthand what this work entails. School counselors and computer science teachers can often help you organize such a meeting.

If you are interested in computer industry careers in general, you should learn as much as possible about computers. Keep up with new technology by talking to other computer users and by reading related magazines, such as *Computer* (http://www.computer.org/portal/web/computer/home). Or visit http://www.computer.org/portal/web/computingnow, which aggregates articles from various IEEE Computer Society publications. You will also find it helpful to join computer clubs and use the Internet to find more information about this field. Visit the Association for Computing Machinery's career Web site, http://computingcareers.acm.org, for information on career paths, a list of suggested high school classes, profiles of computer science students, and answers to frequently asked questions about the field.

Advanced students can put their design ideas and programming knowledge to work by designing and programming their own applications, such as simple games and utility programs.

EDUCATION AND TRAINING REQUIREMENTS
High School

If you are interested in a career in software application development, you should take as many computer, math, and science courses as possible; they provide fundamental math and computer knowledge and teach analytical thinking skills. Classes that focus on schematic drawing and flowcharts are also very valuable. English and speech courses will help you improve your communication skills, which are very important to software application developers who must make formal presentations to management and clients.

Postsecondary Education

A bachelor's degree in computer science, software development, software design, or software engineering, plus

Software application developers discuss solutions to a problematic piece of code. (Stock Rocket. Shutterstock.)

at least one year of experience with a programming language, is required for most software developers. At least one internship is also usually required.

A few colleges offer majors in mobile application design; many offer classes in the field. Rasmussen College was one of the first schools to create a curriculum that focused on mobile application design and programming. It offers an associate's degree in software application development and a bachelor's degree in computer science. Major and core courses include Foundations of Software Design, Introduction to Computer Systems, Mobile Application Development, Fundamentals of Programming, Java, Object Oriented Programming, Discrete Structures for Computer Science, Advanced Algebra, Pre-Calculus, and Calculus. Visit http://www.rasmussen.edu/degrees/technology-design/software-application-development for more information.

In the past, the computer industry has tended to be flexible about official credentials; demonstrated computer proficiency and work experience have often been enough to obtain a good position. However, as more people enter the field, competition has increased, and job requirements have become more stringent. Technical knowledge alone does not suffice in the field of software application development anymore. In order to be a successful developer, you should have at least a peripheral knowledge of the field for which you intend to develop software, such as business, education, or science. Individuals with a degree in education and subsequent teaching experience are much sought after as developers for educational software. Those with bachelor's degrees in computer science with a minor in business or accounting have an excellent chance for employment in developing business or accounting software.

Other Education or Training

The Association for Computing Machinery, International Game Developers Association, Association for Women in Computing, IEEE Computer Society, and the International Webmasters Association offer webinars, on-site classes, workshops, and other continuing education opportunities. Contact these organizations for more information.

■ CERTIFICATION, LICENSING, AND SPECIAL REQUIREMENTS
Certification or Licensing

The IEEE Computer Society offers the designation, certified software development professional, to individuals who meet educational and experience and pass an examination. Certification in software development is also offered by companies such as Hewlett-Packard, IBM, Novell, and Oracle. While not required, certification tells employers that your skills meet industry education and training standards.

■ EXPERIENCE, SKILLS, AND PERSONALITY TRAITS

Aspiring software application developers should participate in at least one internship during college. An internship or other work experience will provide you with a great introduction to the field and allow you to make valuable industry contacts that may come in handy when you are looking for a job. Additionally, you should obtain at least one year of programming experience.

Software application development is project- and detail-oriented, and therefore, you must be patient and diligent. You must also enjoy problem-solving challenges and be able to work under a deadline with minimal supervision. As a software application developer, you should also possess good communication skills for consulting both with management and with clients who will have varying levels of technical expertise.

Software companies are looking for individuals with vision and imagination to help them create new and exciting applications to sell in the ever-competitive software market. Superior technical skills and knowledge combined with motivation, imagination, and exuberance will make you an attractive candidate.

■ EMPLOYMENT PROSPECTS
Employers

Approximately 718,400 software application developers are employed in the United States. Opportunities are best in large cities and suburbs where business and industry are active. Programmers who develop software systems work for software developers and manufacturers, many of whom are in Silicon Valley and San Francisco, in northern California, as well as in Texas, Virginia, Massachusetts, Washington, and New York, among other places. Developers who adapt and tailor the software to meet specific needs of end-users work for those end-user companies, many of which are scattered across the country.

Starting Out

Software development positions are regarded as some of the most interesting, and therefore the most competitive, in the computer industry. Some software application developers are promoted from an entry-level programming position. Software development positions in software companies and large custom software companies will be difficult to secure straight out of college.

Students in technical schools or universities should take advantage of their campus career services offices. They should check regularly for internship postings, job listings, and notices of on-campus recruitment. Career services offices are also valuable resources for resume tips and interviewing techniques. Internships and summer jobs with software corporations are always beneficial and provide experience that will give you the edge over your competition. General computer job fairs are also held throughout the year in larger cities.

There are many online career sites that post job openings, salary surveys, and current employment trends. You can also obtain information from computer organizations such as the IEEE Computer Society. Because this is such a competitive field, you will need to show initiative and creativity that will set you apart from other applicants.

■ ADVANCEMENT PROSPECTS

Those software application developers who demonstrate leadership may be promoted to the position of *project team leader*. Project team leaders develop new software projects and oversee the work done by software application developers and programmers. With experience as a project team leader, a motivated software application developer may be promoted to a position as a *software manager* who runs projects from an even higher level. Individuals with a knack for spotting trends in the software market are also likely to advance.

■ OUTLOOK

Employment for software application developers is expected to grow much faster than the average for all occupations through 2024, according to the *Occupational Outlook Handbook*. Employment will increase as technology becomes more sophisticated and organizations

---

MOST POPULAR TYPES OF APPS   DID YOU KNOW?

1. Social Networking
2. Weather
3. Browser
4. Games
5. Streaming Music
6. Banking
7. Navigation
8. Retail
9. Streaming Video
10. Messaging

Source: The Nielsen Company

---

continue to adopt and integrate these technologies, making for plentiful job openings. Hardware designers and systems programmers are constantly developing faster, more powerful, and more user-friendly hardware and operating systems. As long as these advancements continue, the industry will need software application developers to create software to use these improvements.

The expanding integration of Internet and wireless technologies by businesses has resulted in a rising demand for a variety of skilled professionals who can develop and support a variety of Internet and wireless applications. The health care industry is also using more software applications, which will spur demand for developers. Employment opportunities for the specialty of mobile application developer are expected to be excellent.

■ UNIONS AND ASSOCIATIONS

Software application developers are not represented by unions, but they can obtain useful resources and professional support from the Academy of Interactive Arts & Sciences, Association for Computing Machinery, Association for Women in Computing, Entertainment Software Association, IEEE Computer Society, International Game Developers Association, and the Software & Information Industry Association. The IEEE Computer Society offers certification to software developers.

■ TIPS FOR ENTRY

1. Practice developing your own apps to increase your skills.
2. Apply to small or start-up firms where you will probably receive more responsibility and be asked to handle a wider range of job duties.
3. Visit the following Web sites for job listings:
   - http://apps-jobs.com
   - http://www.elance.com

- http://www.computer.org/portal/web/careers
- http://jobs.acm.org
- http://www.awn.com
- http://www.highendcareers.com
- http://www.dice.com
- http://www.gamejobs.com
- http://www.gamasutra.com

4. Attend industry conferences to network and interview for jobs.

5. Join professional associations such as the IEEE Computer Society to access training and networking resources, industry publications, and employment opportunities.

■ FOR MORE INFORMATION

For information on opportunities in the computer and video game industry, contact

Academy of Interactive Arts & Sciences (AIAS)
11175 Santa Monica Blvd., 4th Floor
Los Angeles, CA 90025
Tel: (310) 484-2552
E-mail: claudio@interactive.org
http://www.interactive.org

For information on careers, contact

Association for Computing Machinery (ACM)
2 Penn Plaza, Suite 701
New York, NY 10121-0701
Tel: (800) 342-6626; (212) 626-0500
Fax: (212) 944-1318
E-mail: acmhelp@acm.org
http://computingcareers.acm.org

For information on career opportunities for women in computing, contact

Association for Women in Computing (AWC)
PO Box 2768
Oakland, CA 94602-0068
E-mail: info@awc-hq.org
http://www.awc-hq.org

For industry information, contact

Entertainment Software Association (ESA)
601 Massachusetts Avenue, NW, Suite 300
Washington, D.C. 20001
E-mail: esa@theesa.com
http://www.theesa.com

For information on careers, certification, education, and student memberships, contact

IEEE Computer Society (IEEE)
2001 L Street, NW, Suite 700
Washington, D.C. 20036-4928
Tel: (202) 371-0101
Fax: (202) 728-9614
E-mail: help@computer.org
http://www.computer.org

For information on careers, contact

International Game Developers Association (IGDA)
19 Mantua Road
Mt. Royal, NJ 08061-1006
Tel: (856) 423-2990
http://www.igda.org

Visit the IWA Web site for information on its voluntary certification program.

International Webmasters Association (IWA)
119 East Union Street, Suite A
Pasadena, CA 91103-3951
Tel: (626) 449-3709
Fax: (866) 607-1773
E-mail: Support@iwanet.org
http://www.iwanet.org

For industry information, contact

Software & Information Industry Association (SIIA)
1090 Vermont Avenue, NW, Sixth Floor
Washington, D.C. 20005-4095
Tel: (202) 289-7442
Fax: (202) 289-7097
http://www.siia.net

Software Designers

■ OVERVIEW

Software designers, also known as *software developers*, create new ideas and design prepackaged and customized computer software. *Systems software designers* create systems software such as computer operating systems, proprietary computer systems for businesses and other organizations, and operating systems that control consumer electronics in cars, big-box appliances, and smartphones. These systems make it possible for computers to complete given tasks and to solve problems. *Software applications designers* create word processing programs, video games, front-end database programs, and spreadsheet programs. Once a need in the market has been identified, software designers first conceive of the program on a global level by outlining what the program will do. Then they write the specifications from which programmers code computer commands to perform the given functions. There are about 1.1 million software developers and programmers employed in the United States. Computer systems design jobs employed 33 percent of them as of May 2015. Software publishers, finance and insurance business, and electronics product manufacturing employed another 24 percent.

■ HISTORY

"In 1983, software development exploded with the introduction of the personal computer. Standard applications included not only spreadsheets and word processors, but graphics packages and communications systems," according to *Events in the History of Computing*, compiled by the Institute of Electrical and Electronics Engineers (IEEE) Computer Society.

Advances in computer technology have enabled professionals to put computers to work in a range of activities once thought impossible. Computer software designers have been able to take advantage of computer hardware improvements in speed, memory capacity, reliability, and accuracy to create programs to do almost anything. With the extensive proliferation of computers in our society, there is a great market for user-friendly, imaginative, and high-performance software. Business and industry rely heavily on the power of computers and use both prepackaged software and software that has been custom-designed for their own specific use. Also, with more people purchasing computer systems for home use, the retail market for prepackaged software has grown steadily. Given these conditions, computer software designing will be an important field in the industry for years to come.

The software industry has many facets, including packaged applications for personal computers (known as "shrink-wrapped software"); operating systems for stand-alone and networked systems; management tools for networks; enterprise software that enables efficient management of large corporations' production, sales, and information systems; software applications and operating systems for mainframe computers; and customized software for specific industry management.

Packaged software is written for mass distribution, not for the specific needs of a particular user. Broad categories include operating systems, utilities, applications, and programming languages. Operating systems control the basic functions of a computer or network. Utilities perform support functions, such as backup or virus protection. Programming software is used to develop the sets of instructions that build all other types of software. The software familiar to most computer users is called application software. This category includes word-processing, spreadsheets, and e-mail packages, commonly used in business, as well as games and reference software used in homes, and subject- or skill-based software used in schools.

■ THE JOB

Without software, computer hardware would have nothing to do. Computers need to be told exactly what to do, and software is the set of codes that gives the computer those instructions. It comes in the form of the familiar prepackaged software that you find in a computer store, such as games, word processing, spreadsheet, and desktop publishing programs, and in customized applications designed to fit specific needs of a particular business. Software designers are the initiators of these complex programs. Computer programmers then create the software by writing the code that carries out the directives of the designer.

Software designers must envision every detail of what an application will do, how it will do it, and how it will look (the user interface). A simple example is how a home accounting program is created. The software designer first lays out the overall functionality of the program, specifying what it should be able to do, such as balancing a checkbook, keeping track of incoming and outgoing bills, and maintaining records of expenses. For each of these tasks, the software designer will outline the design details for the specific

CAREER LADDER

Software Manager

Project Team Leader

Software Designer

Computer Programmer

functions that he or she has mandated, such as what menus and icons will be used, what each screen will look like, and whether there will be help or dialog boxes to assist the user. For example, the designer may specify that the expense record part of the program produce a pie chart that shows the percentage of each household expense in the overall household budget. The designer can specify that the program automatically display the pie chart each time a budget assessment is completed or only after the user clicks on the appropriate icon on the toolbar.

Some software companies specialize in building custom-designed software. This software is highly specialized for specific needs or problems of particular businesses. Some businesses are large enough that they employ in-house software designers who create software applications for their computer systems. A related field is software engineering, which involves writing customized complex software to solve specific engineering or technical problems of a business or industry.

Whether the designer is working on a mass-market or a custom application, the first step is to define the overall goals for the application. This is typically done in consultation with management if working at a software supply company, or with the client if working on a custom-designed project. Then, the software designer studies the goals and problems of the project. If working on custom-designed software, the designer must also take into consideration the existing computer system of the client. Next, the software designer works on the program strategy and specific design detail that he or she has envisioned. At this point, the designer may need to write a proposal outlining the design and estimating time and cost allocations. Based on this report, management or the client decides if the project should proceed.

Once approval is given, the software designer and the programmers begin working on writing the software program. Typically, the software designer writes the specifications for the program, and the applications programmers write the programming codes.

In addition to the duties involved in design, a software designer may be responsible for writing a user's manual or at least writing a report for what should be included in the user's manual. After testing and debugging the program, the software designer will present it to management or to the client.

EARNINGS

Salaries for software designers vary with the size of the company and by location. Salaries may be slightly higher in areas where there is a large concentration of computer companies, such as the Silicon Valley and San Francisco in northern California and Texas, Virginia, Massachusetts, Washington, New York, and other states.

Software developers specializing in systems software earned median salaries of $105,5700 in May 2015, according to the U.S. Department of Labor. The lowest paid 10 percent averaged $64,600 annually, and the highest paid engineers made $159,850 per year or more.

Most designers work for large companies, which offer a full benefits package that includes health insurance, vacation and sick time, and a profit sharing or retirement plan.

WORK ENVIRONMENT

Software designers work in comfortable environments. Many computer companies are known for their casual work atmosphere; employees generally do not have to wear suits, except during client meetings. Overall, software designers work standard weeks. However, they may be required to work overtime near a deadline. It is common in software design to share office or cubicle space with two or three coworkers, which is typical of the team approach to working. As a systems software designer or applications programmer, much of the day is spent in front of the computer, although a software designer will have occasional team meetings or meetings with clients.

Software design can be stressful work for several reasons. First, the market for software is very competitive and companies are pushing to develop more innovative software and to get it on the market before competitors do. For this same reason, software design is also very exciting and creative work. Second, software designers are given a project and a deadline. It is up to the designer and team members to budget their time to finish on schedule. Finally, working with programming languages and so many details can be very frustrating, especially when the tiniest glitch means the program will not run. For this reason, software designers must be patient and diligent.

EXPLORING

Spending a day with an experienced systems software designer or applications programmer will allow you to experience firsthand what this work entails. School counselors can often help you organize such a meeting.

If you are interested in computer industry careers in general, you should learn as much as possible about computers. Keep up with new technology by talking to other computer users and by reading related magazines, such as *Computer* (http://www.computer.org/computer). You will also find it helpful to join computer clubs and use online services and the Internet to find more information about this field.

Advanced students can put their design ideas and programming knowledge to work by designing and programming their own applications, such as simple games and utility programs.

■ EDUCATION AND TRAINING REQUIREMENTS
High School

If you are interested in computer science, you should take as many computer, math, and science courses as possible; they provide fundamental math and computer knowledge and teach analytical thinking skills. Classes that focus on schematic drawing and flowcharts are also very valuable. English and speech courses will help you improve your communication skills, which are very important to software designers who must make formal presentations to management and clients. Also, many technical/vocational schools offer programs in software programming and design. The qualities developed by these classes, plus imagination and an ability to work well under pressure, are key to success in software design.

Postsecondary Training

A bachelor's degree in computer science, plus one year's experience with a programming language, are required for most software designers; however, a master's degree is preferred for some positions.

In the past, the computer industry has tended to be pretty flexible about official credentials; demonstrated computer proficiency and work experience have often been enough to obtain a good position. However, as more people enter the field, competition has increased, and job requirements have become more stringent. Technical knowledge alone does not suffice in the field of software design anymore. In order to be a successful software designer, you should have at least a peripheral knowledge of the field for which you intend to design software, such as business, education, or science. Individuals with degrees in education and subsequent teaching experience are much sought after as designers for educational software. Those with bachelor's degrees in computer science with a minor in business or accounting have an excellent chance for employment in designing business or accounting software.

A software designer plans how a new program will run with an upcoming operating system update. (Stock Rocket. Shutterstock.)

Students also complete an internship or other on-the-job experience as part of their training. A master's degree in software engineering or a related field may be required for some positions. Large computer and consulting firms may offer specialized training in proprietary programs.

Other Education or Training

The Association for Computing Machinery, International Game Developers Association, Association for Women in Computing, IEEE Computer Society, and the International Webmasters Association offer webinars, on-site classes, workshops, and other continuing education opportunities. Contact these organizations for more information.

■ CERTIFICATION, LICENSING, AND SPECIAL REQUIREMENTS
Certification or Licensing

Certification in software development is offered by companies such as Hewlett-Packard, IBM, Novell, Microsoft, and Oracle. While not required, certification tells employers that your skills meet industry education and training standards.

The IEEE Computer Society offers the designation, certified software development professional, to individuals who meet education and experience requirements and pass an examination.

■ EXPERIENCE, SKILLS, AND PERSONALITY TRAITS

Several years' programming experience, plus a college internship or other on-the-job experience, are recommended for aspiring software engineers.

OPEN SOURCE

In the 1960s and 1970s, when computer networks were still in their infancy, groups of "hackers" scattered across the country built the rough framework of what would become the Internet. The hackers enjoyed an extremely collaborative work environment, where everyone shared ideas and built freely on the work of others. However, when large businesses began to realize the value of copyrighting and developing their own software programs, many members of this original group of hackers were lured away by the high salaries and benefits of jobs in private industry. As this trend continued to grow, the free exchange of ideas and code among programmers was becoming a thing of the past.

As a reaction to the "closing off" of the software-development process, small groups of programmers began to develop code and distribute it freely on the Internet. Through newsgroups and bulletin boards, groups of programmers would build on this code, troubleshoot glitches, and, in contrast to the copyrighted code of large businesses, share their code freely with other programmers, thereby creating free software that began to rival many commercial products. This type of software, called open-source software, has come to embody an entire programming philosophy, one that tries to maintain the creative and collaborative vision that gave birth to so much of today's technology.

Software design is project- and detail-oriented, and therefore, you must be patient and diligent. You must also enjoy problem-solving challenges and be able to work under a deadline with minimal supervision. As a software designer, you should also possess good communication skills for consulting both with management and with clients who will have varying levels of technical expertise.

Software companies are looking for individuals with vision and imagination to help them create new and exciting programs to sell in the ever-competitive software market. Superior technical skills and knowledge combined with motivation, imagination, and exuberance will make you an attractive candidate.

■ EMPLOYMENT PROSPECTS
Employers

Around 1.1 million software developers and programmers are employed in the United States. Software designers are employed throughout the United States. Opportunities are best in large cities and suburbs where business and industry are active. Many software manufacturers are headquartered in Silicon Valley and San Francisco in northern California. There are also concentrations of software manufacturers in Texas, Virginia, Massachusetts, Washington, and New York, among other places. Designers who adapt and tailor the software to meet specific needs of end-users work for those end-user companies, many of which are scattered across the country.

Starting Out

Software design positions are regarded as some of the most interesting, and therefore the most competitive, in the computer industry. Some software designers are promoted from an entry-level programming position. Software design positions in software supply companies and large custom software companies will be difficult to secure straight out of college or technical/vocational school.

Entry-level programming and design jobs may be listed in the help wanted sections of newspapers. Employment agencies and online job banks are other good sources.

Students in technical schools or universities should take advantage of their school's career services office. They should check regularly for internship postings, job listings, and notices of on-campus recruitment. Career services offices are also valuable resources for resume tips and interviewing techniques. Internships and summer jobs with such corporations are always beneficial and provide experience that will give you the edge over your competition. General computer job fairs are also held throughout the year in larger cities.

There are many online career sites listed on the World Wide Web that post job openings, salary surveys, and current employment trends. The Web also has online publications that deal specifically with computer jobs. You can also obtain information from computer organizations such as the IEEE Computer Society. Because this is such a competitive field, you will need to show initiative and creativity that will set you apart from other applicants.

■ ADVANCEMENT PROSPECTS

In general, *programmers* work between one and five years before being promoted to *software designer*. A programmer can move up by demonstrating an ability to create new software ideas that translate well into marketable applications. Individuals with a knack for spotting trends in the software market are also likely to advance.

Those software designers who demonstrate leadership may be promoted to *project team leader*. Project team leaders are responsible for developing new software projects and overseeing the work done by software designers and applications programmers. With experience as a project team leader, a motivated software designer may be promoted to a position as a *software manager* who runs projects from an even higher level.

OUTLOOK

Employment of software designers is expected to grow by 17 percent through 2024, according to the U.S. Department of Labor, or much faster than the average for all careers. Increasing demand for software in the health care industry, the expanding integration of software technologies by businesses, the skyrocketing popularity of mobile devices (which require new applications) and computer games, among other factors, are prompting strong growth in this field. Those with advanced education and knowledge of cutting-edge programming tools and languages will have the best job prospects.

UNIONS AND ASSOCIATIONS

Software designers are not represented by unions, but they can obtain useful resources and professional support from the Academy of Interactive Arts & Sciences, Association for Computing Machinery, Association for Women in Computing, Entertainment Software Association, IEEE Computer Society, International Game Developers Association, and the Software & Information Industry Association.

TIPS FOR ENTRY

1. Apply to small or start-up firms where you will probably receive more responsibility and be asked to handle a wider range of job duties.
2. Visit the following Web sites for job listings:
   - http://www.computer.org/portal/web/careers
   - http://jobs.acm.org
   - http://www.awn.com
   - http://www.highendcareers.com
   - http://www.dice.com
   - http://www.gamejobs.com
   - http://www.gamasutra.com
3. Join professional associations to access training and networking resources, industry publications, and employment opportunities.
4. Become certified in order to show employers that you have met the highest standards established by your industry.

FOR MORE INFORMATION

For information on opportunities in the computer and video game industry, contact

Academy of Interactive Arts & Sciences
11175 Santa Monica Blvd, 4th Floor
Los Angeles, CA 90025
Tel: (310) 484-2552
E-mail: claudio@interactive.org
http://www.interactive.org

For information on internships, student membership, and careers, contact
Association for Computing Machinery
2 Penn Plaza, Suite 701
New York, NY 10121-0701
Tel: (800) 342-6626; (212) 626-0500
Fax: (212) 944-1318
E-mail: acmhelp@acm.org
http://www.acm.org

For information on career opportunities for women in computing, contact
Association for Women in Computing (AWC)
PO Box 2768
Oakland, CA 94602-0068
E-mail: Info@awc-hq.org
http://www.awc-hq.org

For industry information, contact
Entertainment Software Association (ESA)
601 Massachusetts Avenue, NW, Suite 300
Washington, D.C. 20001
E-mail: esa@theesa.com
http://www.theesa.com

For information on careers, certification, education, and student memberships, contact
IEEE Computer Society
2001 L Street, NW, Suite 700
Washington, D.C. 20036-4928
Tel: (202) 371-0101
Fax: (202) 728-9614
E-mail: help@computer.org
http://www.computer.org

For information on careers, contact
International Game Developers Association (IGDA)
19 Mantua Road
Mt. Royal, NJ 08061-1006
Tel: (856) 423-2990
http://www.igda.org

For industry information, contact
Software & Information Industry Association (SIIA)
1090 Vermont Ave., NW, 6th Floor
Washington, D.C. 20005-4095
Tel: (202) 289-7442
Fax: (202) 289-7097
http://www.siia.net

Software Engineers

▓ OVERVIEW

Software engineers create or customize existing software programs to meet the needs of a particular business or industry. First, they spend considerable time researching, defining, and analyzing the problem at hand. Then, they develop software programs to resolve the problem on the computer. They may also create software applications that are used for informational purposes or entertainment. There are slightly more than 1 million software designers and developers, which includes software engineers, employed in the United States.

▓ HISTORY

Advances in computer technology have enabled professionals to put computers to work in a range of activities once thought impossible. In the past several years, computer software engineers have been able to take advantage of computer hardware improvements in speed, memory capacity, reliability, and accuracy to create programs that do just about anything. Computer engineering blossomed as a distinct subfield in the computer industry after the new performance levels were achieved. This relative lateness is explained by the fact that the programs written by software engineers to solve business and scientific problems are very intricate and complex, requiring a lot of computing power. Although many computer scientists will continue to focus their research on further developing hardware, the emphasis in the field has moved to software (as a result of the rapid growth of the Internet and mobile telecommunications and computing devices).

▓ THE JOB

Every day, businesses, scientists, and government agencies encounter difficult problems that they cannot solve manually, either because the problem is just too complicated or because it would take too much time to calculate the appropriate solutions. For example, astronomers receive thousands of pieces of data every hour from probes and satellites in space as well as from telescopes here on Earth.

If they had to process the information themselves, compile careful comparisons with previous years' readings, look for patterns or cycles, and keep accurate records of the origin of the data, it would be so cumbersome and lengthy a project as to make it next to impossible. They can, however, process the data with the extensive help of computers. Computer software engineers define and analyze specific problems in business or science and help develop computer software applications that effectively solve them. The software engineers who work in the field of astronomy are well versed in its concepts, but many other kinds of software engineers exist as well.

Software engineers fall into two basic categories. *Systems software engineers* build and maintain entire computer systems for a company. *Applications software engineers* design, create, and modify general computer applications software or specialized utility programs.

Engineers who work on computer systems research how a company's departments and their respective computer systems are organized. For example, there might be customer service, ordering, inventory, billing, shipping, and payroll recordkeeping departments. Systems software engineers suggest ways to coordinate all these parts. They might set up intranets or networks that link computers within the organization and ease communication.

Some applications software engineers develop packaged software applications, such as word processing, graphic design, or database programs, for software development companies. Other applications engineers design customized software for individual businesses or organizations. For example, a software engineer might work with an insurance company to develop new ways to reduce paperwork, such as claim forms, applications, and bill processing. Applications engineers write programs using programming languages like C++ and Java.

Software engineers sometimes specialize in a particular industry such as the chemical industry, insurance, or medicine, which requires knowledge of that industry in addition to computer expertise. Some engineers work for consulting firms that complete software projects for different clients on an individual basis. Others work for large companies that hire full-time engineers to develop software customized to their needs.

Software engineering technicians assist engineers in completing projects. They are usually knowledgeable in analog, digital, and microprocessor electronics and programming techniques. Technicians know enough about program design and computer languages to fill in details left out by engineers or programmers, who conceive of the program from a large-scale perspective. Technicians might also test new software applications with special diagnostic equipment.

Both systems and applications software engineering involve extremely detail-oriented work. Since computers do only what they are programmed to do, engineers have to account for every bit of information with a programming command. Software engineers are thus required to be very well organized and precise. In order to achieve this, they generally follow strict procedures in completing an assignment.

First, they interview clients and colleagues to determine exactly what they want the final program to accomplish. Defining the problem by outlining the goal can sometimes be difficult, especially when clients have little technical training. Then, engineers evaluate the software applications already in use by the client to understand how and why they are failing to fulfill the needs of the operation. After this period of fact gathering, the engineers use methods of scientific analysis and mathematical models to develop possible solutions to the problems. These analytical methods help them predict and measure the outcomes of different proposed designs.

When they have developed a clear idea of what type of program is required to fulfill the client's needs, they draw up a detailed proposal that includes estimates of time and cost allocations. Management must then decide if the project will meet their needs, is a good investment, and whether or not it will be undertaken.

Once a proposal is accepted, both software engineers and technicians begin work on the project. They verify with hardware engineers that the proposed software program can be completed with existing hardware systems. Typically, the engineer writes program specifications and the technician uses his or her knowledge of computer languages to write preliminary programming. Engineers focus most of their effort on program strategies, testing procedures, and reviewing technicians' work.

Software engineers are usually responsible for a significant amount of technical writing, including project proposals, progress reports, and user manuals. They are required to meet regularly with clients to keep project goals clear and learn about any changes as quickly as possible.

When the program is completed, the software engineer organizes a demonstration of the final product to the client. Supervisors, management, and users are generally present. Some software engineers may offer to install the program, train users on it, and make arrangements for ongoing technical support.

■ EARNINGS

Software engineers earned median annual salaries of $64,702 as of January 207, according to Salary.com. The lowest paid 10 percent averaged less than $50,344, and the highest paid 10 percent earned $79,344 or more annually. When software engineers are promoted to *project team leader* or *software manager*, they earn even more. Software engineers generally earn more in geographical areas where there are clusters of computer companies, such as the Silicon Valley in northern California.

Most software engineers work for companies that offer extensive benefits, including health insurance, sick leave, and paid vacation. In some smaller computer companies, however, benefits may be limited.

■ WORK ENVIRONMENT

Software engineers usually work in comfortable office environments. Overall, they usually work 40-hour weeks, but their hours depend on the nature of the employer and expertise of the engineer. In consulting firms, for example, it is typical for software engineers to work long hours and frequently travel to out-of-town assignments. The U.S. Department of Labor reports that more than 25 percent of software developers work more than 40 hours a week.

Software engineers generally receive an assignment and a time frame within which to accomplish it; daily work details are often left up to the individuals. Some engineers work relatively lightly at the beginning of a project, but work a lot of overtime at the end in order to catch up. Most engineers are not compensated for overtime. Software engineering can be stressful, especially when engineers must work to meet deadlines. Working with programming languages and intense details

QUICK FACTS

ALTERNATE TITLE(S)
Applications Software Engineers, Systems Software Engineers

DUTIES
Create new or customize existing software programs to meet the needs and desires of a particular business or industry

SALARY RANGE
$50,344 to $64,702 to $79,344+

WORK ENVIRONMENT
Primarily Indoors

BEST GEOGRAPHIC LOCATION(S)
Silicon Valley in northern California, Texas, Virginia, Massachusetts, Washington, and New York

MINIMUM EDUCATION LEVEL
Bachelor's Degree

SCHOOL SUBJECTS
Computer Science, Mathematics, Physics

EXPERIENCE
Internship; several years' programming experience

PERSONALITY TRAITS
Hands On, Problem-Solving, Technical

SKILLS
Computer, Information Management, Math

CERTIFICATION OR LICENSING
Recommended

SPECIAL REQUIREMENTS
None

EMPLOYMENT PROSPECTS
Excellent

ADVANCEMENT PROSPECTS
Good

OUTLOOK
Much Faster than the Average

NOC
2173

O*NET-SOC
15-1132.00, 15-1133.00, 15-1199.02

CAREER LADDER

Software Manager, or Chief
Information Officer, or
Systems Designer

Software Project Team Leader

Software Engineer

Software Engineering Technician

is often frustrating. Therefore, software engineers should be patient, enjoy problem-solving challenges, and work well under pressure.

■ EXPLORING

Try to spend a day with a working software engineer or technician in order to experience firsthand what their job is like. School counselors can help you arrange such a visit. You can also talk to your high school computer teacher for more information.

In general, you should be intent on learning as much as possible about computers and computer software. You should learn about new developments by reading trade magazines and talking to other computer users. You also can join computer clubs and surf the Internet for information about working in this field.

■ EDUCATION AND TRAINING REQUIREMENTS
High School

A bachelor's or advanced degree in computer science or engineering is required for most software engineers. Thus, to prepare for college studies while in high school, take as many computer, math, and science courses as possible; they provide fundamental math and computer knowledge and teach analytical thinking skills. Classes that rely on schematic drawing and flowcharts are also very valuable. English and speech courses will help you improve your communication skills, which are very important for software engineers.

Postsecondary Training

As more and more well-educated professionals enter the industry, most employers now require a bachelor's degree. A typical degree concentration for an applications software engineer is software engineering, computer science, or mathematics. Systems software engineers typically pursue a concentration in computer science or computer information systems. Students also complete an internship or other on-the-job experience as part of their training. A master's degree in software engineering or a related field may be required for some positions. Large computer and consulting firms may offer specialized training in proprietary programs. If you plan to work in a specific technical field, such as medicine, law, or business, you should receive some formal training in that particular discipline.

Other Education or Training

Several associations offer continuing education opportunities. Student and professional members of the Association for Computing Machinery can access online computing and business courses via the association's Learning Center. The IEEE Computer Society offers career planning webinars and continuing education courses to its members. Other organizations that provide continuing education opportunities include the Association for Women in Computing, Information Architecture Institute, and the International Game Developers Association. Contact these organizations for more information.

■ CERTIFICATION, LICENSING, AND SPECIAL REQUIREMENTS
Certification or Licensing

The IEEE Computer Society offers the certified software development associate credential (for graduating software engineers and entry-level software professionals) and the certified software development professional credential (for experienced software designers and engineers) to individuals who meet education and experience requirements and pass an examination. The Institute for Certification of Computing Professionals also offers certification to computer professionals.

Another option if you're interested in software engineering is to pursue commercial certification. These programs are usually run by computer companies that wish to train professionals to work with their products. Classes are challenging and examinations can be rigorous. New programs are introduced every year.

■ EXPERIENCE, SKILLS, AND PERSONALITY TRAITS

Take as many math and computer science classes as possible and participate in internships and other opportunities to gain experience in the field. Several years of programming experience are recommended for aspiring software engineers.

As a software engineer, you will need strong communication skills in order to be able to make formal business presentations and interact with people having different levels of computer expertise. You must also be detail oriented. Working with programming languages and intense details is often frustrating. Therefore, you should be patient, enjoy problem-solving challenges, have a creative mindset and good analytical skills, and work well under pressure. If you plan to work in a digital media-related field, it is a good idea to have at least some familiarity with your chosen specialty (such as animation or computer and video games).

■ EMPLOYMENT PROSPECTS

Employers

About 1 million software engineers are employed in the United States. Approximately 643,830 work with applications and 373,510 work with systems software. Software engineers work in many industries, including medical, manufacturing, military, communications, aerospace, scientific, and other commercial businesses. About 32 percent of software engineers—the largest concentration in the field—work in computer systems design and related services. Many software engineers work at software firms that are located in Silicon Valley and San Francisco, in northern California, as well as in Texas, Virginia, Massachusetts, Washington, and New York, among other places.

Starting Out

As a student of software engineering, you should work closely with your school's career services office, as many professionals find their first position through on-campus recruiting. Career services office staff are well trained to provide tips on resume writing, interviewing techniques, and locating job leads.

Individuals not working with a school placement office can check the online postings for job openings. They also can work with a local employment agency that places computer professionals in appropriate jobs. Many openings in the computer industry are publicized by word of mouth, so you should stay in touch with working computer professionals to learn who is hiring. In addition, these people may be willing to refer you directly to the person in charge of recruiting.

Check out job-search Web sites such as http://www.dice.com and be sure to create a profile on LinkedIn so that recruiters can learn more about your educational background and skill set.

■ ADVANCEMENT PROSPECTS

Software engineers who demonstrate leadership qualities and thorough technical know-how may become *project team leaders* who are responsible for full-scale software development projects. Project team leaders oversee the work of technicians and engineers. They determine the overall parameters of a project, calculate time schedules and financial budgets, divide the project into smaller tasks, and assign these tasks to engineers. Overall, they do both managerial and technical work.

Software engineers with experience as project team leaders may be promoted to a position as *software manager,* running a large research and development department. Managers oversee software projects with a more encompassing perspective; they help choose projects

Software engineers can create specialized computer systems or modify software applications to help companies become more efficient and productive. (Pixza Studio. Shutterstock.)

to be undertaken, select project team leaders and engineering teams, and assign individual projects. In some cases, they may be required to travel, solicit new business, and contribute to the general marketing strategy of the company.

Other advancement possibilities for software engineers include manager of information systems, chief information officer, systems designer, or independent consultant.

Many computer professionals find that their interests change over time. As long as individuals are well qualified and keep up to date with the latest technology, they are usually able to find positions in other areas of the computer industry.

■ OUTLOOK

Employment opportunities for software engineers are expected to grow 17 percent, much faster than the average for all occupations through 2024, according to the U.S. Department of Labor (DOL). Demands made on computers increase every day and from all industries. Rapid growth in the computer systems design and related industries will account for much of this growth. In addition, businesses will continue to implement new and innovative technology to remain competitive, and they will need software engineers to do this. Software engineers will also be needed to handle ever-growing capabilities of computer networks, e-commerce, and wireless technologies, as well as the security features needed to protect such systems from outside attacks. Growth in mobile technologies and the rapid increase in the number of products that use software will create excellent job opportunities for software engineers.

TIM BERNERS-LEE AND THE WORLD WIDE WEB

Just one person created the World Wide Web. When one considers the millions of Web users and the seemingly limitless amount of information available on the Web, this may seem unbelievable. But it was the work of one man—Tim Berners-Lee—that brought about the invaluable resource that links people and ideas around the world on a daily basis.

You might say that computers are in Berners-Lee's blood. He was born in London in 1955, the child of parents who had met while working on the Ferrant Mark I, the first computer sold commercially. As a student, Berners-Lee was naturally inquisitive and took an early interest in math and physics. One of his favorite books was a Victorian-era encyclopedia entitled *Enquire Within Upon Everything*, which would serve as a major inspiration for his future work.

In 1980, Berners-Lee was working as a software engineer at CERN, the European Laboratory for Particle Physics in Geneva, Switzerland. During this time he began to think of a way to link all of the information in his computer so that he could easily jump from topic to topic, as he had when reading his favorite childhood book. Thus, he wrote a computer program called Enquire Within Upon Everything, which enabled him to do just that. Expanding on this idea, Lee created HTML (hypertext markup language), which enabled him to link information on a limitless number of computers and networks. Berners-Lee then assembled the first Web browser, which enabled a user to view information in an orderly fashion. These were the basic components of the World Wide Web, which would debut on the world scene in 1991.

Although the Web would soar in popularity, Berners-Lee did not make millions from it (although he certainly could have). Instead, he chose to keep his career and invention in the nonprofit sector. He currently works at Massachusetts Institute of Technology and heads the W3 Consortium, which decides on standards for the Web, and founded the Open Data Institute.

Outsourcing of jobs in this field to foreign countries will temper growth somewhat, but overall the future of software engineering is very bright.

Since technology changes so rapidly, software engineers are advised to keep up on the latest developments. While the need for software engineers will remain high, computer languages will probably change every few years and software engineers will need to attend seminars and workshops to learn new computer languages and software design. They also should read trade magazines, surf the Internet, and talk with colleagues about the field. These kinds of continuing education techniques help ensure that software engineers are best equipped to meet the needs of the workplace.

■ UNIONS AND ASSOCIATIONS

Software engineers are not represented by unions, but they can obtain useful resources and professional support from the Academy of Interactive Arts & Sciences, Association for Computing Machinery, Association for Women in Computing, Entertainment Software Association, IEEE Computer Society, Information Architecture Institute, International Game Developers Association, and the Software & Information Industry Association. The Institute for Certification of Computing Professionals and the IEEE Computer Society provide certification.

■ TIPS FOR ENTRY

1. Apply to small or start-up firms where you will probably receive more responsibility and be asked to handle a wider range of job duties.
2. Read publications such as *IEEE Transactions on Software Engineering* and *Computer* (both are available at http://www.computer.org) to learn more about trends in the industry and potential employers.
3. Visit the following Web sites for job listings:
   - http://www.computer.org/portal/web/careers
   - http://jobs.acm.org
   - http://www.awn.com
   - http://www.highendcareers.com
   - http://www.dice.com
   - http://www.gamejobs.com
   - http://www.gamasutra.com
4. Participate in internships or part-time jobs that are arranged by your college's career services office. Additionally, visit http://www.computer.org/portal/web/careers for a list of internship opportunities.

■ FOR MORE INFORMATION

For information on opportunities in the computer and video game industry, contact

Academy of Interactive Arts & Sciences (AIAS)
11175 Santa Monica Blvd., 4th Floor
Los Angeles, CA 900025
Tel: (310) 484-2552
E-mail: claudio@interactive.org
http://www.interactive.org

For information on internships, student membership, and careers, contact

Association for Computing Machinery (ACM)

2 Penn Plaza, Suite 701

New York, NY 10121-0701

Tel: (800) 342-6626; (212) 626-0500

Fax: (212) 944-1318

E-mail: acmhelp@acm.org

http://www.acm.org

For information on career opportunities for women in computing, contact

Association for Women in Computing (AWC)

PO Box 2768

Oakland, CA 94602-0068

E-mail: Info@awc-hq.org

http://www.awc-hq.org

For industry information, contact

Entertainment Software Association (ESA)

601 Massachusetts Avenue, NW, Suite 300

Washington, D.C. 20001

E-mail: esa@theesa.com

http://www.theesa.com

For information on careers, certification, education, and student memberships, contact

IEEE Computer Society (IEEE)

2001 L Street, NW, Suite 700

Washington, D.C. 20036-4928

Tel: (202) 371-0101

Fax: (202) 728-9614

E-mail: help@computer.org

http://www.computer.org

For information about information architecture and educational programs, contact

Information Architecture Institute

800 Cummings Center, Suite 357W

Beverly, MA 01915-6174

E-mail: info@iainstitute.org

http://iainstitute.org

For certification information, contact

Institute for Certification of Computing Professionals (ICCP)

2400 East Devon Avenue, Suite 281

Des Plaines, IL 60018-4602

Tel: (800) 843-8227; (847) 299-4227

E-mail: office2@iccp.org

http://www.iccp.org

For information on careers, contact

International Game Developers Association (IGDA)

19 Mantua Road

Mt. Royal, NJ 08061-1006

Tel: (856) 423-2990

http://www.igda.org

For more information on careers in computer software, contact

Software & Information Industry Association

1090 Vermont Ave., NW, 6th Floor

Washington, D.C. 20005-4095

Tel: (202) 289-7442

Fax: (202) 289-7097

http://www.siia.net

Software Quality Assurance Testers

■ OVERVIEW

Software quality assurance testers, also known as *software quality assurance analysts,* examine new or modified computer software applications to evaluate whether or not they perform as intended. Testers might also verify that computer-automated quality assurance programs function properly. Their work entails trying to crash computer programs by punching in certain characters very quickly, for example, or by clicking the mouse on the border of an icon. They keep very close track of the combinations they enter so that they can replicate the situation if the program does crash. They also offer opinions on the user-friendliness of the program. They report in detail any problems they find or suggestions they have both verbally and in writing to supervisors.

■ HISTORY

The first major advances in modern computer technology were made during World War II. After the war, it was thought that the enormous size of computers, which easily took up the space of entire warehouses, would limit their use to huge government projects. Accordingly, the 1950 census was computer processed.

The introduction of semiconductors to computer technology made possible smaller and less expensive computers. Businesses began adapting computers to their operations as early as 1954. Within 30 years, computers had revolutionized the way people work, play, and shop. Today, computers are everywhere, from businesses of all kinds to government agencies, charitable organizations, and private homes. Over the years, the technology has continued to shrink computer size as their speeds have increased at an unprecedented rate.

Engineers have been able to significantly increase the memory capacity and processing speed of computer hardware. These technological advances enable computers to effectively process more information than ever before. Consequently, more sophisticated software applications have been created. These programs offer extremely user-friendly and sophisticated working environments that would not have been possible on older, slower computers. In addition, the introduction of CD-ROMs and DVD-ROMs to the mass computer market enabled the production of complex programs stored on compact discs. And, today, large computer hard drives and cloud-computing storage allow for the use of very complicated software programs.

As software applications became more complicated, the probability and sheer number of errors increased. Quality assurance departments were expanded to develop methods for testing software applications for errors, or "bugs." Quality assurance is now a branch of science and engineering in its own right. The importance of good testing procedures came

to the forefront of the computer industry in the late 1990s with the emergence of the Year 2000 (Y2K) problems.

The field has changed with the advent of automated testing tools. As technology continues to advance, many quality assurance tests are automated. Quality assurance testers also "test the tests," that is, look for errors in the programs that test the software. There will always be a need for quality assurance testers, however, since they, not another computer, are best suited to judge a program from a user's point of view.

■ THE JOB

Before manufacturers can introduce a product on the consumer market, they must run extensive tests on its safety and quality. Failing to do so thoroughly can be very expensive, resulting in liability lawsuits when unsafe products harm people or in poor sales when products do not perform well. The nature and scope of quality assurance testing varies greatly. High-tech products, such as computers and other electronics, require extremely detailed technical testing.

Computer software applications undergo a specific series of tests designed to anticipate and help solve problems that users might encounter. Quality assurance testers examine new or modified computer software applications to evaluate whether or not they function at the desired level. They also verify that computer automated quality assurance programs perform in accordance with designer specifications and user requirements. This includes checking the product's functionality (how it will work), network performance (how it will work with other products), installation (how to put it in), and configuration (how it is set up).

Some quality assurance testers spend most of their time working on software programs or playing computer games, just as an average consumer might. If it is a game, for example, they play it over and over again for hours, trying to make moves quickly or slowly to "crash" it. A program crashes if it completely stops functioning due to, among other things, an inability to process incoming commands. For other types of programs, such as word processors, quality assurance testers might intentionally make errors, type very quickly, or click the mouse on inappropriate areas of the screen to see if the program can correctly handle such usage.

Quality assurance testers keep detailed records of the hours logged working on individual programs. They write reports based on their observations about how well the program performed in different situations, always imagining how typical, nontechnical users would judge it. The goal is to make the programs more efficient, user-friendly, fun, and visually exciting. Lastly, they keep track of the precise combinations of keystrokes and mouse clicks that made the program crash. This type of record is very important because it enables supervisors and programmers to replicate the problem. Then they can better isolate its source and begin to design a solution.

Programs to be tested arrive in the quality assurance department after programmers, software developers, and software engineers have finished the initial version. Each program is assigned a specific number of tests, and the quality assurance testers go to work. They make sure that the correct tests are run, write reports, and send the program back to the programmers for revisions and correction. Some testers have direct contact with the programmers. After evaluating a product, they might meet with programmers to describe the problems they encountered and suggest ways for solving glitches. Others report solely to a quality assurance supervisor.

When automated tests are to be run, quality assurance testers tell the computer which tests to administer and then ensure that they run smoothly by watching a computer screen for interruption codes and breakdown signals. They also interpret test results, verifying their credibility by running them through special programs that check for accuracy and reliability. They then write reports explaining their conclusions.

Some quality assurance testers have direct contact with users experiencing problems with their software. They listen closely to customer complaints to determine the precise order of keystrokes that led to the problem. They attempt to duplicate the problem on their own computers and run in-depth tests to figure out the cause. Eventually, if the problem is not simply a result of user error, they inform programmers and software engineers of the problems and suggest certain paths to take in resolving them.

Quality assurance testers with solid work experience and bachelor's degrees in a computer-related field might go on to work as *quality assurance analysts*. Analysts write and revise the quality standards for each software program that passes through the department. They also use computer programming skills to create the tests and programs the quality assurance testers use to test the programs. They might evaluate proposals for new software applications, advising management about whether or not the program will be able to achieve its goals. Since they know many software applications inside and out, they might also train users on how to work with various programs.

■ EARNINGS

Software quality assurance analysts had median annual earnings of $52,063 as of January 2017, according to

Salary.com. Salaries ranged from less than $41,394 to $64,472 or more annually. Workers with many years of technical and management experience can earn higher salaries. The Department of Labor reported median earnings of $85,800 as of May 2015 for computer systems analysts, a category that include software quality assurance analysts. The lowest paid 10 percent earned $51,910 or less while the highest paid took home $135,450 or more.

CAREER LADDER

Programmer, or Software Designer, or Engineer

Quality Assurance Supervisor or Quality Assurance Analyst

Experienced Software Quality Assurance Tester

Entry-Level Software Quality Assurance Tester

Testers generally receive a full benefits package as well, including health insurance, paid vacation, and sick leave. As in many industries, people with advanced degrees have the potential to make the most money.

■ WORK ENVIRONMENT

Quality assurance testers work in computer labs or offices. The work is generally repetitive and even monotonous. If a game is being tested, for example, a tester may have to play it for hours until it finally crashes, if at all. This might seem like great fun, but most testers agree that even the newest, most exciting game loses its appeal after several hours. This aspect of the job proves to be very frustrating and boring for some individuals.

Since quality assurance work involves keeping very detailed records, the job can also be stressful. For example, if a tester works on a word processing program for several hours, he or she must be able to recall at any moment the last few keystrokes entered in case the program crashes. This requires long periods of concentration, which can be tiring. Monitoring computer screens to make sure automated quality assurance tests are running properly often has the same effect.

Meeting with supervisors, programmers, and engineers to discuss ideas for the software projects can be intellectually stimulating. At these times, testers should feel at ease communicating with superiors. On the other end, testers who field customer complaints on the telephone may be forced to bear the brunt of customer dissatisfaction, an almost certain source of stress.

Quality assurance testers generally work regular, 40-hour weeks. During the final stages before a program goes into mass production and packaging, however, testers are frequently called on to work overtime.

Software testers use new programs and identify bugs for programmers to fix. (ProStockStudio. Shutterstock.)

■ EXPLORING

Students interested in quality assurance and other computer jobs should gain wide exposure to computer systems and programs of all kinds. Get a computer at home, borrow a friend's, or check out the computer lab at your school. Work on becoming comfortable using Windows programs and learn how to operate all parts of your computer, including the hardware, thoroughly. Look for bugs in your software at home and practice writing them up. Keep up with emerging technologies. If you cannot get hands-on experience, read books on testing and familiarize yourself with methodology, terminology, the development cycle, and where testing fits in. Join a computer group or society. Subscribe to newsletters or magazines that are related to testing or quality assurance. Get involved with online newsgroups that deal with the subject. Check out Web sites that deal with quality assurance.

If you live in an area where numerous computer software companies are located, you might be able to secure a part-time or summer job as a quality assurance tester. In addition, investigate the possibility of spending an afternoon with an employed quality assurance tester to find out what a typical day is like for him or her.

■ EDUCATION AND TRAINING REQUIREMENTS
High School

If you are interested in becoming a quality assurance tester, take as many computer classes as possible to become familiar with how to effectively operate computer software and hardware. Math and science courses are very helpful for teaching the necessary analytical skills.

English and speech classes will help you improve your verbal and written communication skills, which are also essential to the success of quality assurance testers.

Postsecondary Training

It is debatable whether or not a bachelor's degree is necessary to become a quality assurance tester. Some companies require a bachelor's degree in computer science, while others prefer people who come from the business sector who have a small amount of computer experience because they best match the technical level of the software's typical users. If testers are interested in advancement, however, a bachelor's degree is almost a mandate.

Few universities or colleges offer courses on quality assurance testing. As a result, most companies offer in-house training on how to test their particular products

Other Education or Training

The QAI Global Institute offers webinars, seminars, and other training opportunities. Past offerings included "Effective Methods of Software Testing," "Addressing Mobile App Testing Challenges," and "Top Ten Challenges of Test Automation." The Association for Software Testing, IEEE Computer Society, and the International Game Developers Association also provide professional development opportunities. Contact these organizations for more information.

■ CERTIFICATION, LICENSING, AND SPECIAL REQUIREMENTS
Certification or Licensing

As the information technology industry becomes more competitive, the necessity for management to be able to distinguish professional and skilled individuals in the field becomes mandatory, according to the QAI Global Institute. Certification demonstrates a level of understanding in carrying out relevant principles and practices, and provides a common ground for communication among professionals in the field of software quality and testing. The organization offers the designations certified software tester, certified associate in software testing, certified manager of software testing, certified associate in software quality, certified software quality analyst, and certified manager of software quality.

■ EXPERIENCE, SKILLS, AND PERSONALITY TRAITS

Experience as an intern, volunteer, or part-time employee at a software developer is recommended. Some companies recommend testers have some programming skills in languages such as C, C++, SQL, Java, JavaScript, or

Visual Basic. Others prefer testers with no programming ability.

Quality assurance testers need superior verbal and written communication skills. They also must show a proficiency in critical and analytical thinking and be able to critique something diplomatically. Quality assurance testers should have an eye for detail, be focused, and have a lot of enthusiasm because sometimes the work is monotonous and repetitive. Testers should definitely enjoy the challenge of breaking the system.

■ EMPLOYMENT PROSPECTS
Employers
Quality assurance testers are employed throughout the United States. Opportunities are best in large cities and suburbs where business and industry are active. Many work for software manufacturers, a cluster of which are located in Silicon Valley and San Francisco, in northern California. There are also concentrations of software manufacturers in the Pacific Northwest, Boston, Chicago, and Atlanta.

Starting Out
Positions in the field of quality assurance can be obtained several different ways. Many universities and colleges host computer job fairs on campus throughout the year that include representatives from several hardware and software companies. Internships and summer jobs with such corporations are always beneficial and provide experience that will give you the edge over your competition. General computer job fairs are also held throughout the year in larger cities. Some job openings are advertised in newspapers. There are many online career sites listed on the World Wide Web that post job openings, salary surveys, and current employment trends. The Web also has online publications that deal specifically with quality assurance. You can also obtain information from associations for quality professionals, such as the QAI Global Institute, and from computer organizations, including the IEEE Computer Society.

■ ADVANCEMENT PROSPECTS
Quality assurance testers are considered entry-level positions in some companies. After acquiring more experience and technical knowledge, testers might become quality assurance analysts, who write and revise the quality assurance standards or specifications for new programs. They also create the quality assurance examinations that testers use to evaluate programs. This usually involves using computer programming. Some analysts also evaluate proposals for new software products to

decide whether the proposed product is capable of doing what it is supposed to do. Analysts are sometimes promoted to quality assurance manager positions, which require some knowledge of software coding, the entire software production process, and test automation. They manage quality assurance teams for specific software products before and beyond their release.

Some testers also go on to become programmers or software designers or engineers.

■ OUTLOOK
The U.S. Department of Labor predicts that employment for computer analysts in general will grow 21 percent, much faster than the average for all jobs through 2024. Similar growth is forecast for quality testers working in computer systems designs and related services.

In the early days of the computer industry, software companies could make big profits by being the first to introduce a specific kind of product, such as a word processor or presentation kit, to the marketplace. Now, with so many versions of similar software on the market, competition forces firms to focus their energies on customer service. Many companies, therefore, aim to perfect their software applications before they hit the shelves. Searching for every small program glitch in this way requires the effort of many quality assurance testers. Additionally, the sheer number of software applications that are being created for computers, smartphones, and other digital devices is creating strong demand for testers who can manually check software programs or design and oversee automated programs that can handle this important task.

SOFTWARE TESTING BASICS

LEARN MORE ABOUT IT

Hagar, Jon Duncan. *Software Test Attacks to Break Mobile and Embedded Devices.* Boca Raton, Fla.: CRC Press, 2013.

Jorgensen, Paul C. *Software Testing: A Craftsman's Approach,* 4th ed. New York: Auerbach Publications, 2013.

Myers, Glenford J., Corey Sandler, and Tom Badgett. *The Art of Software Testing,* 3rd ed. Hoboken, N.J.: John Wiley & Sons, 2011.

Vance, Stephen. *Quality Code: Software Testing Principles, Practices, and Patterns.* New York: Addison-Wesley Professional, 2013.

Whittaker, James A., Jason Arbon, and Jeff Carollo. *How Google Tests Software.* New York: Addison-Wesley Professional, 2012.

INDEPENDENT TESTING LABS

DID YOU KNOW?

Many quality assurance testers are employed by hardware and software manufacturers. Another venue for employment in this field is independent labs, which provide testing and quality assurance support services to software developers. They are privately held companies that offer comprehensive testing services in test labs and through field consulting and technical training programs. Testers who work for independent labs mostly examine the product's compatibility, functionality, functional localization, installation, interoperability, load, performance, regression, stress, system integration, and test automation. Testers who want to expand their positions can become field consultants who provide information on test automation, test design, planning, and implementation to various corporations. These consultants usually travel to the company's location and conduct much of their work there during the project's duration.

Independent labs also employ technical trainers, who hold classes and suggest appropriate videos to train individuals and entire departments on testing tools, methodologies, and technologies.

Independent labs are located across the country but are usually headquartered in areas that have a significant number of software manufacturers.

This same push toward premarket perfection helps to explain the development of more accurate and efficient quality assurance automation. To stay competitive, companies must refine their quality assurance procedures to ever-higher levels.

■ UNIONS AND ASSOCIATIONS

Software quality assurance testers do not belong to unions. The Association for Software Testing offers membership, professional development opportunities, and additional resources. Other membership organizations for computer professionals include the IEEE Computer Society and the International Game Developers Association. The QAI Global Institute provides certification and continuing education classes and webinars. The Software & Information Industry Association is the main trade association for the software and digital content industry.

■ TIPS FOR ENTRY

1. Talk with software testers about their careers. Ask them for advice on preparing for and entering the field.

2. Attend the QAI Global Institute's Annual International Software Testing Conference (http://www.qaiglobalservices.com) and the Conference of the Association for Software Testing (http://www.associationforsoftwaretesting.org/conference/about-cast) to network and participate in continuing education classes.

3. Read *IEEE Software* (http://www.computer.org/portal/web/computingnow/software) to learn more about the field.

4. Track pros and cons of software programs you use and think of ways to improve them or solve any problems they have.

■ FOR MORE INFORMATION

For information on membership, contact

Association for Software Testing (AST)
http://www.associationforsoftwaretesting.org

For information on scholarships, student memberships, and publications, contact

IEEE Computer Society (IEEE)
2001 L Street, NW, Suite 700
Washington, D.C. 20036-4928
Tel: (202) 371-0101
Fax: (202) 728-9614
E-mail: help@computer.org
http://www.computer.org

For career advice and industry information, contact

International Game Developers Association (IGDA)
19 Mantua Road
Mount Royal, NJ 08061-1006
Tel: (856) 423-2990
http://www.igda.org

For industry information, contact

Software & Information Industry Association (SIIA)
1090 Vermont Ave, NW, Sixth Floor
Washington, D.C. 20005-4095
Tel: (202) 289-7442
Fax: (202) 289-7097
http://www.siia.net

For information on certification, contact

QAI Global Institute
Tel: (407) 363-1111
E-mail: info@qaiworldwide.org
http://www.qaiusa.com

Soil Conservationists and Technicians

■ OVERVIEW

Soil conservationists develop conservation plans to help farmers and ranchers, developers, homeowners, and government officials best use their land while adhering to government conservation regulations. They suggest plans to conserve and reclaim soil, preserve or restore wetlands and other rare ecological areas, rotate crops for increased yields and soil conservation, reduce water pollution, and restore or increase wildlife populations. They assess land users' needs, costs, maintenance requirements, and the life expectancy of various conservation practices. They plan design specifications using survey and field information, technical guides, and engineering field manuals. Soil conservationists also give talks to various organizations to educate land users and the public about how to conserve and restore soil and water resources. Many of their recommendations are based on information provided to them by soil scientists.

Soil conservation technicians work more directly with land users by putting the ideas and plans of the conservationist into action. In their work they use basic engineering and surveying tools, instruments, and techniques. They perform engineering surveys and design and implement conservation practices like terraces and grassed waterways. Soil conservation technicians monitor projects during and after construction and periodically revisit the site to evaluate the practices and plans.

■ HISTORY

In 1908, President Theodore Roosevelt appointed a National Conservation Commission to oversee the proper conservation of the country's natural resources. As a result, many state and local conservation organizations were formed, and Americans began to take a serious interest in preserving their land's natural resources.

Despite this interest, however, conservation methods were not always understood or implemented. For example, farmers in the southern Great Plains, wanting to harvest a cash crop, planted many thousands of acres of wheat during the early decades of the 20th century. The crop was repeated year after year until the natural grasslands of the area were destroyed and the soil was depleted of nutrients. When the area experienced prolonged droughts combined with the naturally occurring high winds, devastating dust storms swept the land during the 1930s. Parts of Oklahoma, Texas, Kansas, New Mexico, and Colorado suffered from severe soil erosion that resulted in desert-like conditions, and this ruined area became known as the Dust Bowl.

As a result of what happened to the Dust Bowl, Congress established the Natural Resources Conservation Service of the U.S. Department of Agriculture in 1935. Because more than 800 million tons of topsoil had already been blown away by the winds over the plains, the job of reclaiming the land through wise conservation practices was not an easy one. In addition to the large areas of the Great Plains that had become desert land, there were other badly eroded lands throughout the country.

Fortunately, emergency planning came to the aid of the newly established conservation program. The Civilian Conservation Corps (CCC) was created to help alleviate unemployment during the Great Depression of the 1930s. The CCC established camps in rural areas and assigned people to aid in many different kinds of conservation. Soil conservationists directed those portions of the CCC program designed to halt the loss of topsoil by wind and water action.

Much progress has been made in the years since the Natural Resources Conservation Service was established. Wasted land has been reclaimed and further loss has been prevented. Land-grant colleges have initiated programs to help farmers understand the principles and procedures of soil conservation. The National Institute of Food and Agriculture (within

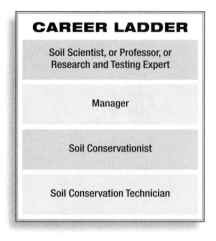

the Department of Agriculture) provides workers who are skilled in soil conservation to work with these programs.

Throughout the United States today there are several thousand federally appointed soil conservation districts. A worker employed by the government works in these districts to demonstrate soil conservation to farmers and agricultural businesses. There are usually one or more professional soil conservationists and one or more soil conservation technicians working in each district.

■ THE JOB

Soil sustains plant and animal life, influences water and air quality, and supports human health and habitation. Its quality has a major impact on ecological balance, biological diversity, air quality, water flow, and plant growth, including crops and forestation. Soil conservationists and technicians help scientists and engineers collect samples and data to determine soil quality, identify problems, and develop plans to better manage the land. They work with farmers, agricultural professionals, landowners, range managers, and public and private agencies to establish and maintain sound conservation practices.

A farmer or landowner contacts soil conservationists to help identify soil quality problems, improve soil quality, maintain it, or stop or reverse soil degradation. Conservationists visit the site to gather information, beginning with past and current uses of the soil and future plans for the site. They consult precipitation and soil maps and try to determine if the way land is being currently used is somehow degrading the soil quality. Conservationists consider irrigation practices, fertilizer use, and tillage systems. At least a five- to 10-year history of land use is most helpful for working in this field.

Site observation reveals signs of soil quality problems. The farmer or landowner can point out areas of concern that occur regularly, such as wet spots, salt accumulation, rills and gullies or excessive runoff water that could indicate erosion, stunted plant growth, or low crop yield. Samples are taken from these areas and tested for such physical, chemical, and biological properties as soil fertility, soil structure, soil stability, water storage and availability, and nutrient retention. Conservationists also look

at plant characteristics, such as rooting depth, which can indicate density or compaction of the soil.

Once all the data are gathered and samples tested, conservationists analyze the results. They look for patterns and trends. If necessary, they take additional samples to verify discrepancies or confirm results. They prepare a report for the farmer or landowner.

A team of conservationists, engineers, scientists, and the landowners propose alternative solutions for soil problems. All the alternatives must be weighed carefully for their possible effects on ecological balance, natural resources, economic factors, and social or cultural factors. The landowner makes the final decision on which solutions to use and a plan is drafted.

After the plan is in place, soil conservationists and technicians continue to monitor and evaluate soil conditions, usually over a period of several years. Periodic soil sampling shows whether progress is being made, and if not, changes can be made to the plan.

These brief examples show how the process works. A farmer has a problem with crop disease. He sees that the yield is reduced and the health of plants is poor. Soil conservationists and technicians consider possible causes and test soil for pests, nutrient deficiencies, lack of biological diversity, saturated soil, and compacted layers. Depending on test results, conservationists might suggest a pest-management program, an improved drainage system, the use of animal manure, or crop rotation.

Another farmer notices the formation of rills and gullies on his land along with a thinning topsoil layer. Soil conservationists' research shows that the erosion is due to such factors as lack of cover, excessive tillage that moves soil down a slope, intensive crop rotation, and low organic matter. Suggested solutions include reducing tillage, using animal manure, planting cover crops or strip crops, and using windbreaks.

Conservationists and technicians who work for the Bureau of Land Management, which oversees hundreds of millions of acres of public domain, help survey publicly owned areas and pinpoint land features to determine the best use of public lands. Soil conservation technicians in the Bureau of Reclamation assist civil, construction, materials, or general engineers. Their job is to oversee certain phases of such projects as the construction of dams and irrigation planning. The bureau's ultimate goal is the control of water and soil resources for the benefit of farms, homes, and cities.

Other soil technicians work as *range technicians*, who help determine the value of rangeland, its grazing capabilities, erosion hazards, and livestock potential. *Physical science technicians* gather data in the field, studying the physical characteristics of the soil, make routine chemical analyses, and set up and operate test apparatus. *Cartographic survey technicians* work with *cartographers* (mapmakers) to map or chart the earth or graphically represent geographical information, survey the public domain, set boundaries, pinpoint land features, and determine the most beneficial public use. *Engineering technicians* conduct field tests and oversee some phases of construction on dams and irrigation projects. They also measure acreage, place property boundaries, and define drainage areas on maps. *Surveying technicians* perform surveys for field measurement and mapping, to plan for construction, to check the accuracy of dredging operations, or to provide reference points and lines for related work. They gather data for the design and construction of highways, dams, topographic maps, and nautical or aeronautical charts.

■ EARNINGS

The Department of Labor reports that median earnings for conservation scientists (the category that includes soil conservationists) were $61,110 in May 2015. Some conservation scientists earned less than $37,380, while others earned $91,830 or more annually.

The salaries of conservationists and technicians working for private firms or agencies are roughly comparable to those paid by the federal government. Earnings at the state and local levels vary depending on the region but are typically lower.

Government jobs and larger private industries offer comprehensive benefits packages that are usually more generous than those offered at smaller firms.

■ WORK ENVIRONMENT

Soil conservationists and technicians usually work 40 hours per week except in unusual or emergency situations. They have opportunities to travel, especially when they work for federal agencies.

Soil conservation is an outdoor job. Workers travel to work sites by car but must often walk great distances to an assigned area. Although they sometimes work from aerial photographs and other on-site pictures, they cannot work from photos alone. They must visit the spot that presents the problem in order to make appropriate recommendations.

Soil conservationists and technicians may spend much of their working time outdoors, but indoor work is also necessary when preparing detailed reports of their work to agency offices.

In their role as assistants to professionals, soil conservation technicians often assume the role of government public relations representatives when dealing with landowners and land managers. They must be able to

A soil technician and scientist collect water samples from a Pennsylvania stream. (Scott Bauer. USDA.)

explain the underlying principles of the structures that they design and the surveys that they perform.

To meet these and other requirements of the job, conservationists and technicians should be prepared to continue their education both formally and informally throughout their careers. They must stay aware of current periodicals and studies so that they can keep up to date in their areas of specialization.

Soil conservationists and technicians gain satisfaction from knowing that their work is vitally important to the nation's economy and environment. Without their expertise, large portions of land in the United States could become barren within a generation.

■ EXPLORING

One of the best ways to become acquainted with soil conservation work and technology is through summer or part-time work on a farm or at a natural

THE SCIENCE OF MANAGING SOIL

LEARN MORE ABOUT IT

Lal, Rattan, and B. A. Stewart. *Principles of Sustainable Soil Management in Agroecosystems.* Boca Raton, Fla.: CRC Press, 2013.

Ohlson, Kristin. *The Soil Will Save Us: How Scientists, Farmers, and Foodies Are Healing the Soil to Save the Planet.* Emmaus, Pa.: Rodale Books, 2014.

Plaster, Edward. *Soil Science and Management,* 6th ed. Independence, Ky.: Cengage Learning, 2013.

Worster, Donald. *Dust Bowl: The Southern Plains in the 1930s.* New York: Oxford University Press, 2004.

park. Other ways to explore this career include joining a local chapter of the 4-H Club or National FFA Organization. Science courses that include lab sections and mathematics courses focusing on practical problem solving will also help give you a feel for this kind of work.

■ EDUCATION AND TRAINING REQUIREMENTS
High School

While in high school, you should take at least one year each of algebra, geometry, and trigonometry. Take several years of English to develop your writing, research, and speaking skills as these are skills you will need when compiling reports and working with others. Science classes, of course, are important to take, including earth science, biology, and chemistry. If your high school offers agriculture classes, be sure to take any relating to land use, crop production, and soils.

Postsecondary Training

Conservationists hold bachelor degrees in areas such as general agriculture, range management, crop or soil science, forestry, and agricultural engineering. Teaching and research positions require further graduate level education in a natural resources field. Though government jobs do not necessarily require a college degree (a combination of appropriate experience and education can serve as substitute), a college education can make you more desirable for a position. Technicians typically hold an associate's degrees or a certificate in applied science or science-related technology.

Typical beginning courses include applied mathematics, communication skills, basic soils, botany, chemistry, zoology, and introduction to range management. Advanced courses include American government, surveying, forestry, game management, soil and water conservation, economics, fish management, and conservation engineering.

Visit https://www.careerplacement.org/colleges for a list of colleges and universities that offer courses and degrees in soil science, agronomy, crop science, and environmental science.

Other Education or Training

Participating in continuing education (CE) classes is a great way to keep your skills up to date and learn about new developments in soil conservation; CE credits may also be required to renew your certification. The Soil and Water Conservation Society offers professional development opportunities at its annual conference and at other events. Past offerings included "Communicating Effectively with Social Media" and "Water Erosion Prediction Project Model Application." The American Society of Agronomy and the Soil Science Society of America also provide CE opportunities. Contact these organizations for more information.

■ CERTIFICATION, LICENSING, AND SPECIAL REQUIREMENTS
Certification or Licensing

No certification or license is required of soil conservationists and technicians; however, becoming certified can improve your skills and professional standing. The American Society of Agronomy offers voluntary certification in soil science. Most government agencies require applicants to take a competitive examination for consideration.

■ EXPERIENCE, SKILLS, AND PERSONALITY TRAITS

Conservationists and technicians must have some practical experience in the use of soil conservation techniques before they enter the field. Many schools require students to work in the field during the school year or during summer vacation before they can be awarded their degree. Jobs are available in the federal park systems and with privately owned industries.

Soil conservationists and technicians must be able to apply practical as well as theoretical knowledge to their work. You must have a working knowledge of soil and water characteristics; be skilled in management of woodlands, wildlife areas, and recreation areas; and have knowledge of surveying instruments and practices, mapping, and the procedures used for interpreting aerial photographs.

Soil conservationists and technicians should also be able to write clear, concise reports to demonstrate and explain the results of tests, studies, and recommendations.

A love for the outdoors and an appreciation for all natural resources are essential for success and personal fulfillment in this job.

■ EMPLOYMENT PROSPECTS
Employers
More than 60 percent of all conservation workers are employed by local, state, and federal government agencies. At the federal level, most soil conservationists and technicians work for the Natural Resource Conservation Service, the Bureau of Land Management, and the Bureau of Reclamation. Others work for agencies at the state and county level. Soil conservationists and technicians also work for private agencies and firms such as banks and loan agencies, mining or steel companies, and public utilities. A small percentage of workers are self-employed consultants that advise private industry owners and government agencies.

Starting Out
Most students gain outside experience by working a summer job in their area of interest. You can get information on summer positions through your school's career services office. Often, contacts made on summer jobs lead to permanent employment after graduation. College career counselors and faculty members are often valuable sources of advice and information in finding employment.

Most soil conservationists and technicians find work with state, county, or federal agencies. Hiring procedures for these jobs vary according to the level of government in which the applicant is seeking work. In general, however, students begin the application procedure during the fourth semester of their program and take some form of competitive examination as part of the process. College career services office personnel can help students find out about the application procedures. Representatives of government agencies often visit college campuses to explain employment opportunities to students and sometimes to recruit for their agencies.

■ ADVANCEMENT PROSPECTS
Soil conservationists and technicians usually start out with a local conservation district to gain experience and expertise before advancing to the state, regional, or national level.

In many cases, technicians hoping to advance their careers continue their education while working by taking evening courses at a local college or technical institute. Federal agencies that employ conservationists and technicians have a policy of promotion from within. Because of this policy, there is a continuing opportunity for such

CREEP, KARST, SCARP, AND MORE — WORDS TO KNOW

Aeration porosity: The fraction of the volume of soil that is filled with air at any given time.

Blowout: A small area from which soil material has been removed by wind.

Creep: Slow mass movement of soil and soil material down steep slopes. Creep is primarily caused by gravity, but aided by saturation with water and by alternate freezing and thawing.

Erosion: The wearing away of soil and other land features by wind, water, and human activities, such as construction and farming.

Fertilizer: Natural and chemical elements that help plants to grow. Chemical fertilizers can be harmful if used in too large quantities.

Gytta: Peat consisting of plant and animal residues from standing water.

Karst: Topography with caves, sinkholes, and underground drainage that is formed in limestone and other rocks by dissolution.

Loam: Soil that contains a variable mixture of sand, silt, and clay.

Macronutrient: A nutrient found in high concentrations in a plant.

Scarp: A cliff or steep slope along the margin of a plateau.

Topsoil: The surface soil that includes the layer where most plants have their roots.

workers to advance through the ranks. The degree of advancement that all conservationists and technicians can expect in their working careers is determined by their aptitudes, abilities, and, of course, their desire to advance.

Workers seeking a more dramatic change can transfer their skills to related jobs outside the conservation industry, such as farming or land appraisal.

■ OUTLOOK
Average growth in employment, 7 percent through 2024, is expected for conservation scientists (a category that includes soil conservationists) and technicians, according to the U.S. Department of Labor (DOL). Most jobs will come from the need to replace those who retire or leave the field for other reasons.

Despite the prediction for static growth, there will continue to be a need for government involvement in protecting natural resources. Job opportunities will be better with local government conservation agencies. The vast majority of America's cropland has suffered from some sort of erosion, and only continued efforts by soil conservation professionals can prevent a dangerous depletion of our most valuable resource: fertile soil.

Some soil conservationists and technicians are employed as research and testing experts for public utility companies, banks and loan agencies, and mining or steel companies. Employment in these areas (which are categorized as "professional, scientific, and technical services" by the DOL) will grow much faster than the average for all careers through 2024.

■ UNIONS AND ASSOCIATIONS

Soil conservationists and technicians who work for government agencies can join the American Federation of Government Employees, a union that represents government workers. Many conservationists and technicians join professional associations such as the American Society of Agronomy, Soil Science Society of America, and the Soil and Water Conservation Society. These organizations provide continuing education classes, publications, networking opportunities, certification, and other resources.

■ TIPS FOR ENTRY

1. To learn more about the field, read:
   - *Journal of Soil and Water Conservation* (http://www.jswconline.org)
   - *Soil Science Society of America Journal* (https://www.soils.org/publications/sssaj)
   - *Crops & Soils* (https://www.agronomy.org/publications/crops-and-soils)
2. Visit the following Web sites for job listings: http://careers.swcs.org and https://www.careerplacement.org.
3. Join the Soil and Water Conservation Society and other professional associations to access training and networking resources, industry publications, and employment opportunities.

■ FOR MORE INFORMATION

For information on soil conservation careers and certification, contact

American Society of Agronomy (ASA)
5585 Guilford Road
Madison, WI 53711-5801
Tel: (608) 273-8080
Fax: (608) 273-2021
E-mail: membership@agronomy.org
http://www.agronomy.org

Contact the NRCS for information on government soil conservation careers. Its Web site has information on volunteer opportunities.

Natural Resources Conservation Service (NRCS)
1400 Independence Ave., SW, Room 5105-A
Washington, D.C. 20250
Tel: (202) 720-7246
Fax: (202) 720-7690
http://www.nrcs.usda.gov

For information on soil conservation, college student chapters, and publications, contact

Soil and Water Conservation Society
945 SW Ankeny Road
Ankeny, IA 50023
Tel: (515) 289-2331
Fax: (515) 289-1227
E-mail: swcs@swcs.org
http://www.swcs.org

For information on education and careers, contact

Soil Science Society of America
5585 Guilford Road
Madison, WI 53711-5801
Tel: (608) 273-8080
Fax: (608) 273-2021
E-mail: membership@soils.org
http://www.soils.org

Soil Scientists

■ OVERVIEW

Soil scientists study the physical, chemical, and biological characteristics of soils to determine the most productive and effective planting strategies. Their research aids in producing larger, healthier crops and more environmentally sound farming procedures. There are approximately 14,690 soil and plant scientists employed in the United States.

■ HISTORY

Hundreds of years ago, farmers planted crops without restriction; they were unaware that soil could be depleted of necessary nutrients by overuse. When crops were poor, farmers often blamed the weather instead of their farming techniques.

Soil, one of our most important natural resources, was taken for granted until its condition became too bad to ignore. An increasing population, moreover, made the United States aware that its own welfare depends on fertile soil capable of producing food for hundreds of millions of people.

Increasing concerns about feeding a growing nation brought agricultural practices into reevaluation. In 1862, the U.S. Department of Agriculture (USDA) was created to give farmers information about new crops and improved farming techniques. Although the department started small, today the USDA is one of the largest agencies of the federal government.

Following the creation of the USDA, laws were created to further promote and protect farmers. The 1933 Agricultural Adjustment Act inaugurated a policy of giving direct government aid to farmers. Two years later, the Natural Resources Conservation Service developed after disastrous dust storms blew away millions of tons of valuable topsoil and destroyed fertile cropland throughout the Midwestern states.

Since 1937, states have organized themselves into soil conservation districts. Each local division coordinates with the USDA, assigning soil scientists and soil conservationists to help local farmers establish and maintain farming practices that will use land in the wisest possible ways.

■ THE JOB

Soil is formed by the breaking of rocks and the decay of trees, plants, and animals. It may take as long as 500 years to make just one inch of topsoil. Unwise and wasteful farming methods can destroy that inch of soil in just a few short years. In addition, rainstorms may carry thousands of pounds of precious topsoil away and dissolve chemicals that are necessary to grow healthy crops through a process called erosion. Soil scientists work with engineers to address these issues.

Soil scientists spend much of their time outdoors, investigating fields, advising farmers about crop rotation or fertilizers, assessing field drainage, and taking soil samples. After researching an area, they may suggest certain crops to farmers to protect bare earth from the ravages of the wind and weather.

Soil scientists may also specialize in one particular aspect of the work. For example, they may work as a *soil mapper* or *soil surveyor*. These specialists study soil structure, origins, and capabilities through field observations, laboratory examinations, and controlled experimentation. Their investigations are aimed at determining the most suitable uses for a particular soil.

Soil fertility experts develop practices that will increase or maintain crop size. They must consider both the type of soil and the crop planted in their analysis. Various soils react differently when exposed to fertilizers, soil additives, crop rotation, and other farming techniques.

All soil scientists work in the laboratory. They examine soil samples under the microscope to determine bacterial and plant-food components. They also write reports based on their field notes and analyses done within the lab.

Soil science is part of the science of *agronomy*, which encompasses crop science. Soil and crop scientists work together in agricultural experiment stations during all seasons, doing research on crop production, soil fertility, and various kinds of soil management.

Some soil and crop scientists travel to remote sections of the world in search of plants and grasses that may thrive in this country and contribute to our food supply, pasture land, or soil replenishing efforts. Some scientists go overseas to advise farmers in other countries on how to treat their soils. Those with advanced degrees can teach college agriculture courses and conduct research projects.

■ EARNINGS

According to the U.S. Department of Labor, median earnings in May 2015 for soil and plant scientists were $60,050. The lowest paid 10 percent earned less than $35,770 and the highest paid 10 percent made more than $105,390. Mean salaries for soil scientists at federal agencies were higher; in May 2015, they made an average of $81,950 a year. Government earnings depend in large part on levels of experience and education. Other than short-term research projects, most jobs offer health and retirement benefits in addition to the annual salary.

■ WORK ENVIRONMENT

Most soil scientists work 40 hours a week. Their job is

QUICK FACTS

ALTERNATE TITLE(S)
Soil Fertility Experts, Soil Mappers, Soil Surveyors

DUTIES
Study the chemical, physical, and biological characteristics of soils to determine the most effective and productive planting strategies

SALARY RANGE
$35,770 to $60,050 to $105,390+

WORK ENVIRONMENT
Indoors/Outdoors

BEST GEOGRAPHIC LOCATION(S)
Opportunities exist throughout the country

MINIMUM EDUCATION LEVEL
Bachelor's Degree

SCHOOL SUBJECTS
Agriculture, Chemistry, Earth Science

EXPERIENCE
Internship; volunteer or part-time experience

PERSONALITY TRAITS
Curious, Problem-Solving, Scientific

SKILLS
Interpersonal, Research, Scientific

CERTIFICATION OR LICENSING
Recommended

SPECIAL REQUIREMENTS
None

EMPLOYMENT PROSPECTS
Good

ADVANCEMENT PROSPECTS
Fair

OUTLOOK
About as Fast as the Average

NOC
2115

O*NET-SOC
19-1013.00

CAREER LADDER

Research Director or College Professor

Soil Scientist

Soil Science Technician

varied, ranging from fieldwork collecting samples, to lab work analyzing their findings. Some jobs may involve travel, even to foreign countries. Other positions may include teaching or supervisory responsibilities for field training programs.

■ EXPLORING

The National FFA Organization can introduce you to the concerns of farmers and researchers. A 4-H club can also give you valuable experience in agriculture. Contact the local branch of these organizations, your county's soil conservation department, or other government agencies to learn about regional projects. If you live in an agricultural community, you may be able to find opportunities for part-time or summer work on a farm or ranch. Visit Web sites that provide more information on soil science and education and careers in the field. One useful site is Careers in Soil Science (https://www.soils.org/careers).

■ EDUCATION AND TRAINING REQUIREMENTS
High School

If you're interested in pursuing a career in agronomy, you should take college preparatory courses covering subjects such as math, science, English, and public speaking. Science courses, such as earth science, biology, and chemistry, are particularly important. Since much of your future work will involve calculations, you should take four years of high school math. You can learn a lot about farming methods and conditions by taking agriculture classes if your high school offers them. Computer science courses are also a good choice to familiarize yourself with using databases, statistical analytical tools, and other software programs. You should also take English and speech courses, since soil scientists must write reports and make presentations about their findings.

Postsecondary Training

A bachelor's degree in agriculture or soil science is the minimum educational requirement to become a soil scientist. Typical courses include physics, geology, bacteriology, botany, chemistry, soil chemistry, plant pathology, soil chemistry, soil and plant morphology, soil fertility, soil classification, and soil genesis.

Research and teaching positions usually require higher levels of education. Most colleges of agriculture also offer master's and doctoral degrees. In addition to studying agriculture or soil science, students can specialize in biology, chemistry, physics, or engineering.

Soil science students should also complete at least one internship as part of their training. Government and private agencies offer a variety of internships to college students who are interested in soil science and conservation. Contact agencies such as the Natural Resources Conservation Service and the Bureau of Land Management for details.

Other Education or Training

The Soil Science Society of America offers professional development opportunities via online courses and webinars and at its annual meeting. Its Fundamentals in Soil Science course features the following breakout sessions: Fundamentals in Soil Genesis, Classification and Morphology, Fundamentals in Soil Chemistry and Mineralogy, Fundamentals in Soil Fertility and Nutrient Management, Fundamentals in Soil Biology and Ecology, Influences and Management of Soil Physical Properties, and Fundamentals in Soil and Land Use Management. The American Society of Agronomy also provides continuing education opportunities. Contact these organizations for more information.

■ CERTIFICATION, LICENSING, AND SPECIAL REQUIREMENTS
Certification or Licensing

Though not required, many soil scientists may seek certification to enhance their careers. The American Society of Agronomy and the Soil Science Society of America offer the following certification designations: certified professional soil scientist/classifier, certified crop adviser, and certified professional agronomist. In order to be accepted into a program, applicants must meet certain levels of education and experience.

■ EXPERIENCE, SKILLS, AND PERSONALITY TRAITS

Those wishing to enter the field of soil science should obtain as much experience as possible in college by participating in internships, volunteering, or working at a part-time job at a state or federal department of agriculture.

Soil scientists must be able to work effectively both on their own and with others on projects, either outdoors or in the lab. Technology is increasingly used in this profession; an understanding of word processing, the Internet, multimedia software, databases, and even computer programming can be useful. Soil scientists spend many hours outdoors in all kinds of weather, so they must be able to endure sometimes difficult and uncomfortable physical conditions. They must be detail-oriented to do accurate research, and they should enjoy solving puzzles—figuring out, for example, why a crop isn't flourishing and what fertilizers should be used.

■ EMPLOYMENT PROSPECTS

Employers

Approximately 14,690 soil and plant scientists are employed in the United States. Most soil scientists work for state or federal departments of agriculture. However, they may also work for other public employers, such as land appraisal boards, land-grant colleges and universities, and conservation departments. Soil scientists who work overseas may be employed by the U.S. Agency for International Development.

Soil scientists are needed in private industries as well, such as agricultural service companies, banks, insurance and real estate firms, food products companies, wholesale distributors, and environmental and engineering consulting groups. Private firms may hire soil scientists for sales or research positions.

Starting Out

In the public sector, college graduates can apply directly to the Natural Resources Conservation Service of the Department of Agriculture, the Department of the Interior, the Environmental Protection Agency, or other state government agencies for beginning positions. University career services offices generally have listings for these openings as well as opportunities available in private industry.

■ ADVANCEMENT PROSPECTS

Salary increases are the most common form of advancement for soil scientists. The nature of the job may not change appreciably even after many years of service. Higher administrative and supervisory positions are few in comparison with the number of jobs that must be done in the field.

Opportunities for advancement will be higher for those with advanced degrees. For soil scientists engaged in teaching, advancement may translate into a higher academic rank with more responsibility. In private business firms, soil scientists have opportunities to advance into positions such as department head or research director. Supervisory and manager positions are also available in state agencies such as road or conservation departments.

■ OUTLOOK

Total employment for soil and plant scientists is expected to grow more than 6 percent for all careers through 2024.

SOIL PORTRAITS
MILESTONES

The appeal of soil study isn't always scientific; sometimes the beauty of soil formation inspires scientists. Hungarian soil scientist Erika Micheli discovered a wavy collection of multicolored soil layers after a surface mining operation had left the ground exposed. Her study of the rippled formations (formed by the burrowing of prehistoric groundhogs, erosion, and pressure from frozen rainwater) led to new precautions for area farmers about the way they use fertilizers and pesticides. In addition, Micheli's discovery inspired her to create lacquered, 3-D portraits of the soil that are suitable for framing.

Job growth will stem from the need to increase the quality and quantity of food produced for a growing population while developing methods to protect the environment. Opportunities in agronomy, including the career of soil scientist, should be especially good.

Careers in this field are often affected by the government's involvement in farming studies; as a result, budget cuts at the federal and state levels may potentially limit funding for this type of job. Employment with federal government agencies is expected to decline by nearly 10 percent through 2024. However, private businesses will continue to demand soil scientists for research and sales positions. Companies dealing with seed, fertilizers, or farm equipment are examples of private industries that hire soil scientists. Job opportunities for soil scientists who work for professional, scientific, and technical services firms are expected to grow 14 percent, much faster than the average for all careers through 2024.

Technological advances in equipment and methods of conservation will allow scientists to better protect the environment, as well as improve farm production. Scientists' ability to evaluate soils and plants will improve with more precise research methods. Combine-mounted yield monitors will produce data as the farmer crosses the field, and satellites will provide more detailed field information. With computer images, scientists will also be able to examine plant roots more carefully.

A continued challenge facing future soil scientists will be convincing farmers to change their current methods of tilling and chemical treatment in favor of environmentally safer methods. They must encourage farmers to balance increased agricultural output with the protection of our limited natural resources.

■ UNIONS AND ASSOCIATIONS

Soil scientists who work for government agencies can join the American Federation of Government Employees. Many scientists join professional associations such as the American Society of Agronomy and the Soil Science Society of America. These organizations provide networking opportunities, certification, continuing education classes, publications, and other resources.

■ TIPS FOR ENTRY

1. Read *Soil Science Society of America Journal* (https://www.soils.org/publications/sssaj) and *Crops & Soils* (https://www.agronomy.org/publications/crops-and-soils) to learn more about the field.
2. Visit the following Web sites for job listings: http://careers.swcs.org and https://www.careerplacement.org.
3. Join the Soil and Water Conservation Society and other professional associations to access training and networking resources, industry publications, and employment opportunities.
4. Talk to a soil scientist about his or her career. The American Society of Agronomy and Soil Science Society of America provide a database of certified members at https://portal.scienceso cieties.org/BuyersGuide/ProfessionalSearch.aspx. Use this database to identify possible interview candidates.

■ FOR MORE INFORMATION

The ASA has information on careers, certification, and college chapters. For details, contact

American Society of Agronomy (ASA)
5585 Guilford Road
Madison, WI 53711-5801
Tel: (608) 273-8080
Fax: (608) 273-2021
E-mail: membership@agronomy.org
http://www.agronomy.org

For information on education and careers, contact

Soil Science Society of America (SSSA)
5585 Guilford Road
Madison, WI 53711-5801
Tel: (608) 273-8080
Fax: (608) 273-2021
E-mail: membership@soils.org
http://www.soils.org

Solar Energy Industry Workers

■ OVERVIEW

Solar energy industry workers perform a wide range of duties, from designing, building, repairing, and maintaining photovoltaic cells and solar power facilities to conducting research on new solar technologies; to assessing and purchasing land for solar facilities. They are also responsible for providing support services to scientific and technical workers and perform many other job duties. As of 2015, approximately 188,000 of the 208,859 solar workers in the United States worked full-time on only solar energy activities, according to The Solar Foundation.

■ HISTORY

People have worshiped the sun and found ways to channel its energy to improve their lives since early times. As far back as 400 B.C., ancient Greeks designed their homes to take advantage of the sun's warmth and light by having the structures face south to capture more heat in the winter. (This is known as "passive solar energy," an old technology that is still used today.) The ancient Romans later improved on these designs by adding more windows to the south side of homes and by putting glass panes in the windows, which allowed more heat and light into buildings. The Romans were also the first to use greenhouses to grow plants and seeds. The Greeks and Romans were among the first to use mirrors to reflect the sun's heat to light fires.

According to a history of solar energy published at the Solar Energy Industries Association's (SEIA) Web site, the artist and inventor Leonardo da Vinci envisioned concentrating collectors that would focus sunlight into a central receiver in the 1500s. Da Vinci even built a rough collector in 1515. More than two centuries after da Vinci's experiments with solar energy, Swiss scientist Horace de Saussure built the world's first working solar collector in 1767. Later, in 1890, French physicist Henri Becquerel discovered the photovoltaic effect, the physical process through which a photovoltaic cell converts sunlight into electricity.

In the following years, many scientists studied photovoltaic technology, but it was not until 1954 that the U.S. company Bell Labs developed the first solar photovoltaic device that produced a useful amount of electricity. In 1956, architect Frank Bridgers used photovoltaic technology to design the Bridgers-Paxton building, the world's first commercial office building featuring solar water heating and passive design. People were finding different opportunities to use solar energy, and in 1958 the SEIA reported that, "solar cells were being used in small-scale scientific and commercial applications, including the space program."

The energy crisis in the 1970s caused the U.S. government to increase research on renewable energy sources, including solar power. Although it was cost-prohibitive at the time to use solar power on a large scale, photovoltaic cells began to be used in remote applications, especially in the telecommunications industry.

The first solar electric generation station plants were built in California's Mojave Desert from 1984 through 1990. They are still in operation today.

Costs to develop solar power technologies have decreased greatly in recent years. State and federal government policies are encouraging the growth of the industry as a means to help the United States gain energy independence from foreign countries and create energy technologies that are more environmentally friendly.

In 2012, solar energy made up 2 percent of all renewable energy in the United States, according to the Energy Information Administration. Its potential as a major energy source is largely untapped.

■ THE JOB

There are different ways to turn the sun's energy into a useful power source. The most common technology today uses photovoltaic (PV) cells. When a PV cell is directly hit by sunlight, the materials inside it absorb this light. Simply put, the activity of absorption frees electrons, which then travel through a circuit. Electrons traveling through a circuit produce electricity. Many PV cells can be linked together to produce unlimited amounts of electricity.

The concentrating solar power (CSP) technologies use mirrors or lenses to focus sunlight onto a receiver. The receiver collects sunlight as heat, which can be used directly or generated into electricity. The four CSP methods used are parabolic trough systems, power towers, parabolic dishes, and compact linear Fresnel systems that concentrate thermal energy to power a conventional steam turbine. Parabolic troughs can produce solar electricity inexpensively compared to the other methods, and they can generate enough power for large-scale projects. Power towers can also generate power for large-scale projects, while parabolic dishes are used for smaller-scale projects. Flat mirrors are used in compact linear Fresnel systems, which allows for more reflectors to be added to a solar array. This technology allows solar infrastructure to use less land surface than other technologies.

Using solar collectors and storage tanks, the sun's energy can be used to heat water for swimming pools or

QUICK FACTS
ALTERNATE TITLE(S) Varies by Profession
DUTIES Design, build, repair, and maintain photovoltaic cells and solar power facilities; conduct research in solar energy technology; provide support to workers who perform the aforementioned tasks
SALARY RANGE $27,540 to $37,830 to $56,670 (solar photovoltaic installers) $40,350 to $75,000 to $157,160+ (scientists and engineers) $47,560 to $75,660 to $101,630+ (plant operators)
WORK ENVIRONMENT Indoors/Outdoors
BEST GEOGRAPHIC LOCATION(S) Opportunities are available throughout the country but are best in California, Arizona, New Jersey, Massachusetts, and New York
MINIMUM EDUCATION LEVEL Bachelor's Degree
SCHOOL SUBJECTS Business, Chemistry, Computer Science
EXPERIENCE Internship; volunteer or part-time experience useful
PERSONALITY TRAITS Conventional, Organized, Technical
SKILLS Building/Trades, Business Management, Computer
CERTIFICATION OR LICENSING Required
SPECIAL REQUIREMENTS Background check, drug screening for some positions
EMPLOYMENT PROSPECTS Good
ADVANCEMENT PROSPECTS Good
OUTLOOK Faster than the Average
NOC 7441
O*NET-SOC 17-2199.03, 17-2199.11, 41-4011.07, 47-1011.03, 47-2231.00, 47-4099.02

buildings. Many schools, hospitals, prisons, and government facilities use solar technology for their water use. This technology can also be used for cooling. Desiccant systems remove moisture from the air, thereby making it more comfortable. Absorption chiller systems are

CAREER LADDER

Manager or Consultant

Experienced Solar Energy
Industry Worker

Entry-Level Solar Energy
Industry Worker

the most common solar cooling systems. These systems produce air-conditioning without using electricity.

A building's design or construction materials can also utilize the sun's energy to provide the building's heating and light through passive solar design, water heating, or with electrical PV cells. *Architects* design structures whose locations are chosen to take advantage of the power of the sun, or they may lay the facilities out so as to avoid excessive heat.

The U.S. Department of Labor breaks the solar energy industry down into the following subsectors: Scientific Research; Solar Power Engineering; Manufacturing for Solar Power; Solar Power Plant Development; Solar Power Plant Construction; Solar Power Plant Operations; Solar Panel Installation and Maintenance; and Support Positions. The following paragraphs provide information on jobs in each subsector. Workers can be employed in more than one subsector. Many of these workers are also employed outside the renewable energy industry.

Scientific Research

Physicists work with scientists and engineers to improve the efficiency of solar panels and find new materials to use for solar panel generation.

Chemists develop new materials to make solar cells, improve existing materials, and work to improve overall solar cell design.

Materials scientists conduct research to find ways to increase the efficiency of solar panels—meaning the amount of energy that is collected by solar cells.

Solar Power Engineering

Solar engineers work in any number of areas of engineering products that help harness energy from the sun. They may research, design, and develop new products, or they may work in testing, production, or maintenance. They may collect and manage data to help design solar systems. Types of products solar engineers work on may include solar panels, solar-powered technology, communications and navigation systems, heating and cooling systems, and even cars. Solar engineers are frequently *electrical, mechanical, civil, chemical, industrial,* or *materials engineers* who are working on solar projects and designing photovoltaic systems.

Computer software developers design and develop software that is used to forecast sunlight and weather patterns to determine whether it will be feasible and cost effective to build solar infrastructure in a particular area. Those who work at power plants develop software that is used to monitor and control plant operations, including adjusting mirrors or photovoltaic panels to increase the amount of energy that is captured as the sun moves in the sky.

Engineering technicians use engineering, science, and mathematics to help solar engineers and other professionals in research and development, quality control, manufacturing, and many other fields.

Manufacturing for Solar Power

Semiconductor processors are highly skilled workers who oversee the process of converting semiconductors (microchips or integrated circuits) into photovoltaic cells.

Computer-controlled machine tool operators run machinery that forms and shapes solar panels or mirror components for concentrating solar plants or the components of photovoltaic panels. Production of these products requires highly precise cutting.

Welding, soldering, and brazing workers use heat to join small cells that are soldered to electric circuitry, which are then combined to make solar panels. These workers may also oversee machinery that performs these tasks.

Glaziers prepare the glass or laminate that sits atop solar panels. They install and secure the glass or laminate, then use rubber, silicone, or vinyl compounds to securely join the materials to the solar panel. They also help manufacture, install, and maintain delicate and expensive mirrors that are used in concentrating solar plants.

Electrical and electronic installers and repairers are responsible for the complex equipment used in solar manufacturing that monitors and controls production processes on the factory floor.

Electrical and electronic equipment assemblers put together complex electrical circuitry in solar panels and the components that connect solar panels.

Industrial production managers plan and coordinate all work activity on the factory floor. They determine what equipment should be used, if new equipment is needed, manage workers and production schedules (including scheduling overtime), and troubleshoot any labor or mechanical problems that emerge in order to keep production running smoothly.

Solar Power Plant Development

Real estate brokers obtain land via purchase or lease on which to build power plants. They have specialized knowledge of property specifications for solar power plants and the rules that have been established to obtain ownership or use of the property.

Atmospheric scientists (including *meteorologists*) study weather patterns and the atmosphere in order to help solar power industry officials decide where to build power plants or large commercial solar projects. They also work for small consulting firms that provide advice to businesses and homeowners that are interested in installing solar power.

Environmental scientists use physical science (such as biology, chemistry, and geology) and social science (including conservation and resource management) to study and assess the environment in relation to the impact human activity has on it, as well as damage incurred through natural interactions. They ensure that environmental laws and regulations are being met, help prevent violations before they occur, and help protect sensitive ecosystems (such as desert environments where many solar facilities are built).

Solar Power Plant Construction

Construction managers oversee the planning and building of solar power plants. They supervise teams made up of construction workers, engineers, and scientists.

Civil engineers use their knowledge of materials science and engineering theory to design and oversee the construction of solar power plants and related infrastructure (such as roads, support structures, and foundations).

The actual construction work is performed by a diverse group of professionals that includes *construction laborers, construction equipment operators, welders, structural iron and steel workers, plumbers,* and *carpenters.*

Solar Power Plant Operations

Power plant operators work in control rooms to monitor the generation and distribution of power. They also conduct periodic inspections of equipment throughout the plant to ensure that it is operating properly.

Electricians install and maintain the equipment and wiring that connects the power plant to the electrical grid, which delivers power to consumers.

Plumbers, pipefitters, and *steamfitters* assemble, install, alter, and repair pipes and pipe systems that carry heat-transfer material—molten salt or synthetic oil—throughout the plant and into heat containment units. Other pipes in the plant carry steam from the heaters to the turbines that create electricity.

Electrical and electronics installers and repairers install, maintain, and repair electronic power equipment that manages and controls substations, generating plants, and monitoring equipment.

A solar energy worker trains two students on panel installation. (bikeriderlondon. Shutterstock.)

Electrical engineers control monitoring transmission and electrical generation devices that are used in power plants.

Solar Panel Installation and Maintenance

The career of *solar photovoltaic installer* is one of the most popular professions in the solar power industry. These workers are specially trained to install commercial and residential solar projects. They use hand and power tools to carefully attach solar panels to the roofs of buildings or to other structures. They make sure that the systems are set up correctly and troubleshoot and repair any problems. Solar photovoltaic installers have comprehensive knowledge of electrical wiring, especially as it relates to the installation of solar panels.

Solar energy installation managers supervise work crews that install solar photovoltaic or thermal systems.

Site assessors study a proposed solar panel installation site to determine how much energy can be collected at the site. They make recommendations on the best type, size, and layout of solar panels that will maximize energy collection. They create installation plans for installers.

Cost estimators use standard estimating techniques to calculate the cost of solar installations, solar power plant construction projects, or the manufacturing of photovoltaic technology.

Electricians install and maintain all the wiring and equipment that is associated with setting up a solar power system at a home or business. They connect the solar panel, inverter (a device that converts the direct current generated by the solar cells into an alternative current that can be used in homes and businesses), and other equipment to the power supply.

Plumbers are responsible for installing solar water heating systems and connecting them to a building's plumbing.

TOP SOLAR STATES BY EMPLOYMENT, 2015

FAST FACTS

State	Estimated Solar Jobs
1. California	75,598
2. Massachusetts	15,095
3. Nevada	8,764
4. New York	8,250
5. New Jersey	7.071
6. Texas	7,030
7. Arizona	6,922
8. Florida	6,560
9. North Carolina	5,950
10. Colorado	4,998

Source: The Solar Foundation

Roofers repair and seal any holes or cuts that were made to the roof as a result of installation of solar panels. They might also help solar photovoltaic installers place structural supports and mounting systems for solar panels on the roof.

Support Positions

Support workers perform clerical duties; supervise workers; manage computer databases; oversee advertising and marketing campaigns; respond to press inquiries; maintain records; educate the public; and do many other tasks. *Secretaries, receptionists, customer service representatives, advertising and marketing workers, media relations specialists, personnel and human resources specialists, lawyers, accountants, information technology workers*, and *educators* are just some of the types of support workers who are employed in this industry. Many of these workers are also employed outside the renewable energy industry.

■ EARNINGS

Solar photovoltaic installers earned median annual salaries of $37,830 in May 2015, according to the U.S. Department of Labor (DOL). Salaries ranged from less than $27,540 to $56,670 or more.

A 2014 survey by the Association of Energy Engineers found their members earned an average salary of $98,847. More than 15 percent of respondents earned less than $60,000, and more than 15 percent earned $100,000 or more.

The DOL does not provide comprehensive salary information for solar energy industry workers (except solar installers). It does provide salary data for engineers, technicians, power plant operators, and environmental

scientists in all industries. It reports that engineers, by specialty, earned the following salary ranges in May 2015: chemical, $59,470 to $157,160+; civil, $52,900 to $129,850+; electrical, $59,240 to $146,280+; industrial, $51,950 to $119,460+; materials, $53,300 to $126,920+; and mechanical, $53,300 to $126,920+.

Electrical and electronics engineering technicians earned salaries that ranged from less than $36,170 to $90,570 or more; civil engineering technicians, $31,400 to $75,550+; industrial engineering technicians, $33,910 to $83,000+; and mechanical engineering technicians, $33,830 to $81,010+.

Power plant operators earned salaries that ranged from less than $47,560 to $101,630 or more in May 2015.

Environmental scientists and specialists earned median annual salaries of $67,460 in May 2015. Ten percent of workers earned less than $40,350, and 10 percent earned $118,070 or more.

Support workers in the solar energy industry earn a wide range of salaries, from starting salaries of $20,000 for clerical support workers, to $200,000 or more for lawyers and top executives.

Benefits for full-time workers include vacation and sick time, health (and sometimes dental), insurance, and pension or 401(k) plans. Self-employed workers must provide their own benefits.

■ WORK ENVIRONMENT

Work environments in the solar energy industry vary by occupation. Clerks, secretaries, receptionists, computer professionals, lawyers, and business managers work indoors in climate-controlled offices. They typically work a standard 40-hour work week. Solar photovoltaic installers often travel from site to site in order to install or maintain equipment needed for solar projects. Installers and roofers often work at great heights on rooftops and ladders. Workers in these positions are at an increased risk of injury. Solar engineers may work indoors or outdoors, depending on the project. They work 40 hours a week, but longer hours may be required when projects are near deadlines. Solar engineers work in office buildings, laboratories, or industrial plants. They may spend time outdoors at solar power plants, and they may also spend time traveling to different plants and work sites in the United States as well as overseas. Semiconductor processors who work in clean rooms must wear "bunny suits," special lightweight garments that keep the cells and circuitry from becoming contaminated by dust and dirt.

■ EXPLORING

One of the best ways to learn more about the solar energy industry is to read solar-related publications. "Careers in

Solar Power," by James Hamilton (U.S. Bureau of Labor Statistics, June 2011, Report 2) is a great resource. It offers information on solar power, educational requirements, career options, and required credentials. It can be accessed at http://www.bls.gov/green/solar_power. Learn more about solar energy by reading magazines such as *Home Power* (http://homepower.com), *Solar Industry* (http://www.solarindustrymag.com), and *Solar Today* (http://solartoday.org). Visit Web sites like Build It Solar (http://www.builditsolar.com) to find all sorts of links to solar projects, designs, and experiments that you might even be interested in doing yourself. You can set up a small solar system at home and see firsthand how it works.

Industry associations and government agencies also hold many competitions designed to promote solar power. You can visit the National Renewable Energy Laboratory's Web site (http://www.nrel.gov) for a list of student programs and competitions held throughout the United States. One such contest is the Junior Solar Sprint/Hydrogen Fuel Cell Car Competition (http://www.nrel.gov/education/jss_hfc.html) held in Colorado for middle school students. The contest calls for the construction and racing of solar- and battery-powered cars. Contestants learn about renewable energy technologies and concepts in a fun, challenging, and exciting setting. Another contest is the U.S. Department of Energy's Solar Decathlon, which "challenges collegiate teams to design, build, and operate solar-powered houses that are affordable, energy-efficient, and attractive." Visit http://www.solardecathlon.gov for more information.

You can also participate in an interview with a solar energy industry professional. Ask your science teacher to help set up an interview, or visit http://www.findsolar.com to search for solar professionals in your area.

■ EDUCATION AND TRAINING REQUIREMENTS
High School

If you plan to work in a technical position in the solar energy industry, you should take classes in computer science, mathematics, physics, and shop. Aspiring science workers will benefit by taking chemistry, earth science, environmental science, physics, and related classes. Those interested in management careers should take business and accounting classes. Communication skills and the ability to use computers are key to success for all workers in the solar energy industry, so be sure to take as many English, speech, and computer science classes as possible.

Postsecondary Education

Educational requirements vary by career. The following paragraphs detail educational requirements for selected workers in the major subsectors of the solar energy industry.

Scientific Research

Most solar engineers have a bachelor of science degree in an engineering specialty, such as electrical, civil, mechanical, or chemical engineering. Engineering programs typically include mathematics, physical and life sciences, and computer or laboratory courses. Classes in social sciences or humanities are usually required as well. Many companies prefer to hire engineers with master of science degrees, so those who pursue advanced degrees may have better odds of securing work. A bachelor's degree is sufficient for many environmental scientist positions; those who work as professors or researchers typically have graduate degrees. Software developers usually have a minimum of a bachelor's degree in computer science, software design, or a related field. Engineering technicians prepare for the field by earning an associate's degree in engineering technology or a related field and completing on-the-job training.

Manufacturing for Solar Power

Most production workers receive on-the-job training, although more skilled workers, such as computer-controlled machine tool operators, obtain their skills via postsecondary technical training or apprenticeships. Industrial production managers usually have bachelor's degrees in industrial technology, business administration, management, or engineering.

Solar Power Plant Development

Real estate brokers usually have at least a bachelor's degree in real estate, business, law, engineering, or a related field. Atmospheric and environmental scientists have bachelor's degrees in earth science, environmental science, meteorology, or related fields. Some positions require applicants to have master's degrees or doctorates.

Solar Power Plant Construction

Construction managers typically have bachelor's degrees in construction management. business management, or management, along with experience in the construction industry. Civil engineers usually possess a bachelor's degree in civil or structural engineering. Lead engineers have a master's degree and specialized training and experience in the construction of solar power plants. Construction workers learn their skills via on-the-job training, through apprenticeships, or by earning technical degrees or certificates.

Solar Power Plant Operations

Power plant operators prepare for the field via a combination of education, on-the-job training, and practical experience.

Solar Panel Installation and Maintenance

Solar photovoltaic installers train for the field in a variety of ways. Many have a background in the construction industry or experience working as electricians. Courses in solar installation are offered by professional associations, trade schools, apprenticeship programs, and photovoltaic module manufacturers. Installers might also learn skills in roofing and plumbing in order to master all the skills needed to complete an installation. Site assessors prepare for the field by receiving on-the-job training and specialized training in site assessment. They also typically have previous experience in roofing, electrical, or solar photovoltaic installation work. Plumbers and electricians train via apprenticeship programs or through technical education at community colleges. Roofers receive on-the-job training or participate in apprenticeship programs.

Support Positions

Training for support workers ranges from on-the-job training for secretaries and receptionists, to a bachelor's degree in computer science or related fields for computer professionals, to a law degree for lawyers.

A small, but growing, number of colleges offer classes, certificates, and degrees in renewable energy. Visit the following Web sites for lists of programs: http://www1.eere.energy.gov/education/educational_professional.html and http://www.irecusa.org/workforce-education.

The Solar Living Institute, a nonprofit organization, offers solar training via online and traditional courses. Visit its Web site, http://www.solarliving.org, for more information. Also, many large solar energy equipment manufacturers offer training and certification programs.

Certification

The Midwest Renewable Energy Association (MREA) offers an entry-level site assessment certificate. According to the MREA, site assessors "evaluate the energy consumption of a household or business, as well as the solar or wind resource at the locations." Certificates in renewable energy technologies are also offered by two- and four-year colleges and universities.

Other Education or Training

The American Solar Energy Society, Solar Electric Power Association, Solar Energy Industries Association, and The Solar Foundation offer continuing education (CE) opportunities via webinars, classes, and conference workshops. The Association of Energy Engineers, Interstate Renewable Energy Council, Midwest Renewable Energy Association, and the National Society of Professional Engineers also provide professional development opportunities. Contact these organizations for more information.

Other professional associations provide CE classes, webinars, and conferences in their particular specialty. For example, the American Institute of Chemical Engineers offers webinars and conference seminars on a variety of topics. Contact the associations for more information.

■ CERTIFICATION, LICENSING, AND SPECIAL REQUIREMENTS
Certification or Licensing

Many technicians choose to become certified by the National Institute for Certification in Engineering Technologies. To become certified, a technician must have a specific amount of job-related experience and pass a multiple-choice examination.

The Society of Manufacturing Engineers offers certification to manufacturing engineers. The Association of Energy Engineers also offers certification in a variety of specialties. To be considered for certification, a candidate must meet eligibility standards such as a minimum of three years of relevant work experience and membership in a professional organization. Most programs consist of classroom work and examination.

Engineers who work on projects that affect the property, health, or life of the public typically pursue licensure. There are two levels of licensing for engineers. Professional Engineers (PEs) have graduated from an accredited engineering curriculum, have four years of engineering experience, and have passed a written exam. Engineering graduates need not wait until they have four years experience, however, to start the licensure process. Those who pass the Fundamentals of Engineering examination after graduating are called Engineers in Training (EITs) or Engineer Interns (EIs). The EIT certification usually is valid for 10 years. After acquiring suitable work experience, EITs can take the second examination, the Principles and Practice of Engineering exam, to gain full PE licensure. For more information on licensing and examination requirements, visit http://www.ncees.org. The National Council of Examiners for Engineering and Surveying (http://www.ncees.org) also provides licensure to engineers.

Many solar installers are licensed as general contractors. Solar thermal installers and photovoltaic installers can also receive voluntary certification from the North American Board of Certified Energy Practitioners (NABCEP). The National Roofing Contractors' Association's Roof Integrated Solar Energy program certifies photovoltaic installers. The Electronics Technicians Association offers three career-track certification pathways in renewable energy technology: installer, integrator, and maintainer. The NABCEP offers certification to photovoltaic technical sales professionals.

Certification and licensing requirements for other jobs in the solar energy industry vary according to the position. Contact professional associations in your area of interest for more information.

The Solar Energy Industries Association reports that "12 states and Puerto Rico require solar-specific licenses in order to engage in solar work. Generally, a solar certification is a specialty area for a general electrical or plumbing license; therefore, a contractor with a general license may engage in solar work." Some atmospheric and environmental scientists may need to be licensed. Those who are employed in positions that may affect the power grid must be certified by the North American Energy Reliability Corporation.

Other Requirements

Some employers may require power plant operators to undergo a background check and submit to periodic drug testing.

■ EXPERIENCE, SKILLS, AND PERSONALITY TRAITS

Any experience you can obtain in the solar energy industry, such as an internship, volunteering, or a part-time job, will be useful.

Ideal skills and personality traits vary for the wide range of workers in the solar energy industry. For example, a passion for solving problems is a key characteristic of all engineers, and particularly for those who work on renewable energy projects. Solar engineers team up with a wide variety of people—from managers, fellow engineers, designers, and construction professionals, to developers, clients, investors, and more—so it's essential to have strong communication skills, a flexible attitude, and the ability to get along well with others. They should also enjoy solving problems and be willing to continue to learn throughout their careers. Solar photovoltaic technicians should have good customer service skills, the ability to use hand-held and power tools, and strong technical skills. They should also be attentive to detail, not be afraid of working at heights, and be able to lift solar panels that weigh between 30 and 40 pounds and batteries that can weigh 60 to 80 pounds. Scientists should enjoy conducting research and solving problems; have inquisitive personalities; and be able to work independently as well as with other members of a team. Office workers need to be detail oriented, punctual, and able to follow instructions.

All workers should have good organizational, communication, and time-management skills; the ability to work independently and as a member of a team when necessary; and a willingness to continue to learn throughout their careers.

■ EMPLOYMENT PROSPECTS
Employers

There are a wide variety of employment opportunities available in the solar energy industry. Contractors, dealers, distributors, builders, utilities, government agencies, manufacturers, installers, and research and development companies can be found throughout the United States. The Southwest has the greatest potential for solar energy, although solar energy development has increased in other areas of the United States. As of November 2013, nearly 142,700 people spent at least 50 percent of their work time on solar-related projects, according to The Solar Foundation. The foundation reports that the top five states for solar jobs are (in descending order): California, Arizona, New Jersey, Massachusetts, and New York.

Manufacturers of solar power components and equipment are located throughout the United States. Large plants are located in California, Colorado, Georgia, Massachusetts, Michigan, New Mexico, Ohio, Oregon, Tennessee, Texas, and Wisconsin.

Starting Out

Many companies recruit on campus or at job fairs. Check with your school's career center for upcoming fairs in your area. Other good job hunting resources are trade journals, some of which may list job advertisements in their classifieds sections. Check out solar energy publications and blogs.

Internships are also a great way to get relevant work experience and to gain valuable contacts. Many of the larger energy companies and nonprofit groups offer internships (either with pay or for course credit) to junior- or senior-level college students. For example, the National Renewable Energy Laboratory offers both undergraduate and graduate students the opportunity to participate in its many research and development programs.

The Solar Energy Industries Association offers a company membership directory at http://www.seia.org/directory. It's a good place to start to learn more about potential employers.

■ ADVANCEMENT PROSPECTS

Advancement opportunities vary by profession. For example, solar panel installers may advance to positions of higher responsibility such as managing other workers. With experience, they may opt to start their own businesses specializing in panel installation and maintenance. Engineers and scientists may start with a position at a small company with local interests and advance to a position of higher responsibility within that same company (for example, director of research and development). Or they may move on to a larger more diverse company such as a public utility, whose interests may cover a broader area. They may also teach at universities and write for various publications.

Trades workers and office workers typically advance by receiving pay raises and managerial duties. By returning to school, construction trades workers can become construction managers or open their own contracting businesses.

■ OUTLOOK

Opportunities in solar energy should be good in the next decade. The Solar Energy Industries Association reports that the number of photovoltaic installations grew by about 41 percent from 2013 to 2015, and solar energy was the "second-largest source of new electricity generating capacity in the U.S., exceeded only by natural gas."

According to the *National Solar Jobs Census 2015*, employers predicted job growth of 14.7 percent in the coming year and similar growth in the near future.

Solar energy use is already well established in high-value markets such as remote power, satellites, and communications. Industry experts are working to improve current technology and lower costs to bring solar-generated electricity, hot water systems, and solar-optimized buildings to the public. The manufacturing of photovoltaic cell systems also presents many employment opportunities.

■ UNIONS AND ASSOCIATIONS

Solar energy technicians, trades workers, and production employees are represented by unions. Some major unions include the International Association of Bridge, Structural, Ornamental and Reinforcing Iron Workers (http://www.ironworkers.org); International Association of Machinists and Aerospace Workers (http://www.goiam.org); International Brotherhood of Electrical Workers (http://ibew.org); International Union of Electronic, Electrical, Salaried, Machine, and Furniture Workers-Communication Workers of America (http://www.iue-cwa.org); International Union of Painters and Allied Trades (http://www.iupat.org); National Association of Plumbing-Heating-Cooling Contractors (http://phccweb.org); United Auto Workers (http://uaw.org); United Association of Journeymen and Apprentices of the Plumbing and Pipefitting Industry of the United States and Canada (http://www.ua.org); United Steelworkers (http://usw.org); and United Union

of Roofers, Waterproofers, and Allied Workers (http://www.unionroofers.com).

Major professional associations for solar energy industry professionals include the American Solar Energy Society, Solar Electric Power Association, Solar Energy Industries Association, and The Solar Foundation. Other renewable energy industry associations of note include the Interstate Renewable Energy Council and the Midwest Renewable Energy Association.

Engineers and technicians can obtain resources and support from the following professional organizations: American Institute of Chemical Engineers (http://www.aiche.org); American Society of Certified Engineering Technicians (http://www.ascet.org); American Society of Civil Engineers (http://www.asce.org); ASME International (http://www.asme.org); Institute of Electrical and Electronics Engineers (http://www.ieee.org); Institute of Industrial Engineers (http://www.iie.ie/); National Society of Professional Engineers (http://www.nspe.org); SAE International (http://www.sae.org); and the Society of Manufacturing Engineers (SME, http://www.sme.org).

The National Council of Examiners for Engineering and Surveying (http://www.ncees.org) provides licensure to engineers. The National Institute for Certification in Engineering Technologies (http://www.nicet.org) offers certification to engineering technicians. The following organizations offer certification to solar photovoltaic installers: Electronics Technicians Association (http://eta-i.org); National Roofing Contractors' Association (http://www.nrca.net); and NABCEP (http://www.nabcep.org). The SME offers certification to manufacturing engineers. The Association of Energy Engineers offers certification in a variety of specialties.

The U.S. Department of Energy's Office of Energy Efficiency and Renewable Energy is a government agency that provides resources for those interested in solar energy.

There are many other professional associations for workers in the solar energy industry. Check the *Encyclopedia of Associations*, which is published by Gale Cengage Learning, for associations in your field of interest. The publication is available in many community and school libraries.

■ TIPS FOR ENTRY

1. Read publications such as *Solar Today* (http://solartoday.org) to learn more about trends in the industry and potential employers.
2. Use social media such as Facebook, LinkedIn, and Twitter to stay up to date on industry developments and learn about job openings.

3. Visit the following Web sites for job listings:
   - http://www.ases.org
   - http://www.seia.org/solar-jobs
   - http://solarliving.jobamatic.com/a/jbb/find-jobs
   - http://www.homepower.com/jobs
   - http://www.nspe.org/resources/career-center
4. Attend the American Solar Energy Society's annual conference, Solar Power International, and other industry events to network and interview for jobs.
5. Join professional associations such as the American Solar Energy Society and the Solar Energy Industries Association to access training and networking resources, industry publications, and employment opportunities.

▓ FOR MORE INFORMATION

For industry news and updates, publications, conferences, career opportunities, and membership information, contact

American Solar Energy Society (ASES)
2525 Arapahoe Ave., Ste. E4-253
Boulder, CO 80302
Tel: (303) 443-3130
E-mail: info@ases.org
http://www.ases.org

For information on careers, employment opportunities, certification, membership, and industry surveys, contact

Association of Energy Engineers (AEE)
3168 Mercer University Drive
Atlanta, GA 30341
Tel: (770) 447-5083
http://www.aeecenter.org

For information about renewable energy, contact

Interstate Renewable Energy Council (IREC)
PO Box 1156
Latham, NY 12110-1156
Tel: (518) 458-6059
E-mail: info@irecusa.org
http://www.irecusa.org

For information on solar tours, energy fairs, industry workshops, and certification, contact

Midwest Renewable Energy Association (MREA)
7558 Deer Road
Custer, WI 54423-9734
Tel: (715) 592-6595
E-mail: info@midwestrenew.org
https://www.midwestrenew.org

For more background information on renewable energy, careers, and internships, contact

National Renewable Energy Laboratory (NREL)
15013 Denver West Parkway
Golden, CO 80401-3305
Tel: (303) 275-3000
E-mail: service.center@nrel.gov
http://www.nrel.gov

For information on careers, certification and licensing, membership benefits, or local chapters, contact

National Society of Professional Engineers (NSPE)
1420 King Street
Alexandria, VA 22314-2794
Tel: (888) 285-6773; (703) 684-2800
Fax: (703) 684-2821
http://www.nspe.org

For general information about the renewable energy industry, contact

Office of Energy Efficiency and Renewable Energy
1000 Independence Avenue, SW
Washington, D.C. 20585
Tel: (877) 337-3463
http://www.eere.energy.gov

For industry information, contact

Solar Electric Power Association (SEPA)
1220 19th Street, NW, Suite 800
Washington, D.C. 20036-2405
Tel: (202) 857-0898
http://www.solarelectricpower.org

For trade news and updates, publications, conferences, career opportunities, and membership information, contact

Solar Energy Industries Association (SEIA)
600 14th Street, NW, Suite 400
Washington, D.C. 20005
Tel: (202) 682-0556
E-mail: info@seia.org
http://www.seia.org

For a variety of resources about solar power, contact

The Solar Foundation
1717 Pennsylvania Avenue, NW, Suite 750
Washington, D.C. 20006
Tel: (202) 469-3750
E-mail: info@solarfound.org
http://www.thesolarfoundation.org

Find out about workshops in sustainable living by visiting
Solar Living Institute (SLI)
PO Box 836, 13771 South Highway 101
Hopland, CA 95449-9607
Tel: (707) 472-2450
E-mail: sli@solarliving.org
http://www.solarliving.org

Solar Engineers

■ OVERVIEW

Solar engineers work in any number of areas of engineering products that help harness energy from the sun. They may research, design, and develop new products, or they may work in testing, production, or maintenance. They may collect and manage data to help design solar systems. Types of products solar engineers work on may include solar panels, solar-powered technology, communications and navigation systems, heating and cooling systems, and even cars. In 2015, solar energy made up 6 percent of all renewable energy in the United States, according to the Energy Information Administration. Renewable energy sources collectively accounted for 10 percent of all U.S. energy consumption.

■ HISTORY

People have worshiped the sun and found ways to channel its energy to improve their lives since early times. As far back as 400 B.C., ancient Greeks designed their homes to take advantage of the sun's warmth and light by having the structures face south to capture more heat in the winter. (This is known as "passive solar energy," an old technology that is still used today.) The Romans later improved on these designs by adding more windows to the south side of homes, and by putting glass panes in the windows, which allowed more heat and light into buildings. The Romans were also the first to use glasshouses to grow plants and seeds. And the Greeks and Romans were among the first to use mirrors to reflect the sun's heat to light fires.

Solar cooking is an ancient practice as well, dating at least as far back as the Essenes, an early sect of Jewish people who used the intense desert sun to bake thin grain wafers. In 1767, Swiss naturalist Horace-Bénédict de Saussure created the first solar oven—an insulated, glazed box with a glass-paned cover, which reached temperatures of 190 degrees Fahrenheit. In the 1950s, to aid communities located near deserts, the United Nations and other agencies funded studies of solar cooking to determine if it was a viable way to reduce reliance on plant life for fuel. The studies proved solar cooking was feasible, and so the UN provided further funding for programs to introduce wooden solar cookers to communities in need, such as in locations where firewood was scarce. Despite the benefits of the cookers, however, most groups ended up sticking with their old cooking methods and turned the cookers into firewood.

Solar cooking is back in force today, though. Solar ovens can now reach temperatures as high as 400 degrees Fahrenheit. Many hobbyists, inventors, and designers have fine-tuned the designs of solar ovens over the years, some turning them into marketable products. And the United Nation's solar cooking idea has been resurrected. In 2006, the nonprofit organizations Jewish Watch International, KoZon Foundation, and Solar Cookers International successfully launched a program to bring solar cookers to Darfur refugees. Civil war started in 2003 in Darfur (located in Western Sudan, Africa) and violence has raged in the years since. Since 2003, approximately 400,000 people have lost their lives and 3 million have been displaced. As simple an idea as it seems, solar cookers could actually save lives, because women and girls would no longer need to leave the safety of numbers to head off alone in search of firewood.

■ THE JOB

Solar engineering, while an ancient practice, is still a relatively new industry that has caught more mainstream attention only within the past 20 years. With forecasts of fossil fuels' eventual extinction and the focus shifting to sustainable business practices, more engineers are researching and developing solar-powered products as a means to conserve energy.

There are two types of solar energy: *passive solar energy* and *active solar energy*. Passive solar energy, as the name suggests, means that no mechanical devices are needed to gather energy from the sun. Positioning buildings to face the sun is one example of passive solar energy. In direct contrast, mechanical devices are used for active solar energy—to collect, store, and distribute solar energy throughout buildings. For instance, mechanical equipment such as pumps, fans, and blowers are used to gather and distribute solar energy to heat the space inside a home. Active solar energy is just one area in which solar engineers work. They help create active solar-space heating systems that are liquid (e.g., water tanks) or air based (e.g., rock bins that store heat), and active solar-water heating systems that use pumps to circulate and heat fluids.

Solar engineers are frequently electrical, mechanical, civil, chemical, or even petroleum engineers who are working on solar projects and designing photovoltaic systems.

Solar engineers may be responsible for such things as reviewing and assessing solar construction documentation; tracking and monitoring project documentation; evaluating construction issues; meeting with other engineers, developers, and investors to present and review project plans and specifications; participating in industry forums; and possibly even dealing with clients directly. One general requirement for most solar engineering positions is a working knowledge of mechanical and electrical engineering, and an understanding of a range of engineering concepts (such as site assessment, analysis, and design, and energy optimization).

▪ EARNINGS

The U.S. Department of Labor (DOL) reports the engineers most frequently employed in the solar industry earned the following average salary ranges as of May 2015, with the lowest 10 percent earning $50,900 or less and the highest ten percent earning $157,480 or more:

- materials engineers: $53,120 to $91,310 to $144,720
- chemical engineers: $59,470 to $97,360 to $157,160
- electrical engineers: $59,240 to $93,310 to $146,820
- industrial engineers: $53,300 to $83,470 to $126,920
- mechanical engineers: $53,640 to $83,590 to $128,430

Solar engineers who work for a company usually receive benefits such as vacation days, sick leave, health and life insurance, and a savings and pension program. Self-employed engineers must provide their own benefits.

▪ WORK ENVIRONMENT

Solar engineers may work indoors or outdoors, depending on the project. Work hours are generally 40 per week, with longer hours required when projects near deadline dates. Solar engineers may work in office buildings, laboratories, or industrial plants. They may spend time outdoors at solar power plants, and may also spend time traveling to different plants and work sites in the United States as well as overseas.

▪ EXPLORING

Learn more about solar energy by reading magazines such as *Home Power* (http://homepower.com) and *Solar Today* (http://solartoday.org), and visit Web sites like Build It Solar (http://www.builditsolar.com) to find all sorts of links to solar projects, designs, and experiments that you might even be interested in doing yourself. You can set up a small solar system at home and see firsthand how it works. To get an idea about the types of engineering jobs that are out there, visit such Web sites as Intech.net (http://www.intech.net) and Simply Hired (http://www.simplyhired.com).

▪ EDUCATION AND TRAINING REQUIREMENTS
High School

Take classes in math (e.g., algebra, calculus, geometry), science, natural science, communications, and computers. Engineering schools tend to favor students who have taken advanced placement and honors classes, so do your best to pursue course work at this high level.

Postsecondary Training

Most solar engineers have a bachelor of science in an engineering specialty, such as electrical, civil, mechanical, or chemical engineering. Engineering programs typically include mathematics, physical and life sciences, and computer or laboratory courses. Classes in social sciences or humanities are usually required as well. Many companies prefer to hire engineers with master of science degrees, so those who pursue advanced degrees may have better odds of securing work. Be sure to attend an engineering program that has been accredited by ABET (http://www.abet.org).

Certification

Certificate programs in renewable energy are provided by colleges and universities,

QUICK FACTS

ALTERNATE TITLE(S)
None

DUTIES
Use science and engineering principles to research, design, and develop new solar energy products; may also work in testing, production, or maintenance

SALARY RANGE
$50,900 to $91,310 to $157,480+

WORK ENVIRONMENT
Primarily Indoors

BEST GEOGRAPHIC LOCATION(S)
Opportunities are available throughout the country but are best in California, Arizona, New Jersey, Massachusetts, and New York

MINIMUM EDUCATION LEVEL
Bachelor's Degree

SCHOOL SUBJECTS
Earth Science, Mathematics, Physics

EXPERIENCE
Internship

PERSONALITY TRAITS
Conventional, Problem-Solving, Technical

SKILLS
Math, Mechanical/Manual Dexterity, Scientific

CERTIFICATION OR LICENSING
Required

SPECIAL REQUIREMENTS
None

EMPLOYMENT PROSPECTS
Good

ADVANCEMENT PROSPECTS
Good

OUTLOOK
Little Change or More Slowly than the Average

NOC
2131, 2132, 2133, 2134

O*NET-SOC
17-2199.03, 17-2199.11

CAREER LADDER

> Manager, or Consulting Firm Owner, or Professor

> Solar Engineer

> Solar Engineering Technician

professional associations (such as the Midwest Renewable Energy Association), and private organizations (such as National Solar Trainers). Contact these providers for more information.

Other Education or Training

Continuing education (CE) opportunities are offered by many professional associations. For example, the Solar Electric Power Association offers webinars, a Utility Solar Conference, and solar procurement workshops. Past webinars included "Predicting Solar Power Production"; "Solar, Storage and Demand Response"; and "Concentrating Solar Power: Technologies, Storage and the New Era of Projects."

Other organizations that offer professional development classes, webinars, conference workshops, and other opportunities include the American Institute of Chemical Engineers, American Solar Energy Society, Association of Energy Engineers, Interstate Renewable Energy Council, Midwest Renewable Energy Association, National Society of Professional Engineers, SAE International, Society of Women Engineers, Solar Energy Industries Association, and The Solar Foundation.

■ CERTIFICATION, LICENSING, AND SPECIAL REQUIREMENTS
Certification or Licensing

The Society of Manufacturing Engineers offers certification to manufacturing engineers. The Association of Energy Engineers also offers certification in a variety

An engineer adjusts solar panels at a SunEdison testing facility. (Dennis Schroeder. U.S. Department of Energy.)

of specialties. Contact these organizations for more information.

All 50 states and the District of Columbia require engineers who offer their services to the public to be licensed as professional engineers (PEs). To be designated as a PE, engineers must have a degree from an engineering program accredited by ABET, four years of relevant work experience, and successfully complete the state examination.

■ EXPERIENCE, SKILLS, AND PERSONALITY TRAITS

Take as many math and science classes as possible and participate in internships to gain experience in the field.

A passion for solving problems is a key characteristic of all engineers, and particularly of those who work on renewable energy projects. Solar engineers team up with a wide variety of people—from management, fellow engineers, designers, and construction professionals, to developers, clients, investors, and more—so it's essential to have strong communication skills, a flexible attitude, and the ability to get along well with others.

■ EMPLOYMENT PROSPECTS
Employers

Solar engineering is a growing field. While many engineers are working on solar projects, there are no statistics available yet regarding the number of solar engineers who are working full time in America. According to the U.S. Department of Labor, in May 2015, there were 34,300 chemical engineers; 178,400 electrical engineers; 241,100 industrial engineers; 25,300 materials engineers; and 277,500 mechanical engineers, employed in the United States.

Power systems companies, solar cell and module manufacturers, solar panel companies, and companies that provide energy-saving services (such as heating and cooling systems, energy audits, etc.) to commercial and residential customers are just a few examples of the types of companies that hire engineers to work on solar projects.

Most engineers, in general, work in architectural, engineering, and related services. Some work for business consulting firms and manufacturing companies that produce electrical and electronic equipment, business machines, computers and data processing companies, and telecommunications parts. Others work for companies that make automotive electronics, scientific equipment, and aircraft parts; consulting firms; public utilities; and government agencies. Some may also work as private consultants.

IMPORTANT DEVELOPMENTS AND HIGHLIGHTS IN SOLAR ENERGY

MILESTONES

1839: French physicist Alexandre-Edmond Becquerel discovers the photovoltaic effect (from Greek, "photo" meaning light, and "voltaic" meaning electricity), which is when certain materials produce small amounts of electricity when exposed to light.

1883: American inventor Charles Fritts creates the first working solar cell (a device that converts solar energy directly into electricity), by coating semiconductor-material selenium with a thin layer of gold. (Efficiency rate was a minuscule 1 to 2 percent.)

1921: Albert Einstein wins the Nobel Prize in Physics for his theories about the photovoltaic effect.

1947: Because energy is scarce during World War II, the United States builds more passive solar buildings.
- The book *Your Solar House*, published by Libby-Owens-Ford Glass Company, also sparks interest in solar energy.

1954: Bell Laboratories invents the "solar battery"—the first practical silicon solar cell with a sunlight energy-conversion efficiency of about 6 percent. Bell demonstrates its invention by powering a toy Ferris wheel and a solar-powered radio transmitter.

1955: Mechanical engineer Frank Bridgers designs the first commercial office building to use solar water heating and passive solar design. The Solar Building, located in Albuquerque, is now a designated historic landmark.
- Western Electric begins selling commercial licenses for silicon photovoltaic technologies.

1959: Explorer VI satellite is launched with a photovoltaic (PV) array of 9,600 solar cells. ("Array" means an interconnected system of PV modules that function as one unit that produces electricity.)

1960: Hoffman Electronics achieves PV cells with 14 percent efficiency.

1963: Sharp starts producing PV modules. (A module is a group of individual PV cells that are used to harness solar radiation for energy.)

1969: A solar furnace is built in Odeillo, France, featuring an eight-story parabolic mirror to capture sun energy.

1970s: The Solar Energy Industries Association and the Solar Energy Research Institute (now the National Renewable Energy Laboratory) are formed.
- Thin-film photovoltaic research begins. (In thin-film solar technology, non-silicon semiconductor materials such as copper, indium, gallium and selenium [CIGS] are used to create photovoltaic cells that convert sunlight into electricity.) Solar cell prices drop from about $100 per watt to about $20 per watt.

1980s: ARCO Solar becomes the first company to produce more than 1 megawatt (1000 kilowatts) of photovoltaic modules in one year.
- American inventor Paul MacCready builds the Solar Challenger, the first solar-powered aircraft, and flies it from France to England across the English Channel.
- Solar One, a 10-megawatt solar-power demonstration project, begins operations (1982–88), and proves the feasibility of power tower systems.

1990s: National Renewable Energy Laboratory produces a solar cell with 30 percent conversion efficiency.
- The tallest skyscraper built in the 1990s in New York City is completed. The building—Four Times Square—has more energy-efficient features than any other commercial skyscraper, including building-integrated photovoltaic panels on floors 37 through 43 (on the south- and west-facing facades) to produce part of the building's power.
- Worldwide-installed PV capacity reaches 1000 megawatts.

2000s: Home Depot begins selling residential solar power systems in San Diego, California.
- Helios, NASA's solar-powered aircraft, sets a new world altitude record for non-rocket-powered craft: 96,863 feet (more than 18 miles up).
- University of Colorado (CU) students build an energy-efficient solar home for the Solar Decathlon, a competition sponsored by the U.S. Department of Energy, and win first prize. (Students integrated aesthetics and modern conveniences with maximum energy production and optimal efficiency.) The houses are transported to the National Mall in Washington, D.C.

2012: Solar energy makes up 2 percent of all renewable energy in the United States.

2013: Nearly 142,700 people spend at least 50 percent of their work time on solar-related projects.

Starting Out

See if you can get an internship with a company that provides solar energy services. You can also learn more about the industry by visiting the Web sites of professional associations such as the Institute for Electrical and Electronic Engineers and the American Solar Energy Society. If there's an upcoming meeting or event in your area, it may be a good opportunity to meet solar energy professionals, find out about the latest trends, and learn where the job market is heading.

■ ADVANCEMENT PROSPECTS

Solar engineers who work for companies can advance by taking on more projects, managing more people, and moving up to senior-level positions. They may start their own companies and expand their business by offering more services and opening up branches in other locations. They may also teach at universities and write for various publications.

■ OUTLOOK

The U.S. Department of Labor forecasts varying employment outlooks for engineers through 2024. Little change or slower-than-average growth is expected for chemical, electrical, industrial, and materials engineers. Employment for mechanical engineers should grow by about 5 percent, as fast as the average for all jobs. Engineers working in solar energy may find it somewhat easier to obtain employment in the years to come, especially if more governments invest money into alternative-energy research and development. The Solar Energy Industries Association reports that the number of photovoltaic installations (measured bu installed solar capacity) grew by more than 41 percent from 2013 to 2015, and solar energy was the "second-largest source of new electricity generating capacity in the U.S., exceeded only by natural gas."

■ UNIONS AND ASSOCIATIONS

Some engineers may be represented by the International Federation of Professional and Technical Engineers (http://www.ifpte.org) and other unions. The Association of Energy Engineers represents the professional interests of engineers who are employed in the renewable energy industry. Major professional organizations for solar engineers include the American Solar Energy Society, Institute of Electrical and Electronics Engineers, Solar Electric Power Association, Solar Energy Industries Association, and The Solar Foundation. Other professional organizations include the Interstate Renewable Energy Council and the Midwest Renewable Energy Association. The National Renewable Energy Laboratory is a federal laboratory that conducts research in renewable energy and energy efficiency.

■ TIPS FOR ENTRY

1. Read publications such as *Solar Industry* (http://www.solarindustrymag.com) and *Solar Today* (http://solartoday.org) to learn more about the field.
2. Visit the following Web sites for job listings:
   - http://www.nspe.org/resources/career-center
   - http://www.seia.org/solar-jobs
   - http://solarliving.jobamatic.com/a/jbb/find-jobs
3. Participate in internships or part-time jobs that are arranged by your college's career services office. Visit http://energy.gov/eere/education/clean-energy-jobs-and-career-planning for information on internships, fellowships, and scholarships.
4. Visit http://energy.gov/eere/education/explore-clean-energy-careers for comprehensive information on careers in renewable energy.

■ FOR MORE INFORMATION

For industry news and updates, publications, conferences, career opportunities, and membership information, contact

American Solar Energy Society (ASES)
2525 Arapahoe Avenue, E4-253
Boulder, CO 80302-6720
Tel: (720) 420-7937
E-mail: info@ases.org
http://www.ases.org

For information on careers, employment opportunities, membership, and industry surveys, contact

Association of Energy Engineers (AEE)
3168 Mercer University Drive
Atlanta, GA 30341
Tel: (770) 447-5083
http://www.aeecenter.org

For information on careers in electrical and electronics engineering, contact

Institute of Electrical and Electronics Engineers (IEEE)
2001 L Street, NW, Suite 700
Washington, D.C. 20036-4910
Tel: (202) 785-0017
E-mail: ieeeusa@ieee.org
http://www.ieee.org

For information about renewable energy, contact
Interstate Renewable Energy Council (IREC)
PO Box 1156
Latham, NY 12110-1156
Tel: (518) 458-6059
E-mail: info@irecusa.org
http://www.irecusa.org

For information on energy fairs and industry workshops, contact
**Midwest Renewable Energy
   Association (MREA)**
7558 Deer Road
Custer, WI 54423-9734
Tel: (715) 592-6595
E-mail: info@midwestrenew.org
https://www.midwestrenew.org

For more background information on renewable energy, careers, and internships, contact
National Renewable Energy Laboratory (NREL)
15013 Denver West Parkway
Golden, CO 80401-3111
Tel: (303) 275-3000
E-mail: service.center@nrel.gov
http://www.nrel.gov

For industry information, contact
Solar Electric Power Association (SEPA)
1220 19th Street, NW, Suite 401
Washington, D.C. 20036-2405
Tel: (202) 857-0898
http://www.solarelectricpower.org

For trade news and updates, publications, conferences, career opportunities, and membership information, contact
Solar Energy Industries Association (SEIA)
600 14th Street, NW, Suite 400
Washington, D.C. 20005
Tel: (202) 682-0556
E-mail: info@seia.org
http://www.seia.org

For a variety of resources about solar power, contact
The Solar Foundation
600 14th Street, NW, Suite 400
Washington, D.C. 20005
Tel: (202) 469-3750
E-mail: info@solarfound.org
http://www.thesolarfoundation.org

Find out about workshops in sustainable living by visiting
Solar Living Institute (SLI)
PO Box 836, 13771 South Highway 101
Hopland, CA 95449-9607
Tel: (707) 472-2450
E-mail: sli@solarliving.org
http://www.solarliving.org

Solutions Architects

■ OVERVIEW

Solutions architects design, plan, and deliver technology strategies that help companies and other organizations solve problems or launch new products, systems, or services. They oversee projects from the brainstorming phase to the finished product or implementation of the solution. Solutions architects work for a variety of companies and organizations ranging from Google and Apple, to the U.S. Departments of Education and Defense, to colleges and universities. They are also known as *information technology architects* and *project architects*.

■ HISTORY

Solutions architects have helped companies organize information technology (IT) resources and solve problems ever since companies and other organizations have used IT to build infrastructure and create products and services. In 2002, the International Association for Software Architects (which is now known as Iasa Global) was founded to improve the quality of the IT architecture industry. It has approximately 80,000 members in more than 50 countries.

■ THE JOB

Iasa Global defines the role of IT architects as "the technology strategist for the business…[who has] a broad understanding of technology that spans programming and development of custom applications, the infrastructure environment that the solution must reside in, and the operational environment that provides support." Solutions architects (SAs) are specialized IT architects who devise "big picture" plans and strategies on how technology and IT professionals in various disciplines will be utilized to solve business problems (e.g., upgrading antiquated online customer service systems, addressing security breaches and implementing security infrastructure to avoid future problems, etc.) and launch new products and services. Before they begin a project, they ask questions such as:

- What are the development concerns and goals of the various stakeholders (clients, colleagues, executives, outside vendors)?
- How much money and time is available to complete the project?
- Should the organization buy or build a solution to the problem?
- What technology platform should be used?
- How will I leverage the skill sets of in-house and contract IT workers to solve the problem?
- How will the solution be scaled to meet expected user demand?
- How will the proposed solution integrate with existing IT systems?
- What are the risks associated with the proposed solution, and how can they be ameliorated?

Once these and other questions are answered, the solutions architect gets to work on the project. Job responsibilities for solutions architects vary by employer and project, but most SAs perform the following duties:

- create a concrete software architecture specification (i.e., the overall design of the IT system and interrelationships between its components) and design artifacts (documents, reports, analyses, models that support the specification)
- test technology that will play a critical role in the architecture to ensure that it will work correctly when work on the project begins
- review patterns that might be useful to the architecture (patterns are previously described and validated approaches to commonly occurring problems in software architecture)
- explain the architecture to members of the team to help them understand and "buy into" the proposed plan
- participate in reviews of the prototypes, designs, and other technical deliverables to ensure that they meet project requirements
- consult with development team members to address issues relating to performance, security, supportability, risk, etc. and identify options and recommend solutions
- refine architectural decisions related to the infrastructure, application architecture, data architecture, patterns and designs, and other criteria
- reduce risk to their employer by working with risk managers to identify and address issues that may affect the success of the project, profitability, etc.
- act as a key member of the project team and provide leadership in both application design and development
- resolve problems and serve as the go-to technical expert for the development team
- participate in solution design reviews and other project milestones

■ EARNINGS

Solutions architects earned median annual salaries of $113,751 in March 2016, according to PayScale.com. Wages ranged from $76,220 to $148,856.

Solutions architects who held the Amazon Web Services certified solutions architect-associate credential had average salaries of $125,871 in 2016, according to a survey of Information IT professionals by Global Knowledge Training LLC, a for-profit education provider.

Benefits for solutions architects include paid holidays, vacation, and sick and personal days; retirement and pension plans; and medical, dental, and life insurance. Some employers offer a 401(k) plan match, paid sabbaticals and maternity and paternity leave, the opportunity to purchase company stock at a discounted price, and reimbursement for the completion of certification and continuing education programs.

■ WORK ENVIRONMENT

Approximately 40 percent of computer and information systems managers worked more than 40 hours per week in 2014, according to the U.S. Department of Labor. Solutions architects spend much of their days in meetings with company executives, managers, business analysts and other members of their team. The work can be stressful when deadlines loom and disagreements arise between members of the team. Solutions architects sometimes travel to client sites or satellite offices to oversee various projects.

■ EXPLORING

Iasa Global provides several ways to explore the field. First, check out the What is IT Architecture? section (http://iasaglobal.org/itabok/what-is-it-architecture) of its Web site to learn about IT architecture career paths (including solutions architects), read a glossary of commonly used terms, and access other resources. If you're a full-time college student, consider participating in its IT Architecture Competition, in which student teams devise and present an end-to-end architecture solution for a real-world business problem. Additionally, the association offers a discounted membership category for college students, as well as a free membership category for those who just want to explore the field. "Free" members receive access to an online membership directory and the organization's virtual library, the opportunity to attend networking and social events with fellow architects, and discounts on e-books, videos, and print publications.

Other ways to explore this career and develop project management experience include reading books about the field (such as *IT Architecture For Dummies,* by Kalani Kirk Hausman and Susan L. Cook), talking with solutions architects about their careers, and taking on management roles in school clubs and other organizations.

■ EDUCATION AND TRAINING REQUIREMENTS
High School

In high school, take courses in business management, mathematics, programming, database management, computer science, English, speech, government, and social studies.

Postsecondary Education

A minimum of a bachelor's degree is required to enter the field, although some employers prefer applicants with graduate degrees. Solutions architects have a wide variety of educational backgrounds. Some have degrees in computer science, management information systems, database management, systems analysis, software engineering, software development, or network engineering. Others have degrees in project management. Many project management programs are accredited by the Global Accreditation Center for Project Management Education Programs. To view a list of accredited U.S. and international programs that offer bachelor's, master's, and doctorate degrees in project management, visit http://www.pmi.org/gac/directory-accredited-programs.aspx.

Other Education or Training

Iasa Global offers both self-paced and instructor-led continuing education (CE) opportunities for IT architects. Recent classes include Business Technology Strategy, Business Architecture, Software Architecture, Effective Meetings, Intro to Leadership, Presentation Skills, Comparing Frameworks and Methodologies, Universal Modeling Language, and Business Process Management. Professional associations (such as Association for Computing Machinery, IEEE Computer Society, and Project Management Institute) and for-profit educational and consulting companies (such as Nielsen Norman Group) also offer CE classes, webinars, and workshops. Contact these organizations to learn more.

Certification

The University of Washington in Seattle, Washington, offers a certificate in solutions architecture. According to the university's Web site, participants will learn "solution development taxonomy, including the development life cycle and modeling system aspects; techniques for analyzing solution alternatives; systems integration strategies and methods for blending a set

CAREER LADDER

CEO or Chief Operating Officer

Chief Information Officer

Chief Technology Officer

Lead Solutions Architect

Solutions Architect

Information technology workers discuss a new computer network for their expanding business with a solutions architect. (Maksym Poriechkin. Shutterstock.)

INS AND OUTS OF INFORMATION TECHNOLOGY ARCHITECTURE

LEARN MORE ABOUT IT

Bell, Michael. *Incremental Software Architecture: A Method for Saving Failing Information Technology Implementations.* Hoboken, N.J.: John Wiley & Sons, 2016.

Bowman, Courtney, and Ari Gesher. *The Architecture of Privacy: On Engineering Technologies that Can Deliver Trustworthy Safeguards.* Sebastopol, Calif.: O'Reilly Media, 2015.

Burd, Stephen D. *Systems Architecture,* 7th ed. Farmington Hills, Mich.: Course Technology PTR, 2015.

Englander, Irv. *The Architecture of Computer Hardware, Systems Software, and Networking: An Information Technology Approach,* 5th ed. Hoboken, N.J.: John Wiley & Sons, 2014.

Erl, Thomas. *Cloud Computing Design Patterns.* Upper Saddle River, N.J.: Prentice Hall, 2015.

Grzech, Adam, Leszek Borzemski, et al. (eds.) *Information Systems Architecture and Technology: Proceedings of 36th International Conference on Information Systems Architecture and Technology.* New York: Springer, 2016.

Hausman, Kalani Kirk, and Susan L. Cook. *Information Technology Architecture for Dummies.* Hoboken, N.J.: For Dummies, 2010.

Hughes, Ralph. *Agile Data Warehousing for the Enterprise: A Guide for Solution Architects and Project Leaders.* Burlington, Mass.: Morgan Kaufmann, 2015.

Resmini, Andrea, and Luca Rosati. *Pervasive Information Architecture: Designing Cross-Channel User Experiences.* Burlington, Mass.: Morgan Kaufmann, 2011.

Stackowiak, Robert, and Art Licht. *Big Data and The Internet of Things: Enterprise Information Architecture for a New Age.* New York: Apress Media LLC, 2015.

Turban, Efraim, and Linda Volonino. *Information Technology for Management: Advancing Sustainable, Profitable Business Growth,* 9th ed. Hoboken, N.J.: John Wiley & Sons, 2013.

of interdependent systems; techniques and deliverables of the Architecture Development Method; and an introduction to TOGAF, EA^3, and Zachman enterprise architecture frameworks." Visit https://www.pce.uw.edu/certificates/solutions-architecture for more information.

Many colleges and universities provide undergraduate and graduate certificates in computer science, project management, software development, software product management, agile development, and other IT-related fields that will be of interest to solutions architects. Contact schools in your area to learn about available programs.

■ CERTIFICATION, LICENSING, AND SPECIAL REQUIREMENTS
Certification or Licensing

Iasa Global offers the certified IT architect credential at four experience levels (foundation, associate, specialist, and professional) to those who complete educational requirements and pass an examination. Visit http://iasa-global.org/certifications for more information.

Many tech companies—such as Microsoft, IBM, Amazon Web Services, HP, and Cisco—provide certification credentials for solutions architects that are tied to their specific products or services.

Some architects earn project management–related credentials. The most-popular credential, project management professional, is offered by the Project Management Institute. According to the institute, those who hold the project management professional credential earn 20 percent more than their non-certified peers. Here are a few other popular certification credentials for project managers:

- Associate in project management, professional in project management, certified project director (offered by the Global Association for Quality Management)
- Master project manager (American Academy of Project Management)
- Project management in information technology security (EC-Council)
- Project+ (CompTIA)

■ EXPERIENCE, SKILLS, AND PERSONALITY TRAITS

Solutions architects need at least five years of experience (more at large companies) in software engineering, IT infrastructure, telecommunications engineering, systems or database administration, project management, or in lower-level solutions architecture positions.

The ability to communicate effectively with people who have various levels of technical knowledge is extremely important for solutions architects. Other key traits include strong analytical and problem solving skills, leadership ability, a detail-oriented personality, initiative, self-motivation, good organizational and planning ability, and strong teaching and mentoring skills in order to educate and guide others regarding architectural principles, standards, and methodologies. Finally, SAs must be proficient in the use of workflow management tools, various hardware platforms (mainframes, desktop computers, mobile devices, and distributed platforms), service-oriented architecture, object-oriented programming concepts, enterprise service business systems, data management and data quality tools, Agile development and systems development life cycle methodologies, and programming languages such as HTML, Java, C#, C++, XML, .NET, and ColdFusion.

▣ EMPLOYMENT PROSPECTS

Employers

Solutions architects work for any company or organization that has a technology-related problem that needs to be solved, including companies of all sizes, colleges and universities, government agencies, and nonprofit organizations. Opportunities are available throughout the country, but are best in large cities.

Starting Out

Some solutions architects start their career as programmers or software application developers. Others enter the profession by working in lower-level IT architecture positions.

Popular job-search strategies include participating in internships, attending career fairs and networking events, joining professional associations and utilizing their job-search resources, working with recruiters, and using the resources of your college's career services office. Additionally, check out the following Web sites for job listings:

- http://iasahome-jobs.careerwebsite.com/jobseeker/search/results
- https://www.linkedin.com/jobs/senior-solutions-architect-jobs
- http://www.careerbuilder.com/jobs/keyword/solution-architect
- http://www.crunchboard.com

▣ ADVANCEMENT PROSPECTS

In the course of their work, solutions architects have many opportunities to work with senior and executive management, and those who make a good impression can advance rapidly at their employers. An experienced solutions architect can advance to the position of *lead solutions architect,* who oversees other SAs and takes on more complex project management duties. Lead solutions architects can become *chief technology officers,* who

assess new technology and determine how it can help their organizations. Chief technology officers with both business and technological acumen can become *chief information officers* (CIO), who are responsible for all aspects of their organization's Information Technology. A highly experienced CIO might become the CEO or chief operating officer of his or her company.

▣ OUTLOOK

The U.S. Department of Labor (DOL) does not provide an employment outlook for solutions architects, but as managers, they can be categorized under the DOL's more general heading of "computer and information systems managers." Employment for workers in this category is expected to grow 15 percent through 2024, or much faster than the average for all careers. The DOL reports that "prospects should be favorable in this occupation because older computer and information systems managers will retire over the next decade. Because innovation is fast paced in IT, opportunities should be best for those who have extensive work experience and knowledge of the newest technology."

The career and recruiting site GlassDoor.com selected the occupation of solutions architect as the third-best job in the United States in 2016. Careers that make GlassDoor's annual list have the highest overall Glassdoor Job Score, which is determined by combining three key factors: the number of job openings, salary, and career opportunities.

▣ UNIONS AND ASSOCIATIONS

Solutions architects do not belong to unions. Some join professional associations such as Iasa Global, which has chapters in nine U.S. cities and Canada and other countries, provides the certified IT architect credential at four levels, offers various membership options (including one for college students), publishes extensive information about careers in information architecture at its Web site, and hosts a monthly e-summit, where experts discuss trends in the field. The Association for Computing Machinery, IEEE Computer Society, and Project Management Institute also provide many useful resources.

▣ TIPS FOR ENTRY

1. Visit https://generalassemb.ly/get/the-absolute-beginners-guide-to-getting-a-job-in-tech to access *The Absolute Beginner's Guide to Getting a Job in Tech* (Note: e-mail sign-up is required).
2. Use social media to stay up to date on industry developments and learn about job openings. Many professional associations use social media to stay in touch with their members and others who are interested in

careers in information technology. For example, Iasa Global has a presence on Facebook, LinkedIn, and Twitter. You should also join solutions architecture groups on LinkedIn such as SharePoint-Enterprise Solutions Architects, Oracle Solutions Architects Group, and IBM SOA Solutions Architects.

3. Become certified to show employers that you've met the highest standards established by your industry.

FOR MORE INFORMATION

For information on education and careers in Information Technology, contact

Association for Computing Machinery
2 Penn Plaza, Suite 701
New York, NY 10121-0799
Tel: (800) 342-6626
http://www.acm.org

For information on careers, certification, membership, and continuing education, contact

Iasa Global
12325 Hymeadow Drive, Suite 2-200
Austin, TX 78750-1847
Tel: (866) 399-4272
E-mail: contactus@iasaglobal.org
http://www.iasaglobal.org

For information on careers and professional development opportunities, contact

IEEE Computer Society
2001 L Street, NW, Suite 700
Washington, D.C. 20036-4928
Tel: (202) 371-0101
E-mail: help@computer.org
http://www.computer.org

To learn more about certification, visit

Project Management Institute
14 Campus Boulevard
Newtown Square, PA 19073-3299
Tel: (855) 746-4849
http://www.pmi.org

Songwriters

OVERVIEW

Songwriters write the words and music for songs, including songs for recordings, advertising jingles, and theatrical performances. We hear the work of songwriters every day, and yet most songwriters remain anonymous, even if a song's performer is famous. Many songwriters perform their own songs. Songwriters are also known as *composers* and *lyricists*.

HISTORY

Songwriting played an important part in the growth of the United States. The early pioneers wrote songs as a way to socialize and relax. Some of the difficult experiences of traveling, fighting over land, farming, and hunting for food were put into words by early songwriters, and the words set to music, for the guitar, banjo, piano, and other instruments. Francis Scott Key became famous for writing the words to the "Star Spangled Banner," set to a popular drinking tune.

Toward the end of the 19th century, sheet music was sold by hundreds of publishing companies centered in New York City in what became known as Tin Pan Alley. This name was coined by a songwriter and journalist named Monroe Rosenfeld. The name referred to the sounds of many voices and pianos coming from the open windows on the street where many of the music publishers were located. By the 1880s, sheet music was sold in the millions; most songs were introduced on the stages of musical theater, vaudeville, and burlesque shows. Radio became an important medium for introducing new songs in the 1920s, followed by the introduction of sound movies in the 1930s. Sheet music became less important as musical recordings were introduced. This presented difficulties for the songwriter and publisher, because the sales of sheet music were easier to control. In the 1940s, the first associations for protecting the rights of the songwriters and publishers were formed; among the benefits songwriters received were royalties for each time a song they had written was recorded, performed, or played on the radio or in film.

By the 1950s, Tin Pan Alley no longer referred to a specific area in New York but was a term used nationwide to denote popular songs in general, and especially a type of simple melody and sentimental and often silly lyrics that dominated the pop music industry. The rise of rock and roll music in the 1950s put an end to Tin Pan Alley's dominance. Many performers began to write their own songs, a trend that became particularly important in the 1960s. In the late 1970s, a new type of songwriting emerged. Rap music, featuring words chanted over a musical background, seemed to bring songwriting full circle, back to the oral traditions of its origins.

THE JOB

There are many different ways to write a song. A song may begin with a few words (the lyrics) or with a few notes of a melody, or a song may be suggested by an idea, theme, or product. A song may come about in a flash of inspiration or may be developed slowly over a long period of time. Songwriters may work alone, or as part of a team, in which one person concentrates on the lyrics while another person concentrates on the music. Sometimes there may be several people working on the same song.

Most popular songs require words, or lyrics, and some songwriters may concentrate on writing the words to a song. These songwriters are called *lyricists*. Events, experiences, or emotions may inspire a lyricist to write lyrics. A lyricist may also be contracted to write the words for a jingle or musical, or to adapt the words from an existing song for another project.

Some songwriters do no more than write the words to a potential song, and leave it to others to develop a melody and musical accompaniment for the words. They may sell the words to a music publisher, or work in a team to create a finished song from the lyric. Some lyricists specialize in writing the words for advertising jingles. They are usually employed by advertising agencies and may work on several different products at once, often under pressure of a deadline.

In songwriting teams, one member may be a lyricist, while the other member is a *composer*. The development of a song can be a highly collaborative process. The composer might suggest topics for the song to the lyricist; the lyricist might suggest a melody to the composer. Other times, the composer plays a musical piece for the lyricist, and the lyricist tries to create lyrics to fit with that piece.

Composers of popular music generally have a strong background in music, and often in performing music as well. They must have an understanding of many musical styles, so that they can develop the music that will fit a project's needs. Composers work with a variety of musical and electronic equipment, including computers, to produce and record their music. They develop the different parts for the different musical instruments needed to play the song. They also work with musicians who will play and record the song, and the composer conducts or otherwise directs the musicians as the song is played.

Songwriters, composers, and musicians often make use of MIDI (musical instrument digital interface) technology to produce sounds through synthesizers, drum machines, and samplers. These sounds are usually controlled by a computer, and the composer or songwriter can mix, alter, and refine the sounds using mixing boards and computer software. Like analog or acoustic instruments, which produce sounds as a string, reed, or drum head vibrates with air, MIDI creates digital "vibrations" that can produce sounds similar to acoustic instruments or highly unusual sounds invented by the songwriter.

Synthesizers and other sound-producing machines may each have their own keyboard or playing mechanism, or be linked through one or more keyboards. They may also be controlled through the computer, or with other types of controls, such as a guitar controller, which plays like a guitar, or foot controls. Songs can be stored on a computer, or copied onto a digital storage device.

Many, if not most, songwriters combine both the work of a lyricist and the work of a composer. Often, a songwriter will perform his or her own songs as well, whether as a singer, a member of a band, or both.

For most songwriters, writing a song is only the first part of their job. After a song is written, songwriters usually produce a "demo" of the song, so that the client or potential purchaser of the song can hear how it sounds. Songwriters contract with recording studios, studio musicians, and recording engineers to produce a version of the song. The songwriter then submits the song to a publishing house, record company, recording artist, film studio, or others, who will then decide if the song is appropriate for their needs. Often, a songwriter will produce several versions of a song, or submit several different songs for a particular project. There is always a chance that one, some, or all of their songs will be rejected.

■ EARNINGS

Songwriters' earnings vary widely, from next to nothing to many millions of dollars. A beginning songwriter may work for free, or for low pay, just to gain experience. A songwriter may sell a jingle to an advertising agency for $1,000 or may receive many thousands of

QUICK FACTS

ALTERNATE TITLE(S)
Composers, Lyricists

DUTIES
Write the words and music for songs

SALARY RANGE
$21,070 to $49,820 to $114,530+

WORK ENVIRONMENT
Primarily Indoors

BEST GEOGRAPHIC LOCATION(S)
New York City, Los Angeles, Nashville, and Chicago

MINIMUM EDUCATION LEVEL
High School Diploma

SCHOOL SUBJECTS
English, Music, Theater/Dance

EXPERIENCE
Experience with a variety of song styles recommended

PERSONALITY TRAITS
Artistic, Creative, Outgoing

SKILLS
Interpersonal, Performance, Music, and Acting, Writing

CERTIFICATION OR LICENSING
None

SPECIAL REQUIREMENTS
None

EMPLOYMENT PROSPECTS
Fair

ADVANCEMENT PROSPECTS
Fair

OUTLOOK
Little Change or More Slowly than the Average

NOC
5132

O*NET-SOC
27-2041.00, 27-2041.04

Hit Songwriter, or Jingle House
Owner, or Musician

Songwriter

Aspiring Songwriter

dollars if his or her work is well known. Royalties from a song may reach $20,000 per year or more per song, and a successful songwriter may earn $100,000 or more per year from the royalties of several songs. A songwriter's earnings may come from a combination of royalties earned on songs and fees from commercial projects.

Those starting as assistants in music production companies or jingle houses may earn as little as $20,000 per year. Experienced songwriters at these companies may earn $50,000 per year or more.

According to the U.S. Department of Labor, in May 2015 salaried writers and authors, a category that includes songwriters, had earnings that ranged from less than $29,230 to more than $114,530, with a median of $60,250. Composers had salaries that ranged from less than $21,070 to more than $101,150 annually, with a median of $49,820.

Because most songwriters are freelance, they will have to provide their own health insurance, life insurance, and pension plans. They are usually paid per project, and therefore receive no overtime pay. When facing a deadline, they may have to work more than eight hours a day or 40 hours a week. Also, songwriters are generally responsible for recording their own demos and must pay for recording studio time, studio musicians, and production expenses.

■ WORK ENVIRONMENT

Songwriters generally possess a strong love for music and, regardless of the level of their success, usually find fulfillment in their careers because they are doing what they love to do. As freelancers, they will control how they spend their day. They will work out of their own home or office. They will have their own instruments, and possibly their own recording equipment as well. Songwriters may also work in recording studios, where conditions can range from noisy and busy to relaxed and quiet.

Writing music can be stressful. When facing a deadline, songwriters may experience a great deal of pressure while trying to get their music just right and on time. They may face a great deal of rejection before they find someone willing to publish or record their songs. Rejection remains a part of the songwriter's life, even after success.

Many songwriters work many years with limited or no success. On the other hand, songwriters experience the joys of creativity, which has its own rewards.

■ EXPLORING

The simplest way to gain experience in songwriting is to learn to play a musical instrument, especially the piano or guitar, and to invent your own songs. Joining a rock group is a way to gain experience writing music for several musicians. Most schools and communities have orchestras, bands, and choruses that are open to performers. Working on a student-written musical show is ideal training if you want to be a songwriter.

If you have your own computer, consider investing in software, a keyboard, and other devices that will allow you to experiment with sounds, recording, and writing and composing your own songs. While much of this equipment is expensive, there are plenty of affordable keyboards, drum machines, and software programs available today. Your school's music department may also have such equipment available.

■ EDUCATION AND TRAINING REQUIREMENTS
High School

You should take courses in music that involve singing, playing instruments, and studying the history of music. Theater and speech classes will help you to understand the nature of performing, and involve you in writing dramatic pieces. You should study poetry in an English class, and try your hand at composing poetry in different forms. Language skills can also be honed in foreign-language classes and by working on student literary magazines. An understanding of how people act and think can influence you as a lyricist, so take courses in psychology and sociology.

Postsecondary Training

There are no real requirements for entering the field of songwriting. All songwriters, however, will benefit from musical training, including musical theory and musical notation. Learning to play one or more instruments, such as the piano or guitar, will be especially helpful in writing songs. Not all songwriters need to be able to sing, but it can be helpful.

Songwriting is an extremely competitive field. Despite a lack of formal educational requirements, prospective songwriters are encouraged to continue their education through high school and preferably toward a college degree. Much of the musical training a songwriter needs, however, can also be learned informally. In general, you should have a background in music theory, and in arrangement and orchestration for multiple instruments.

You should be able to read music, and be able to write it in the proper musical notation. You should have a good sense of the sounds each type of musical instrument produces, alone and in combination. Understanding harmony is important, as well as a proficiency in or understanding of a variety of styles of music. Studies in music history will also help develop this understanding.

On the technical side, you should understand the various features, capabilities, and requirements of modern recording techniques. You should be familiar with MIDI and computer technology, as these play important roles in composing, playing, and recording music today.

There are several organizations that help lyricists, songwriters, and composers. The Songwriters Guild of America (http://www.songwritersguild.com) offers weekly song evaluation workshops in select cities. The Nashville Songwriters Association International (http://www.nashvillesongwriters.com) offers workshops, seminars, and other services, as well as giving annual awards to songwriters. The Songwriters and Lyricists Club provides contacts for songwriters with music-business professionals. These, and other organizations, offer songwriting workshops and other training seminars.

Other Education or Training

The American Society of Composers, Authors, and Publishers provides workshops that cover topics such as songwriting, film scoring, and musical theatre scoring. The American Composers Forum offers workshops and other learning opportunities. Past workshop topics included writing music for film and copyright law. The Society of Composers & Lyricists offers seminars and other continuing education opportunities on music technology, industry trends, and other topics. The Songwriters Guild of America provides songwriting workshops in a variety of cities, and the Nashville Songwriters Association International offers worksokps and other educational opportunities. Contact these organizations for more information.

■ CERTIFICATION, LICENSING, AND SPECIAL REQUIREMENTS
Certification or Licensing

There are no certification or licensing requirements for songwriters.

■ EXPERIENCE, SKILLS, AND PERSONALITY TRAITS

Practice writing songs in a variety of genres—such as rock, rap, jazz, and country. This will help you gain experience working with different styles and musical approaches.

Singer Ne-Yo is also a songwriter who has written popular songs for Beyoncé and Rihanna. (Helga Esteb. Shutterstock.)

Many elements of songwriting cannot really be learned but are a matter of inborn talent. A creative imagination and the ability to invent melodies and combine melodies into a song are essential parts of a songwriting career. As you become more familiar with your own talents, and with songwriting, you'll learn to develop and enhance your creative skills.

■ EMPLOYMENT PROSPECTS
Employers

Most songwriters work freelance, competing for contracts to write songs for a particular artist, television show, movie, video game, or for contracts with musical publishers and advertising agencies. They meet with clients to determine the nature of the project and to get an idea of what kind of music the client seeks, the budget for the project, the time in which the project is expected to be completed, and in what form the work is to be submitted.

WRITING AND SELLING SONGS
LEARN MORE ABOUT IT

Austin, Dave, Jim Peterik, and Cathy Austin. *Songwriting For Dummies,* 2nd ed. New York: For Dummies, 2010.

Freese, Cris (ed.). *2016 Songwriter's Market,* 39th ed. New York: Writer's Digest Books, 2015.

Pattison, Pat. *Songwriting Without Boundaries: Lyric Writing Exercises for Finding Your Voice.* New York: Writer's Digest Books, 2012.

Simos, Mark. *Songwriting Strategies: A 360 Approach.* Boston: Berklee Press, 2014.

Many songwriters work under contract with one or more music publishing houses. Usually, they must fulfill a certain quota of new songs each year. These songwriters receive a salary, called an advance or draw, which is often paid by the week. Once a song has been published, the money earned by the song goes to pay back the songwriter's draw. A percentage of the money earned by the song over and above the amount of the draw goes to the songwriter as a royalty. Other songwriters are employed by so-called "jingle houses," companies that supply music for advertising commercials. Whereas most songwriters work in their own homes or offices, these songwriters work at the jingle house's offices. Film, television, and video production studios may also employ songwriters on their staff.

Starting Out

Songwriting is a very competitive career and difficult to break into for a beginner. The number of high-paying projects is limited. Beginning songwriters often start their careers writing music for themselves or as part of a musical group. They may also offer their services to student films, student and local theater productions, church groups, and other religious and nonprofit organizations, often for free or for a low fee.

Many songwriters get their start while performing their own music in clubs and other venues; they may be approached by a music publisher, who contracts them for a number of songs. Other songwriters record demos of their songs and try to interest record companies and music publishers. Some songwriters organize showcase performances, renting a local club or hall and inviting music industry people to hear their work. Songwriters may have to approach many companies and publishers before they find one willing to buy their songs. A great deal of making a success in songwriting is in developing contacts with people active in the music industry.

Some songwriters get their start in one of the few entry-level positions available. Songwriters aspiring to become composers for film and television can find work as orchestrators or copyists in film houses. Other songwriters may find work for music agents and publishers, which will give them an understanding of the industry and increase their contacts in the business, as they develop their songwriting skills. Those interested in specializing in advertising jingles may find entry-level work as music production assistants with a jingle house. At first, such jobs may involve making coffee, doing paperwork, and completing other clerical tasks. As you gain more exposure to the process of creating music, you may begin in basic areas of music production, or assist experienced songwriters.

■ ADVANCEMENT PROSPECTS

It is important for a songwriter to develop a strong portfolio of work and a reputation for professionalism. Songwriters who establish a reputation for producing quality work will receive larger and higher-paying projects as their careers progress. They may be contracted to score major motion pictures, or to write songs for major recording artists. Ultimately, they may be able to support themselves on their songwriting alone and also have the ability to choose the projects they will work on.

In order to continue to grow with the music industry, songwriters must be tuned into new musical styles and trends. They must also keep up with developments in music technology. A great deal of time is spent making and maintaining contacts with others in the music industry.

Songwriters specializing in jingles and other commercial products may eventually start up their own jingle house. Other songwriters, especially those who have written a number of hit songs, may themselves become recording artists.

For many songwriters, however, success and advancement is a very personal process. A confidence in your own talent will help you to create better work.

■ OUTLOOK

Most songwriters are unable to support themselves from their songwriting alone and must hold other part-time or full-time jobs while writing songs in their spare time. The music industry is very competitive, and there are many more songwriters than paying projects. This situation is expected to continue into the next decade.

There are a few bright spots for songwriters. The recent rise of independent filmmaking has created more venues for songwriters to compose film scores. Cable television also provides more opportunities for songwriting, both in the increased number of advertisements and in the growing trend for cable networks to develop their own original programs. Many computer games and software feature songs and music, and this area should grow rapidly in the next decade. Another boom area is the World Wide Web. As more and more companies, organizations, and individuals set up multimedia Web sites, there will be an increased demand for songwriters to create songs and music for these sites. Songwriters with MIDI capability will be in the strongest position to benefit from the growth created by computer uses of music. In another field, legalized gambling has spread to many states in the country, a large number of resorts and theme parks have opened, and as these venues produce their own musical theater and shows, they will require more songwriters.

The number of hit songs is very small compared to the number of songwriters trying to write them. Success in songwriting therefore requires a combination of hard work, industry connections, and good luck.

■ UNIONS AND ASSOCIATIONS

Professional musicians generally hold membership in the American Federation of Musicians of the United States and Canada. The following organizations represent the professional interests of songwriters: the American Composers Forum; the American Society of Composers, Authors, and Publishers; Broadcast Music Inc.; Nashville Songwriters Association International; the National Association of Composers, USA; and the Songwriters Guild of America.

■ TIPS FOR ENTRY

1. Write songs in as many genres as possible. This will increase your skill and improve your chances of getting a song published.
2. Participate in songwriting workshops and seminars to hone your skills and make valuable industry contacts.
3. Join music associations and organizations. Many provide helpful resources that will help you break into the industry.
4. Apply for internships and fellowships with music companies and organizations.
5. Record demos of your songs and try to interest music publishers and companies.

■ FOR MORE INFORMATION

For professional and artistic development resources, contact

American Composers Forum (ACF)
522 Landmark Center, 75 West 5th Street
Saint Paul, MN 55102-1439
Tel: (651) 228-1407

Fax: (651) 291-7978
E-mail: PMarschke@composersforum.org
http://www.composersforum.org

For membership information, contact

American Society of Composers, Authors and Publishers (ASCAP)
1900 Broadway
New York, NY 10023-7004
Tel: (212) 621-6000
Fax: (212) 621-8453
http://www.ascap.com/songwriter.aspx

Visit the Songwriter's section of the BMI Web site to learn more about performing rights, music publishing, copyright, and the business of songwriting.

Broadcast Music Inc. (BMI)
7 World Trade Center
250 Greenwich Street
New York, NY 10007-0030
Tel: (212) 220-3000
E-mail: newyork@bmi.com
http://www.bmi.com

For information on membership and workshops, contact

Nashville Songwriters Association International (NSAI)
1710 Roy Acuff Place
Nashville, TN 37203-3222
Tel: (800) 321-6008; (615) 256-3354
Fax: (615)256-0034
E-mail: reception@nashvillesongwriters.com
http://members.nashvillesongwriters.com

To learn about the annual young composer's competition and other contests, contact

National Association of Composers, USA (NAC)
PO Box 49256
Barrington Station
Los Angeles, CA 90049-0256
http://www.music-usa.org/nacusa/

The SGA offers song critiques and other workshops in select cities. Visit its Web site for further information on such events.

Songwriters Guild of America (SGA)
5120 Virginia Way, Suite C22
Brentwood, TN 37027-7594
Tel: (800) 524-6742
http://www.songwritersguild.com

Spa Attendants

OVERVIEW

Spa attendants work in hotels, resorts, and salons. They are specially trained in facial, body, and water treatments. They assist massage therapists and estheticians, and prepare and clean the treatment rooms and tables. They provide spa customers with refreshments, towels, washcloths, and robes. According to the International SPA Association, approximately 359,300 people were employed in the U.S. spa industry in May 2016.

HISTORY

Fossils prove that even the mammoths of over 20,000 years ago enjoyed a good spa treatment. The town of Hot Springs, a small resort village nestled in the hills of South Dakota, features a fossil excavation site. This site serves as evidence that mammoths were attracted to the area's pools of warm water. Humans share this attraction. Native Americans considered natural hot springs to be sacred healing grounds. Throughout Europe, the ancient Romans built colossal spas, including the Baths of Caracalla. Only its ruins remain, but these baths once featured hot and cold baths, a swimming pool, a gymnasium, shops, art galleries, and acres of gardens.

Although spas fell out of favor during the Middle Ages, by the 17th and 18th centuries they had once again become popular in Europe. An interest in making use of natural resources for healing and relaxation spread. By the late 1800s there was hardly a well of natural spring water in the United States that a businessman had not capitalized upon. At the turn of the century in the United States, people visited resorts and spas (with or without natural hot springs) for exercise and relaxation. By the 1920s spas had become popular retreats for the wealthy. Since that time, spas have diversified their services and attracted a wide range of visitors. Today's spas have clients ranging from busy professionals looking for several hours of stress reduction, to families looking for healthy vacations, to pregnant women seeking relaxation, to men looking to keep fit. According to the International SPA Association, there were 160 million spa visits in the United States in 2012.

THE JOB

From the ylang-ylang plant to the *lomilomi* massage, spa attendants are teaching vacationers a new language of health and rejuvenation. Although there were only 30 spas in the United States in the late 1970s, the number now has grown to nearly 20,000. More than half of these are day spas, where clients can check in for an afternoon of relaxation and rejuvenation. The remainder are resort/hotel spas, which welcome clients for longer visits.

Spas and resorts have cropped up around natural hot springs, the seaside, the desert, the mountains, and even the plains. Some spas are designed to meet very specific needs, such as weight management and holistic wellness. While most spas offer the usual facials, body wraps, and massages, many are expanding to include "mind/body awareness" as people flock to spas for both physical and spiritual needs.

In some spas, you can schedule hypnosis, yoga, and dream therapy sessions right after your horseback riding, tennis game, and round of golf. So the duties of a spa attendant can vary greatly from location to location.

Spa attendants are also finding work outside of the vacation industry, at salons and day spas, as cosmetologists recognize the need to expand into other areas of beauty care. In addition to actually performing treatments, spa attendants devise special treatment plans for individual clients. They also schedule appointments, order and sell products, launder linens, and clean all spa areas. They offer advice on treatments and skin care products.

A resort often capitalizes on its location. Spa attendants at a resort in Hawaii, for example, would give treatments with fresh seawater, sea salt, seaweed, and Hawaiian plants. In a different kind of environment, a spa and resort may provide very different services. Mud baths, natural hot spring whirlpools, volcanic mineral treatment—resort owners around the world develop their spas with the natural surroundings in mind. This results in very specific training for spa attendants.

EARNINGS

Salaries for spa attendants vary greatly across the country. Spa attendants make from minimum wage to around $10 per hour. Annual salaries with this pay scale would range from $15,080 to $20,800. Salaries vary according to work environment (a large resort will pay more than a small salon) and the spa attendant's responsibilities. Spa attendants are either paid by the hour or by commission (a percentage of the spa treatments performed). Spa attendants also receive tips of between 10 and 15 percent. Some spas automatically bill guests an additional percentage to cover the tip, so that the guest doesn't have to worry about having the money on hand to give to the attendant. With tips from a wealthy clientele and a commission on higher-priced services, a spa attendant at a fine hotel will make much more than an attendant in a smaller day spa.

SimplyHired.com cited the average average salary for spa attendants nationwide in May 2017 as $21,000.

According to the U.S. Department of Labor, in May 2013 the earnings for locker room, dressing room, and coatroom attendants, a category that includes spa attendants, ranged from $8.44 an hour ($17,560 annually) to $17.35 an hour ($36,100 annually), with a median of $10.44 an hour ($21,720 annually).

Employees of spas are likely to receive better benefits than many of their counterparts in the cosmetology field. Spa attendants working at hotels may also receive a variety of perks, such as discounted spa treatments, guest rooms, meals in the hotel restaurants, and travel packages.

■ WORK ENVIRONMENT

Working among vacationers in a sunny, scenic part of the world can be very enjoyable. Most spa attendants work within well-decorated, temperature-controlled buildings, with soothing music piped through the speaker systems. Fresh fruit, tea, and other refreshments are often readily available. Spa attendants work directly with a public that has come to a resort to alleviate stress and other worries, making for very relaxed interactions. Some hotel spa attendants even live on the premises in special employee quarters, or in nearby housing, allowing them to live close to the beaches, mountains, or whatever natural beauty surrounds the resort.

Because spas usually open in the wee hours of the morning and close after dark, spa attendants may have to work long, irregular hours. Depending on the codes of the spa, they wear uniforms and jackets. They also wear gloves if their skin is sensitive to some of the products.

In a local beauty salon, a spa attendant tries to maintain a similarly relaxed environment in the few rooms dedicated to spa treatment. The rest of the salon, however, may be noisy with waiting customers, hair dryers, electric clippers, and music. The salon may also affect those with allergies to chemicals in hair treatment products.

Day spas, which may be located in large cities, typically strive to maintain a serene environment for the clientele, from the reception area, with soft music playing in the background, to the private treatment rooms, which may have soft lighting. While the spa attendant may work in these areas, he or she is also part of the activity behind the scenes, often working with damp laundry, cleaning supplies, and spa products.

■ EXPLORING

One of the best ways to explore this type of work is to get a part-time or summer job at a spa. You may be surprised by the number of spas in your area. There may even be a resort on the outskirts of your city. Search online for "Beauty Salons and Services" as well as "Health Clubs" and "Massage." (Many of the listings under "Spa" are only for hot tub dealerships.) Visit a salon or day spa and ask to interview someone who works as a spa attendant. Some attendants may allow you to shadow them for a day or two. Larger salons may have openings for part-time attendants, allowing you to gather firsthand experience.

Many resorts across the country advertise nationally for summer help. Check the classified advertisements of vacation and travel magazines, and visit http://www.resortjobs.com for a listing. You could also select a resort and spa from the pages of tourism publications, such as *Resort+Recreation* (http://www.resort-recreation.com), and call the hotel directly to request information about summer jobs. You can also find a directory of spas by visiting http://www.spafinder.com.

If you are unable to find a job at a spa, consider a part-time or summer job at a local hotel, beauty salon, or tanning salon. In any of these locations you will gain experience working with guests and providing for their comfort. Nursing homes and hospitals also employ high school students to provide clients or patients with personal care services. Working at a retail store specializing in products for skin care and beauty, aromatherapy, and massage can teach you about various spa treatments and products and help you decide if you are interested in this line of work.

If you have the money, consider making an appointment for yourself at a spa in your area. You may not be able to afford a vacation or full-day treatment, but even an hour spent as a client at a spa can give you an impression

QUICK FACTS

ALTERNATE TITLE(S)
None

DUTIES
Administer facial, body, and water treatments to clients in spas

SALARY RANGE
$17,560 to $21,720 to $36,100+

WORK ENVIRONMENT
Primarily Indoors

BEST GEOGRAPHIC LOCATION(S)
Opportunities are available throughout the country

MINIMUM EDUCATION LEVEL
High School Diploma

SCHOOL SUBJECTS
Biology, Chemistry, Health

EXPERIENCE
Any experience one can obtain working at a spa in any capacity will be useful

PERSONALITY TRAITS
Hands On, Helpful, Outgoing

SKILLS
Interpersonal, Mechanical/Manual Dexterity

CERTIFICATION OR LICENSING
Recommended

SPECIAL REQUIREMENTS
None

EMPLOYMENT PROSPECTS
Good

ADVANCEMENT PROSPECTS
Good

OUTLOOK
About as Fast as the Average

NOC
N/A

O*NET-SOC
39-3093.00

CAREER LADDER

Spa Manager or Spa Program Director

Massage Therapist

Nail Technician or Cosmetician

Experienced Spa Attendant

Spa Attendant Trainee

of what working in such an environment would be like.

■ EDUCATION AND TRAINING REQUIREMENTS
High School

To prepare for work as a spa attendant, take high school courses in anatomy, physiology, and biology. These classes will give you an understanding of the human body and muscle systems. Chemistry will prepare you for the use and preparation of skin care products. Health courses will teach you about nutrition, fitness, and other issues of importance to the health-conscious patrons of resorts and spas. Because so many spas offer treatment for both the body and the mind, take some psychology courses to learn about the history of treating depression, anxiety, and other mental and emotional problems. Finally, take computer classes, because if in your future job you need to keep track of spa supplies, you will probably be using a computer to do so.

In addition to these classes, you will benefit from having CPR and first aid training. Check with your high school to find out if it offers such training or contact organizations such as your local Red Cross. Many spas require attendants to know CPR and first aid, and your training will give you an advantage when looking for a job.

Postsecondary Training

Currently no specific postsecondary training program exists for spa attendants. Most spas put new hires through their own attendant training programs. Any work experience that you already have in a spa, therefore, will make you an appealing job candidate. During your high school years, try to get a summer job at one of the many resorts across the country. Spas often hire extra help to deal with the increased number of guests during this peak vacation period. Although you may only be working with the laundry, you will have the opportunity to see how a spa or resort is run and find out about the many different jobs available.

Some spas require their attendants to be certified cosmeticians or massage therapists. In such cases, education beyond high school is required. If you know of a specific spa at which you wish to work, ask about the hiring policy for attendants. Cosmeticians receive their training from cosmetology schools; massage therapists are educated at schools of massage therapy.

Other Education or Training

The International Spa Association and the Day Spa Association offer a variety of continuing education classes and webinars to spa professionals. Contact these organizations for more information.

■ CERTIFICATION, LICENSING, AND SPECIAL REQUIREMENTS
Certification or Licensing

There are no specific certification or licensing requirements for spa attendants; however, licensing requirements for cosmeticians and massage therapists vary by state, and you should know what these requirements are before you begin a program of study.

Some spas require their attendants to be certified cosmeticians or massage therapists. In such cases, education beyond high school is required. If you know of a specific spa at which you wish to work, ask about the hiring policy for attendants. Cosmeticians receive their training from cosmetology schools; massage therapists are educated at schools of massage therapy. Licensing requirements for these professionals vary by state, and you should know what these requirements are before you begin a program of study.

The International Spa Association offers the certified spa supervisor designation to spa managers who pass an examination and meet other requirements. Contact the association for more information.

■ EXPERIENCE, SKILLS, AND PERSONALITY TRAITS

Any experience one can obtain working at a spa in any capacity will be useful for aspiring spa attendants.

Guests of resorts and spas expect to be pampered and welcomed and can only fully relax during a spa treatment if the attendant is calm and considerate. Be prepared to serve your clients and to remain friendly and helpful.

Any shyness and excessive modesty may also prevent you from performing your spa duties properly. You'll be applying lotions and oils to the naked skin of your guests—if you are uncomfortable, your clients will detect it and become uncomfortable themselves. You must take a professional approach so that your clients feel safe and at ease. You should have a good "bedside manner"—the calm, comforting approach health care professionals use. Self-confidence is also important; you must convey to your client that you're knowledgeable about the treatment.

■ EMPLOYMENT PROSPECTS

Employers

The International SPA Association estimates that, as of May 2016, 359,300 people worked in the spa industry in the United States, which is up from 232,700 in 2007, a more than 32 percent increase. The primary employers of spa attendants are hotels, resorts, salons, and, naturally, spas. Increasing numbers of salons are adding spas to their facilities to maintain a competitive edge; this will lead to increased opportunities for spa attendants throughout the country, mostly in larger cities and metropolitan areas. The same is true for hotel spas. Many spas, however, are clustered in resort areas with attractions like hot springs and consistently pleasant climates.

Starting Out

Many spa attendants receive their training on the job, but some background experience in health care or cosmetology may help you in landing that first job as a spa attendant. If you are not particular about your geographic location, check travel publications for listings of resorts and spas, or visit http://www.spafinder.com for lists of spas according to their specialties and locations.

A degree from a cosmetology or massage therapy school can be valuable when looking for a job in a spa. Many of these degree programs require fieldwork, or hands-on experience, and will put you in touch with salons and fitness centers. Without a degree, you may be limited in the spa treatments you are allowed to perform. But as more and more individual hair stylists and beauty salons open day spas to accommodate all the needs of their clients, both licensed and unlicensed spa attendants will find more job opportunities.

■ ADVANCEMENT PROSPECTS

The longer an attendant works in a spa, the more he or she will learn about the services provided there. The attendant will also have more opportunities to expand upon the on-the-job training and potentially be allowed to perform more treatments. Though attendants typically start off with only an hourly wage, they can eventually receive commissions and tips. The more guests an attendant works with, the better tips and commission he or she will make. In a salon or day spa situation, the clientele will include regular customers. If they are happy with an attendant's work, they will request that attendant's services specifically and thus increase the attendant's income.

Attendants who complete further formal education also become qualified for more advanced positions. Those who attend cosmetology school to become *cosmeticians* typically take classes such as anatomy, chemistry,

A spa attendant maintains the cleanliness and the amenities of the facility. (Blend Images. Shutterstock.)

and physiology. They are qualified to work on the skin, giving facials, body wraps, and makeup applications, and may also do hair removal by waxing or plucking. Nail technician programs offered through cosmetology schools or nail schools qualify the graduate to give manicures and pedicures. Attendants who are particularly interested in fitness may want to consider advancement by getting an associate's degree from a fitness program. Courses for such programs include muscle conditioning, nutrition, and injury prevention. Those interested in massage may seek advancement by completing a massage therapy school program, which will qualify them to give different types of massage. These programs include course work in anatomy and physiology as well as provide hands-on training.

Some attendants advance to become *spa managers* or *spa program directors*. As program directors, they are responsible for adding new services, training spa attendants, determining what skin products to use, and controlling other details of the spa's daily practices. Those who wish to run their own business may eventually open their own spa.

THE ROOTS OF TODAY'S SPA EXPERIENCE

Public baths date back over 4,500 years. They have been found in Pakistan, ancient Babylon (modern-day Iran and Iraq), and Egypt. The medieval Turks created the five stages of the spa bath still practiced today: dry heat, moist heat, massage, cold, and rest. Some cultural contributions to the spa experience have gained popularity more than others: Asian and European massages and whirlpools are all the stuff of the modern-day spa; the Finnish sauna practice of beating one another with tree branches, however, has failed to take the world by storm.

■ OUTLOOK

The International SPA Association reports that spa visits are on the rise in the United States, with clients making nearly 179 million spa visits in 2015, up from 176 million visits in 2014. This increase in visits can be attributed to the growing appreciation for the benefits of spa visits, the increased number of day spas, and increased popularity of spas among men. In fact, many spas are adding treatments specifically for men. These expanding facilities and new treatment options should translate into job opportunities for everyone working in this industry, including spa attendants.

In addition, the public is becoming more health conscious, and people are looking to spas for both enjoyable and educational vacations. Some spas are specializing in teaching guests new patterns of diet, exercise, and

SPA TRENDS

According to the International SPA Association, the spa industry generated $16.3 billion in revenues in 2015 alone. Part of this success is spa employees' attention to customer demands and new trends. The following are some popular trends in the spa industry:

- Eastern/Asian influences in spa design, products, and services
- Medical-type products and services
- Food- and plant-based treatments and products
- Day-spa services that can fit into clients' busy schedules
- Tea and alkaline water bars
- Weightless flotation tanks, chambers, and pools
- More wellness retreats located in urban areas

skin care. A number of health care professionals are even predicting that spas will be covered by health insurance plans; doctors will write prescriptions to patients for spa treatments. To compete with other spas, and to satisfy returning guests, spas are likely to offer even more diverse lists of services and treatments. The spa attendant will have to keep ahead of health and beauty trends and be capable of adapting to new programs and methods.

Anticipating a future of one-stop beauty treatment, the owners of hair and beauty salons are dedicating rooms to spa treatments. For the cost of a little remodeling, hair salons can stay competitive with local day spas, as well as generate more business. Spa attendants may find their best job opportunities at these salons, where they can earn a good commission and establish a client base.

■ UNIONS AND ASSOCIATIONS

Spa attendants are not represented by unions. The International SPA Association and the Day Spa Association are the major professional organizations for spa professionals. The Green Spa Network is a group of ecofriendly spas.

■ TIPS FOR ENTRY

1. Read publications such as *Pulse* (http://expe rienceispa.com/pulse/current-issue) to learn more about trends in the industry and potential employers.
2. Visit the following Web sites for job listings:
   - http://experienceispa.com/job-bank -search-openings
   - http://www.careerbuilder.com
   - http://www.indeed.com
3. Join the International Spa Association (ISPA), Day Spa Association, and other organizations to access training and networking resources, industry publications, and employment opportunities.
4. Attend the annual ISPA Conference & Expo (http://attendispa.com/) to network and to interview for jobs.
5. Contact spas directly to inquire about job opportunities. The ISPA offers a member database at http://www.experienceispa.com/spa-goers/search.

■ FOR MORE INFORMATION

For information on ecofriendly spas, contact

Green Spa Network
PO Box 15428
Atlanta, GA 30333-0428
Tel: (800) 275-3045
E-mail: jessica@greenspanetwork.org
http://greenspanetwork.org

For more information on the spa industry, contact

International SPA Association

2365 Harrodsburg Road, Suite A325

Lexington, KY 40504-3366

Tel: (888) 651-4772; (859) 226-4326

Fax: (859) 226-4445

E-mail: ispa@ispastaff.com

http://www.experienceispa.com

For Information on membership, contact

Spa Industry Association (SIA)

Tel: (952) 283-1252

E-mail: info@dayspaassociation.com

http://www.dayspaassociation.com

Special and Visual Effects Technicians

◼ OVERVIEW

Special and visual effects technicians are crafts persons who use technical skills to create effects, illusions, and computer-generated images for the entertainment industry. They work with a variety of materials and digital techniques to produce the fantastic visions and seemingly real illusions that add dimension to motion picture, theater production, television broadcast, and video game.

◼ HISTORY

At the turn of the century a French magician-turned-filmmaker named Georges Melies invented motion picture special effects. To film futuristic space flight in *A Trip to the Moon*, he made a model of a rocket and fired it from a cannon in front of a painted backdrop. By the 1920s, special effects, or "tricks," had become a department of the major film studios, and technicians were steadily inventing new techniques and illusions. For a tornado scene in *The Wizard of Oz*, a miniature house was filmed falling from the studio ceiling, and when the film was reversed it became Dorothy's house flying into the air. Also in the *Wizard of Oz*, a 90-pound costume transformed actor Bert Lahr into the cowardly lion and extensive makeup and metalwork turned actor Jack Haley into the tin man. Effects departments still make extensive use of miniature models, which are easy to work with and save money.

In 1950, the Supreme Court broke up the movie studio monopolies. Independent, low-budget films began to proliferate and to affect audience tastes. They helped to make realistic, on-site shoots fashionable, and studio special effects departments became virtually extinct. It was not until the 1970s, when George Lucas brought his imagination to *Star Wars*, that special effects were revived in force. The crew that Lucas assembled for that project formed the company Industrial Light & Magic (ILM), which still remains a leader in a field that now includes hundreds of large and small visual and special effects companies. ILM has created visual effects for nearly 300 feature films, including 10 of the top 15 box office hits in movie history.

The industry experimented with computer-generated imagery (CGI) in the 1980s, with such films as *Tron* and *Star Trek II*. By the 1990s, the movie-going public was ready for an effects revolution, which began with James Cameron's *The Abyss* and *Terminator 2: Judgment Day*, and reached full-force with 1993's *Jurassic Park*. *Twister* in 1996, *Titanic* in 1997, and *The Matrix* in 1999 raised the stakes for movie effects, and *Star Wars: Episode I—The Phantom Menace* used 2,000 digital shots (compared to *Titanic*'s 500). Digital inking and painting, along with a software program called Deep Canvas, gave Disney's *Tarzan* its great depth and dimension and detail unlike any other film in the history of animation. *Sky Captain and the World of Tomorrow* (2004), *Sin City* (2005), and *Avatar* (2009) featured settings entirely generated by computers and blended with the performances of live actors. *Avatar* was unique in

QUICK FACTS

ALTERNATE TITLE(S)
Mechanical Effects Specialists, Pyrotechnic Effects Specialists, Special and Visual Effects Coordinators

DUTIES
Create effects, illusions, and computer-generated images for the entertainment industry

SALARY RANGE
$38,520 to $65,300 to $115,960+

WORK ENVIRONMENT
Indoors/Outdoors

BEST GEOGRAPHIC LOCATION(S)
Los Angeles, New York; opportunities throughout the country

MINIMUM EDUCATION LEVEL
Bachelor's Degree

SCHOOL SUBJECTS
Art, Computer Science, Technical/Shop

EXPERIENCE
Internship; volunteer, or part-time experience

PERSONALITY TRAITS
Creative, Hands On, Technical

SKILLS
Building/Trades, Digital Media, Drawing/Design

CERTIFICATION OR LICENSING
Required

SPECIAL REQUIREMENTS
None

EMPLOYMENT PROSPECTS
Fair

ADVANCEMENT PROSPECTS
Good

OUTLOOK
Much Faster than the Average

NOC
5226

O*NET-SOC
27-1014.00

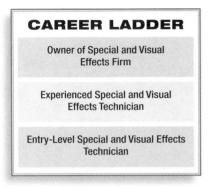

CAREER LADDER

Owner of Special and Visual
Effects Firm

Experienced Special and Visual
Effects Technician

Entry-Level Special and Visual Effects
Technician

its use of a virtual camera system during filming, which displays the CGI reality on a monitor and places the actor's visual counterparts into their digital surroundings in real time; this allows the director to adjust and direct scenes as if producing live action without the need for repeated lighting setups or costume or makeup changes. According to James Cameron, the film's director, the film is composed of 60 percent computer-generated elements and 40 percent live action. In fact, the quality of computer-generated characters and scenery is so good in some movies (such as *Avatar),* that audiences have not been able to tell the difference between live action and computer-generated elements. *Avatar* won the Academy Award for Visual Effects in 2009.

■ THE JOB

This article focuses on two types of effects technicians: special effects technicians and visual effects technicians. Both types create effects that amaze viewers as they watch movies, but they use different methods to go about creating movie magic. Special effects technicians deal with practical constructs and "in camera" effects—meaning those that are shot while the camera is rolling during a scene. Visual effects technicians use computer software programs to create scenes digitally or to add or improve effects after a film is made. The following paragraphs provide more information on these two effects sectors.

Special Effects

Special effects technicians are crafts persons who build, install, and operate equipment used to produce the effects called for in scripts for motion picture, television, and theatrical productions. They read the script before filming to determine the type and number of special effects required. Depending on the effects needed for a production, they will mix chemicals, build large and elaborate sets or models, and fabricate costumes and other required backdrops from materials such as wood, metal, plaster, and clay.

What's known generally as special effects is actually a number of specialized trades. There are companies—known in the industry as special effects shops or houses—that offer specialized services in such diverse areas as computer animation, makeup, and mechanical effects. A special effects shop might provide just one or a combination of these services, and the crafts persons who work at the shops are often skilled in more than one area.

Makeup effects specialists create elaborate masks for actors to wear in a film or theatrical production. They also build prosthetic devices to simulate human—or nonhuman—limbs, hands, and heads. They work with a variety of materials, from latex plastic to create a monster's mask, to human hair they weave into wigs, to plain cotton cloth for a costume. They are skilled at sewing, weaving, applying makeup, and mixing colored dyes.

Mechanical effects specialists create effects such as rain, snow, and wind during movie productions. They may also build small sections of sets and backdrops that have an effect in them. They might also create moving or mechanized props, such as a futuristic automobile for a science fiction film. Because of a production's budget constraints, they are often required to construct miniature working models of such things as airplanes or submarines that, on film, will appear to be life- or larger-than-life-sized. Mechanical effects specialists are usually skilled in a number of trades, including plumbing, welding, carpentry, electricity, and robotics. At some film studios, the construction department may be responsible for some of the more labor-intensive responsibilities of mechanical effects specialists.

Pyrotechnic effects specialists are experts with munitions and firearms. They create carefully planned explosions for dramatic scenes in motion pictures and television broadcasts. They build charges and mix chemicals used for explosions according to strict legal standards.

Most professionals working in the field of special effects offer their services as freelance technicians. Some also work for special effects shops. The shops are contracted by motion picture or television broadcast producers and theatrical productions to provide the effects for a specific production. After reviewing the script and the type and number of the special effects required, the shop will send a special effects team to work on the production, or hire freelance technicians to assist on the job. Depending upon their level of expertise, many freelance technicians work for several shops.

Often, nonunion team members are required to help out with tasks that fall outside an area of expertise during the production. This may involve setting up and tearing down sets, moving heavy equipment, or pitching in on last-minute design changes. Union technicians are contracted to provide a specific service and rarely perform work outside an area of expertise.

Visual Effects

Visual effects technicians, also known as *animators* and *multimedia artists,* use high-tech computer programs to create entire movies, scenes in movies, or effects that are otherwise impossible or too costly to build by traditional means. They typically work in an office, separate from the actual filming location. Because much of the technology they use is on the cutting edge of the industry, computer animation specialists are highly skilled in working with and developing unique computer applications and software programs.

Visual effects technicians often work as freelancers; some own their own businesses. Others may be employed as salaried workers by visual effects, animation, and film studios.

Special and visual effects coordinators lead teams of special effects or computer animation specialists to provide effects for motion pictures, television shows, and commercials.

Special effects team members set up pyrotechnics for a film shoot. (CREATISTA. Shutterstock.)

■ EARNINGS

Some technicians have steady, salaried employment, while others work freelance for an hourly rate and may have periods with no work. The average daily rate for beginning freelance technicians is $100 to $200 per day, while more experienced technicians may earn $300 per day or more. According to Indeed.com, in January 2017 special effects technicians had median average earnings of $16.14 per hour or about $33,000 to $35,000 annually for those employed full time. The U.S. Department of Labor reported salaries for multimedia artists and animators, the category that includes special effects technicians, as ranging from less than $38,520 to more than $115,960.

Those working freelance will not have the benefits of full-time work, having to provide their own health insurance. Those working for special and visual effects houses have the usual benefit packages including health insurance, bonuses, and retirement.

■ WORK ENVIRONMENT

Special and visual effects is an excellent field for someone who likes to dream up fantastic monsters and machines and has the patience to create them. Special and visual effects technicians must be willing to work long hours, and have the stamina to work under strenuous conditions. Twelve-hour days are not uncommon, and to meet a deadline technicians may work for 15 hours a day. Many special and visual effects technicians work freelance, so there can be long periods of no work (and no pay) between jobs.

Because motion picture scripts often call for filming at various locations, special effects technicians may travel a great deal. Work environments can vary considerably; a technician may remain in a shop or at a computer off set, or may go on location for a film or television shoot and work outdoors.

■ EXPLORING

Students who like to build things, who tend to be curious about how things work, or who enjoy working with computers, might be well suited to a career in special and visual effects. To learn more about the profession, visit your school or public library and bookstores to read more about the field. Read Hollywood trade magazines and other related material on your area of interest. *Animation Journal* (http://www.animationjournal.com), *ANIMATIONWorld* (http://www.awn.com/animationworld), *Cinefex* (http://www.cinefex.com), *Variety* (http://www.variety.com), and *The Hollywood Reporter* (http://www.hollywoodreporter.com) are all good places to start.

Since experience and jobs are difficult to get in the film and television industry, it is important to learn about the career to be sure it is right for you. Working on high school drama productions as a stagehand, "techie," or makeup artist can be helpful for learning set and prop design, methods of handling equipment, and artistry. Community theaters and independent filmmakers can provide volunteer work experience; they rely on volunteers because they have limited operating funds.

Alternatively, if you find you are adept in computer classes and curious about advances in computer animation, you may wish to pursue this field by continuing your learning and exploration of computer techniques.

■ EDUCATION AND TRAINING REQUIREMENTS
High School

Special effects technicians rely on a mix of science and art. To prepare for this career, take all the art courses you can, including art history; many filmmakers look to

AND THE OSCAR GOES TO...

Films that have been awarded Oscars in the category of Visual Effects include the following:

2016: *The Jungle Book*
2015: *Ex Machina*
2014: *Interstellar*
2013: *Gravity*
2012: *Life of Pi*
2011: *Hugo*
2010: *Inception*
2009: *Avatar*
2008: *The Curious Case of Benjamin Button*
2007: *The Golden Compass*
2006: *Pirates of the Caribbean: Dead Man's Chest*
2005: *King Kong*
2004: *Spider-Man 2*
2003: *The Lord of the Rings: The Return of the King*
2002: *The Lord of the Rings: The Two Towers*
2001: *The Lord of the Rings: The Fellowship of the Rings*
2000: *Gladiator*
1999: *The Matrix*
1998: *What Dreams May Come*
1997: *Titanic*
1996: *Independence Day*

historic art when composing shots and lighting effects. Photography courses will help you understand the use of light and shadow. Chemistry can give you some insight into the products you will be using. Working on high school drama productions can also be helpful for learning lighting, set, and prop design. Students who are interested in pursuing careers in visual effects should take computer science, animation, and other related classes.

Postsecondary Training

Because of the technical expertise required for multimedia artists and animators, including special and visual effects technicians, most positions now require a bachelor's degree. Some universities have film and television programs that include courses in special effects. Some special effects technicians major in theater, art history, photography, and related subjects. Many colleges and universities offer masters of fine arts degrees. These are studio programs in which you will be able to gain hands-on experience in theater production and filmmaking with a faculty composed of practicing artists.

Many of the skills required to work in mechanical effects can be gained by learning a trade such as carpentry, welding, plumbing, or hydraulics and applying those skills by building sets or props for community theater productions.

■ CERTIFICATION, LICENSING, AND SPECIAL REQUIREMENTS
Certification or Licensing

A mechanical special effects technician who works with fire and explosives generally needs a pyrotechnics operator's license issued by the state. A federal pyrotechnics license is also available.

■ EXPERIENCE, SKILLS, AND PERSONALITY TRAITS

Experience as a special or visual effects intern, volunteer, or part-time employee at an effects firm is recommended.

Special effects work is physically and mentally demanding. Technicians must be able to work as members of a team, following instructions carefully in order to avoid dangerous situations. They often work long days, so they must have high stamina. In addition, the work on a set can be uncomfortable. For example, a mechanical effects specialist may have to work under adverse weather conditions or wait patiently in a small space for the cue to operate an effect. Makeup effects specialists spend most of their time working in a trailer on the set or in a shop where they construct and adjust the items required by the actors. Freelance technicians will often have to provide their own tools and equipment, which they either own or rent, when hired for a job.

Visual effects specialists should have patient personalities since they often sit for long hours in front of a computer, performing meticulous and sometimes repetitive work. Other important skills include the ability to work under deadline pressure, strong communication skills, and the ability to accept constructive criticism of their work.

Special and visual effects technicians must work both carefully and quickly; a mistake or a delay can become very expensive for the production company.

■ EMPLOYMENT PROSPECTS
Employers

The top special effects technicians work for special effects houses. These companies contract with individual film productions; one film may have the effects created by more than one special effects company. Industrial Light and Magic is the top company, having done the effects for such films as *Star Wars: Episodes I & II*, *Harry Potter & the Prisoner of Azkaban*, *Pearl Harbor*, and *Avatar*. Other major companies include Digital Domain (*Lord of the Rings: The Fellowship of the Ring, The Day After Tomorrow, Charlie and the Chocolate Factory, Iron Man 3*), and Rhythm & Hues Studios (*Aliens in the Attic, Night at the Museum, Life of Pi,* and *The Hunger Games).* Some special and visual effects technicians own their own effects company or work on a freelance basis. Freelance technicians may work in several areas, doing theater work, film and television productions, and commercials.

Starting Out

Networking is an important aspect of finding work in the entertainment industry. The Internet Movie Database (http://www.imdb.com) is an extensive listing of professionals in many aspects of the industry. Another good resource is Variety411 (http://variety411.com), an online directory of film industry professionals. Aspiring visual effects technicians can visit http://jobs.awn.com to obtain a list of potential employers.

Internships are another very good way to gain experience and make yourself a marketable job candidate. Film, television, and theater companies are predominantly located in Los Angeles or New York City, but there are opportunities elsewhere. Again, since theater and lower budget film and television productions operate with limited funds, you could find places to work for course credit or experience instead of a salary.

Special effects shops are excellent places to try for an internship. You may find them in books and trade magazines, or try searching online for theatrical equipment, theatrical makeup, theatrical and stage lighting equipment, or animation services. Even if one shop has no opportunities, it may be able to provide the name of another that takes interns.

You should keep a photographic record of all the work you do for theater and film productions, including photos of any drawings or sculptures you have done for art classes. It is important to have a portfolio or demo reel (a reel of film demonstrating your work) to send along with your resume to effects shops, makeup departments, and producers. If you want to work as a visual effects technician, you should create a demo CD or a Web site that features your work.

■ ADVANCEMENT PROSPECTS

Good special and visual effects technicians will acquire skills in several areas, becoming versatile and therefore desirable employees. Since many work on a freelance basis, it is useful to develop a good reputation and maintain contacts from past jobs. Successful technicians may be chosen to work on increasingly prestigious and challenging productions. Once they have a strong background and diverse experience, technicians may start their own shops.

■ OUTLOOK

The U.S. Department of Labor reports that employment of multimedia artists and animators (which includes visual effects technicians) varies by industry. Employment in the motion and picture industries is expected to grow by about 16 percent through 2024 (much faster than the average for all careers). Job opportunities for multimedia artists and animators who work in the television industry will grow by 8 percent (or about as fast as the average), and employment for those who work in the software industry will increase by 27 percent (or much faster than the average). Overall, competition for jobs is very strong since many people view this field as an exciting potential career path.

For over 20 years now, films of all genres have incorporated computer graphics and high-tech effects, inspiring a whole generation of young people with computers and imaginations. Many of today's top effects professionals credit their love of *Star Wars* with directing them toward careers in the industry. As the cost of powerful computers continues to decrease, even more people will be able to experiment with computer graphics and develop their skills and talents.

Though some special and visual effects companies are very profitable, others are struggling to make enough money to meet their expenses. Production companies are attempting to tighten their budgets and to turn out movies and television shows quickly. Therefore, a contract for special effects goes to the lowest bidding effects company. The costs of the effects, including salaries for top technicians, are increasing, while producers decrease their special effects budgets. This situation will either be corrected by effects companies demanding more money, or only a few of the very top companies will be able to thrive.

Digital technology will continue to change the industry rapidly. Experts predict that within 10 years, film will be eliminated and movies will be shot and projected digitally, enhancing computer effects. Filmmakers will edit their movies over the Internet. And it may not be long before filmmakers are able to make entire movies with CGI, employing only digital actors. Some companies are experimenting with taking screen images of past and present film stars and digitally creating new films and performances.

■ UNIONS AND ASSOCIATIONS

Special and visual effects technicians may choose to join a union; some film and television studios will only hire union members. Two of the major unions for special and visual effects technicians are the International Alliance of Theatrical Stage Employees, Moving Picture Technicians, Artists of the Allied Trades of the United States, Its Territories and Canada and Animators Guild Local 839. To get into the union, a technician must complete a training program, which includes apprenticing in a prop-making shop and passing an examination. Union members work under a union contract that determines their work rules, pay, and benefits.

Some special and visual effects technicians join the American Film Institute, Visual Effects Society, and Women in Animation.

■ TIPS FOR ENTRY

1. Visit the following Web sites for job listings:
   - http://jobs.awn.com
   - http://mandy.com
   - https://www.creativeheads.net
   - http://www.visualeffectssociety.com/job-board
2. Read the *Bring It On* career blog at http://www.awn.com/tag/careers to get tips on how to break into the field.
3. Start developing a digital portfolio of your work, or create your own Web site, so that you are ready to begin looking for jobs once you graduate. Include only your best work.
4. Visit http://aidb.com for a database of thousands of animation-related companies.
5. Learn about job opportunities in your state by visiting the Association of Film Commissioners International's Web site, http://www.afci.org.

■ FOR MORE INFORMATION

For information about colleges with film and television programs of study, and to read interviews with filmmakers, visit the AFI Web site.

American Film Institute (AFI)
2021 North Western Avenue
Los Angeles, CA 90027-1657
Tel: (323) 856-7600
Fax: (323) 467-4578
E-mail: information@AFI.com
http://www.afi.com

For extensive information about the digital effects industry, visit the AWN Web site. The site includes feature articles, a guide to education-related resources, and a career section.

Animation World Network (AWN)
13300 Victory Blvd. Suite 365
Van Nuys, CA 91401

Tel: (818) 786-5402
Fax: (818) 786-5417
E-mail: info@awn.com
http://www.awn.com

The guild represents the interests of animation professionals in California. Visit its Web site for information on training, earnings, and the animation industry.

Animators Guild Local 839
1105 North Hollywood Way
Burbank, CA 91505-2528
Tel: (818) 845-7500
Fax: (818) 843-0300
http://www.animationguild.org

For information on union membership, contact

International Alliance of Theatrical Stage Employees, Moving Picture Technicians, Artists of the Allied Trades of the United States, Its Territories and Canada
207 West 25th Street, 4th Floor
New York, NY 10001-7119
Tel: (212) 730-1770
Fax: (212) 730-7809
http://www.iatse-intl.org

For information about festivals and presentations, and news about the industry, contact

Visual Effects Society
5805 Sepulveda Boulevard, Suite 620
Sherman Oaks, CA 91411-2543
Tel: (818) 981-7861
Fax: (818) 981-0179
E-mail: info@visualeffectssociety.com
http://www.visualeffectssociety.com

This nonprofit organization represents the professional interests of women (and men) in animation. Visit its Web site for industry information, links to animation blogs, details on membership for high school students, and its quarterly newsletter.

Women in Animation
c/o Perry, Neidorf & Grassl, LLP, Attn: Marine Hekimian
11400 W. Olympic Blvd., #590
Los Angeles, CA 90064
E-mail: wia@womeninanimation.org
http://www.womeninanimation.org

Special Education Teachers

■ OVERVIEW

Special education teachers teach students ages three to 21 who have a variety of disabilities. They design individualized education plans and work with students one-on-one to help them learn academic subjects and life skills. Approximately 450,700 special education teachers are employed in the United States, mostly in public schools.

■ HISTORY

Modern special education traces its origins to 16th century Spain, where Pedro Ponce de Leon and Juan Pablo Bonet taught deaf students to read and write. It was not until the late 18th century that education for the blind was initiated. An early example was an institute for blind children in Paris that was founded by Valentin Huay. The first U.S. schools for the blind were founded in 1832 in Boston and New York.

By the early 19th century, attempts were made to educate the mentally handicapped. Edouard Sequin, a French psychiatrist, established the first school for the mentally handicapped in 1939 in Orange, New Jersey.

In the first half of the 20th century, special education became increasingly popular in the United States. By the 1960s and early 1970s, parents began to lobby state and local officials for improved special education programs for their children with disabilities. To address continuing inequities in the public education of special needs students, Congress passed the Education for All Handicapped Children Act (Public Law 94-142) in 1975. The act required public schools to provide disabled students with a "free appropriate education" in the "least restrictive environment" possible. The act was reauthorized in 1990 and 1997, and renamed the Individuals with Disabilities Education Act. This act allows approximately six million children (roughly 10 percent of all school-aged children) to receive special education services from highly trained special education teachers.

■ THE JOB

Special education teachers instruct students who have a variety of disabilities. Their students may have physical disabilities, such as vision, hearing, or orthopedic impairment. They may also have learning disabilities or serious emotional disturbances. Although less common, special education teachers sometimes work with students who are gifted and talented, children who have limited proficiency in English, children who have communicable diseases, or children who are neglected and abused.

In order to teach special education students, these teachers design and modify instruction so that it is tailored to individual student needs. Teachers collaborate with school psychologists, social workers, parents, and occupational, physical, and speech-language therapists to develop a specially designed Individualized Education Program (IEP) for each of their students. The IEP sets personalized goals for a student based on his or her learning style and ability, and it outlines specific steps to prepare him or her for employment or postsecondary schooling.

Special education teachers teach at a pace that is dictated by the individual needs and abilities of their students. Unlike most regular classes, special education classes do not have an established curriculum that is taught to all students at the same time. Because student abilities vary widely, instruction is individualized; it is part of the teacher's responsibility to match specific techniques with a student's learning style and abilities. They may spend much time working with students one-on-one or in small groups.

Working with different types of students requires a variety of teaching methods. Some students may need to use special equipment or skills in the classroom in order to overcome their disabilities. For example, a teacher working with a student with a physical disability might use a computer that is operated by touching a screen or by voice

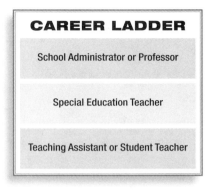

CAREER LADDER

School Administrator or Professor

Special Education Teacher

Teaching Assistant or Student Teacher

commands. To work with hearing-impaired students, the teacher may need to use sign language. With visually impaired students, he or she may use teaching materials that have Braille characters or large, easy-to-see type. Gifted and talented students may need extra challenging assignments, a faster learning pace, or special attention in one curriculum area, such as art or music.

In addition to teaching academic subjects, special education teachers help students develop both emotionally and socially. They work to make students as independent as possible by teaching them functional skills for daily living. They may help young children learn basic grooming, hygiene, and table manners. Older students might be taught how to balance a checkbook, follow a recipe, or use the public transportation system.

Special education teachers meet regularly with their students' parents to inform them of their child's progress and offer suggestions of how to promote learning at home. They may also meet with school administrators, social workers, psychologists, various types of therapists, and students' general education teachers.

The current trend in education is to integrate students with disabilities into regular classrooms to the extent that it is possible and beneficial to them. This is often called "mainstreaming." As mainstreaming becomes increasingly common, special education teachers frequently work with general education teachers in general education classrooms. They may help adapt curriculum materials and teaching techniques to meet the needs of students with disabilities and offer guidance on dealing with students' emotional and behavioral problems.

In addition to working with students, special education teachers are responsible for a certain amount of paperwork. They document each student's progress and may fill out any forms that are required by the school system or the government.

■ EARNINGS

In May 2015, the median annual salary for special education teachers working in kindergartens and elementary schools was $55,810, according to the U.S. Department of Labor. Special education teachers working in middle schools had median annual earnings of $57,280, and those in secondary schools earned $58,500. The lowest paid 10 percent of all special education teachers made less than $37,410 a year, and the highest paid 10 percent made more

than $90,260. In some school districts, salaries for special education teachers follow the same scale as general education teachers. Private school teachers usually earn less than their public school counterparts. Teachers can supplement their annual salaries by becoming an activity sponsor, or by summer work. Some school districts pay their special education teachers on a separate scale, which is usually higher than that of general education teachers.

Regardless of the salary scale, special education teachers usually receive a complete benefits package, which includes health and life insurance, paid holidays and vacations, and a pension plan.

■ WORK ENVIRONMENT

Special education teachers usually work from 7:30 or 8:00 A.M. to 3:00 or 3:30 P.M. Like most teachers, however, they typically spend several hours in the evening grading papers, completing paperwork, or preparing lessons for the next day. Altogether, most special education teachers work more than the standard 40 hours per week.

Although some schools offer year-round classes for students, the majority of special education teachers work the traditional 10-month school year, with a two-month vacation in the summer. Many teachers find this work schedule very appealing, as it gives them the opportunity to pursue personal interests or additional education during the summer break. Teachers typically also get a week off at Christmas and for spring break.

Special education teachers work in a variety of settings in schools, including both ordinary and specially equipped classrooms, resource rooms, and therapy rooms. Some schools have newer and better facilities for special education than others. Although it is less common, some teachers work in residential facilities or tutor students who are homebound or hospitalized.

Working with special education students can be very demanding, due to their physical and emotional needs. Teachers may fight a constant battle to keep certain students, particularly those with behavior disorders, under control. Other students, such as those with mental impairments or learning disabilities, learn so slowly that it may seem as if they are making no progress. The special education teacher must deal daily with frustration, setbacks, and classroom disturbances.

These teachers must also contend with heavy workloads, including a great deal of paperwork to document each student's progress. In addition, they may sometimes be faced with irate parents who feel that their child is not receiving proper treatment or an adequate education.

The positive side of this job is that special education teachers help students overcome their disabilities and learn to be as functional as possible. For a special education teacher, knowing that he or she is making a difference in a child's life can be very rewarding and emotionally fulfilling.

■ EXPLORING

There are a number of ways to explore the field of special education. One of the first and easiest is to approach a special education teacher at his or her school and ask to talk about the job. Perhaps the teacher could provide a tour of the special education classroom or allow you to visit while a class is in session.

You might also want to become acquainted with special-needs students at your own school or become involved in a school or community mentoring program for these students. There may also be other opportunities for volunteer work or part-time jobs in schools, community agencies, camps, or residential facilities that will allow you to work with persons with disabilities.

■ EDUCATION AND TRAINING REQUIREMENTS
High School

If you are considering a career as a special education teacher, you should focus on courses that will prepare you for college. These classes include natural and social sciences, mathematics, and English. Speech classes would also be a good choice for improving your communication skills. Finally, classes in psychology might help you understand the students you will eventually teach and prepare you for college-level psychology course work.

Postsecondary Training

All states require that teachers have at least a bachelor's degree and that they complete a prescribed number of subject and education credits. It is increasingly common for special education teachers to complete an additional fifth year of training after they receive their bachelor's degree. Many states require special education teachers to get a master's degree in special education.

Hundreds of colleges and universities in the United States offer programs in special education, including undergraduate, master's, and doctoral programs. These programs include general and specialized courses in special education, including educational psychology, legal issues of special education, child growth and development, and knowledge and skills needed for teaching students with disabilities. The student typically spends the last year of the program student teaching in an actual classroom, under the supervision of a licensed teacher.

Certification

The American Academy of Special Education Professionals offers a certificate of advanced professional development

---

SUCCEEDING IN SPECIAL EDUCATION
LEARN MORE ABOUT IT

Billingsley, Bonnie S., et al. *A Survival Guide for New Special Educators.* Hoboken, N.J.: Jossey-Bass, 2013.

Golden, Cindy, and Juane Heflin. *The Special Educator's Toolkit: Everything You Need to Organize, Manage, and Monitor Your Classroom.* Baltimore, Md.: Brookes Publishing Co., 2012.

Rohrer, Marcia W., and Nannette M. Samson. *10 Critical Components for Success in the Special Education Classroom.* Thousand Oaks, Calif.: Corwin Press, 2014.

Shelton, Carla F., and Alice B. Pollingue. *The Exceptional Teacher's Handbook: The First-Year Special Education Teacher's Guide to Success.* New York: Skyhorse Publishing, 2014.

---

to teachers who "wish to demonstrate a commitment to excellence to employers, peers, administrators, other professionals, and parents." Applicants must complete the following courses to receive the certificate: Review of the Major Principles of Special Education; Principles of IEP Development; Understanding Assessment in Special Education; Understanding Response to Intervention; and Special Education Eligibility. Contact the academy for more information.

Other Education or Training

Workshops, webinars, classes, conferences, and other continuing education options are available from the American Academy of Special Education Professionals, Association for Childhood Education International, Council for Exceptional Children, and the National Association of Special Education Teachers. Contact these organizations for more information. Special education teachers can also seek out continuing education opportunities via professional associations at the state and local levels.

■ CERTIFICATION, LICENSING, AND SPECIAL REQUIREMENTS
Certification or Licensing

The American Academy of Special Education Professionals and the National Board for Professional Teaching Standards offer certification to special education teachers. Contact these organizations for more information on certification requirements.

All states require that special education teachers be licensed, although the particulars of licensing vary by state. In some states, these teachers must first be certified as elementary or secondary school teachers and then meet specific requirements to teach special education. Some states offer general special education licensure; others license several different subspecialties within special education. Some states allow special education teachers to transfer their license from one state to another, but many still require these teachers to pass licensing requirements for that state.

■ EXPERIENCE, SKILLS, AND PERSONALITY TRAITS

One of the best ways to gain experience in the field is to work as a student teacher; this is a requirement of most teacher-education programs.

To be successful in this field, you need to have many of the same personal characteristics as regular classroom teachers: the ability to communicate, a broad knowledge of the arts, sciences, and history, and a love of children. In addition, you will need a great deal of patience and persistence. You need to be creative, flexible, cooperative, and accepting of differences in others. Finally, you need to be emotionally stable and consistent in your dealings with students.

■ EMPLOYMENT PROSPECTS
Employers

Approximately 450,700 special education teachers are employed in the United States. The majority of special education teachers teach in public and private schools. Others work in state education agencies, homebound or hospital environments, or residential facilities.

Starting Out

Because public school systems are by far the largest employers of special education teachers, this is where you should begin your job search.

You can also use your college's career services office to locate job leads. This may prove a very effective place to begin. You may also write to your state's department of education for information on placement and regulations, or contact state employment offices to inquire about job openings. Applying directly to local school systems can sometimes be effective. Even if a school system does not have an immediate opening, it will usually keep your resume on file should a vacancy occur.

■ ADVANCEMENT PROSPECTS

Advancement opportunities for special education teachers, as for regular classroom teachers, are fairly limited. They may take the form of higher wages, better facilities, or more prestige. In some cases, these teachers advance to become supervisors or administrators, although this

may require continued education on the teacher's part. Another option is for special education teachers to earn advanced degrees and become instructors at the college level.

■ OUTLOOK

The field of special education is expected to grow by 6 percent through 2024, according to the U.S. Department of Labor (DOL), or more slowly than the average for all careers. The DOL reports that job opportunities may be better for those with "experience with early childhood intervention and skills in working with students who have multiple disabilities, severe disabilities, or autism spectrum disorders."

Demand will grow for special education teachers because of the increase in the number of special education students needing services. Medical advances resulting in more survivors of illness and accidents, a rise in birth defects, increased awareness and understanding of learning disabilities, and general population growth are also significant factors for strong demand. Because of the rise in the number of youths with disabilities under the age of 21, the government has given approval for more federally funded programs. Growth of jobs in this field has also been influenced positively by legislation emphasizing training and employment for individuals with disabilities and a growing public awareness and interest in those with disabilities.

Employment for special education teachers at the preschool level will grow faster than the average through 2024, about 9 percent, because children with disabilities are being identified earlier and placed into special education programs.

Finally, there is a fairly high turnover rate in this field, as some special education teachers find the work too stressful and switch to mainstream teaching or change jobs altogether. Many job openings will arise out of a need to replace teachers who leave their positions. There is a shortage of qualified teachers in rural areas and in the inner city. Jobs will also be plentiful for teachers who specialize in speech and language impairments, learning disabilities, and early childhood intervention. Bilingual teachers with multicultural experience will be in high demand.

■ UNIONS AND ASSOCIATIONS

Most special education teachers belong to unions, which help them secure fair working hours, salaries, and working conditions. Teachers may join unions such as the American Federation of Teachers and the National Education Association. Many special education teachers are members of the National Association of Special Education Teachers and the American Academy of Special Education Professionals (AASEP). The National

Board for Professional Teaching Standards and the AASEP offer certification to special education teachers. The Association for Childhood Education International provides research about the field. Other useful organizations include the Council for Exceptional Children and the Council of Administrators of Special Education.

◼ TIPS FOR ENTRY

1. Visit the following Web sites for job listings and career information: http://jobboard.specialedcareers.org and http://aasep.org/career-center/special-education-positions-available-through-aasep.
2. Read industry publications, such as *Teaching Exceptional Children* and *Exceptional Children* (both are available at http://www.cec.sped.org/Publications/CEC-Journals), to learn more about trends in the profession.
3. Become certified by the American Academy of Special Education Professionals and/or the National Board for Professional Teaching Standards in order to show employers that you have met the highest standards set by your profession.
4. Participate in student-teaching opportunities or volunteer as a tutor.

◼ FOR MORE INFORMATION

For information on certification, contact
American Academy of Special Education
  Professionals
3642 E. Sunnydale Drive
Chandler Heights, AZ 85142 85142
Tel: (800) 754-4421, ext 106
Fax: (800) 424-0371
E-mail: info@aasep.org
http://aasep.org

For information about careers, education, and union membership, contact
American Federation of Teachers (AFT)
555 New Jersey Avenue, NW
Washington, D.C. 20001-2029
Tel: (202) 879-4400
http://www.aft.org

To order publications or read current research and other information, contact
Association for Childhood Education
  International
1200 18th Street, NW, Suite 700
Washington, D.C. 20036

Tel: (800) 423-3563; (202) 372-9986
http://www.acei.org

For general information about special education, contact
Council for Exceptional Children
2900 Crystal Drive, Suite 1000
Arlington, VA 22202-3557
Tel: (888) 232-7733
http://www.cec.sped.org

For information on current issues, legal cases, and conferences, contact
Council of Administrators of Special Education
Osigian Office Centre, 101 Katelyn Circle, Suite E
Warner Robins, GA 31088-6484
Tel: (478) 333-6892
Fax: (478) 333-2453
E-mail: lpurcell@casecec.org
http://www.casecec.org

For information on special education online degree programs, visit
eLearners.com
http://www.elearners.com/online-degrees/special-education.htm

For information on careers, contact
National Association of Special Education
  Teachers
1250 Connecticut Avenue, NW, Suite 200
Washington, D.C. 20036-2643
Tel: (800) 754-4421
E-mail: contactus@naset.org
http://www.naset.org

For information on certification, contact
National Board for Professional Teaching
  Standards
1525 Wilson Boulevard, Suite 500
Arlington, VA 22209-2451
Tel: (800) 22TEACH
E-mail: NBPTSCandidateSupport@Pearson.com
http://www.nbpts.org

For information on union membership, contact
National Education Association (NEA)
1201 16th Street, NW
Washington, D.C. 20036-3290
Tel: (202) 833-4000
Fax: (202) 822-7974
http://www.nea.org

Special Procedures Technologists

■ OVERVIEW

Special procedures technologists operate medical diagnostic imaging equipment such as computer tomography (CT) and magnetic resonance imaging (MRI) scanners and assist in imaging procedures such as angiography and cardiac catheterization (CC). They are employed in various health care settings such as hospitals, clinics, and imaging centers. Their skills are in high demand as the population ages and cancer and heart disease continue to be major health concerns.

■ HISTORY

Advances in medical technology have resulted in more sophisticated patient testing using more complex equipment. As this technology has become more complex, the need for trained personnel to assist physicians and specially trained technologists to operate this equipment became apparent. In addition, trained personnel became essential to perform and document the testing procedures, as well as to assist with the patients. The career of special procedures technologist evolved from this need. Technologists are trained to understand the operation of some of the testing equipment and to assist medical personnel as they perform these tests. They are also taught how to position patients during the testing and how to deal with any fears and anxieties patients might have during the procedures.

■ THE JOB

Special procedures technologists' duties vary depending on the training they have with specific diagnostic equipment and testing procedures. Job requirements also vary with the degree of assistance required for certain testing and diagnostic procedures.

Radiologic technologists operate equipment that creates images of a patient's body tissues, organs, and bones for the purpose of medical diagnoses and therapies. These images allow physicians to know the exact nature of a patient's injury or disease, such as the location of a broken bone or the confirmation of an ulcer. Technologists position a patient for examination, immobilize them, prepare the equipment, and monitor the equipment and the patient's progress during the procedure.

Diagnostic medical sonographers, or *sonographers,* use advanced technology in the form of high-frequency sound waves similar to sonar to produce images of the internal body for analysis by radiologists and other physicians.

Nuclear medicine technologists prepare and administer chemicals known as radiopharmaceuticals (radioactive drugs) used in the diagnosis and treatment of certain diseases. These drugs are administered to a patient and absorbed by specific locations in the patient's body, thus allowing technologists to use diagnostic equipment to image and analyze their concentration in certain tissues or organs. Technicians also perform laboratory tests on patients' blood and urine to determine certain body chemical levels.

An *angiographer* is a special procedures technologist who assists with a procedure called an angiogram, which shows any changes that may have occurred to the blood vessels of the patient's circulatory system. The special procedures technologist may assist with many aspects of this test. Similarly, some special procedures technologists may assist cardiologists with the invasive procedure called cardiac catheterization by correctly positioning the patients and explaining to them the procedures performed. They may also monitor and document the patients' vital signs such as blood pressure and respiration and enter that information directly into a computer that controls testing procedures.

Some special procedures technologists assist with CT scanning (also known as CAT scanning), which combines X-rays with computer technology to create clear, cross-section images that provide more details than standard X-rays with minimal radiation exposure. The *CT technologist* might enter data into the scanner's computer control, which includes the type of scan to be performed, the time required, and the thickness of the cross section. The technologist might also observe and reassure the patient while the testing procedure is performed.

Another imaging procedure called MRI produces the most detailed and flexible images among the various imaging techniques. A special procedures technologist often assists with this procedure by explaining the test to the patient and making certain that the patient is not carrying any metal objects that could be hazardous to the patient during the test and could also damage the equipment. The *MRI technologist* might enter the necessary data, such as patient information, the orientation of the scan, and the part of the body to be scanned into the computer. The technologist might initiate the scan and observe the patient through a window in the control room and on a closed-circuit video display, while maintaining voice contact and reassuring the patient.

Other special procedures technologists include *bone densitometry technologists, cardiovascular-interventional technologists, mammographers, quality management technologists, medical dosimetrists,* and *radiation therapists.*

EARNINGS

Salaries for special procedures technologists vary by type of procedure, geographic location, type of employer, and experience level.

The U.S. Department of Labor reports that radiologic technologists, a specialized type of special procedures technologist, made a median annual salary of $56,670 in May 2015. The lowest paid 10 percent earned less than $38,110, and the highest paid 10 percent made more than $81,660 a year. Magnetic resonance imaging technologists earned median annual salaries of $67,720. Salaries ranged from less than $46,690 to $94,450 or more. Cardiovascular technologists and technicians earned median annual salaries of $54,880. Ten percent earned less than $28,420, while the most experienced workers earned $87,170 or more. Salaries for sonographers ranged from less than $48,720 to $97,390, while earnings for nuclear medicine technologists ranged from $52,950 to $100,080.

Benefits vary widely. Most benefit packages, however, include paid vacation and holidays, as well as sick leave, and medical and dental insurance. Some employers may offer additional benefits such as on-site day care and tuition reimbursement.

WORK ENVIRONMENT

Special procedures technologists usually work in one of several departments within a hospital or medical testing facility or clinic. These departments have rooms set up to perform specific tests, such as cardiac catheterization, MRIs, or CAT scans. The testing is usually done as part of a medical team; however, some of the setup may have to be done independently, so technologists may be required to make critical decisions.

Daily schedules and shifts may vary according to the size of the hospital, the number of patients requiring testing, and the type of imaging techniques performed. Although a technologist may be scheduled to work an eight-hour shift, the health care environment is often unpredictable and longer hours may be required. Because technologists deal with sick and dying people, and medical personnel are often required to make life and death decisions, the job can be quite stressful.

EXPLORING

If you are interested in entering the health care field, you can begin your involvement while still in high school. Most hospitals, nursing homes, mental health centers, and other treatment facilities have volunteer programs

QUICK FACTS

ALTERNATE TITLE(S)
Angiographers, Bone Densitometry Technologists, Cardiovascular-Interventional Technologists, CT Technologists, Diagnostic Medical Sonographers, MRI Technologists, Mammographers, Medical Dosimetrists, Nuclear Medicine Technologists, Quality Management Technologists, Radiation Therapists, Radiologic Technologists

DUTIES
Operate medical diagnostic imaging equipment such as computer tomography scanners and assist in imaging procedures such as cardiac catheterization

SALARY RANGE
$38,110 to $67,720 to $100,080+

WORK ENVIRONMENT
Primarily Indoors

BEST GEOGRAPHIC LOCATION(S)
Opportunities are available throughout the country

MINIMUM EDUCATION LEVEL
Associate's Degree

SCHOOL SUBJECTS
Biology, Health, Mathematics

EXPERIENCE
Internship

PERSONALITY TRAITS
Hands On, Helpful, Technical

SKILLS
Interpersonal, Math, Scientific

CERTIFICATION OR LICENSING
Required

SPECIAL REQUIREMENTS
None

EMPLOYMENT PROSPECTS
Excellent

ADVANCEMENT PROSPECTS
Fair

OUTLOOK
Much Faster than the Average

NOC
3215, 3217

O*NET-SOC
29-2034.00, 29-2035.00, 29-2099.06

that allow you to explore the health care environment and gain insight into medicine and patient care. You may be able to get a paid part-time or summer position working as a nurse's aide or home health care helper. In addition to these possibilities, ask your school counselor or

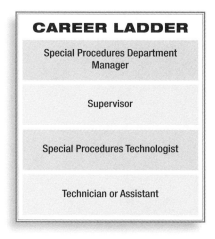

CAREER LADDER

Special Procedures Department Manager

Supervisor

Special Procedures Technologist

Technician or Assistant

a science teacher to help you arrange for a special procedures technologist to give a career talk to interested students. You may also be able to meet a special procedures technologist by contacting a local hospital or imaging center and asking for an information interview with this person. Another possibility is to ask if you can spend part of a day "shadowing" the individual in the workplace.

■ EDUCATION AND TRAINING REQUIREMENTS
High School

High school classes that will help you prepare for further education as a special procedures technologist include advanced courses in anatomy, physiology, and math. Science courses, including biology, chemistry, and physics, are also helpful. Classes in communication such as speech and English, and classes that reinforce written and verbal skills are also helpful. Because most imaging specialties depend heavily on computer technology, you should gain a good understanding of the use of computers. Studies regarding various cultures will also help you deal with patients from various backgrounds. In addition, you might consider studying a foreign language, so as to be able to communicate with patients whose understanding of English is not strong.

Postsecondary Training

The most common way to enter this field is to get an associate's degree in radiology. Some people choose to get a bachelor's degree, but this route is mainly for those interested in going into administrative or teaching positions. Associate degree programs can be found at community colleges, vocational and technical training schools, or in the military. When deciding on which program to attend, look for those accredited by the Joint Review Committee on Education in Radiologic Technology or the Commission on Accreditation of Allied Health Education Programs; a degree from an accredited school will aid you in your job search. Your course of study will include both classroom instruction and clinical experience. Courses will cover topics such as medical terminology, medical ethics, radiation physics, and positioning of patients. In all cases, special procedures technologists must complete additional training, usually offered

through a hospital, medical center, college, or vocational or technical training school, in their specialty area.

Other Education or Training

The American Society of Radiologic Technologists offers continuing education (CE) courses on patient care, leadership, and practice areas such as magnetic resonance, mammography, and computed tomography. The Society of Diagnostic Medical Sonography and the Society of Nuclear Medicine and Molecular Imaging also provide CE classes and webinars. Contact these organizations for more information.

■ CERTIFICATION, LICENSING, AND SPECIAL REQUIREMENTS
Certification or Licensing

Special procedures technologists can become certified through the American Registry of Radiologic Technologists (ARRT) after graduating from an accredited program. After becoming certified, many technologists choose to register with the ARRT. Registration is an annual procedure required to maintain the certification. Registered technologists meet the following three criteria: They agree to comply with the ARRT rules and regulations, comply with the ARRT standards of ethics, and meet continuing education requirements every two years. Although registration and certification are voluntary, many jobs are open only to technologists who have acquired these credentials. In addition to receiving primary certification in various imaging disciplines, special procedures technologists can receive advanced qualifications in mammography, computed tomography, magnetic resonance imaging, quality management, bone densitometry, cardiac-interventional radiography, vascular-interventional radiography, sonography, vascular sonography, or breast sonography.

Certification or registration is also available through the Nuclear Medicine Technology Certification Board, American Registry of Magnetic Resonance Imaging Technologists, and the American Registry of Diagnostic Medical Sonography.

Licensing requirements for special procedures technologists vary by state, although most states and Puerto Rico do require some form of licensing. The ARRT provides general information on state requirements and also notes that licensure legislation is under consideration in several states. Contact your state's licensing board for specific information about requirements in your area.

■ EXPERIENCE, SKILLS, AND PERSONALITY TRAITS

Participation in radiologic technology, computed tomography, magnetic resonance imaging, or other imaging/

therapy-related internships while in college will provide useful experience for aspiring special procedures technologists.

You should have an interest in medicine and compassion for patients to be a successful special procedures technologist. You should have an aptitude for science and math and have strong communication skills. In addition, you should be conscientious, responsible, efficient, and have the ability to work under stress and in emergency situations. You should also work well with people, both independently and as a part of a team. Manual dexterity and stamina are also required. Many employers also require technicians to have up-to-date cardiopulmonary resuscitation (CPR) training.

■ EMPLOYMENT PROSPECTS
Employers
Special procedures technologists are employed in a variety of health care settings. Hospitals are the most likely source for employment, especially for technologists who perform CT and MRI scanning, which require costly equipment. Health maintenance organizations and other health care clinics and centers also hire personnel trained to carry out the variety of testing procedures needed for medical care. Diagnostic imaging centers that are specifically dedicated to performing special imaging procedures are also likely employers. Also, the U.S. government employs radiologic and other imaging personnel, usually through the Department of Veterans Affairs or as members of the armed forces.

Starting Out
Most special procedures technologists begin their careers as radiology technicians or assistants and then receive additional training in their special procedure. Many new graduates find employment through their school's career services office. Some trade journals and area newspapers also list job opportunities. Applying directly to health care and imaging facilities may also produce results.

■ ADVANCEMENT PROSPECTS
Advancement in special procedures fields is generally limited as these specialties already represent advanced areas of radiology. With experience, however, a special procedures technologist may advance to greater responsibilities and to supervisory positions. Some people advance in this field by completing a bachelor's degree in radiology and moving into administrative or teaching positions. In addition, special procedures work may be a valuable bridge to a more advanced medical career, such as a doctor. Skills of a special procedures technologist are in demand in the United States and other countries

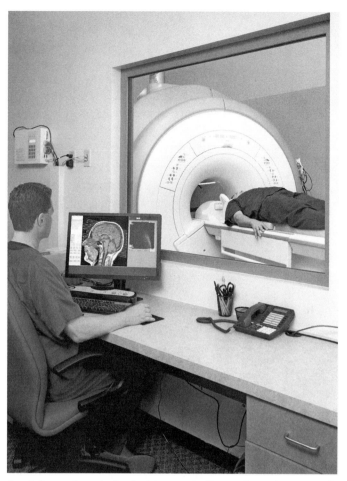

Special procedures technologists operate diagnostic equipment, such as magnetic resonance imaging (MRI) machines. (James Steidl. Shutterstock.)

as well, so there is a possibility of travel to, or employment in, other countries that recognize U.S. training and certification.

■ OUTLOOK
Job opportunities for special procedures technologists are expected to be excellent. The U.S. Department of Labor reports the following employment outlooks through 2024 by specialty: cardiovascular technologists and technicians (job growth of 22 percent), diagnostic medical sonographers (+26 percent), magnetic resonance imaging technologists (+10 percent), and radiologic technologists (+9 percent). Those job candidates who are skilled in multiple specialization areas, such as MRI and CT, will have the best chances of finding jobs. Employers like to hire candidates who can handle a variety of procedures, as this keeps their costs down and streamlines their staffs.

As the population ages and heart disease and cancer continue to be among the primary health concerns in the United States, there will continue to be a high demand

Top Employers of Magnetic Resonance Imaging Technologists and Mean Annual Earnings, May 2015

FAST FACTS

- Medical and diagnostic laboratories: $68,080
- Offices of physicians: $67,680
- Hospitals; State, Local and Private: $67,380

Source: Bureau of Labor Statistics

for skilled technologists who can assist in the diagnosis, prevention, and treatment of these and other conditions. Also, as more and more sophisticated testing and imaging procedures are developed, and as new techniques become available, the demand for skilled special procedures technologists to operate, perform, and assist in these procedures will continue to grow.

■ UNIONS AND ASSOCIATIONS

Special procedures technologists who work for government agencies can join the American Federation of Government Employees and the American Federation of State, County and Municipal Employees, unions that represent government workers. Other unions for health care professionals include the National Union of Healthcare Workers and Service Employee International Union. Major membership organizations for special procedures technologists include the American Society of Radiologic Technologists, Society of Diagnostic Medical Sonography, and the Society of Nuclear Medicine and Molecular Imaging. The American Registry of Radiologic Technologists, Nuclear Medicine Technology Certification Board, American Registry of Magnetic Resonance Imaging Technologists, and the American Registry of Diagnostic Medical Sonography offer certification or registration.

■ TIPS FOR ENTRY

1. Visit http://www.healthecareers.com/asrt and http://www.sdms.org/career/jobboard.asp for job listings.
2. Join the American Society of Radiologic Technologists (ASRT) and other professional associations to access member-only career advice, scholarships, publications, discounts on conferences, and other resources.
3. The ASRT offers detailed information on career paths at http://www.asrt.org/main/careers/careers-in-radiologic-technology.

■ FOR MORE INFORMATION

For information on certification and registration, contact
American Registry of Radiologic Technologists
1255 Northland Drive
St. Paul, MN 55120-1139
Tel: (651) 687-0048
http://www.arrt.org

For information on special procedures technologist careers, contact
American Society of Radiologic Technologists
15000 Central Avenue, SE
Albuquerque, NM 87123-3909
Tel: (800) 444-2778; (505) 298-4500
Fax: (505) 298-5063
E-mail: memberservices@asrt.org
http://www.asrt.org

For information on accredited programs, contact
Joint Review Committee on Education in Radiologic Technology
20 North Wacker Drive, Suite 2850
Chicago, IL 60606-3182
Tel: (312) 704-5300
Fax: (312) 704-5304
E-mail: mail@jrcert.org
http://www.jrcert.org

For information on nuclear medicine, professional development, and education, contact
Society of Nuclear Medicine and Molecular Imaging
1850 Samuel Morse Drive
Reston, VA 20190-5316
Tel: (703) 708-9000
Fax: (703) 708-9015
E-mail: feedback@snmmi.org
http://www.snmmi.org

For information about education and careers, contact
Society of Diagnostic Medical Sonography
2745 Dallas Parkway, Suite 350
Plano, TX 75093-8730
Tel: (800) 229-9506; (214) 473-8057
Fax: (214) 473-8563
http://www.sdms.org

Speech-Language Pathologists and Audiologists

OVERVIEW

Speech-language pathologists and *audiologists* help people who have speech and hearing disorders. They identify the problem and use tests to further evaluate it. Speech-language pathologists, who are also called *speech therapists*, try to improve the speech and language skills of clients with communications disorders. Audiologists perform tests to measure the hearing ability of clients, who may range in age from the very young to the very old. Since it is not uncommon for clients to require assistance for both speech and hearing, pathologists and audiologists may frequently work together to help clients. Some professionals decide to combine these jobs into one, working as speech-language pathologists or audiologists. Audiologists and speech-language pathologists may work for school systems, in private practice, and at clinics and other medical facilities. Other employment possibilities for these professionals include teaching at universities, and conducting research on what causes certain speech and hearing disorders. There are approximately 135,400 speech-language pathologists and 13,200 audiologists employed in the United States.

HISTORY

The diagnosis and treatment of speech and hearing defects is a new part of medical science. In the past, physicians were not able to help patients with these types of problems because there was usually nothing visibly wrong, and little was known about how speech and hearing were related. Until the middle of the 19th century, medical researchers did not know whether speech defects were caused by lack of hearing, or whether the patient was the victim of two separate ailments. And even if they could figure out why something was wrong, doctors still could not communicate with the patient.

Alexander Graham Bell, the inventor of the telephone, provided some of the answers. His grandfather taught elocution (the art of public speaking), and Bell grew up interested in the problems of speech and hearing. It became his profession, and by 1871 Bell was lecturing to a class of teachers of deaf people at Boston University. Soon afterward, Bell opened his own school, where he experimented with the idea of making speech visible to his pupils. If he could make them see the movements made by different human tones, they could speak by learning to produce similar vibrations. Bell's efforts not only helped deaf people of his day, but also led directly to the invention of the telephone in 1876. Probably the most famous deaf person was Helen Keller, whose teacher, Anne Sullivan, applied Bell's discoveries to help Keller overcome her blindness and deafness.

THE JOB

Even though the two professions seem to blend together at times, speech-language pathology and audiology are very different from one another. However, because both speech and hearing are related to one another, a person competent in one discipline must have familiarity with the other.

The duties performed by speech-language pathologists and audiologists differ depending on education, experience, and place of employment. Most speech-language pathologists provide direct clinical services to individuals and independently develop and carry out treatment programs. In medical facilities, they may work with physicians, social workers, psychologists, and other therapists to develop and execute treatment plans. In a school environment, they develop individual or group programs, counsel parents, and sometimes help teachers with classroom activities.

Clients of speech-language pathologists include people who cannot make speech sounds, or cannot make them clearly; those with speech rhythm and fluency

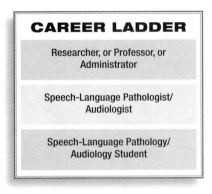

problems such as stuttering; people with voice quality problems, such as inappropriate pitch or harsh voice; those with problems understanding and producing language; and those with cognitive communication impairments, such as attention, memory, and problem-solving disorders. Speech-language pathologists may also work with people who have oral motor problems that cause eating and swallowing difficulties. Clients' problems may be congenital, developmental, or acquired, and caused by hearing loss, brain injury or deterioration, cerebral palsy, stroke, cleft palate, voice pathology, mental retardation, or emotional problems.

Speech-language pathologists conduct written and oral tests and use special instruments to analyze and diagnose the nature and extent of impairment. They develop an individualized plan of care, which may include automated devices and sign language. They teach clients how to make sounds, improve their voices, or increase their language skills to communicate more effectively. Speech-language pathologists help clients develop, or recover, reliable communication skills.

People who have hearing, balance, and related problems consult audiologists, who use audiometers and other testing devices to discover the nature and extent of hearing loss. Audiologists interpret these results and may coordinate them with medical, educational, and psychological information to make a diagnosis and determine a course of treatment.

Hearing disorders can result from trauma at birth, viral infections, genetic disorders, or exposure to loud noise. Treatment may include examining and cleaning the ear canal, fitting and dispensing a hearing aid or other device, and audiologic rehabilitation (including auditory training or instruction in speech or lip reading). Audiologists provide fitting and tuning of cochlear implants and help those with implants adjust to the implant amplification systems. They also test noise levels in workplaces and conduct hearing protection programs in industrial settings, as well as in schools and communities.

Audiologists provide direct clinical services to clients and sometimes develop and implement individual treatment programs. In some environments, however, they work as members of professional teams in planning and implementing treatment plans.

In a research environment, speech pathologists and audiologists investigate communicative disorders and their causes and ways to improve clinical services. Those teaching in colleges and universities instruct students on the principles and bases of communication, communication disorders, and clinical techniques used in speech and hearing.

Speech-language pathologists and audiologists keep records on the initial evaluation, progress, and discharge of clients to identify problems and track progress. They counsel individuals and their families on how to cope with the stress and misunderstanding that often accompany communication disorders.

■ EARNINGS

The U.S. Department of Labor reports that in May 2015 speech-language pathologists earned a median annual salary of $73,410. Salaries ranged from to less than $46,000 to more than $114,840. Audiologists earned a median annual salary of $74,890. The lowest paid 10 percent of these workers earned less than $49,760, while the highest paid 10 percent earned $111,450 or more per year. Geographic location and type of facility are important salary variables. Almost all employment situations provide fringe benefits such as paid vacations, sick leave, and retirement programs.

■ WORK ENVIRONMENT

Most speech-language pathologists and audiologists work 40 hours a week at a desk or table in clean comfortable surroundings. Speech-language pathologists and audiologists who focus on research, however, may work longer hours. The job is not physically demanding but does require attention to detail and intense concentration. The emotional needs of clients and their families may be demanding.

■ EXPLORING

Although the specialized nature of this work makes it difficult for you to get an informal introduction to either profession, there are opportunities to be found. Formal training must begin at the college or university level, but it is possible for you to volunteer in clinics and hospitals. As a prospective speech-language pathologist or audiologist, you may also find it helpful to learn sign language or volunteer your time in speech, language, and hearing centers. Finally, ask your school counselor to help arrange an information interview with a speech-language pathologist or audiologist.

■ EDUCATION AND TRAINING REQUIREMENTS
High School

Since a college degree is a must for practicing in this profession, make sure your high school classes are geared toward preparing you for higher education. Health and science classes, including biology, are very important. Mathematics classes and English classes will help you develop the math, research, and writing skills you will need in college. Because speech-language pathologists and audiologists work so intensely with language, you may also find it beneficial to study a foreign language, paying special attention to how you learn to make sounds and remember words. Speech classes will also improve your awareness of sounds and language as well as improve your speaking and listening skills.

Postsecondary Training

Most states require a master's degree in speech-language pathology or audiology for a beginning job in either profession. Forty-seven states require speech-language pathologists to be licensed if they work in a health care setting. Typical majors for those going into this field include communication sciences and disorders, speech and hearing, or education.

Regardless of your career goal (speech-language pathologist or audiologist), your undergraduate course work should include classes in anatomy, biology, physiology, physics, and other related areas, such as linguistics, semantics, and phonetics. It is also helpful to have some exposure to child psychology.

Accredited graduate programs in speech-language pathology are available at approximately 260 colleges and universities. Graduate-level work for those in speech-language pathology includes studies in evaluating and treating speech and language disorders, stuttering, pronunciation, and voice modulation. To be eligible for certification, which most employers and states require, you must have at least a master's degree from a program accredited by the American Speech-Language-Hearing Association (ASHA).

All states require audiologists to be licensed to practice and 20 states require audiologists to earn a doctorate in order to be certified. Currently there are about 75 accredited doctoral programs in audiology. Graduate-level course work in audiology includes such studies as hearing and language disorders, normal auditory and speech-language development, balance, and audiology instrumentation.

Students of both disciplines are required to complete supervised clinical fieldwork or practicum. It is in your best interest to contact the ASHA or the Council on Academic Accreditation (CAA) for a listing of accredited programs before you decide on a graduate school to attend. Some schools offer graduate degrees only in speech-language pathology or graduate degrees only in audiology. A number of schools offer degrees in both fields.

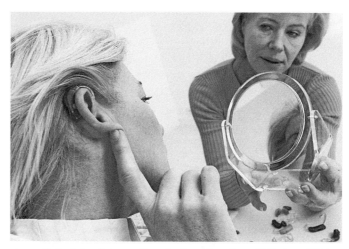

An audiologist assists a patient during a hearing-aid fitting. (JPC-PROD. Shutterstock.)

If you plan to practice in some states or go into research, teaching, or administration, you will need to complete a doctorate degree.

Other Education or Training

The American Speech-Language-Hearing Association offers continuing education courses, Web/telephone seminars, live and self-study Web workshops, and conferences. Topics include practice issues, legal documentation, technology, ethics, language and literacy, and working with children who do not speak English as a first language. The American Auditory Society and the Educational Audiology Association also provide professional development opportunities. Contact these organizations for more information.

■ CERTIFICATION, LICENSING, AND SPECIAL REQUIREMENTS
Certification or Licensing

To work as a speech pathologist or audiologist in a public school, you will be required to be a certified teacher and you must meet special state requirements if treating children with disabilities. Forty-seven states required speech-language pathologists to be licensed if they work in a health care setting, and 12 states require the same license to practice in a public school. In order to become licensed, you must have completed an advanced degree in the field (generally a master's degree, but a doctorate is becoming the new standard for audiologists), pass a standardized test, and complete 300 to 375 hours of supervised clinical experience and nine months of postgraduate professional clinical experience. Audiologists must be licensed in all states. Nearly 20 states require audiologists to have a doctorate degree in order to be licensed. Some states permit audiologists to dispense

FACTS ABOUT STUTTERING

DID YOU KNOW?

Stuttering or stammering while speaking is among the most common speech defects. In many cases, stuttering can be cured through therapy. The following are some facts about stuttering from the Stuttering Foundation of America:

- More than three million Americans stutter.
- Stuttering most frequently occurs in children ages 2 to 4. Boys are four times more likely to stutter than girls.
- Although little is known about the exact causes of stuttering, researchers have discovered much about its development through studies in genetics, neuropsychology, and family dynamics. As a result, there have been many advances in the prevention of stuttering in young children.
- Stuttering usually becomes a more pronounced problem during the teen years.
- James Earl Jones, an actor in high demand for voiceover work, has dealt with stuttering problems. Other well-known people who have faced and conquered stuttering problems include Emily Blunt, Winston Churchill, Marilyn Monroe, Carly Simon, and King George VI.

For more information, visit the American Speech-Language-Hearing Association Web site, http://www.asha.org/public/speech/disorders/stuttering.

hearing aids under an audiology license. Specific education and experience requirements, type of regulation, and title use vary by state.

Many states base their licensing laws on American Speech-Language-Hearing Association (ASHA) certification requirements. ASHA offers speech-language pathologists the certificate of clinical competence in speech-language pathology and audiologists the certificate of clinical competence in audiology. To be eligible for these certifications, you must meet certain education requirements, such as the supervised clinical fieldwork experience, and have completed a postgraduate clinical fellowship. The fellowship must be no less than 36 weeks of full-time professional employment or its part-time equivalent. You must then pass an examination in the area in which you want certification. Credentialing is also available from the American Board of Audiology.

■ EXPERIENCE, SKILLS, AND PERSONALITY TRAITS

Speech-language pathology and audiology college students can gain valuable practical experience by completing a supervised clinical fieldwork or a practicum, and completion of this fieldwork is usually a requirement for graduation.

Naturally, speech-language pathologists and audiologists should have strong communication skills. Note, though, that this means more than being able to speak clearly. You must be able to explain diagnostic test results and treatment plans in an easily understood way for a variety of clients who are already experiencing problems. As a speech-language pathologist or audiologist, you should enjoy working with people, both your clients and other professionals who may be involved in the client's treatment. In addition, you need patience and compassion. A client's progress may be slow, and you should be supportive and encouraging during these times.

■ EMPLOYMENT PROSPECTS

Employers

According to the U.S. Department of Labor, about 135,400 speech-language pathologists and 13,200 audiologists are employed in the United States. About 44 percent of speech-language pathologists are employed in elementary and secondary schools, while 50 percent of audiologists work in offices of physicians and other health care practitioners. Other professionals in this field work in state and local governments, hearing aid stores (audiologists), and scientific research facilities. A small but growing number of speech-language pathologists and audiologists are in private practice, generally working with patients referred to them by physicians and other health practitioners.

Some speech-language pathologists and audiologists contract to provide services in schools, hospitals, or nursing homes, or work as consultants to industry.

Starting Out

If you want to work in the public school systems, your college's career services office can help you with interviewing skills. Professors sometimes know of job openings and may even post these openings on a centrally located bulletin board. It may be possible to find employment by contacting a hospital or rehabilitation center. To work in colleges and universities as a specialist in the classroom, clinic, or research center, it is almost mandatory to be working on a graduate degree. Many scholarships, fellowships, and grants for assistants are available in colleges and universities giving courses in speech-language pathology and audiology. Most of these and other assistance programs are offered at the graduate level. The U.S. Rehabilitation Services Administration, the Children's Bureau, the U.S. Department of Education, and the National Institutes of Health allocate funds for teaching and training grants to colleges and universities with graduate study programs. In addition, the Department of Veterans Affairs provides stipends (a fixed allowance) for predoctoral work.

ADVANCEMENT PROSPECTS

Advancement in speech-language pathology and audiology is based chiefly on education. Individuals who have completed graduate study will have the best opportunities to enter research and administrative areas, supervising other speech-language pathologists or audiologists either in developmental work or in public school systems.

OUTLOOK

Population growth, lengthening life spans, growing awareness of speech-language disorders (such as stuttering) in young children, and increased public awareness of the problems associated with communicative disorders indicate a highly favorable employment outlook for well-qualified personnel. The U.S. Department of Labor predicts that employment for speech-language pathologists will grow much faster than the average, 21 percent, and audiologists will grow even faster, 29 percent, through 2024. Much of this growth depends on economic factors, additional funding by health care providers and third-party payers, and legal mandates requiring services for people with disabilities. Additionally, the passage of the Affordable Care Act is expected to expand the number of people who are eligible for insurance coverage for speech-language pathology or audiology services.

Many of the new jobs emerging through the end of the decade are expected to be in speech and hearing clinics, physicians' offices, and outpatient care facilities. Speech-language pathologists and audiologists will be needed in these places, for example, to carry out the increasing number of rehabilitation programs for stroke victims and patients with head injuries.

Substantial job growth will continue to occur in elementary and secondary schools because of the Education for All Handicapped Children Act of 1975 (which was renamed the Individuals with Disabilities Education Act and amended in 1990, 1997, and 2004). This law guarantees special education and related services to minors with disabilities.

Many new jobs will be created in hospitals, nursing homes, rehabilitation centers, and home health agencies; most of these openings will probably be filled by private practitioners employed on a contract basis. Opportunities for speech-language pathologists and audiologists in private practice should increase in the future. There should be a greater demand for consultant audiologists in the area of industrial and environmental noise as manufacturing and other companies develop and carry out noise-control programs. Speech-language pathologists and audiologists who are fluent in a foreign language (such as Spanish) should have especially strong employment prospects.

UNIONS AND ASSOCIATIONS

The U.S. Department of Labor reports that approximately 40 percent of speech-language pathologists and 15 percent of audiologists are union members or covered by union contracts. They also may join professional associations such as the American Auditory Society, Educational Audiology Association, and the American Speech-Language-Hearing Association (ASHA). The National Student Speech Language Hearing Association offers resources for college students. Certification is offered by the ASHA and the American Board of Audiology.

TIPS FOR ENTRY

1. Visit http://www.asha.org/careers for job listings. This Web site also offers career advice, salary data, and information about working abroad.
2. Join the American Speech-Language-Hearing Association (ASHA), the American Auditory Society, and other professional associations to access training and networking opportunities, industry publications, and employment opportunities. If you're a college student, be sure to join the National Student Speech Language Hearing Association.
3. Attend the Career Fair at the annual convention of the ASHA to network and interview for jobs.
4. Volunteer with a local organization to help people with hearing disabilities.

FOR MORE INFORMATION

The American Auditory Society is concerned with hearing disorders, how to prevent them, and the rehabilitation of individuals with hearing and balance dysfunction.

American Auditory Society
PO Box 779
Pennsville, NJ 08070-0779
Tel: (877) 746-8315
Fax: (650) 763-9185
E-mail: amaudsoc@comcast.net
http://www.amauditorysoc.org

For information on certification, contact
American Board of Audiology
11480 Commerce Park Drive, Suite 220
Reston, VA 20191-1518
Tel: (800) 881-5410
Fax: (703) 485-3555
E-mail: aba@audiology.org
http://www.boardofaudiology.org

This professional, scientific, and credentialing association offers information about communication disorders and career and membership information.

**American Speech-Language-Hearing
Association (ASHA)**
2200 Research Boulevard
Rockville, MD 20850-3289
Tel: (800) 638-8255
Fax: (301)296-8580
E-mail: nsslha@asha.org
http://www.asha.org

To learn more about audiologists who work in education and other settings, contact

Educational Audiology Association
700 McKnight Park Drive, Suite 708
Pittsburgh, PA 15237
Tel: (800) 460-7322
Fax: (888) 729-3489
E-mail: admin@edaud.org
http://www.edaud.org

This association is for undergraduate and graduate students studying human communication and is the only such group recognized by the American Speech Language Hearing Association. For news related to the field and to find out about regional chapters, contact

**National Student Speech, Language, and Hearing
Association**
2200 Research Boulevard, #322
Rockville, MD 20850-3289
Tel: (800) 638-8255
Fax: (301) 296-8580
E-mail: nsslha@asha.org
http://www.asha.org/nsslha

Sporting Goods Production Workers

■ OVERVIEW

Sporting goods production workers are involved in manufacturing, assembling, and finishing sporting goods equipment such as golf clubs, fishing tackle, basketballs, footballs, skis, and baseball equipment. Their tasks range from operating machines to fine handcrafting of equipment.

■ HISTORY

Throughout history, every society and culture has developed games and sports for relaxation and competition.

Bowling, for example, has been around for centuries; a stone ball and nine stone pins were found in the ancient tomb of an Egyptian child. Polo is believed to have originated in Asia and was brought back to England and America by British officers returning from India in the 1800s. Native American peoples played lacrosse with webbed sticks and hard wooden balls centuries ago. Soccer, arguably the world's most popular sport, was invented in England, where a version of the game was played nearly 2,000 years ago.

Some of the most popular sports in America have a relatively recent history. Basketball was invented in 1891 by Dr. James Naismith in Springfield, Massachusetts; its popularity grew so quickly that it became an Olympic event in 1936. Ice hockey as we know it was invented in Canada in the 1870s. It quickly became popular in northern countries and was inaugurated as an Olympic sport in 1920. In the 1870s, football started as a college sport that mixed elements of soccer and rugby and soon developed its own set of rules. Although folklore attributes the invention of baseball to Abner Doubleday in 1839, people were playing it for many years before then.

Some games, both ancient and modern, have changed little since the time they were first played. Soccer, for instance, has remained popular in part because of its simplicity; the only equipment needed to play is a ball. Other sports have grown to require more elaborate equipment. Modern technology has been applied to many aspects of sport and given us such improvements as better protective padding, livelier tennis rackets, and stronger golf balls. Computers are used to improve the design and composition of sports gear. The equipment used in each sport is unique in design and manufacture and is put together by skilled specialists.

■ THE JOB

Every sport involves its own equipment, and each kind of equipment is made somewhat differently. Basketballs and volleyballs are made by approximately the same process, which differs from the processes for making footballs and baseballs. But the manufacturing processes for sporting goods and for other products are also similar in many ways.

As in the manufacturing of other products, *machine operators* control large machine tools, such as presses, and smaller tools, such as saws and sewing machines. After they have done their tasks, they may pass the work on to different kinds of assemblers. *Floor assemblers* operate large machines and power tools; *bench assemblers* work with smaller machines to complete a product and perhaps to test it; *precision assemblers* perform highly skilled assembly work. They may work closely with engineers and technicians to develop and test new products and designs. These general categories can be applied to many of the occupations involved in sporting goods manufacturing, although the job titles vary with different kinds of products.

In the manufacturing of golf equipment, for example, the shaft of a golf club and the head, or club end, are made separately and are then assembled, weighted, and balanced. *Golf-club assemblers* do much of the work. They use bench-mounted circular saws to cut the shaft for a club to a specified length, depending on the model of club being made. *Golf-club head formers* hammer precast metal club heads to the correct angle and then glue the proper club head onto a shaft and secure the head by drilling a small hole and inserting a pin. Wooden clubs are glued together the same way, except that once the assembly has dried, the weight of the club is checked and adjusted for the model type. *Assemblers* or *golf-club weighters* can adjust the weight by drilling a hole into the head and adding molten lead or threaded cylindrical metal weights.

Grip wrappers attach the handle of the golf club. They insert a club in a rotating machine, brush adhesive on the shaft, attach a leather strap, and then carefully spin the shaft to cover it tightly and evenly with the leather strap. When they are finished, they trim the excess leather and fasten the grip in place with tape or a sleeve. Finally, *golf-club head inspectors* examine the head to verify that it conforms to specifications.

The manufacturing of fishing equipment is another instance of a production process involving a series of workers. It begins with *fishing-rod markers,* who mark the places on rod blanks where the line guides and decorative markings should be put. After this, *fishing-rod assemblers* use liquid cement to attach the hardware, such as reel seats, handles, and line guides, onto the rods. Line guides can also be attached with thread by *guide winders,* who decorate the rods by winding thread around them at intervals. Finally, *fishing-reel assemblers* assemble the parts of the intricate reel mechanisms, test the reels, and then attach them to rods.

Some processes used in manufacturing sporting goods, such as lathing (which is used in making baseball bats) and vulcanizing (which is used in making hockey pucks), are commonly used in making many other products as well. But other processes are more specialized. To make basketballs, volleyballs, and soccer balls, for example, *ball assemblers* cement panels of rubberized fabric onto a hollow, spherical frame made of wax. A door opening is left in the ball carcass so that the wax frame can be broken and removed piece by piece. Once this is done, a bladder is inserted into the ball and inflated to a

specific pressure. The flaps of the door opening are then aligned with the other seams of the ball and cemented onto the bladder, and the ball is complete.

Some baseball equipment is still made by hand, much the same way it was many years ago. Many wooden bats are hand-turned to the specifications of each player.

QUICK FACTS

ALTERNATE TITLE(S)
Ball Assemblers, Baseball Glove Shapers, Fishing-Reel Assemblers, Fishing-Rod Assemblers, Fishing-Rod Markers, Golf-Club Assemblers, Golf-Club Head Formers, Golf-Club Head Inspectors, Golf-Club Weighters, Grip Wrappers, Guide Winders, Hand Baseball Sewers, Lining Inserters, Lining Reversers

DUTIES
Manufacture, assemble, and finish sporting goods equipment such as golf clubs, footballs, and skis

SALARY RANGE
$19,240 to $32,000 to $50,420+

WORK ENVIRONMENT
Primarily Indoors

BEST GEOGRAPHIC LOCATION(S)
Opportunities are available throughout the country

MINIMUM EDUCATION LEVEL
High School Diploma

SCHOOL SUBJECTS
Mathematics, Physical Education, Technical/Shop

EXPERIENCE
On-the-job training

PERSONALITY TRAITS
Conventional, Hands On, Technical

SKILLS
Interpersonal, Mechanical/Manual Dexterity

CERTIFICATION OR LICENSING
None

SPECIAL REQUIREMENTS
None

EMPLOYMENT PROSPECTS
Fair

ADVANCEMENT PROSPECTS
Fair

OUTLOOK
Decline

NOC
9619

O*NET-SOC
51-9199.00

CAREER LADDER

Product Inspector or Supervisor

Experienced Sporting Goods
Production Worker

Entry-Level Sporting Goods
Production Worker

Baseballs themselves are assembled by *hand baseball sewers,* who cement the leather hide of the ball to the core and sew the sections of hide together using a harness needle and waxed linen thread. To make baseball gloves, *lacers* sew precut pieces of leather together, working with the glove inside out. Then *lining inserters* put a lining in place, and *reversers* turn the glove right-side out on a series of posts. Next, *baseball glove shapers* use a heated, hand-shaped form to open and stretch the finger linings. With various rubber mallets, they hammer the seams smooth and form the glove pocket. Finally, they try on the glove and pound the pocket to make sure that it fits comfortably.

As these examples show, the manufacturing of sporting goods involves ordinary industrial processes that are adapted to suit each product. Within the limits of sports safety and economical operation of their plants, sporting goods manufacturers are constantly trying to improve designs and manufacturing processes to make equipment that is reliable and durable and maximizes athletic performance.

■ EARNINGS

According to the U.S. Department of Labor, the median hourly wages of cutting, punching, and press machine setters, operators, and tenders, metal and plastic, ranged from $10.00 to $23.25 in May 2015 ($20,800 to $48,350 annually for full-time work). Team assemblers had earnings than ranged from $9.25 an hour to $24.24 or more per hour ($19,240 to $50,420 annually for full-time work). Wages are generally higher for skilled, experienced machine operators. Most workers also get fringe benefits, such as health insurance, paid holidays and vacation days, and pension plans. Some firms offer stock options to employees.

■ WORK ENVIRONMENT

Conditions in plants vary, with some factories having modern, well-equipped, well-lit work stations for employees. Other plants provide less comfortable working conditions. In some jobs, employees have to sit or stand in one place for the entire work shift, while other jobs require heavy lifting, hammering, or other physically strenuous activities. People who operate presses, molds, and other heavy machinery may have to load and remove heavy work pieces made of leather, metal, fiberglass, plastic, and other materials. Almost all workers have production quotas to meet, which can be stressful at times.

Heat, noise, dust, or strong odors are unavoidable in many production jobs. Workers may need to wear safety glasses, hard hats, earplugs, or other protective clothing.

Sports equipment production workers average 40 hours of work per week. Many factories operate two or three shifts a day, so employees may be required to work days, evenings, nights, or weekends.

■ EXPLORING

To learn something about what the work is like in the sporting goods production business, you can try to get a summer job working in a nearby sports equipment factory. Such a job is likely to be in a warehouse or in custodial services, but it may still offer you a chance to observe the manufacturing processes firsthand and to talk with experienced employees about their jobs. Working part time can also be an opportunity to show an employer that you are dependable and have good work habits, and it could lead to permanent employment in the future. Since an interest in sports is helpful, a knowledge of sports and sports equipment gained through actual participation would be beneficial.

■ EDUCATION AND TRAINING REQUIREMENTS
High School

High school courses that can help prepare students for working in the sporting goods equipment industry include shop, basic mathematics, blueprint reading, sewing, and other classes that provide practice in following written instructions and diagrams or making items by hand. Speech classes will also be helpful.

Postsecondary Training

Electronic devices are used more and more in sports for purposes such as timing skiers and runners. As more applications are developed for electronic and electrical equipment, more manufacturing workers will be needed who have the kind of knowledge and training that is available at technical schools. Also, design, precision assembly, and production jobs increasingly rely on machinery that is controlled by computers. For these reasons, a background that includes training in electronics and computer applications is very important for many jobs in this industry.

■ CERTIFICATION, LICENSING, AND SPECIAL REQUIREMENTS
Certification or Licensing

There are no certification or licensing requirements for sporting goods production workers.

EXPERIENCE, SKILLS, AND PERSONALITY TRAITS

No experience is needed to work in entry-level production jobs, but those with prior work experience will increase their chances of landing a job, getting promoted, and possibly earning higher pay.

Sports equipment production workers generally need good eyesight and manual dexterity to work with small parts and operate machines. Interest in sports can be an advantage. For example, it helps for workers who shape baseball gloves to have experience playing baseball and using gloves, so they know the feel of a good fit. Other important traits include strong communication, organizational, interpersonal, and communication skills.

EMPLOYMENT PROSPECTS
Employers

The Sports & Fitness Industry Association represents more than 1,000 sporting goods equipment manufacturers, retailers, and marketers in the United States. They employ more than 375,000 people at over 3,000 businesses, manufacturing plants, and distributions centers located throughout the United States and may be small companies or large conglomerates. The recent trend toward mergers has affected this industry; fewer companies are employing more workers.

Starting Out

Job seekers in this field can contact sporting goods manufacturers directly to learn whether or not they have any job openings. Other possibilities for job leads include checking the listings at the local offices of the state employment service and in the classified sections of newspapers. School counselors can provide information about local companies that are looking for workers.

ADVANCEMENT PROSPECTS

Newly hired employees in sporting goods factories usually are assigned simple tasks. Trainees may acquire their job skills informally as they work beside and watch more experienced workers. Others may enter into a formal training program. Workers who have completed training for their job category and have shown they can meet production requirements may be able move into higher paying production jobs as they become available.

In companies that are large and diversified, workers may advance to jobs in other divisions. Qualified employees may also move to positions as product inspectors or supervisors of other production workers. Moving into management jobs usually requires further experience, technical training, and formal education in business subjects.

THE MOST POPULAR SPORTS IN AMERICA — DID YOU KNOW?

As of January 2015, Harris Interactive, Inc. reported on the favorite sports of Americans age 18 and over. Their survey showed the following top 10 choices:

- National Football League (cited by 32 percent of respondents)
- Major League Baseball (16 percent)
- College Football (10 percent)
- Auto Racing (7 percent)
- National Basketball Association (6 percent)
- National Hockey League (6 percent)
- Major League Soccer (6 percent)
- Men's College Basketball (3 percent)
- Boxing (2 percent)
- Men's Golf (2 percent)

Some knowledgeable, experienced people with new product ideas or an urge for independence may decide to start their own sporting goods production company. Setting up a new business in any field is a risky venture, however, and anyone who is interested in taking this step needs first to take a hard and informed look at the high costs involved, in addition to the potential benefits.

OUTLOOK

As sports and fitness become more popular among health-conscious Americans, the market for sporting goods is expected to continue to grow. Exports of American-made goods may also increase in coming years. This does not mean, however, that the number of jobs in sporting goods manufacturing will also increase.

The manufacture of many kinds of sports gear is very labor-intensive, and to keep labor costs down, manufacturers have moved some of their operations to plants in other countries, where workers can be paid lower wages. In addition, advances in automation, robotics, and computer-aided manufacturing are allowing companies to phase out certain production jobs. In the future, the need will be for employees who can program machines, supervise production, and manage resources. Workers will also be needed to test product safety and quality. In general, employment of cutting, punching, and press machine setters, operators, and tenders, metal and plastic, is forecast to decline by nearly 30 percent through 2024 and by 6 percent for team assemblers, reductions that will certainly include jobs in the sporting goods industry.

The sporting goods manufacturing industry is generally a solid but not expanding business. Job turnover is fairly high among production and assembly workers, so most new workers will be hired to replace people who leave their jobs.

■ UNIONS AND ASSOCIATIONS

Some sporting goods production workers may belong to a number of labor unions depending on their specific job. The Sports & Fitness Industry Association represents more than 1,000 sporting goods equipment manufacturers, retailers, and marketers in the United States. The National Sporting Goods Association is a membership organization for sports manufacturers.

■ TIPS FOR ENTRY

1. Visit http://www.sportscareers.com and http://www.sportjobsource.com for job listings.
2. Read *Sporting Goods Intelligence* (http://www.sginews.com) to learn more about the field.
3. Try to land an internship or entry-level job at a sporting goods manufacturer.

■ FOR MORE INFORMATION

Visit the following Web site for information on careers:

Get in the Game: Developing a Career in the Sporting Goods Industry
Tel: (847) 296-6742
http://www.getinthegamecareers.org

For industry information, contact
National Sporting Goods Association
1601 Feehanville Drive, Suite 300
Mount Prospect, IL 60056-6042
Tel: (800) 815-5422
Fax: (847) 391-9827
E-mail: info@nsga.org
http://www.nsga.org

For industry information and job listings, contact
Sports & Fitness Industry Association
8505 Fenton Street, Suite 211
Silver Spring, MD 20910-4499
Tel: (301) 495-6321
Fax: (301) 495-6322
E-mail: info@sfia.org
http://www.sfia.org

Sports Agents

■ OVERVIEW

Sports agents act as representatives for professional athletes in many different types of negotiations, providing advice and representation concerning contracts, endorsement and advertisement deals, public appearances, and financial investments and taxes, among other areas. They may represent only one athlete or many, depending on the sport, the size of their agency, and the demands of the client or clients they represent. There are approximately 13,230 agents and managers employed in the United States. However, that figure includes literary and talent agents, as well as sports agents.

■ HISTORY

People have been entertained by the spectacular feats and athletic skills of individuals and teams even before gladiators performed in front of thousands in the Colosseum in ancient Rome. In the 20th and 21st centuries, sports have consumed a large share of people's free time. Sports figures, like movie stars, have become internationally recognized celebrities, renowned not only for their athletic prowess, but also for their charismatic personalities. Instead of closing deals with a simple handshake, sports teams now "sign" new athletes to contracts. Like movie stars, athletes began to realize the need to have talented representation—or agents—to protect and promote their interests during contract negotiations. The role of a sports agent has expanded to include many more duties than contract negotiation, although that area remains a crucial responsibility. Today, sports agents handle most, if not all, aspects of a professional athlete's career, from commercial endorsements to financial investments to postretirement career offers.

■ THE JOB

The sports agent's primary duties consist of negotiating contracts and finding endorsements for his or her clients. Contract negotiations require great communication skills on the part of the sports agent. He or she must clearly summarize the athlete's salary and benefit requirements and have a clear vision of the athlete's future—and how any given contract might affect it. Agents usually represent their clients for the duration of their clients' careers, which sometimes means finding work for athletes once their athletic careers are over. For example, an agent may be able to build into the contract a coaching position, in the event that athlete is injured or otherwise unable to complete the contract. Having a good sense of timing helps the agent as well. Part of understanding a bargaining situation means knowing when to stand your ground and when to cut a deal.

Endorsements and public appearance deals bring additional income to the athlete, but they also have the potential to create a great deal of media attention around the athlete. It is the role of the sports agent to ensure that this media attention is positive and works to the benefit of the athlete. Marketing the public image of an athlete is increasingly difficult in today's media-saturated world; in the past, all an athlete needed to do to be considered a winner was be successful at his or her sport. Today, an athlete who wants to attract top endorsements and public appearances must have incredible charisma and a blemish-free image in addition to being a top athletic performer. Generally speaking, agents must be extremely careful when choosing endorsements for their clients.

Often, a great deal of "schmoozing" is necessary to achieve the kind of contacts that will help clients. For example, an agent for a tennis player might court the attention of executives whose companies manufacture items related to tennis, like tennis racquets, balls, and clothing. By developing friendly business relationships with these individuals, the agent has a direct line to those in charge of dispersing product endorsements. If and when those companies decide to use an athlete to help promote their products, the agent's athlete hopefully will be the first considered. Networking like this is part of the sports agent's everyday work routine. In between reviewing contracts and financial arrangements, he or she might be on the phone, chatting to an advertiser, scheduling lunch with a sports scout to uncover fresh talent, or handling some other aspect of the athlete's life, such as renting an apartment for the athlete during spring training.

Financial advising is a growing part of the agent's job. Successful new athletes suddenly have a great deal of money. In order to manage those funds, the agent needs to know a reliable financial adviser or act as the athlete's financial adviser. Creating or finding tax shelters, investing money, and preparing for the athlete's retirement are all duties that agents routinely perform for their clients.

Other duties, which are sometimes so small and trivial as to be deceptively insignificant, are many times what keeps a client happy and convinced that the agent has only the client's best interests in mind. This might mean making sure the athlete's mother always has a great seat at home games, or pestering a talk-show host for months to schedule the agent's client for a post-game interview on a popular sports radio program.

■ EARNINGS

Sports agents can earn phenomenal amounts of money by representing a single star athlete like LeBron James, Venus Williams, or Tiger Woods. Athletes of this stature earn $50 million a year or more in salary and endorsements. A 5 percent commission on such earnings would net the agent approximately $2.5 million a year. Agent commissions, or percentages, at top management firms run anywhere from 5 to 10 percent of the player's earnings, and up to 25 percent for endorsements the agency negotiates on behalf of the athlete.

Although these are high salaries, anyone interested in pursuing a career in this field should understand that most of the athletes the typical sports agent represents are not of the rare star-like variety. This means that they will earn significantly less than agents who represent premier athletes. According to the U.S. Department of Labor, agents and business managers for performers, artists, and athletes earned a median annual salary of $62,940 in May 2015. The lowest paid 10 percent earned $28,060 or less, while the highest paid 25 percent earned $111,370 or more annually.

According to one insider, the sky's the limit; if an agent is extremely ambitious and the agent's contacts within the sports world are fruitful, he or she can earn well over a million dollars a year. People entering the field of sports management should know the realities of the job—the million-dollar scenario is as likely for agents as it is for athletes. It takes ambition, talent, timing, and lots of luck to make it big in this field. Enjoyment of the work, then, is crucial to job satisfaction.

Working for an agency, an experienced agent will

QUICK FACTS

ALTERNATE TITLE(S)
None

DUTIES
Represent the business interests of professional athletes; negotiate contracts; find product endorsements and other business opportunities for their clients

SALARY RANGE
$28,060 to $62,940 to $2.5 million+

WORK ENVIRONMENT
Primarily Indoors

BEST GEOGRAPHIC LOCATION(S)
Opportunities are available throughout the country

MINIMUM EDUCATION LEVEL
Bachelor's Degree

SCHOOL SUBJECTS
Business, Mathematics, Psychology

EXPERIENCE
Internship; experience as an assistant

PERSONALITY TRAITS
Enterprising, Organized, Outgoing

SKILLS
Business Management, Financial, Interpersonal

CERTIFICATION OR LICENSING
Required

SPECIAL REQUIREMENTS
None

EMPLOYMENT PROSPECTS
Fair

ADVANCEMENT PROSPECTS
Fair

OUTLOOK
Little Change or More Slowly than the Average

NOC
1123

O*NET-SOC
13-1011.00

CAREER LADDER

Owner of Sports Management Firm or
Manager/Supervisor

Experienced Sports Agent

Entry-Level Sports Agent

receive health and retirement benefits, bonuses, and paid travel and accommodations. Self-employed agents must provide their own benefits.

■ WORK ENVIRONMENT

Sports agents work with athletes in various stages of their careers, often before those careers even take off. Agents may spend time with the athlete at practice, hours on the telephone in the office, a day or two scouting out new talent, and lunches and dinners with potential advertisers or employers of the athlete.

Sports agents spend most of their time on the telephone, arranging meetings, discussing prospects, networking connections, keeping in touch with the industry trends and issues, and most of all, speaking with their client about strategies and whatever problems the client is dealing with, from negotiating a raise in salary to helping the player through a slump.

■ EXPLORING

Finding jobs in this field is as challenging for those just starting out as it is for those at the top. Even intern positions and entry-level jobs are hard to get, because so many people are struggling to enter the field. Insiders recommend starting as early as possible and taking any job that gives you exposure to athletes. High school students can start by shagging balls at tennis tournaments, golf caddying, or applying for coveted ballboy/girl and batboy/girl or clubhouse assistant positions with major league baseball teams.

College internships are probably the most valuable introduction to the field, especially when you consider that many of the top management firms that hire agents do not accept younger applicants. These firms are looking for men and women who are eager and willing to learn about the field. Insiders believe the internship is crucial to getting a solid start because it may be the last time when anyone will let you close enough to see how the job is done; once someone passes the internship stage, they are viewed by other agents as competition and the avenues of communication close up. Although young recruits in an agency receive some informal training on the job, the secrets of the trade are highly individualized and are developed by the truly successful among the agents.

■ EDUCATION AND TRAINING REQUIREMENTS
High School

High school courses that will be helpful include business, mathematics, English, and speech. Business courses will provide the financial knowledge an agent needs to act as financial adviser and contract negotiator.

Postsecondary Training

No educational requirements exist for sports agents, but it is increasingly difficult to enter the field without at least a bachelor's degree in business administration, marketing, or sports management. Many who eventually become agents also go on to pursue a graduate degree in law or business, two areas which increase but do not guarantee your chances at success. Contract law and economics are courses that can help an agent improve the client's chances, and his or her own chances, for successful negotiations.

■ CERTIFICATION, LICENSING, AND SPECIAL REQUIREMENTS
Certification or Licensing

Many sports agents obtain a license or professional certification or registration as demonstration of their commitment and integrity. Although these are not yet mandatory, it is one way for athletes to determine who, among agents, is legitimate and therefore a better person to hire. Agents working for clients who belong to unions, such as the National Football League Players Association (NFLPA), are required to obtain certification or a union franchise. Basically, agents who obtain certification or a franchise agree to abide by the standards created by the union to protect its members. To become certified by the NFLPA, for example, agents must pay an application fee of $2,500, have an undergraduate and post-graduate degree (master's or law), participate in a two-day seminar, and pass a written examination.

Agents who start their own firms may need a business license in certain states. Contact your state's department of professional regulation for information on requirements in your state.

■ EXPERIENCE, SKILLS, AND PERSONALITY TRAITS

Working for an agent as an intern, volunteer, or assistant is a great experience that will look good on your resume. Contact agents in your area to learn more about the opportunities that are available.

Contacts and exposure to athletes are the unofficial requirements for sports agents. Simply put, without knowing or having access to athletes, it is next to impossible to represent them. Insiders say that often, a successful agent's first client is his or her college roommate—later hired when the college athlete turned professional.

The sports industry generates revenue in the hundreds of billions of dollars, only a portion of which actually goes to the athlete, so everyone who comes to the bargaining table—from management to athlete to advertiser—has a lot at stake. Sports agents must be able to handle tension and stress well, arguing effectively for their client's interests whether the opponent is the head of an international shoe manufacturer or the local real estate agent trying to sell the athlete a new house.

Finally, a large part of the sports agent's job is talking, making contacts, and then using those contacts to improve a client's position. This type of interaction is the bread and butter of a sports agent's career. As one insider put it, being just this side of annoying, obnoxious, or brash helps in this business. Often, the agent with the most name recognition is the one who ends up with the job.

■ EMPLOYMENT PROSPECTS
Employers
Agents are employed by the professional athletes they represent. They are also employed by top management firms, such as IMG Worldwide.

Starting Out
If you do not know an athlete, have no connections or access to athletes, and have had no experience prior to applying to agencies, chances are you will find yourself changing fields pretty quickly. Just as there are no professional organizations and no formal training to do this job, there is no one way to do it, which only makes getting started more difficult. The best way of breaking into the field is to start early and obtain a good internship—one that gives you some exposure to agents and athletes, as well as a chance to develop those contacts. Add to this any information or hot tips you might have on new, fresh talent and you may have a chance. IMG Worldwide, a top employer of sports agents, has summer and semester internship programs for young people interested in this career. For more information, visit http://www.img.com/careers.aspx.

Most people who become agents get involved with a sport, either because they once played it, or a sibling did, or they have followed it so closely as to have made important or solid contacts in the field. Coaches, scouts, and the athletes themselves would all be considered good contacts. So, too, are sportscasters, sportswriters, athletic

Andre Farr is the CEO of the Black Sports Agent Association. (Ira Bostic. Shutterstock.)

trainers, even sports physicians; in short, anyone who can introduce you to athletes is a potential contact.

■ ADVANCEMENT PROSPECTS
In the field of sports management, advancement comes with success, the formula for which is pretty straightforward: If an agent's athletes are successful (and the agent handles the careers of those athletes well), then the agent is successful—financially as well as in terms of reputation. A good, solid reputation will, in turn, garner that agent more successful clients. Some very successful agents launch their own sports management firms.

■ OUTLOOK
The U.S. Department of Labor predicts that employment for agents and business managers of artists, performers, and athletes is expected to grow slower than the average

REPRESENTING PROFESSIONAL ATHLETES   **LEARN MORE ABOUT IT**

Carfagna, Peter A. *Representing the Professional Athlete,* 2nd ed. Eagan, Minn.: West Academic, 2013.

Epstein, Adam. *Sports Law.* Independence, Ky.: Cengage Learning, 2012.

Lewis, Michael. *Moneyball.* New York: W. W. Norton & Company, 2004.

Steinberg, Leigh, and Michael Arkush. *The Agent: My 40-Year Career Making Deals and Changing the Game.* New York: Thomas Dunne Books, 2014.

for all careers through 2024. The sports industry is thriving and there is nothing to suggest that the public's interest in it will dwindle. The increasing popularity of women's sports leagues, such as the Women's National Basketball Association, also accounts for the rapid growth in this field. Also, as cable television brings greater choices to the viewer, it is possible that less-publicized sports will gain in popularity through the increased exposure, thus breathing life and revenues into those sports and creating new demand.

Despite this positive outlook, it's important to remember that the number of sports agents is very small, and it is extremely difficult to build a lucrative career representing star athletes. Agents with extensive experience and graduate-level training in business, finance, or law will have the best job prospects.

■ UNIONS AND ASSOCIATIONS

Sports agents do not belong to unions, and there are no professional associations that represent their interests. An aspiring agent might consider joining business associations at the local, state, and national levels. Those who are lawyers often join the American Bar Association.

■ TIPS FOR ENTRY

1. Participate in internships or part-time jobs at sports management firms that are arranged by your college's career services office. These are excellent ways to obtain experience and get your foot in the door.
2. Learn as much as you can about sports. Try to make contacts with agents and sports trainers, physicians, and reporters to expand your professional network.
3. Conduct information interviews with agents and ask them for advice on breaking into the field.

4. Earn advanced degrees in business management, law, and finance to improve your chances of landing a job.

■ FOR MORE INFORMATION

The following is one of the top management firms in the world, a good source for internships and jobs, with headquarters in Beverly Hills and many other cities around the globe:

International Management Group
9601 Wilshire Boulevard
Beverly Hills, CA 90210
Tel: (310) 285-9000
http://www.img.com/careers.aspx

Sports Broadcasters and Announcers

■ OVERVIEW

Sports broadcasters, or *sportscasters,* for radio and television stations select, write, and deliver footage of current sports news for the sports segment of radio and television news broadcasts or for specific sports events, channels, or shows. They may provide pre- and postgame coverage of sports events, including interviews with coaches and athletes, as well as play-by-play coverage during the game or event.

Sports announcers are the official voices of the teams. At home games it is the sports announcer who makes pre-game announcements, introduces the players in the starting lineups, and keeps the spectators in the stadium or arena abreast of the details of the game by announcing such things as fouls, substitutions, and goals, and who is making them.

■ HISTORY

Radio signals, first transmitted by Guglielmo Marconi in 1895, led to early experimentation with broadcasting in the years preceding World War I. After the war began, however, a ban on nonmilitary radio broadcasts delayed radio's acceptance. In 1919, when the ban was lifted, hundreds of amateur stations sprang up. By 1922, 500 were licensed by the government. Codes and domestic broadcast wavelengths were assigned by the government, which created a traffic jam of aerial signals. Eventually, more powerful stations were permitted to broadcast at a higher wavelength, provided these stations only broadcast live music. This move by the government quickly brought entertainment from large, urban areas to the small towns and rural areas that characterized most of the United States at the time.

In the early days of radio broadcasts, anyone who operated the station would read, usually verbatim, news stories from the day's paper. Quickly, station managers realized that the station's "voice" needed as much charisma and flair as possible. Announcers and journalists with good speaking voices were hired. With the arrival of television, many of those who worked in radio broadcasting moved to this new medium.

Corporate-sponsored radio stations weren't long in coming; Westinghouse Corporation and American Telephone and Telegraph (AT&T) raced to enter the market. Westinghouse engineer Frank Conrad received a license for what is viewed as the first modern radio station, KDKA, in Pittsburgh, Pennsylvania. KDKA broadcast music programs, the 1920 presidential election, and sports events. The next year, Westinghouse began to sell radio sets for as little as $25. By 1924, the radio-listening public numbered 20 million.

Meanwhile, as early as 1929, Vladimir Kosma Zworykin, a Soviet immigrant employed by Westinghouse, was experimenting with visual images to create an all-electronic television system. By 1939, the system was demonstrated at the New York's World Fair with none other than President Franklin D. Roosevelt speaking before the camera. World War II and battles over government regulation and AM and FM frequencies interrupted the introduction of television to the American public, but by 1944, the government had determined specific frequencies for both FM radio and television.

In 1946, there were 6,000 television sets in use; by 1951, the number had risen to an astonishing 12 million sets. The stage had been set for a battle between radio and television. In the ensuing years, expert after expert predicted the demise of radio. The popularity of television, with its soap operas, family dramas, and game shows, was believed by nearly everyone to be too strong a competitor for the old-fashioned, sound-only aspect of radio. The experts were proved wrong; radio continues to flourish.

The national radio networks of the early days are gone, but satellites allow local stations to broadcast network shows anywhere with the equipment to receive the satellite link. The development of filmed and video-recorded television, cable, and satellite transmissions, Internet radio and television stations, broadcasting deregulation, and an international market through direct broadcast satellite systems has drastically changed the face and future of both radio and television.

Today's sports broadcasters in radio and television have all these technological tools and more at their fingertips. Want to see an instant replay of the game-winning three-point shot by LeBron James? As the sportscaster describes it, a technician is playing it back for the viewing public. Have to travel to Costa Rica for a business trip, but hate to miss that Yankees game? No problem. A sportscaster is giving the play-by-play to an AM network station that is, in turn, sending it via satellite to a Costa Rican client-station.

■ THE JOB

One of the primary jobs of most sportscasters for both radio and television stations is to determine what sports news to carry during a news segment. The sportscaster begins working on the first broadcast by reading the sports-related stories that come in over the various news wire services, such as Associated Press and United Press International. To follow up on one of these stories, the sportscaster might telephone several contacts, such as a coach, scout, or athlete, to see if he or she can get a comment or more information. The sportscaster also might want to prepare a list of upcoming games, matches, and other sports events. Athletes often make public appearances for charity events and the sportscaster might want to include a mention of the charity and the participating athlete or athletes.

After deciding which stories to cover and the lineup of the stories that will be featured in the first of the day's broadcasts, sportscasters then review any audio or video clips that will accompany the various stories. Sportscasters working for radio stations choose audio

QUICK FACTS

ALTERNATE TITLE(S)
Baseball Announcers, Sportscasters

DUTIES
Provide coverage of sporting events for the sports segment of radio and television news broadcasts or for specific sports events, channels, or shows (broadcasters); make announcements during live sporting events (announcers)

SALARY RANGE
$18,000 to $46,410 to $86,780+

WORK ENVIRONMENT
Indoors/Outdoors

BEST GEOGRAPHIC LOCATION(S)
Opportunities are available throughout the country, but are best in large, urban areas

MINIMUM EDUCATION LEVEL
Some Postsecondary Training

SCHOOL SUBJECTS
English, Journalism, Speech

EXPERIENCE
Several years experience needed

PERSONALITY TRAITS
Athletic, Outgoing, Talkative

SKILLS
Interpersonal, Performance, Music, and Acting, Public Speaking

CERTIFICATION OR LICENSING
Recommended

SPECIAL REQUIREMENTS
None

EMPLOYMENT PROSPECTS
Fair

ADVANCEMENT PROSPECTS
Fair

OUTLOOK
Little Change or More Slowly than the Average

NOC
5231

O*NET-SOC
27-3011.00, 27-3012.00

CAREER LADDER

Sports Broadcaster or Announcer in a
Large Media Market

Sports Broadcaster or Announcer in a
Medium-Sized Media Market

Sports Broadcaster or Announcer in a
Small Media Market

Sports Copywriter

clips, usually interviews, that augment the piece of news they will read. Sportscasters working for television stations look for video footage—the best 10 seconds of this game or that play—to demonstrate why a certain team lost or won. Sometimes sportscasters choose footage that is humorous or poignant to illustrate the point of the news item.

After they decide which audio or video segments to use, sportscasters then work with sound or video editors to edit the data into a reel or video, or they edit the footage into an audio or video clip themselves. In either case, the finished product will be handed over to the news director or producer with a script detailing when it should play. The news producer or director will make certain that the reel or video comes in on cue during the broadcast.

Frequently a sportscaster will make brief appearances at local sports events to interview coaches and players before and after the game, and sometimes during breaks in the action. These interviews, as well as any footage of the game that the station's camera crews obtain, are then added to the stock from which sportscasters choose for their segments.

Usually, the main broadcast for both radio and television sportscasters is the late-evening broadcast following the evening's scheduled programming. This is when most of the major league sports events have concluded, the statistics for the game are released, and final official scores are reported. Any changes that have occurred since the day's first sports broadcast are updated and new footage or sound bites are added. The final newscast for a television sportscaster will most likely include highlights from the day's sports events, especially dramatic shots of the most impressive plays or winning points scored.

In televised sports news the emphasis is on image. Often sportscasters, like other newscasters, are only on camera for several seconds at a time, but their voices continue over the video that highlights unique moments in different games.

For many sportscasters who work in television, preparing the daily sportscasts is their main job and takes up most of their time. For others, especially sportscasters who work in radio, delivering a play-by-play broadcast of particular sports events is the main focus of their job. These men and women use their knowledge of the game

or sport to create a visual picture of the game for radio listeners with words, as it is happening. The most common sports for which sportscasters deliver play-by-play broadcasts are baseball, basketball, football, hockey, and soccer. A few sportscasters broadcast horse races from the racetrack and sometimes these broadcasts are carried by off-track betting facilities.

Sportscasters who give the play-by-play for a basketball game, for example, usually arrive an hour or so before the start of the game. Often they have a pre-game show that features interviews with, and a statistical review of, the competing teams and athletes. To broadcast a basketball game, sportscasters sit courtside in a special media section so that they can see the action up close. During football, baseball, hockey, and soccer games sportscasters usually sit in one of the nearby media boxes. Throughout the game sportscasters narrate each play for radio listeners using rapid, precise, and lively descriptions. During timeouts, halftimes, or other breaks in play, sportscasters might deliver their own running commentaries of the game, the players' performances, and the coaching.

A sportscaster who specializes in play-by-play broadcasts needs to have an excellent mastery of the rules, players, and statistics of a sport, as well as the hand signals officials use to regulate the flow of a game. Some sportscasters provide play-by-play broadcasts for several different teams or sports, from college to professional levels, requiring them to know more than one sport or team well.

Some sportscasters, who are often former athletes or established sports personalities, combine two aspects of the job. They act as *anchors* or *co-anchors* for sports shows and give some play-by-play commentary. They may also provide their television or radio audience with statistics and general updates.

Sports announcers provide spectators with public address announcements before and during a sports event. For this job, announcers must remain utterly neutral, simply delivering the facts—goals scored, numbers of fouls, or a time-out taken. Sports announcers may be sportscasters or they may be *professional announcers* or *emcees* who make their living recording voice-overs for radio and television commercials and for businesses or stores.

Sports announcers usually give the lineups for games, provide player names and numbers during specific times in a contest, make public announcements during time-outs and pauses in play, and generally keep the crowd involved in the event (especially in baseball). *Baseball announcers* may try to rally the crowd or start the crowd singing or doing the wave.

■ EARNINGS

Salaries in sportscasting vary, depending on the medium (radio or television), the market (large or small, commercial or public), and whether the sportscaster is a former athlete or recognized sports celebrity, as opposed to a newcomer trying to carve out a niche.

According to the U.S. Department of Labor, the average salary of radio and television announcers was $46,410 in May 2015. The lowest paid 10 percent earned $18,000 or less and the highest paid 10 percent earned $86,780 or more. Broadcasters for spectator sports reported mean annual earnings of $82,730.

Sportscasting jobs in radio tend to pay less than those in television. Beginners will find jobs more easily in smaller stations, but the pay will be correspondingly lower than it is in larger markets.

Salaries are usually higher for former athletes and recognized sports personalities or celebrities, such as ex-quarterback Terry Bradshaw. These individuals already have an established personality within the sports community and may thus have an easier time getting athletes and coaches to talk to them. Salaries for such recognizable personalities can be $2 million or more per year.

■ WORK ENVIRONMENT

Sportscasters usually work in clean, well-lit booths or sets in radio or television studios. They also work in special soundproof media rooms at the sports facility that hosts sports events.

Time constraints and deadlines can create havoc and add stress to an already stressful job; often a sportscaster has to race back to the studio to make the final evening broadcast. Sportscasters who deliver play-by-play commentary for radio listeners have the very stressful job of describing everything going on in a game as it happens. They cannot take their eyes off the ball (or puck) and the players while the clock is running, and this can be nerve-wracking and stressful.

On the other hand, sportscasters are usually on a first-name basis with some of the most famous people in the world, namely, professional athletes. They quickly lose the star-struck quality that usually afflicts most spectators and must learn to ask well-developed, concise, and sometimes difficult questions of coaches and athletes.

Sports announcers usually sit in press boxes near the action so they can have a clear view of players and their numbers when announcing. Depending on the type of sport, this may be an enclosed area or they may be out in the open air. Sports announcers start announcing before the event begins and close the event with more announcements, but then are able to end their workday. Because sporting events are scheduled at many different

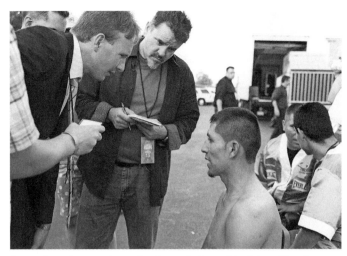

Sports broadcasters interview boxer before a big fight. (Randy Miramontez. Shutterstock.)

times of the day, announcers sometimes must be available at odd hours.

■ EXPLORING

High school and college students have many opportunities to investigate this career choice, but the most obvious way is to participate in a sport. By learning a sport inside and out, you can gain valuable insight into the movements and techniques that, as a sportscaster, you will be describing. In addition, firsthand experience and a love of the sport itself makes it easier to remember interesting trivia related to the sport and the names and numbers of the pros who play it.

If you do not have the coordination or skill for the sport itself, you can volunteer to help out with the team by shagging balls, running drills, or keeping statistics. The latter is perhaps the best way to learn the percentages and personal athletic histories of athletes.

An excellent way to develop the necessary communications skills is to take a journalism course, join the school's speech or debate team, deliver the morning announcements, work as a deejay on the school radio station, or volunteer at a local radio station or cable television station.

Finally, you can hone your sportscasting skills on your own while watching your favorite sports event by turning down the sound on your television and video-recording your own play-by-play deliveries.

■ EDUCATION AND TRAINING REQUIREMENTS
High School

Graduating from high school is an important first step on the road to becoming a sports broadcaster or announcer. While in school, take classes that will allow you to work

SUCCESSFUL SPORTSCASTING

LEARN MORE ABOUT IT

Lewin, Josh, and Josh Hamilton. *Ballgame!: A Decade Covering the Texas Rangers from the Best Seat in the House.* Chicago: Triumph Books, 2012.

Smith, Curt. *A Talk in the Park: Nine Decades of Baseball Tales from the Broadcast Booth.* Dulles, Va.: Potomac Books, Inc., 2011.

Vitale, Dick, and Dick Weiss. *Dick Vitale's Living A Dream: Reflections on 25 Years Sitting in the Best Seat in the House.* New York: Sports Publishing, 2013.

Wolff, Bob. *Bob Wolff's Complete Guide to Sportscasting: How to Make It in Sportscasting With or Without Talent.* New York: Skyhorse Publishing, 2011.

Zumoff, Marc, and Max Negin. *Total Sportscasting: Performance, Production, and Career Development.* New York: Focal Press, 2014.

on your speaking and writing skills. Classes in speech, English, journalism, and foreign languages, such as Spanish and French, will be helpful. You may also find it helpful to take courses in drama and computer science.

Postsecondary Training

Educational requirements for sportscasting positions vary depending on the position. Competition for radio and television sports broadcasting positions is especially fierce, so any added edge can make the difference.

Television sportscasters who deliver the news in sports usually have bachelor's degrees in communications, broadcasting, or journalism. However, personality, charisma, and overall on-camera appearance are so important to ratings that station executives often pay closer attention to the audition recordings they receive from prospective sportscasters than to the items on resumes. Prepare for the job by learning a sport inside and out, developing valuable contacts in the field through internships and part-time or volunteer jobs, and earning a degree in journalism or communications. It also should be noted that the industry is finicky and subjective about looks and charisma.

It is not as crucial for sportscasters who deliver play-by-play broadcasts for radio stations to have the journalistic skills that a television sportscaster has, although good interviewing skills are essential. Instead, they need excellent verbal skills, a daunting command of the sport or sports that they will be covering, and a familiarity with the competing players, coaches, and team histories. To draw a complete picture for their listeners, sportscasters often reach back into history for an interesting detail or statistic, so a good memory for statistics and trivia involving sports history are helpful.

■ CERTIFICATION, LICENSING, AND SPECIAL REQUIREMENTS
Certification or Licensing
The National Association of Sports Public Address Announcers offers certification to announcers who complete an online exam. Contact the association for more information.

■ EXPERIENCE, SKILLS, AND PERSONALITY TRAITS
At least several years experience is needed to work as a broadcaster or announcer for a professional sports team. Aspiring broadcasters and announcers typically start out with minor-league sports teams, gradually gaining enough experience to become qualified to work at the professional level.

A nice speaking voice, excellent verbal and interviewing skills, a pleasant appearance, a solid command of sports in general as well as in-depth knowledge of the most popular sports (football, basketball, baseball, hockey, and soccer), and an outgoing personality are all necessary for a successful career in sportscasting.

In addition, you need to have a strong voice, excellent grammar and English usage, and the ability to ad-lib if and when it is necessary.

■ EMPLOYMENT PROSPECTS
Employers
Most sports broadcasters work for television networks or radio stations. The large sports networks also employ many broadcasters. Radio sportscasters are hired by radio stations that range from small stations to mega-stations.

Sports announcers work for professional sports arenas, sports teams, minor league and major league ball teams, colleges and universities, and high schools. Because sports are popular all over the country, there are opportunities everywhere, although the smaller the town, the fewer the opportunities.

Starting Out
Although an exceptional audition recording might land you an on-camera or on-air job, most sportscasters get their start by writing copy, answering phones, operating cameras or equipment, or assisting the sportscaster with other jobs. Internships or part-time jobs will give you the opportunity to become comfortable in front of a camera or behind a microphone. Of course, contacts within the industry come in handy. In many cases, it is simply an

individual's devotion to the sport and the job that makes the difference—that and being in the right place at the right time.

Put together an audio recording (if you are applying for a radio job or an announcer position) or a video (for television jobs) that showcases your abilities. On the recording, give your account of the sports events that took place on a certain day.

ADVANCEMENT PROSPECTS

In the early stages of their careers, sportscasters might advance from a *sports copywriter* position to become an actual broadcaster. Later in their careers, sportscasters advance by moving to larger and larger markets, beginning with local television stations and advancing to one of the major networks.

Sportscasters who work in radio may begin in a similar way; advancement for these individuals might come in the form of a better time slot for a sports show, or the chance to give more commentary.

Sports announcers advance by adding to the number of teams for whom they provide public address announcements. Some sports announcers also may start out working for colleges and minor leagues and then move up to major league work.

OUTLOOK

The U.S. Department of Labor's predicts that employment for sports announcers will grow by 5 percent through 2024, or more slowly than the average for all careers. Few new radio and television stations are expected to enter the market, and most job openings will come as sportscasters leave the market to retire, relocate, or enter other professions. In general, employment in this field is not affected by economic recessions or declines; in the event of cutbacks, the on-camera sports broadcasters and announcers are the last to go.

Competition for jobs in sportscasting will continue to be fierce, with the better paying jobs in larger markets going to experienced sportscasters who have proven they can keep ratings high. Sportscasters who can easily substitute for other on-camera newscasters or anchors may be more employable.

Employment of announcers in general is projected to shrink 11 percent through 2024. This is a small occupational field, and only the most skilled and experienced announcers will land jobs with professional sports teams.

UNIONS AND ASSOCIATIONS

Union membership may be required for employment with large stations in major cities. The largest talent union is SAG-AFTRA. Some sports broadcasters and announcers may also be members of the National Association of Broadcast Employees and Technicians. Most small stations and minor league sports teams, however, hire nonunion workers. Membership organizations for announcers include the American Sportscasters Association, Association for Women in Sports Media, and the National Association of Sports Public Address Announcers. These organizations provide mentoring and internship programs, scholarships, publications, and networking opportunities. Other useful organizations for announcers include the Broadcast Education Association, the National Association of Broadcasters, and the Radio Television Digital News Association. The Federal Communications Commission regulates interstate and international communications by radio, television, satellite, cable, and wire in all 50 states, the District of Columbia, and U.S. territories.

TIPS FOR ENTRY

1. Work on your high school or college radio station to obtain experience.
2. Contact sports teams to inquire about internship opportunities. Additionally, the Association for Women in Sports Media offers an internship program that has placed more than 120 female college students interested in sports media careers in paid internships. Visit http://awsmonline.org/internship-scholarship for more information.
3. Make a demo recording of your work as a sports announcer and submit it to sports teams.
4. Visit http://www.americansportscastersonline.com/jobbank.html and https://www.naspaa.net for job listings.
5. For a small fee, you can submit a demo recording of your work to the National Association of Sports Public Address Announcers' Announcers' Critique and Evaluation Service. This is a great way to assess your skill level and receive suggestions to improve your delivery (tone, pitch, pace, etc.).

FOR MORE INFORMATION

To read more about the sportscasting field, including current news, interviews with working professionals, and profiles of all-time sportscasting greats, visit

American Sportscasters Association
225 Broadway, Suite 2030
New York, NY 10007-3742
Tel: (212) 227-8080
Fax: (212) 571-0556
E-mail: inquiry@americansportscastersonline.com
http://www.americansportscastersonline.com

For information on membership and its internship program, contact
Association for Women in Sports Media
7742 Spalding Drive, #377
Norcross, GA 30092-4207
E-mail: info@awsmonline.org
http://awsmonline.org

For a list of schools that offer programs and courses in broadcasting, contact
Broadcast Education Association (BEA)
1771 N Street, NW
Washington, D.C. 20036-2891
Tel: (202) 602-0584
Fax: (202) 609-9940
E-mail: HELP@BEAweb.org
http://www.beaweb.org

For information on FCC licenses, contact
Federal Communications Commission (FCC)
445 12th Street, SW
Washington, D.C. 20554-0004
Tel: (888) 225-5322
Fax: (888) 418-0232
http://www.fcc.gov

To get general information about broadcasting, contact
National Association of Broadcasters
1771 N Street, NW
Washington, D.C. 20036-2800
Tel: (202) 429-5300
E-mail: nab@nab.org
http://www.nab.org

For information on certification, mentoring, membership, and careers, visit
National Association of Sports Public Address Announcers
E-mail: brumble@naspaa.net
https://www.naspaa.net

For scholarship and internship information, contact
Radio Television Digital News Association (RTDNA)
529 14th Street, NW, Suite 425
Washington, D.C. 20045-2520
Fax: (202) 223-4007
http://www.rtnda.org

For information on union membership, contact
SAG-AFTRA
5757 Wilshire Boulevard, 7th Floor
Los Angeles, CA 90036-3600
Tel: (855) 724-2387; (312) 954-1600
E-mail: sagaftrainfo@sagaftra.org
http://www.sagaftra.org

Sports Equipment Managers

■ OVERVIEW

Sports equipment managers are responsible for maintaining, ordering, and inventorying athletic equipment and apparel. They deal with everything from fitting football shoulder pads to sharpening hockey skates to doing the team's laundry. The majority of equipment managers employed in the United States work for collegiate and high school teams.

■ HISTORY

Sports cannot be played without using some sort of equipment. Keeping that equipment in good working condition and safe for players to use is the job of equipment managers. One of the major reasons for the emergence of professional equipment managers was the need for qualified athletic personnel to fit football helmets, according to the Athletic Equipment Managers Association (AEMA). It was not until the advent of the plastic shell helmet, which contributed to a more intense-contact game, that the number of injuries in sports rose. The National Operating Committee on Standards for Athletic Equipment began developing standards for football helmets. This increased attention also focused on the need for properly fitted equipment and specially trained personnel to perform the sizing.

■ THE JOB

The responsibilities of equipment managers vary greatly, depending on whether they work for high schools, colleges, universities, or professional teams. Duties are also different from sport to sport, because some have more participants than others. Sports equipment managers at the collegiate level may be responsible for budgeting for all of the university's sports and requisitioning of equipment; some may steer clear of the finances and focus on fitting football equipment and doing laundry. Other duties include purchasing, maintenance, administration and organization, management, professional relations and education, and keeping inventory of all the equipment.

Sports equipment managers are responsible for ordering all the equipment (including uniforms) for their team or school's sports programs. Once the equipment arrives, they make sure that it properly fits each player. Poorly fitting equipment or uniforms can cause discomfort, a lack of mobility, a reduction of vision or hearing, and even injury. After use, equipment managers keep the equipment in good working order. They inspect and clean each piece of equipment to ensure that it meets safety standards. Equipment managers are also responsible for equipment control, which includes pre- and postseason inventory, use, and storage.

Equipment managers need good communication and personnel management skills because they work with coaches, athletic directors, and their staffs.

■ EARNINGS

Average annual earnings for sports equipment managers were $42,000, according to Simplyhired.com. Equipment managers' salaries depend a great deal on if they work for a professional team or the local high school as well as seniority and ranged from $28,000 to $65,000. Depending on their employers, most full-time sports equipment managers enjoy a full complement of benefits, including vacation and sick time as well as holidays and medical and dental insurance.

■ WORK ENVIRONMENT

Equipment managers spend most of their time in schools or in professional team offices during the off-season. Travel is generally limited to football equipment managers, but some schools might have the equipment manager travel with the basketball team.

Equipment managers who work for professional teams usually travel with those teams and coordinate shipping of their team's gear to each game site. Some football equipment managers might also travel to training camp.

■ EXPLORING

One great way to obtain experience is to work as an assistant to your high school's sports equipment manager. Talk to equipment managers about their careers. Questions to ask include: What do you like and dislike about your career? What high school and college classes should I take to prepare for this career? What's the best way to break into this field?

■ EDUCATION AND TRAINING REQUIREMENTS
High School

High school courses that will be helpful include computer science, mathematics, and business. Serving as the equipment manager of one of your high school athletic teams or clubs will give you a great introduction to work in this field.

Postsecondary Training

Many equipment managers have completed at least some postsecondary training. Business and accounting classes can help you prepare to handle equipment budgets and negotiate contracts with manufacturers such as Nike, Reebok, and Adidas. Other recommended classes include computer science, mathematics, English, and speech.

Other Education or Training

To maintain their certification, sports equipment managers must complete continuing education classes and workshops. These opportunities are provided by the Athletic Equipment Managers Association at its annual convention and other events. Contact the association for more information.

■ CERTIFICATION, LICENSING, AND SPECIAL REQUIREMENTS
Certification or Licensing

The Athletic Equipment Managers Association (AEMA) began a professional certification program in 1991. To become a professional equipment manager, applicants must meet one of the following criteria: (1) have a high school/GED degree and five years of paid, nonstudent employment in athletic equipment management; (2) have a four-year college degree and two years paid, nonstudent employment in athletic equipment management; or (3) have a four-year college degree and 1,400 hours as a student equipment manager. They also must be 21 years of age and be a member in good standing with the AEMA. Once these requirements have been met, candidates must take and

QUICK FACTS

ALTERNATE TITLE(S)
None

DUTIES
Maintain, order, and inventory athletic equipment and apparel for high school, college, and professional sports teams

SALARY RANGE
$28,000 to $42,000 to $65,000

WORK ENVIRONMENT
Indoors/Outdoors

BEST GEOGRAPHIC LOCATION(S)
Opportunities exist in all regions

MINIMUM EDUCATION LEVEL
High School Diploma

SCHOOL SUBJECTS
Business, Mathematics, Physical Education

EXPERIENCE
Assistant equipment manager experience required

PERSONALITY TRAITS
Conventional, Hands On, Organized

SKILLS
Business Management, Interpersonal, Organizational

CERTIFICATION OR LICENSING
Recommended

SPECIAL REQUIREMENTS
None

EMPLOYMENT PROSPECTS
Fair

ADVANCEMENT PROSPECTS
Fair

OUTLOOK
About as Fast as the Average

NOC
6722

O*NET-SOC
N/A

CAREER LADDER

Athletic Director

Equipment Manager, Professional Sports Team

Equipment Manager, College Sports Team

Equipment Manager, High School

Assistant Equipment Manager

pass a certification examination. The certification process also includes continuing education, such as annual conventions, workshops, seminars, and meetings.

■ EXPERIENCE, SKILLS, AND PERSONALITY TRAITS

Few people are hired for head equipment manager jobs without first obtaining experience as an assistant equipment manager or working in related positions.

Excellent organizational skills and the ability to get along with many people are critical qualities for equipment managers. Managers must also be able to handle criticism, be creative and responsible, and have some basic computer skills. Sports equipment managers must also be willing to work overtime during the relevant sport's season.

■ EMPLOYMENT PROSPECTS
Employers

High schools, colleges, universities, and professional sports teams throughout the country hire equipment managers, although the number of positions with professional teams is limited, and they are very difficult to

obtain. Several sports need the help of equipment managers, including football, basketball, baseball, hockey, and lacrosse.

Starting Out

Some equipment managers began exploring the field in high school, where they served as volunteers for their sports teams. Others worked in that position in college, which is helpful for developing contacts for potential employment after graduation. An assistant equipment manager might start out doing a team's laundry or helping to fit shoes and helmets for a particular sport, advance to ordering equipment for all the sports, and finally help with budgeting and contracts with athletic equipment suppliers.

■ ADVANCEMENT PROSPECTS

Sports equipment managers can be promoted to more advanced positions in the athletic department, including athletic director and administrative assistant, and some can land positions with sporting goods companies. In this industry, it is important to work your way up through the system.

■ OUTLOOK

For college and university equipment managers, the profession is changing and growing significantly. Athletic Equipment Managers Association certification has led to greater acceptance of the need for skilled equipment managers on the part of athletic directors and other administrators. The addition of computerized inventory programs, university-wide contracts with dealers, and the high-stakes business atmosphere of athletics have increased demands on equipment managers as they are being called on to broaden their skill sets. Qualified equipment managers will be needed to meet these challenges. The Bureau of Labor Statistics forecasts 6 percent growth for the closely related professions of coaches and sports scouts, suggesting equipment managers will experience average employment growth through 2024.

■ UNIONS AND ASSOCIATIONS

Sports equipment managers do not belong to unions. The Athletic Equipment Managers Association is a membership organization for equipment managers. It offers certification, continuing education classes and workshops, networking opportunities, and publications. The National Operating Committee on Standards for Athletic Equipment seeks to reduce the number of injuries in athletics by developing performance standards for protective equipment used in a variety of sports.

PUTTING FOOTBALL HELMETS TO THE TEST
DID YOU KNOW?

According to the National Operating Committee on Standards for Athletic Equipment, standard safety testing for football helmets includes mounting the helmet on a synthetic head and dropping, which is then dropped at predetermined speeds onto steel anvil padded with rubber. The full test requires 29 impacts. Of these, 16 are done at 12.2 mph against six selected locations on the helmet and one random point. Additional impacts occur at lower speeds or at higher temperatures. These circumstances are intended to exceed conditions players encounter on the field to assure safety. A helmet's protection deteriorates with use, giving most football helmets a limited lifespan. In some cases they may be reconditioned, pass testing, and put back into play.

■ TIPS FOR ENTRY

1. Join the Athletic Equipment Managers Association to receive member-only access to online forums and educational opportunities, publications, and other resources. Student (high school and college) and professional memberships are available.
2. Visit http://equipmentmanagers.org/community/ad-jobs for job listings.
3. Talk with sports equipment managers about their careers. Ask them for advice on landing your first job.

■ FOR MORE INFORMATION

For information on scholarships and certification, contact

Athletic Equipment Managers Association
207 E. Bodman
Bement, IL 61813
Tel: (217) 678-1004
Fax: (217) 678-1005
http://equipmentmanagers.org

For information on sports equipment standards, contact

National Operating Committee on Standards for Athletic Equipment
11020 King Street, Suite 215
Overland Park, KS 66210-1201
Tel: (913) 888-1340
Fax: (913) 498-8817
E-mail: Mike.Oliver@NOCSAE.ORG
http://www.nocsae.org

Sports Executives

■ OVERVIEW

Sports executives, sometimes known as *team presidents*, *CEOs*, and *general managers*, oversee the business operations of professional, collegiate, and minor league sports teams. They are responsible for the teams' finances, as well as overseeing the other departments within the organization, such as marketing, public relations, accounting, ticket sales, advertising, sponsorship, and community relations. Sports executives also work on establishing long-term contacts and support within the communities where the teams play.

■ HISTORY

The sports industry has matured into one of the largest industries in the United States. Professional teams are the most widely recognized industry segment in sports. Professional teams include all of the various sports teams, leagues, and governing bodies for which

individuals get paid for their performance. Some of the most notable organizations include the National Football League, National Basketball Association, National Hockey League, and Major League Baseball. These are commonly known as the four majors. During recent decades, more professional leagues have started, such as the Women's National Basketball League, the Arena Football League, and Major League Soccer. There are also many minor league and collegiate organizations.

■ THE JOB

The two top positions in most sports organizations are *team president* and *general manager*. Depending on the size of the franchise, these two positions might be blended together and held by one person.

Team presidents are the chief executive officers of the club. They are responsible for the overall financial success of the team. Presidents oversee several departments within the organization, including marketing, public relations, broadcasting, sales, advertising, ticket sales, community relations, and accounting. Since team presidents must develop strategies to encourage fans to attend games, it is good if they have some experience in public relations or marketing. Along with the public relations manager, team presidents create giveaway programs, such as cap days or poster nights.

Another one of the team president's responsibilities is encouraging community relations by courting season ticket holders, as well as those who purchase luxury box seats, known as skyboxes. Usually, this involves selling these seats to corporations.

QUICK FACTS

ALTERNATE TITLE(S)
Chief Executive Officers, General Managers, Team Presidents

DUTIES
Oversee the business operations of professional, collegiate, and minor league sports teams

SALARY RANGE
$20,000 to $110,140 to $1 million+

WORK ENVIRONMENT
Primarily Indoors

BEST GEOGRAPHIC LOCATION(S)
Opportunities are available throughout the country

MINIMUM EDUCATION LEVEL
Bachelor's Degree

SCHOOL SUBJECTS
Business, Mathematics, Physical Education

EXPERIENCE
At least ten years experience required

PERSONALITY TRAITS
Enterprising, Organized, Problem-Solving

SKILLS
Business Management, Financial, Leadership

CERTIFICATION OR LICENSING
None

SPECIAL REQUIREMENTS
None

EMPLOYMENT PROSPECTS
Fair

ADVANCEMENT PROSPECTS
Fair

OUTLOOK
Little Change or More Slowly than the Average

NOC
0513

O*NET-SOC
11-1011.00, 11-1021.00

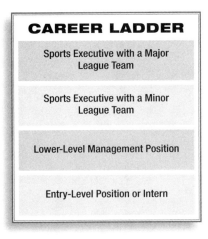

CAREER LADDER

Sports Executive with a Major League Team

Sports Executive with a Minor League Team

Lower-Level Management Position

Entry-Level Position or Intern

General managers handle the daily business activities of the teams, such as hiring and firing, promotions, supervising the scouting department, making trades, and negotiating player contracts. Of course, general managers who are employed by professional sports teams have marketing, finance, and human resources experts that assist them in these and other duties. All sports teams have general managers, and usually the main functions of the job are the same regardless of the team's professional level. However, some general managers that work with minor league teams might also deal with additional job duties, including managing the souvenir booths or organizing the ticket offices. The most important asset the general manager brings to an organization is knowledge of business practices.

■ EARNINGS

General managers, team presidents, and other sports executives may earn salaries that range from $68,600 to more than $187,200 per year. Those in the minor leagues earn far less, only $20,000 to $50,000 while star managers can top 1 million in the majors. According to the U.S. Department of Labor, general and operations managers for sports organizations earned average annual salaries of $110,140 in May 2015. Chief executive officers earned an average of $217,280 while earnings for managers of departments, such as advertising, human resources, marketing, and sales ranged between $100,000 and $125,000.

Most sports executives are eligible for typical fringe benefits including medical and dental insurance, paid sick days and vacation time, and access to retirement savings plans.

■ WORK ENVIRONMENT

Sports executives work mostly in offices. Sports team management is a fickle industry. When a team is winning, everyone loves the general manager or team president. When the team is losing, fans and the media often take out their frustrations on the team's executives. Sports executives must be able to handle that pressure. This industry is extremely competitive, and executives might find themselves without a job several times in their careers. Sports executives sleep, eat, and breathe their jobs, and definitely love the sports they manage.

■ EXPLORING

One way to start exploring this field is to volunteer to do something for your school's sports teams, for example, chart statistics or take on the duties of equipment manager. This is a way to begin learning how athletic departments work. Talk to the general manager of your local minor league baseball club, and try to get a part-time job with the team during the summer. When you are in college, try to get an internship within the athletic department to supplement your course of study. Any experience you gain in any area of sports administration will be valuable to you in your career as a sports executive. You may also find it helpful to read publications such as *Sports Business Journal* (http://www.sportsbusinessjournal.com).

■ EDUCATION AND TRAINING REQUIREMENTS
High School

High school courses that will help you to become a sports executive include business, mathematics, and computer science. English, speech, and physical education courses will also be beneficial. Managing a school club or other organization will give you a general idea of the responsibilities and demands that this career involves.

Postsecondary Training

To become a sports executive, you will need at least a bachelor's degree. Remember, even though this is a sport-related position, presidents and general managers are expected to have the same backgrounds as corporate executives. Most have master's degrees in sports administration, and some have master's degrees in business administration. Typical classes in a sports administration program include Fundamentals of Sport Marketing, Sport Facility and Event Management, Finance and Economics of Sport, and the Legal Aspects of Sport.

Visit http://www.nassm.com/Programs/Academic Programs for a list of colleges and universities that offer degrees in sports management.

■ CERTIFICATION, LICENSING, AND SPECIAL REQUIREMENTS
Certification or Licensing

There are no certification or licensing requirements for sports executives.

■ EXPERIENCE, SKILLS, AND PERSONALITY TRAITS

Sports executives are the all-stars of the sports management world, and it takes many years of experience (some might call it time honing one's skills in the minor leagues) to reach this career pinnacle. You should first participate in at least one internship while in college to obtain enough experience to be hired for entry-level positions in the sports industry. Once hired, you'll need to work three to five years in a support position to qualify for a management-level job, and then about seven years in that position to be considered for executive-level jobs. These experience requirements pertain to jobs at top professional levels; aspiring executives in the minor leagues often need less experience.

Sports executives must create a positive image for their teams. In this age of extensive media coverage (including the frequent public speaking engagements that are required of sports executives), excellent communications skills are a must. Sports executives need to be dynamic public speakers. They also need a keen business sense, excellent leadership skills, and an intimate knowledge of how to forge a good relationship with their communities. They also should have excellent organizational skills, be detail oriented, and be sound decision makers.

■ EMPLOYMENT PROSPECTS
Employers
Employers include professional, collegiate, and minor-league football, hockey, baseball, basketball, soccer, and other sports teams. They are located across the United States and the world.

Starting Out
A majority of all sports executives begin their careers as interns. Interning offers the opportunity to gain recognition in an otherwise extremely competitive industry. Internships vary in length and generally include college credits. They are available in hundreds of sports categories and are offered by more than 90 percent of existing sports organizations. If you are serious about working in the sports industry, an internship is the most effective method of achieving your goals.

Entry-level positions in the sports industry are generally reserved for individuals with intern or volunteer experience. Once you have obtained this experience, you are eligible for thousands of entry-level positions in hundreds of sports-related fields. Qualified employees are hard to find in any industry, so the experience you have gained through internships will prove invaluable at this stage of your career.

■ ADVANCEMENT PROSPECTS
The experience prerequisite to qualify for a management-level position is generally three to five years in a specific field within the sports industry. At this level, an applicant should have experience managing a small to medium-sized staff and possess specific skills, including marketing, public relations, broadcasting, sales, advertising, publications, sports medicine, licensing, and specific sport player development.

The minimum experience to qualify for an executive position is generally seven years. Executives with proven track records in the minors can be promoted to positions in the majors. Major league executives might receive promotions in the form of job offers from more prestigious teams.

■ OUTLOOK
The U.S. Department of Labor predicts that employment for chief executives in the sports industry will decline almost 6 percent through 2024 while jobs for general managers are forecast to grow by almost 5 percent, about as fast as the average for all jobs.

Although there are more sports executive positions available due to league expansion and the creation of new leagues, only a limited number of positions exist, and the competition for these jobs is very fierce. Being a sports executive demands both above-average business and leadership skills, in addition to a solid understanding of the demands and intricacies of a professional sports team. Those who obtain these jobs usually do so after many years of hard work. For that same reason, the rate of turnover in this field is low.

■ UNIONS AND ASSOCIATIONS
Sports executives are not represented by unions, but some may join the North American Society for Sport Management, which represents professionals working in the fields of sport, leisure, and recreation.

INSIDE SPORTS MANAGEMENT · LEARN MORE ABOUT IT

Carson, Mike. *The Manager: Inside the Minds of Football's Leaders.* New York: Bloomsbury Publishing, 2013.

Hoye, Russell, et al. *Sport Management: Principles and Applications,* 3rd ed. New York: Routledge, 2012.

Lussier, Robert, and David Kimball. *Applied Sport Management Skills,* 2nd ed. Champaign, Ill.: Human Kinetics, 2013.

Masteralexis, Lisa P., Carol Barr, and Mary Hums. *Principles and Practice of Sports Management,* 4th ed. Burlington, Mass.: Jones and Bartlett Learning, 2011.

■ TIPS FOR ENTRY

1. Read the *Journal of Sport Management* (http://www.nassm.com/Journals/JSM) and *Sports Business Journal* (http://www.sportsbusinessjournal.com) to learn more about the field.
2. Visit http://www.teamworkonline.com for job listings.
3. Try to land an entry-level job in the sports industry to build your skills and make networking contacts.

■ FOR MORE INFORMATION

Visit the society's Web site for information on membership for college students and a list of colleges and universities that offer sports management programs.

North American Society for Sport Management
135 Winterwood Drive
Butler, PA 16001-7335
Tel: (724) 482-6277
E-mail: businessoffice@nassm.com
http://www.nassm.com

To learn more about sports executives, contact
Teamwork Online LLC
22550 McCauley Road
Shaker Heights, OH 44122-2718
Tel: (216) 360-1790
E-mail: info@teamworkonline.com
http://www.teamworkonline.com

Sports Facility Managers

■ OVERVIEW

Sports facility managers, sometimes called *arena managers, stadium managers, general managers,* or *stadium operations executives,* are responsible for the day-to-day operations involved in running a sports facility. They are involved in sports facility planning, including the buying, selling, or leasing of facilities; facility redesign and construction; and the supervision of sports facilities, including the structures and grounds, as well as the custodial crews. In 2015, the indoor sports facilities management industry consisted of more than 3,800 businesses and generated about $900 million in revenue, as reported by the market research group IBISWorld.

■ HISTORY

Sports date back to ancient Greece and Rome, when athletic games were performed in arenas to entertain the crowds. Today's stadiums or arenas provide much more than a playing field and seats for sports and event spectators. The modern sports facility usually has one or more of the following: practice areas, home and visiting team locker rooms, physical therapy areas, sports equipment storage, press rooms, press boxes, facility maintenance equipment storage, cafeterias, food vendor areas, upscale restaurants, and offices for those who run the various aspects of the facility and teams who play there. Those who manage these venues for sports events are responsible for ensuring that everything runs smoothly for the athletes, the fans, the advertisers, the media, and their own staff.

According to the International Facility Management Association (IFMA), the facility management profession was initially a job based on reactions: When something at the facility broke or wasn't working correctly, facility managers were called upon to assess, fix, and/or replace it. It was in the 1980s, when the IFMA was established, that the scope of the facility manager expanded. Today the job entails ensuring the proper operation of the facility, which includes focusing on sustainability and cost-effective environments that are compliant with corporate and government regulations.

■ THE JOB

Stadium, arena, and facility managers are responsible for the day-to-day operations involved in running a sports facility. In the simplest terms, the manager of a sports facility, like other facility managers, must coordinate the events that occur in the facility with the services and people who make those events possible.

The manager of a sports facility, stadium, or arena spends most of his or her time in the office or somewhere in the facility itself, supervising the day-to-day management of the facility. The manager usually determines the organizational structure of the facility and establishes the personnel staffing requirements, setting up the manner in which things will be done and by whom. The facility manager is constantly analyzing how many different workers are needed to run the various areas of the facility efficiently, without sacrificing quality. The manager addresses staffing needs as they arise, setting the education, experience, and performance standards for each position. Depending on the size of the facility and the nature of the manager's assigned responsibilities, they may hire a personnel director to screen prospective employees, or the manager personally screens job candidates when a position opens up. Usually, all policies and procedures having to do with the morale, safety, service, appearance, and performance of facility employees (and which are not determined by the organization itself) are determined by the manager.

The manager of a sports facility is also responsible for assisting with the development and coordination of the facility's annual operating calendar, including activity schedules, dates and hours of operation, and projections for attendance and revenue. Often, a manager for a sports facility directs and assists with the procurement of activities and events to take place at the facility, depending on the size of the facility. A large, multipurpose stadium, for example, will probably have at least one individual devoted to event planning and the acquisition of activities. Even in this case, however, the sports facility manager must be involved in coordinating the event with all the other aspects of the facility.

The sports facility manager handles the negotiations, contracts, and agreements with industry agents, suppliers, and vendors. Jobs that once were handled in-house by staff employees are now contracted out to private companies that specialize in that aspect of the event. Food service and security, for example, are two areas that are usually privately managed by outside vendors and firms. It is the responsibility of the sports facility manager to hire such contractors and to monitor the quality of their work.

Finally, it is the manager's duty to make certain that the facility, its workers, and the services it offers are in accordance with federal, state, and local regulations.

Although certain responsibilities are shared, the job description for a sports facility manager varies according to the type of sport played and the level of the organization that employs the manager. For example, the duties of a manager for a parks and recreation facility in a medium-sized town will differ considerably from those of the general manager of Churchill Downs in Louisville, Kentucky; the former will perform many of the duties that the latter would most likely delegate to others.

The type of sports stadium, arena, or auditorium in which sports facility managers work also varies, from race tracks to natatoriums to large, multipurpose stadiums that host football games and rock concerts.

Some sports facility managers may be involved with sports facility planning, including the buying, selling, or leasing of facilities; facility redesign and construction; and the supervision of sports facilities, including the structures and grounds, as well as the custodial crews. This may mean months, sometimes even years, of research and long-term planning. Crucial resources and issues the manager might investigate include: sports facility design firms; prospective sites for the new facility and analyses of neighborhood support for a facility; and zoning laws or other federal, state, and local regulations concerning the construction of new buildings. Politics can play a key part in this process; the manager might be involved in these political meetings, as well. Once ground is broken on the new site, a sports facility manager may then divide his or her time between the construction site and the existing site, supervising both facilities until the new one is completed.

■ EARNINGS

Earnings for sports facility managers vary considerably depending on their experience and education, as well as the level of the facility that employs them. Administrative services managers (the category under which the U.S. Department of Labor classifies sports facility managers) earned median annual salaries of $86,110 in May 2015. The lowest paid 10 percent earned less than $46,430, and the highest paid 10 percent earned $153,570 or more per year. Facility managers who are certified earn higher salaries than those who are not certified.

Benefits for full-time workers include vacation and sick time, health, and sometimes dental, insurance, and pension or 401(k) plans.

■ WORK ENVIRONMENT

One of the perks of the profession is the glamorous atmosphere that the job promotes; sports facility managers work to provide a unique environment for amateur and professional athletes, sometimes even celebrities and other performers. Although their work most often is behind-the-scenes, they may have indirect or direct contact with the high-profile personalities who perform in large venues. Sports facility managers usually work in clean, comfortable offices. Their work often involves other activities, such as construction, so they may also spend a great deal of time on construction

QUICK FACTS

ALTERNATE TITLE(S)
Arena Managers, General Managers, Stadium Managers, Stadium Operations Executives

DUTIES
Oversee the day-to-day operations involved in running a sports facility; hire and oversee staff; may be involved in sports facility planning

SALARY RANGE
$46,430 to $86,110 to $153,570+

WORK ENVIRONMENT
Indoors/Outdoors

BEST GEOGRAPHIC LOCATION(S)
Metropolitan areas

MINIMUM EDUCATION LEVEL
Bachelor's Degree

SCHOOL SUBJECTS
Business, English, Mathematics

EXPERIENCE
Five years experience

PERSONALITY TRAITS
Hands On, Organized, Outgoing

SKILLS
Business Management, Interpersonal, Leadership

CERTIFICATION OR LICENSING
Recommended

SPECIAL REQUIREMENTS
None

EMPLOYMENT PROSPECTS
Fair

ADVANCEMENT PROSPECTS
Fair

OUTLOOK
About as Fast as the Average

NOC
0714

O*NET-SOC
11-3011.00

CAREER LADDER

Manager of Large Sports Facility or Multiple Facilities

Manager of Medium-Sized Sports Facility

Manager of Small Sports Facility

Assistant Manager

Administrative, Marketing, or Public Relations Position

sites and in trailers, supervising the construction of a new facility.

The management of a sports arena or stadium naturally involves promotional events, both for the building and the teams or events that are staged there. To be successful in their work, facility managers must maintain regular contact with the members of other departments, such as marketing and public relations.

A sports facility manager's job can be stressful. Construction, renovation, and cleaning and maintenance deadlines must all be met in order to ensure the efficient operation of a sports facility, let alone one in which major sports events occur. Depending on the level of the facility and the nature of events that are staged there, the responsibilities of the manager often require more hours on the job than the typical 9-to-5 day allows. Additional work may be necessary, but is often uncompensated.

■ EXPLORING

If you aren't actively involved with a sport as a participant, you can get involved with sports administration and management by volunteering for positions with your own high school teams. Any and all experience helps, beginning with organizing and managing the equipment for a football team, for example, all the way up to working as a team statistician. You can also work with their local booster club to sponsor events that promote athletics within the school district. These activities demonstrate your interest and devotion and may help you in the future by providing you with an edge when searching for an internship.

Part-time or summer jobs as ushers, vendors, ball boys or girls, for example, not only provide firsthand experience for both high school and college students, but can lead to other contacts and opportunities.

College students interested in sports facility management can often locate valuable internships through contacts they have developed from part-time jobs, but the placement centers in undergraduate or graduate programs in business administration and facility management are also good places to consult for information on internships. The professional leagues and associations for specific sports, the National Hockey

League, the National Football League, and the National Basketball Association, for example, all offer summer internships. Competition for positions with these organizations is keen, so interested students should send for application materials well in advance, study them, and apply early.

Professional organizations within the field also sponsor opportunities to learn on the job. The International Association of Venue Managers (IAVM) offers internships to qualified students. Typically, participating facilities that serve as sites for IAVM internships are responsible for the selection of their interns. While some of these facilities aren't specifically geared toward sporting events, much of the management skills and responsibilities are shared and will provide you with a wonderful opportunity to learn firsthand.

■ EDUCATION AND TRAINING REQUIREMENTS
High School

High school courses that provide a general background for work in sports facility management include business, mathematics, government, and computer science. Speech and writing classes will help hone communication skills. Managing a school club or other organization will give an introduction to overseeing budgets and the work of others.

Postsecondary Training

Most employers prefer to hire sports facility managers with a bachelor's degree. In the past it wasn't necessary, but the competition for jobs in sports administration and facility management is so keen that a bachelor's degree is nearly mandatory. In fact, in many instances, a master's degree in sports administration or sports facility management is increasingly required of managers.

Other Education or Training

The International Association of Venue Managers offers webinars, leadership institutes, and other professional development opportunities. The International Facility Management Association also provides continuing education classes. Contact these organizations for more information.

■ CERTIFICATION, LICENSING, AND SPECIAL REQUIREMENTS
Certification or Licensing

Certification in facility management is not mandatory but is becoming a distinguishing credential among the managers of the largest, most profitable venues. A sports stadium or arena brings its owners a lot of revenue, and these owners aren't willing to trust the management of such lucrative venues to individuals who are not qualified to run them; certification is one way an administration can ensure that certain industry standards in facility management are met. The International Facility Management Association, probably the industry leader in certification, offers the designations certified facility manager, facility management professional, and sustainability facility professional. The International Association of Venue Managers offers the certified facilities executive designation.

■ EXPERIENCE, SKILLS, AND PERSONALITY TRAITS

Most organizations want their facility managers to have, at a minimum, five years of experience in the field or industry. This may include participation in a sport at the professional level, marketing or promotions work, or related management experience that can be shown as relevant to the responsibilities and duties of a sports facility manager.

Successful sports facility managers have excellent strategic, budgetary, and operational planning skills; the day-to-day operations of the sports facility will run on their decisions, so they must be capable of juggling many different tasks.

Leadership and communication skills are also essential. In the course of an average day, sports facility managers might review designs for a new stadium with top-level executives, release a statement to members of the press about the groundbreaking ceremony for the new stadium, and interview prospective foremen for maintenance work. Solid communication skills are needed to clearly express their ideas and share information and goals, regardless of the audience.

■ EMPLOYMENT PROSPECTS
Employers

Sports facility managers may work for a single team, a multisports arena or stadium, or they may work for a city or state organization, such as a parks and recreation department. According to the market research group IBISWorld, there were approximately 3,834 indoor sports facilities management businesses, with 22,566 employees, in 2015.

Starting Out

Graduates of programs in sports administration and sports facility management usually find jobs through internships, personal contacts , or job listings in career services departments.

MANAGING SPORTS FACILITIES AND EVENTS — LEARN MORE ABOUT IT

Aicher, Thomas J., Amanda L. Paule-Koba, and Brianna Newland. *Sport Facility and Event Management.* Burlington, Mass.: Jones & Bartlett Learning, 2015.

Fried, Gil. *Managing Sports Facilities, 3rd ed.* Champaign, Ill.: Human Kinetics, 2015.

Hall, Stacey, Walter Cooper, Lou Marciani, and Jim McGee. *Security Management for Sports and Special Events: An Interagency Approach to Creating Safe Events.* Champaign, Ill.: Human Kinetics, 2011.

Lussier, Robert, and David Kimball. *Applied Sport Management Skills,* 2nd ed. Champaign, Ill.: Human Kinetics, 2013.

Masterman, Guy. *Strategic Sports Event Management, 3rd ed.* New York: Routledge, 2014.

Nagel, Mark S., Richard M. Southall, and Robin Ammon. *Sport Facility Management: Organizing Events and Mitigating Risks,* 3rd ed. Morgantown, W. Va.: Fitness Information Technology, 2016.

Parent, Milena M., and Sharon Smith-Swan. *Managing Major Sports Events: Theory and Practice.* New York: Routledge, 2013.

Schwarz, Eric C., et al. *Managing Sports Facilities and Major Events*, 2nd ed. New York: Routledge, 2016.

Entry-level jobs may be in facility management or in a related field. Most organizations promote from within, so it is common for someone with a bachelor's or graduate degree in facility management who is working in, for example, public relations, to be considered first for an opening in the sports facility department. Associate- or assistant-level positions are the most likely entry point for graduates, but those with exceptional education and experience may qualify for managerial positions after graduation, although this is rare. As the field becomes more popular, it will be increasingly difficult to enter a sports facility management position without a bachelor's degree and a solid internship experience, at the very least.

Those who find entry-level jobs are helped by mentors. Mentoring is an industry-supported method in which an older, experienced member of a facility management team helps a younger, less-experienced individual to learn the ropes. This process helps the person learn and aids the organization by reducing problems caused by inexperienced beginners.

◼ ADVANCEMENT PROSPECTS

Experience and certification are the best ways for someone to advance in this field. Years of successful on-the-job experience count for a great deal in this industry; the owners and administrations of professional teams and sports venues look for someone who has demonstrated the ability to make things run smoothly. Certification is becoming another way in which success can be gauged; more and more frequently, certification garners salary increases and promotions for those who hold it. Increasingly, firms are asking for certified facility managers when they begin job searches. Since certification goes hand-in-hand with experience, it is assumed that those individuals who are certified are the best in their field.

Outside of experience and certification, a willingness and eagerness to learn and branch into new areas is a less objective manner for gauging which managers will land top jobs. Those who are willing to embrace new technology and are open to new ideas and methods for improving efficiency will very likely advance in their careers.

Advancement might also mean changing specialties or developing one. Sports facility managers who are interested in other areas of management may decide to leave the field and involve themselves with different venues, such as auditoriums, performing arts centers, or convention centers, to name just a few. Still others might advance to manage international venues.

◼ OUTLOOK

The Department of Labor forecasts 8 percent employment growth through 2024 for administration services managers overall, which is about as fast as the average for all occupations. In general, the future for facilities managers is much brighter than it is for those in other administrative services. This relatively young field is growing quickly and, especially in the private sector, is not as subject to cost-cutting pressures or as vulnerable to government cutbacks. Demand for jobs in sports administration is great, and the newer field of sports facility management is quickly catching up. Sports facility managers with knowledge of sustainable business operations and practices will also be in demand in the coming years.

◼ UNIONS AND ASSOCIATIONS

Sports facility managers do not belong to unions. Some join the International Association of Venue Managers and the International Facility Management Association, which provide certification, networking opportunities, continuing education classes, publications, and other resources.

◼ TIPS FOR ENTRY

1. Join the International Association of Venue Managers and the International Facility Management Association to access networking opportunities, continuing education classes, publications, and other resources.
2. Read *Facility Manager* (http://magazine.iavm.org/) to learn more about the field.
3. Participate in the International Association of Venue Managers' Mentor Program (http://iavm.org/mentor-connector-program) to build your professional skills and make networking contacts.

◼ FOR MORE INFORMATION

The International Association of Venue Managers has a mission to educate, advocate for, and inspire public assembly venue members worldwide.

International Association of Venue Managers (IAVM)
635 Fritz Drive, Suite 100
Coppell, TX 75019-4442
Tel: (800) 935-4226; (972) 906-7441
Fax: (972) 906-7418
http://www.iavm.org

The International Facility Management Association offers professional development support, educational programs, networking opportunities, and other benefits for facility management professionals.

International Facility Management Association (IFMA)
800 Gessner Road, Suite 900
Houston, TX 77024-4257
Tel: (713) 623-4362
Fax: (713) 623-6124
E-mail: ifma@ifma.org
http://www.ifma.org

The Stadium Managers Association offers education, networking opportunities, job postings, and research for stadium managers.

Stadium Managers Association (SMA)
6919 Vista Drive
West Des Moines, IA 50266-9309
Tel: (515) 282-8192
Fax: (515) 282-9117
http://www.stadiummanagers.org

Sports Instructors and Coaches

▧ OVERVIEW

Sports instructors demonstrate and explain the skills and rules of particular sports, like golf or tennis, to individuals or groups. They help beginners learn basic rules, stances, grips, movements, and techniques of a game. Sports instructors often help experienced athletes to sharpen their skills.

Coaches work with a single, organized team or individual, teaching the skills associated with that sport. A *head coach,* or *manager,* prepares her or his team for competition. During the competition, he or she continues to give instruction from a vantage point near the court or playing field.

Approximately 224,110 coaches and scouts are employed in the United States.

▧ HISTORY

Coaches and instructors have taught players the rules of the game and performance techniques ever since the first athletes and teams competed. The word coach was used in the academic world first, in the 1830s in Oxford University; it described a tutor who "carried" or "coached" a student. It wasn't until the 1860s that coach was used to describe the person who taught and guided athletes and sports teams. Today, the sports industry is an exciting and lucrative field that employs many instructors and coaches to help athletes reach top levels of performance.

Americans have more leisure time than ever and many have decided that they are going to put this time to good use by getting or staying in shape. This fitness boom, as well as a trend toward more sports competitions, has created employment opportunities for many sports-related occupations. Health clubs, community centers, parks and recreational facilities, and private business now employ sports instructors who teach everything from tennis and golf to scuba diving.

As high school and college sports become even more organized, there continues to be a need for coaches qualified to teach the intricate skills associated with athletics today.

▧ THE JOB

The specific job requirements of sports instructors and coaches vary according to the type of sport and athletes involved. For example, an instructor teaching advanced skiing at a resort in Utah will have different duties and responsibilities than an instructor teaching beginning swimming at a municipal pool. Nevertheless, all instructors and coaches are teachers. They must be knowledgeable about rules and strategies for their respective sports. They must also have an effective teaching method that reinforces correct techniques and procedures so their students or players will be able to gain from that valuable knowledge. Also, instructors and coaches need to be aware of and open to new procedures and techniques. Many attend clinics or seminars to learn more about their sport or even how to teach more effectively. Many are also members of professional organizations that deal exclusively with their sport.

Safety is a primary concern for all coaches and instructors. Coaches and instructors make sure their students have the right equipment and know its correct use. A major component of safety is helping students feel comfortable and confident with their abilities. This entails teaching the proper stances, techniques, and movements of a game, instructing students on basic rules, and answering any questions.

While instructors may tutor students individually or in small groups, a coach works with all the members of a team. Both use lectures and demonstrations to show students the proper skills, and both point out students' mistakes or deficiencies.

Motivation is another key element in sports instruction. Almost all sports require stamina, and most coaches will tell you that psychological preparation is every bit as important as physical training.

Coaches and instructors also have administrative responsibilities. College coaches actively recruit new

QUICK FACTS

ALTERNATE TITLE(S)
Sports Managers

DUTIES
Teach people skills associated with a particular sport; prepare athletes and/or teams for competition; provide advice and encouragement during competition

SALARY RANGE
$17,930 to $31,000 to $7 million+

WORK ENVIRONMENT
Indoors/Outdoors

BEST GEOGRAPHIC LOCATION(S)
Nationwide

MINIMUM EDUCATION LEVEL
Bachelor's Degree

SCHOOL SUBJECTS
Biology, Health, Physical Education

EXPERIENCE
Several years experience recommended

PERSONALITY TRAITS
Athletic, Helpful, Outgoing

SKILLS
Coaching/Physical Training, Interpersonal, Teaching

CERTIFICATION OR LICENSING
Required

SPECIAL REQUIREMENTS
None

EMPLOYMENT PROSPECTS
Good

ADVANCEMENT PROSPECTS
Fair

OUTLOOK
About as Fast as the Average

NOC
5252

O*NET-SOC
27-2022.00

CAREER LADDER

Head Coach or Athletic Director

Instructor or Coach

Assistant Coach

players to join their team. Professional coaches attend team meetings with owners and general managers to determine which players they will draft the next season. Sports instructors at health and athletic clubs schedule classes, lessons, and contests.

■ EARNINGS

Earnings for sports instructors and coaches vary considerably depending on the sport and the person or team being coached. The coach of a Wimbledon champion commands much more money per hour than the swimming instructor for the tadpole class at the municipal pool.

The U.S. Department of Labor (DOL) reports that the median earnings for sports coaches and scouts were $31,000 in May 2015. The lowest paid 10 percent earned less than $17,930, while the highest paid 10 percent earned more than $70,050. Often, much of the work is part time, and part-time employees generally do not receive paid vacations, sick days, or health insurance.

Instructors who teach group classes for beginners through park districts or at city recreation centers can expect to earn around $6 per hour. An hour-long individual lesson through a golf course or tennis club averages $75. Coaches for children's teams often work as volunteers.

Many sports instructors work in camps teaching swimming, archery, sailing and other activities. These instructors generally earn between $1,000 and $2,500, plus room and board, for a summer session.

Most coaches who work at the high school level or below also teach within the school district. Besides their teaching salary and coaching fee—either a flat rate or a percentage of their annual salary—school coaches receive a benefits package that includes paid vacations and health insurance.

In 2016, college head football coaches in the NCAA's top-level, 124-school Football Bowl Subdivision earned salaries that ranged from $360,000 to more than $7 million per year, depending on their experience and the school, according to *USA Today*. NCAA basketball tournament coaches earned salaries that ranged from $124,000 (North Carolina Asheville) to to more than $7 million (Duke), while coaches of women's teams at the same level average considerable less at about $850,000 a year, but can make as much as $1 million to $2 million.

Many larger and more successful universities pay more. Coaches also earn bonuses, and many popular coaches augment their salaries with personal appearances and endorsements.

■ WORK ENVIRONMENT

An instructor or coach may work indoors, in a gym or health club, or outdoors, perhaps at a swimming pool. Much of the work is part time. Full-time sports instructors generally work between 35 and 40 hours per week. During the season when their teams compete, coaches can work 16 hours each day, five or six days each week.

It is common for coaches or instructors to work evenings or weekends. Instructors work then because adult students are available for instruction at these hours. Coaches work nights and weekends because this is when their teams compete.

One significant drawback to the job is the lack of job security. A club may hire a new instructor on very little notice, or may cancel a scheduled class for lack of interest. Athletic teams routinely fire coaches after losing seasons.

Sports instructors and coaches should enjoy working with a wide variety of people. They should be able to communicate clearly and possess good leadership skills to effectively teach complex skills. They can take pride in the knowledge that they have helped their students or their players reach new heights of achievement and training.

■ EXPLORING

Try to gain as much experience as possible in all sports and a specific sport in particular. It is never too early to start. High school and college offer great opportunities to participate in sporting events as a player, manager, trainer, or in intramural leagues.

Most communities have sports programs such as Little League baseball or track and field meets sponsored by the recreation commission. Get involved by volunteering as a coach, umpire, or starter.

Talking with sports instructors already working in the field is also a good way to discover specific job information and find out about career opportunities.

■ EDUCATION AND TRAINING REQUIREMENTS
High School

To prepare for college courses, high school students should take courses that teach human physiology. Biology, health, and exercise classes would all be helpful. Courses in English and speech are also important to improve or develop communication skills.

There is no substitute for developing expertise in a sport. If you can play the sport well and effectively explain to other people how they might play, you will most likely be able to get a job as a sports instructor. The most significant source of training for this occupation is gained while on the job.

Postsecondary Training

Postsecondary training in this field varies greatly. College and professional coaches often attended college as athletes, while others attended college and received their degrees without playing a sport. To become a high school coach, you will need a college degree because you will most likely be teaching as well as coaching. At the high school level, coaches spend their days teaching everything from physical education to English to mathematics, and so the college courses these coaches take vary greatly. Coaches of some youth league sports may not need a postsecondary degree, but they must have a solid understanding of their sport and of injury prevention.

The U.S. Department of Labor reports that courses in exercise and sports science, physiology, kinesiology, nutrition and fitness, physical education, and sports medicine may be required to become a coach.

Other Education or Training

The Society of Health and Physical Educators, American Football Coaches Association, National Soccer Coaches Association of America, and the Women's Basketball Coaches Association offer online classes and webinars, workshops, and seminars.

■ CERTIFICATION, LICENSING, AND SPECIAL REQUIREMENTS
Certification or Licensing

Many facilities require sports instructors to be certified. Information on certification is available from any organization that deals with the specific sport in which one might be interested.

Most high school coaches also work as teachers, and those interested in this job should plan to obtain teacher certification in their state.

■ EXPERIENCE, SKILLS, AND PERSONALITY TRAITS

Try to get experience as a coach or instructor. Contact local sports leagues to see if any assistant positions are available.

Coaches have to be experts in their sport. They must have complete knowledge of the rules and strategies of the game, so that they can creatively design effective plays and techniques for their athletes. But the requirements for this job do not end here. Good coaches are able to communicate their extensive knowledge to the athletes in

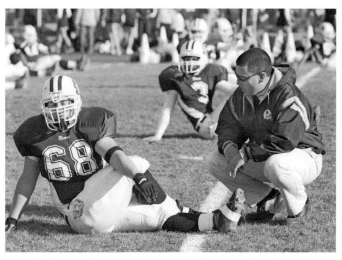

A high school football coach watches a player stretch before a game. (Larry St. Pierre. Shutterstock.)

a way that not only instructs the athletes, but also inspires them to perform to their fullest potential. Therefore, coaches are also teachers who are patient. Patience can make all the difference between an effective coach and one who is unsuccessful.

Coaches and instructors should have optimistic personalities—even if their team is on a losing streak or a player is not performing up to expectations. They must encourage their players to believe that they can win. An optimistic attitude on and off the playing field or court sends a message that the coach believes in their team. Coaches also must be able to work under pressure, guiding teams through games and tournaments that carry great personal and possibly financial stakes for everyone involved.

Discipline is important for athletes, as they must practice plays and techniques over and over again. Coaches who cannot demonstrate and encourage this type of discipline will have difficulty helping their athletes improve.

■ EMPLOYMENT PROSPECTS
Employers

Approximately 224,110 coaches and scouts are employed in the United States. Besides working in high schools, coaches are hired by colleges and universities, professional sports teams, individual athletes such as tennis players, and by youth leagues, summer camps, and recreation centers.

Starting Out

People with expertise in a particular sport, who are interested in becoming an instructor, should apply directly to the appropriate facility. Sometimes a facility will provide training.

TOP INDUSTRIES EMPLOYING SPORTS COACHES AND SCOUTS AND MEAN ANNUAL SALARIES, MAY 2015

FAST FACTS

- Elementary and secondary schools: 58,810 jobs, $34,800
- Other schools of instruction: 47,980 jobs, $33,240
- Other amusement and recreation industries: 47,040 jobs, $39,760
- Colleges, universities, and professional schools: 39,410 jobs, $55,210
- Spectator sports: 7,070 jobs, $59,730
- Civic and social organizations: 6,890 jobs, $30,740

Source: U.S. Department of Labor

For those interested in coaching, many colleges offer positions to *graduate assistant coaches*. Graduate assistant coaches are recently graduated players who are interested in becoming coaches. They receive a stipend and gain valuable coaching experience.

ADVANCEMENT PROSPECTS

Advancement opportunities for both instructors and coaches depend on the individual's skills, willingness to learn, and work ethic. A sports instructor's success can be measured by their students' caliber of play and the number of students they instruct. Successful instructors may become well known enough to open their own schools or camps, write articles and books, or produce how-to videos.

Some would argue that a high percentage of wins is the only criteria for success for professional coaches. However, coaches in the scholastic ranks have other responsibilities and other factors that measure success; for example, high school and college coaches must make sure their players are getting good grades. All coaches must try to produce a team that competes in a sportsmanlike fashion regardless of whether they win or lose.

Successful coaches are often hired by larger schools. High school coaches may advance to become college coaches, and the most successful college coaches often are given the opportunity to coach professional teams. Former players sometimes land assistant or head coaching positions. Some coaches advance by becoming athletic directors.

OUTLOOK

Americans' interest in health, physical fitness, and body image continues to send people to gyms and playing fields. This fitness boom has created strong employment opportunities for many people in sports-related occupations.

Health clubs, community centers, parks and recreational facilities, and private business now employ sports instructors who teach everything from tennis and golf to scuba diving.

According to the U.S. Department of Labor, this occupation will grow about as fast as the average for all careers through 2024. Job opportunities will be best in high schools and in amateur athletic leagues. More sports instructors and coach jobs are expected to open up in colleges also, as more schools will be expanding their sports programs and adding new teams. Health clubs, adult education programs, and private industry will require competent, dedicated instructors. Those with the most training, education, and experience will have the best chance for employment.

The creation of new professional leagues, as well as the expansion of current leagues, will open some new employment opportunities for professional coaches, but competition for these jobs will be very intense. There will also be openings as other coaches retire or are terminated. However, there is very little job security in coaching, unless a coach can consistently produce a winning team.

UNIONS AND ASSOCIATIONS

Coaches and instructors who also work as teachers may join unions such as the American Federation of Teachers or the National Education Association. Other useful organizations for coaches include the American Baseball Coaches Association, American Football Coaches Association, American Hockey Coaches Association, National Association of Basketball Coaches, National High School Athletic Coaches Association, National Soccer Coaches Association of America, Society of Health and Physical Educators, and the Women's Basketball Coaches Association.

TIPS FOR ENTRY

1. Look for job listings on the Web sites of professional associations as well as high school and college Web sites.
2. Join professional associations in the area of interest. For example, if interested in coaching baseball, join the American Baseball Coaches Association.
3. Volunteer to coach a youth league or work as camp counselor during the summer. This will provide experience in coaching and with athletes and young people.
4. Conduct information interviews with high school and college coaches and ask them for advice on breaking into coaching.

▨ FOR MORE INFORMATION

The American Baseball Coaches Association provides information on membership and baseball coaching education.

American Baseball Coaches Association (ABCA)

4101 Piedmont Parkway, Suite C

Greensboro, NC 27410-8151

Tel: (888) 733-8556; (336) 821-3140

Fax: (336) 886-0000

http://www.abca.org

The American Football Coaches Association is dedicated to improving football coaches through ongoing education, interaction, and networking.

American Football Coaches Association (AFCA)

100 Legends Lane

Waco, TX 76706-1243

Tel: (254) 754-9900

Fax: (254) 754-7373

E-mail: info@afca.com

http://www.afca.com

The American Hockey Coaches Association maintains the highest possible standards in hockey and the hockey profession.

American Hockey Coaches Association (AHCA)

7 Concord Street Gloucester

Gloucester, MA 01930-2300

Tel: (781) 245-4177

Fax: (781) 245-2492

E-mail: ahcahockey@comcast.net

http://www.ahcahockey.com

The National High School Athletic Coaches Association provides educational programs and career support for high school athletic coaches.

National High School Athletic Coaches Association (NHSACA)

PO Box 10277

Fargo, ND 58106-0277

Tel: (701) 570-1008

http://www.hscoaches.org

The Society of Health and Physical Educators is a membership organization for health and physical education professionals.

Society of Health and Physical Educators (SHAPE America)

1900 Association Drive

Reston, VA 20191-1598

Tel: (800) 213-7193; (703) 476-3400

Fax: (703) 476-9527

http://www.shapeamerica.org

The National Association of Basketball Coaches promotes integrity, sportsmanship, and teamwork among basketball coaches and players.

National Association of Basketball Coaches (NABC)

1111 Main Street, Suite 1000

Kansas City, MO 64105-2136

Tel: (816) 878-6222

Fax: (816) 878-6223

http://www.nabc.org

The National Soccer Coaches Association of America provides educational programs, job listings, and other resources for professional soccer coaches.

National Soccer Coaches Association of America (NSCAA)

30 West Pershing Road, Suite 350

Kansas City, MO 64108-2463

Tel: (816) 471-1941

E-mail: info@nscaa.com

https://www.nscaa.com

The Women's Basketball Coaches Association provides career support, advocacy, and community for women's basketball coaches and their players.

Women's Basketball Coaches Association (WBCA)

4646 Lawrenceville Highway

Lilburn, GA 30047-3620

Tel: (770) 279-8027

Fax: (770) 279-8473

https://wbca.org

Sports Photographers

▨ OVERVIEW

Sports photographers are specialists hired to shoot pictures of sporting events and athletes. They work for newspapers, magazines, Web sites, and photo stock agencies to bring photos of events of all sizes (from a Little League game to the Olympics) to the pages of periodicals, the Internet, or other publications. Their pictures should clearly capture the movements, skill, and emotions of athletes.

QUICK FACTS

ALTERNATE TITLE(S)
None

DUTIES
Take pictures of sporting events
and athletes

SALARY RANGE
$18,850 to $31,710 to
$72,200+

WORK ENVIRONMENT
Indoors/Outdoors

BEST GEOGRAPHIC LOCATION(S)
Opportunities are available
throughout the country, but are
best in large, urban areas

MINIMUM EDUCATION LEVEL
Some Postsecondary Training

SCHOOL SUBJECTS
Art, Computer Science,
Journalism

EXPERIENCE
Two to three years experience

PERSONALITY TRAITS
Artistic, Organized, Realistic

SKILLS
Business Management, Digital
Media, Interpersonal

CERTIFICATION OR LICENSING
Recommended

SPECIAL REQUIREMENTS
None

EMPLOYMENT PROSPECTS
Fair

ADVANCEMENT PROSPECTS
Fair

OUTLOOK
Little Change or More Slowly
than the Average

NOC
5221

O*NET-SOC
27-4021.00

HISTORY

The Olympic Games are generally credited as being the first organized sports. However, popular support for organized sports developed slowly. Prior to the 19th century, most sports were not officially organized; there were no official rules, competitions, or standards of play. During the 19th century, however, many sports underwent a transition from invented pastime to official sport. Rules governing play, the field of play, and competitions were agreed upon. The first modern track-and-field meet, for example, was held in England in 1825. Meanwhile, in the United States the English game of rugby evolved into American football. The first game was played between Rutgers and Princeton in 1869.

As organized sports grew in popularity, governing bodies and organizations were created to oversee the fair play of each sport. With this organization came public interest in the games. Gradually, coverage of sporting events on radio and in newspapers began to grow until sports quite literally became the national pastime for Americans. Newspapers assigned specialized reporters to capture sporting events to ensure complete and thorough coverage. Trained photographers were also sent to local and national events to capture pictures that evoked the achievements of the sporting world's greatest athletes. Sports photographers are still hired to take pictures of all levels of sports, from neighborhood tee-ball to the World Series. The advent of digital photography and smartphones has enabled more people to capture sports in action, but professionally trained photographers continue to be needed by sports-related media companies.

THE JOB

Sports photographers are hired to shoot quality photos of sporting events, athletes, and crowds cheering on their home teams. Their work is published in newspapers, magazines (such as *Sports Illustrated*), Web pages, books, and other sources.

They are usually trained as photographers but also must have thorough knowledge of the sports they are assigned to shoot. Many sports photographers specialize in shooting one or two sports, such as soccer and hockey—both fast-moving, unpredictable sporting events to capture on film.

To be able to capture quick movements and subtle details on the athletes' faces, sports photographers must have good equipment. They need cameras with fast shutter-speed abilities, tripods to hold cameras steady, and lenses of varying lengths to achieve appropriate depth of field for the intended image.

Sports photographers also need to be at the right place at the right time to get the best shots. Location is key when shooting sporting events. If photographers are too close to the action, they might get injured or, at the very least, interrupt play. If they are too far from the action, they will inevitably miss shots. They need to know where to position themselves to be able to capture the best moments of the game, such as a winning goal or a perfect header in soccer.

In addition to taking pictures, most sports photographers also spend some time developing film and printing photos. However, many now use digital cameras, which eliminate the need for separate developing and printing time. These photographers shoot a sporting event and then head back to their office to download the pictures onto a computer for printing or editing.

EARNINGS

The earning potential for any photographer varies depending on the sports event and the publishing or media company. Typically, the more important the sporting event is, the higher the pay for sports photographers. Photographers shooting a college football game will earn less than those hired to shoot the Super Bowl.

The U.S. Department of Labor reports that photographers in general earned a median salary of $31,710 in May 2015. The lowest paid 10 percent earned $18,850 or less, while the highest paid 10 percent earned $72,200 or more. During the same year, photographers working for newspapers, books, and other publishers earned an average of $45,310 annually.

Salaried sports photographers usually receive benefits such as vacation days, sick leave, health and life insurance, and a savings and pension program. Self-employed photographers must provide their own benefits.

■ WORK ENVIRONMENT

Sports photographers work in an exciting environment that is constantly changing depending on their assignments. One day they may work in the bleachers at a hockey game, and the next day they may roam the sidelines of a soccer match in the driving rain. One thing to note about sports photographers' work environment is the risk of injury. Their close proximity to the playing field means that sports photographers have to be extremely careful when trying to get close enough for the best shots. The work entails continual attention to the game along with attention to their equipment and photographic settings as well as awareness of their environment. For example, they may be concentrating deeply on capturing a great moment of a football game and must be able to move themselves and their expensive equipment if a 275-pound linebacker is suddenly heading their way.

In addition to shooting on location, sports photographers also spend time at computers, editing and transmitting photos to their employers. Self-employed photographers work out of their own offices or home studios and spend part of their time marketing their work and negotiating contract terms.

■ EXPLORING

Participate on a sports team to learn a sport well and build skills. This will later help when sitting on the sidelines and positioning to capture the best images.

Photography clubs provide good practice for shooting and editing pictures and to meet others with similar interests. Joining the school newspaper or yearbook staff is also a great way to gain experience in shooting sporting events. Most yearbooks and newspapers cover their team sports in detail, and photos are what make the stories stand out.

Start a blog that features your photographs of sports events and commentary about sports and the photographic process, or post your photos to the Internet using Instagram or other photo-sharing apps. Be sure to understand the terms of usage before posting photographs for public viewing on social media sites; it is always a good idea to include terms about usage permission. Professional associations can provide language for copyright protection. Another way to explore the field is by talking to sports photographers about their careers. Finally, consider becoming a high school- or college-level member of American Photographic Artists.

■ EDUCATION AND TRAINING REQUIREMENTS
High School

While in high school, take photography classes and any other art classes that are offered. Painting classes, for example, teach composition and balance, which are both important when shooting pictures. Physical education classes introduce the rules of various sports, which will also come in handy when trying to capture images. For self-employed photographers, essential classes include business, accounting, advertising, and marketing classes. English and speech will help to develop communication skills.

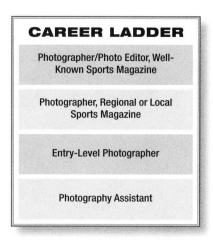

CAREER LADDER

Photographer/Photo Editor, Well-Known Sports Magazine

Photographer, Regional or Local Sports Magazine

Entry-Level Photographer

Photography Assistant

Postsecondary Training

Most sports photographers earn college or art school degrees in photography to increase their skills and knowledge, build a portfolio, and improve their attractiveness to potential employers.

However, in this line of work, experience is more important than formal training. Only the well-practiced photographer is skilled enough to capture a soccer header or two athletes in mid-air fighting for a rebound. These shots require a lot of trial and error before getting the timing down, not to mention the right camera settings.

Other Education or Training

Continuing education events, seminars, classes, and other activities are offered by many professional associations, including American Photographic Artists, American Society of Media Photographers, American Society of Picture Professionals, and Professional Photographers of America.

■ CERTIFICATION, LICENSING, AND SPECIAL REQUIREMENTS
Certification or Licensing

The Professional Photographic Certification Commission, which is affiliated with Professional Photographers of America, offers certification to general photographers. Visit http://www.ppa.com/cpp for more information.

■ EXPERIENCE, SKILLS, AND PERSONALITY TRAITS

The best way to obtain experience in the field is to work as an assistant to a sports photographer. Contact photographers in your area to inquire about opportunities.

In addition to knowing the ins and outs of photography, sports photographers need to know their game and photo

Sports photographers work on the sidelines during a soccer match. (Ververidis Vasilis. Shutterstock.)

subjects in order to be successful. For example, a football player who is known for a post-touchdown victory dance would make a good subject for a post-touchdown photo. Other players might be known for facial expressions, special moves, or other qualities that would be good to get on film. If possible, photographers should study individual athletes or teams for possible photo opportunities.

Sports photographers need to be thorough and patient when shooting pictures because even the smallest detail could make or wreck a photo. A photographer might shoot a hundred photos in the course of a game, but might only get a few good photos—so photographers needs plenty of patience.

■ EMPLOYMENT PROSPECTS
Employers
Sports photographers work for newspapers, sports magazines, Web sites, sports card companies, photo stock agencies, and wire services. Like many other types of photographers, sports photographers are often self-employed and sell their photos to various sources for use in print and online publications. Approximately 60 percent of photographers are self-employed.

Starting Out
Beginning a career in photography can be an uphill battle. The equipment and materials are expensive, there are a lot of risk and competition involved in getting the right photo, and the pay may not be enough to support the photographer's craft. For this reason, many photographers hold other jobs in related fields, such as journalism or editing, and shoot pictures on the side. Others start out as assistants to experienced photographers in order to hone their skills.

Starting out, the photographer's main responsibilities should be to build a portfolio and make contacts in the area in which they would like to publish work. College internships with newspapers or magazines are a great way to accomplish both these tasks. An internship with a newspaper or sports magazine is a good way to meet potential employers and build a body of work.

■ ADVANCEMENT PROSPECTS
Sports photographers advance by selling their work to highly respected publications (such as *ESPN the Magazine*) and commanding more pay for their work. Some photographers become so well known for their work that they are requested by news organizations to shoot international or national sports events, such as the Olympics or the Super Bowl, year after year. Some sports photographers become photo editors or managers at their newspaper or magazine. Others teach photography classes.

■ OUTLOOK
The U.S. Department of Labor predicts that employment of photographers overall will grow by 3 percent through 2024, which is slower than the average for all occupations. The outlook is not good for those who work for news publishers, with 41 percent employment decline predicted in the coming years. Self-employed photographers will do best, with 9 percent job growth expected through 2024. Talented and experienced sports photographers will continue to be needed by popular media outlets and top-selling newspapers and magazines, but competition will continue to be intense for this work. Sports photographers who have a varied portfolio, are experienced with the latest digital camera equipment, and have a mastery of digital photo editing software and capturing digital video will have the best job prospects.

■ UNIONS AND ASSOCIATIONS
Sports photographers may be members of The Newspaper Guild-Communication Workers of America. The following organizations provide membership and other resources: American Photographic Artists, American Society of Media Photographers, American Society of Picture Professionals, National Press Photographers Association, and Professional Photographers of America.

■ TIPS FOR ENTRY
1. Start developing a portfolio of your work so that you are ready to begin looking for jobs once you graduate. Include only your best work.
2. Create your own Web site that showcases your sports photography and advertises your services;

be sure to include terms of usage, including a permission form, on your images.

3. Read industry publications such as *The Picture Professional* (http://aspp.com/the-picture-professional/) to learn more about trends in the industry and potential employers.

■ FOR MORE INFORMATION

The American Photographic Artists offers education, advocacy, and career support for professional photographers.

American Photographic Artists (APA)
2055 Bryant Street
San Francisco, CA 94110-2125
Tel: (800) 272-6264, ext 10
http://apanational.com

The American Society of Media Photographers promotes the rights of photographers, educates its members in business practices, and promotes high standards of ethics.

American Society of Media Photographers (ASMP)
P.O. Box 1810
Traverse City, MI 49685-1810
Tel: (877) 771-2767
Fax: (231) 946-6180
http://www.asmp.org

The American Society of Picture Professionals offers regional chapters, national programs, publications and blogs, and networking opportunities for photography professionals.

American Society of Picture Professionals (ASPP)
201 East 25th Street, #11c
New York, NY 10010-3007
http://aspp.com

The National Press Photographers Association provides advocacy and education for working news photographers, videographers, and multimedia journalists.

National Press Photographers Association (NPPA)
120 Hooper Street
Athens, GA 30602-3018
Tel: (706) 542-2506
E-mail: aramsess@nppa.org
https://www.nppa.org

The Newspaper Guild is a labor union that represents journalists and other media workers in North America.

The Newspaper Guild-Communication Workers of America (TNG-CWA)
501 3rd Street, NW
Washington, D.C. 20001-2797
Tel: (202) 434-7177

PHOTOGRAPHY ON THE FIELD AND THE COURT — LEARN MORE ABOUT IT

Ang, Tom. *Digital Photography Masterclass.* New York: DK ADULT, 2013.

Buckland, Gail. *Who Shot Sports: A Photographic History, 1843 to the Present.* New York: Knopf, 2016.

Frakes, Bill. *Sports Photography: From Snapshots to Great Shots.* San Francisco: Peachpit Press, 2013.

Kelby, Scott. *The Best of the Digital Photography Book Series.* San Francisco: Peachpit Press, 2015.

Martin, Bob. *1/1000th: The Sports Photography of Bob Martin.* Surrey, UK: Vision Sports Photography, 2015.

Miller, Peter Read. *Peter Read Miller on Sports Photography: A Sports Illustrated Photographer's Tips, Tricks, and Tales on Shooting.* San Francisco: New Riders, 2013.

Fax: (202) 434-1472
E-mail: guild@cwa-union.org
http://www.newsguild.org

The Professional Photographers of America provides education and training, publishes its own magazine, and offers various services for its members.

Professional Photographers of America (PPA)
229 Peachtree Street, NE, Suite 2200
Atlanta, GA 30303-1608
Tel: (800) 786-6277; (404) 522-8600
Fax: (404 614-6400
E-mail: csc@ppa.com
http://www.ppa.com

Sports Shooter is an online group of sports photographers that offers firsthand information about sports photography work.

SportsShooter
PO Box 335
New York, NY 10156
http://www.sportsshooter.com

The Society for Photographic Education is a nonprofit association that offers educational programs and scholarships to promote a broader understanding of photography.

Society for Photographic Education (SPE)
2530 Superior Avenue, #403
Cleveland, OH 44114-4230
Tel: (216) 622-2733
Fax: (216) 622-2712
https://www.spenational.org

Sports Physicians

▨ OVERVIEW

Sports physicians, also known as *team physicians*, treat patients who have sustained injuries to their musculoskeletal systems during the play or practice of an individual or team sporting event. Sports physicians also do pre-participation tests and physical exams. Some sports physicians create educational programs to help athletes prevent injury. Sports physicians work for schools, universities, hospitals, and private offices; some also travel and treat members of professional sports teams.

▨ HISTORY

The field of sports medicine, and nearly all the careers related to it, owes its foundation to experiments and studies conducted by Aristotle, Leonardo da Vinci, and Étienne-Jules Marey. Aristotle's treatise on the gaits of humans and animals established the beginning of biomechanics. In one experiment, he used the sun as a transducer to illustrate how a person, when walking in a straight line, actually throws a shadow that produces not a correspondingly straight line, but a zigzag line. Leonardo da Vinci's forays into the range and type of human motion explored a number of questions, including grade locomotion, wind resistance on the body, the projection of the center of gravity onto a base of support, and stepping and standing studies.

However it was Marey, a French physiologist, who created much more advanced devices to study human motion. In fact, sports medicine and modern cinematography both claim him as the father of their respective fields. Marey built the first force platform, a device that was able to visualize the forces between the foot and the floor. English photographer Eadweard Muybridge's serial photographs of a horse in motion inspired Marey's invention of the chronophotograph. In contrast to Muybridge's consecutive frames, taken by several cameras, Marey's pictures with the chronophotograph superimposed the stages of action onto a single photograph; in essence, giving form to motion. By 1892, Marey had made primitive motion pictures, but his efforts were quickly eclipsed by those of film pioneers Louis and Auguste Lumiere.

Following both World Wars I and II, Marey's and others scientists' experiments with motion would combine with medicine's need to heal and/or completely replace the limbs of war veterans. To provide an amputee with a prosthetic device that would come as close as possible to replicating the movement and functional value of a real limb, scientists and doctors began to work together at understanding the range of motion peculiar to the human body.

Sports can be categorized according to the kinds of movements used. Each individual sport uses a unique combination of basic motions, including walking, running, jumping, kicking, and throwing. These basic motions have all been rigidly defined for scientific study so that injuries related to these motions can be better understood and treated. For example, sports that place heavy demands on one part of an athlete's body may overload that part and produce an injury, such as "tennis elbow" and "swimmer's shoulder." Baseball, on the other hand, is a throwing sport and certain injuries from overuse of the shoulder and elbow are expected. Athletes who play volleyball or golf also use some variation of the throwing motion, and therefore also sustain injuries to their shoulders and elbows.

Today, sports medicine concentrates on the treatment and prevention of injuries sustained while participating in sports. Sports medicine is not a single career but a group of careers that is concerned with the health of the athlete. For its specific purposes, the field of sports medicine defines *athlete* as both the amateur athlete who exercises for health and recreation, and the elite athlete who is involved in sports at the collegiate, Olympic, or professional level. Sports physicians treat people of all ages and abilities, including those with disabilities.

Among the professions in the field of sports medicine are the *trainer, physical therapist, physiologist, biomechanical engineer, nutritionist, psychologist,* and *physician*. In addition, the field of sports medicine also encompasses the work of those who conduct research to determine the causes of sports injuries. Discoveries made by researchers in sports medicine have spread from orthopedics to almost every branch of medicine.

Arthroscopic surgery falls into this category. It was developed by orthopedic surgeons to see and operate on skeletal joints without a large open incision. The arthroscope itself is a slender cylinder with a series of lenses that transmit the image from the joint to the eye. The lens system is surrounded by glass fibers designed to transfer light from an external source to the joint. Inserted into the joint through one small, dime- to quarter-sized incision, the arthroscope functions as the surgeon's "eyes" to allow pinpoint accuracy when operating. The surgical elements, themselves, are inserted through other small incisions nearby. In the 1970s, only a few surgeons used the techniques of arthroscopy and did so as an exploratory measure to determine whether or not traditional surgery had a good chance of succeeding. Today, arthroscopy is the most commonly performed orthopedic surgery performed in the United States; instead of being an exploratory procedure, 80 percent of all arthroscopic surgeries are performed to repair tissue damage.

■ THE JOB

Sports physicians treat the injuries and illnesses of both the amateur and elite athlete. They are often referred to as team physicians. Depending upon the level of athlete they are treating, sports physicians are usually either practitioners in family practice as medical doctors (*M.D.'s*) or *orthopedic surgeons*. More often than not, the individual who works as the team physician for a professional sports team is too busy tending to the health needs of the team to have time for a private practice as well.

At the scholastic level, the team physician is usually the *school physician* and is appointed by the school board. Athletic programs at the collegiate level are usually capable of supporting a staff of one or more physicians who cater to the needs of the athletic teams. The size of the school and athletic program also determines the number of full-time physicians; for example, a state university basketball team might have one physician, even an orthopedic surgeon, dedicated wholly to that team's needs.

Professional teams, of course, have the necessary resources to employ both a full-time physician and an orthopedic surgeon. Generally, their presence is required at all practices and games. Often, professional teams have a sports medicine department to handle the various aspects of treatment, from training to nutrition to mental health. If they don't have their own department, they take advantage of the specialists at university hospitals and private care facilities in the area.

To fully understand the nature of a particular sports injury, sports physicians study the athlete as well as the sport. The musculoskeletal system is a complex organization of muscle segments, each related to the function of others through connecting bones and articulations. Pathological states of the musculoskeletal system are reflected in deficits (weaknesses in key muscle segments) that may actually be quite distant from the site of the injury or trauma. The risk factors for any given sport can be assessed by comparing the performance demands that regularly produce characteristic injuries with the risk factors that might predispose an athlete to injury.

Strength and flexibility, for example, are requirements for nearly every sport. Stronger muscles improve an athlete's performance, and deficits in strength can leave him or her prone to injury. Rehabilitation under the supervision of a sports physician focuses on rebuilding lost muscle strength. Likewise, an athlete who lacks flexibility may be subject to muscle strains or pulls. For this athlete, rehabilitation would center on warming and stretching the isolated muscles, as well as muscle groups, to reduce or alleviate such muscle strains. In both cases, it is the responsibility of the sports physician to analyze the potential for injury and work with other sports health professionals to prevent it, as well as to treat the injury after it happens. The goal of every sports physician is to keep athletes performing to the best of their ability and to rehabilitate them safely and quickly after they are injured.

To prevent injuries, as well as treat them, sports physicians administer or supervise physical examinations of the athletes under their care to determine the fitness level of each athlete prior to that athlete actively pursuing the sport. During the exams, sports physicians note any physical traits, defects, previous injuries, or weaknesses. They also check the player's maturity, coordination, stamina, balance, strength, and emotional state. The physical examination accomplishes many different goals. It quickly establishes the athlete's state of health and allows the sports physician to determine whether that athlete is physically capable of playing his or her sport. On the basis of the physical exam, the sports physician advises the coach on the fitness level of the athlete, which in turn determines a great deal about the athlete's position on the team. Furthermore, the exam alerts the sports physician to signs of injury, both old and new. Old or existing injuries can be noted and put under observation, and weaknesses can be detected early so that coach and trainers can implement proper conditioning and training patterns.

Depending upon the results of their physical examinations, the sports physician may advise athletes to gain or lose weight, change their eating, drinking, and sleeping habits, or alter their training programs to include more strength or cardiovascular exercises.

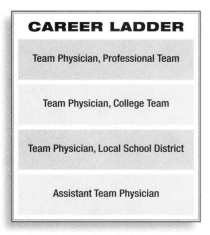

CAREER LADDER

Team Physician, Professional Team

Team Physician, College Team

Team Physician, Local School District

Assistant Team Physician

Routine physical checkups are also a common way of evaluating an athlete's performance level throughout a season, and many sports physicians will administer several exams to gauge the effect of their advice, as well as to ensure that the athlete is making the suggested changes in habits or training.

Preventing injuries is the sports physician's first goal and conditioning is probably the best way to accomplish that goal. Sports physicians are often responsible for developing and supervising the conditioning and training programs that other sports health professionals will implement. The sports physician may work with the coaching staff and athletic trainers to help athletes develop strength, cardiovascular fitness, and flexibility, or the sports physician may advise the coaching and training staff members of the overall safety of a practice program. For example, the sports physician may evaluate the drills and practice exercises that a football coach is using on a given day to make certain that the exercises won't exacerbate old injuries or cause new ones. Sports physicians may even be involved in the selection of protective gear and equipment. The degree of their involvement, again, depends on the size of the team and the nature of the physicians' skills or expertise, as well as on the number of other people on the staff. Large, professional teams tend to have equally large staffs on which one person alone is responsible for ordering and maintaining the protective gear.

Sports physicians are often in attendance at practices (or they are nearby, in case of an injury), but their presence at games is mandatory. If a player shows signs of undue fatigue, exhaustion, or injury, the sports physician needs to be there to remove the athlete from the competition.

After an athlete is injured, the sports physician must be capable of immediately administering first aid or other procedures. They first examine the athlete to determine the gravity and extent of the injury. If the damage is extreme enough (or cannot be determined from a manual and visual exam), the sports physician may send the athlete to the hospital for X-rays or other diagnostic examinations. Later, the team physician may perform surgery or recommend treatment or surgery by a specialist. Some of the most common types of injuries are stress fractures, knee injuries, back injuries, shoulder injuries, and elbow injuries.

The sports physician oversees the athlete's recuperation and rehabilitation post injury, including the nature and timing of physical therapy. The athlete's return to practice and competition is determined by the sports physician's analysis of the athlete's progress. Frequent physical examinations allow the physician to judge if the athlete is fit enough to return to full activity. The decision to allow an athlete to compete again following an injury is a responsibility that sports physicians take seriously; whether the athlete is an amateur or an elite professional, the future health and well-being of the athlete is at stake and cannot be risked, even for an important championship game.

A developing area of the sports physician's responsibilities is the diagnosis and treatment of substance-abuse and doping problems. Unfortunately, even as research on the field of sports medicine has produced new methods and medications that mask pain and decrease inflammation—which shortens recovery time and lengthens athletic careers—some also produce unnatural performance enhancement. Most notable of these are anabolic steroids—synthetic modifications of the male hormone, testosterone—which have become widely abused by athletes who use them to better their performances. When taken while on a high-protein diet and an intensive exercise regimen, these drugs can increase muscle bulk, which in turn can produce increased strength, speed, and stamina. The side effects of these drugs, however, include aggression, sterility, liver problems, premature closure of the growth plates of the long bones, and in women, male pattern baldness and facial hair. These side effects are usually irreversible and pose a significant health risk for young athletes.

Another method also banned from use in competition-level athletics is the withdrawal of an athlete's blood several weeks prior to competition. The blood is stored and then, just before the athlete competes, the blood is transfused back into his or her bloodstream. This process, blood doping, also has serious, even fatal, side effects, including heart failure and death.

Finally, professional athletes sometimes develop substance-abuse problems, such as alcohol or drug abuse. Sports physicians are responsible for detecting all of these problems and helping the athlete return to a healthy lifestyle, which may or may not include competing in their sport.

In addition to the responsibilities and duties outlined above, many sports physicians also perform clinical studies and work with researchers to determine ways of improving sports medicine practices. The results of such studies and research are often published in medical journals and popular magazines.

EARNINGS

Sports physicians' earnings vary depending upon their responsibilities and the size and nature of the team. The private sports physician of a professional individual athlete, such as a figure skater or long-distance runner, will probably earn far less than the team physician for a professional football or basketball team, due to the high earnings and larger budget of the team. On the other hand, the team physician for the professional basketball team probably wouldn't have time for a private practice, although the sports physician for the figure skater or runner would, in all likelihood, also have a private practice or work for a sports health facility.

According to the U.S. Department of Labor, general practitioners and family practice physicians earned an annual median income of $184,390 in May 2015. Ten percent of these physicians earned less than $65,630 annually in that same year, and some earned significantly more. This general figure does not include the fees and other income sports physicians receive from the various athletic organizations for whom they work. Again, these fees will vary according to the size of the team, the location, and the level of the athletic organization (high school, college, or professional, being the most common). The income generated from these fees is far less than what they earn in their private practices. Team physicians who are employed full time by a professional organization typically outearn their nonprofessional sports counterparts, by as much as $1 million or more.

Sports physicians who work as salaried employees of medical practices receive benefits such as health and life insurance and a savings and pension program. Self-employed physicians must provide their own benefits.

WORK ENVIRONMENT

Sports physicians must be ready for a variety of work conditions, from the sterile, well-lighted hospital operating room to the concrete bleachers at an outdoor municipal swimming pool. The work environment is as diverse as the sports in which athletes are involved. Most of their day-to-day responsibilities will be carried out in clean, comfortable surroundings, but on game day sports physicians are expected to be where the athletes are, and that might be a muddy field (football, baseball, and soccer); a snow-covered forest (cross-country skiing); a hot, dusty track (track and field); or a steamy ring (boxing). Picture the playing field of any given sport and that is where you will find sports physicians. They are also expected to travel with the athletes whenever they go out of town.

A sports physician sprays an athlete's injury on the soccer field. (Olga Dmitrieva. Shutterstock.)

This means being away from their home and family, often for several days, depending on the nature, level, and location of the competition.

EXPLORING

A good way to learn more about the sports physicians field is by working with the physician, coach, or athletic trainer for a school's team. Firsthand experience is the best way to gain fresh perspective into the role of the team physician. Later on, when applying for other paid or volunteer positions, it will help to have already had sports-related experience. Try to work with a physician in your target practice area, such as with a college team or with a professional sports team. Observing physicians in their offices or on the sidelines as they treat athletes will give you a good introduction to the field.

EDUCATION AND TRAINING REQUIREMENTS
High School

During high school, take as many health and sports-related classes as possible. Biology, chemistry, health, psychology, computer science, and English are important core courses. High grades in high school are important for anyone aspiring to join the medical profession, because competition for acceptance into medical programs at colleges and universities is always tough.

Postsecondary Training

Sports physicians have either an M.D. (medical doctor degree) or a D.O. (doctor of osteopathy degree). Each

TREATING SPORTS INJURIES

WORDS TO KNOW

Anterior cruciate ligament (ACL): A key ligament that is one of the four major ligaments of the human knee; tears of the ACL are a very common injury for athletes.

Arthography: A diagnostic technique in which the physician injects a dye into an injured joint, which then reveals in an X-ray the exact site and extent of the injury.

Arthroplasty: Procedures and artificial materials used to treat joint problems.

Arthroscopy: A diagnostic or surgical tool. As a diagnostic tool, a tiny camera is inserted into the injured area to reveal the extent of the damage. As a surgical tool, it is used to remove torn cartilage or bone fragments from an injured joint.

Clinical examination: Doctors determine the history of an injury by examining the patient.

Computerized tomography: A computerized diagnostic tool that combines X-ray images of the injured joint to create a detailed view of the injured area.

Hard casts: Casts made of plaster or plastic that immobilize broken bones.

Immobilization: A common treatment that allows an injury to settle and healing to begin.

Magnetic resonance imaging (MRI): A computerized technique that uses magnetic fields to provide a picture of an injury.

Soft casts: Bandage wraps.

involves completing four years of college, followed by four years of medical school, study, and internship at an accredited medical school, and up to six years of residency training in a medical specialty, such as surgery. Many physicians also complete a fellowship in sports medicine either during or after their residency.

During the first two years of medical school, medical students usually spend most of their time in classrooms learning anatomy, physiology, biology, and chemistry, among other subjects. In their last two years, they begin seeing patients in a clinic, observing and working with doctors to treat patients and develop their diagnostic skills. Some medical schools are beginning to alter this time-honored tradition by having medical students begin to work with patients much sooner than two years into their schooling, but this method of combining classroom and clinical experiences is not yet fully accepted or integrated into the curriculum.

After medical school, the new doctors spend a year in an internship program, followed by several years in a residency training program in their area of specialty. Most sports physicians complete this stage of their training by working in orthopedics or general practice.

The fellowship portion of a doctor's training is essential if he or she has chosen to specialize. For example, the doctor specializing in general surgery and interested in sports medicine would probably seek an orthopedics fellowship providing further training in orthopedic surgery techniques.

Other Education or Training

The American College of Sports Medicine offers a team physician course to help physicians prepare to work with athletes. The American Medical Association, American Osteopathic Association, American Orthopaedic Society for Sports Medicine, American College of Sports Medicine, and the National Athletic Trainers' Association also provide professional development opportunities.

■ CERTIFICATION, LICENSING, AND SPECIAL REQUIREMENTS

Certification or Licensing

Board certification is granted by many medical boards such as the American Board of Internal Medicine, American Board of Physical Medicine and Rehabilitation, and the American Board of Surgery. These credentials, though voluntary, signify that the physician is highly qualified in a particular practice area.

All states requires physicians to be licensed and requirements vary by state. To become licensed, doctors must have completed postsecondary training in accordance with the guidelines and rules of their chosen area or specialty. Beyond the formal requirements, this usually involves a qualifying written exam, followed by in-depth oral examinations designed to test the candidate's knowledge and expertise.

■ EXPERIENCE, SKILLS, AND PERSONALITY TRAITS

There is no way to obtain direct experience in high school, but it's a good idea to take as many health and science classes as possible and participate in science clubs. Medical students gain experience by completing residency training in a medical specialty, such as surgery, and a fellowship in sports medicine.

Sports physicians must be able to learn and remember all the many parts of the human body and how they function together. Knowledge of different sports and their demands on an athlete's body is also important. Like all medical doctors, sports physicians must also be able to communicate clearly to their patients with compassion and understanding.

■ EMPLOYMENT PROSPECTS

Employers

Most sports physicians are in private practice, so they work for themselves or with other medical doctors. Some sports physicians, however, may work for sports clinics, rehabilitation centers, hospitals, and college/university teaching hospitals. Still other sports physicians travel with professional baseball, basketball, football, hockey, and soccer teams to attend to those specific athletes. Sports physicians are employed all over the country.

Starting Out

Many sports physicians begin by joining an existing practice and volunteering with a local sports organization. After several years they may apply to the school board for consideration as a team physician for their local school district. Later, they may apply for a position with a college team until they ultimately seek a position with a national or international professional athletics team or organization. This gradual climb occurs while the individual also pursues a successful private practice and builds a strong, solid reputation. Often, the sports physician's established reputation in an area of specialty draws the attention of coaches and management looking to hire a physician for their team.

Others take a more aggressive and ambitious route and immediately begin applying for positions with various professional sports teams as an assistant team physician. As in other professions, contacts can be extremely useful, as are previous experiences in the field. For example, a summer internship during high school or college with a professional hockey team might lead to a job possibility with that hockey team years later. Employment opportunities depend on the job candidate's skill and ambitions.

■ ADVANCEMENT PROSPECTS

Advancement paths vary depending on the nature of an aspiring sports physician's affiliation with athletic organizations (part time or full time). For most sports physicians, advancement will accompany the successful development of their private practices. For those few sports physicians who are employed full time by professional athletic organizations, advancement from assistant to team physician is usually accompanied by increased responsibilities and a corresponding increase in salary.

■ OUTLOOK

Coaches and management are aware of the benefits of good health and nutrition for their athletes after years of watching them close down the bars after a game. Proper nutrition, conditioning, and training prevent injuries to athletes, and preventing injuries is the key when those athletes are making their owners revenues in the billions of dollars. A top sports physician has become, and continues to be, a worthwhile investment for any professional team. The outlook for sports physicians remains strong, but it should be noted that this is a highly competitive profession. The number of physicians who provide services to professional sports teams is extremely small, and it is challenging to land a job at this level.

Even outside the realm of professional sports, amateur athletes require the skills and expertise of talented sports physicians to handle the aches and pains that come from pulling muscles and overtaxing aging knees. Athletes of all ages and abilities take their competitions seriously and are as prone to injury as any professional athlete, if not more, because amateur athletes in general spend less time conditioning their bodies. The U.S. Department of Labor predicts that employment for physicians and surgeons will grow by 14 percent, much faster than the average for all careers, through 2024.

■ UNIONS AND ASSOCIATIONS

Sports physicians do not belong to unions. The American Medical Association and the American Osteopathic Association are the largest membership organizations in the United States for physicians. They provide a wealth of resources for those interested in careers in medicine. Other membership organizations include the American Orthopaedic Society for Sports Medicine, American College of Sports Medicine, and the National Athletic Trainers' Association.

■ TIPS FOR ENTRY

1. Join the American Medical Association, American Osteopathic Association, American Orthopaedic Society for Sports Medicine, and the American College of Sports Medicine to access career information, job listings, publications, and continuing education and networking opportunities.
2. Visit the JAMA Career Center Web site, http://www.jamacareercenter.com, for job listings.
3. Talk to sports physicians about their careers. Ask friends and family members if they know a sports physician they could recommend for an informational interview.
4. Become board certified to show employers that you have met the highest standards established by the medical profession.
5. Read *Medicine & Science in Sports & Exercise* and *Current Sports Medicine Reports* (both are available at http://www.acsm.org/join-acsm/who-should-join/clinicians) and the *American Journal of Sports*

Medicine (http://ajs.sagepub.com/content/current) to learn more about the field.

■ FOR MORE INFORMATION

The American College of Sports Medicine is an association of sports medicine, exercise science, and health and fitness professionals that is dedicated to helping people live longer, healthier lives.

American College of Sports Medicine (ACSM)
401 West Michigan Street
Indianapolis, IN 46202-3233
Tel: (317) 637-9200
Fax: (317) 634-7817
E-mail: publicinfo@acsm.org
http://www.acsm.org

The American Medical Association promotes the arts and science of medicine and the betterment of public health.

American Medical Association (AMA)
330 North Wabash Avenue
Chicago, IL 60611-5885
Tel: (800) 621-8335
http://www.ama-assn.org/ama

The American Orthopaedic Society for Sports Medicine provides education, research, communication, and fellowship for sports medicine specialists.

**American Orthopaedic Society for Sports
   Medicine (AOSSM)**
9400 West Higgins Road, Suite 300
Rosemont, IL 60018-4975
Tel: (877) 321-3500; (847) 292-4900
Fax: (847) 292-4905
E-mail: info@aossm.org
http://www.sportsmed.org/aossmimis

The American Osteopathic Association is the certifying body for osteopathic doctors and the accrediting agency for all osteopathic medical schools.

American Osteopathic Association (AOA)
142 East Ontario Street
Chicago, IL 60611-2864
Tel: (800) 621-1773; (312) 202-8000
Fax: (312) 202-8200
http://www.osteopathic.org

The National Athletic Trainers' Association represents, fosters, and engages the growth and development of professional athletic trainers.

National Athletic Trainers' Association (NATA)
1620 Valwood Parkway, Suite 115
Carrollton, TX 75006-8321
Tel: (860) 437-5700; (214) 637-6282
Fax: (214) 637-2206
http://www.nata.org

Sports Psychologists

■ OVERVIEW

In general, *sports psychologists* work with amateur and professional athletes to improve their mental and physical health, as well as athletic performances, by using goal setting, imagery, focus strategies, and relaxation techniques, among others. Sports psychologists also strive to help athletes to mentally prepare for competition. There are approximately 105,600 psychologists employed in the United States, although sports psychologists comprise only a small segment of this number.

■ HISTORY

In the 17th century, French philosopher René Descartes described his belief that human behaviors could be classified in two ways—voluntary and involuntary. Those behaviors which were completely mechanical, instinctual, and similar to those of animals, he characterized as involuntary; behaviors which required or submitted to reason were characterized as voluntary. Based on this early model, and the subsequent work of others, including John Locke, James Mill, and John Stuart Mill, later philosophers and scientists experimented with sensation and perception, culminating with an introspective analysis of the many elements of an individual's experience.

William James advanced modern psychology by asserting the theory of a stream of thought; G. Stanley Hall, a contemporary of James, established the first true laboratory of psychology at Clark University in 1883. Sigmund Freud introduced the medical tradition to clinical psychology. A physician and neurologist, Freud's methods of psychoanalysis included word association techniques and later, inkblot techniques as developed by Hermann Rorschach.

After World War II, psychology became formally recognized as a profession. The American Psychological Association (APA) has developed standards of training for psychologists, and certification and licensing laws have been passed to regulate the practice of professional psychology.

Since psychology deals with human behavior, psychologists apply their knowledge and techniques to a wide range of endeavors including human services, management, law, and sports.

■ THE JOB

Sport and exercise psychology is the scientific study of the psychological factors that are associated with participation and performance in sport, exercise, and other types of physical activity. In general, sports psychologists work with amateur and professional athletes to improve their mental and physical health, as well as athletic performances, by using goal setting, imagery, focus strategies, and relaxation techniques, among others. Sports psychologists also strive to help athletes to mentally prepare for competition.

Sports psychologists are divided into three categories: clinical, educational, and research. *Clinical sports psychologists* work mainly with individuals who are experiencing emotional problems that are usually, but not always, somehow connected to their sport. *Educational sports psychologists* have two roles, one as a classroom instructor and the other as a consultant. In the classroom, they teach students methods and techniques related to sports psychology. On the field, they usually function as members of the coaching staff. Just as the coach teaches physical skills, the sports psychologist teaches mental skills. *Research sports psychologists* conduct studies that provide the clinical and educational sports psychologists with scientific facts and statistics.

All sports psychology professionals are interested in two main objectives: helping athletes use psychological principles to improve performance (performance enhancement) and understanding how participation in sport, exercise, and physical activity affects an individual's psychological development, health, and well-being throughout the life span.

Sports psychologists work with individual athletes and entire teams. They may concentrate on the problems the athlete is having with the sport, from a bad slump to the feelings of low self-esteem that come when the crowd jeers the athlete's performance. Sports psychologists also work to help the individual athlete to overcome feelings of depression, drug or substance abuse, and violence.

They work with teams in many ways, the most notable of which is creating a feeling of cohesion among the many different personalities that constitute a team. Team members are also counseled when they are traded to another team or released.

Sports psychologists also work with individual athletes and team members on improving their level of performance, concentration, and mental attitude. The phrase "a winning attitude" derives its power from the fact that sports psychologists can help the athletes with whom they work to actually visualize a winning shot or a perfect golf swing and then execute that vision.

Sports psychologists don't work with only exceptional, elite athletes or teams; most sports psychologists, in fact, work with college athletes or amateur athletes, and many teach in academic settings or offer motivational lecture series. Some sports psychologists have their own columns in specialized sports magazines and others work in athletic training facilities, hired full time by the owners to work with the athletes who come there to train.

■ EARNINGS

Specific salary statistics for sports psychologists are not readily available. In general, psychologists' salaries depend on their area of their expertise, the location of their practice, and whether or not they practice alone or in a partnership. The U.S. Department of Labor reports that median annual earnings for all psychologists were $70,580 in May 2015. The lowest paid 10 percent earned less than $40,920, and the highest paid 10 percent earned more than $116,960. Be forewarned, however, that with the higher salary comes long years of study in order to attain the educational background necessary to practice. In fact, in order to stay current with topics ranging

QUICK FACTS

ALTERNATE TITLE(S)
Clinical Sports Psychologists, Educational Sports Psychologists, Research Sports Psychologists

DUTIES
Work with amateur and professional athletes to improve their mental and physical health, as well as their athletic performances

SALARY RANGE
$40,920 to $70,580 to $116,960+

WORK ENVIRONMENT
Primarily Indoors

BEST GEOGRAPHIC LOCATION(S)
Nationwide; most opportunities available in major metropolitan areas

MINIMUM EDUCATION LEVEL
Doctorate

SCHOOL SUBJECTS
Biology, Health, Psychology

EXPERIENCE
Internship or supervised experience required

PERSONALITY TRAITS
Helpful, Problem-Solving, Scientific

SKILLS
Coaching/Physical Training, Interpersonal, Scientific

CERTIFICATION OR LICENSING
Required

SPECIAL REQUIREMENTS
None

EMPLOYMENT PROSPECTS
Fair

ADVANCEMENT PROSPECTS
Good

OUTLOOK
About as Fast as the Average

NOC
4151

O*NET-SOC
19-3031.00, 19-3031.02, 19-3031.03

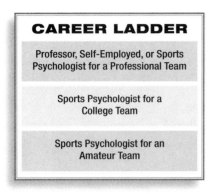

CAREER LADDER

Professor, Self-Employed, or Sports Psychologist for a Professional Team

Sports Psychologist for a College Team

Sports Psychologist for an Amateur Team

from treatment to medication, psychologists must continue to learn and study their field for as long as they intend to practice.

Benefits for full-time workers include vacation and sick time, health, and sometimes dental, insurance, and pension or 401(k) plans. Self-employed psychologists must provide their own benefits.

■ WORK ENVIRONMENT

Sports psychologists spend most of their time working in office and hospital environments, but some of their time is spent in the same environments as the athletes they counsel. This may mean spending several hours on a golf course, on a ski slope, or in the gymnasium. Much depends on the type of psychologist. For example, the clinical psychologist would probably spend most of their time with athletes in the relative comfort of an office setting and the psychologist would meet with athletes during a regular nine-to-five day. Educational sports psychologists would be more likely to be in the gym or on the golf course, working side-by-side with the rest of the coaching staff. Depending on the nature of the study, a research sports psychologist might spend some time with athletes while they are practicing, but in general, they would spend most of the workday in an office or laboratory setting, reviewing or studying the data from their studies.

Sports psychologists need to stay up to date with developing theories and research. To accomplish this, they may have to spend additional time reading journals, books, and papers; conducting research in the library; or attending conferences on relevant issues. They may need to take additional course work to stay abreast of new theories and techniques, as well as to maintain current certification or licensing. Sports psychologists spend a lot of time with the athletes they're helping, but they also spend large amounts of time working alone.

■ EXPLORING

Gain experience in this field by volunteering to work for research programs at area universities or by working in the office of a psychologist. Another option is to learn more about sports by working as a gofer or intern with the sports medicine departments of college, university, or professional athletic teams. Participating in a sport in high school or college can provide insight into the mental and emotional stresses and demands placed upon athletes.

In addition, students should begin their understanding of psychology by taking as many courses in the field as possible.

Joining professional associations is a good way to learn more about the field. The American Psychological Association, for example, offers an affiliate member category for high school and college students.

■ EDUCATION AND TRAINING REQUIREMENTS
High School

High school students should take a college preparatory curriculum that concentrates on English, mathematics, and sciences. Classes in a foreign language, especially French and German, are also important because reading comprehension of these languages is one of the usual requirements for obtaining a doctoral degree. Participation in sports will give you the background necessary to effectively understand the athletes you work with in your practice.

Postsecondary Training

A doctoral degree is generally required for employment as a psychologist, but there are two different degrees that psychologists can seek at the doctorate level. The first degree is the Ph.D., and psychologists with this degree qualify for a wide range of teaching, research, clinical, and counseling positions in universities, elementary and secondary schools, and private industry. The second degree is the Psy.D. (doctor of psychology); psychologists with this degree qualify mainly for clinical positions. The Ph.D. culminates in a dissertation based on original research, while the Psy.D. is usually based on practical work and examinations rather than a dissertation. In clinical or counseling psychology, the requirements for a doctoral degree usually include a year or more of internship or supervised experience.

Individuals who have only a master's degree in psychology are allowed to administer tests as psychological assistants and, if they are under the supervision of doctoral-level psychologists, they can conduct research in laboratories, conduct psychological evaluations, counsel patients, and perform administrative duties. They are also allowed to teach in high schools and two-year colleges and work as school psychologists or counselors.

Those individuals with only a bachelor's degree in psychology can assist psychologists and other professionals and work as research or administrative assistants, but without further academic training they cannot advance further in psychology.

Having said all of this, it will perhaps come as a shock that there are no sports psychology doctoral programs accredited by the American Psychological Association (APA). One of the controversies behind this is whether professionals working with athletes in applied areas of sports psychology should be required to have doctoral training in clinical or counseling psychology—training which would qualify them to provide psychological treatment to athletes as well. The solution reached by the APA, along with the Association for Applied Sport Psychology (AASP) and North American Society for the Psychology of Sport and Physical Activity, is that any practitioners of sports psychology who do not also have doctoral-level clinical or counseling training should refer athletes who need treatment to licensed professionals. Sports psychologists who work with Olympic athletes are required to have doctoral-level degrees.

Those students who are interested in academic teaching and research in sports psychology can earn doctoral degrees in sport sciences and take additional courses in psychology or counseling. Over 50 schools in the United States offer this type of program, including the University of North Carolina–Greensboro (http://kin.wp.uncg.edu/graduate/areas-of-study/sport-exercise-psychology/) and the University of Florida (http://www.hhp.ufl.edu). Typical subjects covered include sports psychology, performance enhancement, concentration skills, stress and attention management, and motivation.

Those students who want more emphasis on psychology in their training can pursue a psychology doctorate in areas such as group procedures, psychotherapy, learning, education, and human development or motivation, with a subspecialty in sports psychology. At most universities, students take courses like these in the sport sciences department, while it is possible to take similar courses through the psychology department of some schools.

Students who wish to provide clinical services to athletes can pursue a doctoral degree in APA-accredited clinical or counseling psychology programs, with a concentration in sports psychology. This track offers students the widest range of job opportunities, from teaching and research in sports and psychology to counseling athletes as well as the general population. Institutions where this mode of study is typical include the University of Wisconsin-Madison (http://www.wisc.edu) and the University of North Texas (http://www.unt.edu).

For those students who are interested primarily in educating people about the health benefits of exercise or in helping student athletes, a master's degree is an option. Many sport sciences departments offer a master's degree in areas related to sports psychology.

SPORTS PSYCHOLOGY FUNDAMENTALS

LEARN MORE ABOUT IT

Aoyagi, Mark, and Arthur Pozwardowski. *Expert Approaches to Sport Psychology*. Morgantown, W.Va.: Fitness Information Technology, 2012.

American College of Sports Medicine. *ACSM's Behavioral Aspects of Physical Activity and Exercise*. Philadephia: Lippincott Williams & Wilkins, 2013.

Cox, Richard. *Sport Psychology: Concepts and Applications,* 7th ed. New York: McGraw-Hill, 2011.

Keegan, Richard. *Being a Sport Psychologist*. New York: Palgrave Macmillan, 2015.

Murphy, Shane. (ed.) *The Oxford Handbook of Sport and Performance Psychology.* Oxford University Press, USA, 2012.

Weinberg, Robert, and Daniel Gould. *Foundations of Sport and Exercise Psychology,* 6th ed. Champaign, Ill.: Human Kinetics, 2014.

Williams, Jean, and Vikki Krane. *Applied Sport Psychology: Personal Growth to Peak Performance*, 7th ed. New York: McGraw-Hill, 2014.

For more detailed information on graduate programs in psychology and sports psychology, look for *The Directory of Graduate Programs in Applied Sport Psychology*, edited by Michael L. Sachs, Kevin L. Burke, and Sherry L. Schweighardt.

Other Education or Training

Professional associations such as the Association for Applied Sports Psychology, the American Psychological Association, and the North American Society for the Psychology of Sport and Physical Activity offers webinars and other professional development courses online and through their conferences.

■ CERTIFICATION, LICENSING, AND SPECIAL REQUIREMENTS
Certification or Licensing

In addition to educational requirements, most states require that all practitioners of psychology meet certification or licensing requirements if they are in independent practice or involved in offering patient care of any kind (including clinical and counseling). Once the educational requirements are fulfilled, a sports psychologist should contact the Association for Applied Sport Psychology and the American Board of Professional Psychology for details about certification and licensing requirements, as they usually vary from state to state.

■ EXPERIENCE, SKILLS, AND PERSONALITY TRAITS

At least a year or more of internship or supervised experience is required to work as a clinical or counseling psychologist.

Various personal attributes apply to different psychology positions because sports psychology is such a broad field. Clinical sports psychologists should be able to relate to others and have excellent listening skills. Educational sports psychologists should have strong communication skills in order to convey ideas and concepts to students and clients. Research sports psychologists should be analytical, detail oriented, and have strong writing and mathematics skills.

■ EMPLOYMENT PROSPECTS

Employers

Approximately 105,600 psychologists are employed in the United States, although sports psychologists comprise only a small segment of this number. Sports psychologists are employed by athletes at the amateur, college, or professional level and by owners of professional, college, and private organizations. They may also work at colleges and universities as teachers and researchers.

Starting Out

Along the road toward a Ph.D. or Psy.D., students of all levels can get involved in the research or educational aspects of psychology, either as a volunteer subject or a paid helper. These positions will gradually increase in responsibility and scope as the student's education progresses. Eventually, the student will be eligible for internships that will, in turn, provide valuable contacts in the field.

Graduates can explore job opportunities with a wide variety of employers, from the university research branch of psychology or sport sciences to the world of elite athletes. Finding work with the latter, however, can prove extremely difficult.

■ ADVANCEMENT PROSPECTS

Sports psychologists advance in several ways, but primarily by increasing the scope and caliber of their reputations in the field. This is accomplished, of course, by consistently helping athletes to improve their athletic performance and to reduce the emotional and/or mental strain placed upon them. Advancement might come in the form of a new position, such as working for a professional team, or it might come in the form of a solid private practice.

Sports psychologists who make their living largely in the academic world do so by successfully publishing the results of studies, research, or theories in specialized medical journals.

■ OUTLOOK

While employment in the general field of psychology is expected to grow much faster than the average for all occupations through 2024, it is hard to say how this prognosis affects the subspecialty of sports psychology. Few people leave the field entirely because so much time is required for training. Many stay in the general field of psychology and merely move around, switching specialties, but even this is rare.

Competition is keen for positions with elite athletes, most experts believe that other areas of sports psychology will continue to offer a substantial number of jobs to new graduates, especially in academe.

Sports psychology can lack the steady income of a private practice or academic teaching post because practitioners are frequently only on call, not steadily billing for their time. It can also be difficult to get work because while they might have a great, famous athlete for a client, chances are pretty good that the athlete doesn't want the public to know they are getting counseling for a bad marriage, a slump, or a drug problem. This forces the sports psychologist to rely on referrals, which they may not receive all that often when athletes and their agents are trying to keep the athlete's therapy a secret.

■ UNIONS AND ASSOCIATIONS

Sports psychologists do not typically belong to unions, but they can obtain useful resources and professional support from the American Psychological Association, Association for Applied Sports Psychology (AASP), and the North American Society for the Psychology of Sport and Physical Activity. The American Board of Professional Psychology and AASP offer certification to psychologists.

■ TIPS FOR ENTRY

1. Attend the annual conference of the Association for Applied Sports Psychology to network and participate in professional development opportunities.
2. Read *Sport, Exercise, and Performance Psychology* and the *Exercise and Sport Psychology Newsletter* (both are available at http://www.apa.org/about/division/div47.aspx) and the *Journal of Applied Sport Psychology* (http://www.appliedsportpsych.org/publications/journal-of-applied-sport-psychology) to learn more about the field.
3. Learn more about the types of jobs being offered for sports psychologists by searching the job listings posted on professional association's Web sites.
4. Become certified by the Association for Applied Sports Psychology and the American Board of Professional Psychology in order to show

employers that you have met the highest standards set by your profession.

■ FOR MORE INFORMATION

The American Board of Professional Psychology provides education and certification of professional psychologists.

American Board of Professional Psychology (ABPP)
600 Market Street, Suite 201
Chapel Hill, NC 27516-4056
Tel: (919) 537-8031
Fax: (919) 537-8034
E-mail: office@abpp.org
http://www.abpp.org

The American Psychological Association provides education, career support, and publications and databases for psychology professionals and students.

American Psychological Association (APA)
750 First Street, NE
Washington, D.C. 20002-4242
Tel: (800) 374-2721; (202) 336-5500
http://www.apa.org/index.aspx

The Association for Applied Sport Psychology promotes the development of science and ethical practice in the field of sport psychology.

Association for Applied Sport Psychology (AASP)
8365 Keystone Crossing, Suite 107
Indianapolis, IN 46240-2685
Tel: (317) 205-9225
Fax: (317) 205-9481
E-mail: info@appliedsportpsych.org
http://www.appliedsportpsych.org

The North American Society for the Psychology of Sport and Physical Activity offers membership benefits, events and conferences, publications, job listings, and other resources.

North American Society for the Psychology of Sport and Physical Activity (NASPSPA)
E-mail: qalmeida@wlu.ca
http://naspspa.com

Sports Publicists

■ OVERVIEW

There are two types of public relations specialists who work as *sports publicists*: those who work for professional and amateur teams and those who work for individual professional athletes. *Sports team publicists* handle the daily press operations for the organization. They handle the media relations, set up interviews with players, ensure that the correct information is distributed to the press, and write press releases and social media posts. *Individual sports publicists*, who work for individual players, try to enhance their client's image by casting them in a positive light via various media outlets. Sports publicists are sometimes called *sports information directors*, *press agents*, *public relations (PR) directors*, *public relations specialists*, *marketing directors*, or *directors of communication*.

■ HISTORY

The field of public relations and publicity was recognized as a profession starting in the 1920s and 1930s, when private public relations firms were established by Ivy Lee and Edward Bernays. Lee wrote the "Declaration of Principles," expressing his ideas about public relations' professionals' obligations and standards of practice in relation to the media and the public. Bernays, a nephew of Sigmund Freud, applied psychology theories to his corporate public relations practice. Specialties within public relations and publicity developed throughout the 20th century, including that of sports publicist.

Sports is one of our nation's largest businesses, and professional teams are the most widely recognized industry segment in sports. This includes all of the various sports teams, leagues, and governing bodies for which athletes get paid for

QUICK FACTS

ALTERNATE TITLE(S)
Directors of Communication, Individual Sports Publicists, Marketing Directors, Press Agents, Public Relations Directors, Public Relations Specialists, Sports Information Directors, Sports Team Publicists

DUTIES
Manage the daily press operations for sports teams and individual athletes

SALARY RANGE
$20,000 to $56,770 to $250,000+

WORK ENVIRONMENT
Primarily Indoors

BEST GEOGRAPHIC LOCATION(S)
Opportunities are available throughout the country, but are best in large, urban areas

MINIMUM EDUCATION LEVEL
Bachelor's Degree

SCHOOL SUBJECTS
English, Journalism, Speech

EXPERIENCE
Internships; volunteer and part-time experience

PERSONALITY TRAITS
Organized, Outgoing, Realistic

SKILLS
Business Management, Public Speaking, Writing

CERTIFICATION OR LICENSING
Recommended

SPECIAL REQUIREMENTS
None

EMPLOYMENT PROSPECTS
Fair

ADVANCEMENT PROSPECTS
Fair

OUTLOOK
About as Fast as the Average

NOC
1123

O*NET-SOC
27-3031.00

CAREER LADDER

Publicist, Major-League Team

Publicist, Minor-League Team

Assistant Publicist

Intern

their performance. The National Football League, National Basketball League, National Hockey League, and Major League Baseball, commonly known as the four majors, are the most notable of the professional leagues in the United States and are connected to many minor league and collegiate organizations. During recent decades, more professional leagues have started, such as the Women's National Basketball League, the Arena Football League, and Major League Soccer.

The sports industry has grown into an extremely lucrative business, and sports publicists are needed to help promote their respective teams or individual players.

■ THE JOB

Sports publicists perform a variety of duties during the course of a typical workday. They are responsible for all of the team's publicity, which includes news and feature releases, news conferences and background information, photography, videos, social media sites and the team or athlete's main Web site, media interviews, and media tours. They also create and update the team's publications, including media guides, programs for all home games, schedule cards, recruiting kits, annual reports, and booster club newsletters.

Sports publicists also deal with game management, which includes announcers, scoreboard operations, telephone hook-ups, scorers, officiating facilities, press box seating and credentials, broadcast facilities, video facilities, and travel and lodging. They are in charge of generating crowd participation by developing promotions, giveaways, half-time exhibitions, and music. Publicists may help design the team's uniform insignia and team banners.

Sports information directors might have other responsibilities, such as creating and placing advertising, attending league meetings, conventions, and workshops, coordinating booster club activities, fund-raising, fan surveys, budgets, equipment negotiations, licensing, and merchandising. Unlike other public relations practitioners, most sports information directors promote their competition as well as the team they work for. The better the opposition, the better the fan interest and ticket sales.

Collegiate publicists might not be affiliated with the college or university's public relations department, but instead might be housed under the athletic department.

Publicists who work for athletes constantly create publicity and news events to get their clients into the spotlight. Many publicists try to show their clients in a positive light by having the athletes participate in goodwill appearances or work with organizations like the United Way. Maintaining a positive image increases the athletes' potential income and market value.

■ EARNINGS

Sports publicists can earn anywhere from $20,000 to more than $250,000 per year. People just starting out might make less, while those with proven track records command higher salaries. Publicists who work for individual athletes can earn more money.

According to the U.S. Department of Labor, in May 2015 public relations specialists overall had median annual earnings of $56,770. The lowest paid 10 percent earned less than $31,690 and the highest paid 10 percent earned $110,080 or more.

Depending on their employers, most sports publicists enjoy a full complement of benefits, including vacation and sick time as well as holidays and medical and dental insurance. Self-employed workers must provide their own benefits.

■ WORK ENVIRONMENT

During the season, sports publicists may work 12- to 20-hour days, seven days a week. Since most sporting events take place in the evening or on weekends, and half are played on the road, sports publicists spend a lot of time on the job. Some publicists travel with their teams, while others do not. Either way, this job is time consuming.

■ EXPLORING

An informational interview with a publicist is a great way to learn more about this type of work and have your questions answered directly. Volunteer to handle various public relations-type duties for a school team or local sports teams or clubs. Run for student council or another leadership position at school to gain experience with public speaking and management. Read publications such as *Sports Illustrated* (http://www.si.com) and *Sports Business Journal* (http://www.sportsbusinessdaily.com/Journal.aspx), and attend sporting events to stay current on sports knowledge. It is also a good idea to volunteer to assist your school's athletic department (in high school or college); you may be able to have a hand in developing a team's media guide or programs. Cover sports for your college newspaper so that you will have some clips to show employers.

■ EDUCATION AND TRAINING REQUIREMENTS
High School

Sports publicists are the voice of the athlete or team they represent, so being an effective communicator is essential. Take classes in English and journalism to hone writing skills, and take speech classes to learn how to compose ideas and thoughts and convey them to an audience. Also take other college preparatory classes, such as math, science, and foreign language. Since sports publicists deal with the public, a general knowledge of history, sociology, psychology, and current events will be especially important.

Postsecondary Training
Most publicists working in the sports industry are college graduates with degrees in public relations, marketing, communications, journalism, or sports administration. A college degree is essential to success as a publicist.

Other Education or Training
The Public Relations Society of America offers continuing education (CE) classes, webinars, seminars, and workshops on crisis communications strategy, public relations writing, digital media, social media, and other topics. The International Association of Business Communicators and College Sports Information Directors of America also provide CE resources. Contact these organizations for more information.

▣ CERTIFICATION, LICENSING, AND SPECIAL REQUIREMENTS
Certification or Licensing
The Public Relations Society of America offers voluntary certification through the Universal Accreditation Board to public relations specialists. While this certification is not sports-related, it will help show prospective employers that you possess a high level of knowledge and experience. Candidates who pass a written and oral examination are designated as accredited in public relations. Voluntary accreditation is also offered by the International Association of Business Communicators to those who meet the education and work experience requirements and pass a written exam.

▣ EXPERIENCE, SKILLS, AND PERSONALITY TRAITS
Any experience one can obtain in the field of sports public relations (internships, volunteer opportunities, a part-time job, etc.) will be useful for aspiring publicists.

Successful sports publicists are outgoing and able to get along with many different types of people. Participate in sports or be a team manager in high school or college so that you become familiar with the lifestyle of an athlete and you can relate to it. Strong organizational skills and the ability to work well under stress are also required, particularly when dealing with big-name clients.

Sᴘᴏʀᴛꜱ Pᴜʙʟɪᴄɪᴛʏ

LEARN MORE ABOUT IT

Favorito, Joe. *Sports Publicity: A Practical Approach,* 2nd ed. New York: Routledge, 2012.

Fields, Sarah K. *Game Faces: Sport Celebrity and the Laws of Reputation*. Champaign, Ill.: University of Illinois Press, 2016.

Futterman, Matthew. *Players: The Story of Sports and Money, and the Visionaries Who Fought to Create a Revolution*. New York: Simon & Schuster, 2016.

L'Etang, Jacquie. *Sports Public Relations.* Thousand Oaks, Calif.: SAGE Publications Ltd., 2013.

Scott, David Meerman. *The New Rules of Marketing and PR: How to Use Social Media, Online Video, Mobile Applications, Blogs, News Releases, and Viral Marketing to Reach Buyers Directly,* 5th ed. Hoboken, N.J.: John Wiley & Sons, 2015.

Stoldt, G. Clayton, et al. *Sport Public Relations: Managing Stakeholder Communication,* 2nd ed. Champaign, Ill.: Human Kinetics, 2012.

▣ EMPLOYMENT PROSPECTS
Employers
Sports publicists work in one of three areas. Some work for public relations firms that handle athletes or sports-oriented events. Others work directly for sports teams in their front offices. Some are self-employed, working directly with clients.

Starting Out
The best way to enter public relations at the professional sports level is by gaining experience at the collegiate ranks. There are many internships available at this level, and getting one is the best way to get a foot in the door. Interns may be asked to contribute to publications and to write and prepare press releases or even help contribute to social media posts. This is a great opportunity not only to learn how to generate all of this material, but also to begin collecting writing samples and clips, which prospective employers will want to see as proof of journalistic and PR writing skills.

There are also training programs within established public relations companies.

▣ ADVANCEMENT PROSPECTS
Sports publicists advance by moving from employment at minor-league teams to opportunities with higher-level teams, culminating with a position with a major-league team. Some publicists develop a multifaceted skill set that

allows them to become assistant general manager or general manager, or get promoted to marketing manager or executive. A publicist at the college-level might advance by moving from working at a small, private school to a flagship state university. Some publicists open their own public relations firms. Others leave the field to teach public relations at colleges and universities.

▣ OUTLOOK

The field of sports publicity is very competitive, and even though it is expanding as more teams and leagues form, it is still difficult to land a job. The U.S. Department of Labor predicts that employment of public relations specialists will grow about as fast as the average for all careers, by 6 percent, through 2024. The number of applicants with degrees in the communications fields (journalism, public relations, and advertising) is expected to exceed the number of job openings. Sports publicists with strong knowledge of social media and who keep up with the latest communications technologies will continue to be in demand in the the coming years.

▣ UNIONS AND ASSOCIATIONS

Sports publicists do not typically belong to unions. The Public Relations Society of America (PRSA) is the major membership organization for publicists. Membership benefits include the opportunity to view free webinars, discounts on PRSA conferences and events, networking opportunities, and access to discussion boards and member directories. The society also has an Entertainment and Sports section for its members. Other membership organizations for publicists include the International Association of Business Communicators and College Sports Information Directors of America.

▣ TIPS FOR ENTRY

1. Read industry-related publications that are published and available through associations such as the Public Relations Society of America. Also check out *Sports Business Journal* (http://www.sportsbusinessdaily.com/Journal.aspx) to learn more about the sports industry.
2. Visit the career center of the Public Relations Society of America Web site, http://www.prsa.org/Jobcenter/career_resources/career_level/entry_level, to learn more about public relations careers.
3. For job listings, visit:
   • http://forms.cosida.com/jobs.aspx
   • http://www.prsa.org/jobcenter
   • http://jobs.iabc.com
4. Visit http://www.prsa.org/Network/FindAFirm/ Search for a database of PR firms, including those that specialize in sports and leisure.

▣ FOR MORE INFORMATION

College Sports Information Directors of America is a membership organization of sports public relations and related media and communications professionals.

College Sports Information Directors of America (CoSIDA)
PO Box 78718
Greenwood, IN 46142-6427
http://www.cosida.com

The International Association of Business Communicators provides education, certification, publications, conferences, and other resources for business communications professionals.

International Association of Business Communicators (IABC)
155 Montgomery Street, Suite 1210
San Francisco, CA 94104-4117
Tel: (800) 776-4222; (415) 544-4700
Fax: (415) 544-4747
E-mail: member_relations@iabc.com
https://www.iabc.com

The Public Relations Society of America provides professional development and sets standards of excellent for public relations and communications professionals.

Public Relations Society of America (PRSA)
33 Maiden Lane, 11th Floor
New York, NY 10038-5150
Tel: (212) 460-1400
E-mail: membership@prsa.org
https://www.prsa.org

Sports Scouts

▣ OVERVIEW

Sports scouts observe athletic contests and athletes to gather information that will help the team that employs them. They may attend a game in the hopes of recruiting a player, or they may accumulate information about an opponent's players and strategies. There are approximately 224,110 scouts and coaches employed in the United States, according to the Department of Labor.

▣ HISTORY

In the first part of the 20th century, baseball became popular as a professional sport. Large eastern cities like New York and Boston were home to some of the best and most popular teams. While these teams competed in baseball stadiums, their scouts were competing to find talented, young players. Traveling by train through the South and Midwest, baseball scouts rushed from town to town in hopes of discovering the next Cy Young or Cap Anson.

Some scouts worked for professional teams while others signed players to personal contracts, hoping to sell those contracts to the owners of professional teams. As baseball became more organized, scouts began to work almost exclusively for one professional team. Soon, young prospects no longer were sent directly to Major League Baseball teams but played in the minor leagues or farm teams. These teams were set up to teach players, who already possessed excellent abilities, the subtle nuances of the game.

These new teams created a need for even more scouts. In addition to locating and signing talented young players, other scouts were assigned the task of watching these players develop and deciding when they were ready to advance to the next level.

As football, basketball, and soccer became popular sports, professional teams began to hire scouts to evaluate the talent of players and the strengths and weaknesses of other teams.

■ THE JOB

Sports scouts attend sporting events and record their findings for pay. They may travel from city to city watching other teams from their league play, or they may attend games for the purpose of recruiting players for their own team. Scouts are an extension of the coaching staff of a team, and in many cases, assistant coaches have scouting responsibilities.

There are two general tasks assigned to scouts. One is recruitment, the other is to gather information about an opposing team. *Recruitment scouts* attend high school and college games to look for talented young players. Coaches or general managers from professional teams may inform scouts about specific personnel needs. For example, a basketball coach may need a guard who can handle the ball well and shoot jump shots. A scout attends numerous college games and then returns to the coach with a list of players who meet the description. In most cases the list will rate the individual players and include some additional information, such as the players' ages, heights, and weights. Notes or impressions from an interview the scout conducted with the player would also be included. Recruitment scouts may attend a game to see a particular individual play but will also make notes on other players. Scouts may see 10 or more games a week, so they must keep detailed notes. Scouts must also be

comfortable with statistics, both compiling and understanding them. Scouts examine statistics like earned run average, yards per carry, and field goal percentage in order to assist them in their deliberations concerning players.

A scout may need to see a player more than once to determine if they have the ability to play at the next level. Scouts report their findings back to the coach or general manager, and it is up to that person to act on the scout's recommendations.

Recruitment scouts need to see numerous games so that they acquire the ability to accurately assess talent. Scouts distinguish between players who have sound, fundamental skills and an understanding of the game and players who are natural athletes but have not yet acquired the finer skills.

Many professional sports leagues have minor leagues or developmental leagues in which players not yet good enough to play at the highest professional level hone their skills. Professional baseball has minor leagues, or a farm system, that consists of players who have talent but are still maturing or learning skills. Many scouts are assigned to these leagues to keep a watchful eye on players as they develop. For example, a Major League Baseball team may employ both full- and part-time scouts, most of whom concentrate on players already playing in the minor leagues. They also receive a daily report compiled by the Major League Scouting Bureau (MLSB). The MLSB is a professional scouting organization that is overseen by the Commissioner's Office of Major League Baseball. It employs approximately 34 full-time and 13 part-time

QUICK FACTS

ALTERNATE TITLE(S)
Recruitment Scouts

DUTIES
Attend high school, college, and professional games to gather information about athletes; study the opponent's players and strategies to help their team win games

SALARY RANGE
$17,930 to $31,000 to $70,050+

WORK ENVIRONMENT
Indoors/Outdoors

BEST GEOGRAPHIC LOCATION(S)
Opportunities are available throughout the world

MINIMUM EDUCATION LEVEL
Bachelor's Degree

SCHOOL SUBJECTS
Foreign Language, Physical Education, Psychology

EXPERIENCE
Experience as an athlete, coach, or manager required

PERSONALITY TRAITS
Curious, Organized, Outgoing

SKILLS
Coaching/Physical Training, Interpersonal, Organizational

CERTIFICATION OR LICENSING
Required

SPECIAL REQUIREMENTS
None

EMPLOYMENT PROSPECTS
Fair

ADVANCEMENT PROSPECTS
Fair

OUTLOOK
About as Fast as the Average

NOC
5252

O*NET-SOC
27-2022.00

CAREER LADDER

Director of Scouting

Scouting Supervisor

Professional League Scout

College Scout

High School Scout

scouts across the United States, Canada, and Puerto Rico. Other professional sports leagues have similar systems. For example, the National Basketball Association has a developmental league. Sports scouts are also assigned to these leagues to evaluate talent.

Assistant coaches and scouts often attend opponents' games to find out about players' abilities and team strategies. They watch the game, diagram set plays, and note players' tendencies. During practice the following week, scouts share their findings and, when possible, detail plans to help offset an opponent's strength.

■ EARNINGS

According to the U.S. Department of Labor, sports scouts and coaches had median annual earnings of $31,000 in May 2015. Beginning sports scouts and coaches earned a salary of $17,930 or less, while the most experienced scouts with many success stories earned more than $70,050. Sports scouts also are reimbursed for travel expenses and meals. Another fringe benefit is free admission to countless sporting events.

Full-time sports scouts typically receive benefits such as paid vacation and sick days, health insurance, and pension plans.

■ WORK ENVIRONMENT

Sports scouts travel an average of three weeks out of every month, and they are away from home most nights and weekends. While on the road, they stay in hotels and eat most of their meals in restaurants. They travel often by car or bus and also frequently by plane.

Workdays on the road are quite long. A sports scout may be on the road by 7:00 A.M. to drive four hours to meet with a player and watch an afternoon game. There may be another game to see that night in another location, or the evening may be spent reviewing video of games attended over the last few days.

Long hours and near constant travel are typical of work as a sports scout, and more often than not, there is little reward for the effort. A scout may recommend several hundred players over the course of his or her career and only a handful of those players will ever make it to the professional level. Despite this, dedicated sports scouts continue to visit isolated diamonds, tiny high school and college gyms, and the cracked concrete of the urban ball court looking for the next superstar.

■ EXPLORING

Individuals interested in a career as a sports scout should participate in sporting events at the high school and college level. Participate either as a player or as an assistant to players or coaches. Read a variety of books by coaches and athletes to learn fundamentals and strategies, and regularly visit the Web sites and social media sites of sports teams, athletes, coaches, and scouts to keep up with news and issues. Also, take part in community sports programs to interact with a variety of players and observe different styles of play.

■ EDUCATION AND TRAINING REQUIREMENTS
High School

A general high school education will give the basic skills needed to succeed in sports scouting. Speech and English courses will help ease communication with prospects as well as with conveying findings to coaches, managers, and front office workers. Learn Spanish or Japanese to help connect with foreign players, who are increasingly sought after by Major League Baseball teams. Finally, take physical education classes and join sports teams—especially the sport for which you want to scout.

Postsecondary Training

There are no colleges and universities that offer classes in sports scouting. Professional baseball teams send promising employees to a "scout school" that is sponsored by the Major League Scouting Bureau. Employees learn the basics of scouting and how to judge talent. The most famous graduate of the school is former scout and current White Sox executive vice president Kenny Williams.

The U.S. Department of Labor reports that scouts typically have a bachelor's degree, with some pursuing degrees in business, marketing, sales, or sports management. An increasing number of scouts have degrees, but there are still many who have just earned a high school diploma or completed some postsecondary training.

■ CERTIFICATION, LICENSING, AND SPECIAL REQUIREMENTS
Certification or Licensing

There are no specific certification or licensing requirements for professional sports scouts. However, scouts who also work as coaches at public high schools or universities may have to meet state certification requirements.

■ EXPERIENCE, SKILLS, AND PERSONALITY TRAITS

Previous experience as a collegiate or professional athlete, coach, or manager is usually required to enter the field.

First and foremost, a person who would like to become a sports scout should have vast knowledge of a particular sport. For a sports scout, an athletic contest is not only something to enjoy, but also something to study. Sports scouts must be detail oriented and methodical in order to understand the rules, regulations, fundamentals, strategies, and personality types that are best suited to athletic competition.

Above-average organizational skills are also essential. More often than not, sports scouts will attend several games before reporting to a supervisor. They must be able to organize their thoughts and notes so they can compare players from several games to come to conclusions about their abilities.

Communication skills are important. Sports scouts must be able to write and speak well, particularly because they interact with other coaches and players on a daily basis. If they work as a recruitment scout, they are in contact with younger players, and thus work well with and understand younger people. A proficiency in a foreign language, especially Spanish or Japanese, will also be of great help, since sports scouts will be sent to foreign countries to monitor the development of promising athletes.

A sports scout must also be a team player, a good judge of talent and character, and be able to recognize ability and mental toughness in others.

■ EMPLOYMENT PROSPECTS

Employers

Sports scouts are employed by major league organizations throughout North America and the world. Others work for professional scouting organizations, such as the Major League Scouting Bureau. Scouts also work for high school and college athletic teams.

Starting Out

Many sports scouts are retired athletes who use their knowledge of the game to scout for younger talent. Not only do athletes gain knowledge from years of competition, but they make valuable contacts in the sporting world.

An aspiring sports scout should become familiar with local sports activity and keep track of talented young players. Meeting people who are active in the sports community is a great help. Sports scouts are part of a vast network of people who gather, compile, and exchange

Former Mets player John Stearns attends a game to scout for the Seattle Mariners. (Debby Wong. Shutterstock.)

information about sports. Coaches, broadcasters, and journalists are also members of this group.

■ ADVANCEMENT PROSPECTS

Sports scouts who provide accurate and concise reports often have the opportunity to observe more talented athletes. A professional baseball scout, for example, may begin scouting college players. As the scout gains experience in providing reliable information, they may be assigned to a minor league division, and eventually may become a scouting supervisor, and then director of scouting for a Major League team.

Scouts who succeed and advance are organized, honest, and effective communicators. Sports scouts build their reputations by identifying players who will be successful at the professional level. Advancement is often based on the success of the players whom the scout has selected.

SCOUTING FOR TALENT ON THE COURT AND FIELD

LEARN MORE ABOUT IT

Austin, Daniel L. *Baseball's Last Great Scout: The Life of Hugh Alexander.* Lincoln, Nebr.: University of Nebraska Press, 2013.

Bodet, Gib, and P.J. Dragseth. *Major League Scout: Twelve Thousand Baseball Games and Six Million Miles.* Jefferson, N.C.: McFarland, 2013.

Calvin, Michael. *The Nowhere Men: The Unknown Story of Football's True Talent Spotters*. Kingston upon Thames: Random House UK, 2014.

Dragseth, P.J. (ed.) *Eye for Talent: Interviews with Veteran Baseball Scouts.* Jefferson, N.C.: McFarland, 2009.

Feinstein, John. *Where Nobody Knows Your Name: Life In the Minor Leagues of Baseball.* New York: Anchor Books, 2015.

Malloy, Shane, and Brian Burke. *The Art of Scouting: How The Hockey Experts Really Watch The Game and Decide Who Makes It.* Hoboken, N.J.: John Wiley & Sons, 2011.

■ OUTLOOK

According to the U.S. Department of Labor (DOL), employment opportunities for scouts and coaches are expected to grow about as fast as the average for all careers through 2024, but competition for jobs will be stiff. The sports scouts field is small and most work for professional teams. Baseball is the sport that employs the greatest number of scouts. Due to the limited number of professional scouts, most job opportunities will be found with lower-level sports, such as with high school and college athletic teams. The DOL reports that the "growing interest in college and professional sports will also increase demand for scouts. In addition, as college tuition increases and scholarships become more competitive, high school athletes will hire scouts directly, in an effort to increase their chances of receiving a college scholarship."

A recent concept in the industry is pool scouting. The concept involves a group of scouts who collect data on a great many players and provide that information to several teams. The scouts are not employed by any one team, but by professional scouting organizations, such as the Major League Scouting Bureau.

If professional leagues add expansion teams and the talent pool diminishes, there will be more opportunities for sports scouts to travel and work in foreign countries. On the other hand, if professional sports leagues contract, there will be fewer job opportunities for scouts.

■ UNIONS AND ASSOCIATIONS

Scouts do not belong to unions. Scouts may become affiliated with industry organizations and employers within their sport. For example, baseball scouts may work for the Major League Scouting Bureau.

■ TIPS FOR ENTRY

1. Talk to sports scouts about their careers. Ask them for advice on breaking into the field.
2. Participate in sports in high school and college. Learn as much you can about the sport for which you'd like to work as a scout.
3. Land an entry-level job with a collegiate or professional sports team to obtain experience and make industry contacts.

■ FOR MORE INFORMATION

The Major League Baseball Scouting Bureau aims to provide the best information on prospects to help baseball clubs make more educated selections in the draft.

Major League Baseball Scouting Bureau (MLB Scouting Bureau)
3500 Porsche Way, Suite 100
Ontario, CA 91764-4941
Tel: (909) 980-1881
Fax: (909) 980-7794
http://mlb.mlb.com/mlb/official_info/about_mlb/scouting_overview.jsp

Major League Soccer provides a variety of soccer information on its Web site, from competitions and conferences to league leaders and trending players.

Major League Soccer (MLS)
E-mail: feedback@mlssoccer.com
http://www.mlssoccer.com

The National Basketball Association includes basketball games and stats, stories, and more on its Web site.

National Basketball Association (NBA)
http://www.nba.com

The National Football League offers football news, videos, schedules, team standings, and more on its Web site.

National Football League (NFL)
http://www.nfl.com

Watch live hockey games, find schedules and information about players, and get stats through the National Hockey League's Web site.

National Hockey League (NHL)
Tel: (800) 559-2333; (412) 386-2646

E-mail: customersupport@web.nhl.com
http://www.nhl.com

Learn more about women's national basketball teams and players, the stats, game schedules, and more through the Women's National Basketball Association's Web site.

**Women's National Basketball
Association (WNBA)**
645 Fifth Avenue
New York, NY 10022
http://www.wnba.com

Sports Trainers

■ OVERVIEW

Sports trainers, also referred to as *athletic trainers*, *certified sports medicine trainers*, and *certified sports medicine therapists*, help amateur and professional athletes prevent injuries, give first aid when an injury occurs during a practice or event, and manage the rehabilitation programs and routines of injured athletes.

Athletic trainers often consult with physicians during all stages of athletic training to ensure that athletes under their care are physically capable of participating in competition. According to the Department of Labor, there are approximately 23,450 athletic trainers employed in the United States.

■ HISTORY

Aristotle, Leonardo da Vinci, and Étienne-Jules Marey all conducted experiments and studies involving motion and the human body, but it was the 19th-century French physiologist Marey whose devices to study human motion really advanced the field of biomechanics and sports medicine. In fact, both modern cinematography and sports medicine claim him as the father of their respective fields. Marey's first contribution was the first force platform, a device that was able to visualize the forces between the foot and the floor. Marey's pictures with another device, the chronophotograph, superimposed the stages of action onto a single photograph; in essence, giving form to motion and allowing scientists to study it frame by frame, motion by motion. By 1892, Marey had even made primitive motion pictures, but his cinematic efforts were quickly eclipsed by those by Louis and Auguste Lumière.

Following both World Wars I and II, Marey's and other scientists' experiments with motion would combine with the need to heal and/or completely replace the limbs of war veterans. In order to provide an amputee with a prosthetic device that would come as close as possible to replicating the movement and functional value of a real limb, scientists and doctors began to work together to understand the range of motion and interrelationships peculiar to each part of the human body.

Mechanically, sports can be categorized according to the kinds of movements used. Each individual sport utilizes a unique combination of basic motions, including walking, running, jumping, kicking, and throwing. These basic motions have all been rigidly defined for scientific study so that injuries related to these motions can be better understood and treated. For example, sports that place heavy demands on one part of an athlete's body may overload that part and produce an injury, such as tennis elbow and swimmer's shoulder. Baseball, on the other hand, is a throwing sport, and certain injuries from overuse of the shoulder and elbow are expected. Athletes who play volleyball or golf also use some variation of the throwing motion and therefore also sustain injuries to their shoulders and elbows.

Today, sports trainers are part of the team of sports medicine professionals that treat the injuries of both the amateur and elite athlete. Like sports physicians, certified sports medicine therapists are responsible for preventing injuries as well as treating them, and they use their knowledge of the human body and its wide range of motions to discover new ways of reducing stress and damage from athletic activities. They work in high schools, secondary schools, colleges, and universities, and a smaller number

---

QUICK FACTS

ALTERNATE TITLE(S)
Athletic Trainers, Certified Sports Medicine Therapists, Certified Sports Medicine Trainers

DUTIES
Help athletes prevent injuries; provide first aid when injuries occur; supervise rehabilitation programs of injured athletes

SALARY RANGE
$28,480 to $44,670 to $68,300+

WORK ENVIRONMENT
Indoors/Outdoors

BEST GEOGRAPHIC LOCATION(S)
Opportunities exist in all regions

MINIMUM EDUCATION LEVEL
Bachelor's Degree

SCHOOL SUBJECTS
Biology, Health, Physical Education

EXPERIENCE
Internship; volunteer or part-time experience

PERSONALITY TRAITS
Hands On, Helpful, Organized

SKILLS
Coaching/Physical Training, Interpersonal, Organizational

CERTIFICATION OR LICENSING
Required

SPECIAL REQUIREMENTS
None

EMPLOYMENT PROSPECTS
Good

ADVANCEMENT PROSPECTS
Good

OUTLOOK
Much Faster than the Average

NOC
3144

O*NET-SOC
29-9091.00

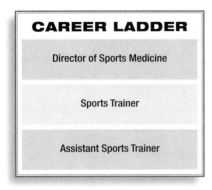

work for professional teams. Many work in health clubs, sports medicine clinics, and other athletic health care settings. In 1990, the American Medical Association (AMA) recognized athletic training as an allied health profession.

■ THE JOB

Sports trainers help amateur and professional athletes prevent injuries through proper exercises and conditioning; provide immediate first-aid to injuries when they occur during a practice or event; and lead injured athletes safely through rehabilitation programs and routines. For the most part, sports trainers are not medical doctors, and are not allowed to conduct certain procedures or provide advanced types of medical care, such as prescribing or administering drugs. Some trainers, however, are trained physicians. If an individual is also trained as an *osteopathic physician*, for example, he or she is licensed as a medical doctor and can conduct more advanced procedures and techniques, including diagnosis, surgery, and the prescription of drugs.

In order to prevent injuries, sports trainers organize team physicals, making certain that each player is examined and evaluated by a physician prior to that athlete's participation in the sport. Along with the team physician, they help to analyze each athlete's overall readiness to play, fitness level, and known or existing weaknesses or injuries. When necessary, they recommend stretching, conditioning, and strengthening exercises to aid the athlete in preventing or exacerbating an injury. This may involve developing specific routines for individual athletes. Finally, athletic trainers work with coaches, and sometimes team physicians, to choose protective athletic equipment. Before games and practice, they often inspect the playing field, surface, or area for any flagrant or subtle risks of injury to the athlete.

Prior to a practice or competition, the athletic trainer may help an athlete conduct special stretching exercises or, as a preventive measure, he or she might tape, wrap, bandage, or brace knees, ankles, or other joints, and areas of the athlete's body that might be at risk for injury. The trainer routinely treats cuts, scratches, and abrasions, among other minor injuries. They may tape, pad, or wrap injuries, and install face guards. When serious injuries do occur, whether in practice or during a competition, the athletic trainer's role is to provide prompt and accurate first-aid treatment to the athlete to ensure that athlete's full recovery. They are trained in emergency procedures and prepared to provide emergency treatment for conditions such as shock, concussion, or bone fracture, stabilizing the athlete until they reach a hospital or trauma center. Often, the trainer will accompany the injured athlete to the hospital, making certain the team physician or an assistant trainer is still on hand to address the health concerns and needs of those athletes who are still competing.

Working in concert with the team physician and several other health professionals, athletic trainers often supervise the therapeutic rehabilitation of athletes under their care. They analyze the athlete's injury and create individualized therapy routines. The trainer may advise the athlete to wear a protective brace or guard to minimize damage while the athlete is recuperating from an injury. Athletic trainers in charge of every level of athlete should be licensed to perform specific medical functions and operate certain devices and equipment.

■ EARNINGS

Earnings vary depending on the level of athletics in which the trainer is involved, the trainer's education and credentials, and the number and type of responsibilities. Those considering a career as an athletic trainer should keep all aspects of the job and salary in perspective; the slight increase in salary of a trainer working for a college team might be offset by the higher stress levels and longer hours away from home. Trainers who work with professional athletes are away from home a great deal, including evenings, weekends, and holidays.

The U.S. Department of Labor reports that athletic trainers earned median salaries of $44,670 in May 2015. The highest paid 10 percent earned more than $68,300, while the lowest paid 10 percent earned less than $28,480.

Depending on their employers, most sports trainers enjoy a full complement of benefits, including vacation and sick time as well as holidays and medical and dental insurance. Self-employed workers must provide their own benefits.

■ WORK ENVIRONMENT

Athletes train year round and so do the sports trainers who supervise their conditioning and rehabilitation programs. Depending on the level and size of an athletic program, trainers may work with athletes in one or more sports. Sports trainers who work in high schools often act as the trainer for several, or all, of the athletic teams. A lot also depends on the school's budgetary restrictions. Most schools generally have a separate trainer for men's and women's sports. Trainers in professional sports work only in one sport and for one team.

Most of the trainer's time is spent at an athletic facility, either in preparation for work or in conditioning or rehab sessions. Athletic trainers are on a schedule similar to that of their athletes; they go to practices, schedule weight and rehab sessions, and attend games. They are expected to travel when and where the team travels.

■ EXPLORING

Most trainers, like other professionals who work with athletes, were first drawn to sports as participants. High school and college students can gain valuable experience by actively participating in a sport. Such experience lends a prospective trainer added insight into the injuries typical of a given sport, as well as the compassion and empathy necessary to comfort an injured athlete who is forced to sit out a game. Most teams need help with everything from equipment to statistics, so plenty of opportunities exist to explore a variety of sports-related positions. Good experience can be gained by working with and learning beside a trainer or team physician. This type of experience is a helpful foundation for a future internship or job; successful candidates are usually those with the most experience and on-the-job training.

■ EDUCATION AND TRAINING REQUIREMENTS
High School

Participation in sports while in high school, either as an athlete or as assistant trainer or manager for a school team, is a good way to learn more about sports training. Take classes in physical education, health, anatomy, and physiology. Students with an interest in becoming athletic trainers will want to become certified in CPR and first aid.

Postsecondary Training

Sports trainers usually earn a bachelor's degree from a college or university program in athletic training that is accredited by the Commission on Accreditation of Athletic Training Education (http://caate.net/search-for-accredited-program/). Students then intern with a certified athletic trainer. Another option is to earn a bachelor's degree or even a master's or professional degree in a related health field, such as osteopathy, and then intern with a certified athletic trainer. The number of hours required for clinical study and the internship phase will vary, depending on the program and the professional organization.

Most accredited programs in athletic training include course work in the prevention and evaluation of athletic injuries and illnesses, first aid and emergency care,

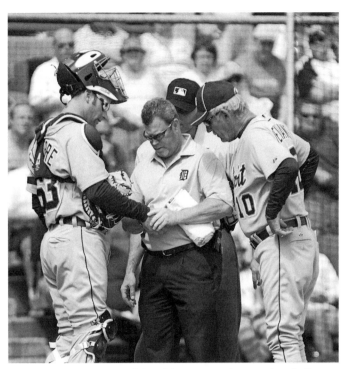

A trainer checks a catcher's hand for injuries during a baseball game. (Aspen Photo. Shutterstock.)

therapeutic exercises, therapeutic modalities, administration of athletic training programs, human anatomy, human physiology, exercise physiology, kinesiology, nutrition, psychology, and personal and community health.

Other Education or Training

Participating in continuing education classes is a great way to keep your skills up to date and learn about new developments in athletic training. The National Athletic Trainers' Association and the American College of Sports Medicine provide professional development workshops and seminars.

■ CERTIFICATION, LICENSING, AND SPECIAL REQUIREMENTS
Certification or Licensing

Nearly all states require athletic trainers to be licensed or registered, which requires certification by the Board of Certification (BOC) for the Athletic Trainer. Different membership organizations and their respective certifying bodies have different eligibility requirements; individuals choose which organization best characterizes their ultimate goal.

For example, the National Athletic Trainers' Association requires that each member have a bachelor's degree (in any field), be either a graduate of an accredited program in athletic training or complete an

TOP INDUSTRIES EMPLOYING SPORTS TRAINERS AND MEAN ANNUAL SALARIES, MAY 2015

FAST FACTS

- Colleges, universities, and professional schools: 4,800 jobs, $47,660
- Offices of other health practitioners: 3,890 jobs, $43,690
- General medical and surgical hospitals: 3,720 jobs, $46,600
- Other amusement and recreation industries: 3,150 jobs, $43,490+
- Elementary and secondary schools: 2,580 jobs, $55,420

Source: U.S. Department of Labor

internship, and pass a certification exam consisting of three sections—written, simulation, and oral practical.

■ EXPERIENCE, SKILLS, AND PERSONALITY TRAITS

Experience as an intern, volunteer, or part-time employee with a professional and amateur sports teams, sports medicine clinic, school, or another organization that employs sports trainers is highly recommended.

Workers in this field need an understanding of human anatomy and physiology, both in terms of physical capabilities and injury treatment and prevention. Sports trainers are not squeamish when it comes to blood, broken bones, or other wounds. Athletes do get hurt, and a trainer who is unable to cope well with this aspect of sports may have a difficult time succeeding in the career. The ability and knowledge to handle medical emergencies is especially important for certified athletic trainers, whose work focuses on injury prevention and treatment.

■ EMPLOYMENT PROSPECTS
Employers

There are approximately 23,450 athletic trainers in the United States. Sports trainers are employed by professional and amateur sports teams, private sports organizations, sports facilities, sports medicine clinics, hospitals, secondary and intermediate schools, the military, educational institutions, and by individual athletes. Other possible athletic-training employment opportunities can be found in corporate health programs, health clubs, clinical and industrial health care programs, and athletic training curriculum programs.

Starting Out

Athletic trainers, regardless of the professional organization they join, are usually required to complete a period of training with a certified athletic trainer or sports medicine therapist. These internships provide students with the foundation for future networking possibilities. Many students find full-time jobs with the teams, organizations, or school districts with which they interned. At the very least, these internships offer students the chance to make valuable contacts and gain valuable on-the-job experience.

Most accredited programs in athletic training also have career services departments that host recruitment seminars with major organizations, provide career counseling services, and put students in contact with prospective employers.

Finally, one of the benefits to belonging to a professional organization is that these associations publish newsletters and maintain Web sites, both of which list job openings. Through these media, as well as through meetings, seminars, and continuing education, students and trainers can make new contacts that will help them locate work and add to their base of knowledge. The National Athletic Trainers' Association, for example, offers job openings in all athletic training settings and locations at its Web site, http://jobs.nata.org.

■ ADVANCEMENT PROSPECTS

Acquiring additional training and education is the most common way of advancing in the field of sports training. Those trainers who have spent years working in the field and who update their skills each year by taking continuing education courses, sometimes even returning to school for an advanced degree, will be among the first to receive promotions.

Management responsibilities are the other way in which athletic trainers can advance in their field. Large universities often employ several trainers to serve the many different teams, with one trainer acting as the *head trainer*, sometimes also called the *director of sports medicine*. This individual coordinates the daily activities and responsibilities of the other trainers and works closely with the coaches of the school's various teams to ensure that all the demands are being met. Most often, trainers advance by working for several years at one school and then move on to another school when an opening is announced that will mean greater responsibilities and benefits.

■ OUTLOOK

The U.S. Department of Labor predicts that employment for athletic trainers will grow by 21 percent, much faster than the average for all careers, throughout 2024. The increasing number of amateur and school sports teams accounts for some of this growth, as does the public's increasing interest in health and fitness. Increased awareness of sports-related injuries, particularly concussions, has increased the demand for athletic trainers. Strong growth is also expected to continue in the health care industry, according to the DOL, as "advances in injury prevention and detection and more sophisticated treatments are projected to increase the demand for athletic trainers." Opportunities should also be good with the military, which is hiring civilian sports trainers to help personnel reduce the risk of injury during exercise and to help rehabilitate those who have been injured.

Competition for the more glamorous jobs is tough; positions with professional athletes and teams are extremely difficult to find and those working in them usually have years and years of experience. More opportunities exist for certified athletic trainers who work with high school athletes, especially if trainers have other skills that make them more employable. For example, the athletic trainer wishing to work with high school athletes who also can teach biology, math, physical education, or other school subjects most likely will find a position sooner than the candidate with only a background in athletic training. The reasoning is simple: With school budgets being cut back, those individuals who perform double-duty will be more attractive to school boards looking to cut costs.

Positions at the college and university level offer the athletic trainer greater stability, with little turnover. Competition for these spots is also tough, however, and many schools are now requiring candidates to have a master's degree in order to be considered.

■ UNIONS AND ASSOCIATIONS

Athletic trainers do not belong to unions, but many join professional associations such as the National Athletic Trainers' Association (NATA) and the American College of Sports Medicine. These organizations provide networking opportunities, professional development classes, publications, and members-only job-search resources. The Board of Certification for the Athletic Trainer provides voluntary certification.

■ TIPS FOR ENTRY

1. Read the *Journal of Athletic Training* (http://nata-journals.org) and the *Athletic Training Education Journal* (http://nataej.org) to learn more about the field.
2. Visit http://jobs.nata.org for job listings.
3. Attend the National Athletic Trainers' Association's Clinical Symposia & Athletic Training Expo to network and participate in continuing education classes.

4. Visit http://www.nata.org/professional-interests/emerging-settings for information on emerging practice areas for sports trainers.

■ FOR MORE INFORMATION

The American College of Sports Medicine provides continuing education, certification, career development, and other resources for sports medicine professionals.

American College of Sports Medicine (ACSM)
401 West Michigan Street
Indianapolis, IN 46202-3233
Tel: (317) 637-9200
Fax: (317) 634-7817
E-mail: publicinfo@acsm.org
http://www.acsm.org

The Board of Certification for the Athletic Trainer is the only accredited certification program for athletic trainers in the United States.

Board of Certification for the Athletic Trainer (BOC)
1415 Harney Street, Suite 200
Omaha, NE 68102-2250
Tel: (877) 262-3926
Fax: (402) 561-0598
E-mail: BOC@bocatc.org
http://www.bocatc.org

The National Athletic Trainers' Association provides a directory of accredited athletic training programs, job listings, and information on careers and certification.

National Athletic Trainers' Association (NATA)
1620 Valwood Parkway, Suite 115
Carrollton, TX 75247-6916
Tel: (860) 427-5700; (214) 637-6282
Fax: (214) 637-2206
http://www.nata.org

Sportswriters

■ OVERVIEW

Sportswriters are reporters who cover the news in sports for newspapers and magazines. They research original ideas or follow up on breaking stories, contacting coaches, athletes, and team owners and managers for comments or more information. Sometimes a sportswriter is fortunate enough to get their own column, in which the sportswriter editorializes on current news or developments in sports. Sportswriters also write

QUICK FACTS

ALTERNATE TITLE(S)
Magazine Sportswriters,
Newspaper Sportswriters,
Sports Columnists, Sports
Reporters, Stringers

DUTIES
Write about sporting events,
athletes, and other sports-
related topics; conduct
interviews and research

SALARY RANGE
$21,390 to $36,360 to
$81,580+

WORK ENVIRONMENT
Indoors/Outdoors

BEST GEOGRAPHIC LOCATION(S)
Opportunities exist in all regions

MINIMUM EDUCATION LEVEL
Bachelor's Degree

SCHOOL SUBJECTS
English, Journalism, Physical
Education

EXPERIENCE
Any writing or sports experience
helpful

PERSONALITY TRAITS
Creative, Curious, Organized

SKILLS
Interpersonal, Organizational,
Writing

CERTIFICATION OR LICENSING
None

SPECIAL REQUIREMENTS
None

EMPLOYMENT PROSPECTS
Fair

ADVANCEMENT PROSPECTS
Fair

OUTLOOK
Decline

NOC
5121

O*NET-SOC
27-3022.00, 27-3043.00

for online publications and social media.

■ HISTORY

Throughout the world there are thousands of daily newspapers and far more semiweeklies, biweeklies, and weeklies, circulating millions of copies on a regular basis. In the international context, the average newspaper is usually heavy with sensational news, light on serious criticism, and burdened by all types of problems (especially economic). Outside Western Europe and North America there are very few ultra-serious, newspapers. Most of the world's newspapers are privately owned, but some degree of government control is evident in many countries.

Magazine journalism has been a potent force in the United States (and internationally) for decades, appealing mainly to the elite, the well educated, and opinion leaders. At least this is true in the sense of "journalistic" magazines. Generally more incisive, more articulate, and more interpretive and comprehensive than newspapers, magazines have supplied an important intellectual dimension to news-oriented journalism. Whereas the main function of newspaper journalism is to inform or summarize in brief fashion, the aim of most magazine journalism is to fill gaps—to explain, interpret, criticize, and comment. Magazine journalism in its many types and styles supplements newspapers and fleshes out the bare bones of newspaper journalism.

Most magazines and newspapers have sections that focus on sports; others, such as *Sports Illustrated* and *ESPN The Magazine*, focus entirely on sports reporting. In either

case, sportswriters are needed to write articles about athletes, teams, and sports competitions. Sportswriters are employed by both newspapers and magazines throughout the United States.

Today, the growth of the Internet and social media have created increasing opportunities for sportswriters to publish their work on blogs, newspaper and magazine Web sites, and other digital venues.

■ THE JOB

The sportswriter's primary job is to report the outcomes of the sports events that occurred that day. Since one newspaper can't employ enough reporters to cover, in person, every single high school, college, and professional sports event that happens on any given day, let alone sports events happening in other cities and countries, sportswriters use the wire news services to get the details. The entire body of statistics for tennis matches, hockey games, and track-and-field events, for example, can be digitally available so that sportswriters can include the general story and the vital statistics in as condensed or lengthy a form as space allows. Major national and international wire services include Reuters, Associated Press, United Press International, Agence France-Presse, and ITAR-TASS.

Sportwriters reviews the local, national, and international news that comes in over the wire news services and then fleshes out the top or lead story, perhaps putting a local perspective on it. An example of a lead story might be the comeback of a professional tennis star; the underdog victory of a third-rate, much-maligned football team; the incredible pitching record of a high school athlete; or the details of a football running back who blew out his knee in a crucial last-minute play. The sportswriter then calls or interviews in person coaches, athletes, scouts, agents, promoters, and sometimes, in the case of an athletic injury, a physician or team of physicians.

Depending on the edition of the newspaper or magazine, the sportswriter might report events that happened anywhere from the day before to events that took place within that week or month. For example, a sportswriter who writes for a magazine such as *Sports Illustrated* probably won't write articles with the same degree of detail per game. Instead, they write articles, commonly called features, that explore an entire season for a team or an athlete. The *magazine sportswriter* might take the same story of the running back with the damaged knee ligaments and follow that athlete through his surgery and rehabilitation, interviewing the running back as well as his wife, doctors, coaches, and agent. This stage of gathering information is the same for both newspaper and magazine sportswriters, the only difference is the timeline. A *newspaper sportswriter* may have only a few hours to conduct research and call around for comments, while the sportswriter for a magazine may have anywhere from several weeks to several months to compose the story.

Regardless of whether the sportswriter works for a newspaper or magazine, the next step for the sportswriter is to write the story. The method will vary depending on the medium. Most sportswriters for newspapers are subject to the constraints of space, and these limits can change at any moment. On a dull day, up until the hour before the paper is published, the sportswriter might have a quarter of a page to fill with local sports news. At the last minute, however, a breaking story might warrant more space. To maintain this required flexibility, sportswriters, like other reporters who write for daily newspapers, compose their stories with the most crucial facts contained within the first one or two paragraphs of the story. Most newspapers now also have Web sites, which allow sportswriters to write longer stories and/or sports editors to use content that didn't make the newspaper's print edition.

Sportswriters for magazines are not as prone to having their stories cut down at the last minute, but their writing is subject to more careful editing. Magazines usually have story meetings weeks or months in advance of the relevant issue, giving sportswriters ample time to plan, research, and write their articles. As a result of the different timetable, the presentation of the story will change. The sportswriter will not cram all the essential facts into an opening paragraph or two, and has greater leeway with the introduction and the rest of the article. The sportswriter will want to set a mood in the introduction, developing the characters of the individuals being interviewed. Details can hinder a newspaper sports story from accomplishing its goal of getting across the facts in a concise form, while in a magazine sports article, those extraneous, revealing details actually become part of the story.

Even with the help of news services, sportswriters still couldn't have all the sports news at their fingertips without the help of other reporters and writers, known in the world of reporting as *stringers*. A stringer covers an event that most likely would not be covered by the wire services, events such as high school sports events, as well as games in professional sports that are occurring simultaneously with other major sports events. The stringer attends the sports event and conveys the scores by e-mail or phone.

Sportswriters for magazines don't necessarily specialize in one area of sports, whereas sportswriters for newspapers usually specialize. Many only cover a particular sport, such as baseball. Others are assigned a beat, or specific area, and like other reporters must cover all the events that fall into that beat. For example, a sportswriter assigned to the high school football beat for a newspaper in Los Angeles, California, would be expected to cover all area high school football games. Since football is seasonal, they might be assigned to the high school basketball beat during the winter season. A sportswriter working in Lexington, Kentucky, might be assigned coverage of all the high school sports in the area, not simply one sport. Assignments are based on experience as well as budget and staffing constraints.

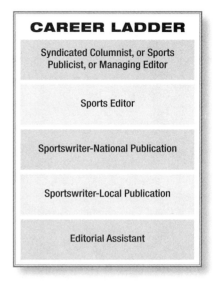

CAREER LADDER

Syndicated Columnist, or Sports Publicist, or Managing Editor

Sports Editor

Sportswriter-National Publication

Sportswriter-Local Publication

Editorial Assistant

■ EARNINGS

According to the U.S. Department of Labor, reporters and correspondents, a category that includes sportswriters, had median annual earnings of $36,360 in May 2015. The lowest paid 10 percent of all reporters earned less than $21,390, while the highest paid 10 percent earned more than $81,580. Reporters and correspondents that worked for newspapers, magazines, and other periodicals earned an average of $40,860.

Sportswriters who cover major sports events, who have their own column, or who have a syndicated column can expect to earn more than the salaries above. Sportswriters who write for major magazines can also expect to earn more, sometimes per article, depending on their reputations and the contracts worked out by themselves or their agents.

■ WORK ENVIRONMENT

Like other journalists, sportswriters work in a variety of conditions, from the air-conditioned offices of a newsroom or magazine publisher to the sweaty, humid locker room of a professional basketball team, to the arid and dusty field where a baseball team's spring training is held. Sportswriters work irregular hours, putting in as much or as little time as the story requires, often traveling to small towns and out-of-the-way locales to cover a team's away games.

For the individuals who love sports, the job offers the chance to cover sports events every day, to immerse themselves in the statistics and injury lists and bidding

STORIES FROM THE SPORTS DESK

LEARN MORE ABOUT IT

Deford, Frank. *Over Time: My Life As a Sportswriter.* New York: Grove Press, 2013.

Finney, Peter. *The Best of Peter Finney, Legendary New Orleans Sportswriter*. Baton Rouge, La.: Louisiana State University Press, 2016.

Geltner, Ted. *Last King of the Sports Page: The Life and Career of Jim Murray.* Columbia, Mo.: University of Missouri Press, 2012.

Lipstye, Robert. *An Accidental Sportswriter.* New York: Ecco, 2011.

Perkins, Dave. *Fun and Games: My 40 Years Writing Sports*. Toronto: ECW Press, 2016.

Telander, Rick, and Glenn Stout. *The Best American Sports Writing 2016.* New York: Mariner Books, 2016.

wars of professional and amateur sports, and to speak, sometimes one-on-one, with talented athletes.

■ EXPLORING

Gain experience by writing for high school and college papers. The experience can be related to sports, but any journalistic experience will help develop the basic skills useful to any reporter, regardless of the subject area.

Increase employment prospects by applying to colleges or universities with renowned academic programs in journalism. Most accredited programs have a required period of training through internships with major newspapers, during which student-interns are responsible for covering a beat.

It is also helpful to read the sports section of your local newspaper or other publications that are related to this field, such as *Sports Illustrated* and *Sports Business Journal* , and visit Web sites such as the Associated Press Sports Editors (http://apsportseditors.com).

■ EDUCATION AND TRAINING REQUIREMENTS
High School

Classes in English, journalism, and speech are most important for honing writing skills. Speech classes are helpful for interacting with others. Be sure to take physical education classes and participate in organized sports, whether as competitor, team manager, or assistant. Also join the school paper or yearbook staff as this gives opportunities to cover and write about school sports teams or other school activities.

Postsecondary Training

Sportswriters need at least a bachelor's degree, although many go on to study journalism at the graduate level.

Most sportswriters concentrate on journalism while in college, either by attending a program in journalism or by taking whatever courses are available outside of a specialized program. It's possible to become a sportswriter without a degree in journalism, but having a degree helps because competition for sportswriting jobs is incredibly fierce. Sportswriters with a specialized degree have improved job prospects. Some may have degrees in communications or English, among other majors.

Learning HTML, a Web site authoring language, can also be helpful to sportswriters who write for the Web, and this skill may qualify you for other writing opportunities. All writers should learn the most popular software programs and office tools that relate to their specialty. Social media savvy is also required for many sportswriting jobs.

Other Education or Training

A variety of webinars, conference seminars, digital journalism training sessions, and other continuing education opportunities are offered by various professional associations such as the American Society of Journalists and Authors, Associated Press Sports Editors, Association for Women in Sports Media, MPA–The Association of Magazine Media, National Society of Newspaper Columnists, and the Society of Professional Journalists. Topics include writing, editing, interviewing, social media, and technology.

■ CERTIFICATION, LICENSING, AND SPECIAL REQUIREMENTS
Certification or Licensing

There are no specific certification or licensing requirements for sportswriters.

■ EXPERIENCE, SKILLS, AND PERSONALITY TRAITS

Any volunteer or paid experience as a writer will be useful for those who aspire to enter the field. Contact community organizations, religious groups, or local businesses, and other organizations that require the skills of writers. Work as a sports reporter for your high school and college newspaper.

The ability to write well and concisely is a key requirement for the job of the sportswriter. Writers must also have a solid understanding of the rules and play of many different sports. To specialize in the coverage of one particular sport, knowledge of that sport must be equal to that of anyone coaching or playing it at the professional level.

Sportwriters must be able to elicit information from a variety of sources, as well as to determine when information being leaked is closer to promotional spin than to fact. There will be more times when a coach or agent will not want to comment on a story than the times when they will want to make an on-the-record comment, so the sportswriter must be assertive in pressing the source for more information.

■ EMPLOYMENT PROSPECTS
Employers

Sportswriters are employed by newspapers, magazines, and Web sites throughout the world. They may cover professional teams based in large cities or high school teams located in tiny towns. Sportswriters also work as freelance writers. According to the Department of Labor, there were 41,050 reporters and correspondents, including sportswriters, employed in the United States in May 2015.

Starting Out

Many sportswriters begin their careers by working as stringers covering the games or matches that no else wants to or can cover. Stringers don't earn much money, but the experience may lead to covering bigger and better games and teams. Some sportswriters make a living out of covering sports for very small towns; others only work at those jobs until they have gained the experience to move on.

Most journalists start their careers by working in small markets—little towns and cities with local papers. After a year or two they move on to larger papers in bigger towns and cities. Sportswriters for newspapers follow the same routine, and many pursue areas other than sports because there are few job openings in sports. The lucky few who hang on to a small sports beat can often parlay that beat into a better position by sticking with the job and demonstrating a devotion to the sport, even cultivating a following of loyal fans. This could lead to a full-time column.

Entry-level sportswriters take advantage of opportunities to learn more about athletes and sports in general. Becoming an expert on a little-known but rapidly growing sport may be one way to do this. For example, learning about mountain biking, and getting a job with a magazine on mountain biking.

Competition for full-time jobs with magazines as a sportswriter is just as keen as it is for major newspapers. Sportswriters will write articles and pitch them to major magazines, hoping that when an opening comes, they will have first crack at it. Still, most sportswriters move into the world of sports magazines after they've proven themselves in newspaper sportswriting. It is possible, however, to get a job with a sports magazine straight from college or graduate school, but usually starting as an intern or assistant working up from there.

■ ADVANCEMENT PROSPECTS

The constraints of budget, staffing, and time—which make a sportswriters' job difficult—are also often what can help a sportswriter rise through the ranks. For example, the writer asked to cover all the sports in a small area may have to hustle to cover the beat alone, but that writer also won't have any competition when covering the big events. They gain valuable experience and bylines writing for a small paper, whereas in a larger market, the same sportswriter would have to wait much longer to be assigned an event that might result in a coveted byline.

Sportswriters advance by gaining the top assignments and covering the major sports in feature articles, as opposed to the bare bones summaries of events. They also advance by moving to larger papers, by getting columns, and finally, by getting a syndicated column—that is, a column carried by many papers around the country or even around the world.

Sportswriters for magazines advance by moving up the publishing ladder, from *editorial assistant* to *associate editor* to *writer*. Often, an editorial assistant might be assigned to research a story for a sports brief—a quirky or short look at an element of the game. For example, *Sports Illustrated* might have a page devoted to new advances in sports equipment for the amateur athlete. The editorial assistant might be given the idea and asked to research it, or specific items. A writer might eventually write it up, using the editorial assistant's notes. Advancement is in being listed as the author of the piece.

In the publishing worlds of both newspapers and magazines, sportswriters can advance by becoming editors of a newspaper's sports page or of a sports magazine. There are also *sports publicists* and *sports information directors* who work for the publicity and promotions arms of colleges, universities, and professional sports teams. These individuals release statements, write and disseminate to the press articles on the organizations' teams and athletes, and arrange press opportunities for coaches and athletes.

■ OUTLOOK

Employment of reporters and correspondents, including sportswriters, who work for newspaper, periodical, book, and directory publishers is projected to decline through 2024, according to the U.S. Department of Labor. This steep decline is due to industry consolidations, a drop in advertising revenue leading to layoffs, and other factors. Some job openings will arise from the need to replace workers who retire or move into other lines of work. Publications increasing their Internet presence may create opportunities for those working as online sportswriters. Sportswriters with expertise in Web design and programming should have improved job prospects. Opportunities will also be better at small, local newspapers and regional magazines.

■ UNIONS AND ASSOCIATIONS

Sportswriters may obtain union representation from the National Writers Union and The Newspaper Guild-Communication Workers of America. Writers may also join the following professional associations: American Society of Journalists and Authors, Associated Press Sports Editors, Association for Women in Sports Media, Football Writers Association of America, National Society of Newspaper Columnists, and the Society of Professional Journalists. Other useful organizations for sportswriters include the Dow Jones News Fund, MPA–The Association of Magazine Media, and the Newspaper Association of America.

■ TIPS FOR ENTRY

1. Write often and create a portfolio of work to show potential employers. Attend sporting events and read sports-related publications to learn as much possible about the industry.
2. Apply for entry-level jobs at newspapers and magazines in order to gain experience in the field.
3. Talk to sportswriters about their careers. Ask them for advice on entering the field.
4. The American Society of Journalists and Authors (ASJA) offers a mentoring program for freelance writers. Visit http://www.asja.org/for-writers/personal-mentoring-program for more information. The ASJA also offers *The ASJA Guide to Freelance Writing* for a small fee.
5. Visit the following Web sites for job openings:
   - http://www.editorandpublisher.com
   - http://www.magazine.org/magazine-careers
   - http://www.the-efa.org/job/joblist.php

■ FOR MORE INFORMATION

The American Society of Journalists and Authors is a membership organization that provides various benefits to published authors.
American Society of Journalists and Authors (ASJA)
355 Lexington Avenue, 15th Floor
New York, NY 10017-6603
Tel: (212) 997-0947
http://asja.org

Associated Press Sports Editors is a membership organization that strives to improve print journalistic standards in sports newsrooms.
Associated Press Sports Editors (APSE)
http://apsportseditors.com

The AWSM provides membership benefits and career-support resources for those employed in sports writing, editing, broadcast and production, public relations, and sports information.
Association for Women in Sports Media (AWSM)
7742 Spalding Drive, #377
Norcross, GA 30092-4207
E-mail: info@awsmonline.org
http://awsmonline.org

The Dow Jones News Fund offers internships, scholarships, and literature for college students.
Dow Jones News Fund (DJNF)
PO Box 300
Princeton, NJ 08543-0300
Tel: (609) 452-2820
Fax: (609) 520-5804
E-mail: djnf@dowjones.com
https://www.newsfund.org

Football Writers Association of America is a membership organization for professional writers who cover football.
Football Writers Association of America (FWAA)
E-mail: tiger@fwaa.com
http://www.sportswriters.net/fwaa

MPA-The Association of Magazine Media offers news, resources, events, and advocacy for magazine media professionals.
MPA-The Association of Magazine Media
757 Third Avenue, 11th Floor
New York, NY 10017-2194
Tel: (212) 872-3700
E-mail: mpa@magazine.org
http://www.magazine.org

The National Society of Newspaper Columnists is an organization for columnists and writers of serial essays.
National Society of Newspaper Columnists
PO Box 411532
San Francisco, CA 94141-1532
Tel: (415) 488-6762
Fax: (484) 297-0336
E-mail: director@columnists.com
http://www.columnists.com

The National Writers Union represents all types of writers working in print, electronic, and multimedia formats.

National Writers Union (NWU)
256 West 38th Street, Suite 703
New York, NY 10018-9807
Tel: (212) 254-0279
Fax: 212-254-0673
E-mail: nwu@nwu.org
https://nwu.org

The News Media Alliance represents diverse news organizations in the United States and Canada.
News Media Alliance (NMA)
4401 Wilson Boulevard, Suite 900
Arlington, VA 22203-4195
Tel: (571) 366-1000
E-mail: info@newsmediaalliance.org
https://www.newsmediaalliance.org

The Newspaper Guild-Communication Workers of America represents journalists and other media workers in digital and traditional news organizations.
The Newspaper Guild-Communication Workers of America
501 Third Street, NW, 6th Floor
Washington, D.C. 20001-2797
Tel: (202) 434-7177
Fax: (202) 434-1472
E-mail: guild@cwa-union.org
http://www.newsguild.org

Part of the American Society of News Editors' Youth Journalism Initiative, School Journalism provides information on journalism careers, summer programs, and college journalism programs.
School Journalism
Missouri Interscholastic Press Association, University of Missouri
132 Neff Annex
Columbia, MO 65211
Tel: (573) 882-6031
E-mail: mipajourno@gmail.com
http://www.schooljournalism.org/

This organization for journalists has campus and online chapters.
Society of Professional Journalists (SPJ)
Eugene S. Pulliam National Journalism Center
3909 North Meridian Street
Indianapolis, IN 46208-4011
Tel: (317) 927-8000
Fax: (317) 920-4789
http://www.spj.org

Stadium Ushers and Vendors

▬ OVERVIEW

Stadium ushers take tickets, escort spectators to their seats, and provide spectators with information and direction upon request.

Stadium vendors sell a variety of food items and other wares either by walking around and calling out the name of the food or product they are selling, or by operating small booths or kiosks. Sometimes vendors are hired by the food service franchise that is licensed to sell food in a stadium or sports facility.

▬ HISTORY

As long as people have been gathering in places such as theaters or sporting events, there has been a need for crowd control. Ushers direct the audience or spectators to their seats, take care of complaints, and keep order among enthusiastic spectators. Whether in a Roman amphitheater or at a modern domed stadium, ushers have been present to help people find their seats. In ancient times, it was customary among Roman dignitaries to have a servant called an *ustiarius*, from which the word usher is derived, standing at the door to announce the arrival of their guests. Vendors have an ancient tradition as well. The Latin word *vendre* literally means to sell. A stadium vendor is an independent, licensed operator selling to the stadium crowds.

▬ THE JOB

The work of stadium ushers and vendors varies with the place, the event, and the audience, but their duties while working sports events are similar. The main job of the usher is to seat patrons. Other duties for the usher might include finding empty available seats for patrons, locating lost items, helping children find their parents, paging people, answering questions, giving directions, attempting to control unruly or ill-behaved people, and settling arguments about seat assignments. In the event that spectators grow unreasonably unruly or out of control, it is the responsibility of ushers to notify security of the disturbance. Ushers watch exits and show patrons to restrooms, drinking fountains, and telephones. They keep aisles clear of objects that might cause patrons to slip or fall.

Similarly, a vendor sells food and other items at a variety of sports events, although the amounts and items sold might vary depending on the event. For example, a vendor selling beer would probably sell more beers during

QUICK FACTS

ALTERNATE TITLE(S)
None

DUTIES
Collect or scan tickets and direct spectators to their seats (ushers); sell a variety of food items and other wares to spectators (vendors)

SALARY RANGE
$13,103 to $19,180 to $28,007+

WORK ENVIRONMENT
Indoors/Outdoors

BEST GEOGRAPHIC LOCATION(S)
Metropolitan areas

MINIMUM EDUCATION LEVEL
High School Diploma

SCHOOL SUBJECTS
Business, Mathematics, Speech

EXPERIENCE
None

PERSONALITY TRAITS
Enterprising, Organized, Outgoing

SKILLS
Interpersonal, Math, Sales

CERTIFICATION OR LICENSING
Required

SPECIAL REQUIREMENTS
Age requirements vary by license type

EMPLOYMENT PROSPECTS
Good

ADVANCEMENT PROSPECTS
Fair

OUTLOOK
About as Fast as the Average

NOC
6623, 6711, 6742

O*NET-SOC
35-3041.00, 39-3031.00

a hockey or football game than during a figure-skating competition; in many cases, they might not even sell beer at such competitions. The vendor may be either an independent seller, licensed by the local government to sell his or her wares, or a vendor working as a freelance operator under license by the owner of the site. For example, the manager of the sports facility allows freelance operators to sell hot dogs, sodas, ice cream, and all the other foods and services enjoyed during a ball game. Or, a vendor might be employed by the franchise licensed to sell T-shirts, caps, and other sports paraphernalia at sports events.

Food vendors are often responsible for preparing the food for sale (and sometimes this just means placing a hot dog inside a bun), as well as handling the sale, making change, and providing any additional items necessary to the consumption of the food, such as napkins, straws, and condiments.

EARNINGS

Hourly rates vary from job to job. Most ushers work at their job for such a short time that they seldom earn more than the starting wage. Median hourly wages for all ushers, lobby attendants, and ticket takers in May 2015 were $9.22 (or $19,180 annually), according to the U.S. Department of Labor. Salary.com reported that salaries for ushers and ticket takers employed in October 2016 ranged from $13,103 to more than $28,007. The pay rate has increased slightly in the past few years due to the demand for this type of worker in most cities. Experienced ushers in metropolitan areas earn the highest wages. For vendors, the amount earned is usually on

a commission basis and the competition can be fierce to get the most desired concessions in the park (hot dogs, ice cream, and so on).

For many ushers and vendors the real reward in working these jobs comes from the chance to be a part of a large-scale event, such as a baseball or football game, where they can be an integral part of the production of the event as well as enjoy the sport.

■ WORK ENVIRONMENT

Stadium ushers and vendors working in domed stadiums or indoor arenas or other indoor sports facilities don't have to brave the elements, while ushers and vendors who work baseball games deal predominately with the heat and those who work football games need to dress warmly, as they frequently work in cold, sometimes miserable conditions. Ushers spend most of their working time standing or walking up and down aisles. In stadiums, ushers and vendors may do considerable climbing up and down stairs or tiers to seat patrons. Work can be stressful when patrons complain or when a crowd gets out of hand.

Three-fourths of all stadium ushers and vendors work part time or seasonally. The range of weekly hours is from 20 to 50 hours.

■ EXPLORING

Labor unions represent many ushers in stage production theaters, ballparks, and sports arenas and usually welcome the opportunity to talk with young people about working as an usher or vendor. Another option is to call the ballpark or stadium directly to find out more about being an usher or vendor. When you learn of special events coming to your town, contact the coordinator and volunteer your services to get a taste for the job.

Although these jobs are not the most glamorous, they will give you a chance to learn about sport facility management and concessions, experience which may come in handy later if you are serious about exploring either career option.

■ EDUCATION AND TRAINING REQUIREMENTS
High School

High school students fill many of the usher and vendor positions in theaters and stadiums, although there is an age requirement for vendors who sell alcoholic beverages. Good standing in high school or a high school degree is usually required. Employers will strongly consider your school attendance record, so regular and prompt attendance is advised.

Postsecondary Training

Vendors and ushers are not required to have college-level education or training. Most training is conducted on the job for a brief time and new employees are used to fill the less responsible jobs and quieter locations. While the trainees are learning, they are shifted to different parts of the stadium as the need arises.

■ CERTIFICATION, LICENSING, AND SPECIAL REQUIREMENTS
Certification or Licensing

Ushers and vendors are not required to be certified, but those who sell alcohol or certain other items must have a license.

Other Requirements

Vendors applying for licenses may need to meet age requirements to sell certain wares.

■ EXPERIENCE, SKILLS, AND PERSONALITY TRAITS

No experience is needed to work as an usher or vendor, but those with prior work experience will increase their chances of landing a job, getting promoted, and possibly earning higher pay.

To be a successful stadium usher or vendor, you need to be affable and friendly. Strong oral communication skills are needed in order to interact successfully with the general public. Strong math skills will help in dealing with the transfer of money. Ushers and vendors should be physically fit because they are on their feet during much of their shift. They must also be willing to work outdoors in sometimes harsh weather conditions, such as extreme cold or heat, driving rain, sleet, or snow.

■ EMPLOYMENT PROSPECTS
Employers

Ushers are employed anywhere that a large group of people gather to watch some type of event or show. Movie theaters, sports stadiums, and colleges/universities are the largest employers of ushers. According to the U.S. Department of Labor, there are approximately 114,000 ushers, lobby attendants, and ticket takers employed in the United States.

Vendors are also employed wherever large groups of people gather to view an event or a show, but with one small difference. During these events, the people must have the time and the ability to spend money on food, drink, and souvenirs. For example, while a cotton candy vendor is right at home at the circus or ballpark, he or she might stick out like a sore thumb at the opera.

Starting Out

Check with local theaters, ballparks, convention centers, and colleges to inquire about possible openings. There is

a lot of turnover in this business, so openings are usually plentiful but are snatched up quickly.

Positions in stadiums are usually part time and seasonal; jobs as ushers or vendors in a stadium used only for baseball end in the fall; if the stadium is domed, there might be additional opportunities to usher or vend during concerts or conventions. Depending on whether or not the vendor is independent or employed by a food or clothing franchise, the vendor may have opportunities year-round. Also, the contacts one makes in these jobs can lead to better jobs in the future.

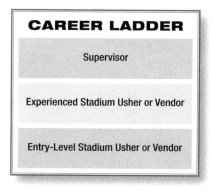

CAREER LADDER

Supervisor

Experienced Stadium Usher or Vendor

Entry-Level Stadium Usher or Vendor

■ ADVANCEMENT PROSPECTS

Stadium ushers or vendors with the most experience usually receive the positions with greater responsibilities, such as handling emergency evacuation procedures. Frequently, ushers and vendors work in crews of three or more, with one individual acting as the supervisor for that crew or team.

In addition to advancing within the categories of ushers and vendors, individuals who have interests in other areas of the game—from public relations to marketing—can make contacts with people who work full time in

A stadium vendor sells cotton candy during a baseball game. (Melissa Bouyounan. Shutterstock.)

those areas and possibly arrange an internship or part-time job. Many people who now work for major sports franchises in a variety of front-office jobs once spent a summer working as a stadium usher or vendor.

■ OUTLOOK

The U.S. Department of Labor predicts 5 percent employment growth, about as fast as the average, for ushers, lobby attendants, and ticket takers through 2024. Stadium revenue rises and falls with the success and failure of the home team; if the team is doing well, crowds swell and fill the stands. Jobs will always exist for ushers and vendors in sports facilities, and these skills are applicable to other venues that use ushers and vendors, such as music halls and theaters.

Turnover in this work is high. Most openings arise as people leave the field for different reasons. Many leave to take better paying jobs. Students working part time usually leave when they graduate from high school or college.

■ UNIONS AND ASSOCIATIONS

Labor unions such as the Service Employees International Union represent many ushers in stage production theaters, ballparks, and sports arenas. The International Association of Venue Managers and the International Facility Management Association can provide information about major convention and assembly management companies.

■ TIPS FOR ENTRY

1. Talk with stadium ushers and vendors about their careers. Ask them for advice on breaking into the field.
2. Join the Service Employees International Union to increase your chances of landing a job and receiving fair pay for your work.

3. Find a volunteer or part-time job opportunity that requires interaction with customers and the public.

■ FOR MORE INFORMATION

The International Association of Venue Managers provides information about major convention and assembly management companies.

International Association of Venue Managers (IAVM)
635 Fritz Drive, Suite 100
Coppell, TX 75019-4442
Tel: (800) 935-4226; (972) 906-7441
Fax: (972) 906-7418
http://www.iavm.org

The International Facility Management Association provides education and career development support for facility management professionals.

International Facility Management Association (IFMA)
800 Gessner Road, Suite 900
Houston, TX 77024-4257
Tel: (713) 623-4362
Fax: (713) 623-6124
E-mail: ifma@ifma.org
https://www.ifma.org

The Service Employees International Union is a labor union dedicated to improving the lives of workers and their families.

Service Employees International Union (SEIU)
1800 Massachusetts Avenue, NW
Washington, D.C. 20036-1216
Tel: (202) 730-7000
http://www.seiu.org

Stage Directors

■ OVERVIEW

Stage directors, or directors, bring theatrical productions to life. They take the words in scripts written by playwrights and help actors interpret them visually for the audience. They also oversee the design and production of the set, props, and costumes, either following descriptions in the script or creating their own vision for the play. They coordinate all creative aspects, including music, lighting, and other elements, and prepare shows for opening.

HISTORY

In ancient Greek times the *choragus,* or head of the chorus, coordinated the singing and movements of people in a theatrical production. Often playwrights staged and cast their plays, but it's uncertain if they "unified" their production. In ancient Roman culture, wealthy citizens organized plays and may or may not have taken part in directing the productions. Reports from the Medieval era (following the fall of the Roman empire through the 15th century) indicate that specialists helped produce special stage effects for productions and may have also managed them. Most Medieval theater in Western civilization related to religion and the Church. Many communities staged local productions of mystery plays (depicting Bible stories), morality plays (allegories for the virtues of moral life over evil), passion plays (dramatizations of the Passion of Jesus Christ).

Professional acting companies emerged in the Elizabethan era and the time of William Shakespeare and the Globe Theater. By the 1800s the first professional directors appeared on the scene. Actors, playwrights, theater owners, and theater managers frequently remained more prominent in connection with productions, however, until the 20th century when directors earned their current status.

Today stage directors are an essential part of every production. Musicals, dramas, comedies, and all other types of plays, whether produced on Broadway, in summer stock, or even community theater, are guided by a stage director. Each director's individual artistic and creative vision drives the play and may turn a production into a hit.

THE JOB

Stage directors oversee all aspects of putting on a play. They bring their creative vision and style to the production and guide cast and crew along the process of staging a dynamic and entertaining show. Directors sometimes work closely with playwrights to interpret a script for the stage. Other times they make a play uniquely their own by imprinting their personal vision onto it.

Stage directors make or consult on all key decisions of a production, including casting, staging, set design, lighting, costumes and makeup, props, music, and other elements. They work closely with the cast to polish and perfect their performances and direct how they deliver dialogue and move around onstage or in the theater to depict each scene. They also manage the crew, who create and revise costumes, sets, and props, and work the curtains and lighting during performances.

Stage directors have input with virtually every creative aspect of a play to give the play a unified look and tone. They work very long hours during rehearsals, determining what lines, actions and moves best convey the vision of the script as well as many hours in production, getting shows ready for opening night. Directors may call for and oversee changes along the way if an aspect of production is not working out.

Once the play is rehearsed and opens, the director's work is largely done. Sometimes directors remain with a production after opening to fine-tune or change aspects of the play based on audience reaction. Mostly, they move on to another project although they may be called back to rehearse new cast members if the play runs for an extended period of time.

Much hinges on the director's work. His or her casting choices, staging decisions, and creative vision for a play can often be the deciding factor in whether the play is a hit or a flop.

EARNINGS

Due to the nature of the job, the earnings of stage directors vary widely. Payment may be a weekly salary or a set fee to direct a particular show. Some stage directors negotiate deals where they are paid a fee plus royalties derived from each production so that they earn more from successful, long-running shows.

Stage directors are not guaranteed work year round. Once the stage director has brought a production to its opening, he or she looks for another job. A successful director who is in demand may obtain employment directing the same play in another location or may quickly

QUICK FACTS

ALTERNATE TITLE(S)
Directors

DUTIES
Visually interpreting the script; guiding actors and actresses in their performances; coordinating all creative aspects of production; conducting rehearsals and preparing a show to open

SALARY RANGE
$31,780 to $68,440 to $181,780+

WORK ENVIRONMENT
Primarily Indoors

BEST GEOGRAPHIC LOCATION(S)
Opportunities exist throughout the United States, with high demand in culturally active cities such as New York City, Boston, Los Angeles, Las Vegas, and Philadelphia

MINIMUM EDUCATION LEVEL
Bachelor's Degree

SCHOOL SUBJECTS
English, Music, Theater/Dance

EXPERIENCE
Several years experience

PERSONALITY TRAITS
Artistic, Creative, Helpful, Organized

SKILLS
Drawing/Design, Leadership, Performance, Music, and Acting

CERTIFICATION OR LICENSING
None

SPECIAL REQUIREMENTS
None

EMPLOYMENT PROSPECTS
Fair

ADVANCEMENT PROSPECTS
Fair

OUTLOOK
About as Fast as the Average

NOC
0512

O*NET-SOC
27-2012.00

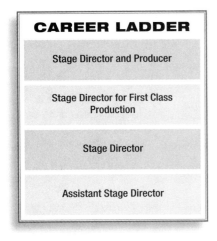

CAREER LADDER

Stage Director and Producer

Stage Director for First Class Production

Stage Director

Assistant Stage Director

be hired to direct another new production. Stage directors may work for theaters or production companies for an entire season, directing multiple plays. These individuals may be paid a salary. Aspiring directors may go years without earning any income from their profession until they become established. Others may work consistently by seeking employment on a range of productions from Broadway to summer stock to community theater, going where the work is.

Many stage directors belong to the Stage Directors and Choreographers Society (SDCS). This labor union negotiates minimum basic agreement rate schedules for stage directors. These vary by type of theater, such as Broadway theaters, dinner theaters, regional theaters, and so on. Agreements also depend on whether the production is a drama or a musical or another type of play. In addition to earnings, the union negotiates minimum rates for benefits including pensions, health benefits, and per diems.

As of September 2016, the minimum rate for individuals working on a Broadway musical include a fee and advance of $68,365. They additionally receive a .75 percent royalty of gross which is equivalent to $1,059 minimum plus 4 percent NOP (net operating profits) between 100-120 percent of the production's "break even" point.

According to the Bureau of Labor Statistics (BLS), the median annual wage for producers and directors in 2015 was $68,440. Half of these workers earned more than that amount and half earned less. The lowest 10 percent earned $31,780 or less, and the highest 10 percent earned $181,780 or more. These statistics apply to producers and directors working in theater, television, and movies. Many directors cross over among these fields or aspire to move from one to the other to increase their earnings.

■ WORK ENVIRONMENT

Stage directors work in theaters around the country. They may work in large or small theaters, and some successful directors work on Broadway. Others may work in regional theaters, dinner theaters, community theaters, summer stock, and so on. Since directors must go where the work is, travel is a common part of the job, especially if they are directing a touring production. Work hours may be long and irregular. The unpredictable nature of the work makes it difficult for stage directors to work a standard work week. Most work is conducted in the theater or in rehearsal studios.

The creative and deadline aspects of the work create stress. The need to manage the personalities of stars, producers, and others with ideas that differ from the director's about how the play should be staged can also create frustration and tension.

■ EXPLORING

Individuals interested in pursuing a career in this field should participate in every experience they can related to theater. Get involved in the school drama club, school theatrical productions, and/or community theater groups to hone your skills and knowledge. Attend a variety of theatrical shows to see how they are staged and performed.

Take classes in drama, theater, and English. As the majority of stage directors are self-employed, business classes will also prove useful. Many community colleges also offer non-credit courses in theater, acting and directing. These are a great way to learn new skills and meet others interested in theater.

Read books about drama and stage productions. Read classic plays. Talk to crew members and directors in your school and local community theater groups about what they do.

■ EDUCATION AND TRAINING REQUIREMENTS
High School

While in high school, take classes in English, speech, art, and theater if offered. Participate in school productions and theater arts programs.

Postsecondary Education

It is not absolutely necessary to have a college degree to become a stage director, but it is helpful. A degree provides credibility and better prepares one to face both the competition in the industry and the opportunities that appear.

There are some directors who have no college background, and others who hold a master's degree. Good choices for majors include theater arts, acting, and arts management.

Classes in directing, play writing, set design, costume design, and acting will be helpful. Some directors earn a degree in theater and go on to receive a Master of Fine Arts (MFA) degree. The National Association of Schools of Theatre accredits more than 180 programs in theater arts. Visit them online at https://nast.arts-accredit.org.

Other Education and Training

Training in the form of practical experience is necessary to get a job and be successful at it. This experience

BACKSTAGE DIALOGUE

all call: A request for volunteers to help with a production.

apron: The part of the stage located between the curtain and the orchestra pit.

batten: Pipes above a stage that are part of the system on which the scenery and lights are hung.

blocking: Directions telling actors where to stand or move on stage during a production.

booth: Where the stage manager and sound and light crew sit during a production.

bump: Also called a zero count fade; This term indicates that the light and sound on stage go on or off without delay.

call time: This is the actual time that actors and crew need to be in the theater.

cue to cue run-through: A rehearsal where it starts at the beginning of the play and leaves out bits of dialogue where there are no cues because there is nothing technical occurring. It skips forward to the next part of the production where there is something happening and a cue is needed.

curtain call: When actors come out to take bows at the end of a show.

down stage: Part of the stage closest to the audience.

dress parade: Also called costume parade. The actors put on their new costumes and stand in front of the costume designer and artistic director to see how they look.

fade: A light or sound level change over a certain number of seconds.

off-book: This is when an actor no longer needs to use the script to deliver lines.

on-book: This is the assistant stage manager, stage manager, or artistic director following the script when actors recite their lines so that they can correct mistakes or give lines.

production meetings: A weekly gathering of all of the theatrical departments discussing how preparations are going for opening night.

set dressing: These are paintings, backdrops, and props that make the set look real.

speed through: This is the final rehearsal. It is done without sound or lights. The cast sits around a table and says their lines rapidly with the proper emotion to assure the accuracy of lines and to bring the tempo of the show up.

---

can be obtained by working as an intern, assistant, or in almost any area of the theater. School, summer stock, and regional theaters are all good training grounds. Many stage directors get their training watching other directors do their job or assisting them.

■ CERTIFICATION, LICENSING, AND SPECIAL REQUIREMENTS

There are no certification or licensing requirements necessary to become a stage director.

■ EXPERIENCE, SKILLS, AND PERSONALITY TRAITS

There is no clear career path for stage directors. Individuals need experience in theater, which they may gain by working as assistant directors. Others began their careers as actors, actresses, stage managers, or even playwrights.

Stage directors must be creative people with a vision. They need to guide actors and actresses in their speech and physical movements. A knowledge of theater, staging, and acting is imperative. Knowing stage jargon is also necessary.

Directors must be good at coordinating the various aspects preparing a production since most of their job is spent doing that. They need to be detail oriented and have the ability to manage many aspects of a production at one time.

Directors need to have a lot of patience as they must constantly explain their creative vision to those interpreting it. They must also be determined and good at working with people.

■ EMPLOYMENT PROSPECTS
Employers

Employment prospects are fair for stage directors who are willing to work in a variety of theaters in various locations. These venues might include summer stock, regional theaters, Off Broadway, and Off-Off Broadway. Prospects become more difficult for individuals when they aspire to work as stage directors on Broadway or other first class productions.

While New York city is the major theatrical capital of the United States, the job market there is so competitive that it is often necessary to find work in other culturally active cities first to gain experience and build a reputation.

Starting Out

The Bureau of Labor Statistics (BLS) reports that in 2016, producers and directors held 114,510 jobs in the United States. This also includes individuals working in motion pictures and television.

Employment depends on a number of factors including the talent and experience of the individual. Other important factors include contacts and networking, being in the right place at the right time, and luck.

Stage directors without a great deal of experience can often find employment at summer stock and dinner theaters around the country. There are also opportunities in casinos and hotels which host stage productions.

■ ADVANCEMENT PROSPECTS

Stage directors advance their careers in a number of ways. The most common is by directing more prestigious productions or directing a show in a more prestigious theater. Most producers would rather hire a well-known stage director or one who has some experience than one who has little background in the field. While on the surface advancement prospects appear poor for stage directors, that is not always the case. In some cases an individual directs a production which is reviewed very well or even turns into a hit. As each director builds on his or her successes, they may find themselves in greater demand.

■ OUTLOOK

The Bureau of Labor Statistics (BLS) includes stage directors in with producers and directors of film, stage, and television. There were 114,510 jobs in this field in the United States as of 2016. That employment is projected to grow by 9 percent through 2024, faster that the average for all occupations. Theatrical producers and directors who work in small and medium-sized theaters may see slower job growth, because many of those theaters have difficulty finding funding as the fewer tickets are sold. Large theaters in big cities, such as New York and Los Angeles, which usually have more stable sources of funding, should provide more opportunities.

■ UNIONS AND ASSOCIATIONS

Stage directors may be members of the Stage Directors and Choreographers Society (SDCS). This is a bargaining union working in theater which negotiates minimum earnings as well as assuring good working conditions and helping provide protection for individual's work.

In some cases, individuals may belong to Actor's Equity, a union which negotiates minimum salaries and working conditions for their members. They may also learn more about the career by contacting the American Association of Community Theater. Visit them at http://www.aact.org/.

For those interested in looking into programs in theater arts, the National Association of Schools of Theatre accredits over 180 programs in theater arts.

■ TIPS FOR ENTRY

1. Make as many contracts in the theatrical industry as possible. You cannot audition to be a stage director. Networking is the key in this field.
2. When you land jobs, do your best to make a good impression on your coworkers. The theater world is small and a good reputation will follow you everywhere.
3. Volunteer to work in your local community theater as an assistant to the director if possible. If not, work in the theater in any capacity.
4. Look for an internship working in theater. Contact schools, colleges, art councils, theater groups, organizations, and associations about availabilities. Once you locate an internship get involved. Do more than you are asked to and learn as much as possible.
5. Many summer theaters offer part-time or summer jobs to students learning their craft. Send your resume with a short cover letter asking for an interview.

■ FOR MORE INFORMATION

Actor's Equity is a theatrical union which negotiates minimum salaries and working conditions for their members.

Actor's Equity (EQUITY)
165 West 46th Street
New York, NY 10036
Tel: (212) 869-8530
Fax: (212) 719-9815
http://www.actorsequity.org/

The American Association of Community Theatre provides expertise, assistance, and support to community theaters.

American Association of Community Theatre (AACT)
1300 Gendy Street
Fort Worth, TX 76107-4036
Tel: (817) 732-3177
Fax: (817) 732-3178
E-mail: info@aact.org
http://www.aact.org

The National Association of Schools of Theatre accredits over 180 programs in theater arts.

> **National Association of Schools of Theatre (NAST)**
> 11250 Roger Bacon Drive, Suite 21
> Reston, VA 20190-5248
> Tel: (703) 437-0700
> Fax: (703) 437-6312
> E-mail: info@arts-accredit.org
> https://nast.arts-accredit.org/

The Stage Directors and Choreographers Society (SDCS) is a theatrical union that negotiates contracts and agreements for stage directors and choreographers throughout the country.

> **Stage Directors and Choreographers**
> **Society (SDCS)**
> 321 West 44th Street, Suite 804
> New York, NY 10036-5477
> Tel: (800) 541-5204
> Fax: (212) 302-6195
> E-mail: info@SDCweb.org
> http://sdcweb.org

Stage Managers

■ OVERVIEW

The stage manager, or production stage manager or assistant stage manager, takes over the responsibilities of the director of a theatrical production when his or her job is done. The job begins before the production's first rehearsal. During that time, the stage manager acts as the representative of the director as well as a liaison between the cast and crew and the production's management. He or she also coordinates when happens on stage.

■ HISTORY

In general, playwrights and actors handled the work of the stage manager until the Elizabethan era. The job appeared in the 17th century when professional theaters and acting troupes became more common. The Globe Theater produced William Shakespeare's plays in that era, and established theaters appeared in other parts of Europe too. As theaters became more professional, the need for better management emerged. At first, actors, playwrights, and others still undertook these new management tasks. But the work eventually became sufficient to justify a dedicated worker.

The term "stage manager" was coined in England in the 18th century, coinciding with the practice of hiring someone other than an actor or playwright as the stage

QUICK FACTS
ALTERNATE TITLE(S) Production Stage Managers; Assistant Stage Managers
DUTIES Coordinate what happens on stage; schedule and plan rehearsals; attend auditions; assure things go smoothly during performance; call the show; write reports regarding the show; coordinate between the cast and crew and the production management
SALARY RANGE $15,000 to $38,753 to $68,000+
WORK ENVIRONMENT Primarily Indoors
BEST GEOGRAPHIC LOCATION(S) Opportunities exist in all regions, with high demand in major cities, such as New York, Las Vegas, and Los Angeles
MINIMUM EDUCATION LEVEL Bachelor's Degree
SCHOOL SUBJECTS Business, Music, Theater/Dance
EXPERIENCE Several years experience
PERSONALITY TRAITS Artistic, Organized, Problem-Solving
SKILLS Interpersonal, Leadership, Performance, Music, and Acting
CERTIFICATION OR LICENSING None
SPECIAL REQUIREMENTS None
EMPLOYMENT PROSPECTS Fair
ADVANCEMENT PROSPECTS Good
OUTLOOK Faster than the Average
NOC 0512
O*NET-SOC 27-2012.00

manager. The growth of interest in theater, increasingly technical aspects of stage production, and more sophisticated presentations drove the expansion of the profession. Today, stage manager is a common job in theaters. Many theatrical pros such as playwrights, directors, and even actors began work as theater assistant stage managers to learn their craft.

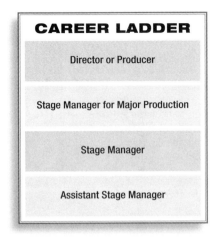

CAREER LADDER

Director or Producer

Stage Manager for Major Production

Stage Manager

Assistant Stage Manager

■ THE JOB

The stage manager or production stage manager or assistant stage manager, as the job might be known as, takes over the responsibilities of the director in a theatrical production when his or her job is done. The job usually begins before the projection's first rehearsal. The individual's main function is to act as the representative of the director. He or she acts as a liaison between the cast and crew and the production's management. He or she additionally coordinates when happens on stage.

Every production has a stage manager. Very elaborate productions may also have assistants. The stage manager has many responsibilities. He or she may attend auditions to provide input into casting decisions. He or she will also keep records of the actors, actresses, singers and dancers who have auditioned.

The stage manager is required to schedule and plan rehearsals and make sure that actors and actresses are there on time to do this, the individual may prepare a written schedule or might instead verbally inform cast members. The stage manager is required to be present at rehearsals.

The individual is responsible for updating the script as changes are made and then making sure that the cast members are given the new script. Another function of the stage manager is to block the show. This means that he or she will verbally tell or physically tape the stage to illustrate where actors or actresses should be at certain times and where props and scenery should be placed.

Part of the responsibility of the stage manager is making sure that the show goes on the way the director intended it to. If, during rehearsals or the actual production, the stage manager sees that an actor or actress is performing his or her part differently than agreed upon, he or she will talk to the individual to get things back on track.

The stage manager also must be on hand to make sure that things are running smoothly among the cast and crew members. He or she may be required to settle both professional and personal disputes.

The stage manager has a great many responsibilities during a performance. The individual does what is referred to as "calling the show." He or she will call cues for the the sound, lighting, and scenic technicians. If actors or actresses need a line, he or she will give it to them. The stage manager will make absolutely sure that everything goes according to the script and schedule.

During the performance, the stage manager is responsible for everything that goes on backstage. He or she will make sure that everyone does their job and does it properly. After each performance the stage manager will write a report regarding the show. In this report, he or she will document activities and discuss things that went well, things that went wrong, and other occurrences. Any accidents or injuries must also be reported. The stage manager's job ends about one week after closing. In the time period between the last performance and the final day of work, he or she will do required paperwork, get necessary files in order, and load the show out of the theater.

The stage manager works many hours in his or her job. When finished, the only people who know if the stage manager performed well or not are the cast, crew, and director.

■ EARNINGS

The earnings of stage managers vary greatly depending on an individual's experience, responsibilities, reputation, the type of theater and production, the company, location, and industry staging the production, and sometimes even the number of seats in a theater. Individuals working in union situations have their earnings negotiated by Actor's Equity. Each type of Equity theater has a different contract. Minimum earnings are higher for those involved in Broadway musicals, for example, than those working in summer stock.

For example, according to the current Equity contract effective through November 6, 2016, the minimum weekly earnings for stage managers working on an off-Broadway show is $664 for theaters with 100-199 seats; $776 for theaters with 200-250 seats; $898 for theaters with 251 to 299 seats; $1,051 for theaters with 300 to 350 seats, and $1,179 for individuals working in theaters with 351-499 seats. This is the minimum. Professionals in demand or highly regarded in the community may often negotiate better deals.

Payscale.com reports that in 2016, the median annual compensation for stage managers was $38,753 with the lowest 10% of individuals earning $15,000 and the highest 90% earning $68,000. Stage managers do not always work every week of the year. Employment is tied to the length of an engagement and typically ends when a show closes, leaving the stage manager to seek new opportunities.

■ WORK ENVIRONMENT

Stage managers work in a variety of theaters, including summer stock, regional theaters, Off-Broadway, Off-Off

Broadway, and Broadway. Some work for touring companies. Stage managers also work at large stadiums, casinos or hotel showrooms, and other venues that host live music or variety acts.

Individuals may work afternoons, nights, and weekends depending on when productions are scheduled. Those that travel with a touring production will have to leave home for extended periods of time.

Stage managers, like others in theater, often work under pressure and put in long hours. They may face tight deadlines with people who may be stressed themselves.

■ EXPLORING

Take drama classes in school. Get involved in your school theater club and take part in theatrical productions. Learn every aspect you can about putting on a play. Join or volunteer at your local community theater group, summer stock, or dinner theater.

Meet with the director and/or stage manager from a local community or summer stock theater. Tell him or her about your future career aspirations and ask about the possibility of interning or at least acting as an assistant or a runner. You will learn a lot about the job, have some great experience to put on your resume, and make contacts.

■ EDUCATION AND TRAINING REQUIREMENTS
High School

While in high school, take classes in English, speech, art, and theater. Participate in school productions and any local theater arts programs. Business classes can help develop managerial skills.

Postsecondary Education

There is no formal educational requirement for a stage manager. A college degree is not mandatory, but may be helpful and is recommended. A degree offers basic background opportunities for experience and making contacts and a degree of credibility. Good choices for majors include theater arts or arts management. Classes in directing, play writing, set design, costume design, and acting will be helpful. Many individuals complete a degree in theater and go on to receive a Master of Fine Arts (MFA) degree. The National Association of Schools of Theatre accredits more than 180 programs in theater arts. Visit them online at https://nast.arts-accredit.org.

Other Education and Training

Training in the form of practical experience is necessary to get a job and be successful at it. This experience can be obtained by working as an intern, assistant, or in almost any area of the theater. School, summer stock, and regional theaters are all good training grounds.

■ CERTIFICATION, LICENSING, AND SPECIAL REQUIREMENTS

There are no certification or licensing requirements for stage managers.

■ EXPERIENCE, SKILLS, AND PERSONALITY TRAITS

Stage managers must have a great deal of experience working in the theater. Most, but not all, have acted as assistant stage managers before obtaining their first position, and many have worked other types of theater jobs, which helps them understand all the elements of a successful production. Stage managers must know a little about everything in the theater, including acting, directing, set design, lighting, costuming, and more. The more knowledgeable the stage manager is, the more successful he or she will be in the job.

Individuals must be personable and get along well with people. In many circumstances, the stage manager must deal with others who are tense, worried, and/or nervous about openings or acting in general. The individual must be compassionate and have the ability to calm people down and make them feel comfortable. He or she must be diplomatic in all situations.

The stage manager should be detail oriented and have the ability to work on many projects at once. He or she must always remain calm in the eye of a storm.

■ EMPLOYMENT PROSPECTS
Employers

Employment prospects are fair for stage managers who are willing to work in a variety of theaters in various locations. These venues might include summer stock, regional theaters, Off-Broadway and Off-Off Broadway. Prospects become more difficult for individuals when they aspire to work as stage managers in Broadway productions. While New York City is the major theatrical capital, there is so much competition that it may be easier to find work in other culturally active cities.

Starting Out

Stage managers without a great deal of experience, can often find employment at summer stock and dinner theaters around the country. There are also opportunities in casinos and hotels which host stage productions.

■ ADVANCEMENT PROSPECTS

Advancement prospects are good for stage managers who are proficient at their jobs. Individuals may take a number of paths to advancement. Stage managers who want to stay in their profession may obtain similar jobs with more prestigious productions. They may also find

MANAGING A PRODUCTION

AEA: An acronym for Actors Equity Association.

Act: The subdivision between sections of a play. May also refer to what actors and actresses do.

Act change: This refers to a change of scenery, props, lighting, costumes, between acts of a theatrical production.

Actor: May also be called an actress. The man or woman whose role is to play a character (other than him/herself) in a theatrical production.

Amateur: This is a member of a theatrical company who is not a professional.

Angel: A person who gives money or backs a theatrical production.

Assistant stage manager: Also called the ASM. This is a junior member of the stage management team.

Blocking: The onstage movements suggested by the director for actors or actresses in a theatrical production.

Cue: A signal for an actor, actress, or production person to take a specific action or an instruction given by a stage manager or director.

Curtain line: The line on a stage where the curtain for each act falls.

Dress rehearsal: The rehearsal in a theatrical production in which everything including costumes, makeup, lighting, sound, and special effects is tried out just as if the play was actually going on in front of an audience.

Equity: Actors' Equity Association.

LRT: An acronym for League of Resident Theaters.

Matinee: This is the afternoon performance of a theatrical production.

Non-resident theater: A theater for which actors are hired on a per-performance basis.

Preview: A performance of a production that is given before the actual opening of a show.

Prompt book: This is a master copy of the script which contains all the actors moves as well as technical cues. It is used by the stage manager to run rehearsals and control performances. It may be referred to as the book.

Resident theater: Seasonal theater for which a group of actors is hired to perform during the entire season and is assigned set rules.

Stage presence: This is the way an actor or actress stands and moves while on stage.

Union card: A card that is used to identify members of specific unions.

---

a steady stream of employment possibilities resulting in higher annual earnings. Stage managers who prefer a career change may become a director. Some stage managers obtain as much experience as possible then go on to become producers.

■ OUTLOOK

The Bureau of Labor Statistics does not specifically discuss the occupational outlook for stage managers. For the related professions of producers and directors, the BLS reported there were 114,510 jobs in the United States in 2016. Employment is projected to grow 9 percent through 2024, faster that the average for all occupations. This also includes individuals working in motion pictures and television, but it indicates likely growth for stage managers too since the professions are so closely related.

■ UNIONS AND ASSOCIATIONS

Stage managers in unionized settings must belong to Actor's Equity. This union negotiates minimum salaries and working conditions for their members.

Individuals may also learn more about the career by contacting the American Association of Community Theater. Visit them at http://www.aact.org/.

Those interested in looking into programs in theater arts should visit the National Association of Schools of Theater, which accredits more than 180 programs in theater arts.

■ TIPS FOR ENTRY

1. Learn as much as you can about all aspects of theater. This knowledge will be useful in obtaining a job and being successful.
2. Look for internships and apprenticeships to obtain on-the-job training. These can often be found at community and regional theaters.
3. Try to locate a job in summer stock. It doesn't matter what position you get. The experience will help you learn as well as provide an opportunity to make important contacts that might help you during the rest of your career.
4. Volunteer at your local community theater. This is another way to learn more about the theater industry.

■ FOR MORE INFORMATION

Stage Managers working in unionized settings must belong to Actor's Equity. This union negotiates minimum salaries and working conditions for their members.

Actor's Equity (EQUITY)
165 West 46th Street
New York, NY 10036

Tel: (212) 869-8530

Fax: (212) 719-9815

http://www.actorsequity.org/

The American Association of Community Theatre provides expertise, assistance and support to community theaters.

American Association of Community Theatre (AACT)

1300 Gendy Street

Fort Worth, TX 76107-4036

Tel: (817) 732-3177

Fax: (817) 732-3178

E-mail: info@aact.org

http://www.aact.org

The National Association of Schools of Theatre accredits over 180 programs in theater arts.

National Association of Schools of Theatre (NAST)

11250 Roger Bacon Drive

Suite 21

Reston, VA 20190-5248

Tel: (703) 437-0700

Fax: (703) 437-6312

E-mail: info@arts-accredit.org

https://nast.arts-accredit.org/

Stage Production Workers

■ OVERVIEW

Stage production workers handle the behind-the-scenes tasks that are necessary for putting on theatrical performances. Their responsibilities include costume and set design, installing lights, rigging, sound equipment, and scenery, and set building for events in parks, stadiums, arenas, and other places. During a performance they control the lighting, sound, and various other aspects of a production that add to its impact on an audience. These technicians work in close cooperation with the stage director, lighting director, actors, and various prop people. In addition, they work directly with theater shops in the construction of sets. Others are involved in the management of the theater or production. In 2014, approximately 135,000 artists, administrators, and technical production staff were employed by nonprofit theaters, according to the Theatre Communications Group.

QUICK FACTS

ALTERNATE TITLE(S)
Carpenters, Costume Workers, Electricians, Lighting Designers, Lighting-Equipment Operators, Prop Makers, Riggers, Sound Technicians

DUTIES
Handle behind-the-scenes tasks that make theatrical performances a success such as designing and building sets and installing lighting

SALARY RANGE
$23,660 to $43,910 to $63,670+

WORK ENVIRONMENT
Primarily Indoors

BEST GEOGRAPHIC LOCATION(S)
Opportunities exist in all regions, with high demand in New York, Los Angeles, Chicago, Branson (Missouri), and Las Vegas

MINIMUM EDUCATION LEVEL
High School Diploma

SCHOOL SUBJECTS
Art, Technical/Shop, Theater/Dance

EXPERIENCE
Any related experience helpful

PERSONALITY TRAITS
Artistic, Creative, Technical

SKILLS
Building/Trades, Drawing/Design, Interpersonal

CERTIFICATION OR LICENSING
None

SPECIAL REQUIREMENTS
None

EMPLOYMENT PROSPECTS
Fair

ADVANCEMENT PROSPECTS
Fair

OUTLOOK
About as Fast as the Average

NOC
5226, 5227

O*NET-SOC
27-1022.00, 39-3092.00, 39-5012.00, 39-5091.00

■ HISTORY

Theatrical performance is among the most ancient of human art forms. Primitive societies wore masks and costumes during ritual ceremonies designed to ward off evil spirits and to promote the welfare of the society.

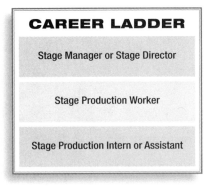

CAREER LADDER

Stage Manager or Stage Director

Stage Production Worker

Stage Production Intern or Assistant

Greek theater also made use of masks and costumes. As Greek theater developed, its costumes became more elaborate and were used to emphasize characters' status within the world of the play. Greek theater was originally performed in a large circle, and the scenery was minimal; around 460 B.C. a wood *skene*, or stage structure, was added to the back of the circle through which the actors could enter or exit the circle. Painted scenery was attached to the *skene*; special effects included cranes for flying actors over the stage. As theater became more professional, people began to specialize in the different areas of theater, such as controlling the scenery, directing the action, and creating the costumes. An important development in early theater was the addition of the raised stage.

By the time of the Romans, theaters were freestanding structures that could be covered and held large audiences. Scenery was often mounted on three-sided prism-like structures that could be rotated to change the scenery during a performance. Medieval performances were often extremely elaborate. Performances were generally held outdoors, and sometimes on wagon stages that moved through a town during the performance. Special effects were often spectacular, with flames and smoke, flood, and realistic massacres complete with flowing blood, hangings, crucifixions, and the like.

Nonreligious theater rose into prominence during the 16th century. The first dedicated theater was built in 1576 in London, followed by many other theaters, including the famous Globe Theater where the works of William Shakespeare were performed. Costumes, primarily representing contemporary dress, were often highly elaborate and quite costly.

The Renaissance and the rediscovery of Greek and Roman theater brought scenery back into prominence in the theater. The development of perspective techniques in painting and drawing led to more realistic settings as backdrops for the performance. More methods were developed for changing the scenery during the performance, although these scene changes continued to be made in front of the audience. Flying machines and other special effects were added; and, as theater moved indoors, stages were lighted by candles and oil lamps.

Many of the features of present-day theater evolved during the 17th and 18th centuries. A new profession emerged: that of stage designer. One of the most influential of these designers was Giacomo Torelli, who invented a mechanical system for raising and lowering settings. Earlier settings, however, were not generally designed for a specific performance, and costumes were not often historically accurate. By the end of the 18th century, stage direction, which had generally been given by the playwright or by one of the leading actors, became a more recognized part of preparing a theatrical performance.

Lighting and scenery developed rapidly in the 19th century. Gas lamps replaced candles and oil lamps, and innovations such as the limelight (a stage light consisting of an oxyhydrogen flame directed on a cylinder of lime and usually equipped with a lens to concentrate the light in a beam) and the spotlight were introduced. Stages began to feature trap doors, and scenery could be raised from below the stage or lowered from above the stage. Many theaters incorporated hydraulic lifts to raise and lower scenery, props, and actors through the trap doors.

The look of a theater production, in its costumes, settings, and props, became at once more realistic and more historically accurate. Settings became increasingly more elaborate, and the introduction of panoramas gave motion effects to the stage. Special effects included the use of real animals on stage, volcanic eruptions, sinking ships, and storms complete with wind and rain. During this period, it became more common that a play would remain in the same theater through many performances. These elaborately planned and staged productions required dedicated directors to oversee the entire production. Another innovation of the 19th century was the use of a curtain to hide the stage during scene changes.

The art of stage production changed considerably with the introduction of electricity to theaters at the end of the 19th century. It became possible to use lighting effects as a major interpretive element in stage productions. Stage machinery became more elaborate, even to the point of moving a whole stage, so that sets could be transformed in new ways. In the 20th century, recording and amplification techniques introduced a wider range of musical and sound effects than ever before. These changes added new dimensions to the tasks of stagehands and other workers.

Today, stage production workers are involved not only in theater performances, but also in film and television performances, which utilize many of the same techniques. As they do on theater stages, workers in television and film do such tasks as building and changing sets and controlling lighting and sound effects.

■ THE JOB

For small productions with fewer employees, stage workers must be able to do a variety of tasks. In larger productions (such as those on Broadway), responsibilities are divided among many different workers, each with a special area of expertise. The following paragraphs describe some of these areas of responsibility.

Stage technicians include many different workers, such as *carpenters, prop makers, lighting designers, lighting-equipment operators, sound technicians, electricians, riggers,* and *costume workers.*

When installing stage equipment, stage technicians begin with blueprints, diagrams, and specifications concerning the stage area. They confer with the stage manager to establish what kinds of sets, scenery, props, lighting, and sound equipment are required for the event or show, and where each should be placed.

Then the technicians gather props provided by the production company and build other props or scenery using hammers, saws, and other hand tools and power tools. If they are working in a theater, they climb ladders or scaffolding to the grid work at the ceiling and use cables to attach curtains, scenery, and other equipment that needs to be moved, raised, and lowered during performances. They may need to balance on and crawl along beams near the ceiling to connect the cables.

Stage technicians also position lights and sound equipment on or around the stage. They clamp light fixtures to supports and connect electrical wiring from the fixtures to power sources and control panels.

The sound equipment used on and around stages usually includes microphones, speakers, and amplifiers. Technicians position this equipment and attach the wires that connect it to power sources and to the sound-mixing equipment that controls the volume and quality of the sound.

During rehearsals and performances, stage technicians in some theaters may follow cues and pull cables that raise and lower curtains and other equipment. Sometimes they also operate the lighting and sound equipment.

Costume designers choose the costumes necessary for a production, including their style, fabric, color, and pattern. They may do research to design clothes that are historically and stylistically authentic. They discuss their ideas with the stage director and make sketches of costumes for the director's approval. They check stores and specialty clothing shops for garments that would meet their needs. If appropriate items are not found, designers may have the costumes made from scratch. They oversee the purchasing of fabric and supervise the workers who actually create the costumes. Costume designers also work with actors to make sure that costumes fit properly. In a large production, they may supervise several assistants who help in all aspects of the job, including locating hard-to-find items.

Stage technicians put away set pieces after a show. (Jakez. Shutterstock.)

Other workers help to complete the desired appearance of the performers. *Hairstylists* and *makeup artists* use cosmetics, greasepaint, wigs, plastics, latex, and other materials to change the look of their hair and skin. Once costumes have been made for a show, *wardrobe supervisors* keep them in good condition for each performance by ironing, mending, and cleaning them, and doing any necessary minor alterations. *Dressers* help performers to get dressed before a show and change quickly between scenes.

■ EARNINGS

Earnings vary widely according to the worker's experience, job responsibilities, the geographic location of the theater, and the budget of the performance. In addition, the International Alliance of Theatrical Stage Employees reports that different local chapters have different pay scales, although its members, who are mostly employed at the largest commercial houses and on Broadway, generally earn more than nonmembers. Set and lighting designers generally work on a freelance basis and are paid widely varying fees on a per-project basis.

The pay of costume designers is often based on the number of costumes designed. Experienced designers working in major markets such as New York and Chicago earn more than those in other markets. Local unions often determine salary scales. Some costume designers working in summer theaters earn around $500 or more a week, but others may earn substantially less. The U.S. Department of Labor (DOL) reports that fashion designers—a group that includes costume designers—made a median annual hourly wage of $30.61 in May 2015. For full-time work, this translates into a yearly income of approximately $63,670. Costume attendants

NONPROFIT THEATER BY THE NUMBERS

FAST FACTS

According to a 2014 survey by Theatre Communications Group:

- Nonprofit theaters contributed more than $2 billion to the United States economy in the form of salaries, benefits, and payments for goods and services.
- Nearly 1.5 million Americans subscribed to a nonprofit theater season.
- Approximately 32.8 million people attended 216,000 performances of 22,000 nonprofit theatrical productions.
- There were an estimated 1,770 nonprofit theaters in the United States, employing 135,000 total paid workers.
- Sixty-seven percent of the nonprofit theater workforce were artistic professionals, 22 percent were production/technical workers; and 11 percent were administrative staff.

Source: Theatre Facts 2014

earned an average hourly wage of $21.40, or $44,500 annually.

Mean hourly earnings for other stage production workers in May 2015, according to the DOL, include: carpenters, $21.11 ($50,380 annually for full-time work); sound engineering technicians, $25.94 ($53,960 annually); riggers, $21.58 ($43,910 annually); makeup artists, $27.06 ($62,180 annually); and hairstylists $11.38 ($23,660 annually).

Most full-time workers receive health insurance and other benefits, as established by the local union contract. Because workers are hired for a particular time period, vacations are rarely provided.

■ WORK ENVIRONMENT

Working conditions in theaters vary from the lavish in a few theaters to small, simply equipped facilities in many community theaters. Many theaters are hot and stuffy during performances, or drafty and cold when empty. Stage production workers can expect to work long hours and spend much time on their feet. Many work evenings and weekends. People who work behind the scenes in theaters must be concerned about safety. Those who work with lights and electric cables risk burns, while those who climb rigging or scaffolding need to use care to avoid falls.

Costume designers work in design shops sketching and designing costumes, in theaters fitting performers, and in libraries and other locations researching costume

possibilities. They spend long hours preparing for a show, with most of their work done before and during the rehearsal period.

■ EXPLORING

A great deal can be learned by becoming involved in high school or college theatrical performances. If possible, gain experience in many different capacities, including acting, stage design, lighting, and special effects. Another way to get experience is by working as a volunteer for amateur community theater productions or special benefit events. This sort of broad experience may lead to a paid or volunteer summer job assisting in a professional theater.

Experiences gained in other fields may be helpful background for some stage production jobs. For example, aspiring costume designers can learn by working for clothes designers in the fashion industry.

■ EDUCATION AND TRAINING REQUIREMENTS
High School

Requirements vary for different kinds of stage production workers and technicians. In general, a high school diploma is necessary and a college degree is highly recommended. High school students interested in careers in theatrical production should take college preparatory courses such as English, history, and mathematics. In addition, they should take drama courses and participate in school theatrical performances in a variety of ways, such as acting or working on sets to helping with promotion.

Postsecondary Training

Those who want to work in technical fields such as lighting and sound design would benefit by taking courses in history and art, as well as subjects such as electricity, electronics, computers, mathematics, and physics. Craft workers such as carpenters and electricians do not need a college degree, and they often learn their work skills through apprenticeships. Makeup artists need to study anatomy and art subjects like sculpture and portrait painting. Costume designers ought to have a graduate degree in design or fine arts, and a well-developed artistic sense.

■ CERTIFICATION, LICENSING, AND SPECIAL REQUIREMENTS
Certification or Licensing

No certification or licensing is available for stage production workers.

■ EXPERIENCE, SKILLS, AND PERSONALITY TRAITS

It will be easier to break into the field with prior experience working on school or community theatrical productions. Learn as many skills as possible—such as set design, electronics, or sound work—in order to increase job prospects.

Passion for theater as an art form is essential to bear with the long hours and often low pay associated with these professions. The ability to get along well with others is also important, since stage technicians often work in teams. Patience and flexibility will be needed as directors and designers may change their minds about set plans or demand a stage, lighting effect, or costume piece that might seem difficult or challenging creatively as well as financially.

■ EMPLOYMENT PROSPECTS
Employers
The Theatre Communications Group reports that approximately 135,000 artists, administrators, and technical production staff were employed in nonprofit theatres in 2014. Stage production workers and technicians may be employed by theater, dance, music, and other performing arts companies. They more often receive full-time employment from companies that have their own facilities, although companies that tour year-round often need to keep technical workers on staff. In addition, managers of performing arts facilities, such as theaters, opera houses, arenas, or auditoriums, may hire full-time technicians. Often, technical workers are not hired by a single employer; many find work with different companies and/or facility managers on a freelance basis.

Starting Out
Competition is keen for nearly all positions associated with theatrical productions, so get as much experience and become as versatile a worker as possible. It is often necessary to begin working on a volunteer basis or start in a position unrelated to the desired field. Many people who want to work in stage production end up in other professions because of the great difficulty in securing satisfying jobs.

Job seekers should not be discouraged by the tight labor market. In New York, Chicago, and Los Angeles, publications specifically about local activities in the theater and television industries are an excellent source of information that may lead to jobs. In many cities, local newspapers regularly list production plans for area community theater groups. Sometimes college internships in theater jobs or recommendations from drama teachers can lead to permanent employment.

■ ADVANCEMENT PROSPECTS
Advancement opportunities vary according to the type of work performed. Workers advance by moving to different theaters where they handle greater responsibilities associated with more complicated productions. Those who

---

DIMMERS, FOOTLIGHTS, AND GOBOS

WORDS TO KNOW

Dimmers: The apparatus that electrically controls the brightness of lights.

Ellipsoidal: The type of reflector used in many profile spotlights.

Floodlights or **floods:** Lights that give a general fixed spread of light.

Focusing: The process of setting up exact areas to be lit by each light onstage.

Follow spot: Light directed at actors that follows all movements.

Footlights: Lights set into the stage floor that throw strong general light into the performers' faces.

Fresnel: Type of spotlight with a lens that gives an even field of light with soft edges.

Gel: Colored medium inserted in front of the light to alter color of beam.

Ghost: A beam of light that inadvertently leaks from a light and falls where it is not wanted.

Gobo: A screen placed in front of a stage light to cast a particular image on stage.

Iris: A device within a lamp that allows a circular beam to be altered through a range of sizes.

Lamp (or **lantern):** Unit of lighting equipment.

Luminaire: International term for lighting equipment (not restricted to theatrical lighting).

Patch border panel: A panel at which the circuits governed by individual lighting dimmers can be changed.

---

develop good reputations in the industry may be sought out by other employers to do similar jobs in new settings.

Costume designers can work on larger theatrical productions or for television production companies. Alternatively, they may establish independent consulting firms and work for a variety of clients.

Competition for the best positions is so strong that many workers remain in the same job and consider salary increases as evidence of their success.

■ OUTLOOK
The outlook for jobs in theater companies varies depending on the job. For example, the Department of Labor predicts that makeup artists will have much faster than average employment growth through 2024, whereas carpenters will have average employment growth in that same timeframe. According to the Theatre Communications Group, there has been a slight increase in revenue in the

theater industry in recent years, due mainly to growth in contributions. Theater attendance has been down, though, and government funding has also decreased. Many nonprofit theaters continue to operate under a deficit. There are few new or small theaters that can pay living wages for stage production workers and technicians, which is why many people working in theater production—especially at small or nonprofit theaters—supplement their incomes with other sources of work.

Today, theaters tend to be concentrated in large metropolitan areas, so the number of job possibilities is greatest there, but so too is the competition for those jobs. Many stage workers start out instead with small theatrical groups. After they develop skills and a local reputation, they may be able to move to bigger, better-paying markets. They may have to work part time, do volunteer work in amateur theater, or support themselves in unrelated fields for extended periods while waiting for better theater jobs.

For the foreseeable future, stage productions, even among the larger theaters, are likely to become less elaborate to lower operating costs. These factors could limit the need for new stage production employees. However, theater remains a popular form of entertainment and an important cultural resource. Those who are skilled in a variety of production areas stand the best chance of employment. For example, someone who knows about both lighting and sound systems, or both set design and props, is more likely to get a desirable position in theater.

■ UNIONS AND ASSOCIATIONS

Many stage production workers belong to unions. Union membership may be required to get a job, although requirements vary in different areas and even in different theaters in the same city. For example, various theater workers belong to the United Scenic Artists or the International Alliance of Theatrical Stage Employees. Some unions require members to pass a competency test before they can begin work. Prospective stage production workers need to investigate union requirements, if any, that apply in their field of interest in their local area. The Theatre Communications Group is another good source of information for stage production workers.

■ TIPS FOR ENTRY

1. Learn as many skills as possible to increase your chances of being hired.
2. Volunteer to work on school and community theater productions.
3. Apply for internships or volunteerships with theater companies.
4. Look for job listings in local newspapers and theater-oriented Web sites. You can also subscribe to ARTSEARCH (http://www.tcg.org/artsearch) to access job listings in the theater industry.
5. Read *American Theatre* (https://www.tcg.org/Publications/AmericanTheatreMagazine.aspx) to learn more about the field.

■ FOR MORE INFORMATION

The IATSE represents technicians, artisans, and craftspersons in the entertainment industry, including live theater, film, and television production.

International Alliance of Theatrical Stage Employees, Moving Picture Technicians, Artists and Allied Crafts (IATSE)
207 West 25th Street, 4th Floor
New York, NY 10001-7119
Tel: (212) 730-1770
Fax: (212) 730-7809
http://www.iatse-intl.org

The Theatre Communications Group provides information on educational programs, surveys, publications, and careers.

Theatre Communications Group (TCG)
520 Eighth Avenue, 24th Floor
New York, NY 10018-4156
Tel: (212) 609-5900
Fax: (212) 609-5901
E-mail: info@tcg.org
http://www.tcg.org

This union represents stage production workers, art directors, and other film industry professionals working in film, television, industrial shows, theater, opera, ballet, commercials, and exhibitions.

United Scenic Artists Local 829
29 West 38th Street, 15th Floor
New York, NY 10018-5504
Tel: (877) 728-5635; (212) 581-0300
Fax: (212) 977-2011
https://www.usa829.org

Stationary Engineers

■ OVERVIEW

Stationary engineers operate and maintain boilers, engines, air compressors, generators, and other equipment used in providing utilities such as heat, ventilation, light, and power for large buildings, industrial plants, and other facilities. They are called stationary engineers because the equipment they work with is similar to equipment on ships or locomotives, except that it is stationary rather than located on a moving vehicle. There are approximately 34,630 stationary engineers employed in the United States.

HISTORY

During the Industrial Revolution of the 18th and 19th centuries, many new inventions changed the ways in which people lived and worked. Some of these inventions used new energy sources, including steam engines, coal, electricity, and petroleum. When this power was applied to the new machines, many aspects of life began to alter dramatically.

As the Industrial Revolution spread, new, large factories were built. Sometimes working conditions for the construction and stationary workers were not good. Employees were required to work 60 to 90 hours per week, and their wages were low considering the number of hours they put in. So in 1896, a small group of stationary engineers met in Chicago to form the National Union of Steam Engineers of America. Each was from a small local union and all shared the skill of being able to operate the dangerous steam boilers of the day. This ability also made the steam engineers vital to the construction industry, which used steam-driven equipment at the turn of the century. As members began working with internal combustion engines, electric motors, hydraulic machinery, and refrigerating systems, as well as steam boilers and engines, the union changed its name to the International Union of Operating Engineers (IUOE). Today, the IUOE sponsors apprenticeship programs and is the primary union to which stationary engineers belong.

Wherever big equipment installations are located, stationary engineers are needed to operate and maintain the equipment. Once again, their jobs are changing. Equipment is becoming increasingly automated and operators now use computerized controls.

THE JOB

Stationary engineers are primarily concerned with the safe, efficient, economical operation of utilities equipment. To do their job, they must monitor meters, gauges, and other instruments attached to the equipment. They take regular readings of the instruments and keep a log of information about the operation of the equipment. This might include the amount of power produced; the amount of fuel consumed; the composition of gases given off in burning fuel; the temperature, pressure, and water levels inside equipment; and temperature

and humidity of air that has been processed through air-conditioning equipment. When instrument readings show that the equipment is not operating in the proper ranges, they may control the operation of the equipment with levers, throttles, switches, and valves. They may override automatic controls on the equipment, switch to backup systems, or shut the equipment down.

Periodically, stationary engineers inspect the equipment and look for any parts that need adjustment, lubrication, or repair. They may tighten loose fittings, replace gaskets and filters, repack bearings, clean burners, oil moving parts, and perform similar maintenance tasks. They may test the water in boilers and add chemicals to the water to prevent scale from building up and clogging water lines. They keep records of all routine service and repair activities.

Stationary engineers try to prevent breakdowns before they occur. If unexpected trouble develops in the system, they must identify and correct the problem as soon as possible. They may need only to make minor repairs, or they may have to completely overhaul the equipment, using a variety of hand and power tools.

In large plants, stationary engineers may be responsible for keeping several complex systems in operation. They may be assisted by other workers, such as *boiler tenders, heating and cooling technicians, turbine operators*, and *assistant stationary engineers*. In small buildings, a single stationary engineer may be in charge of operating and maintaining the equipment.

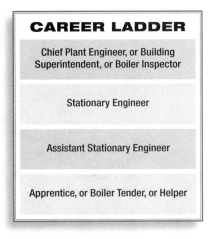

CAREER LADDER

Chief Plant Engineer, or Building
Superintendent, or Boiler Inspector

Stationary Engineer

Assistant Stationary Engineer

Apprentice, or Boiler Tender, or Helper

Often the instruments and equipment with which stationary engineers work are computer controlled. This means that stationary engineers can keep track of operations throughout a system by reading computer outputs at one central location, rather than checking each piece of equipment. Sensors connected to the computers may monitor factors such as temperature and humidity in the building, and this information can be processed to help stationary engineers make decisions about operating the equipment.

Boiler tenders may be responsible for taking care of steam boilers on their own in building or industrial facilities. In some cases, they tend boilers that produce power to run engines, turbines, or equipment used in industrial processes. Boiler tenders may feed solid fuel, such as coal or coke, into a firebox or conveyor hopper, or they may operate controls and valves. They may also be responsible for maintenance, minor repairs, and cleaning of the boiler and burners.

■ EARNINGS

Earnings of stationary engineers vary widely, but ranged from less than $35,400 to $91,260 or more annually in May 2015, according to the U.S. Department of Labor. The median annual salary was $58,530. In metropolitan areas, where most jobs are located, earnings tend to be higher than other areas.

New apprentices earn 45 to 60 percent of the journey-level rate. As their training progresses, they receive pay increases. By the final year of apprenticeship, wages are typically 80 to 95 percent of the journey-level rate.

Most stationary engineers receive fringe benefits in addition to their regular wages. Benefits may include life and health insurance, paid vacation and sick days, employer reimbursement for work-related courses, and retirement plans. Benefits for boiler tenders are similar.

■ WORK ENVIRONMENT

Stationary engineers usually work eight-hour shifts, five days a week. The plants where they work may operate 24 hours a day, so some stationary engineers regularly work afternoon or night shifts, weekends, or holidays. Some work rotating shifts. Occasionally overtime hours are necessary, such as when equipment breaks down or new equipment is being installed.

Most boiler rooms, power plants, and engine rooms are clean and well lighted, but stationary engineers may still encounter some uncomfortable conditions in the course of their work. They may be exposed to high temperatures, dirt, grease, odors, and smoke. At times they may need to crouch, kneel, crawl inside equipment, or work in awkward positions. They may spend much of their time on their feet. There is some danger attached to working around boilers and electrical and mechanical equipment, but following good safety practices greatly reduces the possibility of injury. By staying constantly on the alert, stationary engineers can avoid burns, electrical shock, and injuries from moving parts.

■ EXPLORING

A good way to learn about this work is to get a part-time or summer job in an industrial plant or another large facility where utility equipment is run by a stationary engineer. Even an unskilled position, such as a custodian in a boiler room, can provide an opportunity to observe the work and conditions in this occupation. Talking with a stationary engineer or a union representative may also prove helpful.

■ EDUCATION AND TRAINING REQUIREMENTS
High School

A high school diploma or its equivalent is required to become an apprentice stationary engineer. Courses in computer science, mathematics, physics, chemistry, shop, and mechanical drawing are good introductions to the field, along with vocational training in machinery operation.

Postsecondary Training

Stationary engineers learn the skills they need by completing an apprenticeship or through informal, on-the-job training, often in combination with course work at a vocational or technical school. Because of the similarities between marine and stationary power plants, training in marine engineering during service in the U.S. Navy or Merchant Marines can be an excellent background for this field. However, even with such experience, additional training and study are necessary to become a stationary engineer.

Apprenticeships are administered by local committees that represent both company management and the union to which many stationary engineers belong, the International Union of Operating Engineers. Apprenticeships usually last four years. In the practical-experience part of their training, apprentices learn how to operate, maintain, and repair stationary equipment such as blowers, generators, compressors, motors, and refrigeration machinery. They become familiar with precision measurement devices; hand and machine tools; and hoists, blocks, and other equipment used in lifting heavy machines. In the classroom, apprentices study subjects such as practical chemistry and physics, applied mathematics, computers, blueprint reading, electricity and electronics, and instrumentation.

People who learn their skills on the job work under the supervision of experienced stationary engineers. They may start as *boiler tenders* or *helpers*, doing simple tasks that require no special skills, and learn gradually through practical experience. They eventually move on to more complicated tasks such as repairing cracks or ruptured tubes for high-pressure boilers. The process may go more quickly if they take courses at a vocational or technical school in subjects such as computerized controls and instrumentation.

Other Education or Training

Stationary engineers should continue to take short courses to keep their knowledge current, even after they are well trained and experienced in their field. Employers often pay for this kind of additional training. When new equipment is installed in a building, representatives of the equipment manufacturer may present special training programs. Additionally, the National Association of Power Engineers offers online courses such as "Basic Boiler Plant Operation," "Advanced Boiler Plant Operation," "Gas Turbine & Cogeneration," and "Steam Turbines."

■ CERTIFICATION, LICENSING, AND SPECIAL REQUIREMENTS

Certification or Licensing

The National Association of Power Engineers offers voluntary certification in basic boiler operation, advanced boiler operation, and A/C refrigeration operation to those who pass an examination and meet other requirements.

Most states and cities require licensing for stationary engineers to operate equipment. There are several classes of license, depending on the kind of equipment and its steam pressure or horsepower. A first-class license qualifies workers to operate any equipment, regardless of size or capacity. Stationary engineers in charge of large equipment complexes and those who supervise other workers need this kind of license. Other classes of licenses limit the capacities or types of equipment that the license holders may operate without supervision.

A stationary engineer refers to his checklist when monitoring gauges. (Kzenon. Shutterstock.)

The requirements for obtaining these licenses vary from place to place. In general, applicants must meet certain training and experience requirements for the class of license, pass a written examination, and be at least 18 years old and a resident of the city or state for a specified period of time. When licensed stationary engineers move to another city or state, they may have to meet different licensing requirements and take another examination.

■ EXPERIENCE, SKILLS, AND PERSONALITY TRAITS

Experience as an apprentice, helper, or boiler tender is required to enter the field. The training period may last several years. For example, apprenticeship programs that are sponsored by the International Union of Operating Engineers last four years and include 8,000 hours of on-the-job training and require 600 hours of technical instruction.

Stationary engineers possess mechanical aptitude and manual dexterity, and are in good physical condition. They like keeping track of details and understand the importance of following schedules and routines. A prospective stationary engineer should be able to work independently, without direct supervision. Other important traits include a good work ethic, a willingness to continue to learn throughout one's career, and strong organizational and time-management skills.

■ EMPLOYMENT PROSPECTS
Employers

Stationary engineers hold about 34,630 jobs in the United States. They work in a wide variety of places, including factories, hospitals, airports, power plants, hotels, breweries, office and apartment buildings, schools, and shopping malls. Some are employed as contractors to a building or plant. They work throughout the country, generally in the more heavily populated areas where large industrial and commercial establishments are located.

Starting Out

If they do not start out as apprentices, stationary engineers often enter the field by working as a boiler tender or helper, or as a craftsworker in another field. Information about job openings, apprenticeships, and other training may be obtained through the local offices of the state employment service or the International Union of Operating Engineers. State and city licensing agencies can give details on local licensure requirements and perhaps possible job leads.

■ ADVANCEMENT PROSPECTS

Experienced stationary engineers may advance to jobs in which they are responsible for operating and maintaining larger or more complex equipment installations.

Such job changes may become possible as stationary engineers obtain higher classes of licenses. Obtaining these licenses, however, does not guarantee advancement. Many first-class stationary engineers must work as assistants to other first-class stationary engineers until a position becomes available. Stationary engineers may also move into positions as boiler inspectors, chief plant engineers, building superintendents, building managers, or technical instructors. Additional training or formal education may be needed for some of these positions.

■ OUTLOOK

Employment for stationary engineers is expected to show little or no change through 2024, according to the U.S. Department of Labor (DOL), as a result of declining job demand in manufacturing. Industrial and commercial development will continue, and thus more equipment will be installed and need to be operated by stationary engineers, but much of the new equipment will be automated and computerized. The greater efficiency of such controls and instrumentation will tend to reduce the demand for stationary engineers. On the other hand, the DOL reports that strong job growth is expected for stationary engineers who work in educational services and in health care facilities, due to more buildings being constructed to accommodate a growing population in need of these services.

Employment opportunities for stationary engineers will be best for those with apprenticeship training or vocational school courses covering systems operations using computerized controls and instrumentation, and those who are licensed to practice where the job is located. Even with that training, workers will face competition for job openings.

Job openings will also develop when workers transfer to other jobs or leave the workforce, but turnover in this field is low, due in part to its high wages.

■ UNIONS AND ASSOCIATIONS

Many operating engineers are members of the International Union of Operating Engineers. The National Association of Power Engineers is a membership organization for operating engineers that provides certification, publications, continuing education courses, and networking opportunities. The National Association of Stationary Operating Engineers also offers resources and information on the stationary engineer field.

■ TIPS FOR ENTRY

1. Read *International Operating Engineer* (http://www.iuoe.org/iuoe-magazine) and *National Engineer* (http://powerengineers.com) to learn more about the field.

2. Visit the Web sites of professional associations to find job listings.

3. Join the International Union of Operating Engineers to increase your chances of landing a job and receiving fair pay for your work.

■ FOR MORE INFORMATION

The International Union of Operating Engineers provides information about careers, apprenticeships, and vocational training.

International Union of Operating Engineers (IUOE)
1125 17th Street, NW
Washington, D.C. 20036-4786
Tel: (202) 429-9100
http://www.iuoe.org

The National Association of Power Engineers provides educational courses, training, and other resources for power engineers.

National Association of Power Engineers (NAPE)
One Springfield Street
Chicopee, MA 01013-3065
Tel: (413) 592-6273
Fax: (413) 592-1998
E-mail: nape@powerengineers.com
http://www.powerengineers.com

The National Association of Stationary Operating Engineers provides information about licensing and certification for stationary engineers

National Association of Stationary Operating Engineers (NASOE)
212 Elmwood Avenue Extension, Suite 500
Gloversville, NY 12078-5905
Tel: (518) 620-3683
E-mail: admin@nasoe.org
http://www.nasoe.org

▶ FASTEST GROWING JOBS

Statisticians

■ OVERVIEW

Statisticians use mathematical theories to collect and interpret information. This information is used to help various agencies, industries, and researchers determine the best ways to produce results in their work. There are approximately 33,440 statisticians in the United States, employed in a wide variety of work fields, including government, industry, and scientific research.

■ HISTORY

One of the first known uses of statistical technique was in England in the mid-1800s, when a disastrous epidemic of cholera broke out in a section of London. A local physician named John Snow decided to conduct a survey to determine what sections of the city were affected by the disease. He then constructed a map showing how the infection was distributed and interviewed people who had survived the illness about their living habits. He discovered that everyone who had contracted the illness had drawn water from a certain pump in the area. Once the pump was sealed, the cholera epidemic subsided. Snow's research enabled medical professionals to learn that cholera was transmitted through an infected water supply. His use of statistical methods therefore uncovered a fact that has since saved countless lives.

In its simplest form, statistics is a science that organizes many facts into a systematized picture of data. Modern statistics is based on the theory of probability, and the work of statisticians has been greatly enhanced by the invention of computers.

The need for statisticians has grown by leaps and bounds in modern times. Since 1945, the number of universities with programs leading to graduate degrees in statistics has jumped from a half-dozen to more than 140. One reason for the increased demand is that statistical methods have many important uses. For example, methods similar to those used

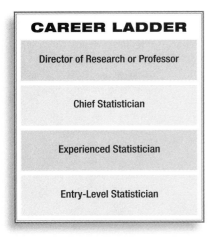

CAREER LADDER

Director of Research or Professor

Chief Statistician

Experienced Statistician

Entry-Level Statistician

to study waves from distant galaxies can also be used to analyze blood hormone levels, track financial market fluctuations, and find concentrations of atmospheric pollutants. Experts predict that the demand for such useful statistical methodology will continue to grow.

Statistics are now used in all areas of science as well as in industry and business. Government officials are especially dependent on statistics—from politicians to education officials to traffic controllers.

■ THE JOB

Statisticians use their knowledge of mathematics and statistical theory to collect and interpret information. They determine whether data are reliable and useful and search for facts that will help solve scientific questions.

Most statisticians work in one of three kinds of jobs: They may teach and do research at a large university, they may work in a government agency (such as the U.S. Census Bureau), or they may work in a business or industry. A few statisticians work in private consulting agencies and sell their services to industrial or government organizations. Other statisticians work in well-known public opinion research organizations. Their studies help us understand what groups of people think about major issues of the day or products on the market.

There are two major areas of statistics: mathematical statistics and applied statistics. *Mathematical statisticians* are primarily theoreticians. They develop and test new statistical methods and theories and devise new ways in which these methods can be applied. They also work on improving existing methods and formulas.

Applied statisticians apply existing theories or known formulas to make new predictions or discoveries. They may forecast population growth or economic conditions, estimate crop yield, predict and evaluate the result of a marketing program, or help engineers and scientists determine the best design for a jet airline.

In some cases, statisticians actually go out and gather the data to be analyzed. Usually, however, they receive data from individuals trained especially in research-gathering techniques. In the U.S. Census Bureau, for example, statisticians work with material that has been compiled by thousands of census takers. Once the census takers have gathered the data, they turn the information

over to statisticians for organization, analysis, and conclusions or recommendations.

Statisticians are employed in many sectors of society. One of the largest employers of statisticians is the government, because many government operations depend on detailed estimates of activities. Government data on consumer prices, population trends, and employment patterns, for example, can affect public policy and social programs.

Statistical models and methods are also necessary for all types of scientific research. For example, a geoscientist estimating earthquake risks or ecologists measuring water quality both use statistical methods to determine the validity of their results. In business and industry, statistical theories are used to figure out how to streamline operations, optimize resources, and, as a result, generate higher profits. For instance, statisticians may predict demand for a product, check the quality of manufactured items, or manage investments.

The insurance industry also uses statisticians to calculate fair and competitive insurance rates and to forecast the risk of underwriting activities.

Statisticians who collect and study data for pharmaceutical companies, public health agencies, or hospitals are known as *biostatisticians* or *biometricians*. They use statistics to help study disease outbreaks, ascertain the effectiveness of medical treatments or drug trials, and perform analytical tasks that help their employers improve efficiency or reduce costs.

■ EARNINGS

The U.S Bureau of Labor Statistics reports that the median annual salary for statisticians was $80,110 in May 2015; the highest paid group earned more than $130,630, while the lowest paid group earned less than $44,900. Statisticians employed by the federal government earned mean annual salaries of $100,960.

The income for statisticians working in colleges and universities differs, depending on their position and their amount of experience. According to the 2013–2014 Salary Report of Academic Statisticians from the American Statistical Association, the median salary for assistant professors working in research universities was between $75,500 to $85,600, based on years of experience. Full professors at research universities earned median salaries that ranged from $109,600 to $162,300.

Most statisticians receive a benefits package from their employer that typically includes paid sick and vacation time, health insurance, and some sort of retirement plan.

■ WORK ENVIRONMENT

Most statisticians' jobs will involve a substantial amount of time on a computer. They usually work under pleasant circumstances, with regular work hours. In private industry or government, statisticians work in an office setting. Some may travel to collaborate on larger research projects. In academia, statisticians often split their time between teaching and conducting research.

■ EXPLORING

While in high school, ask math teachers to give some simple statistical problems, perhaps related to grades or student government. This will allow you to practice the kinds of techniques that statisticians use. To explore the profession further, visit a local insurance agency, the local office of the Internal Revenue Service, or a nearby college and talk to people who use statistical methods.

College students can frequently obtain jobs as student assistants in the offices of faculty members who are engaged in some kind of research. Although these jobs may seem to carry little responsibility, undergraduate students can gain some insight into and practice in research methods.

■ EDUCATION AND TRAINING REQUIREMENTS
High School

A master's degree is typically required for qualification for many jobs in statistics. Take classes that provide a good foundation for college education. Focus on mathematics, computers, and science classes, but don't neglect other college preparatory courses such as English and a foreign language.

Postsecondary Training

Statisticians usually graduate from college with strong mathematics and computer backgrounds. Bachelor's degrees in statistics, mathematics, or biostatistics are available at many colleges and universities in the United States. Classes include differential and integral calculus, mathematical modeling, statistical methods, and probability. Other students major in the field they hope to work in, such as chemistry, agriculture, or psychology.

A master's degree in statistics, mathematics, or survey methodology is the minimum needed for most statistician jobs, but chances for success and advancement are better with a doctorate. Positions in research and academia require a doctorate.

Other Education or Training

The American Statistical Association, Mathematical Association of America, Association for Women in Mathematics, Society for Industrial and Applied Mathematics, and the Statistical Society of Canada offer professional development classes, workshops, and webinars.

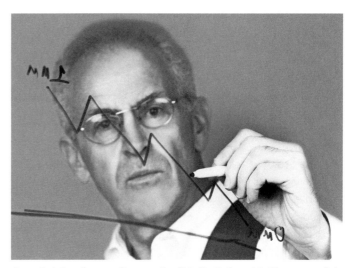

A statistician draws a line graph. (Media Bakery13. Shutterstock.)

■ CERTIFICATION, LICENSING, AND SPECIAL REQUIREMENTS
Certification or Licensing

The American Statistical Association offers two levels of voluntary accreditation—accredited professional statistician (PSTAT) and graduate statistician (GSTAT)—to members who meet education and experience requirements.

■ EXPERIENCE, SKILLS, AND PERSONALITY TRAITS

Aspiring statisticians should take as many math and computer science classes as possible and participate in internships to gain experience in the field.

Prospective statisticians should be able to think in terms of mathematical concepts. The ability to think logically is also important, as statisticians must be able to effectively process and interpret statistics. Statisticians should also have a strong curiosity that will prompt them

---

FLORENCE NIGHTINGALE   MOVERS AND SHAKERS

You probably know Florence Nightingale as a nurse and pioneer in British health care reform in the 19th century. What you may not know is that she was also a statistician. For example, when she was serving as a nurse during the Crimean War, she collected data using applied statistical techniques to determine how many British soldiers died because of unsanitary hospital conditions. She used this information to demonstrate why hospital conditions needed to be changed. By doing this, Florence Nightingale showed how statistics can be used to improve medical and surgical practices.

STATISTICS AND SPORTS

DID YOU KNOW?

Love to follow sports? Consider this: Every time you glance at the stats box for your favorite team, you are looking at the work of a statistician. A sports statistician may work for a particular team, as a consultant, or for a sports data collection firm such as STATS LLC. Depending upon the job, he or she may record statistics as events happen, prepare mid-game and final stats for league records or the media, keep up to date on changes in statistical scoring rules, compile records on various teams or individual players, and analyze how different equipment and stadiums may affect athlete performance.

to explore any given subject. Finally, a good statistician should be detail oriented and able to handle stress well.

■ EMPLOYMENT PROSPECTS

Employers

There are approximately 33,440 statisticians employed in the United States. About 17 percent of these workers are employed by the federal government, such as the Departments of Commerce, Health and Human Services, and Agriculture, the Census Bureau, the Bureau of Economic Analysis, the National Agricultural Statistics Service, and the Bureau of Labor Statistics. Another 8 percent work for state and local governments. Of the remaining statisticians, most work in private industry. Private-industry employers include insurance companies, research and testing services, management and public relations firms, computer and data processing firms, manufacturing companies, and the financial services sector. Statisticians also work in colleges and universities in teaching and research positions.

Jobs for statisticians can be found throughout the United States but are concentrated most heavily in large metropolitan areas such as New York, Chicago, Los Angeles, and Washington, D.C.

Starting Out

Most new graduates find positions through their college career services offices. For those students who are particularly interested in working for a government agency, jobs are listed with the Office of Personnel Management. Some government jobs may be obtained only after the successful passing of a civil service examination. College-level teaching is normally only open to candidates with doctorates. College teaching jobs are usually obtained by making a direct application to the dean of the school or college in which the statistics department is located.

■ ADVANCEMENT PROSPECTS

Advancement may be seen more in terms of gradually increased pay rather than greater job responsibilities. After having acquired experience on the job and value to the employer, the statistician may be promoted to chief statistician, director of research, or, in teaching positions, full professor. Advancement can take many years, and it usually requires returning to graduate school or a special technical school to achieve a higher degree or more skills. Statisticians who advance most rapidly to positions of responsibility are usually those with advanced degrees.

■ OUTLOOK

Employment for statisticians is expected to grow by 34 percent, much faster than the average for all careers, through 2024 according to the U.S. Department of Labor (DOL). We live in a world of data these days as a result of Internet searching and the use of social media, smartphones, and other mobile devices. Businesses and nonprofit organizations will increasingly need statisticians to organize, analyze, and sort this data. This growth will be due to more widespread use of statistical analysis to make informed business, health care, and policy decisions.

The federal government will continue to need statisticians for various agencies (for example, in Social Security, environmental protection, and demography), though competition is predicted to be high for jobs. Private industry will continue to need statisticians, especially in the pharmaceutical industry, as well as in engineering and in the physical and life sciences.

Statisticians with a master's degree, knowledge of computer science and data analytics, and a strong background in a related discipline, such as finance, engineering, biology, or computer science, should have the best job prospects. These candidates can also teach in junior colleges and small four-year colleges. The employment outlook will also be good for those with doctorates in statistics. These individuals are eagerly sought by large corporations as consultants, and they are also in demand by colleges and universities.

■ UNIONS AND ASSOCIATIONS

Statisticians are not typically represented by unions. Membership organizations for statisticians include the American Statistical Association, Mathematical Association of America, Association for Women in Mathematics, Society for Industrial and Applied Mathematics, and the Statistical Society of Canada. These organizations provide salary data, lists of accredited postsecondary programs, information on career paths, networking opportunities, and professional development classes, workshops, and webinars.

■ TIPS FOR ENTRY

1. Read *Amstat News* (http://magazine.amstat.org) to learn more about the field.
2. Visit http://www.amstat.org/ASA/Your-Career/home.aspx to read Careers in Statistics.
3. Visit the following Web sites for job listings:
   - http://www.amstat.org/ASA/Your-Career/JobWeb.aspx
   - https://sites.google.com/site/awmmath/awm-resources/career/awm-job-ads
   - http://www.siam.org/careers

■ FOR MORE INFORMATION

The American Statistical Association offers educational programs, meetings, publications, membership benefits, advocacy, and other resources for statisticians.

American Statistical Association (ASA)
732 North Washington Street
Alexandria, VA 22314-1943
Tel: (888) 231-3473; (703) 684-1221
Fax: (703) 684-2037
E-mail: asainfo@amstat.org
http://www.amstat.org

The Association for Women in Mathematics provides information on educational and employment opportunities in statistics and related fields.

Association for Women in Mathematics (AWM)
11240 Waples Mill Road, Suite 200
Fairfax, VA 22030-6078
Tel: (703) 934-0163
Fax: (703) 359-7562
E-mail: awm@awm-math.org
https://sites.google.com/site/awmmath/home

The Mathematical Association of America aims to advance the mathematical sciences, particularly at the collegiate level.

Mathematical Association of America (MAA)
1529 18th Street, NW
Washington, D.C. 20036-1358
Tel: (800) 741-9415; (202) 387-5200
Fax: (202) 265-2384
E-mail: maahq@maa.org
http://www.maa.org

The Society for Industrial and Applied Mathematics aims to build cooperation between mathematics and the worlds of science and technology, through publications, research, and community.

Society for Industrial and Applied Mathematics (SIAM)
3600 Market Street, 6th Floor
Philadelphia, PA 19104-2688
Tel: (215) 382-9800
Fax: (215) 386-7999
E-mail: service@siam.org
http://www.siam.org

The Statistical Society of Canada encourages the development and use of statistics and probability.

Statistical Society of Canada (SSC)
210 - 1725 St. Laurent Boulevard
Ottawa, ON K1G 3V4
Canada
Tel: (613) 733-2662, ext. 755
Fax: (613) 733-1386
E-mail: info@ssc.ca
http://www.ssc.ca

Steel Industry Workers

■ OVERVIEW

Steel industry workers melt, mold, and form iron ore and other materials to make the iron and steel used in countless products. These workers operate furnaces, molding equipment, and rolling and finishing machines to make iron pipes, grates, steel slabs, bars, billets, sheets, rods, wires, and plates. Iron and steel products range from carpentry nails to building girders and from cars to guitar strings. The U.S. steel industry operates more than 100 facilities that employ approximately 142,000 people, according to the American Iron and Steel Institute.

■ HISTORY

Civilization changed forever when people first learned to heat and hammer iron ore into iron objects about 3,000 years ago. The first raw iron used was probably that found in meteorites on the surface of the earth. Smelting of iron ore from under the earth's surface came later. People already knew how to make metal alloys (bronze, an alloy of copper and tin, had been in use since 3800 B.C.), and about 500 years after iron became widely used, steel was being made in India. Until modern times, however, steel was fairly rare. Now steel is one of the most ubiquitous substances in our civilization. Modern blast furnaces

QUICK FACTS

ALTERNATE TITLE(S)
Blast Furnace Keepers and Helpers, Bottom Makers, Charger Operators, Coiler Operators, Computer-Controlled Machine Tool Operators, Computer Numerically Controlled Machine Tool Programmers, Draw-Bench Operators, Finishing Operators, Furnace Operators, Guide Setters, Hot-Mill Tin Rollers, Hot-Top Liners, Kiln Operators, Mill Recorders, Mill Utility Workers, Pig-Machine Operators, Primary Mill Rollers, Rail-Tractor Operators, Reeling-Machine Operators, Roll Builders, Roller-Leveler Operators, Rolling Attendants, Roll-Tube Setters, Rougher Operators, Roughers, Screwdown Operators, Sinter Workers, Speed Operators, Steel Pourers, Stove Tenders, Table Operators, Tube Drawers, Tubing-Machine Operators

DUTIES
Operate machinery that melts, molds, and forms iron ore and other materials to make the iron and steel used in countless products

SALARY RANGE
$20,000 to $45,530 to $65,000+

WORK ENVIRONMENT
Primarily Indoors

BEST GEOGRAPHIC LOCATION(S)
Alabama, Arkansas, Illinois, Indiana, Michigan, Ohio, Pennsylvania, and Texas, but jobs exist throughout the country

MINIMUM EDUCATION LEVEL
Apprenticeship

SCHOOL SUBJECTS
Chemistry, Mathematics, Technical/Shop

EXPERIENCE
Apprenticeship; experience as production helper

PERSONALITY TRAITS
Conventional, Hands On, Technical

SKILLS
Computer, Math, Mechanical/Manual Dexterity

CERTIFICATION OR LICENSING
Recommended

SPECIAL REQUIREMENTS
None

EMPLOYMENT PROSPECTS
Fair

ADVANCEMENT PROSPECTS
Fair

OUTLOOK
Decline

NOC
9412

O*NET-SOC
47-2221.00, 51-4023.00, 51-4051.00

duplicate many of the processes used by the ancients, but in quantities of which they never could have dreamed.

Since the 1970s, public policy issues regarding the environment and energy have affected the steel industry. More research and attention has been paid in the decades since to the way steel is manufactured and to recycling and sustainability. The American Iron and Steel Institute reports that steel is the most recycled material in the world: Each year more than 60 million tons of steel are recycled or exported for recycling, and 97 percent of steel by-products can also be re-used or recycled.

■ THE JOB

Today most molten iron goes into steel. Elements such as chromium, nickel, and manganese are added to the iron. The material is then tempered—heated and cooled to make it hard and tough. Forged—hammered or squeezed—steel is strong and dense. To produce iron and steel in traditional, integrated mills, the iron is first melted in huge blast furnaces, often more than 10 stories tall. These furnaces are water-cooled steel cylinders heated by blasts from other, dome-topped cylinders that heat air for melting ore.

Skip operators fill railroad cars with raw materials, such as iron ore, coke, and limestone, work controls that hoist the cars up to the top of the furnace, and dump the contents in layers into the furnace. *Stove tenders* heat air in the domed cylinders (or stoves) until it is the correct temperature and open valves to blast the heated air into the furnace. At temperatures exceeding 3000 degrees Fahrenheit, the materials burn and melt. The limestone purifies the iron, and pure molten iron collects at the bottom of the furnace, while the limestone and impurities float on the top as slag.

Blast furnace keepers and helpers then tap the furnace to remove the molten metal. They drill tapholes in the furnace's fire-brick lining and allow the slag to run out of the furnace. The liquid iron flows through a taphole that is drilled lower into torpedo or bottle cars that keep the iron heated. Keepers and helpers then shoot clay into the tapholes to plug them. One furnace can make as many as 8,000 tons of molten iron per day.

Pure molten iron may be cast into molded forms called "pigs," which are used to make engine blocks and other items. *Pig-machine operators* and their helpers run machines that position molds under ladles holding the molten iron. By moving controls, they tilt the ladles and allow the iron to flow into the molds. Workers spray the molds with lime to keep iron from sticking.

Most iron is made into steel in one of three kinds of furnaces: the basic oxygen furnace, the open-hearth furnace, and the electric furnace. To make steel, *kiln operators* heat minerals such as lime, chromium, or manganese before they are mixed with iron. *Mixer operators* transfer molten iron from bottle cars to mixers and mix the iron and other elements together. *Furnace operators* regulate the temperature and flow of coolant in furnaces into which charging-machine operators dump loads of iron and other elements. Using controls that move mechanical arms to pick up boxes of materials and rotate them, the operators spill the contents into the furnace.

When the steel is ready, the furnace is tilted or tapped to allow the molten metal to run into ladles. Next the steel is formed by pouring it into molds to make ingots. Hot-metal crane operators control cranes that pick up the ladles and hold them above molds. *Steel pourers* and their helpers assemble the stoppers used to plug these ladles. Other workers maintain the molds. *Hot-top liners* and helpers line the mold covers with firebrick and mortar. *Mold workers* remove the ingots from the molds and clean and coat the molds for the next casting.

The steel ingots then go to soaking pits for further processing. In the soaking pits, the ingots are reheated so that they may be rolled. *Charger operators* and helpers move steel through soaking-pit furnaces, where it stays heated at temperatures of up to 2450 degrees Fahrenheit for as long as 14 hours. The ingots are then ready for rolling or shaping into billets, blooms, and slabs. *Bottom makers* reline the bottom of the soaking pits with coke dust to keep oxide scale from forming on ingots. The soaking pits are then ready for more ingots.

Rail-tractor operators transport hot ingots and slabs from soaking pits to conveyors that take them to rolling mills. There, massive steel rollers squeeze the hot ingots into specified shapes. In five minutes, a 25" x 27" ingot can be rolled into a bloom with a 9" x 9" cross section or into a 4" billet. *Roll builders* and *mill utility workers* set up rollers for steel to pass through. *Guide setters* adjust rollers according to the type of shape required. *Mill recorders* control the scheduling of rolling ingots and record production data. *Manipulators* operate mechanisms that guide the ingots into the rolling mills. *Primary mill rollers* and *rolling attendants* operate machines that perform the first rolling operations. *Roll-tube setters* adjust machines that roll ingots into shapes for pipes and tubing.

Some rolled steel goes to foundries to be made into tools, heavy equipment, and machine gears. Most, however, goes to finishing mills to be made into sheet steel, piping, wire, and other types of steel. *Hot-mill tin rollers* run machines that roll slabs into sheets and strips. *Roller-leveler operators* run machines that remove wrinkles from sheets. *Roughers*, *rougher operators*, *speed operators*, *screwdown operators*, and *table operators* set up and operate mills that reduce billets, blooms, and slabs to various shapes, depending on requirements. Some *finishing operators* make seamless tubing by piercing steel billets lengthwise and rolling them into tubing. *Reeling-machine operators* then round out and burnish the inner and outer surfaces of these tubes. As steel strips are made, *coiler operators* wind them into coils, checking for defects and cutting them into specified lengths. *Tubing-machine operators* roll metal ribbon into tubes and solder the seams to form conduit. *Finishers* roll strips, sheets, and bars to specified gauges, shapes, and finishes.

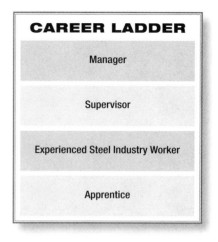

Most rods and tubes and other solid and hollow objects are formed through extruding and drawing hot metal through a die. *Draw-bench operators* and their helpers adjust dies to specified dimensions and draw hot metal rods through them to give them a specified shape and diameter. *Tube drawers* do the same in forming steel tubes.

Other workers process metal that is recovered in powder form from other iron and steel making processes. Much of this powder comes from dust in furnace flues. *Batch makers* tend equipment that recovers powdered metal and separates it from impurities. *Mixers* blend batches of powdered metal, and *sinter workers* make sinter cake, a mass of powdered metal formed without melting. This powder is processed by *press setters and operators* to make bearings, gears, filters, and rings.

The introduction of technology into the manufacturing process has increased productivity, but reduced the number of workers needed to operate certain types of machinery in steel manufacturing plants. *Computer-controlled machine tool operators* oversee computer-controlled machines or robots during the steel manufacturing process. *Computer numerically controlled machine tool programmers* design software programs that control the machining or processing of steel.

Steel production is recorded by workers to assure that procedures are carried out correctly. *Inspectors* and *assorters* check steel products to make sure they meet customers' specifications. Other workers test samples of metal to measure their strength, hardness, or ductility.

The industry also employs various mechanics and construction workers, including *bricklayers* who line furnaces with firebrick and refractory tile and repair

A steel industry worker cuts steel at a factory. (maroti. Shutterstock.)

cracked or broken linings. *Millwrights* install and maintain equipment and machinery. *Electricians* install and repair computer controls for machine tools and other equipment. *Industrial engineers* determine the most efficient and cost-effective methods for production. *Mechanical engineers* often work in management positions to solve mechanical issues on the production line. *Environmental engineers* design, build, and maintain systems to control air and water pollution. *Metallurgical engineers* try to improve or alter the properties of steel, as well as find new uses for the metal. *General laborers* are employed to feed, unload, and clean machines; to move supplies and raw materials; to hoist materials for processing; and to perform a variety of other unskilled tasks. Other workers bale scrap metal or strap coils.

EARNINGS

Most steel mills operate 24 hours a day. Workers work one of three shifts: day, night, or graveyard. Late-shift workers receive premium pay, as do those who work overtime (more than 40 hours per week), or on Sundays and holidays.

According to the U.S. Department of Labor, mean annual earnings for production occupations in steel manufacturing in May 2015 were $45,530. It reports the following mean salaries for workers: first-line supervisors/managers of production and operating workers, $59,930; machinists, $40,250; metal-refining furnace operators and tenders, $48,150; crane and tower operators, $49,890; rolling machine setters, operators, and tenders, metal and plastic, $48,510; inspectors, testers, sorters, samplers, and weighers, $41,520; pourers and casters, metal, $46,690; cutting, punching, and press machine setters, operators, and tenders, metal and plastic, $36,690; and

production work helpers, $33,650. In general, salaries range from $20,000 to $65,000 or more.

Workers receive paid holidays, paid vacations, sick leave, retirement plans, health and life insurance, and other fringe benefits. Many benefits are determined by contracts between the representative union and company management.

WORK ENVIRONMENT

Safety is a great concern in steel mills. Furnaces create incredibly high temperatures, and machines handle mountains of materials. Yet the steel industry is one of the safest in America. While steelworkers of the past worked in searing, dangerous conditions, today's workers often work in air-conditioned spaces and come no closer to machinery than pressing a button. Those who work in close proximity to machines and molten metal wear safety clothing and equipment (hard hats, safety glasses, protective aprons, and so on) provided by the company. Still, some workers are exposed to heat and great amounts of noise. The industry, however, is focused on making mills as safe as possible for workers.

EXPLORING

One of the best ways to learn about the steel industry is to visit a steel mill. If this is not feasible, you may be able to invite a union or industry representative to your school to speak with students about careers in the steel industry. Reading publications, such as *Iron & Steel Technology* (http://www.aist.org/publications/iron-steel-technology), published by iron and steel associations is a good way to become more familiar with the industry and current trends.

EDUCATION AND TRAINING REQUIREMENTS
High School

In the past, some employers hired workers without high school diplomas, but today most prefer high school graduates. Classes to take in high school include English, communications, general mathematics, computer science, and mechanical drawing as well as shop courses.

Postsecondary Training

Most steelworkers learn their skills on the job or through apprenticeships. Apprenticeships are open to high school graduates who are at least 18 years old. Apprentice programs generally last four to five years and teach skills through classroom lectures and on-the-job training. Some employers pay for workers to take additional courses in subjects they can use on the job—chemistry, management, and metallurgy, for example. Other education is available through home-study courses, technical schools, and colleges. In general, those planning to work in administrative, managerial, technical, and engineering positions will need a college degree.

Other Education or Training

The Association for Iron and Steel Technology hosts specialty training conferences annually that allow steel industry professionals to hone their skills and stay up to date on industry developments. Past conferences include The Making, Shaping and Treating of Steel: 101 and Maintenance Solutions: A Practical Training Seminar.

■ CERTIFICATION, LICENSING, AND SPECIAL REQUIREMENTS

Certification or Licensing

The National Institute for Metalworking Skills (NIMS) offers certification in 24 operational areas including metalforming (stamping, press brake, roll forming, laser cutting) and machining (tool and die making; machine building and machine maintenance, etc.)

■ EXPERIENCE, SKILLS, AND PERSONALITY TRAITS

Aspiring steel industry workers must complete an apprentice program that lasts four to five years; previous experience as a production helper will also be useful.

Many of the jobs in this industry are physically demanding, and workers need to be in good health and have strength and endurance. Traits that employers look for include good mechanical skills and computer aptitude, and strong reading comprehension, oral communication, and math skills.

■ EMPLOYMENT PROSPECTS

Employers

In 2015, the U.S. steel industry operated more than 100 facilities employing 142,000 people, according to the American Iron and Steel Institute. Many steel manufacturing plants are located in Alabama, Arkansas, Illinois, Indiana, Michigan, Ohio, Pennsylvania, and Texas.

Starting Out

State employment agencies, online employment agencies, and newspapers' classifieds sections sometimes list openings in steel mills. Job seekers should also apply directly at the mills' personnel offices. Workers who would like to begin as an apprentice should contact a local union or a state apprenticeship bureau.

■ ADVANCEMENT PROSPECTS

Entry-level steelworkers and those new to a plant may start in a pool of unskilled laborers. Steelworkers have a

---

ELECTRONIC ARC FURNACE MILLS   DID YOU KNOW?

Electronic arc furnace (EAF) mills are cost-saving minimills that create steel by using scrap metal from old automobiles, bridges, and appliances. They require smaller startup and operational costs than traditional integrated mills. Unlike integrated mills, which have to be located near raw material deposits, EAF mills can be built anywhere in the country. EAF mills account for about 50 percent of all steel production in the United States.

Source: U.S. Department of Labor

---

strong union, which is why advancement is often dependent on seniority. As workers gain skills and seniority, they may move into more difficult but higher-paying jobs. Workers may take five years to learn the work of supervisors or rollers but then have to wait much longer for openings to occur. With further education and training, workers may advance into management positions.

■ OUTLOOK

Strong foreign competition, an increase in imported steel, decreases in domestic manufacturing, the increasing use of labor-saving machinery (such as computer numerically-controlled [CNC] machine tools and robots), and overproduction of steel on the world market has negatively affected the U.S. steel industry and its workers. The U.S. Department of Labor (DOL) predicts that employment in the steel industry will decline through 2024. Opportunities will be slightly better for workers employed at electronic arc furnace mills, which are more cost-effective than traditional steel mills. The DOL predicts that job opportunities for CNC machine programmers will be strong through 2024.

One growth area for steel manufacturers is the field of renewable energy. According to the American Iron and Steel Institute, "steel is at the core of the green economy...it is the main material used in delivering renewable energy—solar, tidal and wind; and the only material that reduces greenhouse gas emissions in all phases of an automobile's life: manufacturing, driving and end-of-life."

■ UNIONS AND ASSOCIATIONS

Many steel industry professionals are members of United Steelworkers, a union with members in the United States, Canada, and the Caribbean. The American Iron and Steel Institute and Steel Manufacturers Association are membership organizations for steel manufacturing companies and suppliers. The Association for Iron and Steel

Technology is a membership organization for metal industry professionals.

■ TIPS FOR ENTRY

1. Read *Iron & Steel Technology* (http://www.aist.org/publications/iron-steel-technology) to learn more about the field.
2. Visit http://apps.aist.org/jobsasp/jobs_list.asp and http://www.steel.org/about-aisi/members.aspx for job listings and to learn more about the different types of steel companies in operation today.
3. Join the Association for Iron and Steel Technology to access networking opportunities, continuing education resources, and resources for young professionals.

■ FOR MORE INFORMATION

The American Iron and Steel Institute provides advocacy, education, research, and other resources for the steel industry.

American Iron and Steel Institute (AISI)
25 Massachusetts Avenue, NW, Suite 800
Washington, D.C. 20001-1413
Tel: (202) 452-7100
http://www.steel.org

The Association for Iron and Steel Technology aims to advance the technological development, production, processing, and application of iron and steel.

Association for Iron and Steel Technology (AIST)
186 Thorn Hill Road
Warrendale, PA 15086-7528
Tel: (724) 814-3000
Fax: (724) 814-3001
E-mail: memberservices@aist.org
http://www.aist.org

The National Institute for Metalworking Skills offers certification and training programs as well as professional development workshops for apprenticeships.

National Institute for Metalworking Skills (NIMS)
10565 Fairfax Boulevard, Suite 10
Fairfax, VA 22030-3135
Tel: (844) 839-6467; (703) 352-4971
Fax: (703) 352-4991
https://www.nims-skills.org

The Steel Manufacturers Association facilitates the exchange of information and ideas, and promotes public policies that enable North American steelmakers to compete globally.

Steel Manufacturers Association (SMA)
1150 Connecticut Avenue, NW, Suite 1125
Washington, D.C. 20036-4104
Tel: (202) 296-1515
Fax: (202) 296-2506
E-mail: stefanec@steelnet.org
http://steelnet.org

The United Steelworkers provides information on apprenticeship programs and union membership.

United Steelworkers
60 Boulevard of the Allies, Suite 902
Pittsburgh, PA 15222-1258
Tel: (412) 562-2400
http://www.usw.org

Stenographers

■ OVERVIEW

Stenographers take dictation using either shorthand notation or a stenotype machine, then later transcribe their notes into business documents. They may record people's remarks at meetings or other proceedings and later give a summary report or a word-for-word transcript of what was said. General stenographers may also perform other office tasks such as typing, filing, answering phones, and operating office machines. There are approximately 17,670 court reporters, including stenographers, employed in the United States, according to the Department of Labor.

■ HISTORY

People throughout history have experimented with methods and symbols for abbreviating spoken communications because of the need for accurate records of speeches, meetings, legal proceedings, and other events. Contemporary shorthand systems are based on the phonetic principle of using a symbol to represent a sound. Stenographers use a special keyboard called a steno keyboard or shorthand machine to "write" what they hear as they hear it.

Shorthand began to be applied to business communications with the invention of the typewriter. The stenotype, the first machine that could print shorthand characters, was invented by an American stenographer and court reporter named Ward Stone Ireland around 1906. Unlike a traditional typewriter keyboard, the steno keyboard allows more than one key to be pressed at a time. The basic concept behind machine shorthand is phonetic, where combinations of keys represent sounds, but the actual theory used is much more complex than straight phonetics.

Today, stenographers, in addition to using stenotype machines, use Dictaphones or computer-based systems to transcribe reports, letters, and official records of meetings or other events. Their careful and accurate work is essential to the proper functioning of various organizations of law, business, and government.

■ THE JOB

Stenographers take dictation and then transcribe their notes on a typewriter or word processor. They may be asked to record speeches, conversations, legal proceedings, meetings, or a person's business correspondence. They may either take shorthand manually or use a stenotype machine.

In addition to transcription tasks, general stenographers may also have a variety of other office duties, such as typing, operating photocopy and other office machines, answering telephones, and performing general receptionist duties. They may sit in on staff meetings and later transcribe a summary report of the proceedings for use by management. In some situations, stenographers may be responsible for answering routine office mail.

Experienced and highly skilled stenographers take on more difficult dictation assignments. They may take dictation in foreign languages or at very busy proceedings. Some work as *public stenographers*, who are hired out to serve traveling business people and unique meetings and events.

Steno pool supervisors supervise and coordinate the work of stenographers by assigning them to people who have documents to dictate or by giving stenographers manuscripts or recordings to transcribe. They also check final typed copy for accuracy.

Skilled stenographers who receive additional training may learn to operate computer-aided transcription (CAT) systems—stenotype machines that are linked directly to a computer. Specialized computer software instantly translates stenographic symbols into words. This technology is most frequently used by real-time captioners or others doing computer-aided real-time translation in courtrooms, classrooms, or meetings. This area of specialization is also known as computer aided real-time transcription or communication access real-time translation (CART). The use of this technology requires a more sophisticated knowledge of computer systems and English grammar, along with enhanced technical skills. Other areas of specialization for stenographers include the following:

Transcribing-machine operators listen to recordings (often through earphones or earplugs) and transcribe the material. They can control the speed of the recording so that they can type every word they hear at a comfortable speed. Transcribing-machine operators may also have various clerical duties, such as answering the telephones and filing correspondence.

Technical stenographers may specialize in medical, legal, engineering, or other technical areas. They should be familiar with the terminology and the practice of the appropriate subject. For example, a *medical transcriptionist* must be a medical language expert and be familiar with the processes of patient assessment, therapeutic procedures, diagnoses, and prognoses.

Court reporters specialize in taking notes for and transcribing legal and court proceedings. *Real-time captioners* operate CAT stenotype systems to create closed captions for live television broadcasts. It should be noted that the body of knowledge required to perform the tasks of a court reporter or real-time captioner is greater than that which a stenographer needs to know. While a court reporter or captioner could readily perform the tasks of an office stenographer, the stenographer would be unable to perform either job without additional training.

Those with training as court reporters may also work as *broadcast captioners*, transcribing the dialogue from television programs onto television monitors for viewers who are deaf or hard of hearing and for shows that are aired in public places. Broadcast captioners may work in real time during the broadcasts or in post production.

QUICK FACTS

ALTERNATE TITLE(S)
Court Reporters, Medical Transcriptionists, Public Stenographers, Real-Time Captioners, Technical Stenographers, Transcribing-Machine Operators

DUTIES
Take dictation using either shorthand notation or a stenotype machine, then later transcribe their notes into business documents

SALARY RANGE
$27,180 to $37,841 to $90,510+

WORK ENVIRONMENT
Primarily Indoors

BEST GEOGRAPHIC LOCATION(S)
Opportunities are available throughout the country, but are best in large, urban areas

MINIMUM EDUCATION LEVEL
Some Postsecondary Training

SCHOOL SUBJECTS
Business, Computer Science, English

EXPERIENCE
On-the-job training

PERSONALITY TRAITS
Hands On, Organized, Technical

SKILLS
Computer, Interpersonal, Writing

CERTIFICATION OR LICENSING
Recommended

SPECIAL REQUIREMENTS
None

EMPLOYMENT PROSPECTS
Fair

ADVANCEMENT PROSPECTS
Good

OUTLOOK
Little Change or More Slowly than the Average

NOC
1241, 1242, 1243, 1251

O*NET-SOC
23-2091.00, 31-9094.00, 43-6014.00

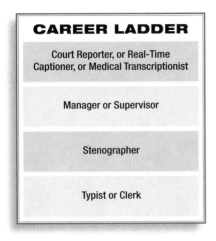

CAREER LADDER

Court Reporter, or Real-Time Captioner, or Medical Transcriptionist

Manager or Supervisor

Stenographer

Typist or Clerk

◼ EARNINGS

Salaries for stenographers vary widely, depending on their skill, experience, level of responsibility, and geographic location. According to Salary .com, stenographers earned average salaries of $37,841 in September 2016; salaries ranged from $30,996 to $46,750. According to the U.S. Department of Labor, in May 2015, court reporters (stenographers who have advanced training) earned annual salaries that ranged from $27,180 to $90,510 or more, with a median salary of $49,500. Full-time workers also receive paid vacation, health insurance, and other benefits.

◼ WORK ENVIRONMENT

Relatively few office stenographers work in the evenings or on weekends. (This is not true of court reporters, real-time captioners, or those who freelance their services, as they often work long and irregular hours.) Some stenographers take on part-time or temporary work during peak business periods.

The physical work environment is usually pleasant and comfortable, although stenographers may sometimes have to work under extreme deadline pressure. Stenographers may also be subject to repetitive stress injury, a prevalent industrial hazard for those who perform repeated motions in their daily work. Carpal tunnel syndrome is a type of repetitive stress injury that stenographers can sometimes develop, causing a prickling sensation or numbness in the hand and sometimes a partial loss of function. Stenographers generally perform their jobs while seated and so must be conscious of correct posture and proper seating.

The majority of stenographers are not required to travel; however, some may accompany their employers on business trips to provide dictation services.

◼ EXPLORING

Gain experience in the stenography field by assuming clerical and typing responsibilities with a school club or other organization. In addition, some school work-study programs may have opportunities with businesses for part-time, on-the-job training. It may also be possible to get a part-time or summer job in a business office by contacting offices directly. Another good idea is to get training in word processing software and office machinery through evening or continuing education courses offered by business schools and community colleges.

◼ EDUCATION AND TRAINING REQUIREMENTS
High School

Stenographers should have a high school diploma. Some high school students follow a business education curriculum and take courses in typing, shorthand, and business procedures. These students may later enter a business school or college for more advanced technical training. Other students may follow a general education program and take courses in English, history, mathematics, computer science, and the sciences, intending to undergo all of their technical training after graduation.

Postsecondary Training

Some students with a business curriculum background are able to obtain jobs immediately after graduation from high school, but those with a college degree, advanced technical training, or some specialization have better job opportunities and higher salaries. In many instances, training at a business school, vocational school, or college may be required. The more advanced career of court reporter or real-time captioner requires a two-year degree in court and conference reporting, although a four-year degree that includes courses in computers and English is preferable.

Numerous opportunities for advanced training exist. Hundreds of business schools and colleges throughout the country offer technical or degree programs with both day and evening classes.

◼ CERTIFICATION, LICENSING, AND SPECIAL REQUIREMENTS
Certification or Licensing

To work for the federal government, stenographers must pass a civil service test and be able to take dictation at the rate of 80 words per minute and type at least 40 words per minute. Tests of verbal and mathematical ability are also required. Employers in the private sector may require similar tests. Certification is available for advanced jobs such as court reporters, real-time captioners, and medical transcriptionists.

◼ EXPERIENCE, SKILLS, AND PERSONALITY TRAITS

No experience is needed for entry-level stenography positions, but those wanting to work in advanced specialties—such as court reporting—will need to complete postsecondary training.

Stenographers should have good reading comprehension and spelling skills, as well as good finger and hand dexterity. They should also find systematic and orderly work appealing, and they should like to work on detailed tasks. Other personal qualifications include dependability, trustworthiness, and a neat personal appearance, given their high degree of visibility.

■ EMPLOYMENT PROSPECTS
Employers
Stenographers, including those who have developed special skills through training, are employed in various organizations of law; business; and federal, state, and local government. Some specialist stenographers work in medical, legal, engineering, or other technical areas. Some stenographers develop their own freelance businesses.

Starting Out
High school counselors and business education teachers may be helpful in locating job opportunities for would-be stenographers. Additionally, business schools and colleges frequently have career services offices to help their trainees and graduates find employment. Those interested in securing an entry-level position can also contact individual businesses or government agencies directly. Jobs may also be located through online employment organizations.

Many companies administer aptitude tests to potential employees before they are hired. Speed and accuracy are critical factors in making such evaluations. Individuals who are initially unable to meet the minimum requirements for a stenographer position may want to take jobs as typists or clerks and, as they gain experience and technical training, try for promotion to the position of stenographer.

■ ADVANCEMENT PROSPECTS
Skilled stenographers can advance to secretarial positions, especially if they develop their interpersonal communications skills. They may also become *heads of stenographic departments* or in some cases be promoted to *office manager*. In some instances, experienced stenographers may go into business for themselves as *public stenographers* serving traveling business people and others. Stenographers who complete advanced training may become *court reporters*, *real-time captioners*, or *medical transcriptionists*.

■ OUTLOOK
Audio recording equipment and the use of personal computers by managers and other professionals has greatly reduced the demand for stenographers in office settings. Continued technological advances, such as computer-aided equipment that can print out what is being said by a spoken voice, will limit demand for basic stenographers without specialized skills and training.

Employment growth for court reporters is expected to be slower than the average through 2024, according to the Department of Labor. There will be more jobs, however, for broadcast captioners, due to new federal regulations that require expanded use of captioning for television, the Internet, and other technologies. Job opportunities will be best in the coming years for computer-aided transcription (CAT) system operators in real-time settings. The trend to provide instantaneous captions for the deaf and hearing-impaired and the growing use of CAT technology in courtroom trials should strengthen the demand for real-time reporters and other specialists.

■ UNIONS AND ASSOCIATIONS
Some stenographers, especially those who work for the federal government, may belong to a union such as the Office and Professional Employees' International Union. Professional associations such as the National Court Reporters Association and the National Verbatim Reporters Association offer educational programs, certification, networking opportunities, and other resources for stenographers and court reporters.

■ TIPS FOR ENTRY
1. Talk with stenographers about their careers. Ask them for advice on preparing for and entering the field.
2. Visit the following Web sites for job listings:
   - http://www.careerbuilder.com
   - http://www.indeed.com

STENOTYPE
DID YOU KNOW?

Stenographers do not use a standard typewriter or computer keyboard for their work. Instead, they use either shorthand or a shorthand machine with 22 keys to record speech much faster. A skilled stenographer can typically capture 225 to more than 300 words per minute at extremely high accuracy. A shorthand machine, or stenotype, has two rows of consonants, with a row of vowels below operated by the thumbs. Keys are pressed simultaneously to capture syllables phonetically, with abbreviations used to quicken the process. Modern stenotypes use computer-aided transcription to re-translate their typing back to English.

- http://www.simplyhired.com
- http://www.monster.com

3. Pursue advanced education in court reporting, medical transcription, or real-time reporting to increase your chances of landing a job and earning higher pay.

■ FOR MORE INFORMATION

The Office and Professional Employees International Union is a labor union that represents office and professional employees.

Office and Professional Employees International Union (OPEIU)
80 Eighth Avenue, 20th Floor
New York, NY 10011-7144
Tel: (800) 346-7348
http://www.opeiu.org

The National Court Reporters Association provides certification programs, advocacy, and other resources for court reporters.

National Court Reporters Association (NCRA)
12030 Sunrise Valley Drive, Suite 400
Reston, VA 20191-3484
Tel: (800) 272-6272; (703) 556-6272
Fax: (703) 391-0629
E-mail: msic@ncra.org
https://www.ncra.org/

The National Verbatim Reporters Association offers support and benefits, certification, conferences, and newsletters for verbatim reporters.

National Verbatim Reporters Association (NVRA)
629 North Main Street
Hattiesburg, MS 39401-3429
Tel: (601) 582-4345
E-mail: membership@nvra.org
https://nvra.org/

Stevedores

■ OVERVIEW

Stevedores, commonly known as *longshore workers* or *dockworkers*, handle cargo at ports, often using materials-handling machinery and gear. They load and unload ships at docks and transfer cargo to and from storage areas or other transports, such as trucks and barges. Members of the water transportation industry, stevedores are employed at ports all over the United States.

The concentration of jobs is at the large ports on the coasts, and experienced skilled workers hold most of the positions.

■ HISTORY

There have been stevedoring workers in North America since colonial times. Long ago, when a sailing vessel arrived at the docks of a settlement, criers would go up and down the nearby streets summoning workers with a call like, "Men along the shore!" Stevedores, or longshore workers, came quickly in hopes of a chance to make some extra cash by helping to unload the ship's cargo. Often, these longshore workers lived in town near the port and had other occupations. Ships arrived too infrequently for them to make a living at the docks. But as the volume of shipping increased, a group of workers developed who were always available at the docks for loading and unloading activities.

Ship owners usually wanted to have cargos moved through ports as soon as possible. They preferred to pick temporary workers from a large labor pool at the time there was work to be done. However, this practice produced unfavorable wages, hours, and working conditions for many workers. In the 19th century, longshore workers were among the first groups of American workers to organize labor unions to force improvements in working conditions.

In ancient times, a ship's cargo was handled in single "man-loads." Grain, a common item of cargo, was packed in sacks that could be carried on and off the ship on a man's shoulders. As methods progressed, the ship's rigging was used for hoisting cargo. The first cargo to need a special type of handling was fuel, which used to be transported in barrels. As the volume of fuel increased, barrels became inadequate. Since the late 19th century, oil products have been shipped in bulk, with no packaging, pumped directly into the hull cells of tankers.

Cargo handling has thus depended on the type of cargo shipped. Vehicles are simply rolled on and off; dry bulk like coal and grain is often poured into cargo holds. In the first part of the 20th century, longshore work slowly became mechanized, relying less on human labor and more on machines. Since the 1960s, containerization of cargos has been a major factor in ocean shipping. This method of transporting goods involves putting freight into large sealed boxes of standard sizes, sometimes fitted as truck trailers. The containers, which can be carried on ships that are specially built to hold them, are easily and quickly moved on and off ships at ports, thus keeping the cost of transport well below that for uncontainerized cargo. Such changes have greatly reduced the demand for stevedoring workers to do manual loading and unloading.

THE JOB

Stevedores perform tasks involved in transferring cargo to and from the holds of ships and around the dock area. They may operate power winches or cranes to move items such as automobiles, crates, scrap metal, and steel beams, using hooks, magnets, or slings. They may operate grain trimmers (equipment that moves bulk grain through a spout and into the hatch of receiving containers). Stevedores may drive trucks along the dock or aboard ships to transfer items such as lumber and crates to within reach of winches. They may drive tractors to move loaded trailers from storage areas to dockside. They may load and unload liquid cargoes, such as vegetable oils, molasses, or chemicals, by fastening hose lines to cargo tanks. Stevedores also do other manual tasks such as lashing cargo in place aboard ships, attaching lifting devices to winches, and signaling to other workers to raise or lower cargo. They may direct other dockworkers in moving cargo by hand or with hand trucks or in securing cargo inside the holds of ships.

Some stevedoring workers perform just one category of specialized tasks. For example, *boat loaders* may load liquid chemical and fuel cargoes such as petroleum, gasoline, heating oil, and sulfuric acid by connecting and disconnecting hose couplings. At each stage in the process, they make sure various conditions are safe. Other boat loaders tend winches and loading chutes to load iron ore onto boats and barges. *Winch drivers* operate steam or electric winches to move various kinds of cargo in and out of a ship's hold. They may alternate jobs with *hatch tenders*, who signal to winch drivers when the cargo is secured and ready for transfer. *Gear repairers* fix gear that is used in lifting cargo and install appropriate equipment depending on the current cargo-handling needs on a particular vessel. Among the many other workers in the dock area are *drivers*, who drive rolling stock (including forklifts, trucks, and mobile cranes), and *carpenters*, who repair pallets and construct braces and other structures to protect cargo in holds or on deck.

Headers or *gang bosses* supervise stevedores. They assign specific duties and explain how the cargo should be handled and secured and how the hoisting equipment should be set up. They may estimate the amount of extra materials that will be needed to brace and protect the cargo, such as paper or lumber.

Stevedoring superintendents coordinate and direct the loading and unloading of cargo. Before loading begins, they study the layout of the ship and the bill of lading to determine where to stow cargo and in what order. Freight that must come out first is usually the last to be loaded. Stevedoring superintendents estimate the time and number of workers they need for the job and give orders for hiring. They make sure that the available equipment is appropriate for the cargo load, and they may direct workers who are handling special materials, such as explosives. Stevedoring superintendents prepare reports on their operations and may create bills, all while keeping in touch with the company representatives from whom they get their directions.

Pier superintendents manage business operations at freight terminals. They determine what cargo various vessels will be carrying and notify stevedoring superintendents to plan to have workers and dock space available for loading and unloading activities. They compute costs; oversee purchasing of cargo handling equipment and hiring of trucks, tractors, and railroad cars; and make sure that the terminal facilities and the company's equipment are properly maintained.

Shipping operations require individuals who have good record-keeping and accounting skills as well. Workers who do these tasks include *shipping clerks*, who maintain information on all incoming and outgoing cargo, such as its quantity and condition, identification marks, and container size. *Location workers* keep track of where cargo is located on piers. *Delivery clerks* and *receiving clerks* keep records on the loading and discharging of vessels and on transferring cargo to and from truckers. *Timekeepers* record the work time of all workers on the pier for billing and payroll purposes.

EARNINGS

The U.S. Department of Labor reports that tank car, truck, and ship loaders made a median hourly wage

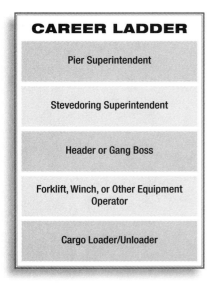

CAREER LADDER

Pier Superintendent

Stevedoring Superintendent

Header or Gang Boss

Forklift, Winch, or Other Equipment Operator

Cargo Loader/Unloader

of $16.63, or $36,660 a year, in May 2015. Salaries ranged from less than $22,370 to $69,820 or more. Those who worked in the water transportation industry earned an average salary of $39,640. Stevedores receive extra pay for handling certain difficult or dangerous cargoes and for working overtime, nights, or holidays. In addition to earnings, full-time workers usually receive good benefits packages that may include pension plans, paid holiday and vacation days, and health insurance.

▨ WORK ENVIRONMENT

Some parts of piers are covered by sheds, yet many stevedores work outdoors much of the time, including in bad weather. Working around materials-handling machinery can be noisy. At times, hours may be very long, such as when it is important that a lot of cargo be moved on and off piers quickly. Stevedores work under stress to meet deadlines. Some work is strenuous, involving lifting heavy material. Stevedores must use care to avoid injury from falls, falling objects, and machines. Some workers, such as those in certain supervisory positions, move about fairly constantly.

▨ EXPLORING

To find out more about stevedoring occupations, contact the offices of the longshore workers' union in local areas. Union representatives can provide information about the likely conditions and prospects for local jobs, as well as answer questions and provide an insider's view of the field. Students in coastal areas have an advantage over others because they can visit ports and ask questions about what is involved in being a dockworker.

▨ EDUCATION AND TRAINING REQUIREMENTS
High School

A well-rounded education while in high school is a good foundation for future stevedore work. Good communication skills and physical fitness are important in this type of job. Take classes in mathematics and English as well as shop and physical education to help prepare for the different aspects of the workload.

Postsecondary Training

Often, no special preparation is needed for this kind of work, as many stevedores learn what they need to know, such as equipment operations, on the job. However, experience operating similar equipment is likely to be an advantage to any applicant and may result in more rapid advancement.

Workers in some positions need clerical or technical skills that can be learned in high school or vocational school. For administrative occupations, college-level training or experience as a ship's officer is often desirable. Supervisory personnel generally need an understanding of the whole process of loading and unloading a vessel. They must be able to deal with a labor force that may include inexperienced workers and that changes in number from day to day.

▨ CERTIFICATION, LICENSING, AND SPECIAL REQUIREMENTS
Certification or Licensing

There are no certification or licensing requirements for stevedores.

Other Requirements

Stevedores must be able to lift and carry at least 50 pounds.

▨ EXPERIENCE, SKILLS, AND PERSONALITY TRAITS

No experience is needed to work in entry-level stevedore positions, but those with prior work experience operating materials-handling machinery will increase their chances of landing a job, getting promoted, and earning higher pay.

Stevedores who work on the docks need to be agile and physically fit. Their work may be strenuous, sometimes requiring lifting weights of up to 50 pounds. Good eyesight and dexterity are essential. Some jobs can be adapted to some extent for workers with disabilities. Stevedores may work in situations that are potentially dangerous, so they must be able to think clearly and quickly and be able to follow orders. Longshore work is a team effort, so it is essential that stevedores work well with others.

▨ EMPLOYMENT PROSPECTS
Employers

Stevedores are employed at all U.S. ports. The bulk of jobs are concentrated on the coasts, and larger companies employ greater numbers of longshore workers. Usually, applicants must be union members to secure a position with one of the larger companies.

Starting Out

To find a job as a stevedore, contact the local union offices or shipping companies to find out whether workers are being hired. Those who would like eventually to work in an administrative position, such as pier superintendent, should consider entering one of the maritime academies (schools that train officers and crew for merchant vessels). Another possibility for people interested in administrative work is to enter a training program conducted by a port authority, which is an organization at a port that controls harbor activities.

Many stevedoring jobs are open only to union workers. In some ports, jobs are allocated based on seniority, so newcomers may be left with the least desirable jobs.

■ ADVANCEMENT PROSPECTS

Dockworkers may start out doing basic labor, such as loading trucks or following instructions to load cargo in holds. Later, if they prove to be responsible and reliable, they may learn how to operate equipment such as winches or forklifts. In general, this kind of advancement depends on the need for workers to do particular tasks, as well as on the individual's abilities. Those who demonstrate strong abilities, leadership, and judgment may have an opportunity to become gang bosses and supervise a crew of other workers. Advancement into administrative positions may require additional formal education.

■ OUTLOOK

The employment outlook for stevedoring workers varies by profession, but, in general, it is expected to be weak in coming years—although certain large ports will experience growth and require larger numbers of specialized workers.

Employment of crane and tower operators in water transportation is projected to grow by 8 percent through 2024, according to the U.S. Department of Labor, about as fast the average for all careers. Global shipping volume is increasing, and operators will be needed to load and unload large cargo ships. Employment of hoist and winch operators in water transportation is projected to grow by only 2 percent through 2024.

A number of factors are contributing to a lack of growth for many longshore occupations, including increased automation and containerization, and the combining of jobs in the industry. Increasing retirement among union members will assure a certain number of new jobs each year. Also, to remedy labor disagreement problems at smaller ports, union officials have devised a travel plan for longshore workers in smaller ports who have decided to work at bigger ports whenever positions are available.

A stevedore signals to a coworker while loading cargo. (potowizard. Shutterstock.)

The trends toward automated materials-handling processes and containerizing cargo are well established. In the future, fewer people may be hired for manual loading and unloading tasks, and the stevedoring workforce will probably be highly skilled, well trained, and will consist mostly of full-time workers.

■ UNIONS AND ASSOCIATIONS

Many stevedoring jobs are open only to union workers. Unions to which stevedores belong are the International Longshoremen's Association and the International Longshore and Warehouse Union. The National Maritime Safety Association provides research and resources to promote the safety and health of longshore workers.

■ TIPS FOR ENTRY

1. Read *The Dispatcher* (http://www.ilwu.org/the-dispatcher-newspaper/current-issue) to learn more about union-related issues.
2. Talk to stevedores about their careers. Ask them for advice on breaking into the field.

3. Land a part-time job at a water transportation firm or related employer to hone your skills and make industry contacts.

FOR MORE INFORMATION

The International Longshore and Warehouse Union provides information on stevedoring occupations.

International Longshore and Warehouse Union (ILWU)
1188 Franklin Street, 4th Floor
San Francisco, CA 94109-6800
Tel: (415) 775-0533
Fax: (415) 775-1302
http://www.ilwu.org

The International Longshoremen's Association is a labor union that represents maritime workers in North America.

International Longshoremen's Association (ILA)
5000 West Side Avenue
North Bergen, NJ 07047-6439
Tel: (212)-425-1200
Fax: (212)-425-2928
http://www.ilaunion.org

The National Maritime Safety Association has a mission to aid, advance, assist, encourage, promote, and support safety in the marine cargo handling operations.

National Maritime Safety Association (NMSA)
1200 19th Street, NW, 3rd Floor
Washington, D.C. 20036-2412
Tel: (202) 587-4830
E-mail: mto@nmsa.us
http://www.nmsa.us

Stock Clerks

OVERVIEW

Stock clerks receive, unpack, store, distribute, and record the inventory for materials or products used by a company, plant, or store. More than 1.9 million stock clerks and order fillers are employed in the United States.

HISTORY

The stock clerk profession has existed for as long as businesses have been engaged in meeting consumers' demands with supplies. Almost every type of business establishment imaginable—shoe store, restaurant, hotel, auto repair shop, hospital, supermarket, or steel mill—buys materials or products from outside distributors and uses these materials in its operations. A large part of the company's money is tied up in these inventory stocks, but without them operations would come to a standstill. Stores would run out of merchandise to sell, mechanics would be unable to repair cars until new parts were shipped in, and factories would be unable to operate once their basic supply of raw materials ran out.

To avoid these problems, businesses have developed their own inventory-control systems to store enough goods and raw materials for uninterrupted operations, move these materials to the places they are needed, and know when it is time to order more. These systems are the responsibility of stock clerks.

THE JOB

Stock clerks work in just about every type of industry, and no matter what kind of storage or stock room they staff—food, clothing, merchandise, medicine, or raw materials—the work of stock clerks is essentially the same. They receive, sort, put away, distribute, and keep track of the items a business sells or uses. Their titles sometimes vary based on their responsibilities.

When goods are received in a stockroom, stock clerks unpack the shipment and check the contents against documents such as the invoice, purchase order, and bill of lading, which lists the contents of the shipment. The shipment is inspected, and any damaged goods are set aside. Stock clerks may reject or send back damaged items or call vendors to complain about the condition of the shipment. In large companies, shipping and receiving clerks may do this work.

Once the goods are received, stock clerks organize them and sometimes mark them with identifying codes or prices so they can be placed in stock according to the existing inventory system. In this way the materials or goods can be found readily when needed, and inventory control is much easier. In many firms stock clerks use handheld scanners and computers to keep inventory records up to date.

In retail stores and supermarkets, stock clerks may bring merchandise to the sales floor and stock shelves and racks. In stockrooms and warehouses, they store materials in bins, on the floor, or on shelves. In other settings, such as restaurants, hotels, and factories, stock clerks deliver goods when they are needed. They may do this on a regular schedule or at the request of other employees or supervisors. Although many stock clerks use mechanical equipment, such as forklifts, to move heavy items, some perform strenuous and laborious work. In general, the work of a stock clerk involves much standing, bending, walking, stretching, lifting, and carrying.

When items are removed from the inventory, stock clerks adjust records to reflect the products' use. These records are kept as current as possible, and inventories are periodically checked against these records. Every item is counted, and the totals are compared with the records on hand or the records from the sales, shipping, production, or purchasing departments. This helps identify how fast items are being used, when items must be ordered from outside suppliers, or even whether items are disappearing from the stockroom. Many retail establishments use computerized cash registers that maintain an inventory count automatically as they record the sale of each item.

The duties of stock clerks vary depending on their place of employment. Stock clerks working in small firms perform many different tasks, including shipping and receiving, inventory control, and purchasing. In large firms, responsibilities may be more narrowly defined. More specific job categories include *inventory clerks*, *stock control clerks*, *material clerks*, *order fillers*, *merchandise distributors*, and *shipping and receiving clerks*.

At a construction site or factory that uses a variety of raw and finished materials, there are many different types of specialized work for stock clerks. *Tool crib attendants* issue, receive, and store the various hand tools, machine tools, dies, and other equipment used in an industrial establishment. They ensure that the tools come back in reasonably good shape and keep track of those that need replacing. *Parts orderers* and stock clerks purchase, store, and distribute the spare parts needed for motor vehicles and other industrial equipment. *Metal control coordinators* oversee the movement of metal stock and supplies used in producing nonferrous metal sheets, bars, tubing, and alloys. In mining and other industries that regularly use explosives, *magazine keepers* store explosive materials and components safely and distribute them to authorized personnel. In the military, *space and storage clerks*

keep track of the weights and amounts of ammunition and explosive components stored in the magazines of an arsenal and check their storage condition.

Many types of stock clerks can be found in other industries. *Parts clerks* handle and distribute spare and replacement parts in repair and maintenance shops. In eyeglass centers, *prescription clerks* select the lens blanks and frames for making eyeglasses and keep inventory

QUICK FACTS

ALTERNATE TITLE(S)
Inventory Clerks, Material Clerks, Merchandise Distributors, Order Fillers, Parts Clerks, Prescription Clerks, Shipping and Receiving Clerks, Stock Control Clerks

DUTIES
Receive, unpack, store, distribute, and track items for their employer

SALARY RANGE
$17,720 to $23,220 to $38,850+

WORK ENVIRONMENT
Primarily Indoors

BEST GEOGRAPHIC LOCATION(S)
Opportunities available throughout the country

MINIMUM EDUCATION LEVEL
High School Diploma

SCHOOL SUBJECTS
Business, English, Mathematics

EXPERIENCE
One to two years experience; on-the-job training

PERSONALITY TRAITS
Conventional, Hands On, Organized

SKILLS
Interpersonal, Mechanical/Manual Dexterity, Organizational

CERTIFICATION OR LICENSING
None

SPECIAL REQUIREMENTS
None

EMPLOYMENT PROSPECTS
Good

ADVANCEMENT PROSPECTS
Good

OUTLOOK
Little Change or More Slowly than the Average

NOC
1411, 6622

O*NET-SOC
43-5081.00, 43-5081.01, 43-5081.02, 43-5081.03, 43-5081.04

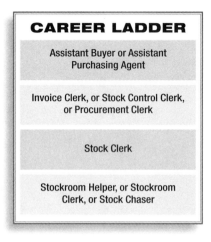

CAREER LADDER

Assistant Buyer or Assistant Purchasing Agent

Invoice Clerk, or Stock Control Clerk, or Procurement Clerk

Stock Clerk

Stockroom Helper, or Stockroom Clerk, or Stock Chaser

stocked at a specified level. In film and television production companies, *property custodians* receive, store, and distribute the props needed for shooting. In hotels and hospitals, *linen room attendants* issue and keep track of inventories of bed linen, tablecloths, and uniforms, while *kitchen clerks* verify the quantity and quality of food products being taken from the storeroom to the kitchen. Aboard ships, the *clerk* in charge of receiving and issuing supplies and keeping track of inventory is known as the *storekeeper*.

■ EARNINGS

Beginning stock clerks usually earn the minimum wage or slightly more. The U.S. Department of Labor reports that stock clerks earned a median hourly wage of $11.17 in May 2015. Based on a 40-hour workweek, this is an annual salary of $23,220. The lowest paid 10 percent earned $17,720 ($8.52 per hour) annually and the highest paid 10 percent earned $38,850 ($18.68 per hour), with time-and-a-half pay for overtime. Average earnings vary depending on the type of industry and geographic location. Stock clerks working in the retail trade generally earn wages in the middle range. In warehousing, motor vehicle manufacturing, transportation, utilities, and wholesale businesses, earnings usually are higher; in finance, insurance, real estate, and other types of office services, earnings generally are lower.

Those working for large companies or national chains may receive excellent benefits. After one year of employment, some stock clerks are offered one to two weeks of paid vacation each year, as well as health and medical insurance and a retirement plan.

■ WORK ENVIRONMENT

Stock clerks usually work in relatively clean, comfortable areas. Working conditions vary considerably, however, depending on the industry and type of merchandise being handled. For example, stock clerks who handle refrigerated goods must spend some time in cold storage rooms, while those who handle construction materials, such as bricks and lumber, occasionally work outside in harsh weather. Most stock clerk jobs involve much standing, bending, walking, stretching, lifting, and carrying.

Some workers may be required to operate machinery to lift and move stock.

Stock clerks are employed in many different types of industries and the amount of hours worked every week depends on the type of employer. Stock clerks in retail stores usually work a five-day, 40-hour week, while those in industry work 44 hours, or five and one-half days, a week. Many others are able to find part-time work. Overtime is common, especially when large shipments arrive or during peak times such as holiday seasons.

■ EXPLORING

The best way to learn about the responsibilities of a stock clerk is to get a part-time or summer job as a *sales clerk*, *stockroom helper*, *stockroom clerk*, or, in some factories, *stock chaser*. These jobs are relatively easy to get and can help you learn about stock work, as well as about the duties of workers in related positions. This sort of part-time work can also lead to a full-time job.

■ EDUCATION AND TRAINING REQUIREMENTS
High School

There are no specific educational requirements for beginning stock clerks but employers prefer to hire high school graduates. Reading and writing skills and a basic knowledge of mathematics are necessary; typing and filing skills are also useful. As more companies install computerized inventory systems, a knowledge of computer science (especially database management) will be important.

Postsecondary Training

Short-term, on-the-job training is the most common method by which stock clerks learn their jobs. Stock clerks are typically trained by senior stock clerks or managers.

■ CERTIFICATION, LICENSING, AND SPECIAL REQUIREMENTS
Certification or Licensing

There are no certification or licensing requirements for stock clerks.

■ EXPERIENCE, SKILLS, AND PERSONALITY TRAITS

No experience is needed to work as a stock clerk, but those with prior work experience will increase their chances of landing a job, getting promoted, and possibly earning higher pay.

Good health and good eyesight are important. A willingness to take orders from supervisors and others is necessary for this work, as is the ability to follow directions. Organizational skills also are important, as is neatness.

Extra training or certification may be required for stock clerks who handle certain types of materials. Generally those who handle jewelry, liquor, or drugs must be bonded.

■ EMPLOYMENT PROSPECTS
Employers

More than 1.9 million people work as stock clerks. About 69 percent of stock clerks work in retail and general merchandise; approximately 11 percent work in wholesale firms; and the remainder work in hospitals, factories, government agencies, schools, and other organizations. Nearly all sales-floor stock clerks are employed in retail establishments, especially supermarkets and department stores.

Starting Out

Job openings for stock clerks often are listed in newspaper and online classified ads. Job seekers should contact the personnel office of the firm looking for stock clerks and fill out an application for employment. School counselors, parents, relatives, and friends also can be good sources for job leads and may be able to give personal references if an employer requires them.

Stock clerks usually receive on-the-job training. New workers start with simple tasks, such as counting and marking stock. The basic responsibilities of the job are usually learned within the first few weeks. As they progress, stock clerks learn to keep records of incoming and outgoing materials, take inventories, and place orders. As wholesale and warehousing establishments convert to automated inventory systems, stock clerks need to be trained to use the new equipment. Stock clerks who bring merchandise to the sales floor and stock shelves and sales racks need little training.

■ ADVANCEMENT PROSPECTS

Stock clerks with ability and determination have a good chance of being promoted to jobs with greater responsibility. In small firms, stock clerks may advance to sales positions or become assistant buyers or purchasing agents. In large firms, stock clerks can advance to more responsible stock handling jobs, such as invoice clerk, stock control clerk, and procurement clerk.

Furthering one's education can lead to more opportunities for advancement. By studying at a technical or business school or taking home-study or online courses, stock clerks can prove to their employer that they have the intelligence and ambition to take on more important

A stock clerk inventories bottles of wine at a shop. (erwinova. Shutterstock.)

tasks. More advanced positions, such as warehouse manager and purchasing agent, are usually given to experienced people who have post-high school education.

■ OUTLOOK

Slow employment growth is anticipated for stock clerks through 2024, according to the U.S. Department of Labor. Increased automation and other productivity improvements that enable clerks to handle more stock will lead to fewer in opportunities in some industries, such as manufacturing and wholesale trade, which are making the greatest use of automation. In addition to computerized inventory control systems, firms in these industries are expected to rely more on sophisticated conveyor belts, automatic high stackers to store and retrieve goods, radio frequency identification tags (which allow clerks to count or find an item or inventory more quickly than in the past), and automatic guided vehicles that are battery-powered and driverless. Sales-floor stock clerks in grocery stores and department stores will probably be less affected by automation than clerks employed in manufacturing, as most of their work is difficult to automate.

This occupation employs a large number of workers and many job openings will occur each year to replace stock clerks who transfer to other jobs and leave the labor force. Stock clerk jobs tend to be entry-level positions, so vacancies will be created by normal career progression to other occupations.

■ UNIONS AND ASSOCIATIONS

Stock clerks may be required to join a union, depending on where they work, such as the United Food & Commercial Workers International Union or the International Brotherhood of Teamsters. This is especially true of stock clerks who are employed by industry and who work in large cities with a high percentage of union-affiliated companies. The National Retail Federation is the world's largest retail trade association. It represents discount and department stores, Main Street merchants, grocers, home goods and specialty stores, wholesalers, and other retailers from the United States and more than 45 countries.

■ TIPS FOR ENTRY

1. Visit the National Retail Federation's Retail Careers Center (https://nrf.com/career-center) for job listings, information on retail education programs, an overview of retail career paths, and career advice.
2. Talk to stock clerks about their careers. Ask them what they like and dislike about their jobs and the best way to break into the field.
3. Join unions to increase your chances of landing a job and receiving fair pay for your work.

■ FOR MORE INFORMATION

The International Brotherhood of Teamsters is a union with a mission to organize and educate workers toward a higher standard of living.

International Brotherhood of Teamsters
25 Louisiana Avenue, NW
Washington, D.C. 20001-2130
https://teamster.org

The National Retail Federation provides information on education and careers in the retail industry.

National Retail Federation (NRF)
1101 New York Avenue, NW, Suite 1200
Washington, D.C. 20005-4348
Tel: (800) 673-4692; (202) 783-7971
Fax: (202) 737-2849
https://nrf.com

United Food and Commercial Workers is a union that organizes and advocates for food and commercial workers.

United Food and Commercial Workers International Union (UFCW)
1775 K Street, NW, BSMT
Washington, D.C. 20006-1598
Tel: (202) 223-3111
http://www.ufcw.org

Strength and Conditioning Coaches

■ OVERVIEW

Strength and conditioning coaches help athletes attain optimum performance through strength training, exercise, and nutritional programs. They work with athletes at all levels, as well as members of the general public who wish to improve their strength, speed, agility, and endurance.

■ HISTORY

Strength and conditioning coaching evolved as a distinct career path in the 1970s when collegiate and professional sports programs began looking for ways to increase the performance and competitiveness of their athletes. Soon after, high schools, as well as individual athletes, also began seeking the services of strength and conditioning coaches to help improve athletic performance. Today, strength and conditioning coaches are key members of athletic programs.

The National Strength and Conditioning Association was formed in 1978 to represent the professional interests of strength and conditioning coaches at all levels. It has more than 45,000 members.

The Collegiate Strength & Conditioning Coaches Association was founded in 2000. While it primarily represents coaches at the collegiate level, it also offers membership to coaches of professional athletic teams.

■ THE JOB

It's no longer enough for an athlete to rely on natural athletic ability. Most athletes turn to strength and conditioning coaches to bring them to the top of their game. Such coaches identify an athlete's weaknesses, and create a conditioning plan to improve strength, form, speed, agility, and endurance.

The conditioning plan will be determined based on the individual athlete, and the sport in question. For example, basketball players may require workouts for stronger leg muscles and core, while golfers may concentrate on more powerful arm and shoulder muscles. The first step is a thorough assessment of the athlete. Equipment such as treadmills, free weights, and weight machines may be used to gauge speed and strength. Oftentimes, the athlete is hooked up to an EKG machine in order to measure his or her heart rate during the workout. Other equipment and technology may also be used to assess the health and overall conditioning level of the athlete.

After the initial assessment, coaches design and implement a sport-specific program while addressing the goals of each athlete. The time of year, whether or not the sport is in season, may also play a part in designing the program. Conditioning sessions may be scheduled more frequently during the off-season when players do not have regular team practices and games. Coaches use their knowledge of anatomy, physiology, and kinesiology to suggest exercises to develop strong leg muscles, powerful arm muscles, a strong core, and cardiovascular endurance. These exercises may include free weights, stationary weight machines, and bands. Coaches supervise all sessions to ensure exercises are performed properly. This may prove demanding, especially if the coach is responsible for managing several athletes at one time. Coaches may prescribe plyometrics, or explosive movement exercises, to develop muscular power, which in turn improves an athlete's speed and agility. In addition to building muscle strength, coaches also make sure athletes are in top form in order to avoid injury. They may monitor an athlete's nutrition regimen, and suggest changes in diet or lifestyle.

A coach who oversees an entire strength and conditioning program is known as the *lead coach* or the *head strength and conditioning coach*. Depending on the size of the athletic program, they may supervise one or more assistant coaches to help with physical fitness and development. This is especially true if the strength and conditioning coaches are responsible for multiple sports disciplines. The lead coach is also responsible for managing the fitness facility, budgeting for new equipment, overseeing the maintenance and repair of existing equipment, and hiring assistants as needed. The lead coach also works closely with head coaches to ensure that specific strength and conditioning goals are met.

■ EARNINGS

Earnings for strength and conditioning coaches vary considerably depending on the sport and the person or team being coached. The U.S. Department of Labor reports that the median earnings for all sports coaches were $31,000 in May 2015. The lowest paid 10 percent earned less than $17,930, while the highest paid 10 percent earned more than $70,050. Sports instructors and coaches who worked at colleges and universities earned a mean annual salary of $55,210, while those employed by elementary and secondary schools earned $34,800. Strength and conditioning coaches at the professional level can earn more than $100,000 a year.

Depending on their employers, most full-time strength and conditioning coaches enjoy a full complement of benefits, including vacation and sick time as well as holidays and medical and dental insurance. Self-employed workers must provide their own benefits.

■ WORK ENVIRONMENT

Strength and conditioning coaches may work indoors, in a gym or health club, or outdoors, perhaps at a swimming pool. Coaches for collegiate and professional sports teams may work 50 to 60 hours a week (including evenings), six to seven days a week when athletes are in competition. Some travel may be involved for games played away from home.

■ EXPLORING

Learn more about strength and conditioning coaching by visiting the Web sites of college and professional sports teams. Read industry publications such as *Strength and Conditioning Journal* and the *Journal of Strength and Conditioning Research;* these journals are published by the National Strength and Conditioning Association (https://www.nsca.com/Publications). Talk to physical education teachers and sports coaches about strength and conditioning training, and ask for them to arrange

---

QUICK FACTS

ALTERNATE TITLE(S)
None

DUTIES
Help people attain optimum performance through strength training, exercise, and nutritional programs

SALARY RANGE
$17,930 to $31,000 to $100,000+

WORK ENVIRONMENT
Indoors/Outdoors

BEST GEOGRAPHIC LOCATION(S)
Opportunities exist in all regions

MINIMUM EDUCATION LEVEL
Bachelor's Degree

SCHOOL SUBJECTS
Biology, Health, Physical Education

EXPERIENCE
Internship, volunteer, or part-time job

PERSONALITY TRAITS
Athletic, Hands On, Helpful

SKILLS
Coaching/Physical Training, Interpersonal, Organizational

CERTIFICATION OR LICENSING
Recommended

SPECIAL REQUIREMENTS
None

EMPLOYMENT PROSPECTS
Good

ADVANCEMENT PROSPECTS
Good

OUTLOOK
About as Fast as the Average

NOC
5252

O*NET-SOC
27-2022.00, 39-9031.00

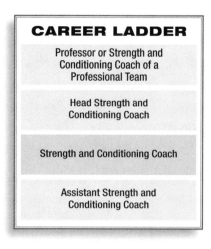

CAREER LADDER

Professor or Strength and Conditioning Coach of a Professional Team

Head Strength and Conditioning Coach

Strength and Conditioning Coach

Assistant Strength and Conditioning Coach

an information interview with a professional in the field. Volunteer to work as a coach for one or more high school sports teams.

■ EDUCATION AND TRAINING REQUIREMENTS
High School

To prepare for this career, take courses in human physiology, exercise science, biology, psychology, and health in high school. Courses in English and speech will help develop communication skills.

Postsecondary Training

Strength and conditioning coaches have a variety of educational backgrounds. Most earn a bachelor's degree in physical education, kinesiology, exercise physiology, or a related area. The National Strength and Conditioning Association recognizes collegiate strength and conditioning or sport performance programs that have met educational guidelines established by the association. Visit https://www.nsca.com/Programs/Education-Recognition-Program/Recognized-ERP-Schools for a list of recognized programs. Some top employers may require strength and conditioning coaches to have a master's degree.

Other Education or Training

Participating in continuing education (CE) classes is a great way to keep skills up to date and learn about new developments in the field; CE credits are also required to renew one's certification. The Collegiate Strength

A strength coach observes an athlete perform a deadlift. (Vince Little. The Bayonet. U.S. Army.)

& Conditioning Coaches Association offers CE clinics and workshops at its annual conference. Past offerings included "Secrets to Success in Strength Training," "Protecting the Health & Safety of the Athlete," and "Empowering, Developing, and Advancing a Successful Career in Athletics." The National Strength and Conditioning Association also provides professional development opportunities.

■ CERTIFICATION, LICENSING, AND SPECIAL REQUIREMENTS
Certification or Licensing

The National Strength and Conditioning Association offers the certified strength and conditioning specialist, certified special populations specialist, and tactical strength and conditioning-facilitators designations to applicants who pass a rigorous examination.

The Collegiate Strength & Conditioning Coaches Association offers two levels of voluntary certification. Coaches who have a bachelor's degree, pass an examination, have certification in cardiopulmonary resuscitation (CPR), and satisfy other requirements are eligible for the strength and conditioning coach certified designation. Those who have worked as full-time, collegiate and/or professional strength and conditioning coaches for a minimum of 12 years, have earned the strength and conditioning coach certified designation, and satisfy other requirements may receive the master strength and conditioning coach designation.

Some employers may require that strength and conditioning coaches be certified in CPR.

■ EXPERIENCE, SKILLS, AND PERSONALITY TRAITS

Several years' experience as an intern, volunteer, or part-time employee with a collegiate or professional sports program, or with a self-employed strength and conditioning coach, is recommended.

Coaches must be experts regarding weight training, conditioning, nutrition, and exercise. They must also be strong communicators in order to effectively educate athletes regarding the benefits of weight training and conditioning, as well as communicate with other coaching professionals regarding the performance and conditioning of athletes. Coaches must be willing to work long hours when their teams compete, and be willing to learn about new strength and conditioning techniques throughout their careers.

■ EMPLOYMENT PROSPECTS
Employers

The majority of employment opportunities exist at the professional and collegiate levels. All professional and collegiate teams, from baseball to soccer to football, have strength and conditioning coaches on staff. Employers at this level expect candidates to have a master's degree in a health science, as well as work experience. Those holding a bachelor's degree and having little work experience may still find employment, but only at an assistant's level.

Coaches working with high school teams may be required to hold an education degree as some schools require their coaching staff to teach classes as well as condition athletes.

A growing number of employment opportunities can be found with private clients. Many intramural teams encourage their players to attend camps to work on speed, agility, and overall fitness. Such companies offer private sessions and group camps to help athletes from many different sport backgrounds improve their overall sports performance. They tailor their programs to meet the specific demands of each sport. Their clientele includes adults as well as children as young as 11 years old.

Starting Out

Participating in an internship program while in college is an excellent way to make contacts and land your first job in the field. Internships may be arranged by your college or offered by professional associations. The National Strength and Conditioning Association and Collegiate Strength & Conditioning Coaches Association both offer internship programs to student members, as well as offer job listings at their Web sites.

■ ADVANCEMENT PROSPECTS

Advancement for strength and conditioning coaches depends on the individual's position, skills, and work ethic. Success for coaches can also be quantified by the success of the individuals they coach (for example, a basketball player who is able to double his or her playing time and scoring because he or she is in better condition), the number of athletes they coach (advancing to coach college athletes in multiple sports), or the type of employer (moving from the collegiate level to employment as a coach for a Major League Baseball team). Some coaches may advance by becoming well known enough to write books or produce how-to videos. Others may become college professors.

■ OUTLOOK

Employment for all fitness trainers and instructors is expected to grow by 8 percent, about as fast as the average for all occupations, through 2024, according to the U.S. Department of Labor. Strength and conditioning coaches will be increasingly relied upon to provide athletes with the extra edge during competition. Despite

BENEFITS OF STRENGTH TRAINING — DID YOU KNOW?

Strength training can help people increase their cardiovascular health by maintaining or increasing lean body mass and producing slight decreases in the relative percentage of body fat. It also increases bone mineral density and may delay or prevent osteoporosis. Strength training may reduce depression and anxiety and encourage overall psychological well-being.

According to the Mayo Clinic, strength training is beneficial for people of all ages, with the key benefits also being that it enhances quality of life, making it easier to do everyday activities and enabling people to live independently longer due to improved fitness. Strength training also sharpens thinking skills and helps improve the management of chronic conditions such as arthritis and heart disease.

Strength training was cited as one of the top 20 fitness trends of 2015, according to a survey of fitness professionals by the American College of Sports Medicine.

Visit the following Web sites for advice from the Centers for Disease Control on recommended daily physical activity (which includes strength training):

- http://www.cdc.gov/physicalactivity/basics/children/index.htm
- http://www.cdc.gov/physicalactivity/basics/adults/index.htm

Sources: Centers for Disease Control and Prevention; Mayo Clinic; National Strength and Conditioning Association

this prediction, there will be strong competition for positions—especially at the collegiate and professional levels. Strength and conditioning coaches who are certified and who have considerable experience will have the best chances for employment.

■ UNIONS AND ASSOCIATIONS

Strength and conditioning coaches do not belong to unions. Many join the National Strength and Conditioning Association, Collegiate Strength & Conditioning Coaches Association, and the Society of Health and Physical Educators.

■ TIPS FOR ENTRY

1. Read *Strength and Conditioning Journal, NSCA Coach,* and the *Journal of Strength and Conditioning Research* (all available at https://www.nsca.com/Publications) to learn more about the field.
2. Join the Collegiate Strength & Conditioning Coaches Association (CSCCa) and National

Strength and Conditioning Association (NSCA) to take advantage of networking resources, publications, and member-only benefits. The NSCA, for example, offers a members-only video career development series.

3. Talk with strength and conditioning coaches about their careers.

4. The CSCCa and NSCA offer mentorship programs for young coaches. They are a great way to develop your professional and personal skills and make valuable industry contacts.

5. Visit the following Web sites for job listings: http://cscca.org/careers and https://www.nsca.com/Membership/Career-Services.

■ FOR MORE INFORMATION

The Collegiate Strength and Conditioning Coaches Association provides information on internships, job opportunities, and certification.

Collegiate Strength and Conditioning Coaches Association (CSCCA)
PO Box 7100
Provo, UT 84602-7100
Tel: (801) 375-9400
E-mail: info@cscca.org
http://www.cscca.org

The National Strength and Conditioning Association provides education, certification, publications, and other resources for elite strength coaches, personal trainers, and researchers and educators.

National Strength and Conditioning Association (NSCA)
1885 Bob Johnson Drive
Colorado Springs, CO 80906-4000
Tel: (800) 815-6826; (719) 632-6722
Fax: (719) 632-6367
E-mail: nsca@nsca.com
https://www.nsca.com

The Society of Health and Physical Educators is committed to empowering children to lead healthy, active lives through effective health and physical education programs.

Society of Health and Physical Educators (SHAPE)
1900 Association Drive
Reston, VA 20191-1598
Tel: (800) 213-7193; (703) 476-3400
Fax: (703) 476-9527
http://www.shapeamerica.org

Stunt Performers

■ OVERVIEW

Stunt performers, also called *stuntmen* and *stuntwomen*, are actors who perform dangerous scenes in motion pictures and on television shows. They may fall off tall buildings, get knocked from horses and motorcycles, imitate fistfights, and drive in high-speed car chases. They must know how to set up stunts that are both safe to perform and believable to audiences. In these dangerous scenes, stunt performers are often asked to double, or take the place of, a star actor.

■ HISTORY

There have been stunt performers since the early years of motion pictures. Frank Hanaway, believed to be the first stunt performer, began his career in the 1903 film *The Great Train Robbery*. A former U.S. cavalryman, Hanaway had developed the skill of falling off a horse unharmed. Until the introduction of sound films in the 1920s, stunt performers were used mostly in slapstick comedy films, which relied on sight gags to entertain the audience.

The first stuntwoman in motion pictures was Helen Gibson, who began her stunt career in the 1914 film series *The Hazards of Helen*. Chosen for the job because of her experience performing tricks on horseback, Gibson went from doubling for Helen Holmes, the star actress, to eventually playing the lead role herself. Among her stunts was jumping from a fast-moving motorcycle onto an adjacent moving locomotive.

Despite the success of Helen Gibson, most stunt performers were men. For dangerous scenes, actresses were usually doubled by a stuntman wearing a wig and the character's costume. Audiences could not tell that the switch had been made because films usually showed stunts at a distance.

Discrimination in the film industry also resulted in few minorities working as stunt performers. White men doubled for American Indians, Asians, Mexicans, and African Americans by applying makeup to their skin.

As the motion picture industry grew, so did the importance of stunt performers. Injury to a star actor could end a film project and incur a considerable financial loss for the studio, which is why producers would allow only stunt performers to handle dangerous scenes. Even so, star actors would commonly brag that they had performed their own stunts. Only a few, such as Helen Gibson and Richard Talmadge (initially a stunt double for Douglas Fairbanks), actually did.

Beginning in the 1950s, the growth in the number of independent, or self-employed, producers brought new opportunities for stunt performers. In general, independent producers were not familiar with stunt work and came to rely on experienced stunt performers to set up stunt scenes and to find qualified individuals to perform them. Stunt performers who did this kind of organizational work came to be called stunt coordinators.

The Stuntmen's Association, the first professional organization in the field, was founded in 1960. Its goal was to share knowledge of stunt techniques and safety practices, to work out special problems concerning stunt performers, and to help producers find qualified stunt performers. Other organizations followed, including the International Stunt Association, the Stuntwomen's Association, the United Stuntwomen's Association, Stunts Unlimited, and Drivers Inc. As a result of these organizations, stunt performers are now better educated and trained in stunt techniques.

An increasing number of women and minorities have become stunt performers since the 1970s. SAG-AFTRA, the union that represents stunt performers, has been at the vanguard of this change. In the 1970s SAG-AFTRA banned the practice of using face paint to have stuntmen play other races, thus forcing producers to find, for example, an African-American stuntman to double for an African-American actor. SAG-AFTRA also began to require that producers make an effort to find female stunt performers to double for actresses. Only after showing that a number of qualified stuntwomen have declined the role can a producer hire a stuntman to do the job.

Over the years, new technology has changed the field of stunt work. Air bags, for example, make stunts safer, and faster cars and better brakes have given stunt performers more control. Stunt performers, however, still rely on their athletic ability and sense of timing when doing a dangerous stunt.

■ THE JOB

Stunt performers work on a wide variety of scenes that have the potential for causing serious injury, including car crashes and chases; fist and sword fights; falls from cars, motorcycles, horses, and buildings; airplane and helicopter gags; rides through river rapids; and confrontations with animals, such as in a buffalo stampede. They are hired as actors, but they rarely perform a speaking role. Some stunt performers specialize in one type of stunt.

There are two general types of stunt roles: double and nondescript. The first requires a stunt performer to "double"—to take the place of—a star actor in a dangerous scene. As a double, the stunt performer must portray the character in the same way as the star actor. A nondescript role does not involve replacing another person and is usually an incidental character in a dangerous scene. An example of a nondescript role is a driver in a freeway chase scene.

The idea for a stunt usually begins with the screenwriter. Stunts can make a movie not only exciting, but also profitable. Action films, in fact, make up the majority of box-office hits. The stunts, however, must make sense within the context of the film's story.

Once the stunts are written into the script, it is the job of the director to decide how they will appear on the screen. Directors, especially of large, action-filled movies, often seek the help of a *stunt coordinator*. Stunt coordinators are individuals who have years of experience performing or coordinating stunts and who know the stunt performer community well. A stunt coordinator can quickly determine if a stunt is feasible and, if so, what is the best and safest way to perform it. The stunt coordinator plans the stunt, oversees the setup and construction of special sets and materials, and either hires or recommends the most qualified stunt performer. Some stunt coordinators also take over the direction of action scenes. Because of this responsibility, many stunt coordinators are members not only of the SAG-AFTRA but also of the Directors Guild of America.

A stunt may last only a few seconds on film but preparations for the stunt can take several hours or even days. Stunt performers work with such departments as props, makeup, wardrobe, and set design. They also work closely with the special effects

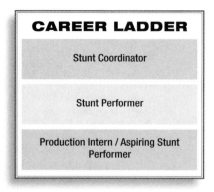

CAREER LADDER

Stunt Coordinator
Stunt Performer
Production Intern / Aspiring Stunt Performer

team to resolve technical problems and ensure safety. The director and the stunt performer must agree on a camera angle that will maximize the effect of the stunt. These preparations can save a considerable amount of production time and money. A carefully planned stunt can often be completed in just one take. More typically, the stunt person will have to perform the stunt several times until the director is satisfied with the performance.

Stunt performers do not have a death wish. They are dedicated professionals who take great precautions to ensure their safety. Air bags, body pads, or cables might be used in a stunt involving a fall or a crash. Stunt performers who must enter a burning building wear special fireproof clothing and protective cream on their the skin. Stunt performers commonly design and build their own protective equipment.

Stunt performers are not only actors but also athletes. Thus, they spend much of their time keeping their bodies in top physical shape and practicing their stunts.

■ EARNINGS

The earnings of stunt performers vary considerably by their experience and the difficulty of the stunts they perform. As of July 2016, the minimum daily salary of

A stunt performer hangs on to the roof of a speeding car during a stunt. (PhotoStock10. Shutterstock.)

stunt performers and stunt coordinators who were SAG-AFTRA members was $933. Stunt performers and coordinators working on a weekly basis in motion pictures or television earned a minimum of $3,479 per week. Stunt coordinators who bargained for "flat deal" rates earned a weekly minimum of $4,231. Calculating an average annual salary for stunt performers is difficult because the work is not necessarily steady. Salaries can range from as low as $15,000 if little work is secured, to $50,000 for a moderately productive year, to more than $150,000 for a year with many bookings.

Stunt performers usually negotiate their salaries with the stunt coordinator. In general, they are paid per stunt; if they have to repeat the stunt three times before the director likes the scene, the stunt performer gets paid three times. If footage of a stunt is used in another film, the performer is paid again. The more elaborate and dangerous the stunt, the more money the stunt performer receives. Stunt performers are also compensated for overtime and travel expenses. Stunt coordinators negotiate their salaries with the producer.

■ WORK ENVIRONMENT

The working conditions of a stunt performer change from project to project. It could be a studio set, a river, or an airplane thousands of feet above the ground. Like all actors, stunt performers are given their own dressing rooms.

Careers in stunt work tend to be short. The small number of jobs is one reason, as are age and injury. Even with the emphasis on safety, injuries commonly occur, often because of mechanical failure, problems with animals, or human error. The possibility of death is always present. Despite these drawbacks, a large number of people are attracted to the work because of the thrill, the competitive challenge, and the chance to work in motion pictures or television.

■ EXPLORING

There are few means of gaining experience as a stunt performer prior to actual employment. Involvement in high school or college athletics is helpful, as is acting experience in a school or local theater. As an intern or extra for a film production, there may be opportunities to see stunt people at work. Theme parks and circuses also make much use of stunt performers; some of these places allow visitors to meet the performers after shows. Finally, read *SAG-AFTRA* magazine (https://www.sagaftra.org/SAG-AFTRA) to learn more about the film and television industries and union membership.

■ EDUCATION AND TRAINING REQUIREMENTS
High School

Take physical education, dance, and other courses that will involve you in exercise, weight lifting, and coordination. Participation in sports teams can help develop the athletic skills needed. English classes are useful for improving communication skills. Theater classes are also recommended for learning to take direction as well as the opportunity to perform for an audience.

Postsecondary Training

There is no minimum educational requirement for becoming a stunt performer. Most learn their skills by working for years under an experienced stunt performer. A number of stunt schools, however, do exist, including the United Stuntmen's Association International Stunt School. You can also benefit from enrolling in theater classes.

Among the skills that must be learned are specific stunt techniques, such as how to throw a punch; the design and building of safety equipment; and production techniques, such as camera angles and film editing. The more a stunt performer knows about all aspects of filmmaking, the better that person can design effective and safe stunts.

Other Education or Training

SAG-AFTRA offers workshops and seminars to members via its locals across the United States. Topics include obtaining health insurance, contract negotiation, and other employment-related issues.

■ CERTIFICATION, LICENSING, AND SPECIAL REQUIREMENTS
Certification or Licensing

There is no certification or licensing available for stunt performers.

■ EXPERIENCE, SKILLS, AND PERSONALITY TRAITS

Stunt work requires excellent athletic ability. Many stunt performers were high school and college athletes, and some were Olympic or world champions. Qualities developed through sports such as self-discipline, coordination, common sense, and coolness under stress are essential to becoming a successful stunt performer. Stunt performers must exercise regularly to stay in shape and maintain good health. An understanding of the mechanics of the stunts is also helpful since they may be working with ropes, cables, and other equipment, you.

FAMOUS DAREDEVILS
MOVERS AND SHAKERS

Stunt performers have been around much longer than the film industry. Throughout the 19th century, circus performers leapt from buildings, hung from their necks, walked tightropes, swallowed swords, and contorted themselves into tiny boxes. Harry Houdini is one of the most famous showmen in entertainment history. Bess Houdini assisted her husband Harry in many famous tricks, including one that ended with her bound and sealed in a trunk. Other "daredevils," as they were known, included Samuel Gilbert Scott, who demonstrated "extraordinary and surpassing powers in the art of leaping and diving" — after swinging about a ship's riggings or jumping from a 240-foot cliff, he'd pass around a hat for contributions. The more dangerous the stunt, the more money he received. His final stunt took place at Waterloo Bridge — while performing pre-dive acrobatics with a rope about his neck, he slipped and strangled to death.

The stunts of women daredevils in the 19th century drew as many spectators as those of the men. Signora Josephine Girardelli was promoted as the "Fire-Proof Lady," a title she earned by holding boiling oil in her mouth and hands, and performing other feats of stamina. May Wirth was a talented equestrian credited as "The Wonder Rider of the World" for her somersaults and other stunts while atop a rushing horse. Even amateurs got into the act — Annie Taylor, a 63-year-old Michigan schoolteacher, became the first person to go over the Niagara Falls in a barrel.

It is helpful to have a common body type because much of the work involves being a stunt double for a star actor. Exceptionally tall or short people, for example, may have difficulty finding roles.

■ EMPLOYMENT PROSPECTS
Employers

Most stunt performers work on a freelance basis, contracting with individual productions on a project-by-project basis. Stunt performers working on TV projects may have long-term commitments if serving as a stand-in for a regular character. Some stunt performers also work in other aspects of the entertainment industry, taking jobs with theme parks, and live stage shows and events.

Starting Out

Most stunt performers enter the field by contacting stunt coordinators and asking for work. Coordinators and stunt associations can be located in trade publications. To be of interest to coordinators, stunt performers promote any special skills they have, such as stunt driving, skiing, and diving. Many stunt performers also have agents who locate work for them, but an agent can be very difficult to get without stunt experience. If you live in New York or Los Angeles, volunteer to work as an intern for an action film; you may have the chance to meet some of the stunt performers, and make connections with crew members and other industry professionals. If you attend a stunt school, you may develop important contacts in the field.

ADVANCEMENT PROSPECTS

New stunt performers generally start with simple roles, such as being one of 40 people in a brawl scene. With greater experience and training, stunt performers can get more complicated roles. Some stunt associations have facilities where stunt performers work out and practice their skills. Stunt performers with a great deal of experience may be invited to join a professional association such as the Stuntmen's Association of Motion Pictures, which gives them opportunities to network with others in the industry.

About five to 10 years of experience are usually necessary to become a stunt coordinator. Some stunt coordinators eventually work as a director of action scenes.

OUTLOOK

More than 7,700 stunt performers belong to SAG-AFTRA, but only a fraction of those can afford to devote themselves to film or television work full time. Stunt coordinators will continue to hire only very experienced professionals, making it difficult to break into the business.

The future of the profession may be affected by computer technology. In more cases, filmmakers may choose to use special effects and computer-generated imagery for action sequences. Not only can computer effects allow for more ambitious images, but they're also safer. Safety on film and television sets has always been a serious concern; despite innovations in filming techniques, stunts remain extremely dangerous. However, using live stunt performers can give a scene more authenticity, so talented stunt performers will always be in demand.

UNIONS AND ASSOCIATIONS

Stunt performers working for film and TV production companies or studios who are guild signatories must belong to the Screen Actors Guild. As a member of a union, stunt performers receive special benefits, such as better pay and compensation for overtime and holidays. Stunt performers also join professional associations such as the Stuntmen's Association of Motion Pictures, Stuntwomen's Association of Motion Pictures, International Stunt Association, and the United Stuntwomen's Association. The United Stuntmen's Association provides stunt training.

TIPS FOR ENTRY

1. Try to get as much acting experience as possible—whether in school or community productions or as a film or television extra.
2. Work hard to improve your physical endurance, strength, flexibility, and overall health. Since work as a stunt performer is very demanding, you will need to be in top shape to land jobs.
3. Apply for a job as a production assistant. Once on the job, network with casting directors, producers, directors, stunt coordinators, and others to let them know you are interested in working as a stunt performer.
4. Attend stunt school and try to obtain job leads with the assistance of instructors and fellow students.
5. Look for jobs and/or market your services at Mandy.com. Other useful sites includes Infolist.com and EntertainmentCareers.net.

FOR MORE INFORMATION

The International Stunt Association provides information on stunt work in film and television industries.

International Stunt Association (ISA)
Tel: (818) 501-5225
Fax: (818) 501-5656
http://www.isastunts.com

SAG-AFTRA, which is the Screen Actors Guild and American Federation of Television and Radio Artists, is the labor union that represents media artists of various specialties.

SAG-AFTRA
5757 Wilshire Boulevard, 7th Floor
Los Angeles, CA 90036-3600
Tel: (855) 724-2387; (323) 954-1600
E-mail: sagaftrainfo@sagaftra.org
http://www.sagaftra.org

The Stuntmen's Association of Motion Pictures is a by invite-only membership association of highly trained stunt coordinators, stuntmen, and second-unit directors.

Stuntmen's Association of Motion
    Pictures (SAMP)
5200 Lankersheim Boulevard, Suite 190
North Hollywood, CA 91601-3100
Tel: (818) 766-4334
Fax: (818) 766-5943
E-mail: hq@stuntmen.com
http://www.stuntmen.com

The Stuntwomen's Association of Motion Pictures is a membership association for professional stuntwomen.
    Stuntwomen's Association of Motion Pictures
        (SWAMP)
3760 Cahuenga Boulevard, Suite 104
Studio City, CA 91604-3579
Tel: (818) 762-0907
E-mail: info@stuntwomen.com
http://www.stuntwomen.com

The United Stuntmen's Association provides information on the International Stunt School.
    United Stuntmen's Association (USA)
PO Box 80084
Seattle, WA 98108-0084
Tel: (206) 349-8339
E-mail: iboushey@gmail.com
http://www.stuntschool.com

The United Stuntwomen's Association is an association of working, professional stuntwomen, stunt coordinators, and second-unit directors.
    United Stuntwomen's Association (USA)
26893 Bouquet Cyn Road, Suite C, Box#218
Saugus, CA 91350-3500
Tel: (818) 508-4651
E-mail: usastunts@usastunts.com
http://www.usastunts.com

Supermarket Workers

■ OVERVIEW

Supermarket workers are a diverse group. Each supermarket worker is employed in one or more areas of a grocery store, from the checkout lane to the deli counter to the back stock room. Nearly 2.7 million people work as wage and salary employees of grocery stores, according to the U.S. Bureau of Labor Statistics. Supermarkets are located in cities and towns across the nation and include large chains and locally owned stores.

■ HISTORY

Grocery stores have existed in the United States since the 1800s. Those early stores did not carry a wide variety of merchandise and brands. Many specialized in one area such as bread, fish, or meat. Even these early stores needed workers to help run their businesses. At the time, the workers were less specialized; often, the same person who helped wrap the meat at a butcher shop might be found later in the day sweeping out the store.

In the early 1900s, small "mom and pop" stores opened. These stores were the beginning of the modern grocery industry. Soon, some of the stores expanded into chains, and the role of the supermarket worker became even more important. With bigger stores, more merchandise, and more customers, the stores needed more staff.

Technology (such as bar codes, digital ordering systems, etc.) has improved efficiency and customer service at supermarkets, but people are still needed to do most of the jobs in a grocery store. One exception is the job of cashier. Self-serve, automated checkout systems have allowed some stores to reduce the number of cashiers they employ. The growing popularity of online grocery shopping also threatens to reduce employment in the industry, but even online ordering involves order takers, delivery personnel, stock room personnel, inventory control workers, and more.

■ THE JOB

There are so many different types of work to do in a grocery store that each job can be very different from the next. One of the first positions most people think of in a grocery store is the cashier. *Cashiers* are a store's front line for customer service, since they interact with customers all day and ensure order accuracy. Cashiers greet customers, scan merchandise, record coupons, present totals, take payments, and help bag groceries. It is each cashier's responsibility to keep his or her work area clean and to ensure that the cash drawer balances at the end of his or her shift. If merchandise is marked incorrectly or damaged, the cashier calls the appropriate department to assist the customer.

Along with the cashiers, *clerks* help to bag the groceries, and, if necessary, they help the customers transport the grocery bags to their vehicles. *Courtesy clerks*, sometimes called *bag boys* or *baggers*, also collect carts from the parking lots and help provide maintenance for those carts.

QUICK FACTS

ALTERNATE TITLE(S)
Bag Boys, Baggers, Bakers, Butchers, Cashiers, Courtesy Clerks, Deli Workers, Stock Clerks

DUTIES
Perform a variety of duties at grocery stores such as take payment from customers (cashiers) and stock goods on shelves (stock clerks)

SALARY RANGE
$15,080 to $26,950 to $50,000+

WORK ENVIRONMENT
Primarily Indoors

BEST GEOGRAPHIC LOCATION(S)
Opportunities exist throughout the country

MINIMUM EDUCATION LEVEL
High School Diploma

SCHOOL SUBJECTS
Business, English, Mathematics

EXPERIENCE
On-the-job training

PERSONALITY TRAITS
Conventional, Organized, Outgoing

SKILLS
Interpersonal, Organizational, Sales

CERTIFICATION OR LICENSING
Required

SPECIAL REQUIREMENTS
None

EMPLOYMENT PROSPECTS
Good

ADVANCEMENT PROSPECTS
Good

OUTLOOK
About as Fast as the Average

NOC
6211, 6611, 6622, 6331, 9617

O*NET-SOC
41-1011.00, 41-2011.00, 43-5081.00

Stock personnel, or *stock clerks,* play an important behind-the-scenes role in supermarkets. They help unload trucks, inspect merchandise, stock shelves, and track inventory. Late at night, these workers prepare for the next day's customers.

Specialization is an important trend in the grocery industry. Since the industry is very competitive, stores are adding more services and conveniences to attract and keep customers. Some of the specialized departments have historically been part of grocery stores, such as bakeries and meat markets, while others, such as restaurants and baby-sitting services, are new.

Each area requires workers with specialized knowledge and training as well as experience in the grocery industry. *Butchers*, *bakers*, and *deli workers* are generally dedicated to their individual departments in the store, while other workers may "float" to the areas where they are needed.

Other supermarket workers are responsible for certain areas such as produce or dairy. While there is no preparation work involved such as there is in the bakery or deli departments, these workers regularly inspect merchandise, check expiration dates, and maintain displays.

Many supermarkets now include restaurants or food courts that require *food preparers, servers, wait staff,* and *chefs.*

Many larger chain supermarkets have a pharmacy on-site. *Pharmacists* fill prescriptions for customers and offer counseling on both prescription and over-the-counter medications. *Pharmacy technicians* assist the pharmacist by filling prescriptions, taking inventory, and handling the cash register.

There are also specialized support positions in supermarkets. *Store detectives* assist with security measures and loss prevention. *Human resource workers* handle personnel-related issues, such as recruiting and training, benefits administration, labor relations, and salary administration. These are important members of the supermarket team, since the average large grocery store employs 250 people. Supermarkets also require qualified *accounting and finance workers, advertising workers, marketing workers, information technology professionals,* and *community and public relations professionals.*

Supermarket workers report to either a *department* or *store manager.* Supermarket managers have to attend weekly departmental meetings and must communicate well with their management, which is usually at the district level. Because many supermarket workers deal directly with the customers, their managers depend on them to relay information about customer needs, wants, and dissatisfactions.

Many supermarket workers work part time. For workers with school, family, or other employment, hours are scheduled at the time they are available, such as evenings and weekends. Employees may work during the day or evening hours since many grocery stores are open 24 hours a day. Weekend hours are also important, and most grocery stores are open on holidays as well.

All supermarket jobs are customer-driven. Grocery sales nationwide continue to climb, and customer service is highly important in the grocery business as in all retail businesses. The primary responsibility of all supermarket workers is to serve the customer. Secondary duties, such as keeping work areas clean, collecting carts from the parking lot, and checking produce for freshness, are also driven by this main priority.

■ EARNINGS

According to the U.S. Department of Labor, the average grocery store employee earned a mean hourly wage of $12.96 (or $26,950 annually) in May 2015. The following are mean hourly rates and salaries for supermarket workers by specialty in May 2015: first-line supervisors of retail sales workers, $19.94 ($41,470 annually); butchers and meat cutters, $14.79 ($30,760 annually); stock clerks and order fillers, $11.64 ($24,200 annually); and cashiers, $10.45 ($21,730 annually). Some employees may make less per hour, down to the current minimum wage of $7.25 per hour (approximately $15,080 annually), while specialized workers in some departments may earn more. Department managers can earn $50,000 or more annually.

Many supermarket workers are part-time employees and do not receive fringe benefits; full-time employees often receive medical benefits and vacation time. Supermarket workers often are eligible for discounts at the stores in which they work, depending on their company policy. The United Food & Commercial Workers International Union represents many supermarket workers concerning pay, benefits, and working condition issues.

■ WORK ENVIRONMENT

Grocery stores are often open 24 hours a day, so workers are required for a variety of shifts. Many supermarket workers are part-time employees and work a varied schedule that changes each week. Depending on the time of day they work, the store may be bustling or quiet. Most of the work is indoors, although some outdoor work may be required to deliver groceries, collect carts, and maintain outside displays. Schedules are usually prepared weekly, and most will include weekend work.

Supermarket workers work in shifts and must work with the managers and other workers in a supervisory environment. These managers may be within their department or within the entire store. They must follow directions and report to those managers when required.

■ EXPLORING

The best way to find out about what it's like to be a supermarket worker is to become one. Openings for high school students are usually available, and it's a great way to find out about the industry.

Take a class relating to a supermarket specialty. For example, if interested in the bakery, take a cake-decorating class to find out if this work is a good fit.

Help out with inventory. Many grocery and retail stores offer limited short-term employment (a day or two a week) for people who can help with inventory during key times of the year. This is a good opportunity to learn more about the work without making a greater commitment.

Talk to your friends or even your parents. Chances are that at some time, they have worked in a grocery store. Find out what they liked and didn't like about the work. Another source for information is your local grocery store. Talk with the people there about their jobs.

■ EDUCATION AND TRAINING REQUIREMENTS
High School

Many workers in the supermarket industry are recent high school graduates or are currently in high school. There is a large turnover in the field, as many workers

CAREER LADDER
Store Manager
Department Manager
Entry-Level Position Such as Cashier or Stock Clerk

A supermarket cashier rings up a customer's transaction.
(bikeriderlondon. Shutterstock.)

The Universal Product Code

Few innovations have helped the grocery store as much as the bar code, or Universal Product Code. This coded group of bars, dashes, and numbers is on nearly every product and enables groceries to better track inventory, ring up sales, and deduct coupons. Check out how supermarkets changed from the ring of the cash register to the beep of the scanner:

1948—Bernard Silver and Joseph Woodland develop the first linear bar code, using movie soundtracks and Morse code as inspiration. They filed for a patent in 1949.

1952—The patent was granted. Woodland's employer, IBM, refused to buy the patent at his price.

1962—Philco bought the patent and sold it to RCA in 1971.

1960s—While the original bar code machines used 500-watt light bulbs, lasers were developed that made the idea more feasible.

1972—RCA began an 18-month test in a Kroger store in Cincinnati.

1973—The UPC (Universal Product Code) was adopted and provided for uniform codes.

Today—UPC codes are found on a variety of products and packaging from groceries to clothing, shipping packages to airline tickets.

move on to other careers. Take English, mathematics, business, and computer science classes to learn the basic skills for most supermarket jobs.

Postsecondary Training

Postsecondary training is not required in the supermarket industry but may be encouraged for specific areas, such as the bakery, or for management positions. Stores offer on-the-job training and value employees who are able to learn quickly while they work.

Other Education or Training

The National Retail Federation offers classes and other continuing education opportunities. Topics include customer service, management issues, purchasing, sales training, store operations, merchandising, and marketing.

■ CERTIFICATION, LICENSING, AND SPECIAL REQUIREMENTS
Certification or Licensing

The National Retail Federation Foundation offers certification programs in customer service and sales, advanced

customer service and sales, and retail management to retail workers who successfully pass an assessment and meet other requirements.

To protect the public's health, bakers, deli workers, and butchers are required by law in most states to possess a health certificate and undergo periodic physical exams. These examinations, usually given by the state board of health, make certain that the individual is free from communicable diseases and skin infections.

■ EXPERIENCE, SKILLS, AND PERSONALITY TRAITS

No experience is needed to work in entry-level positions such as stock clerk. Managers and department heads must have at least three years of experience in lower-level supervisory positions.

The most important requirement for a supermarket worker is the ability to work with people. Workers are required to work with both the public, fellow workers, and their own management, so having communication and customer service skills are important. The ability to follow directions as well as being accurate and honest are qualities that all supermarket workers should possess.

■ EMPLOYMENT PROSPECTS
Employers

Nearly 2.7 million people work as wage and salary employees of grocery stores, according to the U.S. Bureau of Labor Statistics. In 2015, there were over 38,015 supermarkets in the United States with more than $2 million in annual sales, according to *Progressive Grocer* magazine. They are located across the nation, in towns and cities. Some are part of a large chain such as Kroger, Wal-Mart Superstores, and Safeway. Other stores are part of smaller chains or are independently owned.

Workers will have more employment opportunities in cities and large towns where several stores are located. In smaller towns, only one or two stores may serve the area.

Starting Out

Groceries use walk-in applications, job drives, and newspaper ads to attract new employees. Some supermarket jobs require little education and pay a modest hourly rate, so there are often openings as workers move on to other positions or career fields. Dress neatly and have good manner when applying for supermarket jobs in person. Be prepared to fill out application materials at the office. Many of today's grocery managers started out as high school clerks or cashiers. It is possible to turn a part-time job into a full-time career.

ADVANCEMENT PROSPECTS

There are opportunities to advance to more specialized and better-paying positions for those who are dedicated and hard working. Supermarkets rely heavily on experienced workers, so while a college education might be helpful, it is certainly not required to advance in the field. Relevant experience and hard work are just as beneficial to advancement.

OUTLOOK

Employment for supermarket workers is good. The field has a large turnover with workers leaving to pursue other careers. Many part-time employees are seasonal and must be replaced often.

As supermarkets add more conveniences for customers, workers will be needed to staff those areas. For example, adding restaurants to a supermarket creates a need for a whole new set of food service workers.

During the past 10 years, the number of grocery stores and supermarkets has declined. Many small chains and local groceries have been purchased by larger chains, and others have gone out of business in the face of competition. Grocery store and supermarket workers will continue to be needed, however, in many areas of the business.

UNIONS AND ASSOCIATIONS

The United Food & Commercial Workers International Union represents many supermarket workers concerning pay, benefits, and working condition issues. The Food Marketing Institute, Retail Industry Leaders Association, and the National Retail Federation are membership organizations for food and beverage trailers, suppliers, and related organizations.

TIPS FOR ENTRY

1. Visit the National Retail Federation's Retail Careers Center (https://nrf.com/career-center) for job listings, information on retail education programs, an overview of retail career paths, and career advice.
2. Participate in retail-oriented internships or part-time jobs that are arranged by your high school or college's career services office.
3. Become certified by the National Retail Federation in order to show employers that you have met the highest standards set by your industry.

FOR MORE INFORMATION

The Food Marketing Institute represents food retailers and wholesalers, providing advocacy and leadership for the food and consumer product industry worldwide.

Food Marketing Institute (FMI)
2345 Crystal Drive, Suite 800
Arlington, VA 22202-4813
Tel: (202) 452-8444
Fax: (202) 429-4519
http://www.fmi.org

The National Retail Federation is a trade association that represents retailers from the United States as well as other countries.

National Retail Federation (NRF)
1101 New York Avenue, NW
Washington, D.C. 20005-4348
Tel: (800) 673-4692; (202) 783-7971
Fax: (202) 737-2849
https://nrf.com

The Retail Industry Leaders Association provides advocacy, education, and networking opportunities for retailers.

Retail Industry Leaders
     Association (RILA)
1700 North Moore Street, Suite 2250
Arlington, VA 22209-1933
Tel: (703) 841-2300
Fax: (703) 841-1184
https://www.rila.org

The United Food and Commercial Workers International Union provides information about union membership in the food industry.

United Food and Commercial Workers
     International Union (UFCW)
1776 K Street, NW, BSMT
Washington, D.C. 20006-1598
Tel: (202) 223-3111
http://www.ufcw.org

Supply Chain Managers

OVERVIEW

Supply chain managers coordinate and manage the production, transportation, and delivery of goods and products. They oversee inventory control, purchasing, and product development. They analyze the production process and make recommendations to improve the efficiency of the workflow and quality of the products while cutting costs. They make sure there are sufficient materials and supplies on hand for production and that there is sufficient inventory to meet customers' demands.

Supply chain managers may have titles such as industrial production managers, distribution managers, or logisticians, depending on the company. The Department of Labor reports that there were 169,390 industrial production managers, 109,210 transportation, storage, and distribution managers, and 133,770 logisticians employed in the United States in May 2015.

■ HISTORY

The Industrial Revolution brought about machinery that could mass produce products and goods, laying the groundwork for the supply chain field. Manufacturing processes became more efficient as machinery was introduced that required fewer workers. For instance, the cotton gin sped up the removal of seeds from cotton and the spinning jenny sped up the production of yarn. Developments in transportation, such as steamships, railroads, and airplanes, also helped to expand the manufacturing industry, making it possible for materials, supplies, and products to be procured and transported to more regions of the United States and around the world.

One area of supply chain managers' work is logistics. The term that emerged from military operations in the 1900s. The military used logistics to transport the correct number of men, machinery, and supplies to the correct place and at the correct time during campaigns. By the 1950s, logistics had entered the business world, with companies applying the analysis and coordination tactics to business operations to improve production and material handling.

In the 1960s, freight that had to be delivered within certain time frames was transported by trucks rather than railways. This gave rise to what became known as "physical distribution" and cemented the need for professionals who could coordinate and manage the production process, material handling, freight transportation, and warehousing. The National Council of Physical Distribution Management was established at this time to help create standards and guidelines for this new area of business. Starting in the 1970s, distribution, transportation, and supply managers used computers for transactions, truck routing and scheduling, supply and product inventory, record keeping, and other aspects of management and coordination. The growth of personal computers in the 1980s gave business managers even more

computer-based tools to help them in their work, including software for spreadsheets and map-based interfaces for supply chain management and logistics.

The National Council of Physical Distribution Management changed its name to the Council of Logistics Management in the 1980s to reflect the business focus at that time. Companies included training programs for logistics and operations planning in their budgets, and software was introduced for logistics planning, such as Material Requirements Planning (MRP), Enterprise Resource Planning (ERP), and Advanced Planning and Scheduling (APS) systems.

The manufacturing industry grew further in the 1990s and early 2000s, with especially dramatic growth in U.S. imports from China (from $45 billion in 1995 to more than $280 billion in 2006). This growth increased the need for professional supply chain managers to coordinate and manage complex business processes, particularly those that conduct business in different countries.

Supply chain management gained ground as a distinct business discipline. To reflect this new focus, the Council of Logistics Management became the Council of Supply Chain Management Professionals in 2005. The distinction between logistics and supply chain management, as the Council describes it, is: "Logistics is that part of the supply chain process that plans, implements, and controls the efficient, effective forward and reverse flow and storage of goods, services, and related information between the point of origin and the point of consumption in order to meet customers' requirements. ... Supply Chain Management is the systemic, strategic coordination of the traditional business functions and the tactics across these business functions within a particular company and across businesses within the supply chain for the purposes of improving the long-term performance of the individual companies and the supply chain as a whole."

■ THE JOB

Supply chain managers coordinate and manage companies' supply chains, making sure that the production and distribution process flows smoothly, from the point of product acquisition through to delivery to consumers. Their work involves logistics, transportation, production, shipping, distribution, and warehousing. They analyze the production and distribution process and make recommendations for ways to streamline workflows and cut costs while still delivering quality products. They work closely with managers in other departments, such as procurement, production, sales, warehousing, marketing, and research and design. They use computers and supply chain management software to manage supply chain relationships and execute transactions.

A reliable supply chain is essential to success for many businesses. Raw materials must be available in the correct quantities when production is ready to begin or workers and equipment may stand idle. Once finished products roll out of a factory or other production facility, it's essential that transportation be ready to move them to warehouses and distribution facilities in order to convey goods to the consumer. Any disruption or delay can increase costs for the company, lead to losses, or even diminish consumer demand. Supply chain managers assess all aspects of these steps and work with individuals within their company and at other companies to ensure success.

■ EARNINGS

The average annual salary for supply chain managers in August 2016 was $103,739, according to Salary.com. Salaries ranged from $90,190 to $122,346 or more. Industrial production managers earned slightly lower salaries on average, but a small percentage earned far more than supply chain managers. The Department of Labor reported that in May 2015, the average annual salary for these workers was $93,940, with the lowest 10 percent earning $56,640 and the highest 10 percent earning $162,240 or more. Transportation, storage, and distribution managers had an average annual salary of $86,630; salaries ranged from $50,840 to $149,770 or more. Logisticians earned an average annual salary of $74,260, with salaries ranging from $45,830 to $115,960 or more.

■ WORK ENVIRONMENT

Supply chain managers work in offices in corporations and manufacturing companies. They spend part of their work day on the computer, using spreadsheets and tracking schedules and inventory sheets. They also spend a percentage of their day e-mailing and speaking with suppliers, warehouse managers, and other department managers. Their work schedule is generally business hours during weekdays, but there may be times when they need to work evenings, weekends, and sometimes holidays to make sure production process deadlines are met.

■ EXPLORING

There are many different ways to learn more about supply chain management. Start by visiting the Web sites of professional associations such as the Council of Supply Chain Management Professionals and APICS. Read the

QUICK FACTS

ALTERNATE TITLE(S)
Distribution Managers, Industrial Production Managers, Logisticians

DUTIES
Coordinate and manage companies' supply chains; oversee logistics, production, transportation, shipping, distribution, and warehousing of products; analyze production process and make recommendations for improvements

SALARY RANGE
$50,840 to $93,940 to $122,346+

WORK ENVIRONMENT
Primarily Indoors

BEST GEOGRAPHIC LOCATION(S)
Opportunities exist in all regions; the states with the highest employment of transportation, storage, and distribution managers are California, Texas, Illinois, Ohio, and New Jersey

MINIMUM EDUCATION LEVEL
Bachelor's Degree

SCHOOL SUBJECTS
Business, Economics, Mathematics

EXPERIENCE
At least five years experience

PERSONALITY TRAITS
Hands On, Organized, Problem-Solving

SKILLS
Business Management, Interpersonal, Organizational

CERTIFICATION OR LICENSING
Recommended

SPECIAL REQUIREMENTS
None

EMPLOYMENT PROSPECTS
Good

ADVANCEMENT PROSPECTS
Good

OUTLOOK
About as Fast as the Average

NOC
1215

O*NET-SOC
11-9199.04, 13-1081.00

research and news sections to learn more about trends and issues in the supply chain management industry. Explore the careers section to see what kind of jobs are available. Get a foot in the door by working as an intern or in a part-time position in a department where

CAREER LADDER

Supply Chain Department Head

Supply Chain Manager

Assistant Supply Chain Manager

Intern

supply chain managers or related professionals work. This will give you the chance to be immersed in the production process and observe firsthand the day-to-day responsibilities of a supply chain manager.

■ EDUCATION AND TRAINING REQUIREMENTS
High School

Supply chain managers need good business management skills and the ability to communicate clearly with a variety of people. Classes in math, business, English, and computers are helpful in this type of work.

Postsecondary Education

Many companies prefer to hire supply chain managers with a bachelor's degree in supply chain management, business, or systems engineering. Courses in operations and database management, as well as logistics, accounting, English, and computers are essential. Classes in marketing and product development may also be useful.

■ CERTIFICATION, LICENSING, AND SPECIAL REQUIREMENTS

Some companies prefer to hire supply chain managers who have certification in certain specialties. Supply chain managers who meet certification program requirements and pass an exam can improve their chances of securing work. APICS is among the organizations that provides certification programs, with designations that include Certified in Production and Inventory Management (CPIM), Certified Supply Chain Professional (CSCP); Certified in Logistics, Transportation, and Distribution (CLTD); and Supply Chain Operations Reference Professional (SCOR-P).

■ EXPERIENCE, SKILLS, AND PERSONALITY TRAITS

Supply chain managers must be excellent communicators, multitaskers, and managers. The job requires the ability to analyze operations and determine ways to improve production processes while cutting costs and not affecting product quality. Companies often seek supply chain managers with experience in manufacturing settings and success in creating lean manufacturing processes. The job requires strong leadership, problem-solving, critical-thinking, time-management,

organizational, and interpersonal skills. Knowledge of logistics and supply chain management software is essential.

■ EMPLOYMENT PROSPECTS
Employers

Supply chain managers work in manufacturing, federal government; professional, scientific, and technical consulting services; management of companies and enterprises; and wholesale trade. Some examples of companies that use supply chain management professionals are Amazon, DHL, Dell Computers, and Wal-Mart, to name only a few. The Department of Labor does not provide data specifically for supply chain managers. Jobs that overlap supply chain managers include logisticians (133,770 employed), industrial production managers (169,390 employed), and transportation, storage, and distribution managers (109,210 employed.) Memberships to professional associations can also give some idea of the scope of the field. For example, the Council of Supply Chain Management Professionals has more than 8,500 members and APICS, another association for supply chain professionals, has more than 45,000 members.

Starting Out

Supply chain managers start their careers in various ways. Their first job may be as an intern or in an entry-level position in a supply management department of a company. They may also gain entry to supply management through work in the industrial production department or other related departments.

■ ADVANCEMENT PROSPECTS

Supply chain managers may start as coordinators or analysts and work their way up through the ranks. Managers with at least five or more years of experience and certification may advance to become department heads. Those with a master's degree in supply chain management, business, or other related major may be department heads, managing larger groups. Some supply chain managers may leave full-time positions to start their own consulting companies.

■ OUTLOOK

Supply chain managers will continue to be needed to manage and improve production processes. Competition for work will be keen so those with a bachelor's degree in supply chain management and certification will have the best job prospects. The manufacturing, transportation, and warehousing industries are expected to have slow growth through 2024, according to the Department of Labor. Companies will be looking for ways to create leaner manufacturing processes and supply chain managers with experience in this area will be in demand. Job growth for supply chain managers may be tempered, however, by the increasing popularity of retaining third-party agents to provide supply assessments and product and market research.

The wholesale trade sector will offer opportunities for supply chain managers in the coming years. This sector is part of the supply chain of manufacturing, retail trade, and other sectors. The management, scientific, and technical consulting services industry is expected to have some employment growth (2.4 percent) through 2024, and will need supply chain managers for help with lowering costs and improving business operations.

Industrial production managers are projected to have a decline in employment the next few years, but some recent "reshoring" activities by manufacturers may create more job opportunities. Reshoring is when companies and workers that had been located overseas are relocated to the United States. "Domestic sourcing," in which manufacturing plants and businesses are built in lower cost areas of the United States, has also been growing recently, which may offer more jobs for industrial production managers.

■ UNIONS AND ASSOCIATIONS

Supply chain managers belong to professional associations such as APICS, the Council of Supply Chain Management Professionals, and the Institute for Supply Management. They each offer educational programs, certification, events, publications, and other resources in support of supply chain management professionals. Other associations that provide useful information and resources for supply chain management professionals include the Material Handling Industry of America and the Warehousing Education and Research Council.

■ TIPS FOR ENTRY

1. Get an internship or entry-level job in a manufacturing company or a corporation with a supply chain management department.
2. Learn more about supply chain management by visiting the Web sites of professional association such as APICS and Council of Supply Chain Management Professionals.
3. Attend or volunteer at a networking event hosted by a professional association; check the Web sites for a list of upcoming events that may interest you.
4. Read *Supply Chain Quarterly* (http://www.supplychainquarterly.com) for industry news, insights, and analysis, and to learn more about various supply chain organizations.

BEST PRACTICES FOR SUPPLY CHAIN MANAGEMENT — DID YOU KNOW?

Many supply chain organizations adopt best practices to establish a strong foundation for supply chain management. An article in *Supply Chain Quarterly*, a publication by the Council for Supply Chain Management Professionals, discusses some top recommended best practices in the industry.

The first recommended practice is to establish a supply chain council that is tasked with governing and aligning the company's strategy for supply chain management. Next is to properly align and staff the supply chain organization, the structure of which will vary depending on the organization. For instance, a growing trend is that companies are placing procurement, logistics, contract management, forecast/demand planning, and other management functions under the supply chain leader. The third best practice is to choose technology, software, and workflow processes that best fit the company.

Other best practices include establishing alliances with key suppliers, engaging in collaborative strategic sourcing, and focusing on total ownership, not price. It's also recommended that supply chain managers optimize the inventory that the company owns, establish levels of control that are appropriate, minimize risk, and pay attention to social responsibility and "green" initiatives. Today, buyers and consumers pay close attention to suppliers' effect on the environment. Consumers and workers are also well aware of corporate social responsibility policies, so it's important to have these policies in place in supply chain organizations.

Source: Council for Supply Chain Management Professionals' *Supply Chain Quarterly*

■ FOR MORE INFORMATION

APICS provides education, research, and certification programs for supply chain management professionals.

APICS
8430 West Bryn Mawr Avenue, Suite 1000
Chicago, IL 60631-3417
Tel: (800) 444-2742; (773) 867-1777
Fax: (773) 639-3000
E-mail: service@apics.org
http://www.apics.org

The Council of Supply Chain Management Professionals is an international association dedicated to the advancement and dissemination of research and knowledge on supply chain management.

Council of Supply Chain Management
  Professionals (CSCMP)
333 East Butterfield Road, Suite 140
Lombard, IL 60148
Tel: (630) 574-0985
Fax: (630) 574-0989
E-mail: membership@cscmp.org
https://cscmp.org

The Institute for Supply Management offers educational and certification programs, study and training guides, and other resources for supply chain management professionals.

Institute for Supply Management (ISM)
2055 East Centennial Circle
Tempe, AZ 85284-1802
Tel: (800) 888-6276; (480) 752-6276
Fax: (480) 752-7890
https://www.instituteforsupplymanagement.org

The Material Handling Industry of America offers education and career-support resources for supply chain professionals.

Material Handling Industry of America (MHIA)
8720 Red Oak Boulevard, Suite 201
Charlotte, NC 28217-3996
Tel: (704) 676-1190
Fax: (704) 676-1199
http://www.mhi.org

The Warehousing Education and Research Council focuses exclusively on distribution and warehouse management and its role in the supply chain.

**Warehousing Education and Research
  Council (WERC)**
1100 Jorie Boulevard, Suite 170
Oak Brooks, IL 60523-4413
Tel: (630) 990-0001
Fax: (630) 990-0256
E-mail: wercoffice@werc.org
http://www.werc.org

HIGHEST PAYING JOBS

Surgeons

■ OVERVIEW

Surgeons are physicians who make diagnoses and provide preoperative, operative, and postoperative care in surgery affecting almost any part of the body. These doctors also work with trauma victims and the critically ill. Approximately 41,600 surgeons are employed in the United States.

■ HISTORY

Surgery is perhaps the oldest of all medical specialties. Evidence from ancient Egypt, Greece, China, and India suggests that humans have always performed and worked on developing surgical procedures.

The field of surgery advanced during the 18th century when knowledge of anatomy increased through developments in pathology. At this time, common procedures included amputations as well as tumor and bladder stone removal. Surgery patients were usually tied down or sedated with alcoholic beverages or opium during the procedures.

The late 19th century brought major developments that advanced surgical procedures. Anesthesia was introduced in 1846. Also, Louis Pasteur's understanding of bacteria later resulted in the development of antiseptic by Joseph Lister in 1867. The introduction of anesthesia coupled with the use of antiseptic methods resulted in the new phase of modern surgery.

Surgical advances during the 20th and early 21st century include the separation of surgical specialties, the development of surgical tools and X-rays, as well as continued technological advances that create alternatives to traditional procedures such as laproscopic surgery with lasers. Another recent breakthrough is robotic surgery, in which a surgeon uses a computer to control a robotic arm to perform certain types of surgical procedures (such as coronary artery bypass; cutting away cancer tissue from sensitive parts of the body such as blood vessels, nerves, or important body organs; and hip replacement).

■ THE JOB

The work of a surgeon varies according to the work environment and specialty. For example, a general surgeon who specializes in trauma care would most likely work in a large, urban hospital where they would spend a great deal of time in the operating room performing emergency surgical procedures at a moment's notice. On the other hand, a general surgeon who specializes in hernia repair would probably have a more predictable work schedule and would spend much of the time in an ambulatory (also called outpatient) surgery center.

The surgeon is responsible for the diagnosis of the patient, for performing operations, and for providing patients with postoperative surgical care and treatment. In emergency room situations, the patient typically has an injury or severe pain. If the patient needs surgery, the on-duty general surgeon will schedule the surgery. Surgery may be scheduled for the following day, or the patient will be operated on immediately, depending on the urgency of the situation.

A surgeon sees such cases as gunshot, stabbing, and accident victims. Other cases that often involve emergency surgery include appendectomies and removal of kidney stones. When certain problems, such as a kidney stone or inflamed appendix, are diagnosed at an early stage, the surgeon can perform nonemergency surgery.

There are several specialties of surgery and four areas of subspecialization of general surgery. For these areas, the surgeon can receive further education and training leading to certification. A few of these specializations include *neurosurgery* (care for disorders of the nervous system), *plastic and reconstructive surgery* (care for defects of the skin and underlying musculoskeletal structure), *orthopaedic surgery* (care for musculoskeletal disorders that are present at birth or develop later), and *thoracic surgery* (care for diseases and conditions of the chest). The subspecializations for general surgery are: *general vascular surgery, pediatric surgery, hand surgery,* and *surgical critical care.*

■ EARNINGS

According to the U.S. Department of Labor, surgeons earned mean annual salaries of $247,520 in May 2015. Even the lowest paid 10 percent of surgeons earned incomes over $111,420. According to Salary.com, surgeons earned median annual salaries of $362,472 in October 2016. Salaries ranged from less than $306,535 to $430,198 or more.

Incomes may vary from specialty to specialty. Other factors influencing individual incomes include the type and size of practice, the hours worked per week, the geographic location, and the reputation a surgeon has among both patients and fellow professionals.

Benefits for surgeons include vacation and sick time, health, and sometimes dental, insurance, and pension or 401(k) plans.

■ WORK ENVIRONMENT

Surgeons work in sterile operating rooms that are well equipped, well lighted, and well ventilated. They meet patients and conduct all regular business in clean, brightly lit offices. There are usually nurses, laboratory technicians, medical assistants, administrative assistants, bookkeepers, and receptionists available to assist surgeons.

Surgeons usually see patients by appointments that are scheduled according to individual requirements.

They may reserve all mornings for hospital visits and minor surgery. They may see patients in the office only on certain days of the week. Surgeons may also visit patients in nursing homes, hospices, and home-care settings. Many surgeons work 60 or more hours a week.

■ EXPLORING

If you are interested in becoming a surgeon, pay special attention to the work involved in your science laboratory courses. Obviously, working on a living human being is a much weightier prospect than dissecting a pig or a frog, but what you learn about basic handling and cleaning of tools, making incisions, and identifying and properly referring to the body's structures will prove invaluable in your future career. Also ask your science teacher or career counselor to get a surgeon to speak to your biology class, so that they can help you understand more of what the job involves.

■ EDUCATION AND TRAINING REQUIREMENTS
High School

Training to become a surgeon or physician is among the most rigorous of any profession, but the pay is also among the highest. To begin preparing for the demands of college, medical school, and an internship and residency in a hospital, be sure to take as many science and mathematics courses as possible. English, communication, and psychology classes will help prepare for the large amount of reporting and interacting with patients and staff that surgeons do on a daily basis.

Postsecondary Training

Many students who want to become a physician or surgeon enroll in premedical programs at a college or

CAREER LADDER

Professor or Surgical Fellow

Surgeon

Surgical Resident

university. Premedical students take classes in biology, organic and inorganic chemistry, physics, mathematics, English, and the humanities. Some students who major in other disciplines go on to pursue a medical degree, but they generally have to complete additional course work in math and science. All students must take the standardized Medical College Admission Test (MCAT) and then apply to medical schools to pursue the M.D. degree. Note that medical school admissions are fiercely competitive, so developing strong study habits, attaining good grades, and pursuing extracurricular activities are all important characteristics for a medical school applicant to have.

Students can also attend an osteopathic medical program leading to the Doctor of Osteopathic Medicine degree.

Physicians wishing to pursue general surgery must complete a five-year residency in surgery according to the requirements set down by the Accreditation Council for Graduate Medical Education. Throughout the surgery residency, residents are supervised at all levels of training by assisting on and then performing basic operations, such as the removal of an appendix. As the residency years continue, residents gain responsibility through teaching and supervisory duties. Eventually the residents are allowed to perform complex operations independently. Subspecialties require from one to three years of additional training.

Other Education or Training

Keeping up with cutting-edge surgical techniques is key to success as a surgeon. The following professional associations provide continuing education opportunities: Association of Women Surgeons, American Academy of Orthopaedic Surgeons, American Association of Neurological Surgeons, Society of Thoracic Surgeons, American Medical Association, American Osteopathic Association, and the American Society for Aesthetic Plastic Surgery.

■ CERTIFICATION, LICENSING, AND SPECIAL REQUIREMENTS
Certification or Licensing

The American Board of Surgery (ABS) administers board certification in surgery. Certification is a voluntary procedure but it is highly recommended. Most hospitals will

not grant privileges to a surgeon without board certification. HMOs and other insurance groups will not make referrals or payments to a surgeon without board certification. Also, insurance companies are not likely to insure a surgeon for malpractice if he or she is not board certified.

To be eligible to apply for certification in surgery, a candidate must have successfully completed medical school and the requisite residency in surgery. Once a candidate's application has been approved, the candidate may take the computer-based examination. After passing the computer-based exam, the candidate may then take the oral exam.

Certification in surgery is valid for 10 years. To obtain recertification, surgeons must apply to the ABS with documentation of their continuing medical education activities and of the operations and procedures they have performed since being certified, and submit to a review by their peers. They must also pass a written exam.

Certification is available in a number of surgical specialties, including plastic surgery, colon and rectal surgery, neurological surgery, orthopedic surgery, and thoracic surgery. The American Board of Medical Specialties and the American Medical Association recognizes 24 specialty boards that certify physicians and surgeons.

All physicians and surgeons must be licensed by the state in which they work.

■ EXPERIENCE, SKILLS, AND PERSONALITY TRAITS

There is no way to obtain direct experience in high school, but it's a good idea to take as many health and science classes as possible and participate in science clubs. Medical students gain experience by completing a five-year residency and possibly a fellowship (for those interested in pursuing subspecialties).

Successful surgeons are able to think quickly and act decisively in stressful situations, enjoy helping and working with people, are patient, have strong organizational skills, are able to give clear instructions, have good hand-eye coordination, and are able to listen and communicate well.

■ EMPLOYMENT PROSPECTS
Employers

Approximately 41,600 surgeons are employed in the United States. Many licensed physicians and surgeons in the United States work in private solo or group practices. About 10 percent work for hospitals, and others work for federal and state government offices, educational services, and outpatient care facilities.

Starting Out

Many new physicians and surgeons choose to join existing practices instead of attempting to start their own. Establishing a new practice is costly, and it may take time to build a patient base. In a clinic, group practice, or partnership, physicians share the costs for medical equipment and staff salaries, and of establishing a wider patient base.

Surgeons who hope to join an existing practice may find leads through their medical school or residency. During these experiences, they work with many members of the medical community, some of whom may be able to recommend them to appropriate practices.

Another approach would be to check the various medical professional journals, which often run ads for physician positions. Aspiring physicians can also hire a medical placement agency to assist them in the job search.

Physicians who hope to work for a managed care organization or government sponsored clinic should contact the source directly for information on position availability and application procedures.

■ ADVANCEMENT PROSPECTS

Surgeons typically advance by expanding their skill and knowledge, increasing the number of patients they treat, and by increasing their income. They may become fellows in a professional specialty or serve on the board of a medical association. Others achieve recognition by conducting research in new surgical procedures and treatments and publishing their findings in medical journals. Some become professors.

■ OUTLOOK

The wide-ranging skills and knowledge of the surgeon will always be in demand, whether or not the surgeon has a subspecialty. According to the *Occupational Outlook Handbook*, employment for physician and surgeons is expected to grow by 14 percent, much faster than the average for all occupations, through 2024. Many industry experts are now predicting a shortage of general surgeons in the coming years as more students enter nonsurgical specialties, such as anesthesiology and radiology, which require less intensive training. Also, more surgeons will be required to meet medical needs of the growing and aging population. Those who specialize in such areas as cardiology and radiology will be in demand as the older population has increased risk of heart disease and cancer.

■ UNIONS AND ASSOCIATIONS

Most surgeons do not belong to unions, but some may be represented by the Doctors Council SEIU

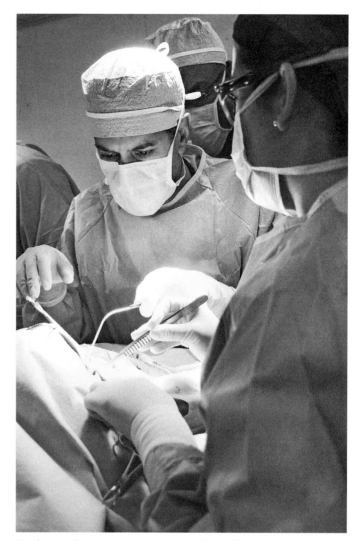

Dr. Sanjay Gupta, a neurosurgeon and award-winning CNN correspondent, operates on a patient. (Mass Communication Specialist 2nd Class Michael C. Barton. U.S. Navy.)

and the Union of American Physicians and Dentists. The American Medical Association and American Osteopathic Association are the major professional associations for physicians and surgeons. They provide publications, information on medical school and careers, networking opportunities, and other resources. Other membership organizations for surgeons include the Association of Women Surgeons, American Academy of Orthopaedic Surgeons, American Association of Neurological Surgeons, Society of Thoracic Surgeons, and the American Society for Aesthetic Plastic Surgery.

Many surgeons receive board certification from the American Board of Surgery, American Board of Medical Specialties, American Board of Cosmetic Surgery, and the American Board of Plastic Surgery.

The Association of American Medical Colleges represents all accredited U.S. and Canadian medical schools,

SURGICAL TOOLS AND TECHNIQUES

WORDS TO KNOW

Drape: Sterile cloth used to surround and isolate the actual site or location of the operation on the patient's body.

Endoscope: An instrument used to visually examine the interior of a hollow organ.

Forceps: An instrument that looks like cooking tongs; used by surgeons to hold back skin or other soft tissue.

Heart-lung machine: A device that maintains circulation during open heart surgery. Blood is diverted from the heart and lungs, oxygenated, and returned to the body.

Scalpel: A thin-bladed knife that is used in surgery.

Scrubbing: The cleaning of the hands, wrists, and forearms of the surgeon and all surgical staff before surgery. This is done to kill germs and harmful bacteria.

Sterile field: The sterile area in which the surgery takes place; any object or person entering this area must be sterilized, or completely free of germs and bacteria.

Sterilize: A procedure in which living microorganisms are removed from an area or instrument.

Surgical debridement: The use of a sharp instrument, such as a scalpel, to remove dead, dying, damaged, or infected tissue.

Suture: The stitches used to close a wound or surgical incision.

major teaching hospitals and health systems, and academic and scientific societies. The American Association of Colleges of Osteopathic Medicine is an organization of osteopathic medical schools.

■ TIPS FOR ENTRY

1. Check out the *The AWS Pocket Mentor* (https://www.womensurgeons.org/aws-pocket-mentor-now-available-as-e-book/), a handbook that aims to ease the transition from medical student to resident to surgeon.

2. Visit https://www.ama-assn.org/education/becoming-physician to read the requirements for "Becoming a Physician."

3. Visit the following Web sites for job listings:
   - https://www.healthecareers.com/aans
   - http://www.sts.org/misc/career-connections
   - http://www.jamacareercenter.com

4. Talk to surgeons about their careers. Many medical surgical associations provides lists of members at their Web sites, which can be referenced for possible interview candidates.

5. Some associations, such as the American Association of Neurological Surgeons, offer resident mentoring programs or other support programs for medical students and new surgeons. Contact associations in your practice area for more information.

■ FOR MORE INFORMATION

The American Academy of Orthopaedic Surgeons provides information and resources for orthopaedic surgeons.

American Academy of Orthopaedic Surgeons (AAOS)
9400 West Higgins Road
Rosemont, IL 60018-4975
Tel: (847) 823-7186
Fax: (847) 823-8125
http://www.aaos.org

The American Association of Colleges of Osteopathic Medicine provides advocacy, education, research, and other resources for osteopathic medical professionals.

American Association of Colleges of Osteopathic Medicine (AACOM)
5550 Friendship Boulevard, Suite 310
Chevy Chase, MD 20815-7231
Tel: (301) 968-4100
Fax: (301) 968-4101
E-mail: aacomasinfo@liaisoncas.com
http://www.aacom.org

The American Association of Neurological Surgeons is dedicated to advancing the specialty of neurosurgery.

American Association of Neurological Surgeons (AANS)
5550 Meadowbrook Drive
Rolling Meadows, IL 60008-3852
Tel: (888) 566-2267; (847) 378-0500
Fax: (847) 378-0600
E-mail: info@aans.org
http://www.aans.org

The American Board of Cosmetic Surgery sets the highest standards for training, expertise, and ethical practice of cosmetic surgery.

American Board of Cosmetic Surgery (ABCS)
8840 Calumet Avenue, Suite 205
Munster, IN 46321-2546
Tel: (219) 836-8585
Fax: (219) 836-5525
http://www.americanboardcosmeticsurgery.org

The American Board of Medical Specialties provides information on certification in medical specialties.

American Board of Medical Specialties (ABMS)
353 North Clark Street, Suite 1400
Chicago, IL 60654-3454
Tel: (312) 436-2600
http://www.abms.org

The American Board of Plastic Surgery has information on certification for plastic surgeons.

American Board of Plastic Surgery (ABPS)
1635 Market Street, Suite 400
Philadelphia, PA 19103-2204
Tel: (215) 587-9322
Fax: (215) 587-9622
E-mail: info@abplasticsurgery.org
https://www.abplasticsurgery.org

The American Board of Surgery provides information on training and certification in various surgical specialties.

American Board of Surgery (ABS)
1617 John F. Kennedy Boulevard, Suite 860
Philadelphia, PA 19103-1821
Tel: (215) 568-4000
Fax: (215) 563-5718
http://www.absurgery.org

The American Medical Association provides information on education and careers in medical fields.

American Medical Association (AMA)
330 North Wabash Avenue, Suite 39300
Chicago, IL 60611-5885
Tel: (800) 621-8335
https://www.ama-assn.org

The American Osteopathic Association provides information on osteopathic medicine.

American Osteopathic Association (AOA)
142 East Ontario Street
Chicago, IL 60611-2864
Tel: (800) 621-1773
Fax: (312) 202-8000
E-mail: (312) 202-8200
http://www.osteopathic.org

The American Society for Aesthetic Plastic Surgery is a professional association for board-certified plastic surgeons.

American Society for Aesthetic Plastic Surgery (ASAPS)
11262 Monarch Street
Garden Grove, CA 92841-1437

Tel: (800) 364-2147; (562) 799-2356
Fax: (562) 799-1098
E-mail: asaps@surgery.org
http://www.surgery.org

The Association of American Medical Colleges provides information about careers in medicine and how to apply to medical schools.

Association of American Medical Colleges (AAMC)
655 K Street, NW, Suite 100
Washington, D.C. 20001-2399
Tel: (202) 828-0400
https://www.aamc.org

The Association of Women Surgeons is a not-for-profit professional and educational organization for women surgeons.

Association of Women Surgeons (AWS)
35 East Wacker Drive, Suite 850
Chicago, IL 60601-2101
Tel: (312) 224-2575
Fax: (312) 644-8557
E-mail: info@womensurgeons.org
https://www.womensurgeons.org

The Society of Thoracic Surgeons represents thoracic surgeons, researchers, and allied health care professionals.

Society of Thoracic Surgeons (STS)
633 North Saint Clair Street, Suite 2320
Chicago, IL 60611-3658
Tel: (312) 202-5800
Fax: (312) 202-5801
http://www.sts.org

Surgical Technologists

■ OVERVIEW

Surgical technologists, also called *surgical technicians* or *operating room technicians*, are members of the surgical team who work in the operating room with surgeons, nurses, anesthesiologists, and other personnel before, during, and after surgery. They ensure a safe and sterile environment. To prepare a patient for surgery, they may wash, shave, and disinfect the area where the incision will be made. They arrange the equipment, instruments, and supplies in the operating room according to

QUICK FACTS

ALTERNATE TITLE(S)
Circulators, Operating Room Technicians, Private Scrubs, Scrub Persons, Surgical First Assistants, Surgical Technicians

DUTIES
Prepare patients and the operating room (OR) for surgery, assist doctors and other health care professionals during surgical procedures, and prepare the OR after surgery for the next patient

SALARY RANGE
$31,410 to $44,330 to $63,410+

WORK ENVIRONMENT
Primarily Indoors

BEST GEOGRAPHIC LOCATION(S)
Nationwide; most opportunities available in major metropolitan areas

MINIMUM EDUCATION LEVEL
High School Diploma, Some Postsecondary Training

SCHOOL SUBJECTS
Biology, Chemistry, Health

EXPERIENCE
Supervised clinical experience required

PERSONALITY TRAITS
Helpful, Scientific, Technical

SKILLS
Mechanical/Manual Dexterity, Organizational, Scientific

CERTIFICATION OR LICENSING
Required

SPECIAL REQUIREMENTS
None

EMPLOYMENT PROSPECTS
Good

ADVANCEMENT PROSPECTS
Good

OUTLOOK
Much Faster than the Average

NOC
3219

O*NET-SOC
29-2055.00

the preference of the surgeons and nurses. During the operation, they adjust lights and other equipment as needed. They count sponges, needles, and instruments used during the operation, hand instruments and supplies to the surgeon, and hold retractors and cut sutures as directed. They maintain specified supplies of fluids (for example, saline, plasma, blood, and glucose), and may assist in administering these fluids. Following the operation, they may clean and restock the operating room and wash and sterilize the used equipment using germicides, autoclaves, and sterilizers, although in most larger hospitals these tasks are done by other central service personnel. There are approximately 100,270 surgical technologists employed in the United States.

■ HISTORY

The origins of surgery date back to prehistoric times, yet two scientific developments made modern surgery possible. The first was the discovery of anesthesia in the mid-19th century. Because the anesthesia eliminated the patient's pain, surgeons were able to take their time during operations, enabling them to try more complex procedures.

The second important discovery was that of the causes of infection. Until Louis Pasteur's discovery of germs and Joseph Lister's development of aseptic surgery in the 19th century, so many people died of infection after operations that the value of surgery was extremely limited.

During World War II, the profession of surgical technology grew when there was a critical need for assistance in performing surgical procedures and a shortage of qualified personnel. Shortly after, formal educational programs were started to teach these medical professionals.

Throughout the last century, the nature of most surgical procedures, with all of their sophisticated techniques for monitoring and safeguarding the patient's condition, has become so complex that more and more people are required to assist the surgeon or surgeons. Many of the tasks that are performed during the operation require highly trained professionals with many years of education, but there are also simpler, more standardized tasks that require people with less complex training and skills. Over the years, such tasks have been taken care of by people referred to as orderlies, scrub nurses, and surgical orderlies.

Today, such people are referred to as surgical technologists, operating room technicians, or surgical technicians. For the most part, these medical professionals have received specialized training in a community college, vocational or technical school, or a hospital-sponsored program. They are eligible to earn certificates of competence, diplomas, and associate degrees, and, in general, enjoy a higher degree of professional status and recognition than did their predecessors.

■ THE JOB

Surgical technologists are health professionals who work in the surgical suite with surgeons, anesthesiologists, registered nurses, and other surgical personnel delivering surgical patient care.

In general, the work responsibilities of surgical technologists may be divided into three phases: preoperative (before surgery), intraoperative (during surgery), and postoperative (after surgery). Surgical technologists may work as the *scrub person, circulator,* or *surgical first assistant.*

In the preoperative phase, surgical technologists prepare the operating room by selecting and opening sterile supplies such as drapes, sutures, sponges, electrosurgical devices, suction tubing, and surgical instruments. They assemble, adjust, and check nonsterile equipment to ensure that it is in proper working order. Surgical technologists also operate sterilizers, lights, suction machines, electrosurgical units, and diagnostic equipment.

When patients arrive in the surgical suite, surgical technologists may assist in preparing them for surgery by providing physical and emotional support, checking charts, and observing vital signs. They properly position the patient on the operating table, assist in connecting and applying surgical equipment and monitoring devices, and prepare the incision site by cleansing the skin with an antiseptic solution.

During surgery, surgical technologists have primary responsibility for maintaining the sterile field. They constantly watch that all members of the team adhere to aseptic techniques so the patient does not develop a postoperative infection. As the scrub person, they most often function as the sterile member of the surgical team who passes instruments, sutures, and sponges during surgery. After "scrubbing," which involves the thorough cleansing of the hands and forearms, they put on a sterile gown and gloves and prepare the sterile instruments and supplies that will be needed. After other members of the sterile team have scrubbed, they assist them with gowning and gloving and applying sterile drapes around the operative site.

Surgical technologists must anticipate the needs of surgeons during the procedure, passing instruments and providing sterile items in an efficient manner. Checking, mixing, and dispensing appropriate fluids and drugs in the sterile field are other common tasks. They share with the circulator the responsibility for accounting for sponges, needles, and instruments before, during, and after surgery. They may hold retractors or instruments, sponge or suction the operative site, or cut suture material as directed by the surgeon. They connect drains and tubing and receive and prepare specimens for subsequent pathologic analysis.

Surgical technologists most often function as the scrub person, but may function in the nonsterile role of circulator. The circulator does not wear a sterile gown and gloves, but is available to assist the surgical team. As a circulator, the surgical technologist obtains additional supplies or equipment, assists the anesthesiologist, keeps a written account of the surgical procedure, and assists the scrub person.

Surgical first assistants, who are technologists with additional education or training, provide aid in retracting tissue, controlling bleeding, and other technical functions that help surgeons during the procedure.

After surgery, surgical technologists are responsible for preparing and applying dressings, including plaster or synthetic casting materials, and for preparing the operating room for the next patient. They may provide staffing in postoperative recovery rooms where patients' responses are carefully monitored in the critical phases following general anesthesia.

Some of these responsibilities vary, depending on the size of the hospital and department in which the surgical technologist works; they also vary based on geographic location and health care needs of the local community.

CAREER LADDER

Central Service Manager, or Surgery Scheduler, or Materials Manager

Surgical First Assistant

Experienced Surgical Technologist

Entry-Level Surgical Technologist

EARNINGS

Salaries vary greatly in different institutions and localities. According to the U.S. Department of Labor, the average salary for surgical technologists was $44,330 in May 2015, and ranged from $31,410 to $63,410 or more a year (excluding overtime). Some technologists with experience earn much more. Most surgical technologists are required to be periodically on call—available to work on short notice in cases of emergency—and can earn overtime from such work. Graduates of educational programs usually receive salaries higher than technologists without formal education. In general, technologists working on the East Coast and West Coast earn more than surgical technologists in other parts of the country. Surgical first assistants and *private scrubs* employed directly by surgeons tend to earn more than surgical technologists employed by hospitals.

Benefits for full-time workers include vacation and sick time, health, and sometimes dental, insurance, and pension or 401(k) plans.

WORK ENVIRONMENT

Surgical technologists naturally spend most of their time in the operating room. Operating rooms are cool, well

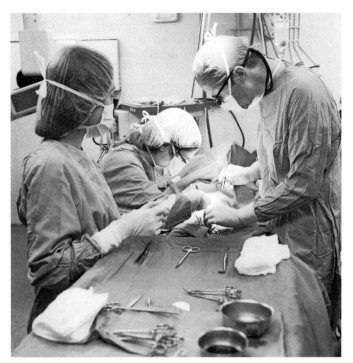

A surgical technologist holds gauze for a surgeon during an operation. (Franck Boston. Shutterstock.)

lighted, orderly, and extremely clean. Technologists are often required to be on their feet for long intervals, during which their attention must be closely focused on the operation.

Members of the surgical team, including surgical technologists, wear sterile gowns, gloves, caps, masks, and eye protection. This surgical attire is meant not only to protect the patient from infection but also to protect the surgical team from any infection or blood-borne diseases that the patient may have. Surgery is usually performed during the day; however, hospitals, clinics, and other facilities require 24-hour-a-day coverage. Most surgical technologists work regular 40-hour weeks, although many are required to be periodically on call.

■ EXPLORING

It is difficult to gain any direct experience on a part-time basis in surgical technology. The first opportunities for direct experience generally come in the clinical and laboratory phases of educational programs. However, interested students can explore some aspects of this career in several ways. Arrange a visit to a hospital, clinic, or other surgical setting in order to learn about the work. Also visit a school with a program accredited by the Commission on Accreditation of Allied Health Education Programs. During such a visit, discuss career plans with an admissions counselor. In addition, volunteering at a local hospital or nursing home can provide insight into the health care environment and help you evaluate your aptitude to work in such a setting.

■ EDUCATION AND TRAINING REQUIREMENTS
High School

During high school, take courses that develop basic skills in mathematics, science, and English. Also take all available courses in health and biology.

Postsecondary Training

Surgical technology education is available through postsecondary programs offered by community and junior colleges, vocational and technical schools, the military, universities, and structured hospital programs in surgical technology. A high school diploma is required for entry into any of these programs.

Many of these programs are accredited by the Commission on Accreditation of Allied Health Education Programs (CAAHEP, http://www.caahep.org/Find-An-Accredited-Program). The Accrediting Bureau of Health Education Schools (http://www.abhes.org) also accredits surgical technology programs. The accredited programs vary from nine to 12 months for a diploma or certificate, to two years for an associate's degree. Students can expect to take courses in medical terminology, communications, anatomy, physiology, microbiology, pharmacology, medical ethics, and legal responsibilities. They also gain thorough knowledge of patient preparation and care, surgical procedures, surgical instruments and technical or robotic equipment, and principles of asepsis (how to prevent infection). In addition to classroom learning, students receive intensive supervised clinical experience in local hospitals, which is an important component of your education.

Other Education or Training

The Association of Surgical Technologists provides a variety of professional edevelopment opportunities, including education sessions at its annual conference. Past sessions included "Interaction Between Surgeon and Scrub Tech," "Microsurgical Solutions to Wound Problems," and "Finding Your Voice–Advocating for Your Patient, Yourself and Our Profession."

■ CERTIFICATION, LICENSING, AND SPECIAL REQUIREMENTS
Certification or Licensing

Increasing numbers of hospitals are requiring certification as a condition of employment. Surgical technologists may earn a professional credential by passing a nationally administered certifying examination. To take the examination, you must be currently or previously certified or be a graduate of a CAAHEP- or ABHES-accredited program. The National Board of Surgical Technology and Surgical Assisting (NBSTSA) is the certifying agency for the profession. Those who pass the exam and fulfill education and experience requirements are granted the designation of certified surgical technologist (CST). To renew one's certification, the CST must earn continuing education credits or retake the certifying examination. The NBSTSA also offers an advanced credential for surgical first assistants; this exam awards the designation of certified surgical first assistant.

Another certification for surgical technologists can be obtained from the National Center for Competency Testing. To take the certification exam, candidates must either complete an accredited surgical technology training program, or have three years of experience in the field, or meet other experience or training criteria. Upon passing the exam, surgical technologists receive the designation of tech in surgery – certified (NCCT). This certification must be renewed every five years either through reexamination or continuing education.

The National Surgical Assistant Association and the American Board of Surgical Assistants also offer certification for surgical first assistants.

Some states, such as Illinois and Washington, require surgical technologists to be licensed.

■ EXPERIENCE, SKILLS, AND PERSONALITY TRAITS

Completion of a supervised clinical experience in a local hospital or other health care setting is required for aspiring surgical technologists.

Surgical technologists must possess an educational background in the medical sciences, a strong sense of responsibility, a concern for order, and an ability to integrate a number of tasks at the same time. They need good manual dexterity to handle awkward surgical instruments with speed and agility. In addition, physical stamina is required to stand through long surgical procedures.

Surgical technologists must be able to work under great pressure in stressful situations. The need for surgery is often a matter of life and death, and one can never assume that procedures will go as planned. If operations do not go well, nerves may fray and tempers flare. Technologists must understand that this is the result of stressful conditions and should not take this anger personally.

In addition, surgical technologists should have a strong desire to help others. Surgery is performed on

SURGICAL TECHNOLOGY — WORDS TO KNOW

-Ectomy: Surgery that involves the partial or complete removal of an organ, as in appendectomy (removal of the appendix).

Edema: Excessive buildup of fluids in body tissues.

Elective surgery: Nonemergency surgery that can be scheduled by choice by the doctor or patient. An example of an elective surgery might be a hip replacement procedure.

Emergency surgery: A type of surgery that must be performed as soon as possible to save the patient's life. Medical situations that would prompt emergency surgery include a gunshot wound or a burst appendix.

On call: The shifts when surgical assistants and other medical personnel remain available via pager to come to work on a moment's notice in case of an emergency.

-Otomy: Surgery that involves the perforation or incision of organs or tissue, as in radial keratotomy (laser surgery performed on the eye).

-Plasty: Surgery to restore, reconstruct, or refigure body parts, as in rhinoplasty (surgery to reshape the nose).

Scrub: The process of thoroughly washing the hands and forearms before surgery to ensure sterility.

Sterile field: The part of the operating room where the instruments, equipment, and surfaces are entirely free of germs.

Videoscopes: Fiber-optic tubes that can be inserted deep into the body through nearly invisible incisions. Various scopes are named for the areas of the body in which they are generally used. Laparoscopes are used in the abdomen, arthroscopes in the joints, thoracoscopes or endoscopes in the chest, and angioscopes inside the walls of blood vessels.

people, not machines. Patients literally entrust their lives to the surgical team, and they rely on them to treat them in a dignified and professional manner. Individuals with these characteristics find surgical technology a rewarding career in which they can make an important contribution to the health and well-being of their community.

■ EMPLOYMENT PROSPECTS
Employers

Approximately 100,270 surgical technologists are employed in the United States. Most surgical technologists are employed in hospital operating and delivery rooms, clinics, and surgical centers. They also work in offices of physicians or dentists who perform outpatient surgery, hospital emergency departments, outpatient care centers, and central supply departments. Surgical technologists may also be employed directly by surgeons as private scrubs or as surgical first assistants.

Starting Out

Graduates of surgical technology programs are often offered jobs in the same hospital in which they received their clinical training. Programs usually cooperate closely with hospitals in the area, which are usually eager to employ technologists educated in local programs. Available positions are also advertised on employment agency Web sites and in newspaper classifieds.

■ ADVANCEMENT PROSPECTS

Experienced surgical technologists can serve in management roles in surgical services departments and may work as *central service managers*, *surgery schedulers*, and *materials managers*. The role of surgical first assistant on the surgical team requires additional training and experience and is considered an advanced role.

Surgical technologists must function well in a number of diverse areas. Their competency with multiple skills is demonstrated by their employment in organ and tissue procurement/preservation, cardiac catheterization laboratories, medical sales and research, and medical-legal auditing for insurance companies. A number are *instructors* and *directors* of surgical technology programs.

■ OUTLOOK

The field of surgical technology is projected to experience rapid job growth through 2024, according to the U.S. Department of Labor. Population growth, increasing life spans, and improvement in medical and surgical procedures have all contributed to a growing demand for surgical services and hence for surgical technologists. As long as the rate at which people undergo surgery continues to increase, there will continue to be a need for this profession. Also, as surgical methods become increasingly complex, more surgical technologists will likely be needed. Surgical technologists who are certified will have the best employment opportunities.

An increasing number of surgical procedures are being performed in the offices of physicians and ambulatory surgical centers, requiring the skills of surgical technologists. As a result, employment opportunities for technologists in these non-hospital settings should grow much faster than for those who work in hospitals.

■ UNIONS AND ASSOCIATIONS

Surgical technologists do not belong to unions, but many join the Association of Surgical Technologists, which provides professional development and networking opportunities. The National Board of Surgical Technology and Surgical Assisting and the National Center for Competency Testing provide certification to surgical technologists.

■ TIPS FOR ENTRY

1. Visit http://careercenter.ast.org/jobseekers and http://jobs.nbstsa.org for job listings.
2. Join the Association of Surgical Technologists (AST) to access networking and opportunities, continuing education classes, and other resources.
3. Attend the AST's Annual National Conference (http://www.ast.org/AboutUs/Conference) to network and participate in continuing education opportunities.
4. Read *The Surgical Technologist* (http://www.ast .org/Publications/The_Surgical_Technologist) to learn more about the field.

■ FOR MORE INFORMATION

The Association of Surgical Technologists offers education, publications, advocacy, and other resources for surgical technologists.

Association of Surgical Technologists (AST)
6 West Dry Creek Circle, Suite 200
Littleton, CO 80120-8031
Tel: (800) 637-7433; (303) 694-9130
Fax: (303) 694-9169
http://www.ast.org

The National Board of Surgical Technology and Surgical Assisting is the certifying body for surgical technologists.

National Board of Surgical Technology and
    Surgical Assisting (NBSTSA)
6 West Dry Creek Circle, Suite 100
Littleton, CO 80120-8031
Tel: (800) 707-0057
Fax: (303) 325-2536
E-mail: mail@nbstsa.org
http://www.nbstsa.org

The National Center for Competency Testing is a credentialing organization for health care professionals and instructors.

National Center for Competency Testing (NCCT)
7007 College Boulevard, Suite 385
Overland Park, KS 66211-1558
Tel: (800) 875-4404
Fax: (913) 498-1243
https://www.ncctinc.com

Surveying and Mapping Technicians

■ OVERVIEW

Surveying and mapping technicians help determine, describe, and record geographic areas or features. They are usually the leading assistant to the *professional surveyor, civil engineer,* or *cartographer.* They operate modern surveying and mapping instruments and may participate in other operations. Technicians must have a basic knowledge of the current practices and legal implications of surveys to establish and record property size, shape, topography, and boundaries. They often supervise other assistants during routine surveying conducted within the bounds established by a professional surveyor. There are approximately 53,620 surveying and mapping technicians working in the United States.

■ HISTORY

Since ancient times, people have needed to define their property boundaries. Marking established areas of individual or group ownership was a basis for the development of early civilizations. Landholding became important in ancient Egypt, and with the development of hieroglyphics, people were able to keep a record of their holdings. Eventually, nations found it necessary not only to mark property boundaries but also to record principal routes of commerce and transportation. For example, records of the Babylonians tell of their canals and irrigation ditches. The Romans surveyed and mapped their empire's principal roads. In the early days of colonial exploration, surveyors and their technical helpers were among the first and most-needed workers. They established new land ownership by surveying and filing claims. Since then, precise and accurate geographical measurements have been needed to determine the location of a highway, the site of a building, the right-of-way for drainage ditches, telephone, and power lines, and for the charting of unexplored land, bodies of water, and underground mines.

Early surveying processes required at least two people. A technical scientist served as the leader, or professional surveyor. This scientist was assisted by helpers to make measurements with chains, tapes, and wheel rotations, where each rotation accounted for a known length of distance. The helpers held rods marked for location purposes and placed other markers to define important points.

As measuring instruments have become more complex, the speed, scope, and accuracy of surveying have

QUICK FACTS

ALTERNATE TITLE(S)
Assistant Field Technicians, Chain Workers, Chief Instrument Workers, Exploration Geology Technicians, Highway Technicians, Mining Surveying Technicians, Photogrammetric Technicians, Rod Workers

DUTIES
Operate surveying and mapping instruments to determine, describe, and record geographic areas or features as instructed by surveyors; write reports that detail their findings

SALARY RANGE
$26,060 to $42,010 to $68,160+

WORK ENVIRONMENT
Primarily Outdoors

BEST GEOGRAPHIC LOCATION(S)
Nationwide

MINIMUM EDUCATION LEVEL
Some Postsecondary Training, Apprenticeship

SCHOOL SUBJECTS
Computer Science, Geography, Mathematics

EXPERIENCE
Internships; on-the-job training

PERSONALITY TRAITS
Hands On, Organized, Technical

SKILLS
Computer, Math, Scientific

CERTIFICATION OR LICENSING
Recommended

SPECIAL REQUIREMENTS
None

EMPLOYMENT PROSPECTS
Good

ADVANCEMENT PROSPECTS
Good

OUTLOOK
Decline

NOC
2254

O*NET-SOC
17-3031.00, 17-3031.01, 17-3031.02

improved. Developments in surveying and mapping technology have made great changes in the planning and construction of highway systems and structures of all kinds. For roadway route selection and design, technicians increasingly use photogrammetry, which uses plotting machines to describe routes from aerial

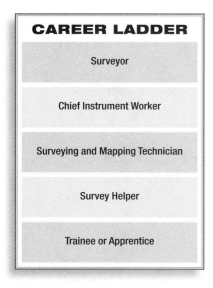

CAREER LADDER

Surveyor

Chief Instrument Worker

Surveying and Mapping Technician

Survey Helper

Trainee or Apprentice

photographs of rural or urban areas. Route data obtained by photogrammetry may then be processed through computers to calculate land acquisition, grading, and construction costs. Photogrammetry is faster and far more accurate than former methods. In addition, new electronic distance-measuring devices have brought surveying to a higher level of precision. Technicians can measure distance more quickly, accurately, and economically than was possible with tapes, rods, and chains.

In addition to photogrammetry, the use of computers in data processing has extended surveying and mapping careers past the earth's surface. Technicians now help to make detailed maps of ocean floors and the Moon. Every rocket fired from the Kennedy Space Center is tracked electronically to determine if it is on course through the use of maps made by surveyors. The technological complexity of such undertakings allows surveyors to delegate more tasks than ever to technicians.

THE JOB

As essential assistants to civil engineers, surveyors, and cartographers, surveying and mapping technicians are usually the first to be involved in any job that requires precise plotting. This includes highways, airports, housing developments, mines, dams, bridges, and buildings of all kinds.

The surveying and mapping technician is a key worker in field parties and major surveying projects and is often assigned the position of chief instrument worker under the surveyor's supervision. Technicians use a variety of surveying instruments, including the theodolite, transit, level, and other electronic equipment, to measure distances or locate a position. Technicians may be *rod workers,* using level rods or range poles to make elevation and distance measurements. They may also be *chain workers,* measuring shorter distances using a surveying chain, metal tape, or electronic distance-measuring equipment. During the survey, it is important to accurately record all readings and keep orderly field notes to check for accuracy.

Surveying and mapping technicians may specialize if they join a firm that focuses on one or more particular types of surveying. Technicians who work in firms that specialize in land surveying are highly skilled in technical measuring and tasks related to establishing township, property, and other tract-of-land boundary lines. They help the professional surveyor with maps, notes, and title deeds. They help survey the land, check the accuracy of existing records, and prepare legal documents such as deeds and leases.

Similarly, technicians who work for highway, pipeline, railway, or power line surveying firms help to establish grades, lines, and other points of reference for construction projects. This survey information provides the exact locations for engineering design and construction work.

Technicians who work for geodetic surveyors help take measurements of large masses of land, sea, or space. These measurements must take into account the curvature of Earth and its geophysical characteristics. Their findings set major points of reference for smaller land surveys, determining national boundaries, and preparing maps.

Technicians may also specialize in hydrographic surveying, measuring harbors, rivers, and other bodies of water. These surveys are needed to design navigation systems, prepare nautical maps and charts, establish property boundaries, and plan for breakwaters, levees, dams, locks, piers, and bridges.

Mining surveying technicians are usually on the geological staffs of either mining companies or exploration companies. In recent years, costly new surveying instruments have changed the way they do their jobs. Using highly technical machinery, technicians can map underground geology, take samples, locate diamond drill holes, log drill cores, and map geological data derived from boreholes. They also map data on mine plans and diagrams and help the geologist determine ore reserves. In the search for new mines, technicians operate delicate instruments to obtain data on variations in Earth's magnetic field, its conductivity, and gravity. They use their data to map the boundaries of areas for potential further exploration.

Surveying and mapping technicians may find topographical surveys to be interesting and challenging work. These surveys determine the contours of the land and indicate such features as mountains, lakes, rivers, forests, roads, farms, buildings, and other distinguishable landmarks. In topographical surveying, technicians help take aerial or land photographs with photogrammetric equipment installed in an airplane or ground station that can take pictures of large areas. This method is widely used to measure farmland planted with certain crops and to verify crop average allotments under government production planning quotas.

A large number of survey technicians are employed in construction work. Technicians are needed from start to finish on any job. They check the construction of a structure for size, height, depth, level, and form specifications. They also use measurements to locate the critical construction points as specified by design plans, such as corners of buildings; foundation points; center points for columns, walls, and other features; floor or ceiling levels; and other features that require precise measurements and location.

Technological advances such as the Global Positioning System (GPS) and Geographic Information Systems (GIS) have revolutionized surveying and mapping work. Surveying teams use these systems to track points on the Earth with radio signals transmitted from satellites and store this information in computer databases.

A surveying technician assists a surveyor in identifying property lines. (ilkercelik. Shutterstock.)

▩ EARNINGS

According to the U.S. Department of Labor, the May 2015 median hourly salary for all surveying and mapping technicians, regardless of the industry, was $20.20 (amounting to $42,010 for full-time work). The lowest paid 10 percent earned less than $12.53 ($26,060 for full-time work), and the highest paid 10 percent earned over $32.77 an hour ($68,160 for full-time work). Technicians working for the public sector in federal, state, and local governments generally earn more per hour than those working in the private sector for engineering and architectural services. Surveying and mapping technicians working for state government agencies made an average of $44,380 per year.

Benefits for salaried surveying and mapping technicians depend on the employer; however, they usually include such items as health insurance, retirement or 401(k) plans, and paid vacation days. Self-employed workers must provide their own benefits.

▩ WORK ENVIRONMENT

Surveying and mapping technicians usually work about 40 hours a week except when overtime is necessary. The peak work period for many kinds of surveying work is during the summer months when weather conditions are most favorable. However, surveying crews are exposed to all types of weather conditions.

Some survey projects involve certain hazards depending upon the region and the climate as well as local plant and animal life. Field survey crews may encounter snakes and poison ivy. They are subject to heat exhaustion, sunburn, and frostbite. Some projects, particularly those being conducted near construction projects or busy highways, impose dangers of injury from cars and flying debris. Unless survey technicians are employed for office assignments, their work location changes from survey to survey. Some assignments may require technicians to be away from home for varying periods of time.

While on the job, technicians who supervise other workers must take special care to observe good safety practices. Construction and mining workplaces usually require hard hats, special clothing, and protective shoes.

▩ EXPLORING

One of the best opportunities for experience is to work part time or during summer break for a construction firm or a company involved in survey work. Even if the job does not involve direct contact with survey crews, there is opportunity to observe their work and converse with them to discover more about their daily activities. Another possibility is to work for a government agency overseeing land use. The Bureau of Land Management, for example, has employment opportunities for students who qualify, as well as many volunteer positions. The Forest Service also offers temporary positions for students.

▩ EDUCATION AND TRAINING REQUIREMENTS
High School

Take mathematics courses, such as algebra, geometry, and trigonometry, as well as mechanical drawing in high school. Physics, chemistry, and biology are other valuable classes that will help you gain laboratory experience. Reading, writing, and comprehension skills as well as knowledge of computers are also vital in surveying and mapping, so English and computer science courses are also highly recommended.

GETTING YOUR FEET WET

DID YOU KNOW?

The following are examples of entry-level technician positions:

- *Survey helpers or drafters* operate surveying instruments to gather numerical data. They calculate tonnage broken, map mine development, and provide precise directions and locations for the work crew. Under the supervision of an experienced surveyor, they conduct studies on operations and equipment to improve methods and reduce costs.
- *Assistant field or exploration geology technicians* operate a variety of geophysical instruments to obtain data on variations in the earth's magnetism, conductivity, and gravity. They map the data and analyze stream waters, soils, and rocks to search for ore occurrences. These technicians often work in remote areas.
- *Highway technicians* help plan, lay out, and supervise the construction and maintenance of highways. Under the direction of a surveyor, they help make surveys and estimate construction costs.
- *Photogrammetric technicians* use aerial photographs to prepare maps, mosaics, plans, and profiles.

Postsecondary Training

Though not required to enter the field, graduates of accredited postsecondary training programs for surveying, photogrammetry, geomatics, and mapping are in the best position to become surveying and mapping technicians. Postsecondary training is available from institutional programs and correspondence schools. These demanding technical programs generally last two years with a possible field study in the summer. First-year courses include English, composition, drafting, applied mathematics, surveying and measurements, construction materials and methods, applied physics, statistics, and computer applications. Second-year courses cover subjects such as technical physics, advanced surveying, photogrammetry and mapping, soils and foundations, technical reporting, legal issues, and transportation and environmental engineering. ABET offers a list of accredited programs at http://main.abet.org/aps/Accreditedprogramsearch.aspx.

With additional experience and study, technicians can specialize in geodesy, topography, hydrography, geographic information systems, or photogrammetry. Many graduates of two-year programs later pursue a bachelor's degree in surveying, engineering, or geomatics.

Aspiring surveying and mapping technicians who do not attend college can train for the field by completing an apprenticeship with an experienced technician or surveyor.

Other Education or Training

The American Society for Photogrammetry and Remote Sensing, National Society of Professional Surveyors, Geographic Land and Information Society, and state-level organizations offer webinars, seminars, and other continuing education opportunities.

■ CERTIFICATION, LICENSING, AND SPECIAL REQUIREMENTS
Certification or Licensing

Many employers prefer certified technicians for promotions into higher positions with more responsibility. The National Society of Professional Surveyors offers the voluntary survey technician certification at four levels. With each level, the technician must have more experience and pass progressively challenging examinations. Technicians must be specially certified to work as surveyors in their state.

The American Society for Photogrammetry and Remote Sensing offers voluntary certification for technicians who specialize in photogrammetry, remote sensing, and geographic information systems (GIS)/land information systems.

Technicians who use GIS technology in their work can receive voluntary certification from the GIS Certification Institute. Applicants must have a baccalaureate degree in any field, complete course work and other documented education in GIS and geospatial data technologies, have work experience in a GIS-related position, and participate in conferences or GIS-related events. Applicants who meet all certification requirements may use the designation certified GIS professional. Certification must be renewed every five years.

■ EXPERIENCE, SKILLS, AND PERSONALITY TRAITS

No experience is required, but any surveying and mapping experience obtained via internships or other learning opportunities will be useful.

Successful surveying and mapping technicians are patient, orderly, systematic, accurate, and objective in their work. They must be willing to work cooperatively and have the ability to think and plan ahead. Because of the increasing technical nature of their work, surveying and mapping technicians must have computer skills to be able to use highly complex equipment such as GPS and GIS technology.

■ EMPLOYMENT PROSPECTS

Employers

Approximately 53,620 surveying and mapping technicians are employed in the United States. About 60 percent of technicians find work with engineering or architectural service firms. The federal government also employs technicians to work for the U.S. Geological Survey, the Bureau of Land Management, the National Oceanic and Atmospheric Administration, the National Geospatial-Intelligence Agency, and the Forest Service. State and local governments also hire surveying and mapping technicians to work for highway departments and urban planning agencies. Construction firms and oil, gas, and mining companies also hire technicians.

Starting Out

Those entering surveying straight from high school may first work as an apprentice. Through on-the-job training and some classroom work, apprentices build up their skills and knowledge of the trade to eventually become surveying and mapping technicians.

If you plan to attend a technical institute or four-year college, check out your school's career services office for help in arranging examinations or interviews. Employers of surveying technicians often send recruiters to schools before graduation and arrange to employ promising graduates. Some community or technical colleges have work-study programs that provide cooperative part-time or summer work for pay. Employers involved with these programs often hire students full time after graduation.

Many cities have employment agencies that specialize in placing technical workers in positions in surveying, mapping, construction, mining, and related fields. Find these services through an online search as well as through local newspaper postings.

■ ADVANCEMENT PROSPECTS

Possibilities for advancement are linked to levels of formal education and experience. As technicians gain experience and technical knowledge, they can advance to positions of greater responsibility and eventually work as chief surveyor. To advance into this position, technicians will most likely need a two- or four-year degree in surveying and many years of experience. Licensing requirements for surveyors vary by state, requiring varying amounts of experience, schooling, and examinations.

Regardless of the level of advancement, all surveying and mapping technicians must continue studying to keep up with the technological developments in their field. Technological advances in computers, lasers, and microcomputers will continue to change job requirements. Studying to keep up with changes combined with progressive experience gained on the job will increase the technician's opportunity for advancement.

■ OUTLOOK

Surveying and mapping technicians are expected to have improved job prospects if they are skilled in using new digital surveying and mapping technologies such as GPS and GIS. Overall, however, employment in this field is expected to decline by 8 percent through 2024, according to the *Occupational Outlook Handbook (OOH)*. The advancements in surveying technology enable technicians to accomplish more work in less time, which reduces the number of technicians needed for the job.

There will continue to be some job opportunities for surveying technicians due to growth in urban and suburban areas. New streets, homes, shopping centers, schools, and gas and water lines will require property and boundary line surveys. Surveying and mapping technicians will also be needed for state and federal highway improvement programs and urban redevelopment programs. The expansion of industrial and business firms and the relocation of some firms in large undeveloped areas are require surveying services.

Job opportunities for surveying and mapping technicians are closely tied to construction activity and local economic conditions, and will vary depending on geographic location. The need to replace workers who have either retired or transferred to other occupations will continue to provide opportunities. In general, technicians with more education and skill training will have more job options.

■ UNIONS AND ASSOCIATIONS

Surveying and mapping technicians may belong to unions such as the American Federation of Government Employees. Technicians can obtain useful resources and professional support from the American Society for Photogrammetry and Remote Sensing, Cartography and Geographic Information Society, Geographic Land and Information Society, GIS Certification Institute, and National Society of Professional Surveyors.

■ TIPS FOR ENTRY

1. Learn more about what surveyors do by reading interviews with surveyors at http://www.beasurveyor.com/meet-the-professional-surveyors.
2. Join professional associations such as the National Society of Professional Surveyors to access training and networking opportunities, industry publications, and employment opportunities.

3. Participate in internships or part-time jobs that are arranged by your college's career services office.

■ FOR MORE INFORMATION

The American Society for Photogrammetry and Remote Sensing aims to advance knowledge and improve understanding of mapping science.

> **American Society for Photogrammetry and Remote Sensing (ASPRS)**
> 5410 Grosvenor Lane, Suite 210
> Bethesda, MD 20814-2160
> Tel: (301) 493-0290
> Fax: (301) 493-0208
> E-mail: asprs@asprs.org
> http://www.asprs.org

The Bureau of Land Management has a mission to sustain the health, diversity, and productivity of America's public lands for the use and enjoyment of present and future generations.

> **Bureau of Land Management (BLM)**
> 1849 C Street, NW, Room 5665
> Washington, D.C. 20240-0001
> Tel: (202) 208-3801
> Fax: (202) 208-5242
> E-mail: blm_wo_newmedia@blm.gov
> http://www.blm.gov

The Cartography and Geographic Information Society is a network of professionals who work in education, research, and practice in cartography and geographic information science.

> **Cartography and Geographic Information Society (CaGIS)**
> E-mail: cagisxd@gmail.com
> http://www.cartogis.org

The North American Cartographic Information Society supports and coordinates activities with professional organizations and institutions involved in cartographic information.

> **North American Cartographic Information Society (NACIS)**
> 2311 East Hartford Avenue
> Milwaukee, WI 53211-3175
> Tel: (414) 229-6282
> Fax: (414) 229-3624
> E-mail: business@nacis.org
> http://nacis.org

The Geographic Land and Information Society provides information on education, membership, and publications on geographic and land information systems.

> **Geographic Land and Information Society (GLIS)**
> c/o CBI, 6300 Ocean Drive, Unit 5868
> Christi, TX 78412-5868
> Tel: (361) 825-2750
> Fax: (361) 825-5848
> E-mail: president@g-lis.org
> http://www.g-lis.org

The GIS Certification Institute provides information on certification in geographic information systems.

> **GIS Certification Institute**
> 701 Lee Street, Suite 680
> Des Plaines, IL 60016-4508
> Tel: (847) 824-7768
> Fax: (847) 824-6363
> E-mail: info@gisci.org
> https://www.gisci.org

The National Society of Professional Surveyors provides advocacy, education, certification, and other resources for professional surveyors.

> **National Society of Professional Surveyors (NSPS)**
> 5119 Pegasus Court, Suite Q
> Frederick, MD 21704-7248
> Tel: (240) 439-4615
> Fax: (240) 439-4952
> http://www.nsps.us.com

Surveyors

■ OVERVIEW

Surveyors make exact measurements and locations of elevations, points, lines, and contours on or near Earth's surface. They measure distances between points to determine property boundaries and to provide data for mapmaking, construction projects, and other engineering purposes. There are approximately 43,140 surveyors employed in the United States.

■ HISTORY

As the United States expanded from the Atlantic to the Pacific, people moved over the mountains and plains into the uncharted regions of the West. They found it necessary to chart their routes and to mark property lines and borderlines by surveying and filing claims.

The need for accurate geographical measurements and precise records of those measurements has increased over the years. Surveying measurements are needed to determine the location of a trail, highway, or road; the site of a log cabin, frame house, or skyscraper; the right-of-way for water pipes, drainage ditches, and telephone lines; and for the charting of unexplored regions, bodies of water, land, and underground mines.

As a result, the demand for professional surveyors has grown and become more complex. New computerized systems are now used to map, store, and retrieve geographical data more accurately and efficiently. This new technology has not only improved the process of surveying but extended its reach as well. Surveyors can now make detailed maps of ocean floors and the moon's surface.

■ THE JOB

On proposed construction projects, such as highways, airstrips, and housing developments, it is the surveyor's responsibility to make necessary measurements through an accurate and detailed survey of the area. The surveyor usually works with a field party consisting of several people. Instrument assistants, called *surveying and mapping technicians*, handle a variety of surveying instruments including the theodolite, transit, level, surveyor's chain, rod, and other electronic equipment. In the course of the survey, it is important that all readings be recorded accurately and field notes maintained so that the survey can be checked for accuracy.

Surveyors may specialize in one or more particular types of surveying.

Construction surveyors make surveys for construction projects, such as highways, bridges, airstrips, shopping centers, and housing developments. They establish grades, lines, and other points of reference for construction projects. This survey information is essential to the work of the numerous engineers and the construction crews who build these projects.

Land surveyors establish township, property, and other tract-of-land boundary lines. They use maps, notes, or actual land title deeds to survey the land, checking for the accuracy of existing records. This information is used to prepare legal documents such as deeds and leases.

Land surveying managers coordinate the work of surveyors, their parties, and legal, engineering, architectural, and other staff involved in a project. In addition, these managers develop policy, prepare budgets, certify work upon completion, and handle numerous other administrative duties.

Highway surveyors establish grades, lines, and other points of reference for highway construction projects.

QUICK FACTS

ALTERNATE TITLE(S)
Cartographers, Construction Surveyors, Forensic Surveyors, Geodesists, Geodetic Computers, Geodetic Surveyors, Geophysical Prospecting Surveyors, Highway Surveyors, Hydrographic Surveyors, Land Surveying Managers, Land Surveyors, Marine Surveyors, Mine Surveyors, Oil-Well Directional Surveyors, Photogrammetric Engineers, Photogrammetrists, Pipeline Surveyors, Surveying and Mapping Technicians

DUTIES
Use surveying and mapping instruments to record exact measurements and locations; study data and write reports; supervise surveying and mapping technicians

SALARY RANGE
$32,850 to $58,020 to $95,800+

WORK ENVIRONMENT
Primarily Outdoors

BEST GEOGRAPHIC LOCATION(S)
Opportunities exist in all regions

MINIMUM EDUCATION LEVEL
Bachelor's Degree

SCHOOL SUBJECTS
Earth Science, Geography, Mathematics

EXPERIENCE
Two to four years experience required

PERSONALITY TRAITS
Hands On, Problem-Solving, Technical

SKILLS
Interpersonal, Math, Scientific

CERTIFICATION OR LICENSING
Required

SPECIAL REQUIREMENTS
None

EMPLOYMENT PROSPECTS
Good

ADVANCEMENT PROSPECTS
Good

OUTLOOK
Decline

NOC
2154

O*NET-SOC
17-1022.00, 17-1022.01

This survey information is essential to the work of the numerous engineers and the construction crews who build the new highway.

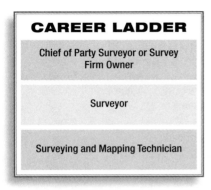

Geodetic surveyors, also known as *geodesists,* measure large masses of land, sea, and space that must take into account the curvature of Earth and its geophysical characteristics. Their work is helpful in establishing points of reference for smaller land surveys, determining national boundaries, and preparing maps. *Geodetic computers* calculate latitude, longitude, angles, areas, and other information needed for mapmaking. They work from field notes made by an engineering survey party and also use reference tables and a calculating machine or computer.

Marine surveyors, also known as *hydrographic surveyors,* measure harbors, rivers, and other bodies of water. They determine the depth of the water through measuring sound waves in relation to nearby land masses. Their work is essential for planning and constructing navigation projects, such as breakwaters, dams, piers, marinas, and bridges, and for preparing nautical charts and maps.

Mine surveyors make surface and underground surveys, preparing maps of mines and mining operations. Such maps are helpful in examining underground passages within the levels of a mine and assessing the volume and location of raw material available.

Geophysical prospecting surveyors locate and mark sites considered likely to contain petroleum deposits. *Oil-well directional surveyors* use sonic, electronic, and nuclear measuring instruments to gauge the presence and amount of oil- and gas-bearing reservoirs. *Pipeline surveyors* determine rights-of-way for oil construction projects, providing information essential to the preparation for and laying of the lines.

Photogrammetric engineers, also known as *photogrammetrists,* determine the contour of an area to show elevations and depressions and indicate such features as mountains, lakes, rivers, forests, roads, farms, buildings, and other landmarks. Aerial, land, and water photographs are taken with special equipment able to capture images of very large areas. From these pictures, accurate measurements of the terrain and surface features can be made. These surveys are helpful in construction projects and in the preparation of topographical maps. Photogrammetry is particularly helpful in charting areas that are inaccessible or difficult to travel.

Cartographers prepare maps, charts, and drawings from aerial photographs and survey data. They also conduct map research, developing new mapping techniques and investigating topics such as how people use maps.

Forensic surveyors serve as expert witnesses in legal proceedings that involve industrial, automobile, or other types of accidents. They gather, analyze, and map data that is used as evidence at a trial, hearing, or lawsuit. These professionals must have extensive experience in the field and be strong communicators in order to explain technical information to people who do not have a background in surveying.

■ EARNINGS

In May 2015, surveyors earned a median annual salary of $58,020, according to the U.S. Department of Labor. The middle 50 percent earned between $43,380 and $77,230 a year. The lowest paid 10 percent were paid less than $32,850, and the highest paid 10 percent earned over $95,800 a year. In general, the federal government paid the highest wages to its surveyors, $84,490 a year.

Most positions with the federal, state, and local governments and with private firms provide life and medical insurance, pension, vacation, and holiday benefits.

■ WORK ENVIRONMENT

Surveyors work 40-hour weeks except when overtime is necessary to meet a project deadline. The peak work period is during the summer months when weather conditions are most favorable. However, it is not uncommon for the surveyor to be exposed to adverse weather conditions.

Some survey projects may involve hazardous conditions, depending on the region and climate as well as the plant and animal life. Survey crews may encounter snakes, poison ivy, and other hazardous plant and animal life, and may suffer heat exhaustion, sunburn, and frostbite while in the field. Survey projects, particularly those near construction projects or busy highways, may impose dangers of injury from heavy traffic, flying objects, and other accidental hazards. Unless the surveyor is employed only for office assignments, the work location most likely will change from survey to survey. Some assignments may require the surveyor to be away from home for periods of time.

■ EXPLORING

Become familiar with surveyor terms, projects, and tools used in this profession by reading books and magazines on the topic. Professional associations publish various newsletters and magazines that are helpful. One of the best opportunities for experience is a summer job with a construction outfit or company that requires survey work. Even if the job does not involve direct contact with survey crews, it will offer an opportunity to observe surveyors and talk with them about their work.

Some colleges have work-study programs that offer on-the-job experience. These opportunities, like summer or part-time jobs, provide helpful contacts in the field that may lead to future full-time employment. Volunteering at an appropriate government agency is another way to explore the field. The U.S. Geological Survey and the Bureau of Land Management usually have volunteer opportunities in select areas.

■ EDUCATION AND TRAINING REQUIREMENTS
High School

Prepare for this career by taking plenty of math and science courses in high school. Take algebra, geometry, and trigonometry to become comfortable making different calculations. Earth science, chemistry, and physics classes are also helpful. Geography will help you learn about different locations, their characteristics, and cartography. Benefits from taking mechanical drawing and other drafting classes include an increased ability to visualize abstractions, exposure to detailed work, and an understanding of perspectives. Taking computer science classes will prepare you for working with technical surveying equipment.

Postsecondary Training

It has become the industry standard for surveyors to earn a bachelor's degree in surveying or engineering combined with on-the-job training. Other entry options include obtaining more job experience (sometimes as an apprentice) combined with a one- to three-year program in surveying and surveying technology offered by community colleges, technical institutes, and vocational schools.

Other Education or Training

The American Society for Photogrammetry and Remote Sensing, Geographic Land and Information Society, and state-level organizations offer webinars, seminars, and other continuing education opportunities.

■ CERTIFICATION, LICENSING, AND SPECIAL REQUIREMENTS
Certification or Licensing

The National Society of Professional Surveyors (NSPS) has partnered with the Federal Emergency Management Agency to create a certification program for floodplain surveyors. The NSPS has also partnered with the Bureau of Land Management to create the certified federal surveyors program.

A surveyor works with a technician on a highway project. (CandyBox Images. Shutterstock.)

The American Society for Photogrammetry and Remote Sensing offers voluntary certification for surveyors who specialize in photogrammetry and GIS. Certification is also provided by the GIS Certification Institute.

All 50 states and the District of Columbia require that surveyors making property and boundary surveys be licensed or registered. The requirements for licensure vary, but most require a degree in surveying or a related field, a certain number of years of experience, and passing of examinations in land surveying. Generally, the higher the degree obtained, the less experience required. Those with bachelor's degrees may need four years of on-the-job experience, while those with a lesser degree may need up to 10 years of prior experience to obtain a license. State licensure departments provide information on the requirements. Those seeking employment in the federal government must take a civil service examination and meet the educational, experience, and other specified requirements for the position.

■ EXPERIENCE, SKILLS, AND PERSONALITY TRAITS

Licensed surveyors must have four years' experience in the field and hold a bachelor's degree. The ability to work with numbers and perform mathematical computations accurately and quickly is essential. Other helpful qualities are the ability to visualize and understand objects in two and three dimensions (spatial relationships) and the ability to discriminate between and compare shapes, sizes, lines, shadings, and other forms (form perception).

Surveyors walk a great deal and carry equipment over all types of terrain so endurance and coordination are important physical assets. In addition, surveyors direct and supervise the work of their team, so you should be

TOP INDUSTRIES EMPLOYING SURVEYORS AND MEAN ANNUAL SALARIES, MAY 2015

FAST FACTS

The following industries employed the highest number of surveyors in May 2015:

- Architectural, engineering, and related services: 30,980 jobs, $60,870
- Local government agencies: 2,640 jobs, $62,420
- State government agencies: 1,870 jobs, $71,370
- Highway, street, and bridge construction: 1,350 jobs, $62,940
- Nonresidential building construction: 810 jobs, $63,050

Source: U.S. Bureau of Labor Statistics

good at working with other people and demonstrate leadership abilities.

■ EMPLOYMENT PROSPECTS
Employers

There are approximately 43,140 surveyors employed in the United States. According to the U.S. Department of Labor, about 70 percent of surveyors in the United States are employed in engineering, architectural, and surveying firms. Federal, state, and local government agencies are the next largest employers of surveying workers, and the majority of the remaining surveyors work for construction firms, oil and gas extraction companies, and public utilities. Only a small number of surveyors are self-employed.

Starting Out

Apprentices with a high school education can enter the field as equipment operators or surveying assistants. Those who have postsecondary education can enter the field more easily, beginning as surveying and mapping technicians.

College graduates can learn about job openings through their schools' career services offices or through potential employers that may visit their campus. Many cities have employment agencies that specialize in seeking out workers for positions in surveying and related fields.

■ ADVANCEMENT PROSPECTS

Experienced workers advance through the leadership ranks within a surveying team. Workers begin as assistants and then can move into positions such as senior technician, party chief, and, finally, licensed surveyor. Because surveying work is closely related to other fields,

surveyors can move into civil engineering or specialize in drafting.

■ OUTLOOK

The U.S. Department of Labor predicts that employment for surveyors will decline by about 2 percent through 2024. Job prospects will be best for surveyors who have college degrees and advanced field experience, and work in industries such as oil and gas mining. The widespread use of technology, such as the Global Positioning System and Geographic Information Systems, will provide jobs to surveyors with strong technical and computer skills. This same technology, however, will also reduce the numbers of surveyors needed, because the technology enables them to accomplish more work in less time.

Growth in urban and suburban areas (with the need for new streets, homes, shopping centers, schools, gas and water lines) will provide employment opportunities. State and federal highway improvement programs and local urban redevelopment programs also will provide jobs for surveyors. The expansion of industrial and business firms and the relocation of some firms to large undeveloped tracts will also create job openings. The construction industry will also provide job opportunities for surveyors. It should be noted, however, that construction projects are closely tied to the state of the economy, so employment may fluctuate from year to year. Job opportunities will not be as strong with government agencies due to budget cuts.

■ UNIONS AND ASSOCIATIONS

Surveyors are not represented by unions, but they can obtain useful resources and professional support from the American Society for Photogrammetry and Remote Sensing, Cartography and Geographic Information Society, Geographic Land and Information Society, GIS Certification Institute, and the National Society of Professional Surveyors.

■ TIPS FOR ENTRY

1. Read journals and magazines about the surveying profession, which can be found through the Surveying Engineering section of Penn State University Libraries' Web site: http://guides.libraries.psu.edu/c.php?g=378978&p=2568678.
2. Join professional associations such as the National Society of Professional Surveyors to access training and networking opportunities, industry publications, and employment opportunities.
3. Search for job listings on professional associations' Web sites and through online employment sites such as Indeed.com and Monster.com.

■ FOR MORE INFORMATION

The American Society for Photogrammetry and Remote Sensing provides education, news, events, and other resources on photogrammetry and mapping science professionals.

American Society for Photogrammetry and Remote Sensing (ASPRS)
5410 Grosvenor Lane, Suite 210
Bethesda, MD 20814-2160
Tel: (301) 493-0290
Fax: (301) 493-0208
E-mail: asprs@asprs.org
http://www.asprs.org

The Bureau of Land Management provides information on volunteer and employment opportunities with the federal government.

Bureau of Land Management (BLM)
1849 C Street, NW
Washington, D.C. 20240-0001
Tel: (202) 208-3801
Fax: (202) 208-5242
E-mail: blm_wo_newmedia@blm.gov
http://www.blm.gov

The Cartography and Geographic Information Society is a network of professionals who work in education, research, and practice in cartography and geographic information science.

Cartography and Geographic Information Society (CaGIS)
E-mail: cagisxd@gmail.com
http://www.cartogis.org

The Geographic Land and Information Society provides information on education, membership, and publications on geographic and land information systems.

Geographic Land and Information Society (GLIS)
c/o CBI, 6300 Ocean Drive, Unit 5868
Christi, TX 78412-5868
Tel: (361) 825-2750
Fax: (361) 825-5848
E-mail: president@g-lis.org
http://www.g-lis.org

The GIS Certification Institute provides information on certification in geographic information systems.

GIS Certification Institute
701 Lee Street, Suite 680
Des Plaines, IL 60016-4508
Tel: (847) 824-7768
Fax: (847) 824-6363
E-mail: info@gisci.org
http://www.gisci.org

The National Society of Professional Surveyors provides advocacy, education, certification, and other resources for professional surveyors.

National Society of Professional Surveyors (NSPS)
5119 Pegasus Court, Suite Q
Frederick, MD 21704-7248
Tel: (240) 439-4615
Fax: (240) 439-4952
http://www.nsps.us.com

The U.S. Geological Survey provides information on volunteer and employment opportunities with the federal government.

U.S. Geological Survey (USGS)
12201 Sunrise Valley Drive
Reston, VA 20192
Tel: (888) 275-8747
https://www.usgs.gov

Swimming Pool Servicers

■ OVERVIEW

Swimming pool servicers clean, adjust, and perform minor repairs on swimming pools, hot tubs, and their auxiliary equipment. There are millions of pools across the country in hotels, parks, apartment complexes, health clubs, and other public areas. These public pools are required by law to be regularly serviced by trained technicians. In addition, the number of homeowners with pools is increasing, and these private pools also need professional servicing.

■ HISTORY

Swimming pools date back to the bathhouses in the palaces of ancient Greece. These bathhouses were elaborate spas, complete with steam rooms, saunas, and large pools. Swimming was a popular pastime even among those who did not have access to bathhouses; many swam in the rivers, oceans, and the lakes of the world. The plagues of medieval Europe made people cautious about swimming in unclean waters, but soon swimming regained popularity. Swimmers swam with their heads above water in a style developed when many people were still afraid of water contamination. This swimming style

QUICK FACTS

ALTERNATE TITLE(S)
None

DUTIES
Clean, adjust, and perform minor repairs on swimming pools, hot tubs, and their auxiliary equipment

SALARY RANGE
$16,871 to $26,557 to $41,804+

WORK ENVIRONMENT
Indoors/Outdoors

BEST GEOGRAPHIC LOCATION(S)
Opportunities available throughout the country

MINIMUM EDUCATION LEVEL
High School Diploma, Some Postsecondary Training

SCHOOL SUBJECTS
Biology, Chemistry, Technical/Shop

EXPERIENCE
On-the-job training

PERSONALITY TRAITS
Hands On, Problem-Solving, Technical

SKILLS
Business Management, Interpersonal, Mechanical/Manual Dexterity

CERTIFICATION OR LICENSING
Required

SPECIAL REQUIREMENTS
None

EMPLOYMENT PROSPECTS
Good

ADVANCEMENT PROSPECTS
Fair

OUTLOOK
Little Change or More Slowly than the Average

NOC
7441

O*NET-SOC
49-9099.00

changed in the mid-1800s when Native Americans introduced an early version of the modern "crawl." Swimming in natural spring waters was even recommended as a health benefit, inspiring hospitals and spas to develop around hot springs.

The first modern Olympics held in 1896 in Athens, Greece, featured swimming as one of the nine competitions. Swimming as both a sport and a pastime has continued to develop along with the technology of pool maintenance. By the 1960s, the National Swimming Pool Foundation had evolved to support research in pool safety and the education of pool operators. Today, the U.S. swimming pool cleaning services industry generates approximately $3 billion in revenue and consists of more than 51,000 businesses, according to the market research group IBISWorld.

■ THE JOB

Swimming pool servicers usually travel a regularly scheduled route, visiting several pools a day. They are responsible for keeping pools clean and equipment operating properly. In general, a pool that receives routine maintenance develops fewer problems.

Cleaning is one of the regular duties of pool servicers. Leaves and other debris need to be scooped off the surface of the water with a net on a long pole. To clean beneath the surface, servicers use a special vacuum cleaner on the pool floor and walls. They scrub pool walls, tiles, and gutters around the pool's edge with stainless steel or nylon brushes to remove layers of grit and scum that collect at the water line. They also hose down the pool deck and unclog the strainers that cover the drains.

After cleaning the pool and its surroundings, servicers test the bacterial content and pH balance (a measure of acidity and alkalinity) of the water. The tests are simple and take only a few minutes, but they are critical. A sample of the pool water is collected in a jar and a few drops of a testing chemical are added to the water. This chemical causes the water to change colors, indicating the water's chemical balance. Swimming pool servicers use these results to determine the amount of chlorine and other chemicals that should be added to make the water safe. The chemicals often used, which include potassium iodide, hydrochloric acid, sodium carbonate, chlorine, and others, are poured directly into the pool or added through a feeder device in the circulation system. These chemicals, when properly regulated, kill bacteria and algae that grow in water.

High levels of chemicals can cause eye or skin irritation. As a result, pool servicers must wear gloves and use caution when working. The chemical makeup of every pool is different and can change daily or even hourly, so servicers keep accurate records of the levels of chemicals added to the pool during their visit. Pool owners or managers take up the responsibility of testing the water between visits from the servicer. The water in home pools is usually tested several times a week, but large public pools are tested hourly.

Swimming pool servicers also inspect and perform routine maintenance on pool equipment, such as circulation pumps, filters, and heaters. In order to clean a filter, servicers force water backwards through it to dislodge any debris that has accumulated. They make sure there are no leaks in pipes, gaskets, connections, or other parts. If a drain or pipe is clogged, servicers use a steel snake, plunger, or other plumbing tool to clear it. They also adjust thermostats, pressure gauges, and other controls to make the pool water comfortable. Minor repairs to machinery, such as fixing or replacing small components, may be necessary. When major repairs are needed, servicers first inform the pool owner before making any repairs.

Another major task for swimming pool servicers in most regions of the country is closing outdoor pools for the winter. In the fall, servicers drain the water out of the pool and its auxiliary equipment. Openings into the pool are plugged, and all pool gear, such as diving boards, ladders, and pumps, is removed, inspected, and stored. The pool is covered with a tarpaulin and tied or weighted in place. In warmer climates where water does not freeze, pools are usually kept full and treated with special chemicals through the winter.

Extra work is also required when a pool is reopened in the spring. After the pool is uncovered and the tank and pool deck are swept clean, swimming pool servicers inspect for cracks, leaks, loose tiles, and broken lamps. They repair all minor problems and make recommendations to the owner about any major work they feel is necessary, such as painting the interior of the pool. Equipment removed in the fall, such as ladders and diving boards, is cleaned and installed. Servicers test water circulation and heating systems to make sure they are operating properly, and then fill the pool with water. Once filled, the pool water is tested and the appropriate chemicals are added to make it safe for swimming.

For every job, servicers keep careful records of the maintenance work they have done so they can inform the company and the customer.

EARNINGS

The amount of money swimming pool servicers make depends upon the region of the country in which they work (which determines the length of the swimming season), services provided by the business, and levels of experience. According to SimplyHired.com, in 2016, pool technicians earned average salaries of $26,557, with salaries ranging from $16,871 to $41,804 or higher. Experts in the business estimate that an experienced pool service owner can average $40,000 to $50,000 a year. Beginning servicers just starting to build a clientele or those who work in an area of the country that allows for only a few months of swimming may earn less than $20,000 a year.

Servicers who work full-time for pool servicing companies usually receive benefits such as vacation days, sick leave, health and life insurance, and a savings and pension program. Self-employed pool servicers must provide their own benefits.

CAREER LADDER

Swimming Pool Service Owner

Swimming Pool Servicer

Assistant Pool Servicer

WORK ENVIRONMENT

Swimming pool servicers generally work alone and sometimes have little client contact. Most of the work is not particularly strenuous, though kneeling, bending, and carrying equipment from a van or work truck to the pool is necessary. Servicers work both indoors and outdoors and usually perform their duties in pleasant weather. They must handle chemicals, requiring the use of protective gloves and possibly a breathing mask to guard against fumes.

Pool servicing can be an excellent career option for those who enjoy spending time outside. Many servicers find the work relaxing and like the idea that this job keeps them from working in a typical office setting.

EXPLORING

A summer or part-time job with a school, park district, community center, or local health club can provide opportunities to learn more about servicing swimming

A servicer checks the pH balance of a swimming pool. (ruzanna. Shutterstock.)

POOL MAINTENANCE

LEARN MORE ABOUT IT

Hardy, Dan. *The Complete Pool Manual for Homeowners and Professionals: A Step-by-Step Maintenance Guide,* 2nd ed. Ocala, Fla.: Atlantic Publishing Company, 2013.

International Code Council. *2015 International Swimming Pool and Spa Code.* New York: ICC, 2015.

National Swimming Pool Foundation. *Pool & Spa Operator Handbook: 2014 Edition.* Colorado Springs, Colo.: National Swimming Pool Foundation, 2014.

O'Keefe, John and Alan Sanderfoot. *What Color Is Your Swimming Pool? A Homeowner's Guide to Troublefree Pool, Spa & Hot Tub Maintenance.* North Adams, Mass.: Storey Publishing, 2003.

Tamminem, Terry. *The Ultimate Guide to Pool Maintenance,* 3rd ed. New York: McGraw-Hill Professional, 2007.

pools. Hotels, motels, apartment buildings, and condominium complexes also frequently have pools and may hire summer or part-time workers to service them. Such a job could offer firsthand insight into the duties of swimming pool servicers, and may help in obtaining full-time employment with a pool maintenance company later.

AQUA Magazine is a good source of technical information concerning pool service. Visit http://aquamagazine.com to read selected articles.

■ EDUCATION AND TRAINING REQUIREMENTS
High School

Take science courses such as chemistry and biology to gain understanding of the chemicals used in testing pool water. Shop courses with lessons in electrical wiring and motors will help to develop skills for repairing and servicing machines and equipment. Bookkeeping and accounting courses are also helpful to learn how to keep financial and tax records. Also learn about spreadsheet and database software programs for future file maintenance of profits and expenses, customers, equipment, and employees. Finally, serving as an assistant on a swim team can teach firsthand about the requirements of maintaining a regulation pool.

Postsecondary Training

Most of the technical training needed for this career can be gained while on the job. Working with another trained professional provides an understanding of the basics of pool maintenance within a few months. Those

considering running their own business should further their knowledge by enrolling in college courses in sales, math, accounting, and small business management. People who are interested in a pool maintenance career should also take advanced courses in electrical applications, electronics, plumbing, and hydraulics.

Other Education or Training

The Association of Pool and Spa Professionals offers professional development classes, workshops, and webinars. Recent offerings included "Safe Storage and Handling of Pool and Spa Chemicals," "Oxidation and Demand," and "Reinvent My Business." The Independent Pool and Spa Service Association also provides continuing education classes and webinars.

■ CERTIFICATION, LICENSING, AND SPECIAL REQUIREMENTS
Certification or Licensing

Certification is available from the National Swimming Pool Foundation, the Association of Pool & Spa Professionals, and by service franchisers. Certification programs consist of a set number of classroom hours and a written exam. Certification is not required but it does indicate that pool technicians have reached a certain level of expertise and skill, and it can help promote their business.

Swimming pool servicers who operate their own businesses will need to be licensed and possibly receive certification from their state's department of health.

■ EXPERIENCE, SKILLS, AND PERSONALITY TRAITS

Prior work as an assistant to a swimming pool servicer is useful in the pool and spa technician field. Servicers often work alone with minimum supervision, which requires self-discipline and a responsible attitude. Inner drive and ambition determine the success of a pool technician's business as they work to attract new clients. They also need to keep up with the technology of swimming pool maintenance to stay knowledgeable about new equipment and services available to their clients. Other important traits include a strong work ethic, persistence, and good communication skills.

■ EMPLOYMENT PROSPECTS
Employers

A majority of swimming pool servicers are self-employed. According to the Association of Pool & Spa Professionals, there are more than 10 million residential swimming pools in the United States, which means that pool service owners can find clients in practically every neighborhood. In addition to servicing residential pools, workers service the pools of motels, apartment complexes, and public parks.

Some servicers choose to work with a franchise service company. These franchisers often offer training and usually provide an established client base.

Starting Out

Once servicers have the training and the money to invest in equipment, they work on pursuing clients. This may involve promoting their business through advertising, flyers, the Internet (including social media), and word of mouth. They may be able to get referrals from local pool and spa construction companies.

■ ADVANCEMENT PROSPECTS

Advancement is usually shown through a growth in business. More area pool construction, positive feedback from customers, and some years in the business will attract more clients and more routes to service. If a business does really well, swimming pool servicers may choose to hire additional employees to do most of the service work, allowing more time to focus on office work and administrative details. Servicers may also expand their business to include the sale of pools, spas, and maintenance equipment. Some servicers may even decide to get a contractor's license and build pools for clients.

■ OUTLOOK

The employment outlook for swimming pool servicers is tied to the health of the economy. When the economy is strong, existing pool owners are more willing to pay for pool cleaning services, and more people are interested in installing swimming pools. The opposite is true when the economy is weak. As the economy strengthens, more people will return to work and have less time to clean and maintain their pools. According to IBISWorld, the swimming pool cleaning service industry grew at an annual rate of nearly 4 percent from 2011 to 2016, and growth is expected to continue in the coming years.

There are more than 10 million existing residential swimming pools and about 309,000 public pools in the United States, and demand will remain for professionals trained to maintain and repair them. The establishment of pool laws benefits servicers because they are often hired to help owners comply with safety regulations. A growing awareness among pool owners about the need to keep pools and hot tubs clean to prevent infection will continue to keep servicers in business.

Technological developments will also create more work for servicers. The need to maintain and repair new

---

ALGAE, ALKALINITY, AND SKIMMER NETS

WORDS TO KNOW

Algae: Harmless, microscopic forms of plant life that discolor the water and can grow on pool walls and floors.

Alkalinity: A measure of the carbonate, bicarbonate, and hydroxide compounds present in the water.

Capacity: The total number of gallons of water a pool can contain.

Corrosion: The eating away of metal parts by acidity and very soft water conditions.

Cyanuric acid: Chemical used to prevent ultraviolet light from decomposing the chlorine in a pool.

Dry acid: A granular chemical, safer to handle than liquid acid, used to lower alkalinity.

Oxidizing: The process of breaking down organic wastes often found in standing water.

Rate of flow: The quantity of water that flows past a designated point in a pool during a specific time period.

Skimmer net: A net that is attached to a telescopic pole that is used to clean debris in a pool.

Sanitizer: A chemical, such as chlorine, which kills algae and bacteria, and causes oxidation.

---

equipment, such as solar heaters, automatic timers, pool covers, and chemical dispensers, will keep pool services in demand.

■ UNIONS AND ASSOCIATIONS

Swimming pool servicers do not belong to unions. Some join professional organizations such as the Association of Pool and Spa Professionals, Independent Pool and Spa Service Association, and the National Swimming Pool Foundation, which provide certification, industry publications, networking opportunities, and other resources.

■ TIPS FOR ENTRY

1. Read *Pool and Spa Industry News* (http://www.poolspanews.com) and *AQ Magazine* and *Recreational Water Quality Newsletter* (both available at http://apsp.org/About/Publications.aspx) to learn more about the field.

2. Visit the Association of Pool & Spa Professionals' career center at http://jobs.apsp.org for job listings.

3. Talk to swimming pool servicers about their careers. Ask them for advice on breaking into the field.

■ FOR MORE INFORMATION

This magazine covers news and issues affecting the swimming pool industry.

AQUA Magazine
22 E. Mifflin St., Suite 910
Madison, WI 53703
Tel: (608) 249-0186
http://aquamagazine.com

The Association of Pool and Spa Professionals provides information on education and certification.

Association of Pool and Spa Professionals (APSP)
2111 Eisenhower Avenue, Suite 500
Alexandria, VA 22314-4695
Tel: (703) 838-0083
Fax: (703) 549-0493
E-mail: memberservices@apsp.org
http://apsp.org

The Independent Pool and Spa Service Association is a membership organization for pool and spa service providers.

Independent Pool and Spa Service Association (IPSSA)
10842 Noel Street, Suite 107
Los Alamitos, CA 90720-2582
Tel: (888) 360-9505
Fax: (888) 368-0432
E-mail: info@ipssa.com
http://www.ipssa.com

The National Swimming Pool Foundation offers education, training programs, conferences, and other resources for pool and spa service professionals.

National Swimming Pool Foundation (NSPF)
4775 Granby Circle
Colorado Springs, CO 80919-3131
Tel: (719) 540-9119
E-mail: service@nspf.org
https://www.nspf.org

Systems Setup Specialists

■ OVERVIEW

Systems setup specialists install new computer systems and upgrade existing ones to meet the specifications of the client. They install hardware, such as memory, sound cards, fax/modems, fans, microprocessors, and systems boards. They also load software and configure the hard drive appropriately. Some systems setup specialists install computer systems at the client's location. Installation might include normal hard drive or network server configurations as well as connecting peripherals such as printers, phones, scanners, modems, and numerous terminals. They might also be involved with technical support in providing initial training to users. Systems setup specialists work for computer manufacturing companies or computer service companies nationwide, or they may be employed as part of the technical support department of many businesses. Systems setup specialists are sometimes called *technical support technicians*, *desktop analyst/specialists*, and *PC setup specialists*.

■ HISTORY

Several big companies like IBM, Apple, Microsoft, Google, and Intel have been the driving force behind various stages of the computer revolution. As technology advances, however, increasingly new companies spring up to compete with them. For example, IBM's first competitive challenge came when other companies decided to produce IBM-compatible PC clones.

Today, the market for computers is saturated with different brands that offer similar features. As a result, many companies are attempting to distinguish themselves from the competition by providing extra service to clients. Offering customized hardware and software is one way for them to do this. Systems setup specialists, therefore, are very important to sales. They ensure that clients receive exactly what they need and want. If the computer system is not set up correctly to begin with, clients might take their business elsewhere. As competition in the computer industry grows even fiercer, the customer service roles of systems setup specialists will become even more important.

■ THE JOB

Most businesses and organizations use computers on a daily basis. In fact, it is difficult to find an office or store that does not use computer technology to help them with at least one business task. One thing is certain: There are so many different ways in which a business or individual can use computer technology that it would be impossible to count them. The wide variety could translate into big problems for computer companies if they tried to sell identical computer systems to every client. For example, a freelance writer would probably not be interested in math software used for advanced mathematical calculations on personal computers. Likewise, a bank or insurance company has different database needs than a law firm.

In order to meet clients' various needs, many computer manufacturers, retailers, and service centers offer to customize commercial hardware and software for each client. Systems might differ by quantity of random access memory (RAM), speed and type of fax/modem, networking capabilities, and software packages. Systems setup specialists install new computer systems and upgrade existing ones to meet the specifications of the client. The main differences among setup specialists are their clients (individuals or businesses) and the level of systems they are qualified to work on.

Some specialists work in-house for large computer manufacturers, retailers, or service centers. Their clients are typically individuals buying for home use as well as small- to medium-sized businesses with minimal computing needs.

In the setup lab, specialists receive orders that list system specifications. They follow instructions on how to set up the computer properly, and install hardware, such as memory chips, sound cards, fax/modems, fans, microprocessors, and system boards. They also install any software requested by the client. Next, they configure the hard drive so it knows exactly what hardware and software is connected to it. Finally, they run diagnostic tests on the system to make sure everything is running well.

The main goal is to eliminate the need for clients to do any setup work on the computer once they receive it. Clients should be able to plug it in, turn it on, and get it to work right away. In some cases, specialists even at this level will be sent to a client's location to install the system and provide some initial training on how to use it.

Other systems setup specialists work for companies that sell predominately to medium- and large-sized businesses. These specialists split their time between the employer's setup lab and the client's location. In the lab, they make initial preparations for installation. Some of the computer equipment might come from other manufacturers or suppliers, and so they have to verify that it is free of defects. They also check that they have all the necessary hardware parts, software, etc., before going to the client's location.

Depending on the size and complexity of the system to be installed, they might travel to the client's location one or more times before installation in order to map out the required wiring, communications lines, and space. They plan these details carefully. If wires are hard to reach, for example, future repairs and upgrade will be difficult. If the system is large, setup specialists might recommend and build a raised floor in the client's computer center. The paneled floor allows easy access to the complex electrical and communications wiring.

Once thorough preparations have been made, setup specialists move the equipment to the clients' location to begin installation. Their on-site work might include configuring hard drives or network servers. They also connect peripherals: printers, phones, fax machines, modems, and numerous networked terminals. When everything is in place, they run extensive diagnostic tests to ensure that the system is running well. Invariably, they encounter problems. One terminal may not be able to send files to another, for example. Another terminal might be unable to establish fax communications outside the company. Solving problems requires consulting flow charts, other computer professionals, and technical manuals. The next round of testing occurs when the users begin working on the system. Some clients might prefer to simulate normal use while setup specialists stand by to correct problems. Large business installations can take days or even weeks to complete.

Sometimes, setup specialists are involved with technical support in training client users on the new system. They must be well versed in the details of how to use the system properly and be able to explain it to individuals who might not know much about computers.

■ EARNINGS

According to PayScale.com, the average annual salary for technical support specialists in October 2016 was $47,000. Salaries ranged from $34,000 to more than $72,000.

Most full-time setup specialists work for companies that provide a full range of benefits, including health insurance, sick leave, and paid vacation. In addition, many employers offer tuition reimbursement programs to employees who successfully complete course work in the field. Setup specialists

QUICK FACTS

ALTERNATE TITLE(S)
Desktop Analysts/Specialists, PC Setup Specialists, Technical Support Technicians

DUTIES
Install new computer systems and upgrade existing ones to meet the specifications of the client

SALARY RANGE
$34,000 to $47,000 to $72,000+

WORK ENVIRONMENT
Primarily Indoors

BEST GEOGRAPHIC LOCATION(S)
Opportunities are available throughout the country, but are best in large, urban areas

MINIMUM EDUCATION LEVEL
High School Diploma, Associate's Degree

SCHOOL SUBJECTS
Business, Computer Science, Mathematics

EXPERIENCE
Internship, or part-time or volunteer experience recommended

PERSONALITY TRAITS
Hands On, Problem-Solving, Technical

SKILLS
Business Management, Computer, Math

CERTIFICATION OR LICENSING
Recommended

SPECIAL REQUIREMENTS
None

EMPLOYMENT PROSPECTS
Good

ADVANCEMENT PROSPECTS
Good

OUTLOOK
Faster than the Average

NOC
2171

O*NET-SOC
15-1151.00

CAREER LADDER

Computer Engineer or Consulting Business Owner

Manager

Systems Setup Specialist

Intern

who operate their own businesses are responsible for providing their own benefits.

■ WORK ENVIRONMENT

Systems setup specialists work primarily indoors, in a comfortable environment. This is not a desk job; specialists move around a lot either in the lab or at the client's site. Travel to client locations is required for many setup specialists. The work also requires some lifting of heavy machinery, which can be avoided if an individual physically cannot perform this task. Given the nature of the work, dress is casual, although those who install systems at the client's site must be dressed in presentable business attire.

Setup specialists usually work a regular 40-hour week. However, they might be asked to work overtime when big installations are reaching final phases. They might have to work during off-hours if the client requires installation to be done then.

■ EXPLORING

There are several ways to obtain a better understanding of what it is like to be a setup specialist. One way is to try to organize a career day through school or friends and relatives. This is a good way to spend a day on the job with setup specialists and experience firsthand what the work entails.

Another option is to work part time for a computer repair shop. Repair shops usually do many upgrades that involve the installation of new hardware, like faster modems and microprocessors and more memory. Working in such a shop after school or on weekends will give the opportunity to observe or practice the precision work of a setup specialist.

Depending on your level of computer knowledge, you may want to volunteer to set up new personal computers for friends or charitable organizations in your neighborhood. Try installing software or customizing some features of the operating system to better meet the needs of the user. To keep up to date on technology developments and get ideas for customizing, read computer magazines, such as *Computerworld* (http://www.computerworld .com) and *PC Magazine* (http://www.pcmag.com).

■ EDUCATION AND TRAINING REQUIREMENTS
High School

Take any mechanics and electronics classes that focus on understanding how complex machinery works. These

classes will provide the basics of reading flow charts and schematic drawings and understanding technical documents. The ability to read these documents efficiently and accurately is a prerequisite for computer setup work. Also take computer classes, especially those that explain the basic functioning of computer technology. English and speech classes will also help build communication skills, which is another important quality because setup specialists often work closely with many different people. Take business classes to become familiar with practices of the business world.

Postsecondary Training

A high school diploma is a minimum educational requirement for most systems setup specialist positions. However, the competitive nature of this industry is increasing the importance of postsecondary education, such as an associate's degree. Computer technology is advancing so rapidly that without a solid understanding of the basics, setup specialists cannot keep up with the changes. Also, many aspiring computer professionals use system setup positions as a springboard to higher-level jobs in the company. Formal computer education, along with work experience, gives them a better chance for advancement.

Other Education or Training

Keeping up with industry developments is key to success as a systems setup specialist. Professional associations often provide continuing education opportunities. For example, student and professional members of the Association for Computing Machinery can access online computing and business courses via the association's Learning Center. Visit http://learning.acm.org for details. The IEEE Computer Society offers career planning webinars and continuing education courses to its members. Visit https://www.computer.org/web/education for more information.

■ CERTIFICATION, LICENSING, AND SPECIAL REQUIREMENTS
Certification or Licensing

A number of companies, such as Microsoft and Cisco, offer certification programs in the use of their products. There are also independent companies that provide training programs leading to certification. Generally these certifications are voluntary. Some employers may pay for part or all of the training cost.

■ EXPERIENCE, SKILLS, AND PERSONALITY TRAITS

Experience as an intern, volunteer, or part-time employee at a hardware or software firm is recommended. Good manual dexterity is required since manual work is performed on large and small scales. For example, sometimes thick cables and communications lines must be installed; other times tiny memory chips or microprocessors are needed.

Systems setup specialists are also curious about how things work. They are typically the kind of people who tinker around the house on DVD players, televisions, small appliances, and computers. Genuine curiosity of this type is important because they are constantly challenged to learn about new equipment and technologies. When things go wrong during installation, setup specialists are called on as electronics and computer problem-solvers and must be prepared with a solid understanding of the basics.

Installation work can be tedious. There are many details involving wiring, communications, and configurations. Setup specialists must therefore be patient and thorough, and troubleshooting can be frustrating at times. They must work well under stress and be able to think clearly about how to resolve the issues. If setup specialists are also involved in user training, they must communicate clearly and be understanding of others' problems.

A systems setup specialist installs a hard drive. (Kjetil Kolbjornsrud. Shutterstock.)

■ EMPLOYMENT PROSPECTS
Employers

Many top computer companies are located throughout the United States, and with them come a number of employment opportunities. Some computer hardware powerhouses include Apple, Dell, and HP Inc. Many mid- to small-sized companies may not have the need for a specific department devoted to computer setup. In such situations, other computer professionals may be assigned setup duties besides their regular job descriptions.

A number of jobs may also be found with smaller companies that contract their services to retail stores or offer them directly to the public. Services may include hardware and software installation, upgrading, and repair.

Starting Out

Most positions in systems setup are considered entry level. Those new to the field with little experience may get their start through networking with working computer professionals for potential employment opportunities. Companies advertise job openings for systems setup professionals in the careers section of their Web sites. Job listings are also found through online employment sites such as Monster, Indeed, and SimplyHired, as well as through school career services offices.

■ ADVANCEMENT PROSPECTS

Systems setup specialists may advance by working on increasingly complex systems installations and by having supervisory or managerial responsibility for the setup department. Other specialists choose to pursue promotion in different functional areas, such as technical support, computer engineering, or systems analysis.

Setup specialists who demonstrate strong ability and drive are often assigned to larger and more complex installations. Instead of installing commercial software, for example, the specialist might now be responsible for constructing flow charts or other drawings as part of the overall installation plan. Also, a specialist who at first works on relatively small departmental networks might be asked to work on company-wide networks.

Computer professionals who use systems setup as a springboard to other positions usually have formal education in a certain field, such as software or hardware engineering. They seek promotion by keeping an eye on job openings within their respective fields.

If specialists show leadership ability, they might be promoted to supervisory and then managerial positions. These positions require more administrative duties and less hands-on work. For example, supervisors are usually in charge of scheduling installation jobs and assigning different jobs to various individuals, taking into account their level of expertise and experience. With more formal education, managers might be involved with the strategic planning of a computer company, deciding what level of service the company is willing to offer to clients.

Specialists may also decide to start their own computer business. Many office supply and electronic stores contract with area computer companies to provide customers with services such as setup and installation, upgrading, and technical support. Those who follow this career path should be familiar with the basics of operating a small business, such as doing accounting, marketing, and inventory.

COMPUTER WORKERS

Nearly 1.9 million people are employed in the computer systems design and related services industry. In 2015, the top industries that employed computer user support specialists, and accompanying average salaries, were:

- Computer systems design and related services: 125,440 employed; $54,360
- Management of companies and enterprises: 31,440 employed; $53,150
- Elementary and secondary schools: 30,630 employed; $44,990
- Employment services: 30,180 employed; $49,290
- Colleges, universities, and professional schools: 26,400 employed; $49,280

Source: U.S. Bureau of Labor Statistics

■ OUTLOOK

Industry experts predict that demand for systems setup specialists will grow faster than the average for all other occupations. The U.S. Department of Labor reports that computer support specialists will have 12 percent employment growth through 2024. This outlook, however, may be somewhat tempered by the economic fluctuations in the technology industry as a whole. Nevertheless, the outlook remains good for systems setup specialists.

The ability to network and share information within the company allows businesses to be productive and work more efficiently. As new technology is developed, companies may upgrade, or replace their systems altogether. Skilled workers will be in demand by companies to staff their technical support departments and provide services ranging from setup and installation to diagnostics.

Also, because of falling hardware and software prices, it has become more affordable for consumers to purchase technology for use in the home. Although advances in software technology have made program installation easy, computer companies will continue to offer installation services as a way to win customers from competitors. In addition, fierce competition will push companies to provide increasingly specialized service in terms of customization of computer systems. As computers become more sophisticated, highly trained setup specialists will be needed to install them correctly. It will essential for setup specialists to stay up to date with technological advances through continuing education, seminars, or work training.

■ UNIONS AND ASSOCIATIONS

Systems setup specialists are not represented by unions, but they can obtain useful resources and professional support from the Association of Support Professionals, Association for Computing Machinery, and the IEEE Computer Society.

■ TIPS FOR ENTRY

1. Join professional associations such as the Association of Support Professionals and the Association for Computing Machinery to access training and networking resources, industry publications, and employment opportunities.
2. Visit the following Web sites for job listings:
   - http://www.dice.com
   - https://www.computer.org/portal/web/careers
   - http://jobs.acm.org
3. Read *ACM Career News* at http://www.acm.org/membership/careernews/current to keep up to date on career trends and get job-search tips.

■ FOR MORE INFORMATION

The Association for Computing Machinery provides education, publications, conferences, and career resources for computing machinery professionals.

Association for Computing Machinery (ACM)
2 Penn Plaza, Suite 701
New York, NY 10121-0701
Tel: (800) 342-6626; (212) 626-0500
Fax: (212) 944-1318
E-mail: acmhelp@acm.org
http://www.acm.org

The Association of Support Professionals publishes research reports on topics that include compensation, fee-based support, and services marketing.

Association of Support Professionals (ASP)
38954 Proctor Boulevard, #396
Sandy, OR 97055-8039
Tel: (503) 668-9004
http://www.asponline.com

The IEEE Computer Society provides education, conferences and events, job postings, volunteer opportunities, and other resources for computer science and technology professionals and students.

IEEE Computer Society
2001 L Street, NW, Suite 700
Washington, D.C. 20036-4928
Tel: (202) 371-0101
Fax: (202) 728-9614
https://www.computer.org

Tailors and Dressmakers

■ OVERVIEW

Tailors and *dressmakers* cut, sew, mend, and alter clothing. Typically, tailors work only with menswear, such as suits, jackets, and coats, while dressmakers work with women's clothing, including dresses, blouses, suits, evening wear, wedding and bridesmaids gowns, and sportswear. Tailors and dressmakers are employed in dressmaking and custom-tailor shops, department stores, and garment factories; others are self-employed. Tailors, dressmakers, and custom sewers hold about 19,980 jobs in the United States.

■ HISTORY

The practice of making and wearing clothing evolved from the need for warmth and protection from injury. For example, in prehistoric times, people wrapped themselves in the warm skins of animals they killed for food. Throughout history, clothing has been made by both men and women, in all cultures and every economic and social class.

Early clothing styles developed according to the climate of the geographical area: skirts and loose blouses of thin fabrics in warmer climates, pants and coats of heavier fabrics in cold climates. Religious customs and occupations also influenced clothing styles. As civilizations grew more and more advanced, clothing as necessity evolved into clothing as fashion.

The invention of the spinning wheel, in use in the 12th century, sped the process of making threads and yarns. With the invention of the two-bar loom, fabric making increased, styles became more detailed, and clothing became more widely available. Fabric production further increased with other inventions, such as the spinning jenny that could spin more than one thread at a time, power looms that ran on steam, and the cotton gin. The invention of the sewing machine tremendously sped the production of garments, although tailors and dressmakers were never completely replaced by machines.

During the Industrial Revolution, factories replaced craft shops. High-production apparel companies employed hundreds of workers. Employees worked 12- to 14-hour workdays for low hourly pay in crowded rooms with poor ventilation and lighting. The poor working conditions of these factories, known as "sweatshops," led to the founding of the International Ladies Garment Workers Union in 1900 and the Amalgamated Clothing Workers of America in 1914; these unions protected workers' rights, ensured their safety, and led to greatly improved working conditions.

Today, the precise skills of tailors and dressmakers are still in demand at factories, stores, and small shops. The limited investment required to cut and sew garments, the wide availability of fabrics, and the demand for one-of-a-kind, tailor-made garments are factors that continue to provide opportunities for self-employed tailors and dressmakers.

■ THE JOB

Some tailors and dressmakers make garments from start to completion. In larger shops, however, each employee usually works on a specific task, such as measuring, patternmaking, cutting, fitting, or stitching. One worker, for example, may only sew in sleeves or pad lapels. Smaller shops may only measure and fit the garment, then send piecework to outside contractors. Some tailors and dressmakers specialize in one type of garment, such as suits or wedding gowns. Many also do alterations on factory-made clothing.

Tailors and dressmakers may run their own business, work in small shops, or work in the custom-tailoring section of large department stores. Some work out of their home. Retail clothing stores, specialty stores, bridal shops, and dry cleaners also employ tailors and dressmakers to do alterations.

Tailors and dressmakers first help customers choose the garment style and fabric, using their knowledge of the various types of fabrics. They take the customer's measurements, such as height, shoulder width, arm

CAREER LADDER

Shop Owner or Fashion Designer

Tailor/Dressmaker

Sewer or Alterer

length, and waist, and they note any special figure problems. They may use ready-made paper patterns or make one of their own. The patterns are then placed on the fabric, and the fabric pieces are carefully cut. When the garment design is complex, or if there are special fitting problems, the tailor or dressmaker may cut the pattern from inexpensive muslin and fit it to the customer; any adjustments are then marked and transferred to the paper pattern before it is used to cut the actual garment fabric. The fabric is pieced together first and then sewn by hand or machine. After one or two fittings, which confirm that the garment fits the customer properly, the tailor or dressmaker finishes the garment with hems, buttons, trim, and a final pressing.

Some tailors or dressmakers specialize in a certain aspect of the garment-making process. *Bushelers* work in factories to repair flaws and correct imperfect sewing in finished garments. *Shop tailors* have a detailed knowledge of special tailoring tasks. They use shears or a knife to trim and shape the edges of garments before sewing, attach shoulder pads, and sew linings in coats. *Skilled tailors* put fine stitching on lapels and pockets, make buttonholes, and sew on trim.

■ EARNINGS

Salaries for tailors and dressmakers vary widely, depending on experience, skill, and location. The median annual

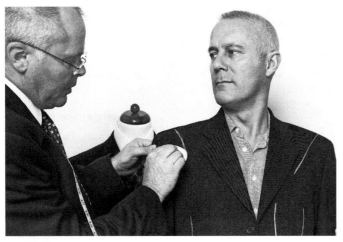

A tailor makes chalk marks on a suit during a fitting. (RTimages. Shutterstock.)

salary for tailors, dressmakers, and custom sewers reported by the U.S. Department of Labor in May 2015 was $25,830 for full-time work. The lowest paid 10 percent earned less than $18,520 a year, while the highest paid 10 percent earned more than $41,390 annually.

Workers employed by large companies and retail stores receive benefits such as paid holidays and vacations, health insurance, and pension plans. They are often affiliated with UNITE HERE, the major labor union in the industry. Self-employed tailors and dressmakers and small-shop workers usually provide their own benefits.

■ WORK ENVIRONMENT

Tailors and dressmakers in large shops work 40 to 48 hours a week, sometimes including Saturdays. Union members usually work 35 to 40 hours a week. Those who run their own businesses often work longer hours. Spring and fall are usually the busiest times.

Since tailoring and dressmaking require a minimal investment, some tailors and dressmakers work out of their homes. Those who work in the larger apparel plants may find the conditions less pleasant. The noise of the machinery can be nerve-wracking, the dye from the fabric may be irritating to the eyes and the skin, and some factories are old and not well maintained.

Much of the work is done sitting down, in one location, and may include fine detail work that can be time consuming. The work may be tiring and tedious and occasionally can cause eyestrain. In some cases, tailors and dressmakers deal directly with customers, who may be either pleasant to interact with, or difficult and demanding.

This type of work, however, can be very satisfying to people who enjoy using their hands and skills to create something. It can be gratifying to complete a project properly, and many workers in this field take great pride in their workmanship.

■ EXPLORING

Take sewing classes at school. Also, check with the local library, community center, or fabric and craft stores—they often offer lessons year-round. Find summer or part-time employment at a local tailor shop. This will give you valuable work experience. Contact schools regarding their programs in fashion design. If their course descriptions sound interesting, take a class or two. You can also create and sew your own designs or offer mending and alteration services to family and friends. Finally, visit department stores, clothing specialty stores, and tailor's shops to observe workers involved in this field.

EDUCATION AND TRAINING REQUIREMENTS
High School

Get as much experience as possible by taking any sewing, tailoring, and clothing classes offered by vocational or family and consumer science departments. There are also a number of institutions that offer either on-site or home-study courses in sewing and dressmaking. Art classes in sketching and design are also helpful. Math classes, such as algebra and geometry, will help hone abilities to work with numbers and to visualize shapes.

Postsecondary Training

Tailors and dressmakers must have at least a high school education, although employers prefer college graduates with advanced training in sewing, tailoring, draping, pat-ternmaking, and design. A limited number of schools and colleges in the United States offer this type of training, including Philadelphia University, the Fashion Institute of Technology in New York City, and Parsons The New School for Design, also in New York. Students who are interested in furthering their career, and perhaps expand-ing from tailoring into design, may want to consider study-ing in one of these specialized institutions. It is, however, entirely possible to enter this field without a college degree.

Some aspiring tailors and dressmakers train for the field by completing apprenticeships with experienced workers.

CERTIFICATION, LICENSING, AND SPECIAL REQUIREMENTS
Certification or Licensing

There are no certification or licensing requirements for tailors and dressmakers.

EXPERIENCE, SKILLS, AND PERSONALITY TRAITS

Try to obtain experience sewing and creating garments. Some aspiring tailors and dressmakers complete appren-ticeships with experienced workers.

Workers in this field must have the ability to sew very well, both by hand and machine, follow directions, and measure accurately. In addition to these skills, tailors and dressmakers must have a good eye for color and style. They need to know how to communicate with and satisfy customers. Strong interpersonal skills will help tailors and dressmakers get and keep clients.

EMPLOYMENT PROSPECTS
Employers

Tailors, dressmakers, and custom sewers hold about 19,980 jobs in the United States. Those interested in high fashion should check out haute couture houses such as

---

INVENTING THE SEWING MACHINE
MILESTONES

It took more than one individual's ingenuity to develop the greatest sewing invention of all time—the sewing machine.

- Thomas Saint designed a machine in 1790 that could work with leather and canvas. However, he built only a patent model and never mass-produced his invention.
- Barthélemy Thimonnier's invention, built in 1829, is considered the first practical sewing machine. Made entirely of wood, and using a barbed needle, this machine was able to sew a chain stitch. Thimonnier mass-produced his machines and was under contract with the French government to sew army uniforms. Local tailors, afraid of the competition, raided his shop and destroyed his sewing machines. Thimonnier was able to save one machine and fled to America.
- Elias Howe is mistakenly credited with inventing the first practical sewing machine in 1844 and patenting it in 1846. After marketing his machine abroad, Howe returned to America and found many other companies had infringed on his patent. He successfully sued.
- Isaac Merritt Singer did much for the industry by mass-producing the first practical sewing machine. He also allowed the public to purchase machines on credit and implemented an aggressive sales campaign. Today, Singer Corporation continues to manufacture and sell consumer sewing machines.

Chanel or Yves Saint Laurent. These industry giants deal with expensive fabrics and innovative designs. They also cater to a high level of clientele. Be prepared for stiff com-petition, because such businesses will consider only the most experienced, highly skilled tailors and dressmakers.

Tailors and dressmakers employed at retail depart-ment stores make alterations on ready-to-wear clothing sold on the premises. They may perform a small task, such as hemming pants or suit sleeves, or a major project such as custom fitting a wedding dress.

Experienced tailors or dressmakers may start their own businesses by making clothes and taking orders from those who like their work. Capital needed to start such a venture is minimal, since the most important equip-ment, such as a sewing machine, iron and ironing board, scissors, and notions, are widely available and relatively inexpensive. Shop space will need to be rented, unless it's a home business. Careful planning is needed to prepare for a self-owned tailoring or dressmaking business, and

TYPES OF PINS

DID YOU KNOW?

Most modern pins are made of brass, nickel-plated steel, or stainless steel. There are different kinds of pins, each designed for a specific sewing purpose.

- *Dressmaker pins* are considered all-purpose pins, though usually not used for fine materials such as silk. They have regular, glass, or plastic heads.
- *Silk pins* make only small puncture holes, so they are best suited for fine silk and synthetic materials.
- *Ballpoint pins* are designed to slide between fibers, so they are best suited for knits.
- *Pleating pins* are designed for light- to medium-weight woven and knit fabrics.
- *Quilting pins* are longer and heavier pins used for heavy, bulky fabrics.
- *T-pins* are used for crafts and for pinning heavy fabrics. Their heads are long and flat, giving the pin a T shape.
- *Sequin* pins are short and are primarily used for pinning sequins and beads.

knowledge of bookkeeping, accounting, and inventory is essential. Marketing is also important since the owner of a business must know how to attract customers.

Starting Out

Custom-tailor shops or garment-manufacturing centers sometimes offer apprenticeships to students or recent graduates, which give them a start in the business. As a beginner you may also find work in related jobs, such as a *sewer* or *alterer* in a custom-tailoring or dressmaking shop, garment factory, dry-cleaning store, or department store. Apply directly to such companies and shops and monitor local newspaper ads for openings as well. Check with your school's career center for industry information or job leads. Trade schools and colleges that have programs in textiles or fashion often offer their students help with job placement.

■ ADVANCEMENT PROSPECTS

Workers in this field usually start by performing simple tasks. As they gain more experience and their skills improve, they may be assigned to more difficult and complicated tasks. However, advancement in the industry is typically somewhat limited. In factories, a production worker might be promoted to the position of line supervisor. Tailors and dressmakers can move to a better shop that offers higher pay or open their own business.

Some workers may find that they have an eye for color and style and an aptitude for design. With further training at an appropriate college, these workers may find a successful career in fashion design and merchandising.

■ OUTLOOK

According to the U.S. Department of Labor, employment prospects in this industry are expected to decline through 2024. Attributing factors include the low cost and ready availability of factory-made clothing and the invention of labor-saving machinery such as computerized sewing and cutting machines. In fact, automated machines are expected to replace many sewing jobs in the next decade. In addition, the apparel industry has declined domestically as many businesses choose to produce their items abroad, where labor is cheap and, many times, unregulated.

Tailors and dressmakers who do reliable and skillful work, however, particularly in the areas of mending and alterations, should be able to find employment. This industry is large, employing thousands of people. Many job openings will be created as current employees leave the workforce due to retirement or other reasons.

■ UNIONS AND ASSOCIATIONS

UNITE HERE is a union that represents the professional interests of tailors and dressmakers. Other organizations that provide useful resources and professional support include the American Apparel & Footwear Association and Custom Tailors and Designers Association. The Distance Education Accrediting Commission provides a list of home-study institutions offering sewing and dressmaking courses.

■ TIPS FOR ENTRY

1. Visit the following Web sites for job listings:
   - http://fashioncareers.jobs.careercast.com
   - https://www.fashion.net/jobs
   - http://www.creativejobscentral.com/fashion-jobs
   - http://www.careerbuilder.com
   - http://www.fashion-jobs.biz
2. Join UNITE HERE to increase your chances of landing a job and receiving fair pay for your work.
3. Participate in information interviews with tailors and dressmakers. Ask them for some tips on how to best break into the field.

■ FOR MORE INFORMATION

The American Apparel and Footwear Association represents apparel, footwear, and other sewn products companies and their suppliers.

**American Apparel and Footwear
   Association (AAFA)**
740 6th Street, NW
Washington, D.C. 20001-3798
Tel: (202) 853-9080
https://www.wewear.org

*The Association of Sewing and Design Professionals offers
seminars, classes, meetings, and other resources.*
**Association of Sewing and Design
   Professionals (ASDP)**
2885 Sanford Aveue SW, #19588
Grandville, MI 49418-1342
Tel: (877) 755-0303
E-mail: admin@sewingprofessionals.org
http://www.sewingprofessionals.org

*The Custom Tailors and Designers Association is a profes-
sional membership organization for custom tailors and
designers.*
**Custom Tailors and Designers
   Association (CTDA)**
229 Forest Hills Road
Rochester, NY 14625-1948
Tel: (888) 248-2832
E-mail: info@ctda.com
http://www.ctda.com

*The Distance Education Accrediting Commission provides
information on accredited distance education institutions
and home-study programs.*
**Distance Education Accrediting
   Commission (DEAC)**
1101 17th Street, NW, Suite 808
Washington, D.C. 20036-4704
Tel: (202) 234-5100
Fax: (202) 332-1386
http://www.deac.org

*The Fashion Institute of Design and Merchandising offers
bachelor's and associate's degree programs in design and
creative business.*
**Fashion Institute of Design and
   Merchandising (FIDM)**
919 South Grand Avenue
Los Angeles, CA 90015-1421
Tel: (800) 624-1200
http://fidm.edu

*The Fashion Institute of Technology offers college classes in
garment design and sewing.*

Fashion Institute of Technology (FIT)
227 West 27th Street
New York, NY 10001-5992
Tel: (212) 217-7999
http://www.fitnyc.edu

*Parsons - The New School of Design offers classes in gar-
ment design and sewing.*
Parsons - The New School of Design
66 West 12th Street
New York, NY 10011-8603
Tel: (212) 229-8989
E-mail: thinkparsons@newschool.edu
http://www.newschool.edu/parsons

*Philadelphia University offers fashion design and other
related courses.*
Philadelphia University
4201 Henry Avenue
Philadelphia, PA 19144-5409
Tel: (215) 951-2700
http://www.philau.edu

*This union fights for workers' rights and represents workers
in various industries, including basic apparel and textiles.*
UNITE HERE!
275 7th Avenue
New York, NY 10001-6708
Tel: (212) 265-7000
http://unitehere.org

Talent Agents and Scouts

■ OVERVIEW

An *agent* is a salesperson who sells artistic or athletic
talent. *Talent agents* act as representatives for actors,
directors, writers, models, athletes, and other people
who work in the arts, advertising, sports, and fashion.
Agents promote their clients' talent and manage their
legal contractual business. *Talent scouts* work for production companies, sports teams, or music producers and
recruit talented people to perform in movies, television
shows, or theatrical productions.

■ HISTORY

The wide variety of careers that exists in the film and
television industries today evolved gradually. In the

QUICK FACTS

ALTERNATE TITLE(S)
Acting Agents, Artist's Agents, Broadcasting Agents, Literary Agents, Modeling Agents, Sports Agents

DUTIES
Promote performing arts talent to film and television studios, recording companies, advertising firms, publishers, and other organizations; manage the careers of talent

SALARY RANGE
$28,060 to $62,940 to $187,200+

WORK ENVIRONMENT
Primarily Indoors

BEST GEOGRAPHIC LOCATION(S)
Los Angeles, New York City, Nashville, and other cities with major entertainment industries

MINIMUM EDUCATION LEVEL
Bachelor's Degree

SCHOOL SUBJECTS
Business, English, Mathematics

EXPERIENCE
Internship; entry level experience required

PERSONALITY TRAITS
Enterprising, Organized, Outgoing

SKILLS
Business Management, Interpersonal, Sales

CERTIFICATION OR LICENSING
Required

SPECIAL REQUIREMENTS
None

EMPLOYMENT PROSPECTS
Fair

ADVANCEMENT PROSPECTS
Fair

OUTLOOK
About as Fast as the Average

NOC
1123

O*NET-SOC
13-1011.00

19th century in England and America, leading actors and actresses developed a system, called the "actor-manager system," in which the actor both performed and handled business and financial arrangements. Over the course of the 20th century, responsibilities diversified. In the first decades of the century, major studios took charge of the actors' professional and financial management.

In the 1950s, the major studio monopolies were broken, and control of actors and contracts came up for grabs. Resourceful, business-minded people became agents when they realized that there was money to be made by controlling access to the talent behind movie and television productions. They became middlemen between actors (and other creative people) and the production studios, charging commissions for use of their clients.

Currently, commissions range between 10 and 15 percent of the money an actor earns in a production. In more recent years, agents have formed revolutionary deals for their stars, making more money for agencies and actors alike. Powerful agencies such as Creative Artists Agency, International Creative Management, and the William Morris Agency (now called William Morris Endeavor Entertainment) are credited with (or, by some, accused of) heralding in the age of the multimillion-dollar deal for film stars. This has proved controversial, as some top actor fees have inflated to more than $20 million per picture; some industry professionals worry that high actor salaries are cutting too deeply into film budgets, while others believe that actors are finally getting their fair share of the profits. Whichever the case, the film industry still thrives, and filmmakers still compete for the highest priced talent. And the agent, always an active player in the industry, has become even more influential in how films are made.

In the 1960s, a number of models became popular celebrity figures, such as Jean Shrimpton, Twiggy, and Varushka, who were noted not only for their modeling work but also for the image and lifestyle they portrayed. In the early days of the fashion industry, models were the products of modeling schools, which also monitored their work schedules. However, as the industry grew and individual models became successful, models often needed, and relied, on someone to manage and organize their careers. Thus, modeling agencies developed to fill this niche. Ford Models Inc., an agency founded in 1946 by Eileen and Jerry Ford, was one of the first modern agencies devoted to promoting the career of the fashion model. The agency made fashion history by negotiating the first big-money contract between model Lauren Hutton and Revlon. Today, Ford Models is an industry leader, employing many talented agents and scouts internationally to represent hundreds of the world's top models.

Sports figures, like movie stars and models, have become internationally recognized figures, renowned not only for their athletic prowess, but also for their charismatic personalities. Like movie stars, athletes began to realize the need to have talented representation—or agents—to protect and promote their interests during contract negotiations. In addition, today's sports agents handle most, if not all, aspects of a professional athlete's career, from commercial endorsements to financial investments to post-retirement career offers.

■ THE JOB

Talent agents act as representatives for actors, writers, artists, models, and others who work in performing and visual arts, fashion, and advertising. They look for clients who have potential for success and then work aggressively to promote their clients to film and television directors, casting directors, production companies, advertising companies, publishers, catalog companies, photographers, galleries, and other potential employers. Agents work closely with clients to find assignments that will best achieve clients' career goals.

Agents find clients in several ways. Those who work for an agency might be assigned a client by the agency, based on experience or a compatible personality. Some agents also work as talent scouts and actively search for new clients, whom they then bring to an agency. Or the clients themselves might approach agents who have good reputations and request their representation. The methods agents use to locate talent are different, depending on each agent's specialty. *Modeling, acting,* and *broadcasting agents* review portfolios, screen tests, and audio recordings to evaluate potential clients' appearance, voice, personality, experience, ability to take direction, and other factors. A *literary agent* reads scripts, books, articles, short stories, and poetry submitted by writers. An *artist's agent* looks at portfolios and original works of art, visits galleries, attends art fairs, and visits student exhibitions. All agents consider a client's potential for a long career—it is important to find people who will grow, develop their skills, and eventually create a continuing demand for their talents.

When an agent agrees to represent a client, they both sign a contract that specifies the extent of representation, the time period, payment, and other legal considerations.

When agents look for jobs for their clients, they do not necessarily try to find as many assignments as possible. Agents carefully choose assignments that will further their clients' careers. For example, an agent might represent an actor who wants to work in film, but is having difficulty finding a role. The agent looks for roles in commercials, music videos, or voice-overs that will give the actor some exposure. A model's agent might find shooting assignments for fashion catalogs while searching for a high-profile assignment with a beauty and fashion magazine.

Agents also work closely with the potential employers of their clients. They need to satisfy the requirements of both parties. Agents who represent actors have a network of directors, producers, advertising executives, and photographers that they contact frequently to see if any of their clients can meet their needs. Models' agents are in touch with magazine and catalog publishers, advertising firms, fashion designers, and event planners. Literary agents have contacts in the publishing world, including small and large presses, magazines, and newspapers. Artists' representatives know gallery owners, art dealers, and art book publishers.

When agents see a possible match between employer and client, they speak to both and quickly organize meetings, interviews, or auditions so that employers can meet potential hires and evaluate their work and capabilities. Agents must be persistent and aggressive on behalf of their clients. They spend time on the phone with employers, convincing them of their clients' talents and persuading them to hire their clients. There may be one or several interviews, and the agent may coach clients through this process to make sure clients understand what the employer is looking for and adapt their presentations

accordingly. When a client achieves success and is in great demand, the agent receives calls, scripts, and other types of work requests and passes along only those that are appropriate to the interests and goals of the client.

When an employer agrees to hire a client, the agent helps negotiate a contract that outlines salary, benefits, promotional appearances, and other fees, rights, and obligations. Agents have to look out for the best interests of their clients and at the same time satisfy employers in order to establish continuing, long-lasting relationships.

CAREER LADDER

Movie Studio or Music Company Head

Talent Agency Head

Senior Agent

Talent Agent and Scout

Assistant to Agent

In addition to promoting individuals, agents may also work to make package deals—for example, combining a writer, director, and a star to make up a package, which they then market to production studios. The agent charges a packaging commission to the studio in addition to the commissions agreed to in each package member's contract. A strong package can be very lucrative for the agency or agencies who represent the talent involved, since the package commission is often a percentage of the total budget of the production.

Agents often develop lifelong working relationships with their clients. They act as business associates, advisers, advocates, mentors, teachers, guardians, and confidantes. Because of the complicated nature of these relationships, they can be volatile, so a successful relationship requires trust and respect on both sides, which can be earned only through experience and time. Agents who represent high-profile talent make up only a small percentage of agency work. Most agents represent lesser known or locally known talent.

The largest agencies are located in Los Angeles and New York City, where film, theater, advertising, publishing, fashion, and art-buying industries are centered. There are modeling and theatrical agencies in most large cities, however, and independent agents are established throughout the country.

■ EARNINGS

Earnings for agents vary greatly, depending on the success of the agent and his or her clients. An agency receives 10 to 15 percent of a client's fee for a project. An agent is then paid a commission by the agency as well

Actor James Franco poses with his agent Kevin Huvane, managing partner and director of Creative Arts Agency. (Helga Esteb. Shutterstock.)

as a base salary. According to the U.S. Department of Labor (DOL), agents and business managers of artists, performers, and athletes earned a median annual salary of $62,940 in May 2015. The lowest paid 10 percent earned less than $28,060 a year, while the highest paid 10 percent earned more than $187,200 annually.

Salaries for fashion model agents depend on the agent's experience, the size and location of the agency, and the models represented. An agent with previous agency experience can earn about $50,000 per year or more. Agents at the top of the industry may make in the hundreds of thousands of dollars. Some agencies choose to pay their agents a commission based on fees generated by model/client bookings. These commissions normally range from 10 to 15 percent of booking totals.

Literary agents also generally earn median salaries of $50,000, with a rare few making hundreds of thousands of dollars a year. Commissions range from 4 to 20 percent of their clients' earnings.

Talent agents and scouts working in the motion picture and video industries earned mean annual salaries of $113,120 in May 2015, according to the DOL. Those working for smaller companies generally earn less.

Experienced agents who work full time at agencies typically receive health and retirement benefits, bonuses, and paid travel and accommodations.

■ WORK ENVIRONMENT

Work in a talent agency can be lively and exciting. It is rewarding for agent's to watch a client attain success with their help. The work may seem glamorous, allowing agents to rub elbows with the rich and famous and make contacts with the most powerful people in entertainment, sports, fashion, or publishing. Most agents, however, represent less-famous actors, artists, models, authors, and athletes.

Agents' work requires a great deal of stamina and determination in the face of setbacks. The work can be extremely stressful, even in small agencies. It often demands long hours, including evenings and weekends. To remain successful, agents at the top of the industry must constantly network. They spend a great deal of time on the telephone, with both clients and others in the industry, and attending industry functions.

■ EXPLORING

Learn as much as possible about the industry that interests you. If it's film, read publications agents read, such as *Variety* (http://variety.com), The *Hollywood Reporter* (http://www.hollywoodreporter.com), and *Entertainment Weekly* (http://www.ew.com). Watch current movies to get a sense of the established and up-and-coming talents in the film industry. Track the careers of actors whom you like, including their early work in independent films, commercials, and stage work.

For sports, watch games and pay attention to the negotiations for players. Read media reports on the management, coaching, and team-building strategies for professional sports.

To explore the world of fashion and modeling, read *Vogue* (http://www.vogue.com), and other beauty and glamour magazines. Attend fashion shows. Learn about fashion photography.

If interested in art or literature, study both historical and current trends. There are numerous art and literary review publications in the library and on newsstands. Look for *Art Business News Magazine* (http://artbusinessnews.com) and *Communication Arts* (http://www.commarts.com).

If you live in Los Angeles or New York, you may be able to volunteer or intern at an agency to find out more about the career. If you live outside Los Angeles and New York, search the Web for listings of local agencies. Most major cities have agents who represent local performing artists, actors, and models. Contact them to see if they can offer some insight into the nature of talent management in general.

■ EDUCATION AND TRAINING REQUIREMENTS
High School

Take courses in business, mathematics, and accounting to prepare for the management aspects of an agent's job. Take English and speech courses to develop good communication skills because an agent must be gifted at negotiation. Agents also need a good eye for talent, so it's important to develop some expertise in film, theater, art, literature, advertising, or another specialty field.

Postsecondary Training

There are no formal requirements for becoming an agent, but a bachelor's degree is strongly recommended. Advanced degrees in law and business are becoming increasingly prevalent; law and business training are useful because agents are responsible for writing contracts according to legal regulations. However, in some cases an agent may obtain this training on the job. Agents come from a variety of backgrounds; some have worked as actors or other creative professionals and then shifted into agent careers because they enjoyed working in the industry. Agents who have degrees from law or business schools have an advantage when it comes to advancing their careers or opening a new agency.

Other Education or Training

The Association of Talent Agents offers symposiums on entertainment law and other industry-related topics.

■ CERTIFICATION, LICENSING, AND SPECIAL REQUIREMENTS
Certification or Licensing

Many states require agents who operate their own businesses to be licensed. Contact officials in the state in which you are interested in working for specific requirements.

■ EXPERIENCE, SKILLS, AND PERSONALITY TRAITS

Several years of prior experience as an intern or volunteer at a talent agency is helpful. This experience provides an advantage when it comes to landing a job.

It is most important to be willing to work hard and aggressively pursue opportunities for clients. Talent agents and scouts should have a good head for business; contract work requires meticulous attention to detail. They also need a great deal of self-motivation and

---

TALENT MANAGEMENT

LEARN MORE ABOUT IT

Burr, Sherri L. *Entertainment Law in a Nutshell,* 3rd ed. Eagan, Minn.: West Publishing, 2012.

Janson, Kimberly. *Demystifying Talent Management: Unleash People's Potential to Deliver Superior Results.* Palmyra, Va.: Maven House, 2015.

Kemper, Tom. *Hidden Talent: The Emergence of Hollywood Agents*. Berkeley, Calif.: University of California Press, 2009.

Litwak, Mark. *Contracts for the Film & Television Industry,* 3rd ed. Silman-James Press, 2012.

Thompson, Anne. *The $11 Billion Year: From Sundance to the Oscars, an Inside Look at the Changing Hollywood System.* New York: HarperCollins Publishers, 2014.

---

ambition to develop good contacts in industries that may be difficult to break into. Successful agents and scouts are comfortable talking with all kinds of people and are able to develop relationships easily. It helps to be a good general conversationalist in addition to being knowledgeable about the field in which they specialize.

■ EMPLOYMENT PROSPECTS
Employers

Talent agencies are located throughout the United States, handling a variety of talents. Those agencies that represent artists and professionals in the film industry are located primarily in Los Angeles. Some film agencies, such as William Morris Endeavor (WME), are located in New York City. An agency may specialize in a particular type of talent, such as minority actors, extras, or TV commercial actors. The top three film agencies that employ agents are the Creative Artists Agency, ICM Partners, and WME. The Association of Authors' Representatives has a list of member agencies, and the vast majority are located in New York City. The top modeling agencies, such as Wilhelmina, Ford, and Elite, have offices in New York City, Los Angeles, and Miami, but there are talent/modeling agencies in all metropolitan areas.

Starting Out

The best way to enter this field is through an internship with an agency. Many talent agents and scouts get their start through an internship with an agency. Those who live in Los Angeles or New York have access to opportunities for internships, part-time jobs, and even volunteer work. Search the Web sites of talent agencies as well as SAG-AFTRA for current listings of available internships and job openings. There are also employment agencies that focus specifically on certain media, such as film and entertainment, and deal with talent agencies; these can be found through online searches.

ADVANCEMENT PROSPECTS

Assistants in talent agencies gain skills and advance their careers by working closely with agents to learn the ropes. They may be able to read contracts and listen in on phone calls and meetings. They begin to take on some of their own clients as they gain experience. Agents who wish to advance must work aggressively on behalf of their clients as well as seek out quality talent to bring into an agency. Those who are successful command more lucrative salaries and may choose to open their own agencies. Some agents find that their work is a good stepping-stone toward a different career in the industry.

OUTLOOK

Employment in the arts and entertainment field is expected to grow rapidly in response to the demand for entertainment from a growing population. However, the numbers of artists and performers also continues to grow, creating fierce competition for all jobs in this industry. This competition will drive the need for more agents and scouts to find talented individuals and place them in the best jobs. This trend will also create strong competition for jobs. Many agents have trouble breaking into the business and holding full-time positions. Many, frustrated by the strong competition, leave the field for other jobs.

The film industry is expected to have steady growth at the box office in the coming years. Markets overseas are expanding, so even the films that don't do well domestically can still turn a tidy profit. As a result, agents at all levels in the film industry will continue to be needed. Also, more original cable television programming and shows for on-demand and streaming video services will lead to more actors and performers seeking representation.

The fashion and modeling industries fluctuate slightly with the economy. During recession periods, consumers are likely to spend less, and advertisers plan more modest campaigns. There is stiff competition among the vast numbers of hopeful models for the relatively few available positions, and it takes skillful agents to find the best assignments for their clients.

Artists' and authors' agents play an important role in getting their clients' work seen and read. Most book publishers will not even consider a manuscript unless it is submitted through a reputable agent.

UNIONS AND ASSOCIATIONS

Talent agents are not represented by unions, but they can join professional associations such as the Association of Talent Agents, Association of Authors' Representatives, and North American Performing Arts Managers and Agents.

TIPS FOR ENTRY

1. Attend industry events to network.
2. Apply for an entry-level position at a talent agency. The Association of Talent Agents offers a list of agents at its Web site, http://www.agentassociation.com.
3. Participate in internships or part-time jobs at talent agencies to build your skills and make networking contacts.

FOR MORE INFORMATION

This organization's Web site lists member agencies, offers a newsletter and blog, and provides links to other literary sites.

Association of Authors' Representatives (AAR)
302A West 12th Street, #122
New York, NY 10014-6036
E-mail: administrator@aaronline.org
http://www.aaronline.org

The Association of Talent Agents is a trade association for talent agencies across the United States.

Association of Talent Agents (ATA)
9255 Sunset Boulevard, Suite 930
Los Angeles, CA 90069-3317
Tel: (310) 274-0628
Fax: (310) 274 - 5063
E-mail: info@agentassociation.com
http://www.agentassociation.com

The North American Performing Arts Managers and Agents promotes the best interests of performing arts agents and managers through professional development, leadership, and alliances in the industry.

North American Performing Arts Managers and Agents (NAPAMA)
459 Columbus Avenue, Suite 133
New York, NY 10024-5129
http://www.napama.org

The SAG-AFTRA Web site provides information about acting and a list of talent agencies.

SAG-AFTRA
5757 Wilshire Boulevard, 7th Floor
Los Angeles, CA 90036-3600
Tel: (855) 724-2387
http://www.sagaftra.org

Tax Preparers

OVERVIEW

Tax preparers prepare income tax returns for individuals and small businesses for a fee, for either quarterly or yearly filings. They help to establish and maintain business records to expedite tax preparations and may advise clients on how to save money on their tax payments. There are approximately 72,060 tax preparers employed in the United States.

HISTORY

President Franklin D. Roosevelt once said, "Taxes are the dues that we pay for the privileges of membership in an organized society." Although most people grumble about paying income taxes and filling out tax forms, everyone carries a share of the burden, and it is still possible to keep a sense of humor about income taxes. As Benjamin Franklin succinctly said, "In this world nothing can be said to be certain, except death and taxes."

Personal income tax may be the most familiar type of taxation, but it is actually a relatively recent method of raising revenue. To raise funds for the Napoleonic Wars between 1799 and 1816, Britain became the first nation to collect income taxes, but a permanent income tax was not established there until 1874. In the same manner, the United States first initiated a temporary income tax during the Civil War. It wasn't until 1913, however, with the adoption of the 16th Amendment to the Constitution, that a tax on personal income became the law of the nation. In addition to the federal income tax, many states and cities have adopted income tax laws. Income taxes are an example of a "progressive tax," one that charges higher percentages of income as people earn more money.

Technology has made it possible to file taxes electronically. Electronic tax filing is a method by which a tax return is converted to a computer-readable form and sent via the Internet to the Internal Revenue Service. Electronically filed tax returns are more accurate than paper filed returns because of the extensive checking performed by the electronic filing software. Detecting and correcting errors early also allows the tax return to flow smoothly through the IRS, speeding up the refund process. Computer software is also available that assists individuals with preparing and filing their own taxes.

THE JOB

Tax preparers help individuals and small businesses keep the proper records to determine their legally required tax and file the proper forms. They must be well acquainted with federal, state, and local tax laws and use their knowledge and skills to help taxpayers take the maximum number of legally allowable deductions.

The first step in preparing tax forms is to collect all the data and documents that are needed to calculate the client's tax liability. The client has to submit documents such as tax returns from previous years, wage and income statements, records of other sources of income, statements of interest and dividends earned, records of expenses, property tax records, and so on. The tax preparer then interviews the client to obtain further information that may have a bearing on the amount of tax owed. If the client is an individual taxpayer, the tax preparer will ask about any important investments, extra expenses that may be deductible, contributions to charity, and insurance payments; events such as marriage, childbirth, and new employment are also important considerations. If the client is a business, the tax preparer may ask about capital gains and losses, taxes already paid, payroll expenses, miscellaneous business expenses, and tax credits.

Once the tax preparer has a complete picture of the client's income and expenses, the proper tax forms and schedules needed to file the tax return can be determined. Some taxpayers have complex finances that take a long time to document and calculate, while others have typical, straightforward returns that take less time. Often the tax preparer can calculate the amount a taxpayer owes, fill out the proper forms, and prepare the complete return in a single interview. When the tax return is more complicated, the tax preparer may have to collect all the data

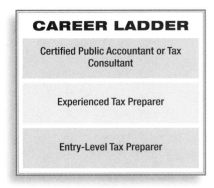

CAREER LADDER

Certified Public Accountant or Tax Consultant

Experienced Tax Preparer

Entry-Level Tax Preparer

during the interview and perform the calculations later. If a client's taxes are unusual or complex, the tax preparer may have to consult tax law handbooks and bulletins.

Computers are the main tools used to figure and prepare tax returns. The tax preparer inputs the data onto a spreadsheet, and the computer calculates and prints out the tax form. Computer software can be versatile and may even print data summary sheets that can serve as checklists and references for the next tax filing.

Tax preparers often have another tax expert or preparer check their work, especially if they work for a tax service firm. The second tax preparer will check to make sure the allowances and deductions taken were proper and that no others were overlooked. They also make certain that the tax laws are interpreted properly and that calculations are correct. It is very important that a tax preparer's work is accurate and error-free, and clients are given a guarantee covering additional taxes or fines if the preparer's work is found to be incorrect. Tax preparers are required by law to sign every return they complete for a client and provide their Social Security number or federal identification number. They must also provide the client with a copy of the tax return and keep a copy in their own files.

■ EARNINGS

According to the U.S. Department of Labor, the median annual income for tax preparers was approximately $36,450 in May 2015. Salaries ranged from less than $19,330 to more than $79,460 annually. Incomes vary widely, however, due to a number of factors.

Tax preparers generally charge a fee per tax return, which may range from $30 to $1,500 or more, depending on the complexity of the return and the preparation time required. The number of clients a preparer has, as well as the difficulty of the returns, can affect the preparer's income. The amount of education a tax preparer has also affects their income. Seasonal or part-time employees, typically those with less education, usually earn minimum wage plus commission. Enrolled agents, certified public accountants, and other professional preparers, typically those with college degrees or more, usually charge more.

Fees also vary widely in different parts of the country. Tax preparers in large cities and in the western United

States generally charge more, as do those who offer year-round financial advice and services.

■ WORK ENVIRONMENT

Tax preparers generally work in office settings that may be located in neighborhood business districts, shopping malls, or other high-traffic areas. Employees of tax service firms may work at storefront desks or in cubicles during the three months preceding the April 15 tax-filing deadline. In addition, many tax preparers work at home to earn extra money while they hold a full-time job.

The hours and schedules that tax preparers work vary greatly, depending on the time of year and the manner in which workers are employed. Because of the changes in tax laws that occur every year, tax preparers often advise their clients throughout the year about possible ways to reduce their tax obligations. The first quarter of the year is the busiest time, and even part-time tax preparers may find themselves working long hours. Workweeks can range from as little as 12 hours to 40 or 50 or more, as tax preparers work late into the evening and on weekends. Tax service firms are usually open seven days a week and 12 hours a day during the first three months of the year. The work is demanding, requiring heavy concentration and long hours sitting at a desk and working on a computer.

■ EXPLORING

Gain some experience by completing income tax returns for yourself and for your family and friends. These returns should be double-checked by the actual taxpayers who will be liable for any fees and extra taxes if the return is prepared incorrectly. Look for internships or part-time jobs in tax service offices and tax preparation firms. Many of these firms operate nationwide, and extra office help might be needed as tax deadlines approach and work becomes hectic. The IRS also trains people to answer tax questions for its 800-number telephone advisory service; they are employed annually during early spring.

Become familiar with the tax preparation software available on the Internet and utilize Web sites to keep abreast of changing laws, regulations, and developments in the industry.

■ EDUCATION AND TRAINING REQUIREMENTS
High School

There are no specific postsecondary educational requirements for tax preparers, but having a high school diploma is helpful. Take mathematics classes. Accounting, bookkeeping, and business classes will also give a good introduction to working with numbers and show the importance of accurate work. In addition, take computer classes. You will need to be comfortable using computers, since much tax work is done using this tool. English classes will help with research, writing, and speaking skills—important communication skills to have when working with clients.

Postsecondary Training

Once high school is completed, it may be possible to find a job as a tax preparer at a large tax-preparing firm. These firms, such as H & R Block, typically require their tax preparers to complete a training program in tax preparation. A college education can mean improved job prospects for tax preparers. Many universities offer individual courses and complete majors in the area of taxation. Another route is to earn a bachelor's degree or master's degree in business administration with a minor or concentration in taxation. Some universities offer master's degrees in taxation.

Other Education or Training

In addition to formal education, tax preparers must continue their professional education. Both federal and state tax laws are revised every year, and the tax preparer is obligated to thoroughly understand these new laws by January 1 of each year. Major tax reform legislation can increase this amount of study even further. One federal reform tax bill can take up thousands of pages, and this can mean up to 60 hours of extra study in a single month to fully understand all the intricacies and implications of the new laws. The National Association of Tax Professionals offers more than 300 live nationwide workshops every year, as well as webinars and other continuing education opportunities. Past classes included "Introduction to Tax Preparation," "Ethics," and "Ins and Outs of Social Security Benefits." Continuing education courses are also provided by the National Society of Tax Professionals and state and local tax associations. Additionally, tax service firms provide classes that explain tax preparation to both professionals and individual taxpayers.

■ CERTIFICATION, LICENSING, AND SPECIAL REQUIREMENTS
Certification or Licensing

Licensing requirements for tax preparers vary by state. They must meet the requirements for the state in which they plan to practice. In general, they must be 18 years of age and have a certain number of hours of formal education and instruction in the tax preparation field.

The Internal Revenue Service (IRS) offers an examination for tax preparers. Those who complete the test

A tax preparer checks her spreadsheet calculations. (Andrey_Popov. Shutterstock.)

successfully are called enrolled agents and are entitled to legally represent any taxpayer in any type of audit before the IRS or state tax boards. Those with prior experience working for the IRS as an auditor or in a higher position may also become enrolled agents without taking the exam. There are no education or experience requirements for taking the examination, but the questions are roughly equivalent to those asked in a college course. Study materials and applications may be obtained from local IRS offices. The IRS does not oversee seasonal tax preparers but local IRS offices may monitor some commercial tax offices.

The Institute of Tax Consultants offers a certification program and the Accreditation Council for Accountancy and Taxation offers the accredited tax preparer, accredited tax advisor, and other credentials.

■ EXPERIENCE, SKILLS, AND PERSONALITY TRAITS

Several years of prior experience at a tax preparation firm is helpful. Tax preparers should have an aptitude

TOP-PAYING INDUSTRIES EMPLOYING TAX PREPARERS AND MEAN ANNUAL EARNINGS, MAY 2015

FAST FACTS

- Other financial investment activities: 200 jobs; $75,530
- Management of companies and enterprises: 100 jobs; $67,720
- Employment services: 130 jobs; $56,160
- Legal services: 430 jobs; $55,190
- Accounting, tax preparation, bookkeeping, and payroll services: 69,090 jobs; $44,560

Source: U.S. Bureau of Labor Statistics

for math and an eye for detail. They should have strong organizational skills and the patience to sift through documents and financial statements. The ability to communicate effectively with clients is also key to be able to explain complex tax procedures and to make customers feel confident and comfortable. Tax preparers also need to work well under the stress and pressure of deadlines. They must be honest, discreet, and trustworthy in dealing with the financial and business affairs of their clients.

EMPLOYMENT PROSPECTS
Employers
There are approximately 72,060 tax preparers employed in the United States. Tax preparers may work for tax service firms that conduct most of their business during tax season. Other tax preparers may be self-employed and work full or part time.

Starting Out
Tax work is seasonal, and most tax firms begin hiring tax preparers in December for the upcoming tax season. Some tax service firms will hire tax preparers from among the graduates of their own training courses. Tax preparers often find job listings through tax preparation firms' Web sites, such as H&R Block, as well as through private and state employment agencies.

There are a large number of Internet sites for this industry, many of which offer job postings. Large tax preparation firms, such as H & R Block, have their own Web sites.

ADVANCEMENT PROSPECTS
Some tax preparers continue their academic education and work toward becoming *certified public accountants*. Others specialize in certain areas of taxation, such as real estate, corporate, or nonprofit work. Tax preparers who specialize in certain fields are able to charge higher fees for their services.

Experienced tax preparers may advance their careers by establishing a private consulting business. They may work alone or grow their business by hiring and managing other tax preparers and support staff.

OUTLOOK
The U.S. Department of Labor predicts that employment for tax preparers will grow more slowly than the average for all occupations through 2024. Tax laws are constantly changing and growing more complex, however, so there will be continued need for tax professionals. Recent surveys of employers in large metropolitan areas have found an adequate supply of tax preparers; prospects for employment may be better in smaller cities or rural areas.

The Patient Protection and Affordable Care Act, enacted in 2010, created job opportunities for tax preparers. Job opportunities will continue for tax professionals who understand the intricacies of the law and who can help clients comply with these regulations and tax provisions.

Tax laws are constantly evolving and people look to tax preparers to save time, money, and frustration, but new tax programs and online resources are easing the process of preparing taxes, lessening the need for outside help. People can easily find information online about tax laws and regulations. Tax tips are readily available, as are online seminars and workshops.

The IRS also offers taxpayers and businesses the option to "e-file," or electronically file their tax returns on the Internet. In tax year 2015, a total of more than 128 million tax returns were e-filed, and of those, 51 million were e-filed by taxpayers from their homes.

UNIONS AND ASSOCIATIONS
Tax preparers do not belong to unions. The National Society of Tax Professionals and the National Association of Tax Professionals are membership organizations that provide continuing education classes, publications, and other resources. The Accreditation Council for Accountancy and Taxation and the Institute of Tax Consultants offer certification.

TIPS FOR ENTRY
1. Join professional associations such as the National Association of Tax Professionals and the National Society of Tax Professionals for access to classes, publications, news and other resources.
2. Get a job or internship at large tax-preparation firms.
3. Talk to tax preparers about their careers. Ask them for tips on breaking into the field.

4. Attend industry conferences—such as the National Association of Tax Professionals' National Conference and Expo—to network and to interview for jobs.

■ FOR MORE INFORMATION

The Accreditation Council for Accountancy and Taxation provides information on exams and credentials for tax preparers.

Accreditation Council for Accountancy and Taxation (ACAT)
1313 Braddock Place, Suite 540
Alexandria, VA 22314-1694
Tel: (888) 289-7763
Fax: (703) 549-2984
http://www.acatcredentials.org

H&R Block offers education and training programs for tax preparers.

H&R Block
Tel: (800) 472-5625
https://www.hrblock.com

The Institute of Tax Consultants offers certification programs for tax consultants.

Institute of Tax Consultants (ITC)
7500 212th SW, Suite 205
Edmonds, WA 98026-7617
Tel: (425) 774-3521
E-mail: kraemerc@juno.com
http://taxprofessionals.homestead.com/welcome.html

The Internal Revenue Service offers certification requirements and other information for tax professionals.

Internal Revenue Service (IRS)
Tel: (800) 829-1040
https://www.irs.gov/for-tax-pros

The National Association of Tax Professionals provides information on educational programs, publications, and online membership.

National Association of Tax Professionals (NATP)
PO Box 8002
Appleton, WI 54912-8002
Tel: (800) 558-3402
Fax: (800) 747-0001
E-mail: natp@natptax.com
https://www.natptax.com

The National Society of Tax Professionals provides education and resources for tax professionals as well as the general public.

National Society of Tax Professionals (NSTP)
11700 NE 95th Street, Unit #100
Vancouver, WA 98682-2411
Tel: (800) 367-8130; (360) 695-8309
Fax: (360) 695-7115
E-mail: taxes@nstp.org
http://www.nstp.org

Taxi Drivers

■ OVERVIEW

Taxi drivers, also known as *cab drivers*, operate automobiles and other motor vehicles to take passengers from one place to another for a fee. This fee is usually based on distance traveled or time as recorded on a taximeter. There are currently about 180,960 taxi drivers and chauffeurs in the United States.

■ HISTORY

Today's taxis are the modern equivalent of vehicles for hire that were first introduced in England in the early 1600s. These vehicles were hackneys, four-wheeled carriages drawn by two horses that could carry up to six passengers. By 1654, there were already 300 privately owned hackneys licensed to operate in London. In the next century, hackneys were introduced in the United States. Around 1820, a smaller vehicle for hire, the cabriolet, became common in London. At first it had two wheels, with room only for a driver and one passenger, and one horse drew it. Some later cabriolets, or cabs, as they were soon called, were larger, and by mid-century, a two-passenger version, the hansom cab, became the most popular cab in London. Hansom cabs were successfully brought to New York and Boston in the 1870s.

Toward the end of the 19th century, motorized cabs began to appear in the streets of Europe and America. From then on, the development of cabs paralleled the development of the automobile. The earliest motorized cabs were powered by electricity, but cabs with internal combustion engines appeared by the early 20th century. Along with the introduction of these vehicles came the need for drivers, thus creating the cab driver profession. In 1891, a device called a "taximeter" (tax is from a Latin word meaning "charge") was invented to calculate the fare owed to the driver. Taximeters found their first use in the new horseless carriages for hire, which were soon called "taxicabs" or just "taxis."

The use of taxis has increased especially in metropolitan areas, where there is dense traffic, increasing population, and limited parking. Modern taxis are often

QUICK FACTS

ALTERNATE TITLE(S)
Cab Drivers, Cabbies

DUTIES
Operate automobiles and other motor vehicles to take passengers from one place to another for a fee

SALARY RANGE
$17,830 to $23,510 to $50,000

WORK ENVIRONMENT
Primarily Indoors

BEST GEOGRAPHIC LOCATION(S)
Opportunities are available throughout the country, but are best in urban and suburban areas

MINIMUM EDUCATION LEVEL
High School Diploma, Some Postsecondary Training

SCHOOL SUBJECTS
Business, English, Mathematics

EXPERIENCE
Driving experience is helpful

PERSONALITY TRAITS
Conventional, Helpful, Outgoing

SKILLS
Interpersonal, Math, Mechanical/Manual Dexterity

CERTIFICATION OR LICENSING
Required

SPECIAL REQUIREMENTS
Must be 21 years of age in most places; pass background check

EMPLOYMENT PROSPECTS
Good

ADVANCEMENT PROSPECTS
Poor

OUTLOOK
Faster than the Average

NOC
7513

O*NET-SOC
53-3041.00

four-door passenger cars that have been specially modified. Depending on local regulations, the vehicles may have such modifications as reinforced frames or extra heavy-duty shock absorbers. Taxi drivers may be employees of taxi companies, driving cars owned by the company; they may be lease drivers, operating cars leased from a taxi company for a regular fee; or they may be completely independent, driving cars that they own themselves.

■ THE JOB

Taxicabs are an important part of the mass transportation system in many cities, so drivers need to be familiar with as much of the local geographical area as possible. Taxicab drivers are often required to do more than simply drive people from one place to another. They also help people with their luggage. Sometimes they pick up and deliver packages. Some provide sightseeing tours for visitors to a community.

Taxi drivers who are employed by, or lease from, a cab service or garage report to the garage before their shift begins and are assigned a cab. They receive a trip sheet and record their name, date of work, and identification number. They also perform a quick cursory check of the interior and exterior of the car to ensure its proper working condition. They check fuel and oil levels, brakes, lights, and windshield wipers, reporting any problems to the dispatcher or company mechanic.

Taxi drivers locate passengers in several ways. Customers requiring transportation may call the cab company with the approximate time and place where they wish to be picked up, or the customer may make a reservation via a mobile application. The dispatcher uses a two-way radio system to notify the driver of this pick-up information. Other drivers pick up passengers at cabstands and taxi lines at airports, theaters, hotels, and railroad stations, and then return to the stand after they deliver the passengers. Drivers may pick up passengers while returning to their stands or stations. Another manner of pick-up for taxi drivers is by cruising busy streets to service passengers who hail or "wave them down." Customers may also arrange for cab pick-ups through online services such as Uber.

When a destination is reached, the taxi driver determines the fare and informs the rider of the cost. Fares consist of many parts. The drop charge is an automatic charge for use of the cab. Other parts of the fare are determined by the time and distance traveled. A taximeter is a machine that measures the fare as it accrues. It is turned on and off when the passenger enters and leaves the cab. Additional portions of the fare may include charges for luggage handling and additional occupants. Commonly, a passenger will offer the taxi driver a tip, which is based on the customer's opinion of the quality and efficiency of the ride and the courtesy of the driver. The taxi driver also may supply a receipt if the passenger requests it.

Taxi drivers are required to keep accurate records of their activities. They record the time and place where they picked up and delivered the passengers on a trip sheet. They also have to keep records on the amount of fares they collect.

There are taxis and taxi drivers in almost every town and city in the country, but most are in large metropolitan areas.

■ EARNINGS

Earnings for taxi drivers vary widely, depending on the number of hours they work, the method by which they are paid, the season, the weather, and other factors. Median hourly earnings of salaried taxi drivers and chauffeurs, including tips, were $11.30 in May 2015, according to the U.S. Department of Labor. This translates to about $23,510 annually for full-time work. Hourly wages ranged from less than $8.57 to more than $18.25 an hour. This range translates to an annual wage range of between $17,830 and $37,970 for full-time work.

Limited information suggests that independent owner-drivers can average anywhere between $20,000 to $30,000 annually, including tips. This assumes they work the industry average of eight to 10 hours a day, five days a week. Many chauffeurs who worked full time earned from about $25,000 to $50,000, including tips.

Many taxi drivers are paid a percentage of the fares they collect, often 40 to 50 percent of total fares. Other drivers receive a base amount plus a commission related to the amount of business they do. A few drivers are guaranteed minimum daily or weekly wages. Drivers who lease their cabs may keep all the fare money above the amount of the leasing fee they pay the cab company. Tips are also an important part of the earnings of taxi drivers. They can equal 15 to 20 percent or more of total fares. Most taxi drivers do not receive company-provided fringe benefits, such as pension plans.

Earnings fluctuate with the season and the weather. Winter is generally the busiest season, and snow and rain almost always produce a busy day. There is also a relationship between general economic conditions and the earnings of taxi drivers, because there is more competition for less business when the economy is in a slump.

▣ WORK ENVIRONMENT

Many taxi drivers put in long hours, working from eight to 12 hours a day, five or six days a week. They do not receive overtime pay. Approximately 20 percent of drivers work part time. Drivers may work Sundays, holidays, or evening hours.

Taxi drivers must be able to get along with their passengers, including those who try their patience or expect too much. Some people urge drivers to drive fast, for example, but drivers who comply may risk accidents or arrests for speeding. Drivers may have to work under other difficult conditions, such as heavy traffic and bad weather. Taxi drivers must be able to drive safely under pressure, and for long periods of time. In some places, drivers must be wary because there is a considerable chance of being robbed.

▣ EXPLORING

Take a ride in a taxi to experience the career firsthand. Speak with cab drivers during the ride to learn more about their work and the pros and cons of the job. Learn more about industry news and find information about upcoming meetings and events through the Taxicab, Limousine & Paratransit Association: http://www.tlpa .org.

▣ EDUCATION AND TRAINING REQUIREMENTS
High School

Taxi drivers do not usually need to meet any particular educational requirements, but a high school education will help you adequately handle the record-keeping part of the job. Also take courses in driver education, business math, and English.

Postsecondary Training

The primary form of postsecondary education is a period of on-the-job training provided to new drivers by most taxi companies, which is required by law in some jurisdictions. Training includes how to operate the taximeter and other communication equipment, how to complete required paper work, driver safety, and customer service. Training may also cover the safe, non-emergency transport of elderly or disabled passengers. Additionally, the Taxicab, Limousine & Paratransit Association offers online training courses for taxi drivers.

CAREER LADDER

Manager or Independent Operator

Lead Driver

Experienced Taxi Driver

Entry-Level Taxi Driver

▣ CERTIFICATION, LICENSING, AND SPECIAL REQUIREMENTS
Certification or Licensing

Those interested in becoming a taxi driver must have a regular driver's license. In most large cities, taxi drivers also must have a special taxicab operator's license—commonly called a hack's license—in addition to a chauffeur's license. Police departments, safety departments, or public utilities commissions generally issue these special licenses. To secure the license, drivers must pass special examinations including questions on local geography, traffic regulations, accident reports, safe driving practices, and insurance regulations. Some companies help their job applicants prepare for these examinations by providing them with specially prepared booklets. The operator's license may need to be renewed annually. In some cities (New York, for example), new license applications can take several months to be processed because the applicant's background must be investigated. Increasingly, many cities and municipalities require a test on English usage. Those who do not pass must take a course in English sponsored by the municipality.

Other Requirements

Most municipalities require taxi drivers to be 21 years of age or older and have a clean driving record and no criminal record. Check with your local taxi commission or regulating agencies for details.

▣ EXPERIENCE, SKILLS, AND PERSONALITY TRAITS

No experience is needed to work as a taxi driver, but any driving experience will be useful.

TOP EMPLOYERS OF TAXI DRIVERS CHAUFFEURS AND MEAN ANNUAL SALARIES, MAY 2015

DID YOU KNOW?

- Taxi and limousine services: 50,630 jobs, $27,050
- Other transit and ground passenger transportation: 24,720 jobs, $24,600
- Automobile dealers: 14,230 jobs, $22,650
- Automotive equipment rental and leasing: 10,310 jobs, $22,900
- Traveler accommodation: 8,260 jobs, $23,920

Source: Bureau of Labor Statistics

Taxi drivers should be in reasonably good health and have a good driving record and no criminal record. In general, they must be 21 years of age or older to drive a taxicab. While driving is not physically strenuous, they will occasionally be asked to lift heavy packages or luggage. They should have especially steady nerves if they work in a big city because they will spend considerable time driving in heavy traffic. They must also be courteous, patient, and able to get along with many different kinds of people.

Taxi drivers who own their own cab or lease one for a long period of time are generally expected to keep their cab clean. Large companies have workers who take care of this task for all the vehicles in the company fleet.

■ EMPLOYMENT PROSPECTS

Employers

Approximately 180,960 taxi drivers and chauffeurs are employed in the United States. Taxi drivers are often employed by a cab service and drive cars owned by the company. Some drivers pay a fee and lease cabs owned by a taxi company, while others own and operate their own cars.

Starting Out

Usually people who want to be taxi drivers apply directly to taxicab companies that may be hiring new drivers. Taxicab companies can be found through online searches and the Yellow Pages. It may take some time to obtain the necessary license to drive a cab, and some companies or municipalities may require additional training, so it may not be possible to begin work immediately. People who have sufficient funds may buy their own cab, but they usually must secure a municipal permit to operate it.

■ ADVANCEMENT PROSPECTS

Taxi drivers have limited advancement opportunities. Some may become managers or independent operators. Others may become *lead drivers,* who train new drivers, while also still working regular driving shifts.

■ OUTLOOK

There will always be a need for taxi drivers. Job opportunities for taxi drivers are expected to grow by 13 percent, faster than the average for all careers, through 2024, according to the U.S. Department of Labor. The high turnover rate in this occupation means that many of the new job openings that develop in the future will come when drivers leave their jobs to go into another kind of work. In addition, as the American population increases and traffic becomes more congested, the need for taxi drivers will increase, especially in metropolitan areas. At present many drivers work on a part-time basis, and that situation is likely to continue.

The emergence of ride-sharing companies (such as Uber and Lyft) may reduce job growth in the taxi industry. These firms typically charge less per ride than traditional taxi companies and operate under little or no government regulation. Many municipalities are developing regulations that may require ride-share companies to conduct regular criminal background checks and drug tests on driver applicants, implement formal driver training programs, and obtain comprehensive commercial liability insurance for vehicles. If regulation of the ride-sharing industry increases, job opportunities will be even better for cab drivers.

■ UNIONS AND ASSOCIATIONS

In large cities, some taxi drivers belong to labor unions. The union to which most belong is the International Brotherhood of Teamsters. The Taxicab, Limousine & Paratransit Association is an organization of more than 1,000 transportation companies, industry suppliers, and regulatory agencies. It offers an online taxi driver education program.

■ TIPS FOR ENTRY

1. Try to obtain as much driving experience as you can.
2. Talk to taxi drivers about their careers. Ask them for advice on breaking into the field.
3. Contact taxi companies to inquire about job opportunities.

■ FOR MORE INFORMATION

The Taxicab, Limousine and Paratransit Association provides education, events, and other resources for the passenger transportation industry.

Taxicab, Limousine and Paratransit
   Association (TLPA)
3200 Tower Oaks Boulevard, Suite 220
Rockville, MD 20852-4265
Tel: (301) 984-5700
Fax: (301) 984-5703
E-mail: info@tlpa.org
http://www.tlpa.org

*The National Limousine Association provides membership
benefits, advocacy, events, and other resources for limousine owners and operators.*

National Limousine Association (NLA)
49 South Maple Avenue
Marlton, NJ 08053-
Tel: (800) 652-7007
Fax: (856) 596-2145
E-mail: info@limo.org
http://www.limo.org

Taxidermists

■ OVERVIEW

Taxidermists preserve and prepare animal skins and parts
to create lifelike animal replicas. Taxidermists prepare
the underpadding and mounting to which the skin will
be attached, model the structure to resemble the animal's body, and then attach appropriate coverings, such
as skin, fur, or feathers. They may add details, such as
eyes or teeth, to make a more realistic representation. The
animals they mount or stuff may be for private or public display. Museums frequently display creations from
taxidermists to exhibit rare, exotic, or extinct animals.
Hunters also use taxidermists' services to mount fishing
and hunting trophies for display.

■ HISTORY

Animal tanning and skin preservation has been practiced over the millennia for clothing, decoration, and
weapons. Native Americans used tanned hides to make
their lodgings. Trophies from hunts of dangerous animals were often worn to display the bravery of the
hunter. Tanning methods included stringing skins up to
dry, scraping them, and perhaps soaking them in water
with tannins from leaves. Animal skins were preserved
for many different purposes, but not specifically from
interest in the natural sciences until the 18th century.
Tanning methods improved during this time. Displaying
the skin on models stuffed with hay or straw became
popular for museums and private collections. Animals

were posed realistically, and
backgrounds were added to the
display areas in museums to
show the habitat of the animal.

By the 19th century, taxidermy was a recognized discipline for museum workers. In
Paris, Maison Verreaux became
the chief supplier of exhibit animals. Carl Akeley, who worked
for Ward's Natural Science
Establishment in New York,
mastered a taxidermic technique that allowed for realistic
modeling of large animals such
as bears, lions, and elephants.
His works are still on display in
The Field Museum (Chicago)
and the American Museum of
Natural History (New York). In
recent years, several taxidermy
supply companies have developed lifelike mannequins to be
used as the foundations for fish,
birds, and fur-bearing animals.
Such new techniques in the art
and science of taxidermy continue to be developed and used.

■ THE JOB

Taxidermists use a variety of
methods to create realistic,
lifelike models of birds and
animals. Specific processes
and techniques vary, but most
taxidermists follow a series of
basic steps.

First, they must remove the
skin from the carcass of the animal with special knives, scissors, and pliers. The skin must
be removed very carefully to
preserve the natural state of the
fur or feathers. Once the skin is
removed, it is preserved with a
chemical solution.

Some taxidermists still make
the body foundation, or skel-
eton, of the animal. These foundations are made with
a variety of materials, including clay, plaster, burlap,
papier-mâché, wire mesh, and glue. Other taxidermists,
however, use ready-made forms, which are available

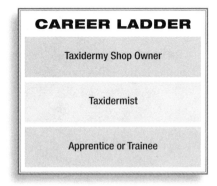

in various sizes; taxidermists simply take measurements of the specimen to be mounted and order the proper size from the supplier. Metal rods are often used to achieve the desired mount for the animal.

The taxidermist uses special adhesives or modeling clay to attach the skin to the foundation or form. Then artificial eyes, teeth, and tongues are attached. Sometimes taxidermists use special techniques, such as airbrushing color or sculpting the eyelids, nose, and lips. They may need to attach antlers, horns, or claws. Finally they groom and dress the fur or feathers with styling gel, if necessary, to enhance the final appearance of the specimen.

Taxidermists work with a variety of animal types, including one-cell organisms, large game animals, birds, fish, and reptiles. They even make models of extinct animal species, based on detailed drawings or paintings. The specific work often depends on the area of the country where the taxidermist is employed, since the types of animals hunted vary by region.

■ EARNINGS

A taxidermist's level of experience, certification, speed, and quality of work are all factors that significantly affect income. Most taxidermists will charge by the inch or the weight of the animal. Fees can range from $100 to $2,500, depending on the size of the animal and the style of the mount. Difficult mounts or unusual background accessories may add significantly to the final price. For example, an open mouth on an animal, as opposed to a droopy mouth or a closed mouth, can add about $100 to the price of a mounting. In addition, the region of the country and the type of game typically hunted and mounted are important variables.

According to SalaryExpert.com, the average annual salary for taxidermists employed in the United States in 2016 was $48,031. Most new taxidermists might expect to earn about $15,000 annually. Those with five to 10 years of experience and proven skills can earn $30,000 or more. Some exceptional taxidermists can earn $50,000 or more annually. Museum workers might also expect to average $25,000 to $30,000 yearly.

Most taxidermists are self-employed or work for a small operation, so they many not have any sort of benefits package. Those who work in museums, however, may be offered health insurance and paid vacations and sick leave.

■ WORK ENVIRONMENT

Most taxidermists work 40 hours a week, although overtime is not uncommon during certain times of the year. Taxidermists with their own shops may have to work long hours, especially when first starting out. They often work with strong chemicals, glues, hand and power tools, and possibly diseased animals. They can sit or stand if working on smaller animals. However, creating larger mammal displays requires more physical work, such as climbing or squatting.

Taxidermists find it satisfying to see a project from beginning to completion. There is also the element of pride in good craftsmanship; it can be gratifying for workers to use their talents to recreate extremely realistic and lifelike animal forms.

■ EXPLORING

Taxidermy is a specialized field, so there are few opportunities for part-time or summer work for students, although some larger companies hire apprentices to help with the workload. It may be possible to learn more by ordering or downloading videos and practicing with mounting kits to experience the mounting process. Other good learning opportunities include speaking to a museum taxidermist or writing to schools or associations that offer courses in taxidermy. Check with the National Taxidermists Association for upcoming conventions and seminars that are open to the public. Time spent at such an event would provide not only a solid learning experience, but also a chance to meet and mingle with the pros.

■ EDUCATION AND TRAINING REQUIREMENTS
High School

High school classes in art, woodworking, and metal shop may help develop the skills necessary for this career. Also, a class or classes in biology might be helpful for learning the bodily workings of certain animals.

Postsecondary Training

In the United States, several schools offer programs or correspondence courses in taxidermy. Courses often last from four to six weeks, and subjects such as laws and legalities, bird mounting, fish mounting, deer, small mammals, diorama-making, airbrush painting, and form-making are covered. Taxidermists who hope to work in museums should expect to take further training and acquire additional skills in related subjects, which they can learn in museum classes. Some aspiring taxidermists train for the field by apprenticing with an experienced taxidermist.

Self-employed taxidermists need accounting, advertising, and marketing courses to help in the management of a business, including maintaining an inventory of chemicals and supplies, advertising and promotion, and pricing their work.

Other Education or Training

The National Taxidermists Association and the United Taxidermist Association offer professional development opportunities at their annual conferences.

■ CERTIFICATION, LICENSING, AND SPECIAL REQUIREMENTS
Certification or Licensing

Taxidermists are required to be licensed in most states, with specific licensing requirements varying from state to state. Many taxidermists choose to become members of national or local professional associations. The largest of these, the National Taxidermists Association, offers the designation of certified taxidermist to members who have met specific requirements. Members may be certified in one or all four categories of specialization: mammals, fish, birds, and reptiles. Certification indicates that they have reached a certain level of expertise and may allow them to charge a higher price for their work.

■ EXPERIENCE, SKILLS, AND PERSONALITY TRAITS

Previous experience as a taxidermy hobbyist, apprentice, or an assistant to a taxidermist is required to enter the field.

Successful taxidermy requires many skills. You must have good manual dexterity, an eye for detail, knowledge of animal anatomy, and training in the taxidermy processes. Taxidermists who operate their own business must have good business management, finance, and marketing skills. Clear communication skills are also important for interacting with customers.

■ EMPLOYMENT PROSPECTS
Employers

Taxidermists can be found throughout the United States and abroad. Experienced and established taxidermists, especially those with a large client base, will often hire apprentices, or less experienced taxidermists, to assist with larger projects or undertake smaller jobs. The majority of taxidermists, about 70 to 80 percent, are self-employed.

Starting Out

Taxidermy is a profession that requires experience. Most workers start out as hobbyists in their own homes, and eventually start doing taxidermy work part time professionally. Later, after they have built up a client base, they may enter the profession full time. Jobs in existing

---

GAMEHEADS

DID YOU KNOW?

Gameheads, composed of the head, and sometimes shoulders and neck, of a specimen, are the most popular type of mount. Most gameheads are mounted for wall display, though artistic taxidermists often mount gameheads on pedestals, allowing them to be viewed from a 360-degree angle.

Here is the much-simplified step-by-step process of mounting a gamehead:

1. Carefully remove the skin from the specimen. Preserve with chemicals or tan into leather.
2. Prepare the mannequin—the form used to shape the specimen—by installing natural antlers and glass eyes.
3. Glue the prepared skin over the mannequin. Adjust as necessary to create a natural look.
4. Add finishing touches to the eyes, ears, nose, mouth, and antler burrs to make them look natural. Use mediums such as paint, glue, and gel.
5. Sew the incision closed. Groom hair.
6. Allow the mount to dry.

---

taxidermy shops or businesses are difficult to find because most taxidermists are self-employed and prefer to do the work themselves. However, in some cases, it may be possible to become a journeyman or apprentice and work for an already established taxidermist on either an hourly basis or for a percentage of the selling price of the work they are doing.

Jobs in museums are often difficult to obtain; applicants should have a background in both taxidermy and general museum studies. Taxidermy schools primarily train their students to become self-employed but may sometimes offer job placement as well.

■ ADVANCEMENT PROSPECTS

Advancement opportunities are good for those with the proper skills, education, and experience. Taxidermists who can work on a wide range of projects will have the best chances of advancing. Since larger game animals bring more money, one method of advancing would be to learn the skills necessary to work on these animals. Taxidermists who develop a large customer base may open their own shop. Workers employed in museums may advance to positions with more responsibilities and higher pay.

■ OUTLOOK

The job outlook for taxidermists should be good over the next decade. Although jobs in museums may be scarce,

CARL ETHAN AKELEY: INNOVATIVE TAXIDERMIST

MOVERS AND SHAKERS

If it weren't for Carl Ethan Akeley, taxidermists would be bored stiff preparing the same mounted head after mounted head. Akeley was a U.S. taxidermist, inventor, explorer, and sculptor who was innovative in the taxidermy field. While employed as a museum taxidermist in the early 20th century, Akeley used his personal technique–the hollow-model method–to display specimens in habitat groups, posing animals in their natural settings. This artistic rendering was adopted by museums worldwide, and eventually trickled down to commercial taxidermy. His mounts are still displayed today, most notably at the American Museum of Natural History in New York and The Field Museum of Natural History in Chicago.

the demand for hunting and fishing trophies continues to provide work for taxidermists. It is not unusual for qualified taxidermists to have a year's worth of work backlogged. In addition, many museums and other educational institutions actively seek models of animal and bird species that are nearing extinction. Talented taxidermists who can take on a variety of projects should be able to find steady employment. Those with an eye for unique poses and mounts, or unusual expressions, will be in high demand.

■ UNIONS AND ASSOCIATIONS

Taxidermists do not belong to unions, but many become members of the National Taxidermists Association and the United Taxidermist Association. These organizations provide professional development opportunities, certification, and taxidermy competitions.

■ TIPS FOR ENTRY

1. Talk to a taxidermist about his or her career. The National Taxidermists Association provides a list of its members on its Web site, http://nationaltaxi dermists.com, which can be used to identify possible interview candidates.
2. Attend the United Taxidermist Association Expo and Competition (http://www.unitedtaxidermyas sociation.com/uta-expo.html) and the National Taxidermists Association Annual Convention and Competition (http://nationaltaxidermists.com/ 2016-convention-schedule/) to participate in continuing education classes, enter taxidermy competitions, and network.
3. Read *Taxidermy Today* (http://www.taxidermyto day.com) to learn more about the field.

■ FOR MORE INFORMATION

The National Taxidermists Association provides information on certification, taxidermy schools, trade magazines, association membership, and career opportunities.

National Taxidermists Association (NTA)
PO Box 384
Pocahontas, IL 62275-0384
Tel: (618) 669-2929
Fax: (618) 669-2909
E-mail: info@NationalTaxidermists.com
http://www.nationaltaxidermists.com

Taxidermy.net provides information on training in taxidermy, including a list of schools, workshops, books, magazines, videos, and links to state taxidermy associations.

Taxidermy.net
E-mail: ken@taxidermy.net
http://www.taxidermy.net

United Taxidermist Association unites, promotes, and champions the needs of taxidermists.

United Taxidermist Association (UTA)
5617 E 30th Street
Tuscon, AZ 85711-6601
Tel: (715) 785-7828
http://www.unitedtaxidermyassociation.com

Teacher Aides

■ OVERVIEW

Teacher aides perform a wide variety of duties to help teachers run a classroom. They prepare instructional materials, help students with classroom work, and supervise students in the library, on the playground, and at lunch. They perform administrative duties such as photocopying, keeping attendance records, and grading papers. There are more than 1.2 million teacher aides employed in the United States. Teacher aides are also known as *teacher assistants, instructional aides, paraprofessionals*, and *paraeducators*.

■ HISTORY

As formal education became more widely available in the 20th century, teachers' jobs became more complex. The size of classes increased, and a growing educational bureaucracy demanded that more records be kept of students' achievements and classroom activities. Advancements in technology, changes in educational theory, and a great increase in the amount and variety of teaching materials available all contributed to the time required to prepare materials and assess student progress, leaving teachers less time for the teaching for which they had been trained.

To remedy this problem, teacher aides began to be employed to take care of the more routine aspects of running an instructional program. Today, many schools and school districts employ teacher aides, to the great benefit of hardworking teachers and students.

■ THE JOB

Teacher aides work in public, private, and parochial preschools and elementary and secondary schools. Their duties vary depending on the classroom teacher, school, and school district. Some teacher aides specialize in one subject, and some work in a specific type of school setting. These settings include bilingual classrooms, gifted and talented programs, classes for learning disabled students and those with unique physical needs, and multiage classrooms. These aides conduct the same type of classroom work as other teacher aides, but they may provide more individual assistance to students.

No matter what kind of classroom they assist in, teacher aides will likely copy, compile, and hand out class materials, set up and operate audiovisual equipment, arrange field trips, and type or word-process materials. They organize classroom files, including grade reports, attendance, and health records. They may also obtain library materials and order classroom supplies.

Teacher aides may be in charge of keeping order in classrooms, school cafeterias, libraries, hallways, and playgrounds. Often, they wait with preschool and elementary students coming to or leaving school and make sure all students are accounted for. When a class leaves its home room for such subjects as art, music, physical education, or computer lab, teacher aides may go with the students to help the teachers of these other subjects.

Another responsibility of teacher aides is correcting and grading homework and tests, usually for objective assignments and tests that require specific answers. They use answer sheets to mark students' papers and examinations and keep records of students' scores. In some large schools, an aide may be called a *grading clerk* and be responsible only for scoring objective tests and computing and recording test scores. Often using an electronic grading machine or computer, the grading clerk totals errors found and computes the percentage of questions answered correctly. The clerk then records this score and averages students' test scores to determine their grades for the course.

Under the teacher's supervision, teacher aides may work directly with students in the classroom. They listen to a group of young students read aloud or involve the class in a special project such as a science fair, art project, or drama production. With older students, teacher aides provide review or study sessions prior to exams or give extra help with research projects or homework. Some teacher aides work with individual students in a tutorial setting, helping in areas of special need or concern. They may work with the teacher to prepare lesson plans, bibliographies, charts, or maps. They may help to decorate the classroom, design bulletin boards and displays, and arrange workstations. Teacher aides may also participate in parent-teacher conferences to discuss students' progress.

■ EARNINGS

Teacher aides are usually paid on an hourly basis and usually only during the nine or 10 months of the school calendar. Salaries vary depending on the school or district, region of the country, and the duties the aides perform. Median annual earnings of teacher assistants in May 2015 were $24,900, according to the U.S. Department of Labor. Salaries ranged from less than $17,920 to more than $38,000.

Benefits such as health insurance and vacation or sick leave may also depend on the school or district as well as the number of hours a teacher aide works. Many schools employ teacher aides only part time and do not offer such benefits. Other teacher aides may receive the same health and pension benefits as the teachers in their school and be covered under collective bargaining agreements.

QUICK FACTS

ALTERNATE TITLE(S)
Grading Clerks, Instructional Aides, Paraeducators, Paraprofessionals, Teacher Assistants

DUTIES
Assist teachers; prepare classroom materials; help students with class work; supervise students; perform administrative duties

SALARY RANGE
$17,920 to $24,900 to $38,000+

WORK ENVIRONMENT
Primarily Indoors

BEST GEOGRAPHIC LOCATION(S)
Opportunities are available throughout the country, but are best in large, urban areas

MINIMUM EDUCATION LEVEL
High School Diploma, Some Postsecondary Training

SCHOOL SUBJECTS
English, History, Mathematics

EXPERIENCE
Experience working with young people is highly recommended

PERSONALITY TRAITS
Helpful, Organized, Social

SKILLS
Computer, Interpersonal, Teaching

CERTIFICATION OR LICENSING
Recommended

SPECIAL REQUIREMENTS
None

EMPLOYMENT PROSPECTS
Good

ADVANCEMENT PROSPECTS
Good

OUTLOOK
About as Fast as the Average

NOC
4413

O*NET-SOC
25-9041.00

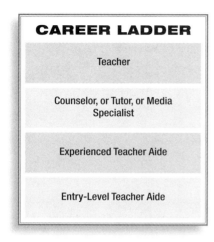

CAREER LADDER

Teacher

Counselor, or Tutor, or Media Specialist

Experienced Teacher Aide

Entry-Level Teacher Aide

■ WORK ENVIRONMENT

Teacher aides work in a well-lit, comfortable, wheelchair-accessible environment, although some older school buildings may be in disrepair with unpredictable heating or cooling systems. Most of their work will be indoors, but teacher aides spend some time outside before and after school, and during recess and lunch hours, to watch over the students. They are often on their feet, monitoring the halls and lunch areas and running errands for teachers. This work is not physically strenuous, but working closely with children can be stressful and tiring.

Teacher aides find it rewarding to help students learn and develop. The pay, however, is not as rewarding.

■ EXPLORING

Gain experience working with children by volunteering to help with religious education classes at your place of worship. You may volunteer to help with scouting troops or work as a counselor at a summer camp. You may have the opportunity to volunteer to help coach a children's athletic team or work with children in after-school programs at community centers. Babysitting is a common way to gain experience in working with children and to learn about the different stages of child development.

A teacher aide works with a group of students during an art session. (Monkey Business Images. Shutterstock.)

■ EDUCATION AND TRAINING REQUIREMENTS
High School

Courses in English, history, social studies, mathematics, art, drama, physical education, and the sciences will provide a broad base of knowledge. This knowledge will enable you to help students learn in these same subjects. Knowledge of a second language can be an asset, especially when working in schools with bilingual student, parent, or staff populations. Courses in child care, family and consumer science, and psychology are also valuable for this career. Gain some experience working with computers; students at many elementary schools and even preschools do a large amount of computer work, and computer skills are important in performing clerical duties.

Postsecondary Training

Postsecondary requirements for teacher aides depend on the school or school district and the kinds of responsibilities the aides have. In districts where aides perform mostly clerical duties, applicants may need only to have a high school diploma or a general equivalency diploma (GED). Those who work in the classroom may be required to take some college courses and attend in-service training and special teacher conferences and seminars. Some schools and districts may help you pay some of the costs involved in attending these programs. Often community and junior colleges have certificate and associate's programs that prepare teacher aides for classroom work, offering courses in child development, health and safety, and child guidance.

Newly hired aides participate in orientation sessions and formal training at the school. In these sessions, aides learn about the school's organization, operation, and philosophy. They learn how to keep school records, operate audiovisual equipment, check books out of the library, and administer first aid.

Many schools prefer to hire teacher aides who have some experience working with children; some schools prefer to hire workers who live within the school district. Schools may also require that you pass written exams and health physicals. Teacher aides must be able to work effectively with both children and adults and should have good verbal and written communication skills.

Other Education or Training

The Association for Childhood Education International offers professional development courses to its members. Teacher aides can also seek out continuing education opportunities via professional education associations at the state and local levels.

CERTIFICATION, LICENSING, AND SPECIAL REQUIREMENTS
Certification or Licensing

Most states now have core performance, skills, and competency standards for education paraprofessionals, including voluntary certification, based on the 2001 federal No Child Left Behind Act. Requirements vary by state and by school, so teacher aides must find out the specific job requirements for the school, school district, or state department of education in the area where they want to work. It is important to remember that an aide who is qualified to work in one state, or even one school, may not be qualified to work in another. The National Resource Center for Paraeducators provides state certification information on its Web site: http://www.nrcpara .org/states.

EXPERIENCE, SKILLS, AND PERSONALITY TRAITS

Experience working at a day care center or caring for younger siblings is highly recommended for aspiring teacher aides.

Teacher aides must enjoy working with children and be able to handle their demands, problems, and questions with patience and fairness. They must be willing and able to follow instructions, but also should be able to take the initiative in projects. Flexibility, creativity, and a cheerful outlook are definite assets for anyone working with children.

EMPLOYMENT PROSPECTS
Employers

More than 1.2 million workers are employed as teacher assistants in the United States. About 40 percent of teacher assistants work part time. Aides can find work in just about any preschool, elementary, or secondary school in the country. Teacher aides also assist in special education programs and in group-home settings. Aides work in both public and private schools.

Starting Out

You can apply directly to schools and school districts for teacher aide positions. Many school districts and state departments of education maintain job listings, bulletin boards, and hotlines that list available openings. Teacher aide jobs are often advertised on the Web sites of school districts. Once hired, teacher aides spend the first months in special training and receive a beginning wage. After six months or so, they have regular responsibilities and possibly a wage increase.

PARA-TO-TEACHER PROGRAMS   DID YOU KNOW?

"Para-to-teacher" programs across the country are helping members of minority groups become teachers. With the field of teaching in desperate need of minority representatives, programs such as the University of Southern California Latino and Language Minority Teacher Projects in Los Angeles, California, are stepping in to offer stipends, mentors, and other assistance to teacher aides seeking teacher certification. The United Federation of Teachers offers the Leap to Teacher program for paraprofessionals who work for the Department of Education to help them advance to teaching careers. *The Guide to Developing Paraeducator-to-Teacher Programs* provides useful information and resources for transitioning from paraeducator to teacher, http://cmmr.usc.edu/paraed/ RNTtoolkit.pdf.

ADVANCEMENT PROSPECTS

Teacher aides usually advance only in terms of increases in salary or responsibility, which come with experience. Aides in some districts may receive time off to take college courses. Some teacher aides choose to pursue bachelor's degrees and fulfill the licensing requirements of the state or school to become teachers.

Aides who find that they enjoy the administrative side of the job may move into school or district office staff positions. Others choose to get more training and then work as *resource teachers, tutors, guidance counselors*, or *reading, mathematics, or speech specialists*. Some teacher aides go into *school library work* or become *media specialists*. While it is true that most of these jobs require additional training, the job of teacher aide is a good place to begin.

OUTLOOK

The U.S. Department of Labor predicts that this field will grow by 6 percent through 2024, which is about as fast as the average for all occupations. The field of special education (working with students with specific learning, emotional, or physical concerns or disabilities) is expected to grow rapidly, and more aides will be needed in these areas.

Several other factors should spur growth in this field. The number of students for whom English is a second language is increasing, which will create demand for teacher aides who are proficient in a second language, such as Spanish. Additionally, teacher aides will play an increasing role in preparing students for standardized testing and helping students who perform poorly academically.

PARAEDUCATOR CAREERS

LEARN MORE ABOUT IT

Ashbaker, Betty Y., and Jill Morgan. *Paraprofessionals in the Classroom: A Survival Guide,* 2nd ed. Upper Saddle River, N.J.: Pearson, 2012.

Carlson, John S., and Richard Carlson. *101 Careers in Education.* New York: Springer Publishing Company, 2015.

Cipani, Ennio. *Decoding Challenging Classroom Behaviors: What Every Teacher and Paraeducator Should Know!* Springfield, Ill.: Charles C. Thomas Publisher Ltd., 2011.

Fitzell, Susan. *Paraprofessionals and Teachers Working Together: Highly Effective Strategies for the Inclusive Classroom,* 2nd ed. Manchester, N.H.: Cogent Catalyst Publications, 2010.

Teacher aides who want to work with young children in day care or extended day programs will have a relatively easy time finding work because more children are attending these programs while their parents are at work. Because of increased responsibilities for aides, state departments of education will likely establish standards of training.

Teacher aides who have at least two years of postsecondary experience, are experienced with working with special education students, and who are fluent in a foreign language will have the best employment prospects.

Areas with rapid population growth, including communities in the South and West will have additional demand for teacher aides. As the number of students in schools increases, new schools and classrooms will be added, and more teachers and teacher aides will be hired. A shortage of teachers will cause administrators to hire more aides to help with larger classrooms. During school budget cuts, however, teacher aide jobs are typically the first to be eliminated.

Teachers will continue to need aides to help students prepare for standardized testing and assist those students who perform poorly on standardized tests. Also, there is high turnover in the teacher aide field due to the low pay, so job opportunities will arise from the need to replace those who move on to other positions or leave the work force.

■ UNIONS AND ASSOCIATIONS

Many teacher aides are represented by unions or are covered by a union contract—mainly the American Federation of Teachers and the National Education Association. Other useful organizations for teacher aides include the Association for Childhood Education International and the National Resource Center for Paraeducators.

■ TIPS FOR ENTRY

1. Join professional associations to access training and networking resources, industry publications, and employment opportunities.
2. Join the National Education Association and the American Federation of Teachers to increase your chances of landing a job and receiving fair pay for your work.
3. Contact school districts directly regarding potential job openings.

■ FOR MORE INFORMATION

This American Federation of Teachers/Paraprofessionals and School-Related Personnel provides information on current issues affecting paraprofessionals in education.

American Federation of Teachers/ Paraprofessionals and School-Related Personnel (AFT/PSRP)
555 New Jersey Avenue, NW
Washington, D.C. 20001-2029
Tel: (202) 879-4400
http://www.aft.org/psrp

The Association for Childhood Education International is a global association of educators and advocates who unite knowledge, experience, and perspective.

Association for Childhood Education International (ACEI)
1200 18th Street, NW, Suite 700
Washington, D.C. 20036-2506
Tel: (800) 423-3563; (202) 372-9986
http://www.acei.org

The National Education Association is a professional employee association for educators.

National Education Association (NEA)
1201 16th Street, NW
Washington, D.C. 20036-3290
Tel: (202) 833-4000
Fax: (202) 822-7974
http://www.nea.org/home/1604.htm

The National Resource Center for Paraeducators provides information about training programs and other resources for paraeducators.

National Resource Center for Paraeducators (NRCP)
http://www.nrcpara.org

Technical Support Specialists

■ OVERVIEW

Technical support specialists investigate and resolve problems in computer functioning. They listen to customer complaints, walk customers through possible solutions, and write technical reports based on their work. Technical support specialists have different duties depending on whom they assist and what they fix. Regardless of specialty, all technical support specialists must be knowledgeable about the products with which they work and be able to communicate effectively with users from different technical backgrounds. There are approximately 585,060 computer support specialists employed in the United States.

■ HISTORY

The first major advances in modern computer technology were made during World War II. After the war, it was thought that the enormous size of computers, which easily took up the space of entire warehouses, would limit their use to huge government projects. The 1950 census, for example, was computer-processed.

The introduction of semiconductors to computer technology made possible smaller and less expensive computers. Businesses began adapting computers to their operations as early as 1954. Within 30 years, computers had revolutionized the way people work, play, and shop. Today, computers are everywhere, from businesses of all kinds to government agencies, charitable organizations, and private homes. Over the years, technology has continued to shrink computer sizes and increase processing speed at an unprecedented rate.

Technical support has been around since the development of the first computers for the simple reason that, like all machines, computers always experience problems at one time or another. Several market phenomena explain the increase in demand for competent technical support specialists. As more companies enter the computer hardware, software, and peripheral market, the intense competition to win customers has resulted in many companies offering free or reasonably priced technical support as part of the purchase package. A company uses its reputation and the availability of a technical support department to differentiate its products from those of other companies, even though the tangible products like a hard drive, for example, may actually be physically identical.

Personal computers and related technology are ubiquitous in private homes, and the sheer quantity of users has risen so dramatically that more technical support specialists are needed to field their complaints. In addition, technological advances hit the marketplace in the form of a new processor or software application so quickly that quality assurance departments cannot possibly identify all the glitches in programming beforehand. Given the great variety of computer equipment and software on the market, it is often difficult for users to reach a high proficiency level with each individual program. When they experience problems, often due to their own errors, users call on technical support to help them.

The goal of many computer companies is to release a product for sale that requires no technical support, so that the technical support department has nothing to do. Given the speed of development, however, this is not likely to occur anytime soon. Until it does, there will be a strong demand for technical support specialists. A growing tendency among companies to outsource technical support jobs overseas will dampen job growth in the United States.

The growth of the Internet and e-commerce is also creating employment opportunities for technical support specialists. Many people who purchase goods or services on the Internet need assistance during the purchasing process. User support specialists answer site users' questions via live-chat features at company Web sites, as well as respond to customer concerns via telephone and e-mail.

■ THE JOB

Most companies rely on computers for a variety of business functions: daily operations,

QUICK FACTS

ALTERNATE TITLE(S)
Help Desk Specialists, Help Desk Technicians, Technical Support Specialists, User Support Specialists

DUTIES
Investigate and resolve problems in computer and Internet functioning; listen to user complaints; walk users through possible solutions; write technical reports based on their work

SALARY RANGE
$28,990 to $48,620 to $81,260+

WORK ENVIRONMENT
Primarily Indoors

BEST GEOGRAPHIC LOCATION(S)
Opportunities exist throughout the country

MINIMUM EDUCATION LEVEL
Associate's Degree

SCHOOL SUBJECTS
Computer Science, English, Mathematics

EXPERIENCE
Internships, volunteer or part-time experience

PERSONALITY TRAITS
Helpful, Problem-Solving, Technical

SKILLS
Computer, Interpersonal, Math

CERTIFICATION OR LICENSING
Recommended

SPECIAL REQUIREMENTS
None

EMPLOYMENT PROSPECTS
Good

ADVANCEMENT PROSPECTS
Good

OUTLOOK
Faster than the Average

NOC
2282

O*NET-SOC
15-1151.00

CAREER LADDER

Software Engineer

Technical Support Manager

Experienced Technical Support Specialist

Entry-Level Technical Support Specialist

such as employee time clocks; monthly projects, such as payroll and sales accounting; and major re-engineering of fundamental business procedures, such as form automation in government agencies, insurance companies, and banks. As a result, it has become increasingly critical that computers function properly all the time. Computer downtime can be extremely expensive, in terms of work left undone and sales not made, for example. When employees experience problems with their computer system, they call technical support for help. Technical support specialists investigate and resolve problems in computer functioning.

Technical support consists of three distinct areas, although these distinctions vary greatly with the nature, size, and scope of the company. The two most prevalent areas are user support and technical support. Most technical support specialists perform some combination of the tasks explained below.

The jobs of technical support specialists vary according to whom they assist and what they fix. Some specialists help private users exclusively; others are on call to a major corporate buyer. Some work with computer hardware and software, while others help with printer, modem, and fax problems. *User support specialists*, also known as *help desk specialists*, work directly with users themselves, who call when they experience problems. The support specialist listens carefully to the user's explanation of the precise nature of the problem and the commands entered that seem to have caused it. Some companies have developed complex software that allows the support specialist to enter a description of the problem and wait for the computer to provide suggestions about what the user should do.

The initial goal is to isolate the source of the problem. If user error is the culprit, the technical support specialist explains procedures related to the program in question, whether it is a graphics, database, word processing, or printing program. If the problem is in the hardware or software, the specialist asks the user to enter certain commands in order to see if the computer makes the appropriate response. If it does not, the support specialist is closer to isolating the cause. The support specialist consults supervisors, programmers, and others in order to outline the cause and possible solutions.

Some technical support specialists conduct live chats online with customers who are having difficulty using a company's Web site, accessing content, or making an online purchase. They also interact with online customers via instant messaging software, e-mail, or telephone.

Some technical support specialists who work for computer companies are mainly involved with solving problems whose cause has been determined to lie in the computer system's operating system, hardware, or software. They make exhaustive use of resources, such as colleagues or books, and try to solve the problem through a variety of methods, including program modifications and the replacement of certain hardware or software.

Technical support specialists employed in the information systems departments of large corporations do this kind of troubleshooting as well. They also oversee the daily operations of the various computer systems, Local Area Networks, Wide Area Networks, and other systems in the company. Sometimes they compare the system's work capacity to the actual daily workload in order to determine if upgrades are needed. In addition, they might help out other computer professionals in the company with modifying commercial software for their company's particular needs.

All technical support work must be well documented. Support specialists write detailed technical reports on every problem they work on. They try to tie together different problems on the same software, so programmers can make adjustments that address all of the issues. Record keeping is crucial because designers, programmers, and engineers use technical support reports to revise current products and improve future ones. Some support specialists help write training manuals. They are often required to read trade magazines and company newsletters in order to keep up to date on their products and the field in general.

■ EARNINGS

Technical support specialist jobs are plentiful in areas where clusters of computer companies are located, such as northern California and Seattle, Washington. Median annual earnings for computer user support specialists were $48,620 in May 2015, according to the U.S. Department of Labor. The lowest paid 10 percent earned $28,990, while the highest paid 10 percent earned $81,260 or more per year. Those who have more education, responsibility, and expertise have the potential to earn much more.

Technical support specialists earned the following mean annual salaries by industry in May 2015 (according to the U.S. Department of Labor): software publishers, $58,070; computer systems design and related services, \$54,360; management of companies and enterprises, \$53,150; data processing, hosting, and related services, \$55,680; wireless telecommunications carriers, \$51,790; and colleges, universities, and professional schools, \$49,280.

Most technical support specialists work for companies that offer a full range of benefits, including health insurance, paid vacation, and sick leave. Smaller service or start-up companies may hire support specialists on a contractual basis.

■ WORK ENVIRONMENT

Technical support specialists work in comfortable business environments. They generally work regular, 40-hour weeks. For certain products, however, they may be asked to work evenings or weekends or at least be on call during those times in case of emergencies. Some Web sites may offer customer service hours in the evening. If they work for service companies, they may be required to travel to clients' sites and log overtime hours.

Technical support work can be stressful, since specialists often deal with frustrated users who may be difficult to work with. Communication problems with people who are less technically qualified may also be a source of frustration. Patience and understanding are essential for handling these problems.

Technical support specialists are expected to work quickly and efficiently and be able to perform under pressure. The ability to do this requires thorough technical expertise and keen analytical ability.

■ EXPLORING

Arrange an informational interview with a technical support specialist. Local computer repair shops that offer technical support service might be a good place to contact. Also contact major corporations and software firms directly.

Work and play on computers as much as possible; many computer professionals became computer hobbyists at a very young age. Surf the Internet and seek out the assistance of an online support specialist if assistance is needed with a video game or other computer problem. Read computer magazines and join school or community computer clubs.

Another good way to explore this field is through a computer technology course at a local technical/vocational school. This would give hands-on exposure to typical technical support training. In addition, if you experience problems with your own hardware or software, call technical support; pay careful attention to how the support specialist handles the call and ask as many questions as the specialist has time to answer.

A technical support specialists talks a customer through a problem with her computer. (Dragon Images. Shutterstock.)

■ EDUCATION AND TRAINING REQUIREMENTS
High School

Take technical classes such as computer science, schematic drawing, or electronics, as these can help develop the logical and analytical thinking skills necessary to be successful in this field. Courses in math and science are also valuable for this reason. Strong verbal and written communication skills are needed since technical support specialists have to deal with computer programmers and software designers as well as computer users who may not be technologically savvy. Learning a foreign language, such as Spanish, will be useful for working with customers who do not speak English as a first language.

Postsecondary Training

Individuals interested in pursuing a job in this field should first determine what area of technical support most appeals to them and then honestly assess their level of experience and knowledge. Large corporations often prefer to hire people with a bachelor's degree in computer science, computer engineering, or information system and some experience, although other employers may only require their workers to have associate's degrees. They may also be impressed with commercial certification in a computer field, such as networking. Those hired within the company will be considered more for their work experience than education.

Employed individuals looking for a career change may want to commit themselves to a program of self-study to qualify for technical support positions. Many computer professionals learn a lot of what they know by playing around on computers, reading trade magazines, and talking with colleagues. Self-taught individuals should learn how to effectively demonstrate their knowledge and

COMPUTER SUPPORT SPECIALTIES

LEARN MORE ABOUT IT

Beisse, Fred. *A Guide to Computer User Support for Help Desk and Support Specialists,* 6th ed. Florence, Ky.: Course Technology Cengage Learning, 2014.

Knapp, Donna. *A Guide to Customer Service Skills for the Service Desk Professional,* 4th ed. Florence, Ky.: Cengage Learning, 2014.

Knapp, Donna. *A Guide to Service Desk Concepts,* 4th ed. Florence, Ky.: Cengage Learning, 2013.

Patterson, David A., and John L. Hennessy. *Computer Organization and Design: The Hardware/ Software Interface,* ARM ed. Philadelphia: Morgan Kaufmann, 2016.

proficiency on the job or during an interview. Besides self-training, employed individuals should investigate tuition reimbursement programs offered by their company.

Once hired, technical support specialists also receive on-the-job training that can last from one week to one year. Most training lasts an average of three months.

Other Education or Training

The Association of Computer Support Specialists offers training seminars. Student and professional members of the Association for Computing Machinery can access online computing and business courses via the association's Learning Center. The IEEE Computer Society offers career planning webinars and continuing education courses to its members.

■ CERTIFICATION, LICENSING, AND SPECIAL REQUIREMENTS
Certification or Licensing

Certification is voluntary and highly recommended. Organizations such as HDI and CompTIA offer certification programs. To become certified, you will need to pass a written test and in some cases may need a certain amount of work experience. Certification shows commitment to the technical support profession and demonstrates levels of expertise. In addition, certification may qualify applicants for certain jobs and lead to new employment opportunities.

■ EXPERIENCE, SKILLS, AND PERSONALITY TRAITS

Experience working with common software, hardware, and operating systems via internships, volunteer opportunities, or part-time jobs will be useful.

Technical support is similar to solving mysteries, so support specialists should enjoy the challenge of problem solving and have strong analytical thinking skills. They must be patient and professional with frustrated users and be able to perform well under stress. Strong, effective communication skills are required for this type of work. This is a rapidly changing field and technical support specialists should be naturally curious and enthusiastic about learning new technologies as they are developed.

■ EMPLOYMENT PROSPECTS
Employers

Technical support specialists work for computer hardware and software companies, as well as in the information systems departments of large corporations and government agencies. There are approximately 585,060 technical support specialists employed in the United States.

Starting Out

Most technical support positions are considered entry-level, employed mainly in computer companies and large corporations. Job opportunities are found directly through the careers sections of companies' Web sites as well as through online employment sites such as Monster, Indeed, SimplyHired, among others. Technical support specialists also learn about jobs through word of mouth. School career services offices may also provide job lists, help with resume and cover letter writing, interview tips, and other resources.

Employees who want to make a career change into technical support can contact the human resources department of the company or speak directly with appropriate management. In companies that are expanding their computing systems, it is often helpful for management to know that current employees would be interested in growing in a computer-related direction. They may even be willing to finance additional education.

■ ADVANCEMENT PROSPECTS

Technical support specialists who demonstrate leadership skills and a strong aptitude for the work may be promoted to supervisory positions within technical support departments. Supervisors are responsible for the more complicated problems that arise, as well as for some administrative duties such as scheduling, interviewing, and job assignments.

Further promotion requires additional education. Some technical support specialists may become commercially certified in computer networking so that they can install, maintain, and repair computer networks. Others may prefer to pursue a bachelor's degree in computer science, either full time or part time. The range of careers available to college graduates varies widely. *Software engineers* analyze industrial, business, and scientific problems and develop software programs to handle them effectively. *Quality assurance engineers* design automated quality assurance tests for new software applications. *Internet quality assurance* specialists work specifically with testing and developing companies' Web sites. *Computer systems/ programmer analysts* study the broad computing picture for a company or a group of companies in order to determine the best way to organize the computer systems.

There are limited opportunities for technical support specialists to be promoted into managerial positions. Doing so would require additional education in business but would probably also depend on the individual's advanced computer knowledge.

OUTLOOK

The U.S. Department of Labor (DOL) predicts that employment for technical support specialists will grow by 12 percent, which is faster than the average for all occupations, through 2024. Each time a new computer product is released on the market or another system is installed, problems arise, whether from user error or technical difficulty. Technical support specialists will continue to be needed to solve the problems. Since technology changes so rapidly, it is very important for these professionals to keep up to date on advances. They should read trade magazines, surf the Internet, and talk with colleagues in order to know what is happening in the field.

The DOL reports that employment will be strong in health care industries because the "field is expected to greatly increase its use of information technology, and support services will be crucial to keep everything running properly." Also, the growth of cloud computing is increasing technical support specialists' productivity at some companies, which will temper some of the job growth. Those who work at computer systems design and related firms, however, will have 31 percent job growth through 2024, much faster than the average.

Some companies stop offering technical support on old products or applications after a designated time, so the key is to be flexible with your understanding of technology. The industry as a whole will require more technical support specialists in the future, but it may be the case that certain computer companies go out of business. It can be a volatile industry for start-ups or young companies dedicated to the development of one product. Technical support specialists interested in working for computer companies should therefore consider living in areas in which many such companies are clustered. In this way, it will be easier to find another job if necessary.

Those with a bachelor's degree, work experience, and good technical and communication skills will have the best job prospects.

UNIONS AND ASSOCIATIONS

Computer support specialists are not represented by unions, but they can obtain useful resources and professional support from the Association for Computing Machinery, Association of Support Professionals, CompTIA, HDI, IEEE Computer Society, and the Technology Services Industry Association.

TIPS FOR ENTRY

1. Join professional associations such as the Association of Support Professionals and the Association for Computing Machinery to access training and networking resources, industry publications, and employment opportunities.
2. Read *ACM Career News* at http://www.acm.org/membership/careernews/current to keep up to date on career trends and get job-search tips.
3. Visit the Web sites of the corporations that interest you and check the careers sections for technical support job openings.

FOR MORE INFORMATION

The Association for Computing Machinery provides education, publications, conferences, and other resources for computing machinery professionals.

Association for Computing Machinery (ACM)
2 Penn Plaza, Suite 701
New York, NY 10121-0701
Tel: (800) 342-6626; (212) 626-0500
Fax: (212) 944-1318
E-mail: acmhelp@acm.org
http://www.acm.org

The Association of Support Professionals provides information regarding salary expectations, employment opportunities nationwide, and industry news.

Association of Support Professionals (ASP)
38954 Proctor Boulevard, #396
Sandy, OR 97055-8039
Tel: (503) 668-9004
http://www.asponline.com

CompTIA offers education, certification programs, and other resources for IT professionals.

CompTIA
3500 Lacey Road, Suite 100
Downers Grove, IL 60515-5439
Tel: (630) 678-8300; (866) 835-8020
https://www.comptia.org

The Computing Research Association offers publications, education, job postings, and other information for computing professionals.

Computing Research Association (CRA)
1828 L Street, NW, Suite 800
Washington, D.C. 20036-4632
Tel: (202) 234-2111
Fax: (202) 667-1066
E-mail: info@cra.org
http://cra.org

For more information on this organization's training courses and certification, contact

Help Desk Institute (HDI)
121 South Tejon, Suite 1100
Colorado Springs, CO 80903-2254
Tel: (800) 248-5667; (719) 955-8180
Fax: (719) 955-8114
E-mail: Support@ThinkHDI.com
http://www.thinkhdi.com

The IEEE Computer Society provides information on careers, education, publications, and other resources for computer professionals.

IEEE Computer Society
2001 L Street, NW, Suite 700
Washington, D.C. 20036-4928
Tel: (202) 371-0101
Fax: (202) 728-9614
https://www.computer.org

The Technology Services Industry Association provides best practices research and data insights for the tech industry.

Technology Services Industry Association (TSIA)
17065 Camino San Bernardo, Suite 200
San Diego, CA 92127-5737
Tel: (858) 674-5491
https://www.tsia.com

Technical Writers and Editors

■ OVERVIEW

Technical writers, sometimes called *technical communicators*, express technical and scientific ideas in easy-to-understand language. *Technical editors* revise written text to correct any errors and make it read smoothly and clearly. They also may coordinate the activities of technical writers, technical illustrators, and other staff in preparing material for publication and oversee the document development and production processes. Technical writers hold about 49,700 jobs and editors, including technical editors, hold about 96,690 jobs in the United States.

■ HISTORY

Humans have used writing to communicate information for over 5,500 years. Technical writing, though, did not emerge as a specific profession in the United States until the early years of the 20th century. Before that time, engineers, scientists, and researchers did any necessary writing themselves.

During the early 1900s, technology expanded rapidly. The use of machines to manufacture and mass-produce a wide number of products paved the way for more complex and technical products. Scientists and researchers were discovering new technologies and applications for technology, particularly in electronics, medicine, and engineering. The need to record studies and research, and report them to others, grew. Also, as products became more complex, it was necessary to provide information that documented their components, showed how they were assembled, and explained how to install, use, and repair them. By the mid-1920s, writers were being used to help engineers and scientists document their work and prepare technical information for nontechnical audiences.

Editors had been used for many years to work with printers and authors. They check copies of a printed document to correct any errors made during printing, to rewrite unclear passages, and to correct errors in spelling, grammar, and punctuation. As the need for technical writers grew, so too did the need for technical editors. Editors became more involved in documents before the printing or digital publishing stage, and today work closely with writers as they prepare their materials. Many editors coordinate the activities of all the people involved in preparing technical communications and manage the document development and production processes.

The need for technical writers grew further with the growth of the computer industry beginning in the 1960s. Originally, many computer companies used computer programmers to write user manuals and other documentation. It was widely assumed that the material was so complex that only those who were involved with creating computer programs would be able to write about them. Computer programmers had the technical knowledge, but many were not able to write clear, easy-to-use manuals. Complaints about the difficulty of using and understanding manuals were common. By the 1970s, computer companies began to hire technical writers to write computer manuals and documents. Today, this is one of the largest areas in which technical writers are employed.

The need for technical marketing writers also grew as a result of expanding computer technology. Many copywriters who worked for advertising agencies and marketing firms did not have the technical background to be able to describe the features of the technical products that were coming to market. Thus developed the need for writers who could combine the ability to promote products with the ability to communicate technical information.

The nature of technical writers' and technical editors' jobs continues to change with emerging technologies. Today, the ability to store, transmit, and receive information through computers and digital means is changing the very nature of documents. Traditional books and paper documents are being replaced by e-books, CD-ROMs, interactive multimedia documents, and other types of digital products.

■ THE JOB

Technical writers and editors prepare a wide variety of documents and materials. The most common types of documents they produce are manuals, technical reports, specifications, and proposals. Some technical writers also write scripts for videos and audiovisual presentations and text for multimedia programs. Technical writers and editors prepare manuals that give instructions and detailed information on how to install, assemble, use, service, or repair a product or equipment. They may write and edit manuals as simple as a two-page leaflet that gives instructions on how to assemble a bicycle or as complex as a 500-page document that tells service technicians how to repair machinery, medical equipment, or a climate-control system. One of the most common types of manuals is the computer software user manual, which informs users on how to load software on their computers, explains how to use the program, and gives information on different features.

Technical writers and editors also prepare technical reports on a multitude of subjects. These reports include documents that give the results of research and laboratory tests and documents that describe the progress of a project. They also write and edit sales proposals, product specifications, quality standards, journal articles, in-house style manuals, and newsletters.

The work of a technical writer begins when they are assigned to prepare a document. The writer meets with members of an account or technical team to learn the requirements for the document, the intended purpose or objectives, and the audience. During the planning stage, the writer learns when the document needs to be completed, approximately how long it should be, whether artwork or illustrations are to be included, who the other team members are, and any other production or printing requirements. A schedule is created that defines the different stages of development and determines when the writer needs to have certain parts of the document ready.

The next step in document development is the research, or information gathering, phase. During this stage, technical writers gather all the available information about the product or subject, read and review it, and determine what other information is needed. They may research the topic by reading technical publications, but in most cases they will need to gather information directly from the people working on the product. Writers meet with and interview people who are sources of information, such as scientists, engineers, software developers, computer programmers, managers, and project managers. They ask questions, listen, and take notes or record interviews. They gather any available notes, drawings, or diagrams that may be useful.

After writers gather all the necessary information, they sort it out and organize it. They plan how they are going to present the information and prepare an outline for the document. They may decide how the document will look and prepare the design, format, and layout of the pages. In some cases, this may be done by an editor rather than the writer. If illustrations, diagrams, or photographs will be included, either the editor or writer makes arrangements for an illustrator, photographer, or

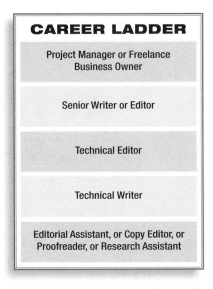

CAREER LADDER

Project Manager or Freelance
Business Owner

Senior Writer or Editor

Technical Editor

Technical Writer

Editorial Assistant, or Copy Editor, or
Proofreader, or Research Assistant

art researcher to produce or obtain them.

Then, the writer starts writing and prepares a rough draft of the document. If the document is very large, a writer may prepare it in segments. Once the rough draft is completed, it is submitted to a designated person or group for technical review. Copies of the draft are distributed to managers, engineers, or other experts who can easily determine if any technical information is inaccurate or missing. These reviewers read the document and suggest changes.

The rough draft is also given to technical editors for review of a variety of factors. The editors check that the material is organized well, that each section flows with the section before and after it, and that the language is appropriate for the intended audience. They also check for correct use of grammar, spelling, and punctuation. They ensure that names of parts or objects are consistent throughout the document and that references are accurate. They also check the labeling of graphs and captions for accuracy. Technical editors use special symbols, called proofreader's marks, to indicate the types of changes needed.

The editor and reviewers return their copies of the document to the technical writer. The writer incorporates the appropriate suggestions and revisions and prepares the final draft. The final draft is once again submitted to a designated reviewer or team of reviewers. In some cases, the technical reviewer may do a quick check to make sure that the requested changes were made. In other cases, the technical reviewer may examine the document in depth to ensure technical accuracy and correctness. A walk-through, or test of the document, may be done for certain types of documents. For example, a walk-through may be done for a document that explains how to assemble a product. A tester assembles the product by following the instructions given in the document. The tester makes a note of all sections that are unclear or inaccurate, and the document is returned to the writer for any necessary revisions.

For some types of documents, a legal review may also be necessary. For example, a pharmaceutical company that is preparing a training manual to teach its sales representatives about a newly released drug needs to ensure that all materials are in compliance with Food and Drug Administration (FDA) requirements. A member of the legal department who is familiar with these requirements will review the document to make sure that all information in the document conforms to FDA rules.

Once the final draft has been approved, the document is submitted to the technical editor, who makes a comprehensive check of the document. In addition to checking that the language is clear and reads smoothly, the editor ensures that the table of contents matches the different sections or chapters of a document, all illustrations and diagrams are correctly placed, all captions are matched to the correct picture, consistent terminology is used, and correct references are used in the bibliography and text.

The editor returns the document to the writer, who makes any necessary corrections. This copy is then checked by a *proofreader*. The proofreader compares the final copy against the editor's marked-up copy and makes sure that all changes were made. The document is then prepared for printing or digital publication. In some cases, the writer is responsible for preparing digital files for printing purposes, and in other cases, a print production coordinator prepares all material to submit to a printer.

Some technical writers specialize in a specific type of material. *Technical marketing writers* create promotional and marketing materials for technological products. They may write the copy for an advertisement for a technical product, such as a computer workstation or software, or they may write press releases about the product. They also write sales literature, product flyers, Web pages, and multimedia presentations.

Other technical writers prepare scripts for videos and films about technical subjects. These writers, called *scriptwriters*, need to have an understanding of film and video production techniques.

Some technical writers and editors prepare articles for scientific, medical, computer, or engineering trade journals. These articles may report the results of research conducted by doctors, scientists, or engineers or report on technological advances in a particular field. Some technical writers and editors also develop textbooks. They may receive articles written by engineers or scientists and edit and revise them to make them more suitable for the intended audience.

Technical writers and editors may create documents for a variety of media. Digital media, such as e-books and content at Web sites, are increasingly being used in place of print books and paper documents. Technical writers may create materials that are accessed through bulletin board systems and the Internet or create computer-based resources, such as help menus on computer programs. They also create interactive, multimedia documents that are distributed on compact discs or on the Internet. Some of these media require knowledge of special computer programs that allow material to be hyperlinked, or electronically cross-referenced.

■ EARNINGS

Median annual earnings for salaried technical writers were $70,240 in May 2015, according to the Bureau of Labor Statistics. Salaries ranged from less than $41,610 to more than $112,220. Editors of all types earned a median salary of $56,010. The lowest paid 10 percent earned $29,230 or less and the highest paid 10 percent earned $109,760 or more.

Technical writers who worked for business, professional, labor, political, and similar organizations earn the highest salaries; the annual mean salary was $91,980 in May 2015. Technical editors who work for security and commodity contracts intermediation and brokerage companies earn top salaries, with the annual mean salary of $102,070 in May 2015.

Most companies offer benefits that include paid holidays and vacations, medical insurance, and 401(k) plans. They may also offer profit sharing, pension plans, and tuition assistance programs.

■ WORK ENVIRONMENT

Technical writers and editors usually work in an office environment, with well-lit and quiet surroundings. They may have their own offices or share workspace with other writers and editors. They may be able to utilize the services of support staff who can word process revisions, make photocopies, e-mail and fax material, and perform other administrative functions or they may have to perform all of these tasks themselves.

Some technical writers and editors work out of home offices and use computer modems and networks to send and receive materials electronically. They may go into the office only on occasion for meetings and gathering information. Freelancers and contract workers may work at a company's premises or at home.

The standard workweek is 40 hours, although many technical writers and editors frequently work 50 or 60 hours a week. Job interruptions, meetings, and conferences can prevent writers from having long periods of time to write. Therefore, many writers work after hours or bring work home. Both writers and editors frequently work in the evening or on weekends in order to meet a deadline.

In many companies there is pressure to produce documents as quickly as possible. Both technical writers and editors may feel at times that they are compromising the quality of their work due to the need to conform to time and budget constraints. In some companies, technical writers and editors may have increased workloads due to company reorganizations or downsizing. They may need to do the work that was formerly done by more than one person. Technical writers and editors also are increasingly assuming roles and responsibilities formerly performed by other people and this can increase work pressures and stress.

Despite these pressures, most technical writers and editors gain immense satisfaction from their work and the roles that they perform in producing technical communications.

■ EXPLORING

Make writing a daily activity. Writing is a skill that develops over time and through practice. Keep journals, join writing clubs, and practice different types of writing, such as scriptwriting and informative reports. Sharing writing with others and asking them to critique it is especially helpful. Comments from readers on what they enjoyed about a piece of writing or difficulty they had in understanding certain sections provides valuable feedback that helps to improve writing style.

Reading a variety of materials is also helpful. Reading exposes you to both good and bad writing styles and techniques, and helps to identify why one approach works better than another.

Experience can also be gained by working on a literary magazine, student newspaper, or yearbook (or starting one of your own if one is not available), or starting a blog (visit Blogger.com and WordPress.com to start your own blog). Both writing and editing articles and managing production give the opportunity to learn new skills and to see what is involved in preparing documents and other materials.

Students may also be able to get internships, cooperative education assignments, or summer or part-time jobs as proofreaders or editorial assistants that may include writing responsibilities.

■ EDUCATION AND TRAINING REQUIREMENTS
High School

Take composition, grammar, literature, creative writing, speech, journalism, social studies, math, statistics, engineering, computer science, and as many science classes as possible. Business courses are also useful as they explain the organizational structure of companies and how they operate.

TOP INDUSTRIES AND ANNUAL EARNINGS FOR TECHNICAL WRITERS, MAY 2015

FAST FACTS

Here are the industries that employed the most technical writers and editors as of 2015 and the mean annual salary in each one:

- Computer systems design and related services: 9,450 jobs, $76,950
- Management, scientific, and technical consulting services: 4,100 jobs, $76,150
- Employment services: 3,890 jobs, $74,140
- Architectural, engineering, and related services: 3,630 jobs, $70,960
- Software publishers: 2,380 jobs, $76,800

Source: U.S. Bureau of Labor Statistics

Postsecondary Training

Most employers prefer to hire technical writers and editors who have a bachelor's or advanced degree. Many technical editors graduate with degrees in the humanities, especially English or journalism. Technical writers typically need to have a strong foundation in engineering, computers, or science. Many technical writers graduate with a degree in engineering or science and take classes in technical writing.

Many different types of college programs are available that prepare people to become technical writers and editors. A growing number of colleges offer degrees in technical writing. Schools without a technical writing program may offer degrees in journalism or English. Programs are offered through English, communications, and journalism departments. Classes vary based on the type of program. In general, classes for technical writers include a core curriculum in writing and classes in algebra, statistics, logic, science, engineering, and computer programming languages. Useful classes for editors include technical writing, project management, grammar, proofreading, copyediting, and print and digital production.

Many technical writers and editors earn a master's degree. In these programs, they study technical writing in depth and may specialize in a certain area, such as scriptwriting, instructional design, or multimedia applications. In addition, many nondegree writing programs are offered to technical writers and editors to hone their skills. Offered as extension courses or continuing education courses, these programs include courses on indexing, editing medical materials, writing for trade journals, and other related subjects.

Technical writers, and occasionally technical editors, are often asked to present samples of their work. College students should build a portfolio during their college years in which they collect their best samples from work that they may have done for a literary magazine, newsletter, or yearbook.

Technical writers and editors should be willing to pursue learning throughout their careers. As technology changes, technical writers and editors may need to take classes to update their knowledge. Changes in printing and computer technology will also change the way technical writers and editors do their jobs, and writers and editors may need to take courses to learn new skills or new technologies.

Other Education or Training

The Society for Technical Communication provides webinars, online courses, and seminars. Past courses included "Project Management and the Technical Communicator," "Don't Write—THINK!," and "Technical Editing Fundamentals." The National Association of Science Writers offers professional development workshops at its annual conference. Contact these organizations for more information.

■ CERTIFICATION, LICENSING, AND SPECIAL REQUIREMENTS
Certification or Licensing

There are no certification or licensing requirements for technical writers and editors. The Society for Technical Communication offers professional certification for those who meet educational requirements and pass tests and evaluations of work products

■ EXPERIENCE, SKILLS, AND PERSONALITY TRAITS

Any experience volunteering, interning, or working part time as a writer will be useful for those who aspire to enter the field. Contact community organizations, religious groups, or local businesses, and other organizations that require the skills of writers. Technical writers and editors should also have experience with a technical subject, such as computer science, engineering, or Web design.

Technical writers need to have good communications skills, science and technical aptitudes, and the ability to think analytically. Technical editors also need to have good communications skills and judgment, as well as the ability to identify and correct errors in written material. They need to be diplomatic, assertive, and able to explain tactfully what needs to be corrected to writers, engineers, and other people involved with a document.

Technical editors should be able to understand technical information easily, but they need less scientific and technical background than writers. Both technical writers and editors need to be able to work as part of a team and collaborate with others on a project. They need to be highly self-motivated, well organized, and able to work under pressure.

■ EMPLOYMENT PROSPECTS

Employers

The Department of Labor reports that the following metropolitan areas offer the best opportunities for technical communicators:

- Washington-Arlington-Alexandria, D.C., Virginia, Maryland, West Virginia
- New York-Jersey City-White Plains, New York, New Jersey
- Los Angeles-Long Beach-Glendale, California
- Boston-Cambridge-Newton, Massachusetts
- San Jose-Sunnyvale-Santa Clara, California

There are approximately 49,770 technical writers currently employed in the United States. Editors of all types (including technical editors) hold 96,690 jobs.

Employment may be found in many different types of places, such as in the fields of aerospace, computers, engineering, pharmaceuticals, and research and development, or with the nuclear industry, medical publishers, government agencies or contractors, and colleges and universities. The aerospace, engineering, medical, and computer industries hire significant numbers of technical writers and editors. The federal government, particularly the Departments of Defense and Agriculture, the National Aeronautics and Space Administration (NASA), and the Energy Research and Development Administration, also hires many writers and editors with technical knowledge.

Starting Out

Many technical writers start their careers as scientists, engineers, technicians, or research assistants and move into writing after several years of experience in those positions. Technical writers with a bachelor's degree in a technical subject such as engineering may be able to find work as a technical writer immediately upon graduating from college, but many employers prefer to hire writers with some work experience.

Technical editors who graduate with a bachelor's degree in English or journalism may find entry-level work as *editorial assistants*, *copy editors*, *research assistants*, or *proofreaders*. From these positions they are able to move into technical editing positions. Beginning workers may find jobs as technical editors in small companies or those with a small technical communications department.

To work for the federal government, writers and editors need to pass an examination. Information about examinations and job openings is available at federal employment centers. Job openings may also be found through career services offices and employment agencies. Another job-hunt route is to research companies that hire technical writers and editors and apply directly to them. Many libraries provide useful job resource guides and directories that provide information about companies that hire in specific areas.

■ ADVANCEMENT PROSPECTS

Technical writers and editors with experience move into more challenging and responsible positions. They may initially work on simple documents or sections of a document. As they demonstrate their proficiency and skills, they are given more complex assignments and are responsible for more activities.

Technical writers and editors with several years of experience may move into project management positions, where they are responsible for the entire document development and production processes. They schedule and budget resources and assign writers, editors, illustrators, and other workers to a project. They monitor the schedule, supervise workers, and ensure that costs remain in budget.

Technical writers and editors who show good project management skills, leadership abilities, and good interpersonal skills may become supervisors or managers. Both technical writers and editors can move into senior writer and senior editor positions. These positions involve increased responsibilities and may include supervising other workers.

Many technical writers and editors seek to develop and perfect their skills rather than move into management or supervisory positions. As they gain a reputation for their quality of work, they may be able to select choice assignments. They may learn new skills as a means of being able to work in new areas. For example, a technical writer may learn a new desktop program in order to become more proficient in design. Or, a technical writer may learn HyperText Markup Language (HTML) in order to be able to create a multimedia program. Technical writers and editors who broaden their skill base and capabilities can move to higher-paying positions within their own company or at another company. They also may work as freelancers or set up their own communications companies.

■ OUTLOOK

The writing and editing field is generally very competitive. Each year, there are more people trying to enter this field than there are available openings. The field of technical writing and editing, though, offers more opportunities than other areas of writing and editing, such as book publishing or journalism. Employment opportunities for technical writers are expected to grow faster than the average for all occupations through 2024. Job opportunities for editors who work for software publishers are expected to grow faster than the average during this period.

Demand is increasing for technical writers who can produce well-written computer manuals and content for the Web. In addition to software publishers and computer systems design and related services firms, management, scientific, and technical consulting services firms are showing an increased need for technical writers. Continued growth in the high technology and electronics industries and the Internet will create a continuing demand for people to write users' guides, instruction manuals, and training materials. Technical writers will be needed to produce copy that describes developments and discoveries in law, medicine, science, and technology for a more general audience.

Writers may find positions that include duties in addition to writing. A growing trend is for companies to use writers to run a department, supervise other writers, and manage freelance writers and outside contractors. In addition, many writers are acquiring responsibilities that include desktop publishing and print production coordination.

The demand for technical writers and editors is significantly affected by the economy. During recessionary times, technical writers and editors are often among the first to be laid off. Many companies today are continuing to downsize or reduce their number of employees and are reluctant to keep writers on staff. Such companies prefer to hire writers and editors on a temporary contractual basis, using them only as long as it takes to complete an assigned document. Technical writers and editors who work on a temporary or freelance basis need to market their services and continually look for new assignments. They also do not have the security or benefits offered by full-time employment.

■ UNIONS AND ASSOCIATIONS

Some writers and editors may obtain union representation from the National Writers Union and The Newspaper Guild-Communication Workers of America. The Society for Technical Communication and the National Association of Science Writers are the leading organizations for technical writers and editors. They provide career resource, professional development classes and webinars, annual conferences, and publications.

■ TIPS FOR ENTRY

1. Write often and create a portfolio of work to show potential employers.
2. To learn more about the field, read publications by the Society for Technical Communication, found at https://www.stc.org/publications, and the National Association of Science Writers' publication, *ScienceWriters* at https://www.nasw.org/sciencewriters.
3. Attend the Technical Communication Summit (http://www.stc.org/education) to network and participate in continuing education opportunities.
4. The American Society of Journalists and Authors (ASJA) offers a mentoring program for freelance writers, at http://asja.org/for-writers/personal-mentoring-program, as well as other resources.

■ FOR MORE INFORMATION

The American Medical Writers Association provides career-support resources and membership benefits for medical writers.

American Medical Writers Association (AMWA)
30 West Gude Drive, Suite 525
Rockville, MD 20850-4347
Tel: (240) 238-0940
Fax: (301) 294-9006
E-mail: amwa@awma.org
http://www.amwa.org

The National Association of Science Writers provides information on writing and editing careers in the field of science communications.

National Association of Science Writers (NASW)
PO Box 7905
Berkeley, CA 94707-0905
Tel: (510) 647-9500
E-mail: webmaster@nasw.org
https://www.nasw.org

The Society for Technical Communication offers education, certification, publications, networking opportunities, and other resources for professional technical communicators.

Society for Technical Communication (STC)
9401 Lee Highway, Suite 300
Fairfax, VA 22031-1803
Tel: (703) 522-4114
Fax: (703) 522-2075
E-mail: stc@stc.org
https://www.stc.org

Telecommunications Network Engineers

■ OVERVIEW

Telecommunications network engineers design the communication systems of companies. They design, install, and oversee the voice, data, and video communication systems, as well as decide on the appropriate hardware and software for telecommunications. They may also be known as computer network architects. The Department of Labor reports that in May 2015, there were approximately 146,600 computer network architects employed in the United States.

■ HISTORY

Telecommunications is the combination of electronics and electrical engineering that brings telephone and high-speed data services to people. The field of telecommunications network engineering has roots in the telegraph industry and later the radio and telephone industries. In the 1800s, the electrical telegraph was used to transmit messages over electrical signals over wires between stations, with the first successful transatlantic telegraph sent in 1866. Alexander Graham Bell introduced his invention, the telephone, in the 1870s, and the use of telephones as a major mode of communication grew in the following decades. The first coast-to-coast long-distance telephone call was made in 1915, between Bell in New York City and a former assistant in San Francisco, California.

The radio was introduced in the late 1800s and early 1900s, with Guglielmo Marconi's invention of wireless telegraphy system and the first wireless transmission between Britain and Newfoundland. Communication satellites were first used in the 1950s and 1960s, for government and NASA projects. Since then, commercial telephone services use communication satellites for long-distance services.

Telecommunications is also tied into computers and computer networking. Computers date back to the 1940s, but were initially used only for government and military purposes. Semiconductors were introduced in the 1950s, and by the late 1970s and early 1980s, smaller, more powerful computers were available to the general public. In the early days, the computer system consisted of several large mainframe computers that were located in computer rooms and terminals throughout companies' office spaces. This system had some drawbacks, however, including delays in information updates from one computer to the next, which is why many companies have turned to network servers instead. The computer network system relies on a network server that is the central processor for all of the computers and related equipment.

Today, telephone services are offered by cable providers through broadband connections, as well as through the Internet on computers. AT&T, Verizon, and other such telephone companies are the main providers of data services via Wi-Fi for computers, tablets, smartphones, and other mobile devices. Another recent service added to the telecommunications industry is voice over Internet protocol (VoIP), which enables phone calls from computers, tablets, and other devices through the Internet, without need of a cellular connection or direct landline. Companies such as Vonage and Skype provide these services.

■ THE JOB

Telecommunications network engineers plan and design telecommunications networks according to companies' business plans and goals. This includes networks and equipment for telephones, voicemail, video, and data communication. They design and build communication networks for data, setting up and evaluating such things as the local area networks (LANs) and the wide area networks (WANs). Their work may involve setting up an internal network, such as networking between the computers in several offices within the same building, or creating an international communication network using a cloud infrastructure to provide service for many customers in multiple locations.

QUICK FACTS

ALTERNATE TITLE(S)
Computer Network Architects

DUTIES
Design and build data communication networks for companies; upgrade hardware and software to keep computer networks operating efficiently; research new networking technologies

SALARY RANGE
$47,446 to $75,408 to $109,348+

WORK ENVIRONMENT
Primarily Indoors

BEST GEOGRAPHIC LOCATION(S)
Opportunities exist in all regions; highest employment levels in Florida, California, Texas, Virginia, and New York

MINIMUM EDUCATION LEVEL
Bachelor's Degree

SCHOOL SUBJECTS
Business, Computer Science, Mathematics

EXPERIENCE
Five to 10 years experience

PERSONALITY TRAITS
Organized, Problem-Solving, Technical

SKILLS
Computer, Information Management, Organizational

CERTIFICATION OR LICENSING
Recommended

SPECIAL REQUIREMENTS
None

EMPLOYMENT PROSPECTS
Good

ADVANCEMENT PROSPECTS
Good

OUTLOOK
Faster than the Average

NOC
5121, 5122

O*NET-SOC
27-3041.00, 27-3042.00

CAREER LADDER

Telecommunications Manager

Telecommunications Network Engineer

Telecommunications Engineer

Internship

Telecommunications network engineers use network drivers and hardware such as cables, hubs, and routers in their work, upgrading hardware and software to ensure computer networks operate efficiently and safely. They install new communications equipment, perform equipment and verification tests, and troubleshoot and solve any networking problems that arise. They keep their department supervisors and managers apprised of network operations. They research new networking technologies for future uses for clients and also keep information security issues in mind when doing their work. Telecommunications network engineers may also be responsible for training other network engineers.

■ EARNINGS

PayScale.com reported the average annual salary for telecommunications network engineers as $75,408 in January 2016; salaries ranged from $47,446 to $109,348 or more. The average annual salary for computer network architects in May 2015 was $100,240, according to the Department of Labor. The lowest 10 percent earned $56,230 and the highest 10 percent earned $155,250 or more. Those who worked for wired telecommunications carriers earned an average annual salary of $105,990.

■ WORK ENVIRONMENT

Telecommunications network engineers work indoors in offices, spending much of their work day on computers and also testing telecommunications equipment. Some travel may be required at times to work in clients' offices. They may work in companies' server rooms where they access the hardware for the computer and information network. The majority of telecommunications network engineers work full time and about 25 percent work more than 40 hours per week.

■ EXPLORING

An internship or part-time job with a telecommunications company is a good way to learn more about the telecommunications network engineering. Search for job listings posted through professional associations, on employment Web sites such as Indeed.com and Monster.com, and also direct postings on telecommunications companies' Web sites. Visit the Association of Computing Machinery's online learning center to find courses and publications on telecommunications networking, http://www.acm.org/education/learning-center.

■ EDUCATION AND TRAINING REQUIREMENTS
High School

Telecommunications network engineers must have strong knowledge of computers, information systems, and electronics. While in high school, take classes in computer science, mathematics, and business. Classes in English and writing are also helpful for the communication skills needed in this field.

Postsecondary Education

Most employers prefer telecommunications network engineers have, at minimum, a bachelor's degree in a computer-related field, and some require a Master of Business Administration (MBA) with a concentration in information systems. Bachelor's degree programs may be in computer science, information systems, engineering, or a similar area of study. Coursework includes laboratory work in database design and network security, preparing students for future work in the diverse technologies used in telecommunications networks.

■ CERTIFICATION, LICENSING, AND SPECIAL REQUIREMENTS

Certification is offered by various professional associations as well as product vendors and software firms. Certification is voluntary and can help advance telecommunications professionals' skills and employment opportunities. Associations such as the National Center for Women & Information Technology and the Association for Computing Machinery, among others, offer certification programs

■ EXPERIENCE, SKILLS, AND PERSONALITY TRAITS

Telecommunications network engineers are usually required to have five to 10 years of prior experience in information technology (IT) systems. Most employers prefer to hire engineers who have experience as telecommunications engineers or network and computer system administrators. Strong analytical skills are required to evaluate telecommunications networks and advise clients on the ways to make the systems more efficient and safe. Attention to detail is needed to design and build network plans and organizational and interpersonal skills are needed to coordinate and communicate with different types of employees at all levels.

■ EMPLOYMENT PROSPECTS
Employers
Telecommunications network engineers work for computer systems design and related services, finance and insurance companies, telecommunications carriers, and government agencies. The Department of Labor reported that there were 146,600 computer network architects, including telecommunications network engineers, employed in the United States in May 2015.

Starting Out
Many telecommunications network engineers get their start through internships and work their way up to the network engineer position. Jobs can be found through postings on professional association's Web sites and through general employment Web sites. Entry-level positions should be available in the coming years as companies continue to expand their telecommunications networks.

■ ADVANCEMENT PROSPECTS
Telecommunications network engineers usually have five to 10 years of prior work experience as telecommunications engineers, computer systems administrators, or related job titles. After several or more years in the network engineer role, they may advance to become department supervisors or managers.

■ OUTLOOK
The outlook for telecommunications network engineers is bright. The Department of Labor predicts faster than average employment growth (9 percent) for computer network architects and related workers through 2024. More companies are expected to expand their telecommunications networks in the coming years; demand will likewise increase for help with designing and building these networks, as well as upgrading existing networks. In 2015, CNNMoney.com ranked telecommunications network engineer among the top 100 careers for big growth, great pay, and satisfying work, predicting 15 percent job growth through 2025. Telecommunications network engineers with a bachelor's degree in computer science or related field, prior relevant experience, certification, and knowledge of the latest technologies will have the best job prospects.

■ UNIONS AND ASSOCIATIONS
The Association for Computing Machinery provides educational programs, conferences, networking

TODAY'S TELECOMMUNICATIONS NETWORKS   DID YOU KNOW?

Telecommunications networks consist of computer networks, telephone networks, and the Internet. The telecommunications network engineer helps to establish the infrastructure and controls that are needed for the transfer and exchange of communications, which includes phone calls, e-mails, text messages, videos, images, and other data, over long distances. In the early days, telecommunications systems were built without computers; today, computers are essential in telecommunications.

Telecommunication network engineers are responsible for connecting not only computer networks and telephone networks for companies, but also ensuring that people can access data on smartphones, tablets, laptops, and other mobile devices. Many companies use telecommunications networks in their offices as well as wireless networks, video conferencing, and other communications technologies. For large companies, telecommunications network engineers network computer systems, phone and video conferencing technology, and the Internet, to increase the efficiency of the companies' meetings of global offices.

opportunities, publications and journals, and other resources for computing practitioners. CompTIA is a nonprofit trade association that offers education and certification programs, advocacy, and philanthropy for the information technology industry. The Computing Research Association provides events and resources for organizations that are involved in computer science, information, and engineering, including industry, government, and academia. The National Center for Women and Information Technology is a nonprofit organization that aims to advance women's participation from early education through to corporate and entrepreneurial careers.

■ TIPS FOR ENTRY
1. Get an internship or part-time job in a telecommunications network service provider to gain experience in this industry.
2. Visit the Web sites of professional associations and read the news sections and publications to learn more about the computing profession.
3. Meet others in the field by attending networking events and conferences offered by trade

organizations such as the Association for Computing Machinery or the National Center for Women & Information Technology, among others.

■ FOR MORE INFORMATION

The Association for Computing Machinery provides education and resources to advance computing as a science and profession.

> **Association for Computing**
> **Machinery (ACM)**
> 2 Penn Plaza, Suite 701
> New York, NY 10121-0701
> Tel: (800) 342-6626; (212) 626-0500
> Fax: (212) 944-1318
> E-mail: acmhelp@acm.org
> http://www.acm.org

CompTIA is a nonprofit trade association that advances the global interests of Information Technology professionals and organizations.

> **CompTIA**
> 3500 Lacey Road, Suite 100
> Downers Grove, IL 60515-5439
> Tel: (866) 835 - 8020; (630) 678-8300
> E-mail: techvoice@comptia.org
> https://www.comptia.org

The Computing Research Association joins together industry, government, and academia to strengthen research and advanced education in computing.

> **Computing Research**
> **Association (CRA)**
> 1828 L Street, NW, Suite 800
> Washington, D.C. 20036-4632
> Tel: (202) 234-2111
> Fax: (202) 667-1066
> http://cra.org

The National Center for Women & Information Technology provides education programs as well as publications, networking events, and other resources for technology and computing students and professionals.

> **National Center for Women & Information**
> **Technology (NCWIT)**
> Campus Box 417 UCB
> Boulder, CO 80309
> Tel: (303) 735-6671
> Fax: (303) 735_6606
> E-mail: info@ncwit.org
> https://www.ncwit.org

Telemarketers

■ OVERVIEW

Telemarketers make and receive phone calls on behalf of a company in order to sell its goods, market its services, gather information, receive orders and complaints, solicit donations, and/or handle other miscellaneous business.

Telemarketing professionals might work directly for one company or for several companies that use the same service. In addition to selling, telemarketers place and receive calls in order to raise funds, conduct marketing research surveys, or raise public awareness. Accordingly, a wide variety of organizations in many industries employ telemarketers. There are approximately 226,730 people who work part time or full time as telemarketers.

■ HISTORY

It is no exaggeration to say that the telephone has become an indispensable part of our daily lives. The speed of communicating by phone and the ability to reach the exact people with whom we want to speak have drastically changed the way business has been conducted over the past hundred years.

Since World War II, many companies have turned to marketing in order to expand business. Marketing involves finding the most likely customers for a product or service and then targeting those customers for sales, investment, or other business activity. A popular form of marketing is telemarketing, or the use of phone calls to sell a product or service, to find out about potential customers, to stay in touch with current customers, or to provide consumers with the most current information on new products and services. Telemarketing allows callers direct contact with potential customers.

■ THE JOB

Telemarketers generally work for one of two types of businesses. Some telemarketers are part of the in-house staff of a company or corporation and make and receive calls on behalf of that company. Others work for a telemarketing service agency and make or receive calls for the clients of the agency. Telemarketing agencies are useful for companies that don't want to or can't keep a full-time telemarketing staff on the payroll or that need telemarketing services only occasionally. Both large corporations and small firms employ telemarketing agencies, which sometimes specialize in particular fields, such as fund-raising, product sales, and insurance.

Telemarketers are generally responsible for either handling incoming calls or placing calls to outside parties. Incoming calls may include requests for information or orders for an advertised product, such as clothing, magazines, appliances, or books. Telemarketers also staff the phones that handle toll-free "800" numbers, which customers call to ask questions about the use of a product or to register complaints. Airline reservations, concert and sports tickets, and credit card problems are all transactions that can be handled by telemarketers. Newspapers often employ classified ad clerks to transcribe classified ads from callers. A person whose sole job is taking orders from callers over the phone is sometimes called an *order clerk*.

Telemarketers place outside calls for many purposes as well. One of the most important reasons to make such calls is to sell products and services to consumers. The phone numbers of the people that telemarketers call usually come from a prepared list of previous customers, the phone book, reply cards from magazines, or a list purchased from another source. Sometimes randomly dialed "cold calls" are made. Once made, these calls often serve as a source of potential leads for the company's regular sales staff. A wide range of products—from newspaper subscriptions and credit cards to time-share resort condominiums and long-distance service—can be successfully sold in this way. Once a sale is made, the telemarketer records all necessary information, such as the buyer's name and address, product choices, and payment information, so that order fillers can prepare the product for shipment.

Cultural organizations, such as ballet and opera companies, public television stations, and theater troupes, use telemarketers to solicit subscriptions and donations. Charity fund-raising also relies heavily on telemarketing.

In addition to selling, telemarketers make calls for other reasons. They may conduct marketing surveys of consumers to discover the reasons for their buying decisions or what they like and dislike about a certain product. They may call to endorse a candidate in an upcoming election or tell citizens about an important vote in their city council. When making calls business-to-business, telemarketers may try to encourage attendance at important meetings, assist a company in recruitment and job placement, or collect demographic information for use in an advertising campaign.

When making outbound calls, telemarketers usually work from a prepared script that they must follow exactly. This is especially true of market-research surveys because people need to be asked the same questions in the same way if the survey data are to be valid. Often when a customer tries to resist a sales pitch, the telemarketer will read a standard response that has been prepared in anticipation of potential objections. At other times, the telemarketer must rely on persuasive sales skills and quick thinking to win over the customer and make the sale. Telemarketers have to be a little more skillful when selling business-to-business because these customers usually have a clear idea of the needs of their businesses and will ask specific questions related to them.

■ EARNINGS

Telemarketers' earnings vary with the type of work they do. The pay can range from the minimum wage ($7.25 per hour, which is $15,080 annually) to more than $18 per hour (more than $38,000 annually). Pay may be higher for those who deliver more elaborate sales presentations, work weekends, or make business-to-business calls. As telemarketers gain experience and skills, their pay increases. The median hourly wage for telemarketers was $11.31 in May 2015, according to the Bureau of Labor Statistics. This translates to median annual earnings of $23,530, and salaries ranged from less than $17,730 to more than $38,450.

Telemarketing workers also frequently enjoy such employee benefits as health and life insurance, paid vacation and sick days, and profit sharing. With such a wide range of organizations for which telemarketers can work, the benefits offered depend entirely on the employer.

■ WORK ENVIRONMENT

The offices in which telemarketers work can range from the very basic, with standard phones and desks, to the highly advanced, with computer terminals, the latest in phone technology, and machines that automatically dial numbers from a database. There may be just four or five telemarketers in a smaller office or more than 100 working at

---

QUICK FACTS

ALTERNATE TITLE(S)
None

DUTIES
Make and receive phone calls on behalf of a company in order to sell its goods, market its services, gather information, and perform other tasks

SALARY RANGE
$15,080 to $23,530 to $38,450+

WORK ENVIRONMENT
Primarily Indoors

BEST GEOGRAPHIC LOCATION(S)
Opportunities are available throughout the country, but are best in large, urban areas

MINIMUM EDUCATION LEVEL
High School Diploma

SCHOOL SUBJECTS
Business, Speech

EXPERIENCE
Experience recommended

PERSONALITY TRAITS
Enterprising, Outgoing, Talkative

SKILLS
Interpersonal, Public Speaking, Sales

CERTIFICATION OR LICENSING
None

SPECIAL REQUIREMENTS
None

EMPLOYMENT PROSPECTS
Good

ADVANCEMENT PROSPECTS
Fair

OUTLOOK
Decline

NOC
6623

O*NET-SOC
41-9041.00

a larger office. The work is not strenuous but it can be very repetitive. The amount of supervision depends on the employer and the region of the country. California and a few other states, for example, have laws that prohibit recording calls or monitoring by supervisors unless both the telemarketer and the person being called are aware of it.

Telemarketing requires many hours of sitting and talking on the phone. Customer rejections, which range from polite to rude, can cause a great deal of stress. As a result, many telemarketers work only four- or five-hour shifts. Telemarketing is an ideal job for people looking for part-time work because workweeks generally run from 24 to 30 hours. Many agencies need staff at unusual hours, so telemarketers are often able to find positions offering schedules that match their lifestyles. There is also 24-hour staffing in many agencies, to handle such calls as airline reservations and reports of stolen credit cards. Telemarketers who make business-to-business calls work during normal business hours, while those who call consumers make most of their calls in the evening and on weekends, when more people are at home.

■ EXPLORING

There are many ways to gain practice and poise in telemarketing. Many organizations use volunteer phone workers during campaigns and fund drives. One of the

In-house telemarketers usually work out of call centers. (Goodluz. Shutterstock.)

most visible of these is public television stations, which conduct fund-raising drives several times a year and are always looking for volunteer help to staff the phone banks. Other groups that routinely need volunteer telemarketers include local political campaigns, theaters and other arts groups, churches, schools, environmental organizations, and nonprofit social organizations, such as crisis centers and inner-city recreation programs.

■ EDUCATION AND TRAINING REQUIREMENTS
High School
The skills and education needed to become a telemarketer depend on the firm. A high school diploma is usually required for any type of position, while some employers hire only people who have earned a college degree.

Telemarketers must be able to speak persuasively and listen to customers carefully, so classes in English, communications, speech, drama, and broadcasting are particularly useful. Business and sales classes, as well as psychology and sociology, are also valuable. In addition, since many telemarketing positions require the use of computers for entering data, familiarity and experience with technology in general and data processing in particular are pluses.

Postsecondary Training
A college degree is not absolutely necessary for many telemarketing positions, but some employers hire only college graduates. Courses in English, speech, drama, and communication are especially useful for those aspiring to the job of telemarketer. In addition, general business classes, such as marketing, advertising, and sales, are valuable. Also, courses in psychology and human behavior can help telemarketers gain insight to the wide variety of people that they often speak to during the course of a typical workday.

Other Education or Training
The Direct Marketing Association (DMA) offers seminars, courses, and webinars to help marketing professionals keep their skills up to date. One past course, "Direct Marketing 101," covered when and how to use telemarketing in direct marketing campaigns.

■ CERTIFICATION, LICENSING, AND SPECIAL REQUIREMENTS
Certification or Licensing
There are no certification or licensing requirements for telemarketers, but some states have guidelines or legislation to regulate the activities of telemarketers. In California, for example, certain types of telemarketing agencies must register each year with the state, although

most business-to-business telemarketing is exempt because sales are usually not the main goal of such calls.

Telemarketers covered by the National Do Not Call Registry are required to access the registry every 31 days to obtain updates to the list, and then are required to remove those phone numbers from their call lists.

■ EXPERIENCE, SKILLS, AND PERSONALITY TRAITS

Previous experience in customer service or sales is recommended for aspiring telemarketers. They must be able to deal well with other people, even in telephone conversations. This work requires the ability to sense how customers are reacting, to keep them interested in the sales pitch, to listen carefully to their responses and complaints, and to react tactfully to impatient and sometimes hostile people. Telemarketers must be able to balance sensitivity to their company's concerns with the needs of the customer.

To succeed in telemarketing, telemarketers must have a warm, pleasant phone voice that conveys sincerity and confidence. They must be detail-oriented as well. They have to take orders while on the phone, get other important information, and fill out complete sales records, all of which requires an accurate and alert mind.

Many federal, state, and local laws have been enacted governing the sort of language and sales tactics that can be used with phone solicitation. Such legislation is intended to protect consumers from unscrupulous telemarketers operating phone scams. Telemarketers must be aware of these laws and conduct their phone sales in an honest and unambiguous manner. To bolster the industry's image in the eyes of the public, several professional organizations exist to further the cause of ethical and effective telemarketing.

■ EMPLOYMENT PROSPECTS

Employers

Approximately 226,730 people work part time or full time as telemarketers. Work is available at a wide variety of establishments, from large multinational corporations, educational publishers, and government agencies to nonprofit organizations, retail catalog outlets, and service businesses. Jobs in telemarketing can be found nationwide, but the cost of operating call centers varies, depending on their location. Some of the most expensive cities in which to operate call centers, for example, are San Francisco, Washington, D.C., and New York, while the least expensive cities include Columbia, South Carolina, and Mobile, Alabama. Large corporations often house their telemarketing centers in cities where both operating costs and salaries are low.

TELEMARKETING TOOLS: FROM PHONE TO SMARTPHONE

ON THE CUTTING EDGE

In the early 1870s, Alexander Graham Bell began experimenting with sound. With the assistance of a young repair mechanic and model maker named Thomas Watson, Bell devised an apparatus for electrically transmitting sound. On March 7, 1876, the U.S. Patent Office granted him patent number 174,465, which covered: "The method of, and apparatus for, transmitting vocal or other sounds telegraphically…by causing electrical undulations, similar in form to the vibrations of the air accompanying the said vocal or other sounds." The telephone was born!

Smartphones have evolved since their first introduction in the late 1990s. They have since become smaller yet more powerful, offering a variety of features. There is now more wireless coverage than in the past, which has increased smartphone use in more locations across the United States as well as around the world. Many smartphones include video conferencing capabilities, speakerphone, digital camera, social media applications, music player and library, Web browsing ability, e-mail, and more. Smartphones can be as light as 113 grams. Users have the ability to customize their smartphone's settings, display, and ring tones.

Starting Out

Agencies that hire telemarketers usually advertise for new employees through employment agencies, many of which specialize in placing telemarketers with firms. It is important to note that employers of telemarketers sometimes interview job applicants over the phone, judging a person's telephone voice, personality, demeanor, and assertiveness. Being prepared for such an interview before contacting an agency can make the difference between getting the job and having to continue to look.

Employees undergo a great deal of on-the-job training after they have been hired. Trainers instruct novice telemarketers on the use of equipment, characteristics of the product or service they will be selling, and proper sales techniques and listening skills. They rehearse with the trainees using the script that has been prepared and guide them through some practice calls.

If a telemarketer's phone calls focus on a complex product or service, as is the case with many business-to-business calls, people trained in the specific field involved may be hired and then instructed in telephone and sales techniques.

■ ADVANCEMENT PROSPECTS

Employees at telemarketing agencies can advance to jobs as *telemarketing managers*. These professionals have a

THE NATIONAL DO NOT CALL REGISTRY

DID YOU KNOW?

Activated on June 27, 2003, the National Do Not Call (DNC) Registry offers a free service to individuals who wish to remove their cell phone and landline numbers from telemarketers' call lists. People who add their phone number to the DNC Registry will receive fewer telemarketer calls. One study of consumers who added their numbers to the list found that they received an average of 30 telemarketing calls per month before registering, and after registering received only six per month. Telemarketers that call a number on the no-call list can be fined up to $16,000 per call.

As of November 2016, the FTC had brought 105 enforcement actions against companies and telemarketers for Do Not Call, abandoned call, robocall, and registry violations. It reports that "80 of these enforcement actions have been resolved, and in those cases the agency has recovered over $41 million in civil penalties and $33 million in redress or disgorgement."

variety of responsibilities, including preparing reports, writing telephone scripts, setting goals and objectives, implementing new service programs, monitoring and analyzing inquiries and complaints, recruiting, scheduling, and training. Telemarketing managers may also enjoy rapidly increasing salaries because they can often earn commissions on the net sales achieved by the agency.

Some telemarketers move into telephone-sales training, either with agencies or as independent consultants. Experienced telemarketers can sometimes find new jobs with higher paying firms, while others start their own telemarketing agencies.

■ OUTLOOK

Employment for telemarketers is expected to decline by 3 percent through 2024, according to the U.S. Department of Labor. In the past, the career of telemarketer consistently ranked as a fast-growing occupation, but growth has slowed in recent years as a result of the movement of call-center jobs overseas and the implementation of the National Do Not Call Registry. The National Do Not Call Registry, a free service offered by the Federal Trade Commission since June 2003, allows consumers to add their cell phone and landline phone numbers to a do-not-call list, from which telemarketers may not call. Telemarketers with experience and a proven track record of generating sales will have the best job prospects. There

is also high turnover in this field so there will be ongoing need to replace workers who leave the job for other opportunities.

■ UNIONS AND ASSOCIATIONS

Telemarketers do not belong to unions. The Direct Marketing Association, American Marketing Association, and the Professional Association of Customer Engagement provide information on telemarketing and customer service careers. The Customer Service Group offers training resources and publications.

■ TIPS FOR ENTRY

1. Read *The Customer Communicator* (http://www .customerservicegroup.com/the_customer_com municator.php) to learn more about developing strong communication skills.
2. Visit http://careercenter.thedma.org/jobseekers for job listings.
3. Contact telemarketing firms to learn more about job opportunities.

■ FOR MORE INFORMATION

The American Marketing Association is an internal professional society of individual members with an interest in the practice, study, and teaching of marketing.

American Marketing Association (AMA)
130 East Randolph Street, 22nd Floor
Chicago, IL 60601-6207
Tel: (800) AMA-1150; (312) 542-9000
Fax: (312) 542-9001
https://www.ama.org

The International Customer Management Institute provides education and career-support resources for customer management professionals.

International Customer Management Institute (ICMI)
121 South Tejon Street, Suite 1100
Colorado Springs, CO 80903-2216
Tel: (800) 672-6177; (719) 955-8149
Fax: (719) 955-8146
E-mail: icmi@icmi.com
http://www.icmi.com

The Customer Service Group provides training and other resources for customer service professionals.

Customer Service Group (CSG)
36 Midvale Road, Suite 2E
Mountain Lakes, NJ 07046-1353

Tel: (973) 265-2300
Fax: (973) 402-6056
http://www.customerservicegroup.com

The Direct Marketing Association is the largest trade association for individuals interested in database marketing.

Direct Marketing Association (DMA)
1333 Broadway, Suite 301
New York, NY 10018-7204
Tel: (212) 768-7277
https://thedma.org

The Professional Association of Customer Engagement is an industry advocacy group that offers professional education opportunities.

Professional Association of Customer Engagement (PACE)
8445 Keystone Crossing, Suite 106
Indianapolis, IN 46240-2454
Tel: (317) 816-9336
http://www.paceassociation.com

Telephone and PBX Installers and Repairers

■ OVERVIEW

Telephone and private branch exchange (PBX) installers and repairers install, service, and repair telephone and PBX systems in customers' homes and places of business. Approximately 219,100 radio and telecommunications equipment installers and repairers are employed in the United States.

■ HISTORY

In 1876, the first practical device for transmitting speech over electric wires was patented by Alexander Graham Bell. The telephone device Bell invented functioned on essentially the same principle as the telephones that are familiar to us today. Both transmit the vibrations of speech sounds by transferring them to solid bodies and converting them to electrical impulses, which can travel along wires. However, technological advances in telephone systems over the past century have turned telephones into powerful instruments for communication.

Within a few years after its introduction, many customers were having the new devices installed and were being connected into local telephone systems. Four years after Bell's patent, there were 30,000 subscribers to 138 local telephone exchanges. By 1887, there were 150,000 telephones in the United States. Long distance service developed slowly because of problems with distortion and signal loss over longer transmission lines. Over time, advances such as amplifiers on transmission lines, microwave radio links, shortwave relays, undersea cables, and earth satellites that amplify and relay signals have so improved service that today's telephone customers expect that their telephone can be quickly linked to one of many millions of other telephones around the globe.

As telephones became a crucial part of 20th-century life, a need arose for workers who specialized in installing, removing, and repairing telephone instruments and related devices. But today's technology has advanced to the point where fewer of these workers are needed than in the past. Once basic wiring is in place, customers can handle much of their own installation work, and telephones can be manufactured so cheaply that it is often simpler to replace instead of repair malfunctioning equipment.

■ THE JOB

When calls go from one telephone to another, they usually go through a telephone company facility that houses automatic switching equipment. For telephone calls to go through, an array of wires, cable, switches, transformers, and other equipment must be installed and in good operating order. *Central office workers*, *cable splicers*, and *line repairers* are among the workers who work on telephone

QUICK FACTS

ALTERNATE TITLE(S)
Cable Splicers, Installers and Repairers, Line Repairers, Station Installers, Systems Technicians, Telecommunications Equipment

DUTIES
Install, service, and repair telephone and PBX systems

SALARY RANGE
$30,210 to $54,570 to $78,400+

WORK ENVIRONMENT
Indoors/Outdoors

BEST GEOGRAPHIC LOCATION(S)
Opportunities exist throughout the country

MINIMUM EDUCATION LEVEL
High School Diploma, Some Postsecondary Training

SCHOOL SUBJECTS
Computer Science, Mathematics, Technical/Shop

EXPERIENCE
Previous experience required

PERSONALITY TRAITS
Conventional, Hands On, Technical

SKILLS
Computer, Interpersonal, Mechanical/Manual Dexterity

CERTIFICATION OR LICENSING
Required

SPECIAL REQUIREMENTS
None

EMPLOYMENT PROSPECTS
Fair

ADVANCEMENT PROSPECTS
Fair

OUTLOOK
Decline

NOC
7246

O*NET-SOC
49-2022.00

equipment away from the customer's premises. *Telephone and PBX installers and repairers* are workers who service the systems on the customer's premises.

When customers request a new telephone line or equipment, *telephone installers*, also called *station installers*, do the necessary work. They often travel to the customer's home or business in a vehicle that contains a variety of tools and equipment. If they must make a new connection, they may have to work on roofs, ladders, or at the top of a telephone pole to attach an incoming wire to the service line. They install a terminal box and connect the appropriate wires. On some jobs, they may have to drill through walls or floors to run wiring. In large buildings, they may connect service wires or terminals in basements or wire closets. After installing equipment, they test it to make sure it functions as it should. Telephone installers may also install or remove telephone booths, coin collectors, and switching key equipment, in addition to private and business phones.

Wear and deterioration may cause telephones to function improperly. *Telephone repairers* can determine the cause of such problems, sometimes with the assistance of *testboard workers* or *trouble locators* in the central office, and then repair the problem and restore service.

Some larger users of telephone services, such as some businesses or hotels, have a single telephone number. Calls that come in may be routed to the proper telephone with PBX switching equipment located on the customer's premises. Outgoing calls also go through what is in effect a private telephone system within the building. In addition to handling regular phone calls, PBX equipment is often used for specialized services such as electronic mail. *PBX installers*, also called *systems technicians*, set up the necessary wiring, switches, and other equipment to make the system function, often creating customized switchboards. These workers often work as part of a crew because the communications equipment they work with is heavy, bulky, and complex.

PBX repairers, with the assistance of *testboard workers*, locate malfunctions and repair PBX and other telephone systems. They may also maintain related equipment, such as power plants, batteries, and relays. Some PBX repairers service and repair mobile radiophones, microwave transmission equipment, and other sophisticated telecommunications devices and equipment.

Some experienced workers can handle a range of installation and repair work. They may put their skills to use handling special jobs, such as investigating unauthorized use of telephone equipment.

■ EARNINGS

In comparison with workers in other craft fields, telephone and PBX installers and repairers are generally well paid. Their actual pay rates vary with their job responsibilities, geographical region, their length of service with the company, and other factors. According to the U.S. Bureau of Labor Statistics, median hourly earnings of telecommunications equipment installers and repairers were $26.24 (or $54,570 annually) in May 2015. Wages ranged from less than $14.53 to more than $37.69 (or $30,210 to $78,400 annually). Mean hourly earnings in the wired telecommunications industry were $27.15 (or $56,460). Workers in this occupation generally have a low turnover rate; therefore, many workers are in the higher wage categories. Fringe benefits for these workers usually include paid holidays and vacations, sick leave, health and disability insurance, and retirement plans.

■ WORK ENVIRONMENT

Telephone installers and repairers often do their work independently, with a minimum of supervision. Especially during emergency situations they may need to work at night, on weekends, or on holidays to restore service. Most installers are on-call 24 hours a day. Most of the work is done in the field, in the homes and offices of clients. Some installation work is done outside, including work on poles, ladders, and rooftops, and some work requires stooping, bending, reaching, and working in awkward or cramped positions.

PBX installers and repairers frequently work as part of crews. Most of their work is indoors, and it may involve crouching, crawling, and lifting.

■ EXPLORING

High school courses in physics, mathematics, blueprint reading, and shop can help you gauge your aptitudes and interest in these occupations. Building electronic kits and assembling models tests manual dexterity and mechanical ability as well as providing experience in following drawings and plans. Direct work experience in this field is probably unavailable on a part-time or summer job basis, but it may be possible to arrange a visit to a telephone company facility to get an overall view of the company's operations.

■ EDUCATION AND TRAINING REQUIREMENTS
High School

Math courses will help you prepare for the technical nature of this career, along with vo-tech, electronics, and other courses that involve hands-on experiments. Computer courses will also be valuable. Take English, speech, and other courses that will help develop communication skills.

Postsecondary Training

As telecommunications technology becomes more complex, postsecondary education in electronics and computer technology is increasingly becoming the standard requirement for employment in this field. Some employers may require an associate's or bachelor's degree in an area such as engineering. Installers may be required to take continuing education courses, either as part of in-house training or through a college program, due to the rapid advancements of telecommunications technology.

Some telephone companies may still hire applicants who have no previous experience with another telephone company and then train the beginners to work with the equipment used in their own system. Companies generally prefer applicants who are high school or vocational school graduates and who have mechanical ability and manual dexterity.

Other Education or Training

The Society of Cable Telecommunications Engineers and Women in Cable Telecommunications provide continuing education classes and webinars. Contact these organizations for more information.

■ CERTIFICATION, LICENSING, AND SPECIAL REQUIREMENTS
Certification or Licensing

Certification may be required, depending on the job position and the equipment being worked on. Some certification is required to enter the occupation, while other certifications reinforce the skills and abilities of candidates for employment and enhance their opportunities for advancement within the profession.

Certifications offered by the Society of Cable Telecommunications Engineers include the broadband premises installer, broadband premises technician, and broadband premises expert. Certification Partners offers the industry-standard certifications convergence technologies professional and certified in convergent network technologies credentials. Certification requires completing training programs and passing competency examinations.

A repairman works on telephone wires to restore service after a storm. (FEMA. Marilee Caliendo.)

■ EXPERIENCE, SKILLS, AND PERSONALITY TRAITS

Previous experience with electronics and computer technology is recommended for aspiring telephone and PBX installers and repairers. Many telecom companies are increasingly hiring in-house employees for installer and repairer positions.

Installers and repairers deal with company customers, so they should have a neat appearance and a pleasant manner. Good eyesight and color vision are needed for working with small parts and for distinguishing the color-coding of wires. Good hearing is necessary for detecting malfunctions revealed by sound.

■ EMPLOYMENT PROSPECTS
Employers

Approximately 219,100 telecommunications equipment installers and repairers are employed in the United States. Telephone installers work for telecommunications companies. They also work for companies that provide phone equipment and services for hotels. Companies that install and service security systems for homes and businesses also employ installers.

Starting Out

Job seekers in this field should contact the employment offices of local telephone companies. Pre-employment tests may be given to determine your knowledge and aptitude for the work.

Newly hired workers learn their skills in programs that last several months. The programs may combine on-the-job work experience with formal classroom instruction and self-instruction using materials such as videos and training manuals. Trainees practice such tasks as connecting telephones to service wires in classrooms that simulate real working conditions. They also accompany experienced workers to job sites and observe them as they work. After they have learned how to install telephone equipment, workers need additional training to become telephone repairers, PBX installers, or PBX repairers.

If there are no openings in the training program at the time they are hired, new workers are assigned instead to some other type of job until openings develop. It is common for openings for installer and repairer positions to be filled by workers who are already employed in other jobs with the same company. In the future, it probably will be even more difficult for workers coming in from outside to get these jobs.

■ ADVANCEMENT PROSPECTS

More experienced telephone installers may, with additional training, move into jobs as PBX installers or as telephone repairers. Similarly, additional training may allow telephone repairers to become PBX repairers. Some experienced workers become *installer-repairers*, combining installation and repair work on telephone company or PBX systems. Some workers may advance to supervisory positions, in which they coordinate and direct the activities of other installers or repairers.

■ OUTLOOK

Employment of telecommunications equipment installers and repairers is expected to decline by 4 percent through 2024, according to the U.S. Department of Labor. Sweeping technological changes are making it possible to install and maintain phone systems with far fewer workers than in the past. New computerized systems are very reliable and have self-diagnosing features that make it easy for repairers to locate problems and replace defective parts. As older, less reliable equipment is taken out of service and new equipment is installed in its place, the need for repairers and installers will decline even further. Once the basic wiring is installed in a building, customers need only buy telephones and plug them into jacks wherever they want them. Customers can readily do some interior wiring and installation work without any help from the telephone company. These effects may be offset, however, by increased demand for a variety of services from phone and cable companies, including upgrading internal lines in businesses and homes and wiring new homes with fiber optic lines. The wide use of the Internet and fax machines has led to a number of homes with multiple lines. Because much business is now conducted through telephone lines, repairs during storms and other emergencies must be done more quickly and efficiently, requiring the skills of experienced installers and repairers.

Installers and repairers with additional training may be able to find work with the growing number of businesses that connect office computers and networks. Those with degrees in engineering can assist in the design for the cabling of business complexes, colleges, and other institutions requiring up-to-date communication services.

Central office and PBX installers and repairers who are experienced in current technology should find very good employment opportunities due to a growing demand for telecommunications networks that offer multimedia services such as VoIP (Voice over Internet Protocol), broadband Internet, and video on demand.

■ UNIONS AND ASSOCIATIONS

Many telephone employees are members of unions, and union membership may be required. The Communications Workers of America and International Brotherhood of Electrical Workers are two unions representing many workers. The Society of Cable Telecommunications Engineers and Women in Cable Telecommunications are membership organizations for telecommunications professionals that offer continuing education classes, networking opportunities, and other resources. The Telecommunications Industry Association is a trade association for information and communications technology companies.

TIPS FOR ENTRY

1. Visit https://www.wict.org/careerdev/jobcenter/Pages/default.aspx to search job listings.
2. Be willing to relocate. It may open more job opportunities.
3. Join a union to increase your chances of landing a job and receiving fair pay for your work.

FOR MORE INFORMATION

The Communications Workers of America represents workers in private and public sector employment.

Communications Workers of America (CWA)
501 Third Street, NW
Washington, D.C. 20001-2797
Tel: (202) 434-1100
http://www.cwa-union.org

The International Brotherhood of Electrical Workers represents workers in utilities, construction, telecommunications, broadcasting, manufacturing, railroads, and government.

International Brotherhood of Electrical Workers (IBEW)
900 Seventh Street, NW
Washington, D.C. 20001-3886
Tel: (202) 833-7000
Fax: (202) 728-7676
http://ibew.org

The Society of Cable Telecommunications Engineers provides information about membership, training programs, and certification.

Society of Cable Telecommunications Engineers (SCTE)
140 Philips Road
Exton, PA 19341-1318
Tel: (800) 542-5040; (610) 363-6888
Fax: (610) 884-7237
E-mail: info@scte.org
http://www.scte.org

The Telecommunications Industry Association provides standards development, policy initiatives, business opportunities, market intelligence, and networking events.

Telecommunications Industry Association (TIA)
1320 North Courthouse Road, Suite 200
Arlington, VA 22201-2598
Tel: (703) 907-7700
Fax: (703) 907-7727
http://www.tiaonline.org

Women in Cable Telecommunications offers career development, conferences, special programs, and membership benefits for women employed in the cable industry.

Women in Cable Telecommunications (WICT)
2000 K Street, NW, Suite 350
Washington, D.C. 20006-1889
Tel: (202) 827-4794
Fax: (202) 450-5596
http://www.wict.org

Telephone Operators

OVERVIEW

Telephone operators help people using phone company services, as well as other telephone users, to place calls and to make connections. There are approximately 112,400 switchboard operators, 9,750 telephone operators, and 2,010 other communications equipment operators employed in the United States.

HISTORY

In the years since Alexander Graham Bell was granted a patent for his invention in 1876, the telephone has evolved from being a novelty gadget to an indispensable part of our daily lives. It is now possible to talk to someone in virtually any corner of the world on the telephone. Technological breakthroughs have allowed us to replace inefficient telephone cables with fiber optic lines and satellites for transmitting signals. Some phone features that we take for granted, such as conference calls, call waiting, and automatic call forwarding, have been developed only in the past few decades.

Technology has also changed the job of the telephone operator. In the past, operators had to connect every phone call by hand, wrestling with hundreds of different cables and phone jacks and trying to match the person making the call to the number being dialed. Today, telephone switchboards are electronic, and the operator can connect many more calls by merely pushing buttons or dialing the proper code or number. Computers have replaced many of the old duties of telephone switchboard operators, such as directory assistance and the "automatic intercept" of nonoperating numbers. Still, telephone operators are needed to perform special duties and add a human touch to telecommunications.

THE JOB

It is now possible to make a collect call, check a bank account balance over the phone, or leave a phone message for someone in a large company without the assistance of

QUICK FACTS

ALTERNATE TITLE(S)
Directory Assistance Operators,
    Switchboard Operators

DUTIES
Help people use phone company
    services, as well as other
    telephone users, to place calls
    and to make connections

SALARY RANGE
$21,860 to $35,880 to
    $63,320+

WORK ENVIRONMENT
Primarily Indoors

BEST GEOGRAPHIC LOCATION(S)
Opportunities are available
    throughout the country

MINIMUM EDUCATION LEVEL
High School Diploma

SCHOOL SUBJECTS
English, Foreign
    Language, Speech

EXPERIENCE
No experience required

PERSONALITY TRAITS
Outgoing, Social, Talkative

SKILLS
Interpersonal, Public Speaking

CERTIFICATION OR LICENSING
None

SPECIAL REQUIREMENTS
None

EMPLOYMENT PROSPECTS
Poor

ADVANCEMENT PROSPECTS
Fair

OUTLOOK
Decline

NOC
1414

O*NET-SOC
43-2011.00, 43-2021.00

an operator. With automation, computers, and voice synthesizers, people can now place a call directly and get all the information needed, saving phone companies, and other businesses, time and money. The demand for telephone operators has dropped considerably from the days when operators were needed to physically connect and disconnect lines at a switchboard. AT&T has laid off thousands of operators in the last 20 years, but people can still find work with telecommunications companies and in corporations that handle a number of calls.

When a call comes into the phone company, a signal lights up on the switchboard, and the telephone operator makes the connection for it by pressing the proper buttons and dialing the proper numbers. If the person is calling from a pay phone, the operator may consult charts to determine the charges and ask the caller to deposit the correct amount to complete the call. If the customer requests a long-distance connection, the operator calculates and quotes the charges and then makes the connection.

Directory assistance operators, also called *information operators*, answer customer inquiries for local telephone numbers by using computerized alphabetical and geographical directories. The directory assistance operator types the spelling of the name requested and the possible location on a keyboard, then scans a directory to find the number. If the number can't be found, the operator may suggest alternate spellings of the name and look for those. When the name is located, the operator often doesn't need to read the number to the caller; instead, a computerized recording will provide the answer while the operator takes another call.

Telephone operators wear headsets that contain both an earphone and a microphone, leaving their hands free to operate the computer terminal or switchboard at which they are seated. They are supervised by *central-office-operator supervisors*.

Other types of switchboard supervisors perform advisory services for clients to show them how to get the most out of their phone systems. *Private branch exchange advisers* conduct training classes to demonstrate the operation of switchboard and teletype equipment, either at the telephone company's training school or on the customer's premises. They may analyze a company's telephone traffic loads and recommend the type of equipment and services that will best fit the company's needs. *Service observers* monitor the conversations between telephone operators and customers to observe the operators' behavior, technical skills, and adherence to phone company policies. Both of these types of workers may give advice on how operators can improve their handling of calls and their personal demeanor on the phone.

■ EARNINGS

The wages paid to telephone operators vary by city, state, and region. The types of duties performed by the employee also affect the salary.

According to the U.S. Department of Labor, median hourly earnings of switchboard operators, including answering service, were $13.19 ($27,440 annually) in May 2015. Median hourly earnings of telephone operators were $17.25 ($35,880 annually), with wages ranging from less than $10.51 to more than $30.44 (or $21,860 and $63,320 annually). The median hourly earnings for all other communications equipment operators were $19.30 ($40,330 annually); hourly earnings ranged from $12.67 to more than $28.58 (or $26,360 to $59,440 or more annually).

Operators are usually paid time-and-a-half for Sunday work and may receive an extra day's pay for working on legal holidays. Some additional remuneration is usually paid when employees work split shifts or shifts that end after 6:00 P.M. Time-and-a-half pay is generally given if operators work more than a five-day week. Choice of work hours is usually determined on the basis of seniority. Pay increases in most instances are determined on the basis of periodic pay scales.

Fringe benefits for these employees usually include paid annual vacations and group insurance plans for sickness, accident, and death; the majority also have retirement and disability pension plans available.

■ WORK ENVIRONMENT

The telephone industry operates around the clock, giving the public 24-hour daily service. Operators may, therefore, be required to work evening hours, night shifts, and on Sundays and holidays. Some operators are asked to work split shifts to cover periods of heavy calling. Telephone company operators generally work between 32 and 38 hours per week.

The telephone operator's job demands good physical health for punctual and regular job attendance; the work, however, is not physically strenuous or demanding. While working, operators are at the switchboard and are allowed to take periodic rest breaks. General working conditions are usually in pleasant surroundings with relatively little noise or confusion. Many telephone company operators work at video display terminals, which may cause eyestrain and muscle strain if not properly designed.

The work of a telephone operator can be very repetitive and is closely supervised. Calls are monitored by supervisors to check that operators are courteous and following company policies. Some operators find this stressful. In addition, telephone companies track the number of calls handled by each operator, and there is an increasing emphasis on operators handling a greater number of calls in order to improve cost efficiencies. This need for higher productivity can also create stress for some workers. Many times the atmosphere becomes stressful and hectic during peak calling times, and operators need to manage a high volume of calls without becoming distressed.

■ EXPLORING

Explore this career by arranging a visit to a local or long-distance telephone company to observe operators at work. There you may also have the chance to talk with operators about the job. Also learn about new developments in telephone technology and services by visiting the Web site of USTelecom Association (https://www .ustelecom.org).

Part-time office jobs may give students experience with in-company phone exchanges and switchboards, in addition to general office experience. While telephone company operations are more complex, applicants with previous experience in handling phone calls may be given preference in hiring.

■ EDUCATION AND TRAINING REQUIREMENTS
High School

Take speech, drama, and other classes that will help with oral communication skills. Typing and computer fundamentals courses will prepare you for the demands of running a modern switchboard and for handling special services such as TDD, which is telecommunications device for the hearing impaired. Learn a foreign language to help with international calls.

Postsecondary Training

Many telephone companies prefer to hire people who are high school graduates. Most of the training for the job will be from the employer, which may include classes in-house or telecommunications courses at a community college.

■ CERTIFICATION, LICENSING, AND SPECIAL REQUIREMENTS
Certification or Licensing

A company may have its own training program leading to certification, there is no national certification for telephone operators.

■ EXPERIENCE, SKILLS, AND PERSONALITY TRAITS

No experience is needed to work as a telephone operator, but those with prior work experience will increase their chances of landing a job, getting promoted, and possibly earning higher pay.

Manual dexterity is an asset to the telephone operator; however, the degree of dexterity needed is about the same as that required for the operation of any type of office equipment. Personal qualifications include tact, patience, a desire to work with people and to be of service to others, a pleasing phone voice, an even-tempered disposition, and good judgment. Operators must also have legible handwriting and must be punctual and dependable in job attendance.

■ EMPLOYMENT PROSPECTS
Employers

There are approximately 112,400 switchboard operators, 9,750 telephone operators, and 2,010 other communications equipment operators employed in the United States. Operators are still needed in telephone companies, but most find jobs handling the phone lines of hotels, retail stores, and other businesses with large numbers of employees. The customer service departments of companies and stores employ telephone operators to handle transactions, make courtesy calls, and answer customers' questions.

Starting Out

Individuals may enter this occupation by applying directly to telephone companies and long-distance

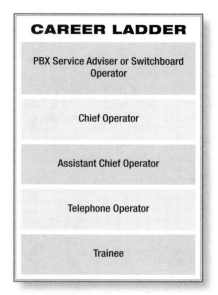

CAREER LADDER

PBX Service Adviser or Switchboard Operator

Chief Operator

Assistant Chief Operator

Telephone Operator

Trainee

A telephone operator uses a computer to help direct calls and provide information. (wavebreakmedia. Shutterstock.)

carriers. In some cities, telephone offices maintain an employment office, while elsewhere employment interviews are conducted by a chief operator or personnel manager. Other job openings may be discovered through state or private employment agencies, employment agencies, or career services offices in schools.

New telephone company employees are usually given a combination of classroom work and on-the-job practice. In the various telephone companies, classroom instruction usually lasts up to three weeks. The nation's time zones and geography are covered so that operators can understand how to calculate rates and know where major cities are located. Recordings are used to familiarize trainees with the various signals and tones of the phone system as well as give them the chance to hear their own phone voices and improve their diction and courtesy. Close supervision continues after training is completed.

Telephone operators continue to receive on-the-job training throughout their careers as phone offices install more modern and automated equipment and as the methods of working with the equipment continue to change. Service assistants are responsible for instructing the new operators in various other types of special operating services.

■ ADVANCEMENT PROSPECTS

Telephone operators may have opportunities for advancement to positions as service assistant, and later to group or assistant chief operator. Chief operators plan and direct the activities of a central office, as well as personnel functions and the performance of the employees. Service assistants may sometimes advance to become PBX service advisers, who go to individual businesses, assess their phone needs, and oversee equipment installation and employee training. Some telephone operators take other positions within a telephone company, such as a clerical position, and advance within that position.

Opportunities for advancement usually depend on the employee's personal initiative, ability, experience, length of employment, and job performance, as well as the size of the place of employment and the number of supervisors needed. Most telephone company operators are members of a union, and the union specifies the time and steps to advance from one position to another. However, many operators can become qualified for a higher-level position but then need to wait for years for an available opening. Some telephone operators become private branch exchange or switchboard operators in corporations and large businesses.

■ OUTLOOK

Employment of telephone and switchboard operators is expected to decline rapidly through 2024, according to the U.S. Department of Labor. During the past 30 years, employment of operators in telephone companies has declined sharply due to automation, which increases the productivity of these workers.

Direct dialing and computerized billing have eliminated the need for many operators. Voice-recognition technology, which gives computers the capacity to understand speech and to respond to callers, now offers directory assistance and helps to place collect calls. Voice response equipment, which allows callers to communicate with computers through the use of touch-tone signals, is used widely by most large companies. Using a combination of voice response equipment, voice mail and messaging systems, and automated call distribution, incoming phone calls can be routed to their destination without the use of an operator. People now use the Internet and e-mail to communicate, neither of which require operators. Directory assistance services are also available on the Internet and provide phone numbers, addresses, maps, and e-mail addresses.

Operators will find most job opportunities outside the phone companies, with customer service departments, telemarketing firms, reservation ticket agencies, hotel switchboards, and other services that field a number of calls. TDD, phone services for the deaf, also requires operators, and the Americans with Disabilities Act is allowing people better access to such services. Unions have tried to make sure that companies reduce unemployment either through attrition or through retraining and reassigning workers. Many telephone companies, however, continue to make workforce reductions by eliminating telephone operator positions or by sending jobs to foreign countries in an attempt to cut operating costs. There will be limited opportunities for employment as a telephone operator in the future.

■ UNIONS AND ASSOCIATIONS

Many telephone operators belong to local union chapters of such organizations as Communications Workers of America (CWA). CWA assists workers in obtaining fair wages, benefits, and working conditions. USTelecom Association is a membership organization of the nation's telecommunications companies.

■ TIPS FOR ENTRY

1. Develop good communication and customer service skills to increase your chances of landing a job.
2. Talk to telephone operators about their careers. Ask them for advice on landing a job.
3. Contact telecom companies directly to inquire about employment opportunities.

■ FOR MORE INFORMATION

The Communications Workers of America provides information about union membership and issues affecting jobs in telecommunications.

Communications Workers of America (CWA)
501 Third Street, NW
Washington, D.C. 20001-2797
Tel: (202) 434-1100
http://www.cwa-union.org

USTelecom Association is a trade association that represents broadband service providers and suppliers.

USTelecom Association
607 14th Street, NW, Suite 400
Washington, D.C. 20005-2073
Tel: (202) 326-7300
Fax: (202) 326-7333
http://ustelecom.org

The Telecommunications Industry Association provides education, career development, events, and other resources for telecom professionals.

Telecommunications Industry Association (TIA)
1320 North Courthouse Road, Suite 200
Arlington, VA 22201-2598

Tel: (703) 907-7700
Fax: (703) 907-7727
https://www.tiaonline.org

THE GHOST OF PHONE SERVICES PAST

DID YOU KNOW?

With call waiting, voice mail, cell phones, pagers, and all the other phone services available, it's hard to imagine a time when receiving a call wasn't so easy. Here are a few facts about the past:

■ To make a long-distance call before 1910, a special operator assisted in conversation. The caller would tell the operator what they wanted to say to the other party, and the operator, known as a "repeater," would then repeat their message into the long-distance phone.

■ The letters on the phone are frequently used for advertising purposes, but they were once used more regularly. Early "telephone exchanges" (or groups of service subscribers) were given the names of their towns, or locations within the city. To dial, callers would use the first two letters of the exchange name before dialing the subscriber's individual number.

■ "Party lines" were used by more than one household— when one subscriber was making a call, another couldn't. Not only that, but subscribers could easily listen in on the phone conversations of other subscribers. (The classic Doris Day movie *Pillow Talk* illustrates this complication.)

Temporary Workers

■ OVERVIEW

Employees who work on an assignment or contractual basis are called *temporary workers*. They usually work through agencies, staffing offices, or placement centers that place qualified workers in jobs that last from one day to months according to their educational background, work experience, or profession.

People work as temps for several reasons. The majority of people temp because they are between full-time positions. Some enjoy the flexibility that temporary assignments offer. Others use the opportunity to try out different occupations or companies in hopes of being hired in a permanent capacity. Companies from almost every industry hire temporary workers to fill in when regular staff members are ill or on vacation. Special

QUICK FACTS

ALTERNATE TITLE(S)
Contract Workers, Temps

DUTIES
Work on an assignment or contractual basis for a variety of for-profit and nonprofit employers

SALARY RANGE
$20,080 to $35,360 to $104,000+

WORK ENVIRONMENT
Primarily Indoors

BEST GEOGRAPHIC LOCATION(S)
Opportunities are available throughout the country

MINIMUM EDUCATION LEVEL
Associate's Degree

SCHOOL SUBJECTS
Business, English, Mathematics

EXPERIENCE
Prior occupational experience required

PERSONALITY TRAITS
Conventional, Enterprising, Organized

SKILLS
Business Management, Interpersonal

CERTIFICATION OR LICENSING
Required

SPECIAL REQUIREMENTS
None

EMPLOYMENT PROSPECTS
Good

ADVANCEMENT PROSPECTS
Good

OUTLOOK
About as Fast as the Average

NOC
N/A

O*NET-SOC
N/A

projects and seasonal work are other reasons for employment. According to the U.S. Department of Commerce, the temporary help services industry accounted for 2.4 percent of all private sector jobs in the United States, with a record high of nearly 3 million temporary jobs in May 2015.

■ HISTORY

Throughout time, some people earned at least part of their income taking short jobs when the work was available. People even traveled to other towns for work, leaving their families behind. The National Association of Personnel Services dates the earliest private employment services to 14th-century Germany, though no detail is available regarding the type of work. Kelly Services Inc. was one of the first temporary staffing agencies in the United States. In 1946 its founder, William Russell Kelly, realized there was a great demand for office and clerical help in Detroit, Michigan. Businesses throughout town needed reliable help, though not on a daily basis. Kelly's first employees were housewives and students—two groups with very flexible schedules. They were able to accept or decline assignments as their schedules allowed.

Soon other temporary agencies were placing qualified workers in a variety of businesses. The first temps were mainly receptionists or clerical help; many had no skills other than those associated with secretarial work. Temporary workers are better prepared today—most are computer savvy and have solid work experience. Also, a large number of temps are professionals with backgrounds in law, accounting, or health care,

and there is a growing trend for placement agencies to focus on one specific occupational group.

■ THE JOB

The largest category of temporary workers is *administrative and clerical workers*, comprising almost half of all temporary workers in the United States. Reception, secretarial, and administrative work are some assignments in this category. In the past, collating, answering phones, typing, and filing were the major duties of temporary workers. Today, many administrative temporaries are skilled in word processing, various computer programs, and other procedures. Other administrative workers, such as *medical secretaries*, *legal secretaries*, and *bookkeepers*, have additional training and skills to help them better perform special duties.

Industrial workers are also employed as temporaries. Assignments may include inspecting, labeling, packaging, and record keeping in factories, warehouses, and docks. Staff shortages or seasonal peak periods are some reasons for contracting temporary help. Most businesses prefer temporary workers to have past work experience, though a majority of industrial assignments do not require advanced training or skills,.

Managerial temporaries come from a variety of backgrounds. This group includes retired businesspeople, recent M.B.A. graduates, and freelance business consultants. Many businesses hire managerial temporaries for short-term projects. For example, consultants may analyze a company's performance record, suggest and implement changes, and exit the project soon afterward. They are also hired to motivate staff or to expedite the release of a product or service. Temporaries hired in this field usually have degrees in business or related subjects; some have advanced degrees. Managerial temporaries with solid work experience or reputable references are highly desired.

Computer programmers, *systems analysts*, and *hardware and software engineers* are just some of the information technology (IT) specialists that work as temporaries. Often referred to as "techsperts," they are contracted to help meet deadlines or work on short-term projects. Companies find it more cost effective to hire temporary IT people than to train existing employees on the latest computer technology, especially when deadlines are short. *Web designers* are also in demand to design and create new company Web sites or tweak existing ones. *Help desk specialists* are often enlisted to provide support for a company's IT department.

Professional occupations also provide abundant opportunities for those interested in short-term assignments. In recent years, companies have increasingly relied on contracting *accounting professionals* to compile financial reports, perform audits, and prepare company tax reports. Installing new accounting systems and training permanent staff in the use of such systems are other tasks completed by accounting temporaries. Businesses often hire temporary workers to work on short-term projects or during seasonal peak periods. Smaller businesses, especially, rely on temporaries to provide manpower to their accounting departments. Accounting temps must have a degree in accounting, taxation, or business administration; many are certified public accountants.

Engineers or *scientists* are often hired to work on special projects or new research. Companies contract engineers to design and develop a new product from start to finish or a portion of the manufacturing process. Pharmaceutical companies need scientists of varying specialties to research, test, and develop new medicines. Temporary workers in this field are highly specialized. All are college graduates; most have advanced degrees and work experience in their specialties.

For special projects or to provide assistance in complicated legal cases, law firms often contract *lawyers* on a short-term basis to work alongside their existing legal team. Lawyers may be assigned to write and file briefs, take depositions, prepare witnesses for trial, or provide litigation support. Paralegals may also work on temporary assignments to research cases, prepare documents, or provide other legal assistance.

Health professionals are enjoying great growth in temporary services. *Nurses*, especially, are in high demand. Agencies are actively recruiting nurses for assignments ranging in length from one day to months at a time. Hospitals and nursing homes are often short staffed and rely on *registered nurses, licensed practical nurses,* and *certified nursing attendants* to work the less desirable night and weekend shifts. Health professionals may also be assigned to care for home health patients. Hospitals in rural towns or remote locations rely heavily on health professionals to work short-term contracts. *Physical therapists, radiological technicians, dialysis technicians, medical assistants,* and *medical records clerks* may also work on temporary assignments.

■ EARNINGS

Temporary workers are paid hourly or per project by the agency or personnel supply firm. In turn, the agency bills the client company for every hour of work, including any fees or commission. According to the American Staffing Association (ASA), temps receive a little more than 70 percent of the billable rate; the agency keeps the remainder. For example, if the temp is paid $21 an hour,

CAREER LADDER

Manager

Salaried Worker

Temporary Worker

the agency actually bills the client $30 per hour and keeps the remaining $9 as its commission. A 30 percent commission may seem high, but from this amount, the agency needs to pay the temp's Social Security, any training costs, job counseling, and office operating and administrative costs.

The hourly rate varies greatly depending on the type of work or occupation. In general, temporary or contract workers may make as little as $10 per hour (or $20,080 annually). Many make about $17 an hour ($35,360 annually), according to the ASA. A few may earn more than $100 per hour ($208,000 annually), depending upon the skills and experience required. Some agencies offer $50 an hour ($104,000 annually) or more for contract nurses. These estimated annual earnings only apply to temps who remain employed full time throughout the year. It's not uncommon for temporary workers to experience breaks of unemployment between jobs. In addition, a stipend is offered to cover expenses such as travel and housing. This is often the case when the nurse or other health professional is assigned outside of their home base.

For most kinds of temporary work, the hourly rate is much higher than that offered to permanent employees. This is possible because benefits such as paid vacation, sick time, health insurance, and other perks are not usually offered to temporary workers. Some agencies may offer benefits to temporary workers after they log in a specific number of working days. Benefits may include medical coverage and short-term disability insurance, but the employee contribution for such benefits is usually higher compared to the contribution paid by full-time, permanent workers. Many temps receive insurance benefits from other sources, most often a spouse working in a full-time job.

■ WORK ENVIRONMENT

The work environment depends on the particular assignment. Industrial work most often takes place at factories or outdoor facilities. Most office assignments are indoors. Some agencies ask clients to provide temporary workers with desks or designated workspaces, especially if the project is long term.

Workdays and hours also vary from assignment to assignment. Usually temporary workers follow the company's work hours. However, if a project deadline

Businesses such as online retailers and distribution centers will hire temporary workers during busy seasons. (bikeriderlondon. Shutterstock.)

is looming, temporary workers may be asked to work overtime or on weekends.

Temporary workers are not usually given preferential treatment by their clients. Work spaces may be small, and interaction with permanent staff, both on professional and social levels, may be limited. Projects are likely to be the ones no one else wants to do. Support staff temporaries, especially, may be faced with mountains of papers to collate, staple, and hand out, while simultaneously answering a bank of phones. On the other hand, some offices may view temporary workers as much needed and appreciated help to meet tough deadlines.

■ EXPLORING

One of the major appeals of temporary work is the great flexibility and variety that it provides. Almost every industry employs temporary workers, so the options for exploring the field are vast. Apply for a summer job or seasonal work during holidays. Usually, businesses look for extra help during busy times. Visit a temporary placement office and shadow a recruiter for the day. You'll see firsthand what recruiters look for when interviewing potential temporary workers. Do they have the proper skills and work experience? Do they look and act professional?

There are many Web sites devoted to the world of temporary work. Read personal work experiences, advice columns on how to survive new office politics, and tips on interviewing. See Protecting Temporary Workers (https://www.osha.gov/temp_workers) for more information.

■ EDUCATION AND TRAINING REQUIREMENTS
High School

Very few students plan their high school curriculum based on the goal of working on a temporary basis. Most people follow a chosen career path and find along the way that temporary work suits their personal lives, educational goals, or professional ambitions better than a full-time, long-term position.

High school courses in business, word processing, computers, math, and English will prepare you to work as an administrative or clerical temp. Otherwise, study the subjects that fit with your chosen career field.

Postsecondary Training

To work as a temp in any professional capacity, such as nursing, accounting, law, or information technology, you must complete the educational requirements for that profession and have some work experience. Many clients require temporary workers to have college degrees or solid training before offering non-entry-level assignments such as managerial or technical projects. Good computer and communication skills are a must.

For students with some postsecondary training, working in a temporary, entry-level position can provide paid work experience and contacts that may help in later job searches.

Other Education or Training

Temporary workers must continue to update their skills throughout their careers by pursuing continuing education classes, workshops, webinars, and other learning opportunities. These resources are provided by professional associations, industry vendors, and colleges and universities.

■ CERTIFICATION, LICENSING, AND SPECIAL REQUIREMENTS
Certification or Licensing

Certification or licensing is required for some professional temporary work. For example, a traveling nurse must have a license to practice in the state or country where the assignment is located. Likewise, lawyers must have a valid license to practice in the assigned location. Agencies will usually help temporary candidates apply for additional licenses or seek reciprocity.

■ EXPERIENCE, SKILLS, AND PERSONALITY TRAITS

Temporary employment firms require most applicants to have prior occupational experience in their specialty, although general office workers or laborers may just need a high school diploma.

The transient nature of temporary work is not for everyone. Imagine having to adapt to a different set of coworkers with each assignment, not to mention a new office environment and the politics that go with it. In addition to adaptability, other important traits for temp workers include strong communication, organizational, and time-management skills, the ability to follow instructions, and a talent for working both independently and as part of a team, when necessary.

■ EMPLOYMENT PROSPECTS
Employers
One of the greatest advantages of temporary work is that employment opportunities exist nationwide. Most temporary workers use an employment agency or staffing service to find assignments. Agencies such as Kelly Services or ManpowerGroup place individuals with basic office and administrative skills. Both are known in the business world for having pools of dependable office support workers as well as highly trained professionals such as technical workers and engineers.

There are also agencies that cater to specialized fields. Accountemps, for example, assigns certified public accountants and other accounting professionals to work on short-term and long-term projects throughout the United States, as well as in Europe and Australia. Special Counsel, a nationwide legal staffing agency, places lawyers, paralegals, and legal assistants in temporary assignments. Clients include top law firms needing extra help for large projects, or corporations needing legal expertise.

Starting Out
Most temps work through an agency or placement center. The agency first conducts a screening interview to assess candidates' skills and work experience. Requirement include an updated resume, any certification or licensing papers, and a list of references. Be prepared to let the agency know of any preferences you may have in terms of assignments—type of project, location, hours, and any physical accommodations you may need. You may have to take several tests depending on the type of temp work for which you are applying. For example, administrative workers may have to take a test to measure their keyboarding speed or computer knowledge. Training is sometimes encouraged to keep temps current with software programs and systems as demanded by clients. The agency may make security or professional checks, verify school transcripts, or order drug testing before you are given an assignment. Search the Internet for employment agencies and placement centers.

STAFFING STATISTICS
FAST FACTS

- More than 3 million people are employed by staffing companies each week.
- 76 percent of staffing employees work full time, a percentage that is nearly identical to the rest of the work force.
- In 2015, the staffing industry generated $147 billion from temporary and contract staffing.
- There are about 20,000 staffing firms operating from 39,000 offices across the United States.
- Staffing firms hire 16 million temporary and contract workers annually, and many staffing firms provide free training to their employees.

Source: American Staffing Association

■ ADVANCEMENT PROSPECTS
Many people view temporary work assignments as a great way to develop industry contacts. Solid work performance may catch the attention of management and result in a temp-to-hire situation. A temporary worker may also view advancement in terms of choice assignments with good companies offering higher pay.

Most agencies offer additional training, at no cost, to their employees. According to a survey conducted by the American Staffing Association, many temporary workers acquire new skills while on assignments. As temporary workers gain knowledge with new equipment and software programs and acquire other highly desirable skills, they can progress to different temporary jobs, many with a better pay scale.

■ OUTLOOK
Almost every industry—from manufacturing to health care—uses temporary workers or consultants, so employment opportunities abound. Most new jobs will occur in the largest occupational groups: office and administrative support, production, and transportation and material moving. There will also be many opportunities in specialized fields such as nursing, health care, accounting, and information technology.

In order to stay competitive, companies must be cost effective. Temporary workers can give companies the power of additional manpower to meet important deadlines or work on special projects and provide support when they are short staffed. Businesses save money with temps because they do not have to pay costly benefits that they pay full-time employees. Also, companies can save time by contracting with temps already trained in a particular computer program instead of retraining existing employees. The American Staffing Association expects that temps in professional and technical occupations, especially health care, law, and engineering, will be in the strongest demand. New jobs will occur in federal, state, and local governments that will continue to contract many of its projects.

Many people enjoy working in a temporary work environment because it allows them the flexibility of choosing when and where to work. Others take advantage of temp work because it gives them access to free training. People who are unsure of their career path view temp work as a chance to audition different industries before committing to one. However, a majority of temporary workers are between jobs or are using their temporary assignments as a possible bridge to full-time employment.

Flexibility is a major perk associated with temporary work but it can also be a serious disadvantage. Once an assignment is complete, temporary workers are usually the first to be let go during a slow economy. Businesses with a smaller working budget tend to manage with existing employees instead of contracting additional help. Also, the notion of hiring temporary workers when a company is downsizing its workforce is considered bad office politics.

◼ UNIONS AND ASSOCIATIONS

Temporary workers do not belong to unions. The American Staffing Association and the National Association of Personnel Services are membership organizations for staffing and recruiting firms.

◼ TIPS FOR ENTRY

1. Contact Kelly Services, ManpowerGroup, Robert Half, and other staffing firms directly to learn more about job opportunities.
2. Become certified in your profession to improve your chances of landing a job.
3. Talk to temporary workers about the best strategies to land a job.

◼ FOR MORE INFORMATION

Accountemps, of Robert Half, places temporary accounting professionals.

Accountemps
Tel: (855) 401-6188
https://www.roberthalf.com/accountemps

The American Staffing Association provides industry information and trends.

American Staffing Association (ASA)
277 South Washington Street, Suite 200
Alexandria, VA 22314-3675

Tel: (703) 253-2020
Fax: (703) 253-2053
https://americanstaffing.net

Kelly Services offers temporary, temp-to-hire, and direct-hire employment opportunities.

Kelly Services
999 West Big Beaver Road
Troy, MI 48084-4782
Tel: (248) 362-4444
E-mail: kfirst@kellyservices.com
http://www.kellyservices.com

ManpowerGroup connects people with employment opportunities in various industries.

ManpowerGroup
http://www.manpowergroup.com

The National Association of Personnel Services offers professional development, membership benefits, networking opportunities, news, and other resources.

National Association of Personnel Services (NAPS)
78 Dawson Village Way, Suite 410-201
Dawsonville, GA 30534-5641
Tel: (844) NAPS-360
http://www.naps360.org

Special Counsel provides information on temporary employment opportunities in the law industry.

Special Counsel
Tel: (800) 737-3436
http://www.specialcounsel.com

Test Drivers

◼ OVERVIEW

Test drivers drive, evaluate, and grade new automobiles and other vehicles before they are made available for sale to the public. They spend many hours driving their assigned model in various driving situations, climates, and speeds. As members of a new product development team, test drivers make suggestions for specific alterations to the car's design, function, and performance. Test drivers are employed by auto manufacturers worldwide, though some may work for contractors specializing in automotive testing or development. Others work as automobile writers and reviewers for trade publications.

HISTORY

There has been a need for test drivers to ensure that vehicles perform well, are safe, and meet other performance criteria ever since the first automobile was manufactured in the late 1800s. In the early days of the automotive industry, cars were tested by engineers, designers, and automotive company owners.

Early test drives were often conducted on the streets of Detroit, Michigan, the headquarters of many automotive manufacturers. Charles B. King, an automotive industry pioneer, became the first person in the United States to test drive a gasoline-powered automobile on American streets (in Detroit) on March 6, 1896. The *Detroit Free Press* commented the next morning: "The first horseless carriage seen in this city was out on the streets last night. It is the invention of Charles B. King, a Detroiter, and its progress up down Woodward Avenue about 11 o' clock caused a deal of comment, people crowding around it so that its progress was impeded. The apparatus seemed to work all right, and went at the rate of five or six miles an hour at an even rate of speed."

As competition between automotive manufacturers grew and more models were produced, a need emerged for specially trained drivers who could assess the performance of vehicles under a variety of road conditions. Much of this testing took place on the highways and byways of America—allowing the public, as well as automotive competitors, to witness great successes and failures.

It soon became clear that while road testing was important, there was also a need for private testing grounds where automotive companies could test their vehicles under controlled conditions and in secret.

In 1924, General Motors established the first private proving ground, or test track, in the industry in Milford, Michigan. Other companies such as Packard, Studebaker, and Nash (later American Motors) soon followed with their own proving grounds.

Approximately two dozen proving tracks are in operation today in the United States, and test drivers continue to play an important role in the automotive industry—testing vehicles on these tracks as well as on public roads and highways.

THE JOB

Automobiles have certainly come a long way in the last few decades. They run smoother, faster, and have more bells and whistles with each new model. However, before auto manufacturers can make new models available to the public, they must ensure that all new features and improvements are safe and reliable. Test drivers are employed by auto manufacturers to drive, evaluate, and grade new cars.

Their work varies depending on the task at hand. Test drivers may be assigned to evaluate the vehicle's dynamics on different types of roads. To gauge the car's performance and handling in high traffic, the driver may travel on highways. Rural or winding roads are often used to test how the car hugs curves and sharp turns, or its handling on rough terrain. Sometimes the driver may use controlled situations such as a closed airport runway, test track, or racing oval to test the car's performance and mileage accumulation at extreme speeds of 150 mph or more.

Test drivers also monitor for any problems and malfunctions with the car's mechanics such as the engine, steering, and brake systems. The driver may take note of any changes in the power and pickup during different stages of the test.

Durability is another component of a driving test. Drivers observe the wear of the car's brakes, tires, bumpers, and other systems with time and usage. Often the car is driven through severe conditions such as damaged roads, inclement weather, and chemicals to test the NVH (noise, vibration, and harshness) engineering, strength of tires and their alignment, shock absorbers, or paint finish.

Test drivers also evaluate the car's ergonomics. They note the comfort of seats, positioning of the steering wheel, and accessibility of other controls ranging from turn signals, to heater and air-conditioning controls, to the car's navigation tools (such as GPS systems). Drivers provide feedback on options such as the number and location of cup

QUICK FACTS

ALTERNATE TITLE(S)
None

DUTIES
Drive, evaluate, and grade new automobiles and other vehicles before they are made available for sale to the public

SALARY RANGE
$20,160 to $41,610 to $128,430+

WORK ENVIRONMENT
Primarily Outdoors

BEST GEOGRAPHIC LOCATION(S)
Opportunities exist throughout the country, but the Big Three automakers—Ford Motor, Fiat Chrysler, and General Motors—are headquartered in Michigan

MINIMUM EDUCATION LEVEL
Bachelor's Degree

SCHOOL SUBJECTS
English, Mathematics, Technical/Shop

EXPERIENCE
Several years experience

PERSONALITY TRAITS
Hands On, Realistic, Technical

SKILLS
Math, Mechanical/Manual Dexterity, Writing

CERTIFICATION OR LICENSING
Required

SPECIAL REQUIREMENTS
None

EMPLOYMENT PROSPECTS
Fair

ADVANCEMENT PROSPECTS
Fair

OUTLOOK
Little Change or More Slowly than the Average

NOC
9522

O*NET-SOC
N/A

CAREER LADDER

Head Driver for an Auto Manufacturer

Experienced Test Driver

Entry-Level Test Driver

holders, vanity mirrors, or storage bins. Once testing is complete, drivers may meet with a team of engineers or members of the product development department to make specific changes or alterations. Test drivers may spend years working to help bring a concept design from prototype to an actual product for general consumption.

Test drivers may also participate in special tests to gauge driver fatigue or performance as a result of sleep deprivation or distractions such as cell phone usage or texting. Some auto manufacturers may use professional test drivers to participate in advertising campaigns, company videos, press release photos, or product brochures.

Test drivers can also find employment as writers and editors at publications serving the automobile industry such as *Motor Trend* or *Car and Driver*. Test drivers working in this capacity review new models of cars and compare or evaluate them against similar models offered by other manufacturers. Auto manufacturers loan publications new car models for a short period of time—usually a week. Drivers are allowed to use these cars as they would their own vehicle, keeping notes on their performance. Sometimes drivers are allowed to drive a model for up to a year to review the car's long-term functionality and reliability.

Test drivers who are employed in publishing often have access to new car models a few months before the general public to allow for the lead time needed for writing, editing, and publishing the review. Auto manufacturers try to maintain good relationships with trade publications as a favorable review is valuable for future car sales.

■ EARNINGS

The U.S. Department of Labor (DOL) does not provide salary information for test drivers. Some test drivers have backgrounds in mechanical engineering. The DOL reports that mechanical engineers employed in motor vehicle parts manufacturing earned mean annual wages of $78,830 in May 2015. Salaries for all mechanical engineers ranged from less than $53,640 to $128,430 or more.

Reporters and correspondents, which includes newspaper and magazine writers, earned salaries that ranged from less than $21,390 to more than $81,580 in May 2015, according to the DOL. Earnings of technical writers ranged from less than $41,610 to $112,220 or more.

According to Glassdoor.com, in November 2016, test drivers earned average salaries of $20,160.

Benefits for full-time workers include vacation and sick time, health, and sometimes dental, insurance, and pension or 401(k) plans. Self-employed test drivers must provide their own benefits.

■ WORK ENVIRONMENT

Test drivers spend the majority of their workday behind the wheel of a car. They are often assigned to drive various types of roads to gauge the car's performance in different situations. Travel is sometimes necessary if the car is manufactured abroad. After a performance test, drivers may meet other team members in an office setting to give reports or brainstorm new alterations. Test drivers writing for a trade publication may take notes during performance testing for use when writing their articles or new product reviews.

Work conditions can occasionally be hazardous. Test drivers often drive their vehicles at top speeds in difficult terrain or less-than-optimal weather conditions. It's important that drivers take every step to protect themselves from injury by wearing seat belts or other protective gear such as helmets, driving gloves, and fireproof clothing.

■ EXPLORING

If of age, get a driver's license to gain experience driving on roads and highways. If not of age for a driver's license, there are other ways to hone driving skills. Visit a go-karting venue and test your driving performance navigating around other drivers and tricky hairpin turns. Computer and video driving-oriented games will also provide a good introduction to the field.

Tinker around with your own car after gaining some driving experiences. It's a great way to know how a finely tuned car works and runs. Don't forget to browse trade publications such as *Road & Track* (http://www.roadandtrack.com) for car and performance reviews—you'll become familiar with what drivers look for when testing a new model.

Another way to explore this industry is by attending auto shows. You will be able to see new vehicles, as well as prototypes of cars of the future.

■ EDUCATION AND TRAINING REQUIREMENTS
High School

Taking auto mechanics courses is a great way to prepare for a career in test driving. It's important to know the mechanics of a car before pushing it to its limits. Be sure to do well in the driver's education program as test drivers put safety and rules of the road before speed during any driving test.

Test drivers need strong communication skills to be able to convey their test data and observations to team members after every test. Hone these skills by taking speech and writing classes. Take writing class or any classes that require writing projects—especially if you want to work on the editorial side of auto test driving.

Postsecondary Training

Many successful test drivers are mechanical engineers with a background in automotive engineering. Others have degrees in automotive technology. Additional classes in auto design or manufacturing will also be helpful. If you aspire to write for an industry trade magazine, a degree in journalism, while not necessary, will give you an edge over other employment candidates.

Other Education or Training

Test drivers stay up to date on current automotive trends and issues through workshops, courses, and conferences. SAE International offers a variety of automotive-related continuing education classes, workshops, and webinars.

■ CERTIFICATION, LICENSING, AND SPECIAL REQUIREMENTS
Certification or Licensing

A valid driver's license is a prerequisite for employment in this field, as well as a clean driving record. Automotive manufacturers may also offer in-house certification programs for test drivers.

■ EXPERIENCE, SKILLS, AND PERSONALITY TRAITS

Many test drivers are mechanical engineers with a background in automotive engineering; others have degrees in automotive technology.

A good test driver will know the mechanics of a car—its power-to-weight ratio, how quickly it changes gears, and how an engine reacts and sounds at various levels of performance. This knowledge is essential in identifying the strengths and weaknesses of a car's design. Test drivers must have a high tolerance for long periods behind the wheel. They often spend many hours driving their assigned cars in difficult situations and at top speeds. Drivers need to stay focused, have presence of mind, and excellent reflexes to avoid potentially dangerous accidents and crashes

A passion for cars and expert driving abilities are not the only skills needed for this career. Test drivers working on the editorial side must have, along with automotive expertise, the ability to write proficiently. While a journalism background is not a prerequisite for this job, candidates with a writing background will certainly have an edge.

JOE OLDHAM, TEST DRIVER — MOVERS AND SHAKERS

Test car driver, photographer, and journalist Joe Oldham plied his trade in the 1970s, putting American muscle cars like Pontiac's Catalina and Trans Am, and Chevrolet's Corvette, and Italy's *primo* sports cars, Ferraris, through metal-grinding, brake-squealing tests. It was his job to drive these cars hard and describe the pros and cons of everything about them, from performance to appearance and features. He wrote about the cars and their performance for car enthusiasts and readers of automotive magazines such as *Cars, Speed & Supercar,* and *Supercars Annual.* To learn more about Oldham and his career as a sports car test driver, check out his book, *Muscle Car Confidential: Confessions of a Muscle Car Test Driver* (St. Paul, Minn.: Motorbooks, 2007).

■ EMPLOYMENT PROSPECTS
Employers

Test drivers are employed by major auto manufacturers. Coveted spots include working as high performance drivers for the Big Three automakers—Ford, Chrysler, and General Motors—though many test drivers vie for positions with major foreign manufacturers such as BMW, Toyota, and Ferrari. Some test drivers are employed by automotive publishing companies.

Starting Out

Test drivers may find work through their career services office or through automotive technology trade schools. Test drivers who are new to the field may be asked to perform basic tests on how well individual systems work, such as the heating and cooling system or the braking system. Or they may assist in setting up a racing course or other testing site. New test drivers are often assigned lower-end cars, or less demanding test routes such as highways or local roads.

■ ADVANCEMENT PROSPECTS

Test drivers with enough experience may be promoted to head driver for an auto manufacturer. Head drivers often test the higher end, luxury models or may be asked to race a manufacturer's concept or muscle car models. Seeking employment at a larger manufacturer or one specializing in exotic cars, such as Ferrari or Aston Martin, is another form of career advancement.

Test drivers who work in the publishing industry can find employment with larger magazines, or may seek additional freelance opportunities for Web sites, e-zines, or local papers.

■ OUTLOOK

Automobile manufacturers will continue to create new models and improve upon existing vehicles, making them faster, more manageable, and better performing. New models must be thoroughly tested before being made available to the public, so employment opportunities for test drivers will continue to be good—although this is a very small field. Trade magazines will also continue to need good writers with knowledge of the industry and automotive technology for their print publications and Web sites.

■ UNIONS AND ASSOCIATIONS

Test drivers do not belong to unions, but many join SAE International, a membership organization for engineers and related technical experts in the aerospace, automotive, and commercial-vehicle industries.

■ TIPS FOR ENTRY

1. Earn a mechanical engineering degree with a specialization in automotive engineering or technology to improve your chances of landing a job.
2. Apply for entry-level jobs with automotive manufacturers.
3. Talk with test drivers about their careers. Ask them for advice on breaking into the field.

■ FOR MORE INFORMATION

SAE International provides education and resources for technical experts in the aerospace, automotive, and commercial vehicle industries.

SAE International
400 Commonwealth Drive
Warrendale, PA 15096-0001
Tel: (877) 606-7323; (724) 776-4841
Fax: (724) 776-0790
http://www.sae.org/automotive

Visit the BMW Web site to learn more about the company, its cars, and careers.

BMW
300 Chestnut Ridge Road
Woodcliff Lake, NJ 07677-7731
Tel: (800) 831-1117
http://www.bmw.com

Visit Fiat Chrysler's Web site for information about test-driving facilities and to learn more about the company and its cars.

Fiat Chrysler
Tel: (800) 247-9753
http://www.chrysler.com

Visit Ford Motor Company's Web site to learn more about the company.

Ford Motor Company
Tel: (800) 392-3673
http://www.ford.com

General Motors Company provides information about its company and careers on its Web site.

General Motors Company (GMC)
http://www.gm.com

Visit Toyota Motor Corporation's Web Site to learn more about the company and careers.

Toyota Motor Corporation
P.O. Box 259001
Plano, TX 75025-9001
Tel: (800) 331-4331
Fax: (310) 468-7814
http://www.toyota.com

Textile Manufacturing Workers

■ OVERVIEW

Textile manufacturing workers prepare natural and synthetic fibers for spinning into yarn and manufacture yarn into textile products that are used in clothing, in household goods, and for many industrial purposes. Among the processes that these workers perform are cleaning, carding, combing, and spinning fibers; weaving, knitting, or bonding yarns and threads into textiles; and dyeing and finishing fabrics. There are approximately 137,510 workers employed in apparel manufacturing and 16,560 textile, apparel, and furnishings workers, according to the Department of Labor.

■ HISTORY

Archaeological evidence suggests that people have been weaving natural fibers into cloth for at least 7,000 years. Basketweaving probably preceded and inspired the weaving of cloth. By about 5,000 years ago, cotton, silk, linen, and wool fabrics were being produced in several areas of the world. Ancient weavers used procedures and equipment that seem simple by today's standards, but some of the cloth they made was of fine quality and striking beauty.

Over time, the production of textiles grew into a highly developed craft industry with various regional centers that were renowned for different kinds of textile products. Yet, until the 18th century, the making of fabrics was largely a cottage industry in which no more than a few people, often family groups, worked in small shops with their own equipment to make products by hand. The Industrial Revolution and the invention of machines such as the cotton gin and the power loom made it possible for a wide variety of textiles to be produced in factories at low cost and in large quantities. Improvements have continued into the 20th century, so that today many processes in making textiles are highly automated.

Other changes have revolutionized the production of fabrics. The first attempts to make artificial fibers date to the 17th century, but it was not until the late 19th and early 20th centuries that a reasonably successful synthetic, a kind of rayon, was developed from the plant substance cellulose. Since then, hundreds of synthetic fibers have been developed from such sources as coal, wood, ammonia, and proteins. Other applications of science and technology to the textile industry have resulted in cloth that has various attractive or useful qualities. Many fabrics that resist creases, repel stains, or are fireproof, mothproof, antiseptic, nonshrinking, glazed, softened, or stiff are the product of modern mechanical or chemical finishing.

Only about half of the textiles produced in the United States are used for clothing. The rest are used in household products (towels, sheets, upholstery) and industrial products (conveyor belts, tire cords, parachutes).

■ THE JOB

Most *textile workers* operate or tend machines. In the most modern plants, the machines are often quite sophisticated and include computerized controls.

Workers in textile manufacturing can be grouped in several categories. Some workers operate machines that clean and align fibers, draw and spin them into yarn, and knit, weave, or tuft the yarn into textile products. Other workers, usually employees of chemical companies, tend machines that produce synthetic fibers through chemical processes. Still other workers prepare machines before production runs. They set up the equipment, adjusting timing and control mechanisms, and they often maintain the machines as well. Another category of workers specializes in finishing textile products before they are sent out to consumers. The following paragraphs describe just a few of the many kinds of specialized workers in textile manufacturing occupations.

In the transformation of raw fiber into cloth, *staple cutters* may perform one of the first steps. They place

QUICK FACTS

ALTERNATE TITLE(S)
Beam-Warper Tenders, Cloth Testers, Dye-Range Operators, Frame Spinners, Loom Operators, Screen Printers, Spinneret Operators, Staple Cutters, Textile Production Workers, Weavers

DUTIES
Operate machinery that produces textile products that are used in clothing, in household goods, and for many industrial purposes

SALARY RANGE
$18,850 to $25,580 to $50,000+

WORK ENVIRONMENT
Primarily Indoors

BEST GEOGRAPHIC LOCATION(S)
Opportunities exist in all regions, but many jobs are in North Carolina, Virginia, Georgia, California, and New Jersey

MINIMUM EDUCATION LEVEL
High School Diploma, Some Postsecondary Training

SCHOOL SUBJECTS
Family and Consumer Science, Technical/Shop

EXPERIENCE
On-the-job training

PERSONALITY TRAITS
Hands On, Realistic, Technical

SKILLS
Interpersonal, Mechanical/Manual Dexterity

CERTIFICATION OR LICENSING
None

SPECIAL REQUIREMENTS
None

EMPLOYMENT PROSPECTS
Poor

ADVANCEMENT PROSPECTS
Fair

OUTLOOK
Decline

NOC
9616

O*NET-SOC
51-6061.00, 51-6062.00, 51-6063.00, 51-6064.00, 51-6099.00

opened bales of raw stock or cans of sliver (combed, untwisted strands of fiber) at the feed end of a cutting machine. They guide the raw stock or sliver onto a conveyor belt or feed rolls, which pull it against the cutting blades. They examine the cut fibers as they fall from the blades and measure them to make sure they are the required length.

CAREER LADDER

Plant Manager

Supervisor

Trainer

Experienced Textile
Manufacturing Worker

Entry-Level Textile
Manufacturing Worker

Spinneret operators oversee machinery that makes manufactured fibers from such nonfibrous materials as metal or plastic. Chemical compounds are dissolved or melted in a liquid, which is then extruded, or forced, through holes in a metal plate, called a spinneret. The size and shape of the holes determine the shape and uses of the fiber. Workers adjust the flow of fiber base through the spinneret, repair breaks in the fiber, and make minor adjustments to the machinery.

Frame spinners, also called *spinning-frame tenders*, tend machines that draw out and twist the sliver into yarn. These workers patrol the spinning-machine area to ensure that the machines have a continuous supply of sliver or roving (a soft, slightly twisted strand of fiber made from sliver). They replace nearly empty packages of roving or sliver with full ones. If they detect a break in the yarn being spun, or in the roving or sliver being fed into the spinning frame, they stop the machine and repair the break. They are responsible for keeping a continuous length of material threaded through the spinning frame while the machine is operating.

Spinning supervisors supervise and coordinate the activities of the various spinning workers. From the production schedule, they determine the quantity and texture of yarn to be spun and the type of fiber to be used. Then they compute such factors as the proper spacing of rollers and the correct size of twist gears, using mathematical formulas and tables and their knowledge of spinning machine processes. They examine the spun yarn as it leaves the spinning frame to detect variations from standards.

A *textile production worker* adjusts the tension on one of the rapier weaving machines. Once the fiber is spun into yarn or thread, it is ready for weaving, knitting, or tufting. Woven fabrics are made on looms that interlace the threads. Knit products, such as socks or women's hosiery, are produced by intermeshing loops of yarn. The tufting process, used in making carpets, involves pushing loops of yarn through a material backing.

Beam-warper tenders work at high-speed warpers, which are machines that automatically wind yarn onto beams, or cylinders, preparatory to dyeing or weaving.

A creel, or rack of yarn spools, is positioned at the feed end of the machine. The workers examine the creel to make sure that the size, color, number, and arrangement of the yarn spools correspond to specifications. They thread the machine with the yarn from the spools, pulling the yarn through several sensing devices and fastening the yarn to the empty cylinder. After setting a counter to record the amount of yarn wound, they start the machine. If a strand of yarn breaks, the machine stops, and the tenders locate and tie the broken ends. When the specified amount of yarn has been wound, they stop the machine, cut the yarn strands, and tape the cut ends.

Weavers or loom operators operate a battery of automatic looms that weave yarn into cloth. They observe the cloth being woven carefully to detect any flaws, and they remove weaving defects by cutting out the filling (cross) threads in the area. If a loom stops, they locate the problem and either correct it or, in the case of mechanical breakdown, notify the appropriate repairer.

After the fabric is removed from the loom, it is ready for dyeing and finishing, which includes treating fabrics to make them fire-, shrink-, wrinkle-, or soil-resistant.

Dye-range operators control the feed end of a dye range, which is an arrangement of equipment that dyes and dries cloth. Operators position the cloth to be dyed and machine-sew its end to the end of the cloth already in the machine. They turn valves to admit dye from a mixing tank onto the dye pads, and they regulate the temperature of the dye and the air in the drying box. They start the machine, and when the process is complete, they record yardage dyed, lot numbers, and the machine running time. *Colorists*, *screen printing artists*, *screen makers*, and *screen printers* print designs on textiles.

Cloth testers perform tests on "gray goods"—raw, undyed, unfinished fabrics—and finished cloth samples. They may count the number of threads in a sample, test its tensile strength in a tearing machine, and crease it to determine its resilience. They may also test for such characteristics as abrasion resistance, fastness of dye, flame retardance, and absorbency, depending on the type of cloth.

■ EARNINGS

Earnings of textile industry workers vary depending on the type of plant where they are employed and the workers' job responsibilities, the shift they work, and seniority. Workers at plants located in the North tend to be paid more than those in the South.

In May 2015, textile knitting and weaving machine setters, operators, and tenders earned median wages of $10.91 an hour (or $23,680 annually). Textile winding, twisting, and drawing out machine setters, operators, and tenders earned a median wage of $12.11 an hour ($26,040 annually). Textile bleaching and dyeing machine operators and tenders earned a median wage of $11.36 an hour ($26,170 yearly). Median hourly earnings for textile cutting machine setters, operators, and tenders were $11.52 (or $25,580 annually). Salaries for workers in these four occupational groups ranged from $18,850 to $48,480 or more. Inspectors, testers, sorters, samplers, and weighers who worked at textile and fabric finishing and fabric coating mills earned a mean wage of $13.74 an hour ($28,580 annually). Textile employees with supervisory responsibilities can make more than $50,000 a year. Most workers with a year or more of service receive paid vacations and insurance benefits. Many are able to participate in pension plans, profit sharing, or year-end bonuses. Some companies offer their employees discounts on the textiles or textile products they sell.

■ WORK ENVIRONMENT

Work areas in modern textile plants are largely clean, well-lighted, air-conditioned, and humidity controlled. Older facilities may be less comfortable, with more fibers or fumes in the air, requiring some workers to wear protective glasses or masks. Some machines can be very noisy, and workers near them must wear ear protectors. Workers also must stay alert and use caution when working around high-speed machines that can catch clothing or jewelry. Those who work around chemicals must wear protective clothing and sometimes respirators. Increased attention to worker safety and health has forced textile manufacturing companies to comply with tough federal, state, and local regulations.

Workweeks in this industry average 40 hours in length. Depending on business conditions, some plants may operate 24 hours a day, with three shifts a day. Production employees may work rotating shifts, so that they share night and weekend hours. Some companies have a four-shift continuous operating schedule, consisting of a 168-hour workweek made of up of four daily shifts totaling 42 hours a week. This system offers a rotating arrangement of days off. During production cutbacks, companies may go to a three- or four-day workweek, but they generally try to avoid layoffs during slow seasons.

Machine operators are often on their feet during much of their shift. Some jobs involve repetitive tasks that some people find boring.

■ EXPLORING

High school courses in subjects such as shop, mechanical drawing, and chemistry and hobbies involving model building and working with machinery can be

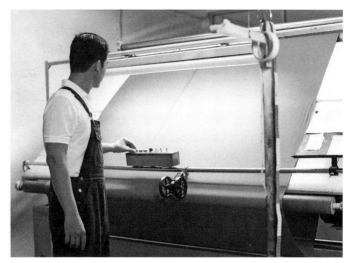

A worker monitors a machine at a textile factory. (Kzenon. Shutterstock.)

good preparation for many jobs in the textile manufacturing field. Students may be able to find summer employment in a textile plant. If that cannot be arranged, a machine operator's job in another manufacturing industry may provide a similar enough experience that it is useful in understanding something about textile manufacturing work.

■ EDUCATION AND TRAINING REQUIREMENTS
High School

For some textile production jobs, a high school education is desirable but may not be necessary. Workers who operate machines are often hired as unskilled labor and trained on the job. However, with the increasingly complex machinery and manufacturing methods in this industry, more and more often a high school diploma plus some technical training is expected of job applicants. High school students interested in a textile career should take courses in physics, chemistry, mathematics, and English. Computer skills are necessary, since many machines are now operated by computer technology.

Postsecondary Training

Even those with postsecondary school education generally must go through a period of on-the-job training by experienced workers or representatives of equipment manufacturers, where they learn the procedures and systems of their particular company. Some companies have co-op programs with nearby schools. Participants in these programs work as interns during their academic training with the agreement that they will work for the sponsoring company upon graduation. A two-year associate's degree in textile technology is required for technicians, laboratory testers, and supervisory personnel.

SPECIAL USES FOR TEXTILES

DID YOU KNOW?

Textiles are used for a wide variety of products and purposes. Some interesting facts about textiles include:

- Recycled soda bottles and plastic food containers are being used to make fabric, such as denim.
- The Jarvik-7 artificial heart is made up of more than 50 percent textile fiber.
- The artificial kidney used in dialysis is made up of about 5,000 to 10,000 hollow fibers, yet it is only about two inches in diameter.
- More than 75 percent of a tire's strength comes from textiles.
- The U.S. military purchases more than 8,000 different textile products each year.

Sources: American Textile Manufacturers Institute; National Council of Textile Organizations

■ CERTIFICATION, LICENSING, AND SPECIAL REQUIREMENTS
Certification or Licensing

There are no certification or licensing requirements for textile manufacturing workers.

■ EXPERIENCE, SKILLS, AND PERSONALITY TRAITS

No experience is needed to work in most textile manufacturing positions, but those with prior work experience will increase their chances of landing a job, getting promoted, and possibly earning higher pay.

Many machine operators need physical stamina, manual dexterity, and a mechanical aptitude to do their job. Changes are underway in the industry that make other kinds of personal characteristics increasingly important, such as the ability to assume responsibility, to take initiative, to communicate with others, and to work well as a part of a team.

■ EMPLOYMENT PROSPECTS
Employers

There are approximately 137,510 workers employed in apparel manufacturing and 16,560 textile, apparel, and furnishings workers in the United States. Most textile production workers are employed either in mills that spin and weave gray goods, or in finishing plants, where gray goods are treated with processes such as dyeing and bleaching. Some textile companies combine these two stages of manufacturing under one roof.

Employment opportunities for textile manufacturing workers are concentrated in the southeastern states. Many of the jobs in this industry are located in North Carolina, Virginia, and California

Starting Out

Most textile production workers obtain their jobs by employment postings through online agencies and newspapers or by applying directly to the personnel office of a textile plant. A new worker usually receives between a week and several months of on-the-job training, depending on the complexity of the job.

Graduates of textile technology programs in colleges and technical institutes may be informed about job openings through their school's career services office. They may be able to line up permanent positions before graduation. Sometimes students in technical programs are sponsored by a local textile company, and upon graduation, they go to work for the sponsoring company.

■ ADVANCEMENT PROSPECTS

Production workers in textile manufacturing who become skilled machine operators may be promoted to positions in which they train new employees. Other workers can qualify for better jobs by learning additional machine-operating skills. Usually the workers with the best knowledge of machine operations are those who set up and prepare machines before production runs. Skilled workers who show that they have good judgment and leadership abilities may be promoted to supervisory positions, in charge of a bank of machines or a stage in the production process. Some companies offer continuing education opportunities to dedicated workers.

Laboratory workers may advance to supervisory positions in the lab. If their educational background includes such courses as industrial engineering and quality control, they may move up to management jobs where they plan and control production.

■ OUTLOOK

The U.S. Department of Labor (DOL) predicts a steep decline in employment for this field through 2024, even as the demand for textile products increases. Changes in the textile industry will account for much of this decline. Factories are reorganizing production operations for greater efficiency and installing equipment that relies on more highly automated and computerized machines and processes. Such technology as shuttleless and air-jet looms and computer-controlled machinery allows several machines to be operated by one operator while still increasing speed and productivity.

Another factor that will probably contribute to a reduced demand for U.S. textile workers is an increase in imports of textiles from other countries. There is a continuing trend toward freer world markets and looser trade restrictions. The DOL predicts that employment at textile mills and textile product mills will decline by 7 percent through 2024.

While fewer workers will be needed to operate machines, there will continue to be many job openings each year as experienced people transfer to other jobs or leave the workforce. Workers who have good technical training and skills will have the best job opportunities.

■ UNIONS AND ASSOCIATIONS

Some textile production workers belong to UNITE HERE and other unions. The National Council of Textile Organizations provides data on textile industry employment and revenue.

■ TIPS FOR ENTRY

1. Talk to textile manufacturing workers about their careers. Ask them for advice on breaking into the field.
2. Visit the following Web sites for job listings:
   - http://www.indeed.com/q-textile-jobs.html
   - http://www.careerbuilder.com/jobs-textiles
   - http://www.gettextilejobs.com
3. Join UNITE HERE to increase your chances of landing a job and receiving fair pay for your work.
4. Be willing to relocate. North Carolina, Virginia, Georgia, and California are employment hubs for this industry.

■ FOR MORE INFORMATION

The College of Textiles offers undergraduate, graduate, and continuing education programs in textiles.

College of Textiles
North Carolina State University, College of Textiles
1020 Main Campus Drive
Raleigh, NC 27606
Tel: (919) 515-6640
https://textiles.ncsu.edu

The National Council of Textile Organizations provides information on textile industry news and issues, educational programs, membership benefits, and other resources.

National Council of Textile Organizations (NCTO)
1701 K Street, NW, Suite 625
Washington, D.C. 20006-1503
Tel: (202) 822-8028
Fax: (202) 822-8029
http://www.ncto.org

Textile Technology Center of Gaston Colleges offers degree and continuing education programs in textile technology.

Textile Technology Center (TTC)
Gaston College
7220 Wilkinson Boulevard
Belmont, NC 28012
Tel: (704) 825-3737
http://www.gaston.edu/textile-technology-center

This union fights for workers' rights and represents workers in various industries, including basic apparel and textiles.

UNITE HERE!
275 Seventh Avenue
New York, NY 10001-6708
Tel: (212) 265-7000
http://unitehere.org

Theater Managers

■ OVERVIEW

Theater managers oversee all activities occurring in a theater. They have diverse duties depending on the specific theater. They supervise general maintenance, what events and productions take place in the theater, and ensure profitability of the theater. Their vision, actions, and decisions can mean the difference between the theater staying open or closing. They oversee the theater's organizational structure and run the day to day activities and operations. They coordinate marketing, fundraising, budgeting, accounting, and staffing. They may work in large theaters, dinner theaters, regional theaters, summer stock theaters, or small, local theaters. Some work in theaters in hotels and casinos. Others may work in concert halls or other venues which put on an array of theatrical productions, concerts, and other events. Theater managers may also be referred to as hall managers, directors of theater operations, or venue managers.

■ HISTORY

The first theater built in America is generally believed to have been constructed in Williamsburg, VA in 1716. William Levingston, who managed a dance school, erected it. Two of the stars of the dance school were Charles Stagg and his wife Mary. A contract dating back to July 11, 1716 shows Livingston and the Staggs agreed to build a theater in Williamsburg and to provide the actors, scenery and music from England to enact comedies and tragedies in the city. In November of 1716, Levingston purchased three lots and built a house, kitchen, and stable as well as a bowling alley and a theater.

QUICK FACTS

ALTERNATE TITLE(S)
Directors of Theater Operations,
Hall Managers, Venue
Managers

DUTIES
Overseeing activities in theater;
handling general maintenance
and profitability; overseeing
organizational structure;
staffing; marketing; assuring
compliance with union
agreements; negotiating
contacts

SALARY RANGE
$24,000 $38,225 to $92,560+

WORK ENVIRONMENT
Primarily Indoors

BEST GEOGRAPHIC LOCATION(S)
Opportunities exist in all regions,
with high demand in New York,
Las Vegas, and Los Angeles

MINIMUM EDUCATION LEVEL
Bachelor's Degree

SCHOOL SUBJECTS
Business, Music, Theater/Dance

EXPERIENCE
Three to five years experience

PERSONALITY TRAITS
Creative, Organized,
Problem-Solving

SKILLS
Business Management,
Leadership, Performance,
Music, and Acting

CERTIFICATION OR LICENSING
None

SPECIAL REQUIREMENTS
None

EMPLOYMENT PROSPECTS
Fair

ADVANCEMENT PROSPECTS
Fair

OUTLOOK
About as Fast as the Average

NOC
0512

O*NET-SOC
11-1021.00; 11-9199.00

There are no records of what plays were presented at the theater. However, a number of years later, the property entered foreclosure. By 1735 and 1736, the theater served amateur productions by students of William and Mary College, though reports indicate a company of professional players also acted there.

One of the obstacles to theaters at this time was a lack of support by the wealthy. No records exist of any other performances after 1736. In 1745 the playhouse/theater was bought by some prominent men of the Virginia Colony and given to Williamsburg as a town hall.

Following this, theaters started popping up around the country, and eventually many became successful. Today, there are theaters in almost every community, big or small, and each needs a theater manager.

■ THE JOB

Theater managers determine the overall success or failure of the theater. How they choose to run the theater, what productions or acts they decide to stage, and how they promote their venue and performers ultimately decides whether the theater thrives or closes. They manage the theater's organizational structure, coordinate day-to-day activities and operations, and plan and manage marketing, fundraising, budgeting, accounting, and staffing.

Theater managers deal with actors, actresses, directors, production personnel, technical crew, musicians, caterers, maintenance workers, theater staff, and anyone else associated professionally with their theater.

They are expected to resolve audience-related issues and problems, and they work with the artistic, production, and facilities departments of a theater to coordinate an annual calendar of activities and shows.

Theater managers oversee the staffing of the theater. This includes recruiting, hiring, and training ushers, security guards, box office and concession clerks, and custodians. If the theater is small, the manager may handle payroll directly. In larger theaters, the individual may simply oversee a payroll department or service.

Theater managers develop marketing plans and strategies to generate ticket sales and assure that large audiences attend shows at the theater. This may include advertising campaigns and publicity. They may develop, design, and write marketing pieces, press releases, and brochures for the theater and any productions. In some instances, the theater manager will oversee an employee or an outside consultant who handles these duties.

Theatrical productions cost a lot of money to produce. Theater managers develop fund-raising strategies to ensure that the production is adequately funded. They create and approve operating, production, and marketing budgets and oversee production expenses including royalty fees, marketing materials, lighting, set design, and props as well as production staff, performers, box office staff, and other workers. In many cases, the manager will negotiate contracts for services and performers.

The theater manager coordinates the activities between all theater staff and stage performances. He or she works to keep the theater booked consistently, make sure performers and acts are paid, and, if the theater is unionized, complies with union rules and regulations. It is essential in unionized settings that the theater manager have good relationships with all of the unions involved. These may include Equity, United Scenic Artists (USA), and the Stage Directors and Choreographers Society (SDC).

Theater managers must handle all types of crises without panicking. Potential problems might include dealing with extreme inclement weather on the day of a performance, patrons falling ill during a performance, patrons becoming unruly, or union workers going on strike.

Theater managers work long irregular hours and often work weekends, holidays, and evenings when theatergoers frequently attend shows.

■ EARNINGS

The earnings of a theater manager vary depending on the size, type, and prestige of the theater as well as the geographic location. Other variables include the experience, qualifications, and duties of the individual.

According to Payscale.com the median annual earnings of theater managers was approximately $38,225.

The lowest 10 percent of individuals in this job earned approximately $24,000 and the highest 10 percent of individuals earned approximately $61,000.

With that being said, according to the Bureau of Labor Statistics, the average annual earnings for all management positions within theater companies and dinner theaters was $92,560.

◼ WORK ENVIRONMENT

Theater managers may work in a variety of settings including large theaters, dinner theaters, regional theaters, summer stock theaters, university theaters, and others. Some work in theaters in hotels and casinos. Others may work in concert halls or other venues which put on an array of theatrical productions, concerts, and other types of events. The environment at a theater may often be stressful before performances or when worrying that ticket sales are up to par and the theater is profitable.

◼ EXPLORING

Take classes in business, math, theater, writing, etc. to hone business skills. Participate in your school's drama club in any capacity. Go to your local community theater group and volunteer. Contact theaters in your area and inquire about summer internships. These activities will give you skills and knowledge and help you make important contacts.

◼ EDUCATION AND TRAINING REQUIREMENTS
High School

A high school diploma or GED is generally the minimum educational requirement for this job. While in school take classes in theater arts, drama, math, English and business. All will help you learn the basics and hone skills. Be sure to participate in your school's drama club, theatrical productions and activities. These will give you experience that will prove helpful later in your career.

Postsecondary Education

While a high school diploma is the minimum educational requirement, it should be noted that most people who hold jobs as theater managers have postsecondary education with degrees in areas such as music, theater arts, drama, business management, or marketing.

A college education provides experience that individuals might not otherwise have as well as the opportunity for internships and the ability to make important contacts.

◼ CERTIFICATION, LICENSING, AND SPECIAL REQUIREMENTS

There are no certification or licensing requirements for theater managers.

◼ EXPERIENCE, SKILLS, AND PERSONALITY TRAITS

CAREER LADDER

General Manager

Theater Manager at Larger Theater

Theater Manager

Assistant Theater Manager

Many theater managers work their way up the career ladder to management positions. They start at the bottom in the theater and after obtaining experience, move up the ranks. Some managers work their way up to management positions, while others earn degrees that prepare them for high-level jobs in the industry.

Theater managers need an array of skills. They must be creative individuals with a vision in order to make their theater (and its productions) successful. Individuals should have marketing skills, accounting skills, business skills, and more. The ability to get along well with people is mandatory. Communications skills, both written and verbal are essential. The ability to multi-task effectively and keep a cool head at all time is also necessary. A knowledge of theater production is required.

◼ EMPLOYMENT PROSPECTS
Employers

Theater managers may work in a variety of employment settings including dinner theaters, regional theaters, large or small theaters, summer stock theaters, and university theaters. Some also work in theaters in hotels and casinos. There are also opportunities in theme parks such as Disneyworld, Disneyland, Dollywood, Six Flags, and many others. Still others may work in concert halls or other venues which put on an array of theatrical productions, concerts and other types of events.

The Bureau of Labor Statistics (BLS) estimates that in 2015 there were 3,470 people working in theater management in theatrical companies and dinner theaters.

Starting Out

Aspiring theater managers may find it easier to break in by locating positions as assistant theater managers of smaller theaters. As theater managers in these types of venues often leave for better jobs, there is a greater chance of moving up the career ladder quickly.

◼ ADVANCEMENT PROSPECTS

There are a number of ways theater managers can advance their careers. The most common is for individuals to

THEATER TALK

Audition: Also known as tryouts for a particular part in a play.

Auditorium: The main area of theater seating, where the audience sits to watch a performance.

Aulaeum: This is a term for the main curtain which separates the audience from the stage.

Box office: The ticket booth. This is the area where tickets are sold, generally found either in or adjoining the lobby of a theater.

Cabaret: Entertainment presented to an audience in theaters, clubs, hotel-restaurants, or similar settings.

Call board: These are bulletin boards near the stage door entrance of a theater posting auditions, casting calls, rehearsal schedules

Community theater: Amateur theater groups or organizations which produce and perform plays.

Curtain call: Refers to the appearance of the cast of a theatrical production at the end of a play to receive the applause of the audience.

Green room: Room or space near stage used by actors and actresses while waiting to go on stage.

Musical: A play in which the story is told through a combination of spoken dialogue and musical numbers.

Playbill: These may be either large posters which are used to promote a play or theatrical performance or a program or booklet containing information about a particular production.

Properties: Also called props. These are all the physical things which are on a stage with the exception of the scenery. For example they might include chairs, books, lamps, etc.

Read: May refer to auditioning or "reading" for a part; or how a prop or action on stage may be perceived by an audience.

Review: A critic's or reporter's analysis of a play or production; often done at the first performance of a play.

Run through: This is a type of rehearsal in which an entire play (or act) is rehearsed without interruption.

Theater in the round: A type of presentation of a play or other production in which the stage is surrounded by the audience on all sides.

Source: http://tctwebstage.com/glossary.htm

option is for the individual to locate positions in auditorium or venue management.

■ OUTLOOK

The Bureau of Labor Statistics (BLS) reports that the projected job growth for theater managers in theatrical companies and dinner theaters is about 6 percent through 2024. This is about average when compared to other occupations.

■ UNIONS AND ASSOCIATIONS

Depending on the specific employment situation, some theater managers may belong to the International Association of Venue Managers (IAVM). Individuals may also have to deal with a variety of performing arts unions including the American Federations of Musicians (AFM) Actors' Equity, United Scenic Artists (USA), and the Stage Directors and Choreographers Society (SDC) among others.

■ TIPS FOR ENTRY

1. If you are inexperienced, look for a job in a small theater or a city to get your foot in the door.
2. Find an internship through your college or other theatrical program in theater management.
3. In addition to looking for jobs in traditional theaters, dinner theaters, regional theaters and on Broadway, look for openings at theaters in casinos, theme parks, hotels, and other venues.
4. Try to find a job as an assistant theater manager in a small theater. Job turnover is higher in these types of venues and you will have a better chance of promotion in a shorter span of time.

■ FOR MORE INFORMATION

Actors' Equity is an American labor union representing the world of live theatrical performance.

Actors' Equity (EQUITY)
165 West 46th Street
New York, NY 10036
Tel: (212) 869-8530
Fax: (212) 719-9815
http://www.actorsequity.org

The International Association of Venue Managers is the primary professional organization for managers of performance, sports, and meeting facilities.

International Association of Venue Managers (IAVM)
635 Fritz Drive, Suite 100
Coppell, TX 75019-4442
Tel: (972) 906-7441
Fax: (972) 906-7418
http://iavm.org/

find similar jobs in larger, more prestigious theaters. That in turn leads to increased responsibilities and earnings. Another option is for the individual to move into the general management of a theater company. A third

The Stage Directors and Choreographers is the theatrical union that unites, empowers, and protects professional Stage Directors and Choreographers throughout the United States.

Stage Directors and Choreographers Society (SDC)
1501 Broadway
Suite 1701
New York, NY 10036
Tel: (800) 541-5204; (212) 391-1070
Fax: (212) 302-6195
E-mail: LPenn@SDCweb.org
http://sdcweb.org

United Scenic Artists, Local USA 829 is a labor union and professional association of designers, artists and craftspeople organized to protect craft standards, working conditions and wages for the entertainment and decorative arts industries.

United Scenic Artists (USA)
29 West 38th Street, 15th Floor
New York, NY 10018
Tel: (212) 581-0300
Fax: (212) 977-2011
E-mail: CeciliaF@usa829.org
https://www.usa829.org

Tire Technicians

■ OVERVIEW

Tire technicians, employed by tire manufacturers, test tires to determine their strength, durability (how long they will last), and any defects in their construction. According to the market research group IBISWorld, there were approximately 364 tire manufacturers in operation in the United States, with nearly 50,000 employees, as of April 2016.

■ HISTORY

Wheels were banded by metal before tires came into use. Copper bands were used on chariot wheels in the Middle East as early as 2000 B.C. Strips of metal were widely used on wheels in medieval and early modern times.

The Scottish engineer Robert Thomson patented the first pneumatic tire for carriages in 1845. Thirty-three years later, the Scottish inventor John Dunlop patented a pneumatic tire for automobiles and bicycles and created a company for the manufacture of such tires. Early automobiles used solid rubber tires or narrow pneumatic tires similar to inner-tube or single-tube bicycle tires.

As automobiles grew heavier and as vehicle size and speed increased, tire manufacturers developed better and more durable tires. After World War II, synthetic rubber and synthetic fibers were used for most tire construction. In the following years, the tubeless automobile tire, puncture-sealing tires, and radial-ply tires were introduced for American trucks, cars, planes, and other vehicles. Throughout the last 150 years of tire innovation, tire technicians have been called upon to test and monitor the quality and durability of these tires.

■ THE JOB

Most tire technicians work either with experimental models of tires that are not yet ready for manufacturing or with production samples as they come out of the factory. Technicians who are involved mostly with testing tires from the factory are called *quality-control technicians*.

There are mainly two types of testing performed by tire technicians: dedicated and free-flowing, or general, testing. Dedicated testing is a high-tech, electronically run procedure that measures rolling resistance. This is the resistance at which a tire meets force and momentum (the force acting against the tire). Dedicated testing requires the technician to be present at all times during the procedure, monitoring the machines, programming variables, and collecting data. Free-flowing testing is a durability type testing. It may last for days or even weeks and covers many different operations that test the tire's durability. A tire technician might test 45 tires at once using different procedures.

QUICK FACTS

ALTERNATE TITLE(S)
None

DUTIES
Test tires to determine their strength and durability, and for any defects in their construction

SALARY RANGE
$21,140 to $36,310 to $62,150+

WORK ENVIRONMENT
Primarily Indoors

BEST GEOGRAPHIC LOCATION(S)
Opportunities available throughout the country

MINIMUM EDUCATION LEVEL
High School Diploma, Some Postsecondary Training

SCHOOL SUBJECTS
Mathematics, Physics, Technical/Shop

EXPERIENCE
Internship

PERSONALITY TRAITS
Conventional, Hands On, Technical

SKILLS
Building/Trades, Mechanical/Manual Dexterity

CERTIFICATION OR LICENSING
None

SPECIAL REQUIREMENTS
None

EMPLOYMENT PROSPECTS
Fair

ADVANCEMENT PROSPECTS
Fair

OUTLOOK
Little Change or More Slowly than the Average

NOC
9423

O*NET-SOC
51-9061.00, 51-9197.00

CAREER LADDER

Tire Test Engineer or Information
Processor

Tire Testing Supervisor

Experienced Tire Technician

Entry-Level Tire Technician

To perform testing, tire technicians inflate the tires and mount them on testing machines. These machines re-create the stresses of actual road conditions, such as traveling at high speeds, carrying a heavy load, or going over bumpy roads. The technicians can adjust the machines to change the speed, the weight of the load, or the bumpiness of the road surface. Then they use pressure gauges and other devices to detect whether any parts of the tire are damaged and to evaluate tire uniformity, quality, and durability. This is done either while the tire is on the machine or after it is taken off. Technicians continue testing the tire until it fails or until it has lasted for some specified period of time.

A tire technician loosens the nuts on a wheel during a tire change. (Tyler Olson. Shutterstock.)

Another test involves cutting cross-sections from brand new or road-tested tires. Technicians use power saws to cut up tires and then inspect the pieces to assess the condition of the cords, the plies (which are rubbery sheets of material inside the tire), and the tread.

Throughout the testing, tire technicians keep careful records of all test results. Later, they prepare reports that may include charts, tables, and graphs to help describe and explain the test results. If a flaw is found, the technician records the data collected and reports it to the supervisor or the engineer in charge. The safety of all vehicles riding on all types of tires is dependent upon the role the tire technician plays in the tire manufacturing process.

In August 2000, the large tire manufacturer Firestone recalled 6.5 million tires, costing the company millions of dollars. As a result of this and more recent smaller tire recalls, people have become more aware of tire problems and have begun to pay closer attention to tire maintenance. This has increased demand for qualified tire technicians.

■ EARNINGS

Tire technicians are classified with inspectors, testers, and graders. According to the U.S. Department of Labor, median hourly earnings of inspectors, testers, sorters, samplers, and weighers who worked in motor vehicle parts manufacturing were $17.46 in May 2015 (for a mean annual, full-time salary of $36,310). Wages for all inspectors ranged from less than $10.16 an hour to more than $29.88 an hour, or from less than $21,140 to more than $62,150 for full-time work.

Employees of large manufacturing facilities are usually eligible for paid vacations, holidays, sick days, and insurance. Many facilities operate around the clock, and opportunities to work off-shifts, Sundays, and holidays bring time-and-a-half and double-time compensation.

■ WORK ENVIRONMENT

Many plants operate 24 hours a day. Newly hired technicians may have to work off-shifts, nights, and weekends. More experienced tire technicians usually get a choice of shifts.

Tire technicians are responsible for filling out reports, making charts and graphs, and relaying important information, both verbally and in writing. As a result, they are under considerable stress to provide accurate, detailed information in a timely manner. They also must frequently work on several projects simultaneously and be able to change projects midstream to address changing deadlines. Tire technicians can be proud that they are relied on to make decisions that affect both multimillion-dollar businesses and the driving public.

■ EXPLORING

Students can get a general overview of the tire industry by reading the annual publication from the Tire and Rim Association (TRA), the *TRA Year Book*, or the magazine *Tire Review* (http://www.tirereview.com). A high school science teacher or guidance counselor may also be able to arrange a presentation by an experienced tire technician. Students may gain indirect experience by working part time or in the summer at a plant where tires are manufactured and tested.

■ EDUCATION AND TRAINING REQUIREMENTS
High School

Tire technicians need to be high school graduates. While in high school, students interested in this career should take courses in science and mathematics, including algebra and geometry; English courses that improve reading and writing skills; and shop or laboratory science courses that introduce measuring devices, electrical machinery, and electronic testing equipment. Training in typing will also allow tire technicians to quickly input and deliver information.

Postsecondary Training

Increasingly, many employers prefer applicants with postsecondary training in a field related to manufacturing or product testing. For example, some tire manufacturers require a two-year technical certificate or an associate's degree in electronics for those seeking employment. You can receive this kind of training at a vocational school or a community or junior college.

■ CERTIFICATION, LICENSING, AND SPECIAL REQUIREMENTS
Certification or Licensing

There are no certification or licensing requirements for tire technicians.

■ EXPERIENCE, SKILLS, AND PERSONALITY TRAITS

Take as many math and science classes as possible and participate in internships at tire manufacturers to gain introductory experience to the field.

Tire technicians must have good written and oral communications skills in order to relay results to other technicians, engineers, managers, and supervisors. They need to be skillful in writing reports and adept at reading and producing charts and graphs. They must also be familiar with computers and able to collect and record data accurately and precisely. Other important traits include attentiveness to detail and strong organizational skills.

TOP GLOBAL TIRE MANUFACTURERS, 2015

FAST FACTS

1. Continental A.G. (Germany)
2. Bridgestone Corporation (Japan)
3. Groupe Michelin (France)
4. Goodyear Tire & Rubber Company (United States)
5. Sumitomo Rubber Industries (Japan)
6. Pirelli & C SpA (Italy)
7. Hankook Tire Company (South Korea)
8. Yokohama Rubber Corporation (Japan)
9. Giti Tire Pte. Ltd. (Singapore)
10. Cheng Shin Rubber/Maxxis (Taiwan)

Source: Tire Review, August 2015

■ EMPLOYMENT PROSPECTS
Employers

Tire technicians are employed by tire manufacturers. The large manufacturing companies, such as Goodyear, Dunlop, and Michelin, all employ technicians to conduct testing on new tires.

Starting Out

A good way to find employment is to apply directly at personnel offices of tire manufacturers. Career services offices at technical institutes and vocational schools also will be good sources of information. Employers looking for qualified technicians often contact these schools when there are job openings.

■ ADVANCEMENT PROSPECTS

Experienced tire technicians may also find opportunities in engineering. Those with advanced training in engineering may become *tire test engineers* or *information processors*. Those with considerable tenure with one company and proven organizational and communications skills may advance to management positions. Advanced tire technicians may become supervisors in the tire testing area or in other sections of the facility.

Experience as a tire technician may also provide a good background for work in quality control, which involves examining a product after it is produced. Quality control personnel can be found in many environments, from factories to offices.

■ OUTLOOK

The U.S. Department of Labor predicts that employment for inspectors, testers, and graders in rubber products manufacturing will show little or no change through 2024. Slow employment growth is expected due to the increased use of computer software and automated systems to run the machines that test tires.

Some job growth may arise due to recent problems with tire quality in the tire industry, which has been leading to changes in manufacturing processes and to tougher auto safety laws. Also, tire manufacturers have become more focused on proving to consumers that their tires are safe, well designed, and thoroughly tested. Many tire companies are investing in new equipment, upgrading testing areas, and expanding research and development centers. As consumers and the government demand more consistent quality checks, the tire industry will likely rely on the skills of well-trained tire technicians.

■ UNIONS AND ASSOCIATIONS

Some tire technicians are members of unions such as United Steelworkers and the International Brotherhood of Teamsters. The Rubber Manufacturers Association is an association for manufacturers of tires, tubes, roofing, sporting goods, mechanical, and industrial products. The Tire Industry Association represents tire manufacturers, repairers, suppliers, and related companies. ASTM International develops standards to improve product quality and safety.

■ TIPS FOR ENTRY

1. Read *Rubber World* (http://www.rubberworld .com/RWmagazine.asp) to learn more about the field.
2. Visit http://us-tra.org/directory.html for a list of tire manufacturers.
3. Conduct information interviews with tire technicians and ask them for advice on preparing for and entering the field.

■ FOR MORE INFORMATION

ASTM International provides information on technical standards and training programs.

ASTM International
100 Barr Harbor Drive, PO Box C700
West Conshohocken, PA 19428-2959
Tel: (877) 909-2786
Fax: (610) 8329555
E-mail: service@astm.org
http://www.astm.org

Rubber Manufacturers Association represents tire manufacturers that produce tires in the United States.

Rubber Manufacturers Association (RMA)
1400 K Street, NW, Suite 900
Washington, D.C. 20005-2403

Tel: (202) 682-4800
E-mail: info@rma.org
http://www.rma.org

The Tire Industry Association offers training programs and publications.

Tire Industry Association (TIA)
1532 Pointer Ridge Place, Suite G
Bowie, MD 20716-1883
Tel: (800) 876-8372
Fax: (301) 430-7283
https://www.tireindustry.org

Title Searchers and Examiners

■ OVERVIEW

Title searchers and examiners conduct searches of public records to determine the legal chain of ownership for a piece of real estate. *Searchers* compile lists of mortgages, deeds, contracts, judgments, and other items pertaining to a property title. *Examiners* determine a property title's legal status, abstract recorded documents (mortgages, deeds, contracts, and so forth), and sometimes prepare and issue policy guaranteeing a title's legality. There are about 54,620 title searchers, examiners, and abstractors working in the United States.

■ HISTORY

To mortgage, sell, build on, or even give away a piece of real estate, the ownership of the land must be first proven and documented. This ownership is known as a title. Establishing a clear title, however, is not an easy task. Land may change hands frequently, and questions often arise as to the use and ownership of the property.

In the United States, most major real estate dealings are publicly recorded, usually with the county recorder, clerk, or registrar. This system began in colonial Virginia and has spread throughout the rest of the country, giving the nation a unique method for keeping track of real estate transactions. In some areas of the country, a title can be traced back 200 years or more.

Over that length of time, a parcel of land may change ownership many times. Owners divide large pieces of land into smaller parcels and may sell or lease certain rights, such as the right to mine beneath a property or run roads and irrigation ditches over it, separately from the land itself. Official records of ownership and interests in land might be contradictory or incomplete. Because of the profitability of the real estate business, the industry has devised methods of leasing and selling property, which makes the task of identifying interests in real property even more complicated and important.

■ THE JOB

Clients hire title searchers and examiners to determine the legal ownership of all parts and privileges of a piece of property. The client may need this information for many reasons: In addition to land sales and purchases, a lawyer may need a title search to fulfill the terms of someone's will; a bank may need it to repossess property used as collateral on a loan; a company may need it when acquiring or merging with another company; or an accountant may need it when preparing tax returns.

The work of the title searcher is the first step in the process. After receiving a request for a title search, the title searcher determines the type of title evidence to gather, its purpose, the people involved, and a legal description of the property. The searcher then compares this description with the legal description contained in public records to verify such facts as the deed of ownership, tax codes, tax parcel number, and description of property boundaries.

This task can take title searchers to a variety of places, including the offices of the county tax assessor, the recorder or registrar of deeds, the clerk of the city or state court, and other city, county, and state officials. Title searchers consult legal records, surveyors' maps, and tax rolls. Companies who employ title searchers also may keep records called indexes. These indexes are kept up to date to allow fast, accurate searching of titles and contain important information on mortgages, deeds, contracts, and judgments. For example, a law firm specializing in real estate and contract law probably would keep extensive indexes, using information gathered both in its own work and from outside sources.

While reviewing legal documents, the title searcher records important information on a standardized worksheet. This information can include judgments, deeds, mortgages (loans made using the property as collateral), liens (charges against the property for the satisfaction of a debt), taxes, special assessments for streets and sewers, and easements. The searcher must record carefully the sources of this information, the location of these records, the date on which any action took place, and the names and addresses of the people involved.

Using the data gathered by the title searcher, the title examiner then determines the status of the property title. Title examiners study all the relevant documents on a property, including records of marriages, births, divorces, adoptions, and other important legal proceedings, to determine the history of ownership. To verify certain facts, they may need to interview judges, clerks, lawyers, bankers, real estate brokers, and other professionals. They may summarize the legal documents they have found and use these abstracts as references in later work.

Title examiners use this information to prepare reports that describe the full extent of a person's title to a property; that person's right to sell, buy, use, or improve it; any restrictions that may exist; and actions required to clear the title. If employed in the office of a title insurance company, the title examiner provides information for the issuance of a policy that insures the title, subject to applicable exclusions and exceptions. The insured party then can proceed to use the property, having protection against any problems that might arise.

In larger offices, a title supervisor may direct and coordinate the activities of other searchers and examiners.

■ EARNINGS

According to the U.S. Bureau of Labor Statistics, median annual earnings of title examiners, abstractors, and searchers were $44,370 in May 2015. Salaries ranged from less than $27,120 to more than $78,230. Title searchers and examiners may receive such fringe benefits as vacations, hospital and life insurance, profit sharing, and pensions, depending on their employers.

■ WORK ENVIRONMENT

Title searchers and examiners generally work a 40-hour week. Most public records offices are

QUICK FACTS

ALTERNATE TITLE(S)
None

DUTIES
Compile lists of mortgages, deeds, contracts, and other items pertaining to a property title (title searcher); determine a property title's legal status and abstract recorded documents (title examiner)

SALARY RANGE
$27,120 to $44,370 to $78,230+

WORK ENVIRONMENT
Primarily Indoors

BEST GEOGRAPHIC LOCATION(S)
Opportunities available throughout the country

MINIMUM EDUCATION LEVEL
High School Diploma, Some Postsecondary Training

SCHOOL SUBJECTS
Business, English, Government

EXPERIENCE
Internship or part-time experience recommended

PERSONALITY TRAITS
Organized, Outgoing, Technical

SKILLS
Information Management, Organizational, Research

CERTIFICATION OR LICENSING
Required

SPECIAL REQUIREMENTS
None

EMPLOYMENT PROSPECTS
Good

ADVANCEMENT PROSPECTS
Good

OUTLOOK
Little Change or More Slowly than the Average

NOC
4211

O*NET-SOC
23-2093.00

CAREER LADDER

Department Supervisor or Senior Title Searcher/Examiner

Title Examiner

Title Searcher

Trainee

open only during regular business hours, so title searchers and examiners usually will not put in much overtime work, except when using private indexes and preparing abstracts.

The offices in which title searchers and examiners work can be very different in terms of comfort, space, and equipment. Searchers and examiners spend much of their day poring over the fine print of legal documents and records, so they may be afflicted occasionally with eyestrain and back fatigue. Generally, however, offices are pleasant, and the work is not physically strenuous.

Title searchers and examiners usually must dress in a businesslike manner because the work is often conducted in a business environment. Dress codes, however, have become more casual recently and vary from office to office.

■ EXPLORING

There may be opportunities for temporary employment during the summer and school holidays at title companies, financial institutions, or law firms. Such employment may involve making copies or sorting and delivering mail, but it offers an excellent chance to see the work of a title searcher or examiner firsthand. Some law firms, real estate brokerages, and title companies provide internships for students who are interested in work as a title searcher or examiner. Information on the availability of such internships is usually available from the regional or local land title association or school counselors.

■ EDUCATION AND TRAINING REQUIREMENTS
High School

A high school diploma is required to begin a career as a title searcher. Helpful classes include business, business law, English, social studies, real estate, real estate law, computer science (especially database management), and typing. In addition, skills in reading, writing, and research methods are essential.

Postsecondary Training

Title examiners usually must have completed some college course work, but a college degree is generally not a requirement. Pertinent courses for title searchers and examiners include business administration,

office management, real estate law, and other types of law. In some locales, attorneys typically perform title examinations.

Most title searchers and examiners also receive on-the-job training.

Other Education or Training

The American Land Title Association offers continuing education opportunities via its Land Title Institute, as well as through distance learning, team training, and telephone seminars.

■ CERTIFICATION, LICENSING, AND SPECIAL REQUIREMENTS
Certification or Licensing

A few states require title searchers and examiners to be licensed or certified. The American Land Title Association offers the national title professional designation to applicants who meet educational and experience requirements.

■ EXPERIENCE, SKILLS, AND PERSONALITY TRAITS

Previous experience performing title search, abstraction, and examination work is recommended for aspiring title searchers and examiners.

Title searchers and examiners must be methodical, analytical, and detail-oriented in their work. They need to be thorough as they study many hundreds of documents that may contain important data. Overlooking important points can damage the accuracy of the final report and may result in financial loss to the client or employer. It is important not to lose sight of the reason for the title search, in addition to remembering the intricacies of real estate law.

In addition to detailed work, title searchers and examiners may have to deal with clients, lawyers, judges, real estate brokers, and other people. This task requires good communication skills, poise, patience, and courtesy.

■ EMPLOYMENT PROSPECTS
Employers

Approximately 54,620 title searchers, examiners, and abstractors are employed in the United States. Title searchers and examiners work in a variety of settings. Some work for law firms, title insurance companies, financial institutions, or companies that write title abstracts. Others work for various branches of government at the city, county, or state level. Title insurance companies, while frequently headquartered in large cities, may have branches throughout the United States.

Starting Out

Title searchers or examiners may get their start by sending resumes and letters of application to local firms that employ these types of workers. Other leads for employment opportunities are local real estate agents or brokers, government employment offices, and local or state land title associations. Graduates from two- and four-year colleges usually have the added advantage of being able to consult their college career services offices for additional information on job openings.

■ ADVANCEMENT PROSPECTS

Title searchers and examiners learn most of their skills on the job. They may gain a basic understanding of the title search process in a few months, using public records and indexes maintained by their employers. Over time, employees must gain a broader understanding of the intricacies of land title evidence and record-keeping systems. This knowledge and several years of experience are the keys to advancement.

With experience, title searchers can move up to become *tax examiners*, *special assessment searchers*, or *abstracters*. With enough experience, a searcher or examiner may be promoted to *title supervisor* or *head clerk*. Other paths for ambitious title searchers and examiners include other types of paralegal work or, with further study, a law degree.

■ OUTLOOK

Employment of title searchers and examiners is expected to show little or no change through 2024, according to the *Occupational Outlook Handbook*. The health of the title insurance business is directly tied to the strength of the real estate market. In prosperous times, more people buy and sell real estate, resulting in a greater need for title searches. While the real estate business in America continues to operate during periods of recession, activity does slow a little. In general, title searchers and examiners can find consistent work in any area of the country with an active real estate market.

■ UNIONS AND ASSOCIATIONS

Title searchers and examiners who work for a state, county, or municipal government may belong to a union representing government workers, such as the American Federation of Government Employees. Many title searchers and examiners are members of the American Land Title Association and regional or state title associations. These groups maintain codes of ethics and standards of practice among their members and conduct educational programs.

TOP EMPLOYERS OF TITLE SEARCHERS AND EXAMINERS AND MEAN ANNUAL EARNINGS, MAY 2015

FAST FACTS

- Legal services: 24,330 jobs, $45,130
- Insurance carriers: 14,350 jobs, $50,370
- Real estate-related activities: 3,840 jobs, $54,560
- Oil and gas extraction: 2,610 jobs, $85,830
- Other financial investment activities: 1,030 jobs, $53,860
- Offices of real estate agents and brokers: 820 jobs, $49,300
- Federal government agencies: 190 jobs, $63,930

Source: U.S. Bureau of Labor Statistics

■ TIPS FOR ENTRY

1. Apply for an entry-level position at a real estate company that does title and examination work. Tell your manager that you are interested in becoming a title searcher or examiner.
2. Visit http://www.alta.org/about/state-land-title-associations.cfm for a list of land title associations in your state.
3. Join the American Land Title Association to access training and networking opportunities, industry publications, and employment opportunities.

■ FOR MORE INFORMATION

The American Land Title Association provides advocacy and education for title insurance professionals.

American Land Title Association (ALTA)
1800 M Street, NW, Suite 300S
Washington, D.C. 20036-5828
Tel: (202) 296-3671
Fax: (202) 2235843
E-mail: service@alta.org
http://www.alta.org

The American Federation of Government Employees represents federal and government employees nationwide and overseas.

American Federation of Government Employees (AFGE)
80 F Street, NW
Washington, D.C. 20001-1528
Tel: (202) 737-8700
E-mail: comments@afge.org
https://www.afge.org

The National Association of Land Title Examiners and Abstractors provides education, training, events, and other resources for land title examiners and abstractors.

National Association of Land Title Examiners and Abstractors (NALTEA)
7490 Eagle Road
Waite Hill, OH 44094
Tel: (404) 256-2404
Fax: (440) 256-2404
E-mail: info@naltea.org
http://www.naltea.org

Tobacco Products Industry Workers

■ OVERVIEW

Tobacco products industry workers manufacture cigars, cigarettes, chewing tobacco, smoking tobacco, and snuff from leaf tobacco. They dry, cure, age, cut, roll, form, and package tobacco in products used by millions of people in the United States and in other countries around the world. Approximately 13,310 people are employed in the tobacco manufacturing industry.

■ HISTORY

The use of tobacco has been traced back to Mayan cultures of nearly 2,000 years ago. As the Mayas moved north, through Central America and into North America, tobacco use spread throughout the continent. When Christopher Columbus arrived in the Caribbean in 1492, he was introduced to tobacco smoking by the Arawak tribe, who smoked the leaves of the plant rolled into cigars. Tobacco seeds were brought back to Europe, where they were cultivated. The Europeans, believing tobacco had medicinal properties, quickly adopted the practice of smoking. Sir Walter Raleigh popularized pipe smoking around 1586, and soon the growing and use of tobacco spread around the world.

Tobacco growing became an important economic activity in America beginning in the colonial era, in part because of the ideal growing conditions found in many of the Southern and Southeastern colonies. Tobacco quickly became a vital part of the colonies' international trade.

Tobacco use remained largely limited to small per-person quantities until the development of cigarettes in the mid-1800s. The invention of the cigarette-making machine in 1881 made the mass production of cigarettes possible. Nevertheless, the average person smoked only 40 cigarettes per year. It was only in the early decades of the 20th century that cigarette consumption, spurred by advertising campaigns, became popular across the country. Soon, the average person smoked up to 40 cigarettes per day.

By the 1960s, it became increasingly apparent that tobacco use was detrimental to people's health. In 1969, laws were passed requiring warning labels to be placed on all tobacco products. During the 1970s, increasing agitation by the antismoking movement led to laws, taxes, and other regulations being placed on the sale and use of tobacco products. Many other countries followed with similar laws and regulations. The number of smokers dropped by as much as 30 percent, and those who still smoked, smoked less. In response, the tobacco industry introduced products such as light cigarettes and low-tar and low-nicotine cigarettes. In the late 1990s, the tobacco industry was at the center of debate, controversy, and subsequent state lawsuits over addictive substances and cancer-causing agents contained in cigarettes. This controversy and the declining numbers of smokers in the United States and much of the West have had a strong impact on the employment levels in the tobacco industry.

■ THE JOB

Various kinds of tobacco plants are cultivated for use in tobacco products. After harvesting, the different types of tobacco are processed in different ways. Using one method or another, all tobacco is cured, or dried, for several days to a month or more in order to change its physical and chemical characteristics. *Farmers* sometimes air-cure tobacco by hanging it in barns to dry naturally. Other curing methods are fire-curing in barns with open fires and flue-curing in barns with flues that circulate heat. Some tobacco is sun-cured by drying it outdoors in the sun.

Cured tobacco is auctioned to tobacco product manufacturers or other dealers. The first step in the manufacturing process is separating out stems, midribs of leaves, and foreign matter. Usually this is done by workers who feed the tobacco into machines. Once stemmed, the tobacco is dried again by *redrying-machine operators*, who use machines with hot-air blowers and fans.

The tobacco is then packed for aging. In preparation for packing, workers may adjust the moisture content of the dry tobacco by steaming the leaves or wetting them down with water. The tobacco is prized, or packed, into large barrels or cases that can hold about a thousand pounds of tobacco each. Workers, including *bulkers*, *prizers*, and *hydraulic-press operators*, pack the containers, which go to warehouses to be aged. The aging process, which may take up to two years, alters the aroma and flavor of the tobacco. After it is aged, workers take the tobacco to factories, where it is removed from the containers.

The tobacco is further conditioned by adding moisture. *Blenders* then select tobacco of various grades and kinds to produce blends with specific characteristics or for specific products, such as cigars or snuff. They place the tobacco on conveyors headed for processing. Blending laborers replenish supplies of the different tobaccos for the blending line. Blending-line attendants tend the conveyors and machines that mix the specified blends.

Some tobacco is flavored using casing fluids, which are water-soluble mixtures. *Casing-material weighers, casing-machine operators, wringer operators, casing cookers*, and *casing-fluid tenders* participate in this flavoring process by preparing the casing material, saturating the tobacco with it, and removing excess fluid before further processing.

The tobacco is ready to be cut into pieces of the correct size. Tobacco for cigars and cigarettes is shredded and cleaned in machines operated by *machine filler shredders* and *strip-cutting-machine operators. Snuff grinders and snuff screeners* tend machines that pulverize chopped tobacco into snuff and sift it through screens to remove oversized particles. *Riddler operators* tend screening devices that separate coarse pieces of tobacco from cut tobacco.

Once cut, the tobacco is made into salable products. Cigarettes are made by machines that wrap shredded tobacco and filters with papers. Workers feed these machines, make the filters, and run the machines, which also print the company's name and insignia on the rolling papers.

Cigar making is similar, except that the filler tobacco is wrapped in tobacco leaf instead of paper. The filler is held together and formed into a bunch in a binder leaf, and the bunch is rolled in a spiral in a wrapper leaf. Various workers sort and count appropriate wrapper leaves and binder leaves. They roll filler tobacco and binder leaves into bunches by hand or using machines. The bunches are pressed into cigar-shaped molds, and bunch trimmers trim excess tobacco from the molds before the bunches are wrapped.

Other workers operate machines that automatically form and wrap cigars. They include auto rollers and wrapper layers, who wrap bunches with sheet tobacco or wrapper leaves. Some workers wrap bunches by hand. *Cigar-head piercers* use machines to pierce draft holes in the cigar ends. Some cigars are pressed into a square shape by tray fillers and press-machine feeders before they are packaged in cigar bands and cellophane. *Patch workers* repair defective or damaged cigars by patching holes with pieces of wrapper leaf.

QUICK FACTS

ALTERNATE TITLE(S)
Benders, Bulkers, Case Packers, Case Sealers, Casing Cookers, Casing-Fluid Tenders, Casing-Machine Operators, Casing-Material Weighers, Cellophaners, Cigar-Head Piercers, Cigar Packers, Hand Banders, Hydraulic-Press Operators, Machine Banders, Machine Filler Shredders, Patch Workers, Prizers, Redrying-Machine Operators, Riddler Operators, Snuff-Box Finishers, Snuff Grinders, Snuff Screeners, Strip-Cutting-Machine Operators, Tobacco Farmers, Tobacco Inspectors, Wringer Operators

DUTIES
Dry, cure, age, cut, roll, form, and package tobacco for use in a variety of products

SALARY RANGE
$19,140 to $28,060 to $55,550+

WORK ENVIRONMENT
Primarily Indoors

BEST GEOGRAPHIC LOCATION(S)
Primarily North Carolina, South Carolina, Georgia, Virginia

MINIMUM EDUCATION LEVEL
High School Diploma

SCHOOL SUBJECTS
Agriculture, Earth Science, Technical/Shop

EXPERIENCE
On-the-job training

PERSONALITY TRAITS
Conventional, Hands On, Realistic

SKILLS
Business Management, Interpersonal, Mechanical/Manual Dexterity

CERTIFICATION OR LICENSING
None

SPECIAL REQUIREMENTS
None

EMPLOYMENT PROSPECTS
Fair

ADVANCEMENT PROSPECTS
Fair

OUTLOOK
Little Change or More Slowly than the Average

NOC
9617

O*NET-SOC
51-3091.00

Some tobacco is made into other products, such as plugs, lumps, and twists. These products are chewed instead of smoked. Twists and some plugs may be made

CAREER LADDER

Tobacco Buyer or Tobacco Grader

Supervisor or Manager

Experienced Tobacco Products Industry Worker

Entry-Level Tobacco Products Industry Worker

by hand, while most plugs and lumps are made by machine. The machines slice, mold, press, and wrap the tobacco, and various workers are responsible for feeding, regulating, and cleaning the machines.

Many workers are employed in packaging the manufactured tobacco products. *Cigar packers*, *hand banders*, *machine banders*, and *cellophaners* package cigars. *Cigar banders* stamp trademarks on cigar wrappers. *Cigarette-packing-machine operators* pack cigarette packs into cartons. *Case packers* and *sealers* pack the cartons into cases and seal them. Other workers pack snuff, chewing tobacco, and other products into cartons, tins, and other packaging. *Snuff-box finishers* glue covers and labels on boxes of snuff.

Finally, *tobacco inspectors* check that the products and their packaging meet quality standards, removing items that are defective. The industry also employs a variety of workers to maintain equipment; load, unload, and distribute materials; prepare tobacco for the different stages of processing; salvage defective items for reclamation; and maintain records of tobacco bought and sold.

■ EARNINGS

Wages for tobacco production workers are generally higher than for most other producers of consumable goods. Earnings vary considerably with the plant and the workers' job skills and responsibilities.

According to the U.S. Bureau of Labor Statistics, median annual earnings of food and tobacco roasting, baking, and drying machine operators and tenders were $28,060 in May 2015. Salaries ranged from $19,140 to more than $46,960. Tobacco packaging and filling machine operators and tenders had mean earnings of $45,840, and tobacco inspectors, testers, sorters, samplers, and weighers had mean earnings of $41,080. The mean annual salary for all tobacco production workers was $55,550.

Tobacco products workers usually receive benefits that include health and life insurance, paid holiday and vacation days, profit-sharing plans, pension plans, and various disability benefits.

■ WORK ENVIRONMENT

In most plants, worker comfort and efficiency are important concerns. Work areas are usually clean, well lighted, and pleasantly air-conditioned. Manufacturing processes are automated wherever possible, and the equipment is designed with safety and comfort in mind. On the downside, much of the work is highly repetitive, and people can find their work very monotonous. Also, tobacco has a strong smell that bothers some people. Some stages of processing produce large quantities of tobacco dust.

■ EXPLORING

Part-time or seasonal tobacco processing jobs may be available for people who are interested in this field. Some plants where tobacco products are manufactured may allow visitors to observe their operations.

■ EDUCATION AND TRAINING REQUIREMENTS
High School

The minimum requirement for all tobacco workers is a high school diploma. Maintenance and mechanical workers often need to be high school graduates with machine maintenance skills or experience. They may need to learn additional skills on the job.

Postsecondary Training

The most common form of postsecondary training for tobacco workers is short-term, on-the-job training, during which new employees learn how to operate various machines and perform other necessary job-related tasks by watching and helping experienced workers.

■ CERTIFICATION, LICENSING, AND SPECIAL REQUIREMENTS
Certification or Licensing

There are no certification or licensing requirements for workers in the tobacco products industry.

A farmer checks his tobacco crop after drying the leaves. (branislavpudar. Shutterstock.)

▪ EXPERIENCE, SKILLS, AND PERSONALITY TRAITS

No experience is needed to work in most tobacco production positions, but those with prior work experience will increase their chances of landing a job, getting promoted, and possibly earning higher pay. Workers such as tobacco buyers or graders who must judge tobacco based on its smell, feel, and appearance usually need at least several years' experience working with tobacco to become familiar with its characteristics.

Important traits for tobacco products industry workers include the ability to concentrate for long periods of time and perform repetitive tasks, good hand-eye coordination, a detail-oriented personality, strong communication skills, the ability to work as a member of a team, and physical strength and stamina.

▪ EMPLOYMENT PROSPECTS
Employers

Approximately 13,310 people are employed in the tobacco manufacturing industry. Most jobs in this industry are located in factories close to tobacco-growing regions, especially in the South and Southeast. The U.S. tobacco industry is primarily located in the southeastern states of North Carolina, Georgia, Virginia, South Carolina, Kentucky, and Tennessee. Many cigar factories are in Florida and Pennsylvania.

Starting Out

Job seekers should apply in person at local tobacco products factories that may be hiring new workers. Leads for specific job openings may be located through the local offices of the state employment service and through union locals. Employment Web sites and newspaper classified ads may also carry listings of available jobs.

▪ ADVANCEMENT PROSPECTS

In the tobacco products industry, advancement is related to increased skills. Machine operators may advance by learning how to run more complex equipment. Experienced workers may be promoted to supervisory positions. With sufficient knowledge and experience, some production workers may eventually become *tobacco buyers* for manufacturers or *tobacco graders* with the U.S. Department of Agriculture.

▪ OUTLOOK

The U.S. Department of Labor predicts slower than average employment growth for food and tobacco processing workers through 2024. Employment in the tobacco industry has decreased in recent decades, mainly the result of increased automation in manufacturing processes.

THE TOBACCO INDUSTRY   LEARN MORE ABOUT IT

Brandt, Allan. *The Cigarette Century: The Rise, Fall, and Deadly Persistence of the Product that Defined America.* New York: Basic Books, 2009.

Eriksen, Michael, Judith Mackay, and Hana Ross. *The Tobacco Atlas,* 4th ed. Atlanta, Ga.: American Cancer Society, 2013.

Fox, Georgia L. *The Archaeology of Smoking and Tobacco,* reprint ed. Gainesville, Fla.: University Press of Florida, 2016.

Korstad, Robert Rodgers. *Civil Rights Unionism: Tobacco Workers and the Struggle for Democracy in the Mid-Twentieth-Century South.* Chapel Hill, N.C.: University of North Carolina Press, 2003.

Pampel, Fred C. *Tobacco Industry and Smoking,* 2nd Rev. ed. New York: Facts on File, 2009.

Manufacturers have also cut back operations due to declining domestic sales and the increasing number of health-related lawsuits. However, while Americans are generally using less tobacco, exports of American-made tobacco products are increasing, especially to the former Soviet Union and Eastern Europe, the Middle East, and Asia. Most future demand for workers in this industry will probably be because of a need to replace workers who have moved to other jobs or left the workforce entirely.

▪ UNIONS AND ASSOCIATIONS

Most tobacco products industry workers are members of the Bakery, Confectionery, Tobacco Workers and Grain Millers International Union.

▪ TIPS FOR ENTRY

1. Join the Bakery, Confectionery, Tobacco Workers and Grain Millers International Union to increase your chances of landing a job and receiving fair pay for your work.
2. Be willing to relocate. Many tobacco manufacturing plants are located in the southern and southeastern United States.
3. Talk with tobacco workers about their careers. Ask them for advice on preparing for and entering the field.

▪ FOR MORE INFORMATION

Tobacco.org provides news and information about the tobacco industry.

Tobacco.org
http://www.tobacco.org

The Bakery, Confectionery, Tobacco Workers and Grain Millers International Union represents manufacturing, production, maintenance, and sanitation workers in the United States and Canada.

Bakery, Confectionery, Tobacco Workers and Grain Millers International Union (BCTGM)
10401 Connecticut Avenue, Floor 4
Kensington, MD 20895-3900
Tel: (301) 933-8600
http://www.bctgm.org

Tobacco Reporter provides global coverage of the tobacco business.

Tobacco Reporter
3101 Poplarwood Court, Suite 115
Raleigh, NC 27604-1010
Tel: (919) 872-5040
Fax: (919 876-6531
http://www.tobaccoreporter.com

Toll Collectors

■ OVERVIEW

Toll collectors receive payments from private motorists and commercial drivers for the use of highways, tunnels, bridges, or ferries.

■ HISTORY

Throughout history, the upkeep and maintenance of roads around the world usually fell to the reigning powers. However, in 1663, three counties in England obtained authority to levy tolls on users to pay for the improvement of a major road linking York and London. By the 18th century, all major roads in Great Britain incorporated tolls, or turnpike trusts, to pay for maintenance.

In 1785, Virginia built a turnpike and other states quickly followed suit. The very first hard-surfaced road of any great length in the United States was the Lancaster Turnpike, completed in 1794. Almost 150 years later, the first successful U.S. toll road for all types of motor vehicles was built in that same state.

The United States contains more than 4 million miles of paved and unpaved streets, roads, and highways. With the wear and tear brought on by harsh weather conditions and constant use, these road surfaces need to be repaired frequently. The construction and repair of streets and highways are funded primarily by state gasoline taxes, vehicle registrations, and other operating fees. However, some highway, bridge, and other transportation improvements are paid for by individual user fees known as tolls. The fees for using turnpikes and toll roads usually depend on the distance a motorist travels. Trucks, trailers, and other heavy vehicles pay more for using these roads than passenger cars because their extra weight puts more strain on pavements and necessitates more frequent road repair,

■ THE JOB

Toll collectors have two main job responsibilities: accepting and dispensing money and providing personal service and information to motorists. Primarily, toll collectors act as cashiers, collecting revenue from motorists and truck drivers who use certain roads, tunnels, bridges, or auto ferries. They accept toll and fare tickets that drivers may have previously purchased or received. They check that the drivers have given them the proper amount and return correct change when necessary.

When handling money, toll collectors begin with a change bank containing bills and coins so they can make change for motorists who lack the exact change. Toll collectors organize this money by denomination, so they are able to make change quickly and accurately, especially during rush-hour traffic. At the end of their shift, they calculate the amount of revenue received for the day by subtracting the original amount in the change bank from the total amount of money now in the till. Toll collectors also prepare cash reports, commuter ticket reports, and deposit slips that report the day's tallies. Many toll collectors become skilled at spotting counterfeit currency immediately.

In addition to their cash-handling duties, toll collectors have a wide range of administrative duties that provide service to motorists and keep the toll plaza operating at peak efficiency. Drivers may ask for directions, maps, or an estimate of the distance to the nearest rest stop or service station. Toll collectors are sometimes the only human link on a particularly long stretch of highway, so they may need to lend assistance in certain emergencies or contact police or ambulance support. They may also notify their supervisors or the highway commission concerning hazardous roads, weather conditions, or vehicles in distress.

Toll collectors also may be responsible for filling out traffic reports and inspecting the toll plaza facility to make sure that the area is free of litter and that toll gates and automatic lanes are working properly. Sometimes toll collectors handle supervisory tasks such as monitoring automatic and nonrevenue lanes, relieving fellow employees for lunch or coffee breaks, or completing violation reports. They are often in contact with state police patrols to watch for drivers who have sped through the toll gate without paying.

In many situations, commercial trucks have to pay more when they are hauling larger loads. Toll collectors are able to classify these vehicles according to their size and calculate the proper toll rates. These workers also have to be aware of and enforce the safety regulations governing their area. Tanker trucks carrying flammable cargoes, for example, are usually barred from publicly used tunnels. Toll operators are responsible for the safety of everyone on the road and must enforce all regulations impartially. Toll collectors who operate ferries may direct the vehicles that are boarding and monitor the capacity of the ferry, as well as collect fares.

■ EARNINGS

Wages for full-time toll collectors vary with the area and state where the collector is employed. Average earnings vary by state and municipality. For example, Indeed.com reports that toll collectors in New York City earned median salaries of $33,000, while collectors in Harris County, Texas, earned $27,000, with a top salary of $41,000. Managerial responsibilities also increase compensation. Part-time employees are usually paid by the hour and may begin at the minimum wage ($7.25 an hour, or $15,080 per year). Toll collectors who are members of a union generally earn more than those who are not. Collectors who work the later shifts may also earn more, and most employees earn time-and-a-half or double time for overtime or holiday work.

Toll collectors receive vacation time calculated on the number of hours worked in conjunction with their years of employment. Those workers with up to five years of service may receive 80 hours of vacation. This scale can increase to 136 hours of vacation for seasoned workers with nine to 14 years of employment. Benefit packages usually include health and dental insurance coverage for employees and their families, as well as pension and retirement plans. Toll workers often enjoy the generous employee benefits of working in government service.

■ WORK ENVIRONMENT

Toll collectors may either stand or sit on stools in the booths they occupy. Toll collectors are exposed to all types of weather, including hail, sleet, snow, or extreme heat or cold, but booths usually are equipped with space heaters and sliding doors to keep out dampness and cold. Collectors are also exposed to exhaust and other potentially toxic fumes. (Those with respiratory difficulties need to be especially aware of this condition.) Toll collectors sometimes have to interact with stressed, impatient, or irate motorists and must be able to deflect potentially heated situations while maintaining a peak level of service and efficiency. Full-time toll collectors usually work an eight-hour shift, but they may have to work at different times of the day, since many tollbooths need to be staffed around the clock.

Most tollbooth complexes have restroom and shower facilities for their employees. Some may have kitchens and break rooms as well. Some workers have assigned lockers or share lockers with workers on different shifts. Usually the employee facilities are better when no oasis or service stations are adjacent to the toll plaza. Toll stations have communications equipment so that they can notify state police or the state department of transportation of any emergencies, hazardous conditions, or violations of the law.

■ EXPLORING

Contact state and local departments of transportation as well as state highway departments to learn more about toll collector opportunities. School counselors may have additional information on such careers or related agencies to contact about the nature of the work and the applicable job requirements. They may also be able to arrange a talk by an experienced toll collector or supervisor. Many such professionals will be more than happy to share their experiences and detail the everyday duties of those involved in the profession.

■ EDUCATION AND TRAINING REQUIREMENTS
High School

A high school diploma is required to work as a toll collector. Recommended high school courses include mathematics, speech, and English classes. These will help develop the communication skills—listening as well as speaking—that are important in the job of toll collecting.

QUICK FACTS	
ALTERNATE TITLE(S)	Toll Booth Attendants, Toll Clerks
DUTIES	Receive payments from private motorists and commercial drivers for the use of highways, tunnels, bridges, or ferries
SALARY RANGE	$15,080 to $27,000 to $41,000+
WORK ENVIRONMENT	Indoors/Outdoors
BEST GEOGRAPHIC LOCATION(S)	Opportunities are available throughout the country
MINIMUM EDUCATION LEVEL	High School Diploma
SCHOOL SUBJECTS	Business, Mathematics, Speech
EXPERIENCE	On-the-job training
PERSONALITY TRAITS	Hands On, Helpful, Outgoing
SKILLS	Interpersonal, Math
CERTIFICATION OR LICENSING	None
SPECIAL REQUIREMENTS	Must be at least 18 years of age
EMPLOYMENT PROSPECTS	Fair
ADVANCEMENT PROSPECTS	Fair
OUTLOOK	Decline
NOC	6742
O*NET-SOC	41-2011.00

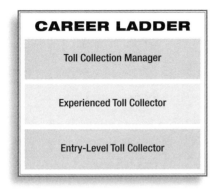

CAREER LADDER

Toll Collection Manager

Experienced Toll Collector

Entry-Level Toll Collector

Postsecondary Training

Toll collectors may have to pass a civil service exam to test their skills and aptitude for the job. When hired, they receive on-the-job training; no formal postsecondary education is required.

■ CERTIFICATION, LICENSING, AND SPECIAL REQUIREMENTS
Certification or Licensing

There are no certification or licensing requirements for toll collectors.

Other Requirements

Toll collectors typically must be 18 years old or older.

■ EXPERIENCE, SKILLS, AND PERSONALITY TRAITS

No experience is needed to work as a toll collector, but those with prior work experience will increase their chances of landing a job, getting promoted, and possibly earning higher pay.

Toll collectors are usually required to be at least 18 years of age, with generally good health and reasonable stamina and endurance. They must have good eyesight and hearing to determine a vehicle's class (and applicable toll), as well as to hear motorists' requests or supervisory instructions in the midst of heavy traffic noise. Manual

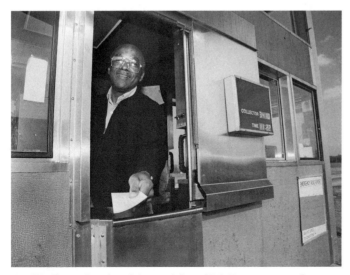

A toll collector hands a driver a ticket. (U.S. Department of Energy.)

dexterity in handling and organizing money and fare tickets, as well as giving change, is also important. Lost or confused motorists rely on the guidance of toll collectors, who should maintain a considerate and helpful attitude. They should also be perceptive and have professional work habits. As with all jobs, honesty is a requirement.

■ EMPLOYMENT PROSPECTS
Employers

Virtually all toll collectors work for a government transport agency, be it local, state, or federal. State departments of transportation employ most toll collectors.

Starting Out

Contact state and local departments of transportation, highway agencies, or civil service organizations for information on education requirements, job prerequisites, and application materials. In those states that require qualification testing, potential applicants should also request information on test dates and preparation materials.

■ ADVANCEMENT PROSPECTS

Advancement for toll collectors may take the form of a promotion from part-time to full-time employment, or from the late evening shift to daytime work. Collectors may also be promoted to supervisory or operations positions, with a corresponding increase in salary and benefits. Most promotions carry additional responsibilities that require further training. Some training may take place on the job, but certain management topics are best learned from an accredited college or training program. Workers who aspire to higher positions may wish to take courses in advance so they will be ready when openings occur. It is important to note that there are few managerial positions compared to the vast number of toll collectors employed—competition for advanced jobs is intense.

■ OUTLOOK

A decline in employment is expected for toll collectors in the coming years, according to an article by the Pew Charitable Trusts. Electronic toll collection (ETC) has adversely affected the employment of toll collectors. In 2015, of the 34 states that had toll roads, 23 of them used ETC in addition to a cash payment system. The electronic technology includes systems that identify and classify vehicles as well as capture video images of license plates that do not have a valid tag. Computerized toll-collecting benefits truck drivers and commuters who frequent the toll roads, but states that have implemented ETC have put a freeze on hiring additional toll collectors or replacing toll collectors who retire or move into other jobs.

Still, a small number of toll collectors will be needed to collect tolls from drivers who do not participate in ETC. Toll collectors may be retrained to monitor and maintain this emerging technology.

■ UNIONS AND ASSOCIATIONS

Some toll collectors are represented by the International Brotherhood of Teamsters and the International Federation of Professional and Technical Engineers. The American Association of State Highway and Transportation Officials and the International Bridge, Tunnel and Turnpike Association can provide information on tollways and career opportunities in the field.

■ TIPS FOR ENTRY

1. Read *Tollways* and *Tollway Express* (both available at http://ibtta.org/ibtta-publications) and TOLLROADSnews (http://tollroadsnews.com) to learn more about the field.
2. Talk to toll collectors about their work. Ask them for advice on breaking into the field.
3. Join unions to increase your chances of landing a job and receiving fair pay for your work.

■ FOR MORE INFORMATION

The American Association of State Highway and Transportation Officials provides education, industry standards, news, and other resources.

American Association of State Highway and Transportation Officials (AASHTO)
444 North Capitol Street, NW, Suite 249
Washington, D.C. 20001-1539
Tel: (202) 624-5800
E-mail: info@aashto.org
http://www.transportation.org

The International Bridge, Tunnel and Turnpike Association offers industry news, events, and membership benefits.

International Bridge, Tunnel and Turnpike Association (IBTTA)
1146 19th Street, NW, Suite 600
Washington, D.C. 20036-3725
Tel: (202) 659-4620
http://www.ibtta.org

The International Brotherhood of Teamsters represents workers in various occupations in the public and private sectors.

International Brotherhood of Teamsters
25 Louisiana Avenue, NW
Washington, D.C. 20001-2130
https://teamster.org

TOLL ROADS IN THE UNITED STATES   FAST FACTS

- In 2015, there were nearly 5.9 million miles of tolled roadways (including bridges and tunnels) in the United States.
- The states with the most miles of tolled roadways were Florida, New York, Oklahoma, Pennsylvania, and New Jersey
- A total of 35 U.S. states and territories have at least one tolled highway, bridge, or tunnel.
- U.S. toll agencies collected $13 billion in toll revenues in 2013.

Sources: Federal Highway Administration; International Bridge, Tunnel and Turnpike Association

---

The International Federation of Professional and Technical Engineers is a union that represents workers in professional, technical, administrative, and associated occupations.

International Federation of Professional and Technical Engineers (IFPTE)
501 3rd Street, NW, Suite 701
Washington, D.C. 20001-2771
Tel: (202) 239-4880
Fax: (202) 239-4881
E-mail: generalinfo@ifpte.org
http://www.ifpte.org

Tour Guides

■ OVERVIEW

Tour guides plan and oversee travel arrangements and accommodations for groups of tourists. They assist travelers with questions or problems, and they may provide travelers with itineraries of their proposed travel route and plans. Tour guides research their destinations thoroughly so that they can handle any unforeseen situation that may occur. There are approximately 35,930 tour guides and escorts, and about 2,810 travel guides employed in the United States.

■ HISTORY

People have always had a certain fascination with unknown or faraway places. Curiosity about distant cities and foreign cultures was one of the main forces behind the spread of civilization. Traveling in the ancient world was an arduous and sometimes dangerous task. Today, however, travel is commonplace. People travel for

QUICK FACTS

ALTERNATE TITLE(S)
Inbound Tour Guides,
    Travel Guides

DUTIES
Plan and oversee travel
    arrangements and
    accommodations for groups of
    tourists; lead tours

SALARY RANGE
$17,790 to $24,110 to
    $65,000+

WORK ENVIRONMENT
Indoors/Outdoors

BEST GEOGRAPHIC LOCATION(S)
Opportunities available
    throughout the world

MINIMUM EDUCATION LEVEL
High School Diploma, Some
    Postsecondary Training

SCHOOL SUBJECTS
Foreign Language, Geography,
    History

EXPERIENCE
Customer service or leadership
    experience

PERSONALITY TRAITS
Helpful, Organized, Outgoing

SKILLS
Interpersonal, Public Speaking,
    Teaching

CERTIFICATION OR LICENSING
Recommended

SPECIAL REQUIREMENTS
None

EMPLOYMENT PROSPECTS
Good

ADVANCEMENT PROSPECTS
Good

OUTLOOK
About as Fast as the Average

NOC
6531

O*NET-SOC
39-7011.00, 39-7012.00

business, recreation, and education. Schoolchildren may take field trips to their state's capitol, and college students now have the opportunity to study in foreign countries. People spend much of their disposable income on recreation and vacation travel.

Early travelers were often accompanied by guides who had become familiar with the routes on earlier trips. When leisure travel became more commonplace in the 19th century, women and young children were not expected to travel alone, so relatives or house servants often acted as companions. Today, tour guides act as escorts for people visiting foreign countries and provide them with additional information on interesting facets of life in another part of the world. In a way, tour guides have taken the place of the early scouts, acting as experts in settings and situations that other people find unfamiliar.

■ THE JOB

Acting as knowledgeable companions and chaperones, tour guides escort groups of tourists to different cities and countries. Their job is to make sure that the passengers in a group tour enjoy an interesting and safe trip. To do this, they have to know a great deal about their travel destination and about the interests, knowledge, and expectations of the people on the tour.

One basic responsibility of tour guides is handling all the details of a trip prior to departure. They may schedule airline flights, bus trips, or train trips as well as book cruises, houseboats, or car rentals. They also research area hotels and other lodging for the group and make reservations in advance. If anyone in the group has unique requirements, such as a specialized diet or a need for wheelchair accessibility, the tour guide will work to meet these requests.

Tour guides plan itineraries and daily activities, keeping in mind the interests of the group. For example, a group of music lovers visiting Vienna may wish to see the many sites of musical history there as well as attend a performance by that city's orchestra. In addition to sightseeing tours, guides may make arrangements in advance for special exhibits, dining experiences, and side trips. Alternate outings are sometimes planned in case of inclement weather conditions.

The second major responsibility of tour guides is, of course, the tour itself. Here, they must make sure all aspects of transportation, lodging, and recreation meet the planned itinerary. They must see to it that travelers' baggage and personal belongings are loaded and handled properly. If the tour includes meals and trips to local establishments, the guide must make sure that each passenger is on time for the various arrivals and departures.

Tour guides provide the people in their groups with interesting information on the locale and alert them to special sights. Tour guides become familiar with the history and significance of places through research and previous visits and endeavor to make the visit as entertaining and informative as possible. They may speak the native language or hire an interpreter in order to get along well with the local people. They are also familiar with local customs so their group will not offend anyone unknowingly. They see that the group stays together so that members do not miss their transportation arrangements or get lost. Guides may also arrange free time for travelers to pursue their individual interests, although time frames and common meeting points for regrouping are established in advance.

Even with thorough preparation, unexpected occurrences can arise on any trip and threaten to ruin everyone's good time. Tour guides must be resourceful to handle these surprises, such as when points of interest are closed or accommodations turn out to be unacceptable. They must be familiar with an area's resources so that they can help in emergencies such as passenger illness or lost personal items. Tour guides often intercede on their travelers' behalf when any questions or problems arise regarding currency, restaurants, customs, or necessary identification.

Inbound tour guides lead short excursions to famous American destinations for foreign or domestic tourists. Inbound tours may last a few hours or overnight. Guides provide an important service to the travel and tourism industry by promoting their specific area.

EARNINGS

Tour guides may find that they have peak and slack periods of the year that correspond to vacation and travel seasons. Many tour guides, however, work eight months of the year. The U.S. Department of Labor reports that in May 2015, median wages ranged from $8.55 per hour to $18.95 per hour (or from $17,790 to $39,410 or more annually), with medium hourly pay of $11.59 (or $24,110 a year). Travel guides earn from $9.59 per hour to $27.55 per hour or more (or $19,940 to $57,300 or more annually). Experienced guides with managerial responsibilities can earn more than $65,000 a year, including gratuities.

Guides receive their meals and accommodations free while conducting a tour, in addition to a daily stipend to cover their personal expenses. Salaries and benefits vary, depending on the tour operators that employ guides and the location in which they are employed. Generally, the states offering the highest compensation are the District of Columbia, Washington, Wyoming, Connecticut, and Alaska.

Tour guides often receive paid vacations as part of their fringe benefits package; some may also receive sick pay and health insurance. Some companies may offer profit sharing and bonuses. Guides often receive discounts from hotels, airlines, and transportation companies in appreciation for repeat business.

WORK ENVIRONMENT

The key word in the tour guide profession is variety. Most tour guides work in offices while they make travel arrangements and handle general business, but once on the road, they experience a wide range of accommodations, conditions, and situations. Tours to distant cities involve maneuvering through busy and confusing airports. Side trips may involve bus rides, train transfers, or private car rentals, all with varying degrees of comfort and reliability. Package trips that encompass seeing a number of foreign countries may require the guide to speak a different language in each city.

The constant feeling of being on the go and the responsibility of leading a large group of people can sometimes be stressful. Unexpected events and uncooperative people have the capacity to ruin part of a trip for everyone involved, including the guide. However, the thrill of travel, discovery, and meeting new people can be so rewarding that all the negatives can be forgotten (or eliminated by pre-planning on the next trip).

EXPLORING

One way to become more familiar with the responsibilities of this job is to accompany local tours. Many cities have their own historical societies and museums that offer tours as well as opportunities to volunteer. To appreciate what is involved with speaking in front of groups and the kind of research that may be necessary for leading tours, you can prepare speeches or presentations for class or local community groups. You may also find it helpful to read publications such as *Courier* (http://ntaonline.com/publication-type/courier-magazine), the National Tour Association's monthly travel magazine.

CAREER LADDER

Tour Agency Owner or Travel Writer

Experienced Tour Guide

Entry-Level Tour Guide

EDUCATION AND TRAINING REQUIREMENTS
High School

A high school diploma is the minimum requirement to be a tour guide. Courses such as speech, communications, art, sociology, anthropology, political science, social studies, and literature often prove beneficial. Some tour guides study foreign languages and cultures as well as geography, history, and architecture.

Postsecondary Training

Some cities have professional schools that offer curricula in the travel industry. Such training may take nine to 12 months and offer job placement services.

A tour guide points out the La Sagrada Familia, an attraction in Barcelona, Spain, to her clients. (funkyfrogstock. Shutterstock.)

TOP EMPLOYERS OF TOUR GUIDES AND MEAN ANNUAL SALARIES, MAY 2015

FAST FACTS

- Museums, historical sites, and similar institutions: 13,350 jobs, $24,470
- Travel arrangement and reservation services: 5,650 jobs, $29,550
- Other amusement and recreation industries: 3,540 jobs, $29,600
- Scenic and sightseeing transportation, land: 2,350 jobs, $30,450
- Local government: 1,190 jobs, $25,060

Source: U.S. Bureau of Labor Statistics

Some two- and four-year colleges offer tour guide training that lasts six to eight weeks. Community colleges may offer programs in tour escort training. Programs such as these often may be taken on a part-time basis. Classes may include history, world geography, psychology, human relations, and communication courses. Sometimes students go on field trips themselves to gain experience. Some travel agencies and tour companies offer their own training so that their tour guides may receive instruction that complements the tour packages the company offers.

Other Education or Training
The National Tour Association offers webinars, networking events, and seminars at its annual conference to help members stay up to date with industry trends.

■ CERTIFICATION, LICENSING, AND SPECIAL REQUIREMENTS
Certification or Licensing
The National Tour Association offers the voluntary certified tour professional designation to candidates who meet education, employment, and service requirements; complete required course work; and complete a learning portfolio.

■ EXPERIENCE, SKILLS, AND PERSONALITY TRAITS
Any experience one can obtain in customer service or leading local tours will be useful.

Successful tour guides are outgoing, friendly, patient, and confident. They must be aware of the typical travelers' needs and the kinds of questions and concerns travelers might have. As a tour guide, they should be comfortable being in charge of large groups of people and have good time-management and organizational skills. They also need to be resourceful and be able to adapt to different environments. Tour guides need to be fun-loving and know how to make others feel at ease in unfamiliar surroundings. Tour guides should enjoy working with people as much as they enjoy traveling.

■ EMPLOYMENT PROSPECTS
Employers
The major employers of tour guides are, naturally, tour companies. Many tour guides work on a freelance basis, while others may own their own tour businesses. Approximately 35,930 tour guides and escorts, and 2,810 travel guides are employed in the United States.

Starting Out
Tour guides may begin as a guide for a museum or state park. This is a good introduction to handling groups of people, giving lectures on points of interest or exhibits and developing confidence and leadership qualities. Zoos, theme parks, historical sites, or local walking tours often need volunteers or part-time employees to work in their information centers, offer visitors directions, and answer a variety of inquiries. When openings occur, it is common for part-time workers to move into full-time positions.

Travel agencies, tour bus companies, and park districts often need additional help during the summer months when the travel season is in full swing. Societies and organizations for architecture and natural history, as well as other cultural groups, often train and employ guides. If you are interested in working as a tour guide for one of these types of groups, submit your application directly to the directors of personnel or managing directors.

■ ADVANCEMENT PROSPECTS
Tour guides gain experience by handling more complicated trips. Some workers may advance through specialization, such as tours to specific countries or to multiple destinations. Some tour guides choose to open their own travel agencies or work for wholesale tour companies, selling trip packages to individuals or retail tour companies.

Some tour guides become *travel writers* and report on exotic destinations for magazines and newspapers. Other guides may decide to work in the corporate world and plan travel arrangements for company executives. With the further development of the global economy, many different jobs have become available for people who know foreign languages and cultures.

■ OUTLOOK

There will be a steady need for tour guides through 2024 because of the many different travel opportunities for business, recreation, and education. Tours designed for special interests, such as to ecologically significant areas and wilderness destinations, continue to grow in popularity. Certain seasons are more popular for travel than others, but well-trained tour guides can keep busy all year long.

Another area of tourism that is on the upswing is inbound tourism. Many foreign travelers view the United States as a dream destination, with tourist spots such as New York City, Disney World, and our National Park System drawing millions of foreign visitors each year. Job opportunities in inbound tourism will likely be more plentiful than those guiding Americans in foreign locations. The best opportunities in inbound tourism are in large cities with international airports and in areas with a large amount of tourist traffic. Opportunities will also be better for those guides who speak foreign languages.

Aspiring tour guides should keep in mind that this field is highly competitive. Tour guide jobs, because of the obvious benefits, are highly sought after, and the beginning job seeker may find it difficult to break into the business. It is important to remember that the travel and tourism industry is affected by the overall economy. When the economy is depressed, people have less money to spend and, therefore, they travel less. The threat of terrorist attacks or civil unrest also adversely affect the travel and tourism industry. If the public perceives that travel is risky, they will travel less and, as a result, tour guides may see reduced employment opportunities.

■ UNIONS AND ASSOCIATIONS

Tour guides are not represented by unions, but they can obtain useful resources and professional support from the following organizations: the National Tour Association and the U.S. Travel Association. The American Society of Travel Agents represents the professional interests of the related career of travel agent.

■ TIPS FOR ENTRY

1. Apply for entry-level jobs with a tour operator to break into the industry.
2. Read publications such as *Courier* (http://ntaon line.com/publication-type/courier-magazine) to learn more about trends in the industry and potential employers.
3. Attend the National Tour Association (NTA) annual convention to network and to interview for jobs.

4. Volunteer at a local museum or park to become a tour guide. This will provide experience with customer service and public speaking.

■ FOR MORE INFORMATION

The American Society of Travel Agents offers advocacy, education, events, publications, and more for travel agents and consumers.

American Society of Travel Agents (ASTA)
675 North Washington Street, Suite 490
Alexandria, VA 22314-1934
Tel: (800) 275-2782
E-mail: askasta@asta.org
http://www.asta.org

The National Tour Association represents tour operators and travel planners.

National Tour Association (NTA)
101 Prosperous Place, Suite 350
Lexington, KY 40509-1891
Tel: (800) 682-8886; (859) 264-6540
Fax: (859) 264-6570
http://ntaonline.com

The U.S. Travel Association provides news, research, educational programs, and other resources for travel industry professionals.

U.S. Travel Association
1100 New York Avenue, NW, Suite 450
Washington, D.C. 20005-3934
Tel: (202) 408-8422
Fax: (202) 408-1255
http://www.ustravel.org

Toxicologists

■ OVERVIEW

Toxicologists design and conduct studies to determine the potential toxicity of chemical, physical, or biological agents on humans, plants, and animals. They provide information on the hazards of these substances to federal, state, and local government agencies, private businesses, and the public. Toxicologists may suggest alternatives to using products that contain dangerous amounts of toxins, often by testifying at official hearings. The Society of Toxicology has more than 7,700 members.

QUICK FACTS

ALTERNATE TITLE(S)
Clinical Toxicologists, Industrial Toxicologists

DUTIES
Design and conduct studies to determine the potential toxicity of chemical, physical, or biological agents on humans, plants, and animals; develop methods to treat poisonings

SALARY RANGE
$44,510 to $82,240 to $250,000+

WORK ENVIRONMENT
Primarily Indoors

BEST GEOGRAPHIC LOCATION(S)
Major metropolitan areas

MINIMUM EDUCATION LEVEL
Master's Degree

SCHOOL SUBJECTS
Biology, Chemistry, Physics

EXPERIENCE
Internships

PERSONALITY TRAITS
Problem-Solving, Scientific, Technical

SKILLS
Math, Research, Scientific

CERTIFICATION OR LICENSING
Recommended

SPECIAL REQUIREMENTS
None

EMPLOYMENT PROSPECTS
Good

ADVANCEMENT PROSPECTS
Good

OUTLOOK
About as Fast as the Average

NOC
2121

O*NET-SOC
N/A

■ HISTORY

The study of the effects of poisons (toxins) began in the 1500s, when doctors documented changes in body tissues of people who died after a long illness. Although research was hampered by the lack of sophisticated research equipment, physicians and scientists continued to collect information on the causes and effects of various diseases over the next 300 years.

As microscopes and other forms of scientific equipment improved, scientists were able to study in greater detail the impacts of chemicals on the human body and the causes of disease. In the mid-1800s, Rudolf Virchow, a German scientist considered to be the founder of pathology (the study of diseased body tissue), began to unlock the mystery of many diseases by studying tissues at the cellular level. His research of diseased cells helped pathologists pinpoint the paths diseases take in the body.

With society's increasing dependence on chemicals (for example, in agriculture, industry, and medicine) and growing use of prescribed (and illegal) drugs, the study of the impact of these potential toxins on public health and environmental quality has become more important. The toxicologist's role in determining the extent of a problem, as well as suggesting possible alternatives or antidotes, plays an important role in society. Toxicologists act as consultants on developing long-term solutions to problems such as air and water pollution, the dumping of toxic waste into landfills, and the recognition of an unusual reaction to a pharmaceutical drug.

■ THE JOB

As scientists, toxicologists are concerned with the detection and effects of toxins, as well as developing methods to treat intoxication (poisonings). A primary objective of a toxicologist is to protect consumers by reducing the risks of accidental exposure to poisons. Toxicologists investigate the many areas in which our society uses potential toxins and documents their impact. For example, a toxicologist may chemically analyze a fish in a local lake to read for mercury, a harmful toxin to humans if consumed in high enough levels. This reading is reported to government or industry officials, who, in turn, write up a legal policy setting the maximum level of mercury that manufacturing companies can release without contaminating nearby fish and endangering consumers.

On many projects, a toxicologist may be part of a research team, such as at a poison control center or a research laboratory. *Clinical toxicologists* may work to help save emergency drug overdose victims. *Industrial toxicologists* and academic toxicologists work on solving long-term issues, such as studying the toxic effects of cigarettes. They may focus on research and development, working to improve and speed up testing methods without sacrificing safety. Toxicologists use the most modern equipment, such as electron microscopes, atomic absorption spectrometers, and mass spectrometers, and they study new research instrumentation that may help with sophisticated research.

Industrial toxicologists work for private companies, testing new products for potential poisons. For example, before a new cosmetic good can be sold, it must be tested according to strict guidelines. Toxicologists oversee this testing, which is often done on laboratory animals. These toxicologists may apply the test article ingredients topically, orally, or by injection. They test the results through observation, blood analysis, and dissection and detailed pathologic examination. Research results are used for labeling and packaging instructions to ensure that customers use the product safely. Although animal experimentation has created a great deal of controversy with animal-rights supporters, humane procedures are stressed throughout toxicology studies.

Toxicologists carefully document their research procedures so that they can be used in later reports on their findings. They often interact with lawyers and legislators on writing legislation. They may also appear at official hearings designed to discuss and implement new policy decisions. Toxicologists must pay careful attention to safety procedures because toxic materials are often handled during research and experimentation.

■ EARNINGS

Toxicologists have good earning potential. Wages vary depending on level of experience, education, and employer. According to Salary.com, in November 2016, the median salary for all toxicologists was $74,116. Salaries ranged from $49,725 or less to $103,517 or more. Toxicologists in executive positions earn more than $150,000, and in the corporate arena they can earn more than $250,000. Those in private industry earn slightly more than those in government or academic positions.

The Department of Labor reports that medical scientists, a profession that includes toxicologists, earned a median salary of $82,240 in 2015, with the lowest 10 percent earning $44,510 or less and the highest 10 percent earning $155,180 or more.

Salaries for toxicologists are, in general, on the rise, but the biggest factor determining earning potential is not location but type of employer. Certification also plays a large role in salary level; toxicologists who are certified earn higher salaries than those who have not earned certification. Comparing gender differences, the salary survey found that women continue to be paid less than their male counterparts.

■ WORK ENVIRONMENT

Toxicologists usually work in well-equipped laboratories or offices, either as part of a team or alone. Research in libraries or in the field is a major part of the job. Some toxicologists work a standard 40-hour workweek, although many work longer hours. Overtime is expected if an important research project is on deadline. Research and experimentation can be both physically and mentally tiring, with much of the laboratory work and analysis done while under time restrictions. Some travel may be required to testify at hearings, to collect field samples, or to attend professional conferences.

Toxicologists often work on research that has important health considerations. At a poison control center, for example, toxicologists may try to find information about the poisonous properties of a product while an overdose victim's life is in danger. Toxicologists' work involves studying the impact of toxic material, so they must be willing to handle contaminated material and adhere to the strict safety precautions required.

■ EXPLORING

Join a science club in addition to taking biology and chemistry courses to further develop laboratory skills. Ask a career counselor to arrange a discussion with a toxicologist to explore career options. Part-time jobs in research laboratories or hospitals are an excellent way to explore science firsthand, although opportunities may be limited and require higher levels of education and experience. Spend time on the Web sites of professional associations for toxicologists, such as the Society of Toxicology, to learn more about the profession and networking opportunities.

■ EDUCATION AND TRAINING REQUIREMENTS

High School

Take courses in both the physical and biological sciences (chemistry and biology, for example), algebra and geometry, and physics. English and other courses that improve written and verbal communication skills will also be useful, since toxicologists must write and report on complicated study results.

Postsecondary Training

Most toxicologists obtain their undergraduate degrees in a scientific field, such as pharmacology or chemistry. Course work should include mathematics (including mathematical modeling), biology, chemistry, statistics, biochemistry, pathology, anatomy, and research methods.

Career opportunities for graduates with bachelor's degrees are limited; the majority of toxicologists go on to obtain master's or doctorate degrees in toxicology. More than 76 percent of toxicologists hold doctorate degrees,

CAREER LADDER

Company Vice-President

Head of Toxicology Department

Toxicologist

Science Technician

Toxicology Intern

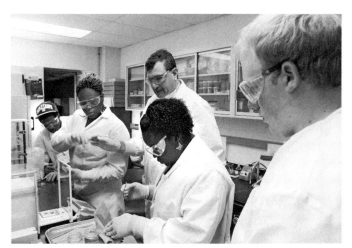

A toxicologist teaches students how to differentiate soils using earthworms. (Jennifer Carroll, U.S. Army Edgewood Chemical Biological Center.)

THE EMERGENCY PLANNING AND COMMUNITY RIGHT-TO-KNOW ACT

DID YOU KNOW?

In 1984, one of the worst chemical industrial disasters in history occurred in Bhopal, India, when a pesticide factory leaked toxic gas, killing more than 4,000 people. In order to protect U.S. citizens from such a chemical disaster, Congress passed the 1986 Emergency Planning and Community Right-to-Know Act requiring industries to immediately report the release of hazardous substances to local and state agencies. The act also mandates that facilities handling or storing hazardous chemicals submit data sheets about these chemicals and inventory forms to state and local officials and local fire departments.

according to the Society of Toxicology. Graduate programs vary depending on field of study, but they may include courses such as pathology, environmental toxicology, and molecular biology. Doctorate programs generally last four to five years.

Other Education or Training

The Society of Toxicology offers continuing education classes at its annual conference. Past classes included "Applications of Computational Systems Biology for Toxicology," "Toxicity of Metals," and "Current Trends in Genetic Toxicology Testing." The American College of Medical Toxicology also provides professional development opportunities.

■ CERTIFICATION, LICENSING, AND SPECIAL REQUIREMENTS
Certification or Licensing

Certification reflects an individual's competence and expertise in toxicology and can enhance career opportunities. The American Board of Toxicology certifies toxicologists who meet educational requirements and pass a comprehensive examination. To be eligible, applicants with a bachelor's degree in an appropriate field must first have 10 years of work experience; with a master's degree, seven years; and with a doctorate degree, three years.

■ EXPERIENCE, SKILLS, AND PERSONALITY TRAITS

Toxicologists gain experience through internships and entry-level roles. They must be hard workers and be dedicated to their field of study. To succeed in their work, they must be careful observers and have an eye for detail. Patience is also necessary, since many research projects

can last months to years and show little results. The ability to work both alone and as part of a team is also needed for research.

Because of the nature of their work, toxicologists must also realize the potential dangers of working with hazardous materials. They must also be comfortable working with laboratory animals and be able to dissect them to examine organs and tissues. Efforts have been made to limit and control live animal experimentation, but research still requires their use to identify toxins and, in turn, protect the consumer public.

■ EMPLOYMENT PROSPECTS
Employers

The Society of Toxicology has more than 7,700 members. Toxicologists work for various consumer products, chemical, and pharmaceutical companies; large universities or medical schools; and government agencies. An increasing number work for consulting firms, providing professional recommendations to agencies, industries, and attorneys about issues involving toxic chemicals. Nonprofit research foundations employ a small number of toxicologists.

Starting Out

Those with the necessary education and experience should contact the appropriate research departments in hospitals, colleges and universities, government agencies, or private businesses. Often, school professors and career services advisers provide job leads and recommendations.

Networking with professionals is another useful way to enter the field. Past work with a team of toxicologists during graduate study may open doors to future research opportunities. Membership in a professional society can also offer more networking contacts. In addition, the Society of Toxicology and the American College of Medical Toxicology both offer career development assistance to members.

■ ADVANCEMENT PROSPECTS

Skilled toxicologists find many advancement opportunities, although specific promotions depend on the size and type of organization where the toxicologist is employed. Those employed at private companies may become heads of research departments. Highly skilled and respected toxicologists may become *vice presidents* or *presidents* of companies because of their involvement in developing important company policy. This type of promotion entails a change in job responsibilities, involving more administrative tasks than research activities.

Toxicologists working for educational institutions may become professors, heads of a department, or deans. Toxicologists who want to continue to research and teach can advance to positions with higher pay and increased job responsibilities. Toxicologists working at universities usually write grant proposals, teach courses, and train graduate students. University positions often do not pay as well as industrial positions, but they offer more independence in pursuing research interests.

OUTLOOK

Employment opportunities for toxicologists are expected to continue to be good. The growing use of chemicals and pharmaceuticals by society has created demand for trained professionals to determine and limit the health risks associated with potential toxins. In addition, new concerns over bioterrorism and the potential use of chemical weapons will create more demand for toxicologists to help develop new vaccines and other antibiotics.

The Department of Labor predicts that medical scientists, including toxicologists, will have employment growth that is as fast as the average for all other occupations through 2024. Job opportunities should be greatest in large urban areas where many large hospitals, chemical manufacturers, and university research facilities are located. Those with the most training and experience will have the best employment prospects.

UNIONS AND ASSOCIATIONS

Toxicologists who work for government agencies can join the American Federation of Government Employees, a union that represents government workers. The Society of Toxicology is the main professional organization for toxicologists. It provides a mentorship program for young members, publications, networking opportunities, and continuing education classes and webinars. The American College of Medical Toxicology is a nonprofit association of physicians with recognized expertise in medical toxicology. The American Board of Toxicology provides voluntary certification to toxicologists.

TIPS FOR ENTRY

1. Read *Toxicological Sciences* and *Communiqué* (both available at https://www.toxicology.org/index.asp) and the *Journal of Medical Toxicology* (http://www.acmt.net/cgi/page.cgi/journals.html) to learn more about the field.
2. Visit https://www.toxicology.org/careers for toxicology career resources.
3. Join the Society of Toxicology (SOT) to participate in Mentor Match (http://www.toxicology.org/

application/jobbank/mentormatch.asp), the society's online mentoring program.
4. Attend the SOT's Annual Meeting & Expo (http://www.toxicology.org/events/am/amToxexpo.asp) to network and participate in continuing education classes and workshops.

FOR MORE INFORMATION

The American Board of Toxicology provides certification programs in professional toxicology.

American Board of Toxicology (ABT)
PO Box 97786
Raleigh, NC 27624-7786
Tel: (919) 841-5022
E-mail: info@abtox.org
http://www.abtox.org

The American College of Medical Toxicology provides education, meetings and forums, publications, and other resources.

POISON TALK

WORDS TO KNOW

Arsenic: A semi-metal element that is tasteless and odorless. Common health effects of excessive arsenic exposure include vomiting, diarrhea, stomach pain, partial paralysis, and blindness. The Environmental Protection Agency has established limits on the acceptable amounts of arsenic in drinking water.

Benign: Referring to a tumor, it means noncancerous.

Carcinogen: A cancer-producing substance.

Control group: A group in an experiment that is not exposed to a procedure or chemical; used to compare with the variable group.

Dissect: To expose, through cutting, the internal organs of an animal for scientific examination.

In vitro: From the Latin, meaning "within glassware," referring to a biological process or experiment that takes place within laboratory equipment such as a test tube.

Malignant: When referring to a cancer, it means highly invasive and quickly spreading.

Metabolism: The combination of chemical processes that take place in a living organism resulting in growth, body functions, or distribution of nutrients.

Risk: The probability that a substance will cause harm under particular conditions of use.

Toxin: A poison produced by a living organism such as a plant.

Anthrax is an acute infectious disease caused by the spore-forming bacterium *Bacillus anthracis*. This bacteria, when dispersed among large groups of people (such as by mail), can be considered an agent of biological warfare. Infection can occur in three forms: cutaneous (skin), inhalation, and gastrointestinal. Anthrax antibiotics, however, have been licensed for use in humans. According to the Center for Disease Control and Prevention (CDC), an anthrax vaccine is reported to be 93 percent effective in protecting against the disease.

Although there have been few deaths from anthrax, police, ambulance workers and the mail-receiving public have been on alert as a result of widespread hoaxes.

Here are some tips from the CDC on handling suspect mail:

- Do not open any suspicious mail.
- Keep mail away from your face when you open it.
- Do not blow or sniff mail or mail contents.
- Avoid vigorous handling of mail, such as tearing or shredding.
- Wash your hands after handling the mail.

Visit http://www.cdc.gov/anthrax for more information on anthrax.

American College of Medical Toxicology (ACMT)
10645 North Tatum Boulevard, Suite 200-111
Phoenix, AZ 85028-3068
Tel: (844) 226-8333
Fax: (844) 226-8333
E-mail: info@acmt.net
http://www.acmt.net

The American Federation of Government Employees represents federal and government employees nationwide and overseas.

American Federation of Government Employees (AFGE)
80 F Street, NW
Washington, D.C. 20001-1528
Tel: (202) 737-8700
E-mail: comments@afge.org
https://www.afge.org

The Society of Toxicology offers educational programs, industry news and events, and membership benefits for toxicology professionals.

Society of Toxicology (SOT)
1821 Michael Faraday Drive, Suite 300
Reston, VA 20190-5348
Tel: (703) 438-3115
Fax: (703) 438-3113
E-mail: sothq@toxicology.org
https://www.toxicology.org

Toy and Game Designers

■ OVERVIEW

Toy and game designers, also known as industrial or commercial designers, come up with the concepts for toys and games. They design products keeping in mind such things as usability, function, aesthetics, safety, production costs, and clients' directions. They sketch their ideas by hand on paper and also create renderings with computer software. There were 31,330 commercial and industrial designers, including toy and game designers, employed in the United States in May 2015, according to the Department of Labor. The U.S. Toy, Doll, and Game Manufacturing industry generates $1 billion in annual revenue, with Hasbro and Mattel continuing to dominate the market.

■ HISTORY

Toys and games date back to early times. Dice is among the oldest games and ancient cultures played a variety of games with dice. Games such as hopscotch and chess are also old; games were used as entertainment, exercise, and to also teach children specific skills.

The first toy and game designers were parents and craftworkers. They made dolls and wooden soldiers from materials that were easy to access at the time, such as clay, wood, and straw. In the 1600s, games were created as part of school instruction. For instance, the precursor to jigsaw puzzles were geographical games made from wood, with countries cut into separate pieces that students had to put together correctly.

The toy manufacturing industry grew in the 1800s, with Germany at the forefront for toy-making, especially known for its wooden and papier-mâché dolls. France became known for its luxury porcelain dolls. England started mass-producing dolls also in the mid-1800s, including Raggedy Ann and Kewpie dolls. By the 1900s, board games for adults and children had grown in popularity. These included Monopoly, Chutes and Ladders, Sorry!, Candyland, among many others. In the 1950s and

1960s, the Barbie, Ken, and G.I. Joe dolls became popular around the world.

Toys and games eventually became more mechanized. Dolls could talk, walk, and move their heads either through battery power or remote controls. Electronic board games enabled people to play without needing a partner.

Computers first appeared in the 1970s, and companies started developing computer games such as Atari's *Pong*, which was based on an arcade game with the same name. Others that became popular included *Space Invaders*, *Road Race*, and *Pac-Man*, to name only a few. Computer and video games have evolved over the decades to be a major, growing segment of the game and toy industry with high-powered gaming consoles such as Xbox One, Playstation 4, Nintendo Switch, and others. But simple and easy-to-use toys, such as balls, hoops, dolls, and yo-yos, continue to be popular.

■ THE JOB

Toy and game designers come up with ideas for toys and games and design them. They may work for toy and game design firms or toy and game manufacturers. They may specialize in certain types of toys and games and/or in creating products for specific age groups. The types of toys and games they create include: arts and crafts, action figures, dolls, electronic toys, mechanical toys, construction toys, toy vehicles, outdoor play toys, plush toys, puzzles and games, scientific toys, toy instruments, toys for animals, and water toys.

Toy and game designers may be assigned a toy or game design by a toy company or they come up with the concept for the product. A market research department may study trends in the toy market, which designers use when determining toy ideas and designs. Toy and game designers make sure that the toys and games they design are age appropriate and meet safety standards. They sketch their ideas by hand on paper and also create models and plans on computers by using computer-aided design software. They work closely with management and design team members throughout the entire toy and game development process.

Self-employed toy and game designers have the added responsibilities of managing and promoting their business, including contacting toy and game manufacturers to pitch ideas and negotiating the sale of toy ideas and products.

■ EARNINGS

The average annual salary for commercial and industrial designers in May 2015 was $67,130, with the lowest 10 percent earning $37,630 and the highest 10 percent earning $104,730 or more. Glassdoor.com reported the average salary for toy designers in May 2016 was $50,000.

QUICK FACTS

ALTERNATE TITLE(S)
Commercial Designers, Industrial Designers

DUTIES
Come up with ideas and create the designs for toys and games; work closely with design department, market research department, and toy manufacturers; sketch ideas and use computer-aided design software to create designs

SALARY RANGE
$37,630 to $67,130 to $104,730+

WORK ENVIRONMENT
Primarily Indoors

BEST GEOGRAPHIC LOCATION(S)
Opportunities exist in all regions with high demand in urban areas, such as New York, Los Angeles, Detroit, Chicago, and San Francisco

MINIMUM EDUCATION LEVEL
Bachelor's Degree

SCHOOL SUBJECTS
Art, Business, Psychology

EXPERIENCE
Entry-level with on-the-job training (assistants); two to three years experience (designers)

PERSONALITY TRAITS
Artistic, Creative, Problem-Solving

SKILLS
Drawing/Design, Interpersonal, Mechanical/Manual Dexterity

CERTIFICATION OR LICENSING
None

SPECIAL REQUIREMENTS
None

EMPLOYMENT PROSPECTS
Fair

ADVANCEMENT PROSPECTS
Good

OUTLOOK
Little Change or More Slowly than the Average

NOC
N/A

O*NET-SOC
N/A

■ WORK ENVIRONMENT

Toy and game designers work in offices in toy and game firms, design companies, or in their own studios. They use computers and computer-aided design software to create models of toys and games. They spend time in

brainstorming meetings with other design team members and market research. They may also spend some time traveling to toy manufacturers' offices, testing facilities, exhibit sites, and design centers.

EXPLORING

Visit the Web sites of professional associations such as the Toy Industry Association to learn more about the trends and news in the toy and game industry. Check the events section to see if there are events coming up that may be worth attending. Working as an intern in a design firm that creates toys and games or in the design department of a toy and game manufacturer is a good way to learn what's involved in the design process. Attend trade shows such as the Toy Fair and Play Fair, held in New York City each year, to see what types of toys and games companies are designing and meet the inventors and designers.

EDUCATION AND TRAINING REQUIREMENTS
High School

Take as many art classes that are offered as possible, including illustration, sculpture, crafts, and graphic design. Classes in computers, English, math, and business are recommended also.

Postsecondary Education

Most entry-level toy and game design jobs require a bachelor's degree, which may be in art, graphic design, industrial design, or other art-related majors. Most toy and game designers need design and illustration skills and knowledge of design software, computer-aided design and drafting, and 3-D modeling. Coursework in business, industrial processes and materials, and manufacturing methods also helps toy and game designers in developing their designs. Art schools require applicants to submit examples of their artistic abilities. Courses in behavioral science, including child psychology, are also beneficial in understanding children better and the impact toys have on their development.

CERTIFICATION, LICENSING, AND SPECIAL REQUIREMENTS

There are no certification or licensing requirements for toy and game designers

EXPERIENCE, SKILLS, AND PERSONALITY TRAITS

Toy and game designers have a bachelor's degree in art, which may include course work in behavioral science, including child psychology. Many designers start in entry-level positions in design firms and after several years may have sufficient experience to design toys and games. They must have an understanding of the age group they design for and the types of games and toys that interest them. Strong drawing skills and knowledge of computer-aided design software is required to do this type of work. An understanding of product functionality and usability is also required, and designers are usually skilled in mechanics, sewing, carpentry, and sometimes even robotics.

EMPLOYMENT PROSPECTS
Employers

Toy and game designers work for toy and game design firms and manufacturers. This is a small field. For example, there are approximately 285 toy, dolls, and game manufacturing businesses in the United States, according to the market research group IBISWorld. The Toy Industry Association represents 900 member organizations. Competition for jobs is keen and employers prefer to hire toy and game designers with prior design experience and strong computer-aided design skills.

Starting Out

A common way to get a foot in the door is through an internship in a design firm or a manufacturing company. Designers may also start in entry-level positions, such as an assistant to the design department. With a year or more of experience they may become junior designers.

ADVANCEMENT PROSPECTS

Toy and game designers with several years of experience may advance to senior-level positions. In larger design firms they may advance to become chief designers and eventually managers of design departments. Some share their experience by teaching in design schools or art schools; they may do this while working full time as designers or move into the education field as a next career. Others may advance by leaving staff positions in large firms and starting their own design studios.

OUTLOOK

Industrial designers will have slower than average employment growth, of 2 percent, through 2024, according to the Department of Labor. The U.S. toy, doll, and game manufacturing industry experienced an annual decline in revenue of nearly 10 percent from 2011 to

2016. Manufacturers face a number of challenges, including competition from low-cost importers and the high costs involved in developing unique toy and game products and protecting the intellectual property rights and trademarks of those products. Creative, innovative games and toys for educational and entertainment purposes will continue to be needed, however. Toy and game designers with knowledge of various computer software programs and prior work experience will have the best job prospects.

■ UNIONS AND ASSOCIATIONS

The Toy Industry Association is a not-for-profit trade association that represents businesses that create and bring entertainment products to children of all ages. The Industrial Designers Society of America has membership chapters across the country for designers as well as students; it hosts educational programs, networking events, awards competitions, and offers publications and other resources. The AIGA provides advocacy and career support for professional designers and design students.

■ TIPS FOR ENTRY

1. A good way to learn firsthand about toy and game design work is through an internship with a design firm or in the design department of a toy and game manufacturing company.

2. Attend a trade show to see what kind of toys and games are being produced and to learn more about the different companies in the industry.

3. Learn more about award-winning toy and game designs and designers by visiting the Toy & Game Inventor Awards Web site, at http://www.tagieawards.com/.

4. Get involved in professional associations for designers such as the Industrial Designers Society of America and the AIGA.

■ FOR MORE INFORMATION

The AIGA offers educational programs, networking opportunities, and career-support resources for design professionals and students.

AIGA
233 Broadway, 17th Floor
New York, NY 10279-0001
Tel: (212) 807-1990
https://www.aiga.org

The Industrial Designers Society of America advances the profession of industrial design by providing advocacy, education, information, and community.

LEGO: PLAY WELL
MOVERS AND SHAKERS

The LEGO company was established in 1932 by Danish carpenter Ole Kirk Christiansen. The word Lego is abbreviated from *leg godt*, which means "play well." Christiansen was a master carpenter and joiner. He opened his woodworking shop in the early 1930s with his 12-year-old son, Godtfred, and started making wooden toys. He named the company LEGO in 1934. By 1943, the company had 40 employees and in 1946, was the first to use a plastic injection-molding machine to produce plastic toys.

In 1949, the LEGO company was producing a wide variety of wooden and plastic toys, including what it called Automatic Binding Bricks, which were the precursors to the LEGO bricks. The Automatic Binding Bricks were modeled on a prototype of British toys called Kiddicraft Self-Locking Building Bricks. The Christiansens' bricks had pegs on the top and the bottoms of the bricks were hollow, allowing children to create any types of designs they liked. Initially the bricks came in four colors. Today LEGO has many product lines, including online games as well as movies, and LEGO products are sold in more than 140 countries.

Source: Lego History, https://wwwsecure.lego.com/en-us/aboutus/lego-group/the_lego_history

Industrial Designers Society of America (IDSA)
555 Grove Street, Suite 200
Herndon, VA 20170-
Tel: (703) 707-6000
http://www.idsa.org

Toy Fair New York is an annual exhibition where inventors and designers exhibit toys and games they have created.

Toy Fair New York
http://www.toyfairny.com

The Toy Industry Association represents businesses that are involved in creating and bringing toys and youth entertainment products to children of all ages.

Toy Industry Association Inc. (TIA)
1115 Broadway, Suite 400
New York, NY 10010-3450
Tel: (212) 675-1141
E-mail: info@toyassociation.org
http://www.toyassociation.org

Toy Industry Workers

■ OVERVIEW

Toy industry workers create, design, manufacture, and market toys and games for adults and children. Their jobs are similar to those of their counterparts in other industries. Some operate large machines, while others assemble toys by hand. According to the U.S. Bureau of Labor Statistics, more than half of all employees in the toy industry work in production. Most toy companies are located in or near large metropolitan areas.

■ HISTORY

Recreational games have roots in ancient cultures. For example, backgammon, one of the oldest known board games, dates back about 5,000 years to areas around the Mediterranean. Chess developed in about the sixth century in India or China and was based on other ancient games.

Dolls and figurines also have turned up among old artifacts. Some seem to have been used as playthings, while others apparently had religious or symbolic importance. More recently, European kings and noblemen gave elaborate dolls in fancy costumes as gifts. Fashion styles thus were spread through other regions and countries. Doll makers in cities such as Paris, France, and Nuremberg, Germany, became famous for crafting especially beautiful dolls. Over the years dolls have been made of wood, clay, china, papier-mâché, wax, and hard rubber, and they have been collected and admired by adults as well as children.

For centuries, most toys were made by hand at home. Mass production began in the 19th century during the Industrial Revolution. In the 20th century, one of the most enduringly popular toys was the teddy bear, named after President Theodore Roosevelt.

Toy companies generally devise their own products or adapt them from perennial favorites, but they occasionally buy ideas for new toys and games from outsiders. One famous example of this was a board game devised during the Great Depression by an out-of-work man in his kitchen. He drew a playing board on his tablecloth using the names of streets in his hometown of Atlantic City and devised a game that let him act out his fantasies of being a real estate and business tycoon. The game, which he called Monopoly, became one of the most popular games of all time.

The popularity of certain toys rises and falls over time. Some toys maintain their popularity with successive generations of children or experience a comeback after a few years. Computer and video games have boomed during the past decade and will undoubtedly continue to become more complex and realistic as technology advances. Still, it is very difficult to predict which new toys will become popular. Introducing a new toy into the marketplace is a gamble, and that adds excitement and pressure to the industry.

■ THE JOB

Taking a toy from the idea stage to the store shelf is a long and complex operation, sometimes requiring a year or two or even longer. Ideas for new toys or games may come from a variety of sources. In large companies, the marketing department and the research and development department review the types of toys that are currently selling well, and they devise new toys to meet the perceived demand. Companies also get ideas from professional inventors, freelance designers, and other people, including children, who write to them describing new toys they would like to see made.

Toy companies consider ideas for production that they sometimes end up scrapping. A toy company has two main considerations in deciding whether to produce a toy: the degree of interest children (or adults) might have in playing with the toy and whether the company can manufacture it profitably.

A toy must be fun to play with, but there are measures of a toy's worth other than amusement. Some toys are designed to be educational, develop motor skills, excite imagination and curiosity about the world, or help children learn ways of expressing themselves.

Often manufacturers test new ideas to determine their appeal to children. *Model makers* create prototypes of new toys. *Marketing researchers* in the company coordinate sessions during which groups of children play with prototype toys. If the children in the test group enjoy a toy and return to play with it more than a few times, the toy has passed a major milestone.

The company also has to ask other important questions: Is the toy safe and durable? Is it similar to other toys on the market? Is there potential for a large number of buyers? Can the toy be mass-produced at a low enough cost per toy to ensure a profit? Such questions are usually the responsibility of research and development workers, who draw up detailed designs for new toys, determine materials to be used, and devise methods to manufacture the toy economically. After the research and development employees have completed their work, the project is passed on to engineers who start production.

Electronic toys, video games, and computer games have skyrocketed in popularity in the past decade. The people who develop them include *computer engineers, technicians, game designers,* and *software programmers. Technical development engineers* work on toys that involve advanced mechanical or acoustical technology. *Plastics engineers* work on plans for plastic toys. They design tools and molds for making plastic toy parts, and they determine the type of molding process and plastic that are best for the job. Plastics engineers who work for large firms may design and build 150 or more new molds each year.

To determine the best way to manufacture a toy, manufacturing engineers study the blueprints for the new product and identify necessary machinery. They may decide that the company can modify equipment it already has, or they may recommend purchasing new machinery. Throughout the engineering process, it is important to find ways to minimize production costs while still maintaining quality.

After selecting the equipment for production, industrial engineers design the operations of manufacturing: the layout of the plant, the time each step in the process should take, the number of workers needed, the ways to measure performance, and other detailed factors. Next, the engineers teach supervisors and assembly workers how to operate the machinery and assemble the new toy. They inform shift supervisors about the rate of production the company expects. Industrial engineers also might be responsible for designing the process of packaging and shipping the completed toys.

As toys are being built on the assembly line, quality control engineers inspect them for safety and durability. Most toy companies adhere to the quality standards outlined in ASTM F963, a set of voluntary guidelines the toy industry has developed for itself. The toy industry is also monitored by the Consumer Product Safety Commission and must adhere to various federal laws and standards that cover the safety of toys under normal use and any foreseeable misuse or abuse.

Finally, getting the toys from the factory to the store shelf is the responsibility of sales and merchandising workers. These employees stay in contact with toy stores and retail outlets and arrange for toy displays and in-store product promotions.

Factory workers on assembly lines mass-produce practically all toys and games. The manufacturing processes can be as unique as the toys themselves. Workers first cast pieces of plastic toys in injection molds and then assemble them. They machine, assemble, and finish or paint wooden and metal toys. They make board games employing many of the same printing and binding processes used for books. They print the playing surface on a piece of paper, glue it to a piece of cardboard of the proper size, and tape the two halves of the board together with bookbinding equipment.

Toy assemblers put together various plastic, wood, metal, and fabric pieces to complete toys. They may sit at a conveyor belt or workbench, where they use small

QUICK FACTS

ALTERNATE TITLE(S)
Computer Engineers, Doll Wigs Hacklers, Game Designers, Hair Finishers, Hand Finishers, Marketing Researchers, Model Makers, Mold Fillers, Plastics Engineers, Rooter Operators, Software Programmers, Technical Development Engineers, Technicians, Toy Assemblers, Toy Designers, Toy Inspectors

DUTIES
Create, design, manufacture, and market toys and games

SALARY RANGE
$21,140 to $36,000 to $126,920+

WORK ENVIRONMENT
Primarily Indoors

BEST GEOGRAPHIC LOCATION(S)
Opportunities exist throughout the country, but are best in California, Texas, Washington, Florida, Ohio, New York, Pennsylvania, Illinois, Michigan, and New Jersey

MINIMUM EDUCATION LEVEL
High School Diploma, Bachelor's Degree

SCHOOL SUBJECTS
Art, Family and Consumer Science, Technical/Shop

EXPERIENCE
On-the-job training (entry level); several years' experience

PERSONALITY TRAITS
Creative, Hands On, Technical

SKILLS
Drawing/Design, Interpersonal, Mechanical/Manual Dexterity

CERTIFICATION OR LICENSING
None

SPECIAL REQUIREMENTS
None

EMPLOYMENT PROSPECTS
Fair

ADVANCEMENT PROSPECTS
Fair

OUTLOOK
About as Fast as the Average

NOC
2252, 9535, 9537, 9619

O*NET-SOC
27-1021.00

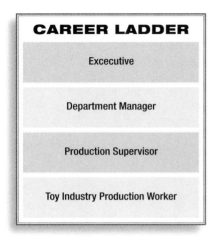

CAREER LADDER

Exccecutive

Department Manager

Production Supervisor

Toy Industry Production Worker

power tools or hand tools, such as pliers and hammers, to fasten the pieces together. Other toy assemblers operate larger machines such as drill presses, reamers, flanging presses, and punch presses. On toys such as wagons that are made on assembly lines, assemblers may do only a single task, such as attaching axles or tires. Other toys may be assembled entirely by one person; for instance, one person at one station on an assembly line may attach the heads, arms, and legs of action figures.

The manufacture of dolls provides a good example of the various manual and mechanical operations that can go into the making of a single toy. Plastic doll *mold fillers* make the head, torso, arms, and legs of the doll in plastic-injection molds. Other workers cure and trim the molded parts and send them off on a conveyor belt. The doll's head may go to a *rooter operator*, who operates a large machine that roots or stitches a specific quantity of synthetic hair onto the head. After attaching the hair in the form of a wig, a *doll wigs hackler* combs and softens synthetic hair by pulling it through a hackle, which is a combing tool with projecting bristles or teeth. Then, a *hair finisher* sets the hair in the specified style by combing, brushing, and cutting. A toy assembler puts together the doll's parts, and a *hand finisher* completes the doll by dressing it in clothes and shoes. An *inspector* examines the completed doll to make sure it meets the original specifications and then sends it on for packaging and shipment.

■ EARNINGS

Earnings in this field vary by the type of job a person does, the size of the employer, and the employer's location. Some production workers are paid on a piecework basis; that is, they are paid according to the number of pieces of work that they complete. Others are paid on a straight salary.

Most production workers work 40-hour work weeks. Machine operators usually earn more than assemblers who work by hand. During the peak production season from July to September, factory workers may have to work long shifts, and they are paid overtime rates for the extra hours. Newly hired production workers may be paid at rates slightly above the federal minimum wage and have annual incomes of approximately $18,890. With experience, they may earn $57,080 or more per year.

According to the U.S. Department of Labor (DOL), inspectors, testers, sorters, samplers, and weighers (a classification including toy inspectors) earned median hourly wages of $17.31 in May 2015. This wage translated to median yearly earnings of approximately $36,000, with a range in salary from a low of $21,140 to a high of $62,150 or more. Most production workers are unionized, and wage scales and conditions for wage increases often are set according to agreements between the union and company management.

Management and engineers are often paid a straight salary. Salary levels for these workers depend on their employer, job responsibilities, experience, seniority, and quality of work. According to the DOL, commercial and industrial designers (including toy designers or model makers) had median yearly earnings of $67,130 in May 2015. Those in the top 10 percent of the salary range earned more than $104,730. The bottom 10 percent of commercial and industrial designers earned less than $37,630. The department also reports the median annual income for industrial engineers as $83,470. The highest paid 10 percent of industrial engineers earned more than $126,920, and the lowest paid 10 percent earned less than $53,300 during that same period.

In addition to wages, many workers receive other benefits, such as health and life insurance coverage, pension plans, and vacations.

■ WORK ENVIRONMENT

The production floor of some toy factories is simply a large room in which workers perform routine tasks. A factory may employ as many as several hundred people to do production work. Some people work at machines, while others sit at tables or assembly lines. Some workers stand throughout much of the work day. Workers often have to meet production schedules and quotas, so they have to keep up a brisk work pace. Some people are bored by the repetition in many production jobs, because they must do the same few tasks over and over for long periods.

In smaller companies, the work may be highly seasonal. Getting the company's products ready for selling in the Christmas season, and to some extent, the Easter season, can mean that employees are asked to put in 10 or more hours of work a day. And if the company makes a product that becomes extremely popular, workers may have to scramble to make enough of the item to keep up with demand. But in the off-peak season, usually the winter months, and in average conditions, production workers may have reduced hours or may be laid off. In many shops, some production workers are employed only five or six months a year. Management and other professional employees work year-round. They may need to put in overtime hours during peak seasons or before trade shows, but they do not earn overtime pay.

■ EXPLORING

One way to find out more about toys and the toy industry is to become familiar with the typical consumer, that is, children. If you have a younger brother or sister, observe what toys he or she plays with most and try to determine why. Think about what toys you enjoyed as a child and figure out what was appealing to you. Spend time at a neighborhood day care center or a children's hospital ward or babysit to learn more about what kids like to play with and why.

Read industry magazines and Web sites to learn more about trends in the business. Playthings (http://www .giftsanddec.com/channel/160-playthings), for example, is one such resource.

A part-time or summer job at a toy store is another good way to explore this field. It gives the opportunity to see what new toys are on the market, how companies advertise and promote their toys, and what types of toys parents and children buy.

Search for jobs at local toy manufacturers. The most likely areas to find jobs are in assembly work, sales, and marketing. A large portion of toys sell in the period before Christmas, so toy companies must have their products ready ahead of time. The months from July through September are usually the busiest in the year, and jobs may be most available during this time.

■ EDUCATION AND TRAINING REQUIREMENTS
High School

A high school diploma is required for many production jobs in the toy industry. Some positions, such as industrial engineer, software programmer, or industrial designer, also require a bachelor's degree. While in high school, be sure to take shop classes that teach how to use machinery. Family and consumer science classes that focus on sewing, using patterns, and picking out materials may also be helpful. Other classes to take include art, basic mathematics, and English.

Postsecondary Training

People with a variety of educational backgrounds are employed in the field. Those in supervisory, research, and design positions may hold bachelor's or graduate degrees in various fields, including art, electronics, engineering, architecture, psychology, business, and the sciences. Those working in production positions, such as rooter operators and toy assemblers, typically learn how

> ### WHAT GOES INTO MAKING A PACKAGE?
> **DID YOU KNOW?**
>
> There are many questions to ask when designing and manufacturing packaging. These are just a few:
>
> - Does it have an appealing design?
> - Is it easy to open and close?
> - Does the package meet government and industry safety regulations?
> - Is it made out of nontoxic materials?
> - Is it packaged so it can be handled safely?
> - Does the package protect the product?
> - Is it environmentally safe?
> - Does the package complement the product?
> - Is the packaging material recyclable?
> - Is the package labeled appropriately?
> - Is the package secure?
> - Is the package durable?
> - Can the package be transported and handled easily?

to do their work during on-the-job training, which lasts anywhere from several days to a few weeks.

Other Education or Training

Both the Toy Industry Association and the American Specialty Toy Retailers Association provide continuing education opportunities at their annual conferences.

■ CERTIFICATION, LICENSING, AND SPECIAL REQUIREMENTS
Certification or Licensing

There are no certification or licensing requirements for workers in the toy industry.

■ EXPERIENCE, SKILLS, AND PERSONALITY TRAITS

No experience is needed for entry-level production positions; several years of industry experience are required for higher-level jobs in management and design.

Production workers need patience and the ability to do repetitive work. Good hand-eye coordination is required for those doing detailed tasks, such as painting designs on toys. The ability to be creative and to understand the consumers' wants are especially important for toy designers. Those operating machinery, such as rooter operators, must be able to complete their work quickly and accurately. Many positions also require that the worker have a good sense of color. Managers must have excellent leadership, business, and finance skills.

CRAYON TRIVIA

DID YOU KNOW?

- Crayons were developed by cousins Edwin Binney and C. Harold Smith and their chemical company, Binney & Smith. They decided that the new wax crayon they had developed to mark crates would be a cheaper and better alternative for American schoolchildren than the charcoal and oil crayons imported from Europe. In 1984, Binney & Smith was purchased by Hallmark Cards, and it is now known as Crayola.
- Edwin Binney's wife, Alice, chose the name "Crayola" from the French word for chalk, *craie*, and *ola*, from oleaginous or oily.
- The first box of eight Crayola crayons appeared on the market in 1903 and sold for about five cents. The eight colors were red, orange, yellow, green, blue, violet, brown, and black.
- Today, Crayolas come in 120 core colors.
- Crayola produces nearly three billion crayons each year, or about 12 million a day.
- Crayons are sold in more than 80 countries and packaged in 12 languages.

■ EMPLOYMENT PROSPECTS

Employers

The following states offer the most job opportunities for toy industry workers: California, Texas, Washington, Florida, Ohio, New York, Pennsylvania, Illinois, Michigan, and New Jersey. In large toy firms, workers with many different titles may be involved in each of the activities described. Sometimes workers are grouped in teams, such as the research and development team, and as a team the members consider research and development aspects of every toy the company makes. In smaller firms, job distinctions may not be so precise and separate. A group of employees may work together on the entire process of developing and marketing a toy from the beginning to the end. The fewer employees in a firm, the more functions they can perform.

Some workers are employed on a temporary basis manufacturing toys during the busiest season, before Christmas.

Starting Out

For entry-level positions in the toy industry, job seekers can contact the personnel offices of toy manufacturers. This is true for most toy factory jobs, whether applicants are looking for engineering, management, marketing, or factory production jobs. Some job listings

and information may be available at the local offices of the state employment service, at local union offices, or through online employment Web sites.

■ ADVANCEMENT PROSPECTS

In general, advancement to better jobs and higher pay depends on acquiring skills, further education, and seniority. Some production workers advance by learning to operate more complex machinery. Reliable, experienced workers in production jobs might be promoted to supervisory positions. Professional and management staff can progress in various ways depending on their areas of expertise, such as by managing more staff or taking on more aspects of business development and marketing.

■ OUTLOOK

According to the Toy Industry Association, sales of traditional toys in the United States totaled $19.48 billion in 2015, a 7 percent increase compared to the previous year. There is always a demand for toys, but this industry is closely linked to the state of the economy. Employment outlooks, however, depend on factors such as the type of job done, the amount of automation introduced into the workplace, and the amount of production that is moved overseas.

Overall, employment for production workers in the U.S. toy industry will probably remain steady or increase slightly as the economy continues to improve. Sales of games and puzzles, arts and crafts, and learning and exploration toys have gone up in the past year, which may create more job opportunities for toy workers with skills or experience in these areas. Additionally, video games that are popular with older children and even adults should make the future bright for this segment of the industry. On the other hand, some video games or game parts are imports from abroad, which may limit the number of new jobs to be found here. Also, if toy preferences change, employment patterns may shift in coming years in ways that are hard to predict now. Nevertheless, there is a fairly high rate of job turnover among production workers due in part to the low pay and repetitive work. Because of this, replacement workers are usually needed.

For those in other areas of the industry, such as design, engineering, and marketing, employment outlooks should follow the overall health of the toy industry as well as the economy.

■ UNIONS AND ASSOCIATIONS

Many toy industry workers belong to the International Union of Allied Novelty and Production Workers or the International Brotherhood of Teamsters. The Toy

Industry Association (TIA) and the American Specialty Toy Retailers Association (ASTRA) represent the professional interests of toy manufacturers, retailers, suppliers, and other organizations that are affiliated with the toy industry. The TIA also provides membership to toy inventors designers, manufacturers' sales representatives, college students, and other individuals in the toy industry. ASTRA provides a membership option for manufacturers' sales representatives.

TIPS FOR ENTRY

1. Attend the American International Toy Fair (http://www.toyfairny.com) to make valuable industry contacts and participate in continuing education opportunities.
2. Read the *Toy Inventor and Designer Guide* (http://www.toyassociation.org/App_Themes/tia/pdfs/resources/inventors/TIAToyInventorDesignerGuide.pdf) for advice on designing toys and bringing them to market.
3. Use social media such as Facebook, LinkedIn, and Twitter to stay up to date on industry developments and learn about job openings. The Toy Industry Association has a presence on Facebook, LinkedIn, Twitter, and YouTube.

FOR MORE INFORMATION

The American Specialty Toy Retailers Association provides resources and support to specialty toy retailers.

American Specialty Toy Retailers Association (ASTRA)
432 North Clark Street, Suite 305
Chicago, IL 60654-4536
Tel: (312) 222-0984
Fax: (312) 222-0986
E-mail: info@astratoy.org
https://www.astratoy.org

The Fashion Institute of Technology offers a bachelor's degree program in toy design.

Fashion Institute of Technology (FIT)
227 West 27th Street
New York, NY 10001-5992
Tel: (212) 217-7999
E-mail: judith_ellis@fitnyc.edu
http://www.fitnyc.edu/toy-design

The Toy Industry Association provides education, news, an annual toy fair, and other resources for the toy industry.

Toy Industry Association (TIA)
1115 Broadway, Suite 400
New York, NY 10010-3466
Tel: (212) 675-1141
E-mail: info@toyassociation.org
http://www.toyassociation.org

Traffic Engineers

OVERVIEW

Traffic engineers, also known as *transportation engineers,* are a branch of civil engineers who study factors that influence traffic conditions on roads and streets, including street lighting, visibility, and location of signs and signals, entrances and exits, and the presence of sites such as factories or shopping malls. They use this information to design and implement plans and electronic systems that improve the flow of traffic. Traffic engineers are often assisted in their work by *traffic technicians.*

HISTORY

During the early colonial days, dirt roads and Native American trails were the primary means of land travel. In 1806, the U.S. Congress provided for the construction of the first federal highway in the United States; it was known as the Cumberland Road, or the National Road. More and more roads were built, connecting neighborhoods, towns, cities, and states. As the population increased and modes of travel began to advance, more roads were needed to facilitate commerce, tourism, and daily transportation. Automobile transportation started in the 1920s, which increased congestion and accidents on the roads. Electric traffic signals were introduced in the United States in 1928 to help control automobile traffic. Because land travel was becoming increasingly complex, traffic engineers were trained to ensure safe travel on roads and highways, in detours and construction work zones, and for special events such as sports competitions and political conventions, among others.

THE JOB

Traffic engineers study factors such as signal timing, traffic flow, high-accident zones, lighting, road capacity, and entrances and exits in order to increase traffic safety and to improve the flow of traffic. In planning and creating their designs, engineers may observe such general traffic influences as the proximity of shopping malls, railroads, airports, or factories, and other factors that affect how well traffic moves. They apply standardized mathematical formulas to certain measurements in order to compute traffic signal duration and speed limits, and they prepare drawings showing the location of new signals or other traffic control devices. They may perform statistical studies of traffic conditions, flow, and volume, and they may—on the basis of such studies—recommend changes in traffic controls and regulations. Traffic engineers design improvement plans with the use of computers and through on-site investigation.

Traffic engineers address a variety of problems in their daily work. They may conduct studies and implement plans to reduce the number of accidents on a particularly dangerous section of highway. They might be asked to prepare traffic impact studies for new residential or industrial developments, implementing improvements to manage the increased flow of traffic. To do this, they may analyze and adjust the timing of traffic signals, suggest the widening of lanes, or recommend the introduction of bus or carpool lanes. In the performance of their duties, traffic engineers must be constantly aware of the effect their designs will have on nearby pedestrian traffic and on environmental concerns, such as air quality, noise pollution, and the presence of wetlands and other protected areas.

Traffic engineers use computers to monitor traffic flow onto highways and at intersections, to study frequent accident sites, to determine road and highway capacities, and to control and regulate the operation of traffic signals throughout entire cities. Computers allow traffic engineers to experiment with multiple design plans while monitoring cost, impact, and efficiency of a particular project.

Traffic engineers who work in government often design or oversee roads or entire public transportation systems. They might oversee the design, planning, and construction of new roads and highways or manage a system that controls the traffic signals by the use of a computer. Engineers frequently interact with a wide variety of people, from average citizens to business leaders and elected officials.

Traffic technicians assist traffic engineers. They collect data in the field by interviewing motorists at intersections where traffic is often congested or where an unusual number of accidents have occurred. They also use radar equipment or timing devices to determine the speed of passing vehicles at certain locations, and they use stopwatches to time traffic signals and other delays to traffic. Some traffic technicians may also have limited design duties.

■ EARNINGS

Salaries for traffic engineers vary widely depending on duties, qualifications, and experience. The U.S. Department of Labor reports that median annual earnings of civil engineers were $82,220 in May 2015. Salaries ranged from less than $52,900 to more than $129,850. In November 2016, Indeed.com reported the average annual salary for traffic engineers was $94,000.

Traffic engineers are also eligible for paid vacation, sick, and personal days, health insurance, pension plans, and in some instances, profit sharing.

■ WORK ENVIRONMENT

Traffic engineers perform their duties both indoors and outdoors, under a variety of conditions. They are subject to the noise of heavy traffic and various weather conditions while gathering data for some of their studies. They may speak to a wide variety of people as they check the success of their designs. Traffic engineers also spend a fair amount of time in the quiet of an office, making calculations and analyzing the data they have collected in the field. They also spend a considerable amount of time working with computers to optimize traffic signal timing, in general design, and to predict traffic flow.

Traffic engineers must be comfortable working with other professionals, such as traffic technicians, designers, planners, and developers, as they work to create a successful transportation system. At the completion of a project they can take pride in the knowledge that their designs have made the streets, roads, and highways safer and more efficient.

■ EXPLORING

Talk to traffic engineers about their careers. Ask them what they like and dislike about their jobs and for advice on preparing for and landing a job in the field. If you're in college, join a student chapter of the Institute of

Transportation Engineers to see if a career in transportation engineering is a good fit for you.

■ EDUCATION AND TRAINING REQUIREMENTS
High School

Traffic engineers must have mathematical skills in algebra, logic, and geometry and a good working knowledge of statistics. Language skills are useful for writing extensive reports that contain statistical data and for presenting these reports to groups of people. Courses in computers and electronics are also helpful. Classes in government are also helpful for a basic understanding of regulations and zoning laws and for future meetings and work with government officials. A high school diploma is the minimum educational requirement for traffic technicians.

Postsecondary Training

Traffic engineers must have at least a bachelor's degree in civil, mechanical, electrical, or general engineering. The field of transportation is vast, which is why many engineers have educational backgrounds in science, planning, computers, environmental planning, and other related fields. Educational courses for traffic engineers may include transportation planning, traffic engineering, highway design, and related courses such as computer science, urban planning, statistics, geography, business management, public administration, and economics.

Traffic engineers acquire some of their skills through on-the-job experience and training conferences and mini-courses offered by their employers, educational facilities, and professional engineering societies. Traffic technicians receive much of their training on the job and through education courses offered by various engineering organizations.

Other Education or Training

The Institute of Transportation Engineers (ITE) provides professional development opportunities via webinars and in-person sessions at conferences and other institute events.

■ CERTIFICATION, LICENSING, AND SPECIAL REQUIREMENTS
Certification or Licensing

The Institute of Transportation Engineers (ITE) offers certification as a professional traffic operations engineer. Requirements include four years of professional practice in traffic operations engineering; a valid license to practice civil, mechanical, electrical or general professional engineering; and passing an examination. The ITE also offers the professional transportation planner designation.

All 50 states and the District of Columbia require engineers that offer their services to the public to be licensed. Licensing typically requires a degree from an ABET-accredited college or university.

CAREER LADDER

Director of Transportation Department or Public Works

Traffic Engineer

Traffic Technician

■ EXPERIENCE, SKILLS, AND PERSONALITY TRAITS

Aspiring traffic engineers should try to gain as much experience as possible by participating in a traffic engineering-related internship or co-op during college. This experience will provide them with an edge when applying for jobs.

Traffic engineers enjoy the challenge of solving problems. They have good oral and written communication skills, since they frequently work with others. They must also be creative and able to visualize the future workings of their designs; that is, how their designs will improve traffic flow, the effects on the environment, and potential problems.

■ EMPLOYMENT PROSPECTS
Employers

Traffic engineers are employed by federal, state, or local agencies or as private consultants by states, counties, towns, and even neighborhood groups. Many teach or engage in research in colleges and universities.

A traffic engineer observes traffic near a construction site. (natalunata . Shutterstock.)

TRAFFIC ENGINEERING BASICS   LEARN MORE ABOUT IT

Currin, Thomas R. *Introduction to Traffic Engineering: A Manual for Data Collection and Analysis,* 2nd ed. Independence, Ky.: Cengage Learning, 2012.

Garber, Nicholas J., and Lester A. Hoel. *Traffic and Highway Engineering,* 5th ed. Independence, Ky.: Cengage Learning, 2014.

ITE. *Transportation Planning Handbook*, 4th ed. Hoboken, N.J.: Wiley, 2016.

Kutz, Myer. *Handbook of Transportation Engineering,* 2nd ed. New York: McGraw-Hill, 2011.

Mannering Fred L., and Scott S. Washburn. *Principals of Highway Engineering and Traffic Analysis,* 6th ed. Hoboken, N.J.: John Wiley & Sons, 2016.

Starting Out

The Institute of Transportation Engineers (ITE) offers the online ITE Community networking site to members. It is an excellent way to build a professional network and learn about job openings. Additionally, student members can get their resumes published in the *ITE Journal.* The journal also lists jobs throughout the country. Most colleges also offer career services programs to help traffic engineering graduates locate their first jobs.

■ ADVANCEMENT PROSPECTS

Experienced traffic engineers may advance to become *directors of transportation departments* or *directors of public works* in civil service positions. A vast array of related employment in the transportation field is available for those engineers who pursue advanced or continuing education. Traffic engineers may specialize in transportation planning, public transportation (urban and intercity transit), airport engineering, highway engineering, harbor and port engineering, railway engineering, or urban and regional planning.

■ OUTLOOK

Employment for civil engineers (including those who specialize in traffic engineering) will increase as fast as the average for all occupations through 2024 according to the U.S. Department of Labor. More engineers will be needed to work with ITS (Intelligent Transportation System) technology such as electronic toll collection, cameras for traffic incidents/detection, and fiber optics for use in variable message signs. As the population increases and continues to move to suburban areas, qualified traffic engineers will be needed to analyze, assess, and implement traffic plans and designs to ensure safety and the steady, continuous flow of traffic. In cities, traffic engineers will continue to be needed to staff advanced transportation management centers that oversee vast stretches of road using computers, sensors, cameras, and other electrical devices.

■ UNIONS AND ASSOCIATIONS

Some traffic engineers may be members of the International Federation of Professional and Technical Engineers, American Federation of Government Employees, and other unions. The Institute of Transportation Engineers is the leading professional membership organization for traffic engineers. It provides certification, members-only networking opportunities, continuing education classes, publications, and other resources. Other noteworthy organizations for traffic engineers include the American Society of Highway Engineers, American Public Transportation Association, and the American Association of State Highway and Transportation Officials. The U.S. Department of Transportation is a federal agency that seeks to "ensure a fast, safe, efficient, accessible and convenient transportation system that meets our vital national interests and enhances the quality of life of the American people, today and into the future."

■ TIPS FOR ENTRY

1. Visit http://jobs.ite.org for job listings.
2. Read *ITE Journal* and the *Journal of Transportation of the Institute of Transportation Engineers* (both available at http://www.ite.org/membership/index.asp) to learn more about the field.
3. Join the Institute of Transportation Engineers (ITE) to access member-only training and networking resources, industry publications, and employment opportunities.
4. Attend the ITE's Technical Conference and Exhibit and Annual Meeting and Exhibit to make industry contacts and participate in continuing education classes.
5. Volunteer for ITE committees, special interest groups, and work groups to raise your profile and make networking contacts.

■ FOR MORE INFORMATION

The American Association of State Highway and Transportation Officials provides education, research, news, and other resources for the transportation industry.

American Association of State Highway and Transportation Officials (AASHTO)
444 North Capitol Street, NW, Suite 249
Washington, D.C. 20001-1539

Tel: (202) 624-5800

E-mail: info@aashto.org

http://www.transportation.org

The American Public Transportation Association aims to improve and strengthen public transportation through advocacy, innovation, and information sharing.

**American Public Transportation
    Association (APTA)**

1300 I Street, NW, Suite 1200 East

Washington, D.C. 20005-3393

Tel: (202) 496-4800

Fax: (202) 496-4324

http://www.apta.com

The American Society of Highway Engineers promotes safe, efficient, and sustainable transportation through education and fellowship.

American Society of Highway Engineers (ASHE)

http://www.ashe.pro

The Institute of Transportation Engineers offers information on membership, careers, and certification.

Institute of Transportation Engineers (ITE)

1627 Eye Street, NW, Suite 600

Washington, D.C. 20006-4087

Tel: (202) 785-0060

Fax: (202) 785-0609

E-mail: ite_staff@ite.org

http://www.ite.org

The U.S. Department of Transportation provides information about the federal transportation system.

U.S. Department of Transportation (DOT)

1200 New Jersey Avenue, SE

Washington, D.C. 20590-0001

Tel: (855) 368-4200

https://www.transportation.gov

Traffic Managers

■ OVERVIEW

Traffic managers coordinate work among account managers, other managers, staff members in other departments, and advertisers at advertising agencies. Some advertising agencies use the titles *project manager* and *project coordinator* to reflect traffic managerial roles. There are 29,340 advertising, promotions, and marketing managers, including traffic managers, employed

in the United States, according to the Department of Labor.

■ HISTORY

The first advertisements in the U.S. appeared in the 1740s in Benjamin Franklin's newspaper, the *Pennsylvanian Gazette*. The ads were mostly about land, transportation,

---

QUICK FACTS

ALTERNATE TITLE(S)
Project Coordinator, Project Manager

DUTIES
Serve as liaison between advertisers and advertising agency staff members; establish project deadlines and make sure work is delivered on time and within budget; communicate changes, problems, or delays to advertisers and advertising project workers

SALARY RANGE
$42,440 to $95,980 to $187,200+

WORK ENVIRONMENT
Primarily Indoors

BEST GEOGRAPHIC LOCATION(S)
Opportunities exist mainly in metropolitan areas, such as New York, Chicago, Los Angeles, Atlanta, Boston, Seattle, and San Francisco

MINIMUM EDUCATION LEVEL
Bachelor's Degree

SCHOOL SUBJECTS
Business, English

EXPERIENCE
Internship; three to four years experience in traffic management or creative services

PERSONALITY TRAITS
Organized, Problem-Solving, Realistic

SKILLS
Interpersonal, Organizational

CERTIFICATION OR LICENSING
None

SPECIAL REQUIREMENTS
None

EMPLOYMENT PROSPECTS
Good

ADVANCEMENT PROSPECTS
Good

OUTLOOK
About as Fast as the Average

NOC
N/A

O*NET-SOC
17-2051.01, 53-6041.00

CAREER LADDER

Senior Traffic Manager

Traffic Manager

Assistant Traffic Manager

Intern

and goods. By the 1800s steam presses were faster and larger, lithography was introduced, paper-making techniques had improved, and color reproduction emerged. Combined, these advances made volume printing affordable for more people. America's population and economy were growing, as was interest in learning about companies' services and products and about news and events. Newspapers sold large advertising spaces in "penny papers," which consumers bought for a cent.

Later in the 1800s, transportation developments such as the steamship and railroad expanded the manufacturing industry. Companies were producing and selling goods in more areas of the country and needed help with advertising to wider groups of people. They contracted advertising agents to choose the newspapers that would most effectively promote sales. The advertising agents coordinated all aspects of the advertisement process, handling some aspects of what today's traffic managers handle. They negotiated rates, selected and guided the printer, confirmed insertions, made sure deadlines were met, and handled payments. Newspapers also hired sales agents to help them with their advertisements. The advertising industry started to grow, expanding to offer not only ad placement services but also ad writing, and marketing and advertising campaign strategies.

New York became a central point for advertising at the turn of the 20th century. Agencies such as BBDO, N.W. Ayer & Son, J. Walter Thompson, and many others set up their headquarters in Manhattan. Advertising copywriters and artists became standard jobs within advertising companies.

The next decades brought radio and television, which advertising agencies embraced as new avenues of revenue. Advertisers continued to keep pace with new technology and innovations in media. Since the 1970s, computers, video games, cable TV, VCRs, DVRs, e-mail, the Internet, social media, mobile devices, wearable technology, On Demand TV, and more have expanded the advertising industry landscape. Companies now have more ways to reach consumers, and advertisers have more ways than ever to strategize and create effective advertising campaigns for them. Advertising and promotion managers, including traffic managers, will continue to be needed to manage and coordinate these increasingly complex, multimedia projects for clients.

THE JOB

Traffic managers work in advertising agencies where they serve as liaisons between advertisers and advertising agency staff members, including creative, production, marketing, sales, and other departments. They may create project schedules using project management software. They establish project deadlines for each step of the advertising campaign and make sure work is completed and delivered on time and within contractually established budgets. When delays arise or if any changes to the work need to be made, they communicate this information immediately to clients and to the staffers involved in the project. They also monitor clients' advertisements and notify them if any errors occur in the writing, data, or images. Advertising traffic managers may also study the advertising project process to determine ways to streamline and improve the process while still delivering quality work.

EARNINGS

The average annual salary for traffic managers was $78,698 in August 2016, according to Salary.com. Salaries ranged from $65,881 to $94,824 or more. Those with a bachelor's degree and more years of experience in the field earn higher salaries. The Department of Labor does not provide data for advertising traffic managers specifically, but does have information on the earnings of advertising, promotions, and marketing managers, which includes traffic managers. In May 2015, the median salary for these workers was $95,890, with the lowest 10 percent earning $42,440 and the highest 10 percent earning $187,200 or more.

WORK ENVIRONMENT

Traffic managers work in offices in advertising agencies. No day is exactly the same, but each day they spend time on computers and mobile devices when away from their desks, checking schedules, e-mails, and communicating with project staff members and advertisers. They meet with project workers to discuss the status of work and update schedules. They may travel to meet with advertisers and staff members working in other cities and regions. Work hours are normally weekdays during business hours but when deadlines approach, they may work overtime during the evenings and weekends.

EXPLORING

Get an internship or entry-level job in an advertising agency. A good place to start may be in the production, marketing, or creative department. The Advertising Educational Foundation offers lists of internship opportunities and other resources for those interested in the advertising industry. Professional associations such as the Association of National Advertisers and the American Association of Advertising Agencies, among many others, also offer information on networking events and educational programs. Explore their Web sites for industry news and trends and to find information about advertising careers.

■ EDUCATION AND TRAINING REQUIREMENTS
High School
Advertising traffic manager work requires strong organizational and communication skills and the ability to manage multiple tasks at one time. Classes in business, math, art, art history, photography, computers, and English will provide a solid foundation for this job.

Postsecondary Education
Many advertising agencies prefer to hire traffic managers with a bachelor's degree; some traffic managers may have a degree in advertising or marketing. Relevant classes include market research, consumer behavior, business management, project management, math, computer science, communication methods and technology, visual arts, and art history.

■ CERTIFICATION, LICENSING, AND SPECIAL REQUIREMENTS
There are no certification or licensing requirements for traffic managers.

■ EXPERIENCE, SKILLS, AND PERSONALITY TRAITS
Traffic managers must have strong organizational and management skills and the ability to communicate clearly with various staff members and advertising agency clients in all levels. Multitaskers who can keep track of schedules as well as information that can change frequently, and also at the last minute, do well in this type of work. Problem-solving skills are frequently called on. Professionalism and diplomacy are also required to effectively work with various personalities to accomplish project goals. Knowledge of project management software and Microsoft Office programs, including Excel and PowerPoint, is required for many traffic manager jobs. Traffic managers usually have several years of prior experience as a coordinator or assistant in traffic management or creative services.

■ EMPLOYMENT PROSPECTS
Employers
Traffic managers work for advertising agencies. They may also work for public relations companies and related

ADVERTISING CONCEPTS AND MANAGEMENT — LEARN MORE ABOUT IT

Applegate, Edd. *The Rise of Advertising in the United States: A History of Innovation to 1960, reprint ed*. New York: Rowman & Littlefield Publishers, 2014.

Barry, Pete. *The Advertising Concept Book: Think Now, Design Later, 3rd ed*. New York: Thames & Hudson, 2016.

Kelley, Larry, and Donal Jugenheimer. *Advertising Account Planning: Planning and Managing an IMC Campaign*, 3rd ed. London: Routledge, 2014.

Kelley, Larry, and Donald Jugenheimer and Kim Sheehan. *Advertising Media Planning: A Brand Management Approach, 4th ed*. London: Routledge, 2015.

Middleton, Kent R., and William E. Lee. *The Law of Public Communication, 9th ed*. London: Routledge, 2015.

Ogilvy, David. *Ogilvy on Advertising*. New York: Vintage, 1985.

Solomon, Robert. *The Art of Client Service: The Classic Guide, 3rd ed*. New York: Wiley, 2016.

Tungate, Mark. *Adland: A Global History of Advertising*. London: Kogan Page, 2013.

Van Dyck, Fons. *Advertising Transformed: New Rules for the Digital Age*. London: Kogan Page, 2014.

Williams, Eliza. *How 30 Great Ads Were Made: From Idea to Campaign*. London: Laurence King Publishing, 2012.

services. In May 2015, approximately 29,340 advertising and promotions managers, including traffic managers, were working in the United States. The majority work in advertising, public relations, and related businesses, while others are employed in radio and TV broadcasting and in newspaper, book, periodical, and directory publishers.

Starting Out
Traffic managers may start as interns or in entry-level positions in traffic management departments and work their way up through the ranks. Most companies prefer to hire traffic managers with at least three or more years of experience in traffic management or creative services.

■ ADVANCEMENT PROSPECTS
Traffic managers with more than four or five years of experience may advance to become senior traffic managers. Their responsibilities may expand to include managing staff and studying the traffic management process and making recommendations to improve efficiencies while cutting costs. Traffic managers may become independent consultants,

working on a project-by-project basis for advertising agencies, public relations companies, and related services.

■ OUTLOOK

The U.S. advertising industry generates $43 billion in revenue and is expected to continue growing relatively well through 2021, as reported by market research group IBISWorld. This growth is being attributed to the continued popularity of digital mediums such as tablets and smartphones, which are providing advertising agencies with additional revenue streams.

Advertising and promotions managers will have average employment growth (5 percent) through 2024, according to the Department of Labor. Companies will continue hiring advertising agencies for help with advertising current products as well as introducing new products to consumers. Many people are interested in working in advertising, however, and competition for jobs is keen. Those with strong knowledge of project management software, MS Office programs such as Excel and PowerPoint, and a bachelor's degree in advertising or marketing will have the best job prospects.

■ UNIONS AND ASSOCIATIONS

The Advertising Educational Foundation offers educational programs and resources for advertising students and professors, advertising professionals, and those interested in the industry. The American Association of Advertising Agencies, commonly known as the 4A's, has been servicing the advertising industry since 1917. Visit its Web site for everything from events and conferences to its careers section, with information on training programs, high school programs, and more. The Association of National Advertisers offers training programs and networking opportunities for advertising professionals.

■ TIPS FOR ENTRY

1. Get a foot in the door by taking an internship in the traffic department or other creative services department of an advertising agency.
2. Explore the Web sites of professional associations such as the 4A's and the Advertising Educational Foundation to learn more about upcoming events and networking opportunities.
3. Find lists of the top advertising agencies by visiting the Redbooks Web site (http://www.redbooks.com/top-ad-agencies/); visit the Web sites of the agencies to learn more about them and to explore job openings.

■ FOR MORE INFORMATION

The American Association of Advertising Agencies has a mission to improve and strengthen the advertising agency business by establishing industry standards, providing advocacy, and fostering professional development.

American Association of Advertising Agencies (4A's)
1065 6th Avenue
New York, NY 10018-1878
Tel: (212) 682-2500
https://www.aaaa.org

The Advertising Educational Foundation is a non-profit foundation with a mission to enrich the understanding of advertising and marketing in society, culture, history, and the economy.

Advertising Educational Foundation (AEF)
708 Third Avenue, 23rd Floor
New York, NY 10017-4201
Tel: (212) 986-8060
Fax: (212) 986-8061
http://www.aef.com

The Association of National Advertisers has a mission to raise the standards of marketers, their companies and brands, and the industry as a whole.

Association of National Advertisers (ANA)
708 Third Avenue, 33rd Floor
New York, NY 10017-4122
Tel: (212) 697-5950
Fax: (212) 687-7310
E-mail: info@ana.net
http://www.ana.net

The International Advertising Association provides advocacy, education, and networking opportunities for branding, communications, and marketing professionals.

International Advertising Association (IAA)
747 Third Avenue, 2nd Floor
New York, NY 10017-2878
Tel: (646) 722-2612
Fax: (646) 722 2501
E-mail: iaa@iaaglobal.org
http://iaaglobal.org

Translators

■ OVERVIEW

Translators focus on translating written materials, such as books, plays, technical or scientific papers, legal documents, laws, treaties, and decrees, from one language to another or multiple languages. There are approximately 49,650 translators and interpreters employed in the United States, according to the U.S. Department of Labor.

HISTORY

Translation has existed as long as there has been written literature. Translations of the Sumerian *Epic of Gilgamesh,* one of the oldest known literary works in the world, have been found in several Southwest Asian languages of the second millennium B.C. Religious, literary, philosophical, and scientific texts were the most commonly translated resources. One of the first recorded translations in the Western world, was the translation of the Old Testament into Greek between 300-200 B.C. This translation became known as the *Septuagint,* a name that references the 70 Jewish scholars who were hired to work on the translation in Alexandria, Egypt. (The term "Septuagint" means seventy in Latin.)

Since the Industrial Revolution, translators have expanded their translation work to business and legal documents, technical manuals, and other nonreligious and nonliterary publications. The growth of the Internet and other technology has greatly expanded job opportunities for translators.

In the last 60 or so years, the field of translation has become a formal discipline, with postsecondary programs in translation and professional associations emerging to serve the needs of those interested in the field. The American Translators Association, one of the leading organizations for translators, was founded in 1959. It has nearly 11,000 members in more than 90 countries. The American Literary Translators Association was founded in 1978. It is the only organization in the United States that is dedicated solely to the art of literary translation.

THE JOB

While interpreters focus on the spoken word, translators work with written language. They read and translate novels, plays, essays, nonfiction and technical works, legal documents, records and reports, speeches, and other written material. Translators generally follow a certain set of procedures in their work. They begin by reading the text, taking careful notes on what they do not understand. To translate questionable passages, they look up words and terms in specialized dictionaries and glossaries. They may also do additional reading on the subject to arrive at a better understanding. Finally, they write translated drafts in the target language.

Most translators use computer-assisted translation tools, in which a computer database of previously translated segments or sentences (called translation

memories) is used to translate new text. These tools help them translate documents faster and receive and submit work electronically. They also use specialized dictionaries and glossaries that are found in print and online to conduct research.

Literary translators translate artistic works such as fiction, journal articles, plays, poetry, and other creative works from one language to another. In addition to simply translating one language to another, it is just as important that literary translators create a translation that reproduces the style of the original text. If possible, they work closely with the original author to clarify meaning and tone in the text to be translated.

Localization translation is a relatively new specialty. *Localization translators* adapt computer software, Web sites, and other business products for use in a different language or culture.

A *sight translator* performs a combination of interpreting and translating by reading printed material in one language while reciting it aloud in another.

EARNINGS

Earnings for translators vary depending on experience, skills, number of languages used, and employers. In government, translators generally begin at the GS-5 rating, earning from $28,262 to $36,740 in 2016. Those with a college degree can start at the higher GS-7 level, earning from $35,009 to $45,512. With an advanced degree, trainees begin at the GS-9 ($42,823 to $55,666), GS-10 ($47,158 to $61,306), or GS-11 level ($51,811 to $67,354).

Translators who work on a freelance basis usually charge by the word, the page, the hour, or the project.

CAREER LADDER

Chief Translator or Reviewer

Experienced Translator

Entry-Level Translator

By the hour, freelance translators usually earn between $15 and $50; however, rates vary depending on the language and the subject matter. Book translators work under contract with publishers. These contracts cover the fees that are to be paid for translating work as well as royalties, advances, penalties for late payments, and other provisions.

The U.S. Department of Labor reports that the median salary for translators and interpreters was $44,190 in May 2015, with salaries ranging from $23,160 to $78,520 or higher. Interpreters and translators who worked for federal government agencies had higher salaries than those offered by other employers, averaging about $74,930 per year in 2015.

Depending on the employer, translators often enjoy such benefits as health and life insurance, pension plans, and paid vacation and sick days.

■ WORK ENVIRONMENT

Translators usually work in offices, although many spend considerable time in libraries and research centers. Freelance translators often work at home, using their own personal computers, the Internet, dictionaries, and other resource materials. Those employed by publishing companies typically work a standard 40-hour week.

■ EXPLORING

For any international field, it is important that you familiarize yourself with other cultures. You can even arrange to regularly correspond with a pen pal in a foreign country or talk to them via e-mail or at a social networking site. You may also want to join a school club that focuses on a particular language, such as the French Club or the Spanish Club. If no such clubs exist, consider forming one. Student clubs can allow you to hone your foreign language speaking and writing skills and learn about other cultures.

Read publications in the foreign language that you are studying in order to improve your skills. Read translations of literary works in their original language and in English to learn more about literary translation techniques. Visit the Web sites of the translation studies programs at colleges and universities to learn more about typical classes and degree requirements. Talk with translators about their careers.

■ EDUCATION AND TRAINING REQUIREMENTS
High School

If you are interested in becoming a translator, you should take a variety of English courses, because most translation work in the United States is from a foreign language into English. The study of one or more foreign languages is vital. If you are interested in becoming proficient in one or more of the Romance languages, such as Italian, French, or Spanish, basic courses in Latin will be useful. Other helpful courses include world history, geography, political science, speech, business, cultural studies, humanities. In fact, any course that emphasizes the written word will be valuable to aspiring translators. In addition, knowledge of a particular subject matter in which you may have interest, such as health, law, and science or a type of literary writing style, will give you a professional edge if you want to specialize. Finally, courses in typing and word processing are recommended.

Postsecondary Training

You'll need a minimum of a bachelor's degree in translation, linguistics, or a related field. Some translators have degrees in literature, history, law, medicine, or other areas related to their professional specialty. Many government or high-level positions require a master's degree.

Hundreds of colleges and universities in the United States offer degrees in languages. In addition, educational institutions now provide programs and degrees specialized for translating. Georgetown University (http://linguistics.georgetown.edu) offers both undergraduate and graduate programs in linguistics. Graduate degrees in translation may be earned at the University of California at Santa Barbara (http://www.ucsb.edu), University of Puerto Rico (http://www.upr.edu), and Middlebury Institute of International Studies at Monterey (http://www.miis.edu). Many of these programs include both general and specialized courses, such as legal translation.

Academic programs for the training of translators can be found in Europe as well. The University of Geneva's Faculty of Translation and Interpreting (http://www.unige.ch/traduction-interpretation/index_en.html) is highly regarded among professionals in the field.

The American Translators Association provides a list of member schools that provide translation and interpreting courses at its Web site, http://www.atanet.org/careers/T_I_programs.php.

Other Education or Training

The American Translators Association offers webinars for freelance translators. Recent topics include how to break into the field of freelance translation, tax issues, and translation environment database tools. It also provides professional development conferences and seminars on topics such as translation tools, business issues, and legal and medical translation. Other organizations that provide conference seminars, webinars, workshops, and other learning opportunities include the American Literary Translators Association, Dictionary Society of North America, and Editorial Freelancers Association. Contact these organizations for more information.

■ CERTIFICATION, LICENSING, AND SPECIAL REQUIREMENTS
Certification or Licensing
Foreign language translators may be granted certification by the American Translators Association (ATA) upon successful completion of required exams. ATA certification is available for translators who translate the following languages into English: Arabic, Croatian, Danish, Dutch, French, German, Italian, Japanese, Polish, Portuguese, Russian, Spanish, Swedish, and Ukrainian. Certification is also available for translators who translate English into the following languages: Chinese, Croatian, Dutch, Finnish, French, German, Hungarian, Italian, Japanese, Polish, Portuguese, Russian, Spanish, Swedish, and Ukrainian.

■ EXPERIENCE, SKILLS, AND PERSONALITY TRAITS
Three to five years of experience with a foreign language and translation is needed to enter the field. Try to participate in volunteer or informal activities that allow you to practice your foreign language and translation skills.

Translators should be knowledgeable of not only the foreign language but also of the culture and social norms of the region or country in which it is spoken. Translators should read daily newspapers in the languages in which they specialize to keep current in both developments and usage. They also should have self-discipline and patience. Above all, they should have an interest in and love of language.

■ EMPLOYMENT PROSPECTS
Employers
There are approximately 44,200 translators and interpreters in the United States. Literary translators are employed by publishing companies and authors. Although many translators work for government or international agencies, some are employed by private firms. Large import-export companies often have translators on their payrolls, although these employees generally perform additional duties for the firm. International banks, companies,

organizations, and associations often employ translators to facilitate communication. In addition, translators work at schools, radio and television stations, airlines, shipping companies, law firms, and scientific and medical operations. Many companies hire freelance or part-time interpreters to help them translate their Web sites into internationally friendly pages.

Many translators work independently in private practice. These self-employed professionals must be disciplined and driven, since they must handle all aspects of the business such as scheduling work and billing clients.

Starting Out
It is difficult to land top translation jobs because the competition for these higher profile positions is fierce. It's a good idea to develop supplemental skills that can be attractive to employers while refining your translating techniques. The United Nations (UN), for example, employs administrative assistants who can take shorthand and transcribe notes in two or more languages. It also might be useful to develop basic interpreting skills to improve your attractiveness to employers.

Most translators begin as part-time freelancers until they gain experience and contacts in the field. Aspiring translators can contact potential employers directly to learn about job openings, use the resources of their college's career services office and language department to identify job leads, and network on social media sites such as LinkedIn and at in-person events.

■ ADVANCEMENT PROSPECTS
Translators can advance to supervisory or managerial positions as they develop a reputation for providing high-quality translation services. Those who work for government agencies advance by clearly defined grade promotions. Translators can also advance to become

ADVICE FROM THE TRENCHES

If you are considering a career as a translator but wondering whether you've got what it takes, here is some advice from those currently in the field.

- Make sure that you love the language and the written and spoken word.
- Keep abreast of new developments affecting your field or business.
- Ask your peers to periodically review your work.
- Learn how to negotiate rates, work within deadlines, and handle revisions.
- Stay in step with advances in online resources, as well as search technologies.
- Invest in dictionaries, grammar books, and other resource materials.
- Have self-discipline and patience.
- Don't bite off more than you can chew.
- Aim for the most accurate translation possible.
- Learn how to type!
- Maintain high professional standards.
- Exhibit cultural sensitivity and awareness.

chief translators or *reviewers,* who check the work of others. Some highly-skilled and business-minded translators launch their own translation agencies.

OUTLOOK

Employment opportunities for translators and interpreters are expected to grow by 29 percent through 2024, according to the U.S. Department of Labor (DOL), or much faster than the average for all careers. The DOL says that "job opportunities should be plentiful for interpreters and translators specializing in health care and law, because of the critical need for all parties to fully understand the information communicated in those fields." The medical field, for example, will provide many jobs for language professionals, translating such products as pharmaceutical inserts, research papers, and medical reports for insurance companies. Opportunities also exist for qualified individuals in law, tourism, trade and business, recreation, and the government.

The DOL predicts that "demand will likely remain strong for translators of frequently translated languages, such as French, German, Portuguese, Russian, and Spanish. Demand also should be strong for translators of Arabic and other Middle Eastern languages and for

the principal Asian languages: Chinese, Japanese, Hindi, and Korean."

UNIONS AND ASSOCIATIONS

Translators who are employed by government agencies may be members of the American Federation of State, County and Municipal Employees and other unions. They can also join professional associations such as the American Translators Association, American Literary Translators Association, National Association of Judiciary Interpreters and Translators, Dictionary Society of North America, and Editorial Freelancers Association. These organizations provide continuing education classes, networking events, and other resources.

TIPS FOR ENTRY

1. Visit http://literarytranslators.org/resources/alta-guides to read *Getting Started in Literary Translation: Making of a Literary Translator* and *Breaking Into Print.*
2. Attend the American Literary Translators Association annual conference (http://literarytranslators.org/conference) to network and learn more about the field.
3. Talk to translators about their careers. The American Translators Association (ATA) offers a list of translators at http://www.atanet.org.
4. Visit the following Web sites for job listings: https://www.state.gov/m/a/ols, http://www.editorandpublisher.com, and http://www.bookjobs.com.
5. The ATA offers a mentorship program for members to help them break into the field. Visit http://www.atanet.org/careers/mentoring.php for more information.

FOR MORE INFORMATION

For information on careers in literary translation, contact
American Literary Translators Association
900 East 7th Street, PMB 266
Bloomington, IN 47405-3201
Tel: (937) 696-0022
E-mail: bpenzer@literarytranslators.org
http://www.literarytranslators.org

For more on the translating and interpreting professions, including information on accreditation, contact
American Translators Association
225 Reinekers Lane, Suite 590
Alexandria, VA 22314-2875

Tel: (703) 683-6100

Fax: (703) 683-6122

E-mail: ata@atanet.org

http://www.atanet.org

This is an organization of lexicographers, writers, linguists, translators, librarians, and others interested in dictionaries. It publishes a semi-annual newsletter, a blog, an annual journal, and a membership directory. Visit its Web site for more information.

Dictionary Society of North America

Department of English CUNY, New York City College of Technology

300 Jay St.

Brooklyn, NY 11201

E-mail: dsnaoffice@gmail.com

http://www.dictionarysociety.com

The EFA is an organization for freelance editors, proofreaders, editors, writers, indexers, and translators. Members receive a newsletter, a free listing in its directory, and daily access to job listings.

Editorial Freelancers Association (EFA)

71 West 23rd Street, 4th Floor

New York, NY 10010-3571

Tel: (866) 929-5425; (212) 929-5400

Fax: (866) 929-5439

E-mail: office@the-efa.org

http://www.the-efa.org

For more information on court interpreting and certification, contact

National Association of Judiciary Interpreters and Translators

2002 Summit Boulevard, Suite 300

Atlanta, GA 30319-6403

Tel: (404) 566-4705

Fax: (404) 566-2301

E-mail: info@najitorg

http://www.najit.org

For information on opportunities with the federal government, contact

U.S. Department of State

Office of Language Services, 2401 E Street, NW, SA-1, 14th Floor

Washington, D.C. 20522-0001

Tel: (202) 261-8800

Fax: (202) 261-8821

https://www.state.gov/m/a/ols

Transplant Coordinators

■ OVERVIEW

Transplant coordinators are involved in practically every aspect of organ procurement (getting the organ from the donor) and transplantation. There are two types of transplant coordinators: *procurement coordinators* and *clinical coordinators*. Procurement coordinators help the families of organ donors deal with the death of a loved one as well as inform them of the organ donation process. Clinical coordinators educate recipients about how to prepare for an organ transplant and how to care for themselves after the transplant.

■ HISTORY

Scientists have been conducting research regarding human and animal organ transplantation since the 18th century. Further research led to refinements in transplant technology, and in 1954 the first successful human kidney transplant was performed in Boston. The 1960s brought many successes in the field of organ transplants, including successful human liver and pancreas transplants. The first heart transplant was performed in 1967.

Despite these successes, many transplants eventually failed because of the body's immune system, which eventually rejected the new organ as a foreign object. Although drugs were designed in the 1960s to help the body accept transplanted organs, it wasn't until the early 1980s that a truly effective immunosuppressant drug, cyclosporin, was available. This drug substantially improved the success rate of transplant surgeries. More precise tissue typing or matching of donor and recipient tissues also helped increase the success rate.

Successful organ transplants have increased, although some transplants still fail over time despite modern drug treatments and closer tissue matching. Research in this area continues with the hope of increasing the rate of successful transplants.

In the United States, more than 500,000 people have received transplants, according to the United Network for Organ Sharing. More than 28,000 Americans receive transplants each year.

■ THE JOB

Transplant coordinators are involved in practically every aspect of organ procurement (getting the organ from the donor) and transplantation. This may involve

QUICK FACTS

ALTERNATE TITLE(S)
Clinical Coordinators,
    Procurement Coordinators

DUTIES
Educate patients and their
    families about the organ
    donation process; procure
    organs after the death of a
    donor; educate transplant
    recipients in how to best
    prepare for organ transplant
    and how to care for
    themselves after the transplant

SALARY RANGE
$45,623 to $70,555 to
    $95,159+

WORK ENVIRONMENT
Primarily Indoors

BEST GEOGRAPHIC LOCATION(S)
Nationwide; most opportunities
    available in major
    metropolitan areas

MINIMUM EDUCATION LEVEL
Bachelor's Degree

SCHOOL SUBJECTS
Biology, Health, Psychology

EXPERIENCE
Several years experience

PERSONALITY TRAITS
Helpful, Organized, Scientific

SKILLS
Interpersonal, Organizational,
    Scientific

CERTIFICATION OR LICENSING
Recommended

SPECIAL REQUIREMENTS
None

EMPLOYMENT PROSPECTS
Good

ADVANCEMENT PROSPECTS
Fair

OUTLOOK
About as Fast as the Average

NOC
3012

O*NET-SOC
N/A

working with medical records, scheduling surgeries, educating potential organ recipients, and counseling donor families.

There are two types of transplant coordinators: procurement coordinators and clinical coordinators. Procurement and clinical coordinators are actively involved in evaluating, planning, and maintaining records, but an important part of their job is helping individuals and families. Procurement coordinators help the families of organ donors deal with the death of their loved one and inform them of the organ donation process.

Clinical coordinators educate recipients in how to best prepare for organ transplant and how to care for themselves after the transplant. Many coordinators, especially clinical coordinators, are registered nurses, but it is not necessary to have a nursing degree to work as a coordinator. Some medical background is important, however. Many transplant coordinators have degrees in biology, physiology, accounting, psychology, business administration, or public health.

Once the donor patient has been declared brain dead and is no longer breathing on their own, the procurement transplant coordinator approaches the donor's family about organ donation. If the family gives its consent, the coordinator then collects medical information and tissue samples for analysis. The coordinator also calls the United Network for Organ Sharing (UNOS), a member organization that includes every transplant program, organ procurement organization (OPO), and tissue typing laboratory in

the United States. The UNOS attempts to match organs with recipients within the OPO's region. If no local match can be made, the coordinator must make arrangements for the organs to be delivered to another state. In either case, the procurement coordinator schedules an operating room for the removal of the organs and coordinates the surgery.

Once the organs have been removed and transported, clinical transplant coordinators take over. Clinical transplant coordinators have been involved in preparing recipients for new organs. It is the clinical coordinators' job to see to the patients' needs before, during, and after organ transplants. This involves admitting patients, contacting surgeons, and arranging for operating rooms, as well as contacting the anesthesiology department and the blood bank. Transplant coordinators educate patients and arrange for blood tests and other tests to make sure patients can withstand the rigors of surgery. They help patients register on organ waiting lists. They ensure that patients have a support system of family, friends, and caregivers in place. After the transplants, coordinators help patients through their recovery by helping them understand their medications, arranging for routine doctor visits and lab tests, and informing them about danger signs of organ rejection.

Another significant aspect of the job of all transplant coordinators is educating the public about the importance of organ donation. They speak to hospital and nursing school staffs and to the general public to encourage donations.

■ EARNINGS

Salaries vary based on educational background, experience, and responsibilities of the coordinator. People who have a degree and work as directors or educators may earn a higher salary than those working at the clinical end. According to PayScale.com, in October 2016, organ transplant coordinators earned salaries that ranged from $45,623 to more than $95,159. The average annual salary was $70,555.

Many transplant coordinators are registered nurses. Salaries are often comparable to those of registered nurses in other fields. Median annual earnings of registered nurses were $67,490 in May 2015 (according to the U.S. Department of Labor), and ranged from less than $46,360 to more than $101,630. Some transplant coordinators are physician assistants, who had median annual earnings of $98,180 in May 2015.

Transplant centers and organ procurement agencies are nonprofit organizations, but transplant coordinators generally receive very good health and retirement benefits that are consistent with other medical professions.

▰ WORK ENVIRONMENT

Transplant coordinators can be found doing their jobs in various environments. They may be in an office completing paperwork, in a hospital visiting with patients, families, or other hospital staff, in a clinic or doctor's office seeing patients, or at a school or business meeting promoting donor awareness. Sometimes coordinators must accompany the organ to the transplant center, and some may be required to be on call and to work long, irregular hours.

▰ EXPLORING

To learn more about the work of transplant coordinator, research the organ transplant process as much as possible. The Internet and local libraries are great resources for information. Talk to your school's guidance counselor about your possible interest in health care. They may be able to suggest different programs to research or, better yet, provide the names of previous students to talk to who have gone on to medical programs. Volunteering at local hospitals or health care clinics provides experience in working with patients.

Much of a transplant coordinator's job involves communicating with patients and their family members during times of high stress, so it is beneficial to explore counseling and social work in addition to medicine.

▰ EDUCATION AND TRAINING REQUIREMENTS
High School

High school courses that will prepare you for a medical-based education will be the most valuable in this profession. Science courses such as biology and chemistry are important, as are courses in psychology, sociology, math, and health.

If you live near a transplant center, there may be volunteer opportunities available at the center or in an outpatient care home for transplant recipients. The local Red Cross also may need volunteers for promoting donor awareness.

Postsecondary Training

There is no specific educational track for transplant coordinators. One transplant coordinator may focus on financing and insurance, while another may work on education and awareness. Another coordinator may perform physical tests and evaluations, while another counsels grieving families. The more experience and education with health care and medicine, the better the job opportunities. A nursing degree isn't required of all coordinators but it does offer a good medical background. A bachelor's degree in one of the sciences, along with experience in a medical setting, will also open up job opportunities.

Some people who work as coordinators may have master's degrees in public health or in business administration. Other coordinators may hold doctorates in psychology or social work.

Other Education or Training

NATCO-The Organization for Transplant Professionals provides an introductory course that is designed to provide basic information to new procurement or transplant professionals, as well as an Organ Preservation Symposium and professional development opportunities at its annual conference. The International Transplant Nurses Society also provides continuing education classes and webinars. Contact these organizations for more information.

▰ CERTIFICATION, LICENSING, AND SPECIAL REQUIREMENTS
Certification or Licensing

Certification, though not required, is available through the American Board for Transplant Certification. Four certification designations are available: certified transplant coordinator, certified procurement transplant coordinator, certified transplant nurse, and certified transplant preservationist. To become certified, applicants must meet work experience requirements and pass an examination.

▰ EXPERIENCE, SKILLS, AND PERSONALITY TRAITS

Previous experience in nursing, transplant support careers, social work, or related areas is typically required to become a transplant coordinator.

Successful transplant coordinators have good organizational skills and are able to work quickly, accurately, and efficiently. They are detail-oriented and have good record-keeping and reporting skills. A transplant coordinator needs to be a compassionate person who is able to communicate well with doctors, patients, donors' families, and the public.

▰ EMPLOYMENT PROSPECTS
Employers

A number of different institutions and organizations require transplant coordinators. There are at least 244 transplant centers across the country and 58 organ procurement organizations; there are also tissue-typing labs.

CAREER LADDER

Senior Transplant Coordinator or Educator

Transplant Coordinator

Registered Nurse or Other Health Care Career

ORGAN TRANSPLANT MYTHS AND FACTS

DID YOU KNOW?

There is a severe organ shortage in this country. Despite continuing efforts at public education, misconceptions and inaccuracies about donation persist. It's a tragedy if even one person decides against donation because they don't know the truth. The following is a list of the most common myths along with the actual facts:

Myth: If emergency room doctors know you're an organ donor, they won't work as hard to save you.

Fact: If you are sick or injured and admitted to the hospital, the number one priority is to save your life. Organ donation can only be considered after brain death has been declared by a physician. Many states have adopted legislation allowing individuals to legally designate their wish to be a donor should brain death occur, although in many states organ procurement organizations also require consent from the donor's family.

Myth: Having "organ donor" noted on your driver's license or carrying a donor card is all you have to do to become a donor.

Fact: A signed donor card and a driver's license with an "organ donor" designation are legal documents, but organ and tissue donation is usually discussed with family members prior to the donation. To ensure that your family understands your wishes, it is important that you tell your family about your decision to donate.

Myth: Only hearts, livers, and kidneys can be transplanted.

Fact: Needed organs include the heart, kidneys, pancreas, lungs, liver and intestines. Tissue that can be donated include the eyes, skin, bone, heart valves, and tendons.

Source: United Network for Organ Sharing

These organizations and centers may be hospital-based, independent, or university-based.

Starting Out

Many transplant coordinators begin their professional careers in other areas such as nursing, business, psychology, social work, or the sciences before they seek a career as a transplant coordinator. Positions for transplant coordinators are advertised nationally in medical publications and on the Internet. NATCO - The Organization for Transplant Professionals also offers job referral information.

■ ADVANCEMENT PROSPECTS

There may be internal advancement opportunities within a clinic such as senior coordinator or senior educator. Other managerial or supervisory positions may also be a way of advancing within the career. There are other aspects of transplantation, such as surgery or hospital administration, which may be available with additional education and experience.

■ OUTLOOK

The number of people waiting for organ donations is growing, but there still is a need to find an increased number of donors. Therefore, a number of organizations have been developed to promote organ donations, particularly among minorities. These efforts require the skills of transplant coordinators. The stress level of the job is high, which means the burnout rate is also high. Also, transplant procurement coordinators' hours can be long and irregular, so many procurement coordinators move on to other positions after only 18 months or less. This means continued job opportunities for those looking for work as coordinators.

■ UNIONS AND ASSOCIATIONS

Transplant coordinators do not typically belong to unions. NATCO - The Organization for Transplant Professionals and the International Transplant Nurses Society are the major membership organizations for transplant coordinators. The American Board for Transplant Certification provides voluntary certification. The United Network for Organ Sharing is the private, nonprofit organization that manages the U.S. organ transplant system under contract with the federal government.

■ TIPS FOR ENTRY

1. Read *Progress in Transplantation* (http://www.natco1.org/Publications/progress-in-transplantation.asp) to learn more about the field.
2. Search the job listings sections of professional associations' Web sites to learn more about the work and potential opportunities.
3. Join NATCO—The Organization for Transplant Professionals and other organizations to access training and networking resources, industry publications, and employment opportunities.
4. Volunteer for NATCO committees, special interest groups, and work groups to raise your profile and make networking contacts.

■ FOR MORE INFORMATION

The American Board for Transplant Certification offers education and certification programs for organ donation and transplant professionals.

**American Board for Transplant
    Certification (ABTC)**
4400 College Boulevard, Suite 220
Overland Park, KS 66211-2341
Tel: (913) 222-8662
Fax: (913) 222-8606
E-mail: abtc-info@KellenCompany.com
http://www.abtc.net

The International Transplant Nurses Society provides education and career-support resources for transplant nurses.
International Transplant Nurses Society (ITNS)
8735 West Higgins Road, Suite 300
Chicago, IL 60631-2738
Tel: (847) 375-6340
Fax: (847) 375-6341
E-mail: info@itns.org
http://www.itns.org

NATCO provides education, advocacy, publications, and other resources for transplant professionals.
**NATCO - The Organization for Transplant
    Professionals**
PO 711233
Oak Hill, VA 20171
Tel: (703) 483-9820
Fax: (703) 879-7544
E-mail: info@natco1.org
http://www.natco1.org

The United Network for Organ Sharing aims to advance organ availability and transplantation to support patients through education, technology, and policy development.
**United Network for Organ
    Sharing (UNOS)**
700 North 4th Street
Richmond, VA 23219-1414
Tel: (804) 782-4800
https://www.unos.org

Travel Agents

■ OVERVIEW

Travel agents assist individuals or groups who will be traveling by planning their itineraries, making transportation, hotel, and tour reservations, obtaining or preparing tickets, and performing related services. There are approximately 66,560 travel agents employed in the United States.

■ HISTORY

The first travel agency in the United States was established in 1872. Before this time, travel as an activity was not widespread due to wars and international barriers, inadequate transportation and hotels, lack of leisure time, the threat of contagious disease, and lower standards of living. Despite the glamour attached to such early travelers as the Italian explorer Marco Polo, people of the Middle Ages and the 17th and 18th centuries were not accustomed to traveling for pleasure.

The manufacturing operations that started during the Industrial Revolution caused international trade to expand greatly. Commercial traffic between countries stimulated both business and personal travel. Yet until the 20th century, travel was arduous, and most areas were unprepared for tourists.

The travel business began with Thomas Cook, an Englishman who first popularized the guided tour. In 1841, Cook arranged his first excursion: a special Midland Counties Railroad Company train to carry passengers from Leicester to a temperance meeting in Loughborough. His business grew rapidly. He made arrangements for 165,000 visitors to attend the Great Exhibition of 1851 in London. The following year, he organized the first "Cook's Tour." Earnest groups of English tourists were soon seen traveling by camel to view the Pyramids and the Sphinx, gliding past historic castles on the Rhine, and riding by carriage to view the wonders of Paris. The "Grand Tour" of Europe soon became an integral part of a young person's education among the privileged classes.

QUICK FACTS

ALTERNATE TITLE(S)
Tour Guides, Tour Organizers, Travel Consultants, Travel Guides

DUTIES
Help clients plan travel; plan itineraries; make transportation, hotel, and tour reservations; obtain or prepare tickets; and perform related services

SALARY RANGE
$20,050 to $35,660 to $60,200+

WORK ENVIRONMENT
Indoors/Outdoors

BEST GEOGRAPHIC LOCATION(S)
Nationwide

MINIMUM EDUCATION LEVEL
High School Diploma, Some Postsecondary Training

SCHOOL SUBJECTS
Business, Geography, Social Studies

EXPERIENCE
Internship, volunteer, or part-time experience

PERSONALITY TRAITS
Helpful, Organized, Realistic

SKILLS
Business Management, Interpersonal, Research

CERTIFICATION OR LICENSING
Required

SPECIAL REQUIREMENTS
None

EMPLOYMENT PROSPECTS
Fair

ADVANCEMENT PROSPECTS
Fair

OUTLOOK
Decline

NOC
6521

O*NET-SOC
41-3041.00

CAREER LADDER

Travel Agency Owner

Travel Agency Manager or Corporate Travel Manager

Travel Agent

Travel Assistant

Over the next century, the development of the railroads, the replacement of sailing ships with faster steamships, the advent of the automobile and the bus, and the invention of the airplane provided an improved quality of transportation that encouraged people to travel for relaxation and personal enrichment. At the same time, cities, regions, and countries began to appreciate the economic aspects of travel. Promotional campaigns were organized to attract and accommodate tourists. Formal organization of the travel industry was reflected in the establishment in 1931 of the American Society of Travel Agents.

In recent years, travel agents to some locations have accommodated a great increase in family travel. This increase is in part a result of greater leisure time. As long as leisure time continues to grow and the nation's standard of living increases, there will be a need for travel agents to help people in planning their vacations wisely.

■ THE JOB

The *travel agent* may work as a *salesperson, travel consultant, tour organizer, travel guide, bookkeeper,* or *small business executive.* If the agent operates a one-person office, they usually perform all of these functions. Other travel agents work in offices with dozens of employees, which allows them to specialize in certain areas. In such offices, one staff member may become an authority on sea cruises, another may work on trips to the Far East, and a third may develop an extensive knowledge of either low-budget or luxury trips. In some cases, travel agents are employed by national or international firms and can draw on extensive resources.

As salespeople, travel agents must be able to motivate people to take advantage of their services. Travel agents study their customers' interests, learn where they have traveled, appraise their financial resources and available time, and present a selection of travel options. Customers are then able to choose how and where they want to travel with a minimum of effort.

Travel agents consult a variety of print and Internet-based sources for information on air transportation departure and arrival times, airfares, and hotel ratings and accommodations. They often base their recommendations on their own travel experiences or those of colleagues or clients. Travel agents may visit hotels, resorts, and restaurants to rate their comfort, cleanliness, and quality of food and service.

As travel consultants, agents give their clients suggestions regarding travel plans and itineraries, information on transportation alternatives, and advice on the available accommodations and rates of hotels and motels. They also explain and help with passport and visa regulations, foreign currency and exchange, climate and wardrobe, health requirements, customs regulations, baggage and accident insurance, traveler's checks or letters of credit, car rentals, tourist attractions, and welcome or tour services.

Many travel agents only sell tours that are developed by other organizations. The most skilled agents, however, often organize tours on a wholesale basis. This involves developing an itinerary; contracting a knowledgeable person to lead the tour; making tentative reservations for transportation, hotels, and side trips; publicizing the tour through descriptive brochures, advertisements, and other travel agents; scheduling reservations; and handling last-minute problems. Sometimes tours are arranged at the specific request of a group or to meet a client's particular needs.

In addition to other duties, travel agents may serve as *tour guides*, leading trips ranging from one week to six months to locations around the world. Agents often find tour leadership a useful way to gain personal travel experience. It also gives them the chance to become thoroughly acquainted with the people in the tour group, who may then use the agent to arrange future trips or recommend the agent to friends and relatives. Tour leaders are usually reimbursed for all their expenses or receive complimentary transportation and lodging. Most travel agents, however, arrange for someone to cover for them at work during their absence, which may make tour leadership prohibitive for self-employed agents.

Agents serve as bookkeepers to handle the complex pattern of transportation and hotel reservations that each trip entails. They work directly with airline, steamship, railroad, bus, and car rental companies. They make direct contact with hotels and sightseeing organizations or work indirectly through a receptive operator in the city involved. These arrangements require a great deal of accuracy because mistakes could result in a client being left stranded in a foreign or remote area. After reservations are made, agents write up or obtain tickets, write out itineraries, and send out bills for the reservations involved. They also send out confirmations to airlines, hotels, and other companies.

Travel agents must promote their services. They present PowerPoint presentations or videos to social and special interest groups, arrange advertising displays, and suggest company-sponsored trips to business managers. They often have a Web site that promotes their services. Many also use social media such as Facebook and Twitter to stay in touch with past and prospective clients.

■ EARNINGS

Travel agencies earn income from commissions paid by hotels, car rental companies, cruise lines, and tour operators. Due to the popularity of Internet travel sites, which enable customers to book their own flights, airlines no longer pay commissions to travel agents. This has been a big blow to those in this career, and it is a trend that will probably continue.

Travel agents typically earn a straight salary. In May 2015, salaries of travel agents ranged from $20,050 to $60,200, with a median annual wage of $35,660, according to the U.S. Department of Labor. In addition to experience level, the location of the firm is also a factor in how much travel agents earn. Agents working in larger metropolitan areas tend to earn more than their counterparts in smaller cities.

Small travel agencies provide a smaller-than-average number of fringe benefits such as retirement, medical, and life insurance plans. Self-employed agents tend to earn more than those who work for others, although the business risk is greater. Also, a self-employed agent may not see much money for the first year or two, since it often takes time to establish a client base that is large enough to make a profit. Those who own their own businesses may experience large fluctuations in income because the travel business is extremely sensitive to swings in the economy.

One of the benefits of working as a travel agent is the chance to travel at a discounted price. Major airlines offer special agent fares, which are often only 25 percent of the regular cost. Hotels, car rental companies, cruise lines, and tour operators also offer reduced rates for travel agents. Agents also get the opportunity to take free or low-cost group tours sponsored by transportation carriers, tour operators, and cruise lines. These trips, called "fam" trips, are designed to familiarize agents with locations and accommodations so that agents can better market them to their clients.

■ WORK ENVIRONMENT

The job of the travel agent is neither as simple nor as glamorous as some might expect. Travel is a highly competitive field. Since almost every travel agent can offer the client the same service, agents must depend on repeat customers for much of their business. Their reliability,

Travel agents assist clients with international paperwork, travel itineraries, accommodations, and group excursions. (Shutterstock. conejota.)

courtesy, and effectiveness in past transactions will determine whether they will get repeat business.

Travel agents also work in an atmosphere of keen competition for referrals. They must resist direct or indirect pressure from travel-related companies that have provided favors in the past (free trips, for example) and book all trips based only on the best interests of clients.

Most agents work a 40-hour week, although this frequently includes working a half-day on Saturday or an occasional evening. During busy seasons (typically from January through June), overtime may be necessary. Agents may receive additional salary for this work or be given compensatory time off.

As they gain experience, agents become more effective. One study revealed that 98 percent of all agents had more than three years' experience in some form of the travel field. Almost half had 20 years experience or more in this area.

■ EXPLORING

Any type of part-time experience with a travel agency is helpful in pursuing this career. A small agency may welcome help during peak travel seasons or when an agent is away from the office. If your high school or college arranges career conferences, you may be able to invite a speaker from the travel industry. Visits to local travel agents will also provide useful information.

Also consider joining the Future Travel Professionals Club, organized by the American Society of Travel Agents (ASTA). Membership offers networking opportunities with professional members of the ASTA, chapter meetings, eligibility for scholarships, and newsletters.

TRAVEL TALK

Airline Reporting Corporation (ARC): An autonomous corporation created by the domestic airlines that appoints travel agencies to sell airline tickets and oversees the financial details of tracking payments to airlines and commission fees to agencies.

Booking: A reservation.

Coach: The economy class on an airline.

Computerized reservation system (CRS): Also known as global distribution system. Any of several computer systems allowing immediate access to fares, schedules, and availability and offering the capability of making reservations and generating tickets. The most commonly used are Amadeus, Sabre, and Travelport.

Confirmation number: An alphanumeric code used to identify and document the confirmation of a booking.

Destination: A place where the traveler is going.

Fam: Abbreviation for "familiarization" trip or tour. A low-cost trip or tour offered to travel agents by a supplier or group of suppliers to familiarize the agents with their destination and services.

Layover: A stop on a trip, usually associated with a change of planes or other transportation.

Luxury class: The most expensive accommodations or fare category.

Satellite ticket printer: A ticket printer that generates airline tickets in an ARC-accredited travel agency.

■ EDUCATION AND TRAINING REQUIREMENTS
High School

A high school diploma is the minimum requirement for becoming a travel agent. Be certain to take computer science courses, as well as typing or keyboarding courses. Since much of the travel agent's job involves computerized reservation systems, it is important to have effective keyboarding skills and to be comfortable working with computers.

Clear communication skills are central to this job, so classes in English or speech are useful. Proficiency in a foreign language is also helpful for work with international travelers. Travel agents who own their own businesses need to market their services to potential customers, so it's a good idea to take advertising and marketing classes. Geography, social studies, and business mathematics are classes that may also help prepare you for various aspects of the travel agent's work.

You can also begin learning about being a travel agent while still in high school by getting a summer or part-time job in travel and tourism. If finding a part-time or summer job in a travel agency proves impossible, you might consider looking for a job as a reservation agent for an airline, rental car agency, or hotel.

Postsecondary Training

Travel courses are available from certain colleges, private vocational schools, and adult education programs in public high schools. Some colleges and universities grant bachelor's and master's degrees in travel and tourism. College training is not required for work as a travel agent, but it can be very helpful and is expected to become increasingly important. It is predicted that in the future most agents will be college graduates. Travel schools provide basic reservation training and other training related to travel agents' functions, which is helpful but not required.

A liberal arts or business administration background is recommended for a career in this field. Useful liberal arts courses include foreign languages, geography, English, communications, history, anthropology, political science, art and music appreciation, and literature. Pertinent business courses include transportation, business law, hotel management, marketing, office management, and accounting. As in many other fields, computer skills are increasingly important.

Certification

The Global Business Travel Association offers a certificate program at locations around the world.

Other Education or Training

The American Society of Travel Agents offers a variety of continuing education classes and webinars, including those that help agents to become specialists in particular countries (such as Jordan and Turkey) or areas (such as North American rail travel). The Travel Institute offers travel agents a number of educational programs such as sales skills development courses and destination specialist courses, which provide a detailed knowledge of various geographic regions of the world. The Global Business Travel Association, National Association of Career Travel Agents, The Travel Institute, and the Society of Government Travel Professionals also offer continuing education classes.

■ CERTIFICATION, LICENSING, AND SPECIAL REQUIREMENTS
Certification or Licensing

To be able to sell passage on various types of transportation, travel agents must be approved by the conferences of carriers involved. These are the Airlines Reporting Corporation, the International Air Transport Association, and the Cruise Lines International Association. To sell tickets for these individual conferences, travel agents must be clearly established in the travel business and have a good personal and business background. Not all travel agents are authorized to sell passage by all of the above conferences. Those who wish to sell the widest range of services should seek affiliation with all three.

Travel agents may choose to become certified by The Travel Institute. The institute offers the designations of certified travel associate, certified travel counselor, and certified travel industry executive to applicants who complete education and experience requirements. Certification is not required but can help travel agents advance in their careers.

The Society of Government Travel Professionals offers the certified government travel professional designation. The Global Business Travel Association provides the global travel professional certification.

Some states require travel agents to be licensed or registered, so it is important to check the requirements for the state in which you plan to work.

■ EXPERIENCE, SKILLS, AND PERSONALITY TRAITS

Aspiring travel agents should try to obtain experience in customer service or actual work at a travel agency via internships, part-time jobs, or volunteer opportunities. Some agencies prefer to hire applicants with experience visiting a particular country or region.

The primary requisite for success in the travel field is a sincere interest in travel. A travel agent's knowledge of and travel experiences with major tourist centers, various hotels, and local customs and points of interest makes them a more effective and convincing source of assistance. Yet the work of travel agents is not one long vacation. They operate in a highly competitive industry.

Travel agents must be able to make quick and accurate use of transportation schedules and tariffs. They must be able to handle addition and subtraction quickly. Almost all agents make use of computers and the Internet to get the very latest information on rates and schedules and to make reservations.

You will work with a wide range of personalities as a travel agent, so skills in psychology and diplomacy are important. You must also be able to generate enthusiasm among your customers and be resourceful in solving any problems that might arise. Knowledge of foreign languages is useful because many customers come from other countries, and you will be in frequent contact with foreign hotels and travel agencies.

■ EMPLOYMENT PROSPECTS
Employers

There are about 66,560 travel agents employed in the United States. Agents may work for commercial travel agents, work in the corporate travel department of a large company, or be self-employed. About 10 percent of agents are self-employed.

In addition to the regular travel business, a number of travel jobs are available with oil companies, automobile clubs, and transportation companies. Some jobs in travel are on the staffs of state and local governments seeking to encourage tourism.

Starting Out

Travel agents may begin by working for companies that are involved with transportation and tourism. A number of positions exist that are particularly appropriate for people who are young and with limited work experience. Airlines, for example, hire flight attendants, reservation agents, and ticket clerks. Railroads and cruise line companies also have clerical positions; the rise in their popularity in recent years has resulted in more job opportunities. Those with travel experience may secure positions as tour guides. Organizations and companies with extensive travel operations may hire employees whose main responsibility is making travel arrangements.

Travel agencies tend to have relatively small staffs, so most openings are filled as a result of direct application and personal contact. While evaluating the merits of various travel agencies, you may wish to note whether the agency's owner belongs to the American Society of Travel Agents (ASTA). This trade group may also help provide career-support resources and job referrals.

■ ADVANCEMENT PROSPECTS

Advancement opportunities within the travel field are limited to growth in terms of business volume or extent of specialization. Successful agents, for example, may hire additional employees or set up branch offices. A travel agency worker with several years of experience may be promoted to become a *travel assistant*. Travel assistants are responsible for answering general questions about transportation, providing current costs of hotel accommodations, and providing other information.

Travel agents may also advance to work as a *corporate travel manager*. Corporate travel managers work for companies, not travel agencies. They book all business travel for a company's employees.

Travel bureau employees may decide to go into business for themselves. Agents may show their professional status by belonging to the American Society of Travel Agents.

▒ OUTLOOK

The U.S. Department of Labor predicts that employment for travel agents will decline by 12 percent through 2024. Most airlines and other travel suppliers now offer consumers the option of making their own travel arrangements through online reservation services, which are readily accessible through the Internet. Travelers are becoming less dependent on agents to make travel arrangements for them. Additionally, airlines have eliminated the flat commission they pay travel agencies. This has reduced the income of many agencies, thereby making them less profitable and less able to hire new travel agents.

Agents who specialize in niche services, such as arranging travel for the corporate world or providing services to disabled travelers or those seeking adventure travel itineraries, will have the best job prospects. There will also be opportunities to plan tour services for foreign visitors vacationing in the United States, and to arrange frequent trips for businesses with overseas offices. Despite the challenges travel agents face, there are still some people who prefer their services over online booking, as they appreciate the efficiency, value, professional knowledge, and face-to-face contact that travel agents provide.

▒ UNIONS AND ASSOCIATIONS

Travel agents are not represented by unions. Major professional associations for travel agents include the American Society of Travel Agents, Global Business Travel Association, National Association of Career Travel Agents, Society of Government Travel Professionals, and The Travel Institute. The U.S. Travel Association provides statistics and other data on travel industry trends.

▒ TIPS FOR ENTRY

1. Visit the publications section of the American Society of Travel Agents' Web site (http://www.asta.org/Publications/index.cfm?navItem Number=11187) to learn more about trends in the industry and potential employers.
2. Visit http://careers.asta.org/jobs for job listings.
3. Join professional associations such as the American Society of Travel Agents to access training and networking resources, industry publications, and employment opportunities.

▒ FOR MORE INFORMATION

The American Society of Travel Agents offers advocacy, education, events, and other resources for travel agents.

American Society of Travel Agents (ASTA)
675 North Washington Street, Suite 490
Alexandria, VA 22314-1934

Tel: (800) 275-2782
E-mail: askasta@asta.org
http://www.asta.org

The Global Business Travel Association provides information on membership, certification, and continuing education.

Global Business Travel Association (GBTA)
123 North Pitt Street
Alexandria, VA 22314-3128
Tel: (703) 684-0836
Fax: (703) 342-4324
E-mail: info@gbta.org
http://www.gbta.org

The National Association of Career Travel Agents, associated with American Society of Travel Agents, represents independent contractors, cruise and tour oriented agents, outside sales agents, and group-oriented travel professionals.

National Association of Career Travel Agents (NACTA)
675 North Washington Street, Suite 490
Alexandria, VA 22314-1934
Tel: (877) 22-NACTA
E-mail: nacta@nacta.com
http://nacta.com

The Society of Government Travel Professionals provides membership benefits, education, and certification for travel professionals.

Society of Government Travel Professionals (SGTP)
PO Box 158
Glyndon, MD 21071-0158
Tel: (202) 241-7487
Fax: (202) 379-1775
http://www.sgtp.org

The Travel Institute provides education and certification programs for travel professionals.

The Travel Institute
945 Concord Street
Framingham, MA 01701-4613
Tel: (800) 542-4282; (781) 237-0280
Fax: (781) 237-3860
http://www.thetravelinstitute.com

The U.S. Travel Association provides events, programs, research, and other information about the U.S. travel and tourism industry.

U.S. Travel Association

1100 New York Avenue, NW, Suite 450

Washington, D.C. 20005-3934

Tel: (202) 408-8422

Fax: (202) 408-1255

https://www.ustravel.org

Truck Dispatchers

■ OVERVIEW

Truck dispatchers coordinate and manage the schedules of truck drivers to ensure products and goods are picked up and delivered in a timely manner. They receive calls for truck services and contact their fleet of truck drivers to arrange the pickups and deliveries. They maintain contact with truck drivers throughout their routes to monitor their progress and to troubleshoot any problems that may arise along the way. They relay information to customers to keep them informed of delivery dates and time estimates. They may work for local or regional trucking companies, either alone or in a team of dispatchers, depending on the size of the company. The Department of Labor reports that there are 196,940 dispatchers employed in the United States.

■ HISTORY

In 1898, the first semi-truck was introduced to the market by Alexandar Winton in Cleveland, Ohio. Prior to trucks, goods and products were delivered by horse-drawn carriages. Winton came up with the idea for the semi so that he could deliver cars that he had manufactured to various locations throughout the United States. The military used trucks in World War I. The trucking industry grew quickly after the war as the government invested money into paving more roads throughout the country.

The 1935 Motor Carrier Act was established to regulate the trucking industry. In the 1950s, the Interstate Highway System was built, with highways and freeways connecting more cities across the United States and increasing the demand for trucks. In 1980, Congress deregulated the trucking industry.

Today there are many different types of trucking companies, from small companies with several trucks for local deliveries to large companies with thousands of trucks that handle cross-country deliveries. Truck dispatchers now use computers, smartphones, tablets, and other mobile devices to arrange and monitor freight and cargo deliveries.

QUICK FACTS

ALTERNATE TITLE(S)
Tour Guides, Tour Organizers, Travel Consultants, Travel Guides

DUTIES
Arrange and coordinate truck drivers and trucks for cargo and freight pickups and deliveries; ensure proper truck driver certification and licensing; maintain contact with customers by phone and e-mail; monitor trucks and schedules by using GPS and satellite tracking technology; troubleshoot problems that may arise.

SALARY RANGE
$22,430 to $37,150 to $61,780+

WORK ENVIRONMENT
Primarily Indoors

BEST GEOGRAPHIC LOCATION(S)
Opportunities exist in all regions with highest demand in New York, Los Angeles, Houston, Chicago, Phoenix, Dallas, Atlanta, and Minneapolis

MINIMUM EDUCATION LEVEL
Associate's Degree

SCHOOL SUBJECTS
Business, Geography, Mathematics

EXPERIENCE
On-the-job training (junior level); several years experience

PERSONALITY TRAITS
Hands On, Organized, Problem-Solving

SKILLS
Business Management, Interpersonal, Organizational

CERTIFICATION OR LICENSING
None

SPECIAL REQUIREMENTS
None

EMPLOYMENT PROSPECTS
Fair

ADVANCEMENT PROSPECTS
Fair

OUTLOOK
Little Change or More Slowly than the Average

NOC
1525

O*NET-SOC
43-5032.00

■ THE JOB

Truck dispatchers assign truck drivers to pick up and deliver freight and cargo according to established schedules. They may arrange for local transport if they work for

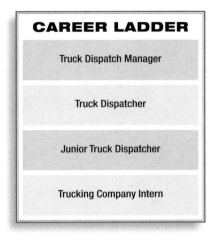

CAREER LADDER

Truck Dispatch Manager

Truck Dispatcher

Junior Truck Dispatcher

Trucking Company Intern

a local trucking company or they may coordinate drivers and schedules for multiple-day trucking in long-haul rigs. They take truck service orders from customers and communicate with them through phone calls and e-mail. The job requires strong communication and organizational skills, especially with keeping recording and tracking freight orders. Dispatchers make sure the truck trailers are filled by consolidating the freight orders, to make the trip as cost-efficient as possible. They also make sure that truck drivers are certified and have the appropriate licensing, particularly to meet specialized freight load transportation requirements. Truck dispatchers use computers, mobile devices, and satellite tracking systems and global positioning system (GPS) technology to monitor the progress of trucks during their delivery routes. They help troubleshoot problems that may arise during the route, such as truck breakdowns, traffic or weather issues, or changes in delivery dates or locations. Truck dispatchers may work alone or they may work in a team, reporting to a dispatch manager or supervisor.

■ EARNINGS

The Department of Labor reported that the average annual salary for dispatchers was $37,150 in May 2015. The lowest 10 percent earned $22,430 and the highest 10 percent earned $61,780 or more. Dispatchers who worked in general freight trucking earned an average of $41,430 per year, which translates to $19.92 per hour. Specialized freight trucking dispatchers had slightly higher incomes: Their average annual salary was $43,620, or $20.97 per hour. Payscale.com reported the median salary for trucking and transportation fleet dispatchers in January 2016 was $41,926, with salaries ranging from $25,023 to more than $56,952.

■ WORK ENVIRONMENT

Truck dispatchers work in trucking company offices and sit for much of their workday. Some independent truck dispatchers may work from their home office. No matter where they work, they use computers, phones, smartphones, and mobile devices. They spend much of their time speaking on the phone with customers and truck drivers, and using computers to arrange trucking schedules and to monitor truck routes. Coordinating schedules

and drivers to meet customers' needs can be stressful, particularly when problems arise that can cause delays in pickups and deliveries. Truck dispatchers may also experience eyestrain and have physical problems from the long hours of sitting and staring at computer screens.

■ EXPLORING

Learn more about the dispatching field by working part-time in a trucking company. An entry-level customer service position is a good way to gain exposure to the types of services a trucking company provides, the clients who use these services, and types of trucks and truck drivers that are used in the business. Another way to explore the field is by visiting the Web sites of various trucking companies. You can find companies by using a search engine and key words such as "top trucking companies."

■ EDUCATION AND TRAINING REQUIREMENTS
High School

Classes in business, English, and math are a good foundation for this field. These subjects help provide students with the organizational, communications, and accounting skills that are needed in trucking dispatch work.

Postsecondary Education

Formal education is not required for most truck dispatcher jobs but applicants with an associate's or bachelor's degree improve their prospects for work. Courses in business, management, accounting, English, and communications provide a good foundation for this field. Classes in computers are also useful.

■ CERTIFICATION, LICENSING, AND SPECIAL REQUIREMENTS

There are no certification or licensing requirements for truck dispatchers.

■ EXPERIENCE, SKILLS, AND PERSONALITY TRAITS

Truck dispatchers must be organized, have clear communication skills, and be able to solve problems quickly and efficiently. There is no specific career track for this job, but some dispatchers have prior experience as junior dispatchers or even as truck drivers. They must be vigilant in staying on top of schedules and monitoring truck drivers' progress throughout the pickup and delivery phases. Knowledge of tracking dispatch software and satellite and global positioning systems is useful. The job also requires strong knowledge of the trucking company's policies and procedures as well as the shipping and driving rules and regulations for both local and regional areas. Truck dispatchers must know the roads and highways they're dispatching trucks to. In addition to all of these skills and knowledge, employers seek dispatchers who are detail oriented, particularly in keeping records of trucking deliveries and pickups for billing. Many trucking companies offer on-the-job training for dispatchers.

■ EMPLOYMENT PROSPECTS
Employers
Truck dispatchers work in local and regional trucking, transportation, and freight companies. They are employed by companies such as United Parcel Service, FedEx, YRC Freight, Schneider National, Roadway Moving, and Crete Carrier Corporation, to name just a few.

Starting Out
Many trucking companies train dispatchers while they are on the job. They also provide dispatch manuals for dispatchers to study and use as reference for the work. Dispatchers may start out in other departments of the trucking company before moving into dispatch. In large trucking companies with a dispatch team, entry may be as a junior or assistant dispatcher.

■ ADVANCEMENT PROSPECTS
Truck dispatchers with four to five years of experience in successfully managing truck deliveries and pickups may advance to senior truck dispatcher or dispatch supervisor positions. They may move up to manage the dispatch department in large trucking and freight companies. They may also move into other senior-level and management roles in the trucking business.

■ OUTLOOK
The Department of Labor (DOL) predicts about 5 percent employment growth in the transportation and material moving industry through 2024. Truck dispatchers will have 4 percent employment growth, which is slower than the average for all other occupations. The DOL also projected that 8,000 new dispatcher jobs will be added between 2014 and 2024. Trucking and transportation companies will continue to need dispatchers to manage and oversee their fleets and delivery schedules. Dispatchers who are flexible to work evening and weekend hours will have better chances of securing work than those who can only work weekday business hours.

■ UNIONS AND ASSOCIATIONS
The American Trucking Associations is a national trade association that provides trucking industry professionals, including dispatchers, access to news, information

TRUCKING INDUSTRY FACTS   DID YOU KNOW?

The trucking industry is a multi-billion dollar business in the United States. As of July 2016, the local freight trucking industry generated $41 billion in revenue. There are nearly 210,000 local trucking businesses that employ more than 263,000 workers. Trucking companies that operate in local freight transport a variety of commodities, most of which are put onto pallets and transported in a container or van trailer. They operate within metropolitan areas, sometimes crossing state lines, but the trips are usually completed within the same day. Local specialized trucking is a $42 billion business, with nearly 57,000 organizations and more than 250,000 workers. Specialized trucking provides specialized transportation for cargo that requires special treatment, such as bulk liquids and gasses and agricultural products.

The biggest income generator in the trucking industry is long-distance freight trucking, which, as of September 2016, generated $182 billion in revenue. There are 360,032 companies and nearly 1.1 million employees in the long-distance freight trucking industry. Long-distance trucks transport various goods and materials between metropolitan areas and regions, often traveling across North American country borders.

Source: IBISWorld

on trends in the trucking business, and industry-related conferences and events. The Federal Motor Carrier Safety Administration enforces safety carrier regulations and works closely with government agencies, the motor carrier industry, and others. The National Association of Small Trucking Companies offers a variety of educational programs, safety and training programs, and networking opportunities for professionals in the small trucking business.

■ TIPS FOR ENTRY
1. Get an internship or part-time job in a trucking company. Working in the customer service department can introduce you to the trucking company's customers and services.
2. Visit trucking companies' Web sites to learn more about their history, products and services, staff, industry news, and employment opportunities.
3. Join a professional association such as the American Trucking Associations for access to educational programs and career support.

■ FOR MORE INFORMATION

The American Trucking Associations provides advocacy and education for trucking industry professionals and policymakers.

American Trucking Associations (ATA)
950 North Glebe Road, Suite 210
Arlington, VA 22203-4181
Tel: (703) 838-1700
E-mail: atamembership@trucking.org
http://www.trucking.org

The Federal Motor Carrier Safety Administration has a mission to ensure safety in motor carrier operations through enforcement of safety regulations.

Federal Motor Carrier Safety Administration (FMCSA)
1200 New Jersey Avenue, SE
Washington, D.C. 20590-3550
Tel: (800) 832-5660
https://www.fmcsa.dot.gov

The National Association of Small Trucking Companies provides advocacy, lobbying, and other services for its small trucking company members.

National Association of Small Trucking Companies (NASTC)
2054 Nashville PIke
Gallatin, TN 37066-3161
Tel: (800) 264-8580; (615) 451-4555
Fax: (615) 451-0041
http://nastc.com

Truck Drivers

■ OVERVIEW

Truck drivers generally are distinguished by the distance they travel. *Over-the-road drivers*, also known as *long-distance drivers* or *tractor-trailer drivers*, haul freight over long distances in large trucks and tractor-trailer rigs that are usually diesel-powered. Depending on the specific operation, over-the-road drivers also load and unload the shipments and make minor repairs to vehicles. *Short-haul drivers* or *pickup and delivery drivers* operate trucks that transport materials, merchandise, and equipment within a limited area, usually a single city or metropolitan area. There are nearly 1.7 million heavy and tractor-trailer truck drivers and 826,510 light truck or delivery service drivers employed in the United States.

■ HISTORY

The first trucks were nothing more than converted automobiles. In 1904, there were only about 500 trucks in the United States. At that time, there was little need for goods to be transported across the country. Manufacturing was such that the same products were produced all over the nation, many in small "mom and pop" operations so that even small towns could supply all the food, clothing, tools, and other materials that people needed. Today, manufacturing is centralized and "mom and pop" stores are all but gone, increasing the need for a way to move consumer goods to every corner of the country.

In World War I, the U.S. Army used trucks for the first time to haul equipment and supplies over terrain that was not accessible by train. After the war, the domestic use of trucks increased rapidly. In the 1920s, the nation became more mobile as streets and highways improved. American businesses and industries were growing at an unprecedented rate, and trucks became established as a reliable way of transporting goods. In fact, trucking companies began to compete with railroads for the business of shipping freight long distances.

Since World War II, other innovations have shaped the trucking industry, including improvements in the designs of truck bodies and the mechanical systems in trucks. Tank trucks were built to carry fuel, and other trucks were designed specifically for transporting livestock, produce, milk, eggs, meat, and heavy machine parts. The efficiency of trucks was further increased by the development of the detachable trailer. Depending on what needed to be shipped, a different trailer could be hooked up to the tractor.

In addition to these technological advances, the establishment of the interstate highway system in 1956 allowed trucks to deliver shipments with increased efficiency. Along with the development of new trucks with better gas mileage, trucking companies now could offer their services to businesses at cheaper rates than railroads.

Trucking today is central to the nation's transportation system, moving dry freight, refrigerated materials, liquid bulk materials, construction materials, livestock, household goods, and other cargo. In fact, nearly all goods are transported by truck at some point after they are produced. Some drivers move manufactured goods from factories to distribution terminals, and after the goods arrive at destination terminals, other drivers deliver the goods to stores and homes. Certain carriers also provide shipping services directly from the supplier to the customer.

■ THE JOB

Truckers drive trucks of all sizes, from small straight trucks and vans to tanker trucks and tractors with multiple trailers. The average tractor-trailer rig is no more than 102 inches wide, excluding the mirrors, 13 feet and six inches tall, and just under 70 feet in length. The engines in these vehicles range from 250 to 600 horsepower.

Over-the-road drivers operate tractor-trailers and other large trucks that are often diesel-powered. These drivers generally haul goods and materials over long distances and frequently drive at night. Whereas many other truck drivers spend a considerable portion of their time loading and unloading materials, over-the-road drivers spend most of their working time driving.

Drivers start their preparations for long-distance runs at the terminal or warehouse where they receive their load. They check over the vehicle to make sure all the equipment and systems are functioning and that the truck is loaded properly and has the necessary fuel, oil, and safety equipment.

Some over-the-road drivers travel the same routes repeatedly and on a regular schedule. Other companies require drivers to do unscheduled runs and work when dispatchers call with an available job. Some long-distance runs are short enough that drivers can get to the destination, remove the load from the trailer, replace it with another load, and return home all in one day. Many runs, however, take up to a week or longer, with various stops. Some companies assign two drivers to long runs, so that one can sleep while the other drives. This method ensures that the trip will take the shortest amount of time possible.

In addition to driving their trucks long distances, over-the-road drivers have other duties. They must inspect their vehicles before and after trips, prepare reports on accidents, and keep daily logs. They may load and unload some shipments or hire workers to help with these tasks at the destination. Drivers of long-distance moving vans, for example, do more loading and unloading work than most other long-haul drivers. Drivers of vehicle-transport trailer trucks move new automobiles or trucks from manufacturers to dealers and also have additional duties. At the plants where the vehicles are made, transport drivers drive new vehicles onto the ramps of transport trailers. They secure the vehicles in place with chains and clamps to prevent them from swaying and rolling. After driving to the destination, the drivers remove the vehicles from the trailers.

Over-the-road drivers must develop a number of skills that differ from the skills needed for operating smaller trucks. Trailer trucks vary in length and number of wheels, so skilled operators of one type of trailer may need to undergo a short training period if they switch to a new type of trailer. Over-the-road drivers must be able to maneuver and judge the position of their trucks and must be able to back their huge trailers into precise positions.

Local truck drivers generally operate the smaller trucks and transport a variety of products. They may travel regular routes or routes that change as needed. Local drivers include delivery workers who supply fresh produce to grocery stores and drivers who deliver gasoline in tank trucks to gas stations. Other local truck drivers, such as those who keep stores stocked with baked goods, may sell their employers' products as well as deliver them to customers along a route. These drivers are known as *route drivers* or *route-sales drivers*.

Often local truck drivers receive their assignments and delivery forms from dispatchers at the company terminal each day. Some drivers load goods or materials on their trucks, but in many situations dockworkers have already loaded the trucks in such a way that the unloading can be accomplished along the route with maximum convenience and efficiency.

Local drivers must be skilled at maneuvering their vehicles through the worst driving conditions, including bad weather and traffic-congested areas. The ability to pull into tight parking spaces, negotiate narrow passageways, and back up to loading docks is essential.

Some drivers have *helpers* who travel with them and assist in unloading at delivery sites, especially if the loads are heavy or bulky or when there are many deliveries scheduled. Drivers of some heavy trucks, such as dump trucks and oil

CAREER LADDER

Owner-Operator

Driver Supervisor, or Dispatcher, or Terminal Manager

Over-the-Road Driver

Local Truck Driver

Driver Helper

tank trucks, operate mechanical levers, pedals, and other devices that assist with loading and unloading cargo. Drivers of moving vans generally have a crew of helpers to aid in loading and unloading customers' household goods and office equipment.

Once a local driver reaches the destination, they sometimes obtain a signature acknowledging that the delivery has been made and may collect a payment from the customer. Some drivers serve as intermediaries between the company and its customers by responding to customer complaints and requests.

Each day, local drivers have to make sure that their deliveries have been made correctly. At the end of the day, they turn in their records and the money they collected. Local drivers may also be responsible for doing routine maintenance on their trucks to keep them in good working condition. Otherwise, any mechanical problems are reported to the maintenance department for repair.

■ EARNINGS

Wages of truck drivers vary according to their employer, size of the truck they drive, product being hauled, geographical region, and other factors. Drivers who are employed by for-hire carriers have higher earnings than those who work independently or for private carriers.

Pay rates for over-the-road truck drivers are often figured using a cents-per-mile rate. Most companies pay between 30 and 50 cents per mile, but large companies are advertising higher rates to attract good drivers. Drivers employed by J. B. Hunt, the nation's largest publicly held trucking company, can earn up to 90 cents a mile and earn an average of $1,000 a week.

Tractor-trailer drivers usually have the highest earnings; average hourly pay generally increases with the size of the truck. Drivers in many southern and mid-Atlantic states have lower earnings than those in the Northeast and West. The U.S. Department of Labor reports that median hourly earnings of heavy truck and tractor-trailer drivers were $19.36 ($40,260 annually) in May 2015. Wages ranged from less than $12.62 to more than $29.81 an hour (or from $26,240 to $62,010 a year for full-time

work). Median hourly earnings of light or delivery services truck drivers were $14.35 ($29,850 annually), and wages ranged from less than $9.07 to more than $29.01 an hour (or $18,860 to $60,350 a year). Median hourly earnings of driver/sales workers, including commission, were $10.79 ($22,450 annually), and wages ranged from less than $8.32 to more than $22.79 an hour (or $17,310 to $47,410 a year).

In addition to their wages, the majority of truck drivers receive benefits, many of which are determined by agreements between their unions and company management. The benefits may include health insurance coverage, pension plans, paid vacation days, and work uniforms.

■ WORK ENVIRONMENT

There is work for truck drivers in even the smallest towns, but most jobs are located in and around larger metropolitan areas. About a third of all drivers work for for-hire carriers, and another third work for private carriers. Some drivers are self-employed.

Driving trucks is often a tiring job, even with modern improvements in cab design. Some local drivers work 40-hour weeks; many work eight hours a day, six days a week, or more. Some drivers, such as those who bring food to grocery stores, often work at night or very early in the morning. Drivers who must load and unload their trucks may do a lot of lifting, stooping, and bending.

It is common for over-the-road truck drivers to work at least 50 hours a week. However, federal regulations require that drivers cannot be on duty for more than 60 hours in any seven-day period. After drivers have driven for 10 hours, they must be off duty for at least eight hours before they can drive again. Drivers often work the maximum allowed time to complete long runs in as little time as possible. In fact, most drivers drive 10 to 12 hours per day and make sure they have proper rest periods. A driver usually covers between 550 and 650 miles daily. The sustained driving, particularly at night, can be fatiguing, boring, and sometimes very stressful, as when traffic or weather conditions are bad.

Local drivers may operate on schedules that easily allow for a social and family life, but long-distance drivers often find that difficult. They may spend a considerable amount of time away from their homes and families, including weekends and holidays. After they try it, many people find they do not want this way of life. On the other hand, some people love the lifestyle of the over-the-road driver. Many families are able to find ways to work around the schedule of a truck-driving spouse. In some cases, the two people assigned to a long-distance run are a husband-and-wife team.

■ EXPLORING

High school students interested in becoming truck drivers may be able to gain experience by working as drivers' helpers during summer vacations or in part-time delivery jobs. Many people get useful experience in driving vehicles while they are serving in the armed forces. It may also be helpful to talk with employers of local or over-the-road truck drivers or with the drivers themselves.

The Internet provides a forum for prospective truck drivers to explore their career options. Two online magazines—*Overdrive* (http://www.etrucker.com) and *Land Line Magazine* (http://www.landlinemag.com)—review news and issues in the trucking industry and answer frequently asked questions for people interested in trucking careers.

■ EDUCATION AND TRAINING REQUIREMENTS
High School

High school students interested in working as truck drivers should take courses in driver training and automobile mechanics. In addition, some bookkeeping, mathematics, and business courses will teach methods that help in keeping accurate records of customer transactions.

Postsecondary Training

Drivers must know and meet the standards set by both state and federal governments for the particular work they do and the type of vehicle they drive. In some companies, new employees can informally learn the skills appropriate for the kind of driving they do from experienced drivers. They may ride with and watch other employees of the company, or they may take a few hours of their own time to learn from an experienced driver. For light truck driving jobs, companies may require new employees to attend classes that range from a few days to about a month. On-the-job training of one to three months is required for new heavy and tractor-trailer truck drivers.

One of the best ways to prepare for a job driving large trucks is to take a tractor-trailer driver training course. Programs vary in the amount of actual driving experience they provide. Programs that are certified by the Professional Truck Driver Institute meet established guidelines for training and generally provide good preparation for drivers. Another way to identify quality programs is to check with local companies that hire drivers and ask for their recommendations. Completing a certified training program helps potential truck drivers learn specific skills, but it does not guarantee a job. Vehicles and the freight inside trucks can represent a

A truck driver updates his log book. (Timothy Epp. Shutterstock.)

large investment to companies that employ truck drivers. Therefore, they seek to hire responsible and reliable drivers in order to protect their investment. For this reason, many employers set various requirements of their own that exceed state and federal standards.

■ CERTIFICATION, LICENSING, AND SPECIAL REQUIREMENTS
Certification or Licensing

Truck drivers must meet federal requirements and any requirements established by the state where they are based. All drivers must obtain a state commercial driver's license. Truck drivers involved in interstate commerce must meet requirements of the U.S. Department of Transportation.

Other Requirements

Candidates must be at least 21 years old and pass a physical examination that requires good vision and hearing, normal blood pressure, and normal use of arms and legs (unless the applicant qualifies for a waiver). Drivers must then pass physicals every two years and meet other requirements, including a minimum of 20/40 vision in each eye and no diagnosis of insulin-dependent diabetes or epilepsy.

■ EXPERIENCE, SKILLS, AND PERSONALITY TRAITS

No experience is needed to work as a truck driver, but those with prior work experience will increase their chances of landing a job, getting promoted, and possibly earning higher pay.

Many drivers work with little supervision, so they need to have a mature, responsible attitude toward their job. In jobs where drivers deal directly with company

No-Zones

Safety is a major concern for truck drivers and should also be for the drivers they share the road with. That's why the Federal Highway Administration launched a campaign to educate other drivers about truck drivers' blind spots and how to avoid them. No-zones are the danger areas around commercial vehicles where crashes are more likely to occur. For example, a truck has a much larger blind spot on both of its sides than a car. When other drivers drive in these no-zones for any length of time, truck drivers can't see them. Also, when cars cut in too soon after passing, then abruptly slow down, truck drivers are forced to compensate with little time or room to spare.

Many trucks carry signs on the back that warn other drivers of wide right turns. Truck drivers sometimes need to swing wide to the left in order to safely negotiate a right turn. Rear blind spots are also a problem because trucks, unlike cars, have deep blind spots directly behind them. A truck driver can't see cars in this position, and the car driver's view of traffic is also severely reduced. Generally speaking, the bigger the truck,

- the bigger its blindspots
- the more room it needs to maneuver
- the longer it takes to stop
- the longer it takes to pass it
- the more likely the car will be the loser in a collision

customers, it is especially important for the drivers to be pleasant, courteous, and able to communicate well with people. Helping a customer with a complaint can mean the difference between losing and keeping a client.

■ EMPLOYMENT PROSPECTS

Employers

Nearly 1.7 million heavy and tractor-trailer truck drivers and 826,510 light truck or delivery services drivers are employed in the United States. Over-the-road and local drivers may be employed by either private carriers or for-hire carriers. Food store chains and manufacturing plants that transport their own goods are examples of private carriers. There are two kinds of for-hire carriers: trucking companies serving the general public (common carriers) and trucking firms transporting goods under contract to certain companies (contract carriers).

Drivers who work independently are known as *owner-operators*. They own their own vehicles and often do their own maintenance and repair work. They must find customers who need goods transported, perhaps through

personal references or by advertising their services. For example, many drivers find contract jobs through "Internet truck stops," where drivers can advertise their services and companies can post locations of loads they need transported. Some independent drivers establish long-term contracts with just one or two clients, such as trucking companies.

Starting Out

Prospective over-the-road drivers can gain commercial driving experience as local truck drivers and then attend a tractor-trailer driver-training program. Driving an intercity bus or dump truck is also suitable experience for aspiring over-the-road truck drivers. Many newly hired long-distance drivers start by filling in for regular drivers or helping out when extra trips are necessary. They are assigned regular work when a job opens up.

Many truck drivers hold other jobs before they become truck drivers. Some local drivers start as *drivers' helpers*, loading and unloading trucks and gradually taking over some driving duties. When a better driving position opens up, helpers who have shown they are reliable and responsible may be promoted. Members of the armed forces who have gained appropriate experience may get driving jobs when they are discharged.

Job seekers may apply directly to firms that use drivers. Listings of specific job openings are often posted at local offices of the state employment service and through employment agency Web sites. Many jobs, however, are not posted. Looking in the Yellow Pages under trucking and moving and storage can provide names of specific companies to solicit. Also, large manufacturers and retailing companies sometimes have their own fleets. Contact them directly by e-mail or phone. Personal visits, when appropriate, sometimes get the best results.

■ ADVANCEMENT PROSPECTS

Some over-the-road drivers who stay with their employers advance by becoming *safety supervisors, driver supervisors,* or *dispatchers*. Many over-the-road drivers look forward to going into business for themselves by acquiring their own tractor-trailer rigs. This step requires a significant initial investment and a continuing good income to cover expenses. Like many other small business owners, *independent drivers* sometimes have a hard time financially. Those who are their own mechanics and have formal business training are in the best position to do well.

Local truck drivers can advance by learning to drive specialized kinds of trucks or by acquiring better schedules or other job conditions. Some may move into positions as dispatchers and, with sufficient experience, they eventually become supervisors or terminal managers.

Other local drivers decide to become over-the-road drivers to receive higher wages.

■ OUTLOOK

Employment for heavy and tractor-trailer truck drivers is expected to increase about as fast as the average rate for all other occupations through 2024, according to the U.S. Department of Labor. Job opportunities are expected to remain strong for drivers in the oil and gas extraction and construction industries. Employment growth for light and delivery truck drivers will be slower than the average during this period as a result of improved routing technology that make drivers more productive.

The need for trucking services is directly linked to the growth of the nation's economy. During economic downturns, when the pace of business slows, some drivers may receive fewer assignments and thus have lower earnings, or they may be laid off. Drivers employed in some vital industries, such as food distribution, are less affected by an economic recession. On the other hand, people who own and operate their own trucks usually suffer the most.

A large number of driver jobs become available each year. Most openings develop when experienced drivers transfer to other fields or leave the workforce entirely. There is a considerable amount of turnover in the field. Beginners are able to get many of these jobs. Competition is expected to remain strong for the more desirable jobs, such as those with large companies or the easiest routes.

■ UNIONS AND ASSOCIATIONS

Some truck drivers may be members of the International Brotherhood of Teamsters and other unions. American Trucking Associations is a national trade association for the trucking industry; it consists of a federation of affiliated state trucking associations and industry-related conferences and councils. The Professional Truck Driver Institute certifies entry-level truck driver training courses and motor carrier driver-finishing programs.

■ TIPS FOR ENTRY

1. Visit http://www.landlinemag.com for job listings.
2. Contact trucking companies directly to learn more about job opportunities.
3. Talk to truck drivers about their careers. Ask them for advice on breaking into the field.

■ FOR MORE INFORMATION

The American Trucking Associations provides education, conferences, and other resources for the trucking industry.

American Trucking Associations (ATA)
950 North Glebe Road, Suite 210
Arlington, VA 22203-4181

COMMERCIAL DRIVER'S LICENSE   DID YOU KNOW?

The first step in becoming a truck driver is obtaining a commercial driver's license (CDL). The commercial driver's license test is not an easy one, and many people must take it more than once before they are successful. The written/computerized portion of the test consists of seven parts. They are: General Knowledge Test (all CDL applicants must take this test); Passenger Vehicle Test (for drivers who will be driving a vehicle with more than 15 people); Hazardous Material Test (required for hauling hazardous materials in quantities large enough to require placards); Doubles and Triples Test (required for Class A drivers pulling doubles and triples); Tank Vehicles Test (required if hauling tankers with liquids or gases); Combination Vehicle Test (to test a driver's knowledge of how to operate tractor-trailers and semitrailers) and Air Brake Test (required to operate vehicles with air brakes.) An example of a general knowledge question is: You should use your high beams: (A) at all times at night, (B) during the day but never at night, (C) any time when on a divided highway, and (D) whenever possible and when legal. [(D) is correct.]

The second part of the exam consists of a road test in which the test-taker is assessed by an experienced driver/proctor. The test proctor looks for how well the test-taker handles passing situations, turns in both directions, intersections, multi-lane roads, and railroad crossings.

Tel: (703) 838-1700
E-mail: atamembership@trucking.org
http://www.trucking.org

The International Brotherhood of Teamsters represents freight drivers, warehouse workers, and other trucking industry professionals.

International Brotherhood of Teamsters
25 Louisiana Avenue, NW
Washington, D.C. 20001-2130
Tel: (202) 624-6800
https://teamster.org

The Professional Truck Driver Institute offers education and certification programs for truck-driver training.

Professional Truck Driver Institute (PTDI)
2460 W 26th Ave, Ste. 245-C
Denver, CO 80211
Tel: (720) 575-7444
Fax: (720) 221-7242
E-mail: info@ptdi.org
http://www.ptdi.org

QUICK FACTS

ALTERNATE TITLE(S)
Mentors

DUTIES
Help students perform better in school (tutor); educate, train, and supervise tutors and mentors (trainer)

SALARY RANGE
$18,000 to $26,080 to $52,000+ (tutors); $55,850 to $102,640 to $180,360+ (trainers)

WORK ENVIRONMENT
Primarily Indoors

BEST GEOGRAPHIC LOCATION(S)
Opportunities available throughout the country

MINIMUM EDUCATION LEVEL
Bachelor's Degree

SCHOOL SUBJECTS
English, History, Mathematics

EXPERIENCE
Expertise or several years experience

PERSONALITY TRAITS
Hands On, Helpful, Social

SKILLS
Interpersonal, Public Speaking, Teaching

CERTIFICATION OR LICENSING
Recommended

SPECIAL REQUIREMENTS
None

EMPLOYMENT PROSPECTS
Good

ADVANCEMENT PROSPECTS
Good

OUTLOOK
About as Fast as the Average

NOC
4021, 4216

O*NET-SOC
13-1151.00, 25-3099.02

Tutors and Trainers

OVERVIEW

Tutors help people reach their full potential in many areas of study including reading, mathematics, and science. *Trainers* educate, train, and supervise tutors and other volunteers according to the mission of the organization to which they belong.

HISTORY

Tutors have helped people master academic subjects and learn life skills for thousands of years. They have helped those who would be kings, the children of politicians and noblemen, and more recently, the disadvantaged, attain knowledge and live better lives through education.

Tutors work for schools and private organizations to help students improve their study skills and master classroom concepts. Tutoring and mentoring youth rank among the five most-popular activities for volunteers, according to the Corporation for National and Community Service. Tutors have many different educational, vocational, and societal backgrounds. What they do have in common is a sense of obligation to help those challenged by their lack of education or financial or social status. Trainers educate tutors regarding proper teaching methods, as well as teach other volunteers about their organization's mission, goals, and services.

Many tutors and trainers belong to the National Tutoring Association (NTA), an organization representing tutors and trainers throughout the United States and 13 other countries.

THE JOB

Tutors work in various capacities. Many elementary schools, high schools, and for-profit schools employ tutors to help in the instruction of their students. Tutors encourage the understanding of standard school subjects such as reading and math, assist with questions regarding homework, and work to improve a student's level of literacy. More importantly, tutors help students develop good learning habits. Many tutors associated with schools are paid employees; most have college degrees applicable to the subjects they tutor, such as a degree in education, mathematics, or English.

Tutors may also find positions with community organizations, such as the YMCA, which has locations throughout the United States, or local special interest groups. Since many of these operations are nonprofit, tutors either volunteer or are paid a small hourly wage.

Colleges and universities also hire tutors to help students. For example, some schools may hire tutors to work with student athletes to help them gain a better understanding of their courses, and become more organized and independent learners. Academic success is important for all students, but more so with student athletes, since grades determine their athletic eligibility.

Mentors are specialized tutors who go beyond educational help and serve as advisers and role models for young people from disadvantaged backgrounds or others who may be new to a career or field of study.

Trainers work for educational centers, schools, and advocacy groups. They provide orientation, instruction, and scheduling for tutors, mentors, and other volunteers. Trainers prepare prospective tutors by teaching the basic concepts of tutoring, such as setting goals, lesson planning, communication skills, and positive reinforcement. They may also suggest different techniques based on the personality or age level of the student. For example, they may recommend that the tutor incorporate study with playtime for young children, and the use of multimedia technology with adults.

EARNINGS

Glassdoor.com reports that in November 2016, salaried tutors earned average salaries of $26,080. Earnings ranged from less than $18,000 to $52,000 or more.

According to the U.S. Department of Labor, training and development managers had median annual earnings of $102,640 in May 2015. The lowest-paid training and development managers earned less than $55,850 and the highest paid earned $180,360 or more. These salaries are mainly for those employed by for-profit companies; trainers who work for nonprofits have much lower earnings.

Full-time tutors and trainers may receive benefits such as paid vacation days, sick leave, and health insurance.

■ WORK ENVIRONMENT

Tutors often need to travel in order to meet their students—especially if the student is a child without the means for transportation. They often meet at a mutually designated location, such as a classroom, library, bookstore, or at a tutoring center. Meeting places should be comfortable for both the student and tutor, and provide a quiet environment in which to learn. Some tutors may take their students on field trips to museums, zoos, workplaces, or cultural events to enhance a lesson. Trainers typically work in comfortable office settings, but may travel offsite to monitor the work of tutors.

■ EXPLORING

One way to begin exploring this field now is to talk to someone who is a tutor or trainer. Ask the following questions: What are your primary and secondary job duties? What are the typical work hours? What do you like most and least about your job? How did you train for this field? What advice would you give to young people who are interested in this career? Also get involved in speech or drama clubs. Any experiences that you can get doing presentations or performing in front of a group will help you prepare for the field. Finally, volunteer to work as a tutor at your school or for a local community organization, or mentor a younger child at your school. This will give you a chance to learn about these careers while helping someone improve their academic and life skills.

■ EDUCATION AND TRAINING REQUIREMENTS
High School

Take a well-rounded college preparatory curriculum. If you know the field that you'd like to tutor in, take as many classes as you can in that subject. For example, if you want to eventually tutor in math, take algebra, geometry, calculus, and any other math classes that are available. Taking speech and English courses will also help you hone communication skills, which will be important when you work with students. Taking a foreign language, such as Spanish, will help you to work with those who do not speak English as a first language.

Postsecondary Training

Tutors and trainers have a variety of educational backgrounds. Most tutors have a bachelor's degree or higher—usually in a field that is related to the area in which they tutor.

Other Education or Training

The National Tutoring Association offers specialized workshops to help tutors keep their skills up to date. Past workshops included: "Implementing The Common Core Standards: Practical Strategies & Effective Lessons," "Understanding Learning Preferences and The Holistic Dialogue," "Mathematics Workshop: Pathway To Competence," and "Tutors: Understanding Compassion Fatigue." The Association for Talent Development also provides continuing education classes and webinars.

CAREER LADDER

Director of Tutoring

Trainer

Tutor

■ CERTIFICATION, LICENSING, AND SPECIAL REQUIREMENTS
Certification or Licensing

Certification is not required to work as a tutor or trainer but can enhance skills and employment opportunities. The National Tutoring Association and the Association for Talent Development offer voluntary certifications to tutors and related professionals.

■ EXPERIENCE, SKILLS, AND PERSONALITY TRAITS

Any experience teaching young people that you can obtain while in school will be useful in these careers. Trainers usually have several years of experience as tutors.

A tutor helps a students with homework. (Black Rock Digital. Shutterstock.)

TUTORING AND MENTORING BASICS

LEARN MORE ABOUT IT

Chin, Tiffani, Jerome Rabow, and Jeimee Estrada. *Tutoring Matters: Everything You Always Wanted to Know About How to Tutor,* 2nd ed. Philadelphia: Temple University Press, 2011.

Garvey, Bob, Paul Stokes, and David Megginson. *Coaching and Mentoring: Theory and Practice,* 2nd ed. Thousand Oaks, Calif.: SAGE Publications Ltd., 2014.

Guptan, Sunil Unny. *Mentoring: A Practitioners Guide to Touching Lives.* Thousand Oaks, Calif.: SAGE Publications Ltd., 2014.

Lipsky, Sally A. *A Training Guide for College Tutors and Peer Educators.* Hoboken, N.J.: Pearson, 2015.

O'Rourke, Liz. *Teacher, Trainer, Tutor: Empowering the Learning Process by Improving the Relationships between Learners, Teachers, Trainers, and Tutors.* Lake Charles, La.: Global Management Enterprises, 2011.

Zachary, Lois J. *The Mentor's Guide: Facilitating Effective Learning Relationships,* 2nd ed. Hoboken, N.J.: Jossey-Bass, 2011.

Besides being skilled in the topics they teach, the best tutors are excellent communicators and are poised, friendly, and instantly at ease around new people. Tutors must also have great patience, especially if their student is having difficulty with a subject. Well-trained tutors will find other methods or approaches for teaching the lesson until the student understands the topic.

Successful tutors are also creative, oftentimes calling upon new inventive ways of instructing and inspiring their students. They must have strong communication skills, be organized, and enjoy teaching others.

■ EMPLOYMENT PROSPECTS

Employers

Tutors and trainers are employed by nonprofit organizations, corporations, and schools of all sizes. Although positions are available throughout the United States, the best opportunities can be found in large cities such as Chicago, New York, Washington, D.C., and Los Angeles.

Starting Out

Many nonprofit organizations and corporations offer opportunities to tutor, mentor, or train; most positions are voluntary or provide a small stipend. You can research possible tutor positions on the Internet or ask a local charity or advocacy group if they need volunteers.

■ ADVANCEMENT PROSPECTS

Tutors often advance by working with larger groups of students. However, they are most rewarded by having a student reach a hard-earned goal—becoming an accomplished reader, graduating from high school, or learning how to be a responsible adult. Some tutors with a passion for this line of work can become trainers for an organization or nonprofit group.

Trainers can advance by being assigned more tutors to train, by being promoted to higher-level positions within their organization, or by moving on to work at larger and more prestigious organizations.

■ OUTLOOK

Tutors and trainers will always be in demand, but those wishing to enter these careers should know that these jobs—except positions with large school systems, large for-profit tutoring organizations, and major foundations and nonprofit organizations—are often part time and low paying. Most tutors and trainers enter the field not for monetary gain, but because they want to help improve the lives of others. Job opportunities will be more readily available in large cities such as New York, Los Angeles, and Chicago that have many nonprofit organizations. Opportunities and pay will be better for tutors and trainers employed by for-profit organizations and companies.

■ UNIONS AND ASSOCIATIONS

Tutors and trainers are not typically members of unions, although those who work as teachers might be members of the National Federation of Teachers or the National Education Association. The National Tutoring Association represents the professional interests of tutors. It offers certification, continuing education, and other resources. The Association for Talent Development provides membership, certification, and publications.

■ TIPS FOR ENTRY

1. Offer to tutor neighborhood children. If their parents like your work, ask them to refer your talents to others.
2. Visit http://www.indeed.com and http://www.careerbuilder.com for job listings.
3. Join the National Tutoring Association (NTA) to access training and networking resources.
4. Become certified by the NTA in order to show employers that you've met the highest standards set by your profession.

FOR MORE INFORMATION

The Association for Talent Development provides information about membership, employment opportunities, and certification in the professional training and development field.

Association for Talent Development (ATD)
1640 King Street, Box 1443
Alexandria, VA 22313-1443
Tel: (800) 628-2783; (703) 683-8100
Fax: (703) 683-1523
E-mail: customercare@td.org
https://www.td.org

The Corporation for National and Community Service is a federal agency that helps Americans improve the lives of their fellow citizens through service.

Corporation for National and Community
Service (CNCS)
250 E Street, SW
Washington, D.C. 20024-3208
Tel: (800) 833-3722
E-mail: info@cns.gov
http://www.nationalservice.gov

The National Tutoring Association offers information on tutoring, including professional training programs and certification.

National Tutoring Association (NTA)
PO Box 6840
Lakeland, FL 33807-6840
http://www.ntatutor.com

Typists and Word Processors

OVERVIEW

Using typewriters, personal computers, and other office machines, *typists* and *word processors* convert handwritten or otherwise unfinished material into clean, readable, typewritten copies. Typists create reports, letters, forms, tables, charts, and other materials for all kinds of businesses and services. Word processors create the same types of materials using a computer that stores information electronically instead of printing it directly onto paper. Other typists use special machines that convert manuscripts into Braille, coded copy, or typeset copy. Typists and word processors hold about 68,660 jobs in the United States.

HISTORY

The invention of the typewriter in 1829 by William Austin Burt greatly increased business efficiency and productivity. The typewriter's benefits grew as typists became skilled at quickly transforming messy handwritten documents into neat, consistently typed copies.

More recently, the introduction of word processing into the workplace has revolutionized typing. This task may be done on a personal computer, a computer terminal hooked up to a network, or a computer that strictly handles word processing functions. By typing documents on a computer screen, workers can correct errors and make any necessary changes before a hard copy is printed, thus eliminating the need for retyping whole pages to correct mistakes. The computer stores the information in its memory, so workers can return to it as often as needed to make copies or changes.

The term *word processing* entered the English language in 1965, when International Business Machines, more commonly known as IBM, introduced a typewriter that put information onto magnetic tape instead of paper. Corrections could be made on this tape before running the tape through a machine that converted the signals on the tape into characters on a printed page. Today, word processing software and personal computers have virtually replaced typewriters in the office.

THE JOB

Some typists perform few duties other than typing. These workers spend approximately 75 percent of their time at the

QUICK FACTS

ALTERNATE TITLE(S)
None

DUTIES
Convert handwritten or otherwise unfinished material into clean, readable, typewritten or digital copies

SALARY RANGE
$25,290 to $37,610 to $53,760+

WORK ENVIRONMENT
Primarily Indoors

BEST GEOGRAPHIC LOCATION(S)
Opportunities best in large, urban areas

MINIMUM EDUCATION LEVEL
High School Diploma

SCHOOL SUBJECTS
Computer Science, English, Speech

EXPERIENCE
On-the-job training; three to six months experience (word processors)

PERSONALITY TRAITS
Conventional, Hands On, Organized

SKILLS
Interpersonal, Mechanical/ Manual Dexterity

CERTIFICATION OR LICENSING
Recommended

SPECIAL REQUIREMENTS
None

EMPLOYMENT PROSPECTS
Fair

ADVANCEMENT PROSPECTS
Fair

OUTLOOK
Decline

NOC
1411

O*NET-SOC
43-9022.00

CAREER LADDER

Office Manager or Word Processing Business Owner

Supervisor

Secretary or Receptionist

Word Processor

Typist

keyboard. They may input statistical data, medical reports, legal briefs, addresses, letters, and other documents from handwritten copies. They may work in pools, dividing the work of a large office among many workers under the supervision of a typing section chief. These typists may also be responsible for making photocopies of typewritten materials for distribution.

Beginning typists may start by typing address labels, headings on form letters, and documents from legible handwritten copy. More experienced typists may work from copy that is more difficult to read and requires the use of independent judgment when typing; they may be responsible for typing complex statistical tables, for example.

Clerk-typists spend up to 50 percent of their time typing. They also perform a variety of clerical tasks such as filing, answering the phone, acting as *receptionists*, and operating copy machines.

Many typists type from audio recordings instead of written or printed copy. *Transcribing-machine operators* sit at keyboards and wear headsets, through which they hear the spoken contents of letters, reports, and meetings. Typists can control the speed of the recording so they can comfortably type every word they hear. They proofread their finished documents and may erase dictated recordings for future use. Some typists in this subspecialty pursue advanced education to become medical transcriptionists or court reporters.

Most typists today are *word processors*. These employees put documents into the proper format by entering codes into the word processing software, telling it which lines to center, which words to underline, where the margins should be set, and how the document should be stored and printed. Word processors can edit, change, insert, and delete materials instantly just by pressing keys. Word processing is particularly efficient for form letters, in which only certain parts of a document change on each copy. When a word processor has finished formatting and keying in a document, the document is sent electronically to a printer for a finished copy. The document is normally saved on a removable hard drive or the computer's hard drive so that any subsequent changes to it can be made easily and new copies

produced immediately. Word processors also can send electronic files via e-mail or modems to people in different locations.

Braille typists and *Braille operators* use special typewriter-like machines to transcribe written or spoken English into Braille. By pressing one key or a combination of keys, they create the raised characters of the Braille alphabet. They may print either on special paper or on metal plates, which are later used to print books or other publications.

■ EARNINGS

The U.S. Department of Labor reports that median annual earnings of word processors and typists were $37,610 in May 2015. Salaries ranged from less than $25,290 to more than $53,760. Word processors and typists employed by wired telecommunications carriers made the highest mean annual salaries: $51,290. Other top-paying employers were rail transportation companies, $49,380; scientific research and development services, $47,030; and legal services, $44,300.

Typists and word processors occasionally may work overtime to finish special projects and may receive overtime pay. In large cities workers usually receive paid holidays, two weeks' vacation after one year of employment, sick leave, health and life insurance, and a pension plan. Some large companies also provide dental insurance, profit sharing opportunities, and bonuses.

■ WORK ENVIRONMENT

Typists and word processors usually work 35 to 40 hours per week at workstations in clean, bright offices. They usually sit most of the day in a fairly small area. The work is detailed and often repetitious, and approaching deadlines may increase the pressure and demands placed on typists and word processors.

Recent years have seen a controversy develop concerning the effect that working at video display terminals (VDTs) can have on workers' health. Working with these screens in improper lighting can cause eyestrain, and sitting at a workstation all day can cause musculoskeletal stress and pain. The computer industry is paying closer attention to these problems and is working to improve health and safety standards in VDT-equipped offices.

Another common ailment for typists and word processors is carpal tunnel syndrome, a painful ailment of the tendons in the wrist that is triggered by repetitive movement. If left unchecked, it can require corrective surgery. However, proper placement of the typing keyboard can help prevent injury. Several companies have designed desks, chairs, and working spaces that accommodate the physical needs of typists and word processors in the best manner currently known.

The nature of this work lends itself to flexible work arrangements. Many typists and word processors work in temporary positions that provide flexible schedules; they may also work part time. Some offices allow word processors and typists to telecommute from home, whereby they receive and send work on home computers via modems. These jobs may be especially convenient for workers with disabilities or family responsibilities, but often they do not provide a full range of benefits and lack the advantages of social interaction on the job.

■ EXPLORING

As with many clerical occupations, a good way to gain experience as a typist is through high school work-study programs. Students in these programs work part time for local businesses and attend classes part time. Temporary agencies also provide training and temporary jobs for exploring the field. Another way to gain typing experience is to volunteer to type for friends and family, local community groups, religious groups, or other organizations and to create your own digital reports.

■ EDUCATION AND TRAINING REQUIREMENTS
High School

Most employers require that typists and word processors be high school graduates and able to type accurately at a rate of at least 40 to 50 words per minute. Typists need good knowledge of spelling, grammar, and punctuation and may be required to be familiar with standard office equipment. Recommended high school classes include English, speech, typing, computer science, and business.

Postsecondary Training

You can learn typing and word processing skills through courses offered by colleges, business schools, and home-study programs. Some people learn keyboarding through self-teaching materials such as software programs or books. Business schools and community colleges often offer certificates or associate's degrees for typists and word processors.

For those who do not pursue such formal education, temporary agencies will often train workers in these skills. Generally, it takes a minimum of three to six months of experience to become a skilled word processor.

Word processors must be able to type 45 to 80 words per minute and should know the proper way to organize such documents as letters, reports, and financial statements. Increasingly, employers are requiring that employees know how to use various software

A typist reviews a document before entering it into the computer. (wavebreakmedia. Shutterstock.)

programs for word processing, spreadsheet, and database management tasks.

Other Education or Training

The Association of Executive and Administrative Professionals offers classes and webinars. The International Association of Administrative Professionals offers education and training programs for administrative professionals.

■ CERTIFICATION, LICENSING, AND SPECIAL REQUIREMENTS
Certification or Licensing

There are no specific certifications available for typists and word processors, but the International Association of Administrative Professionals offers the certified administrative professional (CAP) designation that might be of interest. Certification is awarded to applicants who meet experience/education requirements and pass a rigorous exam covering a number of general secretarial-related topics. The association also offers a technology applications specialty designation to those who have already earned the CAP designation.

■ EXPERIENCE, SKILLS, AND PERSONALITY TRAITS

Typing ability is key to landing a job as a typist. Generally, it takes a minimum of three to six months of experience to become a skilled word processor.

To be a successful typist and word processor, you need manual dexterity and the ability to concentrate. Typists and word processors should be alert, efficient, and attentive to detail. They often work directly with other people, so they need good interpersonal skills, including a courteous and cheerful demeanor. Good listening skills are important in order to transcribe recorded material.

EMPLOYMENT PROSPECTS
Employers

Typists and word processors are employed in almost every kind of workplace, including banks, law firms, factories, schools, hospitals, publishing firms, department stores, and government agencies. They may work with groups of employees in large offices or with only one or two other people in small offices.

There are approximately 68,660 word processors and typists working in the United States. Most of these workers are employed by firms that provide business services, including temporary help, word processing, and computer and data processing. Many also work for federal, state, and local government agencies. Some typists and word processors telecommute, working on client projects from their own home offices.

Starting Out

Business school and college students may learn of typing or word processing positions through their schools' career services offices. Some large businesses recruit employees directly from these schools. High school guidance counselors also may know of local job openings.

People interested in typing or word processor positions can find job listings through online employment agencies and business journals. They can apply directly to the personnel departments of large companies that hire many of these workers. They also can register with temporary agencies. To apply for positions with the federal government, job seekers should apply at the nearest regional Office of Personnel Management, or they can visit its Web site, http://www.usajobs.gov. State, county, and city governments may also have listings for such positions.

ADVANCEMENT PROSPECTS

Typists and word processors usually receive salary increases as they gain experience and are promoted from junior to senior positions. These are often given a classification or pay scale designation, such as typist or word processor I or II. They may also advance from *clerk-typist* to *technical typist*, or from a job in a typing pool to a typing position in a private office.

A degree in business management or executive secretarial skills increases a typist's chances for advancement. In addition, many large companies and government agencies provide training programs that allow workers to upgrade their skills and move into other jobs, such as *secretary, statistical clerk*, or *stenographer*.

Once they have acquired enough experience, some typists and word processors go into business for themselves by working from home and providing typing services to business clients. They may find work typing reports, manuscripts, and papers for professors, authors, business people, and students.

The more word processing experience an employee has, the better the opportunities to move up. Some may be promoted to word processing supervisor or selected for in-house professional training programs in data processing. Word processors may also move into related fields and work as *word-processing equipment salespeople or servicers* or *word-processing teachers* or *consultants*.

OUTLOOK

The U.S. Department of Labor reports that employment in the typing and word processing field is expected to decline by 16 percent through 2024 due to the increasing automation of offices and increased outsourcing of word-processing jobs. Technological innovations such as scanners, voice-recognition software, and electronic data transmission are being used in more workplaces, reducing the need for typists and word processors. Many office workers now do their own word processing because word processing and data entry software has become so user-friendly.

More companies today are contracting out their data entry and word processing projects to temporary help and staffing services firms. Most openings will be with these types of firms, and jobs will go to workers who have the best technical skills and knowledge of several word processing programs.

UNIONS AND ASSOCIATIONS

Some typists and word processors may be represented by the Office & Professional Employees International Union and other unions, and some may join the Association of Executive and Administrative Professionals and the International Association of Administrative Professionals. These associations offer career information, certification, continuing education classes, and networking opportunities.

■ TIPS FOR ENTRY

1. Read *OfficePro* (http://www.iaap-hq.org/page/OfficeProMagazine) and *The Executary* (http://www.theaeap.com/newsletters) to learn more about careers in general secretarial work.
2. Talk to typists and word processors about their jobs. Ask them for advice on preparing for and entering the field.
3. Visit the following Web sites for job listings: http://jobs.theaeap.com and http://careers.iaap-hq.org.

■ FOR MORE INFORMATION

The Association of Executive and Administrative Professionals offers educational programs, seminars, newsletters, and membership benefits.

Association of Executive and Administrative Professionals (AEAP)
900 South Washington Street, Suite G-13
Falls Church, VA 22046-4009
Tel: (703) 237-8616
Fax: (703) 533-1153
E-mail: headquarters@theaeap.com
http://www.theaeap.com

The International Association of Administrative Professionals provides education, certification programs, and other resources for administrative professionals.

International Association of Administrative Professionals (IAAP)
10502 North Ambassador Drive, Suite 100
Kansas City, MO 64153-1291
Tel: (816) 891-6600
Fax: (816) 891-9118
http://www.iaap-hq.org

The Office & Professional Employees International Union represents employees and independent contractors in various industries.

Office & Professional Employees International Union (OPEIU)
80 Eighth Avenue, 20th Floor
New York, NY 10011-7144
Tel: (800) 346-7348
http://www.opeiu.org

Umpires and Referees

■ OVERVIEW

Umpires and *referees* ensure that competitors in athletic events follow the rules. They make binding decisions and have the power to impose penalties upon individuals or teams that break the rules. Umpires, referees, and other sports officials hold about 18,620 jobs in the United States.

■ HISTORY

The history of sport goes back to the time of the ancient Olympic games, ritualistic ball games of Central and South America, and gladiator battles of Rome. Since gladiator battles were fights to the death, there were no rules to be observed and no need for umpires or referees to ensure fairness.

As athletics became more organized, if not less violent, rules were established, and umpires and referees were needed to enforce these rules and regulations. Boxing, soccer, and rugby were the first sports to have trained officials. With the advent of professional sports such as baseball and basketball, officiating became a career option.

■ THE JOB

Every sport has its own set of rules and regulations. Even the same game played on different levels may have its own distinct rules. For example, in professional basketball, the team in possession of the ball has 24 seconds to take a shot on goal. On the college level the shot clock is set at 35 seconds for men's competition and 30 seconds for women's competition, and in the game played by most high school teams, there is no shot clock at all.

Sports officials are the experts on the playing field. They know all the rules for the sport they officiate. They observe players while the ball or puck is in play and penalize those who break the rules. They are the decision makers and the arbiters of disputes between the competing teams.

When an official spots an infraction of the rules, they blow a whistle to stop play. The penalty is communicated to the official scorer, the penalty is assessed, and play continues.

Major League Baseball utilizes four *umpires* for each game (except in the playoffs, when six umpires are used). The *home plate umpire* works behind home plate and is responsible for determining whether each pitched ball is thrown within the strike zone. The home plate umpire

QUICK FACTS

ALTERNATE TITLE(S)
None

DUTIES
Enforce rules and regulations during sporting events

SALARY RANGE
$17,890 to $24,870 to $300,000

WORK ENVIRONMENT
Indoors/Outdoors

BEST GEOGRAPHIC LOCATION(S)
Opportunities available throughout the country

MINIMUM EDUCATION LEVEL
High School Diploma

SCHOOL SUBJECTS
Physical Education, Psychology, Speech

EXPERIENCE
Several years amateur league experience recommended

PERSONALITY TRAITS
Athletic, Outgoing, Realistic

SKILLS
Interpersonal, Leadership, Public Speaking

CERTIFICATION OR LICENSING
Required

SPECIAL REQUIREMENTS
None

EMPLOYMENT PROSPECTS
Fair

ADVANCEMENT PROSPECTS
Fair

OUTLOOK
About as Fast as the Average

NOC
5253

O*NET-SOC
27-2023.00

also rules whether runners crossing home plate are safe or out and keeps track of the ball/strike count on each batter.

Other umpires are responsible for the three bases. They decide whether runners are safe or out at their respective bases. *First- and third-base umpires* also must observe whether a ball, batted to the outfield, lands on the playing field within the foul line.

It is not uncommon for a single official to work a Little League game. When this is the case, the umpire stands behind the plate. The umpire is responsible for calling balls and strikes, keeping track of the number of outs and the ball/strike count, watching the foul line, and ruling on runners at the bases.

Three officials work National Basketball Association games. They are more active than baseball umpires. *Basketball referees* run up and down the court, following both the ball and the players. They must not only watch the ball, but must keep an eye out for illegal contact between players.

If three officials are supervising the game, one stands near the basket of the offensive team, another stands at the free throw line extended, and the third stands on the opposite side of the court (from the second official) halfway between midcourt and the free throw line. Each official watches different parts of the court for infractions. For instance, the official near the basket makes sure that no offensive player stands inside the free throw lane for more than three seconds.

High school and college games have two or three officials. Grade school and amateur league games generally have two. Again, the rules may be slightly different, and the athletic ability may vary, but the game is still basketball.

Football games use between four and seven officials. Like other referees, *football officials* each have specific areas to observe. The referee, who is ultimately in charge, is positioned behind the offensive team. Football referees are responsible for watching the offensive backfield for illegal movement before the ball is put into play, and they also communicate all penalties to the coaches and official scorer.

Another official observes the line of scrimmage for offsides penalties and marks the progress of the ball. The football umpire stands on the defensive team's side, five yards off the line of scrimmage, and watches for illegal blocks in the line. Other officials stand in the defensive backfield and observe defenders and receivers for illegal contact or interference.

Hockey games have three officials who skate up and down the ice. The *hockey referee*, who is in charge, stands between the other hockey umpires and assesses penalties. The umpires call offsides and icing violations. Off the ice, the *penalty time keeper* keeps track of penalty time served, and two *goal judges* determine whether shots on goal have eluded the goalie and entered the net.

■ EARNINGS

Umpire and referee salaries vary greatly, depending on the sport and the level at which it is played. Typically, the closer an official gets to the top of a professional sports league, the higher the wages, but this is not always the case. For example, some college basketball referees might earn more money than a non-lead official in a less popular professional sport.

The U.S. Department of Labor reports median annual earnings of $24,870 for umpires, referees, and related workers in May 2015. Salaries ranged from less than $17,890 to more than $57,750. Those employed in spectator sports earned mean annual salaries of $37,810.

According to the Major League Baseball's Umpire Development Program, annual salaries range from $84,000 to as much as $300,000 a year.

Minor League Baseball reports that its umpires earned the following monthly salaries by level of competition: Triple-A: $2,600-$3,500 per month; Double-A: $2,300-$2,700 per month; Class A Full Season: $2,000-$2,400 per month; and Class A Short-Season & Rookie: $1,900-$2,100 per month.

Professional basketball officials' salaries ranged from $90,000 to about $225,000, depending on the experience of the official. Those officiating at the college level earned an average of $2,000 per game.

Officials in the National Football League earned salaries ranging from $25,000 to $70,000 per season. College-level football referees earned from $500 to $980 per game.

National Hockey League referees are among the top earners, with entry-level officials making an average of $115,000 annually and those with many years of experience earning $220,000 or more.

In professional sports, umpires and referees are typically given additional money for travel, hotel, and food expenses. These officials also receive extra payment if they are invited to work special events such as the World Series, Stanley Cup Finals, or the Super Bowl.

Umpires and referees at the college, amateur, and youth levels are paid by the game. College officials earn between $500 and $980 per game or more, depending on the sport, and high school and middle school officials earn considerably less.

■ WORK ENVIRONMENT

Professional officials work in front of huge crowds. Their judgments and decisions are scrutinized by the fans in the stadium and by millions of fans watching at home.

Professional football officials work one game a week, while baseball umpires may work up to six games a week. Some football stadiums are outdoors, and football officials may have to work through inclement weather. Baseball umpires may work outside also, but they can stop the game because of rain.

Being an official at any level can be stressful. Officials must make split-second, unbiased decisions. Rulings are bound to be unpopular, at least to the team or player that is penalized, and even an eight-year-old Little Leaguer can be quite vocal.

Professional officials travel extensively throughout the season. They may be away from home for weeks at a time. Airplane flights, hotel food, and living out of a suitcase are some of the things that professional sports officials must endure.

At any level and with any sport, the work can be physically demanding. Baseball umpires must crouch behind the catcher to call balls and strikes, and can occasionally be struck by a wayward pitch or a foul tip. Basketball referees must run up and down the court, just as hockey officials must skate the rink. Football officials run the risk of colliding with heavily protected, helmeted 350-pound linemen.

However, if a person enjoys travel and can withstand the verbal abuse from players, coaches, and fans, the job can be very rewarding. Actual hours spent officiating are relatively short. The duration of most games is less than three hours.

Many people become officials because they enjoy sports. When an athlete's playing days are over, becoming an official is one way to maintain an active and important role in the sporting world. Most high school and junior high umpires and referees will tell you that they officiate not for the money, but because they enjoy it.

■ EXPLORING

A great way to find out if you enjoy being an umpire or referee is to officiate for a Little League team or at a summer camp. Locate a sports official in your area and set up an informational interview. Also, you should continue to watch and participate in sports to learn more.

■ EDUCATION AND TRAINING REQUIREMENTS
High School

Learn as much as you can about sports and their rules. You will also want to get in the physical shape necessary to keep up with the athletes during an event. The best way to accomplish these goals is to participate in school sports.

Take classes in English grammar and also other languages if you are interested in working as a baseball umpire or hockey official. Speech, debate, or theater courses will build your self-confidence and teach you the diction skills you need to be understood clearly.

Finally, sports bring together many kinds of people, and as an umpire or referee you must be diplomatic with all of them. Classes in sociology, history, and psychology can help you learn about the different cultures and ways of thinking of people from all parts of the world. Taking a foreign language such as Spanish or Japanese will help you to communicate with players from foreign countries.

Postsecondary Training

Umpires and referees are not required to attend four-year colleges or universities, but many do have college degrees. Often sports officials are former college athletes who decided to pursue a career in sports in a nonperformance capacity. Attending college and participating in college athletics is an excellent way to reinforce knowledge of a sport and its rules while receiving a solid education.

The International Association of Approved Basketball Officials has several schools that run each summer in different places in the United States. There, referees learn rules and work games at the players' camps that are held in conjunction with the schools. Officials for the National

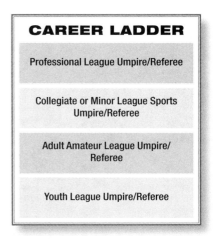

CAREER LADDER

Professional League Umpire/Referee

Collegiate or Minor League Sports Umpire/Referee

Adult Amateur League Umpire/Referee

Youth League Umpire/Referee

Umpire calls a runner safe at home plate. (Photo Disc.)

Football League (NFL) may attend the NFL Officiating Academy to hone their skills.

In almost all cases, officials must attend special training schools or courses. These can vary from the two schools (The Umpire School and the Wendelstedt Umpire School) endorsed by Major League Baseball's Umpire Development Program all the way to the training courses offered to officials in amateur softball. These schools and training courses can be contacted through professional and amateur leagues, college athletic conferences, and state interscholastic commissions. These organizations can also inform you of minimum age requirements (usually 18 and out of high school) and other criteria that vary between leagues and sports.

Other Education or Training

The National Association of Sports Officials offers continuing education seminars at its annual Sports Officiating Summit. Past seminars included "Player Safety Rules and Enforcements: Are They Working?," "It's Your Game: Sport-By-Sport Interactive Clinics," and "Calls Worth Talking About." The International Association of Approved Basketball Officials and associations at the local and state levels also provide continuing education classes.

■ CERTIFICATION, LICENSING, AND SPECIAL REQUIREMENTS
Certification or Licensing

The special training programs that umpires and referees attend act as their certification. Without these, they are not eligible to officiate. These courses may vary, ranging from those in the official training schools of professional umpires to courses taken through a state interscholastic athletic commission for middle school volleyball officials.

■ EXPERIENCE, SKILLS, AND PERSONALITY TRAITS

Previous experience as a sports official is highly recommended. Experience is gained by working as an umpire, referee, or other type of sports official in high school and other amateur leagues. Many umpires and referees obtain knowledge of the rules of their particular sport by competing in that sport at the professional and/or amateur levels.

Different sports have different physical requirements. For example, hockey officials need to be accomplished skaters and should be in excellent health. General physical requirements include good vision, to some extent good hearing, and good physical health.

Sports officials must have good communication skills and the ability to make split-second decisions. Many calls that an official makes will be unpopular, so they need courage to make the correct call and confidence to stand behind their judgment. An easily intimidated official won't last long in any league, which is why the ability to remain cool under pressure is important. Often, games are played in front of large crowds, and fans can be vocal in their criticism of players, coaches, and especially sports officials.

Umpires and referees must also have a thorough understanding of the sport they officiate. They need to be informed about changes to the rules. Sports officials keep informed by attending clinics and seminars sponsored by professional associations.

■ EMPLOYMENT PROSPECTS
Employers

There are approximately 18,620 sports officials employed in the United States. They work for professional and semiprofessional leagues, sports organizations, youth leagues, and schools at all levels.

Starting Out

A person interested in becoming a referee or umpire should begin officiating Little League or amateur league games on weekends and at night. Many umpires and referees also get their start by volunteering. For a paid position, beginners need to pass a written examination and join the state association of officials for each sport they choose to officiate.

■ ADVANCEMENT PROSPECTS

The natural progression for umpires and referees is to begin by officiating young peoples' games and advance to amateur adults' contests. Those with talent and determination may move on to college games or professional minor leagues.

Many officials who would like to move to the professional level attend umpire or referee camps. Many of these camps are conducted by actual professional officials. These programs feature a rigorous review of rules and regulations and often include game situations.

The minor leagues in baseball are a testing ground for prospective umpires. On average, umpires spend six to eight years at the minor-league level before they are even considered for a major-league position. Football officials must have 10 years of officiating experience, five years of which must have been at a collegiate varsity or minor professional level, before they can work in the NFL.

■ OUTLOOK

Employment for umpires, referees, and other sports officials is expected to grow about as fast as the average for all careers through 2024, according to the U.S. Department of Labor (DOL). The growth outlook for the field of sports officiating depends on the sport and the league worked. Umpires and referees are almost always needed at the youth, high school, and amateur levels, and people who are interested in supplementing their incomes this way or simply learning about the field of officiating should find plenty of opportunities for work, especially part-time work. Participation in college sports is also projected to increase in the coming years, especially at smaller colleges and in women's sports.

In professional sports the market is much tighter. Umpires in the major leagues rarely leave the job except to retire. In fact, during a 10-year period, the American League hired only three new umpires. When an opening does occur, an umpire moves up from triple-A baseball, creating an opening for an umpire from double-A, and so on. Professional sports without minor leagues offer even fewer employment opportunities for officials at the professional level. The creation of new leagues and expansion teams does occasionally offer additional job opportunities for professional sports officials.

The outlook for women sports officials has improved over the years with the creation of women's professional basketball leagues such as the WNBA, offering positions to women officials, as well as coaches, trainers, and professional athletes. Additionally, in 1997, two women, Dee Kantner and Violet Palmer, became the first female referees to officiate NBA basketball games—a first for the all-male U.S. major sports leagues. Since then, more opportunities have opened up for women officials in other leagues.

■ UNIONS AND ASSOCIATIONS

Umpires and referees may be represented by local and national unions. They also join professional

SPORTS OFFICIATING

LEARN MORE ABOUT IT

American Sport Education Program. *Successful Sports Officiating,* 2nd ed. Champaign, Ill.: Human Kinetics, 2011.

Clark, Al, and Dan Schlossberg. *Called Out But Safe: A Baseball Umpire's Journey.* Lincoln, Nebr.: University of Nebraska Press, 2014.

Feinstein, John. *Where Nobody Knows Your Name: Life In the Minor Leagues of Baseball.* New York: Anchor Books, 2015.

MacMahon, Clare, et al. *Sports Officials and Officiating: Science and Practice.* New York: Routledge, 2014.

Stern, Jeffrey. *Football Officiating Mechanics Illustrated: Four and Five Person High School Crews.* Racine, Wisc.: Referee Enterprises, Inc./National Association of Sports Officials, 2016.

organizations such as the National Association of Sports Officials, the International Association of Approved Basketball Officials, and associations at the local and state levels.

■ TIPS FOR ENTRY

1. Visit http://mlb.mlb.com/mlb/official_info/ umpires/how_to_become.jsp to read "How to Become an Umpire."
2. Read *Referee* magazine (http://www.naso.org/ MemberBenefits/RefereeMagazine.aspx) to learn more about the field.
3. Attend the National Association of Sports Officials' Sports Officiating Summit to participate in continuing education classes and build your professional network.

■ FOR MORE INFORMATION

The International Association of Approved Basketball Officials provides information on training schools, requirements, and other information for becoming a basketball official.

International Association of Approved Basketball Officials (IAABO)
PO Box 355
Carlisle, PA 17013-0355
Tel: (717) 713-8129
Fax: (717) 718-6164
http://www.iaabo.org

The Jim Evans Academy of Professional Umpiring provides training for aspiring baseball umpires.

Jim Evans Academy of Professional Umpiring
200 South Wilcox Street, #508
Castle Rock, CO 80104-1913
Tel: (303) 290-7411
http://www.umpireacademy.com

John Skilton's Baseball Links offers links to amateur and professional baseball umpiring associations throughout the world.
John Skilton's Baseball Links
http://www.baseball-links.com

This Web site provides information about umpire training schools and career-related resources.
Major League Baseball Umpire Camps
245 Park Avenue, 34th Floor
New York, NY 10167-0002
Tel: (212) 931-7537
E-mail: mlbumpirecamps@mlb.com
http://mlb.mlb.com/mlb/official_info/umpires/camp/
    about_us.jsp

This Web site offers a wealth of information on baseball umpiring, including how to become an umpire, and rules and measurements of the game.
Major League Baseball: Umpires
http://www.mlb.com/mlb/official_info/umpires/index
    .jsp

The Minor League Baseball Umpire Training Academy offers training programs in minor league baseball officiating.
Minor League Baseball Umpire Training Academy
PO Box A
St. Petersburg, FL 33731-1950
Tel: (877) 799-UMPS
Fax: (727) 456-1745
E-mail: Info@MiLBUmpireAcademy.com
https://www.milbumpireacademy.com

The National Association of Sports Officials provides information on how to become a sports official in various sports and offers a wide variety of officiating training publications and videos.
National Association of Sports Officials (NASO)
2017 Lathrop Avenue
Racine, WI 53405-3758
Tel: (262) 632-5448
Fax: (262) 632-5460
E-mail: cservices@naso.org
http://www.naso.org

The Wendelstedt School for Umpires is recognized by Major League Baseball for the Umpire Development Program.
Wendelstedt Umpire School
325 West Gaines Street, Suite 1414
Tallahassee, FL 32399-0400
Tel: (888) 224-6684
http://www.umpireschool.com

Urban and Regional Planners

■ OVERVIEW

Urban and regional planners assist in the development and redevelopment of a city, metropolitan area, or region. They work to preserve historical buildings, protect the environment, and help manage a community's growth and change. Planners evaluate individual buildings and city blocks, and are also involved in the design of new subdivisions, neighborhoods, and even entire towns. There are approximately 35,480 urban and regional planners working in the United States.

■ HISTORY

Cities have always been planned to some degree. Most cultures, from the ancient Greeks to the Chinese to the Native Americans, made some organized plans for the development of their cities. By the fourth century B.C., theories of urban planning existed in the writings of Plato, Aristotle, and Hippocrates. Their ideas concerning the issues of site selection and orientation were later modified and updated by Vitruvius in his book *De architectura*, which appeared after 27 B.C. This work helped create a standardized guide to Roman engineers as they built fortified settlements and cities throughout the vast empire. Largely inspired by Vitruvius, 15th-century Italian theorists compiled enormous amounts of information and ideas on urban planning. They replaced vertical walls with angular fortifications for better protection during times of war. They also widened streets and opened up squares by building new churches, halls, and palaces. Early designs were based on a symmetrical style that quickly became fashionable in many of the more prosperous European cities.

Modern urban planning owes much to the driving force of the Industrial Revolution. The desire for more sanitary living conditions led to the demolition of slums. Laws were enacted to govern new construction and monitor the condition of old buildings. In 1848, Baron George-Eugène Haussmann organized the destruction and replacement of 40 percent of the residential quarters in Paris, France, and created new boulevards and neighborhood park systems. In England, the 1875 Public Health Act allowed municipalities to regulate new construction, the removal of waste, and newly constructed water and sewer systems.

■ THE JOB

Urban and regional planners assist in the development or maintenance of carefully designed communities. Working for a government agency or as a consultant, planners are involved in integrating new buildings, houses, sites, and subdivisions into an overall city plan. Their plans must coordinate streets, traffic, public facilities, water and sewage, transportation, safety, and ecological factors such as wildlife habitats, wetlands, and floodplains. Planners are also involved in renovating and preserving historic buildings. They work with a variety of professionals, including architects, artists, computer programmers, engineers, economists, landscape architects, land developers, lawyers, writers, and environmental and other special interest groups.

Urban and regional planners also work with unused or undeveloped land. They may help design the layout for a proposed building, keeping in mind traffic circulation, parking, and the use of open space. Planners are also responsible for suggesting ways to implement these programs or proposals, considering their costs and how to raise funds for them.

Schools, churches, recreational areas, and residential tracts are studied to determine how they will fit into designs for optimal usefulness and beauty. As with other factors, specifications for the nature and kinds of buildings must be considered. Zoning codes, which regulate the specific use of land and buildings, must be adhered to during construction. Planners need to be knowledgeable of these regulations and other legal matters and communicate them to builders and developers.

Some urban and regional planners teach in colleges and schools of planning, and many do consulting work. Planners today are concerned not only with city codes, but also with environmental problems of water pollution, solid waste disposal, water treatment plants, and public housing.

Planners work in older cities or design new ones. Columbia, Maryland, and Reston, Virginia, both built in the 1960s, are examples of planned communities. Before plans for such communities can be developed, planners must prepare detailed maps and charts showing the proposed use of land for housing, business, and community needs. These studies provide information on the types of industries in the area, the locations of housing developments and businesses, and the plans for providing basic

needs such as water, sewage treatment, and transportation. After maps and charts have been analyzed, planners design the layout to present to land developers, city officials, housing experts, architects, and construction firms.

The following short descriptions list the wide variety of planners within the field.

Human services planners develop health and social service programs to upgrade living standards for those

QUICK FACTS

ALTERNATE TITLE(S)
Economic Development Planners, Historic Preservation Planners, Housing and Community Development Planners, Human Services Planners, International Development Planners, Transportation Planners, Urban Design Planners

DUTIES
Develop growth and redevelopment plans for communities; work closely with government officials, developers, and others

SALARY RANGE
$42,940 to $68,220 to $102,200+

WORK ENVIRONMENT
Primarily Indoors

BEST GEOGRAPHIC LOCATION(S)
Opportunities are available throughout the country

MINIMUM EDUCATION LEVEL
Master's Degree

SCHOOL SUBJECTS
English, Government, Social Studies

EXPERIENCE
Several years' experience required

PERSONALITY TRAITS
Organized, Problem-Solving, Realistic

SKILLS
Information Management, Interpersonal, Organizational

CERTIFICATION OR LICENSING
Recommended

SPECIAL REQUIREMENTS
None

EMPLOYMENT PROSPECTS
Good

ADVANCEMENT PROSPECTS
Good

OUTLOOK
About as Fast as the Average

NOC
2153

O*NET-SOC
19-3051.00

CAREER LADDER

Planning Director or Consultant

Senior Planner

Planner

Planning Aide or Assistant

lacking opportunities or resources. These planners frequently work for private health care organizations and government agencies.

Historic preservation planners use their knowledge of the law and economics to help preserve historic buildings, sites, and neighborhoods. They are frequently employed by state agencies, local governments, and the National Park Service.

Transportation planners, working mainly for government agencies, oversee the transportation infrastructure of a community, keeping in mind local priorities such as economic development and environmental concerns.

Housing and community development planners analyze housing needs to identify potential opportunities and problems that may affect a neighborhood and its surrounding communities. Such planners are usually employed by private real estate and financial firms, local governments, and community development organizations.

Economic development planners, usually employed by local governments or chambers of commerce, focus on attracting and retaining industry to a specific community. They communicate with industry leaders who select sites for new plants, warehouses, and other major projects.

Environmental planners advocate the integration of environmental issues into building construction, land use, and other community objectives. They work at all levels of government and for some nonprofit organizations.

Urban design planners work to design and locate public facilities, such as churches, libraries, and parks, to best serve the larger community. Employers include large-scale developers, private consulting firms, and local governments.

International development planners specialize in strategies for transportation, rural development, modernization, and urbanization. They are frequently employed by international agencies, such as the United Nations, and by national governments in less developed countries.

■ EARNINGS

Earnings vary based on position, work experience, and the population of the city or town the planner serves. According to the Bureau of Labor Statistics, median annual earnings of urban and regional planners were $68,220 in May 2015. The lowest paid 10 percent earned

less than $42,940, and the highest paid 10 percent earned more than $102,200. Mean annual earnings in local government, the industry employing the largest numbers of urban and regional planners, were $69,330.

Many planners work for government agencies, so they usually have sick leave and vacation privileges and are covered by retirement and health plans. Many planners also have access to a city-owned automobile.

Planners who work as consultants are generally paid on a fee basis. Their earnings are often high and vary greatly according to their reputations and work experience. Their earnings will depend on the number of consulting jobs they accept.

■ WORK ENVIRONMENT

Planners spend a considerable amount of time in an office setting. However, in order to gather data about the areas they develop, planners also spend much of their time outdoors examining the surrounding land, structures, and traffic. Most planners work standard 40-hour weeks, but they may also attend evening or weekend council meetings or public forums to share upcoming development proposals.

Planners work alone and with land developers, public officials, civic leaders, and citizens' groups. Occasionally, they may face opposition from interest groups or local citizens against certain development proposals and, as a result, they must have the patience needed to work with disparate groups. The job can be stressful when trying to keep tight deadlines or when defending proposals in both the public and private sectors.

■ EXPLORING

Research the origins of your city by visiting your county courthouse and local library. Check out early photographs and maps of your area to give you an idea of what went into the planning of your community. Visit local historic areas to learn about the development and history behind old buildings. You may also consider getting involved in efforts to preserve local buildings and areas that are threatened.

With the help of a teacher or academic adviser, arrange to interview a planner to learn about his or her job. Another good way to see what planners do is to attend a meeting of a local planning commission, which by law is open to the public. Interested students can find out details about upcoming meetings through their local paper or planning office.

■ EDUCATION AND TRAINING REQUIREMENTS
High School

Take courses in government and social studies to learn about past and present organizational structures of cities and counties. Good communication skills are needed to work with people in a variety of professions, so take courses in speech and English composition. Drafting, architecture, and art classes will familiarize you with the basics of design. Become active on your student council so that you can be involved in implementing changes for the school community. Computer science classes will teach you how to use databases, conduct online research, and use software programs.

Postsecondary Training

A master's degree is the minimum requirement for most trainee jobs with federal, state, or local government boards and agencies. Typical courses include geography, public administration, political science, law, engineering, architecture, landscape architecture, real estate, finance, and management. Computer courses and training in statistical techniques are also essential. Most masters' programs last a minimum of two years and require students to participate in internships with city planning departments.

When considering schools, check with the American Planning Association's *Guide to Undergraduate and Graduate Education in Urban and Regional Planning,* http://www.acsp.org/search/custom.asp?id=3757. The association also provides information on scholarship and fellowship programs available to students enrolled in planning programs.

Other Education or Training

The American Planning Association offers audio/web conferences, workshops, self-directed study options, online courses, and other continuing education opportunities. Other organizations that provide professional development classes that will be useful to urban and regional planners include the American Institute of Architects, American Society of Civil Engineers, International City/County Management Association, and the Canadian Institute of Planners.

■ CERTIFICATION, LICENSING, AND SPECIAL REQUIREMENTS
Certification or Licensing

Certification in urban and regional planning is not required but can lead to more challenging, better-paying positions. The American Institute of Certified Planners, a division of the American Planning Association (APA), grants certification to planners who meet certain academic and professional requirements and successfully complete an examination. The exam tests for knowledge of the history and future of planning, research methods, plan implementation, and other relevant topics.

Regional planners use blueprints and models to manage a community's growth. (auremar. Shutterstock.)

As of 2015, the state of New Jersey required planners to be licensed. The state of Michigan required those who want to practice under the title of "community planner" to be licensed. Contact these states' departments of labor for more information on licensing requirements.

■ EXPERIENCE, SKILLS, AND PERSONALITY TRAITS

Aspiring planners should obtain several years' of experience in the planning field as assistants, interns, or in other positions.

In addition to being interested in planning, urban and regional planners should have design skills and a good understanding of spatial relationships. Good analytical skills help them in evaluating projects. Planners must be able to visualize the relationships between streets, buildings, parks, and other developed spaces and anticipate potential planning problems. As a result, logic and problem-solving abilities are also important.

PLANNING SPECIALIZATIONS FOR URBAN PLANNERS

DID YOU KNOW?

Urban planners may specialize in any of the following areas:

- Community Activism/Empowerment
- Community Development
- Economic Development
- Environmental/Natural Resources Planning
- Historic Preservation
- Housing
- Land Use & Code Enforcement
- Parks & Recreation
- Planning Management/Finance
- Transportation Planning
- Urban Design

Source: American Planning Association

■ EMPLOYMENT PROSPECTS

Employers

There are approximately 35,480 urban and regional planners working in the United States. About 66 percent of planners work for local governments; others work for state agencies, the federal government, and in the private sector.

Many planners are hired for full-time work where they intern. Others choose to seek opportunities in state and federal governments and nonprofit organizations. Planners work for government agencies that focus on particular areas of city research and development, such as transportation, the environment, and housing. Urban and regional planners are also sought by colleges, law firms, the United Nations, and even foreign governments of rapidly modernizing countries.

Starting Out

Those with a bachelor's degree may find employment opportunities as an assistant at an architectural firm or construction office or working as city planning aides in regional or urban offices. New planners research projects, conduct interviews, survey the field, and write reports on their findings. Those with a master's degree enter the profession at a higher level, working for federal, state, and local agencies.

Previous work experience in a planning office or with an architectural or engineering firm is useful before applying for a job with city, county, or regional planning agencies. Membership in a professional organization is also helpful in locating job opportunities.

These include the American Planning Association, the American Institute of Architects, the American Society of Civil Engineers, and the International City/County Management Association. Most of these organizations host student chapters that provide information on internship opportunities and professional publications.

Many planning staffs are small and directors are usually eager to fill positions quickly. As a result, job availability can be highly variable. Students are advised to apply for jobs before they complete their degree requirements. Most colleges have career services offices to assist students in finding job leads.

■ ADVANCEMENT PROSPECTS

Beginning assistants can advance within the planning board or department to eventually become planners. The positions of *senior planner* and *planning director* are successive steps in some agencies. Frequently, experienced planners advance by moving to a larger city or county planning board, where they become responsible for larger and more complicated projects, make policy decisions, or become responsible for funding new developments. Other planners may become *consultants* to communities that cannot afford a full-time planner. Some planners also serve as *city managers*, *cabinet secretaries*, and *presidents of consulting firms*.

■ OUTLOOK

The U.S. Department of Labor (DOL) expects the overall demand for urban and regional planners will grow about as fast as the average for all occupations through 2024. Communities turn to professional planners for help in meeting demands resulting from urbanization and the growth in population. Urban and regional planners are needed to zone and plan land use for undeveloped and rural areas as well as commercial development in rapidly growing suburban areas. Urban planners will be needed to develop revitalization projects within cities and to address problems that stem from population growth, population diversity, environmental degradation, and resource scarcity. Planners will also be needed in suburban areas and municipalities to tackle issues affected by population changes, such as housing needs and transportation systems.

There will be jobs available with nongovernmental agencies that deal with historic preservation and redevelopment. Opportunities also exist in maintaining existing bridges, highways, and sewers, and in preserving and restoring historic sites and buildings.

There will also be job opportunities in the private sector—mainly at companies that provide professional, scientific, and technical services. Planners will work with architecture and engineering firms regarding land use, development site design, and building design. Real estate developers and governments will also continue to contract out various planning services.

Factors that may affect job growth include government regulation regarding the environment, housing, transportation, and land use. The continuing redevelopment of inner-city areas and the expansion of suburban areas will serve to provide many jobs for planners. However, when communities face budgetary constraints, planning departments may be reduced before other services, such as police forces or education.

■ UNIONS AND ASSOCIATIONS

Urban planners are not represented by unions. The major professional organization for planners is the American Planning Association. It offers information on education and careers, professional journals, continuing education opportunities, and other resources. Other useful organizations include the American Institute of Architects, American Society of Civil Engineers, and the International City/County Management Association. Planners who live in Canada often join the Canadian Institute of Planners. The Association of Collegiate Schools of Planning is a consortium of colleges and universities that offer degrees in urban and regional planning.

■ TIPS FOR ENTRY

1. Visit https://www.planning.org/jobs/search for job listings.
2. Join professional associations, such as the American Planning Association (APA), to access industry publications, training and networking opportunities, and career resources. The APA offers great resources at its Web site, http://www.planning.org/onthejob.
3. Participate in internships or part-time jobs that are arranged by your college's career services office.
4. Conduct information interviews with planners and ask them for advice on landing a job.

■ FOR MORE INFORMATION

The American Institute of Architects provides advocacy, education, and various career-support resources for architects.

American Institute of Architects (AIA)
1735 New York Avenue, NW
Washington, D.C. 20006-5292
Tel: (800) 242-3837
Fax: (202) 626 7547
E-mail: infocentral@aia.org
https://www.aia.org

The American Planning Association offers certification and accredited planning programs for planners.

American Planning Association (APA)
205 North Michigan Avenue, Suite 1200
Chicago, IL 60601-5927
Tel: (312) 431-9100
Fax: (312) 786-6700
https://www.planning.org

The American Society of Civil Engineers offers education programs, networking opportunities, and other membership benefits.

American Society of Civil Engineers (ASCE)
1801 Alexander Bell Drive
Reston, VA 20191-5467
Tel: (800) 548-2723
http://www.asce.org

The Association of Collegiate Schools of Planning provides information on planning careers and undergraduate and graduate training in planning.

Association of Collegiate Schools of Planning (ACSP)
http://www.acsp.org

The Canadian Institute of Planners is a membership organization that advocates for planners nationally and internationally.

Canadian Institute of Planners (CIP)
141 Laurier Avenue West, Suite 1112
Ottawa, ON K1P 5J3
Canada
Tel: (800) 207-2138; (613) 237-7526
Fax: (613) 237-7045
http://www.cip-icu.ca

The International City/County Management Association aims to create excellence in local governance by developing and fostering professional management to build better communities.

International City/County Management Association (ICMA)
777 North Capitol Street, NE, Suite 500
Washington, D.C. 20002-4201
Tel: (800) 745-8780; (202) 962-3680
Fax: (202) 962-3500
E-mail: membership@icma.org
http://icma.org

Urologists

■ OVERVIEW

Urologists are physicians and surgeons who specialize in the treatment of medical and surgical disorders of the adrenal gland and of the genitourinary system. They deal with the diseases of both the male and female urinary tract and of the male reproductive organs. According to the Department of Labor, there were approximately 48,920 internists, including urologists, employed in the United States in May 2015.

■ HISTORY

Medieval "healers" who specialized in the surgical removal of bladder stones could be considered the first urologists. The Spanish surgeon Francisco Diaz is the recognized founder of modern urology, however, due to his 1588 treatises on urethra, bladder, and kidney diseases.

Advancements in urology came during the 19th century, when flexible catheters were invented to examine and empty the bladder. In 1877, Max Nitze developed the lighted cytoscope, which is used to view the interior of the bladder. By the 20th century, diseases of the urinary tract could be diagnosed by X-ray.

■ THE JOB

Technically, urology is a surgical subspecialty, but because of the broad range of clinical problems they treat, urologists also have a working knowledge of internal medicine, pediatrics, gynecology, and other specialties.

Common medical disorders that urologists routinely treat include prostate cancer, testicular cancer, bladder cancer, stone disease, urinary tract infections, urinary incontinence, and impotence. Less common disorders include kidney cancer, renal (kidney) disease, male infertility, genitourinary trauma, and sexually transmitted diseases (including AIDS).

The management and treatment of malignant diseases constitute much of the urologist's practice. Prostate cancer is the most common cancer in men and the second leading cause of cancer deaths in men. If detected early, prostate cancer is treatable, but once it has spread beyond the prostate it is difficult to treat successfully.

Testicular cancer is the leading cause of cancer in young men between the ages of 15 and 34. Major advances in the treatment of this cancer, involving both surgery and chemotherapy, now make it the most curable of all cancers. Bladder cancer occurs most frequently in men age 70 and older, and treatment for it also has a high success rate.

Young and middle-aged adults are primarily affected by stone diseases, which represent the third leading cause of hospitalizations in the United States. Kidney stones, composed of a combination of calcium and either oxalate or phosphate, usually pass through the body with urine. Larger stones, however, can block the flow of urine or irritate the lining of the urinary system as they pass. What has become standard treatment today is called extracorporeal shock wave lithotripsy (ESWL). In ESWL, high-energy shock waves are used to pulverize the stones into small fragments that are carried from the body in the urine. This procedure has replaced invasive, open surgery as the preferred treatment for stone disease.

Urologists also consult on spina bifida cases in children and multiple sclerosis cases in adults, as these diseases involve neuromuscular dysfunctions that affect the kidneys, bladder, and genitourinary systems.

The scope of urology has broadened so much that the American Urological Association has identified the following subspecialties: pediatric urology, male infertility, urologic oncology (cancer), renal transplantation, calculi (urinary tract stones), female urology, and neurourology (voiding disorders, erectile dysfunction or impotence, and other disorders).

■ EARNINGS

According to the U.S. Department of Labor, the mean annual salary for physicians who specialized in internal medicine was $187,200 in May 2015. Some internists earn less than $62,520. Very experienced urologists can earn more than $325,000 annually.

Urologists who work for hospitals and other employers usually receive benefits such as vacation days, sick leave, health and life insurance, and a savings and pension program. Self-employed urologists must provide their own benefits.

■ WORK ENVIRONMENT

Like other physicians and surgeons, urologists typically work in small private offices or clinics with a staff of nurses and administrative support employees. When performing surgery, urologists work in well-lighted, sterile environments. Most work long, irregular hours. Those who work in a group setting, such as in a health care organization or group practice, may have less work stress than in a solo practice because they can coordinate patient care with other practitioners. Those who run their own independent practice have responsibilities that extend beyond medical practice, such as overseeing the business management and operations.

■ EXPLORING

There are no opportunities to work as a urologist until medical training is completed, but it can be helpful to speak with a urologist about the career. Ask a school counselor to arrange an information interview with a urologist practicing in your area. Be sure to make a list of questions to ask during the interview, such as: Why did you choose urology? What do you like most and least about your job? What do you think are the most important attributes for someone considering a career in urology? Also learn about the field by visiting the Web sites of professional associations, such as the American Urological Association (https://www.auanet.org/).

■ EDUCATION AND TRAINING REQUIREMENTS
High School

A medical degree is required to be a urologist, so be sure to take a college preparatory program. In addition to courses in English, algebra, and geometry, take biology, chemistry, health, and physics. Courses in communication, history, a foreign language, and psychology can also help you prepare for college, medical school, and an internship and hospital residency.

Postsecondary Training

Students must first earn an M.D. or D.O. degree and become licensed to practice medicine. They then complete a five- or six-year residency in urology, of which the first two years are typically spent in general surgery, followed by three to four years of clinical urology in an approved residency program, with the remaining year spent in general surgery, urology, or other clinical disciplines that are related to urology. The American Urological Association's Web site, http://www.auanet.org, provides information on residency programs.

Many urologic residency training programs are six years in length, with the final year spent in either research or additional clinical training, depending on the orientation of the program and the resident's focus.

The vast majority of urologists enter into clinical practice after completing their residency program. However, fellowships exist in various subspecialties, including pediatrics, infertility, sexual dysfunction, oncology, and transplantation.

Other Education or Training

Keeping up with cutting-edge medical research is key to success as a urologist. Professional associations often provide continuing education opportunities. For example, the American Urological Association offers webinars and in-person classes on topics such as advanced robotic urology and hands-on urologic ultrasound.

The American Osteopathic Association and the American Medical Association also provide professional development classes.

■ CERTIFICATION, LICENSING, AND SPECIAL REQUIREMENTS
Certification or Licensing

Certification by the American Board of Urology is for a 10-year period, with recertification required after that time. Certification requires the successful completion of a qualifying written examination, which must be taken within three years of completing the residency in urology. Certification requirements are subject to change and details can be seen on the American Board of Urology's Web site, https://www.abu.org.

At an early point in their residency period, all students are required to pass a medical licensing examination administered by the board of medical examiners in each state. The length of the residency depends on the specialty chosen.

■ EXPERIENCE, SKILLS, AND PERSONALITY TRAITS

There is no way to obtain direct experience in high school, but it's a good idea to take as many health and science classes as possible and participate in science clubs. During medical training, students gain experience by completing a five- to six-year residency in urology and possibly a fellowship in a subspecialty such as pediatrics or oncology.

Urologists need to enjoy working with people and to have a strong interest in promoting good health through preventive measures such as diet and exercise.

QUICK FACTS

ALTERNATE TITLE(S)
None

DUTIES
Treat patients who have medical and surgical disorders of the adrenal gland and of the genitourinary system

SALARY RANGE
$62,520 to $187,200 to $325,000+

WORK ENVIRONMENT
Primarily Indoors

BEST GEOGRAPHIC LOCATION(S)
Nationwide; most opportunities available in major metropolitan areas

MINIMUM EDUCATION LEVEL
Medical Degree

SCHOOL SUBJECTS
Biology, Chemistry, Health

EXPERIENCE
Residency

PERSONALITY TRAITS
Helpful, Problem-Solving, Scientific

SKILLS
Interpersonal, Research, Scientific

CERTIFICATION OR LICENSING
Required

SPECIAL REQUIREMENTS
None

EMPLOYMENT PROSPECTS
Good

ADVANCEMENT PROSPECTS
Fair

OUTLOOK
Faster than the Average

NOC
3111

O*NET-SOC
29-1069.12

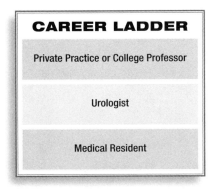

CAREER LADDER

Private Practice or College Professor

Urologist

Medical Resident

The urologist diagnoses and treats conditions of a very personal nature. Many patients are uncomfortable talking about problems relating to their kidneys, bladder, or genitourinary system. The urologist must show compassion and sensitivity to dispel the patient's fears and put them at ease.

Excellent communication skills are essential to patient-physician interactions. Urologist should be able to clearly articulate both the patient's problem and the recommended forms of treatment, including all of the options and their attendant risks and advantages. Urologists frequently consult with other physicians, so they also need to develop good working relationships with other medical specialists.

Like all surgeons, urologists should be in good physical condition; they must remain steady and focused while standing for hours. Urologists who work in hospital trauma units should be prepared for the frenetic pace and tension of split-second decision making.

■ EMPLOYMENT PROSPECTS
Employers

Many licensed physicians and surgeons, including urologists, are partners in or wage-and-salary employees of group practices. Others work in hospitals or for federal, state, and local governments, outpatient care services, and educational services. Some urologists are self-employed in their own practices. According to the American Medical Association, about 75 percent practice

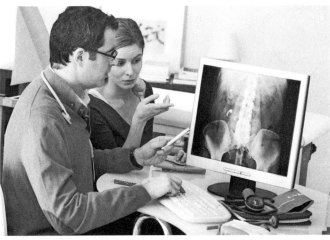

A patient asks questions as her urologist reviews an X ray with her. (Image Point Fr. Shutterstock.)

in metropolitan areas and the remaining 25 percent are located in rural communities.

Starting Out

Many new physicians and surgeons, including urologists, choose to join existing practices instead of attempting to start their own. Establishing a new practice is costly, and it may take time to build a patient base. In a clinic, group practice, or partnership, physicians share the costs for medical equipment and staff salaries, and of establishing a wider patient base.

Urologists who hope to join an existing practice may find leads through their medical school or residency. Another approach is to check the various medical professional journals, which often run ads for available positions. Urologists just starting out can also hire a medical placement agency to assist them in the job search.

Urologists who hope to work for a managed care organization or government sponsored clinic should contact the source directly for information on position availability and application procedures.

■ ADVANCEMENT PROSPECTS

Advancement for urologists generally comes by establishing a reputation of exceptional skills and expertise among their peers and with their patients. Some urologists establish their own private practices, while others choose to teach in universities or medical schools.

■ OUTLOOK

According to the *Occupational Outlook Handbook*, employment for all physicians and surgeons is expected to grow much faster than the average for all occupations through 2024. Employment prospects for urologists are good. The demographics of American society illustrate that the growth in the aging population will increase demand for services that cater, in large part, to them. With baby boomers aging, the need for qualified urologists will continue to grow. In recent years, the implementation of the Patient Protection and Affordable Care Act increased the number of people who are covered by health insurance—and created more demand for urologists and other physicians.

■ UNIONS AND ASSOCIATIONS

Most urologists do not belong to unions, but some may be represented by the Doctors Council SEIU and the Union of American Physicians and Dentists. The American Urological Association, American Medical Association, and American Osteopathic Association are the major professional associations for general practitioners. They provide publications, information on medical school and careers, networking opportunities, and other resources. Many urologists receive board certification from the American Board of Urology.

■ TIPS FOR ENTRY

1. Visit http://www.auanet.org/about/careers-in -urology.cfm for job listings.
2. Join the American Urological Association (AUA) and the American Medical Association to access training and networking resources, industry publications, and employment opportunities.
3. Attend the AUA's annual meeting to network and participate in continuing education classes.
4. Read the *Journal of Urology* (http://www.auanet .org) to learn more about the field.

■ FOR MORE INFORMATION

The American Board of Urology establishes and maintains standards of certification for urologists.

American Board of Urology (ABU)
600 Peter Jefferson Parkway, Suite 150
Charlottesville, VA 22911-8850
Tel: (434) 979-0059
Fax: (434) 979-0266
http://abu.org

The American Medical Association works to enhance the delivery of care and enable physicians and health teams to partner with patients to achieve better health.

American Medical Association (AMA)
AMA Plaza
330 North Wabash Avenue, Suite 39300
Chicago, IL 60611-5885
Tel: (800) 621-8335
https://www.ama-assn.org

The American Osteopathic Association is the accrediting agency for osteopathic medical schools.

American Osteopathic Association (AOA)
142 East Ontario Street
Chicago, IL 60611-2864
Tel: (800) 621-1773; (312) 202-8000
Fax: (312) 202-8200
http://www.osteopathic.org

The American Urological Association provides education, research, scholarly exchange, and advocacy.

American Urological Association (AUA)
1000 Corporate Boulevard
Linthicum, MD 21090-2260
Tel: (866) 746-4282; (410) 689-3700

TOP EMPLOYERS OF INTERNISTS AND ANNUAL MEAN WAGES, MAY 2015   FAST FACTS

- Offices of Physicians: 33,100, $212,200
- General Medical and Surgical Hospitals: 11,140, $149,830
- Outpatient Care Centers: 2,370, $208,670
- Colleges, Universities, and Professional Schools: 1,150, $161,970
- Home Health Care Services: 220, $212,190

Source: Department of Labor

Fax: (410) 689-3800
E-mail: aua@auanet.org
http://www.auanet.org

User Experience Designers

■ OVERVIEW

User experience designers create user interfaces for systems software, applications software, Web sites, and other types of technology. They use their knowledge of design, programming, marketing, and human behavior to ensure that the user has a positive experience with the technology. User experience designers are also known as *UX designers* and *user experience architects*.

■ HISTORY

User experience design traces its origin to the field of ergonomics, which aims to increase human productivity, comfort, safety, and health through the design of human-centered equipment, furniture, techniques, and work methods.

Some also trace the beginnings of the UX design movement to the publication of *Designing for People* in 1955 by the industrial designer Henry Dreyfuss. In it, he wrote "When the point of contact between the product and the people becomes a point of friction, then the industrial designer has failed. On the other hand, if people are made safer, more comfortable, more eager to purchase, more efficient—or just plain happier—by contact with the product, then the designer has succeeded."

As computers and other technology grew in popularity starting in the 1970s, major companies began incorporating human-focused design principles into their products. In 1970, Xerox created PARC, a research and development lab that developed enduring tools of human-computer interaction such as the mouse, the graphical user interface, and computer-generated bitmap graphics. Both Apple and Microsoft incorporated the work of PARC into their products.

In 1995, Donald Norman—an engineer, cognitive scientist, and the author of *The Design of Everyday Things* (1988)—began working at Apple to improve the usability and appearance of its products. He asked to be called a *user experience architect,* which many consider the first use of the job title.

Apple was already well-known for creating visually appealing and user-friendly products, but its 2007 release of the iPhone established even higher user experience and design standards throughout the tech industry, and in other industries that used technology. In the last decade, demand has grown for UX designers as a result of the continuing popularity of the Internet and the rapid adoption of smartphones and other mobile computing devices.

■ THE JOB

"User experience design as a discipline is concerned with all the elements that together make up that interface, including layout, visual design, text, brand, sound, and interaction," according to the User Experience Professionals Association (UXPA). "User experience works to coordinate these elements to allow for the best possible interaction by users."

According to the UXPA, the typical user experience design process is broken down into four phases: Analysis, Design, Implementation, and Deployment.

Analysis Phase

- meet with key stakeholders (e.g., clients, executives, programmers, marketing workers, engineers, quality assurance specialists, and other UX designers) to establish goals and the budget for the project
- conduct field studies in which data is collected about users, user needs, and product requirements; these studies involve both interviewing users and observing their behavior when they use similar products
- investigate similar products offered by competitors
- document user scenarios (i.e., every way in which users might potentially utilize the product)
- document user performance requirements (i.e., what they expect in regard to layout, visual design, text, sound, etc.)
- develop a task analysis (i.e., the steps that must be taken to create the product)

Design Phase

- brainstorm design concepts and metaphors (graphic elements that mimic or copy real-life objects like buttons)
- develop screen flow (the order in which users will see various interfaces as they navigate the product) and navigation models (which define where users start, how they navigate through the product, and all of the major elements of the product such as screens)
- develop a wireframe (a basic outline of navigation and content elements that make up a user interface)
- experiment with and test design concepts
- create prototypes on paper (these are known as low fidelity prototypes)
- conduct usability testing on low-fidelity prototypes
- convert approved low-fidelity prototypes to digital prototypes (which are known as high-fidelity prototypes)
- conduct usability testing again
- document standards and guidelines
- create design specifications for review by executives and customers

Implementation Phase

- conduct ongoing heuristic evaluations (a usability inspection method for software or hardware in which the interface is compared against accepted usability principles, commonly referred to as heuristics) to identify areas in which the product does not follow those principles

- fix design issues and any other problems that have been identified
- work closely with programmers, clients, and executives on various aspects of the design
- conduct usability testing

Deployment Phase

- use surveys to obtain user feedback
- conduct field studies to gather information about real-time use
- check objectives using usability testing
- when objectives are met, production of the finished product is started

▣ EARNINGS

According to the User Experience Professionals Association, user experience designers earned median salaries of $87,643 in 2014. The lowest 25 percent of all UX professionals earned $67,000, and the highest 25 percent earned $120,000. The UXPA reports that UX professionals received the following median annual salaries by level of experience:

- 0–1 years: $59,544
- 5–7 years: $85,000
- 11–15 years: $110,000
- 21+ years: $135,528

User experience designers receive a wide range of benefits, including paid holidays, vacations, and sick and personal days; retirement and pension plans; and medical, dental, and life insurance. In areas where there is a shortage of qualified UX designers, companies offer signing bonuses, stock options, and flexible work schedules to attract candidates.

▣ WORK ENVIRONMENT

User experience designers typically enjoy a casual work environment—except, of course, when deadlines loom or when disagreements occur about the design process. Designers spend much of their work days at the computer and in meetings with other members of the design team. Some UX designers work from home offices. Travel is required during field studies.

▣ EXPLORING

Here are some interesting ways to explore the field of UX design:

- Read publications about UX design such as *User Experience* (http://uxpamagazine.org) and the *Journal of Usability Studies* (http://uxpajournal.org).
- Design the user interface for an imaginary product, or identify an existing product that needs improvement and create your own design/interface. Ask your friends and family to rate the usability of your designs.
- Learn how to use UX design tools; visit http://uxmastery.com/resources/tools for a list of useful resources.
- Talk with user experience designers about their careers. Ask them what a typical day is like on the job and how they broke into the field.
- Visit the User Experience Awards' Web site, https://userexperienceawards.com, which lists the top winners for user design. By reviewing winning designs, you can get an idea of the interesting and groundbreaking work of UX designers.
- Check out Designing the User Experience (http://www.mprove.de/script/00/upa/_media/upaposter_11x17.pdf) to learn more about the UX design process from start to finish.

CAREER LADDER

Chief Technology Officer

User Experience Design Manager

Senior User Experience Designer

User Experience Designer

User experience designers must consider how Web sites and applications will function on different devices. (Monika Wisniewska. Shutterstock.)

KEY TERMS AND IDEAS FOR UX DESIGN
LEARN MORE ABOUT IT

Accessibility: The features of a product that allow people with limited hearing, vision, dexterity, cognition, or physical mobility to effectively use the product.

Efficiency: In relation to usability, the ability to accomplish a task in a software program or on a Web site in minimum amount of time with a minimum amount of effort.

Information architecture: The process of organizing information to make it easy for users to find, understand, and manage.

Parallel design: A strategy in which several designers or design groups are asked to create designs for the same product. The goal is to incorporate the best aspects of each design into the final product.

Participatory design: A design strategy in which the opinions of designers, business representatives, and users are incorporated into the final design to ensure that it is attractive and easy to use.

Readability: The complexity of the vocabulary and sentences used in the text that appears in a product; it can also refer to the font, point size, and other visual design elements of the text.

Site map: A visual summary of the information that can be found on a Web site or of a system.

Storyboard: Drawings, sketches, pictures, and sometimes words that illustrate an interaction between a person and a product (or multiple people and multiple products). Storyboards help designers and clients visualize the end-product as it is being created.

Usability: The degree to which software, hardware, or any other product is easy to use.

Wireframe: A rough plan that summarizes the navigation and content elements that comprise the user interface.

Source: User Experience Professionals Association

■ EDUCATION AND TRAINING REQUIREMENTS
High School

In high school take courses in programming, graphic and web design, marketing, psychology, English, speech, business, and social studies.

Postsecondary Education

User experience designers must have a minimum of a bachelor's degree to enter the field. Designers have degrees in human-computer interaction, graphic design, web design, industrial design, communication, psychology, engineering psychology, human factors/ergonomics, or marketing. Some colleges and universities offer specializations in human-computer interaction, information design, user interface design, and user experience research and design.

Other Education or Training

It's important that user experience designers keep their skills up to date throughout their careers. Webinars, workshops, seminars, and classes are provided by professional associations and tech companies. For example, the User Experience Professionals Association offers webinars such as UX Doesn't Happen on a Screen, It's in the Mind; Psychology 101: Revisiting the Basics of Human Behavior to Optimize User Experience Design; and Using Automated Testing Tools to Empower Your UX Research. The Nielsen Norman Group, a provider of user experience consulting services, offers more than 40 courses on topics such as human-computer interaction, information architecture, user behavior, user testing, and web usability. General Assembly, a global education company, provides courses on design, coding, and digital marketing. The Association for Computing Machinery, Human Factors and Ergonomics Society, and IEEE Computer Society also provide continuing education opportunities.

Certification

A growing number of colleges and universities—including Bentley University, California State University at Fullerton, University of California at San Diego, San Francisco State University, University of Baltimore, University of Washington, and Southern Methodist University—provide undergraduate and graduate certificates in user experience design and related fields. Contact schools in your area to learn about available programs.

■ CERTIFICATION, LICENSING, AND SPECIAL REQUIREMENTS
Certification or Licensing

Human Factors International, which bills itself as "the world's largest company specializing in user experience design," offers the certified usability analyst credential to those who complete four courses and pass an examination. It offers certification courses in cities throughout the United States and the world. Visit http://www.humanfactors.com for more information. The Nielsen Norman Group offers the certified user experience designation to those who complete at least 30 hours of training and pass five exams. Visit https://www.nngroup.com/ux-certification to learn more.

■ EXPERIENCE, SKILLS, AND PERSONALITY TRAITS

The completion of an internship or co-operative educational experience at a firm that employs user experience designers is required for entry-level positions.

User experience designers must have excellent design skills, but they also need a good understanding of psychology and marketing. The ability to communicate effectively and work well with others are also important because UX designers frequently work as a member of a team and interact with a wide range of people—from fellow UX designers, to programmers, clients, and top executives. Other key traits include creativity; the ability to multitask; problem-solving, time-management, and organizational skills; and pragmatism when it comes to design decisions (i.e., knowing how to balance good design with budgetary and time constraints). Finally, UX designers should have knowledge of HTML, CSS, Perl, XML/XSL, Adobe Creative Suite, JQuery, JavaScript, and other software, as well as experience with Agile development methodology.

■ EMPLOYMENT PROSPECTS
Employers

User experience designers are employed by tech and Web services companies. They also work for any organization (such as a sports team, government agency, or a Big Four accounting firm) that wants to create a software application, Web site, or other tech product. Some designers work as freelancers, providing contract services to companies, nonprofit organizations, and government agencies.

Starting Out

One excellent way to break into the field is by completing an internship during college. Many tech companies offer UX design internships. Contact tech companies directly or visit the following Web sites to learn more about internship opportunities:

- https://www.linkedin.com/jobs/user-experience
  -design-internship-jobs
- http://www.hfes.org/Web/EducationalResources/
  internships.html
- http://www.vault.com/internship-rankings/
  top-10-internships

If you're in college, become a student member of the User Experience Professionals Association to access its International Mentorship Program and receive a listing in its membership directory. Taking advantage of these membership benefits will help you to connect with UX designers and learn about job openings.

Other job-search strategies include utilizing employment sites, attending career fairs and networking events, working with recruiters, and using the resources of your college's career services office.

■ ADVANCEMENT PROSPECTS

User experience designers with several years of experience can advance to the position of senior UX designer, and then to UX design manager. Those with strong business skills may advance to executive-level positions such as chief technology officer, CEO, or chief operating officer. Some UX designers launch their own consulting firms.

■ OUTLOOK

Employment for industrial designers (a career that is related to that of UX designer) is expected to grow by 2 percent through 2024, according to the U.S. Department of Labor. Job opportunities for graphic designers (another related career) in computer systems design and related services are projected to grow 21 percent during the same time period. Opportunities for UX designers should most closely mirror those of graphic designers in computer systems design and related services. Tech companies have realized that creating user-friendly products gives them an edge over their competition; the popularity of visually attractive and user-friendly products from Apple is one example of this trend.

According to The Creative Group, a marketing and creative industry staffing agency, "User experience designers are in particular demand. Firms now consider strong user interface design a must, not just a plus. Responsive design also is becoming a greater priority for businesses that want to provide customers with optimal experiences on their devices and browsers of choice."

■ UNIONS AND ASSOCIATIONS

User experience designers do not belong to unions. Some join professional associations such as the User Experience Professionals Association, which publishes *User Experience* and the *Journal of Usability Studies*, hosts an annual conference, offers webinars and other continuing education opportunities, and has a membership category for college students. The Association for Computing Machinery provides information on education and careers at its Web site and has a Special Interest Group on Computer-Human Interaction. Other noteworthy organizations include the Human Factors and Ergonomics Society, IEEE Computer Society, and Interaction Design Association.

■ TIPS FOR ENTRY

1. Visit http://uxmastery.com/how-to-get-started -in-ux-design to read How to Get Started in UX Design.
2. Check out the following Web sites for job listings:
   - https://uxpa.org/job-bank
   - https://www.hfes.org/web/CareerCenter/ Career.aspx
   - http://www.ixda.org/page/job-board
   - http://www.uxjobsboard.com
3. Attend annual conferences held by the User Experience Professionals Association (http:// uxpa2016.org) and the Interaction Design Association (http://www.ixda.org/page/interac tion) to network, participate in continuing education opportunities, and learn best practices from global UX experts.

■ FOR MORE INFORMATION

For information on its Special Interest Group on Computer-Human Interaction, contact

Association for Computing Machinery
2 Penn Plaza, Suite 701
New York, NY 10121-0799
Tel: (800) 342-6626
http://www.acm.org

For information on education and careers, contact

Human Factors and Ergonomics Society
PO Box 1369
Santa Monica, CA 90406-1369
https://www.hfes.org

For information on computer careers, contact

IEEE Computer Society
2001 L Street, NW, Suite 700
Washington, D.C. 20036-4928
Tel: (202) 371-0101
E-mail: help@computer.org
http://www.computer.org

For information on education and careers, contact

Industrial Designers Society of America
555 Grove Street, Suite 200
Herndon, VA 20170-4728
Tel: (703) 707-6000
http://www.idsa.org

For information on membership and careers, contact

Interaction Design Association
http://www.ixda.org

To learn more about User Experience Magazine and membership, visit

User Experience Professionals Association
Tel: (470) 333-8972
E-mail: office@uxpa.org
https://uxpa.org

Venture Capital Accountants and Auditors

■ OVERVIEW

Accountants compile, analyze, verify, and prepare financial records. *Auditors* ensure that financial records are accurate, complete, and in compliance with local, state, and federal laws. More than 1.3 million people are employed as accountants and auditors; only a tiny fraction of this number are employed in the venture capital industry.

■ HISTORY

In recent years, demand has grown for accountants (especially certified public accountants, or CPAs) and auditors as a result of the growing complexity of business transactions and the passage of a variety of laws (such as the Dodd-Frank Wall Street Reform and Consumer Protection Act) that require companies to be more transparent regarding their finances. "During the last 20-odd years, CPAs have become some of the most important decision makers in business," according to Start Here, Go Places, an accounting career Web site created by the American Institute of Certified Public Accountants. "If it wasn't for CPAs, businesses wouldn't know when to invest more capital. Or when to grow. Or downsize. They might even be out of compliance with current laws. Their superhuman ability to create, analyze, and interpret financial info makes them the first to know where the company stands and where it's headed."

■ THE JOB

Accountants and auditors are important behind-the-scenes players in the business world. Smart executives know that their organizations are only as good as their accounting and auditing departments.

Job responsibilities for accountants in the venture capital industry vary by the size of the employer, the stage of the fund's investments, and other factors, but major responsibilities include:

- working closely with partners during the launch and set-up of new funds, during the acquisition of portfolio companies, and during exits (i.e., mergers, the sale of the company, or an initial public offering)
- maintaining and updating financial data in investment databases
- reconciling cash received from investors and investments
- managing general ledgers for the firm and its portfolio companies
- documenting financial variances and responding to investor inquiries
- determining the fair value of the firm's portfolio for limited partners (fair value is defined by the Financial Accounting Standards Board as "the price that would be received to sell an asset or paid to transfer a liability in an orderly transaction between market participants at the measurement date")
- preparing financial statements (e.g., assets and liabilities, operations for the latest investment period, cash flows, and changes in net assets)
- preparing tax returns and being responsible for other tax-related issues
- providing monthly or quarterly accounting of investor contributions and withdrawals and computing profit and losses for the accounting period
- preparing semi-annual and annual reports for limited partners
- overseeing monthly fund transactions (e.g., interest calculation, investor subscriptions, invoice payments, expense accruals tracking, etc.)
- collecting and preparing data for regulatory filings
- working closely with external and internal auditors during year-end reporting
- assisting the chief financial officer with the preparation of financial forecasts
- providing accounting services, as needed, to the firm's portfolio companies

Specialized accountants known as auditors ensure that financial records comply with government regulations and that they have been prepared according to generally accepted accounting principles. Those who work as salaried employees of companies or other organizations are known as *internal auditors*. "The role of internal audit is to provide independent assurance that an organization's risk management, governance, and internal control processes are operating effectively," according to the Chartered Institute of Internal Auditors. The work of internal auditors is checked and verified by *independent*

QUICK FACTS

ALTERNATE TITLE(S)
Corporate Accountants, Independent Auditors, Internal Auditors, Management Accountants

DUTIES
Compile, analyze, verify, and prepare venture capital firm financial records (accountants); make sure that financial records are accurate, complete, and in compliance with laws (auditors)

SALARY RANGE
$40,850 to $78,620 to $191,750+

WORK ENVIRONMENT
Primarily Indoors

BEST GEOGRAPHIC LOCATION(S)
Opportunities are best in San Francisco and other cities with a large number of start-ups

MINIMUM EDUCATION LEVEL
Bachelor's Degree

SCHOOL SUBJECTS
Business, Computer Science, Mathematics

EXPERIENCE
Internship or co-op at public accounting firms or venture capital portfolio companies; at least one year of experience for venture capital firms

PERSONALITY TRAITS
Hands On, Organized, Problem-Solving

SKILLS
Financial, Information Management, Math

CERTIFICATION OR LICENSING
Recommended

SPECIAL REQUIREMENTS
None

EMPLOYMENT PROSPECTS
Good

ADVANCEMENT PROSPECTS
Fair

OUTLOOK
Much Faster than the Average

NOC
1111

O*NET-SOC
13-2011.00, 13-2011.01, 13-2011.02

auditors, who are typically employed by public accounting firms. Major duties for auditors include:

- reviewing the general ledger and other financial documents for accuracy

CAREER LADDER

Partner or Chief Executive Officer

Chief Financial Officer

Controller or Director of Finance

Chief Accountant/Auditor

Accountant/Auditor

- identifying and addressing client issues discovered during the audit process
- recommending improvements on internal controls, operating efficiencies, and profitability to management
- conducting due diligence on a company the client is considering acquiring
- validating financial and nonfinancial data for internal and external review
- performing an annual risk assessment of the business and continuous monitoring of the firm's risk management plan based on its risk analysis

EARNINGS

Accountants and auditors earned median annual salaries of $78,620 in May 2014, according to the U.S. Department of Labor. Salaries ranged from less than $40,850 to $115,950 or more.

Public accounting firm accountants and auditors who provide audit/assurance services to businesses earned salaries that ranged from $49,500 to $191,750 in 2015, according to Robert Half Accounting & Finance's *2016 Salary Guide.*

Accountants and auditors receive a variety of benefits, including health insurance, savings and pension plans, paid vacation and sick days, tuition reimbursement, and performance bonuses.

WORK ENVIRONMENT

Unlike some of the more high-profile VC jobs (such as venture capitalists), accountants and auditors enjoy a good work/life balance. Their work hours are pretty standard (i.e., 9-to-5, Monday-Friday). Advances in technology even allow some accounting and auditing professionals to work at home or in other remote locations (such as at a coffee shop or even on the beach). Some employers offer flexible work schedules (e.g., Fridays off during the summer in exchange for longer hours during the rest of the week).

EXPLORING

To familiarize yourself with the basics of accounting and auditing and the venture capital industry, check out the following resources:

- *Accounting For Dummies* (For Dummies, 2013)
- *Principles of Auditing & Other Assurance Services* (McGraw-Hill Education, 2015)
- Some Basics of Venture Capital: http://zoo.cs.yale.edu/classes/cs155/fall01/kearns.pdf
- Venture Capital 101: https://www.youtube.com/watch?v=Wq8jKqHyd4o

Additionally, talk to venture capital accountants and auditors about their jobs. Ask your counselor or business teacher for help arranging an interview.

EDUCATION AND TRAINING REQUIREMENTS
High School

Does high school matter for aspiring VC accountants and auditors? The answer is a resounding yes. High school classes help you to grow intellectually and as a person, and excelling in your courses will help you to earn a high GPA, which will get you into a top college. And since venture capital partners prefer to hire applicants who attended top colleges, you can now see why your high school education is important.

In addition to obvious classes such as accounting, statistics, economics, and mathematics, you should also take English and speech courses because, in addition to being able to crunch numbers, you'll also need to write reports and discuss financial issues with limited partners, your department manager, and partners in the firm. Other important classes include government, social studies, and science.

Postsecondary Education

A minimum of a bachelor's degree in accounting, economics, finance, or business administration is required to work as an accountant or auditor in the venture capital industry. *U.S. News & World Report* provides a list of the best undergraduate accounting programs in the United States at http://colleges.usnews.rankingsandreviews.com/best-colleges/rankings/business-accounting. Some partners prefer candidates who have a master's degree in accounting, economics, business administration, or finance.

AACSB International accredits colleges and universities that offer undergraduate and graduate degrees in accounting and business. Visit http://www.aacsb.edu/accreditation/accreditedmembers.asp for a list of accredited programs. An additional list of postsecondary accounting programs (associate through graduate level) can be accessed at https://www.thiswaytocpa.com/education/college-search.

The Institute of Internal Auditors has created a formal endorsement program for colleges and universities that offer an internal auditing curriculum within a degree program (undergraduate or postgraduate). Visit https://na.theiia.org/about-us/about-ia/pages/participating-iaep-program-schools.aspx for a list of schools that offer this curriculum.

Other Education or Training

Many accountants and auditors participate in continuing education (CE) classes, workshops, and webinars to improve their job skills, to stay up to date with industry trends, and, if they're certified, to satisfy CE requirements for recertification. Many professional associations provide these opportunities. For example, the Institute of Internal Auditors offers seminars and e-learning opportunities on audit report writing, finance and compliance fraud, operational/performance auditing, risk issues, technology, and personal development (communication, strategic thinking, and problem-solving). Other opportunities are provided by the American Institute of Certified Public Accountants, CFA Institute, Chartered Institute of Management Accountants, Institute of Management Accountants, and the National Venture Capital Association.

Many top public accounting firms provide classroom-based and online learning. For example, PricewaterhouseCoopers offers self-study classes such as Venture Capital Funds, Overview of Investment Companies: Fund Accounting Concepts, and Taxation for Regulated Investment Companies.

Certification

The American Institute of Certified Public Accountants offers a certificate in International Financial Reporting Standards to those who complete 25 online, self-study training courses. Topics include financial statements, interim reporting, and cash flows; investments in associates and joint ventures; and fair value measurement. Certificate programs are also offered by the Chartered Institute of Management Accountants (business accounting) and the Association of Chartered Certified Accountants (international auditing and international financial reporting).

■ CERTIFICATION, LICENSING, AND SPECIAL REQUIREMENTS

Certification or Licensing

Many accountants and auditors become certified to improve their skills and demonstrate to potential employers that they've met the highest standards established by their industry. Becoming certified can also translate into higher earnings. According to the Institute of Management Accountants, those who hold the certified management accountant (CMA) credential earned

---

METROPOLITAN STATISTICAL AREAS

FAST FACTS

In 2015, venture investors deployed capital to 3,662 companies in 133 Metropolitan Statistical Areas (MSAs), according to the *MoneyTree Report* by PricewaterhouseCoopers LLP and the National Venture Capital Association (NVCA). "Contrary to popular belief you don't have to be an entrepreneur living in San Francisco, New York, or Boston to receive venture capital funding," said Bobby Franklin, president and CEO of the NVCA in a press release at the organization's Web site. "There are pockets of innovation all across the United States, and as long as you have a groundbreaking idea with high-growth potential you are well positioned to attract venture capital funding to help grow your business."

The San Francisco-Oakland-Fremont, CA, MSA ranked as the top MSA for venture capital investment, with 797 companies attracting $21.0 billion in 2015. The New York-Northern New Jersey-Long Island, NY/NJ /PA MSA ranked second with 416 startups attracting $7.0 billion. Here are the top 15 MSAs by the number of companies invested in:

1. San Francisco-Oakland-Fremont, CA: 797 start-ups
2. New York-Northern New Jersey-Long Island, NY/NJ/PA: 416 start-ups
3. Boston-Cambridge-Quincy, MA/NH: 348 start-ups
4. San Jose-Sunnyvale-Santa Clara, CA: 321 start-ups
5. Los Angeles-Long Beach-Santa, Ana, CA: 240 start-ups
6. Seattle-Tacoma-Bellevue, WA: 95 start-ups
7. Washington-Arlington-Alexandria, DC/VA/MD/WV: 93 start-ups
8. Philadelphia-Camden-Wilmington, PA/NJ/DE/MD: 93 start-ups
9. San Diego-Carlsbad-San Marcos, CA: 83 start-ups
10. Pittsburgh, PA: 83 start-ups
11. Chicago-Naperville-Joliet, IL/IN/WI: 81 start-ups
12. Austin-Round Rock, TX: 78 start-ups
13. Atlanta-Sandy Springs-Marietta, GA: 58 start-ups
14. Denver-Aurora, CO: 41 start-ups
15. Baltimore-Towson, MD: 37 start-ups

---

63 percent more in total compensation than non-CMAs in 2014. Robert Half Accounting & Finance reports that the CMA credential is one of four certification designations that are in especially strong demand. The other credentials include:

- certified internal auditor (Institute of Internal Auditors)

- certified public accountant (American Institute of Certified Public Accountants, AICPA)
- chartered global management accountant (a joint venture of the AICPA and the Chartered Institute of Management Accountants)

Additionally, some accountants and auditors earn the following certifications:

- credited business accountant/advisor, accredited tax preparer, accredited tax advisor (Accreditation Council for Accountancy and Taxation)
- certification in control self-assessment, certified financial services auditor, certification in risk management assurance (Institute of Internal Auditors)
- certified financial manager (Institute of Management Accountants)
- certified treasury professional, certified corporate financial planning and analysis professional (Association of Financial Professionals)

A large percentage of accountants are certified public accountants (CPAs). Those who receive this designation have passed a qualifying examination and hold a certificate issued by the state in which they wish to practice. The Uniform CPA Examination, which is administered by the AICPA, is used by all states. Nearly all states require at least two years of public accounting experience or the equivalent before a CPA certificate can be earned.

■ EXPERIENCE, SKILLS, AND PERSONALITY TRAITS

Completion of at least one internship in college is highly recommended to prepare for entry-level accounting and auditing positions at public accounting firms. Jobs at venture capital firms require at least one year of experience at an investment bank, a portfolio company of a VC firm, or at a public accounting firm that provides services to the VC industry.

According to the American Institute of Certified Public Accountants, certified public accountants need a combination of strong leadership ability, communications skills, tech know-how, and business savvy. At the organization's Web site, http://www.startheregoplaces.com/students/why-accounting/cpa-skills, you can learn about the steps to take to develop these qualities. Other important traits include a detail-oriented, organized, and analytical personality, strong problem-solving skills, the ability to work both independently and as a member of a team, and honesty and strong ethics. Accountants and auditors must be proficient in the use of financial-related software and databases (such as Microsoft Dynamics

Great Plains, Oracle PeopleSoft, and SAP) and office software (PowerPoint, Excel, and Word).

■ EMPLOYMENT PROSPECTS
Employers

Accountants and auditors are employed by venture capital firms, which are headquartered throughout the United States, but especially in cities and states with strong start-up communities such as New York, Boston, and California. They also work for public accounting firms (including the Big Four: Deloitte, EY, KPMG, and PricewaterhouseCoopers) that provide services to VC firms. Additionally, there are many employment opportunities for accountants and auditors outside the alternative investments industry—with Fortune 500 companies, small- and medium-sized business, at nonprofits, and at government agencies such as the U.S. Government Accountability Office and the U.S. Department of Commerce.

Starting Out

Many aspiring VC accountants and auditors break into the industry by first working at a public accounting firm (such as PricewaterhouseCoopers) that provides services to the VC industry. Pursuing this strategy will provide you with good experience before you seek out job opportunities at VC firms.

To learn about employment opportunities, visit the Web sites of public accounting firms. At some Web sites, you can even apply for jobs. Many firms have a strong presence on college campuses via career fairs or through career exploration programs. They also offer internship programs, during which you can try out accounting jobs and make networking contacts that can lead to a permanent position.

Check out the American Institute of Certified Public Accountants Web site (https://www.thiswaytocpa.com/career-tools/articles) for information on job-search strategies, career paths, writing effective resumes and cover letters, and preparing for and performing well during job interviews.

■ ADVANCEMENT PROSPECTS

Large venture capital firms and public accounting firms provide the best advancement prospects because they employ a large number of accountants and auditors, and provide a clear-cut promotion path to their employees. At a VC firm, an experienced accountant can advance to the position of chief accountant, and then to controller, and chief financial officer (CFO). Highly experienced and skilled CFOs may be offered a partnership stake. Accountants and auditors at public accounting firms can advance to managerial positions and then to executive-level careers such as chief financial officer, CEO, or chief operating officer.

OUTLOOK

Employment for accountants and auditors who work with funds, trusts, and other financial vehicles will grow by more than 18 percent through 2024, according to the *Occupational Outlook Handbook*. It reports that "as more companies go public, there will be greater need for public accountants to handle the legally required financial documentation. The continued globalization of business may lead to increased demand for accounting expertise and services related to international trade and international mergers and acquisitions."

Despite these positive predictions, it's important to remember that it's extremely difficult to land a job in the venture capital industry. Those with advanced degrees, certification, and experience in some area of alternative investments (e.g., hedge funds, private equity, etc.) will have the best job prospects.

UNIONS AND ASSOCIATIONS

Venture capital accountants and auditors are not members of unions. The accounting industry has many professional associations at the national, state, and local levels that provide membership, career resources, educational opportunities, and networking events. For example, accountants and auditors in California (a hotbed of the venture capital industry) can join the California Society of CPAs and the Society of California Accountants, among other organizations. At the national level, the American Institute of Certified Public Accountants (AICPA) is the leading professional association for accounting professionals. It administers the Uniform CPA Examination, and, in cooperation with the Chartered Institute of Management Accountants, offers the chartered global management accountant credential. The AICPA has a membership category for college students, and its Web site features a job board and many career development resources. The National Venture Capital Association is a trade organization of 300 of the leading venture capital firms. The Western Association of Venture Capitalists is a membership organization of more than 90 VC firms that are headquartered in Washington, Oregon, California, Nevada, and Arizona. Other noteworthy organizations include the CFA Institute, Chartered Alternate Investment Analyst Association, Chartered Institute of Management Accountants, Institute of Internal Auditors, and the Institute of Management Accountants.

TIPS FOR ENTRY

1. Become a certified public accountant. It will give you an edge over other applicants.
2. Check out The Edge (http://www.aicpa.org/InterestAreas/YoungCPANetwork/TheEdge), an online newsletter that provides advice to young professionals about job hunting and networking.
3. Use LinkedIn to network with people in the venture capital industry.
4. Become active in your school's business or finance club.

FOR MORE INFORMATION

For information on scholarships, membership, careers, and certification, contact

American Institute of Certified Public Accountants
1211 Avenue of the Americas
New York, NY 10036-8775
Tel: (212) 596-6200
E-mail: service@aicpa.org
http://www.aicpa.org

Visit the institute's Web site for information on certification for financial analysts.

CFA Institute
915 East High Street
Charlottesville, VA 22902-4868
Tel: (800) 247-8132
E-mail: info@cfainstitute.org
http://www.cfainstitute.org

For information on certification, contact

Chartered Alternate Investment Analyst Association
Tel: (413) 253-7373
E-mail: info@caia.org
https://www.caia.org

For information on careers and certification, contact

Chartered Institute of Management Accountants
E-mail: vision@cimaglobal.com
http://www.cimaglobal.com

For information on membership, certification, and continuing education, contact

Institute of Internal Auditors
247 Maitland Avenue
Altamonte Springs, FL 32701-4201
Tel: (407) 937-1111
https://na.theiia.org

For information on certification, careers, continuing education, and its online professional network, contact

Institute of Management Accountants
10 Paragon Drive, Suite 1
Montvale, NJ 07645-1760
Tel: (800) 638-4427
E-mail: ima@imanet.org
http://www.imanet.org

For more information on venture capital, contact

National Venture Capital Association
25 Massachusetts Avenue, NW, Suite 730
Washington, D.C. 20001-1430
Tel: (202) 864-5920
http://www.nvca.org

Venture Capital Analysts

■ OVERVIEW

Venture capital analysts are entry-level professionals who conduct due diligence and deal sourcing, and perform a variety of administrative and support duties. They are typically hired only by large venture capital firms.

■ HISTORY

The venture capital (VC) industry as we know it today began in 1946 when Georges Doriot (who is often considered the "father of venture capital") and others started American Research and Development Corporation (ARDC), the first publicly owned VC firm. During that same year, three wealthy families established professional VC operations (Rockefeller Brothers Inc., J. H. Whitney, and Payson & Trask) in New York City. From 1946 through 1957, ARDC and the three family operations engaged in VC investing, but no other VC firms were founded.

Technological, political, financial, and regulatory events fueled growth in the VC industry starting in the late 1950s onward. One major milestone during this period was the funding of the first venture-backed start-up (Fairchild Semiconductor) in 1957.

Many well-known VC firms were founded in California and on the East Coast in the 1960s and early 1970s—including Sutter Hill Ventures (1962), Greylock Partners (1965), Kleiner, Perkins, Caufield & Byers (1972), and Sequoia Capital (1972).

As the industry grew, venture capitalists began to form professional associations to represent their interests in Washington, D.C., and in foreign capitals, and to assist venture capitalists in their work. In 1969, the first official nonprofit VC organization in the world—the Western Association of Venture Capitalists—was founded. Today, it is comprised of more than 100 venture firms and more than 1,000 venture capitalists. In 1973, the National Venture Capital Association was founded in the offices of the Heizer Corporation, a leading VC firm. It has more than 300 members.

Today, there are more than 800 venture capital firms in the United States alone.

■ THE JOB

Many industry experts describe the job of venture capital analyst as an "in-and-out position" because it is not a partner-track position and analysts must leave the firm after a few years of employment to earn their MBAs, launch a start-up, or otherwise obtain operational and entrepreneurial experience to become qualified for an upper-level position at a VC firm.

The primary duties of analysts are to help associates, principals, and partners conduct due diligence and deal sourcing. They also have administrative and support duties.

During due diligence, the analyst might be asked to screen 20 business plans, selecting the most promising one or two to send up the pipeline to partners. To make this decision, they review financial data, talk with the founders of start-ups, investigate competitors, try out prototypes of start-ups' products or services (if available), talk with their network of friends in the business world, and read industry publications, blogs, and Web sites.

Analysts also source deals, which means that they identify investment opportunities. They attend trade shows and investment conferences, read business journals, talk with business experts and entrepreneurs, and use other sources to identify promising companies. When they discover a good target, they prepare a report on their findings and pass this information along to their manager for review and consideration by the firm's partners.

Lastly, analysts perform administrative and support duties. These range from serving as a "gofer" (fetching coffee or lunch and making photocopies) for partners, to organizing and reviewing basic financial data for associates or principals.

■ EARNINGS

Financial analysts earned median annual salaries of $78,620 in May 2014, according to the U.S. Department of Labor. Salaries ranged from $48,170 to $154,680 or more. Analysts usually receive benefits such as paid vacation days and sick leave, health and life insurance, a 401(k) or other retirement savings plan, and closing bonuses (for sourcing or doing due diligence for an investment deal that is closed). They do not receive carry (a small percentage of the profits the firm makes) or the opportunity to co-invest (invest their own money alongside the firm in some deals).

■ WORK ENVIRONMENT

Although it's understood that they will have to leave their firm after a few years on the job to earn an MBA, most analysts still view their position as a chance to impress the partners and win a coveted invitation to get on the partner track. What does this entail? A lot of grunt work, repetitive job duties, and long hours—including at night and on weekends. In fact, 51 percent of venture capital and private equity professionals—typically associates and analysts, but sometimes managers—worked at least 70 hours a week in 2014, according to the *2015 Private Equity and Venture Capital Compensation Report*. Analysts also travel to meet with the founders of prospective portfolio companies and to attend industry conferences and networking events.

■ EXPLORING

Check out the following resources to learn about the work of analysts and the venture capital industry:

- *Financial Analysts Journal*: http://www.cfapubs .org/loi/faj
- *Venture Capital Journal*: http://www.privatemar kets.thomsonreuters.com/Venture-capital-journal
- Venture Capital Post: http://www.vcpost.com

In college, join venture capital and finance clubs, which offer job shadowing opportunities, investment competitions, networking events, peer industry panels and coffee chats, and mentoring programs. Check with your school to see what types of clubs and programs are available.

■ EDUCATION AND TRAINING REQUIREMENTS
High School

Exceptional grades are needed to get into an elite college, so you need to be very dedicated to your studies in high school. Take as many classes as possible in business, microeconomics, macroeconomics, statistics, accounting, mathematics, computer science, foreign language, English, and speech. Any classes and activities that help you to develop your critical-thinking, analytical, and communication skills will be useful.

Postsecondary Education

Since there are so few analyst positions available, your educational credentials must be outstanding (i.e., a degree from an Ivy League or other top tier school, excellent grades, active participation in business and investment clubs, and participation in at least one internship at a top VC firm, investment bank, Big Four accounting firm, or other prominent employer). Analysts typically have bachelor's degrees in business, finance, entrepreneurism, or a related major.

Other Education or Training

Many professional associations provide continuing education classes, webinars, and workshops. For example, the Market Technicians Association offers webcasts such as Building a Career Using Technical Analysis and U.S. Financial Market Update. Such educational offerings give you an opportunity to build your skills and impress hiring managers. Professional development classes and webinars are also provided by the CFA Institute and the National Venture Capital associations. Contact these organizations for more information.

Certification

The Investment Management Consultants Association offers the Fundamentals of Alternative Investments Certificate Program. In this online, self-paced course, you'll learn about the differences between traditional and alternative investments, due diligence, risk management, investment returns and risks, venture capital and private equity, and other topics. Visit https://www.imca.org/pages/ Fundamentals-Alternative -Investments-Certificate for more information.

QUICK FACTS

ALTERNATE TITLE(S)
None

DUTIES
Conduct due diligence of investment opportunities, deal sourcing, and a variety of administrative and support duties

SALARY RANGE
$48,170 to $78,620 to $154,680+

WORK ENVIRONMENT
Primarily Indoors

BEST GEOGRAPHIC LOCATION(S)
Opportunities are best in San Francisco and other cities with a large number of start-ups

MINIMUM EDUCATION LEVEL
Bachelor's Degree

SCHOOL SUBJECTS
Business, Economics, Mathematics

EXPERIENCE
Internship at a top venture capital firm, investment bank, Big Four accounting firm, or other prominent employer

PERSONALITY TRAITS
Enterprising, Hands On, Outgoing

SKILLS
Financial, Interpersonal, Research

CERTIFICATION OR LICENSING
Recommended

SPECIAL REQUIREMENTS
None

EMPLOYMENT PROSPECTS
Fair

ADVANCEMENT PROSPECTS
Poor

OUTLOOK
Faster than the Average

NOC
1112

O*NET-SOC
13-2051.00, 13-2099.01

CAREER LADDER

Managing Partner

General Partner

Principal

Associate

Analyst

■ CERTIFICATION, LICENSING, AND SPECIAL REQUIREMENTS

Certification or Licensing

Becoming certified is an excellent way to demonstrate your skills and knowledge to prospective employers. Many certification programs are available, but some are only open to those with several years of on-the-job experience. One credential that's available to those with either a bachelor's degree or those who are in the last year of undergraduate study is the three-level chartered financial analyst (CFA) program, which is administered by the CFA Institute. Although it takes an average of four years to complete the CFA program, pursuing this credential will impress potential employers and provide you with excellent knowledge about financial analysis. Another useful certification is the chartered alternate investment analyst credential, which is offered by the Chartered Alternate Investment Analyst Association. Applicants must have a bachelor's degree, and have more than one year of professional experience, or alternatively, have at least four years of professional experience.

■ EXPERIENCE, SKILLS, AND PERSONALITY TRAITS

Aspiring venture capital analysts must complete at least one internship or co-operative educational experience at a top venture capital firm, Big Four accounting firm, investment bank, or other prestigious employer.

Communication and interpersonal skills rank among the most-important traits for analysts, who frequently meet with start-up founders, industry experts, and others to source deals and conduct due diligence on potential investments. Analysts need to work well as a member of a team, and be able to effectively communicate their opinions to principals and partners. Other important traits include a strong work ethic; good research, organizational, and analytical skills; the ability to multi-task; and familiarity with financial statements and data.

■ EMPLOYMENT PROSPECTS

Employers

Venture capital firms are located throughout the United States and the world. Analysts are typically only hired by large firms. They can also work for the portfolio companies of VC firms, investment and commercial banks, in other alternative investment sectors such as private equity, and for any other employer that requires financial analysis.

Starting Out

The best way to land an analyst position is to participate in an internship or cooperative educational experience at a venture capital firm. You can find such opportunities by visiting the Web sites of large VC firms, utilizing the resources of your college's career services office, and visiting job-search sites such as https://www.linkedin.com/jobs/venture-capital-intern-jobs and http://www.efinancialcareers.com. Interns compile performance and financial data, help partners prepare for monthly meetings/calls with portfolio companies, create spreadsheets to streamline processes and better analyze data, and work on other projects as directed by partners or the chief financial officer.

■ ADVANCEMENT PROSPECTS

Unlike principals and some associates, analysts are not on the partner track. Most analysts typically work at a venture capital firm for two to three years before leaving to earn their MBAs, work in operation roles at a portfolio company, or found a start-up.

An analyst who earns an MBA and obtains some operational and entrepreneurial experience might return to a VC firm as an associate or principal. After years of experience, they can advance to the position of general partner, and then managing partner. Some choose to work at portfolio companies or other businesses, with the most skilled gradually advancing to the positions of chief financial officer, CEO, and chief operating officer.

Venture capital firms rely on analysts to assess companies for investment. (Rawpixel.com. Shutterstock.)

OUTLOOK

It's extremely difficult to land an analyst position at a venture capital firm because the industry is so tiny and only a small percentage of firms hire analysts. Those with superior educational credentials, multiple internships at prestigious employers, and a large network of industry contacts will have the best prospects of landing a job.

Outside the VC industry, job opportunities are good for financial analysts. The U.S. Department of Labor (DOL) predicts that employment for financial analysts will grow by 12 percent through 2024, or faster than the average for all careers. The DOL reports that "having certifications and a graduate degree can significantly improve an applicant's prospects."

UNIONS AND ASSOCIATIONS

Venture capital analysts are not members of unions, but they can join professional associations such as the Association for Financial Professionals, CFA Institute, Chartered Alternate Investment Analyst Association, and the Market Technicians Association. These organizations provide certification, publications, continuing education classes and webinars, career support, networking events, and other resources. The National Venture Capital Association is the leading trade association of the U.S. venture capital industry. It has more than 300 member firms, and offers white papers, a blog, industry statistics, and webinars at its Web site. Women.VC, the Association of Women in Alternative Investing, and the Women's Association of Venture and Equity are membership organizations that seek to increase the number of women in the venture capital and other alternative investment industries.

TIPS FOR ENTRY

1. Visit the following Web sites for job listings:
   - http://www.iaqf.org/job-board
   - http://www.jobsearchdigest.com
   - http://www.ventureloop.com
2. Join the International Association for Quantitative Finance (IAQF) and other professional organizations to participate in networking events, take continuing education classes and webinars, and receive discounts on conferences and publications. The IAQF offers membership options for college students and young practitioners.
3. Networking is key to landing a job in the VC industry. Visit http://www.jobsearchdigest.com/private_equity_jobs/career_advice/networking_vc_job to read "Successful Networking for a Venture Capital Job."

SPOTTING GOOD INVESTMENTS — DID YOU KNOW?

How do you spot a good investment? That's a frequent question asked by aspiring venture capitalists. If this could be definitively answered, venture capital would be a secure business indeed! Multiple VC firms rejected many of today's most successful companies. And many companies that have received $10 million, $40 million, and even $400 million in venture capital money have disappeared (remember Webvan, Procket, and Optiva?).

The "perfect investment" has:

- A complete management team who you enjoy spending time with. They are loved by their employees, have experience and integrity, and are respected by the investment community.
- A clearly defined, large, and unexploited market opportunity.
- A finished product that works and addresses a clear market need.
- A set of customers with money to spend, and the ability and desire to spend it.
- A company that is located in a place where it is easily monitored.
- A low price.
- No other institutional investors, or excellent early-stage investors.
- A leading position in the targeted market.
- A unique set of capabilities that will keep the company ahead of the competition, with or without patents (otherwise known as barriers to entry).

All other opportunities are defined as "hairy," displaying some element of risk. But what doesn't?

FOR MORE INFORMATION

For information on earnings, careers, and certification, contact

Association for Financial Professionals
4520 East-West Highway, Suite 750
Bethesda, MD 20814-3574
Tel: (301) 907-2862
http://www.afponline.org

AWAI is a membership organization for women in the venture capital, hedge fund, and private equity industries.

Association of Women in Alternative Investing
AWAI
E-mail: info@altinvesting.org
http://www.altinvesting.org

Visit the institute's Web site for information on certification for financial analysts.

CFA Institute
915 East High Street
Charlottesville, VA 22902-4868
Tel: (800) 247-8132
E-mail: info@cfainstitute.org
http://www.cfainstitute.org

For information on certification, contact

**Chartered Alternate Investment Analyst
    Association**
Tel: (413) 253-7373
E-mail: info@caia.org
https://www.caia.org

For information on education and careers in financial engineering, contact

**International Association for Quantitative
    Finance**
http://www.iaqf.org

For information on certification, continuing education, and networking, contact

Market Technicians Association
61 Broadway, Suite 514
New York, NY 10006-2733
Tel: (646) 652-3300
http://www.mta.org

For more information on venture capital, contact

National Venture Capital Association
25 Massachusetts Avenue, NW, Suite 730
Washington, D.C. 20001-1430
Tel: (202) 864-5920
http://www.nvca.org

For information on membership, contact

Women's Association of Venture and Equity
10 Winton Farm Road
Newtown, CT 06470-2653
Tel: (855) 928-3606
E-mail: wavecoordinator@gmail.com
https://women-wave.org

Women.VC describes itself as an "independent nonprofit organization aiming to strengthen and develop the world investment industry by introducing women professionals who bring real value."

Women.VC
http://www.women.vc

Venture Capital Associates

◼ OVERVIEW

Venture capital associates are entry-level professionals who source deals, perform due diligence on potential investments, and support their firm's portfolio companies. Associates may also be known as *researchers* and *deal sourcers.*

◼ HISTORY

The venture capital (VC) industry as it is known today began in 1946 when Georges Doriot (who is often considered the "father of venture capital") and others started American Research and Development Corporation, the first publicly owned VC firm. Arguably its best investment was the $70,000 it spent in 1957 to help fund Digital Equipment Corporation. Eleven years later, that investment was valued at more than $355 million after the company's initial public offering.

Associates are the "foot soldiers" of venture capital firms. Their primary duties are to source deals and perform due diligence to support the partners so they can deploy more money in profitable investments.

◼ THE JOB

Associates have three main functions at venture capital firms: 1) sourcing deals, 2) performing due diligence on potential investments, and 3) supporting the portfolio companies. Here's a breakdown of their duties in each category:

Sourcing Deals

In an early stage VC firm, you will be expected to source deals. You need to reach out into the world and bring investment opportunities to the firm. This amounts to calling and visiting companies to ascertain their attractiveness and interest in raising capital. This isn't as easy as it sounds. Deal sourcers will go to trade shows, talk with their networks of friends, read the trade press, work with other venture capitalists, attend local networking events and investment conferences, read unsolicited business plans, and talk to portfolio company managers. There are hundreds of deal sourcers at work at any given time—and being the first venture capitalist to contact a company matters. When sourcing deals, schmoozing is key. Any acquaintance or friend might give you the next lead on a company. Venture capital associates must build personal relationships with business partners to increase the level of trust and interdependence.

Conducting Due Diligence

Associates support partners in the due diligence analysis of an investment opportunity. Later-stage companies are normally no secret (they're typically large enough to have attracted press and other attention). The goal is not to uncover the investment opportunity, but to get a company to take your money. Consequently, the partner is usually the one to source later-stage deals. Associates perform due diligence: building spreadsheets and running sensitivity analyses, calling references, investigating competitors, validating legal contracts, visiting remote locations, coordinating with other investors, and so on. Ultimately, associates and partners must decide how best to use the most precious resource: time. Which markets to research? Which company to work on? Which entrepreneur to call back? Which spreadsheet model to build? Which references to call? Which trip to take, which meeting to make? As an apprentice venture capitalist, associates must make decisions all day long. Many of those decisions have to do with which potential assignments to pursue. A venture firm is responsible for the money in its fund, and the clock is ticking.

Supporting Portfolio Companies

In this role, you'll conduct research about target portfolio companies and assist partners during the acquisition process (including negotiating and working with investment bankers, raising more money from other equity sources, negotiating with banks for debt financing, etc.). Once a company is acquired, you'll attend board of directors meetings, help locate and screen potential additions to a company's management team, convince new recruits that they should work with your portfolio company, support the management team (this can be anything from being a friend to "handholding"), and keep partners up-to-date on changes, problems, and successes. You'll also analyze potential exit opportunities for portfolio companies.

■ EARNINGS

Venture capital associates earned median annual salaries of $96,347 in 2015, according to Payscale.com. Salaries ranged from $52,151 to $169,416.

Venture capital associates usually receive a generous benefits package, including vacation days, sick leave, health and life insurance, and a 401(k) or other retirement savings plan. Associates may also receive a closing bonus (for sourcing or doing due diligence for an investment deal that is closed), the opportunity to co-invest (invest their own money alongside the firm in some deals), and sometimes receive a small percentage of carry (the profits the firm makes).

■ WORK ENVIRONMENT

In 2014, 51 percent of venture capital and private equity professionals—typically associates and analysts, but sometimes managers—worked at least 70 hours a week, according to the *2015 Private Equity and Venture Capital Compensation Report*. Associates frequently travel to meet with representatives of potential portfolio companies and investment banks and attend trade events, industry conferences, and networking events. This career can be extremely stressful because associates face constant pressure to generate a steady flow of new investment prospects. Associates often work on nights and weekends to meet with business contacts or catch up on office work that they were unable to complete during regular office hours as a result of being out in the field working on deals.

■ EXPLORING

There are many ways to learn more about venture capital and careers in the field. The U.S. Small Business Administration offers a concise overview of venture capital at https://www.sba.gov/content/venture-capital. You should also check out venture capital blogs such as the *Wall Street Journal*'s Venture Capital Dispatch, http://blogs.wsj.com/venturecapital. Talk to venture capital associates about their careers. Try to develop relationships on LinkedIn or ask your professors to recommend some venture capitalists who would be willing to discuss their careers and what a typical day on the job is like for associates.

QUICK FACTS	
ALTERNATE TITLE(S)	Deal Sourcers, Researchers
DUTIES	Source deals, perform due diligence on potential investments, and support their firm's portfolio companies
SALARY RANGE	$52,151 to $96,347 to $169,416
WORK ENVIRONMENT	Primarily Indoors
BEST GEOGRAPHIC LOCATION(S)	Opportunities are best in New York City, San Francisco, and in other cities with large financial sectors
MINIMUM EDUCATION LEVEL	Bachelor's Degree, Master's Degree
SCHOOL SUBJECTS	Business, Economics, Mathematics
EXPERIENCE	Two or more years of experience in management consulting, investment banking, or private equity
PERSONALITY TRAITS	Enterprising, Hands On, Outgoing
SKILLS	Financial, Interpersonal, Math
CERTIFICATION OR LICENSING	Recommended
SPECIAL REQUIREMENTS	None
EMPLOYMENT PROSPECTS	Good
ADVANCEMENT PROSPECTS	Good
OUTLOOK	Much Faster than the Average
NOC	1112
O*NET-SOC	13-2051.00, 13-2099.01

CAREER LADDER

Managing Partner

General Partner

Principal

Senior Associate

Associate/Analyst

■ EDUCATION AND TRAINING REQUIREMENTS
High School

You'll need at least a bachelor's degree—and preferably a master's degree—to work as a venture capital associate, so be sure to pursue a college-preparatory curriculum in high school. Recommended classes include business, microeconomics, macroeconomics, accounting, mathematics, foreign language, and computer science. English and speech classes will help you to develop strong communication skills to source deals and network with others in the VC industry.

Postsecondary Education

Many venture capital associates have master's degrees in business, finance, or a related major—typically from Ivy League schools or other prestigious colleges. Some are able to enter the field with just a bachelor's degree in one of these majors.

Other Education or Training

Executive education programs in venture capital and private equity are offered by the University of California-Berkeley, Harvard University, and other schools. The CFA Institute offers a class on general capital that focuses on concepts such as general partner due diligence, determining investor

Venture capital associates talk over new business candidates for backing. (Zurijeta. Shutterstock.)

cash flows, and assessing fees. Continuing education classes are also provided by professional associations such as the Alternative Investment Management Association, Financial Management Association International, and the International Association for Quantitative Finance. Contact these organizations for more information.

Certification

The Investment Management Consultants Association offers the Fundamentals of Alternative Investments Certificate Program. In this online, self-paced course, you'll learn about the differences between traditional and alternative investments, investment returns and risks, due diligence, risk management, venture capital and private equity, hedge funds, and other topics. Visit https://www.imca.org/pages/Fundamentals-Alternative-Investments-Certificate for more information.

■ CERTIFICATION, LICENSING, AND SPECIAL REQUIREMENTS
Certification or Licensing

There are no specific certification designations for venture capital associates, but some earn financial certifications that provide them with additional expertise as they do their work. Some popular certifications include:

- chartered financial analyst (administered by the CFA Institute)
- chartered alternate investment analyst (Chartered Alternate Investment Analyst Association)
- certified investment management analyst (Investment Management Consultants Association)
- certified treasury professional, certified corporate financial planning and analysis professional (Association for Financial Professionals)
- certified investment management analyst (Investment Management Consultants Association)

■ EXPERIENCE, SKILLS, AND PERSONALITY TRAITS

Most associates have two or more years of experience in management consulting, investment banking, or private equity—ideally in acquisition due diligence or deal making. A small percentage of associates are hired straight out of college, but have internship or co-op experience at a venture capital, private equity, investment banking, or financial consulting firm.

To be a successful associate, you need excellent communication and interpersonal skills—and a high degree of self-confidence—because you'll need to constantly be reaching out to source deals, interact with your colleagues and managers, and work with the management of portfolio companies. Other important traits include project management, organizational, and analytical skills; a strong work ethic; the ability to effectively manage multiple tasks at one time; and familiarity with financial statements and data.

■ EMPLOYMENT PROSPECTS
Employers

Venture capital firms are located throughout the United States and the world. Many U.S.-based firms are headquartered on the East Coast and in California. Many venture capital firms have fewer than 15 employees. Associates can also find work at corporations that have VC divisions, at the portfolio companies of venture capital firms, and in related industries such as private equity.

Starting Out

Venture capital firms are inundated with requests for interviews and information interviews. The time of venture capitalists is precious. If a VC firm lets it be known they have a single summer internship available, they can expect 300 resumes from people at the top 10 business schools. Now that you're more aware of what you are up against, here's a glint of hope—as a whole, venture capital firms are always hiring.

Your chances of landing a job greatly increases if you already have an MBA and have operational or deal making experience in a related industry (e.g., private equity, investment banking). If you don't, it helps to develop a strong professional network—ideally, with current associates or other in the industry, since many job leads are obtained through word of mouth and in-house referrals. To build your network, attend venture capital conferences, become active on LinkedIn, and volunteer with venture capital—or general business—organizations. One such organization is the VC Taskforce (http://www.vctaskforce.com), which provides networking and educational events—panels, workshops, conferences, and roundtable meetings—for venture capitalists and entrepreneurs seeking funding. According to its Web site, VC Taskforce is looking for volunteers with one or more of the following skills: writing and editing, public relations and marketing communications, event management, sales and business development, research and interviewing, social media, corporate relationship building, and program development and management. A six-month commitment is required.

■ ADVANCEMENT PROSPECTS

Most associates do not make partner because 1) the majority of firms are too small to offer advancement

opportunities to their associates, and 2) most managing partners prefer their principals and general partners to have some sort of entrepreneurial experience before being trusted to make investments. As a result, most associates typically work at a venture capital firm for two to three years before being leaving to earn their MBAs, work in operation roles at a portfolio companies, or found a startup.

For associates lucky enough to be on the partner track, the typical advancement path goes from associate, to senior associate, principal, general partner, and then managing partner.

■ OUTLOOK

The U.S. Department of Labor (DOL) does not provide an employment outlook for private equity associates, but it does report that job opportunities for financial analysts who work for securities, commodities, and other financial investment and related firms are expected to grow much faster than the average for all careers through 2024, according to the U.S. Department of Labor.

■ UNIONS AND ASSOCIATIONS

Venture capital associates do not belong to unions. The National Venture Capital Association, the flagship trade association of the U.S. venture capital industry, has more than 300 member firms. The CFA Institute, Chartered Alternate Investment Analyst Association, Investment Management Consultants Association, Association for Financial Professionals, and Investment Management Consultants Association provide financial-related certifications and continuing education classes and webinars. The Association of Women in Alternative Investing, Women's Association of Venture and Equity, and Women. VC are membership organizations that seek to increase the number of women who are employed in venture capital and other alternative investment industries.

■ TIPS FOR ENTRY

1. Visit http://www.jobsearchdigest.com/private _equity_jobs/career_advice/how_to_get_a_vc _job to read "How to Get a Job in Venture Capital."
2. Become active in your school's business or finance club.
3. Be willing to relocate to venture capital hubs in California and on the East Coast. It will provide more opportunities.

■ FOR MORE INFORMATION

AWAI is a membership organization for women in the venture capital, hedge fund, and private equity industries.

Association of Women in Alternative Investing (AWAI)
E-mail: info@altinvesting.org
http://www.altinvesting.org

For more information on venture capital, contact
National Venture Capital Association
25 Massachusetts Avenue, NW, Suite 730
Washington, D.C. 20001-1430
Tel: (202) 864-5920
http://www.nvca.org

For information on membership, contact
Women's Association of Venture and Equity
10 Winton Farm Road
Newtown, CT 06470-2653
Tel: (855) 928-3606
E-mail: wavecoordinator@gmail.com
https://women-wave.org

Women.VC describes itself as an "independent nonprofit organization aiming to strengthen and develop the world investment industry by introducing women professionals who bring real value."
Women.VC
http://www.women.vc

Venture Capital Chief Financial Officers

■ OVERVIEW

Chief financial officers manage the accounting and financial reporting functions of venture capital firms and their portfolio companies. They also provide strategic business advice to partners and the founders of start-ups.

■ HISTORY

In the early days of the venture capital (VC) industry, founders managed the accounting and financial reporting functions of their firms. As the number of VC firms grew and assets under management increased, founders became too busy to handle these duties. As a result, VC firms began hiring accountants, controllers, and chief financial officers (CFOs) from the corporate world to take on these responsibilities.

Increasingly complex financial transactions, a trend toward more government regulation, and growing demand by investors for transparency and more due diligence information have prompted VC managing partners to rely ever-more on chief financial officers. "The modern CFO has publicly emerged as not only a financial leader, but also a business leader," according to TechCrunch.com. "She is not just a number cruncher, but also a power player in the C-suite. No longer taking a back seat in business discussions, the modern CFO acts as a key driver for evaluating strategic opportunities for a business."

■ THE JOB

The financial management team at a large venture capital firm typically consists of a chief financial officer, a financial controller (or director of finance), an accounting manager (or chief accountant), and one or more accountants and auditors. Chief financial officers are typically employed by medium and large venture capital firms. At a start-up VC firm, hiring a CFO may not be practical, and the firm's founder may be responsible for financial duties or he or she may hire lower-level accounting professionals (such as accountants or controllers) to handle these duties. Major responsibilities of CFOs include:

- handling various financial management tasks, such as tracking cash flow, capital expenditure planning, reconciling bank accounts, and allocating income to limited and general partners in accordance with terms of partnership agreements
- analyzing financial data and providing strategic advice to partners
- preparing quarterly financial reports for investors. These reports contain balance sheets (that list the portfolio companies and their fair market value, as well as cash on hand), profit and loss statements, cash-flow statements, and a schedule of investments.
- working closely with the CFOs of the firm's portfolio companies, or serving as the temporary or permanent CFO of a portfolio company
- overseeing the firm's annual financial budgeting, forecasting, and review process
- developing and implementing financial control processes (in order to ensure operational efficiency and effectiveness, reliable financial reporting, and compliance with laws and regulations
- conducting financial due diligence on potential VC investments and prospective limited partners
- serving as the liaison to internal auditing firms during the auditing process
- overseeing employee benefits programs (including health insurance and retirement fund plans)
- working with risk managers to assess and address areas of financial risk
- assuming responsibility for a variety of other areas at the firm, including information technology, digital security, human resources, and business development functions

■ EARNINGS

Chief financial officers who were employed by venture-backed technology companies earned base salaries of $225,000 in 2014, according to the *2014 VC Executive Compensation Survey Trend Report for Technology Companies* from Advanced-HR, Inc., a private company compensation consulting firm. They also received average incentive pay (i.e., bonuses) of $55,000.

Chief financial officers in the finance and accounting sector earned salaries that ranged from $155,000 to $275,000 in 2015, according to financial recruiter Robert Half Accounting & Finance's *2016 Salary Guide*.

Venture capital CFOs receive benefits such as health and life insurance, a 401(k) or other retirement savings plan, and paid vacation and sick leave. In 2014, CFOs who were employed by venture-backed technology companies received an average of 1 percent of equity (stock options) in the company, according to Advanced-HR, Inc.

■ WORK ENVIRONMENT

Expect to work long hours as a venture capital CFO. In fact, accounting and finance managers logged an average of 47 hours per week in 2013, according to a survey by Robert Half and the Financial Executives Research Foundation. The work environment can be extremely busy. Some CFOs manage several funds at once, which sometimes entails interaction with a different set of investors, the preparation of different quarterly reports, conducting separate audits, and having other unique responsibilities based on the size and type of the fund. Chief financial officers frequently travel to meet with investors, to assist with road shows, and to attend industry conferences and business development events.

QUICK FACTS

ALTERNATE TITLE(S)
None

DUTIES
Manage their employer's accounting and financial reporting functions and provide strategic advice to executives; track and analyze financial data; oversee budgeting and financial controls

SALARY RANGE
$155,000 to $225,000 to $280,000

WORK ENVIRONMENT
Primarily Indoors

BEST GEOGRAPHIC LOCATION(S)
Opportunities are best in San Francisco and in other cities with a large number of start-ups

MINIMUM EDUCATION LEVEL
Bachelor's Degree, Master's Degree

SCHOOL SUBJECTS
Business, Economics, Mathematics

EXPERIENCE
Ten years of experience in lower-level accounting and finance positions

PERSONALITY TRAITS
Organized, Problem-Solving, Realistic

SKILLS
Financial, Information Management, Leadership

CERTIFICATION OR LICENSING
Recommended

SPECIAL REQUIREMENTS
None

EMPLOYMENT PROSPECTS
Fair

ADVANCEMENT PROSPECTS
Fair

OUTLOOK
Much Faster than the Average

NOC
0013, 0111

O*NET-SOC
11-1011.00, 11-3031.01

CAREER LADDER

Partner or Chief Executive Officer

Chief Financial Officer

Controller

Chief Accountant

Accountant/Auditor

■ EXPLORING

There are many blogs that provide useful information about the venture capital industry and the work of chief financial officers, including the following:

- CFO Report: http://blogs.wsj.com/cfo/tag/venture-capital
- Samuel's CFO Blog: http://dergelcfo.com/blog
- Venture CFO: http://theventurecfo.com

Read the bios of VC-fund chief financial officers to learn about their job duties and the educational and professional steps they took to become CFOs. Visit the National Venture Capital Association's Web site, http://nvca.org/about-nvca/members, for a list of members.

Other ways to explore this career include joining finance and venture capital clubs in college, asking your professors for advice about pursuing a career in venture capital, and using LinkedIn to locate VC finance professionals who might be interested in participating in information interviews about their careers.

■ EDUCATION AND TRAINING REQUIREMENTS
High School

Key classes for aspiring CFOs include accounting, business, economics, mathematics, statistics, and computer science (especially database management). English and speech classes are also recommended since chief financial officers frequently write reports, give presentations, and meet with colleagues. Other useful courses include social studies, government, science, and foreign language.

Postsecondary Education

You'll need a minimum of a bachelor's degree in finance, accounting, economics, or business administration to work as a chief financial officer. If you earn a degree in business administration, you should also minor or double major in accounting or a related field. Many venture capital partners require applicants to have a master's degree in business or accounting.

AACSB International accredits colleges and universities that offer undergraduate and graduate degrees in accounting and business. Visit http://www.aacsb.edu/accreditation/accreditedmembers.asp for a list of accredited programs. An additional list of postsecondary accounting programs (associate through graduate level) can be accessed at https://www.thiswaytocpa.com/education/college-search.

Other Education or Training

Continuing education classes, workshops, seminars, and webinars are provided by accounting and finance associations at the national, state, and local levels. The Association of Financial Professionals, for example, provides in-person seminars and webinars on financial risk management, advanced financial statements and credit analysis, cost leadership, and cash flow forecasting. The Chartered Institute of Management Accountants offers more than 200 accounting, finance, business, and skill development (on leadership, communication, negotiation, etc.) courses. It's CFO of the Future master course features the following one-day workshops: Finance Leadership, Strategic Management, Cost and Profitability Analysis, Flexible Planning and Rolling Forecasts, and Best Practice Measurement and Reporting. Other opportunities are provided by the American Institute of Certified Public Accountants, CFA Institute, Financial Executives International, Institute of Internal Auditors, Institute of Management Accountants, and the National Venture Capital Association.

Several universities and organizations provide classes on venture capital deal structure, terms, due diligence, and other topics, including:

- University of California-Berkeley Venture Capital Executive Program: http://executive.berkeley.edu/programs/venture-capital-executive-program
- Venture Capital Institute: http://www.vcinstitute.org
- University of Michigan Center for Venture Capital and Private Equity Finance: http://www.zli.bus.umich.edu/vc_pe
- Venture Capital institute: http://www.vcinstitute.org/Venture_Capital_Institute.html

Certification

Certificate programs allow participants to build their skills in a particular practice area. They typically last less than two years, and more than 50 percent take less than a year to finish. Online and in-person options are usually available. Earning a certificate comes in handy if you need additional information about a field that is not covered in detail by the classes in your degree program. For example, you might pursue a certificate in business management if your major was in accounting or finance to make yourself a better job candidate.

Certificates are offered by accounting and finance associations such as the Chartered Institute of Management Accountants (business accounting), the Association of Chartered Certified Accountants (international auditing and international financial reporting), and the American Institute of Certified Public Accountants (International Financial Reporting Standards). Colleges and universities offer certificates in areas such as accounting, finance, auditing, and business management.

▆ CERTIFICATION, LICENSING, AND SPECIAL REQUIREMENTS
Certification or Licensing

Becoming certified helps you to demonstrate to potential employers that you've met the highest standards established by your industry. It's also a good way to keep your skills up to date because most certifications need to be renewed by completing continuing education classes and webinars. Here are some of the most-popular certifications:

- accredited business accountant/advisor, accredited tax preparer, accredited tax advisor (Accreditation Council for Accountancy and Taxation)
- certification in control self-assessment, certified financial services auditor, certification in risk management assurance (Institute of Internal Auditors)
- certified financial manager, certified management accountant (Institute of Management Accountants)
- certified internal auditor (Institute of Internal Auditors)
- chartered global management accountant (a joint venture of the American Institute of Certified Public Accountants and the Chartered Institute of Management Accountants)
- certified treasury professional, certified corporate financial planning and analysis professional (Association of Financial Professionals)

Many CFOs earn the certified public accountant (CPA) designation. The Uniform CPA Examination, which is administered by the American Institute of Certified Public Accountants, is used by all states.

▆ EXPERIENCE, SKILLS, AND PERSONALITY TRAITS

A minimum of 10 years of experience in lower-level accounting and finance positions is required to become a chief financial officer.

Key personality traits for CFOs include strong communication, interpersonal, organizational, and time-management skills; leadership ability; an analytical and

VENTURE CAPITAL--A SNAPSHOT   FAST FACTS

In 2014:

- There were 804 venture capital (VC) firms in the United States—down from 985 in 2004.
- A total of 257 VC funds in the U.S. raised money—an increase of 47 funds since 2004.
- The average fund size was $111 million, up from $95.3 million in 2004 and $55.9 million in 1994.
- Venture capital firms invested approximately $30 billion into 3,665 companies.
- A total of 345 VC funds closed; they raised $51.1 billion in capital. The median fund size was $60 million.
- Corporate venture capital groups participated in more than one in six venture deals.

In 2015:

- More than $126 million in venture capital was invested worldwide. There were 12,371 deals, and the median deal size was $2.25 million. Sixty-six percent of deals occurred in North America, 19 percent in Europe, and 15 percent in the rest of the world.
- Worldwide, 1,415 VC funds closed; they raised $85.3 billion in capital. The median fund size was $47 million.
- The most-popular exit areas were in software (36 percent of exits), commercial services (13 percent), health care services and supplies (9 percent), and pharmaceuticals and biotechnology (9 percent).

Sources: National Venture Capital Association *Yearbook 2015;* PitchBook

detail-oriented personality; strong ethics; the ability to multitask and change gears as project requirements evolve; and a willingness to continue to learn throughout their careers. Chief financial officers must be familiar with venture capital funding accounting rules, reporting practices, and valuation methodology; have experience in project/deal financing; and be proficient in the use of financial-related software and databases such as Microsoft Dynamics Great Plains, Oracle PeopleSoft, and SAP; data management software such as Microsoft Excel; and presentation software such as Microsoft PowerPoint.

▆ EMPLOYMENT PROSPECTS
Employers

Chief financial officers are employed by venture capital firms (there are about 800 in the U.S.), the portfolio companies of VC firms, and accounting firms that provide services to VC funds. In addition, CFOs work for other businesses, government agencies, and nonprofit organizations.

Starting Out

Since it's so difficult to land a job at a venture capital firm, many aspiring CFOs begin their careers working as accountants and auditors at accounting firms (preferably at one of the Big Four) that have VC practices, portfolio companies of VC firms, regulatory agencies such as the Securities & Exchange Commission, or the accounting/ internal auditing departments of corporations. After obtaining a few years of experience, they can transition to entry-level accounting or auditing jobs at a VC firm.

You can learn about job openings by networking online (via LinkedIn, discussion boards of professional associations, etc.) and by attending in-person events held by trade organizations, your school's career service office, and casual networking groups that list events on Web sites such as MeetUp.com.

■ ADVANCEMENT PROSPECTS

A chief financial officer at a venture capital firm may be asked to become a partner or the managing partner. A few highly-skilled CFOS start their own VC funds. Those employed by corporations or public accounting firms can advance to the positions of chief operating officer or chief executive officer.

■ OUTLOOK

Job opportunities for financial managers (including chief financial officers) who work with funds, trusts, and other financial vehicles will grow by nearly 19 percent through 2024, according to the *Occupational Outlook Handbook.* Despite this prediction, it will be tough to land a job. The venture capital industry is small and only a finite number of positions are available. Some smaller firms do not have CFOs on staff, and there is only one CFO per firm at the firms that do employ these professionals.

Employment prospects are better at the portfolio companies of VC firms—especially those that the firm plans to take public. "A CFO with experience taking a company public is in the catbird seat these days," according to an article on the trend at CFO.com. Chief financial officers with IPO experience are in short supply because the number of IPOs is down overall in the past decade, and many CFOs who have guided companies through the demanding and timely process do not want to take on another IPO.

■ UNIONS AND ASSOCIATIONS

Venture capital CFOs do not belong to unions, but many join finance and accounting associations. These organizations provide excellent career and professional development resources. For example, members of the Association for Financial Professionals receive access to virtual seminars and complimentary webinars, a member directory, discussion boards, and research papers. The association also provides certification and professional development opportunities. Other noteworthy organizations include the American Institute of Certified Public Accountants, Chartered Institute of Management Accountants, Financial Executives International, Financial Management Association International, Institute of Management Accountants, and the Private Equity CFO Association. The National Venture Capital Association is the leading trade association for VC firms in the United States. It offers webinars, publications such as *Venture Capital Review,* industry statistics, and other resources at its Web site. It also has a CFO Task Force.

■ TIPS FOR ENTRY

1. Attend the annual National Venture Capital Association/EY CFO Development Summit (http://nvca.org/events/category/official-nvca -event) to network and participate in continuing education opportunities.
2. Visit the following Web sites for job listings:
   - https://www.glassdoor.com
   - http://www.cfojobsearch.com
   - http://www.efinancialcareers.com
   - https://www.linkedin.com
3. Join professional associations such as the American Institute of Certified Public Accountants and the Association for Financial Professionals to access training and networking resources, industry publications, and employment opportunities.

■ FOR MORE INFORMATION

For information on scholarships, membership, careers, and certification, contact

American Institute of Certified Public Accountants
1211 Avenue of the Americas
New York, NY 10036-8775
Tel: (212) 596-6200
E-mail: service@aicpa.org
http://www.aicpa.org

For information on earnings, careers, and certification, contact

Association for Financial Professionals
4520 East-West Highway, Suite 750
Bethesda, MD 20814-3574
Tel: (301) 907-2862
http://www.afponline.org

Visit the institute's Web site for information on certification for financial analysts.

CFA Institute
915 East High Street
Charlottesville, VA 22902-4868
Tel: (800) 247-8132
E-mail: info@cfainstitute.org
http://www.cfainstitute.org

For information on certification, contact

Chartered Alternate Investment Analyst Association
Tel: (413) 253-7373
E-mail: info@caia.org
https://www.caia.org

For information on careers and certification, contact

Chartered Institute of Management Accountants
E-mail: vision@cimaglobal.com
http://www.cimaglobal.com

This organization represents the professional interests of senior-level financial executives. Visit its Web site for more information.

Financial Executives International
1250 Headquarters Plaza, West Tower, 7th Floor
Morristown, NJ 07960
Tel: (973) 765-1000
http://www.financialexecutives.org

For information on certification, careers, continuing education, and its online professional network, contact

Institute of Internal Auditors
247 Maitland Avenue
Altamonte Springs, FL 32701-4201
Tel: (407) 937-1111
https://na.theiia.org

For information on certification, careers, continuing education, and its online professional network, contact

Institute of Management Accountants
10 Paragon Drive, Suite 1
Montvale, NJ 07645-1760
Tel: (800) 638-4427
E-mail: ima@imanet.org
http://www.imanet.org

For more information on venture capital and its CFO Task Force, contact

National Venture Capital Association
25 Massachusetts Avenue, NW, Suite 730
Washington, D.C. 20001-1430

Tel: (202) 864-5920
http://www.nvca.org

For information on membership for those who are responsible for the financial management of venture capital, private equity, and fund of funds firms, contact

Private Equity CFO Association
c/o Citizens Financial Group
28 State Street, 15th Floor
Boston, MA 02109-5714
http://www.privateequitycfo.org

Venture Capital Investor Relations Specialists

▓ OVERVIEW

Investor relations specialists are experts in communications, public relations, marketing, and finance. They help venture capital firms manage relationships with current investors and market funds to prospective investors (e.g., high-wealth individuals, funds of funds, pension funds, insurance companies, and family offices).

▓ HISTORY

The field of investor relations (IR) was traditionally considered a specialization of public relations. That changed in the 1950s when General Electric hired staff to communicate financial information to shareholders. Other companies also began to hire IR professionals, and these workers focused solely on providing financial information and responding to inquiries from shareholders. In the early 2000s, a series of corporate scandals (e.g., Enron, WorldCom, etc.) prompted the job responsibilities of IR professionals to expand. In the face of increased media scrutiny and growing investor calls for transparency, executives began to rely on IR professionals to not only handle financial communications, but also to serve in a strategic management function.

Within the venture capital (VC) industry, the need for IR professionals has grown as a result of the escalating competition between VC funds for the chance to fund hot start-ups and increasing demand by limited partners and potential investors for financial information.

▓ THE JOB

Investor relations (IR) specialists play two important roles at venture capital firms. They work with the firm's partners to attract new investors, and they keep current

QUICK FACTS

ALTERNATE TITLE(S)
Heads of Investor Relations, Investor Relations Associates, Investor Relations Directors, Investor Relations Managers, Investor Relations Officers

DUTIES
Market venture capital funds to prospective investors while managing relationships with current investors; answer investor questions; provide market intelligence to management; fostering strong communications within the firm and with investors

SALARY RANGE
$100,000 to $149,999 to $249,999+

WORK ENVIRONMENT
Primarily Indoors

BEST GEOGRAPHIC LOCATION(S)
Opportunities are best in San Francisco and in other cities with a large number of start-ups

MINIMUM EDUCATION LEVEL
Bachelor's Degree

SCHOOL SUBJECTS
Business, Economics, Speech

EXPERIENCE
Five years of investor relations experience for management positions; two years of public relations or marketing experience for associates

PERSONALITY TRAITS
Enterprising, Hands On, Outgoing

SKILLS
Financial, Interpersonal, Public Speaking, Sales

CERTIFICATION OR LICENSING
Recommended

SPECIAL REQUIREMENTS
None

EMPLOYMENT PROSPECTS
Good

ADVANCEMENT PROSPECTS
Fair

OUTLOOK
Much Faster than the Average

NOC
0013, 0111, 1113

O*NET-SOC
11-2021.00, 13-1161.00, 13-2051.00, 27-3031.00

investors (who are known as *limited partners*) up-to-date on the fund's performance. "Taking a disciplined approach to regular communications with current investors is crucial," advises JobSearchDigest.com, an employment and career advice site for venture capital, private equity, hedge fund, and investment banking professionals. "In good times, when the fund is performing well, it can lead to increased investment. In tough times, such as the recent economic downturn, the trust and good will built over time can convince investors to stick with their investments and the firm."

Investor relations specialists are in strongest demand during the initial public offering (IPO) stage of the exit process (during which the VC firm seeks to turn the equity it owns in a company back into cash). During the IPO, investor relations specialists educate investors and members of the media about the company with an overall goal of ensuring that its stock is valued as highly as possible. They develop press kits, Web sites, social media campaigns, and other investor materials. They also accompany managing partners and company executives on presentations (called *road shows*) to analysts, fund managers, and investors to generate excitement about the IPO and the products or services offered by the company. The IR specialists may also create a multimedia presentation of the road show to post online. During this time, IR professionals also write reports on the status of the IPO for limited partners, as well as prepare information for potentially thousands of new shareholders.

Other major duties of investor relations professionals include:

- responding to questions from limited partners about the performance of a fund and general market conditions
- working closely with the entire fund management team, including the fund manager, controller, chief financial officer, and fund analysts and associates
- assisting the senior management team by providing market intelligence, summarizing analysts' reports, and providing information on investors' perceptions about the company/IPO
- coordinating with the finance team to respond to due diligence requests from potential investors
- helping senior staff conduct due diligence on potential investors to ensure eligibility and compliance with federal anti-money laundering requirements
- serving as the liaison between limited partners and the firm
- creating and updating the firm's customer relations management database to track interactions with current and potential investors
- overseeing firm-wide media relations activities, including developing its media strategy, writing

press releases and other promotional materials, and managing its Web site and social media accounts

- identifying any potential financial or firm management issues that might be a concern to limited partners and prospective investors and mitigating these issues in advance

■ EARNINGS

Investment relations officers earned average salaries that ranged from $100,000 to $149,999, in 2014, according to the *IR Magazine Global Investor Relations Practice Report 2014*. The average head of investor relations earned between $200,000 and $249,999 a year. Ninety-five percent received a yearly bonus that averaged 35 percent of their base salary.

As in other careers, there are significant pay disparities between men and women. The average male head of investor relations earned between $200,000 and $249,999 a year in 2014, according to *IR Magazine, while women in the same position earned between $150,000 to $199,000.*

Investor relations professionals receive benefits such as health and life insurance, paid vacation days and sick leave, and a 401(k) or other retirement savings plan.

■ WORK ENVIRONMENT

Investor relations professionals travel frequently to meet with current and potential investors. A road show can last anywhere from five to 10 days, and this series of presentations and schmoozing sessions with fund managers, analysts, and investors can be draining. The job can be stressful during busy times such as when a firm is implementing its exit strategy (i.e., IPO, merger, selling the company) or when limited partners are unhappy with the performance of the fund or the firm's investment strategies. On the other hand, many IR specialists enjoy this career because it provides a lot of variety (i.e., road shows in different cities or even countries, meetings with all types of people, creating marketing campaigns, crunching numbers, etc.).

■ EXPLORING

There are many ways to learn more about a career in investor relations and the venture capital industry. Check out books such as *Investor Relations: Principles and International Best Practices in Financial Communications* to learn more about the art of investor relations. Venture Capital 101 (http://blog.pitchbook.com/category/knowledge-center/venture-capital-101) is a good place to learn about the VC funding lifecycle, key industry terms, and other VC-related topics. And publications such as *Investor Relations Update* (https://www.niri.org/resources/publications/ir-update) and *IR Magazine* (http://www.irmagazine.com) provide information

on the latest IR trends, developments, and best practices.

It will also be beneficial to learn as much as you can about the business world. *The Wall Street Journal* (http://www.wsj.com) is a good source of information about major companies, breaking business deals, and government regulations that affect the VC industry. Take marketing and public relations classes in high school. Offer to create a marketing campaign for a school fund-raiser, play, or sports tournament.

CAREER LADDER

Partner

Investor Relations Director

Investor Relations Manager

Investor Relations Associate

■ EDUCATION AND TRAINING REQUIREMENTS
High School

Business, economics, accounting, marketing, public relations, English, and speech classes will provide you with good preparation for college and an eventual career in investor relations. Other recommended courses include history, social studies, computer science, and foreign language.

Postsecondary Education

You'll need at least a bachelor's degrees in marketing, communications, public relations, finance, accounting, or business to work as an investor relations specialist. Many IR professionals have master's degrees in one of these majors. Fordham University offers the only master's degree program in investor relations in the United States. Venture capital partners can be very picky about whom they hire, so you should definitely attend an Ivy League or another top-tier college.

Other Education or Training

Many investor relations specialists keep their skills up to date by participating in continuing education classes, workshops, and webinars, which are offered by professional associations such as the American Marketing Association, Canadian Investor Relations Institute, National Investor Relations Institute, and the Public Relations Society of America.

Several organizations and colleges and universities offer short-term training programs for those who want to learn more about venture capital, including:

- University of California-Berkeley Venture Capital Executive Program: http://executive.berkeley.edu/programs/venture-capital-executive-program

Prospective venture capital investors discuss opportunities with an investor relations specialist. (Kinga. Shutterstock.)

- Venture Capital Institute: http://www.vcinstitute.org
- University of Michigan Center for Venture Capital and Private Equity Finance: http://www.zli.bus.umich.edu/vc_pe
- Venture Capital Institute: http://www.vcinstitute.org/Venture_Capital_Institute.html

Certification

Seneca College (http://www.senecacollege.ca/alumni/perks/irm.pdf) in Toronto, Canada, offers a certificate program in investor relations. Classes focus on media relations, crisis management, financial literacy, social media, ethics, and tools for professional success. The University of California-Irvine (http://www.unex.uci.edu/pdfs/brochures/INVESTOR_brochure.pdf) also offers an investor relations certificate. In addition, students can earn certificates in public relations and marketing at many U.S. and Canadian colleges.

■ CERTIFICATION, LICENSING, AND SPECIAL REQUIREMENTS
Certification or Licensing

Investor relations specialists must be experts in finance, communications, marketing, and public relations. To obtain this expertise, many become certified by professional associations. The certification process typically requires a combination of educational and work experience and the successful completion of an examination. Here are some popular certifications for IR professionals:

- investor relations charter (provided by the National Investor Relations Institute)
- certified professional in investor relations (Canadian Investor Relations Institute)
- professional certified marketer (American Marketing Association)
- accreditation in public relations (Public Relations Society of America)
- chartered financial analyst designation (CFA Institute)
- certified public accountant (American Institute of Certified Public Accountants)
- chartered alternate investment analyst (Chartered Alternate Investment Analyst Association)
- certified investment management analyst (Investment Management Consultants Association)
- certified treasury professional, certified corporate financial planning and analysis professional (Association for Financial Professionals)
- certified investment management analyst (Investment Management Consultants Association)

■ EXPERIENCE, SKILLS, AND PERSONALITY TRAITS

Investor relations managers must have at least five years of relevant work experience in investor relations, public relations, finance, and marketing. Associates need about two years of experience (which can involve a combination of both internship and on-the-job training) at a public relations or marketing firm—ideally one that provides services to the venture capital industry.

Excellent written and oral communication skills and sales ability are needed to prosper in this occupation. Investor relations specialists must be able to translate complex investing and business concepts into plain English in order to convince potential investors to invest in their firm's fund, provide clear and concise information to limited partners who may be worried about the performance of the fund, and interact daily with their colleagues in meetings and via telephone calls, web conferences, and e-mails. Other important traits include:

- a strong work ethic
- excellent business judgment
- an organized and detail-oriented personality
- strong Microsoft Office skills, especially in PowerPoint
- well-developed project management skills
- discretion and the ability to manage highly confidential and sensitive information
- the ability to work under pressure and tackle multiple tasks and projects

■ EMPLOYMENT PROSPECTS
Employers
Investor relations specialists are employed by venture capital firms and also public relations and marketing firms that provide investor relations services to VC firms. There are approximately 800 VC firms in the United States—and many more throughout the world. Many U.S.-based firms are headquartered on the East Coast and in California. In addition to working in the VC industry, IR specialists are employed by many public companies. Many work in related fields such as public relations and marketing.

Starting Out
It's a challenge to land an investor relations job at a venture capital firm because the field is small and many managing partners prefer to hire people they've worked with or those who have been recommended by colleagues.

One strategy to raise your profile is to seek out job opportunities at a marketing or public relations firm that provides investor relations services to VC firms. Once hired, you'll work as a member of a team that works closely with a VC firm's partners or its chief financial officer (who sometimes handles investor relations if a full-time employee is not on staff). Making a good impression could translate into a job offer down the road—or at least some good experience to put on your resume.

Some people find jobs via traditional job-search strategies such as employment sites, recruiters, networking on LinkedIn and other social media sites, and using the resources of their university's career services office.

Many professional associations provide job listings, networking groups, and articles on finding a job at their Web sites. For example, the American Marketing Association's Web site offers job listings and articles such as "Preparing Thoroughly for the Interview Process" and "15 Ways to Describe Yourself in a Job Interview."

■ ADVANCEMENT PROSPECTS
An investor relations associate at a large venture capital firm with a clearly defined career ladder can advance to the position of IR manager, and then IR director. Those with exceptional financial knowledge and experience could become partners at the firm. At smaller firms, there may be only one investor relations professional, and advancement is more difficult. Some IR professionals transition into jobs as public relations and marketing managers with corporations, or they work for government agencies and nonprofits. Others become financial controllers or chief financial officers.

PLANNING YOUR CAREER IN VENTURE CAPITAL   ONLINE RESOURCES

CFA Institute
http://www.cfainstitute.org/community/careers
This professional association's Web site provides job listings and a resources library that covers topics such as the job search, career management, soft skills, and investment industry issues and trends.

EFinancialCareers
http://www.efinancialcareers.com
EFinancialCareers provides venture capital employment listings, job-search articles, and industry news. Users can also create an online profile to help them get noticed by recruiters and hiring managers.

LinkedIn
https://www.linkedin.com
Every aspiring venture capital professional should create a free profile at this popular employment social networking site. LinkedIn also features job listings and information about employers and groups for those interested in VC careers.

Mergers & Inquisitions
http://www.mergersandinquisitions.com
Mergers & Inquisitions offers a wealth of free articles and videos about breaking into and succeeding in the venture capital and other alternative investment industries. The site also offers fee-based courses and coaching.

PE HUB
https://www.pehub.com
This Web site provides venture capital and private equity job listings and career advice, access to selected articles from *Venture Capital Journal,* and the latest industry news.

Private Equity Jobs Digest
http://www.jobsearchdigest.com
Visit this site to access job listings and useful articles such as "What You Need to Know About Venture Capital Jobs" and "How to Get a Job in Venture Capital."

VentureLoop
http://www.ventureloop.com
This Web site provides tens of thousands of venture capital job listings.

■ OUTLOOK
The U.S. Department of Labor does not provide an employment outlook for investor relations specialists,

but it does report that job opportunities for marketing managers and public relations specialists who work in the catch-all category of "other financial investment activities" are expected to grow by 36 percent through 2024. The National Venture Capital Association reports that the number of venture capital firms decreased from 985 firms in 2004 to 803 in 2014, which has fueled competition between firms to convince start-ups to accept their investment funds. Additionally, investors are requiring more information about funds, their performance, and other data, which is creating demand for IR specialists.

UNIONS AND ASSOCIATIONS

Venture capital IR specialists do not belong to unions. The National Investor Relations Institute (NIRI) is a major membership organization for investor relation specialists, although it reports that only 11 percent of its members are employed in the finance industry. Members receive *IR Update,* NIRI's flagship monthly magazine; access to a sample document library (e.g., guidance for corporate disclosure, model job descriptions, and sample investor relations plans); free webinars; discounts on conferences, seminars, and webinars; and access to eGroups, NIRI's private social networking forum. The Canadian Investor Relations Institute is a membership organization for IR professionals in Canada. The work of investor relations specialists also requires considerable knowledge of marketing and public relations, so membership in the American Marketing Association and the Public Relations Society of America will also be useful. The National Venture Capital Association is a major trade organization for venture capital firms. It has about 300 members.

TIPS FOR ENTRY

1. Hone your skills by participating in internships and entry-level jobs at public relations and marketing firms that provide services to the venture capital industry.
2. Check out "best" or "top" company lists to identify potential employers, including:
   - *Entrepreneur*'s VC 100: The Top Investors in Early-Stage Startups list: http://www.entrepreneur.com/article/242702
   - CB Insight: Healthcare's Top Venture Capital Firms: https://www.cbinsights.com/blog/healthcare-venture-capital-top-mosaic
   - Tech.Co's 25 Top VC Firms list: http://tech.co/top-vc-firms-to-pitch-your-startup-to-2015-02
3. Visit the following Web sites for job listings:
   - https://www.niri.org/career-center
   - http://www.efinancialcareers.com
   - http://www.jobsearchdigest.com

FOR MORE INFORMATION

For information on continuing education, publications, careers, and certification, contact

American Marketing Association
130 East Randolph Street, 22nd Floor
Chicago, IL 60601-6207
Tel: (800) AMA-1150
https://www.ama.org

For information on certification and career opportunities in Canada, contact

Canadian Investor Relations Institute
601, 67 Yonge Street
Toronto, ON M5E 1J8
Canada
Tel: (416) 364-8200
E-mail: enquiries@ciri.org
https://www.ciri.org

For information on certification and job listings, visit the institute's Web site.

National Investor Relations Institute
225 Reinekers Lane, Suite 560
Alexandria, VA 22314-2875
Tel: (703) 562-7700
https://www.niri.org/career-center

For more information on venture capital, contact

National Venture Capital Association
25 Massachusetts Avenue, NW, Suite 730
Washington, D.C. 20001-1430
Tel: (202) 864-5920
http://www.nvca.org

For information on careers and its Financial Communication Section, contact

Public Relations Society of America
33 Maiden Lane, 11th Floor
New York, NY 10038-5149
Tel: (212) 460-1400
https://www.prsa.org, https://www.prsa.org/network/communities/financialcommunications

Venture Capitalists

OVERVIEW

Venture capitalists are highly skilled business professionals who identify investment opportunities, evaluate target companies, negotiate the terms of investments, help build successful portfolio companies, and liquidate investments.

HISTORY

The first publicly owned venture capital firm (American Research and Development Corporation) was launched in 1946. Many believe its best investment was the $70,000 it spent in 1957 to help fund Digital Equipment Corporation. Eleven years later, that investment was valued at more than $355 million after the company's initial public offering.

In 1969, the first official nonprofit venture capital (VC) organization in the world—the Western Association of Venture Capitalists—was founded. Today, it is comprised of more than 100 venture firms and more than 1,000 venture capitalists. In 1973, the National Venture Capital Association (NVCA) was founded in the offices of the Heizer Corporation, a leading VC firm. According to a 1973 news story in *SBIC/Venture Capital,* the NVCA was founded "as a means for venture capital organizations throughout the country to work together on mutual interests and problems. Membership is by invitation and open only to venture capital groups, corporate managers, and individual venture capitalists that are responsible for investing private capital in young companies on a professional basis."

Today, there are more than 800 venture capital firms in the United States alone. Corporations are once again focusing on venture capital—either expanding their existing units or launching new ones. In 2014, 1,100 corporations had VC units—double the number in 2009, according to *Global Corporate Venturing.*

THE JOB

Many people view a career in venture capital as exciting, lucrative, rewarding, and a bit mysterious. Some think venture capitalists literally fall into deals and spend most of their time jet-setting around the world passing out money while enjoying the good life. While there's definitely a lot of money to be made for highly-skilled venture capitalists, this career involves many long hours, occasional frustration when deals fall through or when profits don't match expectations, and a lot of hard work.

Venture capitalists have five main duties: identifying investment opportunities, evaluating target companies, negotiating the terms of investments, helping to build successful portfolio companies, and liquidating investments.

Venture capitalists—especially those who are new to a firm—must generate a steady stream of investment possibilities for their employers. They identify business opportunities by reaching out to their network of friends and acquaintances, which may include contacts they

made when they worked at a portfolio company or at a firm that provided professional services (e.g., accounting, auditing, legal, consulting, etc.) to VC firms, their portfolio companies, or to corporations. Additionally, venture capitalists (such as Steve Jurvetson at Draper Fisher Jurvetson) may be so well-known in the VC industry or in

CAREER LADDER

Managing Partner

Partner

Principal

Senior Associate

Associate/Analyst

their previous industries (Information technology, for example) that they're inundated with pitches from entrepreneurs or young companies that need investment.

Once investment opportunities are identified, the venture capitalist spends a considerable amount of time determining if his or her firm should invest in the company. They conduct research, build financial models to determine the potential financial return on the investment, interview the founders of the company, meet with risk managers and lawyers, and perform other types of due diligence. They study (and try out, if possible) the target company's products or services (and the technologies and manufacturing processes that are used to create them), the market and the company's marketing plan for the products or services, the quality of the company's management team and its finances, and other criteria to make a decision. At any one time, a venture capital firm may be considering anywhere from 25 to 50 potential deals, so the due diligence process can be time-consuming, and, sometimes frustrating, because only a handful of companies will meet all the firm's criteria for investment.

Once the venture capital firm chooses to invest in a company, venture capitalists, in close collaboration with lawyers, negotiate the terms of the investment.

The deal is done. The investment has been made in the target company. Many people may think that the work of the venture capitalist is complete, but this is far from reality. Venture capitalists provide many types of assistance to the portfolio company's founders and management team. For example, they help the founders establish and review the company's strategic focus. He or she may think that the founders are marketing to the wrong demographic or launching a service in a too-small geographic area, or perhaps they believe that the price of a product is too low. Venture capitalists also help recruit and hire senior management such as chief financial officers, and provide advice on compensation structures. Many take a seat on the company's board of directors to ensure that it's being run properly.

Finally, when they believe the company is ready and market conditions are favorable, the venture capitalist works to liquidate the investment. This is typically done by completing an initial public offering (IPO) that takes the portfolio company "public," generating additional capital to improve or expand the company. In this situation, investors do not immediately receive a return on their investment. They typically must sign lock-up agreements that prohibit them from cashing out their shares for at least six months. Instead of an IPO, the venture capital firm can choose to merge the company with a larger existing private or public company. In this situation, shareholders receive an immediate financial payout based on the terms of their investment agreement.

In addition to these duties, some venture capitalists serve as the *managing partners* of their firms, or, at a large firm, share these duties with another partner.

One of the main responsibilities of a managing partner is to fund-raise. He or she must constantly look for new investors (and stay connected with past limited partners) who are a good match for the firm's particular focus (i.e., investment stage, industry, geographical area, and size). Managing partners work with the firm's marketing and accounting professionals to create a private placement memorandum for investors that provides information on the firm's track record with previous funds, biographical data about the partners, the investment terms for the fund, and other information. Then they meet with potential investors to pitch the fund. In addition to fund-raising, managing partners also:

- make the final decision regarding a particular investment or investment strategies
- prepare an annual budget for their firm
- work with lawyers to prepare and manage legal documentation for the partnership
- manage partnership expenses
- prepare reports for partners
- recruit and manage staff
- work with in-house or third-party accounting and compliance staff to pay taxes and prepare and submit compliance documents to the Securities & Exchange Commission and other regulatory bodies

■ EARNINGS

Venture capital professionals with an MBA had average earnings (base pay plus bonus) of $296,155 in 2014, according to the 2015 Private Equity and Venture Capital Compensation Report. Those without MBAs received $264,464. Earnings varied by the size of the firm. Venture capital professionals who worked at firms with up to five employees received average earnings (base pay plus bonus) of $266,000; 6 to 9 employees, $248,000; 10 to 24 employees, $291,000; 25 to 49 employees, $306,000; 50

to 99 employees, $313,000; and 100 or more employees, $276,000.

Venture capitalists also can also invest their own money alongside the firm in some deals (this is called co-investment). If a fund is successful, the return on their investment can far exceed salary and bonuses. Venture capitalists also receive carry, which is a percentage of the profits the firm makes. A partner might start with 0.5 percent and move to 4 percent over his/her career. For example, if a firm has a $100 million fund and triples it over eight years, profit might be $200 million. A 1 percent carry would thus be worth $2 million.

In addition to salary, co-investment, and carry, venture capitalists receive benefits such as vacation days, sick leave, health and life insurance, and a 401(k) or other retirement savings plan.

■ WORK ENVIRONMENT

Venture capital firms are loaded with highly-intelligent, creative, and passionate people with Type-A personalities. If this description fits you, then you'll be a good fit and enjoy the work environment. If not, you might want to reconsider pursuing a career in this ultra-competitive industry. A typical day for a venture capitalist might consist of a meeting with an analyst to review financial data, another meeting with partners to discuss the pros and cons of a potential investment, time at one's desk to crunch numbers and handle administrative duties, lunch with an entrepreneur who is seeking funding, and attendance at yet another meeting, this time with the board of directors of one of the firm's portfolio companies. The work hours for venture capitalists can be long. In 2014, 51 percent of venture capital and private equity professionals worked at least 70 hours a week, according to the *2015 Private Equity and Venture Capital Compensation Report.*

■ EXPLORING

Learn as much as you can about venture capital by reading professional journals, books, and other resources. CNBC offers recent articles about developments in the VC industry at http://www.cnbc.com/venture-capital. Another good resource: *The Little Book of Venture Capital Investing: Empowering Economic Growth and Investment Portfolios* (John Wiley & Sons, 2014).

In college, you can get exposure to the world of venture capital by joining a venture capital club. These student-managed organizations offer mentoring opportunities, presentations by leading VC industry figures, and the chance to compete in regional or national investment competitions. Some schools provide even more opportunities. In addition to its

Venture capitalists often choose to back companies that excite them or bring innovation to the market. (Kinga. Shutterstock.)

Entrepreneurship & Venture Capital Club, the Darden School of Business at the University of Virginia offers a VC incubator, which "supports the development and growth of promising seed and early-stage business ventures by providing them with funding, faculty and student support, office space, access to technological expertise, and free legal services; a Venture Capital Bootcamp, a three-day workshop for students who are interested in venture capital and entrepreneurship; and the Batten Venture Internship Program, which links students with summer internships at VC firms and their portfolio companies."

■ EDUCATION AND TRAINING REQUIREMENTS
High School

Classes that will provide good preparation for college and a career in venture capital include business, economics, accounting, English, speech, computer science, marketing, and psychology. Participation in business and debate clubs will also be useful.

Postsecondary Education

Many venture capitalists have master's degrees in business management, Information Technology, engineering, health care management, or even the liberal arts from Ivy League schools or other prestigious colleges. Some have law or medical degrees.

Other Education or Training

Venture capitalists may think they know it all, but as the groundbreaking physicist Albert Einstein once said, "Intellectual growth should commence at birth and cease only at death." Many venture capitalists are smart enough to follow Einstein's advice and pursue continuing

BEN HOROWITZ, CO-FOUNDER OF ANDREESSEN HOROWITZ

MOVERS AND SHAKERS

Ben Horowitz is the co-founder (along with Marc Andreessen) of the venture capital firm Andreessen Horowitz, an industry leader with more than $4 billion under assets. Before launching Andreessen Horowitz, he was the co-founder and CEO of Opsware (formerly Loudcloud), which was acquired by HP, and a vice president at Netscape Communications. Horowitz has a bachelor of arts in computer science from Columbia University and a master's of science in computer science from the University of California at Los Angeles.

While highly respected and skilled as a VC investor, Horowitz has become a sort of cult hero of the venture capital (VC) industry and the business worlds as a result of the publication of his *book The Hard Thing About Hard Things: Building a Business When There Are No Easy Answers* (HarperBusiness, 2014), a fascinating and sometimes brutally honest look at the business and life lessons he learned at Opsware, Netscape, and Andreessen Horowitz, and in his personal life. He also publishes a popular blog (http://www.bhorowitz.com). Horowitz is an aficionado of rap and hip-hop and uses quotes from Nas, Jay-Z, Too $hort, Lil Wayne, and others to accentuate his points about business and management strategy.

Horowitz has a notable record of philanthropy. In 2012, he and the other partners at Andreessen Horowitz announced that they would donate at least half of their incomes from their VC careers to philanthropic causes during their lifetimes. On his blog, he explained their decision: "We are fortunate to work with some of the best entrepreneurs and technologists in the world, and in the process help create great and valuable companies. That activity, done well over decades, can generate a lot of money that can then be productively deployed philanthropically back into the society that makes it all possible. We love participating in this process, and we hope that our philanthropy can, over time, help make the world a better place."

Sources: Andreessen Horowitz; TechCrunch

Review of Securities & Exchange Commission's Pay-to-Play Rules; IPO Readiness: Are You Ready to Take Every Step of the IPO Journey?; What Limited Partners Really Think About the VC Fundraising Environment; and VC Firms in Transition.

There are also programs that provide supplementary training in everything from successful due diligence to valuation methodologies. Here are some well-known programs:

- University of California-Berkeley Venture Capital Executive Program (http://executive.berkeley.edu/programs/venture-capital-executive-program). This five-day course covers topics such as deal structuring, terms and due diligence, venture capital economics and career decisions, and achieving liquidity and accelerating return.
- Venture Capital Institute (http://www.vcinstitute.org). Probably one of the better-known training programs in the United States.
- University of Michigan Ross School of Business, Center for Venture Capital and Private Equity Finance (http://www.zli.bus.umich.edu/vc_pe). University-sponsored conferences and seminars on investing and entrepreneurial finance.

Certification

Aspiring venture capitalists should consider participating in the Fundamentals of Alternative Investments Certificate Program, which is offered by the Investment Management Consultants Association. The online program provides participants with an introduction to venture capital and other alternative assets classes, due diligence, risk management, and other topics. Visit https://www.imca.org/pages/Fundamentals-Alternative-Investments-Certificate for more information.

◼ CERTIFICATION, LICENSING, AND SPECIAL REQUIREMENTS
Certification or Licensing

Some venture capitalists earn financial certifications that provide them with additional expertise as they do their work. Some popular certifications include:

- chartered financial analyst (administered by the CFA Institute)
- chartered alternate investment analyst (Chartered Alternate Investment Analyst Association)
- certified investment management analyst (Investment Management Consultants Association)

education opportunities throughout their careers. Who knows? Maybe the seminar they take on emerging markets in South America will provide just the kernel of knowledge that helps them to identify a good investment opportunity in Brazil. Continuing education opportunities are offered by professional associations and at industry conferences. For example, the National Venture Capital Association offers webinars such as Annual

- certified treasury professional, certified corporate financial planning and analysis professional (Association for Financial Professionals)
- certified investment management analyst (Investment Management Consultants Association)

■ EXPERIENCE, SKILLS, AND PERSONALITY TRAITS

Aspiring venture capitalists need five to 10 years of professional success as a serial entrepreneur, or high-level executive experience at a portfolio company, or experience in a high-profile position in Information Technology, engineering, health services, or biotechnology.

A variety of skills are needed to be a successful venture capitalist, including financial acumen, an analytical mind, excellent negotiation abilities, and keen business judgment. They also need strong communication and interpersonal skills, and the ability work as a member of a team. Venture capital firms are tiny compared to most other professional entities. They are high-pressure partnerships where the alchemy of strong personalities becomes critical to the success of the firm.

■ EMPLOYMENT PROSPECTS
Employers

Venture capitalists are employed by VC firms and corporations (such as Google, Intel, and Novartis) that have VC departments. Venture capital firms are located throughout the United States and the world. Many U.S.-based firms are headquartered in California and on the East Coast. Some top U.S. firms have offices in foreign countries.

Starting Out

"Even if you have a desired skill set, it's not easy to become a venture capitalist," advises *Inc.* "It takes networking, business acumen, plus founding a startup (or two), in order to be seriously considered." There are several ways to work your way into a career at a venture capital firm:

- You could start from the ground up after obtaining two or more years of experience in a related industry such as management consulting, investment banking, or private equity, OR entering after graduating from college with an MBA (some firms hire workers who are currently pursuing an MBA). You'll work as an *associate,* sourcing deals, performing due diligence on potential investments, and supporting the portfolio companies. Others enter at this position after working for a VC-funded start up.

- Obtaining extensive experience in the Information Technology, engineering, health services, or biotech sectors. After at least five years (and the completion of an MBA), you would enter the firm as a *principal* or *partner.*
- Successful entrepreneurs may be asked to join a venture firm as a partner in their 30s or 40s.

■ ADVANCEMENT PROSPECTS

Venture capitalists hold the top spots at their firms so there are few advancement opportunities. Very experienced and skilled partners can move into the position of managing partner, or decide to leave their current employers to launch new VC funds. Some venture capitalists become well-known in the industry by presenting at investor events, speaking at entrepreneurship conferences, serving as mentors, and being active on social media. Some become professors at business schools.

■ OUTLOOK

It's very difficult to land a job as a venture capitalist. A commonly used analogy compares the size of the VC industry with that of Major League Baseball. It's estimated that there are approximately 6,000 professional baseball players (750 in the Major Leagues and 5,250 players in the minor leagues)—and the VC industry is about the same size. So, in short, it's extremely difficult to become a pro ballplayer (even if you are a stellar athlete) and just as difficult to land a partner-track position at a VC firm. Still, some baseball players—and aspiring venture capitalists—do the hard work, get a few opportunities to demonstrate their talent, and eventually fulfill their dreams. And experienced and well-financed aspiring venture capitalists can do one thing that baseball players can't do—start their own firms.

■ UNIONS AND ASSOCIATIONS

Venture capitalists do not belong to unions. Some have founded or are employed by firms that are members of the National Venture Capital Association (NVCA), which bills itself as the "voice of the U.S. venture capital community." The NVCA offers professional development webinars, model legal documents, an industry events calendar, statistical research, a blog, and a list of regional and state VC associations at its Web site. Membership organizations for women in the VC industry include the Association of Women in Alternative Investing, Women's Association of Venture and Equity, and Women.VC.

■ TIPS FOR ENTRY

1. You can break into the field by working in lower-level positions at a venture capital firm. A list of venture

capital firms and corporate venture groups that are members of the National Venture Capital Association can be found at http://nvca.org/about-nvca/members.

2. To get noticed by a venture capital firm, raise your visibility in the start-up community by speaking at entrepreneur events, participating in accelerator programs, and being active on social media (e.g., blogging, Tweeting, etc.)

3. Obtaining operating experience at an early-stage, venture-backed company will make you a good candidate for employment at a VC firm.

■ FOR MORE INFORMATION

AWAI is a membership organization for women in the venture capital, hedge fund, and private equity industries.

Association of Women in Alternative Investing (AWAI)
E-mail: info@altinvesting.org
http://www.altinvesting.org

For more information on venture capital, contact
National Venture Capital Association
25 Massachusetts Avenue, NW, Suite 730
Washington, D.C. 20001-1430
Tel: (202) 864-5920
http://www.nvca.org

For information on membership, contact
Women's Association of Venture and Equity
10 Winton Farm Road
Newtown, CT 06470-2653
Tel: (855) 928-3606
E-mail: wavecoordinator@gmail.com
https://women-wave.org

Women.VC describes itself as an "independent nonprofit organization aiming to strengthen and develop the world investment industry by introducing women professionals who bring real value."
Women.VC
http://www.women.vc

Venture Capital Lawyers

■ OVERVIEW

Venture capital (VC) lawyers are specialized attorneys who provide legal services and advice to VC firms about fund formation and liquidation, fund-raising, due diligence, regulatory compliance, investment strategies, portfolio company management, intellectual property, tax issues, litigation and dispute resolution, and other issues. The top lawyers at venture capital firms are known as *chief legal officers* or *general counsels*. There are 778,700 lawyers employed in the United States. Venture capital lawyers comprise a tiny fraction of this total.

■ HISTORY

Venture capital partners have always needed lawyers to help draft legal agreements, negotiate investment terms, and otherwise represent their interests. Until the mid-2000s, only the largest VC firms with more than $1 billion in assets under management had in-house attorneys. Most medium-sized and small firms had an in-house chief financial officer or hired law firms to handle these issues. In the past decade or so, this has changed because technology is becoming more complex, regulation of the industry is increasing, and managing partners have realized that by bringing on chief legal officers to handle legal issues they can free themselves up to focus on what they're good at—the business side of the industry—rather than three-hour conference calls with opposing attorneys over legal minutiae.

■ THE JOB

Venture capital consists of funds obtained from investors (e.g., endowment funds, high-wealth individuals, pension plans, and family trusts) that are invested in young, innovative companies in exchange for an equity stake that can be translated into a profit when the company goes public or is sold to or merged with another company. Some of America's best-known companies—including Facebook, Whole Foods Market, Google, and Intel—were founded with the help of venture capital.

According to an article about venture capital on BetaKit, a news site about start-ups and tech innovation, lawyers (along with venture capitalists, entrepreneurs, and limited partners) are the key players in the VC industry. Venture capital lawyers can be generalists or they can specialize in areas such as transactional expertise, due diligence, intellectual property, and tax law. They also may work for VC firms that focus on funding start-ups in specific industries (technology, medical science, renewable energy, energy, real estate, etc.). Although job responsibilities vary by employer, typical job duties for VC lawyers include:

- drafting venture capital financing documents such as term sheets, certificates of incorporation, indemnification agreements, investor rights agreements, management rights letters, voting agreements, and stock purchase agreements

- providing counsel at all investment stages, from initial funding through IPOs and mergers (including fundraising strategy, due diligence, and business model issues)
- serving as the liaison between the investment staff and outside counsel during transactions
- advising clients on intellectual property (including patent and trademark) issues
- assisting compliance professionals about reporting and documentation obligations pertaining to compliance with Securities & Exchange Commission (SEC) regulations, and interpreting SEC rules, regulations, and laws that are applicable to VC firms
- reviewing vendor and employee contracts, nondisclosure agreements, and firm marketing materials, among other documents
- designing and negotiating compensation and benefits plans for executives and employees at both VC firms and their portfolio companies

■ EARNINGS

The staffing firm Robert Half Legal publishes an annual salary guide for workers in the legal profession. According to its 2016 guide, in-house corporate lawyers had the following salary ranges by years of experience and size of employer in 2015:

Zero to Three Years of Experience

- Small Company: $81,500 to $156,500
- Midsize Company: $97,750 to $132,000
- Large Company: $121,500 to $156,500

Ten or More Years of Experience

- Small Company: $126,250 to $251,500
- Midsize Company: $143,500 to $225,000
- Large Company: $179,000 to $251,500

Salaries for attorneys at venture capital firms are usually higher—especially if they're also partners and receive carry (which is a percentage of the profits the firm makes). At the largest firms, they can earn $5 million or more annually.

Lawyers also receive fringe benefits such as paid vacation and sick leave, health and life insurance, and a 401(k) or other retirement savings plan. Some receive performance bonuses.

■ WORK ENVIRONMENT

Busy. Intellectually challenging. Demanding. Sometimes contentious and stressful. Smart and interesting coworkers. Rewarding work. Regular office hours. Top of the line technology and office equipment. These are some of the typical ways in which VC lawyers describe their work environment, although environments vary by the size and investment strategies of the firm, the management philosophies of the managing partners of the firm, and other factors. Lawyers should expect to travel to meetings with their counterparts at target companies, legal proceedings, industry conferences, and other events.

■ EXPLORING

There are many resources that will help you to learn more about venture capital and law. First, check out books such as *Venture Capital For Dummies* (For Dummies, 2013) to learn the basics of venture capital. Next, visit the American Bar Association's Legal Career Central (http://www.abalcc.org) to read career profiles, get advice on taking the bar exam, and check out entries in its Career Advice Series. Finally, visit the National Venture Capital Association's Web site, http://nvca.org/resources/model-legal-documents, to read sample legal documents (e.g., term sheet, indemnification agreement, management rights letter) that are used in the VC industry. Reviewing these documents will provide you with an inside look at the types of issues VC lawyers deal with and a glimpse at the complexity of the field.

QUICK FACTS

ALTERNATE TITLE(S)
Associates, Attorneys, Chief Legal Officers, General Counsels, Managing Attorneys

DUTIES
Provide legal counsel to venture capital firms; draft agreements and other legal documents; advise clients on legal issues

SALARY RANGE
$81,500 to $251,500 to $5 million+

WORK ENVIRONMENT
Primarily Indoors

BEST GEOGRAPHIC LOCATION(S)
Opportunities are best in San Francisco and in other cities with a large number of start-ups

MINIMUM EDUCATION LEVEL
Law Degree

SCHOOL SUBJECTS
Business, Economics, Speech

EXPERIENCE
Five years of legal experience in the corporate and financial world

PERSONALITY TRAITS
Hands On, Organized, Problem-Solving

SKILLS
Financial, Organizational, Research

CERTIFICATION OR LICENSING
Required

SPECIAL REQUIREMENTS
None

EMPLOYMENT PROSPECTS
Fair

ADVANCEMENT PROSPECTS
Fair

OUTLOOK
About as Fast as the Average

NOC
4112

O*NET-SOC
23-1011.00

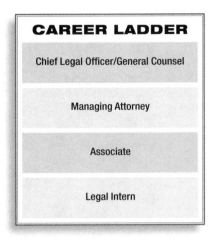

CAREER LADDER

Chief Legal Officer/General Counsel

Managing Attorney

Associate

Legal Intern

Talk to VC lawyers about their careers. Perhaps an attorney will be open to being job shadowed for a day. Joining venture capital or finance clubs while in college or law school will allow you to meet venture capitalists, investigate career paths, and participate in investing competitions.

■ EDUCATION AND TRAINING REQUIREMENTS

High School

In high school, take classes that help to develop your writing, public speaking, critical thinking, and research skills. Such courses include English, speech, foreign languages, social studies, and government. Lawyers need to be logical and analytical, so classes in science, philosophy, mathematics, and computer science will also be useful. Take finance and economics classes because venture capital attorneys need expertise in the financial markets and alternative investments. Be sure to excel in your high school courses, and take as many Advanced Placement classes, as possible. The higher your grades, the better your chances of being accepted by an elite college. Venture capital firms typically seek job candidates who've attended top law schools.

Postsecondary Education

The first step to becoming a lawyer is to earn a bachelor's degree. Many lawyers have undergraduate degrees in prelaw or legal studies, while others (especially those interested in working in the VC industry) earn degrees in finance, business, or accounting, or at least minor or double major in one of these majors. Some colleges and universities offer courses in alternative investments.

To get into law school, you'll need to take the Law School Admission Test (LSAT), which assesses your critical thinking, reasoning, and writing abilities. The Law School Admission Council provides information about preparing for and taking the LSAT at http://www.lsac.org.

More than 220 law schools in the United States are approved by the American Bar Association. A degree of juris doctor (J.D.) or bachelor of laws (LL.B.) is usually granted upon graduation.

Some law schools offer venture capital classes. For example, law students at Duke University can take Venture Capital Financing, which provides an overview of the legal and economic structure of VC transactions and legal agreements. Stanford University and Santa Clara University also provide VC-related classes.

The Association of American Law Schools, a nonprofit association of 180 law schools, offers resources for prospective law students at http://www.aals.org/prospective-law-students.

Other Education or Training

Managing partners often cite the lack of industry knowledge and experience as major factors that disqualify recent law school graduates from consideration for employment. This fact makes it extremely important that aspiring VC lawyers learn as much as they can about capital deal sourcing, investment strategies, contracts, mergers, and other venture capital–related topics in order to become more attractive job candidates. Current VC attorneys also benefit by participating in continuing education classes, seminars, and webinars because the industry is constantly changing.

The following colleges and universities, private organizations, and professional legal and VC associations provide training:

- The University of California-Berkeley Venture Capital Executive Program (http://executive.berkeley.edu/programs/venture-capital-executive-program) offers a five-day program that covers topics such as deal structuring, terms and due diligence, venture capital economics and career decisions, and achieving liquidity and accelerating return.
- The Venture Capital Institute (http://www.vcinstitute.org) provides a four-day program that features seminars such as Mezzanine and Later Stage Investments: An Overview, Early Stage Venture Capital Investments, and Term Sheets for Structuring and Negotiating Deals.
- The University of Michigan's Center for Venture Capital and Private Equity Finance (http://www.zli.bus.umich.edu/vc_pe) provides conferences and seminars on investing and entrepreneurial finance.
- The American Bar Association's Business Law Section offers webinars on venture capital issues.
- The Association of Corporate Counsel provides online and in-person professional development classes and webinars on contract negotiation, ethics, litigation, project management, and basic practice skills.

Certification

Some venture capital attorneys choose to earn a master of laws (LL.M) degree, an advanced law certification that

Local Venture Capital Organizations

There are many venture capital associations at the local, state, and regional levels that can provide networking opportunities, member meet-ups, fellowship and internship programs, mentoring services, continuing education classes, information on start-up events, and other resources for VC professionals. Check the following list for organizations in your area:

- Council for Entrepreneurial Development (North Carolina): http://cednc.org
- Crossroads Venture Group (Connecticut): http://www.cvg.org
- Florida Venture Forum: http://www.flventure.org
- Greater Philadelphia Alliance for Capital & Technologies: http://philadelphiapact.com
- Hawaii Venture Capital Association: http://www.hvca.org
- Illinois Venture Capital Association: http://www.illinoisvc.org
- Iowa Venture Capital Association: http://www.iowaventure.org
- Los Angeles Venture Association: http://www.lava.org
- Michigan Venture Capital Association: http://michiganvca.org
- Mid-Atlantic Venture Association: http://mava.org
- Minnesota Venture Capital Association: http://www.mnvca.org
- MVF (Missouri): http://www.mvfstl.org
- New England Venture Capital Association: http://www.newenglandvc.org
- New Mexico Venture Association: http://www.nmvca.org
- New York City Venture Capital Association: http://www.nyvca.org
- Ohio Venture Association: http://www.ohioventure.org
- Pittsburgh Venture Capital Association: https://thepvca.org
- Rocky Mountain Venture Capital Association: http://www.rockymountainvca.com
- San Diego Venture Group: http://www.sdvg.org
- Southern Capital Forum (southeastern U.S.): http://southerncapitalforum.org
- Texas Venture Capital Association: http://www.txvca.org
- Upstate Venture Association of New York: http://www.uvany.org
- Venture Club of Indiana: http://www.ventureclub.org
- VentureOhio: http://www.ventureohio.org
- Western Association of Venture Capitalists (Arizona, California, Nevada, Oregon, Washington): http://www.wavc.org

helps them advance professionally. LL.M programs, which typically last one year, are offered in many areas—such as banking and finance law, business law, corporate law/corporate governance/corporate compliance, and regulatory compliance. A first law degree is required for admission to LL.M programs. Visit http://www.lsac.org/llm for more information. A list of LL.M specialties and the law schools that offer them is available at http://www.americanbar.org/groups/legal_education/resources/accreditation.html.

■ CERTIFICATION, LICENSING, AND SPECIAL REQUIREMENTS
Certification or Licensing

Lawyers must be admitted to the bar of the state where they want to practice. Applicants must graduate from an American Bar Association (ABA)-approved law school and pass a written examination. The ABA provides an overview of the process at http://www.americanbar.org/groups/legal_education/resources/bar_admissions/basic_overview.html.

■ EXPERIENCE, SKILLS, AND PERSONALITY TRAITS

You will need a minimum of five years of work experience in the corporate world (ideally at investment banks and portfolio companies of VC firms) to be considered for most VC legal positions.

It takes a wide range of skills to be successful as a VC attorney. Since they frequently prepare legal documents, write memos, and meet with partners and the lawyers of start-ups (as well as occasionally represent their clients in court), VC lawyers need top-notch oral and written communication skills and the ability to interact well with others. Lawyers also need strong powers of persuasion, confidence, excellent negotiation skills, strong ethics, creativity, and financial, deal sourcing, and fund-raising expertise.

■ EMPLOYMENT PROSPECTS
Employers
Venture capital lawyers work for VC firms, the portfolio companies of VC firms, corporations that have venture capital departments, and legal practices that provide services to VC firms. Some lawyers are employed by fund investors (e.g., endowment funds, pension plans, high-wealth individuals, and family trusts).

Vault.com publishes an annual list of the best law firms for venture capital law (as ranked by associates). Some of the top firms in 2016 were:

- Latham & Watkins LLP
- Barnes & Thornburg LLP
- Choate Hall & Stewart LLP
- Cooley LLP
- DLA Piper LLP

Visit http://bestlawfirms.usnews.com/search .aspx?practice_area_id=38&page=1 to view the complete list.

In addition to working in the VC industry, lawyers are employed in nearly every other industry, at nonprofits, and by government agencies.

Starting Out
It's extremely difficult for new graduates to land a job in the venture capital industry, typically because they don't have the following: a well-developed network of contacts in the business world; expertise in venture capital deal flow, due diligence, and investment agreements and other contracts; and experience founding a start-up or at least providing services to one. Lawyers who take the time to develop these skills and this experience in the alternative investment industry and in the corporate world (including at investment banks and portfolio companies of VC firms) will become stronger job candidates. Also, it never hurts to earn an MBA and take a few classes in venture capital.

Venture capital partners like to work with people they know (or who've been recommended by trusted colleagues), so unless you're a member of the "in crowd," your skills and achievements may not mean much. So how do you get noticed by VC partners? One common strategy is to approach partners and offer to work for free—helping with due diligence, contracts, intellectual property, or deal flow. If you make a good impression, you might be offered a job. You can also raise your profile by volunteering at venture capital associations or at entrepreneurial events, attending industry conferences, working in the legal department of a VC portfolio company or at a law firm that provides services to VC firms, and starting a blog that discusses legal issues in the VC industry.

■ ADVANCEMENT PROSPECTS
Most venture capital firms are small and don't have large legal departments. In fact, some small firms may only have a chief legal officer on staff or they may only employ contract attorneys. At a large VC firm or a law firm that provides services to the VC industry, new hires might begin as associates or principals, then advance to the positions of managing attorney and chief legal officer. Some attorneys become partners, or even managing partners. With experience, a highly skilled lawyer who works for a VC portfolio company might become the chief financial officer, CEO, or chief operating officer.

■ OUTLOOK
It's very difficult to land a job as a lawyer at a venture capital firm because the industry is extremely small and most managing partners are unwilling to hire attorneys who they do not know personally or who have not been recommended by colleagues. Still, there will always be a need for skilled VC lawyers to help firms perform due diligence, draft legal documents, and protect intellectual property. "Business today is knowledge-based and technology-focused, making the protection of patents and trademarks a thriving practice area," according to national staffing firm Robert Half Legal's *2016 Salary Guide for the Legal Field.*

It will be easier to land a job at a corporation (such as Qualcomm, GE, or Johnson & Johnson) that has a venture capital unit. In 2014, 1,100 corporations had VC units—double the number in 2009, according to *Global Corporate Venturing.*

There are many opportunities for lawyers outside the venture capital industry. Employment for all lawyers, regardless of industry, is expected to grow by 6 percent through 2024, according to the U.S. Department of Labor, or about as fast as the average for all careers. Nearly 44,000 new attorney jobs are expected to be added to the U.S. economy during this time span.

■ UNIONS AND ASSOCIATIONS
Venture capital lawyers are not represented by unions. Many become members of national, state, and local

professional associations to take advantage of networking opportunities, career assistance, continuing education (CE) classes and webinars, and other resources. The American Bar Association (ABA) is the leading legal association in the United States. It offers educational and career information as well as statistics on the legal industry; accredits law schools; publishes journals such as *Business Lawyer, Student Lawyer,* and *ABA Journal;* and has a Private Equity and Venture Capital Committee, Institutional Investors Committee, and Business Law Section. The Association of Corporate Counsel is a membership organization for in-house counsel in the United States and more than 50 other countries. It offers information on careers, publishes *ACC Docket,* hosts an annual meeting, and provides professional development opportunities. The National Venture Capital Association is a trade organization of 300 of the leading venture capital firms. At its Web site, you can find information on CE webinars, samples of commonly-used VC legal documents, a blog, and a list of regional and state VC associations at its Web site.

■ TIPS FOR ENTRY
1. Visit the following Web sites for job listings:
   - http://www.abalcc.org
   - http://www.acc.com/jobline
   - http://www.ventureloop.com
2. Once you've become a lawyer and gained experience, volunteer your services to a venture capital firm. Managing partners love free help, and volunteering might help you get your "foot in the door" at the firm.
3. Participate in an internship at a law firm that provides services to the VC industry to obtain experience and build your network.
4. To learn more about the industry, check out The Venture Alley (https://www.theventurealley.com), a blog about legal and business issues that are important to entrepreneurs, startups, venture capitalists, and angel investors.

■ FOR MORE INFORMATION
For information about law education and careers and its Private Equity and Venture Capital Committee, Institutional Investors Committee, and Business Law Section, contact

American Bar Association
321 North Clark Street
Chicago, IL 60654-7598
Tel: (800) 285-2221
http://www.americanbar.org

For information on continuing education and membership, as well as job listings, visit the association's Web site.

Association of Corporate Counsel
1025 Connecticut Avenue, NW, Suite 200
Washington, D.C. 20036-5425
Tel: (202) 293-4103
http://www.acc.com

For more information on venture capital, contact

National Venture Capital Association
25 Massachusetts Avenue, NW, Suite 730
Washington, D.C. 20001-1430
Tel: (202) 864-5920
http://www.nvca.org

Venture Capital Marketing Specialists

■ OVERVIEW
Venture capital marketing specialists plan, organize, direct, and coordinate their employer's marketing operations. They work to present a positive image of the firm, its partners, and its funds to the public and potential investors via press releases, social media Web sites (including blogs), interviews with members of the media, fund marketing materials, and other strategies. At smaller funds, the role of marketing specialist is often combined with that of investor relations specialist. Marketing specialists may also be known as *chief marketing officers, market research analysts, marketing partners, marketing associates,* and *marketing managers.* Nearly 690,000 marketing managers, specialists, and research analysts are employed in the United States. Venture capital marketing specialists comprise a very small portion of this total.

■ HISTORY
Companies have used marketing campaigns to reach customers ever since the first product or service was sold to the public. But unlike most businesses, venture capital firms have traditionally been loath to tout their funds or disclose their financials to the media or general public, instead preferring to operate under levels of secrecy more akin to the CIA than a typical business.

In recent years, many VC firms have become more like traditional businesses (at least in some respects), hiring marketing and public relations workers to tell their story, promote their funds, and counteract any negative

QUICK FACTS

ALTERNATE TITLE(S)
Chief Marketing Officers, Market Research Analysts, Marketing Associates, Marketing Managers, Marketing Partners

DUTIES
Plan, organize, direct, and coordinate their employer's marketing operations; create a brand for the firm; interact with members of the business media

SALARY RANGE
$33,460 to $125,000 to $297,000

WORK ENVIRONMENT
Primarily Indoors

BEST GEOGRAPHIC LOCATION(S)
Opportunities are best in San Francisco, Los Angeles, Boston, Washington, D.C., and in other cities with a large number of start-ups

MINIMUM EDUCATION LEVEL
Bachelor's Degree

SCHOOL SUBJECTS
Business, English, Speech

EXPERIENCE
One year of marketing experience for entry-level ; five years of lower-level management experience for executives

PERSONALITY TRAITS
Creative, Enterprising, Hands On

SKILLS
Research, Sales, Writing

CERTIFICATION OR LICENSING
Recommended

SPECIAL REQUIREMENTS
None

EMPLOYMENT PROSPECTS
Good

ADVANCEMENT PROSPECTS
Fair

OUTLOOK
Much Faster than the Average

NOC
0013, 4163

O*NET-SOC
11-2021.00, 13-1161.00

press or comments on social media. This sea change is occurring because the number of venture capital firms has declined in recent years, and a smaller group of firms is trying to raise funds from investors. Additionally, the *New York Times* reports that the best entrepreneurs are courted by the venture capitalists, not the other way around…the most promising entrepreneurs do careful due diligence—on Twitter, in blogs, and in the media—before agreeing to take coffee with a venture capitalist."

■ THE JOB

"Marketing is the name we use to describe the promise a company makes, the story it tells, the authentic way it delivers on that promise," according to the author, entrepreneur, and marketing expert Seth Godin. As competition between VC firms increases to fund the next hot start-up, many partners are hiring marketing professionals to help tout the achievements of the firm and tell its story. At some of the top firms, marketing is so highly valued that marketing specialists are being made partners. Job responsibilities of VC marketing specialists vary by firm, but most perform the following duties:

- creating a brand for the firm and telling its "story" to the media and potential investors. This involves everything from sharing inspiring stories about the founders and the formation of the firm, to touting past fund successes, to communicating the idea that the firm is "entrepreneur-friendly" and offers a wealth of expertise in a particular industry sector (technology, green energy, biotechnology, health care products, etc.)
- pitching story ideas about the firm, its partners, and its portfolio companies to influential VC bloggers and members of the business media
- helping the firm's portfolio companies with their marketing and public relations needs
- conducting market research and analyzing data to make the firm's marketing efforts more targeted and effective
- setting up blogs and other social media accounts (LinkedIn, Twitter, etc.) for partners (who use these platforms to tout their firm and its portfolio companies, what they look for in start-ups and founders, and the types of investment strategies that they use)
- creating and implementing strategies to drive traffic to the firm's Web site and the blogs and social media accounts of its founders via search engine optimization and other approaches
- creating and promoting press releases, annual reports, web videos, and other types of communications
- working with investor relations professionals to create password-protected data rooms (Web site portals) for prospective investors. These portals list investments made by predecessor funds, audited

financial statements of predecessor funds, and other due diligence–related content

- working closely with managing partners, freelance or in-house web and publication designers, and colleagues from other departments

EARNINGS

Market research analysts and marketing specialists earned median annual salaries of $61,290 in May 2014, according to the U.S. Department of Labor. Ten percent earned $33,460, and 10 percent earned $116,740 or more. Marketing managers had earnings that ranged from less than $65,980 to $171,390 or more.

Chief marketing officers who were employed by venture-backed technology companies earned base salaries of $235,000 in 2014, according to the *2014 VC Executive Compensation Survey Trend Report for Technology Companies* from Advanced-HR, Inc., a private company compensation consulting firm. They also received average incentive pay (i.e., bonuses) of $62,000.

Marketing specialists receive benefits such as paid vacation and sick leave, health and life insurance, and a 401(k) or other retirement savings plan. In 2014, chief marketing officers who were employed by venture-backed technology companies received an average of 0.88 percent of equity (stock options) in the company, according to Advanced-HR, Inc.

WORK ENVIRONMENT

A typical day for a marketing specialist may consist of brainstorming sessions with the firm's partners to discuss a new marketing campaign and the launch of a new blog, phone conversations with members of the media to tout one of the firm's portfolio companies, several hours of writing press releases and editing copy for the firm's Web site, and after-hours dinners with well-known industry bloggers or reporters. Approximately 40 percent of advertising managers worked more than 40 hours per week in 2014, according to the U.S. Department of Labor.

EXPLORING

For an introduction to marketing concepts and techniques, check out *Marketing For Dummies* (For Dummies, 2014) and *Social Media Marketing For Dummies* (For Dummies, 2014). For a brief overview of venture capital, visit http://www.entrepreneur.com/encyclopedia/venture-capital.

Consider joining a high school or college chapter of DECA (http://www.deca.org), a nonprofit organization that hosts competitions, educational conferences, and leadership training programs for students who are interested in careers in marketing, finance, hospitality, and management.

Others methods to explore this occupation include talking with marketing professionals about their careers, studying past advertising campaigns to see why they were successful or failed, creating a marketing campaign for a real or imaginary product (and testing it out on your friends and family), and visiting the Web sites of professional marketing associations.

CAREER LADDER

Marketing Partner

Marketing Manager

Marketing Specialist

Marketing Associate

EDUCATION AND TRAINING REQUIREMENTS
High School

Helpful high school courses include marketing, business, statistics, mathematics, English, speech, computer science (especially web design), microeconomics, macroeconomics, psychology, and foreign language.

Postsecondary Education

Marketing professionals typically have bachelor's degrees in marketing or advertising. Others have degrees in journalism, speech communications, English, economics, or business administration. Since marketing specialists frequently use social media, it's a good idea to take social media marketing classes. A small, but growing, number of colleges and universities offer degrees or specializations in social media marketing or social media, including Lewis University (Romeoville, Ill.), DePaul University (Chicago, Ill.), Newberry College (Newberry, S.C.), Pace University (New York, N.Y.), and the University of Florida (Gainesville, Fla.).

U.S. News & World Report publishes a list of colleges and universities that offer the best marketing programs in the United States at http://colleges.usnews.rankingsandreviews.com/best-colleges/rankings/business-marketing.

Other Education or Training

Many professional associations provide continuing education programs to help their members keep up to date with industry developments and learn new skills. For example, the eMarketing Association offers online courses in basic emarketing, advanced search engine optimization, and advanced Web site design. The American Marketing Association, Internet Marketing Association,

THE BUSINESS OF VENTURE CAPITAL

LEARN MORE ABOUT IT

Cumming, Douglas. *The Oxford Handbook of Venture Capital.* New York: Oxford University Press, 2012.

Demaria, Cyril. *Introduction to Private Equity: Venture, Growth, LBO, and Turn-Around Capital,* 2nd ed. Hoboken, N.J.: John Wiley & Sons, 2013.

Draper, William H. *The Startup Game: Inside the Partnership Between Venture Capitalists and Entrepreneurs.* New York: St. Martin's Griffin, 2012.

Gerken, Louis C., and Wesley A. Whittaker. *The Little Book of Venture Capital Investing: Empowering Economic Growth and Investment Portfolios.* Hoboken, N.J.: John Wiley & Sons, 2014.

Gottlieb, Richard. *The Directory of Venture Capital & Private Equity Firms 2015: Domestic & International,* 19th ed. Amenia, N.Y.: Grey House Publishing, 2015.

Gravagna, Nicole, and Peter K. Adams. *Venture Capital For Dummies.* Hoboken, N.J.: For Dummies, 2013.

Klonowski, Darek. *The Venture Capital Investment Process: Principles and Practice.* New York: Palgrave Macmillan, 2013.

Lerner, Josh, Ann Leamon, and Felda Hardymon. *Venture Capital and Private Equity: A Casebook,* 5th ed. Hoboken, N.J.: John Wiley & Sons, 2012.

Levin, Jack S., and Donald E. Rocap. *Structuring Venture Capital, Private Equity and Entrepreneurial Transactions.* New York: Wolters Kluwer Law & Business, 2015.

Maynard, Therese, and Dana M. Warren. *Business Planning: Financing the Start-Up Business and Venture Capital,* 2nd ed, New York: Wolters Kluwer Law & Business, 2014.

Ramsinghani, Mahendra. *The Business of Venture Capital: Insights from Leading Practitioners on the Art of Raising a Fund, Deal Structuring, Value Creation, and Exit Strategies,* 2nded. Hoboken, N.J.: John Wiley & Sons, 2014.

Romans, Andrew. *The Entrepreneurial Bible to Venture Capital: Inside Secrets from the Leaders in the Startup Game.* New York: McGraw-Hill Education, 2013.

Marketing Research Association, and National Venture Capital Association offer webinars, workshops, and other professional development opportunities. Contact these organizations to learn more.

Marketing specialists who want to learn more about the financial and deal-making aspects of the venture capital industry can participate in one or more of the following programs that are offered by universities and private organizations:

- University of California-Berkeley Venture Capital Executive Program: http://executive.berkeley.edu/programs/venture-capital-executive-program
- Venture Capital Institute: http://www.vcinstitute.org
- University of Michigan Center for Venture Capital and Private Equity Finance: http://www.zli.bus.umich.edu/vc_pe
- Venture Capital institute: http://www.vcinstitute.org/Venture_Capital_Institute.html

Certification

Undergraduate- and graduate-level marketing and social media marketing certificates are offered by colleges and universities. The American Marketing Association offers the digital marketing e-learning certificate, which features four modules: Social Media, Email Marketing, Web & Digital Analytics, and Digital Content Marketing. Two other modules—Online Advertising and Mobile Marketing—will be launched soon. Visit https://www.ama.org/events-training/eLearning/Pages/eLearning.aspx to learn more.

■ CERTIFICATION, LICENSING, AND SPECIAL REQUIREMENTS
Certification or Licensing

Some VC marketing specialists complete certification programs that are offered by professional associations. For example, the American Marketing Association offers the professional certified marketer credential to applicants who pass a comprehensive online exam that covers core marketing concepts. To be eligible for certification, applicants must have either: 1) a bachelor's degree and two years of professional marketing experience, or 2) a master's degree and one year of professional marketing experience. Visit https://www.ama.org/events-training/Certification/Pages/us-pcm.aspx for more information.

Certification credentials are also provided by the Internet Marketing Association (certified Internet marketer), Marketing Research Association (professional researcher), and the eMarketing Association (certified mobile marketer, certified e-marketing associate, certified e-marketer, certified social marketing associate).

■ EXPERIENCE, SKILLS, AND PERSONALITY TRAITS

Marketing partners and managers need at least five years of experience in leadership positions in marketing departments at the portfolio companies of VC firms, at marketing firms, or in the VC departments of corporations. Entry-level marketing professionals must have at least one year of marketing experience at a well-known corporation or in a related alternative investment sector (e.g., private equity, hedge funds).

Marketing specialists must be able to write informative and interesting press releases, social media posts, and other communications. A "gift for gab" and the ability to schmooze will come in handy because marketing specialists are in frequent contact with reporters, bloggers, and current and potential investors. Other important traits include an eye for detail, the ability to multitask, a positive personality, and creativity. Marketing specialists need to be proficient in the use of venture capital terminology and investment strategies and be able to use Microsoft PowerPoint, Excel, and Word; enterprise collaboration software such as Intralinks and Qumu; and customer relationship management software such as Microsoft Dynamics. They should also be skilled at using social media and search engine optimization techniques.

■ EMPLOYMENT PROSPECTS

Employers

Marketing specialists are employed by venture capital firms, marketing firms that provide services to VC firms, and the portfolio companies of VC firms. They also work for corporations such as Google and Intel that have VC departments.

Venture capital firms are located throughout the United States, with most located in or near large cities such as New York, Los Angeles, San Francisco, Boston, Chicago, San Diego, and Washington, D.C. Many VC firms have offices abroad, especially in Europe and the Far East. For example, Accel (a VC funder of Facebook, Etsy, and Spotify) is headquartered in Palo Alto, California, but it also has offices in the United Kingdom and India.

Starting Out

A good way to break into the venture capital industry is to apply for entry-level jobs with the portfolio companies of VC firms or at marketing firms that provide services to the VC industry. In these positions, you'll work closely with VC partners and get to know the typical marketing needs of the firm. In time, this combination of networking contacts, experience, and industry know-how will allow you to transition into a job at a VC firm.

Visit the Web sites of venture capital firms and VC-related employers to learn about internship opportunities and full-time jobs. Be sure to create a LinkedIn profile and become active on its marketing and venture capital message boards. You can also learn about job opportunities through your school's career services office, at career fairs and other networking events, and at the job boards of marketing association Web sites.

You can access a list of venture capital firms and corporate venture groups that are members of the National Venture Capital Association by visiting http://nvca.org/about-nvca/members.

Checking out "best" or "top" company lists is another good strategy to identify potential employers. Here are several best/top company lists:

- *Entrepreneur*'s VC 100: The Top Investors in Early-Stage Startups list: http://www.entrepreneur.com/article/242702
- *Fortune*'s various industry best lists: http://fortune.com/rankings (some of these companies have venture capital divisions)
- CB Insight: Healthcare's Top Venture Capital Firms: https://www.cbinsights.com/blog/health care-venture-capital-top-mosaic
- Tech.Co's 25 Top VC Firms list: http://tech.co/top-vc-firms-to-pitch-your-startup-to-2015-02

■ ADVANCEMENT PROSPECTS

Large venture capital firms are most likely to have dedicated marketing departments. At smaller firms, there may be just a marketing partner or marketing manager to handle all the firm's marketing needs. At a large firm, entry-level marketing associates can advance to become marketing coordinators/managers. Highly-skilled and experienced managers may be asked to become marketing partners, who make investment decisions and get a share of the firm's profits.

■ OUTLOOK

Employment for market research analysts and marketing specialists who work in the finance and insurance industries is expected to grow much faster than the average for all careers through 2024, according to the U.S. Department of Labor.

There will continue to be demand for venture capital marketing specialists. In recent years, major VC firms such as Draper Fisher Jurvetson; Kleiner Perkins Caufield & Byers; and True Ventures have added dedicated marketing and public relations to their staffs. Venture capital firms are also touting their in-house marketing, public relations, and communications experience as a means to convince hot start-ups to accept their funding.

Additionally, the Jumpstart Our Business Startups Act (commonly known as the JOBS Act), which allows VC firms to advertise and perform general solicitations, is expected to increase marketing efforts at some firms.

UNIONS AND ASSOCIATIONS

Venture capital marketing specialists do not belong to unions. Many professional associations provide useful resources to aspiring and current marketing specialists. For example, the American Marketing Association offers membership options for young professionals and college students, a student job board, professional development opportunities, an annual conference, the professional certified marketer certification, publications such as *Marketing News* and *Marketing Insights,* and many other resources. The National Venture Capital Association represents the interests of U.S. VC firms and corporations that have VC departments. It has a Strategic Communications Group for marketing, public relations, communications, and investor relations professionals from member firms as well as their consultants. Other noteworthy organizations include the eMarketing Association, Internet Marketing Association, and the Marketing Research Association.

TIPS FOR ENTRY

1. Check to see if your college has a chapter of Pi Sigma Epsilon (https://www.pse.org), a coed marketing and sales fraternity that offers networking opportunities, competitions, and conferences.

2. Attend the American Marketing Association International Collegiate Conference to participate in professional development opportunities, competitions, and networking events. Visit https://www.ama.org/events-training/Conferences/Pages/AMA-International-Collegiate-Conference.aspx for more information.

3. Visit the following Web sites for job listings:

   - http://imanetwork.org/career-exchange
   - http://www.emarketingassociation.com/career-center.html
   - http://www.efinancialcareers.com
   - https://www.pehub.com

FOR MORE INFORMATION

For information on marketing education and careers, contact
American Marketing Association
311 South Wacker Drive, Suite 5800
Chicago, IL 60606-6629
Tel: (800) AMA-1150
https://www.ama.org

For information on certification, contact
eMarketing Association
40 Blue Ridge Drive
Charlestown, RI 02813-2746

Tel: (800) 496-2950
E-mail: ema@eMarketingAssociation.com
http://www.emarketingassociation.com

For information on certification, contact
Internet Marketing Association
http://www.imanetwork.org

For information on certification, education, and training, contact
Marketing Research Association
1156 15th Street, NW, Suite 302
Washington, D.C. 20005-1745
Tel: (202) 800-2545
http://www.marketingresearch.org

For more information on venture capital and its Strategic Communications Group, contact
National Venture Capital Association
25 Massachusetts Avenue, NW, Suite 730
Washington, D.C. 20001-1430
Tel: (202) 864-5920
http://www.nvca.org

Venture Capital Principals

OVERVIEW

Venture capital principals assist managing partners and partners by identifying investment opportunities for the fund, conducting due diligence of target companies, helping to manage portfolio companies, and performing a variety of other duties. This position is often considered "partner track."

HISTORY

Venture capital as a structured, formalized investment strategy began in 1946 when Georges Doriot and others started American Research and Development Corporation (ARDC), the first publicly owned venture capital (VC) firm. Also in 1946, three wealthy families established professional VC operations (Rockefeller Brothers Inc., J. H. Whitney, and Payson & Trask) in New York City. From 1946 through 1957, ARDC and the three family entities engaged in VC investing, but no other VC firms were founded. From the late 1950s onward, a series of technological, political, financial, and regulatory events fueled growth in the VC industry. The industry really took off in the late 1980s and early 1990s as a result of the tech boom. Since then, there have been a series of booms and busts, with the most recent bust occurring as a result of the Great Recession of the late 2000s. The industry is currently on the upswing, but it has not regained its pre-recession mojo. In fact, the number of principals employed by VC firms declined by 63 percent from 2004 to 2014, according to the National Venture Capital Association.

THE JOB

Principals are key players at venture capital firms. As partners-in-training, they assist more experienced venture capital professionals, providing everything from deal sourcing, to assistance with due diligence, and portfolio company management. Their major duties include:

- identifying and assessing potential investment opportunities from their network of contacts (business colleagues, venture incubators and accelerators, etc.) and new sources
- preparing industry and competitive research on financing targets and presenting this information to the firm's investment committee
- working closely with managing partners to conduct due diligence (market, management, product, legal, accounting, etc.) on target companies to assess the strength of investment proposals (this includes screening potential business plans and helping to value the company using market comparable and discounted cash flow benchmarking exercises)
- constructing financial models to assess a target company's operation, financing, valuation, etc.
- building relationships with entrepreneurs and venture capitalists at other funds
- participating in the deal process (e.g., drafting term sheets and letters of intent, negotiation, audit, tax, legal, closing)
- providing support to portfolio companies by conducting research, advising senior management, assisting with financing and acquisition activities, and attending board meetings
- analyzing credit issues and equity opportunities at portfolio companies
- serving on the boards of portfolio companies (or functioning as a board observer)
- identifying and negotiating with potential buyers of the fund's portfolio businesses
- assisting partners during the exit process (i.e., initial public offering or merger)
- supporting and mentoring junior staff at the firm

EARNINGS

In 2014, venture capital professionals with an MBA received average earnings (base pay plus bonus) of $296,155, according to the *2015 Private Equity and Venture Capital Compensation Report*. New hires don't make that much money. They earn about $165,000 in base salary.

Principals receive benefits such as vacation days, sick leave, health and life insurance, and a 401(k) or other retirement savings plan. In addition, they are eligible for lucrative perks such as co-investment opportunities, carry, and closing bonuses. Co-investment is the opportunity for the principal to invest his or her own money alongside the firm in some deals. If a fund is successful, the return on their investment can greatly exceed salary and bonuses. Some principals also receive carry, which is a percentage of the profits the firm makes. Finally, principals may receive closing bonuses for sourcing or doing due diligence when an investment is closed. Most early stage firms do not give this lower-level bonus, although some do.

WORK ENVIRONMENT

A career as a principal is fast-paced, sometimes stressful, but usually rewarding. During a typical week, you'll review dozens of pitches, meet with potential investors, attend board meetings, and spend hours and hours at your desk analyzing target companies, responding to issues at portfolio companies, drafting reports and answering e-mails, and creating financial models. Many principals work 50 to 60 hours a week, including at night and on weekends. Principals

CAREER LADDER

Managing Partner

Partner

Principal

Senior Associate

Associate/Analyst

travel frequently to meet with current and potential investors and the executives of portfolio companies, as well as to industry conferences, panels, and other events.

■ EXPLORING

One easy way to learn more about venture capital is to read books and journals about the field, as well as check out Web sites. Here are some useful resources:

- *The Business of Venture Capital: Insights from Leading Practitioners on the Art of Raising a Fund, Deal Structuring, Value Creation, and Exit Strategies,* by Mahendra Ramsinghani
- *Venture Capital Review:* http://www.ey.com/Publication/vwLUAssets/EY-venture-capital-review/$FILE/EY-venture-capital-review.pdf
- Ventureblogs: A List of Venture Capital Blogs: http://www.ventureblogs.com

Do you know the meaning of VC words and phrases such as accredited investor, greenfield, and Series A round? If not, you should peruse PitchBook's Private Equity & Venture Capital Glossary (http://pitchbook.com/news/articles/private-equity-and-venture-capital-glossary) to familiarize yourself with industry jargon.

In college, join venture capital and business clubs. Talk with your professors about VC investment strategies, funding stages, and potential careers. Perhaps he or she can connect you with venture capitalists who would be willing to discuss their careers and the best ways to break into the field.

■ EDUCATION AND TRAINING REQUIREMENTS
High School

Business, accounting, economics, and mathematics classes will provide you with good preparation for the financial aspects of a career as a venture capital principal. Speech and English classes will allow you to become a top-notch communicator as you source deals, debate strategy with your colleagues, and prepare oral and written reports. Other important courses include foreign language, social studies, psychology, and computer science.

Postsecondary Education

An MBA is usually a prerequisite for this career, and a science/engineering undergraduate or graduate degree is even more valuable among many firms. Some partners have law or medical degrees. Most VC professionals on the partner track have degrees from Ivy League schools or other prestigious colleges.

Other Education or Training

The artist and inventor Leonardo da Vinci once said that "learning never exhausts the mind," and aspiring or current VC principals would be wise to heed this observation. The world of venture capital is constantly changing and those who stay up to date will prosper. Those interested in expanding their knowledge can view webinars (such as VC Firms in Transition Debt and Non-Dilutive Capital Raising Solutions) from the National Venture Capital Association or enroll in short-term training programs offered by colleges, universities, and nonprofit and for-profit organizations. Here are some popular programs:

- University of California-Berkeley Venture Capital Executive Program: http://executive.berkeley.edu/programs/venture-capital-executive-program
- Venture Capital Institute: http://www.vcinstitute.org
- University of Michigan Center for Venture Capital and Private Equity Finance: http://www.zli.bus.umich.edu/vc_pe
- Venture Capital institute: http://www.vcinstitute.org/Venture_Capital_Institute.html

Certification

Many colleges and universities offer short-term certificates in business, finance, and economics. Additionally, the Investment Management Consultants Association offers the Fundamentals of Alternative Investments Certificate Program (https://www.imca.org/pages/Fundamentals-Alternative-Investments-Certificate), an online program that introduces participants to venture capital and other alternative assets classes, due diligence, risk management, and other topics. The program features 20 modules. Each module has several video chapters and a quiz—and applicants must pass all of the quizzes to complete the certificate program.

■ CERTIFICATION, LICENSING, AND SPECIAL REQUIREMENTS
Certification or Licensing

Since you'll need a strong finance background to be successful as a principal, it's a good idea to become certified by professional associations. One of the most popular credentials is the chartered financial analyst (CFA) designation, which is offered by the CFA Institute. To enroll in the CFA Program and register for the first exam (there are three levels of certification), applicants must satisfy one of the following requirements:

- have a bachelor's (or equivalent) degree or be in the final year of their bachelor's degree program
- have four years of professional work experience (which does not have to be investment related)
- have a combination of professional work experience and education that totals at least four years.

The certificate program covers topics such as ethical and professional standards, quantitative methods, financial reporting and analysis, corporate finance, equity investments, and alternative investments. Visit https://www.cfainstitute.org/programs/cfaprogram for more information.

Other popular certifications include:

- chartered alternate investment analyst (Chartered Alternate Investment Analyst Association)
- certified investment management analyst (Investment Management Consultants Association)
- certified treasury professional, certified corporate financial planning and analysis professional (Association for Financial Professionals)

■ EXPERIENCE, SKILLS, AND PERSONALITY TRAITS

Principals typically have two to six years of experience as venture capital associates, or they have extensive industry experience (e.g., telecommunications, medical devices, consumer products, engineering, software). Most importantly, they need to provide evidence of their expertise in deal sourcing and structuring, due diligence, and business planning (including financial modeling).

Principals need excellent communication and interpersonal skills because they frequently attend investment meetings, interact with senior-level professionals at banks and equity groups as well as with current and prospective investors, and prepare written reports and financial documents. Other important traits include strong analytical capabilities, financial modeling proficiency, intellectual curiosity, high ethical standards, confidence, good organizational skills, curiosity, creativity, impeccable schmoozing talents, and the ability to excel in a fast-paced and demanding work environment.

BOOTSTRAPPING, DRIVE-BY DEAL, AND VAPORWARE

WORDS TO KNOW

Accelerator (also **incubator**): a center where start-ups are nurtured, or incubated, via mentorship, free work space, and sometimes cash.

Boot-strapping: the strategy of using the cash of family and friends to launch a business.

Burn rate: the rate at which a start-up with little or no revenue uses available funds to cover its expenses.

Cats and dogs: slang for lower-level investors who sometimes participate in early-stage deals alongside professional investors.

Crater: a company that received venture capital and subsequently went bankrupt.

Dog (also **walking dog**):a company that received venture capital but is failing or going nowhere.

Drive-by deal: jargon used to designate a venture capital deal entered into with the intent to make a quick exit from the venture (i.e., a quick sell-off).

League table: rankings of companies based on revenue, earnings, deals, or any other relevant criteria. They are used for comparing companies.

Living dead: start-ups who have received multiple rounds of funding, but will not receive more funding and who will be unable to bring their products or services to market.

Runway: the period of time the start-up has until its cash runs out and it must close.

T-rex: slang for a very large and powerful venture capital fund.

Vaporware: a product that is sold by a start-up, but that has not actually been manufactured (and may never be). Vaporware is used to test market demand. Many people believe this strategy is unethical.

■ EMPLOYMENT PROSPECTS
Employers

Venture capital firms are located throughout the United States and the world. Many U.S.-based firms are headquartered in California and on the East Coast. Most VC firms have fewer than 15 employees. The National Venture Capital Association reports that companies in 47 states and the District of Columbia received VC funding in 2014. Fifty-seven percent of venture capital investment was concentrated in start-ups in California. The next most-popular states for VC investment were Massachusetts, New York, Texas, Washington, Illinois, Florida, Colorado, Utah, and Pennsylvania.

Starting Out

Most people either break into the field by working as associates for two to six years or by accruing extensive experience in a specific industry (e.g., telecommunications, medical devices, consumer products, engineering, software).

You can break into the field as an associate by networking with venture capitalists at industry conferences, seminars, and business development events; participating in an internship at a VC firm; and volunteering with professional VC associations. Another good option is to participate in the Kauffman Fellows Program. The mission of the two-year fellowship is to increase the number of well-trained venture capitalists in the U.S. by placing and paying top candidates to work as associates in well-known venture capital firms. Visit http://www.kauffman fellows.org for more information.

▒ ADVANCEMENT PROSPECTS

Principals who demonstrate their ability to generate good deals and strong returns on investment are promoted to the position of partner, who have similar duties as principals, but focus on big-picture issues and have the authority to approve investments and exits. A highly skilled partner can eventually become a managing partner, who oversees the entire firm. Some venture capitalists may leave the field and become chief financial officers, CEOs, or chief operating officers.

▒ OUTLOOK

Activity level in the VC industry is roughly half of what it was at its 2000-era peak (before the Great Recession). Venture capital firms had $156.5 billion in capital under management in 2014, according to the National Venture Capital Association (NVCA). During that same year, investment levels reached their highest amount ($49.3 billion) since 2000, up from $30.1 billion in 2013.

Despite these partially positive statistics, it is still very difficult to land a job in the venture capital industry because there are fewer firms than in the past (803 in 2014 as compared to 985 firms in 2004) and staffing levels have declined (the NVCA reports that the average VC firm had 7.1 principals in 2014, down from nearly 9 principals in 2007). Opportunities will be best for those with certification, a solid track record of deal sourcing/structuring, and a well-developed roster of business and VC contacts.

▒ UNIONS AND ASSOCIATIONS

Venture capital principals do not belong to unions. Some are members of firms that belong to the National Venture Capital Association, which offers webinars, industry statistics, publications such as *Corporate Venture Connection* and *Venture Capital Review,* and other resources at its Web site. Membership organizations for women in the VC industry include the Association of Women in Alternative Investing, Women's Association of Venture and Equity, and Women.VC.

▒ TIPS FOR ENTRY

1. Read the following publications to learn more about the business world:
   - *Barron's:* http://www.barrons.com
   - *Bloomberg Business:* http://www.bloomberg.com/businessweek
   - *Forbes:* http://www.forbes.com
   - *Fortune:* http://www.fortune.com
2. Take the Venture Capital Aptitude Test, http://guykawasaki.com/the_venture_cap, to see if you're a good fit for a career in venture capital.
3. Volunteer with a venture capital or business organization to do some good, but also make valuable networking contacts that could lead to a job. Here are a few options:
   - VC Taskforce: http://www.vctaskforce.com
   - MBAs Without Borders: http://www.pyxera global.org/signature-initiatives/mbas-without-borders
   - High Water Women Foundation: http://www.highwaterwomen.org

▒ FOR MORE INFORMATION

AWAI is a membership organization for women in the venture capital, hedge fund, and private equity industries.
Association of Women in Alternative Investing (AWAI)
E-mail: info@altinvesting.org
http://www.altinvesting.org

For more information on venture capital, contact
National Venture Capital Association
25 Massachusetts Avenue, NW, Suite 730
Washington, D.C. 20001-1430
Tel: (202) 864-5920
http://www.nvca.org

For information on membership, contact
Women's Association of Venture and Equity
10 Winton Farm Road
Newtown, CT 06470-2653
Tel: (855) 928-3606
E-mail: wavecoordinator@gmail.com
https://women-wave.org

Women.VC describes itself as an "independent nonprofit organization aiming to strengthen and develop the world investment industry by introducing women professionals who bring real value."

Women.VC

http://www.women.vc

Venture Capital Risk Managers

◼ OVERVIEW

Risk managers identify, analyze, and seek to reduce or eliminate risks (e.g., technology, management, product, etc.) that will affect the profitability of venture capital firms and their portfolio companies. They are also known as *risk officers* and *chief risk officers.*

◼ HISTORY

Venture capital (VC) investments are very risky. Studies by the Ewing Marion Kauffman Foundation and the U.S. Bureau of Labor Statistics show that approximately 60 percent of venture capital–funded start-ups survive to age three and only about 35 percent survive to age 10. (The studies focused on only incorporated companies with employees.) Almost anything can go wrong—from a poor management team, to issues with technology, and market saturation.

Venture capitalists have focused on risk ever since the first publicly owned VC firm (American Research and Development Corporation) was founded in 1946. As technology has become more complex and a wider array of risk factors have emerged in recent years, venture capitalists have created stand-alone risk management departments or, at the minimum, created the position of chief risk officer to address these challenges.

◼ THE JOB

Effective risk management practices at a venture capital firm can translate into millions—and even billions—of dollars in profits. On the other hand, ineffective risk management strategies can be both a disaster for the VC firm and its portfolio companies. Major areas of risk in venture capital (and questions typically asked by risk professionals when assessing risk) include:

- Technology: Are there research and development issues that may delay the launch of the company? Does the company have strong Information

QUICK FACTS
ALTERNATE TITLE(S) Chief Risk Officers, Risk Analyst, Risk Officers
DUTIES Identify, analyze, and mitigate risks; creating risk management strategies; implementing risk management protocols; following market developments that affect risk
SALARY RANGE $76,694 to $124,938 to $161,243+
WORK ENVIRONMENT Primarily Indoors
BEST GEOGRAPHIC LOCATION(S) Opportunities are best in San Francisco and in other cities with a large number of start-ups
MINIMUM EDUCATION LEVEL Bachelor's Degree
SCHOOL SUBJECTS Business, Economics, Mathematics
EXPERIENCE Ten years in risk management positions for executives; five years of risk-related work experience or one to two years internship experience for managers and analysts
PERSONALITY TRAITS Organized, Problem-Solving, Realistic
SKILLS Business Management, Financial, Interpersonal
CERTIFICATION OR LICENSING Recommended
SPECIAL REQUIREMENTS None
EMPLOYMENT PROSPECTS Good
ADVANCEMENT PROSPECTS Fair
OUTLOOK Much Faster than the Average
NOC 0111
O*NET-SOC 13-2099.02

Technology security protocols in place that protect its intellectual assets?

- Disruption: Are there any unforeseeable events (e.g., a recession, a sudden spike in the cost of energy, etc.) that could doom or delay the introduction of the product?

CAREER LADDER

Managing Partner

Partner

Chief Risk Officer

Risk Manager

Risk Management Analyst

- Market: What is the market for the product or service like? Are there many competitors? If there's a lot of competition, is there time to build market share before funding runs out? Is it the right time to launch the product or service (i.e., many products or services that are successfully launched today might not have been successful a decade ago)? Are there other major barriers to entry?
- Financial: Will the portfolio company have enough capital to reach the end stage of selling the product or service—allowing the VC firm to profitably exit the investment? Are the unit economics (the direct revenues and costs associated with the business model for the product or service) feasible? What is the overall financial condition of the company? Are strong accounting and auditing practices in place?
- Management: Does the portfolio company employ the right people to ensure that it will meet its goals? Do the founders have a strong track record of success? Is the company's management receptive to feedback? Is it transparent about its financials and staffing issues? If the VC firm deems that changes are needed, are the company's founders amenable to bringing on experts, as needed?
- Legal: How will government regulation affect the company and its products and services? Are there any potential patent or copyright infringement issues?

Major duties of venture capital risk managers include:

- identifying, analyzing, assessing, and ranking all risks by using the scorecard method (which uses a mathematical formula to assess and identify the top areas of concern), software models, and other tools
- working with financial professionals to conduct a complete audit of the target portfolio company to assess whether it will have the necessary funding to bring products or services to market
- meeting with general partners and the board of directors to create a risk management strategy

that defines the risk appetite the firm has for each investment, and drafting an investment diversification plan that reduces risk if serious issues arise regarding a specific investment
- designing and implementing risk management protocols
- implementing and monitoring stress tests, back-tests, and sensitivity analysis for portfolio companies and firm assets
- meeting with portfolio company founders during the life-cycle of the investment to assess previously identified risk-related issues and identify new areas of concern
- keeping up-to-date on market developments and assessing their potential positive or negative effects on portfolio companies

■ EARNINGS

Risk managers earned median annual salaries of $102,059 in January 2016, according to Salary.com. Wages ranged from $76,694 to $134,679 or more. Risk management directors had average earnings of $124,938. The lowest 10 percent earned $94,017 or less, while the top 10 percent earned $161,243 or more.

Venture capital risk managers usually receive a generous benefits package, including vacation days, sick leave, health and life insurance, and a 401(k) or other retirement savings plan.

■ WORK ENVIRONMENT

Risk management professionals typically work a standard 9 to 5, Monday through Friday schedule, but may need to occasionally work at night and on weekends during busy periods. This job can be stressful because there are many risk areas to monitor and failure to identify them can result in the loss of millions of dollars. A typical day for a risk manager might involve research and analysis in his or her office; meetings with partners and members of the compliance, legal, and financial departments regarding risk management issues; and travel to meetings with executives at portfolio companies or those that are candidates for investment.

■ EXPLORING

Talk with your high school principal or a college risk management (RM) officer about the RM protocols that are in place at the institutions. Risk management plans may also be available at these organization's Web sites. Learn as much as you can about risk management; http://www.dummies.com/search.html?query=risk+management is a good source of introductory information. After you've read a few articles, create a risk management plan for an imaginary product or service that you'd like to launch, or for a school function (dance, field trip, science fair) that you're organizing. To learn more about venture capital, check out the Illinois Venture Capital Association's Web site, http://www.illinoisvc.org/faqs-about-venture-capital-private-equity, and the sites of other venture capital associations.

■ EDUCATION AND TRAINING REQUIREMENTS
High School

Risk managers need a comprehensive understanding of both business and financial principles, so it's a good idea to take as many business, economics, mathematics, and accounting classes in high school as possible. English and speech classes will help you to develop strong communication skills, which you'll need to write detailed reports and convey your findings and recommendations to managing partners. Other important classes include computer science, history, and government.

Postsecondary Education

If you want to work at a venture capital firm, you'll need to attend a top-tier college and earn excellent grades. A minimum of a bachelor's degree in risk management, insurance, accounting, finance, economics, or business is required to work as a risk manager. Some venture capital managing partners like to hire those with a master's in risk management or business management.

Fewer than 65 colleges and universities in the United States and Canada offer degrees in risk management. Visit http://www.aria.org/RMI_Programs.htm for a list of schools that offer certificates and bachelor's and graduate degrees in the field.

Other Education or Training

Many risk managers participate in continuing education classes to keep their skills up to date and qualify for certification or re-certification. These opportunities are provided by professional associations at the national, state, and local levels. For example, the Global Association of Risk Professionals offers classes such as Foundations of Financial Risk (for entry-level professionals) and Financial Risk and Regulation (for mid-to-senior level professionals). The Professional Risk Managers' International Association, RIMS—The Risk Management, and the Public Risk Management Association also provide professional development opportunities. Risk managers can also take classes at colleges and universities to keep up on the latest risk management strategies.

Certification

Many professional associations offer short-term certificate programs, which provide novices with a chance to

A risk manager notes potential pitfalls for a start-up requesting backing from his venture capital firm. (BlueSkyImage. Shutterstock.)

learn about the field or help experienced practitioners keep their skills up to date. Most involve a combination of online study/in-person classes and the successful completion of multiple-choice and written examinations. For example, the Professional Risk Managers' International Association offers the associate professional risk manager; credit and counterparty manager; market, liquidity, and asset liability management risk manager; and operational risk manager certificates. Visit http://www.prmia.org/certificate-programs to learn more. Here are a few other risk management/alternative investment certificates:

- International certificate in risk management (offered by the Institute of Risk Management, https://www.theirm.org/qualifications/ international -certificate-in-risk-management)
- Fundamentals of alternative investments (Investment Management Consultants Association, https://www.imca.org/pages/Fundamentals -Alternative-Investments-Certificate)

■ CERTIFICATION, LICENSING, AND SPECIAL REQUIREMENTS
Certification or Licensing

Several associations offer certification programs for risk management professionals, including:

- Global Association of Risk Professionals (financial risk manager, http://www.garp.org/#!/frm)
- RIMS—The Risk Management Society (RIMS-certified risk management professional, http://www.RIMS.org/certification)
- Professional Risk Managers' International Association (professional risk manager, http://www.prmia.org/certificate-programs)

BREAKING INTO VENTURE CAPITAL

How to Get Into Venture Capital

http://www.financewalk.com/2014/venture-capital

This short article answers the following questions:

- What kind of people do venture capital firms typically prefer to hire?
- How important are headhunters in the venture capital firm's recruitment process?
- How are resumes and interviews for venture capital different from those in investment banking or private equity?
- What is the best way to enter the industry?

How to Break Into Venture Capital

http://www.mergersandinquisitions.com/break-into-venture-capital

This article features an interview with an investment banker who broke into the venture capital industry. It features a lot of useful information.

What Are Unconventional Ways to Get an Entry-Level Job at a Venture Capital Firm?

http://fortune.com/2015/07/30/quora-vc-firm-jobs

This article provides four strategies that will help you to get noticed by venture capital partners.

Resume Advice: Private Equity & Venture Capital

http://mbaexeccm.wharton.upenn.edu/wp-content/uploads/files/Wharton_Resume_Advice_Private_Equity_Venture_Capital.pdf

This short guide from the University of Pennsylvania's Wharton School, the world's first collegiate business school, offers advice on how to address specific job requirements and demonstrate transaction experience on one's resume. It also covers VC-specific resume themes and VC resume best practices.

Successful Networking for a Venture Capital Job

http://www.jobsearchdigest.com/private_equity_jobs/career_advice/networking_vc_job

"Entering into a venture capital career absolutely depends upon how well you network," advises the Private Equity Jobs Digest, which provides this tip sheet to help aspiring VC professionals build their networks.

Venture Capital Career Resources

http://www.johngannonblog.com/vc-careers

This spot aggregates all types of job-search information for the venture capital industry. It features links to venture capitalists talking about their jobs, blogs about the VC business, networking and interviewing tips, and job listings.

- CFA Institute (chartered financial analyst credential, http://www.cfainstitute.org/programs/cfaprogram).

■ EXPERIENCE, SKILLS, AND PERSONALITY TRAITS

Chief risk officers need at least 10 years of experience in lower-level risk management positions or in other venture capital careers. Risk managers must have at least five years of experience in risk management, and risk analysts need a year or two of experience (a combination of an internship, co-op, or part-time job) in a risk management position at a corporation or in an another alternative investment sector such as private equity or hedge funds.

You will need excellent judgment, strong communication and interpersonal skills, and confidence in order to effectively convey and support your recommendations regarding risk areas—especially because other members of the firm may not always agree with your conclusions. Other important traits include good problem-solving skills, intellectual curiosity, strong quantitative skills, and the ability to use risk management software.

RIMS—The Risk Management Society provides a detailed summary of key skills, abilities, and knowledge areas for risk managers by level of experience at https://www.rims.org/quality.

■ EMPLOYMENT PROSPECTS
Employers

Risk professionals have many employment options. In the venture capital industry, they can work for VC firms, the portfolio companies of VC firms, and third-party vendors (including investment banks) that specialize in providing risk management services to VC firms. A list of venture capital firms and corporate venture groups that are members of the National Venture Capital Association is available at http://nvca.org/about-nvca/members. Additionally, risk managers work for insurance companies, airlines, banks, manufacturers, hospitals, and for any other business that needs risk management services. They also are employed by the U.S. military, government agencies, and nonprofits.

Starting Out

The venture capital industry is very difficult to break into—especially if you lack prior experience (internships, co-ops, etc.) or if don't have industry contacts. A common strategy is to obtain two to three years of risk management experience at a major corporation, a portfolio company of a venture capital firm, or at a third-party provider of risk management services to VC firms. A combination of this experience, certification, and a degree from a top university will enhance your chances of landing a job. During this time, you should also make contacts with venture capital professionals at networking events (which are sponsored by professional associations or listed on social networking sites such as MeetUp.com). Finally, consider volunteering at a VC association or a finance- or venture capital–related nonprofit to catch the attention of well-known venture capitalists. One such organization is VC Taskforce (http://www.vctaskforce.com), which provides networking and educational events—panels, workshops, conferences, and roundtable meetings—for venture capitalists and entrepreneurs seeking funding. Other job-search methods include using the services of recruiters, checking out employment Web sites, attending career fairs, and applying directly to companies that employ risk professionals.

ADVANCEMENT PROSPECTS

There are few advancement opportunities at small venture capital firms because most have a single risk management staff member or outsource this work to a third-party firm. At large firms, a skilled and experienced risk analyst might advance to the position of risk manager and then to chief risk officer. Some risk management professionals are asked to become partners.

OUTLOOK

Job opportunities for financial managers who work for firms that manage funds, trusts, and other financial vehicles will grow by 19 percent through 2024, according to the U.S. Department of Labor. The venture capital industry has bounced back in recent years (although the activity level in the industry is roughly half of what it was at its 2000-era

peak). In 2014, venture capital firms invested about $30 billion into 3,665 companies, and new commitments to VC funds in the United States increased to $30 billion, up significantly from $17.7 billion in 2013, according to the National Venture Capital Association. With so much investment money flowing, there is a strong need for risk managers to identify threats to the success of portfolio companies and ensure a strong return on investment for VC firms.

UNIONS AND ASSOCIATIONS

Venture capital risk managers do not belong to unions. Professional associations can be excellent resources for risk management professionals—providing everything from certification programs and publications, to networking events and career seminars. For example, the Global Association of Risk Professionals, which has more than 150,000 members in 195 countries, offers the financial risk manager credential, professional development classes and webinars, job listings at its Web site, networking opportunities via chapter events and at its annual Risk Management Convention, and other resources. The National Venture Capital Association is the leading trade organization of the U.S. venture capital industry, with more than 300 member firms. The Women's Association of Venture and Equity and Women.VC are membership organizations that advocate to increase the number of women in the field (women are still vastly underrepresented in the VC industry as compared to their percentage of the U.S. population). Other helpful organizations include the American Risk and Insurance Association, Professional Risk Managers' International Association, Public Risk Management Association, RIMS—The Risk Management Society, and RMA-The Risk Management Association.

TIPS FOR ENTRY

1. Check out the Career Tools section of the RIMS Web site, https://www.rims.org/resources/CareerCenter/Resources/Pages/default.aspx. It features articles on resume writing, networking, career success, and other topics.
2. Visit http://jobs.prmia.org and https://www.linkedin.com/jobs/venture-capital-jobs for job listings.
3. Visit http://www.johngannonblog.com/vc-careers to access a variety of venture capital career resources.

FOR MORE INFORMATION

For information on membership and networking, contact
Global Association of Risk Professionals
111 Town Square Place, 14th Floor
Jersey City, NJ 07310-1755
Tel: (201) 719-7210
http://www.garp.org

For more information on venture capital, contact
**National Venture Capital
    Association**
25 Massachusetts Avenue, NW, Suite 730
Washington, D.C. 20001-1430
Tel: (202) 864-5920
http://www.nvca.org

For information on certification and continuing education, contact
**Professional Risk Managers' International
    Association**
400 Washington Street
Northfield, MN 55057-2027
Tel: (612) 605-5370
http://www.prmia.org

For information on membership, certification, and continuing education, contact
**RIMS—The Risk Management
    Society**
5 Bryant Park, 13th Floor
New York, NY 10018
Tel: (212) 286-9292
https://www.rims.org

For information on membership and continuing education, contact
**RMA-The Risk Management
    Association**
1801 Market Street, Suite 300
Philadelphia, PA 19103-1628
Tel: (800) 677-7621
http://www.rmahq.org

For information on membership, contact
**Women's Association of Venture
    and Equity**
10 Winton Farm Road
Newtown, CT 06470-2653
Tel: (855) 928-3606
E-mail: wavecoordinator@gmail.com
https://women-wave.org

Women.VC describes itself as an "independent nonprofit organization aiming to strengthen and develop the world investment industry by introducing women professionals who bring real value."
Women.VC
http://www.women.vc

Veterinarians

■ OVERVIEW

The *veterinarian*, or *doctor of veterinary medicine*, diagnoses and controls animal diseases, treats sick and injured animals medically and surgically, prevents transmission of animal diseases, and advises owners on proper care of pets and livestock. Veterinarians are dedicated to the protection of the health and welfare of all animals and to society as a whole. There are about 65,650 veterinarians in the United States.

■ HISTORY

The first school of veterinary medicine was opened in 1762 in Lyons, France. Nearly 100 years later, a French physician and veterinarian named Alexandre Francois Liautard emigrated to the United States and became a leader in the movement to establish veterinary medicine as a science. Through his efforts, an organization was started in 1863 that later became the American Veterinary Medical Association. By the late 1800s, veterinarians started to focus their attention on the study and control of animal diseases that affected human health and food supplies. For example, cattle were first tested for tuberculosis in the 1890s.

Initially, veterinary medicine was concerned with the health of horses and farm animals, particularly because agriculture was a major factor in the economy. Pet ownership has grown in the years since and concern for other animals such as dogs, cats, birds, guinea pigs, etc., has expanded veterinary practice. Veterinary medicine has made great strides since its introduction in this country, one advance being the significant reduction in animal diseases contracted by humans.

■ THE JOB

Veterinarians care for pets—large and small. They ensure a safe food supply by maintaining the health of food animals. They also protect the public from residues of herbicides, pesticides, and antibiotics in food. Veterinarians may be involved in wildlife preservation and conservation and use their knowledge to increase food production through genetics, animal feed production, and preventive medicine.

About 74 percent of veterinarians are employed in solo or group veterinary medicine practices. Some veterinarians treat all kinds of animals, but more than half limit their practice to companion animals such as dogs, cats, and birds. A smaller number of veterinarians work mainly with horses, cattle, pigs, sheep, goats, and poultry. Today, a veterinarian may be treating llamas, catfish, or ostriches as well. Others are employed by wildlife management groups, zoos, aquariums, ranches, feed lots, fish farms, and animal shelters.

Veterinarians in private practice diagnose and treat animal health problems. During yearly checkups, the veterinarian records the animal's temperature and weight; inspects its mouth, eyes, and ears; inspects the skin or coat for any signs of abnormalities; observes any peculiarities in the animal's behavior; and discusses the animals eating, sleeping, and exercise habits at length with the owner. The veterinarian will also check the animal's vaccination records and administer inoculations for rabies, distemper, and other diseases if necessary. If the veterinarian or owner notes any special concerns, or if the animal is taken to the veterinarian for a specific procedure, such as spaying or neutering, dental cleaning, or setting broken bones, the animal may stay at the veterinarian's office for one or several days for surgery, observation, or extended treatments. If a sick or wounded animal is beyond medical help, the veterinarian may, with the consent of the owner, have to euthanize the animal.

During office visits and surgery, veterinarians use traditional medical instruments, such as stethoscopes, thermometers, and surgical instruments, and standard tests, such as X-rays and diagnostic medical sonography, to evaluate the animal's health. Veterinarians may also prescribe drugs for the animal, which the owner purchases at the veterinarian's office.

Some veterinarians work in public and corporate sectors. Many are employed by city, county, state, provincial, or federal government agencies that investigate, test for, and control diseases in companion animals, livestock, and poultry that affect both animal and human health. Veterinarians also play an important public health role. For example, veterinarians played an important part in conquering diseases such as malaria and yellow fever.

Pharmaceutical and biomedical research firms hire veterinarians to develop, test, and supervise the production of drugs, chemicals, and biological products such as antibiotics and vaccines that are designed for human and animal use. Some veterinarians are employed in management, technical sales and services, and marketing in agribusiness, pet food companies, and pharmaceutical companies. Still other veterinarians are engaged in research and teaching at veterinary medical schools, working with racetracks or animal-related enterprises, or working within the military, public health corps, and space agencies.

Veterinarians in private clinical practice become specialists in surgery, anesthesiology, dentistry, internal medicine, ophthalmology, or radiology. Many veterinarians also pursue advanced degrees in the basic sciences, such as anatomy, microbiology, and physiology. Veterinarians who seek specialty board certification in one of 40 specialty fields must complete a two- to five-year residency program and must pass an additional examination. Some veterinarians combine their degree in veterinary medicine with a degree in business (M.B.A.) or law (J.D.).

The U.S. Department of Agriculture offers opportunities for veterinarians in the Food Safety and Inspection Service and the Animal and Plant Health Inspection Service, notably in the areas of food hygiene and safety, animal welfare, animal disease control, and research. Veterinarians also are employed by the Environmental Protection Agency to deal with public health and environmental risks to the human population.

Veterinarians are often assisted by *veterinary technicians*, who may conduct basic tests, record an animal's medical history for the veterinarian's review, and assist the veterinarian in surgical procedures.

■ EARNINGS

The U.S. Department of Labor reports that median annual earnings of veterinarians were $88,490 in May 2015. Salaries ranged from less than $53,210 to more than $158,260. The average annual salary for veterinarians working for the federal government was $88,220.

According to a survey by the American Veterinary Medical Association, the average starting salary for veterinary medical college graduates (excluding graduates entering advanced education) was approximately $52,000 in 2014.

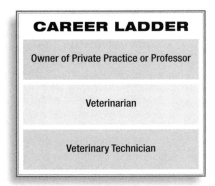

CAREER LADDER

Owner of Private Practice or Professor

Veterinarian

Veterinary Technician

Benefits include paid vacation, health, disability, life insurance, and retirement or pension plans. Self-employed veterinarians must provide their own benefits.

■ WORK ENVIRONMENT

Veterinarians usually treat companion and food animals in hospitals and clinics. Those in large animal practice also work out of well-equipped trucks or cars and may drive considerable distances to farms and ranches. They may work outdoors in all kinds of weather. The chief risk for veterinarians is injury by animals; however, modern tranquilizers and technology have made it much easier to work on all types of animals.

Some veterinarians work long hours, sometimes more than 50 hours a week. Although those in private clinical practice may work nights and weekends, the increased number of emergency clinics has reduced the amount of time private practitioners have to be on call. Large animal practitioners tend to work more irregular hours than those in small animal practice, industry, or government. Veterinarians who are just starting a practice tend to work longer hours.

■ EXPLORING

High school students interested in becoming veterinarians may find part-time or volunteer work on farms, in small-animal clinics, or in pet shops, animal shelters, or research laboratories. Participation in extracurricular activities such as 4-H are good ways to learn about the care of animals. Such experience is important because, as already noted, many schools of veterinary medicine have established experience with animals as a criterion for admission to their programs. Other methods of exploration include talking to a veterinarian about their career, reading books and magazines about veterinary science, and visiting the Web sites of veterinary associations and veterinary medical colleges.

■ EDUCATION AND TRAINING REQUIREMENTS
High School

For the high school student who is interested in admission to a school of veterinary medicine, a college preparatory course is a wise choice. A strong emphasis on science classes such as biology, chemistry, and anatomy is highly recommended.

Postsecondary Training

The doctor of veterinary medicine (D.V.M.) degree requires a minimum of four years of study at an accredited college of veterinary medicine. Although many of these colleges do not require a bachelor's degree for admission, most require applicants to have completed 45–90 hours of undergraduate study. It is possible to obtain pre-veterinary training at a junior college, but since admission to colleges of veterinary medicine is an extremely competitive process, most students receive degrees from four-year colleges before applying. In addition to academic instruction, veterinary education includes clinical experience in diagnosing disease and treating animals, performing surgery, and performing laboratory work in anatomy, biochemistry, and other scientific and medical subjects.

There are 30 colleges of veterinary medicine in the United States that are accredited by the Council on Education of the American Veterinary Medical Association. Visit https://www.avma.org/ProfessionalDevelopment/Education/Accreditation/Colleges/Pages/colleges-accredited.aspx for a list of programs. Each college of veterinary medicine has its own pre-veterinary requirements, which typically include basic language arts, social sciences, humanities, mathematics, chemistry, and biological and physical sciences.

Applicants to schools of veterinary medicine usually must have grades of "B" or better, especially in the sciences. Applicants must take the Medical College Admission Test (MCAT) or the Graduate Record Examination (GRE). Fewer than half of the applicants to schools of veterinary medicine may be admitted, due to small class sizes and limited facilities. Most colleges give preference to candidates with animal- or veterinary-related experience. Colleges usually give preference to in-state applicants because most colleges of veterinary medicine are state-supported. There are regional agreements in which states without veterinary schools send students to designated regional schools.

Veterinary medicine students typically participate in one or more internships during their college careers. The internships allow them to learn more about career options in the field and make industry contacts. Some new veterinary graduates enter one-year internship programs to obtain experience in particular practice specialties such as zoo veterinary science.

Other Education or Training

Nearly all states require veterinarians to attend continuing education courses in order to maintain their licenses. The American Veterinary Medical Association offers continuing education (CE) opportunities at its annual conference. Recent sessions included "Veterinary Financial Planning," "Fees: Shortchanging your Practice or Right on the Money?," and "Shake Things Up: Creative Ideas to Grow your Practice." Many other veterinary organizations provide CE opportunities, including the American Animal Hospital Association, American Association of Equine Practitioners, American Association of Zoo Veterinarians, Association of Exotic Mammal Veterinarians, and the Canadian Veterinary Medical Association.

■ CERTIFICATION, LICENSING, AND SPECIAL REQUIREMENTS
Certification or Licensing

Veterinarians who seek specialty board certification in one of 40 specialty fields must complete a two- to five-year residency program and pass an additional examination. Some veterinarians combine their degree in veterinary medicine with a degree in business or law. The AVMA American Board of Veterinary Specialties provides the details (https://www.avma.org/ProfessionalDevelopment/Education/Specialties).

All states and the District of Columbia require that veterinarians be licensed to practice private clinical medicine. To obtain a license, applicants must have a D.V.M. degree from an accredited or approved college of veterinary medicine. They must also pass one or more national examinations and an examination in the state in which they plan to practice.

Few states issue licenses to veterinarians already licensed by another state. Thus, if a veterinarian moves from one state to another, he or she will probably have to go through the licensing process again. Veterinarians may be employed by a government agency (such as the U.S. Department of Agriculture) or at some academic institution without having a state license.

■ EXPERIENCE, SKILLS, AND PERSONALITY TRAITS

There is no way to obtain direct experience in high school, but it's a good idea to take as many science classes as possible and participate in science clubs. During veterinary training, students gain experience by completing a two- to five-year residency program. Some new veterinary graduates enter 1-year internship programs to obtain experience in particular practice specialties such as equine veterinary science.

Individuals who are interested in veterinary medicine should have an inquiring mind and keen powers of observation. Aptitude and interest in the biological sciences

Veterinarians examine and administer medical treatment to all types of animals, from pet dogs to exotic reptiles. (Shutterstock. In Tune.)

are important. Veterinarians need a lifelong interest in scientific learning as well as a liking and understanding of animals. Veterinarians should be able to meet, talk, and work well with a variety of people. An ability to communicate with the animal owner is as important in a veterinarian as diagnostic skills.

Veterinarians use state-of-the-art medical equipment, such as electron microscopes, laser surgery, radiation therapy, and ultrasound, to diagnose animal diseases and to treat sick or injured animals. Although manual dexterity and physical stamina are often required, especially for farm vets, important roles in veterinary medicine can be adapted for those with disabilities.

Interaction with animal owners is a very important part of being a veterinarian. The discussions between vet and owner are critical to the veterinarian's diagnosis, so they must be able to communicate effectively and get along with a wide variety of personalities. Veterinarians may have to euthanize (that is, humanely kill) an animal that is very sick or severely injured and cannot get well. When a beloved pet dies, the veterinarian must deal with the owner's grief and loss.

■ EMPLOYMENT PROSPECTS
Employers

Approximately 65,650 veterinarians are employed in the United States. Veterinarians work for schools and universities, wildlife management groups, zoos, aquariums, ranches, feed lots, fish farms, pet food or pharmaceutical companies, and the government (mainly in the U.S.

SALARY DISPARITIES BETWEEN VETERINARIANS AND PHYSICIANS

DID YOU KNOW?

Although education, training, and licensing for veterinarians is rigorous and demanding like that for physicians, pay for veterinarians lags far behind the pay of other medical professionals. Until the latter part of the 20th century, salaries for vets and doctors were closer to the same level; today, vets earn a median salary of approximately $88,000 a year while median annual salaries for physicians fall around $240,000. While it is common for physicians to specialize in various branches of medicine, vets tend to treat a wide variety of animals and health issues. Factors contributing to the disparity include the prioritization of human well-being over that of animals and the much greater availability of health insurance for people compared to pets.

Source: Occupational Outlook Handbook

Department of Agriculture and the U.S. Food and Drug Administration's Center for Veterinary Medicine, but also for the Department of Homeland Security). The vast majority, however, are employed by veterinary clinical practices or hospitals. Many successful veterinarians in private practice are self-employed and may even employ other veterinarians. An increase in the demand for veterinarians is anticipated, particularly for those who specialize in areas related to public health issues such as food safety and disease control. Cities and large metropolitan areas will probably provide the bulk of new jobs for these specialists, while jobs for veterinarians who specialize in large animals will be focused in remote, rural areas.

Starting Out

The only way to become a veterinarian is through the prescribed degree program, and vet schools are set up to assist their graduates in finding employment. Veterinarians who wish to enter private clinical practice must have a license to practice in their particular state before opening an office. Licenses are obtained by passing the state's examination.

Information about employment opportunities can be obtained by contacting employers directly or through career services offices of veterinary medicine colleges. Additionally, professional associations such as the American Association of Zoo Veterinarians, the American Association of Wildlife Veterinarians, the Association of American Veterinary Medical Colleges, and the American Veterinary Medical Association offer job listings at their Web sites.

■ ADVANCEMENT PROSPECTS

New graduate veterinarians may enter private clinical practice, usually as employees in an established practice, or become employees of the U.S. government as meat and poultry inspectors, disease control workers, and commissioned officers in the U.S. Public Health Service or the military. New graduates may also enter internships and residencies at veterinary colleges and large private and public veterinary practices or become employed by industrial firms.

The veterinarian who is employed by a government agency may advance in grade and salary after accumulating time and experience on the job. For the veterinarian in private clinical practice, advancement usually consists of an expanding practice and the higher income that will result from it or becoming an owner of several practices.

Those who teach or do research may obtain a doctorate and move from the rank of instructor to that of full professor, or they may advance to an administrative position.

■ OUTLOOK

Employment of veterinarians is expected to grow faster than the average for all occupations through 2024. The number of pets is expected to increase slightly because of rising incomes and an increase in the number of people aged 34 to 59, among whom pet ownership has historically been the highest. Approximately 65 percent of U.S. households owned a pet in 2015–2016, according to the American Pet Products Association. Many single adults and senior citizens have come to appreciate animal ownership. Pet owners also may be willing to pay for more elective and intensive care than in the past.

Emphasis on scientific methods of breeding and raising livestock, poultry, and fish and continued support for public health and disease control programs will contribute to the demand for veterinarians.

The outlook is good for veterinarians with specialty training. Demand for specialists in toxicology, laboratory animal medicine, and pathology is expected to increase. Most jobs for specialists will be in metropolitan areas. Prospects for veterinarians who concentrate on environmental and public health issues, aquaculture, and food animal practice appear to be excellent because of perceived increased need in these areas. Positions in small animal specialties will be competitive. Opportunities in farm animal specialties will be better, since most such positions are located in remote, rural areas, where many veterinarians do not want to practice.

Despite the availability of additional jobs, competition among veterinarians is likely to be stiff. First-year enrollments in veterinary schools have increased, and the number of students in graduate-degree and board-certification programs has risen dramatically.

■ UNIONS AND ASSOCIATIONS

Veterinarians do not typically belong to unions, but there are many professional associations at the national, state, and local levels that represent their interests. The American Veterinary Medical Association is the leading professional organizations for veterinarians. It provides career information, job listings, publications, educational conferences, and other resources. There are also many other specialized associations for veterinarians, including the American Animal Hospital Association, American Association of Equine Practitioners, American Association of Wildlife Veterinarians, American Association of Zoo Veterinarians, Association of Exotic Mammal Veterinarians, and the Canadian Veterinary Medical Association. The Association of American Veterinary Medical Colleges accredits veterinary training programs. The Animal and Plant Health Inspection Service is a federal agency that offers employment opportunities for veterinarians.

■ TIPS FOR ENTRY

1. Read the *Journal of the American Veterinary Medical*, *The Rural Vet*, *Journal of Zoo & Wildlife Medicine*, and the *Journal of Exotic Pet Medicine* to learn more about the field.
2. Visit the careers sections of professional associations' Web sites to search for job listings.
3. Join the American Veterinary Medical Association to access member-only career and practice development resources, publications, continuing education and networking opportunities, and other resources.
4. Participate in internships, externships, and residencies to obtain valuable experience. For information on internships, visit: https://www.avma .org/ProfessionalDevelopment/Education/Pages/ Veterinary-Internships.aspx.
5. Visit https://www.avma.org/ProfessionalDevelop ment/Personal/Pages/working-diagnosis.aspx for topics on finding a job, crafting a resume, and the interview process.

■ FOR MORE INFORMATION

The American Animal Hospital Association represents the professional interests of veterinarians who primarily treat companion animals.

American Animal Hospital Association (AAHA)
12575 West Bayaud Avenue
Lakewood, CO 80228-2021

THE VETERINARIAN'S OATH   DID YOU KNOW?

Being admitted to the profession of veterinary medicine, I solemnly swear to use my scientific knowledge and skills for the benefit of society through the protection of animal health and welfare, the prevention and relief of animal suffering, the conservation of animal resources, the promotion of public health, and the advancement of medical knowledge.

I will practice my profession conscientiously, with dignity, and in keeping with the principles of veterinary medical ethics.

I accept as a lifelong obligation the continual improvement of my professional knowledge and competence.

Source: American Veterinary Medical Association Web site

Tel: (800) 252-2242; (303) 986-2800
Fax: (303) 986-1700
E-mail: info@aaha.org
https://www.aaha.org

The American Association of Equine Practitioners provides information on equine veterinary science.

American Association of Equine Practitioners (AAEP)
4075 Iron Works Parkway
Lexington, KY 40511-8483
Tel: (800) 443-0177; (859) 233-0147
Fax: (859) 233-1968
E-mail: aaepoffice@aaep.org
http://www.aaep.org

The American Association of Wildlife Veterinarians offers job listings and information about wildlife veterinarians.

American Association of Wildlife Veterinarians (AAWV)
http://www.aawv.net

The American Association of Zoo Veterinarians provides education, networking opportunities, and other resources for zoo veterinarians and students.

American Association of Zoo Veterinarians (AAZV)
581705 White Oak Road
Yulee, FL 32097-2169
Tel: (904) 225-3275
Fax: (904) 225-3289
E-mail: admin@aazv.org
http://www.aazv.org

The American Veterinary Medical Association provides information on careers, schools, and resources for veterinarians.

American Veterinary Medical Association (AVMA)
1931 North Meacham Road, Suite 100
Schaumburg, IL 60173-4360
Tel: (800) 248-2862
Fax: (847) 925-1329
https://www.avma.org

The Animal and Plant Health Inspection Service provides information on veterinary opportunities in the federal government.

Animal and Plant Health Inspection Service (APHIS)
4700 River Road
Riverdale, MD 20737-1228
Tel: (844) 820-2234
https://www.aphis.usda.gov

The Association of American Veterinary Medical Colleges provides information on educational programs in veterinary medicine.

Association of American Veterinary Medical Colleges (AAVMC)
655 K Street, NW, Suite 725
Washington, D.C. 20001-2385
Tel: (202) 371-9195
Fax: (202) 842-0773
http://www.aavmc.org

The Association of Exotic Mammal Veterinarians offers education, conferences, publications, and other resources for exotic mammal veterinarians and students.

Association of Exotic Mammal Veterinarians (AEMV)
618 Church Street, Suite 220
Nashville, TN 37219-2453
E-mail: info@aemv.org
http://www.aemv.org

The Canadian Veterinary Medical Association provides information on veterinary careers in Canada.

Canadian Veterinary Medical Association (CVMA)
339 Booth Street
Ottawa, ON K1R 7K1
Canada
Tel: (800) 567-2862; (613) 236-1162
Fax: (613) 236-9681
E-mail: admin@cvma-acmv.org
http://www.canadianveterinarians.net

Veterinary Technicians

■ OVERVIEW

Veterinary technicians provide support and assistance to veterinarians. They work in a variety of environments, including zoos, animal hospitals, clinics, private practices, kennels, and laboratories. Their work may involve large or small animals or both. Most veterinary technicians work with domestic animals, but some professional settings may require treating exotic or endangered species. There are approximately 95,970 veterinary technicians and technologists employed in the United States.

■ HISTORY

As the scope of veterinary practices grew and developed, veterinarians began to need assistants. At first the role was informal, with veterinary assistants being trained by the doctors they worked for. However, in the latter half of the 20th century, the education, and thus the profession, of veterinary assistants became formalized. Professional associations that offer standards for professional practice as well as education and advocacy for veterinary technicians have since grown. For example, the North American Veterinary Technician Association (now known as the National Association of Veterinary Technicians in America) was established in the 1980s, with the goal of giving veterinary technicians a voice in national issues concerning the veterinary profession. Today, veterinary technicians are an indispensable part of a veterinary practice.

■ THE JOB

Many pet owners depend on veterinarians to maintain the health and well-being of their pets. Veterinary clinics and private practices are the primary settings for animal care. In assisting veterinarians, veterinary technicians play an integral role in the care of animals within this particular environment.

A veterinary technician is the person who performs much of the laboratory testing procedures commonly associated with veterinary care. In fact, approximately 50 percent of a veterinary technician's duties involve laboratory testing. Laboratory assignments usually include taking and developing X-rays, performing parasitology tests, and examining various samples taken from the animal's body, such as blood and stool. A veterinary technician may also assist the veterinarian with necropsies in an effort to determine the cause of an animal's death.

In a clinic or private practice, a veterinary technician assists the veterinarian with surgical procedures. This generally entails preparing the animal for surgery by shaving the incision area and applying a topical antibacterial agent. Surgical anesthesia is administered and controlled by the veterinary technician. Throughout the surgical process, the technician tracks the surgical instruments and monitors the animal's vital signs. If an animal is very ill and has no chance for survival, or an overcrowded animal shelter is unable to find a home for a donated or stray animal, the veterinary technician may be required to assist in euthanizing it.

During routine examinations and checkups, veterinary technicians will help restrain the animals. They may perform ear cleaning and nail clipping procedures as part of regular animal care. Outside the examination and surgery rooms, veterinary technicians perform additional duties. In most settings, they record, replenish, and maintain equipment and other supplies.

Veterinary technicians also may work in a zoo. Here, job duties, such as laboratory testing, are quite similar, but practices are more specialized. Unlike in private practice, the *zoo veterinary technician* is not required to explain treatment to pet owners; however, they may have to discuss an animal's treatment or progress with zoo veterinarians, zoo curators, and other zoo professionals. A zoo veterinary technician's work also may differ from private practice in that it may be necessary for the technician to observe the animal in its habitat, which could require working outdoors. Additionally, zoo veterinary technicians usually work with exotic or endangered species. This is a very competitive and highly desired area of practice in the veterinary technician field. There are only a few zoos in each state; thus, a limited number of job opportunities exist within these zoos. To break into this area of practice, veterinary technicians must be among the best in the field.

Veterinary technicians also work in research. Most research opportunities for veterinary technicians are in academic environments with veterinary medicine or medical science programs. Again, laboratory testing may account for many of the duties; however, the veterinary technicians participate in very important animal research projects from start to finish.

Technicians are also needed in rural areas. Farmers require veterinary services for the care of farm animals such as pigs, cows, horses, dogs, cats, sheep, mules, and chickens. It is often essential for the veterinarian and technician to drive to the farmer's residence because animals are usually treated on-site.

Another area in which veterinary technicians work is that of animal training, such as at an obedience school or with show business animals being trained for the circus or movies. Veterinary technicians may also be employed in information systems technology, where information on animals is compiled and provided to the public via the Internet.

No matter what the setting, a veterinary technician must be an effective communicator and proficient in basic computer applications. In clinical or private practice, it is usually the veterinary technician who conveys and explains treatment and subsequent animal care to the animal's owner. In research and laboratory work, the veterinary technician must record and discuss results among colleagues. In most practical veterinary settings, the veterinary technician must record various information on a computer.

■ EARNINGS

Earnings are generally low for veterinary technicians in private practices and clinics, but pay scales are steadily climbing due to the increasing demand. Better-paying jobs are in zoos, in research, and with the federal government. Those fields of practice are very competitive (especially zoos) and only a small percentage of highly qualified veterinary technicians are employed in them.

Most veterinary technicians are employed in private or clinical practice and research. The U.S. Department of Labor reports that the median annual salary for veterinary technicians and technologists was $31,800 in May 2015. The lowest paid 10 percent made less than $21,890 annually, and the highest paid 10 percent made more than $47,410 annually. Earnings vary depending on practice setting, geographic location, level of education, and years of experience. Benefits vary and

---

QUICK FACTS

ALTERNATE TITLE(S)
Veterinary Technologists, Zoo Veterinary Technicians

DUTIES
Provide support and assistance to veterinarians

SALARY RANGE
$21,890 to $31,800 to $47,410+

WORK ENVIRONMENT
Primarily Indoors

BEST GEOGRAPHIC LOCATION(S)
Opportunities are available throughout the country

MINIMUM EDUCATION LEVEL
Associate's Degree

SCHOOL SUBJECTS
Biology, Chemistry, Mathematics

EXPERIENCE
Completion of a veterinary clinical practicum required

PERSONALITY TRAITS
Organized, Problem-Solving, Scientific

SKILLS
Interpersonal, Organizational, Scientific

CERTIFICATION OR LICENSING
Required

SPECIAL REQUIREMENTS
None

EMPLOYMENT PROSPECTS
Good

ADVANCEMENT PROSPECTS
Good

OUTLOOK
Much Faster than the Average

NOC
3213

O*NET-SOC
29-2056.00

CAREER LADDER

Veterinarian

Veterinary Technologist

Veterinary Technician

Veterinary Assistant or Helper

depend on each employer's policies.

■ WORK ENVIRONMENT

Veterinary technicians generally work 40-hour weeks, although some technicians work more than 50 hours a week. These hours may include a few long weekdays, night shifts, and alternated or rotated Saturdays. Hours may fluctuate, as veterinary technicians may need to have their schedules adjusted to accommodate emergency work.

A veterinary technician must be prepared for emergencies. In field or farm work, they often have to overcome weather conditions in treating the animal. Injured animals can be very dangerous, and veterinary technicians have to exercise extreme caution when caring for them. A veterinary technician also handles animals that are diseased or infested with parasites. Some of these conditions, such as ringworm, are contagious, so the veterinary technician must understand how these conditions are transferred to humans and take precautions to prevent the spread of diseases.

People who become veterinary technicians care about animals. For this reason, maintaining an animal's

A veterinary technician moves a dog after root canal. (U.S. Air Force. Senior Airman Dennis Sloan.)

well-being or helping to cure an ill animal is very rewarding work. In private practice, technicians get to know the animals they care for. This provides the opportunity to actually see the animals' progress. In other areas, such as zoo work, veterinary technicians work with very interesting, sometimes endangered, species. This work can be challenging and rewarding in the sense that they are helping to save a species and continuing efforts to educate people about these animals. Veterinary technicians who work in research gain satisfaction from knowing their work contributes to promoting both animal and human health.

■ EXPLORING

High school students can acquire exposure to the veterinary field by working with animals in related settings. For example, a student may be able to work as a part-time animal attendant or receptionist in a private veterinary practice. Paid or volunteer positions may be available at kennels, animal shelters, and training schools. However, direct work with animals in a zoo is unlikely for high school students.

■ EDUCATION AND TRAINING REQUIREMENTS
High School

Veterinary technicians must have a high school diploma. High school students who excel at math and science have a strong foundation on which to build. Those who have had pets or who simply love animals and would like to work with them also fit the profile of a veterinary technician.

Postsecondary Training

The main requirement is the completion of a two- to four-year college-based accredited program. Upon graduation, the student receives an associate's or bachelor's degree. Those who earn an associate's degree are considered veterinary technicians (who often work in private clinical practices under the guidance of a licensed veterinarian). Those who complete a bachelor's degree are typically known as *veterinary technologists*. Many technologists work in advanced research-related jobs, usually under the supervision of a scientist and sometimes a veterinarian. Currently, about 231 veterinary technology programs are accredited by the American Veterinary Medical Association (AVMA). AVMA-accredited programs are found in most states. A few states do their own accrediting, using the AVMA and associated programs as benchmarks.

Most accredited programs offer thorough course work and preparatory learning opportunities to the aspiring veterinary technician. Typical courses include mathematics, chemistry, humanities, biological science, communications, microbiology, liberal arts, ethics/jurisprudence, and basic computers.

Once the students complete this framework, they move on to more specialized courses. Students take advanced classes in animal nutrition, animal care and management, species/breed identification, veterinary anatomy/physiology, medical terminology, radiography and other clinical procedure courses, animal husbandry, parasitology, laboratory animal care, and large/small animal nursing.

Veterinary technicians must be prepared to assist in surgical procedures. In consideration of this, accredited programs offer surgical nursing courses. In these courses, a student learns to identify and use surgical instruments, administer anesthesia, and monitor animals during and after surgery.

In addition to classroom study, accredited programs offer practical courses. Hands-on education and training are commonly achieved through a clinical practicum, or internship, where the student has the opportunity to work in a clinical veterinary setting. During this period, a student is continuously evaluated by the participating veterinarian and encouraged to apply the knowledge and skills learned.

Other Education or Training

To keep abreast of new technology and applications in the field, practicing veterinary technicians may be required to complete a determined number of annual continuing education courses. Professional development seminars, webinars, workshops, and classes are provided by the American Association of Equine Veterinary Technicians, American Veterinary Medical Association, Canadian Veterinary Medical Association, and the National Association of Veterinary Technicians in America. Contact these organizations for more information.

■ CERTIFICATION, LICENSING, AND SPECIAL REQUIREMENTS
Certification or Licensing

The American Veterinary Medical Association (AVMA) determines the majority of the national codes for veterinary technicians, but state codes and laws vary. Most states offer registration or certification, and the majority of these states require graduation from an AVMA-accredited program as a prerequisite for taking the Veterinary Technician National Examination or a similar state or local examination. Most colleges and universities assist graduates with registration and certification arrangements. The American Association for Laboratory

TOP EMPLOYERS OF VETERINARY TECHNOLOGISTS AND TECHNICIANS AND MEAN ANNUAL EARNINGS, MAY 2015   FAST FACTS

- Other professional, scientific, and technical services: 88,170 jobs, $32,760
- Colleges, universities, and professional schools: 2,640 jobs, $41,300
- Social advocacy organizations: 1,620 jobs, $32,590
- Scientific research and development services: 910 jobs, $41,350
- Federal government agencies: 560 jobs, $48,910

Source: U.S. Bureau of Labor Statistics

Animal Science offers certification to veterinary technicians who are interested in working in research settings. The American Association of Equine Veterinary Technicians and the Academy of Veterinary Emergency and Critical Care Technicians also offer certification.

■ EXPERIENCE, SKILLS, AND PERSONALITY TRAITS

Completion of a postsecondary degree and a clinical practicum are required to become a veterinary technician.

As a veterinarian technician, you should be able to meet, talk, and work well with a variety of people. An ability to communicate with the animal owner is as important as diagnostic skills. In clinical or private practice, it is usually the veterinary technician who conveys and explains treatment and subsequent animal care to the animal's owner. Technicians may have to help euthanize (that is, humanely kill) an animal that is very sick or severely injured and cannot get well. As a result, they must be emotionally stable and able to help pet owners deal with their grief and loss.

■ EMPLOYMENT PROSPECTS
Employers

Approximately 95,970 veterinary technicians and technologists are employed in the United States. Veterinary technicians are employed by veterinary clinics, animal hospitals, zoos, schools, universities, and animal training programs. In rural areas, farmers hire veterinary technicians as well as veterinarians. Jobs for veterinary technicians in zoos are relatively few, since there are only a certain number of zoos across the country. Veterinary technicians with an interest in research work at schools with academic programs for medical science or veterinary medicine. The majority of veterinary technicians find employment in animal hospitals or private veterinary practices, which exist all over the country. However, there are more job opportunities for veterinary technicians in more densely populated areas.

Starting Out

Veterinary technicians who complete an accredited program and become certified or registered by the state in which they plan to practice are often able to receive assistance in finding a job through their college's career services office. Students who have completed internships may receive job offers from the place where they interned.

Veterinary technician graduates may also learn of clinic openings through online classified ads. Opportunities in zoos and research facilities are usually listed in specific industry periodicals such as *Veterinary Technician Magazine* and *AZVT News*, a newsletter published by the Association of Zoo Veterinary Technicians.

■ ADVANCEMENT PROSPECTS

There are various career paths veterinary technicians may follow, based on their interests and training. The opportunities are unlimited. With continued education, veterinary technicians can move into allied fields such as veterinary medicine, nursing, medical technology, radiology, and pharmacology. By completing two more years of college and receiving a bachelor's degree, a veterinary technician can become a veterinary technologist. Advanced degrees can open the doors to a variety of specialized fields.

■ OUTLOOK

Employment for veterinary technicians will grow much faster than the average for all occupations through 2024, according to the U.S. Department of Labor (DOL). Veterinary medicine is a field that is not adversely affected by the economy, so it does offer stability. The public's love for pets coupled with higher disposable incomes will encourage continued demand for workers in this occupation. There should be strong opportunities for veterinary technicians in clinics, animal hospitals, biomedical facilities, humane societies, animal control facilities, diagnostic laboratories, wildlife facilities, drug or food manufacturing companies, and food safety inspection facilities.

The DOL reports that veterinary technicians will have good opportunities in areas such as public health, food and animal safety, national disease control, and biomedical research on human health problems. Veterinary technicians who assist veterinarians who treat farm animals will be in strong demand. Competitions for jobs in aquariums and zoos is expected to be very strong as a result of low turnover, the attractiveness of these positions, and slow growth in the construction of new facilities.

■ UNIONS AND ASSOCIATIONS

Veterinary technicians do not typically belong to unions. Membership organizations include the Academy of Veterinary Emergency and Critical Care Technicians, American Association for Laboratory Animal Science, American Association of Equine Veterinary Technicians, American Veterinary Medical Association, Association of Zoo Veterinary Technicians, Canadian Veterinary Medical Association, and the National Association of Veterinary Technicians in America.

■ TIPS FOR ENTRY

1. Visit the career sections of professional associations' Web sites to find job listings for veterinary technicians.
2. Attend conferences held by the Association of Zoo Veterinary Technicians, National Association of Veterinary Technicians in America, and the American Association of Equine Veterinary Technicians to network and participate in continuing education classes and workshops.
3. Read *The NAVTA Journal* (http://www.navta.net/?page=overview) and the *Journal of the American Veterinary Medical Association* (https://www.avma.org/News/Journals) to learn more about the field.

■ FOR MORE INFORMATION

The Academy of Veterinary Emergency and Critical Care Technicians provides information on certification and membership.

Academy of Veterinary Emergency and Critical Care Technicians (AVECCT)
6335 Camp Bullis Road, Suite 12
San Antonio, TX 78257-9720
E-mail: info@avecct.org
http://www.avecct.org

The American Association for Laboratory Animal Science provides education, certification, journals, and other resources.

American Association for Laboratory Animal Science (AALAS)
9190 Crestwyn Hills Drive
Memphis, TN 38125-8538
Tel: (901) 754-8620

Fax: (901) 753-0046
E-mail: info@aalas.org
https://www.aalas.org

The American Association of Equine Veterinary Technicians and Assistants offers education and career-support resources for equine veterinarian technicians and assistants.

American Association of Equine Veterinary Technicians and Assistants (AAEVT)
http://www.aaevt.org

The American Veterinary Medical Association provides information on education and careers in veterinary medicine.

American Veterinary Medical Association (AVMA)
1931 North Meacham Road, Suite 100
Schaumburg, IL 60173-4360
Tel: (800) 248-2862
Fax: (847) 925-1329
https://www.avma.org

The Association of Zoo Veterinary Technicians promotes and improves professional standards among zoo veterinary technicians.

Association of Zoo Veterinary Technicians (AZVT)
http://azvt.org

The Canadian Veterinary Medical Association provides information on veterinary careers in Canada.

Canadian Veterinary Medical Association (CVMA)
339 Booth Street
Ottawa, ON K1R 7K1
Canada
Tel: (800) 567-2862; (613) 236-1162
Fax: (613) 236-9681
E-mail: admin@cvma-acmv.org
http://www.canadianveterinarians.net

The National Association of Veterinary Technicians in America provides education, publications, and membership benefits for veterinary technicians.

National Association of Veterinary Technicians in America (NAVTA)
PO Box 1227
Albert Lea, MN 56007-1227
Tel: (888) 996-2882
Fax: (507) 489-4518
http://www.navta.net

Video Game Art Directors

■ OVERVIEW

Video game art directors play a key role in every stage of the creation of a video game, from formulating concepts to supervising production. They work with 2-D and 3-D artists, animators, modelers, and other artistic staff to coordinate all the visual images used in a game. Video game art directors supervise both in-house and off-site staff, handle management issues, and oversee the entire artistic production process.

■ HISTORY

The artistic elements of computer and video games have come a long way from *Pong* graphics, where a simple moving blip on the screen entertained early gamers. Today's games not only have to be challenging, engaging, and fun, but they must be visually interesting, realistic, and flashy. While some games still incorporate "cute" characters in the vein of *Q*bert* or *Pac-Man,* the majority of game characters are now human. Figures are pictured with bulging muscles, realistic wounds, or, in the case of many *Final Fantasy* characters, have sex appeal. This realism is the work of huge teams of talented artists that all work together on the completion of a single game. As these teams grew, someone was needed to direct the efforts of these workers and ensure the process, quality, and productivity of the department. Thus, the career of art director developed to oversee this important aspect of game creation.

■ THE JOB

Video game art directors make sure that all visual aspects of a computer or video game meet the expectations of the producers, and ultimately, the client. The art director works directly and indirectly with all artists on a project, such as 2-D and 3-D artists, model makers, texture artists, and character animators. Depending on the size of the company, the director may work as a staff artist in addition to handling managerial tasks. But generally, the director's main responsibilities focus on planning meetings rather than design work.

Video game art directors must be skilled in and knowledgeable about design, illustration, computers, research, and writing in order to supervise the work of their department. They need to be skilled in classic art forms, such as illustration and sculpture, while still familiar with computer art tools.

To coordinate all artistic contributions of a computer or video game, video game art directors may begin with the client's concept or develop one in collaboration with the executive producer. Once the concept is established, the next step is to decide on the most effective way to create it. If the project is to create a sequel to a preexisting game, past animations and illustrations must be taken into consideration and reevaluated for use in the new game.

After deciding what needs to be created, video game art directors must hire talented staff that can pull it off. Because the visual aspects of a game are so important, the art department can be quite large, even just for the making of a single game.

The process of creating a computer or video game begins in much the same way that a television show or film is created. The art director may start with the client's concept or create one in-house in collaboration with staff members. Once a concept has been created, the art director sketches a rough storyboard based on the producer's ideas, and the plan is presented for review to the creative director. The next step is to develop a finished storyboard, with larger and more detailed frames (the individual scenes) in color. This storyboard is presented to the client for review and used as a guide for the executive producer.

Technology plays an increasingly important role in the art director's job. Most video game art directors, for example, use a variety of computer software programs, including Adobe InDesign, FrameMaker, Illustrator, and Photoshop; as well as more specialized 3-D game creation tools such as Lightwave, 3ds Max, and Maya. Video game art directors may work on more than one game at a time and must be able to keep numerous, unrelated details straight. They often work under pressure of a deadline and yet must remain calm and pleasant when dealing with clients and staff. Video game art directors are responsible for supervising the production process and staff, so they are often called upon to resolve problems with projects as well as with employees.

■ EARNINGS

Art directors who worked for software publishers earned mean annual salaries of $99,160 in May 2015, according to the U.S. Department of Labor. Salaries for all art directors ranged from less than $47,320 to $172,900 or more.

Most companies employing video game art directors offer insurance benefits, a retirement plan, and other incentives and bonuses.

■ WORK ENVIRONMENT

Video game art directors usually work in studios or office buildings. Their work areas are ordinarily comfortable, well lit, and ventilated. Most art directors work a standard 40-hour week. Many, however, work overtime during busy periods in order to meet deadlines.

Video game art directors work independently while reviewing video games in development, but much of their time is spent collaborating with and supervising a team of employees, often consisting of game designers, producers, writers, and executives.

■ EXPLORING

High school students can get an idea of what an art director does by working on the staff of the school newspaper, magazine, or yearbook. Developing your own artistic talent is important, and this can be accomplished through self-training (reading books about animation and video games and then applying it on your own) or through formal training in animation, painting, drawing, and other creative arts. At the very least, develop your "creative eye," that is, your ability to develop ideas visually. Any art classes will help to develop these skills.

Another way to explore is by researching the career on the Internet. Visit the Web site of the International Game Developers Association (https://www.igda.org) to check out the community and resources sections for information about video game careers.

■ EDUCATION AND TRAINING REQUIREMENTS
High School

A bachelor's degree is a requirement for video game art directors. A variety of high school courses will give you both a taste of college-level offerings and an idea of the skills necessary for video game art directors on the job. These courses include art, drawing, art history, graphic and digital design, illustration, and computer science. Other useful courses that you should take in high school include business, math, technical drawing, and social science.

Postsecondary Training

Video game art directors often have degrees in art, design, game design, or related fields. A growing number of schools offer courses or degrees in game design and other gaming areas. Animation World Network offers a database of animation schools at its Web site, http://schools.awn.com. Another good source of schools can be found at the Game Career Guide Web site, http://www.gamecareerguide.com.

It is essential for video game art directors to have a thorough understanding of how computer animation and layout programs work. In smaller companies, the art director may be responsible for doing some of this work; in larger companies, staff artists, under the direction of the art director, may use these programs. In either case, the director must be familiar with imaging software and how to use it to best create the intended visual effect.

In addition to course work at the college level, many universities and professional art and design schools offer graduates or students in their final year a variety of workshop projects or internships. These opportunities provide students with the chance to work on real games, develop their personal styles, and add to their work experience.

Other Education or Training

The International Game Developers Association offers webinars for new members on a variety of game-related topics, as well as workshops at industry events. The IEEE Computer Society, Women in Games International, and other associations at the national, state, and local levels also provide continuing education opportunities.

■ CERTIFICATION, LICENSING, AND SPECIAL REQUIREMENTS
Certification or Licensing

There are no certification or licensing requirements for video game art directors.

■ EXPERIENCE, SKILLS, AND PERSONALITY TRAITS

Art directors usually obtain years of experience working in lower-level jobs (assistant art director, game designer, etc.) before becoming qualified to supervise projects.

The work of an art director requires creativity, imagination, curiosity, and a sense of adventure. Video game art directors must be able to work with all sorts of specialized computer software as well as communicate their ideas to other directors, producers, designers, and clients.

The ability to work well with different people and situations is a must for video game art directors. They must always be up to date on new techniques, trends, and attitudes. Deadlines are a constant part of the work, so an ability to handle stress and pressure well is key.

CAREER LADDER

Video Game Producer or Art Director at a More Prestigious Company

Video Game Art Director

Assistant Video Game Art Director

The visual aspects of a computer or video game can be the very things that make it sell. For this reason, accuracy and attention to detail are important parts of the art director's job. When the visuals are innovative and clean, the public either clamors for it or pays no notice. But when a project's visuals are done poorly or sloppily, people will notice, even if they have had no artistic training, and the game will not sell.

Other requirements for video game art directors include time-management and organization skills.

■ EMPLOYMENT PROSPECTS
Employers

Video game art directors are involved in computer and video game design work all over the country for game companies large and small. The largest employers are located in California, Texas, Washington, New York, and Massachusetts. Electronic Arts is the largest independent publisher of interactive entertainment, including several development studios. Big media companies such as Disney also have interactive entertainment departments. Jobs should be available at these companies as well as with online services and interactive networks, which are growing rapidly.

Starting Out

Since an art director's job requires a great deal of experience, it is usually not considered an entry-level position. Typically, a person on a career track toward art director is hired as an assistant to an established director. Recent graduates wishing to enter the game industry should develop what is called a demo reel. This is a type of portfolio in which the work is interactive and shows moving animations and backgrounds as opposed to pictures of static images. Demo reels can show your skill in composition, color, light, motion, presentation, and craftsmanship. It should reflect a wide breadth of styles and show work in more than just one genre of game. This will show that you are versatile as well as creative.

Video game art directors have prior experience in lower positions before advancing to the level of director,

THE ART OF VIDEO GAMES

LEARN MORE ABOUT IT

Anthropy, Anna, and Naomi Clark. *A Game Design Vocabulary: Exploring the Foundational Principles Behind Good Game Design.* New York: Addison-Wesley Professional, 2014.

Bossom, Andy, and Ben Dunning. *Video Games: An Introduction to the Industry.* New York: Fairchild Books, 2016.

Chandler, Heather Maxwell. *The Game Production Handbook,* 3rd ed. Burlington, Mass.: Jones & Bartlett Learning, 2013.

Novak, Jeannie. *Game Development Essentials: An Introduction,* 3rd ed. Independence, Ky.: Cengage Learning, 2011.

Solarski, Chris. *Drawing Basics and Video Game Art: Classic to Cutting-Edge Art Techniques for Winning Video Game Design.* New York: Watson-Guptill, 2012.

so be willing to do your time and acquire credentials by working on various projects. Starting out as an intern or assistant in an art department is a good way to get experience and develop skills.

ADVANCEMENT PROSPECTS

Video game art directors are not entry-level workers. They usually have years of experience working at lower-level jobs in the field before gaining the knowledge needed to supervise projects. This experience will help them manage their artistic staff and solve problems quickly when necessary.

Some may be content upon reaching the position of art director, but many video game art directors take on even more responsibility within their organizations, and become game producers, develop original multimedia programs, or create their own games.

Many people who get to the position of art director do not advance beyond the title but move on to work at more prestigious game developers. Competition for positions at companies that have strong reputations continues to be keen because of the sheer number of talented people interested in the field. At smaller game developers, the competition may be less intense, since candidates are competing primarily against others in the local market.

OUTLOOK

Computer and video game developers will always need talented artists to produce their programs. People who can quickly and creatively generate new concepts and ideas will be in high demand. The International Game Developers

Association reports that as art and design teams grow larger, the need for skilled video game art directors will grow as well. Game visuals have become more technical in nature, blurring the line between programmer and artist. Video game art directors, too, need to become more technical and be able to stay on top of emerging technologies that allow for cutting-edge visual effects.

UNIONS AND ASSOCIATIONS

Video game art directors are not represented by unions, but they can obtain useful resources and professional support from the Academy of Interactive Arts & Sciences, Entertainment Software Association, IEEE Computer Society, International Game Developers Association, and Women in Games International.

TIPS FOR ENTRY

1. Visit http://aidb.com for a database of thousands of animation-related companies.
2. Visit the following Web sites for job listings:
   - Animation World Network (http://www.awn.com)
   - CreativeHeads.net (http://www.highendcareers.com)
   - GameJobs.com (http://www.gamejobs.com)
   - Gamasutra (http://www.gamasutra.com)
   - Dice (http://www.dice.com)
3. Attend the Game Developers Conference (http://www.gdconf.com) to network and participate in continuing education opportunities.

FOR MORE INFORMATION

The Academy of Interactive Arts & Sciences is dedicated to the advancement and recognition of the interactive arts.
Academy of Interactive Arts & Sciences (AIAS)
11175 Santa Monica Boulevard, 4th Floor
Los Angeles, CA 90025-3330
Tel: (310) 484-2560
http://www.interactive.org

The Entertainment Software Association provides information about career opportunities in the video game industry.
Entertainment Software Association (ESA)
601 Massachusetts Avenue, NW, Suite 300
Washington, D.C. 20001-3743
E-mail: esa@theesa.com
http://www.theesa.com

Gamasutra provides articles related to all areas of the game industry.
Gamasutra
http://www.gamasutra.com

The IEEE Computer Society offers information on careers and education, publications, conferences, and student membership.

IEEE Computer Society
2001 L Street, NW, Suite 700
Washington, D.C. 20036-4928
Tel: (202) 371-0101
Fax: (202) 728-9614
E-mail: help@computer.org
https://www.computer.org

The International Game Developers Association provides career advice and industry information.

International Game Developers Association (IGDA)
19 Mantua Road
Mount Royal, NJ 08061-1006
Tel: (856) 423-2990
http://www.igda.org

Women in Games International, composed of both female and male professionals, aims to promote the inclusion and advancement of women in the global games industry.

Women in Games International (WIGI)
E-mail: info@getwigi.com
http://www.womeningamesinternational.org

Video Game Producers

■ OVERVIEW

Video game producers are the liaison between the creative side of video game development, and the business side of marketing and selling the final product. They oversee all steps and processes needed in the creation of a video game, including the hiring, training, and management of staff, checking to see that progress is proceeding according to plan, making sure that the project stays within its budget, and finally, shopping around the final product to potential game distributors.

■ HISTORY

Much has happened in the gaming industry since Atari introduced *Pong* in the early 1970s. Since then, new consoles have come out, including some forgotten hits, such as Intellivision and ColecoVision; more recent names include Nintendo, Sega, Sony PlayStation, and Microsoft Xbox. The industry has become a billion-dollar venture,

with much to win in the case of a hot game (think of *Super Mario Brothers* in its heyday), but also much to lose in the case of a financial sinker (think of *E.T. the Extra Terrestrial*—a game so unpopular it actually ended the life of the Atari 2600 console). This financial risk created the need for better oversight and management in the video game production process, which is why the job of producer was born. Video game producers oversee the creative people working away on the details of the game, while ensuring that client and consumer interest will make the project financially viable from the start and marketable in the future.

■ THE JOB

Producers oversee and manage the development of video games and computer games. They do not generally handle the technical aspects of projects, but they are responsible for coordination, management, and overall quality of the final product. At some companies, however, the producer will take on more technical duties, including serving as the lead designer. Most often, the producer is the liaison or "middle man" between the publisher and the game-development team.

Producers must have widely varied knowledge of all aspects of the computer and video game industry. Whether their background is in computers, business, or art, producers must efficiently manage all steps of the development process. They assist the game development staff in the licensing of software, artwork, sound, and other intellectual properties.

QUICK FACTS

ALTERNATE TITLE(S)
None

DUTIES
Oversee all of the steps and processes needed to create a video game, including managing staff, developing and overseeing budgets, and supervising the marketing of the product

SALARY RANGE
$31,780 to $91,480 to $181,780+

WORK ENVIRONMENT
Primarily Indoors

BEST GEOGRAPHIC LOCATION(S)
Opportunities are available throughout the country, but many software publishers are located in California, Texas, Washington, New York, and Massachusetts

MINIMUM EDUCATION LEVEL
Bachelor's Degree

SCHOOL SUBJECTS
Art, Business, Computer Science

EXPERIENCE
Several years' experience required

PERSONALITY TRAITS
Enterprising, Organized, Problem-Solving

SKILLS
Business Management, Computer, Digital Media

CERTIFICATION OR LICENSING
None

SPECIAL REQUIREMENTS
None

EMPLOYMENT PROSPECTS
Good

ADVANCEMENT PROSPECTS
Fair

OUTLOOK
Faster than the Average

NOC
5131

O*NET-SOC
27-2012.01

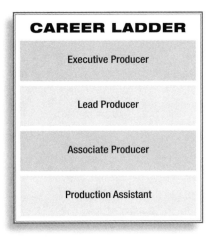

CAREER LADDER

Executive Producer

Lead Producer

Associate Producer

Production Assistant

Producers have many administrative duties, including scheduling meetings and managing documentation. They are also responsible for general business management duties, including hiring and firing of staff. It is essential that producers are excellent communicators, as they work with and manage all different types of personalities. There are two very different sides to the video game industry—the business side and the creative side. Both executive, financial-minded professionals and creative, art-minded professionals must communicate their ideas to the producer, who is then responsible for collaborating these ideas effectively.

The highest-level producing job is that of the *executive producer*, or *senior producer*. This individual trains, mentors, and manages other producers. The executive producer resolves project conflicts, and may have extended contact with clients. In addition to overseeing all other producers and workers on a project, the executive producer is responsible for obtaining funding, updating clients on the progress of projects, and submitting the final work to the client for approval.

Directly under the executive producer are *lead producers*. These professionals have nontechnical duties, but still work closely with the development team. Lead producers oversee tasks including voiceovers, music, effects, and casting.

Associate producers' main responsibilities are overseeing research and product testing. They gather information for the development team, as well as manage video game testers. Associate producers also do more "busy work" such as making client deliveries and taking meeting notes. This may be an entry-level position. Associate producers may have authority over testers, but usually not over any other employees.

Assistant producers, which are also known as *production assistants,* serve as aides to higher-level producers. This occupation is a step toward becoming a producer, but assistants typically do not have much, if any, decision-making authority.

■ EARNINGS

Earnings vary based on skill, experience, and ability to produce high-quality, top-selling games on time and within budget. Producers who worked for software

publishers earned mean annual salaries of $91,480 in May 2015, according to the U.S. Department of Labor. Salaries for all producers ranged from less than $31,780 to $181,780 or more.

Video game producers who work full-time for video game firms usually receive benefits such as vacation days, sick leave, health and life insurance, and a savings and pension program. Self-employed producers must provide their own benefits.

■ WORK ENVIRONMENT

Producers work in bustling, hectic environments that may be viewed as exciting to some, but stressful to others. To succeed at this job, producers need to be able to juggle many tasks at once and work with varying personalities, from game developers and testers who want to make the game as innovative as possible, to the client or upper management whose only interest may be the bottom line. Balancing these (often opposing) priorities can make for a trying, but also exciting, work environment.

■ EXPLORING

To explore this career, make sure to cultivate a love of video games and technology in general. Many schools and communities host computer science clubs that have special chapters catering to avid gamers. If you cannot find such a club, start one with your friends. Schedule tournaments, discuss the best and worst games you've discovered, and think about what makes a game fly off the shelves. This is what a producer has to worry about every day at the office, while still maintaining a passion for playing.

Learn more about the industry and its employers by visiting the Web site of E3, the Electronic Entertainment Expo (http://www.e3insider.com), an annual trade show for computer and video game manufacturers from around the world. The site will give you an idea of the different types of video game companies.

■ EDUCATION AND TRAINING REQUIREMENTS
High School

An interest in playing video games is obviously a requirement, but producers need to know a lot more about the technical side of game development and testing. Create a good foundation by taking math and computer science classes while in high school. Art classes are also useful to stimulate and develop your creative sensibilities, such as illustration—both by hand and with computer drawing tools.

Postsecondary Training

Most larger game developers require producers as well as programmers, testers, and other entry-level workers to have a college degree. A bachelor's degree in computer science with an emphasis in programming, game design, or Web design is preferred, though many enter the industry with business degrees that can come in handy when dealing with clients, balancing the budget, and developing a strong business plan.

Other Education or Training

The International Game Developers Association offers webinars for new members on a variety of game-related topics, as well as workshops at industry events. Women in Games International and other software and computer associations also provide continuing education opportunities.

■ CERTIFICATION, LICENSING, AND SPECIAL REQUIREMENTS
Certification or Licensing

There are no certification or licensing requirements for video game producers.

■ EXPERIENCE, SKILLS, AND PERSONALITY TRAITS

Having a bachelor's degree can help get you in the door of the larger companies, but experience is what really counts in the gaming industry. Several years of experience as an assistant to a producer, as an art director, or in other management positions are required to become a video game producer.

The job of producer includes much administrative work, so producers should have working knowledge of basic commercial software, such as Microsoft Office programs and FileMaker Pro. Familiarity with industry software used in game development is also often a requirement, since producers are heavily in the mix of designers, programmers, and testers.

Higher-level producers such as executive producers will need many years of experience managing teams of workers. Communication and mediating skills are a must in this job, as producers are often forced to solve problems among staff members and make decisions based on varying opinions and priorities, such as those of the developer and those of the client.

■ EMPLOYMENT PROSPECTS
Employers

Video game producers work for game developers of all sizes. Software publishers (such as Electronic Arts and Activision Blizzard) are found throughout the country, though most are located in California, Texas, Washington, New York, and Massachusetts.

VIDEO GAME INDUSTRY HISTORY
LEARN MORE ABOUT IT

Brathwaite, Brenda. *Breaking into the Game Industry: Advice for a Successful Career from Those Who Have Done It.* Independence, Ky.: Cengage Learning, 2011.

Chandler, Heather Maxwell. *The Game Production Handbook,* 3rd ed. Burlington, Mass.: Jones & Bartlett Learning, 2013.

Harris, Blake J. *Console Wars: Sega, Nintendo, and the Battle that Defined a Generation*, reprint ed. New York: Dey Street Books, 2015.

Melissinos, Chris, and Patrick O'Rourke. *The Art of Video Games: From Pac-Man to Mass Effect.* New York: Welcome Books, 2012.

Parkin, Simon. *An Illustrated History of 151 Video Games.* London, U.K.: Lorenz Books, 2014.

Weiss, Brett. *The 100 Greatest Console Video Games: 1977-1987.* Atglen, Penn.: Schiffer Publishing, 2014.

Starting Out

Work experience is valued highly in this industry, so the best bet for landing a first job is with a small, start-up developer. These companies may be more willing to hire less experienced workers in the hopes that they will stay on staff longer than an experienced (and more sought after) producer.

Job listings are easy to find online; most employers post job openings on their company Web sites or with large job search engines. However, because of the industry's popularity, many open positions do not remain open for long. Jobs often are filled internally or through connections before there ever is a need to post a job classified.

■ ADVANCEMENT PROSPECTS

The jobs of *assistant producer* or *associate producer* are entry-level positions, especially if one has worked previously as a *game tester* or *programmer*. Advancement comes in the form of higher-level producing jobs—the top position being that of the *executive producer*, who is responsible for the entire project, beginning to end.

■ OUTLOOK

The Entertainment Software Association reports that 65 percent of American households play video games, and sales of computer and video game software have grown steadily over the years, from $15.2 billion in 2012, to $16.5 billion in 2015, with growth expected to continue. This increasing demand for challenging and entertaining games creates a steady job market for game producers. Overall, employment in this job should grow at a faster than average rate through the coming decade.

One caveat: This is a very popular industry. Talented, artistic, business-minded individuals will be drawn to the business of making and selling computer and video games, causing an influx of applicants for limited numbers of jobs. Individuals with more experience will have the advantage in the job market. However, with the industry's growth, individuals who are hard working, flexible, and passionate about gaming will be able to find entry-level jobs in computer and video game production.

■ UNIONS AND ASSOCIATIONS

Video game producers are not represented by unions, but they can obtain useful resources and professional support from the Academy of Interactive Arts & Sciences, Entertainment Software Association, International Game Developers Association, and Women in Games International.

■ TIPS FOR ENTRY

1. Visit http://aidb.com for a database of thousands of animation-related companies.
2. Visit the following Web sites for job listings:
   - Animation World Network (http://www.awn.com)
   - CreativeHeads.net (http://www.highendcareers.com)
   - GameJobs.com (http://www.gamejobs.com)
   - Gamasutra (http://www.gamasutra.com)
   - Dice (http://www.dice.com)
3. Attend the Game Developers Conference (http://www.gdconf.com) to network and participate in continuing education opportunities.career ladder

■ FOR MORE INFORMATION

The Academy of Interactive Arts & Sciences provides information on opportunities in the computer and video game industry.

Academy of Interactive Arts & Sciences (AIAS)
11175 Santa Monica Boulevard, 4th Floor
Los Angeles, CA 90025-3330
Tel: (310) 484-2560
E-mail: claudio@interactive.org
http://www.interactive.org

This trade show features some of the largest and best-known gaming manufacturers in the world.

Electronic Entertainment Expo (E3)
https://www.e3expo.com

The Entertainment Software Association provides information about career opportunities in the video game industry.

Entertainment Software Association (ESA)
601 Massachusetts Avenue, NW, Suite 300
Washington, D.C. 20001-3743
E-mail: esa@theesa.com
http://www.theesa.com

Gamasutra provides articles related to all areas of the game industry.

Gamasutra
http://www.gamasutra.com

The International Game Developers Association provides career advice and industry information.

International Game Developers Association (IGDA)
19 Mantua Road
Mount Royal, NJ 08061-1006
Tel: (856) 423-2990
http://www.igda.org

Women in Games International, composed of both female and male professionals, aims to promote the inclusion and advancement of women in the global games industry.

Women in Games International (WIGI)
E-mail: info@getwigi.com
http://www.womeningamesinternational.org

Video Game Testers

■ OVERVIEW

Video game testers examine new or modified video game applications to evaluate whether or not they perform at the desired level. Testers also verify that different tasks and levels within a game function properly and progress in a consistent manner. Their work entails trying to find glitches in games and sometimes crashing the game completely. Testers keep very close track of the combinations they enter so that they can replicate the situation in order to remedy it. Testers also offer opinions on the user-friendliness of video and computer games. Any problems they find or suggestions they have are reported in detail both verbally and in writing to supervisors. *Video game testers* act as *quality assurance testers* who specialize in testing video games.

■ HISTORY

Over the years, technology has continued to shrink computer size and increase speed at an unprecedented rate. The video game industry first emerged in the 1970s. Early engineers included Ralph Baer and Steve Russell. Magnavox first manufactured Russell's TV game console, *The Odyssey*, in 1972.

Atari and Sega were the prominent manufacturers of video games throughout the 1970s and 1980s. Nintendo gained popularity in the mid-1980s, and continues to be a dominant player in the industry. Although gaming is a relatively new industry, companies such as Magnavox and Nintendo are more than a century old.

The field of testing and quality assurance has changed with the advent of automated testing tools. There will always be a need for video game testers, however, since they, not a computer, are best suited to judge a game from a user's point of view.

THE JOB

The primary responsibilities of video game testers are game testing and report writing. Testers work with all sorts of games, including handheld electronic devices, computer programs, and traditional video games, which are played on the television screen. As technology advances, testers are responsible for games on more compact electronic devices, such as mobile telephones and palm-sized electronic organizers, as well as online games.

Before video game manufacturers can introduce a game to the consumer market, they must run extensive tests on its quality and effectiveness. Failing to do so thoroughly can be very expensive, resulting in poor sales when games are defective or do not perform well. Video and computer games require extremely detailed technical testing.

Games to be tested arrive in the testing department after programmers and software engineers have finished the initial version. Each game is assigned a specific number of tests, and the video game testers go to work. To test a game, testers play it over and over again for hours, trying to make moves quickly or slowly to "crash" it. A program crashes if it completely stops functioning due to, among other things, an inability to process incoming commands. Testers spend the majority of their time identifying smaller glitches or discrepancies in games, which are known as "bugs."

Video game testers must clearly report any bugs that they find in a game. They keep detailed records of the hours logged working on individual programs. These are called bug reports, and they are based on the tester's observations about how well the game performed in different situations. Testers must always imagine how typical, nontechnical users would judge it. Video game testers can also make suggestions about design improvements.

Prior to being employed in this field, it is important for potential video game testers to carefully observe how different types of people play games. This will help to ensure that suggestions and evaluations reflect more than just personal bias.

In addition, testers verify that video games perform in accordance with designer specifications and user requirements. This includes checking not only the game's functionality (how it will work), but also its network performance (how it will work with other products), installation (how to put it in), and configuration (how it is set up).

Once video game testers make sure that the correct tests are run and the reports are written, they send the game back to the programmers for revisions and correction. Some testers have direct contact with the programmers. After evaluating a product, they might meet with programmers to describe the problems they encountered and suggest ways for solving glitches. Others report solely to a game testing coordinator or supervisor.

The goal is to make the video games and computer programs more efficient, user-friendly, fun, and visually exciting. Testers keep track of the precise combinations of controller movements, keystrokes, and mouse clicks that made the program err or crash. These records must be very precise because they enable supervisors and programmers to replicate the problem. Then they can better isolate its source and begin to design a solution.

Video game testers work closely with a team of development professionals. *Computer and video game developers* and *designers* create and develop

QUICK FACTS

ALTERNATE TITLE(S)
Quality Assurance Testers

DUTIES
Examine new or modified video games to evaluate whether or not they perform at the desired level

SALARY RANGE
$21,140 to $46,790 to $64,345+

WORK ENVIRONMENT
Primarily Indoors

BEST GEOGRAPHIC LOCATION(S)
Opportunities are available throughout the country, but many software publishers are located in California, Texas, Washington, New York, and Massachusetts

MINIMUM EDUCATION LEVEL
Bachelor's Degree

SCHOOL SUBJECTS
Art, Computer Science, Mathematics

EXPERIENCE
Internship; volunteer or part-time experience

PERSONALITY TRAITS
Hands On, Organized, Technical

SKILLS
Computer, Digital Media, Writing

CERTIFICATION OR LICENSING
Recommended

SPECIAL REQUIREMENTS
None

EMPLOYMENT PROSPECTS
Good

ADVANCEMENT PROSPECTS
Good

OUTLOOK
Much Faster than the Average

NOC
N/A

O*NET-SOC
15-1199.01

CAREER LADDER

Game Testing Coordinator, or Game Designer or Programmer

Experienced Video Game Tester

Entry-Level Video Game Tester

new games. They delegate responsibilities to *artists, writers,* and *audio engineers* who work together to produce the developer's desired vision of each game. These professionals creatively collaborate their ideas of style and flow to make each game a polished and engaging finished project. *Programmers* have to reproduce the bugs before they fix them. *Producers* keep the video game's progress on schedule and within budget.

EARNINGS

Testers who worked for software publishers earned mean annual salaries of $46,790 in May 2015, according to the U.S. Department of Labor. Salaries for all testers ranged from less than $21,140 to $62,150 or more.

Software quality assurance analysts had median annual earnings of $51,960 in November 2016, according to Salary.com. Salaries ranged from less than $41,315 to $64,345 or more annually.

Most testers receive paid vacation and sick leave and are eligible to participate in group insurance and retirement benefit plans.

WORK ENVIRONMENT

Video game testers work in game development studios. They play games for a living, and this work can be very fun and entertaining. However, the work is also generally repetitive and even monotonous. If a game is being

tested, for example, a tester may have to play it for hours until it finally crashes, if at all. Most testers agree that even the newest, most exciting game loses its appeal after several hours. This aspect of the job proves to be frustrating and boring for some individuals.

Video game developers may put in long hours in order to meet deadlines. Their work hours usually include nights or weekends. Testers are also frequently called on to work overtime during the final stages before a game goes into mass production and packaging.

Video game testing work involves keeping detailed records, so the job can also be stressful. For example, if a tester works on a game for several hours, they must be able to recall at any moment the last few moves or keystrokes entered in case the program crashes. These long periods of concentration can be tiring.

Meeting with supervisors, programmers, and developers to discuss ideas for the games can be intellectually stimulating. Testers should feel at ease communicating with superiors. On the other end, testers who field customer complaints on the telephone may be forced to bear the brunt of customer dissatisfaction, an almost certain source of stress. The video game industry is always changing, so testers should be prepared to work for many companies throughout their careers.

EXPLORING

Students interested in video game testing and other computer jobs should gain wide exposure to computer systems and video games of all kinds. Become a power user. Get a computer at home, borrow a friend's, or check out the computer lab at your school. First, work on becoming comfortable using the Windows programs and learn how to operate all aspects of computers, including the hardware, thoroughly. Look for bugs in your software at home and practice writing them up.

Secondly, play as many video and computer games as you can. Get good at all different types of games. Learn the differences between games and become familiar with all commands, tasks, and shortcuts.

Keep up with emerging technologies. If you cannot get much hands-on experience, read about the industry. Join a computer group or society. Read books on testing and familiarize yourself with methodology, terminology, the development cycle, and where testing fits in. Subscribe to newsletters or magazines that are related to video game testing, programming, animation, and game design, such as *Computer Graphics World* (http://www.cgw.com). Get involved with online newsgroups that deal with the subject, such as Gamasutra (http://www.gamasutra.com).

GAMERS BY THE NUMBERS   FAST FACTS

- Sixty-three percent of American homes have at least one person who plays video games regularly.
- Thirty-one percent of game players are women age 18 years or older.
- The average age of the most frequent game purchaser is 38.
- Thirty-six percent of gamers play on a smartphone, and 31 percent play on their wireless devices.
- On average, adult gamers have been playing for 13 years.
- About 48 percent of gamers play social games.

Source: Entertainment Software Association

Secure a part-time or summer job as a video game tester if you live in an area where numerous video game development companies are located. An internship with a game development company or any computer-related internship will be a helpful learning experience.

If possible, save up to attend the Game Developers Conference (http://www.gdconf.com) when you are a sophomore or junior in high school. This is a great chance to network with the industry and make yourself known. In addition, investigate the possibility of spending an afternoon with a video game tester to find out what a typical work day is like.

■ EDUCATION AND TRAINING REQUIREMENTS
High School

Take as many computer classes as possible to become familiar with how to effectively operate computer software and hardware. Math and science courses are beneficial for teaching the necessary analytical skills. English and speech classes will help improve verbal and written communication skills, which are also essential to the success of video game testers.

Postsecondary Training

It is debatable whether or not a bachelor's degree is necessary to become a video game tester. Many companies require a bachelor's degree in computer science, while others prefer people who come from the business sector who have a small amount of computer experience because they best match the technical level of the software's typical users. Courses in computer science and psychology are beneficial. Some companies require job seekers to submit a short writing sample when applying for a testing position.

A bachelor's degree is almost certainly a requirement for advancement in the field. Few universities or colleges offer courses on video game testing. As a result, most companies offer in-house training on how to test their particular games. A few specialized schools, like the Academy of Game Entertainment Technology, offer associate's degrees in entertainment technology. A very small number of schools, including DigiPen Institute of Technology, exist solely to train digital entertainment developers.

Other Education or Training

The QAI Global Institute offers webinars, seminars, and other training opportunities. Recent offerings included "Effective Methods of Software Testing" and "Top Ten Challenges of Test Automation." The Association for Software Testing, IEEE Computer Society, and the

---

TOP VIDEO GAMES OF ALL TIME — **MILESTONES**

IGN.com (http://www.ign.com/lists/top-100 -games) named the top 100 computer and video games of all time. Here are the top 10. Give them a try, see what you think, and then look at the rest of the list.

1. *Super Mario Bros. 3* (NES, Nintendo), Released 1990
2. *The Legend of Zelda: A Link to the Past* (SNES, Nintendo), Released 1992
3. *Doom* (id Software), Released 1993
4. *Super Mario Bros.* (NES, Nintendo), Released 1985ish
5. *Portal 2* (Valve), Released 2011
6. *Half-Life 2* (Valve), Released 2004
7. *Super Metroid* (SNES, Nintendo), Released 1994
8. *The Legend of Zelda: Ocarina of Time* (N64, Nintendo), Released 1998
9. *Halo 2* (Bungie Studios), Released 2004
10. *Tetris* (Alexey Pajitnov, NES, Nintendo), Released 1984

International Game Developers Association also provide professional development opportunities.

■ CERTIFICATION, LICENSING, AND SPECIAL REQUIREMENTS
Certification or Licensing

As the gaming industry becomes more competitive, it is increasingly important for video game testers to demonstrate professionalism in the workplace. Some game development companies encourage testers to earn certification. The QAI Global Institute offers various designations for certified software testers, associate testers, and managers. Applicants must pass an examination and satisfy other requirements.

■ EXPERIENCE, SKILLS, AND PERSONALITY TRAITS

Experience as an intern, volunteer, or part-time employee at a game developer is recommended. Some companies recommend testers have some skills in computer programming languages. Others prefer testers with no programming ability.

Video game testers need strong verbal and written communication skills. They also must show a proficiency in critical and analytical thinking and be able to critique a product diplomatically. Video game testers should have an eye for detail, be focused, and have a lot of enthusiasm because sometimes the work is monotonous and repetitive. Testers should definitely enjoy the challenge of breaking the system.

The most important thing is that testers understand the gaming business and the testing tools with which they are working. Video game testers should also be creative problem solvers.

■ EMPLOYMENT PROSPECTS
Employers

Video game testers are employed by computer and video game manufacturers, and no two gaming companies are organized in the same way. Opportunities are best in large cities and suburbs where business and industry are active. Many testers work for video game manufacturers, a cluster of which are located in California, Texas, Washington, New York, and Massachusetts.

Starting Out

Positions in the field of video game testing can be obtained several different ways. Many universities and colleges host computer job fairs on campus throughout the year that include representatives from hardware and software companies. Internships and summer jobs with such corporations are always beneficial and provide experience that will give you the edge over your competition. General computer job fairs are also held throughout the year in larger cities. Job opportunities and industry information can also be found through online employment agencies and trade associations.

■ ADVANCEMENT PROSPECTS

Video game testers are considered entry-level positions in most companies. After acquiring experience and industry knowledge, testers might advance to any number of professions within the gaming industry. *Project managers*, *game test coordinators*, *game designers*, *developers*, and *programmers* are among the possibilities. Video game testers can also move to other areas of the software industry as *quality assurance testers*.

■ OUTLOOK

The U.S. Department of Labor predicts that employment for software developers, including testers, will grow much faster than the average for all careers through 2024. The push toward pre-market perfection will help to keep the video game testing profession strong. To stay competitive, companies are refining their procedures to ever-higher levels. The video game industry is expected to continue growing in the years to come, offering more employment opportunities for experienced video game testers.

■ UNIONS AND ASSOCIATIONS

Video game testers do not belong to unions. The Association for Software Testing offers membership, professional development opportunities, and additional resources. Other membership organizations for computer professionals include the IEEE Computer Society and the International Game Developers Association. The QAI Global Institute provides certification and continuing education classes and webinars. The Software & Information Industry Association is the main trade association for the software and digital content industry. The Academy of Interactive Arts & Sciences is a nonprofit organization that seeks to promote the interactive arts.

■ TIPS FOR ENTRY

1. Talk with software testers about their careers. Ask them for advice on preparing for and entering the field.
2. Attend the QAI Quality Engineered Software and Testing Conference (http://www.qaiglobalservices.com) and the Conference of the Association for Software Testing (http://www.associationforsoftwaretesting.org/conference/about-cast) to network and participate in continuing education classes.
3. Read *IEEE Software* (https://www.computer.org/software-magazine) to learn more about the field.
4. Visit the following Web sites for job listings:

   - Animation World Network (http://www.awn.com)
   - CreativeHeads.net (http://www.highendcareers.com)
   - GameJobs.com (http://www.gamejobs.com)
   - Gamasutra (http://www.gamasutra.com)
   - Dice (http://www.dice.com)

■ FOR MORE INFORMATION

The Academy of Interactive Arts & Sciences is dedicated to the advancement and recognition of the interactive arts.

Academy of Interactive Arts & Sciences (AIAS)
11175 Santa Monica Boulevard, 4th Floor
Los Angeles, CA 90025-3330
Tel: (310) 484-2560
http://www.interactive.org

The Association for Software Testing provides education and training programs, publications, conferences, and other resources.

Association for Software Testing (AST)
https://www.associationforsoftwaretesting.org

The Entertainment Software Association provides information about career opportunities in the video game industry.

Entertainment Software Association (ESA)
601 Massachusetts Avenue, NW, Suite 300
Washington, D.C. 20001-3743
E-mail: esa@theesa.com
http://www.theesa.com

GameDev.Net provides video game reviews, information about classic games, articles, forums, and other resources related to game development.

GameDev.Net
E-mail: support@gamedev.net
http://www.gamedev.net

The IEEE Computer Society provides education programs, conferences, publications, professional development, and job listings.

IEEE Computer Society
2001 L Street, NW, Suite 700
Washington, D.C. 20036-4928
Tel: (202) 371-0101
Fax: (202) 728-9614
E-mail: help@computer.org
http://www.computer.org

The International Game Developers Association provides information on careers in the computer and game development industry.

International Game Developers Association (IGDA)
19 Mantua Road
Mount Royal, NJ 08061-1006
Tel: (856) 423-2990
http://www.igda.org

The QAI Global Institute offers certification and training programs for professionals in various industries.

QAI Global Institute
Tel: (407) 363-1111
http://qaiusa.com

The Software & Information Industry Association offers events, newsletters, and various membership benefits.

Software & Information Industry Association (SIIA)
1090 Vermont Ave, NW, 6th Floor
Washington, D.C. 20005-4905
Tel: (202) 289-7442
Fax: (202) 289-7097
http://www.siia.net

Wastewater Treatment Plant Operators and Technicians

■ OVERVIEW

Wastewater treatment plant operators control, monitor, and maintain the equipment and treatment processes in wastewater (sewage) treatment plants. They remove or neutralize the chemicals, solid materials, and organisms in wastewater so that the water is not polluted when it is returned to the environment. There are approximately 114,770 water and wastewater treatment plant and system operators currently working in the United States.

Wastewater treatment plant technicians work under the supervision of wastewater treatment plant operators. Technicians take samples and monitor treatment to ensure treated water is safe for its intended use. Depending on the level of treatment, water is used for human consumption or for nonconsumptive purposes, such as field irrigation or discharge into natural water sources. Some technicians also work in labs, where they collect and analyze water samples and maintain lab equipment.

■ HISTORY

Water systems and the disposal of wastes are ancient concerns. Thousands of years ago, the Minoans on the island of Crete built some of the earliest known domestic drainage systems. Later, the Romans created marvelous feats of engineering, including enclosed sewer lines that drained both rain runoff and water from the public baths. Urban sanitation methods, however, were limited. Garbage and human wastes were collected from streets and homes and dumped into open watercourses leading away from the cities.

These processes changed little until the 19th century. The health hazards of contact with refuse were poorly understood, but as populations grew, disease outbreaks and noxious conditions in crowded areas made sanitation an important issue. Problems worsened with the Industrial Revolution, which led to both increased population concentrations and industrial wastes that required disposal.

Early efforts by sanitation engineers in the 19th century attempted to take advantage of natural processes. Moderate amounts of pollutants in flowing water go through a natural purification that gradually renders them less harmful. Operators of modern wastewater treatment plants monitor the process that does essentially the same thing that occurs naturally in rivers to purify water, only faster and more effectively. Today's plants are highly sophisticated, complex operations that may utilize biological processes, filtration, chemical treatments, and other methods of removing waste that otherwise may allow bacteria to colonize (live in) critical drinking supplies.

Wastewater treatment operators and technicians must comply with stringent government standards for removing pollutants. Under the Federal Water Pollution Control Act of 1972 and later reauthorizations, it is illegal to discharge any pollutant into the environment without a permit. Industries that send wastes to municipal treatment plants must meet minimum standards and pretreat the wastes so they do not damage the treatment facilities. Standards are also imposed on the treatment plants, controlling the quality of the water they discharge into rivers, streams, and the ocean.

■ THE JOB

Wastewater from homes, public buildings, and industrial plants is transported through sewer pipes to treatment plants. The wastes include both organic and inorganic substances, some of which may be highly toxic, such as lead and mercury. Wastewater treatment plant operators and technicians regulate the flow of incoming wastewater by adjusting pumps, valves, and other equipment, either manually or through remote controls. They keep track of the various meters and gauges that monitor the purification processes and indicate how the equipment is operating. Using the information from these instruments, they control the pumps, engines, and generators that move the untreated water through the processes of filtration, settling, aeration, and sludge digestion.

Wastewater treatment plant operators and technicians also operate chemical-feeding devices, collect water samples, and perform laboratory tests, so that the proper level of chemicals, such as chlorine, is maintained in the wastewater. Technicians may record instrument readings and other information in logs of plant operations. These logs are supervised and monitored by operators. Computers are commonly used to monitor and regulate wastewater treatment equipment and processes. Specialized software allows operators to store and analyze data, which is particularly useful when something in the system malfunctions.

The duties of operators and technicians vary somewhat with the size and type of plant where they work. In small plants one person per shift may be able to do all the necessary routine tasks. But in larger plants, there may be a number of operators, each specializing in just a few activities and working as part of a team that includes engineers, chemists, technicians, mechanics, helpers, and other employees. Some facilities are equipped to handle both wastewater treatment and treatment of the clean water supplied to municipal water systems, and plant operators may be involved with both functions.

Other routine tasks that plant operators and technicians perform include maintenance and minor repairs on equipment such as valves and pumps. They may use common hand tools such as wrenches and pliers and special tools adapted specifically for the equipment. In large facilities, they also direct attendants and helpers who take care of some routine tasks and maintenance work. The accumulated residues of wastes from the water must be removed from the plant, and operators may dispose of these materials. Some of this final product, or sludge, can be reclaimed for uses such as soil conditioners or fuel for the production of electricity.

Technicians may also survey streams and study basin areas to determine water availability. To assist the engineers they work with, technicians prepare graphs, tables, sketches, and diagrams to illustrate survey data. They file plans and documents, answer public inquiries, help train new personnel, and perform various other support duties.

Plant operators and technicians sometimes have to work under emergency conditions, such as when heavy rains flood the sewer pipes, straining the treatment plant's capacity, or when there is a chlorine gas leak or oxygen deficiency in the treatment tanks. When a serious problem arises, they must work quickly and effectively to solve it as soon as possible.

■ EARNINGS

Salaries of wastewater treatment plant operators and technicians vary depending on factors such as the size of the plant, the workers' job responsibilities, and their level of certification. According to the U.S. Department of Labor, water and wastewater treatment plant operators earned median annual salaries of $44,790 in May 2015. The lowest paid 10 percent earned $27,120 or less, while the highest paid 10 percent earned $70,940 or more a year. Plant operators who worked in local government earned a mean salary of $46,570.

In addition to their pay, most operators and technicians receive benefits such as life and health insurance, a pension plan, and reimbursement for education and training related to their job.

■ WORK ENVIRONMENT

Plant operators in small towns may only work part time or may handle other duties as well as wastewater treatment. The size and type of plant also determine the range of duties. In larger plants with many employees, operators and technicians usually perform more specialized functions. In some cases, they may be responsible for monitoring only a single process. In smaller plants, workers likely will have a broader range of responsibilities. Wastewater treatment plants operate 24 hours a day, every day of the year. Operators and technicians usually work one of three eight-hour shifts, often on a rotating basis so that employees share the evening and night work. Overtime is often required during emergencies (such as severe weather conditions and natural disasters).

The work takes operators and technicians both indoors and outdoors. They must contend with noisy machinery and may have to tolerate unpleasant odors, despite the use of chlorine and other chemicals to control odors. The job involves moving about, stooping, reaching, and climbing. Operators and technicians often get their clothes dirty. Slippery sidewalks, dangerous gases, and malfunctioning equipment are potential hazards on the job, but by following safety guidelines, workers can minimize their risk of injury.

■ EXPLORING

It may be possible to arrange to visit a wastewater treatment plant to observe its operations. It can also be helpful to investigate courses and requirements of any programs in wastewater technology or environmental resources programs offered by a local technical school or college. Part-time or summer employment as a helper in a wastewater treatment plant could be a beneficial experience, but such a job may be hard to find. However, a job in any kind of machine shop can provide an opportunity to become familiar with handling machinery and common tools.

Ask wastewater plant operators or technicians in your city if you can interview them about their jobs. Learning about water conservation and water quality in general can be useful. Government agencies or citizen groups dedicated to improving water quality or conserving water can educate you about water quality and supply in your area.

Additionally, visit http://www.wef.org/communications to read *Following the Flow: An Inside Look at Wastewater Treatment.*

■ EDUCATION AND TRAINING REQUIREMENTS
High School

A high school diploma or its equivalent is required for a job as a wastewater treatment plant operator or technician, and additional specialized technical training is generally preferred for both positions. A desirable background for this work includes high school courses in chemistry, biology, mathematics, and computers; welding or electrical training may be helpful as well. Other characteristics that employers look for include mechanical aptitude and the ability to perform mathematical computations easily. You should be able to work basic algebra and statistics problems. Future technicians may be required to prepare reports containing statistics and other scientific documentation. Communications, statistics, and algebra are useful for this career path. Such courses enable the technician to prepare graphs, tables, sketches, and diagrams to illustrate surveys for the operators and engineers they support.

Postsecondary Training

As treatment plants become more technologically complex, workers who have previous training in the field are increasingly at an advantage. Employers generally prefer to hire candidates with specialized education in wastewater technology available in two-year programs that lead to an associate's degree and one-year programs that lead to a certificate. Such programs, which are offered

CAREER LADDER

Plant Supervisor or Superintendent

Wastewater Treatment Plant Operator

Wastewater Treatment Plant Technician

Wastewater Treatment Attendant or Operator-in-Training

A wastewater treatment technician conducts regular system checks at a wastewater treatment plant. (Avatar_023. Shutterstock.)

at some community and junior colleges and vocational-technical institutes, provide a good general knowledge of water pollution control and will prepare you to become an operator or technician. Beginners must still learn the details of operations at the plant where they work, but their specialized training increases their chances for better positions and later promotions.

Many operators and technicians acquire the skills they need during a period of long-term on-the-job training. Newly hired workers often begin as attendants or operators-in-training. Working under the supervision of experienced operators, they pick up knowledge and skills by observing other workers and by doing routine tasks such as recording meter readings, collecting samples, and general cleaning and plant maintenance. In larger plants, trainees may study supplementary written material provided at the plant, or they may attend classes in which they learn plant operations.

Other Education or Training

Wastewater treatment plant operators and technicians often have various opportunities to continue learning about their field. Most state water pollution control agencies offer training courses for people employed in the field. Subjects covered by these training courses include principles of treatment processes and process control, odors and their control, safety, chlorination, sedimentation, biological oxidation, sludge treatment and disposal, and flow measurements. Correspondence courses on related subject areas also are available. Some employers help pay tuition for workers who take related college-level courses in science or engineering.

Professional associations also provide continuing education opportunities. The American Water Works Association offers seminars at its annual conference and other association events, as well as webinars. Recent webinars included "Biological Drinking Water Treatment: Busting the Myths," "Tools for Water Loss Control: The Next Generation," and "High Technology Tools for Operators." The Water Environment Federation and the National Rural Water Association also provide continuing education classes and webinars.

■ CERTIFICATION, LICENSING, AND SPECIAL REQUIREMENTS
Certification or Licensing

Workers who control operations at wastewater treatment plants must be certified by the state in which they are employed. To obtain certification, operators must pass an examination given by the state. There is no nationwide standard, so different states administer different tests. Many states issue several classes of certification, depending on the size of the plant the worker is qualified to control. While some states may recognize certification from other states, operators who relocate may have to re-certify in the new state.

■ EXPERIENCE, SKILLS, AND PERSONALITY TRAITS

Experience as an intern or part-time employee at a wastewater treatment plant is recommended.

Operators and technicians must be familiar with the provisions of the federal Clean Water Act and various state and local regulations that apply to their work. Whenever they become responsible for more complex processes and equipment, they must become acquainted with a wider scope of guidelines and regulations. In larger cities and towns especially, job applicants may have to take a civil service exam or other tests that assess their aptitudes and abilities.

■ EMPLOYMENT PROSPECTS
Employers

About 78 percent of 114,770 water and wastewater treatment plant and system operators currently working in the United States are employed by local governments; others work for the federal government, utility companies, or private sanitary services that operate under contracts with local governments. Jobs are located throughout the country, with the greatest numbers found in areas with high populations.

Wastewater treatment plant operators and technicians can find jobs with state or federal water pollution control agencies, where they monitor plants and provide technical assistance. Examples of such agencies are the Army Corps of Engineers and the Environmental

Protection Agency. These jobs normally require vocational-technical school or community college training. Other experienced wastewater workers find employment with industrial wastewater treatment plants, companies that sell wastewater treatment equipment and chemicals, large utilities, consulting firms, or vocational-technical schools.

Starting Out

Graduates of most postsecondary technical programs and some high schools can get help in locating job openings from the career services office of the school they attended. Another source of information is the local office of the state employment service. Job seekers may also directly contact state and local water pollution control agencies and the personnel offices of wastewater treatment facilities in desired locations.

In some plants, a person must first work as a wastewater treatment plant technician before becoming an operator or working in a supervisory position. Wastewater treatment plant technicians have many of the same duties as a plant operator but less responsibility. They inspect, study, and sample existing water treatment systems and evaluate new structures for efficacy and safety. Support work and instrumentation reading make up the bulk of the technician's day.

Operators and technicians also find job leads as well as internship and trainee positions through the Web sites of professional associations, such as the Water Environment Federation (http://www.wef.org), offer job listings in the wastewater field on their Web sites. Also, an Internet search using the words "wastewater treatment plant operator or technician" will generate a list of Web sites that may contain job postings and internship opportunities.

■ ADVANCEMENT PROSPECTS

Operators with skills and experience are assigned tasks that involve more responsibility for more complex activities. Some technicians advance to become operators. Some operators advance to become *plant supervisors* or *plant superintendents*. The qualifications that superintendents need are related to the size and complexity of the plant. In smaller plants, experienced operators with some postsecondary training may be promoted to superintendent positions. In larger plants, educational requirements are increasing along with the sophistication and complexity of their systems, and superintendents usually have bachelor's degrees in engineering or science.

Some operators and technicians advance by transferring to a related job. Such jobs may require additional education or training to specialize in water pollution

---

MORE PEOPLE, LESS WATER

DID YOU KNOW?

Recycling things such as aluminum cans, paper, and glass is a great way to help preserve our environment. But many of us don't think about the importance of recycling one of our most important renewable resources—water. We have been recycling water for years, and it is an ideal recyclable because it is never used up. Every glass of water you drink contains water molecules that have been used countless times before, perhaps in someone else's glass of water, a swimming pool, or even a fire hydrant. That's why wastewater treatment plants are so important—they make sure the water we drink is clean and safe, no matter where it's been.

As the world's population grows, wastewater treatment plants will become more important to our environment because the supply of cheap, easily available water will shrink. Even in the United States, which as a nation has plenty of fresh water, groundwater is being used at a rate 25 percent higher than its replenishment rate. Areas with fast-growing populations and limited water supplies, such as parts of California, Florida, and Texas, face the highest risk for water shortages in the 21st century. Conserving water in those areas by finding new ways to use less water and make better use of the water we have is something that can be done now. Using effluent (partially treated) water for nonconsumptive purposes, such as irrigation of golf courses, is something that is being done now in Florida. This is a good example of how wastewater treatment plants are vital tools for conserving our environment.

---

control, commercial wastewater equipment sales, or teaching wastewater treatment in a vocational or technical school.

■ OUTLOOK

Employment in this field is expected to grow about as fast as the average for all occupations through 2024, according to the U.S. Department of Labor (DOL). Despite the prediction for average growth, job opportunities will be excellent. The number of job applicants in this field is generally low due to the unclean and physically demanding nature of the work. This relative lack of competition means that workers can enter the field with ease, providing they have adequate training and experience.

The growth in demand for wastewater treatment will be related to the overall growth of the nation's population and economy. New treatment plants will be built, and existing ones will be upgraded, requiring additional trained personnel to manage their operations. Employment demand will also grow because of the need to ensure compliance with increased safety and environmental regulations. Other openings will arise when experienced workers retire or transfer to new occupations. The DOL says that "job prospects will be best for those with training or education in water or wastewater systems and good mechanical skills."

Workers in wastewater treatment plants are rarely laid off, even during a recession, because wastewater treatment is essential to public health and welfare. In the future more wastewater professionals will probably be employed by private companies that contract to manage treatment plants for local governments.

■ UNIONS AND ASSOCIATIONS

Wastewater treatment plant operators and technicians may belong to unions. Membership organizations such as the American Water Works Association and Water Environment Federation provide networking opportunities, publications, continuing education classes and webinars, and other resources. The National Rural Water Association represents rural and small water utilities.

■ TIPS FOR ENTRY

1. Read the *Journal of the American Water Works Association* and *Opflow* (both are available at http://www.awwa.org) and *Rural Water* (http://naylornetwork.com/nrw-nxt) to learn more about the field.
2. For job listings, visit:
   - http://www.awwa.org/resources-tools/career-center.aspx
   - http://epi9-prod.wef.org/about/careers/job-bank/
   - http://careers.waterprocommunity.org
3. Attend the American Water Works Association's Annual Conference and Exhibition (http://www.awwa.org/conferences-education/conferences/annual-conference.aspx) to network and participate in professional development classes and workshops.
4. Visit Work for Water (http://workforwater.org) for information on careers.
5. Use social media to stay up to date on industry developments and learn about job openings. Many professional associations use Facebook, YouTube, and Twitter connect with members and others who are interested in wastewater treatment.

■ FOR MORE INFORMATION

The American Water Works Association provides education programs, conferences, publications, and membership benefits.

American Water Works Association (AWWA)
6666 West Quincy Avenue
Denver, CO 80235-3098
Tel: (800) 926-7337; (303) 794-7711
Fax: (303) 347-0804
http://www.awwa.org

The National Rural Water Association is dedicated to training, supporting, and promoting the water and wastewater professionals that serve small communities across the United States.

National Rural Water Association (NRWA)
2915 South 13th Street
Duncan, OK 73533-9086
Tel: (580) 252-0629
Fax: (580) 255-4476
http://nrwa.org

The Water Environment Federation is a technical and educational organization that represents water quality professionals around the world.

Water Environment Federation (WEF)
601 Wythe Street
Alexandria, VA 22314-1994
Tel: (800) 666-0206
Fax: (703) 684-2400
E-mail: inquiry@wef.org
http://www.wef.org

Watch and Clock Repairers

■ OVERVIEW

Watch and clock repairers clean, adjust, repair, and regulate watches, clocks, chronometers, electronic timepieces, and related instruments. Watch and clock repairers work in department and jewelry stores, at home, or in repair shops. Currently there are approximately 2,200 watch and clock repairers in the United States.

■ HISTORY

Keeping track of time has always been important to people. Ancient devices for measuring the passage of time included sundials and hourglasses. People also measured time through watching water drip at a steady pace until it filled a fixed container or by burning candles with regularly spaced marks on the side. The earliest mechanical clocks were built in Europe in the 1300s. Made of iron and driven by the energy of slowly dropping weights, they were so large and heavy that they had to be fitted into towers, and could indicate the hours only approximately. Improvements in clock mechanisms made them smaller, and a few household versions of weight-driven clocks began to appear by the end of the 1300s.

Portable clocks and watches became possible in the early 1500s, when a coiled mainspring replaced weights as a means for driving the mechanism. Early watches were about four to five inches in diameter, three inches deep, and so heavy that they had to be carried in the hand. A long series of advances refined the size of watches and clocks and improved their performance. By 1809, a watch belonging to the Empress Josephine of France was small enough to be made into the first wristwatch, although wristwatches were not very successful for nearly another century. Among the many changes that improved clocks and watches were parts made of brass and steel, then later of special metal alloys, the introduction of the pendulum in clocks, and the invention of the hairspring to regulate the motion of the balance wheel in watches. More recently, electric and electronic devices have brought further miniaturization and helped increase timekeeping accuracy.

Until the 1800s, timepieces were made by hand, one by one, by skilled artisans. In the early United States, a few clockmakers copied European clocks of the era, and clock towers were built in city public places. Not many people owned watches prior to the 1800s. In that century, however, large numbers of clocks and pocket watches were made using factory methods. Prices became more reasonable, and watches and clocks became popular as people led more active lives and traveled more. Today's watches and clocks are almost always mass-produced in factories, but workers skilled in adjusting and repairing precision parts are still needed to work on electric and mechanical timepieces.

■ THE JOB

Watches and clocks are complex machines with many small parts, and repairing them requires precision and delicacy. The ability to locate and correct defects is an important and necessary skill for watch and clock repairers. They employ a standard, systematic procedure to track down defects, sometimes using information from customers about the history and previous repairs of the timepiece. Some problems arise from incorrect replacement or improper fitting of parts. Careless pushing, pulling, or turning the winding device can also cause problems by making parts too tight or too loose, or permitting dust to enter the mechanism.

QUICK FACTS	
ALTERNATE TITLE(S)	None
DUTIES	Clean, adjust, repair, and regulate watches, clocks, electronic timepieces, and related instruments
SALARY RANGE	$19,320 to $34,750 to $58,220+
WORK ENVIRONMENT	Primarily Indoors
BEST GEOGRAPHIC LOCATION(S)	Opportunities are available throughout the country, but are best in large, urban areas
MINIMUM EDUCATION LEVEL	Some Postsecondary Training
SCHOOL SUBJECTS	Business, Mathematics, Technical/Shop
EXPERIENCE	One to three years' postsecondary training required
PERSONALITY TRAITS	Hands On, Problem-Solving, Technical
SKILLS	Business Management, Mechanical/Manual Dexterity, Organizational
CERTIFICATION OR LICENSING	Recommended
SPECIAL REQUIREMENTS	None
EMPLOYMENT PROSPECTS	Fair
ADVANCEMENT PROSPECTS	Fair
OUTLOOK	Decline
NOC	6344
O*NET-SOC	49-9064.00

The first step is usually opening the case to examine the mechanism. Often with the aid of a magnifying eyeglass, or loupe, repairers check for defective parts and dirt and inspect the springs for rust and incorrect alignment. They may repair or replace such parts as the mainspring, hairspring, jewels or pivots, and escapements. With older timepieces, they may have to make parts in order for the device to function properly. They may clean the mechanism with

CAREER LADDER

Watch/Clock Repair Shop Owner

Supervisor or Service Manager

Watch and Clock Repairer

Watch/Clock Repair Shop Helper

a cleaning solution or ultrasonic sound waves. Timepieces that must be oiled need a delicate touch because excessive amounts of oil, or oil placed in the wrong spots, can cause the mechanism to operate improperly. When the work is complete, the timepiece must be reassembled so that parts fit properly.

Repairers use a number of specialized tools and devices in their work. A timing machine is used to check the accuracy of timepieces. Watches and clocks that show erratic timekeeping are checked for magnetism and may be demagnetized. When diagnosing problems in electric and electronic timepieces, watch and clock repairers may use various meters and other testing equipment. They may also use hand tools, such as pliers, files, pin vises, tweezers, turns, and lathes in their work.

Many watch and clock repairers, especially those who are self-employed or work in a retail store, also repair jewelry and sell items such as clocks, watches, jewelry, china, and silverware. Those working in large stores and shops may have managerial or supervisory duties as well. Repairers who have their own shops often must order parts and merchandise, keep accounts, arrange for advertising, and perform other tasks required to maintain an efficient and profitable business.

■ EARNINGS

According the U.S. Department of Labor, the median annual salary for watch and clock repairers was $34,750 in May 2015. Salaries ranged from less than $19,320 to more than $58,220. In some stores, part of watch and clock repairers' earnings is commissions on the items they service. Someone working 40 hours a week for a company or business can usually expect general benefits.

Repairers who operate their own businesses often earn considerably more than those who are employed by other businesses.

■ WORK ENVIRONMENT

Watch and clock repairers work in a variety of settings, including home businesses, department stores, shopping centers, jewelry stores, or repair shops. Work areas are typically clean, well lighted, and comfortable. Repairers often work individually and sit at a workbench much of the time. Repairs consist of close work with fine tools and

delicate instruments, causing some people to experience eyestrain, especially at the start of their training or career. They can minimize this by using the right equipment and following proper procedures.

Some repairers work a standard 40-hour workweek, while others work as much as 45 to 48 hours a week. Self-employed people may work longer hours, depending on the amount of business.

■ EXPLORING

Learn about this field by getting a part-time job in a shop where watches and clocks are repaired and sold. Even a basic job, such as helping with cleaning and stock deliveries, can provide a good opportunity to observe a skilled watch or clock repairer at work. Jewelry shops often hire high school or college students for part-time jobs during the holiday seasons.

Hobbies and shop courses that require dexterity and patience in using hand tools can provide another way of exploring similar activities and developing manual skills. Some students explore their interest in detailed crafts by learning to repair precision instruments while serving in the military.

The American Watchmakers-Clockmakers Institute and your local library are good sources of information about watch repair history and the profession.

■ EDUCATION AND TRAINING REQUIREMENTS
High School

A high school diploma is desirable for prospective watch and clock repairers. Classes that provide good preparation for this career include shop courses that introduce the use of various tools and electronics classes to learn about circuits and electrical test equipment. Mathematics or accounting classes that teach business math and courses that help develop verbal communication skills are also beneficial. If you plan to operate your own business, take classes in business, accounting, and computer science.

Postsecondary Training

Few people learn this trade on the job. Instead, the best way to learn watch and clock repairing skills is to a school of horology (the art of making and repairing timepieces) that is accredited by the Research and Education Council. Visit http://www.awci.com/education-certification for a list of these schools. Training programs typically take one to three years and include instruction in disassembling and reassembling, cleaning and oiling, and replacing or repairing parts in various kinds of timepieces. Students learn to use such devices as demagnetizers, lathes, and electronic timing equipment. Additional training may be obtained in servicing electronic watches, calendars, chronometers, and timers. Once employed, watch and clock repairers usually take refresher courses to learn about new products that come on the market.

Other Education or Training

The American Watchmakers-Clockmakers Institute provides continuing education bench training courses throughout the United States. Past classes included "Balance Staff & Timing," "Timing & Adjustments," "Quality Control," "Quartz Watch Repair & Diagnostics," "Mechanical Chronographs," "Modern Wristwatch Oiling Procedures," and "Servicing ETA Quartz Chronographs." The National Association of Watch and Clock Collectors also provides professional development classes.

■ CERTIFICATION, LICENSING, AND SPECIAL REQUIREMENTS

Certification or Licensing

The American Watchmakers-Clockmakers Institute offers the following certification designations to watch and clock repairers who pass a written examination and a practical test of repairing skill: certified watchmaker of the 21st century, certified master watchmaker of the 21st century, certified clockmaker of the 21st century, and certified master clockmaker of the 21st century.

■ EXPERIENCE, SKILLS, AND PERSONALITY TRAITS

Aspiring watch and clock repairers must complete a post-secondary training program that lasts from one to three years. During their training, they can also obtain experience by working as an assistant to a watch or clock repairer.

Watch and clock repairers need a combination of personal characteristics. They must have the ability to work independently with a high degree of precision. They need to be able to perceive tiny details in objects and make fine visual discriminations. They must have good manual dexterity, the finger sensitivity to feel small shapes, and steady hands so they can deftly place and work with small parts. They need orderly work habits and the ability to make judgments using set standards. Repairers who are in charge of their own shops need to be tactful, courteous, and able to communicate well with the public and employees. They also need at least a basic understanding of operating a business.

■ EMPLOYMENT PROSPECTS

Employers

Approximately 2,200 watch and clock repairers are employed throughout the country. Jewelry and department stores and service outlets employ watch and clock

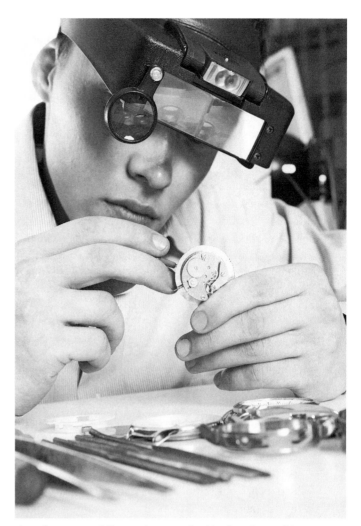

A craftsman carefully repairs a watch. (Andrey Burmakin. Shutterstock.)

repairers. Watch and clock manufacturers may also hire repairers to work in their service departments. Many people with these skills operate their own repair businesses either in a storefront or in their own homes.

Starting Out

Job seekers might check the listings for "jewelers" or "watch repair" in their local Yellow Pages or online and apply directly to any establishments that seem likely. Watch manufacturers can be contacted directly regarding job openings. Graduates of watch and clock repair training programs may get job search assistance from their school's career services office. Local newspaper classified ads also post job openings in the field.

Associations post job openings or offer referral networks on their Web sites. Explore the sites and consider joining a local chapter to better access job leads, make contacts in the industry, and learn about developments in horology.

Seth Thomas, Clock Maker   MOVERS AND SHAKERS

U.S. clock manufacturer Seth Thomas was a pioneer in applying mass-production methods to clock making in the early 19th century. Thomas, born in Wolcott, Connecticut, was a carpenter and joiner by trade. He entered into partnership with Eli Terry and Silas Hoadley in 1807 to make clocks. In 1812, he founded a clock factory in Plymouth, Connecticut, and began the mass production of low-priced clocks. He started making tall clocks with wooden movements, and then added shelf and mantel clocks to the product line. The Seth Thomas Clock Company became one of the world's leading clock manufacturers. In 1875, the part of Plymouth containing the factory was made a separate town named Thomaston in his honor.

■ ADVANCEMENT PROSPECTS

Watch repairers who work in stores and shops may be promoted to positions as *supervisors* or *service managers*. Experienced repairers can go into business for themselves by opening their own repair shop and perhaps eventually expanding it into a retail store selling items such as jewelry and silver in addition to clocks and watches. Some repairers get further training in engraving, jewelry repair, design, or stone setting. Such additional skills may open new avenues for advancement.

Another possibility for some workers is to apply their precision skills in another field. For example, past experience as a watch or clock repairer may be marketable to a company that manufactures aircraft components with small parts. Such job changes, however, are likely to require additional training.

■ OUTLOOK

A decline in employment is expected for watch and clock repairers through 2024, according to the U.S. Department of Labor. Many watches and clocks produced today cost as much or more to repair as to replace, so owners tend to discard their old or broken items. However, sales of high-grade watches (such as Rolex) have made a comeback.

In addition, the American Watchmakers-Clockmakers Institute reports that the average age of a watch/clockmaker is over 60 years old. In the coming decade, some openings will result from the need to replace these retiring workers. This trend, coupled with the fact that there are few people entering this field, means that watch and clock repairers with precision skills should find ample employment opportunities.

■ UNIONS AND ASSOCIATIONS

Watch and clock repairers do not belong to unions, but many join the American Watchmakers-Clockmakers Institute and the National Association of Watch and Clock Collectors. These organizations provide networking opportunities, continuing education workshops and webinars, publications, and other resources.

■ TIPS FOR ENTRY

1. Read the *Horological Times* (http://www.awci.com/horological-times) and *Watch and Clock Bulletin* (http://www.nawcc.org/index.php/publications-home) to learn more about the field.
2. Visit http://awci-jobs.careerwebsite.com for job listings.
3. Talk to a watch repairer about his or her career. The American Watchmakers-Clockmakers Institute provides a database of watchmakers at https://members.awci.com/AWCIWEB/AWCISearch/MemberSearch.aspx, which can be used to identify possible interview candidates.

■ FOR MORE INFORMATION

The American Watchmakers-Clockmakers Institute provides education, certification, a list of horology schools and programs, and other resources.

American Watchmakers-Clockmakers Institute (AWCI)
701 Enterprise Drive
Harrison, OH 45030-1696
Tel: (866) 367-2924, ext 301; (513) 367-9800, ext. 301
Fax: (513) 367-1414
E-mail: awci@awci.com
http://www.awci.com

Horology is the study of measuring time and creating time pieces. This Web site, a vast online collection of horological resources, has many links of interest to watchmakers.

Horology—The Index
http://www.nawcc-index.net

The National Association of Watch and Clock Collectors offers education, publications, local chapter activities, and other resources.

National Association of Watch and Clock Collectors (NAWCC)
514 Poplar Street
Columbia, PA 17512-2130
Tel: (717) 684-8261
Fax: (717) 684-0878
http://www.nawcc.org

Wealth Management Accountants

▨ OVERVIEW

Wealth management firms oversee the financial affairs of high-net-worth individuals—typically defined as those who have liquid assets of more than $1 million (not including the value of one's primary residence). The most prestigious private banks and wealth management firms, such as those attached to major investment companies like Citigroup or Goldman Sachs, have much higher minimums, more than $5 million in some cases. *Accountants* oversee and manage the financial records and operations of their employers. Those in the wealth management (WM) sector are employed directly by WM firms, by accounting firms that provide contracted services to WM firms, and also high-net-worth individuals.

▨ HISTORY

Accountants and auditors have assisted wealth managers ever since the first wealth management firm was founded in the 1860s. Demand has grown rapidly for accounting and auditing professionals as a result of recent financial crises and legislation passed by Congress. In 2002, Congress passed the Sarbanes-Oxley Act, which requires higher levels of financial accounting and disclosure from all publicly held companies. In 2010, Congress passed the Dodd-Frank Wall Street Reform and Consumer Protection Act, which requires wealth management firms with more than $150 million in assets under management to register with the Securities & Exchange Commission and provide higher levels of financial reporting. In addition, investors are placing more pressure on wealth management firms to tighten their accounting standards and provide more transparency, which has also created demand for accounting professionals.

▨ THE JOB

Accountants at wealth management firms are sometimes forgotten amidst the high-stakes work of portfolio managers. But WM firms would be in big trouble if they lacked skilled professionals to ensure the integrity of their financial infrastructure, prepare financial statements, analyze data for tax filings, and perform a variety of other tasks. Job responsibilities for accountants vary by the size of the employer, their job titles, and other factors, but most perform the following duties:

- providing monthly or quarterly accounting of investor contributions and withdrawals and computing profit and losses for the accounting period

QUICK FACTS	
ALTERNATE TITLE(S)	Corporate Accountants, Management Accountants
DUTIES	Compile, analyze, verify, and prepare financial records
SALARY RANGE	$40,500 to $75,000 to $118,000+
WORK ENVIRONMENT	Primarily Indoors
BEST GEOGRAPHIC LOCATION(S)	Opportunities are best in areas where a large number of high-net-worth individuals reside
MINIMUM EDUCATION LEVEL	Bachelor's Degree
SCHOOL SUBJECTS	Business, Computer Science, Mathematics
EXPERIENCE	Completion of an internship or co-op at a bank, wealth management firm, public accounting firm, or corporation; three to five years of experience for management positions
PERSONALITY TRAITS	Hands On, Organized, Realistic
SKILLS	Financial, Information Management, Math
CERTIFICATION OR LICENSING	Recommended
SPECIAL REQUIREMENTS	None
EMPLOYMENT PROSPECTS	Good
ADVANCEMENT PROSPECTS	Good
OUTLOOK	Much Faster than the Average
NOC	1111
O*NET-SOC	13-2011.00, 13-2011.01, 13-2011.02

- monitoring cash account balances on a daily and weekly basis
- maintaining monthly end market value reconciliations
- communicating with the trading desk, portfolio managers, and custodian banks to resolve accounting-related transaction and reporting issues

CAREER LADDER

Partner

Chief Financial Officer

Controller

Chief Accountant/Auditor

Accountant/Auditor

- preparing and submitting quarterly or annual tax filings, and being responsible for other tax-related issues
- working with the compliance department to respond to inquiries from regulators such as the Securities & Exchange Commission
- working with auditors during the year-end audit process
- helping the chief financial officer with the preparation of financial forecasts and reports and on ad-hoc projects
- providing advice to partners regarding tax, compliance, financial risk, and other issues
- calculating net asset value and management fees, and preparing statements that detail this information
- preparing and reviewing quarterly and annual financial statements in accordance with generally accepted accounting principles

Auditors are specially trained accountants who ensure that financial records are accurate, complete, and in compliance with local, state, and federal laws. Those who work as salaried employees of a company or other organization are known as *internal auditors.* Those who work for public accounting firms that provide auditing services to wealth management companies are known as *external auditors.*

■ EARNINGS
Salaries for accountants vary based on their job title, level of experience, and geographic region; size and type of employer; and other factors. The staffing firm Robert Half Finance & Accounting reports the following salary ranges for general accountants at large corporations in 2015 by level of experience:

- manager: $84,500 to $118,000
- senior level: $68,750 to $87,750
- one to three years: $53,750 to $69,500
- up to one year: $42,250 to $55,250

At small companies, the salary ranges were:

- manager: $67,000 to $88,750
- senior level: $57,500 to $70,000

- one to three years: $45,500 to $59,000
- up to one year: $40,500 to $47,250

Accountants and auditors receive a variety of benefits. At some employers, especially large banks, benefits can be excellent. For example, Northern Trust (which ranks among the top 20 banks worldwide in assets under management), provides paid vacation and sick days; health insurance, child care, adoption leave, alternative/flexible work options, savings and pension plans, professional development opportunities, lifestyle coaching, and fitness/wellness discounted memberships.

■ WORK ENVIRONMENT
Most accountants and auditors in the wealth management industry enjoy a good work/life balance (i.e., a 9 to 5 schedule, little work on weekends, flexible hours, and telecommuting options). The majority of accountants find their careers rewarding. Nearly seven out of 10 accountants surveyed by the staffing firm Accountemps in 2015 said that they would remain in accounting if given the opportunity to go back and choose a different career.

■ EXPLORING
Talk with wealth management accountants, or those working in other industries, about their careers. Ask your accounting teacher to help arrange some information interviews. Join business and finance clubs in high school and college. Offer to manage the finances of a school club to get experience working with budgets, paying bills, and managing financial records. Check out the career Web sites of major wealth management banks such as UBS, Morgan Stanley, J.P. Morgan, and Bank of America Merrill Lynch to learn about potential career paths, key skills for work success, and typical work environments. Finally, check out the following resources to learn more about WM and accounting.

- *Accounting Today*-Wealth Management: http://www.accountingtoday.com/wealth-management
- Start Here, Go Places: http://www.startherego places.com
- *Accounting For Dummies* (For Dummies, 2013)
- *Accounting Glossary: http://www.startheregoplaces.com/students/games-tools/glossary*

■ EDUCATION AND TRAINING REQUIREMENTS
High School
Accountants and auditors are numbers crunchers, so you should be sure to take accounting, statistics, and mathematics classes. But they are also increasingly being asked

to use their critical-thinking and analytical skills to provide strategic advice to WM partners. Courses that will help you to develop these skills include government, social studies, philosophy, and science. Joining the debate team will also be useful. English and speech classes will help you to build your oral and written communication skills. Computer science courses (especially database management) will help you to learn how to manage and utilize data.

Postsecondary Education

You'll need a minimum of a bachelor's degree in accounting, economics, finance, or business administration to work as an accountant or auditor at a wealth management firm. Some employers prefer candidates who have a master's degree in accounting, business administration, economics, or finance.

U.S. News & World Report provides a list of the best undergraduate accounting programs in the United States at http://colleges.usnews.rankingsandreviews.com/best -colleges/rankings/business-accounting.

Make sure that the college you attend is accredited by a national or international accrediting agency. "Earning a degree from an accredited school helps when applying for jobs," according to the American Institute of Certified Public Accountants. "Employers will often look at what schools you attended and if they are accredited."

AACSB International and the Association of Collegiate Business Schools and Programs accredit colleges and universities that offer degrees in accounting and business. Visit www.startheregoplaces.com/stu dents/games-tools/college-search for a list of accredited programs.

The Institute of Internal Auditors has created a formal endorsement program for colleges and universities that offer an internal auditing curriculum within a degree program (undergraduate or postgraduate). Visit https:// na.theiia.org/about-us/about-ia/pages/participating -iaep-program-schools.aspx for a list of schools that offer this curriculum.

Other Education or Training

Many associations provide professional development classes, seminars, workshops, and webinars. Completion of continuing education credits is often required to become certified and renew one's certification. For example, the American Institute of Certified Public Accountants offers more than 350 self-study courses, web events, and more than 60 annual conferences and workshops. Recent offerings included Securities & Exchange Commission Reporting, Financial Forecasting and Decision Making, Budgeting Process, and Advanced Excel: Practical Applications for the Accounting

Accountants at wealth management firms ensure that every cent is tracked and recorded. (Robert Kneschke. Shutterstock.)

Professional. The Institute of Internal Auditors provides on-site seminars and webinars such as Data Analysis for Internal Auditors, Audit Report Writing, Communication Skills for Auditors, Leadership Skills for Auditors, and Project Management Techniques. The American Bankers Association, Chartered Institute of Management Accountants, and the Institute of Management Accountants and Institute of Internal Auditors also provide professional development opportunities. Contact these organizations for more information.

Additionally, many wealth management firms offer online and classroom-based learning for new and experienced employees.

Certification

The Chartered Institute of Management Accountants offers a certificate in business accounting that can serve as an entry-level credential for new accountants or as a refresher course for experienced professionals. Other certificate programs are provided by the Association of Chartered Certified Accountants (international auditing and international financial reporting) and the American Institute of Certified Public Accountants (International Financial Reporting Standards).

■ CERTIFICATION, LICENSING, AND SPECIAL REQUIREMENTS
Certification or Licensing

Many certification programs are available for accountants and auditors. Those who are certified typically earn higher salaries and receive more opportunities for promotion than those who are not certified. According

ALL ABOUT ACCOUNTING

FAST FACTS

■ Forty-five percent of accountants surveyed by the staffing firm Accountemps in 2015 said that the "nature of the work and job duties" were the top reason why they chose accounting as a career. Twenty-one percent cited the "employment outlook," and 20 percent said "the variety of career paths within the field."

■ The careers of accountant and auditor frequently rank at the top of "best career" lists. In 2015, for example, *U.S. News & World Report* selected the career of accountant as the 3rd-best business job in the United States.

■ The careers of accountant and auditor rank third among the top 20 occupations adding the most new jobs for those with a bachelor's degree from 2014-24. Approximately 142,400 new jobs will be added during this time span.

■ Accountants and auditors earned mean annual salaries of $73,670 as of May 2014, according to the U.S. Department of Labor. This is much higher than the mean salary ($47,230) for all workers. Mean annual wages for accountants and auditors were highest in the District of Columbia, New York, New Jersey, Maryland, and Massachusetts.

■ In 2014, 63 percent of accountants and auditors in the financial services industry in the United States were women, according to Catalyst, but females comprised only 29.3 percent of executive/senior level officials and managers.

to Robert Half Accounting & Finance's *2016 Salary Guide,* in-demand professional credentials include:

- Certified information systems auditor (ISACA)
- Certified internal auditor (Institute of Internal Auditors)
- Certified management accountant (Institute of Management Accountants)
- Certified public accountant (American Institute of Certified Public Accountants, AICPA)
- Chartered global management accountant (a joint venture of the AICPA and the Chartered Institute of Management Accountants)
- Project management professional (Project Management Institute)

Additionally, some accountants and auditors earn the following certifications:

- Accredited business accountant/advisor, accredited tax preparer, accredited tax advisor (Accreditation Council for Accountancy and Taxation)
- Certification in control self-assessment, certified financial services auditor, certification in risk management assurance (Institute of Internal Auditors)
- Certified financial manager (Institute of Management Accountants)
- Certified treasury professional, certified corporate financial planning and analysis professional (Association of Financial Professionals)

Many accountants are certified public accountants (CPAs). To earn this designation, you must pass a qualifying examination and hold a certificate issued by the state in which you wish to practice. The Uniform CPA Examination, which is administered by the AICPA, is used by all states. Nearly all states require at least two years of public accounting experience or the equivalent before a CPA certificate can be earned.

■ EXPERIENCE, SKILLS, AND PERSONALITY TRAITS

Entry-level accountants and auditors should have completed at least one internship or co-operative educational experience at a wealth management firm or a major public accounting firm during college. "In the absence of experience [for entry-level hires], employers focus more on a candidate's work ethic and fit with the corporate culture," according to Robert Half Accounting & Finance's *2016 Salary Guide.* For management-level positions, you'll need at least three to five years of accounting or auditing experience at a WM firm, a bank, Big Four public accounting firm, or a Fortune 500 corporation.

Successful accountants and auditors have strong communication, project management, organizational, time-management, and problem-solving skills; mathematical and analytical acumen; honesty and strong ethics; and the ability to work both independently and as a member of a team. They also must have knowledge of Generally Accepted Accounting Principles, financial reporting and financial products (e.g., equities, futures, etc.). and the use of accounting software and databases and office software (e.g., PowerPoint, Excel, and Word).

Accountants and auditors must also keep abreast of constantly changing technology. According to Robert Half Accounting & Finance, "businesses are struggling to keep pace with technology and understand the associated risks and opportunities. In response, they seek individuals proficient in enterprise resource planning systems, integrated financial reporting systems, cloud-computing platforms, and information security and data-mining tools, as well as professionals to help with systems conversion projects."

■ EMPLOYMENT PROSPECTS
Employers

Accountants and auditors work for wealth management firms, banks, robo-advisory firms, and independent wealth managers. They also are employed by public accounting firms (such as Deloitte, Ernst & Young, PricewaterhouseCoopers, and KPMG) that provide accounting services to WM companies. Outside the WM industry, many accountants and auditors work for businesses of all sizes, at nonprofits, and for government agencies such as the U.S. Government Accountability Office and the U.S. Department of Commerce.

Starting Out

A good way to break into the field is to participate in an internship at a wealth management firm or a bank that has a WM department. Participating in internships allows you to try out different jobs, build your network, and have the opportunity to impress the internship director and your managers with your work-ethic and enthusiasm for a career in wealth management. Your college's career services office has information on internships. Additionally, the American Institute of Certified Public Accountants provides advice on landing an internship at https://www.thiswaytocpa.com/career-tools/jobs -internships. The Career Tools section of its Web site (https://www.thiswaytocpa.com/career-tools/articles) provides details on job-search strategies, writing effective resumes and cover letters, and preparing for job interviews.

Visit the Web sites of wealth management employers to learn about job opportunities. At many sites, you can apply for jobs. Some new accounting graduates hire recruiters to assist them in the job search.

■ ADVANCEMENT PROSPECTS

Skilled accountants and auditors with several years of experience can advance to the position of chief accountant or auditor, or become *controllers,* who prepare financial reports and oversee the accounting and audit departments of their organizations. Experienced accounting and auditing professionals can become *chief financial officers,* who are responsible for the accuracy of their employer's financial reporting and focus on issues such as compliance, budgeting, and financial strategy. Some become CEOs or chief operating officers at corporations, or partners.

■ OUTLOOK

Job opportunities for accountants and auditors who work with funds, trusts, and other financial vehicles will grow by more than 18 percent through 2024, according to the U.S. Department of Labor. It reports that "globalization, a growing overall economy, and an increasingly complex tax and regulatory environment are expected to lead to strong demand for accountants and auditors."

More opportunities will emerge for accountants and auditors because the number of wealthy people who need wealth management services continues to grow. The number of U.S. households with a net worth of $1 million reached a record high of 10.1 million by late 2014, according to Spectrem Group's *Market Insights Report 2015.* This was an increase of nearly 500,000 households from 2013.

■ UNIONS AND ASSOCIATIONS

Wealth management accountants do not belong to unions. Some join professional associations, which offer many resources that are useful to job seekers and experienced accountants and auditors. For example, the Institute of Management Accountants (IMA) has its own proprietary online social network called LinkUp IMA (http://linkup.imanet.org), which is available to IMA members. LinkUp IMA can be used to locate jobs, find local networking events, and communicate with other members about the certification process or the job search. Another member resource is Career Driver, which allows users to assess their technical and leadership competencies and match their skills with up to 40 management accounting roles. The IMA also provides the certified management accountant credential, offers job listings at its Web site, and publishes *Strategic Finance and Management Accounting.* Other noteworthy organizations include the American Bankers Association, American Institute of Certified Public Accountants, Chartered Institute of Management Accountants, and Institute of Internal Auditors.

■ TIPS FOR ENTRY

1. Read *Start Here Magazine* (http://www.startherego places.com/students/games-tools/start-here -magazine) for tips on becoming an accountant.
2. Visit the following Web sites for job listings and career advice:
   - http://www.pionline.com/section/careers
   - http://www.accountingjobstoday.com
   - http://www.efinancialcareers.com
   - http://www.accountingcrossing.com
   - http://www.pionline.com/section/careers
3. Check out The Edge (http://www.aicpa.org/ InterestAreas/YoungCPANetwork/TheEdge), an online newsletter that provides advice to young professionals about job hunting and networking.

4. Use LinkedIn to network and search for jobs. Consider joining groups such as Accounting and Finance Professionals, Accounting & Audit, and Asset/Wealth Management Careers.

■ FOR MORE INFORMATION

Visit the ABA's Web site for job listings and information on continuing education, its Wealth Management & Trust Conference, and the banking industry.

American Bankers Association (ABA)

1120 Connecticut Avenue, NW

Washington, D.C. 20036-3902

Tel: (800) 226-5377

http://www.aba.com

For information on scholarships, membership, careers, and certification, contact

American Institute of Certified Public Accountants

1211 Avenue of the Americas

New York, NY 10036-8775

Tel: (212) 596-6200

E-mail: service@aicpa.org

http://www.aicpa.org

For information on careers and certification, contact

Chartered Institute of Management Accountants

E-mail: vision@cimaglobal.com

http://www.cimaglobal.com

For information on careers, certification, and continuing education, contact

Institute of Management Accountants

10 Paragon Drive, Suite 1

Montvale, NJ 07645-1760

Tel: (800) 638-4427

E-mail: ima@imanet.org

http://www.imanet.org

For information on certification, careers, continuing education, and its online professional network, contact

Institute of Internal Auditors

247 Maitland Avenue

Altamonte Springs, FL 32701-4201

Tel: (407) 937-1111

https://na.theiia.org

Wealth Management Analysts

■ OVERVIEW

Wealth management analysts are entry-level professionals who assist associates and partners by conducting financial research, performing basic financial modeling, and handling a variety of administrative and support duties (i.e., creating PowerPoint presentations, organizing presentation materials, fetching lunch, making photocopies, etc.).

■ HISTORY

During the latter half of the 19th century in the United States, increasing industrialization and liquidity prompted growing concentrations of paper money in individual hands. This increasing amount of paper wealth (as opposed to the traditional wealth of land and property) precipitated demand for private wealth managers. With growing confidence in the banking system, more and more wealthy people turned to wealth management professionals, who worked either for banks or for brokerage firms, to help them invest and protect their capital.

Analysts have helped private wealth managers to effectively manage and invest the money of high-wealth-individuals ever since these early days. Financial analysts are in demand by a variety of industries. In 2015, *U.S. News & World Report* selected the career of financial analyst as the 13th-best business job in the United States.

■ THE JOB

"Wealth management is the consultative process of meeting the needs and wants of affluent clients by providing the appropriate financial products and services," according to *Forbes*.

Wealth management analysts are entry-level professionals who typically receive a "tryout" of two to three years at a wealth management (WM) firm or in the WM department of a major investment bank before being promoted to the position of associate or leaving the firm to earn their MBAs or pursue other employment opportunities. Typical duties for analysts include:

- preparing routine financial statements
- processing and analyzing financial data for client portfolios
- creating asset allocation reviews and financial plans

- conducting research on a variety of client issues for partners (e.g., assessing a client's tax status, analyzing the merits of a hedge fund investment with a specific strategy, etc.)
- developing analytic/quantitative financial models
- researching a wide variety of financial products (and occasionally being asked to provide their opinions to associates and partners)
- contacting clients (or most likely their assistants) to confirm appointments with the associates
- assisting in pre-client meeting tasks such as preparation of meeting agendas, client paperwork, investment policy statements, financial and tax preparations, and other data
- assisting/participating during client meetings (i.e., getting coffee, running PowerPoint presentations, presenting their own research to a client on behalf of an associate)
- maintaining client records by using document management software such as Redtail CRM and NetDocuments
- creating strategy reports and other types of documents for associates to use with clients and prospective clients
- identifying new business opportunities, including prospecting clients through cold calling and via financial seminars

■ EARNINGS

New college graduates with a bachelor's degree in finance and financial management services earned average starting salaries of $54,086 in spring 2015, according to the National Association of Colleges and Employers.

The U.S. Department of Labor reports that financial analysts earned median annual salaries of $78,620 in May 2014. Salaries ranged from less than $48,170 to $154,680 or more in May 2014.

Employers offer a variety of fringe benefits, which can include the following: paid holidays, vacations, and sick days; personal days; medical, dental, and life insurance; profit-sharing plans; 401(k) plans; retirement and pension plans; and educational reimbursement (continuing education, training, conference attendance, etc.). Some analysts receive performance bonuses that range from $15,000 to $30,000.

■ WORK ENVIRONMENT

Wealth management analysts work long hours—8 A.M. to 8 P.M. can be typical. They may travel with partners to meet investors or to attend conferences. At investment banks, analysts will have use of the latest office equipment and financial software to do their work. Many top firms place a strong emphasis on creating a positive work environment that encourages diversity. For example, Morgan Stanley has more than 25 networking groups that help keep its employees engaged and that promote a culture of inclusion, including the Wealth Management Multicultural Employee Networking Group, Wealth Management Women's Employee Networking Group, and Pride (LGBT) and Ally Employee Networking Group. You can learn about a company's work environment by visiting their Web sites or by checking out Web sites such as GlassDoor.com, which provide employee reviews of major companies.

■ EXPLORING

One way to learn more about the basics of wealth management is to read books, Web sites, and magazines about WM, business, and finance. Here are a few suggestions:

- *Wealth Management Unwrapped* (Rosetta Books, LLC, 2014)
- Charles Schwab *OnInvesting*: http://insights.schwab.com/category/on-investing/%20
- *The Wall Street Journal*: http://www.wsj.com

Learn as much as you can about investing. Follow the stock market and create a real or mock investment portfolio. Many investment and brokerage Web sites will allow you to set up a mock portfolio. In high school and college,

QUICK FACTS

ALTERNATE TITLE(S)
None

DUTIES
Conduct research, perform basic financial modeling, and provide administrative support to wealth managers

SALARY RANGE
$48,170 to $78,620 to $154,680+

WORK ENVIRONMENT
Primarily Indoors

BEST GEOGRAPHIC LOCATION(S)
Opportunities are best in areas where a large number of high-net-worth individuals reside

MINIMUM EDUCATION LEVEL
Bachelor's Degree

SCHOOL SUBJECTS
Business, Economics, Mathematics

EXPERIENCE
An internship or a summer analyst program at a wealth management firm, investment bank, or other financial employer

PERSONALITY TRAITS
Enterprising, Hands On, Organized

SKILLS
Financial, Math, Research

CERTIFICATION OR LICENSING
Recommended

SPECIAL REQUIREMENTS
None

EMPLOYMENT PROSPECTS
Good

ADVANCEMENT PROSPECTS
Good

OUTLOOK
Faster than the Average

NOC
1112, 1114

O*NET-SOC
13-2051.00, 13-2052.00, 13-2099.01

CAREER LADDER

Managing Director

Partner

Chief Investment Officer/Lead
Portfolio Manager

Associate

Analyst

participate in business and finance clubs, which often provide the chance to participate in investment competitions and job shadowing opportunities.

■ EDUCATION AND TRAINING REQUIREMENTS
High School

In high school, take classes in business, economics, computer science, mathematics, English, and speech to prepare for a career as a wealth management analyst. Courses such as sociology, psychology, and science that help you to develop your research and critical-thinking skills will also be useful.

Postsecondary Education

A minimum of a bachelor's degree in finance, mathematics, economics, business, financial engineering, or quantitative finance is required to work as a wealth management analyst. Some analysts have master's degrees, typically in business.

Many banks and large wealth management firms have internship programs. For example, J.P. Morgan offers several summer analyst internship programs for college students who will enter their senior years the following fall. Participants receive hands-on experience and get the opportunity to learn more about J.P. Morgan and network with fellow interns and experienced colleagues.

Other Education or Training

Many professional associations provide educational opportunities to analysts to help them build their skills and, if they're certified, to qualify for re-certification. For example, the American Bankers Association (ABA) offers online and in-person classes on topics such as investment products, asset allocation and portfolio management, minimizing fiduciary risk and litigation, and ethics. Those who have earned the association's certified trust and financial advisor credential must complete 45 continuing education credits every three years. This requirement can be met by completing CE classes provided by the ABA or by other providers. Other continuing education classes, webinars, and workshops are provided by the American Institute of Certified Public Accountants, Association for Financial Counseling and Planning Education, Association for Financial Professionals, CFA Institute, Chartered Alternate Investment Analyst Association, Institute for Private Investors, International Association for Quantitative Finance, International Association of Registered Financial Consultants, Market Technicians Association, New York Society of Security Analysts, Securities Industry and Financial Markets Association, and Women in Insurance and Financial Services.

Many wealth management firms offer in-house educational opportunities that cover topics such as new tax legislation, ethics, emerging investment vehicles and opportunities, and career development.

Certification

The Chartered Institute of Management Accountants offers a certificate in business accounting. The program has five components: fundamentals of management accounting, fundamentals of financial accounting, fundamentals of business mathematics, fundamentals of business economics, and fundamentals of ethics, corporate governance, and business law. Other certificate programs are provided by the Association of Chartered Certified Accountants (international auditing and international financial reporting) and the American Institute of Certified Public Accountants (International Financial Reporting Standards).

Many colleges and universities offer certificates in financial planning, accounting, finance, and related fields. Contact schools in your area for more information.

■ CERTIFICATION, LICENSING, AND SPECIAL REQUIREMENTS
Certification or Licensing

Becoming certified is a good way to expand your financial knowledge and impress potential employers. It's important to note that some certification programs are only open to those with several years of on-the-job experience, but you can earn some credentials starting during your last year of college, right after you graduate, or with just a year or two of work experience. One such program is the three-level chartered financial analyst (CFA) credential, which is administered by the CFA Institute. Those with either a bachelor's degree or those who are in the last year of undergraduate study can apply for the program. Here are a few additional programs to consider:

- Accredited investment fiduciary, accredited investment fiduciary analyst, professional plan consultant (fi360)

ANALYZING WEALTH MANAGEMENT

Beyer, Charlotte B. *Wealth Management Unwrapped.* New York: RosettaBooks, LLC, 2014.

Brunel, Jean L. P. *Goals-Based Wealth Management: An Integrated and Practical Approach to Changing the Structure of Wealth Advisory.* Hoboken, N.J.: John Wiley & Sons, 2015.

Butler, Jason. *The Financial Times Guide to Wealth Management: How to Plan, Invest, and Protect Your Financial Assets,* 2nd ed. Upper Saddle River, N.J.: FT Press, 2015.

Carlson, Ben. *A Wealth of Common Sense: Why Simplicity Trumps Complexity in Any Investment Plan.* New York: Bloomberg Press, 2015.

Chhabra, Ashvin B. *The Aspirational Investor: Taming the Markets to Achieve Your Life's Goals.* New York: HarperBusiness, 2015.

Curtis, Gregory. *Family Capital: Working With Wealthy Families to Manage Their Money Across Generations.* Hoboken, N.J.: John Wiley & Sons, 2016.

Daniell, Mark Haynes, and Tom McCullough. *Family Wealth Management: Seven Imperatives for Successful Investing in the New World Order.* Hoboken, N.J.: John Wiley & Sons, 2013.

Gray, Wesley R., and Jack R. Vogel. *DIY Financial Advisor: A Simple Solution to Build and Protect Your Wealth.* Hoboken, N.J.: John Wiley & Sons, 2015.

Greenwald, Bruce C. N., Judd Kahn, Paul D. Sonkin, and Michael van Biema. *Value Investing: From Graham to Buffett and Beyond,* 2nd ed. Hoboken, N.J.: John Wiley & Sons, 2016.

Hallman, G. Victor, and Jerry Rosenbloom. *Private Wealth Management: The Complete Reference for the Personal Financial Planner,* 9th ed. New York: McGraw-Hill Education, 2015.

Kingsbury, Kathleen Burns. *How to Give Financial Advice to Couples: Essential Skills for Balancing High-Net-Worth Clients' Needs.* New York: McGraw-Hill Education, 2013.

Rice, Bob. *The Alternative Answer: The Nontraditional Investments That Drive the World's Best-Performing Portfolios.* New York: HarperBusiness, 2013.

Rosplock, Kirby. *The Complete Family Office Handbook: A Guide for Affluent Families and the Advisors Who Serve Them.* New York: Bloomberg Press, 2014.

Tyson, Eric. *Investing For Dummies.* Hoboken, N.J.: For Dummies, 2014.

Vento, John J. *Financial Independence: An Advisor's Guide to Comprehensive Wealth Management.* Hoboken, N.J.: John Wiley & Sons, 2013.

Widger, Charles, and Daniel Crosby. *Personal Benchmark: Integrating Behavioral Finance and Investment Management.* Hoboken, N.J.: John Wiley & Sons, 2014.

LEARN MORE ABOUT IT

- Certified international wealth manager diploma (Association of International Wealth Management)
- Chartered alternate investment analyst (Chartered Alternate Investment Analyst Association)
- Chartered market technician (Market Technicians Association)

Wealth management professionals with at least three years of experience providing direct client contact in investment management, administrative, tax, legal, and marketing services can apply for the certified trust and financial advisor credential, which is offered by the American Bankers Association Institute of Certified Bankers.

Some analysts are licensed as certified public accountants (CPAs). The Uniform CPA Examination, which is administered by the American Institute of Certified Public Accountants, is used by all states.

■ EXPERIENCE, SKILLS, AND PERSONALITY TRAITS

Aspiring wealth management analysts should complete an internship or a summer analyst program at a wealth management firm, investment bank, or other financial employer.

Analysts need excellent communication skills because they frequently write reports that summarize their findings, prepare and explain PowerPoint presentations, participate in meetings with colleagues, and convey financial information to investors in user-friendly language. They also need the ability to analyze and interpret financial data and an understanding of financial statements. Other important traits include strong organizational and time-management skills, curiosity, the ability to work both independently and as a member of a team, confidence, the ability to work well under pressure, and strong ethics.

Proficiency in the use of PowerPoint, Microsoft Excel, and Word, as well as financial modeling software, is also required.

■ EMPLOYMENT PROSPECTS
Employers

There are more than 3,190 wealth management businesses in the United States alone. These range from major banks such as Morgan Stanley with large wealth-management divisions, to broker/dealers, to mom-and-pop firms with fewer than 10 employees, to independent wealth managers. Many of the largest U.S. companies also have offices in foreign countries.

Starting Out

The best way to break into the wealth management industry is by participating in a summer analyst internship program at an investment bank—such as Morgan Stanley, J.P. Morgan, and Wells Fargo—that offers WM services. Many companies use these programs to identify promising candidates for full-time employment. Visit the Web sites of banks and large wealth management firms to learn more. Independent advisors and smaller firms may not have formal programs, but they may be willing to create an internship for an especially enthusiastic student.

Additionally, you can learn more about analyst jobs by using job-search sites, checking out employment listings at the Web sites of professional associations, attending career fairs and other networking events, and networking online at social media sites such as LinkedIn.

■ ADVANCEMENT PROSPECTS

Analysts who perform well during their two- to three-year tryouts are asked to become *associates,* the cornerstones of private wealth management. Associates manage client assets and build their own client bases. After many years on the job, an associate can advance to the position of chief investment officer for the firm, which typically also involves being made a partner at the firm.

Those who ultimately do not receive an offer to become an associate are typically encouraged by partners to pursue an MBA, consider other roles at the company (since there's always a new crop of recent graduates competing for analyst positions), or to seek opportunities at other firms.

■ OUTLOOK

Employment for financial analysts is expected to grow by 12 percent through 2024, according to the U.S. Department of Labor (DOL). It reports that demand is growing because "investment portfolios are becoming more complex, and there are more financial products available for trade.

A growing range of financial products and the need for in-depth knowledge of geographic regions are expected to lead to strong employment growth."

■ UNIONS AND ASSOCIATIONS

Wealth management analysts do not belong to unions. Many join associations, which provide certification, professional development opportunities, career resources, networking events, publications, and other benefits. For example, the Association of International Wealth Management is a membership organization for wealth managers, portfolio managers, investment advisors, asset managers, and trust and estate practitioners. It offers the certified international wealth manager diploma, seminars on financial and wealth management issues, and networking opportunities. The New York Society of Security Analysts provides membership, career resources, and Alternative Investments, Career Development, Global Investing, Private Wealth Management, and Student Interest Groups. The CFA Institute provides certification and continuing education opportunities. Other noteworthy organizations include the American Bankers Association, American Institute of Certified Public Accountants, Association for Financial Counseling and Planning Education, Association for Financial Professionals, Certified Financial Planner Board of Standards, Chartered Alternate Investment Analyst Association, Institute for Private Investors, International Association for Quantitative Finance, International Association of Registered Financial Consultants, Market Technicians Association, New York Society of Security Analysts, Securities Industry and Financial Markets Association, and Women in Insurance and Financial Services.

■ TIPS FOR ENTRY

1. Visit the following Web sites for career advice:
   - Bank of America: Recruitment Tips: http:// careers.bankofamerica.com/us/working-here/ recruitment-tips.aspx
   - HSBC: Application Hints and Tips: http://www .hsbc.com/careers/application-hints-and-tips
   - UBS: Interview Preparation: https://www.ubs .com/global/en/about_ubs/careers/graduate -and-intern/interview-preparation.html
2. Use "best company" lists to identify potential employers. For example, *Pensions & Investments* publishes an annual list of the best places to work in money management at http://www.pionline .com/article/20151210/ONLINE/151219977/ best-places-to-work-in-money-management.
3. Attend the American Bankers Association's Wealth Management and Trust Conference (http://www

.aba.com/Training/Conferences/Pages/WMT .aspx) to network and participate in continuing education opportunities.

■ FOR MORE INFORMATION

The ABA represents the "nation's $15 trillion banking industry, which is composed of small, regional and large banks that together employ more than 2 million people, safeguard $11 trillion in deposits and extend more than $8 trillion in loans." Visit its Web site for job listings and information on continuing education, its Wealth Management & Trust Conference, and the banking industry.

American Bankers Association (ABA)
1120 Connecticut Avenue, NW
Washington, D.C. 20036-3902
Tel: (800) 226-5377
http://www.aba.com

For information on certification, membership, and job listings, contact

Association for Financial Counseling and Planning Education
1940 Duke Street, Suite 200
Alexandria, VA 22314-3452
Tel: (703) 684-4484
http://www.afcpe.org

For information on earnings, careers, and certification, contact

Association for Financial Professionals
4520 East-West Highway, Suite 750
Bethesda, MD 20814-3574
Tel: (301) 907-2862
http://www.afponline.org

For information on membership and certification, contact

Association of International Wealth Management
E-mail: info@aiwm.org
http://www.aiwm.org

Visit the institute's Web site for information on certification for financial analysts.

CFA Institute
915 East High Street
Charlottesville, VA 22902-4868
Tel: (800) 247-8132
E-mail: info@cfainstitute.org
http://www.cfainstitute.org

For information on certification and professional development opportunities, contact

Chartered Alternate Investment Analyst Association
Tel: (413) 253-7373
E-mail: info@caia.org
https://www.caia.org

For information on certification, contact

Institute of Business and Finance
4141 Jutland Drive, Suite 330
San Diego, CA 92117-3649
Tel: (800) 848-2029
E-mail: info@icfs.com
http://www.icfs.com

Visit the society's Web site for information on membership for college students, a list of top employers of financial analysts, and scholarships for graduate students.

New York Society of Security Analysts
1540 Broadway, Suite 1010
New York, NY 10036-4083
Tel: (212) 541-4530
http://www.nyssa.org

For information on education and careers, contact

Securities Industry and Financial Markets Association
120 Broadway, 35th Floor
New York, NY 10271-3599
Tel: (212) 313-1200
http://www.sifma.org

For information on membership and continuing education, contact

Women in Insurance and Financial Services
136 Everett Road
Albany, NY 12205-1418
Tel: (866) 264-9437
E-mail: office@wifsnational.org
http://www.wifsnational.org

Wealth Management Associates

■ OVERVIEW

Wealth management associates manage the investment portfolios of high-net-worth clients and use their entrepreneurial and sales skills to attract new clients.

QUICK FACTS

ALTERNATE TITLE(S)
Personal Financial Advisors, Private Bankers, Wealth Managers

DUTIES
Manage the investment portfolios of clients and work to attract new clients; monitor client portfolios; analyzing financial data and projections

SALARY RANGE
$48,170 to $78,620 to $154,680+

WORK ENVIRONMENT
Primarily Indoors

BEST GEOGRAPHIC LOCATION(S)
Opportunities are best in areas where a large number of high-net-worth individuals reside

MINIMUM EDUCATION LEVEL
Bachelor's Degree, Master's Degree

SCHOOL SUBJECTS
Business, Economics, Mathematics

EXPERIENCE
Two to three years of experience as an analyst at a wealth management, hedge fund, private equity, or venture capital firm, or in financial sales and trading positions

PERSONALITY TRAITS
Enterprising, Hands On, Outgoing

SKILLS
Financial, Interpersonal, Research

CERTIFICATION OR LICENSING
Required

SPECIAL REQUIREMENTS
None

EMPLOYMENT PROSPECTS
Good

ADVANCEMENT PROSPECTS
Good

OUTLOOK
Much Faster than the Average

NOC
1112, 1114

O*NET-SOC
13-2051.00, 13-2052.00, 13-2099.01

Associates may also be known as *private bankers, personal financial advisors,* and *wealth managers.*

■ HISTORY

Private wealth management is a specialized branch of the investment community that provides one-stop shopping for a whole host of products and services needed by the wealthy—typically defined as those who have liquid assets of more than $1 million (not including the value of one's primary residence). Many prestigious private banks and wealth management firms have much higher minimums, more than $5 million in some cases, and provide services only to the richest of the rich.

The National Banking Act of 1863 provided the basis of a national banking system in the United States and the establishment of a national currency, which prompted growing confidence in our nation's financial systems. As the U.S. became more industrialized, a growing number of wealthy industrialists, bankers, and other high-wealth individuals began to seek out the services of wealth managers to manage and grow their capital.

In subsequent decades, demand for wealth management professionals grew rapidly, but declined during financial crises—such as the Great Depression (1929–39) and the Great Recession (December 2007 to June 2009)—and various banking and financial scandals.

In recent years, the wealth management industry has resumed its strong growth as the number of millionaires and billionaires increases. In 2014, total assets under management (AUM) reached a record $74 trillion worldwide, according to The Boston Consulting Group, a professional services and consultancy firm. Between 2007 and 2014, total AUM grew by about 26 percent—and industry profits reached a historic peak of $102 billion, matching their 2007 high before the financial crisis.

■ THE JOB

Have you heard the famous proverb, "the art is not in making money, but in keeping it." Smart high-net-worth individuals realize there's a big difference between making money and properly managing it, and therefore hire highly skilled and dedicated wealth management associates to protect and grow their wealth and leave as much as possible for their children and grandchildren. Duties for associates vary by firm, but typically include:

- working closely with clients to create an overall financial strategy that encompasses not only investment, but income management, taxes, small business partnerships, a budget, real estate holdings, and estate planning aspects
- taking and placing client orders in advisory and brokerage accounts
- assisting with trading and rebalancing of client investment accounts
- regularly monitoring clients' portfolios and providing them with regular updates about their

status—and being available via telephone, e-mail, and in-person meetings to discuss any issues that arise

- preparing and analyzing balance sheets, financial projections, and other data
- analyzing current economic trends and applying this information to the management of their clients' portfolios
- following up with clients' other advisors (certified public accountants, lawyers, etc.) as needed
- generating new business through recommendations by current clients, via good old-fashioned networking at financial conferences and charitable events, by participating in clubs and organizations that have a large membership of high-net-worth individuals, and by cold calling potential clients

■ EARNINGS

Entry-level wealth management associates earned median salaries of $65,689 in February 2016, according to Salary.com. Earnings ranged from $47,030 to $84,862. Experienced associates received median salaries of $112,594. Ten percent earned less than $81,876, and 10 percent earned $144,220 or more.

Many associates receive bonuses, which can vary depending on how the firm structures compensation. Some private bankers receive bonuses solely on selling the client new services and the company's investment products, receiving a percentage of the business the private bank brings in from that client. Others have more complex metrics, measuring performance against the client's stated goals.

At a top employer, associates can expect to earn $500,000 per year or more, most of it coming from bonuses or commissions rather than salary. In 10 to 15 years, that can reach at least $1 million per year.

Wealth management firms offer a variety of fringe benefits, such as paid holidays, vacations, and sick days; personal days; medical, dental, and life insurance; profit-sharing plans; 401(k) plans; retirement and pension plans; educational reimbursement; and licensing reimbursement (to complete Series 7, 63, and/or 66 licensing from the Financial Industry Regulatory Authority).

■ WORK ENVIRONMENT

The U.S. Department of Labor reports that 30 percent of personal financial advisors worked more than 40 hours per week in 2014. Associates often work on nights and weekends to meet with current and potential clients in their homes, at financial conferences, and at social events. This career can be stressful because associates—especially those who are new to the job—are under

considerable pressure to bring new clients to their firms. Despite the constant pressure to build a client pipeline, many associates find this job very fulfilling. They value the relationships they build with investors and the chance to help preserve and grow their capital.

CAREER LADDER

Managing Director

Partner

Chief Investment Officer/Vice President

Associate

Analyst

■ EXPLORING

Learn as much as you can about investing strategies and the stock market. The following books provide a good introduction to these topics: *Investing For Dummies* (For Dummies, 2014) and *Stock Market Investing for Beginners: Essentials to Start Investing Successfully* (Tycho Press, 2013). You can also develop your money management and stock-picking skills by managing the finances of a school club or by participating in investment competitions during high school and college. The Wharton School at the University of Pennsylvania offers the Knowledge@Wharton High School Investment Competition (http://kwhs.wharton .upenn.edu/competitions), a free, global, online investment simulation for students, ages 14–18, and teachers.

■ EDUCATION AND TRAINING REQUIREMENTS
High School

If a career as a wealth management associate sounds interesting, take as many business, economics, accounting, and mathematics classes as possible. Because your daily work will involve frequent oral and written communication with your colleagues and clients, it's a good idea to take English and speech classes. Sign-up for computer science, database management, and other technology-related courses because associates use customer relationship management databases, financial modeling software, and a variety of in-house and online databases to do their work. Psychology classes will help you to understand human behavior, and foreign language courses will come in handy if you work with clients who do not speak English fluently.

Postsecondary Education

Wealth management associates have bachelor's degrees (and sometimes advanced degrees) in finance, mathematics, accounting, economics, business, entrepreneurism, financial engineering, or quantitative finance. Some

BEAR MARKET, BULL MARKET, AND ALTERNATIVE INVESTMENT

WORDS TO KNOW

Alternative investments: Financial assets outside traditional investment classes—stocks, bonds, or cash. They are typically owned by institutions or high-net worth individuals. The alternative investing category encompasses investments such as private equity, hedge funds, and real estate.

Bear market: A time in which the prices of stocks in the market are declining or are expected to decline.

Bull market: A time in which the prices of stocks in the market are rising or are expected to rise.

Hedge fund: A private, unregistered investment pool encompassing all types of investment funds, companies and private partnerships that can use a variety of investment techniques such as borrowing money through leverage, selling short, derivatives for directional investing, and options.

Mainstream investments: Refers mainly to mutual funds or other investments that everyone can invest in (without needing a certain net worth to do so).

Mutual fund: A professionally managed investment pool sold to the public through sale of shares representing an ownership interest. These funds have a board of directors or trustees to make sure it is managed for the benefit of investors.

Net worth: The value of an individual's or company's assets minus liabilities.

Private equity: Equity investment in companies not traded on a public stock exchange.

Real estate funds: Investment funds that invest in business and residential properties.

Venture capital: The process of investing in start-up or early-stage companies that have undeveloped or developing products or revenue.

may have degrees, double majors, or minors in sales or marketing. Others have law degrees. A degree from an Ivy League or other top-tier college is required if you want to work at a large investment bank or other top employer.

Other Education or Training

Most professional associations provide continuing education (CE) classes, webinars, workshops, and seminars. These are great ways to keep your skills up to date. For example, the Institute for Private Investors offers five-day wealth management programs in collaboration with The Wharton School at the University of Pennsylvania. The Investment Management Consultants Association, American Bankers Association, American Institute of Certified Public Accountants, Association for Financial Counseling and Planning Education, Association for Financial Professionals, Association of International Wealth Management, Certified Financial Planner Board of Standards, CFA Institute, and other organizations provide CE opportunities. Contact these organizations for more information.

Many investment banks provide ongoing training for associates to help them learn about developments in the wealth management industry, keep their financial skills up to date, and hone their soft skills.

Certification

The Investment Management Consultants Association offers the online Essentials of Investment Consulting Certificate Program, which covers core topics in the investment consulting process such as the various types of investments and the mathematics of managing money and building portfolios. It also provides the Applied Behavioral Finance Certificate Program and the Fundamentals of Alternative Investments Online Certificate Program.

■ CERTIFICATION, LICENSING, AND SPECIAL REQUIREMENTS
Certification or Licensing

Many employers require applicants to have (or currently be pursuing) the certified financial planner (CFP) or chartered financial consultant (ChFC) credentials. To receive the CFP mark of certification, which is offered by the CFP Board, candidates must meet education and experience requirements, pass an examination, and agree to follow the CFP Board's Code of Ethics and Professional Responsibility, Rules of Conduct, and Financial Planning Practice Standards. The American College of Financial Services offers the ChFC designation. To receive this credential, candidates must complete certain course work stipulated by The American College, meet experience requirements, and agree to uphold The American College's Code of Ethics and Procedures.

Several other organizations offer certification to financial planning professionals, including:

- Association for Financial Counseling and Planning Education (accredited financial counselor)
- fi360 (accredited investment fiduciary, accredited investment fiduciary analyst, professional plan consultant)

- Institute of Business and Finance (certified fund specialist, certified annuity specialist, certified estate and trust specialist, certified income specialist, certified tax specialist)
- Investment Adviser Association (chartered investment counselor)
- Investment Management Consultants Association (certified investment management analyst, chartered private wealth advisor).

Associates are usually required to obtain their Series 7 and Series 63 or 66 credentials from the Financial Industry Regulatory Authority, the self-regulatory arm of the investment industry. The Series 7, or General Securities Representative certification, allows you to buy or sell, or solicit the purchase or sale, of all securities products, including corporate securities, municipal securities, municipal fund securities, options, direct participation programs, investment company products, and variable contracts. It's the most basic form of certification for anybody involved with the markets. The majority of firms will also require a Series 63 registration, which requires knowledge of state securities laws and allows you to be a securities agent. Other firms may require the Series 66, which covers the same ground as a Series 63, but also certifies you to act as a registered investment adviser.

■ EXPERIENCE, SKILLS, AND PERSONALITY TRAITS

To become an associate, you'll need two to three years of experience as an analyst at a wealth management, hedge fund, private equity, or venture capital firm, or experience in sales and trading positions with a financial employer.

According to research conducted by global wealth market research and strategy consultancy firm Scorpio Partnership, both young and older investors agree that the most important qualities for a financial advisor are integrity, professionalism, and intelligence. But one interesting difference emerges based on the age group of the investors. Investors who were under the age of 40 placed more emphasis on the importance of soft skills as compared with investors who were over age 60. "Under 40" investors rated the following soft skills as important: creativity, patience, empathy, and sociability. Advisors who provide services to younger clients should take note of these evolving skill sets, especially given the fact that Generation X investors surveyed by professional services firm EY cited "advisor relationship" as the second-most important factor (after portfolio performance) as to why they remain with a particular advisor.

Other important traits for associates include excellent communication, persuasive, problem-solving,

interpersonal, and organizational skills; a passion for the field of investing; impeccable ethics and a willingness to puts the needs of the client before those of their firm; strong attention to detail; and the ability to understand and explain sophisticated financial concepts and issues to investors. They should also be proficient in financial modeling, customer relationship management, and basic office (e.g., Microsoft Excel, PowerPoint, and Word) software.

■ EMPLOYMENT PROSPECTS
Employers

Approximately 47,206 people were employed in private banking services in 2015, according to IBISWorld. They work at major banks, regional and boutique firms, broker/dealers, robo advisory firms, and independent wealth management firms. The four largest employers (UBS, Morgan Stanley, Bank of America Merrill Lynch, and Credit Suisse) hold about 47 percent of industry assets under management. Many firms have fewer than 10 employees.

Starting Out

There are two main entry pathways for aspiring associates. Some enter the field after graduating with an MBA. They complete on-the-job training that lasts anywhere from two to six months, and then they can begin working with clients. Others are promoted to the position of associate after working as an analyst for two to three years.

There are many ways to learn more about job opportunities in the wealth management industry. Many large investment banks recruit on campus, and some offer summer analyst or associate training programs (basically internships) that teach participants about the industry, job responsibilities, and client interaction. Check the Web sites of these companies for recruiting schedules, descriptions of potential career paths, tips on preparing resumes and interviewing, and information on summer programs. College career services offices often maintain lists of employers that are hiring or that are coming to campus for career fairs. Other ways to discover jobs include employment sites, networking online on LinkedIn and other social networking sites, and using the networking and career-assistance resources of professional associations.

■ ADVANCEMENT PROSPECTS

Advancement time frames and paths for associates vary by firm and how each firm measures success. Some associates advance by being asked to join the firm's market strategy team, become a supervisor, or open a new branch office in another city. If you move into any of these positions, you'll also likely be promoted to vice president.

Some associates who are unsatisfied with their career progression leave their companies to work in similar positions at other firms. Others pursue a variety of Wall Street jobs. For example, some choose to work for a hedge fund, or become a more traditional broker/dealer, or even parlay their entrepreneurial abilities into a career as an independent advisor. Associates who do not yet have their MBAs can enroll in graduate school.

■ OUTLOOK

Employment for personal financial advisors (a career category that includes wealth management associates) is expected to grow by 30 percent through 2024, according to the U.S. Department of Labor, or much faster than the average for all careers. Those with certification and advanced degrees will have the best job prospects.

Opportunities should continue to be good for wealth management associates because of the increasing number of wealthy people in the U.S. who need WM services. The number of U.S. households with a net worth of $1 million reached a record high of 10.1 million by late 2014, according to Spectrem Group's *Market Insights Report 2015*. This was an increase of nearly 500,000 households from 2013.

■ UNIONS AND ASSOCIATIONS

Wealth management associates do not belong to unions, but there are many professional associations that provide continuing education (CE) classes and webinars, networking events, publications, and career resources. For example, the American Bankers Association offers extensive CE programs and a job bank, publishes the *ABA Banking Journal*, and hosts the Wealth Management & Trust Conference. According to its Web site, Women in Insurance and Financial Services is "dedicated to attracting capable women to the insurance and financial services sector, developing their talents, and advancing them toward their fullest potential." It offers a mentoring program, a national conference, webinars, discussion groups on social media sites, and other resources. Members of the Association for Financial Counseling and Planning Education receive discounted pricing for continuing education opportunities, publications such as the *Journal of Financial Counseling & Planning* and the *Standard* quarterly newsletter, access to networking opportunities, and other resources. Other noteworthy organizations include the American Institute of Certified Public Accountants, Association for Financial Professionals, Certified Financial Planner Board of Standards, CFA Institute, Chartered Alternate Investment Analyst Association, Institute for Private Investors, International Association

for Quantitative Finance, International Association of Registered Financial Consultants, New York Society of Security Analysts, and the Securities Industry and Financial Markets Association.

■ TIPS FOR ENTRY

1. Visit http://news.efinancialcareers.com/us-en/ 1913/seven-interview-questions-for-wealth -management-associates to read "Seven Interview Questions for Wealth Management Associates."
2. Visit the following Web sites for career advice:
   - CFP Board: Preparing for an Interview: http:// www.cfp.net/career-center/resources-for-job -seekers/preparing-for-an-interview
   - Citigroup: Tools and Tips: https://www.citi .com/oncampus/index/#/toolstips
3. Check out the following Web sites for job listings:
   - http://careers.afcpe.org
   - http://www.cfp.net/career-center
   - http://www.efinancialcareers.com

■ FOR MORE INFORMATION

Visit the ABAs Web site for job listings and information on continuing education, its Wealth Management & Trust Conference, and the banking industry.

American Bankers Association (ABA)
1120 Connecticut Avenue, NW
Washington, D.C. 20036-3902
Tel: (800) 226-5377
http://www.aba.com

For information on certification, membership, and job listings, contact

Association for Financial Counseling and Planning Education
1940 Duke Street, Suite 200
Alexandria, VA 22314-3452
Tel: (703) 684-4484
http://www.afcpe.org

For information on earnings, careers, and certification, contact

Association for Financial Professionals
4520 East-West Highway, Suite 750
Bethesda, MD 20814-3574
Tel: (301) 907-2862
http://www.afponline.org

For information on membership and certification, contact

Association of International Wealth Management
E-mail: info@aiwm.org
http://www.aiwm.org

For information on certification and careers, contact
Certified Financial Planner Board of Standards
1425 K Street, NW, #800
Washington, D.C. 20005-3673
Tel: (800) 487-1497
E-mail: mail@cfpboard.org
http://www.cfp.net

For information on certification, contact
Chartered Alternate Investment Analyst Association
Tel: (413) 253-7373
E-mail: info@caia.org
https://www.caia.org

For information on membership, continuing education, and certification, contact
Investment Management Consultants Association
5619 DTC Parkway, Suite 500
Greenwood Village, CO 80111-3044
Tel: (303) 770-3377
E-mail: imca@imca.org
http://www.imca.org

Visit the NYSSA Web site for information on membership for college students, a list of top employers of financial analysts, and scholarships for graduate students.
New York Society of Security Analysts (NYSSA)
1540 Broadway, Suite 1010
New York, NY 10036-4083
Tel: (212) 541-4530
http://www.nyssa.org

For information on education and careers, contact
Securities Industry and Financial Markets Association
120 Broadway, 35th Floor
New York, NY 10271-3599
Tel: (212) 313-1200
http://www.sifma.org

For information on membership and continuing education, contact
Women in Insurance and Financial Services
136 Everett Road
Albany, NY 12205-1418
Tel: (866) 264-9437
E-mail: office@wifsnational.org
http://www.wifsnational.org

Wealth Management Compliance Professionals

■ OVERVIEW

Compliance professionals make sure that their firms are in compliance with laws and regulations that have been established by the federal government (such as the Investment Advisers Act of 1940 and the Dodd-Frank Wall Street Reform and Consumer Protection Act of 2010), state governments, and voluntary investor-protection organizations such as the Financial Industry Regulatory Authority. They also ensure that their firms comply with internal systems that have been established to ensure compliance with government and voluntary regulators.

■ HISTORY

The federal government has regulated the U.S. banking and financial services industry ever since the first banks were founded. After the stock market crash of 1929, Congress passed a series of laws (including the Securities Act of 1933, the Securities Exchange Act of 1934, and the Investment Advisers Act of 1940) to more closely regulate the industry. The global financial crisis in the late 2000s prompted sweeping regulatory changes in the banking and financial services industry. "The wave of change since the global financial crisis has constituted the most far-reaching revision of regulatory requirements in decades, significantly increasing compliance requirements," according to *Global Risk Management Survey,* 9th edition, a report from Deloitte University Press.

Many wealth management (WM) firms—especially small and mid-size organizations—worry that these regulations will have a negative effect on the performance of their businesses. According to a survey conducted by insurance giant Aon and detailed in its *2015 Global Risk Management Survey,* banks see regulatory/legislative changes as the top issue that can impact their bottom line. As a result, many banks and financial services firms are expanding their compliance departments to reduce regulatory risk.

■ THE JOB

Job duties for compliance professionals vary by employer, job title, and other criteria, but most perform the following duties:

- overseeing the firm's registrations and annual filings with the Financial Industry Regulatory Authority

QUICK FACTS

ALTERNATE TITLE(S)
Chief Compliance Officers, Compliance Analysts, Compliance Directors, Compliance Officers, Senior Compliance Analysts

DUTIES
Create, implement, and oversee compliance monitoring programs at wealth management firms; manage annual regulatory filings; advising managers and partners; keeping current with regulations

SALARY RANGE
$30,000 to $150,000 to $240,750+

WORK ENVIRONMENT
Primarily Indoors

BEST GEOGRAPHIC LOCATION(S)
Opportunities are best in areas where a large number of high-net-worth individuals reside

MINIMUM EDUCATION LEVEL
Bachelor's Degree

SCHOOL SUBJECTS
Business, Economics, Government

EXPERIENCE
Five to 10 years experience for chief compliance officers; internship or co-op for entry-level jobs

PERSONALITY TRAITS
Enterprising, Hands On, Realistic

SKILLS
Financial, Leadership, Organizational

CERTIFICATION OR LICENSING
Recommended

SPECIAL REQUIREMENTS
None

EMPLOYMENT PROSPECTS
Good

ADVANCEMENT PROSPECTS
Fair

OUTLOOK
About as Fast as the Average

NOC
0013, 0111, 1114

O*NET-SOC
11-9199.02

---

and the Securities and Exchange Commission, as well as state notice filings
- developing and implementing a compliance risk management program that identifies and manages compliance risks

- providing advisory support to wealth managers, partners, risk managers, and information technology professionals on regulatory rules
- assisting in regulatory reviews—including internal audits, exams, and inquiries—to ensure that compliance procedures are followed
- designing and overseeing compliance training programs for the firm's employees
- working with the legal department to identify and analyze emerging legal and regulatory issues
- discussing current or emerging compliance issues with the firm's management
- maintaining databases of the firm's compliance activities (such as complaints received, the firm's responses, and investigation outcomes)
- reviewing communications such as securities sales advertising to make sure that there are no violations of regulations
- staying abreast of regulatory developments by reading industry publications and reports and press releases from regulators
- using reporting, compliance program management, portfolio monitoring, electronic communication archiving and review, and other software to collect information for regulatory filings and firm records

■ EARNINGS

The International Compliance Association reports that compliance managers earn salaries that ranged from $53,000 to $105,000. Earnings for compliance officers range from $30,000 to $65,000.

Chief compliance officers at small companies earned salaries that ranged from $116,500 to $156,000, according to Robert Half's *2016 Salary Guide Accounting & Finance*. At large firms, earnings ranged from $169,500 to $240,750.

Wealth management employers offer a variety of benefit packages. For example, the financial services firm Janney Montgomery Scott provides paid holiday, vacation, and sick days; medical, dental, vision, and life insurance; tuition reimbursement; adoption assistance and leave benefits; flexible spending accounts; and a profit-sharing and savings plan.

■ WORK ENVIRONMENT

Compliance professionals work in typical office settings, with standard work hours (Monday-Friday, 9 to 5). This job can be occasionally stressful if the compliance professional fails to identify risk areas that result in a negative outcome for his or her firm. On the other hand, many compliance professionals enjoy their work immensely—valuing the great responsibility they have to steer their firm clear of regulatory pitfalls and areas of risk.

■ EXPLORING

If the terms "asset allocation," "index," "mid caps," and "blue chips" seem like a foreign language to you, then a glossary is a good place to start as you explore the world of wealth management. The investment bank UBS offers a useful glossary of WM terms at https://www.ubs.com/global/en/asset_management/glossary. A short compliance glossary can be found at https://www.idology.com/resources/compliance-glossary-terms. Visit your local library to check out books such as *Essential Strategies for Financial Services Compliance* (John Wiley & Sons, 2015), which provides a detailed overview of the types of issues compliance professionals face every day. Another good resource is the ComplianceX blog, http://compliancex.com. Talk to compliance professionals about their careers. Ask them the following questions:

- What do you like most and least about your career?
- What's the best strategy for people to land jobs in the industry?
- What's the best way to network in this industry?
- How is the wealth management industry changing? What can students do now to improve their chances of landing a job?
- Can you recommend anyone else that I can talk to about career paths and the job search?

■ EDUCATION AND TRAINING REQUIREMENTS
High School

High school classes that will help to prepare you for a career in compliance include English, speech, business, economics, accounting, computer science, database design and management, computer security, social studies, history, and foreign language.

Postsecondary Education

Entry-level compliance professionals typically have bachelor's degrees in business, finance, accounting, or pre-law. Some employers prefer to hire those with graduate degrees in these areas, or those who have law degrees. A few colleges, such as Loyola University Chicago, offer master's degree concentrations in compliance studies. Law schools—such as the Seton Hall Law School—are beginning to offer concentrations in compliance. The Regulatory Compliance Association's College of Regulatory Compliance provides a law and master's concentration in asset management practice, compliance, and regulation. The International Compliance

Association offers postgraduate diplomas in governance, risk, and compliance; financial crime compliance; and other areas.

Other Education or Training

Most wealth management firms provide ongoing training for their employees, which includes classes that focus on specific career areas (e.g., compliance, risk management, portfolio management) and personal and professional development (e.g., leadership, teamwork, and technology skills).

Professional associations also offer a wealth of continuing education (CE) workshops, webinars, seminars, and classes. For example, the Society of Corporate Compliance and Ethics provides webinars such as The ABC's of Professional Development for Compliance Practitioners and Update on Global Data Privacy Laws and Frameworks. It also offers the Basic Compliance and Ethics Academy, a three-and-a-half-day intensive program that covers topics such as compliance standards, policies, and procedures; ethics; communications, education, and training; and risk assessment. The program is offered in cities around the world. Professional development opportunities are also provided by the

A compliance professional points out changes in a wealth management firm's investment plan. (Kinga. Shutterstock.)

ANNUITY, BLUE CHIP, AND DIVIDENDS

WORDS TO KNOW

Annuity: An interest-bearing contract between a life insurance company and an individual that promises periodic payments to the individual during a specific period of time.

Asset allocation: The practice of distributing a portfolio's assets among various types of investments—stocks, bonds, cash, etc.—to achieve a desired investment return at acceptable level of risk.

Asset management: Professional management of investments to achieve attractive returns; also known as **investment management.**

Assets under management: The net asset value of investments under management.

Blue chip: A well-established company with a good record of earnings, sought by investors seeking relative safety and stability.

Bond: A long-term debt instrument with the promise to pay a specified interest and return of the original investment on a stated maturity date.

Commodities: Goods such as corn, oil, live cattle, gold, and coffee that are traded on a commodity exchange.

Commodity funds: An investment fund that invests primarily in tradable commodities.

Dividends: Payments made by a company to those who own its stocks. These payments, which are taxable, are paid annually, quarterly, or monthly.

Stock: A representation of financial ownership in a company; the value of a stock can rise or fall based on a company's performance or other factors. Sometimes called a **share** by investment professionals outside the United States.

International Compliance Association, Regulatory Compliance Association, American Bar Association, and the American Bankers Association. Contact these organizations for more information.

Certification

A few colleges offer undergraduate and graduate certificates in compliance. Typical classes in these programs focus on risk management, ethics, leadership, and accounting systems. Contact the following colleges for more information about their programs:

- University of South Florida: http://www.usf.edu/innovative-education/graduate-certificates/programs/compliance-risk-anti-money-laundering.aspx

- San Francisco State University: http://cob.sfsu.edu/graduate-programs/ethics-compliance-certificate

The International Compliance Association (http://www.int-comp.org/qualifications/all-certificates-and-diplomas) offers certificates that focus on compliance, anti-money laundering, financial crime prevention, due diligence, risk management, and other areas.

■ CERTIFICATION, LICENSING, AND SPECIAL REQUIREMENTS
Certification or Licensing

Several associations and a college have developed certification programs for compliance professionals. The Society of Corporate Compliance and Ethics' Compliance Certification Board awards the certified compliance and ethics professional, the certified compliance and ethics professional fellow, and other credentials to those who pass a certification exam and meet educational and experience requirements. The Regulatory Compliance Association offers the chartered regulatory counsel and the certified compliance officer designations. The American Bankers Association provides the certified regulatory compliance manager credential to applicants who have at least three years of industry experience, earn 80 continuing education credits, and pass an examination.

The Lubin School of Business at Pace University and the Association of International Bank Auditors have partnered to offer the certified compliance and regulatory professional credential. The program covers three main areas: Corporate Governance in Financial Institutions; Regulatory Affairs Within International Financial Institutions; and Developing, Implementing and Leading a Compliance Program.

■ EXPERIENCE, SKILLS, AND PERSONALITY TRAITS

For entry-level positions, you'll need to complete a compliance-related internship or participate in a cooperative educational experience during college. This can be at a wealth management firm, in the compliance department of a corporation, or at a regulator such as the Securities and Exchange Commission. To become a chief compliance officer (CCO), you will need five to 10 years of compliance experience; at least half of this time should be in a managerial position. Some wealth management firms prefer to hire CCOs who have law degrees.

A successful compliance professional has a good understanding of his or her firm's business and its financial products, expertise in federal and state securities laws, and the ability to assess risks that may affect the firm's ability to comply with these laws. Compliance workers must be excellent communicators because they frequently interact with wealth managers, risk managers, government regulators, and their fellow compliance professionals. Strong analytical and problem-solving skills are necessary to identify and mitigate areas of risk. Other important traits include first-rate organizational skills, personal integrity, curiosity, creativity, good presentation skills, excellent judgment, a detail-oriented personality, and the ability to work both independently and as a member of a team.

■ EMPLOYMENT PROSPECTS
Employers

Compliance professionals are employed by major banks, broker/dealers, regional and boutique firms, robo advisory firms, and independent wealth managers. They also work for law firms that provide compliance services to WM firms. There are more than 3,190 wealth management businesses in the United States.

Opportunities in compliance are available in many other industries, including in telecommunications, health care, banking, higher education, oil and gas extraction, and pharmaceuticals. Compliance workers are also employed by government agencies such as the Securities & Exchange Commission.

Starting Out

Participating in an internship is a good way to break into the field if you lack work experience. Many large banks and investment firms have internship programs. If participating in an internship doesn't lead to a job, try to land a job in the operations department of a bank or in positions that deal with anti-money laundering and due diligence controls. Employers like to hire people who have hands-on experience and knowledge of issues that affect their operations. Wealth management firms also seek out applicants who have experience with regulators such as the Financial Industry Regulatory Authority, Securities and Exchange Commission, Federal Reserve, Office of the Comptroller of Currency, as well as state regulatory agencies.

Other job-search strategies include applying to WM firms directly, using the resources of your college's career services office, working with a recruiter (such as the Compliance Search Group), and networking online and at in-person events (many of which are sponsored by professional associations).

■ ADVANCEMENT PROSPECTS

After a few years of experience, a compliance analyst can advance to the position of senior compliance analyst,

and then gradually be promoted to higher-level positions such as compliance officer, compliance director, and chief compliance officer. As they advance, compliance professionals receive salary increases and performance bonuses. Top performers may be asked to become partners in their firms.

■ OUTLOOK

Employment for compliance professionals will be strong during the next decade as a result of increasing government regulation of the financial services industry. "Professionals with risk and compliance backgrounds are seeing steady demand for their expertise, especially in financial services," advises the staffing firm Robert Half Finance and Accounting in its *2015 Salary Guide: Accounting and Finance.* Those with a law degree or a master's degree, certification, and extensive experience will have the best job prospects.

■ UNIONS AND ASSOCIATIONS

Wealth management compliance professionals do not belong to unions. There are three main professional organizations for those who work in compliance: the Regulatory Compliance Association (RCA), Society of Corporate Compliance and Ethics (SCCE), and the International Compliance Association (ICA). The RCA provides the chartered regulatory counsel credential and continuing education (CE) opportunities. The SCCE offers professional development opportunities, provides membership for students and practicing compliance professionals, publishes *Compliance & Ethics Professional* and *Corporate Compliance Weekly News,* and provides various compliance certifications. The ICA offers membership and a variety of certificate and diploma programs. Additionally, the Securities Industry and Financial Markets Association—which represents the interests of securities firms, banks, and asset managers—has a Compliance and Legal Society for individual members. The American Bankers Association's Center for Regulatory Compliance offers CE classes and webinars, and publishes *Bank Compliance.*

■ TIPS FOR ENTRY

1. Visit the following Web sites for job listings:
   * http://www.corporatecompliance.org/CareerCenter/JobBoard.aspx
   * http://www.efinancialcareers.com
   * http://www.pionline.com/section/careers
   * http://compliancejobs.com
2. Participate in a compliance-related internship to learn more about the field and build your network. Visit http://www.corporatecompliance.org/

CareerCenter/Internship.aspx and https://www
.linkedin.com/jobs/compliance-intern-jobs for
internship listings.

3. Attend the American Bankers Association
Regulatory Compliance Conference (http://www
.aba.com/Training/Conferences/Pages/RCC.aspx)
to take advantage of a variety of professional development opportunities and to build your network.

4. Visit http://news.efinancialcareers.com/us-en/
140343/how-to-get-a-job-in-compliance to read
"How to Get a Job in Compliance With Little or
No Experience."

■ FOR MORE INFORMATION

*Visit the ABA's Web site for job listings and information
on continuing education, its Wealth Management & Trust
Conference, and the banking industry.*

American Bankers Association (ABA)
1120 Connecticut Avenue, NW
Washington, D.C. 20036-3902
Tel: (800) 226-5377
http://www.aba.com

*For information on membership and continuing educa-
tion, contact*

International Compliance Association
E-mail: ict@int-comp.com
http://www.int-comp.org

*For information on certification and continuing education,
contact*

Regulatory Compliance Association
Tel: (800) 306-6133
https://www.rcaonline.org

*For information on education and careers and its
Compliance and Legal Society, contact*

**Securities Industry and Financial Markets
Association**
120 Broadway, 35th Floor
New York, NY 10271-3599
Tel: (212) 313-1200
http://www.sifma.org

For information on certification and membership, contact

**Society of Corporate Compliance
and Ethics**
Tel: (888) 277-4977
E-mail: service@corporatecompliance.org
http://www.corporatecompliance.org

Wealth Management Investor Relations Specialists

■ OVERVIEW

Wealth management investor relations specialists use
their skills in public relations, marketing, and finance to
market wealth management services to high-net-worth
individuals, as well as manage relationships with current
investors.

■ HISTORY

Since the 1950s, corporations have employed investor
relations (IR) specialists to provide financial information
to shareholders. But the field really began to grow in the
2000s, after a series of corporate scandals (e.g., Enron,
WorldCom, Lehman Brothers, Bear Stearns, AIG, etc.)
prompted increased government scrutiny of corporations
and the banking industry and fueled growing investor
calls for financial transparency. Two major pieces of federal legislation—The Sarbanes-Oxley Act of 2002 and The
Dodd–Frank Wall Street Reform and Consumer Protection
Act of 2010—instituted much more stringent regulatory
control over the financial industry (including requiring
investment firms to provide more documentation regarding their operations to both regulators and investors). As a
result, demand greatly increased for IR specialists.

The National Investor Relations Institute was founded
in 1969. It is the largest professional investor relations
association in the world, with more than 3,300 members.
The Canadian Investor Relations Institute was founded
in 1997. It has more than 550 members.

■ THE JOB

Job duties for investor relations professionals vary by the
size of their employer. At medium-size and large firms,
there's usually a dedicated IR/marketing professional—
and often an entire department—that handles investor
relations duties. At small funds, the firm's owner might
be responsible for investor relations/marketing, or he or
she might hire an outside public relations/marketing firm
to perform these duties. At some smaller funds, the role
of investor relations specialist is combined with that of
marketing specialist.

Major duties of investor relations specialists include:

- serving as the primary point of contact for existing
investors and working with other members of the
IR department to identify new investors

- creating and updating marketing materials (such as offering memos, fact sheets, portfolio manager bios, and investor presentations)
- maintaining their firm's Web site and social media accounts
- creating due diligence materials such as private placement memorandums and investor questionnaires (to ensure eligibility and compliance with federal anti-money laundering requirements)
- preparing presentations for road shows, investor meetings, conferences, and other events
- maintaining an investor management database to track communications with investors and progress in the sales pipeline
- conducting regular qualitative and quantitative research about the wealth management industry and the firm's competitors
- creating pitch books (a document or presentation that is sent to potential investors to provide information on the firm and its major players, its investment strategies, its risk management strategies and reporting systems, and other data)

■ EARNINGS

New college graduates with a bachelor's degree in marketing earned average starting salaries of $43,123 in spring 2015, according to the National Association of Colleges and Employers.

Investment relations officers earned average salaries that ranged from $100,000 to $149,999 in 2014, according to *IR Magazine's Global Investor Relations Practice Report 2014*. The typical head of an IR department earned between $200,000 and $249,999 in 2014. Ninety-five percent received a yearly bonus that averaged 35 percent of their base salary. Investor relations professionals receive benefits such as health and life insurance, paid vacation days and sick leave, and a 401(k) or other retirement savings plan.

■ WORK ENVIRONMENT

A job in investor relations will be a good fit for someone who likes the world of finance, but who also enjoys interacting with people. A typical work week might involve in-person and phone meetings with current and potential investors, attending road shows and investor meetings with partners, and a lot of brainstorming with IR colleagues and designers to create marketing materials, update the firm's Web site or social media accounts, or prepare quarterly reports. Work hours for IR specialists are fairly standard (i.e., 9 to 5, Monday through Friday)— unless they're traveling on a road show (which can last several days and include work at night and on weekends).

QUICK FACTS

ALTERNATE TITLE(S)
Assistant Investor Relations Managers, Heads of Investor Relations, Investor Relations Directors, Investor Relations Managers, Investor Relations Officers

DUTIES
Manage relationships with current investors while marketing to prospective investors; preparing and giving presentations; research

SALARY RANGE
$43,123 to $150,000 to $250,000+

WORK ENVIRONMENT
Primarily Indoors

BEST GEOGRAPHIC LOCATION(S)
Opportunities are best in areas where a large number of high-net-worth individuals reside

MINIMUM EDUCATION LEVEL
Bachelor's Degree

SCHOOL SUBJECTS
Business, Economics, Speech

EXPERIENCE
Two years of experience in investor relations, marketing, planning and development, finance, or corporate communication or consulting firm for entry-level positions; more than five years for mid-level jobs; more than 10 years for executive-level careers

PERSONALITY TRAITS
Enterprising, Hands On, Outgoing

SKILLS
Financial, Interpersonal, Public Speaking, Sales

CERTIFICATION OR LICENSING
Recommended

SPECIAL REQUIREMENTS
None

EMPLOYMENT PROSPECTS
Good

ADVANCEMENT PROSPECTS
Fair

OUTLOOK
Much Faster than the Average

NOC
0013, 0111, 1113

O*NET-SOC
11-2021.00, 13-1161.00, 27-3031.00

■ EXPLORING

Learn as much as you can about business and investing by checking out these and other publications: *Barron's*

CAREER LADDER

Partner

Investor Relations Director

Investor Relations Manager

Assistant Investor Relations Manager

Investor Relations Associate

(http://www.barrons.com), *Bloomberg Business* (http://www.bloomberg.com/businessweek), and *Private Asset Management* (http://www.pammagazine.com).

Follow the financial markets, and create a real or mock stock portfolio based on your research. Join finance clubs in high school and college. Many clubs compete in investing competitions. If your school doesn't offer a finance club, ask your business teacher to start one.

Talk with investment relations specialists about their jobs. Ask the following questions:

- How did you break into the field?
- What bachelor's degree should I pursue—one in public relations or marketing, or one in finance? Should I also earn a master's degree?
- How important is certification for career success?
- How will the field of investor relations change in the next five to 10 years, and what can I do in college to prepare for these changes?

■ EDUCATION AND TRAINING REQUIREMENTS
High School

High school classes that provide good preparation for a career in investor relations include English, speech, finance, marketing, business, economics, accounting, and mathematics. Other recommended courses include computer science, psychology, history, social studies, and foreign language.

Postsecondary Education

A minimum of a bachelor's degree in marketing, public relations, finance, accounting, business, or a related field is required to work in investor relations. Many IR specialists have master's degrees. Fordham University in New York City offers the only master's degree in investor relations (MSIR) in the United States. According to Fordham's Web site, the MSIR curriculum covers "basic skills in financial accounting, financial theory, and investment practices, as well as issues surrounding the regulatory environment; information technologies that support and influence investor relations; clear and

effective business communication, including the use of media; and business ethics, legal considerations, and strategic relationship management." Visit https://www.fordham.edu/info/22947/investor_relations for more information.

Other Education or Training

Throughout their careers, savvy IR specialists participate in educational seminars and workshops, self-paced courses, and webcasts to expand their knowledge of investor relations, develop their communication and interpersonal skills, and otherwise learn about the fields of IR, marketing, and public relations. Many associations at the national, state, and local levels provide these opportunities. For example, the National Investor Relations Institute offers webinars such as IR as a Career vs. Stepping Stone, Crisis Management at the Annual Meeting, Social Media Strategies for IR, and Communicating the Company's Strategy. The institute also offers professional development classes at its annual conference and self-paced, online courses. Visit https://www.niri.org/professional-development for more information. The American Marketing Association, Canadian Investor Relations Institute, and the Public Relations Society of America also provide continuing education opportunities.

Certification

The University of California-Irvine offers an investor relations certificate program, which, according to its Web site, is "designed for both entry-level and experienced corporate and communication professionals who want to broaden their expertise by gaining a solid practical understanding of how investor relations' activities can benefit the firm." To earn the certificate, participants must complete the following classes:

- Introduction to Investor Relations
- The Capital Markets
- The Investment Process
- The Corporate Environment
- Communications for the Investor Relations Professional
- The Practice of Investor Relations.

Visit http://www.unex.uci.edu/pdfs/brochures/INVESTOR_brochure.pdf for more information.

Seneca College in Toronto, Canada, also offers a certificate program in investor relations. See http://www.senecacollege.ca/alumni/perks/irm.pdf to learn more. Additionally, many colleges offer undergraduate and graduate certificates in public relations and marketing.

■ CERTIFICATION, LICENSING, AND SPECIAL REQUIREMENTS

Certification or Licensing

Some investor relations specialists become certified in order to demonstrate their mastery of job skills and improve their chances of landing a job. In some instances, those who are certified earn higher salaries than those who are not certified. To become certified, you'll typically need to satisfy education and experience requirements and pass an examination—but criteria vary by program. Here are a few popular certifications for IR professionals:

- Accreditation in public relations (Public Relations Society of America)
- Certified professional in investor relations (Canadian Investor Relations Institute)
- Certified public accountant (American Institute of Certified Public Accountants)
- Chartered financial analyst (CFA Institute)
- Investor relations charter (National Investor Relations Institute)
- Professional certified marketer (American Marketing Association)

■ EXPERIENCE, SKILLS, AND PERSONALITY TRAITS

According to the National Investor Relations Institute, entry-level IR relations specialists should have at least two years of experience in investor relations, marketing, planning and development, finance, or corporate communication at a public company or consulting firm. Mid-level professionals need more than five years of experience, and IR executives need more than 10 years of work experience in one or more of these aforementioned areas.

You'll need excellent written and oral communication skills to be successful in this career because IR specialists frequently write copy for marketing materials, the firm's Web site, and investor reports; present information about their firms, their investment portfolio managers, and their investment strategies to potential investors at road shows and at investor conferences; and regularly meet with colleagues to discuss the firm's marketing strategies and a variety of other topics. Investor relations specialists must be knowledgeable about common investment strategies and financial concepts in order to effectively convey complex financial information to potential and current investors in an easy-to-understand manner. Other important traits include:

- excellent analytical and quantitative skills
- strong Microsoft Office skills, especially in PowerPoint

An investor relations specialist explains the financial expertise and benefits his wealth management firm offers. (Shutterstock. goodluz)

- confidence and a persuasive personality
- the ability to manage multiple tasks and projects
- a strong work ethic
- an organized and detail-oriented personality
- the ability to meet deadlines and work well under pressure

■ EMPLOYMENT PROSPECTS

Employers

There are more than 3,190 wealth management businesses (e.g., banks, investment firms, broker/dealers, family offices, solo practitioners) in the United States alone. Investor relations specialists also work for marketing and public relations firms that offer IR services. Opportunities are found throughout the United States, but are concentrated in geographic areas where a large number of affluent people live.

Starting Out

A good way to break into an investor relations position at a wealth management firm is to first obtain experience in IR, marketing, or public relations at a corporation or consulting firm. Most large corporations have extensive career Web sites that provide information on potential career paths, internship programs, and tips on resume writing and interviewing. At many sites, you can apply for jobs. Many professional associations—including the American Marketing Association (http://jobs.ama.org) and the Public Relations Society of America (http://www.prsa.org/jobcenter)—offer job listings and career development resources at their Web sites. Your college's career services

EQUITY, FAMILY OFFICE, AND RISK TOLERANCE

WORDS TO KNOW

Country fund: An investment fund that invests chiefly in the equities of a specific country.

Diversification: An investment strategy that helps to reduce, but not eliminate risk, by allocating a client's investment funds among several assets or asset classes.

Equities: Shares in a corporation (in the form of common stock or preferred stock) that are issued to investors that represent a claim over a proportion of its assets and profit.

Equity fund: A mutual fund that invests primarily in stocks. It is also known as a **stock fund.**

Estate tax: State and/or federal taxes that may be levied on the assets of a deceased person upon his or her death.

Family office: A firm that manages investments, assets, and trusts for a high-wealth family.

Investment policies: The strategies a wealth management firm uses to reach investment goals (stock selection, cash holdings, timing, etc.).

Investment return: The profit or loss on an investment over a certain period of time.

Portfolio: A collection of investments (stock shares, bonds, convertibles, cash, real estate, etc.). Owning a portfolio reduces risk by holding different types of investments and spreading out the risk.

Risk: In regard to the wealth management industry, factors such as chancy investment strategies, poor firm leadership, ineffective information security protocols, and failure to comply with government regulations that may affect the performance of the investment fund or the wealth management firm.

Risk tolerance: The level of risk that an investor is willing to accept to reach his or her investment goals.

counselors can provide information on networking events, career fairs, and related resources. You can build your professional network by joining professional associations such as the National Investor Relations Institute and by attending informal networking events that are advertised on MeetUp.com. Don't forget to utilize social networking sites such as LinkedIn to build your network, interact with recruiters, and learn about job openings.

■ ADVANCEMENT PROSPECTS

With experience, an entry-level IR associate at a large firm can advance to the position of assistant investor

relations manager, then to IR manager, and finally IR director. A highly-skilled and -experienced investor relations director might be asked to become a partner at the firm. Additionally, there are many opportunities outside the wealth management industry—typically in the IR, marketing, and public relations departments of major corporations. Others work in the marketing or public relations departments of nonprofit organizations or government agencies.

■ OUTLOOK

Employment opportunities for marketing managers and public relations specialists who work in the catch-all industry category of "other financial investment activities" are expected to grow by 36 percent through 2024, according to the U.S. Department of Labor. Competition is extremely strong for the investment dollars of high-net-worth individuals, and wealth management partners realize that they need skilled IR specialists on staff to interact with current investors and to convince new investors to choose their firms. Investor relations specialists with advanced degrees, certification, and considerable experience will have the best job prospects.

■ UNIONS AND ASSOCIATIONS

Wealth management investor relations specialists do not belong to unions, but there are many IR, marketing, public relations, finance, and banking associations in the United States and throughout the world that provide useful resources to aspiring and current IR professionals. For example, the National Investor Relations Institute (NIRI) offers membership for IR specialists who work in the United States. Members receive *IR Update,* NIRI's flagship monthly magazine; discounts on conferences, seminars, and webinars; access to eGroups, NIRI's private social networking forum; access to a sample document library (e.g., guidance for corporate disclosure, model job descriptions, and sample investor relations plans); and free webinars. The Canadian Investor Relations Institute is a membership organization for IR professionals in Canada. It offers a mentorship program that links new IR professionals with experienced practitioners, publications such as *IR leader,* an annual conference, and the certified professional in investor relations credential. The CFA Institute offers certification and continuing-education opportunities. The American Bankers Association, American Marketing Association, and the Public Relations Society of America also provide many useful resources.

■ TIPS FOR ENTRY

1. Read financial publications such as *Investor Relations Update* (https://www.niri.org/resources/

publications/ir-update) and *IR Magazine* (http://www.irmagazine.com) to learn more about the field.

2. A strong background in English, speech, marketing, and economics is helpful in this field; take classes in these areas.

3. Visit the following Web sites for job listings:

- http://www.efinancialcareers.com
- https://www.niri.org/career-center (open to members only)
- https://www.ciri.org/MemberServices/JobListings.aspx (open to members only)
- http://aba.careerbank.com

■ FOR MORE INFORMATION

Visit the ABA's Web site for job listings and information on continuing education, its Wealth Management & Trust Conference, and the banking industry.

American Bankers Association (ABA)
1120 Connecticut Avenue, NW
Washington, D.C. 20036-3902
Tel: (800) 226-5377
http://www.aba.com

For information on continuing education, publications, careers, and certification, contact

American Marketing Association
130 East Randolph Street, 22nd Floor
Chicago, IL 60601-6207
Tel: (800) AMA-1150
https://www.ama.org

For information on certification, continuing education, and career opportunities in Canada, contact

Canadian Investor Relations Institute
601, 67 Yonge Street
Toronto, ON M5E 1J8
Canada
Tel: (416) 364-8200
E-mail: enquiries@ciri.org
https://www.ciri.org

For information on certification and job listings, contact

National Investor Relations Institute
225 Reinekers Lane, Suite 560
Alexandria, VA 22314-2875
Tel: (703) 562-7700
https://www.niri.org/career-center

For information on careers and its Financial Communication Section, contact

Public Relations Society of America
33 Maiden Lane, 11th Floor
New York, NY 10038-5149
Tel: (212) 460-1400
https://www.prsa.org, https://www.prsa.org/network/communities/financialcommunications

Wealth Management Lawyers

■ OVERVIEW

Wealth management lawyers provide a variety of legal services to wealth management (WM) firms—ranging from assistance with setting up trusts, to advice on regulatory compliance and tax and real estate issues, and representing their employer during litigation and dispute resolution. Some WM lawyers work for law firms that provide legal services to WM firms. Others are employed directly by high-net-worth individuals. The top attorneys at wealth management firms or banks with WM divisions are known as *chief legal officers* or *general counsels*.

■ HISTORY

Lawyers have provided legal advice to corporations ever since the first corporation (the Stora Kopparberg Mining Company in Falus, Sweden) was chartered by King Magnus Eriksson in 1347.

As of 1880 in the United States, there were 335 chartered business corporations, most having been chartered after 1790, according to *Essays in the Earlier History of Modern Corporations,* by Joseph S. Davis. Most of the new corporations chartered in the early 1800s were involved in public services of some kind, such as banking and insurance.

In the latter half of the 19th century, the number of wealthy people grew as a result of the industrial revolution and other factors, and a variety of wealth management firms (including banks that offered these services) were founded to serve the needs of the affluent. These firms and high-net-worth individuals hired lawyers to provide advice on estate planning, contracts, tax issues, and other financial-related issues.

The growth of international business, the increasing government regulation of WM firms, and the rising number of high-net-worth individuals is fueling strong demand for wealth management lawyers.

■ THE JOB

Job duties for wealth management lawyers vary by the size of the employer, the number of lawyers it has on staff, and other factors. At a small WM firm, there may be just a chief legal officer who handles everything from contracts and due diligence, to regulatory compliance and risk management issues, and employment law and labor issues. At a large WM company, the chief legal officer will be assisted by lower-level attorneys as well as a team of paralegals and legal secretaries. There will also be distinct human resources, risk, and compliance departments. Typical duties for wealth management lawyers include:

- advising partners on the structuring and formation of investment funds
- providing general legal advice on the firm's investment activities, products, and services
- drafting agreements such as client agreements, confidentiality agreements, vendor services agreements, and custody agreements
- structuring estates and trusts, business succession plans, and wills for high-net-worth individuals
- providing advice on tax minimization during the transfer of wealth
- reviewing and negotiating contracts with third-party service providers
- preparing required legal filings
- overseeing and handling litigation, arbitration, and other proceedings that involve the firm
- providing research and due diligence on legal, financial, regulatory, and other areas of risk
- assisting senior leadership to develop, document, and implement processes and policies to ensure compliance with the legal and regulatory environment
- advising clients regarding laws such as the Securities Act of 1933, Securities Exchange Act of 1934, Commodity Exchange Act of 1936, Investment Advisers Act of 1940, Investment Company Act of 1940, Dodd–Frank Wall Street Reform and Consumer Protection Act of 2010, and other national and state securities laws
- responding to inquiries and enforcement actions by the Securities & Exchange Commission and the U.S. Department of Justice

■ EARNINGS

In-house corporate lawyers with zero to three years of experience who worked at small companies earned salaries that ranged from $81,500 to $109,250 in 2015, according to national staffing firm Robert Half Legal's *2016 Salary Guide for the Legal Field.* At large companies, they earned between $121,500 to $156,500.

Attorneys with 10 or more years on the job who worked at small companies had earnings that ranged from $126,250 to $181,000. At large companies, attorneys earned salaries that ranged from $179,000 to $251,500.

Earnings for wealth management lawyers who are also partners can exceed $1 million.

Many large WM firms provide excellent benefits. For example, employees of the global investment management firm Legg Mason receive comprehensive medical, dental, and vision coverage; paid time off for vacation, illness, and personal and family needs; access to a 401(k) plan; tuition reimbursement and the opportunity to take in-house classes and training; merit pay and bonuses; access to institutional shares of its funds, as well as its stock; profit sharing; and life insurance and disability benefits.

◾ WORK ENVIRONMENT

Wealth management lawyers spend much of their work day in the office, conducting legal research, studying and interpreting new government regulations, and attending meetings with partners and members of the risk management, compliance, portfolio management, and other departments. Litigation is a fact of life in the business world, and lawyers occasionally represent their clients in court and at other legal proceedings. Overall, the work environment can be busy and stressful at times due to the large amounts of money at risk, increasing regulatory requirements, and the high expectations of both the firm's partners and investors.

◾ EXPLORING

The American Bar Association (ABA) offers useful information on education and careers at its Web site, http://www.abalcc.org. If you're already in law school, consider becoming a student member of the ABA.

Participate in mock trial competitions in high school and college, which allow you to practice your courtroom skills and meet other people who are interested in legal careers. One such competition is the National High School Mock Trial Championship (http://www.nationalmocktrial.org).

Many colleges and universities host summer programs for high school students who are interested in careers in law. For example, the University of Pennsylvania Law School offers a three-week Pre-College Summer Academy in which participants attend lectures and presentations from Penn Law faculty and guest speakers, visit law firms and trial and appellate courts, and work in teams to prepare for Penn Law's Summer Academy Moot Court Competition.

◾ EDUCATION AND TRAINING REQUIREMENTS
High School

Lawyers must be excellent writers and oral communicators, so it's important to take as many English and speech classes as possible. Joining the debate club will also be useful. Wealth management attorneys are experts in business and finance. To build your skills in these areas, take economics, accounting, business, finance, and mathematics courses. Foreign language classes will come in handy if you work for a firm that does business internationally. Other important classes include government, computer science, history, psychology, and social studies.

Postsecondary Education

The American Bar Association (ABA) does not recommend any particular undergraduate majors to prepare for law school. It reports that "students are admitted to law school from almost every academic discipline. You may choose to major in subjects that are considered to be traditional preparation for law school, such as history, English, philosophy, political science, economics, or business, or you may focus your undergraduate studies in areas as diverse as art, music, science and mathematics, computer science, engineering, nursing, or education."

Most law schools require that applicants take the Law School Admission Test (LSAT). The Law School Admission Council offers detailed information about preparing for and taking the LSAT at http://www.lsac.org.

The ABA has approved more than 220 law schools in the United States. Law school graduates receive either a degree of juris doctor (J.D.) or a bachelor of laws (LL.B.). Some law schools offer classes in family wealth management or related areas.

Other Education or Training

Continuing education classes, seminars, and webinars that are offered by professional associations provide lawyers with an excellent way to keep their skills up to date. For example, the ABA offers Essentials—a series of introductory-level programs that cover the basics of core practice areas. Recent offerings included Legal Research: Top Tips That Will Turbocharge Your Skills, LinkedIn for Lawyers Reloaded, and Recent Cases and Developments in Derivatives Litigation. The ABA Young Lawyers Division provides career development videos and webinars such as Volunteering to Enhance Your Career and Millennial Lawyers: Improve Your Professionalism and Jumpstart Your Career. The Association of Corporate Counsel provides in-person

A lawyer finalizes contracts for clients of his wealth management firm. (goodluz. Shutterstock.)

and online continuing education. Topics include ethics, litigation, compliance, contract negotiation, and basic practice skills. Contact these organizations for more information.

Certification

Some attorneys choose to earn a master of laws (LL.M) degree, an advanced law certification that provides specialized information on topics such as banking and finance law, business law, corporate law/corporate governance/corporate compliance, and regulatory compliance. A first law degree is required for admission to LL.M programs, which typically last one year. For a list of LL.M specialties and the law schools that offer them, visit http://www.americanbar.org/groups/legal_educa tion/resources/accreditation.html.

■ CERTIFICATION, LICENSING, AND SPECIAL REQUIREMENTS
Certification or Licensing

Lawyers must be admitted to the bar of the state where they want to practice. Applicants must graduate from an American Bar Association-approved law school and pass a written examination. The ABA provides an overview of the process at http://www.americanbar.org/groups/ legal_education/resources/bar_admissions/basic_over view.html.

A lawyer who has extensive compliance responsibilities might consider earning the chartered regulatory counsel designation or the certified compliance officer credential from the Regulatory Compliance Association. Attorneys might also want to earn financial-related certifications such as the certified financial planner credential (which is offered by the CFP Board) and the chartered

financial consultant designation (American College of Financial Services).

■ EXPERIENCE, SKILLS, AND PERSONALITY TRAITS

Wealth management associates need a minimum of three to five years of experience with a major law firm, bank, securities regulator, or broker/dealer. Chief legal officers need seven to 10 years of experience.

Successful wealth management lawyers should have excellent problem-solving and analytical skills, confidence, the ability to multitask in a fast-paced work environment, keen business/legal judgment, strong communication skills, and organizational and problem-solving ability.

In 2015, the Association of Corporate Counsel surveyed chief legal officers regarding the non-legal skills they would like their legal department employees to develop. The most-cited skills were:

1. executive presence (cited by 51 percent of respondents)
2. business management (50 percent)
3. communication/listening (48 percent)
4. project management skills (48 percent)

■ EMPLOYMENT PROSPECTS
Employers

Lawyers work for major banks, broker/dealers, regional and boutique firms, robo advisory firms, and independent wealth managers. Others are employed by law firms that provide contracted services to these employers. Vault.com publishes an annual list of the 25 Best Law Firms for Banking & Financial Services (as ranked by associates). The top five firms in 2016 were:

1. Davis Polk & Wardwell LLP
2. Sullivan & Cromwell LLP
3. Cravath, Swaine & Moore LLP
4. Skadden, Arps, Slate, Meagher & Flom LLP and Affiliates
5. Simpson Thacher & Bartlett LLP

Visit http://www.vault.com/company-rankings/law/ best-law-firms-in-each-practice-area/?sRankID=324 to check out the list.

Starting Out

Most wealth management firms don't hire lawyers straight out of law school. Instead, they prefer to hire attorneys who have obtained several years of experience with a major law firm, a large bank, or other major financial employer. Some firms seek lawyers who have experience with a government regulator such as the Securities & Exchange Commission.

There are many ways to land an entry-level job in law. Many major employers recruit on campus, so check with your school's career services office for a schedule of recruiting visits. The campus interviewing process can be very challenging, and it's important to be well prepared. Visit the following Web site to learn more about how to ace campus interviews: http://www.chambers-associate.com/where-to -start/on-campus-interviews.

Other ways to learn more about job opportunities include using social media, attending networking events, joining professional associations and utilizing their career development resources, volunteering with legal aid associations, and attending industry conferences. Finally, contact law firms directly or visit their Web sites for information on career paths and methods of entry. Use the NALP Directory of Legal Employers (http://www.nalpdirectory.com) to search for employers by location, employer type, practice areas, and other criteria.

Unsure about what to do during the actual job-search (i.e., resumes, interviewing, etc.)? If so, the Association of Corporate Counsel is a good resource. It offers answers to frequently asked questions about resumes, cover letters, networking, interview strategies and preparation, and other job-search topics at http://www.acc.com/jobline.

■ ADVANCEMENT PROSPECTS

At a large wealth management firm, an associate with several years of experience can advance to the position of *managing attorney,* who supervises the work of other lawyers, paralegals, and legal secretaries. After seven to 10 years on the job, managing attorneys may advance to the position of *chief legal officer,* the top legal professional at the firm. Some chief legal officers eventually become partners or advance to become their organization's CEO or chief operating officer, or join corporate boards.

■ OUTLOOK

Employment for lawyers who work for firms that deal with funds, trusts, and other financial vehicles is expected to grow by 30 percent through 2024, according to the *Occupational Outlook Handbook (OOH).* Increasing government regulation is creating strong demand for lawyers to help wealth management partners navigate these often complex rules.

Many businesses are expanding their in-house legal departments to cut costs. "For many companies," according to the *OOH,* "the high cost of hiring outside counsel

ADVICE AND NEWS FOR CAREER SUCCESS

ONLINE RESOURCES

Career Success: Navigating the New Work Environment
http://www.cfapubs.org/toc/car/2015/2015/1
Career Success, which is both a book and a Web site, offers a detailed examination of the changing financial industry work environment, key skills that help one become successful, and strategies that readers can implement to reach their career goals. It also features interviews with more than 10 investment professionals.

eFinancialcareers
http://www.efinancialcareers.com
Visit this Web site for thousands of wealth management, accounting, compliance, risk management, private equity, and venture capital job listings. It also features articles about education and careers in a variety of financial sectors.

Futures in Finance
http://www.afponline.org/pub/store/pubs/fif.html
Futures in Finance is a free monthly newsletter that offers useful resources for those interested in finance and treasury careers. Each issue features job listings, articles on interviewing and finding a job, spotlights on hot careers, and information on compensation trends and incentive packages.

The gateway: business and careers newspaper for students
http://thegatewayonline.com
The gateway offers information on careers in banking, asset management, accounting, law, consulting, and technology. It also features internship and job listings.

Pensions & Investments
http://www.pionline.com/section/careers
Pensions & Investments, which bills itself as the "international newspaper of money management," has been published for more than 40 years. It provides job listings and information about the institutional investment market.

Private Asset Management
http://www.pammagazine.com
This resource provides breaking news about developments in the asset management industry. There is a cost to subscribe, but a two-week trial is free.

lawyers and their support staff makes it more economical to shift work to their in-house legal department. This will lead to an increase in the demand of lawyers in a variety of settings, such as financial and insurance firms, consulting firms, and health care providers."

■ UNIONS AND ASSOCIATIONS

Wealth management lawyers do not belong to unions, but many join professional associations that offer networking opportunities, continuing education (CE) classes and webinars, career assistance, specialty membership groups, publications, and other resources. Many legal professionals join the American Bar Association, one of the world's largest voluntary professional organizations with nearly 400,000 members. It accredits law schools; offers educational and career information; publishes journals such as *Business Lawyer, Student Lawyer,* and *ABA Journal;* and has an Institutional Investors Committee, Young Lawyers Division, and Business Law Section. The Association of Corporate Counsel is a membership organization for in-house counsel in the United States and more than 50 other countries. It publishes *ACC Docket* and the *Chief Legal Officers Survey,* offers information on careers, hosts an annual meeting, and provides professional development opportunities. The Association of American Law Schools, a nonprofit association of 180 law schools, offers information for prospective law students at http://www.aals.org/prospective-law-students. The American Bankers Association offers a variety of resources for those engaged in the practice of banking law, including *Banking Docket* and professional development classes and webinars. The Law School Admission Council and the National Association for Law Placement also provide many resources for law students and lawyers. Other useful organizations include the Minority Corporate Counsel Association, and the National Association of Women Lawyers.

Some lawyers join state and local bar associations to take advantage of networking opportunities, continuing education (CE) classes and webinars, career assistance, and other resources. For example, New York–based attorneys might join the New York State Bar Association, New York County Lawyers' Association, or the New York City Bar Association.

■ TIPS FOR ENTRY

1. Visit http://www.chambers-associate.com/where-to-start/compare-firms for a list of well-known law firms. At the site, you can compare firms by a variety of criteria, including starting salary, firm size and revenue, and diversity.
2. Become a student member of the American Bar Association to receive *Student Lawyer,* a magazine that contains useful information for aspiring lawyers, and other career and job-search resources. Sample articles from the magazine can be read at http://www.americanbar.org/groups/law

_students/publications.html. The ABA also offers a Before the Bar Blog and The Law Student Podcast.
3. Visit the following Web sites for job listings:
   - http://www.abalcc.org
   - http://www.acc.com/jobline
   - http://www.indeed.com/q-Wealth-Management-Attorney-jobs.html

■ FOR MORE INFORMATION

Visit the ABA's Web site for job listings and information on continuing education, its Wealth Management & Trust Conference, and the banking industry.

American Bankers Association (ABA)
1120 Connecticut Avenue, NW
Washington, D.C. 20036-3902
Tel: (800) 226-5377
http://www.aba.com

For information about law education and careers and its Young Lawyers Division, Institutional Investors Committee, and Business Law Section, contact

American Bar Association
321 North Clark Street
Chicago, IL 60654-7598
Tel: (800) 285-2221
http://www.americanbar.org

For information on continuing education and membership, contact

Association of Corporate Counsel
1025 Connecticut Avenue, NW, Suite 200
Washington, D.C. 20036-5425
Tel: (202) 293-4103
http://www.acc.com

Wealth Management Managing Directors

■ OVERVIEW

Wealth management managing directors are top-level executives who play a key role in formulating investment and business strategy for their firms, managing and developing staff, overseeing budgets, and maximizing profits, and managing expenses. Many also oversee the investment portfolios of the firm's top clients, as well as work with vice presidents, associates, and investor relations specialists to attract new clients. Managing directors are also known as *managing partners.*

HISTORY

The modern U.S. banking system can trace its roots to the time of the Civil War. It took a lot of money to maintain a large modern army, and the Union increasingly turned to modern methods of financing, including massive printing of paper money and issuing long-term debt with the help of financier Jay Cooke. Cooke sold more than $1.3 billion in federal bonds to help finance the war, and his agents penetrated even the smallest towns across the country, selling not just an investment return from the bonds, but banking as a patriotic institution. Together with the National Banking Act of 1863, the bonds provided the basis for a national banking system and established a national currency.

The new banking system helped foster rapid industrial transformation in the United States during the latter half of the 19th century. With increased industrialization and liquidity came increased concentrations of paper money in individual hands, often known as wealth. Unlike land, handling paper wealth requires private wealth managers. With increasing confidence in the banking system, more and more wealthy people turned to professionals, who worked either for banks or for brokerage firms, helping clients invest and protect their capital.

With total assets under management (AUM) reaching a record $74 trillion worldwide in 2014, according to The Boston Consulting Group, demand has only increased for skilled wealth management professionals, including managing directors.

THE JOB

Managing directors rank among the top decision makers in their firms. They help to establish and implement their company's overall investment strategy, client focus, and/or new business strategy. Their duties vary by employer. Many managing directors still work with clients, although they are typically the most high-profile, high-net-worth customers that the firm has—or the problem clients whose money is just too valuable for the firm to lose. Managing directors also oversee staff, serve on the firm's executive committees, and they may be asked to supervise a branch office or even the firm's main office. In specialty positions, managing directors may serve as their firm's chief investment officer, chief fiduciary officer, or general counsel.

Duties performed by managing directors include:

- working with the firm's board of directors to devise, implement, and maintain investment policies and strategies
- providing investment recommendations to the firm's financial advisors

QUICK FACTS
ALTERNATE TITLE(S) Managing Partners
DUTIES Formulate investment and business strategy for their firms, manage and develop staff, oversee budgets, manage the investment portfolios of clients, work to attract new clients
SALARY RANGE $100,000 to $250,000 to $5 million+
WORK ENVIRONMENT Primarily Indoors
BEST GEOGRAPHIC LOCATION(S) Opportunities are best in areas where a large number of high-net-worth individuals reside
MINIMUM EDUCATION LEVEL Bachelor's Degree, Master's Degree
SCHOOL SUBJECTS Business, Economics, Mathematics
EXPERIENCE At least 10 years of management and investment experience and a proven record bringing in new business
PERSONALITY TRAITS Enterprising, Hands On, Organized
SKILLS Business Management, Financial, Leadership
CERTIFICATION OR LICENSING Required
SPECIAL REQUIREMENTS None
EMPLOYMENT PROSPECTS Fair
ADVANCEMENT PROSPECTS Poor
OUTLOOK About as Fast as the Average
NOC 0013, 0111
O*NET-SOC 11-1011.00, 11-9199.03

- designing and maintaining financial portfolios
- working with the firm's top clients to develop wealth and investment management strategies that match their goals and risk tolerance levels
- participating in the development of new business, including the creation of presentation materials for prospective customers

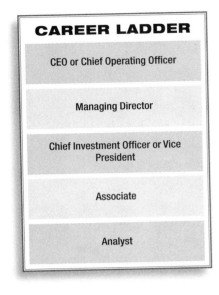

CAREER LADDER

CEO or Chief Operating Officer

Managing Director

Chief Investment Officer or Vice President

Associate

Analyst

- conducting investment research and preparing investment reports for the board
- ensuring that various departments (e.g., risk, accounting, investor relations, compliance, etc.) function effectively
- leading weekly meetings with the investment team and other departments
- managing staff resources to ensure proper client service
- establishing and managing departmental policies and procedures relating to the operational control environment
- maintaining and overseeing the work of third-party service providers
- managing operational risks and legal and compliance issues
- visiting branch offices, as necessary, to ensure their proper functioning
- coaching and mentoring wealth management advisors to help them meet service benchmarks and sales goals
- developing and maintaining financial research programs to ensure that the firm remains on the cutting-edge
- preparing and managing an annual budget, ensuring that revenue flows are maximized and fixed costs are effectively managed

■ EARNINGS

Managing directors in the asset management industry earned median annual salaries of $143,987 in February 2016, according to PayScale.com. It also reports that managing directors earned bonuses that ranged from $4,966 to $195,743, average profit sharing compensation of $15,000, and average commission on sales of $30,000.

Experienced managing directors at large firms can earn $500,000 to $5 million or more (including bonuses).

Wealth management firms, especially large ones, offer a variety of exceptional benefits. For example, Ameriprise Financial (a financial services firm with more than $800 billion in assets under management and administration) offers medical, dental, and vision insurance; annual performance-based incentives; tuition reimbursement; a 401(k) plan with a company match; life and disability insurance; an on-site health services clinic and an on-site fitness center (at its Minneapolis headquarters), and flexible work arrangements, among other benefits.

■ WORK ENVIRONMENT

A day in the life of a managing director can be very busy, involving lots of meetings with the investment team, phone calls and in-person consultations with current and potential investors, and hours at their desks brainstorming new investment, marketing, or staff training ideas. Managing directors are often supported by administrative staff (secretaries, clerks, etc.), and they usually have large offices that are equipped with the latest office equipment and computer technology. Approximately 50 percent of top executives worked more than 40 hours a week in 2014, according to the U.S. Department of Labor.

■ EXPLORING

Some of the easiest ways to learn more about the wealth management industry are to read books and journals about the field. Here are a few suggestions:

- *InvestmentNews:* http://www.investmentnews.com
- *Chief Investment Officer:* http://www.ai-cio.com
- *The Financial Times Guide to Wealth Management: How to Plan, Invest, and Protect Your Financial Assets* (FT Press, 2015)
- *Financial Independence: An Advisor's Guide to Comprehensive Wealth Management* (John Wiley & Sons, 2013)
- *Worth:* http://worth.com

Consider joining Future Business Leaders of America (FBLA, http://www.fbla-pbl.org), a membership organization for middle school and high school students. Its sister organization, Phi Beta Lambda, is available for college students. FBLA offers co-curricular educational programs, networking events with accomplished business professionals, community service projects, and academic events that cover public speaking, business, finance, technology, management, and more.

Goldman Sachs offers a free career newsletter for aspiring wealth management professionals. You can sign up at http://www.goldmansachs.com/careers/why-goldman-sachs/our-culture/newsletter-signup.

■ EDUCATION AND TRAINING REQUIREMENTS
High School

Most WM firms prefer to hire wealth managers who attended an Ivy League college or other elite university, so be sure to work hard in high school in order to earn stellar grades that will increase your chances of being accepted by a top college. In high school, take classes in business, economics, accounting, statistics, and mathematics. Managing directors need strong communication skills so take as many English and speech classes as possible—and join your school's debate club. Other recommended classes include computer science, history, social studies, and foreign language.

Postsecondary Education

Some smaller firms may hire managing directors with only a bachelor's degree in finance, mathematics, accounting, economics, business, entrepreneurism, financial engineering, or quantitative finance, but top firms typically require applicants to have a master's degree in one of these disciplines.

Other Education or Training

The writer Louis L'Amour was on the mark when he said, "No one can get an education, for of necessity education is a continuing process." Most wealth management professionals will discover soon after college that they'll need to update their industry knowledge and skills throughout their careers.

Many professional associations offer continuing education opportunities via webinars at seminars and workshops at conferences, and in other settings. For example, the American Bankers Association offers workshops, seminars, and webinars on accounting, compliance, cybersecurity, legal, and risk management issues. It also provides educational opportunities related to trust/wealth management via its Center for Securities, Trust and Investments. Recent classes included Basic Administrative Duties of a Trustee, Introduction to Trust Products and Services, and Asset Allocation and Portfolio Management.

Other opportunities are provided by the Association of International Wealth Management, Investment Management Consultants Association, American Institute of Certified Public Accountants, Association for Financial Counseling and Planning Education, Association for Financial Professionals, Certified Financial Planner Board of Standards, CFA Institute, and the Institute for Private Investors.

Certification

As they climb the WM industry career ladder, many aspiring managing directors earn educational certificates that provide a general overview of a particular field or a specific topic. Here are a few popular certificates:

- certificate in business accounting (Chartered Institute of Management Accountants)

The managing director of a wealth management firm discusses his investment philosophy with staff. (dotshock. Shutterstock.)

- essentials of investment consulting, applied behavioral finance, fundamentals of alternative investments (Investment Management Consultants Association)
- international auditing and international financial reporting (Association of Chartered Certified Accountants)
- international financial reporting standards (American Institute of Certified Public Accountants).

Many colleges and universities offer certificates in finance, financial planning, accounting, business management, and related fields. Contact schools in your area to learn more.

■ CERTIFICATION, LICENSING, AND SPECIAL REQUIREMENTS
Certification or Licensing

Managing directors do not need to be certified, but many employers require those in lower-level positions to be certified. With competition extremely strong for jobs, it's a good idea to earn a certification or two to increase your attractiveness to potential employers. Many organizations offer certification to wealth management professionals, including:

- American Bankers Association (certified trust and financial advisor, certified corporate trust specialist, certified IRA services professional, certified retirement services professional, certified securities operations professional)
- American College of Financial Services (chartered financial consultant)
- Association for Financial Counseling and Planning Education (accredited financial counselor)

ALEXANDRA LEBENTHAL, CO-CEO OF LEBENTHAL HOLDINGS, CEO OF LEBENTHAL WEALTH ADVISORS, LLC, AND CEO OF LEBENTHAL & CO., LLC

MOVERS AND SHAKERS

Alexandra Lebenthal is the co-chief executive officer (CEO) of Lebenthal Holdings, CEO of Lebenthal Wealth Advisors, LLC, and CEO of Lebenthal & Co., LLC, which her grandparents founded in 1925. She launched her career in the municipal bond department at Kidder Peabody Inc., a well-known securities firm. Lebenthal has received many awards for her work, including being named one of the "50 Most Influential Women in Private Wealth" by *Private Asset Management* in 2015. She is also the author of *The Recessionistas,* a novel that satirizes the "challenges" faced by ultra-wealthy investment bankers and their trophy wives after the financial crisis in the late 2000s.

Lebenthal is a strong supporter of women in the private wealth management industry. She serves on the board of The Committee of 200, which lobbies for increased leadership positions for women in business, and a board member of Savvy Ladies, a nonprofit organization that provides financial education and resources for women. She also founded *Sayra* (which is named after her grandmother who founded her firm), a magazine for female financial advisors. (Visit http://www.lebenthal.com/sayra to read the latest issue.) Lebenthal is a leading advocate for increasing the number of women in private wealth management—especially in family offices. "The family office environment is very conducive for women wanting to work in the private wealth industry," she told *Private Asset Management*. "It allows professionals to be involved in so many different aspects of finance and management, and when managing one family's vast amounts of wealth, it is a very unique working environment….it is always a section of the industry I suggest women explore."

Sources: Lebenthal & Co.; *Private Asset Management*

- CFP Board (certified financial planner)
- fi360 (accredited investment fiduciary, accredited investment fiduciary analyst, professional plan consultant)
- Institute of Business and Finance (certified fund specialist, certified annuity specialist, certified estate and trust specialist, certified income specialist, certified tax specialist)
- Investment Adviser Association (chartered investment counselor)

- Investment Management Consultants Association (certified investment management analyst, chartered private wealth advisor).

Wealth managers are usually required to obtain their Series 7 and Series 63, 65, or 66 credentials from the Financial Industry Regulatory Authority, which is the self-regulatory arm of the investment industry. The Series 7, or General Securities Representative certification, allows you to buy or sell, or solicit the purchase or sale, of all securities products, including corporate securities, municipal securities, municipal fund securities, options, direct participation programs, investment company products, and variable contracts. It's the most basic form of certification for anybody involved with the markets. The majority of firms will also require a Series 63 registration, which requires knowledge of state securities laws and allows you to be a securities agent. Other firms may require the Series 66 (which covers the same ground as a Series 63, but also certifies you to act as a registered investment adviser) and the Series 65 (which certifies you to act as an investment adviser representative).

■ EXPERIENCE, SKILLS, AND PERSONALITY TRAITS

At least 10 years of management and investment experience and a proven track record of generating new business are required to work as a managing director.

Leadership skills are extremely important for managing directors because they must inspire their staff to meet performance goals and set an example of professionalism that permeates their firm—from the vice presidents who report to them to analysts straight out of college. They also must be strategic and analytical thinkers; have excellent communication, customer service, and sales skills; possess expertise regarding financial planning concepts (including comprehensive knowledge of their firm's products and services); and have good organizational, problem-solving, and time-management skills.

■ EMPLOYMENT PROSPECTS
Employers

There are more than 3,190 wealth management businesses in the United States alone. Many U.S.-based firms are headquartered in New York and other major cities such as Boston, Chicago, Dallas, Denver, Houston, Los Angeles, and San Francisco. Many large U.S. firms have offices in foreign countries.

Global wealth market research and strategy consultancy firm Scorpio Partnership reports that the 10 largest private banks (based on assets under management) in the world as of December 31, 2014, were:

1. UBS ($2.035 trillion)
2. Morgan Stanley ($2.025 trillion)
3. Bank of America Merrill Lynch ($1.984 trillion)
4. Credit Suisse ($883 billion)
5. Royal Bank of Scotland ($704 billion)
6. Citi ($550 billion)
7. J.P. Morgan Chase ($428 billion)
8. BNP Paribas ($370 billion)
9. HSBC ($365 billion)
10. Goldman Sachs ($363 billion)

Starting Out

The career of managing director is not entry-level, and it takes many years of experience in lower-level positions (analysts, associates, portfolio managers, vice presidents) to become qualified to enter this occupation.

While in college, use the resources of your school's career services office to locate jobs, improve your resume, and practice your interviewing skills. Many wealth management firms recruit on college campuses. Check with your career counselor or visit the Web sites of WM firms for recruiting schedules.

Participating in an internship at a WM firm is an excellent way to break into the field. Many of the largest firms have internship programs in place, which they use to identify promising candidates for full-time employment. For example, the well-known financial services firm Edward Jones offers several internship programs (http://careers.edwardjones.com/explore -opportunities/students)—including a Financial Advisor Internship Program, Financial Advisor Career Development Program, and internships at the firm's headquarters. Each year, Vault.com ranks the best internship programs (including those offered by the financial services industry). Visit http://www.vault.com/ internship-rankings/top-10-internships/?&rYear=2016 for the latest list.

Other job-search strategies include using social networking sites (such as LinkedIn), hiring recruiters for assistance in the job search, using job sites, and applying for jobs at the Web sites of potential employers.

■ ADVANCEMENT PROSPECTS

Managing directors sit at the top of the management structure at WM firms, so there are not a lot of advancement opportunities. Directors who are not already partners at their firms can advance by becoming partners. Others may leave their firms to work in identical positions at companies with more assets under management or higher industry prestige. Some managing directors move on to work as chief financial officers, CEOs, and chief operating officers at corporations.

■ OUTLOOK

Employment for top executives is expected to grow by 6 percent through 2024, according to the U.S. Department of Labor (DOL). The DOL reports that "top executives are expected to face very strong competition for jobs. The high pay and prestige associated with these positions attract many qualified applicants." Since most wealth management firms have one or only a handful of managing directors, it is extremely difficult to ascend to this top position. Wealth management professionals with extensive managerial experience, an excellent track record of generating strong investment returns for clients, and who keep the new investor pipeline flowing will have the best job prospects.

■ UNIONS AND ASSOCIATIONS

Wealth management managing directors do not belong to unions. Some join or utilize the resources of professional associations such as the American Bankers Association, Association for Financial Counseling and Planning Education, Association for Financial Professionals, Association of International Wealth Management, Certified Financial Planner Board of Standards, CFA Institute, Chartered Alternate Investment Analyst Association, Institute for Private Investors, International Association for Quantitative Finance, International Association of Registered Financial Consultants, New York Society of Security Analysts, and the Securities Industry and Financial Markets Association. These organizations offer everything from certification and professional development opportunities, to networking events and career blogs, to publications and annual conferences.

■ TIPS FOR ENTRY

1. Work in lower-level positions in the wealth management industry to obtain experience.
2. Visit the following Web sites for advice on landing an entry-level career in the WM industry:
   - JPMorgan Advice Center: http://careers.jpmor gan.com/student/jpmorgan/careers/us/advice
   - Raymond James: Career Advice Center: http:// raymondjames.com/careers/students.htm
   - Standard Life Investments: http://www.stan dardlifeinvestments.com/careers/recruitment _process/index.html
3. Participate in continuing education classes throughout your career and become certified to prepare yourself for work at the top levels of the WM industry.
4. Join the American Bar Association Trust Network (http://www.aba.com/Tools/Function/Trust), an

online discussion forum for wealth management professionals.

■ FOR MORE INFORMATION

Visit the ABA's Web site for job listings and information on continuing education, its Wealth Management & Trust Conference, and the banking industry.

American Bankers Association (ABA)
1120 Connecticut Avenue, NW
Washington, D.C. 20036-3902
Tel: (800) 226-5377
http://www.aba.com

For information on certification, membership, and job listings, contact

Association for Financial Counseling and Planning Education
1940 Duke Street, Suite 200
Alexandria, VA 22314-3452
Tel: (703) 684-4484
http://www.afcpe.org

For information on earnings, careers, and certification, contact

Association for Financial Professionals
4520 East-West Highway, Suite 750
Bethesda, MD 20814-3574
Tel: (301) 907-2862
http://www.afponline.org

For information on membership and certification, contact
Association of International Wealth Management
E-mail: info@aiwm.org
http://www.aiwm.org

For information on certification and careers, contact
Certified Financial Planner Board of Standards
1425 K Street, NW, #800
Washington, D.C. 20005-3673
Tel: (800) 487-1497
E-mail: mail@cfpboard.org
http://www.cfp.net

Visit the institute's Web site for information on certification for financial analysts.
CFA Institute
915 East High Street
Charlottesville, VA 22902-4868
Tel: (800) 247-8132
E-mail: info@cfainstitute.org
http://www.cfainstitute.org

This trade organization promotes the professional education of financial advisors and planners.

International Association of Registered Financial Consultants
The Financial Planning Building
PO Box 42506
Middletown, OH 45042-0506
Tel: (800) 532-9060
http://www.iarfc.org

Visit the NYSSA Web site for information on membership for college students, a list of top employers of financial analysts, and scholarships for graduate students.

New York Society of Security Analysts (NYSSA)
1540 Broadway, Suite 1010
New York, NY 10036-4083
Tel: (212) 541-4530
http://www.nyssa.org

For information on education and careers, contact
Securities Industry and Financial Markets Association
120 Broadway, 35th Floor
New York, NY 10271-3599
Tel: (212) 313-1200
http://www.sifma.org

For information on membership and continuing education, contact
Women in Insurance and Financial Services
136 Everett Road
Albany, NY 12205-1418
Tel: (866) 264-9437
E-mail: office@wifsnational.org
http://www.wifsnational.org

Wealth Management Risk Managers

■ OVERVIEW

Risk managers use their quantitative, financial, analytical, and technology skills to identify, study, and work to reduce risks (e.g., risky investment strategies, Information Technology, and compliance) at wealth management firms. They are also known as *chief risk officers, risk officers,* and *risk analysts.*

■ HISTORY

Businesses have utilized risk management strategies ever since the first product or service was created. In the 1950s, risk management emerged as a specialty due to the growing complexity of business operations and manufacturing processes.

In the wealth management industry, demand for chief risk officers (CROs) grew rapidly after the Great Recession (December 2007-June 2009) as a result of increasing government regulation of the financial sector and escalating concerns by investors regarding risk factors that could affect their investments. In 2014, 92 percent of financial services organizations surveyed by professional services firm Deloitte reported that they had a CRO or equivalent position on staff—a sharp increase from the 65 percent of companies that said so in 2002.

■ THE JOB

Developing and maintaining effective risk management (RM) practices is key to the success of any wealth management business. While wealth management partners have used RM strategies since the early days of the industry, more emphasis is being placed on RM due to increasing government regulation and growing competition between WM firms for the investment dollars of high-net-worth individuals. "The wealth management industry is centered on trust," according to *10 Disruptive Trends in Wealth Management,* a report from Deloitte & Touche LLP. "One 'risk event' such as a cyber-attack or a major regulatory fine, can destroy that trust, and in turn, the reputation of the institution."

According to Deloitte & Touche LLP, the most common types of risk in the wealth management industry relate to the following areas:

- trading practices
- compliance
- portfolio management
- regulatory reporting
- information management and security
- middle/back office oversight
- branch supervision
- client on-boarding

Major duties of risk management professionals include:

- designing and implementing an enterprise risk management program to assess and manage risks
- managing the risk management process, including implementing and monitoring stress tests, back-tests, and sensitivity analysis for funds and firm assets
- reviewing, testing, and implementing various risk models and producing model review reports

QUICK FACTS

ALTERNATE TITLE(S)
Chief Risk Officers, Risk Analysts, Risk Officers

DUTIES
Identify, analyze, and mitigate risks; design and implement a risk management program; coordinate with compliance officers and managers

SALARY RANGE
$49,000 to $178,000 to $206,000+

WORK ENVIRONMENT
Primarily Indoors

BEST GEOGRAPHIC LOCATION(S)
Opportunities are best in areas where a large number of high-net-worth individuals reside

MINIMUM EDUCATION LEVEL
Bachelor's Degree

SCHOOL SUBJECTS
Business, Economics, Mathematics

EXPERIENCE
At least 10 years in risk management positions for chief risk officers; five years of risk-related experience for managers; one to two years of work or internship experience for risk analysts

PERSONALITY TRAITS
Organized, Problem-Solving, Realistic

SKILLS
Business Management, Financial, Interpersonal

CERTIFICATION OR LICENSING
Recommended

SPECIAL REQUIREMENTS
None

EMPLOYMENT PROSPECTS
Good

ADVANCEMENT PROSPECTS
Fair

OUTLOOK
Much Faster than the Average

NOC
0111

O*NET-SOC
13-2099.02

- developing and monitoring risk information systems and technology infrastructure
- gathering client information to identify, present, and mitigate risks
- working closely with the firm's chief compliance officer to ensure that regular compliance

CAREER LADDER

Managing Director

Partner

Chief Risk Officer

Risk Manager

Risk Management Analyst

filings are made to regulatory bodies

- documenting and reporting risk policy issues to the firm's risk committee
- constantly working to identify new and emerging risks

■ EARNINGS

Chief risk officers earned median annual salaries of $178,000 in 2013, according to RIMS-The Risk Management Society. The lowest 25 percent earned $148,500 or less, while the top 25 percent earned $206,000 or more. Chief risk officers also received average yearly bonuses of $55,500. Salaries for risk management analysts ranged from $49,000 to $80,000 or more, with an average bonus of $6,000.

Risk managers receive benefits such as paid vacation and sick days, health and life insurance, pensions, and stock options. Benefits can be very generous at top investment banks. For example, Credit Suisse (which ranks among the four largest firms in the industry) offers flexible work schedules and job sharing, family-focused programs (e.g., adoption leave, childcare services, eldercare services), on-site fitness centers, work/life coaching, and employee discounts on various products and services (such as bank and insurance products).

■ WORK ENVIRONMENT

Approximately 33 percent of financial managers (including risk managers) worked more than 40 hours per week in 2014, according to the U.S. Department of Labor. This career can be both rewarding (when risk managers are able to identify areas of risk that could have caused major issues for their firm) and sometimes stressful (when the firm's executives do not agree with the opinions of the risk manager, or if he or she fails to identify a major area of risk before it causes the firm to lose money or clients). Some risk managers travel to conduct on-site risk assessments at third-party service providers, and to attend industry conferences, road shows, and other events.

■ EXPLORING

There are many ways to learn about a career in risk management. One of the easiest ways to do so is by reading books about the field. Here are two suggestions: *The Essentials of Risk Management* (McGraw-Hill Education,

2014) and *Risk Management and Financial Institutions* (John Wiley & Sons, 2015).

Some colleges have risk management clubs for business students. Check with your school to see if it has such a club, or at least a business club, that you can join. Consider competing in the Spencer-RIMS Risk Management Challenge (https://www.rims.org/member ship/Students/Pages/RIMSRiskManagementChallenge. aspx), a competition for college students in the U.S. and Canada that will help you to develop your risk management skills.

Nearly every organization—whether it's a university, wealth management firm, government agency, or a corporation—has risk management protocols in place (many of which are posted online). After reviewing a few of these plans (and the aforementioned RM books), try to create a risk management plan for a school event.

■ EDUCATION AND TRAINING REQUIREMENTS
High School

In high school, take classes that help you to develop your communication skills (including those in English, speech, and creative writing), financial and business acumen (economics, mathematics, accounting, and business), computer skills (database management, computer and information security), and critical-thinking abilities (philosophy, history, and social studies).

Postsecondary Education

You'll need a minimum of a bachelor's degree in risk management, insurance, accounting, finance, economics, business, computer science, or management information systems to work in risk management, although some employers prefer to hire those with graduate degrees. Be sure to augment your studies in one of these areas with classes in financial planning or wealth management so that you can obtain a working understanding of the financial aspects of the business.

Fewer than 65 colleges and universities in the United States and Canada—including Baylor University, Kent State University, Temple University, and the University of Pennsylvania—offer degrees in risk management. Visit http://www.aria.org/RMI_Programs.htm for a list of schools that offer certificates and bachelor's and graduate degrees in the field.

Other Education or Training

Professional associations offer a wealth of continuing education classes, workshops, and webinars that help risk managers keep their skills up to date. For example, the Global Association of Risk Professionals offers Foundations of Financial Risk, a class for entry-level professionals that details how banks operate, how they're governed, and how they're regulated. RIMS-The Risk Management Society provides webinars such as "Cybersecurity Risks in a Mobile Device and Internet of Things World" and "Continuity Risk Management: What Every Risk Professional Should Know." The Public Risk Management Association and the American Bankers Association also provide professional development opportunities.

Certification

The Professional Risk Managers' International Association offers the associate professional risk manager; credit and counterparty manager; market, liquidity, and asset liability management risk manager; and operational risk manager certificates. Visit http://www.prmia.org/certificate-programs to learn more. The Institute of Risk Management offers the international certificate in risk management to applicants who pass multiple-choice and written examinations. Visit https://www.theirm.org/qualifications/international-certificate-in-risk-management for more information.

■ CERTIFICATION, LICENSING, AND SPECIAL REQUIREMENTS
Certification or Licensing

Several associations offer certification programs for risk management professionals. For example, the Global Association of Risk Professionals offers the financial risk manager (FRM) credential. According to the association, "earning the FRM signals to employers that you are serious about risk management and that you have had your knowledge validated against international professional standards." To receive the FRM credential, candidates must pass a two-part examination and have two years of qualified work experience. Visit http://www.garp.org/#!/frm for more information. Other certification credentials are offered by the:

- National Alliance for Insurance Education & Research (certified risk manager, https://www.scic.com/courses/CRM)
- RIMS—The Risk Management Society (RIMS-certified risk management professional, http://www.RIMS.org/certification)
- Professional Risk Managers' International Association (professional risk manager, http://www.prmia.org/certificate-programs)

Some firms seek risk managers who have earned the chartered financial analyst credential, which is administered by the CFA Institute (http://www.cfainstitute.org/programs/cfaprogram).

RISK STRATEGIES FOR MANAGING WEALTH

LEARN MORE ABOUT IT

Brown, Aaron. *Financial Risk Management For Dummies.* Hoboken, N.J.: For Dummies, 2015.

Crouhy, Michel, Robert Mark, and Dan Galai. *The Essentials of Risk Management,* 2nd ed. New York: McGraw-Hill Education, 2014.

Ferguson, Niall. *The Ascent of Money: A Financial History of the World.* New York: Penguin Books, 2009.

Hubbard, Glenn P., and Anthony P. O'Brien. *Money, Banking, and the Financial System,* 2nd ed. Upper Saddle River, N.J.: Prentice Hall, 2013.

Mills, Annie, and Peter Haines. *Essential Strategies for Financial Services Compliance,* 2nd ed. Hoboken, N.J.: John Wiley & Sons, 2015.

Peterson, Steven. *Investment Theory and Risk Management.* Hoboken, N.J.: John Wiley & Sons, 2012.

Piketty, Thomas. *Capital in the Twenty-First Century.* Cambridge, Mass.: Belknap Press, 2014.

Pritchard, Carl L. *Risk Management: Concepts and Guidance,* 5th ed. New York: Auerbach Publications, 2014.

Sehgal, Kabir. *Coined: The Rich Life of Money and How Its History Has Shaped Us.* New York: Grand Central Publishing, 2015.

Shiller, Robert J. *Irrational Exuberance,* 3rd ed. Princeton, N.J.: Princeton University Press, 2015.

Smith Jr., Winthrop H. *Catching Lightning in a Bottle: How Merrill Lynch Revolutionized the Financial World.* Hoboken, N.J.: John Wiley & Sons, 2014.

Weatherall, James Owen. *The Physics of Wall Street: A Brief History of Predicting the Unpredictable.* Boston: Mariner Books, 2014

■ EXPERIENCE, SKILLS, AND PERSONALITY TRAITS

Chief risk officers must have a minimum of 10 years of experience in lower-level risk management positions. Risk managers need at least five years of experience in risk management, and risk analysts need a year or two of experience (a combination of an internship, co-operative education experience, or part-time job) in a risk management position at a corporation.

To be a successful risk management professional, you'll need excellent communication and interpersonal skills, confidence, and an independent mindset to effectively interact with colleagues who may not always agree with your risk assessments; expertise in risk identification and analysis techniques; strong quantitative skills and the ability to use risk management software; excellent analytical and problem-solving skills; creativity; and intellectual curiosity.

■ EMPLOYMENT PROSPECTS

Employers

Risk managers work for banks, investment firms, broker/dealers, and family offices. They also are employed by accounting and consulting firms that provide risk management services to banks and other wealth management companies.

Chief risk officers are most likely to be employed by large institutions. In 2014, 100 percent of large financial services organizations surveyed by professional services firm Deloitte reported that they had a chief risk officer (CRO). Ninety-seven percent of medium-size institutions reported having a CRO, compared to 69 percent of small companies.

In addition to employment in the wealth management industry, risk managers work for corporations of all types, government agencies, the U.S. military, and nonprofit organizations.

Starting Out

Professional associations provide many excellent job-search resources. For example, RIMS—The Risk Management Society offers a Career Tools section on its Web site (https://www.rims.org/resources/CareerCenter/Resources) that features articles on resume writing, networking, career success, and other topics. Its site also provides job listings, information on the Spencer-RIMS Risk Management Challenge (which will allow you to start building your skills and your professional network), and details on its annual conference.

Other job-search strategies include networking at career fairs and on social media sites, using the resources of your college's career services office, participating in internships, using the services of recruiters, and applying for jobs directly at the Web sites of potential employers.

■ ADVANCEMENT PROSPECTS

At an investment bank or a large wealth management firm, a skilled risk analyst can advance to the position of risk manager after five years on the job, and then to chief risk officer (after working as a risk manager for 10 years). Some risk management professionals become partners, receiving an ownership stake in the firm.

In addition to working in risk management positions at corporations, risk managers also can work as independent consultants. Some leave the profession to become teachers at colleges and universities.

■ OUTLOOK

Employment for financial managers who work for firms that manage funds, trusts, and other financial vehicles will grow by 19 percent through 2024, according to the U.S. Department of Labor, or much faster than the average for all careers.

Increasing regulation of the wealth management industry and growing interest by investors in assessing the quality of risk management programs in place at WM firms are creating demand for risk managers. According to Deloitte & Touche LLP's *Global Risk Management Survey,* "Financial institutions are adjusting to the new environment for risk management. Most institutions will need to enhance their risk management programs to stay current—improving analytical capabilities, investing in risk data and information systems, attracting risk management talent, fostering an ethical culture, and aligning incentive compensation practices with risk appetite. They will find that business strategies and models must be reassessed in response to changed regulations more often than before. Perhaps most important, institutions will need to develop the flexibility to respond nimbly to the 'new normal' risk management environment of unceasing regulatory change."

■ UNIONS AND ASSOCIATIONS

Wealth management risk managers do not belong to unions. Some become members of professional associations that provide certification and continuing education programs, publications, and career resources. For example, the Professional Risk Managers' International Association offers the professional risk manager credential and the associate professional risk manager certificate, provides career webinars, publishes *Intelligent Risk* (a quarterly journal for its members), and offers more than 200 meetings each year through its local chapters. The American Bankers Association represents the "nation's $15 trillion banking industry, which is composed of small, regional and large banks that together employ more than 2 million people." It provides extensive continuing-education programs, hosts the Wealth Management & Trust Conference, and publishes the *ABA Banking Journal.* Other noteworthy organizations include the American Risk and Insurance Association, Global Association of Risk Professionals, Public Risk Management Association, RIMS-The Risk Management Society, and RMA-The Risk Management Association.

■ TIPS FOR ENTRY

1. Get certified. It will give you the edge over other applicants.
2. Visit the following web sites for job listings:
   - http://jobs.prmia.org/home/index.cfm?site_id=13141

- http://www.careerbuilder.com/jobs/keyword/risk-manager
- http://www.pionline.com/section/careers
- http://www.riskmanagementweb.com
3. Attend industry conferences to network and learn more about the field. RIMS-The Risk Management Society offers information on its annual conference, as well as regional conferences and summits, at its Web site, https://www.rims.org.

■ FOR MORE INFORMATION

Visit the ABA's Web site for job listings and information on continuing education, its Wealth Management & Trust Conference, and the banking industry.

American Bankers Association (ABA)
1120 Connecticut Avenue, NW
Washington, D.C. 20036-3902
Tel: (800) 226-5377
http://www.aba.com

For information on membership and networking, contact
Global Association of Risk Professionals
111 Town Square Place, 14th Floor
Jersey City, NJ 07310-1755
Tel: (201) 719-7210
http://www.garp.org

For information on certification and continuing education, contact
Professional Risk Managers' International Association
400 Washington Street
Northfield, MN 55057-2027
Tel: (612) 605-5370
http://www.prmia.org

For information on membership, certification, and continuing education, contact
RIMS-The Risk Management Society
5 Bryant Park, 13th Floor
New York, NY 10018
Tel: (212) 286-9292
https://www.rims.org

For information on membership and continuing education, contact
RMA-The Risk Management Association
1801 Market Street, Suite 300
Philadelphia, PA 19103-1628
Tel: (800) 677-7621
http://www.rmahq.org

Wealth Management Vice Presidents

■ OVERVIEW

Wealth management vice presidents are highly skilled upper-level managers who oversee the investment portfolios of clients, work to attract new clients, manage associates and analysts, and play a major role in formulating strategy for their firms. They are also known as *private bankers* and *wealth managers.*

■ HISTORY

In the 1860s and 1870s, the growing number of affluent people (fueled by industrialization and profits made via rebuilding towns and infrastructure after the Civil War), and increasing trust in the U.S. banking system spurred the wealthy to search for skilled financial professionals to manage their fortunes and grow their capital. Since then, the wealth management industry has grown steadily, only declining during financial crises—such as the Great Depression (1929–39) and the Great Recession (December 2007 to June 2009)—and banking and financial scandals.

The number of millionaires and billionaires worldwide has grown rapidly in the last three decades. From 1987 to 2012, the number of billionaires in the United States increased tenfold, from 41 billionaires in 1987 to 425 billionaires in 2012. Worldwide, the number of billionaires reached 2,325 in 2014, according to the Wealth X-UBS Billionaire Census, an increase of 7 percent from 2013. The Census predicts that the global billionaire population will surpass 3,800 by 2020. This growth bodes well for wealth management professionals.

■ THE JOB

Job duties for vice presidents (VPs) vary by firm. At some firms, VPs manage client portfolios and prospect for new investors, while also playing a major decision-making role regarding the firm's investment strategies and products, marketing, risk issues, compliance, etc., as well as overseeing the work of associates, analysts, and other staff. At other firms, VPs may no longer manage portfolios and prospect for new investors, but rather specialize in a particular type of investment (equity mutual funds, bonds, real estate investment trusts, etc.), assisting other private bankers with their work in these areas. Others may be asked to launch and manage a new branch office in another city. Major duties of the typical vice president include:

QUICK FACTS

ALTERNATE TITLE(S)
Private Bankers, Wealth Managers

DUTIES
Manage the investment portfolios of clients, work to attract new clients, oversee associates and analysts, and collaborate with other executives to formulate strategy for the firm

SALARY RANGE
$95,112 to $144,962 to $3 million+

WORK ENVIRONMENT
Primarily Indoors

BEST GEOGRAPHIC LOCATION(S)
Opportunities are best in areas where a large number of high-net-worth individuals reside

MINIMUM EDUCATION LEVEL
Bachelor's Degree, Master's Degree

SCHOOL SUBJECTS
Business, Economics, Mathematics

EXPERIENCE
Ten years investment experience and a proven record of bringing in new business

PERSONALITY TRAITS
Enterprising, Hands On, Organized

SKILLS
Business Management, Financial, Leadership

CERTIFICATION OR LICENSING
Required

SPECIAL REQUIREMENTS
None

EMPLOYMENT PROSPECTS
Good

ADVANCEMENT PROSPECTS
Fair

OUTLOOK
Faster than the Average

NOC
0013, 0111

O*NET-SOC
11-1011.00, 11-9199.03

- creating comprehensive wealth management plans for high-net-worth individuals and families
- developing and recommending investment ideas to managing directors
- monitoring capital market developments and conducting investment-related research in order to develop investment opportunities
- developing quantitative models to measure the effectiveness of investment decisions
- developing portfolio strategic asset allocation and tactical asset location strategies
- working with risk managers on risk management issues (i.e., liquidity, compliance, etc.)
- creating and maintaining a pipeline of high-net-worth individuals and families and successfully transitioning prospects into clients
- working with wealth managers to make sure that potential new clients are properly on-boarded (i.e., the process of gathering new client information and inputting that data, as well as conducting due diligence on the client)
- partnering with the human resources department to create and implement training programs to teach core customer service skills to team members
- working with other top-level executives to develop product and service offerings, create sales and marketing strategies, and establish budgets
- working with the compliance department to ensure that compliance requirements for products and services have been met

■ EARNINGS

Senior vice presidents who were employed in the asset management industry earned median annual salaries of $144,962 in February 2016, according to PayScale.com. Salaries ranged from $95,112 to $231,054. PayScale.com also reports that senior vice presidents earned bonuses that ranged from $4,500 to $101,471, average profit sharing compensation of $10,174, and average commission on sales of $20,000.

After years of service, the best-performing vice presidents can have income (i.e., salary, bonuses, profit sharing, and commissions) that exceeds $3 million.

Wealth management firms offer a variety of fringe benefits, such as medical, dental, and life insurance; paid holidays, vacations, and sick days; personal days; profit-sharing plans; 401(k) plans; retirement and pension plans; educational reimbursement; and licensing reimbursement (to complete licensing examinations from the Financial Industry Regulatory Authority).

■ WORK ENVIRONMENT

Vice presidents often work long hours. In fact, approximately 50 percent of top executives worked more than 40 hours a week in 2014, according to the U.S. Department of Labor. This job can be stressful because there is a constant need to demonstrate results (e.g., strong returns for investors, a steady pipeline of new investors), as well as make wise decisions about a firm's products, investment strategies, levels of risk, and other critical areas. Vice presidents travel to participate in roadshows, meet with current and prospective investors, and attend industry conferences and other events.

■ EXPLORING

Participate in mock investing competitions and simulations to obtain risk-free experience in the financial markets. One such resource is the Investopedia Stock Simulator (http://www.investopedia.com/simulator), which gives participants the chance to invest $100,000 in virtual cash in the stock market and compete with hundreds of thousands of people around the world to see who is the best investor.

In high school and college, join business and investing clubs, many of which offer networking events, investment competitions, guest speakers from the wealth management industry, and job shadowing opportunities.

Talk with wealth management professionals about their careers. Ask your business teacher and career counselor for help arranging interviews.

Finally, check out the following books to learn more about wealth management:

- *The Financial Times Guide to Wealth Management: How to Plan, Invest, and Protect Your Financial Assets* (FT Press, 2015)
- *Private Wealth Management: The Complete Reference for the Personal Financial Planner* (McGraw-Hill Education, 2015)

■ EDUCATION AND TRAINING REQUIREMENTS
High School

Recommended high school classes include business, economics, computer science, English, speech, mathematics, statistics, accounting, history, social studies, and foreign language.

Postsecondary Education

A bachelor's degree in finance, mathematics, accounting, economics, business, entrepreneurism, financial engineering, or quantitative finance is the minimum educational requirement to enter the field, but many firms require their vice presidents to have master's degrees in business, finance, or related areas. Some vice presidents have law degrees.

Other Education or Training

Many professional associations provide continuing education (CE) classes, workshops, webinars, and seminars to help members and non-members keep their skills up to date and qualify for certification and re-certification. For

CAREER LADDER

Managing Director

Partner

Chief Investment Officer/Vice President

Associate

Analyst

example, the Association of International Wealth Management offers online courses such as The Gold Market: An Industry Overview and Investment Options, Understanding High-Frequency Trading, and The Crude Oil Market: An Industry Overview and Investment Options. Other opportunities are provided by the Investment Management Consultants Association, American Bankers Association, American Institute of Certified Public Accountants, Association for Financial Counseling and Planning Education, Association for Financial Professionals, Certified Financial Planner Board of Standards, CFA Institute, and the Institute for Private Investors.

Many wealth management firms provide ongoing training opportunities to help their employees keep their financial skills up to date and develop their soft skills.

Certification

The Investment Management Consultants Association (IMCA) offers the Essentials of Investment Consulting Certificate Program. According to the association's Web site, the online program "covers fundamental concepts and applications including: the mathematics of managing money and building portfolios; understanding the various types of investments; how to select managers, measure performance, and monitor results; and how to set and implement investment strategies using investment policy statements as a guide." The program has 12 learning modules: Algebra and Statistics, Time Value of Money and Rates of Return, Fixed Income-Duration and Yield, Measuring Risk, Performance Measurement, Capital Markets, Asset Allocation, Alternative Investments, Investment Policy, Manager Search and Selection, Due Diligence, and Portfolio Evaluation.

The IMCA also provides the Applied Behavioral Finance Certificate Program and the Fundamentals of Alternative Investments Online Certificate Program.

■ CERTIFICATION, LICENSING, AND SPECIAL REQUIREMENTS
Certification or Licensing

Several organizations offer certification to wealth management professionals, including:

MARIA ELENA LAGOMASINO, CEO, MANAGING PARTNER, AND FOUNDER OF WE FAMILY OFFICES

MOVERS AND SHAKERS

Maria Elena Lagomasino is the chief executive officer (CEO), managing partner, and founder of financial advisory firm WE Family Offices, a global family office serving ultra-high-net-worth families. Before founding WE Family Offices, Lagomasino served as the chairman and CEO of JPMorgan Private Bank, as well as worked at Chase Manhattan Private Bank; Growth Capital Tei Portfolio, LLC; Citibank; and GenSpring Family Offices, LLC. Lagomasino earned a bachelor's degree in French literature from Manhattanville College, and earned graduate degrees at Columbia University (library science) and Fordham University (business administration).

Lagomasino was born in Havana, Cuba, in 1949, and emigrated with her family to the United States at the age of 11—fleeing the Communist revolution led by Fidel Castro. She says that two core values were instilled in her as a result of her family having to flee Cuba (and leaving behind her parents' properties and her grandparents' businesses): the value of family and the value of private capital. "These core values have been integral parts of each and every decision I've made throughout my career and personal life," she explains on her LinkedIn page. "In my career I have been honored to help the families I work with navigate their own challenges of life with wealth, and my life's work has been dedicated to nurturing family dynamics and economic empowerment."

Lagomasino has received many awards during her career, including being named one of the "50 Most Influential Women in Wealth Management" by *Private Asset Management* in 2015, and one of the "Top 25 Women in Finance" by *American Banker* in 2012. She is also the founder of the Institute for the Fiduciary Standard.

Sources: WE Family Offices; *New York Times*; LinkedIn.com

- American College of Financial Services (chartered financial consultant)
- Association for Financial Counseling and Planning Education (accredited financial counselor)
- CFP Board (certified financial planner)
- fi360 (accredited investment fiduciary, accredited investment fiduciary analyst, professional plan consultant)
- Institute of Business and Finance (certified fund specialist, certified annuity specialist, certified estate and trust specialist, certified income specialist, certified tax specialist)
- Investment Adviser Association (chartered investment counselor)
- Investment Management Consultants Association (certified investment management analyst, chartered private wealth advisor).

Like anyone else involved in investing, wealth managers and their activities come under the regulatory aegis of the Financial Industry Regulatory Authority and are generally considered broker-dealers, much like your average broker, and while there may be a handful of esoteric regulations that deal with private wealth management, most experts say private banks and wealth management firms are treated much the same as your local TD Ameritrade or Charles Schwab branch.

Vice presidents are usually required to obtain their Series 7 and Series 63, 65, or 66 credentials from the Financial Industry Regulatory Authority, the self-regulatory arm of the investment industry. The Series 7, or General Securities Representative certification, allows you to buy or sell, or solicit the purchase or sale, of all securities products, including corporate securities, municipal securities, municipal fund securities, options, direct participation programs, investment company products, and variable contracts. It's the most basic form of certification for anybody involved with the markets. The majority of firms will also require a Series 63 registration, which requires knowledge of state securities laws and allows you to be a securities agent. Other firms may require the Series 66 (which covers the same ground as a Series 63, but also certifies you to act as a registered investment adviser) and the Series 65 (which certifies you to act as an investment adviser representative).

■ EXPERIENCE, SKILLS, AND PERSONALITY TRAITS

At least 10 years of investment experience and a proven record of generating new business are required to work as a vice president.

Vice presidents need excellent communication and interpersonal skills to interact effectively with investors, potential clients, and partners, as well as to closely supervise and mentor associates and analysts. They should have strong sales and business acumen, leadership ability, good judgment, excellent quantitative and project management skills, a detail-oriented personality, creativity, the ability to work in a fast-paced environment, and a keen interest in and knowledge of the investment industry, investment strategies, and financial products.

■ EMPLOYMENT PROSPECTS
Employers
There are more than 3,190 wealth management businesses in the United States alone. Major employers include:

- investment firms (e.g., Goldman Sachs, Morgan Stanley, and JPMorgan Chase & Co.)
- national broker/dealers (e.g., Bank of America Merrill Lynch, Edward Jones, Wells Fargo Advisors, UBS Wealth Management)
- regional and boutiques (e.g., Legg Mason, Janney Montgomery Scott, Ameriprise Financial, and Raymond James)
- family offices (i.e., firms that manages investments, assets, and trusts for a high-wealth family)
- independents (i.e., small mom-and-pop businesses)
- robo advisory firms (e.g., Wealthfront, Betterment, Assetbuilder, and Covester)

Starting Out
Many people are promoted to the position of vice president after excelling as associates and in other lower-level positions at their employers or other wealth management firms. Others enter this career after working in the hedge fund, private equity, or venture capital sectors, or after working at financial consulting firms or in the financial departments of corporations.

You can learn more about career opportunities by using traditional job-search strategies such as visiting the Web sites of potential employers, meeting with recruiters on campus, utilizing the services provided by your college's career counselors, signing on with wealth management recruiters, and using social networking sites (such as LinkedIn) to prospect for job leads.

Additionally, participation in internships programs, which are provided by wealth management firms, is an excellent way to break into the field. For example, industry leader HSBC offers a 10-week Global Private Banking Internship Program (http://www.hsbc.com/careers/students-and-graduates/programmes/global-private-banking-internship) for penultimate-year bachelor's or master's degree students. The program provides participants with an understanding of what it takes to become an investment counselor, relationship manager, or product specialist. The most-promising interns are asked to participate in its Global Private Banking Global Graduate Programme (http://www.hsbc.com/careers/students-and-graduates/programmes/global-private-banking-global-graduate-programme), a 24-month program for final-year bachelor's or master's degree students that teaches them how to manage relationships with the bank's high-net-worth clients and provide financial product expertise. Participation in these programs can translate into a full-time position at the company.

■ ADVANCEMENT PROSPECTS
High-performing vice presidents who are able to bring a large number of high-net-worth investors to their firms and manage their portfolios effectively may be tapped to become *managing directors,* one of the top decision makers at a wealth management firm. In this role, you'll be responsible for "big picture" issues such as your company's overall investment strategy, client focus, and/or new business strategies. Some managing directors continue to manage client portfolios—typically those of the firm's most high-profile, high-net-worth customers.

Vice presidents are also well-qualified to work as chief financial officers, CEOs, and chief operating officers at corporations.

■ OUTLOOK
Employment for personal financial advisors (including wealth managers) is expected to grow by 30 percent through 2024, according to the U.S. Department of Labor. Job opportunities for top executives will grow by 6 percent during this same time span. Demand is increasing as a result of the growing numbers of Americans who are classified as being extremely wealthy. The number of households earning between $5 million and $25 million (not including primary residence) grew by 60,000 from 2013 to 2014, to 1,168,000 households, according to Spectrem Group, an investor research analytics firm. And the number of households with more than $25 million increased by 10,000 to 142,000 total households during this same time period.

■ UNIONS AND ASSOCIATIONS
Wealth management vice presidents are not members of unions. A variety of professional associations provide resources to WM professionals. The Certified Financial Planner Board of Standards provides the certified financial planner credential, publishes the *Financial Planning Competency Handbook,* and offers job listings and career-development webinars at its Web site. The Securities Industry and Financial Markets Association is a trade organization for broker-dealers, banks, and asset managers. It offers the Securities Industry Institute, an executive development program for securities industry professionals that is held at The Wharton School of the University

of Pennsylvania. Women in Insurance and Financial Services offers a mentoring program, webinars, discussion groups on social media sites, a national conference, and other resources. Other noteworthy organizations include American Bankers Association, Association for Financial Counseling and Planning Education, Association for Financial Professionals, Association of International Wealth Management, CFA Institute, Chartered Alternate Investment Analyst Association, Institute for Private Investors, International Association for Quantitative Finance, International Association of Registered Financial Consultants, and the New York Society of Security Analysts.

■ TIPS FOR ENTRY

1. Read the following publications to learn more about the field: *Journal of Financial Counseling and Planning* (http://www.afcpe.org/publications) and the *Journal of Portfolio Management* (http://www.iijournals.com).

2. Participate in internships and related job-training programs at banks and other employers to obtain experience and get your "foot in the door" at target companies. Vault.com publishes a list of the best investment bank internships at http://www.vault.com/internship-rankings/best-investment-bank-internships.

3. The CFP Board offers several job-search webinars at http://www.cfp.net/career-center/resources-for-job-seekers/recorded-webinars-for-job-seekers. Recent topics included How to Write Successful Resumes and Cover Letters, Networking 101: Why It's So Important to Your Job Search, and Interviewing Skills for the Financial Services Industry.

■ FOR MORE INFORMATION

Visit the ABA's Web site for job listings and information on continuing education, its Wealth Management & Trust Conference, and the banking industry.

American Bankers Association (ABA)
1120 Connecticut Avenue, NW
Washington, D.C. 20036-3902
Tel: (800) 226-5377
http://www.aba.com

For information on certification, membership, and job listings, contact
Association for Financial Counseling and Planning Education
1940 Duke Street, Suite 200
Alexandria, VA 22314-3452

Tel: (703) 684-4484
http://www.afcpe.org

For information on earnings, careers, and certification, contact
Association for Financial Professionals
4520 East-West Highway, Suite 750
Bethesda, MD 20814-3574
Tel: (301) 907-2862
http://www.afponline.org

For information on membership and certification, contact
Association of International Wealth Management
E-mail: info@aiwm.org
http://www.aiwm.org

For information on certification and careers, contact
Certified Financial Planner Board of Standards
1425 K Street, NW, #800
Washington, D.C. 20005-3673
Tel: (800) 487-1497
E-mail: mail@cfpboard.org
http://www.cfp.net

Visit the institute's Web site for information on certification for financial analysts.
CFA Institute
915 East High Street
Charlottesville, VA 22902-4868
Tel: (800) 247-8132
E-mail: info@cfainstitute.org
http://www.cfainstitute.org

This trade organization promotes the professional education of financial advisors and planners.
International Association of Registered Financial Consultants
The Financial Planning Building
PO Box 42506
Middletown, OH 45042-0506
Tel: (800) 532-9060
http://www.iarfc.org

Visit the NYSSA Web site for information on membership for college students, a list of top employers of financial analysts, and scholarships for graduate students.
New York Society of Security Analysts (NYSSA)
1540 Broadway, Suite 1010
New York, NY 10036-4083
Tel: (212) 541-4530
http://www.nyssa.org

For information on education and careers, contact

Securities Industry and Financial Markets Association
120 Broadway, 35th Floor
New York, NY 10271-3599
Tel: (212) 313-1200
http://www.sifma.org

For information on membership and continuing education, contact

Women in Insurance and Financial Services
136 Everett Road
Albany, NY 12205-1418
Tel: (866) 264-9437
E-mail: office@wifsnational.org
http://www.wifsnational.org

Webmasters

■ OVERVIEW

Webmasters design, implement, and maintain Internet Web sites for corporations, educational institutions, nonpofit organizations, government agencies, or other institutions. Webmasters have working knowledge of network configurations, interface, graphic design, animation, software development, business, writing, marketing, and project management. The function of a webmaster encompasses many different responsibilities, which is why the position is often held by a team of individuals in a large organization. *Webmasters* are also known as *Web developers, Web site managers,* and *Web site administrators.* According to the Department of Labor, there are approximately 127,070 Web developers employed in the United.

■ HISTORY

The Internet developed from ARPANET, an experimental computer network established in the 1960s by the U.S. Department of Defense. By the late 1980s, the Internet was being used by many government and educational institutions.

The World Wide Web was the brainchild of physicist Tim Berners-Lee. Although Berners-Lee formed his idea of the Web in 1989, it was another four years before the first Web browser (Mosaic) made it possible to navigate the Web simply. Businesses quickly realized the commercial potential of the Web and soon developed their own Web sites.

No one person or organization is in charge of the Internet and what's on it. However, each Web site needs an individual, or team of workers, to gather, organize, and maintain online content. These specialists, called webmasters, manage sites for businesses of all sizes, nonprofit organizations, schools, government agencies, and private individuals.

■ THE JOB

The webmaster's job responsibilities depend on the goals and needs of the particular organization for which they work. There are, however, some basic duties that are common to almost all webmasters.

Webmasters, specifically site managers, first secure space on the Web for the site they are developing. This is done by contracting with an Internet service provider. The provider serves as a sort of storage facility for the organization's online information, usually charging a set monthly fee for a specified amount of megabyte space. The webmaster may also be responsible for establishing a uniform resource locator, or URL, for the Web site they are developing. The URL serves as the site's online "address" and must be registered with Internet Corporation for Assigned Names and Numbers, the Web URL registration service.

The webmaster is responsible for developing the actual Web site for their organization. In some cases, this may involve actually writing the text content of the pages. More commonly, however, the webmaster is given the text (and other content) to be used and is merely responsible for programming it in such a way that it can be displayed on a Web page. In larger companies webmasters specialize in content, adaptation, and presentation of data.

QUICK FACTS	
ALTERNATE TITLE(S)	Web Developers, Web Site Administrators, Web Site Managers
DUTIES	Design, implement, and maintain Web sites for companies, government agencies, and nonprofit organizations; monitor performance and usage of Web sites
SALARY RANGE	$51,536 to $71,231 to $91,550+
WORK ENVIRONMENT	Primarily Indoors
BEST GEOGRAPHIC LOCATION(S)	Opportunities are available throughout the country, but are best in large, urban areas
MINIMUM EDUCATION LEVEL	Associate's Degree
SCHOOL SUBJECTS	Art, Computer Science, English
EXPERIENCE	Two years experience
PERSONALITY TRAITS	Creative, Problem-Solving, Technical
SKILLS	Computer, Digital Media, Writing
CERTIFICATION OR LICENSING	Recommended
SPECIAL REQUIREMENTS	None
EMPLOYMENT PROSPECTS	Good
ADVANCEMENT PROSPECTS	Good
OUTLOOK	Much Faster than the Average
NOC	2175
O*NET-SOC	15-1134.00

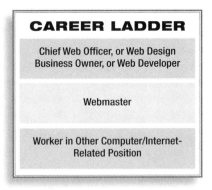

CAREER LADDER

Chief Web Officer, or Web Design
Business Owner, or Web Developer

Webmaster

Worker in Other Computer/Internet-
Related Position

In order for text to be displayed on a Web page, it must be formatted using hypertext markup language (HTML). HTML is a system of coding text so that the computer that is "reading" it knows how to display it. For example, text could be coded to be a certain size or color or to be italicized or boldface. Paragraphs, line breaks, alignment, and margins are other examples of text attributes that must be coded in HTML.

Although it is less and less common, some webmasters code text manually, by actually typing the various commands into the body of the text. This method is time consuming, however, and mistakes are easily made. More often, webmasters use a software program that automatically codes text. Some word processing programs, such as Microsoft Word, even offer HTML options. The majority of coding is now automated by computer processes, but webmasters are still needed to supervise the coding process and ensure that all items have been posted to the Web site as intended. In addition to HTML, webmasters must be familiar with computer languages such as XML and Java and Common Gateway Interface technology (which helps send Web resources to site visitors).

Along with coding the text, the webmaster must lay out the elements of the Web site in such a way that it is visually pleasing, well organized, and easy to navigate. They may use various colors, background patterns, images, tables, or charts. These graphic elements can come from image files already on the Web, software clip art files, or images scanned into the computer with an electronic scanner. In some cases, when an organization is using the Web site to promote its product or service, the webmaster may work with a marketing specialist or department to develop a page.

Some Web sites have several directories or "layers." That is, an organization may have several Web pages, organized in a sort of "tree," with its home page connected, via hypertext links, to other pages, which may in turn be linked to other pages. The webmaster is responsible for organizing the pages in such a way that a visitor can easily browse through them and find what he or she is looking for. Such webmasters are called *programmers* and *developers*; they are also responsible for creating Web tools and special Web functionality.

For webmasters who work for organizations that have several different Web sites, one responsibility may be making sure that the "style" or appearance of all the pages is the same. This is often referred to as "house style." In large organizations, such as universities, where many different departments may be developing and maintaining their own pages, it is especially important that the webmaster monitor these pages to ensure consistency and conformity to the organization's requirements. In almost every case, the webmaster has the final authority for the content and appearance of their organization's Web site. They must carefully edit, proofread, and check the appearance of every page.

Besides designing and setting up Web sites, most webmasters are charged with maintaining and updating existing sites. Most sites contain information that changes regularly. Some change daily or even hourly. Depending on the employer and the type of Web site, the webmaster may spend a good deal of time updating and remodeling the page. They are also responsible for ensuring that the hyperlinks contained within the Web site lead to the sites they should. It is common for links to change or become obsolete, so the webmaster usually performs a link check every few weeks. They may also use specialized software that automates this task.

Other job duties vary, depending on the employer and the position. Most webmasters are responsible for receiving and answering e-mail messages from visitors to the organization's Web site. Some webmasters keep logs and create reports on when and how often their pages are visited and by whom. Depending on the company, Web sites count anywhere from 300 to 1.4 billion visits, or "hits," a month. Some create and maintain order forms or online "shopping carts" that allow visitors to the Web site to purchase products or services. Others have live customer service features that allow customers who are having problems with the site or just want more information about a product or service to communicate online with a "live" individual regarding these issues. Some may train other employees on how to create or update Web pages. Finally, webmasters may be responsible for developing and adhering to a budget for their departments.

■ EARNINGS

According to the National Association of Colleges and Employers, the average starting salary for graduates with a bachelor's degree in computer science was approximately $64,891 in December 2016.

According to Salary.com, webmasters earned average annual salaries of $71,231 in November 2016. Salaries ranged from less than $51,536 to more than $91,550. However, many webmasters move into the position from another position within their company or have taken on the task in addition to other duties. These employees are often paid approximately the same salary they were already making.

Depending on the organization for which they work, webmasters may receive a benefits package in addition to salary. A typical benefits package would include paid vacations and holidays, medical insurance, and perhaps a pension plan.

■ WORK ENVIRONMENT

Webmasters usually spend much of the workday alone, but they still must be able to communicate and work well with others. They may have periodic meetings with Web designers, marketing specialists, search engine optimization specialists, writers, or other professionals who have input into Web site development. In many larger organizations, there is a team of webmasters rather than just one. Although each team member works alone on his or her own specific duties, the members may meet frequently to discuss and coordinate their activities.

The job is constantly evolving because technology is always changing. Webmasters must spend time reading and learning about new developments in online communication. They may be continually working with new computer software or hardware. Their actual job responsibilities may even change, as the capabilities of both the organization and the World Wide Web itself expand. It is important that these employees be flexible and willing to learn and grow with the technology that drives their work.

Most webmasters are allowed to wear fairly casual attire and to work in a relaxed atmosphere because they don't have much interaction with the general public. In most cases, the job calls for standard working hours, although there may be times when overtime is required.

■ EXPLORING

One of the easiest ways to learn about what a webmaster does is to spend time surfing the Web. By examining a variety of Web sites to see how they look and operate, you can begin to get a feel for what goes into a home page.

An even better way to explore this career is to design your own personal Web page. Many Internet servers offer their users the option of designing and maintaining a personal Web page for a very low fee. A personal page can contain virtually anything that you want to include, from snapshots of friends, to blogs, photographs and video, audio files of favorite music, and hypertext links to other favorite sites.

■ EDUCATION AND TRAINING REQUIREMENTS
High School

High school students who are interested in becoming webmasters should take as many computer science

Webmasters work with clients to help them design, launch, and maintain Web sites. (Viacheslav Nikolaenko. Shutterstock.)

classes as possible, including those in programming, digital design, and animation. Mathematics classes are also helpful. Writing skills are important in this career, so English classes are good choices. Those who plan to start their own businesses should take business and marketing classes.

Postsecondary Training

A number of community colleges, colleges, and universities offer classes and certificate programs for webmasters, but there is no standard educational path or requirement for becoming a webmaster. An associate's degree or certification may suffice, but a computer-related bachelor's degree may be required for more advanced jobs. Many webmasters have bachelor's degrees in computer science, information systems, digital media, or computer programming, but liberal arts degrees, such as English, are not uncommon. There are also webmasters who have degrees in engineering, mathematics, and marketing.

Certification

The International Web Association offers professional certificates for Web professionals. Many colleges, universities, and technical schools throughout the United States also offer webmaster certification programs. Programs vary in length, anywhere from three weeks to nine months or more. Topics covered include client/server technology, Web development, programs, and software and hardware.

Other Education or Training

The International Web Association and the World Organization of Webmasters provide continuing education classes, webinars, and workshops.

WWW Basics

Blog: A Web site that is written and maintained by an individual or group of bloggers.

Browser: User-friendly software that makes Internet searches quicker and more efficient.

Flash: A multimedia platform (incorporating text, audio, video, animation, and interactivity) that has become a popular method of adding animation and interactive features to Web pages; it is also widely used for broadcast animation work.

Homepage: A Web page that introduces the site and guides the user to other pages at the site.

HTML (hypertext markup language): A code that helps control the way information on a Web page is transferred and presented and the way that hypertext links appear on the page.

Mobile browser: A browser that is designed to be used on a mobile device such as smartphone.

Search engine: A specialized Web site containing computer-maintained lists of other Web sites; lists are usually organized by subject, name, content, and other categories. Users request searches by typing in keywords, or topical words and phrases, and the search engine displays a list of links to related Web sites.

Search engine optimization: The process of finding keywords or phrases that will be picked up by search engines.

Web 2.0: The second generation of Web sites that allow people with little or no technical skill to create, edit, and publish their own creative content; popular Web 2.0 Web sites include Flickr, Blogger, and Wikipedia.

Widget: A stand-alone application on a Web site that has a specific purpose (such as presenting news) and that is constantly being updated; also called an **applet, badge,** or **gadget.**

■ CERTIFICATION, LICENSING, AND SPECIAL REQUIREMENTS
Certification or Licensing

Certification is not required but can enhance a candidate's chance at landing a webmaster position. The International Web Association and World Organization of webmasters offer voluntary certification programs.

■ EXPERIENCE, SKILLS, AND PERSONALITY TRAITS

Aspiring webmasters should obtain at least two years of experience with Internet technologies. What most webmasters have in common is a strong knowledge of computer technology. Most people who enter this field are already well versed in computer operating systems, programming languages, computer graphics, and Internet standards. In some cases, employers require that candidates already have experience in designing and maintaining Web sites. It is, in fact, most common for someone to move into the position of webmaster from another computer-related job in the same organization.

Webmasters should be organized, creative, and technically savvy. It is important for a Web page to be designed well in order to attract attention. Good writing skills and an aptitude for marketing are also excellent qualities for anyone considering a career in Web site design. Webmasters should also be willing to stay up to date regarding changing Internet technologies during their careers.

■ EMPLOYMENT PROSPECTS
Employers

There are approximately 127,070 Web developers employed in the United States. The majority of webmasters working today are full-time employees. They are employed by Web design companies, businesses, schools or universities, not-for-profit organizations, government agencies—in short, any business or organization that requires an online presence. Webmasters may also work as freelancers or operate their own Web design businesses.

Starting Out

Most people become webmasters by moving into the position from another computer-related position within the same company. All large organizations already use computers for various functions, and they may employ a person or several people to serve as computer specialists. If these organizations decide to develop their own Web sites, they frequently assign the task to one of these employees who is already experienced with the computer system. Often, the person who ultimately becomes an organization's webmaster initially takes on the job in addition to their other, already established duties.

Another way that individuals find jobs in this field is through online postings of job openings. Many companies post webmaster position openings online because the candidates they hope to attract use the Internet for job searches. Prospective webmasters search for jobs through job-related newsgroups and Web search engines.

■ ADVANCEMENT PROSPECTS

Experienced webmasters employed by a large organization may be able to advance to the position of *chief Web officer. Chief Web officers* supervise a team of webmasters and are responsible for every aspect of a company's presence on the Web. Others might advance by starting their own business, designing Web sites on a contractual basis for several clients rather than working exclusively for one organization.

Opportunities for webmasters of the future are endless due to the continuing development of online technology. As understanding and use of the Web increase, there may be new or expanded job duties for individuals with expertise in this field.

■ OUTLOOK

The field of computer systems design and related services is among the fastest-growing industries, according to the U.S. Department of Labor (DOL). As a result, employment for webmasters is expected to grow much faster than the average for all careers through 2024.

One thing to keep in mind, however, is that when technology advances extremely rapidly, it tends to make old methods of doing things obsolete. If current trends continue, the responsibilities of the webmaster will be carried out by a group or department instead of a single employee, in order to keep up with the demands of the position. It is also possible that, like desktop publishing, user-friendly software programs will make Web site design so easy and efficient that it no longer requires an "expert" to do it well. Webmasters who are concerned with job security should be willing to continue learning and using the very latest developments in technology, so that they are prepared to move into the future of online communication, whatever it may be. The DOL reports that webmasters who have knowledge of multiple programming languages and digital media tools, such as Flash and Photoshop, will have the best job prospects.

■ UNIONS AND ASSOCIATIONS

Webmasters are not represented by unions. The two major professional associations for webmasters are the International Web Association and the World Organization of Webmasters. They provide certification, continuing education classes and webinars, networking events, publications, and other resources.

■ TIPS FOR ENTRY

1. Create and manage Web sites for community organizations. If they like your work, ask them to spread the word about your talents.
2. Read publications such as *Website Magazine* (http://www.websitemagazine.com) to learn more about industry trends.
3. Join the International Web Association and the World Organization of Webmasters (WOW) to

access training and networking resources, industry publications, and employment opportunities.
4. Read the WOW blog (http://webprofessionals.org/blog) to learn about trends in the field.
5. Conduct information interviews with webmasters and ask them for advice on preparing for and entering the field. Visit http://webprofessional.org for a database of Web professionals.

■ FOR MORE INFORMATION

The Computing Research Association provides advocacy, education, networking opportunities, and other resources for the computing research industry.

Computing Research Association (CRA)
1828 L Street, NW, Suite 800
Washington, D.C. 20036-4632
Tel: (202) 234-2111
Fax: (202) 667-1066
E-mail: info@cra.org
http://cra.org

The International Web Association provides certification and continuing education programs.

International Web Association (IWA)
119 East Union Street, Suite #A
Pasadena, CA 91103-3951
Tel: (626) 449-3709
Fax: (866) 607-1773
E-mail: Support@iwanet.org
http://iwanet.org

The World Organization of Webmasters, also known as WebProfessionals.org, is dedicated to the support of individuals and organizations who create, manage, or market Web sites.

World Organization of Webmasters (WOW)
PO Box 584
Washington, IL 61571-0584
Tel: (662) 493-2776
E-mail: membership@webprofessionals.org
http://webprofessionals.org

Wedding and Party Consultants

■ OVERVIEW

From directing the bride to the best dress shops and cake decorators to pinning on the corsages the day of the wedding, *wedding and party consultants*, sometimes

QUICK FACTS

ALTERNATE TITLE(S)
Event Professionals, Wedding
and Party Planners

DUTIES
Plan weddings, receptions,
and other large celebrations
and events

SALARY RANGE
$22,204 to $41,434 to
$74,323+

WORK ENVIRONMENT
Indoors/Outdoors

BEST GEOGRAPHIC LOCATION(S)
Opportunities available
throughout the country but
best in large, urban areas

MINIMUM EDUCATION LEVEL
High School Diploma,
Apprenticeship

SCHOOL SUBJECTS
Family and Consumer Science,
Music, Theater/Dance

EXPERIENCE
Previous planning experience
required

PERSONALITY TRAITS
Enterprising, Organized, Social

SKILLS
Business Management,
Interpersonal, Organizational

CERTIFICATION OR LICENSING
Recommended

SPECIAL REQUIREMENTS
None

EMPLOYMENT PROSPECTS
Good

ADVANCEMENT PROSPECTS
Fair

OUTLOOK
Faster than the Average

NOC
6561

O*NET-SOC
13-1121.00

called *event professionals* and *wedding and party planners*, assist in the planning of weddings, receptions, and other large celebrations and events. Most consultants deal in weddings. They generally have home-based businesses, but spend a great deal of time visiting vendors and reception and wedding sites.

HISTORY

Weddings have long provided good careers for musicians, photographers, florists, printers, caterers, and others. Marriage brokers—men and women who made their livings pairing up brides with grooms for nicely "arranged" marriages—were once considered prominent members of some cultures. Wedding consulting, however, has only emerged in recent years.

In the years before wedding consultants, brides divided up responsibilities among cousins and aunts—a family gathered together to lick invitation envelopes assembly-line style, a favorite aunt mixed batches of butter mints, a married sister with some recent wedding experience helped the bride pick a dress and china pattern. Usually it was not until after the event that the bride really had a sense of how to plan a wedding. The profession of wedding consultant as a serious business began in the early 1980s. Recognizing how a bride can benefit a great deal from a knowledgeable guide, men and women hired themselves out as wedding and party experts. It has only been during the last few years that the major wedding magazines and publications have given serious consideration to wedding consultants. Now most wedding experts consider a consultant a necessity in planning a perfect and cost-efficient wedding.

THE JOB

Wedding consultants help brides with decisions such as whether to have butterflies or doves released at the wedding, how to get married on a boat, and which chef to hire to prepare the reception dinner. Even if the requests are more mainstream than these, it can be difficult choosing reliable florists and other vendors, and staying within a budget. The average wedding costs nearly $33,000 (including the dress but not the engagement ring or honeymoon), but many brides end up frustrated and disappointed with their ceremonies.

Wedding consultants help brides save money and avoid stress by offering their services at the earliest stages of planning. They provide the bride with cost estimates, arrange for ceremony and reception sites, order invitations, and help select music. They also offer advice on wedding etiquette and tradition. Consultants then stay on call for their brides through the ceremonies and receptions, pinning on flowers, instructing ushers and other members of the wedding parties, taking gifts from guests, and organizing the cake-cutting and bouquet toss.

Some consultants sell a variety of services, from candles and linens to hand-calligraphed invitations to party favors. A consultant may even own a complete bridal boutique. Some consultants specialize in only "destination" weddings. They set up services in exotic locales, like Hawaii, and handle all the details for an out-of-town bride who will only be arriving the week of the wedding. Consultants also arrange for special wedding sites like historic homes, public gardens, and resorts.

A consultant can also introduce a bride to a number of "extras" that she may not have been aware of before. In addition to arranging for the flowers, candles, and cakes, a consultant may arrange for horse-and-carriage rides, doves to be released after the ceremony, wine bars for the reception, goldfish in bowls at the tables, and other frills. Some brides rely on consultants to meet difficult requests, such as booking special kinds of musicians, or finding alternatives to flowers. Weddings on TV and in the movies often inspire brides. For example a candlelit wedding in a condemned, half-demolished church on the TV show *Friends* sent wedding consultants scurrying to re-create the site in their own cities.

EARNINGS

Due to the fairly recent development of wedding consulting as a career, there haven't been any comprehensive salary surveys. Also, the number of uncertified consultants and consultants who only plan weddings part time make it difficult to estimate average earnings. According to Payscale.com, in October 2016, wedding planners earned average salaries of $41,434. Earnings ranged from less than $22,204 to $74,323 or more.

Though consultants typically make between 10 to 15 percent of a wedding's expense, consultants generally charge a flat rate. A consultant may also be hired to oversee all the pre-wedding administrative details for an agreed-upon fee.

In a large city, an experienced consultant can realistically expect to have a wedding planned for every weekend. Consulting fees for destination weddings tend to be lower because destination weddings are usually much smaller than traditional weddings.

■ WORK ENVIRONMENT

For someone who loves weddings, parties, and meeting new people, consulting can be an ideal career. Clients may be stressed out occasionally, but most of the time they are going to be enthusiastic about planning their weddings and parties. During the week, wedding and party consultants' hours will be spent meeting with vendors, taking phone calls, and working at the computer. Weekends will be a bit faster paced, among larger crowds, and they will get to see the results of their hard work—they will be at the wedding and party sites, fussing over final details and making sure everything goes smoothly.

Their office hours won't be affected by weather conditions, but on the actual wedding and party days they are expected to get easily and quickly from one place to the other. Bad weather on the day of an outdoor wedding or party can result in more work as they move everything to the "rain site." One of the perks of wedding and party consulting is taking an active part in someone's celebration; part of the job is making sure everyone has a good time. But they also must be present for parties, weddings, receptions, and rehearsal dinners, which means they will be working weekends and occasional evenings.

■ EXPLORING

Bridal magazines publish many articles on wedding planning, traditions, and trends. Subscribe to a bridal magazine, such as *Brides, Bridal Guide,* or *Martha Stewart Weddings* to get a sense of what's involved in wedding consulting. Visit the Web sites of professional associations, as well as the Web sites of wedding planners. Sites featuring questions and answers from professionals can give you a lot of insight into the business.

For more hands-on experience, contact the professional organizations for the names of consultants in your area and pay them a visit. Some consultants hire assistants occasionally to help with large weddings. A part-time job

with a florist, caterer, or photographer can also give you a lot of experience in wedding and party planning.

■ EDUCATION AND TRAINING REQUIREMENTS
High School

To be a wedding consultant, you have to know about more than wedding traditions and etiquette. Above all, wedding consulting is a business, so take courses in accounting and business management. Wedding and party consultants are expected to stay well within their client's budget, so they need to be able to balance a checkbook and work with figures. A sense of style is also very important in advising a bride on colors, flowers, and decorations—take courses in art and design. A home economics course may offer lessons in floral arrangement, menu planning, fashion, tailoring, and other subjects of use to a wedding planner.

CAREER LADDER

Consultant With a Large Clientele

Experienced Wedding and Party Consultant

Entry-Level Wedding and Party Consultant

Event Coordinator or Planner

A wedding consultant shows a bride the champagne glasses selected for her table. (oliveromg. Shutterstock.)

WEDDINGS WITH A TWIST

Wedding consultants may specialize in weddings and celebrations that are off the beaten path. Some people choose unusual sites to make their events unique and memorable. For instance, many couples have tied the knot at Bridal Cave in Thunder Mountain Park, Missouri. The spot is located at "Lover's Leap," known for the Native American legend of Wasena, who leaped to her death rather than marry Conwee, the Osage Indian who dragged her and her companion Irona from their village. Irona later married Conwee's brother Prince Buffalo in a ceremony in the mountain cave. Today, people say their "I do's" beneath stalactites and onyx formations.

Others have taken the plunge at the Jules' Undersea Lodge in Key Largo, Florida. Couples dive 21 feet to the hotel, enter through an opening in the bottom of the habitat, and a notary public conducts the service amid the resident tropical fish. The wedding couple must be certified SCUBA divers.

Castle weddings are also popular. For example, some couples have married at the Dalhousie Castle of Edinburgh, Scotland, built in the 1400s and recently converted into a hotel. It includes a wedding chapel and many great photo opportunities, such as on the staircase leading to the dungeon. Receptions can be held in a suite once visited by Queen Victoria.

Gain leadership and planning experience by participating in a school organization. Join prom and homecoming committees, and various school fund-raising events. You will develop budgeting skills while also learning about booking bands, photographers, videographers, and other vendors.

Postsecondary Training

A good liberal arts education can be valuable to a wedding and party consultant, but may not be necessary. Community college courses in small business operation can help you learn about marketing and bookkeeping. Some colleges offer courses in event planning. Courses in art and floral design are valuable, and be sure to take computer courses to learn how to use databases and graphic design programs.

The best experience is gained by actually planning weddings and parties, which may not happen until after you've received some referrals from a professional organization. Various professional organizations, such as the Association of Bridal Consultants and the Association of

Certified Professional Wedding Consultants, offer home study programs, conferences, and seminars for wedding consultants. Speak to representatives of the organizations to learn more about their programs, and to determine which one would be best for you.

■ CERTIFICATION, LICENSING, AND SPECIAL REQUIREMENTS
Certification or Licensing

Certification isn't required to work as a consultant but it can help build business quickly. Brides often contact professional associations directly, and the associations refer the brides to certified consultants in their area. The American Association of Certified Wedding Planners, Association of Bridal Consultants, Association of Certified Professional Wedding Consultants, National Bridal Service, and Weddings Beautiful Worldwide provide voluntary certification to wedding consultants.

■ EXPERIENCE, SKILLS, AND PERSONALITY TRAITS

Previous experience as an event planner, caterer, or in another position that involves organizational and planning acumen is highly recommended for aspiring wedding and party consultants.

Good people skills are very important—much of the consultant's success depends on their relationships with vendors, musicians, and others they hire for weddings and parties. Good word-of-mouth from previous clients also improves their business. Wedding and party consultants should be good at helping people make decisions; moving clients in the right direction is an important part of the job. Patience is necessary, as consultants need to create a stress-free environment for the bride or party host. Other important traits include good organizational skills, creativity, and an interest in helping others.

■ EMPLOYMENT PROSPECTS
Employers

Most consultants are self-employed. In addition to working for brides and other individuals planning large celebrations, consultants work with museums and other nonprofit organizations to plan fund-raising events. They also work for retail stores to plan sales events, and plan grand-opening events for new businesses. Hotels, resorts, and restaurants that host a number of weddings sometimes hire consultants in full-time staff positions. Large retail stores also hire their own full-time events coordinators.

Consultants work all across the country, but are most successful in large cities. In an urban area, a consultant may be able to fill every weekend with at least one wedding. Consultants for "destination" weddings settle in popular vacation and wedding spots such as Hawaii, Mexico, and Las Vegas.

Starting Out

Many people find their way to wedding consulting after careers as event coordinators and planners, or after working weddings as caterers, florists, and musicians. Those who have already developed relationships with area vendors and others involved in the planning of weddings may be able to start their own business without the aid of a professional organization. Those new to the business can benefit from a training program for certification, where they receive not only instruction and professional advice, but also referrals from the organization.

With guidance, training, and a clear understanding of the responsibilities of the job, a wedding consultant can command a good fee from the onset of a new business. Start-up costs are relatively low, since work can be done from home with a computer, an extra phone line, and some advertising. Consultants may invest in basic software to maintain a database, to make attractive graphics for presentation purposes, and to access the Internet. Owning formal and semi-formal dress wear is also important, as the job entails attending many different kinds of weddings and parties.

■ ADVANCEMENT PROSPECTS

Wedding and party consultants with experience can expand their business and clientele. They develop relationships with area vendors that result in more referrals and better discounts. With a bigger business, they can hire regular staff members to help with planning, running errands, and administrative duties. Some consultants expand their services to include such perks as hand-calligraphed invitations and specially designed favors for receptions. Many consultants maintain Web sites to promote their businesses and provide wedding advice. Some start blogs or write books about wedding planning.

■ OUTLOOK

The U.S. Department of Labor predicts that employment for event planners (a category that includes those who plan weddings and parties) will increase faster than the average for all careers through 2024. The average price of a wedding continues to rise, and wedding consultants will be in demand to help couples save money. Additionally, couples are increasingly seeking out the services of wedding planners to help make their weddings memorable. Certified consultants with a strong track record of saving clients money and planning successful and unique weddings will have the best job prospects.

> ## WILD WEDDINGS, PART II
> **DID YOU KNOW?**
>
> If you're ready to get married and, as they say, "take the plunge," here's a great wedding idea for you. Get married underwater at the Jules' Undersea Lodge in Key Largo, Florida. The lodge bills itself as the only underwater hotel in the world. Couples dive 21 feet to the hotel, enter through an opening in the bottom of the habitat, and say their "I do's," while watching the tropical fish that reside in the lagoon that surrounds the hotel. The ceremony is usually conducted by a notary public, who dives down for the nuptial service. According to the hotel, "a toast and the cutting of the cake follow the ceremony. Dinner offers a shrimp cocktail appetizer, a choice of lobster or steak, two hot vegetables, fresh salad and dessert. The hotel "mer-chef" scuba dives to the hotel to prepare the meal and serve the newlyweds." Total cost of this wedding package: $1,750 plus tax. Guests cost extra. The wedding couple must be certified SCUBA divers. Visit http://jul.com for more information.

More people are celebrating their anniversaries by renewing their vows with large events. Wedding consultants will want to capitalize on this trend, as well as expand into other ceremonies like bar and bat mitzvahs.

■ UNIONS AND ASSOCIATIONS

Wedding and party consultants do not belong to unions. Membership organizations for wedding and party consultants include the American Association of Certified Wedding Planners, Association for Wedding Professionals International (AWPI), Association of Bridal Consultants, Association of Certified Professional Wedding Consultants, June Wedding Inc., National Bridal Service, and Weddings Beautiful Worldwide. These organizations provide continuing education opportunities, networking events, certification (except the AWPI), and career information.

■ TIPS FOR ENTRY

1. Talk to wedding and party consultants about their careers. Many wedding planning associations offer member lists at their Web sites. Use these lists to find interview candidates.
2. Use social media to stay up to date on industry developments and learn about job openings. Many professional associations, such as the Association of Certified Professional Wedding Consultants, use Facebook, Twitter, and Pinterest to connect with people.

WILD WEDDINGS, PART III

The Dalhousie Castle of Edinburgh, Scotland, was built over 700 years ago, and was recently converted into a hotel. It includes a wedding chapel and many great photo opportunities. Pose in your wedding gown on the steps of a staircase spiraling down from the "keep" to the dungeon, where you can still see the score marks made by prisoners on the walls. Have your reception in a suite once visited by Queen Victoria, and dine on Scottish salmon, venison, and grouse. Visit http://www.dalhousiecastle.co.uk to learn more.

3. Apply for entry-level jobs at wedding and party planning firms.

■ FOR MORE INFORMATION

The American Association of Certified Wedding Planners provides information on certification and membership.

American Association of Certified Wedding Planners (AACWP)
210 West College Street, Suite 400
Grapevine, TX 76051-5255
Tel: (844) 202-2297
http://aacwp.org

The Association for Wedding Professionals International is an international community of wedding and special event professionals, providing marketing resources and exposure to members, education opportunities, and support for the wedding industry.

Association for Wedding Professionals International (AFWPI)
2929 35th Street, Suite 5598
Sacramento, CA 95817-4008
Tel: (916) 392-5000
http://afwpi.com

The Association of Bridal Consultants offers seminars, webinars, and other resources for bridal consultants.

Association of Bridal Consultants (ABC)
56 Danbury Road, Suite 11
New Milford, CT 06776-3415
Tel: (860) 355-7000
Fax: (860) 354-1404
http://www.bridalassn.com

The Association of Certified Professional Wedding Consultants provides information on membership, certification, and training programs.

Association of Certified Professional Wedding Consultants (ACPWC)
Tel: (408) 227-2792
Fax: (408) 226-0697
E-mail: dmoody@acpwc.com
http://acpwc.net

The National Association for Catering and Events has a mission to advance the catering and events industry and its professionals.

National Association for Catering and Events (NACE)
10440 Little Patuxent Parkway, Suite 300
Columbia, MD 21044-
Tel: (410) 290-5410
Fax: (410) 630-5768
http://www.nace.net

The National Bridal Service provides education and certification programs.

National Bridal Service (NBS)
2225 Grove Avenue
Richmond, VA 23220-4444
Tel: (804) 342-0055
Fax: (804) 342-6062
http://www.nationalbridal.com

Weddings Beautiful Worldwide offers education and certification programs.

Weddings Beautiful Worldwide (WBW)
1004 North Thompson Street, Suite 101
Richmond, VA 23220-4444
Tel: (804) 342-6061
Fax: (804) 342-6062
http://www.weddingsbeautiful.com

Welders and Welding Technicians

■ OVERVIEW

Welders operate a variety of special equipment to join metal parts together permanently, usually using heat and sometimes pressure. They work on constructing and repairing automobiles, aircraft, ships, buildings, bridges, highways, appliances, and many other metal structures and manufactured products. *Welding technicians* are the link between the welder and the engineer and work to improve a wide variety of welding processes. As part of their duties, they may supervise, inspect, and find applications for the welding processes. Approximately 386,240 welders, cutters, solderers, and brazers are employed in the United States.

■ HISTORY

Some welding techniques were used more than 1,000 years ago in forging iron blades by hand, but modern welding processes were first employed in the latter half of the 1800s. From experimental beginnings, the pioneers in this field developed a wide variety of innovative processes. These included resistance welding, invented in 1877, in which an electric current is sent through metal parts in contact. Electrical resistance and pressure melt the metal at the area of contact. Gas welding, also developed in the same era, is a relatively simple process using a torch that burns a gas such as acetylene to create enough heat to melt and fuse metal parts. Oxyacetylene welding, a version of this process developed a few years later, is a common welding process still used today. Arc welding, first used commercially in 1889, relies on an electric arc to generate heat. Thermite welding, which fuses metal pieces with the intense heat of a chemical reaction, was first used around 1900.

In the last century, the sudden demand for vehicles and armaments and a growing list of industrial uses for welding that resulted from the two world wars have spurred researchers to keep improving welding processes and also have encouraged the development of numerous new processes. Today, there are more than 80 different types of welding and welding-related processes. Some of the newer processes include laser-beam welding and electron-beam welding.

Automated welding, in which a robot or machine completes a welding task while being monitored by a welder, welding technician, or machine operator, is becoming an increasingly popular production method. This development is not expected to greatly affect the employment of welders since the machinery must be operated by someone who has knowledge of welding in order to ensure that a proper weld has been made.

■ THE JOB

Welders use various kinds of equipment and processes to create the heat and pressure needed to melt the edges of metal pieces in a controlled fashion so that the pieces may be joined permanently. The processes can be grouped into three categories. The arc welding process derives heat from an electric arc between two electrodes or between an electrode and the workpiece. The gas welding process produces heat by burning a mixture of oxygen and some other combustible gas, such as acetylene or hydrogen.

The resistance welding process obtains heat from pressure and resistance by the workpiece to an electric current. Two of these processes, the arc and gas methods, can also be used to cut, gouge, or finish metal.

Depending on which of these processes and equipment they use, welders may be designated *arc welders*, *plasma welders*, or *acetylene welders*; *combination welders* (meaning they use a combination of gas and arc welding); or *welding machine operators* (meaning they operate machines that use an arc welding process, electron-beam welding process, laser-beam welding process, or friction welding process). Other workers in the welding field include *resistance machine welders*; *oxy-gas cutters*, who use gas torches to cut or trim metals; and *arc cutters*, who use an electric arc to cut or trim metals.

Skilled welders usually begin by planning and laying out their work based on drawings, blueprints, or other specifications. Using their working knowledge of the properties of the metal, they determine the proper sequence of operations needed for the job. They may work with steel, stainless steel, cast iron, bronze, aluminum, nickel, and other metals and alloys. Metal pieces to be welded may be in a variety of positions, such as flat, vertical, horizontal, or overhead.

In the manual arc welding process (the most commonly used method), welders grasp a holder containing a suitable electrode and adjust the electric current supplied to the electrode. Then they strike an arc (an electric discharge across a gap) by touching the electrode

QUICK FACTS

ALTERNATE TITLE(S)
None

DUTIES
Operate a variety of special equipment to join metal parts together permanently, usually using heat and sometimes pressure (welder); provide assistance to welders (technician)

SALARY RANGE
$25,940 to $38,150 to $60,000+

WORK ENVIRONMENT
Indoors/Outdoors

BEST GEOGRAPHIC LOCATION(S)
Opportunities are available throughout the country

MINIMUM EDUCATION LEVEL
High School Diploma, Apprenticeship

SCHOOL SUBJECTS
Mathematics, Physics, Technical/Shop

EXPERIENCE
Postsecondary training or apprenticeship

PERSONALITY TRAITS
Conventional, Hands On, Technical

SKILLS
Building/Trades, Math, Mechanical/Manual Dexterity

CERTIFICATION OR LICENSING
Required

SPECIAL REQUIREMENTS
None

EMPLOYMENT PROSPECTS
Good

ADVANCEMENT PROSPECTS
Good

OUTLOOK
Little Change or More Slowly than the Average

NOC
2212, 7237

O*NET-SOC
51-4121.00, 51-4121.06, 51-4122.00

CAREER LADDER

Welding Supervisor, or Inspector, or or
Instructor

Welder

Welding Technician

Apprentice or Trainee

to the metal. Next, they guide the electrode along the metal seam to be welded, allowing sufficient time for the heat of the arc to melt the metal. The molten metal from the electrode is deposited in the joint and, together with the molten metal edges of the base metal, solidifies to form a solid connection. Welders determine the correct kind of electrode to use based on the job specifications and their knowledge of the materials.

In gas welding, welders melt the metal edges with an intensely hot flame from the combustion of fuel gases in welding torches. First, they obtain the proper types of torch tips and welding rods, which are rods of a filler metal that goes into the weld seam. They adjust the regulators on the tanks of fuel gases, such as oxygen and acetylene, and they light the torch. To obtain the proper size and quality of flame, welders adjust the gas valves on the torch and hold the flame against the metal until it is hot enough. Then they apply the welding rod to the molten metal to supply the extra filler needed to complete the weld.

Maintenance welders, another category of welding workers, may use any of the various welding techniques. They travel to construction sites, utility installations, and other locations to make on-site repairs to metalwork.

Some workers in the welding field do repetitive production tasks using automatic welding equipment. In general, automatic welding is not used where there are critical safety and strength requirements. The surfaces that these welders work on are usually in only one position. Resistance machine welders often work in the mass production of parts, doing the same welding operations repeatedly. To operate the welding machine, they first make adjustments to control the electric current and pressure and then feed in and align the workpieces. After completing the welding operation, welders remove the work from the machine. Welders must constantly monitor the process in order to make sure that the machine is producing the proper weld.

To cut metal, oxygen cutters may use hand-guided torches or machine-mounted torches. They direct the flame of burning oxygen and fuel gas onto the area to be cut until it melts. Then, an additional stream of gas is released from the torch, which cuts the metal along previously marked lines. Arc cutters follow a similar procedure in their work, except that they use an electric arc as the source of heat. As in oxygen cutting, an additional stream of gas may be released when cutting the metal.

Welding technicians fill positions as *supervisors*, *inspectors*, *experimental technicians*, *sales technicians*, *assistants to welding engineers*, and *welding analysts* and *estimators*. Some technicians work in research facilities, where they help engineers test and evaluate newly developed welding equipment, metals, and alloys. When new equipment is being developed or old equipment improved, they conduct experiments on it, evaluate the data, and then make recommendations to engineers. Other welding technicians, who work in the field, inspect welded joints and conduct tests to ensure that welds meet company standards, national code requirements, and customer job specifications. These technicians record the results, prepare and submit reports to welding engineers, and conduct welding personnel certification tests according to national code requirements.

Some beginning welding technicians are employed as *welding operators*. They perform manual, automatic, or semiautomatic welding jobs. They set up work, read blueprints and welding-control symbols, and follow specifications set up for a welded product.

As *welding inspectors*, welding technicians judge the quality of incoming materials, such as electrodes, and of welding work being done. They accept or reject pieces of work according to required standards set forth in codes and specifications. A welding inspector must be able to read blueprints, interpret requirements, and have a knowledge of testing equipment and methods.

Closely related to this work is that of the *welding qualification technician*. This person keeps records of certified welders and supervises tests for the qualification of welding operators.

Other welding technicians work as *welding process-control technicians*. These technicians set up the procedures for welders to follow in various production jobs. They specify welding techniques, types of filler wire to be used, ranges for welding electrodes, and time estimates. Welding technicians also provide instructions concerning welding symbols on blueprints, use of jigs and fixtures, and inspection of products.

Equipment maintenance and sales technicians work out of welding supply houses. They set up equipment sold by their company, train welding operators to use it, and troubleshoot for customers.

■ **EARNINGS**

The earnings of welding trades workers vary widely depending on the skills needed for the job, industry, location, and other factors. The U.S. Department of Labor reports that median annual earnings of welders in May 2015 were $38,150. Salaries ranged from $25,940 to $60,000 or more. In addition to wages, employers often provide fringe benefits, such as health insurance plans, paid vacation time, paid sick time, and pension plans. Salaries for welding technicians vary according to the individual's function and level of education as well as the geographic location of the business.

WORK ENVIRONMENT

Welders may spend their workday inside in well-ventilated and well-lighted shops and factories, outside at a construction site, or in confined spaces, such as in an underground tunnel or inside a large storage tank that is being built. Welding jobs can involve working in uncomfortable positions. Sometimes welders work for short periods in booths that are built to contain sparks and glare. In some jobs, workers must repeat the same procedure over and over.

Welders often encounter hazardous conditions and may need to wear goggles, helmets with protective faceplates, protective clothing, safety shoes, and other gear to prevent burns and other injuries. Many metals give off toxic gases and fumes when heated, and workers must be careful to avoid exposure to such harmful substances. Other potential dangers include explosions from mishandling combustible gases and electric shock. Workers in this field must learn the safest ways of carrying out welding work and always pay attention to safety procedures. Various trade and safety organizations have developed rules for welding procedures, safety practices, and health precautions that can minimize the risks of the job. Operators of automatic welding machines are exposed to fewer hazards than manual welders and cutters, and they usually need to use less protective gear.

EXPLORING

With the help of a teacher or a guidance counselor, students may be able to arrange to visit a workplace where they can observe welders or welding machine operators on the job. Ideally, such a visit can provide a chance to see several welding processes and various kinds of welding work and working conditions, as well as an opportunity to talk with welders about their work. Another way to explore this field is by visiting the Web sites of trade associations, such as the American Welding Society.

EDUCATION AND TRAINING REQUIREMENTS
High School

High school graduates are preferred for trainee positions for skilled jobs. Useful courses for prospective welders include mathematics, blueprint reading, mechanical

A metalworker adds a new weld to a section of a trailer. (Sgt. John Jackson. U.S. Marines.)

drawing, applied physics, and shop. If possible, the shop courses should cover the basics of welding and working with electricity.

Postsecondary Training

Many welders learn their skills through formal training programs in welding, such as those available in many community colleges, technical institutes, trade schools, and the armed forces. Some programs are short term and narrow in focus, while others provide several years of thorough preparation for a variety of jobs.

A high school diploma or its equivalent is required for admission into these programs. Beginners can also learn welding skills in on-the-job training programs. The length of such training programs ranges from several days or weeks for jobs requiring few skills to a period of one to three years for skilled jobs. Trainees often begin as helpers to experienced workers, doing very simple tasks. As they learn, they are given more challenging work. To learn some skilled jobs, trainees supplement their on-the-job training with formal classroom instruction in technical aspects of the trade.

Various programs sponsored by federal, state, and local governments provide training opportunities in some areas. These training programs, which usually stress the fundamentals of welding, may be in the classroom or on the job and last from a few weeks to a year. Apprenticeship programs also offer training. Apprenticeships that teach a range of metalworking skills, including the basics of welding, are run by trade unions such as the International Association of Machinists and Aerospace Workers.

Other Education or Training

The American Welding Society offers a variety of webinars and in-person courses. Recent classes include

WELDING BASICS

LEARN MORE ABOUT IT

Geary, Don, and Rex Miller. *Welding,* 2nd ed.
    New York: McGraw-Hill Professional, 2011.

Jeffus, Larry. *Welding: Principles and Applications,* 8th ed.
    Independence, Ky.: Cengage Learning, 2016.

Lipton, Tom. *Metalworking Sink or Swim: Tips and
    Tricks for Machinists, Welders and Fabricators.* South
    Norwalk, Conn.: Industrial Press, 2009.

McCoy, Kristi Richardson. *The Art of Sculpure Welding:
    From Concept to Creation*. Norwalk, Conn.: Industrial
    Press, 2015.

Morley, Jackson. *The TAB Guide to DIY Welding: Hands-
    on Projects for Hobbyists, Handymen, and Artists.*
    New York: McGraw-Hill/TAB Electronics, 2013.

Pearce, Andrew. *Farm and Workshop Welding: Everything
    You Need to Know to Weld, Cut, and Shape Metal.*
    East Petersburg, Pa.: Fox Chapel Publishing, 2012.

"Welding Fundamentals," "Safety in Welding," "Math for Welders," and "Metallurgy."

■ CERTIFICATION, LICENSING, AND SPECIAL REQUIREMENTS
Certification or Licensing
To do welding work where the strength of the weld is a critical factor (such as in aircraft, bridges, boilers, or high-pressure pipelines), welders may have to pass employer tests or standardized examinations for certification by government agencies or professional and technical associations (such as the American Welding Society).

■ EXPERIENCE, SKILLS, AND PERSONALITY TRAITS
Most employers prefer to hire welding professionals who have completed postsecondary training or an apprenticeship program.

Welders and welding technicians should be in good enough physical condition to bend, stoop, and work in awkward positions. They also need manual dexterity, good eye-hand coordination, and good eyesight, as well as patience and the ability to concentrate for extended periods as they work on a task.

■ EMPLOYMENT PROSPECTS
Employers
Approximately 386,240 welders, cutters, solderers, and brazers are employed in the United States. Workers in welding occupations work in a variety of settings. About 60 percent of welders are employed in manufacturing plants that produce fabricated metal products, transportation equipment, machinery, and architectural and structural metals. Most of the remaining welders work for repair shops or construction companies that build bridges, large buildings, pipelines, and similar metal structures. All welding machine operators work in manufacturing industries.

Starting Out
Graduates of good training programs in welding often receive help in finding jobs through their schools' career services offices. Online job postings and the classified ads sections of newspapers often carry listings of local job openings. Information about openings for trainee positions, apprenticeships, and government training programs, as well as jobs for skilled workers, may be available through the local offices of the state employment service and local offices of unions that organize welding workers. Job seekers also can apply directly to the personnel offices at companies that hire welders.

■ ADVANCEMENT PROSPECTS
Advancement usually depends on acquiring additional skills. Workers who gain experience and learn new processes and techniques are increasingly valuable to their employers. Welders can become *welding supervisors* and take on the responsibility of assigning jobs to workers and showing them how the tasks should be performed. They must supervise job performance and ensure that operations are performed correctly and economically. Others may become *welding instructors*, teaching welding theory, techniques, and related processes. Some welders advance to the position of *welding production manager*, responsible for all aspects of welding production: equipment, materials, process control, inspection, and cost control. Finally, some experienced welders go into business for themselves and open their own welding and repair shops.

■ OUTLOOK
Overall employment for welders is expected to grow more slowly than the average for all careers through 2024, according to the U.S. Department of Labor (DOL). Despite this prediction, there should be plenty of opportunities for skilled welders, since many employers have difficulty finding qualified applicants. The DOL reports that there will be a "need for welders in manufacturing because of the importance and versatility of welding as a manufacturing process. The construction of new power generation facilities and, specifically, pipelines

transporting natural gas and oil will also result in new jobs." Additionally, welders will be needed to rebuild bridges, highways, and buildings.

In construction, wholesale trade, and repair services, more skilled welders will be needed as the economy grows because the work tends to be less routine in these industries, and automation is not likely to be a big factor. During periods when the economy is in a slowdown, many workers in construction and manufacturing, including some welders, may be laid off. Most job openings will develop when experienced workers leave their jobs.

■ UNIONS AND ASSOCIATIONS

Many people in welding and related occupations belong to one of the following unions: the International Association of Machinists and Aerospace Workers; the International Brotherhood of Boilermakers, Iron Ship Builders, Blacksmiths, Forgers and Helpers; the International Union, United Automobile, Aerospace and Agricultural Implement Workers of America; the United Association of Journeymen and Apprentices of the Plumbing and Pipe Fitting Industry of the United States, Canada and Australia; or the United Electrical, Radio, and Machine Workers of America.

The American Welding Society is a membership organization for welding professionals. It offers continuing education classes, certification, career information, and other resources.

■ TIPS FOR ENTRY

1. Visit http://search.jobsinwelding.com for job listings.
2. Join the American Welding Society to access training and networking resources, industry publications, and employment opportunities.
3. Talk to welding professionals about their careers. Ask them for advice on breaking into the field.
4. Check out Careers in Welding (http://careersin welding.com) for information on career paths, education, welding videos, and profiles of welders.

■ FOR MORE INFORMATION

The American Welding Society provides information about careers and certification in welding.

American Welding Society (AWS)
8669 NW 36th Street, #130
Miami, FL 33166-6672
Tel: (800) 443-9353; (305) 443-9353
http://www.aws.org

The International Association of Machinists and Aerospace Workers is a labor union that represents workers from various industries.

International Association of Machinists and Aerospace Workers
9000 Machinists Place
Upper Marlboro, MD 20772-2687
Tel: (301) 967-4500
E-mail: info@iamaw.org
https://www.goiam.org

The International Brotherhood of Boilermakers is a labor union that represents workers employed in heavy industry, shipbuilding, manufacturing, railroads, cement, mining, and related industries.

International Brotherhood of Boilermakers, Iron Ship Builders, Blacksmiths, Forgers and Helpers
753 State Avenue
Kansas City, KS 66101-2516
Tel: (913) 371-2640
http://www.boilermakers.org

> **FASTEST GROWING JOBS**

Wind Energy Industry Workers

■ OVERVIEW

Wind energy industry workers perform a wide range of duties, from designing, building, repairing, and maintaining wind turbines and wind farms, to assessing and purchasing land for wind farms, protecting wildlife (especially birds) from the potentially harmful effects of wind turbines, and providing support services to scientific and technical workers. Approximately 88,000 people are employed in the wind energy industry, according to the American Wind Energy Association.

■ HISTORY

The power of the wind has been utilized for thousands of years. As early as 5000 B.C. wind energy propelled boats on the Nile River in Ancient Egypt. By 200 B.C., according to a history of wind energy from the U.S. Department of Energy, "simple windmills in China were pumping water, while vertical-axis windmills with woven reed sails were grinding grain in Persia and the Middle East."

Windmills were used extensively in the Middle East for food production by the 11th century. European traders and religious crusaders brought this technology back to Europe. The Dutch refined the design of the windmill and used it to drain marshes and lakes. (Today, when we think of Holland, we think of windmills and tulips.)

European colonists brought windmill technology to the Americas. Settlers used windmills to pump water for ranches and farms. Eventually, windmills were used to generate electricity.

The Industrial Revolution caused a decline in the use of windmills in Europe and the United States. Steam engines replaced water-pumping windmills. Inexpensive electricity became available to rural areas in the United States.

Although industrialization caused a decline in the number of windmills being used, it prompted the development of larger windmills, known as wind turbines, to create large amounts of electricity. Wind turbines were constructed in Denmark as early as 1890. Wind turbines were also constructed in the United States.

The energy crisis in the 1970s prompted increased research into wind energy and other renewable energy technologies. Scientists and other researchers sought ways to reduce costs and streamline wind energy technology.

The use of wind energy has grown by leaps and bounds in the United States since the first windmill was erected by colonists. The U.S. Department of Energy reports that in the United States, installed wind electricity capacity has been growing steadily since 2000, and is expected to continue growing throughout the states.

■ THE JOB

The wind turbine is the modern, high-tech equivalent of yesterday's windmill. A single wind turbine can harness the wind's energy to generate enough electricity to power a house or small farm. Wind farms, also called wind plants, are a collection of high-powered turbines that can generate electricity for tens of thousands of homes. In addition to development on land, wind projects are also being developed offshore.

The U.S. Department of Labor breaks the wind energy industry down into three subsectors: Research & Development/Manufacturing, Project Development, and Operation & Maintenance. In addition, support workers such as clerks, lawyers, and database managers provide assistance to workers in these subsectors. Workers can be employed in more than one subsector, and many are also employed outside the renewable energy industry.

Research & Development/Manufacturing

The wind industry is very competitive. There are hundreds of companies that manufacture turbines and related components. Companies are constantly seeking ways to make wind turbines more reliable, efficient, and powerful while keeping costs manageable. In order to achieve these improvements, many different technical workers are employed in research and development. *Aerospace, civil* (with specializations in construction, geotechnical, structural, and transportation engineering), *computer, electrical, environmental, health and safety, industrial, materials,* and *mechanical engineers* design and test the turbines. *Meteorologists* and other *atmospheric scientists* help to identify prime locations for new project sites and may serve as consultants throughout the duration of a project. They also work for small consulting firms that provide advice to businesses and homeowners that are interested in installing wind power. *Materials scientists* design windmill components that can withstand mechanical and environmental stresses. *Engineering technicians* use engineering, science, and mathematics to help wind engineers and other professionals in research and development, manufacturing, quality control, and many other tasks.

Wind turbines have more than 8,000 component parts, but the three major parts are: the blades (which are made of fiberglass and often more than 100 feet in length), the tower (steel segments that are stacked on one another), and the nacelle (a rectangular box atop the tower that contains the turbine's gears, generator, other mechanical components, and electrical components). The manufacturing of the three major pieces of a wind turbine and other components is a complicated process, requiring many types of skilled production workers.

Precision machinists use machine tools, such as drill presses, lathes, and milling machines, to produce metal and plastic parts for wind turbines that meet precise specifications. These parts are too small to be produced by automated machinery.

Computer-controlled machine tool operators run machinery that forms and shapes turbine components, such as those that are part of the drive train or generator.

Assemblers use hand or power tools to put together wind turbine parts into larger components. *Electrical and electronic equipment assemblers* put together complex electrical circuitry in the wind turbine and the components that connect wind turbines to the power grid or other devices.

Welders use heat to join metal pieces, such as cylinders of rolled steel that form turbine tower segments. These workers may also oversee machinery that performs these tasks.

Quality-control inspectors make sure that manufactured parts and systems meet industry and government quality standards and work correctly. Since wind turbines are so expensive and massive, it is extremely important that manufacturing errors are caught and addressed before the wind turbines are actually assembled and installed.

Industrial production managers plan and coordinate all work activity on the factory floor. They determine the types of equipment that should be used and if new equipment is needed, manage workers and production

schedules (including scheduling overtime), and troubleshoot any labor or mechanical problems that emerge in order to keep production running smoothly.

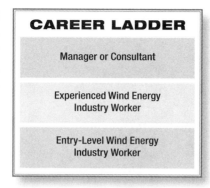

CAREER LADDER

Manager or Consultant

Experienced Wind Energy Industry Worker

Entry-Level Wind Energy Industry Worker

Project Development

The U.S. Department of Energy reports that "building a wind farm is a complex process. Site selection alone requires years of research and planning. And the proposed site must meet several criteria, such as developable land, adequate wind, suitable terrain, and public acceptance. In addition, wind turbines must be deemed safe for wildlife, particularly birds, and be sited away from populated areas because of noise and safety concerns." A variety of skilled workers select the site, ensure that it will not adversely affect the surrounding environment, and install turbines and support structures.

Land acquisition specialists create and implement land acquisition plans for new wind development sites. They work closely with government officials, community organizations, and landowners to generate support for proposed projects. Not everyone may want a wind turbine or wind farm in their "backyard," and land acquisition specialists must address the concerns of reticent individuals and organizations in order to convince them to allow construction. Land acquisition specialists also work with scientists, engineers, and *site assessors* to ensure that the area is appropriate for developing wind technology. Once the land is selected, land acquisition specialists work with *lawyers* and *permitting specialists* to lease or purchase the land.

Asset managers are responsible for the financial aspects of the project during its early stages. They make sure that the project's owner will earn maximum profits, and they manage the project's budget and finances.

Logisticians keep the transportation supply line working efficiently. They make sure that turbine components and building materials are delivered on time so that construction is not delayed and money is not wasted.

Wildlife biologists study the wind farm's potential effect on local wildlife, especially birds and bats. They create reports that detail the environmental impact of proposed wind energy products on local wildlife and provide suggestions on how builders can eliminate or reduce harm to local wildlife.

Geologists study the topography of proposed wind farms in order to make sure that the ground can support

A worker performs tests on an experimental wind turbine. (U.S. Department of Energy.)

massive and heavy wind turbines. They offer advice on where to place the turbines and how to build the foundations.

Environmental scientists help wind farm developers comply with environmental regulations and policies. They ensure that sensitive natural areas near proposed wind farms are protected.

Once the site is selected and the land purchased or leased, construction of the wind turbine or wind farm can begin.

Construction laborers prepare the site for erection of the wind turbines. They clear debris, trees, and vegetation from the site; build surrounding infrastructure such as roads or storage buildings (with the help of *construction equipment operators* and *trades workers)* and break up the ground in preparation for construction.

Crane operators use cranes to lift the turbine components off the trucks when they arrive. They place the first segment on the ground, and then gradually stack the other components atop one another, as they are joined by other workers. Once the tower has been erected, crane operators place the nacelle on top of the tower and then attach the blades.

Electricians connect the turbine's electrical components to the power grid. To do this, they use power tools such as saws and drills, and hand tools such as pliers, screwdrivers, wire strippers, and conduit benders.

Construction managers oversee the planning and building of wind turbines or wind farms. They manage workers, organize and supervise the various construction phases, order supplies, arrange deliveries, and otherwise keep everything running smoothly.

Operation & Maintenance

Wind turbines are expensive and complex pieces of machinery. It is extremely important that they are kept in top condition via regular maintenance, sensor calibration, and general upkeep. A broken or malfunctioning wind turbine means the loss of energy generation and the loss of earnings for its owner. Due to its large size and speed, a faulty turbine can also damage nearby turbines or injure or kill people on the ground. *Wind turbine service technicians,* sometimes called *windsmiths,* are responsible for this maintenance and upkeep. They climb the towers to perform maintenance, repair broken components, and otherwise bring malfunctioning turbine components back to working order. They may be responsible for regular maintenance of anywhere from one turbine to hundreds of turbines on a large wind farm.

Support Positions

Support workers perform clerical duties; supervise workers; manage computer databases; oversee advertising and marketing campaigns; respond to press inquiries; maintain records; educate the public; and do many other tasks. *Secretaries, receptionists, customer service representatives, advertising and marketing workers,media relations specialists, personnel and human resources specialists, lawyers, accountants, information technology workers,* and *educators* are just some of the types of support workers who are employed in this industry.

■ EARNINGS

The Association of Energy Engineers conducted a survey of its members in 2015. It found that they earned an average salary of $98,975. More than 10 percent of respondents earned more than $130,000, and more than 20 percent of respondents earned less than $60,000.

The U.S. Department of Labor (DOL) reports that wind turbine service technicians earned median annual salaries of $51,050 in May 2015. Earnings ranged from less than $37,010 to $71,820 or more.

The DOL does not provide salary information for other wind energy industry workers. It does provide salary ranges for engineers, other specialized technicians, and environmental scientists in all industries. The salaries for engineers employed in the United States in May 2015 ranged from about $50,230 or less to $146,820 or more; this includes civil, electrical, environmental, industrial, materials, and mechanical engineers.

Electrical and electronics engineering technicians earned salaries that ranged from less than $36,170 to $90,570 or more in May 2015, with $61,130 as the median salary. Salaries for civil, environmental, industrial, and mechanical engineering technicians ranged from about $29,270 to $81,010 or more.

Environmental scientists earned median annual salaries of $66,460 in May 2015. Ten percent of workers earned less than $40,350, and 10 percent earned $118,070 or more. Wildlife biologists earned salaries that ranged from less than $39,180 to $97,390 or more, with a median salary of $59,680.

Construction workers and managers had the following salary ranges by specialty in May 2015: construction laborers and helpers, $20,640 to $61,070+; crane operators, $31,410 to $82,760+; electricians, $31,410 to $88,130+; and welders, $25,940 to $60,000+.

Support workers in the wind energy industry earn a wide range of salaries—from starting salaries of $20,000 for receptionists, secretaries, and other office and clerical support workers, to $200,000 or more for experienced lawyers and top executives.

Benefits for full-time workers include vacation and sick time, health (and sometimes dental) insurance, and pension or 401(k) plans. Self-employed workers must provide their own benefits.

■ WORK ENVIRONMENT

Work environments in the wind industry vary by career. For example, engineers travel frequently to inspect turbine installations or wind turbine manufacturing processes. They often travel overseas because many of the biggest turbine manufacturers are located abroad. They also spend time working indoors in offices and laboratories.

Environmental scientists often travel to proposed and existing wind farm sites to study and catalog wildlife populations and prepare reports that suggest ways to protect such populations. Construction sites are often dusty or muddy, depending on weather conditions. Trades workers work outdoors in all types of weather. Wind turbine service technicians must climb wind turbines to conduct regular maintenance and repairs. The work can be dangerous and cramped (nacelles, where technicians do most of their work, are cramped), and technicians must take great care to avoid injury. Technicians wear safety harnesses while working and take other safety precautions.

Wind farms are often located far away from urban areas. This requires workers to travel great distances and live away from home for extended periods of time during the development or construction process. Field workers often work more than 40 hours a week, including on weekends. Workers in support positions, such as lawyers, secretaries, and computer professionals, spend their time in climate-controlled offices. They typically work a standard 40-hour week.

WIND, BY THE NUMBERS   FAST FACTS

The American Wind Energy Association cited the following data for wind capacity:

- U.S. wind energy capacity represents about 18 percent of global wind energy capacity.
- In 2014, wind energy provided 4.4 percent of the nation's electricity.
- The top states for new wind power capacity installed were California, Kansas, Michigan, Texas, and New York.
- From 2005 to 2015, wind energy investment in new wind projects totaled $128 billion.
- Wind energy provided electricity for 20 million American homes in 2015.
- Forty U.S. states, plus Puerto Rico, have utility-scale wind installations.
- There are approximately 48,880 operating utility-scale wind turbines.

Source: American Wind Energy Association

■ EXPLORING

One of the best ways to learn more about the wind energy industry is to read wind-related publications. "Careers in Wind Energy," by James Hamilton, U.S. Bureau of Labor Statistics, is a great resource. It offers information on wind power, educational requirements, career options, and required credentials: http://www.bls.gov/green/wind_energy. Learn more about wind energy by reading magazines such as *Windpower Monthly* (http://www.windpowermonthly.com). You can also talk to wind energy industry workers about their careers. Ask your science teacher or school counselor for help setting up an interview.

■ EDUCATION AND TRAINING REQUIREMENTS
High School

If you plan to work in a science-related position in the wind energy industry, take earth science, environmental science, mathematics, physics, and related classes in high school. Aspiring engineers and technicians should take mathematics, physics, and shop. Since many engineers travel overseas to turbine manufacturers, it would be useful to take a foreign language. Those interested in management careers should take accounting and business classes. All workers will benefit by taking English, speech, and computer science classes.

Postsecondary Education

Educational requirements vary by career. The following paragraphs detail educational requirements for selected workers in the major subsectors of the wind energy industry.

Research & Development/Manufacturing

Most wind engineers have a bachelor of science in an engineering specialty, such as electrical, civil, environmental, industrial, materials, or mechanical engineering. Many companies prefer to hire engineers with master of science degrees, so those who pursue advanced degrees may have better odds of securing work. Engineers also receive extensive on-the-job training.

Engineering technicians prepare for the field by earning a certificate or an associate's degree in engineering technology or a related field and completing on-the-job training.

Most manufacturing workers receive on-the-job training, although more skilled workers, such as computer-controlled machine tool operators, obtain their skills via postsecondary technical training or apprenticeships.

Industrial production managers usually have bachelor's degrees in industrial technology, business administration, management, or industrial engineering, although some work their way up from entry-level positions. Once they are hired, production managers also learn production methods for wind turbine components and the general business policies of their company.

Project Development

Asset managers and land acquisition professionals have at least a bachelor's degree in real estate, law, business, engineering or a related field, plus knowledge of the permit application process and tax and accounting rules.

Most logisticians have bachelor's degrees in engineering, economics, or business, and augment this education with postgraduate study in supply chain management or logistics. They also receive on-the-job training regarding logistics issues in the wind energy industry.

Atmospheric and environmental scientists usually have bachelor's degrees in earth science, geology, environmental science, meteorology, or related fields. The U.S. Department of Energy reports that "a Ph.D. is desirable for scientists in certain fields who oversee environmental impact and site suitability studies and provide expert guidance to ensure that wind turbines are constructed for optimal efficiency and minimal environmental impact."

Construction managers typically have bachelor's degrees in construction management, business management, or management, along with experience in the construction industry and with wind farm construction.

Construction workers learn their skills via on-the-job training, through apprenticeships, or by earning technical degrees or certificates.

Operation & Maintenance

Wind turbine service technicians train for the field in a variety of ways. Some enter the industry from technician or electrician positions in other industries, learning the specialized skills necessary to work in the field via on-the-job training or at technical schools. Many high school graduates who are interested in the field attend community colleges and technical schools, which offer one-year certificates and two-year degrees in wind turbine maintenance.

Support Positions

Training for support workers ranges from on-the-job training for secretaries and receptionists, to a bachelor's degree in computer science or related fields for computer professionals, to a law degree for lawyers.

Online databases of wind energy educational programs can be found on the U.S. Department of Energy's Web site at http://apps2.eere.energy.gov/wind/windex change/schools/education/education_training.asp.

Certification

Certificate programs in renewable energy are provided by colleges and universities, professional associations (such as the Midwest Renewable Energy Association), and private organizations.

Other Education or Training

The American Wind Energy Association offers educational sessions at its annual conference that cover technical, scientific, and business issues. The Association of Energy Engineers, Interstate Renewable Energy Council, Midwest Renewable Energy Association, and the National Society of Professional Engineers also provide continuing education opportunities.

■ CERTIFICATION, LICENSING, AND SPECIAL REQUIREMENTS
Certification or Licensing

The Midwest Renewable Energy Association certifies renewable energy site assessors in wind technology (home-sized systems). The North American Board of Certified Energy Professionals offers certification to small wind power installers.

Many engineering technicians choose to become certified by the National Institute for Certification in Engineering Technologies. To become certified, a technician must have a specific amount of job-related experience and pass a multiple-choice examination. The Electronics Technicians Association International offers certification for small wind tower installers.

SME offers certification to manufacturing engineers. The Association of Energy Engineers also offers certification in a variety of specialties. To be considered for certification, a candidate must meet eligibility standards such as a minimum of three years of relevant work experience and membership in a professional organization. Most programs consist of classroom work and an examination.

Engineers who work on projects that affect the property, health, or life of the public typically pursue licensure. There are two levels of licensing for engineers. Professional Engineers (PEs) have graduated from an accredited engineering curriculum, have four years of engineering experience, and have passed a written exam. Engineering graduates need not wait until they have four years of experience, however, to start the licensure process. Those who pass the Fundamentals of Engineering examination after graduating are called Engineers in Training (EITs) or Engineer Interns (EIs). The EIT certification usually is valid for 10 years. After acquiring suitable work experience, EITs can take the second examination, the Principles and Practice of Engineering exam, to gain full PE licensure. For more information on licensing and examination requirements, visit http://ncees.org.

Certification and licensing requirements for other jobs in the wind energy industry vary according to the position. Contact professional associations in your area of interest for more information.

Some atmospheric and environmental scientists may need to be licensed. Wind energy industry workers who are employed in positions that may affect the power grid must be certified by the North American Energy Reliability Corporation.

■ EXPERIENCE, SKILLS, AND PERSONALITY TRAITS

Prior experience in the wind energy industry, such as an internship, volunteering, or a part-time job, is useful.

Desirable skills and personality traits vary for the wide range of workers in the wind energy industry. For example, wind turbine technicians need strong mechanical skills, good hand-eye coordination, good communication skills, and no fear of heights or working in confined spaces. Engineers and scientists must be creative, good problem solvers, and strong communicators, enjoy conducting research, and have excellent technical and scientific ability.

Key traits of all successful workers include strong communication skills, good organizational and time-management skills, the ability to work as a member of a team, and a willingness to continue to learn throughout one's career.

■ EMPLOYMENT PROSPECTS
Employers

Approximately 88,000 people are employed in the wind energy industry, according to the American Wind Energy Association (AWEA). Although wind is everywhere, different regions of the United States are windier than others. For this reason, wind-related projects tend to be most concentrated in the Midwest, Southwest, and Northeast regions of the United States. The top five U.S. states by total installed wind capacity (in descending order) are Texas, Indiana, California, Oklahoma, and Illinois.

There are more than 500 wind-related manufacturing facilities in the United States. Much wind turbine manufacturing is located in the Midwest and Southeast. Large manufacturers include GE Wind, Siemens, Gamesa, and Vestas.

Starting Out

Many wind energy industry workers obtain their first jobs in the field as a result of contacts made through volunteerships, internships, or part-time positions. Others learn about job openings via trade associations, industry publications, career fairs, networking events, or the services of their colleges' career services offices. Useful information about careers in the renewable-energy industry can be found at the U.S. Department of Energy's Clean Energy Jobs Web page, http://energy.gov/eere/education/education-homepage.

■ ADVANCEMENT PROSPECTS

Advancement prospects vary by career. For example, wind turbine service technicians advance by earning higher salaries, taking on managerial responsibilities, or becoming engineers (after the completion of a bachelor's degree in engineering). Engineers and scientists might open their own consulting firms or seek employment with larger companies. With a Ph.D., engineers and scientists can become college professors or oversee environmental-impact and site suitability studies. Trades workers and office workers typically advance by receiving pay raises and managerial duties. By returning to school, construction workers such as electricians or welders can become construction managers or open their own contracting businesses.

■ OUTLOOK

The wind industry is one of the fastest-growing sectors of the renewable-energy industry. This growth can be attributed primarily to lower production costs. Better technology and equipment have lowered the cost of wind-generated electricity by about 80 percent in the past 20 years; this almost matches the cost of electricity generated by conventional sources such as coal or nuclear power. The American Wind Energy Association estimates that the U.S. wind energy industry will continue to enjoy strong growth in the next decade. According to the Department of Labor, wind turbine service technicians will have 108 percent employment growth through 2024. This is a small field, however, so competition for jobs will still be keen. There will also be good opportunities for engineers, meteorologists, electricians, and others in the wind industry.

■ UNIONS AND ASSOCIATIONS

Wind energy technicians, trades workers, and production employees are represented by unions. Some major unions include the International Association of Bridge, Structural, Ornamental and Reinforcing Iron Workers (http://www.ironworkers.org); International Association of Machinists and Aerospace Workers (https://www.goiam.org); International Brotherhood of Electrical Workers (http://ibew.org); International Union of Electronic, Electrical, Salaried, Machine, and Furniture Workers-Communication Workers of America (http://iue-cwa.org); United Auto Workers (https://uaw.org); and United Steelworkers of America (http://www.usw.org).

The American Wind Energy Association is the major professional association for wind energy industry professionals. Other renewable energy industry associations of note include the Interstate Renewable Energy Council and the Midwest Renewable Energy Association (MREA).

Engineers and technicians can obtain resources and support from the following professional organizations: Amercan Institute of Aeronautics and Astronautics (http://www.aiaa.org); American Society of Certified Engineering Technicians (http://www.ascet.org); American Society of Civil Engineers (http://www.asce.org); ASME International (https://www.asme.org); Association for Computing Machinery (http://www.acm.org); Electronics Technicians Association International (http://eta-i.org); Institute of Electrical and Electronics Engineers (http://www.ieee.org); Institute of Industrial and Systems Engineers (http://www.iienet2.org); IEEE Computer Society (http://www.computer.org); National Society of Professional Engineers (https://www.nspe.org); SAE International (http://www.sae.org); and the Society of Manufacturing Engineers (SME, http://www.sme.org).

The National Council of Examiners for Engineering and Surveying (http://www.ncees.org) provides licensure to engineers. The National Institute for Certification in Engineering Technologies (http://www.nicet.org) offers certification to engineering technicians. The SME offers certification to manufacturing engineers. The Association of Energy Engineers offers certification in a variety of specialties. The North American Board of Certified Energy Practitioners certifies small wind power installers. The MREA certifies renewable energy site assessors in wind technology (home-sized systems).

The U.S. Department of Energy's Office of Energy Efficiency and Renewable Energy is a government agency that provides resources for those interested in wind energy.

There are many other professional associations for workers in the wind energy industry. Check the *Encyclopedia of Associations*, which is published by Gale Cengage Learning, for associations in your field of interest. It is available in many community and school libraries.

■ TIPS FOR ENTRY

1. Read publications such as *Windpower Monthly* (http://www.windpowermonthly.com) to learn more about trends in the industry and potential employers.
2. Use Facebook, LinkedIn, Twitter, and other social media to stay up to date on industry developments and learn about job openings.
3. Join the American Wind Energy Association and other professional associations to access training and networking resources, industry publications, and employment opportunities.
4. Search for job listings at http://awea-jobs.career website.com/?navItemNumber=8205 and http://www.nspe.org/resources/career-center, as well as through online employment Web sites.

■ FOR MORE INFORMATION

The American Wind Energy Association provides industry news and updates, publications, conferences, career opportunities, and membership information.

American Wind Energy Association (AWEA)
1501 M Street, NW, Suite 1000
Washington, D.C. 20005-1769
Tel: (202) 383-2500
Fax: (202) 383-2505
http://www.awea.org

The Association of Energy Engineers offers information on careers, employment opportunities, certification, membership, and industry surveys.

Association of Energy Engineers (AEE)
3168 Mercer University Drive
Atlanta, GA 30341-5630
Tel: (770) 447-5083
E-mail: info@aeecenter.org
http://www.aeecenter.org

The Interstate Renewable Energy Council provides education, credentialing, and information about renewable energy.

Interstate Renewable Energy Council (IREC)

PO Box 1156

Latham, NY 12110-1156

Tel: (518) 621-7379

E-mail: info@irecusa.org

http://www.irecusa.org

The Midwest Renewable Energy Association provides training and events for renewable energy professionals.

Midwest Renewable Energy
Association (MREA)

7558 Deer Road

Custer, WI 54423-9734

Tel: (715) 592-6595

E-mail: info@midwestrenew.org

https://www.midwestrenew.org

The National Renewable Energy Laboratory provides research, publications, and information about careers in renewable energy.

National Renewable Energy
Laboratory (NREL)

15013 Denver West Parkway

Golden, CO 80401-3111

Tel: (303) 275-3000

http://www.nrel.gov

The National Society of Professional Engineers provides information on careers, certification and licensing, membership benefits, and local chapters.

National Society of Professional Engineers (NSPE)

1420 King Street

Alexandria, VA 22314-2794

Tel: (888) 285-6773

Fax: (703) 684-2821

https://www.nspe.org

The Office of Energy Efficiency and Renewable Energy provides information about wind energy and other renewable energy resources.

Office of Energy Efficiency and Renewable Energy

U.S. Department of Energy

Mail Stop EE-1

Washington, D.C. 20585

Tel: (877) 337-3463

E-mail: eereic@ee.doe.gov

http://energy.gov/eere/office-energy-efficiency-
renewable-energy

Wireless Service Technicians

■ OVERVIEW

Wireless service technicians are responsible for maintaining a specified group of cell sites, including the radio towers, cell site equipment, and often the building and grounds for the sites. Technicians routinely visit and monitor the functioning of the on-site equipment, performing preventive testing and maintenance. They also troubleshoot and remedy problems that might arise with any of their sites. Most wireless service technicians spend their work time at various locations, visiting each of their cell sites as necessary.

■ HISTORY

The concept of cellular communication, as it is used today, was developed by Bell Laboratories in the late 1940s. However, it was based on a much older concept: using radio waves to transmit signals over distances. The concept of communicating via radio waves dates back to the late 1800s, when Italian inventor Guglielmo Marconi discovered that radio signals could be transmitted for more than a mile. By 1905, many ships at sea were routinely using Marconi's invention to communicate with the shore.

Cellular radio, which is essentially today's cellular phone service, was first tested in two U.S. markets in the 1970s. This system, a miniature version of large radio networks, was named "cellular" because its broadcast area is divided into smaller units called cells. Each cell was equipped with its own radio tower, with a range of between 1 and 2.5 miles. As a mobile "radiophone" moved through the network of cells, its calls were switched from one cell to another by a computerized system. As long as the radiophone stayed within this network of cells, wireless communication was possible; once outside the system of cells, however, the connection was lost. After its initial tests in Chicago and Washington, D.C., the cellular network was soon duplicated in other towns and cities. As more and more areas throughout the country became "covered" with these networks of cells, it became possible to use cellular phones in more places, and the use of these phones became increasingly widespread.

In 1981, the Federal Communications Commission (FCC) announced that the wireless industry would be regulated. By FCC orders, only two competing wireless service providers could be licensed to operate in each geographic market. The FCC also announced that it would begin licensing in 306 large metropolitan areas first. Licensing in rural service areas would come shortly thereafter. As licensing got underway and cellular service was provided in more areas, the number of wireless service users grew at a rapid pace. By the end of the 1980s, there were almost 4 million cellular subscribers in the United States. By 1992, there were more than 10 million users, 9,000 cell sites, and 1,500 cellular systems throughout the country.

Also in 1992, Ameritech began the country's first commercial trials of digital wireless technology. Digital wireless technology changed the voice to numeric computer code before transmitting it, providing better sound quality and clarity than the traditional, or analog, cellular technology, which carried the voice through radio waves. With continued improvements, digital technology has largely replaced analog cellular technology.

The wireless industry experienced a major change in 1993, when the Omnibus Reconciliation Act was passed. This legislation opened up competition among wireless providers by allowing as many as nine wireless companies to operate in a single market, instead of the two that were previously allowed. With the rapid growth of wireless service throughout the United States, there has been an increased need for qualified, trained people to manage and service the equipment. Each cell site for each wireless carrier requires constant maintenance and troubleshooting to ensure that wireless coverage is not interrupted. The responsibility for maintaining this highly important and expensive equipment is the job of the wireless service technician—a key player in the wireless industry.

■ THE JOB

Wireless service technicians are sometimes also called *cell site technicians*, *field technicians*, or *cell site engineers*. These workers maintain cell sites—which consist of a radio tower and computerized equipment. Each cell site covers a geographic territory that varies in size. When someone places a wireless call within a particular cell site's geographic territory, radio waves are transmitted to that cell site's antenna. The antenna picks up the radio waves and transmits them through cables to computerized equipment that is typically located in a building adjacent to the antenna. This equipment then reads the radio waves, turns them into a computerized code, and sends the information on to a switching center. The call is then transferred to its destination—which might be another wireless phone or a traditional wireline phone.

The equipment at each cell site—the antenna and computerized equipment—are important pieces of the wireless telecommunications network. If a cell site stops functioning for some reason, wireless users within that site's coverage area may not be able to use their mobile phones. Many people rely on these devices to receive or transmit important or emergency information, so a lapse in coverage can be serious. Wireless service technicians are responsible for maintaining and troubleshooting the equipment and operations of the cell sites. The data transmission equipment may be a separate, peripheral part of the cell site equipment, and the technician is responsible for maintaining it as well.

Wireless service technicians typically perform both routine, preventive maintenance and troubleshooting of equipment that has malfunctioned. Routine maintenance might include scheduled visits to each cell site to check power levels and computer functions. Technicians often carry laptop computers, which contain sophisticated testing software. They connect their laptop computers to the cell site equipment to test equipment and ensure it is functioning correctly. Wireless carriers may also have backup equipment, such as generators and batteries, at their cell sites to ensure that even if the primary system fails, wireless coverage is still maintained. Technicians may periodically check this backup equipment to make sure it is functional and ready to be used in case of emergency.

In addition to maintaining the actual cell site computer equipment, wireless service technicians may be responsible for routine and preventive maintenance of the radio tower itself and the building and grounds of the site. Technicians do not perform the actual physical maintenance on the tower and grounds themselves. Rather, they contract with other service providers to do so and are then responsible for ensuring that the work meets appropriate standards and is done when needed.

The frequency of the scheduled visits to individual cell sites depends on the technician's employer and the number of sites the technician is responsible for. For example, a technician who is responsible for 10 to 15 sites might be required to visit each site monthly to perform routine, preventive maintenance. These sites may be close together—perhaps within blocks of each other. In less populated areas the sites may be more than 20 miles apart.

When cell site equipment malfunctions, wireless service technicians are responsible for identifying the problem and making sure that it is repaired. Technicians run diagnostic tests on the equipment to determine where the malfunction is. If the problem is one that can be easily solved—for example, by replacing a piece of equipment—the technician handles it. If it is something more serious, such as a problem with the antenna or with the local wireline telecommunications system, the technician calls the appropriate service people to remedy the situation.

In addition to routine maintenance and troubleshooting responsibilities, wireless service technicians may have a range of other duties. They may test the wireless system by driving around the coverage area while using a mobile phone. They may work with technicians in the switching center to incorporate new cell sites into the network and make sure that the wireless calls are smoothly transmitted from one cell to another.

■ EARNINGS

There is a demand for qualified and dependable employees in the wireless field, so experienced wireless technicians can expect to receive a good salary. According to the U.S. Department of Labor, mean annual earnings for wireless telecommunications installers and repairers (a related field) were $59,940 in May 2015. Salaries for all radio, cellular, and tower equipment installers and repairers ranged from less than $30,490 to $77,690 or more.

The job generally comes with other benefits as well. Many wireless companies provide their service technicians with company vehicles. Cellular phones and laptop computers, which technicians need to perform their work, are also common perks. Finally, most major wireless service providers offer a benefits package to their employees, which often includes health insurance, paid vacation, holiday, and sick days, and a pension or 401(k) plan.

■ WORK ENVIRONMENT

Cell site technicians who are in charge of several cell sites spend their workweek visiting the different sites.

Depending on how far apart the sites are, this may mean driving a substantial distance. While the actual computer equipment is located inside a building at each cell site location, any work or routine checking of the radio tower requires outside work, in varying kinds of weather. Most technicians are assigned a home base—either an office or one of the cell sites—from which they travel out to maintain the other sites. However, their "offices" are really completely portable: from their cellular phones and laptop computers, they can do their work anywhere. They truly live in a wireless, mobile environment.

This is important because the management of cell sites is a 24-hour-a-day, seven-day-a-week business. If an alarm system goes off in the middle of the night, a cell site technician must respond. The ability to access the system remotely from a laptop computer may save the technician an actual trip to the site. The sites must be maintained continuously, so wireless service technicians may work unusual hours.

Most wireless service technicians are not very closely supervised. They generally set their own schedules (with management concurrence) and work alone and independently. They may, however, have to work closely at times with other company employees to integrate new sites into the system, make modifications to the system, or troubleshoot problems.

■ EXPLORING

Become familiar with electronics, which is a key part of the technician's job. There are numerous books and Web sites on electronics and electronic theory, geared to various levels of expertise. Check with your high school or local public library to see what you can find on this topic. In addition, many hobby shops or specialty science stores have electronics kits and experiments that provide hands-on experience with how electronic circuits work.

To find out more about wireless communications specifically, you might again check for books or magazine articles on the subject through an online search as well as in local libraries. You might also contact a wireless provider in your area and ask to talk with a cell technician about their job.

Wireless service technicians repair a faulty cell phone tower.
(Henryk Sadura. Shutterstock.)

■ EDUCATION AND TRAINING REQUIREMENTS
High School

Take classes that will prepare you for further schooling in electronics. Physics classes provide the background necessary to understand the theory of electronics. Wireless service technician jobs are heavily computer-oriented, so computer classes are also excellent choices. Other important classes are those that will provide basic abilities needed in college and in the workplace—such as English, speech, and mathematics courses.

Postsecondary Training

A two-year associate's degree in a technical field is the minimum educational level needed to become a wireless service technician. Many technicians obtain degrees in electronics or electronic technology. Course work includes classes and laboratory work in circuit theory, digital electronics, microprocessors, computer trouble-shooting, telecommunications, and data communications technology. Other students might opt for degrees in telecommunications management or computer science. Take classes on local area networks, advanced networking technologies, network management, and programming. Computer science courses cover programming, operating systems, computer languages, and network architecture. Most wireless service technicians have two-year degrees, but some may have four-year degrees in computer science, telecommunications, electronic engineering, or other similar subjects.

The National Coalition for Telecommunications Education and Learning (NACTEL), in partnership with Pace university, offers degree programs in telecommunications: http://www.nactel.org.

No matter what sort of educational background new technicians have, they have to learn about the specific equipment used by their employers. Most wireless carriers send their technicians through formal education programs, which are typically offered by equipment manufacturers. In these programs, new technicians learn the operating specifics of the equipment they will be maintaining. A new technician is usually given a smaller number of cell sites to manage when he or she first begins and may be paired with a more experienced technician who can answer questions and conduct on-the-job training.

Certification

The NACTEL, in partnership with Pace University, offers an advanced certification program in emerging telecommunications technology to those who meet education requirements, http://www.nactel.org/programs/cert-emerge.html.

■ CERTIFICATION, LICENSING, AND SPECIAL REQUIREMENTS
Certification or Licensing

There are no certification or licensing requirements for wireless service technicians.

Other Requirements

Much of the wireless service technician's job involves traveling between cell sites, so a technician must have a valid driver's license and good driving record.

■ EXPERIENCE, SKILLS, AND PERSONALITY TRAITS

Any experience one can obtain in the field—such as an internship, co-op, or a part-time job—will be useful for aspiring wireless service technicians.

The ability to work independently is one of the most important characteristics of a good wireless service technician. Most technicians work on their own, traveling from site to site and performing their duties with little or no supervision. Technicians should have the discipline and self-motivation to make their own schedules and set their own priorities. It is also important that technicians be highly responsible. The willingness to learn and to adapt to change is another key personality trait of successful wireless service technicians.

■ EMPLOYMENT PROSPECTS
Employers

There are dozens of wireless service providers, both large and small, all over the United States. Anywhere that there is wireless service—that is, anywhere that you can use a cellular phone—there is a cell site, owned and maintained by a wireless provider. Some of the largest wireless providers are AT&T Wireless, Verizon Wireless, Sprint, T-Mobile, and U.S. Cellular. All of these companies have Web sites, and most maintain a listing of available jobs on their site. Wireless service technicians also work for local and regional wireless carriers.

Starting Out

Wireless service technicians find jobs through the Web sites of wireless providers. Many wireless companies maintain jobs sections on their sites, which list available positions. They also learn about opportunities through wireless industry publications, such as *Wireless Week* (https://www.wirelessweek.com).

Technical job fairs, expos, or exchanges offer opportunities to network and learn more about the industry. Technically and technologically skilled employees are so much in demand the communities frequently have events to allow employers to network with and meet potential employees. Check local newspapers for similar events in your community.

Another excellent source of job leads is your college's career services office. Many wireless companies visit schools that offer the appropriate degree programs to recruit qualified students for employees. Some companies even offer a co-op program, in which they hire students on a part-time basis while they are still in school.

■ ADVANCEMENT PROSPECTS

Wireless service technicians with experience may advance to *switch technician* or *switch engineer*. The switch technician works at the switching center, which controls the routing of the wireless phone calls.

Another avenue of advancement might be to move into system performance. System performance workers strive to maximize the performance of the wireless system. They run tests and make adjustments to ensure that the system is providing the best possible coverage in all areas and that signals from the different cell sites do not interfere with each other.

■ OUTLOOK

Employment in the telecommunications industry is expected to decline through 2024, according to the U. S. Department of Labor. This is mainly due to vast improvements in telecommunications equipment and the automation of system monitoring and repair. However, rising demand for wireless services and the creation of new wireless networks should ensure some job opportunities for workers.

WIRELESS BY THE NUMBERS   FAST FACTS

- In 2015, approximately 48 percent of U.S. households were wireless only, an increase over the 38.2 percent wireless online in 2012.
- There were nearly 378 million wireless subscriber connections in December 2015, an increase over the 208 million in 2005.
- Worldwide mobility revenue is expected to reach 1.7 trillion by 2020.
- Mobile accounts are used for more than half of e-commerce.
- One in five people under 50 read e-books with their cellphones.
- Wireless professionals earn pay that is 65 percent higher than the national average for other workers.

Source: CTIA—The Wireless Association

In recent years there has also been an increase in the number of wireless companies. This growth was spurred by the Federal Communications Commission's partial deregulation of the industry in 1993, which allowed for as many as nine carriers in a geographic market. This competition has added some jobs for technicians and is expected to continue to do so. Job opportunities will also arise due to the need to replace workers who leave their positions or retire from the field.

■ UNIONS AND ASSOCIATIONS

Wireless service technicians may belong to Communications Workers of America, the International Brotherhood of Electrical Workers, and other unions. The National Coalition for Telecommunications Education and Learning, in cooperation with Pace University, offers certificate and degree programs for wireless professionals. Other useful organizations for technicians include CTIA - The Wireless Association, Telecommunications Industry Association, Wireless Industry Association, and the Canadian Wireless Telecommunications Association.

■ TIPS FOR ENTRY

1. Visit http://www.vividfuture.org for job listings and information on telecommunications careers.
2. Join the Communications Workers of America and the International Brotherhood of Electrical Workers to increase your chances of landing a job and receiving fair pay for your work.

3. Talk with wireless service technicians about their careers. Ask them for advice on preparing for and entering the field.

■ FOR MORE INFORMATION

The Canadian Wireless Telecommunications Association provides information on the wireless industry in Canada.

Canadian Wireless Telecommunications Association (CWTA)
80 Elgin Street, Suite 300
Ottawa, ON K1P 6R2
Canada
Tel: (613) 233-4888
Fax: 613-233-2032
E-mail: info@cwta.ca
https://www.cwta.ca

The Communications Workers of America is a labor union that represents telecommunications workers.

Communications Workers of America (CWA)
501 3rd Street, NW
Washington, D.C. 20001-2797
Tel: (202) 434-1100
http://www.cwa-union.org

CTIA—The Wireless Association provides industry information and facts about wireless technology.

CTIA—The Wireless Association
1400 16th Street, NW, Suite 600
Washington, D.C. 20036-2225
Tel: (202) 736-3200
http://www.ctia.org

The International Brotherhood of Electrical Workers provides information on union membership.

International Brotherhood of Electrical Workers (IBEW)
900 Seventh Street, NW
Washington, D.C. 20001-3886
Tel: (202) 833-7000
Fax: (202) 728-7676
http://ibew.org

The Telecommunications Industry Association represents the global information and communications technology industry through standards development, policy initiatives, business opportunities, market intelligence, and networking events.

Telecommunications Industry Association (TIA)
1320 North Courthouse Road, Suite 200
Arlington, VA 22201-2598
Tel: (703) 907-7700
Fax: (703) 907-7727
http://www.tiaonline.org

The Wireless Technology Forum is a platform for industry professionals to learn about the business of emerging wireless and mobile technologies and to network with others in the field.

Wireless Technology Forum
6300 Powers Ferry Road, Suite 600-140
Atlanta, GA 30339-2919
E-mail: info@wirelesstechnologyforum.org
http://wirelesstechnologyforum.org

Wood Science and Technology Workers

■ OVERVIEW

Wood scientists and technologists experiment to find the most efficient ways of converting forest resources into useful products for consumers. Toward this end, they explore the physical, biological, and chemical properties of wood and the methods used in growing, processing, and using it. Wood science is conducted for both academic and industrial research and is carried out both in labs and on forest grounds.

■ HISTORY

Wood is one of the oldest and most versatile raw materials. It has provided shelter, tools, and furniture since prehistoric times. Since the technological revolution, scientists have found ways to treat and process wood in more innovative ways, which has allowed it to be used in many products—everything from plywood to wood plastics—that were unheard of only a few decades ago. The field of wood science technology was developed from these efforts to find better ways of using wood. Experimentation during World War II marked its modern beginnings, and the field has advanced remarkably since then. Today, more than 5,000 different products use wood as their primary raw material and there are 400 identified species of lumber.

Wood must first be processed before it can be used in the making of products. This process can include drying, finishing, seasoning, gluing, machining, or treating for preservation. Wood scientists and technologists study these techniques, in conjunction with the chemical and structural properties of wood, to discover new ways to utilize and enhance wood's strength, endurance, and versatility.

Like metallurgy and plastics manufacturing, wood science is concerned with materials engineering. While wood is one of the earth's few renewable resources, it must be wisely grown, harvested, and used to maximize its benefit. Lumber companies have to plan when and which trees to harvest, and what types of trees to plant now for harvesting in 30 years, so as to get the greatest use of the timberlands. Manufacturers of wood products must use the most efficient methods of converting wood into useful products, so as to achieve the least amount of waste and greatest durability. Wood science helps to fulfill these goals as it works toward more economical and efficient ways to satisfy people's need for wood products.

■ THE JOB

Some workers in wood science and technology are involved in research. They work for large wood product firms, universities, or the government on various research projects, ranging from the development of new wood plastics to the designing of methods to cut wood without producing sawdust.

Another area of work in wood and science technology is manufacturing. This is the most diverse area of the field, with jobs encompassing product and process development, quality control, production control, engineering, personnel relations, and general management.

Some wood and science technology careers are in the area of technical service. Technical service representatives for wood industry suppliers use their knowledge of wood to enhance the efficiency of their clients' operations. They may work for a chemical company, a machinery manufacturer, or another service-oriented business. State and federal governments also hire workers in this capacity.

Specialists who work in these areas typically fall into one of three categories of workers: *wood scientists*, *wood technologists* or *wood products engineers*, and *wood products technicians*.

Wood scientists explore the chemical, biological, and physical properties of different woods. They try to find ways to make wood last longer and work better. They also look for faster, more efficient ways to turn wood into lumber, plywood, chemicals, paper, and other products. For example, they develop and improve ways to season or chemically treat wood to increase its resistance to wear, fire, fungi, decay, insects, or marine borers.

All wood must be dried before it can be put to any permanent use in construction or furniture. Wood scientists experiment with methods of drying or curing wood, firing it in kilns at different temperatures and for varying lengths of time, to find ways that will save energy and toughen the wood against warping and other defects.

Wood scientists are able to recommend which woods are most appropriate for certain uses because of their thorough knowledge of different wood types' properties—pliability, strength, and resistance to wear. They can tell what hard and soft woods will make useful lumber and what fast-growing trees can be harvested for plywood and particleboard.

While wood scientists often work in the research area of the industry, wood technologists work primarily for industry. Like scientists, they are also knowledgeable about the scientific properties of wood, but they look at the subject from a business perspective. These specialists work toward finding new ways to make wood products, with a minimum waste of wood, time, and money. Their jobs may combine responsibilities in areas that are usually considered the exclusive domain of either business or science, including materials engineering, research, quality control, production, management, marketing, or sales.

In many ways, wood technologists carry on the work of the wood scientists, by investigating the differing qualities of woods. As employees of paper mills, sawmills, or plywood mills, they may test woods as well as new kilns and new sawmill machines. They may cooperate with foresters who grow and harvest wood. If working for a wood products manufacturer, technologists may experiment with new methods of drying, joining, gluing, machining, and finishing lumber. They may also direct and oversee the activity of other workers, accumulate and analyze data, and write reports.

QUICK FACTS

ALTERNATE TITLE(S)
Wood Products Engineers, Wood Products Technicians, Wood Scientists, Wood Technologists

DUTIES
Conduct research and experiments to find the most efficient ways of converting forest resources into useful products for consumers

SALARY RANGE
$36,048 to $62,160 to $76,880+

WORK ENVIRONMENT
Indoors/Outdoors

BEST GEOGRAPHIC LOCATION(S)
Most opportunities exist along the Eastern Seaboard, in the North Central States, in the Pacific Northwest, and in the southern states from Virginia to eastern Texas

MINIMUM EDUCATION LEVEL
Bachelor's Degree

SCHOOL SUBJECTS
Biology, Chemistry, Mathematics

EXPERIENCE
On-the-job training or internship

PERSONALITY TRAITS
Hands On, Outgoing, Scientific

SKILLS
Information Management, Mechanical/Manual Dexterity, Scientific

CERTIFICATION OR LICENSING
None

SPECIAL REQUIREMENTS
None

EMPLOYMENT PROSPECTS
Good

ADVANCEMENT PROSPECTS
Good

OUTLOOK
Faster than the Average

NOC
2112

O*NET-SOC
N/A

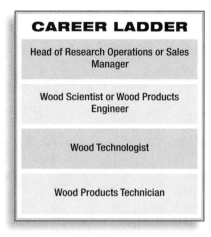

CAREER LADDER

Head of Research Operations or Sales Manager

Wood Scientist or Wood Products Engineer

Wood Technologist

Wood Products Technician

Wood technologists also work closely with their clients, who may be wood manufacturers or the buyers and distributors of wood products. If a sporting goods manufacturer is looking for light, resilient woods for making skis, for example, the wood technologist machines, treats, and supplies this wood. The technologist may even direct scientific research into new methods of improving the quality of wood for making skis. The wood technologist also knows how to test the wood for the qualities the buyer needs. New tooling machines may need to be designed, new processing techniques might need to be perfected, and workers may need to be hired or specially trained to accomplish the end goal. The wood technologist often coordinates all of these activities for both the company's purposes and the advancement of wood science.

Wood technologists often oversee the work of wood products technicians, who also add to the efficiency and profitability of their companies through their knowledge of wood and its properties. Wood products technicians operate kilns, plywood presses, and other machines used in the processing and treating of wood. They may also work in product testing and quality control, helping technologists and engineers overcome problems and expand the horizons of wood science.

Almost all careers in wood science and technology involve a substantial amount of paperwork. Project documentation, as with any scientific study, is extensive and constant. Typically, scientists and technologists spend about half of their time working in the lab and the rest of their time writing proposals, designing layouts, studying processes, and communicating with clients and other project members.

■ EARNINGS

Salary levels in the wood sciences depend on the individual's employer, experience, level of education, and work performed. According to Salary.com, the average starting salary for wood technologists was $40,263 in December 2016. Salaries ranged from $36,048 to $50,068. Indeed .com reports that wood scientists earned average salaries of $58,000 in December 2016.

Engineers employed in wood product manufacturing earned mean annual salaries of $72,150 in May 2015, according to the U.S. Department of Labor. Life and physical scientists averaged from $62,160 to $76,880.

Usually wood scientists, wood technologists, and wood products technicians receive fringe benefits, including health insurance, pension plans, and paid vacations.

■ WORK ENVIRONMENT

Depending on the type of work they perform, wood science specialists operate in a variety of settings, from the office to the open forest. Wood scientists and researchers work in laboratories and, if they are on university faculty, in classrooms. Their experimental work may take them to tree farms and forests. Wood technologists and technicians may work in offices, manufacturing plants, sawmills, or research facilities. Those technologists who are involved in sales often need to travel.

Work may be solitary or as part of a team, depending on the position and the project. And workers in the lab may use a wide variety of equipment—anything from a table saw to a word processing program to a chemical analytical device.

These types of employees work a normal 40-hour week, but extra hours may be required in certain situations. Technologists who supervise technicians and other production workers may have to work second and third shifts. Administrators may also have to put in extra hours. Workers paid by the hour often get overtime pay, but salaried employees do not get extra monetary compensation for their extra hours.

Wood science and technology specialists have a difficult but rewarding job: applying scientific principles such as chemistry, physics, and mathematics to a commonplace raw material and finding new ways for society to use wood in more productive, efficient ways. Many who work in this field enjoy the challenge it presents and feel fulfilled by helping to better understand and more efficiently utilize one of the earth's most necessary resources.

■ EXPLORING

High school counselors should be able to provide you with information on careers in this field. If you live near a college that offers a wood science and technology degree, or near a logging industry or manufacturer of wood products, you may be able to talk with students, professors, or employees who can explain the field more fully. It may even be possible to find a part-time or summer job in the wood industry. Any experience in working with wood and wood products will provide you with valuable insight and education. Take woodworking classes offered in your school or community. By working with wood, you can begin to understand the differences in wood types and how they respond to various kinds of woodworking procedures.

■ EDUCATION AND TRAINING REQUIREMENTS
High School

Many different specialties are contained within the wood science field. Therefore, a broad understanding of many subjects will prove more useful than extensive study of a single discipline. Take as many science classes as possible. Biology, chemistry, and earth sciences will be especially helpful. Mathematics is another important focus area for career preparation. Many jobs in this industry are engineering jobs, which require a solid grasp of advanced math skills. Written and oral communication are important in scientific research, so English and speech classes are good choices to help you develop these skills.

Postsecondary Training

A bachelor's degree is required for employment as a wood scientist or wood technician. Many colleges in the United States offer degrees in wood science, wood technology, forestry, or forest products. Courses of study in these programs may include wood physics, wood chemistry, wood-fluid relationships, wood machinery, and production management. Degree programs in chemistry, biology, physics, mechanical engineering, materials science, or civil engineering can also be very useful if combined with courses in wood science.

A master's degree or doctorate is usually required for more advanced work as a researcher. Advanced studies include such topics as pulp and paper science, business administration, production management, and forestry-wood sciences.

Visit http://www.swst.org/edu/schooldirectory.html for a list of colleges and universities that offer baccalaureate and graduate programs in wood science and technology.

Apprenticeships used to be the most common method of training for wood products technicians, but today most earn a certificate or associate's degree from a two-year college. Their course work in wood science includes the identification, composition, and uses of wood. It also covers wood design, manufacturing, seasoning and machining, and methods and materials for making wood products. Some business courses may also be included. Some students may wish to earn a two-year degree first and then transfer to another school to earn a bachelor's degree.

Other Education or Training

The Society of Wood Science and Technology offers professional development opportunities at

As employees of paper mills or sawmills, wood technologists must be familiar with all types of wood and wood products. (Zurijeta. Shutterstock.)

its annual international convention. Recent sessions included "Hardwood Research and Utilization," "Products, Design, and Manufacturing Technologies," and "Energy, Fuels, Chemicals." The Forest Products Society, Society of American Foresters, and the Canadian Wood Council also provide classes and seminars.

■ CERTIFICATION, LICENSING, AND SPECIAL REQUIREMENTS
Certification or Licensing

There are no certification or licensing requirements for wood scientists and technologists.

■ EXPERIENCE, SKILLS, AND PERSONALITY TRAITS

No experience is required for entry-level wood science workers. Scientists and engineers must earn a degree and complete an internship or receive other on-the-job training.

The main personal requirement for success in this field is the ability to communicate well. The ability to understand and use scientific theory is also important in this career, as are curiosity and persistence in your work habits. Finally, an interest in wood and conservation issues is a plus. Workers in this industry should be environmentally aware, as their industry is contingent on the preservation and proper use of wood as a renewable resource.

■ EMPLOYMENT PROSPECTS
Employers

Most wood scientists and technologists are employed in private industry. Firms that deal with forest products, such as mills, manufacturers of wood products, suppliers to the

UNDERSTANDING WOOD

LEARN MORE ABOUT IT

Carlsen, Spike. *A Splintered History of Wood: Belt-Sander Races, Blind Wood-workers, and Baseball Bats.* New York: Harper Perennial, 2009.

Green, Harvey. *Wood: Craft, Culture, History.* New York: Penguin Group, 2007.

Hoadley, Bruce R. *Understanding Wood: A Craftsman's Guide to Wood Technology,* Rev. ed. Newtown, Conn.: The Taunton Press, 2000.

Mayo, Joseph. *Solid Wood: Case Studies in Mass Timber Architecture, Technology and Design.* London: Routledge, 2015.

Porter, Terry. *Wood Identification and Use: A Field Guide to More than 200 Species.* Newtown, Conn.: The Taunton Press, 2012.

Shmulsky, Rubin, and P. David Jones. *Forest Products and Wood Science,* 6th ed. Hoboken, N.J.: Wiley-Blackwell, 2011.

wood products industry, forest products associations, and paper and pulp companies all hire these kinds of workers. Independent contract research firms may also be sources of employment. Universities and federal and state agencies, such as the Extension Service, hire wood science and technology experts to work on various research projects.

Geographically, careers in wood science and technology tend to be situated near large wood-producing forests and mills. Most wood science technologists work along the Eastern Seaboard, in the North Central States, in the Pacific Northwest, and in the southern states from Virginia to eastern Texas.

Starting Out

Wood science and technology jobs are not hard for qualified applicants to come by. Many forestry firms recruit new employees during visits to campus, and new graduates of wood science and technology programs often learn about employment opportunities through their colleges' career services offices. Other sources of information are professional groups, which may maintain job referral or resume services, and trade magazines, which often carry want ads for job openings. Information on jobs with the federal government can be obtained from the Office of Personnel Management.

■ ADVANCEMENT PROSPECTS

Moving ahead in the wood science field depends on ingenuity, skills, and the ability to handle important projects.

There is no typical career path, and advancement can come in the form of promotions, pay raises, or more important assignments. People with management skills may rise to become sales managers, division chiefs, or directors, although the size of the company often dictates the opportunities for advancement. Larger companies obviously offer more places within the organization, so advancement may be quicker than in a smaller company.

A master's degree or a Ph.D. can be the ticket to advancement for those working in research; workers in this field may be granted permission to conduct independent research or be promoted to heads of research operations. Wood science and technology employees in the business area of the industry may find that additional schooling makes them better candidates for higher administrative positions. Wood products technicians may find that earning a bachelor's degree can help them move up to the position of wood technologist.

■ OUTLOOK

Wood technology is a relatively new science, with breakthroughs in products and technology occurring frequently. It is also a field in which the supply of qualified wood scientists and technologists is short of the demand. Therefore, the employment outlook for workers in this field is expected to be very good.

The demand for wood products is increasing rapidly. At the same time, the costs of growing and harvesting timber and processing wood products are rising rapidly. Wood manufacturers need the skills of wood science specialists to keep their operations profitable and efficient and to help them compete with plastics manufacturers and the makers of other wood substitutes.

Conservation programs will affect the industry both positively and negatively. Pressure to reduce lumber harvests will continue to increase, particularly in threatened areas, such as the rainforest. Those pressures, however, will force increased study of ways to better utilize wood currently being harvested.

Although the employment outlook for wood science and technology workers is expected to be strong, it is heavily tied to the overall economy. The bulk of all forest products is used in the construction industry, so a downturn in new construction means a downturn in all forest-related careers.

■ UNIONS AND ASSOCIATIONS

Some wood science workers may belong to the International Brotherhood of Teamsters and other unions. The Society of Wood Science and Technology, Forest Products Society, and the Society of American Foresters provide membership, networking opportunities, publications, career information, job listings, and continuing education classes. The National Hardwood Lumber Association and the Canadian Wood Council are membership organizations for lumber companies, wood science firms, and related organizations.

■ TIPS FOR ENTRY

1. Read *Wood and Fiber Science, Forest Products Journal,* and *Wood Design Focus* to learn more about the field.
2. Visit the following Web sites for job listings:
   - http://www.swst.org/careers
   - http://jobs.forestprod.org
   - http://nhla.com/jobs
   - http://careercenter.eforester.org
3. Visit http://www.swst.org/careers/profession .html to read Careers in Pulp & Paper, Exploring a Profession in Forest Products, and Careers in Applied Science and Engineering.

■ FOR MORE INFORMATION

The Canadian Wood Council provides information on marketing and manufacturing careers in wood products.

Canadian Wood Council (CWC)
99 Bank Street, Suite 400
Ottawa, ON K1P 6B9
Canada
Tel: (613) 747-5544
Fax: (613) 747-6264
http://cwc.ca

The Forest Products Society offers technical periodicals, newsletters, and directories covering a broad range of topics related to wood and wood fiber properties, products, and markets.

Forest Products Society
15 Technology Parkway South, Suite 115
Peachtree Corners, GA 30092-8200
Tel: (855) 475-0291
http://www.forestprod.org

The National Hardwood Lumber Association offers training, education, and membership benefits.

National Hardwood Lumber Association (NHLA)
PO Box 34518
Memphis, TN 38184-0518
Tel: (901) 377-1818
E-mail: membership@nhla.com
http://www.nhla.com

The Society of American Foresters has a mission to advance sustainable management of forest resources through science, education, and technology.

Society of American Foresters (SAF)
10100 Laureate Way
Bethesda, MD 20814-2198
Tel: (866) 897-8720; (301) 897-8720
Fax: (301) 897-3690
E-mail: membership@safnet.org
http://www.eforester.org

The Society of Wood Science and Technology offers education, networking opportunities, and career-support resources.

Society of Wood Science and Technology (SWST)
PO Box 6155
Monona, WI 53716-6155
Tel: (608) 577-1342
Fax: (608) 254-2769
E-mail: vicki@swst.org
http://www.swst.org

Writers

■ OVERVIEW

Writers express, edit, promote, and interpret ideas and facts in written form for books, magazines, trade journals, newspapers, company newsletters, radio and television broadcasts, and advertisements. They develop fiction and nonfiction ideas for plays, novels, poems, and other related works; report, analyze, and interpret facts, events, and personalities; review art, music, film, drama, and other artistic presentations; and persuade the general public to choose or favor certain goods, services, and personalities. There are approximately 43,380 salaried writers and authors employed in the United States.

■ HISTORY

The skill of writing has existed for thousands of years. Papyrus fragments with writing by ancient Egyptians date from about 3000 B.C. and archaeological findings show that the Chinese had developed books by about 1300 B.C. A number of technical obstacles had to be overcome before printing and the profession of writing evolved. Books of the Middle Ages were copied by hand on parchment. The ornate style that marked these books helped ensure their rarity. Also, few people were able to read.

The development of the printing press by Johannes Gutenberg in the middle of the 15th century and the liberalism of the Protestant Reformation, which encouraged a wide range of publications, greater literacy, and the

QUICK FACTS

ALTERNATE TITLE(S)
Bloggers, Columnists, Continuity
  Writers, Copy Writers, Critics,
  Editorial Writers, News Writers,
  Novelists, Playwrights, Poets,
  Screenwriters, Short Story
  Writers, Technical Writers

DUTIES
Write about a variety of topics;
  perform research; conduct
  interviews

SALARY RANGE
$29,230 to $60,250 to
  $114,530+

WORK ENVIRONMENT
Primarily Indoors

BEST GEOGRAPHIC LOCATION(S)
Opportunities are available in
  all regions but are best in
  New York City; Los Angeles;
  Washington, D.C.; Chicago;
  and Boston.

MINIMUM EDUCATION LEVEL
Bachelor's Degree

SCHOOL SUBJECTS
English, History, Journalism

EXPERIENCE
Any writing experience helpful

PERSONALITY TRAITS
Artistic, Creative, Organized

SKILLS
Organizational, Research, Writing

CERTIFICATION OR LICENSING
None

SPECIAL REQUIREMENTS
None

EMPLOYMENT PROSPECTS
Good

ADVANCEMENT PROSPECTS
Good

OUTLOOK
Little Change or More Slowly
  than the Average

NOC
5121

O*NET-SOC
27-3042.00, 27-3043.00, 27-
  3043.04, 27-3043.05

creation of a number of works of literary merit, prompted the development of the publishing industry. The first authors worked directly with printers.

The modern publishing age began in the 18th century. Printing became mechanized, and the novel, magazines, and newspapers developed. The first newspaper in the American colonies appeared in the early 18th century, but it was Benjamin Franklin who, as editor and writer, made the *Pennsylvania Gazette* one of the most influential in setting a high standard for his fellow American journalists. Franklin also published the first magazine in the colonies, *The American Magazine*, in 1741.

Advances in the printing trades, photoengraving, retailing, and the availability of capital produced a boom in newspapers and magazines in the 19th century. Further mechanization in the printing field, such as the use of the Linotype machine, high-speed rotary presses, and special color reproduction processes, set the stage for still further growth in the book, newspaper, and magazine industry.

In addition to the print media, the broadcasting industry has contributed to the development of the professional writer. Film, radio, and television are sources of entertainment, information, and education that provide employment for thousands of writers.

Today, the growth of the Internet and social media have created an increasing number of opportunities for writers to work as *bloggers*, online journalists, social media professionals, and writers for online videos.

The increasing popularity of electronic books is good news for writers, who now have many additional outlets to reach potential readers outside of the mainstream publishing industry (although some writers believe that publishing companies are taking too large of a cut of profits from e-book sales).

■ THE JOB

Writers work in the field of communications. Specifically, they deal with the written word, whether it is destined for the printed page, broadcast, computer screen, or live theater. The nature of their work is as varied as the materials they produce: books, magazines, trade journals, newspapers, company newsletters and other publications, advertisements, speeches, scripts for motion picture and stage productions, and scripts for radio and television broadcast. Writers develop ideas and write for all media.

Prose writers for newspapers, magazines, and books share many of the same duties. First they come up with an idea for an article or book from their own interests or are assigned a topic by an editor. The topic is of relevance to the particular publication. (For example, a writer for a magazine on parenting may be assigned an article on car seat safety.) Then writers begin gathering as much information as possible about the subject through library research, interviews, the Internet, observation, and other methods. They keep extensive notes from which they draw material for their project. Once the material has been organized and arranged in logical sequence, writers prepare a written outline. The process of developing a piece of writing is exciting, although it can also involve detailed and solitary work. After researching an idea, a writer might discover that a different perspective or related topic would be more effective, entertaining, or marketable.

When working on assignment, writers submit their outlines to an editor or other company representative for approval. Then they write a first draft of the manuscript, trying to put the material into words that will have the desired effect on their audience. They often rewrite or polish sections of the material as they proceed, always searching for just the right way of imparting information or expressing an idea or opinion. A manuscript may be reviewed, corrected, and revised numerous times before a final copy is submitted. Even after that, an editor may request additional changes.

Writers for newspapers, magazines, or books often specialize in their subject matter. Some writers might have an educational background that allows them to give critical interpretations or analyses. For example, a *health or science writer* for a newspaper typically has a degree in biology and can interpret new ideas in the field for the average reader.

Columnists or *commentators* analyze news and social issues. They write about events from the standpoint of their own experience or opinion. *Critics* review literary, musical, or artistic works and performances. *Editorial writers* write on topics of public interest, and their comments, consistent with the viewpoints and policies of their employers, are intended to stimulate or mold public opinion. *Newswriters* work for newspapers, radio, or TV news departments, writing news stories from notes supplied by reporters or wire services.

Corporate writers and *writers for nonprofit organizations* have a wide variety of responsibilities. These writers may work in such places as a large insurance corporation or for a small nonprofit religious group, where they may be required to write news releases, annual reports, speeches for the company head, or public relations materials. Typically they are assigned a topic with length requirements for a given project. They may receive raw research materials, such as statistics, and they are expected to conduct additional research, including personal interviews. These writers must be able to write quickly and accurately on short deadlines, while also working with people whose primary job is not in the communications field. The written work is submitted to a supervisor and often a legal department for approval; rewrites are a normal part of this job.

Copywriters write copy that is primarily designed to sell goods and services. Their work appears as advertisements in newspapers, magazines, and other publications or as commercials on radio and television broadcasts. Sales and marketing representatives first provide information on the product and help determine the style and length of the copy. The copywriters conduct additional research and interviews; to formulate an effective approach, they study advertising trends and review surveys of consumer preferences. Armed with this information, copywriters write a draft that is submitted to the account executive and the client for approval. The copy is often returned for correction and revision until everyone involved is satisfied. Copywriters, like corporate writers, may also write articles, bulletins, news releases, sales letters, speeches, and other related informative and promotional material. Many copywriters are employed in advertising agencies. They also may work for public relations firms or in communications departments of large companies.

Technical writers can be divided into two main groups: those who convert technical information into material for the general public, and those who convey technical information between professionals. Technical writers in the first group may prepare service manuals or handbooks, instruction or repair booklets, or sales literature or brochures; those in the second group may write grant proposals, research reports, contract specifications, or research abstracts.

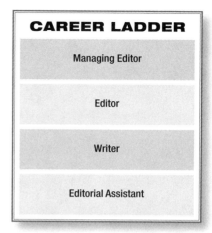

Screenwriters prepare scripts for motion pictures or television. They select or are assigned a subject, conduct research, write and submit a plot outline and narrative synopsis (treatment), and confer with the producer and/or director about possible revisions. Screenwriters may adapt books or plays for film and television dramatizations. They often collaborate with other screenwriters and may specialize in a particular type of script or writing.

Playwrights do similar writing for the stage. They write dialogue and describe action for plays that may be tragedies, comedies, or dramas, with themes sometimes adapted from fictional, historical, or narrative sources. Playwrights combine the elements of action, conflict, purpose, and resolution to depict events from real or imaginary life. They often make revisions even while the play is in rehearsal.

Continuity writers prepare the material read by radio and television announcers to introduce or connect various parts of their programs.

Novelists and *short story writers* create stories that may be published in books, magazines, or literary journals. They take incidents from their own lives, from news events, or from their imaginations and create characters, settings, actions, and resolutions. *Poets* create narrative, dramatic, or lyric poetry for books, magazines, or other publications, as well as for special events such as commemorations. These writers may work with *literary agents* or *editors* who help guide them through the writing process, which includes research of the subject matter and an understanding of the intended audience. Many universities and colleges offer graduate degrees in creative writing. In these programs, students work intensively with published writers to learn the art of storytelling.

Digital writers research, write, and create content that is published on Web sites, smartphones, and other mobile devices, and in e-publications. Bloggers are employed by companies to positively promote their products and services via the written word (blog). Others are

Television writer and author of the Hunger Games *series Suzanne Collins attends the premiere of the film* Catching Fire. *(Helga Esteb. Shutterstock.)*

self-employed and host their own blogs and sell advertisements to earn revenue.

Writers can be employed either as in-house staff or as freelancers. Pay varies according to experience and the position, but freelancers must provide their own office space and equipment such as computers and fax machines. Freelancers also are responsible for keeping tax records, sending out invoices, negotiating contracts, and providing their own health insurance.

■ EARNINGS

In May 2015, median annual earnings for salaried writers and authors were $60,250 a year, according to the Bureau of Labor Statistics. The lowest paid 10 percent earned less than $29,230, while the highest paid 10 percent earned $114,530 or more. Some specialties pay better than others. For example, writers who work in newspaper, periodical, directory, and book publishing earned mean annual salaries of $59,860, while those employed in advertising, public relations, and related services earned mean annual salaries of $77,450.

Salary.com reported that Web writers with up to three years of experience earned median annual salaries of $50,563 in December 2016. The lowest paid 10 percent earned less than $39,631, while the highest paid 10 percent earned $54,506 or more. Full-time bloggers earned an average salary of $51,000 in December 2016, according to Indeed.com. Some bloggers earn stipends based on the number of "hits" their blogs receive. Others sell advertising space at their Web sites, which helps them generate revenue.

In addition to their salaries, many writers earn some income from freelance work. Part-time freelancers often charge by the hour and rates vary based on the project. Fees may range from $42 to $85 an hour for writing Web copy to $45 to $95 an hour for writing newsletters, brochures, or articles. Rates may be as much as $100 or more per hour for writing grants and business proposals. Freelance earnings vary widely. Full-time established freelance writers may earn $50,000 a year or more.

■ WORK ENVIRONMENT

Working conditions vary for writers. Their workweek usually runs 35 to 40 hours, but many writers work overtime. A publication that is issued frequently has more deadlines closer together, creating greater pressures to meet them. The work is especially hectic on newspapers and at broadcasting companies, which operate seven days a week. Writers often work nights and weekends to meet deadlines or to cover a late-developing story.

Most writers work independently, but they often must cooperate with artists, print and digital designers, photographers, rewriters, and advertising people who may have widely differing ideas of how the materials should be prepared and presented.

Physical surroundings range from comfortable private offices to noisy, crowded newsrooms filled with other workers typing and talking on the telephone. Some writers must confine their research to the library or telephone interviews, but others may travel to other cities or countries or to local sites, such as theaters, ballparks, airports, factories, or other offices.

The work is arduous, but most writers are seldom bored. Some jobs, such as that of the foreign correspondent, require travel. The most difficult element is the continual pressure of deadlines. People who are the most content as writers enjoy and work well with deadline pressure.

■ EXPLORING

Test your interest and aptitude in the field of writing by serving as a reporter or writer on school newspapers, yearbooks, and literary magazines. Various writing courses and workshops will provide the opportunity to sharpen your writing skills.

Small community newspapers and local radio stations often welcome contributions from outside sources, although they may not have the resources to pay for them. Jobs in bookstores, magazine shops, and even newsstands will offer you a chance to become familiar with various publications.

You can also obtain information on writing as a career by visiting local newspapers, publishers, or radio and television stations and interviewing some of the writers who work there. Career conferences and other guidance programs frequently include speakers on the entire field of communications from local or national organizations.

■ EDUCATION AND TRAINING REQUIREMENTS
High School

Build a broad educational foundation by taking courses in English, literature, foreign languages, history, general science, social studies, computer science, and typing. The ability to type is almost a requisite for all positions in the communications field, as is familiarity with computers.

Postsecondary Training

Competitive writing jobs almost always demand the background of a college education. Many employers prefer you have a broad liberal arts background or majors in English, literature, history, philosophy, or one of the social sciences. Other employers desire communications or journalism training in college. Occasionally a master's degree in a specialized writing field may be required. A number of schools offer courses in journalism, and some of them offer courses or majors in book publishing, publication management, and newspaper and magazine writing.

Learning HTML, a Web site authoring language, can also be helpful to digital writers and may qualify you for other writing opportunities. All writers should learn the most popular software programs and office tools that relate to their specialty.

In addition to formal course work, most employers look for practical writing experience. Those who have served on high school or college newspapers, yearbooks, or literary magazines, or worked for small community newspapers or radio stations, even in an unpaid position, are attractive candidates. Many book publishers, magazines, newspapers, and radio and television stations have summer internship programs that provide valuable

W. H. AUDEN, 20TH CENTURY POET

MOVERS AND SHAKERS

Wystan Hugh Auden is considered one of the most influential 20th-century poets. As the leader of a group of Marxist authors in the 1930s that included Christopher Isherwood and Stephen Spender, Auden wrote many poems brilliantly satirizing middle-class values and attacking Nazism and Fascism. His main concern, however, was with the individual—especially the artist—and his early writings include such simple and moving lyrics as "In Memory of W. B. Yeats" and "Lullaby." His later poetry shows a break with Marxist ideology and an increasing interest in religion and philosophy.

Auden's long poem *The Age of Anxiety* (1947, Pulitzer Prize 1948), about four people in a bar examining life, loneliness, and hope, was also performed on stage. The title became a catchword for the postwar era. In 1956, Auden was given the National Book Award for *The Shield of Achilles*. He received the National Medal for Literature in 1967. In addition to lyric and narrative poems, he wrote verse plays, essays, and librettos. He also edited a number of poetry collections.

training if you want to learn about the publishing and broadcasting businesses. Interns do many simple tasks, such as running errands and answering phones, but some may be asked to perform research, conduct interviews, or even write some minor pieces.

Writers who specialize in technical fields may need degrees, concentrated course work, or experience in specific subject areas. This applies frequently to engineering, business, or one of the sciences. Also, technical communications is a degree now offered at many universities and colleges.

To enter positions with the federal government, applicants must take a civil service examination and meet certain specified requirements, according to the type and level of position.

Other Education or Training

A variety of webinars, conference seminars, workshops, and other continuing education opportunities are offered by professional associations such as the American Society of Journalists and Authors, Association of American Publishers, Association of Opinion Journalists, Editorial Freelancers Association, MPA–The Association of Magazine Media, National Association of Science Writers, National Society of Newspaper Columnists, Online News Association, Society for Technical Communication, and the Society of Professional Journalists. Topics include writing, editing, interviewing, social media, and technology.

■ CERTIFICATION, LICENSING, AND SPECIAL REQUIREMENTS
Certification or Licensing

Certification is available for some types of writers, such as medical writers, offered by the American Medical Writers Association, and technical writers, offered by a number of groups. Be sure to carefully research the value of a specific certification for your career before obtaining one.

■ EXPERIENCE, SKILLS, AND PERSONALITY TRAITS

Any experience volunteering as a writer will be useful for those who aspire to enter the field. Contact community organizations, religious groups, or local businesses, and other organizations that require the skills of writers.

To be a writer, you should be creative and able to express ideas clearly, have a broad general knowledge, be skilled in research techniques, and be computer literate. Other assets include curiosity, persistence, initiative, resourcefulness, and an accurate memory. For some jobs—on a newspaper, for example, where the activity is hectic and deadlines are short—the ability to concentrate and produce under pressure is essential.

■ EMPLOYMENT PROSPECTS
Employers

There are approximately 43,380 writers and authors currently employed in the United States. About 10 percent of salaried writers and authors work in the information sector, which includes newspapers, magazines, book publishers, film companies, and radio and television broadcasting. Writers also work for advertising agencies and public relations firms and work on journals and newsletters published by business and nonprofit organizations, such as professional associations, labor unions, and religious organizations. Other employers are government agencies and film production companies. About 66 percent of writers and authors are self-employed.

Starting Out

A fair amount of experience is required to gain a high-level position in the field. Most writers start out in entry-level positions. These jobs may be listed with college career services offices, or they may be obtained by applying directly to the employment departments of the individual publishers or broadcasting companies. Graduates who previously served internships with these companies often have the advantage of knowing someone who can give them a personal recommendation. Want ads in newspapers and trade journals, in print and online, are another source for jobs. Few vacancies are listed with public or private employment agencies, however, because of the competition for positions.

Employers in the communications field usually are interested in samples of published writing, and usually prefer to see these samples in a digital portfolio. Bylined or signed articles are more credible (and, as a result, more useful) than stories whose source is not identified.

Entry-level positions as a *junior writer* usually involve library and Internet research, preparation of rough drafts for part or all of a report, cataloging, and other related writing tasks. These are generally carried on under the supervision of a senior writer.

Many firms now hire writers directly upon application or recommendation of college professors and career services offices.

■ ADVANCEMENT PROSPECTS

Most writers find their first jobs as editorial or production assistants. Advancement may be more rapid in small companies, where beginners learn by doing a little bit of everything and may be given writing tasks immediately. In large firms, duties are usually more compartmentalized. Assistants in entry-level positions are assigned such tasks as research, fact checking, and copyrighting, but it generally takes much longer to advance to full-scale writing duties.

Promotion into more responsible positions may come with the assignment of more important articles and stories to write, or it may be the result of moving to another company. Mobility among employees in this field is common. An assistant in one publishing house may switch to an executive position in another. Or a writer may switch to a related field as a type of advancement.

Freelance or self-employed writers earn advancement in the form of larger fees as they gain exposure and establish their reputations.

■ OUTLOOK

The employment of writers is expected to grow more slowly than the average for all careers through 2024, according to the U.S. Department of Labor (DOL). Competition for writing jobs has been and will continue to be competitive, but certain fields will offer better opportunities than other areas. The growth of online publishing on company Web sites and other online services will create a demand for many talented writers. The DOL says that "writers and authors who have adapted to online media and are comfortable writing for and working with a variety of electronic and digital tools should have an advantage in finding work." The fields of advertising and public relations should also provide job opportunities.

Employment for writers at newspapers, periodicals, and book publishers will continue to decline through 2024.

Employment opportunities for technical writers are expected to grow faster than the average for all occupations through 2024. In addition to software publishers and computer systems design and related services firms, management, scientific, and technical consulting services firm are showing an increased need for technical writers.

The major book and magazine publishers, broadcasting companies, advertising agencies, public relations firms, and the federal government account for the concentration of writers in large cities such as New York, Chicago, Los Angeles, Boston, Philadelphia, San Francisco, and Washington, D.C. Opportunities with small newspapers, corporations, and professional, religious, business, technical, and trade publications can be found throughout the country.

People entering this field should realize that the competition for jobs is extremely keen. Beginners may have difficulty finding employment. Of the thousands who graduate each year with degrees in English, journalism, communications, and the liberal arts, intending to establish a career as a writer, many turn to other occupations when they find that applicants far outnumber the job openings available. College students would do well to keep this in mind and prepare for an unrelated alternate career in the event they are unable to obtain a position as writer; another benefit of this approach is that they can become qualified as writers in a specialized field. The practicality of preparing for alternate careers is borne out by the fact that opportunities are best in firms that prepare business and trade publications and in technical writing. Job candidates with good writing skills and knowledge of a specialized area such as economics, finance, computer programming, or science will have the best chances of finding jobs.

Potential writers who end up working in a different field may be able to earn some income as freelancers, selling articles, stories, books, and possibly TV and movie scripts, but it is usually difficult for writers to support themselves entirely as independent writers.

■ UNIONS AND ASSOCIATIONS

Writers may obtain union representation from the National Writers Union and The Newspaper Guild-Communication Workers of America. Writers may also join the following professional associations: American

Society of Journalists and Authors, Association of Opinion Journalists, Editorial Freelancers Association, National Association of Science Writers, National Society of Newspaper Columnists, Online News Association, Society of Professional Journalists, and the Society for Technical Communication. Other useful organizations for writers include the Association of American Publishers, MPA–The Association of Magazine Media, and the Newspaper Association of America.

■ TIPS FOR ENTRY

1. Write as often as you can and create a portfolio of your work to show potential employers. Visit Blogger.com and WordPress.com to start your own blog.
2. Talk to writers about their careers. Ask them for advice on entering the field.
3. Visit the following Web sites for job openings:
   - http://www.editorandpublisher.com
   - https://www.stc.org/about-stc/job-bank
   - http://www.magazine.org/magazine-careers
   - http://www.bookjobs.com
   - http://www.the-efa.org/job/joblist.php
4. The American Society of Journalists and Authors (ASJA) offers a mentoring program for freelance writers. Visit http://www.asja.org/for-writers/personal-mentoring-program for more information. The ASJA also offers *The ASJA Guide to Freelance Writing* for a small fee.
5. Apply for entry-level jobs in the book, newspaper, or magazine publishing industry in order to gain experience in the field.

■ FOR MORE INFORMATION

The American Society of Journalists and Authors provides education, networking opportunities, professional development, and membership benefits.

American Society of Journalists and Authors (ASJA)
355 Lexington Avenue, 15th Floor
New York, NY 10017-6603
Tel: (212) 997-0947
http://asja.org

This organization of book publishers offers an extensive Web site to learn about the book business.

Association of American Publishers (AAP)
71 Fifth Avenue, Second Floor
New York, NY 10003-3004
Tel: (212) 255-0200
Fax: 212-255-7007
http://publishers.org

The American Society of News Editor provides a variety of resources on journalism education and careers in journalism.

American Society of News Editor (ASNE)
209 Reynolds Journalism Institute
Columbia, MO 65211
Tel: (573) 882-2430
Fax: (573) 884-3824
http://asne.org

The Editorial Freelancers Association provides resources and education for freelance editors.

Editorial Freelancers Association (EFA)
71 West 23rd Street, 4th Floor
New York, NY 10010-4102
Tel: (866) 929-5425; (212) 929-5400
Fax: (866) 929-5439
E-mail: office@the-efa.org
http://www.the-efa.org

The MPA - The Association of Magazine Media provides education, events, and advocacy for magazine professionals.

MPA—The Association of Magazine Media
757 Third Avenue, 11th Floor
New York, NY 10017-2194
Tel: (212) 872-3700
E-mail: mpa@magazine.org
http://www.magazine.org

The National Association of Science Writers offers information on science writing and editing careers.

National Association of Science Writers (NASW)
PO Box 7905
Berkeley, CA 94707-0905
Tel: (510) 647-9500
https://www.nasw.org

The National Society of Newspaper Columnists promotes professionalism and camaraderie among columnists and other writers.

National Society of Newspaper Columnists
PO Box 411532
San Francisco, CA 94141-1532
Tel: (415) 488-6762
Fax: (484) 297-0336
E-mail: director@columnists.com
http://www.columnists.com

The National Writers Union is a labor union that provides education, advocacy, and resources for journalists and writers.

National Writers Union (NWU)
256 West 38th Street, Suite 703
New York, NY 10018-9807
Tel: (212) 254-0279
Fax: (212) 254-0673
E-mail: nwu@nwu.org
https://nwu.org

The News Media Alliance provides information on careers in newspapers and industry facts and figures.

News Media Alliance (NMA)
4401 Wilson Boulevard, Suite 900
Arlington, VA 22203-4195
Tel: (571) 366-1000
E-mail: info@newsmediaalliance.org
https://www.newsmediaalliance.org

The guild is a union for journalists, sales workers, and other media professionals.

The Newspaper Guild, Communication Workers of America
501 3rd Street, NW
Washington, D.C. 20001-2797
Tel: (202) 434-7177
Fax: (202) 434-1472
E-mail: guild@cwa-union.org
http://www.newsguild.org

The Online News Association is a membership organization for digital journalists.

Online News Association
1111 North Capitol Street, NE, 6th Floor
Washington, D.C. 20002-7502
Tel: (646) 290-7900
E-mail: support@journalists.org
http://journalists.org

The Society for Technical Communication provides education, certification, and other resources for technical writers.

Society for Technical Communication (STC)
9401 Lee Highway, Suite 300
Fairfax, VA 22031-1803
Tel: (703) 522-4114
Fax: (703) 522-2075
E-mail: stc@stc.org
https://www.stc.org

The Society of Professional Journalists offers job listings, training opportunities, educational resources, discussion boards and blogs, and much more.

Society of Professional Journalists (SPJ)
3909 North Meridian Street
Indianapolis, IN 46208-4011
Tel: (317) 927-8000
Fax: (317) 920-4789
http://www.spj.org

Yoga and Pilates Instructors

■ OVERVIEW

Yoga and Pilates instructors lead specialized exercise, stretching, and meditation classes for people of all ages. They demonstrate techniques in front of the class and then watch members perform the movements, making suggestions and form adjustments as needed. Classes range from introductory to intermediate to advanced, and they may be aimed at specific groups, such as children or the elderly. *Yoga instructors* lead their class through a series of asanas, or poses, aimed at building strength, flexibility, and balance. *Pilates instructors* teach a series of movements that are more fluid than the poses used in yoga. Pilates also builds strength and flexibility but focuses on training the individual's core, or center.

■ HISTORY

Yoga and Pilates have existed in other cultures for many years, but they have become more popular in the United States only in the last few decades.

Yoga, which literally means to yoke together, is an ancient practice. According to the American Yoga Association, early stone carvings and illustrations dating back 5,000 years reveal depictions of people in yoga positions. Contrary to popular belief, yoga is not rooted in Hinduism. In fact, Hinduism was established much later, and early Hindu leaders adopted and promoted certain yoga beliefs and practices for their followers.

One of the earliest known yoga teachers and promoters was a man named Patanjali, who wrote about his yoga practice in a work called Yoga Sutras. His writings covered the basic philosophy and techniques that later became Hatha Yoga. Within Hatha are many styles, such as Iyengar, Ashtanga, Integral, Kripalu, and Jiva Mukti. Ashtanga Yoga, one of the most popular branches, incorporates eight elements: restraint, observance, breathing exercises, physical exercises, preparation for meditation,

concentration, meditation, and self-realization. Most modern yoga instructors focus on just a few of these elements, leading classes through physical poses, breathing techniques, and preparation for meditation.

Pilates (pronounced puh-lot-eez) was developed by Joseph Pilates in the early 1900s. A German living in England during the start of World War I, Pilates was forced into a camp with other foreign nationals. During this time, Pilates encouraged his fellow cellmates to keep moving, even those who were bedridden. According to Katherine Robertson, author of *Pilates...the Intelligent, Elegant, Workout*, Joseph Pilates developed exercise equipment specifically for the injured, converting hospital beds to "bednasiums," which encouraged health and healing through resistance exercise.

This early rehabilitation work led to the machinery behind Pilates exercise. In addition to floor work, Joseph Pilates also incorporated complex equipment consisting of belts, loops, chains, and springs designed to strengthen and lengthen the core muscles of the body.

Today, Pilates is still practiced in its original form, with both mat work and equipment, though many instructors, because of the cost of equipment, offer classes consisting of just floor exercises.

■ THE JOB

Yoga and Pilates instructors teach alternatives to the more traditional exercises of aerobics, weight training, or interval training classes. With yoga, the instructors' methods vary greatly based on the type of yoga they teach. Some instructors begin class seated or even lying down, encouraging class members to relax their

---

QUICK FACTS

ALTERNATE TITLE(S)
None

DUTIES
Lead specialized exercise, stretching, and meditation classes for people of all ages

SALARY RANGE
$18,690 to $36,160 to $101,616+

WORK ENVIRONMENT
Primarily Indoors

BEST GEOGRAPHIC LOCATION(S)
Nationwide

MINIMUM EDUCATION LEVEL
High School Diploma, Some Postsecondary Training

SCHOOL SUBJECTS
Biology, Health, Physical Education

EXPERIENCE
Volunteer or part-time experience

PERSONALITY TRAITS
Athletic, Helpful, Social

SKILLS
Coaching/Physical Training, Interpersonal, Teaching

CERTIFICATION OR LICENSING
Recommended

SPECIAL REQUIREMENTS
None

EMPLOYMENT PROSPECTS
Good

ADVANCEMENT PROSPECTS
Good

OUTLOOK
About as Fast as the Average

NOC
5254

O*NET-SOC
39-9031.00

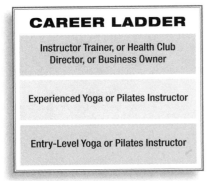

CAREER LADDER

Instructor Trainer, or Health Club Director, or Business Owner

Experienced Yoga or Pilates Instructor

Entry-Level Yoga or Pilates Instructor

muscles and focus on their breathing. After a few minutes of breathing exercises, the instructor leads the class into the various asanas, or yoga poses. These poses have Sanskrit names, though the instructor may use the English terminology for the benefit of the class, instructing students to get into the downward dog position or child's pose. Again, depending on the yoga method, poses may be fluid, with quicker movement from position to position, or instructors may tell class members to hold poses for as long as three or four minutes, encouraging strength and control.

Most yoga classes are done barefoot on the floor, using a thin, rubber mat to keep class members from slipping while in poses. Other equipment, such as foam blocks, ropes, or cloth straps, may also be used in the poses, usually to help with form or assist in the tougher positions.

During the class, yoga instructors verbally describe and demonstrate moves in front of the class. They also walk around and survey the movements of class members, making slight adjustments to members' form to prevent injury, encourage good practice, and improve their skills.

Pilates is similar to yoga in that class participants are led through different motions. However, unlike yoga poses that are often held for minutes at a time, Pilates encompasses more fluid movement of the arms and legs using what is called core strength. This strength comes

from the body's torso, from the top of the rib cage to the lower abdomen.

The job of the Pilates instructor is similar to that of a yoga teacher. Pilates teachers also demonstrate and describe motions and check class members' form and technique. Some classes include equipment such as an apparatus called The Reformer, which is a horizontal framework of straps and strings that is used for more than 100 exercises. Class members can tone, build, lengthen, and strengthen muscles by adjusting the equipment's springs to create different levels of resistance.

Both yoga and Pilates instructors have to prepare for their classes ahead of time to choose the exercises and equipment to be used or whether to focus on one method or area of the body. Good instructors are available after class for questions and advice. Instructors should also be open to class suggestions and comments to make the class the best it can be.

■ EARNINGS

According to the U.S. Bureau of Labor Statistics, in May 2015 the median annual earnings for salaried fitness trainers and aerobics instructors, the classification that includes yoga and Pilates instructors, was $36,160. Salaries ranged from less than $18,690 to $70,180 or more.

Payscale.com reports that in October 2016, yoga instructors earned a median hourly wage of $24.00, or $48,000 per year. Earnings ranged from $24,331 to $101,616. Payscale.com also reports that annual earnings for certified Pilates instructors ranged from $25,169 to $94,713 or more.

A compensation survey by IDEA Health & Fitness Association reports that many employers offer health insurance and paid sick and vacation time to full-time employees. They also may provide discounts on products sold in the club (such as shoes, clothing, and equipment) and free memberships to use the facility.

■ WORK ENVIRONMENT

Yoga and Pilates classes are generally held indoors, in a studio or quiet room, preferably with a wooden floor. Classes can get crowded and hectic at times. Instructors need to keep a level head and maintain a positive personality in order to motivate class participants. They need to lead challenging, yet enjoyable, classes so that members return for more instruction.

■ EXPLORING

The best way to explore these careers is to experience a yoga or Pilates class firsthand. Attend several classes to

A yoga teacher leads an outdoor class. (Mass Communication Specialist 2nd Class Johansen Laurel. U.S. Navy.)

learn the basics of the practice and build your skills. Ask to talk to the instructor after class about their job and how to get started. The instructor may recommend a certification program or give you names of other professionals to talk to about the practice.

You may also want to see if a local gym or community center has part-time positions available. Even if you are just working at the front desk, you will be able to see if you enjoy working in a health facility.

■ EDUCATION AND TRAINING REQUIREMENTS
High School

A high school diploma is the minimum requirement to work as a yoga or Pilates instructor. Take anatomy, biology, psychology, and physical education. In addition, get involved in weight lifting, dance, sports, and other activities that will help you to stay fit and learn more about exercise.

Postsecondary Training

The demand for yoga and Pilates instructors has grown faster than the number of available experienced teachers, leading to unskilled, untrained teachers causing an increase in injuries among students. Consequently, yoga and Pilates instructors must now receive specialized training in their field before they can teach. Standards that include 200 hours of training have been established by the Pilates Method Alliance and the Yoga Alliance. Both organizations also maintain a list of approved training schools that are registered and meet specified requirements. Additional useful college courses include anatomy, physiology, psychology, kinesiology, biomechanics, chemistry, physics, first aid and safety, health, and nutrition. The Pilates Center also provides teacher training programs.

Other Education or Training

Yoga and Pilates instructors must take continuing education workshops and seminars to keep their certification current. These opportunities are offered by American Fitness Professionals and Associates, IDEA Health & Fitness Association, Integral Yoga Teachers Association, The Pilates Center, Pilates Method Alliance, and the Yoga Alliance.

■ CERTIFICATION, LICENSING, AND SPECIAL REQUIREMENTS
Certification or Licensing

Most qualified yoga and Pilates instructors become certified through a professional association, such as the Yoga Alliance or the Pilates Method Alliance (PMA). For example, the PMA offers a comprehensive program consisting of training on proper form, the purpose of each exercise, how to assess and adjust class members' posture and form, and how to properly pace the class to create an effective and comprehensive class. Those who complete a minimum of 450 hours of documented training and and pass a multiple-choice examination receive the certified Pilates teacher designation. The American Fitness Professionals and Associates also provides certification.

It is important to note that there are no nationally recognized standards for either yoga or Pilates instruction. "Certified" training can be as short as a weekend course or as long as a multi-year program that is the equivalent of a college degree. According to the American Yoga Association, because yoga was historically passed down from teacher to student on an individual basis (creating many varieties and methods), it is unlikely that a standard training program for instruction will be created. Be sure to investigate your yoga or Pilates training program to ensure that it is a quality program, and one suited to your own approach. The National Commission for Certifying Agencies accredits certification programs, including the one established by the Pilates Method Alliance.

■ EXPERIENCE, SKILLS, AND PERSONALITY TRAITS

Any volunteer or paid experience you can obtain teaching yoga or Pilates classes will be useful.

Yoga and Pilates instructors are expected to be flexible and physically fit, but they do not have to be in superhuman shape. The American Yoga Association has established a list of strict qualities that instructors should adhere to (maintain a vegetarian diet, act ethically), but the basic qualities of every good instructor are the same: to be knowledgeable and passionate about your craft and be a patient and thorough instructor.

■ EMPLOYMENT PROSPECTS
Employers

Yoga and Pilates instructors work in fitness centers, gymnasiums, spas, dance studios, and community centers. Most employers are for-profit businesses, but some are community-based, such as the YMCA or a family fitness center. Other job possibilities can be found in corporate fitness centers, colleges, nursing homes, hospitals, and resorts. In smaller towns, positions can be found in health care facilities, schools, and community centers.

Starting Out

If you have been attending yoga or Pilates classes regularly, ask your instructor for ideas on training programs and if he or she knows of any job leads.

BOOKS ON YOGA AND PILATES   LEARN MORE ABOUT IT

Freedman, Francoise Barbira, et al. *Yoga & Pilates for Everyone.* London: Southwater, 2016.

Gibbs, Bel, et al. *The Practical Encyclopedia of Yoga & Pilates.* London, U.K.: Anness Publishing Ltd., 2012.

Isacowitz, Rael. *Pilates,* 2nd ed. Champaign, Ill.: Human Kinetics, 2014.

Kaminoff, Leslie, and Amy Matthews. *Yoga Anatomy,* 2nd ed. Champaign, Ill.: Human Kinetics, 2011.

Staugaard-Jones, Jo Ann. *The Anatomy of Exercise and Movement For the Study of Dance, Pilates, Sports, and Yoga.* Berkeley, Calif.: North Atlantic Books, 2011.

Often, facilities that provide training or internships will hire or provide job assistance to individuals who have completed programs. Students can also find jobs through online employment sites, classified ads, and by applying to health and fitness clubs, YMCAs, YWCAs, community centers, local schools, park districts, religious groups, and other fitness organizations. Many companies now provide fitness facilities to their employees. As a result, students should consider nearby companies for prospective instructor positions.

■ ADVANCEMENT PROSPECTS

Yoga and Pilates instructors who have taught for several years and have the proper training can move into an instructor trainer position or, if they have the necessary capital, they may choose to establish their own private studio. To own a yoga or Pilates studio, the instructor should be confident in his or her ability to attract new clients or be willing to ask old clients to move from their old class location to the new studio. With a bachelor's degree in either sports physiology or exercise physiology, instructors can advance to the position of health club director or to teach corporate wellness programs.

■ OUTLOOK

Health professionals have long recommended daily aerobic exercise and resistance training to maintain weight, build strength, and improve overall health. Recently, health professionals have added another recommendation: work on flexibility, posture, and stress reduction. These new concerns have given yoga and Pilates a boost in popularity.

The U.S. Department of Labor predicts that employment for fitness trainers and instructors will grow about as fast as the average for all careers through 2024. As the average age of the population increases, yoga and Pilates instructors will find more opportunities to work with the elderly in retirement homes and assisted-living communities. Large companies and corporations, after realizing the stress reduction benefits of these "softer" forms of exercise, also hire yoga and Pilates instructors to hold classes for their employees.

■ UNIONS AND ASSOCIATIONS

Yoga and Pilates instructors are not represented by unions, but they can obtain useful resources and professional support from American Fitness Professionals and Associates, American Yoga Association, IDEA Health & Fitness Association, Integral Yoga Teachers Association, The Pilates Center, Pilates Method Alliance, and the Yoga Alliance.

■ TIPS FOR ENTRY

1. Search for job listings at http://www.afpafitness.com/careers/find-a-job and http://pilatesmethodalliance-jobs.careerwebsite.com/home/index.cfm?site_id=9541.

2. Attend the Pilates Method Alliance's annual meeting and the Yoga Alliance's Annual Conference to network and participate in continuing education workshops.

3. Talk to yoga and Pilates instructors about their careers. The Pilates Method Alliance provides a database of its members at http://www.pilatesmethodalliance.org, which can be used to identify possible interview candidates.

4. Inquire about work-study opportunities at your local yoga or Pilates studios. This will provide an opportunity to learn how to maintain a studio, meet with other students, and take classes.

■ FOR MORE INFORMATION

American Fitness Professionals and Associates provides information on continuing education and certification for fitness professionals.

American Fitness Professionals and Associates (AFPA)
1601 Long Beach Boulevard
Box 214
Ship Bottom, NJ 08008-0234
Tel: (800) 494-7782; (609) 978-7583
E-mail: afpa@afpafitness.com
https://www.afpafitness.com

The American Yoga Association offers information about the practice, teaching, and origin of yoga.

American Yoga Association

PO Box 19986

Sarasota, FL 34276-2986

E-mail: info@americanyogaassociation.org

http://www.americanyogaassociation.org

IDEA: The Health and Fitness Association offers education, articles, conferences, job listings, and other resources for health and fitness professionals.

IDEA: The Health and Fitness Association

10190 Telesis Court

San Diego, CA 92121-2719

Tel: (800) 999-4332, ext. 7; (858) 535-8979, ext. 7

Fax: (619) 344-0380

E-mail: contact@ideafit.com

http://www.ideafit.com

The Integral Yoga Teachers Association is a membership organization that provides education, career support, news, and other resources for yoga teachers, centers, and institutes.

Integral Yoga Teachers Association (IYTA)

108 Yogaville Way

Buckingham, VA 23921-2229

Tel: (434) 969-3121, ext. 177

E-mail: membership@iyta.org

http://iyta.org

The Pilates Center provides education, training, and certification information for Pilates instructors.

The Pilates Center

5500 Flatiron Parkway, Suite 110

Boulder, CO 80301-2955

Tel: (303) 494-3400

E-mail: info@thepilatescenter.com

http://www.thepilatescenter.com

The Pilates Method Alliance is the professional association and certifying agency for Pilates teachers.

Pilates Method Alliance (PMA)

1666 Kennedy Causeway, Suite 402

North Bay Village, FL 33141-4178

Tel: (866) 573-4945; (305) 573-4946

Fax: (305) 573-4461

E-mail: info@pilatesmethodalliance.org

http://www.pilatesmethodalliance.org

The Yoga Alliance offers education, certification, advocacy, community, and other resources for yoga instructors.

Yoga Alliance

1560 Wilson Boulevard, Suite 700

Arlington, VA 22209-2463

Tel: (888) 921-9642

E-mail: info@yogaalliance.org

https://www.yogaalliance.org

Zoo and Aquarium Curators and Directors

■ OVERVIEW

Zoos are wild kingdoms, and aquariums are underwater worlds. The word *zoo* comes from the Greek for *living being* and is a shortened term for zoological garden or zoological park. This may imply that zoos are created just for beauty and recreation but the main functions of modern zoos are education, conservation, and the study of animals. The term *aquarium* comes from the Latin for *source of water*; in such places, living aquatic plants and animals are studied and exhibited. These land and water gardens are tended by people with an affinity for animals.

Zoo and aquarium directors, or *chief executive officers*, are administrators who coordinate the business affairs of these centers. Directors execute the institution's policies, usually under the direction of a governing authority. They are responsible for the institution's operations and plans for future development and for such tasks as fund-raising and public relations. They also serve as representatives of, and advocates for, their institutions and their entire industry. *Zoo and aquarium curators* are the chief employees responsible for the day-to-day care of the creatures. They oversee the various sections of the animal collections, such as birds, mammals, and fishes.

■ HISTORY

Prehistoric humans did not try to tame animals; for purposes of survival, they hunted them to avoid danger as well as to obtain food. The full history of the establishment of zoos and aquariums can probably be traced as far back as the earliest attempts by humans to domesticate animals. After realizing that they could live with animals as fellow creatures, humans attempted to domesticate them. The precise timing of this phenomenon is not known; it apparently occurred at different times in different parts of the world.

Ancient Sumerians kept fish in manmade ponds around 4,500 years ago. By 1150 B.C. pigeons, elephants, antelope, and deer were held captive for taming in such areas as the Middle East, India, and China. In 1000 B.C. a Chinese emperor named Wen Wang built a zoo and called it the Garden of Intelligence. Also around this time, the Chinese and Japanese were breeding and raising goldfish and carp for their beauty in a garden setting.

Zoos were abundant in ancient Greece; animals were held in captivity for purposes of study in nearly every city-state. In early Egypt and Asia, zoos were created mainly for public show, and during the Roman Empire, fish were kept in ponds and animals were collected both for arena showings and for private zoos. Hernando Cortes, the Spanish conqueror, created a fantastic zoo in Mexico in the early 16th century. The zoo had 300 keepers taking care of birds, mammals, and reptiles.

Zoo and aquarium professions as we know them today began to be established around the mid-18th century with the construction of various extravagant European zoos. The Imperial Menagerie of the Schönbrunn Zoo in Vienna, Austria, was opened in 1765 and still operates to this day. One of the most significant openings occurred in 1828 at the London Zoological Society's Regent's Park. The London Zoo continues to have one of the world's most extensive and popular collections of animals, with more than 750 species, including some of the rarest animals. The world's first public aquarium was also established at Regent's Park, in 1853, after which aquariums were built in other European cities. In the United States, P. T. Barnum was the first to establish a display aquarium, which opened in New York in 1856.

Today's zoos and aquariums are built around habitat-based, multi-species exhibits designed to immerse the visitor in an experience simulating a visit to the wild places from which the animals came. The keeping and breeding of captive animals is no longer an end in itself, but a means of educating and communicating a strong conservation imperative to the public. The public has embraced this change, with visitor numbers rising steadily each year.

Along with this expanded public role has come a professionalization of the industry, marked by advances in animal husbandry, veterinary care, nutrition, and exhibit technology that have greatly improved the conditions under which animals are held. These advances have been costly, and the rise in operating expenses reflects these increased costs. Zoos and aquariums today are big business.

Today, curators have a host of responsibilities involved with the operation of zoos and aquariums. Although many zoos and aquariums are separate places, there are also zoos that contain aquariums as part of their facilities. There are both public and private institutions, large and small, and curators often contribute their knowledge to the most effective methods of design, maintenance, and administration for these institutions.

The director's job has changed radically in the past 15 years, reflecting the overall maturity of the zoo and aquarium business. Directors no longer have direct responsibility for working with animals or managing the people who care for them. The director's role has broadened from animal management to overall management, with a focus that has shifted from the day-to-day details of running the facility to ensuring the ongoing success of the entire operation.

■ THE JOB

General curators of zoos and aquariums oversee the management of an institution's entire animal collection and animal management staff. They help the director coordinate activities, such as education, collection planning, exhibit design, new construction, research, and public services. They meet with the director and other members of the staff to create long-term strategic plans. General curators may have public relations and development responsibilities, such as meeting with the media and identifying and cultivating donors. In most institutions, general curators develop policy; other curators implement policy.

Animal curators are responsible for the day-to-day management of a specific portion of a zoo's or aquarium's animal collection (as defined taxonomically, such as mammals or birds, or ecogeographically, such as the Forest Edge or the Arizona Trail); the people charged with caring for that collection, including assistant curators, zookeepers, administrative staff such as secretaries, as well as researchers, students, and volunteers; and the associated facilities and equipment.

For example, the curator in charge of the mammal department of a large zoo would be responsible for the care of such animals as lions, tigers, monkeys, and elephants. They might oversee nearly 1,000 animals representing about 200 different species, manage scores of employees, and have a multimillion-dollar budget.

Assistant curators report to curators and assist in animal management tasks and decisions. They may have extensive supervisory responsibilities.

Curators have diverse responsibilities and their activities vary widely from day to day. They oversee animal husbandry procedures, including the daily care of the animals, establish proper nutritional programs, and manage animal health delivery in partnership with the veterinary staff. They develop exhibits, educational programs, and visitor services and participate in research and conservation activities. They maintain inventories of animals and other records, and they recommend and implement acquisitions and dispositions of animals. Curators serve as liaisons with other departments.

Curators prepare budgets and reports. They interview and hire new workers. When scientific conferences are held, curators attend them as representatives of the institutions for which they work. They are often called on to write articles for scientific journals and perhaps provide information for newspaper reports and magazine stories.

They may coordinate or participate in on-site research or conservation efforts. To keep abreast of developments in their field, curators spend a lot of time reading.

Curators meet with the *general curator*, the *director*, and other staff to develop the objectives and philosophy of the institution and decide on the best way to care for and exhibit the animals. They must be knowledgeable about the animals' housing requirements, daily care, medical procedures, dietary needs, and social and reproduction habits. Curators represent their zoos or aquariums in collaborative efforts with other institutions, such as the Association of Zoos and Aquariums (AZA) Species Survival Plans that target individual species for intense conservation efforts by zoos and aquariums. In this capacity, curators may exchange information, negotiate breeding loans, or assemble the necessary permits and paperwork to affect the transfers. Other methods of animal acquisition coordinated by curators involve purchases from animal dealers or private collectors and collection of nonendangered species from the wild. Curators may arrange for the quarantine of newly acquired animals. They may arrange to send the remains of dead animals to museums or universities for study.

Curators often work on special projects. They may serve on multidisciplinary committees responsible for planning and constructing new exhibits. Curators interface with colleagues from other states and around the world in collaborative conservation efforts.

Working under the supervision of a governing board, *directors* are charged with pulling together all the institution's operations, development of long-range planning, implementation of new programs, and maintenance of the animal collection and facilities. Much of the director's time is spent meeting with the volunteer governing board and with departmental staff who handle the institution's daily operations.

Directors plan overall budgets, which include consideration of fund-raising programs, government grants, and private financial support from corporations, foundations, and individuals. They work with the board of directors to design major policies and procedures, and they meet with the curators to discuss animal acquisitions, public education, research projects, and developmental

CAREER LADDER

Zoo or Aquarium Director

Assistant Zoo or Aquarium Director

Zoo or Aquarium Curator

Assistant Zoo or Aquarium Curator

Zookeeper or Aquarist

Zoo and aquarium directors coordinate activities and events as well as maintain public relations and operations at their facilities. (Pavel L Photo and Video. Shutterstock.)

activities. In larger zoos and aquariums, directors may give speeches, appear at fund-raising events, and represent their organizations on television or radio.

A major part of the director's job is seeing that his or her institution has adequate financial resources. Zoos and aquariums were once funded largely by local and state governments. However the amount of tax money available for this purpose is dwindling. Generally, zoos and aquariums need to generate enough revenue to pay for about two-thirds of their operating expenses from sources such as donations, membership, retail sales, and visitor services.

As zoos and aquariums endeavor to improve facilities for animals and visitors alike and to present the message of conservation to the public in a more effective manner, renovation of existing structures and construction of new exhibits is an ongoing process. Directors spend much of their time working with architects, engineers, contractors, and artisans on these projects.

Directors are responsible for informing the public about what is going on at the zoo or aquarium. This involves offering interviews with the media, answering questions from individuals, and even resolving complaints. Directors also write for in-house newsletters and annual reports or for general-circulation magazines and newspapers.

The director is not directly involved in animal management but may play a significant role in conservation at a regional, national, or international level. They may be involved at high levels of the Association of Zoos and Aquariums, working on such things as accreditation of other institutions, developing professional ethical standards, or long-range planning. Directors work with other

conservation groups as well and may serve in leadership positions for them too.

As zoos and aquariums expand their conservation role from only the management of captive animals to supporting the preservation of the habitats from which those animals came, directors are working with universities and field biologists to support research.

Other directorial personnel include *assistant directors* and *deputy directors*. Like curators, these workers are responsible for a specific duty or department, such as operations, education, or animal management. They also manage certain employees, supervise animal care workers, and take care of various administrative duties to help the director.

In some smaller zoos and aquariums, the director also serves as the curator, handling the duties of both positions.

■ EARNINGS

Salaries of zoo and aquarium curators and directors vary widely depending on the size and location of the institution, whether it is privately or publicly owned, the size of its endowments and budget, and job responsibilities, educational background, and experience. Generally, zoos and aquariums in metropolitan areas pay higher salaries.

The U.S. Department of Labor reports that the median annual earnings for all curators were $51,520 in May 2015, with salaries ranging from less than $25,970 to more than $83,940. Directors tend to be the highest paid employees at zoos and aquariums; the range of their salary is from approximately $110,000 to more than $150,000 per year, with some directors at major institutions earning considerably more than that. SalaryExpert.com reported $135,010 as the average salary for zoo directors in 2016.

Most zoos and aquariums provide benefits packages including medical insurance, paid vacation and sick leave, and generous retirement benefits. As salaried employees, directors and curators are not eligible for overtime pay, but they may get compensatory time for extra hours worked. Larger institutions may also offer coverage for prescription drugs, dental and vision insurance, mental health plans, and retirement savings plans. Private corporate zoos may offer better benefits, including profit sharing.

■ WORK ENVIRONMENT

The work atmosphere for curators and directors of animal facilities will always center on the zoo or aquarium in which they work. Curators spend most of their time indoors at their desks, reading e-mail, talking on the phone, writing reports, meeting deadlines for budgets, planning exhibits, and so forth. Particularly at large institutions, the majority of their time is spent on administrative duties rather than hands-on interaction with animals. Like other zoo and aquarium employees, curators often work long hours tending to the varied duties to which they are assigned.

When the unexpected happens, curators get their share of animal emergencies. They may find themselves working late into the night with keepers and veterinarians to help care for sick animals or those that are giving birth.

Curators are sometimes required to travel to conferences and community events. They might also travel to other zoos throughout the country or lead trips for zoo members to wilderness areas in the United States and abroad. Despite the tedium and the long hours, zoo and aquarium curators derive great personal satisfaction from their work.

Directors tend to spend a great deal of time in their offices conducting business affairs, but directors are also sometimes required to travel to conferences and community events. They might also travel to other institutions throughout the country or abroad to attend meetings of professional organizations and conservation groups or to discuss animal transfers and other matters. Often, directors lead groups on trips around the United States or to developing countries.

■ EXPLORING

Reading about animals or surfing the Internet, taking classes at local zoos and aquariums, or joining clubs, such as 4-H or Audubon, can help you learn about animals. Taking time to learn about ecology and nature in general will prepare you for the systems-oriented approach used by modern zoo and aquarium managers.

Volunteering at zoos or aquariums, animal shelters, wildlife rehabilitation facilities, stables, or veterinary hospitals demonstrates a serious commitment to animals and provides firsthand experience with them.

Professional organizations, such as Association of Zoos and Aquariums (AZA) and the American Association of Zoo Keepers, have special membership rates for students and nonprofessionals. Associate members receive newsletters and can attend workshops and conferences.

The AZA offers practical advice for students who are considering animal facility jobs such as that of the director. Visit zoos and aquariums and learn how they operate, decide on a specific interest, attend events and meetings planned by zoos and aquariums in your area, and continue to read books and journals on animals and nature.

■ EDUCATION AND TRAINING REQUIREMENTS
High School

High school students who want to prepare for careers in upper management in zoos and aquariums should take classes in the sciences, especially biology, microbiology, chemistry, and physics, as well as in mathematics, computer science, business, language, and speech.

Extracurricular activities for students interested in becoming zoo and aquarium curators and directors should focus on developing leadership and communication skills: these include student body associations, service clubs, debate teams, and school newspapers.

Postsecondary Training

The minimum formal educational requirement for curators is a master's degree. Course work should include biology, invertebrate zoology, vertebrate physiology, comparative anatomy, organic chemistry, physics, microbiology, and virology. Electives are just as important, particularly writing, public speaking, computer science, and education. Even studying a second language can be helpful.

Typically, an advanced degree is required for curators employed at larger institutions; many curators are required to have a doctoral degree. But advanced academic training alone is insufficient; it takes years of on-the-job experience to master the practical aspects of exotic animal husbandry. Also required are management skills, supervisory experience, writing ability, research experience, and sometimes the flexibility to travel.

A few institutions offer curatorial internships designed to provide practical experience. Several major zoos offer formal keeper training courses as well as on-the-job training programs to students who are studying areas related to animal science and care. Such programs could lead to positions as assistant curators. The Association of Zoos and Aquariums provides information about which schools and animal facilities are involved in internship programs.

A director's education and experience must be rather broad, with a solid foundation in animal management skills. Therefore, a good balance between science and business is the key to finding a position in this field. Directors need courses in zoology or biology as well as business courses, such as economics, accounting, and general business, and humanities, such as sociology.

Most directors have a master's degree; many at larger institutions have doctoral degrees. Directors continue their education throughout their careers by taking classes as well as by reading and learning on their own.

ZOOS: BY THE NUMBERS

FAST FACTS

- As of 2016 there were 232 AZA-accredited zoos and aquariums in the United States with a combined annual attendance of 186 million visitors.
- These zoos and aquariums featured 750,000 animals from 6,000 species.
- AZA zoos and aquariums consist of nonprofits, public facilities, and a small percentage of for-profit entities.
- There are more than 500 cooperatively managed Animal Programs, including Species Survival Plan Programs.
- From 2010 through 2014, marine mammals were the most frequently targeted species for conservation projects and received the most funding.

Source: Association of Zoos and Aquariums (AZA)

Certification

The Association of Zoos and Aquariums (AZA) offers certificate programs in management and operations, education and interpretation, and other areas. Those wishing to earn the management and operations certificate must meet educational and work experience requirements.

Other Education or Training

The Association of Zoos and Aquariums (AZA) offers professional training courses such as "Institutional Record Keeping," "Principles of Program Animal Management," and "Managing for Success: Organizational Development."

■ CERTIFICATION, LICENSING, AND SPECIAL REQUIREMENTS
Certification or Licensing

There are no certification or licensing requirements for zoo and aquarium curators and directors.

■ EXPERIENCE, SKILLS, AND PERSONALITY TRAITS

The positions of curator and director are not entry level. Aspiring curators and directors must have at least several years of experience in lower-level positions (preferably as assistant directors and curators) in zoos and aquariums to be considered for these top-level careers.

Curators who work for zoos and aquariums must have a fondness and compassion for animals. Strong interpersonal skills are also extremely important in managing people, including conflict management and negotiating. Curators spend a lot of time making deals with people inside and outside of their institutions. They must have recognized leadership ability, good coaching skills, and the ability to create and maintain a team atmosphere and build consensus.

Curators also need excellent oral and written communication skills. They must be effective and articulate public speakers. They need to be good at problem solving.

Curators should have an in-depth knowledge of every species and exhibit in their collections and how they interact. Modern zoo and aquarium buildings contain technologically advanced, complex equipment, such as environmental controls, and they often house mixed-species exhibits. Not only must curators know about zoology and animal husbandry, they must understand the infrastructure as well.

Zoo and aquarium directors are leaders and communicators. Inspiring others and promoting their institution are among their most important tasks. Their most important traits include leadership ability, personal charisma, people skills, and public speaking ability.

Directors need to be politically savvy. They interact with many different groups, each with their own agendas. They must be able to build bridges between these various groups and put together a consensus. They need to be flexible and open-minded without losing sight of their role as advocate for their institution. Directors must have outstanding time-management skills, and they must be willing and able to delegate.

A fondness and compassion for animals is not all that is needed to become a successful zoo or aquarium director. Directors must also be articulate and sociable. They must be able to communicate effectively with people from all walks of life. Much of their time is spent cultivating prospective donors. They must be comfortable with many different types of people, including those with wealth and power.

■ EMPLOYMENT PROSPECTS
Employers

There are so few zoos and aquariums in the country, so most positions will be the result of turnover, which is low. While a few new zoos and aquariums may open and others may expand their facilities, the number of new curator and director positions available will be extremely low, particularly compared to the number of interested job seekers. The number of curators and directors employed by each facility depends on the size and budget of the operation and the range of animal types they house.

Starting Out

The position of zoo and aquarium curator and the position of director are not entry-level jobs. Most curators start their careers as zookeepers or aquarists and move up through the animal-management ranks.

Competition for zoo and aquarium jobs is intense but there are several ways to pursue such positions. Getting an education in animal science is a good way to make contacts that may be valuable in a job search. Professors and school administrators often can provide advice and counseling on finding jobs as a curator. The best sources for finding out about career opportunities at zoos and aquariums are trade journals (the Association of Zoos and Aquariums' *Connect* or American Association of Zoo Keepers' *Animal Keepers' Forum*), the Web sites of specific institutions, and special-focus periodicals. Most zoos and aquariums have internal job postings. A few zoos and aquariums have job lines. People in the profession often learn about openings by word of mouth.

Working on a part-time or volunteer basis at an animal facility could provide an excellent opportunity to improve your eligibility for higher-level jobs in later years. Moving up from supervisory keeper positions to curator and director positions usually involves moving to another institution, often in another city and state. Today's zoo and aquarium directors often began their careers in education, marketing, business, research, and academia as well as animal management.

ADVANCEMENT PROSPECTS

Curatorial positions are often the top rung of the career ladder for many zoo and aquarium professionals. Curators do not necessarily wish to become zoo or aquarium directors, although the next step for specialized curators is to advance to the position of general curator. Those who are willing to forego direct involvement with animal management and complete the transition to the business of running a zoo or aquarium will set as their ultimate goal the position of zoo or aquarium director. Curators and directors who work for a small facility may aspire to a position at a larger zoo or aquarium, with greater responsibilities and a commensurate increase in pay. Most directors remain at the same institution, reflecting the strong identification of the director with the institution that he or she leads.

Advancing to executive positions requires a combination of experience and education. General curators and zoo directors often have graduate degrees in zoology or in business or finance. Continuing professional education, such as the Association of Zoos and Aquariums' courses in applied zoo and aquarium biology, conservation education, institutional record keeping, population management, and professional management, can be helpful. Attending workshops and conferences sponsored by professional groups or related organizations and making presentations is another means of networking with colleagues from other institutions and professions and becoming better known within the zoo world.

OUTLOOK

Only 230 zoos, aquariums, wildlife parks, and oceanariums in the U.S. are accredited by the Association of Zoos and Aquariums. Considering the number of people interested in animal careers, this is not a large number. Therefore, it is expected that competition for jobs as curators and directors, as well as for most zoo and aquarium jobs, will continue to be very strong.

The employment outlook for zoo directors is not favorable. There will be few job openings because of the slow growth in new zoos and in their capacity to care for animals. The prospects for aquarium directors are somewhat better due to planned construction of several new aquariums.

Employment for curators employed at museums, historical sites, and similar institutions is expected to increase at an average pace through 2024, according to the U.S. Department of Labor, due to growing public interest in zoos, aquariums, and museums. Despite this prediction, it's important to remember that the number of zoo and aquarium curators is small, turnover rates are low, and competition for jobs is very strong.

One area with greater growth potential than conventional zoos and aquariums is privately funded conservation centers.

UNIONS AND ASSOCIATIONS

Zoo and aquarium curators and directors are not members of unions, but many join the Association of Zoos and Aquariums, which provides networking opportunities, continuing education classes, publications, career information, job listings, and other resources. The Alliance of Marine Mammal Parks and Aquariums is a membership organization for zoological parks and aquariums.

TIPS FOR ENTRY

1. Visit https://www.aza.org/jobs and https://www.aazk.org/job-listings/all for job and internship listings.

2. Attend the Association of Zoos and Aquariums' annual conference (https://www.aza.org/conferences-meetings) to network, learn about industry trends, and participate in professional development workshops and seminars.

3. Contact zoos and aquariums directly to learn more about job opportunities. The AZA offers a database of zoos and aquariums at https://www.aza.org/find-a-zoo-or-aquarium.

FOR MORE INFORMATION

The Alliance of Marine Mammal Parks and Aquariums is dedicated to the concerns and issues that affect the public display of marine mammals.

Alliance of Marine Mammal Parks and Aquariums (AMMPA)
E-mail: executivedirector@ammpa.org
http://www.ammpa.org

The Association of Zoos and Aquariums offers education, certification, job listings, and other resources.

Association of Zoos and Aquariums (AZA)
8403 Colesville Road, Suite 710
Silver Spring, MD 20910-3314
Tel: (301) 562-0777
Fax: (301) 562-0888
https://www.aza.org

Friends University of Wichita offers a degree program in zoo science.

Friends University of Wichita
2100 West University Avenue
Wichita, KS 67213-3379
Tel: (800) 794-6945; (316) 295-5000
https://www.friends.edu/undergraduate/natural
-science-mathematics/zoo-science

Santa Fe College offers a zoo animal technology program.

Santa Fe College
3000 Northwest 83rd Street
Gainesville, FL 32606-6210
Tel: (352) 395-5000
http://www.sfcollege.edu/zoo/?section=zoo
_technology_program

Zookeepers

OVERVIEW

Zookeepers provide the day-to-day care for animals in zoological parks. They prepare the diets, clean and maintain the exhibits and holding areas, and monitor the behavior of animals that range from the exotic and endangered to the more common and domesticated. Zookeepers interact with visitors and conduct formal and informal educational presentations. They sometimes assist in research studies, and depending upon the species, may also train animals. Zookeepers may also be known as *animal caretakers.*

HISTORY

Humans have put wild animals on display since ancient times. Around 1500 B.C. Queen Hatshepsut of Egypt established the earliest known zoo. Five hundred years later, the Chinese emperor Wen Wang founded a zoo that covered about 1,500 acres. Rulers seeking to display their wealth and power established small zoos in northern Africa, India, and China. The ancient Greeks established public zoos, while the Romans had many private zoos. During the Middle Ages, from about 400 to 1500 A.D., zoos became rare in Europe.

By the end of the 1400s, European explorers returned from the New World with strange animals, and interest in zoos renewed. During the next 250 years, a number of zoos were established. Some merely consisted of small collections of bears or tigers kept in dismal cages or pits. They were gradually replaced by larger collections of animals that received better care.

In 1752, what is now the oldest operating zoo, the Schönbrunn, opened in Vienna, Austria. Other European zoos followed. In the United States, the Central Park Zoo in New York City opened in 1864, followed by the Buffalo Zoo in New York in 1870, and Chicago's Lincoln Park Zoo in 1874.

Workers were needed to care for the animals in even the earliest zoos. However, this care probably consisted only of giving the animals food and water and cleaning their cages. Little was known about the needs of a particular species. If an animal died, it was replaced by another animal from the wild. Few zoos owned more than one or two animals of a rare species, so the keepers did not need to be involved in observations or research on an animal's lifestyle, health, or nutrition.

The modern zoo is a far cry from even the menageries of earlier eras. Today's zoos are still in the entertainment field, but they have assumed three additional roles: conservation, education, and research. Each of these roles has become vital due to the increasing pressures on the world's wildlife.

THE JOB

Zookeepers are responsible for providing the basic care required to maintain the health of the animals in their care. Daily tasks include preparing food by chopping or grinding meat, fish, vegetables, or fruit; mixing prepared commercial feeds; and unbaling forage grasses. Administering vitamins or medications may be necessary as well. In addition, zookeepers fill water containers in the cages. They clean animal quarters by hosing, scrubbing, raking, and disinfecting.

Zookeepers must safely shift animals from one location to another. They maintain exhibits (for example, by planting grass or putting in new bars) and modify them to enhance the visitors' experience. They also provide enrichment devices for the animals, such as ropes for monkeys to swing on or scratching areas for big cats. They regulate environmental factors by monitoring temperature and humidity or water-quality controls and maintaining an inventory of supplies and equipment. They may bathe and groom animals.

Zookeepers must become experts on the species—and the individuals—in their care. They must observe and understand all types of animal behaviors, including courtship, mating, feeding, aggression, sociality, sleeping, moving, and even urination and defecation. Zookeepers must be able to detect even small changes in an animal's appearance or behavior. They must maintain careful records of these observations in a logbook and file daily written or digital reports. Often, they make recommendations regarding diet or modification of habitats and implement those changes. In addition, they assist the veterinarian in providing treatment to sick animals and may be called on to feed and help raise infants. Zookeepers may capture or transport animals. When an animal is transferred to another institution, a keeper may accompany it to aid in its adjustment to its new home.

The professional zookeeper works closely with zoo staff on research, conservation, and animal reproduction. Many keepers conduct research projects, presenting their findings in papers or professional journals or at workshops or conferences. Some keepers participate in regional or national conservation plans or conduct field research in the United States and abroad.

Keepers may assist an animal trainer or instructor in presenting animal shows or lectures to the public. Depending on the species, keepers may train animals to shift or to move in a certain way to facilitate routine husbandry or veterinary care. Elephant keepers, for example, train their charges to respond to commands to lift their feet so that they may provide proper foot care, including footpad and toenail trims.

Zookeepers must be able to interact with zoo visitors and answer questions in a friendly, professional manner. Keepers may participate in formal presentations for the general public or for special groups. This involves being knowledgeable about the animals in one's care, the animals' natural habitat and habits, and the role zoos play in wildlife conservation.

Keepers must carefully monitor activity around the animals to discourage visitors from teasing or harming them. They must be able to remove harmful objects that are sometimes thrown into an exhibit and tactfully explain the "no feeding" policy to zoo visitors.

Taking care of animals is hard work. About 85 percent of the job involves custodial and maintenance tasks, which can be physically demanding and dirty. These tasks must be done both indoors and outdoors, in all types of weather. In addition, there is the risk of an animal-inflicted injury or disease. Although direct contact with animals is limited and strictly managed, the possibility for injury exists when a person works with large, powerful animals or even small animals that possess sharp teeth and claws.

Animals require care every day, so keepers must work weekends and holidays. They also may be called on to work special events outside their normal working hours.

In large zoological parks, keepers often work with a limited collection of animals. They may be assigned to work specifically with just one taxonomy, such as primates, large cats, or birds, or with different types of animals from a specific ecogeographic area, such as the tropical rainforest or Africa. In smaller zoos, keepers may have more variety and care for a wider range of species.

■ EARNINGS

Most people who choose a career as a zookeeper do not do so for the money, but because they feel compassion for and enjoy being around animals.

Salaries vary widely among zoological parks and depend on the size and location of the institution, whether it is publicly or privately owned, the size of its endowments and budget, and whether the zookeepers belong to a union. Generally, the highest salaries tend to be in metropolitan areas and are relative to the applicant's education and responsibilities.

QUICK FACTS

ALTERNATE TITLE(S)
Animal Caretakers

DUTIES
Provide daily care for animals in zoos

SALARY RANGE
$17,160 to $21,010 to $34,780+

WORK ENVIRONMENT
Indoors/Outdoors

BEST GEOGRAPHIC LOCATION(S)
Opportunities are available throughout the country

MINIMUM EDUCATION LEVEL
Associate's Degree

SCHOOL SUBJECTS
Biology, Chemistry, Speech

EXPERIENCE
Previous experience as a keeper or trainer required

PERSONALITY TRAITS
Hands On, Problem-Solving, Scientific

SKILLS
Interpersonal, Scientific, Teaching

CERTIFICATION OR LICENSING
None

SPECIAL REQUIREMENTS
None

EMPLOYMENT PROSPECTS
Good

ADVANCEMENT PROSPECTS
Fair

OUTLOOK
About as Fast as the Average

NOC
2221

O*NET-SOC
39-2021.00

CAREER LADDER

Zoologist or Curator

Area Supervisor or Assistant Curator

Senior Keeper

Zookeeper

Zookeeper Trainee

The zookeeper's salary can range from slightly above minimum wage to more than $30,000 a year, depending on the keeper's background, grade, and tenure and the zoo's location. Certain areas of the country pay higher wages, reflecting the higher cost of living there. City-run institutions, where keepers are lumped into a job category with less-skilled workers, pay less. On average, aquarists earn slightly more than zookeepers.

The U.S. Bureau of Labor Statistics reported annual average salaries for animal caretakers, a category that includes zookeepers, in May 2015 were $21,010. Salaries ranged from $17,160 to $34,780 or more.

Most zoos provide benefits packages that include medical insurance, paid vacation and sick leave, and generous retirement benefits. Keepers at larger institutions may also have coverage for prescription drugs, dental and vision insurance, mental health plans, and 401(k) plans. Those who work on holidays may receive overtime pay or comp time. A few institutions offer awards, research grants, and unpaid sabbaticals. Private corporate zoos may offer better benefits, including profit sharing.

WORK ENVIRONMENT

Cleaning, feeding, and providing general care to the animals are a necessity seven days a week, sometimes outdoors and in adverse weather conditions. The zookeeper must be prepared for a varied schedule that may include working weekends and holidays. Sick animals may need round-the-clock care. A large portion of the job involves routine chores for animals that will not express appreciation for the keeper's efforts.

Some of the work may be physically demanding and involve lifting heavy supplies such as bales of hay. The cleaning of an animal's enclosure may be unpleasant and smelly. Between the sounds of the animals and the sounds of the zoo visitors, the work setting may be quite noisy.

Zookeepers may be exposed to bites, kicks, diseases, and possible fatal injury from the animals they attend. They must practice constant caution because working with animals presents the potential for danger. Even though an animal may have been held in captivity for years or even since birth, it can be frightened, become stressed because of illness, or otherwise revert to its wild behavior. The keeper must know the physical and mental abilities of an animal, whether it be the strength of an ape, the reaching ability of a large cat, or the intelligence of an elephant. In addition, keepers must develop a healthy relationship with the animals in their care by respecting them as individuals and always being careful to observe safety procedures.

Being a zookeeper is an active, demanding job. The tasks involved require agility and endurance, whether they consist of cleaning quarters, preparing food, or handling animals.

Many keepers would agree that the advantages of the job outweigh the disadvantages. A chief advantage is the personal gratification of successfully maintaining wild animals, especially rare or endangered species. A healthy, well-adjusted animal collection provides a keeper with a deep sense of satisfaction.

EXPLORING

High school students can explore the field of animal care in several ways. They can learn about animals by reading about them and taking classes in biology and zoology. Most zoos have Web sites containing information about the institution and its programs and career opportunities, as well as about the industry in general. Hobbies such as birding and wildlife photography can expand your knowledge of animals.

Many institutions offer classes about animals and conservation or educational programs, such as Keeper Encounters, where students can learn firsthand what a zookeeper's job is like.

Some have part-time or summer jobs that can give a good overview of how a zoo operates. Many zoos offer volunteer opportunities for teens, such as Explorers or Junior Zookeeper programs, which are similar to programs for adult volunteers but with closer supervision. Most volunteer programs require a specific time commitment. Opportunities vary between institutions and run the gamut from cleaning enclosures to preparing food to handling domesticated animals to conducting tours or giving educational presentations.

Prospective zookeepers can volunteer or work part time at animal shelters, boarding kennels, wildlife rehabilitation facilities, stables, or animal hospitals. They may get a feel for working with animals by seeking employment on a farm or ranch during the summer. Joining a 4-H club also allows hands-on experience with animals. Experience with animals is invaluable when seeking a job and provides opportunities to learn about the realities of work in this field.

Professional organizations have special membership rates for nonprofessionals. Reading their newsletters provides an insider's look at what zoo careers are like. Attending local workshops or national conferences offers an opportunity to network and gather information for charting a career path.

■ EDUCATION AND TRAINING REQUIREMENTS
High School

Take as many science classes while in high school as possible. A broad-based science education including courses in biology, ecology, chemistry, physics, and botany, coupled with mathematics and computer science, will be helpful. Courses in English and speech will help you develop your vocabulary and hone your public speaking skills.

Postsecondary Training

Most entry-level positions require at least an associate's degree. Many zookeepers earn a four-year college degree. Animal management has become a highly technical and specialized field. Zookeepers do much more than care for animals' bodily comforts: Many of today's zookeepers are trained *zoologists*. They must be able to perform detailed behavioral observations, record keeping, nutrition studies, and health care. Their increased responsibilities make their role an essential one in maintaining a healthy animal collection.

Degrees in animal science, zoology, biology, marine biology, conservation biology, wildlife management, and animal behavior are preferred. Electives are just as important, particularly writing, public speaking, computer science, education, and even foreign languages. Applicants with interdisciplinary training sometimes have an advantage. A few colleges and junior colleges offer a specialized curriculum for zookeepers. Those seeking advancement to curatorial, research, or conservation positions may need a master's degree. Animal care experience such as *zoo volunteer, farm or ranch worker,* or *veterinary hospital worker* is a must.

Smaller zoos may hire *keeper trainees,* who receive on-the-job training to learn the responsibilities of the *zookeeper.* Several major zoos offer formal keeper training courses, as well as on-the-job training programs, to students who are studying areas related to animal science and care. The Association of Zoos and Aquariums provides information about which schools and animal facilities are involved in internship programs. Such programs could lead to full-time positions.

Many institutions offer unpaid internships for high school and college students interested in investigating a career in animal care. Internships may involve food preparation, hands-on experience with the animal collection,

A zookeeper holds a boa constrictor. (Alfred Wekelo. Shutterstock.)

interpretive services for the public, exhibit design and construction, or the collection and analysis of data. The length of the internships varies. The minimum age for most of these programs is 18.

Visit https://www.aazk.org/zoo-keeping-as-a-career for a list of postsecondary training programs for aspiring zoo keeping professionals.

Other Education or Training

The Association of Zoos and Aquariums (AZA) offers professional training courses such as "Best Practices in Animal Keeping," "Creating Successful Exhibits," and "Crocodilian Biology and Captive Management." Contact the AZA for more information.

■ CERTIFICATION, LICENSING, AND SPECIAL REQUIREMENTS
Certification or Licensing

There are no certification or licensing requirements for zookeepers.

The Smithsonian National Zoo

DID YOU KNOW?

In 1889, an act of Congress established the Smithsonian National Zoo (https://nationalzoo.si.edu) in Washington, D.C., "for the advancement of science and the instruction and recreation of people." The zoo encompasses 163 acres and is home to more than 1,500 animals representing 300 different species. More than 2 million people from all over the world visit the National Zoo annually. A staff of 200, including animal caretakers, veterinarians, and scientists, take care of the animals. Other facts about the National Zoo:

- Almost one-quarter of the animals housed in the zoo are endangered species, including giant pandas, Asian elephants, and western lowland gorillas.
- On the zoo grounds there are different species of trees, woody shrubs and herbaceous plants, grasses, and bamboo.
- Among the animals visitors can see are Sumatran tigers and African lions.
- The zoo was among the first zoos to establish a scientific research program to study animals in the wild and in captivity.

Source: Smithsonian National Zoo & Conservation Biology Institute

■ EXPERIENCE, SKILLS, AND PERSONALITY TRAITS

Previous experience as a keeper trainer and/or a degree in a zoology-related field are required to become a zookeeper. Zookeepers must first and foremost have a fondness and empathy for animals. The work of the zookeeper is not glamorous. It takes a special kind of dedication to provide care to captive animals that require attention 24 hours a day, 365 days a year.

Keepers need excellent interpersonal skills to work together and to interact with visitors and volunteers. Strong oral and written communication skills are also required. They should be detail-oriented and enjoy paperwork and record keeping.

They must be able to work well independently and as part of a team. Keepers rely on each other to get their jobs done safely. A calm, stable nature, maturity, good judgment, and the ability to adhere to established animal handling and/or safety procedures is essential. Being in a bad mood can interfere with concentration, endangering the keeper and coworkers.

Keepers must have keen powers of observation and, due to the physical demands of the job, keepers must be physically fit. Psychological fitness is important too. Zookeepers have to be able to handle the emotional impact when animals with which they have built a relationship go to another institution or die. They cannot be squeamish about handling body wastes or live food items or dealing with sick animals.

■ EMPLOYMENT PROSPECTS

Employers

Only 232 zoos, aquariums, wildlife parks, and oceanariums in the U.S. are accredited by the Association of Zoos and Aquariums (AZA). Most facilities are located in or near large population areas.

Starting Out

Competition for jobs at zoos is intense despite the low pay and challenging working conditions. There are many more candidates than available positions. Most zookeepers enjoy their work, and turnover is low. The majority of new jobs result from the need to replace workers who leave the field. A limited number of jobs are created when new zoos open. Entry-level applicants may find it easier to start out in small zoos in smaller communities, where the pay is usually low, and then move on once they have gained some experience. There are many such small-town zoos in the Midwest.

The days when zookeepers were hired off the street and trained on the job are a thing of the past. Today, most institutions require a bachelor's degree. Practical experience working with animals is a must. This experience can involve volunteering at a zoo or wildlife rehabilitation center, caring for animals in a kennel or animal hospital, or working on a farm or ranch.

Part-time work, summer jobs, or volunteering at a zoo increases an applicant's chances of getting full-time employment. Many zoos fill new positions by promoting current employees. An entry-level position, even if it does not involve working directly with animals, is a means of making contacts and learning about an institution's hiring practices.

Zoos that are municipally operated accept applications through municipal civil service offices. At other zoos, an application is made directly at the zoo office.

Occasionally zoos advertise for personnel in the local newspapers. Better sources of employment opportunities are trade journals (AZA's *Connect* or the American Association of Zoo Keepers Inc.'s *Animal Keepers' Forum*), the Web sites of specific institutions, or special-interest periodicals. A few zoos even have job lines.

Most zoos have internal job postings. People in the profession often learn about openings by word of mouth. Membership in a professional organization can be helpful when conducting a job search.

Some zoos require written aptitude tests or oral exams. Applicants must pass a physical exam, as keepers must be physically able to do such demanding work as lifting heavy sacks of feed or moving sick or injured animals.

■ ADVANCEMENT PROSPECTS

Job advancement in zoos is possible, but the career path is more limited than in some other professions requiring a college degree. The possibility for advancement varies according to a zoo's size and operating policies and an employee's qualifications.

Continuing professional education is a must to keep current on progress in husbandry, veterinary care, and technology, and in order to advance. The Association of Zoos and Aquariums offers formal professional courses in applied zoo and aquarium biology, conservation education, elephant management, institutional record keeping, population management, professional management, and studbook keeping. Attending workshops and conferences sponsored by professional groups or related organizations, such as universities or conservation organizations, is another means of sharing information with colleagues from other institutions and professions.

Most zoos have different levels of animal management staff. The most common avenue for job promotion is from *keeper* to *senior keeper* to *head keeper*, then possibly to *area supervisor* or *assistant curator* and then *curator*. On rare occasions, the next step will be to *zoo director*. Moving up from the senior keeper level to middle and upper management usually involves moving out to another institution, often in another city and state.

In addition to participating in daily animal care, the senior keeper manages a particular building on the zoo grounds and is responsible for supervising the keepers working in that facility. An area supervisor or assistant curator works directly with the curators and is responsible for supervising, scheduling, and training the entire keeper force. In major zoological parks, there are head keepers for each curatorial department.

The curator is responsible for managing a specific department or section within the zoo, either defined by taxonomy, such as mammals, birds, or reptiles, or by habitat or ecogeography, such as the Forest Edge or African savannah. The curator of mammals, for example, is in charge of all mammals in the collection and supervises all staff who work with mammals. Usually, an advanced degree in zoology and research experience is required to become a curator, as well as experience working as a zookeeper and in zoo management.

Many zookeepers eschew advancement and prefer to remain in work where they have the most direct interaction with and immediate impact on the lives of animals.

■ OUTLOOK

The U.S. Department of Labor predicts that job opportunities for animal care and service workers who are employed at museums, historical sites, and similar institutions will grow as fast as the average for all careers through 2024. Employment prospects for zoo animal care workers will not be as strong because the field is so small and competition for jobs is very high. Each year, there are many more applicants than positions available.

Opportunities arise mainly through attrition, which is lower than in many other professions, or the startup of a new facility. For example, the opening in 1998 of Disney's Animal Kingdom and the Long Beach Aquarium created a ripple effect throughout the entire industry as experienced personnel migrated to Florida and California, respectively, and jobs for new hires and promotions opened up at dozens of institutions.

As the preservation of animal species becomes more complicated, there will be a continuing need for zoo staff to work to preserve endangered wildlife and educate the public about conservation. The demand will increase for well-educated personnel who will be responsible for much more than simply feeding the animals and cleaning their enclosures. Zookeepers will need more knowledge as zoos expand and become more specialized. The amount of knowledge and effort necessary to maintain and reproduce a healthy animal collection will keep zookeepers in the front line of animal care.

Pursuing a job in this area is well worth the effort for those who are dedicated to providing care for rapidly diminishing animal species and educating the public about the fate of endangered animals and the need to preserve their natural habitats.

■ UNIONS AND ASSOCIATIONS

Union membership is more common at publicly operated zoos, but zookeepers may be unionized at privately run institutions as well. There is no single zookeepers' union, and a variety of different unions represent the employees at various zoos and aquariums. Some zookeepers join the American Association of Zoo Keepers and the Association of Zoos and Aquariums, which provide networking opportunities, publications, career information, continuing education classes, job listings, and other resources.

TIPS FOR ENTRY

1. Visit https://www.aazk.org/zoo-keeping-as-a-career to read "So You Want to be a Keeper, Trainer, or Aquarist?"

2. Visit http://www.aza.org/jobs and https://www.aazk.org/job-listings/all for job and internship listings.

3. Attend conferences held by the American Association of Zoo Keepers and the Association of Zoos and Aquariums to network, learn about industry trends, and participate in professional development workshops and seminars.

4. Contact zoos directly to learn more about job opportunities. The AZA offers a database of zoos at https://www.aza.org/find-a-zoo-or-aquarium.

FOR MORE INFORMATION

The American Association of Zoo Keepers provides information on careers and membership.

American Association of Zoo Keepers (AAZK)
8476 East Speedway Boulevard, Suite 204
Tucson, AZ 85710-1728
Tel: (520) 298-9688
E-mail: visitor@aazk.org
https://www.aazk.org

The Association of Zoos and Aquariums offers education, certification, job listings, and other resources.

Association of Zoos and Aquariums (AZA)
8403 Colesville Road, Suite 710
Silver Spring, MD 20910-3314
Tel: (301) 562-0777
Fax: (301) 562-0888
http://www.aza.org

The Wildlife Society is an international organization committed to addressing national and international issues that affect the current and future status of wildlife in North America and throughout the world.

The Wildlife Society (TWS)
425 Barlow Place, Suite 200
Bethesda, MD 20814-2170
Tel: (301) 897-9770
E-mail: tws@wildlife.org
http://wildlife.org

Zoologists

OVERVIEW

Zoologists are biologists who study animals. They often select a particular type of animal to study, and they may study an entire animal, one part or aspect of an animal, or a whole animal society or ecosystem. There are many areas of specialization from which a zoologist can choose, such as origins, genetics, characteristics, classifications, behaviors, life processes, and distribution of animals. There are approximately 17,910 zoologists and wildlife biologists employed in the United States.

HISTORY

Human beings have always studied animals. Knowledge of animal behavior was a necessity to prehistoric humans, whose survival depended on their success in hunting. Those early people who hunted to live learned to respect and even revere their prey. Among the earliest known paintings are those located in the Lascaux Caves in France, which depict animals, demonstrating the vital importance of animals to early humans. Most experts believe that the artists who painted those images viewed the animals they hunted not just as a food source, but also as an important element of spiritual or religious life.

The first important developments in zoology occurred in Greece, where Alcmaeon, a philosopher and physician, studied animals and performed the first known dissections of humans in the sixth century B.C. Aristotle, however, is generally considered to be the first real zoologist. Aristotle, who studied with the great philosopher Plato and tutored the world-conquering Alexander the Great, had the lofty goal of setting down in writing everything that was known in his time. In an attempt to extend that knowledge, he observed and dissected sea creatures. He also devised a system of classifying animals that included 500 species, a system that influenced scientists for many centuries after his death. Some scholars believe that Alexander sent various exotic animals to his old tutor from the lands he conquered, giving Aristotle unparalleled access to the animals of the ancient world.

With the exception of important work in physiology done by the Roman physician Galen, the study of zoology progressed little after Aristotle until the middle of the 16th century. Between 1555 and 1700, much significant work was done in the classification of species and in physiology, especially regarding the circulation of blood, which affected studies of both animals and humans. The invention of the microscope in approximately 1590 led to the discovery and study of cells. In the 18th century, Swedish botanist Carl Linnaeus developed the system of classification of plants and animals that is still used.

Zoology continued to develop at a rapid rate, and in 1859, Charles Darwin published *On the Origin of Species*, which promoted the theory of natural selection, revolutionized the way scientists viewed all living creatures, and gave rise to the field of ethology, the study of animal behavior. Since that time, zoologists throughout the world have made innumerable advances.

The rapid development of technology has changed zoology and all sciences by giving scientists the tools to explore areas that had previously been closed to them. Computers, submersibles, spacecraft, and tremendously powerful microscopes are only a few of the means that modern zoologists have used to bring new knowledge to light. In spite of these advances, however, mysteries remain, questions go unanswered, and species remain undiscovered.

■ THE JOB

Zoology is a single specialty within the field of biology, but it is a vast specialty that includes many major subspecialties. Some zoologists study a single animal or a category of animals, whereas others may specialize in a particular part of an animal's anatomy or study a process that takes place in many kinds of animals. A zoologist might study single-cell organisms, a particular variety of fish, or the behavior of groups of animals such as elephants or bees.

Many zoologists are classified according to the animals they study. For example, *entomologists* are experts on insects, *ichthyologists* study fish, *herpetologists* specialize in the study of reptiles and amphibians, *mammalogists* focus on mammals, and *ornithologists* study birds. *Embryologists*, however, are classified according to the process that they study. They examine the ways in which animal embryos form and develop from conception to birth.

Within each primary area of specialization there is a wide range of subspecialties. An ichthyologist, for example, might focus on the physiology, or physical structure and functioning, of a particular fish; on a biochemical phenomenon such as bioluminescence in deep-sea species; on the discovery and classification of fish; on variations within a single species in different parts of the world; or on the ways in which one type of fish interacts with other species in a specific environment. Others may specialize in the effects of pollution on fish or in finding ways to grow fish effectively in controlled environments in order to increase the supply of healthy food available for human consumption.

Some zoologists are primarily *teachers*, while others spend most of their time as *researchers*, performing original research. Teaching jobs in universities and other facilities are probably the most secure positions available, but zoologists who wish to do extensive research may find such positions restrictive. Even zoologists whose primary function is research, however, often need to do some teaching in the course of their work, and almost everyone in the field has to deal with the public at one time or another.

Students often believe that zoological scientists spend most of their time in the field, observing animals and collecting specimens. In fact, most researchers spend no more than two to eight weeks in the field each year. Zoologists spend much of their time at a computer or on the telephone.

It is often the case that junior scientists spend more time in the field than do senior scientists, who study specimens and data collected in the field by their younger colleagues. Senior scientists spend much of their time coordinating research, directing younger scientists and technicians, and writing grant proposals or soliciting funds in other ways.

Raising money is an extremely important activity for zoologists who are not employed by government agencies or major universities. The process of obtaining money for research can be time consuming and difficult. Good development skills can also give scientists a flexibility that government-funded scientists may lack. Government money is sometimes available only for research in narrowly defined areas that may not be those that a scientist wishes to study. A zoologist who wants

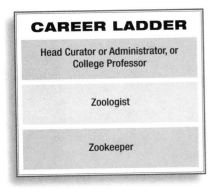

CAREER LADDER

Head Curator or Administrator, or College Professor

Zoologist

Zookeeper

to study a particular area may seek his or her own funding in order not to be limited by government restrictions.

■ EARNINGS

A study conducted by the National Association of Colleges and Employers determined that in September 2016 beginning salaries averaged $62,985 for holders of bachelor's degrees in math and the sciences (including zoologists).

According to the U.S. Department of Labor, the median annual wage for zoologists and wildlife biologists was $59,680 in May 2015. Salaries ranged from less than $39,180 a year to more than $97,390 a year, depending on the zoologist's education and experience.

The benefits that zoologists receive as part of their employment vary widely. Employees of the federal government or top universities tend to have extensive benefit packages, but the benefits offered by private industry cover a wide range, from extremely generous to almost nonexistent.

■ WORK ENVIRONMENT

There is much variation in the conditions under which zoologists work. Professors of zoology may teach exclusively during the school year or may both teach and conduct research. Many professors whose school year consists of teaching spend their summers doing research. Research scientists spend some time in the field, but most of their work is done in the laboratory. There are zoologists who spend most of their time in the field, but they are the exceptions to the rule.

Zoologists who do fieldwork may have to deal with difficult conditions. A gorilla expert may have to spend her time in the forests of Rwanda; a shark expert may need to observe his subjects from a shark cage. For most people in the field, however, that aspect of the work is particularly interesting and satisfying.

Zoologists spend much of their time corresponding with others in their field, studying the latest literature, reviewing articles written by their peers, and making and returning phone calls. They also log many hours working with computers, using computer modeling, performing statistical analyses, recording the results of their research, or writing articles and grant proposals.

No zoologist works in a vacuum. Even those who spend much time in the field have to keep up with developments within their specialty. In most cases, zoologists

deal with many different kinds of people, including students, mentors, the public, colleagues, representatives of granting agencies, private or corporate donors, reporters, and science writers. For this reason, the most successful members of the profession tend to develop good communication skills.

■ EXPLORING

One of the best ways to find out if you are suited for a career as a zoologist is to talk to zoologists and find out exactly what they do. Contact experts in your field of interest. If you are interested in birds, find out whether there is an ornithologist in your area. If there is not, find an expert in some other part of the country. Read books, magazines, and journals to find out who the experts are. Do not be afraid to write or call people and ask them questions.

One good way to meet experts is to attend meetings of professional organizations. If you are interested in fish, locate organizations of ichthyologists by searching in the library or on the Internet. If you can, attend an organization's meeting and introduce yourself to the attendees. Ask questions and learn as much as you can.

Become an intern or volunteer at an organization that is involved in an area that you find interesting. Most organizations have internships, and if you look with determination for an internship, you are likely to find one.

■ EDUCATION AND TRAINING REQUIREMENTS
High School

To prepare for a career in zoology, make sure to get a well-rounded high school education. A solid grounding in biology and chemistry is an absolute necessity, but facility in English will also be invaluable. Writing monographs and articles, communicating with colleagues both orally and in writing, and writing persuasive fund-raising proposals are all activities at which scientists need to excel. Also be sure to read widely, not merely relying on books on science or other subjects that are required by the school. The scientist-in-training should search the library for magazines and journals dealing with areas that are of personal interest. Developing the habit of reading will help to prepare you for the massive amounts of reading involved in research and keeping up with the latest developments in the field. Computer skills are also essential, since most zoologists not only use the computer for writing, communication, and research, but they also use various software programs to perform statistical analyses.

Postsecondary Training

A bachelor's degree is the minimum requirement to work as a zoologist; advanced degrees are needed for research or administrative work. Courses typically include ecology, anatomy, wildlife management, and cellular biology, as well as botany, physics, chemistry, math, and statistics. Students also take classes that focus on specific animals, such as herpetology (reptiles and amphibians) or ornithology (birds). They may also study applied techniques in habitat analysis and conservation. Academic training, practical experience (via internships and externships), and the ability to work effectively with others are the most important prerequisites for a career in zoology.

Other Education or Training

Keeping up with industry developments is key to success as a zoologist. Professional associations at the national, state, and local levels often provide continuing education opportunities. Organizations that provide classes, seminars, webinars, and workshops include American Association of Zoo Keepers, American Institute of Biological Sciences, Society for Integrative and Comparative Biology, and the Zoological Association of America.

■ CERTIFICATION, LICENSING, AND SPECIAL REQUIREMENTS

Certification or Licensing

There are no certification or licensing requirements for zoologists.

■ EXPERIENCE, SKILLS, AND PERSONALITY TRAITS

Experience as an intern, volunteer, or part-time employee at a zoo, aquarium, or other employer of zoologists is recommended.

Success in zoology requires tremendous effort. It would be unwise for a person who wants to work an eight-hour day to become a zoologist, since hard work and long hours (sometimes 60 to 80 hours per week) are the norm. Also, although some top scientists are paid extremely well, the field does not provide a rapid route to riches. A successful zoologist finds satisfaction in work, not in a paycheck. The personal rewards, however, can be tremendous. The typical zoologist finds their work satisfying on many levels.

A successful zoologist must be patient and flexible. A person who cannot juggle various tasks will have a difficult time in a job that requires doing research, writing articles, dealing with the public, teaching students, soliciting funds, and keeping up with the latest publications in the field. Flexibility also comes into play when funding for a particular area of study ends or is unavailable. A zoologist whose range of expertise is too narrowly focused will be at a disadvantage when there are no

Zoologist identifies gene fragments from a parasite. (Peggy Greb/ USDA ARS Photo Unit.)

opportunities in that particular area. A flexible approach and a willingness to explore various areas can be crucial in such situations, and too rigid an attitude may lead a zoologist to avoid studies that they would have found rewarding.

An aptitude for reading and writing is a must for any zoologist. A person who dislikes reading would have difficulty keeping up with the literature in the field, and a person who cannot write or dislikes writing would be unable to write effective articles and books. Publishing is an important part of zoological work, especially for those who are conducting research.

■ EMPLOYMENT PROSPECTS

Employers

Approximately 17,910 zoologists and wildlife biologists are employed in the United States. Zoologists work for a wide variety of institutions, not just zoos. Many

TOP EMPLOYERS OF ZOOLOGISTS AND WILDLIFE BIOLOGISTS AND MEAN ANNUAL EARNINGS, MAY 2015

FAST FACTS

- State government agencies: 6,540 jobs, $55,400
- Federal government agencies: 4,180 jobs, $80,710
- Management, scientific, and technical consulting services: 1,560 jobs, $61,670
- Scientific research and development services: 1,290 jobs, $65,920
- Colleges, universities, and professional schools: 1,160 jobs, $65,460

Source: U.S. Bureau of Labor Statistics

zoologists are teachers at universities and other facilities, where they may teach during the year while spending their summers doing research. A large number of zoologists are researchers; they may be working for nonprofit organizations (requiring grants to fund their work), scientific institutions, or the government. There are also many zoologists who are employed by zoos, aquariums, and museums. Jobs for zoologists exist all over the country, but large cities that have universities, zoos, and museums will provide far more opportunities for zoologists than in rural areas.

Starting Out

It is possible to find work with a bachelor's degree, but those starting out will need to continue their education to advance further in the field. Competition for higher paying, high-level jobs among those with doctoral degrees is fierce; as a result, it is often easier to break into the field with a master's degree than it is with a Ph.D. Many zoologists with their master's degree seek a mid-level job and work toward a Ph.D. on a part-time basis.

You will be ahead of the game if you have made contacts as an intern or as a member of a professional organization. It is an excellent idea to attend the meetings of professional organizations, which generally welcome students. At those meetings, introduce yourself to the scientists you admire and ask for their help and advice.

Don't be shy, but be sure to treat people with respect. Ultimately, it's the way you relate to other people that determines how your career will develop.

■ ADVANCEMENT PROSPECTS

Higher education and publishing are two of the most important means of advancing in the field of zoology. The holder of a Ph.D. will make more money and have a higher status than a zoologist with a bachelor's or master's degree. The publication of articles and books is important for both research scientists and professors of zoology. A young assistant professor who does not publish cannot expect to become a full professor with tenure, and a research scientist who does not publish the results of their research will not become known as an authority in the field. In addition, the publication of a significant work lets everyone in the field know that the author has worked hard and accomplished something worthwhile.

Zoology is not a career with high turnover in jobs, which is why people generally move up within an organization. A professor may become a full professor; a research scientist may become known as an expert in the field or may become the head of a department, division, or institution; a zoologist employed by an aquarium or a zoo may become an administrator or head curator. In some cases, however, scientists may not want what appears to be a more prestigious position. A zoologist who loves to conduct and coordinate research, for example, may not want to become an administrator who is responsible for budgeting, hiring and firing, and other tasks that have nothing to do with research.

■ OUTLOOK

Employment for zoologists and wildlife biologists will grow more slowly than the average for all careers through 2024, according to the *Occupational Outlook Handbook (OOH)*. Despite this prediction, the *OOH* says that "zoologists and wildlife biologists should have good job opportunities. In addition to job growth, many job openings will be created by zoologists and wildlife biologists who retire, advance to management positions, or change careers." Growth in the biological sciences should continue to increase in the coming years, spurred partly by the need analyze and offset the effects of pollution on the environment. Zoologists will continue to be needed to manage animal populations and conservation plans.

Those who are most successful in the field in the future are likely to be those who are able to diversify. Those entering the field would be wise to stay open-minded, maintain a wide range of contacts, and keep an eye out for what is occurring in related fields.

■ UNIONS AND ASSOCIATIONS

Some zoologists may be represented by the International Federation of Professional and Technical Engineers and other unions. Zoologists can obtain useful resources, such as certification, continuing education, and information on education and careers, from the Alliance of Marine Mammal Parks and Aquariums, American Association of

Zoo Keepers, American Institute of Biological Sciences, Society for Integrative and Comparative Biology, and the Zoological Association of America.

■ TIPS FOR ENTRY

1. Participate in internships or part-time jobs that are arranged by your college's career services office.
2. Visit the following Web sites for job and internship listings:
   - http://www.zaa.org/job-board
   - https://www.aza.org/jobs
   - http://jobs.sciencecareers.org
   - http://www.aibs.org/classifieds
3. Attend the annual conferences of the Zoological Association of America and the Association of Zoos and Aquariums to network, learn about industry trends, and participate in professional development workshops and seminars.
4. Contact zoos directly to learn more about job opportunities. The Association of Zoos and Aquariums (AZA) offers a database of zoos at https://www.aza.org/find-a-zoo-or-aquarium.

■ FOR MORE INFORMATION

The Alliance of Marine Mammal Parks and Aquariums is dedicated to the concerns and issues that affect the public display of marine mammals.

Alliance of Marine Mammal Parks and Aquariums (AMMPA)
E-mail: executivedirector@ammpa.org
http://www.ammpa.org

The American Association of Zoo Keepers provides information on careers and membership.

American Association of Zoo Keepers (AAZK)
8476 East Speedway Boulevard, Suite 204
Tucson, AZ 85710-1728
Tel: (520) 298-9688
E-mail: visitor@aazk.org
https://www.aazk.org

The American Institute of Biological Sciences promotes the use of science to inform decision-making that advances biology for the benefit of science and society.

American Institute of Biological Sciences (AIBS)
1313 Dolley Madison Boulevard, Suite 402
McLean, VA 22101-3926
Tel: (703) 790-1745
Fax: (703) 790-2672
https://www.aibs.org

The Association of Zoos and Aquariums offers education, certification, job listings, and other resources.

Association of Zoos and Aquariums (AZA)
8403 Colesville Road, Suite 710
Silver Spring, MD 20910-3314
Tel: (301) 562-0777
Fax: (301) 562-0888
https://www.aza.org

The Society for Integrative and Comparative Biology fosters research, education, public awareness, and understanding of living organisms from molecules and cells to ecology and evolution.

Society for Integrative and Comparative Biology (SICB)
1313 Dolley Madison Boulevard, Suite 402
McLean, VA 22101-3953
Tel: (800) 955-1236; 703) 790-1745
Fax: (703) 790-2672
E-mail: Questions@SICB.org
http://www.sicb.org

The Zoological Association of America provides education, accreditation, conferences, job listings, and other resources.

Zoological Association of America (ZAA)
PO Box 511275
Punta Gorda, FL 33951-1275
Tel: (941) 621-2021
Fax: (941) 621-6571
E-mail: info@zaa.org
http://www.zaa.org

Job Title Index

Entries and page numbers in **bold** indicate titles of career articles.

C